DIRECTORY OF

Historical Figures

Directory of Historical Figures

compiled and edited by
The Editors of Salem Press

Salem Press, Inc.
Pasadena, California Hackensack, New Jersey

For information address the publisher:
Salem Press, Inc.
P.O. Box 50062
Pasadena, California 91115

∞ The paper used in these volumes conforms to the American National Standard for Permanence of Paper for Printed Library Materials, Z39.48-1992 (R1997).

Library of Congress Cataloging-in-Publication Data

Directory of historical figures / compiled and edited by the editors of Salem Press.
p. cm.
ISBN 0-89356-334-X (alk. paper)
1. Biography — Dictionaries. I. Salem Press.

CT103.D57 2000
920.02 21—dc21 99-044231

First Printing

PRINTED IN THE UNITED STATES OF AMERICA

Publisher's Note

This single-volume reference source, *Directory of Historical Figures*, is designed specifically for the reference librarian and provides an easy-to-use listing of thousands of persons who have played a prominent role in history. Unlike other general biographical directories, which tend to focus on people from the Western world and who have died, the *Directory of Historical Figures* excels in its coverage of ethnic Americans and people still living and active.

The directory includes more than 8,000 persons: nobility, diplomats, politicians, actors, athletes, artists, musicians, scientists, inventors, and people who achieved prominence in many other fields of endeavor. The vast amount of information presented here is easily accessible through the directory's simple, logical, consistent formats, putting within arm's reach the names, birth/death dates and places, and fields in which the individual excelled, including a brief description of the individual's achievements.

Each directory listing begins with the person's name as it is most commonly known in the United States. Alphabetization is word-by-word unless a chronological order (Sr. before Jr.) or numerical order (Henry I, Henry II, Henry III, etc.) is more appropriate. Also, initials are spelled as separate words (H. D. precedes Haan). Alternate names by which the person is known follow. *Full* provides the most complete version of the individual's name—for example, for Richard Pryor, *full:* Richard Franklin Lennox Thomas Pryor. *Né* (used for both men and women) applies when the person is best known by a pseudonym, changed name, or married name; the person's given name would then appear after *né*—for example, for Rita Hayworth, *né:* Margarita Carmen Cansino. *Pseudo.* and *aka* list, respectively, pseudonyms and any (other) names by which the person may be known (alternate spellings, other variations, other names, nicknames)—for Edna St. Vincent Millay, *pseudo.:* Nancy Boyd; for Mao Zedong, *aka:* Mao Tse-tung. Given names, pseudonyms, and alternate names also appear alphabetically throughout the volume as cross-references to the main entry.

The name information is followed by the person's date of birth and place of birth, followed by the death date and place of death, if appropriate. Each entry also includes a "fields" line, listing the individual's primary areas of achievement. Each directory entry concludes with a brief description of the person's significance.

The names included in this directory were compiled by the Editors of Salem Press during the past ten years, based on repeated reference inquiries about correct spellings and dates. While preparing both biographical and encyclopedic reference works for Salem Press and other publishers, it became apparent that checking various published and online reference sources often turned up a variety of name spellings and dates. This led the Editors to compile a style manual for biographical research, with name spellings and transliterations carefully chosen to reflect those that are most commonly presented to the North American audience. Unlike other print sources, the *Directory of Historical Figures* includes living individuals, the subject of many library inquiries and the group for which much inconsistent information will often be found. The *Directory of Historical Figures* is designed as an easy-to-use, one-stop source for this frequently requested biographical information.

DIRECTORY OF
Historical Figures

Aaliyah
b. January 16, 1979
Brooklyn, N.Y.
fields: Music (rhythm and blues singer)

African American rhythm and blues singer; Aaliyah, identified by her sexy, velvet voice and her brand of gangster femininity, debuted in 1994, with the album *Age Ain't Nothing but a Number*.

Aalto, Alvar
full: Hugo Alvar Henrik Aalto
b. February 3, 1898
Kurotane, Finland
d. May 11, 1976
Helsinki, Finland
fields: Architecture

Aalto was one of the founding fathers of the so-called International Style in architecture, but he went beyond the geometrical cubism that was the hallmark of the International Style by incorporating into his mature work classical and Romantic elements. In the process, Aalto became not only Finland's most famous architect but also a national hero, even the symbol of the Finnish ideal of *sisu* (fortitude).

Aaron
b. c. 1395 B.C.E.
Egypt
d. c. 1272 B.C.E.
Moserah or Mount Hor, Sinai
fields: Religion and Theology

The founder of the Jewish priesthood, Aaron serves as the prototype of the ideal religious leader.

Aaron, Hank
full: Henry Louis Aaron
b. February 5, 1934
Mobile, Ala.
fields: Sports (baseball)

Professional African American baseball player. Hank Aaron was a powerful right-handed batter and outfielder who started on all-black teams but spent most of his major league career with the Braves in Milwaukee (1954-1965) and Atlanta (1966-1974); broke Babe Ruth's career record of 714 home runs (1974); was traded to the Milwaukee Brewers (1975-1976); hit 755 career home runs; held eighteen major league records; elected to the Baseball Hall of Fame (1982); took a position as an Atlanta Braves executive in 1976 and was promoted to senior vice president in 1989; sponsored the Hank Aaron Celebrity Bowling Tournament for Sickle Cell Anemia (1972); elected president of No Greater Love, a humanitarian organization (1974) and organized a scholarship fund for talented poor youngsters; state chairman of the Wisconsin Easter Seal Society (1975); wrote two autobiographies, *Aaron* (1974) and *I Had a Hammer* (1991).

Abahai
aka: Hung Taiji
b. November 28, 1592
Hetu Ala
d. September 21, 1643
Sheng-ching, Manchuria
fields: Government and Politics, Military Affairs

Abahai consolidated and then expanded the empire begun by his father, Nurhachi, and established the foundations for Manchu rule over China during the Ch'ing Dynasty (1644-1911).

Abano, Pietro d'
aka: Peter of Abano
aka: Petrus de Apono
aka: Petrus Aponensis
b. c. 1250
Abano, near Padua, Italy
d. 1316
Padua, Italy
fields: Medicine, Philosophy

Pietro founded the Paduan school of medicine, introducing elements of Arabic knowledge into Italy. While a successful professor of medicine, he worked toward a synthesis of medieval, classical, Arabic, and Jewish philosophy.

Abbas, Ferhat
b. October 24, 1899
Tahar, Algeria
d. December 24, 1985
Algiers, Algeria
fields: Government and Politics, Diplomacy

Abbas was the first Premier of the Provisional Government of Algeria (1958-1961). Regarded as the "grand old man of Algerian politics," he was an assimilationist in the 1930's and nonviolent radical nationalist in the 1940's whose so-called Manifesto of the Algerian People marked a turning point in the development of an Algerian national independence movement. Realizing that peaceful means would not bring an end to colonialism, Abbas became a revolutionary nationalist, joined the National Liberation Front in 1956, and quickly became its international spokesman.

ʿAbbās the Great
b. January 27, 1571
Iran
d. January 19, 1629
Ashraf, Mazandaran, Iran
fields: Government and Politics

The most famous of all Islamic era monarchs of Iran, ʿAbbās the Great was the chief architect of the modern Iranian state. His legacy also includes great achievements in architecture, literature, textiles, and painting.

Abbott, Berenice
né: Bernice Abbott
b. July 17, 1898
Springfield, Ohio
d. December 9, 1991
Monson, Maine
fields: Photography

Abbott devoted her life to photographing the products of human ingenuity and creativity. She also became one of the earliest "experts" in the field of photography, a lecturer on its philosophy and technique, an inventor of photographic equipment, and a promoter of photography as a form of both art and communication.

Abbott, Edith
b. September 26, 1876
d. July 28, 1957
Grand Island, Nebr.
fields: Social Reform, Women's Rights

Edith Abbott was dean of the School of Social Service Administration. An expert on working-class women and the poor, she wrote *Women in Industry* (1910) and *The Tenements of Chicago* (1936). Grace Abbott was her sister.

Abbott, Grace
b. November 17, 1878
Grand Island, Nebr.
d. June 19, 1939
Chicago, Ill.
fields: Social Reform

Grace Abbott was a social worker specializing in child labor conditions. She was the director of the Child Labor Division of the U.S. Children's Bureau, 1921-1934. She published *The Child and the State* in 1938. Edith Abbott was her sister.

Abbott, Maude
full: Maude Elizabeth Seymour Abbott
b. Mar. 18, 1869
St. Andrews East, Quebec, Canada
d. Sept. 2, 1940
Montreal, Quebec, Canada
fields: Medicine

Maude Abbott was a leader in congenital heart disease research. In 1907, she organized the first meeting of the International Association of Medical Museums. In 1936, she received honorary membership in the all-male Osler Society.

Abbott, Robert Sengstacke

b. Nov. 24, 1870
St. Simons Island, Ga.
d. Feb. 29, 1940
Chicago, Ill.
fields: Publishing, Journalism

African American publisher. In 1905 Robert Sengstacke Abbott, who had graduated from Kent College, Chicago, with a degree in law, founded the *Chicago Defender*, an influential semiweekly newspaper aimed at the African American community. Under Abbott it grew to be the third largest black newspaper in the United States. In 1956, John H. Sengstacke, Abbott's nephew, transformed the paper to a daily with a circulation topping two hundred thousand.

ʿAbd al-Mu'min

b. 1094
Tagra, Algeria
d. May 2, 1163
Rabat, Morocco
fields: Warfare and Conquest, Government and Politics, Patronage of the Arts

Through military prowess and administrative skill, ʿAbd al-Mu'min founded the Almohad empire in North Africa and the Iberian Peninsula, initiating a period of thriving commerce and artistic creativity.

ʿAbd al-Rahman III al-Nasir

b. 891
Córdoba, Spain
d. 961
Córdoba, Spain
fields: Government and Politics

Sound administrative, fiscal, and religious policies, military successes, astute diplomacy, and patronage of learning characterized ʿAbd al-Rahman's reign, which marked the apex of Islamic power in Spain.

Abdelkader

full Arabic: ʿAbd al-Qādir ibn Muḥyī ad-Dīn ibn Muṣṭafā al-ḥasanī al-Jazāʾirī
b. September 26, 1807
Guetna, Ottoman Empire
d. May 26, 1883
Damascus, Ottoman Empire
fields: Government and Politics, Military Affairs

After the French landed in Algiers in 1830, Abdelkader carved a semiautonomous state out of the remnants of the former Turkish possessions in Algeria. He achieved lasting fame for his various campaigns against the French, whom he fought until his surrender in 1847.

ʿAbduh, Muhammad

b. c. 1849
Mahallat Nasr, Gharbiyyah Province, Egypt
d. July 11, 1905
Alexandria, Egypt
fields: Education, Journalism, Government and Politics

ʿAbduh was a major figure in the articulation of modern political, ethical, and social values in an Islamic context. His writings were a major stimulus to the development of Egyptian nationalism and, in a wider sense, to the elaboration of social and political thought throughout Islam.

Abdul Rahman

full: Tunku (Prince) Abdul Rahman Putra Alhaj
b. February 8, 1903
Alor Setar, Kedah, Malaya (now Malaysia)
d. December 6, 1990
Kuala Lumpur, Selangor, Malaysia
fields: Government and Politics

Abdul Rahman was the first prime minister of independent Malaya (1957-1963) and subsequently of the Federation of Malaysia (1963-1979). Led Alliance Party. Negotiated for Malayan independence from England in 1956 (independence declared by Malaya on August 31, 1957). In 1963 Rahman helped negotiate the union of Malaya with Singapore, North Borneo, and Sarawak to form the Federation of Malaysia that year.

Abdul-Jabbar, Kareem

né: Lewis Ferdinand Alcindor, Jr.
aka: Lew Alcindor
b. April 16, 1947
New York, New York
fields: Sports (basketball)

One of history's greatest basketball players; Kareem Abdul-Jabbar, named Lew Alcindor until his conversion to Islam in 1968, was an African American high school star in New York City; at the University of California, Los Angeles (1965-1969), he averaged 26.4 points per game, was named the country's best college player twice, and led his team to three National Collegiate Athletic Association (NCAA) championships; professional career began with a $1.4 million contract with the Milwaukee Bucks (1969-1975) and the Los Angeles Lakers (beginning in 1975); *Sports Illustrated* Sportsman of the Year (1985); also acted in films and on television; co-authored an autobiography, *Giant Steps* (1983); inducted into the Basketball Hall of Fame in 1995.

Abdumajid, Iman. *See* Iman

Abe, Masao

b. February 9, 1915
Osaka, Japan
fields: Philosophy, Religion and Theology

As the foremost exponent of Zen Buddhism for the West and a member of the influential Kyoto School, Masao Abe has been instrumental in promoting and fostering interfaith dialogue between Western theology (both Jewish and Christian) and Buddhist philosophy. His thought is expounded in such works as *Zen and Western Thought* (1985), *The Emptying God* (1990), *Buddhism and Interfaith Dialogue* (1995), and *Zen and Comparative Studies* (1997).

Abe, Tokunosuke

b. 1885
Iwate Prefecture, Japan
d. Jan. 3, 1941
San Diego, Calif.
fields: Business and Industry

Tokunosuke Abe, a Japanese immigrant in Southern California, challenged state laws stipulating that only U.S. citizens were eligible to receive commercial fishing licenses. The state supreme court ruled in *Abe v. Fish and Game Commission* (1935) that the code violated the equal protection clause of the Fourteenth Amendment of the U.S. Constitution.

Abeel, John. *See* Cornplanter

Abel, Niels Henrik

b. August 5, 1802
Finnøy, Norway
d. April 6, 1829
Froland, Norway
fields: Mathematics

Abel was instrumental in the evolution of modern mathematics, especially in the field of algebra. Regarded as one of the foremost analysts of his time, he insisted on a rigorous approach to mathematical proof which was critical for the further development of abstract mathematics.

Abelard, Peter

b. 1079
Le Pallet, Brittany
d. April 21, 1142
the Priory of Saint-Marcel, near Chalon-sur-Saône, Burgundy
fields: Philosophy, Religion and Theology

In philosophy Abelard developed the theory of conceptualism to reconcile Platonic idealism with nominalism. His use of the dialectic to explore Scripture helped shape Scholasticism, and many of his religious views, condemned as heretical in his own lifetime, subsequently influenced church doctrine.

Abernathy, Ralph David

b. March 11, 1926
Linden, Alabama
d. April 17, 1990
Atlanta, Georgia
fields: Civil Rights, Social Reform

Abernathy, one of the greatest African American civil rights leaders of the twentieth century, led the Montgomery bus boycott with Martin Luther King, Jr., and Edward Nixon, helped found the Southern Christian Leadership Conference (SCLC), and organized the Poor People's Campaign after King's assassination.

Abiko, Kyutaro

b. June 23, 1865
Suibara, Kita-Kambara-Gun, Japan
d. May 31, 1936
San Francisco, Calif.
fields: Publishing, Civil Rights, Social Reform

Japanese American labor contractor, banker, and publisher; Kyutaro Abiko was founder, publisher, and editor of the San Francisco Japanese newspaper *Nichibei Shimbun* (1899: *Japanese American News*), which became the most influential Japanese newspaper in the United States by 1910. In 1906 Abiko formed the American Land and Produce Company, through which he organized the Yamato Colony, located near Livingston, California. Abiko (with a European American) purchased additional land in the area in 1919, forming the Cortez Colony. Abiko cofounded the Japanese American Industrial Corporation of San Francisco (1902), which contracted immigrant labor.

Abiko, Yasuo

b. 1910
d. 1988
fields: Journalism

Yasuo Abiko, Japanese American and son of the editor of the *Nichibei Shimbun*, edited the paper's English section at the start of World War II. After the war, he kept the bilingual English-Japanese paper operating, producing it himself if necessary.

Abraham

b. c. 2050 B.C.E.
Ur, Chaldea
d. c. 1950 B.C.E.
Macpelah, Mesopotamia
fields: Religion and Theology

According to Hebrew tradition and biblical record, Abraham is the ancient ancestor of the people of Israel to whom God first promised territory, nationhood, and spiritual blessing. He is therefore the key patriarch in the history of Judaism and of extreme importance as well to the development of both Christianity and Islam.

Abū Bakr

b. c. 573
d. August 23, 634
fields: Religion and Theology, Philosophy, Government and Politics

Abū Bakr supported the Prophet Muhammad in Mecca at the time he declared his prophethood and supposedly accompanied him on his flight from Mecca to Medina, helping him to become established there. He succeeded Muhammad as the first caliph, expanding the nascent Muslim empire by conquering neighboring states.

Abu Hanifah

full: Abu Hanifah Al-Nu ʿMan ibn Thabit
b. c. 699
Kufa, Iraq
d. 767
Baghdad, Iraq
fields: Law, Religion and Theology

Abu Hanifah, celebrated eighth century Muslim jurist and theologian, was the founder of the first of four orthodox schools of Islamic law, the Hanifite. His brilliant use of reason and his gift for systematic thought provided Muslim civilization with a coherent and applicable system of law.

Abū Naṣr al-Fārābī. *See* Fārābī, Muḥammad ibn Muḥammad ibn Ṭarkhān al-

Abuba, Ernest

b. Aug. 25, 1947
Honolulu, Hawaii
fields: Acting, Drama

Ernest Abuba, a leading Asian American actor and director, received the 1983 Best Actor Obie Award for his performance in R. A. Shiomi's *Yellow Fever* (pr. 1982). He directed and performed in many productions while senior artist with the Pan Asian Repertory Theatre of New York. His *Cambodia Agonistes* (pr. 1992), a musical drama, was the first U.S. play to address the Kampuchean genocide.

Abul Wefa

b. June 10, 940
either Buzshan, Khorasan Province, or Buzadhan, Kuhistan Province, Iran
d. July 1, 998
Baghdad
fields: Mathematics, Astronomy

Abul Wefa played a major role in the development of sines and cosines as they apply to the field of trigonometry. These he used to correct astronomical calculations carried forward from classical into Islamic times.

Abzug, Bella

né: Bella Savitzky
b. July 24, 1920
New York, New York
d. March 31, 1998
New York, New York
fields: Government and Politics

One of the most colorful and well-known members of Congress in the 1970's, Abzug has been an aggressive spokesperson for women's rights throughout her life.

Aceves, José

b. 1909
Chihuahua, Mexico
d. 1968
fields: Art (painter, muralist)

Latino painter and muralist. Born in Mexico, José Aceves and his family moved to El Paso, Texas, in 1915. Taught himself how to paint using the history and landscape of the American Southwest, as well as the stylistic traditions of Mexican muralists, for inspiration. The murals he painted from the mid-1930's through the early 1940's for the Federal Art Project of the Works Progress Administration helped introduce Latino art to mainstream America.

Acham, Bernard Ivan Felix. *See* Chen, Jack

Achebe, Chinua

full: Chinualomagu Albert Achebe
b. November 16, 1930
Ogidi, Nigeria
fields: Literature

Achebe was one of the first African writers to achieve international literary success. His use of a mixture of simple English and Ibo phrases reflected a uniquely African heritage and inspired many other African writers to lend their voices to different types of Western literature.

Acheson, Dean

full: Dean Gooderham Acheson
b. April 11, 1893
Middletown, Connecticut
d. October 12, 1971
Sandy Spring, Maryland
fields: Government and Politics

As secretary of state from 1949 to 1953, Acheson conducted negotiations leading to the establishment of the North Atlantic Treaty Organization and dealt with crises involving the victory of Communism in China and American participation in the Korean War; his policies determined the basic framework of the United States' security commitments in Europe and Asia during the Cold War.

Acosta, Manuel Gregorio

b. May 9, 1921
Villa Aldama, Veracruz, Mexico
d. Oct. 25, 1989
Houston, Texas
fields: Art (painter, muralist, sculptor)

Latino painter, muralist, and sculptor. After emigrating to Texas as a child, Manuel Gregorio Acosta studied at the University of Texas at El Paso and at the Chouinard Art Institute in Los Angeles, California. Began painting murals depicting the people and history of the American Southwest. Commissioned in the 1950's to paint historical murals in New Mexico and Texas. The appearance of his portrait of labor activist César Chávez on the cover of *Time* magazine in 1969 brought him national recognition.

Acosta, Zeta

full: Oscar Acosta
b. Apr. 8, 1936
El Paso, Tex.
fields: Literature, Law

Latino writer and lawyer. Zeta Acosta was an important figure in the 1960's and 1970's Chicano movement. In 1966, after spending time in the Air Force and in college, he became a lawyer and gained fame defending Mexican American clients in several widely publicized trials. He wrote two novels—*The Autobiography of a Brown Buffalo* (1972) and its sequel *The Revolt of the Cockroach People* (1973)—in which he documented his struggle to define his own ethnic identity. In 1974 Acosta disappeared without a trace.

Acosta-Belén, Edna

b. Jan. 14, 1948
Hormigueros, Puerto Rico
fields: Education, Civil Rights, Women's Rights

Latina educator. Edna Acosta-Belén immigrated to the United States from Puerto Rico in 1967 to complete her education. Received her Ph.D. from Columbia University in 1977 and became an associate professor of Latin American and Caribbean studies at SUNY, Albany, in 1981. Became an advocate for the education and the civil rights of Puerto Ricans in the United States and helped pioneer the ethnic and women's study movements at SUNY, Albany. Also wrote several books concerning Puerto Rican women and Puerto Ricans in the United States, including *The Hispanic Experience in the United States* (1988) and *Researching Women in Latin America and the Caribbean* (1993).

Acton, Lord

full: John Emerich Edward Dalberg Acton
b. January 10, 1834
Naples, Italy
d. June 19, 1902
Tegernsee, Bavaria, Germany
fields: Historiography

Although he never succeeded in finishing his planned monumental "History of Liberty," Acton was one of the most learned scholars and probing intellects of his time. While a devout Roman Catholic, he was for much of his life at odds with the church hierarchy because of what he saw as its authoritarian tendencies. Acton was first and foremost a moralist, and his most passionate commitment was to the defense of individual freedom.

Acuña, Rudy

full: Rodolfo Francis Acuña
b. May 18, 1932
Los Angeles, Calif.
fields: Education, Civil Rights

Latino educator and activist. After earning a Ph.D. in Latin American history at the University of Southern California, Rudy Acuña began teaching at California State University, Northridge, in 1968, where he founded the department of Chicano studies and became active in the Chicano movement. Possibly the first person to teach a course in Mexican American history (at Mount St. Mary's College in Los Angeles in 1966). Best known for his book *Occupied America: The Chicano's Struggle Toward Liberation* (1972).

Adair, John L.

full: John Lynch Adair
b. 1828
northern Georgia
d. Oct. 21, 1896
Tahlequah, Okla.
fields: Native American Affairs, Government and Politics

Cherokee tribal leader John L. Adair played an important role in Cherokee affairs during the difficult years following the Trail of Tears; worked with a U.S. government commissioner in determining the boundaries between the Cherokee Nation and surrounding states.

Adam, James

b. July 21, 1732
Edinburgh, Scotland
d. October 20, 1794
London, England
fields: Architecture

Robert Adam, one of the greatest British architects, created a new approach to building design in the eighteenth century, which linked the architecture and the interior design of his buildings into a single design scheme. He is equally famous for a significant new style of decorative design that was named for him, the Adam style. His brother James Adam contributed to the Adam enterprise as a close family associate and business partner, and to a lesser degree as an architect and designer on his own merit.

Adam, Robert

b. July 3, 1728
Kirkcaldy, Fifeshire, Scotland
d. March 3, 1792
London, England
fields: Architecture

Robert Adam, one of the greatest British architects, created a new approach to building design in the eighteenth century, which linked the architecture and the interior design of his buildings into a single design scheme. He is equally famous for a significant new style of decorative design that soon was named for him, the Adam style. His brother James contributed to the Adam enterprise as a close family associate and business partner, and to a lesser degree as an architect and designer on his own merit.

Adam de la Halle

aka: Adam d'Arras
aka: Adam le Boscu d'Arras
aka: Adam le Bossu
b. c. 1250
probably Arras, France
d. c. 1285-1288
Naples, Italy, possibly after 1306, England
fields: Music, Literature

One of the few medieval musicians who composed both monophonic and polyphonic music, Adam de la Halle produced musical and literary works in virtually every genre of the thirteenth century.

Adams, Abigail

né: Abigail Smith
b. November 22, 1744
Weymouth, Massachusetts
d. October 28, 1818
Quincy, Massachusetts
fields: Women's Rights

An early proponent of humane treatment and equal education for women, Abigail Adams wrote eloquent, insightful letters which provide a detailed social history of her era and her life with John Adams.

Adams, Ansel

full: Ansel Easton Adams
b. Feb. 20, 1902
San Francisco, Calif.
d. Apr. 22, 1984
Carmel, Calif.
fields: Photography, Environmentalism

Photographer and environmentalist Ansel Adams published numerous collections of photographs of national parks and monuments, including Yosemite, and the Japanese Americans interned at Manzanar. He became a fellow of the American Academy of Arts and Sciences in 1966 and received the Presidential Medal of Freedom in 1980.

Adams, Faye

né: Faye Scruggs
b. c. 1936
fields: Music (rhythm-and-blues singer)

African American rhythm-and-blues singer. In 1953, at age seventeen, Faye Adams signed with the independent label Herald Records and produced her million-selling single "Shake a Hand." She followed this with the number-one hit "I'll Be True," selling 850,000 copies, and "Hurts Me to My Heart," her number one rhythm-and-blues hit of 1954. Adams moved from the Herald label to Imperial Records in 1957, but she was unable to rekindle her earlier popularity. She retired from the recording business in 1963.

Adams, Gerry

full: Gerard Adams
b. October 6, 1948
Belfast, Northern Ireland
fields: Government and Politics

Leader of Northern Ireland's Sinn Féin party. Gerry Adams became president of the party in 1983. Elected that year as a minister of Parliament from West Belfast, but refused to take seat because it would require his taking an oath of allegiance to the British queen. Behind-the-scenes figure in Protestant-Catholic peace negotiations from 1997 to 1999.

Adams, Henry

full: Henry Brooks Adams
b. February 16, 1838
Boston, Massachusetts
d. March 27, 1918
Washington, D.C.
fields: History, Literature

Adams was a first-rate historian who wrote several biographies and the monumental nine-volume *History of the United States of America* (1889-1891), covering the administrations of Thomas Jefferson and James Madison. His two most famous works are interconnected and autobiographical: *Mont-Saint-Michel and Chartres* (1904) and *The Education of Henry Adams* (1907).

Adams, John

b. October 30, 1735
Braintree, Massachusetts
d. July 4, 1826
Quincy, Massachusetts
fields: Government and Politics

As a member of the Continental Congress, Adams helped bring the American Colonies to the point of independence in 1776. As one of the new nation's first diplomats, he helped negotiate the treaty that ended the American War of Independence. He was the second president of the United States, 1797-1801.

Adams, John Quincy

b. July 11, 1767
Braintree, Massachusetts
d. February 23, 1848
Washington, D.C.
fields: Government and Politics

As diplomat, secretary of state, president (1825-1829), and member of the House of Representatives, in a career spanning the early national period to nearly the time of the Civil War, John Quincy Adams helped to shape America's major foreign and domestic policies, always in the direction of strengthening the nation as a unified whole.

Adams, Numa Pompilius Garfield

b. Feb. 26, 1885
Delaplane, Va.
d. Aug. 29, 1940
Chicago, Ill.
fields: Medicine (physician)

African American physician. Numa Pompilius Garfield Adams established a private medical practice in Chicago in 1925. On June 4, 1929, he accepted a position as dean of Howard University Medical College, the first African American to fill this role. Adams was a professor of medicine at Howard University until his death in 1940.

Adams, Oleta

b. 1961?
fields: Music (rhythm-and-blues singer)

African American rhythm-and-blues vocalist; Oleta Adams's powerful voice is capable of wide-ranging rhythm-and-blues styles; featured vocalist on British pop group Tears for Fears' 1989 album *Sowing the Seeds of Love*; Adams's 1990 debut album with Fontana\Polygram Records, *Circle of One*, contained the hit single "Get Here."

Adams, Robert Bradshaw

b. ?
Buffalo, N.Y.
fields: Military Affairs

African American military officer; Robert Bradshaw Adams received a B.A. in business administration from Canisius College and an M.B.A. focusing on automated data processing from George Washington University; Army administration postings have included finance officer, comptroller, commander for integration at Fort Benjamin Harrison and at the U.S. Army Administration Center, and commandant of the U.S. Army Institute of Administration; awards include the Legion of Merit, the Bronze Star, and the Army commendation Medal; after twenty-five years of service, rose to the rank of brigadier general.

Adams, Samuel

b. September 27, 1722
Boston, Massachusetts
d. October 2, 1803
Boston, Massachusetts
fields: Government and Politics

Strategically placed in Boston, the center of resistance to British colonial policies, Adams was one of the most significant organizers of the American Revolution.

Adams-Ender, Clara Leach

b. ?
fields: Military Affairs, Medicine

African American military officer; Clara Leach Adams-Ender received a B.S. in nursing from North Carolina Agricultural and Technical State University, an M.S. focusing on medical surgical nursing from the University of Minnesota, a degree from the Army War College, and an M.S. in military science from the Army Command and General Staff College; U.S. Army postings have included chief of nurse recruiting and inspector general; military awards include the Expert Field Medical Badge (first woman to receive it), the Meritorious Service Medal, and the Legion of Merit; rose to the rank of brigadier general.

Adario

aka: Kondiaronk
aka: Sastaretsi
aka: Gaspar Soiga
aka: Le Rat
b. c. 1650
Ontario, Canada
d. Aug. 1, 1701
Montreal, Canada
fields: Diplomacy, Government and Politics, Native American Affairs

Native American leader. Petun leader Adario skillfully thwarted a late seventeenth century French-Iroquois alliance.

Addams, Jane

b. September 6, 1860
Cedarville, Illinois
d. May 21, 1935
Chicago, Illinois
fields: Social Reform

In hundreds of books and articles and as cofounder and director of the Hull House settlement in Chicago, Addams promoted a variety of Social Reforms designed to facilitate the adjustment to urban, industrial America from 1890 to 1935.

Adderley, Cannonball

full: Julian Edwin Adderley
b. Sept. 15, 1928
Tampa, Fla.
d. Aug. 8, 1975
Gary, Ind.
fields: Music (jazz alto saxophonist)

African American jazz alto saxophonist. After directing a high school band, performing in U.S. Army bands, and playing in small ensembles, Julian Edwin "Cannonball" Adderley joined the Miles Davis Quintet in 1957. An ensemble formed two years later with his brother Nat, featuring hard bop and soul jazz, would thrive until Cannonball's death by stroke during a concert in 1975. Adderley incorporated blues and gospel stylings into his music, and his alto saxophone playing was said to be similar to that of Charlie Parker. He personally generated more than a dozen recordings, including the 1966 hit *Mercy, Mercy, Mercy! Live at "the Club,"* as well as five with the Miles Davis ensembles. He spent his final years performing, teaching, and lecturing.

Adderley, Nat, Sr.

full: Nathaniel Adderley, Sr.
b. Nov. 25, 1931
Tampa, Fla.
fields: Music (jazz trumpeter and cornetist)

African American trumpeter and cornetist. Nat Adderley, Sr., brother of Julian "Cannonball" Adderley, performed in an ensemble with his brother from the mid-1950's to 1975. After his brother's death, he formed his own ensemble. His most famous compositions include "Shout up a Morning," "Jive Samba," and "Work Song."

Addison, Adele

b. July 24, 1925
New York, N.Y.
fields: Music (soprano opera singer)

African American soprano opera singer. A Boston, Mass., debut in 1948 and an engagement in New York City in 1952 launched Adele Addison on a career featuring performances with major U.S. opera companies and orchestras. Addison has been an advocate of contemporary music but her specialty is baroque music. In 1963 she toured the Soviet Union. The institutions at which she has taught include the Eastman School, Rochester, New York, and the State University of New York.

Addison, Joseph

b. May 1, 1672
Milston, Wiltshire, England
d. June 17, 1719
London, England
fields: Literature, Journalism

With Richard Steele, Addison wrote *The Tatler* and *The Spectator*, whose combination of literature and journalism established the magazine as an important medium of cultural expression.

Adelard of Bath

b. c. 1075
Bath, England
d. after 1142-1146
fields: Mathematics (applied math and geometry)

Adelard of Bath helped establish classical and Arabic mathematics, especially geometry and astronomical math, in Western Europe. Wrote *De eodem et diverso* (c. 1116), *Quaestiones naturales* (c. 1107-1133), and *On the Astrolabe* (c. 1142-1146). Translated Euclid's *Elements* (c. 1107-1133). Taught in France, Sicily, Syria, and Palestine.

Adenauer, Konrad

b. January 5, 1876
Cologne, Germany
d. April 19, 1967
Rhöndorf, West Germany
fields: Government and Politics

Between 1917 and 1933, Adenauer served his country as Lord Mayor of Cologne, becoming, after 1945, founder of the Federal Republic of Germany and its first chancellor.

Adler, Alfred

b. February 7, 1870
Penzing, Austria
d. May 28, 1937
Aberdeen, Scotland
fields: Medicine, Social Sciences

Adler, the founder of individual psychology, introduced such fundamental mental-health concepts as "inferiority feeling," "life-style," "striving for superiority," and "social interest." The first to occupy a chair of medical psychology in the United States, Adler pioneered the use of psychiatry in both social work and early childhood education.

Adler, Felix

b. August 13, 1851
Alzey, Hesse-Darmstadt (now Germany)
d. April 24, 1933
New York, New York
fields: Education, Social Reform

Adler founded the Ethical Culture Society, whose goal was to overcome the divisions created by religious creeds and unite all people in ethical deeds.

Adoltay. *See* Big Tree

Adorno, Theodor

né: Theodor Wiesengrund
b. September 11, 1903
Frankfurt am Main, Germany
d. August 6, 1969
Visp, Switzerland
fields: Philosophy, Sociology, Literature, Language and Linguistics

A major figure in the Frankfurt School of Marxist social philosophy, Theodor Adorno tried to fuse philosophy and sociology, developing his concept of "negative dialectic" (in *Negative Dialectics*, 1966) designed to advance philosophical materialism. Adorno was among the first to propose a consistent theory of popular culture and to analyze the modern cultural market, mass cultural consumption, and what he and Max Horkheimer called the "culture industry"; he describes the need of the masses for distraction as both a product and a result of the existing capitalist economy. Known for critiques and analyses of the works of Bertolt Brecht, Jean-Paul Sartre, Franz Kafka, Samuel Beckett, Marcel Proust, James Joyce, other authors. Challenged traditional Marxist criticism and better equipped it to assess both the modernist revolt and the crisis of liberal bourgeois society in the postwar era.

Adouette. *See* Big Tree

Adrian IV

né: Nicholas Breakspear
aka: Nicholas Brekespere
b. c. 1110
near St. Albans, Hertfordshire, England
d. September 1, 1159
Anagni, Italy
fields: Religion and Theology, Diplomacy

Adrian IV served as Vatican diplomat to Scandinavia and later established policies and direction that led the medieval papacy to its thirteenth century zenith of power (Pope Adrian IV, 1154-1159).

Aduja, Peter Aquino

b. Oct. 19, 1920
Vigan, Ilocos Sur, the Philippines
fields: Government and Politics, Business and Industry

Peter Aquino Aduja, a lawyer and businessman, was the first Filipino American to be elected to the Hawaiian legislature prior to statehood. Aduja served as deputy attorney general 1957-1960 and as a Hawaii district court judge 1960-1962. In 1966, Aduja began the first of three terms as a representative of the district of Windwar on Oahu in the state legislature.

Aeken, Jeroen van. *See* Bosch, Hieronymus

Aeschylus

b. 525-524 B.C.E.
Eleusis, Greece
d. 456-455 B.C.E.
Gela, Sicily
fields: Theater and Entertainment

Aeschylus' dramaturgy marks a major stage in the development of Western theater, especially tragedy.

Aesop

b. Probably early sixth century B.C.E.
Thrace, Greece
d. Probably sixth century B.C.E.
Delphi, Greece
fields: Literature

Aesop is reputed to have been a prolific inventor of fables, in which animals are endowed with human speech, for the purpose of illustrating a moral (or immoral) lesson. He probably wrote nothing himself but was rather a famous teller of tales that were later set down. As other fables were invented and collected, the authority of his name became attached to them.

Afonso I

b. c. 1108
Guimarães, Portugal
d. December 6, 1185
Coimbra, Portugal
fields: Monarchy, Government and Politics

Through astute leadership in military victories over Muslims and Christian Iberian neighbors, Afonso created the independent monarchy of Portugal and became its first king.

Agassiz, Elizabeth Cabot Cary

né: Elizabeth Cabot Cary
b. December 5, 1822
Boston, Massachusetts
d. June 27, 1907
Arlington, Massachusetts
fields: Education

First president and cofounder of Radcliffe College, Agassiz helped create a college for women taught by the faculty of Harvard University.

Agassiz, Louis

full: Jean Louis Rodolphe Agassiz
b. May 28, 1807
Motier-en-Vuly, Switzerland
d. December 14, 1873
Cambridge, Massachusetts
fields: Natural History, Education

Agassiz created an awareness of the importance of the study of natural history in the United States with his founding of the Museum of Comparative Zoology at Harvard University. He was an early pioneer in making scientific studies an integral part of the curriculum at American colleges and universities.

Agesilaus II

b. c. 444 B.C.E.
Sparta
d. c. 360 B.C.E.
Cyrene, Libya
fields: Government and Politics, Warfare and Conquest

By common consent the most powerful and illustrious Greek leader of his day, Agesilaus took Sparta to its peak of influence. Unfortunately, his policies led to a devastating defeat at Leuctra in 371, and at his death he left an impoverished and weakened kingdom that would never again play a dominant role in Greek affairs.

Agins, Michell

b. 1956
fields: Photography

African American photographer. Following studies at Loyola University, Chicago, Illinois, Michell Agins accepted a position in 1983 as the mayor of Chicago's official photographer. She also is noted as the first black woman to become a member of the International Photographers of the Motion Picture and Television Industries Union.

Agnesi, Maria Gaetana

b. May 16, 1718
Milan, Italy
d. Jan. 9, 1799
Milan, Italy
fields: Mathematics (algebra, applied math, calculus, and geometry)

Maria Gaetana Agnesi is considered the first female mathematician in modern Western civilization. She unified calculus, spoke seven languages, defended education for women, published *Propositiones philosophicae* (1738), was elected to Bologna Academy of Science, was appointed chair of mathematics and natural philosophy at University of Bologna.

Agnew, Spiro T.

b. November 9, 1918
Baltimore, Maryland
d. September 17, 1996
Berlin, Maryland
fields: Government and Politics

Richard M. Nixon's controversial vice president from 1968 to 1973. Spiro T. Agnew resigned from office in shame in 1973 after admitting to tax fraud.

Agricola, Georgius

né: Georg Bauer
b. March 24, 1494
Glauchau, Saxony
d. November 21, 1555
Chemnitz, Saxony
fields: Geology

Agricola was the forerunner of the new period of scientific investigation involving study and description of natural phenomena (especially geological in nature), preparation of metals from ores, and the development of mechanical procedures. He is regarded as the father of modern mineralogy.

Agrippa, Marcus Vipsanius

b. c. 63 B.C.E.
place unknown
d. March, 12 B.C.E.
Rome
fields: Government and Politics, Warfare and Conquest

Agrippa's military genius, on both land and sea, provided Augustus with the support he needed to establish the Roman principate. His gift for planning and building contributed to the improvement of Rome's roads, water supply, and major public buildings.

Aguilar, Robert Peter

b. Apr. 15, 1931
Maderas, Calif.
fields: Law

Latino attorney and U.S. district court judge. Robert Peter Aguilar earned a law degree at Hastings College of Law in San Francisco and practiced law from 1960 to 1979. In 1979 he began serving as the California Superior Court Judge for Santa Clara County. Appointed in 1980 to serve as a federal judge for the U.S. District Court in San Francisco. In 1990 Aguilar was found guilty of illegally disclosing wiretap information, a decision that was overturned by the U.S. Court of Appeals for the Ninth Circuit on April 19, 1994.

Aguilera-Hellweg, Max

b. 1955
Fresno, Calif.
fields: Photography

Latino photographer. Max Aguilera-Hellweg gained fame for his unusual photographic portraits of a wide range of subjects. After photographing a neurosurgeon in the operating room in 1989, Aguilera-Hellweg worked on a book of photographs of surgery. In the 1990's, he began photographing people in the motion picture and entertainment industry and was commissioned, along with seventy-four other people, to photograph celebrities for the book *A Day in the Life of Hollywood* (1992).

Aguinaldo, Emilio

full: Emilio Aguinaldo y Famy
b. March 23, 1869
near Cavite, Luzon, Philippines

d. February 6, 1964
Manila, Philippines
fields: Government and Politics

Filipino revolutionary and guerrilla leader. Though Aguinaldo has been criticize for his execution of revolutionary leader Andres Bonifacio and for the help he gave to the Japanese when they invaded in 1941, he is widely regarded as a national hero by Filipinos and honored as the nation's first president.

Agwelius (Swift). *See* Bruce, Louis R.

Ah-Sing, Norman. *See* Assing, Norman

Ahmad, Sayyid

full: Sayyid Ahmad Khan
aka: Sir Sayyid Ahmad Khan
b. October 17, 1817
Delhi, India
d. March 27, 1898
Alīgarh, India
fields: Education, Literature, Religion and Theology

Sayyid Ahmad's theological writings summarized a number of important trends within Islamic thought and attempted to redirect religious thinking to meet the challenges of the modern, European-dominated, world. His religious views were, however, too controversial to be widely influential. Yet in the field of education he founded the Muhammadan Anglo-Oriental College, and in literature he created modern Urdu prose.

Ahmad ibn Hanbal

né: Ahmad ibn Muhammad
aka: Ibn Hanbal
b. December, 780
Baghdad, Iraq
d. July, 855
Baghdad, Iraq
fields: Law, Theology

Ibn Hanbal sought to conjoin jurisprudence closely with the study of texts recording the teachings and practices of the Prophet Muhammad. Ibn Hanbal's ideas and his example of steadfast resistance to political persecution inspired the formation of the fourth classical school of Islamic law.

Ahn Chang-ho

b. Nov. 9, 1878
Pyongan, Korea
d. Mar. 10, 1938
Korea
fields: Government and Politics

U.S.-educated Korean political activist who worked for Korean sovereignty after Japan established a protectorate there and then annexed the nation in 1910. The acting prime minister of the Korean provisional government, Ahn Chang-ho was arrested by the Japanese police in Korea in 1935 and charged with anti-Japanese activities. He was tortured while in prison and died shortly after his release.

Ahn, Philip

b. March 29, 1911
Los Angeles, Calif.
d. February 28, 1978
Los Angeles, Calif.
fields: Theater and Entertainment

Korean American actor. The son of Korean immigrants, Ahn was graduated from the University of Southern California and in 1936 embarked on a film career in *The General Died at Dawn*. Over the next four decades, Ahn appeared in more than fifty films, including *Thank You, Mr. Moto* (1937), *The Good Earth* (1937), *Love Is a Many Splendored Thing* (1955), and *The World's Greatest Athlete* (1973). He became known for his portrayal of stereotypically cold, cunning Asian American villains, especially in World War II films. Ahn was familiar to television audiences as the master Kan in the *Kung Fu* series (1972-1975). He was the first Asian American actor to be honored with a star on the "Walk of Fame" by the Hollywood Chamber of Commerce.

Ai

né: Florence Anthony
b. Oct. 21, 1947
Albany, Texas
fields: Poetry

This multiracial poet—half Japanese, one-fourth black, one-eighth Choctaw, one-sixteenth Irish, and one-sixteenth unknown—is known for dramatic monologues, some that assume the voice of public figures such as Alfred Hitchcock and James Dean. Ai's books include *Cruelty* (1973), *Killing Floor* (1979), *Sin* (1986), *Fate* (1991), and *Greed* (1993).

Aiken, Kimberly Clarice

b. 1975?
Columbia, S.C.
fields: Theater and Entertainment (beauty pageant winner)

African American former Miss America. On September 18, 1993, Kimberly Clarice Aiken was crowned as the seventy-third Miss America. At eighteen, she was one of the pageant's youngest title holders; the fifth African American woman to win the crown; and the first African American contestant from the South to receive this honor.

Aiken, Loretta Mary. *See* Mabley, Moms

Ailey, Alvin, Jr.

b. January 5, 1931
Rogers, Tex.
d. Dec.1, 1989
New York, N.Y.
fields: Dance

African American modern dancer, choreographer, and artistic director. Alvin Ailey studied dance while attending various California colleges, 1949-1953, and became a dancer and choreographer with the pioneering Lester Horton Dancers, 1951-1953. After Ailey settled in New York he studied modern dance under well-known artists such as Martha Graham, Hanya Holm, Anna Sokolow, and Charles Weidman; he studied ballet with Karel Shook. He founded Alvin Ailey American Dance Theater in 1958 in New York. For the company's debut Ailey choreographed *Blues Suite*, which has been hailed as an important step in the development of African American dance. Tours abroad during the 1960's brought unprecedented acclaim for an American company. Ailey's unique jazz style has been called "stark," "violent," and "beautiful." Among his many honors, he has received the United Nations Peace Medal.

Aiso, John

b. Dec. 14, 1909
Burbank, Calif.
d. Dec. 29, 1987
Los Angeles, Calif.
fields: Jurisprudence, Military Affairs

John Aiso, a second-generation Japanese American and Harvard-educated lawyer, was drafted into the U.S. Army during World War II, where he earned the rank of lieutenant colonel. He was appointed to the Los Angeles Superior Court in 1958 and ten years later was appointed to the California Court of Appeals.

Aitken, William Maxwell. *See* Beaverbrook, Lord

Akaka, Daniel Kahikina

b. Sept. 11, 1924
Honolulu, Territory of Hawaii
fields: Government and Politics

Daniel Kahikina Akaka, a native Hawaiian and a Democrat, was elected in 1976 to the U.S. House of Representatives. He served seven consecutive terms in Congress and, in 1990, was appointed to the U.S. Senate. That fall, he was elected to the Senate over popular moderate Republican Patricia Saiki, largely because of his popularity among native Hawaiians and the working class.

Akalaitis, Joanne

b. June 29, 1937
Cicero, Illinois
fields: Theater and Entertainment (drama)

Akalaitis is one of the preeminent American theatrical directors of the late twentieth century. Unlike most directors on the commercial stage, she develops her productions using a collaborative method. Her work as a playwright and a director is considered eclectic and avant-garde.

Akbar

full: Abū-ul-Fath Jahāl-ud-Dīn Muhammad Akbar
b. October 15, 1542
Umarkot, Sind
d. October 17, 1605
Āgra, India
fields: Monarchy

As one of India's greatest Mughal emperors (1562-1605), Akbar conquered and unified northern India under his rule. In addition to military conquest, his most significant achievements include the development of an efficient bureaucratic structure, patronage of the arts, and enlightened policies of religious toleration.

Akhenaton

né: Amenhotep IV
aka: Amenophis IV
aka: Ikhnaton
b. c. 1390 B.C.E.
Egypt
d. c. 1360 B.C.E.
Akhetaton (modern Tel el Amarna), Egypt
fields: Government and Politics, Religion and Theology

Akhenaton is credited with the establishment of monotheism in Egypt; he built a new capital, Akhetaton, in honor of Aton, the sun god.

Akhmatova, Anna

né: Anna Andreyevna Gorenko
b. June 23, 1889
Bol'shoy Fontan, near Odessa, Ukraine, Russian Empire
d. March 5, 1966
Domodedovo, near Moscow, U.S.S.R.
fields: Literature

Akhmatova was one of the most acclaimed and revered poets of twentieth century Russia, struggling throughout her life to express with intimacy and insight the plight of a woman in an adversive society. For long periods she was forbidden to publish her works, but by the end of her life her constant poetic inspiration of others had earned for her the International Taormina Poetry Prize (Italy, 1964) and an honorary degree from the University of Oxford (England, 1965).

Akiba ben Joseph

aka: Aqiba ben Joseph
b. c. 40 C.E.
probably near Lydda (modern Lod), Palestine
d. c. 135 C.E.
Caesaria, Palestine
fields: Religion and Theology, Government and Politics

The most influential rabbi in the formation of Jewish legal tradition and Mishnah, Akiba is the one scholar most often quoted in the text. He espoused the unsuccessful cause of Simeon Bar Kokhba and died a martyr. The legends about Akiba have been almost as influential as his teachings and life.

Akihito

b. December 23, 1933
Tokyo, Japan
fields: Government and Politics

By linking the ancient traditions of Japan to the modern age, Emperor Akihito, Japan's nonpolitical head of state, symbolizes his nation's commitment to democracy while Japan learns from its militaristic past.

Akiyoshi, Toshiko

b. December 12, 1929
Ryoyo, Manchuria, China
fields: Music

A composer, bandleader, and pianist who has significantly enriched jazz through a blend of Eastern and Western instruments, techniques, and textures. Akiyoshi has created an entire library of her own compositions and arrangements and has organized virtuoso jazz orchestras to play them, resulting in a series of unique recordings.

Alanbrooke, First Viscount

né: Alan Francis Brooke
aka: Sir Alan Francis Brooke
b. July 23, 1883
Bagnères de Bigorre, France
d. June 17, 1963
Hartley Wintney, Hampshire, England
fields: Military Affairs

Brooke became the chief spokesman for British strategic priorities. More than any other English military man, he helped to shape the strategy which brought victory to the Western Allies in World War II.

Alarcón, Norma

b. 1943?
Monclova, Mexico
fields: Literature

Latina writer. Chicana feminist scholar Norma Alarcón is known primarily for her essays and her translations of literary criticism and feminist essays into Spanish—including, with Ana Castillo, the influential collection *Esta puente, mi espalda: Voces de mujeres tercermundistas en los Estados Unidos* (1988; *This Bridge Called My Back: Writings of Radical Women of Color*, 1988). Other published works include the scholarly books *Bibliography of Hispanic Women Writers* (1980), with Sylvia Kossnar, and *The Sexuality of Latinas* (1989) and *Chicana Critical Issues* (1993), which she edited with Cherríe Moraga and Ana Castillo.

Alatorre, Richard

b. May 15, 1943
Los Angeles, Calif.
fields: Government and Politics

California politician. After earning degrees from California State University, Los Angeles, and the University of Southern California, Richard Alatorre served in the California state assembly from 1972 to 1985. He then was elected to the Los Angeles City Council, where he served as chairman of the budget committee and became an influential member of the Metropolitan Transportation Authority (MTA) governing board.

Albee, Edward

full: Edward Franklin Albee
b. March 12, 1928
Virginia
fields: Theater and Entertainment, Literature

Edward Albee was one of the most significant and productive American playwrights since the presentation of his first play, *The Zoo Story*, in 1959. Writing with a sure hand and balanced sense of the dramatic, he forged new ground with his tightly constructed absurdist plays, often surrealistic in their execution. His controversial 1962 play *Who's Afraid of Virginia Woolf?* questions many of America's most cherished values and traditions, such as beliefs about the family and the child-parent relationship. Although the play was nominated for a Pulitzer Prize, its controversial nature, language, and iconoclasm mitigated against that; he subsequently won a Pulitzer Prize for *A Delicate Balance* (1966). In 1980, he received the gold medal in drama from the American Academy and Institute of Arts and Letters and in 1985 was inducted into the Theater Hall of Fame. In 1994, he received the Lifetime Achievement Award from the William Inge Festival.

Albert Edward. *See* Edward VII

Albert Frederick Alfred George. *See* George VI

Alberti, Leon Battista

b. February 18, 1404
Genoa

d. April, 1472
Rome
fields: Architecture, Philosophy

Alberti is identified by Renaissance historians as an archetype of the universal man. He established a leading reputation as a theorist and practitioner of the visual arts, notably in the field of architecture. As a Humanist, he was the author of numerous moral dialogues.

Albertus Magnus, Saint

b. c. 1200
Lauingen, Swabia
d. November 15, 1280
Cologne
fields: Education, Science

Albertus expanded scientific knowledge through experimentation and observation. As an Aristotelian, he reconciled reason with revelation.

Albizu, Olga

b. 1924
Ponce, Puerto Rico
fields: Art (painter)

Latina painter. In 1948 Olga Albizu graduated from the University of Puerto Rico, where she studied under Spanish painter Estéban Vicente. In 1956 she moved to the United States and held her first exhibit of abstract expressionist paintings. Her painting *Growth* (1960) gained national recognition and was used on the cover of an album by bossa nova musician Stan Getz. Albizu continued to paint album covers for other musicians, which further increased her popularity.

Albizu Campos, Pedro

b. Sept. 12, 1891
Ponce, Puerto Rico
d. Apr. 21, 1965
San Juan, Puerto Rico
fields: Social Reform, Civil Rights

Latino nationalist leader. After earning a law degree from Harvard University in 1923, Pedro Albizu Campos returned to Puerto Rico and joined the Nationalist Party, which sought independence for Puerto Rico. In 1930 he became head of the party but lost the 1932 elections, prompting him to reject democracy in favor of revolution. In 1936 he was arrested and convicted of conspiracy in the United States. Albizu returned to Puerto Rico in 1948 and continued his revolutionary work. Albizu was jailed again in 1954 after Nationalists opened fire at the visitors' gallery of the U.S. House of Representatives but was moved to a hospital in 1956 because of failing health.

Alboin

b. Sixth century
Pannonia (modern northwest Hungary)
d. 572
Verona, Italy
fields: Monarchy, Government and Politics, Military Affairs

As a powerful and aggressive king of the Lombards in Pannonia, Alboin successfully invaded northern Italy in 568, countering the Byzantines and establishing a kingdom that lasted for more than two centuries.

Albright, Gerald

b. Aug. 30, 1957
Los Angeles, Calif.
fields: Music (saxophonist)

African American saxophonist. Gerald Albright began playing bass at the University of Redlands, California. Maceo Parker of the James Brown group was his primary influence. Albright has played with a host of well-known performers including Cab Calloway, Les McCann, Patrice Rushen, Anita Baker, and Janet Jackson. He has also worked with groups such as Third World and the Temptations.

Albright, Madeleine

né: Madeleine Korbel
b. May 15, 1937
Prague, Czechoslovakia
fields: Diplomacy, Government and Politics

As ambassador to the United Nations and as the first woman to hold the office of secretary of state, Albright helped to shape a foreign policy emphasizing an activist role for the United States.

Albuquerque, Afonso de

b. 1453
Alhandra, near Lisbon, Portugal
d. December 15, 1515
at sea, near Goa Harbor
fields: Government and Politics, Military Affairs

Albuquerque, called "the Great" and "the Portuguese Mars," conquered Goa in India (1510) and Malacca on the Malay Peninsula (1511), ended the Arabian trade monopoly in Asia, made Goa a center of the Portuguese colonial government and commerce in that area, and developed colonial administration using native officials. He served as the second Portuguese governor of India. His most lasting contribution was the foundation of the Portuguese colonial empire in the East.

Alcayaga, Lucila Godoy. *See* Mistral, Gabriela

Alcibiades

b. c. 450 B.C.E.
Athens?, Greece
d. 404 B.C.E.
Phrygia, Asia Minor
fields: Government and Politics, Warfare and Conquest

Although it might be argued that Alcibiades was a demagogue, a traitor, a heretic, and morally dissolute, he was a gifted politician and military leader—and certainly one of the most romantic figures of the Peloponnesian War.

Alcindor, Lew. *See* Abdul-Jabbar, Kareem

Alcmaeon

b. c. 510 B.C.E.
Croton, Magna Graecia (southern Italy)
d. c. 430 B.C.E.
place unknown
fields: Medicine, Philosophy

Alcmaeon was one of the earliest Greeks known to have written on medicine and the first to have practiced scientific dissection. He held that the brain is the central organ of sensation and that health is the result of an equilibrium of qualities or forces in the body.

Alcorn, George Edward

b. March 22, 1940
fields: Physics, Invention and Technology (nuclear physicist, inventor, and educator)

African American nuclear physicist, inventor, and educator; George Edward Alcorn invented an imaging X-ray spectrometer while working at the National Aeronautics and Space Administration (NASA); received the 1984 NASA/Goddard Space Flight Center Inventor of the Year Award.

Alcott, Bronson

full: Amos Bronson Alcott
b. November 29, 1799
Wolcott, Connecticut
d. March 4, 1888
Concord, Massachusetts
fields: Education, Philosophy

Alcott was a teacher and a prominent member of New England's Transcendental community. His educational methods focused on moral, spiritual, and imaginative development and encouraged independent thought. He also founded a short-lived utopian community called Fruitlands. He is perhaps most famous as the father of author Louisa May Alcott.

Alcott, Louisa May

b. November 29, 1832
Germantown, Pennsylvania
d. March 6, 1888
Boston, Massachusetts

fields: Literature

Assuming financial responsibility for the support of her family, Louisa May Alcott launched a literary career as a prolific writer of works for both adult and juvenile audiences. Her writing reveals the vitality of everyday life, with the family being her most frequent subject.

Alcuin

né: Alhwini
aka: Albinus
b. c. 735
probably near York, Yorkshire, England
d. May 19, 804
Tours, France
fields: Education, Literature, Religion and Theology, Monarchy

Although an Englishman, Alcuin became court tutor and educational and religious adviser to Charlemagne, King of the Franks and Lombards. Reforms inspired by him made an indelible impression on the later traditions and practices of the Catholic church.

Aldrich, Abby Greene. *See* Rockefeller, Abby Aldrich

Aldridge, Ira Frederick

b. c. 1807
New York, N.Y., or Belair, Md.
d. Aug. 10, 1867
Lodz, Poland
fields: Theater and Entertainment (actor)

African American actor; nineteenth century Shakespearean actor who found success on the European continent; Ira Frederick Aldridge left the U.S. for England in 1824 or 1825 and there claimed Senegal as his birthplace; best known for roles in *Othello*, *Titus Andronicus*, *Richard III*, *King Lear*, and *Macbeth*; toured Great Britain, Belgium, Germany, Austria, France, Turkey, Poland, Sweden, Switzerland, and Russia, where he reportedly introduced the Russian public to *Richard III*, *Macbeth*, and *King Lear*; became a naturalized British citizen in 1863.

Aleekchea'ahoosh. *See* Plenty Coups

Aleksandrov, Pavel Sergeevich

b. May 7, 1896
Bogorodsk (now Noginsk), Russia
d. Nov. 16, 1982
Moscow, Soviet Union
fields: Mathematics (topology)

Pavel Sergeevich Aleksandrov's work in the field of mathematics includes calculating the cardinality of the Borel sets, creating the homological dimension theory, proving fundamental duality theorems for open sets, giving the definitive form of the axioms of a topological space, and laying the foundations for the homology theory of general topological spaces. He published the classic textbook *Topologie* (1935) with Heinz Hopf. Member of US National Academy of Sciences and Academy of Sciences of the USSR; vice president of the International Congress of Mathematicians.

Alekseyev, Konstantin Sergeyevich. *See* Stanislavsky, Konstantin

Alembert, Jean le Rond d'

aka: Jean-Baptiste Daremberg
b. November 17, 1717
Paris, France
d. October 29, 1783
Paris, France
fields: Mathematics, Physics, Philosophy, Music

A pioneer in the use of differential calculus, d'Alembert applied his mathematical genius to solve problems in mechanics. He provided valuable assistance with the *Encyclopédie* and wrote a number of treatises on musical theory.

Alexander I

b. December 23, 1777
St. Petersburg, Russia
d. December 1, 1825
Taganrog, Russia
fields: Government and Politics

As czar of Russia (1801-1825), Alexander I initiated a series of educational, social, and political reforms early in his reign. He was instrumental in forming the coalition that defeated Napoleon I and played a major role in the Congress of Vienna following the Napoleonic Wars.

Alexander II

né: Alexander Nikolayevich Romanov
b. April 29, 1818
Moscow, Russia
d. March 13, 1881
St. Petersburg, Russia
fields: Government and Politics

Czar of Russia, 1855-1881. Called the czar liberator, Alexander emancipated the serfs in 1861, the first of political and legal reforms designed to quicken the pace of modernization in Russia. Despite the reforms, rising expectations caused dissidents to become radicalized. Hence, Alexander's life was ended by political assassins, and reforms were suspended by his successor.

Alexander III

né: Roland Bandinelli
b. Early twelfth century
Siena, Italy
d. August 30, 1181
Città Castellana, Italy
fields: Religion and Theology

Despite decades of controversy, through patience, moderation, and practicality, Alexander III established administrative and legal reforms that strengthened the papal monarchy and contributed to the development of canon law. Although exiled from Rome for much of his papacy, he was recognized as the head of the church by most European leaders from 1160-1181.

Alexander VI

né: Rodrigo de Borja y Doms
aka: Rodrigo Borgia
b. 1431
Játiva, Valencia
d. August 18, 1503
Rome
fields: Politics, Government and Politics, Religion and Theology

Pope Alexander VI, 1492-1503. Alexander VI's policies contributed to the growth of papal temporal power in the Papal States. A discriminating patron of the arts, he employed a number of noteworthy artists, including Pinturicchio and Michelangelo.

Alexander, Archie Alphonso

b. May 14, 1888
Ottumwa, Iowa
d. Jan. 4, 1958
Des Moines, Iowa
fields: Architecture

African American architectural engineer. Archie Alphonso Alexander specialized in the design and construction of bridges and tunnels located throughout the United States. He attended the University of Iowa and in 1912 obtained a B.S. in civil engineering. From 1954 to 1955 he acted as governor of the U.S. Virgin Islands, the first Republican to hold this position.

Alexander, Clifford L., Jr.

b. Sept. 21, 1933
New York, N.Y.
fields: Government and Politics, Military Affairs

African American government official. After graduating from Harvard and Yale, Clifford L. Alexander, Jr., served under the Lyndon Johnson administration as chair of the Equal Employment Opportunity Commission. In 1977 he accepted President Jimmy Carter's appointment as secretary of the Army. As the first African American to run a military department, Alexander increased the progress of ongoing Army desegregation and improved the readiness of the troops. He served in this position until 1980.

Alexander, Lenora Cole

b. Mar. 9, 1935
Buffalo, N.Y.
fields: Government and Politics

African American political appointee. Lenora Cole Alexander earned B.S. (1957), master's of education (1969), and Ph.D. (1974) degrees from the State University of New York at Buffalo. She worked her way through various college administration jobs (1969-1981). In 1981 Alexander accepted an appointment under the Reagan administration as director of the Women's Bureau of the Department of Labor. She also served on the advisory committee on women veterans' affairs for the U.S. Veterans Administration (1983-1986), and on the international front as U.S. representative to the International Commission on the Status of Women (1983) and to the United Nations Conference on the Decade for Women (1985). In 1986 she returned to academia.

Alexander Nevsky

b. c. 1220
Northern Pereiaslavl, Vladimir-Suzdal
d. November 14, 1263
Gorodets, Vladimir-Suzdal
fields: Government and Politics, Warfare and Conquest

Alexander strengthened the Republic of Novgorod by defeating Swedish, Livonian, and German invaders. By skillful diplomacy and appeasement policies, he also secured limited autonomy for the entire Grand Duchy of Vladimir-Suzdal from the Tatars of the Golden Horde.

Alexander the Great

b. 356 B.C.E.
Pella, Macedonia
d. June 13, 323 B.C.E.
Babylon
fields: Government and Politics, Warfare and Conquest

By military genius, political acumen, and cultural vision, Alexander unified and Hellenized most of the civilized ancient world and in so doing became a legendary figure in subsequent ages.

Alfonso X

b. November 23, 1221
probably Burgos, Castile
d. April 4, 1284
Seville, Andalusia
fields: Monarchy, Government and Politics, Literature, Law, Historiography

Alfonso's wide-ranging interests earned for him the title "el Sabio," or "the Wise." In literature, law, historiography, and science, this King of Castile and León sponsored numerous advances of lasting consequence for Spanish culture.

Alfonso, Carlos

b. 1950
Havana, Cuba
d. Feb. 19, 1991
Miami, Fla.
fields: Art (painter)

Latino painter. Carlos Alfonso was already well known in Cuba when he moved to the United States in 1980. His abstract paintings, which have been compared to the surrealistic work of Spanish painter Pablo Picasso, are characterized by mysterious images (many of which have been borrowed from Christianity and Afro-Cuban religions) that explore themes of oppression and exile. After moving to the United States, Alfonso exhibited his work in several group shows and won numerous awards for his art.

Alford, Thomas Wildcat

aka: Gaynwawpiahsika
b. July 15, 1860
near Sasakwa, Okla.
d. Aug. 3, 1938
Shawnee, Okla.
fields: Education, Native American Affairs

Shawnee educator, lobbyist, and government official. Drawing on knowledge of white customs gained from his education with whites, Thomas Wildcat Alford counseled Indians about their land rights and helped them to cope with rapid cultural changes.

Alfred the Great

b. 849
Wantage, Berkshire, England
d. October 26, 899
place unknown
fields: Government and Politics

Through courage, leadership, and practical good sense, Alfred preserved the English kingdom of Wessex from Viking armies and laid the foundation for the later reconquest and unification of all England.

Alfvén, Hannes

full: Hannes Olof Gösta Alfvén
b. May 30, 1908
Norrköping, Sweden
d. Apr. 2, 1995
Djursholm, Sweden
fields: Astronomy, Physics

Hannes Alfvén is the founder of magnetohydrodynamics. He was instrumental in the development of several modern fields of physics, such as plasma physics, the physics of charged particle beams, and interplanetary and magnetospheric physics. He initially proposed a galactic magnetic field, and he codiscovered the source of astronomical radio waves. He won the Nobel Prize in Physics in 1970. In 1990, the Alfvén Laboratory was founded at the Royal Institute of Technology.

Algarín, Miguel

b. Sept. 11, 1941
Santurce, Puerto Rico
fields: Literature

Latino writer. Miguel Algarín, an important figure in New York City's Puerto Rican literary community, refers to himself as "Nuyorican" (a combination of "New" from New York and "rican" from Puerto Rican). He teaches English literature and helped found a Puerto Rican studies program at Rutgers University in New Brunswick, New Jersey. He also promoted Nuyorican culture by opening the Nuyorican Poets' Café and, along with Miguel Piñero, collecting the writings of Nuyoricans in *Nuyorican Poetry: An Anthology of Puerto Rican Words and Feelings* (1975). Algarín's own Nuyorican poetry books include *On Call* (1980) and *Time's Now/Ya es tiempo* (1985).

Algaze, Mario

b. Oct. 4, 1947
Havana, Cuba
fields: Photography

Latino photographer. After fleeing Cuba in 1960, Mario Algaze's family settled in Miami. In the late 1960's Algaze worked as an apprentice to a professional photographer and began taking photographs that captured the architecture and the people of Little Havana in Miami. Beginning in the 1970's, he traveled frequently to Latin America and photographed people going about their daily business, capturing the charming aspects of life in such countries as Ecuador, Colombia, and Mexico. In 1991 Algaze showed his Latin American work in a solo exhibit called Portfolio Latinoamericano.

Alger, Horatio

full: Horatio Alger, Jr.
b. January 13, 1832
Chelsea, Massachusetts
d. July 18, 1899
Natick, Massachusetts
fields: Literature

Alger was a writer of books for juveniles who popularized business as a career for young boys, while at the same time motivating the poor to work hard in hopes of success. Because of the popularity of his books, the story of anyone who became successful in real life became known as a "Horatio Alger story."

Alhazen

né: Abu ʿAli al-Hasan ibn al-Haytham

b. 965
Basra, Iraq
d. 1039
Cairo, Egypt
fields: Physics, Astronomy, Mathematics, Medicine

Alhazen, Islam's greatest scientist, devoted his life to physics, astronomy, mathematics, and medicine. His treatise *Optics*, in which he deftly used experiments and advanced mathematics to understand the action of light, exerted a profound influence on many European natural philosophers.

Ali, Muhammad

né: Cassius Marcellus Clay, Jr.
aka: Cassius Clay
b. January 17, 1942
Louisville, Kentucky
fields: Sports (boxing)

Ali is probably the greatest as well as the best-recognized sports personality of the twentieth century. He brought heavyweight boxing matches to areas of the world never before regarded as important in boxing circles.

Ali, Noble Drew

né: Timothy Drew
b. Jan. 8, 1886
North Carolina
d. July 20, 1929
Chicago, Ill.
fields: Religion and Theology

African American founder of the Moorish Science movement. After discovering Islam during international travels, Noble Drew Ali returned to the United States as a self-proclaimed messenger from Allah. He preached to African Americans that empowerment over racial and economic oppression was possible if they would acknowledge that their group identity had been stolen by Anglo-Christians and embrace Islam as their rightful religion and Morocco as the homeland from which they had emerged. He established the first Moorish Science Temple in 1913, and the movement grew to a membership of twenty to thirty thousand. After Ali died while awaiting trial for murder, the movement split into factions, one segment of which followed former member Wallace D. Fard and went on to become the Nation of Islam.

ʿAlī ibn Abī Ṭālib

b. c. 600
Mecca, Arabia
d. 661
Kūfa, Iraq
fields: Religion and Theology, Philosophy, Government and Politics

Last of the four caliphs of Islam after the death of the Prophet Muhammad and one of the first converts to Islam, ʿAlī ibn Abī Ṭālib was a brave warrior and a scholar. Shiʿites contend that ʿAlī should have been chosen as the first caliph after the death of Muhammad.

Alice, Mary

né: Mary Alice Smith
b. December 3, 1941
Indianola, Miss.
fields: Theater andf Entertainment (actress)

African American actress; in 1979, Mary Alice received Obie awards for her roles in *Julius Caesar* and *Nongogo*; was cast as a professor and college dorm adviser on the hit NBC television series *A Different World* in 1987; received an Emmy Award for her recurring role on the series *I'll Fly Away*.

Alicia, Juana

né: Juana Alicia Montoya
b. 1953
fields: Art (painter)

Latina painter. Juana Alicia uses her art to express her personal experiences and the social concerns of Latinos. She grew up as a farmworker in Salinas, California, and participated in the local labor rights movement. During the 1980's she painted several murals in San Francisco's Mission District, including *Las Lechugeras* (1983; the lettuce workers), an expression of her past as a farmworker that also criticized the overuse of pesticides; *Para las Rosas* (1986; for the roses); and, along with three other artists, *Illuminations* (1986).

Allalimya Takanin. *See* Looking Glass

Allegri, Antonio. *See* Correggio

Allen, Betty Lou

b. Mar. 17, 1930
Campbell, Ohio
fields: Music (mezzo-soprano opera singer)

African American mezzo-soprano. In a career that has included performance and teaching, Betty Lou Allen has been a guest vocalist with numerous choirs and opera companies, performing in such works as Virgil Thomson's *Four Saints in Three Acts* (1952), *Show Boat* (1954), Julia Perry's *Stabat Mater* (1958), and Scott Joplin's *Treemonisha* (1975). After serving on the faculties of the Manhattan School of Music and the North Carolina School of the Arts, she accepted the executive directorship at the Harlem School of the Arts in 1979.

Allen, Byron

b. Apr. 22, 1961
Detroit, Mich.
fields: Theater and Entertainment (comedian)

African American comedian. In a career that has comprised writing and performance, Byron Allen has provided comedy material to such comedians as Freddie Prinze and Jimmie "J.J." Walker. From 1979 to 1984, Allen cohosted the television series *Real People*. He has also made guest appearances on *The Tonight Show*.

Allen, Debbie

b. Jan 16, 1950
Houston, Tex.
fields: Dance, Theater and Entertainment, Television, Film

African American dancer, actress, choreographer, director, and producer. Debbie Allen's abundant theater credits include a Tony award nomination for her title role in *Sweet Charity* (1986), and a Drama Desk Award for her role as Anita in *West Side Story*. Her television credits include choreographer of many Academy Awards presentations, choreographer/actress in the 1982-1987 series *Fame*, producer/director of the 1988 series *A Different World*, and acting in or directing several television movies. Her various film appearances include *Ragtime* (1981) and *Jo Jo Dancer, Your Life Is Calling* (1986). In 1991 she received a star on the Hollywood Walk of Fame. She coproduced the 1997 film *Amistad* with Steven Spielberg.

Allen, Ethan

b. January 21, 1738
Litchfield, Connecticut
d. February 12, 1789
Burlington, Vermont
fields: Military Affairs

Patriot Ethan Allen led Vermont settlers' fight for land rights and secured the first military victory of the American Revolution at Fort Ticonderoga.

Allen, Gracie

full: Grace Ethel Cecile Rosalie Allen
b. July 26, 1900
San Francisco, California
d. August 27, 1964
Hollywood, California
fields: Theater and Entertainment (drama), Radio, Film, Television

Gracie Allen was the first woman to star in a radio program and one of the first woman comedians whose career successfully spanned vaudeville, films, radio, and television.

Allen, Horace Newton

b. Apr. 23, 1858
Delaware, Ohio
d. Dec. 11, 1932
Toledo, Ohio

fields: Medicine, Religion and Theology, Government and Politics

Horace Newton Allen, a Presbyterian missionary and physician, established a hospital in Seoul in 1885. He was appointed secretary for the U.S. embassy in Seoul in 1890, then became the U.S. minister to Korea in 1897. Through his efforts, some seven thousand Koreans emigrated to Hawaii between 1902 and 1905 to work on sugar plantations.

Allen, Jules

b. 1947

fields: Photography

African American photographer. Photographer for production of Ntozake Shange's choreopoem "for colored girls who have considered suicide/ when the rainbow is enuf." Jules Allen's work, which has looked at the various ways that African Americans take photographs, has been exhibited at the Studio Museum of Harlem.

Allen, Marcus

b. Mar. 26, 1960
San Diego, Calif.

fields: Sports (football)

African American football player. Marcus Allen distinguished himself at the University of Southern California in 1981 as the first running back in NCAA history to break the 2,000-yard barrier with 2,342 yards. That same year he left his college career with a Heisman Trophy, a Maxwell Memorial Award, and a United Press International Player of the Year Award, among others. In 1982, Allen was named *The Sporting News* Rookie of the Year for leading the NFL with fourteen touchdowns for the Oakland Raiders. He was named most valuable player in Super Bowl XVIII. In 1985 he led the NFL in rushing and received the National Football League's Most Valuable Player award. After retiring from football in 1998, Allen became a commentator for CBS.

Allen, Milton Burk

b. Dec. 10, 1917
Baltimore, Md.

fields: Law, Government and Politics

African American attorney and public official. Following receipt of a B.A. (1938) and an LL.B. (1948), Milton Burk Allen worked in Baltimore as a defense attorney for twenty-three years. He earned his J.D. in 1971 and that same year was elected to serve as Baltimore states attorney, the first African American to achieve this. He held this position until 1975. In 1976 he accepted appointment as associate judge for the Supreme Bench in Baltimore.

Allen, Paula Gunn

b. Oct. 24, 1939
Cubero, N.Mex.

fields: Literature, Education

Laguna Pueblo writer Paula Gunn Allen's works of poetry, fiction, and literary criticism have brought an influential lesbian and feminist perspective to American Indian literature. Allen's best-known works include a novel, *The Woman Who Owned the Shadows* (1983); a book of essays, *The Sacred Hoop: Recovering the Feminine in American Indian Traditions* (1986); and an anthology, *Spider Woman's Granddaughters: Traditional Tales and Contemporary Writing by Native American Women* (1989).

Allen, Richard

b. Feb. 14, 1760
Philadelphia, Pa.

d. Mar. 26, 1831
Philadelphia, Pa.

fields: Religion and Theology

Founder of the African Methodist Episcopal (AME) church. After gaining freedom from slavery (c. 1781) Richard Allen became the first African American ordained by the Methodist Society to preach. After being granted membership in but denied the right to racially integrated worship at the predominantly white St. George's Methodist Episcopal Church in Philadelphia, Allen founded the Bethel Church, dedicated in 1794. Although Allen was ordained the first African American deacon in 1799, he was barred from Methodist Conference meetings. In 1816 the Pennsylvania Supreme Court settled the controversy over white versus black Methodist control by granting Bethel Church independence from Methodist control. In 1830 Allen led the first meeting of what would become the Negro Convention Movement.

Allen, Richie

full: Richard Anthony Allen

b. Mar. 8, 1942
Wampum, Pa.

fields: Sports (baseball)

African American baseball player. Richie Allen's career in the major leagues spanned fifteen seasons. He played for five teams beginning in 1963. In 1972, playing for the Chicago White Sox, Allen led the league in runs batted in (113) and home runs (37) and won the American League's Most Valuable Player award. He retired in 1967 with 351 home runs and a lifetime batting average of .292.

Allen, Winifred Hall

b. ?
Jamaica

fields: Photography, Journalism

African American photojournalist active during the 1930's. At age eighteen Winifred Hall Allen moved to New York City and began working in a photography studio run by William Woodard in Harlem. She opened the Winifred Hall Photography Studio when Woodard moved to Chicago. Allen's photography captured the lives of Harlem residents.

Allen, Woody

né: Allen Stewart Konigsberg

b. December 1, 1935
Brooklyn, New York

fields: Film, Theater and Entertainment, Literature

At the end of the 1960's, performer, humorist, and playwright Woody Allen emerged as a filmmaker and actor of international stature with such films as *Take the Money and Run* (1969), *Annie Hall* (1977), *Broadway Danny Rose* (1985), and many others. His personal life caused a stir in the 1990's when he acknowledged dating Soon-Yi Farrow, the adopted daughter of actress Mia Farrow, with whom he had had a long-term relationship and a son; Allen married Soon-Yi in 1998.

Allenby, Lord

né: Edmund Henry Hynman Allenby

aka: Edmund Henry Hynman, first viscount Allenby

b. April 23, 1861
Brackenhurst, near Southwell, Nottinghamshire, England

d. May 14, 1936
London, England

fields: Military Affairs

After a career of some note that involved him in the Boer War and the Western Front of World War I, Allenby achieved signal successes for Allied arms by commanding the military forces that captured Jerusalem, Damascus, and Aleppo during the Middle Eastern campaigns of 1917 and 1918.

Allende, Isabel

b. Aug. 2, 1942
Lima, Peru

fields: Literature (novelist)

Latina novelist. Isabel Allende was a journalist in Chile until Chilean president Salvador Allende (her father's first cousin) was assassinated in 1973. While in exile she began writing creatively and in 1982 published *La casa de los espíritus* (*The House of the Spirits*, 1985) to worldwide critical acclaim. The book combined Magical Realism with feminism to create a unique vision of the world. Among Allende's other published works are the fictional books *De amor y de sombra* (1984; *Of Love and Shadows*, 1987) and *The Stories of Eva Luna* (1991), and a collection of essays titled *The Infinite Plan*

(1993). Her 1999 book *Aphrodite: A Memoir of the Senses* detailed how food can arouse the senses.

Allende, Salvador

full: Salvador Allende Gossens
b. June 26, 1908
Valparaíso, Chile
d. September 11, 1973
Santiago, Chile
fields: Government and Politics

Salvador Allende, a socialist, was president of Chile from 1970 to 1973; his government appropriated land and nationalized banks, mines, and some industries; overthrown by the Chilean military, led by Augusto Pinochet, with some covert help from the CIA.

Allensworth, Allen

b. Apr. 7, 1842
Louisville, Ky.
d. Sept. 14, 1914
Allensworth, Calif.
fields: Business and Industry, Exploration and Colonization

African American founder of Allensworth, Calif. After escaping from slavery in 1862 and enlisting in the Navy during the Civil War, Allen Allensworth studied for the ministry and became an Army chaplain, retiring in 1906. He moved to California in 1908 and formed a company which assisted African Americans who wished to migrate to California. The company sold lots which eventually formed the town of Allensworth.

Allport, Gordon

b. November 11, 1897
Montezuma, Ind.
d. October 9, 1967
Boston, Mass.
fields: Psychiatry and Psychology

Psychologist; on faculty at Harvard University, 1930-1967; helped establish department of social relations at Harvard; wrote path-breaking studies on the development of personality; wrote many books, including *Personality: A Psychological Interpretation* (1937), *Nature of Personality* (1950), *Nature of Prejudice* (1954).In his work on personality and social ethics, Allport emphasized the unique constellation of traits, values, and sentiments that characterize each individual.

Almeida, Laurindo

b. Sept. 2, 1917
São Paulo, Brazil
d. July 26, 1995
Los Angeles, Calif.
fields: Music (composer, Spanish acoustic guitarist)

Latino composer and Spanish acoustic guitarist. Laurindo Almeida moved to the United States in 1947 and played guitar with Stan Kenton before forming his own trio in Los Angeles. He wrote music for several films—including *Viva Zapata!* (1952) and *The Old Man and the Sea* (1958)—and gained popularity when his album *Viva Bossa Nova* (1962) reached number thirteen on the charts. In 1964 he won a Grammy Award for the album *Guitar from Ipanema*. In the late 1960's he added classical guitar to his repertoire and subsequently recorded many popular classical and Latin jazz albums.

Alomar, Roberto

full: Roberto Alomar y Velazquez
b. Feb. 5, 1968
Ponce, Puerto Rico
fields: Sports (baseball player)

Latino baseball player. Roberto Alomar, son of Sandy Alomar, Sr., played second base for the Padres from 1988 to 1990 before being traded to the Toronto Blue Jays. By the end of the 1993 season he had earned a lifetime batting average of .297 and had helped the Blue Jays win consecutive world championships in 1992 and 1993. He won several Gold Glove Awards and was named the most valuable player of the 1992 American League Championship Series. From 1996 to 1998, he played for the Baltimore Orioles. For the 1999 baseball season, he played with his brother Sandy on the Cleveland Indians.

Alomar, Sandy, Sr.

full: Santos Alomar y Conde
b. Oct. 19, 1943
Salinas, Puerto Rico
fields: Sports (baseball player)

Latino baseball player. Sandy Alomar, Sr., grew up in Puerto Rico and moved to the United States to play baseball in the big leagues, which he did from 1964 to 1978. He achieved his greatest success as a second baseman for California Angels and was named to the American League All-Star Team in 1970. Alomar also played for several other teams, played every position but pitcher and catcher, and, as a switch hitter, earned a lifetime batting average of .245. He coached baseball during the winter in Puerto Rico and was coaching the San Diego Padres when his sons, Sandy, Jr., and Roberto, joined that team in the late 1980's.

Alomar, Sandy, Jr.

full: Santos Alomar y Velazquez
b. June 18, 1966
Salinas, Puerto Rico
fields: Sports (baseball player)

Latino baseball player. Sandy Alomar, Jr., son of Sandy Alomar, Sr., was the catcher for the San Diego Padres and Cleveland Indians. He won a Gold Glove Award and the American League Rookie of the Year Award in 1990. By the end of 1993 he had a .263 lifetime batting average and had played in three All-Star games. When healthy, Alomar was one of the American League's leading catchers.

Alonso, Luis Antonio Dámaso de. *See* Roland, Gilbert

Alonso, Maria Conchita

b. 1957
Cuba
fields: Theater and Entertainment (acting)

Latina actor. When she was five years old, Maria Conchita Alonso moved with her family to Venezuela, where she became Miss Teenager of the World in 1971 and Miss Venezuela in 1975, acted in films and soap operas, and recorded one platinum and four gold albums. After moving to Los Angeles, she appeared in such films as *Moscow on the Hudson* (1984), *The Running Man* (1987), *Colors* (1988), *Predator 2* (1990), and *The House of the Spirits* (1994). Her television work includes the miniseries *An American Cousin*, the television film *Blood Ties*, and the 1991 series *McBain*. Alonso was also twice nominated for Grammy awards for rock albums she recorded in the late 1980's.

Alou, Felipe

full: Felipe Rojas y Alou
b. May 12, 1935
Santo Domingo, Dominican Republic
fields: Sports (baseball player)

Latino baseball player. Felipe Alou, brother of Matty Alou and Jesús Alou, played outfield and first base in the big leagues from 1958 through 1974. Named to the National League All-Star Team in 1962, 1966, and 1968. His best year was 1966 with the Atlanta Braves: His batting average was .327 (second only to his brother Matty's .342), he led the league in hits (218) and runs scored (122), and he hit 31 home runs. In 1992 he began managing the Montreal Expos and was named National League Manager of the Year in 1994. In 1967 Felipe wrote *Felipe Alou: My Life and Baseball* in which he recounted the difficulties he faced as a Latin American baseball player in the United States. His son, Moises Alou, also became a major league baseball player.

Alou, Jesús

full: Jesús María Rojas y Alou
b. Mar. 24, 1942
Haina, Dominican Republic
fields: Sports (baseball player)

Latino baseball player. Jesús Alou, brother of Felipe Alou and Matty Alou, played major league baseball from 1963 to 1979. Among the teams he played for were the San Francisco Giants, Houston Astros, Oakland Athletics, and New York Mets. His lifetime batting average was .280, and he played for the Athletics during their world championship victories in 1973 and 1974.

Alou, Matty

full: Mateo Rojas y Alou
b. Dec. 22, 1938
Haina, Dominican Republic
fields: Sports (baseball player)

Latino baseball player. Matty Alou began playing baseball in the major leagues in 1960, two years after his brother Felipe began his career. As an outfielder for the San Francisco Giants and Pittsburgh Pirates, he earned a lifetime batting average of .307, the highlight being 1966, when he had a batting average in .342, the highest in the major leagues. Matty was named to the All-Star team in 1968 and 1969. He retired in 1974.

Alou, Moises

b. July 3, 1966
Atlanta, Ga.
fields: Sports (baseball player)

Latino baseball player. Moises Alou, son of Filipe Alou, began playing outfield for the Montreal Expos outfielder in 1992. In 1993 he broke his leg during the season, but not before he had earned a batting average of .286, hit 18 home runs, and amassed 85 runs batted in. He helped the Florida Marlins win the 1997 World Series. In 1998, he played for the Houston Astros.

Alp Arslan

né: Adud al-Dawla Abu Shuja Muhammad ibn Daud Chaghrï Beg
b. c. 1030
Central Asia
d. 1072
near Tirmidh (modern Termez)
fields: Government and Politics, Warfare and Conquest

The second sultan of the Seljuk dynasty, Alp Arslan consolidated and extended the conquests of his predecessor, Toghrïl Beg; his reign, together with that of his son Malik-Shah, constituted the zenith of the empire of the Great Seljuks.

Alston, Charles

b. Nov. 28, 1907
Charlotte, N.C.
d. Apr. 27, 1977
New York, N.Y.
fields: Art, Education

African American artist and educator. Charles Alston created figurative and abstract paintings, sculptures, and other works. He received popular notice for his illustrations on the covers of *The New Yorker* and *Collier's* magazines. In the 1930's he taught at the Harlem Art Workshop and encouraged the development of muralism as a genre of black art. Alston captured the black experience in his paintings of African American families in the 1950's and 1960's.

Altamirano, Ignacio Manuel

b. Nov. 13, 1834
Tixtla, Mexico
d. Feb. 13, 1893
San Remo, Italy
fields: Literature

Latino writer. At different times in his life Ignacio Manuel Altamirano worked as a lawyer, chief justice, historian, professor, literary critic, orator, and diplomat, but he ultimately became Mexico's most important nineteenth century novelist and the originator of the modern Mexican novel. He wrote three major novels—*Clemencia* (1869; *Clemency*, 1907), *La Navidad en las montañas* (1871; *Christmas in the Mountains*, 1961), and *El Zarco, espisodio de la vida mexicana en 1861-63* (1901; *El Zarco, the Bandit*, 1957)—as well as novellas and literary criticism.

Altgeld, John Peter

b. December 30, 1847
Niederselters, Prussia
d. March 12, 1902
Joliet, Illinois
fields: Government and Politics

Altgeld furnished American political life with a high standard of moral courage and, during a crucial historical period, helped to establish the principle that maintenance of the welfare society is an obligation of government.

Althusser, Louis

b. October 16, 1918
Birmendrëis, Algeria
d. October 22, 1990
near Paris, France
fields: Philosophy, Langauge and Linguistics

Combining linguistic structuralism and concepts from Freudian psychoanalysis, Louis Althusser formulated a modern version of scientific and antihumanist Marxism in which structures and process take precedence over individual subjects in accounting for history. During the 1960's and 1970's he influenced leftist sociologists, economists, political theorists, and literary theorists in France and Great Britain; in the United States, the concept of the reproduction of society through education had a great impact on the sociology of education. In 1980, struggling with a severe depression, he strangled his wife, and his name became anathema to many feminists who had earlier used his ideas. After Althusser's incarceration and the decline of communist and socialist movements during the 1980's, many ex-Althusserians became postmodernists, sometimes denouncing Althusser but mining his texts for useful ideas. The posthumously published *The Future Lasts Forever* (1992) summarizes his life and philosophy.

Altman, Sidney

b. May 7, 1939
Montreal, Quebec, Canada
fields: Biology, Chemistry, Genetics

Sydney Altman, a molecular biologist, discovered the catalytic properties of ribonucleic acid (RNA). For this he won the Nobel Prize in Chemistry in 1989. He was a member of the National Academy of Sciences and the American Philosophical Society.

Alurista

né: Alberto Baltazar Urista-Heredia
b. Aug. 8, 1947
Mexico City, Mexico
fields: Literature, Civil Rights

Latino poet and activist. In 1967, while attending San Diego State University, Alurista helped establish the Movimiento Estudiantil Chicano de Aztlán (MECHA), a Chicano student group that later spread to other U.S. campuses. He also helped organize the Chicano studies program (1968) and the Centro de Estudios Chicanos (1969) at the same university. Alurista has also published poetry, which deals with ethnic identity and liberation issues; he writes in both English and Spanish, often mixing languages in a single poem. His poetry collections include *Timespace Huracán: Poems 1972-1975* (1976), *Return: Poems Collected and New* (1982), and *Spik in Glyph?* (1981).

Alva, duke of

full: Fernando Álvarez de Toledo, third duke of Alva
aka: Duke of Alba
b. October 29, 1507
Piedrahita, Spain
d. December 12, 1582
Lisbon, Portugal
fields: Diplomacy, Military Affairs

One of the greatest European soldiers and diplomats of the 1500's, Alva fought for and represented the Hapsburg emperor Charles V and his son King Philip II of Spain.

Alvarado, Juan Bautista

b. 1800
d. 1882
fields: Government and Politics

Latino politician. In 1836 Juan Bautista Alvarado fought Mexican general Antonio López de Santa Anna's attempt to put California under the control of a new centralist government in Mexico. Alvarado's successful rebellion allowed California to remain independent until the federal government was restored in Mexico City, at which time Alvarado became governor of the autonomous province until 1842. His policy of encouraging Americans to settle the area helped the United States take control of California in 1846. After the Mexican American War, Alvarado became a ranchero despite offers from the U.S. government to become either interim governor or secretary of state.

Alvarado, Pedro de

b. 1485
Badajoz, Spain
d. 1541
northern Mexico
fields: Exploration and Colonization

Alvarado was a key subordinate to Hernán Cortés in the sixteenth century Spanish exploration and conquest of Mexico and Central America.

Alvarez, Cecilia Concepción

b. 1959
fields: Art (painter)

Latina artist. Cecilia Concepción Alvarez's art is inspired by Latino art, Chicana politics and social issues, and her own personal vision of beauty, both internal and external. These concerns are brought together in such paintings as *Las Cuatas Diego* (1979). Alvarez believes that artists have an obligation to be socially conscious and to work toward improving humanity in general.

Alvarez, Julia

b. Mar. 27, 1950
New York, N.Y.
fields: Literature

Latina writer. In 1960, Julia Alvarez moved with her family from the Dominican Republic to the United States, where she earned literature and creative writing degrees and taught at Middlebury College in Vermont. She wrote several volumes of poetry before achieving critical and popular success with her first novel, *How the García Girls Lost Their Accents* (1991), which won the 1991 PEN Oakland/Josephine Miles Book Award and which *Library Journal* selected as one of the best books of 1991. Among her other works are *The Housekeeping Book* (1984), *Homecoming* (1984), and *In the Time of the Butterflies* (1994).

Alvarez, Luis Walter

b. June 13, 1911
San Francisco, Calif.
d. September 1, 1988
Berkeley, Calif.
fields: Physics

Latino physicist. Luis Alvarez did most of his work at the University of California, Berkeley, from 1936 until his death in 1988, serving as associate director of the Lawrence Livermore Laboratory (1954-1959, 1976-1978). His main areas of research were particle physics, astrophysics, optics, geophysics, and air navigation. He was a team member on the Manhattan Project; was awarded the Nobel Prize in Physics in 1968; was part of a team of scientists who postulated that the extinction of the dinosaurs was caused by an asteroid impact.

Álvarez de Pineda, Alonzo

b. ?
fields: Exploration and Colonization

Latino explorer. In 1519 Álvarez de Pineda was commissioned by Francisco de Garay, the governor of Jamaica, to explore Florida. During his journey along the western coast of Florida and the northern coast of the Gulf of Mexico, he discovered that Florida was part of a larger land mass rather than an island, as had previously been believed. He also became the first Spanish explorer to see the Mississippi River before returning to Garay in 1520.

Alverio, Rosa Dolores. *See* Moreno, Rita

Amarazhu. *See* Rain in the Face

Ambartsumian, Viktor A.

full: Viktor Amazaspovich Ambartsumian
b. September 18, 1908
Tiflis, Russia
d. August 12, 1996
Byurakan Observatory, near Yerevan, Armenia
fields: Astronomy

Ambartsumian developed the astrophysics of stars and stellar origins and was instrumental in the theory of gigantic catastrophe formation in galaxies related to the evolution of stars and galaxies. He was the founder of the major school of theoretical astrophysics in the U.S.S.R.

Ambrose, Saint

b. 339
Augusta Treverorum, Gaul
d. April 4, 397
Milan, Italy
fields: Religion and Theology, Government and Politics

By the practical application of Roman virtue and Christian ethics Ambrose established the Nicene Creed as the orthodox doctrine of Christianity and asserted the spiritual authority of the church over the state.

Amenhotep IV. *See* Akhenaton

Amenophis IV. *See* Akhenaton

American Horse

aka: Wasechun-tashunka
b. c. 1801
d. 1876
fields: Native American Affairs, Government and Politics

American Horse was an Oglala Lakota Sioux leader; assisted Oglala chiefs in leading warriors and governing the community; actively resisted white encroachment following the Homestead Act of 1862; killed at the Battle of Slim Buttes in retaliation for the death of Custer at Little Big Horn.

Amerson, Lucius D.

b. ?
fields: Government and Politics (law enforcement)

African American law enforcement official; Lucius D. Amerson elected sheriff of Macon County, Alabama, in 1968, the first black southern sheriff elected since Reconstruction; Amerson and a black deputy arrested and indicted for beating an African American prisoner they had arrested; an all-white jury acquitted the two in May of 1971.

Amherst, Lord

né: Jeffrey Amherst
b. January 29, 1717
Sevenoaks, Kent, England
d. August 3, 1797
Montreal, Kent, England
fields: Military Affairs

One of the greatest heroes of the Seven Years' War, Amherst commanded the British and colonial forces that conquered Canada from the French.

Amin, Idi

full: Idi Amin Dada Oumee
b. c. 1925
Koboko, West Nile Province, Uganda
fields: Government and Politics

Dictator Idi Amin was head of Uganda from 1971-1979; seized power from Milton Obote. Expelled thousands of highly trained Asian workers and professionals, setting back Ugandan development; conducted bloody purges; overthrown after failed invasion of Tanzania.

Amirthanayagam, Indran

b. Nov. 17, 1960
Colombo, Ceylon, now Sri Lanka
fields: Poetry, Diplomacy

Indran Amirthanayagam, the recipient of a 1993 New York Foundation for the Arts fellowship in poetry, published a widely acclaimed books of poems, *The Elephants of Reckoning*, in 1993. His poems draw on his life experiences in Colombo and Jaffna, Sri Lanka, in London, Honolulu, and New York. Amirthanayagam also became a diplomat with the U.S. Information Agency.

Ammons, Albert

b. Sept. 23, 1907
Chicago, Ill.
d. Dec. 2, 1949
Chicago, Ill.
fields: Music (jazz pianist)

African American pianist; Albert Ammons often mentioned in critical studies of jazz music, known best for boogie woogie and blues piano stylings; made many solo and group recordings, first recording "Boogie Woogie Stomp" (1936); noted performances at Carnegie Hall and Cafe Society in New York, and at inauguration of President Harry S Truman; Gene Ammons, his son, is a well-known jazz tenor saxophonist.

Amos, Famous. *See* Amos, Wallace, Jr.

Amos, John

b. Dec. 27, 1939
Newark, N.J.
fields: Theater and Entertainment (actor)

African American actor. A former professional football player and Golden Gloves boxer, John Amos has appeared on television, stage, and film. His television credits include his Emmy-nominated role in the miniseries *Roots* (1977, as the grown Kunta Kinte), *The Mary Tyler Moore Show* (1970-1973), *Maude* (1973-1974), and *Good Times* (1974-1976, as James Evans). His stage appearances include 150 performances at the Ebony Showcase Theater in L.A., California, in *Norman, Is That You?* (nominated for most outstanding performance in 1971 by Los Angeles Drama Critics), on Broadway in *Tough to Get Help*, *The Emperor Jones* (1979), and *Twelfth Night* (1989). His film career began with *Vanishing Point* (1971) and includes *Coming to America* (1988) and *Die Hard II* (1990). Amos wrote, produced, and directed the film *Grambling Takes It All Back Home*. Received 1985 NAACP Image Award nomination for *Split Second*.

Amos, Wallace, Jr.

né: Famous Amos
b. July 1, 1936
Tallahassee, Fla.
fields: Business and Industry

African American entrepreneur. In the 1980's in Chicago, Wallace Amos, Jr., creatively invested a relatively small amount of money into a business baking chocolate chip cookies and developed it into a national chain with cookie stores throughout the United States.

Ampère, André-Marie

b. Jan. 22, 1775
Lyons, France
d. June 10, 1836
Marseilles, France
fields: Chemistry, Mathematics, Physics

André-Marie Ampère founded the science of electrodynamics, the relationship between electrical and magnetic phenomena. In 1814, he was awarded the Cross of the French Legion of Honor.

Amundsen, Roald

full: Roald Engelbregt Gravning Amundsen
b. July 16, 1872
Borge, Norway
d. June 18, 1928?
Arctic Ocean
fields: Exploration and Colonization

Amundsen was the first to navigate the Northwest Passage from Godhavn, Greenland, through the islands of Canada to Fort Egbert, Alaska. In 1911, he was the first explorer to reach the South Pole. His studies of magnetics led to major revisions of theories concerning the magnetic North Pole and greater understanding of the Arctic and Antarctic regions.

Anaxagoras

b. c. 500 B.C.E.
Clazomenae, Anatolia
d. c. 428 B.C.E.
Lampsacus
fields: Philosophy, Natural History, Science

By devising a philosophical system to explain the origins and nature of the physical universe which overcame the paradoxes and inconsistencies of earlier systems, Anaxagoras provided an indispensable bridge between the pre-Socratic philosophers of the archaic period of Greek history and the full flowering of philosophy during the Golden Age of Greece.

Anaximander

b. c. 610 B.C.E.
Miletus, Greek Asia Minor
d. c. 547 B.C.E.
probably Miletus
fields: Natural History, Astronomy, Geography

Anaximander realized that no ordinary physical element could be the source of the world's diversity; instead, he saw that the fundamental stuff much be an eternal, unlimited reservoir of qualities and change.

Anaximenes of Miletus

b. Early sixth century B.C.E.
probably Miletus
d. Second half of the sixth century B.C.E.
place unknown
fields: Philosophy, Science

Anaximenes was the last of the great early pre-Socratic thinkers from Miletus and the first, apparently, to attribute the nature of matter entirely to physical rather than moral laws. Thus, his ideas provided a necessary step from the generalized ideas of Thales to the specific physical ideas of the Atomists of the fifth century.

Anaya, Rudolfo

full: Rudolfo Alfonso Anaya
b. Oct. 30, 1937
Pastura, N.Mex.
fields: Literature

Latino writer; Rudolfo Anaya earned degrees at the University of New Mexico (1963, 1968, 1972); taught in public schools, 1963-1970; on faculty, University of New Mexico, since 1974; wrote of the spirituality of the Chicano tradition in novels such as *Bless Me, Ultima* (1972), *Heart of Aztlan* (1976), *Tortuga* (1979), and *Albuquerque* (1991). He has also written a collection of short stories, *The Silence of the Llano* (1982) and the autobiographical *A Chicano in China*.

Anaya, Toney

b. April 29, 1941
Moriarty, N.Mex.
fields: Government and Politics

Latino politician. Before receiving his law degree from American University in 1967, Toney Anaya worked for Senator Dennis Chávez (D-N.Mex.). He later served as legislative counsel to Senator Joseph Montoya, also of New Mexico. In 1974 Anaya moved back to his home state and successfully ran for attorney general (1975-1978). In 1982 Anaya was elected governor of New Mexico; he served one term. In 1986 Anaya became the center of controversy when he commuted the sentences of all of New Mexico's death row prisoners before leaving office. He was a member of the Democratic National Committee in 1988.

Andersen, Hans Christian

b. April 2, 1805
Odense, Denmark
d. August 4, 1875
Rolighed, near Copenhagen, Denmark

fields: Literature

Andersen is the most well-known Danish writer. His greatest achievement was as the author of universally beloved fairy tales.

Andersen, Patrick W.

b. Dec. 29, 1952
Long Beach, Calif.
fields: Publishing, Journalism

Patrick W. Andersen, a graduate of San Francisco State University, was managing editor of *Asian Week*, a community newspaper in San Francisco, California, 1982-1991. The paper featured articles on Asian American politics, business, and the arts. He also wrote about homosexuality and AIDS in the Asian American community.

Anderson, Carl David

b. Sept. 3, 1905
New York, New York
d. Jan. 11, 1991
San Marino, California
fields: Physics

Carl David Anderson discovered the first antiparticle, called the positron, in 1932. In 1935, he set up a cloud chamber on Pike's Peak near Colorado Springs, Colorado, and discovered the mu-meson, or muon. He won the Nobel Prize in Physics in 1936.

Anderson, Cat

full: William Anderson
b. Sept. 12, 1916
Greenville, S.C.
d. Apr. 29, 1981
Norwalk, Calif.
fields: Music (jazz trumpeter)

African American jazz trumpeter; William "Cat" Anderson best known as a member of the Duke Ellington band (1944-1971); instrumental style included playing in the extreme upper register, as in his own composition "El Gato" (1958); appeared in the 1972 film *Lady Sings the Blues*.

Anderson, Charles Edward. *See* Berry, Chuck

Anderson, Eddie "Rochester"

b. Sept. 18, 1905
Oakland, Calif.
d. Feb 28, 1977
Los Angeles, Calif.
fields: Theater and Entertainment (actor)

African American actor. Although Eddie "Rochester" Anderson toured the United States as a comedian, singer, and dancer, and played small roles in several films, he will be best remembered for his role as Jack Benny's manservant, Rochester. He portrayed this subordinate role with dignity and integrity from 1937 to 1955 on radio and on *The Jack Benny Show* on television from 1950 to 1977.

Anderson, Ivie

b. July 10, 1904
Gilroy, Calif.
d. Dec. 28, 1949
Los Angeles, Calif.
fields: Music (jazz singer)

African American jazz singer. During the swing era, Ivie Anderson appeared with Duke Ellington's orchestra as the featured vocalist (1931-1942). Her singing style, combining lyricism, elegance, and warmth, contributed to the orchestra's popularity.

Anderson, James, Jr.

b. 1946
d. Feb 28, 1967
fields: Warfare and Conquest (soldier)

African American soldier. As a private, first class, serving during the Vietnam War, James Anderson, Jr., sacrificed his own life to save his fellow Marines by throwing himself on an enemy grenade. For this act of heroism he was posthumously awarded the Congressional Medal of Honor.

Anderson, Jim

b. 1929
Harlem, N.Y.
fields: Theater and Entertainment (actor), Philanthropy (community activist)

African American actor and community activist. In addition to acting with the Living Theatre in New York, Jim Anderson supported community self-help programs and cofounded the East Harlem Food Buying Federation. This program supplied low-cost fresh produce and other groceries to neighborhood food cooperatives.

Anderson, Laurie

b. June 5, 1947
Wayne, Illinois
fields: Performance Art, Music

A leading figure in the field of performance art, Anderson's integration of contemporary musical themes and cultural issues popularized the idiom and attracted a larger audience to the genre, and as a result, she became one of the first women to be in the vanguard of the postmodern artistic movement.

Anderson, Marian

b. February 27, 1897
Philadelphia, Pennsylvania
d. April 8, 1993
Portland, Oregon
fields: Music

Anderson was a world-renowned contralto. Her career came to have symbolic meaning in the battle against racial prejudice.

Anderson, Mary

b. 1872
Linkoping, Sweden
d. Jan. 30, 1964
Washington, D.C.
fields: Social Reform, Civil Rights

A trade union activist, Mary Anderson in 1894 became a member of the International Boot and Shoe Workers Union, rapidly reaching the position of local branch president; in 1920, became the first director of the Women's Bureau of the Department of Labor.

Anderson, Philip W.

full: Philip Warren Anderson
b. Dec. 13, 1923
Indianapolis, Indiana
fields: Mathematics, Physics

Philip W. Anderson, a theoretical scientist, is known for furthering the understanding of the electron movements in materials called superconductors and semiconductors. For his work, he won the Nobel Prize in Physics with John Van Vleck and Sir Nevill Mott in 1977, as well as the National Medal of Science in 1982.

Anderson, Roberta Joan. *See* Mitchell, Joni

Anderson, Sarah A.

b. ?
Jacksonville, Fla.
fields: Government and Politics

African American state politician; Sarah A. Anderson served as Philadelphia representative to the Pennsylvania state legislature from 1954 to her retirement in 1972; member of Pennsylvania State Democratic Executive Committee; chairperson of the Health and Welfare Committee of State Legislatures; for eight years, judge of the Twenty-fourth Division Election Board and inspector of the Election Boards.

Anderson, Thomas Jefferson

b. Aug. 17, 1928
Coatesville, Pa.
fields: Music (classical composer)

African American composer. Thomas Jefferson Anderson filled university teaching positions from 1955 to 1969. During this time he composed *Symphony in Three Movements* (1964), *Squares* (1965), *Connections* (1966), *Personals* (1966), *Rotations* (1967), and *Chamber Symphony* (1968). From 1963 to 1969 Anderson served as composer-in-residence with the Atlanta Symphony Orchestra. He became chair of the music department at Tufts University, Mass., in 1973.

Anderson, Webster

b. 1933
fields: Warfare and Conquest (soldier)

African American soldier. Despite being gravely wounded, Webster Anderson commanded his artillery battery to counterattack and defeat a North Vietnamese offense during the Vietnam War (Oct. 15, 1967). For this conspicuous heroism, he won the Congressional Medal of Honor.

Andō Hiroshige. *See* Hiroshige

André, John

b. May 2, 1750
London, England
d. October 2, 1780
Tappan, New York
fields: Military Affairs

Serving as an intelligence officer for the British during the Revolution, André convinced American general Benedict Arnold to turn over the fortress of West Point, thus ensuring British victory in the war. However, André was captured while returning to British lines, and the conspiracy was discovered.

Andrea del Sarto

né: Andrea d'Agnolo
b. July 16, 1486
Florence
d. September 28, 1530
Florence
fields: Art

Andrea del Sarto is considered to be one of the most important Florentine painters of the early sixteenth century and is also a figure of great historical importance. In his own work, he was clearly inspired by the classical ideals of the central Italian High Renaissance, particularly by Raphael and Leonardo da Vinci, but his pupils were to become the creators of the anticlassical style later known as mannerism, which dominated Italian art from about 1520 until 1600.

Andrewes, Lancelot

b. 1555
London, England
d. September 26, 1626
London, England
fields: Religion and Theology

With Jeremy Taylor and Richard Hooker, Andrewes helped establish the Anglican church and through his writings and conduct served as the model of the Anglican cleric.

Andrews, Benny

b. Nov. 13, 1930
Madison, Ga.
fields: Art, Education

African American artist and educator. After graduating with a B.F.A. from the Art Institute of Chicago (1958), Benny Andrews went on to teach at the New School for Social Research in New York. He depicts the cultural displacement of African Americans through his expressionist paintings and collages. He directed the National Arts Program in the 1980's and worked as associate editor in charge of art at *Encore* magazine.

Andrews, Raymond

b. June 6, 1934
Madison, Ga.
d. Nov. 26, 1991
Athens, Ga.
fields: Literature

African American writer; Raymond Andrews began writing novels set in the South at age thirty-two; 1978 James Baldwin Prize for Fiction received for first novel *Apalachee Red* (1978); other novels include *The Last Radio Baby* (1990) and *Jessie and Jesus and Cousin Claire* (1991); artist Benny Andrews his brother.

Andrews, V. C.

b. June 6, 1924(?)
Portsmouth, Virginia
d. December 19, 1986
Virginia Beach, Virginia
fields: Literature

V. C. Andrews wrote popular books for young readers that were controversial because they dealt with incest and graphic family violence. After she died, the head of Simon and Schuster's mass-market division hired a ghostwriter to continue her works.

Andujar, Joaquín

b. Dec. 21, 1952
San Pedro de Macoris, Dominican Republic
fields: Sports (baseball player)

Latino baseball player. Right-handed pitcher Joaquín Andujar played his first season in the major leagues in 1976 with the Houston Astros. He was named to the National League All-Star Team in 1977 and 1979. In 1982, playing for the St. Louis Cardinals, he won the final game of the National League Championship Series and games three and seven of the World Series. In 1984 Andujar led the National League with twenty wins, four shutouts, and 261 innings pitched. The following year he won twenty-one games and again led St. Louis into the World Series. However, his attempt to attack an umpire during the decisive game led to his being traded to the Oakland Athletics in 1986 and then Houston before retiring in 1988.

Anfinsen, Christian B.

full: Christian Boehmer Anfinsen
b. Mar. 26, 1916
Monessen, Pennsylvania
d. May 14, 1995
Randallstown, Maryland
fields: Biology, Chemistry, Medicine (immunology)

Christian B. Anfinsen showed that the primary structure of a protein, the amino acid sequence, contains the information necessary to determine the three-dimensional sequence of the protein. In 1972, he was awarded the Nobel Prize in Chemistry.

Angelico, Fra

né: Guido di Pietro
aka: Guidolino di Pietro
aka: Giovanni da Fiesole
aka: Il Beato Fra Giovanni Angelico
b. c. 1400
Vicchio, Tuscany
d. February 18, 1455
Rome
fields: Art

Fra Angelico is best known for adapting the most advanced artistic techniques of his time (perspective and brilliant use of color and line) to extraordinary evocations of purely spiritual subjects.

Angell, Norman

full: Ralph Norman Angell Lane
b. December 26, 1872
Holbeach, Lincolnshire, England
d. October 7, 1967
Croyden, Surrey, England
fields: Diplomacy (international relations), Social Reform, Journalism

Angell fashioned complex ideas of international relations into simple, catchy depictions that enabled him to lead British peace movements before and after World War I.

Angelou, Maya

né: Marguerite Annie Johnson
b. April 4, 1928
St. Louis, Missouri
fields: Literature

Best known for her poetry and autobiographical works, Angelou has had a multifaceted career, enjoying success as a dancer, actress, and teacher.

Angpetu Tokecha. *See* Otherday, John

Anhalt-Zerbst, Sophie Friederike Auguste von. *See* Catherine the Great

Annan, Kofi

full: Kofi Atta Annan
b. April 8, 1938
Kumasi, Gold Coast (now Ghana)
fields: Diplomacy

Ghanaian diplomat Kofi Annan was named secretary-general of the United Nations in 1996. Announced goal of reforming U.N. and cutting waste; urged United States to pay its back dues; conducted 1998 negotiations to avoid U.S. air strikes against Iraq.

Annawan

b. ?
d. c. 1676
fields: Warfare and Conquest, Government and Politics, Native American Affairs

Native American leader. Wampanoag leader Annawan led the war chiefs under King Philip during King Philip's War in 1675-1676.

Anne, Queen

b. February 6, 1665
London, England
d. August 1, 1714
London, England
fields: Monarchy, Government and Politics

Queen of England, 1702-1714. Through her devotion to the Church of England, Anne maintained the provisions of the Act of Settlement of 1701, thereby fostering the cause of constitutional government while preventing another civil war.

Anpetu Waste (Beautiful Day). *See* Deloria, Ella Cara

Anselm, Saint

b. c. 1033
Aosta, Combardy (now in Italy)
d. April 21, 1109
Canterbury?, Kent, England
fields: Philosophy, Religion and Theology

Combining a tenacious attachment to principle with a penetrating mind, Anselm maintained the independence of the English church while making major contributions to the inductive argument for the existence of God.

Anson, George. *See* Anson, Lord

Anson, Lord

né: George Anson
b. April 23, 1697
Shugborough, Staffordshire, England
d. June 6, 1762
Moor Park, Hertfordshire, England
fields: Military Affairs

Through his achievements on active service at sea and at the Admiralty ashore, Anson was instrumental in making British naval predominance one of the major legacies of the wars of the mid-eighteenth century.

Anthony, Florence. *See* Ai

Anthony, John Francis, III. *See* Pastorius, Jaco

Anthony, Michael

b. Feb. 10, 1932
Mayaro, Trinidad and Tobago
fields: Literature

African American novelist, short story writer, and journalist; Michael Anthony best known for optimistic stories about native life in the Caribbean; novels include *Green Days by the River* (1967).

Anthony, Susan B.

full: Susan Brownwell Anthony
b. February 15, 1820
Adams, Massachusetts
d. March 13, 1906
Rochester, New York
fields: Women's Rights

A gifted and relentless worker for feminist causes, Anthony was for five decades the preeminent voice and inspiration of the women's suffrage movement.

Anthony of Egypt, Saint

b. c. 251
Coma, near Memphis, Egypt
d. Probably January 17, 356
Mount Kolzim, near the Red Sea
fields: Religion and Theology, Monasticism

A Christian hermit renowned for his ascetic labors and Gospel teachings, Anthony became celebrated within Christendom as the founder of the eremitic movement and the father of monasticism.

Anthony of Padua, Saint

né: Ferdinand de Boullion
b. August 15, 1195
Lisbon, Portugal
d. June 13, 1231
Arcella, near Padua, Italy
fields: Religion and Theology, Education

Anthony of Padua was one of the most eloquent Franciscan preachers and the first teacher of the Franciscan School of Theology. He is credited with introducing the theology of Saint Augustine into the order and was named a Doctor of the Church.

Antigonus I Monophthalmos

b. 382 B.C.E.
probably Macedonia
d. 301 B.C.E.
Ipsus, Phrygia, Asia Minor
fields: Government and Politics, Warfare and Conquest

Though Antigonus failed to unify Macedonian conquests after Alexander the Great's death in 323 B.C.E., he did establish an eponymous dynasty (Antigonid), which was to rule Macedonia and exert a great influence on Greek affairs elsewhere until the Roman victory at the Battle of Pydna in 168 B.C.E.

Antiochus the Great

b. 242 B.C.E.
possibly Antioch
d. 187 B.C.E.
Elymais, near Susa
fields: Warfare and Conquest

Antiochus went the furthest of any of the successors of Alexander the Great toward reuniting what had once been the vast Alexandrian empire.

Antisthenes

b. c. 444 B.C.E.
Athens, Greece
d. c. 365 B.C.E.
Athens, Greece
fields: Philosophy

Founder of the philosophical school of classical Cynicism, Antisthenes regarded virtue as the sole basis of happiness and viewed self-control and rejection of materialism as the only means of achieving virtue.

Antonio, Donato di Pascuccio d'. *See* Bramante, Donato

Antonio, Juan

aka: Cooswootna
aka: Yampoochee (He Gets Mad Quickly)
b. c. 1783
Mt. San Jacinto region, Calif.
d. Feb. 28, 1863
San Timoteo Cañon, Calif.
fields: Government and Politics, Native American Affairs

Native American leader. A powerful Cahuilla chief, Juan Antonio aided whites on several occasions in California during the turbulent 1850's.

Antony, Marc

aka: Marcus Antonius
b. c. 82 B.C.E.
place unknown
d. 30 B.C.E.
Alexandria, Egypt
fields: Government and Politics, Warfare and Conquest

The military and political defeat of Antony by Octavian (later known as Augustus) resulted in the demise of the republican form of government in Rome and the creation of the Roman Empire, which would rule much of the known world for some five hundred years.

Anza, Juan Bautista de

b. 1735
Fronteras, Mexico
d. Dec. 19, 1788
Arizpe, Mexico
fields: Warfare and Conquest, Exploration and Colonization

Latino soldier and explorer. Juan Bautista de Anza, who came from a military family, became a soldier in 1753 and was promoted to lieutenant within two years. During the 1760's he captained a garrison that fought against the rebellious Apache, Seri, and Pima Indians in Sonora. Anza was promoted to lieutenant colonel after discovering a land route from Sonora to California in 1774. After 1777 he became governor of New Mexico, a position he retained until his death in 1788.

Anzaldúa, Gloria

b. Sept. 26, 1942
Jesus María, Tex.
fields: Literature

Latina writer. Gloria Anzaldúa is a scholar, educator, and writer whose interdisciplinary approach reflects her Texas upbringing, during which she suffered the hardships of migrant labor, cultural sexism, homophobia, and oppression. She established herself as a leading lesbian feminist and scholar while teaching at various U.S. universities. Her most important book, *Borderlands: The New Mestiza = La Frontera* (1987)—which won the Before Columbus American Book Award for 1987—mixes genres, languages, and academic disciplines in its exploration of borders and boundaries. Anzaldúa has also edited several feminist collections.

Aoki, Brenda Wong

b. July 29, 1953
Salt Lake City, Utah
fields: Performance Art

Brenda Wong Aoki was the first Asian American performance artist featured at the National Storytelling Festival in Jonesborough, Tennessee, in 1988. He works combine Western theater and dance traditions with elements from classical Japanese theater. Her debut album, *Dreams and Illusions: Tales of the Pacific Rim*, won the National Association of Independent Record Distributors award for Best Storytelling and Spoken Word Recording (1990).

Aoki, Dan

b. 1916
Kona, Territory of Hawaii
d. 1986
fields: Politics, Military Affairs

Dan Aoki, a Democrat and Japanese American veteran of World War II, helped destroy the dominance of the Republican Party in Hawaii and worked to increase the rights of nonwhites. For about thirty years, he acted as aide and confidante to Democrat Jack Burns, who became governor of Hawaii in 1962.

Aoki, Rocky

full: Hiroaki Aoki
b. 1940
Tokyo, Japan
fields: Business and Industry

Rocky Aoki, a flamboyant promoter, came to the United States in 1960. He saved enough money from his work as an ice cream vendor in Harlem, New York, to start a small restaurant. That restaurant became a chain of restaurants called Benihana in the United States and Japan. He is known for his passion for the sport of hot-air ballooning.

Aparicio, Luis Ernesto

b. Apr. 29, 1934
Maracaibo, Venezuela
fields: Sports (baseball player)

Latino baseball player. Shortstop Luis Ernesto Aparicio moved from Venezuela to the United States in 1953 to play for the Chicago White Sox. In 1955, his first season in the majors, he won the American League's Rookie of the Year Award. In 1959, he helped the White Sox win the American League pennant. Aparicio was then traded to the Baltimore Orioles and was the starting shortstop for their 1966 world championship team. By the time he retired in 1973, he had earned nine Gold Glove Awards. In 1984, the White Sox retired his uniform number (11), and he became the first Venezuelan to be inducted into the National Baseball Hall of Fame.

Apayaka Hadjo. *See* Arpeika

Apes, William

aka: William Apess
b. Jan. 31, 1798
Colrain, Mass.
d. ?
fields: Literature

Native American writer and political figure; William Apes, a Pequot and a nineteenth century political protest writer, wrote *A Son of the Forest* (1829), the first published autobiography by an American Indian.

Apess, William. *See* Apes, William

Apgar, Virginia

b. June 7, 1909
Westfield, New Jersey
d. August 7, 1974
New York, New York
fields: Medicine

Noted for contributions in anesthesiology, public health, genetics, and basic research, Virginia Apgar is best remembered for the Apgar Newborn Scoring System, a system of health evaluation which has saved the lives of countless infants worldwide.

Apodaca, Jerry

b. Oct. 3, 1934
Las Cruces, N.Mex.
fields: Government and Politics

Latino governor of New Mexico. Jerry Apodaca graduated from the University of New Mexico in 1957 and worked as an educator and in business. From 1966 to 1974, he served in the New Mexico State Senate as a moderate Democrat. In 1974 he became the first Latino since 1920 to serve as the state's governor. He was later appointed as chairman of the President's Council on Physical Fitness and Sports by President Jimmy Carter, then resumed his business career in the early 1980's.

Apollinaire, Guillaume

né: Guillaume Albert Wladimir Alexandre Apollinaire de Kostrowitzky
b. August 26, 1880
Rome, Italy
d. November 9, 1918
Paris, France
fields: Literature

Apollinaire left an enduring mark on the poetry and painting of the twentieth century. He was a spokesman for the symbolists and an exponent of Surrealism; in fact, the word "Surrealist" appeared for the first time in his writing. His poem "La Jolie Rousse" (the pretty redhead) became and has remained the charter of free verse.

Apollonia. *See* Kotero, Patricia

Apollonius of Perga

b. c. 262 B.C.E.
Perga, Asia Minor
d. c. 190 B.C.E.
Alexandria, Egypt
fields: Mathematics, Astronomy

One of the ablest geometers in antiquity, Apollonius systematized the theory of conic sections in a treatise that remained the definitive introduction to this field until modern times. His study of circular motion established the foundation for Greek geometric astronomy.

Aponensis, Petrus. *See* Abano, Pietro d'

Apotheyahola. *See* Opothleyaholo

Appenzeller, Henry G.

b. Feb. 6, 1858
Suderton, Pa.
d. June 11, 1902
Kunsan, Korea
fields: Religion and Theology

Henry G. Appenzeller, a missionary, arrived at Inchon, Korea, in 1885. He encouraged Koreans to work on Hawaiian plantations in the early 1900's, believing that exposure to Western civilization would improve the condition of these immigrants.

Apperson, Phoebe Elizabeth. *See* Hearst, Phoebe Apperson

Appiah, Kwame Anthony

aka: K. Anthony Appiah
b. May 8, 1954
London England
fields: Philosophy, Literature, Social Reform

Kwame Anthony Appiah critically analyzed the racial myths by which European culture views Africa and those that inform the pan-African movement. *In My Father's House* (1992) reevaluates concepts of race, nationality, and culture. The book received the Annisfield-Wolf Award and the Heskovitz Award of the African Studies Association for the best work published in English on Africa. Other works include *Identity Against Culture: Understandings of Multiculturalism* (1994) and *Color Conscious: The Political Morality of Race* (1996, with Amy Gutmann).

Appleseed, Johnny

né: John Chapman
b. September 26, 1774
Leominster, Massachusetts
d. March 18 (?), 1845
Allen County, near Fort Wayne, Indiana
fields: Horticulture

By planting apple seeds at new settlements in Ohio and Indiana, Johnny Appleseed laid the foundation for orchards as part of agricultural development of the Midwest.

Appleton, Edward Victor

full: Sir Edward Victor Appleton
b. Sept. 6, 1892
Bradford, Yorkshire, England
d. Apr. 21, 1965
Edinburgh, Scotland
fields: Science, Physics

Edward Victor Appleton demonstrated the existence of the ionosphere in 1924. He determined the structure and made theoretical models of the ionosphere, giving a basis to the behavior of radio waves. In 1947, he was awarded the Nobel Prize in Physics for his ionosphere studies.

Apushamatahubib (Warrior's Seat Is Finished). *See* Pushmataha

Apushwahite. *See* Looking Glass

Aquinas, Saint Thomas. *See* Thomas Aquinas, Saint

Aquino, Corazon

né: Maria Corazon Cojuangco
aka: Cory Aquino
b. January 25, 1933
Tarlac Province, the Philippines
fields: Government and Politics

Aquino became the first woman president of the Philippines. She led the revolution that ended twenty years of dictatorial rule and restored democratic government.

Aquino, Iva Toguri d'. *See* Tokyo Rose

Arafat, Yasir

né: Mohammed Abd al-Rauf Arafat al Qudwa al-Husseini
b. August 4 or 24, 1929
Cairo, Egypt, or Jerusalem, Palestine
fields: Government and Politics, Military Affairs

Arafat was the founder of al-Fatah, a Palestinian revolutionary and sometimes terrorist organization that became the founding block of the Palestine Liberation Organization (PLO). A controversial figure who is a freedom fighter to his own people and a terrorist to Israelis and others, he has moved the Palestinians from near obscurity in the 1960's to the forefront of the world's attention.

Arago, François

full: Dominique-François-Jean Arago
b. Feb. 26, 1786
Estagel, France
d. Oct. 2, 1853
Paris, France
fields: Astronomy, Physics

François Arago began a lecture series in Paris that helped popularize astronomy in 1812. He encouraged others and published the results of their experiments. He also investigated the orbits of the planets and performed experiments with electricity and light.

Aragón, José Rafael

b. c. 1796
d. 1862
fields: Art (sculptor, painter)

Latino sculptor and painter. José Rafael Aragón, a *santero* (maker of religious images), was one of the most important artists Living in New Mexico between 1820 and 1860. He used cottonwood root and pine, which he covered with plaster and painted, to create unique sculptures of saints, paintings of biblical stories, altar screens, and other religious objects that offered a source of spiritual inspiration for Spanish settlers in New Mexico.

Arai, Clarence Takeya

b. 1901
d. 1964
fields: Law, Social Reform

Japanese American lawyer, activist; Clarence Takeya Arai earned law degree from University of Washington in 1924; president, Seattle Progressive Citizens League, 1928, leading to foundation of the National Council of Japanese American Citizens League in 1930; interned during World War II at a camp in Idaho.

Arai, Ryoichiro

b. July 19, 1856
Japan
fields: Business and Industry

Ryoichiro Arai came to New York from Japan in 1876 and began a fifty-year career as a silk trader. He was one of the first Japanese to settle in New York. In 1939, the Japanese government named Arai as a Fourth Class National Treasure.

Arango, Doroteo. *See* Villa, Pancho

Arapoosh

aka: Rotten Belly
aka: Sour Belly
b. c. 1790
northern Wyo.
d. Aug., 1834
fields: Warfare and Conquest, Native American Affairs

Native American leader of the Crow tribe, Arapoosh was revered for his spiritual powers. The foremost warrior among the River Crow who lived along the Big Horn, Powder, and Wind rivers in present-day northern Wyoming and southern Montana, Arapoosh led his people against their traditional Indian enemies, the Blackfeet, Sioux, and Northern Cheyennes.

Arateva. *See* Irateba

Arbus, Diane

né: Diane Nemerov
b. March 14, 1923
New York, New York
d. July 26, 1971
New York, New York
fields: Photography

A pivotal figure in contemporary documentary photography, Diane Arbus created startling images of dwarfs, twins, transvestites, and physically deformed individuals that were always controversial and often misunderstood.

Arce, Julio

pseudo. Jorge Ulica
b. Jan. 9, 1870
Guadalajara, Jalisco, Mexico
d. November, 1926
fields: Journalism

Latino writer. Julio Arce started a neighborhood newspaper when he was ten years old and was editing a student newspaper by the age of fourteen. In his early thirties he edited the newspaper *El diario del pacifico* (Pacific diary) in the city of Culiacán. His opposition to the Mexican Revolution forced him to flee Mexico and settle in San Francisco, California, in 1915, where he worked as a journalist. He became editor of *Hispano-America* and published sharp, satirical sketches called *Crónicas diabólicas* (diabolical chronicles) under the pen name Jorge Ulica that addressed issues of concern to Hispanics in San Francisco.

Archer, Dennis Wayne

b. January 1, 1942
Detroit, Mich.
fields: Government and Politics (attorney and politician)

African American attorney and politician; after serving in a 1986 appointment to the Michigan Supreme Court, Dennis Wayne Archer Court resigned and was elected mayor of Detroit in 1993.

Archibald, Nate "Tiny"

full: Nathaniel Archibald
b. Sept. 2, 1948
New York, N.Y.
fields: Sports (basketball player)

African American basketball player; Nate "Tiny" Archibald (6 feet, 160 pounds) played for Cincinnati Royals; third season (1972-1973) led league in assists and averaged 34 points per game; retired in 1984.

Archimedes

b. 287 B.C.E.
Syracuse, Sicily
d. 212 B.C.E.
Syracuse, Sicily
fields: Science, Mathematics, Engineering

The greatest mathematician of antiquity, Archimedes did his best work in geometry and also founded the disciplines of statics and hydrostatics.

Arden, Elizabeth

né: Florence Nightingale Graham
b. December 31, 1884
Woodbridge, Ontario, Canada
d. October 18, 1966
New York, New York
fields: Business and Industry

An entrepreneur who founded Elizabeth Arden, Inc., a multimillion dollar international cosmetics and beauty salon business, Arden is considered one of the individuals responsible for the creation of the cosmetics industry.

Arenas, Reinaldo

b. July 16, 1943
Holguin, Oriente, Cuba
d. Dec. 7, 1990
New York, N.Y.
fields: Literature

Latino writer. Although Reinaldo Arenas supported Fidel Castro's Cuban revolution of 1959 as a teenager, his second novel, *El mundo alucinante* (1969; *The Ill-Fated Peregrinations of Fray Servando*, 1987), led authorities of the Castro regime to imprison him as a counterrevolutionary from 1974 to 1976. After being forced to live underground because of his homosexuality and his writings, Arenas immigrated to the United States in 1980. He wrote numerous critically acclaimed stories, poems and novel, including *Celestino antes del alba* (1967; *Singing from the Well*, 1987), *The Graveyard of the Angels* (1987), and his autobiography *Before Night Falls* (1993). He committed suicide in 1990 while suffering from AIDS.

Arendt, Hannah

b. October 14, 1906
Hannover, Germany
d. December 4, 1975
New York, New York
fields: Philosophy, Social Science

One of the most challenging political philosophers of the twentieth century, Arendt adopted an Aristotelian approach to explore the origins of totalitarianism, the structure of human consciousness, and the nature of violence and evil.

Aretaeus of Cappadocia

b. Probably second century C.E.
Cappadocia, Roman Empire
d. Date unknown
place unknown
fields: Medicine

Considered by many the greatest ancient physician after Hippocrates, Aretaeus wrote the best and most accurate descriptions of many diseases and made landmark studies of diabetes and neurological and mental disorders.

Arguello, Alexis

b. Apr. 19, 1952
Managua, Nicaragua
fields: Sports (boxer)

Latino Boxer. Alexis Arguello began boxing at the age of fifteen and won his first title in the 126-pound welterweight class in 1974. He then won the junior lightweight (130 pounds) and the lightweight (135 pounds) classes over the next six years. His attempt to win a fourth title, in the junior welterweight class, was thwarted by Aaron Pryor, who defeated Arguello in title bouts in 1982 and 1983. After their second fight, Arguello retired as a national hero. He joined the Contra movement in Nicaragua, then attempted an unsuccessful comeback in 1986.

Argüello, Concepción

b. 1790
San Francisco, Calif.
d. 1857
Convent of Saint Catherine Benicia, Calif.
fields: Religion and Theology, Historical Figure

Latina nun and part of a famous romantic pair. In 1806, Concepción Argüello, daughter of the commandant of San Francisco in the early nineteenth century, fell in love with Nicolai Rezanov, a Russian official who visited San Francisco to obtain food for a Russian colony in Alaska. The two became engaged, but their marriage was contingent on papal approval, which Rezanov was to obtain. He delivered the food he had obtained to Alaska, then set out for Russia in 1807 to report that his mission had succeeded. However, he died en route. Concepción did not learn what happened to him until 1842. In the interim, she became a nun and achieved fame for her kindliness and her charity.

Ari, ha-. *See* Luria, Isaac ben Solomon

Arias, Ronald Francis

b. Nov. 30, 1941
Los Angeles, Calif.
fields: Journalism, Literature

Latino journalist and novelist. Ronald Francis Arias worked as a journalist and published short stories before his debut novel, *The Road to Tamazunchale* (1975), was nominated for the National Book Award in 1976 and brought him widespread recognition as an important Mexican American writer. His style blended American realism, Magical Realism, and journalism. Among Arias's other published works are the nonfiction work *Five Against the Sea* (1989) and the short stories "El mago" (1970), "The Interview" (1974; adapted into a play, *The Wetback*, 1975), and "The Boy Ate Himself" (1980).

Arias Sánchez, Oscar

b. September 13, 1941
Heredia, Costa Rica
fields: Diplomacy, Government and Politics

Oscar Arias Sánchez, president of Costa Rica from 1986 to 1990, was the winner of 1987 Nobel Peace Prize for his Central American peace plan. The plan was termed Esquipulas II, after the Guatemalan city where negotiations began, but is also simply called the Arias peace plan. Guatemala, El Salvador, Honduras, Nicaragua, and Costa Rica signed the agreement in 1987.

Ariosto, Ludovico

b. September 8, 1474
Reggio Emilia
d. July 6, 1533
Ferrara
fields: Literature

Ariosto, although an accomplished Latin poet, made vernacular Italian the established language for serious poetry from lyrics and satires to drama and the epic.

Aripeka. *See* Arpeika

Aristarchus of Samos

b. c. 310 B.C.E.
Samos
d. c. 230 B.C.E.
Alexandria
fields: Astronomy, Mathematics

In the third century B.C.E., Aristarchus of Samos calculated the size of the sun and its distance from the earth. He was first to propose a heliocentric theory of the universe.

Aristide, Jean-Bertrand

b. July 15, 1953
Port Salut, Haiti
fields: Government and Politics

Jean-Bertrand Aristide was president of Haiti in 1991 and again from 1994 to 1996. Overthrown by military in 1991 after being in office seven months; went to United States. Returned to power with help of United States in 1994. After returning in 1994 he dismantled the country's military establishment, long guilty of abuses of power.

Aristippus

b. c. 435 B.C.E.
Cyrene, Cyrenaica (present-day Libya)
d. 365 B.C.E.
Athens, Greece
fields: Philosophy

Departing from the Sophism to which he was exposed as Socrates' student, Aristippus founded the Cyrenaic School of philosophy, the hallmark of which was hedonism.

Aristophanes

b. c. 450 B.C.E.
Athens, Greece
d. c. 385 B.C.E.
Athens, Greece
fields: Theater and Entertainment

Aristophanes' highly entertaining plays provide the only extant examples of Old Comedy, and his last works anticipate the shift to the New Comedy of Menander, Terence, and Plautus. His writings reveal much about not only dramaturgy in late fifth century B.C.E. Athens but also the social, political, and economic conditions of the time.

Aristotle

b. 384 B.C.E.
Stagirus, Chalcidice, Greece
d. 322 B.C.E.
Chalcis, Euboea, Greece
fields: Philosophy, Natural History, Science

Building on Plato's dialogical approach, Aristotle developed what is known as the scientific method. In addition, he founded the Lyceum, the second university-type institution (after Plato's Academy), which, with its vast collections of biological specimens and manuscripts of verse and prose, housed the first research library.

Aristoxenus

b. 375-360 B.C.E.
Tarentum
d. Date unknown
probably Athens
fields: Music

The theoretical writings on music by Aristoxenus established a foundation upon which modern theory is based.

Ariyoshi, George

full: George Ryoichi Ariyoshi
b. Mar. 12, 1926
Honolulu, Hawaii
fields: Government and Politics, Law

Japanese American politician, attorney; George Ariyoshi born in Honolulu, Hawaii, to Japanese immigrants; entered U.S. Army in 1944, working with U.S. military intelligence in Japan after World War II; after earning law degree from University of Michigan Law School in 1952, returned to Hawaii, where he served as a territorial representative, 1954-1958, and a territorial senator, 1958-1959; upon admittance of Hawaii as a state in the union, served as U.S. senator, 1959-1973; senate majority leader, 1965; governor of Hawaii, 1974-1986; first Japanese American to be elected governor of a state.

Ariyoshi, Koji

b. Jan. 30, 1914
Kona, Territory of Hawaii
d. Oct. 25, 1976
Honolulu, Hawaii
fields: Publishing, Journalism

Koji Ariyoshi, a Japanese American, founded the *Honolulu Record*, a left-wing weekly newspaper that supported the unions in their struggles against the big employers of Hawaii in the late 1940's and early 1950's. In 1952, he and six others were convicted of violating the Smith Act, which makes it a criminal offense to advocate the overthrow of any government in the United States by force or violence, a conviction that was reversed six years later.

Arkwright, Richard

b. December 23, 1732
Preston, Lancashire, England
d. August 3, 1792
Cromford, Derbyshire, England
fields: Business and Industry, Invention and Technology

Through exceptional drive, organizational ability, and unbounded confidence, Arkwright synthesized cotton spinning by machine into a continuous process under one roof and thereby established the factory system that was to characterize what came to be called the Industrial Revolution.

Armendáriz, Pedro

b. May 9, 1912
Churubusco, Mexico
d. June 18, 1963
Los Angeles, Calif.
fields: Theater and Entertainment (actor)

Latino actor. Pedro Armendáriz appeared in more than seventy-five films. He began his career acting in such Mexican films as director Emilio Fernández's *María Candelaria* (1943) and *The Pearl* (1945). He later acted in numerous U.S. films, including *The Fugitive* (1947), *Fort Apache* (1948), *We Were Strangers* (1949), *Tulsa* (1949), *The Wonderful Country* (1959), *Francis of Assisi* (1961), and *Captain Sinbad* (1963). Among the major directors he worked for were Luis Buñuel and John Ford. In 1963 he learned he had cancer and shot himself to death. His son, Pedro Armendáriz, Jr., also became an actor.

Armijo, Manuel

b. 1792
Albuquerque, N.Mex.
d. Dec. 9, 1853
fields: Government and Politics

Latino politician. Manuel Armijo was governor of New Mexico from 1827 to 1829 and for most of the period between 1837 and 1846. During the 1840's he promoted private development to discourage American Indians, Texans, and Americans from taking control of the region. During the Mexican American War he ordered his troops to abandon Santa Fe in the face of advancing American troops. It is not clear whether he was bribed by the Americans or feared engaging them in battle. The Mexican government brought charges of treason against Armijo but later dropped them for lack of evidence.

Armiño, Franca de

b. ?
Puerto Rico
fields: Labor Movement, Theater and Entertainment

Latina dramatist and labor organizer. Franca de Armiño (a pseudonym) was a feminist poet, essayist, and playwright who organized and wrote in support of workers' rights during the 1930's and 1940's. Although she is known to have published a play titled *Tragedia puertorriqueña* (Puerto Rican tragedy), a book of essays, and a book of poems, the only surviving work is the play *Los hipócritas: Comedia dramática social* (1937; the hypocrites: a social drama), which was performed in New York City in 1933.

Armistead, James. *See* Lafayette, James Armistead

Armstrong, Edwin H.

full: Edwin Howard Armstrong
b. December 18, 1890
New York, New York
d. January 31, 1954
New York, New York
fields: Invention and Technology (radio electronics), Radio

From the infancy of radio, Armstrong was the leading edge of its technical development, inventing the basic circuitry of modern AM-FM broadcasting.

Armstrong, Henry

né: Henry Jackson, Jr.
b. Dec. 12, 1912
Columbus, Miss.
d. Oct. 24, 1988
Los Angeles, Calif.
fields: Sports (boxer)

African American boxer; Henry Armstrong first boxer to hold three boxing titles simultaneously (featherweight, 1937; welterweight, 1938; and lightweight, 1938).

Armstrong, Lillian Hardin

b. February 3, 1898
Memphis, Tenn.
d. August 27, 1971
Chicago, Ill.
fields: Music (jazz pianist, vocalist, and composer)

African American jazz pianist, vocalist, and composer; Lillian Hardin Armstrong, one of the first female instrumentalists in jazz, was first widely recognized for her work in the early 1920's with Joe "King" Oliver's Creole Jazz Band; in 1924, married Louis Armstrong and played with his Hot Five and Hot Seven groups from 1925 to 1928; recorded jazz classics including "Struttin' with Some Barbeque" (1927) and "West End Blues" (1928); divorced in 1938; suffered a heart attack while performing "St. Louis Blues" in a memorial concert for Louis Armstrong held in Chicago and died shortly thereafter.

Armstrong, Louis

b. August 4, 1901
New Orleans, Louisiana
d. July 6, 1971
New York, New York
fields: Music

Armstrong's importance to the development of jazz is inestimable. Whether played or sung, almost all aspects of jazz style and technique were influenced directly by his innovations of the 1920's. His concepts of range, tone, phrasing, and rhythm, along with his sophisticated choice of pitch, were widely imitated.

Armstrong, Neil

full: Neil Alden Armstrong
b. August 5, 1930
Wapakoneta, Ohio
fields: Avaition and Space Exploration

The first man to walk on the surface of the Moon, on July 20, 1969, Armstrong was commander of *Apollo 11*, the first spacecraft to carry men to the Moon and back to Earth.

Arnaz, Desi, Sr.

full: Desiderio Alberto Arnaz y de Acha III
b. March 2, 1917
Santiago, Cuba
d. December 2, 1986
Del Mar, Calif.
fields: Theater and Entertainment

Cuban American bandleader and actor. In 1933 Desi Arnaz emigrated with his mother from Cuba to Miami, Florida. There he played with such figures as Xavier CUGAT, and by 1938, he led his own band. The following year he moved to California, where he married actress Lucille Ball. His film debut came with *Too Many Girls* in 1940. In 1950, Arnaz and Ball formed Desilu Productions, which pioneered the three-camera film technique that soon became standard in television. Their show, *I Love Lucy*, which featured Arnaz as bandleader Ricky Ricardo and Ball as his zany wife, ran from 1951 to 1961. *I Love Lucy* became a classic of television situation comedy and continued for decades in syndication.

Arnold, Benedict

b. January 14, 1741
Norwich, Connecticut
d. June 14, 1801
London, England
fields: Military Affairs

Despite his skillful leadership of the Colonial forces in the American Revolution, Arnold's betrayal of his country has made his name a synonym for treason.

Arnold, Matthew

b. December 24, 1822
Laleham, England
d. April 15, 1888
Dingle Bank, Liverpool, England
fields: Literature

One of the finest elegiac poets in the English language, Arnold was also Victorian Great Britain's greatest literary and cultural critic.

Arnold, Thomas

b. June 13, 1795
Cowes, Isle of Wight, England
d. June 12, 1842
Rugby, Warwickshire, England
fields: Education, History

Arnold changed British education by his reforms at Rugby School.

Arnold, Wallace Cornelius

b. July 27, 1938
Washington, D.C.
fields: Military Affairs

African American military officer; Wallace Cornelius Arnold served thirty years in Army, achieving rank of major general; posts included director of personnel and inspector general; also held commanding general positions.

Arnold of Villanova

b. c. 1239
Valencia, Aragon? or Provence region, France?
d. September 6, 1311
at sea, near Genoa
fields: Medicine, Religion and Theology

The first great figure of European medicine, physician to kings and popes, Arnold joined Arabic theory to European empiricism. His more than seventy scientific works and translations made him an influential medical theorist down past the sixteenth century, just as his radical theology and stormy life made him lastingly controversial.

Arnolfo di Cambio

b. c. 1245
Colle di Val d'Elsa, Italy
d. Between 1302 and 1310; Florence, Italy
fields: Art, Architecture

As chief architect of Florence during the end of the thirteenth century, Arnolfo directed the construction of some of Florence's principal monuments and brought the Italian classical tradition together with elements of the French Gothic.

Arouet, François-Marie. *See* Voltaire

Árpád

b. c. 850
southern Siberia
d. 907
Old Buda (modern Budapest)
fields: Government and Politics, Military Affairs

Árpád, the first great ruler of a united Hungarian people, led them in a conquest of the land that is present-day Hungary.

Arpeika

aka: Aripeka
aka: Apayaka Hadjo (Crazy Rattlesnake)
aka: Sam Jones
b. c. 1760
Ga.
d. 1860
Fla.
fields: Government and Politics, Native American Affairs

Native American leader. Arpeika was the only Seminole leader successfully to resist removal to the West. Military leader during the Second Seminole War (1835-1842) and Third Seminole War (1855-1858).

Arreola, Juan José

b. Sept. 12, 1918
Ciudad Guzmán, Jalisco, Mexico
fields: Literature

Latino writer. Juan José Arreola was an actor until he gained recognition for his short story "Hizo el bien mientras vivió" (1943), after which he began to focus on creative writing. He won a Rockefeller Foundation scholarship for creative writing in 1950 and the Xavier Villaurrutia prize in 1963. His work is characterized by use of irony and satire, as illustrated by the well-known story "El Guardagujas" (1952; the switchman), which satirizes the Mexican railroad system. Short-story collections include *Varia invención* (1949; varied invention) and *Confabulario* (1952; confabulary); he also wrote the novel *La feria* (1963; *The Fair*, 1977).

Arrhenius, Svante August

b. February 19, 1859
Castle of Vik, near Uppsala, Sweden
d. October 2, 1927
Stockholm, Sweden
fields: Chemistry, Physics

Arrhenius was one of the founders of the interdisciplinary science of physical chemistry. He also aided in establishing the international reputation of the Nobel Prizes, clarified the physical effects of light pressure from the sun, and developed the conception, called "panspermia," that life was introduced on Earth by spores from space. He won the 1903 Nobel Prize in Chemistry.

Arrington, Richard

b. Oct. 19, 1934
Livingston, Ala.
fields: Government and Politics, Education

African American politician and educator; Richard Arrington served as dean of Miles College; for ten years executive director of Alabama Center for Higher Education; in 1979 elected mayor of Birmingham, Alabama; reelected in 1983.

Arriola, Gustavo Montaño

b. July 23, 1917
Florence, Ariz.
fields: Art (cartoonist)

Latino cartoonist. Gustavo Montaño Arriola grew up in Los Angeles, California, and worked in the animation studios of Metro-Goldwyn-Mayer, Screen Gems, and Columbia Pictures during the 1930's. In 1941, Arriola began work on a daily comic strip called "Gordo," which introduced the general public to Mexican culture. Within one year the comic had one million readers. Although publication was interrupted for four years while Arriola served time in the military, "Gordo" became one of the most widely read comic strips of its time when Arriola resumed work on it in 1946.

Arroyo, Martina

b. Feb. 2, 1937?
New York, N.Y.
fields: Music (opera singer)

African American opera singer; in 1959 Martina Arroyo won national Metropolitan Opera audition; debuted with New York Philharmonic (1963); performed at the White House (1977).

Arthur, Chester A.

full: Chester Alan Arthur
b. October 5, 1829
Fairfield, Vermont
d. November 18, 1886
New York, New York
fields: Education, Law, Government and Politics

President of the United States, 1881-1885. Arthur's presidency, virtually free of corruption, comforted a nation grieving over the death of President James A. Garfield, maintained peace and order, promoted economic growth, and demonstrated the stability and adaptability of the American political system, particularly during emergencies.

Artis, William E.

b. Feb. 2, 1914
Washington, N.C.
d. 1977
fields: Art (sculptor), Education

African American sculptor and educator; William E. Artis best known for his sculptural work depicting human aspiration; instructor at Harlem YMCA and Nebraska State Teachers College.

Artist Formerly Known as Prince. *See* Prince

Aruego, Jose Espiritu

b. Aug. 9, 1932
Manila, Philippines
fields: Publishing

Jose Espiritu Aruego draws on his Filipino heritage in writing and illustrating children's books. His *Juan and the Asuangs* (1970) was honored as an outstanding picture book of the year by *The New York Times*. He illustrated Robert Kraus's award-winning book *Whose Mouse Are You?* (1970), and he and his wife, Ariane Dewey, have illustrated many children's books, including *Alligators and Others, All Year Long! A Book of Months* (1993).

Aryabhata

b. C.E. 475 or 476
Kusumapura, India
d. c. C.E. 550
place unknown
fields: Mathematics, Astronomy

Aryabhata, the first great Hindu mathematician-astronomer, in 499 wrote *The Aryabhatiya*, which describes the axial rotation of Earth and presents many innovative rules of arithmetic and planar and spherical trigonometry, and solutions to quadratic equations.

Arzner, Dorothy

b. January 3, 1897
San Francisco, California
d. October 1, 1979
La Quinta, California
fields: Film

An exception within the Hollywood film industry, Arzner was the major woman film director of the Hollywood studio system from the late 1920's through the early 1940's.

Arzola, Marina

b. July 12, 1939
Guayanilla, Puerto Rico
d. December, 1976
Puerto Rico
fields: Literature

Latina poet. While working toward a degree in art at the University of Puerto Rico, Marina Arzola became in involved "El grupo de Guajana" (The Guajana Group), a group of poets associated with the revolutionary literary magazine *Guajana*, founded in 1962. She embraced the militant Marxism and social rebellion of the group and found inspiration in the work of such Latin American poets as Pablo Neruda and César Vallejo. Arzola only published one work, *Pala-bras vivas* (1968), which won the Premio de Club Cívico de Damas de San Juan.

Asaba Waka. *See* Yamada, Waka

Asah, Spencer
aka: Lallo (Little Boy)
b. c. 1908
Carnegie, Okla.
d. May 5, 1954
Norman, Okla.
fields: Art (painter)

Native American painter. Spencer Asah was one of a group of Kiowa artists (the Kiowa Five or Kiowa Six) who initiated the flat style of easel painting, or traditional American Indian painting.

Asante, Molefi Kete
né: Arthur Lee Smith, Jr.
b. Aug. 14, 1942
Valdosta, Ga.
fields: Education

African American scholar; Molefi Kete Asante born Arthur Lee Smith, Jr., but legally changed his name in 1975; after receiving a doctoral degree in communications from the University of California, Los Angeles (UCLA) in 1968, taught at Purdue, UCLA, State University of New York, Howard University, and Temple University; named director of the Center for Afro-American Studies at UCLA; wrote more than two dozen books, including *Afrocentricity: The Theory of Social Change* (1980), *African Culture: The Rhythms of Unity* (1985), and *The Historical and Cultural Atlas of African-Americans* (1991); was founding editor of the *Journal of Black Studies*.

Asawa, Ruth
b. 1926
Norwalk, Calif.
fields: Sculpture

Ruth Asawa, a second-generation Japanese American, is an accomplished sculptor whose work has been exhibitied at the Museum of Modern Art in New York and at other prestigious museums. She was commissioned to create the Japanese American Internment Memorial in San Jose, California. Unveiled on March 5, 1994, the memorial is a visual history of the Japanese American experience.

Asbaje y Ramírez de Santillana, Juana Inés de. *See* Cruz, Sor Juana Inés de la

Asclepiades of Bithynia
b. 124 B.C.E.
Prusa (Cios), Bithynia
d. c. 44 B.C.E.
Rome
fields: Medicine

Asclepiades was the first physician to establish Greek medicine in Rome.

Ash, Mary Kay
né: Mary Kathlyn Wagner
b. May 12, 1915 (?)
Hot Wells, Texas
fields: Business and Industry

As founder and chairman emeritus of Mary Kay Cosmetics, a Fortune 500 company based on direct sales by women who demonstrate beauty products in homes, Mary Kay Ash is famous for her motivational techniques, including awarding pink Cadillacs as prizes.

Ashʿari, al-
full: Abu al-Hasan ʿAli ibn Isma'il al-Ash'ari
b. 873 or 874
Basra, southern Mesopotamia
d. 935 or 936
Baghdad, Iraq
fields: Religion and Theology, Philosophy

Al-Ashʿari initiated a theological movement which gave human reason only a limited role in demonstrating religious truths: Dialectical argument was acceptable if it remained subordinate to revealed facts.

Ashe, Arthur
b. July 10, 1943
Richmond, Virginia
d. February 6, 1993
New York, New York
fields: Sports (tennis)

The first African American man to achieve international prominence in tennis. Arthur Ashe won the 1968 U.S. Open and turned professional the next year. He won 51 of 304 tournaments and was inducted into the International Tennis Hall of Fame in 1985. Ashe used his fame to address a variety of issues dealing with human rights before dying of AIDS, contracted apparently from a blood transfusion, in 1993.

Ashford, Emmett
b. Nov. 23, 1914
Los Angeles, Calif.
d. Mar. 1, 1980
Los Angeles, Calif.
fields: Sports (baseball umpire)

First African American umpire to work a major league baseball game; Emmett Ashford became major league umpire in 1966; called opening game of 1966 season at Griffith Stadium, Washington, D.C.; in 1970, retired from umpiring.

Ashford, Evelyn
b. Apr. 15, 1957
Shreveport, La.
fields: Sports (track and field)

African American track and field athlete; in 1984 Olympic Games Evelyn Ashford won gold medals in the 100-meter run and the 400-meter relay; in 1988 Olympics, received silver medal in 100-meter run.

Ashikaga Takauji
b. 1305
Japan
d. 1358
Kyoto, Japan
fields: Government and Politics, Military Affairs

Through dogged military prowess and ruthless political decisiveness, Takauji prevented Japan from swinging back to an outdated Chinese-style imperial government and placed power fully in the hands of rising new military clans. The Ashikaga shogunate which he founded hastened innovations in politics, culture, and economics that launched Japan's High Middle Ages.

Ashishishe. *See* Curly

Ashurbanipal
aka: Ashur-bani-apli
b. c. 685 B.C.E.
Nineveh, Assyria
d. 627 B.C.E.
Nineveh, Assyria
fields: Government and Politics, Architecture, Art, Literature

The last great king of ancient Assyria, Ashurbanipal lived within a generation of its total annihilation. Inside his exquisitely decorated palace complex at Nineveh, he brought together a magnificent library of cuneiform writing upon clay tablets, which included materials from twenty-five hundred years of achievement by Sumerians, Akkadians, Babylonians, and Assyrians.

Ashurnasirpal II
aka: Ashur-nasir-apli
b. c. 915 B.C.E.
Ashur, Assyria
d. 859 B.C.E.
Kalhu, Assyria
fields: Warfare and Conquest, Government and Politics, Architecture, Art

Ashurnasirpal II created the Neo-Assyrian empire, expanding its boundaries to the Mediterranean coast and into the mountainous regions north and west of the Tigris homeland. At Kalhu, he built an enormous fortress capped by his magnificent palace, which featured the first extensive use of decorated bas-relief.

Asoka the Great

b. c. 302 B.C.E.
probably near Pataliputra, Magadha, India
d. c. 232 B.C.E.
place unknown
fields: Government and Politics, Religion and Theology

Through energetic and enlightened administration of his kingdom, Asoka spread the Buddhist faith in all directions and, by means of his Rock, Pillar, and Cave edicts, provided India, the districts surrounding India, and, ultimately, the entire world with an example of regal compassion that is as admirable as it is rare.

Aspasia

b. c. 475 B.C.E.
Miletus, Asia Minor (modern Turkey)
d. After 428 B.C.E.
probably Athens, Greece
fields: Government and Politics, Philosophy

Aspasia's role as companion to the Athenian statesman Pericles made her the target of contemporary abuse and criticism; that same status and her reputation for skill in rhetoric made her a philosophic and historical ideal of the independent, educated, influential woman.

Asquith, H. H.

full: Herbert Henry Asquith
aka: Herbert Henry, first earl of Oxford and Asquith
b. September 12, 1852
Morley, Yorkshire, England
d. February 15, 1928
The Wharf, Sutton Courtney, Berkshire, England
fields: Government and Politics

Prime Minister of Great Britain from 1908 to 1916, Asquith steered the British government through a period of acute crisis which saw passage of major Social Reform legislation, legal alteration of the constitutional relationship between the two houses of Parliament, severe differences between parties regarding the future position of Ireland within the United Kingdom, and British entry into World War I.

Assad, Hafez al-

b. October 6, 1930
Qardāha, Latakia Province, Syria
fields: Government and Politics

Hafez al-Assad officially took office as president of Syria in 1971 after having seized power in 1970 as the leader of the Ba'th Party. Reelected unopposed by overwhelming majorities in 1978, 1985, and 1992. The long tenure enabled Assad to endow his country with an unaccustomed political stability, but numerous domestic and international problems remained.

Asser, Tobias Michael Carel

b. April 28, 1838
Amsterdam, The Netherlands
d. July 29, 1913
The Hague, The Netherlands
fields: Diplomacy, Law, Government and Politics

Tobias Michael Carel Asser was a Dutch international-law scholar and peace activist. Helped to establish the Permanent Court of Arbitration in 1899 and to initiate and guide the peace conferences held at The Hague in 1893, 1894, 1900, and 1904. Shared Nobel Peace Prize with Alfred H. Fried in 1911. Served as arbitrator in individual disputes, as between Russia and the United States over the Bering Straits (1902) and between the United States and Mexico (1902) over the Pious Fund.

Assing, Norman

aka: Norman Asing
aka: Norman Ah-Sing
aka: Yuan Sheng
fl. c. 1800's
Sanzao, Guangdong Province, China
fields: Business and Industry

Norman Assing, a Chinese American, was a successful merchant and leader of the Chinese community in San Francisco in the mid-1800's. A patriotic American, his strongarm tactics resulted in an 1853 grand jury report charging that the conditions in his companies were repressive. This, combined with a failed move to place four Chinese into his custody, curbed his power.

Astaire, Fred

né: Frederick Austerlitz
b. May 10, 1899
Omaha, Nebraska
d. June 22, 1987
Los Angeles, California
fields: Dance, Film

Astaire was one of the greatest popular dancers of the twentieth century. His films with Ginger Rogers and other partners defined the essence of the American motion picture musical.

Astol, Lalo

full: Leonardo García Astol
b. 1906
Mexico
fields: Theater and Entertainment, Radio

Latino radio personality. Born in Mexico, Lalo Astol began performing in the United States in 1921 in San Antonio, Texas; he survived the Depression doing vaudeville acts. A stint doing comic dialogues on Spanish-language radio in 1938 led, in 1940, to a job as the emcee of a Mexican radio variety show. During the 1950's Astol did radio soap operas and began his struggle to keep plays, vaudeville routines, and Hispanic theater alive in the United States. In the late 1950's and early 1960's, Astol began working in television, writing, directing, and acting in the serial *El Vampiro* (the vampire).

Astor, John J.

full: John Jacob Astor
b. July 17, 1763
Waldorf, near Heidelberg, Germany
d. March 29, 1848
New York, New York
fields: Business and Industry

Combining a shrewd eye for profits with relentless determination, Astor became in turn America's first monopolist, its leading fur trader, its leading trader to China, and "landlord of New York." When he died, he was by far the richest man in the United States.

Astor, Nancy

né: Nancy Witcher Langhorne
b. May 19, 1879
Danville, Virginia
d. May 2, 1964
Grimsthorpe Castle, Lincolnshire, England
fields: Government and Politics, Social Reform

Born a Virginian, Astor was the first woman to sit in the British House of Commons. Always a controversial figure because of her outspoken views on almost every subject from temperance to race relations, she was a zealous campaigner for the rights of women and children.

Astoxkomi. *See* Crowfoot

Atatürk, Kemal

né: Mustafa
aka: Mustafa Kemal
b. May 19, 1881
Salonika, Ottoman Empire (now Thessaloniki, Greece)
d. November 10, 1938
Istanbul, Turkey
fields: Government and Politics, Military Affairs

Through his skills as a politician, general, and statesman, Atatürk founded the modern state of Turkey in 1923 out of the ashes of the old Ottoman Empire.

Athanasius, Saint

b. c. 293
Alexandria, Egypt

d. May 2, 373
Alexandria, Egypt
fields: Religion and Theology, Historiography

For half a century, Athanasius helped to maintain Christian orthodoxy in the Eastern church from his position as Bishop of Alexandria. His defense of the doctrine of the Trinity was influential in the formulation of the Nicene Creed.

Atherton, Gertrude

né: Gertrude Franklin Horn
b. October 30, 1857
San Francisco, California
d. June 14, 1948
San Francisco, California
fields: Literature

A prolific writer known for her California themes, Atherton produced several popular novels featuring strong-willed female protagonists.

Atkins, Cholly

full: Charles Atkins
b. Sept. 30, 1913
Birmingham, Ala.
fields: Dance, Theater and Entertainment

African American dancer and choreographer; Charles "Cholly" Atkins best known as partner of Charles "Honi" Coles in tap dancing duo of Atkins and Coles; in the 1940's they appeared with various well known swing bands and starred at the Apollo Theater in Harlem; in mid-1960's, Atkins choreographed for the Supremes and other Motown groups.

Atkins, David. *See* Sinbad

Atkins, Hannah Diggs

b. Nov. 1, 1923
Winston-Salem, N.C.
fields: Government and Politics

African American state politician and political appointee; Hannah Diggs Atkins served in the Oklahoma state legislature (1968-1980); Oklahoma State secretary of state and cabinet secretary of human resources (1987-1991); founder of National Association of Black State Legislators and of the National Association of Black Women Legislators.

Atkinson, Ti-Grace

b. 1939
Baton Rouge, La.
fields: Women's Rights, Social Reform

Radical feminist; at odds with many traditional women's organizations, Ti-Grace Atkinson has advocated the abolition of marriage and the family in favor of a classless society; was president of the New York chapter of the National Organization for Women (NOW; beginning 1968) but resigned her post in the late 1960's to head The Feminists, a radical organization devoted to a vision of society without patriarchy, sex-related roles, or abortion laws; she left The Feminists in 1970; outspoken on her view of lesbianism as not merely a sexual orientation but a political force in feminism; *Amazon Odyssey* (1974) contains a collection of her speeches and papers.

Atotarho

aka: Tadodaho (Snaky-Headed or His House Blocks the Path)
*b.*fl. 1500's
present-day New York State
fields: Government and Politics, Native American Affairs

Native American leader. Onondaga leader Atotarho was one of three central figures who established the Iroquois Confederacy. Deganawida (the Peacemaker) and Hiawatha were the other two.

Atsidi Sani. *See* Delgadito

Attila

aka: Attila the Hun
b. 406?
Pannonia?
d. 453
probably Jazberin
fields: Government and Politics, Warfare and Conquest

By uniting all the Hunnic tribes from the northern Caucasus to the upper Danube River, rendering the Romans a tributary state, Attila fashioned the most powerful empire of the West in the fifth century.

Attlee, Clement

full: Clement Richard Attlee
b. January 3, 1883
London, England
d. October 8, 1967
London, England
fields: Government and Politics

As prime minister from 1945 to 1951, Attlee led his Labour government as it became a close ally with the United States, granted Indian independence, nationalized major sectors of the economy, established a welfare state, and restructured the postwar economy. With his decisiveness, sound judgment, and managerial abilities, Attlee himself contributed significantly to that success.

Attles, Alvin A., Jr.

b. Nov. 7, 1936
Newark, N.J.
fields: Sports (basketball player and coach)

African American basketball player and coach; after playing eleven seasons with the Philadelphia Warriors, in 1970 Alvin A. Attles, Jr., became their coach and took the 1974-1975 team to the NBA championship; he coached the Warriors through 1983.

Attucks, Crispus

b. 1723
Framingham, Mass.
d. Mar. 5, 1770
Boston, Mass.
fields: Historical Figure

First person killed in the Boston Massacre; on March 5, 1770, Crispus Attucks, a literate former slave, was in a group of colonists that confronted a small group of British troops in Boston; he was the first of five colonists to die when the British fired into the crowd.

Atwood, Margaret

full: Margaret Eleanor Atwood
b. November 18, 1939
Ottawa, Ontario, Canada
fields: Literature

Noted for her witty analysis of modern life, Atwood has become a major figure in North American literature. Her many books of fiction and poetry are widely discussed in relation to both Canadian nationalism and the women's movement.

Auchiah, James

b. 1906
Medicine Park, Okla. Territory
d. Dec. 28, 1974
Carnegie, Okla.
fields: Art (painter)

Native American painter. James Auchiah was one of the Kiowa artists (the Kiowa Five or Kiowa Six) who created the Oklahoma style of Native American painting in the early to mid-twentieth century.

Audubon, John James

b. April 26, 1785
Les Cayes, Saint-Domingue (near Haiti)
d. January 27, 1851
New York, New York
fields: Ornithology, Art

A gifted artist with a love of nature and a passion for discovery, Audubon became the greatest painter of birds of his time, an important natural scientist, and an inspiration to conservationists.

Augusta, Alexander Thomas

b. Mar. 8, 1825
Norfolk, Va.
d. Dec. 21, 1890
Washington, D.C.
fields: Medicine (physician and surgeon)

African American physician and surgeon; in 1856 Alexander Thomas Augusta received his medical degree from a Canadian college because U.S. medical colleges would not admit him; became highest ranking black officer in the Union army with a medical commission (1863); later served in the Howard University medical department.

Augustine, Saint
né: Aurelius Augustinus
b. November 13, 354
Tagaste, Numidia
d. August 28, 430
Hippo Regius, Numidia
fields: Religion and Theology, Philosophy

Renowned for his original interpretations of Scripture and extensive writings—in particular, his *Confessions*—Augustine was the greatest Christian theologian of the ancient world.

Augustus
né: Gaius Octavius
aka: Octavian
b. September 23, 63 B.C.E.
Rome
d. August 19, 14 C.E.
Nola
fields: Government and Politics

Through his political skill and intelligence, Augustus transformed the chaos that followed the assassination of Julius Caesar into the long-lasting Roman Empire.

Aulne, Baron de l'. *See* Turgot, Anne-Robert-Jacques

Aung San Suu Kyi, Daw
b. June 19, 1945
Rangoon, now Yangon, Burma, now Myanmar
fields: Government and Politics, Civil Rights

After 1988, Daw Aung San Suu Kyi, daughter of a Burmese national hero, worked to resist the military regime and fight for democracy and human rights in Myanmar. Although she was placed under house arrest, her opposition party won a decisive victory at the polls in 1990. She received the Nobel Peace Prize in December, 1991.

Aurangzeb
full: Muhī-ud-Dīn Muhammad Aurangzeb
aka: Ālamgīr I
b. November 3, 1618
Dohad, India
d. March 3, 1707
Ahmadnagar, India
fields: Government and Politics

Mughal Emperor of India, 1658-1707. Aurangzeb was the last of the great Mughal emperors who ruled north and central India after 1526. The most pious and ruthless of these rulers, he was a great conqueror, a brilliant administrator, and an extraordinarily cunning statesman.

Aurobindo, Sri
né: Aurobindo Ghose
b. August 15, 1872
Calcutta, India
d. December 5, 1950
Pondicherry, India
fields: Philosophy, Religion and Theology, Government and Politics

Aurobindo was one of the leading politicians and great religious thinkers in twentieth century India. He was a leader of the first national political party with a platform demanding the independence of India from British rule. His writings and actions helped to revitalize India politically and spiritually.

Austen, Jane
b. December 16, 1775
Steventon, Hampshire, England
d. July 18, 1817
Winchester, Hampshire, England
fields: Literature

Austen's realistic rendering of dialogue and her satirical accuracy make her novels a matchless re-creation of upper-class English society in the late eighteenth and early nineteenth centuries. Her novels owe their lasting popularity, however, to Austen's understanding of human nature as it operates in everyday life.

Austerlitz, Frederick. *See* Astaire, Fred

Austin, J. L.
full: John Langshaw Austin
b. March 26, 1911
Lancaster, England
d. February 8, 1960
Oxford, England
fields: Philosophy, Language and Linguistics

In 1936 and 1927, J. L. Austin became the leading spirit of the post-World War II philosophical trend variously called Oxford philosophy, ordinary language philosophy, or analytic philosophy, and the teacher of many leading philosophers and linguists, influencing such thinkers as A. J. Ayer, Isaiah Berlin, and John R. Searle. Austin believed that the best way to reach agreement was through cooperative discussion of well-defined questions among collaborators. Austin's influence is remarkable because he published only seven papers during his lifetime, notably "Other Minds" (1946), "Ifs and Cans" (1956), and "A Plea for Excuses" (1956); three books, *Philosophical Papers* (1961), *Sense and Sensibilia* (1962), and *How to Do Things with Words* (1962), were published posthumously from lecture notes. Austin's work reoriented the research of many philosophers and laid the groundwork for the standard theory of speech acts, directing the course of the philosophy of language.

Austin, Patti
b. Aug. 10, 1948
New York, N.Y.
fields: Music (singer)

African American singer; after gaining early experience as a studio vocalist and singing advertising jingles, Patti Austin's album *Every Home Should Have One* (1981), produced by her godfather Quincy Jones, launched Jones's Qwest record label; she has also recorded songs with George Benson and James Ingram.

Austin, Richard H.
b. May 5, 1913
Stouts Mountain, Ala.
fields: Government and Politics

African American state official and politician; Richard H. Austin served as Michigan's secretary of state for twenty years, first elected in 1970, and reelected for four more consecutive terms.

Austin, Stephen Fuller
b. November 3, 1793
Wythe County, Virginia
d. December 27, 1836
Columbia, Texas
fields: Exploration and Colonization, Government and Politics

Austin established the first Anglo-American colony in Texas and played a significant role in the Texas Revolution, which resulted in that province securing independence from Mexico.

Autels, Guillaume des
b. 1529
d. 1581
fields: Literature

A member of la Pléiade (fl. 1549-1589), a group of loosely organized poets dedicated to raising the level of sophistication of the French language by adding words and genres derived from classical literature. Led by Pierre de Ronsard and Joachim du Bellay, they developed a new form of poetry based on forms such as the sonnet, the ode, epic, and elegy. They also worked to elevate the level of the poet to a position as an intermediary between humanity and the heavens.

Ávalos, David
b. 1947
fields: Art

Latino artist. David Ávalos, a resident of San Diego, California, makes controversial art that challenges racial stereotypes and the treatment of immigrants. In 1988 he helped create bus poster titled *Welcome to America's Finest Tourist Plantation*, which illustrates the disparity between the idyllic image of San Diego used to promote tourism and the harsh life of poor Hispanic people who work in agricultural fields there. *San Diego Donkey Cart* (1985) is a sculpture in the form of a donkey cart that features a wooden backboard depicting a border guard frisking an undocumented worker. The work was placed in front of San Diego's federal courthouse, where cases involving undocumented workers are decided.

Averroës

né: Abu al-Walid Muhammad ibn Ahmad ibn Muhammad ibn Rushd
aka: Ibn Rushd
b. 1126
Córdoba, Spain
d. 1198
Marrakech, Morocco
fields: Scholarship, Philosophy

Jurist, physician, and philosopher, Ibn Rushd was one of the last of a line of medieval Muslim scholars who sought to reconcile the truths of revealed religion and dialectical reasoning. Known to the medieval Christian Schoolmen by the name of Averroës, he exercised an overwhelming influence upon Latin thought through his commentaries on Aristotle.

Avery, Margaret

b. 1940's
Okla.
fields: Theater and Entertainment (actress and singer), Education

African American teacher, actress, and singer; Margaret Avery left teaching to pursue acting in Hollywood; first appeared in television commercials and blaxploitation films; appeared in various television shows and did live theater work; won 1972 L.A. Drama Critics Circle Award for outstanding performance; won best supporting actress Academy Award for role of Shug Avery in the film *The Color Purple* (1985).

Avicenna

né: Abu ʿAli al-Husain ibn ʿAbdallah ibn Sina
b. August or September, 980
Afshena, Transoxiana Province of Bukhara, Persian Empire
d. 1037
Hamadhan, Iran
fields: Philosophy, Medicine, Law, Astronomy, Philology

Avicenna was the first Islamic thinker to synthesize the philosophy of Aristotle and Plato with Islamic traditions. His writings on medicine were studied in Europe as late as the seventeenth century.

Avila, Bobby

né: Roberto Francisco Avila y Gonzalez
b. Apr. 2, 1924
Veracruz, Mexico
fields: Sports (baseball player)

Latino baseball player. In 1949, after switching from soccer to baseball, Bobby Avila joined the Cleveland Indians as a second baseman. He became one of the first Mexican players to succeed in the major leagues. In 1954, despite playing half the season with a broken thumb, he led the American League with a .341 batting average and helped the Indians win the pennant. He was an all-star selections in 1952, 1954, and 1955. In 1960 Avila returned to his homeland a national hero, using his popularity to become a politician and the president of the Mexican League.

Avila, Joaquín

b. 1948
Compton, Calif.
fields: Law

Latino lawyer; Joaquín Avila was Alaska supreme court clerk, 1973-1974; staff attorney, Mexican American Legal Defense and Education Fund (MALDEF), San Francisco, 1974-1976; associate counsel, MALDEF, Texas, 1976-1982; largely responsible for extension of the Voting Rights Act of 1982; served as president, MALDEF, 1982-1985.

Avogadro, Amedeo

b. August 9, 1776
Turin, Kingdom of Sardinia (now Italy)
d. July 9, 1856
Turin, Kingdom of Sardinia (now Italy)
fields: Chemistry, Physics

Avogadro was the first scientist to distinguish between atoms and molecules. Avogadro's law, a hypothesis that relates the volume of a gas to the number of particles present, greatly advanced the understanding of chemical reactions and resolved many chemical problems.

Awa Tside. *See* Dozier, Edward Pasqual

Awa Tsireh

aka: Alfonso Roybal
b. Feb. 1, 1898
San Ildefonso Pueblo, N.Mex.
d. Mar. 12, 1955
San Ildefonso Pueblo, N.Mex.
fields: Art (painter)

San Ildefonso Pueblo painter Alfonso Roybal, who signed his paintings Awa Tsireh, gained widespread recognition as a painter during the 1920's and 1930's; his paintings are included in many major museum collections; won first prize at the opening of the Exposition of Indian Tribal Arts in New York in 1931.

Awoninahku. *See* Lean Bear

Axelrod, Julius

b. May 30, 1912
New York, New York
fields: Chemistry, Medicine

Julius Axelrod explored the function of neurotransmitters and hormones. He showed the relationships between these substances and mental and cardiovascular problems. In 1970, he shared the Nobel Prize in Physiology or Medicine with Bernard Katz and Ulf von Euler.

Axworthy, Lloyd

b. December 21, 1939
North Battleford, Saskatchewan, Canada
fields: Government and Politics

Canadian political figure Lloyd Axworthy was the primary force behind the Ottawa Treaty of 1997, an agreement signed by 120 countries banning the use of land mines. A member of parliament, he served in various other cabinet positions before becoming minister of external affairs in 1996.

Aydid, Muhammad Farah

b. c. 1930
Beledweyne, Italian Somaliland
d. August 1, 1996
Mogadishu, Somalia
fields: Government and Politics

A member of Somalia's largest clan, the Hawiye, rebel leader Muhammad Farah Aydid overthrew Somali leader Muhammad Siad Barre in 1991. He contributed significantly to the famine and anarchy that engulfed Somalia for two years. Aydid gained notoriety when his forces killed American and other foreign troops serving under United Nations command in 1993. Labeled a war criminal by the United Nations.

Ayer, A. J.

full: Alfred Jules Ayer
b. October 29, 1910
London, England
d. June 27, 1989
London, England
fields: Philosophy

A. J. Ayer introduced the Austrian philosophy of logical positivism to the English-speaking world and continued the British empiricist and skeptical tradition of John Locke, George Berkeley, and David Hume. His contributions were primarily to the field of epistemology. *Language, Truth, and Logic* (1936) was the first systematic introduction of logical positivism for the English reader and remains the most accessible source for the ideas advanced by logical positivism, which had an enormous influence in philosophy until the late 1940's and a continuing influence in the social sciences until the 1960's.

Ayers-Allen, Phylicia. *See* Rashad, Phylicia

Ayllón, Lucas Vázquez de. *See* Vázquez de Ayllón, Lucas

Ayonwartha. *See* Hiawatha

Ayrton, Hertha Marks

né: Phoebe Sarah Marks
b. Apr. 28, 1854
Portsea, England
d. Aug. 23, 1923
North Lancing, Sussex, England
fields: Science, Invention and Technology, Physics

Hertha Marks Ayrton invented a line-divider in 1884; published *The Electric Arc* in 1902; explained sand ripples formed under ocean waves; invented drafting and architectural instruments; designed a defensive device, the antigas fan, used during World War I in 1916.

Azaceta, Luis Cruz

b. Apr. 5, 1942
Havana, Cuba
fields: Art (painter)

Latino painter. Luis Cruz Azaceta moved to the United States in 1960 and worked in a factory. From 1966 to 1969, he attended New York's School of Visual Arts. His early paintings featured cartoonlike images of mutilated figures that reflected his nightmarish memories of Cuba and his feelings of alienation. In the 1980's his work focused on the brutality of urban life. He has taught art at universities in California, Louisiana, and New York, and he has received numerous fellowships, including awards from the Guggenheim Memorial Foundation and the National Endowment for the Arts.

Azikiwe, Nnamdi

b. November 16, 1904
Zungeru, Nigeria
d. May 11, 1996
Enugu, Nigeria
fields: Government and Politics

Azikiwe is the father of modern Nigerian nationalism and the leader of Nigeria's independence struggle. He became the first president of the Republic of Nigeria in 1963 and retained that position until ousted during the 1966 coup. He also founded the University of Nigeria at Nsukka and was its first chancellor.

Azikiwe, Nnamdi

b. November 16, 1904
Zungeru, Nigeria
d. May 11, 1996
Enugu, Nigeria
fields: Government and Politics

Nnamdi (born Benjamin) Azikiwe was the first president of independent Nigeria, from 1963 to 1966. Before that, he was an influential journalist in Ghana and Nigeria. Presidency overthrown by army in 1966 coup. He lost subsequent elections for president but remained an Influential and respected figure; retired from politics in 1986.

Azpiazú, Don

b. Jan. 20, 1893
Cienfuegos, Cuba
d. Feb. 11, 1943
Havana, Cuba
fields: Music (bandleader and pianist)

Latino bandleader and pianist. In 1930, Don Azpiazú and his Havana Casino Orchestra recorded "El manisero" ("The Peanut Vendor"). The song became popular in both Europe and the United States and introduced the U.S. audience to Latin music in the rumba style and a wide range of Cuban percussion instruments that had never been heard before by the American public. The following year Azpiazú, along with singer Chick Bullock, recorded "Green Eyes," thought to be the first recorded mixture of American popular song and Cuban music. After the 1930's the American public's interest shifted to other latin bandleaders, and Azpiazú's popularity declined.

Azuela, Mariano

b. Jan. 1, 1873
Lagos de Moreno, Jalisco, Mexico
d. Mar. 1, 1952
Mexico City, Mexico
fields: Literature, Medicine

Latino writer and physician. Although educated as a physician, Mariano Azuela gained fame as one of Mexico's most prolific writers of the twentieth century. He served as a doctor in Francisco "Pancho" Villa's army during the revolution, and, after Villa's defeat at the hands of Venustiano Carranza, Azuela fled to Texas, where he wrote *Los de abajo: Novela de la revolución mexicana* (serialized, 1915; book form, 1916; *The Underdogs: A Novel of the Mexican Revolution*, 1929), about a boy who joins Villa's army. He later returned to Mexico and wrote many more books, including several more about the Mexican Revolution. He received Mexico's National Prize for Literature in 1949.

B

Baade, Walter

full: Wilhelm Heinrich Walter Baade
b. Mar. 24, 1893
Schröttinghausen, Westphalia, Germany
d. June 25, 1960
Bad Salzuflen, Westphalia, Germany
fields: Astronomy, Physics

Walter Baade, in 1920, discovered the asteroid designated 944 Hidalgo; 1922, discovered Comet 1922c (Comet Baade); 1944, presented his findings of two stellar populations; 1948, discovered the asteroid designated 1566 Icarus; discovered there appear to be two major categories of stars; demonstrated that Earth is located in a spiral galaxy; measured the size of the universe.

Baʿal Shem Tov

né: Israel ben Eliezer
b. c. 1700
Okup, Polish Ukraine
d. 1760
probably near Medzhibozh, Polish Ukraine
fields: Religion and Theology

Baʿal Shem Tov brought Eastern European Jewry out of a long period of decay and spread a rejuvenated religious outlook through society. He founded the modern Hasidic branch of Judaism.

Babangida, Ibrahim

full: Ibrahim Badamasi Babangida
b. August 17, 1941
Minna, Nigeria
fields: Government and Politics

Ibrahim Badamasi Babangida was president of Nigeria from 1985 to 1993. In 1985 he helped overthrow the country's military ruler, Alhaji Shagari, and assumed control. Overthrown, in turn, in 1993, after declaring election results void.

Babb, Bella Aurelia. *See* Mansfield, Arabella

Babbage, Charles

b. December 26, 1791
in or near London, England
d. October 18, 1871
London, England
fields: Mathematics, Invention and Technology, Computer Science

Babbage conceptually anticipated many of the developments realized in twentieth century computation science. He contributed to the mathematics of his time and invented several practical devices, including what is considered to be the first computer.

Babel, Isaac Emmanuilovich

b. July 13, 1894
Odessa, Ukraine, Russian Empire
d. March 17, 1941
Siberia, Soviet Union
fields: Literature

A leading Russian writer during the 1920's, Isaac Emmanuilovich Babel became a suspect in the eyes of the Soviet police after publishing *Red Cavalry* (1926), stories about the Russian civil war. The fact he was Jewish contributed to this distrust. Babel refused to write on demand in support of Joseph Stalin's regime and had difficulties publishing his own work. In 1939 he was sent to a concentration camp, where he perished in 1941.

Babeuf, François Noël

b. November 23, 1760
Saint-Quentin, France
d. May 27, 1797
Vendôme, France
fields: Government and Politics

François Noël Babeuf was a French revolutionary leader who was executed because of his outspoken criticism of the new regime. After the 1789 Revolution, he demanded abolition of feudal rights. As the Revolution deepened, he became increasingly at odds with public authorities. He established a journal known as *The Tribune of the People*, in which he attacked the leaders of the Reign of Terror and founded the Society of Equals, which was suppressed. He was later arrested and beheaded.

Bābur

né: Zahīr-ud-Dīn Muhammad
b. February 14, 1483
Fergana
d. December 26, 1530
Āgra, India
fields: Military Affairs, Government and Politics

Emperor of Hindustan, 1526-1530. Bābur, the first of the Mughal rulers in India, spread the Mughal Empire over most of northern India. He was a wise and kind king whose memoirs have revealed much about his life.

Babyface

né: Kenneth Edmonds
b. April 10, 1958
Indianapolis, Ind.
fields: Music (songwriter, producer, singer, and entrepreneur)

African American songwriter, producer, singer, and entrepreneur; in the 1990's, Babyface became one of the most successful and prolific songwriters and producers of popular music; teamed with Antonio "L.A." Reid and produced seventy-five top-ten hits, including Whitney Houston's "I Will Always Love You" ; recorded his own albums including *Tender Lover* (1989), *For the Cool in You* (1993), and *Day* (1996).

Baca, Elfego

b. 1865
Socorro County, N.Mex.
d. Aug., 1945
fields: Historical Figure (folk hero)

Elfego Baca's folk-hero status resulted from an incident that occurred in 1884 in the small village of Frisco, New Mexico, where he was serving as a deputy sheriff. Baca arrested a Texas cowboy and shot another Texan shortly after several Texans had gone on a shooting spree. When angry Texas cattlemen tried to "arrest" him for murder, Baca barricaded himself in a shed and spent thirty-six hours fighting off eighty Texans. He surrendered to a deputy sheriff whom he trusted and was acquitted at the subsequent trial. Baca became a politician in the late 1880's and studied law, gaining admission to the New Mexico bar in 1894.

Baca, Fabiola Cabeza de. *See* Gilbert, Fabiola Cabeza de Baca

Baca, Jimmy Santiago

né: José Santiago Baca
b. Jan. 2, 1952
Santa Fe, N.Mex.
fields: Literature

Latino writer. Jimmy Santiago Baca, who was jailed on a drug conviction when he was twenty years old, taught himself to read and write in prison. Baca's early poems, which he began writing in 1973, caught the eye of poet and editor Denise Levertov, who published his work and encouraged him to begin collecting his poems. The result was *Immigrants in Our Own Land* (1979). His third book, *Martín; &, Meditations on the South Valley* (1986), gained him international recognition and won both the Before Columbus Foundation American Book Award and the Vogelstein Foundation Award. *Black Mesa Poems* (1989) won the Wallace Stevens Poetry Award. During the 1990's, he continued to produce powerful verse.

Baca, Judith F.

b. Sept. 20, 1946
Los Angeles, Calif.
fields: Art, Social Reform

Latina artist and community organizer. Judith F. Baca helped pioneer the Latino mural movement in Southern California. In the early 1970's she became director Citywide Mural Project, supervising the painting of more than 250 murals. The projects often brought youth from warring street gangs together to work on murals. In 1975 she began supervising *The Great Wall of Los Angeles*, a visual history of Los Angeles that stretches across half a mile of a flood channel. In 1976, she helped found the Social and Public Art Resource Center, a nonprofit organization that helps Latino artists.

Baca-Barragán, Polly

b. Feb. 13, 1941
La Salle, Colo.
fields: Government and Politics

Latina legislator. Polly Baca-Barragán became active in Democratic Party politics while attending Colorado State University, from which she graduated in 1963. She directed Spanish-speaking affairs for the Democratic National Committee in 1971 and 1972. In 1974 she was elected to the Colorado state legislature. In 1978 she won a seat in the Colorado State Senate, becoming the first Hispanic woman to do so. She was reelected in 1982 and, in 1984, served as vice chairwoman of the Democratic National Committee.

Baca Zinn, Maxine

b. June 11, 1942
Santa Fe, N.Mex.
fields: Sociology

Latina sociologist; Maxine Baca Zinn was a professor of sociology, University of Michigan at Flint, 1975-1987; research professor in residence, Memphis State University in Memphis, 1987; senior research associate, Julian Samora Research Institute, 1990; professor of sociology, University of Michigan at East Lansing, since 1990; through sociological research on Latino families and Mexican American women, became a pioneer of Chicana feminism in the mid-1970's.

Bacall, Lauren

né: Betty Joan Perske
b. September 16, 1924
New York, New York
fields: Film, Theater and Entertainment

A major performing artist since her screen debut in 1944, Bacall continues to appear in major stage, television, and film roles. The endurance of her popularity and critical acclaim is a testament to Bacall's perseverance and dedicated professionalism.

Bach, Johann Sebastian

b. March 21, 1685
Eisenach, Germany
d. July 28, 1750
Leipzig, Germany
fields: Music

Organist, composer of hundreds of instrumental and choral works, known for his contrapuntal music; founder of a musical dynasty, including four sons: Wilhelm Friedemann, Karl Philipp Emanuel, Johann Christoph Friedrich, and Johann Christian. For three hundred years, Bach has brought joyful, profound, and uplifting music to millions of people the world over. So significant was his contribution to musical composition that some historians characterize music history as "before Bach" and "after Bach."

Bachelard, Gaston

b. June 27, 1884
Bar-sur-Aube, France
d. October 16, 1962
Paris, France
fields: Philosophy, Literature

Philosopher of science and literary analyst, Gaston Bachelard was a major figure in the "criticism of science" school, which argues that scientific activity involves merely observing and analyzing reality. Bachelard pointed out that reality, or the "real world," is constantly changing, and therefore attempts to approximate reality do not involve concrete knowledge of things. Bachelard claimed that daydreaming is not a private matter but part of a collective experience; dreaming and imagining are essential activities with as much value as scientific enterprise. Named a *chevalier* of France's Legion of Honor in 1937. Important works include *The New Scientific Spirit* (1934), *The Psychoanalysis of Fire* (1938), and *The Right to Dream* (1970).

Backus, John

b. Dec. 3, 1924
Philadelphia, Pennsylvania
fields: Mathematics (applied math and mathematical logic)

John Backus was an IBM programmer who developed FORTRAN, a computer language for scientific and engineering computation. He also developed the notation for describing grammatical rules for high-level languages, known as Backus-Naur Form. In 1974 he won the National Medal of Science. In 1977 he introduced a functional programming language called FP.

Bacon, Francis

aka: Sir Francis Bacon
b. January 22, 1561
London, England
d. April 9, 1626
London, England
fields: Philosophy, Science, Government and Politics

A noted statesman of Renaissance England, Francis Bacon defended the divine right theory of monarchy. He became attorney-general in 1613 and lord chancellor in 1618. His political career ended when he was convicted of taking bribes from litigants. After being forced into retirement, he wrote on philosophy and literature. His thirty works include *The Advancement of Learning* (1605, expanded in 1623), *The New Organon and Related Works* (1622), *The New Atlantis* (1626), and several volumes of essays.

Bacon, Nathaniel

b. January 2, 1647
Suffolk, England
d. October 26, 1676
Gloucester County, Virginia
fields: Government and Politics

Bacon died while leading a rebellion against the royally appointed governor of Virginia. A century later, on the eve of the American Revolution, he became a symbol of resistance to tyranny.

Bacon, Roger

b. c. 1220
Ilchester, Somerset, England
d. c. 1292
probably Oxford, England
fields: Science, Education, Philosophy

Bacon was a pioneer in the development of the scientific experimental method, and he advocated educational reform based on secular, scientific disciplines.

Bad Heart Bull, Amos

aka: Tatanka Cante Sica (Bad Heart Buffalo)
aka: Eagle Lance
b. c. 1869
present-day Wyoming
d. 1913
fields: Historiography, Native American Affairs

A member of the Ite Sica band of Oglala Lakota (Sioux), Amos Bad Heart Bull kept an extensive and unique pictographic history of the Oglala Lakota that spanned the last half of the nineteenth century and the beginning of the twentieth.

Baden-Powell, Robert Stephenson Smyth

aka: Sir Robert Stephenson Smyth Baden-Powell
b. February 22, 1857
London, England
d. January 8, 1941
Nyeri, Kenya
fields: Military Affairs, Social Reform

A celebrated hero of the Boer War, Baden-Powell gained universal and lasting fame as the founder of the Boy Scouts and the Girl Guides. He was revered as the "chief scout" of the movement, shaped its ideals, and provided its essential literature.

Badillo, Herman

b. Aug. 21, 1929
Caguas, Puerto Rico
fields: Government and Politics

Born in Puerto Rico; Herman Badillo was sent to the United States as a boy in 1940; gained national recognition during unsuccessful race for mayor of New York City; served as U.S. representative as a New York democrat, 1970-1978; first Puerto Rican elected as a voting member of Congress; appointed deputy mayor of New York City in 1978 (stayed through 1979).

Baeck, Leo

b. May 23, 1873
Lissa, Germany
d. November 2, 1956
London, England
fields: Scholarship, Philosophy, Religion and Theology

Teacher, author, historian of religion, philosophical-theological thinker, and outstanding articulator of modern Judaism, Baeck was the leading rabbi in Germany before World War II and one of the foremost rabbinical scholars of the twentieth century.

Baer, Karl Ernst von

b. February 29, 1792
Piep, near Jerwen, Estonia
d. November 28, 1876
Dorpat, Estonia
fields: Biology, Anthropology, Geology

Baer gained his greatest fame early in his career through his discovery of the mammalian egg and his contributions to the understanding of embryological development. In his later years, Baer would turn his attention to anthropological investigations, including the state of primitiveness of various races, and to geological studies, especially in Russia.

Báez, Alberto Vinicio

b. Nov. 15, 1912
Puebla, Mexico
fields: Physics

Latino physicist. Alberto Vinicio Báez received his B.S. in physics from Drew University in 1933, his M.A. from Syracuse University in 1935, and his Ph.D. from Stanford University in 1960. His primary area of interest was the use of X rays in optical radiation, optics and microscopy, optical images and holography, and instrumentation for astronomy. He taught physics and mathematics and conducted research at several schools, including Cornell University and Stanford University.

Baez, Joan

full: Joan Chandos Baez
b. January 9, 1941
Staten Island, New York
fields: Music, Peace Advocacy

After achieving great success as a folksinger, Baez used her considerable influence to support causes ranging from civil rights to global peace, becoming an icon for the disaffected generation of the 1960's.

Baeza, Braulio

b. Mar. 26, 1940
Panama City, Panama
fields: Sports (jockey)

Latino jockey. Braulio Baeza became a walker at the age of eight and made his first race mount at fifteen. By 1959 he was the leading Panamanian jockey. He moved to the United States in 1960 and continued his success, winning the Belmont Stakes in 1961, 1963, and 1969, and the Kentucky Derby in 1963. Baeza was considered by many to be the sport's finest tactician and became known as the jockey with "a clock in his head" for his ability to closely estimate the times of his runs.

Bahya ben Joseph ibn Pakuda

b. fl. second half of eleventh century
fields: Religion and Theology, Philosophy

Author of *al-Hidāya ilā farāʿid al-gulūb*, better known from the Hebrew translation *Ḥovot ha-levavot* (1161; *Duties of the Heart*, 1962), a classic statement of the inner response necessary for a true commitment of self to the service of God. Despite Arab and Islamic influence (notably, Muslim Sufism and Arabic Neoplatonism), the cosmological, ethical, and eschatological discourses of *Duties of the Heart* are essentially Jewish in both content and character. The work is considered the most popular moral-religious work of the medieval period and left an indelible mark on subsequent generations of Jewish ethical and pietistic writing.

Baier, Annette C.

b. October 11, 1929
Queenstown, New Zealand
fields: Philosophy, Women's Rights

Annette C. Baier's work in traditional philosophical fields demonstrated the worth of women philosophers, and her theory of "appropriate trust" created a middle ground between the male emphasis on justice, order, and obligation and such feminine values as love, caring, and nurturing. In 1998, she became a fellow of the American Academy of Arts and Sciences, one of only four in the philosophy and theology category. Major works include *Postures of the Mind* (1985), *Moral Prejudices* (1994), and *The Commons of the Mind* (1997).

Baïf, Antoine de

full: Jean-Antoine de Baïf
b. 1532
Venice, Italy
d. 1589
fields: Literature

A member of La Pléiade (fl. 1549-1589), a group of loosely organized poets dedicated to raising the level of sophistication of the French language by adding words and genres derived from classical literature. Led by Pierre de Ronsard and Joachim du Bellay, they developed a new form of poetry based on forms such as the sonnet, the ode, epic, and elegy. They also worked to elevate the level of the poet to a position as an intermediary between humanity and the heavens.

Bailey, John B.

b. ?
fields: Photography

African American photographer; active in Boston, Mass., during the 1840's, John B. Bailey specialized in portraiture; teacher of photographer and painter James Presley Ball.

Bailey, Pearl

b. Mar. 29, 1918
Newport News, Va.
d. Aug. 17, 1990
Philadelphia, Pa.
fields: Music (singer), Theater and Entertainment

African American singer and actress, known for her performances of "Bill Bailey, Won't You Please Come Home" and "Toot Toot Tootsie, Good-bye," Pearl Bailey received a Special Tony Award for her starring role in an all-black version of *Hello, Dolly!* (1967); among many stage and screen credits, hosted her own television variety program, *The Pearl Bailey Show* (1971); special delegate to the U.N. under Presidents Ford, Reagan, and Bush.

Bajer, Fredrik

b. April 21, 1837
Vester Egede, Denmark
d. January 22, 1922
Copenhagen, Denmark
fields: Diplomacy, Government and Politics, Peace Advocacy

A Danish diplomat and peace activist, Fredrik Bajer was awarded the 1908 Nobel Peace Prize. Bajer was a delegate at the founding session of the Interparliamentary Union in 1889. First chairman of the International Peace Bureau in 1891. In 1904 and

1905 a primary force in the Danish adoption of peacetime treaties with Portugal, Italy, and the Netherlands.

Baker, Anita

b. Jan. 26, 1958
Toledo, Ohio
fields: Music (rhythm-and-blues singer)

African American rhythm-and-blues singer Anita Baker received six Grammy Awards and three American Music Awards for her mellow love songs, many of which she wrote, arranged, and produced; albums include *The Songstress* (1983), *Giving You the Best That I Got* (1988), and *Compositions* (1990).

Baker, Augusta Braxton

b. Apr. 1, 1911
Baltimore, Md.
d. February 23, 1998
fields: Literature (librarian)

African American librarian; for thirty-seven years, Augusta Braxton Baker served as children's librarian, assistant coordinator of children's services, and storytelling specialist with the New York Public Library system; acquired age-appropriate materials on cultural heritage for children.

Baker, David

b. Apr. 2, 1881
Louisville, Ky.
d. ?
fields: Invention and Technology (inventor)

African American inventor; David Baker's inventions include scales to prevent overloading in elevators, a sanitary cuspidor, and a railway signaling device.

Baker, David

b. Dec. 21, 1931
Indianapolis, Ind.
fields: Music (jazz musician, conductor, and composer), Education

African American educator, jazz musician, conductor, and composer; David Baker has authored compositions and books on music; he has performed with various orchestras and toured with Quincy Jones; headed the jazz program at Indiana University's School of Music.

Baker, Denise

b. ?
Chicago, Ill.
fields: Journalism

African American journalist; Denise Baker first produced a Chicago radio station's late-night talk show (1974); in 1978, worked for a Public Broadcasting Service affiliate in Washington, D.C., covering local and national affairs; received two Emmy Award nominations for her work in public affairs; in 1981, joined NBC News in New York City.

Baker, Dusty

full: Johnnie B. Baker, Jr.
b. June 15, 1949
Riverside, Calif.
fields: Sports (baseball player and manager)

African American baseball player and manager; Dusty Baker retired from the Oakland Athletics in 1986, after nineteen seasons in the major leagues; since 1993, he has managed the San Francisco Giants. He was named National League Manager of the Year in 1993.

Baker, Ella

b. Dec. 13, 1903
Norfolk, Va.
d. Dec. 13, 1986
New York, N.Y.
fields: Civil Rights

African American civil rights activist and officer in several civil rights organizations. While a member of the Southern Christian Leadership Conference, Ella Baker led civil rights protests in the South and helped found the Student Non-Violent Coordinating Committee (SNCC) in 1960. She also helped organize the Mississippi Freedom Democratic Party (MFDP) in 1964 and was active in supporting African liberation movements in Southern Africa.

Baker, George. *See* Father Divine

Baker, Houston Alfred, Jr.

b. March 22, 1943
Louisville, Ky.
fields: Education, Scholarship

African American educator and scholar. Houston Alfred Baker, Jr., taught English at Yale University, the University of Virginia, and the University of Pennsylvania, where he was also director of Afro-American Studies. His numerous scholarly articles and books have focused on African American literature, culture, and aesthetics. Baker is the author of three volumes of poetry and has received many academic awards.

Baker, James E.

b. Jan. 21, 1935
Suffolk, Va.
fields: Government and Politics

African American political appointee; James E. Baker served as State Department foreign service officer in 1960; in 1972, became first African American diplomat appointed to a permanent post in apartheid South Africa; director of U.N. Special Economic Assistance Program (1984).

Baker, Josephine

né: Freda Josephine McDonald
b. June 3, 1906
St. Louis, Missouri
d. April 10, 1975
Paris, France
fields: Dance, Theater and Entertainment, Civil Rights

The first international black woman superstar, Baker achieved phenomenal success as a singer and dancer; offstage, she worked for international peace and civil rights.

Baker, LaVern

b. Nov. 11, 1929
Chicago, Ill.
d. Mar. 10, 1997
New York, N.Y.
fields: Music (rhythm-and-blues singer)

African American singer; LaVern Baker's versatile vocal stylings, gutsy and poignant, gained her a contract with Atlantic Records in 1953 and recognition for such recordings as "That's All I Need," "Shake a Hand," and "Jim Dandy"; in 1991, inducted into the Rock and Roll Hall of Fame.

Baker, Mary Morse. *See* Eddy, Mary Baker

Baker, Philip John. *See* Noel-Baker, Philip John

Bakhtin, Mikhail

full: Mikhail Mikhailovich Bakhtin
b. November 16, 1895
Orel, Russia
d. March 7, 1975
Moscow, U.S.S.R.
fields: Literature

Bakhtin had an impact on literary theory, especially on point of view in the novel; on the philosophy and interrelatedness of language and society; on the extension of areas of linguistics and schools of literary theory; and on modern philosophy, presenting an alternative to systems based on Greek philosophers.

Bakr, Mohammed Ture ibn Abi. *See* Mohammed I Askia

Bakunin, Mikhail

full: Mikhail Aleksandrovich Bakunin
b. May 30, 1814
Premukhino, Russia
d. July 1, 1876
Bern, Switzerland
fields: Philosophy, Social Reform

Bakunin was the foremost anarchist of his time. A relentless revolutionary agitator, he wrote prolifically and inspired a political movement, Nihilism, which survived well into the twentieth century.

Balanchine, George

né: Georgi Melitonovitch Balanchivadze
b. January 22, 1904
St. Petersburg, Russia
d. April 30, 1983
New York, New York
fields: Dance

The foremost choreographer of his time, Balanchine transformed ballet into a diverse, vibrantly contemporary, American medium. He established a training tradition and brought ballet to the forefront of the performing arts in the United States.

Balanchivadze, Georgi Melitonovitch. *See* Balanchine, George

Balboa, Vasco Núñez de

b. 1475
Jeres de los Caballeros, Estremadura Province, Spain
d. January, 1519
Acla, Castillo de Oro, Panama
fields: Exploration and Colonization

Balboa was a Spanish conquistador who participated in the exploration and conquest of the Caribbean and the Central American mainland during the early sixteenth century. In 1513, he "discovered" the Pacific Ocean.

Balch, Emily Greene

b. January 8, 1867
Jamaica Plain, Massachusetts
d. January 9, 1961
Cambridge, Massachusetts
fields: Social Reform, Education, Peace Advocacy

Among the first generation of women to graduate from college in large numbers, Balch authored the frequently cited *Our Slavic Fellow Citizens* (1910) and, as a reward for her peace activities, received the Nobel Peace Prize.

Balch, John A.

b. July 6, 1876
San Francisco, Calif.
d. May 15, 1951
San Francisco, Calif.
fields: Business and Industry

This San Francisco businessperson invested in Hawaiian businesses and became very influential on the islands. John A. Balch purchased the territory's telegraph company in 1906 and built it into a dominant telephone company. He wrote the book *Shall the Japanese Be Allowed to Dominate Hawaii?* (1943).

Baldorioty de Castro, Román

b. 1822
d. 1889
Ponce, Puerto Rico
fields: Literature, Government and Politics

Writer and political figure. During the nineteenth century, Román Baldorioty de Castro supported increased autonomy for Puerto Rico under Spanish colonial rule. As a deputy to the Cortes (the Spanish parliament), to which he was appointed in 1870, he worked to defend colonial rights. In 1872 he founded the newspaper *El Derecho*, whose editorial policy was to support both autonomy and the abolition of slavery. In 1880, he founded another newspaper, *La Crónica*. In 1887 he founded the Partido Autonomista, which worked for Puerto Rican independence. His anti-Spanish sentiment eventually resulted in his imprisonment.

Baldwin, Henry

b. 1780
d. 1844
fields: Law

U.S. Supreme Court justice, 1830-1844 (died while in office); appointed by President Jackson. First justice consistently to write separate opinions expressing his views. Significant opinion: *Holmes v. Jennison*, 39 U.S. 540 (1840). Other publication: *A General View of the Origin and Nature of the Constitution and Government of the United States* (1937).

Baldwin, James

b. August 2, 1924
New York, New York
d. November 30, 1987
St. Paul de Vence, France
fields: Literature

During the racial unrest in the United States in the 1960's, Baldwin was the most visible and respected literary figure in the Civil Rights movement. His best work, including *Go Tell It on the Mountain* (1953) and *The Fire Next Time* (1963), focused on racial concerns and on homosexuality.

Baldwin, Robert

b. May 12, 1804
York, Ontario, Canada
d. December 9, 1858
Toronto, Canada
fields: Government and Politics

Baldwin worked for reform policies which led to responsible government in Upper Canada and, as part of the "Great Ministry" (1848-1851), with Louis Hippolyte La Fontaine, upheld the idea of biculturalism in forging the eventual responsible government established in Canada.

Baldwin, Stanley

b. August 3, 1867
Bewdley, Worcestershire, England
d. December 14, 1947
Astley Hall, Worcestershire, England
fields: Government and Politics

Baldwin was the dominant political figure in British politics during the 1920's and 1930's, was prime minister on three separate occasions, and personified both the attempt to narrow class differences during that era and the unsuccessful policies to avoid a second world war.

Balfour, Arthur

full: Arthur James Balfour
aka: Arthur James, first earl of Balfour
b. July 25, 1848
Whittinghame, East Lothian, Scotland
d. March 19, 1930
Woking, Surrey, England
fields: Government and Politics, Philosophy

As prime minister (1902-1905), and in many other high government offices, Balfour provided leadership to his country and made noteworthy contributions to world peace. Best known for his 1917 Balfour Declaration, advocating a national home in Palestine for the Jewish people.

Balfour, Michael

b. November 22, 1908
Oxford, England
d. September 16, 1995
London, England
fields: Warfare and Conquest, Government and Politics

Michael Balfour was a major figure in British propaganda work during World War II. He later wrote the highly influential book *Propaganda in War, 1939-1945: Organisations, Policies, and Publics in Britain and Germany* (1979).

Baline, Israel. *See* Berlin, Irving

Ball, James Presley

b. 1825
d. 1905
fields: Art (painter), Photography

African American painter and photographer; although James Presley Ball's first daguerrean gallery in Cincinnati, Ohio, failed, he returned to open a successful second gallery, partnering with Alexander Thomas and, later, with his son; moved to Montana in the 1870's and specialized in scenes of African American life and portraits.

Ball, John

b. 1331
Peldon, Essex, England
d. July 15, 1381
St. Albans Abbey
fields: Government and Politics

The rebel John Ball, who described himself as "Sometime Saint Mary priest of York and now of Colchester," was one of the leaders of the Peasants' Revolt of 1381.

Ball, Lucille

full: Lucille Désirée Ball
b. August 6, 1911
Jamestown, New York
d. April 26, 1989
Los Angeles, California
fields: Film, Television

Starring in the television series *I Love Lucy* during the 1950's, Lucille Ball established herself as one of that medium's most popular comedic actresses as well as one of the first women to wield power in the television industry.

Ballard, Robert Duane

b. June 30, 1942
Wichita, Kansas
fields: Archaeology, Oceanography

As a pioneering undersea explorer, Ballard has been responsible for several remarkable discoveries, including the resting place of the *Titanic* and other ships, new life-forms along hot spots in the undersea earth crust, and evidence supporting the theory of plate tectonics.

Baltimore, David

b. Mar. 7, 1938
New York, New York
fields: Biology, Medicine

In 1975 David Baltimore shared the Nobel Prize in Physiology or Medicine for his discovery of the enzyme reverse transcriptase; cofounded the Recombinant DNA Advisory Committee at the National Institutes of Health (NIH) in 1976; named president of the California Institute of Technology in 1997.

Balzac, Honoré de

né: Honoré Balzac
b. May 20, 1799
Tours, France
d. August 18, 1850
Paris, France
fields: Literature

Balzac's novels, assembled under the collective title *The Human Comedy*, form a literary monument composed of some ninety-five works, with more than two thousand characters, which provides a comprehensive survey and analysis of French society and culture at all levels during the first half of the nineteenth century.

Bambara, Toni Cade

né: Miltona Mirkin Cade
b. March 25, 1939
New York, N.Y.
d. December 9, 1995
Wallingford, Pa.
fields: Literature

African American novelist, short-story writer, screenwriter, and activist. Toni Cade Bambara is known for her creative use of Black English in her fiction such as *Gorilla, My Love* (1972), *The Sea Birds Are Still Alive* (1977) and her American Book Award-winning novel *The Salt Eaters* (1980). She collaborated with colleague Louis Massiah on several television documentaries, including an account of the 1985 MOVE firebombing incident entitled *The Bombing of Osage Avenue* and a documentary about the life of W. E. B. Du Bois.

Ban, Shinzaburo

b. 1854
Tokyo, Japan
d. Jan. 18, 1926
fields: Business and Industry

In 1891, Shinzaburo Ban, a Japanese American, formed the S. Ban Company of Portland, a labor-contracting business. The company, one of the region's three biggest firms, brought over many Japanese immigrants to work on U.S. railroads. Ban branched out, opening a number of lumber mills, but went bankrupt in 1924. In 1893 he helped to found Portland Japanese Methodist Church.

Bancroft, Anne

né: Anna Maria Louisa Italiano
b. September 17, 1931
New York, New York
fields: Film, Theater and Entertainment

A successful actor, both on stage and in film, Anne Bancroft has developed women characters of depth, complexity, and variety.

Bancroft, George

b. October 3, 1800
Worcester, Massachusetts
d. January 17, 1891
Washington, D.C.
fields: History, Scholarship, Government and Politics, Diplomacy

Contributing greatly to both scholarly and popular thought in the nineteenth century United States, George Bancroft explained the transformation of the British Colonies into the United States. Served in many capacities in the U.S. government, including Secretary of the Navy (1845-1846), established the U.S. Naval Academy at Annapolis.

Bandaranaike, Sirimavo Ratwatte Dias

b. Apr. 17, 1916
Ratnapura, Ceylon, now Sri Lanka
fields: Government and Politics

A year after the assassination of her husband, Ceylon prime minister Sirimavo Ratwatte Dias Bandaranaike in 1959, Bandaranaike became prime minister. She lost the 1965 election but regained power to hold the office from 1970 to 1977. During her second term, she sought the nationalization of important industries and diplomatic recognition of major communist world powers. Her administration was criticized for its failure to revive the economy and the repressive measures it took. She was again elected prime minister in 1994.

Bandinelli, Roland. *See* Alexander III

Bandini de Couts, Ysidora

b. ?
fields: Historical Figure (rancher)

Latina rancher. Ysidora Bandini de Couts, one of three daughters of Juan Bandini, a pro-American Peruvian rancher living in San Diego, greeted U.S. forces occupying California in 1846 with an American flag she and her sisters made from white muslin sheets striped with red and blue silk from their gowns. Bandini de Couts also worked to restore the deteriorating mission of San Luis Rey.

Banerjea, Surendranath

b. November 10, 1848
Calcutta, India
d. August 6, 1925
Barrackpore, near Calcutta, India
fields: Government and Politics

Banerjea's dedication to moderation in the Indian struggle for liberation from Great Britain served as a political focus during some of the most dangerous times of modern Indian history. His position as one of the most respected Bengali leaders helped to stabilize and concentrate Indian protest into the channel of the Congress Party, which was to inherit Indian government after independence.

Bankhead, Tallulah

full: Tallulah Brockman Bankhead
b. January 31 or February 12, 1902
Huntsville, Alabama
d. December 12, 1968
New York, New York
fields: Film, Theater and Entertainment

A stage, film, and radio personality in the United States and England, Bankhead was instrumental in shifting stage images of women from the demure to the uninhibited.

Banks, Dennis

b. Apr. 12, 1937
Leech Lake Reservation, Minn.
fields: Civil Rights, Social Reform, Native American Affairs

Anishinabe Ojibwa activist; Dennis Banks founded with George Mitchell and Clyde Bellecourt the American Indian Movement (AIM), 1968, to assist Native Americans in securing legal and economic rights; planned the occupation of Alcatraz Island in 1969, day of mourning at Plymouth, Massachusetts, 1970, and the armed occupation of Wounded Knee (1973), site of an 1890 Indian massacre; served fourteen months in a South Dakota penitentiary, 1984-1985, for involvement in a 1973 riot; throughout the 1980's and 1990's raised awareness of the concerns of Native Americans with organized walks and runs; wrote his autobiography, *Sacred Soul* (1988).

Banks, Ernie

full: Ernest Banks
b. Jan. 31, 1931
Dallas, Tex.
fields: Sports (baseball player)

African American baseball player; elected to the Baseball Hall of Fame in 1977, Ernie Banks was the first African American to play for the Chicago Cubs; he was selected to the All-Star team eleven times, twice a home-run leader, and twice elected the National League's Most Valuable Player.

Banks, Joseph

aka: Sir Joseph Banks
b. February 13, 1743
London, England
d. June 19, 1820
Spring Grove, Heston Parish, Isleworth, England
fields: Exploration and Colonization, Natural History, Science

Combining his knowledge of botany and an inherited fortune, Banks led the scientific group on Captain James Cook's expedition in the *Endeavour* and, for forty-one years, as president of the Royal Society, supported and encouraged various scientific activities.

Bannai, Paul

b. July 4, 1920
Delta, Colo.
fields: Government and Politics

In June, 1973, Paul Bannai, a realtor, became the first Japanese American elected to the California state legislature. His previous service was as a member of the Gardena City Planning Commission and as a representative of the Sixty-seventh District on the Los Angeles County Assembly.

Banneker, Benjamin

b. November 9, 1731
Baltimore County, Maryland
d. October 9, 1806
Baltimore, Maryland
fields: Mathematics, Astronomy

Banneker's calculations provided the essential data for almanacs published from 1792 through 1797. A free black in a slave state, Banneker overcame obstacles of rural isolation, little formal education, racial prejudice, and alcoholism to establish himself as a respected scientist, earn a place on the crew that surveyed the District of Columbia, and become a symbol of racial equality (which he defended in his famous correspondence with Thomas Jefferson) in the abolitionist movement.

Bannister, Edward Mitchell

b. c. 1828
St. Andrews, New Brunswick, Canada
d. 1901
Providence, R.I.
fields: Art (painter and sculptor)

African American painter and sculptor; Edward Mitchell Bannister is remembered for his idealistic landscapes; his famous paintings include *Autumn Landscape*, *The Old Ferry*, and *Under the Oaks*, which received Philadelphia's Centennial Exposition Gold Medal in 1876.

Banting, Frederick Grant

aka: Sir Frederick Grant Banting
b. November 14, 1891
Alliston, Ontario, Canada
d. February 21, 1941
near Musgrave Harbor, Newfoundland, Canada
fields: Medicine

Along with Charles Herbert Best, Banting is credited with having discovered insulin, one of the great scientific and humanitarian achievements of the twentieth century. Awarded the Nobel Prize in Physiology or Medicine in 1923.

Bañuelos, Romana Acosta

b. Mar. 20, 1925
Miami, Ariz.
fields: Business and Industry, Government and Politics

U.S. treasurer. In 1949, Romana Acosta Bañuelos opened a tortilla factory that eventually grew into a multimillion-dollar business and resulted in her being named Outstanding Businesswoman of the Year in Los Angeles in 1969. In 1971 President Richard M. Nixon appointed her U.S. treasurer; she was only the sixth woman and the first Mexican American woman to hold that position. In 1974 she returned to her business pursuits.

Baraka, Imamu Amiri

né: LeRoi Jones
b. Oct. 7, 1934
Newark, N.J.
fields: Literature

Poet, playwright; Imamu Amiri Baraka, born LeRoi Jones, founded *Yugen* magazine and Totem Press in 1958 and the Black Arts Repertory Theatre in 1965; achieved fame with honest treatment of racism in plays such as *Dutchman* (1964), which won an Obie Award, *The Slave* (1966), and *Four Revolutionary Plays* (1968); was leading spokesperson for the Black Power movement in Newark, New Jersey, heading the activist Temple of Kawaida; chair of the National Black Political Convention in 1972; renounced Black Nationalism in 1974; turned to Marxist-Leninist-Maoist thought.

Barber, Samuel

b. March 9, 1910
West Chester, Pennsylvania
d. January 23, 1981
New York, New York
fields: Music

Barber developed a style of musical composition which bridged the gap between nineteenth century Romanticism and twentieth century modernism.

Barbieri, Gato

full: Leandro J. Barbieri
b. Nov. 28, 1934
Rosario, Argentina
fields: Music (saxophonist and composer)

Latino saxophonist and composer. Gato Barbieri began establishing his music career in the 1950's by playing in the Lalo Schifrin band and studying Brazilian music. In 1965 he met free-jazz trumpet player Don Cherry, and together they recorded *Complete Communion* (1966). Barbieri's album *Third World* (1969) mixed Latin American rhythms with free jazz. His soundtrack of the film *Last Tango in Paris* (1972) earned a Grammy Award. During the mid-1970's he explored a variety of Latin styles. *Third World Revisited* (1988) further showcased his tenor saxophone solos.

Barbon. *See* Barboncito

Barboncito

aka: Barbon
aka: Bislahani (The Orator)
aka: Hastín Daagii (Man with Whiskers)
aka: Hozhooji Naata (Blessing Speaker)
b. c. 1820
Canyon de Chelly, present-day Ariz.
d. Mar. 16, 1871
Canyon de Chelly, present-day Ariz.

fields: Warfare and Conquest, Native American Affairs, Religion and Theology (religious singer)

Navajo leader Barboncito was a major war chief during the 1863-1866 Navajo War, and he fought with Manuelito; he signed the 1868 treaty establishing the Navajo Reservation. Brother of Delgadito.

Barbosa, José Celso

b. 1857
d. 1921
fields: Government and Politics

Latino political leader. José Celso Barbosa attended the University of Michigan in 1880, returning to San Juan to practice medicine. In 1883 he joined the Liberal Party but split from it after he drafted his own plan for Puerto Rican autonomy from Spain. After the United States gained sovereignty over Puerto Rico in 1898, Barbosa and his followers, known as "Puros," supported federal statehood. Barbosa held several posts on the executive council established by Foraker Act in 1900 as part of the Puerto Rican government under American rule. In the same year Barbosa founded the Partido Republicano, which later became the Partido Estadista Republicano.

Barbour, Billie Louise. *See* Davis, Billie Louise Barbour

Barbour, Philip Pendleton

b. 1783
d. 1841
fields: Law

U.S. Supreme Court justice, 1836-1841 (died while in office); appointed by President Jackson. Significant opinion: *New York v. Miln*, 36 U.S. 102 (1837).

Barca, Pedro Calderón de la. *See* Calderón de la Barca, Pedro

Barcelo, Gertrudes

b. 1800
Sonora, Mexico
d. 1852
Santa Fe, N.Mex.
fields: Business and Industry

Latino entrepreneur. In 1825, Gertrudes Barcelo began operating a gambling house in the Ortiz Mountains in New Mexico. As she became involved with trade and investing, her fame and fortune, as well as her influence in official Mexican circles, increased. In the early 1840's she became Governor Manuel Armijo's friend and political adviser, and some believe his mistress as well. During the U.S. military occupation of New Mexico in 1846, she revealed information about a conspiracy to American authorities and loaned money to U.S. forces for supplies. Before she died, she arranged her own funeral, which was one of the most expensive and flamboyant in Santa Fe's history.

Bardeen, John

b. May 23, 1908
Madison, Wisconsin
d. Jan. 30, 1991
Boston, Massachusetts
fields: Invention and Technology, Physics

John Bardeen was a leader in the development of modern solid-state physics and its application to electronics. In 1956, shared the Nobel Prize in Physics with William Shockley and Walter Brattain; in 1972, shared the Nobel Prize in Physics with J. Robert Schrieffer and Leon N. Cooper.

Barefield, Eddie

full: Edward Emmanuel Barefield
b. Dec. 12, 1909
Scandia, Iowa
fields: Music (jazz musician)

African American musician; Eddie Barefield played alto and tenor saxophones and clarinet with such artists as Cab Calloway, Benny Carter, Duke Ellington, and Ella Fitzgerald; his musical activities included staff musician for ABC radio, pit musician for Broadway plays, film work, and composer/arranger for well-known orchestras.

Barela, Casimiro

b. Mar. 4, 1847
Embudo, N.Mex.
d. Dec., 1920
Colorado
fields: Government and Politics

Latino politician. Between 1869 and 1874, Casimiro Barela served as justice of the peace, county assessor and sheriff, and territorial legislator in southern Colorado. In 1875 he was elected to the state constitutional convention and worked to secure the civil rights of his Hispanic constituents. Elected to the first state senate in 1876 as a Democrat, he switched to the Republican Party in 1900. Known as Colorado's perpetual senator, he served forty consecutive years (twice being elected president of the state senate) until he was defeated in the 1916 election and retired.

Barela, Patrocinio

b. 1908
Bisbee, Ariz.
d. Oct. 24, 1964
Canon de Fernández, Mexico
fields: Art (wood carver, sculptor)

Latino wood carver and sculptor. Patrocinio Barela began carving wood in the early 1930's after he repaired a broken saint figure made of wood for a priest. Barela's stylized and primitive carvings—saints, angels, madonnas, shepherds, animals, family groups, and figures of death—range in size from a few inches to a few feet but always have religious themes, in accordance with the Hispanic tradition of embracing religious objects in daily life. Between 1936 to 1943, he worked for the Federal Art Project of the U.S. government's Works Progress Administration.

Bari, Nina Karlovna

b. Nov. 19, 1901
Moscow, Russia
d. July 15, 1961
Moscow, Soviet Union
fields: Mathematics (set theory and trigonometry)

Nina Karlovna Bari produced important results about functions which can be represented by infinite trigonometric series. She also edited a collection of the works of Nikolai Nikolaevich Luzin and published a treatise on trigonometric series.

Barkley, Charles

full: Charles Wade Barkley
b. Feb. 20, 1963
Leeds, Ala.
fields: Sports (basketball player)

African American basketball player; at six feet, five inches, Charles Barkley played at Auburn University; chosen in the first-round 1984 NBA draft by the Philadelphia Seventy-sixers and became a premier power forward; traded to Phoenix Suns in 1992, was known for his antics and temper tantrums on and off the court; played on the 1992 U.S. Olympic "Dream Team." In 1996 he was traded to the Houston Rockets.

Barksdale, Don Angelo

b. Mar. 31, 1923
fields: Sports (basketball player)

African American basketball player; Don A. Barksdale played for the University of California, Los Angeles, as a six-foot, six-inch forward, moving on to Amateur Athletic Union play and a spot on the 1948 U.S. Olympic gold-medal-winning basketball team; played four NBA seasons with the Baltimore Bullets and the Boston Celtics; after his playing career, Barksdale became a successful record producer.

Barksdale, Richard K.

b. Oct. 31, 1915
Winchester, Mass.
fields: Education, Literature (literary critic)

African American educator and literary critic; acclaimed for his writings on African American poets and writers, Richard K. Barksdale has served as an English professor at various colleges and universities, receiving the 1971 Outstanding Educator of America Award; his two major volumes of literary criticism are *Black Writers of America: A Comprehensive Anthology* (1972), coedited with Kenneth Kinnamon, and *Langston Hughes: The Poet and His Critics* (1977); he has also written fiction, essays, and articles for respected literary journals.

Barnard, Christiaan

full: Christiaan Neethling Barnard
b. November 8, 1922
Beaufort West, South Africa
fields: Medicine

Barnard performed the first successful human-heart transplant on December 3, 1967, followed by his second successful heart transplant on January 2, 1968. His success opened the door for a renewed and prolonged life for many victims of heart disease and brought forth showers of applause upon South Africa.

Barnard, Edward Emerson

b. Dec. 16, 1857
Nashville, Tennessee
d. Feb. 6, 1923
Williams Bay, Wisconsin
fields: Astronomy

Edward Emerson Barnard discovered his first comet in 1881; discovered Amalthea, fifth satellite of Jupiter (1892); concluded that "dark nebulas" are interstellar clouds (1913-1916); discovers stars with fastest known apparent motion (1916).

Barnard, Henry

b. January 24, 1811
Hartford, Connecticut
d. July 5, 1900
Hartford, Connecticut
fields: Education

Combining a high regard for learning and a strong sense of civic responsibility, Barnard stimulated and directed the development of public education during its formative years.

Barnes, Djuna

full: Djuna Chappell Barnes
b. June 12, 1892
Cornwall-on-Hudson, New York
d. June 18, 1982
New York, New York
fields: Literature

A noted member of the American expatriate community in Paris, Djuna Barnes wrote a highly influential experimental novel and pioneered the treatment of lesbianism in literature.

Barnes, Thomas

b. July 23, 1936
Marked Tree, Ala.
fields: Government and Politics

African American mayor of Gary, Ind.; after graduating from DePaul University Law School in 1972, Thomas Barnes worked as a private practice attorney until 1988; elected mayor of Gary, Indiana, in 1987; reelected in 1991.

Barnett, Constantine Clinton

b. Nov. 30, 1869
New Canton, Va.
d. 1935
fields: Medicine

African American physician; in Huntington, West Virginia, Constantine Clinton Barnett founded Barnett Hospital and Nurse Training School; helped found a mental hospital for African Americans in the same state.

Barnett, Ferdinand Lee

b. ?
Alabama
d. ?
fields: Journalism

African American journalist; in 1878, Ferdinand Lee Barnett established the first black newspaper in Illinois—the *Conservator*; in 1895, married Ida B. Wells; became Illinois' first black assistant state's attorney.

Barnett, Ross Robert

b. January 22, 1898
Standing Pine, Mississippi
d. November 6, 1987
Jackson, Mississippi
fields: Government and Politics

The governor of Mississippi in the early 1960's, Ross Robert Barnett was an inflexible segregationist. In 1962 he asked Mississippi's legislature to outlaw the Communist Party, pass a sedition act, and compel state employees to swear allegiance to the United States and Mississippi. He also supported efforts of the Daughters of the American Revolution to purge grammar and high school textbooks failing to teach states' rights, racial integrity, free enterprise, and "Americanism."

Barnum, P. T.

full: Phineas Taylor Barnum
b. July 5, 1810
Bethel, Connecticut
d. April 7, 1891
Bridgeport, Connecticut
fields: Theater and Entertainment, Government and Politics, Writing

With a strong business sense and the ability to take huge risks, P. T. Barnum created the modern museum and the musical concert, converted the tent carnival into the three-ring circus, and ran for a variety of political offices, serving for two terms on the Connecticut legislature and for one as a mayor of Bridgeport.

Baron, Salo Wittmayer

b. May 26, 1895
Tarnow, Austria (now Poland)
d. November 25, 1989
New York, New York
fields: Scholarship, Historiography, Education

Salo Wittmayer Baron was a historian; born in Galicia; earned doctorates in philosophy, law, and political science at the University of Vienna; emigrated to the United States in 1926; joined the faculty of Columbia University in 1926; held the first chair in Jewish history at a U.S. university; placed Jewish history in a broad world context, emphasizing Jewish resourcefulness and creativity; at various times president of American Academy of Jewish Research, the Conference on Jewish Social Studies, and the American Jewish Historical Society; wrote *A Social and Religious History of the Jews* and *The Russian Jew Under the Tsars and Soviets.*

Barraza, Santa

b. Apr. 7, 1951
Kingsville, Tex.
fields: Art

Latina artist. A graduate of the University of Texas at Austin, Santa Barraza helped found Mujeres Artistas del Suroeste, a nonprofit organization that promotes Chicana and Latina artists, in 1976. In 1979 she helped organize the Conferencia Plastica Chicana, a conference that promoted stronger ties between Chicano and Mexican artists. In 1981, she opened Diseño Studio, the first Chicano art gallery in Austin, Texas. In 1988, she became an assistant professor at Pennsylvania State University. Barraza's own art mixes symbols from her Mexican and Indian heritage with Catholic imagery. Her mixed-media *retablos* feature brightly colored folk images painted on sheets of galvanized steel.

Barrera, Lazaro Sosa

b. May 8, 1924
Marianao section of Cuba
d. Apr. 25, 1991
Downey, Calif.
fields: Sports (horse trainer)

Latino horse trainer. Lazaro Sosa Barrera was already well known throughout Mexico and the Caribbean when he moved to the United States and entered racing circles in New York and California in the 1960's. He coached Bold Forbes to Kentucky Derby and Belmont Stakes wins in 1976, and also trained Affirmed, the 1978 Triple Crown winner. Barrera was the top prize-money-winning trainer in horse-racing history and was the only trainer to win four Eclipse Awards as racing's outstanding trainer. He was elected to the Racing Hall of Fame in 1979.

Barrera, Mario

b. Nov. 8, 1939
Mission, Tex.
fields: Education

Latino educator. Mario Barrera earned a B.A. in geology at the University of Texas at Austin in 1961 and an M.A. (1964) and Ph.D. (1970), both in political science, from the University of California, Berkeley. From 1971 to 1976 he was an associate professor at the University of California, La Jolla, and began teaching ethnic studies at the University of California, Berkeley, in 1977. In 1979 he published *Race and Class in the Southwest: A Theory of Racial Inequality*.

Barrett, Brenetta Howell

b. June 28, 1932
Chicago, Ill.
fields: Government and Politics

African American state official; Brenetta Howell Barrett served as director of Illinois' Department of Human Resources beginning 1973; served the Illinois State House Contracts Compliance Commission and the National Volunteers in Service to America (VISTA) program as consultant.

Barrett, Elizabeth. *See* Browning, Elizabeth Barrett

Barretto, Ray

b. Apr. 29, 1929
Brooklyn, N.Y.
fields: Music (drummer, songwriter, bandleader)

Latino drummer, songwriter, and bandleader. Ray Barretto played with José Curbelo's and Tito Puente's bands during the 1950's. In the early 1960's, Barretto recorded a Latin jazz album, *Pachanga with Barretto*, which inspired him to form his own group, Charanga Moderna. One of the most influential Latin jazz musicians of all time, Barretto played with such musicians and groups as Freddie Hubbard, George Benson, the Rolling Stones, and the Average White Band. In the mid-1970's, he was voted best conga player several times and best musician of the year one time by *Latin NY*.

Barrio, Raymond

b. Aug. 27, 1921
West Orange, N.J.
fields: Literature, Art

Latino writer and artist. In 1969, Raymond Barrio, an art teacher, self-published *The Plum Plum Pickers*, his first novel. The proletarian novel about farm labor sold well among supporters of the farmworkers movement (César Chávez's drive to unionize California migrant farm laborers) and became an underground classic. Barrio founded Ventura Press and continued to write essays on art and culture (*Art: Seen*, 1968; *Mexico's Art and Chicano Artists*, 1975; *A Political Portfolio*, 1985) and novels (*Carib Blue*, 1990).

Barroga, Jeannie

b. Sept. 30, 1949
Milwaukee, Wis.
fields: Theater and Entertainment

Asian American playwright Jeannie Barroga's best-known plays are *Eye of the Coconut* (pr. 1987), about a Filipino American growing up in Milwaukee, and *Walls* (pr. 1989), about architect Maya Lin, who designed the Washington, D.C., Vietnam Veterans Memorial. Her other plays include *Kenny Was a Shortstop* (pr. 1991), *The Revered Miss Newton* (pr. 1991), and *Talk Story* (pr. 1991).

Barrow, Joseph Louis. *See* Louis, Joe

Barry, Charles

aka: Sir Charles Barry
b. May 23, 1795
London, England
d. May 12, 1860
London, England
fields: Architecture

The chief architect of the most famous buildings in England, Barry designed the Houses of Parliament, one of the finest examples of the Victorian Gothic Revival.

Barry, Marion

full: Marion Shepilov Barry, Jr.
b. March 6, 1936
Itta Bena, Miss.
fields: Government and Politics

African American mayor of Washington, D.C. A liberal civil rights activist in the 1960's, Marion Barry took office in 1979. Barry lost his position in 1991 when he was convicted and imprisoned for possession of cocaine. He was sentenced to a six-month term in prison. After his release he declared his candidacy for a seat on the District of Columbia City Council. Barry won reelection to the council in November of 1992. He was reelected as mayor in 1995, following a campaign in which he emphasized his African American heritage and his spiritual rebirth.

Barrymore, Ethel

né: Ethel Mae Blythe
b. August 16, 1879
Philadelphia, Pennsylvania
d. June 18, 1959
Beverly Hills, California
fields: Theater and Entertainment (drama)

One of the most distinguished actresses in American and British theater, Barrymore not only performed in classic plays but also created memorable roles in plays written specifically for her.

Barth, Karl

b. May 10, 1886
Basel, Switzerland
d. December 10, 1968
Basel, Switzerland
fields: Religion and Theology

Acclaimed by many as the dominant theologian of the twentieth century, Barth was a Swiss Reformed pastor, professor, and writer best known for his critique of nineteenth century Protestant liberal theology.

Barthé, Richmond

b. Jan. 29, 1901
Bay St. Louis, Miss.
d. Mar. 6, 1989
Pasadena, Calif.
fields: Art (sculptor)

African American sculptor; Richmond Barthé's works include the Booker T. Washington bust for New York University's Hall of Fame, the Arthur Brisbane Memorial monument in New York City, the eagle on the entrance to Washington, D.C.'s Social Security Building, and, in Haiti, statues of Toussaint-Louverture and Jean-Jacques Dessalines.

Barthelemy, Sidney John

b. Mar. 17, 1942
New Orleans, La.
fields: Government and Politics

African American mayor of New Orleans, La.; in 1974, Sidney John Barthelemy became the first African American elected to the Louisiana state senate since Reconstruction; after serving as a New Orleans councilmember-at-large from 1978 to 1986, elected mayor of New Orleans in 1986; in 1988, named vice chair of the Democratic National Committee.

Barthes, Roland

b. November 12, 1915
Cherbourg, France
d. March 26, 1980
Paris, France
fields: Literature, Language and Linguistics

Barthes was one of the most important literary critics of the twentieth century, and he made significant contributions to semiology.

Bartók, Béla

b. March 25, 1881
Nagyszentmiklós, Austro-Hungarian Empire
d. September 26, 1945
New York, New York

fields: Music

Bartók was one of the great champions of Hungarian music. He was responsible for dispelling the misconceptions about Hungarian folk music which prior to Bartók had been commonly associated with Gypsy music.

Barton, Clara

full: Clara Harlowe Barton
b. December 25, 1821
North Oxford, Massachusetts
d. April 12, 1912
Glen Echo, Maryland
fields: Education, Nursing, Social Reform

After half a lifetime devoted to humanitarian pursuits, Barton became the key figure in establishing the American Red Cross.

Barton, Derek H. R.

full: Sir Derek Harold Richard Barton
b. Sept. 8, 1918
Gravesend, Kent, England
d. March 16, 1998
College Station, Texas
fields: Chemistry

Sir Derek H. R. Barton studied steroids and other complex molecules in nature. He won the Nobel Prize in Chemistry in 1969 with his study of the chemical role played by the various geometric patterns that these molecules form.

Barton, Edmund

aka: Sir Edmund Barton
b. January 18, 1849
Sydney, Australia
d. January 7, 1920
Medlow Bath, Australia
fields: Government and Politics, Law

Barton was the leader of the movement to form a federated Australian Commonwealth and was one of the authors of the new nation's constitution. He served as Australia's first prime minister and on the first High Court of Australia.

Basedow, Johann Bernhard

b. September 11, 1723
Hamburg
d. July 25, 1790
Magdeburg, Prussia
fields: Education

A charismatic teacher, Basedow believed that children should be permitted their childhood, and he taught them accordingly, encouraging them to learn through observation and experience more than through books. He insisted on a secular approach to an education that included nature study, physical education, and manual training.

Basie, Count

né: William Basie
b. August 21, 1904
Red Bank, N.J.
d. April 26, 1984
Hollywood, Fla.
fields: Music

African American pianist, bandleader, and composer. One of the major big band and jazz orchestra leaders of the twentieth century, William "Count" Basie was schooled in the stride piano stylings of the 1920's and in the 1930's organized the Barons of Rhythm with Buster Smith. Some key early recordings and compositions are "One O'Clock Jump" (1937), "Jumpin' at the Woodside" (1938), and "Taxi War Dance" (1939). During a brief period in 1950 the Count Basie Orchestra disbanded, and Basie led a smaller group. The reconstituted ensemble began to tour widely in Europe between 1952 and 1954. Basie's orchestra became known for backing prominent vocalists such as Frank Sinatra and for its driving swing sound. Among Basie's significant recordings of the 1950's are *Count Basie Swings and Joe Williams Sings* (1955) and *April in Paris* (1955-1956). One of his notable later recordings is *On the Road* (1979).

Basil the Macedonian

b. 812 or 813
Charioupolis, in Macedonia, Byzantine Empire
d. August 29, 886
Constantinople, Byzantine Empire
fields: Government and Politics, Law

Through his strength, intelligence, and excellent administration, Basil established the 189-year Macedonian dynasty, which brought Byzantium to great heights. He imparted such vitality to an ancient imperial tradition that it has been emulated by modern nations.

Basileus. *See* Porphyry

Baskerville, John

b. January 28, 1706 (baptized)
Wolverly, Worcestershire, England
d. January 8, 1775
Birmingham, England
fields: Business and Industry, Invention and Technology (printing and type founding)

Baskerville designed and produced printing type and printed books which set new standards for fine printing.

Basov, Nikolay Gennadiyevich

b. December 14, 1922
Usman, U.S.S.R.
fields: Physics

Basov played a key role in the invention of quantum microwave amplification devices (masers) and light amplifiers which operate on the principle of stimulated emission of radiation (lasers). He collaborated with Aleksandr Prokhorov, with whom he shared the 1964 Nobel Prize in Physics, to produce the first Soviet maser and did pioneering work on the use of semiconductors in lasers. In his later career, he became a major figure in science administration and policy-making in the U.S.S.R. and continued his work in physics after the breakup of the Soviet Union.

Bass, Charlotta Spears

né: Charlotta Spears
b. Oct. 1880?
Sumter, S.C.
d. Apr. 12, 1969
Los Angeles, Calif.
fields: Government and Politics, Civil Rights (activist), Journalism

African American politician and civil rights activist; for more than forty years, Charlotta Spears Bass edited and published the West Coast's oldest black newspaper, *The California Eagle*; through the newspaper she spoke out against the Ku Klux Klan and called for equal economic and educational opportunities for African Americans; left the Republican Party and was founding member of Progressive Party; in 1952, chosen as Progressive Party vice presidential candidate on ticket with Vincent Hallinan, the first black woman to run for this office; retired from newspaper business in early 1950's.

Bassett, Angela

b. August 16, 1958
New York, N.Y.
fields: Theater and Entertainment, Film (actress)

African American actress; Angela Bassett's credits include stage, television, and film roles; performed on Broadway in *Ma Rainey's Black Bottom* and *Joe Turner's Come and Gone* ; appeared in *F/X* (1986), *Kindergarten Cop* (1990), *City of Hope* (1991), *Boyz 'N the Hood* (1991), *Innocent Blood* (1992), *Passion Fish* (1992), *Malcolm X* (1992), *What's Love Got to Do with It* (1993), *Waiting to Exhale* (1995), and *How Stella Got Her Groove Back* (1998).

Bassey, Shirley

b. Jan. 8, 1937
Cardiff, Wales
fields: Music (singer)

African American vocalist; in 1953, Shirley Bassey launched her career with an appearance in the film *Memories of Al Jolson*; performed throughout Europe and the United States in the 1960's; gained a wider audience for her performance on the soundtrack for the James Bond film *Goldfinger* (1964).

Bassi, Laura

full: Laura Maria Caterina Bassi
b. Oct. 20, 1711
Bologna, Papal States (now Italy)
d. Feb. 20, 1778
Bologna, Papal States
fields: Physics

Laura Bassi taught Newtonian and experimental philosophy during the eighteenth century, proving that a woman could practice science in a university setting.

Bataille, Georges

b. September 10, 1897
Billom, Puy-de-Dôme, France
d. July 8, 1962
Paris, France
fields: Philosophy

Georges Bataille developed a philosophy of excess and exuberance (his concept of transgression), claiming that human beings need to break rules and pass boundaries in order to realize a sense of the sacred. Central figure in the French avant-garde and the Surrealist movement and a founder of the College of Sociology, he helped provide a forum for some of France's most brilliant philosophers and social thinkers and through his journal *Critique* introduced many, such as Jacques Derrida and Michel Foucault, who would later become known as poststructuralists. Critics object to the elements of violence and the rejection of values in his work. *Inner Experience* (1943, rev ed. 1954), *Guilty* (1944), *The Accursed Share* (1949), *Eroticism, Death, and Sensuality* (1957), and *The Tears of Eros* (1962) are among his major works.

Bates, Daisy

b. 1914
Huttig, Ark.
d. 1998
Fountain Inn, South Carolina
fields: Civil Rights (activist)

African American civil rights activist; Daisy Bates will be remembered for standing with the nine African American students who tried to enroll at the all-white Little Rock, Arkansas, high school on September 4, 1957; served as president of the NAACP State Conference of Branches; she and her husband published the *State Press* newspaper in 1941; continued her civil rights work into the 1960's, publishing *The Long Shadow of Little Rock: A Memoir* in 1962.

Bates, Ellas. *See* Diddley, Bo

Bates, Katharine Lee

b. August 12, 1859
Falmouth, Massachusetts
d. March 28, 1929
Wellesley, Massachusetts
fields: Education, Literature

Although she edited critical editions of many literary classics, compiled collections of children's folk and fairy tales, translated ancient Spanish and Icelandic legends and ballads, and authored textbooks on English literature and history that are still in use, Katharine Lee Bates is best remembered for her own poetry—especially "America the Beautiful."

Bates, Peg Leg

full: Clayton Bates
b. Nov. 10, 1907?
Fountain Inn, S.C.
d. Dec. 6, 1998
Fountain Inn, S.C.
fields: Dance (tap dancer)

African American tap dancer; despite losing part of his leg in a childhood accident, self-taught tap dancer Clayton "Peg Leg" Bates became a headliner in nightclub acts and vaudeville and a featured performer in Broadway musicals; performed in all-black cast of *Blackbirds of 1929* at Moulin Rouge in Paris; in 1950's toured with the Ink Spots and the Count Basie orchestra and appeared on *The Ed Sullivan Show* more than any other tap dancer; in 1952 Bates opened a successful resort hotel in upstate New York for African Americans.

Bateson, William

b. Aug. 8, 1861
Whitby, Yorkshire, England
d. Feb. 8, 1926
Merton, London, England
fields: Genetics, Zoology

William Bateson defended and introduced Gregor Mendel's work to Great Britain, and his breeding experiments established basic Mendelian phenomena for plants and animals. In 1910, he founded the *Journal of Genetics* with Reginald Crundall Punnett.

Batista y Zaldívar, Fulgencio

b. January 16, 1901
Banes, Cuba
d. August 6, 1973
Guadalmina, Spain
fields: Government and Politics

Fulgencio Batista y Zaldívar was president of Cuba from 1940 to 1944 and from 1952 to 1959. First ruled behind the scenes from 1933 to 1940. At first popular with common people. Passed laws to improve working conditions and provide safeguards against accidents, unemployment, and poverty among the elderly. In the 1950's, allowed widespread government corruption and abuses. Overthrown by Fidel Castro's 1959 revolution.

Batlle y Ordóñez, José

b. May 21, 1856
Montevideo, Uruguay
d. October 20, 1929
Montevideo, Uruguay
fields: Government and Politics

José Batlle y Ordóñez was president of Uruguay from 1903 to 1907 and from 1911 to 1915. In first term instituted reform program including establishing secondary education in all cities, legalizing divorce, and abolishing some income taxes. In second term established the eight-hour workday and old-age pensions, increased rural credit, and expanded electricity and telephone service.

Batsida Karoosh. *See* White Man Runs Him

Battani, al-

full: ʿAbd Allah Muhammad ibn Jabir ibn Sinan al-Battani al-Harrani al-Sabiʾ
b. 858
near Haran, north-central Syria
d. 929
Kasr al Djiss, region of Samarra, Iraq
fields: Astronomy

Al-Battani examined and corrected, through application of trigonometry, astronomical theories first put forward by the second century Alexandrian Ptolemy.

Battle, Kathleen

b. Aug. 13, 1948
Portsmouth, Ohio
fields: Music (soprano opera singer)

African American soprano opera singer; Kathleen Battle, who made her formal debut in 1972, has received praise for her roles in operas by Strauss, Verdi, and Mozart; her performances of Despina in Mozart's *Cosi Fan Tutte* and Pamina in Mozart's *The Magic Flute* are highly regarded.

Baudelaire, Charles

b. April 9, 1821
Paris, France
d. August 31, 1867
Paris, France
fields: Literature

Baudelaire was instrumental in the transformation from a classical conception of poetry, which concentrated on the subject, to the Romantic focus on the self and presented in his own poetry a heightened sensitivity to the dark dimensions of the beautiful, which served as a consolation for his own awareness of the human inclination toward self-destruction.

Bauer, Georg. *See* Agricola, Georgius

Bauer, Joyce Diane. *See* Brothers, Joyce

Baum, L. Frank

full: Lyman Frank Baum
b. May 15, 1856
Chittenango, New York
d. May 6, 1919
Hollywood, California
fields: Literature

Baum is best known for creating the marvelous land of Oz, a utopian fantasy world chronicled in a series of children's books beginning with the publication of *The Wonderful Wizard of Oz* in 1900. Through his Oz series, Baum created a unique American version of the standard fairy tale.

Baumfree, Isabella. *See* Truth, Sojourner

Baxter, Richard

b. November 12, 1615
Rowton, Shropshire, England
d. December 8, 1691
London, England
fields: Religion and Theology, Government and Politics, Social Reform

Through his preaching, writing, and friendship with many political and church leaders, Baxter aided substantially in making Nonconformity and freedom of conscience a characteristic of the English cultural tradition.

Bayard, Chevalier de

né: Pierre Terrail, lord of Bayard
b. c. 1473
Château de Bayard, Pontcharra, France
d. April 30, 1524
near Roasio, Italy
fields: Military Affairs

The ideal of chivalry, exemplified in Bayard, became a significant element in the education of young men of the upper classes.

Baybars I

full: Baybars I, al-Malik al-Zahir Rukn al-Din Baybars al-Salihi
b. c. 1223
northern shore of the Black Sea
d. July 1, 1277
Damascus
fields: Government and Politics

Through military prowess, administrative skill, courage, and practical good sense, Baybars rose from slavery to become the virtual founder and most eminent representative of the Mamluk (slave) Dynasty in medieval Egypt.

Bayezid II

b. December, 1447, or January, 1448
Demotika, Ottoman Empire
d. May 26, 1512
en route to Demotika, Ottoman Empire
fields: Government and Politics, Military Affairs

Sultan of the Ottoman Empire, 1481-1512. Without being among the great sultans of the Ottoman Empire, Bayezid II filled an important transitional role. The fame of his father, Mehmed II, as well as the symbolic memory of his namesake Bayezid I, would have made it difficult for Bayezid to earn a reputation for strong rule or aggressive foreign policy. That much of Bayezid's time was spent trying unsuccessfully to respond to conflicts toward the East is probably the main historical significance of his reign.

Bayle, Pierre

b. November 18, 1647
Carla-le-Comte, France
d. December 28, 1706
Rotterdam, the Netherlands
fields: Philosophy, Religion and Theology

Pierre Bayle was a skeptic, criticizing philosophical theories both old and new and exposing the weaknesses of Catholic and Protestant theologies. His criticisms helped pave the way for modern toleration and provided the principal arguments for the Enlightenment. One of the central figures in the Republic of Letters, he was in direct contact with many of its leading personalities. In his greatest work, *An Historical and Critical Dictionary* (1697, 1702), he attempted to correct errors in previous dictionaries and encyclopedias and criticized philosophical, scientific, and theological theories.

Bayliss, William Maddock

aka: Sir William Maddock Bayliss
b. May 2, 1860
Wolverhampton, Staffordshire, England
d. August 27, 1924
London, England
fields: Physiology, Biochemistry

Working in the early years of modern physiology, Bayliss made major discoveries in physiology and biochemistry relating to lymph flow, hormones and their actions, principles of enzyme action, and properties of colloidal biological systems.

Baylor, Don

b. June 28, 1949
Austin, Tex.
fields: Sports (baseball player and manager)

African American baseball player and manager; Don Baylor played for five teams, beginning with the Baltimore Orioles in 1970, and in three World Series during his nineteen-season major league career; during the 1979 season, he batted in an American League-leading 139 runs and received the Most Valuable Player award; after retirement in 1988, Baylor worked as a major league batting coach; in 1992, Baylor accepted a position as manager of the Colorado Rockies expansion team; by 1995 he had taken the young team to the National League playoffs.

Baylor, Elgin

b. Sept. 16, 1934
Washington, D.C.
fields: Sports (basketball player)

African American basketball player; for fourteen seasons, Elgin Baylor played as a forward for the Lakers (Minneapolis and Los Angeles); in 1959 he won the Rookie of the Year award and was corecipient of the All-Star game Most Valuable Player award; he retired from playing with records for most points in a half, most career field goals, and most championship series points scored; in 1976 inducted into the Basketball Hall of Fame; Baylor was promoted from assistant coach to head coach of the New Orleans Jazz in 1978; became general manager and executive vice president of the Los Angeles Clippers in 1986.

Beach, Amy Marcy

né: Amy Marcy Cheney
b. September 5, 1867
Henniker, New Hampshire
d. December 27, 1944
New York, New York
fields: Music

Amy Beach was the first American woman to achieve international fame as a composer, and the first major American composer, man or woman, to be trained entirely in the United States. She was, besides, a virtuoso pianist.

Beadle, George Wells

aka: Beets Beadle
b. Oct. 22, 1903
Wahoo, Nebraska
d. June 9, 1989
Pomona, California
fields: Biology, Chemistry, Genetics

George Wells Beadle was a pioneer in the study of the chemical action of genes within cells; helped to demonstrate that genes control specific chemical reactions; in 1958, shared the Nobel Prize in Physiology or Medicine with Edward L. Tatum and Joshua Lederberg.

Beale, Dorothea

b. March 21, 1831
Bishopsgate, London, England
d. November 9, 1906
Cheltenham, England
fields: Education, Social Reform

Combining business acumen, reform enthusiasm, and mystical idealism, Beale shaped an educational breakthrough with her advocacy of intellectual training for girls.

Beals, Jennifer
b. Dec. 19, 1963
Chicago, Ill.
fields: Theater and Entertainment

African American actress; while in her first year at Yale, Jennifer Beals debuted as Alex, the starring role in *Flashdance* (1983), a successful film featuring intense choreography and driving music; she went on to star in *The Bride* (1985) and *The Vampire's Kiss* (1989).

Beamon, Bob
full: Robert Beamon
b. Aug. 29, 1946
New York, N.Y.
fields: Sports (track and field athlete)

African American track and field athlete; in 1968 Bob Beamon received an Olympic gold medal for his long jump performance, which bettered the previous world record by almost 2 feet; his record of 29 feet 2½ inches stood until 1991.

Bear Cub. *See* Passaconaway

Bear Hunter
aka: Wairasuap
aka: Bear Spirit
b. c. 1830
present-day Utah
d. Jan. 27, 1863
near present-day Preston, Idaho
fields: Warfare and Conquest, Native American Affairs

Shoshone war chief Bear Hunter was killed during the Bear River Campaign of 1863, which secured the Great Basin for white expansion.

Bear Spirit. *See* Bear Hunter

Beard, Andrew Jackson
b. 1850
Eastlake, Ala.
d. 1921?
fields: Invention and Technology (inventor)

African American inventor of a railcar coupler; Andrew Jackson Beard earned $50,000 for his patented Jenny Coupler, a device that automatically connected two railcars when they were pushed together.

Beard, Charles A.
full: Charles Austin Beard
b. November 27, 1874
near Knightstown, Indiana
d. September 1, 1948
New Haven, Connecticut
fields: Political Science, History, Scholarship

More than any other twentieth century scholar, Beard shaped how Americans viewed their past through his economic determinism; author of many history books published in the first half of the twentieth century; cofounder of the New School for Social Research.

Beard, Mary Ritter
né: Mary Ritter
b. August 5, 1876
Indianapolis, Indiana
d. August 14, 1958
Phoenix, Arizona
fields: Historiography, Social Reform

An engaged, creative intellectual and suffragist, Beard demonstrated—through her historical research and her writings—women's vital contributions to civilization.

Bearden, Romare
b. Sept. 2, 1914
Charlotte, N.C.
d. Mar. 11, 1988
New York, N.Y.
fields: Art

African American artist; a member of the American Academy of Arts and Letters (1966) and a recipient of the President's National Medal of Arts (1987), Romare Bearden became known as America's finest collagist; he applied collage techniques to African American folk and vernacular elements in an exploration of African American cultural heritage and religious traditions; his *The Painter's Mind: A Study of the Relations of Structure and Space in Painting* (1969), cowritten with Carl Holty, is one of several books to his credit.

Beardsley, Aubrey
b. August 21, 1872
Brighton, England
d. March 16, 1898
Menton, France
fields: Art

Assimilating diverse artistic influences, Beardsley produced black-and-white illustrations for magazines and books that epitomize the achievement of the English Aesthetic movement of the 1890's.

Bear's Heart, James
aka: Nock-ko-ist
b. 1851
d. Jan. 25, 1882
Darlington, Indian Territory
fields: Art, Warfare and Conquest

Cheyenne warrior in his youth and a prolific artist in his later years; James Bear's Heart combined Indian symbolism with formal Western techniques.

Beasley, Delilah Leontium
b. c. 1867
Cincinnati, Ohio
d. Aug. 18, 1934
San Leandro, Calif.
fields: Journalism

African American journalist; after working at newspapers in Cleveland and Cincinnati, Delilah Leontium Beasley moved to California and worked at the *Oakland Tribune*; representing the *Tribune*, she attended the National Convention of Women Voters and the International Council of Women Convention; in 1919 she published a book of pioneer records, *Negro Trailblazers of California*; in the 1920's she fought to abolish the use of racist terminology in journalistic accounts.

Beauharnais, Joséphine de. *See* Joséphine

Beaumarchais, Pierre-Augustin Caron de
b. January 24, 1732
Paris, France
d. May 18, 1799
Paris, France
fields: Theater and Entertainment, Literature

Pierre-Augustin Caron de Beaumarchais was a French dramatist, social critic, and pamphleteer whose plays were suppressed for criticizing the aristocracy. During the 1760's he began writing plays, including *Eugénie* (1767) and *Two Friends* (1770). His first major work was *The Barber of Seville* (1773). Others include *The Marriage of Figaro* (1778) and *Tarare* (1787).

Beaumont, Francis
b. c. 1584
Grace-Dieu, Leicestershire, England
d. March 6, 1616
probably Sundridge, Kent, England
fields: Theater and Entertainment

With their light, witty comedy and melodramatic tragicomedy, Francis Beaumont and John Fletcher introduced a new style and aristocratic outlook into Renaissance English drama.

Beautiful Bird. *See* Irateba

Beauvoir, Simone de
full: Simone Bertrand de Beauvoir
b. January 9, 1908
Paris, France
d. April 14, 1986
Paris, France
fields: Literature, Philosophy, Women's Rights, Social Reform, Civil Rights

De Beauvoir cut across traditional academic fields to produce important works of literature, criticism, and philosophy, while her political activism made her a pioneer of the late twentieth century women's movement as well as a leading figure in the human rights, peace, and social reform movements. Best known for her groundbreaking book *The Second Sex* (1949).

Beaux, Cecilia

b. 1855
Philadelphia, Pennsylvania
d. September 17, 1942
Gloucester, Massachusetts
fields: Art

As a portraitist of the intellectual and social elite of America in the decades surrounding 1900, Beaux served as a model of success in the fine arts.

Beaverbrook, Lord

né: William Maxwell Aitken
aka: First Baron Beaverbrook
b. May 25, 1879
Maple, Ontario, Canada
d. June 9, 1964
Cherkley, Surrey, England
fields: Journalism, Government and Politics

Beaverbrook created the most successful newspaper empire of his day and, in World War II, as minister of aircraft production, was greatly responsible for the victory in the Battle of Britain.

Beavers, Louise

b. Mar. 8, 1902
Cincinnati, Ohio
d. Oct. 26, 1962
Los Angeles, Calif.
fields: Theater and Entertainment

African American actress; Louise Beavers entered films in the 1920's and became typecast in maid and confidante roles; noted for her mixture of calm and humor, she appeared in such films as *Imitation of Life* (1934), *Made for Each Other* (1939), and *Mister Blanding Builds His Dream House* (1948); following Ethel Waters, she took over the title role in the 1950-1953 television series *Beulah*.

Becerra, Xavier

b. Jan. 26, 1958
Sacramento, Calif.
fields: Government and Politics

Latino legislator. Xavier Becerra, who earned a law degree from Stanford University, worked in a legal services office, representing the mentally ill, and worked with State Senator Art Torres before joining the California Department of Justice as a deputy attorney general. In 1990, Becerra moved from Sacramento to Los Angeles and was elected to the state assembly. In 1992, before completing his term, he was elected to represent California's Thirtieth Congressional District and was appointed to committees on education and labor, judiciary and science, and space and technology.

Bechet, Sidney Joseph

b. May 14, 1897
New Orleans, La.
d. May 14, 1959
Paris, France
fields: Music (jazz saxophonist, clarinetist, and composer)

African American jazz saxophonist, clarinetist, and composer; best known for his great technical skill on clarinet and as an early champion of the soprano saxophone, Sidney Joseph Bechet achieved international recognition touring the United States and Europe; he played with such notables as King Oliver and Freddie Keppard in Chicago (1917), and Will Marion Cook's Southern Syncopated Orchestra in Europe; a legendary exponent of New Orleans music, he went on to record with Mamie Smith, Jelly Roll Morton, and Noble Sissle; his recording credits include "The Wildcat Blues" (1923), with Clarence Williams, and "Down in Honky Tonk Town/Coal Cart Blues" (1940), with Louis Armstrong.

Becket, Thomas

aka: Thomas à Becket
b. December 11, 1118
London, England
d. December 29, 1170
Canterbury, Kent, England
fields: Religion and Theology

Becket accepted martyrdom in defending the rights of the medieval church as developed under the Gregorian reforms against the encroachment of the secular power of the state.

Beckett, Samuel

full: Samuel Barclay Beckett
b. April 13, 1906
Foxrock, near Dublin, Ireland
d. December 22, 1989
Paris, France
fields: Literature, Theater and Entertainment

Poet, playwright, novelist, and critic, Beckett created a corpus of drama and fiction that established him as one of the greatest writers of the twentieth century. He won the Nobel Prize in Literature in 1969.

Beckwourth, James Pierson

b. Apr. 26, 1798
Fredericksburg, Va.
d. c. 1867
Denver, Colo.
fields: Exploration and Colonization

African American pioneer; the son of a mulatto slave and her white owner, James Pierson Beckwourth discovered Beckwourth Pass across the Sierra Nevadas while working for the Rocky Mountain Fur Company; he traveled throughout Colorado and California, establishing successful trading posts and ranches.

Becquerel, Alexandre-Edmond

b. March 24, 1820
Paris, France
d. May 11, 1891
Paris, France
fields: Physics, Science

The son of Antoine-César Becquerel and father to Antoine-Henri, Alexandre-Edmond Becquerel also contributed to the study of electrochemistry, electromagnetic radiation, and radioactive decay physics.

Becquerel, Antoine-César

b. March 8, 1788
Châtillon-Coligny, France
d. January 18, 1878
Paris, France
fields: Natural History, Physics

The first of the remarkable Becquerel family, which spans four generations of scientists. Antoine-César Becquerel was a co-creator of the science of electrochemistry; his entire career was spent with the Museum of Natural History in Paris.

Becquerel, Antoine-Henri

b. Dec. 15, 1852
Paris, France
d. Aug. 25, 1908
Le Croisic, Brittany, France
fields: Chemistry, Physics, Science

Antoine-Henri Becquerel published the first evidence of a radioactive transformation in 1901; received the Nobel Prize in Physics in 1903, jointly with Marie and Pierre Curie.

Becton, Julius Wesley, Jr.

b. June 29, 1926
Bryn Mawr, Pa.
fields: Warfare and Conquest, Military Affairs

African American military officer; Julius Wesley Becton, Jr., achieved the rank of lieutenant general during his distinguished Army career; after commanding the First Cavalry Division and the Army Operations, Testing and Evaluation Agency, he went on to command the Army's Seventh Corps in Germany; after retirement from the military in 1985, Becton directed the Federal Emergency Management Agency (FEMA, 1985-1988).

Bede the Venerable, Saint

aka: Baeda
aka: Beda

b. 672 or 673 C.E.
Wearmouth, Northumbria
d. May 25, 735
Jarrow, Durham
fields: Historiography, Literature

Bede is the author of the first worthy extant example of English Christian scholarship. In his own time, Bede set an example by his saintly life and his dedication as a teacher. Today he is known primarily for his *Ecclesiastical History of the English People*, which has earned for him the title "the father of English history."

Beduiat. *See* Victorio

Beecher, Catharine

full: Catharine Esther Beecher
b. September 6, 1800
East Hampton, Long Island, New York
d. May 12, 1878
Elmira, New York
fields: Education, Women's Rights

In pursuit of higher status and influence for women in the domestic arena, Beecher promoted women's education, urging professionalization and appreciation of women's traditional roles.

Beecher, Harriet. *See* Stowe, Harriet Beecher

Beecher, Henry Ward

b. June 24, 1813
Litchfield, Connecticut
d. March 8, 1887
Brooklyn, New York
fields: Religion and Theology

As pastor of Plymouth Church, in Brooklyn, New York, for forty years, Beecher rapidly became one of the most articulate ministers in the United States, breaking with traditional methods of preaching in both style and content. He ushered in a new age of homiletic expertise which went far beyond his podium.

Beekman, Alan

b. Jan. 16, 1913
Utica, N.Y.
fields: Publishing, Journalism

Hawaii resident Alan Beekman wrote extensively on the experiences of Japanese immigrants and Japanese Americans in Hawaii. For eight years, he was a columnist and book reviewer for the *Pacific Citizen* newspaper. His books include *Hawaiian Tales* (1970) and *Crisis: The Japanese Attack on Pearl Harbor and Southeast Asia* (1992).

Beernaert, Auguste-Marie-François

b. July 26, 1829
Ostend, Belgium
d. October 6, 1912
Lucerne, Switzerland
fields: Diplomacy, Government and Politics, Peace Advocacy

A Belgian prime minister and peace activist, Auguste-Marie-François Beernaert was awarded the 1909 Nobel Peace Prize (along with Baron d'Estournelles de Constant of France). Active in the Interparliamentary Union, presided over conferences and committees. At the 1899 International Peace Conference in The Hague, oversaw the first commission on arms limitation.

Beethoven, Ludwig van

b. December 17, 1770 (baptized)
Bonn
d. March 26, 1827
Vienna, Austria
fields: Music

Beethoven contributed greatly to Western classical music. Clearly reflecting the transition from the classical tradition in music to the Romantic, he made numerous innovations in the piano sonata, the string quartet, and the symphony.

Begin, Menachem

b. August 16, 1913
Brest-Litovsk, Russia (now Belarus)
d. March 9, 1992
Tel Aviv, Israel
fields: Government and Politics

Begin placed pressure on the British Mandate government to withdraw from Palestine, enabling Israel to declare its independence and sovereignty over part of Palestine. He also served as a key opposition leader and eventually as prime minister of Israel from 1977 to 1983.

Behring, Emil von

full: Emil Adolf von Behring
b. March 15, 1854
Hansdorf, Prussia (now Germany)
d. March 31, 1917
Marburg, Germany
fields: Medicine

Behring developed vaccinations against tetanus and diphtheria, thereby saving great numbers of lives. He also did important work in bacteriology that led to the modern understanding of infectious disease.

Békésy, Georg von

b. June 3, 1899
Budapest, Austro-Hungarian Empire (now Hungary)
d. June 13, 1972
Honolulu, Hawaii
fields: Medicine, Physics, Physiology

Georg Békésy invented an audiometer to measure hearing loss in 1947; received the Nobel Prize in Physiology or Medicine in 1961 for applying principles of physics to clarify the mechanisms by which sound waves are transmitted to the inner ear and converted into electrical nerve impulses going to the brain.

Belafonte, Harry

full: Harry George Belafonte, Jr.
b. Mar. 1, 1927
New York, N.Y.
fields: Music (singer), Theater and Entertainment

African American singer and actor; musically best known for his 1957 "Day-O (The Banana Boat Song)," Harry Belafonte popularized the music of the West Indies in the United States; also recorded blues and spirituals; received a Tony Award for his performance in the 1953 Broadway revue *John Murray Anderson's Almanac*; Belafonte debuted on film in 1953 with *Bright Road*, and went on to appear in such films as *Island in the Sun* (1957) and *Uptown Saturday Night* (1974); starred in his own hour-long television special and produced the CBS special *Strollin' Twenties*.

Belafonte-Harper, Shari

né: Shari Belafonte
b. Sept. 22, 1954
New York, N.Y.
fields: Theater and Entertainment

African American actress; Shari Belafonte-Harper, daughter of singer and actor Harry Belafonte, held a major role in the television series *Hotel* (1983-1988) and has also appeared in films.

Bell, Alexander Graham

b. March 3, 1847
Edinburgh, Scotland
d. August 2, 1922
Baddeck, Nova Scotia
fields: Invention and Technology, Science, Education

One of the major inventive geniuses of modern times, Bell created and perfected the telephone and greatly advanced the teaching of the deaf.

Bell, Cool Papa

full: James Bell
b. May 17, 1903
Starkville, Miss.
d. Mar. 7, 1991
St. Louis, Mo.
fields: Sports (baseball player)

African American baseball player; an outstanding outfielder and hitter in the Negro Leagues for twenty-five years, "Cool Papa" Bell was elected to the Baseball Hall of Fame in 1974.

Bell, Derrick Albert, Jr.

b. November 6, 1930
Pittsburgh, Pa.
fields: Law, Literature

African American attorney, law professor, and author; in 1992, Derrick Albert Bell, Jr., challenged the hiring practices of Harvard Law School, taking an unpaid leave of absence in protest against the school's refusal to grant tenure to an African American female law professor; he was the university's first African American law professor and the first African American man to receive tenure at the school.

Bell, George

né: Jorge Antonio Bell y Mathey
b. Oct. 21, 1959
San Pedro de Macoris, Dominican Republic
fields: Sports (baseball player)

Latino baseball player. Outfielder George Bell made his major league debut with the Toronto Blue Jays in 1981. In 1984, he hit twenty-six home runs and batted .292. In 1987, he set team records for Toronto for home runs (47), runs batted in (134), and batting average (.605); led the American League in runs batted in; and was named the American League's Most Valuable Player. While playing from Toronto he was twice named to the American League All-Star Team. In 1991 he moved to the Chicago Cubs and made the National League All-Star Team. In 1992 he played for the Chicago White Sox and finished the season with 112 runs batted in. After an injury-plagued 1993 season, Bell was released by the White Sox.

Bell Burnell, Jocelyn

né: Susan Jocelyn Bell
b. July 15, 1943
Belfast, Northern Ireland
fields: Astronomy

Jocelyn Bell Burnell was the first astronomer to note the anomaly that resulted in the discovery of pulsars; also worked in X-ray, infrared, and optical astronomy.

Bellamy, Walt

full: Walter Bellamy
b. July 24, 1939
New Bern, N.C.
fields: Sports (basketball player)

African American basketball player; as a six-foot, eleven-inch, 245-pound center, "Walt" Bellamy received a gold medal as a member of the 1960 U.S. Olympic basketball team; during his twelve-year NBA career, Bellamy played for the Chicago Packers, Baltimore Bullets, New York Knicks, Detroit Pistons, and Atlanta Hawks; he was the NBA Rookie of the Year in 1962, played in four NBA All-Star games, and retired with a career average of 20.1 points and 13.7 rebounds per game.

Belleau, Rémy

b. 1528
Nogent-le-Rotrou, near Chartres, France
d. 1577
fields: Literature

A member of La Pléiade (fl. 1549-1589), a group of loosely organized poets dedicated to raising the level of sophistication of the French language by adding words and genres derived from classical literature. Led by Pierre de Ronsard and Joachim du Bellay, they developed a new form of poetry based on forms such as the sonnet, the ode, epic, and elegy. They also worked to elevate the level of the poet to a position as an intermediary between humanity and the heavens.

Bellini, Giovanni

b. c. 1430
Venice
d. 1516
Venice
fields: Art

As the leading painter of the Republic of Venice over more than two generations, Bellini achieved a synthesis of major currents in art deriving from Italian centers such as Tuscany and Padua as well as from Northern Europe. His conquest of the poetry of light and color was the foundation of the greatness of Venetian painting in the sixteenth century.

Bellow, Saul

b. June 10, 1915
Lachine, Canada
fields: Literature

In writing nine novels and numerous short stories and articles over several decades, Bellow, as an American writer, achieved international recognition signified only in part by his receiving the Nobel Prize in Literature in 1976.

Beltrán, Lola

b. Mar. 7, 1932
El Rosario, Sinaloa, Mexico
d. Mar. 24, 1996
Mexico City, Mexico
fields: Music (singer)

Latina singer. As a teenager, Lola Beltrán moved to Mexico City to become a singer and began to establish herself as an international mariachi star. She became known as *La Reina* (the queen) and spent the next four decades touring Latin America, the United States, and Europe. She recorded more than one hundred albums and such songs as "Black Dove," "Bed of Stone," "Three Days," "To the Four Winds," and "If You Should Return." She also worked in the Mexican cinema, where she starred in more than fifty film musicals.

Ben-Gurion, David

né: David Joseph Gruen
b. October 16, 1886
Płónsk, Poland, Russian Empire (now Poland)
d. December 1, 1973
Tel Aviv, Israel
fields: Government and Politics

David Ben-Gurion was the first prime minister of Israel, serving from 1948 to 1953 and from 1955 to 1963. Chief spokesman for Zionism in 1940's; argued the cause before U.N. Special Commission on Palestine in 1947. On May 14, 1948, Ben-Gurion announced establishment of the new state of Israel. During his ministry Israel grew into a viable country and was victorious in two major wars.

Ben-Jochannan, Yosef

b. Dec. 31, 1918
fields: Historiography

African American historian; Yosef Ben-Jochannan's contention that the ancestors of Egypt's pharaohs came from the source of the Nile River near present-day Tanzania caused controversy among other scholars and historians; authored more than a dozen books including several elementary and secondary school texts; served as chair of the Alkebu-lan Foundation, which published many of his books including *Black Man of the Nile* (1969) and *African Origins of the Major "Western Religions"* (1970); held teaching assignments at universities throughout the United States, South America, and Africa.

Benavides, Santos

b. 1823
Laredo, Tex.
d. Nov. 9, 1891
fields: Government and Politics, Warfare and Conquest

Latino politician and soldier. Santos Benavides participated in the Mexican border separatist movement in the late 1830's and was elected mayor of Laredo and chief justice of Webb County during the 1850's. During the Civil War, he led Mexican American soldiers in protecting the South's cotton trade with Mexico from attack. He was promoted to colonel, the highest military rank earned by a Mexican American during the war. After the conflict ended, Benavides became a successful entrepreneur, was twice elected alderman in Laredo, and served three terms in the state legislature.

Bencivieni di Pepo. *See* Cimabue

Bencomo, Mario

b. July 26, 1953
Pinar del Río, Cuba
fields: Art (painter)

In 1968 Mario Bencomo moved with his family from Cuba to the United States, where he gained fame as a painter of semi-abstract images full of bright, swirling forms. Some paintings, such as *Starry Night* (1986) and *Paradiso Lontano* (1986), depict natural or mythical environments, while others, such as *Extasis de Santa Teresa* (1993), are based on historical people and ideas.

Benedict, Ruth

né: Ruth Fulton
b. June 5, 1887
New York, New York
d. September 17, 1948
New York, New York
fields: Anthropology

Depicting culture as an integrated set of traits chosen from the vast range of behavioral possibilities, Benedict directed the focus of American anthropology in the 1930's and 1940's toward the search for describable cultural configurations.

Benedict of Nursia, Saint

b. c. 480
Nursia, Umbria, Italy
d. c. 547
Monte Cassino, Campania, Italy
fields: Monasticism, Religion and Theology

Over fifty years of his life, Benedict took the Greek pattern for the monastic life and adapted it for systematic use in the Latin church; the resulting *Rule of St. Benedict* became the model for all subsequent monastic movements.

Beneš, Edvard

b. May 28, 1884
Kozlany, Bohemia, Austro-Hungarian Empire
d. September 3, 1948
Sezimovo Ústí, Czechoslovakia
fields: Government and Politics, Education

Beneš helped undermine Austro-Hungarian rule in the Czech and Slovak region during World War I and became foreign minister of the new republic there in 1918. A brilliant statesman, he negotiated numerous agreements, but as president he was unable to prevent the dismemberment of his country at Munich. During World War II, he headed the Czechoslovakian government in exile and after 1945 endeavored unsuccessfully to maintain Czechoslovakia's political freedom in the face of mounting Communist pressures.

Benét, Stephen Vincent

b. July 22, 1898
Bethlehem, Pennsylvania
d. March 13, 1943
New York, New York
fields: Literature

Benét made his major contribution to literature as a poet and primarily as the author of the book-length poem *John Brown's Body* (1928). Benét was a prolific writer in several genres, however, and his canon includes short stories, novels, radio scripts, and nonfiction.

Benincasa, Caterina. *See* Catherine of Siena, Saint

Benitez, David Ismael Concepción y. *See* Concepción, Dave

Benjamin, Walter

b. July 15, 1892
Berlin, Germany
d. September 27, 1940
Port Bou, Spain
fields: Literature

Unappreciated during his own tragic life, Benjamin became a major influence upon modern cultural criticism after World War II when former colleagues and friends began publishing his work. Using messianic and Marxist ideas in a very idiosyncratic manner, Benjamin criticized all attempts to mask the suffering of humanity with an aesthetic illusion.

Benjamin of Tudela

full: Rabbi Benjamin ben Jonah of Tudela
b. Twelfth century
Tudela, Navarre
d. 1173
Castile
fields: Geography

Benjamin's account of his travels presents the best record available of the number, the leaders, and the social, religious, and economic conditions of the Jews in southern Europe and the Middle East during the twelfth century. At the same time, he provides the best documentation of trade and commerce in these areas in the period between the Second and Third Crusades.

Bennett, Belva Ann. *See* Lockwood, Belva A.

Bennett, James Gordon

b. September 1, 1795
Newmill, Keith, Banffshire, Scotland
d. June 1, 1872
New York, New York
fields: Journalism, Publishing

Bennett made the American newspaper an independent enterprise and established the foundations of the profession of journalism.

Bennett, Lerone, Jr.

b. Oct. 17, 1928
Clarksdale, Miss.
fields: Historiography, Journalism, Literature

African American author, editor, and historian; Lerone Bennett, Jr., has worked solely in the African American media; rose from reporter to city editor with the *Atlanta Daily World*; editor of *Jet* magazine and first senior editor at *Ebony* magazine; among other books, produced the best-selling work in popular African American history *Before the Mayflower: A History of the Negro in America, 1619-1962* (1962); in 1978, received the Literature Award from the American Academy of Arts and Letters.

Bennett, Richard Bedford

b. July 3, 1870
Hopewell Hill, New Brunswick, Canada
d. June 26, 1947
Mickleham, Surrey, England
fields: Government and Politics

Richard Bedford Bennett was prime minister of Canada from 1930 to 1935, during the depths of the Great Depression. Imposed high tariffs to protect Canadian products from foreign competitors, a policy that backfired when foreigners chose not to purchase expensive Canadian products.

Bennett, W. A. C.

full: William Andrew Cecil Bennett
b. September 6, 1900
Hastings, Albert County, New Brunswick, Canada
d. February 23, 1979
Kelowna, British Columbia, Canada
fields: Government and Politics

Canadian political leader W. A. C. Bennett was premier of British Columbia from 1952 to 1973. Oversaw development of British Columbia by exploiting cheap energy sources and fostering investment capital and worker productivity. Bennett's many conflicts with Ottawa and Quebec, however, showed that he put British Columbia ahead of Canada as a whole.

Benoît, Jeanne Mathilde. *See* Sauvé, Jeanne

Benson, George

b. Mar. 22, 1943
Pittsburgh, Pa.
fields: Music (jazz guitarist and singer)

African American guitarist and singer; having recorded solely instrumental pieces up to 1976, George Benson moved to Warner Bros. and combined contemporary jazz vocals with guitar to produce *Breezin'*, for which he received three Grammy Awards; *Weekend in L.A.* (1978) led to internationally sold-out performances and earned more

Grammy Awards; continued to collaborate/record with high-profile artists such as Earl Klugh and the Count Basie Orchestra.

Bentham, Jeremy

b. February 15, 1748
London, England
d. June 6, 1832
London, England
fields: Philosophy, Political Science, Social Reform

Jurist and philosopher Jeremy Bentham, in *An Introduction to the Principles of Morals and Legislation* (1789), set forth his "principle of utility," proclaiming that through legislation the government could achieve the greatest good for the greatest number. Out of this background developed politicians known as the Benthamites, sometimes called the Philosophical Radicals or the utilitarians. Bentham influenced philosophers James Mill and his son John Stuart Mill, and he effectively launched a major reform crusade in English politics, the results of which would be realized in the social changes undertaken by English reformers and passed through Parliament as the Reform Bill of 1832.

Benton, Brook

né: Benjamin Franklin Peay
b. Sept. 19, 1931
Camden, S.C.
d. Apr. 9, 1988
New York, N.Y.
fields: Music (singer and songwriter)

African American singer and songwriter; Brook Benton's songs, some in partnership with Mercury Records' artist Clyde Otis and arranger Belford Hendricks, were recorded by such artists as Nat "King" Cole, Patti Page, Roy Hamilton, and Clyde McPhatter; Benton's own recordings included "It's Just a Matter of Time," "The Boll Weevil Song" (1961, charted number two), and his version of Tony Joe White's "Rainy Night in Georgia" (1970, charted in top ten); he earned eighteen gold records during his career.

Benton, Jessie Ann. *See* Frémont, Jessie Benton

Benton, Thomas Hart

b. March 14, 1782
near Hillsboro, North Carolina
d. April 10, 1858
Washington, D.C.
fields: Government and Politics

A prominent United States senator from 1821 to 1851, Benton was a great champion of Western expansion, public land distribution, and "hard money." He was a leading supporter of President Andrew Jackson and his policies.

Benz, Carl

full: Carl Friedrich Benz
b. November 25, 1844; Karlsruhe, Germany
d. April 4, 1929; Ladenburg, Germany
fields: Invention and Technology

As one of the earliest inventors of a practical automobile, Benz developed several features essential to automobile design and function. Founded the engine manufacturer Benz & Co. (1883).

Berdyaev, Nikolai

b. March 6, 1874
Lipky, near Kiev, Ukraine
d. March 23, 1948
Clamart, France
fields: Philosophy, Religion and Theology

The Russian philosopher Nikolai Berdyaev developed Christian existentialism, edited the journal *Put'*(path), founded the Academy of Philosophy and Religion (Berlin, 1922), and wrote *The Origin of Russian Communism* (1937). His Christian existentialism explored the role of freedom in the improvement of humankind and society: If freedom was used in the service of enlarged awareness and capacity, God and humanity became co-creators in a continually progressing universe; if it was turned toward material products instead of being, humanity and society remained in turmoil and confusion.

Berenson, Senda

b. Mar. 19, 1868
Biturmansk, Lithuania
d. Feb. 16, 1954
Santa Barbara, Calif.
fields: Sports, Education

Senda Berenson was an advocate of physical education; was restricted from usual school activity because of a weak back; studied physical education; beginning in 1892 taught physical training to women at Smith College, introducing fencing, folk dance, field hockey, and—most notably—women's line basketball; offered a new view on sports that did not center on competition and that favored intramural sports.

Berg, Alban

b. February 9, 1885
Vienna, Austro-Hungarian Empire
d. December 24, 1935
Vienna, Austria
fields: Music

Berg was one of the pioneers in the creation of atonal and twelve-tone music. Though basing his work on the revolutionary system of his teacher Arnold Schoenberg, Berg established a link between the new style and the Romantic past and demonstrated that atonal and twelve-tone music could still be lyrical and emotionally expressive. As a result, his works gained widespread acceptance and thus encouraged a whole generation of innovative and experimental composers.

Berg, Patty

full: Patricia Jane Berg
b. February 13, 1918
Minneapolis, Minnesota
fields: Sports (golf)

An original organizer of the Ladies Professional Golf Association (LPGA), Berg became the most decorated woman golfer in history and the foremost promoter of golf as the game of a lifetime for professionals and amateurs alike.

Berg, Paul

b. June 30, 1926
Brooklyn, New York
fields: Biology, Genetics, Medicine

Paul Berg created a technique to splice deoxyribonucleic acid (DNA) from different organisms, thereby producing a tool for the study of chromosome structure and the biochemical basis of genetic disease via recombinant DNA technology. Won National Medal of Science in 1983.

Bergius, Friedrich

b. October 11, 1884
Goldschmieden, Germany
d. March 30, 1949
Buenos Aires, Argentina
fields: Chemistry, Engineering, Invention and Technology

Bergius discovered how to obtain liquid hydrocarbon fuels by hydrogenation of coal and how to obtain synthetic sugar from wood cellulose. The fuels made by his processes aided Germany during World War II, and Bergius' methods form the basis for the modern synthetic fuels industry. He won the 1931 Nobel Prize in Chemistry.

Bergman, Ingmar

full: Ernst Ingmar Bergman
b. July 14, 1918
Uppsala, Sweden
fields: Film, Theater and Entertainment

Despite fluctuations in the critical appraisal of his many films, Bergman dominated the Scandinavian filmmaking industry from the mid-1940's until the early 1980's, and his films earned international acclaim. His rapport with actors and his innovative stage techniques also earned for him a reputation as one of the world's foremost theatrical directors.

Bergson, Henri

full: Henri Louis Bergson
b. October 18, 1859
Paris, France

d. January 4, 1941
Paris, France
fields: Philosophy

Bergson, by rejecting the mechanistic view of life held by the noted positivists of his day, focused renewed attention on the importance of the human spirit, its creative potential, and its inherent freedom, thereby opening new intellectual vistas to many creative artists. He was awarded the Nobel Prize in Literature in 1927.

Bering, Vitus Jonassen

b. August 12, 1681
Horsens, Denmark
d. December 19, 1741
Bering Island, Russia
fields: Exploration and Colonization

A sailor in the service of Russia, Bering confirmed the existence of a strait between Asia and North America, led the first European expedition to cross from Siberia to the northwest coast of America, and commanded the Great Northern Expedition of 1733-1742 in its exploration of Siberia.

Berkeley, George

b. March 12, 1685
near Thomastown, Kilkenny, Ireland
d. January 14, 1753
Oxford, England
fields: Philosophy, Religion and Theology, Science

Berkeley put forth a novel theory of sense perception which led to the denial of the existence of physical objects. Serving as the link between John Locke's commonsense materialism and David Hume's skepticism, Berkeley's ideas spanned the philosophical gap between classical traditionalism and the emergence of modern science.

Berliawsky, Leah. *See* Nevelson, Louise

Berlin, Irving

né: Israel Baline
b. May 11, 1888
Temun, Russia
d. September 22, 1989
New York, New York
fields: Music

Berlin, one of the most prolific and recognized American songwriters, had the exceptional ability to make his tunes and rhythms conform to the style and mood of the times in which he lived.

Berlin, Isaiah

full: Isaiah Mendelevich Berlin
b. June 6, 1909
Riga, Latvia, Russian Empire (now Latvia)
d. November 5, 1997
Oxford, England
fields: Philosophy, Political Science

Irving Berlin stressed a pluralistic belief that there is no single, ultimately objective way of viewing the world, human existence, or the goals of individuals or societies. He was awarded the British Order of Merit, designated a Commander of the British Empire, and named a fellow of the British Academy (vice president, 1959-1961; president, 1974-1978). His work earned him the Erasmus, Lippincott, and Agnelli Prizes, along with the Jerusalem Prize for his lifelong defense of civil liberties. In 1957 he was knighted by Queen Elizabeth II and elected to the Chichele Chair of Social and Political Theory at Oxford. His inaugural lecture, "Two Concepts of Liberty," contrasted "negative liberty" (freedom from others) and "positive liberty" (freedom of action), a significant contribution to political thought, the centerpiece of Berlin's best-known work, *Four Essays on Liberty* (1969).

Berlioz, Hector

full: Louis-Hector Berlioz
b. December 11, 1803
La Côte-Saint-André, France
d. March 8, 1869
Paris, France
fields: Music

Berlioz, one of the foremost exponents of Romanticism, extended the art of orchestration in compositions of striking originality. In his writings, which include a treatise on orchestration and a colorful memoir of his life, he made contributions both to musical craft and cultural history. During his lifetime Berlioz's music attained more popularity outside France than within it, where the eccentric notoriety of the man often overshadowed his genius.

Bernadotte, Jean-Baptiste-Jules. *See* Charles XIV John

Bernal, Vicente J.

b. Dec. 15, 1888
Costilla, N.Mex.
d. Apr. 28, 1915
Dubuque, Iowa
fields: Literature (poet)

Latino poet. Vicente J. Bernal, one of the first Hispanic writers from the American Southwest to publish in English, wrote thirty-four English-language poems between 1913 to 1915 while attending Dubuque German College and Academy (now the University of Dubuque) in Dubuque, Iowa. One of the poems was set to music and became the college's alma mater. Bernal died of a brain hemorrhage in 1915, one year before completing his studies. The following year, the *Telegraph-Herald* of Dubuque published his only printed work, a collection of prose and poetry, half of which is in Spanish.

Bernard, Claude

b. July 12, 1813
Saint-Julien, France
d. February 10, 1878
Paris, France
fields: Physiology, Medicine

Bernard is called the "father of physiology," having developed the experimental methods and conceptual framework needed to change physiology from a primarily deductive science based on statistics to one which could discover empirical data using procedures borrowed from chemistry.

Bernard, Jessie Shirley

b. June 8, 1903
Minneapolis, Minn.
d. Oct. 6, 1996
Washington, D.C.
fields: Sociology

After teaching sociology from 1947 to 1964, Jessie Shirley Bernard became a scholar in residence for the U.S. Commission on Civil Rights. Her first book, *American Family Behavior* (1942), suggested that American families were less than perfect. Adopting a more feminist approach in the 1960's, she afterward challenged images of men sacrificing their freedom in marriage to shelter and protect women. Arguing that every marriage was essentially two marriages, offering different expectations and experiences to males and females, she concluded that marriage was often good for men but bad for women.

Bernard of Clairvaux, Saint

b. 1090
Fontaines-les-Dijon, Burgundy
d. August 20, 1153
Clairvaux, Champagne
fields: Religion and Theology, Church Reform

In the first half of the twelfth century, Bernard epitomized the monastic ideal and served as adviser and critic to kings, popes, bishops, abbots, and other leading figures in Western Europe.

Bernays, Edward L.

b. November 22, 1891
Vienna, Austria
d. March 9, 1995
Cambridge, Massachusetts
fields: Psychiatry and Psychology, Warfare and Conquest

Edward L. Bernays was a pioneering public relations counselor whom *Life* magazine named one of the hundred most influential Americans of the twentieth century. He played an important role in drawing the United States into World War I as a member of George Creel's Committee on Public Information. After the war he worked as a publicist who worked to apply human motivation to concepts of mass persuasion. He helped his uncle Sigmund Freud publish his work in English.

Bernini, Gian Lorenzo

b. December 7, 1598
Naples
d. November 28, 1680
Rome
fields: Art, Architecture

The sculpture and architecture of Bernini are considered to be among the most complete expressions of the thought and feeling of the Counter-Reformation. He is also one of the most representative practitioners of the High Baroque style.

Bernoulli, Daniel

b. February 8, 1700
Groningen, the Netherlands
d. March 17, 1782
Basel, Swiss Confederation
fields: Physics, Mathematics, Medicine

Daniel Bernoulli is credited as the founder of mathematical physics. The Bernoulli family contributed to the flowering in the eighteenth century of mathematical analysis, which applied advanced mathematical techniques to problems arising in physics, technology, medicine, and the emerging field of probability theory. Members of the family dominated Continental mathematics from the later seventeenth to the later eighteenth centuries.

Bernoulli, Jakob I

b. December 27, 1654
Basel, Swiss Confederation
d. August 16, 1705
Basel, Swiss Confederation
fields: Mathematics, Physics, Astronomy

Jakob I Bernoulli was the first to prove the law of large numbers and wrote one of the first books on probability. The Bernoulli family contributed to the flowering in the eighteenth century of mathematical analysis, which applied advanced mathematical techniques to problems arising in physics, technology, medicine, and the emerging field of probability theory. Members of the family dominated Continental mathematics from the later seventeenth to the later eighteenth centuries.

Bernoulli, Johann I

b. August 6, 1667
Basel, Swiss Confederation
d. January 1, 1748
Basel, Swiss Confederation
fields: Mathematics

Johann I Bernoulli is best remembered as the inventor of the calculus of variations and the calculus of exponentials. The Bernoulli family contributed to the flowering in the eighteenth century of mathematical analysis, which applied advanced mathematical techniques to problems arising in physics, technology, medicine, and the emerging field of probability theory. Members of the family dominated Continental mathematics from the later seventeenth to the later eighteenth centuries.

Bernstein, Eduard

b. January 6, 1850
Berlin, Prussia
d. December 18, 1932
Berlin, Germany
fields: Social Reform

Bernstein, a German political theorist, socialist politician, and historian, was the originator of Revisionist Socialism. He tried to modify the traditional Marxian prediction of the imminent collapse of capitalism and the subsequent rule of the proletarian class by proposing a theory according to which social-reformist social change would lead to the realization of socialism.

Bernstein, Leonard

b. August 25, 1918
Lawrence, Massachusetts
d. October 14, 1990
New York, New York
fields: Music, Theater and Entertainment, Film

Leonard Bernstein was one of the most important musicians of the latter half of the twentieth century. Both composer and conductor, he bridged a gap between "serious" and show music with such successes as his 1957 musical *West Side Story* and *Candide* (1956). In 1959, he became music director of the New York Philharmonic, a post he would hold through 1969. He helped to popularize serious music with his Young People's Concerts, using his celebrity to promote both cultural and political causes. He revived interest in the music of Gustav Mahler, wrote books about music for the general public (*The Joy of Music*, 1963; *The Infinite Variety of Music*, 1966), and became a political activist during the 1960's, notably conducting an outdoor concert at Jerusalem's Mount Scopus following Israel's Six-Day War of 1967. In his later years, he returned to composing serious music and continued to conduct the great orchestras of the world.

Berrigan, Daniel

full: Daniel Joseph Berrigan
b. May 9, 1921
Virginia, Minnesota
fields: Religion and Theology, Social Reform

Roman Catholic priests Daniel Berrigan and his brother, Philip Francis Berrigan, were leading figures of the anti-Vietnam War movement. They were arrested in May, 1968 for trying to destroy draft board records and were tried as part of the "Catonsville Nine" defendants. Both were sentenced to six years in federal prison, but Daniel Berrigan went underground for four months before he was caught. His reputation was later augmented by his speeches and writings, notably his play, *The Trial of the Catonsville Nine* (1971) and autobiography, *The Dark Night of Resistance*.

Berrigan, Philip

full: Philip Francis Berrigan
b. October 5, 1923
Two Harbors, Minnesota
fields: Religion and Theology, Social Reform

Roman Catholic priests Philip Francis Berrigan and his brother, Daniel Berrigan, were leading figures of the anti-Vietnam War movement. They were arrested in May, 1968, for pouring blood on draft board records and burning documents. Images from their trial—as part of the "Catonsville Nine" defendants—became well-known symbols of the antiwar movement. Both were sentenced to six years in federal prison. In 1971 Philip Berrigan was among those indicted as the "Harrisburg Seven" for plotting to raid government offices, kidnap Henry Kissinger, and sabotage the Pentagon Building. He was eventually convicted only of smuggling love letters to a fellow defendant. After 1979 he continued his antiwar activities and was repeatedly jailed.

Berry, Bertice B.

b. 1960
Wilmington, Del.
fields: Education, Television

African American educator, comedian, and talk show host; a former university professor and stand-up commedian, Bertice B. Berry hosted her own television talk show, *The Bertice Berry Show*, which aired in syndication during the 1993-1994 season; wrote *Bertice: The World According to Me* (1996).

Berry, Chuck

né: Charles Edward Anderson
b. October 18, 1926
St. Louis, Mo.

fields: Music (rock and roll singer and composer)

African American rock and roll singer and composer. Chuck Berry was a pioneer of the rock and roll sound, and his songs helped define the style in the 1950's and influenced a whole generation musicians. Two musicians who influenced Berry's early guitar style are Charlie Christain and blues guitarist T-Bone Walker. His skill at blending blues and country and western into a single, dynamic form helped establish rock music as a focul point of popular culture. Berry recorded many top-selling songs such as "Maybellene," "Roll over Beethoven," "Sweet Little Sixteen," "Reelin' and Rockin'," and "Johnny B. Goode." His awards and honors include the American Music Conference's Music Award (1975), a Grammy Award (1984), and induction into the Rock and Roll Hall of Fame (1986). Berry appeared in *Go, Johnny, Go!* (1958), as well as several other films. Run-ins with the law in his teens and in later life resulted in several periods of incarceration. Berry's life story was published in 1987, *Chuck Berry: The Autobiography*.

Berry, Halle

b. 1969?
Cleveland, Ohio
fields: Theater and Entertainment

African American actress; a former Miss Ohio and first runner-up in the 1986 Miss U.S.A. pageant, Halle Berry appeared in the television series *Living Dolls* and had a continuing role in *Knots Landing*; her film credits include *Jungle Fever* (1991), *Strictly Business* (1992), and *Boomerang* (1992).

Berry, Mary Frances

b. Feb. 17, 1938
Nashville, Tenn.
fields: Education, Government and Politics, Civil Rights

African American educator, government official, and activist; holding B.A., M.A., Ph.D., and J.D. degrees, Mary Frances Berry has taught history and law at various universities; worked her way up to chancellor at University of Colorado; during the Carter administration, served as assistant secretary for education in the U.S. Department of Health, Education, and Welfare (1977-1980) and as commissioner and vice chair of the U.S. Commission on Civil Rights; served as editor of the *Journal of Negro History*; founding member of the Free South Africa Movement.

Berry, Theodore M.

b. Nov. 8, 1905
Maysville, Ky.
fields: Government and Politics

African American mayor of Cincinnati, Ohio; Theodore M. Berry's civil rights work included serving on the board of directors, Cincinnati chapter, of the NAACP (1946-1968) and as chairman of the Ohio Commission on Civil Rights Legislation (1949-1965); elected to Cincinnati city council (1950-1957) and as city alderman (1963-1965); under Johnson administration, served as director of community action programs for the Office of Economic Opportunity (1965-1969); in 1972 Berry was elected the first African American mayor of Cincinnati, a position he held for three years.

Berssenbrugge, Mei-mei

b. Oct. 5, 1947
Beijing, China
fields: Poetry

An American citizen born abroad, Mei-mei Berssenbrugge published several books of poetry, including *Fish Souls* (1971), *Summits Move with the Tide* (1974), *Random Possession* (1979), *The Heat Bird* (1983), *Empathy* (1989), and *Sphericity* (1993). She wrote the one-act play *One, Two Cups* (pr. 1979) and contributed to periodicals such as *East-West Journal*, *Bridge*, and *Conjunctions*.

Berthollet, Claude Louis

b. Dec. 9, 1748
Talloire, Savoy, Italy
d. Nov. 6, 1822
Arcueil, France
fields: Chemistry

Claude Louis Berthollet published *Essai de statique chemique (An Essay on Chemical Statics*, 1804) in 1803, his definitive statement on the laws of affinity; showed that the simple laws of affinity between acidic and basic radicals were not enough to explain all compound formation, and factors such as quantity of material and temperature must be considered. With Pierre Laplace, founded Société d'Arcueil to discuss scientific matters in 1807.

Bertholoff, William Henry Joseph Bonaparte. *See* Smith, Willie

Berzelius, Jöns Jacob

b. Aug. 20, 1779
Väversunda, Östergötland, Sweden
d. Aug. 7, 1848
Stockholm, Sweden
fields: Chemistry

Jöns Jacob Berzelius built a voltaic pile, using its electric current to treat patients, in 1800; discovered element cerium in 1803; isolated element selenium in 1817; discovered element thorium in 1829; and was preeminent in many areas of the new chemistry of the nineteenth century: analysis, atomic and equivalent weights and combining proportions, nomenclature.

Besant, Annie

né: Annie Wood
b. October 1, 1847
London, England
d. September 20, 1933
Adyar, India
fields: Social Reform, Religion and Theology, Government and Politics

After her early work promoting radical reform in England, Besant became leader of the Theosophical Society and was active in the nationalist movement in India.

Beshayeschayecoosis. *See* White Man Runs Him

Beshiltheeni. *See* Delgadito

Bessel, Friedrich Wilhelm

b. July 22, 1784
Minden, Westphalia
d. March 17, 1846
Königsberg, Prussia
fields: Astronomy, Mathematics

Bessel greatly increased the accuracy of the measurements of stellar positions both by using more advanced instruments and by developing methods to account for instrument and observer error. The most famous discovery resulting from these observations was the first accurate determination of the distance to a star.

Bessemer, Henry

aka: Sir Henry Bessemer
b. January 19, 1813
Charlton, Hertfordshire, England
d. March 15, 1898
London, England
fields: Invention and Technology

Bessemer developed and patented the Bessemer process for purifying molten iron. As a result, steel production increased and its cost was cut in half during the 1850's and 1860's, ushering in the "Age of Steel."

Betances, Ramón Emeterio

b. Apr. 8, 1827
Cabo Rojo, Puerto Rico
d. Sept. 18, 1898
Paris, France
fields: Social Reform

Latino revolutionary. Trained as a physician, Ramón Emeterio Betances helped vaccinate poor people in Puerto Rico during the 1855 cholera epidemic. He was also an abolitionist and a leader of the Puerto Rican independence movement, and was expelled from the island several times by Spanish authorities. He was a major force behind the revolt in Lares on September 23, 1868, which, because of a series of misfortunes, was swiftly quelled by Spanish authorities. The Spanish government later declared an amnesty, but Betances settled in France, where he promoted independence for Puerto Rico until his death.

Bethe, Hans Albrecht

b. July 2, 1906
Strasbourg, Alsace-Lorraine
fields: Physics (theoretical), Peace Advocacy

Bethe's work in theoretical nuclear physics explained how stars convert mass to energy and broadened the scientific understanding of subatomic events. Long an influential advocate for restraint in the proliferation of nuclear weapons, he laid the theoretical groundwork for the explosion of the first atom bomb. He was awarded the 1967 Nobel Prize in Physics.

Bethmann Hollweg, Theobald von

full: Theobald Theodor Friedrich Alfred von Bethmann Hollweg
b. November 29, 1856
Hohenfinow, Prussia (now Germany)
d. January 1, 1921
Hohenfinow, Germany
fields: Government and Politics

Theobald von Bethmann Hollweg was chancellor of Germany from 1909 to 1917. Some historians refer to him as giving officials of the Austro-Hungarian Empire a "blank check" to settle their differences with Serbia in July, 1914, leading to World War I. A lifelong conservative, he opposed resumption of unrestricted submarine warfare in February, 1917, realizing that it would probably draw the United States into the war.

Bethune, Blind Tom

full: Thomas Green Bethune
b. May 25, 1849
Columbus, Ga.
d. June 13, 1908
Hoboken, N.J.
fields: Music (pianist)

African American pianist; born a slave and blind from birth, Thomas Green "Blind Tom" Bethune was a misrepresented musical prodigy—he could play difficult piano compositions after hearing them only once; slave-owner Colonel James Bethune exhibited Bethune in performances that included popular ballads, classical pieces, parlor music, and opera; after the Colonel's death, his son John assumed guardianship of Bethune, followed by John's widow—all of whom continued to exhibit Tom in concerts and vaudeville acts until 1904; Bethune is credited with composing more than one hundred original works.

Bethune, Mary McLeod

né: Mary Jane McLeod
b. July 10, 1875
Mayesville, South Carolina
d. May 18, 1955
Daytona Beach, Florida
fields: Education, Social Reform

A leading voice and activist for democratic ideals before World War I and up to the early Civil Rights years, Bethune was instrumental in founding organizations to advance the education and rights of blacks, inspiring others as she was herself inspired.

Beust, Friedrich von

full: Friedrich Ferdinand von Beust
b. January 13, 1809
Dresden, Saxony
d. October 24, 1886
Altenberg Castle, Austro-Hungarian Empire
fields: Diplomacy, Government and Politics

Beust played a leading role from his position in the Saxon government in suppressing the Revolutions of 1848 in the German states and in formulating reactionary policies adopted by the governments of those states over the following two decades. First in the Saxon government, then in the Austrian, he was Otto von Bismarck's most formidable opponent during the Prussian chancellor's attempt to unify the small German states under the leadership of Prussia. Beust was also the architect of the political settlement in 1868 which created the Austro-Hungarian Empire.

Bevan, Aneurin

aka: Nye Bevan
b. November 15, 1897
Tredegar, Monmouthshire, Wales
d. July 6, 1960
Chesham, Buckinghamshire, England
fields: Government and Politics, Social Reform

Bevan was the most eloquent British spokesman of his time for democratic socialism and also the architect of the National Health Service, one of the most important social reforms of the twentieth century.

Bevel, James

b. October 19, 1936
Itta Bena, Miss.
fields: Civil Rights

African American civil rights activist. James Bevel helped found the Student Non-Violent Coordinating Committee (SNCC) in 1960 and served as director of direct action and nonviolent education for the Southern Christian Leadership Conference (SCLC). He became a friend and adviser of Martin Luther King, Jr, while working in the SCLC. He was in Memphis, Tennessee, with King when he was assassinated in 1968. After King's death, Bevel left the organization beacause of disagreements with other SCLC leaders. At this point he retired from the public life of social activism. However he returned to politics in the 1980's as a conservative, campaigning for Ronald Reagan and eventually running for the House of Representatives as Republican. He later founded two advocacy organizations promoting education, nonviolence, and human rights.

Beveridge, Lord

né: William Henry Beveridge
aka: William Henry, First Baron Beveridge of Tuggal
b. March 5, 1879
Rangpur, Bengal, India
d. March 16, 1963
Oxford, England
fields: Economics, Education, Social Reform

As an economist, Beveridge was a pioneer in the study of unemployment and the history of prices. He was the force responsible for building the London School of Economics into one of the world's leading centers of social-science scholarship. He is remembered, however, as the intellectual father of the post-World War II British welfare state.

Bevin, Ernest

b. March 7, 1881
Winsford, Somerset, England
d. April 14, 1951
London, England
fields: Labor Movement, Politics, Diplomacy

Bevin founded, and for eighteen years led, the Transport and General Workers Union, influenced Labour Party policy during the 1930's, served as minister of labour and national service in World War II, and, in the postwar Labour government, was foreign secretary and one of the architects of the Cold War.

Beyle, Marie-Henri. *See* Stendhal

Bhachu, Parminder Kaur

b. Oct. 20, 1953
fields: Scholarship

A scholar of the diaspora experience, Parminder Kaur Bhachu focused on Sikhs in Great Britain, producing works such as *Twice Migrants: East African Sikh Settlers in Britain* (1985). Her coedited works include *Enterprising Women: Ethnicity, Economy, and Gender Relations* (1988, with Sallie Westwood) and *Immigration and Entrepreneurship: Culture, Capital, and Ethnic Networks* (1993, with Ivan Light).

Bhattacharya, Narendranath. *See* Roy, M. N.

Bhonsle, Sivajī. *See* Sivajī

Bhumibol Adulyadej

b. December 5, 1927
Cambridge, Massachusetts
fields: Government and Politics

Bhumibol Adulyadej began his reign as king of Thailand in 1946, a reign longer than that of any other member of the Chakri Dynasty. Maintained Thai unity in spite of fifteen constitutions, seventeen coups, and twenty-one prime ministers. Twice he directly intervened in state affairs to halt or avoid bloodshed.

Bhutto, Benazir

b. June 21, 1953
Karachi, Pakistan
fields: Government and Politics

Benazir Bhutto, daughter of Zulfikar Ali Bhutto, was twice prime minister of Pakistan, from 1988 to 1990 and from 1993 to 1996. Encountered many problems in office; government plagued by corruption and mismanagement. Friends, associates, and family members were accused of financial misdeeds. The government was unable to achieve progress in economic development, and conditions for the poorest people, who traditionally most supported the Bhuttos, worsened.

Bhutto, Zulfikar Ali

b. January 5, 1928
near Larkana, Sind, India (now Pakistan)
d. April 4, 1979
Rawalpindi, Pakistan
fields: Government and Politics

Zulfikar Ali Bhutto led Pakistan as president (1971-1973) and as prime minister (1973-1977). Taking power in 1971, he proclaimed himself president and martial law administrator. Changed his title from president to prime minister in 1973. Despite broad following, widely criticized for Pakistan's economic problems. In 1974, nationalized all the banks and stopped the flow of hard currency abroad. Overthrown in a military coup led by General Mohammad Zia ul-Haq in 1977.

Bias, Len

b. Nov. 18, 1963
Hyattsville, Md.
d. June 19, 1986
College Park, Md.
fields: Sports (basketball player)

African American collegiate basketball star; playing for the University of Maryland, Len Bias became the school's career scoring leader with 2,149 points, was elected an All-American, and as a senior made 224 rebounds and scored an average of 23.2 points per game; died of a cocaine overdose the night after the Boston Celtics selected him as their first pick in the NBA draft.

Biddle, Francis

b. May 9, 1886
Paris, France
d. Oct. 4, 1968
Hayannis, Mass.
fields: Law, Government and Politics

Francis Biddle was a judge on the U.S. Circuit Court of Appeals (1939-1940) who became solicitor general (1940) and attorney general (1941-1945) of the United States, as well as a judge in the Nuremberg Trials (1945-1946). He was angrily criticized by white Americans for not evacuating Japanese Americans during the anti-Japanese American hysteria that arose at the start of World War II.

Biddle, John

b. January 14, 1615 (baptized)
Wotton-under-Edge, Gloucestershire, England
d. September 22, 1662
London, England
fields: Religion and Theology

Biddle was a controversial lay theologian who, through his writings and strong moral leadership, became known as the father of English Unitarianism.

Biddle, Nicholas

b. January 8, 1786
Philadelphia, Pennsylvania
d. February 27, 1844
Philadelphia, Pennsylvania
fields: Banking and Finance

Combining superb managerial skills and a keen understanding of finance and banking, Biddle developed the Bank of the United States into a prototype of the modern central banking system.

Bidu-ya. *See* Victorio

Bierce, Ambrose

full: Ambrose Gwinett Bierce
b. June 24, 1842
Horse Cave Creek, Ohio
d. 1914 (?)
Mexico (?)
fields: Journalism, Literature

A legendary cynic and social satirist, Bierce won local fame in San Francisco, California, as a newspaper and magazine columnist and secured a place in American literature with his nonrealist short stories, many of which are set against the backdrop of the American Civil War.

Bierstadt, Albert

b. January 7, 1830
Solingen, Germany
d. February 18, 1902
New York, New York
fields: Art

Using an exaggerated, romantic style, Bierstadt painted giant landscapes of spectacular Western vistas that helped to shape the myth of the American West, establish the Rocky Mountain School of art, and interest Easterners in preservation of Western scenic areas as national parks.

Big Bear

aka: Mistahimaskwa
b. 1825
near Fort Carlton in present-day Saskatchewan, Canada
d. 1888
near Fort Pitt, present-day Pittsburgh
fields: Native American Affairs

Cree chief during the Second Riel Rebellion of 1885; concerned about the loss of traditional Indian lifestyle, Big Bear refused to sign Treaty Number Six in 1876 and remained off the reservation until 1882 when destruction of the buffalo led to imminent starvation; Big Bear joined Louis Riel, Jr., leader of the Metis uprisings against unremitting white encroachment, particularly during the construction of the Canadian Pacific Railway; in a raid on a settlement at Frog Lake on April 2, 1885, Cree violence that Big Bear tried to prevent resulted in several white mortalities and led to his conviction for treason and a three-year sentence in Stoney Mountain Penitentiary beginning in 1885; he died while imprisoned.

Big Bow

aka: Zipkoheta
b. c. 1830
d. c. 1900
fields: Government and Politics, Warfare and Conquest (Kiowa chief)

Native American leader. During the Central Plains Indian wars, Big Bow was the most militant Kiowa chief and the last to surrender to reservation settlement. After an aggressive U.S. Army campaign to subdue the Kiowa in 1870-1871, Big Bow was the last major war chief to capitulate. In 1874, he joined the Comanches in the Red River War.

Big Crane. *See* Two Leggings

Big Foot

aka: Si Tanka
aka: Spotted Elk
b. c. 1825
d. Dec. 29, 1890
South Dakota

fields: Government and Politics, Warfare and Conquest, Native American Affairs

Minneconjou Sioux leader Big Foot was the leader of the band of nearly two hundred men, women, and children who were killed by the U.S. Seventh Cavalry at Wounded Knee Creek, South Dakota, on December 29, 1890.

Big Mouth. *See* Eskiminzin

Big Tree

aka: Adoltay
aka: Adouette
b. c. 1847
Tex.
d. Nov. 13, 1929
Fort Sill, present-day Okla.
fields: Warfare and Conquest, Native American Affairs

Kiowa tribal leader Big Tree ambushed General William Tecumseh Sherman's wagon train on May 18, 1871, as it was en route to Fort Sill, Texas, during the Kiowa raids.

Big Warrior

aka: Tustennugee Thlucco
b. ?
d. Mar. 8, 1825
Washington, D.C.
fields: Warfare and Conquest, Native American Affairs

Creek tribal leader Big Warrior's decision to fight on the American side in the Creek War of 1813-1814 contributed to the defeat of the Red Sticks faction of Creeks.

Big Winnebago. *See* Crashing Thunder

Biggers, Earl Derr

b. Aug. 26, 1884
Warren, Ohio
d. Apr. 5, 1933
Pasadena, Calif.
fields: Literature

Earl Derr Biggers is best known for six novels featuring Charlie Chan, a Hawaii-based Chinese American detective. All six novels, from *The House Without a Key* (1925) to *Keeper of the Keys* (1932), were serialized in *The Saturday Evening Post.* The humorous mysteries formed the basis for more than thirty films. For many Asian Americans, the Chan character has become a symbol of the racist stereotyping that shaped depictions of Asians and Asian Americans in the media.

Biggers, John

b. 1924
Gastonia, N.C.
fields: Art, Education

African American artist and educator; in 1949, John Biggers founded Texas Southern University's art department; Biggers's sculptures, paintings, murals, and illustrations depict African Americans' accomplishments, rural traditions, and southern roots.

Billingsley, Andrew

b. Mar. 20, 1926
Marion, Ala.
fields: Education, Scholarship

African American university administrator; with a background in social work, Andrew Billingsley came to the University of California as a professor and assistant dean of students (1964), later serving as assistant chancellor for academic affairs (1968-1970); in 1970, served at Howard University as professor of sociology and social work, as vice president of academic affairs, and, in 1975, as graduate professor of social sciences; served as president of Morgan State University (1975-1984); his published works include *Black Families in White America* (1968) and *Black Families and the Struggle for Survival* (1974).

Billops, Camille J.

b. Aug. 12, 1933
Los Angeles, Calif.
fields: Art (sculptor), Education

African American sculptor and educator; Camille J. Billops's ceramic sculptures combine hand-built and wheel-thrown forms; she is also known for her work as a filmmaker, lecturer, and art educator.

Bing, Dave

full: David Bing
b. Nov. 24, 1943
Washington, D.C.
fields: Sports (basketball player)

African American basketball player; "Dave" Bing went from All-American at Syracuse University, N.Y. to being the Detroit Pistons' first pick, second in the 1966 NBA draft; this six-foot, three-inch guard was named the NBA's Rookie of the Year; in his second season, noted as the first guard in twenty years to lead the NBA in scoring; chosen for the All-Star team seven times and named the 1976 All-Star Game's Most Valuable Player, Bing went on to play for the Washington Bullets and the Boston Celtics before ending his professional career in 1978; inducted into the Basketball Hall of Fame in 1990.

Bingham, George Caleb

b. March 20, 1811
Augusta County, Virginia
d. July 7, 1879
Kansas City, Missouri
fields: Art

Bingham was the first American artist to record life on the mid-nineteenth century frontier in paintings of sensitive social commentary and high aesthetic quality.

Biot, Jean-Baptiste

b. Apr. 21, 1774
Paris, France
d. Feb. 3, 1862
Paris, France
fields: Chemistry, Mathematics, Physics

Jean-Baptiste Biot ascended in a balloon in 1804 to demonstrate that the earth's magnetism does not decrease with altitude; demonstrated in 1815 that organic substances rotate polarized light; linked his training in mathematics and physics to develop sophisticated mathematical models of physical systems investigating the speed of sound, electromagnetism, and the polarization of light.

Birkhoff, George David

b. Mar. 21, 1884
Overisel, Michigan
d. Nov. 12, 1944
Cambridge, Massachusetts
fields: Mathematics (applied math)

In 1931 George David Birkhoff published "Proof of the Ergodic Theorem," which led to a solution to the problem of three mutually gravitating bodies. He is known for his work in differential equations, boundary value problems, dynamical systems, and celestial mechanics.

Biruni, al-

full: Abu al-Rayhan Muhammad ibn Ahmad al-Biruni
b. September 973
Khiva, Khwarezm
d. c. 1050
Ghazna, Ghaznavid Afghanistan
fields: Historiography, Science

One of the greatest scholars of medieval Islam, al-Biruni was both a singular compiler of the knowledge and scientific traditions of ancient cultures and a leading innovator in Islamic science.

Bishop, E. Faxon

b. Oct. 27, 1863
Naperville, Ill.
d. Feb. 11, 1943
Honolulu, Territory of Hawaii
fields: Business and Industry, Government and Politics

While president of the Hawaiian Sugar Planters' Association, E. Faxon Bishop negotiated an agreement with the Korean government to bring Korean contract laborers to Hawaii to work on plantations. Because the association paid the laborers before they arrived in the United States, he was charged, in 1903, with illegally assisting the immigration of contract laborers. Later that year, the U.S. district court cleared him of the charge. He was elected to the senate of the Territory of Hawaii in 1904 and became its president in 1907.

Bishop, Elizabeth

b. February 8, 1911
Worcester, Massachusetts
d. October 6, 1979
Boston, Massachusetts
fields: Literature

Elizabeth Bishop wrote some of the most elegantly structured and moving poems in twentieth century American literature.

Bishop, Sanford Dixon, Jr.

b. February 4, 1947
Mobile County, Ala.
fields: Government and Politics

African American politician; Sanford Dixon Bishop, Jr., defeated a white Republican opponent in the 1992 November elections to become a member of the 103rd Congress; was reelected in 1994.

Bislahani. *See* Barboncito

Bismarck, Otto von

full: Otto Eduard Leopold von Bismarck-Schönhausen
aka: Iron Chancellor
b. April 1, 1815
Schönhausen, Prussia
d. July 30, 1898
Friedrichsruh, Germany
fields: Government and Politics

Bismarck, known as the "blood and iron chancellor," occasioned the unification of the several German states into the German Empire of 1871-1918. Though his image is that of the aristocrat in a spiked helmet, he was above all a diplomat and a politician, skillfully manipulating the forces at work within Germany and among the European states to achieve his goals.

Biter. *See* Zotom

Bithorn, Hiram

full: Hiram Gabriel Bithorn y Sosa
b. Mar. 18, 1916
Santurce, Puerto Rico
d. Jan. 1, 1952
El Mante, Mexico
fields: Sports (baseball player)

Latino baseball player. Right-handed pitcher Hiram Bithorn was the first Puerto Rican to play in the major leagues. He debuted with the Chicago Cubs in 1942. In 1943, he led the National League with seven shutouts and compiled an 18-12 record. He returned to the Cubs in 1946 after two years of military service but was traded in 1947 to the Chicago White Sox, where a sore arm ended his major-league career. Bithorn later attempted to play in the Mexican leagues, but he was shot to death on New Year's Day in 1952.

Bizet, Georges

full: Alexandre César Léopold Bizet
b. October 25, 1838
Paris, France
d. June 3, 1875
Bougival, near Paris, France
fields: Music

Bizet is one of the foremost French composers of the nineteenth century and the composer of one of the most popular operas of all time, *Carmen* (1875).

Bjerknes, Vilhelm

full: Vilhelm Frimann Koren Bjerknes
b. March 14, 1862
Christiania (modern Oslo), Norway
d. April 9, 1951
Oslo, Norway
fields: Physics, Oceanography, Meteorology

Bjerknes made some advances in early radio-wave theory, but he is recognized primarily for his extensive work on the formation and behavior of cyclones, polar fronts, squall lines, and other weather phenomena. Under his direction, the Norwegian Weather Forecasting division at Bergen became the world center for meteorological study between 1918 and 1930.

Black, Hugo L.

full: Hugo Lafayette Black
b. February 27, 1886
Harlan, Alabama
d. September 25, 1971
Bethesda, Maryland
fields: Law

As a Justice of the Supreme Court, Black sought to define and in some areas extend constitutional protection of civil liberties, while delineating the prerogatives of government; for more than one-third of a century, he propounded the absolute inviolability of the Constitution as the basis of the nation's jurisprudence.

Black, Joseph

b. Apr. 16, 1728
Bordeaux, France
d. Nov. 10, 1799
Edinburgh, Scotland
fields: Chemistry, Physics

Joseph Black is known as the founder of modern quantitative chemistry; he applied precise measurements to the study of chemical reactions and to the study of heat exchange between substances at different temperatures.

Black, Shirley Temple. *See* Temple, Shirley

Black Elk

aka: Hehaka Sapa
b. c. 1866
S.Dak.
d. Aug. 17, 1950
near Manderson, S.Dak.
fields: Religion and Theology, Philosophy, Warfare and Conquest

Black Elk, one of the greatest of Lakota (Sioux) holy men, witnessed and described many of the most important events of nineteenth century Lakota history. When he was nine years old, Black Elk had a great vision that was to shape his life for many years. The vision was long and complex; it is described in detail in *Black Elk Speaks* (1961), by John Neihardt, which also gives Black Elk's descriptions of the Battle of the Little Bighorn (1876) and the massacre of Big Foot's warriors.

Black Hawk

né: Ma-ka-tai-me-she-kia-kiak
b. 1767
Rock River, Illinois
d. October 3, 1838
near the Des Moines River, Iowa
fields: Native American Affairs, Literature

Black Hawk was a leader in the last Indian war of the old Northwest; he also dictated one of the most interesting Indian autobiographies, *Life of Ma-ka-tai-me-she-kia-kiak, or Black Hawk* (1834).

Black Hoof. *See* Catahecassa

Black Kettle

aka: Moketavato
b. 1803?
d. Nov. 27, 1868
Washita River
fields: Government and Politics, Diplomacy, Native American Affairs

Native American leader. Southern Cheyenne leader Black Kettle, who struggled to maintain peace with white settlers and soldiers, was one of the few survivors of the 1864 Sand Creek Massacre. One of the most noted of the traditional chiefs of the Cheyenne Nation, who were known as "peace chiefs."

Blackburn, Robert

b. 1921
New York, N.Y.
fields: Art (printmaker, painter, and sculptor)

African American printmaker, painter, and sculptor; Robert Blackburn is known for depicting massive figures of strength in his art; established the Printmaking Workshop in 1949 to offer low-cost facilities and programs to artists; in 1988, received the Governor's Art Award for significantly contributing to New York State cultural life.

Blackett, Patrick M. S.

full: Patrick Maynard Stuart Blackett
b. Nov. 18, 1897
London, England
d. July 13, 1974
London, England
fields: Physics

Patrick M. S. Blackett confirmed the existence of the positron in 1933 with Giuseppe Occhialini; won Nobel Prize in Physics in 1948; is considered one of the leaders in the development of modern experimental physics in the twentieth century; worked in diverse fields, including elementary particle physics, geophysics, and the study of cosmic rays.

Blackmore, Amos. *See* Wells, Junior

Blackmun, Harry A.

full: Harry Andrew Blackmun
b. November 12, 1908
Nashville, Illinois
d. March 4, 1999
Arlington, Virginia
fields: Law

U.S. Supreme Court justice, 1970-1994; appointed by President Nixon. Defender of a general constitutional right of privacy. Significant opinions: *Roe v. Wade*, 410 U.S. 113 (1973); *Andresen v. Maryland*, 427 U.S. 463 (1976); *New York v. Burger*, 482 U.S. 691 (1987); *California v. Acevedo*, 500 U.S. 565 (1991).

Blacksnake

aka: Thaonawyuthe
aka: Chain Breaker
b. c. 1760
Cattaraugus, N.Y.
d. Dec. 26, 1859
Cold Spring, N.Y.
fields: Warfare and Conquest, Native American Affairs

Seneca tribal leader Blacksnake was present at, and later recalled in memoirs, many significant events involving the Iroquois between 1775 and 1850. A principal chief of the Seneca, Blacksnake was an honored warrior and leader in combat, but he was not one of the fifty sachems of the confederacy.

Blackstone, William

b. July 10, 1723
Cheapside, London, England
d. February 14, 1780
London, England
fields: Law

Blackstone has remained the most famous jurist in the history of English law. His *Commentaries on the Laws of England* has endured as the most influential work in English legal literature. Blackstone was the last jurist to synthesize the common law of his own age and present it to contemporaries in a cohesive fashion; he succeeded so well that the *Commentaries* still retains its place among the masterpieces of legal writing.

Blackwell, David Harold

b. April 24, 1919
Centralia, Ill.
fields: Statistics, Mathematics, Education

Educator, mathematician, and statistician. Best known for his research involving Markov chains (applications of time sequences that show dependence on earlier events), David Harold Blackwell championed Bayesian inference and made important contributions to game theory. Blackwell was elected president of the Institute of Mathematical Statistics in 1955, and he became the first African American mathematician to be elected to the National Academy of Sciences in 1965. In 1973 Blackwell was named president of the International Association of Statistics in the Physical Sciences, and he received the prestigious Von Neumann Theory Award in mathematics in 1979. Blackwell became a professor of mathematics at Howard University in 1944, but left in 1954 to accept a position as professor of mathematics and statistics at the University of California, Berkeley. He authored of *Basic Statistics* (1969) and coauthored *Theory of Games and Statistical Decisions* (1979).

Blackwell, Elizabeth

b. February 3, 1821
Counterslip, England
d. May 31, 1910
Hastings, England
fields: Medicine

The first woman ever to receive a degree from an American medical school, Elizabeth Blackwell became a leading figure in the drive to open the field of medicine to women.

Blackwell, Scrapper

full: Francis Hillman Blackwell
b. Feb. 21, 1903
Syracuse, S.C.?
d. Oct. 7, 1962
Indianapolis, Ind.
fields: Music (blues singer and lyricist)

African American blues singer and lyricist; Francis Hillman "Scrapper" Blackwell, whose introduction to blues pianist Leroy Carr in 1928 initiated his singing career, is best known for his storytelling or narrative style lyrics.

Blackwood, Ronald A.

b. Jan. 19, 1926
Kingston, Jamaica
fields: Government and Politics

African American mayor of Mount Vernon, N.Y.; after serving on the Mount Vernon city council for fifteen years, Ronald A. Blackwood became the first African American mayor to be elected in the state of New York; in 1988, he was reelected to a four-year term and was recognized by the Department of Housing and Urban Development for his support of minority business ventures.

Blacque, Taurean

né: Herbert Middleton, Jr.
b. May 10, 1946
Newark, N.J.
fields: Theater and Entertainment

African American actor; among Taurean Blacque's numerous television and stage credits is his television role as detective Neal Washington in the series *Hill Street Blues* (1981-1987); he has also appeared in the television serial *Generations*; he debuted on Broadway in a production of *The River Niger*.

Blades, Rubén

b. July 16, 1948
Panama City, Panama
fields: Music, Theater and Entertainment, Law

Panamanian American musician, actor, and attorney. Rubén Blades recorded salsa music albums such as *Buscando America* (1984) and *Escenas* (1985). In 1988 he released his first English-language album, *Nothing but the Truth*. Blades has earned four Grammy Awards as a composer and singer. He has appeared in several films, including *Crossover Dreams* (1985) and *The Milagro Beanfield War* (1988). He was the first Latino to be nominated for Best Actor, for *Dead Men Out* (1988), at the ACE national cable awards. Politically active, Blades helped found the Papa Egoro political party in Panama in 1991.

Blaine, James G.

full: James Gillespie Blaine
b. January 31, 1830
West Brownsville, Pennsylvania
d. January 27, 1893
Washington, D.C.
fields: Government and Politics

Blaine was the most popular Republican politician of the late nineteenth century. Through his personal appeal and his advocacy of the protective tariff, he laid the basis for the emergence of the Republican Party as the majority party in the 1890's.

Blair, Eric Arthur. *See* Orwell, George

Blair, Henry C.

b. 1804
Glenross, Md.
d. 1860
fields: Invention and Technology

African American inventor; Henry C. Blair will be remembered as the first African American to receive a patent on an invention (a corn planting device, 1834); in 1836, he invented a cotton planter.

Blair, John, Jr.

b. 1732
d. 1800
fields: Law

U.S. Supreme Court justice, 1790-1796; appointed by President Washington. Significant opinion: *Chisholm v. Georgia*, 2 U.S. 419 (1793).

Blair, Tony

full: Anthony Charles Lynton Blair
b. May 6, 1953
Edinburgh, Scotland
fields: Government and Politics

Tony Blair took office as prime minister of Great Britain in 1997. Became Labour Party leader in 1994, and revised party's goals with "New Labour" campaign. In office, attempted to establish more peaceable relations with Northern Ireland parties, including Sinn Féin. Created a "welfare-to-work" program to educate welfare recipients; it also gave tax breaks to participating employers and withheld social security from people who refused to work. With other leaders, involved in NATO's bombing campaign against Yugoslavia in 1999.

Blaisdell, Richard Kekuni

b. Mar. 11, 1925
Honolulu, Territory of Hawaii
fields: Medicine, Public Health

Richard Kekuni Blaisdell, the first Native Hawaiian professor at the University of Hawaii's John A. Burns School of Medicine, served as chief hematologist of the Atomic Comb Casualty Commission in Japan between 1959 and 1961. The author of numerous articles on native Hawaiian medicine, he actively participated in the Pro-Hawaiian Sovereignty Working Group and in Ka Pakaukau, another Native Hawaiian sovereignty group.

Blake, Eubie

b. Feb. 7, 1883
Baltimore, Md.
d. Feb. 12, 1983
New York, N.Y.
fields: Music (ragtime pianist and composer)

African American pianist and composer; Eubie Blake made his first recordings in 1917; "I'm Just Wild About Harry" and "Memories of You" are but two of the more than three hundred songs he composed utilizing the highly syncopated rhythms of ragtime; the Dixie Duo, formed by Blake and Noble Sissle in 1915, performed on the vaudeville circuit and toured with bandleader James Europe during World War I; Blake and Sissle composed music for the Broadway musical *Shuffle Along*, which ran from 1921 to 1928; Blake went on to compose for *Blackbirds of 1930* and *Swing It* (1937); Blake performed as a headliner with USO shows during World War II; the 1978 Broadway show *Eubie!* was based on Blake's long and vibrant life; he received the presidential medal of honor in 1981.

Blake, Robert

b. Late August?, 1599
Bridgwater, Somerset, England
d. August 7, 1657
at sea, off Plymouth, Devon, England
fields: Military Affairs, Government and Politics

Combining leadership ability with deep religious faith and a strong sense of duty to his country, Blake was one of the founders and the chief admiral of the English Commonwealth Navy.

Blake, William

b. November 28, 1757
London, England
d. August 12, 1827
London, England
fields: Literature, Art

A gifted and highly original poet, painter, engraver, and draftsman, Blake is regarded as one of the great English Romantic poets.

Blakey, Art

b. Oct. 11, 1919
Pittsburgh, Pa.
d. Oct. 16, 1990
New York, N.Y.
fields: Music (jazz drummer and bandleader)

African American drummer and bandleader; Art Blakey is known as one of the best of the bebop drummers and for incorporating African drumming devices into the jazz form; established a rehearsal band which eventually became The Jazz Messengers, innovators in the funky bebop and soul styles and later known as the best of the hard bop bands; Wayne Shorter, Donald Byrd, and Wynton Marsalis are among the musicians who worked with The Jazz Messengers and benefited from Blakey's tutelage.

Blanc, Louis

b. October 29, 1811
Madrid, Spain
d. December 6, 1882
Cannes, France
fields: Government and Politics, Philosophy

The founder of humanitarian socialism, Blanc developed his dissatisfaction with the misery of the French people into an imperative to transform the basic governmental and economic system to end forever the capitalist exploitation of the working class.

Blanchot, Maurice

b. September 22, 1907
Quain, Saone-et-Loire, France
fields: Philosophy, Literature

A leading novelist and literary critic of the post-World War II generation in France, Maurice Blanchot influenced the work of philosophers such as Jacques Derrida and is widely recognized as a forerunner of the school of literary theory known as deconstruction. Among his works are novels (*Thomas the Obscure*, 1941) and philosophical and theoretical works (*The Work of Fire*, 1949; *The Writing of the Disaster*, 1980).

Bland, Bobby Blue

aka: Blue Boy
b. Jan. 17, 1930
Rosemark, Tenn.
fields: Music (blues singer)

African American blues singer; as a blues vocalist, Bobby "Blue" Bland has performed internationally; more than thirty of his recorded songs have reached the rhythm-and-blues charts top thirty; inducted into the Rock and Roll Hall of Fame in 1992.

Bland, James

b. Oct. 22, 1854
Flushing, N.Y.
d. May 5, 1911
Philadelphia, Pa.
fields: Music (popular composer)

African American composer; James Bland is noted for composing Virginia's state anthem, "Carry Me Back to Old Virginny"; Bland's more than six hundred popular song compositions include "Oh Dem Golden Slippers" and "In the Evening by the Moonlight."

Blassingame, John W.

b. Mar. 23, 1940
Covington, Ga.
fields: Historiography

African American historian; John W. Blassingame is noted as one of the leading historians of the African American experience; his most well known publication, *The Slave Community: Plantation Life in the Antebellum South* (1972), is considered a landmark work in its examination of American slavery; editor of the papers of Frederick Douglass (1979 first volume published).

Blatchford, Samuel

b. 1820
d. 1893
fields: Law

U.S. Supreme Court justice, 1882-1893 (died while in office); appointed by President Arthur. Wrote one of the earliest opinions interpreting the scope of the privilege against self-incrimination. Energetic supporter of substantive due process doctrine. Significant opinions: *Chicago, Milwaukee, and St. Paul Railway Co. v. Minnesota*, 134 U.S. 418 (1890); *O'Neil v. Vermont*, 144 U.S. 323 (1892); *Councilman v. Hitchcock*, 142 U.S. 547 (1892).

Blériot, Louis

b. July 1, 1872
Cambrai, France
d. August 2, 1936
Paris, France
fields: Aviation and Space Exploration

Blériot completed the first overseas flight in a heavier-than-air craft in 1909 and later became a pioneer in the fledgling aeronautics industry. He played a critical role in the French war effort during World War I and the subsequent establishment of commercial aviation.

Bleuler, Eugen

b. April 30, 1857
Zollikon, Switzerland
d. July 15, 1939
Zurich, Switzerland
fields: Psychiatry and Psychology

Bleuler's major achievements were in the study and treatment of schizophrenia, a term he coined in 1908 to denote the splitting of psychological functions that he observed in many of his patients. He also introduced the related terms "autism" and "ambivalence" into psychiatry. He has been admired as much for his tireless and uncompromising devotion to his psychiatric patients as for his important contributions to psychiatric theory.

Bligh, William

b. September 9, 1754
Plymouth, Devonshire, England
d. December 7, 1817
London, England
fields: Botany, Exploration and Colonization, Military Affairs

Notorious for having lost the *Bounty* to mutineers in the South Pacific in 1789, Bligh had a long, distinguished but controversial career in the British navy.

Bloch, Felix

b. Oct. 23, 1905
Zurich, Switzerland
d. Sept. 10, 1983
Zurich, Switzerland
fields: Physics

Felix Bloch joined the Manhattan Project, the government program to develop an atomic bomb, in 1942-1944; won Nobel Prize in Physics in 1952 with Edward Mills Purcell for development of nuclear induction; named the first director of the Conseil Européen pour la Recherche Nucléaire (CERN) in 1954.

Blodgett, Katharine Burr

b. Jan. 10, 1898
Schenectady, New York
d. Oct. 12, 1979
Schenectady, New York
fields: Chemistry, Physics, Invention and Technology

Katharine Burr Blodgett was a research scientist with the General Electric Company; studied thin films, including so-called Langmuir-Blodgett films; General Electric announced her invention of nonreflecting glass in 1938; was first female recipient of the Progress Medal of the Photographic Society of America, 1972.

Blok, Aleksandr

full: Aleksandr Aleksandrovich Blok
b. November 28, 1880
St. Petersburg, Russia
d. August 7, 1921
Petrograd, U.S.S.R.
fields: Literature

Blok is one of Russia's greatest poets. He was called the "last Romantic poet," and his work in literature and drama reflected the profound changes that his country and its people experienced during the era of World War I and the Russian Revolution.

Bloodworth-Thomason, Linda

né: Linda Joyce Bloodworth
b. April 15, 1947
Conway, Arkansas
fields: Television

A powerful force in Hollywood, Bloodworth-Thomason developed television shows, such as *Murphy Brown*, that focused on contemporary issues.

Bloody Knife

b. c. 1840
N.Dak.
d. June 25, 1876
Little Bighorn, Mont.
fields: Warfare and Conquest, Military Affairs, Native American Affairs

A skilled army scout, Bloody Knife, of both Arikara and Hunkpapa Sioux heritage, served with George Armstrong Custer and fought at the Battle of the Little Bighorn (1876).

Bloomer, Amelia Jenks

né: Amelia Jenks
b. May 27, 1818
Homer, New York
d. December 30, 1894
Council Bluffs, Iowa
fields: Journalism, Women's Rights

Bloomer is best remembered for her support of dress reform for women. Her greatest contributions, however, were as publisher of the first women's rights newspaper and leader of the Iowa suffrage campaign.

Bloomer, Elizabeth Ann. *See* Ford, Betty

Blow, Kurtis

né: Kurt Walker
aka: Platinum Prince
b. 1956 or 1957
fields: Music (rap singer)

African American rap singer; considered a pioneer of rap music, Kurtis Blow began composing rap lyrics while working as a private party disc jockey; his 1979 single "Christmas Rappin'" became the first rap hit, selling 500,000 copies; he once described his style as a combination of hardcore street rap and disco influences; in 1984, released the album *Ego Trip* and was featured on the New York Fresh Fest concert tour.

Blowsnake, Sam. *See* Crashing Thunder

Blücher, Gebhard Leberecht von

b. December 16, 1742
Rostock, Mecklenburg-Schwerin
d. September 12, 1819
Krieblowitz, Silesia
fields: Military Affairs

Blücher served the cause of Prussia well throughout his life, especially during the French revolutionary and Napoleonic periods. Although he was not a great strategist, his considerable and undisputed ability as a leader of men and his strong support for military reforms following defeat at Jena in 1806 enabled Prussia to play a major role in the final victory over France, thereby contributing to Prussia's subsequent rise as a major power.

Blue, Vida

b. July 28, 1949
Mansfield, La.
fields: Sports (baseball player)

African American baseball player; a major league pitcher for seventeen seasons, Vida Blue both won the Cy Young Award and was named Most Valuable Player (1971) during his tenure with the Oakland Athletics; he went on to pitch in three World Series, retiring with 209 career victories in 1986.

Blue Boy. *See* Bland, Bobby Blue

Blue Eagle, Acee

aka: Chebona Bula (Laughing Boy)
aka: Alex C. McIntosh
b. Aug. 17, 1907
Wichita Reservation, Okla.
d. June 18, 1959
Muskogee, Okla.
fields: Art, Education (painter, lecturer)

Native American painter. The flamboyant Acee Blue Eagle, part Pawnee and part Creek, is probably the best-known Oklahoma Indian painter; he also taught and lectured widely. Named "Outstanding Indian in the United States" in 1958; created numerous murals.

Bluford, Guion Stewart, Jr.

b. Nov. 22, 1942
Philadelphia, Pa.
fields: Aviation and Space Exploration

African American astronaut; Guion Stewart Bluford, Jr., flew fighter missions in Vietnam and worked as an Air Force test pilot before becoming a mission specialist and flying aboard the space shuttle *Challenger* in August, 1983; the first African American astronaut in space, Bluford boarded the *Challenger* again in October, 1985.

Bluford, Lucile H.

b. ?
fields: Journalism

African American journalist; Lucile H. Bluford's career with the *Kansas City Call* spanned more than forty years; in the late 1930's she was promoted to managing editor; in 1939, after being denied admission to the journalism school at the University of Missouri at Columbia, she unsuccessfully sued the school; her action did result in the establishment of a journalism school at historically black Lincoln University in 1942.

Blum, Léon

b. April 9, 1872
Paris, France
d. March 30, 1950
Jouy-en-Josas, France
fields: Government and Politics

As prime minister of France's Popular Front government in 1936-1937, Blum was responsible for the adoption of landmark social legislation that has permanently affected French political and economic life.

Blume, Judy

b. February 12, 1938
Elizabeth, New Jersey
fields: Literature

Judy Blume has written frank books loved by young readers but loathed by parents, school officials, and watchdog groups because they deal with early teen sexual awareness, menstruation, masturbation, and premarital sex. Her frequently banned books include *Are You There, God? It's Me, Margaret* (1970), *Then Again, Maybe I Won't* (1971), *Deenie* (1973), *Blubber* (1974), *Forever* (1975).

Bly, Nellie

né: Elizabeth Cochran
aka: Elizabeth Cochrane Seaman
b. May 5, 1864
Cochran's Mills, Pennsylvania
d. January 27, 1922
New York, New York
fields: Journalism, Social Reform

Her newspaper writing allowed women to be accepted as journalists and stimulated countless cases of needed reform in living conditions, politics, and businesses in Pittsburgh, Pennsylvania, and New York City.

Blythe, Arthur

b. July 5, 1940
Los Angeles, Calif.
fields: Music (jazz alto saxophonist and composer)

African American alto saxophonist and composer; Arthur Blythe's various performing styles include bop and freer forms; "The Grip" (1977), "In the Tradition" (1979), and "Illusions" (1980) are samples of his recorded work; Blythe formed the group the Leaders in 1984.

Blythe, Ethel Mae. *See* Barrymore, Ethel

Blyton, Enid

b. August 11, 1897
East Dulwich, London
d. November 28, 1968
Hampstead, England
fields: Literature

Enid Blyton hundreds of wrote easy-to-read children's books that were banned by educators and librarians because of their simplistic vocabulary, racial and gender stereotypes, and predictable plots. Her best-known books appeared in the *Noddy*, *Famous Five*, and *Secret Seven* series.

Boadicca

b. First century C.E.
Britain
d. 60 C.E.
Central Britain
fields: Warfare and Conquest

Having endured flogging and the violation of her daughters, Boadicca led a rebellion of the Britons against the Roman invaders. Although the Romans were caught by surprise and lost three cities burned by the rebels, the uprising was quelled, and Boadicca herself died by taking poison.

Boan. *See* Wang Yangming

Boas, Franz

b. July 9, 1858
Minden, Westphalia
d. December 21, 1942
New York, New York
fields: Anthropology

Boas made anthropology a vital discipline in the history of twentieth century social science, and his scholarship, in time, had a significant impact on public policy in the United States.

Boccaccio, Giovanni

b. June or July, 1313
Florence or Certaldo, Italy
d. December 21, 1375
Certaldo, Italy
fields: Literature, Scholarship

Boccaccio was the father of Italian and European narrative. He was also a pioneer of Latin and Greek scholarship in the late Middle Ages and, along with Petrarch, a precursor to the Renaissance Humanists.

Boccherini, Luigi

full: Ridolfo Luigi Boccherini
b. February 19, 1743
Lucca
d. May 28, 1805
Madrid, Spain
fields: Music

Boccherini was one of the most prolific composers of all time, creating almost five hundred instrumental compositions from trios to symphonies. With Joseph Haydn and Wolfgang Amadeus Mozart, he helped to establish the style and structure of the classic string quartet and concerto.

Boccioni, Umberto

b. October 19, 1882
Reggio di Calabria, Italy
d. August 17, 1916
Sorte, near Verona, Italy
fields: Art

Boccioni is the foremost painter and sculptor of the Italian Futurist movement, which developed in the years immediately preceding World War I. Besides producing paintings and sculptures, Boccioni was the leading technical theorist of the movement. His principles of sculpture, in particular, shaped the mixed-media and dynamic productions of the twentieth century.

Boddie, James Timothy, Jr.

b. Oct. 18, 1931
Baltimore, Md.
fields: Military Affairs, Warfare and Conquest

African American military officer; James Timothy Boddie, Jr., attained the rank of U.S. Air Force brigadier general on August 1, 1980; during his military career, served as commandant of cadets at the Tuskegee Institute Air Force Reserve Officers' Training Corps, trained pilots, performed flight testing, flew two hundred combat missions over Vietnam and North Vietnam, commanded a replacement training unit weapons school, and, after graduating from the Air War College in 1975, worked his way through command positions to become deputy director for operations at the National Military Command Center (1980); received many military decorations before retiring in 1983.

Bodhidharma

b. c. 480
Conjeeveram, near Madras, India
d. 520
fields: Religion and Theology

Legendary Buddhist monk who founded Chinese Ch'an (Japanese, Zen) Buddhism. As a missionary, Bodhidharma brought Indian meditation practices to China, teaching that ethical living depends upon understanding and believing that there is no individual self. The text known as *Two Entrances and Four Acts* is thought to expound his thinking.

Bodley, Thomas

aka: Sir Thomas Bodley
b. March 2, 1545
Exeter, Devon, England
d. January 28, 1613
London, England
fields: Diplomacy, Philanthropy, Education

Bodley founded the Bodleian Library at Oxford University, which quickly became one of the world's great research libraries.

Boethius

né: Anicius Manlius Severinus Boethius
b. c. 480
Rome, Italy
d. 524
Pavia, Italy
fields: Philosophy, Religion and Theology, Literature

Adding knowledge of Greek thought to his Christian Roman background, Boethius became one of the most important mediators between the ancient and medieval worlds.

Boffrand, Germain

b. May 7, 1667
Nantes, France
d. March 18, 1754
Paris, France
fields: Architecture

Boffrand developed an approach to interior decoration resulting in rooms where sculpture, architecture, paintings, and furnishings all interacted to convey a unified mood. His most successful rooms, still in existence, are the salons of the Prince and Princess of Soubise at the Hôtel de Soubise in Paris (1732-1739). Boffrand's lively, livable floor plans are best exemplified in his design for the Hôtel Amêlot de Gournay, later Montmorency, of 1712. His concern with the interrelationship of the room, the plan, and the site resulted in works of visual, intellectual, and emotional harmony.

Bogan, Louise

full: Louise Marie Bogan
b. August 11, 1897
Livermore Falls, Maine
d. February 4, 1970
New York, New York
fields: Literature

A woman of rare and severe talent, Bogan left an enduring legacy of lyric poetry and fine criticism.

Bogardus, Emory Stephen

b. Feb. 21, 1882
near Belvidere, Ill.
d. Aug. 21, 1973
Los Angeles, Calif.
fields: Sociology

Latino sociologist. Emory Stephen Bogardus began teaching at the University of Southern California in 1911. He founded the school's sociology department, and he directed the division of social work within that department from 1920 to 1937. Bogardus was regional research director for Southern California for the Pacific Coast Race Relations Survey (1923-1925), was president of the Los Angeles Social Service Commission (1916-1918), and edited the *Journal of Sociology and Social Research* (1916-1961). He wrote numerous books in the fields of literature and sociology, the latter of which focused primarily on race relations and the role of leadership among Mexican Americans.

Bohemond I

b. c. 1052
southern Italy
d. March 7, 1111
Apulia, southern Italy
fields: Warfare and Conquest

Bohemond was one of the leaders of Europe's most successful Crusade to the Holy Land and the founder and first prince of Antioch.

Bohm, David

full: David Joseph Bohm
b. Dec. 20, 1917
Wilkes-Barre, Pennsylvania
d. Oct. 27, 1992
London, England
fields: Physics

David Bohm worked in the fields of quantum mechanical systems and the philosophy of quantum mechanics; published *Quantum Theory*, regarded as one of the best textbooks of its day, in 1951.

Böhme, Jakob

b. April 24, 1575
Alt-Seidenberg, near Görlitz, Silesia
d. November 17, 1624
Görlitz, Silesia
fields: Philosophy, Religion and Theology

In a series of books Böhme developed a profound metaphysical system, rich in myth and symbol, which attempted to explain the nature of God, the origin of the universe and of man, and the Fall of Man and the way of regeneration. His complex and difficult thought influenced many German, French, and English philosophers and poets.

Bohr, Niels

full: Niels Henrik David Bohr
b. October 7, 1885
Copenhagen, Denmark
d. November 18, 1962
Copenhagen, Denmark
fields: Physics, Chemistry

Bohr discovered the fundamental structure and character of the atom, its components and how they interact. For this discovery, he won the Nobel Prize in Physics in 1922. Bohr also made significant contributions to the understanding of how quantum and classical physics unify as a single philosophy in his principle of complementarity.

Bojaxhiu, Agnes Gonxha. *See* Teresa, Mother

Bolden, Buddy

full: Charles Joseph Bolden
b. Sept. 6, 1877
New Orleans, La.
d. Nov. 4, 1931
Jackson, La.
fields: Music (jazz cornetist and bandleader)

African American cornetist and bandleader; information about Charles Joseph

"Buddy" Bolden's life and music is sketchy; known as much for his volatile personality style (alcohol consumption, style of dress, success with women, self-promotion, and trouble with emotional control) as for his musical style (commended for his strong rhythmic drive, "blues tone," and for establishing jazz as a musical form outside the mainstream); around 1895, Bolden began leading his own band in New Orleans; lived in an asylum from 1907 until his death in 1931.

Bolden, Dorothy Lee

b. Oct. 13, 1920
Atlanta, Ga.
fields: Labor Movement

African American labor leader; Dorothy Lee Bolden founded and served as union president for the National Domestic Workers of America; worked with the Department of Health, Education, and Welfare and served on the Commission on the Status of Women (1975); former vice president of the Black Women Coalition of Atlanta; on board of directors for both the Welfare Rights Organization and the NAACP.

Bolden, J. Taber, Jr.

b. Apr. 26, 1926
Cleveland, Ohio
fields: Business and Industry, Television

African American television news executive; J. Taber Bolden, Jr., became NBC's vice president for station affairs in 1976, a position he held into the 1990's, making him the first African American director and station manager for a major television network.

Boleyn, Anne

aka: Anne Bullen
b. c. 1500-1501
probably at Blickling in Norfolk, England
d. May 19, 1536
London, England
fields: Church Reform, Government and Politics

Queen of England, 1533-1536. The desire of England's King Henry VIII to marry Anne Boleyn led to the establishment of the Church of England. Mother of Elizabeth I.

Bolin, Jane Matilda

b. April 11, 1908
Poughkeepsie, N.Y.
fields: Law

First African American woman to serve as a judge in the United States. After graduating from Yale University School of Law in 1931, Jane Matilda Bolin ran her own law practice in New York City until 1937, when she was appointed as an assistant corporation counsel for New York City. She became the first African American woman judge in the United States in July, 1939, when New York City mayor Fiorello La Guardia appointed her to a ten-year term as judge of the Domestic Relations Court of the City of New York. She was reappointed to three additional successive ten-year terms, during which her court was renamed the Family Court of the State of New York. She retired from the bench in 1979, after almost forty years of service. Bolin was a strong advocate of civil and human rights and served on the boards of directors of the Child Welfare League of America, the United Neighborhood Houses, Neighborhood Children's Center, the New York Urban League, and the National Association for the Advancement of Colored People.

Bolingbroke, First Viscount

né: Henry St. John
aka: Baron St. John
b. September 16, 1678
Wiltshire, England
d. December 12, 1751
London, England
fields: Government and Politics

As a Tory politician in Parliament during Queen Anne's reign, Bolingbroke served as secretary of war and later as northern secretary of state. He defended the Church of England and the aristocracy and played a major role in the negotiation of the Treaty of Utrecht. After 1715, he devoted his ability and energy to opposing Robert Walpole. His political writings were both a part of his opposition and an exposition of his political ideas.

Bolívar, Simón

full: Simón José Antonio de la Santisima Trinidad Bolívar
b. July 24, 1783
Caracas, Venezuela
d. December 17, 1830
Villa of San Pedro Alejandrino, near Santa Marta, Colombia
fields: Government and Politics, Military Affairs

The liberator of northern South America, Bolívar epitomized the struggle against Spanish colonial rule. His most lasting contributions include his aid in the liberation of Bolivia, Colombia, Ecuador, Peru, and Venezuela, and his farsighted proposals for hemispheric solidarity among Latin American nations.

Böll, Heinrich

b. December 21, 1917
Cologne, Germany
d. July 16, 1985
Merten, West Germany
fields: Literature

Böll, who was awarded the Nobel Prize in Literature in 1972, remains one of the greatest German authors of the postwar era. His works evince a keen moral sense and a sincere commitment to social change.

Bolles, Donald F., Jr.

b. July 10, 1928
Milwaukee, Wisconsin
d. June 13, 1976
Phoenix, Arizona
fields: Journalism

Donald F. Bolles, Jr., was an investigative reporter who killed by a car bomb while investigating a story. He joined the *Arizona Republic* in 1962 after reporting for the Associated Press and earned a Pulitzer Prize nomination for stories exposing corruption the Arizona state government. He was killed in 1976 while going to meet a man linked to organized crime.

Boltzmann, Ludwig Eduard

b. Feb. 20, 1844
Vienna, Austria
d. Sept. 5, 1906
Duino, near Trieste, Italy
fields: Mathematics, Physics

Ludwig Eduard Boltzmann developed the mathematical kinetic theory of gases by applying the insights of thermodynamics to the molecular universe described by classical mechanics.

Bolyai, János

b. Dec. 15, 1802
Kolozsvár, Hungary (now Cluj, Romania)
d. Jan. 27, 1860
Marosvásárhely, Hungary (now Tîrgu Mures, Romania)
fields: Mathematics (geometry)

János Bolyai is known for discovering the first non-Euclidean geometry while trying to prove Euclid's fifth postulate.

Bolzano, Bernhard

full: Bernhard Placidus Johann Nepomuk Bolzano
b. Oct. 5, 1781
Prague, Bohemia, Austrian Habsburg domain (now Czech Republic)
d. Dec. 18, 1848
Prague, Bohemia, Austrian Habsburg domain
fields: Mathematics (calculus)

Bernhard Bolzano's contribution to the field of mathematics is his discovery of the Bolzano-Weierstrass theorem, a property of sequences of real numbers that can be used to determine if there is at least one number called a limit point near the sequence. Wrote *Wissenschaftslehre* (1837; *Theory of Science,*

1972) and *Paradoxien des Unendlichen* (1851; *Paradoxes of the Infinite*, 1950).

Bombelli, Rafael

b. Jan., 1526
Bologna, Italy
d. 1572
Rome?
fields: Mathematics (algebra)

Rafael Bombelli is known for his work *L'Algebra*, which was first published in 1572 and published in full in 1929. Bombelli systematized the use of complex numbers in the solution of cubic equations.

Bonacich, Edna

b. Mar. 30, 1940
Greenwich, Conn.
fields: Sociology

Edna Bonacich, a sociology professor at the University of California, Riverside, researched the historical and contemporary Asian American experience from a Marxist perspective. Along with coeditor Lucie Cheng, she examined early Asian immigration in the era of America imperialist expansion in *Labor Immigration Under Capitalism* (1984). Other works include *The Economic Basis of Ethnic Solidarity: Small Business in the Japanese American Community* (1980, with John Modell) and *Immigrant Entrepreneurs: Koreans in Los Angeles, 1965-1982* (1988, with Ivan Light).

Bonaparte, Louis Napoleon. *See* Napoleon III

Bonaparte, Napoleon. *See* Napoleon I

Bonaventure, Saint

né: Giovanni di Fidanza
aka: John of Fidanza
b. 1217 or 1221
Bagnoregio, Papal States (now Italy)
d. July 15, 1274
Lyons
fields: Religion and Theology

Bonaventure combined an early commitment to the ideals of Saint Francis of Assisi with great preaching and teaching abilities; he wrote several works on spiritual life and recodified the constitution of the Franciscans. Noted for his ability to reconcile differing groups and individuals, Bonaventure proved himself a defender of both human and divine truth and an outstanding witness for mystic and Christian wisdom.

Bond, Anna Monique

b. ?
fields: Television

African American television newscaster; Anna Monique Bond worked as a reporter and producer at New York City's WABC-TV before moving to NBC-TV's New York City staff in 1982; she later coanchored weekend news broadcasts for the network.

Bond, Horace Mann

b. Nov. 8, 1904
Nashville, Tenn.
d. Dec. 21, 1972
Atlanta, Ga.
fields: Education

African American educational administrator; a leading expert and scholar in the field of education, Horace Mann Bond was head of the department of education, Langston University, Oklahoma (1924-1927), instructor at Fisk University (beginning 1928), head of Fisk University department of education (beginning 1937), president at Fort Valley State College, Georgia (beginning 1939), president of Lincoln University (1945-1957), and dean of Atlanta University school of education (through 1966); the father of civil rights activist Julian Bond.

Bond, Julian

full: Horace Julian Bond
b. Jan. 14, 1940
Nashville, Tenn.
fields: Government and Politics, Civil Rights

African American politician, civil rights activist; Julian Bond was the student founder of the Committee on Appeal for Human Rights; attracted attention of Martin Luther King, Jr., and helped found the Student Nonviolent Coordinating Committee, serving as its first director of communications, 1961-1966; was Democratic member of the Georgia house of representatives, 1965-1975, and the Georgia senate, 1975-1987; helped found the Southern Poverty Law Center in 1971; served as president of the Atlanta branch of the National Association for the Advancement of Colored People (NAACP), 1974-1989; appointed chair of the NAACP in 1998; was host of the television program *America's Black Forum* and narrator of the Public Broadcasting Service civil rights series *Eyes on the Prize.*

Bondfield, Margaret

full: Margaret Grace Bondfield
b. March 17, 1873
Furnam, Somerset, England
d. June 16, 1953
Sanderstead, Surrey, England
fields: Government and Politics, Labor Movement, Social Reform

From humble shop assistant, Bondfield became assistant secretary of the Shop Assistants' Union and chair of the Adult Suffrage Society. Elected to Parliament from Northampton in 1923, she became the first woman chair of the Trades Union Congress in that same year, and the first woman in a British cabinet, in 1929 as minister of labour.

Bonds, Barry

full: Barry Lamar Bonds
b. July 24, 1964
Riverside, Calif.
fields: Sports (baseball player)

African American baseball player; outstanding hitter and outfielder Barry Bonds played for the Pittsburgh Pirates and the San Francisco Giants and was one of the most exciting major league players during the late 1980's and 1990's; was named Most Valuable Player (MVP) in the National League three times (1990, 1992, 1993).

Bonds, Bobby Lee

b. Mar. 15, 1946
Riverside, Calif.
fields: Sports (baseball player)

African American baseball player; father of baseball player Barry Bonds, Bobby Lee Bonds announced his 1968 arrival in the major leagues by hitting a grand slam home run in his first major league game; in five different seasons of his career he stole more than thirty bases and hit more than thirty home runs; won the National League West batting title in 1973.

Bonds, Margaret Allison

b. Mar. 3, 1913
Chicago, Ill.
d. Apr. 26, 1972
Los Angeles, Calif.
fields: Music (pianist and composer)

African American pianist and composer; Margaret Allison Bonds's musical compositions include the musicals *Romey and Julie* and *Shakespeare in Harlem*, *Mass in D Minor*, and the ballet *Migration*; she founded the Chicago-based Allied Arts Academy for ballet and music (1930); directed the Mount Calvary Baptist Church music program in Harlem; worked with the Inner City Repertory Theater in Los Angeles; instructed piano and music theory at the Inner City Institute, Los Angeles.

Bonga, George

b. c. 1802
near Duluth, Minn.
d. 1884
fields: Historical Figure

African American fur trader, interpreter, and guide; in 1820, Governor Lewis Cass hired George Bonga to serve as an interpreter and to negotiate treaties with the Native American tribes in the Lake Superior region of Michigan territory; he completed the Chippewa Treaty of 1837 at Fort Snelling; was known for his manners, powerful physique, and distinct appearance.

Bonhoeffer, Dietrich

b. February 4, 1906
Breslau, Germany (now Wrocław, Poland)
d. April 9, 1945
Flossenbürg, Germany
fields: Philosophy, Religion and Theology

Bonhoeffer defined the concept of Christian discipleship, especially as it related to the Church in Germany during the 1930's. He provided a unique combination of theology and political ethics that made him a leader in German resistance to Adolf Hitler and also led to his untimely death in 1945.

Boniface, Saint

né: Wynfrith
aka: Wynfrid
b. c. 675
Crediton, Devonshire, England
d. June 5, 754
Dokkum, the Netherlands
fields: Religion and Theology, Church Government

Boniface left England to assist in the conversion of pagan Germany. He brought Christianity to many areas and in others set the Church on a new and sounder basis, earning the title "the Apostle of Germany."

Boniface VIII

né: Benedict Caetani
b. c. 1235
probably Anagni, Italy
d. October 12, 1303
Rome, Italy
fields: Religion and Theology, Government and Politics

Though pope for only nine years, Boniface represents both the zenith and nadir of papal power and papal monarchy. In his clash with the secular rulers of Western Europe, Boniface insisted upon the ultimate earthly authority of the Papacy.

Bonilla, Frank

b. ?
New York, N.Y.
fields: Scholarship

Latino scholar. After earning a Ph.D. in sociology (1959) from Harvard University, Frank Bonilla became a member of the American Universities Field Staff (1960-1963), where he investigated the relation between social development and education in Latin America. He taught political science at the Massachusetts Institute of Technology from 1963 to 1967 and was a program adviser in social science to a Ford Foundation project in Brazil (1967-1972). Bonilla then taught political science at Stanford University (1969-1972) and was the first director of the City University of New York (CUNY) Center for Puerto Rican Studies. In 1993, Bonilla became executive director of the Inter-University Program for Latino Research (IUP) at Hunter College of CUNY.

Bonilla, Tony

full: Rubén Bonilla
b. Mar. 3, 1936
Calvert, Tex.
fields: Law

Latino attorney. Tony Bonilla began his legal career in 1960. He was a member of the Texas state legislature (1964-1967) and held a position on the board of directors of the League of United Latin American Citizens (LULAC), serving as president of the organization from 1972 to 1975. In 1986, he served as a representative on the United States Information Agency (USIA) tour of South America to discuss drug issues. From 1973 to 1978, Bonilla chaired of the board of directors of the Corpus Christi Chamber of Commerce and was a member of the coordinating board of the Texas college and university system from 1973 to 1979.

Bonnard, Pierre

b. October 3, 1867
Fontenay-aux-Roses, France
d. January 23, 1947
Le Cannet, France
fields: Art

One of the most independent of Postimpressionist artists, Bonnard created a style and an artistic vision of art as an enchanting celebration of life which, at one and the same time, freed him from his Impressionist predecessors and carried on their tradition of art as a loving record of human and natural beauty.

Bonnin, Gertrude Simmons

aka: Zitkala Sa (Red Bird)
b. Feb. 22, 1875
Pine Ridge Reservation, S.Dak.
d. Jan. 25, 1938
Washington, D.C.
fields: Native American Affairs, Literature

Yankton Sioux educator, writer, activist; a successful author and an influential advocate of Indian policy reform, Gertrude Bonnin moved to Washington, D.C., in 1916, where she spent the rest of her life as an activist, writer, and lecturer; she was elected secretary of the Society of American Indians (SAI) in 1916; opposition to the use of peyote in a religious ceremony led to her split with the SAI in 1920; in the 1920's and 1930's, Bonnin worked with numerous groups involved in reforming Indian policy and, in 1926, she organized the National Council of American Indians; her published works include autobiographical essays and stories based on tribal legends published in *The Atlantic Monthly* and *Harper's* and two books of collected writings, *Old Indian Legends* (1901) and *American Indian Stories* (1921).

Bonnot, Étienne. *See* Condillac, Étienne Bonnot de

Bontemps, Arna

full: Arna Wendell Bontemps
b. Oct. 13, 1902
Alexandria, La.
d. June 4, 1973
Nashville, Tenn.
fields: Literature

African American author; an influential participant in the Harlem Renaissance and a chronicler of black achievement, Arna Bontemps's best known fictional work is *Black Thunder* (1936); during and after the 1940's he wrote primarily nonfiction including *Chariot in the Sky* (1951) and *One Hundred Years of Negro Freedom* (1961); his edited collections include *The Book of Negro Folklore* (1958, with Langston Hughes) and *Great Slave Narratives* (1969); also wrote more than a dozen books for children including biographies and histories; head librarian at Fisk University (1943-1965).

Boole, Alicia. *See* Stott, Alicia Boole

Boole, George

b. Nov. 2, 1815
Lincoln, Lincolnshire, England
d. Dec. 8, 1864
Ballintemple, County Cork, Ireland
fields: Mathematics (mathematical logic)

George Boole was the creator of a new form of algebra, named Boolean algebra, in which logical ideas can be expressed in mathematical terms. His published works include *The Mathematical Analysis of Logic* (1847) and *Treatise on the Calculus of Finite Differences* (1860). Boolean logic set the foundation for computer search programs.

Boone, Daniel

b. November 2, 1734
Berks County, Pennsylvania
d. September 26, 1820
near St. Charles, Missouri
fields: Exploration and Colonizatoin

In addition to opening the trans-Appalachian frontier, Boone became a legendary symbol of the early American frontier.

Boone, Sarah

b. ?
fields: Invention and Technology

African American inventor; Sarah Boone invented the ironing board; it was patented in 1892.

Boone, William. *See* Daniels, Billy

Booth, Edwin

full: Edwin Thomas Booth
b. November 13, 1833
near Bel Air, Maryland
d. June 7, 1893
New York, New York
fields: Theater and Entertainment (acting)

The most talented member of a family of actors, Edwin Booth suffered greatly from identity with his younger brother, the assassin John Wilkes Booth, but came to be admired for his art and his role in advancing the profession of acting in the United States.

Booth, William

b. April 10, 1829
Nottingham, England
d. August 20, 1912
London, England
fields: Religion and Theology, Social Reform

Compelled by his deep Christian faith to seek ways of serving his fellowman, Booth founded the international religious service organization, the Salvation Army, which became established in the United States fifteen years after the Civil War.

Boothe, Ann Clare. *See* Luce, Clare Boothe

Borach, Fanny. *See* Brice, Fanny

Borah, William E.

full: William Edgar Borah
b. June 29, 1865
Jasper Township, Illinois
d. January 19, 1940
Washington, D.C.
fields: Government and Politics

For more than three decades in the United States Senate, Borah was a leading nationalist who spoke and voted courageously for his idealistic view of American democracy.

Borbón, Carlos María Isidro de. *See* Carlos, Don

Borden, Lizzie

b. July 19, 1860
Fall River, Massachusetts
d. June 1, 1927
Fall River, Massachusetts
fields: Law

The legend of Lizzie Borden, axe murderer, endures despite the fact that Borden was acquitted of the August 4, 1892, murder of her father, Andrew Jackson Borden, and stepmother, Abby Durfee Gray Borden.

Borden, Robert Laird

b. June 26, 1854
Grand Pré, Nova Scotia, Canada
d. June 10, 1937
Ottawa, Canada
fields: Government and Politics

As prime minister of Canada during the years of World War I and the Peace at Versailles, Borden played a crucial role in transforming the status of Canada from that of a dominion to that of a nation.

Bordet, Jules

full: Jules-Jean-Baptiste-Vincent Bordet
b. June 13, 1870
Soignies, Belgium
d. Apr. 6, 1961
Brussels, Belgium
fields: Science, Medicine

Jules Bordet isolated the bacterium responsible for whooping cough in 1906; described the germ involved in bovine pleuropneumonia in 1909; won the Nobel Prize in Physiology or Medicine in 1920 for research into the basis of humoral immunity; helped lay the groundwork for the science of immunology.

Borel, Émile

full: Félix-Édouard-Justin-Émile Borel
b. Jan. 7, 1871
Saint-Affrique, France
d. Feb. 3, 1956
Paris, France
fields: Mathematics (calculus, probability, set theory, and statistics)

Émile Borel was president of the Académie des Sciences and won the first gold medal of the National Centre for Scientific Research. He specialized in probability, calculus, divergent series, and theories of measure and functions of real variables.

Borg, Björn

full: Björn Rune Borg
b. June 5, 1956
Södertalje, Sweden
fields: Sports (tennis)

Borg is the only man to win five consecutive Wimbledon championships. He also captured a host of other honors, including six French Open championships.

Borges, Francisco L.

b. Nov. 17, 1951
Santiago, Cape Verde
fields: Government and Politics

African American state politician; after serving on the Hartford, Conn., city council (1981-1985) and as the city's deputy mayor (1983-1985), Francisco L. Borges became state treasurer of Connecticut in 1987.

Borges, Jorge Luis

b. August 24, 1899
Buenos Aires, Argentina
d. June 14, 1986
Geneva, Switzerland
fields: Literature

Author of an important body of stories, poems, and essays, Borges influenced modern fiction and criticism in both South and North America.

Borgia, Rodrigo. *See* Alexander VI

Boris I of Bulgaria

b. 830
probably Pliska, Bulgaria
d. May 15, 907
Preslav, Bulgaria
fields: Government and Politics, Religion and Theology

Under Boris' rule, Bulgaria was brought into the framework of Christian Europe while preserving its political independence and cultural identity. His efforts established Bulgaria as a center of Slavonic Christian culture and laid the foundation for the first Bulgarian Empire.

Borja y Doms, Rodrigo de. *See* Alexander VI

Born, Max

b. Dec. 11, 1882
Breslau, Germany (now Wrocław, Poland)
d. Jan. 5, 1970
Göttingen, West Germany
fields: Physics

Max Born is known as one of the founders of quantum mechanics; work in the dynamics of crystal lattices became the foundation of modern solid-state physics. In 1954, he shared the Nobel Prize in Physics with Hans Albrecht Bethe.

Borodin, Aleksandr

full: Aleksandr Porfiryevich Borodin
b. November 12, 1833
St. Petersburg, Russia
d. February 27, 1887
St. Petersburg, Russia
fields: Music

Borodin made a significant contribution to the repertory of Russian national music, with particular excellence in the domains of opera, symphonic music, chamber music, and song.

Borromini, Francesco

né: Francesco Castelli
b. September 25, 1599
Bissone, near Lake Lugano

d. August 3, 1667
Rome
fields: Architecture

Borromini was one of the most innovative architects of the Baroque era, but his contemporaries were highly critical of his work and believed that it violated the principles of sound architectural design. For this reason, his immediate influence was slight, but he is now considered one of the giants of Baroque architecture.

Bosch, Hieronymus

né: Jeroen van Aeken
b. c. 1450
's-Hertogenbosch, North Brabant
d. 1516
's-Hertogenbosch, North Brabant
fields: Art

Bosch produced strikingly original paintings, whose brilliant style, flickering brushstroke, and fantastic, nightmarish visions influenced twentieth century Surrealists. Bosch's message, however, is rooted in the preoccupations of the early sixteenth century. His obsessions—sin, death, and damnation—reflect orthodox Christian concerns.

Bose, Sudhindra

b. 1883
Keotkhali, Bengal Province, India, now Bangladesh
d. May 26, 1946
Cedar Rapids, Iowa
fields: Scholarship, Journalism

One of the first Asian Indians to receive a Ph.D. degree in the United States, Sudhindra Bose lectured in political science at Iowa State University and was known as an Asia specialist. In 1923, when the U.S. Supreme Court ruled that Asian Indians were ineligible for naturalization, he lost his naturalized citizenship. In 1927, he went to court and regained his U.S. citizenship. He wrote about India and the United States, producing works such as *Some Aspects of British Rule in India* (1916), *Fifteen Years in America* (1920), *Glimpses of America* (1925), and *Mother America* (1934).

Bosomworth, Mary. *See* Musgrove, Mary

Bossuet, Jacques-Bénigne

b. September 27, 1627
Dijon, France
d. April 12, 1704
Paris, France
fields: Religion and Theology, Literature, Historiography

Bossuet was one of the most eloquent orators in seventeenth century France. In his sermons and funeral orations, he expressed profound psychological insights in a very refined and effective style. His major contributions were to rhetoric and sacred oratory.

Boston, Ralph

b. May 9, 1939
Laurel, Miss.
fields: Sports (track and field athlete)

African American track and field athlete; over the course of his career as a long jumper, Ralph Boston set seven world records; he won the 1960 Olympic Games gold medal for a jump of 26 feet 7¾ inches; in 1964 won the silver medal in the long jump; in 1968 won the bronze medal.

Boston Strangler

né: Albert DeSalvo
b. Sept. 3, 1931
Chelsea, Mass.
d. Dec. 27, 1973
Walpole, Mass.
fields: Historical Figure

The "Boston Strangler" is the media epithet given to Albert DeSalvo following his dubious confession to the gruesome murders, between June, 1962, and January, 1964, of eleven Massachusetts women that made him one of the United States' most feared killers in the mid-1960's. In January, 1967, DeSalvo was convicted of armed robbery and rape charges and was sentenced to life imprisonment in a state penitentiary at Walpole, Massachusetts. He was never charged with the Boston Strangler murders. He had served six years of his life sentence when he was stabbed to death in prison in 1973. His murder remains unsolved, and no one has ever been charged with the murders attributed to the Boston Strangler.

Boswell, James

b. October 29, 1740
Edinburgh, Scotland
d. May 19, 1795
London, England
fields: Literature

Boswell was not only the author of the English-speaking world's greatest biography, his *Life of Samuel Johnson* (1791), but also a distinguished autobiographer in his voluminous journals and letters.

Botero, Fernando

b. Apr. 19, 1932
Medellín, Colombia
fields: Art

Latino artist. Fernando Botero graduated from college in Medellín in 1950 and moved to Bogotá, where he had his first solo exhibits. In 1952, he won a national prize for painting. In 1960, he moved to the United States and continued his career. One of his paintings was purchased by the Museum of Modern Art.

Botha, Louis

b. September 27, 1862
near Greytown, Natal
d. August 27, 1919
Pretoria, Transvaal, Union of South Africa
fields: Diplomacy, Government and Politics, Military Affairs

During the Boer War, Botha fought valiantly to preserve the independence of the Transvaal. When the war was lost, he worked successfully for a united South Africa under the Crown.

Bothe, Walther

full: Walther Wilhelm Georg Bothe
b. January 8, 1891
Oranienburg, Germany
d. February 8, 1957
Heidelberg, West Germany
fields: Physics

Bothe was awarded the Nobel Prize in Physics (1954) for his invention of the coincidence counting technique and for discoveries made using it, including the nature of cosmic rays and the fashion in which X rays interact with electrons. He was one of Germany's leading atomic scientists and constructed their first cyclotron.

Botticelli, Sandro

né: Alessandro di Mariano Filipepi
b. c. 1444
Florence
d. May, 1510
Florence
fields: Art

Botticelli has been celebrated for the linear flow of his paintings and for the graceful and thoughtful cast of so much of his work. One of the greatest colorists of Renaissance painting, Botticelli created idealized figures that suggest great spirituality and somewhat less interest in humanity than was depicted in the works of many of his contemporaries.

Bottomley, Horatio W.

full: Horatio William Bottomley
b. March 23, 1860
Bethnal Green, London, England
d. May 26, 1933
London, England
fields: Journalism, Banking and Finance, Government and Politics

Born into poverty, Bottomley acquired and squandered three or four fortunes. As editor of the popular newspaper *John Bull*, he became the self-appointed tribune of the British man in the street before and during World War I. His exploits as a superpatriot made him a popular idol until his fraud conviction in 1922.

Bouchard, Lucien

b. December 22, 1938
Saint-Coeur-de-Marie, Quebec, Canada
fields: Government and Politics

Quebec separatist leader. In early 1990's Lucien Bouchard led formation of Quebec separatist party the Bloc Québécois. In the 1993 Canadian election, the bloc won fifty-four ridings (districts) in Quebec and became the official opposition in Ottawa. Campaigned for Quebec independence referendum of 1995; after its narrow defeat, became Quebec premier in 1996. Attempted to maintain the separatist momentum while reversing province's long-established pattern of deficit spending.

Bouchet, Edward Alexander

b. Sept. 15, 1852
New Haven, Conn.
d. Oct. 28, 1918
New Haven, Conn.
fields: Education

African American physicist; having earned a B.A. (1874) and a Ph.D. (1876) from Yale, Edward Alexander Bouchet became the first African American to earn a doctorate degree from an American university; he went on to teach science at various schools.

Boudinot, Elias

aka: Galegina
b. c. 1803
near Rome, Ga.
d. June 22, 1839
Park Hill, Indian Territory
fields: Journalism (editor, writer)

Eastern Cherokee editor and journalist Elias Boudinot was editor of, and a frequent contributor to, the Cherokee newspaper the *Cherokee Phoenix*; he also collaborated in translating parts of the New Testament into Cherokee and was a signer of the Treaty of New Echota in 1835.

Boudinot, Elias Cornelius

b. Aug. 1, 1835
near Rome, Ga.
d. Sept. 27, 1890
fields: Business and Industry, Native American Affairs

Son of Elias Boudinot. Cherokee businessman Elias Cornelius Boudinot, a lawyer and tobacco factory owner, was involved in a Supreme Court case with far-reaching implications. The Court ruled in 1871 that an act of Congress can supersede any treaty previously entered into and that Boudinot's Company could be held *post facto* for unpaid excise taxes. This court decision ended one of the few economic advantages held by the Cherokees.

Bougainville, Louis-Antoine de

b. November 12, 1729
Paris, France
d. August 31, 1811
Paris, France
fields: Exploration and Colonization, Military Affairs

Bougainville is best known as the leader of the first French expedition to sail around the world. He fought the British during the French and Indian Wars and later during the American Revolutionary War.

Boukharouba, Mohammed Ben Brahim. *See* Boumedienne, Houari

Boulez, Pierre

b. March 26, 1925
Montbrison, France
fields: Music

Boulez's compositions, essays, and lectures have changed the direction of Western music. Though he emerged from the French tradition of Debussy, Ravel, and Messiaen, he rejected his roots and redirected his spiritual allegiance to the Austro-German tradition as embodied in Schoenberg, Berg, and Webern. He also became one of the most influential conductors of modern music in both Europe and the United States.

Boulton, Matthew

b. September 3, 1728
Birmingham, England
d. August 18, 1809
Birmingham, England
fields: Business and Industry

Boulton created one of the first factories, made varied housewares of high artistic quality available to the middle class, modernized the coining process, and aided James Watt in manufacturing and merchandising the steam engine.

Boumedienne, Houari

aka: Mohammed Ben Brahim Boukharouba
b. August 23, 1927
Clauzel, near Goulma, Algeria
d. December 27, 1978
Algiers, Algeria
fields: Government and Politics

President of Algeria (1965-1979) Houari Boumedienne led a coup against Algerian president Ahmed Ben Bella in 1965 and established himself as the second president of Algeria. After a failed coup in 1967, affirmed absolute control and established a military dictatorship. In 1971 took control of Algerian oil industry. Influential figure in Third World politics in mid-1970's. In power until 1978.

Bourbaki, Nicolas

b. 1934-1935
conceived in Paris, France
fields: Mathematics (algebra, mathematical logic, set theory, topology)

Nicolas Bourbaki applied an axiomatic approach to organize related areas of theoretical mathematics by identifying and describing common underlying structures. In 1950, he published "The Architecture of Mathematics," an explanation of the intent to identify and describe the structure and fundamental processes of pure mathematics. He also published thirty-three volumes of *Éléments de Mathématique*.

Bourdieu, Pierre

b. August 1, 1930
Denguin, France
fields: Philosophy, Sociology, Anthropology

In the 1960's, social theorist Pierre Bourdieu was director of the École Pratique des Hautes Études (1964), founder and director of the Centre de Sociologie Européene (1968); in 1981, he was named senior chair in sociology at the Collège de France. He developed a theory of human action as practice-based and drew links between social background and academic success, laying the foundation for the sociology of education. Major works include *The Inheritors* (1964, Jean-Claude Passeron), *Outline of a Theory of Practice* (1972), *The Logic of Practice* (1980), *Language and Symbolic Power* (1982), and *An Invitation to Reflexive Sociology* (1992, with Loic Wacquant).

Bourgeois, Léon

full: Léon-Victor-Auguste Bourgeois
b. May 21, 1851
Paris, France
d. September 29, 1925
Château d'Ozer, near Épernay, Marne, France
fields: Diplomacy, Government and Politics

Léon Bourgeois was a French politician, reformer, and diplomat. In 1919, appointed to the commission that drafted the rules of the League of Nations, the forerunner of the United Nations. From 1919 to 1924, Bourgeois was the French spokesman in both the Council and the Assembly of the League of Nations. Winner of 1920 Nobel Peace Prize.

Bourgeois, Louise

b. December 25, 1911
Paris, France
fields: Art

An internationally recognized sculptor, Bourgeois has created works that are characterized by a singular fusion of the intellectual purity of formal abstraction and the unconscious affect of her personal psyche.

Bourguiba, Habib

b. August 3, 1903
Monastir, Tunisia
fields: Government and Politics

Bourguiba organized Tunisians to confront French rule and was the catalyst for independence, leading his people to nationhood in 1956. For thirty-one years, Bourguiba served as Tunisia's only president, until he was toppled from power in a bloodless *coup d'état* in Tunis.

Bourke, Mary Teresa Winifred. *See* Robinson, Mary

Bourke-White, Margaret

b. June 14, 1904
New York, New York
d. August 27, 1971
Stamford, Connecticut
fields: Photography

Margaret Bourke-White was a pioneering news photographer who helped develop and define the field of photojournalism.

Boutros-Ghali, Boutros

b. November 14, 1922
Cairo, Egypt
fields: Diplomacy, Government and Politics, Law

Boutros-Ghali is best known for his extensive involvement in international affairs as a diplomat, jurist, and scholar. An Egyptian statesman who became the first United Nations secretary general from an Arab nation, Boutros-Ghali strongly supported mediation in post-Cold War conflicts, led the international celebration of the United Nations' fiftieth anniversary, and proposed organizational reforms that were opposed by the United States.

Bouvier, Jacqueline Lee. *See* Onassis, Jacqueline Kennedy

Bowdler, Thomas

b. July 11, 1754
Ashley, Somerset, England
d. February 24, 1825
Rhydding, Glamorganshire, Wales
fields: Literature

Thomas Bowdler's *Family Shakspeare* (1818) made him famous and made his name synonymous with the practice of censoring literary texts by omitting verbal vulgarity. When he died in 1825, he left his censored edition of Edward Gibbon's *The History of the Decline and Fall of the Roman Empire* (1776-1788) for posthumous publication.

Bowe, Riddick

b. Aug. 10, 1967
Brooklyn, N.Y.
fields: Sports (boxer)

African American boxer; after turning professional following a controversial loss in the 1988 Seoul Olympics, Riddick Bowe posted a 31-0 record before beating Evander Holyfield to become the world heavyweight champion in November, 1992; lost the heavyweight title to Holyfield in November, 1993; earned World Boxing Organization championship in March, 1995.

Bowen, Clotilde Marian Dent

b. Mar. 20, 1923
Chicago, Ill.
fields: Medicine

African American medical doctor; noted as the first African American woman to graduate from the medical college at Ohio State University (1947), Clotilde Marian Dent Bowen went on to become the first black female U.S. Army physician, rising to the rank of colonel; associate clinical professor of psychiatry in the medical college at the University of Colorado (1971-1985).

Bowl

aka: Diwali
aka: Colonel Bowles
b. 1756
N.C.
d. July 16, 1839
near present-day Overton, Tex.
fields: Warfare and Conquest, Native American Affairs

Leader of a large band of Cherokee militants, Bowl fought Americans throughout his life.

Bowlegs, Billy

aka: Holatamico
aka: Halpatter-Micco
b. c. 1810
northern Fla.
d. 1864
Kans.
fields: Warfare and Conquest, Native American Affairs

Billy Bowlegs was the principal leader of the Seminoles in Florida during the Third Seminole War, 1855-1858. Later, when the Civil War began, he led his group to Kansas from Indian Territory, where they had settled. He became a captain in a Union regiment mustered from among the Indians.

Bowles, Colonel. *See* Bowl

Bowman, Julia. *See* Robinson, Julia Bowman

Bowman, Sister Thea

b. December 29, 1937
Yazoo City, Miss.
d. March 30, 1990
Canton, Miss
fields: Education (nun, evangelist, educator, and musician)

African American nun, evangelist, educator, and musician; Sister Thea Bowman, once the only African member of the community of Franciscan Sisters of Perpetual Adoration, in 1978 became the Director for Intercultural Awareness for the diocese of Jackson, Miss.; helped found the Institute of Black Catholic Studies at Xavier University in New Orleans; received national recognition by "challenging" the Catholic church's provincialism, lobbying for full incorporation of African American ritual, folksong, and dance into the Catholic mass and for black participation in the church's liturgy and leadership.

Box, Charles E.

b. ?
fields: Government and Politics

African American mayor of Rockford, Ill; after practicing law from 1976 to 1981, Charles E. Box served as legal director of the city of Rockford, Illinois; a subsequent position as city administrator ran until 1989; in April of 1989, overwhelmingly elected mayor of Rockford.

Boxley, Hank. *See* Shocklee, Hank

Boyd, Eva Narcissus. *See* Little Eva

Boyd, Nancy. *See* Millay, Edna St. Vincent

Boyd, Robert Fulton

b. July 8, 1858
Pulaski, Tenn.
d. July 20, 1912
Nashville, Tenn.
fields: Medicine

African American physician, dentist, and surgeon; Robert Fulton Boyd established the Boyd Infirmary in Nashville, Tennessee (1893), which also functioned as a teaching hospital for Meharry Medical College; from 1895-1897, first president of the National Medical Association.

Boykin, Otis

b. 1920
Dallas, Tex.
d. 1982
Chicago, Ill.
fields: Science, Invention and Technology (scientist and inventor)

African American scientist and inventor; Otis Boykin was best known for his invention of a variable resistor used in all guided missiles and for a resistor used in computers, radios, and television sets; also invented a control unit for the artificial heart stimulator (pacemaker), a burglar-proof cash register, automatic control devices for airplanes, and a chemical air filter.

Boyle, Robert

b. January 25, 1627
Lismore, County Waterford, Ireland
d. December 31, 1691
London, England
fields: Physics, Chemistry

Boyle discovered Boyle's law, on the relationship between air pressure and volume, and promoted the experimental approach to scientific study, especially in the field of chemistry.

Boza, Juan

b. May 6, 1941
Camagüey, Cuba
d. Mar. 7, 1991
fields: Art

Latino artist. Juan Boza began studying at the Academia de Bellas Artes de San Alejandro in Havana, Cuba, in 1959 on a scholarship but was expelled over political issues. He became an award-winning lithographer and was hired as a designer for the National Council of Culture, a position from which he was fired in 1971. In 1980, he left Cuba for New York City, where he continued his career and won numerous fellowships and awards. His art has been exhibited worldwide.

Bracetti, Mariana

b. c. 1840
d. ?
fields: Historical Figure

Latina revolutionary figure. Mariana Bracetti gained fame by sewing the flag that rebel forces used on September 23, 1868, the day four hundred people in the town of Lares in Puerto Rico rose against Spanish rule. Although the rebellion failed for a variety of reasons, Puerto Rican independence groups hold annual commemorations on the anniversary of the uprising, which is known as El Grito de Lares.

Bracton, Henry de

aka: Henry de Bratton
b. Early thirteenth century
Devon or Somerset, England
d. 1268
probably Exeter, Devon, England
fields: Law

Bracton was the author of a comprehensive account of the common law of England as it had developed down to the middle of the thirteenth century. His book was extremely influential throughout the medieval period and continued to be consulted by legal authorities during the sixteenth and seventeenth centuries.

Bradford, Margarita. *See* Melville, Margarita Bradford

Bradford, Perry

full: John Henry Perry Bradford
aka: Mule Bradford
b. Feb. 14, 1893
Montgomery, Ala.
d. Apr. 20, 1970
New York, N.Y.
fields: Music (jazz pianist, composer, and producer)

African American jazz pianist, composer, and producer; Perry "Mule" Bradford worked as a solo pianist and on the vaudeville circuit before gaining recognition as the composer of "Crazy Blues," a recording by Mamie Smith which sold more than one million copies; also wrote "That Thing Called Love" and "You Can't Keep a Good Man Down"; his musical comedies include *Made in Harlem* (1918) and the Broadway production *Put and Take* (1921); owned his own music publishing company.

Bradford, William

b. March, 1590
Austerfield, England
d. May 19, 1657
Plymouth, Massachusetts
fields: Government and Politics

Bradford was the leader of the Pilgrims once they settled in America, and he was the author of a history of Plymouth colony, one of the great works of early American literature.

Bradley, David

b. Sept. 7, 1950
Bedford, Pa.
fields: Literature, Education

African American novelist and university professor; David Bradley is best known for his novel dealing with the legacy of slavery for African Americans, *The Chaneysville Incident* (1981); *South Street* (1975) looked at the lives of poor African Americans living in Philadelphia.

Bradley, Ed

b. June 22, 1941
Philadelphia, Pa.
fields: Journalism

African American news correspondent; Ed Bradley worked as a radio reporter, a Paris stringer for CBS (1971), a Vietnam War correspondent (1972-1973), a White House correspondent, and as the first African American news anchor on the *CBS Sunday Night News* before becoming the first black correspondent for the television news program *60 Minutes* (1981-); has received several Emmy Awards.

Bradley, F. H.

full: Francis Herbert Bradley
b. January 30, 1846
Clapham, Surrey, England
d. September 18, 1924
Oxford, England
fields: Philosophy

In the history of British philosophy, Bradley represents a point of view that is fundamentally Idealist. He was a vigorous, gifted, brooding critic of England's empirical philosphers.

Bradley, Joseph P.

b. 1813
d. 1892
fields: Law

U.S. Supreme Court justice, 1870-1892 (died while in office); appointed by President Grant. Author of *Boyd v. United States*, 116 U.S. 616 (1886), the first case offering a significant interpretation of the Fourth and Fifth Amendments. Significant opinions: *Legal Tender Cases*, 79 U.S. 603 (1871) (concurring opinion); *Civil Rights Cases*, 109 U.S. 3 (1885); *Munn v. Illinois*, 118 U.S. 557 (1886).

Bradley, Melvin L. P.

b. Jan. 6, 1938
Texarkana, Tex.
fields: Government and Politics

African American government official; from 1980 to 1988, Melvin L. P. Bradley served as senior policy adviser and special assistant to President Ronald Reagan; prior positions included assistant to California governor Reagan (1970-1975), director of public relations at Drew Medical School in Los Angeles, and assistant to the vice president of United Airlines; became a corporate consultant in Washington, D.C., following his service under the Reagan administration.

Bradley, Omar N.

full: Omar Nelson Bradley
b. February 12, 1893
Clark, Missouri
d. April 8, 1981
New York, New York
fields: Military Affairs

Bradley provided stability and continuity within the American military establishment during the critical period following the end of World War II and the onset of the Cold War.

Bradley, Tom

full: Thomas J. Bradley

b. Dec. 29, 1917
Calvert, Tex.
d. Sept. 29, 1998
Los Angeles, Calif.
fields: Government and Politics

African American politician; Tom Bradley held various positions with the Los Angeles Police Department, 1940-1961; after earning a law degree in the 1950's, became the first African American elected to the Los Angeles City Council, 1963-1973; served as mayor of Los Angeles, 1973-1992 (five terms); was a founding member of the Black Achievers Committee of the National Association for the Advancement of Colored People.

Bradman, Donald G.

full: Sir Donald George Bradman
b. August 27, 1908
Cootamundra, New South Wales, Australia
fields: Sports (cricket)

Widely regarded as among the greatest of all cricketers, Bradman shaped the modern game with his complete mastery of the arts of batting and captaincy.

Bradshaw, John

b. June 29, 1933
Houston, Tex.
fields: Psychiatry and Psychology, Television

After going through Alcoholics Anonymous (AA), John Elliot Bradshaw became a successful speaker and consultant on alcohol-related issues whose training as a Roman Catholic priest made him sensitive to the problems of troubled people. While doing local television work in Texas, he was asked by the Public Broadcasting Service to do a miniseries, *Eight Stages of Man* (1982-1984). This was followed by *Bradshaw on the Family* (1986). His book *Homecoming: Reclaiming and Championing Your Inner Child* (1990) popularized the concept of the "inner child"—who incorporates failings of its parents. Bradshaw also introduced "dysfunctional family" into the language.

Bradstreet, Anne

né: Anne Dudley
b. 1612 (?)
Northampton, Northamptonshire, England
d. September 16, 1672
Andover, Massachusetts Bay Colony
fields: Literature

Not only the first American woman poet, Anne Bradstreet ranks as the first true American poet of either sex.

Brady, Mathew B.

b. c. 1823
Warren County, New York
d. January 15, 1896
New York, New York
fields: Photography

Brady brought to the American public a panorama of personalities and scenes through the photographic medium, and he was instrumental in creating a pictorial record of the Civil War.

Bragg, Lawrence

full: William Lawrence Bragg
aka: Sir Lawrence Bragg
b. March 31, 1890
Adelaide, South Australia, Australia
d. July 1, 1971
Ipswich, Suffolk, England
fields: Physics

Bragg used X-ray diffraction to determine the arrangement of atoms in many crystals and helped establish the field of X-ray crystallography. He was awarded the 1915 Nobel Prize in Physics.

Bragg, Robert Henry

full: Robert Henry Bragg, Jr.
b. Aug. 11, 1919
Jacksonville, Florida
d. ?
Nigeria
fields: Physics, Invention and Technology

Robert Henry Bragg examined the structure and properties of different materials, especially various forms of carbon, which led to a better understanding of how these materials could be incorporated into manufactured goods.

Brahe, Tycho

né: Tycho Brahe Ottosøn
b. December 14, 1546
Knudstrup Castle, Scania, Denmark
d. October 24, 1601
Prague, Bohemia
fields: Astronomy

Brahe realized early that the existing means for observing and measuring celestial bodies and their motions were inaccurate. His great achievements are to have significantly improved existing instruments, to have invented some new instruments, and to have made amazingly accurate observations.

Brahmagupta

b. c. 598
Bhillamala, India
d. c. 660
possibly Ujjain, India
fields: Mathematics, Astronomy

Brahmagupta wrote the book in verse entitled *Brahmasphuṭasiddhānta*, which expounds a complex system of astronomy and contains two important chapters on arithmetic, algebra, and geometry. His work on indeterminate equations and introduction of negative numbers greatly influenced the development of science in both India and Arabia.

Brahms, Johannes

b. May 7, 1833
Hamburg
d. April 3, 1897
Vienna, Austro-Hungarian Empire
fields: Music

One of the greatest composers of his century, Brahms left an enduring corpus of works. He demonstrated that the forms and genres of Viennese classicism continued to have artistic validity in the late nineteenth century and that they were not incompatible with the ethos of Romanticism.

Braille, Louis

b. January 4, 1809
Coupvray, near Paris, France
d. January 6, 1852
Paris, France
fields: Invention and Technology, Social Reform

Braille was responsible for the invention of what has become a worldwide system for teaching the blind to read and write.

Brailsford, Marvin Delano

b. Jan. 31, 1939
Burkeville, Tex.
fields: Military Affairs

African American military officer; Marvin Delano Brailsford achieved the rank of U.S. Army lieutenant general during his more than thirty-two years of commissioned service; his postings were in the areas of chemical and nuclear operations and armament research and development; retired from active military service on February 29, 1992.

Braithwaite, William Stanley Beaumont

b. Dec. 6, 1878
Boston, Mass.
d. June 8, 1962
New York, N.Y.
fields: Literature, Journalism

African American poet, editor, and novelist; as a poetry critic for the *Boston Evening Transcript* and as an editor of a variety of poetry anthologies, William Stanley Beaumont Braithwaite introduced outstanding contemporary poetry to the general public during the early decades of the twentieth century; Braithwaite also wrote poetry in the Romantic tradition.

Bramante, Donato

né: Donato di Pascuccio d'Antonio

b. 1444
Monte Asdruvaldo, near Urbino, Papal States
d. April 11, 1514
Rome
fields: Architecture

One of the greatest architects of the Italian Renaissance, Bramante stands out for the pure classicism of his buildings. His influence extended throughout Europe. Except for the long nave, St. Peter's in Rome is basically his design.

Brancusi, Constantin

b. February 19, 1876
Hobitza, Romania
d. March 16, 1957
Paris, France
fields: Art

A craftsman and a poet of forms, Brancusi carried abstraction to its utmost limits, often far beyond the material's own representational element. Renouncing the traditional form, he attempted to extract from the material—whether marble, metal, or wood—its maximum effect. His major contribution to modern sculpture was his unique capacity to render meaning through sheer form.

Brandeis, Louis D.

full: Louis Dembitz Brandeis
b. November 13, 1856
Louisville, Kentucky
d. October 5, 1941
Washington, D.C.
fields: Social Reform, Law

Brandeis was a leading social reformer from 1897 to 1916, gaining the unofficial title of the "people's attorney"; he was the leader of the American Zionist movement from 1914 until 1939 and served as Associate Justice of the United States Supreme Court from 1916 until his retirement in 1939.

Brando, Marlon

full: Marlon Brando, Jr.
b. April 3, 1924
Omaha, Nebraska
fields: Film, Theater and Entertainment (drama)

Known for the behavioral honesty and psychological truthfulness of his acting, Brando's unique style revolutionized film and theater. The mark of his style can be found in virtually every performer today and has earned Brando an important and permanent role in the history of acting.

Brandt, Willy

né: Herbert Ernst Karl Frahm
b. December 18, 1913
Lübeck, Germany
d. October 8, 1992
Unkel, near Bonne, Germany
fields: Government and Politics

Brandt was awarded the Nobel Peace Prize (1971) for his efforts in improving relations between West Germany and Eastern Europe. He was instrumental in creating a competitive political party system in West Germany. In 1985, Brandt received the Albert Einstein Peace Prize and the Third World Prize.

Brant, Joseph

né: Thayendanegea
b. 1742
the Ohio country
d. November 24, 1807
near Brantford, Ontario, Canada
fields: Native American Affairs, Government and Politics

Mohawk; Brant was a military leader for the British during the American Revolution and afterward secured indemnities for the Iroquois and established the first Episcopal church in upper Canada.

Brant, Molly

aka: Mary Brant
aka: Degonwadonti (Many Opposed to One)
aka: Gonwatsijayenni
b. c. 1753
Canajoharie, N.Y.
d. Apr. 16, 1796
Kingston, Ontario, Canada
fields: Diplomacy, Government and Politics, Native American Affairs

Native American (Mohawk) political figure. Molly Brant was a leading Mohawk during the time of the American Revolution. She was instrumental in convincing the Mohawks and the Iroquois Confederacy to side with the British. Sister of Joseph Brant.

Branting, Karl Hjalmar

b. November 23, 1860
Stockholm, Sweden
d. February 24, 1925
Stockholm, Sweden
fields: Government and Politics, Diplomcay

Karl Hjalmar Branting was the Swedish labor movement's greatest leader. When the Social Democratic Party was formed in 1889, he was its uncontested leader. Three-time prime minister of Sweden—in 1920, from 1921 to 1923, and from 1924 to 1925. Swedish delegate to League of Nations beginning in 1920; became known as "the great European." In 1921 awarded the Nobel Peace Prize, jointly with Christian L. Lange of Norway.

Braque, Georges

b. May 13, 1882
Argenteuil, France
d. August 31, 1963
Paris, France
fields: Art

Braque cofounded cubism with his friend, Pablo Picasso. Braque is best known, however, as a master of the still life, which constituted approximately two-thirds of his output. His paintings are famous for their discipline, rationality, classical lines, and subdued colors.

Bratt, Robert K.

b. ?
fields: Government and Politics

As the first director of the U.S. Department of Justice's Office of Redress Administration (ORA), Robert K. Bratt administered the government's redress and reparations program, which made payments to Japanese Americans and others interned during World War II. In his role as executive officer in the Civil Rights Division of the U.S. attorney's office, Bratt helped implement the section of the Civil Liberties Act of 1988 involving restitution for the Japanese internees.

Braudel, Fernand

b. August 24, 1902
Lunéville, France
d. November 28, 1985
Paris, France
fields: Historiography, Geography, Social Sciences

Braudel expanded significantly the nature and scope of historical research by reintegrating history with the social and behavioral sciences and by devising a distinctive analytical theory and methodology to justify and make possible a major shift in the ways in which historical research was conducted.

Braugher, Andre

b. 1963?
Chicago, Ill.
fields: Television, Film, Theater and Entertainment (actor)

African American actor; Andre Braugher's film credits include *Glory* (1989), *Primal Fear* (1996), *City of Angels* (1998), and *Thick as Thieves* (1999); from 1992 to 1998, he played Detective Frank Pembleton on the NBC television series *Homicide: Life on the Streets*. In 1998, he won an Emmy for his work on *Homicide*.

Braun, Carol E. Moseley

b. Aug. 16, 1947
Chicago, Ill.
fields: Government and Politics

African American politician; Carol E. Moseley Braun was assistant U.S. attorney for the northern district of Illinois, 1973-1977; served as Illinois state representative, 1979-1987, establishing a reputation as an ardent supporter of civil rights legislation; was Cook County recorder of deeds, 1987-1993; became first African American woman to be elected to the U.S. Senate (Democrat, Illinois) in 1992.

Braun, Sanford. *See* Koufax, Sandy

Braun, Wernher von

b. March 23, 1912
Wirsitz, Germany
d. June 16, 1977
Alexandria, Virginia
fields: Aviation and Space Exploration

A pioneer in German rocketry and a visionary of space flight, von Braun dominated the early American space program by directing construction of the Saturn rocket which propelled the first astronauts to the Moon.

Brautigan, Richard

full: Richard Gary Brautigan
b. January 30, 1935
Tacoma, Washington
d. September, 1984
Bolinas, California
fields: Literature

American poet and novelist. Richard Brautigan's quirky, often humorous countercultural writing embodied both the Beat and the hippie movements, establishing him as one of the most prominent West Coast writers of the 1960's. Among his best-known works is *A Confederate General from Big Sur* (1964), *Trout Fishing in America* (1967), and *In Watermelon Sugar* (1968).

Brawley, Benjamin Griffith

b. Apr. 22, 1882
Columbia, S.C.
d. Feb. 1, 1939
Washington, D.C.
fields: Education, Literature

African American clergyman, college professor, and author; Benjamin Griffith Brawley served as a professor of English at Morehouse College, Shaw University, and Howard University; published *A Short History of the American Negro* (1913).

Braxton, Toni

b. 1968
Severn, Md.
fields: Music (singer)

African American singer; Toni Braxton released her solo album *Toni Braxton* in 1993; was awarded a Grammy for best new artist and female R&B vocalist for "Another Sad Love Song" in 1994; her sultry, jazz-tinged vocals are often compared to Whitney Houston and Anita Baker. In 1996, she released *Secrets*.

Braxton, William E.

b. 1878
Washington, D.C.
d. 1932
fields: Art

African American painter and illustrator; William E. Braxton may be viewed as the first African American expressionist painter; although his art pieces never brought him financial success, he is remembered for such works as *Seascape* and *The Good Book*.

Brazelton, T. Berry

full: Thomas Berry Brazelton
b. May 10, 1918
Waco, Tex.
fields: Medicine, Psychiatry and Psychology, Sociology

A pediatrician, T. Berry Brazelton began teaching at Harvard University's medical school in 1951. There he developed an interest in infant behavior and parenting and founded the Neonatal Behavioral Assessment Scale (NBAS) to help speed adoption procedures. He also cofounded the Child Development Unit at Boston's Children's Hospital Medical Center. His many books include popular manuals on child rearing. He hosted *What Every Baby Knows* on the Lifetime cable channel and wrote monthly features for *Family Circle* and *Redbook*.

Breakspear, Nicholas. *See* Adrian IV

Brecht, Bertolt

né: Eugen Berthold Brecht
b. February 10, 1898
Augsburg, Germany
d. August 14, 1956
East Berlin, East Germany
fields: Literature

Brecht is generally considered not only Germany's leading dramatist but also one of the central influences on Western theater since World War II.

Breckenridge, Mary

b. Feb. 17, 1881
Memphis, Tenn.
d. May 16, 1965
Wendover, Ky.
fields: Public Health, Nursing

Mary Breckenridge was a midwife and crusader for midwifery. Was a registered nurse and a volunteer for the American Red Cross in France after the Armistice of World War I; in 1923 became a certified midwife in England; in 1925 chose Kentucky as the site for the pioneering Frontier Nursing Service (FNS), funding some of it herself. The FNS substantially lowered the death rate for women in childbirth in Kentucky, established midwifery as an affordable alternative to doctors for poor families.

Bréda, François Dominique Toussaint. *See* Toussaint-Louverture

Breedlove, Sarah. *See* Walker, Madam C. J.

Brennan, William J.

full: William Joseph Brennan, Jr.
b. 1906
d. 1997
fields: Law

U.S. Supreme Court justice, 1956-1990; appointed by President Eisenhower. Author of many important Warren Court-era opinions on individual rights; opposed death penalty. Significant opinions: *Baker v. Carr*, 369 U.S. 186 (1962); *Wong Sun v. United States*, 371 U.S. 471 (1963); *New York Times Co. v. Sullivan*, 376 U.S. 254 (1964); *United States v. Wade*, 388 U.S. 218 (1967); *Warden v. Hayden*, 387 U.S. 294 (1967); *Coleman v. Alabama*, 399 U.S. 1 (1970); *Gregg v. Georgia*, 428 U.S. 153 (1976, dissenting opinion); *Craig v. Boren*, 429 U.S. 190 (1976); *Dunaway v. New York*, 442 U.S. 200 (1979); *Pennsylvania v. Muniz*, 496 U.S. 582 (1990).

Breton, André

b. February 19, 1896
Tinchebray, France
d. September 28, 1966
Paris, France
fields: Literature

A novelist, poet, and founder of the Surrealist movement, Breton embodied the principle that the imagination is the center of the human definition of reality and that his creativity must be permitted to emerge unencumbered by the constraints of logic and reason.

Breuer, Josef

b. January 15, 1842
Vienna, Austria
d. June 20, 1925
Vienna, Austria
fields: Psychiatry and Psychology, Physiology, Medicine

Breuer was one of the foremost physiologists of the nineteenth century and made major contributions to the understanding of the process of respiration and the function of the inner ear. Yet he is remembered primarily for his discovery of the cathartic or "talking out" method of treating neurotic disorders, a discovery that led, through Sigmund Freud, to the development of psychoanalysis.

Breuil, Henri-Édouard-Prosper

b. February 28, 1877
Mortain, France
d. August 14, 1961
L'Îsle-Adam, France
fields: Anthropology

A major figure in prehistoric archaeology, Breuil specialized in prehistoric art, opening new vistas of understanding and establishing the first useful chronologies for this crucial facet of early human cultural activity.

Brewer, David Josiah

b. 1837
d. 1910
fields: Law

U.S. Supreme Court justice, 1890-1910 (died while in office); appointed by President Harrison. Believed many forms of governmental economic and social regulation were unconstitutional under substantive due process doctrine. Significant opinions: *Reagan v. Farmers' Loan & Trust Co.*, 154 U.S. 362 (1894); *In re Debs*, 158 U.S. 564 (1895); *Muller v. Oregon*, 208 U.S. 412 (1908).

Brewster, David

full: Sir David Brewster
b. Dec. 11, 1781
Jedburgh, Roxburghshire, Scotland
d. Feb. 10, 1868
Allerby, Melrose, Scotland
fields: Physics, Science

In 1816, David Brewster invented the kaleidoscope. He also edited several scientific journals. In 1831, he helped found the British Association for the Advancement of Science (BAAS).

Breyer, Steven

full: Steven Gerald Breyer
b. 1938
fields: Law

U.S. Supreme Court justice, began tenure in 1994; appointed by President Clinton.

Brezhnev, Leonid

full: Leonid Ilich Brezhnev
b. December 19, 1906
Kamenskoye, Ukraine, Russian Empire
d. November 10, 1982
Moscow, U.S.S.R.
fields: Government and Politics

Brezhnev directed the Soviet Union for nearly two decades (1964-1982). His administrative record as party chief and head of government was characterized by emphasis on continuity and the status quo in domestic policy, an increase in military strength, and a mixture in foreign policy of cautious adventurism, arms control agreements with the United States, and military intervention in two neighboring states.

Briand, Aristide

full: Aristide Pierre Henri Briand
b. March 28, 1862
Nantes, Breton, France
d. March 7, 1932
Paris, France
fields: Diplomacy, Government and Politics

French foreign minister and eleven-time premier (prime minister). Aristide Briand was determined to maintain post-World War I European cooperation; became a popular international statesman. The Locarno Treaty (1925) was his major achievement. Also helped draft the Kellogg-Briand Pact (1928). Winner of 1926 Nobel Peace Prize with Gustav Stresemann.

Brice, Fanny

né: Fanny Borach
b. October 29, 1891
New York, New York
d. May 29, 1951
Los Angeles, California
fields: Music, Theater and Entertainment

A celebrated singer and comedian whose extensive career extended from vaudeville to radio, Brice defied commonly accepted standards of beauty and created an individual niche in comedy for her own specialized talents.

Brico, Antonia

b. June 26, 1902
Rotterdam, The Netherlands
d. August 3, 1989
Denver, Colorado
fields: Music

Antonia Brico was an internationally recognized conductor who had two careers in her lifetime: the first in the 1930's and 1940's, and the second toward the end of her life in the 1970's and 1980's, after the release of the documentary film *Antonia: A Portrait of the Woman* in 1974. This film was instrumental in showing the severe discrimination suffered by Brico in penetrating the formerly all-male field of conducting.

Bridgman, Percy Williams

b. April 21, 1882
Cambridge, Massachusetts
d. August 20, 1961
Randolph, New Hampshire
fields: Physics, Philosophy

Through his invention and investigations, Bridgman vastly extended the range of high pressure physics. Through his development of the philosophical notion of operational analysis, he greatly aided his colleagues in coping with the new ideas of twentieth century physics. His work contributed significantly to the coming of age of physics in America. He was awarded the 1946 Nobel Prize in Physics.

Briggs, Bunny

b. Feb. 26, 1922
New York, N.Y.
fields: Dance

African American tap dancer; a self-taught tap dancer, Bunny Briggs spent his early career performing in New York clubs and ballrooms and in the private homes of wealthy families (1927-1940's); his 1960's solo appearances with Duke Ellington's band were captured on two Ellington albums; in 1989 he made a solo appearance in the Broadway musical *Black and Blue*; film credits include *Slow Poke* (1933) and *Tap* (1989).

Briggs, Cyril V.

b. May 28, 1887
Chester's Park, Nevis, British West Indies
d. October 18, 1966
Los Angeles, Calif.
fields: Civil Rights

African American civil rights activist; Cyril V. Briggs was the founder and leader of the African Blood Brotherhood (ABB), which advocated a black nationalist and socialist political line, in opposition to the anti-communist orientation of Marcus Garvey. By the mid-1920's, Briggs was attracted to the possibilities of a class alliance with white workers in a common struggle for socialism. Briggs dissolved the ABB, joining the Communist Party of the U.S.A. (CPUSA). He worked within the party until his death.

Bright, John

b. November 16, 1811
Rochdale, Lancashire, England
d. March 27, 1889
Rochdale, Lancashire, England
fields: Government and Politics

Combining moral courage and personal integrity, Bright was instrumental in bringing about many liberal reforms in nineteenth century Great Britain.

Brimmer, Andrew Felton

b. Sept. 13, 1926
Newellton, La.
fields: Economics

African American economist; the author of several books on financial markets and economic development, Andrew Felton Brimmer is noted as the first African American to serve on the Federal Reserve Board (1966-1974); earlier positions included economist for the Federal Reserve Bank of New York City (1955-1958), deputy assistant secretary of commerce (1963-1965), and assistant secretary for economic affairs with the Commerce Department (1965-1966); resigned the Federal Reserve Board to teach at the Harvard Graduate School of Business Administration.

Brindley, James

b. 1716
Turnstead, Derbyshire, England
d. September 27, 1772
Turnhurst, Staffordshire, England
fields: Engineering

The first modern English canal engineer, Brindley designed and engineered the canal network necessary for the industrialization of the Midlands and therefore essential to eighteenth century England's industrial revolution.

Brinson-Pineda, Barbara

b. 1956
San Francisco, Calif.
fields: Literature

Latina poet. Barbara Brinson-Pineda often mixes Spanish and English in her poems. Among her published volumes of poetry are *Nocturno* (1978), *Vocabulary of the Dead* (1984), and *Speak to Me from Dreams* (1989), the last being her best-known work. She has taught creative writing at the University of California, Santa Cruz.

Brisco-Hooks, Valerie

b. July 6, 1960
Greenwood, Miss.
fields: Sports (track and field athlete)

African American track and field athlete; in 1984 Valerie Brisco-Hooks won Olympic gold medals in the 200-meter run, the 400-meter run, and the 400-meter relay; in the 1988 Olympics, she received a silver medal in the 1,600-meter relay and placed fourth in the 400-meter run.

Briscoe, Connie

b. December 31, 1952
Washington, D.C.
fields: Literature (novelist)

African American novelist; Connie Briscoe, whose deafness moved her to begin writing, published *Sisters and Lovers* (1994), *Big Girls Don't Cry* (1996), and *A Long Way from Home* (1999); was the first African American and deaf editor of *American Annals of the Deaf.*

Brito, Aristeo

b. Oct. 20, 1942
Ojinaga, Mexico
fields: Literature

Latino writer. As a professor of Spanish literature, Aristeo Brito has worked to make the American literary canon more inclusive and to establish Chicano literature as a permanent section of the Modern Language Association. He began writing in the early 1970's during the Chicano movement, becoming one of the few Mexican American authors to write exclusively in Spanish. Among his books are *Fomento literario: Cuentos; poemas* (1974) and *El Diablo en Texas* (1976; *The Devil in Texas*, 1990).

Britten, Benjamin

full: Edward Benjamin Britten
b. November 22, 1913
Lowestoft, Suffolk, England
d. December 4, 1976
Aldeburgh, Suffolk, England
fields: Music

The outstanding English composer of the mid-twentieth century, Britten established English opera as a viable form and produced a distinguished body of compositions for both professional and amateur musicians. He was also a skilled pianist and conductor, of both his own works and those of other composers.

Broadus, Calvin. *See* Snoop Doggy Dogg

Brock, Gertha

b. ?
fields: Theater and Entertainment (Costume designer)

African American costume designer; Gertha Brock's costuming work was probably best represented in the 1973 play *Ceremonies in Dark Old Men.*

Brock, Lou

b. June 18, 1939
El Dorado, Ark.
fields: Sports (baseball player)

African American baseball player; noted for his base-stealing, Lou Brock entered the major leagues in 1961 and played nineteen seasons with the Chicago Cubs and the St. Louis Cardinals; in 1974 Brock broke Ty Cobb's single-season record when he stole 118 bases, and he surpassed Cobb's lifetime stolen-base record in 1977; Brock retired in 1979 with 3,023 career hits and 938 stolen bases; he was later inducted into the Baseball Hall of Fame.

Brodribb, John Henry. *See* Irving, Henry

Broglie, Louis de

full: Louis Victor Pierre Raymond de Broglie
b. August 15, 1892
Dieppe, France
d. March 19, 1987
Louveciennes, Yvelines, France
fields: Physics

Through his theory of the wave-matter composition of electrons, Broglie introduced a major and necessary component to quantum theory. He was awarded the 1929 Nobel Prize in Physics.

Brokenburr, Robert Lee

b. Nov. 16, 1886
Phoebus, Va.
d. 1974
fields: Government and Politics

African American state politician and political appointee; after working for many years as a private practice attorney, Robert Lee Brokenburr served two terms as an Indiana state senator; he went on to work in the Indiana state and federal court systems at various levels; appointed by President Dwight D. Eisenhower to serve as alternate delegate to the United Nations (1955-1956).

Bronson, Ruth Muskrat

b. 1897
Whitewater, Okla.
d. June 24, 1982
Tucson, Ariz.
fields: Education

Cherokee educator Ruth Muskrat Bronson taught Native American youth about their culture and heritage. She also worked with the Bureau of Indian Affairs, starting in 1931 as director of the bureau's scholarship program, a position she held until 1943, after which she was executive secretary of the National Congress of American Indians.

Bronstein, Lev Davidovich. *See* Trotsky, Leon

Brontë, Anne

b. January 17, 1820
Thornton, Yorkshire, England
d. May 28, 1849
Scarborough, England
fields: Literature

Not as famous as her older sisters Charlotte and Emily, Anne Brontë published two highly regarded novels, *Agnes Grey* (1847) and *The Tenant of Wildfell Hall* (1848), during her short life but died before she reached her full potential as a writer.

Brontë, Charlotte

b. April 21, 1816
Thornton, Yorkshire, England
d. March 31, 1855
Haworth, Yorkshire, England
fields: Literature

One of the major English writers of the Victorian era, Charlotte Brontë wrote four novels, the first of which, *Jane Eyre* (1847), made her instantly famous.

Brontë, Emily

b. July 30, 1818
Thornton, Yorkshire, England

d. December 19, 1848
Haworth, Yorkshire, England
fields: Literature

One of the major English writers of the Victorian era, although not a famous as her older sister Charlotte, Emily Brontë wrote *Wuthering Heights* (1847), which remains a favorite of both readers and filmmakers.

Brooke, Alan Francis

b. July 23, 1883
Bagnères de Bigorre, France
d. June 17, 1963
Harley Wintney, Hampshire, England
fields: Military Affairs

Alan Francis Brooke commanded the 2nd Corps of the British Expeditionary Force (BEF), sent to France at the start of World War II in 1939. Responsible for building the British army to face the expected German invasion. Perhaps most important, Brooke was also Prime Minister Winston Churchill's closest military adviser.

Brooke, Alan Francis. *See* Alanbrooke, First Viscount

Brooke, Edward William

b. Oct. 26, 1919
Washington, D.C.
fields: Government and Politics

African American politician; liberal-wing Republican Edward William Brooke is noted as the first African American since 1874 to be elected to a full term in the U.S. Senate (1966, reelected in 1972); prior positions included practicing law in Massachusetts, serving as attorney general of Massachusetts (1962); after losing his Senate seat to Paul Tsongas in 1978, Brooke returned to practicing law and also became a lobbyist in Washington, D.C.

Brooks, Avery

b. 1949
Evansville, Ind.
fields: Theater and Entertainment, Education

African American actor, singer, and professor; Avery Brooks's television credits include roles as Hawk in the two series *Spenser: For Hire* (1985-1988) and *A Man Called Hawk* (1989) and as Benjamin Cisco, commander of a Starfleet base, in *Star Trek: Deep Space Nine* (beginning in 1993); stage credits include the opera *X: The Life and Times of Malcolm X* (1985), *Paul Robeson* (1988), and *Othello* (1991); also taught theater arts at his alma mater, Rutgers University, beginning in 1977.

Brooks, Elmer T.

b. Dec. 30, 1932
Washington, D.C.
fields: Military Affairs

African American military officer; during his thirty-year career with the U.S. Air Force (1955-1985), Elmer T. Brooks rose to the rank of brigadier general (1981); his postings included missile combat crew commander and instructor, flight control technologist for the Gemini and Apollo space programs (1965-1968), several positions within the Department of Defense, and deputy director for international negotiations with the Organization of the Joint Chiefs of Staff.

Brooks, Emma Tenayuca. *See* Tenayuca, Emma

Brooks, Gwendolyn

b. June 7, 1917
Topeka, Kansas
fields: Literature

The winner of the Pulitzer Prize for Poetry in 1950, Brooks elevated the image of African Americans from a plain, invisible people to a people with a rich and complex culture.

Brooks, Harry William, Jr.

b. May 17, 1928
Indianapolis, Ind.
fields: Military Affairs, Warfare and Conquest

African American military officer; originally commissioned as a second lieutenant in 1949, Harry William Brooks, Jr., achieved the rank of major general (1974) before retiring from the U.S. Army in 1976; his postings included commanding officer, Second Battalion, Fortieth Artillery, 199th Infantry Brigade in Vietnam, commander of the Seventy-second Field Artillery Group in Europe, and director of the Army's equal opportunity programs (1972) in Washington, D.C.

Brooks, Leo Austin

b. Aug. 9, 1932
Washington, D.C.
fields: Military Affairs

African American military officer; during his thirty-year U.S. Army career (1954-1984), Leo Austin Brooks's assignments included assistant chief of staff for supply for the Army in Vietnam, commander of the Sacramento, California, Army depot, director of industrial operations at Fort Hood, Texas, and commanding general of the U.S. Army Troop Support Agency.

Brooks, Romaine

né: Beatrice Romaine Goddard
b. May 1, 1874
Rome, Italy
d. December 7, 1970
Nice, France
fields: Art

Romaine Brooks's lifestyle, paintings, and drawings exemplify female strength, ingenuity, and power of expression. Her portraits of females provide some of the earliest images of modern and independent women.

Broonzy, Big Bill

né: William Lee Conley
b. June 26, 1893
Scott, Miss.
d. Aug. 14, 1958
Chicago, Ill.
fields: Music (blues singer and guitarist)

African American blues singer and guitarist; following the 1927 release of the instrumental "House Rent Stomp," Big Bill Broonzy went on to become the RCA-Bluebird label's biggest recording star; after receiving acclaim for his role as the primitive bluesman in the 1939 "From Spirituals to Swing" concert at Carnegie Hall, Broonzy made additional recordings and came to be considered one of Chicago's top musicians; during the 1950's, he played to adoring crowds in Europe; with writer Yannick Bruynoghe published his autobiography *Big Bill Blues* (1955).

Brothers, Joyce

né: Joyce Diane Bauer
b. October 20, 1929
New York, New York
fields: Psychiatry and Psychology

Joyce Brothers has filled a void in television programming by offering mass therapy to the dejected, lonely, and troubled with gentleness and sincerity on such matters as sex and child-rearing.

Brougham, Henry

full: Henry Peter Brougham
aka: First Baron Brougham and Vaux
b. September 19, 1778
Edinburgh, Scotland
d. May 7, 1868
Cannes, France
fields: Education, Law, Government and Politics

Known as a British reform politician, Brougham sponsored laws to make slave trade a felony, ensure freedom of the press, and spread universal education.

Brouwer, L. E. J.

full: Luitzen Egbertus Jan Brouwer
b. Feb. 27, 1881
Overschie (now a suburb of Rotterdam), the Netherlands
d. Dec. 2, 1966
Blaricum, the Netherlands
fields: Mathematics (mathematical logic and topology)

L. E. J. Brouwer published his fixed-point theorem in "Über Abbildung von Mannigfaltigkeiten" in 1912. He is considered by many to be the founder of the theory of topology. He also established the doctrine of mathematical intuitionism, a view of math as a process that builds its own universe, without any restrictions other than its basis on fundamental mathematical intuition.

Brower, David

b. July 1, 1912
Berkeley, Calif.
fields: Conservation and Environmentalism

Environmental activist. Brower served as executive director of the Sierra Club from 1952 to 1969. During his tenure, the Sierra Club successfully opposed the construction of dams in the Grand Canyon and in Dinosaur National Monument but could not prevent the building of a dam in Utah's Glen Canyon. A policy dispute prompted his 1969 resignation. He subsequently helped to form Friends of the Earth and the Earth Island Institute.

Brown, Bobby

b. 1969
Boston, Mass.
fields: Music (rap, hip-hop, and soul singer)

African American singer and dancer; known for combining rap and hip-hop with the more traditional rhythm and blues and soul, Bobby Brown debuted recording and performing with the group New Edition; he left the group for a solo career in 1986, and his second solo album *Don't Be Cruel*, containing the top hit "My Prerogative," sold almost six million copies; Brown's hit "On Our Own" was featured in the *Ghostbusters II* film and soundtrack (1989); in 1992, married singer Whitney Houston.

Brown, Charlotte Hawkins

b. June 11, 1883
Henderson, N.C.
d. January 11, 1961
Greensboro, N.C.
fields: Education, Civil Rights

African American educator and civil rights advocate. In 1902 Charlotte Brown founded and presided over the Palmer Memorial Institute in rural North Carolina, an educational institution for African American children; founded the national Council of Negro Women, the North Carolina Federation of Negro Women's Clubs, of which she was president from 1915 to 1936, and the Commision on Interracial Cooperation (1919). She also served on the national board of the Young Women's Christian Association. A prolific writer, Brown earned renown as the "First Lady of Social Graces" with the publication of her book *The Correct Thing to Do, to Say, and to Wear* (1941). She was an ardent champion of civil rights and of efforts to achieve interracial harmony, especially among women.

Brown, Clara

b. 1800?
Kentucky
d. c. 1880
fields: Historical Figure

African American pioneer; a freed slave believed to be the first African American woman to reside in Colorado, Clara Brown established a laundry business in Central City to earn money to buy freedom for enslaved family members; she went on to own several gold mines.

Brown, Claude

b. Feb. 23, 1937
New York, N.Y.
fields: Literature

African American lecturer and author; Claude Brown moved from gang membership, street crime, and reform school to graduating from Howard University with a B.A. (1965); his first book, *Manchild in the Promised Land* (1965), a study of the brutality of ghetto life, achieved sixth place on the best-seller list; he continued to write, producing the 1976 novel *The Children of Ham* and contributing to various periodicals.

Brown, Clifford

aka: Brownie
b. Oct. 30, 1930
Wilmington, Del.
d. June 26, 1956
Pennsylvania
fields: Music (trumpeter)

African American jazz trumpeter; one of the premier trumpeters of the 1950's, Clifford Brown first recorded with Chris Powell's rhythm-and-blues band, the Blue Flames (1952), toured Europe with Lionel Hampton's band (1953), and worked with Art Blakey's Jazz Messengers before achieving his greatest recognition playing with Max Roach in the Brown/Roach Quintet; he demonstrated his formidable and brilliant jazz technique with the quintet, a group which greatly influenced the development of bebop, until his death in an automobile accident.

Brown, Corrine

b. November 11, 1946
Jacksonville, Fla.
fields: Government and Politics (politician and educator)

African American politician and educator; Corrine Brown took office as a freshman representative in the 103rd Congress in January of 1993 and was the first African American elected to represent the state of Florida in Congress. She was reelected in 1994, 1996, and 1998.

Brown, Coverdale, Jr.

b. ?
New Orleans, La.
fields: Military Affairs

African American military officer; by the 1990's, Coverdale Brown, Jr., had achieved the rank of brigadier general; in Vietnam he commanded a military intelligence battalion; at the Defense Intelligence Agency in Washington, D.C., he served in the Directorate for Intelligence Research and was also assistant vice director for estimates and deputy vice director for foreign intelligence.

Brown, Dorothy Lavinia

b. Jan. 7, 1919
Philadelphia, Pa.
fields: Medicine, Education

African American physician and educator; Dorothy Lavinia Brown is noted as the South's first African American general surgeon; from 1960 to 1983, served as clinical professor of surgery at Meharry Medical Center and chief of surgery at Riverside Hospital; as the first African American woman to win a seat in the Tennessee legislature (1966), fought for abortion rights in cases of incest or rape or to save the mother's life; she was not reelected; served as director of student health services at Meharry College and at Nashville's Fisk University.

Brown, Earlene

b. 1934 or 1935
fields: Sports (shot put and discus thrower)

African American shot put and discus thrower; at 250 pounds, Earlene Brown received the 1960 Olympic bronze medal in the shot put for her throw of 53 feet, 10¼ inches; in three consecutive Olympics, 1956, 1960, and 1964, she reached the final in the shot put (the first athlete to do so); the first American woman to throw beyond the fifty foot mark in the shot put.

Brown, Elaine

b. ?
fields: Civil Rights, Social Reform

African American social activist; in November, 1974, Elaine Brown took over leadership of the Black Panther Party following Huey Newton's indictment for murder; under Brown's leadership, a variety of community programs were established in Oakland, California, including health clinics, legal aid agencies, children's programs, and the distribution of free food to the poor; in 1973 and 1975, Brown ran unsuccessfully for a seat on the Oakland city council, but she was appointed to several city commissions; attended the Democratic National Convention as a Jerry Brown delegate in 1976; played a pivotal role in the election of Oakland's first black mayor.

Brown, Ernest

b. ?
fields: Dance, Theater and Entertainment

African American dancer and comedian; as half of the tap team Cook and Brown, four-foot, ten-inch-tall Ernest Brown joined with six-foot-tall Charles "Cookie" Cook in a vaudeville and nightclub act that combined acrobatics with vernacular dance, comedy, and satire; they performed in New York clubs throughout the 1930's and appeared in a number of films including *52nd Street* (1937) and *Toot That Trumpet* (1941); they appeared in the 1948 Broadway musical *Kiss Me Kate*; Brown participated in a tap dance revival at the Newport Jazz Festival in the 1960's.

Brown, Georg Stanford

b. June 24, 1943
Havana, Cuba
fields: Television (actor and director)

African American actor and director; Georg Stanford Brown is credited with many television, theater, and film appearances; nominated for an Emmy for his role in the 1977 television miniseries *Roots*; received an Emmy Award as director of an episode of the television series *Cagney and Lacey*.

Brown, George

b. November 29, 1818
Alloa, Scotland
d. May 9, 1880
Toronto, Canada
fields: Journalism, Publishing, Government and Politics

In 1844, Brown became publisher of the Toronto *Globe* and eventually turned it into a leading Canadian newspaper that backed political reform. Brown became a member of the Canadian Parliament in 1851 and continued to be active in both publishing and politics until his death in 1880.

Brown, George L.

b. July 1, 1926
Lawrence, Kans.
fields: Government and Politics, Business and Industry

African American state legislator and business executive; while working as a writer and editor for the *Denver Post* (1950-1965), George L. Brown was elected to the Colorado State House of Representatives (1955); Colorado state senator (1956-1974); assistant director of the Denver Housing Authority (1965-1969); lieutenant governor of Colorado (1975-1979); rose from vice president of marketing for Grumman Ecosystems (1979) to vice president of their Washington, D.C., office (1981).

Brown, H. Rap

full: Hubert Gerold Brown
aka: Jamil Abdullah Al-Amin
b. Oct. 4, 1943
Baton Rouge, La.
fields: Civil Rights

African American civil rights activist; H. Rap Brown became leader of the Student Nonviolent Coordinating Committee in 1967; charged with inciting riot in Cambridge, Maryland (1967) and convicted of carrying a gun across state lines (1968); officer in the Black Panther Party; published *Die Nigger Die* (1969); while in prison for a robbery conviction, converted to Islam, taking the name Jamil Abdullah Al-Amin; leader of Community Mosque in Atlanta, Georgia.

Brown, Hallie Q.

b. Mar. 10, 1845
Pittsburgh, Pa.
d. Sept. 16, 1949
Wilberforce, Ohio
fields: Education, Civil Rights, Social Reform

African American educator, reformer, and author; as a college student, Hallie Q. Brown traveled extensively crusading for women's rights and demanding an end to racial discrimination; she first taught school on plantations in South Carolina and Mississippi; served as dean at Allen University, South Carolina (1885-1887); principal at Tuskegee Institute, Alabama (1890's); professor of education and English at her alma mater, Wilberforce University, Ohio; president of National Association of Colored Women (1921); compiled and edited *Homespun Heroines and Other Women of Distinction* (1926).

Brown, Helen Gurley

né: Helen Gurley
b. February 18, 1922
Green Forest, Arkansas
fields: Publishing

Author of several books on the single life and editor of *Cosmopolitan* magazine, Brown legitimized and defined the single lifestyle for a generation.

Brown, Helen Hayes. *See* Hayes, Helen

Brown, Henry Billings

b. 1836
d. 1913
fields: Law

U.S. Supreme Court justice, 1891-1906; appointed by President Harrison. Author of "separate but equal" doctrine concerning racial classifications. Significant opinions: *Pollock v. Farmers' Loan & Trust Co.*, 158 U.S. 601 (1895, dissenting opinion); *Plessy v. Ferguson*, 163 U.S. 537 (1896); *Holden v. Hardy*, 169 U.S. 366 (1898).

Brown, Henry "Box"

full: Henry Brown
b. 1816
Richmond, Va.
d. c. 1860
fields: Historical Figure

Escaped African American slave; the autobiography, *Narrative of Henry Box Brown Who Escaped from Slavery Enclosed in a Box Three Feet Long and Two Wide* (1849), describes Henry "Box" Brown's escape from slavery; after Brown's wife and children were sold by his master, Brown enlisted the help of Samuel A. Smith, a white man, who boxed up Brown and freighted him to abolitionists in Philadelphia, Pa.; Brown became a lecturer on the abolitionist circuit but was forced to take refuge in England following passage of the Fugitive Slave Law (1850).

Brown, James

b. May 3, 1933
Barnwell, South Carolina
fields: Music (soul)

Known as the "Godfather of Soul," as well as the "Hardest-Working Man in Show Business," James Brown became a legend in the music business during the 1960's and early 1970's; singles include "Please, Please, Please" (1956), "Try Me" (1958), "Papa's Got a Brand New Bag" (1965), and "Say It Loud, I'm Black and I'm Proud" (1968). Brown's political activism during the 1960's led to much criticism. In 1968, the Internal Revenue Service (IRS) demanded almost two million dollars in back taxes; Brown revived his career in the 1980's with such hits as "Living in America" (1985); from 1988 to 1991, he served time in prison for assault and continued to be dogged by charges from the IRS for an outstanding tax debt of eleven million dollars; in the late 1990's, Brown filed a lawsuit against the U.S. Customs Service for the return of $260,743; inducted into the Rock and Roll Hall of Fame in 1986, the same year he published his autobiography *James Brown: Godfather of Soul*.

Brown, Jesse

b. March 27, 1944
Detroit, Mich.
fields: Government and Politics (military veteran and political appointee)

African American military veteran and political appointee. Jesse Brown, a Vietnam veteran who was awarded the Purple Heart, became the first black executive director of the nonprofit Disabled American Veterans organization. His lobbying skills led to an appointment by President Bill Clinton in 1993 as secretary of the Veterans Affairs Department. He resigned in 1997 to pursue other interests.

Brown, Jim

b. February 17, 1936
St. Simons Island, Georgia
fields: Sports (football)

One of professional football's greatest players. Jim Brown also achieved recognition for his outspoken nature and his social activism; drafted by the Cleveland Browns of the National Football League, for whom he played for nine seasons; named the league's rookie of the year in 1958 and its player of the year in 1958, 1963, and 1965; appeared in such Hollywood films as *The Dirty Dozen* (1967), *Ice Station Zebra* (1968), *Three the Hard Way* (1975), and *I'm Gonna Get You Sucka* (1988); elected to the Pro Football Hall of Fame in Canton, Ohio, in 1971.

Brown, John

b. May 9, 1800
Torrington, Connecticut
d. December 2, 1859
Charlestown, West Virginia
fields: Social Reform (abolitionism)

Brown has come to symbolize the struggle over the abolition of slavery in the United States. He was the catalyst for change from polite debate and parliamentary maneuvering aimed at modification of the institution to physical violence and a direct onslaught on Southern territory and the supporters of slavery.

Brown, John Mitchell, Sr.

b. Dec. 11, 1929
Vicksburg, Miss.
fields: Warfare and Conquest, Military Affairs

African American army officer; during his thirty-three year U.S. Army career (1955-1988), John Mitchell Brown, Sr., achieved the rank of major general; he earned many commendations during combat duty as an infantry battalion commander and as assistant division commander in Korea and Vietnam; during his later career he served as a comptroller.

Brown, Joyce

b. Dec. 1, 1920
New York, N.Y.
fields: Music (conductor)

African American conductor; on March 15, 1970, Joyce Brown became the first African American woman to conduct the opening of a Broadway musical (*Purlie*); she served as musical director for the Alvin Ailey Ballet Company and for singers Diahann Carroll and Norman Atkins and dancers Gower and Marge Champion.

Brown, Lancelot

b. 1716
Kirkharle, Northumberland, England
d. February 6, 1783
London, England
fields: Landscape Architecture

Building on the pioneering work of William Kent, Brown brought to perfection the "natural" school of landscaping. This school, using only trees, water, and lawns, sought to transform the estates of the English gentry into vast prospects which, while appearing to be the work of nature, were meant to be superior, aesthetically, to anything nature could do.

Brown, Les

full: Leslie Calvin Brown
b. February 17, 1945
Miami, Fla.
fields: Social Reform (motivational speaker and author)

African American motivational speaker and author; four years after beginning his public speaking career, former legislator Les Brown was the first African American to receive the prestigious Council of Peers Award for Excellence, in 1989.

Brown, Louise

full: Louise Joy Brown
b. July 25, 1978
England
fields: Historical Figure

Louise Brown was the first baby born to be conceived outside a mother's body. Her parents, Gilbert and Lesley Brown, were childless because Lesley's Fallopian tubes were blocked. To overcome this biological problem, doctors used in vitro technology, in which an egg was surgically removed from the mother and was combined with ejaculated sperm from the father in a laboratory dish to induce conception or fertilization. The fertilized egg was then implanted into the mother's uterus, where its development culminated in the birth of Louise Joy Brown.

Brown, Margaret Wise

b. May 23, 1910
New York, New York
d. November 13, 1952
Nice, France
fields: Literature

The author of one hundred books for children, as well as numerous other works, Brown brought a new vitality and art to the field of juvenile literature.

Brown, Marion

b. Sept. 8, 1935
Atlanta, Ga.
fields: Music (jazz alto saxophone player)

African American jazz alto saxophone player; from 1962 to 1967, Marion Brown played with and was influenced by Sun Ra, Archie Shepp, and John Coltrane; coming from a bebop background, Brown reinterprets standard jazz pieces and uses his own compositions to create new forms.

Brown, Oscar, Jr.

b. Oct. 10, 1926
Chicago, Ill.
fields: Music (singer and songwriter)

African American vocalist and songwriter; Oscar Brown, Jr., performed primarily in theater and nightclub settings; he wrote lyrics for multiple artists including Miles Davis and Nat Adderley; in the year 1960 he recorded *Sin and Soul* and some of his songs were included in *We Insist! Freedom Now Suite*; hosted the television program *Jazz Scene USA* (1962).

Brown, Pete

b. Feb. 2, 1935
Port Gibson, Mo.
fields: Sports (golfer)

African American golfer; with his win at the Waco Turner Open in 1964, Pete Brown became the first African American golfer to win an official PGA tournament; after turning professional in 1954, Brown had won the United Golf Association title and the Negro National Open in both 1961 and 1962; a sudden-death playoff at the 1970 San Diego Open provided his biggest win, over British golfer Tony Jacklin.

Brown, Rachel Fuller

b. November 23, 1898
Springfield, Massachusetts
d. January 14, 1980
Albany, New York
fields: Biochemistry, Medicine

With microbiologist Elizabeth Hazen, Brown discovered and purified the first antifungal antibiotic used to treat human disease. This discovery led to the two scientists' becoming the first women to receive the Chemical Pioneer Award from the American Institute of Chemists.

Brown, Ray

b. Oct. 13, 1926
Philadelphia, Pa.
fields: Music (jazz bassist)

African American bassist; after early work with the pioneers of bebop, participating in recording sessions with Dizzy Gillespie, Charlie Parker, and Bud Powell, Ray Brown went on to direct his own group (primarily backing up his wife, Ella Fitzgerald); from the early 1950's to 1966, he was a double bassist with the Oscar Peterson trio, during which time he also mastered the cello; he later worked as a freelance performer and studio artist, manager, and producer.

Brown, Rita Mae

b. November 28, 1944
Hanover, Pennsylvania
fields: Literature, Women's Rights

Through her novels, poems, essays, and political activity, Rita Mae Brown has brought lesbian existence "out of the closet" and into popular awareness.

Brown, Robert

b. Dec. 8, 1941
Cleveland, Ohio
fields: Sports (football player)

African American football player; after playing tackle for the University of Nebraska, Robert Brown was picked up by the Philadelphia Eagles, the number-one 1964 draft pick of the National Football League; between 1965 and 1972, Brown played in six All-Pro games.

Brown, Ronald H.

full: Ronald Harmon Brown
b. August 1, 1941
Washington, D.C.
d. April 3, 1996
Sveti Ivan, near Dubrovnik, Croatia
fields: Government and Politics

African American politician. Ronald H. Brown became the first African American to head the national organization of either major party. As chairman of the Democratic National Party, Brown downplayed racial questions and other potential sources of division, made particular efforts to win over conservative white voters who had left the party in the 1980's, and pressed efforts to register new Democratic voters. In 1993 President Bill Clinton appointed Brown to serve on his cabinet as secretary of commerce. He was highly regarded and aggressively pursued export opportunities for U.S. businesses abroad.

Brown, Roy

b. Sept. 10, 1925
New Orleans, La.
d. May 25, 1981
Pacoima, Calif.
fields: Music (rock-and-roll musician)

African American rock-and-roll musician; a pioneer rock-and-roll performer during the late 1940's and 1950's, Roy Brown achieved his greatest success with the 1947 release of "Good Rockin' Tonight"; his victimization by unscrupulous managers prevented a rise to fame that he and others thought he deserved.

Brown, Ruth Weston

b. Jan. 30, 1928
Portsmouth, Va.
fields: Music (rhythm-and-blues and pop singer), Theater and Entertainment

African American singer and stage actress; Ruth Weston Brown's fame began in 1949 with such Atlantic rhythm-and-blues recordings as "So Long," "I'll Get Along Somehow," and the biggest hit "Mama He Treats Your Daughter Mean"; her cross over pop hit "Lucky Lips" (1957) assured her 1950's stardom; Brown pursued an acting career in the 1970's, appearing in the civil rights musical *Selma* and on the television sitcom *Hello Larry*; received the 1989 Tony Award for her performance in the jazz musical *Black and Blue*.

Brown, Sterling A.

full: Sterling Allen Brown
b. May 1, 1901
Washington, D.C.
d. Jan. 13, 1989
Takoma Park, Md.
fields: Literature, Education, Language and Linguistics

African American poet and literary and linguistic historian, critic, and teacher, remembered as a champion of the African American author's expression of the black American experience; Sterling A. Brown's poems, which incorporate the themes of black folk epics, dialect, and the rhythms of work songs, have been collected in *Southern Road* (1932), *The Last Ride of Wild Bill and Eleven Narrative Poems* (1975), and *The Collected Poems of Sterling A. Brown* (1980). Brown had a long teaching career of visiting professorships and a permanent position at Howard University (1929-1969); named Poet Laureate of the District of Columbia (1984).

Brown, Tony

full: William Anthony Brown
b. Apr. 11, 1933
Charleston, W.Va.
fields: Television

African American television broadcaster and producer; a winner of many awards for his contributions to the field of public affairs broadcasting, Tony Brown is best known as the host and producer of *Tony Brown's Journal*, the longest running public affairs program on television; founded the Howard University School of Communication and served as its first dean (1971-1974).

Brown, Willa B.

b. ?
Glasgow, Ky.
fields: Aviation and Space Exploration

African American pilot; Willa B. Brown enlisted the backing of Eleanor Roosevelt and gained admittance of African American pilots into the Army Air Force; Brown later served as a Civil Air Patrol lieutenant and ran a flying school in the Chicago, Illinois area.

Brown, William E., Jr.

b. ?
New York, N.Y.
fields: Warfare and Conquest

African American military officer; during his U.S. Air Force career, William E. Brown, Jr., achieved the rank of major general; as a command pilot he flew with fighter-interceptor squadrons and with the New York Air Defense Sector and logged more than forty-nine hundred hours of flying time; commendations include the Legion of Merit, the Distinguished Flying Cross, the Air Force Commendation Medal, the Purple Heart, and the Republic of Korea Presidential Unit Citation.

Brown, William Wells

b. 1815
Lexington, Ky.
d. Nov. 6, 1884
Chelsea, Mass.
fields: Literature, Social Reform

African American author and abolitionist; William Wells Brown is believed to be the first African American to publish a novel, *Clotel: Or, The President's Daughter: A Narrative of Slave Life in the United States* (published in England, 1853); Brown is also credited with two abolitionist plays, one of which, *The Escape: Or, A Leap for Freedom* (1858), is believed to be the first drama published by an African American; his first work, *Narrative of William W. Brown, a Fugitive Slave, Written by Himself*, was created in 1847; following his own escape from slavery in 1834, Brown participated in the Underground Railroad and became an abolitionist lecturer and journalist; he traveling abroad (1849-1854), during which time friends in England purchased his freedom.

Brown, Willie L., Jr.

b. March 20, 1934
Mineola, Tex.
fields: Government and Politics

African American politician and lawyer. Willie L. Brown was elected to the California State Assembly in 1964, beginning thirty years of service there. He was elected speaker of the assembly in 1980 and held that office for nearly fifteen years, leaving in 1995 only because of newly passed term-limit laws. As speaker of the assembly, Brown was responsible for establishing a state holiday in honor of Martin Luther King, Jr.'s birthday, decriminalizing homosexuality, and enacting mandatory seat-belt laws. He introduced laws to compensate crime victims, to regulate health care cost to low-income families, and to reduce costly court delays. He constantly defended the Democratic Party's position on affirmative action, education, and welfare. Brown took the oath of office as the first African American mayor of San Francisco on January 8, 1996.

Browne, Roscoe Lee

b. May 2, 1925
Woodbury, N.J.
fields: Theater and Entertainment, Film, Television

African American actor; Roscoe Lee Browne, who began acting at age thirty-one, has appeared on stage, in film, and on television; theater credits include *Julius Caesar* (1957) and *Benito Cereno* (1974); film credits include *Black Like Me* (1964), *The Cowboys* (1972), and *Legal Eagles* (1986); television credits include *The Defenders* (1963), the miniseries *King* (1979), and *The Cosby Show* (1986).

Browne, Vivian

b. Apr. 26, 1929
Laurel, Fla.
fields: Art (painter), Education

African American painter and educator; incorporating painting and photographic techniques, Vivian Browne is known for creating large, abstract, mixed-media works; before joining the art faculty of Rutgers University in the 1970's, Browne taught at the secondary level; in 1965 she received the 1965 Achievement Award from the National Association of Business and Professional Negro Women.

Brownie. *See* Brown, Clifford

Browning, Elizabeth Barrett

né: Elizabeth Barrett
b. March 6, 1806
Coxhoe Hall, County Durham, England
d. June 29, 1861
Florence, Italy
fields: Literature

Browning was the most respected woman poet of the Victorian age. Her work is known for its formal iconoclasm, impetuosity of tone, and political content.

Brownmiller, Susan

b. February 15, 1935
New York, N.Y.
fields: Journalism, Literature, Women's Rights

A writer and lecturer, Susan Brownmiller is an antipornography activist best known for her book *Against Our Will: Men, Women, and Rape* (1975), in which she argues that men use rape to dominate women and that the fear of rape makes women more submissive; cofounded the New York Radical Feminists (1968); as a freelance journalist and a staff writer for the *Village Voice*, she protested against such traditional women's magazines as *Ladies' Home Journal* for their portrayals of submissive womanhood; named one of *Time* magazine's Women of the Year in 1975; other published works include *Femininity* (1984) and the novel *Waverly Place* (1989), which deals with battered women and child abuse; founded Women Against Pornography.

Broz, Josip. *See* Tito

Bruce, Blanche Kelso

b. Mar. 1, 1841
Farmville, Va.
d. Mar. 17, 1898
Washington, D.C.
fields: Government and Politics

African American politician; Blanche Kelso Bruce was born a slave and after the Civil War built a fortune as a plantation owner; served in various local and state positions in Mississippi; was a U.S. senator from Mississippi (Republican), 1875-1881, became the first African American to serve a full term; was a staunch defender of black, Chinese, and American Indian rights; with U.S. register of treasury, 1881-1889, 1895-1898; worked as recorder of deeds, District of Columbia, 1889-1895.

Bruce, James

b. December 14, 1730
Kinnaird, Stirlingshire, Scotland
d. April 27, 1794
Kinnaird, Stirlingshire, Scotland
fields: Exploration and Colonization

Bruce explored extensively along the Blue Nile and in Ethiopia, and his endeavors did much to direct European attention to the interior of Africa in the late eighteenth century.

Bruce, Lenny

né: Leonard Alfred Schneider
b. October 13, 1925
Mineola, New York
d. August 3, 1966
Los Angeles, California
fields: Theater and Entertainment

One of the most controversial entertainers of the early 1960's. Lenny Bruce satirized political, sexual, religious, and moral attitudes; arrested nineteen times, mostly on obscenity charges (also charged with use and possession of narcotics); though never imprisoned, the controversies surrounding his legal problems resulted in a sharp reduction in his professional engagements; died of a morphine overdose in 1966.

Bruce, Louis R.

aka: Agwelius (Swift)
b. Dec. 30, 1906
Onondaga Reservation near Syracuse, N.Y.
d. May 20, 1989
Arlington, Va.
fields: Native American Affairs, Government and Politics

Oglala Sioux leader and BIA commissioner; Louis R. Bruce served as commissioner of the Bureau of Indian Affairs (BIA) during the late 1960's and early 1970's when Native American activism was strong; from 1935 to 1941, he served as New York state director of Indian projects for the National Youth Administration; in 1957 he created the National American Indian Youth Conference; in 1969 Bruce was named commissioner of the Bureau of Indian Affairs by President Richard Nixon; he appointed Native Americans to influential positions and encountered opposition from interests that had benefited from keeping Indians in subordinate positions; Bruce and most of his top assistants were subsequently fired by Nixon, less than a week before the 1972 presidential election.

Bruce, Robert

b. July 11, 1274
Turnberry Castle, Carrick, Scotland
d. June 7, 1329
Cardross, Scotland
fields: Monarchy, Government and Politics, Diplomacy

Bruce led Scotland to victory in the struggle for independence from English control. As king of Scotland, he consolidated Scottish political autonomy and finally secured English recognition of Scotland as an independent nation in the Treaty of Edinburgh, signed by King Edward III in 1328.

Bruce, Stanley

full: Stanley Melbourne Bruce
b. April 15, 1883
Melbourne, Australia
d. August 25, 1967
London, England
fields: Government and Politics

Prime minister of Australia from 1923 to 1929. Stanley Bruce was Nationalist Party leader and, beginning in 1929, head of coalition Nationalist and Country Party government. The Bruce era was characterized as one of "men, money, markets." Widely seen as antilabor, and in the elections of 1929, the Nationalists lost to the Labor Party by a wide margin. In England during World War II, Bruce mediated between Australian and British concerns regarding troop deployment.

Bruce-Novoa, Juan D.

b. June 20, 1944
San José, Costa Rica
fields: Scholarship

Latino scholar. While working as a professor of Spanish, Juan D. Bruce-Novoa became a renowned figure in Chicano criticism. His published interviews with important Mexican American writers such as Rudolfo Anaya and Tomás Rivera are among his most important contributions to Chicano scholarship. His published works include *Chicano Authors: Inquiry by Interview* (1980), *Chicano Poetry: A Response to Chaos* (1982), *La literatura chicana a través de sus autores* (1983; editor, with José Guillermo Saaverdar), *Antología retrospectiva del cuento chicano* (1988), and *RetroSpace: Collected Essays on Chicano Literature* (1990).

Bruckner, Anton

b. September 4, 1824
Ansfelden, Austro-Hungarian Empire
d. October 11, 1896
Vienna, Austro-Hungarian Empire
fields: Music

Rising from modest rural origins, Bruckner first established himself as one of the leading organists of his time, then persevered in his creative work to produce a great series of choral and symphonic works. Musically eloquent and possessing a unique sense of spiritual aspiration, the finest of Bruckner's large-scale compositions belong to the essential repertoire of nineteenth century music.

Bruegel, Pieter, the Elder

b. c. 1525
near Brée, Brabant
d. September 5, 1569
Brussels
fields: Art

In an era when portraiture dominated, Bruegel teamed his subjects with their larger environment, greatly elevating landscape art. Bruegel's miniaturist style also chronicled the many facets of everyday sixteenth century Flemish life.

Brundtland, Gro Harlem

né: Gro Harlem
b. April 20, 1939
Oslo, Norway
fields: Government and Politics

Gro Harlem Brundtland was the first woman prime minister of Norway, serving in 1981, from 1986 to 1989, and again from 1990 to 1996. Her ideas on the environment and economic development won her an international reputation and gained her the nickname "the mother of sustainable development." In 1998, named head of the World Health Organization.

Brunel, Isambard Kingdom

b. April 9, 1806
Portsmouth, England
d. September 15, 1859
London, England
fields: Engineering

Brunel was the most important developer of iron and steamship construction and the guiding force in the building of the Great Western Railway. Perhaps more important, he continued the tradition begun by his father, Marc Isambard Brunel, of capturing the imagination of the public with great engineering projects. Thus he symbolized the budding age of technology.

Brunel, Marc Isambard

b. April 25, 1769
Hacqueville, France
d. December 12, 1849
London, England
fields: Engineering

Brunel was one of the leaders in mechanizing production during the early nineteenth century. He was also the most famous civil engineer of his day.

Brunelleschi, Filippo

b. 1377
Florence
d. April 15, 1446
Florence
fields: Architecture, Art, Engineering

Brunelleschi's architectural accomplishments, as well as his dedication to the principles of perspective, established a vigorous new classical Renaissance style that influenced building design for centuries.

Bruner, Jerome

full: Jerome Seymour Bruner
b. October 1, 1915
New York, N.Y.
fields: Sociology, Psychiatry and Psychology

While teaching psychology at Harvard University, Jerome Seymour Bruner developed a theory of perception contradicting the law of central tendency, which holds that guesses about size or magnitude err toward the middle. In 1960 he opened Harvard's Center for Cognitive Studies. He also developed the multistage theory of children's cognitive development, which articulated the enactive, iconic, and symbolic modes of representation. He later taught at England's Oxford University, where he examined children's transition from "prelinguistic to linguistic" communication. Bruner's work was instrumental in American educational reform and contributed to establishment of government funded day-care centers and early childhood education programs.

Bruni, Leonardo

b. c. 1370
Arezzo, Republic of Florence
d. March 9, 1444
Florence
fields: Historiography, Literature, Government and Politics

Bruni was a leading Italian Renaissance figure, a Humanist scholar whose work was important in the development of historiography.

Brunner, Emil

full: Heinrich Emil Brunner
b. December 23, 1889
Winterthur, Switzerland
d. April 6, 1966
Zurich, Switzerland
fields: Church Reform, Religion and Theology

A leading and articulate exponent of the "new theology" or "dialectical theology" movement that dominated European theology during the 1920's and 1930's and profoundly influenced American theology, Brunner lectured widely, published frequently, and was an influential and respected theologian, especially in English-speaking religious circles. His work on behalf of such international organizations as the Young Men's Christian Association (YMCA) and the Ecumenical Movement earned for Brunner the reputation of a world Christian theologian.

Bruno, Giordano

né: Filippo Bruno
b. 1548
Nola, near Naples
d. February 17, 1600
Rome
fields: Philosophy, Astronomy

With his daring and speculative theories in astronomy and philosophy, Bruno anticipated many of the achievements of modern science, but his stubborn personality and arcane interests brought him into inevitable conflict with the authorities of his time.

Brutus, Marcus Junius

b. 85 b.c.e.
probably Rome
d. October 23, 42 b.c.e.
Philippi, Greece
fields: Government and Politics, Warfare and Conquest

As leader and conscience of the conspiracy that assassinated the dictator Julius Caesar, Brutus attempted to restore the Roman Republic but instead ushered in the Empire.

Bryan, Andrew

b. 1737
Goose Creek, S.C.
d. 1812
fields: Religion and Theology

African American clergyman; ordained in 1788, Andrew Bryan purchased his own freedom from slavery and established one of Georgia's first African American Baptist churches, the First African/First Bryan Baptist Church in Savannah.

Bryan, William Jennings

b. March 19, 1860
Salem, Illinois
d. July 26, 1925
Dayton, Tennessee
fields: Government and Politics

With his crusader's zeal for righteousness and a determination to champion the cause of the common man, Bryan used his dramatic oratorical skills to gain the leadership of the Democratic Party from 1896 to 1912. Three times he won the Democratic nomination for president, but he lost all three elections.

Bryant, Anita

b. March 25, 1940
Barnsdall, Oklahoma
fields: Music, Social Reform

An American pop singer, Anita Bryant started her entertainment career by performing on local radio and television stations during her teen years. After winning a beauty pageant, she became a runner-up for Miss America. She went on to record several gold records and write a best-selling book. A Christian fundamentalist, she damaged her mainstream recording career in the late 1970's by speaking out aggressively against homosexuality and gay rights.

Bryant, Cunningham Campbell

b. Aug. 8, 1921
Clifton, Va.
fields: Military Affairs, Warfare and Conquest

African American military officer; Cunningham Campbell Bryant served with the U.S. Army (1943-1949, 1969-1971) and with the National Guard; National Guard postings included executive officer of the 140th Engineering Battalion (1952-1958) and commandant at the Officer Candidate School (1964-1967); he achieved the rank of major general.

Bryant, Joyce

b. 1928
San Francisco, Calif.
fields: Music (nightclub singer and opera soprano)

African American nightclub singer and opera soprano; from the mid-1940's to the mid-1950's, Joyce Bryant built a career as a nightclub singer sporting unusual silver-dyed hair; after taking time out to earn a college degree (1955-1959), Bryant pursued operatic voice training; during her three years with the New York City Opera, her most celebrated role was as Bess in *Porgy and Bess* (1961); she appeared with various European opera companies (1967-1977) and returned to the U.S. to perform once again on the nightclub circuit.

Bryant, Louise

né: Anna Louisa Mohan
b. December 5, 1885
San Francisco, California
d. January 6, 1936
Sèvres, France
fields: Journalism

An international correspondent who published extensively on the subject of radical politics, Louise Bryant both witnessed and reported on the Russian Revolution.

Bryant, Wayne Richard

b. November 7, 1947
Camden, N.J.
fields: Law (attorney and county official)

African American attorney and county official; Wayne Richard Bryant received the Award of Merit from the New Jersey County Transportation Association and the Distinguished Service Award from the Camden County Planning Board; in 1992, received the Arthur Armitage Distinguished Alumni Award from the Rutgers University Law School.

Bryant, William Benson

b. Sept. 18, 1911
Wetumpka, Ala.
fields: Law

African American federal judge; after serving in the U.S. Army (1943-1947), William Benson Bryant ran a private law practice in Washington, D.C.; assistant to the U.S. attorney for the District of Columbia (1951-1954); partner in the firm of Houston, Bryant and Gardner (1954-1965); in 1965 became the first African American to serve as a judge at the district court level when he was appointed U.S. district judge for the District of Columbia by President Lyndon B. Johnson; eventually rose to the rank of senior U.S. district judge.

Bryant, William Cullen

b. November 3, 1794
Cummington, Massachusetts
d. June 12, 1878
New York, New York
fields: Literature (poetry), Journalism

As a poet, Bryant is often described as a transitional figure because of his fluency in exploiting Romantic themes drawn from nature in conventional neoclassical verse forms. In his half-century as an editor for the New York *Evening Post*, he was a vigorous spokesman for American liberal thought.

Bryson, Robert Peabo

b. Apr. 13, 1951
Greenville, S.C.
fields: Music (soul ballad singer)

African American singer; Robert Peabo Bryson's most representative work appeared under the Capitol Records label: the classic album *Reaching for the Sky*, the steamy ballad collection *Crosswinds* (1979), and *Can You Stop the Rain* (1991); underappreciated as a musical talent, Bryson produced work that was not funky enough for European audiences and was considered overproduced by American fans of soul music; appeared in the musical comedy *A Woman Like That* (1991).

Brzezinski, Zbigniew

full: Zbigniew Kazimierz Brzezinski
b. March 28, 1928
Warsaw, Poland
fields: Diplomacy, Government and Politics

Zbigniew Brzezinski was a cofounder of the Trilateral Commission (1973) and was U.S. national security adviser during the Jimmy Carter administration (1977-1981). Instrumental in negotiating several important treaties signed between the Soviet Union and the United States, including the Strategic Arms Limitation Talks II (SALT II) treaty in 1979. Influential books by Brzezinski include *The Soviet Bloc: Unity and Conflict* (1960) and *Ideology and Power in Soviet Politics* (1967).

Buaken, Manuel

b. April, 1911
Philippines
fields: Journalism, Publishing

Manuel Buaken, a Filipino, came to the United States in 1927 to attend Princeton University on a scholarship. After his arrival, he gave up the scholarship and instead worked as a domestic servant, janitor, dishwasher, and farmworker. He later served with the U.S. Army's First Filipino Infantry Regiment in World War II. From these experiences, he created *I Have Lived with the American People* (1948), a memoir presenting the poverty, racial prejudice, and mistreatment endured by Filipino immigrants.

Bubbles, John

né: John William Sublett
b. Feb. 19, 1902
Louisville, Ky.
d. May 18, 1986
Baldwin Hills, Calif.
fields: Dance; Theater and Entertainment

African American dancer; considered the father of rhythm tap dancing, John Bubbles teamed with musician Ford Lee "Buck" Washington to form the successful vaudeville team of Buck and Bubbles; following their appearance as headliners on the 1920's Keith vaudeville circuit, they moved on to Broadway musicals, appearing in *Weather Clear-Track Fast* (1927) and *Blackbirds of 1930*; Bubbles debuted the character of Sportin' Life in Gershwin's 1935 opera *Porgy and Bess*; Bubbles's film credits include *Cabin in the Sky* (1943) and *A Song Is Born* (1948); Buck died in 1955, and Bubbles continued as a solo act or teamed with other entertainers in nightclub acts; appeared on USO tour in Vietnam during 1960's.

Buber, Martin

full: Mordecai Martin Buber
b. February 8, 1878
Vienna, Austro-Hungarian Empire
d. June 13, 1965
Jerusalem, Israel
fields: Philosophy, Religion and Theology, Literature

One of the greatest Jewish philosophers of the twentieth century, Buber postulated an interpersonal relationship between God and man. This theoretical relationship, which he called I-Thou, profoundly affected diverse thinkers of all faiths.

Bucareli, Antonio María

b. Jan. 24, 1717
Seville, Spain
d. Apr. 9, 1779
Mexico City, Mexico
fields: Warfare and Conquest, Government and Politics

Latino soldier and administrator. Antonio María Bucareli, a Spanish noble, began his military career as a cadet at the age of fifteen and eventually rose to become viceroy, captain-general, and governor of New Spain (1771-1779). Seen by historians as a man of peace, integrity, and intelligence, his achievements include peacefully keeping England and Russia out of New Spain and authorizing enterprises that led to the discovery of a land route to Alta California (1774), the exploration of San Francisco Bay (1775), and the founding of San Francisco (1776).

Bucer, Martin

b. November 11, 1491
Schlettstadt, Alsace
d. February 28, 1551
Cambridge, England
fields: Church Reform, Religion and Theology

During the Reformation, Bucer served as mediator between Huldrych Zwingli and Martin Luther and attempted to reconcile the Roman Catholic Church and the Protestants. He made lasting contributions to the liturgy of Protestant sects, particularly in England.

Buchan, John

aka: Lord Tweedsmuir
b. August 26, 1875
Perth, Scotland
d. February 12, 1940
Ottawa, Canada
fields: Literature, Government and Politics

A Scottish author, John Buchan began his career as in the British colonial service in South Africa in 1901. After publishing articles on World War I, the British War Office and Foreign Service recruited him as a propagandist. He became best known as an author of espionage novels, such as *The Thirty-nine Steps* (1915), *Greenmantle* (1916), and *The Three Hostages* (1924). He was later raised to the peerage and made governor general of Canada.

Buchanan, James

b. April 23, 1791
Mercerburg, Pennsylvania
d. June 1, 1868
Lancaster, Pennsylvania
fields: Government and Politics

President of the United States, 1857-1861. During the era leading up to the Civil War, Buchanan worked hard to preserve the Union. His presidency was devoted to trying to maintain the Democratic Party's North-South coalition.

Buchanan, Pat

full: Patrick Joseph Buchanan
b. Nov. 2, 1938
Washington, D.C.
fields: Government and Politics

Conservative politician and political commentator. Pat Buchanan served as director of communications for U.S. president Ronald Reagan from 1985 to 1987. He mounted unsuccessful campaigns for the Republican presidential nomination in 1992 and 1996. He received strong support from conservatives, but his controversial views on social issues limited his appeal to mainstream voters.

Buck, Pearl S.

né: Pearl Sydenstricker
b. June 26, 1892
Hillsboro, West Virginia
d. March 6, 1973
Danby, Vermont
fields: Literature

A novelist and Nobel laureate in literature (1938), Buck campaigned tirelessly for freedom and equal rights for all peoples of the world, both East and West.

Buckingham, First Duke of

né: George Villiers
b. August 28, 1592
Brooksby, Leicestershire, England
d. August 23, 1628
Portsmouth, Hampshire, England
fields: Government and Politics

As the personal favorite of James I and Charles I, Buckingham was the most powerful political figure in Great Britain in the 1620's. Under his leadership, British participation in the Thirty Years' War resulted in embarrassing military defeats which caused a dangerous political and constitutional rupture between the Crown and Parliament.

Buckley, William F., Jr.

full: William Frank Buckley, Jr.
b. November 24, 1925
New York, New York
fields: Government and Politics, Political Science, Social Reform

A major spokesman for conservative political viewpoints as author, magazine editor, columnist, speaker, and television host William F. Buckley, Jr., founded the conservative and libertarian *National Review* (1955), serving as its editor in chief until 1990; helped found Young Americans for Freedom in 1960; and, in 1962, began a nationally syndicated newspaper editorial column that gave rise to his celebrity. He ran as Conservative Party candidate for New York City mayor in 1965. In 1966, he created a television talk show, *Firing Line*. He was instrumental in moving conservative politics into the mainstream.

Buddha

né: Siddhārtha Gautama
aka: Siddhārtha
aka: Sākyamuni
b. c. 566 B.C.E.
Lumbinī, Nepal
d. c. 486 B.C.E.
Kusinagara, India
fields: Religion and Theology, Philosophy, Monasticism

By his own example and teaching, Buddha showed that all people can attain an enlightened state of mind by cultivating a combination of compassion (loving-kindness toward all beings without exception) and wisdom (seeing things as they really are).

Buell, Sarah Josepha. *See* Hale, Sarah Josepha

Bueno, María

full: María Ester Audion Bueno
b. Oct. 11, 1939
São Paulo, Brazil
fields: Sports (tennis player)

Latina tennis player. In 1959, María Bueno, a self-taught tennis player, won the singles title at Wimbledon (the first South American to do so), as well as the U.S. National Championship, prompting the Associated Press to name her Athlete of the Year. The following year she won Wimbledon again. She was ranked number one in the world in both years. From May, 1961, to September, 1963, her game suffered from the aftereffects of a bout with hepatitis, but Bueno staged a successful comeback, winning the U.S. National Championship in 1963, 1964, and 1966 and the Wimbledon title in 1964.

Buffalo Bill. *See* Cody, William

Buffalo Hump

aka: Bull Hump
aka: Pochanaw-quoip
b. c. 1800
Indian Territory, present-day Okla.
d. after 1865
fields: Warfare and Conquest, Native American Affairs

Comanche tribal leader. A leader in the early Comanche Wars, Buffalo Hump was most active from the 1830's through the 1850's. Buffalo Hump's son, also named Buffalo Hump, fought with war chief Quanah Parker.

Buffon, Comte de

né: Georges-Louis Leclerc
b. September 7, 1707
Montbard, France
d. April 16, 1788
Paris, France
fields: Biology, Natural History

Buffon wrote one of the earliest multivolume natural histories that saw nature as a complete entity. He also worked toward a concept of evolution and geological change that would contribute to later investigators in the field.

Bugonegijig. *See* Hole-in-the-Day

Buitron, Robert

b. 1953
fields: Photography

Latino photographer. During the late 1970's and early 1980's, Arizona photographer Robert Buitron completed "Family and Photography: A Portrait of a Family in Two Cultures," a series of photographs depicting the diversity of Mexican American culture. The work brought him widespread recognition, and he was one of ten people commissioned to work as official photographers for the 1984 Olympic Games in Los Angeles, California.

Bujones, Fernando

b. March 9, 1955
Miami, Fla.
fields: Dance

Cuban American ballet dancer. Fernando Bujones was a member of the New York City Ballet before joining the American Ballet Theater, becoming its principal dancer from 1974 to 1985. He was awarded the gold medal at the Seventh International Ballet Competition in Varna, Bulgaria, in 1974. A guest artist with ballet and opera companies all over the world, Bujones has danced with La Scala Milano, the Royal Swedish Ballet, and the Paris Opera. His choreographies include *Grand Pas Romantique*, 1984, and *Raymondal*, 1988. Known for his midair turns, precise leg beats, and high elevation, Bujones received a *Dance* Magazine Award in 1982 and a *New York Times* Artistic Award in 1985. In 1987 he was named a permanent international guest artist with the Boston Ballet. May 4, 1990, was proclaimed "Bujones Day" by the governor of Massachusetts. In 1995, he was named director of the Monterrey Ballet, Monterrey, Mexico.

Būkhārī, al-

full: Abū ʿAbdallāh Muḥammad ibn Ismāʿīl al-Būkhārī
b. July 19, 810
Bukhara, Central Asia (now in Uzbekistan)
d. August 3, 870
Khartank, near Samarkand
fields: Religion and Theology

Author of *Al-jami al-sahih* (*The Sound Epitome*), a compendium of traditions (*ḥadīth*) relating to the life and times of Muḥammad and the early Islamic community. Through his establishment of rigorous standards for the evaluation of *ḥadīth*, or traditions, al-Būkhārī helped to place Islamic ethics and jurisprudence on a new, historically documented level. He is said to have examined more than 600,000 *ḥadīth* during his lifetime. Of these, he designed 2,602 as authentic (*sahih*). *Al-jami al-sahih* was intended to provide future generations of Muslims with verified historical, legal, and ethical material from which their societies could draw in times of need. This work still stands as the most respected collection of *ḥadīth* in the Islamic world.

Bukharin, Nikolai Ivanovich

b. October 9, 1888
Moscow, Russia
d. March 15, 1938
Moscow, U.S.S.R.
fields: Government and Politics

Bukharin was a leader of the Bolshevik Revolution of 1917 and the foremost theoretician of the Soviet Communist Party during its early formative years. In 1924, after the death of the Party's founder, Vladimir Ilich Lenin, Bukharin became his heir and successor until he was forced from power by Joseph Stalin in 1928.

Bulfinch, Charles

b. August 8, 1763
Boston, Massachusetts
d. April 4, 1844
Boston, Massachusetts
fields: Architecture, Government and Politics

One of the first American architects to have used drawings extensively for the construction of buildings, Bulfinch exercised a wide influence on the architecture of the early national period of American history, especially in his native New England.

Bulgakov, Mikhail Afanasyevich

b. May 15, 1891
Kiev, Ukraine, Russian Empire
d. March 10, 1940
Moscow, Soviet Union
fields: Literature

Mikhail Afanasyevich Bulgakov lived through Russia's revolution and civil war without taking sides. In the mid-1920's he began publishing such satirical works as the novel *The White Guard* (1926; adapted to stage as *Days of Turbins*) and the play *Zoyka's Apartment* (1926). His novel *The Master and Margarita* (written in the 1940's but not published until 1967) is regarded as perhaps the greatest satire of the Soviet system.

Bull Bear

b. c. 1840
Kans.
d. after 1875
Cheyenne Reservation, Indian Territory
fields: Warfare and Conquest, Native American Affairs

One of the principal leaders of the elite Cheyenne society of warriors known as the Dog Soldiers, Bull Bear participated in numerous battles during the Cheyenne Wars for the Great Plains.

Bull Hump. *See* Buffalo Hump

Bullard, Eugene Jacques

b. Oct. 9, 1894
Columbus, Ga.
d. 1961
fields: Aviation and Space Exploration

African American pilot; believed to be the world's first black combat aviator, Eugene Jacques Bullard left the U.S. to escape discrimination; after being wounded at the front during World War I, fighting with the French Foreign Legion, Bullard then joined the newly established aviator corps before eventually returning to the U.S.

Bullen, Anne. *See* Bolyen, Anne

Bullins, Ed

b. July 2, 1935
Philadelphia, Pa.
fields: Literature, Theater and Entertainment

African American playwright; considered to be one of the most authentic African American writers in contemporary drama, Ed Bullins ignores conventional techniques and writes about and for urban blacks; his works include *The Taking of Miss Janie* (winner of the 1975 New York Drama Critics Circle Award), *The Fabulous Miss Marie* (pr. 1971, pb. 1974; for which Bullins received the 1971 Obie award), and *In New England Winter* (pb. 1969, pr. 1971).

Bullock, Fanny. *See* Workman, Fanny Bullock

Bullock, Star

full: Starmanda Bullock
b. ?
Washington, D.C.
fields: Art (painter)

African American painter; educated at Howard University, the Brooklyn Museum School, and the University of Massachusetts; Star Bullock's works have appeared at the Boston Museum and the Smithsonian Institution; she began teaching painting and design at Howard University in 1969.

Bulosan, Carlos

b. Nov. 24, c. 1911
Binalonan, Luzon, Philippines
d. Sept. 11, 1956
Seattle, Wash.
fields: Literature, Labor Movement

Filipino American writer, labor activist; Carlos Bulosan migrated from the Philippines; worked in an Alaskan cannery and as a migrant field hand before becoming a respected author; best known for three novels, *The Voice of Bataan* (1943), *The Laughter of My Father* (1944), and *America Is in the Heart* (1946).

Bülow, Bernhard von

full: Bernhard Heinrich Martin Karl von Bülow
b. May 3, 1849
Klein-Flottbeck, Holstein
d. October 28, 1929
Rome, Italy
fields: Government and Politics, Diplomacy

During twelve years of high office, first as foreign minister and then imperial chancellor, Bülow virtually shaped the expansionism that Emperor William II of Germany embraced as the guiding principle for both foreign and domestic policy. Bülow believed in *Weltpolitik* as the guarantee of German national security and interest. He acquired the sobriquet "the Eel" for his skill in forwarding this policy.

Bultmann, Rudolf

full: Rudolf Karl Bultmann
b. August 20, 1884
Wiefelstede, Germany
d. July 30, 1976
Marburg, West Germany
fields: Religion and Theology

Bultmann's contributions to New Testament research and Christian theology significantly shaped the methodology and content of both endeavors in the twentieth century. Bultmann's concept of demythologizing and his argument for an existential reading of the New Testament continue to influence much modern discussion about the Bible.

Bumbry, Grace Ann

b. Jan. 4, 1937
St. Louis, Mo.
fields: Music (opera singer)

African American opera singer; Grace Ann Bumbry appeared at many European venues following her operatic debut in 1960; after Bumbry's 1965 debut with the Metropolitan Opera in New York, she became a mainstay there; appeared at the White House; received a Grammy Award in 1979.

Bunche, Ralph

full: Ralph Johnson Bunche
b. August 7, 1904
Detroit, Michigan
d. December 9, 1971
New York, New York
fields: Education, Diplomacy

Bunche played a major role in making Americans conscious of the contradictions between their racial policies and their democratic aspirations. He helped bring better understanding between nations, participating in the drafting of the United Nations Charter, and through diplomatic negotiations helped to maintain peace in the Middle East and Africa, winning the Nobel Peace Prize for his efforts.

Buñuel, Luis

b. February 22, 1900
Calanda, Spain
d. July 29, 1983
Mexico City, Mexico
fields: Film

With his first three films, Buñuel virtually defined the genre of Surrealist cinema. The thirty-two films that he directed (and often coscripted) establish him as one of the century's most gifted film auteurs.

Bunyan, John

b. November 30, 1628 (baptized)
Elstow, Bedfordshire
d. August 31, 1688
London, England
fields: Literature, Religion and Theology

Drawing on the popular culture of England's socially most turbulent period, Bunyan preserved in much of his writing the idiom and images of the less articulate levels of society. As a religious allegory, his *The Pilgrim's Progress* appeals beyond creed to the vision of a life transcending the ordinary.

Burbank, Luther

b. March 7, 1849
Lancaster, Massachusetts
d. April 11, 1926
Santa Rosa, California
fields: Horticulture

As a plant breeder, Burbank introduced more than eight hundred new plants and gave the world a lesson in the value of horticultural science: Make plants work for the benefit of man.

Burbidge, Margaret

né: Eleanor Margaret Peachey
b. Aug. 12, 1919
Davenport, England
fields: Astronomy, Physics

Margaret Burbidge's work increased astronomers' understanding of the synthesis of elements within stars, the rotation of galaxies, and the nature of quasars.

Burciaga, José Antonio

b. Aug. 23, 1940
El Chuco, Tex.
fields: Literature, Art

Writer and artist. José Antonio Burciaga worked as a journalist and freelance writer in the early 1970's, then founded Diseños Literarios, a publishing company in Menlo Park, California, through which he published his first collection of poems and drawings, *Restless Serpents* (1976). Among his published work, which is known for its satire and concern with Chicano cultural issues, is the poetry collection *Undocumented Love* (1992), which won the Before Columbus American Book Award, and the essay collection *Weedee Peepo* (1988). He helped found the comedy group Culture Clash, and his murals have been shown in the United States and Mexico.

Burckhardt, Jacob

b. May 25, 1818
Basel, Switzerland
d. August 8, 1897
Basel, Switzerland
fields: Historiography

Burckhardt, a uniquely gifted historian and literary artist, was a pioneer in the development of modern *Kulturgeschichte*, the study of nonpolitical aspects of civilization. His lasting contribution was in Renaissance historiography, where his work became a model for the treatment of culture in the study of civilization.

Burge, Gregg

b. c. 1960
Merrick, Long Island, N.Y.
fields: Dance, Theater and Entertainment

African American dancer and actor; Gregg Burge appeared in television commercials and on *The Electric Company* as a child actor; appeared as the Scarecrow in the Broadway production of *The Wiz* at age seventeen; debuted as Richie in the 1985 film *A Chorus Line*; established a dance studio in his hometown.

Burger, Warren E.

full: Warren Earl Burger
b. September 17, 1907
St. Paul, Minnesota
d. June 25, 1995
Washington, D.C.
fields: Law

As chief justice of the United States for seventeen years, Burger was viewed as a conservative "law-and-order" judge who many thought would reverse much of the constitutionally revolutionary liberalism of the era of his predecessor, Earl Warren. Instead, the Burger Court consolidated and continued much of the Warren heritage.

Burgess, John M.

b. Mar. 11, 1909
Grand Rapids, Mich.
fields: Church Government, Religion and Theology

First African American bishop of the Episcopal church in the United States (1970); before becoming bishop, John M. Burgess's positions included chaplain at Howard University, canon at the Episcopal Cathedral in Washington, D.C., and superintendent of the Episcopal City Mission in Boston, Mass.; noted for helping to increase minority membership in the Episcopal Church; Burgess retired as bishop of Massachusetts in 1976.

Burgh, Hubert de

b. Late twelfth century
Burgh, Norfolk, England
d. May 12, 1243
Banstead, Surrey, England
fields: Government and Politics

The dominant figure in the early part of the reign of Henry III, de Burgh served as justiciar throughout the king's minority and beyond. It was his policy to strengthen the power and prestige of the monarchy in the face of baronial faction and opposition.

Burgos, Julia de

b. Feb. 17, 1914
Carolina, Puerto Rico
d. July, 1953
New York, N.Y.
fields: Literature

Latina poet. As a poet and a person, Julia de Burgos was concerned with feminist and Puerto Rican nationalist issues. Her first volume of poetry, *Poemas exactos a mí misma* (1937), caught the attention of writers and critics in Puerto Rico. In *Poemas en veinte surcos* (1938), the influence of Chilean poet Pablo Neruda can clearly be seen. *Canción de la verdad sencilla* (1939) won the Premio de Instituto de Literatura Puertorriqueña. Burgos, who suffered from depression and alcoholism, died homeless in New York City but was buried in Puerto Rico. *El mar y tú, otros poemas* (1954) and *Antología Poética* (1967) were published posthumously.

Buridan, Jean

b. c. 1295
Béthune, France
d. c. 1358
Paris, France
fields: Philosophy, Physics

A distinguished natural philosopher, Buridan wrote critical commentaries on the works of Aristotle and laid the foundations of the modern science of mechanics.

Burke, Edmund

b. January 12, 1729
Dublin, Ireland
d. July 9, 1797
Beaconsfield, Buckinghamshire, England
fields: Government and Politics, Philosophy

A parliamentary politician, Burke criticized the abuse of royal power by King George III and his ministers, but he was also critical of theories of radical democracy, which he thought threatened the stability of the social order. He opposed the use of force in dealing with the American Colonies and was an eloquent advocate of responsibility and humanity in dealing with subject peoples. In later life he supported the Crown and other historic institutions of Great Britain when they were challenged by the power and ideology of revolutionary France.

Burke, Jane Margaret. *See* Byrne, Jane

Burke, Selma

b. Dec. 31, 1901
Mooresville, N.C.
fields: Art (sculptor)

African American sculptor and educator; Selma Burke is noted for her sculptures of American leaders, including the portrait of former president Franklin Roosevelt that appears on the U.S. dime (1943) and a statue of Dr. Martin Luther King, Jr.; awards Burke has received include the Pearl S. Buck Award (1987) and an award from *Essence* magazine (1989).

Burke, Yvonne Brathwaite

b. Oct. 5, 1932
Los Angeles, Calif.
fields: Government and Politics

First African American woman elected to Congress from California; a Democratic party activist, Yvonne Brathwaite Burke was elected to three terms (beginning in 1966) in the California state assembly; in 1972, served as vice chair of the Democratic National Convention in Miami, Fla., and was elected to the U.S. House of Representatives, serving six years; elected Los Angeles County Supervisor (1992).

Burleigh, Harry T.

b. Dec. 2, 1866
Erie, Pa.
d. Sept. 12, 1949
Stamford, Conn.
fields: Music (composer and arranger)

African American composer and arranger; the first African American to receive a scholarship to the National Conservatory of Music, Harry T. Burleigh helped familiarize a wider American audience with the Negro spiritual form through his arrangements of spirituals; his "Swing Low, Sweet Chariot" is among the Burleigh arrangements that continue to be used.

Burnell, Enid Muriel. *See* Lyons, Enid Muriel

Burnet, Macfarlane

full: Frank Macfarlane Burnet
aka: Sir Macfarlane Burnet

b. September 3, 1899
Traralgon, Victoria, Australia
d. August 31, 1985
Melbourne, Australia
fields: Medicine

Burnet was awarded the 1960 Nobel Prize for the discovery of acquired immunological tolerance to tissue transplants, but he also discovered a method for identifying bacteria by the viruses that attack them, as well as a technique for cultivating viruses in chicken embryos.

Burnett, Carol

b. April 26, 1936
San Antonio, Texas
fields: Theater and Entertainment, Television

Overcoming a childhood of poverty and abandonment, Carol Burnett launched a career on television, stage, and screen that eventually made her one of the most popular entertainers in the United States.

Burnett, Frances Hodgson

né: Frances Eliza Hodgson
b. November 24, 1849
Manchester, England
d. October 29, 1924
Plandome, Long Island, New York
fields: Literature, Theater and Entertainment

Burnett's immensely popular stories and dramatizations brought pleasure and hope to many people and bridged divides between British and American audiences, the rich and the poor, and children and adults.

Burney, Charles

b. April 7, 1726
Shrewsbury, England
d. April 12, 1814
Chelsea, Middlesex, England
fields: Music

Inspired by the prodigious commentary on music contained in the French *Encyclopédie*, Burney compiled an informative history of music that gave rise to a distinguished tradition of English musical criticism.

Burney, William D., Jr.

b. Apr. 23, 1951
Augusta, Maine
fields: Government and Politics

African American mayor of Augusta, Maine; following graduation with a law degree in 1977, William D. Burney, Jr., worked as project manager of a housing development in Boston, as executive director of Downstreet 82 in Augusta, Maine, and then in a variety of positions with the Maine State Housing Authority; Burney eventually rose to assistant director for housing development before becoming the first African American elected to the Augusta city council; in 1988, he was elected the first African American mayor in Maine's history.

Burnham, Daniel Hudson

b. September 4, 1846
near Henderson, New York
d. June 1, 1912
Heidelberg, Germany
fields: Architecture, Urban Development

Energetic and practical, Burnham was master of the utilitarian, technical, and financial aspects of architecture. He made important contributions to the development of the American skyscraper form, the organization of the modern architectural office, and the encouragement of comprehensive urban and regional planning.

Burns, Anthony

b. May 31, 1834
Stafford County, Va.
d. July 27, 1862
St. Catharines, Ontario, Canada
fields: Historical Figure, Law

Fugitive African American slave; after being arrested and forced to return to slavery in Virginia in 1854, Anthony Burns became the subject of the first test case in Massachusetts of the Fugitive Slave Law of 1850; after black parishioners in Boston purchased his freedom, he was ordained a Baptist minister and moved to Canada, where he served a congregation of freedmen.

Burns, Isaac. *See* Murphy, Isaac

Burns, John Anthony

b. Mar. 30, 1909
Ft. Assiniboine, Mont.
d. April 5, 1975
Honolulu, Hawaii
fields: Government and Politics

John Anthony Burns served as a delegate to Congress from Hawaii from 1956 to 1959 and as governor of Hawaii from 1962 to 1973. A Democrat who helped end the Republican Party's dominance in Hawaii in the 1950's, he sought to bring equality to the people of the state and to end the political, economic, and social dominance enjoyed by white elites. As a delegate to Congress, Burns was instrumental in achieving statehood for Hawaii in 1959.

Burns, Robert

b. January 25, 1759
Alloway, Ayrshire, Scotland
d. July 21, 1796
Dumfries, Scotland
fields: Literature

Burns, writing his poetry and songs at the culmination of Scottish cultural tradition, made a major contribution to preserving Scottish culture, especially the folk song; his universal human appeal made him an internationally recognized as well as an intensely national poet.

Burnside, William

b. July 2, 1852
London, England
d. Aug. 21, 1927
West Wickham, Kent, England
fields: Mathematics (applied math and probability)

William Burnside was a mathematician best known for his contributions to the study of group theory.

Burr, Aaron

b. February 6, 1756
Newark, New Jersey
d. September 14, 1836
Port Richmond, Staten Island, New York
fields: Government and Politics, Law

Burr developed the political organization which assured the presidential victory of Thomas Jefferson, and was the force behind the liberalization of New York's penal codes and political process.

Burrell, Leroy

full: Leroy Russell Burrell
b. Feb. 21, 1967
Philadelphia, Pa.
fields: Sports (track sprinter)

African American track sprinter; in 1990, Leroy Burrell set a new world record for the 100-meter dash (9.90 seconds); at the 1992 Olympics, although he did not medal for his individual performance, he received a gold medal as a member of the U.S. 4 × 100-meter relay team which won with a world record time of 37.4 seconds.

Burrell, Stanley Kirk. *See* Hammer

Burris, Roland W.

b. Aug. 3, 1937
Centralia, Ill.
fields: Government and Politics

African American government official; in a professional career combining finance and law, Roland W. Burris has filled positions including director of the Illinois Department of General Services (1976) and Illinois state comptroller (1978; reelected twice); in 1990, elected state attorney general, the first African American to hold this position; for several years running, named by *Ebony* magazine to its list of one hundred most influential black Americans.

Burroughs, Edgar Rice

b. September 1, 1875
Chicago, Illinois

d. March 19, 1950
Encino, California
fields: Literature

Burroughs was one of the most popular authors of the twentieth century. His romantic adventures set in such places as Africa, the center of the earth, and Mars helped shape modern science fiction, and his heroes John Carter of Mars and Tarzan of the Apes have become enduring cultural icons.

Burroughs, Margaret Taylor Goss

b. Nov. 1, 1917
St. Rose Parish, La.
fields: Art

African American museum director and artist; with a master's degree from the Art Institute of Chicago (1948), Margaret Taylor Goss Burroughs went on to exhibit her own paintings and sculptures; in 1961, she was named director of Chicago's Du Sable Museum of African American History.

Burroughs, Nannie Helen

b. 1883
Washington, D.C.
d. 1961
fields: Education, Social Reform

African American activist and educator; Nannie Helen Burroughs established the Woman's Industrial Club to teach industrial skills to girls; raised funds to open the National Training School for Girls; active member of the National Association of Colored Women's Clubs and the NAACP.

Burrows, Stephen Gerald

b. September 15, 1943
Newark, N.J.
fields: Fashion (fashion designer)

African American fashion designer; after working for designer Henri Bendel, Stephen Gerald Burrows established his own company and line of clothing in 1973.

Burrows, Vinie

b. Nov. 15, 1928
New York, N.Y.
fields: Art (performance), Civil Rights, Social Reform

African American performing artist and sociopolitical activist; as a permanant representative to the U.N., Vinie Burrows advocates for the oppressed, minorities, and African peoples; founder of Women for Racial and Economic Equality; her solo performance *Walk Together Children* (1968) used music, poetry, and prose to explore the African American situation in the United States.

Burton, Harold Hitz

b. 1888
d. 1964
fields: Law

U.S. Supreme Court justice, 1945-1958; appointed by President Truman. Generally, opposed expansion of rights for criminal defendants in state courts. Significant opinions: *Haley v. Ohio*, 332 U.S. 596 (1948, dissenting opinion); *Henderson v. United States*, 339 U.S. 816 (1950); *Louisiana v. Resweber*, 329 U.S. 459 (1947, dissenting opinion).

Burton, LeVar

né: Le Vardis Robert Martyn, Jr.
b. Feb. 16, 1957
Landstuhl, West Germany
fields: Television

African American actor; LeVar Burton is known for playing such television roles as the young Kunta Kinte in the miniseries *Roots* (1977) and in *Roots: The Gift* (1988) and the blind Lieutenant Geordi La Forge in the series *Star Trek: The Next Generation* (1987-1992); he is also known to many children as the host of PBS's award-winning *Reading Rainbow* series.

Burton, Richard Francis

b. March 19, 1821
Torquay, Devonshire, England
d. October 20, 1890
Trieste, Italy
fields: Exploration and Colonization, Scholarship, Diplomacy

Burton was a British explorer and Orientalist who explored in Asia, Africa, and South America. He was famous as an author of travel books and many literary translations, including *The Arabian Nights' Entertainments.*

Busby, Jheryl

b. c. 1949
Los Angeles, Calif.
fields: Music (record company executive)

African American record company executive; Jheryl Busby was hired by MCA Records in 1984 to serve as vice president of the label's black music division; promoted the careers of established black artists such as Patti LaBelle and helped launch the careers of promising new groups such as New Edition; in 1988 became president and chief executive officer of Motown Records.

Busby, Jim

b. July 16, 1944
Houston, Tex.
fields: Government and Politics

African American mayor of Victorville, Calif.; after serving with the U.S. Navy during the Vietnam War, Jim Busby attended the University of Redlands, California, and completed a bachelor of science degree in business and a master's degree in business management, while working with TRW Space and Defense; he stayed with TRW for twenty-two years; in May, 1988, he was elected to the Victorville city council; soon thereafter his fellow councilmembers appointed him mayor pro tem.

Bush, Anita

b. c. 1883
Washington, D.C.
d. Feb. 16, 1974
New York, N.Y.
fields: Theater and Entertainment

African American actress; Anita Bush pioneered the development of African American theater; following membership in the Williams and Walker vaudeville troupe (1903-1909), Bush established one of the twentieth century's first black dramatic groups, the Anita Bush Stock Company (1915), later known as the Lafayette Players; Bush's stage credits include the Broadway musicals *In Dahomey* (1902) and *Abyssinia* (1903); her film credits include *The Crimson Skull* (1921) and *The Bull Doggers* (1922).

Bush, George

full: George Herbert Walker Bush
b. June 12, 1924
Milton, Massachusetts
fields: Government and Politics

As forty-first president of the United States (1989-1993), Bush culminated a career that included service as U.S. ambassador to the United Nations, chairman of the Republican National Committee, director of the Central Intelligence Agency, and vice president to Ronald Reagan.

Bush, George W.

b. c. 1791
Pennsylvania
d. c. 1863
fields: Exploration and Colonization

African American explorer; after fighting with Andrew Jackson at the Battle of New Orleans during the War of 1812, George W. Bush hired on with the Hudson's Bay Company, eventually reaching the Pacific Coast in 1820; in 1845, after twelve years of farming in Missouri, Bush helped lead a group of settlers to the Puget Sound.

Bushyhead, Dennis Wolf

aka: Unáduti
b. Mar. 18, 1826
near Cleveland, Tenn.
d. Feb. 4, 1898
Talequah, Okla.

fields: Government and Politics, Native American Affairs

Cherokee tribal leader Dennis Wolf Bushyhead was one of the leading political figures of the Cherokee Nation during the second half of the nineteenth century. During the 1870's, Dennis helped found the National Independent Party, partly to challenge an attempt by full-bloods to take control of all Cherokee affairs. In 1879, Bushyhead began serving two elected four-year terms as principal chief.

Bussey, Charles David

b. Dec. 8, 1933
Edgefield, S.C.
fields: Military Affairs

African American military officer; after more than thirty-three years of commissioned service with the U.S. Army (1955-1989), Charles David Bussey retired at the rank of major general; he quickly advanced from assistant mess officer through such positions as platoon leader; commander of Company A of the First Battalion, Fifth Cavalry, First Cavalry Division in Korea (1963-1964); manpower analyst in the office of the assistant chief of staff and, later, executive officer in Vietnam; deputy chief of public affairs in the office of the secretary of the Army (1984); and deputy chief of staff for personnel at the U.S. Army Materiel Command in Washington, D.C.

Butcher, Philip

b. Sept. 28, 1918
Washington, D.C.
fields: Education, Literature

African American author and educator; holding A.B. (1942) and M.A. (1947) degrees from Howard University and a Ph.D. (1956) from Columbia University, Philip Butcher eventually became a professor at Morgan State University; he has written two books about George Washington Cable and edited a book of William Stanley Braithwaite readings.

Buthelezi, Mangosuthu Gatsha

b. August 27, 1928
Mahlabatini, Natal, South Africa
fields: Civil Rights, Government and Politics

Mangosuthu Gatsha Buthelezi was an influential South African political leader and anti-apartheid activist in the 1970's and 1980's. In the 1970's, appointed chief minister of South African province of KwaZulu. Buthelezi was a popular leader, and when KwaZulu held its first election in 1978, the Zulu people voted to retain him as chief minister. Conflicts in early 1990's between his Inkatha Freedom Party and the African National Congress (ANC) of Nelson Mandela led to violence and the death of thousands in the early 1990's. His influence waned in 1990's.

Butler, Dorothy. *See* Gilliam, Dorothy Butler

Butler, Jerry

b. Dec. 8, 1939
Sunflower, Miss.
fields: Music (rhythm-and-blues singer)

African American rhythm-and-blues singer; with Curtis Mayfield, Sam Gooden, and brothers Arthur and Richard Brooks, Jerry Butler formed a rhythm-and-blues group called the Impressions; their single, "For Your Precious Love" (cowritten by Butler and the Brooks brothers), hit the *Billboard* top-ten list within five weeks of its release; as a solo artist, Butler's hits included "He Will Break Your Heart" (1960), "Let It Be Me" (1964; a duet with Betty Everett that reached the top ten of the rhythm-and-blues chart), "Hey, Western Union Man" (1968; reached number one on the rhythm-and-blues chart), and "Only the Strong Survive" (1969; a number-one hit); in 1980, Butler founded the Fountain Records label; released the album *Ice and Hot* in 1982.

Butler, Joseph

b. May 18, 1692
Wantage, Berkshire, England
d. June 16, 1752
Bath, Somerset, England
fields: Philosophy, Religion and Theology

Joseph Butler presented the classical theory of the ethics of conscience and the standard critique of psychological egoism, as well as an influential version of the "argument from design" as to the existence of God and a powerful theory of personal identity. Major works: *Fifteen Sermons to Which Are Added Six Sermons Preached on Public[k] Occasions* (1765, revised from an earlier 1726 edition), *The Analogy of Religion Natural and Revealed, to the Constitution and Course of Nature* (1736), and *A Charge Deliver'd to the Clergy of the Diocese of Durham* (1751).

Butler, Nicholas Murray

b. April 2, 1862
Elizabeth, New Jersey
d. December 7, 1947
New York, New York
fields: Education

Butler, organizer of Teachers College (Columbia University) and winner of the 1931 Nobel Peace Prize, was a leading figure in the creation of the modern American university.

Butler, Octavia E.

full: Octavia Estelle Butler
b. June 22, 1947
Pasadena, Calif.
fields: Literature

African American science fiction writer; the winner of two Hugo Awards, the Nebula Award, and a Locus Award (*Locus* Magazine), Octavia E. Butler writes with an economical style, portraying independent black women in multiracial societies that are open to sexual equality; works such as *Kindred* (1979) and *Wild Seed* (1980) have earned her a solid reputation.

Butler, Pierce

b. 1866
d. 1939
fields: Law

U.S. Supreme Court justice, 1923-1939 (died while in office); appointed by President Harding. Opposed most New Deal regulatory measures. Significant opinions: *Olmstead v. United States*, 277 U.S. 438 (1928, dissenting opinion); *United States v. Schwimmer*, 279 U.S. 644 (1929).

Butler, R. A.

full: Richard Austen Butler
b. December 9, 1902
Attock, Seral, India
d. March 8, 1982
Great Yeldham, Essex, England
fields: Education, Government and Politics, Social Reform

As chief architect of the Education Act of 1944, Butler accomplished one of the major educational reforms of the twentieth century, establishing the outlines of contemporary English secondary education. In the realm of politics, Butler was largely responsible for leading the Conservative Party's acceptance of the welfare state and the mixed economy following the Labour Party's triumph in the 1945 general elections.

Buxton, Thomas Fowell

aka: Sir Thomas Fowell Buxton
b. April 1, 1786
Castle Hedingham, Essex, England
d. February 19, 1845
Northrepps Hall, Norfolk, England
fields: Social Reform (abolitionism)

Buxton was for a long time active in a variety of humanitarian causes, including prison reform and charitable relief, but he is best known for his sustained efforts to bring about the abolition of slavery.

Byas, Don

né: Carlos Wesley
b. Oct. 21, 1912
Muskogee, Okla.
d. Aug. 24, 1972
Amsterdam, The Netherlands

fields: Music (jazz tenor saxophonist)

African American tenor saxophonist; a transitional figure in the movement from swing to bebop during the 1940's, Don Byas attempted to combine the musical ideas of Charlie Parker with the tone of Coleman Hawkins; Byas established a reputation as a performer during the 1930's while playing with bands such as those of Lionel Hampton, Buck Clayton, and Andy Kirk; in 1941, Byas replaced the legendary Lester Young in Count Basie's orchestra; Byas performed with, and was influenced by, the emerging "modern" players, but he stayed true to his swing and blues roots; featured soloist at festivals throughout Europe during the 1950's and 1960's.

Byrd, Donald

b. Dec. 9, 1932
Detroit, Mich.
fields: Music (jazz trumpet and flugelhorn player)

African American trumpet and flugelhorn player; during the 1950's, Donald Byrd performed with such major talents as Art Blakey, Max Roach, Sonny Rollins, Arthur Taylor, Lou Donaldson, George Wallington, Jackie McLean, Pepper Adams, and John Coltrane; between 1955 and 1958, Byrd recorded on approximately sixty albums; his later recording credits included *Free Form* (1961), *A New Perspective* (1963), *Electric Byrd* (1970), *Black Byrd* (1972), *Street Lady* (1973), and the fusion funk album, *I Want to Thank You for F.U.M.L.* (1978); holding university degrees in music (B.A., 1954), music education (M.A.), law (1976), and a doctorate from Columbia Teachers College (1982), Byrd taught at Rutgers University, Hampton Institute, Howard University (serving as director of the Jazz Institute, 1968-1972), and Queen's College, New York City (1990's).

Byrd, Henry Roeland. *See* Professor Longhair

Byrd, Melvin Leon

b. Nov. 1, 1935
Suffolk, Va.
fields: Military Affairs

African American military officer; after more than thirty-two years of active service with the U.S. Army (1959-1991), Melvin Leon Byrd retired as a brigadier general; his postings included ordnance adviser with the United States Military Assistance Command in Vietnam (1965-1966), chief of the maintenance management branch at the United States Army Quartermaster School in Va.; deputy director for joint actions in the office of the deputy chief of staff for logistics; and commanding general of the United States Army Materiel Command in Europe (1986-1988).

Byrd, Richard

full: Richard Evelyn Byrd
b. October 25, 1888
Winchester, Virginia
d. March 11, 1957
Boston, Massachusetts
fields: Aviation and Space Exploration, Exploration and Colonization

Byrd played a central role in the development of naval aviation and was a major figure in Arctic and Antarctic exploration, receiving a Medal of Honor for this flight over the North Pole (with Floyd Bennett, 1926) and establishing the Antarctic base Little America (1929).

Byrd, William

b. 1543
possibly Lincoln, Lincolnshire, England
d. July 4, 1623
Stondon Massey, Essex, England
fields: Music

Byrd was the outstanding English composer of the Renaissance, notable both for the variety of forms and styles in which he composed and for the outstanding quality of the individual pieces within each genre. He was apparently the first English composer to understand fully the new technique of imitative polyphony as developed in the Netherlands, and he passed this understanding on to his students, who included the composers Thomas Morley, Thomas Tomkins, and, almost certainly, Orlando Gibbons.

Byrne, Jane

né: Jane Margaret Burke
b. May 24, 1934
Chicago, Illinois
fields: Government and Politics

Active in Democratic politics since 1960 and in Chicago city administration since 1964, Jane Byrne was the first woman to be elected mayor of Chicago.

Byrnes, James Francis

b. 1879
d. 1972
fields: Law

U.S. Supreme Court justice, 1941-1942; appointed by President Franklin D. Roosevelt. Last justice who became a lawyer without attending law school. Resigned from the Court to assist the president in the war effort. Served as secretary of state in the Truman administration.

Byron, Augusta Ada. *See* Lovelace, Augusta Ada

Byron, JoAnne Deborah. *See* Shakur, Assata Olugbala

Byron, Lord

né: George Gordon
full: George Gordon, Lord Byron
b. January 22, 1788
London, England
d. April 19, 1824
Missolonghi, Greece
fields: Literature

Not only did Byron write satirical and lyrical poetry of the highest order, but also his life seemed, to many of his contemporaries, to be the embodiment of the revolutionary spirit of Romanticism. His figure of the "Byronic hero" became vastly influential in nineteenth century European culture.

C

Cabell, James Branch

b. April 14, 1879
Richmond, Virginia
d. May 5, 1958
Richmond, Virginia
fields: Literature

James Branch Cabell was an American author and literary editor who gained international fame in the uproar following publication of his novel *Jurgen* (1919), a medieval romance, which was charged with violating New York state pornography laws. Afterward he remained a central figure of the 1920's American literary avant garde. He published more than fifty books and was an editor of the Richmond literary *Reviewer* and a coeditor of the *American Spectator*.

Cabello, Domingo

b. 1725
Castile, Spain
d. 1801
Nicaragua
fields: Warfare and Conquest, Government and Politics

Latino soldier and administrator. Domingo Cabello joined the Spanish army in 1741 and served in Spain, Portugal, and Cuba. He was awarded governorship of Nicaragua in recognition for bravery at the siege of Havana (1762), then became governor of Texas in 1778 for eight years. During this time he maintained order and helped pacify the Apache and Comanche through fair treatment and sound trade practices. In 1886 he was promoted to subinspector of troops of Cuba. Later, he became a brigadier general and commandant general of Nicaragua.

Cabeza de Baca, Ezequiel

b. 1964
Las Vegas, N.Mex.
d. Feb. 18, 1917
Santa Fe, N.Mex.
fields: Government and Politics, Journalism

Latino politician and journalist. In 1891, Ezequiel became associate editor of the Las Vegas weekly newspaper *La Voz del Pueblo* and nine years later became editor. In 1893, Félix Martínez was elected to the Fourth District Court in San Miguel County, and Ezequiel was appointed his deputy clerk. Ezequiel later became county chairman of the Democratic Party. In 1911 he was elected as the state's first lieutenant governor and won the race for New Mexico's second governor. However, he died during his term.

Cabeza de Baca, Fabiola. *See* Gilbert, Fabiola Cabeza de Baca

Cabeza de Baca, Fernando E.

b. 1937
Albuquerque, N.Mex.
fields: Business and Industry, Civil Rights

Latino businessman and civic leader. During the 1960's and 1970's, Fernando E. Cabeza de Baca served as commissioner of the New Mexico department of transportation and western regional director for the federal Department of Health, Education, and Welfare. In 1974 he was appointed special assistant to the president by Gerald Ford. Cabeza de Baca was involved with the American Legion and the League of United Latin American Citizens. He also worked to promote minority business interests and the free enterprise system.

Cabeza de Vaca, Alvar Nuñez

b. c. 1490
Jerez de la Frontera, Spain
d. c. 1560
Spain
fields: Exploration and Colonization

Cabeza de Vaca's capture by Native Americans in Texas gave him the chance to explore the region in detail and write an invaluable account of the people and topography of Texas and northern Mexico that stimulated further exploration.

Cabot, John

né: Juan Caboto
b. c. 1450
Genoa?, Italy
d. c. 1498
place unknown
fields: Exploration and Colonization

Cabot persuaded Englishmen to explore new lands beyond the western horizon and laid the foundations of England's claim to and eventual control of the North American continent.

Cabrera, Lydia

b. May 20, 1900
Havana, Cuba
d. Sept. 19, 1991
Miami, Fla.
fields: Anthropology (ethnologist)

Latina ethnologist. Lydia Cabrera's interest in Afro-Caribbean culture began when she left Cuba in 1927 to study Asian religions at L'École du Louvre in Paris, France. She began collecting Afro-Cuban folklore and eventually published more than twenty books on the subject, the most well known being her book on Santería religious practices, *El Monte* (1954). Her work is considered an important contribution to the anthropological study of Cuba.

Cabrillo, Juan Rodríguez

b. c. 1500
Portugal or Spain
d. Jan. 3, 1543
San Miguel Island, Calif.
fields: Exploration and Colonization

Latino explorer. Juan Rodríguez Cabrillo, who traveled to the New World at a young age, served first with Pánfilo de Narváez in Cuba and Hernán Cortés in Mexico. In 1542, Cortés sent Cabrillo on an expedition to explore the Pacific coast. Cabrillo sailed farther north than anyone had before and became the first explorer to see the Pacific coast of the United States. During the journey, Cabrillo broke his arm and, in January of 1543, died of complications from the wound.

Cabrini, Frances Xavier

aka: Mother Cabrini
b. July 15, 1850
Sant' Angelo Lodigiano, Lombardy, Italy
d. December 22, 1917
Chicago, Illinois
fields: Religion and Theology, Social Reform

Founder of a religious community dedicated to helping the poor, Mother Cabrini contributed to missions among Italian immigrants to America, eventually establishing convents, schools, and charitable orphanages all over the world.

Cade, Miltona Mirkin. *See* Bambara, Toni Cade

Cadoria, Sherian Grace

b. Jan. 26, 1940
Marksville, La.
fields: Military Affairs

African American military officer; upon retiring from the U.S. Army in 1990, Sherian Grace Cadoria had achieved the rank of brigadier general; her postings included platoon leader for a Women's Army Corps training battalion (1962); chief of the personnel division at Aberdeen Proving Ground in Maryland; commander of the first region of the U.S. Army criminal investigation command; and deputy commanding general and director for mobilization and contingency operations at the Total Army Personnel Command at Alexandria, Va.

Cady, Elizabeth. *See* Stanton, Elizabeth Cady

Cædmon

b. Seventh century
Northumbria, England
d. c. 680
probably Whitby, England

fields: Literature

An unlettered monk of the seventh century, Cædmon is recognized as the first named English poet.

Caemmerer, Hanna von. *See* Neumann, Hanna

Caesar, Adolph

b. 1934?
Harlem, N.Y.
d. Mar. 16, 1986
Los Angeles, Calif.
fields: Theater and Entertainment, Film

African American actor; Adolph Caesar received an Obie and a New York Drama Desk Award for his 1981 performance in *A Soldier's Play*; his film credits include the 1984 film version of *A Soldier's Play*, which garnered him an Oscar nomination, and *The Color Purple* (1985), in which he portrayed the old minister; recipient of the 1985 National Association for the Advancement of Colored People Image Award.

Caesar, Julius

né: Gaius Julius Caesar
b. July 12/13, 100 B.C.E.
Rome
d. March 15, 44 B.C.E.
Rome
fields: Government and Politics, Warfare and Conquest, Literature

With his conquest of Gaul, Caesar expanded Roman rule into northern Europe. He then won a desperate civil war to establish himself as sole ruler of the Roman world, ending the republic and preparing the stage for the empire.

Caesar, Shirley

b. Oct. 13, 1939
Durham, N.C.
fields: Music (gospel singer), Religion and Theology

African American gospel singer and evangelist; a featured singer on thirty albums, five-time Grammy winner, and the recipient of three gold albums, Shirley Caesar began her professional career with the female gospel group the Caravans (1958-1966); after 1966, with "rock gospel," she updated the church-oriented style of gospel to attract young fans of rhythm-and-blues music; songs such as her Grammy Award-winning "Put Your Hand in the Hand of the Man from Galilee" pushed gospel music to the forefront of the American music scene; during this time she also established the Shirley Caesar Outreach Ministries, which provided aid to needy families in Durham, N.C.; in 1983, she became copastor of the Mt. Calvary Holy Church in Winston-Salem, N.C.

Caetani, Benedict. *See* Boniface VIII

Cahan, Abraham

b. July 7, 1860
Vilna, Russian Empire (now Vilnius, Lithuania)
d. August 31, 1951
New York, New York
fields: Journalism

Abraham Cahan was a journalist; born in the Russian empire, fled to the United States escaping czarist persecution; worked for Joseph Pulitzer's *World*; founded Yiddish newspaper *Vorwarts!* (*Jewish Daily Forward*), in 1897, which he edited for fifty years; a staunch socialist, who nevertheless spoke out against the brutality of Stalin's regime in Russia; explored the Jewish immigrant experience in the novels *Imported Bridegroom* (1898), *The White Terror and the Red* (1905), *The Rise of David Levinsky* (1907).

Cahill, Jane Pennington. *See* Pfeiffer, Jane Cahill

Cain, Richard Harvey

b. Apr. 12, 1825
Greenbrier County, Va.
d. Jan. 18, 1887
Washington, D.C.
fields: Government and Politics

African American U.S. congressman from South Carolina during Reconstruction; a pastor of the African Methodist Episcopal (AME) church, Richard Harvey Cain served in the Missouri state senate (1868-1870); elected to the U.S. House of Representatives (1872-1874), served on the House Committee on Agriculture; elected to Congress as South Carolina's Second District representative (1876-1878), served on the House Committee on Private Claims; later served as a bishop of the AME church.

Calamity Jane

né: Martha Cannary
or né: Martha Canary
b. May 1, 1852 (?)
Princeton, Missouri (?)
d. August 1, 1903
Terry, South Dakota
fields: Exploration and Colonization, Military Affairs

Independent and determined to live as she chose in a man's world, Calamity Jane became famous, legendary, and exemplary of the almost mythical character of the American West.

Calder, Alexander

b. July 22, 1898
Lawnton, Pennsylvania
d. November 11, 1976
New York, New York
fields: Art

Calder was an experimental abstract artist who applied engineering concepts to sculpture and other media to create a new understanding of the use of space and form in art.

Calderón, José. *See* Cuba, Joe

Calderón de la Barca, Pedro

b. January 17, 1600
Madrid, Spain
d. May 25, 1681
Madrid, Spain
fields: Theater and Entertainment

Calderón continued the Golden Age of drama after the death of Lope de Vega Carpio, bringing to Spain some of the greatest dramatic literature and *autos sacramentales* in the seventeenth century.

Caldwell, Erskine

b. December 17, 1903
White Oak, Georgia
d. April 11, 1987
Paradise Valley, Arizona
fields: Literature

Erskine Caldwell was an American writer whose books were often attacked for their perceived obscenity, beginning with his first novel, *The Bastard* (1929). His masterpiece, *Tobacco Road* (1932), caused an outcry in his native South. *God's Little Acre* (1933) also prompted censorship. His other books included *Journeyman* (1935).

Caldwell, Sarah

b. March 6, 1924
Maryville, Missouri
fields: Music

A major force in producing, staging, directing, and promoting opera, Sarah Caldwell has broken new ground for women in the arts and has served as a role model for those who followed.

Calhoun, John C.

full: John Caldwell Calhoun
b. March 18, 1782
Abbeville District, South Carolina
d. March 31, 1850
Washington, D.C.
fields: Government and Politics

In addition to wielding great influence in national politics for four decades, Calhoun wrote incisively on the problem of protecting minority rights against majority rule in a democracy.

Caliari, Paolo. *See* Veronese, Paolo

Caligula

né: Gaius Julius Caesar
b. August 31, 12 C.E.
probably Antium (Anzio), Italy
d. January, 41 C.E.
Rome
fields: Government and Politics, Roman Caesars

The third ruler of the Julio-Claudian dynasty, Caligula did much during his short reign to transform the position of Roman emperor into an institution of absolute monarchy.

Callaghan, James

full: Leonard James Callaghan
b. March 27, 1912
Portsmouth, England
fields: Government and Politics

James Callaghan was prime minister of Great Britain from 1976 to 1979. As Labour Party foreign secretary, 1974-1976, helped renegotiate Britain's membership in the EEC. In 1976 Prime Minister Harold Wilson suddenly announced his resignation. Callaghan emerged as party leader and new prime minister. Faced a deteriorating economic situation, with very high inflation and serious unemployment. Agreed on a policy to regulate incomes, cut government spending, and took out international loans. In 1978, however, called for an unpopular 5 percent ceiling for wage increases. Labour's thin majority in Parliament dissolved, and the Labour government fell in the spring of 1979.

Callender, Clive Orville

b. November 16, 1936
New York, N.Y.
fields: Medicine, Education (surgeon and educator)

African American surgeon and educator; Clive Orville Callender, known for his research in organ transplant surgery, wasthe National Medical Association's Physician of the Year in 1989; served on the Advisory Committee to the U.S. Secretary of Health; was elected a member of the American Surgical Association.

Callender, Leroy Nathaniel

b. Feb. 22, 1932
New York, N.Y.
fields: Engineering

African American civil and structural engineer; with a degree from Brooklyn Technical High School and two years experience as a draftsman (1950-1952), Leroy Nathaniel Callender designed buildings for the U.S. Army in Korea; after earning a B.A. in civil engineering, Callender went to work as a project engineer (1959-1968), and was an engineer for the first nuclear power plant built in the East; in 1969 he established his own firm of consulting engineers; in 1975 he founded a second company specializing in waterworks development.

Callender, Red

full: George Sylvester Callender
b. Mar. 6, 1918
Haynesville, Va.
d. Mar. 8, 1992
Saugus, Calif.
fields: Music (string bass and tuba player)

African American string bass and tuba player; beginning in the mid-1930's, Red Callender played with such notable artists as Louis Armstrong (1937), Nat "King" Cole, Erroll Garner's Trio (1946), and Johnny Otis (1947); as one of the first black musicians to break Hollywood's color barrier, Callender's film credits included *I Dood It!* (1943), *New Orleans* (1947, with Louis Armstrong), and *St. Louis Blues* (1958); Henry Fonda's television series *Smith Family* took Callender's 1958 hit song "Primrose Lane" as its theme; in 1985, he published his autobiography, *Unfinished Dream: The Musical World of Red Callender.*

Calleros, Cleofas

b. 1896
d. 1973
El Paso, Tex.
fields: Literature

Latino writer. Cleofas Calleros was a Catholic and a member of the Knights of Columbus who wrote books (many in collaboration with Marjorie F. Graham) and newspaper columns about the early inhabitants and missions of Texas, focusing primarily on the El Paso region. Articles from his newspaper column, titled "Then and Now," were collected in *El Paso-Then and Now* (1954). Other works include *El Paso's Missions and Indians* (1951), *The Mother Mission: Our Lady of Mount Carmel* (1952), and *Seventieth Anniversary of Columbianism in Texas* (1972).

Calles, Plutarco Elías

b. September 25, 1887
Guaymas, Mexico
d. October 19, 1945
Mexico City, Mexico
fields: Government and Politics

Calles was a member of the Sonoran Dynasty, which dominated Mexico's political life between 1920 and 1934. As president and *jefe máximo* (1924-1934), he institutionalized the Mexican Revolution and embarked upon a reform program that laid the foundation for modern Mexico's economic and political growth.

Callimachus

b. c. 305 B.C.E.
Cyrene, Libya
d. c. 240 B.C.E.
Alexandria, Egypt
fields: Literature

Although most of Callimachus' work has been lost, his hymns and epigrams—incorporating drama, sophistication, and a sense of history—survive as masterpieces of their kind. He set an ideal of tone and content which has influenced poets for centuries.

Callis, Eulalia de. *See* Fages, Doña Eulalia

Calloway, Cab

full: Cabell Calloway III
b. Dec. 25, 1907
Rochester, N.Y.
d. Nov. 18, 1994
Hosckessin, Del.
fields: Music (musician)

African American musician; Cab Calloway's career as a master of ceremonies and big band leader began with his directing of the band, the Missourians, later called Cab Calloway and His Orchestra; for a decade at Harlem's Cotton Club, Duke Ellington and Calloway played alternating engagements; Calloway's 1931 signature song, "Minnie the Moocher," with its "hi-de-ho" shout, and his "scat" improvisations of nonsensical but rhythmic syllables gave Calloway his unique style; in 1948, Calloway disbanded his orchestra, but he continued to work as a concert and club headliner into the 1980's and 1990's; Calloway published his *Hipster's Dictionary* (1938; which sold more than two million copies) and an autobiography, *Of Minnie the Moocher and Me* (1976) and appeared on radio shows, stage, and film.

Calmette, Albert

b. July 12, 1863
Nice, France
d. October 29, 1933
Paris, France
fields: Biology, Medicine

Calmette, working with Camille Guérin, was the first to introduce vaccination against tuberculosis. In 1894, he improved the serum used to treat patients with plague that was first prepared by Alexandre Yersin. Calmette was one of the first to introduce a single antiserum against snake venom that was effective against many different types of snakes. His work in public health extended to the introduction of sewage purification as well as the control of many infectious diseases.

Calvin, John

b. July 10, 1509
Noyon, Picardy

d. May 27, 1564
Geneva
fields: Religion and Theology

Calvin was one of the most important theologians of the Protestant Reformation of the sixteenth century. The Reformed church that he established in Geneva became a model for Calvinist churches throughout Europe. Calvinism itself became the most dynamic Protestant religion of the seventeenth century.

Calvin, Melvin

b. Apr. 8, 1911
St. Paul, Minnesota
fields: Botany, Biology, Chemistry

Melvin Calvin won the 1961 Nobel Prize in Chemistry. He demonstrated the path of carbon in photosynthesis, the biochemical process on which all life depends.

Camaekin. *See* Kamiakin

Camarillo, Albert

né: Alberto Michael Camarillo
b. Feb. 9, 1948
Compton, Calif.
fields: Historiography

Latino historian. Albert Camarillo began teaching history at Stanford University in 1975, directed the Stanford Center for Chicano Research from 1980 to 1985, and was executive director of the Inter-University Program for Latino Research from 1983 to 1988. His primary area of interest is the history of Mexican Americans and other minorities in urban areas of the United States. Among his published works are *Chicanos in a Changing Society: From Mexican Pueblos to American Barrios in Santa Barbara and Southern California, 1848-1930* (1979), *Chicanos in California* (1984), and *Latinos in the United States: A Historical Bibliography* (1986).

Cambacérès, Jean-Jacques-Régis de

b. October 18, 1753
Montpellier, France
d. March 8, 1824
Paris, France
fields: Law, Government and Politics

Cambacérès served France as a skilled jurist, an able legislator, and a prudent administrator during the revolutionary period. As second consul to Napoleon I, he effected a new civil code, controlled the media, and served as a moderating influence on the emperor. Without personal political ambitions, he dedicated himself to maintaining Napoleon's power and to serving his country.

Cambridge, Godfrey

b. Feb. 26, 1933
New York, N.Y.
d. Nov. 29, 1976
Hollywood, Calif.
fields: Theater and Entertainment, Film

African American actor; in the 1960's, Godfrey Cambridge became known as an acerbic comedian, stage actor, and film star; his film credits include his portrayal of Grave Digger Jones in *Cotton Comes to Harlem* (1970) and its sequel, *Come Back, Charleston Blue* (1972), and his role as a bigoted white executive who becomes black in *Watermelon Man* (1970); he died of a heart attack at age 44.

Cameron, Donaldina Mackenzie

b. July 26, 1869
New Zealand
d. Jan. 4, 1968
Palo Alto, Calif.
fields: Education, Social Reform, Civil Rights

Donaldina Mackenzie Cameron, who began by working for the Chinese Presbyterian Mission Home in San Francisco's Chinatown in 1895, dedicated her life to aiding, educating, and Christianizing Chinese immigrants, particularly prostitutes and slave girls. She and the mission home endured threats, intimidation, and violence levied against them by the Chinese *tong* associations. She rescued more than three thousand Chinese and Japanese women, and her work helped end the Chinese and Japanese illegal slave trade to the United States.

Cameron, Richard

b. c. 1648
Falkland, Fife, Scotland
d. July 22, 1680
Airds Moss (or Ayrsmoss), near Auchinleck, Ayrshire, Scotland
fields: Religion and Theology

Although Cameron prepared for ordination in the Church of Scotland, he became a zealous Covenanter during the Restoration period in Britain. He was killed during a revolt against the established order, but his followers, the Cameronians, later established the Reformed Presbyterian Church.

Camões, Luís de

aka: Luís de Camoëns
b. c. 1524
probably Lisbon, Portugal
d. June 10, 1580
Lisbon, Portugal
fields: Literature

Camões is the author of *Os Lusíadas* (1572; *The Lusiads*, 1655), the national epic of Portugal. Celebrating the voyage of Vasco da Gama, the poem recites the heroic history of the Portuguese nation.

Campa, Arthur L.

né: Arturo León Campa
b. Feb. 20, 1905
Guaymas, Sonora, Mexico
d. 1978
fields: Scholarship (folklorist)

Latino folklorist. Arthur L. Campa spent ten years working on his doctorate at Columbia University while teaching at the University of New Mexico during the academic year. From 1946 to 1972, he taught in the modern languages department of the University of Denver. Campa was known for his research concerning the legends of the American Southwest and the differences between Anglo and Mexican Americans. Among the books he published were *A Bibliography of Spanish Folklore in New Mexico* (1930), *Treasures of the Sangre de Cristos* (1962), and *Hispanic Culture in the Southwest* (1979).

Campanella, Roy

b. Nov. 19, 1921
Philadelphia, Pa.
d. June 26, 1993
Los Angeles, Calif.
fields: Sports (baseball player)

African American baseball player; after becoming a top star in the Negro Leagues, Roy Campanella was signed in 1946 to the Brooklyn Dodgers; in 1948 he was called up from the minor league team and would remain the Dodgers' regular catcher until an automobile accident in January, 1958, left him a quadriplegic; during his career the Dodgers were five-time National League champions, and he was named National League Most Valuable Player three times (1951, 1953, 1955); during the 1953 season, he set major league records for a catcher with forty-one home runs, 142 runs batted in, and 807 putouts; in 1969, elected to the Baseball Hall of Fame.

Campaneris, Bert

né: Dagoberto Campaneris y Blanco
b. Mar. 9, 1942
Pueblo Nuevo, Cuba
fields: Sports (baseball player)

Latino baseball player. In 1964, shortstop Bert Campaneris became only the third player in the history of baseball to hit a home run on the first pitch thrown to him. He went on to a nineteen-year career in which he led the American League in triples in 1965, in hits in 1968, and in stolen bases in 1965, 1966, 1967, 1968, 1970, and 1972. He was named to the American League All-Star Team in 1965, 1972, 1973, 1974, 1975, and

1977. He also played on the Oakland Athletics' 1972, 1973, and 1974 world championship teams.

Campbell, Alexander

b. September 12, 1788
Balleymena, County Antrim, Ireland
d. March 4, 1866
Bethany, West Virginia
fields: Religion and Theology

Campbell became a leader in a movement that attempted to restore the original structure of the Christian church of the first century, helping spawn both the Disciples of Christ and the Churches of Christ in the process.

Campbell, Aunt Sally

né: Sally Campbell
b. ?
fields: Historical Figure

African American gold miner; in the 1800's, Aunt Sally Campbell mined in Deadwood, South Dakota; it is believed that she was the first non-Native American woman to visit the Black Hills.

Campbell, Bebe Moore

b. 1950
fields: Literature (novelist and journalist)

African American novelist and journalist; Bebe Moore Campbell's writing include *Successful Women, Angry Men—Backlash in the Two-Career Marriage* (1986), *Sweet Summer: Growing Up with and Without My Dad* (1989), *Your Blues Ain't Like Mine* (1992), *Brothers and Sisters* (1994), and *Singing in the Comeback Choir* (1998).

Campbell, Ben Nighthorse

b. Apr. 13, 1933
Auburn, Calif.
fields: Government and Politics, Native American Affairs

Northern Cheyenne senator; after establishing himself as a jewelry designer and quarter-horse rancher in Colorado, Ben Nighthorse Campbell was elected to the Colorado State Legislature (1983-1986); served in Congress as Colorado's third congressional district representative (1987-1992); in 1992 he became the first person of American Indian descent since Charles Curtis to be elected to the Senate. He was reelected in 1998.

Campbell, Bill

full: William Campbell
b. 1954
Raleigh, N.C.
fields: Law, Government and Politics (attorney and politician)

African American attorney and politician; in 1994, Bill Campbell became mayor of Atlanta. While mayor, the Summer Olympics were held in Atlanta in 1996.

Campbell, Chris

b. Sept. 21, 1954
Westfield, N.J.
fields: Sports (wrestler)

African American wrestler; in 1981 at 180.5 pounds, Chris Campbell became the world champion; in 1983 he was national champion; in 1990 he was national champion, world team trials champion, and world silver medalist (at 198 pounds); in 1991 he was again national champion and world team trials champion; he was a member of the 1980 and 1992 Olympic teams.

Campbell, Earl Christian

b. Mar. 29, 1955
Tyler, Tex.
fields: Sports (football player)

African American football player; at the University of Texas, Earl Christian Campbell played as an All-American fullback and running back, winning the Heisman Trophy in 1977; in 1978 he signed with the Houston Oilers as the number-one NFL draft pick; during his career (1978-1981), Campbell scored 74 touchdowns and gained a total of 9,407 yards, leading the NFL in yards gained during those four seasons; in 1991 elected to the Pro Football Hall of Fame.

Campbell, John Archibald

b. 1811
d. 1889
fields: Law

U.S. Supreme Court justice, 1853-1861; appointed by President Pierce. Resigned soon after Alabama's secession from the Union and became assistant secretary of war for the Confederacy. Significant opinion: *Scott v. Sandford*, 60 U.S. 393 (1857) (concurring opinion).

Campbell, Kim

né: Avril Phaedra Campbell
b. March 10, 1947
Port Alberni, British Columbia, Canada
fields: Government and Politics

As Canada's first woman prime minister, Kim Campbell advanced the quest of North American women for high political office.

Campbell, Little Milton. *See* Little Milton

Campbell, Tevin

b. 1977
Dallas, Tex.
fields: Music (singer)

African American singer; as a twelve-year-old in seventh grade, Tevin Campbell was signed by Quincy Jones; at age thirteen, his song "Tomorrow (A Better You, a Better Me) topped the rhythm-and-blues charts; he earned a Grammy nomination for "Round and Round," (1990), a hit cut from the sound track of Prince's movie *Graffiti Bridge*; "Tell Me What You Want Me to Do," the first single from his debut album *T.E.V.I.N.* (1991) reached the top ten; he has made guest television appearances on *Saturday Night Live*, Arsenio Hall's and Oprah Winfrey's talk shows, and on the series *The Fresh Prince of Bel Air* (1991).

Campbell-Bannerman, Henry

né: Henry Campbell
b. September 7, 1836
Glasgow, Scotland
d. April 22, 1908
London, England
fields: Government and Politics

Henry Campbell-Bannerman was prime minister of Great Britain from 1905 to 1908. His government formulated extensive social and economic legislation, but the House of Lords vetoed almost all of it. Some notable objectives were achieved, including the Trade Disputes Act of 1906.

Campeche, José

b. Jan. 6, 1752
San Juan, Puerto Rico
d. Nov. 7, 1809
Puerto Rico
fields: Art, Music, Architecture

Latino painter, sculptor, architect, and musician. José Campeche, considered by many to be Puerto Rico's first great artist, began drawing as a child and honed his painting skills during his twenties by studying with exiled Spanish painter Luis Paret y Alcalzar. Campeche's best-known paintings were portraits of Puerto Rico's upper-class society, most of which were done between 1785 and 1801. He also painted religious images and scenes that captured Puerto Rican life and historic events.

Campusano, Chuy

full: Jesús Campusano
b. 1943
d. 1997
fields: Art (painter)

Latino painter. In 1971, Chuy Campusano, along with Ruben Guzmán and Spain Rodríguez, painted an outdoor mural in San Francisco's Mission District that foreshadowed the Chicano mural movement in California. The early mural was significant because it reflected a new, positive self-image among Latinos, who were beginning to reject the idea of themselves as outsiders in American culture. Campusano also painted murals on the Mission District community center, a library, and a police station, and designed a mural for the Mission District Bank of America.

Camus, Albert

b. November 7, 1913
Mondovi, Algeria
d. January 4, 1960
near Villeblevin, France
fields: Literature, Philosophy

Camus's philosophical and literary writings established his reputation as the moral conscience of France during the 1940's and 1950's. With understated eloquence, he reaffirmed the intrinsic values of individual freedom and dignity in the face of such evils as Nazism, Stalinism, and colonial exploitation. He won the Nobel Prize in Literature in 1957.

Canady, Hortense

b. Aug. 18, 1927
Chicago, Ill.
fields: Education

African American educational administrator; Hortense Canady served two terms as president of the African American women's sorority Delta Sigma Theta (1983-1988); under Canady's leadership the sorority focused on the issues of international human rights, illiteracy, single parenting, acquired immune deficiency syndrome, and drug abuse; she also was a member of the Education Committee of the NAACP; was elected to the Lansing, Michigan, Board of Education (1969); received the Sojourner Truth Award from the Negro Business and Professional Women's Association (1968).

Canal, Giovanni Antonio. *See* Canaletto

Canaletto

né: Giovanni Antonio Canal
b. October 18, 1697
Venice
d. April 20, 1768
Venice
fields: Art

Among the most popular of the Old Masters, Canaletto preserved in his canvases the world of eighteenth century Venice. His realistic portrayal of the commonplace and his brilliant clarity influenced numerous artists in Italy and England.

Cancel Miranda, Rafael

b. 1929
Mayagüez, Puerto Rico
fields: Historical Figure

Latino revolutionary figure. Rafael Cancel Miranda spent two years in prison for refusing to serve in the U.S. Army in the early 1950's. He then moved to New York and met Lolita Lebrón Soto, Andrés Figueroa Cordero, and Irving Flores, Puerto Rican nationalists working to gain independence for their home country. On March 1, 1954, the four opened fire at the U.S. House of Representatives and wounded five congressmen. Cancel Miranda was sentenced to twenty-five to seventy-five years in prison, but all four nationalists were pardoned by President Jimmy Carter in 1979 and returned to Puerto Rico.

Candela, Felix

b. January 27, 1910
Madrid, Spain
fields: Architecture

Candela specialized in thin concrete shells as an architectural form. Although not the first to use them, he carried them to new artistic heights, while maintaining their practicality and economy.

Candelaria, Nash

b. May 7, 1928
Los Angeles, Calif.
fields: Literature

Latino novelist. Nash Candelaria was born in Los Angeles, but much of his writing explores the history of New Mexico, where his ancestors were among the first Spanish settlers. His first three novels—*Memories of the Alhambra* (1977), *Not by the Sword* (1982), and *Inheritance of Strangers* (1984)—are a historical trilogy based in New Mexico. Candelaria also published the short-story collection *The Day the Cisco Kid Shot John Wayne* (1988) and the novel *Leonor Park* (1991).

Canegata, Leonard Lionel Cornelius. *See* Lee, Canada

Cannary, Martha. *See* Calamity Jane

Canning, George

b. April 11, 1770
London, England
d. August 8, 1827
Chiswick, England
fields: Government and Politics

By placing British power behind the national independence movements in Latin America and Greece, Canning helped further Great Britain's own economic and political interests and weakened the forces of reaction in Europe.

Cannon, Annie Jump

b. December 11, 1863
Dover, Delaware
d. April 13, 1941
Cambridge, Massachusetts
fields: Astronomy

In her work at the Harvard College Observatory, Cannon cataloged stars according to their spectral class into the Draper Catalogue and discovered several new variable stars and novas.

Canonchet

aka: Nanuntenoo
b. c. 1630
Apr., 1676
Stonington, Conn.
fields: Government and Politics, Warfare and Conquest, Native American Affairs

Native American leader. Narragansett tribal leader Canonchet is best known for his interactions with the British colonists during King Philip's War (1675-1676).

Canonicus

b. c. 1565
d. June 4, 1647
fields: Diplomacy, Government and Politics, Native American Affairs

Native American leader. Narragansett leader Canonicus kept the Narragansetts at peace with the British colonists for the twenty-seven years between their arrival in 1620 and his death; he befriended Roger Williams, giving him the land on which stands present-day Providence, Rhode Island.

Canova, Antonio

b. November 1, 1757
Possagno, near Venice
d. October 13, 1822
Venice
fields: Art

Canova fixed the ideal style in neoclassical sculpture for generations. His works were considered the standard of international artistic excellence in his day and his name and opinion held great authority.

Canseco, José

né: José Canseco y Capas
b. July 2, 1964
Havana, Cuba
fields: Sports (baseball player)

Latino baseball player. Outfielder José Canseco was named Minor League Player of the Year in 1985 by *The Sporting News* and American League Rookie of the Year in 1986 during his first season in the majors with the Oakland Athletics. In 1988, Canseco led the league with 42 home runs, 40 stolen bases, and a slugging average of .569, winning the league's Most Valuable Player Award. Canseco helped Oakland win 1988, 1989, and 1990 American League championships and the 1989 World Series title. He was selected for the All-Star team in 1986, 1988-1990, and 1992. In 1992 he was traded to the Texas Rangers. During the 1990's, he also played for the Boston Red Sox, Oakland Athletics,

Toronto Blue Jays, and the Tampa Bay Devil Rays.

Cansino, Margarita Carmen. *See* Hayworth, Rita

Cantinflas
né: Mario Moreno Reyes
b. Aug. 12, 1911
Mexico City, Mexico
d. April 20, 1993
Mexico City, Mexico
fields: Theater and Entertainment (actor)

Latino actor. Mario Moreno Reyes ran away from agricultural school to join a traveling tent show. He created the persona "Cantinflas," a man who spoke in gibberish and non sequiturs and who soon came to be known as the Mexican Charlie Chaplin. He began a film career and became one of the biggest stars in Spanish-language cinema. His Mexican films include *No te engañes, corazón* (1936), *Allí está el detalle* (1941), and *Ni sangre ni arena* (1941). He began his own production company in the 1950's and had roles in two Hollywood films: *Around the World in Eighty Days* (1956) and *Pepe* (1960).

Cantor, Georg
full: Georg Ferdinand Ludwig Philipp Cantor
b. Mar. 3, 1845
St. Petersburg, Russia
d. Jan. 6, 1918
Halle, Germany
fields: Mathematics (number theory, set theory, and topology)

In 1874 Georg Cantor published proof that real numbers are uncountable. In 1895, he published "Beiträge zur Begründung der tranfiniten Mengenlehre I" (*Contributions to the Founding of the Theory of Transfinite Numbers*, 1897), which proved the existence of a hierarchy of infinite sets of different sizes. He also created set theory and the infinite cardinal and ordinal numbers. In 1904 he received the Sylvester Medal.

Canute the Great
né: Canute Sveinson
b. c. 995
Jelling?, Denmark
d. November 12, 1035
Shaftesbury, Dorset
fields: Monarchy, Government and Politics

This Dane's conquest and strong kingship (1017-1035) gave England a period of peace and prosperity which began to repair damage, destruction, and demoralization wrought by centuries of Viking attacks (793-1016). A fierce young Viking himself, Canute matured into a ruler who appeared to be the ideal Christian king, lawgiver, and protector of his people, but Canute's very success not only foreshadowed but also helped to bring about the Norman Conquest of 1066.

Capablanca, José Raúl
b. Nov. 19, 1888
Havana, Cuba
d. Mar. 8, 1942
New York, N.Y.
fields: Sports (chess champion)

Latino chess champion. José Raúl Capablanca, who learned to play chess by watching his father play, defeated the champion of Cuba at the age of thirteen. He moved to the United States, dropped out of Columbia University to pursue a chess career, and defeated U.S. champion Frank Marshall in 1909. In 1911 Capablanca won an international tournament in San Sebastian, Spain, after competitors argued that he lacked the experience to compete. In 1921 Capablanca defeated Emanuel Lasker to take the world title and then lost it in 1927 to Alexander Alekhine. Capablanca wrote several chess books, including *My Chess Career* (1920) and *A Primer of Chess* (1935).

Capek, Karel
b. January 9, 1890
Malé Svatoňovice, Bohemia, Austro-Hungarian Empire
d. December 25, 1938
Prague, Czechoslovakia
fields: Literature

Čapek, a practicing journalist, is best remembered as a dramatist who also wrote children's stories, short stories, and novels, many of them satirical. An early master of science fiction, Čapek's most famous play, *R.U.R.: Rossum's Universal Robots* (with Josef Čapek, 1921; English translation, 1923) popularized the word "robot," invented by his brother Josef.

Capetillo, Luisa
b. Oct. 28, 1879
Arecibo, Puerto Rico
d. Apr. 10, 1922
Río Piedras, Puerto Rico
fields: Social Reform, Labor Movement

Latina union leader. Luisa Capetillo believed that many problems faced by working-class women (domestic and otherwise) would disappear if workers earned a fair wage and if women could vote. She joined the Federation of Free Workers and wrote articles for its newspaper. She founded the newspaper *La mujer* (the woman) in 1910, then traveled to Cuba, Florida, and New York, where she wrote for *Cultura obrera* (work culture). She then returned to Puerto Rico and organized labor strikes.

Capone, Al
full: Alphonse Capone
b. January 17, 1899
Brooklyn, New York
d. January 25, 1947
Palm Island, Florida
fields: Law

Through his modern business practices, cruel brutality, and self-promotion, Capone revolutionized organized crime in the United States during the Prohibition era.

Capote, Truman
né: Truman Streckfus Persons
b. September 30, 1924
New Orleans, Louisiana
d. August 25, 1984
Los Angeles, California
fields: Literature

Recognized as one of the leading American authors of the second half of the twentieth century, Capote regarded himself as a stylist, a writer whose mastery of the craft was so absolute that he could adapt his writing style to any media.

Capra, Frank
b. May 18, 1897
Palermo, Italy
d. September 3, 1991
La Quinta, California
fields: Film

As a Hollywood filmmaker, Frank Capra focused on common people and the dangers of demagoguery in a democracy in such films as *Meet John Doe* (1942) and *Mr. Smith Goes to Washington* (1941). During World War II he made such noted documentary films as the *Why We Fight* series and *The Negro Soldier* (1944) for the U.S. government.

Captain Jack
aka: Kintpuash (Having Indigestion)
b. c. 1840
Lost River, Northern Calif.
d. Oct. 3, 1873
Fort Klamath, Oreg.
fields: Native American Affairs, Warfare and Conquest

Modoc tribal chief; after the Modocs ceded their Southwest Oregon and Northern California territory to the U.S. government in 1864 and were required to share a reservation with the more favorably treated Klamath Indians, Kintpuash (nicknamed Captain Jack by whites) led the Modocs back to California in 1865 and refused to return to the reservation; troops sent in November, 1872, to return the Modocs to Oregon became involved in the Modoc War of 1872-1873 in which Kintpuash and his small band of followers retreated to the lava beds near Tule Lake, California, and held off a large number of soldiers for several months; the Modocs were finally overcome, the resisting Modocs were tried without legal defense, and Kintpuash and three other leaders were hanged.

Captain Pipe. *See* Hopocan

Cara, Irene

né: Irene Escalera
b. Mar. 18, 1959
Bronx, N.Y.
fields: Music (popular singer and keyboard player), Film,

African American singer, dancer, and keyboard player; Irene Cara rose to fame with her soundtrack recordings for the 1980 film *Fame*, for which she was nominated for two Grammy Awards and a Golden Globe award; in 1983 she received two Grammy Awards for her top-selling single from the film *Flashdance*; she has also appeared in Broadway musicals and, in 1979, played the role of Bertha Palmer in the television miniseries *Roots: The Next Generations*.

Caraway, Hattie

né: Hattie Ophelia Wyatt
b. Feb. 1, 1878
near Bakerville, Tenn.
d. Dec. 21, 1950
Falls Church, Va.
fields: Government and Politics

Hattie Caraway was the first woman U.S. senator. Took over husband Thaddeus Carway's senator position for Arkansas after his death in 1931. Won renomination in 1932, becoming the first woman elected to the U.S. Senate; elected for a second term in 1938; in 1943 cosponsored the Equal Rights Amendment.

Carbajal, Michael

b. 1968
Arizona
fields: Sports (boxer)

Latino boxer. Michael Carbajal, the son of boxer Manuel Carbajal, was selected as the light-flyweight (106 pounds) member of the U.S. team for the 1988 Seoul Olympics, where he won the silver medal. As a professional he was nicknamed "Little Hands of Stone" and, in July, 1990, won the International Boxing Federation (IBF) light-flyweight title. In February of 1994 he was defeated by Chiquita Gonzalez in the first fight to offer a $1 million purse in a weight class under lightweight. In 1997 he again won the IBF light-flyweight title.

Cardano, Gerolamo (Jerome Cardan)

aka: Girolamo or Geronimo Cardano
aka: Jerome Cardan
b. Sept. 24, 1501
Pavia, Duchy of Milan (now Italy)
d. Sept. 21, 1576
Rome, Papal States (now Italy)
fields: Mathematics (algebra and probability)

Gerolamo Cardano (Jerome Cardan) published his greatest work, *Artis Magnae, sive de Regulis Algebraicis Liber Unus* (*The Great Art: Or, On the Rules of Algebra*, 1968) in 1545. It revealed the algebraic solutions of the cubic and quartic equations. In 1570 he was briefly jailed for charges of heresy. In 1575, he completed his autobiography, *De Vita Propria Liber* (*The Book of My Life*, 1930).

Cárdenas, Lázaro

b. May 21, 1895
Jiquilpan, Mexico
d. October 19, 1970
Mexico City, Mexico
fields: Government and Politics

The energetic and controversial President of Mexico from 1934 to 1940, Cárdenas carried out bold policies intended to benefit peasants and workers. In 1938, he posed a major challenge to the United States and Great Britain by his nationalization of their Mexican oil properties. His assertion of the authority of the Mexican government left an indelible imprint on his times and provided precedents for other developing nations after World War II.

Cardona, Florencia Bisenta de Casillas Martínez. *See* Carr, Vikki

Cardozo, Benjamin Nathan

b. May 24, 1870
New York, New York
d. July 9, 1938
Port Chester, New York
fields: Law

Cardozo's twenty-five-year career on the New York Court of Appeals and the United States Supreme Court made him one of the most admired and respected judges in American history. As a scholar, he illuminated the nature of the judicial process; as a judge, he helped transform American law to meet the needs of a changing, modern society.

Cardozo, Francis Louis

b. Feb. 1, 1837
Charleston, S.C.
d. July 22, 1903
Washington, D.C.
fields: Government and Politics

African American reconstruction statesman; born free and educated in Scotland and England, Francis Louis Cardozo was one of the best-educated African Americans of the Reconstruction era (1865-1877); was a member of the South Carolina constitutional convention; served as secretary of state for South Carolina (appointed 1868; the first African American to be appointed to a cabinet post at the state level); later served as state treasurer.

Cardozo, W. Warrick

full: William Warrick Cardozo
b. Apr. 6, 1905
Washington, D.C.
d. Aug. 11, 1962
Washington, D.C.
fields: Medicine

African American physician; W. Warrick Cardozo was an early pioneer in the investigation of sickle-cell anemia; at Freedmen's Hospital, worked as an associate professor of pediatrics; also served as school medical inspector for the District of Columbia board of health.

Carew, Rod

full: Rodney Cline Carew y Scott
b. Oct. 1, 1945
Gatun, Panama
fields: Sports (baseball player)

African American baseball player; elected to the Baseball Hall of Fame in 1991, Rod Carew held seven batting titles during his career; he had a lifetime batting average of .328 (featuring fifteen consecutive seasons above .300).

Carey, Archibald J., Jr.

b. Feb 29, 1908
Chicago, Ill.
fields: Government and Politics

Local African American politician and political appointee; after serving as pastor of Chicago's Woodlawn African Methodist Episcopal Church (1930-1949) and while working as a private practice attorney (1939-1966), Archibald J. Carey, Jr., was elected to two terms as Chicago's Third Ward alderman (1947-1955); was appointed as alternate delegate to the United Nations by President Dwight D. Eisenhower (1953-1956); later served as vice chairman of the President's Committee on Governmental Employment Policy; in 1989 appointed to serve as Illinois Supreme Court judge.

Carey, Lott

b. 1780?
Charles City County, Va.
d. Nov. 10, 1828
Cape Mesurado, Liberia
fields: Exploration and Colonization

Early African American colonist; after purchasing his freedom from slavery in 1813, Lott Carey traveled to Africa in 1821; an ordained Baptist minister motivated by evangelical Christianity and a nationalist political commitment to build an African American colony, Carey founded several congregations in Africa, including the first Baptist church in Liberia, and served as both vice governor and acting governor of the colony of Liberia; during an armed confrontation with Africans, Carey was killed.

Cariaga, Roman Ruiz

b. 1909
Santo Tomas, Philippines
fields: Anthropology, Journalism, Sociology

Filipino American anthropologist and sociologist Roman Ruiz Cariaga studied Filipinos in Hawaiian plantation communities and in Honolulu between 1932 and 1936, publishing studies about their lives. He also wrote articles on Filipinos in Hawaii and in the Philippines for magazines and daily newspapers. His writings combating widespread stereotypes about Filipinos and provided rich information on their experiences and struggles in both rural and urban settings. His insightful contributions played a significant role in increasing the knowledge and understanding of the Filipino American historical experience in Hawaii.

Caritat, Marie-Jean-Antoine-Nicolas. *See* Condorcet, Marquis de

Carleton, Guy

aka: Lord Dorchester
aka: first Baron Dorchester
b. September 3, 1724
Strabane, County Tyrone, Ireland
d. November 10, 1808
Stubbings, Berkshire, England
fields: Military Affairs, Colonial Administration

Carleton's competent military leadership and adroit political sensitivity helped ease the transition of Canada from its position as conquered French province to prosperous English colony.

Carlin, George

b. May 12, 1937
Bronx, New York
fields: Theater and Entertainment

An American stand-up comedian, George Carlin won fame when the U.S. Supreme Court ruled, in 1979, on a case involving a radio broadcast of a routine he had done using seven forbidden "filthy words."

Carlos, Don

né: Carlos María Isidro de Borbón
b. March 29, 1788
Aranjuez, Spain
d. March 10, 1855
Trieste, Austrian Empire (now Italy)
fields: Government and Politics, Military Affairs

Don Carlos was the first of the Carlist claimants to the throne of Spain. His life was dedicated to disputing the right of his niece, Doña Isabel, to Spain's throne and upholding the principles, laws, and institutions of the Old Regime.

Carlos, John

full: John Wesley Carlos
b. June 5, 1945
New York, N.Y.
fields: Sports (sprinter)

African American sprinter; one of the best sprinters in the world, bronze medalist (in the 200-meter) John Carlos—along with his fellow medalist Tommie Smith— raised his fist in a black power salute during the 1968 Olympics in Mexico City and was ordered off the Olympic team and out of the Olympic Village; won the Amateur Athletic Union and National Collegiate Athletic Association 200-meter run and equaled the world records for the indoor 60 and outdoor 100; participated in the professional International Track Association (1973-1975); also had a brief career in professional football.

Carlson, Chester F.

full: Chester Floyd Carlson
b. February 8, 1906
Seattle, Washington
d. September 19, 1968
New York, New York
fields: Invention and Technology

Working in his own laboratory, Carlson developed the first electrostatic copying device. After being rebuffed many times in his quest for corporate sponsorship, Carlson achieved fame and riches when his invention was developed into the hugely successful Xerox machine.

Carlyle, Thomas

b. December 4, 1795
Ecclefachan, Dumfriesshire, Scotland
d. February 5, 1881
London, England
fields: Historiography, Literature

As the most eminent man of letters in the Victorian age, Carlyle thundered against what he saw as the materialism and moral decadence of the age. The uniqueness of his vivid and emphatic style, and his ability to recreate the flavor and feeling of historical events, have earned for him a place among the masters of English prose.

Carmichael, Stokely

aka: Kwame Toure
b. June 29, 1941
Port of Spain, Trinidad
d. Nov. 15, 1998
Conakry, Guinea
fields: Civil Rights, Social Reform

African American political activist; Stokely Carmichael was born in Trinidad; after attending Howard University, he became an accomplished organizer for the Student Nonviolent Coordinating Committee (SNCC) of which he was elected chair in 1966; popularized the controversial phrase "black power" as well as radical policies, which led to his expulsion from SNCC in 1968; joined the Black Panther Party in 1968, but resigned the following year and moved to Guinea, Africa; since the 1970's consistently supported Pan-Africanism; changed his name in 1978 to Kwame Toure, in honor of African leaders Sékou Touré and Kwame Nkrumah.

Carn, Jean

b. 1948?
fields: Music (jazz vocalist)

African American jazz vocalist; before separating in 1973, Jean Carn and her husband Doug Carn produced three albums, *Infant Eyes*, *Spirit of the New Land*, and *Revelations*; to support her three children, Jean worked as a solo vocalist with the Duke Ellington orchestra; she later toured with Norman Connors and Earth, Wind, and Fire; her first solo album produced the hit single "Free Love"; the albums *Happy to Be With You* and *When I Find You Love* followed.

Carnap, Rudolf

b. May 18, 1891
Ronsdorf, Germany
d. September 14, 1970
Santa Monica, California
fields: Philosophy

Carnap is recognized as a leading figure in the philosophy of logical positivism and made significant contributions to logic, the theory of probability, philosophy of science, and linguistic analysis.

Carnegie, Andrew

b. November 25, 1835
Dunfermline, Scotland
d. August 11, 1919
Lenox, Massachusetts
fields: Business and Industry, Philanthropy

One of the wealthiest men in the world at the time of his retirement from business in 1901, Carnegie achieved great fame for his business success and for his many benefactions, which became the chief interest of his later years.

Carney, Harry

né: Howell Carney
b. Apr. 1, 1910
Boston, Mass.

d. Oct. 8, 1974
New York, N.Y.
fields: Music (jazz baritone saxophonist)

African American baritone saxophonist; a member of the Duke Ellington Orchestra for over forty years, Harry Carney was the most outstanding jazz baritone saxophonist of his era; during a professional career that began in 1925, Carney recorded primarily with Duke Ellington and was a featured soloist on numerous recordings, including "Blue Reverie" (1937), "Chocolate Shake" (1941), the "Black" section from Ellington's *Black, Brown and Beige* (1943), "Sophisticated Lady" (1950) "La Plus Belle Africaine" (1966), and "Chromatic Love Affair" (1971); awards received during his career included the *Esquire* Silver Award (1945 and 1947), the *Down Beat* readers' poll (1944-1948), the *Down Beat* critics' poll (1953 and 1954), and the *Metronome* poll (1944-1948).

Carney, Pat

full: Patricia Carney
b. May 26, 1935
Shanghai, China
fields: Government and Politics

Canadian political figure. Pat Carney was a Member of Parliament for the Progressive Conservative Party from 1980 to 1988, representing the Vancouver, British Columbia, area. Minister for international trade from 1986 to 1988. Subsequently appointed to Canadian Senate.

Carney, William H.

b. 1840
Norfolk, Va.
d. Dec. 9, 1908
Boston, Mass.
fields: Warfare and Conquest

African American military hero; during the Civil War battle of Fort Wagner, S.C. (July 18, 1863), William H. Carney took up the regimental flag from his company's mortally wounded color bearer and, despite being wounded three times, never let the flag touch the ground; for his bravery, he was awarded the Medal of Honor (the first of twenty black soldiers during the Civil War to be so decorated).

Carnot, Lazare

full: Lazare-Nicolas-Marguerite Carnot
b. May 13, 1753
Nolay, Burgundy, France
d. Aug. 2, 1823
Magdeburg, Prussian Saxony (now Germany)
fields: Mathematics (geometry)

Lazare Carnot is known for his major work, *Géométrie de position* (1803). He instituted a generality for modern pure geometry with his investigation of geometric systems in different states that could evolve into each other.

Carpini, Giovanni da Pian del

b. c. 1180
Pian del Carpini (modern Piano della Magione), Umbria
d. August 1, 1252
Italy, possibly Perugia
fields: Religion and Theology, Historiography, Exploration

Combining a deep commitment to the religious ideals of Francis of Assisi with language and teaching abilities, Carpini extended the work of the Franciscans to Saxony, Germany, northern Europe, Spain, and North Africa. Upon his return from the first formal Christian mission to the Mongols, he wrote an important work on the history of the peoples of Central Asia.

Carpio, Lope de Vega. *See* Vega, Lope de

Carr, Edward Hallett

aka: E. H. Carr
b. June 28, 1892
London, England
d. November 3, 1982
Cambridge, England
fields: Scholarship, Warfare and Conquest

Edward Hallett Carr was regarded as Great Britain's finest historian of the Soviet Union, particularly for his three-volume *The Bolshevik Revolution* (1950-1953). His other works include *Britain: A Survey of British Foreign Policy from Versailles to the Outbreak of War* (1939).

Carr, Leroy

b. Mar. 27, 1905
Nashville, Tenn.
d. Apr. 29, 1935
Indianapolis, Ind.
fields: Music (pianist and blues singer)

African American pianist and blues singer; in 1928 Leroy Carr combined his sophisticated piano stylings and warm vocals with Francis "Scrapper" Blackwell's astringent guitar sound to create instant performing and recording success; by 1935 the duo had recorded 162 cuts including "How Long, How Long Blues," "Ain't It a Shame," "I Believe I'll Make a Change," and "Mean Mistreater Mama"; a heavy drinker, Carr died of kidney disease.

Carr, Vikki

né: Florencia Bisenta de Casillas Martínez Cardona
b. July 19, 1940
El Paso, Tex.
fields: Music (singer)

Mexican American singer; Vikki Carr's best-selling records and fifteen gold albums included such hits as "Can't Take My Eyes Off of You" and "It Must Be Him" (charted at number three); she also recorded twelve albums with CBS-Mexico, including *Disculpame* and *Ni Princesa*; named Woman of the Year by the *Los Angeles Times* in 1970; founded the Vikki Carr Scholarship Foundation in 1971 to provide higher education opportunities for young Mexican Americans; received Grammy Awards for her Spanish-language album *Simplemente Mujer* (1985) and for *Cosas Del Amor* (1991; for Best Latin Pop Album).

Carracci, Agostino

b. August 16, 1557
Bologna, Papal States
d. February 23, 1602
Parma
fields: Art

From the mid-1580's onward, the paintings and frescoes of Ludovico, Agostino, and Annibale Carracci of Bologna made their city one of the major centers of reaction against the so-called mannerist style, an elegant and often overrefined style that had dominated Italian art for sixty or seventy years.

Carracci, Annibale

b. November 3, 1560
Bologna, Papal States
d. July 15, 1609
Rome
fields: Art

From the mid-1580's onward, the paintings and frescoes of Ludovico, Agostino, and Annibale Carracci of Bologna made their city one of the major centers of reaction against the so-called mannerist style, an elegant and often overrefined style that had dominated Italian art for sixty or seventy years. When Annibale went to Rome in the early 1590's, his work laid the foundation for the magnificent pictorial accomplishments of the Baroque period.

Carracci, Ludovico

b. April 21 (baptized), 1555
Bologna, Papal States
d. November 13, 1619
Bologna, Papal States
fields: Art

From the mid-1580's onward, the paintings and frescoes of Ludovico, Agostino, and Annibale Carracci of Bologna made their city one of the major centers of reaction against the so-called mannerist style, an elegant and often overrefined style that had dominated Italian art for sixty or seventy years

Carrasco, Barbara

b. 1955

fields: Art

Latina artist. Barbara Carrasco has designed and painted numerous public murals in Los Angeles that focus on minority and feminist issues. She has also painted murals in Armenia and Nicaragua. Controversy has surrounded her work, including the mural *L.A. History—A Mexican Perspective*, which she was commissioned to paint for the 1984 Olympics and which depicted such scenes of minority oppression as the internment of Japanese Americans during World War II.

Carrera, Barbara

b. Dec. 31, 1945
Managua, Nicaragua

fields: Theater and Entertainment (actor), Fashion (model)

Latina actor and model. Barbara Carrera, who began her career as a fashion model, appeared in her first film, *The Master Gunfighter*, in 1975. She has played varied roles in such television miniseries and movies as *Centennial* (1978) and *Sins of the Past* (1984). She played Angelica Nero in the television series *Dallas* in 1985 and 1986. Carrera has also acted in numerous films, including *Embryo* (1976), *The Island of Dr. Moreau* (1977), *Condorman* (1981), *I the Jury* (1982), *Lone Wolf McQuade* (1983), *Never Say Never Again* (1983), *Wild Geese II* (1985), and *Loverboy* (1989).

Carrero, Jaime

b. 1931
Mayagüez, Puerto Rico

fields: Literature

Latino writer. Jaime Carrero's work during the 1950's and 1960's helped lay the foundation for the "Nuyorican" literary movement. His dual education in both New York City and Puerto Rico is reflected in his bilingual writing, which often deals with nationalism and cultural identity. His work includes the novel *Raquelo tiene un mensaje* (1970; Raquelo has a message), which won the Primer Premio del Ateneo Puertorriqueño; the play *Flag Inside* (1966), which won the same award; and the poetry collection *Jet neorriqueño/Neo-Rican Jetliner Poems* (1964).

Carrillo, Eduardo

b. ?
Veracruz, Mexico

fields: Theater and Entertainment

Latino playwright and actor. After Eduardo Carrillo moved to Los Angeles in 1922 as a member of the Gran Compañía Cómico Dramático María Teresa Montoya, he began writing plays that dealt with the expatriate community in Los Angeles. *El Proceso de Aurelio Pompa* (1924), for example, dramatized the persecution of Aurelio Pompa, a Mexican laborer who was eventually executed. Carrillo wrote other *revistas* and one-acts, including *Los Angeles al día* (1922, written with Gabriel Novarro), *Malditas sean los hombres* (1924), and *En las puertas del infierno* (1925); historical plays such as *El zarco* (1924) and *Patria y honor* (1924); and the comedy *Un crimen más* (1938).

Carrillo, Leo

full: Poldo Antonio Carrillo

b. Aug. 6, 1880
Los Angeles, Calif.

d. Sept. 10, 1961
Santa Monica, Calif.

fields: Theater and Entertainment (actor)

Latino actor. Leo Carrillo began his career with a vaudeville act, moved to Broadway, and eventually acted in more than fifty films between 1930 and 1950. In his early films, such as *Love Me Forever* (1935), he played romantic leads but was later found himself playing humorous sidekicks to heroic figures. His most famous role was for television, as the partner of actor Duncan Renaldo in *The Cisco Kid*, released in the late 1950's.

Carroll, Charles

b. September 20, 1737
Annapolis, Maryland

d. November 14, 1832
Baltimore, Maryland

fields: Government and Politics, Law

With a rebellious spirit, a penchant for the law, and an ability to forecast social upheaval, Carroll fought for government reform, helping to bring about independence and religious freedom for an entire nation.

Carroll, Diahann

né: Carol Diahann Johnson

b. July 17, 1935
New York, N.Y.

fields: Theater and Entertainment, Film, Television

African American singer and actress; Diahann Carroll's stage credits include the Broadway musical *House of Flowers* (1954) and the musical *No Strings* (created by composer Richard Rodgers as a vehicle for Carroll, for which she won a Tony award); her film credits include *Carmen Jones* (1954), *Porgy and Bess* (1959), *Paris Blues* (1961), *Hurry Sundown* (1967), *Claudine* (1974; received an Academy Award nomination and an Image Award from the National Association for the Advancement of Colored People), and *The Five Heartbeats* (1991); her television credits include guest star in the *Naked City* series (1961; received two Emmy nominations), star of *Julia* (1968-1971), *The Diahann Carroll Show* (1976), *Roots: The Next Generations* (1979), *I Know Why the Caged Bird Sings* (1979), *Sister, Sister* (1982), and *Dynasty* (1984-1987).

Carroll, Lewis

né: Charles Lutwidge Dodgson

b. January 27, 1832
Daresbury, Cheshire, England

d. January 14, 1898
Guildford, Surrey, England

fields: Literature, Mathematics, Photography

Lewis Carroll wrote stories and poems that fundamentally changed and enlivened children's literature. He also pioneered children's photography and published books that advanced the fields of logic and mathematics.

Carroll, Vinnette Justine

b. Mar. 11, 1922
New York, N.Y.

fields: Theater and Entertainment (director)

African American director; in addition to television and film acting credits, Vinnette Justine Carroll is noted as the first African American female director on Broadway; she wrote and directed the New York City Urban Arts Corps productions of *Don't Bother Me, I Can't Cope* (1972) and *Your Arms Too Short to Box with God* (1975).

Carron, Thomas. *See* Tomah

Carruthers, George R.

b. October 1, 1939
Cincinnati, Ohio

fields: Astronomy, Physics

African American astrophysicist; in 1972 George R. Carruthers developed the lunar surface ultraviolet camera deployed on Apollo 16 and the ultraviolet telescope on OAO 3 (Copernicus); awarded NASA's Exceptional Scientific Achievement Medal (1972); his ultraviolet telescope is deployed on Skylab 4 (1973); becomes a senior astrophysicist at the Naval Research Laboratory (1982); develops far-ultraviolet cameras flown on space shuttle missions (1982, 1991); his electronic imaging devices and techniques for photographing hydrogen molecules in space help advance understanding of how stars are made; they also can monitor pollutants in the atmosphere above large cities.

Carson, Benjamin Solomon

b. Sept. 18, 1951
Detroit, Mich.

fields: Medicine

African American neurosurgeon; as Johns Hopkins Hospital's first African American neurosurgical resident (1978-1982), Benjamin Solomon Carson rose to become director of pediatric neurosurgery at that institution in 1985; he is noted for separating a set of German conjoined-at-the-head twins in 1987.

Carson, Clayborne

b. 1944
New York, N.Y.
fields: Scholarship

African American scholar; Clayborne Carson has written several works in the fields of African American and U.S. history; his publications include *In Struggle: SNCC and the Black Awakening of the 1960s* (1981), a study of the Student Nonviolent Coordinating Committee; his editing projects have included publishing a volume about Malcolm X and the editing of the papers of Martin Luther King, Jr.

Carson, Kit

full: Christopher Carson
b. December 24, 1809
Madison County, Kentucky
d. May 23, 1868
Fort Lyon, Colorado
fields: Exploration and Colonization, Native American Affairs, Military Affairs

As trapper, guide, Indian agent, and soldier, Carson helped open the American West to settlement. His frontier adventures continue to impress those fascinated by the West's romantic era.

Carson, Rachel

full: Rachel Louise Carson
b. May 27, 1907
Springdale, Pennsylvania
d. April 14, 1964
Silver Spring, Maryland
fields: Biology, Literature

A marine biologist and gifted expositor, Rachel Carson wrote many articles as well as three lilting, lyrical books about the sea. She is most remembered, however, for her fourth book, *Silent Spring* (1962), an exhaustively researched exposé that sparked a national furor over the irresponsible use of pesticides in America.

Carter, Benny

full: Bennett Lester Carter
b. Aug. 8, 1907
New York, N.Y.
fields: Music (jazz saxophonist, composer, arranger, and orchestra leader)

African American jazz saxophonist, composer, arranger, and orchestra leader; after forming his own successful orchestra in 1932, self-taught musician Benny Carter relocated to London in 1934 and worked as a staff arranger for the dance orchestra of the British Broadcasting Corporation and wrote such jazz standards as "Blues in My Heart" (1931) and "When Lights Are Low" (1936); in 1941, he returned to the U.S. to form a sextet that included Jimmy Hamilton and Dizzy Gillespie; his recording and arranging for Hollywood films included sound tracks for *Stormy Weather* (1943), *The Gene Krupa Story* (1959), and *An American in Paris* (1951); he has written arrangements for singers Sarah Vaughan, Ella Fitzgerald, and Ray Charles; his albums include *Further Definitions* (1961) and *Benny Carter: A Gentleman and His Music* (1985).

Carter, Betty

né: Lillie Mae Jones
aka: Lorraine Carter
b. May 16, 1930
Flint, Mich.
d. Sept. 26, 1998
Brooklyn, N.Y.
fields: Music (vocalist)

African American vocalist; known as the godmother of jazz because she helped so many young artists, Grammy award-winning Betty Carter was a member of the Lionel Hampton band in 1948; in the early 1960's, she toured with Ray Charles; in 1971 Carter launched Bet-Car Productions, her own record label; *Finally Betty Carter* (1969) and *Whatever Happened to Love?* (1982) are among her recordings.

Carter, Hurricane

né: Rubin Carter
b. May 15, 1937
Clifton, N.J.
fields: Law

African American middleweight boxer convicted of murder but later released; a contender for the world middleweight boxing championship, Hurricane Carter and his friend John Artis were sentenced by an all-white jury for the 1966 murders of three Caucasians in a New Jersey bar, based on the changed testimony of witnesses who could not initially identify them; they were later released on bail and, at a retrial in 1976, they were again convicted; in November, 1985, a federal judge overturned the 1976 conviction citing a racially biased jury and withheld evidence by the prosecution; a 1987 appeal by the prosecution to reinstate the conviction was denied.

Carter, Jimmy

full: James Earl Carter, Jr.
b. October 1, 1924
Plains, Georgia
fields: Government and Politics

Thirty-ninth president of the United States, 1977-1981. President Carter was a conservative in some policies and a liberal in others. On the one hand, he attacked government bureaucracy, moved away from détente with the Soviet Union, and increased military spending; on the other, he supported racial equality, took seriously the problems of underdeveloped countries, and pressured repressive regimes to respect human rights.

Carter, Lisle Carleton, Jr.

b. Nov. 18, 1925
New York, N.Y.
fields: Government and Politics, Education

African American government official and university administrator; after practicing law privately and for the National Urban League, Lisle Carleton Carter, Jr., joined the Department of Health, Education, and Welfare in 1961 and conducted inspections of educational and health conditions in eleven African countries; in January, 1966, he was appointed assistant secretary of HEW by President Lyndon B. Johnson; from 1968 to 1974 Carter taught at the university level, rising to serve as chancellor at Atlanta University Center and, in 1977, as president of the University of the District of Columbia.

Carter, Nell

b. Sept. 14, 1948
Birmingham, Ala.
fields: Music, Theater and Entertainment, Television

African American singer and actress; Nell Carter's Tony Award-winning role in *Ain't Misbehavin'* (1978) initiated her initial critical and popular recognition; she went on to play Nell Harper in the television series *Gimme a Break* (1981-1987) followed by appearances in several less successful television series; despite suffering a brain aneurysm, in 1992 Carter starred in a television pilot, *Maid for Each Other*, appeared in the television drama *Final Shot: The Hank Gaither's Story* as Hank Gaither's mother, and did a voice-over for the animated film *Bebe's Kids* (1992).

Carter, Robert Lee

b. Mar. 11, 1917
Caryville, Fla.
fields: Law

African American federal judge; in 1972, Robert Lee Carter was appointed U.S. district judge for the Southern District of New York by President Richard M. Nixon; prior to his appointment other positions included assistant special counsel for the NAACP (1945-1946), president of the National Committee Against Discrimination in Housing (1966-1972), and special assistant U.S. attorney for the Southern District of New York.

Carter, Ronald Levin

b. May 4, 1937
Ferndale, Mich.
fields: Music (jazz bassist)

African American jazz bassist; one of the leading bassists of his time, Ronald Levin Carter played on critically acclaimed albums such as *Miles Smiles* (1967), *Nefertiti* (1968), and *Filles De Kilimanjaro* (1969); in the 1970's, led his own jazz group and toured with "supergroups," such as V.S.O.P., which included former Miles Davis band members pianist Herbie Hancock, saxophonist Wayne Shorter, and drummer Tony Williams.

Carter, Stephen L.

b. 1954
Washington, D.C.
fields: Literature, Law, Scholarship (educator, lawyer, and author)

African American educator, lawyer, and author; among the nation's leading experts on American constitutional law, Stephen L. Carter wrote *Reflections of an Affirmative Action Baby* (1991), *The Culture of Disbelief: How American Law and Politics Trivialize Religion* (1993), and *The Confirmation Mess: Cleaning Up the Federal Appointments Process* (1994).

Carter, William

b. 1909
St. Louis, Mo.
fields: Art (muralist and painter)

African American muralist and painter; after studying at the Art Institute of Chicago and the University of Illinois, in the 1940's William Carter joined with other African American artists to provide art instruction to black youth in the community centers of Chicago.

Cartier, Jacques

b. c. 1491
St. Malo, Brittany, France
d. September 1, 1557
St. Malo, Brittany, France
fields: Exploration and Colonization

Cartier explored the St. Lawrence River and the Gulf of St. Lawrence, claiming the area for France, and wrote a detailed account of his travels.

Cartier-Bresson, Henri

b. August 22, 1908
Chanteloup, France
fields: Art, Photography

Cartier-Bresson, whose photography is acclaimed for both its immediacy and its human authenticity, has contributed a body of work unique in the history of the craft. Aside from his emphasis on the typical and ordinary in his choice of subjects, his use of the new, smaller hand-held camera and faster films defined the ideas of "the decisive moment" in photography.

Cartwright, Mary Lucy

b. Dec. 17, 1900
Aynho, Northamptonshire, England
fields: Mathematics (calculus)

Mary Lucy Cartwright's work furthered the understanding of mathematical functions containing real and complex variables, especially as they relate to nonlinear oscillation theory. She received the Sylvester Medal in 1964 and the De Morgan Medal of the London Mathematical Society in 1968.

Cartwright, Roscoe Conklin

b. May 27, 1919
Kansas City, Kans.
d. Dec. 1, 1974
Virginia
fields: Military Affairs

African American military officer; after thirty-two years of service in the U.S. Army (1942-1974), Roscoe Conklin Cartwright retired as a brigadier general; his postings included commanding officer of the 108th Artillery Group in the Pacific in Vietnam, deputy commanding officer at the U.S. Army Support Command at Cam Ranh Bay, director of management review and analysis in the office of the comptroller of the Army, and, in 1972, assistant division commander of U.S. military headquarters and the Seventh Army, Third Infantry Division; Cartwright died in an air crash.

Carty, Rico

full: Ricardo Adolfo Jacobo y Carty
b. Sept. 1, 1939
San Pedro de Macoris, Dominican Republic
fields: Sports (baseball player)

Latino baseball player. During his rookie season with the Milwaukee Braves in 1964, Rico Carty had a .330 batting average and twenty-two home runs. His hitting prowess continued, although tuberculosis forced him to miss the 1968 season. In 1969, Carty suffered seven shoulder dislocations but still managed to hit .342. In 1970, he earned a league-leading .366 batting average and made the All-Star team. He spent the 1970's playing for numerous teams but in 1978 hit a career-high thirty-one home runs. He retired after the 1979 season.

Caruso, Enrico

né: Errico Caruso
b. February 27, 1873
Naples, Italy
d. August 2, 1921
Naples, Italy
fields: Music

"The Great Caruso" was hailed by many as the greatest operatic tenor of the twentieth century. With his "voice of gold," he achieved international success that was unparalleled by any singer in his lifetime.

Carver, George Washington

b. July 12, 1861(?)
near Diamond Grove, Missouri
d. January 5, 1943
Tuskegee, Alabama
fields: Science, Education

Through his work with plant diseases, soil analysis, and crop management, Carver enabled many Southern farmers to have greater crop yield and profits. In his role as educator and friend, he motivated hundreds of blacks to improve their lives and inspired white friends to work toward racial equality.

Carwell, L'Ann. *See* McKissack, Patricia

Cary, Elizabeth Cabot. *See* Agassiz, Elizabeth Cabot Cary

Cary, William Sterling

b. Aug. 10, 1927
Plainfield, N.J.
fields: Religion and Theology, Social Reform

African American clergyman and political activist; from 1958 to 1968 William Sterling Cary served as pastor at Grace Congregational Church in New York City; in 1972 he began a three-year term as the first African American president of the National Council of Churches; in this capacity he advocated for low-income housing, strict enforcement of fair employment laws, and welfare reform.

Casals, Pablo

aka: Pau Casals
b. December 29, 1876
Vendrell, Spain
d. October 22, 1973
San Juan, Puerto Rico
fields: Music

Although recognized as a conductor and composer, Casals is best known for his sensational mastery of the cello. He evolved systems of fingering and bowing that are the source of modern playing technique, and his musical interpretation greatly enhanced international appreciation of the cello as an instrument of artistic expression.

Casals, Rosemary

b. Sept. 6, 1948
San Francisco, Calif.
fields: Sports (tennis player)

Latina tennis player. During her first appearance at Wimbledon in 1966, Rosemary

Casals made it to the fourth round. She eventually won eleven professional singles titles and reached the U.S. Open finals two times. She particularly excelled in doubles play. While coupled with Billie Jean King, she won seven Wimbledon doubles titles and the first seven Virginia Slims tournaments. The pair won a total of fifty-six professional titles. Casals won twelve major doubles titles. By the time she won her last professional title in 1988 with Martina Navratilova, Casals had won a record 685 singles and doubles tournaments over more than twenty years.

Casanova, Giovanni Giacomo

aka: Jean-Jacques, chevalier de Seingalt
b. April 2, 1725
Venice, Italy
d. June 4, 1798
Dux, Bohemia (now Duchcov, Czech Republic)
fields: Literature

Although discounted by some as too bawdy to be literature, Casanova's twelve volumes of memoirs serve as a treatise on the manners and mores of society in eighteenth century Europe.

Casas, Bartolomé De las. *See* De las Casas, Bartolomé

Casas, Melesio, II

b. Nov. 24, 1929
El Paso, Tex.
fields: Art (painter)

Latino painter. In 1958, Melesio Casas II earned a master of arts degree from the University of the Americas in Mexico City, Mexico, and eventually became an art instructor at San Antonio College in San Antonio, Texas. During the 1960's he began painting what he called "humanscapes," some of which deal with the way the media influences human behavior, while others address the social, political, and economic problems faced by Chicanos. Casas, who is considered a pioneer of the Chicano art movement, helped found Con Safos, an organizations that aids the development of Mexican American artists.

Casey, Bernie

b. June 8, 1939
Wyco, W.Va.
fields: Film, Television

African American actor; after playing professional football for six years with the San Francisco 49ers and two years with the Los Angeles Rams, Bernie Casey studied drama at the University of California at Berkeley; his television credits include roles in the miniseries *Roots: The Next Generations* (1979) and in the series *Bay City Blues* and *Harris and Company*; his film credits include featured roles in *Guns of the Magnificent Seven* (1969), *Cleopatra Jones* (1973), *Cornbread, Earl, and Me* (1975), *Dr. Black, Mr. Hyde* (1976), *Bill and Ted's Excellent Adventure* (1989), and *I'm Gonna Git You Sucka* (1988); with a master of fine arts degree, he is also a painter and a poet.

Casimir the Great

b. April 30, 1310
Kujawia, Poland
d. November 5, 1370
Kraków, Poland
fields: Government and Politics

Casimir inherited a reunited Poland and shaped it into a major Central European power, which was subsequently nurtured through a brilliant golden age lasting three centuries.

Cassatt, Mary

full: Mary Stevenson Cassatt
b. May 22, 1844
Allegheny City, Pennsylvania
d. June 14, 1926
Château de Beaufresne, France
fields: Art

Using Impressionist techniques to create vivid, unsentimental portraits, Cassatt became America's foremost woman painter at a time when the art world was regarded as an exclusively male domain.

Cassin, René

full: René-Samuel Cassin
b. October 5, 1887
Bayonne, France
d. February 20, 1976
Paris, France
fields: Law

Through his part in encouraging adoption of the Universal Declaration of Human Rights of the United Nations, as well as his activities on behalf of international organizations, Cassin promoted the recognition of an international plane of legal standards to support the rights of the individual.

Cassini, Gian Domenico

b. June 8, 1625
Perinaldo, Imperia, Republic of Genoa (now Italy)
d. Sept. 14, 1712
Paris, France
fields: Astronomy, Science, Physics

Gian Domenico Cassini published tables of the positions of Jupiter's satellites in 1668. Beginning in 1671, he discovered the four satellites of Saturn. In 1671-1673, he calculated the astronomical unit, which established the distance scale for the solar system. In 1675, he observed that the ring around Saturn is divided into at least two concentric rings. In 1693 he charted the movements of the four brightest satellites of Jupiter.

Cassiodorus

full: Flavius Magnus Aurelius Cassiodorus
b. c. 490
Scyllacium, Calabria, Italy
d. c. 585
Vivarium, Calabria, Italy
fields: Government and Politics, Historiography, Monasticism

Cassiodorus lived during the transition period between the late Roman Empire and the early Middle Ages; he aided in the cultural synthesis of Germanic, Greco-Roman, and Christian cultures. Most important, he was a key conservator of ancient manuscripts for later generations.

Cassirer, Ernst

b. July 28, 1874
Breslau, Germany (now Wrocław, Poland)
d. April 13, 1945
New York, New York
fields: Historiography, Philosophy

Cassirer created an innovative and modified form of Kantian philosophy. He published a number of works on the history of philosophy that demonstrated the relevance of philosophy to scientific and humanistic knowledge.

Cassius

né: Gaius Cassius Longinus
b. Date unknown
probably Rome
d. 44 B.C.E.
Philippi
fields: Government and Politics, Warfare and Conquest

As a diehard republican, Cassius distrusted Julius Caesar's ambition to control the Roman government. With his brother-in-law Marcus Brutus and others, Cassius organized Caesar's assassination on the Ides of March in 44 B.C.E.

Castañeda, Antonia I.

b. 1942
Texas
fields: Education

Latina educator. In 1970, Antonia I. Castañeda earned a master's degree in Latin American studies from the University of Washington in 1970. In 1972, she coedited *Chicano Literature: Text and Context*. In 1971, she began teaching courses in Chicano history, Latin American history, and women's history. Among the schools at which she has taught are the University of Washington, Stanford University, and Pomona College. Castañeda has published many research essays and has won fellowships from the Ford Foundation, the American Association of University Women, and the University of California, San Diego. She earned her Ph.D. in American history from Stanford University in 1990.

Castañeda, Carlos

full: Carlos César Aranha Castañeda
b. December 25, 1925?
Cajamarca, Peru?
d. April 27, 1998
Los Angeles, Calif.
fields: Literature

Peruvian American writer; Carlos Castañeda is best known for his autobiographical, anthropological, philosophical narratives which describe his apprenticeship with an American Indian Yaqui *brujo* (medicine man or sorcerer) named Don Juan; his published works include *The Teachings of Don Juan: A Yaqui Way of Knowledge* (1968), *A Separate Reality: Further Conversations with Don Juan* (1971), *Journey to Ixtlan: The Lessons of Don Juan* (1972), and *The Power of Silence: Further Lessons of Don Juan* (1987).

Castañeda, Carlos E.

b. November 11, 1896
Ciudad Camargo, Mexico
d. April 4, 1958
fields: Historiography, Education

Historian and educator; among Carlos E. Castañeda's publications (twelve books and more than eighty articles on Southwest and Mexican history) are *The Mexican Side of the Texas Revolution* (1928), his critical editing of the "lost" *History of Texas* by Fray Juan Morfi (1932), and the six-volume work, *Our Catholic Heritage in Texas* (his best known work, completed between 1936 and 1950); Castañeda served as editor of the *Hispanic American Historical Review*, the *Americas Review*, and *The Handbook of Latin American Studies*; he served as associate professor in the Spanish department at William and Mary College in Virginia and as a librarian and later full professor (1946) in the history department at the University of Texas.

Castellanos, Rosario

b. May 25, 1925
Mexico City, Mexico
d. Aug. 7, 1974
Tel-Aviv, Israel
fields: Literature

Latina writer. After graduating from the National University of Mexico (UNAM), Rosario Castellanos spent ten years as cultural director for the state of Chiapas. In the 1960's she taught at UNAM and in the 1970's was Mexico's ambassador to Israel. Castellanos's writing dealt with such issues as the oppression of women and of indigenous Indians in Chiapas. Among her works were the novels *Balún-Canán* (1957; *The Nine Guardians*, 1959), *Oficio de tinieblas* (1962; service of darkness), and *Los convidados de agosto* (1964; the guests of August) and the essay collection *El uso de la palabra* (1974; the right to speak).

Castelli, Francesco. *See* Borromini, Francesco

Castillo, Ana

full: Ana Hernandez del Castillo
b. June 15, 1953
Chicago, Ill.
fields: Literature

Latina writer. Ana Castillo wrote poetry before her first novel, *The Mixquiahuala Letters* (1986), won the Before Columbus Foundation's 1987 American Book Award. *So Far from God* (1993), her third novel, won the 1993 Carl Sandburg Literary Award. Castillo also published a collection of feminist essays called *Massacre of the Dreamers: Essays on Xicanisma* (1994) and, with Norma Alarcón, translated a collection of essays (*This Bridge Called My Back: Writings by Radical Women of Color*, 1984, edited by Cherríe Moraga and Gloria Anzaldúa) from English into the Spanish. She has also published collections of her poetry, including *The Invitation* (1979), *Women Are Not Roses* (1984), and *My Father Was a Toltec* (1988).

Castillo, Leonel Javier

b. June 9, 1939
Victoria, Tex.
fields: Government and Politics

Latino immigration official. Leonel Javier Castillo worked in the Peace Corps in the Philippines, supervised the Neighborhood Center-Day Care Association in Houston, and worked as controller for Houston and treasurer for the Texas Democratic Party before serving as the first Mexican American commissioner of the United States Immigration and Naturalization Service (INS) from 1977 to 1979. He resigned in the face of controversy over his policy of deemphasizing the deportation illegal immigrants. He started his own business (Castillo Enterprises), became president of Hispanic International University, and to work for immigrants' rights.

Castillo-Speed, Lillian

b. Feb. 15, 1949
La Puente, Calif.
fields: Education (librarian)

Latina librarian. Lillian Castillo-Speed earned her master's degree from the School of Library and Information Studies UC Berkeley in 1983 and began coordinating the Chicano Studies Library at that school the following year. She has worked to maintain autonomous ethnic libraries in universities and establish ethnic research centers in state libraries. Castillo-Speed also edited the *Chicano Periodicals Index* from 1984 to 1988 and the *Chicano Index* beginning in 1989, and began developing the Chicano Database, a CD-ROM research tool, in 1990.

Castle, Irene

né: Irene Foote
b. April 7, 1893
New Rochelle, New York
d. January 25, 1969
Eureka Springs, Arkansas
fields: Dance

A famous ballroom dancer known for her refined style and elegant fashions, Irene Castle popularized ballroom dancing in the second decade of the twentieth century. She also made several silent motion pictures and was an activist in protecting animals from abuse.

Castlereagh, Viscount

né: Robert Stewart
full: Robert Stewart, second marquis of Londonderry
b. June 18, 1769
Dublin, Ireland
d. August 12, 1822
Cray Farm, North Cray, Kent, England
fields: Diplomacy, Government and Politics

Castlereagh's political skills helped pass the Act of Union between Great Britain and Ireland, thus creating the United Kingdom. His role in the peace negotiations following the Napoleonic Wars helped ensure a just and long-lasting peace.

Castro, Fidel

full: Fidel Castro Ruz
b. August 13, 1926 or 1927
near Birán, Cuba
fields: Government and Politics

Castro led a successful revolutionary struggle against the Cuban dictatorship of Fulgencio Batista y Zaldívar in the late 1950's. The revolutionary leader subsequently implemented Latin America's third social revolution of the twentieth century and transformed Cuba into the first communist state of the hemisphere in defiance of the United States.

Castro, George

b. Feb. 23, 1939
Los Angeles, Calif.
fields: Chemistry

Latino chemist. After earning his Ph.D. in chemistry at the University of California, Riverside, in 1965, George Castro, a specialist in research management and physical chemistry, performed research at the University of Pennsylvania from 1965 to 1967 and at the California Institute of Technology from 1967 to 1968. At the IBM Almaden Research Center in San Jose, California, he researched organic photoconductors and the electronic properties of organic solids.

Castro, Raúl Hector

b. June 12, 1916
Cananea, Sonora, Mexico
fields: Government and Politics

Latino politician. President Lyndon B. Johnson appointed Raúl Hector Castro as ambassador to El Salvador in 1965. In 1970, Castro ran for governor of Arizona as a moderate Democrat and lost. Despite the conservative nature of Arizona, he ran again in 1974 and won, mostly because of his efforts to reach Mexican Americans, Navajos, businesspeople, and farmers. In 1977, Castro resigned his governorship to serve as ambassador to Argentina.

Castro, Salvador B.

b. Oct. 25, 1933
Los Angeles, Calif.
fields: Education, Social Reform

Latino teacher and activist. After serving in the Korean War, Salvador B. Castro earned his B.A. at Los Angeles State College in 1962. While there, he became active in the Democratic Party and the Mexican American Political Association. After graduation, he taught history and government in Pasadena and Los Angeles. In March of 1968, Castro became the symbolic leader to about five thousand Mexican American students who left their classrooms during an organized school walkout known as the Blowout. After two weeks of demonstrations, Castro and twelve others were arrested for allegedly organizing the demonstrations, but all were eventually acquitted. Castro was not allowed to teach again until 1973.

Cat, The. *See* Millan, Felix

Catahecassa

aka: Black Hoof
b. c. 1740
Fla.
d. c. 1831
Wapakoneta, Ohio
fields: Warfare and Conquest, Native American Affairs

A Shawnee principal chief and spirited orator, Catahecassa fought against white settlers during several Indian rebellions. Supported Pontiac in pantribal rebellion against the British in 1763; aided Shawnee chief Cornstalk and Tarhe of the Wyandots during Lord Dunmore's War, 1773-1774. He later refused to join Tecumseh in his rebellion during 1809-1811.

Catalá, Rafael

b. Sept. 26, 1942
Las Tunas, Cuba
fields: Literature, Scholarship

Latino poet and scholar. Rafael Catalá immigrated to the United States in 1961, where he earned university degrees that sparked his interest in psychology, Latin American ideology, philosophy, and literature. In 1980, he organized Ometeca, a literary and cultural workshop that mixed the humanities and science. This fusion was explored in his book of poems, *Ciencia poesía* (1986; science poetry). Other poetry collections include *Caminos/Roads* (1972), *Circulo cuadrado* (1974), *Ojo sencillo/Triquitraque* (1975), *Copulantes* (1981), and *Escobas de millo* (1984).

Cather, Willa

full: Willela Sibert Cather
b. December 7, 1873
Back Creek Valley, near Gore, Virginia
d. April 24, 1947
New York, New York
fields: Literature, Journalism

At a time when such careers were nearly unheard of for women, Cather became a celebrated theater and music critic, crusading magazine editor, and accomplished novelist-poet in the tradition of American naturalism.

Catherine de Médicis

b. April 13, 1519
Florence
d. January 5, 1589
Blois, France
fields: Government and Politics

Queen of France, 1547-1559; queen mother, 1559-1589. Catherine de Médicis contributed to maintaining a strong centralized monarchy in spite of challenges from noble and religious factions. Her attempts to balance Roman Catholic and Calvinist interests in France also encouraged at least a minimum of toleration in the seventeenth century.

Catherine of Aragon

né: Catalina of Aragon
b. December 16, 1485
Alcala de Henares, Spain
d. January 7, 1536
Kimbolton, Huntingdonshire, England
fields: Church Reform, Monarchy

Twice married to English princes, Catherine, the first wife of Henry VIII, refused to accept a royal divorce, which led to Henry's expulsion of the Roman Catholic Church and the establishment of the Protestant church in England.

Catherine of Siena, Saint

né: Caterina Benincasa
b. March 25, 1347
Siena, Italy
d. April 29, 1380
Rome, Italy
fields: Religion and Theology, Government and Politics

This patron saint of Italy and Doctor of the Church helped to persuade the Avignon papacy to return to Rome. She is also known for her mystic writings, which advocate a combination of personal ecstatic experience with active service in the world.

Catherine the Great

né: Sophie Friederike Auguste von Anhalt-Zerbst
b. May 2, 1729
Stettin, Pomerania, Prussia
d. November 17, 1796
St. Petersburg, Russia
fields: Monarchy

Empress of Russia, 1762-1796. One of the early englightened monarchs, Catherine attempted to create a uniform Russian government with a modern Westernized code of laws that represented all levels of Russian society with the exception of the serfs. In the forty-four years of her reign, she sculpted Russia into one of the great world powers of the time and laid the foundation for what would become modern Russia.

Catlett, Elizabeth

b. Apr. 15, 1915 or 1919
Washington, D.C.
fields: Art (sculptor and printmaker)

African American sculptor and printmaker; Elizabeth Catlett is known for prints depicting black female laborers, farmworkers, and artists and huge carvings of African American mothers and children; her work focused public attention on black women's struggles and highlighted the social, economic, and political issues affecting African Americans; before moving to Mexico in 1946, she taught at several U.S. colleges.

Catlin, George

b. July 26, 1796
Wilkes-Barre, Pennsylvania
d. December 23, 1872
Jersey City, New Jersey
fields: Native American Affairs, Art, Social Science

Catlin provided some of the earliest paintings showing the culture of the upper Missouri River Valley Indians, and his books include much significant ethnological material about tribal ceremonies.

Cato

b. ?
fields: Historical Figure

African American slave insurrection leader; in September, 1739, Cato led the Stono River, South Carolina, insurrection; encouraged by the promise that Spain would set free any slaves from South Carolina who could reach St. Augustine, Florida, Cato led about one hundred slaves south; after breaking into a weapons storehouse and killing more than twenty white people, the slaves were captured within several hours, and many within the group were executed.

Cato the Censor

né: Marcus Porcius Cato
b. 234 B.C.E.
Tusculum, Italy
d. 149 B.C.E.
Rome, Italy
fields: Government and Politics

Through his personal example, public service, and writings, Cato advocated an ideal of a powerful, prosperous state populated with self-reliant, active citizens.

Cato the Younger

aka: Cato Uticensis
b. 95 B.C.E.
Rome, Italy
d. 46 B.C.E.
Utica, Africa
fields: Government and Politics, Philosophy

Cato the Younger was a Stoic philosopher who represented the conservative Senatorial Party in Roman politics. He sought to preserve the dying Roman Republic at a time of rising military dictatorships.

Catron, John

b. 1786
d. 1865
fields: Law

U.S. Supreme Court justice, 1837-1865 (died while in office); appointed by President Jackson. Significant opinions: *License Cases*, 46 U.S. 504 (1847); *Scott v. Sandford*, 60 U.S. 393 (1857) (concurring opinion).

Catt, Carrie Chapman

né: Carrie Lane
aka: Carrie Chapman
b. January 9, 1859
Ripon, Wisconsin
d. March 9, 1947
New Rochelle, New York
fields: Women's Rights

Recognized as one of the ablest leaders and organizers of the woman suffrage movement, Carrie Chapman Catt brought new life to a faltering National American Woman Suffrage Association (NAWSA) and designed the campaign which won the federal vote for women.

Catullus

b. c. 85 B.C.E.
Verona, Cisalpine Gaul
d. c. 54 B.C.E.
probably Rome
fields: Literature

Catullus was the leader of a group of poets, the *novi poetae*, who created a more native idiom for Roman poetry. Intensely personal, epigrammatic, and more colloquial than epic or dramatic, this style of poetry prepared the way and set the standards for the literary achievements of the Augustan Age.

Cauchy, Augustin-Louis

b. Aug. 21, 1789
Paris, France
d. May 23, 1857
Sceaux, France
fields: Mathematics (algebra, applied math, calculus, geometry, number theory, and probability)

In 1821, Augustin-Louis Cauchy published a text in which he introduced rigor into mathematical analysis. He almost singlehandedly developed the calculus of complex functions.

Cavalcanti, Guido

b. c. 1259
Florence, Italy
d. August 27 or 28, 1300
Florence, Italy
fields: Literature (poetry)

Through his unique treatment of the theme of love, Cavalcanti became one of the major poets of the so-called *dolce stil nuovo* school. He exerted a major influence on Dante and the love poets of the early Renaissance.

Cavalieri, Bonaventura

b. 1598
Milan, Duchy of Milan, Habsburg Empire (now Italy)
d. Nov. 30, 1647
Bologna, Papal States (now Italy)
fields: Mathematics (calculus and geometry)

Bonaventura Cavalieri established the use of indivisibles in studying problems of area and volume.

Cavazos, Lauro

b. Jan. 4, 1927
fields: Education, Government and Politics

Latino educator, government official; Lauro Cavazos dean of Tufts University School of Medicine; president of Texas Tech University; appointed secretary of education by President Ronald Reagan in 1988 and reappointed by George Bush in 1989 (served to 1990), the first Hispanic named to the cabinet; instrumental in the creation of the President's Council on Educational Excellence for Hispanic Americans.

Cavelier, René-Robert. *See* La Salle, Sieur de

Cavell, Stanley

full: Stanley Louis Cavell
b. September 1, 1926
Atlanta, Georgia
fields: Philosophy

Stanley Cavell's work is known for its exploration of skepticism and its preoccupation with issues that arise from everyday experience. He questions the professionalization of philosophy as a discipline. Cavell has demonstrated that philosophy belongs at the center of all the humanities, revealing the relationships among these disciplines and the questions they ask about experience. Among his best-known works are *Must We Mean What We Say?* (1969), *The Claim of Reason* (1979), *Pursuits of Happiness* (1981), *This New Yet Unapproachable America* (1989), *Philosophical Passages* (1995), and *Contesting Tears: The Hollywood Melodrama of the Unknown Woman* (1996).

Cavendish, Henry

aka: Honourable Henry Cavendish
b. October 10, 1731
Nice, France
d. February 24, 1810
London, England
fields: Chemistry, Philosophy

Cavendish was responsible for advances in the chemistry of gases and contributed to the study of electrical phenomena.

Cavendish, Thomas

b. September 19, 1560 (baptized)
Grimston Hall, Suffolk, England
d. c. May, 1592
at sea, near Ascension Island
fields: Exploration and Colonization

A boldly enterprising voyager, Cavendish was the second Englishman to circumnavigate the globe; in the course of his expedition he captured one of the richest prizes in the history of English privateering against Spain.

Cavour, Count

né: Camillo Benso di Cavour
b. August 10, 1810
Turin, French Empire
d. June 6, 1861
Turin, Italy
fields: Government and Politics

As prime minister between 1852 and 1861, Cavour gave Piedmont the economic and diplomatic leadership of Italy and played a key role in the country's political unification. He is generally regarded as the founder of modern Italy.

Caxton, William

b. c. 1422
the weald of Kent, England, possibly in the village of Hadlow
d. c. 1491
London, England
fields: Publishing, Language and Linguistics

In 1476, Caxton set up the first printing press in England, and before he died, around 1491, he had published some hundred items, many of them his own translations, at the same time helping to determine the variety of English in which printing would be done.

Cayetano, Benjamin Jerome

b. Nov. 14, 1939
Honolulu, Territory of Hawaii
fields: Government and Politics

Filipino American Benjamin Jerome Cayetano entered government service almost immediately after earning a J.D. degree from Loyola University Law School in 1971. From 1974 to 1978, he served as a Hawaii state representative, then from 1978 to 1986 as a state senator. He was named lieutenant governor in 1986, the first Filipino American to fill such a position.

Cayley, Arthur

b. Aug. 16, 1821
Richmond, Surrey, England
d. Jan. 26, 1895
Cambridge, England
fields: Mathematics (algebra and geometry)

Arthur Cayley is known for founding the study of many disciplines in mathematics. He also helped to establish university research mathematics in England. The amount of his mathematical output has been matched by very few other mathematicians. In 1859, he was awarded the Royal Medal of the Royal Society of London, in 1883, he was elected president of the British Association for the Advancement of Science.

Cayley, George

aka: Sir George Cayley
b. December 27, 1773
Scarborough, Yorkshire, England
d. December 15, 1857
Brompton, Yorkshire, England
fields: Aviation and Space Exploration, Invention and Technology, Social Reform

Cayley was the first to conceive and publish the modern idea of the airplane: namely, the concept that an airplane should consist of one or more fixed wings, a fuselage, and a tail. Moreover, he was the first to carry out a serious program of aeronautical research.

Ceausescu, Nicolae

b. January 26, 1918
Scornicesti, Romania
d. December 25, 1989
near Bucharest, Romania
fields: Government and Politics

Autocratic president of Romania from 1967 to 1989. Nicolae Ceausescu at first seemed to promise gradual liberalization of Romania, but in 1971 he abandoned this approach and established a cult of personality and despotic rule. Developed the most repressive government of the communist states of the Eastern bloc. Constructed sumptuous villas where his family lived in luxury. In December, 1989, brutal government suppression of riots led to severe unrest. Ceausescu lost control, and open revolt quickly began. Ceausescu and his wife were apprehended, tried, and executed within days.

Cecil, Robert. *See* Salisbury, first earl of

Cecil, Robert. *See* Salisbury, third marquess of

Cecil, William

aka: First Baron Burghley
aka: Lord Burghley
b. September 13, 1520
Bourne, Lincolnshire, England
d. August 4, 1598
London, England
fields: Government and Politics

Combining his enormous capacity for work with his dedication to Elizabeth I, Cecil effectively managed the affairs of the English government for forty years, from 1558 to 1598.

Cedeño, César

full: César Cedeño y Encarnación
b. Feb. 25, 1951
Santo Domingo, Dominican Republic
fields: Sports (baseball player)

Latino Baseball player. In 1970, outfielder César Cedeño made his major league debut with the Houston Astros and stayed with them for twelve seasons. He won Gold Glove Awards every year from 1972 to 1976 and played in four All-Star Games. He was traded to the Cincinnati Reds in 1982 and the St. Louis Cardinals in 1985, helping them win the National League pennant. He retired following the 1986 season, during which he played for the Los Angeles Dodgers, with a .285 career average, 199 home runs, and 550 stolen bases.

Celler, Emanuel

b. May 6, 1888
Brooklyn, N.Y.
d. Jan. 15, 1981
Brooklyn, N.Y.
fields: Government and Politics

Emanuel Celler, of Jewish background and a Democrat, was a U.S. representative from 1922 until 1972. He was a staunch advocate of liberal causes and favored greater immigration from Asia. In 1944, he and Representative Clare Booth Luce introduced legislation permitting Asian Indians to immigrate to the United States and become U.S. citizens. With the addition of a provision that increased the yearly number of Filipino immigrants and extended naturalization rights to them, the bill became the Luce-Celler Bill of 1946. Celler also supported passage of the Immigration and Nationality Act of 1965, with lessened the barriers for Asian immigrants.

Cellini, Benvenuto

b. November 3, 1500
Florence
d. February 13, 1571
Florence
fields: Art, Literature

Cellini is acknowledged as perhaps the finest goldsmith in Renaissance Italy. His sculpture, represented by his bronze *Perseus*, was also superb. He is, however, best known for his lively and spirited autobiography, which transmits his spirit and that of his age.

Celsius, Anders

b. Nov. 27, 1701
Uppsala, Sweden
d. Apr. 25, 1744
Uppsala, Sweden
fields: Astronomy, Mathematics, Physics

Anders Celsius participated in a French expedition in 1737 to measure 1 degree of longitude in the polar region, proving Sir Isaac Newton's theory of Earth flattening at the poles. In 1741, he introduced his 100-degree thermometer scale, which was later named for him. In 1742, he proposed that all scientific measurements of temperature be based on the boiling point and the freezing point of water, two nonvarying, naturally occurring points.

Celsus, Aulus Cornelius

b. c. 25 B.C.E.
possibly near Narbonne on the Mediterranean coast of France
d. c. 50 C.E.
probably Rome
fields: Historiography, Medicine

Celsus wrote the first complete history of medicine and the first comprehensive account of medical and surgical procedures.

Cepeda, Orlando

full: Orlando Manuel Cepeda y Penne
September 17, 1937
Ponce, Puerto Rico

fields: Sports (baseball player)

Puerto Rican baseball player; from 1958 to 1974, first baseman Orlando Cepeda played in the major leagues with six different teams; in his debut year with the San Francisco Giants (1958), Cepeda earned the league's Rookie of the Year Award; Cepeda won the 1967 National League Most Valuable Player Award playing for the St. Louis Cardinals; he retired with a lifetime batting average of .297 with 379 home runs; a ten-month prison sentence for marijuana possession after his retirement may have prevented his election to the Baseball Hall of Fame.

Cerenkov, Pavel. *See* Cherenkov, Pavel Alekseyevich

Cerf, Bennett

b. May 25, 1898
New York, New York
d. August 27, 1971
Mount Kisco, New York
fields: Literature

An American book publisher and editor, Bennett Cerf led the early 1930's battle to have James Joyce's controversial novel *Ulysses* published in the United States. As publisher of the Modern Library edition and cofounder of the Random House publishing company, he published great literature in the United States.

Cervantes, Alfonso Juan

b. Aug. 27, 1920
St. Louis, Mo.
d. June 22, 1983
St. Louis, Mo.
fields: Government and Politics

Mayor of St. Louis. Alfonso Juan Cervantes served two controversial terms as mayor of St. Louis from 1965 to 1973. During this time, he worked to boost tourism and convention business in the city. A convention center bearing his name was built, but two projects tarnished his reputation: the Spanish International Pavilion, forced to close less than one year after it opened because of financial difficulties, and the *Santa Maria*, which was built for the 1965 World Fair but was destroyed by a storm five months after its completion while it sat in the Mississippi River.

Cervantes, Lorna Dee

b. Aug. 6, 1954
San Francisco, Calif.
fields: Literature

Latina poet. Feeling that women's voices were ignored in the early Chicano movement, Lorna Dee Cervantes founded her own press and the poetry magazine (*Mango*) in San Jose, California. She later founded the poetry magazine *Red Dirt* while teaching creative writing at the University of Colorado at Boulder. Her poetry, which often focuses on male-female relationships, feminist issues, and Native American culture, helped lay the groundwork for later female Mexican American poets. Her books of poetry include *Emplumada* (1981) and *From the Cables of Genocide: Poems on Love and Hunger* (1991).

Cervantes, Miguel de

full: Miguel de Cervantes Saavedra
b. September 29, 1547
Alcalá de Henares, Spain
d. April 23, 1616
Madrid, Spain
fields: Literature

Poet, playwright, and novelist, Cervantes is Spain's greatest writer, chiefly because of *Don Quixote de la Mancha*, the first real European novel and one of the supreme works of world literature.

Cervántez, Yreina

b. 1952
Garden City, Kans.
fields: Art (painter, printmaker)

Latina painter and printmaker. In 1975, Yreina Cervántez earned a fine arts degree from the University of California, Santa Cruz. During the 1980's and 1990's she taught drawing, watercolor painting, and Mexican and Chicano art history at various California colleges and was the multicultural coordinator for the Los Angeles Municipal Art Gallery. Her murals, which can be seen in Los Angeles and Managua, Nicaragua, have helped continue the tradition begun by Chicano artists in the 1960's and 1970's.

Césaire, Aimé

b. June 25, 1913
Basse-Pointe, Martinique
fields: Literature, Colonial Administration

Césaire contributed to the spiritual foundation of a number of Afro-American social, intellectual, and literary movements. His poetry and plays embody the idea of *négritude*, a word he created, which became the affirmative basis of the idea that one is black and proud of it. Although a renowned poet, playwright, and essayist, he has functioned as an active politician in the government of his native Martinique.

Cetan Wakan Mani. *See* Little Crow

Cézanne, Paul

b. January 19, 1839
Aix-en-Provence, France
d. October 22, 1906
Aix-en-Provence, France
fields: Art

Cézanne's innovative and brilliant style challenged the conventions of nineteenth century art and had a major influence on twentieth century cubists and abstract artists.

Cha, Theresa Hak Kyung

b. March 4, 1951
Pusan, Republic of Korea
d. Nov. 5, 1982
New York, N.Y.
fields: Theater and Entertainment, Literature

Theresa Hak Kyung Cha, a Korea-born American filmmaker, often explores social and cultural alienation and displacement in her works. Her video productions include *Secret Spill* (1974), *Mouth to Mouth* (1975), *Permutations* (1976), *Re Dis Appearing* (1977), *Passages, Paysages* (1978), and *Exilee* (1980). Her 1982 *Dictee* was a complex, multiform text that addresseds the question of representation against various conditions of exile and displacement.

Chacón, Alicia Rosencrans

b. ?
fields: Government and Politics

Latina government official. Alicia Rosencrans Chacón was the first woman to serve as a county judge in El Paso County, Texas, the first Hispanic judge in that county in more than a century, and the first woman to serve in her county's municipal government (as county clerk). She was also the first woman to serve as regional director of the Small Business Administration, to which President Jimmy Carter appointed her in 1978. She was elected to the El Paso City Council in 1983 and in 1985. In addition, Chacón was chairwoman of the Mexican American Legal Defense and Educational Fund and was a director of the Vista Institute of Hispanic Studies, National Hispanic Leadership Agenda, and National Council of La Raza.

Chacón, Bobby

full: Robert Chacón
b. Nov. 28, 1951
Los Angeles, Calif.
fields: Sports (boxer)

Latino boxer. In 1974, Robert Chacón defeated Alfredo Marcano to win the World Boxing Council (WBC) featherweight title. In 1975 he lost the title to Rubén Olivares and moved into the junior-lightweight class, where he beat Rafael Limon in 1982 to win the WBC title.

Chacón, Eusebio

b. Dec. 16, 1869
Peñasco, N.Mex.
d. Apr. 3, 1948
Trinidad, Colo.
fields: Literature

Latino writer; Eusebio Chacón earned law degree from Notre Dame; wrote passionately of Hispanic culture in works such as *El hijo de la tempestad* (Son of the Storm, 1892) and *Tras la tormenta la calma* (The Calm After the Storm, 1892).

Chacón, Felipe Maximiliano

b. 1873
Santa Fe, N.Mex.
fields: Literature

Latino writer. Felipe Maximiliano Chacón worked as a journalist and an editor of Spanish-language newspapers in New Mexico before publishing his only book, *Obras de Felipe Maximiliano Chacón, "El Cantor Neomexicano": Poesía y Prosa* (1924; works of Felipe Maximiliano Chacón, the New Mexican bard: poetry and prose). A Spanish-language collection of fifty-six poems, three short stories (including "Don Julio Berlanga"), and seven translations of English poems into Spanish, it was one of first Hispanic works to be published in American Southwest.

Chacón, Peter R.

b. June 10, 1925
Phoenix, Ariz.
fields: Government and Politics

State legislator. Peter R. Chacón was born in Arizona and earned his undergraduate degree (1953) and master's degree (1960) at San Diego State University. He was a vice principal and administrator in the San Diego school system before becoming the first Latino from the Seventy-ninth District elected to the California State Assembly in 1970.

Chadwick, Edwin

b. January 24, 1800
Longsight, near Manchester, England
d. July 6, 1890
East Sheen, Surrey, England
fields: Social Reform

The most active and determined of Jeremy Bentham's disciples, Chadwick sought to reform British government with utilitarian rigor and efficiency, in the hope of making it responsive to the massive social problems created by industrialization and urbanization.

Chadwick, James

b. October 20, 1891
Manchester, England
d. July 24, 1974
Cambridge, England
fields: Physics (nuclear)

With the discovery of the neutron, one of the elementary particles of matter, Chadwick opened a new era in nuclear physics research. He was a leader in the investigation of both military and civilian applications of that discovery. He was awarded the 1935 Nobel Prize in Physics.

Chagall, Marc

né: Moishe Shagal
b. July 7, 1887
Vitebsk, Russia
d. March 28, 1985
Saint-Paul-de-Vence, France
fields: Art

Chagall was a master of several artistic media, including stained glass, printmaking, mosaic, stage design, mural, ceramic, and tapestry, but he is best known for his paintings that depict the fantastical states of dreams and memories. The distinctive Chagallian appearance of an artistic work portrays a world of vibrantly colored figures in incongruous juxtaposition and magical abrogation of natural law, the kind of vision that many people experience in their sleep.

Chain Breaker. *See* Blacksnake

Chakravorty, Gayatri. *See* Spivak, Gayatri Chakravorty

Chamberlain, Austen

full: Joseph Austen Chamberlain
b. October 16, 1863
Birmingham, Warwickshire, England
d. March 16, 1937
London, England
fields: Diplomacy, Government and Politics

Austen Chamberlain was a British statesman and diplomat. Chancellor of the Exchequer from 1919 to 1921. Foreign secretary from 1924 to 1928 in the Stanley Baldwin government. Winner of 1925 Nobel Peace Prize for his major role in the Locarno Agreements of 1925, which settled major differences between France and Germany.

Chamberlain, Joseph

b. July 8, 1836
London, England
d. July 2, 1914
Highbury, Birmingham, England
fields: Government and Politics

An influential Victorian politician, Chamberlain supported the British Empire and a strong economic union between its members.

Chamberlain, Neville

full: Arthur Neville Chamberlain
b. March 18, 1869
Birmingham, Warwickshire, England
d. November 9, 1940
Highfield Park, Heckfield, England
fields: Government and Politics

Chamberlain was a major voice in the Conservative Party for two decades, seeking modest and solid social reforms to improve the housing and health of the common people of Great Britain. As prime minister from 1937 to 1940, he sought in vain to avert World War II by appeasing Adolf Hitler.

Chamberlain, Wilt

full: Wilton Norman Chamberlain
b. August 21, 1936
Philadelphia, Pennsylvania
d. October 12, 1999
Los Angeles, California
fields: Sports (basketball)

The greatest single-season scorer in the history of the National Basketball Association. Wilt Chamberlain's accomplishments in basketball represent an unsurpassed career in the sport. During Chamberlain's first season (1959-1960) in the National Basketball Association, he easily broke the league scoring record with an average of 37.6 points per game. He also led the league in rebounds, averaging 27.0 per game. He broke salary records when he signed a contract to play for sixty-five thousand dollars a year, more than any player had received in the history of professional basketball. Playing for the Philadelphia (later San Francisco) Warriors, the Philadelphia 76ers, and the Los Angeles Lakers, he led the NBA in scoring seven years in a row, including a sensational 50.4 per game average in the 1961-1962 season. On March 2, 1962, Chamberlain scored 100 points against the New York Knicks, a record that was unmatched more than thirty years later. Following his retirement in 1973, Chamberlain briefly became the coach of the San Diego Conquistadors of the American Basketball Association.

Chambers, Andrew Phillip

b. June 30, 1931
Bedford, Va.
fields: Military Affairs

African American military officer; after more than thirty-four years of active service in the U.S. Army (1954-1989), Andrew Phillip Chambers retired at the rank of lieutenant general; his postings included commander of the headquarters company of the First Brigade of the Eighth Cavalry Division in Korea, in Europe as chief of the morale and discipline branch of the personnel services division, deputy brigade commander, and battalion commander, commanding general of the Seventh Corps of the United States Army in Europe (1985-1987), and commanding general of the Third U.S. Army, Forces Command, at Fort McPherson, Ga.

Chambers, Julius LeVonne

b. October 6, 1936
Montgomery County, N.C.

fields: Civil Rights, Law (attorney, educator, and civil rights activist)

African American attorney, educator, and civil rights activist. In 1971, Julius LeVonne Chambers argued the case *Swann v. Charlotte-Mecklenburg Board of Education* before the Supreme Court. The Court's landmark busing decision in this case paved the way for further desegregation in school districts around the nation. He was elected to serve as president of the Legal Defense and Educational Fund in 1975 and received a Hall of Fame Award from the NAACP that same year. He became chancellor of North Carolina Central University in 1993.

Chambly. *See* Shábona

Champlain, Samuel de

b. c. 1567
Brouage, France
d. December 25, 1635
Quebec, Canada
fields: Exploration and Colonization

Widely respected as the Father of New France, Champlain represented the French attempt to acquire and settle North America, one of the great might-have-beens of American history.

Chan, Gordon

b. Feb. 11, 1936
Macao
fields: Horticulture

Gordon Chan, who immigrated to the United States in 1947, became a part of his family's chrysanthemum flower-growing business in 1961. After moving to San Jose, California, the business expanded to growing roses. He founded the California Cut Flower Commission. He was the first Chinese American member of the Santa Clara County Farm Bureau and that county's first Chinese American planning commissioner.

Chan, Jeffery Paul

b. Aug. 19, 1942
Stockton, Calif.
fields: Literature, Theater and Entertainment

Jeffery Paul Chan wrote numerous fiction, essays, and plays, many on Asian American themes. His play *Chinatown Gangs* was produced by San Francisco television station KQED in 1972, and *Bunnyhop* was presented at East West Players in 1978. He coedited *Aiiieeeee! An Anthology of Asian-American Writers* (1974) and *The Big Aiiieeeee! An Anthology of Chinese American and Japanese American Literature* (1991).

Chan, Kenyon Sing

b. 1948
Oakland, Calif.
fields: Psychology

Psychologist Kenyon Sing Chan published numerous articles and reports on minority children in the U.S. school system, including *Dropping Out Among Language Minority Youth* (1982) and *Navajo Youth and Early School Withdrawal: A Case Study* (1983). As a consultant for children's television, he focused on the effects of racial stereotypes and violence. Chan was cofounder of the short-lived *Rice Magazine* (1987-1989), which focused on the Asian American community and the Pacific Rim, and helped found the Asian American Studies Department at California State University, Northridge.

Chan, Sucheng

b. April 16, 1941
Shanghai, China
fields: Scholarship, Historiography

Chinese American Sucheng Chan wrote the award-winning *This Bittersweet Soil: The Chinese in California Agriculture, 1860-1910* (1986) and *Asian Americans: An Interpretive History* (1991). She also edited *Entry Denied: Exclusion and the Chinese Community in America, 1882-1943* (1991). This specialist in Asian American studies wrote of her struggle against childhood polio and of living with a physical handicap in the piece "You're Short, Besides!" for *Making Waves: An Anthology of Writings by and About Asian American Women* (1989).

Chan, Wing-tsit

b. Aug. 18, 1901
Guangdong, China
d. Aug. 12, 1994
Pittsburgh, Penn.
fields: Scholarship

Wing-tsit Chan earned a bachelor's degree from Lingnan University in Canton, China, in 1924 and a doctorate from Harvard in 1929. He was a professor at Lingnan University, the University of Hawaii, Dartmouth College, and Columbia University. A Guggenheim Fellow in 1948-1949, Chan has written and edited a number of books and more than a hundred book reviews, and articles.

Chandler, Dana

b. Apr. 7, 1941
Lynn, Mass.
fields: Art (painter), Education

African American painter and educator; recipient of the 1970 Man of the Year Award from the NAACP, Dana Chandler creates art dealing with American racism; his simple designs and vivid colors fill murals of African American ghetto life and politically charged paintings such as *Fred Hampton's Door* (1970).

Chandrasekhar, Subrahmanyan

b. October 19, 1910
Lahore, India
d. August 21, 1995
Chicago, Illinois
fields: Mathematics, Physics

Astrophysicist; in 1930 Subrahmanyan Chandrasekhar formulated the Chandrasekhar limit (stars retaining a mass above a certain limit undergo further collapse and do not necessarily end up as white dwarfs); published *An Introduction to the Study of Stellar Structure* (1939; a full account of his theory of white dwarfs); became managing editor of the *Astrophysical Journal* (1952; serving as sole editor for twenty years); he shared the Nobel Prize in Physics (1983; with California Institute of Technology physicist William A. Fowler) for advancing theories of how stars age and collapse.

Chanel, Coco

né: Gabrielle Chanel
b. August 19, 1883
Saumur, France
d. January 10, 1971
Paris, France
fields: Fashion, Business and Industry

Chanel was the first to dress women in a manner that reflected their increasing liberated status, which began in the first quarter of the twentieth century, and she continued to do so for nearly six decades, reigning as queen of fashion in Paris. Her pioneering genius elevated her above the level of merely a great designer, allowing her to support independently her creative brilliance with a fashion empire that encompassed design, textiles, jewelry, and perfume.

Chaney, James

b. ?
d. June 21, 1964
Neshoba County, Miss.
fields: Civil Rights

James Chaney was one of three civil rights workers murdered by members of the Ku Klux Klan in Mississippi in June, 1964. The outrage over their murders brought unprecedented publicity and pressure for the federal government to enforce civil rights of African Americans in the southern states. On October 20, 1967, an all-white Mississippi jury found seven men guilty of the murder, marking the first time a Mississippi jury ever found a white person guilty of crimes perpetrated on a black person or civil rights worker. After exhausting their appeals, the guilty men all served lengthy prison sentences at various federal penitentiaries.

Chaney, John Griffith. *See* London, Jack

Chang Chih-tung

b. September 2, 1837
Nan-p'i, Chihli, China
d. October 4, 1909
Peking, Chihli, China
fields: Government and Politics, Education

Chang Chih-tung was a leading scholar-official in China during the last half-century of the Ch'ing Dynasty. His educational, military, and economic reforms contributed greatly to the survival of China's last imperial dynasty.

Chang, Diana

b. 1934
New York, N.Y.
fields: Literature, Poetry, Art

Diana Chang was born in the United States to a Chinese father and a Eurasian mother but spent much of her childhood in China. A novelist, poet, and painter, her novels include *The Frontiers of Love* (1956), *A Woman of Thirty* (1959), and *Eye to Eye* (1974). Two of her books of poetry are *The Horizon Is Definitely Speaking* (1982) and *What Matisse Was After* (1984).

Chang, Edward T.

full: Edward Tachan Chang
b. May 6, 1956
Inchon, South Korea
fields: Scholarship, Sociology

Korean American Edward T. Chang, a specialist in ethnic studies, taught at several California universities. His scholarship has focused on interethnic relations, particularly Korean American-African American relations, the subject of his doctoral dissertation. In 1992, he published a Korean-language book on African Americans to foster greater understanding of African Americans and their history among Koreans.

Chang, Gordon

b. June 19, 1948
Hong Kong
fields: Scholarship, Historiography

Chinese American Gordon Chang specializes in U.S.-China relations and foreign policy and is the author of *Friends and Enemies: The United States, China, and the Soviet Union, 1948-1972* (1990). In 1988 he participated in symposia in what was then the Soviet Union and in Korea. Before becoming a member of the Stanford University history department in 1991, he taught Asian American studies and history at Laney College and the University of California, Irvine.

Chang, John M.

né: Chang Myon
b. Aug. 28, 1899
Seoul, Korea
d. June, 1966
Seoul, Republic of Korea
fields: Government and Politics

U.S.-educated John M. Chang led the student revolution that overthrew the twelve-year regime of Syngman Rhee in South Korea. Chang served as prime minister of the Second Republic from 1960 to May, 1961, when Park Chung Hee took control of the nation in a military coup.

Chang, Michael

b. February 22, 1972
Hoboken, N.J.
fields: Sports (tennis player)

Chinese American tennis player; after turning professional at age sixteen, Michael Chang became the youngest male player ever to win the French Open (1989) and the first American to do so in thirty-four years; he also was the youngest player to compete on center court at Wimbledon in 1989; in 1990 Chang helped lead the U.S. team to a Davis Cup championship. For most of the 1990's, Chang continued to be one of the top tennis players in the world.

Chang, Yin-huan

b. Feb. 8, 1837
Fo-shan, China
d. Aug. 20, 1900
Sinkiang, China
fields: Government and Politics

Yin-huan Chang was a Chinese diplomat; in the 1870's worked with the government to fortify Chinese ports after Japan's invasion of Formosa (later Taiwan); 1886-1889, successfully negotiated financial reparations to families of Chinese miners killed in the 1885 Rock Springs Massacre; negotiated a treaty regulating Chinese laborer immigration and seeking to protect Chinese Americans from discrimination and violence; executed in China in 1900 after his return there.

Chang, Yum Sinn

b. Mar. 11, 1888
Guangdong Province, China
d. Sept. 13, 1966
fields: Education

Chinese American Yum Sinn Chang was one of the first two instructors (1911-1915) and later principal (1915-1966) of Mun Lun School in Honolulu, Hawaii. Other positions included board chair (1961-1963) and managing editor (1941-1961) of *New China Daily Press*, president of the Oo Shak Village Club, and adviser to the Chinese Education Association of Hawaii and the Sam Heong Village Club.

Chang-Díaz, Franklin Ramón

b. Apr. 5, 1950
San José, Costa Rica
fields: Aviation and Space Exploration (astronaut)

Latino astronaut. Franklin Ramón Chang-Díaz moved to the United States from Costa Rica when he was eighteen years old to study science, eventually earning a Ph.D. from the Massachusetts Institute of Technology in applied physics in 1977. He then did research on fusion reactors at the Charles Stark Draper Laboratory before being chosen as a mission specialist candidate in 1980. By 1994 he had participated in four NASA space shuttle missions.

Chang In-hwan

b. Mar. 30, 1875
North Pyongan Province, Korea
d. May 22, 1930
San Francisco, Calif.
fields: Government and Politics

One of the first Koreans who immigrated to Hawaii to work on plantations, In-hwan Chang moved to San Francisco in 1905. He became involved in the Korean independence movement, and in 1908, he and a group of Koreans confronted Durham White Stevens, an American acting as foreign affairs adviser to the Korean puppet government installed by Japan. During a struggle, Chang shot and killed Stevens. Convicted of murder, he was sentenced to twenty-five years in prison. He served ten years before being released in 1919.

Channing, William Ellery

b. April 7, 1780
Newport, Rhode Island
d. October 2, 1842
Bennington, Vermont
fields: Religion and Theology

Channing led the attack by Unitarian clergy on New England Congregationalism and helped establish the basis for modern liberal Christianity.

Chanticleer, Raven

b. Sept. 13, 1933
New York, N.Y.
fields: Fashion, Film

African American entertainer and designer; having received training in fashion and design from the Fashion Institute of Technology, the University of Texas, and the University of Paris, Raven Chanticleer has designed fashions for many celebrities including Sarah Vaughan, Della Reese, Josephine Baker, Eartha Kitt, and Mahalia Jackson; he has also worked as a theater, television, and film actor; his film credits include *Carmen Jones* (1954), *Porgy and Bess* (1959), *Cotton*

Comes to Harlem (1970), *Uptown Saturday Night* (1974), and *The Wiz* (1978).

Chao, Elaine L.

full: Elaine Lan Chao
b. 1954
Taiwan
fields: Government and Politics, Business and Industry

After earning an masters in business administration from Harvard University in 1979, Chinese American Elaine L. Chao worked for Gulf Oil and Citicorp. She entered government service full time in 1986, serving as chair of the Federal Maritime Commission in 1988, deputy secretary of transportation 1989-1991, and director of the Peace Corps in 1991. She was the president of the United Way from 1992 to 1996. Since then, she served on the board of directors of various companies.

Chao, Rosalind

b. ?
Orange County, Calif.
fields: Theater and Entertainment

Chinese American Rosalind Chao played roles in a large number of stage, television, and screen productions. In such series as *AfterMASH* (1983-1984) and *Star Trek: The Next Generation* (1987-1994), she was a regular cast member. Her film roles include *Thousand Pieces of Gold* (1991) and *The Joy Luck Club* (1993).

Chao, Stephen

b. 1956
Ann Arbor, Mich.
fields: Theater and Entertainment

Chinese American director and executive Stephen Chao gained a measure of recognition as an innovative but controversial programmer for the Fox network. A graduate of Harvard Business School, Chao worked for the Fox Television Studios in Los Angeles under Barry Diller. Chao was told to develop innovative, low-budget television shows, which he did, ensuring Fox's image as brassy and profane. He became president of Fox television and news in 1992, a post he held briefly. In 1993 he signed a deal to produce independent films for Twentieth Century-Fox. Chao became president of programming and marketing for the USA Network in 1998.

Chao, Yuen Ren

b. Nov. 3, 1892
Tianjin, China
d. 1982
fields: Scholarship, Language and Linguistics

Chinese American Yuen Ren Chao, who received a doctorate from Harvard University in 1918, was a professor of East Asian Languages at the University of California, Berkeley, until his retirement in 1960. A specialist in Chinese grammar and logic, he wrote numerous books, including *A Grammar of Spoken Chinese* (1968) and *Language and Symbolic Systems* (1968).

Chapin, Arthur A.

b. 1915
Philadelphia, Pa.
fields: Government and Politics

African American political appointee; Arthur A. Chapin was appointed by President John F. Kennedy as director of the Equal Employment Opportunity Commission (EEOC) of the Department of Labor; Chapin involved in compiling *The Directory of Negro College Graduates.*

Chaplin, Charles

full: Charles Spencer Chaplin, Jr.
b. April 16, 1889
London, England
d. December 25, 1977
Corsier-sur-Vevey, Switzerland
fields: Film

Through his screen persona of the Tramp, Chaplin represented the American "forgotten man" and presented the image of indomitable courage in the face of overwhelming social and political obstacles.

Chapman, Carrie. *See* Catt, Carrie Chapman

Chapman, George

b. c. 1559
Hitchin, Hertfordshire, England
d. 1634
London, England
fields: Literature, Theater and Entertainment

Best remembered because his translations of Homer's *Iliad* and *Odyssey* inspired John Keats to write a well-known sonnet, George Chapman also was a poet and dramatist whose tragedies reflected his classical background.

Chapman, John. *See* Appleseed, Johnny

Chapman, Tracy

b. Mar. 30, 1964
Cleveland, Ohio
fields: Music (folk singer, songwriter, and guitarist)

African American folk singer, songwriter, and guitarist; the winner of three 1989 Grammy Awards for best new artist, best contemporary folk performance, and best female pop vocal performance, Tracy Chapman is noted for relaying powerful social messages through her lyrics; participated in the 1988 Amnesty International Human Rights Now! Tour.

Char, Tin-Yuke

b. July 4, 1905
Honolulu, Territory of Hawaii
d. June 17, 1990
Honolulu, Hawaii
fields: Historiography, Business and Industry

In the mid-1920's, Tin-Yuke Char began research into the history of his ancestors, the Hakka. In 1939, he began a career in insurance, pursuing his interest in the Chinese in Hawaii on the side. After retiring from the insurance business in 1969, he devoted himself to community service and research, writing *The Hakka Chinese: Their Origin and Folk Songs* (1969) and an autobiography, *The Bamboo Path: Life and Writings of a Chinese in Hawaii* (1977). He compiled and edited *The Sandalwood Mountains: Readings and Stories of the Early Chinese in Hawaii* (1975), *Chinese Historic Sites and Pioneer Families of the Island of Hawaii* (1983). and *Chinese Historic Sites and Pioneer Families of Rural Oahu* (1988).

Chardin, Jean Siméon

b. November 2, 1699
Paris, France
d. December 6, 1779
Paris, France
fields: Art

Perhaps the greatest French painter of the eighteenth century, Chardin drew his inspiration from the Dutch masters and the simple world of the Paris bourgeoisie that he knew so well. Yet he was not merely a genre painter, because many of the techniques that he employed both in his oils and in his pastels would be adopted and developed by generations of painters yet unborn.

Charlemagne

né: Charles
b. 742
Gaul
d. January 28, 814
Aix-la-Chapelle
fields: Government and Politics, Warfare and Conquest, Religion and Theology, Monarchy

By 800, when he was crowned emperor by Pope Leo III, Charlemagne had revived the Roman idea of universal empire, preserved through the Carolingian Renaissance much of the written legacy of the ancient world, and established the foundation for a European civilization distinct from that of ancient Rome and from the contemporary Byzantine and Islamic empires.

Charles I

b. November 19, 1600
Dumferline Castle, Scotland

d. January 30, 1649
London, England
fields: Government and Politics, Law

As King of England (1625-1649), Charles I became involved in a dispute with Parliament over the extent of his prerogative and the ordering of religion, a dispute that resulted in civil war and, by later resolution, in the development of limited monarchy in England.

Charles II

b. May 29, 1630
London, England
d. February 6, 1685
London, England
fields: Government and Politics

King of England, 1660-1685. As the English sought to restore stable government in the aftermath of the Interregnum, Charles II, the eldest surviving son of Charles I, played a crucial role in this process. At ease in any company, he gave the monarchy a human dimension which it had never possessed, and his understanding of the forces that motivated his subjects helped him steer the nation through troubled times.

Charles III

aka: Don Carlos de Bourbon
aka: Charles IV, King of the Two Sicilies
b. January 20, 1716
Madrid, Spain
d. December 14, 1788
Madrid, Spain
fields: Government and Politics

King of Spain, 1759-1788. Charles III's Bourbon Reforms rejuvenated the economic and political administration of Spain and its colonies. While upholding the doctrine of political absolutism, these reforms promoted Enlightenment ideals of humanitarianism, rationalism, and secularism in Spanish government and culture. As a consequence, Charles became the most successful of Europe's "enlightened despots."

Charles IV

b. May 14, 1316
Prague, Bohemia
d. November 29, 1378
Prague, Bohemia
fields: Government and Politics, Monarchy

The greatest ruler of medieval Bohemia and the last important medieval Holy Roman Emperor, Charles was an efficient and effective administrator. He stabilized German political affairs, strengthened the power of his family in Bohemia and in Europe, and influenced the culture of his time.

Charles V

aka: Charles I, King of Spain
b. February 24, 1500
Ghent, Burgundy
d. September 21, 1558
Yuste, Spain
fields: Government and Politics, Religion and Theology

King of Spain, 1516-1556; Holy Roman Emperor, 1519-1556. Charles V initiated 150 years of Habsburg dynastic hegemony in Europe, stopped the Turkish advance in Europe, promoted reform, and expanded Spanish colonization in America.

Charles XII

b. June 17, 1682
Stockholm, Sweden
d. December 11, 1718
Fredriksten, Norway
fields: Military Affairs, Government and Politics

King of Sweden, 1697-1718. As one of the greatest kings of the Vasa Dynasty, Charles XII defended Sweden and won many victories for his country during the Great Northern War against Russia, Poland, and Denmark. He brought Swedish power to a high point and also initiated its decline.

Charles XIV John

né: Jean-Baptiste-Jules Bernadotte
aka: Charles John
b. January 26, 1763
Pau, France
d. March 8, 1844
Stockholm, Sweden
fields: Government and Politics, Military Affairs

Charles XIV lived virtually two distinct lives. He was first a soldier in the French army with strong republican convictions, and then the conservative King of Sweden, 1818-1844.

Charles, Ezzard Mack

b. July 7, 1921
Lawrenceville, Ga.
d. May 28, 1975
Chicago, Ill.
fields: Sports (boxer)

African American boxer; the heavyweight champion from 1949 to 1951, Ezzard Mack Charles beat Jersey Joe Walcott to win the National Boxing Association title and, in 1950, went on to beat Joe Louis to become undisputed champion; in 1951, he lost the title to Walcott; during his career Charles fought 122 bouts, scored 58 knockouts, and won 38 decisions.

Charles, Ray

né: Ray Charles Robinson
b. September 23, 1930
Albany, Georgia
fields: Music

African American musician Ray Charles helped expand the market for black music forms and also helped open creative possibilities for music in general in the 1960's.

Charles, Rupaul Andre. *See* RuPaul

Charles d'Orléans

b. November 24, 1391
Paris, France
d. January 4, 1465
Amboise, France
fields: Literature, Government and Politics

Defeated and taken prisoner while leading French troops at Agincourt, Charles spent twenty-five years in captivity in England writing lyric poetry in French and English. When released, he contributed to peace negotiations and maintained a poetry salon.

Charles Martel

b. 689
near Liège, France
d. October 22, 741
Quierzy-sur-Oise, France
fields: Monarchy, Government and Politics, Military Affairs

Through skill, good fortune, and ruthless ambition, Charles Martel rose to dominate the kingdom of the Franks and its weak Merovingian kings, laying the groundwork for his son Pippin to be recognized as the first Carolingian king of the Franks and for his grandson Charlemagne to emerge as the first Holy Roman Emperor. Charles not only founded the Carolingian dynasty but also led Frankish forces to check the Muslim advance into southern France in 732, achieving fame in the Battle of Tours and earning the surname Martel ("the Hammer").

Charles the Bald

b. June 13, 823
Frankfurt am Main
d. October 6, 877
Avrieux or Brides-les-Bain, France
fields: Monarchy, Government and Politics

Reigning during one of the most turbulent periods in European history, Charles managed to survive and pass the crown of the West Frankish kingdom to his posterity.

Charles the Bold

b. November 10, 1433
Dijon, Burgundy
d. January 5, 1477
near Nancy, Lorraine
fields: Government and Politics

Duke of Burgundy, 1467-1477. Charles the Bold attempted to build the Duchy of Burgundy into a unified kingdom. He was considered a serious threat to the stability and centralization of the French state.

Charleston, Oscar McKinley

b. Oct. 14, 1896
Indianapolis, Ind.
d. Oct. 6, 1954
Philadelphia, Pa.
fields: Sports (baseball player)

African American baseball player; Oscar McKinley Charleston played for the Negro League Indianapolis ABCs from 1915 to 1941; he then managed Negro League teams until 1954; he was said to have had power comparable to Babe Ruth, base running skills like Ty Cobb, and defense instincts comparable to outfielder Tris Speaker; elected to the Baseball Hall of Fame in 1976.

Charlot

aka: Clem-hak-kah (Bear Claw)
aka: Martin Charlot
b. c. 1831
northern Idaho
d. 1900
Jocko Reservation
fields: Government and Politics, Native American Affairs

Native American leader. Flathead/Salish (possibly Kalispel) leader Charlot fought against removal by white settlers. Resisted moving from fertile farms in Bitterroot Mountains area of Montana to Pend d'Oreille reservation; forced to move in 1900.

Charlton, Cornelius H.

b. July 24, 1929
East Gulf, W.Va.
d. June 2, 1951
Chipo-ri, Korea
fields: Warfare and Conquest

African American military hero; on June 2, 1951 during the Korean War, Cornelius H. Charlton took up command of his unit when the commanding officer was shot; he then led an attack on Hill 542; while single-handedly eliminating an emplacement that was standing in the way of his unit, he was mortally wounded by two grenades; for his actions he was posthumously awarded the Medal of Honor.

Charlton, Samuel

b. c. 1761
New Jersey
d. 1843
New York, N.Y.
fields: Warfare and Conquest

African American Revolutionary War soldier; born a slave, teenager Samuel Charlton was sent to fight in the Revolutionary War as a substitute for his master; he survived the battles of Brandywine, Germantown, and Monmouth only to return to his master and slavery following the war; he was freed following the death of his master.

Chartier, Alain

b. c. 1385
Bayeux, France
d. 1429
Avignon, France
fields: Literature, Government and Politics

Chartier's skillful use of the French language and his imaginative, elegant style significantly influenced the development of French poetry in the fifteenth century. As royal secretary to Charles VII of Valois, Chartier played an active role in the complex political world during the Hundred Years' War, a world which he accurately recorded in prose works of extraordinary literary and historical importance.

Chase, James E.

b. b. 1914?
Ballinger, Tex.
d. May 19, 1987
Spokane, Wash.
fields: Government and Politics

African American mayor of Spokane, Wash.; on Nov. 3, 1981, James E. Chase became the first African American mayor of Spokane, a predominantly white city, with 72 percent of the vote; he served until December, 1985; he died of cancer at age seventy-three.

Chase, Margaret Madeline. *See* Smith, Margaret Chase

Chase, Salmon P.

full: Salmon Portland Chase
b. January 13, 1808
Cornish, New Hampshire
d. May 7, 1873
New York, New York
fields: Civil Rights, Law, Government and Politics

As an attorney, politician, and constitutional theorist, Chase contributed to the abolition of slavery. During the 1850's, he served as a United States senator and as governor of Ohio, and he participated in the formation of the Republican Party. He was later appointed secretary of the treasury and was Chief Justice of the Supreme Court (1796-1811).

Chase, Samuel

b. April 17, 1741
Somerset County, Maryland
d. June 19, 1811
Baltimore, Maryland
fields: Law

The only United States Supreme Court justice ever to face an impeachment trial, Chase was both a partisan firebrand and a founding father whose political and legal theory helped shape the republic.

Chase-Riboud, Barbara

b. June 20, 1939
Philadelphia, Pa.
fields: Art (sculptor), Literature

African American sculptor and writer; while still a high school student, Barbara Chase-Riboud won an art prize from *Seventeen* magazine and sold her first prints to the Museum of Modern Art; her sculptures, which have incorporated symbolic forms and fabrics inspired by her time spent in Africa and China and themes from her experiences during the early Civil Rights movement, have been exhibited in European museums, the Betty Parsons Gallery in New York, the Massachusetts Institute of Technology, and the University Art Gallery in Berkeley, California; she has published novels, including *Sally Hemings* (1979), and several volumes of poetry.

Chateaubriand

full: François-August-René de Chateaubriand
b. September 4, 1768
Saint-Malo, France
d. July 4, 1848
Paris, France
fields: Literature

The father of French Romanticism, Chateaubriand popularized the melancholy hero and deeply influenced many other nineteenth and twentieth century writers.

Châtelet, Marquise du

né: Gabrielle-Émilie Le Tonnelier de Breteuil
b. December 17, 1706
Paris, France
d. September 10, 1749
Lunéville, Meurthe-et-Moselle, France
fields: Astronomy, Chemistry, Mathematics, Physics

In 1733 Marquise du Châtelet met the writer Voltaire, and they began what would become a lifelong relationship; in 1738 she published "Lettre sur les éléments de la philosophie de Newton," a popularized account of Newton's natural philosophy, under Voltaire's name; in 1740 she published *Institutions de physique*, a physics textbook; she gave birth to her last child in 1749; *Principes mathématiques de la philosophie naturelle*, her translation into French of Newton's *Philosophiae Naturalis Principia Mathematica* (1687), is published posthumously in 1759.

Chatham, first earl of. *See* Pitt the Elder, William

Chatman, Peter. *See* Memphis Slim

Chatterji, Gadadhar. *See* Ramakrishna

Chattopadhyay, Sarojini. *See* Naidu, Sarojini

Chattopadhyaya, Gadadhar. *See* Ramakrishna

Chaucer, Geoffrey

b. c. 1343
London?, England
d. October 25, 1400
London, England
fields: Literature

A great innovator and a great master of English poetry, Chaucer used his descriptive and narrative skill to express a comic vision of humanity undimmed by the passage of six centuries.

Chávez, César

full: César Estrada Chávez
b. Mar. 31, 1927
near Yuma, Ariz.
d. Apr. 23, 1993
San Luis, Ariz.
fields: Labor Movement

Mexican American farm labor organizer; César Chávez was raised as a migrant worker after his parents lost their farm during the depression; general director, Community Service Organization, 1958-1962; established the National Farm Workers Association, 1962, which merged with another organization to become the United Farm Workers Organizing Committee, 1966, later the United Farm Workers of America; led strikes and boycotts from 1965 to improve wages and working conditions for migrant workers; committed to nonviolent tactics; instrumental to the passage of the Agricultural Labor Relations Act (1975); received Presidential Medal of Freedom.

Chávez, Denise Elia

b. Aug. 15, 1948
Las Cruces, N.Mex.
fields: Literature

Latina writer. Denise Elia Chávez, a prolific Mexican American playwright, had written more than twenty plays by the early 1990's. She has taught theater at several southwestern universities and helped found the National Institute of Chicana Writers. Her plays include *The Wait* (1970), which won New Mexico University's Best Play Award, and *Plaza* (1984). She has also written several novels, including *The Last of the Menu Girls* (1986), which won the Puerto del Sol fiction award for 1985 and the Steele Jones Fiction Award in 1986, and *Face of an Angel* (1990).

Chávez, Dennis

b. Apr. 8, 1888
near Albuquerque, N.Mex.
d. Nov. 18, 1962
Albuquerque, N.Mex.
fields: Government and Politics

Latino politician; Dennis Chávez was born in New Mexico; largely self-educated; earned law degree at Georgetown University in 1920; served as U.S. representative (Democrat), 1931-1935; appointed to the U.S. senate in 1935, then elected, 1937-1962; first Hispanic U.S. senator; opposed U.S. entry into World War II; drafted a bill creating the Fair Employment Practices Commission.

Chávez, Eduardo Arcenio

b. Mar. 14, 1917
Wagon Mound, N.Mex.
fields: Art (painter and sculptor)

Latino painter and sculptor. Although Eduardo Arcenio Chávez considered himself self-taught, he studied art at the Colorado Springs Fine Arts Center. He painted murals for the Works Progress Administration in the 1930's and in 1947 won the Pepsi-Cola Prize for American Painting. In the 1950's and 1960's, his painting became more abstract. Examples of his abstract work include *Xochimilcho* (1965) and *Moon Journey* (1969). Chávez also taught art in New York and Colorado, and was an instructor with the Art Students League from 1954 to 1958.

Chávez, Helen

b. 1928
Brawley, Calif.
fields: Social Reform

Latina union activist. Helen Chávez was the wife of legendary activist César Chávez. She provided emotional support and worked to feed and clothe the couple's eight children while César worked, without pay, to organize workers. Helen was arrested for civil disobedience in 1965 while participating in a labor strike. Also in that year, she and César set up a credit union for the National Farm Workers Association, which Helen managed for years afterward.

Chávez, Julio César

b. July 12, 1962
Ciudád Obregón, Mexico
fields: Sports (boxer)

Latino boxer. In 1984, Julio César Chávez knocked out Mario Martinez to become the super featherweight championship. During the next decade, he won the World Boxing Association (WBA) lightweight title, the International Boxing Federation (IBF) lightweight title, and the World Boxing Council (WBC) super lightweight title. In 1993, he fought Pernell Whitaker to a majority draw. The following year, Chávez received his first loss in ninety-one fights at the hands of Frankie Randall. However, Chávez won the rematch and recaptured the super lightweight title. During the 1990's, he also fought and lost twice to Oscar de la Hoya.

Chavez, Linda

b. June 17, 1947
Albuquerque, New Mexico
fields: Government and Politics

As a Hispanic conservative activist and public official, Chavez broadened the role of women and minorities in American politics.

Chávez, Manuel

aka: Fray Angélico Chávez
b. Apr. 10, 1910
Wagon Mound, N.Mex.
d. Mar. 18, 1996
Santa Fe, N. Mex.
fields: Literature

Latino writer. Manuel Chávez was a former Franciscan monk and Catholic priest who wrote poetry, prose fiction, and historical nonfiction. His poetry was dominated by Catholic themes, while his historical fiction focused on early Hispanics in New Mexico. He won the Catholic Poetry Award in 1948 from the Catholic Poetry Society. His poetry collections include *Clothed with the Sun* (1939), *The Lady from Toledo* (1960), and *Selected Poems, with an Apología* (1969). His prose works include *The Short Stories of Fray Angélico Chávez* (1987), edited by Genaro M. Padilla, and a spiritual autobiography titled *My Penitente Land: Reflections on Spanish New Mexico* (1974).

Chavis, Benjamin

full: Benjamin Franklin Chavis, Jr.
b. Jan. 22, 1948
Oxford, N.C.
fields: Civil Rights

African American civil rights activist; Benjamin Chavis after training as a theologian, became a civil rights organizer for the Southern Christian Leadership Council and the United Church of Christ; indicted in 1971 as one of the Wilmington Ten for the firebombing of a store in Wilmington, Delaware; convicted but granted parole, his conviction was reversed in 1980; appointed executive director of the Commission for Racial Justice in 1985; served as executive director of the National Association for the Advancement of Colored People, 1993-1994, a position from which he was forced to resign because of a financial scandal; turned attention to the National African American Leadership Summit (NAALS); national director of the Million Man March (1995).

Cheatham, Henry Plummer

b. Dec. 27, 1857
near Henderson, N.C.
d. Nov. 29, 1935
Oxford, N.C.
fields: Government and Politics

African American legislator; as a graduate, with honors, from Shaw University in Raleigh, N.C., Henry Plummer Cheatham served in the U.S. House of Representatives, representing the Second Congressional District of North Carolina, from 1888 to 1892; in 1897 the Senate confirmed him as recorder of deeds for the District of Columbia; from 1907 until his death, he served as superintendent of an orphanage for African American children.

Chebona Bula. *See* Blue Eagle, Acee

Chebyshev, Pafnuty Lvovich

b. May 16, 1821
Okatovo, Kaluga, Russia
d. Dec. 8, 1894
St. Petersburg, Russia
fields: Mathematics (algebra, number theory, probability, and statistics)

Pafnuty Lvovich Chebyshev produced a theory on the best approximation of functions. He is also responsible for Chebyshev's theorem, which gives a precise and simple demonstration of the generalized law of large numbers and is fundamental in modern probability.

Checker, Chubby

né: Ernest Evans
b. Oct. 3, 1941
Philadelphia, Pa.
fields: Music (popular singer)

African American singer; most often associated with his recording "The Twist" (1960) and the dance that accompanied it, Chubby Checker was never able to divorce himself from his association in popular culture as the articulator and icon of this one popular movement; through his songs "Pony Time" (1961) and "The Fly" (1961) and their accompanying dances, he tried to continue his success as a dance innovator; both songs reached the top ten but did not generate as much of a following as the Twist; although he had no more hits after 1965, he continued to perform in rock revival shows and to record.

Cheek, James

b. Dec. 4, 1932
Roanoke Rapids, N.C.
fields: Education

African American educator and administrator; a recipient, in 1983, of the Presidential Medal of Freedom, James Cheek has served as president of Shaw University, Raleigh, N.C. (beginning 1963), Howard University, Washington D.C. (1969-1989), and Tennessee Wesleyan College (beginning 1989); he has also served as special consultant to the president on black colleges and universities and as a member of the National Urban Coalition steering committee.

Cheek, King

b. May 26, 1937
Weldon, N.C.
fields: Education

African American educator and lawyer; with degrees in economics and law, King Cheek has served as president of Shaw University and Morgan State College; he has led civic and professional organizations; in 1971 he was awarded the Grand Commander of the Order of the Star of Africa by President William Tubman of Liberia.

Cheema, Boona

b.?
India
fields: Social Reform

After Boona Cheema, a Sikh, arrived in the United States, she settled in the San Francisco Bay Area, where she organized support services for homeless people. Her program served as a model for similar efforts. In 1988, U.S. president George Bush, during his nonmination acceptance speech at the Republican National Convention, cited her as one of the "thousand points of light."

Cheever, John

b. May 27, 1912
Quincy, Massachusetts
d. June 18, 1982
Ossining, New York
fields: Literature

Award-winning novelist and short-story writer John Cheever's vision of the foibles and weaknesses of American society mixes irony, compassion, whimsy, and symbolism. He published stories and novels from 1929 to his death in 1982, earning an O'Henry Award, a National Institute of Arts and Letters Award, and the National Book Award (for *The Wapshot Chronicle*, published in 1957) and establishing himself as a master chronicler of the upper middle class.

Chekhov, Anton

full: Anton Pavlovich Chekhov
aka: Anton Tchekhov
b. January 29, 1860
Taganrog, in the Crimea, Russia
d. July 15, 1904
Badenweiler, Germany
fields: Literature, Theater and Entertainment (drama)

Although Chekhov had a significant impact on the creation of modern drama with his four major plays, his most important influence has been on the development of the modern short story. With his numerous lyrical stories, Chekhov liberated the short story in particular from its adherence to the parable form and fiction in general from the tedium of the realistic novel.

Chen Duxiu

aka: Ch'en Tu-hsiu
b. October 8, 1879
Huaining (now Anqing), Anhui Province, China
d. May 27, 1942
Chiangchin, near Chongqing, China
fields: Government and Politics

Chen Duxiu, cofounder of Chinese Communist Party (CCP) in 1921, had widespread influence on twentieth century China. General secretary of party until being ousted in 1927. Arrested in 1932 for endangering the republic. At highly publicized trial was found guilty and sentenced to fifteen years in prison. Released in a general amnesty in August, 1937,

Chen, Jack

né: Bernard Ivan Felix Acham
b. July 2, 1908
Port-of-Spain, Trinidad
fields: Historiography, Sociology

Jack Chen, the second son of Eugene Chen, former foreign affairs adviser to Sun Yat-sen, was a founding member, in 1983, of the Pear Garden in the West, the San Francisco American Chinese Opera and Performing Arts Center. This authority on Sino-American relations published fifteen books, including *New Earth* (1957), *A Year in Upper Felicity* (1973), *Inside the Cultural Revolution* (1975), and *The Chinese of America* (1980).

Chen, Joan

né: Chen Chong
b. January 3, 1960
Shanghai, People's Republic of China
fields: Theater and Entertainment, Film

Shanghai-born actor and director Joan Chen performed in many films, including *Blade Runner* (1982) and *The Last Emperor* (1987), with starring roles in *Heaven and Earth* (1993) and *Golden Gate* (1994). She was a regular on the television series *Twin Peaks* (1990-1991). She also directed 1999's *Xiu Xiu*.

Chen, King C.

b. Oct. 24, 1926
Fujian Province, China

d. June 9, 1992
Newark, N.J.
fields: Scholarship, Government and Politics

King C. Chen, a specialist in Asian political affairs and international relations who fled Communist China during the revolution, was a professor of political science at Rutgers University for twenty-four years. He served as adviser to the U.S. State Department, on the editorial boards of *Asian Affairs* and the *Central Daily News* in Taipei, and as president of the Chinese-American Academic and Professional Society. His books include *Vietnam and China, 1938-1954* (1969), *China's War Against Vietnam, 1979* (1987), and *China's Policy Toward Taiwan* (1990).

Chen, Lily Lee

b. May 27, 1936
Tianjin, China
fields: Government and Politics

Lily Lee Chen became the first Chinese American woman ever to serve as mayor of a U.S. city when she served as mayor of Monterey Park, California, November, 1983, to September, 1984. Other service includes stints as president of the Chinese American Democratic Club and the Chinese American Political Action Committee, planning committee member of the 1984 Democratic National Convention, and national president of the Organization of Chinese American Women.

Ch'en Tu-hsiu

né: Ch'en Ch'ien-sheng
b. October 8, 1879
Huaining District, Anhwei Province, China
d. May 27, 1942
Chiangching, Szechwan Province, China
fields: Government and Politics, Literature

As the editor of a groundbreaking literary journal and Dean of Arts and Letters at Peking University, Ch'en Tu-hsiu was a central figure in the Chinese "literary renaissance" of 1915-1921 and in the May Fourth Movement of 1919. He founded the Chinese Communist Party with Li Ta-ch'ao in 1921 and served as its chairman from 1921 to 1927.

Chen Xiangmei. *See* Chennault, Anna C.

Ch'en Yi. *See* Hsüan-tsang

Chenault, Kenneth I.

b. June 2, 1951
Hempstead, N.Y.
fields: Business and Industry (corporate executive and attorney)

African American corporate executive and attorney; in 1981, Kenneth I. Chenault joined the American Express Company; in 1984, he was promoted to senior vice president and general manager of merchandise services and oversaw an expansion of the card's direct sales to nearly $400 million by 1986; in the financially-challenged early 1990's he dedicated himself to increasing customer service and maintaining merchant loyalty. From 1995 to 1997, he served as vice chairman of American Express. He became president and COO (chief operating officer) of American Express in 1997. In 1999, he was named CEO (chief executive officer).

Cheney, Amy Marcy. *See* Beach, Amy Marcy

Cheng Ch'eng-kung

b. August 28, 1624
Hirado, near Nagasaki, Japan
d. June 23, 1662
Taiwan
fields: Government and Politics, Military Affairs

Cheng was a Chinese sea lord who fought for the failing Ming Dynasty against the conquering Manchus. He incorporated Taiwan into the Chinese cultural and political systems.

Cheng Ho

né: Ma San-po
b. c. 1371
K'un-yang, Yunnan, China
d. between 1433 and 1436
possibly Calicut, India
fields: Government and Politics, Exploration

An imperial eunuch, Cheng Ho commanded the Ming Dynasty's voyages of exploration in the early fifteenth century, sailing farther than any person in history at that time.

Cheng, Lucie

aka: Lucie Cheng Hirata
b. ?
fields: Scholarship, Sociology

Lucie Cheng was an associate professor of sociology and director of the Center for Pacific Rim Studies at the University of California, Los Angeles. She served as director of the university's Asian American Studies Center and coedited the book *Labor Immigration Under Capitalism* (1984).

Chenier, Clifton

b. June 25, 1925
near Opelousas, La.
d. Dec. 12, 1987
near Opelousas(?), La.
fields: Music (zydeco)

African American known as the king of zydeco; Clifton Chenier recorded "Louisiana Stomp" in mid-1950's; toured with his band Zydeco Ramblers; became internationally known in the 1960's; was featured in documentary *Hot Pepper* (1974).

Chennault, Anna C.

né: Chen Xiangmei
b. June 23, 1925
Beijing, China
fields: Government and Politics, Journalism

Anna C. Chennault was the wife of American aviator Claire Lee Chennault, the legendary commander of the Flying Tigers in China during World War II, and a prominent member of the China lobby in the United States during the Cold War. She was a correspondent for the Chinese Central News Agency in Kunming, where she met her husband, whom she married in 1947. After her husband's death in 1958, Chennault moved to Washington, D.C., and became a lobbyist, using her political connections especially on behalf of the Chinese Nationalists on Taiwan and the anticommunist regime in South Vietnam. Chennault's English-language writings include the autobiographical works *A Thousand Springs* (1962) and *The Education of Anna* (1980).

Chennault, Madelyn

b. July 15, 1934
Atlanta, Ga.
fields: Pschiatry and Psychology, Education

African American educator and psychologist; Madelyn Chennault was Fort Valley State College's Calloway professor of Educational Psychology; advocate for mental-health services and programs for the mentally retarded and the poor.

Cher

né: Cherilyn Sarkisian
b. May 20, 1946
El Centro, California
fields: Music, Film

Cher began her career in the mid-1960's as a pop singer, but gained wider acclaim after turning to acting and starring in a number of successful films.

Cherenkov, Pavel Alekseyevich

aka: Pavel Cerenkov
b. July 28, 1904
Novaya Chigla, Russia
d. Jan. 6, 1990
probably in Moscow, the Soviet Union
fields: Physics

Pavel Alekseyevich Cherenkov found that the light emitted by transparent substances placed near radioactive sources is not emitted symmetrically, discovering what is now called Cherenkov radiation. In 1958 he won the Nobel Prize in Physics with Ilya Frank and Igor Tamm.

Chern, Shiing-Shen

b. Oct. 26, 1911
Jiaxing, Zhejiang Province, China
fields: Mathematics (applied math and geometry)

Shiing-Shen Chern established Chern characteristic classes, which play an important role in math and mathematical physics. He set up the Institute of Mathematics in China in 1945. In 1975 he won the U.S. National Medal of Science, and in 1983 he won the Wolf Prize.

Chesimard, JoAnne Deborah. *See* Shakur, Assata Olugbala

Chesnut, Mary Boykin

né: Mary Boykin Miller
b. March 31, 1823
Mount Pleasant Plantation, near Camden, South Carolina
d. November 22, 1886
Sarsfield, South Carolina
fields: Historiography, Civil Rights

In her Civil War diary and its revisions, Chesnut created—often within the contexts of women's issues—powerful literary works with enduring historical, political, and social implications.

Chesnutt, Charles Waddell

b. June 20, 1858
Cleveland, Ohio
d. Nov. 15, 1932
Cleveland, Ohio
fields: Literature

African American author; Charles Waddell Chesnutt published short stories, including "The Goophered Grapevine"; best-known works are *The Conjure Woman* (1899), a collection of short stories, and *The House Behind the Cedars* (1900), a novel.

Chessman, Caryl

full: Carol Whittier Chessman
b. May 27, 1921
St. Joseph, Michigan
d. May 2, 1960
San Quentin, California
fields: Historical Figure, Law, Social Reform

San Quentin inmate Caryl Chessman, with his many public appeals for the repeal of the death penalty, made capital punishment the subject of national and worldwide scrutiny.

Cheucunsene. *See* Dragging Canoe

Cheung, King-Kok

b. 1954
fields: Literature

King-Kok Cheung, who received a Ph.D. in English from the University of California, Berkeley, coauthored *Asian American Literature: An Annotated Bibliography* (1988), with Stan Yogi. She published *Articulate Silences: Hisaye Yamamoto, Maxine Hong Kingston, Joy Kogawa* (1993) and edited *"Seventeen Syllables"* (1994) by Hisaye Yamamoto, a volume in a series on women writers published by Rutgers University Press. In addition to two stories by Yamamoto, the volume includes critical essays and other materials, including an interview with Yamamoto, conducted by Cheung, who also contributed an introduction and one of the critical essays.

Chiang Kai-Shek

b. October 31, 1887
Chikow, China
d. April 5, 1975
Taipei, Taiwan
fields: Government and Politics

Chiang was the most important man in the Kuomintang government during the Nanking decade. He led the government and Chinese armed forces through eight years of war against Japan (1937-1945) until Allied victory, was elected president, but lost the civil war to the Chinese Communist Party. He and his Kuomintang followers fled in 1949 to Taiwan, where he ruled until his death.

Chiang Soong Mei-ling

né: Soong Mei-ling
b. Apr. 14, 1897
Shanghai, China
fields: Diplomacy, Government and Politics

Widow of the former president of the Republic of China, Chiang Kai-shek, and a leader of Chinese women, Soong Mei-ling Chiang was born in an affluent Chinese Christian family and attended college in the United States. After her marriage in 1927, she acted as her husband's personal secretary and interpreter. She headed a number of women's projects, including relief programs for refugees and shelters for homeless children. She visited the United States to plead the cause of the Chinese Nationalists between 1942 and 1943, charming millions of Americans with her grace and eloquence. After 1949, she lived in Taiwan, then after her husband's death in 1975, she settled in Long Island, New York.

Chicago, Judy

né: Judith Cohen
b. July 20, 1939
Chicago, Illinois
fields: Art

A leader of the Women Artists' Movement of the 1970's, Judy Chicago has produced a body of art and writing that has been extremely influential in promoting acceptance and recognition of women artists of the past and modern times and in encouraging the development of a more expansive, inclusive view of history.

Chichikam Lupalkuelatko. *See* Scarface Charlie

Ch'ien-lung

né: Hung-li
aka: Kao Tsung (temple name)
aka: Ch'un Huang-ti (posthumous name)
b. September 25, 1711
Peking, China
d. February 7, 1799
Peking, China
fields: Government and Politics

Emperor of China, 1735-1796, in the Ch'ing Dynasty. Ch'ien-lung presided over an empire unprecedented in size and power. Under his rule, China reached its apex, enjoying a long span of peace, order, and prosperity.

Chifley, Joseph Benedict

aka: Ben Chifley
b. September 22, 1885
Bathurst, New South Wales (now Australia)
d. June 13, 1951
Canberra, Australian Capital Territory, Australia
fields: Government and Politics

Joseph Benedict Chifley was Labor Party prime minister of Australia from 1945 to 1949. Supported full employment and increased social services; encouraged large-scale immigration. Attempted to nationalize Australia's banks. Trade unions became dissatisfied with government and called large-scale strikes. Chifley employed troops to work at mines during a coal strike, a controversial move.

Child, Lydia Maria

né: Lydia Maria Francis
b. February 11, 1802
Medford, Massachusetts
d. October 20, 1880
Wayland, Massachusetts
fields: Literature, Social Reform (abolitionism)

Child was one of America's first successful women writers and editors, combining popular writing with a lifetime's dedication to the causes of racial equality and general public enlightenment.

Childress, Alice

b. Oct. 12, 1920
Charleston, S.C.
d. Aug. 14, 1994
New York, N.Y.

fields: Literature, Theater and Entertainment

African American dramatist and novelist; Alice Childress wrote the play *Trouble in Mind* (pr. 1955), which won 1956 Obie Award; published popular juvenile novel *A Hero Ain't Nothin' but a Sandwich* (1973).

Chin, Frank

full: Frank Chew Chin, Jr.
b. Feb. 25, 1940
Berkeley, Calif.
fields: Literature

Asian American writer, playwright; Frank Chin produced *The Chickencoop Chinaman* (1972), becoming the first Asian American playwright to reach the New York stage; founded the Asian American Theatre Workshop in San Francisco in 1973; opposed to the Asian American literature of popular authors such as Maxine Hong Kingston and Amy Tan, which he considers to be founded in Western philosophy and tradition; *The Year of the Dragon* (1974) dealt with the disintegration of a Chinese American family; organized Day of Remembrance in 1978, bringing Japanese American leaders and activists together to publicize grievances suffered during World War II; with others edited *Aiiieeeee! An Anthology of Asian American Writers* (1974) (revised and expanded *The Big Aiiieeeee! An Anthology of Chinese and Japanese American Literature* (1991); also published *The Chinaman Pacific and Frisco R.R. Co.* (1988), a collection of short fiction, and *Donald Duk* (1991) a novel.

Chin, John Yehall

b. Mar. 2, 1908
Toishan, China
d. July 11, 1994
San Francisco, Calif.
fields: Education

John Yehall Chin, the first Chinese American elected to a public office in San Francisco, became president of the San Francisco Community College Board. He served as a member of the first Human Rights Commission in Washington, D.C., and as president of the Chinese Six Companies, the Hop Wo Benevolent Association, and the Yee Fung Toy Family Association. He became principal of the Chinese Language School in San Francisco in 1955.

Chin, Marilyn

b. January 14, 1955
Hong Kong
fields: Literature (poetry)

Marilyn Chin received a bachelor's degree in classical Chinese literature and an M.F.A. in 1981 from the University of Iowa. She published two poetry collections, *Dwarf Bamboo* (1987) and *The Phoenix Gone, the Terrace Empty* (1994). Chin received a National Endowment for the Arts Writing Fellowship and a Stegner Fellowship.

Ch'in Shih Huang-ti. *See* Shi Huangdi

Chin, Vincent

b. 1955
d. June 22, 1982
Detroit, Mich.
fields: Historical Figure

Vincent Chin was a Chinese American engineering draftsman who was murdered by anti-Asians Ronald Ebens and stepson Michael Nitz in June of 1982. Ebens and Nitz received light sentences—a $3,780 fine and three years of probation each—outraging the Asian American community and leading to protests and demands for justice. After an FBI investigation, Ebens was sentenced to twenty-five years in prison, but the conviction was reversed on appeal because of judicial errors. The case was retried in 1987; Ebens was freed, but in a subsequent civil suit he was ordered to pay $1.5 million to Chin's estate as part of a court-approved settlement agreement.

Chinda Sutemi

b. 1856
Hirosaki, Japan
d. 1929
fields: Diplomacy

Chinda Sutemi was Japanese consul in San Francisco, beginning in 1890, and served as ambassador from Japan from 1912 until 1916, during the administration of President Woodrow Wilson. While a consul, he became concerned that the immigration of Japanese prostitutes to the West Coast might trigger antiforeign exclusionist activity and urged Japan to tighten the immigrant selection process. His efforts resulted in the Gentlemen's Agreement of 1907, which limited the number of Japanese immigrant laborers to the United States. He lodged a protest against segregation of Japanese students in San Francisco public schools in 1906 and asked Wilson to exert pressure to block passage of California's proposed antialien land bill, but to no avail.

Ch'ing, Chiang. *See* Jiang Qing

Ching, Hung Wai

b. ?
fields: Government and Politics

Hung Wai Ching, a Chinese American civil leader in Hawaii, headed the Morale Section of the Office of the Military Governor shortly after the bombing of Pearl Harbor. As trusted adviser to the Federal Bureau of Investigation and the military governor, Ching unwaveringly stood up for the loyalty of the Japanese Americans. He encouraged Japanese Americans who had been discharged from the Hawaii Territorial Guard in January, 1942, to petition the military governor to accept them for noncombat labor. When Assistant Secretary of War John J. McCloy saw their group, the Varsity Victory Volunteers, at work, Ching took the opportunity to impress on the secretary that the Japanese Americans could be trusted, even in the Army. Eventually Japanese Americans were accepted for combat duty.

Chinh, Kieu

b. c. 1939
Hanoi, Vietnam
fields: Theater and Entertainment

Kieu Chinh, a Vietnamese American, had a strong supporting role in *The Joy Luck Club*, one of the most critically acclaimed and commercially successful films of 1993. She left Hanoi and moved to Saigon in 1954. She became an actress, gaining major roles in many films, including the Hollywood productions *A Yank in Vietnam* (1964) and *Operation C.I.A.* (1965). By the late 1960's Chinh had become the most famous female film star in Southeast Asia. Chinh fled Saigon in 1975, settling in Southern California. In 1987 she quit her job as a translator to renew her acting career. In 1989 Chinh was cast in *Welcome Home* and *Vietnam, Texas*, two feature films with Vietnamese themes. For a time she was also attached to the popular ABC television series *China Beach*.

Chinn, Thomas Wayne

b. July 28, 1909
Marshfield, Oreg.
d. September 11, 1997
San Francisco, Calif.
fields: Business and Industry, Publishing

Thomas Wayne Chinn, businessperson, publisher, and editor, arrived in San Francisco in 1919. The president of his own firm, Gollan Typography, until 1980, he founded and published *Chinese News* and *Chinese Digest*, the first English-language weekly newspaper for Chinese Americans. He published *Bridging the Pacific: San Francisco Chinatown and Its People* in 1989. He was president of the Chinese Historical Society of America, which he helped found.

Chino, Eusebio Francesco. *See* Kino, Eusebio Francisco

Chisholm, Grace. *See* Young, Grace Chisholm

Chisholm, Jesse

b. c. 1805
southeastern Tenn.

d. Mar. 4, 1868
near Norman, Okla.
fields: Diplomacy, Native American Affairs

Multilingual Cherokee trader Jesse Chisholm's work as a trader and his ability as an interpreter carried his influence far beyond the reach of his own tribe. In 1865 he drove a wagon from Texas to his trading post. Texas cattlemen followed the ruts left by Chisholm's wagon to get their cattle to Wichita, and the route became the famous Chisholm Trail.

Chisholm, Shirley

né: Shirley Anita St. Hill
b. November 30, 1924
Brooklyn, New York
fields: Government and Politics

As the first African American woman elected to the U.S. Congress and the first to run as a candidate for the presidency, Shirley Chisholm has been an outspoken advocate for women, children, and ethnic minorities.

Ch'iu, K'ung. *See* Confucius

Chivington, John Milton

b. Jan. 27, 1821
Warren County, Ohio
d. Oct. 4, 1894
Denver, Colo.
fields: Native American Affairs, Warfare and Conquest

John Milton Chivington was a Methodist preacher turned soldier, known as the Fighting Parson. Colonel of the Colorado Volunteers, Chivington led the attack upon Cheyennes at Sand Creek—two hundred American Indians were gunned down, clubbed, or knifed to death, most of them women and children. The massacre spread a wave of revulsion against Chivington and his men and gave the Cheyennes, Sioux, and Arapahos renewed strength in protests. Partly because of Chivington's actions, the U.S. Army spent $30 million in campaigns to subdue the Native Americans.

Cho, Henry

b. 1962
Knoxville, Tenn.
fields: Theater and Entertainment

Korean American Henry Cho began doing stand-up comedy in 1986. His material is largely drawn from growing up as an Asian American in the South. An actor as well as a comedian, he has had roles in films and television programs.

Chock, Eric

b. 1950
fields: Literature (poetry)

Eric Chock cofounded *Bamboo Ridge: The Hawaii Writers' Quarterly*, thus helping the distinctive "local literature" of Hawaii gain recognition. He received a B.A. from the University of Pennsylvania and an M.A. from the University of Hawaii and served as program coordinator for the Hawaii Poets in the Schools program in Honolulu. A collection of his poems, *Last Days Here*, was published in 1990.

Chomsky, Noam

full: Avram Noam Chomsky
b. December 7, 1928
Philadelphia, Pennsylvania
fields: Language and Linguistics, Political Science

By creating and developing a new theory of how language works, Chomsky transformed the study of linguistics. At the same time, he built a worldwide reputation as a radical critic of U.S. foreign policy and media culture.

Chopin, Frédéric

full: Frédéric-François Chopin
b. March 1, 1810
Zelazowa Wola, Poland
d. October 17, 1849
Paris, France
fields: Music

Chopin achieved eminence in two usually distinct areas of music: as a performer and as a composer. He became the foremost pianist of his time, despite the fact that his delicate style and unwillingness to perform in public placed him outside contemporary fashion and practice. His eminence as a composer is equally startling, for unlike every other composer of comparable stature, Chopin devoted himself almost exclusively to keyboard music. Against what some have perceived as the narrowness of his interests, one may posit the brilliance and diversity of his compositions.

Chopin, Kate

né: Katherine O'Flaherty
b. February 8, 1851
St. Louis, Missouri
d. August 22, 1904
St. Louis, Missouri
fields: Literature

Author of the early feminist novel *The Awakening*, Kate Chopin created works that showcased the Louisiana bayou country and often featured women struggling against society's restrictions.

Chosroes. *See* Khosrow I

Chou En-Lai

aka: Zhou Enlai
b. March 5, 1898
Huaian, Jiangsu Province, China
d. January 8, 1976
Beijing, China
fields: Diplomacy, Government and Politics

Chou En-lai was the premier of the new People's Republic of China from its birth in 1949 until his death in 1976. He thereby guided the new China in solidifying the new order, led in domestic reform toward modernization, and was instrumental in having the new government accepted by the international community during trying times.

Chou Shu-jên. *See* Lu Hsün

Chou, Wen-chung

b. June 28, 1923
Chefu, China
fields: Music

After arriving in the United States in 1946, composer Wen-chung Chou attended the New England Conservatory of Music for three years and received a master's degree from Columbia University in 1954. Naturalized in 1958, he began teaching music at Columbia in 1964. He was named Fritz Reiner Professor of Music Composition in 1984 and received honors and award from the Rockefeller Foundation, the National Institute of Arts and Letters, and the National Endowment for the Arts.

Choukeka. *See* Decora, Spoon

Choy, Christine

b. Sept. 17, 1953
Shanghai, People's Republic of China
fields: Film, Theater and Entertainment

Filmmaker Christine Choy was born to a Mongolian mother and a Korean father and lived in her father's country until she was sixteen, when she moved to the United States. Her films include the documentaries *From Spikes Spindles* (1976), about New York's Chinatown; *To Love, Honor, and Obey* (1980), about domestic violence; and *Mississippi Triangle* (1983), an examination of the relationship between the African American and Chinese American communities of the Mississippi Delta. Her best-known film is the documentary *Who Killed Vincent Chin?* (1988).

Choy, Curtis

b. 1951
San Francisco, Calif.
fields: Film, Theater and Entertainment

In 1973, Asian American Curtis Choy founded Chonk Moonhunter, a production company specializing in Asian American images. Choy was a sound-effects specialist for *Year of the Dragon* (1985) and a production mixer for *Dim Sum* (1984), *Chan Is Missing* (1982), and *The Joy Luck Club* (1993).

Choy, Herbert Young Cho

b. Jan. 6, 1916
Hakaweli, Territory of Hawaii
fields: Law

Korean American Herbert Young Cho Choy grew up in Honolulu, receiving a bachelor's degree from the University of Hawaii in 1938. He graduated from Harvard Law School in 1941, returned to Hawaii, and passed the bar examination that same year. He served in the U.S. Army from 1942 to 1946. After his discharge, he went into private practice in Honolulu. He served as attorney general for the Territory from 1957 to 1958. Choy was appointed to serve as a federal judge on the Ninth Circuit of the U.S. Court of Appeals in Honolulu in 1971, the first Asian American to serve as a U.S. federal court judge.

Choy, Philip

b. Dec. 17, 1926
San Francisco, Calif.
fields: Architecture

Philip Choy, an architect, served two terms as president of the Chinese Historical Society of America and helped restore the Angel Island immigration station in San Francisco Bay. One of the first Chinese Americans to teach Chinese American history in the United States, he coauthored, with H. Mark Lai, *Outlines: History of the Chinese in America* (1973) and was assistant editor of *A History of the Chinese in California* (1969).

Chrétien, Jean

full: Joseph-Jacques Jean Chrétien
b. January 11, 1934
Shawinigan, Quebec
fields: Government and Politics

In both the 1993 and 1997 Canadian elections, Chrétien led his Liberal Party to absolute majorities in the Canadian House of Commons. His victory in 1993 put an end to nine years of Conservative Party rule in Canada.

Chrétien de Troyes

b. c. 1140
possibly Troyes, France
d. c. 1190
probably Troyes, France, or Flanders
fields: Literature

Chrétien is one of the great names in early French literature and is known as the principal articulator of many significant medieval Arthurian legends.

Christian, Almeric

b. Nov. 23, 1919
Christiansted, St. Croix
fields: Law

African American federal judge; Almeric Christian was U.S. attorney for the Virgin Islands (1962-1969); appointed to the federal bench in 1969; became chief justice of the District Court for the Territory of the Virgin Islands in 1970.

Christian, Barbara T.

b. Dec. 12, 1943
St. Thomas, U.S. Virgin Islands
fields: Education, Scholarship

African American educator and author; Barbara T. Christian taught at the College of the City University of New York and the University of California, Berkeley; her books include *Black Women Novelists: Development of a Tradition, 1892-1976* (1980) and *Black Feminist Criticism: Perspectives on Black Women Writers* (1985).

Christian, Charlie

full: Charles Christian
b. July 29, 1916
Dallas, Tex.
d. Mar. 2, 1942
New York, N.Y.
fields: Music (jazz)

African American jazz guitarist and seminal bop figure; Charlie Christian was among the first successful amplified acoustic guitarists; recorded with Benny Goodman beginning in 1939; believed to have coined the term "bebop."

Christie, Agatha

né: Agatha Mary Clarissa Miller
b. September 15, 1890
Torquay, Devon, England
d. January 12, 1976
Wallingford, Oxfordshire, England
fields: Literature

Because of her ingenuity in devising plots, her skill in creating characters (particularly detectives such as Miss Marple and Hercule Poirot), and her genial humor, Christie won international fame and a considerable fortune as the best-selling detective story writer in history.

Christina

b. December 8, 1626
Stockholm, Sweden
d. April 19, 1689
Rome
fields: Monarchy, Patronage of the Arts

Queen of Sweden, 1644-1654. Under Christina's short rule, Sweden benefited politically and socially through the Treaty of Westphalia, which brought an end to the devastating Thirty Years' War, and culturally by the importation of many works of art and manuscripts from cultural centers of Europe. During her residence in Rome, Christina was an enthusiastic patron of the arts, founding the learned society Accademia Reale in 1674, a precursor to the Accademia dell'Arcadia of eighteenth century Italy.

Christine de Pizan

b. c. 1365
Venice, Italy
d. c. 1430
probably at the Convent of Poissy, near Versailles, France
fields: Literature

The first woman of letters in France and the first known woman in Europe to earn her living by writing, Christine was a prolific, versatile, and acclaimed lyric poet, didactic writer, and Humanist scholar; she was a precursor to the *femmes savantes* of the Renaissance and to nineteenth and twentieth century feminists.

Christophe, Henri

aka: Henri I
b. October 6, 1767
Island of Grenada, British West Indies
d. October 8, 1820
Sans Souci palace, Haiti
fields: Government and Politics

Christophe was one of the three great black leaders of the Haitian Revolution. With the removal of Toussaint-Louverture to France and the assassination of Jean-Jacques Dessalines, he was chosen president of the Haitian Republic in 1806 (1806-1811); self-proclaimed Henri I, King of Haiti, 1811-1820.

Christopher, Saint

b. place and date unknown
possibly third century Asia Minor
d. c. 250 C.E.
possibly Lycia
fields: Religion and Theology, Saints

Although a legendary figure, Saint Christopher has long been a popular Christian saint, known as the patron of travelers and ferrymen.

Christopher, Warren

b. Oct. 27, 1925
Scranton, N.D.
fields: Governement and Politics, Diplomacy

U.S. diplomat. A lawyer by training, William Christopher served as U.S. deputy attorney general from 1967 through 1969 and as deputy secretary of state from 1977 through 1981. In 1993, he was appointed U.S. secretary of state by President Bill Clinton, and he played a major role in Middle Eastern and Bosnian peace negotiations.

Chrysostom, Saint John

b. c. 354 C.E.
Antioch, Syria
d. September 14, 407 C.E.
Comana, Pontus
fields: Religion and Theology, Oratory

Chrysostom, the greatest homiletic preacher of the Greek church, later became the patron saint of preachers.

Chu Hsi

b. October 18, 1130
Yu-ch'i, Fukien, China
d. April 23, 1200
Chien-yang County, Fukien, China
fields: Philosophy, Education, Government and Politics

Through writings and educational activities, Chu Hsi reformulated Confucianism. His work helped Confucianism regain intellectual ascendancy from Buddhism and Taoism, establishing basic Confucian orientations for centuries and influencing East Asian culture.

Chu, Judy M.

b. July 7, 1953
Los Angeles, Calif.
fields: Government and Politics

Judy M. Chu, city council member and former mayor of Monterey Park, California, helped smooth relations among the city's different ethnic groups during the late 1980's. Her projects include a city-sponsored after-school child care program and the Asian Youth Center. She coauthored *Linking Our Lives: Chinese American Women of Los Angeles* (1984) and was a board member of the Garvey (California) School District.

Chu, Louis H.

b. October 1, 1915
Toishan, China
d. February 27, 1970
Queens, N.Y.
fields: Literature

Chinese American novelist and social worker; Louis H. Chu immigrated to the United States in 1924; is best known for his novel *Eat a Bowl of Tea* (1961; an accurate account of life among New York's Chinatown "bachelor societies" in the early 1940's); Chu also served as director of the Golden Age Club, a day center for older Chinese Americans in New York's Chinatown; between 1951 and 1961, hosted a popular radio program called "Chinese Festival" which aired four nights per week.

Chu, Paul Ching-Wu

b. Dec. 2, 1941
Hunan, China
fields: Science (physics), Education

Paul Ching-Wu Chu moved to the United States in 1963. He earned a master's degree at Fordham University in New York in 1965 and a doctoral degree at the University of California, San Diego, in 1968. In 1979, Chu began teaching at the University of Houston, where he became director of the school's magnetic information research lab in 1984. There, he developed a superconducting ceramic material that brought him numerous honorary degrees and awards, among them election to the prestigious National Academy of Sciences and the American Academy of Arts and Sciences. Chu became the head of the Texas Center for Superconductivity, a multimillion-dollar research complex at the University of Houston dedicated to research and development.

Ch'ü Yüan

b. c. 343 B.C.E.
Ch'u, China
d. 278 B.C.E.
in the Mi-lo River, China
fields: Government and Politics

A skilled statesman who always tried to speak the truth no matter what the cost, Ch'ü Yüan exemplified the Confucian ideal of the virtuous official; his country's first widely known poet, he became one of the founding fathers of Chinese literature.

Chuang Tzu. *See* Zhuangzi

Chuang-tzu. *See* Zhuangzi

Chubb Rock

né: Richard Simpson
b. 1968
Jamaica
fields: Music (rap)

African American rap music artist; Chubb Rock cowrote and coperformed the popular song "Just Ask Me To," from the sound track for the film *Boyz 'N the Hood* (1991).

Chuck, Maurice H.

b. Oct. 5, 1931
Guangdong Province, China
fields: Publishing, Journalism

Maurice H. Chuck, president of the Chinese Journalism Corporation, founded and published the *San Francisco Journal*, a bilingual weekly community newspaper, beginning in 1972. The paper was the first community paper to support normalization of relations between the United States and the People's Republic of China. The paper, which became a daily in 1983, ceased publication in 1986.

Chun Doo Hwan

b. Jan. 18, 1931
Naechonri, Korea
fields: Government and Politics

Chun Doo Hwan seized the presidency of South Korea in a military coup after Park Chung Hee's assassination in 1979. He instituted a law limiting future presidents to a single seven-year term. He was elected president in 1981. In 1987 mass demonstrations erupted because of a lack of reforms leading to direct democratic elections.

Chun Quon

b. Sept. 16, 1867
Gangbei Guangdong Province, China
d. Aug. 11, 1953
Honolulu, Territory of Hawaii
fields: Business and Industry

Chun Quon arrived in Honolulu in 1885 after spending three weeks in San Francisco. He opened Yee Hop meat market in Chinatown in 1887, becoming partners with Lum Hop in 1888. In 1900, a fire forced them to close, but two years later, Chun, Lum, and six others expanded, renaming the store C. Q. Yee Hop. By the 1940's, the business, now a corporation, had assets of more than $1 million. He branched out, managing King Market, founding American Brewing Company in 1933, Hawaiian Hardwood Company in 1939, and Yee Hop Realty Company in 1943. He supported publishing efforts, including Honolulu's *New China Press*, San Francisco's *Chinese World*, and Hong Kong's *Humanities Weekly*.

Chung, Connie

full: Constance Yu-Hwa Chung
b. August 20, 1946
Washington, D.C.
fields: Journalism, Television

A leader in broadcast journalism, Chung advanced through the ranks as a news anchor and hosted several of her own interview news programs before being made the first female coanchor of the *CBS Evening News* in 1993.

Chung, Henry

né: Chung Han Kyung
b. ?
fields: Government and Politics

Henry Chung, a supporter of Korean independence, along with Syngman Rhee and Min Chan-ho, was part of a delegation to represent Korean interests at the 1919 Paris peace conference. Rhee proposed a plan that would make Korea a trustee under the supervision of the League of Nations until an independent government could be created. The Paris peace conference refused to consider the plan. Later that year, Rhee became president of the Korean provisional government, making Chung one of his commissioners. Chung's duties were to conduct diplomatic activities, raise funds, and create support for the provisional government. His book, *The Case of Korea* (1921), helped make many Americans aware of the Japanese annexation of Korea.

Chung Kun Ai

aka: C. K. Ai
b. Nov. 26, 1865
Guangdong Province, China
d. Sept. 30, 1961
Honolulu, Hawaii
fields: Business and Industry, Philanthropy

Chung Kun Ai, an immigrant to Hawaii in 1879 and a classmate of Sun Yat-sen at Iolani College, became a successful businessman and philanthropist. He founded a building-supply firm, the City Mill Company, in 1899. This firm's success allowed him to invest in other commercial undertaking in Hawaii and in China. A philanthropist, he raised money for the Wai Wah Chinese Hospital and the Chinese Palolo Home for aged and indigent laborers. He served as president of the United Chinese Society and on the Young Men's Christian Association and mission boards and was a member of the Chinese and Honolulu chambers of commerce. Chung helped rebuild the Chung ancestral hall and school in his native village. His autobiography, *My Seventy Nine Years in Hawaii* (1960), describes his life and his work.

Chung, Myung-Whun

b. January 22, 1953
Seoul, Korea
fields: Music (classical pianist, conductor)

Korean American conductor and pianist; at the age of seven, Myung-Whun Chung debuted with the Seoul Philharmonic Orchestra; his family immigrated to the United States in late 1961; he took second prize at the Tchaikovsky Piano Competition in Moscow (1974); performed first solo piano recital at New York's Carnegie Hall (1974); in 1978, selected as assistant conductor with the Los Angeles Philharmonic Orchestra, later becoming associate conductor; during the 1980's, conducted and played with orchestras and opera companies in Europe; served as music director for the Opera de la Bastille's gala celebration of the bicentennial of the French Revolution (1989); in 1988 and 1989, won Italy's Abbiata and Toscanini prizes.

Churchill, John. *See* Marlborough, first duke of

Churchill, Pamela Digby. *See* Harriman, Pamela Digby Churchill

Churchill, Winston

full: Winston Spencer Churchill
aka: Sir Winston Churchill
b. November 30, 1874
Bleinheim Palace, Oxfordshire, England
d. January 24, 1965
London, England
fields: Government and Politics, Literature

One of England's greatest prime ministers and war leaders and one of the twentieth century's greatest public figures, Churchill was tremendously influential in both war and peace. He also won the Nobel Prize in Literature in 1953.

Churchland, Patricia Smith

né: Patricia Smith
b. July 16, 1943
Oliver, British Columbia, Canada
fields: Philosophy, Science (neuroscience)

Bridging a gap between philosophy and neuroscience, Patricia Smith Churchland demonstrated that empirical study of the brain is crucial to the philosophy of mind, introducing philosophers to scientific information about the brain and the nervous system, conveying technical neuroscientific results in a fashion accessible to the nonscientist, and extracting the philosophical implications of such research. Awarded a MacArthur Foundation fellowship in 1991. Major works include *Neurophilosophy: Toward a Unified Science of the Mind-Brain* (1986), *The Computational Brain* (1992, with Terrence J. Sejnowski), and *On the Contrary* (1998, with Paul M. Churchland).

Churchland, Paul M.

full: Paul Montgomery Churchland
b. 1942
Vancouver, British Columbia, Canada
fields: Philosophy, Science (neuroscience)

An analytic philosopher of mind, Paul M. Churchland maintained that advances in the neurosciences and artificial intelligence are the key to understanding cognition. A leading defender of scientific realism, he held that scientific theories present a literally true account of the world, especially of the unobservable world. His "eliminative materialism" holds that there are no mental states, only brain states. Major works include *Scientific Realism and the Plasticity of Mind* (1979), *Matter and Consciousness* (1984, rev. ed. 1988), *The Computer That Could: A Neurophilosophical Portrait* (1994), and *The Engine of Reason, the Seat of the Soul: A Philosophical Journey into the Brain* (1995).

Ciccone, Madonna Louise Veronica. *See* Madonna

Cicero

né: Marcus Tullius Cicero
b. January 3, 106 B.C.E.
Arpinum, Latium
d. December 7, 43 B.C.E.
Formiae, Latium
fields: Government and Politics, Law, Oratory, Philosophy, Literature

With courageous and principled statesmanship, Cicero guided Rome through a series of severe crises. While he was not able to save the Republic, he transmitted its political and cultural values in speeches and treatises that became models of style for posterity.

Cid, El

né: Rodrigo Díaz de Vivar
aka: Ruy Díaz
b. c. 1043
Vivar, Spain
d. July 10, 1099
Valencia, Spain
fields: Warfare and Conquest

El Cid, through military skill and leadership, halted the Almoravide advance on the peninsula, and by exemplifying his times' ideals of courage, loyalty, and force of will became the national hero of his people.

Cid, Armando

b. ?
fields: Art, Social Reform

Artist and Chicano activist. Armando Cid's paintings and public murals incorporate pre-Columbian motifs along with representations of Latino life. He is best knnown for having produced posters and murals for the Royal Chicano Air Force, an organization founded in 1970 to promote Chicano culture and make art accessible to ordinary people.

Cimabue

né: Bencivieni di Pepo
b. c. 1240
Florence
d. c. 1302
Florence
fields: Art

Cimabue introduced a more naturalistic depiction of the human body in medieval painting and is commonly regarded as a transition figure between the relatively stiff Byzantine mode and the freer style that evolved in Italy during the fourteenth century.

Cimon

b. c. 510 B.C.E.
place unknown
d. c. 451 B.C.E.
near Citium (modern Larnaca), Cyprus
fields: Government and Politics, Warfare and Conquest

Through skillful military leadership and diplomacy, Cimon became an important force behind the establishment of the Delian League—a Greek alliance against the Persians—and its later transformation into the Athenian Empire. Domestically, he struggled unsuccessfully against the further extension of democracy in ancient Athens.

Cinque, Joseph

aka: Joseph Cinquez
aka: Joseph Cingue
aka: Joseph Singbe
aka: Joseph Jinqua
aka: Joseph Singua
aka: Joseph Shinquaw
b. c. 1811
Mani, Africa
d. 1879
Sierra Leone, Africa
fields: Civil Rights, Historical Figure

Slave mutiny leader from Africa; Joseph Cinque was the leader of the 1839 *La Amistad* slave revolt, in which captured Africans took control of the slave ship. They were later captured, then set free in a Supreme Court decision, in which John Quincy Adams argued their defense.

Cione, Andrea di. *See* Orcagna, Andrea

Cione, Andrea di Michele di Francesco. *See* Verrocchio, Andrea del

Cisneros, Evelyn

b. 1955
Long Beach, Calif.
fields: Dance

Latino ballet dancer; Evelyn Cisneros studied at the San Francisco Ballet School and the School of American Ballet in New York; apprenticed at the San Francisco Ballet (beginning 1971) and joined the company six years later; her starring performances include *Scherzo*, *Romeo and Juliet*, *Cinderella*, *The Comfort Zone*, and *Swan Lake*; her roles in *A Song for Dead Warriors* (1984; nationally televised) and *The Tempest* (1984; nationally televised) were choreographed specifically for her; awards received include those from Hispanic Women Making History (1984), the Mexican American Legal Defense and Education Fund (1985), and the California League of United Latin Citizens (1988); named spokesperson of the Chicano/Latino Youth Leadership Conference in 1989.

Cisneros, Henry

full: Henry Gabriel Cisneros
b. June 11, 1947
San Antonio, Tex.
fields: Government and Politics

Latino politician; Henry Cisneros after earning graduate degrees from Harvard University and George Washington University, joined faculty of University of Texas at San Antonio, 1974; was a member, San Antonio City Council, 1975-1981, emphasizing cooperation between white and Latino residents; served as mayor of San Antonio, 1981-1989, becoming the first Hispanic mayor of a major U.S. city; was secretary of Housing and Urban Development, 1993-1996; indicted for conspiracy and obstruction of justice in 1997.

Cisneros, Sandra

b. Dec. 20, 1954
Chicago, Ill.
fields: Literature

Writer. Sandra Cisneros received her master of fine arts degree in 1978 from the University of Iowa Writers' Workshop; the poet Gary Soto helped her to publish her first collection, *Bad Boys* (1980). Her acclaimed works include *My Wicked Wicked Ways* (1987), *The House on Mango Street* (1984), which won the Before Columbus Foundation's 1985 American Book Award for 1985, *Woman Hollering Creek and Other Stories* (1991), which won the Lannan Literary Award for 1991 and was named a noteworthy 1991 book by *The New York Times*, and *Loose Woman* (1994).

Citroën, André-Gustave

b. February 5, 1878
Paris, France
d. July 3, 1935
Paris, France
fields: Engineering, Business and Industry, Exploration and Colonization

Citroën introduced Henry Ford's mass production techniques to the European automobile industry and founded the company that produced the first car that was affordable to a broad cross section of consumers in Europe. He financed several scientific exhibitions and gave the lighting of the Arc de Triomphe and the Place de la Concorde to the city of Paris.

Cixi

aka: Tz'u-hsi
b. November 29, 1835
Beijing, China
d. November 15, 1908
Beijing, China
fields: Government and Politics

Empress dowager of Qing (Manchu) Dynasty, dominant Chinese political figure from 1861 to the early 1900's. Regent to two young Chinese emperors. Cixi adamantly opposed reforms of Chinese government that would have reduced her power. Instigated a coup in 1898 in which Emperor Guangxu was imprisoned in the Forbidden City until his death ten years later; suspected that Cixi had him poisoned. A day after the Guangxu's death, the empress dowager herself died from dysentery. The dynasty collapsed three years later because of a spontaneous revolution.

Claiborne, Liz

full: Elisabeth Claiborne
b. March 31, 1929
Brussels, Belgium
fields: Fashion

A designer of affordable, casual, mix-and-match sportswear separates for working women, Liz Claiborne has expanded her enterprises to become one of the few women to head a *Fortune 500* company.

Clairaut, Alexis-Claude

b. May 7, 1713
Paris, France
d. May 17, 1765
Paris, France
fields: Mathematics (algebra, applied math, calculus, and geometry)

Alexis-Claude Clairaut is known for writing the first book on analytic geometry in three-dimensional space. Clairaut studied the shape of the earth and the motion of the moon and Halley's comet with Isaac Newton's calculus and law of gravitation. He also improved the telescope and discovered results of differential equations. His publications include *Elémens de géométrie* (1741; *Elements of Geometry*, 1881), *Elémens d'algèbre* (1746), and a memoir on telescopes.

Clarendon, First Earl of

né: Edward Hyde
b. February 18, 1609
Dinton, Wiltshire, England
d. December 9, 1674
Rouen, France
fields: Government and Politics, Literature

The adviser to two kings of England during the English Revolution, Clarendon laid the theoretical and the practical bases for the restoration of both the monarchy and traditional English society. He also wrote a masterpiece of historical literature, based on his experiences.

Clark, Dee

full: Delectus Clark
b. November, 1938
Blythesville, Ark.
fields: Music (rhythm-and-blues)

African American rhythm-and-blues singer; Dee Clark had a number of top-ten hits between 1958 and 1961, including "Raindrops."

Clark, Edward

b. May 6, 1926
New Orleans, La.
fields: Art (painter)

African American painter; Edward Clark was a proponent of the 1950's abstract "action school."

Clark, George Rogers

b. November 19, 1752
near Charlottesville, Virginia
d. February 13, 1818
Louisville, Kentucky
fields: Military Affairs, Urban Development

Clark's successful attack against the British forts at Kaskaskia, Cahokia, and Vincennes in 1778-1779 served as the basis for the American claim to the Northwest Territory during negotiation of the Treaty of Paris of 1783. His leadership of the Northwest campaign led in turn to the founding of Louisville, Kentucky, and Clarksville, Indiana.

Clark, Gloria Marshall. *See* Sudarkasa, Niara

Clark, Joe

full: Charles Joseph Clark
b. June 5, 1939
High River, Alberta, Canada
fields: Government and Politics

Joe Clark was prime minister of Canada for seven months in 1979 and 1980, leading a minority government. Leader of the Progressive Conservative Party, he was the youngest person ever to hold the office. Widely lampooned by media as a weak leader. In Brian Mulroney government, Clark was secretary of state for external affairs from 1984 to 1991. Many regard him as one of Canada's most effective secretaries of state.

Clark, Joe Louis

b. May 7, 1939
Rochelle, Ga.
fields: Education (educator and educational administrator)

African American educator and educational administrator; the 1989 motion picture *Lean on Me* is a dramatized version of Joe Louis Clark's battle to rid Eastside High School of drugs and violence; was honored for academic and disciplinary excellence at a White House ceremony by President Ronald Reagan in 1985.

Clark, Kenneth

full: Kenneth Bancroft Clark
b. July 24, 1914
Panama Canal Zone
fields: Psychiatry and Psychology, Education

In the late 1930's and early 1940's, African American Kenneth Clark, with his wife Mamie, conducted studies on young children's racial preferences by using black and white dolls to test the impact of segregation on the self-awareness, identity, and self-image of African American children. Their research influenced the *Brown v. Board of Education* decision (1954), in which the Court concluded that segregated schooling for African Americans and whites was inherently unequal.

Clark, Mamie

b. October 18, 1917
Hot Springs, Ark.
d. August 11, 1983
Hastings-on-Hudson, N.Y.
fields: Sociology, Psychiatry and Psychology, Education

Psychologist Mamie Clark and her husband, Kenneth Clark, she studied children's racial attitudes and found that young African American children tended to regard the color white and depictions of white persons more positively than black persons. This finding helped influence the Supreme Court in its *Brown v. Board of Education* decision (1954) that outlawed racial segregation in public schools. Meanwhile, in 1946 the Clarks founded what became the Northside Center for Child Development as an alternative to the child-welfare system of New York City.

Clark, Marcia

b. 1954
Berkeley, Calif.
fields: Law

Marcia Clark was the California attorney and lead prosecutor in the criminal murder trial of O. J. Simpson. Working in the L.A. district attorney's office, Clark tried more than twenty murder cases, winning convictions in all but one before the Simpson case; was promoted to assistant director of the Central Operations/Bureau of Central Operations, in which she supervised more than two hundred attorneys. In January, 1997, Clark resigned from the district attorney's office; accepted an advance of more than four million dollars for a book about the Simpson trial, *Without a Doubt* (1997), which she then devoted her time to promoting.

Clark, Mark

b. 1952
Peoria, Ill.
d. Dec. 4, 1969
Chicago, Ill.
fields: Civil Rights

African American member of the Black Panther Party (BPP); Mark Clark was killed by FBI agents during a raid on the home of Black Panther leader Fred Hampton.

Clark, Septima Poinsette

b. May 3, 1898
Charleston, S.C.
d. December 15, 1987
John's Island, S.C.
fields: Civil Rights, Education

African American civil rights activist and educator; Septima Poinsette Clark was instrumental in winning equal pay for black teachers in South Carolina (1945); in the mid-1950's, she was fired from a teaching job in Charleston because of her refusal to give up her NAACP membership; while working with the Southern Christian Leadership Conference, she set up voter registration drives and literacy schools for semiliterate adults; elected to the Charleston school board during the 1970's; Clark published two autobiographies, *Echo in My Soul* (1962) and *Ready from Within: Septima Clark and the Civil Rights Movement* (1986).

Clark, Tom

full: Tom Campbell Clark
b. 1890
d. 1977
fields: Law

U.S. Supreme Court justice, 1949-1967; appointed by President Truman. Author of *Mapp v. Ohio* opinion, which imposed the exclusionary rule on states. Retired from the Court when his son, Ramsey Clark, became attorney general. Significant opinions: *Jenks v. United States*, 353 U.S. 657 (1957) (dissenting opinion); *Mapp v. Ohio*, 367 U.S. 643 (1961); *School District of Abington v. Schempp*, 374 U.S. 203 (1963); *Sheppard v. Maxwell*, 384 U.S. 333 (1966).

Clark, William

b. August 1, 1770
Caroline County, Virginia
d. September 1, 1838
St. Louis, Missouri
fields: Exploration and Colonization, Native American Affairs

William Clark was coleader of the Lewis and Clark Expedition, the first party of white men to cross the North American continent from the Atlantic to the Pacific coast within the geographical limits of the present United States. After the expedition, Clark was for three decades one of the most important administrators of Indian affairs in the nation's history.

Clarke, Aileen. *See* Hernandez, Aileen Clarke

Clarke, John Henrik

b. Jan. 1, 1915
Union Springs, Ala.
fields: Historiography, Literature

African American historian and writer; John Henrik Clarke acheived renown as historian, journalist, editor, anthologist, teacher, poet, writer of fiction, community activist, and lecturer; first president of the African Heritage Studies Association.

Clarke, John Hessin

b. 1857
d. 1945
fields: Law

U.S. Supreme Court justice, 1916-1922; appointed by President Wilson. Resigned from the Court to advocate United States entry into the League of Nations. Significant opinions: *Abrams v. United States*, 250 U.S. 616 (1919); *Hammer v. Dagenhart*, 247 U.S. 251 (1918) (dissenting opinion).

Clarke, Stanley Marvin

b. June 31, 1951
Philadelphia, Pa.
fields: Music (jazz)

African American musician; Stanley Marvin Clarke played bass with a number of prominant musicians, including Stan Getz and Chick Corea.

Claude, Georges

b. September 24, 1870
Paris, France
d. May 23, 1960
St. Cloud, France
fields: Chemistry, Invention and Technology

Claude was the first successfully to liquefy air in quantity independent of Carl von Linde in 1902. A few years later, Claude's Liquid Air Company was separating the components of liquid air and producing high-quality oxygen. Founder of Claude Neon, he held a monopoly on the neon-tube industry in the 1920's.

Claude Lorrain

né: Claude Gellé
aka: le Lorrain
b. 1600
Chamagne, Lorraine, France
d. November 23, 1682
Rome
fields: Art

Claude established landscape in Roman and French painting as a subtle and varied means of artistic expression on an equal level with the older genres of religious and historical painting. He is one of the greatest masters of all time in the ideal landscape.

Claudius I

né: Tiberius Claudius Drusus Nero Germanicus
b. August 1, 10 B.C.E.
Lugdunum, Gaul (modern Lyon, France)
d. October 13, 54 C.E.
Rome, Italy
fields: Government and Politics

Coming to power after the politically and financially devastating reign of Caligula, Claudius I completed the centralizing tendencies of Roman imperial government by creating a bureaucracy that was totally professional in training and totally loyal in its devotion to the imperial concept of government.

Clausewitz, Carl von

b. June 1, 1780
Burg, near Magdeburg, Prussia
d. November 16, 1831
Breslau, Silesia
fields: Military Affairs, Philosophy

Clausewitz played an important role in Prussian military and political history during the Napoleonic Wars. He is best known, however, as the leading philosopher of war. His most famous work, *On War*, has been characterized as "not simply the greatest, but the only great book about war."

Clausius, Rudolf

full: Rudolf Julius Emanuel Clausius
b. Jan. 2, 1822
Köslin, Prussia (now Koszalin, Poland)
d. Aug. 24, 1888
Bonn, Germany
fields: Physics

Rudolf Clausius formulated the second law of thermodynamics, stating the equivalence of heat and work, in 1850. He introduced the term "entropy" to describe various thermodynamic processes.

Clay, Cassius. *See* Ali, Muhammad

Clay, Henry

b. April 12, 1777
Hanover County, Virginia
d. June 29, 1852
Washington, D.C.
fields: Government and Politics

Clay was a dominant figure in American politics during the first half of the nineteenth century. His American System and his efforts to bring compromise in the controversy over slavery helped ease the growing tensions within the Union.

Clay, William Lacy

b. Apr. 30, 1931
St. Louis, Mo.
fields: Government and Politics

African American politician; William Lacy Clay was the first African American congressmen from Missouri.

Clayton, Eva M.

b. September 16, 1938
North Carolina
fields: Government and Politics (politician)

African American politician; in 1993, Eva M. Clayton became one of the first two African Americans to serve in the U.S. Congress as a Representative from North Carolina during the twentieth century.

Clayton, Xernona

b. Aug. 30, 1930
Muskogee, Okla.
fields: Television

African American television executive and talk show host; Xernona Clayton was executive producer for Black History Month programs for the Turner Broadcasting System; hosted *The Xernona Clayton Show* on WGA-TV.

Cleage, Albert Buford, Jr.

b. June 13, 1911
Indianapolis, Ind.
fields: Civil Rights, Religion and Theology

African American theologian and civil rights activist; Albert Buford Cleage, Jr., was an outspoken advocate for black Christian nationalism; in the 1960's, he founded the Black Messiah Movement in Detroit, Mich.; in his published works *The Black Messiah* (1968) and *Black Christian Nationalism: New Directions for the Black Church* (1972), Cleage posits that authentic Christianity has emerged from the black community and calls for political action on the part of that community so that all black peoples may be liberated.

Cleaver, Eldridge

full: Leroy Eldridge Cleaver
b. Aug. 31, 1935
Wabbaseka, Ark.
d. May 1, 1998
Pomona, Calif.
fields: Civil Rights

African American radical leader and member of the Black Panther Party; Eldridge Cleaver was minister of information for the Black Panther Party (BPP); author of *Soul on Ice* (1968); fled to Cuba to avoid being returned to prison; expelled from BPP in 1971 while abroad; surrendered to U.S. authorities in 1975 and founded prison ministry after his 1976 release; ran unsuccessfully as conservative independent candidate for congress in 1984.

Cleaver, Emanuel, II

b. October 26, 1944
Waxahachie, Tex.
fields: Government and Politics (politician, pastor, and civil rights activist)

African American politician, pastor, and civil rights activist; in 1991, Emanuel Cleaver II was elected mayor of Kansas City, Mo., becoming the first African American to hold this office; was reelected in 1995; appointed the first female mayor pro tem of Kansas City.

Cleisthenes of Athens

b. c. 570 B.C.E.
place unknown
d. After 510 B.C.E.
place unknown
fields: Government and Politics, Law

The famous lawgiver and reformer Cleisthenes was the real architect of Athenian democracy. His statesmanship created radical innovations in the constitution: the representative principle and the idea of political equality.

Clemenceau, Georges

b. September 28, 1841
Mouilleron-en-Pareds, France
d. November 24, 1929
Paris, France
fields: Government and Politics

Clemenceau was significant in French politics from 1871 to 1919. Although he influenced the nation's political course several times, Clemenceau is best known for his role as premier during the last eighteen months of World War I, when his determination to win inspired France despite enormous adversity.

Clemens, Samuel Langhorne. *See* Twain, Mark

Clement I

aka: Clemens Romanus
aka: Clement of Rome
b. Date unknown
perhaps Rome
d. c. 99
perhaps in the Crimea
fields: Religion and Theology

Clement was the first of the Apostolic Fathers about whom anything is known and, according to tradition, was the third successor to Peter as Bishop of Rome. Clement was also the author of the earliest and most valuable surviving example of Christian literature not included in the New Testament.

Clement VII

né: Guilio de Medici
b. 1478
Florence
d. September 25, 1534
Rome
fields: Church Reform, Religion and Theology

Pope Clement VII, 1523-1534. While Clement's pontificate was marred with failures, especially with regard to halting the spread of the Protestant Reformation, he did manage to encourage reforms within the Catholic Church through newly established religious orders and did much to enrich the art treasures of the Vatican.

Clemente, Roberto

b. August 18, 1934
Carolina, Puerto Rico
d. December 31, 1972
near Carolina, Puerto Rico
fields: Sports (baseball player)

Latino baseball player; an outfielder with a powerful arm, Roberto Clemente was drafted by the Pittsburgh Pirates (1955; spent entire career with that team); held four National League batting titles; won twelve Gold Glove Awards (1961-1972); named National League Most Valuable Player (1966); named 1971 World Series Most Valuable Player; .317 lifetime batting average with the Pirates; died in a plane crash while delivering relief supplies to Nicaraguan earthquake victims; elected to Baseball Hall of Fame (1973).

Clem-hak-kah. *See* Charlot

Cleomenes I

b. Date unknown
Sparta, Greece
d. c. 490 B.C.E.
Sparta, Greece
fields: Warfare and Conquest

Through a number of military victories and even in defeat, Cleomenes I strengthened Sparta as no ruler had before him.

Cleomenes II

b. Date unknown
Sparta, Greece
d. c. 309 B.C.E.
Sparta, Greece
fields: Government and Politics

Cleomenes II ruled Sparta during a difficult and trying time. He managed to hold a beaten city-state together and ally it with neighboring powers. Cleomenes II's rule gave Sparta time to rebuild without threatening its confidence.

Cleomenes III

b. Date unknown
Sparta, Greece
d. 219 B.C.E.
Alexandria
fields: Government and Politics

Cleomenes III instituted social reforms in Sparta that canceled debt, registered hundreds of new citizens, and redistributed lands.

Cleopatra VII

b. 69 B.C.E.
Alexandria, Egypt
d. 30 B.C.E.
Alexandria, Egypt
fields: Government and Politics

Cleopatra VII, as the last of the Ptolemaic Greek rulers of an independent Egypt, tried to come to terms with the ceaseless expansion of the Roman Empire throughout the Mediterranean and at her death left behind a rich, imperial province which continued to flourish as a center of commerce, science, and learning under Roman rule.

Cleveland, Grover

full: Steven Grover Cleveland
b. March 18, 1837
Caldwell, New Jersey
d. June 24, 1908
Princeton, New Jersey
fields: Government and Politics

Cleveland, who was both the twenty-second (1885-1889) and the twenty-fourth (1893-1897) president of the United States, brought great strength of character and inestimable political courage to the United States during years of political turmoil and economic crisis.

Cleveland, James

b. Dec. 5, 1931
Chicago, Ill.
d. Feb. 9, 1991
Los Angeles, Calif.
fields: Music (gospel)

African American gospel singer, pianist, composer, arranger, producer, and church pastor; James Cleveland won four Grammys and earned sixteen gold records.

Clews, Elsie Worthington. *See* Parsons, Elsie Clews

Clifford, Nathan

b. 1803
d. 1881
fields: Law

U.S. Supreme Court justice, 1858-1881 (died while in office); appointed by President Buchanan.

Clifford, Thomas E.

b. Mar. 9, 1929
Washington, D.C.
fields: Military Affairs

African American military officer; Thomas E. Clifford was a highly decorated officer in the U.S. Air Force.

Cline, Patsy

né: Virginia Patterson Hensley

b. September 8, 1932
Gore, Virginia
d. March 5, 1963
near Camden, Tennessee
fields: Music

A pioneering force in bringing women to the forefront of country music, Patsy Cline proved not only that a female could become a significant star but also that her singing could appeal across many musical boundaries.

Clinton, Bill

né: William Jefferson Blythe IV
b. August 19, 1946
Hope, Arkansas
fields: Government and Politics

A five-term governor of Arkansas who was especially successful in improving education in his state, Clinton was elected the forty-second president of the United States in 1992; in 1996, he became the first Democratic president since Franklin Delano Roosevelt to win election to two full terms. Clinton's presidency oversaw a strong national economy with the unusual combination of low interest rates, low inflation rates, and low unemployment figures; a reduction of the staggering national debt; and a term rocked by scandals and an impeachment vote by the House of Representatives. President of the United States, 1993-2001.

Clinton, DeWitt

b. March 2, 1769
Little Britain, New York
d. February 11, 1828
Albany, New York
fields: Government and Politics

Clinton controlled New York State for his faction of the Republican Party, advocating both social stability and an active role for government. He was an unsuccessful presidential candidate and fought the emerging power of Martin Van Buren. His best-known project is the Erie Canal, concrete and practical, like his approach to politics, and exemplifying a proper resolution of several types of problems in a growing nation.

Clinton, George Wylie

b. Mar. 28, 1859
Cedar Creek, S.C.
d. 1921
fields: Religion and Theology

African American bishop of the African Methodist Episcopal (AME) church; George Wylie Clinton edited *African-American Spokesman* and founded *The AME Zion Quarterly Review.*

Clinton, Henry

aka: Sir Henry Clinton
b. April 16, 1730
Newfoundland
d. December 23, 1795
Gibraltar
fields: Military Affairs

Clinton, the most successful British general during the American Revolution, drafted strategic plans that if properly implemented might have saved Britain's North American colonies. Yet Clinton's failure to command his subordinates was one major reason for Britain's defeat.

Clinton, Hillary Rodham

né: Hillary Diane Rodham
b. October 26, 1947
Chicago, Illinois
fields: Law, Government and Politics

A highly regarded lawyer and activist for children's rights and comprehensive health care, Clinton also became her husband's most important adviser when he served as governor of Arkansas and president of the United States.

Clive, Robert

b. September 29, 1725
Styche, Shropshire, England
d. November 22, 1774
London, England
fields: Government and Politics, Military Affairs

Clive's military success against the French at Arcot and the Bengalese at Plassey, along with his rule over Bengal, created the basis for the vast British Empire in India in the eighteenth century.

Close, Glenn

b. March 19, 1947
Greenwich, Connecticut
fields: Film, Theater and Entertainment (drama)

A talented actress who has received awards for her performances in film, theater, and television, Glenn Close has played characters whose careers, problems, and situations reflect women's social and political issues.

Cloud, Henry Roe

aka: Wonah'ilayhunka
b. Dec. 28, 1884
Thurston County, Nebr.
d. Feb. 9, 1950
Siletz, Oreg.
fields: Native American Affairs, Education, Government and Politics

Winnebago educator and administrator; Henry Roe Cloud was instrumental in expanding Indian educational opportunities; in 1910 he became the first Native American to graduate from Yale University; served as chairman of the Winnebago delegation to President William H. Taft in 1912; was a member of the Commission of Federal Survey of Indian Schools in 1914; in 1915 established the Roe Indian Institute in Wichita, Kansas (which promoted an academic rather than a vocational curriculum with the aim of developing Indian leaders; 1920, became the American Indian Institute); was a member of the Standing Committee of One Hundred on Indian Affairs in 1920; was a co-author of the Meriam Report of 1928; and served as supervisor of Indian education at the Bureau of Indian Affairs from 1936 to 1947.

Clovis

aka: Chlodovech
b. c. 466
probably Tournai
d. November 27, 511
Paris
fields: Government and Politics, Warfare and Conquest, Religion and Theology

In the early sixth century, Clovis extended his Frankish domain by conquest to form the nucleus of France and, in the process, united his interests with those of the orthodox Church in the West, which he saved from the threat of the Arian heresy.

Clyburn, James E.

b. July 21, 1940
Sumter, S.C.
fields: Government and Politics, Civil Rights (politician)

African American politician; in 1992, James E. Clyburn was elected to Congress from South Carolina, the first African American representative from that state since 1897; was reelected in 1994.

Coachman, Alice

b. Nov. 29, 1923
Albany, Ga.
fields: Sports (track and field)

African American athlete; Alice Coachman was the first black woman to win an Olympic gold medal in track and field; set an Olympic record for the high-jump in 1948.

Coacoochee. *See* Wildcat

Coage, Allen James

b. Oct. 22, 1943
New York, N.Y.
fields: Sports (judo)

African American judo athlete; Allen James Coage was the first black person to win an Olympic medal (bronze in 1976) in judo; served as captain of the U.S. Olympic judo team (1976); also won gold medals in the 1967 and 1975 Pan-American Games.

Coates, Dorothy Love

b. ?
Birmingham, Ala.
fields: Music (gospel)

African American gospel singer; Dorothy Love Coates sang with the Harmonettes, a gospel group popular in Birmingham in the 1940's and 1950's.

Cobain, Kurt

b. Feb. 20, 1967
Aberdeen, Wash.
d. April 5, 1994
Seattle, Wash.
fields: Music

Rock musician. Kurt Cobain was the lead singer, guitarist, and songwriter for Nirvana, the most critically successful band of the 1990's "grunge rock" movement. He formed Nirvana in 1987 with bassist Chris Novoselic; they were joined by drummer David Grohl in 1990.) His 1994 suicide secured his popular image as the representative figure of a forlorn generation. He was survived by wife Courtney Love, lead singer of the band Hole, and their daughter, Frances Bean.

Cobb, Jewel Plummer

né: Jewel Plummer
b. Jan. 17, 1924
Chicago, Illinois
fields: Biology

Jewel Plummer Cobb studied the cytology of cancer, assessing the impact of new chemotherapeutic agents; supported opportunities for women and minorities in science; became president of California State University at Fullerton in 1981.

Cobb, Ty

full: Tyrus Raymond Cobb
b. December 18, 1886
Narrows, Georgia
d. July 17, 1961
Atlanta, Georgia
fields: Sports (baseball)

Cobb's aggressive and inventive style of play enabled him to set records in every phase of the game; many believe that he is the greatest player in the history of baseball.

Cobb, William Montague

b. Oct. 12, 1904
Washington, D.C.
fields: Civil Rights, Education, Medicine

African American physician, scholar, and civil rights activist; William Montague Cobb served on the faculty at Howard's medical college beginning in 1928; also active in the National Association for the Advancement of Colored People.

Cobbett, William

b. March 9, 1763
Farnham, Surrey, England
d. June 18, 1835
Normandy Farm, near Guildford, Surrey, England
fields: Journalism and Politics

Cobbett, "the Poor Man's Friend," was the leading radical journalist of his day and was among the more prolific writers in English history. For thirty-three years (1802-1835), *The Political Register* led the popular attack on privilege and corruption in English government.

Cobden, Richard

b. June 3, 1804
Heyshott, Sussex, England
d. April 2, 1865
London, England
fields: Government and Politics, Diplomacy (trade policy)

Cobden was the undoubted champion of free trade in Victorian Britain and a well-known figure in the Manchester school of economic thought. With the Anti-Corn Law League, Cobden led the fight for repeal of the corn and provision laws in 1846. He negotiated the Cobden-Chevalier Treaty with France in 1860.

Cochise

aka: Goci (His Nose)
b. c. 1812
Chiricahua Mountains of present-day southern Ariz.
d. June 8, 1874
Chiricahua Apache Reservation, Ariz. Territory
fields: Native American Affairs, Warfare and Conquest

Chiricahua Apache tribal chief; as principal chief of the eastern Chiricahua Apaches from 1860 to 1872, Cochise orchestrated and led raids against U.S. and Mexican settlements; early in 1861, government troops led by Lieutenant George Nicholas Bascom apparently captured Cochise by treachery during a peace parlay on February 6, 1861; Bascom ordered the execution of three of Cochise's relatives in retaliation for the torture deaths of three U.S. citizens (the Bascom Affair); Cochise escaped and spent the next decade pursuing vengeance; following the Civil War, Cochise evaded the U.S. and Mexican armies for several years; finally, General Oliver Otis Howard negotiated a lasting treaty with Cochise on October 10, 1872, allowing Cochise and his people to live at peace in the Chiricahua Mountains, drawing rations from the U.S. government; in return, Apache raids virtually ceased in Arizona and New Mexico, but continued sporadically in northern Mexico, for the remainder of Cochise's life.

Cochran, Elizabeth. *See* Bly, Nellie

Cochran, Jacqueline

b. c. 1910
Pensacola, Florida
d. August 9, 1980
Indio, California
fields: Aviation and Space Exploration

A pioneer in women's aviation and a savvy businesswoman, Jacqueline Cochran paved the way for female American pilots of the future.

Cochran, Johnnie L., Jr.

b. October 2, 1937
Shreveport, La.
fields: Law

African American lawyer and activist; in 1962 Johnnie L. Cochran, Jr., graduated from the Loyola University School of Law; his cases have included successfully defending several members of the Black Panther Party (1971) who were charged with conspiracy to commit murder, failing to win acquittal for L.A. Black Panther leader Geronimo Pratt who was charged with murder (1972), and leading the victorious defense team in O. J. Simpson's criminal murder trial (1995); the Los Angeles Trial Lawyers Association honored him as Trial Lawyer of the Year in 1990; in 1996 he published his memoirs, *Journey to Justice*. In 1997, Cochran along with the other lawyers of a team got Geronimo Pratt's case reconsidered.

Cocteau, Jean

b. July 5, 1889
Maisons-Laffitte, France
d. October 11, 1963
Milly-la-Forêt, France
fields: Literature, Film, Art

From the years before World War I until his death in 1963, Cocteau enriched the cultural life of France with his highly creative contributions to such diverse fields as literature, ballet, art, and cinema. His works express with great lucidity a pessimistic view of the world that continues to fascinate admirers of Cocteau's films, novels, plays, and poems.

Cody, William

full: William Frederick Cody
aka: Buffalo Bill
b. February 26, 1846
Scott County, Iowa
d. January 10, 1917
Denver, Colorado
fields: Exploration and Colonization, Theater and Entertainment

Capitalizing on the legends created about his prowess as a plainsman, Cody popularized the American West through his Wild West show, which brought the sights of the last frontier to eastern America and to Europe.

Coe, Sebastian
full: Sebastian Newbold Coe
b. September 29, 1956
London, England
fields: Sports (runner)

An Olympic champion in the 1,500-meter run in 1980 and 1984, Coe set world records in four events while establishing himself as Great Britain's greatest middle-distance runner.

Coffin, Lucretia. *See* Mott, Lucretia

Cohen, Elizabeth. *See* Comden, Betty

Cohen, Judith. *See* Chicago, Judy

Cohen, Paul J.
full: Paul Joseph Cohen
b. Apr. 2, 1934
Long Branch, New Jersey
fields: Mathematics (applied math, calculus, mathematical logic, and set theory)

Paul J. Cohen gave proof that the size of the set of real numbers cannot be determined using the standard axioms of set theory. Won National Medal of Science in 1967.

Cohn, Ferdinand Julius
b. January 24, 1828
Breslau, Lower Silesia
d. June 25, 1898
Breslau, Lower Silesia
fields: Botany, Biology

Cohn is considered one of the founders of modern bacteriology. As a botanist, he contributed to understanding the evolutionary position of many microscopic plantlike organisms by elucidating their life histories.

Cojuangco, Maria Corazon. *See* Aquino, Corazon

Coke, Edward
aka: Sir Edward Coke
b. February 1, 1552
Mileham Manor, Norfolk, England
d. September 3, 1634
Stoke Poges, Buckinghamshire, England
fields: Law

During a long and distinguished legal career as barrister, member of the House of Commons, Queen Elizabeth's attorney general, and King James I's Chief Justice, Coke evolved from a king's man to a leading defender of free speech, the rights of Parliament, and the several rights associated with a fair trial. In 1628, he was the principal champion of the Petition of Right, one of the three great documents of English liberty. His written volumes on the law were primary texts for students of English law for nearly three centuries and constituted an important defense of the principles of liberty and the prevention of arbitrary government. His doctrine of judicial voidance was transformed by American colonials into the constitutional doctrine of judicial review.

Coker, Daniel
né: Isaac Wright
b. 1780
Frederick County or Baltimore County, Md.
d. 1846
Freetown, Sierra Leone
fields: Education, Religion and Theology

African American educator and missionary; Daniel Coker helped found the African Methodist Episcopal Zion church; best known as a missionary to Sierra Leone, Africa in 1816.

Colbert, Jean-Baptiste
b. August 29, 1619
Reims, France
d. September 6, 1683
Paris, France
fields: Government and Politics, Patronage of the Arts

Colbert contributed to the reform of the administrative, economic, legal, and cultural foundations of the French monarchy. As the third in a succession of great French ministers of the seventeenth century, he exercised primary responsibility for implementing the system of absolute monarchy that governed France until 1789.

Cole, Johnnetta Betsch
b. Oct. 19, 1936
Jacksonville, Fla.
fields: Education

African American university administrator; Johnnetta Betsch Cole taught anthropology at several university before becoming president of Spelman College.

Cole, Nat King
né: Nathaniel Adams Coles
b. Mar. 17, 1919
Montgomery Ala.
d. Feb. 15, 1965
Santa Monica, Calif.
fields: Music (jazz)

African American singer, pianist, and actor; Nat King Cole made a number of popular recordings, including "Smile," and "Mona Lisa."

Cole, Natalie
b. Feb. 6, 1949
Los Angeles, Calif.
fields: Music (popular)

African American singer; Natalie Cole was the daughter of singer Nat King Cole; made a number of hit recordings in the 1970's; had a come-back in the 1980's with *Unforgettable*, a duet in which she overdubbed her own vocals onto her father's most famous recording.

Cole, Rebecca J.
b. 1846
d. 1922
fields: Medicine

African American medical doctor; Rebecca J. Cole was the first African American woman to practice medicine.

Cole, Thomas W., Jr.
b. Jan. 11, 1941
Vernon, Tex.
fields: Education

African American educational administrator; Thomas W. Cole, Jr. was the first president (1989) of Clark-Atlanta University.

Coleman, Bessie
b. Jan. 26, 1893
Atlanta, Tex.
d. Apr. 30, 1926
Jacksonville, Fla.
fields: Aviation and Space Exploration

African American pilot; Bessie Coleman was the first black woman, and one of the first women, to earn an International Pilots License.

Coleman, Ornette
b. Mar. 19, 1930
Forth Worth, Tex.
fields: Music (jazz)

African American jazz saxophonist; Ornette Coleman was a seminal jazz figure; his recordings include *The Shape of Jazz to Come* (1959) and *Ornette and Prime Time: Opening the Caravan of Dreams* (1985).

Coleman, Wanda
b. November 13, 1946
Los Angeles, Calif.
fields: Literature (poet, journalist, and writer)

African American poet, journalist, and writer; Wanda Coleman was a contributing editor and columnist for the *Los Angeles Times Magazine*; was a staff writer for the NBC soap opera *Days of Our Lives* from 1975 to 1976 and won an Emmy Award during that season.

Coleman, William Thaddeus, Jr.

b. July 7, 1920
Germantown, Pa.
fields: Law, Government and Politics

African American attorney and government official; William Thaddeus Coleman, Jr. served as legal secretary to Supreme Court Justice Felix Frankfurter; was appointed as secretary of transportation by President Gerald Ford.

Coleridge, Samuel Taylor

b. October 21, 1772
Ottery St. Mary, Devonshire, England
d. July 25, 1834
Highgate, London, England
fields: Literature, Religion and Theology

Coleridge wrote several of the finest lyric poems in the English language and is considered one of the most brilliant of literary critics. As a speculative religious thinker, he had a seminal influence on many of the great minds of the nineteenth century.

Coleridge-Taylor, Samuel

b. Aug. 15, 1875
London, England
d. Sept. 1, 1912
London, England
fields: Music (folk)

African American composer, educator, conductor; Samuel Coleridge-Taylor became popular in the United States when he began composing musical themes based on African American folk music.

Coles, Honi

full: Charles Coles
b. 1911
Philadelphia, Pa.
d. Nov. 12, 1992
New York, N.Y.
fields: Dance (tap)

African American tap dancer; Honi Coles was said to have the fastest feet in show business; partnered with Cholly Atkins in the 1940's and 1950's; became production manager of Apollo Theater and president of the Negro Actors Guild.

Coles, Robert

b. October 12, 1929
Boston, Mass.
fields: Sociology, Psychiatry and Psychology

Robert Coles has explored children's lives in different cultures, classes, races, and economic conditions, winning a Pulitzer Prize for *Children of Crisis* (1967-1978). He has also written about migrants, sharecroppers, mountaineers, Eskimos, Chicanos, and Native Americans, as well as privileged children. His books *The Spiritual Life of Children* (1991) and *In God's House: Children's Drawings* (1996) examine how children react to the idea of God. His other books include *The Moral Life of Children* (1991), *When Slow Is Fast Enough: Educating the Delayed Preschool Child* (1993), *The Ongoing Journey: Awakening Spiritual Life in At-Risk Youth* (1997), and *The Youngest Parents: Teenage Pregnancy as It Shapes Lives* (1997).

Colet, John

b. Probably 1466
London, England
d. September 16, 1519
Sheen, Surrey, England
fields: Education, Religion and Theology, Church Reform

As the founder of St. Paul's school and dean of St. Paul's Cathedral, Colet wrote, preached, and led other humanists in educational, social, and religious reform.

Colette

full: Sidonie-Gabrielle Colette
b. January 28, 1873
Saint-Saveur-en-Puisaye, Burgundy, France
d. August 3, 1954
Paris, France
fields: Literature

Colette's work has been called the finest naturalist expressionism of the early twentieth century. Her gift for conveying sensations, emotions, and ambience produces the very personal style that her nom de plume so immediately calls to mind.

Collazo, Oscar

b. 1914
Puerto Rico
d. Feb. 20, 1994
Vega Baja, Puerto Rico
fields: Government and politics

Puerto Rican nationalist. Oscar Collazo and Griselio Torresola fired gunshots at Blair House in Washington, D.C., on November 1, 1950; President Harry S Truman had been staying at Blair House while the White House was being renovated. Truman was not injured in the attack, but Torresola and a presidential guard were killed. Collazo was sentenced to death for his role in the attack, but his sentence was commuted to life imprisonment. In 1979, he was freed in by President Jimmy Carter.

Collier, John

b. 1884
Atlanta, Georgia
d. 1968
fields: Sociology, Education

John Collier was a sociologist and educator; executive secretary, American Indian Defense Association, 1923-1933; editor, *American Indian Life*, 1926-1933; U.S. Commissioner of Indian Affairs, 1933-1945, responsible for passage of Indian Reorganization Act in 1934; director, National Indian Institute, 1945-1950; president, Institute of Ethnic Affairs, 1947-1968; wrote *Indians of the Americas* (1947), *Patterns and Ceremonials of the Indians of the Southwest* (1949).

Collingwood, R. G.

full: Robin George Collingwood
b. Feb. 22, 1889
Cartmel Fell, Lancashire, England
d. January 9, 1943
Coniston, Lancashire, England
fields: Philosophy

Collingwood stimulated international interest with his efforts to harmonize philosophy and history. His effort to explain what was meant by the term "philosophy of history" resulted in its becoming a respected discipline in Great Britain and the United States. Major works: *Religion and Philosophy* (1916), *Speculum Mentis* (1924), *Outlines of a Philosophy of Art* (1925), *An Essay on Philosophical Method* (1933), *The Principles of Art* (1938), *An Autobiography* (1939), *An Essay on Metaphysics* (1940), *The New Leviathan* (1942), *The Idea of Nature* (1945), *The Idea of History* (1946), *Essays in Political Philosophy* (1989).

Collins, Barbara-Rose

né: Barbara Rose Richardson
b. April 13, 1939
Detroit, Mich.
fields: Governement and Politics (politician)

African American politician; Democrat Barbara-Rose Collins was elected to the Michigan House of Representatives in November of 1974; was reelected three times, serving in the state legislature through 1981; was elected to Congress in 1990 and reelected in 1992 and 1994. She was defeated in the election of 1996.

Collins, Cardiss Robertson

b. Sept. 24, 1931
St. Louis, Mo.
fields: Government and Politics

African American congresswoman; Cardiss Robertson Collins was the first woman and the first African American to chair the House Government Operations Subcommittee on Manpower and Housing; elected chair of the Congressional Black Caucus in 1979.

Collins, George Washington

b. Mar. 5, 1925
Chicago, Ill.
d. Dec. 8, 1972
near Chicago, Ill.

fields: Government and Politics

African American congressman; George Washington Collins served as U.S. representative from Illinois' Sixth District in 1972 and served on the House Committee on Government Operations and the House Committee on Public Works; was killed in plane crash and was succeeded, by election, by his wife Cardiss Collins.

Collins, Janet

b. Mar. 2, 1917
New Orleans, La.
fields: Dance

African American dancer and choreographer; Janet Collins was the first African American dancer to perform on the Metropolitan Opera (1951).

Collins, Marva

né: Marva Knight
b. August 31, 1936
Monroeville, Alabama
fields: Education

Founder of the Daniel Hale Williams Westside Preparatory School, Marva Collins has spent her time educating inner-city children who are labeled at risk and ineducable.

Collins, Michael

b. October 16, 1890
Clonakilty, County Cork, Ireland
d. August 22, 1922
Beal-na-Blath, County Cork, Ireland
fields: Government and Politics

As a guerrilla leader, negotiator, finance minister, and head of the provisional government, Collins led Ireland toward independence from Great Britain.

Collins, Norman

full: Norman Richard Collins
b. October 3, 1907
Beaconsfield, Buckinghamshire, England
d. September 6, 1982
London, England
fields: Literature, Publishing, Television

Although Collins wrote fourteen novels and one work of nonfiction in his lifetime (most of which were popular successes), as well as succeeding as a publisher, he is better known for his innovative programming at the British Broadcasting Corporation during the late 1940's, and later for advocating and leading the movement toward commercial television broadcasting in Great Britain.

Collins, Robert Frederick

b. Jan. 27, 1931
New Orleans, La.
fields: Law

African American federal judge; Robert Frederick Collins was appointed by Jimmy Carter to the Eastern District of Louisiana in 1978; first federal judge to be convicted of taking a bribe.

Collins, Wayne Mortimer

b. 1899 or 1900
Sacramento, California
d. July 16, 1974
in an airplane between San Francisco and Honolulu
fields: Law, Civil Rights

Attorney; a California attorney, Wayne Mortimer Collins is noted for defending the civil liberties of Japanese Americans during World War II; his cases included representing World War II exclusion order violator Fred Korematsu (whose case he appealed all the way to the Supreme Court) and Iva Toguri (Tokyo Rose; for whom he made an unsuccessful attempt to win a presidential pardon); Collins also fought against the deportation of Japanese Americans who had renounced their U.S. citizenship while being detained in U.S. internment camps and Japanese Peruvians who had been extradited to the U.S. internment camps during the war.

Colón, Jesús

b. 1901
Cayey, Puerto Rico
d. 1974
New York, N.Y.
fields: Literature

Writer. During his lifetime, Jesus Colón published only a single work, *A Puerto Rican in New York and Other Sketches* (1961), a collection of autobiographical essays chronicling his experiences as an immigrant working in New York City. Hoping to reach a wide audience, he wrote in English; some of his essays were first published in his column for the *Daily Worker*, a Communist Party publication. He also served as president of Editorial Hispánica, a Spanish-language press. Another collection of his essays, *The Way It Was and Other Writings: Historical Vignettes About the New York Puerto Rican Community*, was published in 1993.

Colón, Miriam

b. 1945
Ponce, Puerto Rico
fields: Theater and Entertainment

Director and actress. Miriam Colón attended the University of Puerto Rico and studied at the Erwin Piscator Dramatic Workshop and the Actors' Studio in New York. Her first film was the 1951 Spanish-language feature *Los peloteros*. In 1967, she founded the Puerto Rican Traveling Theater. Among her many stage credits are roles in *The Innkeepers* (1956), *Me, Cándido!* (1965), *The Oxcart* (1966), *Winterset* (1968), *The Passion of Antígone Pérez* (1972), *Julius Caesar* (1979), *Orinoco* (1985), and *Simpson St.* (1985). She received an honorary doctor of letters degreee from Montclair State University in 1989; in 1990, she received the White House Hispanic Heritage Award.

Colón, Willie

full: William Anthony Colón
b. Apr. 28, 1950
New York, N.Y.
fields: Music

Bandleader and trombonist. Willie Colón, the son of Puerto Rican parents, signed a recording contract in 1967 with Fania Records. His first album, *El malo*, was released that year. In 1972, he released *Cosa nuestra*, his first gold-selling album, which included the hit "Che che colé." In 1975, Colón invited Rubén Blades to sing with his band; the result of this collaboration was the *The Good, the Bad, the Ugly* (1975). His 1982 album with Blades, *Canciones del Solar de los Aburridos*, received a Grammy Award.

Colorado. *See* Colorow

Colorow

aka: Colorado (Red)
b. c. 1810
northern Mexico, in present-day northern Colo.
d. Dec. 11, 1888
Uintah Reservation, Utah
fields: Government and Politics, Native American Affairs

Native American leader. Colorow was an influential chief among northern Colorado Ute bands and a leader in an attack on U.S. troops in 1879; he clashed with game wardens while leading his band to hunt off the reservation in 1887.

Colt, Samuel

b. July 19, 1814
Hartford, Connecticut
d. January 10, 1862
Hartford, Connecticut
fields: Invention and Technology

Colt developed the revolving pistol and the revolving rifle and pioneered the mass production of guns with interchangeable parts. Colt firearms played a significant role in nineteenth century U.S. history and also provided a key link in the transformation of weapons of war.

Coltrane, Alice

né: Turiya Sagittinanda
b. Aug. 27, 1937
Detroit, Mich.
fields: Music (jazz)

African American musician; Alice Coltrane founded the Vedantic Center in California in 1972; wife of John Coltrane.

Coltrane, John

b. September 23, 1926
Hamlet, North Carolina
d. July 17, 1967
Huntington, Long Island, New York
fields: Music

Coltrane was one of the most important innovators in American jazz. He was most closely associated with the controversial free jazz movement of the 1960's.

Columbus, Christopher

aka: Cristóbal Colón
b. Between August 25 and October 31, 1451
Genoa
d. May 20, 1506
Valladolid, Spain
fields: Exploration and Colonization

Columbus' discovery of America was the first recorded transatlantic voyage. It led directly to Europe's colonial settlement and exploitation of the New World, and it altered the course of history.

Comcomly

b. c. 1765
Northwest Coast, U.S.
d. 1830
Northwest Coast, U.S.
fields: Government and Politics, Exploration and Conquest (tribal leader)

Native American leader. Chinook leader Comcomly aided white exploration of the Northwest Coast. Assisted Meriwether Lewis and William Clark as they traveled to the mouth of the Columbia River in 1805. In 1811, aided John Jacob Astor's fur traders, who had been shipwrecked. An extraordinarily wealthy man, Comcomly relished extravagant displays. During visits to Vancouver, he was accompanied by three hundred slaves.

Comden, Betty

né: Elizabeth Cohen
b. May 3, 1917
Brooklyn, New York
fields: Film, Music, Theater and Entertainment (drama)

In her lifelong writing partnership with Adolph Green, Betty Comden collaborated as a lyricist, dramatist, and screenwriter for some of the most notable musicals produced on Broadway and in Hollywood, ranging from *On the Town* (1944; film version, 1949) and *Singin' in the Rain* (1952) through *The Will Rogers Follies: A Life in Revue* (1991).

Comer, James P.

full: James Pierpont Comer
b. September 25, 1934
East Chicago, Ind.
fields: Education, Psychiatry and Psychology

The "Comer method" has rehabilitated undisciplined and failing schools and children by teaching mainstream social values, involving parents, and integrating arts and academics, thus fostering interest and self-esteem in students.

Compton, Arthur Holly

b. September 10, 1892
Wooster, Ohio
d. March 15, 1962
Berkeley, California
fields: Physics

Although Compton's most famous discovery was that named for him, the Compton effect, he also carried out important cosmic ray research, contributed significantly to the development of the atom bomb, and was an influential educator. He was awarded the 1927 Nobel Prize in Physics.

Comstock, Anthony

b. March 7, 1844
New Canaan, Connecticut
d. September 21, 1915
Summit, New Jersey
fields: Government and Politics

A career U.S. postal official, Anthony Comstock was a self-styled crusader against what he considered to be pornography. In 1873 he successfully lobbied a sympathetic Congress to make the postal regulations against pornography more restrictive. The resulting Federal Anti-Obscenity Act was commonly known as the "Comstock Law." Thereafter, he worked tirelessly to help enforce that law.

Comte, Auguste

full: Isidore-Auguste-Marie-François-Xavier Comte
b. January 19, 1798
Montpellier, France
d. September 5, 1857
Paris, France
fields: Philosophy, Sociology, Historiography, Religion and Theology

One of the greatest systematic thinkers of nineteenth century France, Comte was the father of positivism, a philosophy which saw the evolution of new ideas as the shaping force in history and regarded the empirical method of science as the only valid basis of knowledge. Comte sought to extend the method of science to the study of man, coining the word "sociology." His later thought took a Romantic swing, emphasizing the primacy of the feelings, glorifying religion in a secular guise, and proposing a highly regulated social order.

Conant, James Bryant

b. March 26, 1893
Dorchester, Massachusetts
d. February 11, 1978
Hanover, New Hampshire
fields: Science, Education, Diplomacy (international)

Conant helped unravel the mysteries of the components of chlorophyll and hemoglobin. He served as an innovative president of Harvard University, United States high commissioner to Germany after World War II, and ambassador to the newly created German Federal Republic.

Concepción, Dave

full: David Ismael Concepción y Benitez
b. June 17, 1948
Aragua, Venezuela
fields: Sports (baseball)

Baseball player. Dave Concepción was a star shortstop for the Cincinnati Reds from 1970 to 1978. A superb infielder, Concepción won five Gold Glove Awards; he was also a solid hitter, with a lifetime batting average of .267 in nineteen seasons. He was selected to nine National League All-Star teams (in 1973 and every year from 1975 to 1982, and he was the All-Star Game's Most Valuable Player in 1982. in 1977, he received the 1977 Roberto Clemente Award as the top Latin American major leaguer.

Concepción de Gracia, Gilberto

b. July 9, 1909
Vega Alta, Puerto Rico
d. Mar. 15, 1968
Santurce, Puerto Rico
fields: Government and politics

Political leader. Gilberto Concepción de Gracia earned a law degree at George Washington University in Washington, D.C., but returned to Puerto Rico to join the struggle for Puerto Rican independence. In 1946, he helped to organize the Popular Independence Party.

Condé, The Great

aka: Louis II de Bourbon, the duke of Enghien
aka: Louis II de Bourbon, fourth Prince de Condé
b. September 8, 1621
Paris, France
d. December 11, 1686
Fontainebleau, France
fields: Military Affairs

Condé played an important role in the struggle for royal absolutism, initially supporting the royal cause during the Fronde, then rebelling against the king. After reconciliation, he continued to serve as a successful and innovative military commander. He was part of the movement to abandon the old feudal levies in exchange for a tightly organized and highly trained and disciplined standing royal army. Condé was an expert tactician in the field.

Condillac, Étienne Bonnot de

né: Étienne Bonnot
b. September 30, 1714
Grenoble, France
d. August 2, 1780
Château Flux, Beaugency, France
fields: Philosophy

In writings famed for precision, clarity, and persuasiveness, Condillac was the only major figure of the French Enlightenment to create a systematic theory of knowledge and exhibit a professional command of the issues of philosophy.

Condorcet, Marquis de

né: Marie-Jean-Antoine-Nicolas Caritat
b. September 17, 1743
Ribemont, France
d. March 29, 1794
Bourg-la-Reine, France
fields: Sociology, Education, Mathematics

Condorcet's works synthesized the thinking of the philosophes of the Enlightenment. He spent his life promoting educational, political, social, and religious change in France.

Cone, James

b. August 5, 1938
Fordyce, Arkansas
fields: Religion and Theology

James Cone is a theologian; faculty member at Union Theological Seminary from 1969; provided systematic case for divine support of the black liberation struggle in the United States and elsewhere; wrote many books, including *Black Theology and Black Power* (1969), *For My People: Black Theology and the Black Church* (1984), and *Martin and Malcolm and America: A Dream or a Nightmare* (1991).

Confucius

né: Kong Qiu
aka: Kongfuzi
aka: K'ung Ch'iu
b. 551 B.C.E.
state of Lu, China
d. 479 B.C.E.
Qufu, state of Lu, China
fields: Philosophy, Education, Ethics

Confucius' teachings had little impact on his own times, but through his disciples and followers Confucianism became the official state philosophy in the second century B.C.E., while its texts became the basis of formal education. Confucianism, modified and developed by succeeding centuries of interpreters, remained the dominant philosophy of China until the early twentieth century and still has a major influence on people throughout East Asia.

Conley, William Lee. *See* Broonzy, Big Bill

Connolly, Maureen

full: Maureen Catherine Connolly
b. September 17, 1934
San Diego, California
d. June 21, 1969
Dallas, Texas
fields: Sports (tennis)

Before a serious injury cut short her dazzling career at the age of nineteen, Maureen "Little Mo" Connolly established herself as one of the most powerful and effective women's tennis players in modern history. She was the first women's tennis player to achieve the Grand Slam in 1953.

Conquering Bear

aka: Mahtoiowa
aka: Whirling Bear
b. ?
d. Aug. 19, 1854
Wyo.
fields: Government and Politics, Native American Affairs

Brule Sioux chief Conquering Bear was killed while attempting to accommodate whites; his death precipitated war in the northern Plains. When he was killed, Conquering Bear's warriors retaliated, killing all but one of Lieutenant John Grattan's detachment. Subsequently, on September 3, 1855, General William S. Harney and his forces attacked a Sioux camp. Thus began the wars of the northern Plains.

Conrad, Barbara

b. Aug. 11, 1945
Pittsburgh, Pa.
fields: Music (opera)

African American opera singer; Barbara Conrad began performing at the Metropolitan Opera in 1982.

Conrad, Joseph

né: Jósef Teodor Konrad Nałę Korzeniowski
b. December 3, 1857
Berdyczów, Podolia, Poland
d. August 3, 1924
Oswalds, BishopBlock, Ksbourne, England
fields: Literature

Although best known as an adventure novelist, Conrad raised the form to new heights, dealing with the issues of human isolation in the face of an overwhelming natural universe, with a psychological realism that revealed the depths of his characters' consciousness and perceptions.

Conroy, Francis Hilary

b. Dec. 31, 1919
Normal, Ill.
fields: Scholarship, Historiography

Francis Hilary Conroy was one of the first historians to study early Japanese immigration to Hawaii. A professor of history at the University of Pennsylvania until his retirement in 1990, he wrote *East Across the Pacific* (1972) with T. Scott Miyakawa.

Consaponaheeso. *See* Musgrove, Mary

Constable, John

b. June 11, 1776
East Bergholt, Suffolk, England
d. March 31, 1837
London, England
fields: Art

Constable combined a passion for nature with his conception of an ideal rural England to create some of the most evocative, poetic landscapes of all time.

Constantine. *See* Cyril, Saint

Constantine, Baron

né: Learie Nicholas Constantine
b. September 21, 1901
Petit Valley, Diego Martinez, Trinidad
d. July 1, 1971
London, England
fields: Sports (cricket), Social Reform, Government and Politics

The outstanding West Indian cricketer of his time, Constantine used his influence to promote racial justice and West Indian independence. He became the first black member of the House of Lords.

Constantine the Great

né: Flavius Valerius Constantinus
b. February 17 or 27, c. 272-285
Naissus (in modern Yugoslavia)
d. May 22, 337
Nicomedia
fields: Warfare and Conquest, Government and Politics, Religion and Theology

As the result of a series of successful wars, Constantine became ruler of Rome and its empire. As the first Christian emperor of Rome, he was primarily responsible for initiating the great changes which in a few decades turned the pagan empire into a Christian one. Finally, Constantine refounded the old Greek city of Byzantium as the New Rome, which, as Constantinople, became Europe's greatest city during the next millennium.

Conway, John Horton

b. Dec. 26, 1937
Liverpool, England
fields: Mathematics (arithmetic, geometry, mathematical logic, and number theory)

John Horton Conway discovered a new simple group, the Conway group, in 1969. In 1970 he introduced the Game of Life. He investigated mathematical games to produce a theoretical foundation for number theory, and he discovered surreal numbers.

Conyers, John, Jr.

b. May 16, 1929
Detroit, Mich.
fields: Government and Politics

African American politician; John Conyers, Jr. was elected as congressman from the First District of Michigan in 1964; nationally influential in representing issues that are important to African Americans; first African American to serve on the House Juciary Committee and participated in the hearings on the impeachment of both Richard Nixon and Bill Clinton.

Cook, Charles Cookie

b. 1914
Chicago, Ill.
d. Aug. 8, 1991
New York, N.Y.
fields: Dance (tap)

African American tap dancer; Charles "Cookie" Cook teamed with Ernest "Brownie" Brown to become an international headline act on vaudeville.

Cook, James

aka: Captain James Cook
b. October 27, 1728
Marton, Yorkshire, England
d. February 14, 1779
Kealakekua Bay, Hawaii
fields: Exploration and Colonization

With his inspired seamanship and his practical grasp of scientific method, Cook added greatly to world knowledge of geography and oceanography and laid the basis for British colonialism in the Pacific.

Cook, Joseph

b. December 7, 1860
Silverdale, Staffordshire, England
d. July 30, 1947
Sydney, New South Wales, Australia
fields: Government and Politics

Prime minister of Australia in 1913 and 1914 as leader of newly formed Liberal Party, Joseph Cook was criticized by many for moving from his Labor roots to a more conservative political position. As prime minister he could accomplish little because his party did not control of the upper house of Parliament.

Cook, Julian Abele, Jr.

b. June 22, 1930
Washington, D.C.
fields: Law

African American federal judge; Julian Abele Cook, Jr. was appointed by Jimmy Carter to the Eastern District of Michigan; promoted to chief justice in 1989.

Cook, Mercer

b. Mar. 30, 1903
Washington, D.C.
d. Oct. 4, 1987
Washington, D.C.
fields: Education, Government and Politics

African American educator, author, poet, and political appointee; Mercer Cook was a professor of romance languages at several universities; served as ambassador to Niger (1961-1964) and Senegal and Gambia (1965-1966).

Cook, Samuel DuBois

b. Nov. 21, 1928
Griffin, Ga.
fields: Education

African American educator; Samuel DuBois Cook taught at several universities; became president of Dillard University in 1975.

Cooke, Jay

b. August 10, 1821
Sandusky, Ohio
d. February 18, 1905
Ogontz, Pennsylvania
fields: Banking and Finance

Cooke was the foremost investment banker during the mid-nineteenth century and pioneered new ways of mobilizing the savings of Americans for productive ends.

Cooke, Sam

né: Samuel Cook
b. Jan. 22, 1931
Clarksdale, Miss.
d. Dec. 11, 1964
Los Angeles, Calif.
fields: Music (gospel, pop)

African American gospel singer; Sam Cooke was the first African American gospel star to achieve success in popular music; lead singer of the Soul Stirrers; pop hits include "You Send Me".

Cooke, William Fothergill

b. May 4, 1806
Ealing, Middlesex, England
d. June 25, 1879
Fearnham, Surrey, England
fields: Invention and Technology (telegraphy)

From the joining of William Fothergill Cooke's entrepreneurial skills and Charles Wheatstone's scientific knowledge came the world's first commercial telegraph network.

Cooley, Thomas

b. January 6, 1824
near Attica, N.Y.
d. September 12, 1898
Ann Arbor, Mich.
fields: Law

American jurist. Thomas Cooley was the author of influential books about law (including *Treatise on the Constitutional Limitations Which Rest upon the Legislative Power of the States of the American Union*, 1868), a judge on the Michigan Supreme Court, a distinguished law teacher, and the first chairman of the Interstate Commerce Commission.

Coolidge, Calvin

full: John Calvin Coolidge
b. July 4, 1872
Plymouth, Vermont
d. January 5, 1933
Northampton, Massachusetts
fields: Government and Politics

Practicing the virtues most Americans seemed to honor in absentia, Calvin Coolidge served as thirtieth president of the United States (1923-1929) during the central years of that extraordinary decade, the 1920's.

Coolidge, Martha

b. August 17, 1946
New Haven, Connecticut
fields: Film

After an early career in documentary filmmaking, Coolidge became a successful feature film director of teen comedies, coming-of-age dramas, and social satires.

Coolidge, Mary Roberts

b. Oct. 28, 1860
Kingsbury, Ind.
d. Apr. 13, 1945
Berkeley, Calif.
fields: Historiography

Mary Roberts Coolidge received an undergraduate degree from Cornell in 1880 and a doctorate from Stanford University in 1896. She taught at Stanford from 1896 to 1903 and, in 1909, published *Chinese Immigration*, one of the first comprehensive analyses of the Chinese in the United States. From 1918 to 1927, Coolidge was professor of sociology at Mills College.

Coomaraswamy, Ananda Kentish

b. Aug. 22, 1877
Colombo, Ceylon

d. Sept. 9, 1947
Needham, Mass.
fields: Scholarship, Art, Philosophy

Ananda Kentish Coomaraswamy, born of a Ceylonese father and British mother, was educated in England. He was appointed a research fellow in Indian, Persian, and Muslim art at the Museum of Fine Arts in Boston in 1917. Coomaraswamy was a critic of commercialism, modernism, and egalitarianism, who saw his task as stewardship of, and piety toward, truth, goodness, and beauty. His writings include *Mediaeval Sinhalese Art* (1908), *Catalogue of the Indian Collections in the Museum of Fine Arts, Boston* (1923-1930), *History of Indian and Indonesian Art* (1927), *The Transformation of Nature in Art* (1934), and *Why Exhibit Works of Art* (1943), reprinted as *Christian and Oriental Philosophy of Art* (1956).

Cooney, Joan Ganz
b. November 30, 1929
Phoenix, Ariz.
fields: Television, Education

After starting journalism, Joan Ganz Cooney got into documentary television work in New York during the 1950's. In 1968 she formed the Children's Television Workshop, which introduced *Sesame Street* for very young children the following year. The Children's Television Workshop also produced *The Electric Company* for older children. In 1989 she was inducted into the Academy of Television Arts and Sciences Hall of Fame.

Cooper, Algernon J.
b. May 30, 1944
Mobile, Ala.
fields: Government and Politics

African American mayor of Prichard, Ala; Algernon J. Cooper also served as president of the Southern Conference of Black Mayors.

Cooper, Anna Julia Haywood
né: Anna Julia Haywood
b. Aug. 10, 1858
Raleigh, N.C.
d. Feb. 27, 1964
Washington, D.C.
fields: Education

African American pioneer in secondary education and civil rights; Anna Julia Haywood Cooper reportedly began student-teaching as a preteen; received degrees from Oberlin in the 1880's and earned doctorate at the Sorbonne in 1925; served as principal of African American Dunbar high school; ran school for unemployed African Americans from her home.

Cooper, Anthony Ashley. *See* Shaftesbury, first earl of

Cooper, Anthony Ashley. *See* Shaftesbury, third earl of

Cooper, Cecil
b. Dec. 20, 1949
Brenham, Tex.
fields: Sports (baseball)

African American baseball player; Cecil Cooper was a first baseman who played for seventeen seasons (1971-1987) with the Boston Red Sox and the Milwaukee Brewers.

Cooper, Chuck
full: Charles H. Cooper
b. 1926
d. Feb. 5, 1984
Pittsburgh, Pa.
fields: Sports (basketball)

African American basketball player; the son of Tarzan Cooper, Chuck Cooper was a star for the Harlem Rens; in 1950 became the first African American to sign a contract to play in the National Basketball Association.

Cooper, J. California
full: Joan California Cooper
b. ?
Berkeley, Calif.
fields: Literature

African American author; J. California Cooper's works include *A Piece of Mine: A New Short Story Collection* (1984) and the novels *Homemade Love* (1986) and *Some Soul to Keep* (1987).

Cooper, James Fenimore
né: James Cooper
b. September 15, 1789
Burlington, New Jersey
d. September 14, 1851
Cooperstown, New York
fields: Literature

Cooper pioneered the historical novel based on American themes and characters. He also wrote the first sea novel. In his fiction and nonfiction, he proved himself an astute social critic of the excesses of democracy.

Cooper, Julia
b. 1921?
Fayetteville, N.C.
fields: Law

African American federal judge; Julia Cooper was appointed by Gerald Ford to the District of Columbia Court of Appeals in 1975.

Cooper, Tarzan
full: Charles Theodore Cooper
b. Aug. 30, 1907
Newark, N.J.
d. Dec. 19, 1980
Philadelphia, Pa.
fields: Sports (basketball)

African American basketball player; Tarzan Cooper played for the Harlem Rens (1929-1939); elected to the Naismith Memorial Basketball Hall of Fame (1963).

Cooper, Vera. *See* Rubin, Vera C.

Coosaponakeesa. *See* Musgrove, Mary

Cooswootna. *See* Antonio, Juan

Coowescoowe. *See* Ross, John

Copernicus, Nicolaus
b. February 19, 1473
Thorn (Toruń), Prussia
d. May 24, 1543
Frauenburg (Frombork), Prussia
fields: Astronomy

Copernicus discarded the Ptolemaic system and introduced the theory that the planets, including the earth, revolve around the sun. He defended the right of learned men to discuss scientific theories, even when they differ from currently accepted beliefs and contradict religious dogma.

Copland, Aaron
b. November 14, 1900
Brooklyn, New York
d. December 2, 1990
North Tarrytown, New York
fields: Music

Copland advanced the cause of music in America through a lifetime of musical composition and an unending concern for and promotion of a distinctly American music.

Copley, John Singleton
b. July 3, 1738
Boston, Massachusetts
d. September 9, 1815
London, England
fields: Art (painting)

Copley achieved a striking realism in his portraits and a vibrant excitement in his historical paintings. In gaining international acclaim, he showed that America could have a distinguished cultural life.

Copps, Sheila
full: Sheila Maureen Copps
b. November 27, 1952
Hamilton, Ontatio, Canada
fields: Government and Politics

Deputy prime minister (1993-1997), minister for the environment (1993-1996), and heritage minister (beginning in 1996) of Canada, Sheila Copps was one of Canada's most recognizable and popular politicians in the latter 1990's. Added considerable land to the national park system and supported Canadian recording artists and television producers on intellectual property (copyright) issues.

Copway, George

aka: Kahgegwagebow (Stands Fast)
b. c. 1818
near the mouth of the Trent River, Ontario, Canada
d. c. 1863
near Pontiac, Mich.
fields: Literature

Native American (Ojibwa) writer George Copway published a number of books on Ojibwa topics. Among them are *The Life, History, and Travels of Kah-ge-ga-gah-bowh* (1847), later revised and reissued as *The Life, Letters and Speeches of Kah-ge-ga-gah-bowh, or G. Copway* (1850), and *The Traditional History and Characteristic Sketches of the Ojibway Nation* (1850), reissued as *Indian Life and Indian History, by an Indian Author* (1858).

Corbusier, Le

né: Charles-Édouard Jeanneret
b. October 6, 1887
La Chaux-de-Fonds, Switzerland
d. August 27, 1965
Cap Martin, France
fields: Architecture

Le Corbusier was one of the most creative, bold, and controversial architects of the twentieth century. He also wrote passionately and powerfully about the nature and configuration of the modern city, thus making him a pioneer in the field of urban planning.

Cordero, Ángel Tomás, Jr.

b. Nov. 8, 1942
Santurce, Puerto Rico
fields: Sports (horse racing)

Jockey. A member of a famous Puerto Rican racing family, Angel Cordero, Jr., won the 1974 Kentucky Derby aboard Cannonade. He won a second Derby a Belmont Stakes in 1976 on Bold Forbes and third in 1985 on Spend a Buck. His record also includes wins in the 1980 and 1984 Preakness Stakes. He was the top money-winning rider in 1976, 1982, and 1983. He amassed more than seven thousand career wins and more than $160 million in prize money.

Cordero, Roque

b. Aug. 16, 1917
Panama City, Panama
fields: Music (classical)

African American composer and conductor; Roque Cordero's works include *Capricho interiorano* (1939) and *Rapsodia campesina* (1953).

Córdova, Arturo de

né: Arturo García
b. May 8, 1908
Mérida, Yucatán, Mexico
d. 1973
Mexico City, Mexico
fields: Theater and Entertainment (actor)

Actor. Arturo de Córdova was a leading Mexican film actor known for his striking good looks. He rose to fame in such Mexican films as *Cielito lindo* (1936), *La Zandunga* (1937), *Que viene mi marido* (1939), *El* (1951), and *Fruto prohibido* (1952). His U.S. films include *For Whom the Bell Tolls* (1943), *Hostages* (1943), *Frenchman's Creek* (1944), *A Medal for Benny* (1945), *Masquerade in Mexico* (1945), *The Flame* (1947), *New Orleans* (1947), *The Adventures of Casanova* (1948), and *Kill Him for Me* (1953). His pairing with Betty Hutton in *Incendiary Blonde* (1945) sparked protests from women's groups and a boycott of the film in Salt Lake City.

Cordova, Dorothy Laigo

b. Feb. 6, 1932
Seattle, Wash.
fields: Historiography

Filipina American Dorothy Laigo Cordova directed the nationwide research project "The Forgotten Asian Americans: Filipinos and Koreans," which received funds from the National Endowment for the Humanities. In 1957, she, her husband, and some others founded Filipino Youth Activities of Seattle. In 1976, she became the executive director of the Demonstration Project for Asian Americans. She served as regent of Seattle University from 1980 to 1981. The next year, she and her husband, Fred, founded the Filipino American National Historical Society, In 1988-1989, she lectured in Asian American studies at the University of Washington.

Cordova, Fred

b. June 3, 1931
Selma, Calif.
fields: Journalism, Publishing, Civil Rights

Fred Cordova, a journalist, is a long-time community advocate. He and his wife helped found Filipino Youth Activities, a program meant to prevent juvenile delinquency, in 1957. He created the youth group's award-winning Princesa Drill Team, Cumbanchero Percussioneers and Mandayan Marchers in 1959, leading the groups for twenty years. Manager of Information Services at the University of Washington beginning in 1974, he wrote *Filipinos: Forgotten Asian Americans* (1983). In 1982, he and his wife founded the Filipino American National Historical Society. He was a visiting faculty scholar at the Smithsonian Institution in 1985.

Corelli, Arcangelo

b. February 17, 1653
Fusignano, Italy
d. January 8, 1713
Rome, Italy
fields: Music

Corelli was one of the most significant violin virtuosos of the late Baroque period. He composed sonatas and concertos for string instruments, which became famous throughout Europe for their pedagogical and musical value.

Cori, Carl F.

full: Carl Ferdinand Cori
b. Dec. 5, 1896
Prague, Austria-Hungary (now Czech Republic)
d. Oct. 20, 1984
Cambridge, Massachusetts
fields: Biology, Chemistry, Physiology

Carl F. Cori, collaborating with his wife, Gerty, determined the essential mechanism of carbohydrate metabolism in animal tissue; the two proposed the chemical methods by which glucose is converted to glycogen and identified the enzymes that catalyze specific chemical steps in the pathway; in 1947, they were awarded the Nobel Prize in Physiology or Medicine.

Cori, Gerty T.

né: Gerty Theresa Radnitz
b. Aug. 15, 1896
Prague, Austria-Hungary (now Czech Republic)
d. Oct. 26, 1957
St. Louis, Missouri
fields: Biology, Chemistry, Physiology

In collaboration with her husband, Carl, Gerty Cori investigated the chemical methods by which the sugar glucose is created in animal tissue; the Coris discovered, isolated, and purified the catalytic enzymes required to create and break up the polymer glycogen, leading to the identification of enzyme-specific diseases. In 1947, the two won the Nobel Prize in Physiology or Medicine.

Coriolis, Gustave-Gaspard de

b. May 21, 1792
Paris, France
d. Sept. 19, 1843
Paris, France
fields: Mathematics, Physics

Gustave-Gaspard Coriolis discovered and studied forces in a rotating system; his work with the Coriolis force influenced mechanical physics and has been used to explain various natural phenomena.

Cormack, Allan M.

full: Allan MacLeod Cormack
b. Feb. 23, 1924
Johannesburg, South Africa
d. May 7, 1998
Winchester, Massachusetts
fields: Mathematics (applied math and calculus)

The first computed tomography (CT) machine was produced in 1971, using Allan M. Cormack's mathematical procedures. Cormack won the 1979 Nobel Prize in Physiology or Medicine for his development of the mathematical procedure used in CT scanning.

Cormier, Robert Edmund

b. January 17, 1925
Leominster, Massachusetts
fields: Journalism, Literature

An American journalist, Robert Edmund Cormier is an essayist and author of young adult novels noted for introducing young readers to a "new" realism, depicting the darker side of life. His popular books include *The Chocolate War* (1974) and its sequel, *Beyond the Chocolate War* (1985). Other noted works include *I Am the Cheese* (1977), *After the First Death* (1979), *The Bumblebee Flies Away* (1983), *Fade* (1988), and *We All Fall Down (1991).*

Corneille, Pierre

b. June 6, 1606
Rouen, France
d. September 30, 1684
Paris, France
fields: Theater and Entertainment

Corneille wrote or collaborated on more than thirty plays during a career spanning forty-five years. His masterpiece, *The Cid*, is the first classical tragedy in French. His work dominated the French stage during the first half of the seventeenth century and helped to define the character of classical theater.

Cornelius, Don

b. September 27, 1936
Chicago, Ill.
fields: Television (television host)

African American television host; from 1970 into the 1990's, Don Cornelius produced and hosted the dance show *Soul Train*; in 1995, the Don Cornelius Productions company produced and syndicated the *Soul Train 25th Anniversary Hall of Fame Special.*

Cornforth, John

full: Sir John Warcup Cornforth
b. Sept. 7, 1917
Sydney, Australia
fields: Chemistry

John Cornforth demonstrated the power of associating a molecule's exact structure, or stereochemistry, with its synthesis in nature. In 1975, he won the Nobel Prize in Chemistry.

Cornish, Samuel Eli

b. 1795
Sussex County, Del.
d. 1858
Brooklyn, N.Y.
fields: Civil Rights, Journalism, Religion, Social Reform

African American abolitionist, editor, and minister; Samuel Eli Cornish made a significant contribution to African American religious culture in from the 1920's through the 1940's; best known for founding a number of important African American newspapers, including *Freedom's Journal*; also founded the New York Anti-Slavery Society.

Cornplanter

aka: Kayehtwanken (By What One Plants)
aka: John Abeel
aka: John O'Bail
b. between 1732 and 1740
Conewaugus, N.Y.
d. Feb. 18, 1836
Cornplantertown, Pa.
fields: Native American Affairs, Warfare and Conquest

Seneca war chief; Cornplanter achieved prominence as an Iroquois war chief fighting for the French in the French and Indian War (1755-1759) and the British in the American Revolution in the Wyoming, Cherry Valley, and Newtown campaigns (1777-1778); at subsequent treaty conferences he emphasized the need for peaceful coexistence between Indians and the United States; he was present at the treaty negotiations at Fort Stanwix (1784) and Fort Harmar (1789), which resulted in the loss of Seneca lands to the U.S. government; in gratitude for his assistance at the Treaty of Fort Harmar, Pennsylvania granted to Cornplanter fifteen hundred acres in 1796, and many Senecas in the Allegany region lived on his grant pending settlement of reservation boundaries in New York; among those with him was his half-brother, the prophet Handsome Lake, whose visions were recorded by resident Quakers; in 1822 the land was declared tax exempt as long as it was held by Cornplanter or his descendants.

Cornstalk

aka: Wynepuechsika
b. c. 1720
western Pa.
d. Nov. 10, 1777
Point Pleasant, W.Va.
fields: Warfare and Conquest, Native American Affairs

Native American leader. Shawnee war chief Cornstalk opposed white settlers in the Ohio Valley and intermittently warred against them from the 1750's to his death in 1777. In 1776, he attempted to form an Indian alliance to drive all whites back across the Appalachians. Despite eloquent appeals, he was unsuccessful.

Cornwallis, First Marquess

né: Charles Cornwallis
b. December 31, 1738
London, England
d. October 5, 1805
Ghazipur, India
fields: Military Affairs, Government and Politics

Cornwallis served his country on three continents, combining military skill with private and public probity as the chief civil administrator in India and Ireland.

Corona, Bert N.

b. May 29, 1918
El Paso, Tex.
fields: Labor movement

Labor leader. Bert Corona worked for some sixty years to improving the situation of Mexican American workers. In the 1930's and 1940's, he organized Mexican Americans in low-paying jobs in Southern California. Later, he helped found the Community Service Organization and the Mexican American Political Association. As an organizer for the National Association of Mexican Americans, he opposed McCarthyism and the McCarran-Walter Immigration Act. He served as an adviser to President Lyndon Johnson in the 1960's and campaigned against the Vietnam War. He also served as president of the Association of California School Administrators.

Coronado, Francisco Vásquez de

b. 1510
Salamanca, Spain
d. September 22, 1554
Mexico City, Mexico
fields: Exploration and Colonization

As leader of the 1540-1542 expedition to the Seven Cities of Cíbola and Quivira, Coronado explored what became Arizona, Texas, New Mexico, Oklahoma, and Kansas and opened the Southwest to Spanish colonization and settlement.

Coronel, Antonio

b. Oct. 21, 1817
Mexico City, Mexico
d. Apr. 17, 1894
California
fields: Education, Government and Politics

Educator and politician. Antonio Coronel, a Mexican schoolteacher who made a small fortune in the California gold fields, became the first superintendent of Los Angeles schools in 1852. In 1853, he became the city's mayor; served as chairman of the Los Angeles County Democratic Committee and as a member of the Los Angeles School Board. During the Civil War, he served four terms on the Los Angeles Common Council, and he became California state treasurer in 1867. Coronel participated in numerous civic causes before retiring from politics in the 1880's. He became a part owner of the weekly newspaper *La Crónica* in 1873, and he remained active in its management for four years.

Corpi, Lucha

b. Apr. 13, 1945
Jáltipan, Mexico
fields: Literature

Poet and writer. Lucha Corpi is an acclaimed writer of poetry and prose. Her poetry, which is written primarily in Spanish, focuses on women's roles. She was a founding member of Aztlán Cultural and the Centro Chicano de Escritores, organizations that extol Mexican American culture and art. Corpi is best known for her series "The Marina Poems," which first appeared in the collection *The Other Voice: Twentieth-Century Women's Poetry in Translation* (1976). Her work is also featured in *Fireflight: Three Latin American Poets* (1976). Her other works include *Palabras de mediodía/Noon Words* (1980) and *Delia's Song* (1988).

Correggio

né: Antonio Allegri
b. c. 1489
Correggio, Duchy of Modena
d. c. March 5, 1534
Correggio, Duchy of Modena
fields: Art

Correggio executed frescoes and paintings of religious and mythological subjects that demonstrate his skills as one of the greatest masters of the High Renaissance. Correggio's innovations in composition, expressiveness, and particularly in the illusionistic foreshortening of figures seen from below (*di sotto in su*) were to have a tremendous influence on later Baroque painters.

Cortázar, Julio

b. Aug. 26, 1914
Brussels, Belgium
d. Feb. 12, 1984
Paris, France
fields: Literature

Writer. Julio Cortázar was reared and educated in Argentina, but he spent much of his life in France. His poetry, short stories, and novels have been praised for their humor, interplay between realistic and fantastic elements, and social activism, and experimental styles. He first earned international acclaim with *Rayuela* (1963), translated into English as *Hopscotch* (1966). His other works include *Libro de Manuel* (1973; *A Manual for Manuel*, 1978), *Alguien que anda por ahi y otros relatos* (1977; *A Change of Light, and Other Stories*, 1980), *Un tal Lucas* (1979; *A Certain Lucas*, 1984), and *Queremos tanto a Glenda* (1980; *We Love Glenda So Much, and Other Tales*, 1983).

Cortés, Ernie

full: Ernesto Cortés, Jr.
b. 1943
San Antonio, Tex.
fields: Labor Movement

Labor organizer. Ernie Cortés used his understanding of union organizing and Roman Catholic theology to assist the poor of Texas. He helped found Communities Organized for Public Service in San Antonio in the 1970's. He became a director of the Industrial Areas Foundation, a politically liberal but socially conservative Catholic group, in 1971. He supervised foundation groups in San Antonio, Houston, and El Paso, employing "liberation theology" in the struggles of immigrant groups. In 1989, he was awarded a John D. and Catherine T. MacArthur Foundation Fellowship.

Cortés, Hernán

b. 1485
Medellín, Extremadura, Spain
d. December 2, 1547
Castilleja de la Cuesta, near Seville, Spain
fields: Exploration and Colonization, Military Affairs

Cortés skillfully led a small band of Spaniards and numerous Indian allies to the heart of the Aztec capital of Tenochtitlán (later Mexico City), and within two years he boldly conquered the powerful Aztec Empire. His most lasting contribution has been to western exploration and conquest of the New World.

Cortez, Gregorio

b. June 22, 1875
Tamaulipas, Mexico
d. 1916
Austin, Tex.
fields: Social Reform

Folk hero. Gregorio Cortez was a Texas farmer and Mexican immigrant to the United States. On June 12, 1901, Karnes County sheriff W. T. Morris attempted to arrest Cortez on charge of horse-theft, but errors made by a translator prompted Cortez to shoot the sheriff. He then embarked on a ten-day, five-hundred-mile journey to Laredo, eluding his pursuers and killing a member of the posse chasing him. He was captured by Texas Rangers and was convicted of murdering the posse member but acquitted of murdering the sheriff. In 1913, the governor of Texas pardoned Cortez, and he later fought in the Mexican Revolution. His exploits have been immortalized in countless folk tales and poems known as *corridos*.

Cortez, Jayne

b. May 10, 1936
Ariz.
fields: Literature, Theater and Entertainment (poet and performer)

African American poet and performer. Jayne Cortez's written work is also available on recordings. Following literature's oral tradition, her poetry is intended to be read aloud. Her works have been publilshed through her own Bola Press to ensure artistic control.

Cortéz, Ricardo

né: Jacob Kranze
or né: Jacob Krantz
b. Sept. 19, 1899
Vienna, Austria
d. Apr. 28, 1977
New York, N.Y.
fields: Theater and Entertainment

Actor. Ricardo Cortéz was born to a Jewish family of Austrian and Hungarian descent, but he immigrated to the United States as a young man and went to Hollywood. With his dark good looks, he was considered a classical "Latin lover"; he adopted the name Ricardo Cortéz and went on to make dozens of films, including *Sixty Cents an Hour* (1923), *Pony Express* (1924), *The Torrent* (1926), *The Sorrows of Satan* (1927), *The Maltese Falcon* (1931), *Melody of Life* (1932), *Talk of the Devil* (1936), *Mr. Moto's Last Warning* (1938), *Masquerade in Mexico* (1945), *Blackmail* (1947), and *The Last Hurrah* (1958). He also directed several features, including *City Girl* (1938) and *Free, Blonde, and Twenty-one* (1940).

Cortina, Juan

b. May 16, 1824
Camargo, Tamaulipas, Mexico
d. 1892
Atzcapotzalco, Mexico
fields: Military Affairs, Warfare and Conquest

Revolutionary. The son of a prominent Mexican landowner, Juan Cortina moved to Texas in the early 1840's. In 1859, he shot a deputy who had arrested a former servant of his family. Cortina then fled and organized an armed force that occupied Brownsville, Texas. He and his men were the scourge of the Lower Rio Grande Valley between 1859 and 1873. In 1875, he was arrested by the Mexican government on rustling charges; he was rearrested a year later and sent to Mexico City. He was not allowed to return to the border area until 1890.

Cortor, Eldzier

b. Jan. 10, 1916
Richmond, Va.
fields: Art (painting)

African American painter, educator, printmaker, and poet; Eldzier Cortor's most famous works are surrealistic paintings of elongated figures of introspective, isolated black women.

Cosby, Bill

full: William Henry Cosby, Jr.
b. July 12, 1937
Germantown, Pa.
fields: Theater and entertainment

African American actor, comedian; Bill Cosby, by the mid-1960's, was playing top nightclubs with his comedy routine and regularly appearing on television; became first African American star of prime time television with three-time Emmy-winning role in *I Spy* (1965-1968); won fourth Emmy for *Bill Cosby Special* (1969); throughout the 1970's appeared in films and television series and in Las Vegas, Reno, and Tahoe nightclubs; *The Cosby Show* (1985-1992) presented upper-middle-class black family life to mainstream American audiences; earned nine Grammy Awards; wrote several books, including *Fatherhood* (1986) and *Time Flies* (1987).

Cose, Ellis Jonathan

b. February 20, 1951
Chicago, Ill.
fields: Journalism (journalist and cultural critic)

African American journalist and cultural critic; Ellis Jonathan Cose published *The Press* (1989), *A Nation of Strangers: Prejudice, Politics, and the Populating of America* (1992), *The Rage of a Privileged Class* (1993), and *A Man's World: How Real Is Male Privilege—And How High Is Its Price?* (1995).

Cosgrave, William T.

full: William Thomas Cosgrave
b. June 6, 1880
Dublin, Ireland
d. November 16, 1965
Dublin, Ireland
fields: Government and Politics

At a crucial period in Irish history Cosgrave's even-handed administration of the Irish Free State government achieved victory in a civil war, while preserving democratic institutions and making possible the future achievements of the Republic of Eire.

Cotera, Martha P.

b. Jan. 17, 1938
Nuevo Casas Grandes, Chihuahua, Mexico
fields: Education, Literature, Scholarship

Writer and librarian. Martha Cotera's extensive body of work provides resource and research materials for Mexican American students and scholars. Most of her writings are informational or bibliographic, but she has also written essays on Hispanic women's roles and struggles. Her works include *The Chicana Feminist* (1977), *Bridging Two Cultures* (1980), *Latina Sourcebook* (1982), *Checklists for Counteracting Race and Sex Bias in Educational Materials* (1982), *Everyone's Guide to Sources on Hispanic Women* (1983), and *Doña Doormat No Está Aquí: Assertion and Communication Techniques for Hispanic Women* (1982).

Cotter, Joseph Seamon, Sr.

b. Feb. 2, 1861
Nelson County, Ky.
d. Mar. 14, 1949
Louisville, Ky.
fields: Literature

African American writer; Joseph Seamon Cotter, Sr., wrote poetry, fiction, drama, tales, short plays, and prose.

Cotter, Joseph Seamon, Jr.

b. Sept. 2, 1895
Louisville, Ky.
d. Feb. 3, 1919
Louisville, Ky.
fields: Literature

African American poet; Joseph Seamon Cotter, Jr., was first inspired to write poetry by the death of his sister from tuberculosis; published collection, *The Band of Gideon, and Other Lyrics* (1918), before dying from tuberculosis himself.

Cotto-Thorner, Guillermo

b. 1916
Juncos, Puerto Rico
fields: Literature, Religion and Theology

Novelist and clergyman. Guillermo Cotto-Thorner was a Baptist minister who wrote in Spanish. His works include a collection of his sermons titled *Camino de victoria* (1945; victory road); his best-known work, the novel *Trópico en Manhattan* (1951; Manhattan tropical), a novel published in Puerto Rico; and another novel, *Gambeta* (1971).

Cotton, John

b. December 4, 1584
Derby, England
d. December 23, 1652
Boston, Massachusetts
fields: Religion and Theology

One of the foremost clergymen who defined the religious practices of early New England, Cotton was one of the architects of Congregationalism.

Coubertin, Pierre de

aka: Pierre, baron de Coubertin
b. January 1, 1863
Paris, France
d. September 2, 1937
Geneva, Switzerland
fields: Sports, Diplomacy

Coubertin was the driving force behind the revival of the Olympic Games on an international scale. Through his efforts, the International Olympic Committee (IOC) was established in 1894, and the first modern international Olympics were held in Athens in 1896; he also oversaw the difficult formative years of the Games until they reached maturity and success.

Coughlin, Father Charles

full: Father Charles Edward Coughlin
b. October 25, 1891
Hamilton, Ontario, Canada
b. October 27, 1979
Bloomfield Hills, Michigan
fields: Religion and Theology, Radio, Social Reform

A Roman Catholic priest and radio broadcaster during the 1930's; Father Charles Coughlin initially advocated a social program that included living wages, private property takings for the common good, labor organization, and the primacy of human rights over property rights to counter the effects of the Great Depression; his CBS program "Golden Hour of the Little Flower" had as many as thirty million listeners; after his outspokenness cost him his program, Coughlin formed his own network; in the 1940's his message became increasingly anticommunist and anti-Semitic until he was again forced off the air.

Coulomb, Charles-Augustin

b. June 14, 1736
Angoulême, France
d. Aug. 23, 1806
Paris, France
fields: Physics

Charles-Augustin Coulomb examined the strength of materials; made major advances in friction, torsion, electricity, and magnetism. Coulomb's law, which allows the calculation of force between charges, and the coulomb, the unit of charge, are named for him.

Couperin, François

b. November 10, 1668
Paris, France
d. September 11, 1733
Paris, France
fields: Music

Couperin was the chief representative of French musical classicism in the waning years of the reign of Louis XIV and the regency which followed.

Courbet, Gustave

b. June 10, 1819
Ornans, France
d. December 31, 1877
La Tour-de-Peilz, Switzerland
fields: Art

Courbet contributed to the formation of modern art by liberating subject matter and style from academic dogma. The most profound aspects of his contribution are the influences his works have had upon the subsequent analysis of realism.

Couric, Katie

full: Katherine Anne Couric
b. January 7, 1957
Arlington, Virginia
fields: Journalism

An award-winning television journalist, Couric has made notable contributions to reporting and producing the news of issues, events, and figures at both national and international levels.

Cousteau, Jacques

full: Jacques-Yves Cousteau
b. June 11, 1910
Saint-André-de-Cubzac, France
d. June 25, 1997
Paris, France
fields: Biology, Zoology, Engineering

Cousteau is the father of underwater exploration, having coinvented (with Émile Gagnon) the self-contained underwater breathing apparatus (SCUBA) in 1943. Cousteau has shared his explorations of the underwater world with millions of people around the world through his films, books, and television productions. Cousteau has also directed the engineering of several underwater living structures and systems as well as the design of an oceangoing vessel using a rigid turbosail for propulsion.

Coverdale, Miles

b. c. 1488
York, Yorkshire, England
d. January 20, 1568
London, England
fields: Religion and Theology

The first translator of the complete and official Bible into English, Coverdale in the late Elizabethan era provided a link between the English Reformation and the first English Puritans.

Covilhã, Pêro da

b. c. 1447
Covilhã, Beira, Portugal
d. After 1526
Abyssinia (modern Ethiopia)
fields: Exploration and Colonization, Geography, Diplomacy

Covilhã was the first Portuguese to visit India, one of the first Europeans to travel extensively in Arabia, the first to visit Sofala in southern Mozambique, and an unwilling resident of Abyssinia for at least thirty-three years. His report on his travels in India, Arabia, and along the coasts of India, Arabia, the Red Sea, and East Africa may have aided and influenced the course of Portuguese penetration of India and East Africa, and his residence in Abyssinia was critical in the opening of diplomatic relations between its emperor and Portugal.

Coward, Noël

full: Noël Peirce Coward
b. December 16, 1899
Teddington, Middlesex, England
d. March 26, 1973
Blue Harbour, Jamaica
fields: Theater and Entertainment, Film, Music

Personifying the essence of sophistication, wit, and style, Coward was one of the most productive and versatile artists in the history of show business as a playwright, composer, actor, singer, and director.

Cowings, Patricia Suzanne

b. December 15, 1948
New York, N.Y.
fields: Psychiatry and Psychology (psychologist and biofeedback researcher)

African American psychologist and biofeedback researcher. Patricia Suzanne Cowings, employed by the National Aeronautics and Space Administration (NASA) since 1977, conducted studies that were focused on aerospace medicine and bioastronautics. Her work was the focus of specific experiments conducted on the space shuttle *Endeavour*'s mission in September of 1992.

Cowlings, Al

b. June 17, 1947
San Francisco, Calif.
fields: Sports (football player)

African American football player. Al Cowlings played defensive end for several professional football teams before retiring in 1979. He gained national attention in 1994 through his involvement with accused murderer O. J. Simpson.

Cox, Allan V.

full: Allan Verne Cox
b. Dec. 17, 1926
Santa Ana, California
d. Jan. 27, 1987
Woodside, California
fields: Science

Geophysicist Allan V. Cox's work in paleomagnetism provided evidence for the many reversals that have occurred in the earth's magnetic field; this phenomenon was later used in the development of the theory of plate tectonics and crustal movement.

Cox, Gertrude Mary

b. Jan. 13, 1900
Dayton, Iowa
d. Oct. 17, 1978
Durham, North Carolina
fields: Mathematics (statistics)

Gertrude Mary Cox was a pioneer statistician. She earned Iowa State College's first M.S. in statistics and was director of the Institute of Statistics from 1945 to 1960. She was made president of the American Statistical Association in 1956. Cox organized information about experimental design principles, mainly for agricultural and biological research.

Cox, Ida

né: Ida Prather
b. Feb. 25, 1896
Toccoa, Ga.
d. Nov. 10, 1967
Knoxville, Tenn.
fields: Music (blues)

African American blues singer; Ida Cox reached the peak of her career in the 1920's with somber blues songs such as "Black Crepe Blues," and "Coffin Blues"; also recorded under the names Jula Powers, Velma Bradley, and Kate Lewis.

Cram, Donald J.

full: Donald James Cram
b. Apr. 22, 1919
Chester, Vermont
fields: Chemistry

Donald J. Cram demonstrated the retention of three-dimensional molecular form in a wide variety of substitution and elimination reactions; concentrated on host-guest chemistry, in which one molecule holds another in a position that leads to a very specific reaction. In 1960, he published *Organic Chemistry*, an influential textbook arranged by reaction mechanism. In 1987, he was awarded the Nobel Prize in Chemistry.

Cramer, Gabriel
b. July 31, 1704
Geneva, Switzerland
d. Jan. 4, 1752
traveling in Bagnols-sur-Cèze, France
fields: Mathematics (algebra)

Gabriel Cramer discovered a simple method, now known as Cramer's rule, for solving a number of equations in the same number of unknowns. In 1750, he published his only book, *Introduction à l'analyse des lignes courbes algébriques* (introduction to the analysis of algebraic curves).

Cranach, Lucas, the Elder
né: Lucas Müller
b. 1472
Kronach, Upper Franconia
d. October 16, 1553
Weimar, Saxony
fields: Art

Cranach established an individual decorative style of paintings, drawings, and prints during his fifty-year career at the court of Wittenberg. A personal friend of Martin Luther, Cranach was one of the first German artists to incorporate elements of early Reformation theology into his pictures. His numerous examples of mythological subjects and portraits can be related to Humanist scholars at the University of Wittenberg and to erudite tastes of the Saxon court.

Crandall, Prudence
b. September 3, 1803
Hopkinton, Rhode Island
d. January 28, 1890
Elk Falls, Kansas
fields: Education, Social Reform, Women's Rights

A Quaker who became devoted to a range of social reforms, Crandall dedicated her life to education, especially for black females, and also to women's suffrage.

Crane. *See* Tarhe

Crane, Hart
full: Harold Hart Crane
b. July 21, 1899
Garrettsville, Ohio
d. April 27, 1932
Gulf of Mexico
fields: Literature

As a visionary artist with an intense, challenging literary style, Crane was the creator of a unique poetic idiom that expressed a personal view of the cultural conditions that fascinated him during the time when the United States was emerging as a technologically advanced world power.

Crane, Stephen
b. November 1, 1871
Newark, New Jersey
d. June 5, 1900
Badenweiler, Germany
fields: Literature

Crane is best remembered for his war novel, *The Red Badge of Courage* (1895); he also wrote estimable poetry and more than a dozen other novels and collections of stories.

Cranmer, Thomas
b. July 2, 1489
Aslacton, Nottinghamshire, England
d. March 21, 1556
Oxford, England
fields: Religion and Theology

Cranmer presided, along with Henry VIII and Thomas Cromwell, Henry's vicegerent in spiritual affairs, over the creation of the Anglican Church in England and separation from the Church of Rome. Cranmer was responsible for giving an English Bible to the English, drafting a new English service via the Book of Common Prayer (1549, 1552), and sealing England's commitment to a Protestant form of worship by his death under Henry's daughter Mary.

Crashing Thunder
aka: Sam Blowsnake
aka: Big Winnebago
aka: Hágaga
b. c. 1865
d. ?
fields: Anthropology

Native American autobiographer. A Winnebago, Crashing Thunder wrote an autobiography filled with cultural information, personal detail, and psychological revelation. His life story—elicited, translated, and published as *Crashing Thunder: The Autobiography of an American Indian*, 1926 by ethnologist Paul Radin— reveals the day-to-day lives and the fundamental beliefs of the Winnebago.

Craven, Martha. *See* Nussbaum, Martha Craven

Crawford, Cheryl
b. September 24, 1902
Akron, Ohio
d. October 7, 1986
New York, New York
fields: Theater and Entertainment (drama)

A prizewinning producer and director with unequaled influence in American theater for more than fifty years, Crawford served as casting director for the Theatre Guild early in her career before going on to help found the Group Theatre, the Actors Studio, and the American Repertory Theatre.

Crawford, Randy
b. 1952
Macon, Ga.
fields: Music (vocalist)

African American singer; Randy Crawford released several albums, including *Miss Randy Crawford*, and *Now We May Begin* (which contained her first solo hit, "One Day I'll Fly Away").

Crawford-Seeger, Ruth
né: Ruth Porter Crawford
b. July 3, 1901
East Liverpool, Ohio
d. November 18, 1953
Chevy Chase, Maryland
fields: Music

A pioneer among innovative twentieth century classical composers, Ruth Crawford-Seeger was active in avant-garde musical circles in the 1920's and 1930's. Later, her scholarly research in the area of American folk music resulted in transcriptions of more than 300 works from the Library of Congress Archives.

Cray, Robert
b. Aug. 1, 1953
Columbus, Ga.
fields: Music (rhythm and blues)

African American musician; Robert Cray emerged in the mid-1980's as an innovative force and an influential artist in rhythm and blues and electric blues; won several Grammys and W. C. Handys.

Crazy Bear. *See* Porter, Pleasant

Crazy Horse
né: Tashunca-uitko
b. 1842?
Black Hills of South Dakota
d. September 5, 1877
Fort Robinson, Nebraska
fields: Native American Affairs

Crazy Horse, the greatest of the Sioux chiefs, led his people in a valiant but futile struggle against domination by the white man and white culture. He fought to the last to hold his native land for the Indian people.

Crazy Snake
aka: Chitto Harjo
aka: Wilson Jones
b. 1846
near Boley, Okla.
d. April 11, 1912
near Smithville, Okla.
fields: Government and Politics, Native American Affairs

Native American leader. Leader of the traditionalist faction of the Creek Nation, Crazy Snake led an unsuccessful Oklahoma uprising to prevent the allotment of tribal lands in 1901. He and his followers attacked Indians who had accepted allotments, as well as white settlers.

Crazy War Hunter. *See* Menewa

Cream, Arnold Raymond. *See* Walcott, Jersey Joe

Creek Mary. *See* Musgrove, Mary

Creel, George

b. December 1, 1876
Lafayette County, Missouri
d. October 2, 1953
San Francisco, California
fields: Journalism, Warfare and Conquest

As head of the U.S. government's Committee on Public Information, George Creel was the leading American propagandist during World War I. He had begun his career as a muckraking journalist and became noted as a noted pioneer of modern public relations before the war began. His best-known book is *How We Advertised America: The First Telling of the Amazing Story of the Committee on Public Information that Carried the Gospel of Americanism to Every Corner of the Globe* (1920).

Cremer, William Randal

b. March 18, 1838
Fareham, Wiltshire, England
d. July 22, 1908
London, England
fields: Diplomacy, Peace Advocacy

A British union activist and peace advocate, William Randal Cremer was winner of the 1903 Nobel Peace Prize. Cremer and Frédéric Passy cofounded the Interparliamentary Union, an international organization to promoted peace through arbitration, in 1889.

Crichlow, Ernest

b. 1914
New York, N.Y.
fields: Art (painting)

African American painter and illustrator; Ernest Crichlow's paintings portray the joys and fears of childhood, adolescence, and motherhood.

Crick, Francis

full: Francis Harry Compton Crick
b. June 8, 1916
Northampton, Northamptonshire, England
fields: Genetics, Biology (molecular)

Francis Crick discovered the structure of deoxyribonucleic acid (DNA), theorized on the sequence hypothesis and mechanism of protein synthesis, and laid the foundation for modern genetics and molecular biology. He won the 1962 Nobel Prize in Physiology or Medicine.

Crim, Alonzo

b. Oct. 1, 1928
Chicago, Ill.
fields: Education

African American educator and educational administrator; Alonzo Crim was the head of the Compton School District (California) between 1970 and 1973; superintendent of Atlanta (Georgia) public schools, where he implemented controversial busing program.

Crite, Allan Rohan

b. Mar. 20, 1910
Plainfield, N.J.
fields: Art (painting)

African American painter and illustrator; Allan Rohan Crite specialized in liturgical art; recorded African American social events during the 1930's.

Croce, Benedetto

b. February 25, 1866
Pescassèroli, Italy
d. November 20, 1952
Naples, Italy
fields: Philosophy, Historiography, Government and Politics

Croce was modern Italy's premier philosopher. His extensive writing on philosophy, history, aesthetics, and literary criticism represents a major contribution to European culture. For his reserved but firm opposition to Benito Mussolini's regime, Croce became recognized worldwide as an anti-Fascist symbol and as the intellectual guardian of Italy's democratic political heritage.

Crocker, Charles

b. Sept. 16, 1822
Troy, N.Y.
d. Aug. 14, 1888
Monterey, Calif.
fields: Banking and Finance, Technology

Railroad magnate and financier Charles Crocker left school at age twelve and bought the agency for a New York newspaper with borrowed funds, selling it at a profit two years later. He went to California in 1849 and became a successful Sacramento merchant. Crocker was one of the founders of the Central Pacific Railroad in the early 1860's. As supervisor on the transcontinental railroad, which was completed in 1869, he brought in large numbers of Chinese immigrants, believing that they were more dependable, productive, and cheaper than white workers.

Crockett, David

b. August 17, 1786
Greene County, Tennessee
d. March 6, 1836
the Alamo, San Antonio, Texas
fields: Exploration and Colonization, Government and Politics, Literature, Military Affairs

Crockett, a congressman from western Tennessee and the author of a best-selling autobiography, became the most celebrated backwoodsman in the United States. His death at the battle of the Alamo turned him into one of America's legendary frontier heroes.

Crockett, George William, Jr.

b. Aug. 10, 1909
Jacksonville, Fla.
d. Sept. 7, 1997
Washington, D.C.
fields: Government and Politics

African American U.S. representative from Michigan. George William Crockett, Jr., was a fair employment labor advocate serving in a number of government positions; won the Michigan house seat of Charles Diggs in 1980 and held it until 1990.

Cromartie, Eugene Rufus

b. Oct. 3, 1936
Wabasso, Fla.
fields: Military Affairs

African American military officer; Eugene Rufus Cromartie served as deputy provost marshal of the U.S. Army in Europe.

Cromwell, Oliver

b. April 25, 1599
Huntingdon, Huntingdonshire, England
d. September 3, 1658
London, England
fields: Government and Politics, Military Affairs

Cromwell was the dominant figure in the Puritan Revolution of 1640-1660, first as a military commander, then as an advocate of the trial and execution of Charles I in 1649, and finally as a political leader trying unsuccessfully to find the formula for a permanent settlement.

Cromwell, Oliver

b. May 24, 1753
Black Horse, N.J.
d. Jan. 24, 1853
Columbus, N.J.
fields: Warfare and Conquest

African American Revolutionary War soldier; Oliver Cromwell crossed the Delaware with George Washington; participated in several major battles in the war.

Cromwell, Thomas

b. 1485?
Putney, England

d. July 28, 1540
London, England
fields: Government and Politics

During the 1530's, one of the most crucial and turbulent decades in English history, the chief minister of Henry VIII was Thomas Cromwell, who helped bring about the king's marriage to Anne Boleyn, the separation of the Church of England from Rome, the dissolution of the monasteries, and the establishment of Protestantism in England.

Cronkite, Walter

full: Walter Leland Cronkite, Jr.
b. November 4, 1916
St. Joseph, Missouri
fields: Journalism, Television

One of the nation's most prominent, respected, and trusted broadcast journalists, Walter Cronkite was a leader in bringing television news into the mainstream of American life. Beginning as a newspaper reporter with United Press (UP) in 1937, he covered World War II from 1942 to 1945 and the subsequent Nuremberg Trials; served as UP's chief correspondent in Moscow (1946-1948), became a Washington, D.C., bureau head for a group of midwestern radio stations (1949), and joined the Columbia Broadcasting System (CBS) as a television news correspondent (1950). In 1962, he became news anchor of *The CBS Evening News*, rising to superstar status as a broadcast journalist and one of the most trusted individuals. In 1981, he ended his career as a news anchor to become a CBS special correspondent. He also hosted cultural and public affairs programs and produced television documentaries for syndication. Setting the standards by which others in television news were judged, he grew to have major influence on public opinion.

Cross, Theodore L.

b. Feb. 12, 1924
Newton, Mass.
fields: Law

African American lawyer; Theodore L. Cross is the author of *Black Capitalism: Strategy for Business in the Ghetto* (1969) and *The Black Power Imperative: Racial Inequality and the Politics of Nonviolence* (1984).

Crosse, Rupert

b. 1928
Nevis, British West Indies
d. Mar. 5, 1973
Nevis, British West Indies
fields: Television, Theater and Entertainment

African American stage, television, and film actor; Rupert Crosse starred in such films as The Reivers (1970), *Too Late Blues* (1961), *Shadows* (1961), and *Ride in the Whirlwind* (1965).

Crosthwait, David Nelson, Jr.

b. May 27, 1898
Nashville, Tenn.
d. Feb. 25, 1976
Michigan City, Ind.
fields: Invention and Technology

African American inventor; David Nelson Crosthwait, Jr., invented such things as the automatic water feeder (Sept. 21, 1920), a thermostat-setting apparatus (Dec. 4, 1928), and the vacuum pump (Apr. 22, 1930).

Crothers, Rachel

b. December 12, 1870
Bloomington, Illinois
d. July 5, 1958
Danbury, Connecticut
fields: Theater and Entertainment (drama)

A prolific and successful playwright and director for more than thirty years, Crothers often focused on the lives of women who faced dilemmas posed by changing sex role expectations.

Crothers, Scatman

full: Benjamin Sherman Crothers
b. May 23, 1910
Terre Haute, Ind.
d. Nov. 22, 1986
Los Angeles, Calif.
fields: Theater and Entertainment

African American actor; Scatman Crothers played with a band that broke the midwestern color barrier in 1930's nightclubs; remembered best as Louie the garbage man on the television show *Chico and the Man* (1974-1978); appeared in a number of films, including *One Flew Over the Cuckoo's Nest* (1975) and *The Shining* (1980).

Crouch, Andrae

b. July 1, 1942
Pacoima, Calif.
fields: Music (gospel)

African American gospel singer, songwriter, record producer, and arranger; Andrae Crouch has sold millions of albums and is internationally popular with Christian music fans; received numerous Grammy Awards and several Dove Awards.

Crow Dog

aka: Kangi Sunka
b. c. 1835
d. 1920
Pine Ridge Reservation, S.Dak.
fields: Warfare and Conquest, Native American Affairs

Brule Sioux war chief Crow Dog was an important figure in the Ghost Dance phenomenon of 1890. He vociferously opposed army occupation of South Dakota Indian reservations and was one of the last holdouts after the massacre at Wounded Knee during December of 1890. Crow Dog had earlier been convicted of murder in a Dakota Territory court, but he was freed on order of the U.S. Supreme Court when it ruled that the territorial government had no jurisdiction over the crime (*Ex parte Crow Dog*, 1883).

Crowder, Jack. *See* Rasulala, Thalmus

Crowdy, William S.

b. ?
d. 1908
fields: Religion

African American clergyman; William S. Crowdy founded the Church of God and Saints of Christ in 1896.

Crowfoot

aka: Isapo-Muxika
aka: Astoxkomi (Shot Close)
b. c. 1830
present-day Calgary, Alberta, Canada
d. April 25, 1890
Canada
fields: Government and Politics, Native American Affairs

Blackfoot tribal leader Crowfoot was a skillful chief who led his people through the difficult twenty-year transition from nomadic freedom to reservation life. Signed a treaty in 1877 giving reservation lands to the Blackfeet Confederacy and ceding some 50,000 acres to whites.

Crowfoot, Dorothy Mary. *See* Hodgkin, Dorothy Crowfoot

Crudup, Big Boy

full: Arthur Crudup
b. 1896?
Forest, Miss.
d. Mar. 28, 1974
Nassawadox, Va.
fields: Music (blues, rock and roll)

African American musician; Big Boy Crudup is widely considered to be the father of rock and roll; guitarist and a prolific songwriter; frequently covered, his "That's All Right" (1946) was Elvis Presley's first big hit.

Crumb, Robert

b. August 30, 1943
Philadelphia, Pennsylvania
fields: Art

Robert Crumb is an American graphic novelist whose work has been attacked as pornographic and obscene. A pioneer in the "underground comics" field, he has written for such publications as *Zap Comix* and *Snatch*, and he was the creator of Felix the Cat.

Crummell, Alexander

b. Mar. 3, 1819
New York, N.Y.
d. Sept. 9, 1898
Point Pleasant, N.J.
fields: Education, Social Reform, Religion and Theology, Literature

African American christian minister, teacher, author; Alexander Crummell was a pioneer and proponent of Pan-African thought and black nationalism; instrumental in establishing a tradition of African American scholarship; after earning a degree at Queens College, Cambridge, in England, served as professor of mental and moral science at the College of Liberia, 1853-1873; was minister of St. Luke's Protestant Episcopal Church, 1876-1898; helped found the American Negro Academy in 1897; published many books, including *Future of Africa* (1862) and *Africa and America* (1891), and *Civilization, the Primal Need of the Race* (1898).

Crumpler, Rebecca Lee

b. 1858?
fields: Medicine

African American physician; Rebecca Lee Crumpler was possibly the first African American woman to practice medicine as a physician in the United States.

Cruz, Celia

b. October 21, 1924
Havana, Cuba
fields: Music

Cuban American singer; Celia Cruz toured the Americas as a soloist with La Sonora Matancera orchestra throughout the 1950's; in 1960, following the Cuban revolution, Cruz and her band emigrated to Mexico, moving again in 1961 to the United States; after recording more than thirty albums during the 1960's, she became known as the "Queen of Salsa" for her salsa music, which incorporated sacred songs from the Caribbean; in 1978 named *Billboard*'s Best Female Vocalist; inducted into *Billboard*'s Latin Music Hall of Fame in 1994.

Cruz, Emilio

b. Mar. 15, 1938
New York, N.Y.
fields: Art (paintings)

African American artist and poet; Emilio Cruz's paintings, such as *Silver Umbrella*, reflect imagination and fantasy.

Cruz, Sor Juana Inés de la

né: Juana Inés de Asbaje y Ramírez de Santillana
aka: Sor Juana
b. November, 1648
San Miguel Nepantla, Mexico
d. April 17, 1695
Mexico City
fields: Literature

Sor Juana is an outstanding poet of Mexico's colonial period. She is recognized as a key figure in Latin American literature and has the stature of an important Spanish poet of the seventeenth century.

Cruz, Nicky

b. Aug. 6, 1954
San Francisco, Calif.
fields: Literature, Religion and Theology

Novelist. Puerto Rican immigrant Nicky Cruz rose to fame for his accounts of his descent into gang violence and his subsequent religious conversion. His first book, *Run, Baby, Run* (1968), written with Jaime Buckingham, depicts Cruz's youth on the streets of New York City; the book's popularity led to the film adaptation *The Cross and the Switchblade* (1970). His other books include *The Lonely Now* (1971), a collection of experiences of runaways, and *Satan on the Loose* (1973), an examination of the devil and demonology.

Cruz, Victor Hernández

b. Feb. 6, 1949
Aguas Buenas, Puerto Rico
fields: Literature

Poet. As a child, Puerto Rican-born Victor Hernandez Cruz moved with his family to the Harlem section of New York City. He produced several collections of poems and served as editor of *Umbra* in the 1960's and 1970's. In 1983, he moved to San Francisco. He has described his poetry as "Afro-Latin".

Cryor, Cary Beth

b. Nov. 19, 1947
Baltimore, Md.
fields: Film

African American photographer and film editor; Cary Beth Cryor worked as a film editor on the feature film *Claudine* (1974).

Ctesibius of Alexandria

b. fl. c. 270 B.C.E.
Alexandria, Egypt
d. Probably after 250 B.C.E.
Alexandria, Egypt
fields: Invention and Technology

One of the great mechanical geniuses and inventors of antiquity, Ctesibius was the father of pneumatics, the first to employ compressed air to run his devices. He is credited with a number of inventions, including a water pump, a water organ, a more precise water clock, and bronze spring and pneumatic catapults.

Cuba, Joe

né: José Calderón
b. 1931
New York, New York
fields: Music

Bandleader and conga drummer. Joe Cuba grew up in Spanish Harlem; he began his musical career with La Alfarona X in 1950. In 1954, he formed the Joe Cuba Sextet, which included piano player Nick Jimenez and voclaists Cheo Feliciano and Jimmy Sabater. The group's hits include "To Be with You," "El Pito," and "Bang Bang," the first *bugalú* song to sell a million copies.

Cueva, Julio José Iglesias de la. *See* Iglesias, Julio

Cuffee, Paul

aka: Paul Cuffe
b. January 17, 1759
Cuttyhunk Island, Mass.
d. September 9, 1817
Westport, Mass.
fields: Business and Industry, Exploration and Colonization, Philanthropy

African American navigator, businessman, philanthropist, and pan-African activist; by the early 1800's, Paul Cuffee had amassed great wealth running his own trading ships along the Atlantic coast of colonial America; Cuffee invested his wealth in various ways to support civil rights and education for blacks; he supported the colonization by black Americans of Sierra Leone in Africa, seeing this effort as a viable solution to their oppression and enslavement; he purchased a house in Freetown, Sierra Leone, to facilitate trade between Africa and America; in 1816, Cuffee personally ferried thirty-eight settlers to Sierra Leone on one of his ships; despite the fact that their arrival was coolly received by the British authorities and that heavy import fees were imposed on his cargo, Cuffee returned to the United States convinced that the plan could succeed; he died after several months of illness and before he could see his plan through.

Cugat, Xavier

full: Francisco de Asis Javier Cugat Mingall de Bru y Deulofeo
b. Jan. 1, 1900
Gerona, Spain
d. Oct. 27, 1990
Barcelona, Spain
fields: Music

Violinist, bandleader, and composer. Born in Spain, Xavier Cugat as a child moved with his family to Cuba, where at the age of twelve he became a violinist with Havana's National Theatre Symphony Orchestra. A prodigy, he studied in Germany, played with the Berlin Symphony Orchestra, and performed at Carnegie Hall in New York City. He later moved to Los Angeles, where he became a film star in the 1930's. In 1933, he became the bandleader at New York's Waldorf-Astoria Hotel, and he helped to popularize Latin rhythms in the United States. His recordings include the 1944 hit "Babalu."

Culbertson, Madame. *See* Natawista

Cullen, Countée

b. May 30, 1903
New York, N.Y.
d. Jan. 9, 1946
New York, N.Y.
fields: Literature

African American poet; Countée Cullen was an important poet of the Harlem Renaissance; works include his first book of poems, *Color* (1925), and *The Ballad of the Brown Girl: An Old Ballad Retold* (1927); best known poem is "Yet Do I Marvel."

Culp, Oveta. *See* Hobby, Oveta Culp

Cummings, E. E.

full: Edward Estlin Cummings
aka: e. e. cummings
b. October 14, 1894
Cambridge, Massachusetts
d. September 3, 1962
Conway, New Hampshire
fields: Literature

Through his unorthodox style of capitalization and punctuation and his innovative use of spacing, cummings helped transform the appearance of modern poetry.

Cummings, Michael A.

b. November 28, 1945
Los Angeles, Calif.
fields: Art (artist and quiltmaker)

African American artist and quiltmaker. Michael A. Cummings's quilts are constructed around themes that depict stories of African American life. His works are displayed in the permanent collections of prominent institutions such as the California Afro-American Museum in Los Angeles, the Atlanta Life Insurance Company, and the Studio Museum of Harlem.

Cunningham, Imogen

b. April 12, 1883
Portland, Oregon
d. June 23, 1976
San Francisco, California
fields: Photography

Cunningham demonstrated that an unqualified humanistic approach to using the camera could celebrate the individual subject as well as the art form.

Cunningham, Randall

b. Mar. 27, 1963
Santa Barbara, Calif.
fields: Sports (football)

African American football quarterback; Randall Cunningham played quarterback for the Philadelphia Eagles. After being out of football during 1996, he joined the Minnesota Vikings in 1997.

Curie, Irène. *See* Joliot-Curie, Irène

Curie, Marie

aka: Madame Curie
né: Marya Skłodowska
aka: Manya Skłodowska
b. November 7, 1867
Warsaw, Poland
d. July 4, 1934
Sancellemoz, near Sallanches, France
fields: Chemistry, Physics, Medicine

Marie and Pierre Curie made some of the most significant scientific advancements in the modern age with the discovery of radium and other radioactive elements. For this work, the Curies and scientist Henri Becquerel received the 1903 Nobel Prize in Physics. Marie alone would win the 1911 Nobel Prize in Chemistry, one of the only individuals ever to win two such awards.

Curie, Pierre

b. May 15, 1859
Paris, France
d. April 19, 1906
Paris, France
fields: Chemistry, Physics, Medicine

Marie and Pierre Curie made some of the most significant scientific advancements in the modern age with the discovery of radium and other radioactive elements. For this work, the Curies and scientist Henri Becquerel received the 1903 Nobel Prize in Physics. Marie alone would win the 1911 Nobel Prize in Chemistry, one of the only individuals ever to win two such awards.

Curly

aka: Ashishishe
b. c. 1859
along the Rosebud River, Mont.
d. May 22, 1923
fields: Warfare and Conquest, Military Affairs, Native American Affairs

A member of the Crow tribe, Curly served as scout for General George A. Custer at the Battle of the Little Bighorn (1876); after Custer's defeat, he escaped and reported the annihilation of Custer's army. (Other Crow scouts told somewhat different versions of the story.)

Curry, Jerry Ralph

b. Sept. 7, 1932
McKeesport, Pa.
fields: Military Affairs, Government and Politics

African American military officer and government official; Jerry Ralph Curry retired from the military in 1984 with the rank of major general; administrator for the National Highway Traffic Safety Administration.

Curtin, John

b. January 8, 1885
Creswick, Victoria, Australia
d. July 5, 1945
Canberra, Australia
fields: Government and Politics

Long a leader in the Australian Labor Party and a champion of social justice, Curtin served as Prime Minister of Australia from 1941 until his death, guiding the country through the darkest days of World War II and preparing it for peace.

Curtis, Austin Maurice, Sr.

b. Jan. 15, 1868
Raleigh, N.C.
d. 1939
Washington, D.C.
fields: Medicine

African American surgeon and hospital administrator; Austin Maurice Curtis, Sr., was the first African American to be appointed (1896) as a surgeon at the Cook County Hospital in Chicago.

Curtis, Benjamin Robbins

b. 1809
d. 1874
fields: Law

U.S. Supreme Court justice, 1851-1857; appointed by President Fillmore. Defense counsel for President Johnson during his impeachment trial. Significant opinions: *Cooley v. Board of Wardens of the Port of Philadelphia*, 53 U.S. 299 (1851); *Scott v. Sandford*, 60 U.S. 393 (1857) (dissenting opinion).

Curtis, Charles

b. Jan. 25, 1860
Topeka, Kans.
d. Feb. 8, 1936
Washington, D.C.

fields: Government and Politics, Native American Affairs

Native American politician. A Kansa, Charles Curtis was the first American of Indian descent to serve in the United States Senate (beginning in 1907) Senate majority leader from 1925 to 1929. Elected vice president of the United States in 1928, serving under President Herbert Hoover from 1929 to 1933. First American Indian to become vice president of the United States.

Curtis, Edward Sheriff

b. Feb. 19, 1868
Madison, Wis.
d. Oct. 19, 1952
Los Angeles, Calif.
fields: Native American Affairs, Art, Photography, Film

Edward Sheriff Curtis was a photographer and writer who documented the lives of American Indians—spanning thirty years, eighty tribes, and forty thousand photographs. Books: *The North American Indian* (1907-1911); *Indian Days of the Long Ago* (1914); *In the Land of the Head Hunters* (1915), a film re-creating the life of the American Indians on the Pacific Northwest coast.

Curzon, George Nathaniel

b. January 11, 1859
Kedleston Hall, Derbyshire, England
d. March 20, 1925
London, England
fields: Government and Politics

British political figure George Nathaniel Curzon was foreign secretary from 1919 to 1924. Previously served as viceroy of India (1898-1905) and in other capacities. A Conservative, in 1916 and 1917 Curzon was one of the members of the inner war cabinet responsible for shaping Britain's World War I policies.

Curzon, Lord

full: George Nathaniel Curzon, marquess Curzon of Kedleston
b. January 11, 1859
Kedleston Hall, Derbyshire, England
d. March 20, 1925
London, England
fields: Government and Politics

Curzon was Viceroy of India from 1898 to 1905 and foreign secretary from 1919 to 1924. He established reforms of the treatment of the Indian people, took an interest in India's cultural and artistic heritage, and in England played an important role in university and parliamentary reform.

Cushing, Caleb

b. January 17, 1800
Salisbury, Massachusetts
d. January 2, 1879
Newburyport, Massachusetts
fields: Diplomacy, Government and Politics, Law

Cushing enhanced the power and status of the attorney general's office through his legal opinions, writings on the historical development and function of that cabinet post, and recommendations for reform of the federal judiciary.

Cushing, Harvey Williams

b. April 8, 1869
Cleveland, Ohio
d. October 7, 1939
New Haven, Connecticut
fields: Medicine (neurosurgery), Physiology (neurophysiology)

Cushing was the founder of modern neurosurgical procedures, introducing into general medicine and surgery the determination of blood pressure and the continuous recording of vital signs during surgery. He made fundamental discoveries about the disorders of the pituitary gland and had a profound influence on the training of surgeons in the United States.

Cushing, Cardinal Richard James

b. August 24, 1895
Boston, Massachusetts
d. November 2, 1970
Boston, Massachusetts
fields: Religion and Theology

Cardinal Richard James Cushing was a Roman Catholic cleric who played a leading role in promoting censorship after World War II. He was archbishop of the Boston diocese from 1944 to 1970 and became a cardinal in 1958.

Cushing, William

b. 1732
d. 1810
fields: Law

U.S. Supreme Court justice, 1790-1810 (died while in office); appointed by President Washington. In more than twenty years of service, wrote only nineteen opinions. Significant opinion: *Ware v. Hylton*, 2 U.S. 282 (1796). Served as chief justice for one week, in 1796, before he decided to decline the office and remain as an associate justice.

Custer, George A.

full: George Armstrong Custer
b. December 5, 1839
New Rumley, Ohio
d. June 25, 1876
Little Big Horn River, Montana Territory
fields: Military Affairs

Although greatly obscured by the events surrounding his death at the Battle of the Little Big Horn, Custer's illustrious Civil War exploits made him one of the nation's most respected military figures and a national idol. After the war, his expeditions into the Yellowstone region and the Black Hills earned for him renown as an explorer and compiler of scientific information.

Custis, Martha Dandridge. *See* Washington, Martha

Cuvier, Georges

full: Georges Léopold Chrétien Frédéric Dagobert Cuvier
b. August 23, 1769
Montbéliard, Württemberg
d. May 13, 1832
Paris, France
fields: Biology

Cuvier was an anatomist who greatly extended the classification system of Linnaeus by dividing living organisms and the fossil record into phyla. He was also an antievolutionist, who adapted the theory that organic changes in the world were shaped by a series of catastrophes.

Cyrano de Bergerac

né: Savinien Cyrano
b. March 6, 1619
Paris, France
d. July 28, 1655
Paris, France
fields: Literature, Military Affairs

Although the real-life Cyrano de Bergerac was a gallant soldier, a fine swordsman, a playwright, and an author, he is best remembered as the hero of numerous romantic but unhistorical legends. Since the nineteenth century, many readers have known him only as the protagonist of a poetic drama by Edmond Rostand.

Cyrano, Savinien. *See* Cyrano de Bergerac

Cyril, Saint

né: Constantine
b. c. 827
Thessalonica, Greece
d. February 14, 869
Rome
fields: Religion and Theology, Linguistics

Through their spiritual commitment, blood brothers Cyril and Methodius expanded Christianity in central and eastern Europe and established the foundations of Slavic culture and literature with the development of the Glagolitic alphabet.

Cyrus the Great

b. c. 601-590 B.C.E.
Media (modern northern Iran)
d. c. 530 B.C.E.
Scythia (southern Russia)
fields: Warfare and Conquest, Government and Politics

Cyrus conquered Media and brought Persia into the arena of world leadership by defeating the Neo-Babylonians (Chaldeans) in Babylon (c. 539 B.C.E.). He created a Persian Empire—the Achaemenian dynastic empire—stretching from Turkey to India. His unusually beneficent treatment of conquered peoples was widely praised throughout the Ancient Near East as well as the later Greco-Roman world.

Czermanik, János Jozsef. *See* Kádár, János

Dabuda. *See* Datsolalee

Dagataga. *See* Watie, Stand

Daguerre, Jacques

b. November 18, 1787
Cormeilles, near Paris, France
d. July 10, 1851
Bry-sur-Marne, France
fields: Invention and Technology

Daguerre's greatest renown rests upon his contribution to the technology of photography. He achieved the earliest fixed-image photograph developed from a latent image. The process discovered by him produced a photograph on a polished iodized silver plate that was patented as the "daguerreotype."

Dahauson. *See* Dohasan

Dahl, Roald

b. September 13, 1916
Llandaff, Wales
d. November 23, 1990
Oxford, England
fields: Literature, Film

Roald Dahl was well known as a screenwriter and as an author of both adult and children's books. Some of his popular children's book, such as *The Witches* (1983), were attacked for their alleged vulgarity and cruelty. Others, such as *Charlie and the Chocolate Factory* (1964) and *The BFG* (1982), were attacked for promoting negative racial stereotypes. His *Revolting Rhymes* (1982) was one of the most frequently banned books in U.S. schools.

Dailey, Ulysses Grant

b. Aug. 3, 1885
Donaldsonville, La.
d. Apr. 22, 1961
Chicago, Ill.
fields: Medicine

African American surgeon; Ulysses Grant Dailey made significant advances in anatomy and surgery.

Daimler, Gottlieb

b. March 17, 1834
Schorndorf (near Stuttgart), Württemberg
d. March 6, 1900
Cannstatt, Germany
fields: Engineering, Invention and Technology

Daimler, as much as any one man, was the inventor of the first high-speed motor; because of his carburetion process and his development of light engine weight his motor became adaptable to driving both motor cars and aircraft.

Dalai Lama

né: Lhamo Dhondrub
aka: Tenzin Gyatso
b. July 6, 1935
Taktser, Amdo, Tibet
fields: Government and Politics, Religion and Theology

The Dalai Lama, the spiritual and temporal head of the traditional Buddhist community of Tibet, is also the winner of the 1989 Nobel Peace Prize. Since the 1950 invasion by China, Tibet has been under Chinese occupation; in 1959 he was forced to flee to India. His leadership of Tibet's government in exile has made him a symbol of religious and ethical opposition to oppression.

Dale, Henry Hallett

full: Sir Henry Hallett Dale
b. June 9, 1875
London, England
d. July 23, 1968
Cambridge, England
fields: Medicine, Physiology

Henry Hallett Dale explained how nerves communicate with nearby cells, including other nerves, by releasing specific chemicals. In 1936, he was awarded the Nobel Prize in Physiology or Medicine jointly with Otto Loewi.

Dalhousie, first marquess of

né: James Andrew Broun Ramsay
b. April 22, 1812
Dalhousie Castle, Midlothian, Scotland
d. December 19, 1860
Dalhousie Castle, Midlothian, Scotland
fields: Government and Politics

Dalhousie's greatest accomplishment was the creation of a communications system linking all of India.

Dalí, Salvador

b. May 11, 1904
Figueras, Spain
d. January 23, 1989
Figueras, Spain
fields: Art

During an active career that spanned more than six decades, Dalí emerged as the most popular and influential painter associated with the Surrealist movement. He became one of the towering figures of twentieth century art, noted not only for his painting but also for numerous other creative endeavors.

Dalrymple, Ian

b. August 26, 1903
Johannesburg, South Africa
d. April 28, 1989
London, England
fields: Film

Ian Dalrymple was a leading figure in British propaganda films during World War II. His prewar work included *Taxi for Two* (1929), *The Divorce of Lady X* (1938), *The Citadel* (1938), and *Pygmalion* (1938)—for whose screenplay he won an Academy Award. After the war began, he worked on such documentaries as *Target for Tonight* (1940), *London Can Take It* (1940), *Ordinary People* (1941), and *The Changing Face of Europe*. After the war he established the independent company Wessex Films. He also was an advisor to British Lion Films and chairman of the British Film Academy.

Dalton, John

b. September 6, 1766
Eaglesfield, Cumberland, England
d. July 27, 1844
Manchester, England
fields: Physics, Chemistry, Meteorology

Dalton was the founder of the modern atomic theory.

Daly, Mary

b. October 16, 1928
Schenectady, N.Y.
fields: Literature, Religion and Theology, Women's Rights

Mary Daly is known for her feminist writings, which challenge antiwoman sentiments in traditional religion, language, and other aspects of culture. Writings such as *Beyond God the Father* (1974) explore misogyny in religion. In such works as *Gyn/Ecology* (1978), and *Webster's First New Intergalactic Wickedary of the English Language* (1987), Daly focused on the need for a woman-identified, nonpatriarchal language women can use to describe female experience and wisdom.

Dalziel, Diana. *See* Vreeland, Diana

Dampier, William

b. August?, 1651
East Coker, Somerset, England
d. March, 1715
London, England
fields: Exploration and Colonization

Dampier was the most accomplished of sailor-scientists in the era between the great voyages of discovery of the Elizabethan period and the planned scientific expeditions of the mid-eighteenth century.

Dandolo, Enrico

b. 1108?
Venice
d. 1205
Constantinople
fields: Government and Politics

As Doge of Venice from 1193 to 1205, Enrico Dandolo presided over the Republic of Venice and founded its commercial, colonial, and maritime empire in the eastern Mediterranean Sea. He was the outstanding leader of the Fourth Crusade, 1201-1204, and played the key role in its diversion from the Holy Land to Constantinople.

Dandridge, Dorothy

b. Nov. 9, 1924
Cleveland, Ohio
d. Sept. 8, 1965
Los Angeles, Calif.
fields: Film

African American actress; Dorothy Dandridge was the first black actress to be presented to the American public as a sex symbol; her films include *Carmen Jones* (1954), *Island in the Sun* (1957), and *Porgy and Bess* (1959).

Dandridge, Robert L., Jr.

b. Nov. 15, 1947
Richmond, Va.
fields: Sports (basketball)

African American basketball player; Robert L. Dandridge, Jr., played forward for thirteen seasons with the Milwaukee Bucks and the Washington Bullets.

Daniel, Peter Vivian

b. 1784
d. 1860
fields: Law

U.S. Supreme Court justice, 1842-1860 (died while in office); appointed by President Van Buren. Consistent advocate of states' rights. Significant opinions: *Cooley v. Board of Wardens of the Port of Philadelphia*, 53 U.S. 299 (1851) (concurring opinion); *Scott v. Sandford*, 60 U.S. 393 (1857) (concurring opinion).

Daniels, Bebe

full: Virginia Daniels
b. Jan. 14, 1901
Dallas, Tex.
d. Mar. 16, 1971
London, England
fields: Theater and Entertainment, Film

Actress. The daughter of a Scottish theatrical manager and a Spanish actress, Bebe Daniels made her film debut at the age of seven in *The Common Enemy* (1910), and she soon began appearing in short comic films by Hal Roach. In 1919, she began working for Paramount; in 1931, she appeared in the first film adaptation of *The Maltese Falcon* opposite Ricardo Cortéz. Other film appearances include *Male and Female* (1919), *Why Change Your Wife?* (1920), *Unguarded Women* (1924), *Monsieur Beaucaire* (1924), *She's a Sheik* (1927), *Rio Rita* (1929), *Alias French Gertie* (1930), *Forty-second Street* (1933), *Counsellor at Law* (1933), *Hi Gang* (1941), *Life with the Lyons* (1953), and *The Lyons in Paris* (1955).

Daniels, Billy

né: William Boone
b. Sept. 12, 1915
Jacksonville, Fla.
d. Oct. 7, 1988
Los Angeles, Calif.
fields: Music (jazz)

African American vocalist; Billy Daniels sang with Erskine Hawkins and Cab Calloway; signature song was "That Old Black Magic."

Daniels, Jimmy

b. c. 1908
Laredo, Tex.
d. June 29, 1984
New York, N.Y.
fields: Music (jazz)

African American singer; Jimmy Daniels was proprietor of a Harlem supper club which featured his own singing.

Daniels, Randy

b. Nov. 30, 1949
Chicago, Ill.
fields: Television

African American television reporter; Randy Daniels became a correspondent for the Columbia Broadcasting System (CBS) in 1972.

Daniels, Roger

b. 1927
New York, N.Y.
fields: Historiography

Historian Roger Daniels received a doctoral degree in 1961 from the University of California, Los Angeles, and became a professor of history at the University of Cincinnati. Daniels became a leading scholar in the history of Asian Americans. His books include *The Politics of Prejudice: The Anti-Japanese Movement in California and the Struggle for Japanese Exclusion* (1962), *American Racism: Exploration of the Nature of Prejudice* (1970; coauthored with Harry H. L. Kitano), *Asian America: Chinese and Japanese in the United States Since 1850* (1988), and *Coming to America: A History of Immigration and Ethnicity in American Life* (1990). He helped make such historical films as *Refugee Road* (1982), *Nisei Soldier* (1984), and *Unfinished Business* (1986). Daniels worked as a consultant for the U.S. Commission on Wartime Relocation and Internment of Civilians during the early 1980's.

Daniels, Virginia. *See* Daniels, Bebe

Danielsen, Karen Clementina Theodora. *See* Horney, Karen

Danielsen, Karen Clementina Theodora. *See* Horney, Karen

Danilova, Alexandra

b. November 20, 1904
Peterhof, Russia
d. July 13, 1997
New York, New York
fields: Dance

An internationally acclaimed ballerina from the 1930's to the 1950's, Danilova carried on the traditions of classical ballet and helped bring them to the United States, where she worked as a master teacher from the 1960's through the 1980's.

Danjon, André-Louis

b. April 6, 1890
Caen, France
d. April 21, 1967
Paris, France
fields: Astronomy

Danjon primarily worked to increase the precision of astronomical instruments in observing stars. The invention of the prismatic 60 degree astrolabe, or the Danjon astrolabe, is his crowning achievement. Toward the end of his career, in the 1950's, he also investigated irregularities in the rotation of Earth.

D'Annunzio, Gabriele

b. March 12, 1863
Pescara, Italy
d. March 1, 1938
Gardone, Italy
fields: Theater and Entertainment, Literature

Gabriele D'Annunzio was an Italian writer, some of whose works were placed on the Roman Catholic *Index Librorum Prohibitorum* in 1911 for celebrating sensual gratification and promoting allegedly non-Christian values. D'Annunzio published his first poetry collection in 1879 and served in Italy's parliament from 1884 to 1904. He was an early advocate of Fascist ideology and introduced the black shirt symbol of the Fascist Party. In 1937 Italian dictator Benito Mussolini appointed D'Annunzio president of the Royal Italian Academy. D'Annunzio's novels included *The Child of Pleasure* (1898), *The Triumph of Death* (1894), and *The Flame of Life* (1900).

Dante

né: Durante Alaghieri
aka: Dante Alagherius
b. May, 1265
Florence, Italy
d. September 13 or 14, 1321
Ravenna, Italy
fields: Literature

Dante's *The Divine Comedy*, written in vernacular Italian *terza rima*, synthesizes classical and medieval thought in a confessional format which is at once universal and intensely personal.

Dantley, Adrian Delano

b. Feb. 28, 1956
Washington, D.C.
fields: Sports (basketball)

African American basketball player; Adrian Delano Dantley was picked up as a 1976 first round draft by the Buffalo Braves; led gold-medal winning U.S. Olympic basketball team in 1976; frequently traded, but spent most of career with Utah Jazz.

Danton, Georges

full: Georges-Jacques Danton
b. October 26, 1759
Arcis-sur-Aube, France
d. April 5, 1794
Paris, France
fields: Government and Politics

Danton was one of the principal leaders and shapers of the French Revolution. He became influential in molding modern conceptions of democracy, revolutionary politics, and the nation-state.

d'Aquino, Iva Toguri. *See* Tokyo Rose

Darby, Abraham

b. c. 1678
Wren's Nest, near Dudley, Worcestershire, England
d. March 8, 1717
Coalbrookdale, Shrophire, England
fields: Business and Industry, Invention and Technology

Darby solved the problem of substituting coal for wood in the making of iron. His use of coke, after further improvements made by his son, Abraham Darby II, and others, changed English ironmaking from a declining industry into the second leading sector, along with cotton production, of the first Industrial Revolution.

Darden, Christopher A.

b. April 7, 1956
Martinez, Calif.
fields: Law

African American attorney Christopher Darden was assistant prosecutor for the Los Angeles County district attorney's office in the O. J. Simpson murder trial. While with the Major Crimes Division, Darden was involved in a number of high profile court cases, including the Reginald Denny beating case. After the conclusion of the Simpson trial, Darden took a leave of absence to teach classes at Southwestern University of Law, where he had been serving as an adjunct professor. He published *In Contempt* (1996), which which reached the top of *The New York Times Book Review*'s best-seller list.

Daremberg, Jean-Baptiste. *See* Alembert, Jean le Rond d'

Darius the Great

b. 550 B.C.E.
place unknown
d. 486 B.C.E.
Persepolis, Persia
fields: Government and Politics, Law

Darius consolidated and expanded the Persian Empire through humane, wise, and judicious administration. He respected the languages, religions, and cultures of his subject nations, and in return they fought his battles, built lavish palaces for him, and brought him precious gifts.

Darrow, Clarence

full: Clarence Seward Darrow
b. April 18, 1857
Kinsman, Ohio
d. March 13, 1938
Chicago, Illinois
fields: Law

The most renowned defense attorney of his time, Darrow won a number of important verdicts in difficult cases while espousing unpopular causes.

Dart, Isom

b. fl. 1800's
fields: Historical figure

African American cowboy in Arkansas; Isom Dart was born a slave but a name for himself as a horse thief; shot to death and buried on Cold Springs Mountain, Wyomimg.

Darwin, Charles

full: Charles Robert Darwin
b. February 12, 1809
Shrewsbury, Shropshire, England
d. April 19, 1882
Downe, Kent, England
fields: Biology, Natural History

Darwin's theory of evolution through natural selection, which he set forth in *On the Origin of Species*, revolutionized biology by providing a scientific explanation for the origin and development of living forms.

Das, Tarak Nath

b. June 15, 1884
near Calcutta, West Bengal, India
d. Dec. 22, 1958
New York City, N.Y.?
fields: Government and Politics

In the early part of the twentieth century, Tarak Nath Das, student activist, author, lecturer, and political revolutionary, campaigned vigorously in the United States on Canadian and American immigration exclusion laws and Indian independence from repressive British rule. He arrived in the United States in 1906, receiving his doctorate from Georgetown in 1924. In 1907, he launched *Free Hindustan*, a radical monthly. After a long struggle, he was naturalized in 1914. He was kept under surveillance for his anti-British activities and was sent to prison for "anti-American" plots. Threatened with deportation, he managed to stay in the United States although the government persisted in trying to revoke his citizenship. In 1927, all pending cases for denaturalization were finally canceled.

Dash, Julie

b. 1952
New York, N.Y.
fields: Film

African American film director; Julie Dash's films include *Daughters of the Dust* (1991)and *Funny Valentines* (1999).

Dasoda-hae. *See* Mangas Coloradas

Datsolalee

aka: Louisa Keyser
aka: Dabuda (Wide Hips)
b. Nov. 1835
Carson Valley, Nev.
d. Dec. 6, 1925
Carson City, Nev.
fields: Art

Native American artist and artisan. A Washoe, Datsolalee (Louisa Keyser) was an accomplished designer and basketmaker. Basketry had long been a fine art among the Washoe, and she was recognized as its most accomplished practitioner.

Datta, Narandranath. *See* Vivekananda

Daugherty, Harry M.

b. January 26, 1860
Washington Court House, Ohio
d. October 12, 1941
Columbus, Ohio
fields: Government and Politics; Law

President Warren G. Harding's attorney general. Harry M. Daugherty curtailed rail union power (1922) and banned branch banking. Forced to resign in 1924 because of

Teapot Dome scandal; prosecuted for fraud in 1927 but not convicted.

Daurat, Jean. *See* Dorat, Jean

Dausset, Jean

full: Jean Baptiste Gabriel Joachim Dausset
b. Oct. 19, 1916
Toulouse, France
fields: Genetics, Medicine

Jean Dausset discovered the major histocompatibility complex in humans, a group of genes responsible for controlling tissue graft rejection. In 1980, she was awarded the Nobel Prize in Physiology or Medicine.

Davenport, Willie D.

b. June 8, 1943
Troy, Ala.
fields: Sports (track and field, bobsledding)

African American track and field athlete and bobsledder; Willie D. Davenport was considered to be the world's best high hurdler in the late 1960's; won a number of Olympic medals and set Olympic record for 110-meter hurdles in 1968; was also on 1980 Olympic bobsled team; elected to the National Track and Field Hall of Fame in 1982 and the Olympic Hall of Fame in 1991.

David

b. c. 1030 B.C.E.
Bethlehem, Judah
d. c. 962 B.C.E.
Jerusalem, Israel
fields: Religion and Theology

According to Hebrew tradition and the biblical record, David was the greatest king of Israel. It was prophesied of him that through his lineage the promise of a latter-day Messiah and other spiritual blessings would be fulfilled, making him a key monarch in the history of Israel and of importance to the development of both Christianity and later Judaism.

David I

aka: David I of Scotland
b. Between 1080 and 1085
Scotland
d. May 24, 1153
Carlisle, Cumberland, England
fields: Monarchy, Government and Politics

By granting feudal tenures to Anglo-Normans, extending the diocesan system, encouraging monastic growth, defeating various Scottish opponents, remodeling his government along patterns found in England and France, and protecting his interests along the Anglo-Scottish border, David created a more united kingdom built upon the thriving European institutions of his day.

David II

né: David Bruce
b. March 5, 1324
Dunfermline, Scotland
d. February 22, 1371
Edinburgh, Scotland
fields: Monarchy, Government and Politics

Although he was King of Scotland during many years of its struggle for independence from the English, David II spent much time in exile or captivity before his return to the kingdom and a period of peace (David II of Scotland, 1331-1371).

David, Jacques-Louis

b. August 30, 1748
Paris, France
d. December 29, 1825
Brussels, Belgium
fields: Art

David was the founder of nineteenth century neoclassicism. His participation in the political events of his time directed not only the course of his own art but that of European painting as well.

Davidson, Donald

full: Donald Herbert Davidson
b. March 6, 1917
Springfield, Massachusetts
fields: Philosophy, Language and Linguistics

Donald Davidson's philosophical investigations into action theory, the ontology of events, and especially the semantics of natural language was groundbreaking throughout the latter third of the twentieth century. His truth-conditional analysis of meaning remains paramount for many philosophers of language as do his views on interpretation and the shared commonality of knowledge and truth. At a time when many proclaimed the fragmentation and even the end of philosophy, Davidson offered a rigorous, systematic attempt to understand people as speakers and agents, as persons. Major works include *Essays on Actions and Events* (1980) and *Inquiries into Truth and Interpretation* (1984), and "The Folly of Trying to Define Truth" (1996).

Davis, Angela Yvonne

b. January 26, 1944
Birmingham, Ala.
fields: Education, Government and Politics, Social Reform

African American human rights activist, author, educator, and political candidate; Angela Yvonne Davis gained fame as an organizer of the Black Power movement, a member of the Communist Party, and a university professor; she has been a controversial figure since the 1960's, advocating revolution and defending Black Power leaders; membership in the Che-Lumumba Club led to her October, 1970, arrest on charges of murder, kidnapping, and conspiracy; she was acquitted of all charges in 1972; her published works include a political autobiography, *Angela Davis* (1974), *If They Come in the Morning* (1971; an edited collection of writing by herself and other African American activists), *Women, Race, and Class* (1981), *Women, Culture, and Politics* (1989), and *Blues Legacies and Black Feminism* (1998); appointed to the University of California Presidential Chair at University of California, Santa Cruz (1995).

Davis, Arthur Paul

b. Nov. 21, 1904
Hampton, Va.
d. April 21, 1999
Washington, D. C.
fields: Education

African American educator and literary critic; Arthur Paul Davis *From the Dark Tower: Afro-American Writers, 1900-1960* (1974); taught at North Carolina College for Negroes (1927-1928), at Virginia Union University (1929-1944), and then at Howard University.

Davis, Benjamin O., Sr.

b. July 1, 1877
Washington, D.C.
d. November 26, 1970
North Chicago, Ill.
fields: Military Affairs

African American military officer; Davis was the first African American to reach the rank of general in the regular army. President Franklin D. Roosevelt promoted him to brigadier general on October 16, 1940. He served in the Spanish-American War and later served in the all-black Ninth Cavalry. He retired from military service in 1948.

Davis, Benjamin O., Jr.

b. December 18, 1912
Washington, D.C.
fields: Military Affairs

African American military officer. Benjamin Davis, Jr., became the first African American U.S. Air Force general on October 27, 1954. He was the second African American general in the armed forces (his father, Benjamin O. Davis, Sr., was the first). He was a decorated pilot and squadron commander during World War II. He commanded Godman Field in Kentucky on June 21, 1945. President Lyndon Johnson promoted him to the rank of lieutenant general on April 16, 1965. That year he was named chief of staff of U.S. forces in Korea.

Davis, Bette

full: Ruth Elizabeth Davis
b. April 5, 1908
Lowell, Massachusetts
d. October 8, 1989
Neuilly-sur-Seine, on the outskirts of Paris, France
fields: Film, Theater and Entertainment (drama)

With a screen persona comprised of equal parts talent, passion, and intelligence, Bette Davis was, at the height of her career, the leading film actress of her generation.

Davis, Billie Louise Barbour

né: Billie Louise Barbour
b. 1906
Kansas City, Mo.
d. 1955
fields: Photography

African American photographer; Billie Louise Barbour Davis is known for her portraits and landscapes.

Davis, Charles Twitchell

b. Apr. 29, 1918
d. Mar. 25, 1981
fields: Education, Scholarship

African American scholar; Charles Twitchell Davis wrote extensively about African American prose, drama, and poetry; Princeton's first black professor (1955-1961); served as professor of English and as chair of Afro-American studies at Yale University until his death.

Davis, Clifton

b. Oct. 4, 1945
Chicago, Ill.
fields: Television, Theater and Entertainment

African American actor, singer, songwriter, and musician; after appearing in a number of theater productions, Clifton Davis starred on the television shows *That's My Mama* (1974-1975) and *Amen*; wrote songs for Motown, notably the hit "Never Can Say Goodbye"; became pastor for Seventh-day Adventist church.

Davis, Collis H., Jr.

b. ?
fields: Photography, Film

African American photographer and filmmaker; Collis H. Davis, Jr., is best known for his photographs of jazz musicians.

Davis, David

b. 1815
d. 1886
fields: Law

U.S. Supreme Court justice, 1862-1877; appointed by President Lincoln. Resigned from the Court to take a seat in the United States Senate. Significant opinion: *Ex parte Milligan*, 71 U.S. 2 (1866).

Davis, Elmer

full: Elmer Holmes Davis
b. January 13, 1890
Aurora, Indiana
d. May 18, 1958
Washington, D.C.
fields: Radio, Journalism, Warfare and Conquest

A well-known radio commentator, Elmer Davis became director of the U.S. Office of War Information during World War II. He helped the government reorganize its system for disseminating news and encouraged President Franklin D. Roosevelt to permit more realistic reporting on the war. His agency promoted war bonds, rationing, victory gardens, secrecy about military movements, and improved labor productivity. After the war he returned to radio broadcasting and won the George Foster Peabody Radio Award in 1951.

Davis, Ernie

b. Dec. 14, 1939
New Salem, Pa.
d. May 18, 1963
Cleveland, Ohio
fields: Sports (football)

African American football player; Ernie Davis was the first African American to win college football's Heisman Trophy; died of leukemia before start of first season he would have played professional football.

Davis, Frances Reed Elliott

b. 1882
Knoxville, Tenn.
d. May 2, 1965
Michigan
fields: Nursing

African American nurse and educator; Frances Reed Elliott Davis was the first African American to join the American Red Cross Nursing Service.

Davis, Geena

full: Virginia Phyllis Davis
b. January 21, 1957
Wareham, Massachusetts
fields: Film, Television

Known for her strong feminist roles as an actor, Davis won an Academy Award as Best Supporting Actress in 1989 for her role in *The Accidental Tourist* (1988) and was nominated in the same category in 1991 for her role as Thelma in *Thelma and Louise* (1990).

Davis, Griffith J.

b. 1923
Atlanta, Ga.
fields: Photography

African American photographer; Griffith J. Davis began his career in 1947 as a professional photographer with *Ebony* magazine; in 1952, began work for the U.S. Agency for International Development involving photography, communications policy, broadcasting, film, and communications training programs.

Davis, Henrietta Vinton

b. 1860
Baltimore, Md.
d. Nov. 23, 1941
Washington, D.C.
fields: Civil Rights, Social Reform

African American political organizer; Henrietta Vinton Davis was a leader of the Universal Negro Improvement Association in the 1920's and 1930's and was elected president of the organization in 1934.

Davis, Jefferson

b. June 3, 1808
Christian County, Kentucky
d. December 6, 1889
New Orleans, Louisiana
fields: Government and Politics

Davis served his country ably as senator and secretary of war; his commitment to the South led him to accept the presidency of the Confederacy and attempt to preserve Southern independence against bitter opposition and overwhelming odds. Reviled or idealized as a symbol of the Confederacy, Davis' consistency of principle and unflagging efforts balance out the fact that he was not well fitted for the demands of the times and the position.

Davis, John

b. c. 1550
Sandridge Barton, Devonshire, England
d. December 29 or 30, 1605
near Singapore
fields: Exploration and Colonization

The most diligent and successful of the English explorers who attempted to find a northwest passage to the Far East, Davis greatly enlarged knowledge of the islands, waters, and coastline of the northern edge of North America.

Davis, John Henry, Jr.

b. Jan. 12, 1921
Smithtown, N.Y.
fields: Sports (weight lifting)

African American weight lifter; John Henry Davis, Jr., remained undefeated between 1938 and 1953; won Olympic gold medals (1948 and 1952).

Davis, Lenwood G.

b. Feb. 22, 1939
Beaufort, N.C.

fields: Education, Scholarship

African American educator; Lenwood G. Davis compiled dozens of lists of sources on topics of special interest to African Americans.

Davis, Miles

full: Davis, Miles Dewey
b. May 25, 1926
Alton, Ill.
d. Sept. 28, 1991
Santa Monica, Calif.
fields: Music (jazz)

African American trumpeter, flugelhornist, and composer; Miles Davis, a seminal jazz figure, began his career during the bebop era (1940's), playing with Charlie Parker; with nine-piece band, was influential in the development of cool jazz (1950's); turned to jazz fusion in the 1970's.

Davis, Ossie

b. Dec. 18, 1917
Cogdell, Ga.
fields: Theater and Entertainment

African American actor, director, and playwright; Ossie Davis acted in the theater in the 1950's; had numerous film and television roles in the 1950's and 1960's; wrote several plays, including *Purlie Victorious* (pr. 1961).

Davis, Pat

b. ?
New York, N.Y.
fields: Photography

African American photographer; Pat Davis's work is distinguished by her analytical images and subjects shot from extreme angles.

Davis, Preston Augustus

b. c. 1925
Norfolk, Va.
fields: Business and Industry

African American management consultant and political appointee; Preston Augustus Davis was a senior management analyst with the Department of Agriculture between 1971 and 1978; appointed by Jimmy Carter to as director of Small Business Affairs at the Department of Agriculture.

Davis, Reverend Gary

full: Gary Davis
b. Apr. 30, 1896
Laurens County, S.C.
d. May 5, 1972
Hammonton, N.J.
fields: Music (blues and folk)

African American blues and folk musician; Reverend Gary Davis was influential as guitar teacher and mentor in the folk revival of the 1960's.

Davis, Rodney M.

b. Apr. 7, 1942
Macon, Ga.
d. Sept. 6, 1967
Quang Nam Province, Republic of Vietnam
fields: Warfare and conquest

African American military hero; Rodney M. Davis was awarded the Congressional Medal of Honor for throwing himself on a grenade to save his fellow Marines.

Davis, Sammy, Jr.

b. December 8, 1925
Harlem, N.Y.
d. May 16, 1990
Beverly Hills, Calif.
fields: Theater and Entertainment, Music (pop)

African American singer, dancer, and actor; Sammy Davis, Jr., began his recording career in 1946; *Metronome* named his "The Way You Look Tonight" the record of the year and also named Davis as "Most Outstanding New Personality" of the year. He opened on Broadway on March 22, 1956, starring in *Mr. Wonderful*, which ran for 383 performances. He starred in or had feature roles in such films as *The Benny Goodman Story* (1956); *Anna Lucasta* (1958); *Porgy and Bess* (1959). In the 1960's, Davis was identified with the "Rat Pack," an entertainment clique led by Frank Sinatra and including Dean Martin, Peter Lawford, Joey Bishop, Tony Curtis, and Henry Silva. Davis died on May 19, 1990, of throat cancer.

Davis, Walter Paul

b. Sept. 9, 1954
Pineville, N.C.
fields: Sports (basketball)

African American basketball player; Walter Paul Davis played in six NBA All-Star Games while with the Suns (drafted in 1977) before finishing his career with the Denver Nuggets; won a gold medal with the U.S. basketball team at the 1976 Montreal Olympics.

Davison, Frederic Ellis

b. Sept. 28, 1917
Washington, D.C.
d. Jan. 24, 1999
Washington, D.C.
fields: Military Affairs

African American military officer; Frederic Ellis Davison was the first African American Army combat general.

Davy, Humphry

aka: Sir Humphry Davy
b. December 17, 1778
Penzance, Cornwall, England
d. May 29, 1829
Geneva, Switzerland
fields: Chemistry, Invention and Technology, Philosophy

As a philosopher of science, brilliant chemist, and president of the Royal Society, Davy advanced the cause of science as few men had before him. He identified the chemical elements barium, chlorine, magnesium, potassium, sodium, and strontium; pioneered anesthesiology with his experiments with nitrous oxide; invented the Davy lamp to save miners from the perils of explosions; made significant contributions to the application of science for the betterment of society in fields such as agricultural chemistry and tanning; and wrote widely read books on philosophy, flyfishing, and travel.

Dawes, Charles G.

full: Charles Gates Dawes
b. August 27, 1865
Marietta, Ohio
d. April 23, 1951
Evanston, Illinois
fields: Government and Politics

A U.S. public official, Charles G. Dawes was U.S. vice president (1925-1929), cocreator of the Dawes Plan (1924), and winner of the 1925 Nobel Peace Prize. The Dawes Plan was intended to help stabilize european economies. It called for a rescheduling of Germany's reparation payments, a new German currency and system of taxation, the end of foreign military occupation, and new loans to Germany. Implemented by 1925, it may have been the United States' most important contribution to world peace and order in the 1920's.

Dawes, Dominique

full: Dominique Margaux Dawes
b. November 20, 1976
Silver Spring, Md.
fields: Sports (gymnast)

African American gymnast; In 1992, Dominique Dawes joined Betty Okino as the first African American females to qualify for spots on the United States Olympic Gymnastics team, which went on to win a bronze medal in the 1992 Summer Olympics. She was a leading member of The Magnificent Seven Gold Medal-winning gymnastics team of the 1996 Olympics Games and also won Bronze medals in uneven bars and floor exercise.

Dawidowicz, Lucy S.

né: Lucy Schildkret

b. June 16, 1915
New York, New York
d. December 5, 1990
New York, New York
fields: Historiography, Education
Dawidowicz was the author of several important studies about the life of Eastern European Jews in the period before World War II and their experiences during the Holocaust perpetrated by the Nazis.

Dawson, Andre
full: Andre Fernando Dawson
aka: The Hawk Dawson
b. July 10, 1954
Miami, Fla.
fields: Sports (baseball)
African American baseball player; Andre Dawson was the first player to reach double figures in home runs and stolen bases for twelve straight seasons; played for Montreal Expos and Chicago Cubs.

Dawson, Daniel D.
b. 1944?
fields: Photography
African American photographer, filmmaker, and curator; Daniel D. Dawson's color photography is marked by abstractions of reality.

Dawson, William Levi
b. Apr. 26, 1886
Albany, Ga.
d. Nov. 9, 1970
Chicago, Ill.
fields: Government and Politics
African American congressman; William Levi Dawson represented the First Congressional District of Illinois from 1943 until his death; first African American to chair a major congressional committee (Government Operations Committee); first African American vice president of the Democratic National Committee.

Day, Dorothy
b. November 8, 1897
Brooklyn, New York
d. November 29, 1980
New York, New York
fields: Journalism, Social Reform
Cofounder of a radical Catholic social movement, the Catholic Worker (CW), and editor and publisher of its paper, Day linked traditional piety to immediate relief for the needy and to nonviolent direct action in order to end injustice and war.

Day, Morris
b. 1957
Springfield, Ill.
fields: Music (funk)
African American singer and actor; Morris Day sang in a flambouyant funk group called Time in the 1980's; played with Prince in *Purple Rain* (1984).

Day, Sandra. *See* O'Connor, Sandra Day

Day, William R.
full: William Rufus Day
b. 1849
d. 1923
fields: Law
U.S. Supreme Court justice, 1903-1922; appointed by President Theodore Roosevelt. Author of the exclusionary rule remedy for Fourth Amendment violations in federal courts. Significant opinions: *Weeks v. United States*, 232 U.S. 383 (1914); *Hammer v. Dagenhart*, 247 U.S. 251 (1918).

Dayal, Har
b. October 14, 1884
Delhi, India
d. March 4, 1939
Philadelphia, Pa.
fields: Government and Politics
Indian political activist and writer Har Dayal was a key figure in the the Asian Indian nationalist movement (1905-1919). He arrived in the United States in 1911 and organized against anti-Indian discrimination and for reform of immigration laws. He published a pro-independence Indian-language newspaper, *Ghadar*, and played a leading role in the formation of the Ghadr Party in San Francisco in 1913. He was deported in 1914. After the World War I, Dayal supported the Indian Home Rule movement. He also authored the following books: *Forty-four Months in Germany and Turkey: February 1915 to October 1918* (1920), *Our Educational Problem* (1922), *The Bodhisattva Doctrine in Buddhist Sanskrit Literature* (1932), *Hints for Self-Culture* (1934), and *Twelve Religions and Modern Life* (1938).

Dayan, Moshe
b. May 4, 1915
Deganiah, Palestine
d. October 16, 1981
Tel Aviv, Israel
fields: Military Affairs, Government and Politics
A native-born Israeli, Dayan helped Israel win its independence and homeland in 1948-1949 and, as chief of staff, helped build the Israeli Defense Forces into one of the most aggressive military forces in the world. He served as defense minister and as foreign minister and was a member of the Knesset.

Days, Drew Saunders, III
b. Aug. 29, 1941
Atlanta, Ga.
fields: Law
African American attorney; Drew Saunders Days III was appointed by Jimmy Carter to the position of assistant attorney general for civil rights, the first African American to serve in that post.

Deák, Ferenc
full: Ferenc Deák, Jr.
b. October 17, 1803
Söjtör, Zala County, Hungary
d. January 28, 1876
Pest, Hungary
fields: Government and Politics
Deák's persuasive and undaunting efforts brought about Hungary's most important compromise, the *Ausgleich.* He also led the liberals in the passage of much needed social reforms and was one of Hungary's greatest codifiers of progressive laws that brought Hungary out of feudalism.

Deakin, Alfred
b. August 3, 1856
Melbourne, Victoria, Australia
d. October 7, 1919
Melbourne, Victoria, Australia
fields: Government and Politics
After serving a ten-year apprenticeship in Victoria's legislative assembly from 1880, Deakin spent the next decade working toward the federation of the Australian colonies. One of the primary founders of the Commonwealth of Australia, he served three times as prime minister, dominating the government during its first, formative decade.

Dean, William Henry
b. 1910
Lynchburg, Va.
d. 1952
fields: Economics
African American economist; William Henry Dean served on the Division of Economic Stability and Development of the United Nations (1946) and was chief of the Africa unit.

de Beauvoir, Simone. *See* Beauvoir, Simone de

Deborah
b. c. 1200 B.C.E.-1125 B.C.E.
central Israel
d. c. 1200 B.C.E.-1124 B.C.E.
central Israel
fields: Biblical Figures, Literature, Religion and Theology, Warfare and Conquest
A Joan of Arc of the Bible, Deborah rallied Israelite tribes to defeat oppressors as

she had prophesied; her victory poem is considered one of Scripture's most ancient texts.

Debs, Eugene V.

full: Eugene Victor Debs
b. November 5, 1855
Terre Haute, Indiana
d. October 20, 1926
Elmhurst, Illinois
fields: Labor Movement, Government and Politics

Debs's work in the organization of labor and the adoption of social welfare legislation had a significant impact on the American economy and government.

Debussy, Claude

full: Achille-Claude Debussy
b. August 22, 1862
Saint-Germain-en-Laye, near Paris, France
d. March 25, 1918
Paris, France
fields: Music

Debussy is the most important and innovative composer of the end of the nineteenth century, laying down the foundation for the transition from the late Romantics such as Wagner to the early modernists such as Stravinsky. His influence was particularly felt in two areas: the suggestion of pictorial and visual effects in music, especially the subtle qualities of Impressionist painters, and the use of nontraditional scales and chords, greatly expanding harmonic possibilities.

Debye, Peter J. W.

né: Petrus Josephus Wilhelmus Dibije
full: Peter Joseph William Debye
b. Mar. 24, 1884
Maastricht, the Netherlands
d. Nov. 2, 1966
Ithaca, New York
fields: Chemistry, Physics

Peter J. W. Debye examined the bonding and structure of compounds; he investigated the polarity of molecules through a study of their dipole moments and from their X-ray diffraction patterns. In 1916, with Paul Scherrer, he developed powder X-ray diffraction. In 1936, he received the Nobel Prize in Chemistry.

DeCarava, Roy

b. 1919
New York, N.Y.
fields: Photography

African American photographer; Roy DeCarava worked with poet Langston Hughes on photodocumentary journal of Harlem titled *The Sweet Flypaper of Life* (1955); photographs appeared in seminal *Family of Man* exhibit and can be found in numerous important collections.

Decatur, Stephen

b. January 5, 1779
Sinepuxent, Maryland
d. March 22, 1820
Bladensburg, Maryland
fields: Military Affairs

Decatur was the most colorful and successful open-sea naval commander and hero of the Barbary Wars and the War of 1812.

Decora, Spoon

aka: Choukeka
b. c. 1730
d. 1816
fields: Government and Politics, Diplomacy, Native American Affairs

Native American leader. Winnebago leader who played a leading role in negotiating the St. Louis Treaty of 1816. Took a leading role in the Winnebagos' conflicts with the Chippewas. Spoon Decora was one of the first of several Winnebago leaders to carry the name "Decora."

Dedekind, Richard

full: Julius Wilhelm Richard Dedekind
b. October 6, 1831
Brunswick
d. February 12, 1916
Brunswick, Germany
fields: Mathematics

Dedekind gave a new definition to the concept of irrational numbers, based exclusively on arithmetic principles. He helped clarify the notions of infinity and continuity and contributed to the establishment of rigorous theoretical foundations for mathematics.

De Diego, José

b. Apr. 16, 1868
Aguadilla, Puerto Rico
d. July 16, 1918
New York, N.Y.
fields: Government and Politics, Literature

Political leader and writer. A precursor of modernism in Puerto Rican literature, José De Diego also symbolizes the ideal of Puerto Rican independence. He emerged as the leader of the Unionist Party, which was founded in 1904 to seek self-rule for the island. In 1907, he met with U.S. president Theodore Roosevelt, and he began to campaign for a 1920 plebiscite on the options of statehood or independence. In November, 1917, he decided to table his proposal while the United States fought in World War I; he became ill and died soon thereafter.

Dee, Ruby

né: Ruby Ann Wallace
b. Oct. 27, 1923
Cleveland, Ohio
fields: Film, Theater and Entertainment

African American actress; Ruby Dee co-starred with Ossie Davis in his comedy *Purlie Victorious* (1961); married Davis in 1948; appeared in the roles of Ruth Younger in *A Raisin in the Sun* (1959), and Lena in *Boesman and Lena* (1970); won an Obie for her performance in *Wedding Band* (1972); inducted in the Broadway Hall of Fame (1988) and the Black Filmmakers Hall of Fame (1975).

Deer, Ada Elizabeth

b. August 7, 1935
Keshena, Wis.
fields: Civil Rights, Social Reform, Native American Affairs

Native American rights activist; Ada Elizabeth Deer began her career as a community services coordinator for the Bureau of Indian Affairs in the 1960's, later working on behalf of the education of women and American Indians in organizations such as the National Women's Education Fund, Planned Parenthood, Common Cause, and the Urban League; in 1970 she led the successful lobbying effort to convince the federal government to repeal the Menominee Termination Act (1954) which had ended the Menominee's official tribal status; President Richard M. Nixon restored federal recognition and benefits to her tribe in 1973; appointed the first woman head of the Bureau of Indian Affairs by President Bill Clinton in 1993.

Defoe, Daniel

né: Daniel Foe
b. 1660
London, England
d. April 24, 1731
London, England
fields: Literature

Because of his inventiveness, his eye for detail, and his stylistic adeptness, Defoe was a great journalist and the creator of fiction that set the standard for the English novel.

De Forest, Lee

b. August 26, 1873
Council Bluffs, Iowa
d. June 30, 1961
Hollywood, California
fields: Invention and Technology (electronics)

De Forest's three hundred patents mark him as a great American inventor. For his most famous invention—the thermionic grid-triode—he was known as the "father of radio."

DeFrantz, Anita Luceete

b. Oct. 4, 1952
Philadelphia, Pa.
fields: Sports (rower)

African American rower; Anita Luceete DeFrantz was the first African American woman to compete for the United States in Olympic rowing and to be named as a member of the International Olympic Committee; won a bronze medal in the 1976 Olympic eight-oared rowing competition; held six national titles; was a vocal critic of the 1984 Olympic boycott; president of the Los Angeles Athletic Association.

Deganawida

b. c. 1550
d. c. 1600
fields: Government and Politics, Diplomacy, Religion and Theology, Native American Affairs

Native American leader. Huron leader Deganawida is said to have founded the Iroquois Confederacy, most likely in the sixteenth century, convincing Hiawatha and other leaders of the Mohawk, Oneida, Seneca, Onondaga, and Cayuga leaders to accept the idea.

Degas, Edgar

b. July 19, 1834
Paris, France
d. September 27, 1917
Paris, France
fields: Art

Degas was one of the great figural painters and draftsmen of the nineteenth century. His work combined a deep understanding of tradition with a commitment to innovative portrayals of modern life. His artistic independence was asserted in his role as one of the leading figures of the Impressionistic exhibitions of 1874-1886.

De Gasperi, Alcide

né: Alcide Degasperi
b. April 3, 1881
Pieve Tesino, Austria (now Italy)
d. August 19, 1954
Sella di Valsugana, Italy
fields: Government and Politics

De Gasperi was the only political leader to preside over Italy's eight consecutive governments from December, 1945, to August, 1953. He led Italy to its post-World War II national reconstruction and aligned it with the West.

de Gaulle, Charles. *See* Gaulle, Charles de

Degonwadonti. *See* Brant, Molly

DeGrate, Dalvin

b. July 23, 1971
Newport News, Va.
fields: Music (rhythm and blues)

A member of the African American rhythm and blues group Jodeci, which is composed of two pairs of brothers, Jo-Jo Hailey, K-Ci Hailey, Dalvin DeGrate, and DeVante Swing DeGrate; Jodeci's albums include *Forever My Lady* (1991), *Diary of a Mad Band* (1993), and *The Show the Party After the Hotel* (1995).

DeGrate, DeVante Swing

né: Donald DeGrate, Jr.
b. September 29, 1969
Newport News, Va.
fields: Music (rhythm and blues)

A member of the African American rhythm and blues group Jodeci, which is composed of two pairs of brothers, Jo-Jo Hailey, K-Ci Hailey, Dalvin DeGrate, and DeVante Swing DeGrate; Jodeci's albums include *Forever My Lady* (1991), *Diary of a Mad Band* (1993), and *The Show the Party After the Hotel* (1995).

De Grazia, Edward

b. February 5, 1927
Chicago, Illinois
fields: Law

An American attorney, Edward De Grazia has been best known as a defender of writers and artists accused of obscenity. His most famous cases have involved such works as Aristophenes' *Lysistrata*, Henry Miller's *Tropic of Cancer*, William S. Burroughs' *Naked Lunch*, and the Swedish film *I Am Curious—Yellow*. De Grazia has also written on censorship, particularly that involving the arts. His books include *Censorship Landmarks* (1969), *Banned Films: Movies, Censors and the First Amendment* (1982; written with Roger K. Newman), and *Girls Lean Back Everywhere: The Law of Obscenity and the Assault on Genius* (1992).

Dekanisora

b. c. 1650
Onondaga, N.Y.
d. c. 1732
Albany, N.Y.
fields: Diplomacy, Government and Politics, Native American Affairs

Native American leader. Onondaga leader Dekanisora was the leading Iroquois orator of his era and a noted neutralist politician and diplomat in Iroquois dealings with the English and French in the Northeast. Played a leading role in engineering major peace settlement of 1701 between the Iroquois, French, and French-allied tribes.

de Klerk, F. W.

full: Frederik Willem de Klerk
b. March 18, 1936
Johannesburg, Transvaal, South Africa
fields: Government and Politics

As president of South Africa, de Klerk initiated the process of dismantling the racist system of apartheid that had existed in his country since 1948. He was central in the negotiations that led to the first truly national elections in South African history.

Delacroix, Eugène

b. April 26, 1798
Charenton-Saint-Maurice, France
d. August 13, 1863
Paris, France
fields: Art

Delacroix, a powerful colorist, became the most important figure in the development of the Romantic painting movement in France in the nineteenth century. A prolific artist, he sought to stir viewers deeply by appealing to their senses even though he chose to explore the dark side of their human emotions.

De la Garza, Kika

full: Eligio De la Garza
b. Sept. 22, 1927
Mercedes, Tex.
fields: Government and Politics

Public official. Kiki De la Garza served in the Texas legislature from 1953 to 1964, and he was elected to the U.S. Congress in 1964. In 1981, he assumed the chairmanship of the House Agriculture Committee, becoming the first Latino to chair a standing subcommittee in the House of Representatives. A staunch protector of farming interests, De la Garza has also been successful in addressing water and sewerage problems in small settlements in the Rio Grande Valley.

De la Hoya, Oscar

b. Feb. 4, 1973
Los Angeles, Calif.
fields: Sports (boxing)

Boxer. Oscar De la Hoya rose to prominence from a childhood in which he was surrounded by gangs and drug dealers. Nicknamed the "Golden Boy," he won the gold medal in the 132-pound class at the 1992 Summer Olympics. He compiled an amateur record of 225 wins and only 5 losses, with 153 knockouts. In November, 1992, he turned professional, and he captured the World Boxing Organization (WBO) junior lightweight title in March, 1994. In July, 1994, he won the WBO lightweight. In May, 1995, he won the International Boxing Federation (IBF) lightweight championship. He won the WBC welterweight title in April, 1997, by defeating Pernell Whitaker.

Delandro, Donald Joseph

b. ?
New Orleans, La.
fields: Military Affairs
African American military officer; Donald Joseph Delandro acheived the rank of brigadier general and was highly decorated.

Delaney, Beauford

b. 1901
Knoxville, Tenn.
d. 1979
Vincennes, France
fields: Art (painter)
African American painter; Beauford Delaney was known for expressionist paintings and abstractions with lavish applications of paint; brother of painter Joseph Delaney.

Delaney, Joseph

b. 1904
Knoxville, Tenn.
fields: Art (painter)
African American painter; Joseph Delaney is best known for his paintings of New York crowd scenes; brother of painter Beauford Delaney.

Delany, Martin Robison

b. May 6, 1812
Charles Town, Va. (now W. Va.)
d. Jan. 24, 1885
Wilberforce, near Xenia, Ohio
fields: Civil Rights, Social Reform, Literature
African American black nationalist and emigrationist, author, abolitionist; Martin Robison Delany was a proponent of black nationalism and emigrationism and promoted black pride and self-sufficiency; edited *The Mystery* and *North Star* in support of the antislavery movement; disappointed with treatment of blacks in the United States, he recommended founding an African American colony in Africa or South America; commissioned first black major in the U.S. Army in 1863; published *The Condition, Elevation, Emigration, and Destiny of the Colored People of the United States, Politically Considered* (1852) and *Principia of Ethnology: The Origin of Races and Color* (1879).

Delany, Samuel R., Jr.

full: Samuel Ray Delany, Jr.
b. Apr. 1, 1942
New York, N.Y.
fields: Literature
African American science fiction writer; Samuel R. Delany, Jr., has won Nebula Awards for *Babel-17* (1966), "Aye, and Gomorrah" and *The Einstein Intersection* (1967), and "Time Considered as a Helix of Precious Stones" (1969).

De la Renta, Oscar

b. July 22, 1932
Santo Domingo, Dominican Republic
fields: Fashion
Oscar de la Renta is known as a Dominican American fashion designer. Worked for Balenciaga and Lanvin, was successively a partner at Jane Derby, Inc., and a designer with Elizabeth Arden. Established his own lines and company in 1969. Considered a leading figure in the international fashion world; won the Nieman-Marcus Award in 1968, election to the Coty Hall of Fame in 1973, the Jack Dempsey Award for Humanitarianism in 1988, and a Lifetime Achievement Award in 1990 from the Council of Fashion Designers of America.

De Large, Robert Carlos

b. Mar. 15, 1842
Aiken, S.C.
d. Feb. 14, 1874
Charleston, S.C.
fields: Government and Politics
African American congressman; Robert Carlos De Large was a U.S. representative from South Carolina during Reconstruction; elected to the state house of representatives (1868) and appointed land commissioner (1870); elected to the U.S. House of Representatives from South Carolina's Second District (1871) in a contested election.

De las Casas, Bartolomé

b. c. August, 1474
Seville, Spain
d. July 17, 1566
Madrid, Spain
fields: Religion and Theology, Exploration and Colonization, Native American Affairs
Spanish missionary and historian. An early Spanish missionary, de las Casas traveled to Hispaniola in the West Indies in 1502. The first person in the New World to be ordained to the Catholic church, he is believed to have received holy orders in 1512 or 1513. In 1515, he returned to Spain, where he spoke out against Spanish abuses of the Indians and was made their protector. He led a failed expedition to colonize Venezuela (abandoned 1522) and took Dominican orders in 1523. He was consecrated as bishop of Chiapas in Guatemala, and he returned to the Spanish court in the 1550's. He is best known for his *Apologética Historia de las Indias*, a chronicle of his experiences that condemned Spanish oppression of native peoples.

Delaunay, Robert

full: Robert-Victor-Felix Delaunay
b. April 12, 1885
Paris, France
d. October 25, 1941
Montpellier, France
fields: Art
Delaunay believed that colors are the painter's actual language, that color is both form and subject of a work of art. His experiments with the interaction of colors and the visual effects of light made him one of the most important pioneers of early twentieth century abstraction.

De Lavallade, Carmen

b. Mar. 6, 1931
Los Angeles, Calif.
fields: Dance (dancer and choreographer)
African American dancer and choreographer; Carmen De Lavallade danced with Alvin Ailey from 1950 to 1954, was premier danseuse the Metropolitan Opera Company (1955-1956); appeared with Josephine Baker in 1964; choreographer and performer-in-residence at the Yale School of Drama.

Delaware Prophet

aka: Neolin (Enlightened One)
b. c. 1725
d. c. 1775
fields: Religion and Theology, Native American Affairs
Lenni Lenape (Delaware). The Delaware Prophet, an important religious leader in the mid-eighteenth century, was known for his renunciation of "white ways". Came into prominence in the 1760's during Pontiac's efforts to unite tribes against the European invaders.

Delbrück, Max

full: Max Ludwig Henning Delbrück
b. Sept. 4, 1906
Grunewald, Berlin, Germany
d. Mar. 9, 1981
Pasadena, California
fields: Genetics, Medicine
Max Delbrück transformed the study of bacterial genetics into an exact science. He was awarded the 1969 Nobel Prize in Physiology or Medicine with Salvador Edward Luria and Alfred Day Hershey for discoveries concerning the replication and genetic structure of viruses.

Del Castillo, Adelaida

b. 1950
Los Angeles, Calif.
fields: Anthropology, Scholarship, Women's Rights
Anthropologist and feminist. Adelaida Del Castillo has focused her work on the

status of Hispanic women. Her works include *Negotiated Lives: The Power and Stigma of Women's Domestic Relations in Mexico City* (1981) and *Between Borders: Essays on Mexicana/Chicana History* (1990). She coedited, with Magdalena Mora, *Mexican Women in the United States: Struggles Past and Present* (1980), and she helped to found the feminist journal *Encuento Feminil.*

De León, Patricia

b. 1775
Soto la Marina, Nuevo Santande, Mexico
d. 1849
Texas
fields: Exploration and Colonization

Rancher. Patricia de la Garza was the wife of Martín de León, whom she married in 1795; they made their home in Gruillas, Texas. In 1824, the Mexican government granted her husband permission to found a colony in Texas. Although he died in 1833, the colony was firmly established.

Deleuze, Gilles

b. January 18, 1925
Paris, France
d. November 4, 1995
Paris, France
fields: Philosophy

Social theorist and Sorbonne professor Gilles Deleuze provided important interpretations of key philosophers, including Immanuel Kant, Friedrich Nietzsche, David Hume, Baruch Spinoza, and Gottfried Wilhelm Leibniz. During the 1970's, he lent his reputation to political causes, supporting the gay rights movement and trying to initiate prison reforms. He has also developed a "philosophy of difference," expounded in *Difference and Repetition* (1968). In the 1990's, Deleuze's books on film were beginning to be studied by film theorists. *Nietzsche and Philosophy* (1962), *Proust and Signs* (1964), *Capitalism and Schizophrenia* (1972-1980, with Félix Guattari, including the sensational *Anti-Oedipus*), *A Thousand Plateaus* (1980, with Guattari), and *What Is Philosophy?* (1991, with Guattari).

Delgadito

aka: Atsidi Sani (Old Smith)
aka: Beshiltheeni (Knife Maker)
b. c. 1830
near Nazlini, N.Mex. Territory
d. c. 1870
near Chinle, N.Mex. Territory
fields: Art (silversmith)

Navajo silversmith. Delgadito was the first Navajo metalsmith; his pride in craftsmanship continues to influence Navajo smiths, and silverwork has become the single most important source of individual income to the tribe. Younger brother of Barboncito. Participated in Navajo War of 1863-1866, supporting Manuelito.

Delibes, Léo

full: Clément-Philibert-Léo Delibes
b. February 21, 1836
Saint-Germain-du-Val, France
d. January 16, 1891
Paris, France
fields: Music

Delibes contributed significantly, as a composer, to the French ballet and opera of the nineteenth century.

Delius, Frederick

né: Fritz Theodor Albert Delius
b. January 29, 1862
Bradford, Yorkshire, England
d. June 10, 1934
Grez-sur-Loing, France
fields: Music

The richness and variety of Delius' harmonic resources are principally displayed in works written for chorus and orchestra. His music evokes the expressiveness of lyric poetry and yet simultaneously challenges the conventions that usually convey such lyricism.

Dellums, Ronald V.

b. Nov. 24, 1935
Oakland, Calif.
fields: Government and Politics

African American congressman; Ronald V. Dellums became U.S. representative from California in 1970; authored legislation banning U.S. trade with apartheid South Africa; chairman of the Congressional Black Caucus and the House Committee on the District of Columbia; campaigned for arms control and against Ronald Reagan's Strategic Defense Initiative; appointed to the House Intelligence Committee over conservative objections. After serving twenty-seven years in Congress, Dellums decided not to seek reelection in 1998.

Deloria, Ella Cara

aka: Anpetu Waste (Beautiful Day)
aka: Anpetu Wate Win (Beautiful Day Woman)
b. Jan. 30, 1888
Yankton Sioux Reservation, S.Dak.
d. Feb. 12, 1971
Tripp, S.Dak.
fields: Native American Affairs, Language and Linguistics

Yankton Sioux ethnographer and linguist; never formally trained as an anthropologist, Ella Cara Deloria collected and translated numerous traditional Sioux stories and beliefs and was a leading authority on Sioux culture; her published works include *Dakota Texts* (1932; a bilingual collection of traditional Sioux stories), *Dakota Grammar* (1941; a collaborative effort with anthropologist Franz Boas to explain Dakota linguistic rules), and *Speaking of Indians* (1944; an exploration of native and non-native differences); at her death, Deloria left hundreds of pages of unpublished manuscripts including a novel, *Waterlily* (1988; drafted during the early 1940's, focuses on women's roles in traditional native life).

Deloria, Vine, Jr.

b. Mar. 26, 1933
Martin, S.Dak.
fields: Native American Affairs, Scholarship

Yankton Sioux or Standing Rock Sioux political scientist and author; Vine Deloria, Jr., served as executive director, National Congress of American Indians, 1964-1967; earned law degree at University of Colorado in 1970; was on faculties at Western Washington State College, 1970-1972, University of California, Los Angeles, 1972-1974, University of Arizona, 1978-1990, and University of Colorado, beginning 1990; chairperson, Institute for the Development of Indian Law, 1970-1978; in his extensive writings presents the case for Indian self-determination; displayed sharp-witted political satire in *Custer Died for Your Sins: An Indian Manifesto* (1969) and *We Talk, You Listen: New Tribes, New Turf* (1970); other published works include *God Is Red: A Native View of Religion* (1973), *Behind the Trail of Broken Treaties: An Indian Declaration of Independence* (1974), *American Indians, American Justice* (1983), *American Indian Policy in the Twentieth Century* (1985).

Delors, Jacques

full: Jacques Lucien Jean Delors
b. July 20, 1925
Paris, France
fields: Banking and Finance, Diplomacy, Government and Politics

French statesman Jacques Delors was centrally important in European economic integration during the 1980's and early 1990's, earning him nickname "Monsieur Europe." From 1985 to 1994, president of the European Commission. Reduced the budget deficit of the European Community (EC). Developed plan for removing trade barriers among member countries of the EC, incorporated into the Act of European Unity in 1985. In 1989, issued a report calling for unified EC monetary system and European central bank. The bank was established in 1998.

Del Rio, Dolores
né: Lolita Dolores Martínez Asunsolo López Negrette
b. Aug. 3, 1905
Durango, Mexico
d. Apr. 11, 1983
Newport Beach, Calif.
fields: Theater and Entertainment

Actress. One of Hollywood's most successful Hispanic actresses, Dolores Del Rio made her film debut in *Joanna* (1925). Her films include *The Loves of Carmen* (1927), *Ramona* (1928), *The Red Dance* (1928), *Girl of the Rio* (1932), *Lancer Spy* (1937), *Journey into Fear* (1942), *María Candelaria* (1943), *Las Abandonadas* (1944), and *The Fugitive* (1947). Known for her grace and beauty, she played French, Polynesian, and Indian roles as well as Latinas. She was banned from the United States in the 1950's for helping anti-Franco refugees from Spain, but she returned to Hollywood in 1960 to act in *Flaming Star*. Her final role was in the 1978 film *The Children of Sanchez*.

Delshay
b. c. 1835
present-day Ariz.
d. c. 1874
Ariz.
fields: Government and Politics, Native American Affairs

Native American leader. Apache leader Delshay was murdered by a bounty hunter, and his head was publicly displayed as a warning to other Apaches who raided white settlements.

Del Valle, Reginaldo F.
full: Reginaldo Francisco Del Valle
b. 1854
Los Angeles, Calif.
d. Sept. 21, 1938
Los Angeles, Calif.
fields: Diplomacy, Government and Politics

Diplomat. Reginaldo Del Valle served as a fact-finding emissary to Mexico for U.S. president Woodrow Wilson. An attorney and former member of the California state legislature, Del Valle was to meet with Mexican revolutionaries Venustiano Carranza and Emiliano Zapata. The mission proved a disaster; Del Valle, who disdained the Mexican masses, was unsympathetic to the revolutionary leaders. Moreover, though his mission was confidential, he gave an interview to a Mexico City newspaper. The U.S. government recalled him, and he returned to California, where he served on numerous government boards and civic committees.

Demby, William
b. December 25, 1922
Pittsburgh, Pa.
fields: Literature (novelist and educator)

African American novelist and educator; William Demby published *Beetlecreek* (1950), *The Catacombs* (1965), and *Love Story Black* (1978).

de Menil, Dominique
né: Dominique Schlumberger
b. March 23, 1908
Paris, France
d. December 31, 1997
Houston, Texas
fields: Patronage of the Arts, Philanthropy

In addition to her influential humanitarian work, Dominique de Menil has commissioned works from and inspired numerous artists of the late twentieth century while also bringing art and art education to the general public.

De Mille, Agnes
b. 1905
New York, New York
d. October 7, 1993
New York, New York
fields: Dance

Agnes de Mille, a pioneer in modern dance, was the first to integrate dance into theatrical productions and to make it accessible to the general public.

DeMille, Cecil B.
né: Cecil Blount deMille
b. August 12, 1881
Ashfield, Massachusetts
d. January 21, 1959
Los Angeles, California
fields: Film

Capturing early twentieth century American values on the screen, DeMille achieved popular, if not critical, success in his film spectacles and sex comedies.

Democritus
b. c. 460 B.C.E.
Abdera, Thrace
d. c. 370 B.C.E.
Abdera, Thrace
fields: Philosophy

Democritus worked out a far-reaching atomism, which he applied to science, metaphysics, and ethics. His view that the world is made up of changing combinations of unchanging atoms was addressed to one of the central questions of his age—"How is change possible?"—and provided a model of reasoning that was mechanistic, materialist, and nonsupernatural.

De Morgan, Augustus
b. June 27, 1806
Madura, Madras Presidency, India
d. Mar. 18, 1871
London, England
fields: Mathematics (algebra and mathematical logic)

Augustus De Morgan developed a logic of relations. His work bridges Aristotle's classical approach to logic to George Boole's mathematical logic. In 1865 he was elected the first president of the London Mathematical Society.

Demosthenes
b. 384 B.C.E.
Athens, Greece
d. 322 B.C.E.
Calauria, Greee
fields: Law, Government and Politics

Demosthenes' life and career as an orator were consumed by his titanic struggle with Philip II of Macedonia and by his efforts to recall Athenian spirit and vigor to its former greatness. The single-mindedness, sincerity, and intense patriotism of Demosthenes—combined with his consummate genius and mastery of oratorical technique—make him one of the most notable personalities of antiquity.

Dempsey, Jack
né: William Harrison Dempsey
b. June 24, 1895
Manassa, Colorado
d. May 31, 1983
New York, New York
fields: Sports (boxing)

Dempsey was one of the greatest sports personalities of the so-called Golden Age of Sports (the 1920's) and the first boxer to make major contributions to sporting life in the United States.

Deng Xiaoping
né: Deng Xexien
b. August 22, 1904
Paifang village, Xiexing township, Guang'an county, Sichuan province, China
d. February 19, 1997
Beijing, China
fields: Government and Politics

Deng was a member of the Central Committee of the Chinese Communist Party until 1987, held various official titles from 1949 to 1989 (including deputy prime minister), and was China's de facto ruler from 1978 until his death in 1997. The rapid economic growth that China experienced after 1979 was largely the result of his economic policies.

Denis, Maurice

b. November 25, 1870
Granville, France
d. November 13, 1943
Paris, France
fields: Art

Denis was the theorist of the Nabi school, a group of artists influenced by Paul Gauguin, as well as one of its more important artists. In the second part of his career, he helped bring about a revival of religious art.

Denis, Saint

né: Dionysius
b. Date unknown
Italy
d. c. 250 C.E.
near Paris
fields: Religion and Theology and Saints

Contribution Saint Denis (pronounced Deh-NEE), a third century bishop and missionary from Italy, converted the Gauls to Christianity around the area of Paris, thereby establishing the foundation of what would later become one of the leading centers of the Christian faith in Europe. Legend has attributed much about his origins and deeds that is misleading and erroneous.

Dennett, Daniel C.

full: Daniel Clement Dennett
b. March 28, 1942
Boston, Massachusetts
fields: Philosophy, Science (neuroscience)

Daniel C. Dennett played a central part in the development of the scientific study of consciousness and in the development of cognitive science. His willingness to draw on the work of psychologists, computer scientists, evolutionary biologists, and physicists helped convince philosophers that these disciplines could contribute to philosophy. *Brainstorms: Philosophical Essays on Mind and Psychology* (1978) set forth his concept of intentional systems and challenged the stimulus-and-response views of behaviorists; the influential and controversial *Consciousness Explained* (1991) sold one hundred thousand copies within five years of publication; *Darwin's Dangerous Idea* (1995), which also reached a large audience, defended strict Darwinian ideas in rebuttal of Darwinian revisionists and creationist theory.

Dennis, Ruth. *See* St. Denis, Ruth

Densmore, Frances

full: Frances Theresa Densmore
b. May 21, 1867
Red Wing, Minnesota
d. June 5, 1957
Red Wing, Minnesota
fields: Anthropology

A pioneer ethnomusicologist who studied American Indian music, Densmore collected several thousand Indian songs by means of recordings and transcriptions.

DePillars, Murry Norman

b. Dec. 21, 1938
Chicago, Ill.
fields: Art (visual artist), Scholarship

African American visual artist and scholar; Murry Norman DePillars's works fall into three phases—satirical works using African American cartoon characters, the brightly colored, spatial-dot Queen Candace series, and stylized jazz portraits; became dean of arts at Virginia Commonwealth University, Richmond.

DePriest, James

b. Nov. 21, 1936
Philadelphia, Pa.
fields: Music (conductor and music director)

African American conductor and music director; James DePriest was assistant conductor for Leonard Bernstein and the New York Philharmonic (1965-1966) before become associate conductor of the National Symphony Orchestra (1971-1975); conducted Oregon Symphony beginning in 1980).

Depriest, Oscar

b. 1871
Florence, Ala.
d. May 12, 1951
Chicago, Ill.
fields: Government and Politics

African American politician; Oscar Depriest was the first African American elected to the United States Congress (1928) since Reconstruction; was active in the Republican Party when concern for legislation favorable to African Americans was shifting to the Democratic Party; lost seat in 1934 to first African American Democrat to serve in the U.S. Congress, Arthur Mitchell.

Der, Henry

b. Dec. 30, 1946
San Francisco, Calif.
fields: Government and Politics

Henry Der, a leading spokesperson in the Asian American community, became executive director of Chinese for Affirmative Action in 1974. As a community advocate, he sought passage of the bilingual election amendments to the 1965 Voting Rights Act and fought to retain the nine Asian American groups in the race question of the 1990 census.

Derby, fourteenth earl of

né: Edward George Geoffrey Smith Stanley
full: Edward George Geoffrey Smith Stanley, fourteenth earl of Derby
b. March 29, 1799
Knowsley Park, Lancashire, England
d. October 23, 1869
Knowsley Park, Lancashire, England
fields: Government and Politics

One of the leading British politicians at a time when Great Britain was at the height of its economic and political power, Derby oversaw the relatively peaceful democratic reform of his country.

De Rivera, José

b. Sept. 18, 1904
West Baton Rouge, La.
d. Mar. 19, 1985
New York, N.Y.
fields: Art

José De Rivera was a Latino sculptor. Made first sculptures in 1930. Known for 1938 *Flight* for New Jersey's Newark Airport and a piece for the U.S. Pavilion at the 1958 Brussels World Fair. Had first one-man show in 1946.

Derrida, Jacques

b. July 15, 1930
El Biar, Algeria
fields: Philosophy, Language and Linguistics, Literature

Derrida is the author and principal exponent of grammatology, a writing-centered theory of language and of the associated critical practice known as deconstruction. As one of the leading figures in poststructuralism and postmodernism, he has argued forcefully against philosophical, scientific, and religious efforts to institutionalize some preferred system of meanings as "truth."

DeSalvo, Albert. *See* Boston Strangler

Desargues, Girard

aka: Gérard Desargues
b. Mar. 2, 1591
baptized in Lyon, France
d. Oct., 1661
France, possibly in Lyon or Paris
fields: Mathematics (geometry)

Girard Desargues was an architect who used projective geometry to create a universal method of perspective.

Descartes, René

b. March 31, 1596
La Haye, Touraine, France
d. February 11, 1650
Stockholm, Sweden
fields: Mathematics, Philosophy, Physics

Descartes' cardinal contribution is the extension of the mathematical method to all fields of knowledge. He is the father of analytic geometry and the author of the most universally appropriate version of mind-body dualism in the history of philosophy.

Deshler, David W.

b. ?
Columbus, Ohio
fields: Business and Industry

David W. Deshler, who established a mining operation in Korea and other enterprises in Japan, helped the Hawaiian Sugar Planters' Association bring Korean workers to Hawaiian sugar plantations in the early 1900's. About seven thousand Korean laborers emigrated to Hawaii between 1902 and 1905, when the Korean government stopped the outflow because of reports of mistreatment of workers and pressure from the Japanese government, whose workers were being displaced. Deshler profited handsomely from his part in the deal, receiving fifty-four dollars per worker.

Desiga, Daniel

b. ?
fields: Art (painter)

Painter. Daniel Desiga's paintings and murals draw attention to labor issues and problems facing Latinos and to the contributions that ethnic groups have made to the development of the Pacific Northwest. His *Campesino* (1976) is an oil painting of a solitary farmworker bent over a row of seedlings in a vast field; its style resembles that used to dignify workers in Depression-era murals. Desiga's mural for the Centro de la Raza in Seattle presents the darker side of agricultural labor, depicting a farmworker nailed to a cross on the ground he has cultivated. Desiga's other murals suggest the physical and natural forces that have shaped the Pacific Northwest.

Deskahe. *See* General, Alexander

De Soto, Rosana

b. Sept. 2, 1950?
San Jose, Calif.
fields: Theater and Entertainment

Actress. Rosana De Soto has performed in plays and light opera in addition to her film work. Her film credits include *The In-Laws* (1979), *Serial* (1980), *Cannery Row* (1982), *The Ballad of Gregorio Cortez* (1983), *American Justice* (1985), *About Last Night* (1986), *Family Business* (1989), and *Face of the Enemy* (1990). In 1987, she starred in two hit films, playing teacher Jaime Escalante's wife in *Stand and Deliver* and singer Ritchie Valens' mother in *La Bamba*

Deulofeo, Francisco de Asis Javier Cugat Mingall de Bru y. *See* Cugat, Xavier

De Valera, Eamon

b. October 14, 1882
New York, New York
d. August 29, 1975
Blackrock, near Dublin, Ireland
fields: Government and Politics

The leading Irish statesman of the twentieth century, de Valera embodied the Irish nationalist movement and served as leader of the independence movement and later as head of the Irish government for twenty-one years.

Devers, Gail

full: Gail Yolanda Devers
b. November 19, 1966
Seattle, Wash.
fields: Sports (track athlete)

African American track athlete; in the early 1980's, Gail Devers became a world-class athlete in hurdles, sprints, and the long jump under the guidance of noted track coach Bob Kersee; was eliminated from the 1988 United States Olympic Team because of health problems later traced to Graves' disease; after treatment, went on to a gold-medal performance at the 1992 Summer Olympics. She won two gold medals at the 1996 Summer Olympics in Atlanta. In 1997, she was named Women's Sports Foundation Athlete of the Year.

Devlin, Bernadette

b. April 23, 1947
Cookstown, Northern Ireland
fields: Government and Politics, Civil Rights

Bernadette Devlin was a Northern Ireland advocate of Roman Catholic civil rights in Northern Ireland. On April 17, 1969, she became the youngest woman ever to be elected to the British Parliament.

Dewey, George

b. December 26, 1837
Montpelier, Vermont
d. January 16, 1917
Washington, D.C.
fields: Military Affairs

Dewey defeated the Spanish in the Battle of Manila Bay on May 1, 1898, and subsequently served as senior officer of the navy until his death.

Dewey, John

b. October 20, 1859
Burlington, Vermont
d. June 1, 1952
New York, New York
fields: Philosophy, Psychiatry and Psychology, Social Reform

In his intellectual concerns and educational interests, Dewey significantly shaped the roles of philosophy and reform in the United States.

Dewey, Melvil

né: Melville Dewey
b. December 10, 1851
Adams Center, New York
d. December 26, 1931
Lake Placid Club South, Florida
fields: Education

Dewey was the single most original and effective American educator in developing modern library organization and the professional training of librarians.

DeWitt, John L.

full: John Lesesne DeWitt
b. January 9, 1880
Fort Sidney, Neb.
d. June 20, 1962
Washington, D.C.
fields: Military Affairs

In 1941, two days after the Japanese attack on Pearl Harbor, Lieutenant John Lesesne DeWitt was appointed Western Defense Commander. The following year, President Franklin Roosevelt's Executive Order 9066 allowed DeWitt to designate restricted zones and establish systematic procedures for the exclusion, evacuation, and relocation of thousands of Japanese Americans to internment camps in California, Utah, Arizona, Idaho, and elsewhere for the duration of World War II.

Dewson, Molly

né: Mary Williams Dewson
b. Feb. 18, 1874
Quincy, Mass.
d. Oct. 21, 1962
Castine, Maine
fields: Social Reform, Women's Rights

Molly Dewson was active in social services committees; wrote "The Delinquent Girl on Parole" (1911) out of concern with the treatment of young female prisoners; research as secretary of the National Consumer's League led to the first minimum wage act in 1912; in 1930 helped pass the New York law limiting women's working hours; in 1933, with the help of Eleanor Roosevelt, organized the Women's Division, a group dedicated to getting women elected to government positions.

Diaghilev, Sergei

b. March 31, 1872
Selistchev Barracks, Novgorod Province, Russia
d. August 19, 1929
Venice, Italy
fields: Dance, Patronage of the Arts

Diaghilev founded and edited an influential journal of the arts and was an impresario in such diverse fields as painting, music, ballet, and opera. In Paris in 1909, he founded the Ballets Russes, which toured throughout the world. Diaghilev is credited with revitalizing ballet as an art.

Diana, princess of Wales

né: Diana Frances Spencer
b. July 1, 1961
Park House, near Sandringham, Norfolk, England
d. August 31, 1997
Paris, France
fields: Peace Advocacy, Social Reform, Monarchy

Through her strong devotion to humanitarian causes, ranging from abolition of land mines to compassionate concern for the terminally ill, Diana revolutionized and uplifted the public image of British royalty in the 1990's.

Dias, Bartolomeu

b. c. 1450
probably near Lisbon, Portugal
d. May 23?, 1500
at sea off the coast of Brazil
fields: Exploration and Colonization

Dias was the first to command a sea expedition around Africa's Cape of Good Hope, a feat that had been attempted for more than fifty years before his success and one that led to the opening of sea trade between Portugal and the Orient.

Díaz, Justino

b. Jan. 29, 1940
San Juan, Puerto Rico
fields: Music

Opera singer. Justino Díaz is one of opera's leading bass singers. He studied at the University of Puerto Rico and the New England Conservatory and first appeared with the New England Opera Theater in 1961. He made his Metropolitan Opera debut in *Rigoletto* in 1963. He has appeared with the American Opera Society, at Puerto Rico's Casals Festival, at the Spoleto Festival, and at the prestigious Salzburg Festival. He sang the role of Antony in *Antony and Cleopatra* at the opening night of New York's Lincoln Center on September 16, 1966, and in 1971 he sang in *Beatrix Cenci* for the inauguration of the opera house at the Kennedy Center in Washington, D.C.

Díaz, Porfirio

full: José de la Cruz Porfirio Díaz
b. September 15, 1830
Oaxaca, Mexico
d. July 2, 1915
Paris, France
fields: Government and Politics

Porfirio Díaz was dictatorial president of Mexico from 1876 to 1911. In 1876, he overthrew Sebastian Lerdo de Tejada and assumed power. Established public security by summarily shooting rebels and bandits upon capture. Instituted economic reforms, constructed railroads and electrical, telephone, and telegraph systems. Regime based on political maneuvering, intimidation, and brute force. Díaz used imprisonment, exile, and assassination to silence opposition. In 1910 Francisco Madero launched an uprising that became the Mexican Revolution; Díaz went into exile in 1911.

Díaz, Ruy. *See* Cid, El

Díaz Valcárcel, Emilio

b. Oct. 16, 1929
Trujillo Alto, Puerto Rico
fields: Literature

Novelist. Emilio Díaz Valcárcel is an award-winning Puerto Rican writer whose works are known for their harshness and frankness. He is also founding editor of the cultural magazine *Cupey* and a professor of Spanish. His works include *Figuraciones en el mes de marzo* (1972; *Schemes in the Month of March*, 1979); *Proceso en diciembre* (1963), short stories based on his experiences as a Puerto Rican soldier in the U.S. Army; a play, *Una sola puerta hacia al muerte* (1957); the short-story collections *"El asedio," y otros cuentos* (1958) and *El hombre que trabajó el lunes* (1966); and *Inventario* (1975) and *Harlem todos los días* (1978), both novels.

Dibije, Petrus Josephus Wilhelmus. *See* Debye, Peter J. W.

Dickens, Charles

full: Charles John Huffam Dickens
b. February 7, 1812
Portsmouth, Hampshire, England
d. June 9, 1870
Gad's Hill, Rochester, Kent, England
fields: Literature

The most popular novelist of his time, Dickens created a fictional world that reflects the social and technological changes of the Victorian era.

Dickerson, Eric

né: Eric Demetric Johnson
b. Sept. 2, 1960
Sealy, Tex.
fields: Sports (football player)

African American football player; while playing for Southern Methodist University, Eric Dickerson teamed with running back Craig James to form the "Pony Express" backfield; led the NFL in rushing in 1983; played for Los Angeles Rams until traded to Indianapolis Colts in 1986; considered a formidable player but a troublemaker for owners, he was traded to Los Angeles Raiders in 1992.

Dickerson, Ernest

b. 1952
Newark, N.J.
fields: Film

African American cinematographer; Ernest Dickerson is best known for his work with Spike Lee, including *She's Gotta Have It* (1986), and *School Daze* (1988).

Dickerson-Thompson, Julee

b. ?
fields: Art (graphic designer and illustrator)

African American graphic designer and illustrator; Julee Dickerson-Thompson has done album covers for the group Sweet Honey in the Rock and, for Africa World Press, the *Brown Spices ABC Coloring Book*; her work has been exhibited in a number of museums.

Dickinson, Emily

full: Emily Elizabeth Dickinson
b. December 10, 1830
Amherst, Massachusetts
d. May 15, 1886
Amherst, Massachusetts
fields: Literature (poetry)

Dickinson, living a reclusive social life, led an inner life of intense, imaginative creativity that made her one of America's greatest poets.

Dickinson, John

b. November 8, 1732
Crosia-dore Plantation, Maryland
d. February 14, 1808
Wilmington, Delaware
fields: Political Science, Government and Politics

At a crucial point in the development of the American Revolution, Dickinson stated the colonists' arguments against England in a new and compelling way and became, for a while, a spokesman for all the Colonies. Later, he helped draft and win ratification of the United States Constitution.

Diddley, Bo

né: Ellas Bates
b. Dec. 30, 1928
McComb, Miss.
fields: Music (rock and roll guitarist and singer)

African American guitarist and singer; Bo Diddley toured with the Alan Freed show in the 1950's and 1960's and became a seminal figure in early rock and roll; his experimentation with guitar feedback influenced later performers such as Jimmy Hendrix.

Diderot, Denis

b. October 5, 1713
Langres, France
d. July 31, 1784
Paris, France
fields: Philosophy, Literature

As editor of and contributor to the *Encyclopedia*, Diderot codified and promulgated the views of the French Enlightenment. His posthumously published fiction has earned for him a prominent place in the pantheon of eighteenth century writers, and his philosophical works remain challenging and influential.

Didion, Joan

b. December 5, 1934
Sacramento, California
fields: Journalism, Literature, Film

One of America's leading novelists and journalists, Joan Didion is also an accomplished screenwriter, hailed for her impressive command of American culture on both the East and West Coasts. Beginning in the mid-1960's, however, her pieces in *The Saturday Evening Post* distinguished her as one of the United States' foremost essayists; she was one of the first to provide incisive and novelistic commentary on the hippies in the Haight-Ashbury section of San Francisco and on related episodes in what she deemed the "California dream." *Slouching Towards Bethlehem* (1968), *Play It as It Lays* (1970), *A Book of Common Prayer* (1977), and *The Last Thing He Wanted* (1996) are among her best-known works, and she has also collaborated with her husband, writer John Gregory Dunne, on numerous screenplays.

Didrikson, Babe. *See* Zaharias, Babe Didrikson

Didymus. *See* Thomas, Saint

Diefenbaker, John G.

full: John George Diefenbaker
b. September 18, 1895
Neustadt, Ontario, Canada
d. August 16, 1979
Ottawa, Ontario, Canada
fields: Government and Politics

John G. Diefenbaker (who acquired the nickname "Dief the Chief") was prime minister of Canada from 1957 to 1963. Brought a strongly nationalistic vision to Canadian politics; in 1960 produced Canada's Bill of Rights. Soon became unpopular as government finances went into debt. Made domestic and foreign-policy miscalculations. Refused to arm U.S. nuclear missiles in Canada during Cuban Missile Crisis; became personal enemy of U.S. president John F. Kennedy.

Diego, José De. *See* De Diego, José

Diego, Juan

b. 1474
Mexico
d. 1548
Mexico
fields: Religion and Theology

Witness to the Virgin Mary. Juan Diego was an Aztec who converted to Christianity in 1523. According to contemporary sources, he first reported seeing the Virgin Mary on December 9, 1531. As a result of his reports, Bishop Juan de Zumarraga agreed to build a church on the site. The apparition came to be known as the Virgin of Guadalupe, a major symbol of Catholicism in Mexico.

Diels, Otto Paul Hermann

b. January 23, 1876
Hamburg, Germany
d. March 7, 1950
Kiel, West Germany
fields: Chemistry

Diels made two fundamental contributions to classical organic chemistry: the selenium dehydrogenation and the diene reaction. The selenium reaction made it possible to establish the structure of a large number of important natural materials, notably the steroids. The diene reaction is unique in its variety, durability, and quality. He won the 1950 Nobel Prize in Chemistry.

Diesel, Rudolf

b. March 18, 1858
Paris, France
d. September 29, 1913
at sea, in the English Channel
fields: Invention and Technology

Diesel invented the diesel engine. His invention has found many applications—in automobiles, trucks, ships, and submarines, and for generating electricity.

Dietrich, Marlene

full: Maria Magdelena Dietrich
b. December 27, 1901
Berlin, Germany
d. May 6, 1992
Paris, France
fields: Film

Marlene Dietrich established herself worldwide in a career that began in the infancy of the film industry, largely on the strength of her image as the modern femme fatale, glamorous, self-confident, erotic, and independent.

Digby, Pamela Beryl. *See* Harriman, Pamela Digby Churchill

Diggs, Charles Coles, Jr.

b. December 2, 1922
Detroit, Mich.
fields: Government and Politics

U.S. Congressman from Michigan. Charles Diggs served in the U.S. House of Representatives for twenty-five years. In 1954, Diggs became the first black congressman from the state of Michigan. In 1963, he asked President John F. Kennedy to send federal troops and National Guard units to Mississippi to protect black voters. By 1970, Diggs had become the most popular and the most effective black member of the House of Representatives. Diggs was the first chairman of the Congressional Black Caucus. In 1971 he resigned from the U.S. delegation to the United Nations to protest the Nixon Administration's policies toward African nations. Diggs was a proponent of home rule for the District of Columbia. He was convicted in 1978 of twenty-nine counts of defrauding the federal government and was charged with making false statements about his use of his congressional payroll. Diggs was censured in the House and retired from Congress in January, 1981. He agreed to repay the government $40,000 and served a half-year term in federal prison.

Dihigo, Martin

b. May 25, 1905
Matanzas, Cuba
d. May 22, 1971
Cienfuegos, Cuba
fields: Sports (baseball)

Baseball player. Martin Dihigo was kept out of the U.S. major leagues because of his race. Dihigo had a long career in Latin American leagues and also played in the U.S. Negro Leagues from 1923 to 1936. A pitcher with a blazing fastball, he was also a powerful hitter who led the Eastern Colored League in home runs in 1926 and the American Negro League in batting in 1929. He led the New York Cubans into the Negro National League playoffs in 1935 as a playing manager. In September, 1937, he pitched the first professional no-hitter on Mexican soil; he also pitched no-hitters in Venezuela and Puerto Rico. He later became Cuba's minister of sports. Dihigo was inducted into the U.S. National Baseball Hall of Fame in 1977, making him the only player to have been elected to the Mexican, Cuban, and U.S. halls of fame.

Dilthey, Wilhelm

b. November 19, 1833
Biebrich am Rhein, near Wiesbaden, Duchy of Nassau (now in Germany)
d. September 30, 1911
Seis am Schlern, near Bozen, Austrian Tirol, Austro-Hungarian Empire
fields: Philosophy

Combining major aspects of German idealism and British empiricism, Wilhelm Dilthey formulated humanistic methods for understanding and interpreting human behavior. He is known for his work to establish a distinction between the methodology of the humanities from that of the natural sciences. Major works include *Einleitung in die Geisteswissenschaften* (1883; *Introduction to the Human Sciences*, 1988), *Das Erlebnis und die Dichtung* (1905), and *Der Aufbau der geschichtlichen Welt in den Geisteswissenschaften* (1910).

DiMaggio, Joe

full: Joseph Paul DiMaggio, Jr.
b. November 25, 1914
Martinez, California
d. March 8, 1999
Hollywood, Florida
fields: Sports (baseball)

DiMaggio was one of the greatest players in major league baseball history. Besides generating impressive career batting and fielding statistics and leading the New York Yankees to ten American League pennants during his thirteen-year career, DiMaggio played with a verve, grace, and style that have made him a symbol of excellence on the baseball diamond as well as an American cultural icon.

Dine, Jim

b. June 16, 1935
Cincinnati, Ohio
fields: Art

Jim Dine is an American "pop" artist whose was confiscated as obscene when he exhibited it in London in 1966. His subject matter focused on such banal and everyday objects as hearts, hand tools, and bathrobes.

Ding, Loni

b. June 8, 1931
San Francisco, Calif.
fields: Film

Loni Ding produced documentaries on Asian American affairs. She cofounded the National Asian American Telecommunications Association (NAATA) and was president of Vox Productions. She won Northern California Emmys for *Nisei Soldier* (1984) and *Bean Sprouts* (1982).

Dinkins, David N.

b. July 10, 1927
Trenton, N.J.
fields: Government and Politics

In 1965 David Dinkins was elected to the New York state assembly. The African American assemblyman began a campaign for racial justice. In 1967 Dinkins's district, however, disappeared in a reapportionment maneuver. In 1985, he was elected president of the Borough of Manhattan, a post he held until 1989. Dinkins faced Rudolph Giuliani in the 1989 New York City mayoral race. His victory was a narrow one, and he lost to Giuliani in the 1993 mayoral election. After his loss, Dinkins began teaching at Columbia University.

Diocles of Carystus

b. c. 375 B.C.E.
Carystus, Greece
d. c. 295 B.C.E.
Athens?, Greece
fields: Medicine

Diocles was a fourth century B.C.E. Greek physician who was regarded in antiquity as second only to Hippocrates. He wrote several medical works, including the first separate treatise on anatomy and the first herbal. His best-known contributions to medicine are in the area of hygiene.

Diocletian

b. c. 245
possibly Salona
d. December 3, 316
Salona
fields: Government and Politics

Diocletian put an end to the disastrous phase of Roman history known as the Military Anarchy or the Imperial Crisis and laid the foundation for the later Roman Empire known as the Byzantine Empire. His reforms ensured the continuity of the Roman Empire in the East for more than a thousand years.

Diogenes

b. c. 412 B.C.E.
Sinope, modern Turkey
d. c. 323 B.C.E.
probably Corinth, Greece
fields: Philosophy, Religion and Theology, Theology

The most famous and colorful of the Cynic philosophers, Diogenes lived in extreme poverty and shunned all comforts in his quest for a virtuous life.

Dionysius. *See* Denis, Saint

Dionysius Exiguus

b. Second half of the fifth century
Scythia
d. First half of the sixth century
Rome
fields: Religion and Theology

Dionysius Exiguus provided a more accurate means to ascertain the date of Easter and initiated the convention of the Christian era by basing the calendar on the year of the birth of Christ.

Diophantus

b. fl. c. 250 C.E.
place unknown
d. Date unknown
place unknown
fields: Mathematics

Diophantus wrote a treatise on arithmetic which represents the most complete collection of problems dating from Greek times involving solutions of determinate and indeterminate equations. This work was the basis of much medieval Arabic and European Renaissance algebra.

Dioscorides, Pedanius

b. c. 40 C.E.
Anazarbus, Roman Cilicia (modern Turkey)
d. c. 90 C.E.
place unknown
fields: Medicine

Through wide travel and much observation, Dioscorides compiled, organized, and published the most comprehensive pharmacological text produced in the ancient world. The work, *De materia medica*, remained a standard reference work for herbalists and physicians for some sixteen hundred years.

Dirac, Paul Adrien Maurice

b. Aug. 8, 1902
Bristol, Gloucestershire, England
d. Oct. 20, 1984
Tallahassee, Florida
fields: Mathematics, Physics

Paul Adrien Maurice Dirac was one of the founders of quantum mechanics; formulated a relativistic model of the electron in 1928; developed early quantum radiation theory. Based on his equations, predicted the existence of the positron, the antiparticle that is the opposite of the electron. In 1933, he was awarded the Nobel Prize in Physics jointly with Erwin Schrödinger.

Dirichlet, Peter Gustav Lejeune

b. Feb. 13, 1805
Düren, French Empire (now Germany)
d. May 5, 1859
Göttingen, Hanover (now Germany)
fields: Mathematics (applied math and number theory)

In 1829, Peter Gustav Lejeune Dirichlet published a paper in which he proved the sufficient conditions for the convergence of a Fourier series. In 1837, he published a paper proving that many arithmetic sequences contain an infinite number of primes. In 1837, he gave a modern view of the concept of a function.

Dirksen, Everett
full: Everett McKinley Dirksen
b. January 4, 1896
Pekin, Illinois
d. September 7, 1969
Washington, D.C.
fields: Government and Politics

Elected Republican minority leader in the U.S. Senate (1959), Everett Dirksen played a crucial role in drafting and passing the civil rights legislation of the 1960's. In 1963, his support of the Nuclear Test Ban Treaty ensured its passage; a year later, his efforts on behalf of the Civil Rights Act of 1964 enabled it to pass despite a filibuster in the Senate. Dirksen became a widely recognized and popular figure because of his television program, in which he appeared with his Republican counterparts in the House.

Disney, Walt
full: Walter Elias Disney
b. December 5, 1901
Chicago, Illinois
d. December 15, 1966
Burbank, California
fields: Film, Television, Theater and Entertainment

More than any other person, Disney was an innovator in the entertainment industry, a chance-taker responsible for what he termed "imagineering," leading the way in children's amusements.

Disraeli, Benjamin
full: Benjamin Disraeli, first earl of Beaconsfield
b. December 21, 1804
London, England
d. April 19, 1881
London, England
fields: Government and Politics, Literature

Disraeli overcame social and political prejudice in nineteenth century Great Britain to become leader of the Conservative Party, served twice as prime minister (1868, 1874-1880), and formulated a "Tory Radicalism" distinctively free from the prevalent Whig-Liberal philosophy of Utilitarianism.

Diwali. *See* Bowl

Dix, Dorothea
full: Dorothea ynde Dix
b. April 4, 1802
Hampden, Maine (then part of Massachusetts)
d. July 17, 1887
Trenton, New Jersey
fields: Social Reform

A crusader for the rights of the mentally ill, Dix devoted her life to establishing psychiatric hospitals to provide proper care for those with mental and emotional problems.

Dixon, Big Willie
full: Willie Dixon
b. July 1, 1915
Vicksburg, Miss.
d. Jan. 29, 1992
Los Angeles, Calif.
fields: Music (blues bassist, singer, and songwriter)

African American bassist, singer, and songwriter; Big Willie Dixon influenced a generation of rock and roll musicians; greatly involved in the early success of Chess Records as the company's in-house bass player and songwriter; hit songs include the standards "Hootchie Coochie Man," and "You Need Love."

Dixon, Charlie
full: Charles Edward Dixon
b. c. 1898
Jersey City, N.J.
d. Dec. 6, 1940
New York, N.Y.
fields: Music (banjoist and jazz arranger and composer)

African American banjoist and jazz arranger and composer; Charlie Dixon joined Fletcher Henderson's band in 1924; left Henderson in 1928, but continued to arrange for him; arranged "Harlem Congo" (1937) for Chick Webb.

Dixon, Dean
b. Jan. 10, 1915
New York, N.Y.
d. Nov. 3, 1976
Zurich, Switzerland
fields: Music (conductor)

African American conductor; Dean Dixon was the first African American conductor of the New York Philharmonic Orchestra; founded the Dean Dixon Symphony Orchestra and the Dean Dixon Choral Society in New York.

Dixon, Ivan, III
b. Apr. 6, 1931
New York, N.Y.
fields: Television, Theater and Entertainment

African American actor; Ivan Dixon III is best known for his role as Sergeant Kinchloe in *Hogan's Heroes* (1965-1970); his theater work includes *The Cave Dwellers* (1957) and *A Raisin in the Sun* (1959); also directed television programs in the 1960's and films, including *The Spook Who Sat by the Door* (1973), which he also produced.

Dixon, Jessy
b. Mar. 12, 1938
San Antonio, Tex.
fields: Music (composer, pianist, and gospel music singer)

African American composer, pianist, and gospel music singer; Jessy Dixon directed the Omega Singers, the Thompson Community Choir, and the Jessy Dixon Singers; achieving success in gospel music, he was chosen to represent contemporary gospel, in 1980, at the Golden Jubilee Year Celebration of Gospel Music.

Dixon, Julian C.
b. Aug. 8, 1934
Washington, D.C.
fields: Government and Politics

African American congressman; Julian C. Dixon, a Democrat, was the first African American to chair a congressional appropriations subcommittee; served in California state assembly (1972-1978); was elected to represent the Twenty-eighth congressional district (1978); chaired the Congressional Black Caucus (1983-1984).

Dixon, Richard Clay
b. ?
Dayton, Ohio
fields: Government and Politics

African American mayor of Dayton, Ohio; Richard Clay Dixon was appointed city commissioner for Dayton (1979); elected mayor (1987).

Dixon, Sharon Pratt. *See* Kelly, Sharon Pratt

Djilas, Milovan
b. June 12, 1911
Podbišće, Montenegro
d. April 20, 1995
Belgrade, Serbia
fields: Government and Politics, Philosophy, Literature

Djilas was a leader of the Partisan forces in the resistance to the Axis and its allies and collaborators in the Yugoslav Revolution during World War II, and he was a founding father of Titoist Yugoslavia. In the process he became a major theoretician and critic of postwar communism as well as a major European writer.

Dobbs, Mattiwilda
b. July 11, 1925
Atlanta, Ga.

fields: Music (opera soprano)
African American opera soprano; Mattiwilda Dobbs debuted with the New York Metropolitan Opera in 1956.

Doby, Larry
full: Lawrence Eugene Doby
b. Dec. 13, 1924
Camden, S.C.
fields: Sports (baseball player)
African American baseball player; Larry Doby was the first African American player in the American League; played for the Cleveland Indians, beginning in 1947, twice leading the league in home runs.

Doctor, Henry, Jr.
b. Aug. 23, 1932
Oakley, S.C.
fields: Military Affairs
Highly decorated African American military officer; Henry Doctor, Jr. served in a number of high ranking positions before retiring from the U.S. Army with the rank of lieutenant general.

Dr. Dre
né: Andre Young
b. February 18, 1965
Los Angeles, Calif.
fields: Music (rap producer, composer, vocalist, and entrepreneur)
African American rap producer, composer, vocalist, and entrepreneur; a founding father of West Coast "gangsta rap," Dr. Dre released hit albums including *Eazy Duz It* (1985), *Straight Outta Compton* (1988), *100 Miles and Runnin'* (1990), *Efil4zaggin* (1991), *The Chronic* (1992), and *Dr. Dre Presents ... The Aftermath* (1996); produced for other artists on his company label, Death Row Records. Formed a new company after Death Row Records went out of business in 1996.

Dr. J. *See* Erving, Julius

Dodds, Johnny
b. Apr. 12, 1892
New Orleans, La.
d. Aug. 8, 1940
Chicago, Ill.
fields: Music (jazz clarinetist and alto saxophonist)
African American jazz clarinetist and alto saxophonist; Johnny Dodds is considered a transitional figure between the older, more formalized style and the improvisation-based playing of other jazz clarinetist such as Sidney Bechet and Jimmie Noone.

Dodge, Annie. *See* Wauneka, Annie Dodge

Dodge, Henry Chee
aka: Hastin Adiits'a'ii (Mr. Interpreter)
b. Feb. 22, 1860
Fort Defiance, Ariz.
d. Jan. 7, 1947
Ganado, Ariz.
fields: Government and Politics, Native American Affairs
Native American leader. A Navajo, Henry Chee Dodge played a central role as an interpreter, businessman, and tribal chairman in more than half a century of dealings between the U.S. government and the Navajos. In 1922, Dodge became a member of the Tribal Business Council. He was elected the tribe's first chairman the following year, serving until 1928.

Dodgson, Charles Lutwidge. *See* Carroll, Lewis

Dodson, Owen
b. Nov. 28, 1914
Brooklyn, N.Y.
d. June 21, 1983
New York, N.Y.
fields: Literature, Education
African American writer; Owen Dodson became head of the Howard University drama department.

Doe, Samuel K.
full: Samuel Kanyon Doe
b. May 6, 1950
Tuzon, Grand Gedeh, Liberia
d. September 9, 1990
Monrovia, Liberia
fields: Government and Politics
President of Liberia from 1980 to 1990. Samuel K. Doe seized power after being involved in the assassination of President William Tolbert in 1980. Biases that had previously favored Americo-Liberians were eliminated. Soon instances of government suppression of dissent as well as the government's murder of opponent Thomas Quiwonkpa sewed unrest. Tribal factionalism between Doe's Krahn tribe and the Gio and Mande grew. By the late 1980's Doe was losing control of Liberia's rural areas; rebel leaders Charles Taylor and Prince Yormie Johnson made gains and advanced on the capital. Johnson apprehended and murdered Doe in 1990; Taylor eventually assumed power.

Dohasan
aka: Little Mountain
aka: Little Bluff
aka: Dahauson
aka: Tohauson
b. c. 1805
d. c. 1866
Indian Territory, present-day Okla.
fields: Warfare and Conquest, Native American Affairs
Native American leader. A Kiowa, Dohasan forged an alliance between independent Kiowa bands, making the tribe a major power in the southern Plains in the 1840's. Signed the Treaty of Fort Atkinson in 1853 and the Little Arkansas Treaty of 1865.

Doi, Isami
b. May 12, 1903
Ewa, Oahu, Territory of Hawaii
d. 1965
fields: Art
After receiving a B.A. in art studies from Columbia University, Isami Doi moved to Paris to study from 1930 until 1931. After returning to New York, he advised and encouraged many Japanese American artists, eventually returning to Hawaii to paint. Various museums and galleries have exhibited his works.

Doi, Nelson Kiyoshi
b. Jan. 1, 1922
Pahoa, Hawaii
fields: Government and Politics
Nelson Kiyoshi Doi, lieutenant governor of Hawaii, 1974-1979, helped the Japanese American Democrats rise to power after World War II. He earned his bachelor's degree from the University of Hawaii and his law degree from the University of Minnesota Law School in 1948. Before serving as lieutenant governor, he was Hawaii state senator, 1959-1969, and senior justice of the Third Circuit Court, Hilo, 1969-1974.

Doi, Yuriko
b. Aug. 13, 1941
Tokyo, Japan
fields: Theater and Entertainment
Yuriko Doi studied theater at Waseda University before emigrating to the United States in 1967. She founded San Francisco's Theatre of Yugen in 1978. This company attempted to cultivate American appreciation for classical Japanese *kyogen* and Noh theater and to create crosscultural theater by combining Western themes and materials with classical Japanese performance techniques.

Dole, Bob
full: Robert Joseph Dole
b. July 22, 1923
Russell, Kansas
fields: Government and Politics
A prominent Republican senator and presidential candidate, Dole was an effective legislator, mediator, and deal maker who sup-

ported legislation for civil rights, farm reform, aid for the disabled, Social Security, and a balanced federal budget.

Dole, Elizabeth
né: Mary Elizabeth Hanford
b. July 29, 1936
Salisbury, North Carolina
fields: Government and Politics

A dedicated government official, Elizabeth Dole served five American presidents in cabinet and other appointed positions, and she made a bid for the U.S. presidency in 2000.

Dolphy, Eric
b. June 20, 1928
Los Angeles, Calif.
d. June 29, 1964
West Berlin, West Germany
fields: Music (alto saxophonist, bass clarinetist, flutist, and composer)

African American alto saxophonist, bass clarinetist, flutist, and composer; Eric Dolphy was one of the major instrumental voices in avant-garde jazz; his appreciation of the musicality of bird song sparked interest among musicians using ecological themes; recordings include *The Complete Prestige Recordings of Eric Dolphy* (1995) and *Out to Lunch* (1964).

Domagk, Gerhard
b. October 30, 1895
Lagow, Germany
d. April 24, 1964
Burgberg, West Germany
fields: Biochemistry, Medicine

Domagk was awarded the Nobel Prize in Physiology or Medicine in 1939 for his discovery that a synthesized dye, prontosil, was an effective treatment for streptococcal infections in mice. This discovery led to the development of sulfa drugs, the first successful chemical means for dealing with bacterial infections.

Domingo, Placido
b. Jan. 21, 1941
Madrid, Spain
fields: Music

Opera singer and conductor. Dynamic opera tenor Placido Domingo made his professional debut in 1961 in Monterrey, Mexico, in *La Traviata*. In 1965, Domingo made his New York City debut with the New York City Opera, and in 1968, he debuted with the New York Metropolitan Opera. In 1975, he began conducting orchestras. He joined José Carreras and Luciano Pavarotti to sing at the 1990 soccer World Cup; in 1994, they performed together again on the eve of the World Cup in Los Angeles, California. In 1996, he assumed the artistic directorship of the Washington Opera.

Dominic, Saint
b. c. 1170
Calaruega, Old Castile, Spain
d. August 6, 1221
Bologna, Italy
fields: Religion and Theology, Monasticism

Through faith, courage, and practicality, Dominic established the Dominican Order in 1215, which revolutionized the monastic movement of the Middle Ages and filled a vital need for apostolic preaching in the Church.

Domino, Fats
full: Antoine Domino
b. Feb. 26, 1928
New Orleans, La.
fields: Music (pianist and singer)

African American pianist and singer; Fats Domino was an influential figure in early rhythm and blues; appeared in the teen films *Shake, Rattle, and Rock* (1956) and *The Girl Can't Help It* (1956); hits include "Ain't That a Shame," (1955), "I'm Walk'n'" (1957), and "Blueberry Hill" (1956).

Don Francisco
né: Mario Kreutzberger
b. 1941
Chile
fields: Television

Television personality. The son of Jewish immigrants who fled Germany and settled in Chile, Mario Kreutzberger is best known as Don Francisco, the uninhibited host of the weekly Univisión network television show *Sábado Gigante*. The show's audience was estimated in 1992 at forty million viewers worldwide. In 1991, he began hosting another Univisión program, *Noche de Gigantes*.

Donatello
né: Donato di Niccolò di Betto Bardi
b. c. 1386
Florence
d. December 13, 1466
Florence
fields: Art

One of the first great European artists to articulate fully the principles of perspective, Donatello has had an incalculable influence on his successors, who have derived their inspiration from his highly naturalistic and intense dramatizations of the human form.

Donehogawa. *See* Parker, Ely Samuel

Dong, Arthur E.
b. October 30, 1953
San Francisco, Calif.
fields: Film, Theater and Entertainment

Arthur E. Dong, educated at the American Film Institute, the Center for Advanced Studies, and San Francisco State University, produced and directed numerous Asian American films and documentaries. His films include *Forbidden City, U.S.A.* (1989), which won nine awards from various film festivals, and *Sewing Woman* (1982), a short film nominated for an Academy Award for its portrayal of a woman's struggle to survive.

Dönitz, Karl
b. September 16, 1891
Grünau, near Berlin, Germany
d. December 24, 1980
Aumühle-Bilenkamp, near Hamburg, West Germany
fields: Military Affairs, Warfare and Conquest

Shortly after the outbreak of World War II in 1939, German admiral Karl Dönitz was named commander of the German submarine (U-boat) fleet. He then commanded the German navy between 1943 and 1945. Steadfast in his commitment to Hitler. Dönitz's "wolf pack" tactics concentrated large numbers of submarines against Allied ship convoys. In a series of major convoy battles, German submarines were destroying Allied ships faster than they could be replaced. By May, 1943, however, the Battle of the Atlantic had turned in favor of the Allies.

Donizetti, Gaetano
b. November 29, 1797
Bergamo, Cisalpine Republic
d. April 8, 1848
Bergamo, Austrian Empire
fields: Music

Donizetti was the most prolific composer of Italian operas in the first half of the nineteenth century. Though his work are uneven in quality, he was, at his best, the greatest and most vital exponent of Italian Romanticism before Giuseppe Verdi.

Donnaconna
b. ?
d. c. 1539
France
fields: Government and Politics, Native American Affairs

Native American leader. A Huron, Donnaconna was the first Indian leader of note to resist French incursion into tribal territory in present-day Canada. However, explorer Jacques Cartier seized Donnaconna, his two sons, and seven other of his villagers in 1536 and forced the captives to sail to France with him. None of them returned to their homeland; all but one died soon after arrival in France.

Donne, John

b. Between January 24 and June 19, 1572
London, England
d. March 31, 1631
London, England
fields: Literature

Capturing the restless, questioning spirit of the early seventeenth century, Donne established the "metaphysical" style—witty, colloquial, and dramatic—in his love poetry, which is both devotional and erotic.

Doob, Leonard W.

b. March 3, 1909
New York, N.Y.
fields: Psychiatry and Psychology

Before World War II Leonard Doob was one of several behavioral scientists associated with the Institute for Propaganda Analysis. In 1940 he joined the Committee for National Morale, designed to foster public morale during the war. He later worked on psychological warfare with the Office of War Information, heading the office's Bureau of Overseas Intelligence. His books include *Propaganda: Its Psychology and Technique* (1935), *Public Opinion and Propaganda* (1948), and *Frustration and Aggression* (1939).

Doolittle, Hilda. *See* H. D.

Dorat, Jean

aka: Jean Daurat
b. 1508
Limoges, France
d. 1588
fields: Literature

A member of la Pléiade (fl. 1549-1589), a group of loosely organized poets dedicated to raising the level of sophistication of the French language by adding words and genres derived from classical literature. Led by Pierre de Ronsard and Joachim du Bellay, they developed a new form of poetry based on forms such as the sonnet, the ode, epic, and elegy. They also worked to elevate the level of the poet to a position as an intermediary between humanity and the heavens.

Dorchester, Lord. *See* Carleton, Guy

Dorgon

b. November 17, 1612
Mukden, Manchuria
d. December 31, 1650
Kharakhotun, China
fields: Military Affairs, Government and Politics

Dorgon devised and implemented the political and military policies which led to the Manchu conquest of China. As regent over the first Ch'ing emperor, his measures contributed to the longevity of Manchu rule.

Dorn, Michael

b. Dec. 9, 1952
Luling, Tex.
fields: Television

African American actor; Michael Dorn played Lieutenant Worf on television series *Star Trek: The Next Generation* (1987-1992) and *Star Trek: Deep Space Nine* (1993-1999).

Dorsett, Tony

full: Anthony Drew Dorsett
b. Apr. 7, 1954
Aliquippa, Pa.
fields: Sports (football player)

African American football player; Tony Dorsett was a first round draft choice in 1977 and played running back for the Dallas Cowboys until 1988.

Dorsey, Thomas Andrew

aka: Georgia Tom
b. July 1, 1899
Villa Rica, Ga.
d. Jan. 23, 1993
Chicago, Ill.
fields: Music (blues musician and gospel music composer)

African American blues musician and gospel music composer; known as the father of gospel music, Thomas Andrew Dorsey was first known as a composer and performer of blues songs; teamed with Tampa Red and Ma Rainey; founded the first gospel choir at Ebenezer Baptist Church in 1931; best known songs are "Tight Like That" (blues) and "Take My Hand, Precious Lord" (gospel).

Dostoevski, Fyodor

full: Fyodor Mihaylovich Dostoevski
b. November 11, 1821
Moscow, Russia
d. February 9, 1881
St. Petersburg, Russia
fields: Literature

One of the world's greatest novelists, Dostoevski summoned to imaginative life areas of psychological, political, and aesthetic experience which have significantly shaped the modern sensibility.

Doug E. Fresh

b. Sept. 17, 1966
fields: Music (Rap vocalist)

African American rap vocalist; Doug E. Fresh was known as "The Human Beat Box"; hits include "The Show," which also featured rapper Ricky "Slick Rick" Walters.

Douglas, Aaron

b. May 26, 1899
Topeka, Kans.
d. Feb. 2, 1979
Nashville, Tenn.
fields: Art (painter and illustrator)

African American painter and illustrator; Aaron Douglas gained recognition in the 1920's and 1930's; adapted art deco to uniquely African American themes and motifs; works include the murals *Aspects of Negro Life* (1934) at the Schomburg Center in the New York Public Library.

Douglas, Helen Gahagan

né: Mary Helen Gahagan
b. November 25, 1900
Boonton, New Jersey
d. June 28, 1980
New York, New York
fields: Theater and Entertainment, Government and Politics

As a congresswoman from California and in her private life, Douglas was an outspoken advocate of civil liberties and opportunities for oppressed minorities.

Douglas, Minnie. *See* Memphis Minnie

Douglas, Stephen A.

full: Stephen Arnold Douglas
b. April 23, 1813
Brandon, Vermont
d. June 3, 1861
Chicago, Illinois
fields: Government and Politics

Endowed with a vision of nationalism, Douglas worked to develop the United States internally and to preserve the Union.

Douglas, Tommy

full: Thomas Clement Douglas
b. October 20, 1904
Falkirk, Scotland
d. February 24, 1986
Ottawa, Canada
fields: Government and Politics

Canadian political leader Tommy Douglas was long-time premier of Saskatchewan, serving from 1944 to 1961. His party's government instituted publicly financed medical care in Saskatchewan, which eventually led to the establishment of Canada's public health-care system. In 1961, Douglas became the first leader of a new national party, the New Democratic Party, which he led for ten years.

Douglas, William O.

full: William Orville Douglas
b. October 16, 1898
Maine, Minnesota

b. January 19, 1980
Washington, D.C.
fields: Law

U.S. Supreme Court justice, 1939-1975; William O. Douglas was appointed by President Franklin D. Roosevelt; during his tenure he championed personal freedom and opposed censorship; significant opinions were *Terminiello v. Chicago*, 337 U.S. 1 (1949); *Griswold v. Connecticut*, 381 U.S. 479 (1965); *Argersinger v. Hamlin*, 407 U.S. 25 (1972). Other writings: *Go East, Young Man* (1974); *The Court Years, 1939-1975* (1980); and more than thirty other books.

Douglas-Home, Alexander

full: Alexander Frederick Douglas-Home
aka: Viscount Dunglass
b. July 2, 1903
London, England
d. October 9, 1995
The Hirsel, Coldstream, Berwickshire, Scotland
fields: Government and Politics

Prime minister of Great Britain in 1963 and 1964, Alexander (Alec) Douglas-Home wrestled, not always successfully, with Britain's economic woes. His brief term as Conservative prime minister was not distinguished, but he was an effective foreign secretary under Prime Minister Harold Macmillan from 1960 to 1963.

Douglass, Frederick

b. February, 1817?
Tuckahoe, Talbot County, Maryland
d. February 20, 1895
Washington, D.C.
fields: Civil Rights, Social Reform

Born a slave, Frederick Douglass' lifelong concerns were with freedom and human rights for all people. He articulated these concerns most specifically for black Americans and women.

Dove, Rita

b. August 28, 1952
Akron, Ohio
fields: Literature (poet, short-story writer, novelist, and educator)

African American poet, short-story writer, novelist, and educator; Rita Dove, the first African American poet laureate of the United States (1993-1995), published *Thomas and Beulah* in 1986, for which she won the Pulitzer Prize in poetry; other poetic works include *The Yellow House on the Corner* (1980), *Mandolin* (1982), *Museum* (1983), *The Other Side of the House* (1988), *Grace Notes* (1989), and *Mother Love* (1995); she has published in other generes as well.

Dove, Ulysses

b. January 17, 1947
Jonesville, S.C.
d. June 11, 1996
New York, N.Y.
fields: Dance (choreographer and dancer)

African American choreographer and dancer; Ulysses Dove debuted in the Alvin Ailey American Dance Theater with the piece *I See the Moon . . . and the Moon Sees Me* (1979); his best-known freelance works include *Vespers* (1986); *Episodes* (1987), and *Serious Pleasures* (1992); his last ballet, "Twilight," was premiered in New York City shortly before his AIDS-related death.

Downer, Alexander

full: Alexander John Gosse Downer
b. September 9, 1951
Adelaide, Australia
fields: Government and Politics

Australian political figure Alexander Downer was briefly Liberal Party leader in 1994; replaced by more popular John Howard. Upon becoming prime minister in 1996, Howard appointed Downer foreign minister. Downer faced a number of Asian and Pacific problems, including New Guinea's Sandline crisis and the severe economic crisis that, among other things, led to the resignation of President Suharto of Indonesia in 1998.

Doyle, Arthur Conan

aka: Sir Arthur Conan Doyle
b. May 22, 1859
Edinburgh, Scotland
d. July 7, 1930
Crowborough, Sussex, England
fields: Literature

Doyle created one of the first and most popular and long-lived of fictional detectives: Sherlock Holmes.

Doyle, Sam

b. 1906
d. 1985
Saint Helena Island, S.C.
fields: Art (painter and wood sculptor)

African American painter and wood sculptor; Sam Doyle, a self-taught artist, was known for his "naive" style. His enamel paintings depict local personalities and his wood sculptures re-create animals with regional as well as spiritual significance.

Dozier, Edward Pasqual

aka: Awa Tside
b. Apr. 23, 1916
Santa Clara Pueblo, N.Mex.
d. May 2, 1971
Tucson, Ariz.
fields: Anthropology

One of the first American Indian professors of anthropology. Edward P. Dozier, a Santa Clara Pueblo, published many important articles and books based on his research among Pueblo people and in the Philippines. Books include *The Tewa of Arizona* (1954) and *Hano: A Tewa Village in Arizona* (1966).

Draco

b. Unknown; perhaps seventh century B.C.E.
perhaps Athens, Greece
d. Unknown; perhaps seventh century B.C.E.
perhaps Athens, Greece
fields: Government and Politics, Law

At the behest of the Athenian Council, Draco produced the first written codification of law for the ancient city-state. His effort is remembered primarily for the harshness of its penalties and for its differentiation between various homicidal acts. Draco was the first to assert that the state should be responsible for the punishment of homicide.

Dragging Canoe

aka: Cheucunsene
aka: Kunmesee
aka: Tsungunsini
b. c. 1730
Running Water Village on the Tennessee River, Tenn.
d. Mar. 1, 1792
Running Water Village, Tenn.
fields: Government and Politics, Warfare and Conquest, Native American Affairs

Native American leader. Cherokee leader Dragging Canoe violently opposed white expansion into Indian land. Unlike his father, Chief Attakullakulla, he was against any form of white encroachment on Cherokee lands. As the Cherokee continued signing away their land, Dragging Canoe maintained his policy of armed resistance until 1784.

Drake, Francis

aka: Sir Francis Drake
b. c. 1540
Crowndale, Devonshire, England
d. January 28, 1596
at sea off Porto Bello, Panama
fields: Exploration and Colonization

A flair for leadership, combined with fearlessness and a powerful spirit of adventure, afforded Drake the most prominent place among those Elizabethan explorers and naval commanders who pioneered England's overseas expansion.

Draper, Louis H.

b. 1935
Richmond, Va.
fields: Photography

African American photographer; Louis H. Draper cofounded the Kamoinge Workshop in Harlem, which subsequently opened the Market Place gallery, a popular gathering place for black writers and artists in the 1960's.

Draves, Vickie

né: Victoria Manalo
aka: Victoria Taylor
b. December 31, 1924
San Francisco, Calif.
fields: Sports (diving)

As a sixteen year old, Vickie Manalo, the daughter of a Filipino man and a British woman, was invited to join a diving club on Nob Hill, which she did although forced to drop her Filipino last name, Manalo, and adopt her mother's maiden name, Taylor. She trained with diving coach Charlie Sava, then with Lyle Draves at Oakland's Athens Club. She stopped training for a time. After World War II, she married Draves, returned to top form and won three consecutive ten-meter platform diving titles at the National Tower Diving Championships between 1946 and 1948 and earned the national springboard title in 1948. As a member of the 1948 U.S. Olympic diving team, Draves earned gold medals in women's platform and springboard diving, becoming the first woman to place first in both diving competitions at the same Olympic games. She was inducted into the International Swimming Hall of Fame in 1969.

Dreiser, Theodore

full: Theodore Herman Albert Dreiser
b. August 27, 1871
Terre Haute, Indiana
d. December 28, 1945
Hollywood, California
fields: Literature

Combining a strong social conscience, a frankly deterministic view of life as a struggle for survival, and an honest representation of human sexuality, Dreiser's fiction helped to shape a generation of American writers and to mute the voice of censorship in American culture.

Drew, Charles Richard

b. June 3, 1904
Washington, D.C.
d. April 1, 1950
near Burlington, N.C.
fields: Medicine

Charles Drew compiled all the existing knowledge on stored, or banked, blood, and added his own research. During World War II, Drew, an African American surgeon and researcher at Howard University was made medical director of the Blood for Britain program, where he refined the emergency use of plasma and developed the practical storage and distribution of blood supplies. Drew also helped establish a similar program for the United States.

Drew, Timothy. *See* Ali, Noble Drew

Drexel, Katherine

b. Nov. 26, 1858
Philadelphia, Pa.
d. Mar. 3, 1955
Cornwells Heights, Pa.
fields: Religion and Theology

The daughter of a wealthy philanthropist, Katherine Drexel founded of the Sisters of the Blessed Sacrament, which served Native Americans and African Americans through its schools and orphanages; beatified in 1988.

Drexler, Clyde

b. June 22, 1962
New Orleans, La.
fields: Sports (basketball player)

African American basketball player; Clyde Drexler played guard for the Portland Trail Blazers, beginning in 1983. He was traded to the Houston Rockets in 1995.

Dreyer, Carl Theodor

b. February 3, 1889
Copenhagen, Denmark
d. March 20, 1968
Copenhagen, Denmark
fields: Film

Dreyer is Denmark's most famous film director, an auteur who had total control over his films. Despite the relatively few films he directed (about one a decade once he was established), he became an international director, whose reputation rests, for the most part, on three films: *The Passion of Joan of Arc, Day of Wrath,* and *Ordet.*

Drinkard, Emily. *See* Houston, Cissy

Driskell, David C.

b. June 7, 1931
Eatonton, Ga.
fields: Art (painter, art historian, art consultant, and educator)

African American painter, art historian, art consultant, and educator; David C. Driskell authored several art catalogs and art history books, including *Two Centuries of Black American Art* (1976).

Driver, Wilsonia Benita. *See* Sanchez, Sonia

D'Rivera, Paquito

b. June 4, 1948
Havana, Cuba
fields: Music

Alto saxophonist. Paquito D'Rivera is one of the leading practitioners of the Latin American "bop" saxophone style and is also an accomplished soprano saxophone, flute, and flugelhorn player. He has played in the Orquesta Cubana de Música Moderna; in the group Irakere; with David Amram, Dizzy Gillespie, and McCoy Tyner; with his own group; and as a studio musician.

Dryden, John

b. August 19, 1631
Aldwinckle, Northamptonshire, England
d. May 1, 1700
London, England
fields: Literature

Poet, playwright, satirist, translator, and critic, Dryden was the central literary figure in the English Restoration period.

D'Souza, Dinesh

b. April 25, 1961
Bombay, India
fields: Literature, Social Reform

Dinesh D'Souza is an author; born in Bombay; came to the United States in 1978 to complete his high school education; while in college edited the *Dartmouth Review* (1981), often perceived as being insensitive to minorities; contributed articles to prominent conservative political journals; assistant to domestic policy chief Gary Bauer during the administration of President Ronald Reagan, 1987-1989; best known for his *Illiberal Education: The Politics of Race and Sex on Campus* (1991), a bestseller that fueled a national debate on political correctness and the best means of creating fair rules for a diverse society.

Du Fu

aka: Tu Fu
b. 712
perhaps Duling, Shaanxi, China
d. 770
Tanzhou (modern Chang sha), Hunan province, China
fields: Literature

Du Fu is considered the greatest of Chinese poets as well as one of the giant figures of world literature.

Duardo, Richard

b. 1952
fields: Art

Artist. Richard Duardo is a silkscreen artist who helped found the Centro de Arte Publico in Los Angeles in the 1970's. He has promoted Chicano style with such silkscreens as *Zoot Suit* (1978) and *Aztlan* (1982).

Duarte, José Napoleon

b. November 23, 1926
San Salvador, El Salvador
d. February 23, 1990
San Salvador, El Salvador

fields: Government and Politics
President of El Salvador from 1984 to 1989. José Napoleon Duarte assumed control of El Salvador in 1980 after a coup against President Carlos Humberto Romero in 1979 created widespred unrest. Subsequently elected president; took office in 1984. El Salvador's bloody civil war began in the early 1980's and did not end until 1992. Right-wing death squads assassinated political opponents Leftists, in turn, killed many local government officials. Some eighty thousand casualties occurred, mostly at the hands of out-of-control government troops.

Duarte, María Eva. *See* Perón, Eva

Dubček, Alexander
b. November 27, 1921
Uhrovec, Czechoslovakia
d. November 7, 1992
Prague, Czechoslovakia
fields: Government and Politics
After becoming first secretary of the Czechoslovakian Communist Party on January 5, 1968, Dubček led the liberalization movement known as the Prague Spring. He attempted, unsuccessfully, to move Czechoslovakian politics and economy away from Stalinist notions of Marxist socialism.

du Bellay, Joachim
b. c. 1522
d. 1560
fields: Literature
A member of la Pléiade (fl. 1549-1589), a group of loosely organized poets dedicated to raising the level of sophistication of the French language by adding words and genres derived from classical literature. Led by Pierre de Ronsard and Joachim du Bellay, they developed a new form of poetry based on forms such as the sonnet, the ode, epic, and elegy. They also worked to elevate the level of the poet to a position as an intermediary between humanity and the heavens.

Du Bois, Shirley Graham
né: Shirley Graham
b. Nov. 11, 1896
Evansville, Ind.
d. Mar. 27, 1977
Beijing, China
fields: Literature
African American writer; Shirley Graham Du Bois was a civil rights activist in the 1940's in addition to being a playwright; married W. E. B. Du Bois in 1951.

Du Bois, W. E. B.
full: William Edward Burghardt Du Bois
b. February 23, 1868
Great Barrington, Massachusetts
d. August 27, 1963
Accra, Ghana
fields: Civil Rights, Journalism
One of the principal founders of the National Association for the Advancement of Colored People and editor of several influential journals, Du Bois was for many years the leading black intellectual in the United States. Through his teaching, writings, and speeches he advocated economic, political, and cultural advancement of blacks not only in the United States but also abroad.

Duccio di Buoninsegna
b. c. 1255
possibly Siena
d. August 3, 1319
Siena
fields: Art
By blending techniques borrowed from French Gothic, Florentine, and Byzantine art, Duccio created a distinct Sienese style of painting. His attempts at three-dimensionality and his inventive use of architectural structures in his painting influenced future generations of Italian and French artists.

Duchamp, Marcel
full: Henri-Robert-Marcel Duchamp
b. July 28, 1887
Blainville, France
d. October 2, 1968
Neuilly, France
fields: Art
Duchamp became the most controversial, provocative, and enigmatic figure in modern art of the twentieth century. A maverick, he began as a painter but spent the rest of his life questioning and testing every convention and premise for art known.

Dudevant, Baronne. *See* Sand, George

Dudley, Anne. *See* Bradstreet, Anne

Dudley, Edward Richard
b. Mar. 11, 1911
South Boston, Va.
fields: Government and Politics, Law
African American political appointee; Edward Richard Dudley was U.S. ambassador to Liberia (1948-1953); borough president of Manhattan (1961-1965); administrative judge of the New York Supreme Court (1971-1985).

Duffy, Marguerite Josephine. *See* Terry, Megan

Duke, Bill
full: William Duke
b. February, 1943
Poughkeepsie, N.Y.
fields: Film, Television
African American actor, director, and writer; Bill Duke appeared in the films *Car Wash* (1976) and *American Gigolo* (1980); directed *The Killing Floor* (1984) for television and *A Rage in Harlem* (1991).

Duke, David
b. July 1, 1950
Tulsa, Oklahoma
fields: Government and Politics
Ku Klux Klan leader, politician; David Duke graduated from Louisiana State University; Grand Dragon, Grand Wizard of the Ku Klux Klan, 1973-1980; ties to the American Nazi Party; founder of the National Association for the Advancement of White People (NAAWP); Louisiana state representative (Republican), 1989-1991; made strong bid for the U.S. senate in 1990 with a message of racial resentment, garnering 44 percent of the vote; ran for U.S. president in 1988; reached run-off election in campaign for governor of Louisiana (1992), receiving 55 percent of the white votes.

Duke, James Buchanan
b. December 23, 1856
Durham, North Carolina
d. October 10, 1925
New York, New York
fields: Business and Industry
From modest beginnings, Duke organized and built up the largest conglomerate of tobacco companies in the nation, comprising the American Tobacco Company and its subsidiaries; he also founded power and textile companies and established the Duke Endowment in support of Duke University as well as other educational and charitable institutions.

Dulbecco, Renato
b. Feb. 22, 1914
Catanzaro, Italy
fields: Biology, Genetics
Renato Dulbecco's researched the interaction of tumor viruses and animal cells, which is essential to an understanding of cancer. In 1975, he shared the Nobel Prize in Physiology or Medicine with David Baltimore and Howard M. Temin. He first proposed the Human Genome Project, which began in 1986.

Dull Knife
aka: Wahiev
aka: Morning Star
aka: Tamela Pashme
b. c. 1810
d. c. 1883
fields: Warfare and Conquest, Government and Politics, Native American Affairs
Northern Cheyenne soldier chief. In 1860's, allied with the Sioux leaders Crazy

Horse, Gall, and Hump. One of the signers of the 1868 Fort Laramie Treaty. With Little Wolf, led the Cheyenne on ill-fated 1,500-mile journey from their exile in Indian Territory to their northern home in Montana in 1878. They were captured, and many were killed while trying to escape from Fort Robinson.

Dulles, John Foster

b. February 25, 1888
Washington, D.C.
d. May 24, 1959
Washington, D.C.
fields: Government and Politics

As secretary of state from 1953 to 1959, a period marked by major crises in Asia and Europe, Dulles advocated a policy of firmly countering Soviet and Chinese Communist advances; in doing so, he enunciated a diplomatic doctrine that had great influence in the Cold War era.

Dumars, Joe, III

b. May 24, 1963
Shreveport, La.
fields: Sports (basketball player)

African American basketball player; Joe Dumars III played guard for the Detroit Pistons beginning in 1985.

Dumas, Alexandre, *père*

b. July 24, 1802
Villers-Cotterêts, France
d. December 5, 1870
Puys, France
fields: Literature, Theater and Entertainment (drama)

Dumas was a major playwright who helped to revolutionize French drama and theater. He was one of the best historical novelists, publishing more than two hundred novels.

Dumas, Henry Lee

b. July 20, 1934
Sweet Home, Ark.
d. May 23, 1968
New York, N.Y.
fields: Literature

African American poet and short-story writer; Henry Lee Dumas was killed at the age of 33; works, the bulk of which was published posthumously, included *Ark of Bones and Other Stories* (1970).

Dumas, Jean-Baptiste-André

b. July 14, 1800
Alais (now Alès), Gard, France
d. Apr. 10, 1884
Cannes, France
fields: Chemistry

Jean-Baptiste-André Dumas developed a method for the quantitative determination of nitrogen in organic compounds in 1833; proposed substitution reactions for organic compounds in 1834; accurately measured the atomic mass of carbon in 1840; also measured molecular masses and nitrogen levels in organic compounds.

DuMetz, Barbara

b. ?
Charleston, W. Va.
fields: Photoghraphy

African American photographer; Barbara DuMetz is best known for her commercial advertising work.

Dummett, Michael

full: Michael Anthony Eardley Dummett
b. June 27, 1925
London, England
fields: Philosophy

Michael Dummett revived interest in the founder of mathematical logic, Gottlob Frege, and vigorously defended the theory of meaning as the only proper method for approaching philosophical problems. Dummett's analysis of the realism/antirealism debate probably is the aspect of his thought that has exerted the greatest influence on contemporary philosophy. Dummett himself suggested that if he had made any worthwhile contribution to philosophy, it was in developing the view that the theory of meaning underlies metaphysics. Major works include *Frege: Philosophy of Language* (1973), *Elements of Intuitionism* (1977), *Truth and Other Enigmas* (1978), *The Interpretation of Frege's Philosophy* (1981), *Frege and Other Philosophers* (1991), *Frege: Philosophy of Mathematics* (1991), *The Logical Basis of Metaphysics* (1991), *The Origins of Analytical Philosophy* (1993), and *The Seas of Language* (1993).

Dun, Dennis

b. Apr. 19, 1952
Stockton, Calif.
fields: Theater and Entertainment

Dennis Dun join the Asian-American Theatre Company in 1977 and acted in more than twenty-five productions there. His other acting work includes appearances on television's *Midnight Caller* (1988-1990) and *Falcon Crest* (1981-1990) and in films including *The Last Emperor* (1987), *Big Trouble in Little China* (1986), *Year of the Dragon* (1985), *Prince of Darkness* (1987) and *A Thousand Pieces of Gold* (1991).

Dunant, Jean-Henri

b. May 8, 1828
Geneva, Switzerland
d. October, 30, 1910
Heiden, Switzerland
fields: Social Reform

Dunant is considered both the father of the International Red Cross and the cofounder of the World's Young Men's Christian Association.

Dunbar, Paul Laurence

b. June 27, 1872
Dayton, Ohio
d. February 9, 1906
Dayton, Ohio
fields: Literature

Born to parents who had both been slaves, Paul Laurence Dunbar's is recognized for providing the most authentic written representations of African American life in the United States during the late nineteenth and early twentieth centuries.

Duncan, Arthur

b. ?
fields: Dance (tap dancer)

African American tap dancer; Arthur Duncan was the only African American dancer to appear regularly on *The Lawrence Welk Show* (1964-1982).

Duncan, Isadora

full: Angela Isadora Duncan
b. May 26, 1877
San Francisco, California
d. September 14, 1927
Nice, France
fields: Dance

Reacting against the strictures of classical ballet and the artificialities of other forms of dance, Duncan was a major innovator and one of the founders of modern dance. In her personal life, Duncan also endeavored to extend women's freedoms.

Duncan, Todd

b. Feb. 12, 1903
Danville, Ky.
d. Feb. 28, 1998, Washington, D.C.
fields: Music, Theater and Entertainment

African American performing artist; Todd Duncan performed in a number of musicals, including *Porgy and Bess*, and *Cabin in the Sky*; won the 1950 Critics Award for best male performance in a Broadway musical; sang at President Lyndon B. Johnson's inaugural.

Duncanson, Robert

b. 1817 or 1821
New York State
d. Dec. 21, 1872
Detroit, Mich.
fields: Art (painter)

African American painter; Robert Duncanson was best known for his landscapes in the romantic style.

Dunglass, Viscount. *See* Douglas-Home, Alexander

Dunham, Katherine

b. June 22, 1909
Chicago, Illinois
fields: Dance, Anthropology, Education

Katherine Dunham, an ethnologist-choreographer-dancer of African and American Indian descent, served as a catalyst and a creative force in theater and dance, translating cultural heritage through theater pieces. Her theories and techniques of movement are used by choreographers and dancers throughout the world.

Dunham, Robert

b. 1932
Kannapolis, N.C.
fields: Business and Industry

African American restaurateur; Robert Dunham was president of the Harlem McDonald's restaurant franchise.

Duns Scotus, John

b. c. March, 1266
Duns, Scotland
d. November 8, 1308
Cologne, Germany
fields: Philosophy, Religion and Theology

With his new, closely woven synthesis of Scholastic philosophical and theological thought, Duns Scotus created the school of Scotism. His rigorous and subtle critical method and fresh theoretical formulations influenced important later thinkers, from his own time to the present.

Dunstable, John

b. c. 1390
England
d. December 24, 1453
probably London, England
fields: Music

Through a strategic use of dissonance and harmonic structure, Dunstable became one of the most influential composers of the fifteenth century, laying the foundation for music in the Renaissance.

Dupin, Amandine-Aurore-Lucile. *See* Sand, George

Duplessis, Maurice

full: Maurice Le Noblet Duplessis
b. April 20, 1890
Trois-Rivières, Quebec, Canada
d. September 7, 1959
Schefferville, Quebec, Canada
fields: Government and Politics

Quebec nationalist and conservative politician. With Paul Gouin, Maurice Duplessis founded the the Union Nationale Party in 1935. Duplessis served as premier of Quebec from 1936 to 1939 and again from 1944 to 1959. From 1944, his government increased the powers of the Quebec provincial government, sometimes acting against the federal government in Ottawa, thus helping set the stage for the later quebec independence movement.

Duplessis-Mornay. *See* Mornay, Philippe de

Du Pont, Eleuthère Irénée

b. June 24, 1771
Paris, France
d. October 31, 1834
Philadelphia, Pennsylvania
fields: Business and Industry

Combining sharp business acumen with innovative technical methods and tenacious moral principles, Du Pont founded E. I. Du Pont de Nemours and Company, which became a powerful American empire.

Duran, Roberto

b. June 16, 1951
Panama City, Panama
fields: Sport (boxing)

Boxer. Roberto Duran won the world lightweight title in June, 1972 and successfully defended it until 1978, when he moved to the welterweight class. His hitting earned him the nickname *Manos de piedra*, or "Hands of Stone." In June, 1980, he bested Sugar Ray Leonard for the welterweight title; in their November, 1980, rematch, however, Duran quit in the eighth round. In 1983, he took the junior middleweight title from Davey Moore, and he captured his fourth championship in 1989 by defeating Ivan Barkley for the World Boxing Council middleweight title. He spent much of the early 1990's seeking an elusive fifth title.

Durant, Ariel

né: Chaya Kaufman
b. May 10, 1898
Proskurov, Russia
d. October 25, 1981
Los Angeles, California
fields: Historiography, Literature

With her husband, Will Durant, Ariel Durant was the author of one of the twentieth century's most ambitious works on the history of civilization: *The Story of Civilization*, 11 volumes, 1935-1975.

Duranty, Walter

b. May 25, 1884
Liverpool, England
d. October 3, 1957
Orlando, Florida
fields: Journalism

Walter Duranty was a journalist whose writings were manipulated by the Soviet Union for propaganda purposes. From the 1920's through 1941 he was a *New York Times* correspondent in the Soviet Union, where he became known as a reliable reporter on local events. After he won a Pulitzer Prize in 1932, his apologetic coverage of Soviet government actions during the Ukrainian famine and Stalinist purges damaged his reputation. His career declined after he left the Soviet Union in 1941.

Dürer, Albrecht

b. May 21, 1471
Nuremberg, Bavaria
d. April 6, 1528
Nuremberg, Bavaria
fields: Art

Dürer has often been called the "Leonardo of the North" because of his diverse talents. Painter, graphic artist, and theorist, he moved in elite intellectual circles that included some of the most famous men of his time. As a graphic artist, Dürer has never been surpassed. He helped bring Italian Renaissance ideas to the art of northern Europe.

Durham, Archer L.

b. June 9, 1932
Pasadena, Calif.
fields: Military Affairs

Highly decorated African American military officer; Archer L. Durham acheived the rank of major general in the U.S. Air Force.

Durham, Eddie

b. Aug. 19, 1906
San Marcos, Tex.
d. Mar. 6, 1987
New York, N.Y.
fields: Music (jazz trombonist, guitarist, and arranger)

African American trombonist, guitarist, and arranger; Eddie Durham played with the likes of Jimmie Lunceford and arranged many songs for popular bands, including Count Basie's and Glenn Miller's.

Durham, first earl of

né: John George Lambton
aka: John George, viscount Lambton and first earl of Durham
b. April 12, 1792
London, England
d. July 28, 1840
Isle of Wight, England
fields: Government and Politics

Known as "Radical Jack" for his advanced ideas of parliamentary reform and later appointed Governor-General of Canada, Lord Durham wrote his famous *Report on the Affairs of British North America* in 1839. Because the report insisted upon British-style responsible government for the colony, it has been regarded as the charter document for the British Commonwealth of Nations.

Durkheim, Émile

b. April 15, 1858
Épinal, France
d. November 15, 1917
Paris, France
fields: Sociology

Along with his contemporary Max Weber, Durkheim was one of the founders of modern sociology. He demonstrated that the discipline was not reducible to psychology or biology and received the first sociology professorship in France. His notion of society as a moral construct has had a great impact on anthropology, history, religion, law, and political theory and, during his own lifetime, had considerable influence on republicans and socialists of the Third Republic.

Du Sable, Jean Baptiste Pointe

b. 1745
St. Marc, Saint-Dominque (now Haiti)
d. 1818
St. Charles, Mo.
fields: Historical figure

African American founder of the city of Chicago, Ill; Jean Baptiste Pointe Du Sable, the son of a French sailor and a slave, built the first house and settlement in Chicago in the 1770's.

Dutt, Narandranath. *See* Vivekananda

Dutton, Charles S.

b. January 30, 1951
Baltimore, Md.
fields: Film, Theater and Entertainment (actor)

African American actor; Charles S. Dutton's credits include stage, screen, and television roles; best known as the lead character on the Fox situation comedy *Roc* (1991-1993); performed in plays including *Ma Rainey's Black Bottom*, *Joe Turner's Come and Gone*, and *The Piano Lesson*; appeared in films such as *No Mercy* (1986), *"Crocodile" Dundee II* (1988), *Jacknife* (1989), *An Unremarkable Life* (1989), *Mississippi Masala* (1992), *Alien* ^{3} (1992), *Menace II Society* (1993), *Get on the Bus* (1996), *Mimic* (1997), and *Cookie's Fortune* (1999).

Duvalier, François

aka: Papa Doc
b. April 14, 1907
Port-au-Prince, Haiti
d. April 21, 1971
Port-au-Prince, Haiti
fields: Government and Politics

François Duvalier, "Papa Doc," was dictatorial president of Haiti from 1957 to 1971. Formed the Volunteers for National Security—the Tonton Macoutes—a private army responsible to him alone, in 1958; the group instilled terror throughout the country. Skillfully used Haitians' belief in voodoo religion to consolidate his power. Outlawed all political parties and unions, attacked the Roman Catholic Church, dissolved the legislature. Arrested and murdered thousands of suspected dissidents. Increasingly paranoid, declared martial law in 1961; created a police state to control Haitians at every level of society. Remained in power until his death and passed presidency on to his son, Jean-Claude Duvalier.

Duvalier, Jean-Claude

aka: Baby Doc
b. July 3, 1951
Port-au-Prince, Haiti
fields: Government and Politics

Jean-Claude Duvalier, "Baby Doc," inherited rule of Haiti at death of his father, François Duvalier, in 1971. Disbanded his father's private palace army, the Tontons Macoutes, and created his own, the Leopard Battalion. Promised, but never delivered, reforms. Drained untold millions of dollars from country's coffers into his own Haitian and overseas accounts. Enraged citizens revolted in 1985-1986, and Duvalier fled to a life of luxury in France in 1986.

Duvall, Gabriel

b. 1752
d. 1844
fields: Law

U.S. Supreme Court justice, 1811-1835; appointed by President Madison. One of the first members of the Court to hold strong antislavery views.

Duve, Christian de

full: Christian René de Duve
b. Oct. 2, 1917
Thames-Ditton, Surrey, England
fields: Biology

Christian de Duve's studies of cell structure and function helped establish the field of cell biology. In 1955, he proposed the existence of the lysosome, a new organelle; in 1974, he was awarded the Nobel Prize in Physiology or Medicine.

du Vigneaud, Vincent

b. May 18, 1901
Chicago, Illinois
d. Dec. 11, 1978
White Plains, New York
fields: Chemistry

Vincent du Vigneaud revealed biotin to be a vitamin; in 1953, he synthesized and determined the structure of oxytocin; in 1955, he was awarded the Nobel Prize in Chemistry; in 1965, he revealed the relationship between hormonal structure and activity.

Dvořák, Antonín

full: Antonín Leopold Dvořák
b. September 8, 1841
Nelahozeves, Bohemia
d. May 1, 1904
Prague, Bohemia
fields: Music

Dvořák was one of the most notable European composers of the nineteenth century. He became one of the chief creators of the Czech national style of music and also had a profound influence on the development of American music.

Dworkin, Andrea

b. September 26, 1946
Camden, New Jersey
fields: Women's Rights

Andrea Dworkin proposed in her book *Pornography: Men Hating Women* (1981) that pornography should be prohibited on the grounds it violates women's civil rights. Other writings include *Woman Hating* (1974), *Intercourse* (1987), and *Letters from the War Zone* (1993).

Dworkin, Ronald

full: Ronald Myles Dworkin
b. December 11, 1931
Worcester, Massachusetts
fields: Philosophy, Law

Ronald Dworkin articulated a liberal philosophy of law that emphasizes the individual's affirmative rights to equal concern and fundamental liberties. Following the publication of *Taking Rights Seriously* (1977), he became one of the most influential philosophers of law in the English-speaking world, and his articles in *The New York Review of Books* attracted a large audience. Dworkin criticized legal positivism and utilitarianism during the Vietnam War, when many people in the West were thirsting for philosophical alternatives that included moral content. He did much to popularize the notion of judicial activism, that judges should look upon abstract legal terms as concepts of political morality. Other major works include *A Matter of Principle* (1985), *Law's Empire* (1986), *Life's Dominion* (1993), and *Freedom's Law* (1996).

Dylan, Bob

né: Robert Allen Zimmerman

b. May 24, 1941
Duluth, Minnesota
fields: Music, Literature

Singer and songwriter Bob Dylan wrote folk and rock music and songs that greatly influenced not only the course of popular music but also political and social attitudes; he is considered one of the seminal figures in the history of popular music. His music evolved from traditional folk to protest songs during the 1960's antiwar era to a fusion of folk and rock that came to be known as "folk rock" to more electric sounds. Among his most important albums are *Bob Dylan* (1962), *The Freewheelin' Bob Dylan* (1963, which contains "Blowin' in the Wind"), *The Times They Are a-Changin'* (1964), *Bringing It All Back Home* (1965), *Highway 61 Revisited* (1965), and *Blonde on Blonde* (1966). In July, 1966, Dylan was in a motorcycle accident and disappeared from public view for a year and a half. He emerged from his isolation to become a born-again Christian for a brief period and to continue to perform and produce albums, both alone and with groups such as Tom Petty and the Heartbreakers and the Grateful Dead. He was inducted into the Rock and Roll Hall of Fame in 1988; in 1998, he won a Grammy Award for best album for *Time Out of Mind.*

Dymally, Mervyn

b. May 12, 1926
Trinidad, British West Indies
fields: Law

African American legislator; Mervyn Dymally was elected to the California State Assembly in 1962; state senator (1967); lieutenant governor of California (1975 to 1979); served in Congress from 1981 to 1992.

Dzhugashvili, Joseph Vissarionovich. *See* Stalin, Joseph

E., Sheila

full: Sheila Escovedo
b. December 12, 1959
Oakland, Calif.
fields: Music

Latina drummer and singer. Sheila E. is the daughter of Peter Escovedo, famous for his conga drumming with the band Santana. She started playing conga drums at age five, and by the early 1970's was performing with her father's band, Azteca. She also worked as a studio musician for Herbie Hancock, Lionel Richie, Diana Ross, and Marvin Gaye. In 1984, she worked for Prince, and then with his encouragement, turned solo. Albums include *The Glamorous Life* (1984), *Romance 1600* (1985), *Sheila E.* (1987), and *Sex Cymbal* (1991). In the late 1990's, she was featured as the musical director on the short-lived *The Magic Hour*.

Eads, James Buchanan

b. May 23, 1820
Lawrenceberg, Indiana
d. March 8, 1887
Nassau, New Providence Island, Bahamas
fields: Business, Invention and Technology, Engineering

Eads revolutionized long-span bridge construction; the Eads Bridge, spanning the Mississippi River at St. Louis, is the only such structure bearing an engineer's name. He was a highly successful capitalist and an inventor of note, with more than fifty patents credited to him.

Eagle Lance. *See* Bad Heart Bull, Amos

Eagle Striking with Talons. *See* Kicking Bird

Eakins, Thomas

b. July 25, 1844
Philadelphia, Pennsylvania
d. June 25, 1916
Philadelphia, Pennsylvania
fields: Art

Eakins produced a handful of major paintings which were to add to the reputation of the United States as a center of art independent of Europe. He was also an important influence on art education in the United States.

Earhart, Amelia

b. July 24, 1897
Atchison, Kansas
d. July 2, 1937?
near Howland Island in the Pacific Ocean
fields: Aviation and Space Exploration

By being the first woman to fly across the Atlantic and by establishing numerous other flying records, Earhart helped to promote commercial aviation and advance the cause of women in aviation.

Earp, Wyatt

full: Wyatt Berry Stapp Earp
b. March 19, 1848
Monmouth, Illinois
d. January 13, 1929
Los Angeles, California
fields: Law

Earp, a lawman in the early cowtowns of the Old West, established a reputation that made him an American legend. To some, he epitomized revenge; to others, he was an American hero.

Eastman, Charles Alexander

aka: Ohiyesa (The Winner)
aka: Hakadah
b. Feb. 19, 1858
near Redwood Falls, Minn.
d. Jan. 8, 1939
Detroit, Mich.
fields: Native American Affairs, Medicine, Literature

Santee Sioux author and physician; Washington, D.C., lobbyist representing Santee Sioux claims, 1897-1900; physician at Crow Creek Reservation, 1900-1903; Indian inspector, Bureau of Indian Affairs, 1923-1925; authored eleven books including *Indian Boyhood* (1902; autobiography), *The Soul of the Indian* (1911), *The Indian Today* (1915), *From the Deep Woods to Civilization* (1916; autobiography), and *Indian Heroes and Great Chieftains* (1918).

Eastman, Crystal

b. June 25, 1881
Marlborough, Mass.
d. July 8, 1928
Erie, Pa.
fields: Social Reform, Women's Rights

Crystal Eastman was a lawyer, industrial reformer, and women's rights advocate. In 1910 she published *Work Accidents and the Law*, which resulted in improved workers' compensation laws; was a member of the Political Equality League (later the Woman's Peace Party); in 1912 founded the Congressional Union for Women's Suffrage; from 1917 to 1921 she and her brother, Max, published the journal *Liberator*.

Eastman, George

b. July 12, 1854
Waterville, New York
d. March 14, 1932
Rochester, New York
fields: Photography, Invention and Technology, Business and Industry, Philanthropy

Through his introduction to his simple-to-operate roll-film Kodak camera, Eastman made photograph-making accessible to virtually all people. He built the Eastman Kodak Company into the world's largest photographic manufacturing establishment by dominating world markets and by pioneering in organized industrial research and development.

Eaton, Edith Maud. *See* Sui Sin Far

Eazy-E

né: Eric Wright
b. September 7, 1963
Compton, Calif.
d. March 26, 1995
Los Angeles, Calif.
fields: Music (rap vocalist and entrepreneur)

African American rap vocalist and entrepreneur; Eazy-E was a founding member of the rap music group NWA (Niggaz With Attitude) and pioneered West Coast "gangsta rap"; final album, *Str8 Off the Streetz of . . . Compton*, was released in 1996.

Eban, Abba

né: Aubrey Solomon
aka: Aubrey S. Eban
aka: Abba Solomon Eban
b. February 2, 1915
Cape Town, South Africa
fields: Diplomacy, Government and Politics

Eban was Israel's Permanent Representative to the United Nations, Ambassador to the United States, and foreign minister. He played an influential role in the negotiations leading to the creation of the state of Israel and in securing its membership in the United Nations. His diplomatic and oratorical talents, used in the service of Israel, gained for him worldwide recognition.

Eberharter, Herman P.

b. Apr. 29, 1892
Pittsburgh, Pa.
d. Sept. 9, 1958
Arlington, Va.
fields: Government and Politics

U.S. Representative Herman P. Eberharter was first elected to the 75th U.S. Congress in 1936, as a Democrat. He served ten consecutive terms. Eberharter was a member of the House Special Committee to Investigate Un-American Activities, known as the Dies Committee. In 1943, this subcommittee set out to prove the disloyalty of Japanese Americans as part of an investigation of the War Relocation Authority. The committee failed to prove any disloyalty, and Eberharter later claimed that the committee was prejudiced and that most of its assertions were unsubstantiated.

Eberst, Jacob. *See* Offenbach, Jacques

Éboué, Félix

full: Adolphe-Félix-Sylvestre Éboué
b. December 26, 1884
Cayenne, French Guiana
d. May 17, 1944
Cairo, Egypt
fields: Government and Politics, Colonial Administration

Éboué rose from the lower ranks of the French colonial service to become the first black governor of Guadeloupe, the first black governor of Chad, and the first black governor-general in French-speaking Africa when he was appointed to head former French Equatorial Africa in 1941.

Eccles, John Carew

aka: Sir John Carew Eccles
b. January 27, 1903
Melbourne, Australia
d. May 2, 1997
Contra, Switzerland
fields: Physiology

Eccles made fundamental discoveries concerning the transmission of nerve impulses and the existence of inhibitory neurons that control the spread of such impulses. He won the 1963 Nobel Prize in Physiology or Medicine.

Eckener, Hugo

b. August 10, 1868
Flensburg, Prussia
d. August 14, 1954
Friedrichshafen, West Germany
fields: Aviation and Space Exploration

Eckener was the most important person associated with zeppelin development during and after World War II. As head of the Zeppelin Airline, he made a number of pioneering flights that made him one of the most famous Germans of his day. He thus became not only the leader of the zeppelin movement but also an important force in reestablishing Germany's reputation in world opinion after World War I.

Eckert, Johanna. *See* Holm, Hanya

Eckhart, Meister

full: Johannes Heinrich Eckhart von Hochheim
b. c. 1260
Hochheim, Franconia (now a province of Thuringia, Germany)
d. 1327 or 1328
Avignon, France?
fields: Philosophy, Religion and Theology

The medieval mystic Scholasticism of Meister Eckhart formed an intellectual bridge between classic Scholasticism and the idealism, Protestantism, and Romanticism of following centuries. He served as provincial prior for the Dominican order for Saxony (1303), vicar general for Bohemia (1307), and head of the Dominican order in Strassburg (1312). Later in life his ideas were challenged by the Church, and a papal bull issued in 1329 condemned several of his propositions. In 1980, a process was initiated by the Dominican order to clear Eckhart's name and received the approval of Pope John Paul II.

Eckstine, Billy

full: William Clarence Eckstine
b. July 8, 1914
Pittsburgh, Pa.
fields: Music (singer, trumpeter, valve trombonist, and bandleader)

African American singer, trumpeter, valve trombonist, and bandleader; Billy Eckstine achieved fame as a singer with the Earl Hines band; his own band consisted of many seminal jazz figures, including Miles Davis, Charlie Parker, and Dizzie Gillespie.

Eddington, Arthur Stanley

full: Sir Arthur Stanley Eddington
b. Dec. 28, 1882
Kendal, England
d. Nov. 22, 1944
Cambridge, England
fields: Astronomy, Physics

Arthur Stanley Eddington researched the motions, distribution, and structures of stars; his measurements during the 1919 solar eclipse were crucial in establishing Albert Einstein's general theory of relativity.

Eddy, Mary Baker

né: Mary Morse Baker
b. July 16, 1821
Bow, New Hampshire
d. December 3, 1910
Chestnut Hill, Massachusetts
fields: Religion and Theology

A deeply religious thinker, Mary Baker Eddy established the Church of Christ, Scientist—the first church movement to be founded in the United States by a woman.

Edelman, Marian Wright

né: Marian Wright
b. June 6, 1939
Bennettsville, South Carolina
fields: Civil Rights, Education, Social Reform

Edelman created a lobbying organization dedicated to improving conditions for children in the United States.

Eden, Anthony

full: Robert Anthony Eden
b. June 12, 1897
Windlestone Hall, near Bishop Auckland, Durham, England
d. January 14, 1977
Alvediston, Wiltshire, England
fields: Government and Politics, Diplomacy

Although his three appointments as foreign secretary, during 1935-1938, 1940-1945, and 1951-1955, brought Eden a high reputation for firmness and diplomatic adroitness, his tenure as prime minister, between 1955 and 1957, ended in humiliation and resignation for his part in the ill-starred invasion of Egypt which brought the Suez crisis to a head.

Ederle, Gertrude

full: Gertrude Caroline Ederle
b. October 23, 1906
New York, New York
fields: Sports (swimming)

An American swimmer, Ederle became the first woman to swim across the English Channel, breaking the time record of the fastest man by one hour and fifty-nine minutes.

Edison, Thomas Alva

b. February 11, 1847
Milan, Ohio
d. October 18, 1931
West Orange, New Jersey
fields: Invention and Technology

With his successful incandescent electric lighting system, Edison transformed the world of American electrical technology. With his myriad other inventions, including a stock ticker, duplex and quadraplex telegraph, phonograph, telephone transmitter, motion-picture camera, and storage battery, he symbolized the ingenious, prolific, heroic, and professional American inventor in an age of invention, innovation, and industrialization.

Edley, Christopher Fairfield, Sr.

b. January 1, 1928
Charleston, W.V.
fields: Philanthropy (attorney, fund-raiser, and education advocate)

African American attorney, fund-raiser, and education advocate; in 1973, Christopher Fairfield Edley, Sr., was chosen to serve as president and chief executive officer of the United Negro College Fund (UNCF); successfully promoted the "A Mind Is a Terrible Thing to Waste" campaign; retired in 1990 and received the George W. Collins Award in 1991.

Edmonds, Kenneth. *See* Babyface

Edmunson, William

b. 1882
Davidson County, Ky.
d. 1951
fields: Art (sculptor)

African American self-taught sculptor; William Edmunson began his career sculpting gravestones for African American patrons; received recognition in 1938 through a solo exhibition at the Museum of Modern Art in New York; works are characterized by fluidity and economy of detail.

Edward I

b. June 17, 1239
Westminster, London, England
d. July 7, 1307
Burgh-upon-the-Sands, Cumberland, England
fields: Monarchy, Government and Politics, Law

King of England, 1272-1307. Although most highly regarded in his own time as a crusader, conqueror of Wales, and Hammer of the stubborn Scots, Edward's more modern historians admire him principally as lawmaker and lawgiver, the monarch who brought Parliament into partnership in the governance of England.

Edward II

aka: Edward II of Caernarvon
b. April 25, 1284
Caernarvon Castle, Caernarvonshire, Wales
d. September 21, 1327
Berkeley Castle, Gloucestershire, England
fields: Monarchy, Government and Politics

King of England, 1307-1327. Edward's ineffectual leadership and weakness of character furthered the growth of representative government in England.

Edward III

b. November 13, 1312
Windsor Castle, Berkshire, England
d. June 21, 1377
Sheen, Surrey, England
fields: Monarchy, Government and Politics

Under Edward's reign (1327-1377), England witnessed an increase in the governing power of Parliament (and especially that of the House of Commons), owing to the necessity for the king to seek parliamentary authority for the money to finance his wars with Scotland and with France. Edward's reign also witnessed the beginning, and the most glorious English campaigns, of the Hundred Years' War.

Edward IV

b. April 28, 1442
Rouen, Normandy, France
d. April 9, 1483
Westminster Palace, England
fields: Government and Politics

King of England, 1461-1470, 1471-1483). Utilizing instruments of government inherited from the Lancastrian kings, as well as molding pragmatic methods which anticipated those of the Tudors, Edward of York restored both the authority and prestige of the English monarchy following the dangers and drift of the reigns of the Lancastrian kings. He was aided in this success by the end of the Hundred Years' War (1453), which had become both a distraction and a financial and military disaster for the English monarchy.

Edward VI

b. October 12, 1537
Hampton Court Palace, London, England
d. July 6, 1553
London, England
fields: Government and Politics

King of England, 1547-1553. Edward's reign definitively established the strong Tudor monarchy and English Protestantism. Despite his youth, the king played a significant role in both.

Edward VII

né: Albert Edward
b. November 9, 1841
Buckingham Palace, London, England
d. May 6, 1910
Buckingham Palace, London, England
fields: Government and Politics

King Edward VII (1901-1910) made the British monarchy fascinating and thereby brought to it an appeal which contributed greatly to its popularity in the twentieth century. He exercised little influence in politics, but he used his natural talents to promote his country's foreign policy.

Edward VIII. *See* Windsor, duke of

Edward the Confessor

b. c. 1005
Islip, Oxfordshire, England
d. January 5, 1066
London, England
fields: Monarchy, Government and Politics

King of England, 1043-1066. Edward served as the focus of a series of events that culminated in one of the most significant episodes in English history, the Norman Conquest of England.

Edward the Elder

b. 870?
place unknown
d. July 17, 924
Farndon-on-Dee, Chester, England
fields: Monarchy, Government and Politics

King of England, 899-924. Building on the success of his father, King Alfred the Great, and working in close collaboration with his sister Ethelflaed, Edward the Elder defeated all Viking kingdoms and coalitions in England and moved toward the political unification of the country.

Edwards, Alfred Leroy

b. Aug. 9, 1920
Key West, Fla.
fields: Education, Government and Politics

African American educator and government official; Alfred Leroy Edwards served as deputy assistant secretary of the United States Department of Agriculture (1963-1974); helped found the University of Nigeria at Nsukka.

Edwards, Cecile Hoover

b. Oct. 20, 1926
East St. Louis, Ill.
fields: Education

African American nutritionist; Cecile Hoover Edwards was dean of the school of human ecology at Howard University in 1974.

Edwards, Jonathan

b. October 5, 1703
East Windsor, Connecticut
d. March 22, 1758
Princeton, New Jersey
fields: Religion and Theology

The greatest Puritan theologian in America, Edwards tried to establish an intellectual foundation for Puritanism, to find a rational interpretation of predestination, and to justify the ways of God to man.

Edwards, Melvin E.

b. May 4, 1937
Houston, Tex.
fields: Art, Education (sculptor and educator)

African American sculptor and educator; Melvin E. Edwards's works are characterized as containing "black humor."

Edwards, Nelson Jack

b. 1917
Lowndes County, Ala.
d. Nov. 2, 1974
Detroit, Mich.
fields: Labor Movement

African American labor union official; Nelson Jack Edwards was the first African American to become president of a UAW union local; in 1962, became first African American to serve on the UAW executive board; vice president of the UAW (1970).

Égalité, Philippe. *See* Orléans, duc d'

Egas Moniz, António

né: António Caetano de Abreu Freire
baptized: António Caetano de Abreu Freire Egas Moniz
b. November 29, 1874
Avança, Portugal
d. December 13, 1955
Lisbon, Portugal
fields: Medicine, Physiology

Moniz made two important contributions to the field of neurology during the 1920's and 1930's. He was the father of cerebral angiography and later developed the prefrontal lobotomy, for which he received the Nobel Prize in Physiology or Medicine in 1949.

Egbert

b. Eighth century
Wessex, in western Britain
d. 839
England
fields: Government and Politics, Military Affairs

Egbert restored the fortunes of Wessex and established the political foundation of the future English state that, under Alfred the Great, would successfully resist Scandinavian dominance in the ninth century.

Egstrom, Norma Deloris. *See* Lee, Peggy

Ehrenfels, Christian von

full: Maria Christian Julius Leopold Karl Freiherr von Ehrenfels
b. June 20, 1859
Rodaun, Austria
d. September 8, 1932
Lichtenau, Austria
fields: Psychiatry and Psychology, Philosophy, Literature

An article published by Ehrenfels in 1890 is the source of modern Gestalt psychology. In his native Austria-Hungary, he was primarily considered a philosopher, especially in the field of value theory and ethics. Controversial in his time, he published a book on sexual ethics; he also wrote on eugenics, music, and mathematics, and was the author of several plays and dramas.

Ehrlich, Eugen

b. September 14, 1862
Czernowitz, Austro-Hungarian Empire
d. May 2, 1922
Vienna, Austria
fields: Law, Philosophy

Ehrlich is generally credited with founding the legal philosophy of the sociology of law. This judicial concept changed the fundamental outlook of legal scholars in the early twentieth century, in both Europe and in the United States, from a purely analytical view of the law to a view that recognized the unique facts and social circumstances of individual cases.

Ehrlich, Paul

b. March 14, 1854
Strehlen, Prussia
d. August 20, 1915
Bad Homburg, Germany
fields: Physiology, Medicine, Chemistry

Ehrlich won a Nobel Prize in Physiology or Medicine (1908) for his work that led to the development of a diphtheria antitoxin dosage. He also devised a method of measuring the effectiveness of serum, and he was praised for his theory of immunity and for his work in histology-produced tissue-staining techniques. Yet he is best remembered for his development of the arsenic compound number 606, which was used as a treatment of syphilis.

Ehrlich, Paul R.

full: Paul Ralph Ehrlich
b. May 29, 1932
Philadelphia, Pennsylvania
fields: Biology, Genetics, Zoology

Paul R. Ehrlich, a biologist and educator, was a leader of the international movement for human population control. In 1968, he helped organize the Zero Population Growth group and published the classic book *The Population Bomb.*

Eichmann, Adolf

full: Karl Adolf Eichmann
aka: Ricardo Klement
b. March 19, 1906
Solingen, Germany
d. May 31, 1962
Ramle, Israel
fields: Historical Figure

One of Nazi Germany's bloodiest war criminals, Adolf Eichmann was in charge of routing millions of Jews to Germany's infamous extermination camps during World War II. After Germany's defeat in 1945, Eichmann escaped from a U.S. Army prison camp and fled to the Middle East. In 1958, he settled in Buenos Aires, Argentina, until his capture by agents of the Israeli Security Service on May 11, 1960. Eichmann was found guilty and was hanged in 1962.

Eikerenkoetter, Frederick Joseph, II. *See* Reverend Ike

Eilberg, Amy

b. October 12, 1954
Philadelphia, Pennsylvania
fields: Religion and Theology

The first woman to be ordained as a rabbi in the Conservative branch of Judaism, Amy Eilberg has served as a chaplain at Methodist Hospital of Indiana in Indianapolis and as a community rabbi for the Jewish Welfare Federation and at the Jewish Healing Center in San Francisco, California.

Einstein, Albert

b. March 14, 1879
Ulm, Germany
d. April 18, 1955
Princeton, New Jersey
fields: Physics (theoretical)

Einstein was the principal founder of modern theoretical physics; his theory of relativity fundamentally changed our understanding of the physical world. His stature as a scientist, together with his strong humanitarian stance on major political and social issues, made him one of the outstanding men of the twentieth century. He was awarded the 1921 Nobel Prize in Physics.

Einthoven, Willem

b. May 21, 1860
Semarang, Java, Dutch East Indies
d. September 28, 1927
Leiden, The Netherlands
fields: Physiology, Medicine

Accomplished in several areas of physiology, physics, and medicine, Einthoven elaborated techniques for measuring minute electrical currents in the human heart, notably the string galvanometer, which became the basis for modern electrocardiography and made possible great advances in combating heart disease. He was awarded the Nobel Prize in Physiology or Medicine in 1924.

Eisenhower, Dwight D.

full: Dwight David Eisenhower
b. October 14, 1890
Denison, Texas
d. March 28, 1969
Washington, D.C.
fields: Military Affairs, Government and Politics

Thirty-fourth president of the United States, 1953-1961. During World War II, Eisenhower served with distinction as Allied Commander for the invasions of North Africa, Italy, and France. He won the presidential elections of 1952 and 1956 and guided the country through eight years of peace and prosperity.

Eisenhower, Milton Stover

b. Sept. 15, 1899
Abilene, Kans.
d. May 2, 1985
Baltimore, Md.
fields: Government and Politics

Eisenhower, the brother of former president Dwight D. Eisenhower, was an educator and adviser to six presidents. As the first director of the War Relocation Authority in 1942, it was his job to move people of Japanese ancestry away from the West Coast. Eisenhower's plan, which included a plea for tolerance, was met with racist responses and a demand for a concentration camp. A surprised Eisenhower resigned shortly afterward.

Eisenstein, Sergei

b. January 23, 1898
Riga, Latvia
d. February 11, 1948
Moscow, U.S.S.R.
fields: Film

Universally regarded as one of the greatest directors in the history of the cinema, and an influential theorist and teacher as well, Eisenstein pioneered a method of film editing known as montage. As the result of political censorship, he completed only six films in his lifetime, three of which—*Potemkin, Alexander Nevsky*, and *Ivan the Terrible*—are considered classics.

Eissner, Clara. *See* Zetkin, Clara

Elder, Lee

full: Robert Lee Elder
b. July 14, 1934
Dallas, Tex.
fields: Sports (golfer)

African American golfer; Lee Elder was the first African American to play in a Masters tournament (1975); the first African American to break the $100,000 mark in yearly earnings (1976); and the first African American member of the U.S. Ryder Cup team (1979).

Elder, Lonne, III

b. Dec. 26, 1931
Americus, Ga.
d. June 11, 1996, Woodland Hills, Calif.
fields: Literature, Theater and Entertainment

African American writer; Lonne Elder III is best known for his play *Ceremonies in Dark Old Men* (1965).

Elder, Rose Harper

b. ?
fields: Sports (Golfer)

African American golfer; Rose Harper Elder's golfing career continued even after she founded Rose Elder and Associates, a firm involved in public relations, marketing, and promotions; married to golfer Lee Elder.

Elders, Joycelyn

b. August 13, 1933
Schaal, Ark.
fields: Medicine, Public Health, Government and Politics

African American health educator and U.S. public official. Joycelyn Elders was appointed surgeon general of the United States in 1993 by President Bill Clinton; first African American and second woman to hold that position; previously director of the Arkansas department of health (1987); as surgeon general, Elders disseminated public health information concerning problems such as teenage pregnancy, sexually transmitted diseases, and aquired immunodeficiency syndrome (AIDS); became unpopular with the powerful liquor and tobacco lobbies when she called for higher taxes on their products; conservatives upset by her advocacy of public funding of condom distribution, sex education, and abortion; others alarmed by her interest in studying the possible impact of legalizing drugs; resigned in 1995 after anger over her suggestion that teaching young people about masterbation might help alleviate problems stemming from teenage sexual activity; returned to the University of Arkansas for Medical Sciences; some lectures and writings published in *Dancing with the Bears* (1994).

Eldridge, Roy

né: David Eldridge
b. Jan. 30, 1911
Pittsburgh, Pa.
d. Feb. 26, 1989
New York, N.Y.
fields: Music (jazz trumpeter)

African American jazz trumpeter; Roy Eldridge played with the likes of Fletcher "Smack" Henderson, Gene Krupa, and "Count" Basie; an important influence on Dizzy Gillespie.

Eleanor of Aquitaine

b. c. 1122
either at Bordeaux or at the nearby castle of Belin, southern France
d. April 1, 1204
the Abbey of Fontevrault
fields: Monarchy, Government and Politics

As Queen of France (1137-1180), Queen of England (1154-1189), and mother to two English kings, Eleanor of Aquitaine was probably the most powerful woman of her time. In addition, she promoted the literary and social style of courtly love and the troubadours.

Elgar, Edward

full: Edward William Elgar
aka: Sir Edward Elgar
b. June 2, 1857
Broadheath, Worcester, England
d. February 23, 1934
Worcester, England
fields: Music

Basically self-taught, Elgar slowly matured into an artist who expressed powerful emotions in music of strong, "masculine" British character; he was one of the last great Romantic composers.

Eliade, Mircea

b. March 9, 1907
Bucharest, Romania
d. April 22, 1986
Chicago, Illinois
fields: Literature, Religion and Theology

Eliade examined the phenomena of diverse religious experiences, drawing upon similarities within each. By looking at individual, sociopsychological manifestations against the "terror of history" in the twentieth century and expressing these in modes conditioned by his own spirituality and imagination, Eliade sought to say what makes religion universal.

Eliezer, Israel ben. *See* Ba'al Shem Tov

Elijah ben Solomon

b. April 23, 1720
Selec, Lithuania
d. October 9, 1797
Vilna, Lithuania
fields: Religion and Theology

Elijah ben Solomon contributed to Talmudic and rabbinic literature by solving the most complicated questions of Jewish law and by writing commentaries and annotations to biblical, Talmudic, and Cabalistic books.

Elion, Gertrude Belle

b. January 23, 1918
New York, New York
d. February 21, 1999
Chapel Hill, North Carolina
fields: Biochemistry

Elion developed new drugs for many serious diseases, including leukemia, herpes, and malaria, by carefully exploiting differences between normal and abnormal cells. She is one of very few women scientists to win a Nobel Prize or to hold a senior position at a major pharmaceutical firm. She was awarded the 1988 Nobel Prize in Physiology or Medicine.

Eliot, Charles William

b. March 20, 1834
Boston, Massachusetts
d. August 22, 1926
Northeast Harbor, Mount Desert, Maine
fields: Education

As president of Harvard College (1869-1909), Eliot combined administrative skill with a readiness to undertake novel and irregular ventures, transforming the structure and function of higher education in the United States.

Eliot, George

né: Mary Ann Evans
aka: Marian Evans
aka: Marian Lewes
b. November 22, 1819
Chilvers Coton, Warwickshire, England
d. December 22, 1880
London, England
fields: Literature

Because of her philosophical profundity and her mastery of fictional technique, Eliot won a reputation as one of the world's great novelists and helped establish the novel as an appropriate vehicle for the serious exploration of ideas.

Eliot, John

b. August 5, 1604 (baptized)
Widford, Hertfordshire, England
d. May 21, 1690
Roxbury, Massachusetts Bay Colony (now Massachusetts)
fields: Religion and Theology

The Puritan clergyman Eliot is known as the Apostle to the Indians for his close to fifty years of work among the Indians of Massachusetts. He assisted in the production of the first book published in North America, the 1640 *Bay Psalm Book*, and translated the first Bible printed in North America, an Algonquian language version.

Eliot, T. S.

full: Thomas Stearns Eliot
b. September 26, 1888
St. Louis, Missouri
d. January 4, 1965
London, England
fields: Literature

Eliot, perhaps the most significant of the new wave of Symbolists of the 1920's, startled the world of poetry and spoke for a lost generation in *The Waste Land*, engaged literary critics with his landmark book of criticism, *The Sacred Wood*, and wrote the most successful verse play of the twentieth century, *The Cocktail Party*. He won the 1948 Nobel Prize in Literature.

Elizabeth I

b. September 7, 1533
Greenwich, England
d. March 24, 1603
Richmond, England
fields: Government and Politics

Queen of England, 1558-1603. The last of the five Tudor monarchs, Queen Elizabeth I earned the respect of her associates and the love of her subjects while ruling her people longer and more capably than most kings of her time.

Elizabeth II

né: Elizabeth Alexandra Mary
b. April 21, 1926
London, England
fields: Government and Politics

Dignified and regal, yet down-to-earth and accessible, Elizabeth II (queen of Great Britain from 1952) embodied the continuing vitality of the British monarchy at the end of the twentieth century. The popularity and esteem in which she is held helped make her an ideal head of state.

Elizabeth of Hungary, Saint

b. 1207
Sárospatak, Hungary
d. November 17, 1231
near Wittenberg, Thuringia
fields: Religion and Theology, Social Reform

Elizabeth, seeking to live according to the Christian ideal, established the first orphanage for homeless children in Central Europe and actively cared for the poor and the unemployed.

Elizondo, Hector

b. Dec. 22, 1936
New York, N.Y.
fields: Theater and Entertainment

Actor. Hector Elizondo starred as a Puerto Rican janitor in the 1960's off-Broadway hit *Steambath*, for which he received an Obie Award. He also appeared in productions of *Drums in the Night*, *Prisoner of Second Avenue*, *The Dance of Death*, *The Great White Hope*, and *The Price*. He made his film debut in 1971 in *Valdez Is Coming*. He was nominated for a Golden Globe Award in 1990 for his supporting role in *Pretty Woman*.

Elizondo, Sergio

full: Sergio Danilo Elizondo Domínguez
b. Apr. 29, 1930
El Fuerte, Mexico
fields: Literature

Writer and scholar. Sergio Elizondo is one of the strongest proponents of Chicano cultural nationalism. His works include the volumes of poetry *Perros y antiperros: Una épica chicana* (1972; dogs and antidogs: a Chicano epic), and *Libro para batos y chavalas chicanas* (1977; a book for Chicano guys and girls); a short-story collection, *Rosa, la flauta* (1980; Rose, the flute); and the novels *Muerte en una estrella* (1984; death on a star) and *Suruma* (1990).

Eller, Carl Lee

b. Jan. 25, 1942
Winston-Salem, N.C.
fields: Sports (football player)

African American football player; Carl Lee Eller was one of football's most respected defensive ends; played for the Minnesota Vikings (1964 to 1978).

Ellerbee, Linda

né: Linda Jane Smith
b. August 15, 1944
Bryan, Texas
fields: Journalism, Television

As a broadcast journalist and author, Ellerbee gained distinction for her direct, witty, and intelligent approach to writing and delivering the news.

Ellington, Duke

né: Edward Kennedy Ellington
b. April 29, 1899
Washington, D.C.
d. May 24, 1974
New York, New York
fields: Music

As a pianist, composer, and bandleader, Ellington made one of the most pervasive contributions to the development of jazz music in the United States.

Ellington, Mercer Kennedy

b. Mar. 11, 1919
Washington, D.C.
d. Feb. 8, 1996
Copenhagen, Denmark
fields: Music (musician)

African American musician; Mercer Kennedy Ellington, the son of Duke Ellington, worked with the likes of Dizzy Gillespie, Charlie Mingus, and Carmen McRae; took over his father's band after Duke Ellington's death; conducted the Broadway musical *Sophisticated Ladies* in the 1980's.

Elliott, Robert Brown

b. Aug. 11, 1842
Boston, Mass.
d. Aug. 9, 1884
New Orleans, La.
fields: Government and Politics

African American politician; Robert Brown Elliott served on the South Carolina constitutional convention after the Civil War; won election to the lower house of the state legislature; served two terms in the U.S. Congress (1871-1874); speaker of the house for the South Carolina legislature for two years.

Ellis, Albert

b. September 27, 1913
Pittsburgh, Pa.
fields: Psychiatry and Psychology

A psychologist, Albert Ellis taught at Rutgers and New York Universities. While gradually turning away from psychoanalytic theory, he developed rational emotive behavior therapy, designed to change behavior by confronting patients with their irrational beliefs and persuading them to adopt rational ones. Ellis published fifty-four books and more than six hundred articles. He is coauthor of such books as *A Guide to a Successful Marriage* (1977) and *How to Raise an Emotionally Healthy, Happy, Child* (1981). His Albert Ellis Institute in New York is a nonprofit humanistic educational organization.

Ellis, Havelock

full: Henry Havelock Ellis
b. February 2, 1859
Croydon, Surrey, England
d. July 8, 1939
Hintlesham, Suffolk, England
fields: Psychiatry and Psychology, Sociology, Journalism

Believing that sex should be discussed openly and seriously, Ellis collected, classified, and wrote about sexual behavior, thus dispelling many of the Victorian prejudices and misconceptions about sex and paving the way for future study.

Ellis, Jimmy

b. Feb. 24, 1940
Louisville, Ky.
fields: Sports (boxer)

African American boxer; Jimmy Ellis began his career as Muhammad Ali's sparring partner; beat Jerry Quarry in 1967 for Ali's vacant spot in a World Boxing Association elimination tournament. Retired in 1975 after losses to Joe Frazier, Ali, and Ernie Shavers.

Ellis, Trey

b. 1962
Washington, D.C.
fields: Literature

African American writer; Trey Ellis wrote his first novel, *Platitudes* (1988), at the age of twenty-three; published *Home Repairs* in 1993 and *Right Here, Right Now* in 1999.

Ellison, Ralph

b. Mar. 1, 1914
Oklahoma, City, Okla.
d. April 16, 1994
New York, N.Y.
fields: Literature

African American writer. Ralph Ellison became a major literary figure on the strength of a single novel, *Invisible Man* (1952), which won the National Book Award in 1953. The basic thesis that guided Ellison's creative vision throughout his career: Within the United States, there exists a surrealistic world created by racism in which black men are alienated and unrecognized by the larger society. Ellison skillfully explored this hypothesis in his greatest work, *Invisible Man*, which has been placed on virtually every list of major novels in modern American literature. Ellison was the Albert Schweitzer Professor at New York University in New York City between 1970 and 1980. After his death extensive notes and previously published sections of a novel in progress were used to create *Juneteenth* (1999, edited by John F. Callahan).

Ellsworth, Oliver

b. April 29, 1745
Windsor, Conn.
d. November 26, 1807
Windsor, Conn.
fields: Law

Chief justice of the United States, 1796-1800. Oliver Ellsworth, one of the United States' founders and an originator of the Great Compromise (establishing the bicameral legislature), was also the main author of the Judiciary Act of 1789, which developed the federal judiciary.

Ellul, Jacques

b. January 6, 1912
Bordeaux, France
d. May 19, 1994
Bordeaux, France
fields: Philosophy

A French philosopher, Jacques Ellul was a critic of modern technology. His most influential books, *La Technique: Ou, L'Enjou du siècle* (1954; *The Technological Society*, 1964) and *Propagandes* (1954; *Propaganda: The Formation of Men's Attitudes*, 1965), argued that technology allowed creation of a total environment of propaganda. Trained as a lawyer, he flirted with communism as a young man. However, by the 1950's his writings evidenced a strong religiosity as he came to believe that ultimately only God could save humanity from the technological systems human beings had unthinkingly constructed.

Éluard, Paul

né: Eugène Grindel
b. December 14, 1895
Saint-Denis, France
d. November 18, 1952
Charenton-le-Pont, France
fields: Literature

As one of the founders of the Surrealist movement, Éluard led the way in finding new poetic means of investigating human nature. He was actively interested in the spheres of literature in general and poetry in particular. Éluard's major contribution to the development of French poetry is his entire poetic work, a blend of avant-garde with classical tradition.

Ely, Richard Theodore

b. April 13, 1854
Ripley, New York
d. October 4, 1943
Old Lyme, Connecticut
fields: Education

Richard Theodore Ely's trial by his university on charges of advocating socialism led to a celebrated affirmation of academic freedom. In 1881 he joined the faculty at Johns Hopkins University and later became head of the School of Economics, Political Science and History at the University of Wisconsin in Madison. His prolific writing on economics expressed sympathy for working men and women, and his concern for labor led to his being accused of promoting socialism to his students by Wisconsin's state superintendent of education in 1894.

Emeneau, M. B.

full: Murray Barnson Emeneau
b. Feb. 28, 1904
Lunenburg, Nova Scotia, Canada
fields: Language and Linguistics, Education

M. B. Emeneau, linguist and professor of languages, served as president of the Linguistic Society of America (1949) and editor of the *Journal of the American Oriental Society* (1947-1951). His honors include Guggenheim Fellowships in 1949 and 1956. Emeneau's most noteworthy works are his translation of Kalidasa's *Shakuntala: Or, The Lost Ring* (c. 45 B.C.E. or c. 395 C.E.) and *A Dravidian Etymological Dictionary* (1961), coauthored with T. Burrow.

Emerson, Ralph Waldo

b. May 25, 1803
Boston, Massachusetts
d. April 27, 1882
Concord, Massachusetts
fields: Literature

Emerson headed the American Transcendentalist movement and was an essayist, poet, and Unitarian minister. His writings laid foundations for American thought and literature, influencing (among others) Henry David Thoreau.

Emi, Frank

full: Frank Seishi Emi
b. 1920's?
Los Angeles, California(?)
fields: Social Reform, Civil Rights

Frank Seishi Emi was a Japanese American political activist who was interned during World War II; protested the loyalty questionnaire posed to all arriving internees at the Heart Mountain Relocation Center in Utah;

in early 1944, after the Selective Service was reinstated for Japanese Americans, Emi was one of sixty-three draftees arrested for refusing to report to their preinduction physicals; along with Kiyoshi Okamoto, was an organizer of the Heart Mountain Fair Play Committee, which demanded restoration of constitutional rights before military conscription; was one of seven protest leaders convicted of conspiracy to violate the Selective Service Act and spent four years in federal prison at Leavenworth.

Emmons, Delos Carleton

b. Jan. 17, 1888
Huntington, W. Va.
d. Oct. 3, 1965
Hillsborough, Calif.
fields: Military Affairs

Military leader. Delos Carleton Emmons graduated from West Point (1909), and served at posts in California, Alaska, New York, and Texas. In 1917 he entered the young field of army aviation. By 1941, he was Chief of the Air Force Control Command, the highest rank in the Army Air Force. Emmons was appointed commander of the Hawaiian Department after the bombing of Pearl Harbor by the Japanese on December 7, 1941, and served as military governor of Hawaii through the end of World War II. Because Emmons believed in their loyalty, Japanese Americans in Hawaii were not subjected to evacuation and internment.

Empedocles

b. c. 490 B.C.E.
Acragas, Sicily
d. c. 430 B.C.E.
in the Peloponnese, Greece
fields: Philosophy, Science, Natural History

Empedocles was one of the earliest of the Greek philosophers to provide a unified theory of the nature of the world and the cosmos.

Empress Dowager. *See* Cixi

Encarnación, César Cedeño y. *See* Cedeño, César

Endo, Mitsuye

b. 1920
Sacramento, Calif.
fields: Civil Rights

Mitsuye Endo was a U.S. citizen who worked for the California Department of Motor Vehicles and was fired after Japan attacked Pearl Harbor. In 1942, Saburo Kido, a lawyer with the Japanese American Citizens League, who had investigated the firing of Japanese American state employees, and James Purcell were searching for an ideal candidate for a *habeas corpus* test case. They found Endo. A *habeas corpus* petition was filed in July, 1942. The case reached the U.S. Supreme Court in October, 1944, and the Court, in December, 1944, unanimously decided in favor of Endo..

Endo, Russell

b. ?
fields: Scholarship

Russell Endo, professor of sociology at the University of Colorado, was influential in the development of Asian American studies. Endo, Stanley Sue, and Nathaniel Wagner edited *Asian-Americans: Psychological Perspectives* (1973), one of the first textbooks on Asian Americans. Endo's other works include articles on bibliographical materials dealing with Asian American studies. He also coedited *Frontiers of Asian American Studies* (1989).

Engels, Friedrich

b. November 28, 1820
Barmen, Prussia
d. August 5, 1895
London, England
fields: Social Reform, Government and Politics

In partnership with Karl Marx, Engels analyzed the origins and nature of industrial capitalist society and worked to bring about the overthrow of that society by a working-class revolution.

English, Diane

b. 1948
Buffalo, New York
fields: Television

A gifted writer and innovative television producer, English has created several television series that have featured strong roles for women, explored social and political issues, and aided the cause of women working within the television industry.

Ennis, Edward J.

b. 1907
d. January 7, 1990
New York, New York
fields: Law, Government and Politics

Edward J. Ennis was an attorney with the U.S. Justice Department during World War II. He opposed the government's plan to place Japanese Americans in detention camps as unconstitutional but was unable to stop the executive order stipulating the relocation of Japanese Americans. He was placed in charge of the Enemy Alien Control Unit, which examined the loyalty of Japanese, German, and Italian residents, and appointed to prosecute cases against Gordon Hirabayashi and Fred Korematsu, who violated wartime curfew regulations. Ennis left the Justice Department in 1955 and worked as an attorney with the American Civil Liberties Union. At congressional hearings held by the Commission on Wartime Relocation and Internment of Civilians during the 1980's, he testified on behalf of Japanese Americans.

Ennius, Quintus

b. 239 B.C.E.
Rudiae, Calabria
d. c. 169 B.C.E.
Rome?
fields: Literature

Known as the father of Latin poetry, Ennius extended the Latin language into areas previously reserved for Greek, offering explanations for Roman origins. He thus paved the way for the Golden Age of Latin poetry and influenced poets as different as Lucretius and Vergil.

Enriquez, Gaspar

b. July 18, 1942
El Paso, Tex.
fields: Art

Artist. Gaspar Enriquez weaves Hispanic themes into prints, sculptures, jewelry, crafts, and mixed-media pieces. His *La Familia IX* (1985) is a mixed-media altar with small doors adorned with family photographs. His other works incorporate photogarphs with crosses and metal sculptures of Southwestern plants.

Enriquez, Rene

b. Nov. 25, 1933
San Francisco, Calif.
fields: Theater and Entertainment

Actor. Latino actor Rene Enriquez has built his career on portrayals of political and authority figures, including Nicaraguan president Anastasio Somoza in the film *Under Fire* (1983) and Lieutenant Ray Calletano in the hit 1980's television series *Hill Street Blues*. His many film credits include *Girl in the Night* (1960), *Bananas* (1971), *Harry and Tonto* (1974), *Night Moves* (1975), *The Evil That Men Do* (1984), and *Bulletproof* (1985). He was nominated for an Emmy Award in 1985 for his role in *Imagen*.

Enver Pasha

b. November 22, 1881
Constantinople, Ottoman Empire (now Istanbul, Turkey)
d. August 4, 1922
near Baldzhuan, Turkistan (now Tajikistan)
fields: Military Affairs, Government and Politics

As a leader of the Young Turks Revolution, Enver undermined the authority of the sultan and, as a member of the triumvirate, ruled the Ottoman Empire from 1913 to 1918. His promotion of Pan-Turkism and Pan-Islamism during this time led Turkey into World War I on the side of the Triple Alliance and, ultimately, into defeat. After 1918, Enver pursued his Pan-Turkist ideology in Central Asia, where he unified and led disparate Basmachi bands against the Soviets.

Epaminondas

b. c. 410 B.C.E.
Thebes
d. 362 B.C.E.
Mantinea, Greece
fields: Government and Politics, Warfare and Conquest

The greatest military tactician of the classical Greek period, Epaminondas broke the hegemony of Sparta and made Thebes the most powerful state in Greece.

Ephron, Nora

b. May 19, 1941
New York, New York
fields: Journalism, Film

Known for her critical, comedic observations in magazine writing and films, Ephron is one of Hollywood's most successful screenwriters and directors.

Epictetus

b. c. 55
Hierapolis, Phrygia
d. c. 135
Nicopolis, Epirus (now Greece)
fields: Philosophy

Epictetus revived early Greek Stoicism, which emphasized rationality and denied the uncertainty of probability, emphasizing tolerance of pain and the freedom of the soul. His teachings were admired by early Christians, who found them consonant with their own reactions to persecution; famous Christian theologians and priests such as Gregory of Nazianzus and Saint Augustine claimed to be admirers of Epictetus's teachings. Epictetus also the philosophical thought of the nineteenth and twentieth centuries, including that of Georg Wilhelm Friedrich Hegel and later philosophers. His thought is set forth in *Discourses* and *Encheridion.*

Epicurus

b. 341 B.C.E.
Greek island of Samos
d. 270 B.C.E.
Athens, Greece
fields: Philosophy

Epicurus founded the Garden School of Greek philosophy, which has had a significant influence on philosophers, statesmen, and literary figures throughout the history of Western culture.

Epstein, Jacob

aka: Sir Jacob Epstein
b. November 10, 1880
New York, New York
d. August 19, 1959
London, England
fields: Art

An unequaled portrait sculptor and an innovator in sculpting techniques, Epstein was the most important British sculptor in the early twentieth century.

Equiano, Olaudah

né: Gustavas Vassa
b. 1745
probably near Onitsha, Nigeria
d. Apr. 31, 1797
England
fields: Literature, Historical Figure

African American author and former slave; Olaudah Equiano wrote the slave narrative *The Interesting Narrative of the Life of Olaudah Equiano, or Gustavas Vassa, the African* (1789).

Erasistratus

b. c. 325 B.C.E.
Iulis, Island of Chios
d. c. 250 B.C.E.
possibly Mycale, Ionia, Asia Minor, or Alexandria, Egypt
fields: Medicine

Erasistratus made numerous physiological and anatomical discoveries, perhaps using—like his contemporary Herophilus—an exceptional combination of human and animal dissection (and possibly vivisection) to explore the structure and workings of the human body. By creating illuminating alternatives to Hippocratic and Aristotelian models of physiopathological explanation, he also paved the way for the influential Asclepiades of Bithynia.

Erasmus, Desiderius

né: Erasmus
b. October 28, 1466?
Rotterdam, Holland (now in the Netherlands)
d. July 12, 1536
Basel, Switzerland
fields: Education, Religion and Theology, Literature

Of the intellectuals who transmitted and adapted the Renaissance spirit to northern Europe, Erasmus was the greatest. Taken together, his writings reflect a rare combination of practical Christian piety, biblical and patristic scholarship, and broad humanistic learning.

Eratosthenes of Cyrene

b. c. 285 B.C.E.
Cyrene
d. c. 205 B.C.E.
Alexandria
fields: Literature, Geography, Mathematics

Through his energetic directorship, Eratosthenes helped make the Library of Alexandria the greatest repository of learning in the Mediterranean world, and his varied contributions made him the most versatile scholar and scientist of the third century B.C.E.

Erdös, Paul

b. Mar. 26, 1913
Budapest, Hungary
d. Sept. 20, 1996
Warsaw, Poland
fields: Mathematics (mathematical logic and number theory)

Paul Erdös was a mathematical pilgrim. He traveled the world posing and solving perplexing problems in number theory and other areas. Erdös popularized the field of combinatorial analysis, or combinatorics. He won the Hungarian State Prize in 1983 and the Wolf Prize (Israel) in 1984.

Erdrich, Louise

b. June 7, 1954
Little Falls, Minnesota
fields: Literature

A poet and novelist of Chippewa and German descent, Erdrich has become one of the most important authors writing Native American fiction in the late twentieth century.

Erhard, Ludwig

b. February 4, 1897
Fürth, Germany
d. May 5, 1977
Bonn, West Germany
fields: Economics, Government and Politics

Erhard developed the idea of the social market economy and transformed the life of postwar West Germany, setting his country on the path to becoming the "economic miracle" of the 1950's. He went on to become his country's minister of economics, vice chancellor, and chancellor between 1949 and 1966.

Erigena, Johannes Scotus

b. c. 810
Ireland
d. c. 877
France or England
fields: Philosophy, Religion and Theology

Johannes Scotus Erigena provided the first Latin translations of and commentaries on the works of the great Greek fathers of the early Christian church. His sometimes controversial Neoplatonic works were a synthesis of medieval theology and philosophy. Major works include *De divina praedestinatione* (851), *De divisione naturae* (c. 862-866), and *Homilia in prologum Sancti Evangelli secondum Joannem* (c. 870).

Erikson, Erik H.

né: Erik Homburger
b. June 15, 1902
near Frankfurt, Germany
d. May 12, 1994
Harwich, Mass.
fields: Psychiatry and Psychology

Erik H. Erikson modernized and extended Freudian theory, postulating eight stages of psychosocial development; he was particularly well known for his description of the identity crisis experienced by adolescents. He began his career teaching in Vienna and came to the United States in 1933, later teaching at Harvard, Yale, and the University of California, Berkeley. His books include *Childhood and Society* (1950), *Young Man Luther* (1958), *Identity, Youth, and Crisis* (1968), and *Gandhi's Truth* (1969), and his theories remain central to many child development textbooks.

Erlach, Johann Bernhard Fischer von. *See* Fischer von Erlach, Johann Bernhard

Ernst, Max

b. April 2, 1891
Brühl, near Cologne, Germany
d. April 1, 1976
Paris, France
fields: Art

The German painter and sculptor Ernst was the cofounder of the Cologne branch of Dada and later became a leading artist of the Surrealist movement. His work contributed much to the broadening of Surrealist artistic and philosophical thinking.

Ernst, Morris Leopold

b. August 23, 1888
Uniontown, Alabama
d. May 21, 1976
New York, New York
fields: Law, Social Reform

An important civil liberties lawyer, Morris Leopold Ernst specialized in censorship law and cases involving literary freedom. After losing a censorship case in 1927, he determined to master this field. As co-general counsel of the American Civil Liberties Union from 1929 to 1954 he vigorously attacked literary censorship. He wrote more than two dozen books and hundreds of articles on the subject. His books include *To the Pure: A Study in Obscenity and the Censor* (1928), *Censored: The Private Life of the Movies* (1930), *The Censor Marches On: Recent Milestones in the Obscenity Laws in the United States* (1940), and *Censorship: The Search for the Obscene* (1964).

Erskine, first Baron

né: Thomas Erskine
b. January, 1750
Edinburgh, Scotland
d. November 17, 1823
Almondell, Linlithgow, Scotland
fields: Law, Government and Politics

Combining eloquence and with strong liberal leanings, Erskine became the most famous and accomplished trial lawyer and defender of individual rights in English history.

Erving, Julius

aka: Dr. J.
b. Feb. 22, 1950
Hempstead, N.Y.
fields: Sports (basketball player)

African American basketball player; Julius Erving was one of pro basketball's leading career scorers, playing first for the Virginia Squires, then for the New York Nets; in 1976, joined the Philadelphia 76ers; retired in 1987.

Erwin, Richard C.

b. Aug. 23, 1923
Marion, N.C.
fields: Law

African American federal judge; Richard C. Erwin was appointed by Jimmy Carter to the Middle District of North Carolina.

Erzberger, Matthias

b. September 20, 1875
Buttenhausen, Germany
d. August 26, 1921
near Bad Griesbach, Germany
fields: Government and Politics

Erzberger was the dominant voice of the progressive wing of the Catholic Center Party in the German parliament during and just after World War I. He led the fight for Germany's acceptance of the 1918 armistice and for Germany's ratification of the Versailles Treaty.

Esaki, Leo

aka: Esaki Reiona
b. Mar. 12, 1925
Osaka, Japan
fields: Physics

In 1973, Leo Esaki shared the Nobel Prize in Physics for his discovery of the tunneling effect in semiconductors. While employed by the Sony Corporation and working toward his doctoral degree from the University of Tokyo, he made breakthrough formulations on tunneling. His experiments led to the discovery of the tunnel diode, a powerful device vital to the operation of modern computers. He went to work for IBM in New York in 1960. In 1965, he was made an IBM Fellow, the firm's highest research honor. His research into superlattices has also won awards.

Escalante, Jaime

b. Dec. 31, 1930
La Paz, Bolivia
fields: Education

Latino educator Jaime Escalante developed an innovative program to teach mathematics at Garfield High School in East Los Angeles. His work was dramatized in the feature film *Stand and Deliver* (1987). He later hosted a television series titled *Futures: Exploring the Role of Mathematics in the Working World* for the Public Broadcasting System. The ARCO Foundation funded a $25,000 grant to honor him and his work, and Escalante received the Jefferson Award from the American Institute for Public Service in 1990.

Escalera, Irene. *See* Cara, Irene

Escalona, Beatriz

aka: La Chata Noloesca
b. Aug. 20, 1903
San Antonio, Tex.
d. 1980
fields: Theater and Entertainment

Actress. Beatriz Escalona was an agile comic actress who rose to fame in Southwestern vaudeville of the 1920's under the stage name La Chata Noloesca. Her stage persona was a fast-talking street character in a maid's or child's costume. By 1930, she had her own theatrical company in Los Angeles; in 1936, the company relocated to San Antonio. Escalona later became an influential theater manager on New York's Hispanic circuit; her daughter Belia Areu also became a stage star.

Escobar, Sixto

b. Mar. 23, 1913
Barceloneta, Puerto Rico
d. Nov. 17, 1979
Barceloneta, Puerto Rico
fields: Sports (boxing)

Boxer. Sixto Escobar took the National Boxing Association bantamweight title from Baby Casanova in 1934 to became the first Puerto Rican world champion. He kept the title for a year before losing it, then regained it three months later. In 1936, he captured the world bantamweight title from Tony Marino; he lost that title in 1937 but regained it in 1938. In 1939, weight problems caused him to vacate the title; he fought his last fight in December, 1940. His career record included twenty-one knockouts in sixty-four fights.

Escovedo, Sheila. *See* E., Sheila

Eshkebugecoshe. *See* Flat Mouth

Eskiminzin

aka: Big Mouth
aka: Hackibanzin
b. c. 1825
Gila region, present-day Ariz.
d. 1890
San Carlos Agency, Ariz.
fields: Government and Politics, Native American Affairs

Aravaipa Apache principal chief. Although a proponent of peace, Eskiminzin was victimized by white settlers seeking retaliation for Apache raids. In 1871, in what became known as the Camp Grant Massacre, 150 Apache, including eight members of Eskiminzin's family, were murdered. After the raiders were tried and acquitted, Apache hostility escalated.

Esparza, Moctezuma Díaz

b. Mar. 12, 1949
Los Angeles, Calif.
fields: Theater and Entertainment

Filmmaker. Longtime Chicano activist Moctezuma Díaz Esparza is a cofounder of Esparza/Katz Productions and a leading producer of films dealing with Hispanic themes. He coproduced *Alambrista!* (1977) and *The Milagro Beanfield War* (1988), produced *Only Once in a Lifetime* (1978) and *Radioactive Dreams* (1986), and directed of *The Ballad of Gregorio Cortez* (1983). He earned an Academy Award nomination as coproducer of *Agueda Martínez*, a 1978 documentary on the elderly of northern New Mexico,

Espinosa, Aurelio Macedonio, Sr.

b. Sept. 12, 1880
Carnero, Colombia
d. Sept. 4, 1958
Stanford, Calif.
fields: Education, Scholarship

Folklorist and educator. Aurelio Espinosa, Sr., produced dozens of textbooks, monographs, and scholarly articles on folklore. Among his best-known works are *Cuentos populares españoles* (1946-1947) and *Romancero de Nuevo Méjico* (1953). He was active in founding the American Association of Teachers of Spanish and served as editor of the group's journal, *Hispania*, from 1918 to 1926. In 1928, he was elected the association's president. He served as editor of the *Journal of American Folklore* from 1914 to 1946 and as associate editor of *Western Folklore* from 1947 to 1953. In 1923 and 1924, he was president of the American Folk-Lore Society.

Espinosa, Paul

b. Aug. 8, 1950
Alamosa, Calif.
fields: Theater and Entertainment, Television

Filmmaker and television producer. Paul Espinosa is specialist in Latino and U.S.-Mexico border topics. His production credits include *The Trail North* (1983), *Ballad of an Unsung Hero* (1984), *The Lemon Grove Incident* (1986), *Uneasy Neighbors* (1990), *The New Tijuana* (1990), *Los Mineros: American Experience* (1991), *1492 Revisited* (1992), and *The Hunt for Pancho Villa: American Experience* (1993). He received an Emmy Award in 1988 for the documentary *In the Shadow of the Law*.

Espiritu, Yen Le

b. February 13, 1963
Saigon, Republic of Vietnam, now Ho Chi Minh City, Socialist Republic of Vietnam
fields: Scholarship

Yen Le Espiritu, a Vietnamese American married to a Filipino American, published *Asian American Panethnicity: Bridging Institutions and Identities* in 1992. In the work, she explored how "previously unrelated groups submerge their differences and assume a common identity." She emphasizes the interethnic cooperation is essential in preserving the rights and interests of all Asian Americans.

Esposito, Giancarlo Giusseppi Alessandro

b. April 26, 1958
Copenhagen, Denmark
fields: Theater and Entertainment, Film (actor)

African American actor; Giancarlo Giusseppi Alessandro Esposito's acting credits include roles on stage and screen; performed in *Lost in the Stars* and a 1980 production of *Zooman and the Sign*, for which he won an Obie award; appeared in films including *Trading Places* (1983), *The Cotton Club* (1984), *School Daze* (1988), *Do the Right Thing* (1989), *Mo' Better Blues* (1990), *Malcolm X* (1992), *Bob Roberts* (1992), *Fresh* (1994), *Smoke* (1995), *The Usual Suspects* (1995), *Nothing to Lose* (1997), and *Twilight* (1998); starred in short-lived television series *Bakersfield P.D.*

Espy, Mike

full: Alphonso Michael Espy
b. Nov. 30, 1953
Yazoo City, Miss.
fields: Government and Politics

African American politician; Mike Espy was the first African American to be elected to the U.S. Congress from Mississippi since Reconstruction; served as U.S. secretary of agriculture under President Bill Clinton; charges of unethical acceptance of gifts resulted in Espy's resignation in 1994; acquitted of all charges in 1999.

Esquivel, Laura

b. 1950
Mexico City, Mexico
fields: Literature, Theater and Entertainment

Novelist and screenwriter. Laura Esquivel's first novel, *Como agua para chocolate* (1989; *Like Water for Chocolate*, 1992), became an international best-seller and a the basis for a critically acclaimed 1989 film. The film version, with a screenplay by Esquivel and directed by Esquivel's husband, Alfonso Arau won eleven Mexican Academy of Motion Pictures Ariel Awards. Esquivel and Arau also collaborated on the hit Mexican film *Chido One*; Esquivel also scripted the children's feature *Little Ocean Star* (1984).

Estefan, Gloria

né: Gloria Fajardo
b. September 1, 1957
Havana, Cuba
fields: Music

A vocalist and songwriter, Gloria Estefan draws from her Cuban origins to attract popular audiences in the United States and Latin America.

Estes, Billie Sol

b. January 10, 1925
near Clyde, Texas
fields: Historical Figure

A fraud perpetrator of the early 1960's, Billie Sol Estes defrauded lending institutions of millions by using nonexistent fertilizer tanks as collateral for loans. Following his release from prison in 1971, Estes in 1979 was indicted on charges that included income-tax evasion and mail fraud; he was convicted of conspiracy to defraud investors and concealment of assets and sentenced to another ten years in prison, and he was paroled in November, 1983. The Estes case had a great impact on auditing procedures in the United States.

Estes, Lydia. *See* Pinkham, Lydia Estes

Estes, Simon

b. Feb. 2, 1938
Centerville, Iowa
fields: Music (opera singer and recitalist)

African American opera singer and recitalist; Simon Estes was well known in European opera before making his Metropolitan Opera debut in 1982.

Esteves, Sandra María

b. May 10, 1948
New York, N.Y.
fields: Literature

Novelist and poet. Puerto Rican poet and artist Sandra Maria Esteves emerged from New York City's 1970's Puerto Rican cultural reawakening. Her poetry volumes include *Yerba Buena* (1980), selected as the best small-press publication of 1981; *Tropical Rains: A Bilingual Downpour* (1984); and *Bluestown Mockingbird Mambo* (1990).

Estevez, Carlos. *See* Sheen, Charlie

Estevez, Emilio

b. May 12, 1962
New York, N.Y.
fields: Theater and Entertainment, Film (actor)

Emilio Estevez, the son of Martin and Janet Sheen, made his motion picture debut in *Tex* (1982) and got his first starring role in *Repo Man* (1984). He went on to star in such films as *The Breakfast Club* (1984), *St. Elmo's Fire* (1985), *Young Guns* (1988), *Young Guns 2* (1990), and *The Mighty Ducks* (1992). He directed the films *Wisdom* (1986), *Men at Work* (1990), and *The War at Home* (1996), and he wrote the screenplays for *That Was Then . . . This Is Now* (1985), *Wisdom*, and *Clear Intent* (1986).

Estevez, Ramón. *See* Sheen, Martin

Estrada, Leobardo

b. May 6, 1945
El Paso, Tex.
fields: Scholarship

Demographer. Leobarda Estrada was one of eight researchers selected to advise U.S. secretary of commerce Robert Mosbacher on undercounting of Latinos in the 1990 U.S. Census. Estrada also drew the redistricting plan accepted by the court in *Garza v. County of Los Angeles, California Board of Supervisors* and has worked as a consultant for the Southwest Voter Registration and Education Project, the state of California, and various public and private research institutes. Following the 1991 beating of Rodney King by police officers, Estrada was a member of the Christopher Commission, which investigated the Los Angeles Police Department.

Estrada Palma, Tomás

b. July 9, 1835
near Bayamo, Cuba
d. Nov. 14, 1908
Oriente Province, Cuba
fields: Government and Politics

Political leader. Tomás Estrada Palma fought for Cuban independence and headed the Cuban government-in-exile that was established in New York after the Ten Years' War (1868-1878). Fluent in English, he was a naturalized U.S. citizen. With U.S. backing, he became the first elected president of Cuba in 1902. His first term saw the expansion of U.S. economic interests in Cuba, and he rigged the 1905 elections to obtain a second term. When his opponents rebelled, he called for U.S. intervention, resigned, and in September, 1906, left the island.

Ethelred II, the Unready

b. 968?
place unknown
d. April 23, 1016
London, England
fields: Monarchy, Government and Politics

King of England, 979-1016. Although the son of a powerful king and a member of one of the most successful and prestigious dynasties of the Dark Ages, Ethelred showed himself unable to cope with repeated Viking assaults and became a byword for military and political ineptitude.

Etokeah. *See* Hump

Etzioni, Amitai

b. Jan. 4, 1929
Cologne, Germany
fields: Sociology

Sociologist and ethicist. A onetime professor at George Washington University, senior U.S. presidential adviser, and president of the American Sociological Association, Amitai Etzioni became a leading figure in the communitarian movement, which seeks to mobilize resources for the understanding and good of all. His books include *The Spirit of Community: Rights, Responsibilities, and the Communitarian Agenda* (1993).

Eu, March Fong

né: March Kong Fong
b. Mar. 29, 1922
Oakdale, Calif.
fields: Government and Politics, Public Health, Medicine

Asian American health worker and politician. In 1966 March Fong Eu was elected to the California State Assembly representing Oakland and Castro Valley. She won election as secretary of state in 1974 by the record-setting margin; she began her fifth term in 1991. As secretary of state, Eu implemented more than four hundred legislative bills and championed women's and human rights. After being ambushed at her home in a robbery attempt, fighting crime became one of Eu's first priorities. After serving for twenty years as California secretary of state, Eu resigned in 1994 to accept the position of U.S. ambassador to Micronesia.

Eucken, Rudolf Christoph

b. January 5, 1846
Aurich, East Friesland
d. September 15, 1926
Jena, Germany
fields: Philosophy

Eucken characterized the malaise of his age as spiritual confusion. His philosophy attempted to bring people out of this state of depression by stressing activism and spirituality as a renovating force. He was awarded the Nobel Prize in Literature in 1908.

Euclid

b. 335 B.C.E.
probably Greece
d. 270 B.C.E.
Alexandria, Egypt
fields: Mathematics

Euclid took the geometry known in his day and presented it in a logical system. His work, the *Elements*, became the standard textbook on the subject down to modern times.

Eudoxus of Cnidus

b. c. 390 B.C.E.
Cnidus
d. c. 337 B.C.E.
Cnidus
fields: Mathematics, Astronomy

Eudoxus and his disciples resolved classical difficulties in the fields of geometry and geometric astronomy. Their approach became definitive for later research in these fields.

Euler, Leonhard

b. April 15, 1707
Basel, Switzerland
d. September 18, 1783
St. Petersburg, Russia
fields: Mathematics, Physics

Euler had a tremendous impact on almost all fields of mathematics, setting his contemporaries and those who followed on new and more fruitful courses. His founding of the field of analysis is particularly important, and his notations are in common use in mathematics today. He was one of the most prolific mathematical writers ever.

Eupalinus of Megara

b. c. 575 B.C.E.
Megara, Greece
d. c. 500 B.C.E.
place unknown
fields: Engineering

Eupalinus was the architect of the tunnel and aqueduct on the island of Samos that bear his name. Probably built for the tyrant Polycrates in the sixth century B.C.E., they still stand today as monuments to the advanced engineering skills of the greeks of the archaic period.

Euripides

b. c. 485 B.C.E.
Phlya, Greece
d. 406 B.C.E.
Macedonia, Greece
fields: Theater and Entertainment, Literature

Ranking with Aeschylus and Sophocles as a master of Attic tragedy, Euripides was the most "modern" of the great Greek tragedians, often criticizing traditional mythology and realistically working out the logical implications of ancient legends.

Europe, James Reese

b. Feb. 22, 1881
Mobile, Ala.
d. May 10, 1919
Boston, Mass.
fields: Music (bandleader, pianist, and violinist)

African American bandleader, pianist, and violinist; James Reese Europe formed the Clef Club Orchestra in 1910, which became the first African American musical ensemble to record with a major label (Victor); collaborated with dance team of Irene and Vernon Castle, introducing a number of popular dances, inluding the foxtrot.

Eusebius of Caesarea

b. c. 260
probably Caesarea, Palestine
d. May 30, 339
Caesarea, Palestine
fields: Historiography, Religion and Theology

Living through both the last major Christian persecutions and the legalization of Christianity under Constantine the Great, Eusebius interpreted human history in terms of an upward process toward a divine purpose. He formulated the political philosophy of unity of church and state under the providence of God that became standard in the East.

Evans, Annie Lillian. *See* Evanti, Lillian

Evans, Ernest. *See* Checker, Chubby

Evans, James Carmichael

b. July 1, 1900
Gallatin, Tenn.
d. 1988
fields: Engineering, Education, Invention and Technology (engineer, educator, and civilian aide)

African American engineer, educator, and civilian aide; James Carmichael Evans served as a civilian aide to Secretary of Defense Louis Johnson and was instrumental in eliminating restrictions that limited the advancement of African Americans in the armed services; helped implement desegregation of the military under Executive Order 9981; received the Meritorious Civilian Service Medal in 1970; also patented a method of using exhaust gases to prevent icing on aircraft.

Evans, Mari

b. July 16, 1923
Toledo, Ohio
fields: Literature (poet)

African American poet; Mari Evans gained fame in the 1960's as a writer of lean, concise verse on racial themes; her best known poem is "Alarm Clark" (1966).

Evans, Mary Ann. *See* Eliot, George

Evans, Melvin Herbert

b. Aug. 7, 1917
Christiansted, St. Croix
d. Nov. 27, 1984
Christiansted, St. Croix
fields: Government and Politics

African American congressional delegate from the Virgin Islands; Melvin Herbert Evans was appointed governor of the Virgin Islands by Richard Nixon (1969); ambassador to Trinidad and Tobago (1981).

Evans, Michael Jonas

b. Nov. 3, 1949
Salisbury, N.C.
fields: Television

African American actor; Michael Jonas Evans is best known for his role as Lionel Jefferson in the television series *All in the Family* (1971-1975) and *The Jeffersons* (1975-1982); helped create the television series *Good Times* in 1974.

Evans, Minnie Jones

b. Dec. 12, 1892
Long Creek, N.C.
d. 1987
fields: Art (folk artist)

African American self-taught folk artist; Minnie Jones Evans worked in oil paints, ink and pencil, and wax crayon.

Evans, William. *See* Lateef, Yusef

Evanti, Lillian

né: Annie Lillian Evans
b. Aug. 12, 1890
Washington, D.C.
d. Dec. 7, 1967
Washington, D.C.
fields: Music (coloratura soprano)

African American coloratura soprano; Lillian Evanti was rebuffed by the Metropolitan Opera in 1932, on racial grounds, after establishing a successful career in Europe; starred with the National Negro Opera company; lobbied for Kennedy Center.

Evatt, Herbert Vere

b. April 30, 1894
East Maitland, Australia
d. November 2, 1965
Canberra, Australia
fields: Law, Scholarship, Government and Politics, Diplomacy (international affairs)

Evatt contributed an intellectual idealism to Australian legal and historical scholarship and to its domestic politics. As minister for external affairs, he directed Australia's first independent foreign policy and was instrumental in drafting the Charter of the United Nations.

Everett, Percival L.

b. December 22, 1956
Fort Gordon, Ga.
fields: Literature (writer)

African American writer; Percival L. Everett's works include the novels *Suder* (1983), *Walk Me to the Distance* (1985), *Cutting Lisa* (1986), *For Her Dark Skin* (1990), *Zulus* (1990), and *God's Country* (1994); a short-story collection, *The Weather and Women Treat Me Fair* (1987); and a children's book, *The One That Got Away* (1992).

Everett, Ron N.. *See* Karenga, Maulana Ron

Evers, Charles

full: James Charles Evers
b. Sept. 11, 1922
Decatur, Miss.
fields: Civil Rights, Government and Politics

Charles Evers succeeded his brother, Medgar Evers, as field secretary for the National Association for the Advancement of Colored People (NAACP) in 1963 and ran for Congress in 1968, losing in the Democratic Party run-off election. The following year he was elected mayor of Fayette, Mississippi, and became a champion of black business development. Unseated in 1981, he was reelected in 1985 and was eventually mayor for four terms. He also conducted unsuccessful campaigns for governor in 1971 and U.S. senator in 1978.

Evers, Medgar

full: Medgar Wylie Evers
b. July 2, 1925
Decatur, Miss.
d. June 12, 1963
Jackson, Miss.
fields: Civil Rights

African American civil rights activist; Medgar Evers was appointed Mississippi field secretary of the National Association for the Advancement of Colored People, 1954; actively fought for enforcement of school integration and advocated the right of blacks to vote and the boycotting of merchants who discriminated against African Americans; when murdered in 1963 became one of the first martyrs of the Civil Rights movement; Byron de la Beckwith tried (1964) but released after two hung juries; Beckwith tried and convicted in 1994.

Evers-Williams, Myrlie

b. March 17, 1933
Vicksburg, Miss.
fields: Civil Rights

African American civil rights activist; Myrlie Evers-Williams was the wife of murdered civil rights activist, Medgar Evers; married again to Walter Edgar Williams in 1976; became the first African American woman to serve as commissioner of public works in Los Angeles, a possition held until 1990; in 1995 was elected the first African American woman to lead the NAACP; served as leader of the NAACP from 1995 to 1998; authored *For Us, the Living* (1967) and an autobiography, *Watch Me Fly* (1999).

Evert, Chris

full: Christine Marie Evert
b. December 21, 1954
Fort Lauderdale, Florida
fields: Sports (tennis)

Chris Evert burst upon the tennis scene in 1971 as the first of the modern teenage stars. During the two decades that followed, she became one of the great champions of the sport and one of the most popular players that tennis has ever known.

Ewing, Patrick

full: Patrick Aloysius Ewing
b. Aug. 5, 1962
Kingston, Jamaica
fields: Sports (basketball player)

African American basketball player; one the of top centers of the 1980's and 1990's, Patrick Ewing was a 1985 first round draft pick of the New York Knicks.

Eyck, Hubert

b. Before 1390
possibly Maastricht, Flanders
d. Probably September 18, 1426
Ghent, Flanders
fields: Art

In paintings of unprecedented accuracy of observation and coherence of form, Jan and Hubert van Eyck achieved a fusion of Christian religious content with a passionate devotion to visual fact.

Eyck, Jan van

b. c. 1390
possibly Maastricht, Flanders
d. July 9, 1441
Bruges, Flanders
fields: Art

In paintings of unprecedented accuracy of observation and coherence of form, Jan and Hubert van Eyck achieved a fusion of Christian religious content with a passionate devotion to visual fact.

Ezekiel

b. c. 627 B.C.E.
Jerusalem
d. c. 570 B.C.E.
Babylonia
fields: Religion and Theology

As a visionary and prophetic leader, Ezekiel was one of a number of individuals who held the Jewish community together during the early years of the Babylonian Exile (586-538 B.C.E.). His visions and consolatory prophecies encouraged those in exile to look toward the day of the restoration of the Temple in Jerusalem.

Ezra

b. Late sixth or early fifth century B.C.E.
southern Mesopotamia
d. Date unknown
probably Jerusalem
fields: Religion and Theology

As a "scribe skilled in the law of Moses," Ezra led a religious reform movement which transformed the identity of the Jewish community which had returned from exile to Jerusalem. This new identity of the Jewish people was premised upon a return to observance of the Law (Torah).

Faber, Sandra
né: Sandra Moore
b. Dec. 28, 1944
Boston, Massachusetts
fields: Astronomy

Sandra Faber studied galaxies' formation, structure, and evolution; discovered a new method for determining the distances to galaxies; investigated the large-scale motion of galaxies; in 1979, concluded that galaxies are surrounded by enormous pockets of invisible matter; in 1990, she helped establish the Keck Observatory.

Fabius
né: Quintus Fabius Maximus
b. c. 275 B.C.E.
place unknown
d. 203 B.C.E.
possibly Rome
fields: Government and Politics, Warfare and Conquest

During the Second Punic War (218-202 B.C.E.) between Carthage and Rome, Fabius, nicknamed "the Delayer," using feint-and-run tactics, carried on a fairly successful war of attrition against Hannibal, the great Carthaginian general whose army ravaged the Italian peninsula and threatened Rome itself.

Fábregas, Virginia
b. 1870
Yautepec, Mexico
d. Nov. 18, 1950
New York, N.Y.
fields: Theater and Entertainment

Actor and manager. The daughter of a Mexican mother and Spanish father, Virginia Fábregas made her stage debut in 1892 and became a leading Los Angeles theatrical manager during the 1920's and 1930's. She retired to Mexico City in 1933 but returned to Hollywood in the late 1930's to star in Spanish-language features. She received the Mexican Medal of Civic Merit in 1945; her son Manuel Sánchez Navarro also became a successful film actor.

Fabrici, Girolamo. *See* Fabricius, Hieronymus

Fabricius, Hieronymus
full: Hieronymus Fabricius ab Aquapendente
aka: Girolamo Fabrici
aka: Geronimo Fabrizio
b. May 20, 1537
Aquapendente, near Orvieto, Italy
d. May 21, 1619
Padua, Italy
fields: Medicine, Physiology

One of the greatest anatomists of the scientific revolution was Hieronymus Fabricius, who discovered the valves in the veins in 1574; carried out detailed studies of embryos. As a teacher, influenced the discoveries of his student William Harvey.

Fackenheim, Emil L.
full: Emil Ludwig Fackenheim
b. June 22, 1916
Halle, Germany
fields: Philosophy, Religion and Theology

Emil L. Fackenheim used Jewish resources to interpret non-Jewish philosophy and Western techniques on Jewish texts and history. He defined an authentic Jewish philosopher, and an authentic Jew, as one who has opened the self to the historical uniqueness of the Holocaust and one who actively supports the building of the State of Israel as past, present, and future home for the Jews. Major works include *Metaphysics and Historicity* (1961), *The Religious Dimension in Hegel's Thought* (1967), *Quest for Past and Future* (1968), *God's Presence in History* (1970), *Encounters Between Judaism and Modern Philosophy* (1973), *The Jewish Return into History* (1978), *To Mend the World* (1982), and *The God Within* (1996).

Fadden, Arthur William
b. April 13, 1894
Ingham, Queensland (now Australia)
d. April 21, 1973
Brisbane, Queensland, Australia
fields: Government and Politics

Arthur William Fadden was prime minister of Australia for a few months in 1941, but his main contribution was as deputy prime minister to Robert Gordon Menzies (1940-1941, 1949-1958): He served as acting prime minister during Menzies's trips abroad. Fadden later figured that he had spent 692 days—nearly two years—as acting prime minister while Menzies was out of the country. Authorized Australian troops to be sent to Korea in 1950.

Fagan, Eleanora. *See* Holiday, Billie

Fages, Doña Eulalia
né: Eulalia de Callis
b. ?
Spain
d. ?
Spain
fields: Colonial Administration

Wife of a California governor. Doña Eulalia Fages was the wife of Pedro Fages, a late-eighteenth century Spanish governor of Alta California. She earned a reputation as a generous woman with a fiery temper; during a 1782 trip to Monterey, California, she allegedly gave away most of her clothing to the town's poor.

Fahd
né: Fahd ibn Abd Al-Aziz al Saud
b. 1922 or 1923
Riyadh, Arabia (now Saudi Arabia)
fields: Government and Politics

King of Saudia Arabia from 1982. Continuing the reign of the Al-Saud family, Fahd has led Saudi Arabia through decades of development and has become a major force in the political and economic affairs of the Arab and Western worlds.

Fahrenheit, Gabriel Daniel
b. May 24, 1686
Danzig (now Gdansk), Poland
d. Sept. 16, 1736
The Hague, the Netherlands
fields: Invention and Technology, Physics

Gabriel Daniel Fahrenheit invented the spirit (alcohol) thermometer in 1709; made first mercury-in-glass thermometer in 1714; established a temperature scale calibrated between 96 and 32 degrees in 1717, named for him; patented a pumping device for draining Dutch lowlands in 1736.

Faidherbe, Louis
full: Louis Léon César Faidherbe
b. June 3, 1818
Lille, France
d. September 29, 1889
Paris, France
fields: Colonial Administration, Military Affairs

Faidherbe, through war and diplomacy, laid the foundation of France's West African empire. He stemmed the Muslim military advance in West Africa but respected Islam. He improved Senegal economically, socially, and culturally. His generalship retrieved France's honor in the Franco-German War.

Fair, Ronald L.
b. Oct. 27, 1932
Chicago, Ill.
fields: Literature

African American novelist and poet; Ronald L. Fair achieved critical praise for works such as his poetry collection *Excerpts* (1975); his best known novel, *Hog Butcher* (1966), was made into a film and republished as *Cornbread, Earl, and Me* (1975).

Fairfax, Third Baron
né: Thomas Fairfax
b. January 17, 1612
Denton, Yorkshire, England

d. November 12, 1671
Nun Appleton, near Bilborough, Yorkshire, England
fields: Military Affairs, Government and Politics

Lord Fairfax commanded the parliamentary army in the crucial phase of the English Civil War, ensuring the defeat of the king.

Faisal

full: Faisal ibn Abdul Aziz
b. c. 1905
Riyadh, Arabia
d. March 25, 1975
Riyadh, Saudi Arabia
fields: Government and Politics

Faisal, as crown prince and eventually King of Saudi Arabia, led his country to its status as a world power through his participation in the Arab oil embargo and the formation of the United Arab Emirates and OPEC. He also advanced many domestic reforms.

Faisal I

b. May 20, 1885
Taif, Arabia (now Saudi Arabia)
d. September 8, 1933
Bern, Switzerland
fields: Government and Politics

After commanding forces that played a prominent part in the Arab revolt of 1916-1918 against Ottoman rule, Faisal became the first king of modern Iraq and ruled from 1921 to 1933; by adopting a position midway between British and nationalist demands, he was able ultimately to win independence for his country.

Faithfull, Marianne

né: Marian Evelyn Faithfull
b. December 29, 1946
London, England
fields: Music, Theater and Entertainment

Known for her delicate singing voice and striking beauty, Marianne Faithfull became a casualty of the rock-and-roll lifestyle through her romantic involvement with the Rolling Stones' lead singer Mick Jagger. She recorded the Jagger/Richards ballad "As Tears Go By" in (1964). Although Faithfull had a handful of hit singles by 1966, she became equally famous for being Jagger's girlfriend while married to another; as part of the "swinging" 1960's, she attended wild parties and became a regular user of drugs. During the early 1970's, Faithfull struggled with her addiction. In 1979, she made a dramatic comeback with the release of the poignant album *Broken English.*

Fajardo, Gloria. *See* Estefan, Gloria

Fakhr al-Din al-Razi

full: Abu ʿAbd Allah Muhammad ibn ʿUmar ibn al-Husayn ibn ʿAli al-Imam Fakhr al Din al-Razi
b. 1148 or 1149
Rayy, Iran
d. 1210
Herat, Khorasan Province, Iran
fields: Religion and Theology

Fakhr al-Din al-Razi was among the last representatives of Islamic theology to espouse the systematic orthodox school founded by al-Ashʿari. An itinerant scholar, al-Razi's personal contributions as a teacher left an indelible mark on the intellectual life of the eastern provinces of the late twelfth and early thirteenth century Islamic Caliphate; his writings were distributed widely, in both the Iranian (eastern) and Arabic (western) provinces of the caliphs' empire.

Falcon, Angelo

b. ?
Bayamón, Puerto Rico
fields: Social Reform, Government and Politics

Political activist and researcher. Angelo Falcon, a graduated by Columbia College and the State University of New York at Albany, founded the Institute for Puerto Rican Policy and served as its president. The New York City-based institute is a nonpartisan, nonprofit center focusing on issues of interest to Puerto Ricans and members of other Latino communities. Falcon also served as one of the principal investigators in the Latino National Political Survey.

Falero, Emilio

b. 1947
Sagua la Grande, Cuba
fields: Art (painter)

Painter. Emilio Falero's detailed figurative paintings that have the look of Renaissance works. His best-known paintings include *The Music Lesson* (1983) and *The Lace Maker* (1979).

Falla, Manuel de

full: Manuel Maria de Falla y Matheu
b. November 23, 1876
Cádiz, Spain
d. November 14, 1946
Alta Garcia, Argentina
fields: Music

Falla, a preeminent composer of Spanish nationalistic music, combined elements of Impressionism with themes and folk melodies of his national and personal style. His art is rooted in the folk songs of Spain, in the purest historical traditions of Spanish music.

Faludi, Susan C.

b. April 18, 1959
New York, N.Y.
fields: Literature, Women's Rights

Journalist and feminist writer. Susan Faludi authored the 1991 best-seller *Backlash: The Undeclared War Against American Women*, which accused the mainstream media of distorting women's issues in retaliation for women's social gains and asserted the need for ongoing feminist activism in American culture. The controversial book received the 1992 National Book Critics Circle award for nonfiction. In 1999, she published *Stiffed: The Betrayal of the American Male.*

Falwell, Jerry

b. August 11, 1933
Lynchburg, Va.
fields: Religion and Theology, Television

Conservative religious leader and popular television evangelist. The Reverend Jerry Falwell became pastor of the Thomas Road Baptist Church in Lynchburg, Virginia, in 1956—broadcast site of *The Old Time Gospel Hour*, the radio and television ministry that brought him to national prominence. In 1979, he created the Moral Majority, an influential but short-lived conservative organization that called for a restoration of the Christian-based moral values of American society. It was disbanded in 1989 and Falwell was eclipsed by the better-financed and well-organized Reverend "Pat" Robertson, founder of the Christian Coalition.

Fang, John T. C.

b. May 27, 1925
Shanghai, China
d. Apr. 27, 1992
San Francisco, Calif.
fields: Journalism, Publishing

Asian American journalist, publisher; John T. C. Fang was born in China, fled to Taiwan when communists assumed power in 1949; served as reporter and associate editor of *New Life Daily News* (Taiwan); settled in the United States in early 1950's; managing editor of *Chinese Daily Post* (San Francisco) in the 1950's and 1960's; in the 1970's published *Young China Daily News*, founded by Sun Yat-sen early in the twentieth century; established *Asian Weekly* (1979), which became the paper of record among Asian Americans; beginning in 1984, prepared special editions during presidential elections, highlighting ethnic concerns.

Fanon, Frantz

full: Frantz Omar Fanon
b. July 20, 1925
Fort-de-France, Martinique

d. December 6, 1961
Bethesda, Maryland
fields: Philosophy, Civil Rights, Social Reform

Psychoanalyst and social philosopher, editor of the Algerian liberation movements newspaper *El Moudjahid*, Frantz Fanon argued that race was the most important factor in colonial relationships and articulated a theory of global revolution for colonized peoples that emphasized the need for each member of society to participate in the decolonization process. His work inspired leaders during the American Civil Rights movement of the 1960's. Major works include *Black Skin, White Masks* (1952), *Studies in a Dying Colonialism* (1959), and *The Wretched of the Earth* (1961).

Fārābī, al-

né: Abū Naṣr al-Fārābī
full: Muḥammad ibn Muḥammad ibn Ṭarkhān ibn Uzalagh al-Fārābī
b. 870
Farab, north of Tashkent in Kazakh-stan
d. 950
Aleppo, Syria
fields: Philosophy, Government and Politics

Author of *The Opinions of the Inhabitants of the Virtuous City* and *The Agreement of Plato and Aristotle*, Muḥammad ibn Muḥammad ibn Ṭarkhān al-Fārābī attempted a reconciliation of Plato, Aristotle, and Neoplatonic thought, creating a political ethics that emphasized good rulers: The virtuous city is well-led, so that its citizens are reminded of a life beyond this one and can achieve moral virtue, which allows reason to govern appetites and passions. Al-Fārābī had an important place in the philosophy of Avicenna, Albertus Magnus, and, through them, Saint Thomas Aquinas.

Faraday, Michael

b. September 22, 1791
Newington, Surrey, England
d. August 25, 1867
Hampton Court, Surrey, England
fields: Physics, Chemistry

Considered by many as the greatest British physicist of the nineteenth century, Faraday's discoveries in electromagnetism were fundamental to the development of field physics. His inventions of the dynamo and electric motor provided the basis for modern electrical industry.

Fard, Wallace D.

aka: Wallace Fard Muhammad
b. c. 1877
d. 1934
fields: Religion and Theology

African American religious leader; Wallace D. Fard founded founded the "First Temple of Islam," later the Nation of Islam.

Farmer, Arthur Stewart

b. Aug. 21, 1928
Council Bluffs, Iowa
fields: Music (jazz trumpeter and flügelhornist)

African American trumpeter and flügelhornist; Arthur Stewart Farmer was the twin of jazz bassist Addison Farmer; collaborated with the likes of Lionel Hampton and Clifford Brown; wrote a number of jazz standards with Benny Golson.

Farmer, Fannie

full: Fannie Merritt Farmer
b. March 23, 1857
Boston, Massachusetts
d. January 15, 1915
Boston, Massachusetts
fields: Education

Farmer was a teacher of cooking and food science. Her 1896 *Boston Cooking-School Cook Book* was the first modern cookbook with clear instructions stressing precise measurements.

Farmer, Forest Jackson

b. January 15, 1941
Zanesville, Ohio
fields: Business and Industry (automotive executive)

African American automotive executive; Forest Jackson Farmer joined the Chrysler Motors Corporation in 1968 and became president of Acustar, Inc. (an independent subsidiary of Chrysler that produces electronic components for automobiles) in 1988.

Farmer, James

full: James Leonard Farmer
b. Jan. 12, 1920
Marshall, Tex.
d. July 9, 1999
Fredericksburg, Va.
fields: Civil Rights

African American civil rights leader; James Farmer was the organizer of the Congress of Racial Equality (CORE), 1942, the first major nonviolent protest organization; staged the first successful sit-in, at a Chicago restaurant in 1943; program director of the National Association for the Advancement of Colored People, 1959-1961; introduced the tactic of the Freedom Ride in 1961 to test principles of desegregation; left CORE in 1966; appointed assistant secretary of Health, Education, and Welfare in 1969 (1969-1970); became associate director of the Coalition of American Public Employees in 1976 (1976-1981).

Farmer, Sarah Jane

b. July 22, 1847
Dover, New Hampshire
d. November 23, 1916
Portsmouth, New Hampshire
fields: Religion and Theology

Founder of Greenacre summer conferences on comparative religion in Eliot, Maine, Farmer later established the first American Bahaʾi community there.

Farnese, Alessandro. *See* Paul III

Farnese, Alessandro

b. August 27, 1545
Rome
d. December 2-3, 1592
Arras, France
fields: Military Affairs

Combining prodigious military ability and political talent, Farnese came close to retaking all of the Netherlands for Spain before imperial distractions and drains on Philip's finances elsewhere combined to undermine his achievements.

Farnham, Marynia

b. Sept. 29, 1899
Red Wing, Minn.
d. May 29, 1979
Brattleboro, Vt.
fields: Sociology

Marynia Farnham was an antifeminist sociologist and psychiatrist, best known for her antifeminist book, *Modern Woman: The Lost Sex* (1947), written with Ferdinand Lundberg, in which she asserts that by leaving traditional family roles, feminists only make themselves and others around them unhappy.

Farragut, David G.

full: David Glasgow Farragut
b. July 5, 1801
Campbell's Station, Tennessee
d. August 14, 1870
Portsmouth, New Hampshire
fields: Military Affairs

The first admiral in the United States Navy, Farragut is most noted for his victory over Confederate forces in the Battle of Mobile Bay.

Farrakhan, Louis

né: Louis Eugene Walcott
full: Louis Abdul Farrakhan
b. May 11, 1933
New York, N.Y.
fields: Social Reform, Religion and Theology

African American minister, leader of the Nation of Islam; Louis Farrakhan was born Louis Eugene Walcott; joined the Nation of Islam in 1955; denounced Malcolm X (following his split with Elijah Muhammad) and succeeded him as leader of the Harlem mosque and national spokesman for the Nation of Islam; stressed discipline, black self-sufficiency, and black separatism; left Nation of Islam when it began to accept whites in the mid-1970's, founding a rival organization, later known by the same name; published the newspaper *The Final Call*; supported Jesse Jackson in the 1984 presidential campaign, marking a turning point in Black Muslim political involvement; criticized for anti-Semitic statements attributed to him and other members of the Nation of Islam; organized 1995 Million Man March.

Farrand, Beatrix Jones

né: Beatrix Cadwalader Jones
b. June 19, 1872
New York City
d. February 27, 1959
Bar Harbor, Maine
fields: Landscape Architecture

The first American woman landscape architect, Farrand was instrumental in the popularizing of a natural style of landscape design.

Farrell, Suzanne

né: Roberta Sue Ficker
b. August 16, 1945
Cincinnati, Ohio
fields: Dance

Farrell was a principal dancer in the New York City Ballet and an interpreter of and collaborator with choreographer George Balanchine.

Farrelly, Alexander A.

b. ?
fields: Government and Politics

African American territorial governor; Alexander A. Farrelly was elected in 1986 as governor of the Virgin Islands.

Farrow, Mia

full: Maria de Lourdes Villiers Farrow
b. February 9, 1945
Los Angeles, California
fields: Theater and Entertainment, Film

Unconventional and a free spirit, Mia Farrow gained fame both for her acting skills and for the men with whom she became involved, including Frank Sinatra, Andre Previn, and Woody Allen. She appeared as Alison McKenzie in the 1960's prime-time television soap opera *Peyton Place*. During the late 1960's and 1970's she appeared in such films as Roman Polanski's classic horror film *Rosemary's Baby* (1968), *John and Mary* with Dustin Hoffman (1969), *The Great Gatsby* with Robert Redford (1974), *A Wedding* (1978), *Death on the Nile* (1978), and in 1982 Woody Allen's *A Midsummer Night's Comedy*, the first of several collaborations as well as the start of their personal relationship. In 1992, Farrow learned that Allen had begun an affair with her adopted daughter Soon-Yi Previn. A long and unseemly custody battle ensued, and in 1993 Farrow was awarded custody of the three Allen children.

Faske, Donna. *See* Karan, Donna

Father Divine

né: George Baker
aka: Major J. Devine
b. May, 1879
Rockville, Md.
d. Sept. 10, 1965
Philadelphia, Pa.
fields: Religion and Theology

Religious leader; Father Divine, probably born George Baker; early life mysterious; joined various Christian sects before returning to native Georgia around 1910 to proclaim himself a "divine messenger;" driven from Georgia, settled in New York City in 1915, where he fed the poor and homeless and established a communitarian religious group based on racial equality; his Peace Mission movement spread in the 1930's and 1940's, becoming a cult in which Father Divine was worshiped as God incarnate on earth; published weekly magazine, "The New Day."

Father MC

b. ?
fields: Music (Rap vocalist)

African American rap vocalist; Father MC helped popularize Love Rap, combining a rhythm-and-blues sound with rap lyrics.

Fāṭima

b. c. 606
Mecca, Arabia
d. 632
Medina, Arabia
fields: Religion and Theology

A model of piety, spiritual purity, and spiritual power in Islam, Fāṭima was the daughter of the Prophet Muhammad and is revered throughout the Islamic world as an exemplary woman. She married Ali ibn Abī Ṭālib, and their descendants became the Fāṭimid dynasty of North Africa.

Fatou, Pierre

full: Pierre Joseph Louis Fatou
b. Feb. 28, 1878
Lorient, France
d. Aug. 10, 1929
Pornichet, France
fields: Mathematics (applied math, calculus, and geometry)

Pierre Fatou published important work on the iteration of functions in 1919-1920. He was one of the founders of what is now known as the theory of chaos. He discovered the Julia set with Gaston Julia and laid the groundwork for the discovery of the Mandelbrot set. He became president of the Mathematical Society of France in 1927.

Faulk, John Henry

b. August 21, 1913
Austin, Texas
d. April 9, 1990
Austin, Texas
fields: Radio, Television

A radio and television personality, John Henry Faulk was blacklisted during the 1950's and won a major libel suit against the organization that accused him of communist sympathies while he was hosting a radio show in New Jersey. While filing suit against the organization, he lost his job and could not find work in the entertainment industry. In 1962 he finally won his suit and was awarded generous damages. His case established that blacklisting occurred throughout the entertainment industry. Afterward he returned to radio and television appearances. His 1964 book, *Fear on Trial*, is a memoir of his legal battles.

Faulkner, William

full: William Cuthbert Faulkner
b. September 25, 1897
New Albany, Mississippi
d. July 6, 1962
Byhalia, Mississippi
fields: Literature

Using the South as his inspiration and setting, Faulkner wrote a series of novels and stories which reflect universal human truths and conditions; he won the Nobel Prize in Literature in 1949 and is regarded as one of the greatest of American novelists.

Fauntroy, Walter

b. Feb. 6, 1933
Washington, D.C.
fields: Government and Politics

African American politician; Walter Fauntroy, a Baptist minister, was director of the SCLC (1960) and helped organize the 1963 March on Washington and the 1965 Selma to Montgomery march; representative in Congress for the District of Columbia (1975); chaired the Congressional Black Caucus (1981-1983).

Fauset, Crystal Bird

b. June 27, 1893
Princess Anne, Md.
d. Mar. 28, 1965
Philadelphia, Pa.
fields: Government and Politics

African American politician; Crystal Bird Fauset was the first African American woman elected to a state legislature (Pennsylvania in 1938); served in Franklin D. Roosevelt's "black cabinet."

Fauset, Jessie Redmon

b. April 27, 1882
Snow Hill, N.J.
d. Apr. 30, 1961
Philadelphia, Pa.
fields: Literature

African American novelist; Jessie Redmon Fauset was the literary editor of *The Crisis*, a publication of the National Association for the Advancement of Colored People; influential in the Harlem Renaissance; best-known works are *The Chinaberry Tree* (1931) and *Plum Bun* (1928).

Favela, Ricardo

b. 1944
fields: Art, Social Reform

Artist and community organizer. Ricardo Favela is best known for his contributions to Chicano art in California. In 1968, he helped to organize the Rebel Chicano Art Front, later dubbed the Royal Chicano Air Force (RCAF). His silkscreened poster *Huelga!* (strike!), which depicts RCAF members dressed as pilots organizing a strike in support of California farmworkers, is typical of his politically charged art.

Fawcett, Millicent Garrett

né: Millicent Garrett
aka: Dame Millicent Garrett Fawcett
b. June 11, 1847
Aldeburgh, Suffolk, England
d. August 5, 1929
London, England
fields: Women's Rights, Social Reform

Dame Millicent Garrett Fawcett was a leader in advancing the causes of women's suffrage, education, and social reform. She also worked to end the double standard in the grounds for divorce, to improve women's rights of guardianship over their children, and to open the legal profession to women. From 1897 to 1919, she was president of the nonviolent National Union of Women's Suffrage Societies.

Fawkes, Guy

b. April 13, 1570
York, England
d. January 31, 1606
Westminster, England
fields: Government and Politics

Guy Fawkes was a key conspirator in the Gunpowder Plot, a secret attempt to destroy the English king and Parliament. Discovery of the plot intensified Protestant suspicions of Catholics and led to a period of reduced tolerance of Catholicism in England.

Fax, Elton

b. Oct. 9, 1909
Baltimore, Md.
fields: Literature, Art

African American author and illustrator; Elton Fax illustrated more than twenty-seven children's volumes, written biographies of artists, and exhibited his own art in major museums.

Fechner, Gustav Theodor

b. April 19, 1801
Gross-Särchen, Prussia
d. November 18, 1887
Leipzig, Germany
fields: Philosophy, Physics

Fechner is widely regarded as the founder of psychophysics, or the science of the mind-body relation, and as a pioneer in experimental psychology. His most important contributions are a number of quantitative methods for measuring absolute and differential thresholds that are still employed by psychologists to study sensitivity to stimulation.

Fedorovich, Grand Duke Peter. *See* Peter III

Feigenbaum, Mitchell Jay

b. Dec. 19, 1944
Philadelphia, Pennsylvania
fields: Mathematics (applied math)

Mitchell Jay Feigenbaum found a universal law that governs the transition from regular to chaotic behavior. He won the MacArthur Foundation Award in 1984 and the Wolf Foundation Prize in Physics in 1986.

Feinstein, Dianne

né: Dianne Goldman
b. June 22, 1933
San Francisco, California
fields: Government and Politics

In each of her elected offices from the presidency of the Board of Supervisors of San Francisco to U.S. Senator from California, Dianne Feinstein has been a pioneer, the first woman to hold that position.

Feleo-Gonzalez, Marina

b. July 22, 1932
Santa Rosa, Philippines
fields: Theater and Entertainment

Playwright, screenwriter, and media consultant Marina Feleo-Gonzalez founded the screenwriters guild of the Philippines and the Radio/TV Writers Guild of the Philippines and received numerous awards for her scripts. She taught for American independent film organizations such as Third World Newsreel, the Film News Now Foundation, and Women Make Movies. She lectured throughout in the United States, on topics such as Asian and Asian American film, video, and culture.

Feliciano, José

full: José Monserrate Feliciano
b. September 10, 1945
Larez, Puerto Rico
fields: Music

Puerto Rican-born musician and singer. Although born blind, he learned the guitar while growing up in the Spanish Harlem, New York City. In 1964, he signed a recording contract with RCA Records and released his first album, *The Voice and Guitar of José Feliciano*. His hit version of the Doors' song "Light My Fire" (1968)— which sold more than a million copies— was featured on *Feliciano!* (1968), his first gold album. Named *Guitar Player* magazine's Best Folk Guitarist in 1973, he went on to appear in various television episodes and received an Emmy Award nomination for the theme to *Chico and the Man*. He amassed more than thirty gold albums and won numerous Grammy Awards. In 1991, he was presented with a lifetime achievement award at the first annual Latin Music Expo. During the 1990's he continued to release albums.

Félix, María

full: María de Los Angeles Félix Guereña
b. Apr. 8, 1914
Alamos, Sonora, Mexico
fields: Theater and Entertainment, Film

Maria Félix was the queen of Mexican films during the 1940's, 1950's, and 1960's. She made her debut in *El peñon de las animas* (1942); her other Mexican film credits include *María Eugenia* (1942), *Doña Bárbara* (1943), *La mujer sin alma* (1943), *El monje blanco* (1945), *La noche del Sábado* (1950), *La pasión desnuda* (1953), *Miércoles de Ceniza* (1958), and *La cucaracha* (1958). She had a limited Hollywood career in such films as *The Devil Is a Woman* (1952) and *French Can-Can* (1955).

Fellini, Federico

b. January 20, 1920
Rimini, Italy
d. October 31, 1993
Rome, Italy
fields: Film

Fellini's achievement, beginning in 1950, was to move Italian cinema away from the realistic chronicle, to concentrate on the private, inner experience and personal memory as the inspiration for art.

Fells, Augusta Christine. *See* Savage, Augusta

Fender, Freddy

né: Baldemar Garza Huerta
b. June 4, 1937
San Benito, Tex.
fields: Music (singer)

Freddy Fender recorded his first hit single, "Wasted Days and Wasted Nights," in 1959; his rockabilly style prompted some critics to label him the "Mexican Elvis." In the 1970's, he had a series of hit singles on the country music charts, including the bilingual "Before the Next Teardrop Falls," a remake of "Wasted Days and Wasted Nights," "Secret Love," "You'll Lose a Good Thing," "Vaya Con Dios," and "Walking Piece of Heaven." He acted in Robert Redford's 1988 film *The Milagro Beanfield War* and in 1989 joined Doug Sahm, Flaco Jiménez, and Augie Meyers in forming the Texas Tornados.

Fenollosa, Ernest Francisco

aka: Tei-Shin
aka: Kano Yeitan Masanobu
b. Feb. 18, 1853
Salem, Massachusetts
d. Sept. 21, 1908
London, England
fields: Art, Poetry

Ernest Francisco Fenollosa, working during the Meiji Restoration, strove to preserve Japan's classical art, which was being neglected as a consequence of the drive toward modernization. He wrote and lectured extensively on Asian art, spurring further scholarship. He went to Japan in 1878, where he lectured in political science, philosophy, and economics until 1886 at Tokyo Imperial University. In 1887, he cofounded the Tokyo Art Academy. In 1890, Fenollosa became curator of Asian art at the Boston Museum of Fine Arts. He taught English language and literature in Tokyo 1897-1900, assuming a professorship at Columbia University upon his return to the United States. His writings include *East and West: The Discovery of America and Other Poems* (1893), *The Masters of Ukioye* (1896), *An Outline of the History of Ukiyo-ye* (1901), *Epochs of Chinese and Japanese Art: An Outline History of East Asiatic Design* (1912), and *The Chinese Written Character as a Medium for Poetry* (1920).

Ferdinand II

aka: Ferdinand el Católico
aka: Ferdinand the Catholic
aka: Ferdinand III
aka: Ferdinand V
b. March 10, 1452
Sos, Spain
d. January 23, 1516
Madrigalejo, Spain
fields: Monarchy, Military Affairs, Government and Politics

King of Sicily, 1468-1516; Ferdinand V, king of Castile, 1474-1504; Ferdinand II, king of Aragon, 1479-1516; Ferdinand III, king of Naples, 1504-1516. With his wife Isabella I, the Catholic monarch directed Spain's transition from medieval diversity to national unity. They achieved governmental and ecclesiastical reform, and established a continuing Spanish presence in Italy, America, and northern Africa.

Ferdinand II

b. July 9, 1578
Graz, Austria
d. February 15, 1637
Vienna, Austria
fields: Monarchy

While Emperor of the Holy Roman Empire from 1619 to 1637, Ferdinand II sought to restore Roman Catholicism to the Protestant areas of the Empire and to assert Habsburg political hegemony throughout the Empire. His efforts directly resulted in the Thirty Years' War in Germany, one of history's most devastating wars.

Ferguson, Adam

b. June 20, 1723
Logierait, Perthshire, Scotland
d. February 22, 1816
St. Andrews, Fife, Scotland
fields: Philosophy

Ferguson was a leading figure of the eighteenth century Scottish Enlightenment. He was not simply the contemporary of David Hume and Adam Smith but also esteemed as their peer. Widely regarded as the founder of modern sociology, he was the forerunner of, and a significant influence upon, such later thinkers as Auguste Comte, Herbert Spencer, and even Karl Marx.

Ferguson, Alonzo L.

b. Jan. 10, 1931
Washington, D.C.
fields: Military Affairs

Highly decorated African American military officer; Alonzo L. Ferguson achieved the rank of brigadier general in the U.S. Air Force.

Ferguson, Clarence Clyde, Jr.

b. Nov. 4, 1924
Wilmington, N.C.
fields: Government and Politics

African American government official; Clarence Clyde Ferguson, Jr. was ambassador to Uganda (1970-1972); U.S. representative to the Economic and Social Council of the United Nations in the 1970's.

Ferlinghetti, Lawrence

b. March 24, 1919
Yonkers, New York
fields: Literature

The most widely read of the poets who came to prominence during the emergence of the Beat movement. Ferlinghetti's use of a kind of beat vernacular made his lyrical and political poetry very popular during the 1960's. Ferlinghetti was tried on obscenity charges after his publishing company, City Lights Books, published a volume by Allen Ginsberg. His own works include *Pictures of the Gone World* (1955), *A Coney Island of the Mind* (1958), *Starting from San Francisco* (1961), *The Secret Meaning of Things* (1968).

Fermat, Pierre de

b. August 17, 1601
Beaumont-de-Lomagne, France
d. January 12, 1665
Castres, France
fields: Mathematics

Fermat, though a lawyer and jurist, made several pivotal discoveries in the foundations of analytical geometry, differential calculus, and probability theory. His main achievements, however, were in number theory, in which he established the basis of the modern theory and formulated two fundamental theorems that still bear his name.

Fermi, Enrico

b. September 29, 1901
Rome, Italy
d. November 28, 1954
Chicago, Illinois
fields: Physics

Fermi's experiments utilizing neutron bombardment led to the production of the first controlled chain reaction, critical to the United States' development of the atom bomb. He was awarded the 1938 Nobel Prize in Physics.

Fernández, Agustín

b. 1928
Havana, Cuba
fields: Art (painter)

Painter. Augustin Fernández's paintings contrast erotic images with precisely rendered metallic objects. Some of his works emulate the cubists' tendency to reduce images to geometric forms; others convey the dreamlike quality of the surrealists.

Fernandez, Carole Fragoza

b. July 1, 1941
New York, N.Y.
fields: Literature (fiction)

Novelist. Carole Fragoza Fernandez is the author of *Sleep of the Innocents* (1991), a novel about a young woman in an unnamed Latin American country whose life is shattered by military violence.

Fernández, Dolores. *See* Huerta, Dolores

Fernández, Joseph A.

b. 1935
New York, N.Y.
fields: Education

Educational administrator. Joseph Fernández was superintendent of Florida's Dade County School System from 1987 to 1989 before becoming chancellor of the New York City's public schools. He has earned him numerous awards, including Dade County Administrator of the Year (1979); a Cuban Teacher in Exile Award of Honor (1987); a National Puerto Rican Coalition Life Achievement Award (1990); a School Administrator of the Year Award from the National Caucus of Hispanic School Board Members (1991); and an Award for Education from the Hispanic Heritage Awards Committee (1991).

Fernández, Manny

full: Manuel José Fernández
b. July 3, 1946
Oakland, Calif.
fields: Sports (football)

Football player. Manny Fernández was an important part the Miami Dolphins defense in the 1970's. During the 1972-1973 season, he played a key role in Miami's undefeated season and Super Bowl victory, and he received the Johnny Unitas Award. He was named five times to the American Football Conference Second Team; he also was named to the United Press International All-Time Super Bowl All-Star Team.

Fernández, Ricardo

b. Dec. 11, 1940
Santruce, Puerto Rico
fields: Education

Educator; Ricardo Fernández was born in Puerto Rico; earned advanced degrees at Princeton University; on faculty at University of Wisconsin, 1973-1990; president, Lehman College of the City University of New York since 1990; president of the board of directors of the Multicultural Training and Advocacy since 1986; president of the National Association for Bilingual Education (1980-1981); produced pioneering reports on Hispanic education; appointed to board of directors of the Puerto Rican Legal Defense and Education Fund; coauthored *Reducing the Risk: Schools as Communities of Support* (1989).

Fernández, Roberto

b. Sept. 24, 1951
Sagua la Grande, Cuba
fields: Literature

Writer and academician. Roberto Fernández was born into a family that left Cuba in 1961 and settled in Florida. His works include two collections of short stories, *Cuentos sin rumbos* (1975; directionless tales) and *El jardín de la luna* (1976; the garden of the moon), and three novels, *La vida es un special. 75* (1981), *La montaña rusa* (1985, the rollercoaster) and *Raining Backwards* (1988).

Fernández, Royes

b. July 15, 1929
New Orleans, La.
d. Mar. 3, 1980
New York, N.Y.
fields: Dance

Dancer. Royes Fernández made his professional debut in 1946 with Colonel W. de Basil's Original Ballet Russe and subsequently danced with companies including the Borovansky Ballet, the San Francisco Ballet, and the London Festival Ballet. He was a principal dancer with the American Ballet Theatre from 1950 to 1953 and again from 1957 through 1972.

Fernandez, Rudy

b. 1948
Trinidad, Colo.
fields: Art

Artist. Rudy Fernandez's paintings and sculptures combine regional and ethnic images with universal and personal symbols. He received a Visual Arts Fellowship in Painting from the Arizona Commission on Arts in 1981, and his work was featured in the traveling show Hispanic Art in the United States in the late 1980's.

Fernandez, Tony

full: Octavio Antonio Fernandez y Castro
b. Aug. 6, 1962
San Pedro de Macoris, Dominican Republic
fields: Sports (baseball)

Baseball player. Switch-hitting shortstop Tony Fernandez made his major league debut with the Toronto Blue Jays in 1983. His 213 hits in the 1986 season represented the highest total by a major league shortstop in the twentieth century. He has won multiple the Gold Glove Awards and has been selected to All-Star teams in both the American and National Leagues.

Ferrar, Nicholas

b. February 22, 1592
London, England
d. December 4, 1637
Little Gidding, Huntingdonshire, England
fields: Religion and Theology

Turning away from his worldly success in London society, business, and politics, Ferrar found a richer life on the borders of the Fen country at Little Gidding in a tiny Christian community which he designed for his extended family. He has been called one of the greatest Christian Englishmen who have ever lived. Although he performed no great deeds, Ferrar's example of religious everyday family life had an impact on future generations.

Ferrari, Enzo

b. February 18, 1898
Modena, Italy
d. August 14, 1988
Modena, Italy
fields: Business and Industry, Engineering, Sports (auto racing)

Ferrari was a designer and builder of sports cars and is among the most significant forces of this century in the manufacturing and racing of sophisticated, high-speed autos. He revolutionized the industry and sport, and for much of the 1950's and 1960's his cars dominated the high-performance racing circuits.

Ferrari, Lodovico

aka: Lodovico Ferraro
b. Feb. 2, 1522
Bologna, Papal States (now Italy)
d. Oct. 5, 1565
Bologna, Papal States
fields: Mathematics (algebra)

Lodovico Ferrari studied under Gerolamo Cardano in 1536-1540. He discovered the solution of the general quartic (fourth-degree) polynomial equation in 1540. In 1545, he published *Ars Magna* with Cardano.

Ferraro, Geraldine

full: Geraldine Anne Ferraro
b. August 26, 1935
Newburgh, New York
fields: Government and Politics

In 1984, Ferraro became the first woman to be nominated to the vice presidency by a major political party.

Ferre, Luis A.

full: Luis Alberto Ferre
b. Feb. 17, 1904
Ponce, Puerto Rico
fields: Government and Politics

Governor of Puerto Rico. A strong advocate of Puerto Rican statehood, Luis Ferre ran unsuccessfully for governor three times on the Statehood Republican Party ticket. In 1965, he was named to the U.S.-Puerto Rico Commission on the Status of Puerto Rico. He organized the United Statehooders Association, which became the New Progressive Party in 1967. In 1968, he was elected to serve as governor.

Ferre, Maurice Antonio

b. June 23, 1935
Ponce, Puerto Rico
fields: Government and Politics

Mayor of Miami, Florida. Maurice Ferre began his political career in the Florida House of Representatives in 1966. From 1967 to 1970, he was a city commissioner in Miami. In 1973, he became mayor of Miami, a position he held until 1985. In 1976, he acted as National Hispanic Co-Chairman of Jimmy Carter's presidential campaign, and he served on various advisory boards and committees during the Carter Administration.

Ferré, Rosario

b. July 28, 1942
Ponce, Puerto Rico
fields: Literature, Publishing

Writer and publisher. Rosario Ferré's work explores the position of women in a male-dominated culture. Her works include *Papeles de Pandora* (1976; *The Youngest Doll*, 1991), *La caja de cristal* (1978; the glass box), and *Maldito amor* (1986; *Sweet Diamond Dust*, 1988). The daughter of a onetime governor of Puerto Rico, she has embraced the cause of Puerto Rican independence.

Ferrell, Frank J.

b. 1800's
New York
fields: Invention and Technology

African American inventor; Frank J. Ferrell was awarded a number of patents for significant inventions, including improved designs for steam engine components.

Ferrer, Fernando

b. Apr. 30, 1950
Bronx, N.Y.
fields: Government and Politics

Public official. Fernando Ferrer became the director of housing for the Bronx Borough President's Office in 1979. In 1982, he was elected to the city council. In 1987, he was appointed as Bronx borough president. He has been an active leader of the Puerto Rican community.

Ferrer, José

full: José Vicente Ferrer de Otero y Cintron
b. January 8, 1912
Santurce, Puerto Rico
d. January 26, 1992
Coral Gables, Fla.
fields: Theater and Entertainment, Film

Puerto Rican actor, director, and producer. José Ferrer's theatrical career spanned half a century and included dozens of stage plays—as actor and/or director—and films. He debuted on Broadway in 1935 in *A Slight Case of Murder* and became known for such performances as Iago opposite Paul Robeson in *Othello* (1943), the title role in *Cyrano de Bergerac* (1946), and Don Quixote in *Man of La Mancha* (1966). He was the first Latino to receive an Academy Award, for the film version of *Cyrano de Bergerac* (1950). In 1981, he was elected to the Theatre Hall of Fame.

Ferrill, Mikki

b. May 12, 1937
Chicago, Ill.
fields: Photography

African American photographer; Mikki Ferrill contributed to such publications as *Time*, *Ebony*, *Jet*, the *Chicago Tribune*, and the *Chicago Defender*.

Fetchit, Stepin

né: Lincoln Theodore Monroe Andrew Skeeter Perry
b. May 30, 1902
Key West, Fla.
d. Nov. 19, 1985
Woodland Hills, Calif.
fields: Film

African American actor and comedian; Stepin Fetchit was Hollywood's first African American star; began his career in minstrel and vaudeville; began work in film in 1927 and became a star in 1929 with *Hearts in Dixie*; appreciated for his superb comic timing, he was criticized for perpetuating the "coon" stereotype of the lazy, dimwitted black servant.

Feuerbach, Ludwig

full: Ludwig Andreas Feuerbach
b. July 28, 1804
Landshut, Bavaria (now Germany)
d. September 13, 1872
Rechenberg, Bavaria
fields: Philosophy, Religion and Theology

Ludwig Feuerbach shifted philosophical concerns from idealism toward scientific positivist and materialist ideas of nineteenth century naturalism. He had a profound influence on Karl Marx and Friedrich Engels, through whom Feuerbach radicalized thought in the modern world. Feuerbach gave philosophical direction to Martin Heidegger with the concept of *Dasein* (human being), theological direction to Martin Buber with ideas of I-Thou relationships, and psychological/psychoanalytical directions to Sigmund Freud and R. D. Laing with notions of human anxiety and existential self-alienation. Major works include *Thoughts on Death and Immortality* (1930), *The Essence of Christianity* (1841), *Principles of the Philosophy of the Future* (1843), *The Essence of Faith According to Luther* (1844), and *Lectures on the Essence of Religion* (1851).

Feynman, Richard P.

full: Richard Phillips Feynman
b. May 11, 1918
New York, New York
d. Feb. 15, 1988
Los Angeles, California
fields: Mathematics, Physics

Richard P. Feynman is best known for his work on the development of the atomic bomb, quantum electrodynamics, and the development of Feynman diagrams. In 1965, he shared the Nobel Prize in Physics.

Fichte, Johann Gottlieb

b. May 19, 1762
Rammenau, Saxony
d. January 27, 1814
Berlin, Prussia
fields: Philosophy

Fichte's philosophy of ethical idealism served as the pivotal theory in the development of Idealism within the German philosophical community. His emendations of Immanuel Kant's conception of the human mind paved the way for the development of Absolute Idealism by Georg Wilhelm Friedrich Hegel.

Ficker, Roberta Sue. *See* Farrell, Suzanne

Field, Marshall

b. August 18, 1834
near Conway, Massachusetts
d. January 16, 1906
New York, New York
fields: Business and Industry, Philanthropy

Founder of Marshall Field and Company, which became the largest wholesale and retail dry-goods store in the world, Field introduced many retailing concepts that set the standard for modern merchandising.

Field, Stephen J.

full: Stephen Johnson Field
b. November 4, 1816
Haddam, Connecticut
d. April 9, 1899
Washington, D.C.
fields: Law (constitutional)

In the last quarter of the nineteenth century, Justice Field's brilliant and ingenious legal opinions protected the United States' entrepreneurs from what they perceived to be the destructive power of popular government.

Fielding, Henry

b. April 22, 1707
Sharpham Park, Somersetshire, England
d. October 8, 1754
Lisbon, Portugal
fields: Literature

Although he was an effective journalist and a successful dramatist, and although with his brother John he was responsible for establishing the London police force which developed into Scotland Yard, Fielding's major contribution was in the development of the novel as a carefully plotted form with fully developed characters, dramatic scenes, and serious intent.

Fields, Barbara Jeanne

b. ?
Charleston, S.C.
fields: Historiography

African American historian; Barbara Jeanne Fields's expertise in nineteenth century American history resulted in her appearance on P.B.S documentaries *The Civil War* (1990) and *The Massachusetts 54th* (1991).

Fields, Cleo

b. November 22, 1962
Louisiana
fields: Government and Politics

African American politician; in 1986, Cleo Fields became Louisiana's youngest senator; elected to the U.S. House of Representatives in 1992; defeated in a run-off election for governor in 1995.

Fields, Dorothy

b. July 15, 1904
Allenhurst, New Jersey
d. March 28, 1974
New York, New York
fields: Music

One of the most gifted lyricists during the golden age of American popular music, Dorothy Fields collaborated with Jerome Kern, Jimmy McHugh, and Cy Coleman on enduring standard songs. She also wrote the libretto for such musicals as *Annie Get Your Gun* (1946) and *Sweet Charity* (1964).

Fields, Mary

b. c. 1832
Tennessee
d. 1914
Montana
fields: Historical Figure

African American pioneer; Mary Fields moved to Montana to work at a mission school for Native American girls; the second woman to drive a U.S. mail route.

Fiesole, Giovanni da. *See* Angelico, Fra

Figueroa, Angelina

b. 1914
Puerto Rico
fields: Music

Pianist. Pianist and music teacher Angelina Figueroa was a member of the renowned Puerto Rican Figueroa family of musicians.

Figueroa, Carmelina

b. 1911
Puerto Rico
d. 1994
fields: Music

Pianist. Pianist and music teacher Carmelina Figueroa was a member of the renowned Puerto Rican Figueroa family of musicians.

Figueroa, Guillermo

b. 1916
Puerto Rico
fields: Music

Violist and conductor. A member of the renowned Puerto Rican Figueroa family of musicians, Guillermo Figueroa earned acclaim as a violist and conductor. In the 1940's, he joined brothers Pepito, Kachiro, Narciso, and Rafael in the Quinteto Figueroa; in 1968, the group was honored with the title of Official Quintet of the Commonwealth of Puerto Rico.

Figueroa, Kachiro

né: Jaime Figueroa
b. 1910
Puerto Rico
fields: Music

Violinist and conductor. A member of the renowned Puerto Rican Figueroa family of musicians, Jaime "Kachiro" Figueroa joined his brothers Pepito, Narciso, Rafael, and Guillermo to form the Quinteto Figueroa in the 1940's; in 1968, the group was honored with the title of Official Quintet of the Commonwealth of Puerto Rico.

Figueroa, Lenore

b. 1908
Puerto Rico
d. 1945
fields: Music

Pianist. A member of the renowned Puerto Rican Figueroa family of musicians, Leonor Figueroa earned acclaim as a pianist and music teacher.

Figueroa, Narciso

b. October 31, 1906
Aguadilla, Puerto Rico
fields: Music

Composer and pianist. The son of Jesús Figueroa Iriarte and Carmen Sanabia Ellinger, Narciso Figueroa distinguished himself as a concert pianist in Europe and as a teacher in the Conservatorio de Música de Puerto Rico. He composed *danzas*, the ballet piano suite *Estampas del San Juan que yo amo*, and a piano concerto premiered by the Orquesta Sinfónica de Puerto Rico.

Figueroa, Pepito

né: José Figuiroa
b. 1905
Puerto Rico
fields: Music

Violinist. The scion of a well-known Puerto Rican musical family, child prodigy Pepito Figueroa began his music lessons with his parents. In 1923, he entered the Real Conservatorio de Madrid in 1923; in 1925, he won the prestigious Sarasate award. He retired in the 1980's as first violinist of the Puerto Rico Symphony Orchestra.

Figueroa, Rafael

b. 1917
Puerto Rico
fields: Music

Cellist. A member of the renowned Puerto Rican Figueroa family of musicians, Rafael Figueroa earned acclaim as a cellist. In the 1940's, he joined brothers Pepito, Kachiro, Narciso, and Guillermo in the Quinteto Figueroa; in 1968, the group was honored with the title of Official Quintet of the Commonwealth of Puerto Rico.

Figueroa Iriarte, Jesús

b. 1878
Puerto Rico
d. 1971
fields: Music

Composer and arranger. The patriarch of a prominent Puerto Rican musical family, Jesús Figueroa Iriarte wrote musical arrangements for dance bands and concert halls. In 1903, he married Carmen Sanabia Ellinger (1882-1954); their children included violinist José "Pepito" (b. 1905), composer and pianist Narciso (b. 1906), pianist and teacher Leonor (1908-1945), violinist and orchestra conductor Jaime "Kachiro" (b. 1910), pianist and instructor Carmelina (1911-1994), piano teacher Angelina (b. 1914), violist and conductor Guillermo (b. 1916), and cellist Rafael (b. 1917). A third generation has carried on the family tradition.

Filipepi, Alessandro di Mariano. *See* Botticelli, Sandro

Fillmore, Millard

b. January 7, 1800
Summerhill, New York
d. March 8, 1874
Buffalo, New York

fields: Government and Politics

President of the United States, 1850-1853. In 1850, President Fillmore pushed for legislation designed to resolve a deadlock between Northern and Southern states over the admission of California to the Union and extension of slavery into new territories. Fillmore's support of the compromise legislation cost him the Whig presidential nomination in 1852; it also may have postponed the Civil War for a decade.

Finley, Clarence C.

b. Aug. 24, 1922
Chicago, Ill.
fields: Business and Industry

African American business executive; Clarence C. Finley's position as executive vice president of Burlington House Products Group made him among the most important black executives in the U.S.

Firdusi

b. Between 932 and 941
Tus, Khorasan Province, Iran
d. Between 1020 and 1025
Tabaran, near Tus, Iran
fields: Literature

Firdusi's *Shahnamah* is the supreme example of the epic in the Persian language. Through centuries of foreign invasion and conquest, it has served as a major means of preserving Iran's cultural identity.

Firestone, Shulamith

b. 1945
Ottawa, Canada
fields: Government and Politics, Social Reform, Women's Rights

Shulamith Firestone became known as a feminist with her book *The Dialectic of Sex: The Case for Feminist Revolution* (1970), one of the founding textes of modern feminism. She is cofounder and editor of the journals *Redstockings* and *Notes for the Second Year.*

Fischer, Bobby

full: Robert James Fischer
b. March 9, 1943
Chicago, Illinois
fields: Sports (chess)

Bobby Fischer was the most renowned chess player in the United States during the 1960's, and one of the strongest players in the history of the game. During the 1960's, Fischer finished first or second in every tournament in which he played except one. In 1972, he played Boris Spassky for the World Championship, winning a twenty-one-game match by four points. Thereafter, Fischer dropped out of competitive chess, forfeiting the championship to Anatoly Karpov in 1975.

Fischer, Edmond H.

b. Apr. 6, 1920
Shanghai, China
fields: Biology, Physiology

Edmond H. Fischer's work in biochemistry led to the discovery of phosphorylation-dephosphorylation regulatory mechanisms in many biological processes. In 1992, he shared the Nobel Prize in Physiology or Medicine with Edwin G. Krebs.

Fischer, Ernst Otto

b. Nov. 10, 1918
Solln, near Munich, Germany
fields: Chemistry

Ernst Otto Fischer shared the Nobel Prize in Chemistry in 1973 with Sir Geoffrey Wilkinson for leading research into the chemistry of organometallic compounds.

Fischer von Erlach, Johann Bernhard

b. July 20, 1656 (baptized)
Graz, Austria
d. April 5, 1723
Vienna, Austria
fields: Architecture

The founder of the Austrian Baroque, Fischer von Erlach was the pivotal figure in the artistic life of late seventeenth century and early eighteenth century Austria, creating an architectural style which embodied the imperial pride of the revived Habsburg Empire.

Fishburne, Laurence John, III

b. July 30, 1961
Augusta, Ga.
fields: Film, Theater and Entertainment (actor)

African American actor; Laurence John Fishburne III's film credits include *Apocalypse Now* (1979), *Rumble Fish* (1983), *The Cotton Club* (1984), *Gardens of Stone* (1987), *The Color Purple* (1983), *School Daze* (1988), and *Class Action* (1990), *Boyz 'N the Hood* (1991), *What's Love Got to Do with It* (1993, for which he earned an Academy Award nomination), *Searching for Bobby Fischer* (1993), *Higher Learning* (1995), *Bad Company* (1995), *Othello* (1995), *Event Horizon* (1997), and *The Matrix* (1999); won a Tony Award in 1992 for the play *Two Trains Running.*

Fisher, Andrew

b. August 29, 1862
Crosshouse, Ayrshire, Scotland
d. October 22, 1928
London, England
fields: Government and Politics

Andrew Fisher was prime minister of Australia three times (1908-1909, 1910-1913, 1914-1915). Reforms instituted by his government between 1910 and 1913 included maternity allowances, aged and invalid pensions, and the founding of the Commonwealth Bank.

Fisher, Brock. *See* Peters, Brock

Fisher, Elijah John

b. Aug. 2, 1858
La Grange, Ga.
d. 1913
fields: Religion and Theology

African American clergyman; Elijah John Fisher gained national attention for publicly criticizing Booker T. Washington for failing to speak out against lynching.

Fisher, Gail

b. Aug. 18, 1935
Orange, N.J.
fields: Television

African American actress; Gail Fisher played Peggy Fair on the *Mannix* television series (1968-1974); the first black actress to win an Emmy (1969).

Fisher, Ronald Aylmer

b. Feb. 17, 1890
London, England
d. July 29, 1962
Adelaide, Australia
fields: Mathematics (statistics)

In 1921-1923 Ronald Aylmer Fisher developed analysis of variance for studying the causes of variation affecting crop yields in agricultural experiments. In 1934, he was elected a Fellow of the Royal Society of London.

Fisher, Rudolph

b. May 9, 1897
Washington, D.C.
d. Dec. 26, 1934
New York, N.Y.
fields: Literature

African American author and physician; Rudolph Fisher was a Harlem Renaissance writer best-known for "High Yaller."

Fisher, Saint John

b. 1469
Beverley, Yorkshire, England
d. June 22, 1535
London, England
fields: Education, Religion and Theology

Fisher strongly contested the views of Martin Luther through his writings, supporting the Catholic faith, the Catholic Church, and the idea of the real presence in the Eucharist. He was canonized as a saint by the Roman Catholic Church in May, 1535.

Fiske, Helen Maria. *See* Jackson, Helen Hunt

Fitch, John

b. January 21, 1743
Windsor (modern South Windsor), Connecticut
d. July 2, 1798
Bardstown, Kentucky
fields: Engineering, Invention and Technology

Fitch was one of the earliest inventors to produce serviceable steamboats.

Fitch, Val L.

full: Val Logsdon Fitch
b. Mar. 10, 1923
near Merriman, Nebraska
fields: Physics

In 1964 Val L. Fitch demonstrated that subatomic particles violate the principle of charge conjugation, parity, and time (CPT) symmetry. He and colleague James W. Cronin won the Nobel Prize in Physics in 1980.

Fitzgerald, Ella

b. April 25, 1917
Newport News, Virginia
d. June 15, 1996
Beverly Hills, California
fields: Music

Described as having perhaps the most extraordinary jazz voice in the world, Fitzgerald was a musical innovator as well as a pioneer in American jazz and popular music.

Fitzgerald, F. Scott

full: Francis Scott Key Fitzgerald
b. September 24, 1896
St. Paul, Minnesota
d. December 21, 1940
Hollywood, California
fields: Literature

With a poetic style and an insight into the lure of and the fallacies within the American Dream, Fitzgerald created some of the most distinctively American fiction.

Fitzgerald, Zelda

né: Zelda Sayre
b. July 24, 1900
Montgomery, Ala.
d. March 11, 1948
Asheville, N.C.
fields: Literature

Zelda Fitzgerald was a writer whose life was enmeshed with that of writer F. Scott Fitzgerald, whom she married in 1920; in 1924 they became expatriates in the south of France; she suffered a series of nervous breakdowns beginning in 1930; wrote *Save Me the Waltz* (1932), painted, drew; spent the rest of her life in and out of a mental hospital, where she died in a fire in 1948.

Fitzpatrick, Joseph

b. Feb. 22, 1913
Bayonne, N.J.
d. March 15, 1995
Bronx, N.Y.
fields: Sociology

Joseph Fitzpatrick's research has focused on Puerto Ricans on the U.S. mainland. His publications include *Puerto Rican Americans: The Meaning of Migration to the Mainland* (1971). He has served as vice president of the Puerto Rican Family Institute and on the board of directors of the Puerto Rican Legal Defense and Education Fund.

Fizeau, Hippolyte

full: Armand-Hippolyte-Louis Fizeau
b. Sept. 23, 1819
Paris, France
d. Sept. 18, 1896
Venteuil, France
fields: Astronomy, Physics

Hippolyte Fizeau, in 1845 with Léon Foucault, took probably the first clear photographs of the surface of the sun; in 1848, he described the effect of motion on light emitted from stars; in 1849, he measured the speed of light; in 1851, he measured the shift in the speed of light through a moving substance such as water.

Flack, Roberta

b. Feb. 10, 1939
Asheville, N.C.
fields: Music (pop singer)

African American singer; Roberta Flack's hit songs include "The First Time Ever I Saw Your Face," "Killing Me Softly with His Song" (1973) and "Feel Like Makin' Love" (1974).

Flack, Rory

b. Apr. 28, 1969
Belleville, Ill.
fields: Sports (ice skater)

African American ice skater; Rory Flack won the first annual Golden Blade Award at the United States Open Professional Championships (1991).

Flake, Floyd Harold

b. Jan. 30, 1945
Los Angeles, Calif.
fields: Government and Politics

African American U.S. representative from New York; Floyd Harold Flake won his House seat in 1986; reelected to two additional full terms as a U.S. representative from New York in 1989 and 1991. He left Congress in 1997 and became a full-time minister.

Flat Mouth

aka: Guelle Plat
aka: Wide Mouth
aka: Eshkebugecoshe
b. 1774
Leech Lake, Minn.
d. 1860
Leech Lake, Minn.
fields: Government and Politics, Native American Affairs

Flat Mouth was an Ojibwa (Chippewa) principal chief during the struggles for control of the upper Mississippi Valley region. He was apparently influenced by Tecumseh's brother, the Shawnee Prophet, (Tenskwatawa) but refused aid to Tecumseh during his pan-Indian rebellion in 1809-1811. Flat Mouth's Chippewas were among the few Indian tribes successfully to resist relocation, remaining on tribal lands.

Flaubert, Gustave

b. December 12, 1821
Rouen, France
d. May 8, 1880
Croisset, France
fields: Literature

The most influential European novelist of the nineteenth century, Flaubert, who is most famous for his masterpiece *Madame Bovary*, is regarded as the leader of the realist school of French literature.

Fleming, Alexander

aka: Sir Alexander Fleming
b. August 6, 1881
Lochfield, Ayrshire, Scotland
d. March 11, 1955
London, England
fields: Medicine, Biology

An exceptional facility for observation combined with excellent training and a careful adherence to the basic principles of the scientific method to enable Fleming to discover lysozyme and penicillin. These discoveries placed him in the vanguard of modern scientists struggling to control infectious diseases among the general population. Awarded 1945 Nobel Prize for Physiology or Medicine.

Fleming, Peggy

full: Peggy Gale Fleming
b. July 27, 1948
San Jose, California
fields: Sports (ice skating)

America's "Ballerina on Ice," Peggy Fleming won the 1968 Olympic gold medal for ladies figure skating at Grenoble, France, and became television's first skating star. During the first live, in-color Olympic telecast, her gold-medal-winning program included the first spread-eagle, double-axel, spread-eagle combination performed by a woman in international competition. After defending her world title, Fleming retired from amateur skating in 1968. As a professional skater, she appeared in numerous television specials and ice shows and worked as a commentator for national and international skating competitions. She maintained her career as a professional skater into the 1990's.

Fleming, Williamina Paton Stevens

né: Williamina Paton Stevens
b. May 15, 1857
Dundee, Scotland
d. May 21, 1911
Boston, Massachusetts
fields: Astronomy

Skilled in the analysis of stellar spectral photographs, Fleming discovered several new variable stars and novae and was the leader of a group of women doing similar work.

Flemister, Fred

b. 1916
Atlanta, Ga.
fields: Art (painter)

African American painter; Fred Flemister won first prize in oils at the American Negro Exposition in Chicago (1940).

Fletcher, Dusty

full: Clinton Fletcher
b. ?
fields: Theater and Entertainment

African American comedian; Dusty Fletcher became best known for the hit comedy song, "Open the Door, Richard"; appeared in a number of Theatre Owners Booking Association shows.

Fletcher, John

b. December, 1579
Rye, Sussex, England
d. August, 1625
London, England
fields: Theater and Entertainment, Literature

With their light, witty comedy and melodramatic tragicomedy, Francis Beaumont and John Fletcher introduced a new style and aristocratic outlook into Renaissance English drama.

Fletcher, Robert E.

b. Dec. 12, 1938
Detroit, Mich.
fields: Photography, Film

African American photographer, filmmaker, and educator; Robert E. Fletcher was staff photographer for the Student Nonviolent Coordinating Committee; contributed to a number of magazines in addition to codirecting films and working as a cameraman on television productions.

Flexner, Abraham

b. November 13, 1866
Louisville, Kentucky
d. September 21, 1959
Falls Church, Virginia
fields: Education

Successfully blending scholarship and administrative ability with reformist zeal, Flexner was responsible for major transformations of American elementary, secondary, medical, and postgraduate education.

Flipper, Henry Ossian

b. Mar. 21, 1856
Thomasville, Ga.
d. May 3, 1940
Atlanta, Ga.
fields: Military Affairs

First African American to graduate from West Point Military Academy (1877).

FloJo. *See* Griffith-Joyner, Florence

Flood, Curtis Charles

b. Jan. 18, 1938
Houston, Tex.
fields: Sports (baseball player)

African American baseball player; Curtis Charles Flood played outfield for the St. Louis Cardinals beginning in 1958; filed suit (unsuccessfully) in 1969 to eliminate the reserve clause that limited the salaries of top players.

Flora, William

b. 1755
Portsmouth, Va.
d. 1820
Portsmouth, Va.
fields: Warfare and Conquest

African American Revolutionary War hero; William Flora was the last Patriot soldier to retreat during the Battle of Great Bridge in 1775.

Flores, Juan

b. Sept. 27, 1943
Alexandria, Va.
fields: Scholarship

Juan Flores is a researcher of Puerto Rican and Latin American topics. He won the Casa de las Americas prize for *The Insular Vision: Pedreira's Interpretation of Puerto Rican Culture* (1978) and the American Book Award for his introduction to and edition of Jesús Colón's *A Puerto Rican in New York* (1984).

Flores, Patricio Fernández

b. July 20, 1929
Ganado, Tex.
fields: Church Government, Civil Rights

Catholic archbishop and Mexican American civil rights advocate. Ordained to the priesthood in 1956, Patricio Fernández Flores was consecrated the first Mexican American bishop in the United States in 1970. Nine years later he became archbishop of San Antonio, Texas. He used his influence to support a number of causes including improved conditions for migrant workers.

Flores, Tom

full: Thomas Raymond Flores
b. March 21, 1937
Fresno, Calif.
fields: Sports (football)

Mexican American football player and coach. Tom Flores began his professional career with the Calgary Stampeders of the Canadian Football League in 1958. In 1959, he played briefly for the Washington Redskins of the National Football League and in 1960, he was starting quarterback for the Oakland Raiders of the American Football League (AFL). He led the AFL in passing percentage in 1960, threw six touchdown passes in a single game in 1963, and earned All-Star status in 1966. After retiring in 1969, he returned to the Raiders in 1972 as an assistant to head coach John Madden, whom he replaced in 1979. He led the Raiders to an 11-5 record and a Super Bowl victory over the Philadelphia Eagles in 1981. After the franchise moved to Los Angeles, he was named Latino of the Year for the City of Los Angeles (1981) and National Football League Coach of the Year (1982). He directed the Raiders to a 38-9 Super Bowl win over the Washington Redskins in 1984, but by 1992 had moved on as head coach of the Seattle Seahawks. He left the Seahawks in 1994.

Flores Magón, Ricardo

b. Sept. 16, 1873
San Antonio Eloxochitlán, Oaxaca, Mexico
d. Nov. 21, 1922
Fort Leavenworth, Kans.
fields: Government and Politics, Military Affairs, Warfare and Conquest

Revolutionary. Ricardo Flores Magón fled to the United States after his 1903 release from a Mexican jail. In St. Louis, he published the revolutionary journal *Regeneración* and formed the Mexican Liberal Party, which called for the overthrow of dictator Porfirio Díaz. Flores Magón also planned raids to Mexico from the United States; on one, he captured and briefly held the city of Tijuana. In 1918, he was sentenced to twenty years in prison for violating U.S. neutrality acts. After the U.S. government approved his return to Mexico in 1922, he died mysteriously in his cell.

Flores Salinas, Juan

b. 1835
d. Feb. 14, 1857
Los Angeles, Calif.
fields: Military Affairs, Warfare and Conquest

Guerrilla. Juan Flores Salinas escaped from San Quentin Prison, where he was serving a term for horse stealing, in 1856; he then assembled more than fifty Mexican Americans into a bandit gang operating out of San Juan Capistrano. He and fifty-two of his men were captured in February, 1857, and he was immediately hanged.

Florey, Baron

né: Howard Walter Florey
b. September 24, 1898
Adelaide, Australia
d. February 21, 1968
Oxford, England
fields: Biology, Medicine

A wide-ranging intellect, extensive training in the sciences upon which medicine has become progressively more dependent, and the capacity for organizing resources and directing efforts effectively made it possible for Florey to unlock the fundamental scientific secrets of Alexander Fleming's discoveries of lysozyme and penicillin and make antibiotic therapy a cornerstone of the practice of modern medicine. His isolation of the active antimicrobial ingredient in *Penicillium notatum* made it readily available to physicians and stands as one of the more significant scientific achievements of this century. Awarded 1945 Nobel Prize for Physiology or Medicine.

Florit, Eugenio

b. Oct. 15, 1903
Madrid, Spain
fields: Literature, Theater and Entertainment

Latino poet, playwright, and critic. Black Cuban poet Eugenio Florit graduated from law school in 1927. He published the books *Treinta y dos poemas brevas* (1927; thirty-two short poems) and *Revista de avance* (1928-1930) privately. After finished school, he helped to organize the second International Conference on Emigration and Immigration and worked in the Cuban Department of State, then published *Reino (Kingdom)* in 1938. He taught at Columbia University, Barnard College, and Middlebury College in Vermont. He was the central figure in the Hispanic literary community in New York in the 1940's and 1950's.

Flory, Paul J.

full: Paul John Flory
b. June 19, 1910
Sterling, Illinois
d. Sept. 9, 1985
Big Sur, California
fields: Chemistry

Paul J. Flory, by studying plastics and rubbers, was a leading contributor to the theory of the physical conformation of the long molecular chains that make up polymers. He won the Nobel Prize in Chemistry for fundamental achievements in macromolecular science in 1974, the same year he won the National Medal of Science, and the Priestley Medal of the American Chemical Society.

Floyd, James A.

b. ?
fields: Government and Politics

African American mayor of Princeton, N.J.; James A. Floyd was the first African American mayor of Princeton.

Flügge-Lotz, Irmgard

né: Irmgard Lotz
b. July 16, 1903
Hameln, Germany
d. May 22, 1974
Stanford, California
fields: Mathematics (applied math)

In 1953 Irmgard Flügge-Lotz published *Discontinuous Automatic Control*, which presented an automatic control theory that was essential for the advancement of aerospace technology. In 1968 she published *Discontinuous and Optimal Control*. She was elected a Fellow of the American Institute of Aeronautics and Astronautics in 1970. That year she also received the Society of Women Engineers' Achievement Award.

Flynn, Elizabeth Gurley

b. August 7, 1890
Concord, New Hampshire
d. September 5, 1964
Moscow, Soviet Union
fields: Labor Movement, Social Reform, Women's Rights

A great orator and champion of the socialist and communist movements in the United States, Flynn dedicated her life to fighting for the rights of the working class and women.

Fodor, Jerry A.

b. April 22, 1935
New York, New York
fields: Philosophy, Psychiatry and Psychology, Language and Linguistics

Attempting to vindicate people's commonsense psychological views, Jerry A. Fodor provided a staunch defense of a representational theory of mind (RTM) and the language of thought that such a theory presupposes. Major works include *RePresentations: Philosophical Essays on the Foundations of Cognitive Science* (1981), *The Modularity of Mind* (1983), *Psychosemantics: The Problem of Meaning in the Philosophy of Mind* (1987), *The Elm and the Expert: Mentalese and Its Semantics* (1994), and *Concepts: Where Cognitive Science Went Wrong* (1998).

Foe, Daniel. *See* Defoe, Daniel

Fogarty, Margaret. *See* Rudkin, Margaret

Foley, Lelia Kasenia Smith

b. 1941
Taft, Okla.
fields: Government and Politics

African American mayor; Lelia Kasenia Smith Foley was the first black woman to serve as mayor in the continental United States; she was elected to the Taft city council and selected to be mayor by her fellow council members; remained on the city council until 1986.

Folger, Lydia. *See* Fowler, Lydia Folger

Fonda, Jane

full: Jane Seymour Fonda
b. December 21, 1937
New York, New York
fields: Film, Social Reform, Business and Industry

Fonda is a high-profile film star who became a political activist and a leading figure in the anti-Vietnam War protest movement of the 1960's, a spokesperson for women's rights, and a hugely successful businesswoman.

Fong, Hiram L.

full: Hiram Leong Fong
b. Oct. 15, 1906
Honolulu, Hawaii
fields: Government and Politics

Asian American politician; Hiram L. Fong was born to Chinese immigrants in Honolulu, Hawaii; earned law degree from Harvard in 1935; rose to rank of major, U.S. Army Air Corps, 1942-1944; Hawaiian territorial representative, 1938-1954; first Asian American elected to the U.S. senate (Republican), 1959-1977; helped establish the University of Hawaii's East West Center; instrumental in framing immigration reforms, 1965; won Horatio Alger Award (1970).

Fong, March Kong. *See* Eu, March Fong

Fong, Walter

b. ?
fields: Business and Industry

Chinese American Walter Fong, owner of the Farmer's Market chain of supermarkets, helped build the Confucius Church of Sacramento. The church, founded for religious, social, cultural, and educational activities in

February, 1961, housed a school and the Chinese Consolidated Benevolent Association.

Fong-Torres, Ben

b. January 7, 1945
Alameda, Calif.
fields: Literature

The first Asian American writer to appear regularly in a national magazine, San Francsico Bay Area-native Ben Fong-Torres started out as editor of *East/West*, a bilingual weekly Chinatown newspaper. From 1968 to 1980 he served as senior editor of *Rolling Stone*, the national music magazine. From 1983 to 1992 he wrote a regular column for the *San Francisco Chronicle*. His memoirs were published as *The Rice Room: Growing Up Chinese-American—From Number Two Son to Rock 'n' Roll* (1994). Other works include *The Motown Album: The Sound of Young America* (1990) and *Hickory Wind: The Life and Times of Gram Parsons* (1991).

Fonteyn, Margot

né: Margaret Evelyn Hookham
aka: Dame Margot Fonteyn
b. May 18, 1919
Reigate, Surrey, England
d. February 21, 1991
Panama City, Panama
fields: Dance

As the first ballerina trained by a British school and company to achieve international status, Fonteyn almost single-handedly developed the Royal Ballet's female repertoire during her thirty years with the company and became the model for the modern ballerina.

Foote, Irene. *See* Castle, Irene

Forbes, James A., Jr.

b. 1935
Burgaw, N.C.
fields: Religion and Theology

African American minister; James A. Forbes, Jr. became the first black senior pastor at Riverside Church in New York City in 1989.

Forbes, Steve

full: Malcolm Stevenson Forbes, Jr.
b. July 18, 1947
Morristown, N.J.
fields: Government and Politics, Publishing, Business and Industry

Publisher and presidential candidate. Steve Forbes, the son of publishing magnate Malcolm Forbes, emerged as a surprise contender for the 1996 Republican presidential nomination. With an estimated personal net worth of $489 million, Forbes compensated for a lack of political experience with a massive advertising campaign that touted his flat-tax proposal to overhaul the nation's tax system. After successes in several early primaries, Forbes was trounced by eventual nominee Bob Dole.

Ford, Aleck. *See* Williamson, Sonny Boy, II

Ford, Barney

b. ?
d. 1902
fields: Business and Industry

African American businessman; Barney Ford ran a station of the Underground Railroad; campaigned to delay statehood for Colorado until African American suffrage had been granted there; built the Inter-Ocean Hotel in Denver after earning considerable wealth in Nicaragua.

Ford, Betty

né: Elizabeth Ann Bloomer
b. April 8, 1918
Chicago, Ill.
fields: Government and Politics

First Lady of the United States, 1974-1977. Betty Ford, whose stances on controversial topics often ran counter to those of husband Gerald Ford's Republican political party, was celebrated for her support of the Equal Rights Amendment (ERA), her outspokeness on social issues such as abortion, and for the publicizing of her own battle with breast cancer. After leaving the White House, she revealed her own struggle with alcoholism and founded the Betty Ford Center for the treatment of alcoholics and chemical dependents. She authored *The Times of My Life*(1978) and *Betty: A Glad Awakening* (1987).

Ford, Eileen

né: Eileen Otte
b. March 25, 1922
New York, New York
fields: Business and Industry

Vice president and cofounder of the prestigious Ford Model Agency, located in New York and Paris, Eileen Ford wrote several books on modeling and is known for her ability to discover and develop talent. Ford has also been instrumental in the standardization of business practices in modeling.

Ford, Gerald R.

né: Gerald Rudolph Ford, Jr.
b. July 14, 1913
Omaha, Nebraska
fields: Government and Politics

Thirty-eighth president of the United States, 1974-1977. Becoming president after Richard M. Nixon's resignation in disgrace, Ford restored integrity to the office of President of the United States and a sense of decency and unity to the nation.

Ford, Harold

b. May 20, 1945
Memphis, Tenn.
fields: Government and Politics

African American politician; in 1974 Harold Ford was the first African American to be elected to Congress from Tennessee; indicted on charges of bribery but reelected in 1990; 1992 embroiled in House check-bouncing scandal. Retiring from Congress in 1996, his son was elected to the seat that he vacated. His son became the first African American to succeed his father in Congress.

Ford, Henry

b. July 30, 1863
Springwells township, Michigan
d. April 7, 1947
Dearborn, Michigan
fields: Business and Industry

Combining ruthlessness with concern for the average worker, Ford revolutionized the early automobile industry by creating a low-priced car, the Model T, through the now famous assembly-line method. He also created the Ford Foundation, a nationwide philanthropy.

Forde, Francis Michael

aka: Frank Forde
b. July 18, 1890
Mitchell, Queensland (now Australia)
d. January 28, 1983
Brisbane, Queensland, Australia
fields: Government and Politics

Australian politician. From 1941 to 1945, during World War II, Francis Michael Forde was deputy prime minister to John Curtin and minister for the army. Played significant role in Curtin's wartime government, which introduced a number of social reforms. Briefly served as acting prime minister, then (upon Curtin's death) prime minister in 1945.

Foreman, Dave

b. Oct. 18, 1946
Albuquerque, N.M.
fields: Conservation and Environmentalism

Environmental activist. In 1980, David Foreman founded Earth First!, one of the most radical of environmental organizations. His books include the 1991 biography *Confessions of an Eco-Warrior*.

Foreman, George

b. Jan. 22, 1948
Marshall, Tex.
fields: Sports (boxer), Theater and Entertainment

African American boxer, minister, and actor; George Foreman became the oldest man ever to win and defend the heavyweight title; won gold medal in 1968 Olympic Games and turned professional in 1969; defeated Joe Frazier for the heavyweight championship of the world in 1973; defended title three times until defeated by Muhammad Ali in 1974; retired from professional boxing in 1977; in 1991 defended and lost title to Evander Holyfield; regained title in 1994 in bout with Michael Moorer; in 1995 won a controversial split decision over German boxer Axel Schultz; became a media personality in the 1990's and starred in short-lived situation comedy *George*; also served as boxing analyst for HBO sports television.

Foreman, Stephen

b. Oct. 22, 1807
Rome, Ga.
d. Dec. 8, 1881
Park Hill, Indian Territory
fields: Religion and Theology, Native American Affairs, Education

A Cherokee and a fully ordained Presbyterian minister, Stephen Foreman served as a spiritual and political leader to the Cherokee. In 1841, he led one of the last Cherokee detachments on the Trail of Tears, continuing his ministry in Oklahoma. Also in 1841, organized a public school system for Cherokee children, and in 1844 was elected to the Cherokee Supreme Court.

Forester, C. S.

né: Cecil Lewis Troughton Smith
b. August 27, 1899
Cairo, Egypt
d. April 2, 1966
Fullerton, California
fields: Literature

One of the most popular novelists of the mid-twentieth century, Forester wrote more than fifty books but is best known for his multivolume saga about British naval hero Horatio Hornblower—an immortal figure in modern literature.

Forman, James

b. October 4, 1929
Chicago, Ill.
fields: Civil Rights

African American James Forman was the executive secretary of the Student Non-Violent Coordinating Committee (SNCC) from 1961 to 1966. He was instrumental in organizing many of the 1960's campaigns of the Civil Rights movement and made an additional impact on the protest movement as the author of numerous books, including *The Making of Black Revolutionaries: A Personal Account* (1972).

Forrest, Edwin

b. March 9, 1806
Philadelphia, Pennsylvania
d. December 12, 1872
Philadelphia, Pennsylvania
fields: Theater and Entertainment

Despite early obstacles, Forrest became the first great American actor, the first to gain international acclaim.

Forster, E. M.

full: Edward Morgan Forster
b. January 1, 1879
London, England
d. June 7, 1970
Coventry, England
fields: Literature

A liberal and a humanist, Forster was more centrist than extreme, and as such, he was an almost perfect embodiment of an early twentieth century realist who accepted the primacy of facts but insisted on balancing them with intuition or spirit.

Forster, William Edward

b. July 11, 1818
Bradpole, Dorsetshire
d. April 5, 1886
London, England
fields: Education, Government and Politics

Forster was most famous for reform in education. He was an "advanced" Liberal, responsible for the Education Act of 1870, the Ballot Act of 1872, and advancement of other Radical causes. He was less revered for his policy of coercion in Ireland.

Fortas, Abe

b. June 19, 1910
Memphis, Tennessee
d. April 5, 1982
Washington, D.C.
fields: Law

U.S. Supreme Court justice, 1965-1969; appointed by President Lyndon B. Johnson. As a lawyer, successfully argued in *Gideon v. Wainwright*, 372 U.S. 335 (1963), that the right to counsel be applied to the states. Longtime adviser and confidant of President Johnson. Nominated for chief justice in 1968, but withdrew. Resigned after disclosure of alleged financial impropriety involving a former client. Significant opinions: *In re Gault*, 381 U.S. 1 (1967); *Tinker v. Des Moines Independent Community School District*, 393 U.S. 503 (1969).

Forte, Johnnie, Jr.

b. ?
New Boston, Tex.
fields: Military Affairs

African American military officer; a decorated U.S. Army career officer, Johnnie Forte, Jr. achieved the rank of brigadier general on May 1, 1979; duty assignments included commander of the Fourth Battalion of the Sixty-first Air Defense Artillery Division and commander of the 108th Air Defense Artillery Group.

Forten, Charlotte

full: Charlotte Lottie Forten
b. August 17, 1837
Philadelphia, Pennsylvania
d. July 22, 1914
Washington, D.C.
fields: Education, Literature, Civil Rights

Charlotte Forten, an African American educator, author, and abolitionist, spent her life furthering the cause of fellow African Americans.

Forten, James

b. Sept. 2, 1766
Philadelphia, Pa.
d. Mar. 4, 1842
Philadelphia, Pa.
fields: Civil Rights

African American abolitionist, entrepreneur; James Forten was born of free parents in Philadelphia, served aboard a privateer during the American Revolution; captured and held prisoner for seven months; while in England became acquainted with abolitionist philosophy; by 1798 owned a prosperous maritime company; became active in the abolitionist movement in the 1830's, including membership in the American Anti-Slavery Society, which he helped to organize; one of the primary contributors of funds for William Lloyd Garrison's newspaper *The Liberator*; founded the American Moral Reform Society.

Fortescue, John

aka: Sir John Fortescue
b. c. 1385
Norris, Somerset, England
d. c. 1479
Ebrington, Gloucestershire, England
fields: Political Science, Law

The first English thinker to recognize that Parliament's power over legislation and taxation had made England a limited rather than an absolute monarchy, Fortescue played a major role in shaping English constitutional concepts.

Fortune, Amos

b. 1710
d. 1801
Jaffrey, N.H.
fields: Business and Industry

African American businessman; Amos Fortune purchased his freedom in 1770 and founded a tannery and book bindery in New

Hampshire; became a wealthy philanthropist who supported the African American causes.

Fortune, T. Thomas

full: Timothy Thomas Fortune
b. Oct. 3, 1856
Marianna, Fla.
d. June 2, 1928
Philadelphia, Pa.
fields: Civil Rights, Journalism

African American journalist and civil rights activist; T. Thomas Fortune worked in various positions for the *New York Sun* from 1878; founded the *New York Age* (1883), the leading black journal of opinion in the United States; crusaded against school segregation; helped organize the National Afro-American League (1890) which opposed all forms of discrimination and demanded full civil rights, better schools, and fair wages; played major role in founding of the National Afro-American Council (1898), a forerunner of the Niagara Movement; joined Booker T. Washington in organizing the National Negro Business League in 1900; wrote *Black and White: Land, Labor, and Politics in the South* (1885) and *The Negro in Politics* (1885); coined the term "Afro-American" as a substitute for "Negro" in the New York press.

Fossey, Dian

b. January 16, 1932
San Francisco, California
d. December 26, 1985
Karisoke Research Institute, Rwanda
fields: Anthropology

Through her firsthand study of Central Africa's mountain gorillas, Fossey established their classification as a subspecies and courageously struggled to forestall their extinction.

Foster, Bob

full: Robert Wayne Foster
b. Dec. 15, 1938
Albuquerque, N.Mex.
fields: Sports (boxer)

African American boxer; Bob Foster, elected to *Ring*'s Boxing Hall of Fame in 1983, used his seventy-nine-inch reach to hold the light heavyweight championship from 1968 to 1974; he fought in the first professional match between black and white fighters in South Africa in 1973.

Foster, George

b. Dec. 1, 1948
Tuscaloosa, Ala.
fields: Sports (baseball player)

African American baseball player; outfielder George Foster played in the major leagues from 1969 to 1986; led National League in home runs twice (1977, 1978); led in runs batted in three times (1976, 1977, 1978); had two World Series wins (1975, 1976); won 1977 Most Valuable Player Award.

Foster, Gloria

b. Nov. 15, 1936
Chicago, Ill.
fields: Theater and Entertainment (actress)

African American actress; Gloria Foster's acting credits include film appearances, and Broadway and Off-Broadway performances in *The Cherry Orchard*, *A Midsummer Night's Dream*, *The Trojan Women*, *Long Day's Journey into Night*, and *Black Visions*; awards include the Obie and the Black Filmmakers Hall of Fame.

Foster, Greg

b. Aug. 4, 1958
Maywood, Ill.
fields: Sports (hurdler)

African American hurdler. Three-time winner of the World Track and Field Championships (1984, 1987, and 1991), Greg Foster also won a silver medal at the 1984 Olympics. A fall prevented his participation in the 1988 Olympic Games.

Foster, Henry, Jr.

b. September 8, 1933
Pine Bluff, Ark.
fields: Medicine, Government and Politics, Public Health

Physician Henry Foster founded a teenage pregnancy prevention program for local at-risk inner city youths in Nashville, Tennessee. That work earned for him President George Bush's recognition as one of the "thousand points of light." Nevertheless, his 1995 nomination by President Bill Clinton to replace Joycelyn Elders as U.S. surgeon general was defeated by the Republican majority in Congress because he had performed abortions during his years of practice as an obstetrician and gynecologist. He subsequently received an appointment as presidential adviser on teenage pregnancy.

Foster, Jodie

né: Alicia Christian Foster
b. November 19, 1962
Los Angeles, California
fields: Film

One of Hollywood's major actresses, Foster won two Academy Awards for Best Actress and a nomination for Best Supporting Actress before she reached the age of thirty.

Foster, Pops

full: George Murphy Foster
b. May 19, 1892
McCall, La.
d. Oct. 30, 1969
San Francisco, Calif.
fields: Music (jazz musician)

African American jazz musician; Pops Foster is considered the first famous double bass player in jazz; recorded with King Oliver Creole Jazz Band in 1930's for Gennett label; recordings reissued in 1980's.

Foster, Rube

full: Andrew Foster
b. Sept. 17, 1879
Galveston, Tex.
d. 1930
Ill.
fields: Sports (baseball player)

African American baseball player; one of baseball's greatest pitchers, Rube Foster founded the Negro National League in 1920; inducted into the Baseball Hall of Fame in 1981.

Foster, Stephen Collins

b. July 4, 1826
Lawrenceville, Pennsylvania
d. January 13, 1864
New York, New York
fields: Music

Working within the most popular, sometimes vulgar, style of the day, Foster wrote works of unaffected simplicity and melodic beauty that became among the finest representatives of the American folk song.

Foucault, Léon

full: Jean-Bernard-Léon Foucault
b. Sept. 18, 1819
Paris, France
d. Feb. 11, 1868
Paris, France
fields: Astronomy, Invention and Technology, Physics

Léon Foucault made the first daguerreotype of the sun's surface in 1845; in 1848, showed how the brain combines two separate colors presented to individual eyes into one image; in 1850, measured the earth's rotation with a swinging pendulum; in 1852, invented the gyroscope; in 1857, developed a method for silvering glass to improve telescope mirrors; in 1862, made the first precise measurement of the velocity of light.

Foucault, Michel

b. October 15, 1926
Poitiers, France
d. June 25, 1984
Paris, France
fields: Philosophy, Psychiatry and Psychology, Language and Linguistics

Michel Foucault was a controversial and seminal theorist and philosopher who taught at the Collège de France (starting in 1970) and examined structures of societal and political power in Western thought and how they related to discourse and language as well as to human sexuality. He is best known for such works as *Madness and Civilization* (1961), *The Order of Things* (1966), *The Discourse on Language* (1971), *Discipline and Punish* (1975), and his three-volume *The History of Sexuality* (1976-1984).

Four Bears. *See* Mato Tope

Fourier, Charles

né: François-Marie-Charles Fourrier
b. April 7, 1772
Besançon, France
d. October 10, 1837
Paris, France
fields: Social Reform, Social Science

Fourier was one of the founding fathers of nineteenth century Utopian socialism. Although the few experiments in building a model community based upon his theories proved short-lived, Fourier's writings have continued to attract interest.

Fourier, Joseph

full: Jean-Baptiste-Joseph Fourier
b. March 21, 1768
Auxerre, France
d. May 16, 1830
Paris, France
fields: Mathematics, Physics

In deriving and solving equations representing the flow of heat in bodies, Fourier developed analytical methods which proved to be useful in the fields of pure mathematics, applied mathematics, and theoretical physics.

Fowler, Lydia Folger

né: Lydia Folger
b. May 5, 1822
Nantucket, Massachusetts
d. January 26, 1879
London, England
fields: Medicine, Women's Rights

The first woman to become a professor at an American medical school, Fowler became a well-known lecturer on physiology, temperance, and women's rights during the years in which the medical field gradually opened to the entry of women.

Fox, Charles James

b. January 24, 1749
London, England
d. September 13, 1806
Chiswick, Devon, England
fields: Government and Politics

Spending decades of his political career in opposition, Fox associated aristocratic Whiggery and the Whig Party he came to lead with the defense of liberty against the exercise of arbitrary power by the king and the king's ministers.

Fox, George

b. July, 1624
Drayton-in-the-Clay (now Fenny Drayton), Leicestershire, England
d. January 13, 1691
London, England
fields: Religion and Theology

Fox founded the Religious Society of Friends (Quakers) and then spent the remainder of his life defending and sustaining the new sect during one of England's most tumultuous periods.

Fox, Terry

b. July 28, 1958
Winnipeg, Manitoba, Canada
d. June 28, 1981
New Westminster, British Columbia, Canada
fields: Sports (runner), Public Health

"Marathon of Hope" runner. In 1977, Terry Fox had his right leg amputated above the knee as a result of cancer. In 1980, he began an attempt to run across Canada to raise money for for cancer research. He traversed more than thirty-two hundred miles before succumbing to a second bout of cancer. The Terry Fox Fund and an annual fund-raising run bear his name.

Foxworthy, Jeff

b. Sept. 6, 1958
Atlanta, Ga.
fields: Theater and Entertainment

American comedian, author, and entertainer whose material has been built on so-called "redneck" humor; Jeff Foxworthy recorded albums of his comedy material and published paperback books; maintained that his work is not political and that he does not promote divisions among people based on class and region; argued that rednecks are everywhere because the term simply means a "glorious absence of sophistication.

Foxx, Redd

né: John Elroy Sanford
b. Dec. 9, 1922
St. Louis, Mo.
d. Oct. 11, 1991
Los Angeles, Calif.
fields: Televison, Theater and Entertainment (comedian and actor)

African American comedian and actor; Redd Foxx moved from bawdy recordings and nightclub routines to television guest appearances in the 1960's; starred in *Sanford and Son* (1972-1977), one of the first shows with a primarily black cast; later shows included *The Redd Foxx Show* (1986) and *The Royal Family* (1991).

Fracastoro, Girolamo

b. c. 1478
Verona, Venetian Republic
d. August 6, 1553
Incaffi, Venetian Republic
fields: Medicine, Philosophy, Astronomy, Literature

Fracastoro clearly described contagious diseases, and his prophetic hypotheses on their causes foreshadowed by centuries the modern understanding of microbial infections.

Fragonard, Jean-Honoré

b. April 5, 1732
Grasse, France
d. August 22, 1806
Paris, France
fields: Art (painter)

One of the foremost painters of the eighteenth century and praised for the gaiety of his style and composition, Fragonard is renowned for his depictions of French high society in the years immediately preceding the Revolution.

Frahm, Herbert Ernst Karl. *See* Brandt, Willy

France, Anatole

né: Anatole François Thibault
b. April 16, 1844
Paris, France
d. October 12, 1924
Saint-Cyr-sur-Loire, France
fields: Literature

Anatole France's reclusive devotion to books turned to militancy in the wake of the Dreyfus affair, and he used his satirical skills thereafter to campaign against intolerance and social injustice. He was awarded the Nobel Prize in Literature in 1921.

Francis I

b. September 12, 1494
Cognac, France
d. March 31, 1547
Rambouillet, France
fields: Monarchy, Patronage of the Arts

King of France, 1515-1547. Francis I, France's Renaissance monarch, increased the power of the Crown within France, led his country in a series of wars against the Habsburgs, created a glittering court, and helped to introduce the Italian Renaissance into France.

Francis, Herbert

b. May 26, 1940
Miami, Fla.
fields: Sports (bicyclist)

African American bicyclist. In 1960, Herbert Francis was the first African American male to compete in Olympic bicycling.

Francis, Josiah

aka: Francis the Prophet
aka: Hayo
aka: Hillis
aka: Hillishago
b. ?
d. c. 1818
St. Marks River, Fla.
fields: Government and Politics, Warfare and Conquest, Native American Affairs, Religion and Theology (shaman)

Native American leader. A Creek and Seminole, Josiah Francis traveled the Mississippi Valley with Tecumseh in 1811, seeking allies for Tecumseh's rebellion. Participated in the Creek War of 1813-1814 and the first Seminole War in 1817-1818. Francis' daughter was Milly Francis.

Francis, Lydia Maria. *See* Child, Lydia Maria

Francis, Milly Hayo

b. c. 1802
Fla.
d. c. 1848
near present-day Muskogee, Okla.
fields: Diplomacy

Milly Hayo Francis was a Creek and Seminole woman. In an incident reminiscent of the legend of Pocahontas and John Smith, she is known for having intervened to save the life of a white soldier, Georgia militiaman George McKinnon. Daughter of Josiah Francis.

Francis Ferdinand

b. December 18, 1863
Graz, Austria
d. June 28, 1914
Sarajevo, Bosnia
fields: Government and Politics

As heir to the Austro-Hungarian throne, Francis Ferdinand attempted to uphold the authority of the Hapsburg dynasty and deal with the nationalities issue that threatened the integrity of the empire. The assassination of the archduke and his wife in Sarajevo by a Serbian nationalist served as the immediate spark for the outbreak of World War I.

Francis Joseph I

né: Francis
b. August 18, 1830
Schönbrunn Palace, near Vienna, Austria
d. November 21, 1916
Schönbrunn Palace, near Vienna, Austria
fields: Government and Politics

Emperor of Austria, 1848-1916. The reign of Francis Joseph I was one of the longest in European history. Ascending the throne at the age of eighteen, he eventually became the living symbol of an imperial ideal of government doomed to vanish at his death, which occurred near the end of World War I.

Francis of Assisi, Saint

né: Francesco di Pietro di Bernardone
b. c. 1181
Assisi, Umbria, Italy
d. October 3, 1226
Assisi, Umbria, Italy
fields: Religion and Theology, Monasticism

Through the rejection of material values and the establishment of the Franciscan Orders, Francis of Assisi contributed to the reform movement of the medieval Church during the early thirteenth century.

Francis the Prophet. *See* Francis, Josiah

Franck, César

full: César Auguste Franck
b. December 10, 1822
Liège, Belgium
d. November 8, 1890
Paris, France
fields: Music

Franck's mastery of the principles of orchestration and the harmonic theories of the nineteenth century made him the acknowledged leader of French music of the era and one of the world's great composers.

Franco, Francisco

full: Francisco Paulino Hermenegildo Teódulo Franco y Bahamonde
b. December 4, 1892
El Ferrol, Spain
d. November 20, 1975
Madrid, Spain
fields: Government and Politics

Franco led the Nationalist forces to victory in the Spanish Civil War (1936-1939), established a stable, although authoritarian, government, kept Spain neutral in World War II, associated Spain with the West in the Cold War, and provided for a smooth transition of power upon his death.

Franco, Julio

full: Julio César Robles y Franco
b. Aug. 23, 1961
San Pedro de Macoris, Dominican Republic
fields: Sports (baseball player)

Latino baseball player. Julio Franco began playing infield with the Philadelphia Phillies in 1982 but was soon traded to the Cleveland Indians, where he played shortstop. In 1989, he was traded to the Texas Rangers, where he made the All-Star team three times and won the American League batting title (.341 average) in 1991. After the 1993 season he signed a one-year, $1 million contract with the Chicago White Sox. After playing in Japan in 1995, he returned to play for the Cleveland Indians (1996) and the Milwaukee Brewers (1997).

Frank, Anne

full: Annelies Marie Frank
b. June 12, 1929
Frankfurt am Main, Germany
d. March, 1945
Bergen-Belsen concentration camp, near Hannover, Germany
fields: Literature, Historical Figure

Frank's personal diary, which documents her family's life as persecuted Jews in Nazi-occupied Amsterdam, Holland, provides intimate details and a perceptive awareness of conditions leading to the Holocaust.

Frank, Barney

b. March 31, 1940
Bayonne, N.J.
fields: Government and Politics

Openly gay U.S. congressman. A member of the Democratic Party, Barney Frank was first elected to Congress in 1980, representing Massachusetts' Fourth Congressional District. In June, 1987, he disclosed to the *Boston Globe* that he was a homosexual and in 1992 he published, *Speaking Frankly* (1992). He was notably outspoken against the impeachment of President Bill Clinton.

Frankenthaler, Helen

b. December 12, 1928
New York, New York
fields: Art

An innovator in painting, printmaking, and sculpture, Frankenthaler is the inventor of stain painting and is recognized as the forerunner of color-field painting.

Frankfurter, Felix

b. November 15, 1882
Vienna, Austria
d. February 22, 1965
Washington, D.C.
fields: Law (constitutional)

Throughout Frankfurter's tenure on the United States Supreme Court, he was committed to the principle of judicial restraint; as a teacher at Harvard Law School for more than twenty-five years, he was one of America's greatest constitutional scholars.

Frankl, Viktor Emil

b. March 26, 1905
Vienna, Austria
d. September 2, 1997
Vienna, Austria
fields: Philosophy, Psychiatry and Psychology

Psychotherapist Viktor Emil Frankl turned his experiences as a prisoner in Nazi concentration camps into an enduring work of survival literature and originated logotherapy, a existential system of psychological treatment emphasizing that the search for meaning in life is the key to psychological health. In a 1991 survey by the Library of Congress and the Book-of-the-Month Club, people who regarded themselves as lifetime general-interest readers rated his *Man's Search for Meaning* (1959) as one of the ten most influential books they had ever read. Other major works include *The Unconscious God: Psychotherapy and Theology* (1975), *The Will to Meaning* (1969), *Psychotherapie für Jedermann* (1971), *Der Wille zum Sinn: Ausgewaehlte Vortraeger über Logotherapie* (1972), and *The Unheard Cry for Meaning: Psychotherapy and Humanism* (1979).

Franklin, Aretha

full: Aretha Louise Franklin
b. March 25, 1942
Memphis, Tenn.
fields: Music (singer)

African American singer; during the 1960's, she established herself as one of the greatest soul singers of any era; in 1987, Aretha Franklin became the first female singer to be inducted into the Rock and Roll Hall of Fame; won her fifteenth Grammy Award in 1988; performed at the inaugural celebration honoring President Bill Clinton in 1993; received a Lifetime Achievement Award from the National Academy of Recording Arts and Sciences in 1994; was selected as the youngest recipient of the Kennedy Center Honors in December of 1994. In 1998, she released one of her best albums in years *A Rose Is Still a Rose.*

Franklin, Benjamin

b. January 17, 1706
Boston, Massachusetts
d. April 17, 1790
Philadelphia, Pennsylvania
fields: Government and Politics

Franklin helped shape most of the important political, social, and intellectual developments in eighteenth century America. He became a veritable symbol of America by the end of his life, both at home and abroad, and he remains an influential folk hero.

Franklin, C. L.

full: Clarence LaVaughn Franklin
b. January 22, 1915
Sunflower County, Miss.
d. July 27, 1984
Detroit, Mich.
fields: Civil Rights

African American minister and civil rights leader, C. L. Franklin's inspirational preaching brought him to national attention through radio broadcasts and the more than twenty record albums of his sermons, some of which were produced and distributed by Motown Records. His daughter, soul singer Aretha Franklin, got her start in the church's choir. A close ally of Martin Luther King, Jr., Franklin worked with the Southern Christian Leadership Conference and Operation PUSH and remained a leader in Detroit's civil rights movement until he was shot in his home during a burglary attempt in 1979. He remained in a coma until his death five years later.

Franklin, John Hope

b. January 2, 1915
Rentiesville, Okla.
fields: Historiography, Scholarship

African American historian and educator. John Hope Franklin is a distinguished author whose specialty is the role of blacks in United States history. His major works include *From Slavery to Freedom: A History of American Negroes* (1947), *The Militant South, 1800-1861* (1956); *Reconstruction: After the Civil War* (1961), *The Emancipation Proclamation* (1963), *Racial Equality in America* (1976), *Race and History: Selected Essays, 1938-1988* (1989), and *George Washington Williams: A Biography* (1985).

Franklin, Rosalind E.

full: Rosalind Elsie Franklin
b. July 25, 1920
London, England
d. Apr. 16, 1958
London, England
fields: Biology, Chemistry, Genetics, Medicine

Rosalind E. Franklin measured deoxyribonucleic acid (DNA) fibers by X-ray diffraction, which was crucial to the model of DNA structure proposed by James D. Watson and Francis Crick—enormously important in the development of molecular biology.

Franks, Gary A.

b. Feb. 9, 1953
Waterbury, Conn.
fields: Government and Politics

African American U.S. representative; in 1990, Republican Gary A. Franks was elected the first African American to represent Connecticut in the U.S. Congress; became a member of the Congressional Black Caucus.

Fraser, Malcolm

full: John Malcolm Fraser
b. May 21, 1930
Melbourne, Victoria, Australia
fields: Government and Politics

Malcolm Fraser was Liberal prime minister of Australia from 1975 to 1983. At first the economy grew under Fraser's prime ministership, but it went into recession in 1982, prompting dissatisfaction. Labor Party leader Robert (Bob) Hawke became prime minister in 1983.

Fraunces, Samuel

b. c. 1722
British West Indies
d. Oct. 10, 1795
Philadelphia, Pa.
fields: Historical Figure

African American patriot. Samuel Fraunces's tavern was a favorite gathering place for patriots such as George Washington during the American Revolution.

Frazer, James George

aka: Sir James George Frazer
b. January 1, 1854
Glasgow, Scotland
d. May 7, 1941
Cambridge, England
fields: Anthropology

Although Frazer's theories are not held in high esteem by most modern anthropologists, he was a pioneer in applying the comparative approach to the study of human institutions. At the same time, his writings had a broader intellectual impact that did much to undermine late Victorian ethnocentrism. His masterwork, *The Golden Bough*, would play a major role in inspiring and shaping twentieth century modernist literature.

Frazier, E. Franklin

full: Edward Franklin Frazier
b. Sept. 24, 1894
Baltimore, Md.
d. May 17, 1962
Washington, D.C.
fields: Sociology, Education

African American sociologist and educator; E. Franklin Frazier was an authority on sociological aspects of African American life; best known for studies of the African American family,including: *The Negro Family in the United States* (1939), *Black Bourgeoisie* (1957).

Frazier, Joe

b. January 17, 1944
Beaufort, South Carolina
fields: Sports (boxer)

The first African American Olympic heavyweight gold medalist, Joe Frazier is best remembered for his three classic fights with Muhammad Ali. Won the heavyweight championship after knocking out Jimmy Ellis in 1970; won by decision in first fight with

Ali in November of the same year; lost title in technical knockout by George Foreman in 1973; defeated again by Ali in 1974, and in highly anticipated 1975 title bout, was defeated by Ali in a ktechnical knockout.

Frazier, Walt

b. Mar. 29, 1945
Atlanta, Ga.
fields: Sports (basketball player)

African American basketball player. Twice voted best defensive player in the National Basketball Association, Walt Frazier retired in 1980 and was inducted into the Basketball Hall of Fame in 1987.

Frederick I

b. July 11, 1657
Königsberg, East Prussia
d. February 25, 1713
Berlin, Prussia
fields: Monarchy, Government and Politics

King of Prussia, 1701-1713. Frederick I is noted principally for having crowned himself in 1701, thus transforming his noncontiguous territories into the Prussian monarchy.

Frederick I Barbarossa

b. c. 1123
Germany
d. June 10, 1190
Seleucia, Armenia
fields: Monarchy, Government and Politics

King of Germany, 1152-1190. For thirty-eight years Frederick ruled over the chaotic area of the Holy Roman Empire. While he failed to unite effectively his German territories with the city-states of northern Italy, he nevertheless imposed his personality and power on a strong German feudal state.

Frederick II

aka: Frederick II of Hohenstaufen
b. December 26, 1194
Iesi, near Ancona
d. December 13, 1250
Castle Fiorentino, Apulia
fields: Monarchy, Government and Politics

Frederick I, king of Sicily, 1197-1250; king of Germany, 1212-1250; Holy Roman Emperor, 1220-1250. An able administrator, Frederick reorganized the government of Sicily to create a centralized monarchy centuries before its time.

Frederick Henry

aka: Frederick Henry, count of Nassau
aka: Frederick Henry, prince of Orange
b. January 29, 1584
Delft, Holland
d. March 14, 1647
The Hague, Holland
fields: Military Affairs, Government and Politics

Frederick Henry succeeded through his military and diplomatic abilities in completing successfully the Eighty Years' War for the Independence of the Dutch United Provinces from Spain and in establishing the House of Orange as the hereditary sovereign of the new nation.

Frederick the Great

aka: Frederick II
b. January 24, 1712
Berlin, Prussia
d. August 17, 1786
Potsdam, Prussia
fields: Government and Politics, Monarchy

As king of Prussia (1740-1786), Frederick II raised the power and prestige of his state from a status of relative obscurity to that of one of Europe's most powerful nations. Through despotic but progressive policies at home and spectacular victories in war, he earned recognition as Frederick the Great.

Frederick William, the Great Elector

b. February 16, 1620
Berlin, Brandenburg-Prussia
d. May 9, 1688
Potsdam, outside Berlin, Brandenburg-Prussia
fields: Government and Politics, Military Affairs

Elector of Brandenburg, 1640-1688. Frederick William was the first gifted ruler of the Hohenzollern family. He was the founder of the Prussian army and bureaucracy, and laid the basis for the future strength of the Brandenburg-Prussian state.

Fredholm, Erik Ivar

b. Apr. 7, 1866
Stockholm, Sweden
d. Aug. 17, 1927
Stockholm, Sweden
fields: Mathematics (applied math and calculus)

In 1903 Erik Ivar Fredholm's work led to the birth of the modern integral equations theory. Fredholm demonstrated that important equations arising from integral calculus could be solved by methods developed for solving algebraic equations.

Freeman, Albert Cornelius, Jr.

b. March 21, 1934
San Antonio, Tex.
fields: Theater and Entertainment, Television

African American actor. Albert Freeman, son of jazz pianist Al Freeman, Sr., appeared in Broadway and Off-Broadway plays, films, and television productions. In 1975 he starred in the television series *Hot L Baltimore*, and by 1995 had also appeared on *Homicide: Life on the Streets* and in the film *Once Upon a Time When We Were Colored.*

Freeman, Alice Elvira. *See* Palmer, Alice Freeman

Freeman, Jewel Virginia Mulligan

b. Nov. 17, 1917
Kansas City, Mo.
fields: Government and Politics, Social Reform

African American social worker. Jewel Virginia Mulligan Freeman served as a clinical social worker and later a civil rights and management specialist with the Federal Aviation Administration.

Freeman, Jordan

b. ?
d. Dec. 6, 1781
New London, Conn.
fields: Warfare and Conquest

African American Revolutionary War soldier; Jordan Freeman killed the British commander in hand-to-hand combat at the Battle of Groton Heights; died in the battle.

Freeman, Morgan

b. June 1, 1937
Greenwood, Miss.
fields: Film, Theater and Entertainment (actor)

African American actor; Morgan Freeman's acting credits include stage, film, and television performances; Broadway debut was in an all-black *Hello, Dolly!* (1967); won Obie awards for *Coriolanus* (1980), *The Gospel at Colonus* (1984), and *Driving Miss Daisy* (1987); film credits include *Johnny Handsome* (1988), *Robin Hood* (1990), *Lean on Me* (1989), *Driving Miss Daisy* (1989), *Glory* (1989), *The Shawshank Redemption* (1994), *and* Amistad (1997);received two Oscar nominations.

Freeman, Roland

b. July 27, 1936
Baltimore, Md.
fields: Photography

African American photographer; Roland Freeman used images to document his participation in the 1963 March on Washington; was the first photographer to be granted a fellowship from the National Endowment for the Humanities, in 1973.

Frege, Gottlob

full: Friedrich Ludwig Gottlob Frege
b. November 8, 1848
Wismar, Mecklenburg-Schwerin (now in Germany)

d. July 26, 1925
Bad Kleinen, Germany
fields: Philosophy

Frege is the founder of modern symbolic logic and the creator of the first system of notations and quantifiers of modern logic. For most of his life, he taught at the University of Jena, where he investigated the foundations of mathematics and produced seminal works in logic. His major works include *Conceptual Notation* (1879) and *The Foundations of Arithmetic* (1884).

Freire, António Caetano de Abreu. *See* Egas Moniz, António

Freire, Paulo

b. September 19, 1921
Recife, Brazil
d. May 2, 1997
São Paolo, Brazil
fields: Education

In the early 1960's, Paulo Freire directed Brazil's national literacy program aimed at teaching not only reading and writing but also critical thinking and citizenship skills. Arrested and jailed for such "subversive" activities in 1964, and thereafter exiled to Chile, where he worked with the Agrarian Reform Training and Research Institute and served as a consultant to the United Nations Educational, Scientific, and Cultural Organization (UNESCO). During the 1970's in Geneva, Switzerland, worked for the World Council of Churches, from which he extended his pedagogical methods throughout the Third World. His best-known work, *Pedagogy of the Oppressed* (1970), was joined by many others, including *Learning to Question* (1989), *Literacy: Reading the Word and the World* (1987, with Donaldo Macedo), and *A Pedagogy for Liberation* (1987, with Ira Shor).

Frémont, Jessie Benton

né: Jessie Ann Benton
b. May 31, 1824
near Lexington, Virginia
d. December 27, 1902
Los Angeles, California
fields: Government and Politics

As the daughter of a powerful senator and wife of an explorer and general, Frémont participated in Jacksonian politics, the opening of the West, abolitionism, and the Civil War. In her behind-the-scenes work, she challenged the constraints of nineteenth century roles for women.

Frémont, John C.

full: John Charles Frémont
b. January 21, 1813
Savannah, Georgia
d. July 13, 1890
New York, New York
fields: Exploration and Colonization, Government and Politics

John C. Frémont's exploits as an explorer helped to propel the American people westward toward Oregon and California. When the continental nation he helped to create was faced with civil war, he fought to maintain the Union and end slavery.

Fresh Prince. *See* Smith, Will

Fresnel, Augustin-Jean

b. May 10, 1788
Broglie, Normandy, France
d. July 14, 1827
Ville-d'Avray, France
fields: Physics

After the time of Sir Isaac Newton, light was thought to consist of particles. Augustin-Jean Fresnel put the wave theory of light on a firm mathematical basis and helped it gain acceptance, stating that light waves are transverse (vibrating "sideways" to the direction of travel).

Fresquez, Carlos

b. 1956
Denver, Colo.
fields: Art (painter)

Latino painter. Carlos Fresquez's colorful, figurative paintings depict the urban life of working-class Mexican Americans. He sometimes mounts painted figures cut from wood onto incongruous backdrops, such as in *Zoot Suit en los Rockies* (1984), which depicts a Mexican American youth wearing a zoot suit against a mountainous backdrop.

Freud, Sigmund

b. May 6, 1856
Freiberg, Moravia, Austrian Empire (now Příbor, Czech Republic)
d. September 23, 1939
London, England
fields: Medicine, Psychiatry and Psychology

Freud was the founder of psychoanalysis and as such has had a tremendous impact upon contemporary thought and popular culture by baring the irrational and subconscious roots of much human action.

Freyssinet, Eugène

full: Marie-Eugène-Léon Freyssinet
b. July 13, 1879
Objat, France
d. June 8, 1962
Saint-Martin-Vésubie, France
fields: Architecture, Engineering

Through craftsmanship and enterprise, Freyssinet brought the aesthetic and practical utilization of modern forms of prestressed concrete (he invented the term in 1933) into international currency as a permanent form of construction. He won renown both in France and in Great Britain as a major architect-engineer who expanded the availability of novel architectural materials, thereby freshening opportunities for each of these professions.

Friedan, Betty

né: Betty Naomi Goldstein
b. February 4, 1921
Peoria, Illinois
fields: Women's Rights

Betty Friedan's first book energized thousands of women and helped to initiate the feminist movement in the late 1960's. Since that time, she has been a leader in the continuing struggle for women's rights.

Friedman, Herbert

b. June 21, 1916
New York, New York
fields: Astronomy, Physics

Herbert Friedman provided the first scientific proof that X rays come from the sun, in 1949; in 1956, discovered evidence for the existence of extrasolar X rays; in 1957, launched the first telescope into space; in 1958, discovered solar sources of X rays and ultraviolet radiation; in 1960, led a team that took the first X-ray photographs of the sun; pioneered rocket astronomy by including sensors on rockets fired high into the atmosphere or into space.

Friedman, Milton

b. July 31, 1912
Brooklyn, N.Y.
fields: Economics

Economist. Milton Friedman received the Nobel Prize for Economic Science in 1976. His books include *Capitalism and Freedom* (1962, reprinted 1981) and *Free to Choose* (1980), both coauthored by his wife Rose. With Anna Jacobson Schwartz, he wrote *A Monetary History of the United States, 1867-1960* (1963) which discusses the U.S. government's control of the money supply. He argues excess money creation is the cause of inflation.

Friedrich Wilhelm Viktor Albert, Prince. *See* William II

Frigerio, Ismael

b. 1955
Santiago, Chile
fields: Art (painter)

Latino painter. Before moving to New York City in 1981 to avoid political struggles in Chile, Ismael Frigerio studied art and philosophy at the University of Chile. His interest in German and American expressionist painters is apparent in his own work, expressionistic paintings that explore themes of identity and loss, and often depict confrontations between Aztec and European cultures. His dark, haunting perspective is apparent in such paintings as *The First Opportunity of Pain* (1985), *Division of Souls* (1987), and *The Lurking Place* (1985).

Frisch, Karl von

b. November 20, 1886
Vienna, Austria
d. June 12, 1982
Munich, West Germany
fields: Zoology

Frisch was awarded the 1973 Nobel Prize in Physiology or Medicine for his achievements in the relatively new science of ethology, which is the study of animal behavior. His studies of the social life of bees and the sensory capabilities of fish are particularly significant.

Frisch, Max

full: Max Rudolf Frisch
b. May 15, 1911
Zurich, Switzerland
d. April 4, 1991
near Zurich, Switzerland
fields: Literature

One of the most widely respected literary figures in the German-speaking world since the 1950's, Frisch has increasingly been recognized as a writer of international stature. Indicative of this recognition are the translations of his works into more than twenty languages, the voluminous secondary literature surrounding his oeuvre, his candidacy for the Nobel Prize, and the receipt of the Neustadt International Prize for Literature in 1986.

Frobenius, Leo

full: Leo Viktor Frobenius
b. June 29, 1873
Berlin, Germany
d. August 9, 1938
Biganzolo, Italy
fields: Anthropology

Frobenius was a pioneer in the study and exploration of African culture. He championed the idea that primitive, nonliterate cultures have preserved forms of thought, behavior, and cultural patterns older than those of the earliest advanced literate civilizations. He also developed a theory explaining the origin of culture, its stages of development, and how all the various cultures of the world are linked by these stages.

Frobisher, Martin

aka: Sir Martin Frobisher
b. c. 1535
Pontefract, Yorkshire, England
d. November 22, 1594
Plymouth, Devon, England
fields: Exploration and Colonization

Frobisher's search for the Northwest Passage failed, but he and his English contemporaries helped establish an English presence in the Atlantic.

Froebel, Friedrich

full: Friedrich Wilhelm August Froebel
b. April 21, 1782
Oberweissbach, Thuringia
d. June 21, 1852
Marienthal, Thuringia
fields: Education

Froebel founded the first kindergarten. He believed in the underlying unity in nature, for him God, and emphasized that schools should provide pleasant surroundings, encourage self-activity, and offer physical training for children.

Froissart, Jean

b. 1337?
Valenciennes, Hainaut, France
d. c. 1404
Chimay, Belgium
fields: Historiography

Froissart was a seminal figure in fourteenth century European historiography. In his *Chronicles*, he offered a vivid panorama of an age in transition that relied for its inspiration on waning codes of chivalry and a growing spirit of Humanism.

Fromm, Erich

b. March 23, 1900
Frankfurt am Main, Germany
d. March 18, 1980
Muralto, Switzerland
fields: Psychiatry and Psychology

Fromm was influential in synthesizing the field of psychology with social, political, and philosophical ideas. Through his many popular books written for the layperson, he explored the theme of the dehumanizing effects of modern society on mankind and the actions man must take to save himself from destruction. Fromm also insisted on a more humanistic approach to psychoanalysis.

Frost, Robert

b. March 26, 1874
San Francisco, California
d. January 29, 1963
Boston, Massachusetts
fields: Literature

Frost helped renew popular interest in American poetry by refusing to write in the academic modernist style that was popular at the time. Instead, he wrote about nature and rural life in a traditional yet complex style that appealed to a wide audience.

Fry, Hedy

b. 1941
Trinidad
fields: Government and Politics

Canadian politician. Before entering politics, Hedy Frey had practiced medicine for twenty-two years in British Columbia. In 1993, defeated sitting prime minister Kim Campbell for her Parliamentary seat. Named secretary of state for multiculturalism and the status of women in 1996.

Fry, Roger

full: Roger Eliot Fry
b. December 14, 1866
London, England
d. September 9, 1934
London, England
fields: Art (painting)

Fry was the preeminent art critic, scholar, and lecturer in England in the first decades of the twentieth century.

Fuentes, Carlos

b. Nov. 11, 1928
Mexico City, Mexico
fields: Literature, Diplomacy

Latino writer and diplomat. Carlos Fuentes, one of Latin America's foremost cultural figures, has written influential novels, short stories, plays, and essays. He has also served Mexico's ambassador to France and has advocated cultural diversity in Mexico. His books include *Los días enmascarados* (1954), *Terra Nostra* (1975; English translation, 1976), *El gringo viejo* (1985; *The Old Gringo*, 1985), *La muerte de Artemio Cruz* (1962; *The Death of Artemio Cruz*, 1964), *Cambio de piel* (1967; *A Change of Skin*, 1968), and *Cristóbal nonato* (1987; *Christopher Unborn*, 1989).

Fuentes, Juan R.

b. 1950
fields: Art

Latino artist. In the 1970's, Juan R. Fuentes taught postermaking at La Raza Graphic Center of San Francisco, and his art was popularized in *The Chicano Calendar*. He is credited with playing an important role in bringing a Cuban poster exhibition to the California Palace of the Legion of Honor, which boosted the Chicano poster movement of the late 1970's and helped popularize Hispanic art.

Fugard, Athol

full: Harold Athol Lannigan Fugard
b. June 11, 1932
Middelburg, South Africa

fields: Literature

Universally acknowledged to be South Africa's foremost dramatist, Fugard is also known as "the conscience of his country" for his plays, which focus on the victims of apartheid, and for his sociopolitical drama, which comments on South Africa's nonwhite population and on the poor and dispossessed who exist on the fringes of society.

Fugita, Stephen S.

b. Apr. 6, 1943
Jerome, Ark.
fields: Scholarship

Stephen S. Fugita received his doctoral degree in psychology at the University of California, Riverside. He was director of the Pacific/Asian Mental Health Research Center at the University of Illinois, Chicago, from 1987 to 1990 and became director of the Ethnic Studies Program and associate professor of psychology at the University of Santa Clara, California. He studied mental-health issues relating to the Asian American community, especially those relating to the World War II internment of Japanese Americans. He wrote *Japanese American Ethnicity: The Persistence of Community* (1991) and coauthored *The Japanese American Experience* (1991).

Fuhr, Grant Scott

b. Sept. 28, 1962
Edmonton, Alberta, Canada
fields: Sports (hockey player)

African American hockey player. As a goalie for Canada's Edmonton Oilers, Grant Scott Fuhr assisted the team in winning five Stanley Cup championships between 1984 and 1990.

Fujimori, Alberto

full: Alberto Kenyo Fujimori
b. July 28, 1938
Lima, Peru
fields: Government and Politics

The son of Japanese immigrants, Alberto Fujimori became the president of Peru in 1990. Winning the election after demonstrating an astute understanding of Peruvian desires and the use of propaganda, he went on to rule as a virtual dictator. In the 1995 presidential election, he found himself hard-pressed to obtain the necessary 50 percent electoral plurality. In April, 1997, his national and international stature was enhanced by the successful resolution of a hostage crisis involving Tupac Amaru rebels that had begun four months earlier.

Fujiwara Michinaga

b. 966
Kyoto, Japan
d. January 3, 1028
Kyoto, Japan
fields: Government and Politics

The greatest statesman of the Heian period, Michinaga maintained absolute control of the throne and court for thirty years and brought the Fujiwara family to the height of its power. He epitomizes Japanese leadership during the formative period of Japanese cultural development.

Fukuda, Mitsuyoshi

b. 1917
fields: Business and Industry

Mitsuyoshi Fukuda became vice president of industrial relations for the Honolulu company Castle & Cooke in 1966, becoming the first Japanese American vice president of a Big Five corporation. He joined the company in 1946 after serving in the all-Nisei 100th Infantry Battalion, where he rose to the rank of infantry major.

Fukui, Kenichi

b. Oct. 4, 1918
Nara, Japan
d. January 9, 1998
Kyoto, Japan
fields: Chemistry, Physics

In the early 1950's, Kenichi Fukui developed the frontier orbitals theory, which predicts the site and rate of a chemical reaction. In 1981, he shared the Nobel Prize in Chemistry with Roald Hoffmann.

Fukunaga, Myles

b. ?
d. Nov. 19, 1929, Honolulu, Territory of Hawaii)
Honolulu, Territory of Hawaii
fields: Historical Figure

Myles Fukunaga, the son of plantation workers who fell into poverty, was captured and charged with the 1928 kidnap/murder of Gill Jamieson, son of the vice president of the Hawaiian Trust Company, the family's primary creditor. The Japanese community tried to ensure that Fukunaga got a fair trial. Fukunaga was convicted and given the death sentence although a psychiatrist testified that the defendant was insane. The Japanese community protested what it believed was an unfair trial, but appeals failed, and Fukunaga was executed.

Fukuyama, Francis

b. Oct. 27, 1952
Chicago, Ill.
fields: Historiography

Francis Fukuyama wrote "The End of History?," a provocative article that drew international attention when it was published in *The National Interest* in 1989. Fukuyama received a B.A. from Cornell University in 1974 and a Ph.D. from Harvard in 1981. He joined the RAND Corporation in 1979. His thesis, also presented in his book *The End of History and the Last Man* (1992), is that the global challenger to liberal democracy and capitalism are gone after the collapse of communism in the Soviet Union, which means that history—the evolving competition between political, social, and economic ideologies—has ended.

Fukuzawa Yukichi

b. January 10, 1835
Buzen, Japan
d. February 3, 1901
Tokyo, Japan
fields: Education

Fukuzawa Yukichi, a prominent educator, expressed his belief in the merits of Westernization and modernization through his many writings. He established schools, including Keio University—a prestigious private institution—and a Tokyo-based newspaper. In his very popular books, he urged Westernization as a means of making Japan a stronger world power. Some Japanese were inspired to emigrate to the United States because of his writings.

Fulbert of Chartres, Saint

b. c. 960
Rome, Italy
d. April 10, 1028
Chartres, France
fields: Education, Church Reform

Fulbert was founder of the cathedral school at Chartres, whose curriculum was based on the seven liberal arts, thus producing the twelfth century renaissance and Christian humanism.

Fulbright, J. William

full: James William Fulbright
b. April 9, 1905
Sumner, Missouri
d. February 9, 1995
Washington, D.C.
fields: Government and Politics

Long-time influential U.S. senator, serving from 1945 to 1974. J. William Fulbright drafted legislation, passed in 1946 (the Fulbright Act), that funded the Fulbright Scholarships. Outspoken opponent of President Johnson's Vietnam War policies, as detailed in his book *Arrogance of Power* (1966).

Fuller, Charles

b. Mar. 5, 1939
Philadelphia, Pa.
fields: Theater and Entertainment, Literature

African American playwright and author; Charles Fuller's *A Soldier's Play* (1981) earned for him the 1982 Pulitzer Prize for Drama; was only the second African American to win this award.

Fuller, Loie

full: Marie Louise Fuller
b. January 15, 1862
Fullersburg, Illinois
d. January 1, 1928
Paris, France
fields: Dance

A pioneer in the art of modern dance, Loie Fuller created choreography that featured the manipulation of fabric and novel lighting effects. Her spectacular dances helped to create an enthusiastic audience for solo American dance performers.

Fuller, Margaret

full: Sarah Margaret Fuller
b. May 23, 1810
Cambridgeport, Massachusetts
d. July 19, 1850
at sea near Fire Island, New York
fields: Journalism, Social Reform

A pioneering feminist far ahead of her time, Margaret Fuller was a perceptive literary and social critic, and America's first woman foreign journalist.

Fuller, Melville Weston

b. February 11, 1833
Augusta, Maine
d. July 4, 1910
Sorrento, Maine
fields: Law

Chief justice of the United States, 1888-1910. Mellville Weston Fuller reached the Supreme Court primarily because he was in the right place at the right time, but once there, he proved himself an able administrator. Refined the role of chief justice as moderator.

Fuller, Meta Vaux Warrick

né: Meta Vaux Warrick
b. June 6, 1877
Philadelphia, Pennsylvania
d. March 13, 1968
Framingham, Massachusetts
fields: Art

As an African American sculptor, Meta Fuller drew upon her heritage for many of the themes in her work. She is recognized as a forerunner of the Harlem Renaissance of the 1920's.

Fuller, R. Buckminster

full: Richard Buckminster Fuller
b. July 12, 1895
Milton, Massachusetts
d. July 1, 1983
Los Angeles, California
fields: Engineering, Architecture, Invention and Technology

Fuller heightened Americans' awareness of how to employ natural resources to full advantage—a principle exemplified in his design of the geodesic dome.

Fuller, S. B.

b. 1905
Monroe, La.
d. Oct. 26, 1988
Blue Island, Ill.
fields: Business and Industry

African American businessman. Founder of the Fuller Products Company, a Chicago-based cosmetics manufacturer, S. B. Fuller also was publisher of the *Pittsburgh Courier*.

Fulton, Robert

full: Robert Fulton, Jr.
b. November 14, 1765
Little Britain Township, Pennsylvania
d. February 24, 1815
New York, New York
fields: Engineering, Invention and Technology

Fulton built the first profitable steamboat, established the traditions that distinguished American steamboats for the remainder of the century, and laid the groundwork for future submarine and torpedo warfare.

Fulton, Ruth. *See* Benedict, Ruth

Fusco, Coco

b. ?
fields: Art, Literature

Latina performance artist and writer. During the 1980's, Coco Fusco began writing articles on Latino art and culture for *Art in America*, *The Nation*, *The Drama Review*, and *The Village Voice*. She also curated the exhibition "Signs of Transition: Eighties Art from Cuba." Her performance art, which explores the U.S. Latino experience, includes *Norte/Sur* (1989, with Guillermo Gómez-Peña), *The New World (B)order* (1993, with Gómez-Peña and Robert Sifuentes), and *Two Undiscovered Aborigines Visit Irvine* (1992).

Futrell, Mary Hatwood

né: Mary Alice Hatwood
b. May 24, 1940
Alta Vista, Virginia
fields: Education

Futrell, a dedicated educator, worked her way up through the ranks to become the first African American to lead the National Education Association (NEA), a national teachers union representing 1.9 million members.

G

Gabler, Mel
b. January 5, 1915
Houston, Texas
fields: Education

Mel Gabler, with his wife Norma Gabler, began a grassroots movement to review school textbook adoptions in the 1960's. They eventually founded Educational Research Analysts, which operated out of their home in Longview, Texas, with the goal of "cleansing" the nation's public schools of ideas that threaten their own conservative religious and patriotic beliefs.

Gabler, Norma
b. 1923?
fields: Education

Norma Gabler, with her husband Mel Gabler, began a grassroots movement to review school textbook adoptions in the 1960's. They eventually founded Educational Research Analysts, which operated out of their home in Longview, Texas, with the goal of "cleansing" the nation's public schools of ideas that threaten their own conservative religious and patriotic beliefs.

Gabor, Dennis
né: Denes Gabor
b. June 5, 1900
Budapest, Hungary
d. Feb. 8, 1979
London, England
fields: Invention and Technology, Physics

Dennis Gabor, in 1947, invented the process of holography and contributed to its development; offered insights into the process of invention and the future of humankind as influenced by technology; in 1971, awarded the Nobel Prize in Physics for his work with holography.

Gabriel
né: Gabriel Prosser
b. c. 1776
near Richmond, Va.
d. Oct. 7, 1800
Richmond, Va.
fields: Historical Figure, Civil Rights

African American slave insurrectionist inspired by the Declaration of Independence; Gabriel—the slave of Thomas Prosser—was a literate coachman and blacksmith who planned and then helped to lead a large, unsuccessful slave revolt in Richmond, Virginia, on August 30, 1800; aimed to free his fellow slaves in Virginia by overpowering whites around Richmond, but bad weather and security leaks doomed the slaves' attack; Gabriel and other rebel leaders were hanged, and the insurrection did much to heighten southern whites' fears of blacks.

Gabrieli, Andrea
b. c. 1520
in or near Venice
d. 1586
Venice
fields: Music

Gabrieli was one of the most versatile musicians of his generation. His compositional output includes sacred vocal music, secular vocal music, instrumental ensemble music, and organ music.

Gabrieli, Giovanni
b. c. 1556
Venice
d. August 12, 1612
Venice
fields: Music

Gabrieli was one of the most gifted of the Venetian school of composers of the Renaissance and Baroque eras. Through his teaching of northern European students, particularly Heinrich Schütz, and the wide circulation of his published music north of the Alps, Gabrieli is considered an important influence on the development of German music during the Baroque period.

Gadamer, Hans-Georg
b. February 11, 1900
Marburg, Germany
fields: Philosophy, Literature

Hans-Georg Gadamer framed a position that became known as philosophical hermeneutics, which stresses meaning and truth in a text and examines the relationship between the text's tradition and its interpreter. His influence peaked after the publication of his most important work, *Truth and Method* (1960). He stressed meaning and truth in a text, as opposed to the epistemological knowledge of the natural sciences. In the 1970's and 1980's, Gadamer's work became a major force in literary criticism in the United States.

Gadsden, James
b. May 15, 1788
Charleston, South Carolina
d. December 26, 1858
Charleston, South Carolina
fields: Business and Industry, Diplomacy, Engineering, Military Affairs

Though Gadsden was an accomplished soldier, engineer, and railroad executive, his lasting fame came as the United States' minister to Mexico in the mid-1850's. While in Mexico City, he negotiated the Gadsden Purchase, the U.S. acquisition of a strip of territory that became the southern portions of Arizona and New Mexico.

Gafford, Alice
b. 1886
Tecumseh, Kans.
fields: Art (painter)

African American painter; Artist and organizer Alice Gafford promoted the careers of African American artists; her most notable painting is *Tea Party* (1986).

Gagarin, Yuri
full: Yuri Alekseyevich Gagarin
b. March 9, 1934
Klushino, near Gzhatsk, Smolensk Oblast, U.S.S.R.
d. March 27, 1968
near Moscow, U.S.S.R.
fields: Aviation and Space Exploration

Gagarin ushered the world into the space age as the first human in space with his orbital mission Vostok 1 on April 12, 1961.

Gage, Matilda Joslyn
né: Matilda Joslyn
b. March 25, 1826
Cicero, New York
d. March 18, 1898
Chicago, Illinois
fields: Women's Rights

Matilda Joslyn Gage's scholarly work provided much of the woman suffrage movement's literature. Her countless speeches and writings on behalf of the movement made her one of its most important leaders.

Gage, Thomas
b. 1721
Firle, Sussex, England
d. April 2, 1787
London, England
fields: Military Affairs

A skillful organizer and an efficient administrator, Gage helped to establish Great Britain's first empire on a solid footing through service as governor at Montreal and military commander in America.

Gahagan, Mary Helen. *See* Douglas, Helen Gahagan

Gaillard, Slim
b. Jan. 4, 1916
Detroit, Mich.
fields: Music (singer, guitarist, pianist)

African American singer, guitarist, and pianist. A popular performer in the 1930's and 1940's, Slim Gaillard specialized in scat singing.

Gaines, Big House. *See* Gaines, Clarence

Gaines, Clarence

aka: Big House Gaines
b. May 21, 1923
Paducah, Ky.
fields: Sports (basketball coach)

African American basketball coach. While coaching at Winston-Salem University from 1947 into the late 1980's, Clarence Gaines became only the second coach in National Collegiate Athletic Association (NCAA) history to win 800 games. He retired in 1993 with a record 828 victories.

Gaines, Ernest J.

b. Jan. 15, 1933
Oscar, La.
fields: Literature

African American author; Ernest J. Gaines's novels include *Catherine Carmier* (1964), *The Autobiography of Miss Jane Pittman* (1971), *A Gathering of Old Men* (1983), and *A Lesson Before Dying* (1993); some of these works were later released on film.

Gaines, Joseph B. *See* Gans, Joe B.

Gaines, LaDonna. *See* Summer, Donna

Gaines, Paul L., Sr.

b. Apr. 20, 1932
Newport, R.I.
fields: Government and Politics

African American mayor of Newport, R.I.; Paul L. Gaines, Sr. was elected the city's first African American mayor in 1981; served until 1983.

Gainsborough, Thomas

b. c. May 14, 1727
Sudbury, England
d. August 2, 1788
London, England
fields: Art

Through his landscapes and portraits, Gainsborough became one of the most creative English painters of his age and an inspiration to many significant artists of the next century.

Gaither, Jake

full: Alonzo Gaither
b. Apr. 11, 1903
d. Feb. 1994
fields: Sports (football coach)

African American football coach; Jake Gaither coached the Florida A&M Rattlers from 1945 to 1969; in 1970, he was the first African American elected to the Orange Bowl Committee;in 1975, he was inducted into the National Football Foundation Hall of Fame.

Gajdusek, D. Carleton

full: Daniel Carleton Gajdusek
b. Sept. 9, 1923
Yonkers, New York
fields: Medicine

D. Carleton Gajdusek aided the discovery that a group of diseases affecting the central nervous system may share a common infectious agent that resembles slow viruses. In 1976, he was awarded the Nobel Prize in Physiology or Medicine.

Gakyō-rōjin. *See* Hokusai

Galarraga, Andres

b. June 18, 1961
Caracas, Venezuela
fields: Sports (baseball player)

Latino baseball player. First baseman Andres Galarraga was signed by the Montreal Expos at the age of seventeen and reached the majors four years later, in 1985. In 1988, he hit twenty-nine home runs, batted .302, led the National League in hits and doubles, and made the National League All-Star Team. In 1989 and 1990, he won Gold Glove Awards. After several lackluster seasons, in 1993, while playing for the Colorado Rockies, he won the National League batting title with an average of .370, made the All-Star Team, and was named the league's Comeback Player of the Year by *The Sporting News*.

Galarza, Ernesto

b. August 15, 1905
Jalcocotán, Nayarit, Mexico
d. Jun. 22, 1984
San Jose, Calif.
fields: Labor Movement, Scholarship

Mexican American activist, labor organizer, and writer; Ernesto Galarza worked in the education and labor divisions of the Pan-American Union (later the Organization of American States; 1936-1947); organized agricultural workers in California through his positions as union secretary and vice president of the National Farm Labor Union and the National Agricultural Workers Union (1947-1963); later lectured and taught at the University of Notre Dame, San Jose State University, and the University of California at San Diego and at Santa Cruz; among his more important publications are *Merchants of Labor: The Mexican Bracero Story* (1964), *Mexican Americans in the Southwest* (1969), *Spiders in the House and Workers in the Field* (1970), his autobiography, *Barrio Boy* (1971), and *Farmworkers and Agribusiness* (1977); first Latino to receive a nomination for the Nobel Prize in Literature.

Galegina. *See* Boudinot, Elias

Galen

b. 129
Pergamum, the capital of Asia
d. c. 199
possibly Rome or Pergamum
fields: Medicine, Physiology, Philosophy

Although not a first-rate philosopher, Galen was influential in formulating a powerful logical empiricism which took scientific axioms as self-evident rather than hypothetical. His greatest contribution was in medicine, where he made the best presentation of anatomical knowledge in the ancient world; his theories and practices remained dominant during the Middle Ages.

Galileo

né: Galileo Galilei
b. February 15, 1564
Pisa, Republic of Florence
d. January 8, 1642
Arcetri, Republic of Florence
fields: Astronomy

Galileo helped establish the modern scientific method through his use of observation and experimentation. His work in mathematics, physics, and astronomy made him a leading figure of the early scientific revolution.

Galimore, Ron

b. 1950's
Tallahassee, Fla.
fields: Sports (gymnast)

African American gymnast; Ron Galimore became the first gymnast to win National Collegiate Athletic Association (NCAA) titles in four different years; he was a member of the 1980 U.S. Olympic team that boycotted the Games; son of Chicago Bears football player Willie Galimore.

Gall

aka: Pizi
aka: Man Who Goes in the Middle
aka: Red Walker
b. c. 1840
near Moreau River in present-day S.Dak.
d. Dec. 5, 1894
Oak Creek, S.Dak.
fields: Warfare and Conquest, Native American Affairs

Native American leader. Gall, a Hunkpapa Lakota (Sioux) leader, was a noted warrior and military tactician in the wars for the Bozeman Trail and the Black Hills in the 1860's and 1870's. He was the principal Indian military strategist at the Battle of the Little Bighorn in 1876.

Gallagher, Frank

pseud.: David Hogan
pseud.: David O'Neill

b. 1893
Cork, Ireland
d. July, 1962
Dublin, Ireland
fields: Literature, Journalism

Frank Gallagher was a chief publicist of the Irish liberation movement, which he joined in 1917. He explained Éamon de Valéra's Fianna Fáil party in *King and Constitution* (1926) and was de Valéra's personal secretary in the late 1920's. He also he wrote for American and other overseas publications and edited Fianna Fáil's journal *The Nation*. Other books by him on the movement include *The Four Glorious Years* (1953) and *Days of Fear* (1928). Gallagher also edited his hometown newspaper and was first editor of the *Irish Press* (1931-1935). He spent his last years preparing the *Dictionary of Irish Biography*. His other books include *Dark Mountain, and Other Stories* (1931) and *The Invisible Land: The History of the Partition of Ireland* (1957).

Gallant, Mavis

né: Mavis de Trafford Young
b. August 11, 1922
Montreal, Quebec, Canada
fields: Literature

One of Canada's best-known writers, Gallant has produced intelligent and subtle stories that have been widely influential.

Gallatin, Albert

full: Abraham Alfonse Albert Gallatin
b. January 29, 1761
Geneva, Switzerland
d. August 12, 1849
Astoria, New York
fields: Banking and Finance, Government and Politics, Science

Drawing upon the social philosophy of the French Enlightenment, Gallatin contributed, as secretary of the treasury to the administrations of Presidents Thomas Jefferson and James Madison, to the fiscal stability of the new nation and, as the first president of the American Ethnological Society, to the development of American anthropology.

Galler, Mrs. Fred. *See* Mourning Dove

Galois, Èvariste

b. October 25, 1811
Bourg-la-Reine, near Paris, France
d. May 31, 1832
Paris, France
fields: Mathematics

Galois produced, with the aid of group theory, a definitive answer to the problem of the solvability of algebraic equations, a problem that had preoccupied mathematicians since the eighteenth century. Consequently, he laid one of the foundations of modern algebra.

Galton, Francis

b. February 16, 1822
Birmingham, near Sparkbrook, England
d. January 17, 1911
Haslemere, Surrey, England
fields: Statistics, Genetics

Galton was responsible for developing modern statistical methods and laid the foundation for modern psychology and for the eugenics movement.

Galvani, Luigi

baptized: Alyosio Domenico Galvani
b. September 9, 1737
Bologna, Papal States
d. December 4, 1798
Bologna, Papal States
fields: Physiology, Physics

Galvani contributed to physiological studies on the electrical stimulation of nerves and muscles. His most important discovery was the production of electric current from the contact of two different metals attached to a frog, which led to the invention by Alessandro Volta of the electric battery.

Gálvez, Bernardo de

b. July 23, 1746
Macharaviaya, Spain
d. Nov. 30, 1786
Mexico City, Mexico
fields: Warfare and Conquest, Government and Politics

Latino soldier and administrator. After serving in the 1762 Spanish-Portuguese War, Bernardo de Gálvez moved to Mexico and fought Apaches in Chihuahua (1769-1771). He moved back to Europe in 1772, then became the governor of Louisiana in 1777. While in office, he helped supply American colonists and captured British ships entering Louisiana. In 1779, his forces defeated the British in Louisiana, Mississippi, Alabama, and Florida. Pensacola Bay was renamed Santa Maria de Gálvez Bay in his honor, and Galveston, Texas, was named for him. He was named the captain general of Louisiana, Florida, and Cuba (1784) and viceroy of New Spain (1785).

Gálvez, Daniel

b. 1953
fields: Art

Latino Artist. Daniel Gálvez's photorealist pastels depict the details and essence of barrios and barrio life. He is aligned with a school of Chicano artists who subvert rather than confront authority.

Gama, Vasco da

b. c. 1460
Sines, Portugal
d. December 24, 1524
Cochin, India
fields: Exploration and Colonization, Military Affairs

Da Gama was the first European during the Age of Discovery to reach India by sailing around Africa. His voyage culminated decades of Portuguese efforts at exploration and began Portugal's era as a spice empire.

Gambetta, Léon

b. April 2, 1838
Cahors, near Toulouse, France
d. December 31, 1882
near Paris, France
fields: Government and Politics

Gambetta, one of the most vocal critics of the Second Empire of Napoleon III in the 1860's, became the virtual dictator of France in 1870 during the resistance to the Prussian invasion. He was one of the most prominent and the most popular republican politicians of the period.

Gamboa, Diane

b. 1957
Los Angeles, Calif.
fields: Art

Latina artist. Diane Gamboa, who many consider too young to have been influenced by the protest years of the 1960's and early 1970's, is more concerned with personal issues, such as the experience of rape. In 1982 she also began designing clothing made of paper and has gained attention for her pachuca and chola fashions. She is the younger sister of artist Harry Gamboa, Jr.

Gamboa, Harry, Jr.

b. 1951
fields: Art, Photography

Latino artist and photographer. Harry Gamboa, Jr., attended Garfield High in East Los Angeles, where he organized student walkouts to protest the poor quality of education at the school. In college, he helped edit and design a magazine called *Regeneration* and became involved in asco ("nausea"), a group of humorous and nihilistic performance artists who often shocked and disgusted spectators. Gamboa was also a founding member of LACE Gallery. He received a National Endowment for the Arts fellowship and he wrote a play called *Jetter's Jinx*. He is artist Diane Gamboa's older brother.

Gamio, Manuel

b. Mar. 2, 1883
Distrito Federal, Mexico

d. July 16, 1960
Mexico City, Mexico
fields: Anthropology, Sociology

Latino anthropologist and sociologist. After earning his bachelor's degree at the National Preparatory School of San Ildefonso, Manuel Gamio attended Columbia University from 1909 to 1911. He served as Mexico's director of anthropology (1917-1924) and as director of the Instituto Indigenista Interamericano (1942-1960). He pioneered the study of Mexican migration to the United States. He advocated the seasonal migration of Mexican workers to the United States under government supervision because he believed that permanent emigration drained Mexico of its most talented people. In 1930 he published *Mexican Immigration to the United States: A Study of Human Migration and Adjustment.*

Gamow, George

b. Mar. 4, 1904
Odessa, Russia
d. Aug. 20, 1968
Boulder, Colorado
fields: Astronomy, Genetics, Physics

George Gamow proposed theories on quantum tunneling in radioactive decay and nucleosynthesis and the big bang; in 1954, he proposed a coding theory by which deoxyribonucleic acid (DNA) directs protein synthesis.

Ganado Mucho

aka: Tótsohnii Hastiin (Man of the Big Water)
b. c. 1809
near Klagetoh, Ariz.
d. 1893
near Klagetoh, Ariz.
fields: Government and Politics, Native American Affairs

Native American leader. Ganado Mucho was a Navajo leader during the tribe's difficult transition to reservation life. Worked with other Navajo headmen such as Manuelito to keep the peace with whites.

Gance, Abel

b. October 25, 1889
Paris, France
d. November 10, 1981
Paris, France
fields: Film

Gance was the first French filmmaker to recognize and realize the full spectacular effect of the cinema, by means of new techniques of editing and montage and by inventions that advanced the art and scope of the cinema.

Gandert, Miguel Adrian

b. Jan. 12, 1956
Española, N.Mex.
fields: Photography

Latino photographer. Miguel Adrian Gandert received both his undergraduate degree (1977) and his master's degree (1983) from the University of Mexico. He has worked primarily in New Mexico and has taught photography at the University of New Mexico at Albuquerque.

Gandhi, Indira

né: Indira Nehru
b. November 19, 1917
Allahabad, India
d. October 31, 1984
New Delhi, India
fields: Government and Politics

By serving as prime minister of India for almost two decades, Gandhi carried on a family tradition of political leadership, maintained her country's nonaligned status, and attempted to enact social reforms to eliminate poverty and hunger in her Third World democracy.

Gandhi, Mahatma

né: Mohandas Karamchand Gandhi
b. October 2, 1869
Porbandar, India
d. January 30, 1948
New Delhi, India
fields: Government and Politics, Civil Rights, Social Reform, Religion and Theology

Gandhi, as one of the main figures of the Indian independence movement, pioneered the use of nonviolent protest; the strategies and tactics he employed have been adapted by many groups struggling to achieve justice, including the Civil Rights movement in the United States. Gandhi also worked to reform traditional Indian society, speaking out for women's rights and for the group known as the untouchables.

Gandhi, Rajiv

full: Rajiv Ratna Gandhi
b. August 20, 1944
Bombay, India
d. May 21, 1991
Sriperumbudur, Tamil Nadu, India
fields: Government and Politics

Prime minister of India from 1984 to 1989, Rajiv Gandhi was the eldest son of Indira Gandhi, herself two-time prime minister (1966-1977, 1980-1984). Ministership often called "ill-starred"; plagued by scandals and crises. Alienated older politicians; kickback scandal in 1987; that same year monsoon failed, causing devastating drought, and Gandhi sent Indian troops into Sri Lanka to defeat the Tamils. Operation was a failure. Escalating violence within India. Lost the prime ministership in the elections of November 29, 1989. Aassassinated in 1991 by a Tamil woman with a bomb; she was a member of a Tamil Tiger team of terrorists.

Ganeodiyo. *See* Handsome Lake

Gans, Joe B.

né: Joseph B. Gaines
b. Nov. 25, 1874
Baltimore, Md.
d. Aug. 10, 1910
Baltimore, Md.
fields: Sports (boxer)

African American boxer. Joe B. Gans, considered the greatest lightweight boxer of all time, was elected to Ring's Boxing Hall of Fame in 1954.

Gantt, Harvey Bernard

b. Jan. 14, 1943
Charleston, S.C.
fields: Government and Politics (mayor)

African American mayor of Charlotte, N.C.; Harvey Bernard Gantt sued Clemson University and, in 1963, became its first African American student; was elected mayor of Charlotte in 1983 and served until 1987; in 1990 became the first African American in North Carolina's history to receive the Democratic nomination but was defeated by Republican Senator Jesse Helms.

Garakontie, Daniel

aka: Harakontie
b. c. 1600
Onondaga, N.Y.
d. c. 1676
Onondaga, N.Y.
fields: Diplomacy (diplomat, orator)

Native American leader. An Onondaga, Garakontie was a highly skilled negotiator between the Onondaga (and other Five Nations Iroquois) and the French in New France. Garakontie did not always enjoy popularity and support among his own people; many eventually denounced him for accepting Christianity and for allying closely with the French.

Garbo, Greta

né: Greta Lovisa Gustafsson
b. September 18, 1905
Stockholm, Sweden
d. April 15, 1990
New York, New York
fields: Film

A major star in early Hollywood, Garbo was able to exert economic, social, and symbolic influence in a way that no other film actress has. Garbo was one of the few performers to survive the transition from silent to sound films.

Garcés, Francisco Tomás

b. Apr. 12, 1738
Aragon, Spain
d. July 18, 1781
near the Gila River, Ariz.
fields: Religion and Theology, Exploration and Colonization

Latino missionary and explorer. In the mid-1760's, Francisco Tomás Garcés moved from Spain to the New World, where he explored the Colorado and Gila Rivers of Arizona and founded Franciscan missions among Pima, Yuma, and Opa tribes. He also discovered a route from Sonora to California. Garcés, along with several other priests and thirty Spanish soldiers, was killed by Yumas during the Yuma Massacre while exploring the mouth of the Gila River.

García, Arturo. *See* Córdova, Arturo de

García, Cristina

b. July 4, 1958
Havana, Cuba
fields: Literature

Latina writer. After moving with her family to the United States when she was two years old, Cristina García earned her bachelor's degree from Barnard College and her master's degree from the Johns Hopkins University School of Advanced International Studies, where she specialized in Latin American studies. García then worked as a reporter and researcher for *Time* magazine, later becoming a bureau chief and correspondent for the magazine. In 1992 she published the novel *Dreaming in Cuban* (1992).

García, Enrique Gay

b. 1928
Santiago de Cuba, Cuba
fields: Art (sculptor and muralist)

Latino sculptor and muralist. Enrique Gay García began exhibiting his artwork in the 1950's. In 1963, he moved from Cuba to Italy, where he studied at the University of Perugia and the Art Institute of Venice before moving to Miami, Florida. He also lived for a time in Mexico, where he studied muralist technique. García's murals, many of which were made in collaboration with David Alfaro Siqueiros, can be found in Puerto Rico and Florida.

García, Gus C.

b. 1916
Laredo, Tex.
d. June 3, 1964
San Antonio, Tex.
fields: Law

Latino lawyer. Gus C. García was an assistant district attorney for Bexar County, Texas, and an assistant city attorney for San Antonio before serving as chief counsel in the Supreme Court case *Hernández v. Texas* (1954), which found that the exclusion of Mexican Americans from trial juries was illegal.

García, Héctor Pérez

b. Jan. 17, 1914
Llera, Tamau-lipas, Mexico
d. July 26, 1996
Corpus Christi, Tex.
fields: Civil Rights

Mexican American civil rights activist; earned medical degree at University of Texas in 1940; founder of the American GI Forum (1948), Latino veterans concerned with civil rights and education; founder of Political Association of Spanish Speaking Organizations; alternative ambassador to the United Nations in 1964; commissioner, U.S. Commission on Civil Rights in 1968; active in many human and civil rights organizations, including League of United Latin American Citizens, Texas Advisory Committee to the U.S. Commission on Civil Rights, and Advisory Council to Veterans Administration; received Presidential Medal of Freedom (1984).

Garcia, Jerry

full: Jerome John Garcia
b. Aug. 1, 1942
San Francisco, Calif.
d. Aug. 9, 1995
Novato, Calif.
fields: Music (singer, songwriter, and guitarist)

Latino singer, songwriter, and guitarist. After his discharge from the U.S. Army in 1959, Jerry Garcia concentrated on his music and formed the Warlocks in 1965, which became the Grateful Dead in 1966. The San Francisco band, which signed a recording contract with Warner Brothers in 1967, helped popularize the psychedelic sound and became a phenomenally popular live act. Garcia also worked on solo music projects and dabbled in visual art.

García, Roberto

b. Jan. 9, 1933
Bronx, N.Y.
fields: Government and Politics

Latino public official. Roberto García was elected to the New York State Assembly in 1966 and became New York's first Puerto Rican state senator in 1967. In 1978, he was elected to Congress. He later served on the House Banking, Finance, and Urban Affairs committee, chaired the subcommittee on Census and Population (which oversaw the 1980 Census), and served on the House Post Office and Civil Service committee and as chairman of the Congressional Hispanic Caucus. In 1990, García was indicted for receiving illegal gratuities and left office. The charges were subsequently dropped.

García, Rupert

b. Sept. 29, 1941
French Camp, Calif.
fields: Art

Latino artist. Rupert García earned an A.A. (1962) in painting from Stockton College, a B.A. (1968) and an M.A. (1970) in painting and printmaking from San Francisco State University, and an M.A. (1981) in art history from the University of California, Berkeley. He became one of the most important graphic and poster artists of the 1960's and 1970's Chicano art movement. He also taught at several colleges, including San Francisco State University; San Francisco Art Institute; the University of California, Berkeley; San Jose State University; and the Mexican Museum in San Francisco.

García Diego y Moreno, Francisco

b. Sept. 17, 1785
Lagos de Moreno, Jalisco, Mexico
d. Apr. 30, 1845
Santa Barbara, Calif.
fields: Religion and Theology, Education

Catholic bishop and educator. Francisco García Diego y Moreno was born in Mexico, joined the Franciscan order in Guadalupe in 1801, and was ordained to the priesthood in 1808. In 1833, he arrived in Santa Clara, California, and began working to restore the deteriorating missions in the area. In 1840, he was ordained as the first bishop of the new diocese of Ambas Californias, establishing the seat of the bishopric in San Diego until he moved it to Santa Barbara in 1842. In 1844, at the mission of Santa Inés, he established the first Catholic seminary in California.

García Lorca, Federico

b. June 5, 1898
Fuentevaqueros, Spain
d. August 19, 1936
Víznar, Spain
fields: Literature

García Lorca is celebrated as a poet and dramatist who was able to weave traditional and folk elements of Spanish literature and culture into highly imaginative and original works. His poems and dramas are replete with startling metaphors and images that are both personal and universal in their focus on life and death, sexual identity, and the conflicts of fantasy and reality.

García Márquez, Gabriel

full: Gabriel José García Márquez
b. March 6, 1928
Aracataca, Colombia
fields: Literature

Nobel laureate García Márquez is one of the best-known and most admired writers of Latin American fiction. His mythic accounts—which reflect a vibrant blending of history, legends, and folktales—have been instrumental in bringing recognition to Latin American authors for their significant contribution to contemporary world literature. He won the 1982 Nobel Prize in Literature.

García-Ramis, Magali

b. Sept. 20, 1946
Santurce, Puerto Rico
fields: Literature

Latina writer. Born in Puerto Rico, Magali García-Ramis graduated from Columbia University in New York City in 1968. While there, she won the Ateneo Puertorriqueño prize for the short story "Todos los domingos." In 1971, she returned to Puerto Rico, worked as a journalist, taught, and published the story "La viuda de Chencho el Loco." In 1976, while living in Mexico, she published the short-story collection *La familia de todos nosotros* (1976). The following year, García-Ramis moved back to Puerto Rico and began working at the School of Public Communications of Puerto Rico. In 1986, she published *Felices días, Tio Sergio* (*Happy Days, Uncle Sergio*, 1995).

García Rivera, Oscar

b. ?
fields: Government and Politics

Latino politician. In 1937, Oscar García Rivera was elected to represent East Harlem in the New York State Assembly, becoming New York's first Puerto Rican assemblyman. In 1938, as the American Labor Party candidate, he defeated the Republican candidate. During his political career, García Rivera worked to defend the rights of migrant agricultural workers and tenement dwellers. He continued working in these areas as a lawyer after leaving office.

García Robles, Alfonso

b. March 20, 1911
Zamora, Michoacán, Mexico
d. September 2, 1991
Mexico City, Mexico
fields: Diplomacy

A Mexican diplomat, Alfonso García Robles was winner of 1982 Nobel Peace Prize (with Alva Myrdal). Peace advocate who cultivated a relationship with the U.S. Responsible for the 1967 Treaty for the Denuclearization of Latin America, known as the Treaty of Tlatelolco, signed by South American countries except Brazil and Argentina.

Gardel, Carlos

né: Charles Romauld Gardes
b. Dec. 11, 1890
Toulouse, France
d. July 6, 1935
Medellín, Colombia
fields: Theater and Entertainment, Music

Latino actor and singer. After moving with his mother from France to Buenos Aires, Argentina, at the age of three, Carlos Gardel developed his dancing, singing, and performing skills. In 1913, he made his first recording, then formed his own singing and dancing group, which toured throughout South America. He made several Spanish-language films for Paramount in New York—including *Cuesta abajo* (1934), *El Tango en Broadway* (1934), *El día que me quieras* (1935), and *Tango Bar* (1935)—which turned him into film star in the Spanish-speaking world. In 1935, he died in a plane crash during a publicity tour of Latin America.

Gardiner, Stephen

b. c. 1497
Bury St. Edmunds, Suffolk, England
d. November 12, 1555
Whitehall Palace, London, England
fields: Religion and Theology, Government and Politics, Diplomacy

As one of the most talented of the defenders of religious conservatism and traditional doctrine in early Tudor England, Gardiner fought the advance of Protestantism in church and state. Although his personal efforts were largely successful, ultimately his cause suffered defeat.

Gardner, Edward

b. Aug. 29, 1907
Lowndes County, Ala.
fields: Civil rights, Church Government

African American clergyman; Reverend Edward Gardner was devoted to the fight for civil rights in Alabama; participated in Project Confrontation (1963); was president of the Alabama Christian Movement for Human Rights (1968).

Gardner, Erle Stanley

b. July 17, 1889
Malden, Massachusetts
d. March 11, 1970
Temecula, California
fields: Literature

Gardner, a prolific writer of detective fiction, created Perry Mason, one of the most well known and popular fictional lawyers in print and on television.

Gardner, Isabella Stewart

né: Isabella Stewart
b. April 14, 1840
New York, New York
d. July 17, 1924
Boston, Massachusetts
fields: Patronage of the Arts

Isabella Stewart Gardner, one of the greatest collectors of European art of her day, built a fascinating museum to house her collections.

Gardner, Martin

b. Oct. 21, 1914
Tulsa, Oklahoma
fields: Mathematics (applied math)

Martin Gardner is known for debunking pseudoscience. He published many math puzzle and games, including *Perplexing Puzzles and Tantalizing Teasers* (1969). He popularized math and science with his books and magazine articles; in 1997, he won the Forum Award for promoting public understanding of the relationship between physics and society.

Garfield, James A.

full: James Abram Garfield
b. November 19, 1831
Orange Township, Ohio
d. September 19, 1881
Elberon, New Jersey
fields: Government and Politics

During his almost two decades, first as congressman, then briefly as president of the United States (1881), Garfield played a key role in every issue of national importance. As party leader, he helped resolve the factionalism within the Republican Party and enabled the Republicans to lead the United States into the twentieth century.

Garibaldi, Giuseppe

b. July 4, 1807
Nice, France
d. June 2, 1882
Caprera, Italy
fields: Military Affairs

Hero of the Risorgimento, Garibaldi inspired Italy to unite under the leadership of Victor Emanuel of Piedmont and Sardinia. His victory over Naples was the key achievement in bringing about a unified Italy and capped a life devoted to wars of liberation.

Garland, Judy

né: Frances Gumm
b. June 10, 1922
Grand Rapids, Minnesota
d. June 22, 1969
London, England
fields: Film, Music

An entertainer with a magnificent voice that attracted a worldwide audience, Judy

Garland appeared in films, on television, and in concert. She is remembered for her powerful singing and dramatic flair.

Garner, Erroll Louis

b. June 15, 1921
Pittsburgh, Pa.
d. Jan. 2, 1977
Los Angeles, Calif.
fields: Music (jazz pianist)

African American jazz pianist; Erroll Louis Garner is known primarily for his 1940's trio work; he developed a unique style of piano playing which involved the use of block chords in a steady rhythmic pattern; recordings include "Erroll's Bounce" (1947),"Easy to Love/Lullaby of Birdland" (1953), and "Misty" (1954).

Garner, James N.

b. ?
fields: Government and Politics

African American mayor of the village of Hempstead, Long Island, N.Y. In 1989, Republican James N. Garner became Long Island's first African American mayor.

Garnet, Henry Highland

b. Dec. 23, 1815
New Market, Md.
d. Feb. 13, 1882
Monrovia, Liberia
fields: Religion and Theology, Civil Rights

African American minister, orator and black nationalist; Henry Highland Garnet, in the vanguard of black abolitionism, used his pastorate of Liberty Street Presbyterian Church in Troy, N.Y., to organize black independent political action; was the first black person to sermonize in the U.S. House of Representatives; appointed U.S. minister and general counsel to Liberia in 1881.

Garnier, Tony

full: Antoine Garnier
b. August 13, 1869
Lyons, France
d. January 19, 1948
La Bédoule, France
fields: Architecture

Garnier gained international distinction during the infancy of grand-scale urban planning for his design of the *Cité Industrielle*, representing the introduction of "functional urbanism" in France, his use of audacious concepts, his exploitation of new structural materials, and his influence on major architects and urban planners.

Garra, Antonio

b. c. 1800
Southern Calif.
d. Dec., 1852
Southern Calif.
fields: Government and Politics, Warfare and Conquest, Native American Affairs

Native American leader. Antonio Garra, a Cupeño and the leader of the Garra Uprising, attempted to halt white migration into California between 1849 and 1851. Had Cahuilla, Chemehuevi, Cocopa, Kamia, Luiseño, Mojave, and Quechan supporters.

Garrett, Millicent. *See* Fawcett, Millicent Garrett

Garrick, David

b. February 19, 1717
Hereford, Herefordshire, England
d. January 20, 1779
London, England
fields: Theater and Entertainment

Garrick raised acting to a new level of expression and respectability, further popularized the plays of William Shakespeare, and brought creative management to Drury Lane.

Garriga, Mariano Simon

b. 1886
Point Isabel, Tex.
d. Feb. 21, 1965
Corpus Christi, Tex.
fields: Religion and Theology

Catholic bishop. Mariano Simon Garriga attended St. Mary's College in Kansas City, Kansas, and St. Francis Seminary in Milwaukee, Wisconsin. He was ordained to the priesthood in 1911, then served as a chaplain during World War I and as a pastor at St. Cecelia's Church in San Antonio, Texas. In 1936, Garriga became the first Mexican American to become a Catholic bishop. In 1959, he was given the honorary title of "Mr. South Texas" in recognition of his work as a bishop and as a cultural historian of Texas. In 1962, he attended the Second Vatican Council (Vatican II) in Rome.

Garrison, William Lloyd

b. December 10, 1805
Newburyport, Massachusetts
d. May 24, 1879
New York, New York
fields: Social Reform (abolitionism)

A crucial figure in the demise of American slavery and the coming of the Civil War, Garrison combined Protestant Evangelicalism, Jeffersonian liberalism, and Quaker humanism into a radical antislavery doctrine that called for the immediate end of the institution of slavery.

Garrison, Zina

b. Nov. 16, 1963
Houston, Tex.
fields: Sports (tennis player)

African American tennis player; Zina Garrison won the U.S. Open and Wimbledon junior titles in 1981; won a bronze medal in singles in the 1988 Olympics and a gold medal in doubles.

Garry, Spokane

b. 1811
near the junction of the Latah Creek and Spokane River, Wash.
d. Jan. 14, 1892
Indian Canyon, near Spokane, Wash.
fields: Government and Politics, Diplomacy, Native American Affairs

Native American leader. A Spokane (Salish), Spokane Garry both led his tribe in battle against whites and sought to Christianize his people. Skillful negotiator. A pacifist, he nonetheless joined other Indian warriors in the 1858 Battle of Four Lakes, losing to Colonel George Wright.

Garvey, Amy Jacques

b. 1896?
Kingston, Jamaica
d. July 22, 1973
Kingston, Jamaica
fields: Social Reform

African American activist; Amy Jacques Garvey, second wife of Marcus Garvey edited two volumes of his work, the *Philosophy and Opinions of Marcus Garvey, Volume I* (1923) and *Volume II* (1925); also wrote *Garvey and Garveyism* (1963).

Garvey, Marcus

full: Marcus Mosiah Garvey
b. August 17, 1887
St. Ann's Bay, Jamaica
d. June 10, 1940
London, England
fields: Civil Rights

Combining his talents of effective journalism and charismatic oratory, Garvey organized the first black mass-protest movement in the history of the United States.

Garvin, Frank. *See* Yerby, Frank

Garza, Catarino

b. November 25, 1859
near Matamoros, Tamaulipas, Mexico
d. 1902
Panama
fields: Journalism, Civil Rights

Journalist and revolutionary; Catarino Garza used editorial pages in the several newspapers he founded during the 1880's to provide guidance and leadership in the fight for Mexican American civil rights; Garza was a well known border rebel who opposed the authoritarian regime of Mexican president

Porfirio Díaz; in 1891 he launched three incursions into Mexico but was turned back each time by the Mexican army; U.S. authorities, fearing a Mexican revolt in the border region, stationed large numbers of troops there to prevent any further guerrilla activities on Garza's part; Garza fled the U.S. for Cuba and later died fighting in Panama's struggle for independence from Colombia.

Garza, Eligio De la. *See* De la Garza, Kika

Garza, Reynaldo

b. July 7, 1915
Brownsville, Tex.
fields: Law

Federal judge. In 1961, Reynaldo Garza was appointed as a U.S. district court judge in Brownsville, Texas, by President John F. Kennedy. In 1979, he was appointed as the senior judge of the U.S. Court of Appeals, Fifth Circuit, by President Jimmy Carter. In 1987, he was appointed to the Emergency Court of Appeals of the United States and later became its chief judge. In 1952, he received the Pro Ecclesi et Pontifice medal. In 1954, Pope Pius XII decorated Garza as a knight in the Order of St. Gregory the Great. The Reynaldo G. Garza School of Law in Edinburg, Texas, was named for him.

Gaskill, Robert Clarence

b. ?
Yonkers, N.Y.
fields: Military Affairs

African American military officer. In 1979, Robert Clarence Gaskill achieved the rank of major general in the United States Army. He retired in 1981.

Gaston, Arthur George

b. July 4, 1892
Demopolis, Ala.
d. Jan. 19, 1999
Birmingham, Ala.
fields: Business and Industry

African American businessman. Self-made millionaire Arthur George Gaston built a business empire with enterprises that included banking, broadcasting, insurance, and real estate.

Gaston, Cito

full: Clarence Edwin Gaston
b. March 17, 1944
San Antonio, Tex.
fields: Sports (baseball)

African American Latino baseball player and manager; from 1967 through 1978, Cito Gaston played as a major league outfielder and first baseman with the Atlanta Braves, San Diego Padres, and Pittsburgh Pirates; beginning 1982 he coached with the Toronto Blue Jays; in 1989 he became manager of the team and led the Blue Jays to American League Eastern Division titles (1989 and 1991) and to World Series championships (1992 and 1993). He was fired in 1997.

Gaston, Mauricio

b. Sept. 10, 1947
Havana, Cuba
d. Sept. 13, 1986
Boston, Mass.
fields: Social Reform, Education

Political activist and educator. After the Cuban Revolution in 1959, Mauricio Gaston moved with is family to the United States. He graduated from Princeton University with a degree in architecture in 1968, then co-founded the Boston tenant organizing group City Life/Vida Urbana, joined the Puerto Rican Socialist Party, worked for Puerto Rican independence, and sought stronger ties between the United States and Cuba. He earned a master's degree in urban planning from the Massachusetts Institute of Technology and worked on urban redevelopment during the 1980's until he died in 1986. The University of Massachusetts established the Mauricio Gaston Institute for Latino Community Development and Public Policy.

Gates, Bill

full: William Henry Gates III
b. Oct. 28, 1955
Seattle, Wash.
fields: Computer Science, Business and Economics

Computer software magnate. Bill Gates founded the Microsoft Corporation, which developed the highly successful Microsoft Disk Operating System; by 1983, 40 percent of all personal computers were running on Microsoft software. The success of Micrsoft products such as the Windows programming system made Gates one of the world's richest men by the 1990's.

Gates, Henry Louis, Jr.

b. Sept. 16, 1950
Keyser, W.Va.
fields: Education, Literature, Journalism

African American educator and editor; an award-winning author and literary critic, Henry Louis Gates, Jr., is also recognized as one of the most prominent scholars in African American Studies; edited *Black Is the Color of the Cosmos: Essays on Afro-American Literature and Culture* (1982) and *Our Nig: Or, Sketches from the Life of a Free Black* (1983); won the 1989 American Book Award for *The Signifying Monkey: A Theory of Afro-American Literary Criticism* (1988) and the Anisfield Book Award for the thirty-volume *The Schomburg Library of Nineteenth-Century Black Women Writers* (1988).

Gates, J. M.

b. c. 1885
Atlanta, Ga.
d. c. 1940
Atlanta, Ga.
fields: Religion and Theology, Music (singer)

African American baptist preacher and singer; J. M. Gates was pastor at Mount Calvary Church in Rock Dale Park, Atlanta, Ga., for more than thirty years; blues-style singing led to commercial recordings of his sermons.

Gaudí, Antonio

full: Antonio Gaudí y Cornet
b. June 25, 1852
in or near Reus, Spain
d. June 10, 1926
Barcelona, Spain
fields: Architecture

Gaudí is generally regarded as the foremost architect produced by Spain, but his place in architectural history is difficult to classify. Although he started out strongly influenced by medieval models, he became a prolific inventor of imaginative forms and innovative structural devices, showed himself to be a master in the handling of building materials, and is justly recognized as a brilliant manipulator of space, color, and light.

Gauguin, Paul

b. June 7, 1848
Paris, France
d. May 8, 1903
Atuana, Marquesas Islands
fields: Art

Gauguin epitomized a rejection of nineteenth century realism and its final phase, Impressionism, in favor of a new approach to painting based on primitive art; a simplification of lines, colors, and forms; and a suppression of detail, all intended to enhance the intellectual-emotional impact of a work of art. His program amounted in fact to a deliberate overthrow of the primacy of the optical sensation that had dictated all art since the Renaissance and is therefore the single most revolutionary thought introduced by a nineteenth century artist.

Gaulle, Charles de

full: Charles André Joseph Marie de Gaulle
b. November 22, 1890
Lille, France
d. November 9, 1970
Colombey-les-Deux-Églises, France
fields: Government and Politics, Military Affairs

Beginning from exile in 1940, de Gaulle became the leader of France against Germany in World War II. In 1958, he was recalled to power, created the Fifth French Republic, extricated France from Algeria and the rest of its overseas empire, and led France into a more independent foreign policy in Europe and the world.

Gauss, Carl Friedrich

b. April 30, 1777
Brunswick, Germany
d. February 23, 1855
Göttingen, Lower Saxony
fields: Mathematics, Astronomy, Physics

Gauss, one of the greatest scientific thinkers of all time, often ranked with Archimedes and Isaac Newton, made significant contributions in many branches of science. Perhaps his greatest achievement was that he arrived at the two most revolutionary mathematical ideas of the nineteenth century, non-Euclidean geometry and noncommutative algebra.

Gautama, Siddhārtha. *See* Buddha

Gautier, Théophile

b. August 31, 1811
Tarbes, France
d. October 23, 1872
Neuilly-sur-Seine, France
fields: Literature

Théophile Gautier was a French writer and critic whose challenges to literary and social values provoked censorship of his writings. As art critic for *La Presse* and literary commentator for *Journal Officiel* and other publications, he rejected prevailing aesthetic notions and attacked the hypocrisy of French culture and morality. His novel *Mademoiselle de Maupin* (1835) was an attack on the mediocrity of the bourgeoisie; it established his reputation for the scandalous, and he was denounced and rejected by the French Academy three times.

Gavin, John

b. Apr. 8, 1932
Los Angeles, Calif.
fields: Film, Business and Industry

John Gavin is known as a Latino actor, diplomat, and corporate executive. From 1955-1974, he was a noted film performer, serving as president of the Screen Actors Guild from 1971 to 1973, an adviser to the Secretary-General of the Organization of American States from 1961 to 1974, president of Gamma Services Corporation from 1968 to 1981; President Ronald Reagan appointed him to serve as U.S. Ambassador to Mexico from 1981 until 1986; vice president with Atlantic Richfield Co. (ARCO), president of Univisa, Inc.

Gay-Lussac, Joseph-Louis

né: Joseph-Louis Gay
b. December 6, 1778
Saint-Léonard-de-Noblat, France
d. May 9, 1850
Paris, France
fields: Chemistry, Physics

A preeminent scientist of his generation, Gay-Lussac helped prepare the way, through his discoveries in chemistry and physics, for the modern atomic-molecular theory of matter. His investigations of gases led to the law describing how they react with each other in simple proportions by volume, and his chemical investigations led to the discovery of a new element, boron, and to the development of new techniques in qualitative and quantitative analysis.

Gaye, Marvin

b. Apr. 2, 1939
Washington, D.C.
d. Apr. 1, 1984
Los Angeles, Calif.
fields: Music

African American motown recording artist; Marvin Gaye had more than twenty hits for MoTown Records; hired in 1960 by Berry Gordy, Jr., as session drummer for Smokey Robinson and the Miracles and backup singer for the Marvelettes; 1970's hits included "What's Going On," "Mercy Mercy Me (the Ecology)," and *Let's Get It On*; left MoTown in 1982 and received Grammy Award for "Sexual Healing"; shot to death by his father in a violent quarrel.

Gayle, Addison, Jr.

b. June 2, 1932
Newport News, Va.
fields: Literature

African American poet, essayist, and biographer; Addison Gayle, Jr.'s autobiography, *Wayward Child: A Personal Odyssey*, was published in 1977; biographies include *Oak and Ivy: A Biography of Paul Laurence Dunbar* (1971) and *Richard Wright: Ordeal of a Native Son* (1983).

Gaynor, Gloria

b. Sept. 7, 1949
Newark, N.J.
fields: Music (singer)

African American singer; Gloria Gaynor was known as the queen of American disco; released first album *Never Can Say Goodbye* in 1975; "I Will Survive." (1979) became a popular feminine-power anthem; released *Gloria Gaynor* in 1982.

Gaynwawpiahsika. *See* Alford, Thomas Wildcat

Geddes, Norman Bel

né: Norman Melancton Geddes
b. April 27, 1893
Adrian, Michigan
d. May 8, 1958
New York, New York
fields: Business and Industry, Theater and Entertainment (drama)

With a remarkable ability to integrate many ideas into an organic whole, Geddes became one of the greatest stage designers of the twentieth century, as well as an industrial designer known as "the father of streamlining."

Gehrig, Lou

full: Henry Louis Gehrig
b. June 19, 1903
New York, New York
d. June 2, 1941
New York, New York
fields: Sports (baseball)

Gehrig was the bulwark of the New York Yankees baseball dynasty of the 1920's, including the famed Murderer's Row team of 1927, and he played in 2,130 consecutive major league games, an endurance record unequaled in baseball history.

Geiger, Hans

full: Johannes Hans Wilhelm Geiger
b. Sept. 30, 1882
Neustadt an der Haardt (now Neustadt an der Weinstrasse), Rheinland-Pfalz, Germany
d. Sept. 24, 1945
Potsdam, Germany
fields: Physics

Hans Geiger created the Geiger counter, which detects subatomic particles by the ionization of gas.

Geiger, Rudolf

full: Rudolf Oskar Robert Williams Geiger
b. August 24, 1894
Erlangen, Germany
d. 1981
place unknown
fields: Meteorology

Geiger is recognized as the founder of a subdiscipline of meteorology that studies the nature of climatic conditions a few meters from the ground.

Geisel, Theodor Seuss. *See* Seuss, Dr.

Geitel, Hans Friedrich

b. July 16, 1855
Brunswick, Germany
d. Aug. 15, 1923
Wolfenbüttel, Germany
fields: Science, Invention and Technology, Physics

Hans Friedrich Geitel, in 1884-1885, discovered the selective photoelectric effect; with Julius Elster, he invented the photoelectric cell; in 1893, patented the first practical photoelectric cell; in 1894, discovered the photoelectric effect for visible light; in 1903, discovered the scintillation effect produced by radioactivity; in 1905-1907, found radioactive substances in lead; in 1911, discovered the photoelectric effect for infrared light.

Gell-Mann, Murray

b. Sept. 15, 1929
New York, New York
fields: Physics

Murray Gell-Mann, in 1953, proposed the property of "strangeness"; in 1962, proposed "the Eightfold Way" of classifying elementary particles; in 1964, applied mathematical group theory to propose that subatomic particles, such as protons and neutrons, are themselves composed of fundamental particles that he named "quarks"; in 1969, awarded the Nobel Prize in Physics.

Gellé, Claude. *See* Claude Lorrain

Geller, Margaret

full: Margaret Joan Geller
b. Dec. 8, 1947
Ithaca, New York
fields: Astronomy, Physics

Margaret Geller studied the distribution of galaxies in space; in 1989, with John P. Huchra, discovered the Great Wall, a long sheet of galaxies that is the largest known structure in the universe.

General, Alexander

aka: Deskahe
aka: Shao-hyowa (Great Sky)
b. c. 1889
Six Nations Reserve, Ontario, Canada
d. 1965
fields: Government and Politics, Scholarship, Native American Affairs

Cayuga, Oneida. Alexander General worked with anthropologists to promote understanding of traditional Iroquois beliefs and the cause of Iroquois nationalism. Instrumental in the organization of the Indian Defense League and the Mohawk Workers, early nationalist movements. Known for his collaboration with Frank Speck on *The Midwinter Rites of the Cayuga Longhouse* (1949).

Genet, Jean

b. December 19, 1910
Paris, France
d. April 15, 1986
Paris, France
fields: Literature

Genet was one of the major innovators in French theater in the period following World War II. His work helped transform concepts of Western drama and marked one of the golden ages of theater.

Genghis Khan

né: Temüjin
b. Between 1155 and 1162
Delyun Boldog, near the Gobi Desert
d. August 18, 1227
Ordos area in northern China
fields: Warfare and Conquest, Government and Politics

Khan of Mongol Empire, 1206-1227. A military genius, Genghis Khan united the clans and tribes of peoples later collectively known as the Mongols, leading them on conquests to the east, south, and west and organizing the Mongol Empire—which under his grandson, Kublai, came to dominate eighty percent of Eurasia.

Genseric

aka: Gaiseric
b. c. 390
probably Slovakia
d. 477
Carthage
fields: Government and Politics, Warfare and Conquest

One of the most important Germanic rulers, the Vandal leader Genseric invaded north Africa, sacked Rome, and hastened the fall of the Western Roman Empire.

Genthe, Arnold

b. January 8, 1869
Berlin, Germany
d. August 9, 1942
Candlewood Lake, Conn.
fields: Photography

German American photographer; known for both his studio portraits and his photographs of urban street life, particularly the rich details of early twentieth century Chinese life in San Francisco's Chinatown, Arnold Genthe worked in San Francisco (1898-1911) and then in New York; his published works include *Rebellion in Photography* (1900), *Pictures of Old Chinatown* (1908), *Old Chinatown* (1913), and his autobiography *As I Remember* (1936).

Gentile, Giovanni

b. May 30, 1875
Castelvetrano, Italy
d. April 15, 1944
Florence, Italy
fields: Philosophy, Education, Government and Politics

Gentile was the most prominent Italian intellectual associated with the Fascist dictatorship of Benito Mussolini. As a government official, Gentile helped shape Fascist educational policies and define the government's role in Italian culture. His neo-idealism and theories on political authoritarianism provided structure for Fascist ideology and philosophical justification for the Fascist state.

Gentili, Alberico

aka: Albericus Gentilis
b. January 14, 1552
Castello di San Ginesio, Ancona, Papal States
d. June 19, 1608
London, England
fields: Law

Gentili, a precursor of Hugo Grotius, brought the study of international law into modern times by recognizing that all the states of Europe belonged to one community of law, by applying the principles of morality to international law and particularly to war, and by separating international law from its religious basis (though not from morality) and placing it instead upon a basis of practicality.

George I

né: George Louis
b. May 28, 1660
Osnabrück, Hanover
d. June 11, 1727
Osnabrück, Hanover
fields: Government and Politics

King of Great Britain and Ireland, 1714-1727. George I became king at a time when the constitutional settlement brought about by the Revolution of 1688-1689 made it necessary for the Crown and Parliament to learn to work together. Although he was not personally popular, his firmness and moderation at a time of bitter partisanship stabilized the Hanoverian dynasty on the British throne. While maintaining the authority of the king in foreign policy and the appointment of ministers, George I was willing to give his ministers wide discretion in domestic policy and public finance, where the major consideration was the support of Parliament. In so doing he contributed to the development of cabinet government.

George II

né: George Augustus
b. November 10, 1683
Herrenhausen Palace, Hanover, Germany
d. October 25, 1760
London, England
fields: Government and Politics

King of Great Britain and Ireland, 1727-1760. George II continued the relationship of Crown and Parliament developed under George I, which gave the king extensive powers in foreign affairs and the appointment of ministers but required him to appoint ministers and follow policies which the Parliament would support. Under George II this system of government was adapted to the needs of a dynamic, expanding nation which, by the end of his reign, had established itself as a major European power and the dominant force in overseas trade and colonies.

George III

b. June 4, 1738
London, England
d. January 29, 1820
Windsor Castle, Berkshire, England
fields: Government and Politics

King George III, 1760-1820. For forty years George III was king of Great Britain and Ireland, which, in 1801, became the United Kingdom of Great Britain and Ireland. His reign covered a period of remarkable political, economic, social, and cultural change. He was conservative in his views, but his efforts to prevent changes in the role of the monarchy were frustrated by forces beyond his control. By standing for traditional values, he helped make the changes of his time more acceptable to his people.

George IV

né: George Augustus Frederick
b. August 12, 1762
St. James' Palace, London, England
d. June 26, 1830
Windsor Castle, Windsor, England
fields: Government and Politics

King of Great Britain, 1820-1830 (regent from 1811). Through his incompetence and disreputable personal behavior, King George IV eroded traditional British respect for and reliance upon the monarchy as a viable, governing institution. Inadvertently, he thus strengthened the powers of Parliament and weakened those of the British king.

George V

né: George Frederick Ernest Albert
b. June 3, 1865
Marlborough House, London, England
d. January 20, 1936
Sandringham, Norfolk, England
fields: Government and Politics

George V (1910-1936) brought stability and prestige to the British monarchy at a time of unprecedented turmoil. He was a model of constitutional propriety, and he fused Victorian and Edwardian elements of kingship to form the popular modern monarchy.

George VI

né: Albert Frederick Alfred George
b. December 14, 1895
Sandringham, Norfolk, England
d. February 6, 1952
Sandringham, Norfolk, England
fields: Government and Politics

As chief of state of Great Britain from 1936 to 1952, King George VI symbolized his country's determination to fight for victory in World War II and to regain its sense of purpose in the war's aftermath.

George, Henry

b. September 2, 1839
Philadelphia, Pennsylvania
d. October 29, 1897
New York, New York
fields: Social Reform, Economics

George's writings and lectures on land, labor, and economic policies expressed a popular radicalism that challenged established economic doctrines and dominant political practices, exercising a profound influence for reform both in the United States and abroad.

George, Nelson

b. September 1, 1957
Brooklyn, N.Y.
fields: Journalism (journalist and cultural critic)

African American journalist and cultural critic; Nelson George published *Where Did Our Love Go?: The Rise and Fall of the Motown Sound* (1985), *The Death of Rhythm and Blues* (1988), *Elevating the Game: Black Men and Basketball* (1992), *Buppies, B-Boys, Baps and Bohos: Notes on Post-Soul Black Culture* (1992), and *Hip Hop* America (1998); wrote a novel entitled *Urban Romance: A Novel of New York in the 80s* (1994).

George, Zelma Watson

b. Dec. 8, 1903
Hearne, Tex.
d. July 3, 1994
fields: Government and Politics

African American government official. Zelma Watson George served as a member of the U.S. delegation to the fifteenth session of the United Nations General Assembly.

Georgia Tom. *See* Dorsey, Thomas Andrew

Georgiou, Tyrone

b. ?
New York, N.Y.
fields: Photography, Education

African American photographer and teacher. Tyrone Georgiou was a designer and photographer for the Architects Renewal Committee in Harlem.

Géricault, Théodore

full: Jean-Louis-André-Théodore Géricault
b. September 26, 1791
Rouen, France
d. January 26, 1824
Paris, France
fields: Art

Géricault helped to move French art away from neoclassicism, which was dominant between the revolutionary and Napoleonic eras, into new, more modern directions. Nineteenth century Romantic and realistic painters alike claimed to have been inspired by his work.

Germain, Sophie

full: Marie-Sophie Germain
b. Apr. 1, 1776
Paris, France
d. June 27, 1831
Paris, France
fields: Mathematics (applied math and number theory)

Sophie Germain won the grand prize of the Académie des Sciences, given for the best essay on the mathematical theory of vibrations of general curved and plane elastic surfaces, in 1816. She was a founder of mathematical physics.

Geronimo

né: Goyathlay
b. c. 1827
near modern Clifton, Arizona
d. February 17, 1909
Fort Sill, Oklahoma
fields: Native American Affairs

For two decades the most feared and vilified individual in the Southwest, Geronimo, in his old age, became a freak attraction at fairs and expositions. His maligned and misunderstood career epitomized the troubles of a withering Apache culture struggling to survive in a hostile modern world.

Geronimo, Cesar

full: Cesar Francisco Geronimo y Zorrilla
b. Mar. 11, 1948
El Seibo, Dominican Republic
fields: Sports (baseball player)

Latino baseball player. Center fielder Cesar Geronimo was signed by the New York Yankees, made his major league debut with Houston in 1969, then moved to the Cincinnati Reds in 1972. He won Gold Glove Awards every year from 1974 to 1977 and earned a .258 batting average, with a high of .307 in 1976. Geronimo was an important member of the Reds teams that won five divisional championships, three National League pennants, and two World Series titles during the 1970's. In 1981, he was traded to the Kansas City Royals, then retired in 1983.

Gershvin, Jacob. *See* Gershwin, George

Gershwin, George

né: Jacob Gershvin
b. September 26, 1898
Brooklyn, New York
d. July 11, 1937
Los Angeles, California
fields: Music

With a relatively untrained but intuitive sense of music techniques, Gershwin composed some of the most lasting popular and serious music of the twentieth century.

Gershwin, Ira

full: Israel Gershwin
b. December 6, 1896
New York, New York
d. August 17, 1983
Beverly Hills, California
fields: Music

From the 1920's to the 1960's, Gershwin helped popularize the American musical by writing lyrics for Broadway productions and motion pictures that combined slang with light verse. Three of his songs were nominated for Academy Awards, and in 1932 he won a Pulitzer Prize for his work in *Of Thee I Sing*.

Gervin, George

aka: Iceman Gervin
b. Apr. 27, 1952
Detroit, Mich.
fields: Sports (basketball player)

African American basketball player. As a member of the San Antonio Spurs, George Gervin became one of the greatest scorers in NBA history, winning four NBA scoring titles before retiring in 1986.

Gervin, Iceman. *See* Gervin, George

Gesell, Arnold

full: Arnold Lucius Gesell
b. June 21, 1880
Alma, Wisconsin
d. May 29, 1961
New Haven, Connecticut
fields: Psychiatry and Psychology, Sociology

Gesell was a pioneer in the study of the physical and mental development of children and the author of a series of popular books that influenced both psychologists and parents for more than thirty years.

Gesner, Conrad

b. March 26, 1516
Zurich, Swiss Confederation
d. December 13, 1565
Zurich, Swiss Confederation
fields: Philology, Medicine, Natural History

Gesner was a Renaissance man, who collected, studied, and published the works of earlier literary, medical, and natural history authorities; he also compiled encyclopedic surveys of earlier scholarship in these fields. Equally as important, however, was Gesner's extension of knowledge, particularly in the fields of philology and natural history.

Gessell, Arnold L.

b. June 21, 1880
Alma, Wis.
d. May 29, 1961
New Haven, Conn.
fields: Psychiatry and Psychology

Trained at Yale University, where he later taught, Arnold L. Gessell developed scales for measuring behavior at different ages and helped devise the development quotient for children. In 1911 he founded the Yale Clinic for Child Development (later the Gessell Institute), which he directed until 1948. He and collaborator L. B. Ames wrote *The Mental Growth of the Pre-school Child* (1925). In 1942 he wrote *Infant and Child in the Culture of Today* Frances Ilg. That book greatly influenced child-rearing practices in the 1940's and 1950's.

Gewirth, Alan

b. November 28, 1912
Union City, New Jersey
fields: Philosophy

Drawing his inspiration from Immanuel Kant, Alan Gewirth attempted to provide a rational basis for a universal system of morality. He taught at many universities, lectured nationally and abroad, and was president of the American Philosophical Association (1973-1974), a senior fellow of the National Endowment for the Humanities (1974-1975), and a Guggenheim fellow (1975-1976). Major works include *Marsilius of Padua and Medieval Political Philosophy* (1951), *The Defensor Pacis* (1956), *Moral Rationality* (1972), *Reason and Morality* (1978), *Human Rights: Essays on Justification and Applications* (1982), *The Community of Rights* (1996), *Self-Fulfillment* (1998).

Ghazan, Mahmud

b. November 5, 1271
Abaskun, Iran
d. May 11, 1304
near Qazvin, northwestern Iran
fields: Government and Politics, Warfare and Conquest

The greatest of the Mongol Il-Khans of Iran, 1295-1394, Mahmud Ghazan was responsible for the conversion of the Il-Khanate to Islam and presided over remarkable flowering of syncretistic Central Asian and Iranian culture.

Ghazzālī, al-

full: Abū Ḥāmid Muḥammad ibn Muḥammad aṭ-Ṭusī al-Ghazzālī
aka: al-Ghazālī
b. 1058
Ṭūs, Khurasan, Iran
d. December 18, 1111
Ṭūs, Khurasan, Iran
fields: Religion and Theology, Philosophy

Author of *Iḥyāʾ ʿUlūm al-Dīn* (c. 1103; *The Revival of Religious Sciences*, 1964), *Mishkāt al-Anwār (The Niche for Lights)*, *al-Tahāfut al-Falāsifa* (*The Incoherence of the Philosophers*, 1958), and an influential spiritual autobiography, *al-Munqidh Min al-Dalāl*. Al-Ghazzali is widely regarded as the greatest theologian of Islam; his thought and writing bridged the gap between the Scholastic and the mystical interpretations of religion and formed an ethical and moral structure that has endured. In 1095, he suffered a severe personal crisis, left the Nizāmiyya, traveled throughout the Middle East, and eventually resettled in his ancestral home, Ṭūs, where he wrote the many treatises that secured his central place in Islamicate thought. After carefully studying the works of numerous Sufis and understanding their principles intellectually, he appears to have had an epiphany in which those principles became experiential. He is best known for his writings on ethics, the proper foundations for ethics, and mysticism.

Ghiberti, Lorenzo

b. c. 1378
Pelago, near Florence
d. December 1, 1455
Florence
fields: Art

Ghiberti's sculpture for the baptistery in Florence is often considered the first example of Renaissance art in Italy.

Ghislieri, Antonio. *See* Pius V

Ghose, Aurobindo. *See* Aurobindo, Sri

Giacometti, Alberto

b. October 10, 1901
Borgonovo, Switzerland
d. January 11, 1966
Chur, Switzerland
fields: Art

Giacometti was not only one of the most important sculptors of the twentieth century but also a distinguished painter and draftsman. His attenuated, gaunt sculptured figures, as well as his paintings and drawings of persons with eyes transfixed in a disturbing stare, have become icons of modern art.

Giauque, William Francis

b. May 12, 1895
Niagara Falls, Ontario, Canada
d. Mar. 28, 1982
Oakland, California
fields: Chemistry, Physics

William Francis Giauque, in 1929 with H. L. Johnston, discovered isotopes of atmospheric oxygen; in 1933, invented adiabatic demagnetization cooling, the first cooling to below 1 degree Kelvin; in 1938, invented a new thermometer for low-temperature measurement; contributed significantly toward the establishment of the third law of thermodynamics; in 1949, was awarded the Nobel Prize in Chemistry.

Gibbon, Edward

b. May 8, 1737
Putney, Surrey, England
d. January 16, 1794
London, England
fields: Historiography

Combining immense learning with a polished style and a gently ironic wit, Gibbon wrote *The History of the Decline and Fall of the Roman Empire*, which proved a durable landmark in historiography.

Gibbons, James

b. July 23, 1834
Baltimore, Maryland
d. March 24, 1921
Baltimore, Maryland
fields: Religion and Theology

As the most influential American archbishop of the late nineteenth century, Gibbons helped establish Catholicism as an important and vital religion in modern American society.

Gibbs, Erna

né: Erna Leonhardt
b. March 5, 1904
Bad Homburg, Germany
d. July 23, 1987
Chicago, Illinois
fields: Medicine

Erna Gibbs, with her husband, Frederic A. Gibbs, played key roles in the use of the electroencephalograph (EEG) as a diagnostic tool. Their application of the EEG was instrumental in understanding the cause of epilepsy.

Gibbs, Josiah Willard

aka: J. Willard Gibbs
b. February 11, 1839
New Haven, Connecticut
d. April 28, 1903
New Haven, Connecticut
fields: Chemistry (physical), Physics (theoretical)

Gibbs established the theoretical basis for modern physical chemistry by quantifying the second law of thermodynamics and developing heterogeneous thermodynamics. This and other work earned for him recognition as the greatest American scientist of the nineteenth century.

Gibson, Althea

b. August 25, 1927
Silver, South Carolina
fields: Sports (tennis)

The first African American to win a Wimbledon singles title, Althea Gibson was an important figure in establishing blacks as equal competitors at the highest levels of the tennis world. She overcame the prejudice of the tennis world at a time when racial barriers in the sport still operated. She should be remembered as one of the stellar performers in the history of women's tennis.

Gibson, Bob

full: Robert Gibson
b. Nov. 9, 1935
Omaha, Neb.
fields: Sports (baseball player)

African American baseball player; playing for the St. Louis Cardinals from 1959 to 1975, Bob Gibson won the Cy Young Award twice, and pitched in eight All-Star games and three World Series; elected to the Hall of Fame in 1981.

Gibson, Jo Ann. *See* Robinson, Jo Ann Gibson

Gibson, Josh

full: Joshua Gibson
b. b. Dec. 21, 1911
Buena Vista, Ga.
d. Jan. 20, 1947
Pittsburgh, Pa.
fields: Sports (baseball player)

African American baseball player; playing from 1930 to 1946, Josh Gibson had the highest lifetime batting average in Negro League history; only player ever to hit a ball out of Yankee Stadium; elected to the Hall of Fame in 1972.

Gibson, Kenneth A.

b. May 15, 1932
Enterprise, Ala.
fields: Government and Politics

African American mayor of Newark, N.J.; in 1970, Kenneth A. Gibson was elected as Newark's first African American mayor; served four consecutive terms until losing in 1986 reelection bid.

Gibson, Truman K., Jr.

b. Jan. 22, 1912
Atlanta, Ga.
fields: Government and Politics

African American government official. From 1943 to 1945, Truman K. Gibson, Jr. was the second person to hold the office of Civilian Aide to the Secretary of War.

Gibson, Walter Murray

b. 1824
S.C.
d. Jan. 21, 1888
San Francisco, Calif.
fields: Government and Politics

Walter Murray Gibson moved to Hawaii in 1861, settled in Lahaina, and won a seat in the legislature in 1878. He supported the importation of Japanese laborers and championed the cause of the native Hawaiians. However, despite his banner policy of "Hawaii for the Hawaiians," he created feelings of racial prejudice because of his extreme insular views. He became premier of the Hawaiian kingdom in 1882. In 1887, reckless use of power by the Hawaiian king led to a nonviolent revolt staged by four hundred white businessmen, who forced the king to expel Gibson.

Giddings, Joshua Reed

b. October 6, 1795
Tioga Point (later Athens), Bradford County, Pennsylvania
d. May 27, 1864
Montreal, Quebec, Canada
fields: Law, Government and Politics, Social Reform

While a member of the U.S. House of Representatives from Ohio in the late 1830's, Joshua Reed Giddings fought against attempts to prevent opponents of slavery from exercising their right to free speech. In 1861 President Abraham Lincoln appointed Giddings U.S. consul general in Canada, where he served until his death.

Gide, André

b. November 22, 1869
Paris, France
d. February 19, 1951
Paris, France
fields: Literature

Through his works, especially his fiction, Gide not only presented the problems and conditions of modern man but also renovated narrative genres and ways of seeing and feeling the world. He won the 1947 Nobel Prize in Literature.

Gilbert, Fabiola Cabeza de Baca

né: Fabiola Cabeza de Baca

b. May 16, 1898
Las Vegas, N.Mex.
fields: Education, Literature

Latina educator and writer. Fabiola Cabeza de Baca Gilbert was a second cousin to Ezequiel Cabeza de Baca. In 1951, using her knowledge of folk diet and customs, she established United Nations nutrition centers for the Tarascan Indians of Lake Pátzcuaro, Mexico. In the 1960's she organized Peace Corps training programs in the same region. She also hosted a radio program on culture and nutrition and wrote a weekly column on New Mexican food, customs, and folklore in the Spanish-language newspaper *El Nuevo Mexicano*. In 1954 she published *We Fed Them Cactus* (1954), a personal history of the Cabeza de Baca family.

Gilbert, Jarobin, Jr.

b. ?
fields: Television

African American broadcast executive. Jarobin Gilbert, Jr., was responsible for planning the National Broadcasting Company's (NBC) 1980 coverage of the Olympic Games in Moscow (which were later boycotted by the United States). Named vice president of NBC in 1981, he brought the Olympics back to the network for the 1988 games.

Gilbert, W. S.

full: William Schwenck Gilbert
b. November 18, 1836
London, England
d. May 29, 1911
Grim's Dyke, Harrow Weald, Middlesex, England
fields: Music, Theater and Entertainment, Literature

In his collaborations with Arthur Sullivan, librettist W. S. Gilbert forged a truly British character for light opera, in the process establishing operetta as a major dramatic subgenre and extending its boundaries to include melodrama, satire, and serious drama.

Gilbert, Walter

b. Mar. 21, 1932
Boston, Massachusetts
fields: Biology, Genetics, Physics

Walter Gilbert worked in molecular biology; isolated the *lac*-repressor; was one of the scientists who discovered the molecular structure of genes; in 1980, was awarded the Nobel Prize in Chemistry.

Gilbert, William

b. May 24, 1544
Colchester, Essex, England
d. Dec. 10, 1603
London or Colchester, England
fields: Astronomy, Physics

William Gilbert was one of the first great modern experimental scientists; demonstrated that magnetism and electricity are distinct phenomena; experimented with spherical magnets and compass needles; theorized that the earth exerts a magnetic influence—a precursor to the modern conception of gravity acting as an attractive force between masses.

Gilcrease, William Thomas

b. Feb. 8, 1890
Robeline, La.
d. May 6, 1962
Tulsa, Okla.
fields: Art (art collector, oilman, civic leader)

William Thomas Gilcrease, a Creek Indian, devoted his life to American Indian art and history, gathering a large collection of artifacts, documents, and artwork. In 1942, he established the Tulsa-based Gilcrease Foundation, whose corporate charter was "to maintain an art gallery, museum, and library devoted to the preservation for public use and enjoyment the artistic, cultural and historical records of the American Indian."

Gillespie, Dizzy

né: John Birks Gillespie
b. October 21, 1917
Cheraw, South Carolina
d. January 6, 1993
Englewood, New Jersey
fields: Music

As a renowned African American jazz trumpeter, bandleader, and composer, Gillespie founded the jazz movement known as "bebop" by combining Latin rhythms with jazz music.

Gilliam, Dorothy Butler

né: Dorothy Butler
b. 1936
Memphis, Tenn.
fields: Journalism

African American editor and newspaper columnist; Dorothy Butler Gilliam was a reporter and editor at *The Washington Post*; wrote *Paul Robeson: All-American* (1976); was married to artist Sam Gilliam.

Gilliam, Sam

b. Nov. 30, 1933
Tupelo, Miss.
fields: Art (painter and sculptor)

African American painter and sculptor; Sam Gilliam specialized in enormous relief works that combined sculpture and painting; awarded the Norman Walt Harris prize and two grants from the National Endowment for the Arts.

Gilman, Charlotte Perkins

né: Charlotte Anna Perkins
b. July 3, 1860
Hartford, Connecticut
d. August 17, 1935
Pasadena, California
fields: Literature, Journalism

In highly original literary and social scientific works, Charlotte Perkins Stetson Gilman addressed both women's contemporary status and the social and economic changes necessary to improve it.

Gilmore, Artis

b. Sept. 21, 1949
Chipley, Fla.
fields: Sports (basketball player)

African American basketball player; Artis Gilmore was the American Basketball Association's (ABA) Rookie of the Year in 1972; was drafted by the Chicago Bulls in 1976, and played in the National Basketball Association (NBA) until 1988.

Gilpin, Charles Sidney

b. Nov. 20, 1878
Richmond, Va.
d. May 6, 1930
Eldridge Park, N.J.
fields: Theater and Entertainment (stage actor)

African American stage actor. Charles Sidney Gilpin was cast as William Custis in *Abraham Lincoln* (1919) and won his greatest acclaim as the title character in Eugene O'Neill's *The Emperor Jones* (1920).

Gilpin, Laura

b. April 22, 1891
Austin Bluffs, Colorado
d. November 30, 1979
Santa Fe, New Mexico
fields: Photography

Gilpin was best known for her photographs of the American Southwest, particularly for her portraits of Pueblo and Navajo Indians, and received considerable acclaim as the most important woman photographer of the southwestern landscape and Native American culture.

Gilson, Étienne

full: Étienne Henri Gilson
b. June 13, 1884
Paris, France
d. September 19, 1978
Cravant, France
fields: Historiography, Philosophy, Religion and Theology

Gilson made the ideas of Saint Thomas Aquinas and other medieval theologians intelligible and relevant for twentieth century scholars. He believed deeply that faith and reason were not incompatible but symbiotic: They were mutual helpmates whose interaction via fundamental principles created a dynamic vitality essential for the proper development of both secular and sacred knowledge.

Gingrich, Newt

full: Newton Leroy Gingrich
b. June 17, 1943
Harrisburg, Pa.
fields: Government and Politics

Arch-conservative U.S. politician. Gingrich was elected to the U.S. House of Representatives from Georgia in 1978; in 1989, he became House minority whip. In 1995, he became the first Republican Speaker of the House in more than forty years. His proposed "Contract with America" called for conservative legislative reforms.

Ginn, Mrs. Glenn. *See* Lee, Rose Hum

Ginsberg, Allen

b. June 3, 1926
Newark, New Jersey
d. April 5, 1997
New York, New York
fields: Literature

One of America's best-known poets. Allen Ginsberg's first collection of poems, *Howl and Other Poems* (1956) was the subject of an obscenity trial in San Francisco in 1957; was a leader of the hippie and antiwar movements during the 1960's.

Ginsburg, Ruth Bader

b. March 15, 1933
Brooklyn, N.Y.
fields: Law

U.S. Supreme Court justice; from 1971 to 1980, Ruth Bader Ginsburg served as counsel for the Women's Rights Project of the ACLU, winning five of the six sex-discrimination cases she argued before the U.S. Supreme Court; appointed to the U.S. Court of Appeals (1980; where she became known as a moderate); in 1993, nominated to the Supreme Court by President Bill Clinton, becoming the first Jewish American since 1969 and only the second woman to sit on the U.S. Supreme Court.

Ginzburg, Ralph

b. October 28, 1929
New York, New York
fields: Journalism

Ralph Ginzburg was a New York magazine publisher whose unsuccessful appeal on a federal obscenity conviction led to the U.S. Supreme Court's amending its test for defining obscenity. In 1963 he was convicted of violating the Comstock Act in a federal court and sentenced to prison after publishing photographs of black and white lovers in his magazine *Eros*. In 1966 the U.S. Supreme Court ruled on his appeal, concluding that Ginzburg was guilty of pandering for having written advertisements for his publication suggesting it was obscene. Ginzburg's conviction was subsequently reduced from five years in prison to three.

Gioberti, Vincenzo

b. April 5, 1801
Turin, Kingdom of Sardinia
d. October 26, 1852
Paris, France
fields: Philosophy, Religion and Theology, Government and Politics

Gioberti contributed the first comprehensive political program for the Risorgimento—the Italian national unification movement. He represented the progressive Catholic political tradition in nineteenth century Italy and sought to redefine the Church's political role in the process of creating the new Italian nation.

Giorgione

né: Giorgio de Castelfranco (?)
aka: Zorzo de Castelfranco
b. c. 1477
Castelfranco, Republic of Venice
d. c. 1510
Venice
fields: Art

The Renaissance celebration of the ordinary human being enjoying the pleasures of the natural life not in the great public paintings, but in the intimacy of the small canvas, suitable for displaying in the simple living room, found its painter in Giorgione, the master of the private moment.

Giotto

b. c. 1266
Vespignano, near Florence, Italy
d. January 8, 1337
Florence, Italy
fields: Art, Architecture

Since his own time, Giotto has been recognized as the first major figure in European painting. He was among the first to concentrate on the individual, an interest later shared by Renaissance artists; his paintings are remarkable for their revelations of human complexity.

Giovanni, Nikki

né: Yolande Cornelia Giovanni
b. June 7, 1943
Knoxville, Tennessee
fields: Literature

An African American poet who first gained fame in the 1960's. Her poetry addresses issues ranging from the black revolution to love and includes *Black Feeling, Black Talk* (1968) and *Black Judgement* (1969), which contained her best-known poem, "Nikki-Rosa"; also published *Gemini: An Extended Autobiographical Statement on My First Twenty-five Years of Being a Black Poet* (1971).

Giovanni di Fidanza. *See* Bonaventure, Saint

Girard, Albert

b. 1595
St. Mihiel, Lorraine, France
d. Dec. 8, 1632
Leiden, the Netherlands
fields: Mathematics (algebra, applied math, number theory, and trigonometry)

Albert Girard was one of the first mathematicians to recognize the importance of negative, imaginary, and repeated solutions to polynomial equations. Credited with being the first to formulate a statement that the number of solutions to an integral polynomial equation equals the degree of the equation.

Giraudoux, Jean

full: Hippolyte-Jean Giraudoux
b. October 29, 1882
Bellac, France
d. January 31, 1944
Paris, France
fields: Literature

Giraudoux's plays dominated the French theater of the 1930's; his work for the stage sustained the aesthetic revolution begun after World War I and anticipated the avant-garde developments of the 1940's. A prolific essayist, Giraudoux wrote novels and short stories that continued the tradition of highly stylized, imagistic fiction established by Symbolist writers.

Girodias, Maurice

b. 1919
Paris, France
d. July 3, 1990
Paris, France
fields: Publishing

Maurice Girodias was a French publisher who published sexually explicit books under the imprint of his Olympia Press, which he established in 1953. Based in Paris, it published works in English such as Terry Southern and Mason Hoffenberg's comic novel *Candy* (1958), Vladimir Nabokov's *Lolita* (1955). and William Burroughs' *Naked Lunch* (1959). Beginning in 1956, Girodias was repeatedly prosecuted for obscenity by the French government. After he moved Olympia Press to New York in 1967, he had only marginal success.

Gish, Lillian

full: Lillian Diana Gish
b. October 14, 1893
Springfield, Ohio
d. February 27, 1993
New York, New York
fields: Film, Theater and Entertainment (drama)

A legendary and versatile performer for nine decades, Lillian Gish was hailed as the First Lady of the Silent Screen, starred in some of Broadway's most memorable productions, and performed regularly on television.

Gist, Carole

b. 1970
Detroit, Mich.
fields: Theater and Entertainment

African American Miss USA of 1990. Representing the state of Michigan, Carole Gist was the first African American to win the Miss USA title. Claiming discrimination, breach of promise, and citing poor working conditions, she later filed an $18 million lawsuit against the pageant.

Givens, Robin

b. November 27, 1965
New York, N.Y.
fields: Film, Television (actress)

African American actress; Robin Givens appeared on the ABC comedy series *Head of the Class* (1986-1991); was briefly married to boxer Mike Tyson in 1988; film credits include *A Rage in Harlem* (1991), *Boomerang* (1992), and *Blankman* (1994).

Gladstone, William Ewart

b. December 29, 1809
Liverpool, England
d. May 19, 1898
Hawarden, Flintshire, England
fields: Government and Politics

For more than half a century, Gladstone was a leading figure in the British Parliament, and he held a number of key cabinet positions, including prime minister, a post he filled four times between 1868 and 1895.

Glashow, Sheldon L.

full: Sheldon Lee Glashow
b. Dec. 5, 1932
New York, New York
fields: Physics

Sheldon L. Glashow worked to improve the equations of Steven Weinberg and Abdus Salam, which unified electromagnetic forces with the weak force responsible for some radioactivity. In 1979, he shared the Nobel Prize in Physics with Weinberg and Salam.

Glass, Cheryl

b. ?
fields: Sports (auto racer)

African American sprint car racer. Cheryl Glass won the track championship at Skagit Raceway in Washington at the age of eighteen, but an accident hampered her bid to become the first black woman to drive in the Indianapolis 500.

Glaudé, Stephen A.

b. July 25, 1954
Washington, D.C.
fields: Government and Politics

African American political appointee; Stephen A. Glaudé's first political appointment came in 1981, when President Ronald Reagan named him to the President's Task Force on Private Sector Initiatives; appointed by President George Bush to serve as assistant for intergovernmental relations and deputy secretary of the Department of Housing and Urban Development.

Glazer, Nathan

b. February 25, 1923
New York, New York
fields: Sociology, Education

Nathan Glazer is a sociologist; on faculty at Harvard's Graduate School of Education, 1968; early books were oriented toward Zionism and socialism, though he became a neoconservative in the 1970's; best known for *Beyond the Melting Pot* (1963), written with Daniel Patrick Moynihan, and *Affirmative Discrimination* (1976).

Glenn, John

full: John Herschel Glenn, Jr.
b. July 18, 1921
Cambridge, Ohio
fields: Aviation and Space Exploration, Government and Politics

U.S. astronaut and senator. John H. Glenn, Jr., was the first American astronaut to circle the earth in space (February 20, 1962), in the the Project Mercury space capsule *Friendship 7*. Elected to U.S. Senate as a Democrat in 1974, held seat until retirement in 1998. Between October 29 and November 7, 1998, at age seventy-seven, Glenn was aboard the space shuttle *Discovery*, becoming the oldest person to have gone into space.

Gleska, Sinte. *See* Spotted Tail

Gloster, Hugh

full: Hugh Morris Gloster
b. May 11, 1911
Brownsville, Tenn.
fields: Education, Scholarship, Literature

African American author and educator; Hugh Gloster wrote *Negro Voices in American Fiction* (1948); was president of Morehouse College from 1967 to 1987; received Fulbright fellowships to Japan (1953-1955) and Poland (1961-1962).

Glover, Danny

b. July 22, 1947
San Francisco, Calif.
fields: Film, Theater and Entertainment (actor)

African American actor; Danny Glover's acting credits include television, stage, and film performances; broke through in televison appearances on *Lou Grant* and *B.J. and the Bear*— major roles were *Mandela* (1987), *A Raisin in the Sun* (1989), *Lonesome Dove* (1989), and *Dead Man Out* (1989); acted in Athol Fugard's *Blood Knot* and *Master Harold . . . and the Boys*; appeared in numerous films including *Places in the Heart* (1984); *Witness* (1985), *Silverado* (1985); *The Color Purple* (1985), *Flight of the Intruder* (1991), *A Rage in Harlem* (1991), *Pure Luck* (1991), *Lethal Weapon* (1987), *Lethal Weapon 2* (1989), *Lethal Weapon 3* (1992), and *Lethal Weapon 4* (1998).

Glover, Savion

b. c. 1974
Newark, N.J.?
fields: Dance

African American tap dancer. Savion Glover played Jelly Roll Morton as a young man in the smash Broadway hit *Jelly's Last Jam* and appeared in the film *Tap* (1989).

Gluck, Christoph

b. July 2, 1714
Erasbach, Upper Palatinate
d. November 15, 1787
Vienna, Austria
fields: Music

Gluck established a new style of opera that marked the end of the Baroque and the beginning of the classical era in music. Many of his stage works represent a turning point in the balance between counterpoint and homophony, between vocal display and musical drama.

Glyn, Elinor

b. October 17, 1864
Jersey, Channel Islands, England
d. September 23, 1943
London, England
fields: Literature, Film

An English novelist, Elinor Glyn wrote a popular novel, *Three Weeks* (1907), that was denounced by a U.S. court as too immoral to be entitled to copyright protection. In 1915 Glyn brought suit for copyright infringement against a burlesque of her novel called *Pim-*

ple's Three Weeks. The court ruled that immoral works did not have copyright protection and urged suppression of Glyn's novel. Glyn also wrote the screenplay for the novel's 1924 Hollywood film version.

Gneisenau, August von

b. October 27, 1760
Schildau, Saxony
d. August 23, 1831
Posen, Pomerania
fields: Military Affairs

As a Prussian field marshal and member of King Frederick William III's Military Reorganization Commission, Gneisenau fashioned the Prussian strategy that finally defeated Napoleon I in the campaigns of 1813 and 1814 and played a key role in reforming the Prussian army into the most professional military force in nineteenth century Europe. Gneisenau's organizational and operational reforms survive today as accepted elements in most of the world's armies.

Gobat, Charles Albert

b. May 21, 1843
Tramelan, Switzerland
d. March, 16, 1914
Bern, Switzerland
fields: Diplomacy, Government and Politics

Swiss public servant and peace activist, Charles Albert Gobat was cowinner of 1902 Nobel Peace Prize. Active in the Interparliamentary Union and, from 1906, the International Peace Bureau. Inspired many to join peace movement.

Goci (His Nose). *See* Cochise

Godard, Jean-Luc

b. December 3, 1930
Paris, France
fields: Film

Godard, along with his colleagues in the Nouvelle Vague (New Wave) of postwar French film, expanded the possibilities of cinematic expression so that traditional narrative patterns could no longer be regarded as limits and was instrumental in locating film at the center of postmodern aesthetics, establishing the cinema as the equal of any form of artistic expression.

Godbolt, James. *See* Slyde, Jimmy

Goddard, Beatrice Romaine. *See* Brooks, Romaine

Goddard, Robert H.

full: Robert Hutchings Goddard
b. October 5, 1882
Worcester, Massachusetts
d. August 10, 1945
Baltimore, Maryland
fields: Aviation and Space Exploration, Invention and Technology

As the deviser of the first successful liquid-fuel rocket and as a tireless explorer of the theoretical and practical problems of rocketry decades before the subject gained substantial support in the United States, Goddard stands as the great American pioneer of space travel.

Gödel, Kurt

b. April 28, 1906
Brünn, Moravia, Austro-Hungarian Empire (now Brno, Czech Republic)
d. January 14, 1978
Princeton, New Jersey
fields: Mathematics, Physics

Mathematician and physicist; in 1940 Kurt Gödel left Austria to become a member of the Institute for Advanced Study in Princeton, New Jersey; from 1944 to 1952, Gödel worked with Albert Einstein on solutions to general relativity equations; became a U.S. citizen in 1948; beginning in 1949, Gödel developed a solution to Einstein's equations using his model of a rotating universe in which closed timelike curves would allow one to return to the past; retired from the Institute for Advanced Study in 1976.

Godfroy, Francis

b. c. 1788
d. c. 1840
fields: Warfare and Conquest, Native American Affairs

Native American leader. Francis Godfroy, a Miami, was an ally of Tecumseh during Tecumseh's Rebellion (1809-1811), attempting to stop white immigration into the Old Northwest. Fought on the side of the British in the War of 1812.

Godkin, Edwin Lawrence

b. October 2, 1831
Moyne, Ireland
d. May 21, 1902
Brixham, England
fields: Journalism

As editor of *The Nation* and, later, of the *Evening Post*, Godkin was one of the most influential voices in post-Civil War American politics.

Godolphin, first earl of

né: Sidney Godolphin
b. June 15, 1645 (baptized)
Breage, Cornwall, England
d. September 15, 1712
St. Albans, Hertfordshire, England
fields: Government and Politics

Without seeking fame or personal compensation, Godolphin created the structural power base which would later become, officially, the office of prime minister, and served as the prototype for this evolution in English government.

Godunov, Boris Fyodorovich

b. c. 1551
place unknown
d. April 23, 1605
Moscow, Russia
fields: Government and Politics

Czar of Russia, 1598-1605. Godunov provided a brief period of stability between the harsh rule of Ivan the Terrible and the unsettled period of the Time of Troubles.

Godwin, Mary. *See* Shelley, Mary Wollstonecraft

Godwin, William

b. March 3, 1756
Wisbech, Isle of Ely, Cambridgeshire, England
d. April 7, 1836
London, England
fields: Philosophy, Government and Politics, Literature

Having evolved in his thinking from a radical Protestant position to the revolutionary, atheistic synthesis of the massive treatise *An Enquiry Concerning Political Justice, and Its Influence on General Virtue and Happiness*, Godwin developed the ideas of libertarian socialism that were to influence profoundly both the individualism of English Romanticism and the later anarchistic, communist ideas of the utopian Robert Owen, the Socialist economist William Thompson, and the young Karl Marx. His friendship with and marriage to Mary Wollstonecraft contributed to early feminist thought, and his ideas stimulated nearly all the Romantic poets.

Godwinson, Harold. *See* Harold II

Goebbels, Joseph

full: Paul Joseph Goebbels
b. October 29, 1897
Rheydt, Germany
d. May 1, 1945
Berlin, Germany
fields: Government and Politics

Goebbels was the propaganda master of the Nazi regime and Adolf Hitler's minister of culture during the twelve-year Third Reich. One of the few intellectuals in the Party leadership, Goebbels was largely responsible for the success of the Nazi program.

Goeppert, Maria Gertrude. *See* Mayer, Maria Goeppert

Goethals, George Washington

b. June 29, 1858
Brooklyn, New York
d. January 21, 1928
New York, New York
fields: Engineering

Goethals was chief engineer of the Panama Canal, which revolutionized maritime transportation and commerce.

Goethe, Johann Wolfgang von

b. August 28, 1749
Frankfurt am Main
d. March 22, 1832
Weimar, Saxe-Weimar-Eisenach
fields: Theater and Entertainment, Literature, Science

Goethe, whose lyric, dramatic, and narrative talents produced literary works of lasting influence on the Western tradition, is considered to be one of the greatest German writers. An amateur scientist and able administrator, Goethe was a truly gifted man of his time.

Gogh, Vincent van

full: Vincent Willem van Gogh
b. March 30, 1853
Zundert, the Netherlands
d. July 29, 1890
Auvers-sur-Oise, France
fields: Art

During his brief artistic career, van Gogh gave expression to a passionate vision of nature and humanity. Following his death, his paintings came to be acknowledged by critics and the public as constituting one of the highest achievements of nineteenth century art.

Gogol, Nikolai

b. March 31, 1809
Sorochintsy, Ukraine, Russia
d. March 4, 1852
Moscow, Russia
fields: Literature

Gogol made an important contribution to the development of modern comic fiction, particularly short fiction. By combining such disparate narrative elements as oral folklore and literary Romanticism, Gogol paved the way for such modernist writers as Franz Kafka.

Goizueta, Roberto C.

b. Nov. 18, 1931
Havana, Cuba
fields: Business and Industry

Roberto C. Goizueta was a Cuban American business executive. Worked for Coca-Cola Company, becoming chairman of the board and chief executive officer in 1981—the first Cuban American with such corporate power; helped turn the company around and recapture the international market during the 1980's; won the Spanish Institute Gold Medal in 1986 and the NAACP Equal Justice Award in 1991.

Goldberg, Arthur Joseph

b. 1908
d. 1990
fields: Law

U.S. Supreme Court justice, 1962-1965; appointed by President Kennedy. Resigned to become ambassador to the United Nations with expectation that he would be permitted to settle the Vietnam War. Significant opinions: *Escobedo v. Illinois*, 378 U.S. 478 (1964); *Aguilar v. Texas*, 378 U.S. 108 (1964); *Griswold v. Connecticut*, 381 U.S. 479 (1965) (concurring opinion).

Goldberg, Whoopi

né: Caryn Johnson
b. November 13, 1949
New York, New York
fields: Theater and Entertainment (drama), Television, Film

Whoopi Goldberg has overcome what many may consider insurmountable obstacles to emerge as a multitalented entertainer, the first African American female to win an Oscar, a Grammy, and a Golden Globe award.

Goldfisch, Samuel. *See* Goldwyn, Samuel

Goldie, George

né: George Dashwood Goldie Taubman
aka: Sir George Taubman Goldie
b. May 20, 1846
Douglas, Isle of Man
d. August 20, 1925
London, England
fields: Colonial Administration

Employing his commercial skills and great administrative abilities, Goldie formed the Royal Niger Company and contributed immensely to the extension of British influence in Nigeria.

Goldman, Dianne. *See* Feinstein, Dianne

Goldman, Emma

b. June 27, 1869
Kovno, Lithuania
d. May 14, 1940
Toronto, Canada
fields: Social Reform

A leading member of the anarchic Left in the early twentieth century, Goldman was a critic of both capitalism and socialism and an advocate of women's rights.

Goldsmith, Oliver

b. November 10, 1728 or 1730
Pallas, County Longford(?), Ireland
d. April 4, 1774
London, England
fields: Literature

As a novelist, poet, dramatist, and essayist, Goldsmith stands in the first rank. His *The Life of Richard Nash, Esq.* (1762) pioneered a new type of biography, and his historical writings helped educate generations of schoolchildren and adults.

Goldstein, Betty Naomi. *See* Friedan, Betty

Goldwater, Barry

full: Barry Morris Goldwater
b. January 1, 1909
Phoenix, Arizona
d. May 29, 1998
Phoenix, Arizona
fields: Government and Politics

One of the founders of the modern conservative movement in the United States, Barry Goldwater helped conservatives capture the Republican Party in the 1960's. Despite losing the 1964 presidential election, his efforts solidified the growing conservative movement; his *Conscience of a Conservative* (1962) sold 3.5 million copies, advocating individualism, limited government, a strict constructionist view of the U.S. Constitution, federalism, and anticommunism. Through public appearances and by chiding many members of the Republican Party for being too liberal and accommodating the growing influence of government in American society, Goldwater gained credibility with party conservatives, and he is remembered by members of both major political parties as a man of impeccable integrity who stood by his ideals.

Goldwyn, Samuel

né: Samuel Goldfisch
b. August 27, 1882
Warsaw, Poland
d. January 31, 1974
Beverly Hills, California
fields: Film

Working as an independent Hollywood producer with his own company and studio, Goldwyn made films that were known for their high quality and good taste, despite his own impoverished upbringing and limited education.

Golgi, Camillo

full: Camillo Bartolomeo Emilio Golgi
b. July 7, 1843
Corteno (now Corteno Golgi), Italy
d. Jan. 21, 1926
Pavia, Italy
fields: Biology, Physiology

Camillo Golgi conducted pioneering research in neuroanatomy; in 1873, proposed the fine, interconnected network of the central nervous system; in 1898, discovered internal reticular apparatuses (called Golgi bodies) in cells; studied malaria; in 1906, awarded the Nobel Prize in Physiology or Medicine.

Gomes, Lloyd H.

b. Feb. 8, 1913
Turlock, Calif.
fields: Warfare and Conquest

Latino military figure. Lloyd H. Gomes, who joined the Army Reserve Corps in 1937 and was commissioned as a second lieutenant in 1938, served in World War II and Korea. Among the awards he earned were the Purple Heart, Bronze Star, Silver Star, and Distinguished Service Cross. In 1952, he was promoted to full colonel. In 1958, he became chief of staff for the Eighty-second Airborne Division at Fort Bragg. In 1965, he was promoted to brigadier general and assigned as a senior adviser to the First Republic Korean Army and as commander of a U.S. Army advisory group. In 1967, he was promoted to major general. Gomes retired on August 31, 1969.

Gomez, Lefty

full: Vernon Louis Gomez
b. Nov. 26, 1908
Rodeo, Calif.
d. Feb. 17, 1989
Greenbrae, Calif.
fields: Sports (baseball player)

Latino baseball player. Left-handed pitcher Lefty Gomez made his major league debut in 1930 with the New York Yankees. He won more than twenty games in a season four times and earned a 6-0 record in five World Series. Gomez drove in the first run in All-Star Game history and went on to play in six more All-Star games. He retired in 1943 with a lifetime 189-102 record. He was elected to the National Baseball Hall of Fame in 1972.

Gomez, Preston

né: Pedro Gomez y Martinez
b. Apr. 20, 1923
Central Preston, Cuba
fields: Sports (baseball player and manager)

Latino baseball player and manager. Although Preston Gomez's major league playing career consisted of only eight games as a reserve infielder with the Washington Senators in 1944, he became manager of the San Diego Padres in 1969 after many years as minor-league manager. The newly formed Padres finished in last place three years in row under his guidance. In 1974, he led the Houston Astros to a fourth-place finish in the National League Western Division. He was hired by the Chicago Cubs in 1980 but was fired when the team performed poorly. As a major-league manager, his overall record was 346-529.

Gómez-Peña, Guillermo

b. September, 1955
Mexico City, Mexico
fields: Art

Latino performance artist. Guillermo Gómez-Peña attended the Universidad Nacional Autonoma de Mexico before moving to the United States in 1978 to attend the California Institute of the Arts. In 1980, he cofounded a performance group focused on cultural and immigration issues called the Poyesis Genetica. He moved to San Diego in 1983 and cohosted a radio show called *Border Dialogues* and published a journal called *The Broken Line/La Línea Quebrada.* In 1985, he cofounded the Border Arts Workshop/El Taller de Arte Fronterizo. Gómez-Peña's controversial performances writings deal with immigration and ethnic issues. In 1991, he was awarded a MacArthur Foundation fellowship.

Gómez-Quiñones, Juan

b. Jan. 28, 1942
Parral, Chihuahua, Mexico
fields: Civil Rights, Literature, Historiography

Mexican American poet, historian, civil rights activist; Juan Gómez-Quiñones was born in Mexico; professor of history, University of California, Los Angeles (UCLA), 1969; director of Chicano Studies Research Center, UCLA (1975-1985); cofounder, United Mexican American Students; cofounder/director, Chicano Legal Defense; published the pioneering work *Sembradores, Ricardo Flores Magón y el Partido Liberal Mexicano: A Eulogy and Critique* (1973) and a poetry collection, *Fifth and Grande Vista: Poems, 1960-1973* (1974).

Gompers, Samuel

b. January 27, 1850
London, England
d. December 13, 1924
San Antonio, Texas
fields: Labor Movement

Gompers helped create the first successful national organization of trade unions in the United States, the American Federation of Labor (AFL), and he led the AFL almost continuously from its creation in 1886 to 1924.

Gondola, Andrea di Pietro della. *See* Palladio, Andrea

Gongsun Long

aka: Kung-sun Lung
b. c. 320 B.C.E.
Chao (now Shanxi), China
d. c. 250 B.C.E.
China
fields: Philosophy

Gongsun Long left the largest corpus of the Chinese School of Names, the dialectician school of philosophers. His *Gongsun Longzi* is the only surviving independent work of logic in Chinese literature.

Gonsalves, Paul

b. July 12, 1920
Boston, Mass.
d. May 14, 1974
London, England
fields: Music (tenor saxophonist)

Latino tenor saxophonist. After World War II, Paul Gonsalves joined Count Basie's band. He played with Dizzy Gillespie's band in 1949 and 1950, then joined the Duke Ellington Orchestra, where he remained for the rest of his career. Gonsalves also worked as a soloist with various groups.

Gonwatsijayenni. *See* Brant, Molly

Gonzáles, Henry Barbosa

b. 1916
fields: Government and Politics, Civil Rights

Henry Barbosa Gonzáles is a politician; born in San Antonio, Texas, to Mexican parents; earned law degree at St. Mary's University in 1943; was a member, San Antonio City Council, 1953-1956; elected to the Texas state senate in 1956, becoming the first Mexican American state senator in 110 years; served as U.S. representative from Texas since 1961; vigorous supporter of civil rights campaigns of Presidents John F. Kennedy and Lyndon B. Johnson in the 1960's.

Gonzáles, Corky

né: Rodolfo Gonzáles
b. June 18, 1928
Denver, Colo.
fields: Civil Rights, Literature

Mexican American social activist and poet; Rodolfo "Corky" Gonzáles founded the Crusade for Justice in 1965 in Denver, providing medical and legal aid to Mexican Americans; led the Chicano contingent of the Poor People's March on Washington, D.C., in 1968; organized annual Chicano Youth Liberation Conferences; instrumental in the launch of the Chicano political party La Raza Unida, in 1970; rejected the idea of assimilation, advocating self-determination and political and economic autonomy for Mexican Americans; his poem "I Am Joaquin" (1967) became a symbol of the emerging Chicano movement.

González, Adalberto Elías

b. ?
Altar, Sonora, Mexico
fields: Literature, Theater and Entertainment

Playwright and actor. Adalberto Elías González attended the Escuela Normal in Hermosillo in Mexico before moving to Los Angeles in 1920 and becoming an important figure in early Hispanic theater in the region. He began working as a film critic for *El Heraldo de México* in 1924 and two years later won a playwriting contest sponsored by the Teatro Hidalgo. Among his plays were *Los amores de Ramona, La asesina del martillo o la mujer tigresa* (1922), *Sangre yaqui* (1924), *La desgracia del pobre* (1926); and *La flor del fandango* (1928).

González, Genaro

b. Dec. 28, 1949
McAllen, Tex.
fields: Literature

Latino writer. Genaro González attended Pan American University in Edinburg, Texas, on a scholarship, as well as Pomona College, the University of California at Riverside, and the University of California at Santa Cruz, where he earned a master's degree and a doctorate in social psychology. He has taught at Pan American University and at the Universidad de las Americas in Mexico. While in college he wrote the short story "Un hijo del sol" (1971; child of the sun) and went on to write *Rainbow's End* (1988), which was nominated for the American Book Award. He also published such noteworthy works as *Only Sons* (1991) and *The Quixote Cult* (1998).

González, Henry Barbosa

b. May 3, 1916
San Antonio, Tex.
fields: Government and Politics, Civil Rights

Mexican American civil rights activist and politician; the first Mexican American to be elected to the Texas state senate (1956) in more than one hundred years, Henry Barbosa González gained national attention for his antisegregation and civil rights work; in 1960 he became the first Mexican American to represent Texas in Congress; in that capacity he rose to the position of chairman of the House Banking Committee. He retired in 1997.

González, José Luis

full: José Luis González Coiscou
b. Mar. 8, 1926
Santo Domingo, Dominican Republic
fields: Literature

Latino writer. José Luis González, whose family moved from the Dominican Republic to Puerto Rico when he was four, graduated from the University of Puerto Rico in 1946. As he student, he published two short-story collections that dealt with the lives of poor people. González studied at the New York School for Social Research in 1947. In 1948, he founded a socialist group in Puerto Rico and published the short-story collection *El hombre de la calle* (man in the street), which concerns the oppression of Puerto Ricans. While living in Mexico he published another collection, *En este lado* (1954; on this side).

González, José Victoriano. *See* Gris, Juan

González, Juan

b. Jan. 12, 1945
Camagüey, Cuba
d. December, 1993
New York, N.Y.
fields: Art

Artist. Juan González left Cuba in 1961 and studied art at the University of Miami in Florida, where he earned bachelor's and master's degrees in fine arts. He later moved to New York City. His art has been featured in solo and group exhibitions throughout the United States.

González, Myrtle

b. Sept. 28, 1891
Los Angeles, Calif.
d. 1919, Los Angeles
Calif.
fields: Theater and Entertainment

Latina actor. Myrtle González started acting in plays in Los Angeles at an early age. During her teenage years, she performed professionally with the Los Angeles Belasco Theater Company, and she went on to become the first Mexican American actress to play the lead in feature films in the United States. After her debut in *Ghosts* (1911), she appeared in more than forty Vitagraph and Universal Pictures films in six years, including *The Chalice of Courage* (1916) and her last film, *Captain Alvarez* (1917). She died from influenza at the age of twenty-seven.

Gonzalez, N. V. M.

full: Nestor Vicente Madali Gonzalez
b. Sept. 8, 1915
Romblon, Philippines
fields: Literature, Journalism, Education

Short-story writer N. V. M. Gonzalez began his career as a journalist in 1934. He published his first collection of short stories, *Seven Hills Away*, in 1947. He studied writing at Stanford University under Wallace Stegner in 1949, then joined the faculty at the University of the Philippines as a visiting lecturer and professor. In 1969, he became professor of English at California State University, Hayward, leaving to become international writer-in-residence at the University of the Philippines. His works include *Children of the Ash-Covered Loam and Other Stories* (1954), *The Bamboo Dancers* (1961), *Look, Stranger, on This Island Now* (1963), *Selected Stories* (1964), and *The Bread of Salt and Other Stories* (1993).

Gonzalez, Pancho

full: Richard Alonzo Gonzalez
b. May 9, 1928
Los Angeles, Calif.
d. July 3, 1995
Las Vegas, Nev.
fields: Sports (tennis player)

Mexican American tennis player; following victories at the U.S. National Championships (1948 and 1949), and capturing doubles titles at Wimbledon and the French Championship (1949; with Frank Parker), Pancho Gonzalez turned professional; largely untrained as a tennis player, he went on to win the U.S. Professional Championship eight times; from 1954 through 1961, Gonzalez held the top ranking in men's tennis; he won the World Professional Championship (1966), the Tournament of Champions (1969), and the World Series of Tennis (1971); elected to the National Lawn Tennis Hall of Fame in 1968; he became a successful trainer and coach after retiring from playing.

González, Pedro J.

b. 1895
northern Mexico
d. Mar. 17, 1995
Lodi, Calif.
fields: Social Reform

Latino radio personality. Pedro J. González served with Pancho Villa's forces in the Mexican Revolution, then moved to Los Angeles in 1923 with his wife. He became the first Spanish-speaking radio announcer in Los Angeles and had his own radio program called *Los Madrugadores* ("early risers"). In 1929, González protested the poor treatment of Mexican Americans and the massive deportation of Mexicans. His enemies fabricated enough evidence to convict him of the rape of a sixteen-year-old girl in 1934, for which he was sentenced to fifty years in prison. Six years later, the girl recanted her story and González was freed but was deported. he resumed his broadcasting career in Tijuana, Mexico. The film *Break of Dawn* (1988) was about his life.

González, Ray

b. Sept. 20, 1952
El Paso, Tex.
fields: Publishing, Literature

Latino editor and poet. In 1975, Ray González earned his bachelor's degree in creative writing from the University of Texas at El Paso. He moved to Colorado, where he taught writing and worked as the editor of the Latino newspaper *La Voz* (the voice) and the poetry editor of the *Bloomsbury Review*. He also began his own press, Mesilla, to promote the work of other poets. In 1988, he was awarded the Four Corners Book Award for Poetry and the Colorado Governor's Award for Excellence in the Arts. In 1989, he began serving as head of the Guadalupe Cultural Arts Center in San Antonio, Texas.

González-Irizarry, Aníbal

b. ?
Puerto Pico
fields: Journalism, Television

Broadcast journalist. When Aníbal González-Irizarry began broadcasting fifteen-minute news segments on the New York television show *El Show Hispano* (1952-1954), he became the first Hispanic television newscaster in the United States. He also worked as a disc jockey and a newscaster on two Spanish-language radio stations in New York City. In 1955, he returned to Puerto Rico and worked for more than twenty years as the most prominent and respected anchorman on Puerto Rican television.

González Parsons, Lucía

b. c. 1852
near Fort Worth, Tex.
d. 1942
fields: Social Reform

Latina labor leader. Lucía González Parsons, along with her husband, journalist Albert Parsons, was active in the Chicago labor movement and in the socialist party late in the nineteenth century. As a member of the Chicago Working Women's Union, she worked for women's rights. When Albert was convicted of being one of the eight leaders of the May 4, 1886, Haymarket Riot, González Parsons worked to save him and the others. The campaign failed, and they were executed. She later helped found the Industrial Workers of the World and the International Labor Defense.

Good Shouting Child. *See* Opothleyaholo

Goode, Eslanda Cardoza. *See* Robeson, Eslanda Cardoza Goode

Goode, Malvin R.

b. Feb. 13, 1908
White Plains, Va.
fields: Journalism

African American reporter. In 1962, Malvin R. Goode became the American Broadcasting Company (ABC) television network's first black reporter.

Goode, Sarah E.

b. fl. 1800's
fields: Historical Figure, Invention and Technology

African American inventor; born a slave, Sarah E. Goode became the most significant black female inventor of the nineteenth century; invented a folding cabinet bed (1885).

Goode, W. Wilson

full: Willie Wilson Goode
b. Aug. 19, 1938
Seaboard, N.C.
fields: Government and Politics

African American mayor of Philadelphia, Pa. In 1984, W. Wilson Goode became the first African American chief executive in the history of Philadelphia.

Gooden, Dwight

full: Dwight Eugene Gooden
aka: Doc Gooden
b. Nov. 11, 1964
Tampa, Fla.
fields: Sports (baseball player)

African American baseball player; in 1984, Pitcher Dwight Gooden became the youngest player in an All-Star game and the National League's youngest Rookie of the Year; in 1985 became youngest Cy Young Award winner; helped the New York Mets clinch their first World Series victory in seventeen years in 1986.

Goodman, Andrew

b. ?
d. June 21, 1964
Neshoba County, Miss.
fields: Civil Rights

Andrew Goodman was one of three civil rights workers murdered by members of the Ku Klux Klan in Mississippi in June, 1964. The outrage over their murders brought unprecedented publicity and pressure for the federal government to enforce civil rights of African Americans in the southern states. On October 20, 1967, an all-white Mississippi jury found seven men guilty of the murder, marking the first time a Mississippi jury ever found a white person guilty of crimes perpetrated on a black person or civil rights worker. After exhausting their appeals, the guilty men all served lengthy prison sentences at various federal penitentiaries.

Goodman, Benny

full: Benjamin David Goodman
b. May 30, 1909
Chicago, Illinois
d. June 13, 1986
New York, New York
fields: Music

A superb jazz clarinetist, Goodman led a series of outstanding dance bands that shaped the character of American swing music between 1935 and 1950.

Goodman, Nelson

full: Henry Nelson Goodman
b. August 7, 1906
Somerville, Massachusetts
fields: Philosophy, Art (aesthetics)

Nelson Goodman's wide range of interests in the philosophy of art, language, and science yielded influential studies of logic, epistemology, metaphysics, and symbolic systems, particularly in the realm of aesthetics. He attracted a large audience of nonspecialists with his humor, concision, and reliance on nontechnical language and commonsense examples, running most of his books through several editions. These include *The Structure of Appearance* (1951), *Fact, Fiction, and Forecast* (1954), *Languages of Art* (1968), *Problems and Projects* (1972), *Ways of Worldmaking* (1978), *Of Mind and Other Matters* (1984), *Reconceptions in Philosophy and Other Arts and Sciences* (1988, with Catherine Z. Elgin), and *A Study of Qualities* (1990).

Goodyear, Charles

b. December 29, 1800
New Haven, Connecticut
d. July 1, 1860
New York, New York
fields: Invention and Technology

Goodyear was the first man to vulcanize rubber, thereby rendering it usable for manufacturing numerous products.

Gorbachev, Mikhail

full: Mikhail Sergeyevich Gorbachev
b. March 2, 1931
Privolnoye, Soviet Union
fields: Government and Politics

Gorbachev, as general secretary of the Communist Party and also President of the Soviet Union, made efforts to implement major improvements in the economy and society, underscoring his genuine belief in the need for long-overdue reforms. The revisions and adjustments in Soviet foreign policy that occurred during the Gorbachev era are noteworthy.

Gorden, Fred Augustus

b. Feb. 22, 1940
Anniston, Ala.
fields: Military Affairs (military officer)

African American military officer; in 1989 Fred Augustus Gorden, winner of numerous military commendations, attained the rank of major general; appointed acting director of military personnel management in the office of the deputy chief of staff for personnel for the United States Army in 1992.

Gordimer, Nadine

b. November 20, 1923
Springs, near Johannesburg, South Africa
fields: Literature

Through her writings, Gordimer has illuminated the troubled history of South Africa with unparalleled clarity, sensitivity, honesty, and art.

Gordon, Charles George

b. January 28, 1833
Woolwich Common, England
d. January 26, 1885
Khartoum, the Sudan
fields: Military Affairs

All the associations one might make with a man of the British Empire during the Victorian age—soldier, statesman, and adventurer—were forcefully expressed in the life of Charles Gordon.

Gordon, Dexter

b. Feb. 27, 1923
Los Angeles, Calif.
d. Apr. 25, 1990
Philadelphia, Pa.
fields: Music (saxophonist, composer), Theater and Entertainment (actor)

African American tenor saxophonist, soprano saxophonist, composer, and actor; Dexter Gordon was one of the most significant bebop saxophonists, influencing musicians such as John Coltrane and Sonny Rollins; his most famous early solo was "Blowing the Blues Away"; recorded for Blue Note in the 1960's; received Academy Award nomination (best actor) for his role as an old jazz musician in *Round Midnight* (1986).

Gordon, Edwin Jason

b. Oct. 10, 1952
Cincinnati, Ohio
fields: Publishing

African American publishing executive; Edwin Jason Gordon was an editor for South-West Publishing and Harcourt Brace Jovanovich (1984) before becoming director of San Diego State University Press (1987-1989); left to become assistant director at Howard University Press.

Gordon, George. *See* Byron, Lord

Gordon, Juliette Magill Kinzie. *See* Low, Juliette Gordon

Gordon, Odetta Holmes Felious. *See* Odetta

Gordon, Ruth

né: Ruth Jones
b. October 30, 1896
Quincy, Massachusetts
d. August 28, 1985
Edgartown, Massachusetts
fields: Theater and Entertainment (drama), Film, Literature

A world-renowned actress, Ruth Gordon was also a playwright, film writer, and novelist. Her acting career included stage, film, and television.

Gordone, Charles

b. Oct. 12, 1925
Cleveland, Ohio
d. Nov. 17, 1995
College Station, Texas
fields: Theater and Entertainment, Literature

African American playwright, actor, director, and producer. In 1970 Charles Gordone was the first African American playwright to receive the Pulitzer Prize for drama, for his play, *No Place to Be Somebody* (1969), which also won the Drama Desk Award and the Critics Circle Award.

Gordy, Berry, Jr.

b. Nov. 28, 1929
Detroit, Mich.
fields: Music, Business and Industry

African American songwriter, producer; Berry Gordy, Jr., served with U.S. Army in Korea (1951-1953); after a number of failed or unsatisfying jobs in Detroit, Michigan, began writing hit songs with his sister Gwen and Billy Davis; formed Motown Record Corporation and a number of related businesses in 1959; by the mid-1960's had brought black soul music to mainstream American audiences with highly polished performances by artists such as the Supremes, Smokey Robinson, the Four Tops, the Marvelettes, Marvin Gaye, the Jackson Five, Lionel Richie, and Stevie Wonder; inducted into the Rock and Roll Hall of Fame in 1988.

Gordy, Kennedy W. *See* Rockwell

Gore, Al

full: Albert Arnold Gore, Jr.
b. March 31, 1948
Washington, D.C.
fields: Government and Politics

Gore has been involved in national government for more than twenty years. He has gained a reputation as an able legislator and effective executive as U.S. vice president. His particular policy contributions have been in the areas of nuclear disarmament, environmental improvements, government efficiency, and government policy with regard to electronic communications.

Gore, Tipper

né: Mary Elizabeth Aitcheson
b. 1949
Arlington, Va.
fields: Government and Politics, Photography

Wife of U.S. vice president Albert Gore, Jr. Tipper Gore is recognized as a photojournalist, writer, and political activist; in 1985 campaigned against sex, drugs, and violence in rock lyrics, calling for the rock industry to label sexually explicit records; published *Raising Kids in an X-Rated Society* (1987), advising parents on how to fight objectionable popular culture; along with other Washington political wives, formed the Parents' Music Resource Center to distribute information to schools and law-enforcement groups; published *Picture This: A Visual Diary* (1996), a collection of photos she took during the 1992 presidential campaign.

Gorenko, Anna Andreyevna. *See* Akhmatova, Anna

Gorgas, William Crawford

b. October 3, 1854
Toulminville, Alabama
d. July 4, 1920
London, England
fields: Public Health

Gorgas, a dedicated humanitarian, led the effort that eliminated yellow fever as one of the major epidemic diseases throughout the world. This feat was accomplished through the diligent and practical application of scientific discoveries concerning the disease.

Göring, Hermann

full: Hermann Wilhelm Göring
b. January 12, 1893
Rosenheim, Germany
d. October 15, 1946
Nürnberg, Germany
fields: Military Affairs, Government and Politics

Göring, a highly decorated fighter pilot in World War I who cultivated contacts with conservative-nationalist elements in Germany before 1933, contributed to Adolf Hitler's rise to power and played a major role in his consolidation of power. After 1935, Göring directed both the massive rebuilding of the German air force and economic efforts to prepare Germany for war. One of the most powerful leaders of the Third Reich until 1942, and Hitler's designated successor, Göring was tried and convicted at Nürnberg in 1946 for his part in the crimes of the Third Reich.

Gorky, Maxim

né: Aleksey Maksimovich Peshkov
b. March 28, 1868
Nizhni Novgorod, Russia

d. June 18, 1936
Gorki, near Moscow, U.S.S.R.
fields: Literature, Social Reform

Gorky is recognized as the founding father of Soviet literature, influencing the development of the Soviet short story and the proletarian novel and drama. His reminiscences of both Anton Chekhov and Leo Tolstoy give valuable, insightful observations about two older contemporaries. Equally important is his contribution to the Bolshevik revolutionary movement as one of its chief supporters and journalists. Because of his close associations with Vladimir Ilich Lenin, Leon Trotsky, and Joseph Stalin, he became the official cultural spokesman for the new government.

Gorman, R. C.

b. July 26, 1933
Chinle, Ariz.
fields: Art

Navajo artist R. C. Gorman was one of the most commercially successful Indian painters. Altered the non-Indian standard of Indian art. He was the first Indian artist to own a gallery. Apolitical images of strong, large women strolling or sitting, often with a child or pottery, drawn with a single line, are his hallmark.

Gorme, Eydie

full: Edith Gorme
b. Aug. 16, 1932
Bronx, N.Y.
fields: Music (singer)

Latina singer. Eydie Gorme first sang on the radio at the age of three. She starred in several school musicals while attending William Taft High School. In 1953, she signed a recording contract with Coral. By the following year she had become a regular on *The Tonight Show*. She married Steve Lawrence on December 29, 1957, and they became a popular club act. Gorme released the single "Blame It on the Bossa Nova" in 1963 with a Latin rhythm. Gorme and Lawrence received Emmy Awards for their television specials, and Gorme won the 1967 Grammy Award as Best Female Vocalist for "If He Walked into My Life." Gorme and Lawrence continued to appear in concert and on television into the 1990's.

Gorton, John Grey

b. September 9, 1911
Melbourne, Victoria, Australia
fields: Government and Politics

John Grey Gorton was prime minister of Australia between 1968 and 1971. Limited number of Australian troops sent to Vietnam, discouraged overseas investment, and extended the federal government's role in education.

Gosset, William Sealy

b. June 13, 1876
Canterbury, England
d. Oct. 16, 1937
Beaconsfield, England
fields: Mathematics (statistics)

William Sealy Gosset established the t-test, which analyzes data from experiments with small numbers of runs.

Gossett, Louis, Jr.

b. May 27, 1936
Brooklyn, N.Y.
fields: Film, Theater and Entertainment (actor)

African American actor; Louis Gossett, Jr.'s credits include stage, film, and television performances; won the Donaldson Award as best newcomer of 1953; made his film debut in the screen adaptation of *A Raisin in the Sun* (1961); performed in Off-Broadway plays such as *The Blacks* (1961), *Tambourines to Glory* (1963), and *The Blood Knot*; was cast in the televison adaptation of *Roots* (1977); won an Academy Award (best supporting actor) for *An Officer and a Gentleman* (1982); founded the Gossett Academy of Dramatic Arts (GADA) and LoGo Entertainment.

Gotanda, Philip Kan

b. Dec. 17, 1949
Stockton, Calif.
fields: Theater and Entertainment, Film

Philip Kan Gotanda, a preeminent Asian American playwright and theater director, is most widely acclaimed for his Japanese American family sagas. Gotanda's first play, *The Avocado Kid*, was based on the Japanese folktale of Momotaro, a boy found inside a peach. His other plays and musicals include *A Song for a Nisei Fisherman* (pr. 1982), *The Wash* (pr. 1986), *Yankee Dawg You Die* (pr. 1988), *Fish Head Soup* (pr. 1991), and *Day Standing on Its Head* (pr. 1993). He wrote the screenplay for the 1989 film version of *The Wash*, and wrote and directed *The Kiss* (1993).

Gothardt, Matthias. *See* Grünewald, Matthias

Goto, Yasuo Baron

b. Nov. 20, 1901
Japan
d. Nov. 19, 1985
Honolulu, Hawaii
fields: Business and Industry

Yasuo Baron Goto was an agriculture expert and a vice chancellor of the Institute for Technical Interchange at the East-West Center in Honolulu, from 1962 to 1969. Before joining the East-West Center, he headed the Hawaii Agricultural Extension service. A professor of agriculture at the University of Hawaii, he helped many Third World economies with agricultural development and served on the boards of many businesses and organizations.

Gottfried von Strassburg

b. fl. c. 1210
Alsace?
d. Date unknown
place unknown
fields: Literature

Gottfried was one of the great writers of the German courtly epic during the High Middle Ages.

Gottschalk, Louis Moreau

b. May 8, 1829
New Orleans, La.
d. Dec. 18, 1869
Rio de Janeiro, Brazil
fields: Music (composer, pianist)

African American composer and pianist; Louis Moreau Gottschalk played "creole" compositions, the precursor of ragtime and jazz.

Gou Bourgell, José

b. ?
Cataluña, Spain
fields: Literature, Journalism

Latino playwright and journalist. José Gou Bourgell worked in Los Angeles and the Calexico area near the border between the United States and Mexico from 1924 to 1937. Among his plays were *La mancha roja* (1924), *El crimen de la virtud* (1924), *El parricida* (1926), *El suicida* (1927), and *Virginidades* (1928). Gou Bourgell also worked as a journalist for the newspaper *El Heraldo de México* in Los Angeles and served as editor of *La Voz* and *El Mundo al Día* in Calexico.

Gould, Stephen Jay

b. Sept. 10, 1941
New York, New York
fields: Biology, Science

Stephen Jay Gould published widely on the origins and diversity of life on Earth; his theory of punctuated equilibrium, a deviation from Darwinism, was highly controversial in the 1970's.

Goulden, Emmeline. *See* Pankhurst, Emmeline

Gounod, Charles

full: Charles-François Gounod
b. June 18, 1818
Paris, France

d. October 18, 1893
St. Cloud, France
fields: Music

Because of his great popularity and stylistic influence on the next generation of composers, Gounod is often considered to be the central figure in French music in the third quarter of the nineteenth century.

Gourdin, Edward Orval

b. Aug. 10, 1897
Jacksonville, Fla.
d. July 21, 1966
Quincy, Mass.
fields: Sports (long jumper)

African American long jumper; in 1921 Edward Orval Gourdin became the first athlete in history to jump more than twenty-five feet in a college international meet; won a silver medal in the 1924 Olympics.

Gourdine, Meredith C.

b. September 26, 1929
Newark, New Jersey
fields: Invention and Technology, Physics

Physicist and engineer; after working as a senior research scientist at the Jet Propulsion Laboratory (JPL), as a laboratory director at Plasmadyne Corporation, and as a chief scientist at Curtiss-Wright Corporation, Meredith C. Gourdine founded his own research and development company, Gourdine Systems (1964-1973) and conducted pioneering research in electrogasdynamics, the conversion of gas to electricity for energy use; among his almost seventy patented inventions are the "Incineraid," which removes smoke from buildings, and a technique for dispersing fog on airport runways; in 1974 he founded the Houston-based company Energy Innovations.

Gourdine, Simon Peter

b. July 30, 1940
Jersey City, N.J.
fields: Law (attorney)

African American attorney; from the 1970's to the 1990's, Simon Peter Gourdine held positions as deputy commisioner of the National Basketball Association (NBA), commissioner of the New York City Department of Consumer Affairs, secretary for the Rockefeller Foundation, and director of labor relations for the New York City Transit Authority.

Gouzenko, Igor Sergeievich

b. 1917
Ottawa, Ontario, Canada
d. June 29, 1982
fields: Government and Politics

Igor Sergeievich Gouzenko was a Soviet government intelligence officer who defected to Canada and exposed a Soviet espionage network. His case caused a public sensation in Canada, raising suspicions that Canadian, American, and British citizens had collaborated with Soviet agents. He lived the rest of his life in seclusion, appearing in public only under the protection of a mask.

Goya, Francisco de

b. March 30, 1746
Fuendetodos, Spain
d. April 16, 1828
Bordeaux, France
fields: Art

A painter and engraver, Goya was not only one of Spain's greatest artists but also one of Western art's most original practitioners. His aesthetic range was so comprehensive that he anticipated all the major artistic schools from the French Romantics to the German Expressionists.

Goyathlay. *See* Geronimo

Graca, Marcelino Manoel de. *See* Grace, Sweet Daddy

Gracchus, Gaius Sempronius

b. 153 B.C.E.
probably Rome
d. 121 B.C.E.
Rome
fields: Government and Politics

Although the Gracchi brothers, Tiberius and Gaius, were born into one of the wealthiest and most influential families in Rome, they dedicated their lives to the service of the people. In the waning years of the Roman Republic, when greed and the lust for power consumed the energies of many from the ruling class, the Gracchi tried through a series of reforms to restore the vigor of popular government; many of their ideas were later adopted by rulers such as Julius Caesar and his nephew and heir, Augustus.

Gracchus, Tiberius Sempronius

b. 163 B.C.E.
probably Rome
d. 133 B.C.E.
Rome
fields: Government and Politics

Although the Gracchi brothers, Tiberius and Gaius, were born into one of the wealthiest and most influential families in Rome, they dedicated their lives to the service of the people. In the waning years of the Roman Republic, when greed and the lust for power consumed the energies of many from the ruling class, the Gracchi tried through a series of reforms to restore the vigor of popular government; many of their ideas were later adopted by rulers such as Julius Caesar and his nephew and heir, Augustus.

Grace, Sweet Daddy

né: Marcelino Manoel de Graca
aka: Charles Emmanuel Grace
b. Jan. 25, 1881
Brava, Cape Verde Islands
d. Jan. 12, 1960
Los Angeles, Calif.
fields: Religion and Theology

African American religious leader; Charles Emmanuel "Sweet Daddy" Grace established the United House of Prayer for All People, with ministry style rooted in faith healing and speaking in tongues around 1921; products such as "Daddy Grace" coffee, tea, and creams were believed to heal; by 1960, his church had some 25,000 adherents in 375 congregations.

Grace, William Gilbert

b. July 18, 1848
Downend, Gloucestershire, England
d. October 23, 1915
Eltham, Kent, England
fields: Sports

Grace's brilliance as a player, coupled with his immense personal popularity, consolidated cricket's position as England's national game. He became a symbol of the manly competitiveness which Victorians regarded as an essential element in the British character.

Gracia, Gilberto Concepción de. *See* Concepción de Gracia, Gilberto

Graham, Billy

full: William Franklin Graham, Jr.
b. November 7, 1918
near Charlotte, North Carolina
fields: Diplomacy, Religion and Theology

Friend and confidante of presidents, popes, and world figures, Billy Graham stands as the twentieth century's best-known and most effective evangelist as well as a rigorous, though unofficial, diplomat. His mass meetings, attended by hundreds of thousands of individuals and televised to reach millions more, have presented the tenets of Christianity on a worldwide scale.

Graham, Florence Nightingale. *See* Arden, Elizabeth

Graham, Gordon

b. 1936
Coshocton, Ohio
fields: Journalism, Television

African American television broadcaster; Gordon Graham's news career started at Los Angeles radio station KGFJ; he began covering the House of Representatives for NBC News in 1971.

Graham, Katharine

né: Katharine Meyer
b. June 16, 1917
New York, New York
fields: Publishing, Journalism

The only woman to serve as publisher of a major American newspaper during the twentieth century, Graham built *The Washington Post* into a national institution and helped bring down an American president. Her paper won numerous Pulitzer prizes over the years, including for its work on the Watergate scandal, but she also won the 1998 Pulitzer Prize for nonfiction with her autobiography, *Personal History*.

Graham, Lawrence Otis

b. December 25, 1962
New York, N.Y.
fields: Literature (attorney, educator, and author)

African American attorney, educator, and author; Lawrence Otis Graham published *Member of the Club: Reflections on Life in a Racially Polarized World* (1995) and *Our Kind of People* (1999).

Graham, Martha

b. May 11, 1894
Allegheny, Pennsylvania
d. April 1, 1991
New York, New York
fields: Dance

Graham is generally accepted as the greatest single figure in American modern dance.

Gramm, Phil

full: William Philip Gramm
b. July 8, 1942
Fort Benning, Ga.
fields: Government and Politics

U.S. senator and presidential candidate. Gramm was elected a U.S. Congressman from Texas as a Democrat in 1978. After a dispute with House Speaker Tip O'Neill, he resigned his seat in 1983 and won reelection as a Republican. In 1984, he was elected to the Senate for the first time. He was a major proponent of the proposed Gramm-Rudman-Hollings balanced-budget amendment, and he contended for the 1996 Republican presidential nomination.

Gramm, Wendy Lee

b. Jan. 10, 1945
Waialua, Territory of Hawaii
fields: Economics, Education, Government and Politics

Korean American Wendy Lee Gramm was on the faculty of Texas A&M University. In 1978, her husband, Philip Gramm, was elected to the House of Representatives. Gramm joined her husband in Washington, D.C., where she accepted a research position with the Institute for Defense Analyses, a Washington-based think tank. She went to work for the Federal Trade Commission in 1982, becoming director of the commission's Bureau of Economics in 1983. She became a Republican in 1983, served as administrator of the Office of Information and Regulatory Affairs at the Office of Management and Budget from 1985 to 1987, and chair of the Commodity Futures Trading Commission beginning in 1988. Resigning from the Commission in 1993, she became a board member of the Chicago Mercantile Exchange.

Gramsci, Antonio

b. January 23, 1891
Ales, Sardinia, Italy
d. April 27, 1937
Rome, Italy
fields: Government and Politics, Political Science

Gramsci gave modern social and political theory and the study of history a new method of social analysis with his writings on culture and hegemony. He was one of the first European communists to establish the theoretical foundations for a Western Marxism free of reliance on the Soviet Union. Gramsci was himself an active revolutionary who produced his most influential work during an eleven-year imprisonment under Benito Mussolini.

Granger, Lester Blackwell

b. Sept. 16, 1896
Newport News, Va.
d. Jan. 9, 1976
Alexandria, La.
fields: Government and Politics

African American government official; from 1941 to 1961, Lester Blackwell Granger was the executive director of the National Urban League.

Grant, Micki

né: M. Louise Perkins
b. June 30, 19??
Chicago, Ill.
fields: Music (composer and singer)

African American composer and singer; Micki Grant's credits include writing the lyrics for the Broadway play *Don't Bother Me, I Can't Cope* (1971), and cowriting the play *Your Arms Too Short to Box with God.*

Grant, Ulysses S.

né: Hiram Ulysses Grant
aka: Ulysses Hiram Grant
b. April 27, 1822
Point Pleasant, Ohio
d. July 23, 1885
Mount McGregor, New York
fields: Government and Politics, Military Affairs

President of the United States, 1869-1877. Grant became the preeminent general of the Civil War, demonstrating the persistence and strategic genius that brought about the victory of the North.

Granville, Evelyn Boyd

b. May 1, 1924
Washington, D.C.
fields: Mathematics, Education

African American mathematician; Evelyn Boyd Granville is noted as one of the first two African American women to earn a Ph.D. in pure mathematics (Yale University, 1949); she worked at spacecraft trajectory and orbit calculations for IBM (1956-1960, 1963), and worked in the group that developed computer programs to compute the orbits of spacecraft at the Computation and Data Reduction Center of Space Technology Laboratories in Los Angeles (1960-1962); served as a member of the mathematics faculty at California State University, Los Angeles (1967-1984); taught at Texas College (1985-1988).

Grass, Günter

b. October 16, 1927
Danzig, Germany
fields: Literature

Grass is to be considered one of the leading figures of German literature since 1945. His writings address social and political issues in a unique manner, and he has consistently stressed the relationship between the artist and society.

Grass, John

aka: Pezi (Grass Field)
aka: Mato Watakpe (Charging Bear)
b. c. 1837
d. May 10, 1918
Standing Rock Reservation, N.Dak.
fields: Government and Politics, Diplomacy, Native American Affairs

John Grass, a Teton Sioux, was a diplomat and political leader of the Sioux during their long struggle against the United States. In an attempt to break Sitting Bull's influence over the Sioux, Indian Agent Major James ("White Hair") McLaughlin set up Grass, Gall, and other Sioux as rival chiefs to Sitting Bull after the latter had surrendered in 1881. For more than three decades, Grass served as head judge in the Court of Indian Offenses of the Standing Rock Reservation.

Gravely, Samuel L., Jr.

b. June 4, 1922
Richmond, Va.
fields: Military Affairs (naval officer)

Naval officer. In 1971, Gravely became the first African American admiral in the U.S. Navy. He earned a B.A. degree in history from Virginia Union University in 1948 and began his naval career in the Naval Reserve, transferring to full-time duty in 1955. He retired in 1980.

Graves, Earl

full: Earl G. Graves, Sr.
b. Jan. 9, 1935
Brooklyn, N.Y.
fields: Business and Industry, Publisher

African American publisher, editor, entrepreneur; Earl Graves was an officer in the, U.S. Army Green Berets, 1957-1960; administrative assistant to Robert F. Kennedy, 1964-1968; launched *Black Enterprise* (1970) to provide African Americans with practical help for succeeding in business; by the late 1990's, *Black Enterprise* had a subscription base of more than 300,000; member of the national Council for Business Opportunity; trustee of the Tuskegee Institute; wrote *How to Succeed in Business Without Being White* (1997).

Graves, Teresa

b. 1949
Houston, Tex.
fields: Film, Theater and Entertainment (actor)

African American actor; Teresa Graves, best known for her television series *Get Christie Love!* (1974-1975), first appeared on *Rowan and Martin's Laugh-In* (1969-1970); her films credits included *That Man Bolt* (1973) and *Black Eye* (1974).

Gray, Asa

b. November 18, 1810
Sauquoit, New York
d. January 30, 1888
Cambridge, Massachusetts
fields: Science

The leading botanical taxonomist in nineteenth century United States and the founder of the discipline of plant geography, Gray was the first advocate of Darwinian evolution in the United States.

Gray, Frizell. *See* Mfume, Kweisi

Gray, Herbert

full: Herbert Eser Gray
b. May 25, 1931
Windsor, Ontario, Canada
fields: Government and Politics

Long-time Liberal member of Canada's Parliament. Herbert Gray held many cabinet posts. Was minister of industry, trade, and commerce (1980 to 1982), solicitor general (1993-1997), and deputy prime minister (beginning 1997). The 1971 Gray Report examined and criticized the amount of control the U.S. was exerting over the Canadian economy.

Gray, Horace

b. 1828
d. 1902
fields: Law

U.S. Supreme Court justice, 1882-1902 (died while in office); appointed by President Arthur. Significant opinions: *Sparf v. Hansen*, 156 U.S. 51 (1895); *United States v. Wong Kim Ark*, 169 U.S. 649 (1898).

Gray, John

b. 1951
Houston, Tex.
fields: Psychiatry and Psychology, Sociology

The author of popular psychology self-help books and a seminar leader and lecturer, John Gray explored practical communication between the sexes. He also had commercial success with such books as *What Your Mother Couldn't Tell You and Your Father Didn't Know* (1994) and *Men, Women, and Relationships: Making Peace with the Opposite Sex* (1993). He is best known for *Men Are from Mars, Women Are from Venus* (1992), followed by *Mars and Venus in Love* (1996), *Mars and Venus Together Forever* (1996), *Mars and Venus in the Bedroom* (1997), and *Mars and Venus on a Date* (1997).

Gray, William H., III

b. Aug. 20, 1941
Baton Rouge, La.
fields: Government and Politics

African American U.S. representative; William H. Gray III took his seat in January of 1979; held appointments on the House Committee on Foreign Affairs, the House Committee on the District of Columbia, and the House Budget Committee; was elected chairman of the House Democratic Caucus (1988) and House Majority Whip (1989), becoming the highest-ranking African American representative in Congress; accepted later position as president of the United Negro College Fund.

Great Sun

b. ?
d. c. 1730
fields: Government and Politics, Native American Affairs

Native American leader. Among the Natchez, "Great Sun" was the hereditary title bestowed upon the tribe's principal chief. The Great Sun who is known to history was the leader of the Natchez Revolt of 1729. In the aftermath of the revolt, the tribal identity of the Natchez was destroyed.

Greco, El

né: Doménikos Theotokópoulos
aka: Il Greco
b. 1541
Candia, Crete
d. April 7, 1614
Toledo, Spain
fields: Art

Adapting principles he learned in Venice and Rome, El Greco achieved a unique artistic style and became Spain's greatest religious artist and one of the world's foremost portrait painters.

Greeley, Horace

b. February 3, 1811
Amherst, New Hampshire
d. November 29, 1872
New York, New York
fields: Journalism, Social Reform

A daring journalist and lecturer, Greeley engaged himself personally with a wide range of social issues—labor rights, abolitionism, territorial expansion, women's rights, and political reform—and his paper, the *New York Tribune*, became a medium for the best thought of his time.

Green, Al

b. Apr. 13, 1946
Forest City, Ark.
fields: Music (singer, songwriter)

African American singer and songwriter; during the 1970's, Al Green was one of the most successful soul music vocalists; hit songs and albums included "Tired of Being Alone" (1971) and "Let's Stay Together" (1971), *Call Me* (1973), and *Al Green Is Love* (1975); became a pastor and gospel music performer in the late 1970's; *The Belle Album* (1977) displayed his transitional work.

Green, Chuck

full: Charles Green
b. 1919?
near Atlanta, Ga.
d. Mar. 7, 1997
Oakland, Calif.
fields: Dance (tap dancer)

African American tap dancer; Chuck Green performed throughout the United States during the 1940's as half of the comedy tap duo, Chuck and Chuckles.

Green, Clifford Scott

b. Apr. 2, 1923
Philadelphia, Pa.
fields: Law (judge)

African American judge; In 1971, Clifford Scott Green became a U.S. district judge in Pennsylvania.

Green, Darrell

b. Feb. 15, 1960
Houston, Tex.
fields: Sports (football player)

African American football player; Darrell Green played in the Pro Bowl in 1984, 1986, 1987, 1990, and 1991; was part of a 4 × 100-meter relay team that set a world record at the World Championships in Helsinki, Finland, in 1983; won a gold medal in the same event at the 1984 Olympics.

Green, Dennis

b. February 17, 1949
Harrisburg, Pa.
fields: Sports (college and professional football coach)

African American college and professional football coach; in 1982, while coaching at Northwestern University, Dennis Green was named Big Ten Coach of the Year; worked as the receivers coach for the San Francisco 49ers from 1986 to 1988; from 1989 to 1992 was head coach of the football program at Stanford University; in 1992 became the head coach of the Minnesota Vikings of the National Football League (NFL).

Green, Ernest G.

b. Sept. 22, 1941
Little Rock, Ark.
fields: Banking and Finance, Government and Politics

African American investment banker and political appointee. Ernest G. Green was one of the "Little Rock Nine" who enrolled in Central High School in 1957 and one of only four to get his diploma. He was appointed by President Jimmy Carter to serve as assistant secretary for employment and training at the Department of Labor (1977-1981) and pursued a career in investment banking.

Green, George

b. July 14, 1793
Baptized in Sneinton, Nottingham, England
d. May 31, 1841
Sneinton, Nottingham, England
fields: Mathematics (applied math)

George Green published *An Essay on the Application of Mathematical Analysis to the Theories of Electricity and Magnetism* in 1828, providing much of the modern mathematical foundation for the theory of electricity and magnetism. Responsible for Green's theorem of multivariable calculus.

Green, Henry Morgan

b. Aug. 26, 1876
Georgia
d. 1939
fields: Medicine

African American physician; from 1921 to 1922, Henry Morgan Green was president of the National Medical Association; helped found the National Hospital Association in 1923.

Green, Katie Beatrice. *See* Hall, Katie Beatrice Green

Green, Thomas Hill

b. April 7, 1836
Birkin, Yorkshire, England
d. March 26, 1882
Oxford, England
fields: Philosophy, Education

Green was both a theorist and a reformer who established the Idealist school of philosophy at Oxford, contributed political ideas that facilitated the movement away from Liberalism, and was a powerful advocate of educational reform.

Greene, Graham

b. October 2, 1904
Berkhamsted, Hertfordshire, England
d. April, 1991
Vevey, Switzerland
fields: Literature

Combining a fascination with the nature of good and evil in the contemporary world and a masterful ability to develop exciting plots about complex yet believable characters caught in real-life situations, Greene created a body of fiction which enjoys a critical and popular appeal unique in twentieth century literature.

Greene, Mean Joe

full: Charles Edward Greene
b. Sept. 24, 1946
Temple, Tex.
fields: Sports (football player)

African American football player; from 1969 to 1981, Mean Joe Greene was a defensive tackle for the Pittsburgh Steelers; was Defensive Rookie of the Year in 1969; led the Steelers to four Super Bowl victories; named to the Pro Football Hall of Fame in 1987.

Greene, Nathanael

b. August 7, 1742
Potowomut, Rhode Island
d. June 19, 1786
Mulberry Grove plantation, Georgia
fields: Military Affairs

Greene was one of George Washington's most trusted subordinates throughout the Revolutionary War, playing a significant role both as a field commander and as the Continental army's quartermaster general.

Greener, Richard

b. 1844
Philadelphia, Pa.
d. May 2, 1922
Chicago, Ill.
fields: Education, Diplomacy, Law, Government and Politics

African American educator, politician, diplomat, and lawyer; in 1870 Richard Greener was the first African American to graduate from Harvard University; he later became dean of law at Howard University and associate editor of *The New National Era*.

Greenfield, Elizabeth Taylor

b. c. 1819
Natchez, Miss.
d. Mar. 31, 1876
Philadelphia, Pa.
fields: Music (concert singer)

African American concert singer; former slave Elizabeth Taylor Greenfield is believed to be the earliest African American concert singer; her New York City debut in 1853 led to a command performance before Queen Victoria in 1854.

Greenlee, Sam

b. July 13, 1930
Chicago, Ill.
fields: Literature

African American author; Sam Greenlee wrote *The Spook Who Sat by the Door* (1969), which earned the British Press Book of the Year Award; other works include *Blues for an African Princess* (1970) and a four-volume autobiography: *D'Jokarta Blues*, *Bagdad Blues*, *Mykonos Blues*, and *Babylon Blues* (1988-1989).

Greenspan, Alan

b. March 6, 1926
New York, New York
fields: Economics, Government and Politics

As chairman of the U.S. Federal Reserve Board, Alan Greenspan has worked to balance economic growth, employment rates, and inflation.

Greenway, Francis

full: Francis Howard Greenway
b. November 20, 1777
Mangotsfield, England
d. September 26, 1837
East Maitland, Australia
fields: Architecture

Although surrounded by controversy, Greenway attempted to legitimate and regulate building practices in Australia during the period when it was regarded as a penal colony. More important, however, he gave to the early buildings aesthetically unique designs combining both beauty and practicality.

Greer, Edward

b. Mar. 8, 1924
Gary, W.Va.
fields: Military Affairs

African American military officer; commissioned as a second lieutenant in 1948, Edward Greer commanded the First Battalion in Korea, the 108th Artillery Group in Vietnam (1970-1971), and was promoted to the rank of major general in 1972; awarded the Silver Star, the Legion of Merit, and the Bronze Star.

Greer, Germaine

b. Jan. 29, 1939
near Melbourne, Australia
fields: Women's Rights

Germaine Greer is known as a feminist writer and critic; first and best-known book is *The Female Eunuch* (1970), one of the bibles of the resurgent feminist movement of the 1960's and 1970's, which describes all women as deformed by the demands of male-dominated society; became director of the Tulsa Center for the Study of Women's Literature in Oklahoma in 1979; in 1992, published *The Change: Women, Aging, and the Menopause*, a major study of the social and psychological effects of menopause.

Gregory VII

né: Hildebrand
b. c. 1020
Sanoa, Tuscany
d. May 25, 1085
Salerno
fields: Religion and Theology, Church Government

Pope Gregory VII, 1073-1085. As the dominant figure in the medieval Papacy, Gregory VII launched a wave of reform which brought about much of the structure of the modern Roman Catholic church. His clash with Henry IV was merely the first in a series of struggles between the lords spiritual and temporal which characterized the Middle Ages.

Gregory IX

né: Ugo of Segni
aka: Ugolino of Segni
b. c. 1170
Anagni, Italy
d. August 22, 1241
Rome, Italy
fields: Religion and Theology, Scholarship

Pope Gregory IX, 1227-1241. With perseverance, courage, and conviction, under difficult circumstances, Gregory IX defended the Church from every perceived threat, encouraging spiritual life and learning within its structure, particularly in canon law.

Gregory, Dick

full: Richard Claxton Gregory
b. October 12, 1932
St. Louis, Missouri
fields: Theater and Entertainment; Civil Rights

A stand-up comedian who promoted civil rights causes in his nightclub acts and college speeches before becoming a prominent civil rights activist. Dick Gregory's involvement in the Civil Rights movement, antiwar campaign, and political arena won him national acclaim.

Gregory, Frederick Drew

b. Jan. 7, 1941
Washington, D.C.
fields: Aviation and Space Exploration

African American astronaut; Frederick Drew Gregory's first mission was pilot of the space shuttle *Challenger* (Apr. 29, 1985); commanded the shuttles *Discovery* (1989) and *Atlantis* (1991); awarded the NASA Outstanding Leadership Award, the Defense Superior Service Medal, two Distinguished Flying Crosses, and sixteen Air Medals; recipient of the National Society of Black Engineers Distinguished National Scientist Award (1979).

Gregory of Nazianzus

b. 329 or 330
Arianzus, Cappadocia
d. 389 or 390
Arianzus, Cappadocia
fields: Oratory, Literature, Religion and Theology

A consummate rhetorician, Gregory produced many orations, poems, and letters which provide much information on the religious and social life of Christianity in the second half of the fourth century. As a theologian, Gregory was influential in the formulation of orthodox doctrine regarding the divinity of the Holy Spirit.

Gregory of Nyssa

b. c. 335
Caesarea, Cappadocia
d. c. 394
Constantinople
fields: Religion and Theology

A profound thinker and theologian, as well as an eloquent preacher, Gregory was one of the brilliant leaders of Christian orthodoxy in the late fourth century. His influence led to the defeat of the Arian heresy and the triumph of the orthodox Nicene position at the Council of Constantinople in 381.

Gregory of Tours

né: Georgius Florentius
aka: Gregory, Bishop of Tours
b. November 30, 539
Auvergne
d. November 17, 594
Tours
fields: Historiography

Gregory provided historians with their prime source of information on Merovingian Gaul for the years 575-591; he also contributed to the Christian tradition an example of living in accord with the best principles of the Church.

Gregory the Great

aka: Saint Gregory I
b. c. 540
Rome, Italy
d. March 12, 604
Rome, Italy
fields: Religion and Theology, Government and Politics, Monasticism

Bishop of Rome and Pope, 590-604. By example and direction, Gregory set the basic patterns for the medieval church of Central and Western Europe in the areas of pastoral administration, interpretation of the Bible, and liturgical usage. He was directly responsible for sending missionaries to England and the consequent organization of the medieval English church. This evangelistic effort was to serve as a model for later missionary activity.

Grenville, Richard

aka: Sir Richard Grenville
b. c. June 15, 1542
Buckland Abbey?, Devonshire, England
d. c. September 3, 1591
at sea, off Flores, the Azores
fields: Military Affairs

Grenville's heroic death in battle against an overwhelming fleet was an inspiration to Elizabethan Englishmen in their war against a powerful Spanish Empire.

Grey, Edward

aka: Sir Edward Grey
aka: Edward, third baronet and viscount Grey of Fallodon
b. April 25, 1862
London, England
d. September 7, 1933
Fallodon, Northumberland, England
fields: Government and Politics

As foreign secretary for more than a decade (1905-1916), Grey set the course of British policy before and during the early years of World War I.

Grey, George Edward

aka: Sir George Edward Grey

b. April 14, 1812
Lisbon, Portugal
d. September 19, 1898
London, England
fields: Government and Politics

Grey, one of the great proconsuls of the British Empire, fused the arrogant, autocratic, decisive man of action with eclectic, radical, and democratic beliefs. He had a particularly profound influence on settlement, political developments, native policy, and ethnography, on three colonial frontiers: South Africa, South Australia, and, most important, New Zealand.

Grey, Jane

aka: Lady Jane Grey
b. October, 1537
Leicestershire, England
d. February 12, 1554
London, England
fields: Monarchy

Queen of England for nine days in 1553. Had her reign as queen of England been fully legal and more lengthy, Jane Grey would have been England's first ruling queen and likely a successful monarch.

Grey, Second Earl

né: Charles Grey
full: Charles, Second Earl Grey
b. March 13, 1764
Fallodon, Northumberland, England
d. July 17, 1845
Howick, Northumberland, England
fields: Government and Politics

Grey recognized that parliamentary reform was necessary in order to maintain the ascendancy of the aristocracy in a rapidly changing English society. He led the government which passed the Reform Bill of 1832.

Grice, Francis

b. ?
Port-au-Prince, Haiti
fields: Photography

African American photographer; Francis Grice was a daguerreotype photographer beginning in the 1850's.

Grieg, Edvard

b. June 15, 1843
Bergen, Norway
d. September 4, 1907
Bergen, Norway
fields: Music

Drawing on Norwegian folk culture for inspiration, Grieg created an original, distinctive music of Romantic nationalism that made him the foremost composer in Norway and the first Scandinavian composer to achieve world renown.

Grier, Pam

b. May 26, 1949
Winston-Salem, N.C.
fields: Film (actor)

African American actor; Pam Grier became known as queen of the 1970's Blaxploitation action films; had title role in *Foxy Brown* (1973); made a successful comeback in 1990's *Jackie Brown* (1997).

Grier, Robert Cooper

b. 1794
d. 1870
fields: Law

U.S. Supreme Court justice, 1846-1870; appointed by President Polk. Significant opinions: *Moore v. Illinois* 55 U.S. 13 (1852); The *Prize Cases* 67 U.S. 635 (1863).

Grier, Rosey

full: Roosevelt Grier
b. July 14, 1932
Cuthbert, Ga.
fields: Sports (football player)

African American football player; Rosey Grier was a star tackle for the New York Giants (1955-1962) and Los Angeles Rams (1963-1968) and became one of the finest defensive linemen in National Football League history; later career included bodyguard to Robert F. Kennedy, singer, actor, and author; wrote *Rosey Grier's Needlepoint for Men* (1973) and *Rosey: An Autobiography* (1986).

Grierson, John

b. April 26, 1898
Deanston, Scotland
d. February 19, 1972
Bath, England
fields: Film

The founder of the British Documentary Film Movement, John Grierson first learned about propaganda by studying yellow journalism in the United States in 1924. In England he got the Empire Marketing Board to establish a documentary film unit, which eventually launched the British Documentary Movement. In 1939 Grierson established the National Film Board of Canada, which he directed through World War II. After the war Grierson found it difficult to find work because of his socialist leanings. He later hosted a television program for Scottish television, taught in Canada, and remained chief spokesman of the documentary movement.

Griffey, Ken, Jr.

full: George Kenneth Griffey, Jr.
b. November 21, 1969
Donora, Pa.
fields: Sports (professional baseball player)

African American professional baseball player; in 1990, Ken Griffey, Jr., became the first Seattle Mariner ever voted to the All-Star game; won Gold Gloves in 1990, 1991, and 1992; 1989 was the first time a father and son had played in the major leagues at the same time. During the 1990's, he established himself as a superstar because of his ability to hit home runs, hit for a good average, and his defensive prowess. In 1998, he won his ninth consecutive Gold Glove.

Griffin, Archie

full: Archie Mason Griffin
b. Aug. 21, 1954
Columbus, Ohio
fields: Sports (football player)

African American football player; Archie Griffin became the first person to win the Heisman Trophy twice (1974, 1975); inducted into the College Football Hall of Fame in 1986.

Griffith, D. W.

full: David Wark Griffith
b. January 22, 1875
Floydsfork, Kentucky
d. July 23, 1948
Hollywood, California
fields: Film

A genius in the exposition of complex plots through revolutionary filmmaking techniques, Griffith was the foremost figure in the development of the American film as an expression of American values and as a commercially successful medium.

Griffith, Delorez Florence. *See* Griffith-Joyner, Florence

Griffith, Mark Winston

b. February 6, 1963
Brooklyn, N.Y.
fields: Banking and Finance (financial entrepreneurs and community development specialists)

Financial entrepreneurs and community development specialists; in 1993, Mark Winston Griffith and Errol T. Lewis founded the Central Brooklyn Federal Credit Union, which provided loans and other much-needed financial services to many low-income customers in the local African American community.

Griffith-Joyner, Florence

né: Delorez Florence Griffith
aka: FloJo
b. Dec. 21, 1959
Mojave Desert, Calif.
d. Sept. 21, 1998
Mission Viejo, Calif.
fields: Sports (sprinter)

African American sprinter; in the 1988 Olympics, Florence "FloJo" Griffith-Joyner won the silver medal in the 200-meter dash; in the 1988 Olympics she took three golds (100-, 200-, and 400-meter dashes) and won a silver medal in the 1,600-meter relay; died at the age of thirty-eight of a heart seizure.

Grimké, Angelina

b. February 20, 1805
Charleston, South Carolina
d. October 26, 1879
Hyde Park, Massachusetts
fields: Social Reform, Women's Rights

Because their genders hindered their activity in the abolitionist movement, the Grimké sisters, Sarah and Angelina, realized the necessity for women's rights and worked to establish them.

Grimké, Sarah

full: Sarah Moore Grimké
b. November 26, 1792
Charleston, South Carolina
d. December 23, 1873
Hyde Park, Massachusetts
fields: Social Reform, Women's Rights

Because their genders hindered their activity in the abolitionist movement, the Grimké sisters, Sarah and Angelina, realized the necessity for women's rights and worked to establish them.

Grimm, Jacob

full: Jacob Ludwig Grimm
b. January 4, 1785
Hanau, near Kassel, Hesse-Kassel (now Germany)
d. September 20, 1863
Berlin, Prussia (now Germany)
fields: Language and Linguistics, Literature

Remembered as the authors of probably the best-known book of fairy tales in the Western world, the Grimm brothers (Jacob and Wilhelm) were two of the most noted philologists of the nineteenth century. They made significant contributions to linguistic theory, folklore, and the study of the German language and its literature.

Grimm, Wilhelm

full: Wilhelm Carl Grimm
b. February 24, 1786
Hanau, near Kassel, Hesse-Kassel (now Germany)
d. December 16, 1859
Berlin, Prussia (now Germany)
fields: Language and Linguistics, Literature

Remembered as the authors of probably the best-known book of fairy tales in the Western world, the Grimm brothers (Jacob and Wilhelm) were two of the most noted philologists of the nineteenth century. They made significant contributions to linguistic theory, folklore, and the study of the German language and its literature.

Grindel, Eugène. *See* Éluard, Paul

Gris, Juan

né: José Victoriano González
b. March 23, 1887
Madrid, Spain
d. May 11, 1927
Boulogne-sur-Seine, France
fields: Art

Despite a relatively short professional career, Gris was one of the founding fathers and most influential artists of the cubist movement in art in the early twentieth century.

Griscom, Elizabeth. *See* Ross, Betsy

Grist, Reri

b. c. 1934
New York, N.Y.
fields: Music (opera singer)

African American opera singer; Soprano Reri Grist debuted in 1959 and performed in major operas throughout the United States and Europe.

Gromyko, Andrei Andreyevich

b. July 18, 1909
Starye Gromyki, Belorussia, Russian Empire (now Belarus)
d. July 2, 1989
Moscow, U.S.S.R.
fields: Government and Politics, Diplomacy

Soviet leader and diplomat Andrei Andreyevich Gromyko served as Soviet Union's foreign minister from 1957 to 1985. Personally met with President Kennedy during Cubam Missile Crisis. Involved in numerous agreements, from the 1963 Nuclear Test-Ban Treaty to the 1974 and 1979 SALT treaties.

Gronk

né: Glugio Gronk Nicandro
b. 1954
Los Angeles, Calif.
fields: Art

Latino artist. Gronk's mother chose his middle name, a Brazilian word meaning "to fly," from a *National Geographic* magazine while she was in labor. From an early age, Gronk wanted to be an artist. He dropped out of school and became a founding member of the street performance group asco, known for protest antics, theater works, and videos. He also became a painter known for improvisational and physical qualities of his work.

Gropius, Walter

full: Walter Adolph Gropius
b. May 18, 1883
Berlin, Germany
d. July 5, 1969
Boston, Massachusetts
fields: Architecture

Considered one of the founders of modern architecture, Gropius worked to make architecture and art responsive to the needs of an urbanized and industrialized society. His major projects were in urban and industrial architecture and in industrial design. He designed educational programs in both modern architecture and industrial design.

Grosz, George

b. July 26, 1893
Berlin, Germany
b. July 6, 1959
West Berlin, West Germany
fields: Art

Noted for its unrelenting exposure of social ills and its scathing depictions of contemporary figures, George Grosz's German Expressionist art was a major target of the Nazis' Degenerate Art Exhibition of 1937.

Grotius, Hugo

aka: Huigh de Groot
b. April 10, 1583
Delft, Holland
d. August 28, 1645
Rostock, Mecklenburg
fields: Law

Grotius' 1625 treatise *On the Law of War and Peace* has gained for him the reputation of the father of international law.

Grove, William Robert

aka: Sir William Robert Grove
b. July 11, 1811
Swansea, Glamorganshire, Wales
d. August 1, 1896
London, England
fields: Invention and Technology, Physics, Law

Though trained as a lawyer, Grove invented the electric cell that bears his name. He also discovered and popularized the conservation of energy principle and helped to reform the Royal Society of London.

Grue, Le Chef. *See* Tarhe

Gruen, David Joseph. *See* Ben-Gurion, David

Grünewald, Matthias

né: Matthias Gothardt
b. c. 1475
Würzburg
d. August, 1528
Halle, Magdeburg
fields: Art

Grünewald was the culmination of the Gothic tradition in German painting while giving evidence of the primacy of individual artistic expression within the tradition of the Italian Renaissance. He employed Gothic principles of expressiveness and Renaissance pictorial conventions, creating a unique style which transcended the limitations of the traditions out of which he worked.

Guarini, Guarino

b. January 17, 1624
Modena
d. March 6, 1683
Milan
fields: Architecture

Guarini's fusion of medieval and Moorish architectural vaulting systems, his theologically symbolic geometric floor plans, and his dramatic use of light allowed him to create structures which are perennially fascinating and influential.

Guaton-bain. *See* Satanta

Guderian, Heinz

full: Heinz Wilhelm Guderian
b. June 17, 1888
Culm, Germany (now Chełmno, Poland)
d. May 15, 1954
Schwangau bei Füssen, West Germany
fields: Military Affairs

Guderian was the tactical innovator who created the modern armored division, using tanks with motorized support as a battle formation. He led German panzers with great success in the early years of World War II.

Guelle Plat. *See* Flat Mouth

Guericke, Otto von

b. November 20, 1602
Magdeburg
d. May 11, 1686
Hamburg
fields: Physics, Invention and Technology, Technology

His experiments with electricity and, especially, air pressure make Guericke an important figure in the era of the scientific revolution.

Guerrero, Pedro

b. June 29, 1956
San Pedro de Macoris, Dominican Republic
fields: Sports (baseball player)

Latino baseball player. In 1981, his first year as a regular player, outfielder Pedro Guerrero helped the Los Angeles Dodgers win the National League pennant and was a cowinner of the World Series Most Valuable Player Award. He made the All-Star team five times. After an injury-plagued 1986 season, he returned in 1987 to win the United Press International Comeback Player of the Year Award. Guerrero was traded to the St. Louis Cardinals during the 1988 season; after several seasons with them, he began playing professionally in Mexico.

Guevara, Che

full: Ernesto Guevara de la Serna
b. June 14, 1928
Rosario, Argentina
d. October 9, 1967
La Higuera, Bolivia
fields: Military Affairs, Government and Politics

Guevara is best known as a theorist and practitioner of revolutionary guerrilla warfare in Latin America. Guevara's writings and his ill-fated military experience in Bolivia have influenced Latin American revolutionary strategy as well as created posthumously a heroic international symbol for those who share his political ideals.

Guggenheim, Daniel

b. July 9, 1856
Philadelphia, Pennsylvania
d. September 28, 1930
Port Washington, New York
fields: Business and Industry, Philanthropy

Through daring business risks and tight family control over his ventures, Guggenheim created one of the first multinational corporations and went a long way toward his goal of controlling the mineral wealth of the entire world.

Guicciardini, Francesco

b. March 6, 1483
Florence
d. May 22, 1540
S. Margherita ia Montici, Florence
fields: Historiography

Guicciardini helped revolutionize history writing by breaking with Humanist conventions. He was one of the first historians to present history as a series of interrelated causes and effects and to treat the history of Italy in the larger context of European affairs.

Guidi, Tommaso di Giovanni di Simone. *See* Masaccio

Guido d'Arezzo

aka: Guido Aretinus
aka: Guy of Arezzo
b. c. 991
possibly Arezzo, Tuscany
d. 1050
Avellana, Italy
fields: Music

Guido is generally credited with reestablishing solmization and with perfecting staff notation. His *Micrologus*, a treatise on musical practice, was one of the most widely copied and read books on music in the Middle Ages.

Guillaume, Charles-Édouard

b. February 15, 1861
Fleurier, Switzerland
d. June 13, 1938
Sèvres, France
fields: Physics

Measurements, and the standards on which they are based, are the foundation of the physical sciences. During his long tenure as assistant director and director of the International Bureau of Weights and Measures at Sèvres, Guillaume was indefatigable as researcher and administrator in refining instruments and methods of measurement to the greatest possible precision, and in publishing to the world the current status of metricization and metric standards. For his efforts, he received the Nobel Prize in Physics in 1920.

Guillaume, Robert

b. Nov. 30, 1937
St. Louis, Mo.
fields: Film, Theater and Entertainment, Music, Television

African American actor and singer; Robert Guillaume's work included stage, film, and television roles; performed in plays such as *Fly Blackbird*, *Kwamina*, *Guys and Dolls*, *Purlie*, *Jacques Brel Is Alive and Living in Paris*, and *Phantom of the Opera*; featured in television series including *Soap* (1977-1981) and *Benson* (1979-1986); film credits included *Wanted Dead or Alive* (1987) and *Lean on Me* (1989).

Guillén, Nicolás

né: Cristobal Guillén y Batista
b. July 10, 1902
Camagüey, Cuba
d. July 16, 1989
Havana, Cuba
fields: Literature (poet)

Latino poet. Nicolás Guillén's poetry, which he began publishing in the 1930's, explores African and Cuban culture. In 1937, he went to Spain to fight for the republican cause, then returned to Cuba to work on behalf of the revolution and Fidel Castro. His published works include *West Indies, Ltd.*, *Poemas* (1934), *España: Poema en cuatro angustias y una esperanza* (1937; Spain: a poem in four anguishes and one hope), *Che comandante* (1967; Che commander), and *La rueda dentada* (1972; the gear or sprocket).

Guinier, Lani
full: Carol Lani Guinier
b. April 19, 1950
New York, N.Y.
fields: Law, Government and Politics, Scholarship (attorney and scholar)

African American attorney and scholar. In 1993, President Bill Clinton nominated Lani Guinier to become his assistant attorney general for civil rights at the Justice Department. The controversial nomination was withdrawn prior to her confirmation hearing before the Senate Judiciary Committee. She later wrote *The Tyranny of the Majority: Fundamental Fairness in Representative Democracy* (1994).

Guipago. *See* Lone Wolf

Guisewite, Cathy
full: Cathy Lee Guisewite
b. September 5, 1950
Dayton, Ohio
fields: Journalism, Art

After building a successful career in advertising, Cathy Guisewite created *Cathy*, an immensely popular comic strip that illustrates the life of a young, single, working woman in contemporary society. In a national poll by newspaper editors for *World Almanac and Book of Facts*, Guisewite has twice been selected as one of "America's Twenty-Five Most Influential Women."

Gulick, Sidney Lewis
b. 1860
Micronesia
d. Dec. 24, 1945
Boise, Ida.
fields: Religion and Theology

Sidney Lewis Gulick, a missionary and peace activist, received a divinity degree from Union Theological Seminary in 1886. He was posted to Kumamoto, Japan, in 1888, where he learned to read and speak Japanese. He became an instructor in theology at Kyoto's Doshisha University and supported the peace movement after the Russo-Japanese War of 1904-1905. In 1913, he returned to the United States because of health problems. Disturbed by the blatant racism expressed toward Japanese residents of the United States, he worked to counteract discriminatory immigration and naturalization laws.

Gullion, Allen
b. Dec. 14, 1880
Carrollton, Ky.
d. June 19, 1946
Washington, D.C.
fields: Military Affairs

Provost marshal general of the U.S. Army and legal counsel for the Army during World War II, Allen Gullion approved of Executive Order 9066, which ordered the forced relocation of Japanese Americans. His rationale for the internment was that the "military necessity" to intern outweighed adherence to constitutional law.

Gumbel, Bryant
full: Bryant Charles Gumbel
b. Sept. 29, 1948
New Orleans, La.
fields: Journalism, Television (sportscaster and broadcast news reporter)

African American sportscaster and broadcast news reporter; in 1972, Bryant Gumbel made his televison debut as a weekend sportscaster for KNBC-TV in Burbank, Calif.; advanced to the role of sports director by 1976; cohosted *Grandstand*; selected as part-time cohost for NBC's *Today Show* in 1980, becoming the network's first full-time cohost (with Jane Pauley) in 1981; earned Emmy Awards (1976, 1977) and the Edward R. Murrow Award from the Overseas Press Club in 1988. After leaving the *Today Show* in 1997, he was involved in various television projects.

Gumm, Frances. *See* Garland, Judy

Gunn, Moses
b. Oct. 2, 1929
St. Louis, Mo.
fields: Theater and Entertainment (actor)

African American actor; Moses Gunn's stage performances led to an Obie Award for Aaron the Moor in *Titus Andronicus* (1967-1968), another Obie for Milton Edwards in *The First Breeze of Summer* (1975), and a Tony nomination for *The Poison Tree* (1976); greatest acclaim was for his portrayal of the title character in *Othello* (1970); televison appearances included *Good Times* (1977) and *A Man Called Hawk* (1989); film work included *The Great White Hope* (1970), *Shaft* (1971),and *Ragtime* (1981).

Gunn, Wendell Wilkie
b. ?
fields: Government and Politics

African American political appointee; Wendell Wilkie Gunn received his first political appointment from President Ronald Reagan in 1982 as special assistant to the president on international trade policy; appointed by President George Bush to serve as chief of staff of the Department of Housing and Urban Development in 1989.

Guo Moruo
aka: Kuo Mo-jo
b. November 10 or 16, 1892
Sha-wan, Sichuan Province, China
d. June 12, 1978
Beijing, China
fields: Government and Politics, Literature

A writer of poems and essays, Guo Moruo joined the Chinese Communist Party in 1927; in 1949 he was part of new Communist government under Mao Zedong. President of Chinese Academy of Sciences. Traveled, publicizing Chinese Communist points of view. Guo was pne of the few who were able to maintain important government posts from 1949 until the late 1970's.

Gupta, Kanta Chandra
b. 1897
Delhi, India
d. Sept. 11, 1982
San Francisco, Calif.
fields: Medicine

Kanta Chandra Gupta, a chiropractor, was the first woman from India to apply for U.S. citizenship and a Ghadr Party activist. When her husband died in 1929, she supported her family through cleaning jobs. In 1931 she completed a nursing degree through correspondence courses offered by the Chicago School of Nursing. Four years later the Los Angeles College of Chiropractic awarded her a chiropractic degree, and she became a successful San Francisco chiropractor. She spoke and wrote extensively about the value of educating women, emphasizing the value of scientific and practical learning. Gupta was an active member of the Ghadr Party, which sought independence from Britain for India.

Gurley, Helen. *See* Brown, Helen Gurley

Gurū. *See* Nānak

Gustafsson, Greta Lovisa. *See* Garbo, Greta

Gustavus II Adolphus
b. December 9, 1594
Stockholm, Sweden
d. November 6, 1632
Lützen, Saxony
fields: Military Affairs, Monarchy, Government and Politics

King of Sweden, 1611-1632. Gustavus was one of the greatest military commanders in the history of warfare. He was responsible for brilliant military innovations in strategy and tactics, and in the development of modern weaponry. Gustavus also transformed Sweden into one of the leading nations in Europe by implementing wide-ranging domestic reforms in the fields of government administration, economic development, and education.

Gutenberg, Johann

né: Johannes Gensfleisch zur Laden
b. 1394-1399
Mainz, Germany
d. Probably February 3, 1468
Mainz, Germany
fields: Invention and Technology

Gutenberg invented printing with movable metal type.

Guth, Alan H.

full: Alan Harvey Guth
b. Feb. 27, 1947
New Brunswick, New Jersey
fields: Astronomy, Physics

Alan H. Guth theorized that early in its life, the universe underwent a sudden inflation—an idea that helped resolve serious dilemmas in cosmology.

Guðjónsson, Halldór Kiljan. *See* Laxness, Halldór

Guthrie, Woody

full: Woodrow Wilson Guthrie
b. July 14, 1912
Okemah, Oklahoma
b. October 3, 1967
New York, New York
fields: Music (folk)

Woody Guthrie established the modern genre of the traveling folk poet while defending himself and his work from a variety of would-be censors. In the mid-1930's, the communist newspaper *The Daily Worker* began publishing a weekly column by Guthrie titled "Woody Sez." In 1940 he began appearing on a popular radio program, *Back Where I Come From*. His songs include "This Land Is Your Land," "Do Re Mi," and "Deportee." Guthrie also wrote a newspaper column for *People's World* and two books, *Seeds of Man* and *Bound for Glory*.

Gutiérrez, Horacio Tomás

b. August 28, 1948
Havana, Cuba
fields: Music (pianist)

Cuban American pianist; at eleven years of age, Horacio Tomás Gutiérrez was a guest soloist with the Havana Symphony; in 1959, following the Cuban Revolution, he immigrated to the U.S. and, in 1967, became a U.S. citizen; after receiving the Silver Medal at the Tchaikovsky Competition in Moscow (1970), Gutiérrez debuted professionally with the Los Angeles Philharmonic Orchestra; he has performed with orchestras around the world, recorded several albums, and has received an Emmy Award and the 1982 Avery Fisher Prize.

Gutiérrez, José Ángel

b. Oct. 25, 1944
Crystal City, Tex.
fields: Civil Rights

Mexican American educator, civil rights activist; José Ángel Gutiérrez was a founder of La Raza Unida Party, 1970; cofounder of Mexican American Unity Council, 1968; cofounder of Mexican American Youth Organization, 1967; served as associate professor, Western Oregon State College, 1982-1986; was executive director, Greater Dallas Legal and Community Development Foundation, 1986; administrative law judge, city of Dallas, Texas, 1990.

Gutierrez, Sidney

b. June 27, 1951
Albuquerque, N.Mex.
fields: Aviation and Space Exploration

Latino Astronaut. Sidney Gutierrez became an astronaut for NASA in 1985 and subsequently flew several space missions, including as a pilot on the nine-day STS-40 Spacelab Life Sciences launch (June, 1991) and as a commander of the STS-59 Space Radar Laboratory in April, 1994. Gutierrez earned the NASA Exceptional Achievement Medal, the NASA Space Flight Medal, the Congressional Hispanic Caucus Award, and the 1992 Hispanic Engineer of the Year Achievement Award. By 1994, Gutierrez had become a colonel in the U.S. Air Force.

Guy, Buddy

full: George Guy
b. July 30, 1936
Lettsworth, La.
fields: Music (guitarist, singer, songwriter, club owner)

African American guitarist, singer, songwriter, and club owner; Buddy Guy, along with "Magic" Sam Maghett and Otis Rush, created a definitive electric guitar style in Chicago known as the "West Side Sound."

Guy, Jasmine

b. Mar. 10, 1964
Boston, Mass.
fields: Theater and Entertainment, Television, Dance

African American dancer and actress; Jasmine Guy's televison credits included principal dancer on *Fame*, the character Whitley Gilbert in the NBC series *The Cosby Show* and its spin-off *A Different World*; trained as a dancer at the Alvin Ailey Dance Center; stage acted in *The Wiz*, *Bubbling Brown Sugar*, *Beehive*, and *Leader of the Pack*; film credits included *School Daze* (1988) and *Harlem Nights* (1989); awarded an Image Award in 1990 by the National Association for the Advancement of Colored People (NAACP).

Guy, Rosa Cuthbert

b. Sept. 1, 1928
Trinidad
fields: Literature

African American author; author of adult and young adult fiction, Rosa Cuthbert Guy wrote *Bird at My Window* (1966), *The Disappearance* (1979), and *And I Heard a Bird Sing* (1987); was founding president of the Harlem Writer's Guild.

Guy de Chauliac

aka: Guigo (or Guido) de Chaulhaco (or Cauliaco, Caillat, or Chaulhac)
b. c. 1290
Chauliac, France
d. July 25, 1368
Avignon, France
fields: Medicine

Guy wrote the most important treatise on surgery during the later Middle Ages. For more than two centuries, he was considered the leading authority on such diverse medical topics as dissection; surgical procedure; professional ethics; leprosy; plague origins, symptoms, and preventions; anatomical structure; pharmaceutical drugs; dental care; and ophthalmology.

Guzmán, Nuño Beltrán de

b. ?
Spain
d. 1544
Spain
fields: Exploration and Colonization

Latino explorer. Nuño Beltrán de Guzmán, Hernán Cortés's rival in the conquest of Mexico, was named governor of the colony of Pánuco in 1527 in Cortés's absence. When Cortés returned from Spain to resume control, Guzmán conquered the northern frontier in 1530 by killing thousands of Indians. He turned the area into the colony of New Galicia and served as its governor until 1537. He was investigated for running an illegal slave trade and for his harsh treatment of Indians. He was imprisoned, then sent to Spain, where spent the rest of his life trying to vindicate his name.

Guzmán, Ralph C.

b. Oct. 24, 1924
Mexico
d. Oct. 10, 1985
Santa Cruz, Calif.
fields: Government and Politics, Scholarship

Latino public official and scholar. Ralph C. Guzmán, one of the foremost Hispanic educators in the United States, wrote several books that displayed his knowledge of Latin American affairs, including *The Mexican-American People: The Nation's Second Largest Minority* (1970) and *The Political*

Socialization of the Mexican American People (1976). In 1978, President Jimmy Carter named Guzmán deputy assistant secretary of state, and he became responsible for much of U.S. policy toward Central and South America. In 1980, he returned to teaching.

Guzmán Aguilera, Antonio

b. Mar. 21, 1894
San Miguel de Mesquital, Mexico
fields: Literature

Playwright. During the 1920's, Antonio Guzmán Aguilera established himself in Los Angeles as a master of the *revista* form of short comedic theater, through which he examined Mexican American culture, current events in Los Angeles, and U.S. politics. He wrote more than 450 works, including the plays *Oro, seda, sangre y sol* (1924) and *María del Pilar Moreno o la pequeña vengadora* (1924), and the *revistas Alma tricolor, Exploración presidenciál*, and *Pierrot mexicano*. In 1927, he established the Compañía Guzmán Aguilera.

Gwynn, Tony

b. May 9, 1960
Los Angeles, Calif.
fields: Sports (baseball player)

African American baseball player; outfielder Tony Gwynn began his professional career with the San Diego Padres in 1982; led the National League in batting eight times (1984, 1987, 1988, 1989, 1994, 1995, 1996, 1997) and won four Gold Gloves. In 1999, he became one of the less than twenty-five players ever to reach at least 3,000 hits in a career.

Gyatso, Tenzin. *See* Dalai Lama

H

H. D.

né: Hilda Doolittle
b. September 10, 1886
Bethlehem, Pennsylvania
d. September 27, 1961
Zurich, Switzerland
fields: Literature

The works of H. D., the first great modernist poet, formed the true core of Ezra Pound's Imagist movement and exercised an extraordinary influence on modern poetics. She explored images taken from classical mythology from a profoundly feminine and personal perspective in spare, taut poems.

Haan, Kil-soo

b. ?
fields: Government and Politics

Kil-soo Haan, named in 1941 as the liaison officer for the Korean Commission, a diplomatic agency of the Korean provisional government in China, represented the Koreans in talks with the U.S. government. He and Syngman Rhee, another member of the commission, held differing opinions and competed to represent Koreans. From 1938 to 1945, when he was a spokesperson for the Sino-Korean People's League in Hawaii, he warned Americans of an impending Japanese attack and accused the Japanese in Hawaii of spying and conducting sabotage for the Japanese government.

Haber, Fritz

b. December 9, 1868
Breslau, Silesia (now Wrocław, Poland)
d. January 29, 1934
Basel, Switzerland
fields: Chemistry

Haber developed a synthetic process, now named for him, for manufacturing ammonia directly from elemental nitrogen and hydrogen. This made the commercial production of artificial fertilizers possible and has had a profound effect on global agriculture and food production. He won the 1918 Nobel Prize in Chemistry.

Habermas, Jürgen

b. June 18, 1929
Dusseldorf, Germany
fields: Philosophy

An important member of the Frankfurt School for Social Research, Jürgen Habermas is best known for his attempts to articulate a comprehensive and emancipatory theory of language, communication, and the evolution of society within an ethical framework. His major contribution to philosophy and sociology lies in his recasting of critical theory to divert attention from the analysis of concrete social and political situations and detail the changing structure of consciousness in modern societies. Major works include *Theory and Practice* (1963), *Knowledge and Human Interests* (1968), *The Theory of Communicative Action* (1981), *Between Facts and Norms* (1992).

Habyarimana, Juvénal

b. March 8, 1937
Gasiz, Gisenyi, Ruanda-Urundi (now Rwanda)
d. April 6, 1994
near Kigali, Rwanda
fields: Government and Politics

Juvénal Habyarimana was president of Rwanda from 1973 to 1994. Repeatedly accused of corruption in the 1980's. Ethnic strife between dominant Hutus (Habyarimana was a Hutu) and rebel Tutsis boiled over in early 1990's, leading to genocide, and Habyarimana made the Tutsis a scapegoat for Rwanda's problems. Killed when his jet shot down by rockets in 1994.

Hackibanzin. *See* Eskiminzin

Hadamard, Jacques-Salomon

b. Dec. 8, 1865
Versailles, France
d. Oct. 17, 1963
Paris, France
fields: Mathematics (algebra, calculus, and mathematical logic)

Jacques-Salomon Hadamard created a function designating the distribution of prime numbers; he provided a solution for Cauchy's problem in linear differential equations.

Hadfield, Robert Abbott

b. November 28, 1858
Attercliffe, Sheffield, England
d. September 30, 1940
Kingston, Surrey, England
fields: Geology (metallurgy), Invention and Technology

Hadfield's discovery of manganese steel ushered in the age of alloy steels, which have proven to be essential to the development of modern industrial technology and weapons.

Hadrian

b. January 24, 76
Italica, Spain
d. July 10, 138
Baiae, Bay of Naples
fields: Government and Politics

Hadrian succeeded in bringing a relatively peaceful period to the Roman Empire, in realizing much-needed domestic and civil reforms, and in leaving, through his architectural and artistic gifts, his personal stamp on Rome, Athens, and Jerusalem.

Haeckel, Ernst

full: Ernst Heinrich Philipp August Haeckel
b. February 16, 1834
Potsdam, Prussia
d. August 9, 1919
Jena, Germany
fields: Biology, Natural History, Zoology, Philosophy

Haeckel studied and classified many marine organisms, especially the radiolaria and the medusae. He is most noted for his refinement of Charles Darwin's theory of evolution, its extension to mankind and the origin of life, the refinement of the biogenetic law, and the development of monism as a religion.

Hafiz

né: Shams al-Din Muhammed
aka: Shams al-Din Muhammed of Shiraz
b. c. 1320
Shiraz, Iran
d. 1389 or 1390
Shiraz, Iran
fields: Literature

The premier lyric poet in more than a millennium of literary expression in the Persian language, Hafiz represents the culmination of lyrical styles and modes that began some five centuries before him and remains a model for Iranian poets today.

Hágaga. *See* Crashing Thunder

Hagedorn, Jessica Tarahata

b. 1949
Manila, Philippines
fields: Literature, Poetry

Jessica Tarahata Hagedorn, novelist, poet, and short-story writer, moved to the United States at the age of fourteen. Her first poetry collection was published in 1975, performing some of her poetry accompanied by the band The West Coast Gangster Choir. She became involved with the performance art scene and moved to New York in 1978, where she began to write short stories. Her first novel, *Dogeaters* (1990), won the National Book Award in 1990. She also published *Danger and Beauty* (1993), a collection of poetry, short fiction, and prose.

Haggins, Jon

b. September 5, 1943
Tampa, Fla.
fields: Fashion (fashion designer)

African American fashion designer; in the 1980's, Jon Haggins offered a collection called "Jungle Fever," featuring animal patterns and rainforest motifs.

Hagler

aka: Haiglar
b. c. 1690
S.C.
d. Aug. 30, 1763
S.C.
fields: Government and Politics, Native American Affairs

Native American leader. Hagler was the most significant of the eighteenth century Catawba chiefs; he established peace with the white colonists of South Carolina and unified his people. Involved in warfare between Catawbas and other eastern tribes. Carolina. Opposed to alcohol and the harm it seemed to be doing to his people.

Hagler, Marvin

aka: Marvelous Marvin Hagler
b. May 23, 1954
Newark, N.J.
fields: Sports (boxer)

African American left-handed professional middleweight boxer; in 1980 Marvin Hagler became world middleweight champion, a title he held until 1987 when he lost to Sugar Ray Leonard.

Hahn, Gloria

né: Kim Ronyoung
b. March 28, 1926
Los Angeles, Calif.
d. Feb., 1987

fields: Art, Literature (fiction)

Gloria Hahn, artist and novelist, depicted the Korean American experience in her novel *Clay Walls* (1986), which was translated into Korean and published in South Korea after her death. Born Kim Ronyoung, she married Richard Hahn at the age of nineteen. She received a bachelor's degree from San Francisco State University in 1975. She created numerous drawings, paintings, and works of calligraphy; wrote for Korean magazines and newspapers; and organized and promoted cultural events within the Korean American community.

Hahn, Kimiko

b. 1955
New York
fields: Literature

Poet and short story writer Kimiko Hahn is the daughter of two artists: Maude Miyako Hamai, from Hawaii, and Walter Hahn, from Wisconsin. Her works include the poetry collections *Air Pocket* (1989) and *Earshot* (1992); She coauthored *We Stand Our Ground: Three Women, Their Vision, Their Poetry* (1988) and coedited *Without Ceremony* (1988), an anthology of writing by Asian American women. Hahn was editor at *Bridge* magazine from 1982 to 1984, and founded Word of Mouth: A Multicultural Arts Project, where she coordinated readings and workshops from 1985 to 1990. She received National Endowment for the Arts fellowships in poetry in 1986 and 1992 and fellowships from the New York Foundation for the Arts in 1987 and 1991.

Hahn, Otto

b. March 8, 1879
Frankfurt am Main, Germany
d. July 28, 1968
Göttingen, West Germany
fields: Chemistry, Physics

A pioneer in understanding the nature of radioactivity, Hahn (with his colleague Fritz Strassmann) is credited with having discovered nuclear fission as well as certain radioactive isotopes and elements. He was awarded the 1944 Nobel Prize in Chemistry and played a major role in reestablishing German science after World War II.

Hahn, Richard S.

b. April 28, 1922
Lincoln, Nebr.
fields: Medicine

Korean American Richard S. Hahn was a cardiothoracic surgeon who developed the prototype of the coronary bypass operation in 1949. He received an M.D. from Northwestern University Medical School in 1947 and worked as a surgeon until 1987, receiving numerous awards and honors. He participated in humanitarian efforts in Peru, Mexico, Central America, Thailand, China, and Bhutan. His wife, Gloria, was the author of *Clay Walls* (1987), a novel about Korean American life.

Hahnemann, Samuel

full: Christain Friedrich Samuel Hahnemann
b. April 10, 1755
Meissen, Saxony (now in Germany)
d. July 2, 1843
Paris, France
fields: Medicine

Hahnemann was the founder of the science of homeopathy, a healing method that follows the principle of treating like with like. That is, diseases are treated with substances that, used on a healthy person, create the very symptoms of the disease, but that, used in minute amounts, cure the symptoms in a sick person.

Haig, Alexander M.

full: Alexander Meigs Haig, Jr.
b. December 2, 1924
Philadelphia, Pennsylvania
fields: Government and Politics, Diplomacy

Alexander M. Haig, with his strong military background, was a security adviser and confidant to U.S. presidents Nixon, Ford, and Reagan. Briefly White House chief of staff under Nixon. President Ronald Reagan's secretary of state from 1981 to 1982; Haig resigned because of frequent clashes with White House policy makers.

Haiglar. *See* Hagler

Haile Selassie I

né: Tafari Makonnen
b. July 23, 1892
near Harer, Ethiopia
d. August 27, 1975
Addis Ababa, Ethiopia
fields: Government and Politics

During his long rule as emperor (1930-1974), Haile Selassie instituted programs for unification and modernization at home, while striving to open up Ethiopia to the world outside its formidable borders.

Hailey, Jo-Jo

né: Joel Hailey
b. June 10, 1971
Charlotte, N.C.
fields: Music (rhythm and blues)

A member of the African American rhythm and blues group Jodeci, which is composed of two pairs of brothers, Jo-Jo Hailey, K-Ci Hailey, Dalvin DeGrate, and DeVante Swing DeGrate; Jodeci's albums include *Forever My Lady* (1991), *Diary of a Mad Band* (1993), and *The Show the Party After the Hotel* (1995).

Hailey, K-Ci

né: Cedric Hailey
b. September 2, 1969
Charlotte, N.C.
fields: Music (rhythm and blues)

A member of the African American rhythm and blues group Jodeci, which is composed of two pairs of brothers, Jo-Jo Hailey, K-Ci Hailey, Dalvin DeGrate, and DeVante Swing DeGrate; Jodeci's albums include *Forever My Lady* (1991), *Diary of a Mad Band* (1993), and *The Show the Party After the Hotel* (1995).

Hakadah. *See* Eastman, Charles Alexander

Hakar Jim. *See* Hooker Jim

Haksigaxunuminka. *See* Mountain Wolf Woman

Haldane, J. B. S.

full: John Burdon Sanderson Haldane
b. Nov. 5, 1892
Oxford, England
d. Dec. 1, 1964
Bhubaneswar, India
fields: Biology, Genetics, Physiology

J. B. S. Haldane proposed new ideas and supporting research in the fields of respiratory physiology, chromosome mapping, sex linkage, and enzyme physiology.

Hale, Clara McBride

b. Apr. 1, 1905
Philadelphia, Pa.
d. Dec. 18, 1992
New York, N.Y.
fields: Social Reform

African American child-care volunteer; in 1969 Clara McBride Hale founded Hale House, a refuge for unwanted and drug-dependent or AIDS-infected infants.

Hale, George Ellery

b. June 29, 1868
Chicago, Illinois
d. Feb. 21, 1938
Pasadena, California
fields: Astronomy, Invention and Technology, Physics

George Ellery Hale invented the spectroheliograph in 1889; founded the *Astrophysical Journal* in 1895; discovered magnetic fields in sunspots in 1908; in 1919, discovered the twenty-two-year sunspot cycle.

Hale, Matthew

b. November 1, 1609
Alderley, Gloucestershire, England
d. December 25, 1676
Alderley, Gloucestershire, England
fields: Law

Hale, a lawyer, scholar, and author, who climaxed a brilliant legal career by serving as Lord Chief Justice of the Court of King's Bench, was one of the three or four most important contributors to the early modern evolution of English common law.

Hale, Sarah Josepha

né: Sarah Josepha Buell
b. October 24, 1788
Newport, New Hampshire
d. April 30, 1879
Philadelphia, Pennsylvania
fields: Literature, Journalism

The author of poetry, novels, plays, and cookbooks, as well as an important history of women, Hale is best known as the editor of *Godey's Lady's Book*, the most popular magazine in the United States before the Civil War. As editor of this women's magazine, Hale encouraged and supported women writers, and she advocated improved opportunities for women's education and work.

Haley, Alex

full: Alex Palmer Haley
b. Aug. 11, 1921
Ithica, N.Y.
d. Feb. 10, 1992
Seattle, Wash.
fields: Journalism, Literature

African American journalist, author; Alex Haley was the chief journalist for the U.S. Coast Guard, 1952-1959; interviewed Malcolm X for *Playboy*, which led to his first book, *The Autobiography of Malcolm X* (1965); spent a dozen of years researching family history, leading to publication of the novel *Roots* (1976), based on the life of a Mandingo youth named Kunta Kinte; the novel led to a twelve-hour television series, hundreds of interviews and articles, instructional packets and tapes, and sparked intense interest in African American genealogy and history; received a special Pulitzer Prize for *Roots* in 1977; a television sequel to *Roots*, *Roots: The Next Generation*, aired in 1979.

Half-King

aka: Tanacharison
b. c. 1700
near Buffalo, N.Y.
d. Oct. 4, 1754
Harrisburg, Pa.
fields: Government and Politics, Native American Affairs

Native American leader. Half-King, an Oneida (although born a Catawba), joined the British forces during the French and Indian War. Fought in the Battle of Great Meadows (1754), the opening salvo of the final British war with the French in North America, which ended in 1763.

Halide Edib Adıvar

b. 1884
İstanbul, Ottoman Empire
d. January 9, 1964
Istanbul, Turkey
fields: Literature, Government and Politics, Women's Rights

Adıvar was a leading Turkish nationalist, writer, and social reformer. She played a prominent role in the Young Turk Revolution of 1908-1909 and an even more important part in the Nationalist Revolution, led by Mustafa Kemal (Atatürk) between 1919 and 1924. As such she was one of the first Turkish women to take an active, indeed militant, interest in national politics. She was the first Turkish graduate of the American College for Girls in İstanbul, and she is credited with writing the first novel in Turkish.

Hall, Arsenio

b. Feb. 12, 1956
Cleveland, Ohio
fields: Theater and Entertainment, Television (comedian, talk show host, actor)

African American african American comedian and talk show host; Arsenio Hall was best known as the late-night talk show host for *The Late Show* (1987) and *The Arsenio Hall Show* (1989-1994); was a televison series regular on *The New Love American Style* (1985), *Motown Revue* (1985), and *Solid Gold* (1987); film credits included *Amazon Women on the Moon* (1987), *Coming to America* (1988), and *Harlem Nights* (1989).

Hall, G. Stanley

b. February 1, 1844
Ashfield, Mass.
d. April 24, 1924
Worcester, Mass.
fields: Psychiatry and Psychology, Education

A pioneer of American psychology, G. Stanley Hall founded the first American psychological journal and was first president of the American Psychological Association. He studied philosophy and physiology in Germany, and in 1878 he became the first American to earn a Ph.D. in psychology. The theory of evolution influenced Hall's psychology, which he called genetic psychology. After popularizing child study, he studied adolescence and published *Adolescence: Its Psychology and Its Relation to Physiology, Anthropology, Sociology, Sex, Crime, Religion and Education* in 1904.

Hall, George Cleveland

b. Feb. 22, 1864
Ypsilanti, Mich.
d. June 17, 1930
Chicago, Ill.
fields: Medicine

African American physician; in 1890 George Cleveland Hall helped organize Provident Hospital in Chicago; founded the Cook County Physicians Association in Illinois.

Hall, Jack

b. Feb. 28, 1915
Ashland, Wis.
d. Jan. 2, 1971
San Francisco, Calif.
fields: Labor Movement

Jack Hall, regional director of the International Longshoremen's and Warehouseman's Union (ILWU) in Hawaii from 1944 until 1969, moved to the West Coast in June, 1969, to become the union's vice president and director of organization. On December 6, 1973, he was elected to Labor's International Hall of Fame. He and six others were arrested on August 28, 1951, on charges of violating the

Smith Act of 1940, which makes it a criminal offense to advocate the overthrow of any government in the United States by force or violence. He was found guilty and sentenced to five years in prison and fined $5,000. In 1958, the U.S. Ninth Circuit Court of Appeals reversed the Honolulu court's decision, acquitting all seven men.

Hall, James Reginald, Jr.

b. July 15, 1936
Anniston, Ala.
fields: Military Affairs

African American military officer; James Reginald Hall, Jr. was a commanding general at the U.S. Army's Fort Sheridan in Illinois and a battalion commander in the Korean War; he achieved the rank of brigadier general.

Hall, Katie Beatrice Green

né: Katie Beatrice Green
b. Apr. 3, 1938
Mound Bayou, Miss.
fields: Government and Politics

African American U. S. representative from Indiana; Katie Beatrice Green Hall became the first African American to represent the state of Indiana in the U.S. Congress in 1983.

Hall, Lloyd Augustus

b. June 20, 1894
Elgin, Ill.
d. January 2, 1971
Altadena, Calif.
fields: Chemistry

African American chemist. Lloyd Augustus Hall's specialty was the preservation and processing of meat and bakery products; his discovery of curing salts had a large impact on the meat-packing industry; earned B.S. in pharmaceutical chemistry from Northwestern University (1916); worked as sanitary chemist at the Chicago Department of Health (1916-1924); employed as chief chemist at John Morrell & Company (1919-1921); served as president and chemical director of the Chemical Products Corporation in Chicago (1922-1925); became consultant at Griffith Laboratories, later becoming technical director and chief chemist (1924-1959); employed with the Illinois Department of Agriculture's State Food Commission (1944-1949); served as chair of the Chicago chapter of the American Institute of Chemists (1954).

Hall, Prince

b. c. 1735
Bridgetown, Barbados
d. December 4, 1807
Boston, Mass.
fields: Civil Rights

African American activist. In 1765 Prince Hall relocated to Boston and became a minister. He enlisted in the Revolutionary militia, promoted equal schools for black children, and organized a fraternal society for freedmen (1775), which became the first group of black masons, African Lodge No. 459 (1787). Hall organized other fraternal societies, agitated for abolition, and was an early supporter of black colonization to Africa.

Hall, Titus C.

b. 1910's
Pflugerville, Tex.
fields: Military Affairs

African American military officer; in 1972, Titus C. Hall became chief avionics engineer for the B-1 strategic manned bomber, serving at the headquarters of the Aeronautical Systems Division at Wright-Patterson Air Force Base in Ohio; was named deputy for reconnaissance and electronic warfare systems in 1978.

Ḥallāj, al-

full: Abū al-Mughīth al-Ḥusayn ibn Mansūr al-Ḥallāj
b. c. 858
Beida, Iran
d. March 26, 922
Baghdad, Iraq
fields: Religion and Theology, Philosophy

By making known his experiences of mystical communion with Allah, al-Ḥallāj promoted a highly controversial and ultimately influential doctrine of divine grace and knowledge. His imprisonment and martyrdom became one of the most celebrated episodes in the development of Sufi history.

Hallalhotsoot. *See* Lawyer

Haller, Albrecht von

full: Victor Albrecht von Haller
b. Oct. 16, 1708
Bern, Switzerland
d. Dec. 12, 1777
Bern, Switzerland
fields: Botany, Physiology

Albrecht von Haller created the use of injection techniques to study blood vessels; proposed the "mechanical automatism" of the heart; pioneered the use of Linnaean classification of Swiss plant life.

Halley, Edmond

b. October 29, 1656
Haggerston, near London, England
d. June 14, 1742
Greenwich, near London, England
fields: Astronomy

Among his many scientific achievements, Halley's best-known accomplishment was to solve the riddle of the orbits of comets. In particular, he predicted that the one seen in 1682 would return in 1759. This comet was later named for him.

Halpatter-Micco. *See* Bowlegs, Billy

Hals, Frans

b. c. 1583
Antwerp, Spanish Netherlands
d. September 1, 1666
Haarlem, United Provinces
fields: Art

Hals was the most celebrated northern painter of his era except for Rembrandt, who was a few years his junior. Hals specialized in painting group scenes and individual portraits in which his highly original use of grays provided his work with a chromatic unity that in the work of artists such as Leonardo da Vinci was achieved through chiaroscuro, the play of light and ark.

Halsey, William F.

full: William Frederick Halsey, Jr.
b. October 30, 1882
Elizabeth, New Jersey
d. August 16, 1959
Fishers Island, New York
fields: Military Affairs

"Bull" Halsey was a colorful and offensive-minded fighter who went by the slogan "hit hard, hit fast, hit often." A proponent of naval aviation and an avowed risk taker, he epitomized the aggressive spirit of the United States Navy during World War II.

Hamada Hikozo. *See* Heco, Joseph

Hamer, Fannie Lou

b. Oct. 6, 1917
Montgomery County, Miss.
d. Mar. 14, 1977
Mound Bayou, Miss.
fields: Civil Rights

African American civil rights activist; Fannie Lou Hamer after forty years of work on the same plantation, lost her job when she tried to vote; began working with the Student Nonviolent Coordinating Committee to register black voters in 1962; helped form the Mississippi Freedom Democratic Party and spoke eloquently in favor of seating black delegates to the Democratic National Convention in 1964; became one of the first delegates to the Democratic convention in 1968; founded Freedom Farms Corporation, 1969; toured and spoke widely on behalf of civil rights legislation.

Hamilton, Alexander
b. January 11, 1755
Nevis, British West Indies
d. July 12, 1804
New York, New York
fields: Government and Politics

Hamilton served as aide-de-camp to Washington during the American Revolution and was a delegate to the Philadelphia Convention of 1787 and signer of the Constitution. An early advocate of a strong national government, he coauthored The Federalist and was the United States' first secretary of the treasury.

Hamilton, Alice
b. February 27, 1869
New York, New York
d. September 22, 1970
Hadlyme, Connecticut
fields: Medicine, Social Reform

A physician turned social reformer, Alice Hamilton became one of the world's leading experts on industrial poisons and pioneered the development of the new field of industrial medicine in the United States.

Hamilton, Charles Vernon
b. Oct. 19, 1929
Muskogee, Okla.
fields: Literature, Civil Rights

African American author, political scientist, educator, and adviser to civil rights organizations; Charles Vernon Hamilton wrote *Black Power: The Politics of Liberation in America* (1967), *The Bench and the Ballot: Southern Federal Judges and Black Votes* (1973), and *Adam Clayton Powell, Jr.: The Political Biography of an American Dilemma* (1991).

Hamilton, Gordon
full: Amy Gordon Hamilton
b. December 26, 1892
Tenafly, New Jersey
d. March 10, 1967
British Columbia, Canada
fields: Education, Sociology

Hamilton was a leader in changing emphases in the training of social workers through her teaching, writings, and practice of the profession. She advocated a better world through social work practice that was informed by the social sciences and psychology as well as scientific approaches to casework.

Hamilton, Virginia Esther
b. March 13, 1936
Yellow Springs, Ohio
fields: Literature (novelist and children's book author)

African American novelist and children's book author. Virginia Esther Hamilton's first book, *Zeely* (1967), won the Nancy Block Memorial Award and was cited as a notable children's book for that year by the American Library Association. She also wrote *M. C. Higgins, the Great* (1974); *The Planet of Junior Brown* (1971); the trilogy *Justice and Her Brothers* (1979), *Dustland* (1980), and *The Gathering* (1981). She received the 1996 Coretta Scott King Author Award for her book *Her Stories* (1995).

Hamilton, William Rowan
b. August 3/4, 1805
Dublin, Ireland
d. September 2, 1865
near Dublin, Ireland
fields: Mathematics, Physics, Optics

Hamilton, while questioning a commonly accepted three-dimensional concept of space on a plane, discovered quaternions and, in doing so, drastically altered the study of algebra, forcing the abandonment of the commutative law of multiplication that was dominant in his day and leading the way to new methods of vector analysis.

Hamlet, James Frank
b. Dec. 13, 1921
Alliance, Ohio
fields: Military Affairs

African American military officer; in 1973 James Frank Hamlet attained the rank of major general in the United States Army.

Hammarskjöld, Dag
full: Dag Hjalmar Agne Carl Hammarskjöld
b. July 29, 1905
Jönköping, Sweden
d. September 18, 1961
near Ndola, Northern Rhodesia
fields: Diplomacy

As secretary-general of the United Nations from 1953 to 1961, Hammarskjöld vastly increased both the influence and the prestige of the United Nations (U.N.). He oversaw the explosive growth of the organization among Third World nations, prevented the U.N. from becoming a pawn of the major Cold War rivals, and initiated the U.N.'s peacekeeping role.

Hammer
né: Stanley Kirk Burrell
b. March 30, 1963
Oakland, Calif.
fields: Music, Theater and Entertainment (rap singer, dancer)

African American rap singer and dancer; Hammer revolutionized rap music by shifting the emphasis from verbal to visual effects with a stage show comprising dancers, backup singers, musicians, and deejays; successful albums included *Feel My Power* (1987; retitled *Let's Get It Started* in 1988), *Please Hammer Don't Hurt 'Em* (1989), *Too Legit to Quit* (1991); won three Grammy Awards in 1990; dropped "M.C." from his stage name in 1991.

Hammerstein, Oscar, II
né: Oscar Greeley Glendenning Hammerstein
b. July 12, 1895
New York, New York
d. August 23, 1960
Doylestown, Pennsylvania
fields: Theater and Entertainment

Working with such composers as Herbert Stothart, Jerome Kern, Sigmund Romberg, and especially Richard Rodgers, Hammerstein wrote books and lyrics which transformed the American musical into an integrated dramatic form and created a number of classics.

Hammon, Jupiter
b. Oct. 17, 1711
Oyster Bay, N.Y.
d. 1806?
Hartford, Conn.
fields: Literature (poet)

African American poet; born a slave, Jupiter Hammon is believed to be the first published African American poet; "An Evening Thought: Salvation by Christ, with Penitential Cries" (1760) is one of his most representative poems.

Hammons, David
b. July 24, 1943
Springfield, Ill.
fields: Art

African American artist; David Hammons incorporated the American flag and everyday objects into prints and mixed media that conveyed the African American experience; works included *Injustice Case* (1970).

Hammurabi
b. c. 1810 B.C.E.
Babylon
d. 1750 B.C.E.
Babylon
fields: Government and Politics, Law

Building upon an Amorite sheikhdom of four generations of ancestors, this long-reigning representative of the dynasty matured gradually in power until he was able to streatch his control over the entire length of the Euphrates and Tigris river valleys. The literary creativity of the age brought into being the Old Babylonian dialect, most fully exemplified in the codification of law remembered under Hammurabi's name.

Hampton, Fred

b. August 31, 1948
Maywood, Ill.
d. December 4, 1969
Chicago, Ill.
fields: Civil Rights

African American civil rights activist and Black Panther Party leader. At nineteen Fred Hampton served as youth council president of his hometown branch of the National Association for the Advancement of Colored People; joined the Black Panther Party (1968); became the chapter's chairman and helped build the chapter into one of the strongest African American organizations in Chicago; believed that the party's focus should be on improving the condition of African Americans as well as all oppressed peoples; shot and killed while sleeping during Chicago police raid of his apartment, December, 1967; federal and state investigations that followed Hampton's death pointed to serious misconduct by the police, and possibly the Federal Bureau of Investigation, in harassing and mistreating members of the Black Panther Party.

Hampton, Henry Eugene, Jr.

b. January 8, 1940
St. Louis, Mo.
fields: Film (documentary filmmaker)

African American documentary filmmaker; Henry Eugene Hampton, Jr., created the award-winning fourteen-hour Civil Rights series *Eyes on the Prize* (covering the years 1954 to 1964) and *Eyes on the Prize II* (following the years 1966 to 1980); also produced *The Great Depression*, a seven-hour series televised in 1993, and *America's War on Poverty* (1995); awarded the Charles Frankel Prize from the National Endowment for the Humanities in 1990.

Hampton, Lionel

b. Apr. 12, 1913
Louisville, Ky.
fields: Music (jazz musician)

African American jazz musician; Lionel Hampton was best known for his use of the vibraphone as an effective instrument of jazz and the jazz ensemble. His recording of "Flying Home" (1942) remains a classic of the big band jazz era.

Hamsun, Knut

né: Knut Pedersen
b. August 4, 1859
Lom, Norway
d. February 19, 1952
Nørholm, Norway
fields: Literature

The author of more than twenty novels, six plays, and numerous essays, poems, and short stories, Hamsun is widely considered to be Norway's greatest novelist. He was the recipient of the Nobel Prize in Literature in 1920.

Han Feizi

aka: Han Fei Tzu
b. 280 B.C.E.
the state of Han, China
d. 233 B.C.E.
the state of Qin, China
fields: Philosophy

Combining the philosophies of the Daoist, Confucius, Mohist, and especially Legalist (*fa*) traditions, Han Feizi synthesized and articulated better than any of his predecessors the complex set of philosophical and practical ideas about government known as Legalism. He advocated promulgation of law to punish criminals severally and to reward good citizens, irrespective of relationship or rank. His influence on Chinese political science is far greater than that on Chinese philosophy because his Legalism addressed political policies for rulers.

Han, Maggie

b. 1959
Providence, R.I.
fields: Theater and Entertainment

Korean American Maggie Han was a fashion model before becoming an actor. She was studying American literature at Harvard University with the intent of becoming a journalist when cast in *Space* (1985), a Columbia Broadcasting Service miniseries. She moved to Los Angeles and began an acting career. Her first screen role was as the courtesan Eastern Jewel in *The Last Emperor* (1987).

Hancock

aka: King Hancock
b. fl. early 1700's
fields: Warfare and Conquest, Government and Politics, Native American Affairs

Hancock, a Tuscarora, led his tribe in North Carolina's bloody Tuscarora War against white settlers in the early 1700's. In 1712, North and South Carolina sent a combined force under the leadership of Colonel John Barnwell against Hancock, destroying his main village of Cotechney. Hancock finally agreed to a peace plan, which was quickly broken by the colonists.

Hancock, Herbie

né: Herbert Jeffrey
b. Apr. 12, 1940
Chicago, Ill.
fields: Music (jazz pianist)

African American jazz pianist; Herbie Hancock played with the Miles Davis quintet in the 1960's, specializing in a blend of blues and hard bop; formed the Herbie Hancock quartet in 1973; won an Academy Award for his score of the film *'Round Midnight* (1986).

Hancock, John

b. January 12, 1737
North Braintree (now Quincy), Massachusetts
d. October 8, 1793
Boston, Massachusetts
fields: Government and Politics

The first signer of the Declaration of Independence, Hancock was a wealthy Boston merchant and a notable example of those more aristocratic patriots who invested much money as well as much time in the cause of liberty. Hancock was a leader in Massachusetts Colonial politics, president of the Second Continental Congress, and Governor of Massachusetts.

Hand, Learned

full: Billings Learned Hand
b. January 27, 1872
Albany, New York
d. August 18, 1961
New York, New York
fields: Law

During a career on the federal bench spanning more than half a century, Hand became one of the most respected and honored jurists in America. His commitment to tolerance and rigorous thought helped transform and modernize American law in the twentieth century.

Handel, George Frideric

b. February 23, 1685
Halle, Saxony
d. April 14, 1759
London, England
fields: Music

One of the most gifted composers in music history, Handel gave to the world some of the most beautiful music ever written, including the *Messiah*, *Water Music*, and *Fireworks Music*.

Handsome Lake

aka: Kaniatario
aka: Ganeodiyo
b. c. 1735
Canawaugus Village on the Genessee River near Avon, N.Y.
d. Aug. 10, 1815
Onondaga, N.Y.
fields: Religion and Theology

Native American religious leader. Handsome Lake, a Seneca, was the founder of the Longhouse religion in the early 1800's; it became widely practiced among the Iroquois. The religious visions of Handsome Lake were the basis for a nearly complete transformation in the religion and practice of the

Seneca. The Longhouse religion was similar to other prophetic movements, such as Wovoka's and John Slocum's.

Handy, John Richard, III

b. Feb. 3, 1933
Dallas, Tex.
fields: Music (alto saxophonist)

African American alto saxophonist; multi-instrumentalist John Richard Handy III was also accomplished on tenor saxophone, flute, and clarinet; played with the Charles Mingus orchestra in the recordings *Jazz Portraits* (1959) and *Mingus ah um* (1959); was a bandleader in the late 1950's; his ensemble performed at the Monterey Jazz Festival, earning a place on the 1965 *Live at the Monterey Jazz Festival* album.

Handy, W. C.

full: William Christopher Handy
b. November 16, 1873
Florence, Ala.
d. March 28, 1958
New York, N.Y.
fields: Music

African American blues composer. W. C. Handy is known as "father of the blues" and is honored with a statue on Memphis' famous Beale Street. A horn player and bandleader, Handy gained fame for writing enduring tunes that popularized the blues. Handy played with minstrel groups during the 1890's and composed "The Memphis Blues" (1909) as a campaign song for the city's political boss. Handy's best-known song is "St. Louis Blues" (1914). He began working in the music publishing business in New York City in 1918. Despite progressive blindness Handy authored an autobiography (1941) and other books.

Hane, Mikiso

b. Jan. 16, 1922
Hollister, Calif.
fields: Historiography

Mikiso Hane, born in the United States, spent 1933 to 1940 in a village in Hiroshima. He was interned in a relocation camp a few years after returning to the United States. A professor of Japanese history at Knox College in Illinois, he wrote *Peasants, Rebels and Outcasts: The Underside of Modern Japan* (1982) and *Japan: A Historical Survey* (1972).

Hanford, Mary Elizabeth. *See* Dole, Elizabeth

Hanihara Masanao

b. 1876
Yamanashi Prefecture, Japan
d. 1932
Japan
fields: Diplomacy

Hanihara Masanao, who served as part of the Japanese embassy staff in Washington, D.C., between 1902 and 1911, became Japanese ambassador to the United States in 1922. He lobbied against congressional legislation designed to prohibit the immigration of Japanese immigrants. His efforts angered Massachusetts Senator Henry Cabot Lodge, who felt Hanihara's remarks were a thinly veiled threat to U.S. security. The Immigration Act of 1924 passed, and Hanihara resigned his post as ambassador in protest.

Hankel, Hermann

b. Feb. 14, 1839
Halle, Prussia (now Germany)
d. Aug. 29, 1873
Schramberg, near Tübingen, Germany
fields: Mathematics (number theory and set theory)

Hermann Hankel helped formulate the theory of complex number systems and the concept of function. He also found certain solutions to Bessel's equation, which are now called Hankel functions. In 1867, he published *Theorie der complexen Zahlensysteme* (theory of complex number systems).

Hankins, Anthony Mark

b. November 10, 1967
Elizabeth, N.J.
fields: Fashion (fashion designer)

African American fashion designer; Anthony Mark Hankins uses bold colors, ethnic prints, and details such as glass beadwork in his signature style; the "Hankins' label has appeared in mainstream outlets and in Vogue-Butterick pattern catalogs.

Hanna, Marcus A.

full: Marcus Alonzo Hanna
b. September 24, 1837
New Lisbon, Ohio
d. February 15, 1904
Washington, D.C.
fields: Government and Politics

Hanna was the close political friend of William McKinley, helped him secure the presidency in 1896, and then served as an influential United States senator until his death.

Hannibal

b. 247 B.C.E.
probably Carthage, North Africa
d. 182 B.C.E.
Libyssa, Bithynia, Asia Minor
fields: Warfare and Conquest

During the Second Punic War, Hannibal led an army of mercenaries across the Alps into Italy, where, for fifteen years, he exhibited superior generalship, defeating the Romans in one battle after another.

Hanno

b. c. 520-510 B.C.E.
place unknown
d. Date unknown
place unknown
fields: Exploration

Hanno successfully founded the first trading colonies along the western African coast and then pushed on to explore the coast at least as far as modern Sierra Leone. His account of his journey provided the only reasonably accurate account of Africa until the time of Prince Henry the Navigator.

Hansberry, Lorraine

full: Lorraine Vivian Hansberry
b. May 19, 1930
Chicago, Illinois
d. January 12, 1965
New York, New York
fields: Literature

A writer and an activist, Lorraine Hansberry was the first African American woman to win the New York Drama Critics' Circle award.

Hansen, Austin

b. 1910
Virgin Islands
d. 1996
New York, New York
fields: Photography

African American photographer; Austin Hansen was introduced to photography by the Virgin Island's official photographer, Clair Taylor, in the early 1920's; learned combat photography in the Navy during World War II, after which he set up a photography business in Harlem, New York.

Harakontie. *See* Garakontie, Daniel

Haralson, Jeremiah

b. Apr. 1, 1846
near Columbus, Ga.
d. 1916?
prob. Colorado
fields: Government and Politics

African American politician; Slave-born Jeremiah Haralson was elected to Congress in 1874 representing Alabama.

Harano, Ross Masao

b. 1942
California
fields: Banking and Finance, Business and Industry, Law

Ross Masao Harano is an activist and businessman; born in California, his family was forcibly relocated to Arkansas; after growing up in Chicago, went into banking and international trade; served as equal opportunity officer, director of advisory councils, and chief of the crime victims division of the Illinois Office of the Attorney General, 1988-1993; president, Illinois Ethnic Coalition; chairperson, Chicago Chapter of the Japanese American Citizens League; president, Chicago World Trade Center.

Hard, Darlene

full: Darlene Ruth Hard
b. January 6, 1936
Los Angeles, California
fields: Sports (tennis)

A tennis champion who achieved the top rank in the sport during the early 1960's, Darlene Hard overcame an impoverished background to master the game. Her skills in doubles earned for her twelve titles at the French Open, U.S. Open, and Wimbledon tournaments from 1957 through 1963; she won a Wimbledon doubles title in 1969. In 1973, she was inducted into the International Tennis Hall of Fame. In retirement, she coached tennis. She is considered partly responsible for the growing popularity of women's tennis at the end of the 1960's.

Hardaway, Penny

né: Anfernee Hardaway
b. July 18, 1971
Memphis, Tenn.
fields: Sports (basketball player)

African American basketball player; playing for the Orlando Magic, Penny Hardaway was a starting point guard in the 1995 All-Star Game. In 1999, he joined the Phoenix Suns.

Hardenberg, Karl von

full: Karl August von Hardenberg
b. May 31, 1750
Essenrode, Hanover
d. November 26, 1822
Genoa, Kingdom of Sardinia
fields: Government and Politics, Diplomacy

Hardenberg played a leading role in the Prussian reform movement. He also directed the foreign policy of his country during the eventful years 1810-1822 and played a pivotal role in forming the coalition of powers that defeated Napoleon. He was the spokesman for Prussia at the Congress of Vienna in 1815, which determined the political fate of Europe for the next fifty years.

Hardie, James Keir

b. August 15, 1856
Legrannock, Lanarkshire, Scotland
d. September 26, 1915
Glasgow, Scotland
fields: Government and Politics, Labor Movement

Through agitation and enthusiasm, Hardie, more than any other person, helped inspire and organize both the Independent Labour Party and then the more broadly based Labour Party, which became one of Great Britain's two major parties after World War I.

Hardin, Lillian. *See* Armstrong, Lillian Hardin

Harding, Vincent

b. July 25, 1931
New York, N.Y.
fields: Civil Rights, Religion and Theology

African American historian, clergyman, and theologian; civil rights activists Vincent Harding and his wife were key coworkers with Martin Luther King, Jr.; in 1981 he chaired the board of the King Center; an outstanding historian of African American life, his books include *The Other American Revolution* (1980), *There Is a River: The Black Struggle for Freedom in America* (1981), and *Hope and History: Why We Must Share the Story of the Movement* (1990).; known for his work as chair of the *Black Heritage* series for public television, he was also senior adviser to *Eyes on the Prize: America's Civil Rights Years* for public television.

Harding, Warren G.

full: Warren Gamaliel Harding
b. November 2, 1865
Caledonia, Ohio
d. August 2, 1923
San Francisco, California
fields: Government and Politics

As twenty-ninth president of the United States from 1921 to 1923, Harding adopted compromise politics in economics and foreign affairs in an attempt to guide the nation through readjustment to great social and economic changes.

Hardison, Inge

b. ?
Portsmouth, Va.
fields: Photography, Art (sculptor)

African American photographer and sculptor; Inge Hardison was a founding member of the Black Academy of Arts and Letters; known for her work in children's portraiture and for a series of historical portraits of African American leaders in cast stone.

Hardison, Kadeem

b. c. 1966
Brooklyn, N.Y.
fields: Theater and Entertainment (actor)

African American actor; on television's *A Different World* (1987), Kadeem Hardison played the role of Dwayne Wayne; also appeared on *The Cosby Show* and in the films *School Daze* (1988) and *White Men Can't Jump* (1992).

Hardouin, Jules. *See* Mansart, Jules Hardouin-

Hardy, Antonio. *See* Kane, Big Daddy

Hardy, G. H.

full: Godfrey Harold Hardy
b. Feb. 7, 1877
Cranleigh, Surrey, near London, England
d. Dec. 1, 1947
Cambridge, England
fields: Mathematics (number theory)

G. H. Hardy supported the cause of pure mathematics. Helped discover the noted Indian mathematician Srinivasa Ramanujan. 1908, published the classic book *A Course of Pure Mathematics*.

Hardy, Thomas

b. June 2, 1840
Higher Bockhampton, Dorset, England
d. January 11, 1928
Dorchester, Dorset, England
fields: Literature

One of the great English novelists and poets of the late nineteenth century, Hardy is representative of the Victorian trauma of the loss of God and the search for a new order.

Hare, Nathan

b. Apr. 9, 1934
Slick, Okla.
fields: Scholarship, Literature, Publishing

African American scholar and writer; an outspoken champion of African American rights, Nathan Hare published *The Black Scholar* in the early 1970's; he wrote *The Endangered Black Family: Coping with the Unisexualization and Coming Extinction of the Black Race* (1984), and *Bringing the Black Boy to Manhood: The Passage* (1987).

Hare, Richard Mervyn

b. March 21, 1919
Backwell, near Bristol, Somerset, England
fields: Philosophy

Author of *The Language of Morals* (1952), *Freedom and Reason* (1963), *Applications of Moral Philosophy* (1972), *Moral Thinking* (1981), *Essays in Ethical Theory* (1989), and *Essays on Political Morality* (1989), Richard Mervyn Hare offers a moral theory, called "universal prescriptivism," based on the idea that moral judgments are universalizable prescriptions. His work is one of the most eclectic efforts in contemporary moral philosophy; his view has certain definite affinities with utilitarianism, with existentialist ethics, with Kantian ethics, and with emotivism. On the practical side of moral philosophy, Hare shows an unusual philosophical interest in problems related to moral education and moral decision making.

Harewood, Dorian

b. Aug. 6, 1950
Dayton, Ohio
fields: Film, Theater and Entertainment (actor)

African American actor; an actor with stage, screen, and television credits, Dorian Harewood toured in *Jesus Christ Superstar* in the early 1970's; was featured in television roles on *Roots: The Next Generations* (1979), *Beulah Land* (1980), and in *The Jesse Owens Story* (1984); film credits included *Against All Odds* (1984), *The Falcon and the Snowman* (1985), *Full Metal Jacket* (1987), and *Change of Heart* (1998).

Hargreaves, James

b. Unknown
possibly Blackburn, Lancashire, England
d. April 22, 1778
Nottinghamshire, England
fields: Invention and Technology

Hargreaves invented the spinning jenny, which greatly multiplied the output of spinners and initiated a period of rapid growth in the textile industry which marked the onset of the British Industrial Revolution.

Hargrove, John R.

b. Oct. 25, 1923
Atlantic City, N.J.
fields: Law (judge), Government and Politics

African American judge; John R. Hargrove was appointed assistant U.S. attorney for the Maryland district in 1955; served as deputy U.S. attorney (1957-1962), associate judge of the Municipal Court of Baltimore City (1968-1971), and judge of Maryland's District Court #1 for Baltimore City (1971-1974); was appointed judge of the Supreme Court of Baltimore City in 1974, a position he held into the 1990's.

Harjo, Chitto. *See* Crazy Snake

Harjo, Joy

b. May 9, 1951
Tulsa, Okla.
fields: Literature

Muscogee Creek poet; member of faculties at University of Colorado, 1985-1988, University of Arizona, 1988-1990, and University of New Mexico beginning 1990; throughout the 1980's worked extensively with the Native American Public Broadcasting Consortium; her widely acclaimed poetry draws upon the symbols and mystical elements of traditional Native American culture; published works include *What Moon Drove Me to This* (1980), *She Had Some Horses* (1983), *Secrets from the Center of the World* (1989), *In Mad Love and War* (1990), and *The Woman Who Fell from the Sky* (1994).

Harjo, Talmuches. *See* McQueen, Peter

Harjo, Talof. *See* Porter, Pleasant

Harlan, John

full: John Marshall Harlan
b. 1833
d. 1911
fields: Law

U.S. Supreme Court justice, 1877-1911 (died while in office); appointed by President Hayes. No other justice has written as many dissenting opinons which later became the law of the land. Significant opinions: *Plessy v. Ferguson*, 163 U.S. 537 (1896) (dissenting opinion); *Pollock v. Farmers' Loan & Trust Co.*, 158 U.S. 601 (1895) (dissenting opinion); *Lochner v. New York*, 198 U.S. 45 (1905) (dissenting opinion); *Berea College v. Kentucky*, 211 U.S. 45 (1908) (dissenting opinion).

Harlan, John Marshall, II

b. 1899
d. 1971
fields: Law

U.S. Supreme Court justice, 1955-1971; appointed by President Eisenhower. Author of the modern approach to the scope of the Fourth Amendment. Significant opinions: *Katz v. United States*, 389 U.S. 347 (1967) (concurring opinion); *Simmons v. United States*, 390 U.S. 377 (1968); *Spinelli v. United States*, 393 U.S. 410 (1969).

Harlem, Gro. *See* Brundtland, Gro Harlem

Harmon, Ellen Gould. *See* White, Ellen G.

Harmsworth, Alfred

full: Alfred Charles William Harmsworth
aka: Alfred Harmsworth, first viscount Northcliffe
aka: Viscount Northcliffe
b. July 15, 1865
Chapelizod, Ireland
d. August 14, 1922
London, England
fields: Journalism, Government and Politics

The brothers Alfred and Harold Harmsworth's innovative approach to newspaper publishing revolutionized the practice of journalism, and both became adept at translating their business acumen into an effective force in the political arena. Lord Northcliffe owned the *Daily Mail* and, after 1906, *The Times of London*. He used his newspapers to encourage the British government to prepare for war against Germany. During World War I Northcliffe headed the British war mission to the United States and worked in the Ministry of Information. After the war, his political influence waned.

Harmsworth, Harold

full: Harold Sidney Harmsworth
aka: Harold Sidney Harmsworth, first viscount Rothermere
aka: Viscount Rothermere
b. April 26, 1868
Hampstead, England
d. November 26, 1940
Hamilton, Bermuda
fields: Journalism, Government and Politics

The brothers Alfred and Harold Harmsworth's innovative approach to newspaper publishing revolutionized the practice of journalism, and both became adept at translating their business acumen into an effective force in the political arena.

Harnack, Adolf von

b. May 7, 1851
Dorpat, Estonia, Russian Empire
d. June 10, 1930
Heidelberg, Germany
fields: Religion and Theology, Scholarship

Harnack's writings on the history of early Christianity remain the standard for all work done in this field. Harnack became an absolute master of the literature of the early Christian era and definitively shaped the perception of this era and its literature not only through his interpretation of the texts but also by his careful editing of the sources.

Harney, Ben

né: Benjamin Robertson
b. March 1, 1871
Middleboro, Ky.
d. March 1, 1938
Philadelphia, Pa.
fields: Music

African American ragtime pianist. Ben Harney arrived in New York in 1896 and is credited with introducing ragtime there. Popular in vaudeville theater and elsewhere, he encouraged imitation and the promotion of ragtime contests, which Harney often won.

Harney, Ben

b. 1953
fields: Theater and Entertainment, Music

African American singer and actor. Harney is credited with numerous Broadway performances, including roles in *The Wiz*, *Ain't Misbehavin*, *Purlie*, and *Pippin*. He won a Tony Award for his role as Curtis Taylor in *Dreamgirls* in 1982.

Harold II

né: Harold Godwinson

b. c. 1022
East Anglia, England
d. October 14, 1066
near Hastings, England
fields: Government and Politics, Military Affairs, Monarchy

Harold Godwinson was elected English king in 1066 and defeated a Norse invasion at Stamford Bridge, but he was himself defeated at Hastings by William the Conqueror and the Normans nine months later.

Harper, Elijah

b. Mar. 3, 1949
Red Sucker Lake, Manitoba, Canada
fields: Native American Affairs, Government and Politics

Cree activist and politician; Elijah Harper helped establish the native Canadian students' association at the University of Manitoba, 1970-1972; elected chief of the Red Sucker Lake Band, 1977-1981; member of the Manitoba legislature, 1981-1997; the only native member of the Manitoba Legislative Assembly, he blocked the adoption of the Meech Lake Accord in June, 1990, because it failed to mention native peoples; helped organize the movement for the establishment of National Aboriginal Day in 1996; he came to symbolize the active defense of aboriginal interests.

Harper, Frances E. W.

b. Sept. 24, 1825
Baltimore, Md.
d. Feb. 22, 1911
Philadelphia, Pa.
fields: Civil Rights (abolitionist), Education, Literature

African American abolitionist, educator, and writer; Frances E. W. Harper worked to expand African American after the Civil War; wrote a novel, *Iola Leroy: Or, Shadows Uplifted* (1892).

Harper, Michael S.

b. Mar. 18, 1938
Brooklyn, N.Y.
fields: Literature (poet)

African American poet; Michael S. Harper authored numerous volumes of poetry, most of which were influenced by jazz, blues, and spiritual music.

Harper, William

b. Dec. 27, 1873
near Cayuga, Canada
d. Mar. 27, 1910
Mexico City, Mexico
fields: Art

African American artist; landscape artist William Harper's most acclaimed works include *Landscape, Autumn Landscape*, and *Afternoon at Montigny*.

Harper, William Rainey

b. July 26, 1856
New Concord, Ohio
d. January 10, 1906
Chicago, Illinois
fields: Education

President of the University of Chicago during its formative years, Harper was a major figure in the reshaping of American higher education.

Harpo, Slim

né: James Isaac Moore
b. Feb. 11, 1924
Port Allen, La.
d. Jan. 31, 1970
Baton Rouge, La.
fields: Music (blues musician)

African American blues musician; Slim Harpo played harmonica and guitar; his most popular recordings included "Rainin' in My Heart" (1961) and "Scratch My Back" (1966).

Harrell, Andre O'Neal

b. 1962?
Bronx, N.Y.
fields: Music (rap performer and record company executive)

African American rap per- former and record company executive; Andre O'Neal Harrell started Uptown Records and was responsible for discovering and producing musical performers such as Heavy D and the Boyz, Jodeci, Al B. Sure!, Father MC, Christopher Williams, and Mary J. Blige; in 1992, signed a new seven-year deal MCA, also expanding his company as Uptown Entertainment; went on to head MCA's Motown Records division.

Harriman, Pamela Digby Churchill

né: Pamela Beryl Digby
aka: Pamela Digby Churchill
aka: Pamela Chruchill Hayward
full: Pamela Beryl Digby Chruchill Hayward Harriman
b. March 20, 1920
Farnborough, England
d. February 5, 1997
Paris, France
fields: Government and Politics

A leading fund raiser for the Democratic Party in the 1980's, Harriman became U.S. Ambassador to France in 1993.

Harriman, William Averell

b. November 15, 1891
New York, New York
d. July 26, 1986
Yorktown Heights, New York
fields: Diplomacy, Government and Politics

One of the chief architects of the containment policy in the 1940's, Harriman lent valuable continuity to American policy toward the Communist world during his nearly forty years of government service.

Harriot, Thomas

b. 1560
Oxford, England
d. July 2, 1621
London, England
fields: Mathematics (algebra, applied math, and trigonometry), Astronomy

Thomas Harriot was mathematical tutor and scientific adviser to Walter Raleigh, holding classes in navigation. In 1609-1610, he made telescopic observations of the moon, Jupiter's satellites, and sunspots. Was influential in the development of algebraic symbolism, equation solving, and navigational mathematics.

Harris, Barbara

b. 1951
Philadelphia, Pa.
fields: Religion and Theology

African American episcopal bishop; Barbara Harris became the first female bishop of the Episcopal church in the United States in 1989.

Harris, Bernard

b. October 13, 1927
New York, N.Y.
fields: Engineering, Education (electrical engineer and educator)

African American electrical engineer and educator. Bernard Harris founded his own electrical engineering company, Harris Scientific Services, in 1979. His major research interest in applications of atmospheric and oceanographic acoustics to such diverse fields as noise pollution and Navy oceanography led to his work on methods of noise control.

Harris, Doug

b. ?
Portsmouth, Va.
fields: Photography, Film, Civil Rights

African American photographer and filmmaker; Doug Harris trained photographers for the Student Nonviolent Coordinating Committee and documented events of the Civil Rights movement throughout the South.

Harris, Franco

b. Mar. 7, 1950
Fort Dix, N.J.
fields: Sports (football player)

African American football player; in 1972 Franco Harris joined the Pittsburgh

Steelers as a running back; helped the team to win the Super Bowl in 1975, 1976, 1979, and 1980; awarded Most Valuable Player in 1975.

Harris, Frank

b. February 14, 1856
County Galway, Ireland
b. August 26, 1931
Nice, France
fields: Literature

Frank Harris is best known for his revealing multivolume autobiography *My Life and Loves* (1922-1926, 1958), a sensational book banned in both Great Britain and the United States. He also published *Elder Conklin, and Other Stories* (1894) and several biographical works, including the four-volume collection *Contemporary Portraits* (1915-1930).

Harris, Frank

b. fl. 1900-1930
fields: Photography

African American photographer. Frank Harris worked in Philadelphia, Pa., between 1900 and 1930, where his studio was one of the largest owned by an African American. Often his subjects were street scenes and portraits in black and white. Harris' work is part of the permanent collection at the Schomburg Center for Research in Black Culture in New York City.

Harris, James, III

aka: Jimmy Jam
b. 1960?
fields: Music (pop songwriter, producer)

African American pop songwriters and producers; James Harris III and Terry Lewis were members of the Time, a Minneapolis rock group discovered by Prince; cowrote and coproduced songs for the group's albums, including *The Time* (1981) and *What Time Is It?* (1982); formed Flyte Tyme Productions after the band broke up in the early 1980's; won first Grammy in collaboration with Janet Jackson on her album *Control* (1986), named best album of the year in 1987; cowrote "I Didn't Mean to Turn You On" for Robert Palmer and worked with Jackson on her follow-up album, *Rhythm Nation 1814*.

Harris, James A.

b. Aug. 25, 1926
Des Moines, Iowa
fields: Education

African American association executive; James A. Harris was president of the National Education Association from 1974 until the 1990's.

Harris, Joel Chandler

b. December 9, 1848
Eatonton, Georgia
d. July 3, 1908
Atlanta, Georgia
fields: Literature

Harris was best known in his day for his collections of Uncle Remus tales, which were not created but recorded by him. When the American Academy of Arts and Letters was founded in 1905, Harris was elected to be one of the inaugural members. With the emergence of the Civil Rights movement, however, and with the portrayal of Uncle Remus as a man among cartoons in Walt Disney's movie *Song of the South*, the figure of Uncle Remus fell into some amount of literary and political disfavor. More recent studies of folklore have, however, established Harris' importance as a folklorist who collected authentic black folk tales.

Harris, Julie

full: Julia Ann Harris
b. December 2, 1925
Grosse Pointe, Michigan
fields: Theater and Entertainment (drama), Film

The outstanding actress of her generation, Harris has performed on stage as well as in films and television. She not only has won awards for her work in all three media but also has encouraged new playwrights to develop roles for women.

Harris, LaDonna

b. Feb. 15, 1931
Temple, Okla.
fields: Native American Affairs, Social Reform

Comanche political activist; LaDonna Harris created Oklahomans for Indian Opportunity, which organized members of sixty tribes in 1965; chair, National Women's Advisory Council of the War on Poverty in 1967 and National Council on Indian Opportunity in 1968; founded Americans for Indian Opportunity in 1970, which promotes economic self-sufficiency for indigenous people and supports self-determination projects for native people at the local, national, and international levels; served as special adviser to the Office for Economic Opportunity during the administration of President Jimmy Carter, 1977-1981, establishing the controversial Council for Energy Resources Tribes.

Harris, Leslie

b. 1961
Cleveland, Ohio
fields: Film (filmmaker)

African American filmmaker; Leslie Harris was credited with being the first African American woman to release her own feature film, *Just Another Girl on the I.R.T.* (1993).

Harris, Lucy

full: Luisa Harris
b. Feb. 10, 1955
Minter City, Miss.
fields: Sports (basketball player)

African American basketball player; Lucy Harris helped the U.S. women's teams win a gold medal at the 1975 Pan-American Games and a silver medal at the 1976 Montreal Olympics; became the first female basketball player ever to be drafted by a professional men's team when she was selected by the New Orleans Jazz of the National Basketball Association (NBA); played for the Houston Angels of the short-lived Women's Professional Basketball League (WPBL) in 1980.

Harris, Margaret R.

b. Sept. 15, 1943
Chicago, Ill.
fields: Music (conductor, pianist, composer)

African American conductor, pianist, and composer; Margaret R. Harris took over as musical director of the musical *Hair* in 1968; also conducted the St. Louis, Los Angeles, and Chicago symphony orchestras.

Harris, Mary. *See* Jones, Mother

Harris, Patricia Roberts

b. May 31, 1924
Mattoon, Ill.
d. Mar. 23, 1985
Washington, D.C
fields: Government and Politics

African American government official; Patricia Roberts Harris was the United States' first black female ambassador. She served as ambassador to Luxembourg under President Lyndon B. Johnson. In 1979 she moved to the post of secretary of Health, Education, and Welfare in the Carter Administration.

Harris, Robert Allen

b. Jan. 9, 1938
Detroit, Mich.
fields: Education, Music (conductor, composer)

African American professor, conductor, and composer; Robert Allen Harris was a faculty member at Wayne State University, Michigan State University, and Northwestern University.

Harris, Shack

full: James Harris
b. July 20, 1947
Monroe, La.
fields: Sports (football player)

African American football player; In 1974, his best season, quarterback Shack Harris led the Los Angeles Rams to the Super Bowl; the team lost to the Minnesota Vikings.

Harris, Spike

full: Middleton A. Harris
b. Jan. 22, 1908
New York, N.Y.
d. 1977
fields: Historiography

African American historian; Spike Harris was president of Negro History Associates; collected copies of government documents and other artifacts that went to the Schomburg Collection in New York City.

Harris, Townsend

b. Oct. 3, 1804
Sandy Hill, N.Y.
d. Feb. 25, 1878
New York, N.Y.
fields: Diplomacy, Government and Politics

Townsend Harris, as the first U.S. consul to reside in Japan, helped open Japan to economic penetration by Western powers. His negotiations resulted in a commercial treaty (signed July 29, 1858) between the United States and Japan. The treaty guaranteed diplomatic and commercial privileges to the United States and opened six Japanese ports to U.S. trade. After resigning from his post as consul in 1861, he involved himself in New York City politics.

Harrison, Benjamin

b. August 20, 1833
North Bend, Ohio
d. March 13, 1901
Indianapolis, Indiana
fields: Government and Politics

As the twenty-third president of the United States (1889-1893), Harrison gave the country an honest and straightforward administration devoted to Republican principles.

Harrison, Earl Grant

b. Apr. 27, 1899
Philadelphia, Pa.
d. July 28, 1955
Indian Lake, N.Y.
fields: Government and Politics

Earl Grant Harrison was director of the Alien Registration Office in Washington, D.C. Under pressure by the Korean American community, he allowed Koreans to register as Koreans, not as Japanese subjects, under the Alien Registration Act of 1940. Korea was annexed by the Japanese in 1910 and remained part of Japan until 1945.

Harrison, Francis Burton

b. Dec. 18, 1873
New York, N.Y.
d. Nov. 21, 1957
Flemington, N.J.
fields: Government and Politics

Francis Burton Harrison graduated from New York Law School in 1897 and was admitted to the bar the next year. In 1902, he was elected to the House of Representatives. After a failed bid to become the state's lieutenant governor, he won election to a congressional seat in 1906, serving two more terms. He opposed imperialism, particularly U.S. policy in the Philippines. He became governor-general of the Philippines in 1913 and began transferring power into the hands of the Filipinos. Many Americans were angered by his acts and were pleased when Harrison was replaced in 1921. Beginning in 1935, Harrison became adviser to Manuel Quezon, president of the Philippines, continuing to serve Quezon during World War II. After the war, Harrison served as U.S. commissioner of civil claims in the Philippines from 1946 to 1947 and continued to act as adviser to the Philippine government.

Harrison, Frederic

b. October 18, 1831
London, England
d. January 13, 1923
Bath, Somerset, England
fields: Social Reform, Philosophy

In his varied career as a professor of law, literary critic, and lecturer, Harrison was one of the staunchest advocates of the philosophy of positivism in mid-Victorian England.

Harrison, George

full: George Harold Harrison
b. February 25, 1943
Liverpool, England
fields: Music (popular)

George Harrison is best remembered as the lead guitarist for the Beatles. More than any other English band before it, the Beatles popularized American rock-and-roll and became not only the major exponent of British rock-and-roll to the world but also one of the greatest popular bands ever. Harrison also wrote songs and had a successful career after the Beatles disbanded.

Harrison, Gloria Macías

b. ?
San Bernardino, Calif.
fields: Education, Publishing

Educational administrator and publisher. In 1969, Gloria Harrison founded *El Chicano Community Newspaper*. In 1987, she became co-owner and copublisher of the *Colton Courier* and *Rialto Records*. From 1966 to 1990, she was an associate professor at San Bernardino Valley College. From 1988 to 1990, she also served as chair of the department of foreign languages. In 1991, she became dean of the humanities division of the same school. Harrison has been a member of the Hispanic Chamber of Commerce, the California State Council for the Humanities, and the California State Commission on the Status of Women. She was a delegate to the 1984 Democratic National Convention.

Harrison, Richard B.

b. Sept. 28, 1864
London, Ontario, Canada
d. Mar. 14, 1935
New York, N.Y.
fields: Theater and Entertainment (actor)

African American shakespearean reader, elocutionist, and actor; Richard B. Harrison organized a drama school at the Agricultural and Technological College in Greensboro, N.C. in 1923; was given a Spingarn Medal for his portrayal of "De Lawd" in the all-black musical *The Green Pastures* (1930) in 1931.

Harrison, William Henry

b. February 9, 1773
near Charles City, Virginia
d. April 4, 1841
Washington, D.C.
fields: Government and Politics, Military Affairs

Harrison became one of the nation's most glamorous military heroes because of his victory over the Indian forces of Tecumseh and the Prophet at the Battle of Tippecanoe in 1811. As a soldier and later governor of the Old Northwest Territory, he became identified with the ideas and desires of the West, eventually riding his military reputation into a brief tenure in the presidency.

Harry, Jackée. *See* Jackée

Harsha

b. c. 590
probably Thanesar, India
d. c. 647
possibly Kanauj, India
fields: Government and Politics, Warfare and Conquest, Religion and Theology, Theater and Entertainment

One of the last great rulers of the classical age of Hindu India, Harsha defended Buddhism in its homeland, established relations with the Chinese Empire, and distinguished himself in classical Sanskrit theater.

Hart, Emma. *See* Willard, Emma

Hart, H. L. A.

full: Herbert Lionel Adolphus Hart
b. July 18, 1907
Harrogate, England
d. December 19, 1992
Oxford, England
fields: Philosophy, Law

Combining the approaches of postwar linguistic philosophy and British analytical jurisprudence, H. L. A. Hart revived the field of philosophy of law after World War II, making distinctive and notable contributions to such issues as the nature of law, the relationships between law and morality, punishment and responsibility, and the concept of rights. His major works include *Causation in the Law* (1959, 2d ed. 1985, with Tony Honoré), *The Concept of Law* (1961, 2d ed. 1994), *Law, Liberty, and Morality* (1963), *Punishment and Responsibility* (1968), *Essays on Bentham* (1982), and *Essays in Jurisprudence and Philosophy* (1983).

Hart, Lorenz

full: Lorenz Milton Hart
b. May 2, 1895
New York, New York
d. November 22, 1943
New York, New York
fields: Theater and Entertainment, Music

The first musical-comedy lyricist to receive equal billing with the composer, Hart was among a small group of early musical-comedy writers who led the way in combining diverse theatrical traditions of romance, spectacle, satire, and musical revue into a distinctly American art form.

Hartline, Haldan Keffer

b. Dec. 22, 1903
Bloomsburg, Pennsylvania
d. Mar. 17, 1983
Fallston, Maryland
fields: Medicine, Physiology

Haldan Keffer Hartline researched the behavior of individual cells in the retina of the eye; won the 1967 Nobel Prize in Physiology or Medicine.

Hartman, Johnny

b. 1922
Chicago, Ill.
d. 1983
fields: Music (ballad-oriented jazz singer)

African American ballad-oriented jazz singer; Johnny Hartman sang with Dizzy Gillespie, Errol Garner, and Earl Hines; made an album with John Coltrane in the early 1960's.

Hartmann, Carl Sadakichi

b. Nov. 8, 1869
Deshima, Japan
d. Nov. 21, 1944
St. Petersburg, Fla.
fields: Art, Drama, Poetry

Son of a German merchant and diplomat and his Japanese wife, who died soon after childbirth, Carl Sadakichi Hartmann was reared by wealthy relatives in Hamburg, Germany. In 1882, he went to the United States; developed an interest in American literature; began writing essays on art during the late 1880's and became a French correspondent for a newspaper in 1892, meeting Stéphane Mallarmé. He published an art magazine *The Art Critic*; launched *Art News* (1896) and *The Stylus* (1910). His works include the plays *Christ* (1893) and *Buddha* (1897), seven collected stories published as *Schopenhauer in the Air* (1899), *Japanese Art* (1904), and his magnum opus, *A History of American Art*. Hartmann became friends with photographer Alfred Stieglitz and promoted photography as an art form.

Hartmann, Nicolai

b. February 20, 1882
Riga, Latvia
d. October 9, 1950
Göttingen, West Germany
fields: Philosophy

Hartmann successfully vindicated ontology as worthy of a scientific study of being to his contemporaries who treated it cavalierly.

Hartmann von Aue

b. c. 1160-1165
Swabia
d. c. 1210-1220
Swabia
fields: Literature

Through its language, style, and literary form, Hartmann's work provided a model for the composition of courtly epic verse and stands at the beginning of the Hohenstaufen renaissance in German literature.

Hartshorne, Charles

b. June 5, 1897
Kittanning, Pennsylvania
fields: Philosophy, Religion and Theology

Charles Hartshorne advanced the idea of "process theology," which held that process or change was the basic characteristic of all beings, including God. This concept had a major influence on American Protestant theology. His major works include *The Divine Relativity* (1948), *A Natural Theology for Our Time* (1967), *Omnipotence and Other Theological Mistakes* (1984), *Creativity in American Philosophy* (1984), *Wisdom as Moderation* (1987), *The Darkness and the Light* (1990), and *The Zero Fallacy and Other Essays in Neoclassical Philosophy* (1997).

Harun al-Rashid

b. February, 766
al-Rayy, northern Iran
d. March 24, 809
probably Khorasan Province, Iran
fields: Government and Politics, Warfare and Conquest

Harun al-Rashid counts among the most famous holders of the office of caliph in the 'Abbasid Dynasty in Baghdad (eighth to thirteenth century). His most notable accomplishments were quelling revolts, establishing peace, and promoting industry and trade.

Harvey, Anne Gray. *See* Sexton, Anne

Harvey, William

b. April 1, 1578
Folkestone, Kent, England
d. June 3, 1657
London, England
fields: Biology, Medicine

Observation, dissection, and experimentation led Harvey to believe that blood follows a circular path through the body: outward through the arteries and back to the heart through the veins.

Hasan al-Basri, al-

full: Abu Sa'id ibn Abi al-Hasan Yasar al-Basri
b. 642
Medina, Arabia
d. 728
Basra, Iraq
fields: Religion and Theology

Al-Hasan was the most famous of Muslim teachers and preachers of the generation that followed the age of the Prophet Muhammad and his Companions. His views on religion and politics in the early stages of the Islamic Empire, as well as his code of conduct, made him the model of the pious Muslim in the formative age of Islam.

Hasanoanda (the Reader, or Coming to the Front). *See* Parker, Ely Samuel

Hashkeh Naabah (Angry Warrior). *See* Manuelito

Hassan II

full: Mawlay Hassan Mohammad ibn Yusuf
b. July 9, 1929
Rabat, Morocco
fields: Government and Politics

Hassan II became king of Morocco in 1961. Built new schools; improved status of women; launched public works projects. Generally was pro-Western during Cold War.

Faced some internal opposition; made enemies. Escaped numerous plots to overthrow him and two serious military assassination attempts. The first was at his forty-second birthday party in 1971, when ninety-eight guests were killed; the second was in 1972, when his official jet was repeatedly strafed upon reentering Moroccan airspace on orders from high-ranking Moroccan military officials.

Hastin Adiits'a'ii. *See* Dodge, Henry Chee

Hastin Ch'ilhajinii (Man of the Black Weeds). *See* Manuelito

Hastín Daagii. *See* Barboncito

Hastings, Warren

b. December 6, 1732
Churchill, Oxfordshire, England
d. August 22, 1818
Daylesford, Worcestershire, England
fields: Government and Politics

As the first governor-general, Hastings consolidated British rule in India by intervening in the internal politics of Indian states and by meeting threats elsewhere in the Indian subcontinent.

Hatcher, Andrew T.

b. June, 1923
Princeton, N.J.
fields: Journalism, Government and Politics

African American journalist, businessman, and political appointee; Andrew T. Hatcher was President John F. Kennedy's associate press secretary in 1960 and the first major African American appointee of Kennedy's New Frontier program.

Hatcher, Charles. *See* Starr, Edwin

Hatcher, John C., Jr.

b. ?
fields: Government and Politics

African American mayor of East Orange, N. J.; John C. Hatcher, Jr. served a four-year term as mayor of East Orange beginning in 1985.

Hatcher, Richard Gordon

b. July 10, 1933
Michigan City, Ind.
fields: Government and Politics

African American lawyer and political leader. Richard Gordon Hatcher was one of the first African Americans to be elected mayor of a major city in the United States. He successfully ran for mayor of Gary, Indiana, in 1967 and remained in office for twenty years (1967-1987). Hatcher had to overcame corrupt machine politics to gain this position. He symbolized the shift "from protest to politics" among African American civil rights leaders in the late 1960's. At the first National Black Political Convention, held in Gary in 1972, Hatcher was the keynote speaker. The convention goal was to help solidify political gains by establishing a "Black Agenda" for Congress and the nation.

Hatchett, Joseph Woodrow

b. Sept. 17, 1932
Clearwater, Fla.
fields: Law (federal judge)

African American federal judge. In 1975 Joseph Woodrow Hatchett was appointed a justice on the Florida Supreme Court, becoming the first African American to be appointed to the highest court of a state since Reconstruction.

Hatchootucknee. *See* Pitchlynn, Peter Perkins

Hathaway, Donny

b. Oct. 1, 1945
Chicago, Ill.
d. Jan. 13, 1979
New York, N.Y.
fields: Music (singer, pianist, composer-arranger, record producer)

African American singer, pianist, composer-arranger, and record producer; in the 1970;s Donny Hathaway produced and worked with acts such as Curtis Mayfield and the Impressions, Roberta Flack, Jerry Butler, and the Staple Singers; albums included *Donny Hathaway* (1971) and *Live* (1972); recorded a popular single, "Where Is the Love," in 1972 with Roberta Flack.

Hathaway, Isaac

b. Apr. 4, 1871
Lexington, Ky.
d. ?
fields: Art (sculptor), Education

African American sculptor and educator; Isaac Hathaway, head of the ceramics department at Alabama State Teachers College in Montgomery, was commissioned by the U.S. Mint to design the memorial coins issued in honor of Booker T. Washington and George Washington Carver.

Hatoyama Ichiro

b. January 1, 1883
Tokyo, Japan
d. March 7, 1959
Tokyo, Japan
fields: Government and Politics

Hatoyama was the architect of the postwar conservative coalition which has ruled Japan as the Liberal Democratic Party (Jiyu-Minshuto) since 1955.

Hatshepsut

aka: Hatshipsitu
b. Mid- to late sixteenth century B.C.E.
probably near Thebes, Egypt
d. c. 1482 B.C.E.
place unknown
fields: Government and Politics

Governing in her own right, Hatshepsut gave to Egypt two decades of peace and prosperity and beautified Thebes with temples and monuments.

Hatta, Mohammad

b. August 12, 1902
Bukittinggi, Sumatra, Dutch East Indies
d. March 14, 1980
Djakarta, Indonesia
fields: Government and Politics

Hatta directed the nationalist movement leading to the independence and final transfer of power to Indonesia at the end of 1949. He consolidated the independent nation's government, military, and economy based on democratic means.

Hattori, James

b. ?
Los Angeles, Calif.
fields: Journalism

Journalist James Hattori worked at local stations in Seattle and Houston before the Columbia Broadcasting Service (CBS) hired him as a network correspondent in Dallas. For a time, Hattori was vice president for broadcast for the Asian American Journalists Association. Hattori became CBS's Tokyo correspondent in 1993.

Hatwood, Mary Alice. *See* Futrell, Mary Hatwood

Haughey, Charles James

b. September 16, 1925
Castlebar, County Mayo, Ireland
fields: Government and Politics

A long-time Irish political figure, Charles James Haughey was three-time prime minister (taoiseach) of Ireland (1979-1981, 1982, 1987-1992). Forced to resign in 1992 following a wire-tapping scandal.

Havel, Václav

b. October 5, 1936
Prague, Czechoslovakia
fields: Theater and Entertainment, Government and Politics

A courageous dissident and important playwright, Václav Havel became the first president of the postcommunist government of the Czech Republic. His plays include *The Garden Party* (1963) and *The Memorandum* (1965). He coauthored Charter 77 in 1977 and, after serving a prison term for his dissidence, *Just a Few Sentences* (1989), a new manifesto demanding civil rights. An alliance of dissident groups collectively called Civic Forum was formed under Havel's leadership and led to the Velvet Revolution—Czechoslovakia's transition to democratic government.

Havens, Richie

né: Richard Pierce
b. Jan. 21, 1941
Brooklyn, N.Y.
fields: Music (folk singer)

African American folk singer and self-taught guitarist; Richie Havens made his recording debut in 1963; biggest hit was a version of George Harrison's "Here Comes the Sun" (1971).

Hawke, Robert

full: Robert James Lee Hawke
b. December 9, 1929
Bordertown, South Australia, Australia
fields: Government and Politics

Robert "Bob" Hawke was Labor Party prime minister of Australia from 1983 to 1991. His government concentrated on economic restructuring in order to combat a deep recession. Agreed on Prices and Incomes Accord with the trade union movement. Hawke and his treasurer, Paul Keating, implemented deregulation of finance and banking, taxation reform, and new approaches to labor relations. Keating replaced him as prime minister in 1991.

Hawking, Stephen W.

full: Stephen William Hawking
b. January 8, 1942
Oxford, England
fields: Astronomy, Physics

Many consider Hawking to be the greatest physicist of the late twentieth century. His work combines the two primary developments of early twentieth century physics—general relativity and quantum mechanics—to explain the origins and structure of the universe.

Hawkins, Coleman

b. Nov. 21, 1904
St. Joseph, Mo.
d. May 19, 1969
New York, N.Y.
fields: Music (jazz tenor saxophonist)

African American jazz tenor saxophonist; Coleman Hawkins promoted the use of the saxophone as a key instrument in jazz.

Hawkins, Connie

full: Cornelius Hawkins
b. July 7, 1942
Bedford-Stuyvesant, N.Y.
fields: Sports (basketball player)

African American basketball player; In 1967 Cornelius Hawkins played for the newly-formed American Basketball Association's (ABA) Pittsburgh Pipers; in 1969 won a court decision that allowed him to play for the National Basketball League (NBA); retired in 1976.

Hawkins, Edwin R.

b. Aug. 18, 1943
Oakland, Calif.
fields: Music (gospel singer)

African American gospel singer; Edwin R. Hawkins and his group, the Edwin Hawkins Singers, had a hit in 1969 with the gospel song "Oh Happy Day."

Hawkins, Erskine

b. July 26, 1914
Birmingham, Ala.
d. Nov. 11, 1993, Willingboro, N.J.
fields: Music (jazz trumpeter and bandleader)

African American jazz trumpeter and bandleader; From the late 1930's to the mid-1950's Erskine Hawkins's band recorded and made radio broadcasts; best known for recording "Tuxedo Junction" (1939).

Hawkins, Jamesetta. *See* James, Etta

Hawkins, Tramaine Davis

b. Oct. 11, 1957
San Francisco, Calif.
fields: Music (gospel music vocalist)

African American gospel music vocalist; Tramaine Davis Hawkins sang with the Edwin Hawkins Singers before going solo in the early 1980's; best-selling albums included *The Joy That Floods My Soul* and *Tramaine Live!*

Hawksmoor, Nicholas

b. c. 1661
probably East Drayton, Nottinghamshire, England
d. March 25, 1736
London, England
fields: Architecture

Overshadowed by Sir Christopher Wren and Sir John Vanbrugh for two centuries, Hawksmoor is now recognized as one of the three greatest English Baroque architects; his daring originality and eccentric brilliance mark him as the innovator *sui generis* of his time.

Hawthorne, Nathaniel

b. July 4, 1804
Salem, Massachusetts
d. May 19, 1864
Plymouth, New Hampshire
fields: Literature

With a series of short stories and novels which bring to life New England's Puritan past, Hawthorne achieved one of the most distinguished literary careers of the nineteenth century.

Hay, Elizabeth Dexter

b. Apr. 2, 1927
St. Augustine, Florida
fields: Biology, Medicine

Elizabeth Dexter Hay researched cell movement to learn how cells migrate correctly—forming embryos, healing wounds, and fighting infections—or abnormally, causing cancers and birth defects.

Hay, John

full: John Milton Hay
b. October 8, 1838
Salem, Indiana
d. July 1, 1905
Newbury, New Hampshire
fields: Diplomacy

After a distinguished career as presidential assistant, poet, novelist, editor, and historian, Hay served as secretary of state from 1898 to 1905, implementing the foreign policy initiatives that resulted in the United States' rise to world power.

Haya de la Torre, Víctor Raúl

b. February 22, 1895
Trujillo, Peru
d. August 2, 1979
Lima, Peru
fields: Government and Politics

Haya de la Torre was the founder of the Alianza Popular Revolucionaria Americana (APRA), an inter-American, democratic political movement that stimulated parties to modernize the old elitist orders in Peru and throughout Latin America.

Hayakawa, S. I.

b. July 18, 1906
Vancouver, British Columbia
d. Feb. 27, 1992
Greenbrae, Calif.
fields: Government and Politics, Education

Japanese American politician, educator; S. I. Hayakawa was born in British Columbia to Japanese immigrants; received degrees from University of Manitoba in 1927 and McGill University in 1928 before moving to United States to earn a doctorate at the University of Wisconsin (1935), where he remained as a member of the English department; as Canadian citizen was spared internment during World War II; president of San Francisco State University, 1968-1972; U.S. senator (Republican) for California, 1977-1983; special adviser to the secretary of state for East Asian and Pacific affairs, 1983-

1990; wrote *Language in Action* (1941), a seminal text in semantics, and *Language in Thought and Action* (1949).

Hayakawa, Sessue

né: Kintaro Hayakawa
b. June 10, 1890
Naaura Township, Honshu, Japan
d. November 23, 1973
Tokyo, Japan
fields: Theater and Entertainment

Japanese American actor. Sessue Hayakawa first came to the United States in 1909 to study political science, but in 1913 he decided to become an actor. Hayakawa appeared in many plays and silent films and even started his own production company in 1918. Hayakawa returned to Japan and became a Buddhist priest during the 1920's. His most notable films include *The Cheat* (1915) and *The Bridge on the River Kwai* (1957). For his role in *The Bridge on the River Kwai* he received an Academy Award nomination and a Golden Globe award. Hayakawa was a devout Buddhist who spoke eight languages and included religious training at his Tokyo drama school. His autobiography, *Zen Showed Me the Way . . . to Peace, Happiness, and Tranquility*, was published in 1960.

Hayashi, Dennis

b. May 31, 1952
Los Angeles, Calif.
fields: Civil Rights, Government and Politics, Law

Dennis Hayashi was born in Los Angeles to Japanese American parents who were interned during World War II; earned law degree at Hastings College in 1978; worked for the Asian Law Caucus, 1979-1991; defended the civil rights of Pacific Islanders, Vietnamese, Japanese, and other Asian Americans; served as co-counsel in the *coram nobis* case *Korematsu v. United States* (1984); selected executive director of the national Japanese American Citizens League (1991); cofounder of National Network Against Anti-Asian Violence; appointed director of the Office of Civil Rights, 1993.

Hayashi, Eric

b. Dec. 28, 1952
San Francisco, Calif.
fields: Theater and Entertainment

Eric Hayashi helped found San Francisco's Asian-American Theatre Workshop, which became the Asian-American Theatre Company in 1977 and produced plays by Frank Chin, David Henry Hwang, Philip Kan Gotanda, Momoko Iko, R. A. Shiomi, Genny Lim, and Warren Kubota. Hayashi became executive director of the company in 1986 and artistic director in 1989. While president of Sansei Productions, Records, and Tapes, he produced the Asian American rock group Noh Buddies (1983-1984), Lane Nishikawa's *Life in the Fast Lane* (pr. 1981), and Charlie Chin's *ABC (American Born Chinese)* (pr. 1983).

Hayashi, Harvey Saburo

né: Hayashi Saburo
b. 1866
Aizuwakamatsu, Japan
d. June 1, 1943
Holualoa, Kona, Territory of Hawaii
fields: Medicine, Publishing

Harvey Saburo Hayashi was the son of a samurai who was exiled for rebelling against the Meiji emperor. He graduated from Hahnemann Hospital and College with a degree in medicine in 1892. He moved to Kona, Hawaii, and opened a practice that treated primarily Japanese plantation workers. He also published a newspaper, the *Kona Hankyo*, for the rural community's residents.

Hayatt, Lester

b. 1948
fields: Fashion (fashion designer)

African American fashion designer; in 1984, Lester Hayatt, founder of Lester Hayatt Sportswear and "Hayatt" retail outlets, was among the ten African Americans honored for their impact on the fashion scene in the sixth annual Tribute to the Black Designer.

Hayden, Ferdinand Vandeveer

b. September 7, 1829
Westfield, Massachusetts
d. December 22, 1887
Philadelphia, Pennsylvania
fields: Exploration and Colonization, Natural History

Hayden organized and led scientific explorations throughout the Rocky Mountains in the 1860's and 1870's. The publicity surrounding his discoveries was a key factor in the creation of Yellowstone National Park, the first such park in the United States.

Hayden, Palmer C.

b. 1893
Wide Water, Va.
d. 1973
fields: Art (painter)

African American painter; Palmer C. Hayden painted the John Henry series; was the first recipient of the Harmon Foundation's Gold Medal for distinguished achievement by an African American in the fine arts.

Hayden, Robert Earl

b. Aug. 4, 1913
Detroit, Mich.
d. Feb. 25, 1980
Ann Arbor, Mich.
fields: Literature (poet)

African American poet; From 1976 to 1978, Robert Earl Hayden was the first African American to serve as consultant in poetry at the Library of Congress; published *Heart-shape in the Dust* (1940), *Words in the Mourning Time* (1968), and *American Journal* (1978).

Haydn, Franz Joseph

b. March 31, 1732
Rohrau, Austria
d. May 31, 1809
Vienna, Austrian Empire
fields: Music

For nearly fifty years, Haydn expressed his joy of life and love of beauty through music. He is considered the father of instrumental music (he developed the form of the string quartet). Haydn's collected works include seventeen operas, sixty-eight string quartets, sixty-two sonatas, and 107 symphonies.

Hayer, Talmadge

b. c. 1943
fields: Historical Figure

African American convicted assassin of Malcolm X; Under controversy, Talmadge Hayer was found guilty on Mar. 11, 1966, and sentenced to life imprisonment on Apr. 14, 1966.

Hayes, Bob

b. Dec. 20, 1942
Jacksonville, Fla.
fields: Sports (sprinter and football player)

African American sprinter and football player; Bob Hayes, nicknamed "the world's fastest human", won gold medals in the 1964 Olympics; played in the National Football League from 1965-1974.

Hayes, Charles Arthur

b. Feb. 17, 1918
Cairo, Ill.
d. April, 1997
Hazel Crest, Ill.
fields: Government and Politics

African American U.S. representative, Illinois; in 1983 Charles Arthur Hayes won the special election held to fill the remaining congressional term of Harold Washington; was reelected to four additional terms in Congress.

Hayes, Darlene

b. 1947
Topeka, Kans.
fields: Television

African American television producer; in 1975 Darlene Hayes was an associate producer for the *Phil Donahue Show*; produced *The Marsha Warfield Show*.

Hayes, Elvin Ernest

b. Nov. 17, 1945
Rayville, La.
fields: Sports (basketball player)

African American basketball player; Elvin Earnest Hayes retired in 1984 after sixteen National Basketball Association (NBA) seasons with San Diego, Houston, Baltimore, and Washington; elected to the Naismith Memorial Basketball Hall of Fame in 1990.

Hayes, Helen

né: Helen Hayes Brown
b. October 10, 1900
Washington, D.C.
d. March 17, 1993
Nyack, New York
fields: Theater and Entertainment (drama)

In more than sixty years on stage and screen, Hayes became the "first lady of the American theater."

Hayes, Ira Hamilton

b. Jan. 12, 1923
Bapchule, near Sacaton, Ariz.
d. Jan. 24, 1955
Bapchule, Ariz.
fields: Warfare and Conquest

Pima Indian U.S. war hero; as a U.S. Marine during World War II, Ira Hamilton Hayes was one of the six servicemen photographed raising the U.S. flag on Iwo Jima's Mount Suribachi on February 23, 1945; after his discharge from the Marines following the war, he found it difficult to cope with civilian life or with the fame resulting from the photograph; with limited education, Hayes had trouble finding work, and he struggled throughout his life with alcoholism; shortly after his thirty-second birthday, he was found dead of exposure in a field not far from his birthplace.

Hayes, Isaac

b. Aug. 20, 1942
Covington, Tenn.
fields: Music (songwriter, singer)

African American musician, songwriter, and singer; in 1964 Isaac Hayes began his creative association with the "Memphis Sound" of soul music at Stax Records; teamed with David Porter in 1966 to write hit songs including "Hold On, I'm Comin'", "Soul Man,", and "B-A-B-Y"; recorded his own hit album, *Hot Buttered Soul* (1969); produced the *Shaft* (11971) sound track.

Hayes, Roland

b. June 3, 1887
Curryville, Ga.
d. Jan. 1, 1977
Boston, Mass.
fields: Music (singer)

African American singer and recitalist; in 1917 Roland Hayes was the first black person to give a recital at Boston's Symphony Hall; sang for King George V in 1921; made his official debut at Carnegie Hall in 1923 and became an international star; last appearance was in 1973.

Hayes, Rutherford B.

full: Rutherford Birchard Hayes
b. October 4, 1822
Delaware, Ohio
d. January 17, 1893
Fremont, Ohio
fields: Government and Politics

President of the United States, 1877-1881. Though an ardent Radical Republican early in the Reconstruction era, Hayes moderated his views and as president ended that era by withdrawing military support for Republican state governments in the South. During his administration, Hayes also opposed inflation, defended the presidency from congressional attacks, and fought for civil service reform.

Haynes, George Edmund

b. May 11, 1880
Pine Bluff, Ark.
d. Jan. 8, 1960
Brooklyn, N.Y.
fields: Social Reform

African American social activist; George Edmund Haynes was the first African American to receive a doctorate from Columbia University; cofounded the Department of Race Relations of the Federal Council of Churches in America.

Haynes, Lemuel

b. July 8, 1753
West Hartford, Conn.
d. Sept. 28, 1833
Granville, N.Y.
fields: Historical Figure, Warfare and Conquest

African American preacher and Revolutionary War soldier; Lemuel Haynes was one of three black soldiers to participate in the taking of Fort Ticonderoga, N.Y., on May 10, 1775; was the first African American to receive a degree from an American college, in 1804.

Haynes, Lloyd

full: Samuel Lloyd Haynes
b. Oct. 19, 1935
South Bend, Ind.
d. Dec. 31, 1986
Coronado, Calif.
fields: Film, Theater and Entertainment (actor)

African American actor; Lloyd Haynes's film credits included *Ice Station Zebra* (1968) and *The Greatest* (1977); best known for his portrayal of history teacher, Pete Dixon, in the television series *Room 222* (1969-1974).

Haynsworth, Clement, Jr.

full: Clement Furman Haynsworth, Jr.
b. October 30, 1912
Greenville, South Carolina
d. November 22, 1989
Greenville, South Carolina
fields: Law

A conservative appeals court judge, Clement Haynsworth, Jr., received the first of two consecutive nominations to the Supreme Court by President Richard Nixon to be rejected by the Senate. When Justice Abe Fortas resigned from the Supreme Court on May 14, 1969, President Richard M. Nixon nominated Haynsworth on August 18, 1969. The American Bar Association rated him "highly qualified," but during Senate hearings he was criticized by representatives of labor and civil rights organizations, who charged him of being racist and antilabor and of participating in cases in which he had a financial interest. Because of these political and ethical uncertainties, the Senate rejected Haynsworth's nomination. Haynsworth then resumed his position on the court of appeals, which he held until his death.

Hayo. *See* Francis, Josiah

Hayslip, Le Ly

né: Phung Thi Le Ly
b. December 19, 1949
Ky La, Vietnam
fields: Literature, Social Reform

Advocating forgiveness and healing on both sides in the wake of the Vietnam War, Le Ly Hayslip created the East Meets West Foundation to build clinics, schools, and rehabilitation centers in Vietnam with the assistance of American veterans and other donors.

Hayward, Pamela Chruchill. *See* Harriman, Pamela Digby Churchill

Haywood, Anna Julia. *See* Cooper, Anna Julia Haywood

Haywood, Bill

full: William Dudley Haywood
aka: Big Bill Haywood
b. February 4, 1869
Salt Lake City, Utah
d. May 18, 1928
Moscow, U.S.S.R.

fields: Labor Movement

A founder of the Industrial Workers of the World (IWW), Bill Haywood began his labor career as a charter member of a western miners' union in 1896 and spent five years leading violence-prone strikes throughout Colorado. In 1905 he presided over the founding convention of the IWW. Tried for sedition for antiwar activities during World War I, he jumped bail in 1921 and fled to the Soviet Union. Afterward, enemies of labor unions often pointed to Haywood's flight as proof that IWW activities had been influenced by communism.

Haywood, Spencer

b. Apr. 22, 1949
Silver City, Miss.
fields: Sports (basketball player)

African American basketball player. Spencer Haywood began his twelve-year National Basketball Association (NBA) career in 1970 and played for the Los Angeles Lakers.

Hayworth, Rita

né: Margarita Carmen Cansino
b. October 17, 1918
Brooklyn, New York
d. May 14, 1987
New York, New York
fields: Film

A dazzling film star, Hayworth was renowned worldwide as one of the favorite pinup queens of American servicemen during World War II.

Head, Edith

né: Edith Claire Posener
b. October 28, 1898(?)
Los Angeles, California
d. October 24, 1981
Hollywood, California
fields: Film, Fashion

A prolific designer of film costumes who helped shape Hollywood's image of women for fifty-eight years, Edith Head was a dominant force in a profession largely defined by men.

Healy, James Augustine

b. Apr. 6, 1830
Macon, Ga.
d. Aug. 5, 1900
Portland, Maine
fields: Church Government, Religion and Theology

African American bishop; James Augustine Healy became the first African American Catholic priest in 1854; became the first African American Catholic bishop in 1875.

Hearns, Thomas

aka: Hit Man Hearns
b. Oct. 18, 1958
Memphis, Tenn.
fields: Sports (professional boxer)

African American professional boxer; the first boxer to win world titles in five different weight categories, Thomas Hearns also received National Golden Gloves and Amateur Boxer of the Year awards.

Hearst, Phoebe Apperson

né: Phoebe Elizabeth Apperson
b. December 3, 1842
Franklin County, Missouri
d. April 3, 1919
Pleasanton, California
fields: Patronage of the Arts

Phoebe Hearst was a leading patron in the areas of women's causes, education, and the arts.

Hearst, William Randolph

b. Apr. 29, 1863
San Francisco, Calif.
d. Aug. 14, 1951
Beverly Hills, Calif.
fields: Publishing, Journalism

Newspaper publisher William Randolph Hearst built circulation for his papers through sensational reporting and color comics. He stirred up public opinion in favor of a war with Spain (1898). Before and during World War II, his papers participated in a determined and systematic campaign to promote anti-Japanese activities and feeling although he published pro-German articles. He strongly supported the internment of Japanese Americans.

Heath, Edward

b. July 9, 1916
Broadstairs, Kent, England
fields: Government and Politics

Rising through the ranks of the Conservative Party to become Prime Minister of Great Britain, Health led his country into partnership with Europe by achieving British admission to the European Economic Community.

Heath, Jimmy

full: James Edward Heath
b. Oct. 25, 1926
Philadelphia, Pa.
fields: Music (saxophonist, flutist, composer)

African American saxophonist, flutist, composer, and educator; in 1947, Jimmy "Little Bird" Heath worked with Dizzy Gillespie's band; met Charlie "Bird" Parker in 1948 and organized his own Philadelphia-based big band; recorded with the Heath Brothers band in the 1970's; composed symphonic works including *Three Ears* (1988).

Heat-Moon, William Least

aka: William Trogdon
b. Aug. 27, 1939
Kansas City, Mo.
fields: Literature

Osage author; a best-selling author and noted lecturer, William Least Heat-Moon taught literature at Stephen's College in Columbia, Missouri, 1965-1978; lectured at the University of Missouri School of Journalism, 1985-1987; his published works include his nonfiction bestsellers *Blue Highways* (1983; travel memoir of a 13,000-mile automobile trek along the backroads of thirty-eight states) and *PrairyErth* (1991; combines natural history, social history, and ecology with life-affirming vignettes of common people who live in the heart of the Kansas Flint Hills); Heat-Moon also contributes articles to a variety of prestigious magazines, such as *Esquire*, *Time*, and *The Atlantic Monthly*.

Heaviside, Oliver

b. May 18, 1850
London, England
d. February 3, 1925
Torquay, Devon, England
fields: Mathematics, Physics

Oliver Heaviside invented vector analysis and operational calculus, which later became the method of Fourier transforms; made important contributions in the theory of propagation of electrical signals along wires and cables; worked as a telegraph operator (1868-1874); proposed method for duplex and multiplex telegraphy (1873); formulated the "telegraphers' equation" (1876); published a reformulation of James Clerk Maxwell's electromagnetic equations (1885); proposed a new system of vector algebra (1885); was elected a Fellow of the Royal Society of London (1891); published the first volume of *Electromagnetic Theory* and papers on operational calculus (1893); postulated the existence of the ionosphere (1902); received the first Faraday Medal of the Institution of Electrical Engineers (1923).

Heavy D.

né: Dwight Myers
b. 1967
Mount Vernon, N.Y.
fields: Music (rap singer)

African American lead singer for the rap group Heavy D; formed in 1986, upbeat Heavy D. and the Boyz recorded *Living Large* (1987), *Big Tyme* (1989), and *Peaceful Journey* (1991).

Heco, Joseph

né: Hamada Hikozo
b. 1837
Harima Province, Japan

d. 1897
fields: Historial Figure

Hamada Hikozo arrived in San Francisco in 1851 after he and a number of other sailors were rescued by an American ship after their ship was disabled on the Pacific Ocean. He received Western education, converted to Christianity, and became Joseph Heco, a U.S. citizen. Heco became an interpreter for Townsend Harris, the first U.S. consul to Japan in 1858. Heco later pursued business interests including a Japanese newspaper that published news translated from foreign papers. He wrote two accounts of his career: *Hyoryuki*, published in Japanese in 1868, describes his experiences as a castaway in the United States; *The Narrative of a Japanese* appeared in English in 1895.

Hector, Edward

b. c. 1744
d. 1834
fields: Historical Figure, Warfare and Conquest

African American revolutionary War soldier; after joining the army in 1777, Edward Hector saved the ammunition wagon he was in charge of at the Battle of Brandywine.

Heezen, Bruce

full: Bruce Charles Heezen
b. Apr. 11, 1924
Vinton, Iowa
d. June 21, 1977
in a submarine near Reykjanes Ridge, southwest of Iceland
fields: Science

Bruce Charles Heezen, in 1956, completed the first physiographic diagram of the North Atlantic Ocean, with Marie Tharp; recognized that deep submarine canyons are created by turbidity currents; discovered a rift zone in the center of the mid-ocean ridge that is related to continental drift; identified the ridge as a submarine mountain range that reaches around the earth; realized that the central rift is seismically active.

Hegel, Georg Wilhelm Friedrich

b. August 27, 1770
Stuttgart, Württemberg
d. November 14, 1831
Berlin, Prussia
fields: Philosophy

Hegel developed many theories of great philosophical importance that over the past century have influenced the social sciences, anthropology, sociology, psychology, history, and political theory. He believed that the mind is the ultimate reality and that philosophy can restore humanity to a state of harmony.

Hehaka Sapa. *See* Black Elk

Heidegger, Martin

b. September 26, 1889
Messkirch, Germany
d. May 26, 1976
Messkirch, West Germany
fields: Philosophy

Though within the Continental tradition of philosophy known as existentialism, Heidegger strove to free philosophy from what he claimed were its millennia-old metaphysical shackles. Using complex and arcane terminology, he sought to penetrate the nature of the confrontation of the human being with being itself and to clear a way for the answer to the age-old question of why there is something rather than nothing.

Height, Dorothy Irene

b. Mar. 24, 1912
Richmond, Va.
fields: Civil Rights, Women's Rights

African American administrator; Dorothy Irene Height, who was active in women's, civil rights, and community service groups, was best known as the fourth president of the National Council of Negro Women.

Hein, Piet

né: Pieter Pieterszoon Heyn
b. November 15, 1577
Delfshaven, Holland
d. June 18, 1629
at sea, near Dungeness, off the coast of Dunkirk
fields: Military Affairs, Diplomacy

Hein aided substantially in the Netherlands' breaking away from Spanish control. He defeated the Spanish and Portuguese several times in naval combat, including the most celebrated capture of treasure ships in the history of the Spanish Main.

Heine, Heinrich

né: Chaim Harry Heine
b. December 13, 1797
Düsseldorf
d. February 17, 1856
Paris, France
fields: Literature

Through his literary and journalistic works, Heine exposed the hypocrisy and oppressiveness of feudal society as it existed in many parts of Europe during the first half of the nineteenth century.

Heine, Heinrich Eduard

b. Mar. 16, 1821
Berlin, Prussia (now Germany)
d. Oct. 21, 1881
Halle, Germany
fields: Mathematics (geometry)

Heinrich Heine formulated the notion of uniform continuity. Laid the foundation for the Heine-Borel covering theorem. 1861, published *Handbuch der Kugelfunctionen, Theorie, und Anwendungen*, a standard work on spherical functions.

Heinkel, Ernst

full: Ernst Heinrich Heinkel
b. January 24, 1888
Grünbach, Germany
d. January 30, 1958
Stuttgart, West Germany
fields: Aviation and Space Exploration

Heinkel was a major figure in the development of European military and commercial aviation in the first half of the twentieth century, noted for advanced designs and the first practical jet- and rocket-propelled aircraft.

Heinmot Hikkih. *See* Yellow Wolf

Heinmot Tooyalakekt. *See* Joseph, Chief

Heisenberg, Werner

b. December 5, 1901
Würzburg, Germany
d. February 1, 1976
Munich, West Germany
fields: Physics

Heisenberg is considered to be one of the most important scientists of the twentieth century, mainly as a result of his creation of quantum mechanics, a theory that has dominated the development of nuclear and atomic physics since 1925. He was awarded the 1932 Nobel Prize in Physics.

Heiss, Carol

b. January 20, 1940
New York, New York
fields: Sports (ice skating)

Ladies figure skating gold medalist Carol Heiss's courage and determination captured America's heart and imagination at the 1960 Winter Olympics. In 1954, she had suffered a career-threatening injury and in 1955 learned that her mother suffered from cancer. Despite these setbacks, she placed second in the 1955 World Championships and finished a very close second at the 1956 Winter Olympics. Finally, in Squaw Valley, California, in 1960, she won an Olympic gold medal, dazzling the world with a spectacular display of skating. Four weeks after her victory, she announced her retirement from amateur skating, married figure skater Hayes Alan Jenkins, and made a film, *Snow White and the Three Stooges* (1961).

Helena, Saint

b. c. 248
Drepanum (modern Herkes) in Bithnyia, Asia Minor
d. c. 328
Nicomedia
fields: Religion and Theology, Saints

Literally the most important woman in the world during her time, Helena was the mother of Constantine the Great, the first Christian Roman emperor. Helena's elevation to sainthood was conferred, according to tradition, because she set out on pilgrimage to Palestine to discover the cross of Christ's crucifixion and, upon doing so, founded the Church of the Nativity and the Church of the Holy Sepulchre in the Holy Land.

Hellman, Lillian

full: Lillian Florence Hellman
b. June 20, 1905
New Orleans, Louisiana
d. June 30, 1984
Martha's Vineyard, Massachusetts
fields: Literature, Film

A leading American playwright and important screenwriter, Hellman published memoirs in the 1960's and 1970's that advanced the growing interest in women's lives and in autobiography.

Helmholtz, Hermann von

full: Hermann Ludwig Ferdinand von Helmholtz
b. August 31, 1821
Potsdam, Prussia
d. September 8, 1894
Berlin, Germany
fields: Physiology, Physics

Helmholtz contributed to the fields of energetics, physiological acoustics and optics, mathematics, hydrodynamics, and electrodynamics. His most important work was in establishing the principle of conservation of energy and in his experimental and theoretical studies of hearing and vision.

Helmont, Jan Baptista van

aka: Johannes Baptista van Helmont
b. Jan. 12, 1580
Brussels, Spanish Netherlands (now Belgium)
d. Dec. 30, 1644
Vilvoorde, near Spanish Netherlands (now Belgium)
fields: Chemistry, Medicine, Physiology

Rejecting ancient medical authority, Jan Baptista van Helmont formulated reasonably accurate descriptions of chemical digestion, the physiological benefit of fever, and the cause of disease; the experiments led him to discover gas and the indestructibility of matter; many of his propositions are condemned by the Spanish Inquisition in 1625.

Helms, Jesse Alexander

full: Jesse Alexander Helms
b. October 18, 1921
Monroe, North Carolina
fields: Government and Politics

A conservative Republican senator from North Carolina, Jesse Helms was elected to his post in 1972 after achieving local celebrity as a radio personality opposing racial integration. In the 1980's he sought to restrict funding of the National Endowment for the Arts by creating grant guidelines aimed at eliminating controversial awards.

Helper, Hinton

b. December 27, 1829
Rowan (later Davie) County, North Carolina
d. March 8, 1909
Washington, D.C.
fields: Literature

Hinton Helper is remembering for writing *The Impending Crisis of the South: How to Meet It* (1857), an attack on slavery that argued free white laborers were doomed to poverty because they had to compete with slaves. After publishing his book, he moved to New York for his own safety, while his book was suppressed in the South. In 1861 President Abraham Lincoln appointed Helper U.S. consul at Buenos Aires, where he served until 1866. Helper's post-Civil War writings made it clear he had not attacked slavery out of compassion for slaves. During the 1870's he worked on a project to build a railroad from Hudson Bay to the Strait of Magellan. Failure to secure support for the idea left him depressed and contributed to his suicide.

Hemingway, Ernest

b. July 21, 1899
Oak Park, Illinois
d. July 2, 1961
Ketchum, Idaho
fields: Literature

Hemingway was one of the most influential writers in the twentieth century, both as a much-imitated stylist and as a larger-than-life celebrity. He won the 1954 Nobel Prize in Literature.

Hemsley, Sherman

b. Feb. 1, 1938
Philadelphia, Pa.
fields: Theater and Entertainment, Television(actor)

African American actor; Sherman Hemsley was best known for his role as George Jefferson in the *All In the Family* (1973-1975) and *The Jeffersons* (1975-1985) television series; also played a church deacon in the *Amen* (1986-1991) series.

Henderson, Arthur

b. September 13, 1863
Glasgow, Scotland
d. October 20, 1935
London, England
fields: Diplomacy, Government and Politics

British politician and diplomat, winner of 1934 Nobel Peace Prize. Arthur Henderson was instrumental in building the British Labour Party and in extending the influence of internationalism in Europe. Involved with the development of the League of Nations and with the Dawes Plan. Britain's foreign secretary from 1929 to 1931.

Henderson, Leroy W.

b. May 27, 1936
Richmond, Va.
fields: Photography, Film, Education

African American photographer, filmmaker, and teacher; since he began freelancing in 1967, Leroy W. Henderson's work for magazines was published internationally and garnered for him numerous awards and honors.

Henderson, Rickey

b. Dec. 25, 1958
Chicago, Ill.
fields: Sports (baseball player)

African American baseball player; considered the best leadoff batter in baseball's history, Rickey Henderson won the Gold Glove Award in 1981; beat Ty Cobb's American League record of 892 stolen bases over a career in 1990.

Henderson, Smack

full: James Fletcher Hamilton Henderson
b. Dec. 18, 1897
Cuthbert, Ga.
d. Dec. 29, 1952
New York, N.Y.
fields: Music (arranger, pianist, bandleader)

African American arranger, pianist, and bandleader; in the 1930's Smack Henderson's orchestral arrangements for big bands were major contributions to the new swing sound; recognized as the first jazz musician to use written arrangements.

Hendricks, Barbara

b. November 20, 1948
Stephens, Ark.
fields: Music (opera singer)

African American opera singer; Barbara Hendricks debuted with the San Francisco Spring Opera in its 1974 production of *Ormindo*; made more than fifty recordings and appeared in the film version of *La Bohème* in 1988.

Hendrix, Jimi

né: Johnny Allen Hendrix
full: James Marshall Hendrix
b. November 27, 1942
Seattle, Washington
d. September 18, 1970
London, England
fields: Music (rock)

Guitarist, singer, and songwriter. Jimi Hendrix's innovations were both technical and creative. His recordings with his band, the Jimi Hendrix Experience, include *Are You Experienced?* (1967), which contained "Purple Haze," "Manic Depression," "Fire," "The Wind Cries Mary," and "Foxy Lady"; *Axis: Bold as Love* (1968), which contained "Little Wing" and "If Six Was Nine"; and *Electric Ladyland* (1968), which contained "Voodoo Chile" and "All Along the Watchtower." He formed the Band of Gypsys, with whom he performed in highly regarded concerts before dying of an overdose in 1970.

Heney, Francis J.

b. Mar. 17, 1859
Lima, N.Y.
d. Oct. 31, 1937
Santa Monica, Calif.
fields: Government and Politics

California State senator Francis J. Heney was one of the sponsors of the Webb-Heney Bill, an alien land law. The 1913 act was the first in a series of laws designed to drive Asian immigrants out of agriculture by prohibiting them from owning property. Many other states followed California's example and created alien land laws of their own.

Hengist

aka: Hengest
b. c. 420 C.E.
probably Jutland
d. c. 488 C.E.
probably Kent, England, or near Knaresborough, Yorkshire
fields: Warfare and Conquest

Hengist is reputed to have led the first Germanic invasion of Britain and to have established the first "English" kingdom in Kent.

Henie, Sonja

b. April 8, 1912
Kristiania (now Oslo), Norway
d. October 12, 1969
in an airplane bound for Oslo, Norway
fields: Sports, Acting

Henie is the only female figure skater to win gold medals in three consecutive Olympics—1928, 1932, and 1936. By combining graceful dance movements with her athletic ability, Henie was largely responsible for creating the huge international interest in figure skating.

Henley, Beth

full: Elizabeth Becker Henley
b. May 8, 1952
Jackson, Mississippi
fields: Literature

Focusing many of her plays on female characters and contemporary women's issues, Beth Henley has broken into the traditional male canon of mainstream American theater, with her plays regularly staged, produced, anthologized, and taught.

Henri I. *See* Christophe, Henri

Henry I

aka: Henry I, King of England
b. c. September, 1068
Selby, Yorkshire, England
d. December 1, 1135
Lyons-la-Forêt, Normandy
fields: Law, Government and Politics, Monarchy

King of England, 1100-1135. Henry I did much to organize and regularize the laws and government of England. Under him, reforms were achieved in judicial and fiscal matters. By his marriage to Matilda of Scotland, a descendant of Edward the Confessor, Henry I won the support of many of his English subjects, although the marriage was less pleasing to Normans.

Henry II

aka: Henry II, King of England
b. March 5, 1133
Le Mans, Maine (now in France)
d. July 6, 1189
near Tours
fields: Law, Government and Politics, Monarchy

King of England, 1154-1189. Beginning his reign after a time of civil war, Henry II began a period of reconstruction. After the reestablishment of order in the realm, Henry sought to build further reforms on those of his grandfather, Henry I; these would include general administration as well as specific reforms in fiscal and judicial affairs. An ardent reader and student, Henry fostered the study of the laws of England and encouraged the study of constitutional law.

Henry II the Saint

aka: Henry II, King of Germany
b. May 6, 973
Abbach, Bavaria
d. July 13, 1024
near Göttingen (in modern West Germany)
fields: Government and Politics, Monarchy

King of Germany, 1002-1024. Using patience, common sense, and a realistic approach to the intrigues and problems of eleventh century Germany and Italy, Henry restored the monarchy north of the Alps and supported and encouraged Church reforms.

Henry III

aka: Henry III, King of England
b. October 1, 1207
Winchester, Hampshire, England
d. November 16, 1272
London, England
fields: Government and Politics, Monarchy

King of England, 1227-1272. Henry's reign witnessed the growing role of the community of the realm in the rule of England: By the end of Henry's reign, the rule of England could no longer be exercised by the king alone.

Henry IV

aka: Henry IV, King of Germany
b. November 11, 1050
Goslar, Saxony
d. August 7, 1106
Liège
fields: Government and Politics, Monarchy

King of Germany, 1056-1106. Henry's struggles with the German nobility and the Papacy had a decisive impact on the future constitutional and political development of Germany. Although his tenacious defense of the rights and prerogatives of the monarchy was largely unsuccessful, it still marked him as one of the greatest of the German kings.

Henry IV

aka: Henry IV, King of England
b. April 3, 1367
near Spilsby, Lincolnshire, England
d. March 20, 1413
London, England
fields: Government and Politics, Monarchy

King of England, 1399-1413. Henry IV usurped the throne of Richard II and placed his family, the Lancastrians, in power, initiating the dynastic struggle between the great aristocratic families of Lancaster and York known as the Wars of the Roses. The manner in which Parliament was allowed to depose Richard and accept Henry as the royal successor provided the opportunity for Parliament to gain more power than it had ever held before: The Lancastrian kings would rule by parliamentary title, and in the fifteenth century political theories would place great stress on the legal limitations of royal power.

Henry IV

aka: Henry of Navarre

b. December 14, 1553
castle of Pau, Basses Pyrenees
d. May 14, 1610
Paris, France
fields: Monarchy, Government and Politics

Henry III, king of Navarre, 1572-1589; king of France, 1589-1610. Henry IV brought peace and national prestige to France within the structure of powerful monarchy after protracted strife, which had included eight civil wars. He settled the long-standing Catholic-Protestant conflict by embracing Catholicism while granting broad toleration to the French Reformed church. He is the most noteworthy of early modern rulers who made religious liberty the law of the state.

Henry V

né: Henry of Monmouth
b. September 16, 1387
Monmouth Castle, England
d. August 31, 1422
Bois de Vincennes, France
fields: Government and Politics

King of England 1413-1422. Henry V gave England justice and stability at home, while his military and political genius enabled him to proceed in the conquest of France and claim to its crown. He left England a strong power in European affairs.

Henry VI

aka: Henry of Windsor
b. December 6, 1421
Windsor, Berkshire, England
d. May 21, 1471
London, England
fields: Government and Politics

King of England and France, 1422-1461, 1470-1471. As the realm recoiled from the confusion of a Continental conflict and a civil war, Henry VI, the third and last Lancastrian king of England, abrogated his role as an effective monarch and became a pawn of his relatives and great nobles.

Henry VII

aka: Henry Tudor
b. January 28, 1457
Pembroke Castle, Pembrokeshire, Wales
d. April 21, 1509
Richmond, Surrey, England
fields: Government and Politics

King of England, 1485-1509. Henry's sense of caution, his flair for public relations, and his knowledge of the importance of timing allowed him to end the Wars of the Roses and lay the foundations of England's Tudor dynasty.

Henry VIII

b. June 28, 1491
Greenwich, England
d. January 28, 1547
London, England
fields: Government and Politics, Religion and Theology

King of England, 1509-1547. Through administrative changes and his break with the Roman Catholic Church, and the subsequent establishment of the Church of England, Henry VIII strengthened the position of the monarch in English society.

Henry, Joseph

b. December 17, 1797
Albany, New York
d. May 13, 1878
Washington, D.C.
fields: Science

As the first secretary of the Smithsonian Institution, president of the National Academy of Sciences, and a leading experimental physicist, Henry was one of the most important molders of an American professional scientific community.

Henry, O.

né: William Sydney Porter
b. September 11, 1862
Greensboro, North Carolina
d. June 5, 1910
New York, New York
fields: Literature

William Sydney Porter advanced the state of American short stories and made his pen name of O. Henry synonymous with surprise endings. In a little more than one decade, he published more than two hundred stories in magazines and books, some of which are still well known one century later.

Henry, Patrick

b. May 29, 1736
Studley Plantation, Hanover County, Virginia
d. June 6, 1799
Red Hill Plantation, Charlotte County, Virginia
fields: Government and Politics

Expressing his libertarian ideas through a uniquely powerful oratory, Henry was a principal architect of the American Revolution.

Henry, Richard B.. *See* Obadele, Imari Abubakari

Henry the Lion

b. 1129
place unknown
d. August 6, 1195
Brunswick, Saxony
fields: Government and Politics

Henry was the most important of the twelfth century German nobles who resisted the authority of the Holy Roman Emperor. He was also a leader in the movement to extend German colonization into Slavic territory.

Henry the Navigator, Prince

aka: Henrique o Navegador
aka: Henry, prince of Portugal
b. March 4, 1394
Porto, Portugal
d. November 13, 1460
Sagres, Portugal
fields: Exploration and Colonization, Warfare and Conquest

Although Prince Henry considered crusading against the North African Muslims to be his primary task, it was his African explorations that later put Portugal at the forefront of the European age of discovery.

Hensley, Virginia Patterson. *See* Cline, Patsy

Henson, Josiah

b. June 15, 1789
Port Tobacco, Md.
d. 1883?
Dresden, Ontario, Canada
fields: Historical Figure

African American escaped slave; Josiah Henson may have been the model for the title character in Harriet Beecher Stowe's *Uncle Tom's Cabin: Or, Life Among the Lowly* (1852).

Henson, Matthew Alexander

b. August 8, 1866
Charles County., Md.
d. March 9, 1955
New York, N.Y.
fields: Exploration and Colonization

African American explorer. Matthew Alexander Henson was an assistant to the Arctic explorer Robert E. Peary for twenty-three years. He was the only American on the North Pole expedition and was the first person actually to reach the pole; he planted the U.S. flag there. Henson went to sea at age twenty, and was an able seaman by 1887 when he first joined Peary, then a U.S. Navy civil engineer, on a trip to Nicaragua. Henson and Peary made eight Arctic voyages together, with Henson serving as interpreter with the Inuits and in many other necessary roles. Peary, Henson, and four Inuits reached the pole on April 6, 1909. Peary sent back five support teams as they neared their goal but kept Henson with him for the final leg of their journey.

Henze, Hans Werner

b. July 1, 1926
Gütersloh, Germany
fields: Music

Henze is one of the most prolific European composers of the postwar era, with a catalog of published compositions numbering more than 150 works in almost every medium. His success as a modern operatic composer is unique.

Hepburn, Katharine

full: Katharine Houghton Hepburn
b. May 12, 1907
Hartford, Connecticut
fields: Film

With a career spanning most of the twentieth century, Katharine Hep- burn has, from her early career days, embodied wit, independence, and charm to the American public. Hepburn was one of the first actresses to break down Hollywood's stereotype of women, and she has served as a model of grit and beauty throughout her career.

Heraclitus of Ephesus

b. c. 540 B.C.E.
Ephesus, Greece
d. c. 480 B.C.E.
place unknown
fields: Philosophy

Heraclitus formulated one of the earliest and most comprehensive theories of the nature of the world, the cosmos, and the soul. His theory that the soul pervaded all parts of the universe and its inhabitants stood in contrast to the ideas of his more mechanistic contemporaries.

Heraclius

b. c. 575
possibly Cappadocia
d. Probably February 11, 641
Constantinople
fields: Government and Politics, Warfare and Conquest, Monarchy

Byzantine Emperor, 610-641. Seizing the East Roman (Byzantine) Imperial throne amid seemingly fatal crises, Heraclius turned back the onslaughts of the Persians and Avars, only to see his work largely undone by the Arab conquests. Nevertheless, he and his successors initiated institutional reorganization that would save and revitalize the empire.

Herder, Johann Gottfried

b. August 25, 1744
Mohrungen, East Prussia
d. December 18, 1803
Weimar, Saxe-Weimar
fields: Philosophy, Literature

Herder was a major figure in the transitional period in German letters encompassing the second half of the eighteenth century. He was a universalist whose writings dealt with many areas of human thought.

Heredia, José María

b. Dec. 31, 1803
Santiago, Cuba
d. May 7, 1839
Mexico City, Mexico
fields: Literature

Latino poet. After earning a law degree from the University of Havana, José María Heredia was forced to leave Cuba for the United States in 1823 for political reasons. He began writing poetry in the Romantic style, earning the titles "the first Hispanic-American romantic" and "the firstborn of Hispanic Romanticism." He published *Poesías* (poems) in 1825. The poem "Meditación en el teocalli de Cholula," which he wrote in 1820 at the age of seventeen, is considered a great achievement of early Spanish-American Romanticism.

Herman, Alexis M.

b. July 16, 1947
Mobile, Ala.
fields: Government and Politics

African American political appointee; in 1977, Alexis M. Herman was the first black woman to be appointed as director of the Women's Bureau of the Labor Department; in 1989 she was chosen by Ron Brown to serve as his chief of staff for the Democratic National Committee.

Hermene Moxmox. *See* Yellow Wolf

Hermite, Charles

b. Dec. 24, 1822
Dieuze, France
d. Jan. 14, 1901
Paris, France
fields: Mathematics (algebra, applied math, calculus, and number theory)

Charles Hermite studied elliptic functions. Finds the general solution of the quintic equation, 1858. Proves that the number e is transcendental, 1873.

Hernandez, Aileen Clarke

né: Aileen Clarke
b. May 23, 1926
Brooklyn, New York
fields: Labor Movement, Social Reform, Women's Rights

As president of the National Organization for Women—the first black woman to hold that post—director of the International Ladies' Garment Workers Union, and commissioner of the Equal Employment Opportunity Commission, Aileen Hernandez has represented the interests of women and minorities in the forefront of social reform.

Hernández, Antonia

b. May 30, 1948
Torreon, Coahuila, Mexico
fields: Law

Mexican American lawyer; Antonia Hernández was born in Coahuila, Mexico; earned law degree at University of California, Los Angeles, in 1974; staff counsel to U.S. Senate Judiciary Committee, 1978-1981; served as staff attorney, Mexican American Legal Defense and Education Fund (MALDEF), Washington, D.C., 1981-1983; employment litigation director, MALDEF, Los Angeles, 1983-1985; became president and general counsel, MALDEF (1985); after 1992 Los Angeles riots, appointed to Rebuild L.A. commission.

Hernández, Ester

b. 1944
Dinuba, Calif.
fields: Art

Latina artist. Ester Hernández, of Native American (Yaqui) and Chicano ancestry, was a farmworker before she cofounded the Mujeres Muralistas art collective. Her art combines her interest in her own heritage, her devotion to the female image, and social criticism. Hernández has worked in many media but is primarily a printmaker. Her most well known print is *Sun Mad*, which she made after she discovered that the water in her hometown, Dinuba, was contaminated with pesticides.

Hernández, Juano

b. 1896
San Juan, Puerto Rico
d. July 17, 1970
San Juan, Puerto Rico
fields: Film, Theater and Entertainment (actor)

African American actor; Juano Hernández played Lucas Beauchamp in *Intruder in the Dust* (1949), the first definitive film portrayal of an African American who did not accommodate and stood in defiance of racial hatred.

Hernandez, Keith

b. Oct. 20, 1953
San Francisco, Calif.
fields: Sports (baseball player)

Latino baseball player. First baseman Keith Hernandez made his major league debut in 1974 with the St. Louis Cardinals. In 1979, he won the National League batting title, led the league in doubles and runs scored, and shared the league's Most Valuable Player Award. The following season, Hernandez again led the league in runs scored. He won the Gold Glove Award for eleven consecutive years beginning in 1978. In 1982, he helped the Cardinals to a World Series victory but was traded to the New York Mets amid rumors of cocaine use. Hernandez overcame his addiction and helped the Mets win the 1986 World Series.

Hernández, Willie

full: Guillermo Hernández y Villanueva
b. Nov. 14, 1954
Aguada, Puerto Rico
fields: Sports (baseball player)

Latino baseball player. Left-handed pitcher Willie Hernández made his major league debut in 1977 with the Chicago Cubs. In 1984, he emerged as a top relief pitcher while helping the Detroit Tigers defeat the San Diego Padres in the World Series. That same season, he was named to his first All-Star team and won the American League's Cy Young and Most Valuable Player awards (only the second reliever to win both). Hernández made the All-Star team again in 1985 and 1986, then retired after the 1988 season.

Hernández de Córdoba, Francisco

b. ?
d. 1517
Havana, Cuba
fields: Exploration and Colonization

Spanish explorer. Francisco Hernández de Córdoba sailed from Havana with three ships in February of 1517 and landed in the Yucatán Peninsula after a storm blew him off course. On the trip back to Cuba, another storm drove his ships to the Florida coast, which he had previously explored with Juan Ponce de León. Upon his return to Cuba, Hernández de Córdoba died of wounds suffered during an Indian attack in Florida. Although he had helped explore the Florida coast, Hernández de Córdoba is primarily remembered for the accounts he gave of the Yucatán Peninsula, which inspired others, including Hernán Cortés, to explore the area.

Herndon, Alonzo F.

b. June 26, 1858
Walton County, Ga.
d. July 21, 1927
Atlanta, Ga.
fields: Business and Industry, Philanthropy

African American businessman; Alonzo F. Herndon earned a fortune with the African American-owned Atlanta Life Insurance Company (founded in 1905); Herndon's son, Norris, established the Alonzo F. and Norris B. Herndon Foundation for philanthropic activities.

Hero of Alexandria

aka: Heron of Alexandria
b. fl. 62 C.E.
Alexandria
d. late first century
Alexandria
fields: Mathematics, Science

Hero wrote about mechanical devices and is the most important ancient authority on them. Some of these were his own inventions, including a rudimentary steam engine and windmill. He also investigated mathematics, where his most noted contribution was a method for approximating square roots.

Herod the Great

b. B.C.E.
probably Idumaea, Palestine
d. Spring, 4 B.C.E.
Jericho
fields: Government and Politics

As a loyal king of Judaea under Roman administration, Herod brought peace, prosperity, and a cultural flowering to the land he ruled. Nevertheless, negative aspects of his reign—including harsh dealings with family members and the inability to placate his Jewish subjects—have tended to overshadow these positive achievements.

Herodotus

b. c. 484 B.C.E.
Halicarnassus, Asia Minor
d. c. 424 B.C.E.
probably Thurii, Italy
fields: Historiography

For having written the first work of history, Herodotus is commonly called "the father of history."

Herophilus

b. c. 335 B.C.E.
Chalcedon, Bithynia
d. c. 280 B.C.E.
probably Alexandria, Egypt
fields: Medicine, Physiology

The first systematic dissector, and possibly vivisector, of the human body, the Greek physician Herophilus made numerous anatomical discoveries and significantly enriched anatomical nomenclature. His knowledge of human anatomy was superior to that of his precursors, and he laid the foundation for subsequent Western anatomy. Herophilus' analysis of the pulse and his dream theory also exercised a strong influence on medicine and psychology in later centuries.

Herrera, Efren

b. July 30, 1951
Guadalajara, Jalisco, Mexico
fields: Sports (football player)

Latino football player. Efren Herrera played soccer in Mexico but switched to football after moving to California during high school. In 1970, he broke ten school records at the University of California, Los Angeles. In 1973, he was named an All-American. Herrera was drafted by the Detroit Lions in 1974 but did not emerge as a top kicker until he played with the Dallas Cowboys. His 69.7 field-goal percentage for the 1970's was the decade's best. He helped the Cowboys win the 1977 Super Bowl, then moved to the Seattle Seahawks in 1978, where he kicked a career-high 100 points. He retired in 1982.

Herrera, Juan Felipe

b. Dec. 27, 1948
Fowler, Calif.
fields: Literature

Latino poet. In 1972, Juan Felipe Herrera earned his bachelor's degree in social anthropology from the University of California, Los Angeles. He abandoned doctoral work at Stanford University in favor of a master's degree from the prestigious Iowa Writers Workshop. Herrera began publishing poetry in the late 1960's. In the early 1970's, he worked on an experimental book with no formal beginning or end, no pagination, no titles, and no conventional cover called *Rebozos of Love*. He formed the theater group Teatro Tolteca in 1968 and published such notable works as *Exiles of Desire* (1983), *Laughing Out Loud, I Fly* (1998), and *Border-crosser with a Lamborghini Dream* (1999).

Herrera, Miguel

b. 1835
d. 1905
fields: Art

Latino artist. Miguel Herrera, a Mexican American who lived in Taos County, New Mexico, created religious figures for the Brotherhood of Penitentes from the 1870's and 1880's. His figures, which were meant to be dressed in fabric clothing, are distinguishable because of their height and because of their ears, which are usually made of seashells and are set lower on the head than those of real people.

Herrera-Sobek, María

b. ?
Mexico
fields: Scholarship (folklorist)

Folklorist. María Herrera-Sobek earned her undergraduate degree in chemistry at California State University at Northridge (1974), her master's degree in Latin American studies from the University of California, Irvine, and her Ph.D. from the University of California, Los Angeles. Her study of Mexican American culture has resulted in such books as *The Bracero Experience: Elitelore Versus Folklore* (1979), *Beyond Stereotypes: The Critical Analysis of Chicana Literature*

(1985), *The Mexican Corrido: A Feminist Analysis* (1990), and *Northward Bound: The Mexican Immigrant Experience in Ballad and Song* (1993).

Herriot, Édouard

b. July 5, 1872
Troyes, France
d. March 26, 1957
Lyons, France
fields: Government and Politics

One of the most important French statesmen of the first half of the twentieth century, Herriot served nearly four decades in the French parliament, headed three governments between 1924 and 1933, held posts in six other cabinets between 1916 and 1936, was mayor of Lyons (France's second-largest city) from 1905 to 1957, and was leader of the Radical-Socialist Party for much of his career.

Herschel, Caroline Lucretia

b. Mar. 16, 1750 (by German calendar, 1751 by British calendar)
Hanover, Hanover (now Germany)
d. Jan. 9, 1848
Hanover, Hanover
fields: Astronomy

Caroline Lucretia Herschel was an observer of comets and star clusters; discovered three new nebulas in 1783; transcribed, reduced, and cataloged astronomical data.

Herschel, John

full: Sir John Herschel
b. Mar. 7, 1792
Slough, Buckinghamshire, England
d. May 11, 1871
Hawkhurst, Kent, England
fields: Astronomy, Chemistry, Mathematics, Invention and Technology

John Herschel, in 1819, discovered hypo (sodium thiosulfate), a fixing agent for use in photography; conducted extensive observations of stars and nebulas;in 1864, published a catalog of 5,079 nebulas and stellar clusters.

Herschel, William

né: Friedrich Wilhelm Herschel
full: Sir Frederick William Herschel
b. Nov. 15, 1738
Hanover, Hanover (now Germany)
d. Aug. 25, 1822
Slough, Buckinghamshire, England
fields: Astronomy

William Herschel, on Mar. 13, 1781, discovered Uranus; in 1781, correctly calculated the rotation time of Mars; in 1785-1789, built the world's largest telescope; in 1787, discovered Mimas and Enceladus, moons of Saturn; in 1787, discovered Titania and Oberon, moons of Uranus; in 1801, proposed the term "asteroid" for bodies between Mars and Jupiter; perfected reflecting telescopes; cataloged 800 double stars and 2,500 star clusters and nebulas; proved the universality of the law of gravity.

Hertz, Gustav

full: Gustav Ludwig Hertz
b. July 22, 1887
Hamburg, Germany
d. October 30, 1975
Berlin, East Germany
fields: Physics

Hertz and his colleague James Franck received the Nobel Prize in Physics in 1925 for their spectroscopic experiments on mercury vapor when bombarded with electrons. Their results were some of the first to confirm empirically the accuracy of Niels Bohr's model of atomic structure as well as the hypothesis of Max Planck and Albert Einstein that atoms absorb energy in discrete quanta rather than continuously.

Hertz, Heinrich

full: Heinrich Rudolf Hertz
b. Feb. 22, 1857
Hamburg, Germany
d. Jan. 1, 1894
Bonn, Germany
fields: Physics

Heinrich Hertz was first to measure electromagnetic waves and their radiation, after James Clerk Maxwell's theories.

Hertzsprung, Ejnar

b. Oct. 8, 1873
Frederiksberg, Denmark
d. Oct. 21, 1967
Roskilde, Denmark
fields: Astronomy, Physics

A pioneer in the detailed study of light from stars, Ejnar Hertzsprung discovered the relationship between the brightness and temperature of stars; made the first measurement of the distance to another galaxy, the Small Magellanic Cloud.

Herzen, Aleksandr

b. April 6, 1812
Moscow, Russia
d. January 21, 1870
Paris, France
fields: Social Reform, Literature

As one of the "fathers" of the Russian intelligentsia, Herzen urged an increased pace of Westernization for Russia, yet harbored a Slavophile attraction for the village commune. From his offices in London, he edited the influential émigré newspaper *Kolokol* (the bell) from 1857 to 1866, thereby helping to shape the direction of Russian radical opinion.

Herzig, Jack

full: John A. Herzig
b. July 30, 1922
Newark, N.J.
fields: Scholarship

John Herzig, consultant to the U.S. Commission on Wartime Relocation and Internment of Civilians, testified before Congress in favor of passage of Japanese American redress legislation. The commission's efforts played an important role in the enactment of the Civil Liberties Act of 1988. He helped execute the terms of the act as principal consultant for the Justice Department's Office of Redress Administration. During the Gordon K. Hirabayashi *coram nobis* case of 1988, the testimony offered by Herzig and his Japanese American wife helped refute allegations of subversive activities by Japanese Americans in World War II. The court overturned Hirabayashi's conviction.

Herzl, Theodor

b. May 2, 1860
Pest, Hungary
d. July 3, 1904
Edlach, Austria
fields: Diplomacy, Journalism

Often called the "father of modern Zionism," Herzl expounded on the need for a Jewish homeland and created an effective organizational framework for this political movement. His diplomatic missions to secure a Jewish state lent worldwide credibility to early Zionism.

Herzog, Chaim

b. September 17, 1918
Belfast, Ireland
d. April 17, 1997
Tel Aviv, Israel
fields: Government and Politics

Chaim Herzog was an Israeli soldier and statesman. Head of military intelligence from 1959 to 1962. Israel's ambassador to United Nations at time of strong anti-Israel sentiment in late 1970's. As Israeli president (a position with limited power) from 1983 to 1993, was heavily involved in coalition-building activities behind the scenes; also traveled and enhanced Israel's standing abroad.

Heschel, Abraham Joshua

b. January 11, 1907
Warsaw, Poland, Russian Empire (now Poland)
d. December 23, 1972
New York, New York
fields: Philosophy, Religion and Theology

Jewish philosopher and theologian Abraham Joshua Heschel was a leader in the Civil Rights and anti-Vietnam War movements of the 1960's and a driving force in improving relations between Christians and Jews. He interpreted Jewish tradition through such works as *Man Is Not Alone* (1951) and lived it through his religious and social activism. He was the first Jewish scholar appointed to the Union Theological Seminary in New York. Other major works include *Man's Quest for God* (1954), *God in Search of Man* (1955), *The Prophets* (1962), *Who Is Man?* (1965), *The Insecurity of Freedom* (1966), and *Between God and Man* (1975).

Hesiod

b. fl. c. 700 B.C.E.
Ascra, Greece
d. Date unknown
Ozolian Locris, Greece
fields: Literature

Hesiod organized and interpreted the Greek myths which form the basis for European civilization and examined with moral conscience the working life of Greek society at the dawn of modern history.

Hess, Harry Hammond

b. May 24, 1906
New York, New York
d. Aug. 25, 1969
Woods Hole, Massachusetts
fields: Science

Harry Hammond Hess connected seemingly unrelated geologic phenomena into a comprehensive theory; proposed a new paradigm for interpreting the structure and mechanics of the earth with his mobile seafloor theory.

Hess, Rudolf

full: Walter Richard Rudolf Hess
b. April 26, 1894
Alexandria, Egypt
d. August 17, 1987
West Berlin, West Germany (now Berlin, Germany)
fields: Government and Politics

Rudolf Hess was Adolf Hitler's secretary and deputy in the 1930's. Devoted follower of Hitler since early 1920's. Eventually displaced by Matin Boorman. Made secret solo night flight to Scotland in 1941 (still not entirely understood) and was captured. Later given a life sentence at the Nuremberg Trials. Died in 1987, the sole remaining Nazi prisoner in Berlin's Spandau prison.

Hess, Victor Franz

b. June 24, 1883
Schloss Waldstein, Styria, Austria
d. Dec. 17, 1964
Mount Vernon, New York
fields: Physics

Victor Franz Hess was a leader in establishing the extraterrestrial origin of cosmic rays; carried out important studies in radioactivity and atmospheric electricity; in 1936, won the Nobel Prize in Physics.

Hesse, Eva

b. January 11, 1936
Hamburg, Germany
d. May 29, 1970
New York, New York
fields: Art (sculpture)

Eva Hesse was a sculptor known for using nontraditional materials and forms in pieces that often have an emotional content and for emphasizing the process of creation. Between 1964 and 1970, she made more than one hundred sculptures designed to hang from ceilings and walls or to be placed on the floor. Nonrepresentational, they nevertheless seem organic in form and are charged with emotion. Diagnosed with a brain tumor in April, 1969, she continued to work until her death in May, 1970, at the age of thirty-four. That year, the School of Visual Arts in New York exhibited a survey of her sculptures. In 1972, the Guggenheim Museum organized a retrospective show.

Hesse, Hermann

b. July 2, 1877
Calw, Germany
d. August 9, 1962
Montagnola, Switzerland
fields: Literature

Writing in the tradition of Romantic individualism, Hesse produced novels and novellas that brought him literary acclaim. Highly autobiographical and confessional, his prose works employ modernist thought and aesthetic principles to narrate the development of existential protagonists. He won the 1946 Nobel Prize in Literature.

Hevesy, Georg von

b. August 1, 1885
Budapest, Hungary
d. July 5, 1966
Frieburg im Breisgau, West Germany
fields: Chemistry, Physics, Biology, Medicine

Hevesy pioneered the use of radioactive isotopes to study chemical processes. For this work, he was awarded the Nobel Prize in Chemistry for 1943 and the Atoms for Peace Award in 1959. He is also known for his discovery in 1923 of the element hafnium.

Hewett, Howard

b. ?
fields: Music (pop vocalist)

African American pop vocalist; Howard Hewett was a founding member of the Solar Records group Shalamar; had a hit single "Dancin' in the Sheets" from the film *Footloose* (1984).

Hewish, Antony

b. May 11, 1924
Fowey, Cornwall, England
fields: Astronomy

Antony Hewish, in 1964, discovered interplanetary scintillation of small radio sources; in 1965, detected a radio source in the Crab nebula; in 1967, discovered the first pulsar; won the Nobel Prize in Physics, along with Sir Martin Ryle, for the development of new techniques in radio astronomy, in 1974; observations of pulsars provided evidence for the existence of neutron stars.

Hewitt, John N. B.

b. Dec. 16, 1859
Lewiston, N.Y.
d. Oct. 14, 1937
Washington, D.C.
fields: Anthropology

Native American anthropologist. John N. B. Hewitt, a Tuscarora (he was perhaps as much as one-quarter Tuscarora), was a leading authority on the Iroquois League and the ceremonials and customs of the Six Nations. Fluent in Tuscarora, Mohawk, and Onondaga; also became well versed in several Algonquian dialects

Heyerdahl, Thor

b. October 6, 1914
Larvik, Norway
fields: Anthropology, Archaeology, Exploration and Colonization

Heyerdahl undertook several successful sea voyages using prehistoric type of craft to demonstrate that early man was skilled in navigation on ocean currents and thus, by transpacific and transatlantic crossings, was able to migrate. He has written numerous books, both popular and scientific, about his voyages and diffusionist theories.

Hiawatha

aka: Hienwentha
aka: Ayonwartha (He Who Combs)
b. c. 1525
Mohawk River valley, N.Y.
d. c. 1575
Mohawk River valley, N.Y.
fields: Diplomacy, Government and Politics, Native American Affairs

Native American leader. Hiawatha, a Mohawk, is credited, along with Deganawida (a Huron), with organizing the League of the Iroquois, or Five Nation Confederacy, in the sixteenth century. Among the Iroquois tribes today, both Hiawatha and Deganawida are highly esteemed figures. Poet Henry Wadsworth Longfellow muddied the historical waters considerably with his 1855 epic poem, *Hiawatha*. His story was based mostly on Chippewa legend, although he borrowed the name Hiawatha for his hero.

Hickok, Lorena

full: Alice Lorena Hickok
b. March 7, 1893
East Troy, Wisconsin
d. May 1, 1968
Rhinebeck, New York
fields: Journalism

One of the first female political analysts in American history, Hickok became perhaps Eleanor Roosevelt's closest friend, the New Deal's primary reporter on Depression conditions, and a leading contributor to the women's movement.

Hickok, Wild Bill

né: James Butler Hickok
b. May 27, 1837
Troy Grove, Illinois
d. August 2, 1876
Deadwood, Dakota Territory (now South Dakota)
fields: Law, Military Affairs

Hickok's prowess with a pistol made him one of the deadliest gunfighters in the American West and one of the most forceful and accomplished lawmen of the Kansas cattle towns. Hickok's exploits as a soldier, scout, gunfighter, and lawman made him one of the most recognized figures from the American frontier.

Hidalgo, Hilda

b. Sept. 1, 1928
Puerto Rico
fields: Social reform, Education

Latino educator, social activist; director, Group Work and Tutorial Division of the Child Service Association, Newark, New Jersey, 1964; founding member, Puerto Rican Congress of New Jersey, 1975; professor of public administration and social work, Rutgers University, 1977-1992; wrote *Rehabilitation in the 80's: Understanding the Hispanic Disabled* (1982); served on editorial boards for *Journal of Gay and Lesbian Psychotherapy*, *Affilia: The Journal of Women and Social Work*, and *Society and Culture*.

Hidalgo y Costilla, Miguel

b. May 8, 1753
Corralejos, Guanajuato, Mexico
d. Aug. 1, 1811
Chihuahua, Mexico
fields: Religion and Theology, Social Reform

Latino priest and revolutionary. Miguel Hidalgo y Costilla was ordained as a priest in 1778. When Napoleon defeated Spain in Europe in 1808, Hidalgo organized a Mexican revolt that began on September 16, 1808. He led his parishioners to seize a prison and capture Guanajuato. He captured several more cities and accumulated almost 100,000 followers before his defeat and capture at Mexico City on January 17, 1811. Hidalgo was defrocked and executed by firing squad. Many view him as the father of Mexican independence.

Hienwentha. *See* Hiawatha

Hieronymus, Eusebius. *See* Jerome, Saint

Higginbotham, A. Leon, Jr.

b. Feb. 25, 1928
Trenton, N.J.
d. Dec. 14, 1998
Boston, Mass.
fields: Government and Politics

African American government official; A. Leon Higginbotham, Jr., was appointed a circuit judge on the U.S. Court of Appeals by President Jimmy Carter in 1977; authored *The Colonial Period* (1978), the first volume in *In the Matter of Color: Race and the American Legal Process.*

Higgins, Chester A., Sr.

b. May 10, 1917
Chicago, Ill.
fields: Journalism, Government and Politics

African American journalist and political appointee; Chester A. Higgins, Sr. wrote for the *Louisville Defender* newspaper and for *Ebony* and *Tan* magazines; named associate editor of *Jet* magazine in 1959; in 1972 became general assistant to Benjamin Hooks, the first African American commissioner of the Federal Communications Agency.

Higgins, Chester, Jr.

b. Nov. 6, 1946
Lexington, Ky.
fields: Photography

African American photographer; Chester Higgins, Jr., photographed the black community during the era after the Civil Rights movement; books include *Black Women* (1970, with text by Harold McDougall) and *Drums of Life: A Photographic Essay on the Black Man in America* (1974).

Higgins, Margaret. *See* Sanger, Margaret

Higgins, Marguerite

b. September 3, 1920
Hong Kong, China
d. January 3, 1966
Washington, D.C.
fields: Journalism

While covering the Korean War, Higgins became the first woman to win a Pulitzer Prize for international reporting.

Higginson, Thomas Wentworth

full: Thomas Wentworth Storrow Higginson
b. December 22, 1823
Cambridge, Massachusetts
d. May 9, 1911
Cambridge, Massachusetts
fields: Literature, Military Affairs, Social Reform, Women's Rights

Higginson wrote prolifically but is best known in the literary world as the discoverer of Emily Dickinson's poetry. He is notable for commanding a regiment of black enlisted men in the Civil War and for laboring in social causes such as the abolition of slavery and women's rights.

Hightower, Dennis Fowler

b. October 28, 1941
Washington, D.C.
fields: Business and Industry (business executive)

African American business executive; in 1995, Dennis Fowler Hightower was named president of Walt Disney Television and Telecommunications, becoming the first African American to ever hold the post and the highest ranking African American executive in the Disney organization at that time.

Hijuelos, Oscar

b. Aug. 24, 1951
New York, N.Y.
fields: Literature

Latino writer. Cuban American writer Oscar Hijuelos earned his undergraduate and M.S. degrees at the City College of the City University of New York. He worked in advertising for several years before he started writing full-time. His books have been described as a combination of realism and Latin American Magical Realism. *Our House in the Last World* (1983), his first novel, won the Rome Fellowship in Literature from the American Academy and Institute of Arts and Letters. *The Mambo Kings Play Songs of Love* (1989) won the 1990 Pulitzer Prize in fiction. He also published such notable works as *The Fourteen Sisters of Emilio Montez O'Brien* (1993) and *Mr. Ives' Christmas* (1995).

Hilbert, David

b. Jan. 23, 1862
Königsberg, Prussia (now Kaliningrad, Russia)
d. Feb. 14, 1943
Göttingen, Germany
fields: Mathematics (algebra, applied math, calculus, geometry, mathematical logic, and number theory)

David Hilbert worked in the theory of algebraic invariants and number fields, geometry, functional analysis, integral equations, mathematical physics, and the calculus of variations; he helped establish the foundations of modern mathematics.

Hildebrand. *See* Gregory VII

Hildebrandt, Johann Lucas von
b. November 14, 1668
Genoa
d. November 16, 1745
Vienna, Austria
fields: Architecture

One of the supreme architects of the Austrian Baroque, Hildebrandt specialized in the design and construction of palaces and pleasure gardens for the Austrian and German nobility. His finest achievement was the Belvedere Palace, built for Prince Eugene in Vienna.

Hildegard von Bingen
b. 1098
Bermersheim, near Alzey, Rheimhessen (now in Germany)
d. September 17, 1179
Rupertsberg, near Bingen (now in Germany)
fields: Religion and Theology, Literature, Music

The first major German mystic, Hildegard, in her prolific writings and extensive preaching, exerted a widespread influence on religious and political figures in twelfth century Europe.

Hill, Amy
b. c. 1953
Seattle, Wash.
fields: Art, Theater and Entertainment

Performance artist Amy Hill's one-woman show "Tokyo Bound" was a critical and box-office success. In her work, she draws on her experience as an Asian American of Japanese and Finnish extraction. She appeared in television shows and films, including *Dim Sum: A Little Bit of Heart* (1984) and *Singles* (1993), and worked with the Cold Tofu and Great Leap performance groups.

Hill, Anita Faye
b. July 30, 1956
Lone Tree, Okla.
fields: Law, Women's Rights

A lawyer and a professor at the University of Oklahoma Law School, Anita Hill entered the national spotlight in 1991 when she testified before the Senate that she had been sexually harassed by Supreme Court justice nominee Clarence Thomas in the 1980's when she worked under him in the Department of Education's Office of Civil Rights (1981-1982) and at the Equal Employment Opportunity Commission (1982-1983); many women were outraged by such alleged behavior and by the hostile manner in which the all-male panel of senators treated Hill. Although Thomas was confirmed as a Supreme Court justice (by a vote of 52 to 48), Hill's thoughtful presentation made her a symbol for feminists, and she continued to speak out on important women's issues.

Hill, Chippie
full: Bertha Hill
b. Mar. 15, 1905
Charleston, S.C.
d. May 7, 1950
New York, N.Y.
fields: Music (singer)

African American singer; Chippie Hill performed with blues artist Ma Rainey, Louis Armstrong, and Thomas Dorsey.

Hill, Herbert
b. January 24, 1924
New York, N.Y.
fields: Civil Rights, Education

African American educator and civil rights activist. Herbert Hill worked as a researcher and organizer for the United Steelworkers of America during 1947-1948 and began his lifelong association with the NAACP in 1948. He served as special assistant to the executive director (1948-1952), then as national labor secretary (1952-1960), and later national labor director. Hill was involved in virtually every NAACP suit filed against workplace (and intraunion) discrimination, against racially biased pay differentials, and against employer antilabor activity which especially affected black workers. Among his publications are *Citizen's Guide to Desegregation: A Study of Social and Legal Change in American Life* (1955, with Jack Greenberg), *No Harvest for the Reaper: The Story of the Migratory Agricultural Worker in the United States* (1960), *Employment, Race, and Poverty* (1967, with Arthur Ross), and *Race, Work, and the Law* (1985), volume one of *Black Labor and the American Legal System.*

Hill, James Jerome
b. September 16, 1838
Rockwood, Ontario
d. May 29, 1916
St. Paul, Minnesota
fields: Business and Industry, Engineering

Hill used his tenacity and entrepreneurial skills to amass a personal fortune and create a railroad empire in the American Northwest. In the process, he substantially contributed to both the region's and the nation's prosperity and growth.

Hill, Octavia
b. December 3, 1838
Wisbech, Cambridgeshire, England
d. August 13, 1912
London, England
fields: Social Reform

Hill sought to cope with the social consequences of slum housing by creating and managing a system of humane and personal contact between landlord and tenant. Concern with the urban environment also led her to preserve open spaces for public use, to fight against smoke pollution, and to assist in the establishment of the National Trust.

Hillary, Edmund
full: Edmund Percival Hillary
aka: Sir Edmund Hillary
b. July 20, 1919
Auckland, New Zealand
fields: Exploration and Colonization

Hillary and his Sherpa guide Tenzing Norgay were the first men to reach the top of Mount Everest. Hillary also was the first man to drive a land vehicle across Antarctica to the South Pole.

Hillery, John Richard
b. Apr. 28, 1874
St. Mary's County, Md.
d. 1940
fields: Invention and Technology

African American inventor; podiatrist John Richard Hillery invented the tarsal arch support; was issued a Scroll of Blessing by the pope for curing a Catholic nun.

Hilliard, Asa Grant, III
b. Aug. 22, 1933
Galveston, Tex.
fields: Education

African American educator; professor Asa Grant Hilliard III studied the learning process of black children; was a member of the board of directors of the National Black Child Development Institute from 1973 to 1975.

Hilliard, David
b. May 15, 1942
Mobile, Ala.
fields: Civil Rights

African American member of the Black Panther Party (BPP); David Hilliard was considered one of the co-founders of the Black Panther Party; wrote *This Side of Glory: The Autobiography of David Hilliard and the Story of the Black Panthers* (1992).

Hilliard, Earl Frederick
b. April 9, 1942
Birmingham, Ala.

fields: Government and Politics (politician and attorney)

African American politician and attorney; in 1983, Earl Frederick Hilliard was elected to serve as a state senator in Alabama; ran for Congress from Alabama's Seventh Congressional District and was elected in 1992; reelected in 1994.

Hillis. *See* Francis, Josiah

Hillis, Margaret

b. October 1, 1921
Kokomo, Indiana
d. February 5, 1998
Evanston, Illinois
fields: Music

One of the twentieth century's leading choral conductors, Margaret Hillis achieved recognition in a field that was one of the last bastions of male domination in the arts. She founded the Chicago Symphony Chorus, and she was the first woman to conduct the Chicago Symphony.

Hillishago. *See* Francis, Josiah

Himes, Chester

full: Chester Bomar Himes
b. July 29, 1909
Jefferson City, Mo.
d. Nov. 12, 1984
Moraira, Spain
fields: Literature

African American novelist, short-fiction writer, essayist, and social analyst; Chester Himes's writing career began in the Ohio State penitentiary; paroled in 1936; published *If He Hollers Let Him Go* (1945), *Lonely Crusade* (1947), and novels such as *Cotton Comes to Harlem* (1965), which feature Grave Digger Jones and Coffin Ed Johnson.

Himmler, Heinrich

b. October 7, 1900
Munich, Germany
d. May 23, 1945
Lüneburg, Germany
fields: Military Affairs, Government and Politics

As Reich leader of the Schutzstaffel (SS) and chief of the German police, Himmler controlled the entire security apparatus of the Third Reich. Entrusted by Adolf Hitler with the implementation of the so-called final solution, Himmler became the principal organizer of the killing of nearly six million Jews.

Hindemith, Paul

b. November 16, 1895
Hanau, Germany
d. December 28, 1963
Frankfurt am Main, West Germany
fields: Music

Hindemith, a neoclassicist, used forms that were popular during the seventeenth and eighteenth centuries. He sought to redefine and assert the principles of tonality in the twentieth century in his writings and to reflect those principles in his compositions.

Hindenburg, Paul von

full: Paul Ludwig Hans Anton von Beneckendorff und von Hindenburg
b. October 2, 1847
Posen, Prussia
d. August 2, 1934
Neudeck, Germany
fields: Military Affairs, Government and Politics

During the years 1916-1918, Hindenburg commanded Germany's armed forces. As the second President of the Weimar Republic, Hindenburg attempted to manage a Germany that was beset by extreme political, economic, and social disorder. As a result of this instability, Hindenburg presided over the rise of Nazi power. On January 20, 1933, he appointed Adolf Hitler as Chancellor of Germany, despite his personal dislike of the man, thereby legally giving Hitler power.

Hine, Darlene Clark

b. Feb. 7, 1947
Moorley, Mo.
fields: Education, Scholarhship, Historiography

African American historian, educator, and college administrator; during the 1980's, Darlene Clark Hine became best known for her scholarship in African American women's history; wrote *Black Victory: The Rise and Fall of the White Primary in Texas* (1979), and *Black Women in White: Racial Conflict and Cooperation in the Nursing Profession, 1890-1950* (1989).

Hines, Charles Alfonso

b. Sept. 4, 1935
Washington, D.C.
fields: Military Affairs

African American military officer; Charles Alfonso Hines achieved the rank of major general in the United States Army in 1988 and received a number of commendations and awards throughout his career.

Hines, Fatha

full: Earl Kenneth Hines
b. Dec. 28, 1905
Duquesne, Pa.
d. Apr. 22, 1983
Oakland, Calif.
fields: Music (pianist, bandleader, composer)

African American pianist, bandleader, and composer; Fatha Hines may be considered the most technically advanced and musically sophisticated of the early jazz pianists; developed a technique with his right hand described as "trumpet" style.

Hines, Gregory

full: Gregory Oliver Hines
b. Feb. 14, 1946
New York, N.Y.
fields: Dance (tap), Theater and Entertainment

African American improvisational tap dancer; Gregory Hines's credits included Broadway, film, and television; received Outer Critics' Circle award for performance in *Eubie!* (1978); received Tony nominations for *Comin' Uptown* and *Sophisticated Ladies*; film successes included *The Cotton Club* (1984) and *White Nights* (1985); starred in *The Gregory Hines Show* (1997-1998).

Hing, Alex

b. ?
fields: Labor Movement

Chinese American Alex Hing, a community and labor organizer in San Francisco and New York, was minister of information for the Red Guards, a radical Chinese American group, founded in 1969, which merged with I Wor Kuen in 1971. He served on the interim steering committee of the Asian Pacific American Labor Alliance (APALA) of the American Federation of Labor-Congress of Industrial Organizations (AFL-CIO) and belonged to the Hotel Employees and Restaurant Employees union. A hotel cook, Hing published articles in *East Wind* and *Amerasia Journal*.

Hinkson, Mary

b. 1930
Philadelphia, Pa.
fields: Dance

African American dancer and choreographer; Mary Hinkson danced with the Martha Graham company and is best-known for the 1963 role created for her in *Circe*.

Hinojosa, Rolando

né: Roland Hinojosa-Smith
b. January 21, 1929
Mercedes, Tex.
fields: Literature

Mexican American writer. Rolando Hinojosa began to write seriously while he was in high school. He completed military service and earned degrees in Spanish. Hinojosa published *Estampas del valle y otras obras/Sketches of the Valley and Other Works* in 1973. It was the first volume in his evolving "Klail City Death Trip" series, focused on residents of a fictional Texas border town. Amidst substantial critical acclaim, Hinojosa became the first Chicano to win an important international literary award and the first citizen of the United States to be honored by the Casa de las Americas panel of Latin American judges.

Hinshelwood, Cyril Norman

full: Sir Cyril Norman Hinshelwood
b. June 19, 1897
London, England
d. Oct. 9, 1967
London, England
fields: Chemistry

Cyril Norman Hinshelwood worked in chemical kinetics, discovering the branching chain mechanism for explosive reactions in 1928. In 1956, shared the Nobel Prize in Chemistry with Nikolai Semenov.

Hinton, Milton J.

b. 1910
Vicksburg, Miss.
fields: Photography, Music

African American photographer and musician; Milton J. Hinton created a comprehensive photographic record of jazz musicians and singers both onstage and offstage.

Hinton, S. E.

full: Susan Eloise Hinton
b. 1950
Tulsa, Oklahoma
fields: Literature

An American author of popular novels for young adults, S. E. Hinton introduced a controversial style characterized by realistic dialogue, unsentimental plots, and violence. She published *The Outsiders* (1967) when she was only eighteen. Her later books included *That Was Then, This Is Now* (1971), *Tex* (1979), *Rumble Fish* (1977), and *Taming the Star Runner* (1988).

Hinton, William Augustus

b. Dec. 15, 1883
Chicago, Ill.
d. Aug. 8, 1959
Canton, Mass.
fields: Medicine, Education

African American physician and educator; William Augustus Hinton became Harvard Medical School's first African American professor in 1949 and received international recognition for discovering a method of testing for syphilis; authored *Syphilis and Its Treatment* (1936), a standard reference work on the subject.

Hipparchus

b. 190 B.C.E.
Nicaea, Bithynia, Asia Minor (modern Iznik, Turkey)
d. 126 B.C.E.
possibly Rhodes
fields: Astronomy, Mathematics, Geography

Hipparchus was the greatest astronomer of ancient times. He was the founder of trigonometry, which he used in a method for determining the distances from Earth to the moon and sun, and the first to use consistently the idea of latitude and longitude to describe locations on Earth and in the sky.

Hippocrates

b. c. 460 B.C.E.
Cos, Greece
d. c. 370 B.C.E.
Larissa, Thessaly
fields: Medicine

Hippocrates is credited with separating the practice of medicine from magic and superstition, inaugurating the modern practice of scientific observation, and setting the guidelines for high standards of ethical medical practice.

Hippolytus of Rome

b. c. 170
place unknown
d. c. 235
Sardinia
fields: Religion and Theology, Philosophy

Initiating Christian commentary on the books of the Old Testament, Hippolytus also provided the first systematic handbook regulating the ordination of the ministry and the conduct of worship. In addition, he elaborated the connections among the Greco-Roman philosophical schools and popular practices and the diversity of opinions which divided the Christian communities.

Hirabayashi, Gordon Kiyoshi

b. Apr. 23, 1918
Seattle, Wash.
fields: Historical Figure

Gordon Kiyoshi Hirabayashi, a twenty-four-year-old University of Washington student when the relocation order for Japanese Americans was issued in February, 1942, felt the law was unjust. He formally refused to register for evacuation in May, 1942. In October, 1942, Hirabayashi was tried for violating both the curfew and exclusion orders. His attorney, Frank Walters of the American Civil Libertise Union, argued that Hirabayashi's Fifth Amendment right to due process was violated by the exclusion order. Hirabayashi was found guilty and appealed. In February, 1943, an appeals court asked the Supreme Court to rule on the legality of the exclusion order, the curfew order, and Public Law 503. In June, 1943, the Court upheld the curfew order but declined to rule on the exclusion order. On January 12, 1988, through a petition for a writ of *coram nobis*, Hirabayashi's conviction was vacated.

Hirabayashi, James

b. Oct. 30, 1926
Meredith, Wash.
fields: Scholarship

Japanese American James Hirabayashi was interned at Tule Lake during World War II. After the war, he became an anthropologist, receiving a Ph.D. from Harvard in 1962. he conducted research in the United States, Japan, and Nigeria. He was part of the faculty at San Francisco State University from 1959 to 1989. He supported the Third World Liberation Front strike in 1969. Not long after the successful strike, he became dean of ethnic studies for six years. In 1989, he became the chief curator of the Japanese American National Museum.

Hirabayashi, Lane Ryo

b. Oct. 17, 1952
Seattle, Wash.
fields: Scholarship

Lane Ryo Hirabayashi, like his father, James Hirabayashi, is an anthropologist and an active supporter of ethnic studies. He received his Ph.D. from the University of Colorado, Boulder, in 1981. His areas of research include the Zapotec Indians of Mexico, the Japanese American internment, and the community of Gardena, California. He also plays blues and folk guitar professionally.

Hirano, Irene Yasutake

full: Irene Ann Yasutake Hirano
b. Oct. 7, 1948
Los Angeles, Calif.
fields: Social Reform

Japanese American administrator, social activist; Irene Yasutake Hirano was born in Los Angeles, her father's family was interned during World War II; cofounder and president of Leadership Education for Asian Pacifics; chair of the National Network of Asian and Pacific Women; president of the Asian Pacific Legal Defense and Education Fund; chair of the California State Superintendent's Council on Asian Pacific Affairs; vice president of the Southern Christian Leadership Conference; associate director of Asian Women's Center, 1972-1975; executive director of T.H.E. Clinic for Women, Los Angeles, providing medical help and counseling to poor women; president, Asian Women's Network, Los Angeles, 1980; became director and president of the Japanese American National Museum (1988).

Hiraoka, Kimitake. *See* Mishima, Yukio

Hirasaki, Jimmy

full: Kiyoshi Hirasaki
b. 1900
Kumamoto Prefecture, Japan

d. 1963
fields: Business and Industry

Jimmy Hirasaki, who arrived in the United States as a teenager, learned how to produce onion and carrot seeds from a farmer in Gilroy, California. After the 1920's, Hirasaki focused on garlic, and by 1941, he was planting fifteen hundred acres of garlic. He was voluntarily relocated to Grand Junction, Colorado, during World War II but returned to Gilroy and re-created the business. He later helped launch the *Hokubei Mainichi* newspaper.

Hirata, Lucie Cheng. *See* Cheng, Lucie

Hirohito

aka: Showa
b. April 29, 1901
Tokyo, Japan
d. January 7, 1989
Tokyo, Japan
fields: Government and Politics

Hirohito (or Showa, more correctly since his death), in an unprecedented action, made the decision that ended World War II in the Pacific. Thereafter, he provided the symbolic leadership that facilitated the recovery of Japan from the devastation of the war, while first renouncing a divine status for himself and then promulgating the new democratic constitution for his nation.

Hiroshige

né: Andō Tokutarō
full: Andō Hiroshige
aka: Utagawa Hiroshige
aka: Ichiyūsai Hiroshige
aka: Ryusai
b. 1797
Edo, Japan
d. 1858
Edo, Japan
fields: Art

Hiroshige was one of the last masters of the *ukiyo-e* woodblock prints in Japan and was famed for his poetic landscapes.

His Eyes Are Dreamy. *See* Two Leggings

Hiss, Alger

b. November 11, 1904
Baltimore, Maryland
d. November 15, 1996
New York, New York
fields: Diplomacy, Law

Hiss was a U.S. diplomat accused of being a Communist spy and became the defendant in two notorious trials that heightened the public's fear of communist infiltration in the government.

Hitchcock, Alfred

full: Alfred Joseph Hitchcock
b. August 13, 1899
Leytonstone (now in London), England
d. April 29, 1980
Bel Air, California
fields: Film

In a film career that lasted more than fifty years, Hitchcock directed numerous thrillers that explored the psychological depths of the human condition. In the process, he created some of the most memorable and influential films of the modern era.

Hitchings, George

full: George Herbert Hitchings, Jr.
b. Apr. 18, 1905
Hoquiam, Washington
d. February 27, 1998
Chapel Hill, North Carolina
fields: Biology, Chemistry, Medicine

George Herbert Hitchings, Jr. was one of the most successful twentieth century practitioners of chemotherapy. He introduced rational drug design and numerous pharmaceuticals to medical use, including, in 1951, the anticarcinogen 6-mercaptopurine; in 1957, the drug azothioprine (Immuran), which is widely used as an immunosuppressant in organ transplantation; and in 1977, the drug acyclovir (Zovirax). In 1988, he was awarded, with Gertrude Belle Elion and James Whyte Black, the Nobel Prize in Physiology or Medicine.

Hitler, Adolf

b. April 20, 1889
Braunau am Inn, Austro-Hungarian Empire
d. April 30, 1945
Berlin, Germany
fields: Government and Politics

As leader of the National Socialist German Workers' Party in Germany and as dictator of the Third Reich, Hitler was responsible for many of the events that led to World War II. His belief in Teutonic racial superiority and his anti-Semitism also resulted in the Holocaust.

Hiura, Barbara

b. Mar. 24, 1950
Chicago, Ill.
fields: Journalism

Barbara Hiura, who earned an M.A. at the University of California, Berkeley, was a reporter for the newspaper *Hokubei Mainichi* in San Francisco. She served as president and board member of the National Association for Ethnic Studies.

Ho Chi Minh

né: Nguyen That Thanh
b. May 19, 1890
Kim Lien, Vietnam, French Indochina
d. September 3, 1969
Hanoi, North Vietnam
fields: Government and Politics

Ho was the chief architect, founder, and leader of the Indochinese Communist Party (1930), an organizer of the Viet Minh (1941), and President of the Democratic Republic of Vietnam (North Vietnam) from 1945 until his death. An ardent proponent of his country's independence, Ho was recognized as one of the twentieth century's greatest anticolonial revolutionaries and most influential Communist leaders.

Ho, Chinn

b. Feb. 26, 1904
Honolulu, Territory of Hawaii
d. May 12, 1987
Honolulu, Hawaii
fields: Banking and Finance

Asian American Chinn Ho pioneered the concept of condominium ownership in Hawaii and was the first Asian American to serve as director of Theo H. Davies, one of the islands' "Big Five" companies. He later served as director of Host International, World Airways, Hawaiian Airlines, Pacific Insurance Co., Pioneer Mill Company, Honolulu Stadium, and the *Honolulu Advertiser.* He assembled a group of investors to buy the *Honolulu Star-Bulletin* and became director of Gannett Pacific Corporation when Gannett took over the paper. He later invested in buildings and land in Guam, Hong Kong, California, and China.

Ho, David

b. November 3, 1952
Taiwan
fields: Medicine

Physician and researcher David Ho became one of the world's foremost authorities on the human immunodeficiency virus (HIV). He was named the head of the newly built Aaron Diamond AIDS Research Center in New York in 1990. Ho demonstrated that the virus is rarely in human saliva and identified the bodily cells that the virus targets for attack. He was the first to isolate the virus in otherwise healthy carriers. He became the personal physician of former National Basketball Association (NBA) star Earvin "Magic" Johnson, following the announcement in late 1991 of Johnson's HIV-positive status.

Ho, Fred

né: Fred Wei-Han Houn
b. 1957
Palo Alto, Calif.
fields: Music

Asian American Fred Ho created a new style of jazz that draws on Asian and African American music and is inspired by a commitment to revolutionary social change. In the early 1980's he formed two multiracial jazz groups, the Asian American Art Ensemble and the Afro-Asian Music Ensemble. His albums include *Blues for the Freedom Fighters* (1985), *Tomorrow Is Now! Suite* (1985), *Bamboo That Snaps Back* (1986), *A Song for Manong* (1988), and *We Refuse to Be Used and Abused* (1988). He created a jazz opera *Chinaman's Chance*, which premiered in San Francisco in 1987 and received a full production in 1989. He received the Duke Ellington Distinguished Artist Lifetime Achievement Award and many other commissions and awards.

Hobbes, Thomas

b. April 5, 1588
Westport, Wiltshire, England
d. December 4, 1679
Hardwick Hall, Derbyshire, England
fields: Government and Politics, Philosophy

A pioneer of modern political principles, Hobbes wrote the English language's first great work of political philosophy.

Hobby, Oveta Culp

né: Oveta Culp
b. January 19, 1905
Killeen, Texas
d. August 16, 1995
Houston, Texas
fields: Government and Politics

As army officer, cabinet member, and business leader, Hobby was a pioneer for American women in many areas of public life.

Hobhouse, Leonard T.

full: Leonard Trelawny Hobhouse
b. September 8, 1864
St. Ive, England
d. June 21, 1929
Alençon, Normandy, France
fields: Sociology, Political Science, Philosophy

Hobhouse helped develop the theoretical basis of modern liberalism and was the founder of sociology as an academic discipline in Great Britain.

Hochheim, Johannes Heinrich Eckhart von. *See* Eckhart, Meister

Hochhuth, Rolf

b. April 1, 1931
Eschwege, Germany
fields: Theater and Entertainment, Literature

A German writer, Rolf Hochhuth used drama to expose the alleged moral shortcomings of world leaders and provoked strong opposition from governments, organizations, and individuals. His first play, *The Deputy* (1963), launched a heated debate over its implications that Pope Pius XII had failed to speak out forcefully against the Jewish Holocaust. His second play, *Soldiers: An Obituary for Geneva* (1967), depicted Britain's Former British prime minister Winston Churchill as having supported terror-bombing of German civilians during World War II. Hochhuth's later plays generated little international interest but repeatedly brought him into conflict with German authorities.

Hochschild, Arlie Russell

b. January 15, 1940
Boston, Mass.
fields: Economics, Sociology

With Anne Machung, Arlie Russell Hochschild wrote *The Second Shift: Working Parents and the Revolution at Home* (1989), which explored how parents used their time away from work, confirming that women spend more time than men on child care and household tasks. Hochschild called for restructuring of the workplace to accommodate family needs. In her book *The Time Bind* (1997) she observed that although a company she studied offered family-friendly work policies, workers chose not to take advantage of them.

Hockney, David

b. July 9, 1937
Bradford, Yorkshire, England
fields: Art

In the forefront since the mid-1960's, his work immensely popular worldwide, Hockney brings to postmodern art a freshness and originality that, although modern, harks back to traditional art sources, employing figurative and narrative elements.

Hodge, Derek M.

b. Oct. 5, 1941
Frederiksted, Virgin Islands
fields: Government and Politics

African American territorial senator; in 1984, Derek M. Hodge served as senate president in the Virgin Islands territorial senate; was elected lieutenant governor in 1986.

Hodges, Johnny

full: John Cornelius Hodges
b. July 25, 1907
Cambridge, Mass.
d. May 11, 1970
New York, N.Y.
fields: Music (saxophonist)

African American alto and soprano saxophonist; Johnny "Rabbit" or "Jeep" Hodges was one of the finest alto saxophonists of all time; played with the Duke Ellington Orchestra from 1928 to 1951, then from 1955 until retirement; recordings included "Yellow Dog Blues/Tishomingo Blues" (1928), "It Don't Mean a Thing" (1932), "Warm Valley" (1940), "Jeep's Blues" (1938) and "Things Ain't What They Used to Be" (1941)."

Hodgkin, Alan Lloyd

full: Sir Alan Lloyd Hodgkin
b. Feb. 5, 1914
Banbury, Oxfordshire, England
d. Dec. 20, 1998
Cambridge, England
fields: Biology, Physiology

Alan Lloyd Hodgkin discovered the chemical processes that control the passage of impulses along individual nerve fibers; in 1963, shared the Nobel Prize in Physiology or Medicine with Andrew F. Huxley and Sir John Carew Eccles.

Hodgkin, Dorothy Crowfoot

full: Dorothy Mary Crowfoot
b. May 12, 1910
Cairo, Egypt
d. July 29, 1994
Shipston-on-Stour, Warwickshire, England
fields: Chemistry, Physics

Dorothy Crowfoot Hodgkin used X-ray crystallography to determine the chemical structure of important substances such as penicillin (1945), vitamin B_{12} (1956), and insulin (1969). In 1964, she won the Nobel Prize in Chemistry.

Hodgson, Frances Eliza. *See* Burnett, Frances Hodgson

Hoffman, Malvina

full: Malvina Cornell Hoffman
b. June 15, 1885
New York, New York
d. July 10, 1966
New York, New York
fields: Art

A leading sculptor who achieved international fame in the 1920's and 1930's, Malvina Hoffman ranked among the foremost American women artists. She contributed greatly to the acceptance of women as professionals.

Hoffman, Ruth. *See* Hubbard, Ruth

Hoffmann, Roald

né: Roald Safran
b. July 18, 1937
Zloczow, Poland (now Ukraine)
fields: Chemistry

Roald Hoffmann was an authority on chemical physics and applied chemical theory; shared the Nobel Prize in Chemistry with Kenichi Fukui in 1981 for his theories concerning chemical reactions.

Hogan, David. *See* Gallagher, Frank

Hogan, Linda

b. July 16, 1947
Denver, Colo.
fields: Literature (poet, novelist)

Native American writer. Through her fiction and poetry, Chickasaw writer Linda Hogan develops unique perspectives on Indian history, nature, and feminism. Her fction includes *Mean Spirit* (1990) and *That Horse* (1985). Poetry volumes include *Calling Myself Home* (1978), *Eclipse* (1983), and *Savings* (1988).

Hogarth, William

b. November 10, 1697
London, England
d. October 26, 1764
London, England
fields: Art

Hogarth's vivid sense of detail and dramatic construction enabled him to create paintings and engravings that were entertainingly comic as well as devastatingly satiric.

Hoggard, James Clinton

b. Aug. 9, 1916
Jersey City, N.J.
fields: Church Government, Religion and Theology

African American clergyman; James Clinton Hoggard was ordained in 1939 and became a bishop in the African Methodist Episcopal Zion church in 1972.

Hohenheim, Philippus Aureolus Theophrastus Bombast von. *See* Paracelsus

Hokeah, Jack

b. c. 1900
Caddo County, Okla.
d. Dec. 14, 1969
Fort Cobb, Okla.
fields: Art (painter)

Native American painter. Jack Hokeah, a Kiowa, was one of the original members of the Kiowa Five, a group of painters who instituted a style of painting based on traditional cultural scenes. Hokeah was also a champion dancer and leader of dance groups. His painting is most known for strong images of dancers in motion.

Hokinson, Helen

full: Helen Elna Hokinson
b. June 29, 1893
Mendota, Illinois
d. November 1, 1949
Washington, D.C.
fields: Art

One of the first women to attain outstanding success as a cartoonist, Hokinson inspired other women to enter the field and to focus on feminine themes and characters.

Hokoyama, J. D.

b. ?
fields: Education

J. D. Hokoyama became president and executive director of Leadership Education for Asian Pacifics (LEAP), a nonprofit Asian American community organization that teaches leadership skills to Asian and Pacific Americans. He helped form LEAP's Asian Pacific American Public Policy Institute in 1992. In 1993, LEAP and the Asian American Studies Center of the University of California, Los Angeles, issued *The State of Asian Pacific America: Policy Issues to the Year 2020.* Hokoyama, who received a B.A. in English literature and an M.Ed. in educational administration from Loyola University of Los Angeles, participated in many Asian American community programs.

Hokusai

né: Kawamura Tokitarō
full: Katsushika Hokusai
aka: Shunrō
aka: Gakyō-rōjin
b. 1760
Edo, Japan
d. 1849
Japan
fields: Art

A versatile, productive artist, Hokusai was one of the last great masters of the woodblock print.

Holatamico. *See* Bowlegs, Billy

Holbein, Hans, the Younger

b. 1497 or 1498
Augsburg
d. 1543
London, England
fields: Art

A master of portraits and an excellent draftsman, Holbein was an important transitional figure in European art. Holbein's portraits offer a revealing look at the personalities of his time.

Holder, Geoffrey Lamont

b. Aug. 1, 1930
Port-of-Spain, Trinidad
fields: Dance, Theater and Entertainment

African American dancer, producer, director, choreographer, and actor; Geoffrey Lamont Holder's credits include stage and film, but he is often associated with his Seven-Up commercials in the 1970's; formed the Geoffrey Holder Dance Company in 1950; directed and designed costumes for the Broadway musical *The Wiz* (1975); appeared in films such as *All Night Long* (1961), *Everything You Always Wanted to Know About Sex (But Were Afraid to Ask)* (1972), *Live and Let Die* (1973), and *Annie* (1982).

Hole-in-the-Day

aka: Bugonegijig
b. 1825
d. June 27, 1868
Crow Wing, Minn.
fields: Diplomacy, Government and Politics, Native American Affairs

Ojibwa (Chippewa). A controversial figure, Hole-in-the-Day made a number of agreements for his people that brought him considerable personal gain. He visited Washington, D.C., several times, and at one point he married a white newspaper reporter there. He was known as a bargainer and a person who would take a percentage of any agreement made on behalf of his people.

Holiday, Billie

né: Eleanora Fagan
b. April 7, 1915
Philadelphia, Pennsylvania
d. July 17, 1959
New York, New York
fields: Music

One of the most influential jazz singers ever recorded, Billie Holiday created the standards by which jazz singers continue to be judged. Her life reflected the racism of a white entertainment industry and the sexism within a male- dominated jazz world.

Holland, Endesha Ida Mae

b. August 29, 1944
Greenwood, Miss.
fields: Theater and Entertainment, Education, Civil Rights (dramatist, educator, and activist)

African American dramatist, educator, and activist. Endesha Ida Mae Holland's play, *From the Mississippi Delta*, opened Off Broadway in 1991. Based on Holland's life experience and that of her mother, it testifies to the ability of African Americans— particularly women—to overcome poverty and abuse.

Holland, Jerome H.

b. Jan. 9, 1916
Auburn, N.Y.
fields: Education, Government and Politics

African American educator and political appointee; in 1953 Jerome H. Holland became president of Delaware State College; in

1960 became president of Hampton Institute; was appointed by President Richard Nixon to serve as U.S. ambassador to Sweden in 1970; in 1972 to became first African American member of the Board of Directors of the New York Stock Exchange.

Holland, John Philip

b. February 29, 1840
Liscannor, County Clare, Ireland
d. August 12, 1914
Newark, New Jersey
fields: Invention and Technology

Holland developed and manufactured the first submarine capable of traveling long distances under water.

Holliday, Jennifer

b. Oct. 19, 1960
Riverside, Tex.
fields: Music (singer)

African American singer; Jennifer Holliday made her Broadway debut in *Your Arms Too Short to Box with God* in 1980; won a Tony for her starring performance in *Dreamgirls* (1981); album *Free My Soul* was released in 1983.

Hollolsotetote. *See* Lawyer

Hollow Horn Bear

aka: Matihehlogego
b. 1850
Sheridan County, Nebr.
d. Mar. 15, 1913
Washington, D.C.
fields: Government and Politics, Warfare and Conquest, Native American Affairs

Native American leader. A Brule Sioux leader, Hollow Horn Bear fought against subjugation until the 1870's, then favored peace with whites. He gained fame as the chief who defeated Lieutenant William Fetterman (who had bragged that he would cut through Sioux country with a handful of troops). He later became something of a celebrity, appearing on a U.S. postage stamp and on a five-dollar bill.

Holloway, Brenda

b. June 21, 1946
Atascadero, Calif.
fields: Music (pop vocalist)

African American pop vocalist; Brenda Holloway recorded on the Tamla label for Motown's Berry Gordy; hits included "I'll Always Love You" (1964), "When I'm Gone," Together Till the End of Time," "Just Look What You've Done," and "Operator"; composed "You've Made Me So Very Happy" (1967); won a judgment against Motown Records in 1972 for reimbursement of royalties.

Holm, Hanya

né: Johanna Eckert
b. 1893
Worms, Germany
d. November 3, 1992
New York, New York
fields: Dance

A pioneer in modern dance, Holm was an outstanding dance educator who adapted the spatial, rhythmic, and expressive focus of German modern dance to encompass a distinctly American sensibility.

Holman, Eddie

b. ?
fields: Music (pop vocalist)

African American pop vocalist; Eddie Holman's hit singles included "Hey There Lonely Girl" (1969), "Don't Stop Now" (1970), and "Cathy Called" (1970).

Holman, John

b. August 24, 1951
Durham, N.C.
fields: Literature (short-story writer)

African American short-story writer; John Holman published *Squabble: and Other Stories* in 1990; nominated for the Pushcart Prize for fiction in both 1983 and 1984.

Holman, M. Carl

b. June 27, 1919
Minter City, Miss.
d. August 9, 1988
Washington, D.C.
fields: Government and Politics, Civil Rights, Literature

African American poet, civil rights leader, and president of the National Urban Coalition; Carl M. Holman is often described as the godfather of the civil rights movement; taught for fourteen-years as an English professor at Clark College in Atlanta, Ga., (1949-1963); was active in the early developments of the Civil Rights movement in the South during the 1950's; served as adviser to civil rights leaders and strategist for student demonstrators; was a published poet and wrote extensively on African American and urban issues for magazines and newspapers; was editor of the *Atlanta Inquirer*; moved to Washington, D.C., in 1962, to become an information officer at the United States Commission on Civil Rights (considered the unofficial African American cabinet of the John F. Kennedy and Lyndon B. Johnson administrations); became special assistant to the staff director (1965) and then deputy director (1966); became president of the National Urban Coalition (1971), a national advocacy organization for a variety of urban interests.

Holmes, Arthur

b. ?
Decatur, Ala.
fields: Military Affairs

African American military officer; in 1981, Arthur Holmes achieved the rank of major general in the United States Army.

Holmes, Hamilton

full: Hamilton Earl Holmes
b. July 8, 1941
Atlanta, Georgia
d. October 26, 1995
Atlanta, Georgia
fields: Civil Rights, Education

On January 10, 1961, Hamilton Earl Holmes and Charlayne Hunter became the first African Americans to desegregate the University of Georgia after federal district court Judge William Bootle ordered that Hunter and Holmes be admitted to the still-segregated university. Both eventually graduated, despite initial threats of violence. Holmes continuing his study at Emory University School of Medicine, receiving his degree in 1967. He remained on staff at the university, garnering recognition for his work as an orthopedic surgeon. He died in 1995.

Holmes, Larry

b. Nov. 3, 1949
Cuthbert, Ga.
fields: Sports (professional boxer)

African American professional boxer; Larry Holmes took the World Boxing Council heavyweight title from Ken Norton in 1978 and held onto it until his defeat by Michael Spinks in 1985.

Holmes, Oliver Wendell

b. August 29, 1809
Cambridge, Massachusetts
d. October 7, 1894
Boston, Massachusetts
fields: Literature, Medicine

Holmes was an American doctor and teacher of medicine who helped pioneer many new medical techniques, including the use of microscopes and anesthesia. He was also a poet and essayist whose writings were dominated by wit and inventiveness.

Holmes, Oliver Wendell, Jr.

b. March 8, 1841
Boston, Massachusetts
d. March 6, 1935
Washington, D.C.
fields: Law

As an associate justice of the U.S. Supreme Court, Oliver Wendell Holmes helped set the stage for the development of modern American jurisprudence.

Holstein, Friedrich von

b. April 24, 1837
Schwedt an der Oder, Pomerania
d. May 8, 1909
Berlin, Germany
fields: Diplomacy

Holstein was a controversial chief adviser on German foreign policy from 1890 to 1906, sometimes blamed for German diplomatic isolation before World War I.

Holt, Harold

full: Harold Edward Holt
b. August 5, 1908
Sydney, Australia
d. December 17, 1967
near Portsea, Victoria, Australia
fields: Government and Politics

Prime minister of Australia in 1966 and 1967. For most of his prime ministership Harold Holt was preoccupied with Vietnam War issues. Stated that Australia would go "all the way with LBJ" in its military commitment in Vietnam. Holt disappeared while swimming at Cheviot Beach on the Mornington Peninsula just before Christmas in 1967. His body was never recovered and he was presumed drowned.

Holte, Patricia Louise. *See* LaBelle, Patti

Holyfield, Evander

b. Oct. 19, 1962
Atmore, Ala.
fields: Sports (boxer)

African American boxer; Evander Holyfield won the bronze medal in the light heavyweight division in the 1984 Olympics; defeated World Boxing Association (WBA) champion Carlos de León to become world cruiserweight champion in 1988; won world heavyweight title in 1990 and lost it to Riddick Bowe in 1992. During his June, 1997, fight with Mike Tyson, Tyson was disqualified for biting Holyfield's ears. Later that same year, he beat Michael Moorer to win the IBF heavyweight title.

Homar, Lorenzo

b. Sept. 10, 1913
Puerta de Tierra, Puerto Rico
fields: Art

Latino artist. Lorenzo Homar studied and worked in New York City from 1928 to 1950 before returning to Puerto Rico. He directed the Division of Community Education's print workshop from 1950 to 1956, then organized and directed the Graphic Arts Workshop of the Institute of Puerto Rican Culture, a position he retained until 1972, when he became an instructor in the School of Plastic Arts run by the institute. Around 1960, Homar gave up painting to concentrate on printmaking and typography, skills he used to produce the silkscreen posters for which he is most well known. He also designed books, record jackets, Christmas cards, and stage sets.

Homer

b. early ninth century B.C.E.
possibly Ionia, Greece
d. late ninth century B.C.E.
Greece
fields: Literature

Homer wrote the *Iliad* and the *Odyssey*, Greek epic poems which played a crucial role in the birth of classical Greek civilization. These works greatly influenced history, theology, and literature in Greece and the entire Western world.

Homer, Winslow

b. February 24, 1836
Boston, Massachusetts
d. September 29, 1910
Prouts Neck, Maine
fields: Art

Homer was an American artist who was known for his luminous watercolors and powerful oils, especially those depicting the power, moods, beauty, and menace of the sea.

Honanisto. *See* Howling Wolf

Honda, Harry K.

b. Aug. 12, 1919
Los Angeles, Calif.
fields: Journalism

Harry K. Honda's landed his first journalism job as a sports writer for the Japanese-language paper *Rafu Shimpo* in 1936. Two years later, he edited the English-language section of the *Sangyo Nippo* (*Japanese Industrial Daily*). He joined the U.S. Army in October, 1941, and served until December, 1945. After receiving a bachelor's degree from Loyola University in Los Angeles in 1950, he became assistant English-language editor of *Shin Nichibei Shimbun* (*New Japanese American News*). In 1952 he was hired as editor for the weekly paper *Pacific Citizen*, climbing the ranks there to become general manager/operations, senior editor, and finally as editor emeritus. Honda was an active member of the Japanese American Citizens League, which adopted *Pacific Citizen* as its official publication on July 27, 1932.

Honda, Soichiro

b. November 17, 1906
Iwata-gun, Japan
d. August 5, 1991
Tokyo, Japan
fields: Business and Industry

Honda's career provides an authentic rags-to-riches story. From the humblest of beginnings as a mechanic and with only the scantiest of formal education, he became an inventor, innovator, and manufacturer in one of the most competitive industries in Japan. The motorcycles and automobiles produced by the company which bears his name are sold throughout the entire world.

Honecker, Erich

b. August 25, 1912
Neunkirchen, Germany
d. May 29, 1994
Santiago, Chile
fields: Government and Politics

Head of East Germany's Communist Party from 1971 to 1989. In 1961 East Germany's Communist Party leader Walter Ulbricht gave Erich honecker the job of overseeing the construction of the Berlin Wall. Honecker's influence increased steadily. Became head of party in 1971 and remained in the post until 1989. Named head of government in 1976. East Germany under Honecker a repressive society but one that provided for people's needs and increased industrial production. Increasingly out of touch in late 1980's, forced to resign in 1989. Brought to trial in 1993 for his role in political repression and abuses, but, his health failing, was released before trial completed.

Hong, Maxine. *See* Kingston, Maxine Hong

Hong Xiuquan

b. Jan. 1, 1814
Fuyuanshui, Guangdong Province, China
d. June 1, 1864
Nanjing, Jiangsu Province, China
fields: Government and Politics

Hong Xiuquan, the leader of the Taiping Rebellion (1850-1864), was first welcomed by foreign powers because of his opposition to the Manchus and his anti-Confucian stance. The foreign powers later rejected him as mad and disruptive, but later Chinese, especially Sun Yat-sen, venerated him as a harbinger of nationalism. Hong persuaded relatives and Hakka villages in Guangxi Province to join his God Worshippers Society and eventually to raise the flag of rebellion in January, 1851. Hong supported universal brotherly love; a prohibition on opium, prostitution, and mixing of the sexes; equal status for women; abolition of landlordism in favor of equal holdings and communal farming; openness to new technology; and equality for all nations. However, he was ineffectual at stopping dissension or implementing programs and in June, 1864, killed himself before the Qing army reached him in Nanjing.

Hongo, Florence M.

b. Nov. 21, 1928
Cressey, Calif.
fields: Social Reform, Education

Japanese American educator, social activist; Florence M. Hongo was born in California; interned in a Colorado camp during World War II; faculty member at the College of San Mateo (1983); general manager and board president of the Japanese American Curriculum Project in 1969 (from 1994, the Asian American Curriculum Project), which produced the controversial *Japanese Americans, the Untold Story* (1970); after the state refused to accept the work as a supplemental textbook, began distributing books, filmstrips, and other literature designed to produce full information about the internment of Japanese Americans; edited *Japanese American Journey* (1985).

Hongo, Garrett Kaoru

b. May 30, 1951
Volcano, Hawaii
fields: Literature

Garrett Kaoru Hongo is known mainly for his poetry, which focuses on the Asian American experience, including the internment of Japanese Americans during World War II; first book of poetry, *Yellow Light*, appeared in 1982; his second, *The River of Heaven* (1988), earned for him the Lamont Poetry Prize and a Pulitzer Prize nomination.

Honor, Edward

b. Mar. 17, 1933
Melville, La.
fields: Military Affairs

African American military officer; after thirty-four years of military service, Edward Honor retired in 1989, having achieved the rank of lieutenant general in the United States Army.

Honore, Charles Edward

b. Apr. 20, 1934
Baton Rouge, La.
fields: Military Affairs

African American military officer; Charles Edward Honore retired in 1990, having attained the rank of major general in the United States Army.

Hood, James Walker

b. May 30, 1831
Kennet, Pa.
d. 1918
fields: Historical Figure, Civil Rights

African American first black missionary to freed slaves in the South; James Walker Hood was influential in making North Carolina a center of the church; wrote *One Hundred Years of the African Methodist Episcopal Zion Church: Or, the Centennial of African Methodism* (1895).

Hooke, Robert

b. July 18, 1635
Freshwater, on the Isle of Wight, England
d. Mar. 3, 1703
London, England
fields: Astronomy, Biology, Invention and Technology

An experimenter, Robert Hooke conducted detailed investigations with the microscope; coined the term "cell" to describe the structural unit of living material; in 1700, invented the marine barometer.

Hooker Jim

aka: Hakar Jim
b. c. 1825
Calif.
d. 1879
Quapaw Agency, Indian Territory
fields: Warfare and Conquest, Government and Politics, Native American Affairs

Native American leader. A Modoc, and a leader of the Modoc War (along with Captain Jack), Hooker Jim resisted relocation to an Oregon reservation in the 1870's.

Hooker, John Lee

b. Aug. 22, 1917?
Clarksdale, Miss.
fields: Music (blues singer and guitarist)

African American blues singer and guitarist. Known for his trademark "boogie" guitar style, John Lee Hooker released his first hit recording, "Boogie Chillen" in 1948. Bands such as Canned Heat in the 1960's and Z. Z. Top in the 1970's based their sounds on his unique style. His collaborative album *The Healer* (1989) won Grammy Awards.

Hookham, Margaret Evelyn. *See* Fonteyn, Margot

Hooks, Bell

né: Gloria Watkins
aka: bell hooks
b. September 25, 1952
Hopkinsville, Ky.
fields: Literature, Education

African American author and educator; a Distinguished Professor of English at the City College of the City University of New York, Bell Hooks has written a series of provocative articles and books on the history of African American women, on the relationships between African American men and women, and on contemporary African American art and music; her published works include *Ain't I a Woman: Black Women and Feminism* (1981), *Feminist Theory: From Margin to Center* (1984), *Talking Back: Thinking Feminist, Thinking Black* (1989), *Yearning: Race, Gender, and Cultural Politics* (1990), *Breaking Bread: Insurgent Black Intellectual Life* (1991), *The Woman's Mourning Song* (1992), *Black Looks: Race and Representation* (1992), *Outlaw Culture* (1994), *Teaching to Transgress: Education and the Practice of Freedom* (1994), *Killing Rage* (1995), *Bone Black* (1996), and *Reel to Real* (1996).

Hooks, Benjamin Lawson

b. Jan. 31, 1925
Memphis, Tenn.
fields: Civil Rights

African American civil rights leader; Benjamin Lawson Hooks was a board member of the Southern Christian Leadership Conference (SCLC); appointed by President Richard Nixon as the first African American to serve on the Federal Communications Commission; in 1977 became executive director of the National Association for the Advancement of Colored People (NAACP), where he vigorously promoted integration, pro-African foreign policy, and employment legislation; retired from this post in 1993.

Hooks, Kevin

b. Sept. 19, 1958
Philadelphia, Pa.
fields: Film, Theater and Entertainment, Television

African American actor and director; son of actor Robert Hooks, Kevin Hooks's first major film roles were in *Sounder* (1972) and *A Hero Ain't Nothin' but a Sandwich* (1978); between 1984 and 1987 directed television episodes of *V*, *Fame*, *Hotel*, *Cutter to Houston*, and *St. Elsewhere*; directed first feature film, *Strictly Business*, in 1991. He also directed *Passenger 57* (1992).

Hooks, Robert

b. Apr. 18, 1937
Washington, D.C.
fields: Theater and Entertainment (actor)

African American actor and cofounder of the Negro Ensemble Company; Robert Hooks debuted on Broadway replacing Louis Gossett, Jr., in *A Raisin in the Sun* (1960) and also performed in *Dutchman* (1964), *Where's Daddy?* (1966), and *Hallelujah Baby!*(1967); cofounded the Negro Ensemble Company (NEC) in 1967; guest-starred on such television series as *Marcus Welby, M.D.*, *WKRP in Cincinnati*, and *Murder, She Wrote;* starred in the series *N.Y.P.D.* (1967-1969); screen credits included *Star Trek III: The Search for Spock* (1984), *Passenger 57* (1992), and *Fled* (1996).

Hoonk-hoo-no-kaw. *See* Little Priest

Hoover, Herbert

full: Herbert Clark Hoover
b. August 10, 1874
West Branch, Iowa
d. October 20, 1964
New York, New York
fields: Government and Politics

As the thirty-first president of the United States (1929-1933), whose presidency ushered in the Great Depression, Hoover has long been castigated as a failure. Nevertheless, his career both before and after his presidency and the accomplishments of his administration give final judgment of Hoover as a great American.

Hoover, J. Edgar

full: John Edgar Hoover
b. January 1, 1895
Washington, D.C.
d. May 2, 1972
Washington, D.C.
fields: Government and Politics

Head of the Federal Bureau of Investigation for forty-eight years (from 1924 to 1972), Hoover was one of the most controversial figures in American politics, the first and most durable leader of the anti-Communist movement that ruled American public life for much of the century.

Hope, Bob

b. May 29, 1903
Leslie Town Eltham, England
fields: Film, Theater and Entertainment

Bob Hope began his show business career on radio during the 1930's and soon moved to films, gaining fame in a series of light comedies with Bing Crosby. During World War II he entertained U.S. troops and appeared in many films for the War Activities Committee. From 1948 to 1972 he lead annual Christmas tours of U.S. military forces abroad. At of eighty-seven he staged a final military tour in 1990 for Gulf War troops.

Hope, John

b. June 2, 1898
Augusta, Ga.
d. February 20, 1936
Atlanta, Ga.
fields: Education (educator and university president)

African American educator and university president; in 1906, John Hope became the first African American president of Atlanta Baptist College (later known as Morehouse College); in 1929, founded and was president of the Atlanta University system—the first African American college consortium, including Atlanta University, Morehouse College, Spelman College, Morris Brown College, Clark College, and Gammon Theological Seminary.

Hopkins, Claude Driskett

b. Aug. 24, 1903
Alexandria, Va.
d. Feb. 19, 1984
New York, N.Y.
fields: Music (jazz)

African American jazz pianist, arranger, and composer. In the 1920's and 1930's, Claude Driskett Hopkins's band played for the Josephine Baker revue and at venues such as the Roseland Ballroom, Asbury Park, Cocoanut Grove, and the Cotton Club. The Claude Hopkins Orchestra appeared in several 1930's films.

Hopkins, Frederick Gowland

full: Sir Frederick Gowland Hopkins
b. June 20, 1861
Eastbourne, Sussex, England
d. May 16, 1947
Cambridge, England
fields: Biology, Chemistry, Medicine, Physiology

Frederick Gowland Hopkins was the main figure in the establishment of biochemistry in Britain; made important contributions to the understanding of the metabolism of living cells and to biochemical research methods; demonstrated need for vitamins in diet in 1912; in 1929, won the Nobel Prize in Physiology or Medicine.

Hopkins, Harry

full: Harry Lloyd Hopkins
b. August 17, 1890
Sioux City, Iowa
d. January 29, 1946
New York, New York
fields: Government and Politics

A superb administrator, Hopkins led the United States in combating unemployment during the Great Depression in the 1930's and the menace of Fascism during World War II.

Hopkins, Sam

aka: Sam Lightnin' Hopkins
b. Mar. 15, 1912
Centerville, Tex.
d. Jan. 30, 1982
Houston, Tex.
fields: Music (blues)

African American blues musician. Sam "Lightnin'" Hopkins devised a guitar style involving jazz-like improvisations while developing a unique vocal approach using his own, often extemporaneous, lyrics rather than traditional blues verses. A documentary film, *The Blues According to Lightnin' Hopkins*, was made in 1968.

Hopocan

aka: Captain Pipe
aka: Konieschguanokee
b. c. 1725
Pa.
d. 1794
Captain Pipe's Village, Upper Sandusky, Ohio
fields: Warfare and Conquest, Native American Affairs

Lenni Lenape (Delaware). A hereditary war chief, Hopocan battled Americans during the French and Indian War, Pontiac's Rebellion (1763), and the American Revolution. Hopocan participated in several councils, signing treaties at Fort Pitt (1778), Fort McIntosh, Ohio (1785), and Fort Harmer (1787).

Hopper, Edward

b. July 22, 1882
Nyack, New York
d. May 15, 1967
New York, New York
fields: Art

Hopper is widely acknowledged as one of the most significant twentieth century American realist painters. His deceptively simple but striking images of the loneliness and alienation of city life have become icons of American popular culture.

Hopper, Grace Murray

né: Grace Brewster Murray
b. December 9, 1906
New York, New York
d. January 1, 1992
Arlington, Virginia
fields: Invention and Technology

A pioneer in programming languages, Hooper developed FLOW-MATIC, the foundation of COBOL, and then standardized all Navy versions.

Horace

né: Quintus Horatius Flaccus
b. December 8, 65 B.C.E.
Venusia, Italy
d. November 27, 8 B.C.E.
Rome, Italy
fields: Literature

The most important Roman lyric poet, Horace took an appealing, deceptively casual approach to poetry. His odes, epistles, and satires became a beloved source of proverbial wisdom and a model for Renaissance and neoclassical poets throughout Europe.

Horn, Gertrude Franklin. *See* Atherton, Gertrude

Hornby, Leslie. *See* Twiggy

Horne, Lena

full: Lena Mary Calhoun Horne
b. June 30, 1917
Brooklyn, N.Y.
fields: Theater and Entertainment

African American actress and singer; Lena Horne was the first African American performer to sign a long-term contract with a major film studio; first film with MGM, *Panama Hattie* (1942); starred in *Cabin in the Sky* (1942) and *Stormy Weather* (1943), among others; blacklisted during the Joseph McCarthy era, but starred in the successful musical *Jamaica* (1957) on Broadway, which ignored the blacklist; active in the Civil Rights movement in the 1960's; participated in the March on Washington (August 28, 1963) and performed at a Carnegie Hall benefit for the Student Nonviolent Coordinating Committee (SNCC) that same year; published autobiography, *Lena* (1965); returned to Broadway in 1981 in a one-woman show entitled *Lena Horne: The Lady and Her Music*; received a Tony Award, a New York Drama Critics' Circle award, and a Kennedy Center award for lifetime achievement in the arts; also received the NAACP's prestigious Spingarn Medal (1982

Horne, Marilyn

b. January 16, 1934
Bradford, Pennsylvania
fields: Music

An internationally famous American trained mezzo-soprano, Marilyn Horne is best known for her performances and revivals of nineteenth century bel canto operatic and recital repertoire, especially the works of Gioacchino Rossini.

Horney, Karen

né: Karen Clementina Theodora Danielsen
b. September 16, 1885
Eilbek, near Hamburg, Germany
d. December 4, 1952
New York, New York
fields: Psychiatry and Psychology

Horney was a leading psychologist who contributed to understanding the psychology of women, emphasized the role of sociocultural factors in producing neurosis, and developed a new noninstinctivist psychoanalytic theory.

Horowitz, Vladimir

b. October 1, 1903
Berdichev, Russia (now Ukraine)
d. November 5, 1989
New York, New York
fields: Music

Horowitz was the foremost twentieth century exemplar of the Russian school of Romantic pianists.

Horse, John

b. c. 1812
Florida
d. Aug. 9, 1882
Mexico City, Mexico
fields: Historical Figure

African American seminole Indian chief also known as Cavallo, Coheia, John Nikla, Gopher John, and Juan Caballo; in 1849, John Horse led an exodus of Seminole blacks to Mexico where, after several relocations, he obtained a land grant near Nacimiento.

Horsford, Anna Maria

b. Mar. 6, 1947
New York, N.Y.
fields: Theater and Entertainment; Television (actor)

African American actress; Anna Maria Horsford's theater credits include *for colored girls who have considered suicide/ when the rainbow is enuf*; best known for the role of Thelma Frye on the television show *Amen* (1986).

Horton, Odell

b. May 13, 1929
Bolivar, Tenn.
fields: Law (judge), Civil Rights

African American federal judge; in 1957, Odell Horton served on a committee responsible for investigating civil rights abuses by the Memphis police department; served as assistant U.S. attorney for the Western District of Tennessee from 1962 to 1967; appointed by President Jimmy Carter in 1979 to serve as U.S. district judge for the Western District of Tennessee.

Hosa. *See* Little Raven

Hosmer, Harriet

full: Harriet Goodhue Hosmer
b. October 9, 1830
Watertown, Massachusetts
d. February 21, 1908
Watertown, Massachusetts
fields: Art

America's first and best neoclassical female sculptor, Hosmer was successful in Europe and the United States, and she inspired other female artists to follow her example.

Hosokawa, William K.

b. Jan. 30, 1915
Seattle, Wash.
fields: Journalism

Journalist William K. Hosokawa wrote two books on the Japanese American Citizens League (JACL), *Nisei: The Quiet Americans* (1969) and *JACL in Quest of Justice* (1982) as well as *Thirty-Five Years in the Frying Pan* (1978), and *They Call Me Moses Masaoka* (1987). Hosokawa and his family were interned at the Puyallup, Washington, assembly center and then at the Heart Mountain concentration camp in Wyoming, where he became editor of the camp newspaper. In 1943 he accepted a position with the *Des Moines Register* in Iowa. Three years later, he left for a position with the *Denver Post* in Colorado, eventually becoming an editor. His awards include the Colorado Society of Professional Journalists' Outstanding Journalist award (1976), the Denver Press Club's Outstanding Colorado Communicator award (1985), and the Decorated Japanese Order of the Rising Run (1987).

Hostos y Bonilla, Eugenio María de

b. Jan. 11, 1839
Rio Cañas, Mayagüez, Puerto Rico
d. Aug. 11, 1903
Santo Domingo, Dominican Republic
fields: Literature

Writer. Eugenio María de Hostos y Bonilla earned a degree from the Central University of Madrid Law School in Spain around 1860. In 1869, he moved to the United States and became a Cuban activist in New York City, traveling to South America to promote the cause. During the 1880's, he founded and served as dean of the Santo Domingo Normal School. He later taught constitutional law at the University of Chile. Among his published writings were *Obras Completas* (1939; *The Complete Works of Eugenio María de Hostos*, 1979) and a criticism of William Shakespeare's *Hamlet, Prince of Denmark* (pb. 1603) that many consider the leading Spanish-language study of that work.

Hotchkiss, Hazel Virginia. *See* Wightman, Hazel

Hothlepoya. *See* Menewa

Hotman, François

b. August 23, 1524
Paris, France
d. February 12, 1590
Basel, Swiss Confederation
fields: Law, Political Science

Hotman, a brilliant French legal scholar and teacher, used his considerable knowledge and writing ability for the Huguenot cause of freedom of conscience, and, in the process, developed a philosophy of limited constitutional monarchy and became one of the first modern revolutionaries.

Hotóakhihoois. *See* Tall Bull

Hotúaeka'ash Tait. *See* Tall Bull

Houn, Fred Wei-Han. *See* Ho, Fred

Hounsfield, Godfrey Newbold

aka: Sir Godfrey Newbold Hounsfield
b. August 28, 1919
Newark, Nottinghamshire, England
fields: Engineering, Invention and Technology, Medicine

Hounsfield invented computed tomography, a method of producing detailed images of internal body tissues that provides physicians with much more information than ordinary X rays can supply. Computed tomography pioneered the development of other advanced methods of medical imaging in the late twentieth century. He was awarded the 1979 Nobel Prize in Physiology or Medicine.

Hountondji, Paulin J.

b. 1942
Abidjan, Ivory Coast, French West Africa
fields: Philosophy, Government and Politics

African philosopher Paulin J. Hountondji, a key figure in postcolonial Dahomey (Benin), criticized "ethnophilosophy" and endorsed a critical, "scientific" understanding of philosophy, thereby compelling a reassessment of traditional African philosophy and an examination of the relationship among philosophy, science, and postcolonial African development. His major works include *Libertés: Contribution à la révolution Dahoméenne* (1973), *Sur la philosophie africaine: Critique de l'ethnophilosophie* (1977), *African Philosophy: Myth and Reality* (1983), and *Recherche théorique africaine et contrat de solidarité* (1978).

Houphouët-Boigny, Félix

b. October 18, 1905
Yamoussoukro, Ivory Coast
d. December 7, 1993
Yamoussoukro, Ivory Coast
fields: Government and Politics

Houphouët-Boigny began serving as President of the Ivory Coast in 1960. Through his guidance and close ties with France, the Ivory Coast became one of the most economically and politically stable nations of Africa.

House, Son

full: Eddie James House
b. Mar. 21, 1902
Riverton, Miss.
d. Oct. 12, 1988
Detroit, Mich.
fields: Music (blues musician)

African American blues musician; Son House began recording his relentless steel guitar style and a powerful voice in 1930; recorded sides for the Library of Congress in 1942.

Houssay, Bernardo Alberto

b. April 10, 1887
Buenos Aires, Argentina
d. September 21, 1971
Buenos Aires, Argentina
fields: Physiology, Biology, Medicine

Houssay was the first South American to receive the Nobel Prize in Physiology or Medicine. He was awarded the prize in 1947 for his discovery of the relation between the pancreas and the pituitary gland. This important work paved the way for further studies of diabetes.

Houston, Charles Hamilton

b. September 3, 1895
Washington, D.C.
d. April 20, 1950
Washington, D.C.
fields: Law, Civil Rights (attorney and educator)

African American attorney and educator; known as the "First Mr. Civil Rights," Charles Hamilton Houston influenced the legal careers of premier lawyers such as William H. Hastie and U.S. Supreme Court Associate Justice Thurgood Marshall; provided the context used to eventually overturn *Plessy v. Ferguson* (1896).

Houston, Cissy

né: Emily Drinkard
b. 1932
Newark, N.J.
fields: Music (singer)

African American singer; Mother of pop diva Whitney Houston and Dionne Warwick's aunt, Cissy Houston was a much-in-demand soul and pop music backup singer for Neil Diamond, Aretha Franklin, Wilson Pickett, Dusty Springfield, Elvis Presley and others.

Houston, Jeanne Wakatsuki

né: Jeanne Toyo Wakatsuki
b. Sept. 26, 1934
Inglewood, Calif.
fields: Publishing

Jeanne Wakatsuki Houston's *Farewell to Manzanar: A True Story of Japanese American Experience During and After the World War II Internment* (1973) drew national attention to the wartime injustice suffered by Japanese Americans. Houston and her family were interned in the Manzanar relocation center in the high-mountain desert of California. At the age of thirty-seven, she chronicled the fear, anxiety, agony, and confusion she had experienced as a child in Manzanar in her book. Her screenplay version of the book, made into a television film in 1976, received the Humanitas Prize, Christopher Award, and an award from the National Women's Political Caucus.

Houston, Sam

full: Samuel Houston, Jr.
b. March 2, 1793
Rockbridge County, Virginia
d. July 26, 1863
Huntsville, Texas
fields: Government and Politics

Houston served as commanding general of the Texan army during the Texas Revolution. He later won election as president of the Republic of Texas, governor of the state of Texas, and United States senator.

Houston, Velina Hasu

b. May 5, 1957
Junction City, Kan.
fields: Theater and Entertainment

The daughter of an African American man and a Japanese woman, Velina Hasu Houston wrote her first play at age twelve. She received a master's degree in theater and playwriting from the University of California, Los Angeles. Frequent themes in her plays are racism, culture clashes, and ethical responsibility. She received numerous awards and honors, including the Lorraine Hansberry Playwriting Award (1982) and various *DramaLogue* Outstanding Achievement in Theater Awards. Houston cofounded the Amerasian League, an organization that seeks to increase awareness of Amerasian culture.

Houston, Whitney

b. Aug. 9, 1963
Newark, N.J.
fields: Music (singer)

African American singer; Pop diva Whitney Houston is known for the exceptional range of her voice; first album, *Whitney Houston* (1985), contained "Saving All My Love for You," which won her a Grammy Award for best female pop vocalist; other albums included *Whitney* (1987), and *I'm Your Baby Tonight* (1990); her film credits included *The Bodyguard* (1992), *Waiting to Exhale* (1995), and *The Preacher's Wife* (1996).

Hovick, Rose Louise. *See* Lee, Gypsy Rose

Hovland, Carl

b. June 12, 1912
Chicago, Illinois
d. April 16, 1961
Hamden, Connecticut
fields: Psychiatry and Psychology

Carl Hovland was a psychologist and propaganda theorist who studied the influence of media, particularly film. During

World War II he worked for the Information and Education Division of the U.S. War Department and helped produce a series of films titled *Why We Fight*. He returned to Yale University after the war and supervised a research program on communication, whose results he summarized in *Communication and Persuasion* (1953).

Howard, Catherine

b. c. 1521
probably at Horsham or Lambeth, England
d. February 13, 1542
London, England
fields: Monarchy

As fifth wife to King Henry VIII, Catherine Howard briefly reigned as queen of England until revelations about her personal life brought about her sudden downfall and execution.

Howard, John

full: John Winston Howard
b. July 26, 1939
Sydney, New South Wales, Australia
fields: Government and Politics

John Howard took office as prime minister of Australia in 1996. Reaffirmed Australia's identity as a pro-Western nation and stressed its alliance with the United States, downplaying role in Asia. Dealt with Australian ramifications of Asian financial crisis of 1997. Judged more sympathetic to white farmers in their legal battles with aboriginals over land rights than was his predecessor, Paul Keating.

Howard, Miki

b. ?
fields: Music (pop vocalist)

African American pop vocalist; Miki Howard's rhythm-and-blues singing style led to a contract on the Atlantic records label in the mid-1980's.

Howard, Oliver O.

full: Oliver Otis Howard
b. November 8, 1830
Leeds, Maine
d. October 26, 1909
Burlington, Vermont
fields: Education, Military Affairs

Oliver Otis Howard was a U.S. army officer; entered army in 1854; fought in the Civil War, being promoted to brigadier general in 1861; commissioner, Bureau of Refugees, Freedmen, and Abandoned Lands, 1865-1874; founder and president of Howard University, 1869-1874; commander in campaign against Chief Joseph, 1877; superintendent at West Point, 1881-1882; considered one of the few "humanitarian" generals who campaigned on behalf of Indian rights.

Howe, Elias

full: Elias Howe, Jr.
b. July 9, 1819
Spencer, Massachusetts
d. October 3, 1867
Brooklyn, New York
fields: Invention

Howe was the first American inventor to build a workable sewing machine and have it successfully patented.

Howe, James Wong

né: Wong Tung Jim
b. August 28, 1899
Guangdong, China
d. July 12, 1976
Hollywood, Calif.
fields: Theater and Entertainment

Chinese American cinematographer. In 1917 James Wong Howe began his career as a cameraman's assistant under director Cecil B. De Mille and shot his own first film, *Drums of Fate*, in 1923. He earned ten Academy Award nominations and two Oscars, for *The Rose Tattoo* (1955) and *Hud* (1963). He also received Look Awards for *Body and Soul* (1947) and *Picnic* (1955) and received the Medal of Honor from the George Eastman Festival of Film Artists. Howe was a member of the Chinese Historical Society.

Howe, Joseph

b. December 13, 1804
Halifax, Nova Scotia, Canada
d. June 1, 1873
Halifax, Nova Scotia, Canada
fields: Publishing, Government and Politics

Joseph Howe was a Canadian newspaper publisher and politician whose acquittal on criminal libel charges set a precedent for freedom of the press throughout North America. While he was publisher of a Halifax newspaper in 1835, he printed an anonymous letter claiming that local government authorities were extorting money from the poor and he was charged with criminal libel. He then took the authorities to court and spoke in his own defense. After he was pronounced not guilty, his trial was praised as a confirmation of true freedom of the press.

Howe, Julia Ward

né: Julia Ward
b. May 27, 1819
New York, New York
d. October 17, 1910
Newport, Rhode Island
fields: Literature, Social Reform

Howe composed the lyrics to the inspiring patriotic song "The Battle Hymn of the Republic" and was an active crusader for women's right to vote.

Howe, Oscar

aka: Nazuha Hoksina (Trader Boy)
b. May 13, 1915
Joe Creek, S.Dak.
d. Oct. 7, 1983
Vermillion, S.Dak.
fields: Art (painter)

Native American painter. Yanktonai Sioux artist Oscar Howe successfully eschewed the prevailing Native American style with his modernist canvases, initiating the modern Indian art movement. His artistic subjects were Sioux stories, hunts, and myths—images shaped by his use of line and color.

Howe, Richard

aka: Admiral Richard Howe
b. March 19, 1726
London, England
d. August 5, 1799
Bath?, England
fields: Military Affairs, Government and Politics

One of England's foremost seamen of the Age of Sail, Howe won several noted victories over the French and Spanish but was unsuccessful in negotiating an end to the American rebellion.

Howe, Samuel Gridley

b. November 10, 1801
Boston, Massachusetts
d. January 9, 1876
Boston, Massachusetts
fields: Education, Philanthropy

A universal reformer, Howe's greatest contribution was to the education of the blind, the deaf-blind, and the mentally retarded. His monumental efforts significantly enhanced social concern for the handicapped in the United States.

Howe, Tina

b. November 21, 1937
New York, New York
fields: Literature

Since 1969, Tina Howe has written plays that use comic absurdity to show the pain underlying domestic life.

Howe, William

aka: William Howe
b. August 10, 1729
London, England
d. July 12, 1814
Plymouth, England
fields: Military Affairs

A model English officer of the eighteenth century, Howe gave his entire adult life to the service of the Crown. Upon such dedication the British Empire would be built.

Howell, Vernon. *See* Koresh, David

Howling Wolf

aka: Honanisto
b. c. 1850
present-day Okla.
d. July 2, 1927
Waurika, Okla.
fields: Warfare and Conquest, Art, Native American Affairs

Howling Wolf was a Cheyenne warrior, war chief, and artist. He became a war chief during the wars for the Plains; following the Red River War of 1874-1875, he surrendered and was sent to Fort Marion, a military prison. While imprisoned, encouraged by Lieutenant Richard Henry Pratt to become an artist. In 1884, he became chief of the Dog Soldiers, a self-styled Cheyenne reservation police force.

Howze, Joseph Lawson

b. Aug. 30, 1923
Daphne, Ala.
fields: Religon and Theology, Church Government

African American bishop; Joseph Lawson Howze was appointed auxiliary bishop of Natchez-Jackson, Miss., in 1973, and in 1977 was named to found the Diocese of Biloxi.

Hoyle, Fred

full: Sir Fred Hoyle
b. June 24, 1915
Bingley, Yorkshire, England
fields: Astronomy, Physics

A controversial figure, Fred Hoyle is the coauthor of the steady state cosmological theory; made key contributions to astrophysics, especially in helping to explain how elements are made in stars and supernovas.

Hoyt, Kenneth

b. ?
fields: Law (judge)

African American judge; in 1988, Kenneth Hoyt was appointed by President Ronald Reagan to serve as U.S. District Judge for Texas.

Hozhooji Naata. *See* Barboncito

Hsia Kuei

b. c. 1180
Ch'ien tang, Chekiang, China
d. c. 1250
Hangchow, Chekiang, China
fields: Art

Together with Ma Yüan, Hsia Kuei formed the Ma-Hsia school of painting, which was extremely influential in the subsequent development of landscape painting in China and Japan.

Hsiang-yang. *See* Mi Fei

Hsieh Ling-yün

b. 385
Commandery of Ch'en, Yang-chia, Honan Province, China
d. 433
Kuang-chou, Nan-hai, China
fields: Literature, Philosophy

Hsieh Ling-yün was the first and greatest of China's nature poets, the founder of the school of *shan-shui* verse. A philosophical syncretist, he blended elements of Confucianism and Taoism with Buddhism to produce a uniquely Chinese synthesis.

Hsu, Francis Lang Kwang

b. Oct. 28, 1909
Zhuanghe, Manchuria, China
fields: Anthropology, Sociology

Francis Lang Kwang Hsu, who received a bachelor's from Shanghai University in 1933 and a doctoral degree from the University of London in 1943, taught anthropology at Northwestern University from 1947 to 1978. He wrote extensively on the Asian American, including *Americans and Chinese: Two Ways of Life* (1953; 3d ed. 1981), *Americans and Chinese: Purpose and Fulfillment in Great Civilizations* (1970), *The Challenge of the American Dream: The Chinese in the United States* (1971), and *Iemoto: The Heart of Japan* (1975).

Hsu, Kai-yu

b. July 5, 1922
China
d. Jan. 4, 1982
fields: Journalism, Education

Kai-yu Hsu worked first as a reporter and then an editor for *The Chinese World Daily* (San Francisco) from 1948 to 1952, leaving to pursue a career as a university professor and administrator. He directed educational projects involving Chinese language and culture. Along with Helen Palubinskas, he coedited *Asian-American Authors* (1972), one of the first anthologies of Asian American writing. He edited and translated *Twentieth Century Chinese Poetry: An Anthology* (1963) and wrote the biography *Chou En-lai: China's Gray Eminence* (1968).

Hsüan-tsang

né: Ch'en Yi
b. c. 602
Lo-yang, Honan, China
d. 664
Ch'ang-an, China
fields: Exploration, Religion and Theology, Literature

A pilgrim and scholar, Hsüan-tsang brought the wisdom of the Sanskrit Buddhist scriptures from India to China, producing a huge legacy of Chinese sutras and a record of his travels. His works stand as testaments to his faith and courage as one of China's greatest travelers in the physical and spiritual quest for religious truth.

Hsün-tzu. *See* Xunzi

Hu Jingnan. *See* Woo, Gilbert Gang Nam

Hu-DeHart, Evelyn

b. Mar. 12, 1947
Chongqing, China
fields: Historiography

Asian American historian Evelyn Hu-DeHart recived two Fulbrights and lectured in the United Kingdom, Mexico, Peru, Cuba, the People's Republic of China, and Taiwan. She wrote two books on the Yaqui Indians of northern Mexico and Arizona. She became professor of history and the director of the Center for Studies of Ethnicity and Race in America at the University of Colorado, Boulder, in 1988.

Huang, Alice S.

full: Alice Shih-hou Huang
b. Mar. 22, 1939
Nanchang, Jianxi, China
fields: Genetics, Medicine

Alice S. Huang researched viral genetics; aided in the discovery of the enzyme reverse transcriptase; studied how abnormal viruses interfere with the reproduction of normal viruses.

Huang Zunxian

b. 1848
Chia-ying (now Meixian), Guangdong Province, China
d. Mar. 28, 1905
Chia-ying, China
fields: Literature, Government and Politics

Huang Zunxian, a poet and diplomat serving the Chinese government, visited Japan, the United States, and England, often incorporating what he gleaned from his travels into his poetry. He incorporated the rhythms and patterns of vernacular Chinese and local folk songs into his verse, making his work very popular. While in Japan in 1876, Huang came to believe that the Japanese might try to claim the Korean peninsula and wrote cautioning the Koreans. He also wrote a history of Japan. In San Francisco, he noticed prejudice against the Chinese, an observation he recorded in numerous poems.

Huáscar

né: Tupac Cusi Huallpa
b. c. 1495
Cuzco, Peru
d. 1532
Andamarca, Peru
fields: Monarchy, Military Affairs

Huáscar, the last ruler of the Incas (1525-1532), has the unenviable renown of losing the mightiest empire in pre-Columbian America.

Hubbard, Ruth

né: Ruth Hoffman
b. Mar. 3, 1924
Vienna, Austria
fields: Biology, Chemistry, Genetics

Ruth Hubbard was a biochemist who became a leading scientific critic of genetic research on gender-role differences and other human traits; in 1974, became the first woman to receive tenure at Harvard in the natural sciences.

Hubbard, William DeHart

b. Nov. 25, 1903
Cincinnati, Ohio
d. June 23, 1976
Cleveland, Ohio
fields: Sports (track and field)

African American long jumper; in 1924 William DeHart Hubbard became the first black person in Olympic history to win an individual gold medal.

Hubble, Edwin Powell

b. Nov. 20, 1889
Marshfield, Missouri
d. Sept. 28, 1953
San Marino, California
fields: Astronomy

Edwin Powell Hubble proved that galaxies consist of ordinary stars; measured the distances of galaxies, showing that more distant ones have larger recession velocities; in 1949, became the first to use the 200-inch telescope at Mount Palomar Observatory, California.

Hubel, David H.

full: David Hunter Hubel
b. Feb. 27, 1926
Windsor, Ontario, Canada
fields: Biology, Chemistry, Medicine

David H. Hubel pioneered the science of vision. He was the first to describe and map the visual cortex, for which he won the Nobel Prize in Physiology or Medicine in 1981.

Huber, Robert

b. Feb. 20, 1937
Munich, Germany
fields: Biology, Chemistry

Robert Huber crystallized the membrane proteins that take part in the chemical process of photosynthesis; in 1988, he won the Nobel Prize in Chemistry.

Hudlin, Reginald

b. 1962
East St. Louis, Ill.
fields: Film

African American film director, writer, and producer; Reginald Hudlin and older brother Warrington produced *House Party* (1991), which was developed from Reginald's Academy-award-winning short film.

Hudlin, Warrington

b. ?
East St. Louis, Ill.
fields: Film

African American film director, writer, and producer; in 1978, Warrington Hudlin cofounded the New York-based Black Filmmaker Forum; created feature films and music videos with his brother, Reginald, and produced *House Party* (1991).

Hudson, Ernie

b. December 17, 1945
Benton Harbor, Mich.
fields: Film, Television (actor)

African American actor; Ernie Hudson's film credits include *Leadbelly* (1976), *Ghostbusters* (1984), *Ghostbusters II* (1989), *Weeds* (1986), *The Basketball Diaries* (1995), *Congo* (1995), *The Hand That Rocks the Cradle* (1992), *The Crow* (1994), and *The Substitute* (1996).

Hudson, Henry

b. 1560's?
England
d. 1611
Hudson Bay?
fields: Exploration and Colonization

Although he failed to find the northwest passage to China that he sought, Hudson did, by his explorations, clarify the contours of present-day Canada's northern territories.

Hudson, Lou

b. July 11, 1944
Greensboro, N.C.
fields: Sports (basketball player)

African American basketball player; during his National Basketball League career, from 1966 to 1979, Lou Hudson averaged more than twenty points per game and played in six All-Star games.

Huerta, Baldemar Garza. *See* Fender, Freddy

Huerta, Dolores

né: Dolores Fernández
b. April 10, 1930
Dawson, New Mexico
fields: Labor Movement

Cofounder of the United Farm Workers Association with César Chávez, Huerta became renowned throughout the labor movement as a tireless and effective negotiator and organizer. Her role as a Chicana labor leader in the male-dominated culture of southwestern farmworkers has made her a champion of the woman's movement in the 1970's and beyond.

Huerta, Jorge

b. Nov. 20, 1942
Los Angeles, Calif.
fields: Theater and Entertainment, Literature

Latino director and writer. Jorge Huerta founded Teatro de la Esperanza during the early 1970's while working on his doctorate in dramatic literature and Chicano and U.S. Latino studies from the University of California, Santa Barbara. He also cofounded Máscara Mágica, San Diego's first independent professional Latino theatrical company. From 1989 to 1991, Huerta directed the nation's first Hispanic American master of fine arts program, at the University of California, San Diego. Huerta wrote *Chicano Theatre: Themes and Forms* (1982) and edited *Necessary Theater: Six Plays About the Chicano Experience* (1990).

Huerta, Victoriano

b. December 23, 1854
Colotán, Jalisco, Mexico
d. January 13, 1916
El Paso, Texas
fields: Government and Politics

Victoriano Huerta was a Mexican revolutionary and was provisional president of Mexico in 1913 and 1914. Maneuvered Francisco Madero out of power in 1913. Faced widespread revolts and unrest; responded with violence and repression. The military and landowners supported the Huerta regime because they knew that they faced the loss of land and the end of the traditional military if the insurgents won. Combined forces of Francisco Villa, Venustiano Carranza, and Alvaro Obregón defeated Huerta's army in the spring of 1914 and forced Huerta to flee to Europe.

Huggins, William

full: Sir William Huggins
b. Feb. 7, 1824
Stoke Newington, London, England

d. May 12, 1910
Tulse Hill, London, England
fields: Astronomy, Physics

William Huggins determined the chemical constitutions of various stars and nebulas by applying the principles of spectrum analysis to stellar light.

Hughes, Charles Evans

b. April 11, 1862
Glens Falls, New York
d. August 27, 1948
Osterville, Massachusetts
fields: Law, Government and Politics

Hughes served America's public interests as secretary of state and chief justice of the United States. He combined reforming zeal with brilliant administrative skills, and few Americans have demonstrated such commitment to the national good.

Hughes, Howard

full: Howard Robard Hughes, Jr.
b. December 24, 1905
Houston, Texas
d. April 5, 1976
in an airplane en route from Acapulco, Mexico, to Houston, Texas
fields: Business and Industry, Aviation and Space Exploration, Theater and Entertainment, Film

A tycoon, financial genius, aviator, filmmaker, and celebrity enigma, Howard Hughes enjoyed fame and fortune equaled by few others during his complex life but endured numerous hardships. By 1938, a world-class pilot and aircraft designer, he held nearly every aviation record, but in 1946, Hughes's XF-11 crashed and sent him to the hospital, where he developed an addiction to morphine that led to other dependencies. In 1947, he suffered from an embarrassing Senate investigation into his wartime financial conduct, which ended after the dramatic flight of his gigantic seaplane, nicknamed *Spruce Goose*. In 1948, an effort to draft Hughes for president failed. Throughout the 1950's, Hughes concentrated on expanding his business empire. He was a billionaire by the mid-1960's, his holdings including a charitable medical institute, media outlets, and Hughes Aircraft Corporation. He languished personally, becoming a reclusive shell of a person, paranoid and dependent, living in a rented hotel room in Las Vegas, Nevada, from which he rarely emerged. From this obscurity, he influenced presidential elections since the early 1960's, some in favor of Republicans and others in favor of Democrats. Rumors of his death were common by the 1970's. In dreadful physical condition, he died while being flown to Houston in 1976.

Hughes, Langston

full: James Mercer Langston Hughes
b. February 1, 1902
Joplin, Missouri
d. May 22, 1967
New York, New York
fields: Literature

While Hughes's greatest achievement was his poetry, which related and celebrated the African American experience, he was also a novelist, dramatist, short story writer, and journalist, making him one of the most versatile black American writers to grow out of the Harlem Renaissance of the 1920's and 1930's.

Hughes, William Morris

b. September 25, 1862
London, England
d. October 28, 1952
Sydney, New South Wales, Australia
fields: Government and Politics

Trade union organizer and wartime leader, Hughes was the first prime minister to put Australia's case on the international scene, especially winning concessions from a reluctant President Woodrow Wilson at the Paris Peace Conference (1919).

Hugo, Victor

full: Victor-Marie Hugo
b. February 26, 1802
Besançon, France
d. May 22, 1885
Paris, France
fields: Literature

Hugo was one of the great authors of the nineteenth century, and by the force of his personality he became one of its great public figures, using his enormous popularity in the service of many political and social causes. His literary career, spanning six of the most turbulent decades in modern European history, encompassed poetry, drama, the novel, and nonfiction writing.

Huineng

b. 638
Southwest Guangdong, China
d. 713
Guangdong, China
fields: Philosophy, Religion and Theology

Although Huineng was the sixth patriarch of Chinese Chan (Zen) Buddhism, most Buddhist practitioners and scholars believe that the true tradition of Chinese Chan began with him. His brand of Buddhism was the first to display distinctly Chinese characteristics. His major work is *Liuzu tan jing* (c. 677; *Sutra Spoken by the Sixth Patriarch*, 1930; better known as *The Platform Sutra of the Sixth Patriarch*, 1967), often referred to as the Platform Sutra or Altar Sutra. The fact that it is called a sutra is significant because the word is most often reserved for the teachings of Shakyamuni, the historical Buddha and founder of Buddhism; Huineng's work is the only one by a Chinese author to be called a sutra, and it is still widely used by Zen practitioners.

Hulbert, Homer B.

b. Jan. 26, 1863
New Haven, Vt.
d. Aug. 5, 1949
Seoul, Republic of Korea
fields: Diplomacy

Diplomat Homer B. Hulbert served in Korea from 1886 to 1905. Adviser to Korea's penultimate king, Kojong, Hulbert led a secret mission to the Second Hague Peace Conference in 1907, at which delegates denied the king's petition asserting the illegality of the 1905 Japanese Protectorate treaty. Hulbert asked President Theodore Roosevelt to help in accordance with the 1882 Korean-American Treaty but was refused Hulbert's works include *The History of Korea* (1905) and *The Passing of Korea* (1906).

Hulbert, Hot Rod

full: Maurice Hulbert
b. ?
Helena, Ark.
fields: Radio, Theater and Entertainment

African American disc jockey and businessman; at station WDIA in Memphis, Tenn., Hot Rod Hulbert developed the fast-talking style that influenced many future disc jockeys and contributed to the unique character of African American radio.

Hull, Agrippa

b. c. 1759
Northampton, Mass.
d. 1848
Stockbridge, Mass.
fields: Historical Figure, Warfare and Conquest

African American soldier; Agrippa Hull was an orderly in the Continental Army and performed amputations and surgery in the field.

Hull, Cordell

b. October 2, 1871
Overton County, Tennessee
d. July 23, 1955
Bethesda, Maryland
fields: Diplomacy, Government and Politics

Serving as secretary of state longer than any man in American history, Hull shaped the world of diplomacy along the lines of his Jeffersonian and Wilsonian principles. His commitment to Woodrow Wilson's dream of a world organization helped make the United Nations a reality.

Humboldt, Alexander von

b. September 14, 1769
Schloss Tegel, near Berlin, Prussia
d. May 6, 1859
Berlin, Prussia
fields: Geography, Meteorology, Geography (planet)

Humboldt, a native of Germany, undertook a famous four-year expedition to the Americas. The outcome of this expedition was the new sciences of geography, plant geography, and meteorology. Humboldt insisted on seeing a geographical site as a whole including climate, elevation, and distribution of plants, animals, and natural resources. He was one of the founders of modern science and scientific methods.

Hume, David

b. May 7, 1711
Edinburgh, Scotland
d. August 25, 1776
Edinburgh, Scotland
fields: Philosophy

Hume's philosophical writings destroyed the earlier reliance on reason as a guide for action and made major advances in the theory of perception and ethics.

Humishuma. *See* Mourning Dove

Hump

aka: Etokeah
b. c. 1848
d. Dec., 1908
Cherry Creek, S.Dak.
fields: Government and Politics, Warfare and Conquest, Native American Affairs

Hump, a Miniconjou Sioux, was an important leader in the Sioux Wars of the 1860's and 1870's. In 1866 led the attack that killed Captain William Fetterman and eighty soldiers outside Fort Kearney in Wyoming. Refusing to sign the Treaty of Fort Laramie, he joined Crazy Horse, Red Cloud, and other Sioux war chiefs. Present at the Battle of the Little Bighorn in 1876. Hump later became a Ghost Dancer. In 1890, he went to Washington, D.C., to negotiate for better treatment of the Sioux people.

Humperdinck, Engelbert

b. September 1, 1854
Siegburg, near Bonn, Prussia (now Germany)
d. September 27, 1921
Neustrelitz, Germany
fields: Music

As the developer and chief exponent of the "fairy-tale" opera, Humperdinck became, for a brief time, the most important German opera composer after Richard Wagner. Although he was soon eclipsed by other composers, his music survives in one enduringly popular work.

Humphrey, Hubert H.

full: Hubert Horatio Humphrey, Jr.
b. May 27, 1911
Wallace, South Dakota
d. January 13, 1978
Waverly, Minnesota
fields: Government and Politics

In the tradition of philosophical pragmatism and New Deal liberalism in the twentieth century, Humphrey became one of the most innovative and effective legislators in United States history.

Humphrey, Melvin

b. Jan. 2, 1921
St. Louis, Mo.
fields: Government and Politics

African American political appointee; Melvin Humphrey was appointed by President Ronald Reagan to serve as director of the Office of Small Business Development at the Department of Transportation.

Hune, Shirley

b. ?
Toronto, Canada
fields: Sociology, Historiography

Professor of urban studies Shirley Hune specializes in U.S. immigration policy, Asian American studies, and global policies and their relationship to Third World states and migrant workers. She received a Ph.D. in American civilization from George Washington University and was a president of the Association for Asian American Studies. She became acting associate dean for Graduate Programs at the University of California, Los Angeles, in 1993.

Hung Hsiu-ch'üan

b. January 1, 1814
Hua-hsien, Kwangtung, China
d. June, 1864
Nanking, China
fields: Government and Politics, Religion and Theology

Hung created and led the first revolutionary movement to shake the traditional Chinese political system. His movement, the T'ai-p'ing Heavenly Kingdom, was a cataclysmic upheaval that greatly influenced both Sun Yat-sen and Mao Tse-tung.

Hung Taiji. *See* Abahai

Hung-li. *See* Ch'ien-lung

Hunt, George

b. c. 1854
Fort Rupert, British Columbia, Canada
d. Sept. 5, 1933
Fort Rupert, British Columbia, Canada
fields: Anthropology (ethnologist)

Native American scholar. Kwakiutl ethnologist George Hunt, who worked with anthropologist Franz Boas, recorded Kwakiutl traditions and lifeways. Maintained the respect of both academicians and his own people. Appeared as coauthor with Boas on *Kwakiutl Tears* (1905) and *Ethnology of the Kwakiutl* (1921).

Hunt, Helen Maria. *See* Jackson, Helen Hunt

Hunt, Richard Howard

b. Sept. 12, 1935
Chicago, Ill.
fields: Art (sculptor, painter)

African American sculptor and painter. Richard Howard Hunt is considered to be one of America's leading sculptors of metal. His abstract style often incorporates figurative or organic forms.

Hunt, Ward

b. 1810
d. 1886
fields: Law

U.S. Supreme Court justice, 1873-1882; appointed by President Grant.

Hunt, William Holman

b. April 2, 1827
London, England
d. September 7, 1910
London, England
fields: Art

As a result of his activity in the Pre-Raphaelite Brotherhood and his artistic success outside the Royal Academy, Hunt exerted a broadening influence on British art, reforming ideas regarding lighting and color and bringing considerations of content back into primary importance in painting.

Hunter, Alberta

b. Apr. 1, 1895
Memphis, Tenn.
d. Oct. 17, 1984
New York, N.Y.
fields: Music (blues singer)

African American blues singer; in the 1920's, Alberta Hunter was one of the first African American women to record the blues; recorded her composition, "Down-Hearted Blues" (1922), for the Paramount label.

Hunter, Eddie

b. Feb. 4, 1888
New York, N.Y.
d. Feb. 14, 1980
New York, N.Y.

fields: Theater and Entertainment (actor), Literature

African American playwright and actor; vaudevillian Eddie "The Fighting Comedian" Hunter wrote and performed in all-black Broadway musicals, including *How Come* (1923) and *My Magnolia* (1926).

Hunter, Kristin Elaine Eggleston

b. Sept. 12, 1931
Philadelphia, Pa.
fields: Literature

African American author. Kristin Elaine Eggleston Hunter won the 1968 National Council on Interracial Books for Children award. Her children's novels include *The Soul Brothers and Sister Lou* (1968) and *Lou in the Limelight* (1981). Her adult fiction includes *God Bless the Child* (1964).

Hunter-Gault, Charlayne

né: Charlayne Alberta Hunter
b. February 27, 1942
Due West, South Carolina
fields: Journalism, Civil Rights

The first African American woman to earn a bachelor's degree from the University of Georgia (1963), Hunter-Gault has had a distinguished career in national broadcast journalism.

Hunton, Benjamin Lacy

b. 1919
Hyattsville, Md.
fields: Military Affairs, Government and Politics

African American military officer and government official; Benjamin Lacy Hunton served on the White House Committee on Civil Rights and Minority Affairs and as a reservist in the Army was elevated to the rank of brigadier general; entered active duty in 1942 as a second lieutenant.

Hunyadi, János

b. c. 1407
place unknown
d. August 11, 1456
Zimony (Zemun)
fields: Warfare and Conquest, Government and Politics

By organizing, financing, and leading the Hungarian and Central European military forces, Hunyadi halted the Ottoman Empire's advance at the Balkan Mountains, postponing for some seventy years the Turkish conquest of central Hungary.

Hunyadi, Mátyás. *See* Matthias I Corvinus

Hurh, Won Moo

b. Sept. 24, 1932
Chungju, Choong-Nam, Korea
fields: Sociology

Won Moo Hurh immigrated to the United States in 1965. A professor of sociology, his fields of interest include Korean immigration, race and ethnic relations, social psychology, and sociological theory. His books include *Comparative Study of Korean Immigrants in the United States: A Typological Approach* (1977), *Korean Immigrants in America: A Structural Analysis of Ethnic Confinement and Adhesive Adaptation* (1984), coauthored with Kwang Chung Kim, and *Assimilation Patterns of Immigrants in the United States* (1978), with Hei Chu Kim and Kwang Chung Kim.

Hurley, George W.

b. 1884
d. 1943
fields: Religion and Theology

African American established Universal Hagar's Spiritual Church in 1923 in Detroit, Mich; George W. Hurley claimed to be the God of the Aquarian Age, creating his own cosmological system and attacking institutional racism.

Hurston, Zora Neale

b. January 7, 1891
Eatonville, Florida
d. January 28, 1960
Fort Pierce, Florida
fields: Literature

The most accomplished African American woman writing in the first half of the twentieth century, Zora Neale Hurston was a major writer of the Harlem Renaissance and an important influence on later generations of women writers.

Hurt, Mississippi

full: John Smith Hurt
b. July 3, 1893
Teoc, Miss.
d. Nov. 2, 1966
Grenada, Miss.
fields: Music (blues singer, harmonica player, guitarist)

African American blues singer, harmonica player, and guitarist; Mississippi Hurt reemerged in the 1960's, rerecording songs that he originally recorded in the 1920's, including "Avalon Blues," "Big Leg Blues," "Candy Man Blues," "Lazy Blues," "Nobody's Dirty Business," "Pera Lee," and "Sliding Delta."

Hus, Jan

b. 1372 or 1373
Husinec, southern Bohemia
d. July 6, 1415
Constance (in modern Germany)
fields: Religion and Theology, Church Reform

Through preaching and writing against the abuses of the medieval church attendant upon the divided Papacy, the greedy and indolent clergy, and the rigid anti-layperson doctrines, Hus laid the foundation for the Protestant Reformation one hundred years later. His martyrdom at the Council of Constance made him a national hero to the Czech people.

Ḥusayn ibn ʿAlī

b. c. 626
Medina, Arabia
d. October 10 [10th of Muharram], 680
Karbala, Iraq
fields: Religion and Theology, Government and Politics

Ḥusayn ibn ʿAlī was grandson of the Prophet Muḥammad and the fourth caliph to succeed him. His assassination in 661 led to a dispute that was one of the formative events in Shīʿa Islam; his martyrdom and its annual remembrance serve as visceral reminders that human lives belong only to God and are to be surrendered to His service.

Hussein I

né: Hussein ibn Talal
b. November 14, 1935
Amman, Transjordan
fields: Government and Politics

Holding power longer than any other world leader, Hussein, King of Jordan, maintained the autonomy of Jordan, contributed to Arab unity, and served as a stabilizing force in the Middle East.

Hussein, Saddam

full: Saddam Hussein al-Tikriti
b. April 28, 1937
Tikrit, Iraq
fields: Government and Politics

President of Iraq (installed 1979). In 1968, Saddam Hussein helped to lead a coup that put the Ba'th party in control of Iraq. Hussein became president in July, 1979. Hussein became a military dictator, relentlessly and brutally suppressing political opposition. One such action was his ordering of chemical-weapons attacks on his country's Kurdish population in the 1980's. After amassing the region's largest military force, Hussein attacked Iran (1980-1988). In 1990, with Iraq's military force partly recovered, Hussein launched an invasion of the small neighboring country of Kuwait. The United States led an international coalition which successfully forced the Iraqi military from oil-rich Kuwait. Iraq was condemned by the United Nations, isolated by a strict trade embargo, and subject to weapons inspections.

Hussein, however, was soon defying the United Nations, continuing to develop weapons of mass destruction, oppressing the Kurdish and Shiite populations within Iraq, and sponsoring terrorism abroad. Frustrated by Hussein's continued refusal to let U.N. inspectors visit suspected weapons sites the United States and Great Britain launched bomb and missile strikes against numerous sites in Iraq in December, 1998.

Husserl, Edmund

b. April 8, 1859
Prossnitz, Moravia, Austrian Empire (now Prostějov, Czech Republic)
d. April 27, 1938
Freiburg im Breisgau, Germany
fields: Philosophy

Husserl is known as the founder of phenomenology, regarded by many as one of the most significant movements of the twentieth century.

Hutchins, Robert M.

full: Robert Maynard Hutchins
b. January 17, 1899
Brooklyn, New York
d. May 14, 1977
Santa Barbara, California
fields: Education, Social Criticism

By working to reform higher education, directing foundation programs, and heading study centers, Hutchins helped preserve, during the twentieth century, the Jeffersonian concept of an educated citizenry in a participatory democracy.

Hutchinson, Anne

né: Anne Marbury
b. 1591
Alford, England
d. August, 1643
Pelham Bay, Dutch New Netherland
fields: Religion and Theology

Through promotion of radical religious beliefs and challenges to the social order, Hutchinson became the focal point of great tensions within Massachusetts Bay Colony, a patriarchal biblical commonwealth.

Hutchinson, Thomas

b. September 9, 1711
Boston, Massachusetts
d. June 3, 1780
near London, England
fields: Government and Politics

As the last civilian to serve as royal governor of Massachusetts, Hutchinson had the tragic experience of watching the union between his province and Great Britain dissolve, in spite of his strenuous efforts. He proved his love of Massachusetts by writing a remarkably objective and thoroughly documented three-volume history of the colony, from its beginning to 1774.

Hutto, J. B.

full: Joseph Benjamin Hutto
b. Apr. 26, 1926
Blackville, S.C.
fields: Music (blues musician)

African American blues musician; in 1953, J. B. Hutto formed his own trio, J. B. Hutto and the Hawks; incorporated the bottleneck guitar work of Delta blues musicians into his style; adapted and recorded "Dust My Broom."

Hutton, Bobby James

b. 1951
Oakland, Calif.
d. Apr. 6, 1968
Oakland, Calif.
fields: Civil Rights, Social Reform

African American member of the Black Panther Party for Self Defense; Bobby James Hutton, one of the first Black Panthers, was killed in a shootout with Oakland police.

Huxley, Aldous

full: Aldous Leonard Huxley
b. July 26, 1894
Laleham, near Godalming, Surrey, England
d. November 22, 1963
Los Angeles, California
fields: Literature

Through far-sighted, iconoclastic thought and prolific, diverse writings, Huxley not only recorded but also transcended his age, greatly enriching intellectual life for the twentieth century and beyond.

Huxley, Thomas Henry

b. May 4, 1825
Ealing, Middlesex, England
d. June 29, 1895
Eastbourne, East Sussex, England
fields: Science, Philosophy

The first and most influential defender of Charles Darwin's theory of evolution, Huxley forcefully articulated its implications in the fields of religion, philosophy, and ethics.

Huygens, Christiaan

b. April 14, 1629
The Hague, the Netherlands
d. July 8, 1695
The Hague, the Netherlands
fields: Physics, Astronomy, Invention and Technology

Huygens was one of the greatest minds of the scientific revolution. His wave theory of light became highly influential in the nineteenth century. He invented the pendulum clock and discovered through his improved telescope the rings of Saturn.

Hwang, David Henry

b. August 11, 1957
Los Angeles, Calif.
Theater and Entertainment, Literature

Chinese American playwright. David Henry Hwang studied English and playwriting at Stanford University and the Yale School of Drama; first succeeded with with *F.O.B.* (1979), about a "fresh off the boat" Chinese American immigrant; won an Obie Award; other plays include *The Dance and the Railroad* (1981), *Family Devotions* (1981), *Sound and Beauty* (1983), and *Rich Relations* (1986); wrote *M. Butterfly* (1988), a provocative variation on the Madame Butterfly story; won Tony and Drama Desk Awards; wrote screenplay for the feature film of *M. Butterfly* (1993) and for the film *Golden Gate* (1994); received Rockefeller, Guggenheim, and National Endowment of the Arts fellowships; served on the boards of both the Dramatists Guild and the Theatre Communications Group; plays included in *Broken Promises: Four Plays by David Henry Hwang* (1983) and in the anthology *New Plays USA* (1982).

Hyde, Edward. *See* Clarendon, First Earl of

Hyde, Ida H.

full: Ida Henrietta Hyde
b. Sept. 8, 1857
Davenport, Iowa
d. Aug. 22, 1945
Berkeley, California
fields: Medicine, Physiology, Zoology

Ida H. Hyde invented the microelectrode. She set up scholarships for other female scientists.

Hyman, Earle

b. Oct. 11, 1926
Rocky Mount, N.C.
fields: Theater and Entertainment, Television (actor)

African American stage actor; Earle Hyman, perhaps best known as Russell Huxtable on television's *The Cosby Show* (1984-1992), received an AUDELCO Pioneers Award in 1980 for his career-long contributions to African Americans in theater.

Hyman, Flo

full: Flora Hyman
b. July 29, 1954
Los Angeles, Calif.
d. Jan. 24, 1986
Matsue, Japan
fields: Sports (volleyball player)

African American volleyball player; spiker Flo Hyman joined the U.S. National Volleyball Team in 1975; led the U.S. Volleyball Team to a silver medal in the 1984 Olympics; won the Outstanding Player award in the 1981 World Cup tournament; died suddenly in 1986 of heart failure (attributed to Marfan's Syndrome); first Flo Hyman Memorial Award presented to Martina Navratilova in 1987.

Hyman, John Adams

b. July 23, 1840
near Warrenton, N.C.
d. Sept. 14, 1891
Washington, D.C.
fields: Government and Politics

African American representative from North Carolina during Reconstruction. John Adams Hyman received the Republican nomination in 1874 and defeated his Democratic opponent in the general election to become the first African American member of the House of Representatives from North Carolina.

Hyman, Phyllis

b. 1950
Philadelphia, Pa.
d. June 30, 1995
New York, N.Y.
fields: Music (singer)

African American singer; Phyllis Hyman's first album, *Phyllis Hyman*, was released 1977; other albums included *Somewhere in My Lifetime* (1979), *You Sure Look Good to Me* (1980), *Can't We Fall in Love Again?* (1981), and *Prime of My Life* (1991); made her Broadway debut in 1981 in *Sophisticated Ladies and* received a Theater World Award.

Hypatia

b. c. 370 C.E.
probably Alexandria
d. 415 C.E.
Alexandria
fields: Mathematics, Philosophy, Science

The last of the great pagan scientists, Hypatia is best known to history for the manner of her death, which has caused her to be regarded as a symbol of courage in the face of an oppressive Christian Church.

Hyun, Peter

b. Aug. 15, 1906
Lihue, Hawaii
d. Aug. 25, 1993
Oxnard, Calif.
fields: Theater and Entertainment, Business and Industry

Peter Hyun is the son of one of the founders of the Korean provisional government in exile, set up in Shanghai in 1920. He graduated from DePauw University in Indiana and became active in theater in New York and Massachusetts. Hyun became director of the Children's Theater of the New York Federal Theater, a Works Progress Administration project, in 1936. He served in Army intelligence during World War II and after 1945 as a liaison officer for the U.S. military government in Korea. After the war, he directed plays, taught, and opened a Chinese restaurant in California. In 1986, he published an autobiography, *Man Sei! The Making of a Korean American.*

I

I, Ālamgīr. *See* Aurangzeb

Ibn al-ʿArabī

full: Muḥyī al-Dīn Abū ʿAbd Allāh Muḥammad ibn ʿAlī ibn Muḥammad ibn al-ʿArabī al-Ḥātīmī al-Ṭāʾī ibn al-ʿArabī
aka: Abū Bakr Muḥammad ibn al-ʿArabī al-Ḥātīmī al-Ṭāʾī
b. July 28, 1165
Murcia, Spain
d. November 16, 1240
Damascus, Syria
fields: Philosophy, Religion and Theology, Monasticism

Ibn al-ʿArabī formulated and made explicit the inner doctrines of Sufism and was the link between the Eastern and Western schools of that philosophy.

Ibn Battutah

full: Abu ʿAbd Allah Muhammad ibn ʿAbd Allah al-Lawati al-Tanji
b. 1304
Tangier, Morocco
d. c. 1377
Morocco
fields: Exploration

Driven by an exceptional wanderlust, Ibn Battutah became the greatest Muslim traveler. His peregrinations through India, Russia, China, the East Indies, North Africa, and the Near and Middle East were recorded in the most famous of all Islamic travelogs, the *Rihlah*.

Ibn Gabirol

full: Solomon ben Yehuda ibn Gabirol
b. c. 1020
probably Málaga, Spain
d. c. 1057
probably Valencia, Spain
fields: Literature and Philosophy

Ibn Gabirol created a form of poetry written in biblical Hebrew. His version of Neoplatonic philosophy came to be integrated within Christian Augustinian thought.

Ibn Hanbal. *See* Ahmad ibn Hanbal

Ibn Khaldun

full: Abu Zayd ʿAbd al-Rahman Ibn Khaldun
b. May 27, 1332
Tunis, Tunisia
d. March 17, 1406
Cairo, Egypt
fields: Historiography

Ibn Khaldun formulated highly original and widely acclaimed theories on the rise and fall of empires and established himself as one of the most distinguished intellectual figures of Western Islam in the late Middle Ages.

Ibn Rushd. *See* Averroës

Ibsen, Henrik

b. March 20, 1828
Skien, Norway
d. May 23, 1906
Christiana, Norway
fields: Theater and Entertainment (drama)

Ibsen is one of the leading figures in modern drama. Moving beyond the melodramas of the nineteenth century, Ibsen created a drama of psychological realism. His dramas helped to create modern realistic theater.

Ice Cube

né: O'Shea Jackson
b. June 15, c. 1969
Los Angeles, Calif.
fields: Music, Film (rap vocalist and actor)

African American rap vocalist and actor; Ice Cube was a founding member of NWA (Niggaz With Attitude), the first nationally known "gangsta rap" group; went solo in 1990 and released albums including *AmeriKKKa's Most Wanted* (1990), *Death Certificate* (1991), *The Predator* (1992), and *Lethal Injection* (1994); film credits include *Boyz 'N the Hood* (1991), *Trespass* (1992), *Higher Learning* (1995), *Dangerous Ground* (1997), *Anaconda* (1997), and *The Players Club* (1998; the first film he directed).

Ice-T

né: Tracey Marrow
b. Feb. 16, 1958
Newark, N.J.
fields: Music (rap singer), Film

African American rap singer, producer, and actor; Ice-T's albums include *Rhyme Pays* (1987), *Power*, and *The Iceberg*; collaborated with Quincy Jones and received a Grammy for *Back on the Block* (1990); his film work included roles in *Colors* (1988), *New Jack City* (1991), and *Ricochet* (1991), *Johnny Mnemonic* (1995), and *Crazy Six* (1998).

Ichihashi, Yamato

b. 1878
Aichi Prefecture, Japan
d. 1965
Stanford, Calif.
fields: Sociology, Historiography

Yamato Ichihashi received his bachelor's degree in economics from Stanford University in 1907 and his master's degree in 1908. He received a doctoral degree from Harvard University in 1913, writing a dissertation on immigration and the Japanese immigrant community in the United States. In 1913, he began to teach Japanese history and politics at Stanford and was granted tenure in 1928. Four years later, Ichihashi published his landmark study *Japanese in the United States*. During World War II, he and his family were interned at Manzanar, Tule Lake, and Granada. After the war, the professor returned to Stanford, where he lived until his death in 1965.

Ichioka, Yuji

b. June 23, 1936
San Francisco, Calif.
fields: Historiography, Sociology

Yuji Ichioka, who received a master's degree in history from the University of California, Berkeley, in 1968, cofounded the Asian American Political Alliance while studying for his master's. Ichioka, who coined the term "Asian American," became associate director of the Asian American Studies Center at the University of California, Los Angeles, in 1969. His 1988 publication, *The Issei: The World of the First Generation Japanese Immigrants, 1885-1924*, won an award from the Association for Asian American Studies.

Ichiyūsai Hiroshige. *See* Hiroshige

Idrisi, al-

full: Abu ʿAbd Allah Muhammad ibn Muhammad ʿAbd Allah ibn Idris al-Hammundi al-Hasani al-Idrisi
b. 1100
Sabtah, Morocco
d. Between 1164 and 1166
near Sabtah, Morocco
fields: Geography, Cartography

A world traveler, al-Idrisi eventually collaborated with the Norman king of Sicily, Roger II, to produce a major geography and several significant maps of the medieval world. These works served as models for productions in the field for more than five hundred years.

Igasaki, Paul M.

b. 1955
fields: Law, Social Reform

Paul M. Igasaki is a lawyer and social activist; born in Chicago; moved to California to attend Martin Luther King, Jr., School of Law at the University of California, Davis; lawyer, Legal Services of Northern California, 1980-1985; Washington, D.C., representative for the Japanese American Citizens League; executive director of the Asian Law Caucus, 1991-1994; chairman of the Equal Employment Opportunity Commission, 1994.

Iglesias, Julio

full: Julio José Iglesias de la Cueva
b. Sept. 23, 1943
Madrid, Spain
fields: Music (singer and songwriter)

Latino singer and songwriter. During his recovery from a serious automobile accident in the summer of 1963, Julio Iglesias learned to play the guitar. He subsequently decided to attempt a career in music. He began to write songs in 1968 and became well known throughout Europe for "Guendoline" (1970). By the early 1970's, Iglesias he had become a top-selling recording artist in Europe, Latin America, Japan, and parts of the Middle East. In 1983, as the world's best-selling recording artist, he won the *Guinness Book of World Records*'s first Diamond Disc Award. In 1987, he won a Grammy Award for Best Latin Popular Performance.

Ignacio

aka: John Lyon
b. 1828
San Juan, Colo.
d. Dec. 9, 1913
Ute Mountain Reservation, Colo.
fields: Government and Politics, Native American Affairs

A Wiminuche Ute, Ignacio was leader of the Southern Ute during negotiations with the U.S. government for a Ute reservation. He counseled cooperation with whites. After the death of Ouray in 1880, Ignacio was recognized as the chief of all the Southern Utes. The town of Ignacio, Colorado, was named for him.

Ignatius of Antioch

b. c. 30 C.E.
Antioch, Syria
d. December 20, 107? C.E.
Rome
fields: Religion and Theology

Ignatius served as Bishop of Antioch from the early 60's to the early 100's and was an important theologian and the exemplary martyr of the early Christian Church. By his writings and example, Ignatius strengthened the office of bishop in the church hierarchy, clarified many central Christian doctrines, such as the Real Presence and the Virgin Birth, and formulated the strategy and tactics of voluntary martyrdom.

Ii Naosuke

b. November 29, 1815
Hikone, Japan
d. March 24, 1860
Edo, Japan
fields: Government and Politics

Ii was a conservative but pragmatic defender of the Tokugawa family's rule (*bakufu*) in nineteenth century Japan. While he temporarily slowed the decline of the *bakufu*, his policies in the long run were ineffective in dealing with either the growing domestic hostility toward the shogun or the Western pressures open Japan to full participation in world trade and politics.

Ikeda, Hayato

b. December 3, 1899
Yoshina, Hiroshima Prefecture, Japan
d. August 13, 1965
Tokyo, Japan
fields: Government and Politics

As Prime Minister of Japan from 1960 to 1964, Ikeda succeeded in restoring Japan's prestige in the eyes of the world after the riots and unrest attending the 1960 renewal of the United States-Japan Security Treaty. Ikeda brokered a cooperative effort between his political party and the bureaucracy, which produced the widely supported Income Doubling Plan and resulted in a high-growth economic pattern that has been maintained ever since.

Ikhnaton. *See* Akhenaton

Iksana, Natawista. *See* Natawista

Imamura, Yemyo

b. 1867
Fukui, Japan
d. 1932
fields: Religion and Theology

Yemyo Imamura, a bishop of the Honpa Hongwanji, landed in Hawaii in 1899. He attempted to bridge the gap between Christianity and Buddhism, working among followers of the Jodo Shinshu Buddhist sect, the largest in the islands. He helped establish a Young Men's Buddhist Association (YMBA), which assisted Japanese immigrants in the new country.

Iman

né: Iman Abdumajid
b. July 25, 1955
Mogadishu, Somalia
fields: Fashion (model), Film

African American model; Known by her first name, Somalia-born Iman became one of the highest paid models in the world and appeared on magazine covers and in films such as *Out of Africa* (1985), *The Human Factor* (1979), *No Way Out* (1987), and *Star Trek VI: The Undiscovered Country* (1991). She married rock legend David Bowie in 1992.

Imari, Brother. *See* Obadele, Imari Abubakari

Imazeki, Howard

b. 1907
Japan
fields: Journalism, Publishing

Howard Imazeki arrived in the United States with his family in 1918 and received a bachelor's degree in journalism in 1934. He was the English-section editor of the *Shin Sekai-Asahi Shimbun* before joining his father in the poultry business. He and his family were removed to the Tule Lake relocation center during the war. He edited the camp newspaper during his internment and worked for the U.S. Navy from 1943 until the end of the war. After the war ended, Imazeki worked in Japan as an interpreter and translator, returning to the United States in 1954 to join the staff of the *Hokubei Mainichi* as the paper's English-section editor.

Imhotep

b. Twenty-seventh century B.C.E.
Egypt
d. Twenty-seventh century B.C.E.
Egypt
fields: Architecture, Medicine

Imhotep, the priest-physician who was deified as the Egyptian god of medicine, was also an architect and is credited with starting the age of pyramid building.

Inada, Lawson Fusao

b. 1938
Fresno, Calif.
fields: Poetry

Lawson Fusao Inada, a third-generation Japanese American born in the central California community of Fresno, was interned during World War II in camps in Arkansas and Colorado. Inada coedited the collection *Aiiieeeee! An Anthology of Asian American Writers* (1974) and its sequel *The Big Aiiieeeee! An Anthology of Chinese American and Japanese American Literature* (1991). His poetry collections include *Before the War: Poems As They Happened* (1971) and *Legends from Camp* (1992).

Ingalls, Laura. *See* Wilder, Laura Ingalls

Ingram, Rex

b. Oct. 20, 1895
Cairo, Ill.
d. Sept. 19, 1969
Los Angeles, Calif.
fields: Theater and Entertainment, Film (stage and film actor)

African American stage and film actor; Rex Ingram's breakthrough film role was "De Lawd" in *The Green Pastures* (1936); played Jim in *The Adventures of Huckleberry Finn* (1939) and was Lucifer, Jr., in the stage performance of *Cabin in the Sky* (1940).

Ingres, Jean-Auguste-Dominique

b. August 29, 1780
Montauban, near Toulouse, France
d. January 14, 1867
Paris, France
fields: Art

Ingres championed sound draftsmanship and inspiration from Greek civilization. His idealized figures and flawless surfaces set an unequaled standard in the first half of the nineteenth century. In elevating aesthetic form and personal expression above orthodoxy, Ingres inadvertently became one of the earliest examples of art for art's sake, a concept which became important for the later modern movements.

Iñigo de Oñaz y Loyola. *See* Loyola, Saint Ignatius of

Inkpaduta

b. c. 1815
S.Dak.
d. c. 1878
fields: Warfare and Conquest, Government and Politics, Native American Affairs

A Wahpekute Sioux, Inkpaduta was the Sioux leader of a bloody outbreak in Iowa (the Spirit Lake uprising) in 1856-1857, during a time of increasing settlement by whites. Warriors under Inkpaduta's leadership killed forty-seven colonists and kidnapped four women, only one of whom was later released.

Inman, Lee

full: Dorothy J. Inman
b. ?
Birmingham, Ala.
fields: Government and Politics

African American mayor of Tallahassee, Fla; Lee Inman was elected as a Tallahassee city commissioner in 1986 and served in that post until becoming mayor in 1988.

Innis, Roy

full: Roy Emile Alfredo Innis
b. June 6, 1934
St. Croix, U.S. Virgin Islands
fields: Civil Rights

African American civil rights leader; Roy Innis joined Congress of Racial Equality (CORE) in 1963, becoming national director in 1968; founded Harlem Commonwealth Council designed to promote black businesses; coedited *Manhattan Tribune*, weekly tabloid covering Harlem and the Upper West Side; proponent of black nationalism and separatism; against school integration; CORE's influence peaked in the late 1960's and declined steadily thereafter.

Innocent III

né: Lothario of Segni
b. 1160 or 1161
Anagni, the Roman Campagna
d. July 16, 1216
Perugia
fields: Religion and Theology, Government and Politics

Pope Innocent III, 1198-1216. At a period of crisis in the Catholic church, Pope Innocent III succeeded in affirming the power of his office against challenges from powerful lay rulers and from the Albigensian heresy, and in so doing became the most powerful pope of the Middle Ages. In addition, through sweeping ecclesiastical reform, he attempted to mute the arguments of the critics of an increasingly venal, poorly educated, and self-indulgent clergy.

Innocent IV

né: Sinibaldo Fieschi
b. c. 1180
Genoa
d. December 7, 1254
Naples
fields: Religion and Theology, Government and Politics

Pope Innocent IV, 1243-1254. Throughout his pontificate, Innocent IV defended the temporal and spiritual authority of the Papacy and upheld its supremacy over secular rulers.

Inönü, Ismet

né: İsmet Pasha
b. September 24, 1884
Smyrna (now İzmir), Ottoman Empire (now Turkey)
d. December 25, 1973
Ankara, Turkey
fields: Government and Politics

İnönü served as the first prime minister of the Turkish Republic from 1923 to 1937 and as its second president from 1938 to 1950. During this time, he worked to maintain his nation's neutrality in international affairs and oversaw its transformation into a modernized state.

Inouye, Daniel

full: Daniel Ken Inouye
b. Sept. 7, 1924
Honolulu, Hawaii
fields: Government and Politics

Japanese American politician; Daniel Inouye was born in Honolulu, Hawaii; joined U.S. Army, where he distinguished himself in combat in Europe, 1943-1945 and lost his arm; earned a law degree at George Washington University Law School in 1952; majority leader in Hawaii territorial house, 1954-1958; U.S. representative (Democrat), 1959-1963; U.S. senator since 1963; strong supporter of President Lyndon B. Johnson's social welfare program; gained national attention as member of the senate Watergate committee in 1973; chair of senate Iran-Contra committee; chaired the Select Committee on Indian Affairs, the Appropriations Subcommittee on Defense, and the Senate Democratic Steering Committee among others; wrote autobiography, *Journey to Washington* (1967).

Inshtatheumba. *See* La Flesche, Susette

Ionesco, Eugène

b. November 26, 1912
Slatina, Romania
d. March 28, 1994
Paris, France
fields: Literature

One of the greatest playwrights of the twentieth century, Ionesco helped develop and popularize the genre of Theater of the Absurd through his then-experimental plays, which expose the emptiness of societal institutions.

Irateba

aka: Arateva
aka: Yaratev
aka: Beautiful Bird
b. c. 1814
near present-day Needles, Calif.
d. June 17, 1878
fields: Diplomacy, Government and Politics, Native American Affairs

Native American leader. During initial white explorations of the Mojave region of California, Irateba, a Mojave, was the principal Indian guide. In 1849-1850 and again in 1856-1858, he aided Lieutenant Joseph Ives's exploration of the Colorado River. Irateba also guided Lieutenant Lorenzo Sitgreaves's expedition to San Diego, 1854, and Lieutenant Amiel Whipple's trek to Los Angeles.

Iredell, James

b. 1751
d. 1799
fields: Law

U.S. Supreme Court justice, 1790-1799 (died while in office); appointed by President Washington. Significant opinion: *Chisholm v. Georgia*, 2 U.S. 419 (1793) (dissenting opinion).

Irenaeus, Saint

b. Between 120 and 140
probably Smyrna, Asia Minor
d. 202
Lugdunum, Gaul (modern Lyons, France)
fields: Religion and Theology

As the first systematic theologian of the Christian church, Irenaeus laid the foundation for the development of church doctrine and effectively ended the threat that Gnosticism might substitute mysticism for faith in the resurrection of Christ.

Irigaray, Luce

b. 1930
Belgium
fields: Philosophy, Psychiatry and Psychology, Language and Linguistics

Luce Irigaray's work in the area of language and its relation to women's oppression in the West is deemed crucial by literary theorists, students of gender theory, sociologists, and linguists. Because she holds that language is inadequate to express certain truths, especially female truths, her unusual and unique use of language is part of her message, although that has both estranged and endeared her readers. Major works include *Speculum of the Other Woman* (1974) and *An Ethics of Sexual Difference* (1984).

Iromagaja. *See* Rain in the Face

Iron Chancellor. *See* Bismarck, Otto von

Irons, Peter

b. Aug. 11, 1940
Salem, Mass.
fields: Jurisprudence, Government and Politics

Attorney and constitutional scholar Peter Irons played a significant part in the landmark *coram nobis* cases, *Korematsu v. United States* (1983) and *Hirabayashi v. United States* (1988). Educated at Antioch College (B.A., 1966), Boston University (Ph.D., 1973), and Harvard Law School (J.D., 1988). In 1993, Irons published *May It Please the Court*, a book and six audiocassettes, consisting of recordings of open arguments in twenty-three key Supreme Court cases. The release of this material provoked controversy because it violated a routine agreement Irons had signed to obtain access to the tapes in the National Archives. Some scholars praised his actions, stating that the restrictions on the tapes, taken from open sessions, were illegitimate.

Irvin, Monte

full: Merrill Monford Irvin
b. Feb. 25, 1919
Columbia, Ala.
fields: Sports (baseball player)

African American baseball player; elected to baseball's Hall of Fame in 1973, Monte Irvin played in the Negro Leagues before signing with the New York Giants in 1949 and starring in two World Series.

Irving, Henry

né: John Henry Brodribb
b. February 6, 1838
Keinton Mandeville, Somerset, England
d. October 13, 1905
Bradford, Yorkshire, England
fields: Theater and Entertainment

Breaking with the conventions of acting and staging current in Victorian England, Irving introduced a more natural acting style, greater reliance on authentic texts, and more realistic production values for the staging of William Shakespeare's plays.

Irving, Washington

b. April 3, 1783
New York, New York
d. November 28, 1859
Tarrytown, New York
fields: Literature (fiction), History, Diplomacy

Washington Irving, America's first international literary success, was responsible for making American letters respectable in the nineteenth century.

Irvis, K. Leroy

b. Dec. 27, 1919
Saugerties, N.Y.
fields: Government and Politics, Literature

African American politician, teacher, and author; K. Leroy Irvis served in the Pennsylvania House of Representatives from 1958 to 1988; authored *This Land of Fire* (1988), a book of poems.

Irwin, Robert Walker

b. 1844
Copenhagen, Denmark
d. 1929
fields: Government and Politics, Business and Industry

Robert Walker Irwin participated in numerous business ventures in Japan and promoted immigration of Japanese to Hawaii. He arrived in Japan in 1866 as agent for the Pacific Mail Steamship Company in Yokohama. Seven years later, he helped establish an import-export company that eventually became Mitsui Bussan Kaisha (Mitsui Trading Company). He became Hawaiian consul-general to Japan in 1880 and helped arrange for Japanese laborers to go to Hawaii to work on sugar plantations, working with the help of the Mitsui Company. In 1893, in response to some immigration difficulties, Irwin tried to obtain for Japanese immigrants the same rights and privileges accorded to other foreigners in Hawaii.

Irwin, Wallace

b. March 15, 1875
Oneida, N.Y.
d. Feb. 14, 1959
Southern Pines, N.C.
fields: Journalism, Literature

Humorist Wallace Irwin published a series of letters in *Collier's Weekly* under the pseudonym "Hashimura Togo" in the early 1900's. The letters, supposedly the work of a Japanese American schoolboy, were written in fractured English and recounted stereotypical Japanese behaviors. The popular letters were collected into books, including *Letters of a Japanese Schoolboy* (1909). Another of Irwin's works was *Seed of the Sun* (1921), a novel about Japan's efforts to make California one of its colonies. Irwin attended Stanford University from 1896 to 1899, leaving to work for the *San Francisco Examiner* and later the *Overland Monthly*.

Isaacs, Alick

b. July 17, 1921
Glasgow, Scotland
d. Jan. 25, 1967
London, England
fields: Biology, Medicine

Alick Isaacs is known for discovering interferon, a protein that explains why only one ribonucleic acid (RNA) virus type can infect the body at a time.

Isabella I

aka: Isabella la Católica
aka: Isabella the Catholic
b. April 22, 1451
Madrigal, Spain
d. November 26, 1504
Medina del Campo, Spain
fields: Monarchy, Military Affairs, Government and Politics

Queen of Castile, 1474-1504. With her husband Ferdinand II, the Catholic monarch directed Spain's transition from medieval diversity to national unity. They achieved governmental and ecclesiastical reform, and established a continuing Spanish presence in Italy, America, and northern Africa.

Isaiah

b. c. 760 B.C.E.
Jerusalem, Judah
d. c. 701-680 B.C.E.
probably Jerusalem, Judah
fields: Religion and Theology

Because of his clear grasp of political reality and the power of his poetic utterances, Isaiah is generally considered to be the greatest of the Old Testament prophets.

Isapo-Muxika. *See* Crowfoot

Isatai

b. c. 1850
northwest Tex.
d. c. 1900
northwest Tex.

fields: Warfare and Conquest, Native American Affairs

Native American (Comanche) leader and medicine man. When Isatai was a young warrior, his claims of supernatural power at first brought hope to his discouraged people. In 1874, using the medicine that Isatai said would protect them in battle, a united force of Comanche, Kiowa, Cheyenne, and Arapaho warriors led by Quanah Parker and other war chiefs attacked Adobe Walls, an old trading post then occupied by white buffalo hunters. Isatai's medicine proved useless against the high-powered buffalo rifles of the hunters. After twelve men had been killed, nine of them Indians, the united force terminated the attack. Quanah Parker and other Comanche leaders never again trusted the power of medicine men.

Ishaynishus. *See* Two Moon

Ishi

b. c. 1862
near Deer Creek, Northern Calif.
d. Mar. 25, 1916
San Francisco, Calif.
fields: Historical Personage (refugee)

Ishi was a California Yahi who became known in the press as the "last wild Indian." In 1911, when Ishi appeared, exhausted and hungry, in the corral of a slaughterhouse near Oroville in Northern California, the Yahi were all thought to have been annihilated many years before. To anthropologists, Ishi was an important source of scientific knowledge. Anthropologists Alfred Kroeber and Thomas Waterman took Ishi to live at the Museum of Anthropology at the University of California, Berkeley. Ishi, In keeping with Yahi etiquette, Ishi would not reveal his name, so Kroeber bestowed the name "Ishi"—a Yana term for "man."

Ishi'eyo. *See* Two Moon

Ishigo, Estelle

b. July 15, 1899
Oakland, Calif.
d. Feb., 1990
Los Angeles, Calif.
fields: Art

Estelle Ishigo, a white woman, was an art student when she met Arthur Shigeharu Ishigo, a San Francisco-born Nisei and aspiring actor. They were married on August 28, 1929. She voluntarily accompanied her husband when he was forced to relocate to a detention camp at Heart Mountain. While there, she created hundreds of sketches and watercolor paintings of life in the camp. An Academy Award-winning documentary, *Days of Waiting* (1990), directed by Steven Okazaki, was made about her experiences.

Isidore of Seville, Saint

b. c. 560
Seville, Spain
d. April 4, 636
Seville, Spain
fields: Education, Literature, Religion and Theology

Through his defense of education, Isidore of Seville not only preserved the classical traditions of his people but also helped to forge a national identity.

Islas, Arturo, Jr.

b. May 24, 1938
El Paso, Tex.
d. Feb. 15, 1991
fields: Literature

Latino novelist. Arturo Islas, Jr., completed his doctorate in English at Stanford University in 1971. He was appointed to a tenure-track position at the university in 1970. As he became more interested in Chicano-related issues, he turned to autobiographical writing, resulting in the highly acclaimed novel *The Rain God: A Desert Tale* (1984). His second novel, *Migrant Souls*, was published in 1990, eight years after it was completed. The year after its publication, Islas died of cancer.

Isocrates

b. 436 B.C.E.
Athens, Greece
d. 338 B.C.E.
Athens, Greece
fields: Philosophy

One of the ten "Attic Orators," Isocrates made significant contributions to the development of rhetorical theory, philosophy, and education in Ancient Greece. Isocrates' model of education grounded in rhetoric guided educators for centuries to follow.

Isonaga Hikosuke. *See* Nagasawa, Kanaye

Isparhecher

aka: Spahecha (Whooping While Taking Off Scalp)
b. 1829
Ala.
d. Dec. 22, 1902
Creek Nation, present-day Okla.
fields: Government and Politics, Native American Affairs

Native American leader. Leader of the traditionalist faction in the Creek Nation, Isparhecher led an unsuccessful attempt to overthrow the tribal government in 1882 (known as Isparhecher's War, or the Green Peach War). Afterward Isparhecher continued to be the leader of tribal conservatives. He served as the Creek chief justice and was elected principal chief in 1895.

Israel, Prince Ashiel Ben

b. ?
fields: Religion and Theology

African American religious leader within the Jewish faith; in the 1980's, Prince Ashiel Ben Israel was director of the American followers of the Original Hebrew Israelite Nation.

Israels, Belle Lindner. *See* Moskowitz, Belle

Italiano, Anna Maria Louisa. *See* Bancroft, Anne

Itliong, Larry Dulay

b. October 25, 1913
d. 1976
Delano, Calif.
fields: Labor Movement

Filipino farm labor organizer Larry Itliong laid the foundations for the California farmworker union movement. In 1956 Itliong founded the Filipino Farm Labor Union (FFLU). Support from the AFL-CIO allowed Itliong to organize field workers under the banner of the Agricultural Workers Organizing Committee (AWOC). AWOC began the Delano grape strike against grape growers in California's San Joaquin Valley in 1965. The National Farm Workers Union (NFWU) led by César Chávez joined the strike, and AWOC and NFWU merged to form the United Farm Workers (UFW) Organizing Committee in 1966. Itliong served as vice president of the UFW until 1971.

Itō Hirobumi

b. September 2, 1841
Tsukari Village, Chōshū, Japan
d. October 26, 1909
Harbin, Manchuria, China
fields: Government and Politics

Itō Hirobumi became counsellor to Emperor Meiji and his home minister in 1878. Four-time prime minister of Japan between 1885 and 1896, drafted the 1885 Meiji Constitution. Waged a successful war against China in 1894-1895 over control of Korea. Assassinated by a Korean nationalist in Manchuria.

Ito, Robert

b. July 2, 1931
Vancouver, British Columbia, Canada
fields: Theater and Entertainment

Japanese American actor Robert Ito was best known for his role as Sam Fujiyama, a medical examiner in the National Broadcasting Company series *Quincy, M. E.* (1976-

1983), a weekly drama about Quincy, a mystery-solving doctor of forensic medicine.

Iturbi, José

b. Nov. 28, 1895
Valencia, Spain
d. June 28, 1980
Hollywood, Calif.
fields: Music (classical pianist and conductor)

Classical pianist and conductor. José Iturbi, the most famous Spanish American pianist of his day, began piano lessons at the age of five. He studied with Victor Staub at the Paris Conservatory, graduating in 1913 with the highest honors. He served as head of the piano department at the Geneva Conservatory in Switzerland from 1919 to 1923. His American piano debut took place in 1929. Iturbi conducted orchestras in Mexico, Europe, and the United States, and led the Rochester Philharmonic Orchestra from 1936 to 1944. In 1950, he became the first classical musician to sell more than a million copies of a single recording.

Itzcóatl

b. c. 1382
place unknown
d. 1440
probably Tenochtitlán (modern Mexico City)
fields: Government and Politics

King of Mexica, 1427?-1440. As the founder of the Mexican state, Itzcóatl was largely responsible both for the strengths which enabled it to survive until the Spanish conquest and for the weaknesses which contributed to its destruction.

Ivan the Great

full: Ivan the Great, grand prince of Muscovy
né: Ivan III Vasilyevich
b. January 22, 1440
Moscow, Russia
d. October 27, 1505
Moscow, Russia
fields: Government and Politics

Grand prince and sovereign of Russia, 1462-1505. Ivan the Great laid the foundation for the political centralization and territorial unification of the Russian national state and the consolidation and growth of imperial autocracy. Known in the history of Russia as "the gatherer of the Russian lands," he united all the Slavic independent and semi-independent principalities and cities under the aegis of the Muscovite rulers and began the long struggle with Poland-Lithuania and Sweden for recovering Russia's "historical" lands of the Ukraine, White Russia, and the Baltic States. Ivan was also the Grand Prince of Muscovy who ended Russia's 240 years of Mongol or Tatar rule and proclaimed the independence of his country.

Ivan the Terrible

aka: Ivan IV Vasilyevich
b. August 25, 1530
Moscow, Russia
d. March 18, 1584
Moscow, Russia
fields: Government and Politics

Czar of Russia, 1547-1584 (ruler under his mother's regency from 1533). Of all the Russian czars, Ivan contributed the most in giving shape to Russian autocracy as it would exist until the end of serfdom in 1861. He also conquered Kazan and Astrakhan, significantly reducing the Tatar threat and securing the important trade routes in the Volga region, and took the first steps toward the incorporation of Siberia.

Ives, Charles

b. October 20, 1874
Danbury, Connecticut
d. May 19, 1954
New York, New York
fields: Music

Using experimental techniques that disregarded traditional musical theories, Ives wrote compositions which expressed American experiences and feelings.

Iwamatsu Jun Atsushi. *See* Yashima, Taro

Iwamatsu, Makoto. *See* Mako

J

Jaar, Alfredo

b. Feb. 5, 1956
Santiago, Chile
fields: Art (sculptor)

Sculptor. Alfredo Jaar creates sculptures that highlight the relationship of the industrialized world to less developed countries and the people who live there. In 1985, he received a John Simon Guggenheim Foundation Grant. During the late 1980's and 1990's his work was shown in several major exhibitions. His sculptures have been purchased by the High Museum of Art in Atlanta, the La Jolla Museum of Contemporary Art in California, and the L'Arche de la Fraternité, La Défense, in Paris.

Jābir ibn Ḥayyān, Abū Mūsā

b. 721
Tus (in modern Iran)
d. 815
Al-Kufa (in modern Iraq)
fields: Chemistry

The greatest alchemist of Islam, Jabir is regarded as the father of Arabian chemistry; his many works considerably influenced later Arabian and European chemists, and his alchemical ideas and recipes helped advance chemical theory and experimentation.

Jackée

né: Jackée Harry
b. Aug. 14, 1957
Winston-Salem, N.C.
fields: Television, Theater and Entertainment, Film (actor)

African American actress; in 1987, Jackée won an Emmy Award for her role as Sandra Clark on the television show *227*; her film credits include *Moscow on the Hudson* (1984) and *The Cotton Club* (1984).

Jackson, Andrew

b. March 15, 1767
Waxhaw area, South Carolina
d. June 8, 1845
the Hermitage, near Nashville, Tennessee
fields: Government and Politics, Military Affairs

Possessing the characteristics of the roughly hewn Western frontiersman as opposed to aristocratic propensities of the Eastern and Virginia "establishment," Jackson came to symbolize the common man in America and the rise of democracy. President of the United States, 1829-1837)

Jackson, Baby

full: Laurence Jackson
b. 1921
Baltimore, Md.
d. 1974
New York, N.Y.
fields: Dance

African American dancer. Baby Jackson performed from the 1930's through the 1950's and is considered to be one of the most original dancers of the jazz, swing, and bebop eras.

Jackson, Benjamin F.

b. fl. 1800's
fields: Invention and Technology

African American inventor; Benjamin F. Jackson developed patents for a steam boiler, a gas burner, and a hydrocarbon burner system (1899).

Jackson, Bo

né: Vincent Edward Jackson
b. Nov. 30, 1962
Bessemer, Ala.
fields: Sports (football and baseball player)

African American football and baseball player; Bo Jackson was one of very few athletes to play two professional sports; won football's Heisman Trophy in 1985; joined the Kansas City Royals baseball team in 1986 and the Los Angeles Raiders football team in 1987; had hip replacement surgery in 1992; also played baseball with the Chicago White Sox and California Angels; retired in 1995.

Jackson, Eugene

b. Sept. 5, 1943
Waukomis, Okla.
fields: Journalism

African American broadcast executive; Eugene Jackson was president of Unity Broadcasting Network.

Jackson, Fay M.

b. ?
fields: Journalism

African American journalist; Fay M. Jackson published *The Flash*, the first black news magazine, in Los Angeles, Calif., in the early 1920's.

Jackson, Freddie

b. 1958
fields: Music (rhythm-and-blues vocalist)

African American rhythm-and-blues vocalist; discovered in 1982 by singer Melba Moore, Freddie Jackson went on to release highly successful albums including *Rock Me Tonight* (1985), *Just Like the First Time* (1987), and *Don't Let Love Slip Away* (1988); received the 1986 American Black Gold Award for Outstanding Male Artist.

Jackson, George

b. Sept. 23, 1941
Chicago, Ill.
d. Aug. 21, 1971
San Quentin, Calif.
fields: Civil Rights, Social Reform, Literature

African American martyr of the radical black prison movement; one of San Quentin's "Soledad Brothers" and a field marshal in the Black Panther Party, George Jackson was a revolutionary dedicated to political agitation within; authored *Soledad Brother: The Prison Letters of George Jackson* (1970) and *Blood in My Eye* (1972); was murdered during a prison disturbance manufactured by police authorities.

Jackson, Helen Hunt

né: Helen Maria Fiske
aka: Helen Maria Hunt
b. October 15, 1830
Amherst, Massachusetts
d. August 12, 1885
San Francisco, California
fields: Literature, Social Reform

Jackson received the first government commission on behalf of American Indians and fought vehemently for their civil rights and liberties.

Jackson, Henry, Jr. *See* Armstrong, Henry

Jackson, Howell Edmunds

b. 1832
d. 1895
fields: Law

U.S. Supreme Court justice, 1893-1895 (died while in office); appointed by President Harrison.

Jackson, Isaiah Allen

b. January 22, 1945
Richmond, Va.
fields: Music (orchestra conductor)

African American orchestra conductor; Isaiah Allen Jackson founded the Juilliard String Ensemble and served as the group's conductor; was the music director for the New York Youth Symphony from 1969 to 1973; became the first American to hold a major post at Britain's Covent Garden when he was appointed principal conductor and later, music director of the Royal Ballet.

Jackson, Janet

b. May 16, 1966
Gary, Ind.
fields: Music, Dance, Television

African American singer, dancer, and actress; Janet Jackson, younger sister of pop star Michael Jackson, recorded hit albums including *Control* (1986), *Janet Jackson's Rhythm Nation 1814* (1989), and *The Velvet Rope* (1997); won American Music Awards as best dance artist, best female pop-rock artist, and best female soul-rhythm-and-blues artist in 1991; appeared on televison shows including *Good Times, A New Kind of Family, Diff'rent Strokes*, and *Fame*; appeared in the film *Poetic Justice* (1993).

Jackson, Jermaine

full: Jermaine La Jaune Jackson
b. Dec. 11, 1954
Gary, Ind.
fields: Music (singer, producer, and bassist)

African American singer, producer, and bassist; one of Motown's Jackson 5 brothers, Jermaine Jackson went on to record solo albums and produce for other artists.

Jackson, Jesse

full: Jesse Louis Jackson
b. October 8, 1941
Greenville, South Carolina
fields: Civil Rights, Government and Politics

Jesse Jackson became one of the most influential, eloquent, and widely known African American political leaders in the United States during the decades after the death of Martin Luther King, Jr.

Jackson, Jesse Louis, Jr.

b. March 11, 1965
Greenville, S.C.
fields: Government and Politics, Civil Rights

Attorney and U.S. congressman Jesse Jackson, Jr., is the son of civil rights leader Jesse Louis Jackson. Jackson served as president of the Keep Hope Alive Political Action Committee, vice president of Operation PUSH, and national outreach director of the National Rainbow Coalition. The youngest appointed member of the Democratic Party's national committee, Jackson was elected to the House of Representatives from the Second District of Illinois in 1995.

Jackson, Joseph Harrison

b. Sept. 11, 1900
Rudyard, Miss.
d. Aug. 18, 1990
fields: Religion and Theology, Church Government

African American religious leader; a Progressive Baptist, Joseph Harrison Jackson was president of the National Baptist Convention from 1953 to 1982.

Jackson, Mahalia

b. October 26, 1911
New Orleans, Louisiana
d. January 27, 1972
Evergreen Park, Illinois (near Chicago)
fields: Music

One of the greatest American singers, Mahalia Jackson introduced black gospel music to an international audience and was a leading figure in the Civil Rights movement.

Jackson, May Howard

b. 1877
Philadelphia, Pa.
d. July 12, 1931
Long Beach, Long Island
fields: Art

Sculptor and educator May Howard Jackson is known for her portraits emphasizing characteristics that Jackson believe to be part of the subject's social conditions. Jackson's reputation rests on her busts of prominent African Americans as Paul Laurence Dunbar and W. E. B. Du Bois.

Jackson, Maynard Holbrook, Jr.

b. March 23, 1938
Dallas, Tex.
fields: Government and Politics

Maynard Holbrook Jackson, Jr., was elected the first African American mayor of Atlanta, Ga., in 1973. He was the first black mayor of any major southeastern city in the United States. He was also Atlanta's youngest mayor as well as the youngest mayor of any major American city. Jackson served two consecutive four-year terms as mayor, practiced law for eight years, and was reelected mayor in 1989 with 79 percent of the votes—significant because Atlanta was only 67 percent African American.

Jackson, Michael

full: Michael Joseph Jackson
b. Aug. 29, 1958
Gary, Ind.
fields: Music (pop singer, songwriter)

African American singer and songwriter; child singer Michael Jackson and the Jackson 5 had their first Motown hit in 1969 with "I Want You Back"; Michael released his first solo album, *Got to Be There* in 1972; the group moved to Epic Records and changed their name to The Jacksons; in 1978 released *Destiny* (1978), which had a hit single "Shake Your Body (Down to the Ground)," written by Michael and brother Randy; became a superstar solo artist with *Off the Wall* (1979) and *Thriller* (1982); appeared in music videos for "Billie Jean" and "Thriller"; cowrote "We Are the World" with Lionel Ritchie; released more hit albums including *Bad* (1987) and *Dangerous* (1991); married Lisa Marie Presley, daughter of the late Elvis Presley, in 1994, only to divorce twenty months later; released *HIStory: Past, Present and Future, Book I* in 1995; married (1996) and had two children (1997 and 1998) with Debbie Rowe.

Jackson, Millie

b. July 15, 1944
Thompson, Ga.
fields: Music (soul singer, songwriter)

African American soul singer and songwriter; Millie Jackson's crossover gospel/pop hit singles included "A Child of God" (1972), "Ask Me What You Want," and "It Hurts So Good," and "(If Loving You Is Wrong) I Don't Want to Be Right," which went gold.

Jackson, Milt

b. Jan. 1, 1923
Detroit, Mich.
fields: Music (jazz vibraphonist)

African American jazz vibraphonist; Milt Jackson established the Modern Jazz Quartet, perhaps the greatest popularizers of post-swing era jazz, in 1952.

Jackson, Nell

b. July 1, 1929
Athens, Ga.
d. Apr. 1, 1988
Vestal, N.Y.
fields: Sports (athlete and coach)

African American athlete and coach; in 1956, former Olympian Nell Jackson became the first black female head coach of the women's Olympic track and field team; was inducted into the Black Athletes Hall of Fame in 1977 and the National Track and Field Hall of Fame in 1989.

Jackson, O'Shea. *See* Ice Cube

Jackson, Reggie

b. May 18, 1946
Wyncote, Pa.
fields: Sports (baseball player)

African American baseball player; Reggie Jackson, nicknamed "Mr. October," started in the major leagues with the Kansas City Athletics (1967) and later played for the Oakland Athletics, the Baltimore Orioles, the New York Yankees, and the California Angels; played in five World Series; retired in 1987.

Jackson, Reginald L.

b. ?
fields: Photography, Anthropology (visual), Education

African American photographer, visual anthropologist, and educator; Reginald L. Jackson photographed communities of people of African descent, noting commonalities; was awarded fellowships from the Ford Foundation and from the National Endowment for the Arts.

Jackson, Robert H.
full: Robert Houghwout Jackson
b. 1892
d. 1954
fields: Law

U.S. Supreme Court justice, 1941-1954 (died while in office); appointed by President Franklin D. Roosevelt. Took a leave from the Court to serve as chief prosecutor in the Nuremberg war crimes trial of Nazi leaders. Publicly feuded with Justice Black over this and other matters. Significant opinion: *West Virginia State Board of Education v. Barnette*, 319 U.S. 624 (1943). Other writings: *The Struggle for Judicial Supremacy* (1941); *The Supreme Court in the American System of Government* (1955).

Jackson, Samuel Charles
b. May 8, 1929
Kansas City, Kans.
fields: Government and Politics

African American political appointee; Samuel Charles Jackson was appointed assistant secretary of the Department of Housing and Urban Development (1969-1973) by President Lyndon Johnson.

Jackson, Samuel L.
b. December 21, 1948
Atlanta, Ga.
fields: Film, Theater and Entertainment (actor)

African American actor; Samuel L. Jackson helped found the Atlanta-based Just Us Theatre Company; theater credits include Yale Repertory Theatre's premieres of *The Piano Lesson* (1987) and *Two Trains Running* (1990); film credits include *School Daze* (1988), *Do the Right Thing* (1989), *Mo' Better Blues* (1990), *Jungle Fever* (1991), *Jurassic Park* (1993), *National Lampoon's Loaded Weapon I* (1993), *Fresh* (1994), *Pulp Fiction* (1994), *Die Hard: With a Vengeance* (1995), *Jackie Brown* (1997), *Eve's Bayou* (1997), *Out of Sight* (1998), *The Negotiator* (1998), *Star Wars Episode One: The Phantom Menace* (1999), and *Deep Blue Sea* (1999).

Jackson, Sheila. *See* Jackson Lee, Sheila

Jackson, Shirley Ann
b. August 5, 1946
Washington, D.C.
fields: Science

Shirley Ann Jackson completed her doctoral studies of theoretical elementary particle physics in 1973; she was the first African American woman to receive a Ph.D. at MIT. In 1976, Jackson began work at AT&T Bell Laboratories researching topics based on theoretical material sciences, her specialty being solid or condensed state physics. President Bill Clinton appointed her to serve as chair of the Nuclear Regulatory Commission in 1995.

Jackson, Stonewall
né: Thomas Jonathan Jackson
b. January 21, 1824
Clarksburg, Virginia
d. May 10, 1863
Guiney's Station, Virginia
fields: Military Affairs

The ablest and most renowned of Lee's lieutenants, Jackson led daring marches and employed do-or-die battle tactics which resulted in key victories by which the Confederacy was sustained during the first two years of the Civil War.

Jackson Lee, Sheila
né: Sheila Jackson
b. January 12, 1950
Queens, N.Y.
fields: Government and Politics, Law

African American judge, attorney, and politician; in 1994, Sheila Jackson Lee was elected to the U.S. House of Representatives as a representative from Texas' Eighteenth Congressional District; in 1997, she became a member of the House Judiciary Committee; as a member of the Committee, she defended President Clinton in 1998 and voted against the articles of impeachment.

Jacob, François
b. June 17, 1920
Nancy, France
fields: Biology, Biochemistry, Genetics

Jacob shared the 1965 Nobel Prize in Physiology or Medicine with André Lwoff and Jacques Monod, for their collaborative discoveries concerning the genetic control of enzyme and virus synthesis. These studies were a landmark in the evolving area of molecular biology. They spanned virology, biochemistry, and microbiology.

Jacob, John Edward
b. December 16, 1934
Trout, La.
fields: Civil Rights

John Edward Jacob was an officer of the National Urban League from 1979 to 1994. In 1982, he succeeded Vernon Jordan as the organization's president, position he held until his departure in 1994.

Jacobi, Karl Gustav Jacob
b. Dec. 10, 1804
Potsdam, Prussia (now Germany)
d. Feb. 18, 1851
Berlin, Prussia
fields: Mathematics (algebra, applied math, calculus, and number theory)

In 1829 Karl Gustav Jacob Jacobi formulated the theory of elliptic functions, which proved important to number theory, complex variables, and applied mathematics; worked with partial differential equations; studied the functional determinant now called the Jacobian.

Jacobs, Lawrence-Hilton
b. Sept. 4, 1953
New York, N.Y.
fields: Television, Film (actor)

African American actor; from 1975 to 1979, Lawrence Hilton Jacobs played Freddie "Boom Boom" Washington in the television series *Welcome Back, Kotter*; film credits included *Serpico* (1973), *Death Wish* (1974), *Cooley High* (1975), *Youngblood* (1978), and *in the Name of the Father* (1993).

Jacobs, Marion Walter. *See* Little Walter

Jacopo della Quercia
b. c. 1374
probably Siena
d. October 20, 1438
Siena
fields: Art

Heir to the late Gothic sculptural style of fourteenth century Italy and influenced by the spatial massing of form found in ancient classical art, Jacopo forged an independent, monumental style of great expressive power. Along with Lorenzo Ghiberti, Donatello, and Nanni di Banco, he is considered one of the most significant sculptors working in the early decades of the Italian Renaissance.

Jadwiga
b. 1373 or 1374
place unknown
d. July 17, 1399
place unknown
fields: Government and Politics, Religion and Theology, Monarchy

Queen of Poland, 1386-1399. Crown Princess of Poland Jadwiga's marriage to Jagiełło, Grand Duke of Lithuania, brought about the unification of Lithuania and Poland and the conversion of the Lithuanian people from paganism to the Roman Catholic faith.

Jagan, Cheddi
full: Cheddi Berret Jagan
b. March 22, 1918
Plantation Port Mourant, British Guiana (now Guyana)
d. March 6, 1997
Washington, D.C.
fields: Government and Politics

Cheddi Jagan founded Guyana's People's Progressive Party (PPP) in 1950 with goals of independence and land reform. Leader of independence movement until independence in 1966. For the next generation, the People's National Congress (PNC) dominated Guyanese politicsm and Jagan led the opposition party. As president of Guyana (1992-1997), sought foreign investment and privatization of industries.

Jaggar, Alison M.

full: Alison Mary Jaggar
b. September 23, 1942
Sheffield, England
fields: Philosophy, Women's Rights

One of the founders of feminist philosophy, Jaggar is noted for bringing rigorous analysis to bear on the claims of various theories about women's subordination. She has been a pathfinder in making "womanspace" within the profession of philosophy itself, as a founding member of the Society for Women in Philosophy and as chair of the American Philosophical Association's Committee on the Status of Women. Among her major works are *Feminist Politics and Human Nature* (1983), *Living with Contradictions* (1994), and *Morality and Social Justice* (1995, with others).

Jagger, Mick

full: Michael Phillip Jagger
b. July 26, 1943
Dartford, Kent, England
fields: Music, Theater and Entertainment

Lead singer of the rock-and-roll group the Rolling Stones, Mick Jagger became one of the most popular and controversial celebrities of rock and roll. Calling themselves "the greatest rock-and-roll band in the world," the Rolling Stones remained as important for what they represented as for their music, more threatening to middle-class values than their contemporaries, the Beatles. Jagger, with his sexually ambiguous stage persona and often-explicit lyrics, was an integral part of the sexual revolution. He was arrested on drug charges in 1967, was involved in several high-profile romances, and in 1969 helped organize the Altamont Speedway rock festival, which proved a disaster when a young African American audience member was murdered during the event. He broke temporarily with the Rolling Stones in the mid-1980's, rejoining them to embark on several successful world tours in the late 1980's and 1990's. Ironically, given his radical image, he was one of the first to encourage corporate sponsorship of rock-and-roll albums and tours, thereby helping to transform rock music from the voice of the counterculture to a billion-dollar industry.

Jagiełło. *See* Władysław II Jagiełło

Jaḥiẓ, al-

full: Abū ʿUthman ʿAmr ibn Baḥr ibn Maḥbūb al-Jaḥiẓ
b. c. 776
Basra, Iraq
d. 868
Basra, Iraq
fields: Language and Linguistics, Literature, Science

As the first important Arabic prose writer, al-Jahiz employed his vast erudition and innovative stylistic technique to free the Arabic language from its theological and philological restraints, making it a tool for the long-term cultural cohesion of the diverse cultures of Islam.

Jaisohn, Philip

né: So Jae-pil
b. Oct. 28, 1866
South Cholla Province, Korea
d. Jan. 5, 1951
Philadelphia, Pa.?
fields: Government and Politics

So Jae-pil fled to the United States in 1884 after participating in a coup staged to reform Korea's political leadership and throw off Japanese control. He completed medical studies at Johns Hopkins Medical School in 1895, then returned to Korea, where he became an adviser to King Kojong, founded the Independence Association, and launched a newspaper called *Tongnip Sinmun* (*The Independent*). Because of these activities, the Korean government sought to arrest So, who fled to the United States in 1898. After becoming a U.S. citizen, he changed his name to Philip Jaisohn. He put together a three-day congress for Korean liberty in 1919, where delegates passed a ten-point resolution that included the demand that the League of Nations recognize Korea as independent from Japan. He became the publicist for the Bureau of Korean Information after the congress, and for three years after Korea was officially liberated from Japanese rule in 1945, Jaisohn advised U.S. occupation forces in Korea.

Jakobson, Roman

full: Roman Osipovich Jakobson
b. October 11, 1896
Moscow, Russia
d. July 18, 1982
Cambridge, Massachusetts
fields: Literature, Language and Linguistics

A prominent and founding member of the linguistic circles of Moscow and Prague, Jakobson was instrumental in the European development of structuralism in linguistics and in literary theory. Arriving in the United States in 1941, he brought extensive knowledge of European linguistics to the American scene, and, through his teaching at Columbia and Harvard universities and his prolific scholarship, he profoundly influenced Slavic studies, poetic analysis, and the development of American phonology.

Jalāl al-Dīn, Maulānā. *See* Rūmī, Jalāl al-Dīn

Jamal, Ahmad

né: Fritz Jones
b. July 2, 1930
Pittsburgh, Pa.
fields: Music (pianist)

African American pianist; known for his spare but fluid and elegant style, Ahmad Jamal and his trio recorded *Ahmad Jamal at the Pershing* (1958), *Ahmad Jamal at the Blackhawk* (1961), *At the Top—Poinciana Revisited* (1968), *Jamal Plays Jamal* (1974), and *Ahmad Jamal Live at Bubba's* (1981).

Jamāl al-Dīn al-Afghānī

full: Jamāl al-Dīn al-Afghānī as-Sayyid Muhammad Ibn-i Safdar al-Husain
b. 1838-1839
Asadābād, Iran
d. March 9, 1897
Istanbul, Ottoman Empire
fields: Philosophy, Government and Politics

Afghānī was the Pan-Islamist politician and teacher whose intense hatred of, and opposition to, British colonial policies focused the energies of Middle Eastern, Central Asian, and Indian Muslim intellectuals on the plight of the masses. His untiring quest for Muslim solidarity influenced Egypt's nationalist movement and Iran's constitutional and Islamic revolutions.

James I

né: James Stuart
aka: James VI of Scotland
b. June 19, 1566
Edinburgh Castle, Edinburgh, Scotland
d. March 27, 1625
Theobalds, Hertfordshire, England
fields: Government and Politics, Monarchy

King of Scotland 1568-1625; king of England, 1603-1625. Overcoming the tragedies which characterized his tumultuous formative years, James I provided continuity in English politics for a generation after the death of Elizabeth I in 1603.

James I the Conqueror

aka: James I, King of Aragon
b. February 2, 1208
Montpellier
d. July 27, 1276
Valencia, Spain
fields: Government and Politics, Warfare and Conquest, Literature, Law, Monarchy

King of Aragon, 1217-1276. James conquered three Islamic principalities in Spain and reorganized his many realms in Mediterranean Spain and Occitania (now southern France) into a great and prosperous state, rivaling Genoa for control of western Mediterranean naval power and trade. An autobiographer, he also founded a university and promulgated the first Romanized law code of general application in Europe.

James II

b. October 14, 1633
London, England
d. September 16, 1701
Saint-Germain, near Paris, France
fields: Government and Politics, Monarchy

King of England, 1685-1688. Although he was not a successful king (he was forced into exile in France in 1688), James II was a distinguished soldier and sailor and an efficient, industrious naval administrator.

James, Alice

b. August 7, 1848
New York, New York
d. March 6, 1892
London, England
fields: Literature

During the last three years of her life, Alice James, invalid sister of novelist Henry James and psychologist William James, kept a diary in which she recorded her impressions of British and American society and provided revealing and intimate portraits of her famous brothers.

James, Avon C., Jr.

b. ?
Hampton, Va.
fields: Military Affairs

African American military officer; Avon C. James, Jr. achieved the rank of brigadier general in the United States Air Force.

James, Chappie

full: Daniel James
b. Feb. 11, 1920
Pensacola, Fla.
d. Feb. 25, 1978
Colorado Springs, Colo.
fields: Military Affairs

African American military officer; Chappie James was the first African American to reach the rank of four-star general in the armed forces.

James, Elmore

b. Jan. 27, 1918
Richland, Miss.
d. May 24, 1963
Chicago, Ill.
fields: Music (blues singer)

African American blues singer; Elmore James, a dramatic and violent guitar player with a strong, rough voice, first recorded in the early 1950's; famous for his recording of "Dust My Broom" (1952).

James, Etta

né: Jamesetta Hawkins
b. Jan. 25, 1938
Los Angeles, Calif.
fields: Music (singer)

African American singer; in the early 1950's, Etta James recorded rhythm-and blues and rock-and-roll-style hits including "Roll with Me, Henry" (later retitled "The Wallflower"), "Good Rockin' Daddy," "I'm a Fool," and "Hey Henry"; inducted into Rock and Roll Hall of Fame in 1993; continued to record strong albums in the 1990's.

James, Henry

b. April 15, 1843
New York, New York
d. February 28, 1916
London, England
fields: Literature

James is one of the most preeminent and influential writers of the modern novel in America. Both his life and his work are closely related to the United States' emergence in the twentieth century as a major world power.

James, Rick

né: James Johnson
b. Feb. 1, 1952
Buffalo, N.Y.
fields: Music

African American singer, instrumentalist, producer, and writer; in the 1980's, Rick James became the "father of punk funk"; albums included *Come Get It* (1978); *Bustin' Out of L Seven* (1979) and *Fire It Up* (1979); *Garden of Love* (1980), and *Street Songs* (1981), with its hit single "Super Freak."

James, Sharpe

b. Feb. 20, 1936
Jacksonville, Fla.
fields: Government and Politics

African American mayor of Newark, N.J.; in 1986, Sharpe James defeated Newark's first African American mayor to become the first Newark city council member to be elected mayor.

James, Sylvester. *See* Sylvester

James, William

b. January 11, 1842
New York, New York
d. August 26, 1910
Chocorua, New Hampshire
fields: Psychiatry and Psychology, Religion and Theology, Philosophy

Seeking to reconcile a deep commitment to scientific thought with man's emotional nature and longing for some kind of religious faith, James helped create and popularize the modern science of psychology and the uniquely American approach to philosophy called pragmatism.

Jamison, Judith

b. May 10, 1943
Philadelphia, Pa.
fields: Dance

African American dancer; Judith Jamison danced with the Alvin Ailey Dance Theater from 1965 to 1980; best-known role was in the Ailey-choreographed dance *Cry*; appeared with the American Ballet Theatre among others, and toured internationally.

Janáček, Leoš

b. July 3, 1854
Hukvaldy, Moravia, Austrian Empire
d. August 12, 1928
Ostrava, Czechoslovakia
fields: Music

As the originator of a unique method of musical composition utilizing Moravian speech patterns and folk music, Leoš Janáček created the ideal medium for the musical expression of Czech folk culture and aspirations, and became one of the few composers to integrate folk art into formal European music.

Janet, Pierre

b. May 30, 1859
Paris, France
d. February 24, 1947
Paris, France
fields: Psychiatry and Psychology

Janet is best known for his work in bringing together clinical psychiatry and academic psychology. He integrated his systematic observations of neurotic disorders, in the description of which he coined the term "subconscious," with more general psychological concepts concerning behavior patterns and thought processes. He has had a considerable impact not only upon French psychiatry but also upon psychiatry as a whole through his influence on Carl Jung, Alfred Adler, and, to some extent, Sigmund Freud.

Jang, Jon

b. Mar. 11, 1954
Calif.
fields: Music

Chinese American pianist and composer Jon Jang fused diverse musical traditions, including Asian and African American, in his avant-garde jazz works that often contain a political message. Among Jang's works are *Tiananmen*, a piece for jazz orchestra which premiered on June 4, 1992, the third anniversary of the Tiananmen Square incident, and *Concerto for Jazz Ensemble and Taiko (Reparations Now!)*, which reflects on the internment of Japanese Americans during World War II and the eventual triumph of the redress movement. His albums include *Jang* (1982), *Are You Chinese or Charlie Chan?* (1983), *Jangle Bells* (1988), *Never Give Up!* (1989), and *Self Defense* (1992).

Janovskaja, Sof'ja Aleksandrovna

né: Sof'ja Aleksandrovna Neimark
b. Jan. 31, 1896
Pruzhany, Poland (now in Belarus)
d. Oct. 24, 1966
Moscow, Soviet Union
fields: Mathematics (mathematical logic)

Sof'ja Aleksandrovna Janovskaja formulated a materialist philosophy of mathematics, of which mathematical logic was an important component.

Jansen, Cornelius Otto

b. November 3, 1585
Accoi, Holland
d. May 6, 1638
Ypres, Spanish Netherlands
fields: Church Reform, Religion and Theology

Jansen created a new and challenging interpretation of the theology of Saint Augustine for the Catholic Reformation. Out of the controversy over his book *Augustinus* emerged Jansenism, a powerful church reform movement bearing his name.

Jao, Frank

b. June 15, 1949
Hai Phong, North Vietnam
fields: Business and Industry

Vietnamese American Frank Jao is the real estate developer behind Little Saigon in Westminister, California. A translator in the South Vietnamese army, he came to the United States in 1975. In 1978, he founded the Bridgecreek Group and has developed more than $250 million worth of commercial and residential properties, including his biggest development, Little Saigon's Asian Garden Mall.

Jaramillo, Cleofas Martinez

b. 1878
Arroyo Hondo, N.Mex.
d. 1956
fields: Scholarship, Literature

Latino folklorist and writer. After her husband died in 1920, Cleofas Martinez Jaramillo became a businesswoman. She wrote a cookbook, and she translated and published twenty-five of her mother's stories. Jaramillo then founded La Sociedad Folklórica, whose goal was to keep Hispanic folklore alive, and published her own books on folklore, including *Shadows of the Past* (1941). In 1955, Jaramillo published the autobiographical *Romance of a Little Village Girl*, which provided a seventy-year record of an upper-class Hispanic woman trying to preserve a vanishing culture.

Jaramillo, Mari-Luci

b. June 19, 1928
Las Vegas, N.Mex.
fields: Education, Diplomacy

Latina educator and diplomat. Mari-Luci Jaramillo, a Mexican American, earned her Ph.D. in 1970 at New Mexico Highlands University. She taught elementary school, concentrating on increasing the educational levels of Latino children, then became a professor in the Department of Elementary Education at the University of New Mexico. Jaramillo eventually became chair of that department. In 1977, President Jimmy Carter appointed her ambassador to Honduras, after which she returned to teaching.

Jaramillo, Pedro

b. c. 1850
near Guadalajara, Mexico
d. July 3, 1907
Paisano, Tex.
fields: Religion and Theology

Latino spiritualist and healer. Pedro Jaramillo, who claimed that God had given him the power to heal the sick, moved from Mexico to the Los Olmos Ranch in southeastern Texas in the 1880's. For thirty years he treated the poor Mexicans and Mexican Americans in the area free of charge. When he died, his grave near present-day Falfurrias, Texas, became a shrine visited by people whose parents or relatives he had helped.

Jarreau, Al

full: Alwyn Lopez Jarreau
b. Mar. 12, 1940
Milwaukee, Wisc.
fields: Music (singer)

African American singer; Al Jarreau first began recording for Warner Bros. Records in the late 1960's; albums included *We Got By* (1975), *Look at the Rainbow* (1978), *Breaking Away* (1981), with the smash single "We're in This Love Together," *Heaven and Earth* (1992), and *Tenderness* (1994); won the Grammy Award for best jazz vocalist (1978 and 1979); recorded the theme song to ABC television's successful *Moonlighting* series.

Jaspers, Karl

full: Karl Theodor Jaspers
b. February 23, 1883
Oldenburg, Germany
d. February 26, 1969
Basel, Switzerland
fields: Philosophy, Medicine

In his early career, Jaspers played an important role in establishing the foundations of clinical psychiatry, and in his mature years he was one of the major philosophers to lay the groundwork for the existential movement. After World War II, he attempted to develop a world philosophy which would promote human unity based on freedom and tolerance.

Jaurès, Jean

full: Auguste-Marie-Joseph-Jean Jaurès
b. September 3, 1859
Castres, France
d. July 31, 1914
Paris, France
fields: Government and Politics

Through the use of his powerful oratorical skills and his philosophical studies, Jaurès became the founding father of French socialism and a leading international advocate for peace prior to World War I.

Jaxon, Frankie

aka: Half-Pint Jaxon
b. Feb. 3, 1895
Montgomery, Ala.
fields: Music (singer, composer)

African American singer and composer; from 1914 to 1926, Frankie Jaxon sang at the Paradise Cafe in Atlantic City, N.J., and at the Sunset Cafe in Chicago, Ill.

Jay, John

b. December 12, 1745
New York, New York
d. May 17, 1829
Bedford, New York
fields: Law, Government and Politics

As president of the Second Continental Congress, ambassador to Spain, foreign secretary under the Articles of Confederation, first chief justice of the United States, and governor of New York, Jay contributed greatly to the political and judicial development of his state and his country.

Jaye, Miles

b. ?
fields: Music (pop vocalist)

African American pop vocalist; Miles Jaye recorded the hit song "Let's Start Love Over" (1987); released such albums as *Miles* (1987), *Irresistible* (1989), and *Strong* (1991).

Jeanneret, Charles-Édouard. *See* Le Corbusier

Jeans, James

full: Sir James Hopwood Jeans
b. Sept. 11, 1877
Ormskirk, Lancashire, England
d. Sept. 16, 1946
Dorking, Surrey, England
fields: Astronomy, Physics

In 1905 James Jeans corrected the derivation of Lord Rayleigh's law explaining the distribution of blackbody radiation; popularized science in Great Britain.

Jefferson, Blind Lemon

full: Lemon Jefferson
b. July 11, 1897
Couchman, Tex.
d. Dec. 1929, or Dec. 1930
Chicago, Ill.
fields: Music (blues singer and guitarist)

African American blues singer and guitarist. Blind Lemon Jefferson was one of the most influential early bluesmen. His vocality (high falsetto, with raspy, taut, nasalized sound) became the standard for many contemporary and future blues musicians, and his guitar playing techniques were also imitated widely.

Jefferson, Louise

b. ?
Washington, D.C.
fields: Photography

African American photographer; A photographer since the 1950's, Louise Jefferson worked as the art director for Friendship Press, the publishing agent of the National Council of Churches, for more than twenty years.

Jefferson, Thomas

b. April 13, 1743
Shadwell, Goochland (later County, Virginia
d. July 4, 1826
Monticello, Albemarle County, Virginia
fields: Government and Politics

Third president of the United States, 1801-1809. A genuine revolutionary, Thomas Jefferson was one of the early and effective leaders of the movement to overthrow British rule in North America; he then labored to create a free, prosperous, enlightened, and agrarian republic.

Jefferson, William J.

b. March 14, 1947
Lake Providence, La.
fields: Government and Politics, Law

African American attorney and politician; in 1990, William J. Jefferson was elected to the U.S. House of Representatives, representing Louisiana's Second Congressional District; began serving his third consecutive congressional term in 1994.

Jeffrey, Herbert. *See* Hancock, Herbie

Jeffrey, Lord

né: Francis Jeffrey
b. October 23, 1773
Edinburgh, Scotland
d. January 26, 1850
Edinburgh, Scotland
fields: Journalism, Law

As founder and editor of the *Edinburgh Review*, Jeffrey created a forceful instrument for critical analysis and the shaping of popular opinion.

Jeffries, Leonard, Jr.

b. January 19, 1937
Newark, New Jersey
fields: Education

Leonard Jeffries became a tenured professor and chairman of the black studies department at the City College of New York (CCNY) in 1972. A proponent of Afrocentrism, he argued a controversial theory that black people, because they have more melanin than whites, are intellectually superior. In July, 1991, he gave a speech in Albany, New York, that many considered antiwhite and, especially, anti-Semitic. The U.S. Supreme Court ruled City College of New York did not violate Jeffries' First Amendment rights when it removed him from chairmanship of his department.

Jemison, Mae C.

full: Mae Carol Jemison
b. Oct. 17, 1956
Decatur, Ala.
fields: Aviation and Space Exploration

African American first black female astronaut; Mae C. Jemison took her first space flight in September of 1992, when she served on the crew of the space shuttle *Endeavor*. After leaving the Astronaut Corps in 1993, she taught at Dartmouth and established Jemison Group, a technologies marketing company.

Jen, Gish

né: Lillian Jen
b. August 12, 1955
New York, N.Y.
fields: Literature

Chinese American writer Lillian Jen changed her name to Gish (for the actress Lillian Gish). Jen published stories in *The New Yorker, The Atlantic Monthly,* and the anthology *Best American Short Stories of 1988*. Her first novel, *Typical American* (1991), describes a Chinese American family's pursuit of the American Dream.

Jenifer, Franklyn Green

b. Mar. 26, 1939
Washington, D.C.
fields: Education

African American educator; in 1990, Franklyn Green Jenifer became the fourth African American and the first alumnus to head Howard University; was its fourteenth president.

Jenkins, Carol Ann

b. Nov. 30, 1944
Montgomery, Ala.
fields: Journalism, Television

African American broadcaster; Carol Ann Jenkins anchored WNBC-TV in New York City in 1990; received Lifetime Achievement Award from the New York Association of Black Journalists that same year.

Jenkins, Ferguson Arthur

b. Dec. 13, 1943
Chatham, Ontario, Canada
fields: Sports (baseball player)

African American baseball player; one of the all-time strikeout leaders in the majors, Ferguson Arthur Jenkins won the Cy Young Award in 1971; was elected to the Baseball Hall of Famein 1991.

Jenkins, Howard, Jr.

b. June 16, 1915
Denver, Colo.
fields: Government and Politics

African American political appointee; Howard Jenkins, Jr. was the first African American lawyer to be admitted to the Colorado State Bar; in 1963, was appointed a member of the National Labor Relations Board by President John F. Kennedy; was reappointed by Lyndon Johnson, Richard Nixon, and Jimmy Carter.

Jenkins, Martin David

b. Sept. 11, 1904
Terre Haute, Ind.
d. 1978
fields: Education

African American educational administrator; Martin David Jenkins served as Morgan State College's president from 1948 to 1970; was a director for the American Council on Education from 1970 to 1975.

Jenkinson, Robert Banks. *See* Liverpool, second earl of

Jenks, Amelia. *See* Bloomer, Amelia Jenks

Jenner, Edward

b. May 17, 1749
Berkeley, Gloucestershire, England

d. January 26, 1823
Berkeley, Gloucestershire, England
fields: Medicine

By discovering the vaccination as a preventive measure against smallpox, Jenner pioneered the concept of using a modified form of a disease to produce immunity.

Jensen, J. Hans D.

full: Johannes Hans Daniel Jensen
b. June 25, 1907
Hamburg, Germany
d. Feb. 11, 1973
Heidelberg, West Germany
fields: Physics

J. Hans D. Jensen, with others, developed the shell model of the atomic nucleus in 1948; explained the "magic numbers" of neutrons and protons associated with the stability of certain elements and their isotopes; in 1963, was awarded the Nobel Prize in Physics jointly with Eugene Wigner and Maria Goeppert Mayer.

Jensen, Joan M.

b. Dec. 9, 1934
St. Paul, Minn.
fields: Historiography

Joan M. Jensen, who received her Ph.D. from the University of California, Los Angeles, in 1962, wrote the first thorough documentation of the Asian Indian immigrant experience in the United States. *Passage from India: Asian Indian Immigrants in North America* (1988) is an account of the emigration of South Asian Indians to North America between 1870 and 1930.

Jeremiah

b. c. 645 B.C.E.
Anathoth, Judaea
d. After 587 B.C.E.
Egypt
fields: Religion and Theology

Though Jeremiah failed to win the people of Judaea to a repentance which might have averted the catastrophe which overwhelmed them, his prophecies remained to comfort later generations of the people of Judah and to stand as a symbol of renewal for all people.

Jerne, Niels K.

full: Niels Kaj Jerne
b. Dec. 23, 1911
London, England
d. Oct. 7, 1994
Pont du Gard, France
fields: Medicine

Niels K. Jerne is considered to be the founder of modern cellular immunology; in 1955, proposed the natural selection theory of antibody formation; in 1971, presented an explanation of immune system discrimination between "self" and "nonself"; in 1974, proposed his immune network theory; won the 1984 Nobel Prize in Physiology or Medicine, with Georges Köhler and César Milstein, for these three major theories explaining the workings of the immune system.

Jerome, Saint

né: Eusebius Hieronymus
b. Between 331 and 347
Stridon, Dalmatia (modern Yugoslavia)
d. Probably 420
Bethlehem, Palestine
fields: Scholarship, Monasticism, Religion and Theology

Because of his scholarship, commentaries on and translation of the Bible into Latin, and role as a propagandist for celibacy and the monastic life, Jerome is numbered with Saint Ambrose, Saint Augustine, and Gregory the Great as one of the Fathers of the Church.

Jesus Christ

b. c. 6 B.C.E.
Bethlehem, Judaea
d. 30 C.E.
Jerusalem
fields: Religion and Theology

As the basis for a religious faith that has attracted many millions of adherents, Jesus' life and teachings have exerted an enormous influence on Western civilization.

Jewett, Sarah Orne

full: Theodora Sarah Orne Jewett
b. September 3, 1849
South Berwick, Maine
d. June 24, 1909
South Berwick, Maine
fields: Literature

Author of twenty books, Jewett was the most accomplished of the American writers associated with literary regionalism and a major force in the creation and development of an American women's literary tradition.

Jhabvala, Ruth Prawer

né: Ruth Prawer
b. May 7, 1927
Cologne, Germany
fields: Literature, Film

Ruth Prawer Jhabvala has demonstrated remarkable staying power as a screenwriter in the film industry, not generally regarded for sustaining careers, particularly for women. At the same time, she continues to be a well-respected novelist and short-story writer.

Jiang Qing

aka: Chiang Ch'ing
b. 1914
Zhucheng, Shandong, China
d. May 14, 1991
Beijing, China
fields: Government and Politics

Chinese Communist political figure. Jiang Qing was the wife of Mao Zedong and a member of the Gang of Four. Powerful and feared political force in latter 1960's during Cultural Revolution; directed Red Guard. Became government censor of art, music, literature, and theater. Arrested after Mao's death in 1976 and tried for complicity in thousands of deaths in 1980. In prison until her death.

Jiang Zemin

aka: Chiang Tse-min
b. August 17, 1926
Yangzhou, Jiangsu Province, China
fields: Government and Politics

Took office as general secretary of Chinese Communist Party in 1989. As general secretary, Jiang Zemin was a moderate with a generally nonauthoritarian style. Initiated an anticrime drive in 1996. In July of 1997, officially reclaimed Hong Kong from Great Britain. In October 1997, became the first Chinese head of state to visit Washington, D.C., in twelve years.

Jiggetts, Charles B.

b. 1926
Henderson, N.C.
fields: Military Affairs

African American military officer; Charles B. Jiggetts was a brigadier general in the United States Air Force.

Jiménez, Flaco

full: Leonardo Jiménez
b. Mar. 11, 1939
San Antonio, Tex.
fields: Music (accordionist and songwriter)

Latino accordionist and songwriter. Flaco Jiménez released several singles in the San Antonio area before his song "Hasta La Vista" became a hit in the mid-1950's. Jiménez's appearance on Doug Sahm's *Doug Sahm and Band* (1973) led to more invitations to work with mainstream recording artists. He played on Ry Cooder's *Chicken Skin Music* (1976), *Showtime* (1977), *The Border* (1982), and *Get Rhythm* (1987). Jiménez's *Ay Te Dejo en San Antonio* (1986) won a Grammy Award. In 1989 he joined Doug Sahm and others to create the Texas Tornados, whose first album, *Texas Tornados* (1990), won a Grammy Award for Best Mexican-American Performance.

Jiménez, Luis Alfonso, Jr.

b. July 30, 1940
El Paso, Tex.

fields: Art

Latino artist. Luis Alfonso Jiménez, Jr., earned a bachelor's degree in fine arts at the University of Texas at Austin in 1964. In the same year, he studied at the Universidad Nacional Autónoma de México on a scholarship. In 1966, he moved to New York City and began showing his fiberglass and epoxy sculptures in one-man and group exhibitions. Jiménez lived in several cities in the 1970's before settling in Hondo, New Mexico. He has also experimented with lithography.

Jiménez de Cisneros, Francisco

né: Gonzalo Jiménez de Cisneros
b. 1436
Torrelaguna, Province of Madrid, Spain
d. November 8, 1517
Roa, Spain
fields: Government and Politics, Religion and Theology, Education

Regent of Spain, 1506-1507, 1516-1517. Jiménez worked to maintain a united Spain at the beginning of the sixteenth century. He founded the University of Alcalá de Henares and sponsored the famous Polyglot Bible.

Jimmy Jam. *See* Harris, James, III

Jinnah, Mohammed Ali

b. December 25, 1876
Karachi, India (now Pakistan)
d. September 11, 1948
Karachi, Pakistan
fields: Government and Politics

Indian Muslim activist and first governor-general of Pakistan (1947-1948). In 1936 Mohammed Ali Jinnah assumed the presidency of the All-India Muslim League. In 1940 the league demanded separate states for India's Muslims. Between 1940 and 1947, Jinnah led a determined campaign to create a new Muslim state, Pakistan. Considered the creator of Pakistan, which was established August 14, 1947.

Joachim of Fiore

b. c. 1135
Celico, Italy
d. 1202
Fiore, Italy
fields: Religion and Theology, Historiography

Joachim developed a persuasive system of historical understanding which evolved through three successive stages culminating in an age of the Holy Spirit filled with bliss and understanding.

Joan of Arc

b. c. 1412
Domremy, France
d. May 30, 1431
Rouen, France
fields: Government and Politics, Religion and Theology

Joan's victories initiated the withdrawal of English troops from France to end the Hundred Years' War, and she made possible the coronation of Charles VII at Reims. As a martyr to her vision and mission, she had as much influence after her death as in her lifetime.

Jobim, Antonio Carlos

b. Jan. 25, 1927
Rio de Janeiro, Brazil
d. Dec. 8, 1994
New York, N.Y.
fields: Music (composer, pianist, guitarist, and singer)

Latino composer, pianist, guitarist, and singer. Antonio Carlos Jobim learned to play the piano as a child. He earned an international repution with the score to the 1959 film *Orfeo Negro* (*Black Orpheus*). During the 1960's he wrote numerous popular songs, such as "A felicidade," "Desafinado," "Agua de beber" ("Drinking Water"), "Garota de Ipanema" ("The Girl from Ipanema"), and "Por causa de você" ("Don't Ever Go Away"). He also wrote the soundtrack for the film *Copacabana Palace* (1963). After the 1960's, he continued to compose music was inducted into the Songwriters Hall of Fame in 1991.

Jobs, Steve

b. Feb. 24, 1955
California
fields: Computer Science, Business and Economics

Corporate computer executive and creator of the Apple computer. In the mid-1970's, Steve Jobs joined with Hewlett-Packard computer engineer Stephen Wozniak in developing the Apple I computer. He served as chairman of Apple Computer Corporation until 1985, when he left to form NeXT corporation.

Jōchō

aka: Kōshō
b. Date unknown
probably Kyoto, Japan
d. 1057
probably Kyoto, Japan
fields: Art

Jōchō established an indigenous Japanese style of wood sculpture using a joined-wood technique.

Jodelle, Étienne

b. 1532
d. 1573
fields: Literature

A member of la Pléiade (fl. 1549-1589), a group of loosely organized poets dedicated to raising the level of sophistication of the French language by adding words and genres derived from classical literature. Led by Pierre de Ronsard and Joachim du Bellay, they developed a new form of poetry based on forms such as the sonnet, the ode, epic, and elegy. They also worked to elevate the level of the poet to a position as an intermediary between humanity and the heavens.

Joe, Kenneth

b. Aug. 14, 1923
China
fields: Banking and Finance

Chinese American banker Kenneth Joe served as editor of several major Chinese newspapers in Hong Kong and the United States and as dean of the Central Chinese School in San Francisco for twelve years. Former vice president and director of Sincere Federal Savings Bank in San Francisco, California, he was regarded as a "walking encyclopedia" of Chinese art and culture in the San Francisco Chinese American community.

Joffre, Joseph-Jacques-Césaire

b. January 12, 1852
Rivesaltes, France
d. January 3, 1931
Paris, France
fields: Military Affairs

Joffre was the chief of staff of the French armies facing the armies of the German Empire in August, 1914. His armies halted the German tide at the First Battle of the Marne, and his actions between August 25 and September 5, 1914, enabled other commanders to blunt, disrupt, and eventually turn back the invading Germans.

Johanan ben Zakkai

b. c. 1 C.E.
Judaea
d. c. 80 C.E.
Beror Heil, west of Jerusalem, Judaea
fields: Religion and Theology

After the destruction of Jerusalem by the Romans in 70 C.E., when the temple cult—the center of Jewish life—lay in ruins, Johanan was responsible for reorienting Jewish life around faithful observance of the Law (Torah).

Johannsen, Wilhelm Ludvig

b. Feb. 3, 1857
Copenhagen, Denmark
d. Nov. 11, 1927
Copenhagen, Denmark
fields: Biology, Botany, Genetics, Physiology

Wilhelm Ludvig Johannsen helped establish the field of genetics; invented the terms "gene," "genotype" and "phenotype" in 1909.

John III Sobieski
né: John Sobieski
b. August 17, 1629
Olesko, Poland
d. June 17, 1696
Castle Wilanów, near Warsaw, Poland
fields: Military Affairs, Monarchy, Government and Politics

King of Poland, 1674-1696. In lifting the Turkish siege of Vienna, Sobieski halted the Ottoman conquest of Europe, preserving Western culture and Christendom. The status of women, in particular, differs so profoundly in Christian societies from that in Islamic societies that the debt of Western women to Sobieski's generalship can hardly be overstated.

John XXIII
né: Angelo Giuseppe Roncalli
b. November 25, 1881
Sotto il Monte, Italy
d. June 3, 1963
Vatican City, Italy
fields: Church Government, Church Reform

Pope John XXIII, 1958-1963. John called the Second Vatican Council, which would modernize the Catholic church, and guided the early planning of the council, which helped ensure its achievements.

John, Augustus
b. January 4, 1878
Tenby, Wales
d. October 31, 1961
Fordingbridge, Hampshire, England
fields: Art

A talented portrait painter, an accomplished etcher, and a notorious bohemian, John became one of the best-known British artists in the twentieth century.

John, Captain. *See* Konkapot, John

John, King
b. December 24, 1166
Oxford, Oxfordshire, England
d. October 18, 1216
Norwich, Norfolk, England
fields: Government and Politics, Monarchy

King of England, 1199-1216. King John's poor statesmanship was primarily responsible for the downfall of the Angevin Empire and the decreased power of the English monarch, as reflected in the Magna Carta.

John Fire. *See* Lame Deer

John Logan. *See* Logan, James

John of Damascus
aka: John Damascene
b. c. 675
Damascus, Syria
d. December 4, 749
near Jerusalem
fields: Religion and Theology, Literature

During the Iconoclastic Controversy of the eighth century, John wrote a series of theological tracts defending the use of images in Christian worship, thus establishing the theological position of Eastern Orthodoxy.

John of the Cross, Saint
né: Juan de Yepes y Álvarez
b. June 24, 1542
Fontiveros, Spain
d. December 14, 1591
Úbeda, Spain
fields: Church Reform, Religion and Theology

Saint John of the Cross contributed to the renewal of monastic life and to the development of mystical theology during the golden age of the Catholic Reformation. His most lasting contribution has been to Western mysticism.

John Paul II
né: Karol Jozef Wojtyła
b. May 18, 1920
Wadowice, Poland
fields: Church Government

Pope John Paul II (elected in 1978) is the 264th pope of the Roman Catholic church and the first non-Italian pope since 1522. The first Slav to be named pope, the first pope from a communist country, and the youngest pope in modern times, John Paul II has a history of political involvement that predates even his religious vocation, having fought attempts first by Nazi Germany and later by the Soviet Union to weaken the power of the Church in Poland. During his reign as pope, he has sought to bring the Church back to some of the traditional values that he believed were lost after the Second Vatican Council.

John the Apostle
b. c. 10 C.E.
probably Capernaum
d. c. 100 C.E.
Ephesus
fields: Religion and Theology

John the Apostle was one of Jesus' most trusted disciples during his lifetime; after his death, John was a leader in the early Church and by his writings made important contributions to Christian theology.

John the Baptist
b. c. 7 B.C.E.
near Jerusalem, Israel
d. c. 27 C.E.
Jerusalem, Israel
fields: Religion and Theology

According to the biblical narrative, John was the cousin of Jesus and played a central role in introducing Jesus' ministry to the people of Palestine; as an austere, prophetic figure in the history of Judaism and Christianity, John was a stern moralist who addressed a generation of outwardly religious but inwardly corrupted people.

Johnny, Shoe Shine. *See* Shines, Johnny

Johnson, Albert
b. March 5, 1869
Springfield, Ill.
d. January 17, 1957
American Lake, Wash.
fields: Journalism, Government and Politics

Albert Johnson was a successful journalist who owned a number of newspapers. In 1912 he won a seat in the U.S. House of Representatives for the state of Washington. He served from 1913 until 1933. In 1919 Johnson became chairman of the House Committee on Immigration and Naturalization, where he spearheaded the congressional effort to establish more severe limits on immigration. In 1924 Johnson introduced the Immigration Act of 1924 (National Origins Act).

Johnson, Andrew
b. December 29, 1808
Raleigh, North Carolina
d. July 31, 1875
near Carter Station, Tennessee
fields: Government and Politics

Johnson was a Tennessee politician, a Civil War military governor of Tennessee, a vice president of the United States, and the seventeenth president of the United States, from 1865 to 1869. His lenient Reconstruction policies toward the South embittered members of Congress and postponed unification of the embattled republic.

Johnson, Anna. *See* Wheeler, Anna Johnson Pell

Johnson, Anne-Marie
b. July 18, 1960
Los Angeles, Calif.
fields: Television (actor)

African American actress; Anne-Marie Johnson appeared televison shows such as *What's Happening Now!!*, *In the Heat of the Night*, and *In Living Color*; appeared in such films as *Hollywood Shuffle* (1987) and *Down in the Delta* (1998).

Johnson, Ben

full: Benjamin Sinclair Johnson, Jr.
b. December 30, 1961
Falmouth, Jamaica
fields: Sports (track)

Ben Johnson emigrated to Canada from Jamaica in 1976. At the 1987 World Track and Field Championships held at Rome, Italy, he edged out U.S. sprinter Carl Lewis to set a world record for the 100-meter event with a time of 9.83 seconds. Johnson was the first Canadian gold medalist at a world championship track meet in fifty-five years. Johnson won the 100-meter event at the 1988 Summer Olympics in Seoul, Korea, with a time of 9.79 seconds. Johnson tested positive for banned substances and was disqualified. His world records in the 100-meter event and indoor 60-meter event were declared invalid. He was banned from the sport after testing positive again for steroid use in 1993.

Johnson, Beverly

b. Oct. 13, 1951
Buffalo, N.Y.
fields: Fashion (model)

African American model; in 1974, supermodel Beverly Johnson became the first African American fashion model to appear on the cover of *Vogue* magazine; named Outstanding U.S. Model in 1975; continued her career into the 1990's.

Johnson, Budd

full: Albert J. Johnson
b. Dec. 14, 1910
Dallas, Tex.
d. Oct. 20, 1984
Kansas City, Mo.
fields: Music (tenor saxophonist, composer, arranger)

African American tenor saxophonist, composer, and arranger; Budd Johnson worked with Earl Hines's band from 1935 to 1942; in the 1940's arranged for Billy Eckstine, Woody Herman, Buddy Rich, and others; his style combined the swing sound with a bebop flavor.

Johnson, Bunk

full: William Geary Johnson
b. Dec. 27, 1879
New Orleans, La.
d. July 7, 1949
New Iberia, La.
fields: Music (cornetist, trumpeter)

African American cornetist and trumpeter; one of the most colorful and controversial figures of the jazz world, Bunk Johnson played in the style of his legendary mentor, Buddy Bolden; was rediscovered and became a focal point of the New Orleans jazz revival of the 1940's.

Johnson, Carol Diahann. *See* Carroll, Diahann

Johnson, Caryn. *See* Goldberg, Whoopi

Johnson, Charles Richard

b. Apr. 23, 1948
Evanston, Ill.
fields: Literature, Art

African American writer and artist; Charles Richard Johnson published two books of drawings, *Black Humor* (1970) and *Half-Past Nation Time* (1972); his written works include *Faith and the Good Thing* (1974), *Oxherding Tale* (1982), and *Middle Passage* (1990), which won a National Book Award.

Johnson, Charles Spurgeon

b. July 24, 1893
Bristol, Va.
d. October 27, 1956
Louisville, Ky.
fields: Education, Social Sciences

Charled Spurgeon Johnson authored the classic study, *The Negro in Chicago: A Study of Race Relations and a Race Riot* (1922), as well as *The Negro in American Civilization* (1930), *Race Relations* (with W. D. Weatherford, 1934), *The Collapse of Cotton Tenancy* (with Will Alexander and Edwin Embree, 1935), and *Growing Up in the Black Belt* (1941). In 1928, Johnson became chair of the social science department at Fisk University. In 1946, he became the first African American president of Fisk.

Johnson, Daniel LaRue

b. 1938
Los Angeles, Calif.
fields: Art (sculptor, painter)

African American sculptor and painter; Daniel LaRue Johnson's early work identified with the Civil Rights movement; his later minimal sculptures contained overtones of the rhythms of American jazz and African music.

Johnson, Eddie Bernice

b. December 3, 1935
Waco, Tex.
fields: Government and Politics

African American nurse and politician; elected in 1972 to the Texas House of Representatives, Bernice Johnson became the first African American woman chosen by the citizens of Dallas to hold public office; in 1986 won election to the Texas State Senate; became one of fifteen African American members of 1993 freshmen legislators in Congress.

Johnson, Emily Pauline

aka: Tekahionwake
b. Mar. 10, 1861
Six Nations Reserve, near Brantford, Ontario, Canada
d. Mar. 7, 1913
Vancouver, B.C., Canada
fields: Literature (poet, writer)

Canadian poet. A Mohawk and one of Canada's leading poets of the late nineteenth century, Emily Pauline Johnson celebrated her Mohawk heritage at a time when it was not fashionable. Wrote about the Canadian landscape from a native perspective. Books include *The White Wampum* (1895) *Canadian Born* (1903) as well as the prose works *Legends of Vancouver* (1911), *The Moccasin Maker* (1913), and *The Shagganappi* (1913). Her most famous poem, "The Song My Paddle Sings," has been learned by generations of Canadian schoolchildren.

Johnson, Eric Demetric. *See* Dickerson, Eric

Johnson, Fenton

b. May 7, 1888
Chicago, Ill.
d. Sept. 17, 1958
Chicago, Ill.
fields: Literature (poet)

African American poet; Fenton Johnson's poetry focuses on racial injustices and, at the same time, depicts the positive aspects of African American life.

Johnson, George Ellis

b. June 16, 1927
Richton, Miss.
fields: Business and Industry

African American business executive; in 1954, George Ellis Johnson founded Johnson Products Company (hair care and cosmetics); in 1972 endowed the George E. Johnson Educational Fund to award business education scholarships to low-income students.

Johnson, Georgia

b. Sept. 10, 1886
Atlanta, Ga.
d. May 14, 1966
Washington, D.C.
fields: Literature

African American poet, dramatist, and composer; Georgia Johnson was best known for her four volumes of poems and numerous poems appearing in periodicals.

Johnson, Gus, Jr.

b. Dec. 13, 1938
Akron, Ohio
d. Apr. 28, 1987
Akron, Ohio
fields: Sports (basketball player)

African American basketball player; Gus Johnson, Jr. was a National Basketball League All-Star in 1968, 1969, 1970, and 1971; played on the NBA All-Defensive Team First Team in 1970 and 1971

Johnson, Guy Benton
b. Feb. 28, 1901
Caddo Mills, Tex.
d. May 23, 1991
Chapel Hill, N.C.
fields: Historiography

African American historian; Guy Benton Johnson's *Folk Culture on St. Helena Island, South Carolina* (1930) studied the source of Negro spirituals.

Johnson, Hazel Winifred
b. ?
West Chester, Pa.
fields: Military Affairs

African American first female African American general in the United States armed forces. Hazel Winifred Johnson retired from military service in 1983. Her military commendations included the Legion of Merit, Army Commendation Medal, and Meritorious Service Medal.

Johnson, Henry
b. 1897
Winston-Salem, N.C.
d. July 2, 1929
Washington, D.C.
fields: Warfare and Conquest, Military Affairs

African American military hero; Henry Johnson was a member of the first black regiment to fight in World War I. Although wounded, he took on a German patrol unit single-handedly and rescued a captured member of his company. He was the first American to win France's Croix de Guerre in World War I; a separate Croix de Guerre was also awarded to his 369th Infantry Division.

Johnson, J. J.
full: James Louis Johnson
b. Jan. 22, 1924
Indianapolis, Ind.
fields: Music (trombonist, composer, arranger)

African American trombonist, composer, and arranger; after playing with the Benny Carter band and the Count Basie Orchestra, J. J. Johnson recorded as a bandleader, producing *Mad Bebop* (1946), *Boneology* (1947), and *Blue Mode* (1949); he is credited with perfecting modern jazz trombone style.

Johnson, J. Rosamond
full: John Rosamond Johnson
b. Aug. 11, 1873
Jacksonville, Fla.
d. Nov. 11, 1954
New York, N.Y.
fields: Music (composer, performer)

African American composer and performer; J. Rosamond Johnson collaborated with his brother, writer James Weldon Johnson, on musical works such as the opera *Toloso* and the song "Lift Every Voice and Sing" (1901); he performed in *Porgy and Bess* (between 1935 and 1942) and in *Blackbirds* (1939), *Mamba's Daughters* (1939), and *Cabin in the Sky* (1940); collaborated with his brother in *The Book of American Negro Spirituals* (1925) and *The Second Book of Negro Spirituals* (1926), and published two collections, *Shout Songs* (1936) and *Rolling Along in Song* (1937).

Johnson, Jack
full: John Arthur Johnson
b. March 31, 1878
Galveston, Texas
d. June 10, 1946
Raleigh, North Carolina
fields: Sports (boxing)

Jack Johnson was a boxer; first black heavyweight champion, 1908-1915; became the center of racial controversy as the public called for Jim Jeffries, the white former champion, to come out of retirement; Johnson defeated Jeffries in 1910.

Johnson, James. *See* James, Rick

Johnson, James Arthur. *See* St. Jacques, Raymond

Johnson, James P.
full: James Price Johnson
b. Feb. 1, 1894
New Brunswick, N.J.
d. Nov. 17, 1955
New York, N.Y.
fields: Music (composer, piano player)

African American composer and piano player; James P. Johnson, one of the leading exponents of New York stride piano, was a major influence on jazz pianists such as Duke Ellington and Art Tatum; compositions included "The Harlem Strut" (1921), "Carolina Shout" (1921), "The Charleston" (1923), *Jingles* (1930), and *You've Got to be Modernistic* (1930).

Johnson, James Weldon
né: James William Johnson
b. June 17, 1871
Jacksonville, Fla.
d. June 26, 1938
Wiscasset, Maine
fields: Civil Rights, Literature, Government and Politics

African American poet, diplomat, civil rights leader; as a young man James Weldon Johnson was known principally as lyricist for popular songs, including "Lift Every Voice and Sing" (1899); served as U.S. consul in Puerto Cabello, Venezuela, 1906-1909, and Corinto, Nicaragua, 1909-1912; contributing editor to the New York Age (1914-1923), an influential black weekly; executive secretary of the National Association for the Advancement of Colored People, 1920-1930; wrote many books, including *The Autobiography of an Ex-Colored Man* (1912), *The Book of American Negro Poetry* (1922), *God's Trombones* (1927), and *Negro Americans, What Now* (1934).

Johnson, Jesse
b. 1961
Rock Island, Ill.
fields: Music (singer, musician)

African American singer and musician; Prince protégé Jesse Johnson appeared in the film *Purple Rain* (1984) and cowrote the hit "Jungle Love"; 1985 hit singles included "I Want To Be Your Man" and "Can You Help Me"; 1989 album *Jesse Johnson's Revue* featured "I Want My Girl."

Johnson, John H.
full: John Harold Johnson
b. Jan. 19, 1918
Arkansas City, Ark.
fields: Publishing, Business and Industry

African American businessman and publisher; John H. Johnson addressed the need for mainstream black publications with the establishment of the *Negro Digest* (1942-1951), *Ebony* (1945), and *Jet* (1951); launched Fashion Fair Cosmetics; elected to the board of Twentieth Century Fox; elected chairman and Chief executive officer of Supreme Life Insurance Company; member of advisory council of Harvard Graduate School of Business; director for the Chamber of Commerce of the United States; published autobiography, *Succeeding Against the Odds* (1989).

Johnson, Judy
full: William Julius Johnson
b. Oct. 20, 1900
Snow Hill, Md.
d. June 15, 1989
Wilmington, Del.
fields: Sports (baseball player)

African American baseball player. Judy Johnson led the Philadelphia Hilldales, one of the top Negro League teams of the time, to Eastern Colored League pennants in 1923, 1924, and 1925, and to victory in the 1925 Negro League World Series. An outstanding defensive third baseman and a powerful hitter, he retired from baseball in 1973 and was inducted into the National Baseball Hall of Fame in 1975.

Johnson, Katherine G.

full: Katherine Coleman Goble Johnson
b. 1918
West Virginia
fields: Physics, Aviation and Space Exploration

African American physicist and space scientist; Katherine G. Johnson worked with the National Aeronautics and Space Administration teams that tracked manned and unmanned orbital missions; pioneered new navigation techniques to determine more practical ways of tracking missions; retired in 1992.

Johnson, Larry Demetric

b. March 14, 1969
Tyler, Tex.
fields: Sports (basketball player)

African American professional basketball player; playing for the University of Nevada at Las Vegas (UNLV), Larry Demetric Johnson was selected as an NCAA first-team All-American in 1990; in 1991 received the Naismith and the Wooden Atwards; played for the Charlotte Hornets starting in 1991; in 1992 was named NBA Rookie of the Year and was chosen for the 1992 NBA All-Rookie first team. In 1996, he was traded to the New York Knicks.

Johnson, Lonnie

full: Alonzo Johnson
b. Feb. 8, 1889
New Orleans, La.
d. June 18, 1970
Toronto, Canada
fields: Music (blues musician)

African American blues musician; in 1926, Lonnie Johnson's first record was issued, "Mr. Johnson's Blues" and "Falling Rain Blues"; in 1939, his Bluebird (RCA Victor) recording, "I'm a Jelly Roll Baker," was a rhythm-and-blues hit; released "Tomorrow Night" in 1947; is credited with popularizing the single-line countermelody to the vocal among performers such as Big Bill Broonzy and B.B. King.

Johnson, Louis

b. Mar. 19, 1933
Stateville, N.C.
fields: Dance

African American choreographer and director; Louis Johnson choreographed performances for the Cincinnati Ballet, the Alvin Ailey Dance Company, the Dance Theater of Harlem, and the Metropolitan Opera Theater Ballet, and such films as *Damn Yankees* (1958) and *The Wiz* (1978); founded and directed the Louis Johnson Dance Theater.

Johnson, Lyndon B.

full: Lyndon Baines Johnson
b. August 27, 1908
near Stonewall, Gillespie County, Texas
d. January 22, 1973
en route to San Antonio, Texas
fields: Government and Politics

An astute, skilled, and compassionate professional politician, Johnson advanced the cause of civil rights and expanded the government's role in social welfare through his Great Society programs. Thirty-sixth president of the United States, 1963-1969.

Johnson, Magic

full: Earvin "Magic" Johnson, Jr.
b. August 14, 1959
Lansing, Mich.
fields: Sports (basketball)

Magic Johnson led Michigan State University to a National Collegiate Athletic Association (NCAA) basketball championship in 1979 and the Los Angeles Lakers to five titles in the National Basketball Association (NBA) in the 1980's. In 1991 he announced that he had been infected with the human immunodeficiency virus (HIV), and he retired from league basketball. He did, however, compete on the 1992 U.S. Olympic "Dream Team" and participated in the 1992 NBA All-Star Game, again capturing most valuable player honors. He returned to the NBA in the 1995-1996 season, helping the Lakers to secure a playoff spot. His continuing visibility at the highest levels of professional sports raised awareness and promoted understanding of AIDS.

Johnson, Malvin Gray

b. Jan. 28, 1896
Greensboro, N.C.
d. Oct. 4, 1934
fields: Art (painter)

African American painter; a commercial artist, Malvin Gray Johnson was one of the first African American artists to experiment with cubism; won the Otto H. Kahn Prize in 1928.

Johnson, Marguerite Annie. *See* Angelou, Maya

Johnson, Michael

b. Sept. 13, 1967
Dallas, Tex.
fields: Sports (track sprinter)

African American track sprinter; Michael Johnson ranked first in the world in both the 200- and 400-meter runs for 1990 and 1991, the first person ever to earn those rankings two years in a row. His is an unorthodox running style, coming out of his mark to stand up straight, with short, choppy strides. He established new world records in the 200-meter event twice in 1994-1995, and won forty-one consecutive 400-meter events between 1990 and 1995. In the 1996 Olympics he won gold medals in both the 200-meter and 400-meter events. At the 1999 World Championship, at the age of thirty-one, he broke the world's record in the 400, with a time of 43.18; he broke the longest standing record for a running event.

Johnson, Rafer

full: Rafer Lewis Johnson
b. Aug. 18, 1935
Hillsboro, Tex.
fields: Sports (decathlon champion)

African American decathlon champion; in 1955, Rafer Johnson won the decathlon in the Pan-American Games and set a world record of 7,758 points later that year; he took the silver medal in the 1956 Olympics and the gold in the 1960 Olympics, setting an Olympic record of 8,392 points. He is named to several halls of fame, garnered numerous awards, served on boards of directors, and lit the torch at the 1984 Olympics.

Johnson, Robert

b. May 8, 1911
Hazlehurst, Miss.
d. Aug. 16, 1938
Greenwood, Miss.
fields: Music (blues singer and guitarist)

African American blues singer and guitarist; Robert Johnson made his best-known recordings for the Vocalion/American Record Company label from 1936 to 1937, including "Come On in My Kitchen," "Dust My Broom," "I'm a Steady Rollin' Man," "Kind Hearted Woman," "Terraplane Blues," "Crossroads Blues," "Me and the Devil Blues," and "Hellhound on My Trail."

Johnson, Samuel

b. September 18, 1709
Lichfield, Staffordshire, England
d. December 13, 1784
London, England
fields: Literature, Language and Linguistics, Journalism

Johnson not only wrote some of the finest poetry, fiction, and essays of his time but also edited the works of William Shakespeare and compiled the first dictionary of the English language.

Johnson, Thomas

b. 1732
d. 1819
fields: Law

U.S. Supreme Court justice, 1791-1793; appointed by President Washington. Wrote only one opinion.

Johnson, Virginia Alma Fairfax

b. Jan. 25, 1950
Washington, D.C.
fields: Dance (ballet)

African American ballet dancer; beginning in 1969, Virginia Alma Fairfax Johnson was principal dancer for the Dance Theater of Harlem for more than twenty years.

Johnson, Virginia E.

b. February 11, 1925
Springfield, Mo.
fields: Medicine, Sociology, Psychiatry and Psychology

Virginia E. Johnson and her husband, William H. Masters, used scientific equipment to record physiological responses to sexual stimulations in men and women engaging in sexual activity. In 1966 the results of their eleven-year research project were published in the best-selling *Human Sexual Response*. Their other books include *Homosexuality in Perspective* (1979), *Crisis: Heterosexual Behavior in the Age of AIDS* (1988), *The Pleasure Bond: A New Look at Sexuality and Commitment* (1975), and *Textbook of Sexual Medicine* (1979).

Johnson, William

b. 1771
d. 1834
fields: Law

U.S. Supreme Court justice, 1804-1834 (died while in office); appointed by President Jefferson. Only member of the Court during this period who directly challenged Chief Justice Marshall's views on the Constitution. Significant opinions: *Gibbons v. Ogden*, 22 U.S. 1 (1824) (concurring opinion); *United States v. Hudson and Goodwin*, 11 U.S. 32 (1832).

Johnson, William Henry

b. 1901
Florence, S.C.
d. Apr. 13, 1970
Long Island, N.Y.
fields: Art (painter)

African American painter; pioneer black modernist William Henry Johnson worked in a variety of styles and even painted murals for the Works Progress Administration.

Johnston, Frances Benjamin

b. January 15, 1864
Grafton, West Virginia
d. May 16, 1952
New Orleans, Louisiana
fields: Photography

A leading portrait photographer, recorder of American life, and chronicler of pre-Civil War southern architecture, Johnston pioneered in a field where women had a chance to establish their own careers. Her pictures provide a valuable record of American life at the beginning of the twentieth century.

Joiner, Charlie

full: Charles Joiner, Jr.
b. Oct. 14, 1947
Many, La.
fields: Sports (football player)

African American football player; after joining the San Diego Chargers in 1976, Charlie Joiner played in the 1976, 1979, and 1980 Pro Bowls; was named NFL Man of the Year in 1983; retired in 1986.

Joliot, Frédéric

b. March 19, 1900
Paris, France
d. August 14, 1958
Paris, France
fields: Chemistry

The Frederic and Irène Joliot-Curie continued the work which Irène's parents, Pierre and Marie Curie, had begun on radioactivity. Frédéric and Irène received the Nobel Prize in Chemistry in 1935 for having discovered the possibility of artificial radioactivity. The resulting new radiosotopes could then be used in research and medicine far more economically than could the rare and expensive radium.

Joliot-Curie, Irène

né: Irène Curie
b. September 12, 1897
Paris, France
d. March 17, 1956
Paris, France
fields: Chemistry

The Irène and Frederic Joliot-Curie continued the work which Irène's parents, Pierre and Marie Curie, had begun on radioactivity. Frédéric and Irène received the Nobel Prize in Chemistry in 1935 for having discovered the possibility of artificial radioactivity. The resulting new radiosotopes could then be used in research and medicine far more economically than could the rare and expensive radium.

Jolliet, Louis

b. A few days before September 21, 1645
probably in Beaupré, near Quebec, New France (French Canada)
d. May, 1700
Quebec Province, New France
fields: Exploration and Colonization

Along with Father Jacques Marquette, Jolliet led an expedition to discover the course of the Mississippi River, descending to the mouth of the Arkansas River before being certain that the Mississippi flowed into the Gulf of Mexico. The journey paved the way for later French exploration of the area.

Jonas, Hans

b. May 10, 1903
Mönchengladbach, Germany
d. February 5, 1993
New Rochelle, New York
fields: Philosophy

Philosopher Hans Jonas attempts to explicate a connection between metaphysics and ethics that in modern philosophy has been largely disavowed. His work on method represents a return to speculative philosophy, which aims toward a sort of comprehensive explanation of the cosmos and the place of humanity in it. At the same time, he integrates scientific principles and disciplines such as evolution and biology into his analysis, resulting in a contemporary and informed philosophy of nature. His early and late works reveal a place in his thinking for God, as understood from a vantage point of liberal Judaism, but he does not believe that the notion of a creator God is fundamentally necessary to the grounding of ethics. Jonas contends that the practice of philosophy should make its practitioners moral, as it did with Socrates. Major works include *The Gnostic Religion* (1958), *The Phenomenon of Life* (1966), *Philosophical Essays: From Ancient Creed to Technological Man* (1974), *The Imperative of Responsibility: In Search of an Ethics for the Technological Age* (1984), and *Mortality and Morality: A Search for the Good After Auschwitz* (1996).

Jones, Absalom

b. Nov. 6, 1746
Sussex, Del.
d. Feb. 13, 1818
Philadelphia, Pa.
fields: Church Government, Religion and Theology

First African American priest of the Protestant Episcopal church; in 1794, Absalom Jones became the first leader of St. Thomas African Episcopal Church; in 1804, was ordained and became the first African American Protestant Episcopal priest in the United States.

Jones, Beatrix Cadwalader. *See* Farrand, Beatrix Jones

Jones, Bill T.

b. Feb. 15, 1952
Bunnell, Fla.
fields: Dance

African American dancer and choreographer; post-modernist Bill T. Jones's perfomances combine stage presence with complex and intricate choreographed movements and verbalizations.

Jones, Bobby

b. 1942?
Farmerville, La.
fields: Music (soul singer)

African American soul singer; during the 1960's and 1970's, Bobby Jones's releases included the ballad "A Certain Feeling," a soul single "Talkin' 'Bout Jones's" (1968), and "I'm So Lonely" (1971), written by the Dells.

Jones, Bobby

full: Robert Tyre Jones
b. March 17, 1902
Atlanta, Georgia
d. December 18, 1971
Atlanta, Georgia
fields: Sports (golf)

Jones climaxed his career in amateur golf in 1930 by winning in a single year the "Grand Slam," the four major American and British open and amateur championships, an achievement still unmatched by the late 1980's. He went on to found the Augusta National Golf Club and the Masters Tournament.

Jones, Carl

b. c. 1955
Tenn.
fields: Fashion (fashion designer)

African American fashion designer. Carl Jones and T. J. Walker, inspired by the appeal of the hip-hop culture and a desire to express their cultural heritage, created the influential Cross Colours clothing line in 1990.

Jones, Claudia

b. 1915?
Port of Spain, Trinidad
d. 1952
England
fields: Government and Politics, Social Reform

African American political activist; Claudia Jones joined the Young Communist League in the early 1930's and became editor of the *Weekly Review* and *Spotlight*, the league's publications; was convicted of violating the Smith Act in 1951; served one year of her prison term, then was deported to England.

Jones, Edith Newbold. *See* Wharton, Edith

Jones, Elvin Ray

b. Sept. 9, 1927
Pontiac, Mich.
fields: Music (drummer)

African American drummer; from 1960 to 1966, Elvin Ray Jones was a principal member of the John Coltrane Quartet, his polyrhythmic percussion style a hallmark of the group's rhythm section; recordings with Coltrane included *Africa/Brass* (1961), *Live at the Village Vanguard* (1961), *Coltrane* (1962), *Live at Birdland* (1963), *A Love Supreme* (1964), and *Ascension* (1965).

Jones, Esther Mae. *See* Phillips, Esther

Jones, Eugene Kinckle

b. July 30, 1885
Richmond, Va.
d. January 11, 1954
New York, N.Y.
fields: Civil Rights

Eugene Kinckle Jones was a National Urban League officer from 1911 to 1950. In 1912 Jones became associate chief executive of the league. As executive secretary (1917-1940) Jones played a large role in shaping the organization. He was one of the founders of Alpha Phi Alpha, the first black college fraternity, which was organized at Cornell University in 1906. He was also instrumental in persuading the Carnegie Foundation to buy Arthur A. Schomburg's collection of books, manuscripts, and art for donation to the New York Public Library. The collection formed the nucleus for the renowned Schomburg Center for Research in Black Culture.

Jones, Frederick McKinley

b. May 17, 1892
Cincinnati, Ohio
d. Feb. 21, 1961
Minneapolis, Minn.
fields: Invention and Technology

African American inventor; Frederick McKinley Jones patented an automatic refrigeration system that revolutionized the trucking and railway industries.

Jones, Gayl

b. Nov. 23, 1949
Lexington, Ky.
fields: Literature

African American feminist author; Gayl Jones, writing in the tradition of Zora Neale Hurston and Alice Walker, published *Corregidora* (1975), *White Rat* (1977), *Song for Anninho* (1981), *Xarque and Other Poems* (1985), and *The Healing* (1998).

Jones, Grace

b. May 19, 1952
Spanishtown, Jamaica
fields: Fashion, Music (singer), Theater and Entertainment (actor)

African American model, actress, and singer; at age seventeen, Grace Jones began working for the Wilhelmina Modeling Agency; posed for the covers of *Vogue*, *Elle*, and appeared in the film *Gordon's War* (1973); became a 1970's cult artist of Paris discos and New York City dance clubs and was hailed as "the Dietrich of the New Decade"; albums included *Warm Leatherette* (1980), *Nightclubbing* (1981)—which included "Walking in the Rain")— *Living My Life* (1982), and *Bulletproof Heart* (1989).

Jones, Hank

full: Henry Jones
b. July 31, 1918
Vicksburg, Miss.
fields: Music (jazz pianist)

African American jazz pianist; Hank Jones began his professional career at age thirteen; worked with jazz greats such as Coleman Hawkins and Billy Eckstine in the 1940's; was an accompanist for Ella Fitzgerald between 1948 and 1953; in 1959, secured a staff position with CBS and worked with the Ray Block Orchestra as part of *The Ed Sullivan Show*; in 1976, became part of the Great Jazz Trio; played on hundreds of recordings with such legendary figures as Milt Jackson, Lester Young, Cannonball Adderley, and Charlie Parker; recorded with his brother Thad and as a soloist; sampling of albums includes *Have You Met Hank Jones?* (1956), *Satin Doll* (1980), *The Great Jazz Trio Revisited: At the Village Vanguard* (1980), *The Oracle* (1989), *A Handful of Keys* (1991), and *Favors* (1997).

Jones, Inigo

b. July 15, 1573
London, England
d. June 21, 1652
London, England
fields: Art, Architecture

Working during the English Renaissance in the fields of theater design and architecture, Jones introduced innovations that contributed greatly to the urban planning done under Charles I and contributed to the creation of a modern drama.

Jones, James Earl

b. January 17, 1931
Arkabutla, Miss.
fields: Theater and Entertainment, Film, Television

James Earl Jones's performance in the Broadway production of *The Great White Hope* in 1969 was a breakthrough for black actors. His theater credits include many Shakesperian roles and acclaimed performances in Athol Fugard's *The Blood Knot* and *Boesman and Lena*. Jones's numerous film credits include *Dr. Strangelove* (1964) and *Star Wars* (1976). He portrayed writer Alex

Haley in the sequel to the television miniseries *Roots*.

Jones, John Paul

né: John Paul
b. July 6, 1747
Arbigland, Scotland
d. July 18, 1792
Paris, France
fields: Military Affairs, Warfare and Conquest

Known in his own time for his daring raids on British territory and spectacular engagements with British vessels during the American Revolutionary War, Jones is now widely regarded as the founder of the United States Navy.

Jones, K. C.

b. May 25, 1932
Tyler, Tex.
fields: Sports (basketball player and coach)

African American basketball player and coach; K. C. Jones joined the Boston Celtics in 1958 and retired in 1967; in 1983, became the Celtics' second African American head coach (after Bill Russell) and coached Boston to NBA championships in 1984 and 1986.

Jones, Lillie Mae. *See* Carter, Betty

Jones, Lois Mailou

b. Nov. 3, 1905
Boston, Mass.
fields: Art, Education

African American artist and educator; Lois Mailou Jones designed fabrics and worked as a costume and stage designer, a painter-illustrator, and a stained glass designer; notable paintings include *Negro Cabin* (1931), *The Ascent of Ethiopia* (1933), and *Jennie* (1943); taught art at Howard University for forty-seven years.

Jones, Mother

né: Mary Harris
aka: Mary Harris Jones
b. May 1, 1830
Cork, Ireland
d. November 30, 1930
Silver Spring, Maryland
fields: Social Reform, Labor Movement

As a labor organizer and fiery orator, Mother Jones inspired workers and breathed life into union organizing efforts in the early twentieth century.

Jones, Nathaniel Raphael

b. May 13, 1926
Youngstown, Ohio
fields: Civil Rights, Law

Nathaniel Raphael Jones practiced law from 1959 to 1961, and he was an assistant United States attorney from 1961 to 1967. From 1966 until 1969 he served as executive director of the Fair Employment Practices Commission in Youngstown. Jones served as the general counsel for the National Association for the Advancement of Colored People (NAACP) between 1969 and 1979. He coordinated an NAACP legal assault on northern school segregation and argued the Supreme Court case of *Bradley v. Milliken*. Jones was appointed as a judge on the U.S. Court of Appeals for the Sixth Circuit in 1979 by President Jimmy Carter.

Jones, Peter

aka: Kahkewaquonaby
aka: Kahkewagwonnaby
b. Jan. 1, 1802
Burlington Heights, Ontario
d. June 29, 1856
Brantford, Ontario, Canada
fields: Native American Affairs, Literature, Religion and Theology

Ojibwa missionary, author, and political activist; Peter Jones was ordained in 1830; as a missionary and also as a political lobbyist, he traveled extensively throughout Ontario and New York State; wrote numerous religious tracts and hymnbooks, translated Ojibwa texts into English, and made earliest translation of Bible from English into Ojibwa; chief of two Ojibwa bands; fought for Indian land rights; *The Life and Journals of Kah-ke-wa-quona-by* (1860) and *A History of the Ojebway Indians* (1861; remains a source for information on Ojibwa customs) published posthumously.

Jones, Quincy

full: Quincy Delight Jones
b. March 14, 1933
Chicago, Ill.
fields: Music

African American composer, arranger, and producer Quincy Jones is the winner of twenty Grammy awards and a four-time Oscar nominee. He has written more than thirty-three film scores, including music for *The Wiz* (1978), *In Cold Blood* (1967), and *The Color Purple* (1985). He played in a number of bands, including those of Ray Charles, Lionel Hampton, and Dizzie Gillespie. Jones was Mercury Records' first black vice-president. He produced the album and video *We Are the World* (1985) and Michael Jackson's best-selling *Thriller* (1982). Jones's own discography includes *You've Got it Bad, Girl* (1973), *Body Heat* (1974), *Mellow Madness* (1975), *I Heard That!* (1976), *The Dude* (1981), and *Quincy Jones, The Best* (1982).

Jones, Richard Myknee

b. June 13, 1889
Donaldsville, La.
d. Dec. 8, 1945
Chicago, Ill.
fields: Music (jazz pianist, songwriter, producer)

African American jazz pianist, songwriter, and producer; Richard Myknee Jones broke into the recording business in the 1920's as a recording director of "race records"; toured and recorded songs with his group the Jazz Wizards, later known as the Chicago Cosmopolitans; in the 1930's, worked as a talent scout for Decca and Mercury Records; best known for songs such as "Jazzin' Babies Blues" (1924), "Riverside Blues" (1925), and the "Trouble in Mind" (1926).

Jones, Ruth. *See* Gordon, Ruth

Jones, Ruth Lee. *See* Washington, Dinah

Jones, Sam. *See* Arpeika

Jones, Sam

full: Samuel Jones
b. June 24, 1933
Wilmington, N.C.
fields: Sports (basketball player)

African American basketball player; in 1957, Sam Jones was drafted by the Boston Celtics of the National Basketball Association (NBA) and became a top guard; played in NBA All-Star Games in 1962, 1964, 1965, 1966, and 1968, and was named to the league's twenty-fifth anniversary team in 1970; elected to the Naismith Memorial Basketball Hall of Fame in 1983.

Jones, Sissieretta

né: Matilda Sissieretta Joyner
b. Jan. 5, 1869
Portsmouth, Va.
d. June 24, 1933
Providence, R.I.
fields: Music (singer)

African American singer; Sissieretta Jones performed at the White House for President Benjamin Harrison in 1892; while touring Europe, was given the nickname "Black Patti" as an affirmation of her rich singing style, similar to that of Italian soprano Adelina Patti; in 1896 was billed as the most popular prima donna of all nations and races while performing in New York City; starred in the revue *A Trip to Africa* (1910).

Jones, Uriah

b. ?
fields: Sports (fencer)

African American fencer; in 1968, Uriah Jones was the first black member of an American Olympic fencing team.

Jones, Wilson. *See* Crazy Snake

Jonson, Ben

full: Benjamin Jonson
b. June 11, 1573
London, England
d. August 6, 1637
London, England
fields: Literature, Theater and Entertainment

The comic plays Jonson wrote in the 1600's remain landmark works of the English Renaissance, and as mentor to younger writers he influenced the course of poetry in the seventeenth century.

Joplin, Janis

b. January 19, 1943
Port Arthur, Texas
d. October 4, 1970
Hollywood, California
fields: Music

Janis Joplin, one of the prime movers in the evolution of rock 'n' roll, demonstrated that white women were capable of singing with as much emotional intensity as that of great black singers such as Bessie Smith.

Joplin, Scott

b. November 24, 1868
Bowie County, near Texarkana, Texas
d. April 1, 1917
New York, New York
fields: Music

Despite humble origins, racial prejudices, and cultural barriers, African American Scott Joplin became a respected piano player and a composer of ragtime music. Known as the "King of Ragtime," his most famous composition, "Maple Leaf Rag" (1899), was the first piece of sheet music to sell one million copies in the United States.

Jordan, Barbara

full: Barbara Charline Jordan
b. February 21, 1936
Houston, Texas
d. January 17, 1996
Austin, Texas
fields: Government and Politics, Law, Education

The first African American elected to the Texas Senate since Reconstruction, Barbara Jordan went on to become a member of the U.S. House of Representatives. She mesmerized the nation during televised coverage of the House Judiciary Committee's investigation considering the impeachment of President Richard Nixon.

Jordan, Camille

full: Marie-Ennemond-Camille Jordan
b. Jan. 5, 1838
Lyon, France
d. Jan. 20 or 21, 1922
probably in Paris, France, but possibly in Milan, Italy
fields: Mathematics (topology)

Camille Jordan formalized the principles of group theory; created the framework for the study of surfaces; published *Traité des substitutions et des équations algébriques* (1870).

Jordan, Jeane Duane. *See* Kirkpatrick, Jeane

Jordan, June

b. July 9, 1936
Harlem, N.Y.
fields: Literature, Journalism, Education

African American educator, novelist, essayist, poet, and activist; June Jordan's first novel, *His Own Where* (1971), made *The New York Times* List of Most Outstanding Books of 1971 and the American Library Association List of Best Books and was a National Book Award Finalist; won the National Black Journalists Achievement Award for International Reporting in 1984 and the MADRE Award for Leadership in 1989. While continuing to produce important works, she became a professor of African American studies at the University of California, Berkeley, in 1997.

Jordan, Michael

full: Michael Jeffery Jordan
b. February 17, 1963
Brooklyn, N.Y.
fields: Sports (basketball)

After being named college player of the year (1983 and 1984) and winning a gold medal in the 1984 Olympic Games, Michael Jordan entered the National Basketball Association (NBA). He was drafted by the Chicago Bulls as the third pick of the first round. The Bulls won NBA championships in 1991-1993 and 1996-1998, Jordan was named Rookie of the Year (1985), Defensive Player of the Year (1988), and League Most Valuable Player (1988, 1991, 1992, 1996, 1998). He led the NBA in points averaged per game for five straight seasons, beginning in 1986-1987. In 1993 Jordan retired from professional basketball at the height his career, shortly after the murder of his father, James Jordan. He signed a minor league baseball contract with the Chicago White Sox organization in 1994, but his baseball career was unspectacular and short-lived. Jordan rejoined the Chicago Bulls in 1995 and led the Bulls to the second round of the NBA play-offs. He retired in 1998.

Jordan, Stanley

b. July 31, 1959
Chicago, Ill.
fields: Music (electric guitarist)

African American electric guitarist; Stanley Jordan's unique approach to jazz electric guitar involves tapping the strings with both hands, allowing him to play two independent lines at the same time; performed to acclaim at the Kool Jazz Festival (1984) and the 1985 Montreux International Jazz Festival; albums include *Touch Sensitive* (1982), *Magic Touch* (1985), *Stolen Moments* (1990), and *Live in New York* (1998).

Jordan, Steve

né: Estaban Jordan
b. ?
fields: Music (accordionist and songwriter)

Latino accordionist and songwriter. In the 1960's, Mexican American accordionist Steve Jordan began recording music that combined the *música norteña* tradition and rock music. He became known as the "Jimi Hendrix of the accordion" and for wearing an eyepatch. He gained popularity after appearing in David Byrne's 1986 film *True Stories*. In the same year, he played on the *Born in East L.A.* soundtrack, and his album *Turn Me Loose* was nominated for a Grammy Award.

Jordan, Vernon

full: Vernon Eulion Jordan, Jr.
b. Aug. 15, 1935
Atlanta, Ga.
fields: Civil Rights, Law

African American lawyer, civil rights leader; Vernon Jordan was the field secretary for the Georgia Branch of the National Association for the Advancement of Colored People, 1962-1964; director of the Voter Education Project of the Southern Regional Council, 1964-1968; appointed executive director of the United Negro College Fund, 1970-1972; served as executive director of the National Urban League, 1972-1981; became political confidante of President Bill Clinton in 1992. Jordan became embroiled in the Monica Lewinsky scandal in 1998 when questions arose concerning his role in securing a job for Lewinsky (a White House intern who had an affair with President Clinton).

Joseph II

b. March 13, 1741
Vienna, Austria
d. February 20, 1790
Vienna, Austria
fields: Monarchy

King of the Romans, 1764-1790. Joseph II contributed to the enlightened reform of the Habsburg monarchy at the end of the eighteenth century, which enabled it to survive as a great power until the end of World War I.

Joseph, Chief

né: Heinmot Tooyalakekt

b. c. 1840
Lapwai Preserve, Wallowa Valley, northeastern Oregon
d. September 21, 1904
Colville Indian Reservation, Washington
fields: Native American Affairs, Civil Rights

Leader of his people in the Nez Perce War of 1877, Chief Joseph attempted to retain for his people the freedoms enjoyed prior to white American interest in their lands.

Joseph, Ronald

b. 1910
St. Kitts, British West Indies
d. 1992
Brussels, Belgium
fields: Art (painter)

African American painter; Ronald Joseph was a member of the Harlem Artists Guild and involved in the Works Progress Administration mural project; considered one of foremost black abstract artists in the United States.

Joséphine

né: Marie-Joséphe-Rose Tascher de la Pagerie
aka: Joséphine de Beauharnais
b. June 23, 1763
Trois-Îlets, Martinique
d. May 29, 1814
Malmaison, France
fields: Government and Politics

Empress of France, 1804-1810. Joséphine's life exemplified the chaos and unpredictability of the French Revolution and subsequent warfare. Popularly loved as "the good Joséphine," her social talents assisted Napoleon Bonaparte in creating stability and reconciliation among the various factions dividing the citizens of France.

Josephson, Brian D.

full: Brian David Josephson
b. Jan. 4, 1940
Cardiff, Glamorgan, Wales
fields: Physics

Brian D. Josephson, while still a graduate student, described supercurrents in the thin barrier region sandwiched between two superconductors, fostering studies of the complexity of superconducting behavior. In 1973, he won the Nobel Prize in Physics, jointly with Leo Esaki and Ivar Giaever.

Josephus, Flavius

aka: Joseph ben Matthias
b. c. 37 C.E.
Jerusalem, Palestine
d. c. 100 C.E.
probably Rome
fields: Historiography, Scholarship

Josephus' history of the Jewish revolt against Rome in 66, the fall of Jerusalem in 70, and the capture of Masada in 73 remains, despite patent exaggerations and questionable reporting, the primary source of information for this segment of world history.

Joslyn, Matilda. *See* Gage, Matilda Joslyn

Joule, James Prescott

b. Dec. 24, 1818
Salford, Lancashire, England
d. Oct. 11, 1889
Sale, Cheshire, England
fields: Physics, Science, Invention and Technology

James Prescott Joule's experiments led to the confirmation of ideas on the kinetic nature of heat and of the representation of heat as a form of energy; in 1852, collaborated with William Thomson (later Lord Kelvin) to verify experimentally the Joule-Thomson refrigeration effect; in 1875, made precision measurements of the mechanical equivalent of heat.

Journeycake, Charles

aka: Neshapanasumin
b. Dec. 16, 1817
Ohio
d. Jan. 3, 1894
Indian Territory
fields: Government and Politics, Native American Affairs, Religion and Theology

Native American leader. Journeycake, a Lenni Lenape, fought for the rights of his people during a number of relocations—first to Kansas, then to land formerly allocated to the Cherokees in northeastern Oklahoma. One of the founders of Bacone College, an Indian school in Oklahoma.

Joyce, James

b. February 2, 1882
Dublin, Ireland
d. January 13, 1941
Zurich, Switzerland
fields: Literature

Author of the germinal modernist novels *Ulysses* and *Finnegans Wake*, Joyce played a central role in the development of the mystique of the inaccessible artist and helped define the course of twentieth century culture.

Joyce, William

aka: Lord Haw Haw
b. April 24, 1906
Brooklyn, New York
d. January 3, 1946
London, England
fields: Radio

Popularly known as "Lord Haw Haw," William Joyce made pro-German broadcasts to Great Britain during World War II and became an object of ridicule. Before the war began, he worked with Oswald Mosley, the British Fascist leader. After having a falling out with Mosley, Joyce went to Germany, where he conducted broadcasts for the Nazi regime. After the war he was tried for treason in England and was hanged.

Joyner-Kersee, Jackie

né: Jacqueline Joyner
b. Mar. 3, 1962
East St. Louis, Ill.
fields: Sports (track and field athlete)

African American track and field athlete; Jackie Joyner-Kersee, called the "World's Greatest Woman Athlete," won a silver medal in the heptathlon in the 1984 Olympics and gold in that event and the long jump in the 1988 Olympics; was awarded the 1986 Sullivan Award as the best athlete in the United States; became the first woman to win the heptathlon in two Olympics in the 1992 Summer Olympics; won a bronze medal at the 1996 Summer Olympics in Atlanta; retired from competition in 1998.

Joyner, Matilda Sissieretta. *See* Jones, Sissieretta

Juan Carlos I

né: Juan Carlos Alfonso Víctor María de Borbón y Borbón
b. January 5, 1938
Rome, Italy
fields: Government and Politics

Juan Carlos I was crowned king of Spain in 1975, two days after the death of dictator Francisco Franco. Established a democratic, constitutional monarchy, managed to maintain military's support for reforms.

Juana, Sor. *See* Cruz, Sor Juana Inés de la

Juárez, Benito

b. March 21, 1806
San Pablo Guelatao, Oaxaca, Mexico
d. July 19, 1872
Mexico City, Mexico
fields: Government and Politics

The dominant figure of mid-nineteenth century Mexican politics, Juárez embodied a liberal vision of a democratic republican form of government, economic development and modernization, virulent anticlericalism, and mandatory public education. Although he was prevented from fully implementing his ambitious agenda by years of warfare against foreign intervention and his policies were anathema to many entrenched conservative elements in Mexico, especially the Catholic church, Juárez's reform program laid the groundwork for a modern Mexican nation.

Juba, Master. *See* Lane, William Henry

Judah ha-Levi

b. c. 1075
Tudela, Spain
d. c. 1141
possibly Jerusalem, Palestine
fields: Literature, Philosophy

Judah ha-Levi, one of the greatest Hebrew poets, was also an important medieval religious philosopher.

Judd, Walter Henry

b. Sept. 25, 1898
Rising City, Nebr.
d. Feb. 13, 1994
Mitchellville, Md.
fields: Government and Politics

Walter Henry Judd, Minnesota congressman from 1942 to 1962, received his medical degree from the University of Nebraska in 1923 and worked in China as a medical missionary 1925-1931 and 1934-1938. Judd was responsible for the passage of the Immigration Act of 1943 (also known as the Magnuson Act), which repealed the Chinese Exclusion Acts in force since 1882. A sympathizer with the Chinese Nationalists, in the late 1940's he headed the China bloc in Congress to pass the China Aid Act of 1948. From 1964 to 1969, he frequently lectured and gave daily radio commentaries on U.S. domestic and foreign policy. He also worked for *Reader's Digest* as a contributing editor from 1963 to 1976.

Judkins, Steveland. *See* Wonder, Stevie

Julia, Raúl

b. Mar. 9, 1940
San Juan, Puerto Rico
d. Oct. 24, 1994
New York, N.Y.
fields: Theater and Entertainment (actor), Film, Television

Latino actor. Raúl Julia's theatrical debut occurred in 1964 in *La vida es sueño* (*Life Is a Dream*). In 1966, he made his first appearance at the New York Shakespeare Festival in *Macbeth*. He debuted on Broadway in *The Cuban Thing* and was nominated for four Tony Awards. Julia's first film appearance was *Stiletto* (1969), after which he played roles in such films as *The Eyes of Laura Mars* (1978), *Kiss of the Spider Woman* (1985), *Tequila Sunrise* (1988), *Presumed Innocent* (1990), and *The Addams Family* (1991), and *Addams Family Values* (1993). He also appeared in the television film *Onassis* and had a recurring role on *Sesame Street*.

Julian, Percy Lavon

b. April 11, 1899
Montgomery, Ala.
d. April 19, 1975
Waukegan, Ill.
fields: Science

African American scientist Percy Lavon Julian taught at Fisk University until 1922, when he attended Harvard University to earn his master's degree in chemistry. In 1934 Julian and his collaborator Josef Pikl presented the results of their research on synthesizing the physostigmine molecule to the American Chemical Society. In 1935 he became director of research for the Glidden Company, where he helped develop the foam fire extinguisher used by the U.S. Navy in World War II and synthetic cortisone for the treatment of rheumatoid arthritis. Julian opened his own research laboratory in Chicago, Ill., in 1954, which he sold in 1961 to the Smith, Kline, and French pharmaceutical firm.

Julien, Max

b. 1941
Washington, D.C.
fields: Film (screenwriter, actor, producer)

African American screenwriter, actor, and producer during Hollywood's Blaxploitation period; Max Julien's credits include screenwriter for *Cleopatra Jones* (1973), star of such films as *The Mack* (1973) and *Thomasine and Bushrod* (1974), and appeared in *How to Be a Player* (1997).

Julius II

né: Giuliano della Rovere
b. December 5, 1443
Albisola, Republic of Genoa
d. February 21, 1513
Rome
fields: Religion and Theology, Military Affairs, Patronage of the Arts

Pope, 1503-1513. Julius II, the Warrior Pope, was the first and only pontiff personally to command and lead a papal army into battle. His military exploits regained large amounts of territory lost to the Papal States in wars with France and small Italian republics. Besides his attempts to strengthen church administration and reduce nepotism, he was also a patron to Michelangelo, Raphael, and Donato Bramante.

Jung, Carl

full: Carl Gustav Jung
b. July 26, 1875
Kesswil, Switzerland
d. June 6, 1961
Küsnacht, Switzerland
fields: Psychiatry and Psychology

Jung, the founder of analytic psychology, is probably best known for his descriptions of the orientations of the personality, "extroversion" and "introversion." His theories of universal symbolic representations have had a far-reaching impact on such diverse disciplines as art, literature, filmmaking, religion, anthropology, and history.

Jurado, Katy

full: María Cristina Jurado García
b. Jan. 16, 1927
Guadalajara, Mexico
fields: Theater and Enertainment (actor), Film

Latina actor. Katy Jurado was film columnist for Mexican publications before her Hollywood debut in *The Bullfighter and the Lady* (1951). In 1952, she played Gary Cooper's jilted lover in *High Noon*. Among her other films were *The Racers* (1955), *The Badlanders* (1958), *Stay Away Joe* (1968), and *Under the Volcano* (1984). She was nominated for an Academy Award for her role in *Barabbas* (1962). Jurado also appeared in several Spanish-language films made in Mexico and Spain, and she had a few television roles, including the film *Evita Peron* and the 1984 series *AKA Pablo*.

Just, Ernest Everett

b. August 14, 1883
Charleston, South Carolina
d. October 27, 1941
Washington, D.C.
fields: Science

Marine biologist Ernest Everett Just conducted pathbreaking research on invertebrate embryos as well as egg fertilization, artificial parthenogenesis, and cell division. He published a primer, *The Biology of the Cell Surface*, in 1939.

Justinian I

b. 483
Illyria
d. November 14, 565
Constantinople
fields: Government and Politics, Law, Monarchy

Emperor, 527-565. A conscientious man of somber judgment and religious zeal, Justinian was the pivotal emperor in the transition from the later Roman Empire to the Byzantine Empire. He has been called the "Last Roman Emperor" and the "First Byzantine Emperor." He left a legacy of great buildings, a legal compilation that became the foundation of European law, and an enhanced autocratic tradition that helped the Byzantine Empire guard against the onslaught of Islam.

Juvenal

né: Decimus Junius Juvenalis
b. c. 60 C.E.
Aquinum
d. c. 130 C.E.
place unknown
fields: Literature

Juvenal expanded the dimensions of poetic satire in savage works that lashed out at man's vices and corruption.

Kacha. *See* Tiger, Jerome R.

Kádár, János
né: János Jozsef Czermanik
b. May 26, 1912
Fiume, Austro-Hungarian Empire (now Rijeka, Croatia)
d. July 6, 1989
Budapest, Hungary
fields: Government and Politics

János Kádár was premier (1956-1958; 1961-1965) and then first secretary (1965-1988) of Communist Hungary. Enacted internal reforms, such as easing economic restrictions and allowing a sort of quasi-capitalism, but supported Soviet foreign policy.

Kadohata, Cynthia
full: Cynthia Lynn Kadohata
b. 1956
Chicago, Ill.
fields: Literature

Japanese American writer Cynthia Kadohata published a number of short stories in prominent literary magazines, including "Charlie O," which appeared in *The New Yorker* in 1985. Her first novel *The Floating World* was released in 1989, followed in 1992 by *In the Heart of the Valley*.

Kafka, Franz
b. July 3, 1883
Prague, Austro-Hungarian Empire
d. June 3, 1924
Kierling, Austria
fields: Literature

Kafka's unique style of narration and the intensely psychological and existential nature of his fiction, letters, and diaries have made him one of the most influential authors of the twentieth century.

Kagan, Jerome
b. February 25, 1929
Newark, N.J.
fields: Psychiatry and Psychology

Best known for his work on shyness in children, Jerome Kagan demonstrated how early childhood behaviors resemble those of of teenagers and adults. In 1987 he was honored with the Award for Distinguished Scientific Contribution by the American Psychological Association.

Kaganovich, Ida. *See* Rosenthal, Ida

Kagawa, Lawrence
b. 1904
d. 1973
fields: Banking and Finance

Insurance executive Lawrence Kagawa got his first job in the field with International Trust Company of Honolulu in 1923. In 1933, he began working for Occidental Underwriters of Hawaii, the first insurance company in Hawaii to employ Asian Americans as agents, to stop charging Asian Americans higher premiums, and to invest in Hawaiian concerns. Kagawa was company president until 1963 when he became chairman and chief executive, a position he held until retirement in 1970.

Kagawa, Toyohiko
b. July 10, 1888
Kobe, Japan
d. April 23, 1960
Tokyo, Japan
fields: Labor Movement, Literature, Journalism, Religion and Theology

Toyohiko Kagawa converted to Christianity and studied theology. He became involved in the Japanese labor movement and led a dockworkers' strike in 1921, insisting it be run on Christian principles. When Japan became militaristic in the 1920's, Kagawa advocated pacifism. In 1928 he founded the National Anti-War League of Japan. Two years later he launched the Kingdom of God movement. His reputation slipped during World War II, however, because he made radio broadcasts condemning the Allied bombings. After the war he called for Japanese repentance and briefly held a position in the government. He supported world federation.

Kagiwada, George
b. July 4, 1931
Los Angeles, Calif.
fields: Sociology

George Kagiwada received a Ph.D. degree from the University of California, Los Angeles, in 1969. He specialized in social adaptation theory and taught sociology at the University of Manitoba, Canada, from 1968 to 1970. He became the first tenured Asian American professor at the University of California, Davis, in 1977. He remained at that institution until his retirement in 1993.

Kahane, Meir
né: Martin David Kahane
aka: Michael King
b. August 1, 1932
New York, New York
d. November 5, 1990
New York, New York
fields: Religion and Theology, Government and Politics

Meir Kahane was a rabbi and Jewish activist; earned law degree from New York University; in 1960's founded Jewish Defense League, advocating use of violence in securing Jewish rights; emigrated to Israel in 1971 and was elected to the Israeli parliament in 1981; assassinated in New York City; wrote *The Jewish Stake in Vietnam* (1967).

Kahgegwagebow. *See* Copway, George

Kahkewaquonaby. *See* Jones, Peter

Kahlo, Frida
full: Magdalena Carmen Frida Kahlo y Calderón
b. July 6, 1907
Coyoacán, Mexico
d. July 13, 1954
Coyoacán, Mexico
fields: Art

Latina artist. Frida Kahlo married muralist Diego Rivera on August 21, 1929. She began painting while recovering from an accident. Her first show was at the Julien Levy Gallery in New York City in 1938. She became one of the founding members of the Seminaria de Cultura Mexicana in 1941 and was appointed a professor of painting at La Esmeralda in 1943. In 1946, Kahlo won the National Prize of Arts and Sciences. Kahlo was political throughout her life: She joined the Mexican Communist Party in 1928 and had a relationship with communist leader Leon Trotsky in 1937. She also supported the Spanish Republicans in the Spanish Civil War (1936-1939).

Kakutani, Michiko
b. Jan. 9, 1955
New Haven, Conn.
fields: Literature, Journalism

Michiko Kakutani received her bachelor's degree in English from Yale University and began working as a reporter for *The Washington Post* in 1976. She was a writer on the staff of *Time* magazine, from 1977 to 1979, when she began to cover cultural news for *The New York Times*. She became a book critic for the newspaper in 1983 and is known for her perceptive critical sense and her writing style. In 1988, Kakutani published *The Poet at the Piano: Portraits of Writers, Filmmakers, and Performers at Work*.

Kalakaua, David
b. Nov. 16, 1836
Honolulu, Hawaii
d. Jan. 20, 1891
San Francisco, Calif.
fields: Government and Politics, Diplomacy

David Kalakaua, the son of a Hawaiian chief, served for thirteen years in the Hawaiian legislative assembly before being elected king of Hawaii on February 12, 1874. He signed the Reciprocity Treaty (1875), which eliminated the U.S. tariff on sugar and led to the rapid expansion of sugar production in Hawaii, producing new demands for immigrant labor and resulting in the construction of an industrial infrastructure. In 1881, Kalakaua helped negotiate a treaty to encourage immigration from Japan. In 1887, upset by government licensing schemes, U.S. businessmen revolted, restricting the king's authority through a new constitution. The businessmen also pressured the king to allow the United States to create a coaling station in Pearl Harbor in order to renew the Reciprocity Treaty. Tired and ill, the king traveled to California, where he died in 1891.

Kālidāsa

b. c. 100 B.C.E. or c. 340 C.E.
India
d. c. 40 B.C.E. or c. 400 C.E.
probably India
fields: Literature

Recognized as the author of no more than three plays and four poems, which fuse together themes of nature and love within the framework of Hinduism, Kālidāsa is generally regarded as India's greatest poet and dramatist. Sometimes characterized as the "Shakespeare of India," he is especially known in the West for his romantic play *Sakuntala* and his metaphysical love poem *The Cloud Messenger*.

Kalish, Sophie. *See* Tucker, Sophie

Kamehameha I

né: Paiea
b. c. 1758
Halawa, North Kohala, the island of Hawaii, Hawaiian Islands
d. May 8, 1819
Kailua, Hawaii
fields: Government and Politics, Military Affairs

Through his prowess, astute leadership in battle, and adroit use of European advisers, ships, and weapons, Kamehameha overcame his adversaries and united the Hawaiian Islands for the first time in their history. In the process, he made himself their king and founded a dynasty. King of all Hawaiian islands, 1804-1819.

Kamerlingh Onnes, Heike

b. Sept. 21, 1853
Groningen, the Netherlands
d. Feb. 21, 1926
Leiden, the Netherlands
fields: Invention and Technology, Physics

Heike Kamerlingh Onnes was a pioneer in the field of low-temperature physics; in 1892, buildt a cascade-type gas liquefaction refrigeration device; in 1906, created liquid hydrogen; in 1908, created liquid helium; in 1911, discovered superconductivity; in 1913, received the Nobel Prize in Physics; in 1924, demonstrated the unusual behavior of helium near 2.2 degrees Kelvin.

Kamiakin

aka: Camaekin (He Will Not Go)
b. c. 1800
near present-day Yakima, Wash.
d. 1877
Rock Lake, Wash.
fields: Government and Politics, Warfare and Conquest, Native American Affairs

Native American leader. Chief Kamiakin of the Yakima led the Yakima Nation during the Yakima War of 1855-1856, a time when they were being overrun by European American settlers.

Kämpfer, Engelbert

b. September 16, 1651
Lemgo, Duchy of Lippe
d. November 2, 1716
Lemgo, Duchy of Lippe
fields: Literature, Medicine, Botany

Based on his own travels, Kämpfer wrote detailed and highly accurate accounts of Japan and other areas of Asia, the Middle East, and Russia. In addition, he wrote on Asian natural history, diseases, and medical practices.

Kanamori, Hiroo

b. Oct. 17, 1936
Tokyo, Japan
fields: Science

Hiroo Kanamori earned his doctoral degree in 1964 at the University of Tokyo and remained there to work at the Earthquake Research Institute. In 1972, he began to teach geophysics at the California Institute of Technology (Caltech) in Pasadena, California. Considered by many to be the world's foremost expert in earthquake seismology, Kanamori became director of Caltech's Seismological Laboratory in 1990. He was named California Scientist of the Year in November, 1993.

Kanazawa, Tooru J.

b. Nov. 12, 1906
Spokane, Wash.
fields: Journalism

After graduating from the University of Washington with a degree in journalism, Tooru J. Kanazawa Journalist. went to work in 1932 for the *Rafu Shimpo,* a Los Angeles Japanese newspaper. He moved to new York in 1940 and served as a volunteer with the U.S. Army's all-Nisei 442nd Regimental Combat Team during World War II, receiving the Bronze Star for meritorious service. In 1989, he published a book, *Sushi and Sourdough: A Novel* (1989), based on his experiences growing up in the frontier gold-mining town of Juneau, Alaska, and the lives of Issei working in the salmon canneries there.

Kandinsky, Wassily

b. December 4, 1866
Moscow, Russia
d. December 13, 1944
Neuilly-sur-Seine, near Paris, France
fields: Art

Both for the quality and influence of his works and for the influence of his theoretical and pedagogical writings, Kandinsky was the most significant figure in the development of nonrepresentational abstract art in the first half of the twentieth century. He was the pioneer among those artists whose aim was not to reproduce the expressive qualities of objects and events in nature but to exploit the intrinsic expressive attributes of artistic materials, particularly pigments, without reference to natural appearances.

Kane, Big Daddy

né: Antonio Hardy
b. 1968
Brooklyn, N.Y.
fields: Music (rapper)

African American rapper, songwriter, producer; Big Daddy Kane's albums include *Long Live the Kane* (1987), *It's a Big Daddy Thing* (1990), *Taste of Chocolate* (1990), and *Prince of Darkness* (1991).

Kanellos, Nicolás

b. Jan. 31, 1945
New York, N.Y.
fields: Scholarship, Publishing

Latino scholar and editor. Nicolás Kanellos founded the magazine *Revista Chicano-Riqueña*, which later became *The Americas Review*, in 1973. The magazine led to the establishment of Arte Público Press in Houston in 1979. Kanellos worked as a professor of Hispanic and classical languages at the University of Houston. He published *The History of Hispanic Theater in the United States: Origins to 1940* (1990) and coauthored *Nuevos Pasos: Chicano and Puerto Rican Drama* (1989, with Jorge Huerta). He edited several books, including *Short Fiction by Hispanic Writers of the United States* (1993). Kanellos received a White House Hispanic Heritage Award for Literature in 1988 and an American Book Award in 1990.

Kanemitsu, Matsumi

b. May 28, 1922
Ogden City, Utah
d. May 11, 1992
Los Angeles, Calif.
fields: Art

Born in the United States and educated in Japan, Matsumi Kanemitsu returned to the United States in 1938 and lived in Utah and Nevada, working as a copper miner while creating his art. He served in the military during World War II and moved to New York City in the early 1950's, where he was influenced by artists such as Mark Rothko and Willem de Kooning and by Japanese brush painting. In 1964, he moved to California.

Kang, Connie Kyonshill

b. Nov. 11, 1942
Hamhung, Korea
fields: Journalism

Korean American Connie Kyonshill Kang is one of the first Asian American women to break into mainstream print media. She has written for the *Los Angeles Times*, *The Wall Street Journal*, *The New York Times*, *The San Francisco Chronicle*, and the *Korea Times*. She cofounded the Korean American Journalists Association in 1985.

Kang, Younghill

b. May 10?, 1903
Song-Dune-Chi, Korea
d. Dec. 11, 1972
Satellite Beach, Fla.
fields: Publishing, Literature

Younghill Kang arrived in the United States in 1921, going to college in Canada and at Harvard University and becoming the first Korea-born comparative literature professor at New York University. His publications include *The Grass Roof* (1931); *East Goes West* (1937); and *The Happy Grove* (1933). He received Guggenheim and Le prix Halperine Kamnisty (1937) awards.

Kang Youwei

b. Mar. 19, 1858
Canton, Guangdong Province, China
d. Mar. 31, 1927
Qingdao, Shandong Province, China
fields: Government and Politics

Kang Youwei founded one of China's first political parties, the Baohuanghui (Chinese Empire Reform Association), in an attempt to revive a weak and corrupt China. The party tried to tap the strength of overseas Chinese and had branches in most Chinese American communities. Kang, a government official, tried to reform the dynasty, reinterpreting Confucianism to promote modernization. Kang gained influence at court during the Reform Movement of 1898 but lost it when the Empress Dowager staged a successful coup d'état. Kang fled China to Canada, where he formed the Constitutionalist Party, which had considerable support in Canada and the United States. After the republican revolution in 1911, Kang returned to China, where he supported an unsuccessful movement to revive the Qing Dynasty. After the failure of the restoration, he left official life and devoted himself to his writing.

Kangi Sunka. *See* Crow Dog

Kangxi

aka: K'ang-Hsi
b. May 4, 1654
Beijing, China
d. December 20, 1722
Beijing, China
fields: Government and Politics

Emperor of China, 1669-1722. Kangxi was the fourth emperor of the Ching Dynasty that ruled China from 1644 to 1912. Blending knowledge and action in his leadership, he consolidated Manchu power and legitimated the Manchus' rule in China.

Kaniatario. *See* Handsome Lake

Kanishka

b. First or second century C.E.
probably west-central Asia
d. Probably second century C.E.
probably northern India
fields: Government and Politics, Religion and Theology, Patronage of the Arts

Kanishka, the greatest ruler of the Kushan Empire, administered an extensive realm that embraced much of modern India and Pakistan and parts of central Asia and China. Kanishka's patronage was responsible for the introduction of Mahayana Buddhism into China and for a remarkable flowering of Buddhist iconography.

Kano Yeitan Masanobu. *See* Fenollosa, Ernest Francisco

Kant, Immanuel

b. April 22, 1724
Königsberg, Prussia
d. February 12, 1804
Königsberg, Prussia
fields: Philosophy

Kant vindicated the authority of science while preserving the autonomy of morals by means of a new system of thought called critical or transcendental philosophy.

Kapitsa, Pyotr Leonidovich

b. July 9, 1894
Kronshtadt, Russia
d. April 8, 1984
Moscow, U.S.S.R.
fields: Physics, Invention and Technology

Kapitsa was both an experimental physicist and a brilliant designer of investigative and industrial equipment. As a tribute to the importance of his research at very low temperatures, he was awarded a Nobel Prize in Physics (1978) for his discovery of the superfluidity of liquid helium and for his invention of apparatuses for the liquefaction of helium and air.

Kaplan, Mordecai M.

full: Mordecai Menahem Kaplan
b. June 11, 1881
Lithuania
d. November 8, 1983
Bronx, New York
fields: Religion and Theology, Education

Mordecai Kaplan was a Conservative Jewish leader; born in Lithuania; immigrated to United States in 1889; graduated from City College of New York in 1900 and Columbia graduate school in 1902; ordained at the Jewish Theological Seminary in 1902, where he joined the faculty in 1909 and became dean of the teachers institute there in 1931; organized the first Jewish center in the United States, in New York, 1916; established the Society for the Advancement of Judaism in 1922; led the Reconstructionist movement, publishing *Judaism as a Civilization* (1934) and the biweekly *The Reconstructionist* (1935); also wrote Judaism in Transition (1936) and *Future of the American Jew* (1948).

Kapp, Joseph Robert

b. Mar. 19, 1938
Santa Fe, N.Mex.
fields: Sports (football player and coach)

Latino football player and coach. Although drafted by the Washington Redskins of NFL in 1959, quarterback Joseph Robert Kapp opted to play in the Canadian Football League (CFL). In 1967, he moved to the NFL and the Minnesota Vikings, leading them to a division title in 1968 and into the 1969 Super Bowl, which they lost after Kapp was injured and taken out of the game. After a contract dispute in 1971, Kapp filed suit against the NFL. In 1974, a U.S. District Court agreed with his claim that the league's policies violated antitrust laws, a decision that set an important precedent for dealings between players and team owners. After retirement, Kapp coached at the University of California at Berkeley.

Kapteyn, Jacobus Cornelius

b. Jan. 19, 1851
Barneveld, the Netherlands

d. June 18, 1922
Amsterdam, the Netherlands
fields: Astronomy

Jacobus Cornelius Kapteyn, in 1904, announced his discovery of "star streaming" at the International Congress of Science in St. Louis; helped organize the systematic collection and cataloging of basic stellar data; investigated the distribution and motions of stars in the system today called the Milky Way.

Karajan, Herbert von

b. April 5, 1908
Salzburg, Austro-Hungarian Empire
d. July 16, 1989
Anif, Austria
fields: Music

Karajan, the finest conductor of the postwar period, was the conductor of the Berlin Philharmonic Orchestra and was named conductor for life of that organization in 1955. He was also the head of the Vienna State Opera, of the Salzburg Festival, and of the Philharmonia Orchestra of London.

Karamanlis, Constantine

b. March 8, 1907
Küpköy (now Próti), Macedonia
d. April 23, 1998
Athens, Greece
fields: Government and Politics

Constantine Karamanlis was two-time prime minister (1955-1963, 1974-1980) and president (1980-1955, 1990-1995) of Greece. Avoided war with Turkey over island of Cyprus in 1970's; subordinated military to civilian control. Conducted 1974 referendum that abolished Greek monarchy.

Karami, Rashid

b. December 30, 1921
Tripoli, Lebanon
d. June 1, 1987
aboard a helicopter traveling from Tripoli to Beirut, Lebanon
fields: Government and Politics

Ten-time prime minister of Lebanon between 1955 and 1987, Rashid Karami was a principal figure in Lebanese politics for some thirty years. Both an Arab nationalist and advocate of Lebanese independence. Engineered cease-fire agreement in Lebanese civil war (1975-1976). Resisted implementation of 1983 Israel-Lebanon agreement after Israel's 1982 invasion of Lebanon. Killed by a bomb placed under his seat in a military helicopter.

Karan, Donna

né: Donna Faske
b. October 2, 1948
New York, New York
fields: Fashion, Business and Industry

By combining her talent for designing clothes with her sharp marketing skills, Donna Karan has built her Donna Karan Company into a multimillion dollar international business.

Karenga, Ron Ndabetta

né: Ronald Everett Karenga
aka: Maulana Ron Karenga
b. 1941
Maryland
fields: Social Reform

African American black nationalist; Ron Ndabetta Karenga founded the United Slaves (US) Cultural Organization (1965) and created the Kwanza holiday and the Kawaida movement. He believed in the power of black art and the need for a separate black aesthetic. While serving time in prison for assault (1971-1975), Karenga wrote many articles on subjects ranging from feminism to Pan-Africanism, which often appeared in *Black Scholar*. His books include *The Black Aesthetic* (1972), *Afro-American Nationalism* (1976), and *Introduction to Black Studies* (1982).

Käsebier, Gertrude

né: Gertrude Stanton
b. May 18, 1852
Des Moines, Iowa
d. October 13, 1934
New York, New York
fields: Photography

Käsebier, a celebrated pictorial photographer, was chosen by Alfred Stieglitz to be one of the founding members of the Photo-Secession, the most famous group of art photographers in the United States at the turn of the century.

Kashiwahara, Ken

b. July 18, 1940
Waimea, Kauai, Hawaii
fields: Journalism

Ken Kashiwahara, who graduated from San Francisco State University with a B.A. in broadcast communications in 1963, was ABC's correspondent in Southeast Asia in 1975 and Hong Kong bureau chief from 1975 to 1978. One of the last reporters to leave Vietnam at the end of the war, Kashiwahara became the San Francisco bureau chief for ABC News in 1978 after working as anchor and reporter for radio and television stations in Honolulu and Los Angeles. In 1986, he won an Emmy Award for a *20/20* segment.

Kaskabel. *See* Padilla, Benjamín

Katayama, Sen

b. 1859
Okayama Prefecture, Japan
d. 1933
Soviet Union
fields: Labor Movement, Government and Politics

Sen Katayama came to the United States to study theology, earning a B.D. from Yale in 1895 and returning to Japan two years later to help establish the country's first labor union. A recruiter and organizer for the Japanese Socialist Association, he established offices in San Francisco and Los Angeles in the early 1900's. He organized the Japanese Labor Federation of America 1915-1916. In 1919, he helped with the organization of the Communist Party of America. Three years later, to escape prosecution he fled to the Soviet Union. He was buried in the Kremlin.

Katlian

b. late 1700's
d. mid-1800's
fields: Warfare and Conquest, Native American Affairs

A Tlingit, Katlian led Tlingit resistance to the Russians in Alaska. The struggle was essentially a sporadic war against Russian freebooters and colonists in the present-day Alaska panhandle. Katlian Led a native raid in Sitka in 1799 that destroyed the first Russian fort in America.

Katsushika Hokusai. *See* Hokusai

Katz, Leandro

b. June 6, 1938
Buenos Aires, Argentina
fields: Art, Film

Latino artist and filmmaker. Leandro Katz moved to the United States in the mid-1960's and studied at the Pratt Graphic Arts Center in New York City from 1965 to 1967. His first U.S. exhibit was in 1964, and his work was later shown at such major museums as the Whitney Museum of American Art, the New Museum of Contemporary Art. He has taught at the School of Visual Arts in New York City, Brown University, and the New School of Social Research in New York City. Katz has won several awards, including a John Simon Guggenheim Memorial Fellowship in 1979.

Kauffmann, Angelica

b. October 30, 1741
Coire, Swiss Confederation
d. November 5, 1807
Rome
fields: Art

Refusing to accept the traditional role for the woman artist as a painter of portraits or still lifes, Kauffmann determined to become a history painter. An early exponent of neoclassicism, she produced some of the finest works done in this style, which helped greatly to popularize the movement throughout Europe and in England.

Kaufman, Chaya. *See* Durant, Ariel

Kaunda, Kenneth

full: Kenneth David Kaunda
b. April 28, 1924
Lubwa, Northern Rhodesia (now Zambia)
fields: Government and Politics

Kenneth Kaunda was an activist and advocate of Northern Rhodesian racial equality and independence from England in the 1950's and early 1960's. Involved in transition government, 1962-1964, briefly prime minister (1964), then elected first president of Zambia (independent Northern Rhodesia's new name) upon independence in October, 1964. Fought war with Southern Rhodesia in 1970's. Economic collapse in 1970's; rule became repressive in 1980's. Agreed to elections and was voted out of office in 1991.

Kautsky, Karl

b. October 16, 1854
Prague, Austro-Hungarian Empire
d. October 17, 1938
Amsterdam, the Netherlands
fields: Government and Politics

Austrian-born Marxist theoretician and author. From the 1890's to the outbreak of World War I (1914), Karl Kautsky was the most influential popularizer of Marxism in Europe. Later highly critical of new Russian Bolshevik government (1917) as not being socialist but establishing a new kind of class society utilizing terror.

Kawabata, Yasunari

b. June 11, 1899
Osaka, Japan
d. April 16, 1972
Zushi, Japan
fields: Literature

Kawabata was the first Japanese writer to be awarded the Nobel Prize in Literature (1968). Considered to be among the most Japanese of Japanese writers, he served as a critic and as a mentor for other writers as well.

Kawabe, Harry Sotaro

b. 1890
Maibara, near Osaka, Japan
d. 1969
fields: Business and Industry

Harry Sotaro Kawabe arrived in Seattle in 1905 and shortly thereafter bought and managed a small business. In 1909, he traveled to Alaska, eventually starting a prosperous steam laundry business. After being interned in a relocation camp during World War II, he returned to Seattle, becoming wealthy through real estate and an import/export business. His work toward improving Japanese-U.S. relations won him public recognition during the latter part of his life. In 1965, he started a company in Alaska that would supply Japan with needed natural resources.

Kawakami, Karl Kiyoshi

né: Kiyoshi Kawakami
b. 1879
Yamagata Prefecture, Japan
d. 1949
fields: Journalism

Socialist Karl Kiyoshi Kawakami immigrated to the United States in 1901 and earned a degree in political science from the University of Iowa. From 1914 to 1920, he headed the Pacific Press Bureau, a news agency operated by the Japanese government. His publications include *American-Japanese Relations: An Inside View of Japan's Policies and Purposes* (1912) and *Asia at the Door: A Study of the Japanese Question in Continental United States, Hawaii, and Canada* (1914). He wrote on behalf of Japanese immigrants in the United States, arguing that they could be completely assimilated, and spoke out against the harsh restrictions on Japanese immigration, including the Immigration Act of 1924. He also called for extending naturalization rights to Japanese immigrants.

Kawamura, Terry Teruo

b. December 10, 1949
Wahiawa, Oahu, Territory of Hawaii
d. March 20, 1969
Camp Radcliff, Republic of Vietnam
fields: Warfare and Conquest

Japanese American Terry Teruo Kawamura was attached to the 173d Engineer Company at Camp Radcliffe in Vietnam. He threw himself atop an explosive, saving the lives of several others in his unit but dying in the effort during an enemy raid. Kawamura was one of only 155 Vietnam veterans to earn the United States' highest military honor, the Congressional Medal of Honor.

Kawano, Jack

b. ?
Pahoa, Hawaii
d. 1984
California
fields: Labor Movement

Jack Kawano helped to found the Honolulu Longshoreman's Association, which merged with the International Longshoreman's and Warehouseman's Union (ILWU) in October of 1937. As an ILWU organizer Kawano helped increase the union's rolls from 970 members in 1944 to some 30,000 members by 1947. In 1951 Kawano provided testimony before the House Committee on Un-American Activities regarding connections between the ILWU and the Hawaii Communist Party. His testimony led to the conviction of the Hawaii Seven.

Kay, John

b. July 16, 1704
Park, Walmersley, near Bury, Lancashire, England
d. c. 1780-1781
France
fields: Invention and Technology

Kay invented the flying-shuttle which helped to mechanize the process of weaving and contributed to the Industrial Revolution.

Kay, Ulysses

b. January 7, 1917
Tucson, Ariz.
d. May 20, 1995
Englewood, N.J.
fields: Music (musician and composer)

African American musician and composer; Ulysses Kay has received many awards for compositions such as *A Short Overture* (1947), *The Boor* (1955), *Concerto for Orchestra* (1953), *Serenade for Orchestra* (1945), and *Sinfonia in E* (1951). He was a graduate of the Universities of Arizona and Rochester as well as being the recipient of various honorary doctorates.

Kay-Shuttleworth, First Baronet

full: James Phillips, First Baronet Kay-Shuttleworth
né: James Phillips Kay
aka: Sir James Phillips Kay-Shuttleworth
b. July 20, 1804
Rochdale, Lancashire, England
d. May 26, 1877
London, England
fields: Education, Government and Politics

One of the earliest civil servants appointed to office in the reformed British government, Kay-Shuttleworth helped to shape both the nature of elementary education and the methods of nineteenth century public administration.

Kayehtwanken (By What One Plants). *See* Cornplanter

Kazantzakis, Nikos

b. February 18, 1883
Heraklion, Crete
d. October 26, 1957
Freiburg, West Germany
fields: Literature

The best-known, most successful, and most controversial Greek writer of the twentieth century, Kazantzakis has written several of the most absorbing and enduring works of his time.

Kean, Edmund

b. November 4, 1787?
London, England
d. May 15, 1833
Richmond, England
fields: Theater and Entertainment

Kean's capacity to identify deeply and sympathetically with the characters he portrayed and his ability to communicate passion to his audiences established him as the foremost tragic actor of his day and assured the dominance of Romantic over classical acting techniques on the nineteenth century British stage.

Kearney, Denis

b. Feb. 1, 1847
Oakmount, Cork County, Ireland
d. Apr. 24, 1907
Alameda, Calif.
fields: Government and Politics

Denis Kearney, as leader of the Workingmen's Party of California during the late 1870's, participated in anti-Chinese and prowhite labor activities. At this time, California was experiencing both economic difficulties and increasing anti-Chinese sentiment. Anti-Chinese riots broke out in 1877, and shortly after, Kearney began promoting the new Workingmen's Party, made largely of white working class people. He attacked the Chinese, calling them morally unfit and a detriment to white labor. His acts contributed to the passage of the Chinese Exclusion Acts of 1882 and 1884. By the mid-1880's, the party was defunct and Kearny had returned to business affairs, although he continued to speak out against the Chinese.

Kearse, Amalya Lyle

b. June 11, 1939
Vauxhall, N.J.
fields: Law (federal judge)

African American federal judge. After becoming a partner in a Wall Street firm, Amalya Lyle Kearse was elected to serve a two-year term on the board of directors of the Legal Defense and Educational Fund of the National Association for the Advancement of Colored People (1977). Then, in 1979, President Jimmy Carter appointed Kearse to serve on the U.S. Court of Appeals, Second Circuit, New York City. She also served on the boards of the National Urban League, the Young Women's Christian Association (YWCA) of New York City, and Big Sisters, Inc.

Keaser, Lloyd Weldon

b. February 9, 1950
Pumphrey, Md.
fields: Sports (wrestler)

African American wrestler. In 1975 Lloyd Weldon Keaser won the Pan-American Games freestyle wrestling championship and the National Greco-Roman title. In the 1976 Olympics he took a silver medal as a lightweight.

Keating, Paul

full: Paul John Keating
b. January 18, 1944
Sydney, New South Wales, Australia
fields: Government and Politics

Prime minister of Australia from 1993 to 1996. Paul Keating was treasurer of government of Robert Hawke from 1983 to 1991; instituted reforms to deal with serious economic recession. In 1991 took over Labor Party leadership from Hawke. As prime minister, supported land rights for Australian Aborigines and stronger ties with Asia. Unpopular with general public. Defeated by Liberal Party in 1996 elections.

Keats, John

b. October 31, 1795
London, England
d. February 23, 1821
Rome, Italy
fields: Literature

Keats, whose works explore the significance of beauty, joy, and imagination in a world of suffering and death, was one of the great poets of the Romantic era and is generally acknowledged to be among the finest writers of personal correspondence in English.

Keith, Damon Jerome

b. July 4, 1922
Detroit, Mich.
fields: Law (federal judge)

African American federal judge. From 1958 to 1963 Damon Jerome Keith was a member of the Wayne County Board of Supervisors, and starting in 1964, he served as chairman of the Michigan Civil Rights Commission. In 1967 President Lyndon B. Johnson appointed Keith to the post of U.S. district judge for the Eastern District of Michigan. President Jimmy Carter appointed Keith to serve as U.S. circuit judge for the Sixth Circuit of the U.S. Court of Appeals (covering Kentucky, Michigan, Ohio, and Tennessee) in 1978.

Keller, Helen

full: Helen Adams Keller
b. June 27, 1880
Tuscumbia, Alabama
d. June 1, 1968
Westport, Connecticut
fields: Social Reform, Education

Blind and deaf since early childhood, Keller exemplified by her life of activism the full empowerment potential of disabled persons who receive appropriate adaptive education. She served as a spokesperson and fund-raiser for the benefit of deaf and blind people.

Kelley, Florence

b. September 12, 1859
Philadelphia, Pennsylvania
d. February 17, 1932
Philadelphia, Pennsylvania
fields: Social Reform, Women's Rights

A longtime campaigner for maximum-hour and minimum-wage legislation, Florence Kelley served as chief factory inspector of Illinois and as general secretary of the National Consumers' League.

Kelley, William Melvin

b. November 1, 1937
Bronx, N.Y.
fields: Literature

African American author and playwright; William Melvin Kelley was the recipient of both the Rosenthal Foundation Award (1963) and Harvard's Dana Reed Prize (1960). He also received the Black Academy of Arts and Letters Prize for *Dunfords Travels Everywheres* (1970). His other works include *A Different Drummer* (1962), *Dancers on the Shore* (1964), *A Drop of Patience* (1965), and *dem* (1967).

Kellogg, Frank B.

full: Frank Billings Kellogg
b. December 22, 1856
Potsdam, New York
d. December 21, 1937
St. Paul, Minnesota
fields: Diplomacy

U.S. senator from Minnesota (1917-1923), then secretary of state under president Coolidge from 1925 to 1929. With French diplomat Aristide Briand, responsible for 1928 Kellogg-Briand Pact. Winner of 1929 Nobel Peace Prize. From 1930 to 1935 served on the Permanent Court of International Justice (the World Court).

Kelly, Jim

b. May 5, 1946
Paris, Ky.
fields: Theater and Entertainment, Sports

African American actor; Jim Kelly used his experience as an international middleweight karate champion (1971) to further his career in martial arts and action films of the 1970's. Some of his better known films include *Enter the Dragon* (1973), *Black Belt Jones* (1974), and *Black Samurai* (1977).

Kelly, Leontine

b. March 5, 1920
Washington, D.C.
fields: Religion and Theology

African American clergywoman; Leontine Kelly entered the ministry in 1969. She became the first black woman to be elected bishop of the United Methodist Church in 1984. Kelly was honored with the Southern Christian Leadership Conference "Drum Major for Justice" award in 1987 for her.

Kelly, Leroy

b. May 20, 1942
Philadelphia, Pa.
fields: Sports (football)

African American running back for the Cleveland Browns. In 1967 and 1968 Leroy Kelly led the National Football League in rushing, 1,205 yards and 1,239 yards respectively. Over the course of his ten year career as a professional, Kelly gained 7,274 yards, had twenty-seven 100-yard rushing games, and went to the Pro Bowl for six straight years, from 1966 to 1971.

Kelly, Patrick

b. September 24, c. 1954
Vicksburg, Miss.
d. January 1, 1990
Paris, France
fields: Fashion (fashion designer)

African American fashion designer; Patrick Kelly, who launched a special line as part of a multimillion dollar deal with Warnaco, became the first American elected to the Chambre Syndicale du Prete-a-Porter, an association of fashion's elite in Paris, France, in 1988.

Kelly, Paula

b. October 21, 1943
Jacksonville, Fla.
fields: Theater and Entertainment

African American actress, singer, and dancer; Paula Kelly graduated from the High School for Performing Arts in New York City and the Juilliard School of Music. For her role in *Sweet Charity*, 1968, she won England's Variety Award for Best Supporting Actress in a Musical. Her film credits include the film version of *Sweet Charity* (1969), *The Andromeda Strain* (1971), *Trouble Man* (1972), and *Uptown Saturday Night* (1974).

Kelly, Sharon Pratt

né: Sharon Pratt
aka: Sharon Pratt Dixon
b. Jan. 30, 1944
Washington, D.C.
fields: Government and Politics

African American politician; Sharon Pratt Dixon was the first African American woman to be elected mayor of a major U.S. city; the first native of Washington, D.C., to serve as mayor, Dixon defeated Marion Barry in the 1990 mayoral race. In 1991, she married James Kelly. She finished third to Barry in the 1994 mayoral primary election.

Kelvin, Lord

né: William Thomson
aka: Sir William Thomson
b. June 26, 1824
Belfast, Ireland
d. December 17, 1907
Largs, Scotland
fields: Physics

Kelvin contributed fundamentally to the mid-nineteenth century revolution in physics.

Kemal, Mustafa. *See* Atatürk, Kemal

Kemble, Fanny

full: Farancis Anne Kemble
b. November 27, 1809
London, England
d. January 15, 1893
London, England
fields: Theater and Entertainment (drama), Social Reform

Kemble was one of the finest actresses on the British and American stage. Her *Journal of a Residence on a Georgian Plantation in 1838-1839* is one of the best firsthand accounts of slavery in the United States.

Kemp, Shawn T.

b. November 26, 1969
Elkhart, Ind.
fields: Sports (basketball player)

African American basketball player; in 1989, Shawn T. Kemp, one of only a handful of players in NBA history who had never played on a college basketball team, was drafted by the Seattle Supersonics; played in the All Star games in 1993, 1994, and 1995, and was a member of the 1994 Dream Team II.

Kenan, Randall G.

b. March 12, 1963
Brooklyn, N.Y.
fields: Literature

African American writer; Randall G. Kenan wrote a novel, *A Visitation of Spirits* (1989), and a short-story collection, *Let the Dead Bury Their Dead and Other Stories* (1992). In 1999, he published *Walking on Water: Black American Lives at the Turn of the Twenty-first Century*.

Kendall, Edward Calvin

b. Mar. 8, 1886
South Norwalk, Connecticut
d. May 4, 1972
Princeton, New Jersey
fields: Chemistry, Physiology

In 1914 Edward Calvin Kendall discovered the thyroid hormone thyroxine; in 1949 discovered the adrenal steroid cortisone; in 1950, awarded the Nobel Prize in Physiology or Medicine.

Kendrew, John Cowdery

b. Mar. 24, 1917
Oxford, England
d. August 23, 1997
Cambridge, England
fields: Biology, Chemistry

Using X-ray diffraction, John Cowdery Kendrew determined the three-dimensional structure of the protein myoglobin; in 1962, received the Nobel Prize in Chemistry with Max Perutz.

Kendrick, Eddie

né: Eddie Kendricks
b. December 17, 1939
Union Springs, Ala.
d. October 5, 1992
Birmingham, Ala.
fields: Music

African American singer and songwriter; Eddie Kendrick was an original member of the Primes, which later became the Temptations. After hits such as "The Way You Do the Things You Do" (1964) with the Temptations, Kendrick began a solo career in 1971. "Can I" (1971), "If You Let Me" (1972), and the number one "Keep on Trucking'" (1973) are among his hit singles. His reunion with the Temptations in 1982 produced the top-ten album *Standing on the Top*, which included a number-one single of the same title.

Kennan, George F.

full: George Frost Kennan
b. February 16, 1904
Milwaukee, Wisconsin
fields: Diplomacy

George F. Kennan was a U.S. diplomat, historian, and expert on Russia. He spent two years in the Soviet Union, working for the U.S. Foreign Service, at the end of World War II. Wrote many books, including *Russia Leaves the War* (1956), the first volume of his *Soviet-American Relations, 1917-1920*; it was the first of two to win Pulitzer Prizes.

Kennedy, Anthony

full: Anthony McLeod Kennedy
b. 1936
fields: Law

U.S. Supreme Court justice, began tenure in 1988; appointed by President Reagan. Expanded administrative search exception to warrant requirement to individuals. Significant opinions: *Skinner v. Railway Labor Executives' Association*, 489 U.S. 602 (1989); *Illinois v. Perkins*, 496 U.S. 292 (1990).

Kennedy, Jacqueline. *See* Onassis, Jacqueline Kennedy

Kennedy, John F.

full: John Fitzgerald Kennedy
b. May 29, 1917
Brookline, Massachusetts
d. November 22, 1963
Dallas, Texas
fields: Government and Politics

Combining intelligence with personal charm, Kennedy became a model to millions around the globe, inspiring them to seek new goals and to work toward those goals with self-confidence. Thirty-fifth president of the United States, 1961-1963. He was assassinated in Dallas, Texas.

Kennedy, Leon Isaac

b. 1949
Cleveland, Ohio
fields: Theater and Entertainment

African American actor; Leon Isaac Kennedy is best known for hi roles in *Penitentiary* (1979), *Penitentiary II* (1982), and *Penitentiary III* (1987) as an underdog boxer. He also played this part in the 1981 remake film *Body and Soul*. Kennedy appeared in *Hollywood Vice Squad* (1986) and *Too Scared to Scream* (1982) and starred in *Knights of the City* in 1987.

Kennedy, Robert F.

full: Robert Francis Kennedy
b. November 20, 1925
Brookline, Massachusetts
d. June 6, 1968
Los Angeles, California
fields: Government and Politics

Kennedy served his brother President John Kennedy as an able and active attorney general; he passionately advocated justice and equality for minorities and the poor in the United States. He was the leading Democratic candidate in the 1968 presidential election campaign when he was assassinated in Los Angeles, by Sirhan Sirhan.

Kennedy, Royal

b. ?
fields: Journalism, Television

African American journalist. After working as a general assignment reporter and local newscast anchor at WDSU-TV in New Orleans in 1971, Royal Kennedy moved to WKYC-TV in 1973, where she won a Cleveland Emmy for "outstanding individual achievement." In 1975 she moved to WMAQ-TV, where, among other things, she anchored local newscasts during the *Today* show telecasts. Though named as an ABC News Chicago correspondent in April of 1978, Kennedy moved to the Los Angeles affiliate of ABC the same year.

Kennedy, Ted

full: Edward Moore Kennedy
b. February 22, 1932
Boston, Massachusetts
fields: Government and Politics

One of the most prominent of U.S. senators, Edward "Ted" Kennedy inherited a political legacy and tradition of public service from his father Joe and mother Rose, becoming a U.S. senator from Massachusetts on November 6, 1962, when he took the seat left vacant by his brother John Fitzgerald, the new president. His other brother, Robert F. Kennedy, became attorney general. He worked hard at being a senator and produced a solid, consistently liberal voting record. The assassinations of his brothers made him heir to the Kennedy tradition, but in July, 1969, he drove his car off a bridge on Chappaquiddick Island, resulting in the death of a young woman, Mary Jo Kopechne. His failure to make a timely report of the accident or to explain his actions severely damaged any presidential aspirations he might have held. Nevertheless, he became both the patriarch of the Kennedy dynasty and the leading symbol of American liberalism as the twentieth century ended, championing liberal causes such as the elimination of poverty, labor issues, and equal rights.

Kennekuk

aka: Kickapoo Prophet
b. c. 1785
along Osage River in Ill.
d. 1852
along Missouri River in present-day Kans.
fields: Government and Politics, Diplomacy, Native American Affairs, Religion and Theology (shaman)

Native American leader. Leader of the peaceful Northern Kickapoo, Kennekuk managed to delay his tribe's relocation for several years (from 1819 to 1833). Advocated return to traditional ways and abstention from alcohol. Urged his tribe to reach a state of holiness and thereby achieve an earthly paradise.

Kent, George E.

b. May 31, 1920
Columbus, Ga.
d. 1982
fields: Education

African American educator; George E. Kent graduated with a B.A. from Savannah State College (1941) and received his M.A. (1948) and Ph.D. (1953) from Boston University. He is the author of *Blackness and the Adventure of Western Culture* (1972) and *A Life of Gwendolyn Brooks* (1989). Kent served as a professor and dean at Delaware State College from 1949 to 1960 and joined the faculty of the University of Chicago in 1969.

Kent, James

b. July 31, 1763
Fredericksburg, New York
d. December 12, 1847
New York, New York
fields: Law

Kent acquired renown as a legal scholar of profound intellect from his law lectures, written judicial opinions, and four-volume *Commentaries on American Law* (1826-1830). His work set the standard by which subsequent legal and constitutional scholarship in the United States was measured.

Kent, Rockwell

pseud. Hogarth, Jr.
b. June 21, 1882
Tarrytown Heights, New York
d. March 13, 1971
Plattsburgh, New York
fields: Art

Rockwell Kent first gained renown through such travel books as *Wilderness* (1920), *Voyaging Southward from the Strait of Magellan* (1924), and *N by E* (1930). Meanwhile, he became a commercial artist, illustrated books, and was a contributing editor of *Colophon* and editor of *Creative Art*. He also tried to organize an artists' union and was president of the International Workers Order, an allegedly communist group. In 1939 he was charged as a communist by the House Committee on Un-American Activities, which later linked him to eighty left-wing groups. In 1960 he gave the Soviet Union many of his paintings and drawings. When the Soviet government awarded him the Lenin Peace Prize in 1967, he donated the money to North Vietnam. Kent also supported the National Association for the Advancement of Colored People.

Kenyatta, Jomo

né: Kamau Ngengi
b. c. 1984
Ichaweri, British East Africa
d. August 22, 1978
Mombasa, Kenya
fields: Government and Politics

Kenyatta wrote the first scholarly book on indigenous African culture from an African perspective, entitled *Facing Mount Kenya: The Tribal Life of Gikuyu* (1938). He became the first Prime Minister of the Republic of Kenya and the symbol of national unity.

Keokuk

b. c. 1783
Saukenuk, modern Rock Island, Ill.
d. Apr., 1848
Franklin County near Pomona, Kans.
fields: Native American Affairs, Diplomacy

Native American leader. Keokuk led the peace band of Sauk in the Rock River Valley of Illinois. Was willing to exchange Sauk and Fox land for personal gain. In 1820's, U.S. government Indian agents promoted the ambitions of Keokuk for prestige among his people. After the Black Hawk War of 1832, emerged as dominant Sauk figure. Negotiated a treaty in which the Sauk, Fox, and Winnebago sold much of their land west of the Mississippi. The Sauk and Fox nations were left with a small reservation along the Iowa River. Participated in 1837 negotiations in which 26.5 million acres of Indian land were ceded to the United States. In 1845, sold the remaining Sauk lands in Iowa, and the Sauks were forced to relocate in Kansas.

Kepler, Johannes

b. December 27, 1571
Weil der Stadt, Swabia
d. November 15, 1630
Regensburg, Bavaria
fields: Astronomy, Physics

Through the application of his exceptional intellect, faith, and tenacity, Kepler created the science of modern astronomy and provided the solid foundation upon which Isaac Newton built his laws of universal gravitation.

Kerensky, Aleksandr Fyodorovich

b. May 2, 1881
Simbirsk (now Ulyanovsk), Russia
d. June 11, 1970
New York, New York
fields: Government and Politics

Kerensky was the leading figure in the short-lived Provisional Government that replaced the deposed Czar Nicholas II and was in turn displaced by the Bolshevik (Communist) Party of Vladimir Ilich Lenin during the Russian Revolution of 1917. He attempted unsuccessfully to establish a liberal democratic government in Russia.

Kerouac, Jack

full: Jean Louis Debris de Kerouac
b. March 12, 1922
Lowell, Massachusetts
d. October 21, 1969
St. Petersburg, Florida
fields: Literature

Kerouac was one of the major figures of the Beat movement in the United States, a literary and cultural reaction against Cold War America. Although Kerouac viewed himself as a naturalistic novelist in the tradition of Thomas Wolfe and William Faulkner, literary and social critics generally view him as one of the more dramatic examples of American countercultural artistic expression, especially in novels such as *On the Road* and *The Dharma Bums*.

Kerr, Louise Año Nuevo

b. Dec. 24, 1938
Denver, Colo.
fields: Education

Latina educator and administrator. Louise Año Nuevo Kerr earned a Ph.D. in history from the University of Illinois, Chicago, in 1976. She taught at Loyola University in Chicago from 1973 to 1980, then became an assistant dean. In 1988, Kerr was named associate vice chancellor for academic affairs at the University of Illinois, Chicago. She became the chair of the Committee on Decent and Unbiased Campaign Tactics in 1989. Besides publishing her own scholarly articles, Kerr helped edit *Aztlan: International Journal of Chicano Studies* from 1981 to 1985. She won the Congressional Hispanic Caucus Humanities Award in 1979.

Kesselring, Albert

b. November 20, 1885
Marktsteft, Germany
d. July 16, 1960
Bad Nauheim, West Germany
fields: Military Affairs

Kesselring was one of Germany's more effective military commanders during World War II, particularly during the 1943-1944 Italian Campaign. He was instrumental in building the *Luftwaffe* into a viable component of the German war machine.

Kevorkian, Jack

b. May 26, 1928
Pontiac, Mich.
fields: Social Reform, Medicine

Known as Dr. Death, Jack Kevorkian advocated the legalization of physician assisted suicide by publicizing the deaths of his patients whom he helped to die. Between 1990 and 1998, he had assisted in at least ninety-three suicides of terminally ill patients and had been arrested and jailed several times. He was twice acquitted of murder by juries after acting as his own defense attorney; his third trial, however, ended with his conviction in March, 1999, on charges of second-degree murder. Sentenced to ten to twenty-five years in prison, he promised to appeal the case all the way to the Supreme Court.

Key, Francis Scott

b. August 1, 1779
Frederick County (now Carroll County), Maryland
d. January 11, 1843
Baltimore, Maryland
fields: Law, Music

Key is most widely known as the author of the song "The Star-Spangled Banner," which became the national anthem of the United States in 1931.

Keyes, Alan

b. Aug. 7, 1950
New York, N.Y.
fields: Government and Politics

Public speaker, newspaper columnist, and author; Alan Keyes represented the United States on the United Nations Economic and Social Council (1981-1987); was president of Citizens Against Government Waste; in 1996 was a black candidate for the Republican presidential nomination; published *Masters of the Dream: The Strength and Betrayal of Black America* (1995).

Keynes, John Maynard

b. June 5, 1883
Cambridge, England
d. April 21, 1946
Tilton, Sussex, England
fields: Economics

Keynes's seminal work, *The General Theory of Employment, Interest, and Money*, created a school that dominated economic thought in the mid-twentieth century and that continues to exercise a potent influence. Concern for world economic health, however, made him equally important in the arena of public affairs from World War I to the creation of the International Monetary Fund and World Bank after World War II.

Keyser, Louisa. *See* Datsolalee

Khachaturian, Aram

b. June 6, 1903
Tiflis, Russian Empire (later Tbilisi, Georgia)
d. May 1, 1978
Moscow, Soviet Union
fields: Music

A Soviet composer, Aram Khachaturian fell established his popularity as the composer of such popular works as the *Violin Concerto* (1940) and the ballet *Gayane* (1942). In 1948 he was named one of the offenders when the Soviet government's Central Committee published a report on the dire state of Soviet music. He was forced to confess his alleged errors and nervously blamed bad advice from critics and a preoccupation with technique. After dictator Joseph Stalin's death in 1953, he argued for greater creative freedom for Soviet artists.

Khan, Ali Akbar

b. Apr. 14, 1922
Shivpur, India, now Bangladesh
fields: Music

Ali Akbar Khan, along with his brother-in-law Ravi Shankar, is known for his popularization of Indian classical music in the United States and elsewhere. He studied the sarod (a long-necked plucked, fretless lute with four melody strings, four drone strings, two rhythm strings, and fifteen resonating strings). Khan debuted as a performer in 1936 and began performing abroad in the 1950's. He founded a second branch of the Ali Akbar Khan College of Music in San Rafael, California, in 1967. Khan coauthored *The Classical Music of North India* (1991), a 367-page introductory text.

Khan, Chaka

né: Yvette Marie Stevens
b. March 23, 1953
Great Lakes, Ill.
fields: Music

African American singer and songwriter; Chaka Khan got her start in the jazz clubs of Chicago, where she later became the singer for Ask Rufus. The group's first major crossover hit, "Tell Me Something Good," a gold record, also won a Grammy for best vocal performance in 1974. Another gold record followed, *Rags to Rufus* (1974). Though she continued to record with Rufus, Khan went solo in 1978, releasing hits such as *I Feel for You* (1984) and the single, "Own the Night" (1985).

Khan, Fazal Muhammad

b. 1910
Punjab, India, now Pakistan
d. Apr. 28, 1972
Butte City, Calif.
fields: Business and Industry

Despite alien land laws, Fazal Muhammad Khan became a highly successful rice farmer in Northern California's Butte County. Khan, a Punjabi, arrived in California in 1926, beginning work as a farm laborer. Three years later, he became the partner of Babu and Naimet Khan who had been rice farmers in Butte County since 1916. The Khans leased and later bought more than four thousand acres of rice-producing land to become one of the larger rice-growing operations in the northern Sacramento Valley. They got around the alien land laws by leasing and buying the land in the name of their attorney, transferring the property into their own names after laws passed in 1946 made it possible for South Asians to become naturalized. Khan became a prominent member of the Pakistani American community, heading the Muslim Association and the Pakistan-America Association and helping found the Muslim mosque in Sacramento, as well as a prominent member of the farming community.

Khan, Mubarak Ali

b. ?
fields: Government and Politics

A farmer and community spokesperson, Mubarak Ali Khan and his associates gathered five thousand signatures from U.S. citizens in support of Asian Indian naturalization rights. Khan arrived in the United States in 1913, settling in a farming community near Phoenix, Arizona. He founded the India Welfare League to assist unemployed Asian Indians in 1937 and advocate their naturalization rights. After the passage of the Luce-Celler Bill of 1946, Khan turned his attention to India, supporting Muslim demands for the separate nation of Pakistan. He created the Pakistan Welfare League of America to present his case to the American public. After the 1947 creation of Pakistan, Khan continued to educate Americans about South Asia and to improve understanding between the peoples of Pakistan and the United States.

Khaury, Herbert. *See* Tiny Tim

Khomeini, Ayatollah

né: Ruhollah Musawi
aka: Ruhollah Khomeini
b. September 24, 1902
Khomein, Iran
d. June 3, 1989
Tehran, Iran
fields: Religion and Theology, Government and Politics

Ruhollah Khomeini was exiled for sixteen years after speaking against the rule of Shah Mohammed Reza Pahlevi in 1963. From France and Iraq he rallied an opposition force that overthrew the Shah in 1979. His theocratic government supported the 1979 seizure of the U.S. embassy and the taking of hostages by militant Iranian students. In 1989 he issued a death warrant against British author Salman Rushdie, whose novel *The Satanic Verses* had been judged blasphemous.

Khosrow I

aka: Chosroes
b. c. 510
probably Ctesiphon, Mesopotamia
d. 579
probably Ctesiphon, Mesopotamia
fields: Government and Politics, Warfare and Conquest

Ruler of Persia, 531-579. Through courage and shrewd practical intelligence, Khosrow I restored and revitalized the threatened Sassanian monarchy, bringing Persian civilization to a peak of wealth, prestige, and security. He also introduced administrative, civil, and military innovations that radically transformed government; thus he earned the title "Anushirvan" (of the Immortal Spirit).

Khrushchev, Nikita S.

full: Nikita Sergeyevich Khrushchev
b. April 17, 1894
Kalinovka, Russia
d. September 11, 1971
Moscow, U.S.S.R.
fields: Government and Politics

Khrushchev ruled the Soviet Union for a tumultuous decade, during which he began de-Stalinization and released millions of his countrymen from the Siberian Gulag. In foreign affairs, the Sino-Soviet split, the suppression of the Hungarian Revolution of 1956, and the Cuban Missile Crisis characterized his time in power.

Khurram. *See* Shah Jahan

Khwārizmī, al-

full: Muḥammad ibn Mūsā al-Khwārizmī
b. c. 780
place unknown
d. c. 850
possibly Baghdad
fields: Mathematics, Astronomy, Geography

Al-Khwārizmī is the author of several important mathematical works. The Latin translations of his writings introduced the concepts of algebra and Hindu-Arabic numerals into the mathematics of medieval Europe. He also compiled a set of astronomical tables widely used in the Islamic Near East.

Kiang, Peter Nien-chu

b. ?
fields: Education, Sociology

Peter Nien-chu Kiang received an Ed.D. degree from the Harvard University Graduate School of Education in 1991. He teaches and publishes on multicultural education and Asian American studies. He made videos and films on the Asian American experience, including *Cahoon Hollow* (1979), an animated work that explored the legacy of the Vietnam War and was exhibited at the Asian American International Film Festival in 1980. From 1980 to 1986 he directed the Boston-based Asian American Resource Workshop, which sponsors educational, cultural, and community advocacy programs for Asian Americans throughout New England.

Kickapoo Prophet. *See* Kennekuk

Kicking Bear

b. fl. latter 1800's
fields: Government and Politics, Religion and Theology, Native American Affairs

An Oglala and Miniconjou Sioux, Kicking Bear fought in the battles of the Little Bighorn (1876) and Rosebud, and in the Black Hills War of 1876-1877. Became an apostle of Wovoka and his Ghost dance religion in the 1880's. Ghost Dance leaders claimed that wearing Ghost Dance shirts would protect the wearers from bullets shot by white men. The Ghost Dance religion essentially died on December 29, 1890, with the massacre at Wounded Knee.

Kicking Bird

aka: Tene-angop'te
aka: Watohkonk
aka: Eagle Striking with Talons
b. c. 1835
Central Plains
d. May 3, 1875
Cache Creek, Okla.
fields: Government and Politics, Peace Advocacy, Native American Affairs

Native American leader. Kicking Bird, a Kiowa leader, earned early reputation as a warrior but led a peace faction during the 1870's Indian wars on the central Plains. Signed Treaty of Little Arkansas River (1865), Treaty of Medicine Lodge (1867).

Kid Chocolate. *See* Sardiñas, Eligio

Kid Frost

né: Arturo Molina, Jr.
b. May 31, 1964
Los Angeles, Calif.
fields: Music (rapper)

Mexican American rapper. Raised in East Los Angeles, Kid Frost was a gang member and low rider before his 1990 single "La Raza," from the album *Hispanic Causing Panic*, became a hit. In 1991, he formed Latin Alliance, a group of rappers of Central American, Cuban, Mexican, and Puerto Rican descent who believe that rap music can act as a unifying force in Latino culture. In 1995, he released *Smile Now, Die Later*.

Kidd, William

b. c. 1645; Greenock, Scotland
d. May 23, 1701; London, England
fields: Government and Politics, Military Affairs

At the time of his death, Kidd was probably the most notorious pirate of the age, but he was also a victim of the changing political and administrative practices of an increasingly modern age.

Kido, Saburo

b. 1902
Hilo, Territory of Hawaii
d. April 4, 1977
fields: Civil Rights

Saburo Kido was cofounder and wartime president of the Japanese American Citizens League (JACL). In the late 1920's, he helped found the New American Citizens League and, as its president, attended the Seattle convention that produced the Japanese American Citizens League in 1930. He was elected president of the JACL in 1940, and his pro-government policy during World War II and the Japanese American internment caused him to be labeled a collaborator.

Kierkegaard, Søren

full: Søren Aabye Kierkegaard
b. May 5, 1813
Copenhagen, Denmark
d. November 11, 1855
Copenhagen, Denmark
fields: Philosophy, Religion and Theology

Søren Kierkegaard's challenge to neat systems of philosophical thought, such as that propounded by Georg Wilhelm Friedrich Hegel, has highlighted his philosophical influence. His predominant assumption, that existence is too multiform to be systematized, created the fabric around which existentialism, and indeed much of Continental philosophy, have been woven.

Kikuchi, Charles

b. 1917
d. Sept. 25, 1988
fields: Social Reform

In 1941, Charles Kikuchi started graduate school in social welfare at the University of California, Berkeley. After the Japanese attacked Pearl Harbor, the Japanese American Evacuation and Resettlement Study, led by Berkeley sociologist Dorothy Swaine Thomas, hired Kikuchi as a researcher. He began to keep a diary, a section of which was published in 1973 as *The Kikuchi Diary: Chronicle of an American Concentration Camp*. At the Tanforan Assembly Center, a temporary detention center in Northern California, and at the Gila River relocation center in Arizona, Kikuchi conducted field surveys. He also recorded the resettlement of camp residents to homes in Chicago. After a stint in the military, he became a social worker with the New York Veterans Administration in 1950, staying in that position until his retirement in 1973.

Kikuchi, Yuriko. *See* Yuriko

Kiliahote. *See* Wright, Allen

Killens, John Oliver

b. January 14, 1916
Macon, Ga.
d. October 27, 1987
Brooklyn, N.Y.
fields: Literature

African American novelist, dramatist, essay writer, and university lecturer; John Oliver Killens wrote plays, *Lower Than the Angels* (pr. 1965) and *Cotillion* (pr. 1975), adapted from his novel, and screenplays, *Odds Against Tomorrow* (1959), written with Nelson Gidding and *Slaves* (1969), written with Herbert J. Biberman, as well as well respected novels such as *Youngblood* (1954), *And Then We Heard the Thunder* (1963), and *The Cotillion: Or, One Good Bull Is Half the Herd* (1971), the latter two being Pulitzer Prize nominees.

Killy, Jean-Claude

b. August 30, 1943
Saint Cloud, France
fields: Sports (skiing)

Killy dominated men's international Alpine skiing competitions from 1965 through 1968. He will also be remembered as the second skier in Olympic history to sweep the Alpine events.

Kim, Bok-lim C.

b. 1930
fields: Sociology, Historiography

In her works, Bok-lim C. Kim described Korean American sociological experiences and history. She wrote *The Asian Americans: Changing Patterns, Changing Needs* (1978) and was a contributing author for *Women in Shadows: A Handbook for Service Providers Working with Asian Wives of U.S. Military Personnel* (1981).

Kim, Charles

né: Kim Ho
b. May 25, 1884
Korea
d. Jan. 5, 1968
fields: Business and Industry, Philanthropy

Charles Kim (born Kim Ho) arrived in the United States in 1914 and settled in California's San Joaquin Valley. He and a friend, Harry Kim (Kim Hyung-soon), established the Kim Brothers Company, which was active in fruit cultivation and distribution as well as nursery management. The business was profitable, and the Kims began donating generously to the Korean American community. Charles Kim chaired the United Korean Committee, which supported the Korean Provisional government, and cofounded the Korean Foundation, which provided scholarships to Korean American students.

Kim, Elaine H.

b. Feb. 26, 1942
New York, N.Y.
fields: Literature, Sociology

Elaine H. Kim, one of the first tenured Asian American women at a major U.S. university, is a specialist in Asian American studies. She wrote *Asian American Literature: An Introduction to the Writings and Their Social Context* (1982) and coedited *Making Waves: An Anthology of Writings by and About Asian American Women* (1989) and *Writing Self, Writing Nation: A Collection of Essays on Theresa Hak Kyung Cha's "Dictee"* (1993). Kim helped found Asian Immigrant Advocates and Asian Women United of California and is a former president of the Association for Asian American Studies.

Kim, Ernie

b. Sept. 2, 1918
Manteca, Calif.
fields: Art

Korean American Ernie Kim is an award-winning ceramist who was graduated from the Ceramics Craft Studio in Mountain View in 1955. He chaired the ceramics department at the San Francisco Art Institute and directed the Richmond Art Center.

Kim, Eugene Eun-Chol

b. May 5, 1928
Wonsan, Korea
fields: Sociology

Eugene Eun-Chol Kim arrived in the United States in 1965, becoming professor of education and ethnic studies and program director of Asian American Studies at California State University, Sacramento. Kim wrote *American Mosaic: Selected Readings for America's Multicultural Heritage* (1993) and *Strangers to This Land: Interdisciplinary Perspective on Ethnic Studies* (1986) and coauthored *A Resource Guide for Secondary School Teaching: Planning for Competence* (1990).

Kim, Haeryen

b. July 14, 1948
Iri Chonpuk, Republic of Korea
fields: Theater and Entertainment

Haeryen Kim moved to the United States in 1985 and studied theater at New York University. Three years later, she founded two Korean American theater companies in New York City: The Seoul Theatre Ensemble, which drew on traditional Korean theater techniques and cultural themes, and the Educational Theatre for Asian Teenagers, which used experimental theater techniques, such as oral histories, collaborative scriptwriting, improvisation, and audience participation. Through The Silk Road, an umbrella organization formed of the two companies, Kim produced intercultural works such as *America Far-Merica* (1988), *Joyness of the Youth* (1989), *Sesame Leaves . . . Sleepwalking in Korea* (1990), and *Peony* (1991). At the LaMama Experimental Theatre Club in New York City, her company produced the dance drama *Deungsinbul*, about the self-immolation of a Korean monk.

Kim, Hyung-chan

b. Nov. 4, 1938
fields: Sociology

Hyung-chan Kim, who received a B.A. from Hankuk University of Foreign Studies in Seoul, South Korea (1961), and B.A. (1964), M.A. (1965), and Ed.D. (1969) degrees from George Peabody College for Teachers, made a major contribution to Asian American studies through his reference works and studies. His works include the *Dictionary of Asian American History* (1986), *Asian Americans and the Supreme Court: A Documentary History* (1992), and *A Legal History of Asian Americans, 1790-1990* (1994). He also edited *Asian American Studies: An Annotated Bibliography and Research Guide* (1989).

Kim Il Sung

né: Kim Song Ju
b. April 15, 1912
near Pyongyang, Korea
d. July 8, 1994
Pyongyang, North Korea
fields: Government and Politics

Kim Il Sung joined the Korean Communist Party in 1931. The following year he led a small anti-Japanese guerrilla regime. In 1946 the Soviet Union installed Kim at the head of a provisional government in northern Korea. Kim was premier of the Democratic People's Republic of Korea from 1948 to 1994. In 1972 he became president as well. With Soviet backing, Kim started the Korean War (1950-1953) by invading the South.

Kim, Illsoo

b. 1944
fields: Sociology

Illsoo Kim, who has a doctoral degree from the Graduate Center of the City University of New York, extensively researched the Korean community of New York. Kim's publications include *New Urban Immigrants: The Korean Community in New York* (1981), *The Koreans: Small Business in an Urban Frontier* (1987), and *Immigrants to Urban America: The Korean Community in the New York Metropolitan Area* (1991).

Kim, Jay C.

né: Kim Chang Joon
b. March 27, 1939
Seoul, Korea
fields: Government and Politics

Jay C. Kim helped found and served as president of the Korean American Political Association. In 1990, Kim was elected to a seat on the Diamond Bar, California, city council. In 1992 he became the first Asian immigrant to win election to the U.S. Congress. In 1994 the Federal Bureau of Investigation (FBI) and Internal Revenue Service (IRS) began an investigation into Kim's finances as part of a probe into alleged violations of campaign-spending laws. In 1997 he pleaded guilty to accepting $230,000 in illegal campaign contributions.

Kim Ku

b. 1876
Hwanghae Province, Korea
d. June 26, 1949
Seoul, Republic of Korea
fields: Government and Politics

Kim Ku headed the Korean provisional government in exile in Shanghai, China, which was established after the March, 1919, rebellion against the Japanese in Korea. Ardently anti-Japanese, Kim helped organize the Korean Independence Party in 1930 and the Korean Nationalist Party in 1936. Twice during World War II, Kim tried to assassinate the Japanese emperor. After Korea was liberated in 1945, he worked with Syngman Rhee to achieve national unity and resist the communists. Rhee and Kim later argued and parted ways. In 1948, after South Korea was formed, Kim headed his own revamped Korean Independence Party until his death.

Kim, Kyu-sik

b. Jan. 27, 1881
Korea
d. 1950
fields: Government and Politics

Kyu-sik Kim was adopted by an American missionary family and came to study in the United States in 1897. Beginning in 1913, Kim held various posts in the Korean provisional government-in-exile in Shanghai. In 1919, he moved to the United States, where he chaired the Korean Commission to Europe and the United States. Conflicts with Syngman Rhee caused him to return to China, where in 1935, he was elected president of the Korean National Revolutionary Party.

Kim, Randall Duk

b. Sept. 24, 1943
Honolulu, Territory of Hawaii
fields: Theater and Entertainment

Randall Duk Kim, an Asian American of Korean Chinese descent, played major roles in many classics and the title roles in Shakespeare's *Titus Andronicus* (1972), *Richard III* (1973; 1974-1975), *Pericles* (1974), *The Tempest* (1974; 1975-1976), and *Hamlet* (1976; 1978-1979) at theaters throughout the United States. He won critical acclaim for his performances as Tam Lum (*The Chickencoop Chinaman*, 1972) and Fred Eng (*Year of the Dragon*, 1974) in the New York premieres of Frank Chin's plays at the American Place Theatre. Along with Charles Bright and Anne Occhiogrosso, in 1977 Kim founded The American Players in Washington, D.C., and later moved the company to Wisconsin. In 1991, he moved to Hawaii, where he continued working in the theater.

Kim, Richard E.

né: Kim Eun Kook
b. Mar. 13, 1932
Hamhung City, Korea
fields: Literature, Education

Richard E. Kim, born as Kim Eun Kook, came to the United States in 1954. He received a bachelor's degree from Middlebury College in 1959, an M.A. from The Johns Hopkins University in 1960, an M.F.A. from Iowa State University in 1962, and an M.A. from Harvard in 1963. He published his first novel, *The Martyred*, in 1964. The novel, based on his wartime experiences, was nominated for the National Book Award in 1964. That same year, Kim became part of the English Department at the University of Massachusetts, Amherst, and received a Guggenheim Fellowship (1964-1965). His other publications include *The Innocent* (1968), a novel, and *Lost Names: Scenes from a Korean Boyhood* (1970), a collection of autobiographical pieces.

Kim Ronyoung. *See* Hahn, Gloria

Kim, Warren Y.

né: Won-yong Kim
b. Dec. 25, 1896
Seoul, Korea
d. ?
Los Angeles, Calif.
fields: Philanthropy

Warren Y. Kim, who arrived in the United States in 1917, was an activist and community leader throughout his lifetime. In 1957, he helped create the Korean Foundation, which provided scholarships to Korean American students, and in 1963 founded the Korean Center, which later became the Korean Association of Southern California. Kim supported the Korean independence movement through his membership in the U.S.-based Korean National Association. He wrote *Chaemi Hanin Osimnyon-sa* (1959), a fifty-year history of the Koreans in America.

Kim, Willa

b. ?
Los Angeles, Calif.
fields: Fashion, Theater and Entertainment

Costume designer Willa Kim, educated at Los Angeles' Chouinard Institute of Art, created standard-setting innovative dance costumes using stretch fabrics and unique approaches to fabric painting. Her designs have been worn by members of the Eliot Feld Ballet, San Francisco Ballet, Joffrey Ballet, Glen Tetley Dance Company, Harkness Ballet, American Ballet Theatre, and Alvin Ailey Dance Theatre. The first Broadway production for which she designed the costumes, Edward Albee's *Malcolm*, was followed by more than one hundred theatrical productions, ballets, operas, and television productions. She received Tony Awards for her designs for Duke Ellington's *Sophisticated Ladies* in 1981 and the musical *The Will Rogers Follies* in 1991.

Kim, Willyce

b. 1946
Honolulu, Territory of Hawaii
fields: Literature (poet)

Korean American poet and novelist Willyce Kim is known for her lesbian themes. She wrote several collections of poetry, including the chapbooks *Curtains of Light* (1971), *Eating Artichokes* (1972), and *Under the Rolling Sky* (1976). Two of her novels are *Dancer Dawkins and the California Kid* (1985) and *Dead Heat* (1988).

Kim, Yong Ik

b. May 15, 1920
Korea
fields: Literature

Writer Yong Ik Kim came to the United States as a student and became a naturalized citizen. He has written many short stories, including "From Below the Bridge" (1958), "The Happy Days" (1960), "The Dividing Gourd" (1962), "The Blue in the Seed" (1964), "Love in Winter" (1964), and "The Shoes from Yan San Valley" (1970).

Kim, Yongjeung

b. Apr. 2, 1898
Kum-san, Korea
fields: Publishing

Yongjeung Kim, one of the founders of the K & S Company, a very prosperous wholesale business in the Korean American Community in Los Angeles, used the media to promote Korean independence. From 1939 until 1943, he was public relations director for the Korean National Association and belonged to the United Korean Committee in America from 1941 until 1943. He helped the U.S. Office of War Information during its World War II broadcasts to Korea and the Far East. From 1943 until 1962, Kim published and edited *The Voice of Korea* as founder and president of the Korean Affairs Institute (Washington, D.C.), advocating the unification of Korea through neutralization.

Kim, Young Oak

b. 1918
Los Angeles, Calif.
fields: Warfare and Conquest

Army officer Young Oak Kim was widely acclaimed as one of the outstanding U.S. Army officers of World War II and the Korean War and one of the most decorated soldiers of his generation. Kim, who was drafted in January, 1941, was ordered to attend Army Officer Candidate School, and was commissioned in January, 1943. Kim was assigned to the newly formed 100th Battalion, made up of Japanese Americans. Because of the enmity between Koreans and Japanese, his superiors offered to have him reassigned, but Kim took command of the Second Platoon, Company B. After Kim arrived in Italy, he personally captured the first three German prisoners of war taken by the 100th Battalion. While in Europe, he received the Silver Star and the Distinguished Service Cross. During the Korean War, Kim commanded the First Battalion, 31st Infantry Division, and his skill as a field commander was widely recognized.

Kimbro, Warren

b. ?
fields: Civil Rights

African American participant in the New Haven chapter of the Black Panther Party; Warren Kimbro pled guilty to the murder of Alex Rackley, a suspected police informant, on January 16, 1970. He testified against Bobby Seale and fellow Panthers who had also been arrested in connection to the crime. He received a life sentence for second-degree murder.

Kimura, Larry

b. June 17, 1946
Waimea, Territory of Hawaii
fields: Education, Music

Asian American Larry Kimura combined his talents as an educator and song writer between 1982 and 1984, when he served as president of *Punana Leo*, a Hawaiian immersion program in which students are taught academic subjects in Hawaiian. Kimura first taught Hawaiian language and culture at the University of Hawaii, Hilo. His songs, written in Hawaiian, have won numerous awards.

Kindī, Abū Yūsuf Yaʿqūb ibn Isḥāq al-

b. c. 800
Kufa, south of Karbala, Iraq
d. 866
Baghdad, Iraq
fields: Philosophy

A prolific author who wrote on many subjects, Abū Yūsuf Yaʿqūb ibn Isḥāq al-Kindī was the first major Arab philosopher, providing the first systematic expression of ethics and moral psychology in Arabic. He argued that the soul is immaterial and is analogous to divine substance; the appetites and passions have their source in the material body and can lead a person into excessive love of physical pleasures. To avoid that development, the soul must be purified through the quest for truth and the rigorous study of philosophy. His work was important in medieval European attempts to understand Aristotle's *De Anima.*

King, B. B.

full: Riley King
b. September 16, 1925
Itta Bena, Miss.
fields: Music

African American blues singer and guitarist; B. B. King was a popular performer on Memphis' Beale Street and worked as a disc jockey on a local radio station as the Beale Street Blues Boy; he began recording in 1949. Considered to be a definitive blues albums, King's *Live at the Regal* was released in 1965. King won a Grammy Award for *There Must Be a Better World Somewhere* in 1981.

King, Ben E.

né: Benjamin Earl Nelson
b. September 28, 1938
Henderson, N.C.
fields: Music

African American soul balladeer and songwriter; Ben E. King cowrote and sang lead for the hit, "There Goes My Baby" (1960), with the Drifters; they also hit the top of the charts with "Save the Last Dance for Me." His solo hits of the 1960's include "Spanish Harlem," "Stand by Me," and "Don't Play That Song." King released the album *Supernatural Thing, Part 1*, in the mid-1970's, and collaborated with the Average White Band for the album *Benny and Us* (1977).

King, Billie Jean

né: Billie Jean Moffitt
b. November 22, 1943
Long Beach, California
fields: Sports (tennis)

In addition to being a superb tennis player, Billie Jean King has been a driving force for the recognition and improvement of women's tennis. Her victory over Bobby Riggs in September, 1973, established her as the preeminent advocate of equity for women tennis players in every phase of their sport.

King, Champagne

full: Evelyn King
b. July 1, 1960
The Bronx, N.Y.
fields: Music

African American singer; Champagne King began her career with a hit single, "Shame," from her first album, *Smooth Talk* (1977). This was followed by a gold album, *Music Box* (1979), *I'm in Love* (1981), and another gold record, *Get Loose* (1982). She released *Face to Face* in 1983 and *Long Time Coming*, featuring the single "Your Personal Touch,"in 1985.

King, Coretta Scott

b. April 27, 1927
Marion, Alabama
fields: Civil Rights

One of the nation's most prominent women of the 1960's, a civil rights activist and lecturer. Coretta Scott King is the widow of slain civil rights leader Martin Luther King, Jr. She was the first woman to give a commencement address at Harvard University in 1968, and founded the Martin Luther King, Jr., Center for Nonviolent Social Change in Atlanta (1980).

King Curtis

né: Curtis Ousley
b. February 7, 1934
Fort Worth, Tex.
d. August 13, 1971
New York, N.Y.
fields: Music

African American saxophonist and bandleader; King Curtis and his band recorded jazz for Prestige records through the latter half of the 1950's. Some of his first mainstream hits included soul standards, such as "Night Train" and "Honky Tonk," and an original piece, "Soul Serenade." He appeared on tracks with Buddy Holly, Nat "King" Cole, and the Coasters, who featured him in "Yakety-Yak," and played backup on singer Aretha Franklin's releases.

King, Emery

b. March 30, 1948
Gary, Ind.
fields: Journalism

African American journalist; Emery King began his career as a radio reporter and then moved into television WBBM's television station in Chicago (1976-1980). He was a Washington news correspondent from 1980 to 1986 and started anchoring WDIV-TV news in Detroit, Mich., in 1986. Among his honors are two Emmy Awards, for 1977 and 1979 reporting.

King, Ernest Joseph

b. November 23, 1878
Lorain, Ohio
d. June 25, 1956
Portsmouth, New Hampshire
fields: Military Affairs, Warfare and Conquest

U.S. chief of naval operations during World War II. After the Japanese attacked Pearl Harbor on December 7, 1941, Ernest Joseph King was named commander in chief of the U.S. fleet. Four months later he was also made chief of naval operations; he held the two positions concurrently. Involved in naval strategy at top levels; member of the Joint Chiefs of Staff from that body's creation in 1942.

King, Helen Dean

b. Sept. 27, 1869
Owego, New York
d. Mar. 7, 1955
Philadelphia, Pennsylvania
fields: Biology, Genetics

Helen Dean King is known for producing standard strains of laboratory rats used worldwide for experimental studies.

King, Jean Sadako

né: Jean Sadako McKillop
b. Dec. 6, 1925
Honolulu, Territory of Hawaii
fields: Government and Politics

Jean Sadako King is the daughter of a postmaster of Scottish descent and a Japanese American woman. She received a B.A. from the University of Hawaii in 1948, she earned an M.A. in history from New York University in 1953 and an M.F.A. from the University of Hawaii in 1968. A Democrat, she served as state representative (1972-1974) and state senator (1974-1978) before becoming the first woman in Hawaii to become lieutenant governor of the state (1978-1982). Her struggle to protect the environment is reflected in the Environmental Protection Act (1972) and the Shoreline Protection Act (1975), enacted under her leadership. She ran unsuccessfully for governor in 1982 and retired from politics.

King, Larry

né: Larry Zeiger
b. Nov. 19, 1933
Brooklyn, N.Y.
fields: Radio, Television, Journalism

Television and radio broadcaster. King rose to prominence in the 1980's as the host of a nationally syndicated late-night radio talk show and a television show on the Cable News Network (CNN). In 1992, his television show became known as the forum via which Ross Perot began his presidential candidacy.

King, Martin Luther, Sr.

né: Michael Luther King
b. December 19, 1899
Stockbridge, Ga.
d. November 11, 1984
Atlanta, Ga.
fields: Civil Rights

Martin Luther King, Sr., was pastor of Ebenezer Baptist Church in Atlanta from 1932 to 1975. In 1936, he led protesters on a march to Atlanta's city hall to demand voting rights. He also fought for the equalization of black and white teachers' salaries, the desegregation of the Atlanta courthouse elevators, and other civil rights. His son and namesake became the foremost leader for African American civil rights.

King, Martin Luther, Jr.

b. January 15, 1929
Atlanta, Georgia
d. April 4, 1968
Memphis, Tennessee
fields: Civil Rights, Social Reform

As founding president of the Southern Christian Leadership Conference, King spearheaded the nonviolent movement that led to the 1964 Civil Rights Act and the 1965 Voting Rights Act. His nonviolent war against racial injustice and poverty was put on the world's stage when King became the youngest person and third black person to win the Nobel Peace Prize, in 1964. His significance to American history is celebrated every January with a national holiday.

King, Melvin H.

b. October 20, 1928
Boston, Mass.
fields: Government and Politics

African American politician and community activist; Melvin H. King mounted his first campaign for mayor of Boston, Mass., in 1979 and a second in 1983. He stressed commitment to increasing the number of jobs, providing better public housing, and the renovation of Boston's aging residential neighborhoods. King had an extended career as a community activist and educator and was elected to the Commonwealth of Massachusetts legislature in 1973 and served until 1982.

King, Michael. *See* Kahane, Meir

King, Rodney

full: Rodney Glenn King
b. 1966
Los Angeles, Calif.
fields: Law, Historical Figure

Rodney King was an African American motorist beaten by Los Angeles police officers in 1991. The beating was videotaped by a spectator and broadcast nationwide. The 1992 acquittal of the four officers charged by a mostly white jury resulted in rioting that lasted four days, from April 30 to May 3, with fifty-eight deaths and property damage of $1 billion.

King, Stephen

full: Stephen Edwin King
b. September 21, 1947
Portland, Maine
fields: Literature, Film

Through his storytelling abilities and vivid imagination, as demonstrated in his novels, short stories, and films, Stephen King has done much to move the horror genre into the forefront of popular literature. He has modernized many gothic or horror themes and techniques.

King, William Lyon Mackenzie

b. December 17, 1874
Berlin, Ontario, Canada
d. July 22, 1950
Kingsmere, Quebec, Canada
fields: Government and Politics

King helped organize Canada's Department of Labour and was the first Canadian political leader concerned with industrial exploitation of workers. As prime minister, he established an independent Canadian policy in world affairs.

King Hancock. *See* Hancock

King Philip. *See* Metacomet

Kingman, Dong Moy Shu

né: Tsang King-man
b. March 31, 1911
Oakland, Calif.
fields: Art

The watercolors of Dong Moy Shu Kingman are represented in permanent collections in Boston's Museum of Fine Arts, New York's Metropolitan Museum of Art and Museum of Modern Art, the Chicago Art Institute, the U.S. State Department, and many other galleries. Kingman, a Guggenheim Fellow in 1942-1943, has illustrated children's books, created murals for hotels, and produced artwork for films such as *Lost Horizon* (1973). He was the (New York) Chinese American Planning Council's Man of the Year in 1981. Kingman published *Paint the Yellow Tiger* in 1991.

Kingsolver, Barbara

b. April 8, 1955
Annapolis, Md.
fields: Literature

Native American writer; Barbara Kingsolver published *The Bean Trees* in 1988, establishing her major themes: discovering self, maintaining a family, and negotiating American life as an American Indian; committed to social responsibility—*Holding the Line: Women in the Great Arizona Mine Strike of 1983* (1989) and autobiographical essays collected in *High Tide in Tucson: Essays from Now or Never* (1995); explored the conflict between tribal responsibilities and individual rights in *Pigs in Heaven* (1993), affirming the ability of human beings to form families and maintain relationships despite differences in culture among them.

Kingston, Maxine Hong

né: Maxine Hong
b. October 27, 1940
Stockton, California
fields: Literature

A writer of memoirs, nonfiction, and fiction, Kingston writes powerfully about the lives of Chinese Americans. Stylistically experimental, her books merge myth and reality, past and present, female and male voices to universalize her own, her family's, and her characters' experiences.

Kino, Eusebio Francisco

aka: Eusebio Francesco Chino
b. August 10, 1645
Segno, Tirol (now Italy)
d. Mar. 15, 1711
Magdalena de Kino, Sonora, Mexico
fields: Religion and Theology, Exploration and Colonization

Latino missionary and explorer. In 1681, Eusebio Francisco Kino was sent by the Jesuit order, which he had joined in 1665, to Mexico. He founded a number of Jesuit missions among the Indians of the Sonoran Desert, beginning with the Nuestra Señora de los Dolores in 1687. Kino explored the Rio Grande and the Gila and Colorado Rivers, taught Arizona's Pima Indians new agricultural methods, and reportedly fought the enslavement of Indians in the silver mines of Mexico. He also made a map of lower California and Pimería Alta that was used for more than one century after his death.

Kinsey, Alfred Charles

b. June 23, 1894
Hoboken, New Jersey

d. August 25, 1956
Bloomington, Indiana
fields: Zoology, Psychiatry and Psychology, Sociology

The greatest pioneer in sex research since Sigmund Freud, Kinsey revolutionized the study of human sexual behavior by applying to it the methodology of scientific empiricism.

Kinsky, Countess. *See* Suttner, Bertha von

Kintpuash (Having Indigestion). *See* Captain Jack

Kipling, Rudyard

b. December 30, 1865
Bombay, India
d. January 18, 1936
London, England
fields: Literature

The author of several books of extraordinary insight about the realm of childhood, as well as some stirring popular poetry sympathetic to the British soldier, Kipling's greatest accomplishment was his depiction of life in India at the close of the nineteenth century.

Kirby, George

b. June 8, 1923
Chicago, Ill.
d. September 30, 1995
Las Vegas, Nev.
fields: Theater and Entertainment

African American actor and entertainer; George Kirby, known for his more than one hundred impersonations, was featured on the short-lived weekly *ABC Comedy Hour* in 1972. His television appearances include *Gimme a Break*, *Murder, She Wrote*, *Fame*, *227*, and *The Perry Como Show*. His film credits include *Leonard Part 6* (1987), *Trouble in Mind* (1985), and *A Man Called Adam* (1966).

Kirchhoff, Gustav Robert

b. Mar. 12, 1824
Königsberg, Prussia (now Kaliningrad, Russia)
d. Oct. 17, 1887
Berlin, Germany
fields: Astronomy, Chemistry, Physics

Gustav Robert Kirchhoff helped established the science of spectrum analysis; in 1857, offered a general theory of the motion of electricity in conductors; in 1859, discovered the law of absorption and emission of radiation by material bodies; in 1860, discovered the elements cesium and rubidium; in 1862, introduced the concept of blackbody radiation.

Kirchner, Ernst Ludwig

b. May 6, 1880
Aschaffenburg, Germany
d. June 15, 1938
near Davos, Switzerland
fields: Art

Kirchner was one of the founders and a leading artist of German expressionism—a major early twentieth century art movement whose basic ideas effectively challenged the then-dominant Impressionistic art and influenced contemporary literature, music, drama, and film.

Kirk, Rahsaan Roland

b. August 7, 1936
Columbus, Ohio
d. December 5, 1977
Bloomington, Ind.
fields: Music (jazz instrumentalist)

African American jazz instrumentalist; Rahsaan Roland Kirk, though primarily a tenor saxophonist, is known for playing such exotic reed instruments as the manzello and stritch, in addition to the clarinet, flute, and trumpet. He recorded mostly as leader, on numerous albums for Mercury and Atlantic records. He also recorded with other people's groups and in the 1960's played with rock guitarists Jimi Hendrix and Frank Zappa.

Kirkpatrick, Jeane

né: Jeane Duane Jordan
b. November 19, 1926
Duncan, Oklahoma
fields: Diplomacy, Government and Politics, Women's Rights

The first woman to serve as American Ambassador to the United Nations (1981-1985), Kirkpatrick also wrote one of the first books on women and American politics, giving that new field of scholarship legitimacy.

Kishi, Kichimatsu

b. January 7, 1872
Nagaoka, Japan
d. 1956
Orange County, Calif.
fields: Business and Industry

Kichimatsu Kishi came to the United States in 1907 and bought a 3,500-acre tract of land in the southeastern part of Texas to produce rice. The large rice colony prospered. When Kishi's farm suffered a setback in 1916, Kishi and his employees branched out into truck farming, livestock, and oil drilling. These successful ventures allowed the rice colony to prosper again, and Kishi built a church and school. In 1931, creditors seized all of Kishi's property, but a few years later, Kishi and his wife, aided by their son, were able to farm again, although on a much smaller scale.

Kissinger, Henry A.

né: Heinz Alfred Kissinger
b. May 27, 1923
Fürth, Germany
fields: Diplomacy, Government and Politics

Both in theory (in his writings as an academic) and in practice (serving as national security adviser and secretary of state), Kissinger advocated a new conception of American foreign policy more closely akin to traditional European balance-of-power politics than to the reformist model to which Americans had become accustomed.

Kitagawa, Daisuke

b. Oct. 3, 1910
Taihoku, now Taipei, Taiwan
d. Mar. 27, 1970
Geneva, Switzerland
fields: Religion and Theology

Daisuke Kitagawa studied theology at the University of Chicago's Divinity School and at General Theological Seminary in New York. He was ordained as an Episcopalian priest in 1939. He was interned at Tule Lake in Northern California during World War II and served as field secretary for the National Council of Churches' Committee on Japanese American Resettlement from 1943 to 1944. He served as a pastor and church administrator in Minnesota for the next ten years, beginning work for the World Council of Churches in Geneva in 1956. Kitagawa wrote *Issei and Nisei: The Internment Years* (1967) and a volume on the impact of Christianity on race relations.

Kitagawa, Sōtatsu. *See* Sōtatsu

Kitano, Harry H. L.

b. Feb. 14, 1926
San Francisco, Calif.
fields: Education

Japanese American scholar; Harry H. L. Kitano was raised in San Francisco; interned in Topaz, Utah, during World War II; earned Ph.D. at University of California, Berkeley, in 1958; on faculty at University of California, Los Angeles, where he has twice been director of the Asian American Studies Center; wrote many important sociological studies of Japanese Americans, including *Japanese Americans: Evolution of a Sub-Culture* (1969), *Race Relations* (1974), and *The Japanese Americans* (1987); coauthored works such as *American Racism: Exploration of the Nature of Prejudice* (1970) and *Japanese Americans, from Relocation to Redress* (1986); developed the theory of the two-category system of race relations and the concept of subculture (with Roger Daniels).

Kitasato, Shibasaburo

b. Dec. 20, 1852
Oguni, Kumamoto, Japan
d. June 13, 1931
Nakanojo, Gumma, Japan
fields: Science, Medicine

A pioneering bacteriologist, Shibasaburo Kitasato investigated tetanus and diphtheria, opening the new discipline of serology, which became immunology; in 1889, produced the first pure culture of *Clostridium tetani.*

Kitchen, Robert Wilson, Jr.

b. 1922?
fields: Diplomacy, Government and Politics (appointee)

Diplomat and political appointee. Kitchen was graduated from Morehouse College in 1943, received his M.S. in business administration from Columbia University in 1946, and received his LL.D. in industrial management and engineering from Chapman College in 1965. Beginning in the early 1950's, Kitchen served as an administrative assistant in the Economic Development Mission to Liberia, rising to become acting director of the mission. He was later economic adviser to the director of the International Cooperative Administration Mission to Pakistan, then Pakistan Desk Officer, and finally Chief of the Special Mission to the Sudan in 1957. He administered the first major Agency for International Development (AID) program in Africa as head of the U.S. Mission to the Sudan from 1958 to 1960. Kitchen also served as deputy representative to the Economic and Social Council of the United Nations (UNESCO) in the 1940's.

Kitchener, Lord

né: Horatio Herbert Kitchener
aka: Horatio Herbert, First Earl Kitchener Khartoum and of Broome
b. June 24, 1850
near Listowel, County Kerry, Ireland
d. June 5, 1916
off the Orkney Islands, Scotland
fields: Military Affairs

Kitchener held many military and imperial positions throughout the Middle East between 1874 and 1899. He was commander in chief of British forces in the South African War, 1900-1902. He served as the secretary of state for war during World War I and was regarded as a symbol of Great Britain's will to victory.

Kitt, Eartha

b. January 26, 1928
North, S.C.
fields: Theater and Entertainment

African American actress and singer; Eartha Kitt got her break as a featured entertainer in the revue *New Faces of 1952*. This led to a starring role in the drama *Mrs. Patterson* (1954), and many other plays followed. Kitt was also a popular recoreding artist with hits such as "C'est Si Bon" (1953) and "Santa Baby" (1953). A frequent guest on television talk and variety shows, she had a recurring role as the Catwoman on the *Batman* series (1967). Her film credits include *St. Louis Blues* (1958), the title role in *Anna Lucasta* (1959), and *Friday Foster* (1975).

Klah, Hosteen

aka: Left Handed
b. Oct., 1867
Bear Mountain, N.Mex. Territory
d. Feb. 27, 1937
near Gallup, N.Mex.
fields: Art, Religion and Theology

Hosteen Klah was an influential Navajo medicine man and an accomplished weaver; as a weaver, he represented his people at two world's fairs. In 1919-1920, Klah wove the first rug based on a sand painting; it was called "The Whirling Log," from the Yeibichai Ceremony. Between 1919 and 1937, he wove twenty-five sand-painting tapestries.

Klee, Paul

b. December 18, 1879
Münchenbuchsee, near Bern, Switzerland
d. June 29, 1940
Muralto-Locarno, Switzerland
fields: Art

Klee was one of the most brilliant, varied, and complex artists of the twentieth century. Klee, whose paintings and graphics were always rooted in physical reality, invented symbols for the formative process of nature. As a teacher and theoretician, he was able to provide significant insights into the meaning of art. His writings include the most complete principles of design devised by a modern artist.

Klein, A. M.

full: Abraham Moses Klein
b. February 14, 1909
Ratno, Volhynia, Russian Empire (now Ratne, Ukraine)
d. August 21, 1972
Montreal, Quebec, Canada
fields: Journalism, Literature

Abraham Moses Klein was a lawyer, poet, writer; born in the Ukraine, raised in the Jewish immigrant district of Montreal; earned a degree from University of Montreal law school in 1933; editor and columnist of the *Canadian Jewish Chronicle* (1938-1955); visiting lecturer in poetry at McGill University, 1945-1948; suffered mental breakdown in early 1950's and gradually withdrew from society; wrote *The Hitleriad* (1944), *The Rocking Chair* (1948) and *The Second Scroll* (1951).

Klein, Felix

full: Christian Felix Klein
b. Apr. 25, 1849
Düsseldorf, Prussia (now Germany)
d. June 22, 1925
Göttingen, Germany
fields: Mathematics (algebra, calculus, and geometry)

Felix Klein proved that the essential properties of a given geometry could be represented by the group of transformations that preserve those properties.

Klein, Ralph

b. November 1, 1942
Calgary, Alberta, Canada
fields: Government and Politics

Ralph Klein became premier of Alberta in 1992. A strict fiscal conservative, he eliminated the province's deficit largely through cuts in public services. He was reelected in 1997.

Kleist, Heinrich von

full: Heinrich Wilhelm von Kleist
b. October 18, 1777
Frankfurt an der Oder, Prussia
d. November 21, 1811
Wannsee bei Potsdam, Prussia
fields: Literature (drama)

Kleist was one of the most important literary figures in the development of the German *Novellen* of poetic realism. Although he is better known in Germany than in English-speaking countries, he is usually acknowledged to have been ahead of his time, a forerunner of the modern literature of the grotesque, usually associated with Franz Kafka a century later.

Klement, Ricardo. *See* Eichmann, Adolf

Klugh, Earl

b. December 16, 1954
Detroit, Mich.
fields: Music (acoustic guitarist)

African American acoustic guitarist; Earl Klugh, who began touring with George Benson in the early 1970's and played on Benson's album *White Rabbit* (1971), joined Benson's group in 1973. Klugh stopped touring, after his gig with Return to Forever, in 1974 to work on his own projects. His album, *One on One* (1979), recorded with Bob James, received a Grammy Award that year.

Klugh, James Richard

b. June 22, 1931
Greenwood, S.C.
fields: Military Affairs

African American military officer. During James Richard Klugh's notable Army career he recieved such honors as the Meritorious Service Medal with oak leaf cluster, the Army Commendation Medal with two oak leaf clusters, and numerous Air Medals. His duty included service in Vietnam (1969-1970) as division chemical officer; operations officer and public information officer with the United States Army Europe (1963-1965); and assistant deputy chief of staff for logistics in Washington, D.C. (1987-1990).

Knauth, Susanne Katherina. *See* Langer, Susanne K.

Kneeland, Abner

b. April 7, 1774
Gardner, Massachusetts
d. August 27, 1844
Salubria, Iowa
fields: Religion and Theology

During the early nineteenth century, Abner Kneeland held ministerial positions in Universalist churches and edited journals advancing liberal Christian views. By 1829 he was estranged from his church, so he resigned his posts, established the First Society of Free Enquirers in Boston, and launched the *Boston Investigator*, a journal devoted to exploring religious rationalism. An 1833 issue of this journal led to his indictment for publishing blasphemy, and he was eventually imprisoned. His court battles secured him wide attention and new support. In 1839 he resettled in Iowa.

Knight, Etheridge

b. April 19, 1931
Corinth, Miss.
d. March 6, 1991
Indianapolis, Ind.
fields: Literature (poet)

African American poet; Etheridge Knight, who began writing in prison, has produced many poetry collections including *Poems from Prison* (1968), *Black Voices from Prison* (1970), *Belly Song and Other Poems* (1973), and *Born of a Woman: New and Selected Poems* (1980). He was honored with a Guggenheim Fellowship in 1974 and held writer-in-residence positions at several universities.

Knight, Marie

b. ?
fields: Music (gospel singer)

African American gospel singer; Marie Knight, who had a fervent and disciplined voice, was in striking contrast to her singing partner Sister Rosetta Tharpe. The combination worked however, and at the height of their popularity, in 1950, they played to an audience of twenty-seven thousand at Griffith Stadium in Washington, D.C. After the duo released a blues album they were shunned by the gospel community, and Knight's career never recovered.

Knight, Marva. *See* Collins, Marva

Knopf, Blanche Wolf

né: Blanche Wolf
b. July 30, 1894
New York, New York
d. June 4, 1966
New York, New York
fields: Publishing

A leading American publisher, Knopf played a key role in shaping the intellectual and cultural climate of the nation. Among other things, she brought Simone de Beauvoir's classic feminist treatise *The Second Sex* to the American public.

Knox, Clinton Everett

b. May 6, 1908
New Bedford, Mass.
d. 1980
fields: Diplomacy

African American diplomat and political appointee; Clinton Everett Knox attended the North Atlantic Treaty Organization (NATO) Defense College in Paris in 1957 and later became first secretary in the U.S. mission to NATO. He was counselor and then deputy chief to the mission at the U.S. embassy in Honduras and was appointed U.S. ambassador to Dahomey in 1964. Knox also served as ambassador to Haiti from 1969 to 1973.

Knox, Frank

b. Jan. 1, 1874
Boston, Mass.
d. Apr. 28, 1944
Washington, D.C.
fields: Military Affairs

Frank Knox was appointed secretary of the navy by President Franklin D. Roosevelt in 1940. Before releasing his official report on the bombing of Pearl Harbor by the Japanese in 1941, he made several statements implying that the Hawaiian Japanese had spied on U.S. military facilities and assisted Japanese Fifth Column (sabotage) activity. The report itself did not contain evidence of any such actions, but his statements made many Americans believe that Japanese Americans were spies.

Knox, John

b. c. 1514
Giffordgate, near Haddington, East Lothian, Scotland
d. November 24, 1572
Edinburgh, Scotland
fields: Religion and Theology

The leading reformer and historian of the Protestant Reformation in Scotland, John Knox gave to Calvinism its Presbyterian expression in both England and Scotland and found in covenant theology the rationale for political militancy.

Koch, Robert

b. December 11, 1843
Clausthal, Prussia
d. May 27, 1910
Baden-Baden, Germany
fields: Medicine

Koch was a pioneer bacteriologist and the first to prove definitively that specific microorganisms cause specific diseases. He identified the bacterium that caused cholera, enabling the virtual elimination of that disease in the Western world. He isolated the causative agent of tuberculosis, eventually leading to the containment of that once-deadly scourge, and he discovered the reproductive cycle of anthrax, providing for the successful combating of that disease.

Kochi, Shinsei Paul

b. Feb. 27, 1889
Nakijin, Kunigashiragun, Okinawa Prefecture, Japan
d. Dec. 20, 1980
fields: Journalism, Social Reform

After Shinsei Paul Kochi arrived in Los Angeles, he worked as a gardener while writing for various publications. He was interned in Heart Mountain, then became part of a resettlement program and moved to Nebraska. He urged other Japanese Americans to leave the camps. In 1943, Kochi began to work for the Office of Strategic Services in New York. His work took him to various parts of Asia, where he saw the effects of war. He organized relief efforts to benefit war-torn Okinawa and published numerous articles about conditions there. Later, Kochi helped establish the Japanese Community Pioneer Center of Los Angeles to help elderly Japanese Americans. He coedited a history of the Okinawan community, *History of the Okinawans in North America* (1988).

Kochiyama, Yuri

b. 1921
San Pedro, Calif.
fields: Social Reform, Civil Rights

Japanese American political activist; Yuri Kochiyama was born in California; interned in Arkansas during World War II; joined National Association for the Advancement of Colored People during the 1950's; moved to Harlem in 1960 during the Civil Rights movement, working for better community education and working conditions; met Malcolm X and joined his Organization for Afro-American Unity in 1964; supported solidarity between Asians, African Americans, and Hispanics.

Koda, Keisaburo

b. 1882
Fukushima, Japan
d. 1964
Japan
fields: Business and Industry

Keisaburo Koda arrived in the United States in 1906. He started a successful wholesale fish distribution company in Southern California, selling his share of the business to become a rice farmer in Sacramento. His farm had grown to ten thousand acres by 1932, and by the late 1930's, he had a personal net worth of several million dollars. He pioneered the use of airplanes to scatter rice seed across large fields. During World War II, Koda was interned in Granada in Colorado. When he returned to California, he found that most of his property had been sold. He fought for its return through the courts while rebuilding his business, aided by his sons. He soon became prosperous again, selling Kokuho rice. Koda died in 1964 before his claim was settled, but in 1965, the U.S. government, under the Japanese American Evacuation Claims Act of 1948, awarded his family more than $360,000 in compensation for losses traceable to the internment. Although the amount was large, most of it went to the lawyers who fought the case.

Kogawa, Joy

b. June 6, 1935
Vancouver, British Columbia, Canada
fields: Literature

Japanese Canadian writer, poet; Joy Kogawa was born in Vancouver, British Columbia; interned in interior British Columbia during World War II; best known for her novel *Obasan* (1981), which realistically portrays the pain and alienation that Japanese Canadians suffered during World War II; published a children's version of *Obasan*, *Naomi's Road*, and a sequel, *Itsuka*, about the redress movement; also wrote poetry books, *The Splintered Moon*, (1967), *A Choice of Dreams* (1974), *Jericho Road* (1977), and *Woman in the Woods* (1985).

Kohl, Helmut

full: Helmut Michael Kohl
b. April 3, 1930
Ludwigshafen am Rhein, Germany
fields: Government and Politics

Kohl strengthened Germany's international position during the late twentieth century, and, in 1990, he aggressively pursued German reunification.

Kohlberg, Lawrence

b. October 25, 1927
Bronxville, N.Y.
d. January 17, 1987
Boston, Mass.
fields: Psychiatry and Psychology, Education

In his pioneering work, Kohlberg extended Jean Piaget's work on cognitive development to study individuals' reasoning in making moral decisions. Authored *Essays on Moral Development* (1981).

Kojong

né: Yi Myong-bok
b. 1852
Korea
d. Jan. 22, 1919
Korea
fields: Government and Politics

Kojong, at age eleven, became the last king in the Yi Dynasty (1392-1910). The Korean king supported the efforts of U.S. missionary Horace N. Allen to increase Korean emigration to Hawaii because of a sense of nationalist pride in Koreans being allowed to enter the United States when Chinese were not. The Japanese forced him to abdicate to his son in 1907.

Kokoschka, Oskar

b. March 1, 1886
Pöchlarn, Austro-Hungarian Empire
d. February 22, 1980
Villeneuve, Switzerland
fields: Art (painter)

Although he was reluctant to be identified with any art movement, Kokoschka is generally considered one of Europe's finest expressionist painters. Excelling at psychologically oriented portraiture, he also produced striking allegorical compositions, lithographs, landscapes, posters, and half a dozen plays.

Kollwitz, Käthe

né: Käthe Schmidt
b. July 8, 1867
Königsberg, East Prussia
d. April 22, 1945
Moritzburg, Germany
fields: Art

Kollwitz was one of the most talented and renowned graphic artists of the early twentieth century. While her art was clearly social and political in meaning, her mastery of light and form resulted in a purely aesthetic statement that has seldom been equaled in the graphic arts.

Kolmogorov, Andrey Nikolayevich

b. Apr. 25, 1903
Tambov, Russia
d. Oct. 20, 1987
Moscow, Soviet Union
fields: Mathematics

Andrey Nikolayevich Kolmogorov was the most honored Russian mathematician of the twentieth century. He is best known for establishing the axiomatic basis for probability theory. Expert in most areas of math, including algebra, applied math, calculus, geometry, mathematical logic, probability, set theory, statistics, topology, and trigonometry.

Kondiaronk. *See* Adario

Kondo Masaharu

b. 1877
Kyoto, Japan
d. 1948
Tokyo, Japan
fields: Business and Industry

Kondo Masaharu, who had studied fisheries and oceanography in Japan, saw a chance to expand the Southern California fisheries industry when he reached Los Angeles in 1908. He started the San Diego-based MK Fishing Company in 1912 and won exclusive rights from the Mexican government to ply the waters of Turtle Bay, off Baja, California. He imported contract fishermen from Japan and introduced new technologies, including the use of flexible and sturdy bamboo fishing poles, more effective lures and use of bait, refrigerated boats, and ways of locating schools of fish using radio-tracking.

Konieschguanokee. *See* Hopocan

Konigsberg, Allen Stewart. *See* Allen, Woody

Konkapot, Captain. *See* Konkapot, John

Konkapot, John

aka: Captain Konkapot
aka: Captain John
b. c. 1700
Housatonic River valley, Mass.
d. c. 1775
Stockbridge, Mass.
fields: Government and Politics, Native American Affairs

Native American leader. John Konkapot was a Christianized Mahican who aided Calvinist missionaries among his band. Massachusetts congregational minister Jonathan Edwards befriended him. Aided British in French and Indian Wars.

Kono, Tommy

full: Tamio Kono
b. June 27, 1930
Sacramento, Calif.
fields: Sports (weightlifting, bodybuilder)

Japanese American Tommy Kono suffered severe asthma as a child. While interned in Tule Lake, his health improved and he took up the sport of weightlifting. After the war, he lifted weights while studying at Sacramento Junior College. He was drafted in 1952 and given duty as a cook in Hawaii in order to continue competing. Kono won his first national title as a lightweight in 1952 and competed on the U.S. Olympic team as a weightlifter in 1952 and 1956, winning gold medals both times. At the 1960 Olympics, he won a silver medal. Kono also competed in bodybuilding events. He won six world weightlifting championships, established twenty-six world records, and won titles as Mr. World and Mr. Universe. He coached various Olympic weight lifting teams in 1968, 1972, and 1976. In 1990, Kono was inducted into the U.S. Olympic Hall of Fame.

Koo, Wellington

né: Ku Wei-Chun
full: Vi Kyun Wellington Koo
b. 1887
Shanghai, China
d. Nov. 14, 1985
New York, N.Y.
fields: Diplomacy

Wellington Koo received a doctoral degree in political science from Columbia in 1912, then returned to China to enter government service. He was minister to the United States from 1915 to 1918. His arguments resulted in China's being elected to the League of Nations council as a nonpermanent member. He participated in the Washington Disarmament Conference (1921-1922) that finalized the Nine-Power Treaty (1922) guaranteeing the administrative and territorial integrity of China. He served as foreign minister and as acting premier of the Beijing government in the mid-1920's. He returned to international diplomacy after Manchuria was seized by the Japanese in 1931. He was appointed China's ambassador to France, then ambassador to Great Britain. He signed the United Nations charter on behalf of China. He also served as ambassador to the United States in Washington, D.C. He sought U.S. aid for China during the Chinese civil war (1946-1949) and negotiated for the Nationalists after they relocated in Taiwan. He served on the International Court of Justice at The Hague from 1957 to 1967.

Kool Moe Dee

b. 1962?
fields: Music (rap artist)

African American rap artist; Kool Moe Dee got his start rapping with the Treacherous Three. His first solo album, *I'm Kool Moe Dee*, was released in 1985, and his second in 1987. He coproduced his third album, *Knowledge Is King* (1989), with Teddy Riley and also collaborated with Quincy Jones on his single "Back on the Block" from the sound track to *Listen Up! The Lives of Quincy Jones* (1990). Kool Moe Dee performed on the single and appeared in the Stop the Violence video of "Self-Destruction," a project to raise money for the National Urban League.

Koopmanschap, Cornelius

b. Feb. 13, 1828
Weesperkarspel, near Amsterdam, The Netherlands
d. 1882
Rio de Janeiro, Brazil
fields: Business and Industry

Cornelius Koopmanschap arrived in California in the early 1850's and began importing goods from China. In the 1860's, he moved to Hong Kong, where he used his connections to become a contractor and importer of Chinese labor to all parts of the world, including the United States. He brought more than thirty thousand Chinese workers into California.

Koquethagechton. *See* White Eyes

Korbel, Madeleine. *See* Albright, Madeleine

Korematsu, Fred

full: Fred Toyosaburo Korematsu
b. 1920?
Oakland, Calif.
fields: Civil Rights

Fred Korematsu was a Japanese American who resisted internment during World War II. He was arrested in 1942 and was persuaded by an ACLU lawyer to serve as a test case. The U.S. Supreme Court ruled in *Korematsu v. United States* (1944) that wartime expedience, not race prejudice, had motivated the government's internment program. In 1983 Korematsu's case was vacated because the government had suppressed evidence in the original court procedings.

Koresh, David

né: Vernon Howell
b. 1959
Houston, Tex.
d. April 19, 1993
Waco, Tex.
fields: Religion and Theology

Religious cult leader. David Koresh was a self-proclaimed Messiah who led a group of followers known as the Branch Davidians. Concerned over reports of child sexual abuse by Koresh and his followers, U.S. government agents stormed the cult's compound in Waco, Texas, after a fifty-one-day siege. The compound was destroyed by fire, and Koresh and most of his followers were killed, provoking criticism and leading to a congressional investigation.

Kornberg, Arthur

b. Mar. 3, 1918
Brooklyn, New York
fields: Biology, Genetics, Medicine

Arthur Kornberg isolated deoxyribonucleic acid (DNA) polymerase, the enzyme in bacteria that catalyzes the replication of genetic material; later used the enzyme to synthesize biologically active DNA in a test tube; was awarded the 1959 Nobel Prize in Physiology or Medicine.

Korolev, Sergei

full: Sergei Pavlovich Korolev
b. December 30, 1907
Nerzhin, Ukraine, Russian Empire
d. January 14, 1966
Moscow, U.S.S.R.
fields: Aviation and Space Exploration

Korolev, known as the "chief designer of rocket-cosmic systems" in the Soviet Union, was the father of the Soviet space program of the 1950's and 1960's. He designed the rocket boosters, the first unmanned Sputnik satellites, and the manned Vostok, Voskhod, and Soyuz spacecraft.

Korzeniowski, Jósef Teodor Konrad Nałę. *See* Conrad, Joseph

Kōshō. *See* Jōchō

Kossel, Albrecht

full: Karl Martin Leonhard Albrecht Kossel
b. Sept. 16, 1853
Rostock, Mecklenburg (now Germany)
d. July 5, 1927
Heidelberg, Germany
fields: Chemistry, Physiology

Albrecht Kossel was a pioneer in the chemistry of nucleic acids; in 1884, identified histone proteins in the nucleus; in 1885, discovered adenine and guanine in nucleic acids; in 1891, identified the presence of a carbohydrate in nucleic acids; in 1894, discovered cytosine and thymine in nucleic acids; in 1896, discovered the amino acid histidine; in 1910, awarded the Nobel Prize in Physiology or Medicine; in 1912, proposed that nuclear proteins are the chemical basis for biological specificity.

Kostrowitzky, Guillaume Albert Wladimir Alexandre Apollinaire de. *See* Apollinaire, Guillaume

Kostyra, Martha. *See* Stewart, Martha

Kotero, Patricia

aka: Apollonia
b. 1959
Mexico City, Mexico
fields: Music, Theater Entertainment

African American singer and actress; Patricia Kotero played the female lead in Prince's film *Purple Rain* (1984). Through that connection she became the lead singer of Vanity 6 (later Apollonia 6). With Kotero as lead vocalist, the group reached the charts with "Sex Shooter" in 1984. Kotero also appeared regularly in television's nighttime serial *Falcon Crest* in 1985 and 1986.

Kotto, Yaphet

b. November 15, 1937
New York, N.Y.
fields: Theater and Entertainment, Film

African American actor; Yaphet Kotto's film credits include *The Liberation of L. B. Jones* (1970), *Live and Let Die* (1973), (1977), *Alien* (1979), *The Star Chamber* (1983), *Midnight Run* (1988) and *Two if by Sea* (1996). His stage appearances include *The Great White Hope*, *The Blood Knot*, *In White America*, *A Good Place to Raise a Boy*, and *Fences*. Among other television appearances Kotto has been seen on *Tour of Duty* and *Homicide: Life on the Streets*. Kotto's autobiography, *The Royalty*, was first published in 1990.

Koufax, Sandy

né: Sanford Braun
b. December 30, 1935
Brooklyn, New York
fields: Sports (baseball)

One of baseball's finest pitchers, Sandy Koufax helped lead the Los Angeles Dodgers to two World Series championships. In 1961, 1963, 1965, and 1966, Koufax led the National League in strikeouts; he won two World Series games in 1963 and received the first of his three Cy Young Awards. The following year, injuries to his pitching arm forced him once again to end his season early. Aided by cortisone shots, Koufax came back in 1965 to a spectacular season that saw him pitch two more winning World Series games and a recordbreaking fourth no-hitter, the only perfect game in Los Angeles Dodger history. By 1966, Koufax had become the highest-paid player in baseball. Plagued by progressive arthritis caused by his injuries, he retired from baseball at the end of the 1966 season, thereafer working as a sports broadcaster following his retirement. In 1972, he became the youngest player ever elected to the Baseball Hall of Fame.

Kountz, Samuel Lee, Jr.

b. October 20, 1930
Lexa, Ark.
d. December 23, 1981
Great Neck, N.Y.
fields: Medicine (physician)

Physician. Kountz is perhaps most famous for performing a televised operation on the *Today Show*. He was an authority on kidney transplantation and taught at several prestigious universities.}}

Kovalevskaya, Sofya

né: Sofya Vasilyevna Korvin-Krukovskaya
aka: Sonya Kovalevsky
b. Jan. 15, 1850
Moscow, Russia
d. Feb. 10, 1891
Stockholm, Sweden
fields: Mathematics (applied math)

Sofya Kovalevskaya was one of the first women to obtain a Ph.D. in mathematics; most widely known Russian mathematician of the late nineteenth century.

Krantz, Jacob. *See* Cortéz, Ricardo

Krasner, Lee

né: Lenore Krassner
aka: Lena Krassner
b. October 27, 1908
New York, New York
d. June 19, 1984
New York, New York
fields: Art

Lee Krasner was a leader in the abstract expressionist movement in the United States. She spoke out for women's rights and became an example of a woman who took her work seriously within a movement that was dominated by males.

Kravitz, Lenny

b. c. 1964
New York, N.Y.
fields: Music

African American singer; Lenny Kravitz albums include *Let Love Rule* (1989), *Mama Said* (1991), *Are You Gonna Go My Way?* (1993), and *5* (1998); Kravitz has an eclectic musical style, with influences ranging from the Beatles through psychedelic sounds of the 1960's and 1970's. Both critics and fans have compared Kravitz to Prince and John Lennon.

Krebs, Hans Adolf

full: Hans Adolf Krebs
b. Aug. 25, 1900
Hildesheim, Germany
d. Nov. 22, 1981
Oxford, England
fields: Biology, Chemistry, Physiology

Hans Adolf Krebs was one of the founders of biochemistry; in 1930-1932, discovered the ornithine-urea cycle; correctly postulated, with limited evidence, the existence of the citric acid cycle, an important metabolic pathway; in 1953, awarded the Nobel Prize in Physiology or Medicine, jointly with Fritz Lipmann, for his work on metabolism.

Krebs, Nicholas. *See* Nicholas of Cusa

Kremer, Gerhard. *See* Mercator, Gerardus

Kreps, Juanita

né: Juanita Morris
b. January 11, 1921
Lynch, Kentucky
fields: Economics, Education, Government and Politics

An economist, higher educational administrator, and secretary of commerce under the Carter Administration, Kreps was dedicated to improving the well-being of people and facilitating the smooth operation of the economy.

Kreutzberger, Mario. *See* Don Francisco

Kripke, Saul

full: Saul Aaron Kripke
b. November 13, 1940
Bay Shore, New York
fields: Philosophy, Language and Linguistics

Saul Kripke provided technical and conceptual advances in modal logic but is more widely known for his work in the philosophy of language, in particular for initiating the causal theory of reference. Among his major works are *Naming and Necessity* (1980) and *Wittgenstein on Rules and Private Language* (1982).

Krishnamurti, Jiddu

b. May 22, 1895
Madanapalle, Andhra Pradesh, India
d. Feb. 17, 1986
Ojai, Calif.
fields: Philosophy, Religion and Theology

Spiritual leader and philosopher Jiddu Krishnamurti spread his message of enlightenment through talks and lectures throughout the world. Krishnamurti began as a lecturer of Theosophy, a Buddhist-Hindu based faith, but gradually evolved his own philosophy. He created schools throughout the world. His publications include *Tradition and Revolution* (1972), *Krishnamurti on Education* (1972), and the series *Commentaries on Liv-*

ing (1967), *The Wholeness of Life* (1978), and *Mind Without Measure* (1984).

Kristeva, Julia

b. June 24, 1941
Silven, Bulgaria
fields: Philosophy, Langauge and Linguistics, Literature

Julia Kristeva linked semiotics and literary criticism by treating literature as a psychological, historical, and political phenomenon. Her analyses employ concepts from both psychology and political philosophy. She treats literature as a psychological, historical, and political phenomenon. Although Kristeva's fundamental theories have evolved and matured, their provenance is not completely forgotten. Though identified with the leftist intellectual movement of France and agreeing with many of its ideals, Kristeva occupies a unique position as a radical anti-Marxist. Among her many works, *Strangers to Ourselves* (1988) is one of her best known.

Krogh, August

full: Schack August Steenberg Krogh
b. November 15, 1874
Grenaa, Denmark
d. September 13, 1949
Copenhagen, Denmark
fields: Physiology, Zoology

Krogh won the 1920 Nobel Prize in Physiology or Medicine for his investigations into how the capillaries regulate the flow of blood, and thus oxygen, in the body. He also made important advances in the understanding of how the lungs exchange oxygen from the air into the bloodstream.

Kronecker, Leopold

b. Dec. 7, 1823
Liegnitz, Prussia (now Legnica, Poland)
d. Dec. 29, 1891
Berlin, Germany
fields: Mathematics (algebra and number theory)

Leopold Kronecker was a proponent of the philosophy of intuitionism, in which all mathematics is based on the natural numbers.

Kropotkin, Peter

b. December 21, 1842
Moscow, Russia
d. February 8, 1921
Dmitrov, Soviet Union
fields: Philosophy

A Russian anarchist, Peter Kropotkin put his faith in what he called "mutualism," a belief that the natural self-interest of the individual dictated cooperation with one's fellows to solve the problems of social living. Because of his views, he was imprisoned in 1874. After a spectacular escape, he fled to Western Europe and published books explaining his anarchist theories. He returned to Russia after the 1917 revolution.

Krupp, Alfred

b. April 26, 1812; Essen, Grand Duchy of Berg
d. July 14, 1887; Essen, Germany
fields: Business and Industry, Invention and Technology

During the period of Germany's unification into one of the most powerful nations in Europe, Krupp expanded his family's steel-making concern into one of the most powerful industrial enterprises of the nineteenth century.

Kryfts, Nicholas. *See* Nicholas of Cusa

Ku Wei-Chun. *See* Koo, Wellington

Kubitschek, Juscelino

full: Juscelino Kubitschek de Oliveira
b. September 12, 1902
Diamantina, Brazil
d. August 22, 1976
Near Resende, Brazil
fields: Government and Politics

Juscelino Kubitschek was president of Brazil from 1956 to 1961 and builder of the nation's capital, Brasília, which was inaugurated in 1960. His policies fostered industrialization but also created serious inflation.

Kublai Khan

b. 1215
Mongolia
d. 1294
Ta-tu (Peking), China
fields: Warfare and Conquest, Government and Politics

Great Khan of the Mongol Empire, 1260-1294. As a Mongol general and the Great Khan, Kublai helped to conquer and came to rule over an empire which encompassed 80 percent of Eurasia. He founded the Yuän Dynasty of China and brought the Mongols to the peak of their power and influence.

Kübler-Ross, Elisabeth

né: Elisabeth Kübler
b. July 8, 1926
Zurich, Switzerland
fields: Psychiatry and Psychology

A leading researcher in the field of thanatology (the study of death), Kübler-Ross is most widely recognized for having identified five stages in the process of dying that have provided a framework for further work by professionals in the area of counseling the terminally ill and their families. Her work has helped remove former taboos from the subject of death and brought a compassionate and humane approach to the care of the dying.

Kuhn, Maggie

b. Aug. 3, 1905
Buffalo, N.Y.
d. Apr. 22, 1995
Philadelphia, Pa.
fields: Government and Politics

Political activist and founder of the Gray Panthers; Margaret E. Kuhn's political work began after she reached the age of sixty-five. In 1970 she and several friends organized against ageism, other forms of age discrimination, and discrimination generally in American society; convener and charismatic leader of the Gray Panthers; fought for social justice through grassroots politics; used street theater, including demonstrations, protest marches, and picketing; rejected special-interest politics, viewing the problems experienced by women, minorities, the elderly, and other economically disadvantaged groups as interconnected; her autobiography, *No Stone Unturned*, was published in 1991.

Kuhn, Thomas S.

full: Thomas Samuel Kuhn
b. July 18, 1922; Cincinnati, Ohio
d. June 17, 1996; Cambridge, Massachusetts
fields: Philosophy, Science

Departing from traditional philosophy of science, Kuhn argued that science evolves not only by the steady accumulation of knowledge but also by periodic conceptual revolutions. He emphasized that in its pursuit of knowledge, science is a social process. His major works include *The Copernican Revolution* (1957), *The Essential Tension* (1977), and *The Trouble with the Historical Philosophy of Science* (1992). His most influenctial book, *The Structure of Scientific Revolutions* (1962), presented the concepts of scientific "paradigms" and "paradigm shifts," terms that entered the vocabulary of popular culture and were often used loosely. Controversies over his ideas testify to his pervasive effect on intellectual discourse. During an Massachusetts Institute of Technology commencement address in 1996, Vice President Al Gore praised Kuhn for clarifying the relation between science and society and thereby helping each person cope with the world's increasingly rich technological culture.

Kuiper, Gerard Peter

b. Dec. 7, 1905
Harenkarspel, the Netherlands
d. Dec. 23, 1973
Mexico City, Mexico
fields: Astronomy

Gerard Peter Kuiper added to the theoretical understanding of the solar system; in

1948, discovered Miranda, a moon of Uranus; in 1949, discovered Nereid, a moon of Neptune; in 1951, proposed that comets originate in a disk, called the Kuiper belt, outside the orbit of Neptune; proposed a model of how the solar system formed.

Kūkai

né: Kōbō Daishi
b. July 27, 774
Byōbugaura, Sanuki Province, Japan
d. April 22, 835
Mt. Kōya, Japan
fields: Religion and Theology, Philosophy

Kūkai, a Buddhist monk, founded the Shingon school of Japanese Buddhism and taught that conformity to social and moral rules constituted the second of the ten rungs on the ladder that leads to true Buddhahood. Some Shingon adherents believe that he exists in the Heaven of the Satisfied, from which he will return with Maitreya, the future Buddha, and many people make pilgrimages to his tomb. After Kūkai's death, the Japanese bestowed on him the title Kōbō Daishi (Great Teacher of Karma).

Kumar, K. V.

b. 1945
fields: Business and Industry, Government and Politics

K. V. Kumar is a businessperson and political activist; born in Bangalore, India; came to United States as a student in 1968, working as messenger for international organizations; priest at Vittala Hindu temple, Washington, D.C.; founded the National Indian American Chamber of Commerce in 1991 to assist more than one hundred thousand Indian-owned or -operated businesses; active in Republican politics.

Kummok'quifiokta. *See* Wooden Leg

Kunitomo, George Tadao

b. 1893
Kurume, Fukuoka Prefecture, Japan
d. 1967
fields: Education

George Tadao Kunitomo, along with Colbert Naoya Kurokawa and Soen Yamashita, advocated the idea that Hawaii belonged to Japan. Kunitomo received a degree from Oberlin College in 1923, then became the first Japanese-language teacher at Honolulu's McKinley High School. He taught at the University of Hawaii for several years, then returned to Japan and in 1939 resigned from the university. During World War II, he embraced the idea that Japan would lead and unite the nations of East Asia and believed that Japan had a right to possession of the Hawaiian Islands.

Kuniyoshi, Yasuo

b. Sept. 1, 1889
Okayama Prefecture, Japan
d. May 14, 1953
New York, N.Y.
fields: Art, Photography

Yasuo Kuniyoshi arrived in Seattle in 1906. From 1916 to 1920, he studied at the Art Students League. His career began to take off in the 1920's; his paintings were being shown in galleries throughout New York, and he also worked as a photographer. Japan's National Museum of Modern Art staged an exhibition of his work in 1931. He created posters for the U.S. War Department and publicly criticized Japan's imperialist policies during World War II. He presented a solo exhibition at the Whitney Museum of American Art in New York in 1948, becoming the first living American artist to do so.

Kunkel, Louis O.

full: Louis Otto Kunkel
b. May 7, 1884
Mexico, Missouri
d. Mar. 20, 1960
Newtown, Pennsylvania
fields: Botany, Medicine

Louis O. Kunkel answered major questions about the transmission and treatment of viral diseases of plants; helped build institutions of research; brought together many of the early leaders in plant virology.

Kunmesee. *See* Dragging Canoe

Kuo Mo-jo

aka: Guo Mor yo
b. November 10 or 16, 1892
Sha-wan, China
d. June 12, 1978
Peking, China
fields: Government and Politics, Literature

Historian and novelist, poet and propagandist, Kuo was perhaps the most prolific Chinese intellectual of the twentieth century. After the founding of the People's Republic of China in 1949, he served in a variety of government posts, including that of President of the Chinese Academy of Sciences. He survived the purges of the Anti-Rightist Campaign (1957) and the Cultural Revolution era (1966-1976) and continued publishing through the 1970's.

Kupka, František

b. September 23, 1871
Opočno, Bohemia, Austro-Hungarian Empire
d. June 24, 1958
Puteaux, France
fields: Art

František Kupka painted what were probably the first abstract modern paintings, beginning around 1911. He was also a talented illustrator of books and magazines and an important theorist of abstract art.

Kuramoto, June Okida

b. July 22, 1948
Saitama-ken, Japan
fields: Music

June Okida Kuramoto moved to the United States with her parents when she was five years old. Kuramoto, a koto player, collaborated with Dan Kuramoto, a jazz flutist and keyboardist. The couple were married in 1971 and soon established Hiroshima, a pop music group known for its blending of traditional Japanese musical elements with jazz and other Western musical rhythms. The group released its first album, *Hiroshima*, in 1979. The band's fifth album, *Go* (1987) spent eight weeks at the top of *Billboard* magazine's Contemporary Jazz Album chart. Kuramoto has also prepared musical scores for television programs and film and performed with a number of other popular musicians, including Stanley Clarke, Teddy Pendergrass, Ravi Shankar, the Manhattan Transfer, and Lou Gramm.

Kurchatov, Igor Vasilyevich

b. January 12, 1903
Sim Mill, in the Ural Mountains, Russia
d. February 7, 1960
Moscow, U.S.S.R.
fields: Physics

Kurchatov was the father of atomic power in the Soviet Union. He played a pivotal role in the introduction and advancement of atomic energy as a peaceful source of power in that country and was a leader in the development of the Soviet Union's atom bomb in the late 1940's.

Kurihara, Joseph Yoshisuke

b. 1895
Kauai, Republic of Hawaii
fields: Social Reform

Joseph Yoshisuke Kurihara, a U.S. citizen, had served in the U.S. Army during World War I. Despite his status as a veteran, he was interned in a detention camp during World War II. Angered that the government would question the loyalty of a veteran, he helped form militant protests at the Manzanar relocation center. He was sent to the segregated relocation center at Tule Lake. In February, 1946, he renounced his U.S. citizenship and moved to Japan.

Kurokawa, Colbert Naoya

b. 1890
Chiba Prefecture, Japan

d. 1978
Japan
fields: Government and Politics

Colbert Naoya Kurokawa came to Hawaii as a teenager. After receiving a degree from Dickinson College in Pennsylvania in 1922, he returned to Hawaii and became the educational secretary for a branch of the Young Men's Christian Association. Among the first Japanese Americans admitted to the Honolulu Lions Club, in 1926, as a delegate to the national convention, he persuaded the Lions to delete the word "white" from its national membership requirements. Two days after the Japanese bombed Pearl Harbor, Kurokawa either had his U.S. passport taken by Japanese officials, was interned, or both. In 1943, he published a report urging the government of Japan to take possession of the Hawaiian islands. In the early 1950's, he moved back to Hawaii, but in 1958 he moved to Japan.

Kuroki, Ben

b. 1918
Nebr.
fields: Warfare and Conquest

Ben Kuroki, aerial gunner and World War II hero, enlisted in the Army Air Corps and was assigned to a bomber squadron operating out of England and North Africa. He was sent home to Nebraska after flying thirty missions but asked to be reassigned to duty in the Pacific theater. Aboard a B-29, he flew nearly thirty additional missions against Japan. A biography of Kuroki, *Boy from Nebraska: The Story of Ben Kuroki*, was published in 1946.

Kurosawa, Akira

b. March 23, 1910
Tokyo, Japan
d. September 5, 1998
Tokyo, Japan
fields: Film

Throughout his long career as one of the greatest directors in the history of the cinema, Kurosawa explored a humane and profound vision of existence with a brilliantly inventive use of the art of film.

Kusatsu, Clyde

b. September 13, 1948
Honolulu, Territory of Hawaii
fields: Theater and Entertainment, Film, Television

Clyde Kusatsu, a graduate of Northwestern University, appeared in many films and on numerous television programs. He had a regular role on the television series *Bring 'Em Back Alive* (1982-1983) and the short-lived *Island Son* (1992). He also had a part in *Dragon: The Bruce Lee Story* (1993).

Kutuzov, Mikhail Illarionovic

b. September 16, 1745
St. Petersburg, Russia
d. April 28, 1813
Bunzlau, Silesia (now Boleslawiec, Poland)
fields: Military Affairs

An innovative Russian military commander, Kutuzov is best known for defeating Napoleon during the French invasion of Russia in 1812 after having lost to him at Austerlitz in 1805.

Kwahnah (Sweet Odor). *See* Parker, Quanah

Kwan, Nancy

b. May 19, 1939
Hong Kong
fields: Theater and Entertainment, Film

Actor Nancy Kwan's most famous role was that of the title character in *The World of Suzie Wong* (1960). In addition , she had roles in She also appeared in *Flower Drum Song* (1961), the first Asian American musical, and in numerous television programs.

Kwong, Peter

b. ?
fields: Journalism

Peter Kwong, a longtime community activist in New York's Chinatown and professor of Asian American studies, wrote studies regarding immigration. He combines historical background with firsthand observations in works such as *The New Chinatown* (1987) and *Chinatown, New York: Labor and Politics, 1930-1950* (1979).

Kwuon, Im Jung

b. 1958
Seoul, South Korea
fields: Journalism, Social Reform

Im Jung Kwuon moved to Los Angeles with her family at the age of four. She struggled greatly as she tried to balance the demands of her traditionalist parents with her desire to belong in American society. She began to use drugs and alcohol, then went into therapy and to college. She received bachelor's degrees in sociology and economics from the University of California, Los Angeles, in 1989 and a master's degree in counseling psychology at the University of Southern California. In 1990, she began writing a "Dear Immy" advice column for the *Korea Times* that deals with social and emotional issues.

L

L. L. Cool J.

né: James Todd Smith
b. 1969?
Queens, N.Y.
fields: Music (rap singer)

African American rap singer; L. L. Cool J.'s first release was "I Need a Beat," which sold more than one hundred thousand copies. His second album, *Radio* (1985), included "I Want You," "I Can Give You More," and "I Can't Live Without My Radio" and went platinum. L.L.'s other albums include *Bigger and Deffer* (1987), which remained on Billboard's Top Ten list for two months, *Walkin' with a Panther* (1989), *Mama Said Knock You Out* (1990), and *Phenomenon* (1997).

L. T. *See* Taylor, Lawrence

Laban, Rudolf

full: Rudolf Jean-Baptist Attila, marquis de Laban de Varalja
b. December 15, 1879
Poszony, Austro-Hungarian Empire
d. July 1, 1958
Weybridge, England
fields: Dance

In Germany Laban is recognized as the father of the Expressive Dance (Ausdruckstanz) Movement. In England his Effort theory has vitally influenced the educational system. In the United States, dance acquired literacy through his system of notation (Labanotation).

Labarthe, Pedro Juan

b. 1906
Puerto Rico
fields: Literature

Latino writer. Pedro Juan Labarthe is known in the United States for his autobiographical book *The Son of Two Nations: The Private Life of a Columbia Student* (1931), which documents his experiences at Columbia University and his efforts to improve his socioeconomic status through assimilation.

Labat, Tony

b. Nov. 14, 1951
Havana, Cuba
fields: Art

Latino artist. Tony Labat moved to the United States in 1965 and earned B.F.A. (1978) and M.F.A. (1980) degrees from the San Francisco Art Institute. His work, which is primarily in the video medium, is in several major museums, including the Centre Pompidou in Paris, France; the Museum of Modern Art in New York City; and the Oppenheim Collection in Bonn, Germany. Labat won National Endowment for the Arts fellowships in 1983 and 1988.

LaBelle, Patti

né: Patricia Louise Holte
b. October 4, 1944
Philadelphia, Pa.
fields: Music

African American singer, songwriter, bandleader, and actress; Patti LaBelle reached the top ten with the *Nightbirds* album in 1973 and number one with the single "Lady Marmalade." While continuing her music career she costarred in a revival of *Your Arms Too Short to Box with God* on Broadway in 1982. A duet with Michael McDonald went to number one on the charts in 1986, and LaBelle won a Grammy in 1991 for her performance of *Burnin'*.

La Brack, Bruce W.

b. July 16, 1941
Troy, N.Y.
fields: Anthropology

Widely published cultural anthropologist Bruce W. La Brack published many works, including pioneering studies of the Sikhs in North America such *The Sikhs of Northern California: 1904-1975* (1988). He received a Ph.D. in 1980 from Syracuse University and, in 1986, was named Professor of Anthropology and International Studies at the University of the Pacific. He has conducted research in South Asian history and ethnology, Sikhs, cross-cultural issues, and postwar Japan.

La Brède de Montesquieu, Baron de. *See* Montesquieu

Lacan, Jacques

full: Jacques Marie Émile Lacan
b. April 13, 1901
Paris, France
d. September 9, 1981
Paris, France
fields: Psychiatry and Psychology, Philosophy, Language and Linguistics

Lacan was the single most important figure in the development of psychoanalysis in twentieth century France. His powerful rereading of Freud's work and rethinking of Freud's fundamental concepts made him a key figure in French intellectual life from the 1950's until his death.

Lafayette, James Armistead

né: James Armistead
b. b. 1760
New Kent County, Va.
d. 1832
fields: Military Affairs

African American soldier; James Armistead Lafayette, though born into slavery, served as a spy behind British lines during the Revolutionary War. In return for his service, Lafayette was freed by the Virginia legislature in 1786, after which he became a landowner.

La Flesche, Francis

aka: Zhogaxe (Woodworker)
b. 1857
d. 1932
fields: Anthropology, Scholarship

Native American advocate and ethnologist. Francis La Flesche, a Ponca, struggled to regain the Ponca homeland in the late 1870's and 1880's. Attended National University Law School in Washington, D.C., graduating in 1892. Collaborated with anthropologist Alice C. Fletcher on *A Study of Omaha Music* (1893) and *The Omaha Tribe* (1911). Wrote other books.

La Flesche, Susan. *See* Picotte, Susan La Flesche

La Flesche, Susette

aka: Josette La Flesche
aka: Inshtatheumba (Bright Eyes)
b. 1854
Omaha reservation, Nebr.
d. 1903
Lincoln, Nebr.
fields: Native American Affairs

Susette La Flesche, a Ponca and a native-rights advocate, lectured in support of the Poncas' regaining their ancestral land in 1879-1880 with her brother Francis and Standing Bear. Coauthored a memoir with Standing Bear, *Ploughed Under: The Story of an Indian Chief* (1832).

La Follette, Robert M.

full: Robert Marion La Follette
b. June 14, 1855
Primrose, Wisconsin
d. June 18, 1925
Washington, D.C.
fields: Government and Politics

As governor of Wisconsin and United States Senator, La Follette combined a strong sense of social justice with an intense commitment to principles as a leader of the reform movement in politics from 1900 to 1925.

La Fontaine, Henri-Marie

b. April 22, 1854
Brussels, Belgium
d. May 14, 1943
Brussels, Belgium

fields: Diplomacy, Government and Politics, Law

La Fontaine was a leader in the European popular peace movement and was awarded the Nobel Peace Prize in 1913. In addition to being an influential pacifist, he was an outstanding jurist, dedicated professor, Belgian senator, social reformer, and prolific author.

La Fontaine, Jean de

b. July 8, 1621
Château-Thierry, Champagne, France
d. April 13, 1695
Paris, France
fields: Literature

La Fontaine is recognized as one of the major writers of the French classical period. He wrote drama, ballet, popular tales, and various forms of poetry, but he is best known in France and abroad for his verse fables, a genre he developed to perfection.

Lafontant, Jewel

b. April 28, 1922
Chicago, Ill.
d. May 31, 1997
Chicago, Ill.
fields: Government and Politics

African American government official; Jewel Lafontant was appointed deputy solicitor general and United Nations representative in 1973. She held the former post until 1975. She was appointed an ambassador and coordinator for refugee affairs in 1989 by President George Bush. Lafontant also served as director of several major corporations and on the National Council of Minority Business Enterprise.

Lagerlöf, Selma

full: Selma Ottiliana Lovisa Lagerlöf
b. November 20, 1858
Mårbacka, Sweden
d. March 16, 1940
Mårbacka, Sweden
fields: Literature

Lagerlöf was the first woman to receive the Nobel Prize in Literature (1909) and the first woman to be elected to the Swedish Academy (1914). During her lifetime, she was loved throughout the world because of both her gift for storytelling and her idealism, which was a welcome change from the pessimistic realism dominating her period. Since her death, she also has been increasingly recognized as a preserver of the folkways and traditions of rural Sweden.

Lagrange, Joseph-Louis

b. January 25, 1736
Turin, Sardinia
d. April 10, 1813
Paris, France
fields: Mathematics

One of the most brilliant mathematicians of the mid- and late eighteenth century, Lagrange accomplished astonishing syntheses of the mathematical innovations of his predecessors, especially in the systems underlying classic physics. Almost as remarkable for his winning personality as his incisive intellect, Lagrange created the mathematical basis of modern mechanics.

La Guardia, Fiorello Henry

b. December 11, 1882
New York, New York
d. September 20, 1947
New York, New York
fields: Government and Politics

Using boundless energy, La Guardia, the son of immigrants, served the public during a thirty-year career that included several terms as a U.S. congressman and three terms as mayor of New York City. He was the first Italian-American elected to these positions.

Laguerre, Enrique A.

b. May 3, 1906
Moca, Puerto Rico
fields: Literature

Latino novelist. Enrique A. Laguerre earned bachelor's and master's degrees from the University of Puerto Rico and performed doctoral work at Columbia University. He taught in rural Puerto Rico in the 1920's, then worked for the Puerto Rico Department of Education, taught at the University of Puerto Rico at Rio Piedras, and was a consultant for the Department of Public Instruction. He also taught in the United States. He wrote ten novels, include *La llamarada* (1935), that deal with problems faced by Puerto Rican both on the island and in the United States.

Lai, Him Mark

b. Nov. 1, 1925
San Francisco, Calif.
fields: Engineering, Sociology

Him Mark Lai, an engineer for the Bechtel Corporation until 1984, wrote *A History Reclaimed: An Annotated Bibliography and Guide of Chinese Language Materials on the Chinese of America* (1986) and coauthored *History of the Chinese in California: A Syllabus* (1969), *Chinese Newspapers in North America, 1854-1975* (1976), and *Chinese of America, 1785-1980: Exhibition Catalog* (1980). Lai coedited *Island: Poetry and History of Chinese Immigrants on Angel Island* (1980), for which he received an American Book Award from the Before Columbus Foundation. Lai lectured in Chinese American history at San Francisco State University and the University of California, Berkeley. He became a member of the editorial board of *Amerasia Journal* in 1979 and *Chinese America: History and Perspectives* in 1986. He received a service award from the Association for Asian American Studies.

Lal, Gobind Behari

b. Oct. 9, 1889
Delhi, India
d. Apr. 2, 1982
San Francisco, Calif.
fields: Journalism

Gobind Behari Lal's 1925 article on cancer research for the *San Francisco Examiner* won him national recognition. He became science editor for the *International News Service* and *The American Weekly*. Lal and three others won the Pulitzer Prize for their work in the Harvard Tercentenary in 1936. Others awards included the George Westinghouse Award in 1946 from the American Association for the Advancement of Science for outstanding journalism and a Guggenheim Fellowship in 1956 for the book *Science in the East and West*. Other publications include *Joseph Mazzini as a Social Reformer* (1915), *Politics and Science in India* (1920), and *Chemistry of Personality* (1932). One of the founding members of the National Association of Science Writers, Lal served as its president in 1940-1941.

Lalawethika. *See* Tenskwatawa

Lallo. *See* Asah, Spencer

Lam, Tony

b. 1930's
Vietnam
fields: Business and Industry, Philanthropy

In November, 1992, restaurateur Tony Lam became the first Vietnamese refugee be elected to office in the United States when he earned a seat on the city council of Westminster, California, a city in Orange County with one of the largest concentrations of Vietnamese Americans in the country. Lam had been a successful businessman in South Vietnam but was forced to flee when Saigon fell in April, 1975. In the United States, Lam worked various positions, including a shipping company supervisor, insurance broker, immigration consultant, and advertising executive, and later bought several Vietnamese restaurants.

Lamar, Joseph Rucker

b. 1857
d. 1916
fields: Law

U.S. Supreme Court justice, 1911-1916 (died while in office); appointed by President Taft. Significant opinion: *Gompers v. Bucks*

Stove and Range Company, 221 U.S. 418 (1911).

Lamar, Lucius Quintus Cincinnatus

b. 1825
d. 1893
fields: Law

U.S. Supreme Court justice, 1888-1893 (died while in office); appointed by President Cleveland. Significant opinions: *In re Neagle*, 135 U.S. 1 (1890) (dissenting opinion); *Field v. Clark*, 143 U.S. 649 (1892) (dissenting opinion).

Lamarck, Jean-Baptiste

full: Jean-Baptiste-Pierre-Antoine de Monet, chevalier de Lamarck
b. Aug. 1, 1744
Bazentin-le-Petit, Picardy, France
d. Dec. 28, 1829
Paris, France
fields: Biology, Botany, Zoology

Jean-Baptiste Lamarck proposed that evolutionary change takes place by the use and disuse of organs; in 1802, published *Hydrogéologie* (*Hydrogeology*, 1964) offering a history of the earth as a series of floods and the building up of deposits to form continents; in 1809, proposed laws governing the ascent of life to higher stages and the inheritance of acquired characteristics; developed a system for the classification of invertebrates based on anatomy; made major contributions to the classification of plants.

Lamas, Fernando

b. October 8, 1915
Buenos Aires, Argentina
d. October 8, 1982
Los Angeles, Calif.
fields: Theater and Entertainment, Television

Latino actor. Fernando Lamas made his first film in 1939 but did not become a star until his fifth film, *Lady Windermere's Fan* (1942). After making more than a dozen Spanish-language films, he moved, in 1949, to the United States, where he was cast in "Latin lover" roles. Among his films were *The Merry Widow* (1952) and *The Girl Rush* (1955). In the late 1950's he began directing, producing, and writing for both television and motion pictures.

Lamas, Lorenzo

b. January 20, 1958
Santa Monica, Calif.
fields: Theater and Entertainment, Television

Latino actor. Lorenzo Lamas, son of Fernando Lamas, appeared in television episodes of *The Love Boat*, *Sword of Justice*, *California Fever*, *Switch*, and *Secrets of Midland Heights*. He also had roles in *Grease* (1978), *Tilt* (1978), *Take Down* (1978), and *Body Rock* (1984). He became a heartthrob when he starred as the villain Lance Cumson in the successful series *Falcon Crest* in 1981. He later hosted a syndicated show called *Dancin' to the Hits*. In the 1990's he starred in his own television series called *Renegade*, in which he plays a Harley-riding fugitive who helps people in distress.

Lamb, The. *See* Sampson, Edgar Melvin

Lamb, William. *See* Melbourne, second viscount

Lambert, Johann Heinrich

b. Aug. 26, 1728
Mülhausen, Alsace, France
d. Sept. 25, 1777
Berlin, Prussia (now Germany)
fields: Mathematics (number theory)

In 1767 Johann Heinrich Lambert proved that pi is an irrational quantity; introduced hyperbolic functions into trigonometry.

Lambert, John

b. September, 1619
Calton, West Riding, Yorkshire, England
d. March, 1684
St. Nicholas Isle, Plymouth Sound, Cornwall, England
fields: Military Affairs, Government and Politics

After serving as one of Parliament's leading officers in England's civil war, Lambert emerged as a central figure in the Protectorate. After Oliver Cromwell's death, Lambert led the army's unsuccessful attempt to maintain a republic and prevent the Stuart restoration.

Lambton, John George. *See* Durham, first earl of

Lame Deer

aka: Tahca Ushte
aka: John Fire
b. c. 1895
near Pine Ridge, S.Dak.
d. Dec. 14, 1976
Denver, Colo.
fields: Native American Affairs, Literature

A Miniconjou Sioux, Lame Deer moved between the white world and the world of the Indian on a reservation; he was a rancher, rodeo rider, reservation policeman, and holy man. Remembered for his autobiography, *Lame Deer: Seeker of Visions* (1976, written with Richard Erdoes). Recounts his life growing up on a reservation and protests against the white culture that robbed Indians of their land and culture.

La Mettrie, Julien Offroy de

b. December 25, 1709
Saint-Malo, Brittany, France
d. November 11, 1751
Berlin, Germany
fields: Philosophy

Julien Offroy de La Mettrie carried Cartesian mechanism to its logical endpoint by positing, on the basis of his medical understanding, that a human being is a mechanism and that happiness arises from the effects of sense stimuli on this mechanism. His major works include *Treatise on the Soul* (1745), *Man a Machine* (1747), *Anti-Seneca* (1747), *Man a Plant* (1748), *Les Animaux plus que machines* (1750), and *Le Petite Homme à longue queue* (1751).

Lamochattee. *See* Weatherford, William

Lancaster, Joseph

b. 1778
London, England
d. October 24, 1838
New York, New York
fields: Education

An advocate of mass education, Lancaster devised an intricate educational system which was economical and replicable, thus promoting its adoption by numerous countries.

Lanchester, Frederick William

b. October 23, 1868
Lewisham, London, England
d. March 8, 1946
Birmingham, England
fields: Invention and Technology

With an intuitive genius, Lanchester designed and built the first truly British motorcar, owing nothing to previous production of a horseless carriage and little or nothing to the pioneering designs of the French and Germans whose works were copied or adapted by other British inventors. In addition, Lanchester developed, ten years before the first heavier-than-air flight, the principles of powered flight and aircraft design.

Land, Edwin Herbert

b. May 7, 1909
Bridgeport, Connecticut
d. Mar. 1, 1991
Cambridge, Massachusetts
fields: Chemistry, Invention and Technology, Physics

Edwin Herbert Land founded the Polaroid Corporationin 1937; patented polarizing filters; introduced instant black-and-white photography in 1947; demonstrated the Land effect in color vision in 1959; created instant color photography in 1963; debuted instant film and camera for motion pictures in 1977.

Landau, Lev Davidovich
b. January 22, 1908
Baku, Azerbaijan, Russian Empire
d. April 1, 1968
Moscow, U.S.S.R.
fields: Physics

Landau contributed to the development of quantum mechanics and its applications to the physical world. Among his major achievements are the development of the theory of phase transitions and his explanation of the behavior of quantum liquids such as liquid helium in the superfluid state. Landau's contributions to the theory of quantum liquids were recognized by the award of the Nobel Prize in Physics in 1962.

Landini, Francesco
aka: Francesco Landino
b. 1325-1335
Fiesole, Italy
d. September 2, 1397
Florence, Italy
fields: Music

Landini was the most highly regarded Italian composer and performer of his time.

Landsteiner, Karl
b. June 14, 1868
Vienna, Austria
d. June 26, 1943
New York, New York
fields: Biology, Genetics, Medicine

Karl Landsteiner was a pioneer in the development of immunology; in 1900-1901, demonstrated the existence of different types of human blood (A, B, and O groups); in 1927-1928, with Philip Levine, discovered additional blood groups (M, N, and MN) in humans; in 1940, with Alexander S. Wiener, reported the existence of Rh blood groups; received the Nobel Prize in Physiology or Medicine in 1930.

Lane, Carrie. *See* Catt, Carrie Chapman

Lane, Charles
b. December 5, 1953
New York, N.Y.
fields: Film (filmmaker and actor)

African American filmmaker and actor; Charles Lane's credits include independent and feature films such as *Place and Time*, *Skins*, *Sidewalk Stories* (1989), and *True Identity* (1991); inducted into the Black Filmmakers Hall of Fame in 1990; received the CEBA Pioneer of Excellence Award (1991) and an award from the National Association for the Advancement of Colored People (1992).

Lane, Dick
full: Richard Lane
aka: Night Train
b. April 16, 1928
Austin, Tex.
fields: Sports (football)

African American football player. After playing on the All-Army team in 1949 and 1950 Dick Lane began his professional football career in 1952, after his discharge. In his rookie year with the Los Angeles Rams Lane set a record for pass interceptions. Named All-Pro defensive back three times, Lane was inducted into the Pro Football Hall of Fame in 1974.

Lane, Isaac
b. March 3, 1834
Jackson, Tenn.
d. December 6, 1937
Jackson, Tenn.
fields: Education, Religion and Theology

African American educator and clergyman; Isaac Lane worked to expand the Christian Methodist Episcopal church to major cities, mostly in the Midwest. He became a bishop in 1873. Lane founded the Lane College in Jackson in 1882, with money he had raised himself.

Lane, William Henry
aka: Master Juba
b. 1825
New York?, N.Y.
d. 1853
London, England
fields: Dance

African American dancer. Through his beautiful and intricate dancing William Henry Lane opened the door for African Americans to perform with Caucasian minstrels and for African Americans to perform in all theaters. Tutored by Jim Lowe, by 1845, Lane was headlining for the Ethiopian Minstrels. He later joined the Georgia Champions, another minstrel group, for a successful tour of New England. He also enjoyed critical acclaim in London, where he had gone in 1848, with Pell's Ethiopian Serenaders.

Laney, Lucy Craft
b. April 13, 1854
Macon, Ga.
d. October 23, 1933
Augusta, Ga.
fields: Education

African American educator; Lucy Craft Laney founded Haines Normal and Industrial Institute (1883), which made valuable contributions to the education of African Americans.

Lang, Fritz
b. December 5, 1890
Vienna, Austro-Hungarian Empire
d. August 2, 1976
Los Angeles, California
fields: Film

Lang was a pioneer in twentieth century filmmaking. The silent films that he directed in Germany in the 1920's established his reputation as a creative innovator and skilled cinematic craftsman. His sound films in the early 1930's and Hollywood films of the 1940's and 1950's demonstrated his remarkable ability to adapt to changing technical and cultural settings without sacrificing cinematic integrity.

Lang, K. D.
full: Kathryn Dawn Lang
aka: k. d. lang
b. November 2, 1961
Edmonton, Alberta, Canada
fields: Music

A songwriter and Grammy-winning singer, Lang has achieved success in the genres of country-western and alternative pop music while challenging stereotypes of female popular entertainers.

Lange, Christian Lous
b. September 17, 1869
Stavanger, Norway
d. December 11, 1938
Oslo, Norway
fields: Diplomacy, Peace Advocacy

Christian Lous Lange, a Norwegian historian, was secretary-general of the Interparliamentary Union from 1909 to 1933. He was awarded the 1921 Nobel Peace Prize along with Swedish prime minister Karl H. Branting. First secretary of Nobel Institute.

Lange, Dorothea
né: Dorothea Margretta Nutzhorn
b. May 26, 1895
Hoboken, New Jersey
d. October 11, 1965
San Francisco, California
fields: Photography, Social Reform

Considered by many to be the country's most distinguished documentary photographer, Dorothea Lange brought her photographic vision to bear most memorably on the living conditions of Depression America's rural poor and Japanese Americans detained in World War II internment camps.

Lange, Ted W., III
b. January 5, 1947
Oakland, Calif.
fields: Theater and Entertainment, Television

African American actor, playwright, and director; Ted W. Lange III made his Broadway debut in the musical production of *Hair* (1969). He also acted with the Colorado Shakespeare Company in productions of *Two*

Gentlemen of Verona, King Henry VI, and *Macbeth*. Lange created the role of bartender Isaac Washington on the hit series *The Love Boat* (1977-1986). Lange also developed screenplays and original plays, produced and directed a production of *Othello*, and starred in a production of *Driving Miss Daisy*.

Langer, Susanne K.

né: Susanne Katherina Knauth
b. December 20, 1895
New York, New York
d. July 17, 1985
Old Lyme, Connecticut
fields: Philosophy, Education

A leading American philosopher in an historically male-dominated field, Langer was one of the major influences on twentieth century thought in the fields of philosophy and aesthetics. Her work in the realm of "symbolic transformation" helped to establish logical philosophical framework for art and social science, areas not formerly thought to adhere to any ordered system of ideas.

Langhorne, Nancy Witcher. *See* Astor, Nancy

Langley, Samuel Pierpont

b. August 22, 1834
Roxbury, Massachusetts
d. February 27, 1906
Aiken, South Carolina
fields: Astronomy, Aviation and Space Exploration, Invention and Technology

Through pioneering research, Langley discovered new portions of the infrared spectrum, while his invention of the bolometer aided in spectral measurements of solar and lunar radiation. He also established the principles of flight and demonstrated the practicability of mechanical flight with self-propelled, heavier-than-air machines.

Langmuir, Irving

b. Jan. 31, 1881
Brooklyn, New York
d. Aug. 16, 1957
Falmouth, Massachusetts
fields: Chemistry, Physics, Invention and Technology

Irving Langmuir was an industrial physical chemist; did pioneering work in electrical technology, surface chemistry, the structure of matter, electrical discharge, thermionic emission, plasma physics, and weather modification; in 1932, won the Nobel Prize in Chemistry.

Langston, John Mercer

b. December 14, 1829
Louisa County, Va.
d. November 15, 1897
Washington, D.C.
fields: Education, Government and Politics

African American educator and public official; John Mercer Langston was one of the first African Americans elected to office. He was founder and president of the National Equal Rights League (1864). Langston served as school inspector general of the Freedmen's Bureau and as professor of law, dean, and acting president of Howard University (1869-1876). He was the United States' minister to Haiti and chargé d'affaires to Santo Domingo (1877-1885) and was elected to the U.S. House of Representatives (1890-1891).

Lanier, Bob

full: Robert Jerry Lanier, Jr.
b. September 10, 1948
Buffalo, N.Y.
fields: Sports (basketball)

African American basketball player; Bob Lanier joined the Detroit Pistons in 1970 after an All-America collegiate career at St. Bonaventure University. During his fourteen-year career in the National Basketball Association, playing with the Detroit Pistons and the Milwaukee Bucks, Lanier averaged more than twenty points and ten rebounds per game.

Lankester, Edwin Ray

aka: Sir Edwin Ray Lankester
b. May 15, 1847
London, England
d. August 15, 1929
London, England
fields: Zoology, Natural History

After studying invertebrates, Lankester systematized the field of embryology, and he researched major groups of living and fossil animals. He wrote more than one hundred scientific essays, mostly dealing with comparative anatomy and paleontology, and his series of books made scientific matters understandable and interesting to laypersons.

Lankford, John Anderson

b. December 4, 1874
Potosi, Mo.
d. ?
fields: Architecture

African American architect; John Anderson Lankford, the first black architect in the United States, designed many churches in the United States, Africa, and South America. He was a supervisor of construction for the U.S. government during World War I.

Lansbury, Angela

full: Angela Brigid Lansbury
b. October 16, 1925
London, England
fields: Theater and Entertainment (drama), Film, Television

Lansbury has been an award-winning actress on stage, screen, and television from the early 1940's through the end of the century.

Lansdowne, Lord

full: Henry Charles Keith Petty-Fitzmaurice, fifth marquess of Lansdowne
né: Henry Charles Keith Petty-Fitzmaurice
b. January 14, 1845
London, England
d. June 3, 1927
Newtown Anmer, Clonmel, Ireland
fields: Government and Politics, Diplomacy

British politician and diplomat. Governor-general of Canada, 1883-1888; viceroy of India from 1888 to 1894. Foreign secretary from 1900 to 1906 and was instrumental in forming major alliances with Japan in 1902 and with France in 1904. In 1917, Lansdowne was disheartened by the ongoing slaughter of World War I. He sent a letter to a London newspaper advocating that the British begin talks with Germany and attempt to negotiate an end to the war. The highly controversial "Lansdowne letter" effectively ended his public career.

Lansing, Robert

b. Oct. 17, 1864
Watertown, N.Y.
d. Oct. 30, 1928
Washington, D.C.
fields: Government and Politics

Robert Lansing, U.S. secretary of state (1915-1920), negotiated the Lansing-Ishii Agreement (1917) between the United States and Japan. The agreement attempted to reconcile the two countries' China policies. The agreement recognized Japan's special interests in China, but it emphasized the continuation of the Open Door policy, or the equal trading rights of all foreign nations, in China.

Lao-tzu. *See* Laozi

Laozi

aka: Lao-tzu
b. 604 B.C.E.
Quren, State of Chu, China
d. Sixth century B.C.E.
place unknown
fields: Philosophy

Laozi is widely recognized as the premier thinker of Taoism, the second of China's great philosophical schools.

la Péruse, Jean de

full: Jean Baslier de la Péruse

b. 1529
Vendômois, France
d. 1554
fields: Literature

A member of la Pléiade (fl. 1549-1589), a group of loosely organized poets dedicated to raising the level of sophistication of the French language by adding words and genres derived from classical literature. Led by Pierre de Ronsard and Joachim du Bellay, they developed a new form of poetry based on forms such as the sonnet, the ode, epic, and elegy. They also worked to elevate the level of the poet to a position as an intermediary between humanity and the heavens.

Laplace, Pierre-Simon

b. March 23, 1749
Beaumont-en-Auge, Normandy, France
d. March 5, 1827
Paris, France
fields: Astronomy, Mathematics, Physics

Laplace made groundbreaking mathematical contributions to probability theory and statistical analysis. Using Isaac Newton's theory of gravitation, he also performed very detailed mathematical analyses of the shape of Earth and the orbits of comets, planets, and their moons.

Lardner, Ring, Jr.

b. August 19, 1915
Chicago, Illinois
fields: Film

The son of humorist Ring Lardner, Ring Lardner, Jr., began his career as a journalist in New York but later became a Hollywood screenwriter. He won Academy Awards for his screenplays of *Woman of the Year* (1942) and *M*A*S*H* (1970). Meanwhile, he underwent a long period of being blacklisted after refusing to testify before the House Committee on Un-American Activities in 1947, when he became known as a member of the so-called "Hollywood Ten." His ostracism finally ended in 1964, when he was hired to write a screenplay for *The Cincinnati Kid*.

Larkins, E. Pat

b. ?
fields: Government and Politics

African American mayor and commissioner for city of Pompano Beach, Florida; E. Pat Larkins served as a commissioner for the city of Pompano Beach before becoming mayor of the city in 1985. She remained mayor through December of 1988.

LaRouche, Lyndon H., Jr.

b. September 8, 1922
Rochester, New Hampshire
fields: Government and Politics

A radical politician, Lyndon H. LaRouche, Jr., became a leader in the Students for a Democratic Society after leaving the Socialist Labor Party. When SDS expelled him in 1969, he formed the National Caucus of Labor Committees (NCLC). His political philosophy used sexism and homophobia. In 1973 he founded the U.S. Labor Party and launched his first of six failed presidential campaigns in 1976. During his 1984 campaign, his front groups committed credit card fraud to raise money, and he and several aides were convicted by a federal court.

Larraz, Julio F.

b. Mar. 12, 1944
Havana, Cuba
fields: Art

Latino artist. Julio F. Larraz moved from Cuba to Miami, Florida, in 1961. Although his training as painter was informal, he began exhibiting his work by 1973. In 1975, he was awarded a Cintas Foundation Fellowship. During the 1980's, Larraz's oil and watercolor paintings were exhibited in numerous group and solo shows in the United States and Latin America. His paintings can be found in the Museo de Arte Moderno in Bogotá, Colombia; the Museo de Monterrey in Mexico; and the collection of the Cintas Foundation.

Lars, Byron

b. 1965?
Oakland, Calif.
fields: Fashion (fashion designer)

African American fashion designer; Byron Lars founded his own design business in 1990; named Rookie of the Year by *Women's Wear Daily* magazine in April of 1991.

LaSalle, Eriq

b. 1962
Hartford, Conn.
fields: Televison, Theater and Entertainment (actor)

African American actor; best known for his role as Dr. Peter Benton on the NBC television medical drama *ER* (1994), Eriq LaSalle also appeared in the films *Coming to America* (1988) and *Color of Night* (1994). In 1996, he directed *Rebound*.

La Salle, Sieur de

né: René-Robert Cavelier
b. November 21, 1643
Rouen, France
d. March 19, 1687
on the Brazos River, Texas
fields: Exploration and Colonization

La Salle was the first European to traverse fully the Mississippi River. He exited into the Gulf of Mexico, where he later attempted unsuccessfully to found a French colony on the Texas coast.

Las Casas, Bartolomé de

b. August, 1474
Seville, Spain
d. July 31, 1566
Madrid, Spain
fields: Religion and Theology, Colonial Administration, Social Reform

Las Casas wrote a history of the early Spanish conquests in the New World and participated in the Spanish conquest of the Caribbean. Concerned with the plight of the Indians, he spent more than fifty years attempting to free the Indians from the oppression of their European conquerors, working to destroy the *encomienda* system and finding new ways of converting the Indians to Christianity.

Lasker, Bruno

b. July 26, 1880
Hamburg, Germany
d. Sept. 9, 1965
Kitsap County, Wash.
fields: Sociology

Bruno Lasker emigrated to the United States in 1914, In 1923, he became a researcher for the Institute of Pacific Relations (IPR), and in 1928, secretary of the Southeast Asian Institute. Lasker was commissioned to do a three-month study of Filipino immigration to the United States and prepare a report for the American Council of the IPR, which was printed as *Filipino Immigration: To Continental United States and to Hawaii*. From 1946 to 1852, Lasker was a member of the United Nations Ad Hoc Committee on Slavery. His works include *People of Southeast Asia* (1944), *Human Bondage in Southeast Asia* (1950), and *Standards of Living in Southern and Eastern Asia* (1954).

Laski, Harold J.

full: Harold Joseph Laski
b. June 30, 1893
Manchester, England
d. March 24, 1950
London, England
fields: Political Science, Education

Laski combined a strong commitment to social democracy with an equally strong faith in education; his career as a professor at the London School of Economics provided him with the opportunity to develop his political theory while also enabling him to influence the intellectual debate about the Labour Party program of the 1930's and 1940's.

Lassalle, Ferdinand

b. April 11, 1825
Breslau, Prussia

d. August 31, 1864
Geneva, Switzerland
fields: Political Science, Economics

Lassalle was one of the founders of the German labor movement and the most important advocate of scientific socialism in Germany after the Revolution of 1848. His theory of evolutionary socialism eventually triumphed within the German Social Democratic Party.

Lasswell, Harold D.

b. February 13, 1902
Donnellson, Illinois
d. December 18, 1978
New York, New York
fields: Scholarship, Philosophy

A professor of political science and law at Yale University, Harold D. Lasswell was director of the war communications research division of the Library of Congress. He built a political philosophy around the question of who gets what, and when and how they get it, and became a leading theorist on propaganda. His books include *Propaganda Technique in the World War* (1927), *Politics: Who Gets What, When, How* (1936), *World Politics and Personal Insecurity* (1937), and *World Revolutionary Propaganda.*

Lasuén, Fermin Francisco de

b. 1720
Vitoria, Spain
d. June 26, 1803
Mission San Carlos, Calif.
fields: Religion and Theology

Latino missionary. Franciscan missionary Fermin Francisco de Lasuén moved to Mexico and took over took over Francisco de Borjia mission in 1767. In 1773, Lasuén was assigned to Mission San Gabriel in Alta California, where he defused trouble with the Indian population. In 1775, he moved to San Diego and helped end the San Diego Indian revolt. In 1785, Lasuén became the president of California's Franciscan missions and remained in that position for eighteen years, during which time nine missions were founded. Point Fermin and Point Lasuén near Los Angeles were named for him.

László I, Saint

aka: Ladislas
b. 1040?
Kraków, Poland
d. July 29, 1095
somewhere near the Moravian border
fields: Government and Politics, Religion and Theology, Monarchy

King of Hungary, 1077-1095 (actually named Regent in 1077, until the crown could be returned for the coronation as king). By means of legislative reforms, diplomacy, and military bravura, László brought for Hungary both internal security and, with the annexation of Croatia, a new, more active role in the affairs of the world.

Lateef, Yusef

né: William Evans
b. October 9, 1920
Chattanooga, Tenn.
fields: Music (multi-instrumentalist and composer)

African American multi-instrumentalist and composer; Yusef Latee, primarily a tenor saxophonist, worked with many well-knowns including Dizzy Gillespie, Charles Mingus, and Cannonball Adderley. Some Lateef recordings: *The Dreamer*, 1959, *Eastern Sounds*, 1961, *Psychicemotus*, 1965, *Yusef Lateef, Suite 16*, 1970, and *In a Temple Garden*, 1979. *Yusef Lateef's Flute Book of the Blues* was published in 1973.

Lathen, John William

b. July 6, 1916
Hackensack, N.J.
fields: Psychiatry and Psychology

African American psychiatrist; John William Lathen, who received his M.D. from the Howard University Medical School (1949), was the first black chemist to be employed at Bendix Corporation (1943). For more than thirty years he ran a private psychiatric practice and became the first black president of the Bergen County, N.J., Mental Health Association.

Lathrop, Julia C.

full: Julia Clifford Lathrop
b. June 29, 1858
Rockford, Ill.
d. April 15, 1932
Rockford, Ill.
fields: Psychiatry and Psychology, Government and Politics, Social Reform

The daughter of suffragist Sarah Potter Lathrop, Julia Clifford Lathrop worked with Jane Addams at Hull House in Chicago. In 1893 Illinois governor John P. Altgeld appointed her to the state Board of Charities. Her reports called for reforming mental institutions and hospitals and placing children elsewhere. In 1909 she helped create the first U.S. juvenile court system in Cook County. Three years later President William Howard Taft named her head of the new Children's Bureau of the Department of Commerce and Labor (1912-1921), designed to enforce the first child-labor laws.

Latimer, Hugh

b. Between 1485 and 1492
Thurcaston, Leicestershire, England
d. October 16, 1555
Oxford, England
fields: Religion and Theology

With his powerful preaching, Latimer helped mobilize popular opinion to support the reformation of the English church.

Latimer, Lewis Howard

b. September 4, 1848
Chelsea, Mass.
d. December 11, 1928
Flushing, N.Y.
fields: Science, Invention and Technology

African American scientist and inventor; Lewis Howard Latimer was a member of Thomas Alva Edison's research team and a major contributor to the development and commercialization of the incandescent light bulb; he improved the quality and lifespan of the carbon filaments then used in all incandescent bulbs. Latimer was also a civil rights advocate and humanitarian who participated in many projects that benefited immigrants and other disadvantaged people.

Latrobe, Benjamin Henry

full: Benjamin Henry Boneval Latrobe
b. May 1, 1764
Fulneck, England
d. September 3, 1820
New Orleans, Louisiana
fields: Architecture, Engineering

Latrobe was the founder of the architectural profession in the United States as the country's first professional architect-engineer.

Lattimer, Agnes Delores

b. May 13, 1928
Memphis, Tenn.
fields: Medicine

African American doctor; Agnes Delores Lattimer received her M.D. from the Chicago Medical School, where she was trained in the department of pediatrics. A distinguished pediatrician, she became a fellow of the American Academy of Pediatrics, and served on the Chicago Board of Health. She is the author of many scholarly articles in her field.

Lattimore, Owen

b. July 29, 1900
Washington, D.C.
d. May 31, 1989
Providence, R.I.
fields: Journalism, Literature

Sinologist and journalist; Owen Lattimore wrote *The Desert Road to Turkestan* (1928); a leading authority on the history, culture, and politics of central Asia; during the early 1940's, was the American adviser to Chinese leader Chiang Kai-shek. In 1950, accused by Senator Joseph McCarthy of being a spy for the Soviet Union—charges were initially dropped due to lack of evidence, but a confessed Communist testified that Lattimore had been a Communist Party member. After being indicted for perjury in 1952, he was eventually cleared of all charges; published an account of his experiences, *Ordeal by Slander* (1950).

Lattisaw, Stacy

b. November 25, 1966
Washington, D.C.
fields: Music

African American singer; Stacy Lattisaw's recordings include *Young and in Love* (1979), *Let Me Be Your Angel* (1980), *With You* (1981), and *Sneakin' Out* (1982). "Let Me Be Your Angel," "Dynamite," "Jump to the Beat," and the remake "Love on a Two-Way Street" were some of her hits. Lattisaw was the youngest person ever honored by the National Council of Negro Women (1981).

Lau, Alan Chong

b. 1948
Calif.
fields: Literature (poet)

Poet Alan Chong Lau, along with poets Lawson Fusao Inada and Garrett Hongo, wrote *The Buddha Bandits Down Highway 99* (1978). He won an American Book Award from the Before Columbus Foundation in 1980 for *Songs for Jadina*. He coedited the anthology *Turning Shadows into Light: Art and Culture of the Northwest's Early Asian/Pacific Community* (1982). He received a Japan-U.S. Creative Artists Fellowship in 1983.

Laud, William

b. October 7, 1573
Reading, Berkshire, England
d. January 10, 1645
London, England
fields: Religion and Theology, Government and Politics

As Archbishop of Canterbury and as a martyr for his conception of the Church of England, Laud contributed powerfully to the Anglo-Catholic tradition in English religion.

Laue, Max von

full: Max Theodor Felix von Laue
b. Oct. 9, 1879
Pfaffendorf, near Kolenz, Germany
d. Apr. 23, 1960
Berlin, West Germany
fields: Science, Physics

In 1912 Max von Laue discovered X-ray diffraction, which proved that X rays are electromagnetic waves and enabled scientists to measure the position of atoms in crystals; in 1914, awarded the Nobel Prize in Physics.

Laurence, Margaret

b. July 18, 1926
Neepawa, Manitoba, Canada
d. January, 1987
Lakefield, Ontario, Canada
fields: Literature

A Canadian novelist, Margaret Laurence was known for her cycle of five books with strong female protagonists. These included *The Stone Angel* (1964), *A Jest of God* (1966), and *The Diviners* (1974)—all of which were denounced by Christian Fundamentalists as immoral.

Laureta, Alfred

b. May 21, 1924
Territory of Hawaii
fields: Law, Government and Politics

Filipino American Alfred Laureta earned a B.Ed. degree from the University of Hawaii in 1947, then attended the law school at Fordham University. He opened a law practice in Honolulu in 1954 in partnership with future Hawaii governor George Ariyoshi. Laureta became the first Filipino director of the Department of Labor and Industrial Relations (1963-1967) under Governor John A. Burns. In 1967, he accepted a position on the state's Circuit Court One.

Laurier, Wilfrid

aka: Sir Wilfrid Laurier
b. November 20, 1841
St. Lin, Canada East (now Quebec, Canada)
d. February 17, 1919
Ottawa, Ontario, Canada
fields: Government and Politics

By transforming Canadian Liberalism and shifting its base to Quebec, Laurier made possible the subsequent dominance of federal politics by the Liberal Party. As the first French-Canadian to become Prime Minister of Canada (1896-1911), he presided over an era of expansion, general prosperity, and increasing Canadian self-awareness.

Laval, François

full: François-Xavier de Laval-Montmorency
b. April 30, 1623
Montigny-sur-Avre, near Chartres, France
d. May 6, 1708
Quebec City, Canada
fields: Religion and Theology

As the first Bishop of Quebec, Laval worked with the governors of New France to Christianize the Native Americans and to establish the parish structure of the Roman Catholic church in Canada. Laval's work also preserved French influence in Canada even after the English conquest in 1763.

Laval, Pierre

b. June 28, 1883
Châteldon, France
d. October 15, 1945
Paris, France
fields: Government and Politics

An opportunistic and controversial politician, Laval held eighteen ministerial offices and was premier of France four times. Following France's early defeat in World War II, he led the Vichy French government in a policy of collaboration with Germany.

Laver, Rod

full: Rodney George Laver
b. August 9, 1938
Rockhampton, Queensland, Australia
fields: Sports (tennis)

An outstanding world tennis player, Laver won the grand slam of tennis in 1962 and in 1969, the first time as an amateur and the second time as a professional. The grand slam of tennis involves winning the four major world singles' titles in the same year: the American, Australian, British, and French championships. Laver is the only player to have accomplished this feat twice, the first to have won the grand slam since the American John Donald Budge in 1938, and the first professional player ever to have won the grand slam.

Laveran, Alphonse

full: Charles Louis Alphonse Laveran
b. June 18, 1845
Paris, France
d. May 18, 1922
Paris, France
fields: Medicine, Zoology

Alphonse Laveran studied causes of malaria; was first to demonstrate that protozoa can cause disease; won the Nobel Prize in Physiology or Medicine in 1907.

Laviera, Tato

full: Jesús Abraham Laviera
b. Sept. 5, 1950
Santurce, Puerto Rico
fields: Literature, Social Reform

Latino poet and community worker. Tato Laviera was involved in directing the Association of Community Services, served on the boards of Madison Neighbors in Action and Mobilization for Youth, and did work for the Jamaica Arts Center, the Puerto Rico Family Institute, and United Bronx Parents. He helped produce the sixteenth Annual Puerto Rico Parade of Chicago and the first and second Latino Book Fair and Writers Festivals, held in Chicago and Houston, respectively. He wrote plays for the Henry Street Settlement New Federal Theater and read his poetry at the White House in 1980. Among his poetry collections are *La Carreta Made a U-Turn* (1979) and *Enclave* (1981).

Lavoisier, Antoine-Laurent
b. August 26, 1743
Paris, France
d. May 8, 1794
Paris, France
fields: Chemistry, Cartography, Economics

Besides important contributions to eighteenth century geology, physics, cartography, and economic reforms, particularly in agriculture and manufacturing, Lavoisier, through his discrediting of the phlogiston theory and his proof of the law of the conservation of matter, is best known as the father of modern chemistry.

Law, Bonar
full: Andrew Bonar Law
b. September 16, 1858
Kingston, New Brunswick, Canada
d. October 30, 1923
London, England
fields: Government and Politics

As leader of the Conservative Party between 1911 and 1923, Bonar Law reorganized the party's structure, thereby creating the modern Tory Party organization. He was a major force in the coalition government of David Lloyd George during and after World War I, and was Prime Minister of Great Britain, 1922-1923.

Lawless, Theodore K.
b. December 6, 1892
New Orleans, La.
d. May 1, 1971
Chicago, Ill.
fields: Medicine

African American medical doctor; Theodore K. Lawless received his M.D. from Northwestern University, making his specialty dermatology. He taught at Northwestern's school of medicine from 1924 to 1941 and made a number of important contributions to the treatment of syphilis and leprosy.

Lawrence, D. H.
full: David Herbert Lawrence
b. September 11, 1885
Eastwood, Nottinghamshire, England
d. March 2, 1930
Vence, France
fields: Literature

Combining brilliant descriptive powers with compelling evocations of natural settings and basic human drives, Lawrence expanded the limits by which romantic-erotic situations could be portrayed in fictional settings.

Lawrence, Ernest Orlando
b. August 8, 1901
Canton, South Dakota
d. August 27, 1958
Palo Alto, California
fields: Physics (nuclear)

The inventor of the cyclotron, Lawrence used this particle accelerator to explore the atomic nucleus and became one of America's most influential scientific statesmen during and after World War II. He was awarded the 1939 Nobel Prize in Physics.

Lawrence, First Baron
né: John Laird Mair Lawrence
aka: John Laird Mair Lawrence, First Baron Lawrence
b. March 4, 1811
Richmond, Yorkshire, England
d. June 26, 1879
London, England
fields: Colonial Administration

Lawrence was one of the builders of British India. His efforts were crucial to the successful establishment of the administration of the Punjab and to the defeat of the great Indian mutiny of 1857. He was viceroy from 1864 to 1869.

Lawrence, Jacob
b. September 7, 1917
Atlantic City, N.J.
fields: Art, Education

African American artist and educator; Jacob Lawrence received a Rosenwald Fellowship, a Guggenheim Fellowship, and an American Academy of Arts and Letters grant, exhibited at the Museum of Modern Art (1963), the Metropolitan Museum (1963), and the Seattle Art Museum (1986), and, in 1990, received the National Medal of Arts. He is known for works such as the Toussaint L'Ouverture series (1937-1938), the Frederick Douglass series (1938-1939), and the Harlem series (1940-1943), as well as *Street Scene #1* (1936), *Three Family Toilet* (1943), and *Eight Sermons from Genesis*.

Lawrence, Martin
b. April 16, 1965
Frankfurt, West Germany
fields: Television, Theater and Entertainment, Film (actor and comedian)

African American actor and comedian; in 1992, Martin Lawrence's weekly comedy, *Martin*, debuted on the Fox television network; appeared in films including *Bad Boys* (1995), *A Thin Line Between Love and Hate* (1996), *Nothing to Lose* (1997), and *Life* (1999).

Lawrence, Robert H., Jr.
b. October 2, 1935
Chicago, Ill.
d. December 8, 1967
Edwards Air Force Base, Calif.
fields: Aviation and Space Exploration

African American first African American astronaut designate. In 1967, as part of the national space program, Robert H. Lawrence, Jr., was selected to begin training for thirty-day space flights. Lawrence had been working at the Air Force Weapons Laboratory at Kirtland Air Force Base in New Mexico as a research scientist. He died in a crash during a routine proficiency flight in an F-104.

Lawrence, T. E.
full: Thomas Edward Lawrence
b. August 16, 1888
Tremadoc, Caenarvonshire, Wales
d. May 19, 1935
Bovington, near Clonds Hill, Dorset, England
fields: Military Affairs, Literature

Lawrence introduced striking innovations when he directed the operations of Arab irregular forces during the desert campaigns of World War I in 1917 and 1918; he then captured the imagination of much of the world by describing his exploits in memoirs that have been called "one of the greatest modern epics in the English language."

Lawrence, Thomas
aka: Sir Thomas Lawrence
b. April 13, 1769
Bristol, England
d. January 7, 1830
London, England
fields: Art

The foremost portrait painter of his day, Lawrence enhanced the reputation of English art. As a collector and adviser to patrons and government, he established and enriched a number of museums.

Lawrence-Lightfoot, Sara
b. Aug., 1944
Nashville, Tenn.
fields: Sociology, Scholarship

African American professor and sociologist; Sara Lawrence-Lightfoot was only the second tenured African American female professor in Harvard's history; wrote *Worlds Apart: Relationships Between Families and Schools* (1978), *Beyond Bias: Perspectives on Classrooms* (1979), *The Good High School: Portraits of Character and Culture* (1983), *Balm in Gilead: Portrait of a Healer* (1988), *I've Known Rivers: Lives of Loss and Liberation* (1994), and *Respect: An Exploration* (1999).

Lawson, Jennifer Karen

b. 1946

fields: Film (editor), Television (executive)

African American film editor, educator, and corporate executive; Jennifer Karen Lawson was hired as executive vice president of national programming for the Public Broadcasting Service (PBS) in 1989; received praise for her work in promoting Ken Burns's acclaimed 1990 documentary, *The Civil War*.

Lawson, John

b. ?

d. ?

fields: Warfare and Conquest

African American military hero; John Lawson entered the Navy during the Civil War and served under Admiral David Farragut aboard the USS *Hartford*. He fought in numerous campaigns, including the battle against Fort Morgan at Mobile Bay, in Alabama. In that battle he was wounded but refused to seek medical treatment, instead remaining at his station; he received the Naval Medal of Honor for his heroism during that battle.

Lawyer

aka: Hallalhotsoot

aka: Hollolsotetote (The Talker)

b. c. 1795

d. Jan. 3, 1876

fields: Government and Politics, Diplomacy, Native American Affairs

Native American leader. Lawyer, a Nez Perce and Flathead, negotiated land-rights treaties in the name of the Nez Perce that were repudiated by Chief Joseph the Younger before his Long March in 1877. Chief Joseph gave Lawyer that name because (as Joseph noted in a speech to Congress in 1879) "he talked too much" and gave away land that did not belong to him.

Laxness, Halldór

né: Halldór Kiljan Guðjónsson

b. April 23, 1902
Reykjavík, Iceland

d. February 8, 1998
near Reykjavík, Iceland

fields: Literature

Laxness, in a period when Iceland was reawakening to its history, became a spokesman for that history and renewed the distinctive art of Icelandic narrative. He received the Nobel Prize in Literature in 1955, a fitting tribute to his contribution to world literature.

Lazaro, Ladislas

b. June 5, 1872
near Ville Platte, La.

d. Mar. 30, 1927
Washington, D.C.

fields: Government and Politics

Latino politician. Mexican American Ladislas Lazaro graduated from a medical school in Louisville, Kentucky, in 1894, then returned to his home state of Louisiana to practice medicine in the town of Washington. In 1913, he became interested in agriculture. Lazaro also served in the Louisiana state senate between 1908 and 1912 and was elected to Congress as a Democrat in 1913, where he served until his death.

Lazarus, Emma

b. July 22, 1849
New York, New York

d. November 19, 1887
New York, New York

fields: Literature, Social Reform

Lazarus began writing poems as a girl and published volumes of poetry, plays, translations, a novel, and many influential essays in *Century* magazine and in the American Jewish press. She is best remembered for her sonnet "The New Colossus," which is engraved on the base of the Statue of Liberty.

Le Duc Tho

b. October 14, 1911
Nam Ha Province, Tonkin (now Vietnam)

d. October 13, 1990
Hanoi, Vietnam

fields: Diplomacy, Warfare and Conquest

Vietnamese revolutionary and a leader of the Viet Cong during the Vietnam War. North Vietnam's chief representative at the Paris Peace Talks, which, after Lee engaged in secret talks with American negotiator Henry Kissinger, instituted a cease-fire in Vietnam on January 7, 1973. Declined 1973 Nobel Peace Prize.

Le Rat. *See* Adario

Le Tonnelier de Breteuil, Gabrielle-Émilie. *See* Châtelet, Marquise du

Le Xuan Khoa

b. 1931

fields: Education, Civil Rights, Social Reform

Le Xuan Khoa is an educator, community leader; born in Vietnam; deputy minister for culture and education in South Vietnam; vice-president, University of Saigon; came to United States as a refugee in 1975; chief executive of Southeast Asia Refugee Action Center since 1980; editor in chief of *The Bridge*, reporting on refugee issues; frequently has testified to U.S. Congress on immigration issues.

Lea, Homer

b. Nov. 17, 1876
Denver, Colo.

d. Nov. 1, 1912
Los Angeles, Calif.

fields: Warfare and Conquest

Military strategist and political activist Homer Lea worked for the reform engineered by Kang Youwei under emperor Guangxu. He later supported Sun Yat-sen's revolution. Lea attempted to channel funds and forces to Sun but was unsuccessful. On January 1, 1912, when Sun became the president of the Republic of China, Lea became Sun's private adviser on military and diplomatic affairs. Lea returned to the United States when Yuan Shikai assumed the presidency. In 1941, long after Lea's death, one of his books, *The Valor of Ignorance* (1909), which had predicted the Japanese attack on the United States, became an instant best-seller.

Leadbelly

né: Huddie Ledbetter

b. January 20, 1889
Mooringsport, La.

d. December 6, 1949
New York, N.Y.

fields: Music (blues singer and guitarist)

African American blues singer and guitarist. Considered to be one of the most important and commercially untainted representatives of African American song traditions, particularly the blues and the work songs of the rural South, Leadbelly is also remembered for his gravelly voice, matter-of-fact spoken discourse to his audiences, and his unique twelve-string guitar playing. He played with musicians such as folk singer and guitarist Blind Lemon Jefferson and virtuoso harmonica player Sonny Terry.

Leakey, L. S. B.

full: Louis Seymour Bazett Leakey

b. August 7, 1903
Kabete, Kenya

d. October 1, 1972
London, England

fields: Anthropology (paleoanthropology)

Leakey's lifelong examinations of the fossil remains near Lake Victoria and in the Olduvai Gorge in East Africa have provided clues as to the origin of the human species among prehistoric primates. This work, as well as his later support of the study of animal behavior in the wild, has significantly advanced understanding of both how evolution occurred and how prehistoric humans managed to survive and eventually to prevail.

Leal, Luis

b. Sept. 17, 1907
Linares, Mexico

fields: Literature, Education

Latino writer and educator. Luis Leal was an instructor at the University of Chicago from 1942 to 1943 and 1946 to 1948, then was promoted to assistant professor of Spanish. In 1952, he became associate professor of modern languages at the University of Mississippi. From 1955 to 1959, he taught Spanish at Emory University, then moved to the University of Illinois at Urbana-Champaign, where he became a professor in 1962 and professor emeritus in 1976. In 1980, he became the acting director of the Center for Chicano Studies at the University of California, Santa Barbara. Leal has written on Mexican folklore, literature, and culture in both Spanish and English, and he has edited several anthologies, including *A Decade of Chicano Literature, 1970-1979: Critical Essays and Bibliography* (1982).

Lean Bear

aka: Awoninahku
aka: Starved Bear
b. c. 1813
d. c. 1864
fields: Government and Politics, Diplomacy, Peace Advocacy, Native American Affairs

A Southern Cheyenne, Lean Bear was one of the principal Plains Indian leaders who strove for peace in the early 1860's. Part of the 1863 delegation to Washington, D.C., that met with President Abraham Lincoln to negotiate a peace. In 1864 his peaceful camp was attacked by by U.S. Cavalry and Lean Bear was shot and killed. On his chest was the peace medal given to him in Washington; in his hand were the papers signed by Lincoln saying that he was a friend to the whites and a keeper of peace. This attack, and the Sand Creek Massacre soon afterward, led to the Cheyenne-Arapaho War (or the Colorado War) of 1864-1865 and to later fighting on the southern Plains.

Lear, Norman

b. July 27, 1922
New Haven, Connecticut
fields: Television (producer)

Norman Lear made his reputation in television with the hit sitcom *All in the Family*, which he adapted from the popular British series *Till Death Do Us Part* in 1971. The success of *All in the Family*, enabled Lear to produce such other top-rated shows as *Maude*, *Good Times*, *The Jeffersons*, and *Sanford and Son*. In 1970 Lear founded the People for the American Way, which became a strong voice against censorship.

Leary, Timothy

b. October 22, 1920
Springfield, Massachusetts
d. May 31, 1996
Beverly Hills, California
fields: Social Reform

The nation's leading proponent of psychedelic drugs. For three years, Leary directed the Harvard Psychedelic Research Project, which involved more than fifty faculty members, graduate students, and distinguished visiting scholars, including Aldous Huxley, Arthur Koestler, Allen Ginsberg, and Jack Kerouac. Leary became a prominent figure in the emerging counterculture, touring the country and expounding on the virtues of hallucinogenic drugs. Leary who coined the 1960's phrase, "Turn on, tune in, and drop out."

Leavitt, Henrietta Swan

b. July 4, 1868
Lancaster, Massachusetts
d. Dec. 12, 1921
Cambridge, Massachusetts
fields: Astronomy

Henrietta Swan Leavitt was a pioneer in the photographic measurements of the brightness of stars; in 1912, proposed the period-luminosity law for Cepheid variable stars, which measured distances to galaxies; in 1917, published "The North Polar Sequence," offering a brightness standard for stars in the Milky Way; in 1920, provided the basis for Harlow Shapley's determination of the size of the universe; discovered 2,400 variable stars.

Lebesgue, Henri-Léon

b. June 28, 1875
Beauvais, France
d. July 26, 1941
Paris, France
fields: Mathematics (calculus)

Henri-Léon Lebesque formulated a theory of integration that greatly extended the number and type of problems that could be solved by integral calculus.

Leblanc, Nicolas

b. December 6, 1742
Ivoy-le-Pré, France
d. January 16, 1806
Saint-Denis, France
fields: Chemistry

Leblanc, an amateur chemist, developed a process that now bears his name for making soda (sodium carbonate) from salt (sodium chloride). His use of limestone (calcium carbonate) to cause this conversion was at the core of his process, which played a fundamental role in creating the modern chemical industry.

Le Bon, Gustave

b. May 7, 1841
Nogent-le-Rotrou, France
d. December 13, 1931
Marnes-la-Coquette, France
fields: Anthropology, Medicine, Sociology

Although Le Bon is known primarily for his unique work in crowd psychology, he is still remembered by some—not always favorably—for his work on the unconscious mind, his writing in medicine, his controversial theories of race, his books on anthropology and archaeology, his treatise on the training of horses, his explorations into black light and the equivalence of matter and energy, and his writing on the composition of tobacco smoke.

Lebrón Soto, Lolita

b. 1919
Lares, Puerto Rico
fields: Social Reform

Puerto Rican nationalist. Lolita Lebrón Soto, a member of Puerto Rico's Nationalist Party, moved to New York in 1940. On March 1, 1954, she led three other nationalists— Andrés Figueroa Cordero, Rafael Cancel Miranda, and Irving Flores—in an armed assault on the U.S. House of Representatives. Five congressmen were wounded. Lebrón was sentenced to serve sixteen to fifty years in prison at Alderson, Virginia. She was allowed to return to Puerto Rico for the funeral of her daughter. President Jimmy Carter pardoned her in 1979.

Leclerc, Georges-Louis. *See* Buffon, Comte de

Lecuona, Ernesto

b. 1895 or 1896
Guanabacoa, Cuba
d. Nov. 29, 1963
Santa Cruz de Tenerife, Canary Islands
fields: Music (bandleader, composer, and pianist)

Latino bandleader, composer, and pianist. Ernesto Lecuona began composing music when he was eleven and gave his first recital in New York City at the age of seventeen. His Palau Brothers Cuban Orchestra was featured in film musical *Cuban Love Song* (1931). During the 1930's, his group, the Lecuona Cuban Boys, toured Europe and recorded for Columbia. Many of his songs—including "Siboney," "Para Vigo Me Voy" ("Say 'Si Si'"), and "Canto Karabali" ("Jungle Drums")—have been rerecorded by such artists as Dizzy Gillespie, Glenn Miller, and the Andrews Sisters.

Ledbetter, Huddie. *See* Leadbelly

Lederberg, Joshua
b. May 23, 1925
Montclair, New Jersey
fields: Genetics, Medicine, Science

Joshua Lederberg worked in bacterial genetics; established the presence of sexual reproduction among bacteria; demonstrated the possibility of genetic manipulation of bacterial genetic material; in 1958, awarded the Nobel Prize in Physiology or Medicine.

Lederman, Leon M.
full: Leon Max Lederman
b. July 15, 1922
the Bronx, New York
fields: Physics

Leon M. Lederman was one of the foremost high-energy physicists of the latter part of the twentieth century; conducted an experiment revealing the existence of the muon neutrino, which led to the postulation of the standard model of physics; in 1956, discovered the neutral K-meson; in 1960-1962, conducted experiments that produced the world's first beam of neutrinos; in 1977, discovered the upsilon particle; in 1988, shared the Nobel Prize in Physics.

Lee, Andrea
b. 1953
Philadelphia, Pa.
fields: Literature, Journalism (fiction)

African American novelist and journalist; Andrea Lee wrote *Russian Journal* (1981) and the semiautobiographical novel *Sarah Phillips* (1984).

Lee, Ang
b. 1954
Republic of China
fields: Film

Ang Lee came to the United States in 1978 and earned a degree in drama from the University of Illinois, Champaign-Urbana and a master's in cinema from New York University. His award-winning 1984 thesis film, *Fine Line*, got Lee an agent at the William Morris artists agency. A Taiwanese film company produced *Pushing Hands* (1992) and *The Wedding Banquet* (1993), which won numerous awards. Lee's *Eat, Drink, Man, Woman* (1993) about a Taiwanese cook was shown extensively in the United States.

Lee, Ann
b. February 29, 1736
Manchester, England
d. September 8, 1784
Niskeyuna, New York
fields: Religion and Theology

Ann Lee was the founder of the United Society of Believers in Christ's Second Coming, a religious sect commonly known as the Shakers. Members of the sect believed Mother Ann to be the female embodiment of Christ and the maternal component of the Father/Mother God.

Lee, Bertram M.
b. January 21, 1939
Lynchburg, Va.
fields: Banking and Finance

African American financier. In July, 1989, Bertram M. Lee and his partner C. B. Bynoe became the first African American owners of a professional sports franchise in the United States when they purchased the Denver Nuggets of the National Basketball Association for $65 million.

Lee, Bruce
né: Lee Jun Fan
b. Nov. 27, 1940
San Francisco, Calif.
d. July 20, 1973
Hong Kong
fields: Film, Sports (martial arts)

Bruce Lee began his film career as a child actor in Hong Kong. In 1954 Lee began studying the martial art of Wing Chun. In 1958 Lee emigrated to the United States. He began teaching Jeet Kune Do, the Way of the Intercepting Fist, in 1964, after publishing *Chinese Gung Fu: The Philosophical Art of Self-Defense* (1963). He appeared as Kato in the television series *The Green Hornet* (1966-1967). In 1971 Lee returned to Hong Kong, where he made three films with producer Raymond Chow: *The Big Boss* (1971; *Fists of Fury*, 1971), *Fist of Fury* (1971; *The Chinese Connection*, 1972), and *Way of the Dragon* (1972; *Return of the Dragon*, 1973). In 1972 Warner Bros. Studios agreed to produce Lee's film *Enter the Dragon* (1973), but Lee died suddenly of cerebral edema before the film was released

Lee, Canada
né: Leonard Lionel Cornelius Canegata
b. May 3, 1907
New York, N.Y.
d. May 9, 1952
New York, N.Y.
fields: Theater and Entertainment, Film

African American actor; Canada Lee first gained major recognition for his role as Bigger Thomas in the stage version of *Native Son* (1941). Lee appeared in Alfred Hitchcock's film *Lifeboat* (1944) and narrated the radio program *New World A-Comin'*. His stage appearances include *The Tempest* (1945), *On Whitman Avenue* (1946), *The Duchess of Malfi* (1946), and *Set My People Free* (1948). He also starred in the film *Cry the Beloved Country* (1951).

Lee, Chin Yang
aka: Chin-yang Li
aka: C. Y. Lee
b. 1917
Xiaoxia Village, Xiangtan, Hunan Province, China
fields: Theater and Entertainment, Music

Chin Yang Lee came to the United States by way of India in the 1940's. He received an M.F.A. in 1947 from Yale Drama School. A short story he submitted to *Readers' Digest* won first prize, so he decided to pursue a career as a writer. His *Flower Drum Song* (1957) became a best-seller. The musical version, created by Richard Rodgers and Oscar Hammerstein II, was a hit on Broadway in 1958. It became a film in 1961. Lee's other publications include *Lovers' Point* (1958), *The Sawbwa and His Secretary* (1959), *Madame Goldenflower* (1960), *Cripple Mah and the New Order* (1961), *The Virgin Market* (1964), *The Land of the Golden Mountain* (1967), *Days of the Tong Wars* (1974), and *China Saga* (1987).

Lee, Chol Soo
b. 1953
Korea
fields: Historical Figure

Chol Soo Lee's experience with the U.S. legal system was the basis for the film *True Believer* (1989). He was arrested by the San Francisco police in 1973 and charged with a murder that he did not commit because the police were unable to distinguish between him and the real perpetrator, another Asian American. Lawyers, aided by community activists, overturned Lee's conviction.

Lee, Chong-sik
b. July 30, 1931
Korea
fields: Government and Politics, Scholarship

Chong-sik Lee immigrated from Korea to the United States after World War II. He wrote *The Politics of Korean Nationalism* (1963) and coauthored *Communism in Korea* (1972) with Robert A. Scalapino, which received the Woodrow Wilson Award.

Lee, Dai-keong
b. Sept. 2, 1915
Honolulu, Territory of Hawaii
fields: Music

Asian American Dai-keong Lee studied under Roger Sessions in New York from 1937 to 1938, Frederick Jacobi at the Julliard Graduate School from 1938 to 1941, and Aaron Copland at the Berkshire Music Center for the summer of 1941. A Guggenheim Fellow in 1945 and 1951, Lee is known for his orchestral, symphonic, and chamber music works.

Lee, David

né: Yi Tae-wi
b. ?
Korea
d. 1928
fields: Government and Politics, Publishing

Korean refugee David Lee cofounded the Chinmok-hoe and Kongnip Hyop-hoe and was president of the Korean National Association from 1913 to 1915 and in 1918. He became editor of *New Korea*, a community weekly newspaper, and invented a typesetting machine for Korean characters in 1915.

Lee, Dennis

b. August 31, 1939
Toronto, Ontario, Canada
fields: Literature

A Canadian poet and author of children's books, Dennis Lee became famous as a writer of poetry for children when he published *Alligator Pie* (1974) and *Garbage Delight* (1977). However, these books and others were charged by some as containing overly violent material. His *Lizzy's Lion* (1984) was Canada's most frequently challenged book from 1985 to 1987.

Lee, Don L.. *See* Madhubuti, Haki R.

Lee, Edward Jae Song

b. May, 1973
Los Angeles, Calif.
d. Apr. 30, 1992
Los Angeles, Calif.
fields: Historical Figure

Edward Jae Song Lee was the only Korean American who died during the 1992 Los Angeles riots. He went to Koreatown to aid store owners but was mistakenly shot by a Korean America who thought he was a looter.

Lee, Evelyn

b. June 25, 1944
Macao
fields: Medicine, Psychiatry and Psychology

Evelyn Lee specializes in mental health and social services for immigrants and Asian Americans. She was executive director of Richmond Area Multi-Services in San Francisco and clinical professor of psychiatry at the University of California, San Francisco. Lee wrote *Ten Principles on Raising Chinese-American Teens* (1988) and served as program director and consultant to various community and mainstream health agencies.

Lee, Gaby. *See* Lincoln, Abbey

Lee, Gus

full: Augustus Lee
b. 1946
San Francisco, Calif.
fields: Literature

Raised in an African American neighborhood in San Francisco and treated harshly by his non-Chinese stepmother, Chinese American Augustus Lee reflected on his life in his autobiographical novels, *China Boy* (1991) and *Honor and Duty* (1994). Lee was director of attorney education for the State Bar of California when his first novel was published.

Lee, Gypsy Rose

né: Rose Louise Hovick
b. January 9, 1914
probably Seattle, Washington
d. April 26, 1970
Los Angeles, California
fields: Theater and Entertainment, Film

Although she began her career in vaudeville and burlesque, Lee's charisma and intelligence brought her success on the stage, in films and television, and as an author.

Lee, Howard N., Jr.

b. July 28, 1934
Lithonia, Ga.
fields: Government and Politics

African American mayor of Chapel Hill, N.C.;Howard N. Lee, Jr., was the first African American man to serve as mayor in Chapel Hill, North Carolina. He held that office from 1969 to 1975.

Lee, Jason Scott

b. 1967
Los Angeles
fields: Film, Theater and Entertainment

Jason Scott Lee studied under acting coach Sal Romeo at the Friends and Artists Theater Ensemble in Los Angeles. He first appeared in *Born in East L. A.* (1987) and starred in *Dragon: The Bruce Lee Story* (1993) and *Map of the Human Heart* (1993). Lee garnered critical acclaim for his versatility and range.

Lee, Joie

né: Joy Lee
b. 1962?
Brooklyn, N.Y.
fields: Film (actor)

African American actor; Joie Lee was featured in her brother Spike's films including *She's Gotta Have It* (1986), *School Daze* (1988), *Do the Right Thing* (1989), and *Mo' Better Blues* (1990); also appeared in *A Kiss Before Dying* (1990) and on the television programs *The Cosby Show* and *Saturday Night Live*; co-wrote *Crooklyn* (1994).

Lee, K. W.

full: Kyung Won Lee
b. June 1, 1928
Kaesong, Korea
fields: Journalism

K. W. Lee, hired by the *Kingsport Times & News* in Tennessee in 1956, became the first Korean immigrant investigative journalist with a mainstream daily. He received the first national Asian American Journalists Association Award of Excellence in 1987 and was editor of the English edition of the *Korea Times* and publisher/editor of *Koreantown Weekly* (1979-1982). He helped found the Korean American Journalists Association in 1985.

Lee Kuan Yew

b. September 16, 1923
Singapore
fields: Government and Politics

Lee became one of the longest-ruling, freely elected prime ministers in the world. His popularity came from his ability to rule fairly, to unite a multiracial society, and to make Singapore, which is only 224 square miles in area with 2.6 million people, into the second busiest port in the world with the third largest oil refinery and a standard of living second only to that of Japan in all of Asia.

Lee, Li-Young

b. 1957
Jakarta, Indonesia
fields: Literature (poet)

Li-Young Lee, great-grandson of Yuan Shikai, president of the Republic of China, wrote two well-regarded collections of poetry, *Rose* (1986) and *The City in Which I Love You* (1990), which was the Lamont Poetry Selection of the Academy of American Poets in 1990. He received a Writer's Award from the Whiting Foundation in 1988 and a Guggenheim fellowship in 1989.

Lee, Lim Poon

b. Dec. 19, 1910
Hong Kong
fields: Business and Industry

Lim Poon Lee, postmaster at San Francisco in 1966, was the first Chinese American to serve in that capacity. A former sergeant in the U.S. Army, he chaired the California Department of Veterans Affairs and belonged to the boards of the Greater Chinatown Community Service Association and the Chinese American Civic Council.

Lee, Ming Cho

b. Oct. 30, 1930
Shanghai, China
fields: Theater and Entertainment

Ming Cho Lee assisted Jo Lielziner, the top American scenic designer, from 1954 to 1958, working on the Broadway productions of *Silk Stockings*, *Cat on a Hot Tin Roof*, *Gypsy*, *The Lark*, *New Girl in Town*, and *The*

World of Suzie Wong. In 1959, Lee began designing for opera at Baltimore's Peabody Arts Theatre. In the 1960's, with the New York Shakespeare Festival, Lee did the scenic designs for more than fifty productions, including the rock musical *Hair* (1967) and Ntozake Shange's *for colored girls who have considered suicide/when the rainbow is enuf* (1976). Lee also created architectural spaces and produced designs for choreographers. His work for Patrick Meyers' play *K-2* earned the 1983 Tony Award for Best Scenic Design.

Lee, Peggy
né: Norma Deloris Egstrom
b. May 26, 1920
Jamestown, North Dakota
fields: Music

After rising to fame as a big band vocalist, Lee achieved lasting success in many other areas of American entertainment.

Lee, Pius
b. Apr. 14, 1937
Zhongshan, China
fields: Business and Industry

Realtor Pius Lee, president of California Realty & Land, was commissioner of the San Francisco Human Rights Commission (1979-1980), the California State Industrial Welfare Commission (1981-1984), and the San Francisco Police Commission (1988-1992). He chaired the Economic Opportunity Council, the San Francisco-Taipei Sister City Committee, the Commission for Economic Development Advisory Council on Asia, and the Hai Sen Benevolent Association. He also served as president of the Chinese Chamber of Commerce and the Chinese Hospital.

Lee, Robert E.
full: Robert Edward Lee
b. January 19, 1807
Stratford, Virginia
d. October 12, 1870
Lexington, Virginia
fields: Military Affairs

Perhaps the finest army tactician of his generation, Lee, by his brilliant command of the Army of Northern Virginia, prolonged the life of the Confederacy during the Civil War.

Lee, Rose Hum
aka: Mrs. Glenn Ginn
b. Aug. 20, 1904
Butte, Mont.
d. Mar. 25, 1964
fields: Sociology

Rose Hum Lee became the first Chinese American to chair the sociology department at the University of Chicago. She wrote *The Chinese in the United States of America* (1960) and participated in organization that helped people in China during the Sino-Japanese War and World War II.

Lee, Sammy
b. Aug. 1, 1920
Fresno, Calif.
fields: Sports (diving)

Korean American Sammy Lee became the first Asian American to win an Olympic gold medal when he received gold medals for platform diving in 1948 and 1952. He also was awarded a bronze medal for springboard diving in 1948. Lee, the first nonwhite recipient, received the James E. Sullivan Memorial Award for outstanding achievement in sports in 1953. In 1990, he was elected to the U.S. Olympic Hall of Fame.

Lee, Spike
full: Shelton Jackson Lee
b. Mar. 20, 1957
Atlanta, Ga.
fields: Theater and Entertainment

African American filmmaker; Spike Lee while attending New York University's Institute of Film and Television, won the Student Award presented by the Academy of Motion Picture Arts and Sciences for *Joe's Bed-Stuy Barbershop: We Cut Heads* (1982); his controversial films, highlighting past and present struggles of African Americans in a land of alien values, include *She's Gotta Have It* (1986), *Do the Right Thing* (1989), *Mo' Better Blues* (1990), *Jungle Fever* (1991), *Malcolm X* (1992), and *He Got Game* (1998).

Lee, T. D.
full: Tsung-Dao Lee
b. Nov. 25, 1926
Shanghai, China
fields: Physics

Chinese American physicist; T. D. Lee, in collaboration with his friend and countryman Chen Ning Yang, successfully challenged the generally accepted "parity principle," ushering in a new era in the field of physics; Yang and Lee shared the 1957 Nobel Prize in Physics (Lee was the second youngest laureate ever) as well as the Albert Einstein Award.

Lee, Thomas Henry
b. May 11, 1923
Shanghai, China
fields: Engineering

Engineer Thomas Henry Lee worked for General Electric from 1959 to 1980, when he became professor of electrical engineering at the Massachusetts Institute of Technology. Lee, who holds more than twenty-nine patents, was responsible for the production of solid-state HUDC transmission and developed power vacuum interrupters.

Lee, Tsung-Dao
b. Nov. 25, 1926
Shanghai, China
fields: Science

In 1957 Tsung-Dao Lee shared the Nobel Prize in Physics with Chen Ning Yang for their research of the parity laws, which led to significant discoveries regarding subatomic particles. Lee and Yang were the first Chinese citizens to be awarded the prize.

Lee, Virginia
né: Virginia Yew
b. May 5, 1927
San Francisco, Calif.
fields: Literature

Virginia Lee became one of the first Chinese American novelists when she published *The House That Tai Ming Built* in 1963. The work received a gold medal from the Commonwealth Club of California in 1963.

Lee-Smith, Hughie
b. September 20, 1915
Eustis, Fla.
d. February 23, 1999
Albuquerque, N.M.
fields: Art (painter)

African American painter; Hughie Lee-Smith's work has been characterized as technically mature and eloquent. He was the recipient of various prizes including the Emily Lowe Award (1957) and the Founders Prize of the Detroit Institute of Arts (1953). He taught at several art schools, the Art Students League in New York City being one.

Leeds, first duke of
né: Thomas Osborne
aka: Thomas Osborne, earl of Danby, marquess of Carmarthen, and first duke of Leeds
b. February 20, 1632
Kiveton, Yorkshire, England
d. July 26, 1712
Easton Neston, Northamptonshire, England
fields: Government and Politics

The heir of a distinguished Royalist family from Yorkshire, Sir Thomas Osborne, Duke of Leeds, became one of the leading politicians of his day. He is regarded as one of the founders of the political faction that evolved into the Tory Party. He was a staunch defender of the monarchy and its prerogative as long as they did not threaten the Church of England and the basic rights of the English people. In many ways he set the pattern for politicians who followed in the next century.

Leeuwenhoek, Antoni van
b. October 24, 1632
Delft, the Netherlands

d. August 26, 1723
Delft, the Netherlands
fields: Biology

Leeuwenhoek took the microscope when it was a new and undeveloped instrument and made it a significant tool for scientific research. He built the best microscopes anyone was to have for another two centuries, and he discovered a new world of living organisms, never before seen by human eyes.

Leffall, LaSalle Doheny, Jr.

b. May 22, 1930
Tallahassee, Fla.
fields: Medicine (physician, oncologist)

African American physician, oncologist, and educator; LaSalle Doheny Leffall, Jr., gained national attention in 1985, when he was asked by the media to explain President Ronald Reagan's impending cancer operation; named Charles R. Drew Professor of Surgery at the Howard University College of Medicine in 1992; received the St. George Medal and Citation from the American Cancer Society in 1977 for his cancer research.

Lefschetz, Solomon

b. Sept. 3, 1884
Moscow, Russia
d. Oct. 5, 1972
Princeton, New Jersey
fields: Mathematics (geometry and topology)

Solomon Lefschetz is responsible for many of the basic ideas of algebraic topology.

Left Hand the First

aka: Nawat
aka: Niwot
b. 1820's
eastern Colo. or western Nebr. or Kans.
d. Nov. 29, 1864
Sand Creek, Colo.
fields: Government and Politics, Peace Advocacy, Native American Affairs

Native American leader. A Southern Arapaho, the first Left Hand was a leading peace chief during the Plains Indian wars.

Left Hand the Second

aka: Nawat
aka: Niwot
b. c. 1840
eastern Colo. or western Nebr. or Kans.
d. June 20, 1911
Geary, Okla.
fields: Government and Politics, Native American Affairs

Southern Arapaho. The second Left Hand was a principal chief. Signed an agreement in 1890 permitting allotment of Arapaho land in Indian Territory in spite of opposition from the Southern Cheyenne, who shared a reservation with the Arapaho.

Left Handed. *See* Klah, Hosteen

Le Gallienne, Eva

b. January 11, 1899
London, England
d. June 3, 1991
Weston, Connecticut
fields: Theater and Entertainment (actor)

A leading actress of classical plays, Le Gallienne also founded a repertory company with which she introduced dramas by Anton Chekhov and Henrik Ibsen to American audiences. Hoping to build an audience, she drastically reduced the price of theater tickets, which was an innovation in its day.

Legendre, Adrien-Marie

b. Sept. 18, 1752
Paris, France
d. Jan. 10, 1833
Paris, France
fields: Mathematics (applied math, calculus, geometry, and number theory)

Adrien-Marie Legendre was active in many mathematical areas in the eighteenth and nineteenth centuries; founded or kept alive other fields until additional mathematicians became interested in those subjects.

Léger, Fernand

b. February 4, 1881
Argentan, France
d. August 17, 1955
Gif-sur-Yvette, France
fields: Art

Léger was known primarily for his depictions of people as machinelike creatures. He was an avid admirer of things modern and strove to reconcile the significance of modern art with an image of the industrial machine society.

Lehn, Jean-Marie

b. Sept. 30, 1939
Rosheim, France
fields: Chemistry, Science, Invention and Technology

Jean-Marie Lehn was instrumental in developing supramolecular chemistry, improving the understanding of how molecules "recognize" one another and opening the door for the synthesis of artificial enzymes, cells, and molecular devices. In 1987, he was awarded the Nobel Prize in Chemistry.

Leibniz, Gottfried Wilhelm

b. July 1, 1646
Leipzig, Saxony
d. November 14, 1716
Hanover
fields: Philosophy, Mathematics

Though never employed as an academic philosopher, Leibniz was one of the greatest intellectuals of his day: He was a metaphysician, theologian, philologist, historian, genealogist, poet, inventor, scientist, mathematician, logician, lawyer, and diplomat. He contributed to the development of rationalist philosophy, and he also corresponded with or personally knew virtually every major European thinker in every field of inquiry.

Leibovitz, Annie

full: Anna-Lou Leibovitz
b. October 2, 1949
Westbury, Connecticut
fields: Photography

A leading photographer since the early 1970's, Leibovitz has become known for her bold portraits of celebrities.

Leif Eriksson

b. c. 970
Iceland, possibly in Haukadal
d. c. 1035
probably near Julianehaab, Greenland
fields: Exploration and Colonization

Though probably not the first European to sight America, Leif made the first deliberate exploration of the North American continent and provided the main stimulus for later, unsuccessful attempts at permanent settlement.

Leighton, Alexander

b. 1568
d. 1649
fields: Religion and Theology

An English Puritan divine and physician, Alexander Leighton was a harsh critic of English bishops and was punished with bodily mutilation and imprisonment. He argued for the removal of the Church of England's bishops in *An Appeal to the Parliament: Or, Sions Plea Against the Prelacie* (1628). Two years later he was arrested, tried, and sentenced to be whipped, have an ear cut off, his nose slit, and his face branded. He also spent eleven years in jail before being released when Puritan Revolution began.

Leland, Mickey

full: George Leland
b. November 27, 1944
Lubbock, Tex.
d. August 7, 1989
near Fugnido refugee camp, Ethiopia
fields: Government and Politics

African American politician; Mickey Leland served as a member of the Texas legislature from 1973 to 1978 and was elected to the United States Congress in 1978; he remained in office until his death. He chaired various congressional committees including the Congressional Black Caucus. He challenged Congress to set new priorities including funds and programs for refugees, the homeless, and the hungry in Africa and throughout the world.

Leloir, Luis F.

full: Luis Federico Leloir
b. Sept. 6, 1908
Paris, France
d. Dec. 2, 1987
Buenos Aires, Argentina
fields: Biology, Chemistry

Luis F. Leloir discovered angiotensin; worked on the biochemistry of carbohydrates, particularly sugar nucleotides and glycogen; in 1970, won the Nobel Prize in Chemistry for his work on the role of sugar nucleotides in carbohydrate biochemistry.

Lemaître, Georges

full: Georges Abbé Lemaître
b. July 17, 1894
Charleroi, Belgium
d. June 20, 1966
Louvain, Belgium
fields: Physics, Mathematics, Astronomy

Building on evidence and theories adduced by several physicists, mathematicians, and cosmologists whose work, like his own, focused upon the provenance and character of the universe, Lemaître, through brilliant synthesis, formulated what has become the generally accepted scientific explanation of the universe's origin, namely, the big bang theory.

Lemon, Meadowlark

né: Meadow George Lemon III
b. April 25, 1932
Wilmington, N.C.
fields: Sports (basketball player)

African American basketball player; Meadowlark Lemon joined the Harlem Globetrotters, a popular African American touring comedy basketball team, in 1954 and quickly became its star attraction. He dazzled audiences for twenty-five years with fancy ball handling and behind-the-back passes, retiring in 1978.

Lemon, Ralph

b. 1952?
Minneapolis, Minn.
fields: Dance (choreographer)

African American choreographer; Ralph Lemon began dancing in college and then turned to choreography. He formed the Ralph Lemon Company, based in New York City, in the mid-1980's.

Lenin, Vladimir Ilich

né: Vladimir Ilich Ulyanov
b. April 22, 1870
Simbirsk, Russia
d. January 21, 1924
Gorki, U.S.S.R.
fields: Government and Politics

Lenin adapted Marxist theory to the politics of late imperial Russia, creating and leading the Communist Party, which eventually seized power in November, 1917. From 1918 until his death in 1924, he was the main architect of the new socialist state that became the model for world communism.

Lennon, John

full: John Winston Lennon
b. October 9, 1940
Liverpool, England
b. December 8, 1980
New York, New York
fields: Music (rock)

John Lennon first received international attention as a member of the Beatles after the release of "Love Me Do" in 1962. Lennon wrote or cowrote with Paul McCartney many of the Beatles' hits. His 1966 remark comparing the popularity of the Beatles with that of Jesus sparked public burnings of Beatles records and calls for banning the group's music, particularly in the religiously conservative American South. He published two books, *In His Own Words* and *A Spaniard in the Works*. He married avant-garde artist Yoko Ono; his personal relationship and artistic collaboration with Ono was widely, though unfairly, blamed for the breakup of the Beatles in 1970. Politically outspoken, Lennon was a counterculture icon whose oppositon to the Vietnam War and advocacy of peace was reflected in such albums as *Live Peace in Toronto* (1969, with Ono), *Imagine* (1971), *Some Time in New York City* (1972), *Mind Games* (1973), and *Walls and Bridges* (1974). *Double Fantasy* (1980, with Ono) was released after a five year absence from the music scene. Lennon was murdered by a fan the same year.

Lenoir, Étienne

b. January 12, 1822
Mussy-la-Ville, Belgium
d. August 4, 1900
La Varenne-Saint-Hilaire, France
fields: Invention and Technology

Lenoir invented a number of useful processes and devices, the most famous being an internal-combustion engine. The quality and significance of his engine are still matters of controversy, but there is little doubt that it stimulated the efforts of the other pioneers of internal-combustion-engine design.

Le Nôtre, André

b. March 12, 1613
Paris, France
d. September 15, 1700
Paris, France
fields: Landscape Architecture

Le Nôtre's designs for great public gardens complement the architecture of many of the most important buildings in seventeenth century France. He virtually created the French formal garden, which subordinated nature to reason and order while maintaining a fascination with and awareness of nature's beauty and delight.

Leo IX

né: Bruno of Egisheim
b. June 21, 1002
Egisheim, Alsace
d. April 19, 1054
Rome
fields: Religion and Theology

Pope Leo IX, 1048-1054. Leo IX was one of the most important of the medieval popes. Coming to the Papacy after a long period of papal and religious decline, and during an era when the authority of the Holy Roman Emperors was at its most influential, Leo instituted a number of significant reforms within the Church which had profound results not only for the Roman church in the West and the Orthodox church in the East but also for the Holy Roman Empire and other kingdoms in Europe.

Leo X

né: Giovanni de' Medici
b. December 11, 1475
Florence
d. December 1, 1521
Rome
fields: Government and Politics, Religion and Theology, Patronage of the Arts

Pope, 1513-1521. As a patron of the arts, Leo X turned Rome into the cultural center of the Western world. As pope, he engaged in secular politics and presided over the period in church history that witnessed the outbreak of the Protestant Reformation.

Leo XIII

né: Vincenzo Gioacchino Pecci
b. March 2, 1810
Carpineto Romano, Italy
d. July 20, 1903
Rome, Italy
fields: Religion and Theology, Church Reform

Pope Leo XIII (1878-1903), considered to be one of the greatest leaders of the Roman Catholic church during a period of crisis, tried to maintain the strength and power of the Church in a world changing through industry, colonization, and governmental upheaval. The fact that he was not always successful is not as significant as the fact that he was a pioneer, aware of the needs of the modern Roman Catholic church.

León, Alonso de

b. 1637
Spain
d. 1691
near San Antonio, Tex.
fields: Warfare and Conquest, Exploration and Colonization

Spanish soldier and explorer. Alonso de León, governor of Coahuila, Mexico, first entered Texas in early 1688 to destroy Fort St. Louis, an East Texas French settlement. He found that it had already been destroyed by local Indians and abandoned. León made four more excursions into the area, during which he laid a foundation for future Spanish settlements in East Texas, crossed and named many of the rivers of Texas, and founded two missions, San Francisco de los Texas and Santa Maria.

Leonard, Buck

full: Walter Fenner Leonard
b. September 8, 1907
Rocky Mount, N.C.
d. November 27, 1997
Rocky Mount, N.C.
fields: Sports (baseball player)

African American baseball player; Buck Leonard signed to play with the Homestead Grays, a top Negro Leagues team, in 1934. He was a powerful first baseman and hitter. His efforts helped the Homestead Grays to ten Negro National League pennants and three Negro League World Series titles. Leonard was chosen to ten East-West Negro League All-Star teams, and in 1972, he was inducted into the National Baseball Hall of Fame.

Leonard, Sugar Ray

full: Ray Charles Leonard
b. May 17, 1956
Wilmington, N.C.
fields: Sports (boxer)

African American boxer; Sugar Ray Leonard won 145 of 150 amateur bouts as well as a gold medal at the 1975 Pan-American Games and a gold medal at the 1976 Olympics. He turned pro in 1977 and went on to win the World Boxing Council (WBC) welterweight crown. Leonard retired from and returned to the ring several times between 1982 and 1987, when he won a disputed twelve-round decision against "Marvelous" Marvin Hagler to become world champion. In 1989 he was able to retain his title in a fight against Roberto Duran. While retiring in 1991, he came out of retirement in 1997 to fight Hector Camacho. After losing to Camacho, Leonard retired in 1997.

Leonardo da Vinci

b. April 15, 1452
Vinci, near Florence
d. May 2, 1519
Cloux Château, near Amboise, France
fields: Art

Leonardo da Vinci was the most outstanding painter of the Italian Renaissance; some authorities consider him the best painter and draftsman of all time. In addition, he made a number of discoveries in botany, anatomy, mechanical engineering, and medicine which were unprecedented and unparalleled until the twentieth century.

Leonardo of Pisa

aka: Leonardo Pissano
aka: Leonardo Fibonacci
b. c. 1170
Pisa, Italy
d. c. 1240
Pisa, Italy
fields: Mathematics

Leonardo provided Western Europe with the earliest and most heralded Latin account of the Hindu-Arabic number system and its computational methods. He helped to render Roman numerals and the abacus obsolete, contributed substantially to the acceptance of the Arabic algebraic system, and created a revolutionary mathematical technique known as the "Fibonacci sequence."

Leong, Charles Lai

b. c. 1911
San Francisco, California
d. Feb. 23, 1984
San Francisco, California
fields: Journalism

Charles Lai Leong founded an English-language paper for Chinese Americans, the California Chinese Press in 1940. He wrote for *East/West*, *Asian Week*, and the *San Francisco Chronicle*. He published *The Eagle and the Dragon* in 1976.

Leong, Russell Charles

b. 1950
San Francisco, Calif.
fields: Journalism, Film, Literature

In 1977, Russell Charles Leong became the editor of *Amerasia Journal*. His poems, stories, and essays have been published in periodicals and anthologies including *Aiiieeeee! An Anthology of Asian-American Writers* (1974), *The New England Review*, *Tricycle: The Buddhist Review*, and *Charlie Chan Is Dead: An Anthology of Contemporary Asian American Fiction* (1993). In 1993, *In the Country of Dreams and Dust*, his first book of poems, appeared. Leong produced video documentaries such as *Morning Begins Here* (1985) and *Why Is Preparing Fish a Political Act? The Poetry of Janice Mirikitani* (1990).

Leonhardt, Erna. *See* Gibbs, Erna

Leonidas

b. c. 510 B.C.E.
Sparta, Greece
d. August 20, 480 B.C.E.
Thermopylae, Thessaly, Greece
fields: Warfare and Conquest

The bravery and supreme sacrifice of Leonidas and his men at Thermopylae sent a surge of pride through all Greece, made the Greeks aware of their heritage, and stiffened their resolve to face—and, eventually, to prevail over—what seemed to be overwhelming odds.

Leopold I

né: Leopold Ignatius
b. June 9, 1640
Vienna, Austria
d. May 5, 1705
Vienna, Austria
fields: Monarchy

Holy Roman Emperor of the German nations, 1658-1705. Leopold I presided over the revival of imperial and Habsburg influence after the defeats of the Thirty Years' War. He consolidated imperial authority in Germany, recovered Hungary from the Turks, and resisted the efforts of Louis XIV of France to achieve European hegemony.

Leopold, Aldo

full: Rand Aldo Leopold
b. January 11, 1887
Burlington, Iowa
d. April 21, 1948
near Baraboo, Wis.
fields: Conservation and Environmentalism

Aldo Leopold caused first U.S. Wilderness Area to be established and wrote the influential *A Sand County Almanac* (1949). He formally stated the "Land Ethic," which placed humanity within, rather than in charge of, the ecosystem, and founded the Wilderness Society in 1935. Leopold made a family project of restoring the ecosystem to its original condition on an abandoned farm he had purchased near Baraboo, Wisconsin.

Le Pen, Jean-Marie

b. June 20, 1928
La Trinité-sur-Mer, France
fields: Government and Politics

French political figure; controversial, even feared, leader of France's far-right National Front party from the 1970's to the

1990's. Jean-Marie Le Pen employed racist rhetoric and played on fears that France was being overrun by foreigners.

Lermontov, Mikhail

full: Mikhail Yuryevich Lermontov
b. October 15, 1814
Moscow, Russia
d. July 27, 1841
Pyatigorsk, Russia
fields: Literature

Lermontov left an impressive legacy as a poet during the Russian Romantic period, writing both lyric and narrative verse of lasting significance. He was also a dramatist and a novelist whose major work, *A Hero of Our Time*, presaged the great realistic psychological novels of Leo Tolstoy and Fyodor Dostoevski.

Lerner, Michael

b. Feb. 7, 1943
Newark, N.J.
fields: Social Reform

American psychologist and social reformer; Michael Lerner helped form the Institute of Labor and Mental Health in 1977 to develop a better understanding between the general working people and therapists; wrote *The Politics of Meaning* (1996) and *Jewish Renewal* (1994), dealing with the nature of Jewish identity and the need for Jews to turn back to Jewish tradition, and he coauthored *Jews and Blacks* (1995) with Cornel West.

Lescot, Pierre

b. 1510?
Paris, France
d. September 10, 1578
Paris, France
fields: Architecture, Art

Lescot was long regarded as the first of France's great architects, chiefly because of his redesign and reconstruction of the original Louvre. Although modern scholarship modifies this estimate, he remains ranked among the premier French architects and designers of the sixteenth century.

Leslie, F. W.

b. 1813
d. 1865
fields: Invention and Technology

African American inventor; F. W. Leslie patented, in 1897, the glue seal for envelopes.

Lesseps, Ferdinand de

full: Ferdinand-Marie de Lesseps
aka: Vicomte de Lesseps
b. November 19, 1805
Versailles, France
d. December 7, 1894
La Chênaie, France
fields: Diplomacy, Business and Industry

Having initiated his career in diplomacy, Lesseps, though never trained as an engineer, is best known for his entrepreneurial abilities that led to the construction of the Suez Canal and the commencement of the transisthmian Panama Canal.

Lessing, Gotthold Ephraim

b. January 22, 1729
Kamenz, Saxony
d. February 15, 1781
Brunswick
fields: Literature, Theater and Entertainment, Philosophy

Lessing contributed to literature through his work in the field of literary criticism and drama, to philosophy in his efforts to bring the ideas of the European Enlightenment to Germany, and to theology in his founding of the philosophy of religion.

Lester, Julius

b. January 27, 1939
St. Louis, Mo.
fields: Literature

African American writer. Known for his militant and controversial politics as well as his confrontations with other African American activists, Julius Lester wrote numerous politically oriented works, including *Lovesong: Becoming a Jew* (1988), *This Strange New Feeling* (1982), *All Is Well* (autobiography, 1976), and *To Be a Slave* (1968). Lester later focused his academic career on Judaic studies after converting to Judaism.

LeTang, Henry

b. 1915?
New York, N.Y.
fields: Dance

African American dancer and choreographer. A teacher as well as performer, Henry LeTang began teaching tap dance in 1937. Some of his students included Lena Horne, Billie Holiday, Lola Falana, Debbie Allen, and Harry Belafonte. He choreographed numbers for such Broadway musicals as *The Wiz* (1975) and *Bubbling Brown Sugar* (1976). In 1978 he choreographed *Eubie!* for which he received both a Tony nomination and a Drama Critics Award.

Le Tellier, François-Michel. *See* Louvois, marquis de

Leung, Peter

b. Mar. 11, 1940
China
fields: Sociology, Historiography

Peter Leung developed the first Cantonese-language program at the University of California, Davis, in 1969. He served on the board of the Sacramento Chinese Community Service Center and wrote *One Day, One Dollar* (1984), a book about the Chinese farming experience in Locke, California. In 1991, he organized a festival commemorating the contributions of nineteenth century Chinese gold miners in Coloma, California.

Leung, Tye

b.?
fields: Historical Figure

Translator Tye Leung, a California resident, became the first Chinese American woman to vote in a U.S. presidential election in 1912. She worked as interpreter and assistant to the matrons of the Angel Island immigration station in San Francisco Bay, which served as a detention center for Asian immigrants awaiting entry to the United States.

Lévesque, René

b. 1922
fields: Government and Politics

French-Canadian politician; René Lévesque was born in Quebec, hosted *Point de Mire* (Point of View), a public affairs television program, 1956-1959; during the 1960's, served in the Quebec legislature; formed the separatist organization that would become the Parti Québécois in 1967, arguing that independence alone could protect French speakers in Canada; premier of Quebec, 1976-1985; his administration passed Bill 101 securing the status of the French language within Quebec.

Levi-Montalcini, Rita

né: Rita Levi
b. Apr. 22, 1909
Turin, Italy
fields: Biology, Physiology

Rita Levi-Montalcini discovered a substance called nerve growth factor, which is crucial to the development of the nervous system; in 1986, shared the Nobel Prize in Physiology or Medicine with Stanley Cohen.

Lévi-Strauss, Claude

b. November 28, 1908
Brussels, Belgium
fields: Anthropology, Language and Linguistics

Lévi-Strauss, one of the founders of structural anthropology, used his discipline to achieve insights into Western civilization by studying non-Western societies. He challenged basic Western assumptions about politics, history, and culture and became one of the major figures in the intellectual history of the twentieth century.

Lévinas, Emmanuel

b. January 12, 1906
Kaunas, Lithuania
d. December 25, 1995
Paris, France
fields: Philosophy

Philosopher and university professor profoundly affected by the Nazi Holocaust of World War II. With the claim that ethics, rather than ontology, is "first philosophy," Emmanuel Lévinas launched a major critique of the Western philosophical tradition, suggesting that philosophy is finally the wisdom of love in the service of love. Edmund Husserl's phenomenology and Martin Heidegger's ontology formed the focus of much of his work. Among his many works, *Totality and Infinity* (1961) and *Otherwise than Being* (1974) are especially important. Lévinas's work is perhaps the most significant attempt to move beyond the phenomenology of Edmund Husserl and Martin Heidegger. He influenced philosophers Paul Ricoeur, Jacques Derrida, Adriaan Peperzak, and Jean-Luc Marion.

Lew, Barzillai

b. November 5, 1743
Groton, Mass.
d. 1793
fields: Warfare and Conquest

African American revolutionary war soldier. During his six years as a soldier in the American Revolution Barzillai Lew served eight months with the Twenty-seventh Massachusetts Regiment, which was at the Battle of Bunker Hill on June 17, 1775. He was also a soldier in the French and Indian Wars. A possible date of death is January 19, 1821.

Lewes, Marian. *See* Eliot, George

Lewis, C. I.

full: Clarence Irving Lewis
b. April 12, 1883
Stoneham, Massachusetts
d. February 3, 1964
Menlo Park, California
fields: Philosophy

One of the leading American philosophers of his generation, C. I. Lewis made an original contribution to logic by inventing modal logic. His work in epistemology helped spread in the United States a major new view of a priori knowledge as wholly analytic. His work on empirical knowledge and on value theory has been less widely influential, but his view of ethics contributed to a renewal of interest in Kantian ethical principles. His major works include *A Survey of Symbolic Logic* (1918), *Mind and the World-Order* (1929), *Symbolic Logic* (1932, with Cooper Harold Langford), *An Analysis of Knowledge and Valuation* (1946), *The Ground and Nature of the Right* (1955), *Our Social Inheritance* (1957), and *Values and Imperatives* (1969).

Lewis, C. S.

full: Clive Staples Lewis
b. November 29, 1898
Belfast, Northern Ireland
d. November, 22, 1963
Oxford, England
fields: Literature, Religion and Theology

Lewis enlarged the understanding of the literature of the Middle Ages and Renaissance. He also composed novels and children's literature of lasting impact and published many insightful books concerning Christianity.

Lewis, Carl

full: Frederick Carlton Lewis
b. July 1, 1961
Birmingham, Ala.
fields: Sports (track and field athlete)

African American track and field athlete. After receiving the Sullivan Award as the best amateur athlete in the United States in 1982, Carl Lewis went on to win four gold medals (long jump, 100- and 200-meter dashes, and 400-meter relay) in the 1984 Olympics, setting Olympic records in the 200-meter dash and the 400-meter relay. He won two gold medals (100-meter dash and long jump) and a silver (200-meter dash) in the 1988 Olympics, with another record-setting time in the 100-meter dash. Making a third Olympic team at the age of thirty-one, Lewis won a gold in the long jump and was part of the gold-medal winning 4 × 100-meter relay team, which set a world record at 37.4 seconds.

Lewis, Charlotte

b. September 10, 1955
Chicago, Ill.
fields: Sports (basketball player)

African American basketball player. A star college player at Illinois State, Charlotte Lewis was chosen as a 1977 National Collegiate Athletic Association (NCAA) Division I women's first-team All-American. She was a member of the U.S. women's basketball team that won a silver medal at the Montreal Olympic Games in 1976.

Lewis, Delano

b. November 12, 1938
Arkansas City, Kans.
fields: Business and Industry (corporate executive), Law

African American attorney and corporate executive; Delano Lewis was promoted to the position of president of the Chesapeake and Potomac Telephone Company in 1988; became president and chief executive officer of National Public Radio (NPR) in 1993.

Lewis, Edmonia

full: Mary Edmonia Lewis
b. 1845(?)
probably near Albany, New York
d. after 1909
probably Rome, Italy
fields: Art

A talented sculptor, Edmonia Lewis drew on her African American and Native American heritage to expand the range of American neoclassic sculpture. Believed to be the first female African American sculptor, Lewis moved to Boston, Mass., in 1862, trained in sculpture with Edmund Brackett, and opened a studio; she most often sculpted in marble and specialized in portrait busts and symbolic groups; her work, which depicted the strength and will of oppressed people in their struggle to be free, included *Forever Free*, *Hagar*, the *Hiawatha* series, *Freedwoman*, *Medallion Head of John Brown*, *Abraham Lincoln*, *Old Indian Arrow Maker and His Daughter*, and *William Lloyd Garrison*. *The Death of Cleopatra* won an award at the 1876 American Centennial Exposition in Philadelphia, Pa.

Lewis, Gilbert N.

full: Gilbert Newton Lewis
b. Oct. 25, 1875
Weymouth, Massachusetts
d. Mar. 23, 1946
Berkeley, California
fields: Chemistry

Gilbert N. Lewis was a pioneer in chemical thermodynamics and an early defender of relativity theory; laid the foundation for the electron theory of valence; extended the concept of acids and bases; was the first to isolate heavy hydrogen.

Lewis, James B.

b. November 30, 1947
Roswell, N.Mex.
fields: Government and Politics

African American state official; James B. Lewis was elected New Mexico state treasurer in 1984, the first African American to hold a major statewide office in New Mexico; as treasurer he held membership on the New Mexico State Board of Finance and the National State Treasurers Association; prior to this office, from 1977 to 1983, he was an investigator and purchasing director for the Albuquerque district attorney's office, and, from 1983 to 1985, he served as treasurer for Bernalillo County.

Lewis, Jerry Lee

b. September 29, 1935
Ferriday, Louisiana
fields: Music

A rock and roll musician, Jerry Lee Lewis became a star during the mid-1950's with such hit records as "Whole Lot of Shakin' Going On" and "Great Balls of Fire." However, when it was publicly learned that he had married his thirteen-year-old cousin in 1957, his career went into a slide. Nevertheless, he continued to perform and record and gradually regained some of his earlier stature over the next four decades.

Lewis, John L.

full: John Llewellyn Lewis
b. February 12, 1880
Lucas, Iowa
d. June 11, 1969
Washington, D.C.
fields: Labor Movement

As president of the United Mine Workers union and founder of the Congress of Industrial Organizations, Lewis dominated the progress of organized labor in the United States from the 1920's through the 1960's.

Lewis, John Robert

b. Feb. 21, 1940
Troy, Ala.
fields: Civil Rights

African American civil rights activist John Robert Lewis was also chairperson of the Student Non-Violent Coordinating Committee (SNCC). In 1960, Lewis initiated the first sit-in protests against segregation at that city's lunch counters. As SNCC's leader, Lewis supported nonviolent protest, a position that was increasingly challenged by more militant members. After resigning from SNCC in 1966, he directed community voter registration projects in Nashville, Tennessee, and Atlanta, Georgia. He was appointed by Jimmy Carter to head ACTION, the federal agency charged with community economic recovery. In 1982 Lewis was elected to the Atlanta city council and to the U.S. House of Representatives.

Lewis, Julian Herman

b. May 26, 1891
Shawneetown, Ill.
d. March, 1989
Dyer, Ind.
fields: Medicine

African American physician; in 1915, Julian Herman Lewis became the first African American to receive a Ph.D. in physiology from the University of Chicago; after earning an M.D. from Rush Medical College (1917), he taught pathology at the University of Chicago (1917-1943); in 1942, he published *The Biology of the Negro*.

Lewis, Meriwether

b. August 18, 1774
Albemarle County, Virginia
d. October 11, 1809
Grinder's Stand, Tennessee
fields: Exploration and Colonization

Meriwether Lewis was coleader of the Lewis and Clark Expedition, the first party of white men to cross the North American continent from the Atlantic to the Pacific coast within the geographical limits of the present United States.

Lewis, Oliver

b. ?
d. ?
fields: Sports (jockey)

African American jockey; in 1875, Oliver Lewis won the first running of the Kentucky Derby, riding a horse named Aristides; he went on to become a trainer in Lexington, Ky.

Lewis, Ramsey Emanuel, Jr.

b. May 27, 1935
Chicago, Ill.
fields: Music (jazz pianist)

African American jazz musician; after releasing a single, "The In Crowd" (1965), which sold millions of copies, followed by a few other recordings, Ramsey Emanuel Lewis, Jr's jazz trio moved from relative obscurity to become one of the most popular jazz combos in the United States; in his recordings and live performances, Lewis sought to bridge the gap between popular music and the more obscure versions of jazz; his arrangements often included strings and voices complementing a small jazz combo, resulting in pleasant, easy-listening music rooted in jazz.

Lewis, Reginald F.

b. December 7, 1942
Baltimore, Md.
d. January 19, 1993
New York, N.Y.
fields: Business and Industry, Law

African American business executive; a graduate of Harvard Law School, Reginald F. Lewis worked as a partner at the first black law firm on Wall Street, Murphy, Thorpe, and Lewis (1970-1973); from 1973 to 1989, he ran a private practice specializing in corporate law; he went on to become president and chief executive officer of TLC Beatrice International Holdings, Inc.

Lewis, Roy

b. ?
fields: Photography

African American photographer; during the 1960's, Roy Lewis began his career working for black periodicals as a photojournalist; having developed a documentary style while training under photographers Lacey Crawford and Ted Williams, he covered civil rights activities, cultural events, and entertainers in and around Chicago, Ill.

Lewis, Samella Sanders

b. February 27, 1924
New Orleans, La.
fields: Art (painter, art historian), Education

African American painter, art historian, educator, and editor; Samella Sanders Lewis has taught art and art history at numerous institutions including Scripps College in California, the California State University, and Florida A&M University; Lewis has produced several films about black artists and has published several books about black art.

Lewis, Sinclair

full: Harry Sinclair Lewis
b. February 7, 1885
Sauk Centre, Minnesota
d. January 10, 1951
Rome, Italy
fields: Literature

The first American to win the Nobel Prize in Literature (1930), Lewis at once painstakingly depicted and satirized previously neglected areas of middle-American life.

Lewis, Terry

b. 1957
fields: Music (pop songwriter, producer)

Pop songwriters and producers. Terry Lewis and James Harris III were members of the Time, a Minneapolis rock group discovered by Prince; cowrote and coproduced songs for the group's albums, including *The Time* (1981) and *What Time Is It?* (1982); formed Flyte Tyme Productions after the band broke up in the early 1980's; won first Grammy in collaboration with Janet Jackson on her album *Control* (1986), named best album of the year in 1987; cowrote "I Didn't Mean to Turn You On" for Robert Palmer and worked with Jackson on her follow-up album, *Rhythm Nation 1814*.

Lewis, W. Arthur

full: Sir William Arthur Lewis
b. January 23, 1915
Castries, St. Lucia, British West Indies
d. June 15, 1991
Bridgetown, Barbados
fields: Economics

African American economist; the first black person to win a Nobel Prize in the sciences, Sir W. Arthur Lewis was corecipient of the 1979 Nobel Prize in Economic Sciences, sharing it with Theodore W. Schultz; following his tenure as vice chancellor of the University of the West Indies (1959-1963), he was knighted (1963); from 1963 to 1983, he worked as a professor at Princeton University; during his 1970 to 1974 leave of absence from Princeton, he helped establish the Caribbean Development Bank; his published works include *The Theory of Economic Growth* (1955) and *Politics in West Africa* (1965).

Lezama Lima, José

full: José María Andres Fernando Lezama Lima
b. Dec. 19, 1910
Campamento Militar de Columbia, Cuba
d. Aug. 9, 1976
Havana, Cuba
fields: Literature

Latino poet and novelist. José Lezama Lima was a member of the generation of writers of the Latin American "Boom." He founded the prerevolutionary journal *Orígenes* and influenced many later poets. He was virtually unknown outside of Cuba until he published his first novel, *Paradiso* (1966, rev. ed., 1988; *Paradise*, 1974), which is considered a classic in Cuban literature. His poetry was considered by some to be counterrevolutionary, and his requests to leave Cuba were repeatedly denied.

Lhamo Dhondrub. *See* Dalai Lama

Li, Chin-yang. *See* Lee, Chin Yang

Li, Choh Hao

b. Apr. 21, 1913
Canton, China
d. Nov. 28, 1987
Berkeley, Calif.
fields: Biology

Biochemist and endocrinologist Choh Hao Li, a longtime professor at the University of California, Berkeley, isolated six of eight hormones known to be secreted by the human pituitary gland and synthesized the pituitary human growth hormone in the early 1970's. He discovered beta-endorphin, a pain killer produced in the brain, in 1978. He also isolated insulin-like growth factor 1, which stimulates the growth of bones and cartilage in the human body. He received numerous honors and awards for his scientific endeavors.

Li Hongzhang

aka: Li Hung-chang
b. February 15, 1823
Hefei, Anhui, China
d. November 7, 1901
Tianjin, China
fields: Government and Politics, Military Affairs

Li played a leading role in the Ch'ing Dynasty, instituting reforms based on a moderate policy of Westernization known as self-strengthening, while in foreign affairs he adopted a firm, but conciliatory attitude.

Li Peng

b. October, 1928
Chengdu, Sichuan Province, China
fields: Government and Politics

Premier of China from 1988 to 1998. Zhou Enlai was Li Peng's friend, father (by adoption), and political mentor. Li Peng lost support of many after the fierce government crackdown on student protesters at Tiananmen Square and elsewhere in 1989.

Li Po

b. 701
Sinkiang Uighur
d. 762
Tan Tu, Anhwei Province, China
fields: Literature

Li's clever, sensuous, and mystical verse has led many to consider him China's foremost lyric poet.

Li Qingzhao

aka: Li Ch'ing-chao
b. 1084
Jinan, Shantong Province, China
d. c. 1155
Hangzhou, Zhejiang Province, China
fields: Literature

The greatest woman lyricist in the history of classical Chinese literature, Li made use of everyday language to explore the subtleties of human emotions, bringing the art of Chinese lyricism close to perfection. Her simple yet elegant style shaped the poetic expressions of the Southern Sung Dynasty and inspired many lyricists—even into the modern age.

Li, Victor H.

b. 1941
Hong Kong
fields: Law

Victor H. Li received a J.D. degree from Harvard Law School in 1964 and an LL.M. degree from Harvard the following year. He taught at the University of Michigan Law School, Columbia Law School, and Stanford Law School. Columbia honored Li as the Harlan Fiske Stone Scholar in 1964, and Li was named a Fulbright-Hays Fellow in 1965-1966. He was director of the East-West Center of Honolulu from 1981 to 1990.

Liang Qichao

b. Feb. 23, 1873
Xinhui, Guangdong Province, China
d. Jan. 19, 1929
Beijing, China
fields: Government and Politics

Intellectual and political reformer Liang Qichao was devoted to the modern transformation of Chinese society. He and reformer Kang Youwei led a short-lived movement to restore the Chinese emperor to the throne in 1898 and were forced to flee to Japan. In 1903, Liang toured Canada and the United States at the invitation of the Baohuanghui, a reform association founded by Kang. His memoirs, published in 1904 in China, provide valuable demographic information on Chinese Americans in the early twentieth century. In 1912, after the revolution, Liang returned to China and worked for the new government for a short time.

Libby, Willard F.

full: Willard Frank Libby
b. Dec. 17, 1908
Grand Valley, Colorado
d. Sept. 8, 1980
Los Angeles, California
fields: Astronomy, Chemistry, Science

Willard F. Libby developed carbon dating, a process by which organisms up to seventy thousand years old can be dated with reasonable accuracy; in 1960, awarded the Nobel Prize in Chemistry.

Lichtenstein, Roy

b. October 27, 1923
New York, New York
d. September 29, 1997
New York, New York
fields: Art (painting, sculpture)

By merging contemporary art, advertising, and popular art (comic strips), Roy Lichtenstein created abstract paintings that document popular American culture. In his paintings, he experimented with comic-book techniques. He used thick, black outlines, primary colors, and Benday dots to present scenes of action, violence, romance, or sentimental idealization. Some of his more famous works are the *Big Party* (1965) and *Whaam* (1963).

Liebig, Justus von

b. May 12, 1803
Darmstadt
d. April 18, 1873
Munich, Germany
fields: Chemistry

Liebig was one of the most important chemists of the nineteenth century. In addition to pioneering experimental research that transformed the basis of modern organic chemistry, his studies on agriculture led to the development of agricultural chemistry, and his systematic processes for training students became institutionalized within the German research university.

Liebknecht, Wilhelm

b. March 29, 1826
Giessen, Hesse-Darmstadt
d. August 7, 1900
Berlin, Germany
fields: Government and Politics

Liebknecht was a founding member of the German Social Democratic Party and an extreme critic of authoritarian government in Germany. He was a delegate to the German Reichstag and editor of the Social Democratic Party newspaper *Vorwärts*. His most important contribution was an effort to promote the ideals of democracy in the nineteenth century European socialist movement.

Lifar, Serge

b. April 2, 1905
Kiev, Russia
d. December 15, 1986
Lausanne, Switzerland
fields: Dance

As a dancer and choreographer, Lifar reestablished the Paris Opéra's leading role in the world of ballet by a series of innovative reforms: enhancing the role of male dancers; bringing modern concepts to the classical repertoire of the Opéra; and making dance the dominant element by emphasizing rhythm independently of music. His ballets are considered modern in subject and decor but classical in structure. In them, he attempts to convey drama through technique and choreography rather than through mime and music.

Light, Ivan

b. Nov. 3, 1941
Chicago, Ill.
fields: Sociology

Ivan Light, a professor of sociology at the University of California, Los Angeles, is a specialist in immigrant entrepreneurs. He wrote *Ethnic Enterprise in America* (1972) and coauthored, with Edna Bonacich, *Immigrant Entrepreneurs* (1988).

Ligot, Cayetano

b. ?
fields: Government and Politics

Leonard Wood, governor-general of the Philippines, in 1921 appointed Cayetano Ligot as labor commissioner to oversee conditions faced by Filipino workers on Hawaiian plantations and Hermenegildo Crus, director of the Philippine Bureau of Labor, to prepare a report on labor conditions in Hawaii. Ligot, who toured Hawaii, agreed with Crus's report, which blamed labor unrest on Filipino workers rather than on the Hawaiian Sugar Planters' Association. The Filipino workers saw Ligot's acts as indicative of his collusion with the planters and as a betrayal of his responsibility to guarantee their safety and well-being.

Liliuokalani

aka: Lydia Kamekaeha Paki
aka: Mrs. John O. Dominis
b. September 2, 1838
Honolulu, Hawaii
d. November 11, 1917
Honolulu, Hawaii
fields: Government and Politics

The last monarch of Hawaii (1891-1892), Liliuokalani witnessed the end of the Hawaiian kingdom and the beginning of the islands' annexation as a territory of the United States.

Lim, Genny

b. Dec. 15, 1946
San Francisco, Calif.
fields: Literature (poet, playwright), Theater and Entertainment

Poet and playwright Genny Lim, along with H. Mark Lai and Judy Yung, translated Chinese poems written on the barracks walls at San Francisco's Angel Island by detained immigrants and published them as *Island: Poetry and History of Chinese Immigrants on Angel Island, 1910-1940* (1980). She helped compile and edit *The Chinese American Experience: Papers from the Second National Conference on Chinese American Studies* (1984). Other works include two plays *Paper Angels* (1982) and *Bitter Cane* (1989). Lim also served as poet-in-residence at the Fine Arts Museums of San Francisco.

Lim, Shirley Geok-lin

*b.*1944
Malacca, Malaysia
fields: Literature (poetry), Scholarship

Poet and scholar Shirley Geok-lin Lim was awarded the Commonwealth Poetry Prize for her first book of poems, *Crossing the Peninsula and Other Poems* (1980). She wrote *Approaches to Teaching Kingston's "The Woman Warrior"* (1991) and coedited *The Forbidden Stitch: An Asian American Women's Anthology* (1989), which received an American Book Award from the Before Columbus Foundation, and *Reading the Literatures of Asian America* (1992), a collection of critical essays.

Lima, José María Andres Fernando Lezama. *See* Lezama Lima, José

Limbaugh, Rush

b. January, 1951
Cape Girardeau, Missouri
fields: Radio

A conservative American radio talk-show host, Rush Limbaugh was instrumental in the elimination of the broadcasting industry's fairness doctrine. Limbaugh's critics pointed to his three divorces and draft evasion in response to his hard-line espousal of Republican "values." Nevertheless, his bellicose delivery of narrow political views tapped into a vein of nationalism and widely held fears about the moral direction of U.S. society. His radio program began in 1988 and by 1996 was heard by more than twenty million Americans on more than six hundred stations. Meanwhile, he expanded his media empire to include a daily syndicated television show, a political newsletter, and two best-selling books, *The Way Things Ought to Be* (1992) and *See, I Told You So* (1993). His television show was canceled in 1996 because of falling ratings.

Limón, José Arcadio

b. Jan. 12, 1908
Culiacán, Mexico
d. Dec. 2, 1972
Flemington, N.J.
fields: Dance

José Arcadio Limón moved to New York in 1927 to study dance with Doris Humphrey, Charles Weidman, and Martha Graham. In 1930, he choreographed *Bacchanale*. Other notable works include *Danzas Mexicanas* (1939), *Chaconne* (1942), and *The Moor's Pavane* (1949). He formed his own dance company in 1945. In 1964, Limón became director of the American Dance Theater in residence at Lincoln Center in New York City.

Lin Biao

aka: Lin Piao
b. December 5, 1907
Huang-kang District, Hupeh Province, China
d. September 12 or 13, 1971
in an airplane crash in Mongolia
fields: Military Affairs, Government and Politics

Lin was a military officer who was an early adherent of Mao Tse-tung's armed rural revolution and achieved notable battlefield successes, especially in the Chinese Civil War from 1947 to 1949. Lin Piao was a champion of Mao's Cultural Revolution, and in 1969 he became Mao's designated successor.

Lin, Maya Ying

b. October 5, 1959
Athens, Ohio
fields: Architecture

Lin designed the Vietnam Veterans Memorial in Washington, D.C., and the Civil Rights Memorial in Montgomery, Alabama.

Lin Yutang

b. October 10, 1895
Zhangzhou, Fujian Province, China
d. March 26, 1976
Hong Kong
fields: Philosophy, Literature

Lin Yutang became the best-known Chinese cultural envoy to the United States. At the peak of his influence during the 1930's and 1940's, his descriptions of Chinese philosophy and character in his nonfiction and novels were major sources through which Western readers learned to appreciate Chinese life and thought. Among his major works are *My Country and My People* (1935), *The Importance of Living* (1937), *The Vigil of a Nation* (1944), and *From Pagan to Christian* (1959).

Lin Zexu

aka: Lin Tse-hsü
b. August 30, 1785
Houguan, Fujian, China
d. November 22, 1850
Chaozhou, Guandong, China
fields: Government and Politics

A respected scholar-official serving the Manchu Ch'ing Dynasty, Lin led the effort to eradicate the sale of opium by foreigners at Canton, a successful campaign that led to the Opium War (1839-1842) and the ignominious 1842 Treaty of Nanking.

Lina, Charleszetta. *See* Waddles, Mother

Lincoln, Abbey

né: Gaby Lee
b. August 6, 1930
Chicago, Ill.
fields: Music (singer and composer)

African American singer and composer; Abbey Lincoln, born Gaby Lee, began performing in the 1950's and took the name Abbey Lincoln in 1956. She first recorded with the Benny Carter Orchestra and sometimes sang with the Sonny Rollins/Max Roach Quartet. She and Roach were married from 1962 to 1970. Though she became widely known as a civil rights activist and actress in the 1960's, Lincoln returned to her roots as a jazz and ballad singer in the 1980's and 1990's.

Lincoln, Abraham

b. February 12, 1809
near Hodgenville, Kentucky
d. April 15, 1865
Washington, D.C.
fields: Civil Rights, Government and Politics

President of the United States, 1861-1865. Abraham Lincoln is generally considered to have been the outstanding figure responsible for the preservation of the federal Union.

Lincoln, C. Eric

full: Charles Eric Lincoln
b. June 23, 1924
Athens, Ala.
fields: Religion and Theology, Education

African American presbyterian minister, scholar, and university teacher. One of America's leading black theologians and sociologists of religion, Eric Lincoln became a frequent international conference speaker while maintaining a formidable output of both academic and popular writing. Some of his works include *The Black Muslims in America* (1961), *The Black Experience in Religion* (1974), and *Race, Religion, and the Continuing American Dilemma* (1984). Lincoln has taught at numerous educational institutions including Clark College, the Boston University School of Theology, Fisk, and Duke University.

Lind, Jenny

né: Johanna Maria Lind
b. October 6, 1820
Stockholm, Sweden
d. November 2, 1887
Wynds Point, Herefordshire, England
fields: Music

Through perseverance, hard work, and her unique charismatic personality, Lind, known as the "Swedish Nightingale," became the most famous female singer of the nineteenth century, an internationally successful touring star, and a role model for her generation.

Lindbergh, Charles A.

full: Charles Augustus Lindbergh
b. February 4, 1902
Detroit, Michigan
d. August 26, 1974
Hana, Maui, Hawaii
fields: Aviation and Space Exploration, Conservation and Environmentalism

Lindbergh's historic New York to Paris solo flight in 1927 was a turning point in aviation history, and he continued to play a major role in both civil and military aviation throughout his life.

Lindner, Belle. *See* Moskowitz, Belle

Ling, Amy

b. 1939
Beijing, China
fields: Literature (poetry), Scholarship

Poet Amy Ling published *Chinamerican Reflections* (1984), a collection of highly personal poems. She wrote *Between Worlds: Women Writers of Chinese Ancestry* (1990), coedited the companion volumes *Imagining America: Stories from the Promised Land* (1991) and *Visions of America: Personal Narratives from the Promised Land* (1993) with Shirley Geok-lin Lim, and edited the essay collection *Reading the Literatures of Asian America* (1992).

Linnaeus, Carolus

aka: Carl von Linné
b. May 23, 1707
Sodra Råshult, Småland, Sweden
d. Jan. 10, 1778
Uppsala, Sweden
fields: Biology, Botany, Zoology

Carolus Linnaeus published *Systema Naturae* (1735; *A General System of Nature*, 1800-1801) and *Species Plantarum* (1753), in which he revealed his system of classification and nomenclature with which he organized and named the known living things. Still the basis for modern classification systems and binomial nomenclature.

Linné, Carl von. *See* Linnaeus

Lion, The. *See* Smith, Willie

Lion, Jules

b. 1810
Paris, France
d. 1866
fields: Photography

African American photographer. One of the first black photographers, Jules Lion became famous for his pictures of New Orleans and his portraits of the city's leaders. He had studied the daguerreotype in Paris. Of his work only one photograph remains.

Liouville, Joseph

b. Mar. 24, 1809
Saint-Omer, Pas-de-Calais, France
d. Sept. 8, 1882
Paris, France
fields: Mathematics (algebra, calculus, and number theory)

Joseph Liouville founded the *Journal de Mathématiques Pures et Appliquées* in 1836; discovered transcendental numbers; studied differential and integral equations.

Lipchitz, Jacques

b. August 22, 1891
Druskieniki, Lithuania
d. May 26, 1973
Capri, Italy
fields: Art

Throughout his long career, Lipchitz made immeasurable contributions to the development of twentieth century sculpture. Beginning with his works of 1913-1930, he was one of the most inventive of the cubist sculptors, creating the sculptural equivalent of the ambiguous spaces and volumes in cubist painting. In his later works, he was less concerned with theory, searching instead for a more personal, expressive formal language.

Lipmann, Fritz Albert

b. June 12, 1899
Königsberg, East Prussia (now Kaliningrad, Russia)
d. July 24, 1986
Poughkeepsie, New York
fields: Biology, Chemistry, Physiology

Fritz Albert Lipmann suggested the central role of high-energy phosphate compounds in metabolism; discovered coenzyme A; in 1953, was awarded the Nobel Prize in Physiology or Medicine jointly with Hans Adolf Krebs.

Lippershey, Hans

b. c. 1570
Wesel, Westphalia
d. c. 1619
Middelburg, Zeeland, United Provinces
fields: Invention and Technology

Lippershey, a lens grinder and spectacle maker, generally receives credit for the invention of the telescope and binoculars in 1608.

Lippmann, Walter

b. September 23, 1889
New York, New York
d. December 14, 1974
New York, New York
fields: Journalism, Political Science, Philosophy

In a career spanning six decades, Lippmann lucidly analyzed current events, advised statesmen, and was author of more than twenty books which perceptively examined the challenges confronting American democracy.

Lipscomb, William N.

full: William Nunn Lipscomb, Jr.
b. July 16, 1919
Cleveland, Ohio
fields: Chemistry

William N. Lipscomb was an authority on chemical physics, X-ray crystallography, and chemical biology; won the Nobel Prize in Chemistry in 1976 for his studies of chemical bonding.

Lisa, Manuel

b. Sept. 8, 1772
New Orleans, La.
d. Aug. 12, 1820
St. Louis, Mo.
fields: Exploration and Colonization, Business and Industry

Latino explorer and trader. In 1802, Manuel Lisa and Pierre Chouteau opened the Missouri Fur Company, which operated trading posts along the Missouri River. After the Louisiana Purchase of 1803, Lisa led several exploration trips and opened more trading posts and forts. In 1812, he opened Fort Lisa, the most important trading post on the Missouri River for the next ten years. In 1814, Lisa became subagent for all the Missouri River Indian tribes located above the mouth of the Kansas River. He is credited with keeping the Western Plains Indians from helping the British in the War of 1812 and with opening the Missouri River to Americans.

Lister, Joseph

b. April 5, 1827
Upton Park, Essex, England
d. February 10, 1912
Walmer, Kent, England
fields: Medicine

Combining skill as a laboratory scientist with great technical ability at surgery, Lister developed and helped to propagate antiseptic surgery.

Liston, Sonny

full: Charles Liston
b. May 8, 1932
near Forrest City, Ark.
d. December 30?, 1970
Las Vegas, Nev.
fields: Sports (boxer)

African American boxer; Sonny Liston beat Floyd Patterson in Chicago, Ill., in 1962, to win the world championship title. He lost the title in 1964 to Cassius Clay (later known as Muhammad Ali).

Liszt, Franz

b. October 22, 1811
Raiding, Hungary
d. July 31, 1886
Bayreuth, Germany
fields: Music

Liszt revolutionized the art of piano playing and thus established the vogue of the recitalist. As a composer, he attempted to reconcile the trends of French and German Romanticism, created the musical genre of the symphonic poem, founded new innovations in harmony and form, and in his late works anticipated many devices of twentieth century music.

Little, Cleavon

full: Cleavon Jake Little
b. June 1, 1939
Chickasha, Okla.
d. October 22, 1992
Sherman Oaks, Calif.
fields: Theater and Entertainment

African American actor; Cleavon Little stage performances include *Narrow Road to the Deep North* (1972), *Same Time Next Year* (1977), *The Sly Fox* (1978), *I'm Not Rappaport* (1985), and *All God's Dangers* (1989). He won a Tony Award for Best Actor in a musical, for his performance in *Purlie* in 1970. He appeared in many films and television series: *Blazing Saddles* (1974), *Cotton Comes to Harlem* (1970), *Greased Lightning* (1977), *Fletch Lives* (1989), *Temperature's Rising* (1972), and *All in the Family*.

Little, Floyd Douglas

b. July 4, 1942
New Haven, Conn.
fields: Sports (football player)

African American football player. A three-time All-American at Syracuse University, Floyd Douglas Little led his team to the Gator Bowl in 1968 and later was inducted into the College Football Hall of Fame. His first years as a professional were with the Denver Broncos (1967-1970). After the AFL and the NFL merged, Little played for three NFL All-Pro teams; he led the NFL in rushing in 1971 and touchdowns in 1973. Little retired after the 1974 season, and the Broncos retired his uniform number, 44.

Little, Joanne

b. May 8, 1954
Washington, N.C.
fields: Historical Figure

African American victim of attempted rape. In August, 1974, Joanne Little stabbed and killed a prison guard in self-defense. Various feminist and civil rights organizations rallied to support her case. As a result a class-action lawsuit was filed asking for protection for female prisoners against sexual abuse by male attendants at the prison, who could see the prisoners undress, bathe, and use the bathroom. Little was acquitted of second-degree murder in August of 1975.

Little, Malcolm. *See* Malcolm X

Little Bluff. *See* Dohasan

Little Boy Blue. *See* Williamson, Sonny Boy, II

Little Chief. *See* Little Priest

Little Crow. *See* Little Raven

Little Crow

aka: Cetan Wakan Mani
aka: Tahatan Wakan Mini (Hawk That Hunts Walking)
aka: Taoyateduta (His Red People)
b. c. 1820
near South St. Paul, Minn.
d. July 1863
near Hutchinson, Minn.
fields: Government and Politics, Native American Affairs

A Mdewakanton (Dakota) Sioux, Little Crow was a leader during the Sioux Minnesota Uprising of 1862. The brief but bloody uprising was ended when the Sioux were defeated at Wood Lake on September 23, 1862.

Little Eva

né: Eva Narcissus Boyd
b. June 29, 1945
Bell Haven, N.C.
fields: Music (singer)

African American singer; Little Eva is best known for her hit "The Loco-Motion" (1962), written by Carole King and Jerry Goffin. She also reached the charts with "Keep Your Hands Off My Baby," "Let's Turkey Trot" (1963), and "Swingin' on a Star" (1963), a duet with Big Dee Irwin which reached number thirty-eight on the American pop chart and made the top ten in Great Britain.

Little Milton

né: James Milton Campbell
aka: Campbell, Little Milton
b. Sept. 7, 1934
Inverness, Miss.
fields: Music (rhythm-and-blues musician)

African American musician; rhythm-and-blues guitarist and singer Little Milton Campbell made recordings with two other labels before scoring his Checker Records hits "Blindman," "Grits Ain't Groceries," and "Sweet Sixteen"; in 1971 his soul-filled blues style was encouraged by Stax Records, for whom he made some of his best recordings, including the album *Waiting for Little Milton*; Campbell has appealed mainly to African American audiences with his Mississippi-church-revival performing style, featuring piercing, loud shrieks from both guitar and voice.

Little Mountain. *See* Dohasan

Little Priest

aka: Hoonk-hoo-no-kaw
aka: Little Chief
b. ?
d. Sept., 1866
fields: Government and Politics, Warfare and Conquest, Native American Affairs

Native American leader. Little Priest was a Winnebago tribal representative and warrior. Supported the Minnesota Uprising of the Sioux that took place from 1862 to 1863 and may have participated in the fighting. Became a scout and company leader for the Omaha, fighting the Sioux between 1866 and 1868 in a war for the control of the Bozeman Trail.

Little Raven

aka: Hosa
aka: Little Crow
b. c. 1825
on the Platte River, Nebr.
d. 1889
Cantonment, Indian Territory
fields: Government and Politics, Diplomacy, Peace Advocacy, Native American Affairs

Native American leader. As principal Arapaho chief, Little Raven supported accommodation and peace with whites. However, retaliating against white encroachment during the Civil War, he led several raids in Kansas and Colorado. In 1865 and 1867, signed the treaties of Little Arkansas and Medicine Lodge.

Little Richard

né: Richard Penniman
b. December 25, 1935
Macon, Ga.
fields: Music

African American influential early rock-and-roll musician; Little Richard's commercial success began with his hit "Tutti Frutti" (1956) and continued with songs such as "Long Tall Sally" (1956), "Lucille" and "Jenny, Jenny" (1957), and "Good Golly Miss Molly" (1958). Artists such as Paul McCartney and John Fogerty were influenced by Little Richard whose style included energetic piano playing and wildly expressive vocals (including squeals, shrieks, and howls).

Little Robe

b. 1828
d. 1886
fields: Diplomacy, Peace Advocacy, Government and Politics, Native American Affairs

Native American leader. A Southern Cheyenne, Little Robe fought against whites in the Cheyenne-Arapaho War. Thereafter advocated peace, joining with Black Kettle and George Bent to bring the militant Dog Soldiers to the signing of the Medicine Lodge Treaty of 1867. Succeeded Black Kettle as leading peace chief of the Southern Cheyenne in 1868.

Little Turtle

aka: Michikinikwa
b. c. 1752
near Fort Wayne, Ind.
d. July 14, 1812
Fort Wayne, Ind.
fields: Native American Affairs, Warfare and Conquest

Miami Tribal chief; noted for his military skill, Little Turtle led a coalition of Indian forces in an attempt to retain the Ohio River as the southern boundary of their land; he organized the defeat of Brigadier General Josiah Harmer and an armed force of fifteen hundred men on the Miami River (1790) and the defeat of General St. Clair and fourteen hundred American soldiers (1791; fewer than six hundred soldiers survived); following the defeat of the Indian forces by General Anthony Wayne at Fallen Timbers (1794), Little Turtle helped to negotiate the Treaty of Greenville (1795) under which the Miami and associated tribes ceded their rights to most of modern Ohio and a large portion of Indiana to the U.S.

Little Walter

né: Marion Walter Jacobs
b. May 1, 1930
Marksville, La.
d. February 15, 1968
Chicago, Ill.
fields: Music (harmonica player)

African American harmonica player; Little Walter is known for developing the harmonica into a lead instrument and for being the first to mimic the sound of saxophone players such as Louis Jordan with the harmonica. With his warm, mournful voice he was a powerful singer and a highly organized band leader with a new innovative sound. Little Walter recorded about one hundred titles for the Chess label, including "Juke," a number-one hit on the rhythm-and-blues charts.

Little Wolf

aka: Ohkom Kakit
aka: Two Tails
b. c. 1820
near the Eel and Blue rivers, Mont.
d. 1904
Tongue River Reservation, Mont.
fields: Government and Politics, Warfare and Conquest, Native American Affairs

Native American leader. A Northern Cheyenne, Little Wolf fought alongside such leaders as Crazy Horse and Gall in the 1860's. In 1878, along with Dull Knife, he led some 350 Cheyennes on a 1,500-mile journey from Indian Territory back to their Montana homeland. Little Wolf's group eluded troops pursuing them until March, 1879, at which time Little Wolf surrendered to W. P. Clark near the mouth of the Powder River. He and his people were taken to Fort Keogh, Montana.

Littleton, Thomas

aka: Sir Thomas Littleton
b. 1422
Frankley, Worcestershire, England
d. August 23, 1481
Frankley, Worcestershire, England
fields: Law

Littleton's fame rests upon a short treatise titled *Tenures*, written toward the end of his life, in which he gives a full and clear account of the several estates, tenures, and doctrines pertaining to landholding that were then known to the English law. *Tenures* is the primary source of the land law of medieval England, and it is considered to be the first great book upon English law not written in Latin and wholly uninfluenced by Roman law.

Litvinov, Maksim Maksimovich

né: Meier Moiseevich Wallach
b. July 17, 1876
Bialystok, Poland, Russian Empire
d. December 31, 1951
Moscow, U.S.S.R.
fields: Diplomacy

Litvinov was the most prominent Soviet diplomat of the interwar period. During the 1920's, he was a leading advocate of world peace through universal disarmament. In the 1930's, he negotiated American recognition of the Soviet Union and became the main spokesman for the Soviet policy of collective security with the Western powers against German, Japanese, and Italian aggression prior to World War II.

Liu, Daniel S. C.

b. Feb. 13, 1908
Honolulu, Territory of Hawaii
fields: Law

Daniel S. C. Liu became the first Chinese American to serve as police chief in Honolulu, in 1948. He became vice president of the International Association of Chiefs of Police in 1957, then served as president from 1963 to 1964. In 1966, he received the J. Edgar Hoover Gold Medal Award, and in 1968, a distinguished service award from the National Police Officers Association.

Liu, Henry Yi

né: Liu Yi-liang
b. Dec. 7, 1932
Liu Jia Tai, Jiangsu Province, China
d. Oct. 15, 1984
Daly City, Calif.
fields: Journalism

The assassination of Henry Yi Liu embarrassed the government of Taiwan, officials of which were implicated in the killing. In 1967 Liu moved to the United States and became a naturalized citizen, writing articles for Chinese-language newspapers and books on Chinese politics. In 1984, a revised edition of his *Biography of Chiang Ching-kuo* was published in the United States. That same year, on October 15, Liu was gunned down at his home.

Liu, Pei Chi

né: Po-chi Liu
b. May 29, 1908
fields: Publishing

Pei Chi Liu became editor of the San Francisco-based *Chinese Nationalist Daily* (*Kuo Min Yat Po*), an organ of the Chinese Nationalist party, in 1940. He organized the Chinatown Anti-Communist League and wrote a two-volume, Chinese-language history of the Chinese in the United States, published 1976-1981.

Liu Shaoqi

aka: Liu Shao-ch'i
b. 1898
Ning-hsiang district, Hunan Province, China
d. November 12, 1969
K'ai-feng, Honan Province, China
fields: Government and Politics

An important first-generation figure of the Chinese Communist Party, Liu was an early advocate of Mao Tse-tung's leadership. After 1949, Liu's management skills were critical to the new People's Republic of China. He served as chairman of the government after 1959, as well as a top party leader.

Liu, William T.

b. May 6, 1930
Nanjing, China
fields: Sociology, Education

William T. Liu became the first Asian American appointed to the Chicago Board of Education in 1988. He directed the Pacific American Research Centre from 1976 to 1989 and taught sociology at the University of Illinois, Chicago, until he retired in 1992. Liu was a board member of the Advisory Council of the Asian American Assembly for Policy Research, the Asian Human Services of Greater Chicago, and the Asian Pacific Health Forum.

Liveright, Horace

b. December 10, 1886
Osceola Mills, Pennsylvania
d. September 24, 1933
New York, New York
fields: Publishing

A partner in the publishing firm of Boni and Liveright, Horace Liveright was at the center of censorship controversy during the 1920's. He and partner Albert Boni reprinted literary works such as Andreas Latzko's pacifist novel *Men in War* (1918) and a new translation of Petronius Arbiter's *The Satyricon* (1922)—some of which drew attacks from right-wing and moralist groups.

Liverpool, second earl of

né: Robert Banks Jenkinson
aka: Robert Banks Jenkinson, second earl of Liverpool
b. June 7, 1770
London, England
d. December 4, 1828
London, England
fields: Government and Politics

As prime minister from 1812 to 1827, Liverpool led Great Britain to victory over Napoleon, rode out the domestic strife of the postwar years, and directed the economic recovery and liberal legislation of the 1820's.

Livingston, Edward

b. May 28, 1764
Clermont, N.Y.
d. May 23, 1836
Rhinebeck, N.Y.
fields: Law, Government and Politics

American lawyer and statesman. Edward Livingston's criminal code for Louisiana, drafted in the 1820's, though never adopted, greatly influenced subsequent thought and practice in criminal justice. Livingston later served as a U.S. congresssman, senator, and secretary of state.

Livingston, George

b. ?
fields: Government and Politics

African American mayor of Richmond, Calif. Following George Livingston's term as a member-at-large on the Richmond city council, he was elected to his first term as mayor of Richmond, in June of 1987. He was reelected to serve through November of 1993.

Livingston, Henry Brockholst

b. 1757
d. 1823
fields: Law

U.S. Supreme Court justice, 1807-1823 (died while in office); appointed by President Jefferson.

Livingstone, David

b. March 19, 1813
Blantyre, Scotland
d. May 1, 1873
Chitambo's village near Lake Bangweulu, Central Africa
fields: Exploration and Colonization, Religion and Theology

Although Livingstone is often thought of primarily as a missionary, in truth he was singularly unsuccessful in this endeavor. His actual importance was as an explorer whose travels, together with moving appeals asking Britons to do something about the slave trade in the African interior, focused the eyes of the civilized world on the "dark continent."

Livy

né: Titus Livius
b. 59 B.C.E.
Patavium (modern Padua), Italy
d. c. 17 C.E.
probably Patavium, Italy
fields: Historiography

Livy preserved many of the early legendary traditions and mythology dealing with the earliest phase of ancient Roman history. Since many of the authors and sources he used have long been lost, his work assumes a greater importance.

Llorens Torres, Luis

b. 1876
Juana Díaz, Puerto Rico
d. 1944
New York, N.Y.
fields: Literature

Latino poet. Luis Llorens Torres grew up in Puerto Rico but began his career as a poet while in Spain. He eventually returned to Puerto Rico, began working for Puerto Rican independence, and founded the literary journal *La Revista de las Antilles*. With the publication of *Al pie de la Alhambra* (1899, at the foot of the Alhambra), Llorens Torres was recognized as an original poet with a "nativist" flavor. He thus came to be known as "the poet of Puerto Rico."

Lloyd George, David

b. January 17, 1863
Manchester, England
d. March 26, 1945
Ty Newydd, near Llanystumdwy, Wales
fields: Government and Politics

While guiding his country through the trials of World War I, Lloyd George ushered in a new era: the age of the common man as world leader.

Lobachevsky, Nikolay Ivanovich

b. December 1, 1792
Nizhny Novgorod, Russia
d. February 24, 1856
Kazan, Russia
fields: Mathematics

Lobachevsky was the boldest and most consistent founder of a post-Euclidean theory of real space. His persistence in holding open his revolutionary line of inquiry into the reality of geometry helped to set the stage for the radical discoveries of twentieth century theoretical physics.

Locke, Alain

full: Alain Leroy Locke
b. Sept. 13, 1886
Philadelphia, Pa.
d. June 9, 1954
New York, N.Y.
fields: Literature, Education

African American philosopher, writer; Alain Locke after study at Harvard University, Oxford University, and the University of Berlin, served on faculty at Howard University, 1912-1953; celebrated black cultural contributions in works such as *The New Negro: An Interpretation* (1925) and a special issue of the journal *Survey Graphic*, which announced the arrival of a "Harlem Renaissance" and published work by Langston Hughes, Zora Neale Hurston, and W. E. B. Du Bois; also wrote or edited *Race Contacts and Inter-Racial Relations* (1916), *Opportunity* (an annual review of the state of black writing), *Negro Art: Past and Present* (1936), and *The Negro and His Music* (1940).

Locke, Gary

b. Jan. 1950
Seattle, Wash.
fields: Government and Politics

Gary Locke was elected to the Washington State House of Representatives in 1982 and served on a number of committees, including house appropriations and judiciary. Locke won the Legislator of the Year award in 1990. He also was a member of the boards of Kin On Chinese Nursing Home and Asian Counseling and Referral Center.

Locke, John

b. August 29, 1632
Wrington, Somerset, England
d. October 26, 1704
Oates, Essex, England
fields: Philosophy

One of the first modern philosophers, Locke combined the rational, deductive theory of René Descartes and the inductive, scientific experimentalism of Francis Bacon and the Royal Society. He gave the Western world the first modern theory of human nature and a new synthesis of the individualistic concept of liberty and the theory of government that was emerging out of the debates over natural law.

Lockhart, Calvin

b. October 8, 1934
Nassau, Bahama Islands
fields: Theater and Entertainment

African American actor; Calvin Lockhart's film credits include *Joanna* (1968), *Cotton Comes to Harlem* (1970), *Uptown Saturday Night* (1974), and *Let's Do It Again* (1975). He appeared in the television series *Dynasty* in the 1980's as one of Diahann Carroll's suitors.

Lockwood, Belva A.

né: Belva Ann Bennett
aka: Belva McNall
b. October 24, 1830
Royalton, New York
d. May 19, 1917
Washington, D.C.
fields: Law, Women's Rights, Peace Advocacy

Lockwood obtained passage of federal legislation giving women equal pay for equal work in government service, became the first woman to be granted the right to plead cases before the U.S. Supreme Court, and was a committed activist for women's rights.

Lockyer, Joseph Norman

aka: Sir Joseph Norman Lockyer
b. May 17, 1836
Rugby, Warwickshire, England
d. August 16, 1920
Salcombe Regis, Devonshire, England
fields: Science, Publishing, Physics (astrophysics)

Lockyer was a pioneering, self-educated astrophysicist who founded in 1869, and edited throughout its first fifty years, the weekly journal *Nature*, which is the world's premier general science periodical.

Lodge, Henry Cabot

b. May 12, 1850
Boston, Massachusetts
d. November 9, 1924
Cambridge, Massachusetts
fields: Government and Politics

Combining integrity, acumen, and strong Republican partisanship, Lodge helped shape the nation's political history throughout his thirty-seven-year tenure as a United States congressman and senator.

Logan, James

aka: Logan the Mingo
aka: John Logan
aka: Tahgahjute
b. c. 1723
Shamokin, present-day Sunbury, Pa.
d. 1780
near Detroit, Mich.
fields: Warfare and Conquest, Native American Affairs

Native American leader. James Logan, a Cayuga (or Mingo, as some Cayugas were known), was a leader in Lord Dunmore's War (1773-1774), aligned with Shawnee leader Cornstalk. Logan on several occasions raided white settlers in the Appalachian region. He became militant after white settlers killed his wife and several children.

Logan, Juan Leon

b. August 16, 1946
Nashville, Tenn.
fields: Art (sculptor)

African American sculptor; Juan Leon Logan worked with metal to explore such formal matters as the representation of volume by means of modern industrial materials; received the Romare Bearden Award for Creativity for Innovation of Medium in 1977.

Logan, Rayford Whittingham

b. January 7, 1897
Washington, D.C.
d. November 4, 1982
Washington, D.C.
fields: Historiography

Lomas Garza, Carmen

b. 1948
Kingsville, Tex.
fields: Art

Latina artist. Carmen Lomas Garza earned a bachelor's degree in art education at Texas A&I University in Kingsville (1972) and master of arts degrees at Antioch Graduate School of Education, Juárez-Lincoln Extension (1973) and San Francisco State University (1980). Her art reflects the racism and discrimination she experienced as a child in South Texas, as well as her upbringing in a rural Chicano community. She was associated with the Chicano movement of the 1960's.

Lombardi, Vince

full: Vincent Thomas Lombardi
b. June 11, 1913
Brooklyn, New York
d. September 3, 1970
Washington, D.C.
fields: Sports (football)

One of the United States' most successful professional football coaches, Vince Lombardi's style of leadership influenced a wide public. In 1954, he entered professional football as offensive coach of the New York Giants. In 1959, he became head coach and general manager of the Green Bay Packers and transformed them into a winning team that dominated the National Football League for the next nine years, winning the league title in 1961, 1962, 1965, 1966, and 1967, and the Super Bowl games of 1967 and 1968. His quest for excellence once led him to say, "Winning isn't everything. It is the only thing." Lombardi retired from coaching in 1968 but remained with the Packers as general manager. In 1969, he moved to Washington, D.C., coaching the Redskins to their first winning season in fourteen years. He died of intestinal cancer the next year.

Lomelí, Francisco

b. Apr. 13, 1947
Sombrerete, Zacatecas, Mexico
fields: Education, Literature

Latino educator, critic, and writer. Francisco Lomelí was born in Mexico but was educated in the United States, then became a professor at the University of California at Santa Barbara. Lomelí has received fellowships from the Fulbright Foundation (1969), the Ford Foundation (1974), Rotary Club International (1983), and the Rockefeller Foundation (1989). He has published literary criticism, edited *Chicano Literature: A Reference Guide* (1985) and *Aztlan: Essays on the Chicano Homeland* (1989), and coedited *Handbook of Hispanic Cultures in the United States: Literature and Art* (1994). He was named to the editorial boards of the journals *The Americas Review*, *The Bilingual Review*, *Discurso Literario*, and *The Latino Studies Journal*.

Lomonosov, Mikhail Vasilyevich

b. November 19, 1711
near Kholmogory, Russia
d. April 15, 1765
St. Petersburg, Russia
fields: Literature, Chemistry, Physics, Historiography

Through his reform of the Russian literary language, his scientific investigations, and his reinterpretation of early Russian history, Lomonosov was at the beginning of modern Russian intellectual history and a founder of Russian nationalism.

London, Jack

né: John Griffith Chaney
b. January 12, 1876
San Francisco, California
d. November 22, 1916
Glen Ellen, California
fields: Literature

London was one of the main exponents of American literary naturalism, a popular writer of adventure stories, and a crusading journalist, socialist, and political novelist who pioneered the role of the twentieth century activist writer.

Lone, John

*b.*October 13, 1952
Hong Kong
fields: Theater and Entertainment

Actor John Lone's first break was a role in David Henry Hwang's 1980 comedy-drama about Chinese American self-identification, *FOB*, at New York's Public Theatre, which earned him Drama League of American and Obie awards. In 1981, Lone starred in Hwang's *The Dance and the Railroad*, created specially for the actor, and in 1983 in Hwang's *Sound and Beauty*. The actor also appeared in films such as *Iceman* (1984), *The Year of the Dragon* (1985), *The Last Emperor* (1987), and *M. Butterfly* (1993).

Lone Wolf

aka: Guipago
b. c. 1820
d. c. 1879
fields: Government and Politics, Warfare and Conquest, Native American Affairs

Native American leader. Lone Wolf was principal chief of the Kiowa from 1866 to 1879 and fought in many major battles against whites. Participated in the Wichita Agency melee in August, 1874, which set off the Red River War on the southern Plains. Surrendered in 1875; exiled to Fort Marion, Florida.

Long, Avon

b. June 18, 1910
Baltimore, Md.
d. February 15, 1984
New York, N.Y.
fields: Theater and Entertainment

African American dancer, singer, and actor; Avon Long danced at the Cotton Club in 1931 and joined the black vaudeville circuit in 1934. He won widespread approval for his performance as Sportin' Life in the 1942 revival of *Porgy and Bess*. Later stage credits include *Don't Play Us Cheap* (1972), a Tony nominated role, and *Bubbling' Brown Sugar* (1975). Long's film credits include *The Sting* (1973) and *Harry and Tonto* (1974), and in 1979 he appeared as Chicken George Moore in *Roots: The Next Generations*.

Long, Huey

full: Huey Pierce Long
b. August 30, 1893
near Winnfield, Louisiana
d. September 10, 1935
Baton Rouge, Louisiana
fields: Government and Politics

Joining a sincere concern for the economic plight of the common people with an overwhelming desire to realize his ideas and plans, Long fashioned a political career of great accomplishment for both good and ill.

Long, James

b. 1954
New York, N.Y.
fields: Sports (jockey)

African American jockey. In 1974 James Long, one of the few black jockeys active at the time, was the first African American jockey to win a race at the Saratoga Springs track in New York.

Long, Jefferson Franklin

b. March 3, 1836
Knoxville, Ga.

d. February 4, 1901
Macon, Ga.
fields: Government and Politics

African American congressman. In 1870, Jefferson Franklin Long was nominated to run for the remaining term of the Forty-first Congress as a representative from Georgia's Fourth District. He won the election and after taking office became the first black representative ever to deliver a speech on the floor of Congress, on February 1, 1871.

Longfellow, Henry Wadsworth

b. February 27, 1807
Portland, Maine
d. March 24, 1882
Cambridge, Massachusetts
fields: Literature

Besides working to establish the study of modern languages and comparative literature in the United States, Longfellow became the most popular of all living poets during his time.

Longworth, Alice Roosevelt

né: Alice Lee Roosevelt
b. February 12, 1884
New York, New York
d. February 20, 1980
Washington, D.C.
fields: Government and Politics

Often referred to as "Washington's other monument," Alice Roosevelt Longworth reigned for more than eight decades as one of the most controversial and influential individuals within the political and social arenas of America's capital city.

Loo, Chalsa M.

b. Mar. 7, 1945
Honolulu, Territory of Hawaii
fields: Psychiatry and Psychology

Chalsa M. Loo, who holds a Ph.D. from Ohio State University, served as clinical psychologist at the Department of Veterans Affairs in Honolulu and professor of psychology at the University of Hawaii. She founded the nonprofit Chinatown Housing and Health Research Project (later the Chinatown Research Center) in San Francisco in 1978, which studied the lives of Chinatown residents, and wrote *Chinatown: Most Time, Hard Time* (1991).

Looking Glass

aka: Allalimya Takanin
aka: Apushwahite
b. c. 1823
near present-day Asotin, Wash.
d. Oct. 5, 1877
Bear's Paw Battlefield, Bear's Paw Mountains, Mont.
fields: Government and Politics, Warfare and Conquest, Native American Affairs

Nez Perce leader Looking Glass, one of the important nontreaty Nez Perce chiefs, served as war leader and guide in the ultimately unsuccessful retreat to Canada in the Nez Perce War of 1877. The Nez Perce were overtaken in the Bear's Paw Mountains (Montana), only 30 miles from Canada, and defeated. Looking Glass was the last casualty of the Nez Perce War, fatally shot in the head.

Loomis, Augustus Ward

b. 1816
Andover, Conn.
d. 1891
fields: Religion and Theology

Augustus Ward Loomis, who had previously served as a missionary in China, established a school in Chinatown in San Francisco to teach English and produce converts to Christianity. His handbook, *English and Chinese Lessons*, was published by the American Tract Society in 1872. Loomis also acted as an advocate for the Chinese American community.

Loos, Anita

full: Corinne Anita Loos
b. April 26, 1888
Sissons, California
d. August 18, 1981
New York, New York
fields: Literature, Film

A pioneering scriptwriter who developed the use of intertitles during the silent film era, Anita Loos also wrote the famous jazz-age novel *Gentlemen Prefer Blondes*.

Lopez, Alfonso Ramon

b. Aug. 20, 1908
Tampa, Fla.
fields: Sports (baseball player and manager)

Latino baseball player and manager. Catcher Alfonso Ramon Lopez spent nineteen years in the major leagues before retiring after the 1947 season. He began managing the Cleveland Indians after the 1950 season and led them to the 1954 American League pennant. When he led the Chicago White Sox to the 1959 American League pennant, he became the only American League manager to lead a team other than the New York Yankees into the World Series from 1949 to 1964. He was named the 1959 American League Manager of the Year. In 1977, Lopez was elected to the Baseball Hall of Fame.

Lopez, Aurelio

full: Aurelio Alejandro Lopez y Rios
b. Oct. 5, 1948
Tecamachalco, Mexico
fields: Sports (baseball player)

Latino baseball player. Pitcher Aurelio Lopez made his major league debut with the Kansas City Royals in 1974. He returned to the Mexican League for three seasons, then signed with the St. Louis Cardinals in 1978. He was traded to the Detroit Tigers one year later, where he became one of the best relievers in the American League. Lopez led American League relievers in wins in 1980 and 1984 and made the 1983 All-Star team. He won the deciding game of the 1984 World Series for the Tigers against the San Diego Padres. Lopez became a free agent in 1985 and played for the Houston Astros before retiring at the end of the 1987 season.

López, Ignacio

b. March, 1908
Guadalajara, Jalisco, Mexico
fields: Journalism

Ignacio López helped to found civic unity leagues, which focused on the problems of poor Mexican Americans, in various Southern California communities. He published the bilingual weekly newspaper *El Espectador* until 1961. López headed the Spanish department in the foreign-language office of the Division of War Information during World War II, and he was also the Spanish-speaking director of the Los Angeles Office of Coordinator of Inter-American Affairs.

López, José Dolores

b. 1868
d. 1937
fields: Art

Latino artist. Between 1917 and 1929, José Dolores López made furniture, window and door frames, coffins, crosses for grave markers, and small wooden figures. He began making santos, or religious figures, during a resurgence of interest in traditional Hispanic art. López's son, George, began carving in the mid-1920's and by the 1960's was considered to be the best active *santero*.

Lopez, Nancy

b. January 6, 1957
Torrance, California
fields: Sports (golf)

Success as an amateur and professional golfer established Nancy Lopez as a predominant figure in the world of golf, and her presence stimulated the growth of women's professional golf in the United States and internationally.

López, Trini

full: Trinidad López
b. May 15, 1937
Dallas, Tex.
fields: Music (singer)

Latino singer. Trini López started a Tex-Mex folk rock band in high school. He later moved to Los Angeles, became a popular solo artist, and signed a recording contract with Reprise Records in 1963. His first album sold more than one million copies, and the single "If I Had a Hammer" became an international hit. López costarred in the popular film *The Dirty Dozen* (1967) and was named Dallas Man of the Year in 1967.

López, Yolanda

b. 1942
San Diego, Calif.
fields: Art

Latina artist. Yolanda López received her master of fine arts degree from the University of California, San Diego, in 1978 and went on to teach painting at the California College of Arts and Crafts. She has made posters, videos, and installation art, and her work often includes such religious figures as Our Lady of Guadalupe. These figures are updated to emphasize Chicano culture and identity. López has also worked to help farmworkers and to improve living and working conditions along the U.S.-Mexico border.

López del Castillo, Gerardo

b. ?
Mexico City, Mexico
d. ?
fields: Theater and Entertainment (actor)

Latino actor. Gerardo López del Castillo began acting at the age of fifteen. In the 1850's, he became the leading actor in and a director for the Compañía de la Familia Estrella, which moved its base to San Francisco in 1862. López del Castillo became president of the Junta Patriótica Méxicana de San Francisco, used some of his performances to raise funds for the revolution in Mexico, and returned to Mexico several times to serve the revolution as a soldier. He returned to Mexico City for good in the 1870's to promote the establishment of a national dramatic literature.

Lorca, Federico García. *See* García Lorca, Federico

Lord, Bette Bao

b. Nov. 3, 1938
Shanghai, China
fields: Literature

Bette Bao Lord's works include *Eighth Moon* (1964), *Spring Moon* (1981), *In the Year of the Boar and Jackie Robinson* (1984), a novel for children, and *Legacies: A Chinese Mosaic* (1990).

Lord Haw Haw. *See* Joyce, William

Lorde, Audre

b. b. February 18, 1934
New York, N.Y.
d. November 17, 1992
St. Croix
fields: Literature (poet and memoirist)

African American poet and memoirist; Audre Lorde wrote about racial injustice, sexism, and parent-child relationships; she waqs also known for her lesbian love poetry. Her writings include *From a Land Where Other People Live* (1973), nominated for a National Book Award in 1974, *Zami: A New Spelling of My Name* (1982), and *Sister Outsider* (1984). *Coal* (1976) and *The Black Unicorn* (1978) are two of Lorde's most important poetic works. *The Cancer Journals* and *A Burst of Light* (1988) chronicle her struggles with cancer. *The Marvelous Arithmetic of Distance* (1993) was her last book of poetry.

Lorentz, Hendrik Antoon

b. July 18, 1853
Arnhem, The Netherlands
d. February 4, 1928
Haarlem, The Netherlands
fields: Physics

Lorentz's work on electromagnetic theory paved the way for the development of relativity theory and quantum mechanics. In 1902, he was awarded the second Nobel Prize in Physics. His scientific research and his efforts to create an international scientific community drew the leading physicists of the early twentieth century to Leiden, making it a leading center for theoretical physics.

Lorenz, Konrad

full: Konrad Zacharias Lorenz
b. November 7, 1903
Vienna, Austro-Hungarian Empire
d. February 27, 1989
Altenburg, Austria
fields: Zoology, Psychiatry and Psychology, Physiology, Medicine

Awarded a Nobel Prize in Physiology or Medicine in 1973, Konrad Lorenz, initially working as a zoologist, became one of the principal founders of the science of ethology through his studies correlating patterns of animal and human behavior and their implied common evolutionary origins.

Lorenzana, Apolinaria

b. 1800
d. 1884
Santa Barbara, Calif.
fields: Religion and Theology

Religious figure. Apolinaria Lorenzana, found abandoned as an infant in 1800, grew up in California's missions. Between 1821 and 1830, she helped Father Antonio Peyri at Mission San Luis Rey, teaching the women to sew and caring for the sick. She later acquired the Jamacho and La Cañada de los Coches Ranches. Lorenzana went blind in later life.

Lorenzetti, Ambrogio

b. c. 1290
probably Siena
d. 1348
probably Siena
fields: Art

The Lorenzetti brothers, Pietro and Ambrogio, recognized the problems of depicting three-dimensional space on a two-dimensional surface. Although they did not fully solve the problems of perspective, their experiments with space provided a necessary stage for the development of Italian Renaissance painting.

Lorenzetti, Pietro

b. c. 1280
probably Siena
d. 1348
probably Siena
fields: Art

The Lorenzetti brothers, Pietro and Ambrogio, recognized the problems of depicting three-dimensional space on a two-dimensional surface. Although they did not fully solve the problems of perspective, their experiments with space provided a necessary stage for the development of Italian Renaissance painting.

Lott, Ronnie

full: Ronald Mandel Lott
b. May 8, 1959
Albuquerque, N. Mex.
fields: Sports (football player)

African American professional football player; Ronnie Lott played for the San Francisco 49ers from 1981 to 1990; went to the Super Bowl four times with the team; joined the Los Angeles Raiders from 1991 to 1993; in 1993, became a member of the New York Jets and was named Defensive Back of the Year by the National Football League Alumni Association; played for the Kansas City Chiefs in 1994 and 1995; he retired and became an NFL analyst for Fox television in 1996.

Lotz, Irmgard. *See* Flügge-Lotz, Irmgard

Louganis, Greg

b. Jan. 29, 1960
El Cajon, Calif.
fields: Sports (diving)

Competitive diver. Greg Louganis earned recognition as one of the world's greatest athletes by winning one silver and four gold medals for the United States in the 1976,

1984, and 1988 Olympic Games. During a dive at the 1988 Olympics, he cut his head on a diving board; the injury bled profusely, but he continued to compete. In 1995, Louganis divulged that he had known that he was infected with the HIV virus at the time of the injury. The disclosure prompted criticism of Louganis, who did not reveal his condition to the doctor who treated his wound.

Louie, David

b. June 19, 1950
Lakewood, Ohio
fields: Journalism

Broadcast journalist. He became the first Asian American reporter hired by KGO-TV, the San Francisco station owned and operated by the American Broadcasting Company (ABC), and the first Asian American news manager while working at WXYZ in Detroit. The winner of two Emmy Awards, he has served as national president of the eleven-hundred-member Asian American Journalists Association (AAJA) and also as president of its San Francisco Bay Area chapter.

Louie, David Wong

b. 1954
Rockville Center, N.Y.
fields: Publishing

David Wong Louie's first book, *The Pangs of Love* (1991), a short-story collection, won critical acclaim, including the *Los Angeles Times* Art Seidenbaum Book Prize for first fiction and the *Ploughshares* John C. Zacharis First Book Award. Louie, a professor of fiction writing and Asian American studied at the University of California, Los Angeles, received fellowships from the National Endowment for the Arts, the California Arts Council, and the McDowell Colony.

Louie, Sinclair

b. May 11, 1922
Canton, China
fields: Business and Industry

Sinclair Louie arrived in the United States in 1932. During World War II, he served under General George Patton. He became the owner of the largest bazaar business chain in San Francisco, including Bargain Bazaar, Canton Bazaar, Ginza, Jade Empire, Empress Fine Arts, Far East Flea Market, and China Bazaar, and made numerous contributions to various Chinatown charitable organizations.

Louis II de Bourbon. *See* Condé, The Great

Louis IX

aka: Saint Louis IX, King of France
b. April 25, 1214
Poissy, France
d. August 25, 1270
near Tunis (modern Tunisia)
fields: Government and Politics, Religion and Theology, Monarchy

King of France, 1236-1270. Louis IX reformed and centralized the French government and judiciary and increased the prestige of the royal house of France through his saintly life. Canonized in 1297.

Louis XI

né: Louis de Valois
b. July 3, 1423
Bourges, France
d. August 30, 1483
Plessis-les-Tours, France
fields: Government and Politics, Monarchy

King of France, 1461-1483. Louis XI rebuilt France from the Hundred Years' War, prevented renewed English invasion, demolished Burgundy as a great power within France, ended the era of feudal dominance, restored the extent and influence of the royal domain, and reorganized medieval France as a modern nation-state, with himself as the prototype of Renaissance despotism.

Louis XIII

b. September 27, 1601
Fontainebleau, France
d. May 14, 1643
Saint-Germain-en-Laye, France
fields: Government and Politics, Military Affairs, Monarchy

King of France, 1610-1643. Louis XIII governed France during an era of conflict. Overshadowed by his father and son, he increased the power of the Crown with the help of Cardinal de Richelieu.

Louis XIV

aka: the Sun King
b. September 5, 1638
Saint-Germain-en-Laye, France
d. September 1, 1715
Versailles, France
fields: Government and Politics, Monarchy

King of France, 1643-1715. Known as *le Roi Soleil*, or "the Sun King," Louis XIV led France to the pinnacle of power and prestige in seventeenth century Europe, and, more than any other monarch, embodied the principle of absolutism in royal authority. Dedicated to bringing glory to France, he sponsored magnificent cultural achievements but left his country bankrupt and weakened through a long series of costly wars.

Louis, Errol T.

b. August 24, 1962
Harlem, N.Y.
fields: Banking and Finance

African American financial entrepreneurs and community development specialists; in 1993, Errol T. Louis and Mark Winston Griffith and founded the Central Brooklyn Federal Credit Union, which provided loans and other much-needed financial services to low-income customers in the local African American community.

Louis, Joe

né: Joseph Louis Barrow
b. May 13, 1914
near Lafayette, Alabama
d. April 12, 1981
Las Vegas, Nevada
fields: Sports (boxing)

World heavyweight boxing champion from 1937 to 1949, Louis was a hero to black Americans of all backgrounds. Although some maintained that a boxer should not have been so celebrated, Louis was perhaps more widely recognized and applauded by the black community than any other individual prior to the modern Civil Rights movement.

Louis, Nikki Nojima

b. Dec. 7, 1937
Seattle, Wash.
fields: Theater and Entertainment

Nikki Nojima Louis began writing for regional theaters in the American northwest, including The Exclusion Act (which became Northwest Asian American Theatre) and the Seattle Group Theatre, in the 1980's. Her plays include *Japanese Voices in America* (1985), *Made in America* (1985), *Breaking the Silence* (1987), *Changing Faces* (1988), *Our Mothers' Stories* (1989), *Winds of Change* (1990), *Most Dangerous Women* (1990), *Gold! Gold! Gold!* (1991), *I Dream a World* (1991), and *Island Dreams* (1993). Her plays incorporate oral histories, improvisation, and other collaborative creative techniques to express multicultural themes and issues.

Louis-Philippe-Joseph. *See* Orléans, duc d'

Louis the German

aka: Louis II the German
b. c. 804
possibly Aquitaine
d. August 28, 876
Frankfurt
fields: Government and Politics, Monarchy

German king, 843-876. As the ruler who founded the kingdom that later became known as Germany, Louis, while supporting the idea of the unity of the Carolingian Empire, protected his kingdom from the covetousness of his relatives, patronized the Church, and defended his lands from numerous attacks by such peoples as the Vikings, Hungarians, Bohemians, Moravians, and Slavs.

Loury, Glenn C.

b. September 3, 1948
Chicago, Ill.
fields: Economics (political), Education

Political economist and educator. Loury earned a B.A. in mathematics from Northwestern University and a Ph.D. in economics from the Massachusetts Institute of Technology. His work has challenged assumptions about costs of affirmative action programs to the African American community. A strong advocate of self-reliance among the African American community, he has commented that the problems of the ghetto cannot be reversed effectively by civil rights policies, and he is critical of civil rights leaders and others who turn to government as the primary source for empowerment. He has taught at Harvard and Boston Universities.

Louvois, Marquis de

né: François-Michel Le Tellier
b. January 18, 1639
Paris, France
d. July 16, 1691
Versailles, France
fields: Military Affairs

Louvois used his administrative genius and harsh discipline to create and maintain France's first military complex. He established unprecedented civilian control over the military and heavily influenced King Louis XIV's foreign policy.

Love, Bob

b. December 8, 1942
Delhi, La.
fields: Sports (basketball player)

African American basketball player; Bob Love found fame after joining the Chicago Bulls during the 1968-1969 season. The National Basketball Association's sixth-highest scorer in the 1970-1971 and 1971-1972 seasons, he averaged more than twenty-five points per game. In 1977 he retired with a career scoring average of 17.6 points per game.

Love, Nat

b. June, 1854
Davidson County, Tenn.
d. 1921
Los Angeles, Calif.
fields: Historical Figure (cowboy)

African American cowboy; Nat Love, known as "Deadwood Dick," was a skilled gun handler and range rider who pursued criminals and fought Indians. He published his autobiography in 1907.

Lovejoy, Elijah Parish

b. November 9, 1802
Albion, Maine
d. November 7, 1837
Alton, Illinois
fields: Journalism, Social Reform

A newspaper publisher, Elijah Parish Lovejoy was killed by a mob for his outspoken opposition to slavery. In 1883 he launched a new newspaper, the *St. Louis Observer*, for a group of Christian business leaders but soon made many enemies in Missouri, as proslavery advocates circulated handbills denouncing Lovejoy as an advocate of miscegenation and advising him to leave St. Louis. In 1837 he was killed while protecting the Illinois warehouse where his press was stored.

Lovelace, Augusta Ada

né: Augusta Ada Byron
b. Dec. 10, 1815
Piccadilly Terrace, Middlesex (now in London), England
d. Nov. 27, 1852
London, England
fields: Mathematics (mathematical logic)

In 1834 Augusta Ada Lovelace translated L. F. Menabrea's paper describing Babbage's Analytical Engine. She linked the Analytical Engine to its potential use for sound and graphics and provided what has come to be termed the first "computer program."

Lovelace, Earl

b. 1935
Trinidad
fields: Literature

African American writer; Earl Lovelace's writings, often set in Trinidadian slums and villages, point to the need for social change and suggest that a combination of individual responsibility and community identity will help diverse peoples live together in harmony.

Low, Charlie

b. June 9, 1901
Winnemucca, Nev.
d. 1991
fields: Business and Industry

Entrepreneur Charlie Low owned the first bar in San Francisco's Chinatown, the Chinese Village, and the well-known Chinese nightclub, the Forbidden City. In 1927, he was involved in the building of the first modern apartment in Chinatown. Low established a stock brokerage, an insurance agency, a real estate firm, an employment service, and a legal advice office.

Low, David

Sir David Low
b. April 7, 1897
Dunedin, New Zealand
d. September 19, 1963
London, England
fields: Journalism, Art

After British cartoonist David Low started life in New Zealand, and came to London in 1919 and later became a staff cartoonist for the *Evening Standard*. where he remained until 1949. He later worked for the *Daily Herald* and *Manchester Guardian*. His cartoons lampooned domestic and international political figures and was particularly tough on Nazi Germany, which banned his work. Low was also the creator of Colonel Blimp.

Low, Harry W.

b. Mar. 12, 1931
Oakdale, Calif.
fields: Law

Chinese American Harry W. Low was presiding justice of the California Court of Appeals when he retired in 1991. Earlier positions included deputy attorney general of California and a judge in the superior, juvenile, and municipal courts. Low was a member of the California Judges Association, the National and San Francisco Lodge of the Chinese American Citizens Alliance, and the San Francisco Police Commission. He edited the California Judges Association's official publication, *Courts Commentary*.

Low, Juliette Gordon

né: Juliette Magill Kinzie Gordon
b. October 31, 1860
Savannah, Georgia
d. January 18, 1927
Savannah, Georgia
fields: Social Reform

The principal founder of the Girl Scouts of the United States of America, Low spent the last fifteen years of her life working for an organization which would be similar to, but independent of, the Boy Scouts of America.

Lowe, Ann

b. December 14, 1898
Clayton, Ala.
d. February 25, 1981
Queens, N.Y.
fields: Fashion (dress designer)

African American dress designer; Ann Lowe was a designer for Neiman Marcus and I. Magnin department stores, among others, and also sold her designs herself. She designed the wedding gown worn by Jacqueline Bouvier for her marriage to John F. Kennedy in 1953.

Lowe, Felicia

b. Dec. 6, 1945
Oakland, Calif.
fields: Journalism, Film

Chinese American Felicia Lowe wrote, produced, and directed the documentaries *China, Land of My Father* (1979) and *Carved in Silence* (1988), the story of Chinese immigrants detained on Angel Island. Her films have been exhibited at the Whitney Museum, the Smithsonian Institution in Washington, D.C., and New York's Museum of Modern Art. Lowe, an Emmy Award-winning broadcast journalist, worked as a reporter for KGO-TV and as a producer for KQED-TV, both San Francisco stations.

Lowe, Pardee

full: George Cooper Pardee Lowe
b. Sept. 9, 1905
San Francisco, Calif.
fields: Publishing

Pardee Lowe's autobiography *Father and Glorious Descendant* (1943), was the first book-length literary work by an American-born Asian. Portions of this work appeared in *The Atlantic Monthly* and *The Yale Review* before it was published as a book, and critics praised Lowe's work. In the work, Lowe displays a desire to assimilate and describes numerous clashes with his father, providing Americans with a glimpse of Asian American life.

Lowell, Amy

b. February 9, 1874
Brookline, Massachusetts
d. May 12, 1925
Brookline, Massachusetts
fields: Literature

A leading poet of her day and leader of the Imagist movement, Amy Lowell also worked enthusiastically to popularize poetry and the other arts. She supported the work of other writers by editing collections of their works and by giving popular lectures on literature.

Lowenstein, Allard

b. Jan. 16, 1929
Newark, N.J.
d. Mar. 14, 1980
New York, N.Y.
fields: Civil Rights, Government and Politics

An opponent of U.S. involvement in the Vietnam War and of President Lyndon B. Johnson's reelection in 1968, Allard Lowenstein also played an important role the Freedom Summer project. He later entered politics and was elected to Congress for one term in 1969. President Jimmy Carter made head of a delegation to the United Nations Commission on Human Rights in 1976.

Lower, Richard

b. c. 1631 (baptized Jan. 29, 1632)
Tremeer, near Bodmin, Cornwall, England
d. Jan. 17, 1691
London, England
fields: Biology, Medicine, Physiology

Richard Lower, in 1665, performed the first transfusion of blood from one animal into another, using dogs; showed that the difference in color between arterial blood and venous blood results when the blood absorbs air as it passes through the lungs.

Lowery, Joseph E.

b. October 6, 1924
Huntsville, Ala.
fields: Civil Rights, Religion and Theology

African American civil rights leader and minister; Joseph E. Lowery was one of the coordinators of the 1955 Montgomery bus boycott and a chief adviser to Martin Luther King, Jr.; in 1957, was a cofounder of the Southern Negro Leaders Conference (later the Southern Christian Leadership Conference, SCLC) in 1957, and in 1977 became its president; in 1995 led the celebrations commemorating the thirtieth anniversary of the Selma to Montgomery march; pastor of the Warren Street Church in Birmingham, Alabama, 1952-1961; pastor of Cascade United Methodist Church in Atlanta from 1986.

Loyola, Saint Ignatius of

né: Iñigo de Oñaz y Loyola
b. 1491
Loyola, Guipúzcoa Province, Spain
d. July 31, 1556
Rome
fields: Religion and Theology

Founder of the Society of Jesus, better known as the Jesuits, Loyola was a dynamic religious leader whose life and writings strongly influenced his times. His religious order has been particularly notable in the field of education. Canonized in 1622.

Lozano, Ignacio Eugenio, Sr.

b. 1887
Marín, Nuevo León, Mexico
d. 1953
San Antonio, Tex.
fields: Publishing (newspaper editor)

Latino newspaper editor. Ignacio Eugenio Lozano, Sr., started the influential Spanish-language newspapers *La Prensa* in 1913 and *La Opinión* in 1926. The newspapers supported workers during labor disputes and provided good coverage of the Latino community. Lozano's son, Ignacio, Jr., began managing *La Opinión* in the 1950's. His son, Jose, served as publisher during the 1980's, and his daughter, Mónica Cecilia, became associate publisher and editor a few years later. In 1990, *La Opinión* was sold to the *Los Angeles Times*.

Lu Xun

aka: Lu Hsün
né: Zhou Shuren
aka: Chou Shu-jên
b. September 25, 1881
Shaoxing, China
d. October 19, 1936
Shanghai, China
fields: Literature, Government and Politics

One of twentieth century China's great men of letters, Lu Hsün pioneered a new literary tradition in China and offered a defiant indictment of Chinese character and traditions. He is honored by the Chinese Communists for his formative impact on young Chinese intellectuals and the revolutionary movement.

Lucas, John Harding, Jr.

b. October 31, 1953
Durham, N.C.
fields: Sports (basketball player and coach)

African American basketball player and coach; John Harding Lucas, Jr., started his professional career in 1976 with the Houston Rockets; in 1986 was cut from the team for cocaine use; a recovering addict, he returned to the NBA in 1987; retired in 1990; bought the Miami Tropics basketball team and hired athletes in recovery; Tropics won the 1992 United States Basketball League championship; head coach of the San Antonio Spurs, 1992-1994; head coach of the Philadelphia 76ers, 1994-1996; published *Winning a Day at a Time* (1994).

Lucas, María Elena

b. Mar. 22, 1941
Matamoros, Mexico
fields: Social Reform, Labor Movement

Latina labor organizer. María Elena Lucas began her life of labor at the age of five. In the late 1970's, she joined farmworkers in Onarga, Illinois, to demand better conditions and became an organizer for the Farm Worker Organizing Committee. In 1988, she was permanently disabled by exposure to pesticides but continued to struggle on behalf of farmworkers.

Lucas, William

b. January 15, 1928
New York, N.Y.
fields: Government and Politics

African American political appointee; William Lucas was nominated to serve as assistant attorney general for civil rights by President George Bush in 1989. The nomination was controversial because he was an opponent of quotas as a method of advancing the career opportunities of minority groups. A tie vote led to the rejection of his nomination.

Luce, Clare Boothe

né: Ann Clare Boothe
b. April 10, 1903
New York, New York
d. October 9, 1987
Washington, D.C.
fields: Journalism, Government and Politics

As a journalist, playwright, and political appointee, Luce became an eminent example of how women could overcome gender stereotypes that limit their goals.

Luce, Henry R.

full: Henry Robinson Luce
b. April 3, 1898
Tengchow (modern P'eng-lai), China
d. February 28, 1967
Phoenix, Arizona
fields: Journalism

Luce established a powerful journalistic empire with magazines such as *Time*, which took survey of all the world, and used this power to influence American politics and foreign policy for almost four decades.

Lucero. *See* Victorio

Lucian

b. c. 120
Samosata, Syria
d. c. 180
probably Egypt
fields: Literature

Lucian turned the philosophical dialogue into a form for satirizing ideas and manners. Lucianic satire became a mainstay of European literature in the Renaissance.

Lucretius

né: Titus Lucretius Carus
b. c. 98 B.C.E.
probably Rome
d. October 15, 55 B.C.E.
Rome
fields: Literature, Natural History, Philosophy

Though he in no sense offered an original philosophical outlook, Lucretius' *On The Nature of Things* synthesized primary tenets of Greek Epicureanism and atomism and offered a rational, nontheological explanation for the constituents of the universe; just as remarkable is the fact that he did this in Latin hexameter verse and developed a philosophical vocabulary required for the task.

Ludendorff, Erich

full: Erich Friedrich Wilhelm Ludendorff
b. April 9, 1865
Kruszewnia, near Posen, Prussia (now Poznan, Poland)
d. December 20, 1937
Munich, Germany
fields: Military Affairs

Ludendorff served as second in command to Field Marshal Paul von Hindenburg during World War I and became the most powerful man in Germany from 1916 to 1918. In the 1920's, he was involved with radical nationalist movements, including the Nazi movement, but eventually became too radical even for Hitler. By the mid-1920's, he had lost his influence with conservative and radical nationalists.

Ludwig, Nikolaus. *See* Zinzendorf, Graf von

Lue Gim Gong

b. 1858
Taishan district, Guangdong Province, China
d. June 3, 1925
fields: Horticulture

Horticulturist Lue Gim Gong came to be known as the "Chinese Burbank." He developed an orange that bears his name and became the mainstay of the Florida citrus industry. In 1911, Gong received the Wilder Silver Medal from the American Pomological Society in recognition of his contribution. In addition, Lue developed a sweet apple that ripened a month earlier than others being cultivated nearby, a salmon-colored raspberry, a peach that ripened shortly before Thanksgiving, and a cherry currant as large as a cherry. A grapefruit bearing his name was another of his unique creations.

Lugard, Lord

né: Frederic John Dealtry Lugard
aka: Frederic John Dealtry, baron Lugard of Abinger
b. January 22, 1858
Madras, India
d. April 11, 1945
Abinger Common, Surrey, England
fields: Exploration and Colonization, Government and Politics

Employing his impressive military and administrative skills, Lugard played a major role in extending British control over Uganda and Nigeria and developed the administrative system known as "indirect rule."

Luis, Juan

b. July 10, 1940
Vieques, Puerto Rico
fields: Government and Politics

Governor of the Virgin Islands. Juan Luis was born in Puerto Rico but was raised on St. Croix in the Virgin Islands. He served in the U.S. Army, taught primary school, and held administrative positions in several local businesses. In 1972, he was elected insular senator as a candidate of the Independent Citizens Movement. Luis served as chairman of the housing and planning committee, as vice chairman of the recreational committee, and as a member of various finance, public safety, health and welfare, and labor and veterans' affairs committees. Luis was elected lieutenant governor in 1974 and governor in 1978.

Luján, Gilbert Sánchez

pseudo. Magu
b. 1940
French Camp, Calif.
fields: Art

Latino artist. Gilbert Sánchez Luján, known professionally as "Magu," grew up near Los Angeles and earned his master's degree in fine arts at the University of California, Irvine. He specialized in ceramics, painted wood sculptures, and pastel paintings. Luján, Beto de la Rocha, Carlos Almaraz, and Frank Romero formed an exhibiting group called Los Four. Their first show, in Irvine in 1974, was later expanded for an exhibition at the Los Angeles County Museum of Art. Luján moved to Fresno, California, in 1974 and taught ethnic studies and served as chair of La Raza Studies Department at Fresno City College. In 1981, he returned to Los Angeles and taught at the Municipal Art Center at Barnsdall Park.

Luján, Manuel, Jr.

b. May 12, 1928
San Ildefonso, N.Mex.
fields: Government and Politics

In 1948 Manuel Luján, Jr., ran unsuccessfully for governor of New Mexico as a moderate Republican. Luján won a seat in Congress in 1968, later serving as the ranking Republican member of the House Interior Committee and the Science, Space, and Technology Committee. He was appointed secretary of the interior by President George Bush in 1989.

Lukács, György

aka: Georg Lukács
b. April 13, 1885
Budapest, Austro-Hungarian Empire
d. June 4, 1971
Budapest, Hungary
fields: Philosophy, Literature

Lukács is one of the most outstanding and respected Marxist philosophers and literary critics from Eastern Europe in the twentieth century.

Luke, Keye

b. June 18, 1904
Canton, China
d. Jan. 12, 1991
Whittier, Calif.
fields: Film, Television

Beginning in 1934 Chinese American Keye Luke appeared in many motion pictures, including *The Good Earth* (1937),

Love Is a Many-Splendored Thing (1955), and *The Hawaiians* (1970), as well as in numerous Charlie Chan films. Luke was best known as Master Po in the television series *Kung Fu* (1972-1975).

Luke, Wing Chong

b. Feb. 25, 1925
Guangdong Province, China
d. May 16, 1965
Snohomish County, Wash.
fields: Government and Politics

Wing Chong Luke successfully ran for city council member in Seattle in 1962. Although accused of being a communist, he won by a landslide. Luke advocated open housing, cultural awareness, civil rights, fishing programs for city residents, historic preservation, kite festivals, and cross-generational activities. He was passionate about cultural pluralism and humanism. He died in a plane accident in 1965 and was honored after his death by the Wing Luke Memorial Museum (later the Wing Luke Asian Museum) devoted to Asian Pacific American history and art.

Lull, Raymond

aka: Ramon Llull
b. c. 1235
Palma de Mallorca
d. early 1316
at Tunis, on Majorca, or on the voyage to Majorca
fields: Literature, Philosophy, Religion and Theology

As the Doctor Illuminatus (enlightened teacher), Lull devised a unique and influential Neoplatonic and non-Scholastic philosophy. As a mystic and lay missionary, he founded a school of Arabic, composed Arabic books, and dialogued with Islamic savants in North Africa. As an author and poet, he helped create the Catalan language. Friend of rulers, prelates, and the powerful, he wandered the courts of Europe relentlessly as a propagandist for his many enterprises.

Lum, Darrell H. Y.

b. 1950
Honolulu, Territory of Hawaii
fields: Literature

Darrell H. Y. Lum writes stories in Hawaiian Creole, an English-based creole that draws on the languages of the diverse immigrants who labored on Hawaii's sugar plantations. His works include *Sun* (1980) and *Pass On, No Pass Back!* (1990), which received the 1992 Outstanding Book Award from the Association for Asian American Studies. Lum, one of the editors of *Bamboo Ridge: The Hawaii Writers' Quarterly*, was a founder of Bamboo Ridge Press.

Lum, Herman Tsui Fai

b. Nov. 5, 1926
Honolulu, Territory of Hawaii
fields: Law

In 1950, Herman Tsui Fai Lum received an LL.B. degree from the University of Missouri and became a member of the Hawaii State Bar. Lum was appointed as a justice of the Honolulu Circuit Court in 1967 and later served as senior justice of the state's family court. He was named to the Hawaii Supreme Court in 1980 and became chief justice in 1983.

Lum, Kalfred Dip

b. Dec. 25, 1899
Honolulu, Territory of Hawaii
d. July 3, 1979
San Francisco, Calif.
fields: Government and Politics

Kalfred Dip Lum received a Ph.D. in government and international law from New York University in 1926 and became a professor at the University of Hawaii in 1928. He served in a number of positions for the Guomindang during the 1930's, continuously working for the Chinese Nationalist cause. In the late 1930's, he moved to Oregon and managed a hotel. He continued to manage hotels and motels until he retired in 1963.

Lum, Mary

b. ?
New York, N.Y.
fields: Theater and Entertainment

Actor Mary Lum worked extensively with New York City's Pan Asian Repertory Theatre and was an original member of New York City's Women's Experimental Theatre Company. Lum created roles in *The Daughters Cycle* (pr. 1979) and *Women's Body and Other Natural Resources* (pr. 1981) at the Interart Theatre in New York City. She appeared before the New York Human Rights Commission, testifying to the marginalization of Asian American women in the performing arts during the 1990 *Miss Saigon* (pr. 1989) controversy.

Lum, Wing Tek

b. 1946
Honolulu, Hawaii
fields: Literature (poet)

Poet Wing Tek Lum was a leading figure in the "local" movement among writers of Hawaii. He wrote *Expounding the Doubtful Points* (1987), a poetry collection that received the 1988 creative literature award from the Association for Asian American Studies.

Lumbly, Carl

b. 1952?
Jamaica, West Indies
fields: Theater and Entertainment

African American actor; Carl Lumbly is best known as Detective Mark Petrie in the television series *Cagney and Lacey*; he also was seen on the series *Tax*. He appeared in the film *Judgment in Berlin* in 1988.

Lumhe Chate. *See* Weatherford, William

Lumière, Auguste

full: Auguste Marie Louis Lumière
b. October 19, 1862
Besançon, France
d. April 10, 1954
Lyons, France
fields: Business and Industry, Invention and Technology, Film

The brothers Auguste and Louis Lumière introduced many successful innovations to the manufacture of photographic materials and won particular renown for the development of the first commercially viable projected motion pictures and for the introduction of the color photographic medium known as the Autochrome process.

Lumière, Louis

full: Louis Jean Lumière
b. October 5, 1864
Besançon, France
d. June 6, 1948
Bandol, France
fields: Business and Industry, Invention and Technology, Film

The brothers Louis and Auguste Lumière introduced many successful innovations to the manufacture of photographic materials and won particular renown for the development of the first commercially viable projected motion pictures and for the introduction of the color photographic medium known as the Autochrome process.

Lumumba, Patrice

full: Patrice Hémery Lumumba
b. July 2, 1925
Onalua, Katako-Kombe Territory, Sankaru District, Kasai, Belgian Congo
d. c. January 17, 1961
Katanga, Congo
fields: Government and Politics

In 1960 Patrice Lumumba became the first prime minister of independent Congo; Joseph Kasavubu was president. The country was in disastrous shape from the beginning, fighting against Belgium and then trying to hold on to two provinces that were seceding. Power struggle between Lumumba and Kasavubu, with Kasavubu winning. Lumumba was arrested and flown to rebellious Katanga province, where he was murdered.

Lunceford, Jimmie

full: James Melvin Lunceford
b. June 6, 1902
Fulton, Mo.
d. July 12, 1947
Seaside, Oreg.
fields: Music (bandleader and instrumentalist)

African American bandleader and instrumentalist; Jimmie Lunceford, who ranked with Count Basie and Duke Ellington as a leader of a big band, led his band to fame with songs such as "White Heat," "Jazznocracy," "Rhythm in Our Business," and Duke Ellington's "Mood Indigo," all recorded in 1934. Other well-known recordings by Lunceford were "Organ Grinder's Swing," "For Dancers Only," "Margie," "Lunceford Special," and "Yard Dog Mazurka."

Lupino, Ida

b. February 4, 1918
London, England
d. August 3, 1995
Burbank, California
fields: Film

After achieving stardom, Ida Lupino became dissatisfied with the limited roles available to Hollywood actresses and went on to pioneer as a director specializing in films about problems of women in a patriarchal society.

Luque, Dolf

full: Adolfo Luque
b. Aug. 4, 1890
Havana, Cuba
d. July 3, 1957
Havana, Cuba
fields: Sports (baseball player and coach)

Latino baseball player and coach. Pitcher Dolf Luque debuted in the major leagues in 1914 with the Boston Red Sox. He joined the Cincinnati Reds in 1918 and spent twelve seasons with them. In 1919, he pitched five scoreless innings in two games of the World Series against the Chicago White Sox, becoming the first Latin American-born player to appear in the World Series. In 1933, Luque won the final game of the 1933 World Series for the New York Giants. He retired after the 1935 season and coached the Giants during the late 1930's and early 1940's.

Luria, Isaac ben Solomon

aka: ha-Ari
b. 1534
Jerusalem
d. August 5, 1572
Safed
fields: Philosophy, Religion and Theology

Luria was the culminating figure in the history of the Jewish mystical tradition known as Cabala, which, originating in southern France in the last quarter of the thirteenth century, reached its height in the sixteenth century. Luria's revision of key Cabalist concepts and his theory of a dynamic creation—catastrophically altered by sin but capable of regeneration and final redemption—had a profound influence on subsequent Jewish thought, including Hasidism, and on messianic movements in both the Jewish and the Christian worlds.

Luria, Salvador Edward

b. Aug. 13, 1912
Turin, Italy
d. Feb. 6, 1991
Lexington, Massachusetts
fields: Biology, Genetics, Medicine

Salvador Edward Luria explained viral replication and gene structure, thus relating virology and biochemistry; in 1969, was awarded the Nobel Prize in Physiology or Medicine.

Lurton, Horace Harmon

b. 1844
d. 1914
fields: Law

U.S. Supreme Court justice, 1910-1914 (died while in office); appointed by President Taft.

Luther, Martin

b. November 10, 1483
Eisleben, Saxony
d. February 18, 1546
Eisleben, Saxony
fields: Philosophy, Religion and Theology, Church Reform

Out of his own personal struggle and his conflict with the Church, Luther developed a theology and a religious movement that rejuvenated the Christian faith and had a profound impact on the social, political, and religious thought of Western society.

Lutuli, Albert

full: Albert John Mvumbi Lutuli
b. c. 1898
near Bulawayo, Rhodesia (now Zimbabwe)
d. July 21, 1967
Stanger, South Africa
fields: Civil Rights, Social Reform, Government and Politics

In 1960, Lutuli became the first African to receive the Nobel Peace Prize. This international honor recognized his commitment to nonviolent means to free South Africans from apartheid and to restore the honor of Africa.

Luu, Jane X.

né: Luu Le Hang
b. July 15, 1963
Saigon, South Vietnam
fields: Astronomy, Physics

Jane X. Luu, in 1992, discovered the first known object in the Kuiper belt, a region of the outer solar system, which led to a greater understanding of the origin of comets.

Luxemburg, Rosa

né: Rozalia Luksenburg
b. March 5, 1871
Zamość, Poland, Russian Empire
d. January 15, 1919
Berlin, Germany
fields: Social Reform, Philosophy, Journalism

Luxemburg was a leading figure in the left wing of the German Social Democratic Party, and she played a key role in the founding of the Polish Social Democratic Party and the German Communist Party. An able, indefatigable journalist and writer, she developed a humanistic version of Marxism that emphasized internationalism, mass participation, a dislike of violence, and opposition to gradual reformism.

Lwoff, André

b. May 8, 1902
Ainay-le-Château, France
d. Sept. 30, 1994
Paris, France
fields: Biology, Genetics, Medicine

André Lwoff, with Marguerite Lwoff, established the role of vitamins as coenzymes in 1936; in 1950, demonstrated the perpetuation of viral deoxyribonucleic acid (DNA) in lysogenic bacteria, playing a significant role in the understanding of the genetic mechanisms of bacterial replication and viral infection; in 1965, was awarded the Nobel Prize in Physiology or Medicine.

Lyell, Charles

aka: Sir Charles Lyell
b. November 14, 1797
Kinnordy, Kirriemuir, Scotland
d. February 22, 1875
London, England
fields: Geology

Lyell gave shape to the emerging science of geology with his theory of Uniformitarianism, explaining past change from currently observable causes.

Lyle, Marcenia. *See* Stone, Toni

Lyman, Stanford

b. June 10, 1933
San Francisco, Calif.
fields: Sociology

Stanford Lyman, a leading scholar in the field of race and ethnicity in American culture, published several studies focusing on Asian

American history and issues, including *Chinese Americans* (1974), *The Asian in the West* (1970), and *The Asian in North America* (1977), and *Color, Culture, Civilization: Race and Minority Issues in American Society* (1994).

Lynch, John Roy

b. September 10, 1847
near Vidalia, La.
d. November 2, 1939
Chicago, Ill.
fields: Government and Politics

African American politician; John Roy Lynch was appointed a local justice of the peace in 1869. The same year, Lynch was elected to the state's House of Representatives. There he became a member of the military affairs and elections committees, and in his second term he was elected Speaker of the House. Lynch served again in the U.S. House of Representatives in 1872 to 1877 and for one term beginning in 1882. His autobiography, *Reminiscences of an Active Life: The Autobiography of John Roy Lynch*, was published in 1970.

Lynd, Helen Merrell

né: Helen Merrell
b. March 17, 1896
La Grange, Illinois
d. January 30, 1982
Warren, Ohio
fields: Sociology, Education

Helen Merrell Lynd is best known for her collaboration with her husband, Robert S. Lynd, in writing the classic studies *Middletown: A Study in Contemporary American Culture* (1929) and *Middletown in Transition: A Study in Cultural Conflicts* (1937). She also made her mark as an innovator in higher education for women, as a historian, and as a social psychologist.

Lynd, Robert

b. September 26, 1892
New Albany, Ind.
d. November 1, 1970
Warren, Conn.
fields: Sociology, Education

Robert Lynd and his wife, Helen Lynd, were pioneers in using the objective techniques of cultural anthropology to analyze a modern city. Their books *Middletown: A Study in Contemporary American Culture* (1929) and *Middletown in Transition: A Study in Cultural Conflicts* (1937) are classics in the field of urban sociology.

Lynk, Miles Vandahurst

b. June 3, 1871
Brownsville, Tenn.
d. December 29, 1957
Memphis, Tenn.
fields: Medicine

African American physician. In 1892 Miles Vandahurst Lynk published the first medical journal issued by a black person in the United States, *Medical and Surgical Observer*. He was founder and president of the University of West Tennessee and helped to establish the National Medical Association, an organization of black physicians.

Lynn, Loretta

né: Loretta Webb
b. April 14, 1935
Butcher Hollow, Kentucky
fields: Music

This "Queen of Country Music" was the first woman to be named Entertainer of the Year by the Country Music Association in 1972. Her popularity and productivity remain unmatched; writing and recording more than fifty records, while achieving sales exceeding twenty million albums.

Lyon, John. *See* Ignacio

Lyon, Mary

full: Mary Mason Lyon
b. February 28, 1797
Buckland, Massachusetts
d. March 5, 1849
South Hadley, Massachusetts
fields: Education

Combining a strong religious faith with a firm belief in the necessity of advanced training for women, Lyon served as the impetus for the creation of Mount Holyoke Female Seminary (later Mount Holyoke College). Insisting on a permanent endowment, she founded what has become the oldest continuing institution of higher learning for women in the United States.

Lyon, Matthew

pseud. Matthew "Ragged Matt the Democrat" Lyon
b. July 14, 1750
County Wicklow, Ireland
d. August 1, 1822
Spadra Bluff, Arkansas
fields: Government and Politics

A Revolutionary War veteran and congressman from Vermont, Matthew Lyon was convicted of criticizing President John Adams under the federal Sedition Act of 1798, which made it a crime to criticize the president, Congress, or the U.S. government to "defame them or bring them into disrepute." Afterward Lyon's political enemies expected him to lose his re-election bid; however, Vermont voters returned him to office by an overwhelming margin.

Lyons, Enid Muriel

aka: Dame Enid Muriel Lyons
né: Enid Muriel Burnell
b. July 9, 1897
Duck River, Tasmania, Australia
d. September 2, 1981
Ulverstone, Tasmania, Australia
fields: Government and Politics

Lyons became the first woman to sit in the Australian House of Representatives (1943-1951) and the first woman to become a federal cabinet minister (1949-1951). Married Joseph Aloysius Lyons.

Lyons, Joseph Aloysius

b. September 15, 1879
Stanley, Tasmania, Australia
d. April 7, 1939
Sydney, New South Wales, Australia
fields: Government and Politics

Winning a reputation as the "financial recovery" leader, first in the Tasmanian state parliament and then at the national level, Lyons broke away from the Australian Labor Party to lead the newly formed United Australia Party to victory in December, 1931, giving the Commonwealth seven years of stable government. Married Enid Muriel Burnell Lyons.

Lyotard, Jean-François

b. August 10, 1924
Versailles, France
d. April 21 1998
Paris, France
fields: Philosophy

Academician and political activist in France during the turbulent 1960's, Jean-François Lyotard wrote on philosophy, politics, and aesthetics, made the link between postmodernism and poststructuralism, engaged the problems of psychoanalysis, Marxism, and deconstruction, and examined the way society legitimizes knowledge and discourse. *Discours, figure* (1971), *Libidinal Economy* (1974), *The Postmodern Condition* (1979), and *The Differend* (1983) are among his most important works.

Lysippus

b. c. 390 B.C.E.
Sicyon, Greece
d. c. 300 B.C.E.
place unknown
fields: Art

A sculptor whose career spanned virtually the entire fourth century B.C.E., Lysippus was not only a major transitional figure between classical and Hellenistic styles but the most renowned portraitist of the century as well.

M. C. Lyte

b. 1970?
fields: Music (rap vocalist)

African American rap vocalist; M. C. Lyte, one of the first female rappers to go solo, was involved in recording the single and video "Self-Destruction" to raise money for the National Urban League. Lyte also has appeared in public service ads about women, birth control, and acquired immune deficiency syndrome (AIDS). *Act Like You Know* (1992), her third album, contained the single "When in Love." Her style includes blunt and direct lyrics about serious social issues such as teenage pregnancy and drug abuse.

Ma, L. Eve Armentrout

b. Dec. 28, 1943
Greenville, S.C.
fields: Education

L. Eve Armentrout Ma, who earned a J.D. from Hastings College of the Law and a Ph.D. in modern Chinese history from the University of California, Davis, specialized in international and constitutional law, Chinese and Japanese history, and U.S. military history. She wrote *Revolutionaries, Monarchists and Chinatowns: Chinese Politics in the Americas and the 1911 Revolution* (1990) and numerous articles in journals such as *The Journal of American-East Asian Relations*, *Amerasia Journal*, and *Modern Asian Studies*. From 1989 until 1991, Ma served as assistant professor of history at Mills College.

Ma, Yo-Yo

b. October 7, 1955
Paris, France
fields: Music (classical)

Chinese American cellist Yo-Yo Ma made his Carnegie Hall debut at the age of nine. He was guest artist with the New York and Los Angeles Philharmonic Orchestras, among others in the United States and Europe. Ma received a number of Grammy Awards and was the first solo winner of the Avery Fisher Prize in 1978.

Ma Yuan

b. c. 1165
He Zhong, Shanxi, China
d. c. 1225
Hangzhou, Zhejiang, China
fields: Art

Together with his somewhat younger contemporary, Xia Gui, Ma Yuan formed the Maxia school of Chinese painting. In some ways, the school served as the prototype for Chinese landscape painting and heavily influenced both Chinese and Japanese painters.

Mabley, Moms

full: Jackie Mabley
né: Loretta Mary Aiken
b. March 19, 1897?
Brevard, N.C.
d. May 23, 1975
White Plains, N.Y.
fields: Theater and Entertainment (comedienne)

African American comedienne; Moms Mabley is best known for her creation of the comic character of a worn-out old woman wearing a funny hat and droopy stockings. Her comedy ranged from domestic issues to race relations and the battle of the sexes and drew from folk wisdom with sly insights. Among other comic albums her most enduring are "Moms Mabley at the U.N." and "Moms Mabley at the Geneva Conference."

Mabovitch, Golda. *See* Meir, Golda

McAdoo, Bob

b. September 25, 1951
Greensboro, N.C.
fields: Sports (basketball player)

African American basketball player; Bob McAdoo, a high-scoring center and forward, won three NBA scoring titles and the 1975 Most Valuable Player award. In 1986 he retired with a lifetime professional scoring average of 22.1 points per game.

MacArthur, Douglas

b. January 26, 1880
Little Rock, Arkansas
d. April 5, 1964
Washington, D.C.
fields: Military Affairs

MacArthur had a greater impact on American military history than virtually any other officer in the twentieth century. Variously gifted, he was a hero to much of the American public but a center of controversy on several occasions.

Macaulay, Thomas Babington

b. October 25, 1800
Rothley Temple, Leicestershire, England
d. December 28, 1859
Holly Lodge, Kensington, England
fields: Government and Politics, Literature, Historiography

Macaulay was a prominent Whig politician and popular essayist, but his greatest achievement was *The History of England from the Accession of James the Second*, a work of enduring popularity and influence.

McCall, James Franklin

b. June 25, 1934
Philadelphia, Pa.
fields: Military Affairs

African American military officer. During his thirty-three years in the Army James Franklin McCall served in Vietnam as an adviser with the United States Military Assistance Command, taught at Fort Knox, and became comptroller of the Army, in the office of the secretary of the Army, his final post. His many decorations include the Distinguished Service Medal with oak leaf cluster and the Meritorious Service Medal. He retired in 1991, a Lieutenant General.

McCall, Nathan Jerome

b. November 25, 1954
Portsmouth, Va.
fields: Literature, Journalism

African American journalist and writer; Nathan Jerome McCall's autobiography, *Makes Me Wanna Holler: A Young Black Man in America* appeared on *The New York Times* best-seller list in 1994 and earned a National Black Image Award in 1995.

McCann, Les

full: Leslie Coleman McCann
b. September 23, 1935
Lexington, Ky.
fields: Music (pianist and singer)

African American pianist and singer; Les McCann released two successful jazz albums in 1960 *Les McCann Plays the Truth* and *The Shout*; performed with Eddie Harris at the 1969 Montreux International Jazz Festival; had a hit single, "Compared to What," from the album recorded at that festival; later focused more on rhythm-and-blues and soul music rather than jazz.

McCarthy, Nobu

b. November 13, 1934
Ottawa, Ontario, Canada
fields: Theater and Entertainment

Actor Nobu McCarthy got her start when she was cast as the female lead opposite Jerry Lewis and Sessue Hayakawa in *The Geisha Boy* (1958). She also appeared in *Tokyo After Dark* (1959) and *Walk Like a Dragon* (1960). Unhappy with the roles she had received, McCarthy joined the East West Players, an Asian American theater group, in the 1970's. Her film credits include the 1976 television film *Farewell to Manzanar*, the Hollywood film *The Karate Kid, Part II* (1986), and the film adaptation of Philip Kan Gotanda's *The Wash* (1988).

McCarthy, Eugene

full: Eugene Joseph McCarthy

b. March 29, 1916
Watkins, Minnesota
fields: Government and Politics

A staunch opponent of the Vietnam War, Eugene McCarthy was a U.S. senator from Minnesota (elected 1958) when he campaigned for the presidency in 1968. The campaign was instrumental in bringing protests against the Vietnam War into the nation's mainstream, and his performance in the New Hampshire primary contributed to President Lyndon Johnson's decision not to seek reelection in 1968. Because of his opposition to the war, McCarthy became a political hero to many young Americans. He chose not to run for reelection to the Senate in 1970. He ran for president as an independent in 1976 but received less than 1 percent of the vote.

McCarthy, Joseph R.

full: Joseph Raymond McCarthy
b. November 14, 1908
Grand Chute, near Appleton, Wisconsin
d. May 2, 1957
Bethesda, Maryland
fields: Government and Politics

McCarthy was the key figure in what came to be labeled "McCarthyism"—a national furor of divisive concern and suspicion regarding alleged Communists in American government. For four years, he was a dominant figure in American political life, striking fear into his opponents and confusion into the public mind.

McCarthy, Mary

full: Mary Therese McCarthy
b. June 21, 1912
Seattle, Washington
d. October 25, 1989
New York, New York
fields: Journalism, Literature

The most prominent woman among what came to be called the New York intellectuals, notorious for her acerbic tongue and for rather stormy relations with her male colleagues, McCarthy brought great vigor and insight and an uncompromising set of standards to American criticism and fiction.

McCartney, Paul

full: James Paul McCartney
b. June 18, 1942
Liverpool, England
fields: Music (popular)

Paul McCartney, with John Lennon, was the principal songwriter for the Beatles. More than any other English band before it, the Beatles popularized American rock-and-roll and became not only the major exponent of British rock-and-roll to the world but also one of the greatest popular bands ever. McCartney continued to be successful after the Beatles disbanded.

McCauley, Rosa Lee. *See* Parks, Rosa

McClatchy, V. S.

full: Valentine Stuart McClatchy
b. Aug. 28, 1857
Sacramento, Calif.
d. May 15, 1938
San Francisco, Calif.
fields: Publishing, Journalism

V. S. McClatchy was co-owner and publisher of *The Sacramento Bee* from 1884 to 1923. An opponent of Japanese immigration, his participation with exclusionist organizations was partly responsible for the enactment of laws preventing all Japanese aliens ineligible for U.S. citizenship from owning or leasing land. McClatchy, who believed that Asian immigrants were a threat to the American way of life, spoke and wrote extensively on his views. He supported the Alien Land Laws of 1913 and 1920, and argued in front of a congressional committee that Japanese should not become citizens, an idea reflected in the Immigration Act of 1924.

McClintock, Barbara

b. June 16, 1902
Hartford, Connecticut
d. September 2, 1992
Huntington, Long Island, New York
fields: Genetics

A pioneer in both classical genetics and molecular genetics, McClintock won the Nobel Prize in Physiology or Medicine in 1983.

McCloy, John Jay

b. Mar. 31, 1895
Philadelphia, Pa.
d. Mar. 11, 1989
Stamford, Conn.
fields: Government and Politics

John Jay McCloy, a 1921 graduate of Harvard Law School, was an influential policymaker and administrator. As assistant secretary of war, he played a significant role in the internment of Japanese Americans during World War II.

McClure, Frederick Donald

b. February 2, 1954
Fort Worth, Tex.
fields: Government and Politics

African American attorney and political appointee; Frederick Donald McClure worked for Senator John Tower of Texas (starting in 1983) as agricultural assistant, state office director, and legal director; became U.S. associate deputy attorney general (1984-1985); served as presidential special assistant for legislative affairs (1985); was hired by Texas Air Corporation as its government affairs staff vice president (1986-1989); was appointed as presidential special assistant for legislative affairs (1989).

McCormick, Cyrus Hall

b. February 15, 1809
Rockbridge County, Virginia
d. May 13, 1884
Chicago, Illinois
fields: Invention and Technology, Philanthropy

McCormick revolutionized American agriculture through his invention of the reaper and through his marketing innovations. He also shaped American theological development by his patronage of a Northwest seminary.

McCovey, Willie

b. January 10, 1938
Mobile, Ala.
fields: Sports (baseball player)

African American baseball player; Willie McCovey began his twenty-two-year major league career with the San Francisco Giants in 1959 and later played for the San Diego Padres and Oakland Athletics. Three times he led the National League in home runs, and he won the league's Most Valuable Player award in 1969. He retired in 1980 with 521 lifetime homers. He was elected to the Baseball Hall of Fame in 1986.

McCoy, Elijah

b. May 2, 1844
Colchester, Ontario, Canada
d. October 10, 1929
Eloise, Mich.
fields: Invention and Technology

African American inventor Elijah McCoy invented and refined automatic lubricators used to oil engines and machinery. The phrase "the real McCoy" may have come into use as a reference to the quality of McCoy's devices.

McCree, Wade Hampton, Jr.

b. July 3, 1920
Des Moines, Iowa
d. August 30, 1987
Detroit, Mich.
fields: Government and Politics

African American political appointee; Wade Hampton McCree, Jr., received his LL.B. degree from Harvard Law School (1944), was admitted to the Michigan State Bar (1948), and became a judge on the Michigan Circuit Court in Wayne County in 1954. Later named judge of the U.S. District Court for the Eastern Michigan District, he was appointed solicitor general in 1977.

McCullers, Carson

né: Lula Carson Smith
b. February 19, 1917
Columbus, Georgia
d. September 29, 1967
Nyack, New York
fields: Literature

A Southern novelist and short-story writer, Carson McCullers presented in her fiction a world of alienated adolescents, misfits, and outcasts, treating themes of human isolation with great sensitivity.

McCullough, Geraldine

b. December 1, 1922
Kingston, Ark.
fields: Art (sculptor and printmaker)

African American sculptor, printmaker, and educator; Geraldine McCullough studied at Art Institute of Chicago, DePaul University, and the University of Illinois. Besides teaching at Rosary College in River Forest, Ill, she has produced commissioned sculptures in Chicago, Ill., and her work has a permanent place in the collections of the Oakland Museum and Howard University.

McCunn, Ruthanne Lum

b. Feb. 21, 1946
San Francisco, Calif.
fields: Literature

Ruthanne Lum McCunn wrote the award-winning *Thousand Pieces of Gold* (1981), a biographical novel from which the 1991 movie of the same name was based; *An Illustrated History of the Chinese in America* (1979); *Pie-Biter* (1983), which won an American Book Award from the Before Columbus Foundation; and *Chinese American Portraits: Personal Histories 1828-1988* (1988). The daughter of a white American father and a Chinese mother, she described the personal and historical experiences of Asian Americans.

McCurdy, Robert C.

b. 1941
Atlantic City, N.J.
fields: Sports (jockey)

African American jockey; Robert C. McCurdy was one of the few black jockeys racing in the 1960's. He was the leading jockey at the Garden State Park fall meet in 1963, winning thirty races. That year he won more than a hundred races. He retired in 1967, with career earnings exceeding one million dollars. He rode more than three thousand mounts to a total of 264 wins.

McDaniel, Hattie

b. June 10, 1895
Wichita, Kans.
d. October 26, 1952
Hollywood, Calif.
fields: Theater and Entertainment, Film

First African American actor to win an Academy Award; Hattie McDaniel appeared in many films, *Blonde Venus* (1932), *Judge Priest* (1934), *Alice Adams* (1935), *The Mad Miss Manton* (1935), *Show Boat* (1936), and *Saratoga* (1937), but is best known for her role as the faithful "Mammy" of the O'Hara household in the classic film *Gone With the Wind* (1939). Her performance earned McDaniel an Academy Award for Best Supporting Actress, the first Oscar awarded to an African American.

McDaniel, Mildred Louise

b. November 4, 1933
Atlanta, Ga.
fields: Sports (high jumper)

African American high jumper; Mildred Louise McDaniel won the Amateur Athletic Union outdoor high jump in 1953 as well as the outdoor and indoor titles in 1955 and 1956; won an Olympic gold medal in the high jump in 1956 (setting an Olympic and world record of five feet nine and one-half inches); won the high jump at the 1959 Pan American Games.

McDonald, Freda Josephine. *See* Baker, Josephine

McDonald, Gabrielle Kirk

b. April 12, 1942
St. Paul, Minn.
fields: Law

African American federal judge; Gabrielle Kirk McDonald served as a staff attorney for the National Association for the Advancement of Colored People Legal Defense and Educational Fund from 1966 to 1969. After starting her own law firm, teaching at Texas Southern University (1970-1977), and lecturing at the University of Texas at Houston (1977-1978), Mcdonald was appointed judge of the U.S. District Court, southern district, in Houston on May 11, 1979.

Macdonald, John Alexander

b. January 11, 1815
Glasgow, Scotland
d. June 6, 1891
Ottawa, Ontario, Canada
fields: Government and Politics

Macdonald not only had a major role in drawing up the British North American Act, which created the Dominion of Canada, but also, as Canada's first prime minister, brought about the new nation's territorial and political expansion from sea to sea. Within the British community, he paved the way for Canadians to determine their own foreign affairs and foreshadowed the British Commonwealth of Nations.

MacDonald, Ramsay

full: James Ramsay MacDonald
b. October 12, 1866
Lossiemouth, Morayshire, Scotland
d. November 9, 1937
at sea
fields: Government and Politics

The most significant figure in the development of the Labour Party, MacDonald guided it through his voluminous political writings, his organizational acumen and skills, and his actions as prime minister of its first two governments. The party became in practice more reformist than Socialist. It grew as a broad-based party aspiring to govern rather than a small pressure group within Parliament; it tapped trade union strength but rebuffed trade union control.

McEwen, Mark

b. September 16, 1954
San Antonio, Tex.
fields: Television, Radio (broadcaster and radio personality)

African American broadcaster and radio personality; hired as a weather reporter for CBS's morning show in 1986, Mark McEwen was the only anchor retained on the revamped *CBS This Morning* show in 1987; became a cohost of *CBS This Morning* in 1996.

McFerrin, Bobby

full: Robert McFerrin, Jr.
b. March 11, 1950
New York, N.Y.
fields: Music (vocalist)

African American vocalist; Bobby McFerrin is best known for his improvised singing. He has a powerful vocal range and makes effective use of his ability to mimic musical instrument with his voice. His concerts often include audience participation and have featured "duets" with horn players Wynton Marsalis and Wayne Shorter. His song "Don't Worry, Be Happy" (1989) was a big hit and was awarded three Grammys. Over the years, he also won several Grammy awards in the Best Male Jazz Vocalist category.

McFerrin, Robert, Sr.

b. March 19, 1921
Marianna, Ark.
fields: Music (opera singer)

African American opera singer; Robert McFerrin, Sr., debuted with the Metropolitan Opera in 1955. As well as performing major roles in many operas, he has also taught voice in the United States and abroad. He is the father of jazz singer Bobby McFerrin.

McGee, Henry Wadsworth, Jr.

b. December 31, 1932
Chicago, Ill.
fields: Government and Politics

African American state politician and educator; Henry Wadsworth McGee, Jr., served as assistant state's attorney for Cook County (1958-1961); became Great Lakes regional director of legal services for the U.S. Office of Economic Opportunity (1966-1967); became legal director of the Juvenile Delinquent Research Program at the University of Chicago's Center for Studies in Criminal Justice (1967); taught at the University of Florence, University of Puerto Rico, the University of Madrid, and the University of California at Los Angeles.

McGee, James Howell

b. November 8, 1918
Berryburg, W.V.
fields: Government and Politics

African American mayor of Dayton, Ohio; James Howell McGee's political career began with his election as city commissioner of Dayton, Ohio, in 1967, a post he kept until 1970. Elected mayor of Dayton in 1980, he served as a member of the advisory board for the National League of Cities and on the board of directors for Sister Cities International.

McGee, Vonetta

b. January 14, 1950?
San Francisco, Calif.
fields: Theater and Entertainment

African American actress; Vonetta McGee's film credits include *Hammer* (1972), *The Big Bust Out,* (1973), *Thomasine and Bushrod* (1974), *The Eiger Sanction* (1975), and *Brothers* (1977). On television she appeared as a regular in the series *Hell Town* (1985) and also was seen in series such as *Cagney and Lacey* (1986), *Diff'rent Strokes* (1980), and *The Yellow Rose* (1984).

McGee, Willie

b. November 2, 1958
San Francisco, Calif.
fields: Sports (baseball player)

African American baseball player; Willie McGee, who played with the Giants, the St. Louis Cardinals, and the Oakland Athletics, was a "line-drive" hitter, who won two batting championships (1985 and 1990). In 1985 he was the National League's Most Valuable Player with a .353 batting average, 216 hits, 18 triples (all three figures led the league), 10 home runs, and 82 runs batted in.

McGillivray, Alexander

b. c. 1759
near Montgomery, Alabama
d. February 17, 1793
Pensacola, Florida
fields: Native American Affairs, Social Reform

McGillivray was one of the earliest mixed-blood Creek leaders to use his bicultural abilities to protect both Indian sovereignty and his own personal power.

McGovern, George

full: George Stanley McGovern
b. July 19, 1922
Avon, South Dakota
fields: Government and Politics

A political leader in the anti-Vietnam War movement, George McGovern was the Democratic presidential candidate in 1972. He was elected to the House of Representatives in 1956; appointed director of the Food for Peace Program in 1961 by President John F. Kennedy; won election to the U.S. Senate in 1962; ran unsuccessfully for the Democratic Party nomination for president in 1968; and in 1972, secured the Democratic nomination for the presidency and campaigned on a platform of opposition to U.S. involvement in Vietnam. He lost a landslide election to Republican Richard M. Nixon. McGovern stayed in the Senate until 1980, when he lost his bid for reelection.

McGriff, Jimmy

b. April 3, 1936
Philadelphia, Pa.
fields: Music (jazz musician)

African American jazz musician; Jimmy McGriff, a jazz organist, had commercial success with "I've Got a Woman" in 1963 and went on to make many more recordings as both a leader and a sideman, as with drummer Buddy Rich in 1974.

McGuffey, William Holmes

b. September 23, 1800
Washington County, Pennsylvania
d. May 4, 1873
Charlottesville, Virginia
fields: Education

As an early nineteenth century college president, professor, and Presbyterian clergyman in the Ohio Valley, McGuffey compiled the most famous series of school textbooks in American history. His six *Eclectic Readers* sold more than 122 million copies between 1836 and 1920, and impressed upon young Americans the virtues of individual morality, thrift, hard work, and sobriety.

McGuire, George A.

b. March 26, 1866
Sweets, Antigua
d. November 10, 1934
New York, N.Y.
fields: Religion and Theology

African American founder and bishop of the African Orthodox church. Racist conflict within the Episcopalian church prompted George A. McGuire to leave to start his own church; he also worked as the chaplain-general of Marcus Garvey's Universal Negro Improvement Association. He lectured and formed churches in the United States, Australia, Canada, Cuba, the Dominican Republic, Antigua, Venezuela, and Uganda. He combated racism and promoted a sense of global pride in black heritage and is remembered for his work among the sick and the poor.

Mach, Ernst

b. Feb. 18, 1838
Chirlitz-Turas, Moravia (now Chrlice-Turany, Czech Republic)
d. Feb. 19, 1916
Vaterstetten, Germany
fields: Physics, Science

Ernst Mach researched projectile motion; stated theory or philosophy of science called positivism; criticized Sir Isaac Newton's conception of absolute space and time, having a tremendous impact on the thought of Albert Einstein.

Machado de Assis, Joaquim Maria

b. June 21, 1839
Rio de Janeiro, Brazil
d. September 29, 1908
Rio de Janeiro, Brazil
fields: Literature

Because of his uniquely modern and boldly experimental contribution to narrative form and technique, as well as the universal appeal of his works, Machado is considered the greatest figure in nineteenth century Brazilian literature and a world master of the short story.

Machaut, Guillaume de

b. c. 1300
Machault, near Reims, France
d. Possibly April, 1377
Reims, France
fields: Music, Literature

Generally acclaimed as the most important figure of the French *ars nova*, Machaut—poet, musician, courtier, and diplomat—was among the first to compose polyphonic settings of the fixed forms of medieval poetry (ballade, rondeau, virelay), to write songs for four voices, and to compose an integrated setting of the entire Ordinary of the Mass.

Machel, Samora Moisès

b. September 29, 1933
Chilembene, Mozambique
d. October 19, 1986
Mbuzini, near Komatipoort, Lebombo Mountains, South Africa
fields: Military Affairs, Government and Politics

Machel is mostly remembered for his able leadership as commander of the guerrilla army of the Mozambique Liberation Front, which fought against the stronger Portuguese army from 1964 to 1974. He was also the first President of the People's Republic of Mozambique, from 1975 to his death in 1986.

McHenry, Donald F.

b. October 13, 1936
St. Louis, Mo.
fields: Government and Politics

African American educator and political appointee; Donald F. McHenry worked for the State Department in the Office of United Nations Political Affairs (1963-1966); worked as assistant to the secretary of state (1968-1969); became special assistant to the counselor of the State Department (1969); received the State Department's Superior Service Award (1966); was appointed as the U.S. permanent representative to the United Nations (1979); wrote *Micronesia, Trust Betrayed: Altruism Versus Self-Interest in American Foreign Policy* (1975).

McHenry, Doug

b. December 15, 1950
fields: Film (producer)

African American film producer; Doug McHenry and his partner George Jackson produced *New Jack City* (1991), *Krush Groove* (1985), *Disorderlies* (1987), and *Jason's Lyric* (1994).

Machiavelli, Niccolò

b. May 3, 1469
Florence
d. June 21, 1527
Florence
fields: Political Science, Historiography, Literature

Machiavelli's posthumous reputation rests primarily on his having initiated a pragmatic mode of political discourse that is entirely independent of ethical considerations derived from traditional sources of moral authority, such as classical philosophy and Christian theology.

McIntosh, Alex C.. *See* Blue Eagle, Acee

McIntosh, William

aka: Tustennugee Hutkee (White Warrior)
b. c. 1775
Coweta, Ga.
d. May 1, 1825
Acorn Town, Ala.
fields: Government and Politics, Native American Affairs

Native American leader. William McIntosh, a Creek, led the pro-American faction of the Creeks during the early nineteenth century, signing treaties ceding much land to the United States. Opposed by the Red Stick faction of Creek traditionalists and fought against them in the Creek War (1813-1814). Signed 1825 Treaty of Indian Springs, ceding most of the tribe's remaining land east of the Mississippi. This violated a decree of the Creek National Council that prescribed the death penalty for any Creek who ceded tribal land without the council's consent. The council ordered McIntosh's execution.

MacIntyre, Alasdair

full: Alasdair Chalmers MacIntyre
b. January 12, 1929
Glasgow, Scotland
fields: Philosophy

Alasdair MacIntyre made philosophical thinking available to nonphilosophers by bringing philosophy in to serve other disciplines and areas of concern, including religious faith, sociology, medicine, psychology, and politics, and by writing in a way accessible to nonexperts, as in *A Short History of Ethics* (1966). Second, he created a foundation whereby he can critique contemporary thought from a traditional viewpoint, while maintaining the reality of modern pluralism and avoiding a reactionary conservatism. This knife-edge endeavor is accomplished by reinterpreting the Thomist enterprise of finding an absolute concept of truth and yet holding the necessity of a historicist approach. People have to philosophize from within time. What students need to be taught is not to dialogue but to engage in conflict. Other works include *Difficulties in Christian Belief* (1959), *Marxism and Christianity* (1968), and *First Principles, Final Ends, and Contemporary Philosophical Issues* (1990).

Mack, Julian William

b. July 19, 1866
San Francisco, Calif.
d. September 5, 1943
New York, N.Y.
fields: Law

American jurist. Julian William Mack, a leading Zionist and progressive reformer, was a pioneer in the development of the juvenile justice system and presided over several highly publicized trials in the 1920's, including the mail fraud trial of Marcus Garvey. One of the originators of the *Harvard Law Review* (1887).

McKay, Claude

b. September 15, 1889
Sunny Ville, Jamaica
d. May 22, 1948
Chicago, Ill.
fields: Literature

African American poet, novelist, and essayist; a key figure in the Harlem Renaissance, Claude McKay is noted primarily for his poetry containing subject matter based on his own experience of American racism; his published poetry works include *Constab Ballads* (1912) and *Songs of Jamaica* (1912), written mostly in Jamaican dialect, and the work which helped establish his reputation as a major figure of the Harlem Renaissance, *Harlem Shadows* (1922); his fiction includes the short stories of *Gingertown* (1932) and the novels *Home to Harlem* (1928), *Banjo: A Story Without a Plot* (1929), and the most artistically successful of his fiction, *Banana Bottom* (1933); he also published an autobiography, *A Long Way from Home* (1937), and the nonfiction *Harlem: Negro Metropolis* (1940).

McKee, Lonette

b. July 21, 1956
Detroit, Mich.
fields: Theater and Entertainment, Film, Music

African American actress and singer; Lonette McKee's film credits include *Sparkle* (1976), the Richard Pryor films *Which Way Is Up?* (1977) and *Brewster's Millions* (1985), *The Cotton Club* (1984), *'Round Midnight* (1986), the Spike Lee films *Jungle Fever* (1991), *Malcolm X* (1992), and *He Got Game* (1998); and her stage work includes the 1981 musical *The First*, *Show Boat* (1983), for which she garnered a Tony nomination for her performance as the octoroon, Julie, and the 1986 Off-Broadway show *Lady Day at Emerson's Bar and Grill*, for which she received rave reviews for her portrayal of Billie Holiday.

McKegney, Tony

b. Feb., 1958
Montreal, Quebec, Canada
fields: Sports (hockey player)

Professional hockey player; as one of the very few black players ever to compete on an National Hockey League (NHL) team, Tony McKegney began playing in the NHL in 1978, after being drafted by the Buffalo Sabres; moved around the league, playing for the Minnesota North Stars, the New York Rangers (where he received the nickname "McKetzky"), the St. Louis Blues, the Detroit

Red Wings, the Quebec Nordiques, and the Chicago Blackhawks. In 1992, he played hockey in Europe.

McKenna, Joseph

b. 1843
d. 1926
fields: Law

U.S. Supreme Court justice, 1898-1925; appointed by President McKinley. In 1924, after old age rendered him incompetent but he remained on the Court, the other justices agreed to decide no case where his vote was the deciding one. Significant opinions: *Hoke v. United States*, 227 U.S. 308 (1913); *Hammer v. Dagenhart*, 247 U.S. 251 (1918) (dissenting opinion); *Gilbert v. Minnesota*, 254 U.S. 325 (1920).

Mackenzie, Alexander

aka: Sir Alexander Mackenzie
b. c. 1764
Stornoway, Scotland
d. March 12, 1820
Mulnain, near Dunkeld, Scotland
fields: Exploration and Colonization

By crossing Canada in 1793, Mackenzie became the first white man north of Mexico to reach the Pacific Ocean via an overland route.

MacKenzie, Frederick Arthur

b. 1869
d. 1931
fields: Literature

Frederick Arthur MacKenzie wrote *Korea's Fight for Freedom* (1920). The work, sponsored by the Korean Commission, received praise in England and influenced the formation of the League of the Friends of Korea in 1920.

Mackenzie, William Lyon

b. March 12, 1795
Springfield, Dundee, Forfarshire, Scotland
d. August 28, 1861
Toronto, Canada
fields: Government and Politics, Journalism

Mackenzie sought to establish for English Canada a political entity independent of British colonialism and devoted his life to a critique of English political authority in Canada and a demand for redress of grievances by English Canadians.

Mackey, Howard Hamilton, Sr.

b. November 25, 1901
Philadelphia, Pa.
d. August 20, 1987
Washington, D.C.
fields: Architecture

African American architect; a teacher of architecture, design, and tropical architecture for almost fifty years at Howard University, Howard Hamilton Mackey, Sr., served as head of Howard's department of architecture for more than thirty of those years; he also served as a consultant to the embassies of Ghana, Nigeria, and India.

McKillop, Jean Sadako. *See* King, Jean Sadako

Mackinder, Halford John

aka: Sir Halford John Mackinder
b. February 15, 1861
Gainsborough, Lincolnshire, England
d. March 6, 1947
Parkstone, Dorset, England
fields: Geography, Government and Politics, Education

Mackinder's contributions in the academic discipline of geography gained early recognition, and significant institutions were created for which he was credited. Mackinder is most noted for the Heartland theory of geopolitics.

McKinley, John

b. 1780
d. 1852
fields: Law

U.S. Supreme Court justice, 1838-1852 (died while in office); appointed by President Van Buren.

McKinley, William

full: William McKinley, Jr.
b. January 29, 1843
Niles, Ohio
d. September 14, 1901
Buffalo, New York
fields: Government and Politics

President of the United States, 1897-1901. By strengthening the powers of the presidency, McKinley's administration prepared the way for forceful executives of the twentieth century such as Woodrow Wilson, Theodore Roosevelt, and Franklin D. Roosevelt. His expansionist policies brought new overseas territories such as Puerto Rico, the Philippines, Guam, and Hawaii into the American empire.

McKinney, Cynthia Ann

b. March 17, 1955
Atlanta, Ga.
fields: Government and Politics, Education

African American educator and government official; in 1992, Cynthia Ann McKinney became the first African American elected to Congress from Georgia in 1992. During her 1988-1992 term in the Georgia state legislature, McKinney also had the distinction of being part of the country's only father-daughter team to serve in the same legislature.

McKinney, Nina Mae

b. 1913
Lancaster, S.C.
d. May 3, 1967
New York, N.Y.
fields: Theater and Entertainment, Film

African American actress; noted as Hollywood's first African American sex symbol, Nina Mae McKinney's stage appearances included the Broadway revue *Blackbirds of 1928*, a starring role as Chick in King Vidor's all-black musical *Hallelujah!* (1929; propelled her to immediate fame), *Sanders of the River* (1939; in England, costarring with Paul Robeson), and the dramas *Good Neighbor* (1941) and *Rain* (1951); her film credits included the black independently produced films *St. Louis Gal* (1938), *Gang Smashers* (1938), *Straight to Heaven* (1939), *The Devil's Daughter* (1939), *Dark Waters* (1944), *Night Train to Memphis* (1946), and *Mantan Messes Up* (1946), and the miscegenation drama *Pinky* (1949); in 1978 posthumously inducted into the Black Filmmakers Hall of Fame.

MacKinnon, Catharine A.

full: Catharine Alice MacKinnon
b. 1946
Minneapolis, Minnesota
fields: Law, Women's Rights

A pioneer in the development of feminist legal theory, MacKinnon formulated the argument that sexual harassment should be viewed as a form of sex discrimination—an argument that later became embedded in law.

McKissack, Fredrick Lemuel

b. August 12, 1939
Nashville, Tenn.
fields: Literature (children's books)

African American children's book authors, Fredrick Lemuel McKissack and Patricia McKissack have written about topics that specifically, but not exclusively, appeal to African American children and young adults. The award-winning team's published works include *A History of the Civil Rights Movement* (1986), *Abram, Abram, Where Are We Going?* (1985); *A Long Hard Journey: The Story of the Pullman Porters* (1990); *Madam C. J. Walker*; and *Christmas in the Big House, Christmas in the Quarters* (1995).

McKissack, Patricia

né: L'Ann Carwell
b. August 9, 1944
Nashville, Tenn.
fields: Literature (children's books)

African American children's book authors, Patricia and Frederick McKissack have written about topics that specifically, but not exclusively, appeal to African American children and young adults. The award-winning team's published works include *A History of the Civil Rights Movement* (1986), *Abram, Abram, Where Are We Going?* (1985); *A Long Hard Journey: The Story of the Pullman Porters* (1990); *Madam C. J. Walker*; and *Christmas in the Big House, Christmas in the Quarters* (1995). As sole author, Patricia McKissack won the 1993 Coretta Scott King Award for *The Dark Thirty: Southern Tales of the Supernatural* (1992), which was also named a 1993 Newbery Honor Book. She also authored other books, including *A Picture of Freedom* (1997).

McKissick, Floyd

full: Floyd Bixler McKissick, Sr.
b. Mar. 9, 1922
Asheville, N.C.
d. Apr. 28, 1991
Durham, N.C.
fields: Civil Rights, Law

African American lawyer, civil rights leader; Floyd McKissick sued the University of North Carolina at Chapel Hill for admission to their Law School and became the first African American to earn a degree there; national director of Congress on Racial Equality, 1966-1968; between 1968 and 1980 worked to establish a new and self-sufficient African American community in Warren County, North Carolina, known as Soul City; appointed to a North Carolina judgeship in 1989; wrote *Three-fifths of Man* (1968).

McKuen, Rod

full: Rod Marvin McKuen
b. April 29, 1933
Oakland, California
fields: Literature, Music

A popular and successful poet, singer, and songwriter, Rod McKuen wrote sentimental poems and songs that earned the love of the masses and the disdain of literary critics. In 1966, *Seasons in the Sun* became an award-winning album in France, and he developed a long-term relationship with French chanson artists such as Jacques Brel. In 1966, after former Limelighters singer Glenn Yarbrough recorded a collection of McKuen poems (including "Stanyan Street") set to music, McKuen self-published *Stanyan Street and Other Sorrows*. The book sold more than sixty thousand copies before publisher Random House acquired it. McKuen's 1967 album, *The Sea*, sold five hundred thousand copies in its first year. During the 1960's, McKuen wrote numerous concertos, symphonies, ballets, and more than a thousand songs. His musical score for the popular 1969 film *The Prime of Miss Jean Brodie* was nominated for an Academy Award. His volumes of poetry include *Listen to the Warm* (1967), *Lonesome Cities* (1968), *The World of Rod McKuen* (1968), *In Someone's Shadow* (1969), and *Twelve Years of Christmas* (1969).

Maclaurin, Colin

b. February, 1698
Kilmodan, Argyll, Scotland
d. January 14, 1746
Edinburgh, Scotland
fields: Mathematics, Physics

Maclaurin, the greatest British mathematician of the eighteenth century, developed and extended Isaac Newton's work in fluxions (calculus) and gravitation and made important new discoveries in geometry and mathematical analysis.

McLean, John

b. 1785
d. 1861
fields: Law

U.S. Supreme Court justice, 1830-1861 (died while in office); appointed by President Jackson. Adamant antislavery justice. Significant opinions: *Prigg v. Pennsylvania*, 41 U.S. 539 (1842) (dissenting opinion); *Ex parte Dorr*, 44 U.S. 103 (1844); *Scott v. Sandford*, 60 U.S. 393 (1857) (dissenting opinion).

Macleod, John J. R.

full: John James Rickard Macleod
b. September 6, 1876
Cluny, Perthshire, Scotland
d. March 16, 1935
Aberdeen, Scotland
fields: Biochemistry, Physiology

As the leader of a physiology research laboratory at the University of Toronto in Canada, Macleod shared the 1923 Nobel Prize in Physiology or Medicine for the discovery of insulin as a treatment for diabetes.

McLeod, Mary Jane. *See* Bethune, Mary McLeod

McLish, Rachel Livia Elizondo

b. 1958
Harlingen, Tex.
fields: Sports (bodybuilder)

Latina bodybuilder. In 1980, Rachel Livia Elizondo McLish won the first U.S. Women's Body Building Championships, as well as the Ms. Olympia title. In 1982, she again won Ms. Olympia and also won the World Championship. She retired during the mid-1980's and became the spokesperson for the Health and Tennis Corporation of America. She wrote several books on drug-free fitness and bodybuilding, marketed a line of workout clothing, and appeared in the film *Iron Eagle III* (1992).

McLuhan, Marshall

full: Herbert Marshall McLuhan
b. July 21, 1911
Edmonton, Alberta, Canada
d. December 31, 1980
Toronto, Ontario, Canada
fields: Communications Theory

With a cryptic, maddeningly epigrammatic style, McLuhan provided the twentieth century with its most provocative critique of the way technology, specifically electronic media, has shaped the modern view of what it means to be human.

McMahon, William

b. February 23, 1908
Sydney, Australia
d. March 31, 1988
Sydney, Australia
fields: Government and Politics

William McMahon was a thirty-three-year Liberal member of Parliament who held several cabinet posts during his career. Prime minister of Australia in 1971 and 1972. Took office when Liberal Party replaced John Gorton with McMahon as party leader. Voted out when Labor Party came to power in 1972.

McMath, Virginia Katherine. *See* Rogers, Ginger

MacMillan, Alexander

b. October 3, 1818
Irvine, Ayrshire, Scotland
d. January 26, 1896
London, England
fields: Publishing

Starting as booksellers, Daniel and Alexander Macmillan, in 1844, founded Macmillan and Company, which would eventually become one of the world's major publishing enterprises.

MacMillan, Daniel

b. September 13, 1813
Island of Arran, Buteshire, Scotland
d. June 27, 1857
Cambridge, England
fields: Publishing

Starting as booksellers, Daniel and Alexander Macmillan, in 1844, founded Macmillan and Company, which would eventually become one of the world's major publishing enterprises.

McMillan, Edwin Mattison

b. September 18, 1907
Redondo Beach, California

d. September 7, 1991
El Cerrito, California
fields: Physics

McMillan discovered the first transuranic element, neptunium, and was codiscoverer of plutonium, an artificially made element which is fundamental to nuclear power and nuclear bombs. He also discovered the important principle of phase stability, which made possible the high-energy accelerators of the late twentieth century producing fundamental advances in man's understanding of the nature of matter. He won the 1951 Nobel Prize in Chemistry.

Macmillan, Harold

full: Maurice Harold Macmillan
b. February 10, 1894
London, England
d. December 29, 1986
Birch Grove, Sussex, England
fields: Government and Politics, Publishing

As British prime minister from 1957 to 1963, Macmillan witnessed a period of unprecedented affluence combined with a diminished role in world affairs for Great Britain. Committed to improving the lot of the average Englishman, to granting independence to the British possessions, and to strong economic policies, he ended his career as prime minister in the wake of ill health, divisions within his party, and scandal.

McMillan, Terry

b. October 18, 1951
Port Huron, Mich.
fields: Literature

African American novelist; Terry McMillan's novels include *Mama* (1987), *Disappearing Acts* (1989), *Waiting to Exhale* (1992), and *How Stella Got Her Groove Back* (1996).

McMillian, Theodore

b. January 28, 1919
St. Louis, Mo.
fields: Law

African American federal judge; after working as a lecturer at St. Louis University Law School and serving on the faculty at Webster College, Theodore McMillian became assistant circuit attorney for the city of St. Louis (1953-1956); from 1972 to 1978, he served as a judge on the Missouri Court of Appeals; in 1978 President Jimmy Carter appointed him to the position of U.S. circuit judge for the Eighth Circuit of the U.S. Court of Appeals.

McNair, Barbara

b. March 4, 1939
Racine, Wis.
fields: Music (popular singer), Film, Television

African American singer and actress; as a singer Barbara McNair released the albums *I Enjoy Being a Girl* (1964), *Here I Am* (1967), and *The Real Barbara McNair* (1970); McNair's television credits include appearances on the mid-1960's television series *Hogan's Heroes*, *Dr. Kildare*, and *I Spy* and as star of her own weekly musical variety show, *The Barbara McNair Show* (1969-1971); her film credits include *A Change of Habit* (1969; with Elvis Presley) and *They Call Me Mister Tibbs* (1970; with Sidney Poitier).

McNair, Ronald E.

b. October 12, 1950
Lake City, S.C.
d. January 28, 1986
Cape Canaveral, Fla.
fields: Aviation and Space Exploration

African American astronaut; after working as a physicist at Hughes Research Laboratories, Ronald E. McNair became a mission specialist astronaut with the National Aeronautics and Space Administration in 1978; McNair was aboard the space shuttle *Challenger* when it exploded, soon after takeoff, on January 28, 1986.

McNamara, Robert

b. June 9, 1916
San Francisco, California
fields: Government and Politics, Military Affairs

One of the nation's chief policymakers in the 1960's. As secretary of defense from 1961 through 1968, McNamara played a key role in such events as the 1961 crisis in Berlin, the 1962 Cuban Missile Crisis, and the Vietnam War.

McNeil, Claudia Mae

b. August 13, 1917
Baltimore, Md.
d. November 25, 1993
Englewood, N.J.
fields: Theater and Entertainment, Television, Film

African American actress; Claudia Mae McNeil's stage credits include her well known role as Lena, the family matriarch, in Lorraine Hansberry's *A Raisin in the Sun* (1959, 1975) and in the musical version, *Raisin* (1981), *Tiger, Tiger Burning Bright* (1962, for which she received a Tony Award nomination), James Baldwin's *The Amen Corner*, *Winesburg, Ohio* (1958), *Something Different* (1968), *Her First Roman* (1968), *The Wrong Way Light Bulb* (1969), and *Contributions* (1970); she has appeared on television in *Simply Heavenly* (1952), in Carson McCullers' *The Member of the Wedding* (1958), and in *The Nurses* (for which she won an Emmy in 1963); her film credits include *The Last Angry Man* (1958) and *Black Girl* (1972).

MacNeil, Lori

b. December 18, 1963
San Diego, Calif.
fields: Sports (tennis player)

African American tennis player; most well known as a doubles player, Lori MacNeil turned professional in 1983; in 1988 she ranked ninth in the world as a doubles player and tenth as a singles player.

McNickle, D'Arcy

b. Jan. 18, 1904
St. Ignatius, Mont.
d. Oct. 18, 1977
Albuquerque, N.Mex.
fields: Native American Affairs, Anthropology, Literature

A Salish and Kutenai Indian of Canadian Cree, French, and Irish American ancestry, D'Arcy McNickle wrote one of the first novels by an American Indian, the largely autobiographical *The Surrounded* (1936). He then worked as an administrator and political organizer and authored works of anthropology and history. Served as a founding member of the National Congress of American Indians in 1944 and, from 1972 to 1977, as director of what is now known as the D'Arcy McNickle Center for the History of the American Indian at the Newberry Library in Chicago.

McPhail, Sharon M.

b. November 6, 1948
Cambridge, Mass.
fields: Law, Government and Politics

African American attorney, activist, and politician; Sharon M. McPhail was division chief of Screening and District Courts for the Wayne County Prosecutor's Office from 1987 to 1994; was a strong candidate but defeated in the 1993 general election for mayor of Detroit.

McPhatter, Clyde

b. November 15, 1933
Durham, N.C.
d. June 13, 1972
New York, N.Y.
fields: Music (popular singer, songwriter, bandleader)

African American singer, songwriter, and bandleader throughout the 1950's and much of the 1960's; Clyde McPhatter performed as the lead tenor of the vocal group the Dominoes; left the Dominoes in 1953 and formed the Drifters, releasing the hits "Money

Honey" (1953) and "Honey Love" (1954); among his many hits reaching the charts as a solo artist was "A Lover's Question" (1959); number one on the U.S. rhythm-and-blues charts, in the top ten in England) which garnered for McPhatter a gold record; later top-ten singles included "Ta-Ta" (1960) and "Lover Please" (1962); in 1987 inducted into the Rock and Roll Hall of Fame.

McPherson, James Alan

b. September 16, 1943
Savannah, Ga.
fields: Literature

In 1978 James Alan McPherson won the Pulitzer Prize for fiction for his novel *Elbow Room.*

McQueen, Butterfly

full: Thelma McQueen
b. January 8, 1911
Tampa, Fla.
d. December 22, 1995
Augusta, Ga.
fields: Theater and Entertainment, Film

African American actress; Butterfly McQueen's stage credits include her debut in George Abbott's musical *Brown Sugar* (1937) followed by a part written specifically for her in Abbott's play *What a Life* (1938), *Swingin' the Dream* (1939), an all-black touring production of *Harvey* (1946), and the pre-Broadway production of *The Wiz* (1975); her film credits, usually playing a domestic, include the role of Prissy in *Gone with the Wind* (1939), *The Women* (1939), *Cabin in the Sky* (1943), *Mildred Pierce* (1945), *Duel in the Sun* (1947), *The Phynx* (1970), *Amazing Grace* (1974), and *Mosquito Coast* (1986); in 1975 inducted into the Black Filmmakers Hall of Fame.

McQueen, Peter

aka: Talmuches Harjo
b. ?
d. 1818
Fla.
fields: Warfare and Conquest, Native American Affairs

Peter McQueen's band of Creek Red Sticks touched off the Creek War (1813-1814) by battling Alabama militia at Burnt Corn Creek. After 1814 McQueen led his followers into northern Florida, where continued friction led to General Andrew Jackson's invasion (the First Seminole War, 1817-1818).

McRae, Carmen

b. April 8, 1922
New York, N.Y.
d. November 10, 1994
Beverly Hills, Calif.
fields: Music (jazz)

Carmen McRae began her singing career in 1946 with the Benny Carter Orchestra. She is known for her unique approach to bebop. *Carmen Sings Monk* (1990) is widely considered her finest album. In 1994 McRae was honored with a National Endowment for the Arts Fellowship Award for lifetime achievement.

Macready, William Charles

b. March 3, 1793
London, England
d. April 27, 1873
Cheltenham, England
fields: Theater and Entertainment

The mid-nineteenth century's most influential actor-manager, Macready laid the foundations for reform in the theater, helping to forge the modern theater; restored uncorrupted Shakespeare texts to the stage; and gave solid encouragement to the contemporary "new drama."

McReynolds, James C.

full: James Clark McReynolds
b. 1862
d. 1946
fields: Law

U.S. Supreme Court justice, 1914-1941; appointed by President Wilson. Arguably the most reactionary and bigoted, and certainly the least congenial, justice ever to serve on the Supreme Court. Opposed use of individual rights in criminal cases and New Deal regulatory measures. Significant opinions: *Berger v. United States*, 255 U.S. 22 (1921) (dissenting opinion); *Carroll v. United States*, 267 U.S. 132 (1925) (dissenting opinion); *Pierce v. Society of Sisters*, 268 U.S. 510 (1925); *Stromberg v. California*, 283 U.S. 359 (1931) (dissenting opinion); *Powell v. Alabama*, 287 U.S. 45 (1932) (dissenting opinion).

McTell, Blind Willie

b. May 5, 1901
Thomson, Ga.
d. August 19, 1959
Milledgeville, Ga.
fields: Music (blues guitarist)

African American blues musician; in 1927 and 1928, Blind Willie McTell had his strongest recording sessions producing "'Tain't Long fo' Day," "Mr. McTell Got the Blues," "Dark Night Blues," and "Statesboro Blues" with Ralph Peer for Victor; because McTell believed he had to imitate more successful artists, he imitated Blind Willie Johnson; McTell sporadically recorded on various labels during the rest of his career, producing occasional masterpieces such as "Dyin' Crapshooter Blues" and "Broke Down Engine Blues"; McTell also recorded under the names Georgia Bill, Barrelhouse Sammy, Red Hot Willie, and Pig 'n' Whistle; McTell died after drinking heavily and being hospitalized for several strokes; death records and his gravestone mistakenly identify him as Eddie McTier.

McVeigh, Timothy

b. April 23, 1967
Lockport, N.Y.
fields: Law (crime)

Principal suspect in the April 19, 1995, Oklahoma City bombing. A former U.S. Army sergeant and Gulf War veteran, McVeigh was convicted in 1997 of participating in the 1995 bombing of the Oklahoma City Federal Building; the explosion took 169 lives. He was sentenced to death.

McWilliams, Carey

b. December 13, 1905
Steamboat Springs, Colo.
d. June 27, 1980
New York, N.Y.
fields: Journalism, Civil Rights

Carey McWilliams's concern with California's labor and land policies led to his appointment as the state's commissioner of immigration and housing in 1939. His book *Factories in the Field* (1939), described the labor conditions of California farmworkers. He also served as president of the Committee for the Protection of the Foreign Born, which was formed to block passage of antilabor bills in Congress. In 1943 he formed a defense committee to assist Mexican Americans convicted in the Sleepy Lagoon case. His novel *Brothers Under the Skin* (1943) called for a "new federal civil rights statute." He served as West Coast contributing editor for *The Nation* magazine beginning in 1945 and became managing editor in 1951. Four years later he was named editor.

Macy, Anne Sullivan

né: Anne Mansfield Sullivan
b. April 14, 1866
Feeding Hills, Massachusetts
d. October 20, 1936
Forest Hills, Long Island
fields: Education

Macy was Helen Keller's teacher and lifelong companion until Macy's death.

Maddox, Lester

full: Lester Garfield Maddox
b. September 30, 1915
Atlanta, Georgia
fields: Government and Politics

Segregationist, restaurant owner, and governor of Georgia from 1967 to 1971, Lester Maddox gained national notoriety by defying the Civil Rights Act of 1964, brandishing a pickax handle at demonstrators in front of his Pickrick restaurant. After losing several suits in federal court, Maddox closed his restaurant rather than serve African American customers. He claimed that his stance was motivated not by racism but by states' rights, free enterprise, and Christianity. In 1966, he parlayed his notoriety into victory in the race for governor. His policies proved surprisingly progressive: He increased funding for education and appointed African Americans to state offices. Maddox was elected lieutenant governor in 1970 but lost a second bid for the governorship in 1974.

Madero, Francisco

full: Francisco Indalécio Madero
b. October 30, 1873
Parras, Coahuila, Mexico
d. February 22, 1913
Mexico City, Mexico
fields: Government and Politics

Madero ushered in the first phase of the Mexican Revolution of 1910. Through his book, political organizing, and his campaign of opposition, he provided the leadership for the opposition to the dictator Porfirio Díaz. When Díaz fell, Madero became the president of Mexico.

Madhubuti, Haki R.

né: Don L. Lee
b. February 23, 1942
Little Rock, Ark.
fields: Literature

African American writer, cultural critic, and educator; Haki R. Madhubuti is a poet concerned with social and political change. His works include *Think Black* (1967), *Don't Cry, Scream* (1969), and *Dynamite Voices: Black Poets of the 1960's* (1971). In 1967 Madhubuti founded the Third World Press, and in 1969, he founded the Institute of Positive Education in Chicago, Ill., which saught to empower through education.

Madikizela, Nomzamo Winifred. *See* Mandela, Winnie

Madison, Dolley

né: Dolley Payne
b. May 20, 1768
Guilford County, North Carolina
d. July 12, 1849
Washington, D.C.
fields: Government and Politics

First Lady Dolley Madison's popularity and social acumen made her a political asset to President James Madison. The leading social figure in the capital city for years, she was arguably the most beloved and important woman of her times and later became a role model for many First Ladies in the United States.

Madison, James

full: James Madison, Jr.
b. March 16, 1751
Port Conway, Virginia
d. June 28, 1836
Montpelier, Virginia
fields: Government and Politics

Madison was the primary architect of the United States Constitution and the fourth President of the United States (1809-1817).

Madonna

né: Madonna Louise Veronica Ciccone
b. August 16, 1958
Bay City, Michigan
fields: Music (pop)

Madonna released her first album, *Madonna*, in 1983. Her next album, *Like a Virgin* (1984), sold seventeen million copies in the United States and another fifteen million worldwide. The albums *True Blue* (1986), *Who's That Girl* (1987, soundtrack), *You Can Dance* (1987, compilation), and *Like a Prayer* (1989) followed. In the early 1990's Madonna released the provocative video "Justify My Love" (1990), which even MTV refused to air. In 1992 the critically acclaimed album *Erotica* was released simultaneously with a critically panned book of erotic photographs of Madonna simply entitled *Sex* (1992). *Bedtime Stories* was released in 1994, followed by *Something to Remember* (1995, compilition) and *Ray of Light* (1998). She also appeared in the films *Desperately Seeking Susan* (1985), *Truth or Dare* (1991), *Shadows and Fog* (1992), *A League of Their Own* (1992), and *Evita* (1996).

Maecenas, Gaius

full: Gaius Maecenas Cilnius
b. April 13, c. 70 B.C.E.
probably Arretium
d. September 30, 8 B.C.E.
Rome
fields: Literature, Government and Politics

Maecenas was one of the most powerful men in Rome of the first century B.C.E., often functioning as diplomatic arbiter and city administrator. His most significant role was as patron to a circle of writers who became known as the poets of the Golden Age of Latin literature.

Magellan, Ferdinand

b. 1480
northern province of Minho, Portugal
d. April, 1521
Mactan Island, the Philippines
fields: Exploration and Colonization

Magellan was the first person to command an expedition that circumnavigated the earth. While doing so, he discovered the southernmost point of South America (later called the Strait of Magellan), was the first to sail across the Pacific Ocean (which he named), and discovered the Philippine Islands. His feat also proved that the earth is indeed round.

Magón, Ricardo Flores

b. 1873
Mexico
d. November 22, 1922
Leavenworth, Kansas
fields: Government and Politics, Journalism

Ricardo Flores Magón was a politician; journalist; founded the Partido Liberal Mexicano (PLM); attempted to invade Mexico from Texas, 1891-1892; fled to Laredo, Texas, 1904; his newspaper *Regeneracion* advocated the overthrow of Porfirio Díaz in Mexico and labor reform in the United States; jailed for violating neutrality laws, 1907-1910; moved to Los Angeles and launched armed invasion of Baja California upon the outbreak of revolution in Mexico, 1910; imprisoned for espionage, 1918-1922.

Magritte, René

full: René François Ghislain Magritte
b. November 21, 1898
Lessines, Belgium
d. August 15, 1967
Brussels, Belgium
fields: Art

Magritte was the most prominent Belgian associated with the modern art movement known as Surrealism. While his concept of the art of painting increasingly diverged from Surrealist theory, the integrity and fascination of his large body of work won for him an extended and devoted audience in the latter part of his career.

Magsaysay, Ramón

b. August 31, 1907
Iba, Philippines
d. March 17, 1957
near Cebu, Philippines
fields: Government and Politics

Ramón Magsaysay was president of the Philippines from 1953 to 1957. A popular leader but unable to institute much-needed reforms. Close ties to U.S., including assistance from CIA.

Magu. *See* Luján, Gilbert Sánchez

Mahathir bin Mohamad, Datuk Seri

b. December 20, 1925
Alor Setar, Kedah, Malaya (now in Malaysia)
fields: Government and Politics

Datuk Seri Mahathir bin Mohamad took office as prime minister of Malaysia in 1981. Generally managed to keep both Chinese and Malay residents satisfied; occasionally resorted to suppression of opponents. Contended with severe currency crisis in 1997.

Mahesh Yogi, Maharishi

né: Mahesh Prasad Varma?
b. October 18, c.1911
Madhya Pradesh, India
fields: Religion and Theology, Philosophy

Maharishi Mahesh Yogi introduced transcendental meditation (TM), a simple form of mantra meditation, to the West. He became the most successful meditation teacher in history through personal charisma, celebrity endorsements, skillful presentation, and fortuitous timing. To propagate his teachings, the Maharishi formed the Spiritual Regeneration Movement, the Students' International Meditation Society, the Maharishi European Research University, and Maharishi International University in Fairfield, Iowa.

Mahfouz, Naguib

b. December 11, 1911
Cairo, Egypt
fields: Literature, Social Reform, Government and Politics

Mahfouz is Egypt's foremost writer and the premier man of letters for the entire Arabic-speaking world. He began publishing in 1939, and his literary output since then can only be described as astounding. In recognition of his contribution to world literature, Mahfouz was awarded the 1988 Nobel Prize in Literature, becoming the first Arab writer to be so honored.

Mahkato. *See* Mankato

Mahler, Gustav

b. July 7, 1860
Kalischt, Bohemia, Austrian Empire
d. May 18, 1911
Vienna, Austria
fields: Music

Mahler had parallel careers as conductor and composer, in each of which he was regarded by many of his contemporaries as the leading musical figure of his generation. His ten symphonies and other varied compositions represent the culmination of romanticism and the beginnings of modern music.

Mahoney, Charles H.

b. March 29, 1886
Decatur, Mich.
d. January 29, 1966
Detroit, Mich.
fields: Government and Politics

African American diplomat and political appointee; After a thirty year career s an attorney in Michigan, Charles H. Mahoney was appointed as delegate to the United Nations by President Dwight Eisenhower; he served from 1954 to 1959.

Mahoney, Mary Eliza

b. May 7, 1845
Dorchester, Mass.
d. January 4, 1926
Boston, Mass.
fields: Nursing

African American professional nurse; Mary Eliza Mahoney, who was graduated in 1879 from the nursing program of the New England Hospital for Women and Children, was the first black professional nurse in America; admitted to the American Nurses' Association (ASA) nursing Hall of Fame in 1976.

Mahthela. *See* Spybuck, Ernest

Mahtoiowa. *See* Conquering Bear

Mailer, Norman

full: Norman Kingsley Mailer
b. January 31, 1923
Long Branch, New Jersey
fields: Literature

One of the most controversial literary figure of his generation, Mailer redefined the art of literary journalism and became one of the most prominent and unpredictable novelists and social critics in the United States.

Maimonides, Moses

b. March 30, 1135
Córdoba, Spain
d. December 13, 1204
Cairo, Egypt
fields: Religion and Theology, Philosophy, Medicine

Through his classification of Jewish law, life, and observance, as defined in the Torah, Mishnah, and Talmud, and his further interpretation of the philosophical bases of Judaism in the light of Aristotelian thought, Maimonides influenced Jewish and Christian scholarship and trends, an influence which continues to the present. His work combining psychology and medicine may be interpreted as one of the early foundations of psychotherapy.

Mainor, Dorothy Leigh. *See* Maynor, Dorothy

Major, Clarence

b. December 31, 1936
Atlanta, Ga.
fields: Literature

African American poet, novelist, and essayist; Clarence Major's novels include *Reflex and Bone Structure* (1975), *Painted Turtle: Woman With Guitar* (1988), *Dirty Bird Blues* (1996), and *All-Night Visitors* (1999). His style is experimental with unorthodox use of syntax, narrative structure, and characterization.

Major, John

full: John Roy Major
b. March 29, 1943
London, England
fields: Government and Politics

After a rapid rise through the ranks of the Conservative Party, John Major succeeded Margaret Thatcher as prime minister of England in November, 1990, and through quiet but pragmatic leadership, kept the party in power for another seven years.

Makarios III

né: Mikhail Khristodolou Mouskos
b. August 13, 1913
Pano Panayia, Paphos, Cyprus
d. August 3, 1977
Nicosia, Cyprus
fields: Government and Politics

First president of Republic of Cyprus, serving from 1959 to 1977. After World War II, Makarios III, as archbishop of Cyprus, became a leader in the struggle for *énosis* (union) with Greece. The island's Turkish population fiercely opposed union. Cyprus became independent after Great Britain, Greece, and Turkey reached an agreement that the country would have a Greek president—Makarios III—and a Turkish vice president. In ensuing years, Makarios struggled to keep Cyprus united, a struggle that was finally lost in 1974.

Ma-ka-tai-me-she-kia-kiak. *See* Black Hawk

Makhpíya-Lúta. *See* Red Cloud

Makino, Fred Kinzaburo

full: Frederick Kinzaburo Makino
b. Aug. 28, 1877
Yokohama, Japan
d. Feb. 17, 1953
Honolulu, Territory of Hawaii
fields: Publisher, Civil Rights

Japanese Hawiian publisher, community leader; Fred Kinzaburo Makino was born in Japan to an English merchant and a Japanese woman; sent to Hawaii in 1899, where he opened a drugstore; played a key role in the Higher Wage Association and the plantation strike of 1909; started the newspaper *Hawaii Hochi* in 1912 in support of Japanese laborers; fought against restrictions on Japanese-language schools in Hawaii.

Mako

né: Makoto Iwamatsu
b. December 10, 1933
Kobe, Japan
fields: Theater and Entertainment

Mako studied acting at the Pasadena Playhouse, then found work with television shows such as *77 Sunset Strip* and *Hawaiian Eye*. His performance in *The Sand Pebbles* (1966) earned him an Academy Award nomination as Best Supporting Actor. In the 1970's, Mako helped form the East West Players, the first Asian American theater company, which served as a forum for presenting drama written and performed by Asian Americans. Mako appeared in films such as *Testament* (1983), *Conan, the Destroyer* (1984), Philip Kan Gotanda's *The Wash* (1988), *Pacific Heights* (1990), and *Rising Sun* (1993). His performance in the Broadway production of the musical *Pacific Overtures* (1976) earned him a Tony nomination. On February 1, 1994, Mako was honored with a star on the Hollywood Walk of Fame.

Makonnen, Tafari. *See* Haile Selassie I

Malamud, Bernard

b. April 26, 1914
Brooklyn, New York
d. March 18, 1986
New York, New York
fields: Literature

Bernard Malamud was a writer who frequently examined the moral strength of Judaism in urban environments; won Pulitzer Prize for fiction for *The Fixer* (1966); on faculty of Oregon State University, 1949-1961, and Bennington College, 1961-1986; also wrote *The Magic Barrel* (1958), *The Natural* (1952), *The Tenants* (1971), *Dubin's Lives* (1979).

Malchus. *See* Porphyry

Malcolm X

né: Malcolm Little
b. May 19, 1925
Omaha, Nebraska
d. February 21, 1965
New York, New York
fields: Civil Rights, Social Reform

Born Malcolm Little, Malcolm X rose from life as a criminal hustler to become the national minister of the Nation of Islam and a popularizer of black nationalism, which emphasized self-defense for African Americans and independence from white America. Malcolm X's separatism served as a political alternative to Martin Luther King, Jr.'s advocacy of nonviolence and desegregation.

Maldonado-Denis, Manuel

b. 1933
Santurce, Puerto Rico
fields: Education, Historiography

Latino educator and historian. After earning his master's degree and doctorate from the University of Chicago, Manuel Maldonado-Denis began teaching at the University of Puerto Rico in Río Piedras in 1959. In 1972 and 1973, he was professor of Puerto Rican studies at Queens College of the City University of New York. Maldonado-Denis has written several books on the history of Puerto Rico and emigration of Puerto Ricans to the United States.

Malebranche, Nicolas

b. August 6, 1638
Paris, France
d. October 13, 1715
Paris, France
fields: Philosophy

Seventeenth century French philosopher Nicolas Malebranche sought to reconcile René Descartes's mechanistic philosophy with the God-filled universe of Saint Augustine and the Neoplatonists, and he held that one cannot know anything outside oneself except through God. His best-known works are *The Search After Truth* (1674-1675) and *Treatise of Nature and Grace* (1680).

Malenkov, Georgi M.

full: Georgi Maksimilianovich Malenkov
b. January 8, 1902
Orenburg, Russia
d. January 14, 1988
Moscow, U.S.S.R.
fields: Government and Politics

Malenkov was a close associate of Joseph Stalin in his bloody terror against the Communist Party of the Soviet Union and Soviet society in general. In 1953, he was Stalin's immediate successor as prime minister of the government and first secretary of the Communist Party, positions that he soon lost in the power struggle with Nikita S. Khrushchev.

Malone, Jeff

b. June 28, 1961
Mobile, Ala.
fields: Sports (basketball player)

African American basketball player. Named an All-American as a senior at Mississippi State University, in 1983 Jeff Malone was the first-round draft choice of the Washington Bullets of the National Basketball Association (NBA). In his six seasons with the Bullets, Malone was an excellent shooter and a consistent 20-point-per-game scorer. He was traded to the Utah Jazz before the 1990-1991 season. He ended his career with the Miami Heat in 1996.

Malone, Karl

b. July 24, 1963
Summerfield, La.
fields: Sports (basketball player)

African American basketball player. His first season with the Utah Jazz Karl Malone averaged 14.9 points and 8.9 rebounds per game; second season averaged 21.7 points and 10.4 rebounds per game; third year averaged 27.7 points and 12.0 rebounds per game and played in first NBA All-Star Game; 1988-1989 season, averaged 29.1 points-per-game and 10.7 rebounds per game and won most valuable player at the NBA All-Star Game; next year scoring average improved to 31.0 points per game; won a gold medal at the Barcelona Olympics (1992) as member of the U.S. "Dream Team." He was named NBA Most Valuable Player for the season in 1997 and 1999.

Malone, Moses

full: Moses Eugene Malone
b. March 23, 1955
Petersburg, Va.
fields: Sports (basketball player)

African American basketball player; Moses Malone led the NBA in rebounding in 1979, 1981, 1982, 1983, 1984, and 1985; was named the league's Most Valuable Player (1979, 1982, and 1983); was chosen to play in twelve consecutive NBA All-Star Games beginning in 1978; helped lead the 76ers to the 1983 NBA title; was chosen as the Most Valuable Player in the 1983 playoffs. Over his career, he played for nine NBA teams. Malone retired in 1995.

Malone, Vivian

b. 1942
Mobile, Alabama
fields: Civil Rights, Education

Vivian Malone was one of two African American students registering at the University of Alabama in June, 1963, despite Governor George Wallace's strong, personal opposition. She became the first African American to graduate from the university in the riots occurring upon her arrival. Malone completed her degree in personnel management and entertained many job offers after graduation. She worked for the Justice Department, the Veterans Administration Hospital in Atlanta, and the Environmental Protection Agency (EPA) as director of civil rights and urban affairs. She also served as executive director of the Voter Education Project in Atlanta. Malone retired from the EPA in 1996. In that year, she met with former governor Wallace, who apologized for the 1963 confrontation, expressing deep regret over his and others' political actions before awarding Malone the first Lurleen B. Wallace Award of Courage, an award honoring women who made major improvements in the state.

Malory, Thomas

aka: Sir Thomas Malory
b. Early fifteenth century
Warwickshire or Cambridgeshire
d. 1469 or 1471
Cambridgeshire or London
fields: Literature

Combining French prose, Arthurian romances, and some English materials with stories of his own invention, Malory set the Arthurian legend in its enduring form in *Le Morte d'Arthur*.

Malpighi, Marcello

b. Mar. 10, 1628
Baptized in Crevalcore, near Bologna, Papal States (now Italy)
d. Nov. 29, 1694
Rome, Papal States
fields: Medicine, Physiology

Marcello Malpighi found the anatomical connections between the venous and arterial vessels; proved William Harvey's concepts of the circulation; researched the small vessels of the kidneys and of other organs; identified the red cell components of blood.

Malraux, André

full: Georges André Malraux
b. November 3, 1901
Paris, France
d. November 23, 1976
Paris, France
fields: Literature, Government and Politics

Malraux was a multifaceted twentieth century intellectual who had significant accomplishments in three worthy pursuits: As a novelist he produced some of the best fiction written in French during the century; in politics, he functioned successfully as a right-hand man to French President Charles de Gaulle; as an art critic, collector, and theorist, he also made noteworthy advancements.

Malthus, Thomas Robert

b. February 13, 1766
the Rookery, near Dorking, Surrey, England
d. December 23, 1834; Claverton, Bath, England
fields: Economics

The original professor of political economy, Malthus will be forever linked to discussions of the population problem. Terms such as "Malthusian economics" and "neo-Malthusianism" have achieved a permanent place in the English language and suggest the high level of controversy which his work engendered.

Man Who Goes in the Middle. *See* Gall

Manalo, Victoria. *See* Draves, Vickie

Mandela, Nelson

full: Nelson Rolihlahla Mandela
b. July 18, 1918
Mvezo, Umtata district, Transkei, South Africa
fields: Civil Rights, Social Reform

Mandela dedicated his life to the struggle to end racial segregation and white minority rule under the apartheid system in South Africa. His contribution to the political education, mobilization, and organization of millions of people against the apartheid system has been unparalleled. In the 1990's the South African government moved to abolish apartheid, and Mandela was elected president in 1994.

Mandela, Winnie

né: Nomzamo Winifred Madikizela
b. September 26, 1934
Bizana, Transkei, South Africa
fields: Civil Rights

South African anti-apartheid activist and political figure; first wife of Nelson Mandela. In the 1970's and 1980's, Winnie Mandela was first jailed, then forced into internal exile in a remote village. In 1991 sentenced to prison for a 1988-1989 violent incident involving her bodyguards; sentence reduced to a fine. Called before South Africa's Truth and Reconciliation Commission (TRC), maintained her innocence of intimidation charges.

Mandelbrot, Benoit B.

b. November 20, 1924
Warsaw, Poland
fields: Mathematics, Physics

Benoit B. Mandelbrot founded the language of fractal geometry to describe forms of nature that are not made up of straight lines, circles, or smooth curves. In 1982 he published *The Fractal Geometry of Nature*.

Manet, Édouard

b. January 23, 1832
Paris, France
d. April 30, 1883
Paris, France
fields: Art

In a relatively short career of just over twenty years, Manet challenged the conventions of European art by creating a body of paintings, drawings, and etchings manifesting novel approaches both to form and to content. His works and his career were the focal points of the struggle for artistic independence waged by a generation of French artists and writers in the mid-nineteenth century.

Mangas Coloradas

aka: Red Sleeves
aka: Dasoda-hae (He Just Sits There)
b. c. 1791
N.Mex.
d. Jan. 19, 1863
fields: Warfare and Conquest, Native American Affairs

An Apache, Mangas Coloradas was an important war chief during the era of the so-called Apache Wars. Father-in-law of Cochise. A leader in the guerrilla warfare waged by the Apaches against the Mexicans. Toward the end of his life, Americans replaced Mexicans as his adversaries.

Mangopeomen. *See* Opechancanough

Mani

b. April 14, 216 C.E.
near Ctesiphon, Babylonia
d. c. February, 277 C.E.
Gundeshapur, Susiana
fields: Religion and Theology

Mani was a Persian religious visionary and founder of Manichaeism. According to Manichaean tradition, in 240 C.E. he was instructed by angelic command to proclaim the true faith. His message spread throughout the Persian realm, with the support of the royal family. However, after Shapur I died in 272 C.E., the Zoroastrian clergy was successful in curtailing Manichaean proselytizing. Mani was charged with converting a Persian notable, convicted, imprisoned, and tortured.

Mankato

aka: Mahkato (Blue Earth)
b. c. 1830
near present-day Minneapolis, Minn.
d. Sept. 23, 1862
Wood Lake, Minn.
fields: Warfare and Conquest, Native American Affairs

A Santee Sioux leader, Mankato was (with Little Crow) a leader of the Minnesota Uprising of 1862, an event which marked the end of the Indian wars in Minnesota. Killed in the Battle of Wood Lake on September 23, struck by a cannonball.

Mankiller, Wilma P.

full: Wilma Pearl Mankiller
b. November 18, 1945
Tahlequah, Oklahoma

fields: Government and Politics

By becoming the first woman to be the principal chief of the Cherokee Nation, or of any major American Indian tribe, Wilma Mankiller renewed a long tradition of female leadership in Cherokee affairs.

Manlapit, Pablo

b. Jan. 17, 1891
Lipa, Butangas, Luzon, Philippines
d. 1969
Philippines
fields: Labor Movement

Pablo Manlapit migrated from the Philippines to Hawaii as a plantation laborer in 1910; founded Filipino Federation of Labor in 1911 and Filipino Unemployed Association in 1913; helped organize sugar strikes of plantation workers in Hawaii in 1920 and 1924, the first major strike involving workers of multiple ethnic groups; convicted in 1924 following strike violence but paroled in 1927 with the requirement of leaving Hawaii; organized Filipino workers in California, 1927-1932; forced to return to the Philippines in 1934.

Manley, Michael

full: Michael Norman Manley
b. December 10, 1924
St. Andrew, Jamaica
d. March 6, 1997
St. Andrew, Jamaica
fields: Government and Politics

Michael Manley was prime minister of Jamaica from 1972 to 1980 and again from 1989 to 1992. Democratic socialist. Established nonaligned foreign policy; maintained close ties with Cuba.

Mann, Horace

b. May 4, 1796
Franklin, Massachusetts
d. August 2, 1859
Yellow Springs, Ohio
fields: Education, Government and Politics, Social Reform

As legislator and educator, Mann initiated the first state mental hospital and the first comprehensive system of public education in the United States.

Mann, Sally

b. 1951
Lexington, Virginia
fields: Photography

An American photographer, Sally Mann is noted for her photographs of her own nude children. Her pictures contain hints of violence and sexual precocity that have inspired calls for their censorship. Her published photograph collections, such as *Immediate Family* (1992) and *Still Time* (1994), show her children dressing, swimming, sleeping, and lounging—often in tattered clothes or completely nude. Conservative critics have demanded an end to National Endowment for the Arts funding of artists such as Mann.

Mann, Thomas

b. June 6, 1875
Lübeck, Germany
d. August 12, 1955
Zurich, Switzerland
fields: Literature

Mann wrote in the tradition of nineteenth century realism, depending upon depth and breadth of treatment rather than stylistic innovation for his effectiveness. After receiving the Nobel Prize in Literature in 1929, he was widely regarded as a sage as well as a great artist.

Mannas, Jimmie

b. September 15, 1941
Newark, N.J.
fields: Photography, Film

African American photographer and filmmaker; Jimmie Mannas studied at the New York Institute of Photography, the School of Visual Arts, and New York University. In the mid-1960's he had workshops in Brooklyn, Manhattan, and The Bronx. In 1971 he moved to Guyana and served as a film adviser to the country's ministry of information and culture for four years. He then returned to the United States to continue his photography and filmmaking career.

Mannerheim, Carl Gustaf

b. June 4, 1867
Louhisaari, Villnas, near Turku, Finland
d. January 27, 1951
Lausanne, Switzerland
fields: Military Affairs, Government and Politics

Mannerheim dominated the political and military history of Finland from the time Finland became independent in 1917 until his retirement in 1946. He fought in both world wars as a military general. As a political figure, he served as president of his nation during a critical period of the 1940's.

Manning, Henry Edward

b. July 15, 1808
Copped Hall, Totteridge, Hertfordshire, England
d. January 14, 1892
London, England
fields: Religion and Theology, Social Reform

Manning combined a deep Christian faith with an active Christian conscience. As an Anglican cleric he was an avid reformer and the leader of the Oxford Movement. In 1851, Manning converted to the Roman Catholic faith and continued his careers as theologian, reformer, and philanthropist. Manning contributed greatly to the rebirth of Roman Catholicism in England.

Manning, Preston

b. June 10, 1942
Edmonton, Alberta, Canada
fields: Government and Politics

Preston Manning founded the conservative Reform Party of Canada in 1987 and was its leader. In 1993 elections the party surprised many observers by winning fifty-two seats in Parliament. Controversial figure; fundamentalist Christian.

Mannix, Daniel

b. March 4, 1864
Charleville, County Cork, Ireland
d. November 6, 1963
Melbourne, Victoria, Australia
fields: Religion and Theology, Government and Politics

Mannix became the hero of working-class Catholics for his articulate and outspoken views in favor of Ireland and against British and Protestant influences in Australia which he believed threatened their rights to equality and justice.

Mansart, François

full: Nicolas-François Mansart
b. January 23, 1598
Paris, France
d. September 23, 1666
Paris, France
fields: Architecture

Mansart is generally recognized, along with Louis Le Vau, as one of the two greatest French architects of the seventeenth century and is credited with reviving classicism in French architecture while retaining enough vestiges of the prevailing Gothic to produce buildings that were truly unique.

Mansart, Jules Hardouin-

né: Jules Hardouin
b. c. April 16, 1646
Paris, France
d. May 11, 1708
Marly-le-Roi, France
fields: Architecture

Hardouin-Mansart contributed extensively to French architecture and city planning in the reign of Louis XIV, especially in designing and in altering the huge complex of Versailles Palace and its environs. His further legacy included his training of other architects, sculptors, stonecutters, Gobelin tapestry weavers, porcelain specialists, and crystal cutters. From his architectural achievements, a more beautiful Paris and Versailles emerged.

Mansfield, Arabella

né: Bella Aurelia Babb
b. May 23, 1846
Sperry Station, near Burlington, Iowa
d. Aug. 2, 1911
Aurora, Ill.
fields: Law, Women's Rights

Arts professor, suffragist, and, in 1869, the first woman to be admitted to the bar in the United States; Arabella Mansfield earned her law degree but did not practice; was active in establishing the Iowa Woman Suffrage Society.

Mansfield, first earl of

né: William Murray
b. March 2, 1705
Scone, Perthshire, Scotland
d. March 20, 1793
London, England
fields: Law

As Chief Justice of the Court of King's Bench, Mansfield made many reforms in procedure and substantive law, virtually initiated the creation of a code of commercial law, and developed an attitude toward judgment consistent with a changing world.

Mantegna, Andrea

b. c. 1431
Isola di Cartura, Republic of Venice
d. September 13, 1506
Mantua
fields: Art

Mantegna contributed to the growth of Renaissance art in northern Italy while at the same time creating an individual style appreciated for its powers of invention, directness of presentation, illusionism, and detailed realism. His most important contributions were centered in his roles as transmitter of the Florentine Renaissance to his northern Italian contemporaries and as artistic interpreter of antiquity for his own and succeeding generations.

Mantle, Mickey

full: Mickey Charles Mantle
b. October 20, 1931
Spavinaw, Oklahoma
d. August 13, 1995
Dallas, Texas
fields: Sports (baseball)

One of the greatest major league baseball players of all time, Mickey Mantle retired after the 1968 season with numerous records and honors. A member of the New York Yankees known for his long home runs, Mantle won a triple crown in 1956 and Most Valuable Player awards in 1956 and 1957. He led the American League in homers in 1960 and batting over .300 the next four years. He challenged Babe Ruth's single-season homer record in 1961, won Most Valuable Player honors in 1962, and played in the World Series from 1960 to 1964. Injuries, alcohol abuse, and age combined to erode his skills after 1964, culminating in his retirement after the 1968 season. Among the records he set were most homers by a switch-hitter (536), most World Series homers (18), and most games played by a Yankee (2,401). In 1974, he was inducted into the National Baseball Hall of Fame. In 1994, he was diagnosed as suffering from a variety of liver ailments; although he received a controversial transplant, he died shortly thereafter.

Manuel I

aka: Manuel the Fortunate
b. May 31, 1469
Alcochete, Portugal
d. December 13, 1521
Lisbon, Portugal
fields: Monarchy

King of Portugal, 1495-1521. Manuel I, known as "the Fortunate," is considered one of Portugal's most illustrious monarchs. His reign represents the zenith of Portuguese imperial strength. Continuing the centralizing trends and overseas expansion policies of his predecessors, Manuel brought both to a climax, while presiding over a court remarkable for its splendor.

Manuel, George

b. February 17, 1921
Chase, British Columbia, Canada
d. 1989
fields: Native American Affairs, Civil Rights

George Manuel was a Shuswap tribal leader and civil rights activist; born in a Shuswap village in southern British Columbia; organized tribes in British Columbia in protest of the Canadian government's decision to stop payment for medical service to native Canadians; formed Aboriginal Native Rights Committee of the Interior Tribes in 1958; president, National Indian Brotherhood, 1970-1976; president of Union of British Columbian Indian Chiefs, 1977-1981, president of World Council of Indigenous Peoples in 1975 and 1981; wrote *The Fourth World* (1974).

Manuel, Herschel Thurman

b. Dec. 24, 1887
Freetown, Ind.
d. Mar. 21, 1976
Austin, Tex.
fields: Education, Psychiatry and Psychology

Educational psychologist. Herschel Thurman Manuel taught at Western State College in Colorado from 1919 to 1925 and at the University of Texas at Austin from 1925 to 1976. He researched problems faced by Spanish-speaking children in English-speaking environments, as well as issues related to bilingual education and testing. He wrote *The Education of Mexican and Spanish-Speaking Children in Texas* (1930) and *Spanish-Speaking Children of the Southwest: Their Education and the Public Welfare* (1965).

Manuelito

aka: Hastin Ch'ilhajinii (Man of the Black Weeds)
aka: Hashkeh Naabah (Angry Warrior)
aka: Pistol Bullet
b. c. 1818
near Bears Ears Peak, Utah
d. 1894
Navajo Reservation, N.Mex.
fields: Native American Affairs, Warfare and Conquest

Navajo resistance leader; a leader in the Navajo War of 1863-1866, which resulted in the Long Walk to Bosque Redondo, Manuelito was one of the last Navajo leaders to surrender; in September, 1866, he led twenty-three starving warriors to join the other Navajo at Bosque Redondo, where many died from disease and lack of food; Manuelito was one of the delegates who went to Washington in 1876 and secured a reservation of 3.5 million acres; in 1872 he became the commander of the new Navajo police.

Manzoni, Alessandro

b. March 7, 1785
Milan, Lombardy
d. May 22, 1873
Milan, Italy
fields: Literature

Among his writings in various genres, Manzoni authored the great Romantic historical novel *The Betrothed*, an acknowledged world masterpiece and much-beloved expression of Italian culture that contributed to the unification of Italy and to the Italian language.

Mao Zedong

aka: Mao Tse-tung
b. December 26, 1893
Shaoshan, Hunan Province, China
d. September 9, 1976
Peking, China
fields: Military Affairs, Government and Politics

Mao, Chairman of the Chinese Communist Party, led the People's Liberation Army to victory over the Chinese government headed by Chiang Kai-shek, leader of the Kuomintang, or Nationalist Party; established the People's Republic of China; and was the key figure in both party and government during most of his remaining years. He also adapted Marxist-Leninist theory and practice to Chinese conditions and, in effect, created a new doctrine that he later viewed as valid on a world scale.

Mapplethorpe, Robert

b. November 4, 1946
New York, New York
b. March 9, 1989
Boston, Massachusetts
fields: Photography

Robert Mapplethorpe gained notoriety during the 1970's for his homoerotic photographs exploring New York's gay subculture. His images included portraits and still-life work—particularly flower studies, in addition to homoerotic work. Some critics considered him to be the finest studio photographer of his generation. In 1988 controversy surrounding a traveling exhibition of Mapplethorpe's work spurred debate about the use of government funds to support art and led to changes in the granting process of the National Endowment for the Arts (NEA). He died of AIDS in 1989.

Maqui-banasha. *See* Young Bear

Marable, Manning

b. May 13, 1950
Dayton, Ohio
fields: Education, Literature

African American educator and author; Manning Marable's writings include *From the Grassroots: Essays Toward Afro-American Liberation* (1980), *How Capitalism Underdeveloped Black America: Problems in Race, Political Economy, and Society* (1983), and *Race, Reform and Rebellion: The Second Reconstruction in Black America, 1945-1990* (1991). He has taught at Tuskegee Institute (1976), the Africana Studies and Research Center at Cornell University (1979), and Fisk University (1982).

Marat, Jean-Paul

b. May 24, 1743
Boudry, Switzerland
d. July 13, 1793
Paris, France
fields: Journalism, Government and Politics

As a revolutionary journalist and a deputy to the National Convention, Marat was notorious for his support of popular violence and his advocacy of dictatorship.

Marble, Alice

b. September 28, 1913
Beckwourth, California
d. December 13, 1990
Palm Springs, California
fields: Sports (tennis)

Alice Marble was the foremost woman tennis player in the United States between 1936 and 1945. Her style of play and her lifestyle helped change the image of the female sports star.

Marbury, Anne. *See* Hutchinson, Anne

Marc, Franz

b. February 8, 1880
Munich, Germany
d. March 4, 1916
near Verdun, France
fields: Art

Known for symbolic paintings of horses and other animals and as a founder of the Blue Rider group of German expressionist artists, Marc contributed to the development of modern abstract art.

Marcel, Gabriel

b. December 7, 1889
Paris, France
d. October 8, 1973
Paris, France
fields: Philosophy, Literature

Marcel was a major figure in the mid-twentieth century development of French philosophy, as well as a significant dramatist. He was the first French thinker to explore phenomenological and existential themes in depth and, along with Maurice Merleau-Ponty, Jean-Paul Sartre, and Albert Camus, became a key influence on the post-World War II French intellectual scene.

Marchbanks, Vance Hunter

b. 1905
Fort Washikie, Wyo.
d. 1973
fields: Aviation and Space Exploration; Military Affairs

African American physician and military officer; Vance Hunter Marchbanks joined the Air Force in 1941 as a member of the Tuskegee Airmen; awarded the Bronze Star during World War II; achieved the rank of colonel and the rating of chief flight surgeon; contributed to the Air Force's understanding of flight fatigue; assigned to the National Aeronautics and Space Administration (NASA) as part of its Project Mercury program from 1960 to 1963; was responsible for tracking astronouat John Glenn's sensory responses during the 1962 orbital mission of *Friendship 7*.

Marciano, Rocky

né: Rocco Francis Marchegiano
b. Sept. 1, 1923
Brockton, Massachusetts
d. August 31, 1969
near Newton, Iowa
fields: Sports (boxing)

Marciano retired as the only undefeated heavyweight champion in boxing history. The son of poor Italian immigrants, he dignified the legendary belt and brought great pride to the Italian American community.

Marconi, Guglielmo

b. April 25, 1874
Bologna, Italy
d. July 20, 1937
Rome, Italy
fields: Invention and Technology

Marconi, who shared the 1909 Nobel Prize in Physics with Karl Ferdinand Braun, was recognized for his pioneering work in physics that led to the invention of devices for sending signals wirelessly, thereby revolutionizing telegraphic and radio transmission over long distances.

Marcos, Ferdinand

full: Ferdinand Edralin Marcos
b. September 11, 1917
Sarrat, Philippines
d. September 28, 1989
Honolulu, Hawaii
fields: Government and Politics

Marcos was regarded in the 1960's as a reformer dealing with long-standing national problems, such as corruption, smuggling, and poverty. Marcos was regarded throughout the 1960's as a staunch American ally, even sending Philippine troops to fight in Vietnam. His increasingly autocratic style of governing from 1972 onward, combined with his family's extravagant corruption, began to erode his popularity to the point at which he had to flee the country in February, 1986.

Marcus Aurelius

né: Marcus Aurelius Verus
full: Marcus Aurelius Antoninus
b. April 26, 121
Rome
d. March 17, 180
Sirmium or Vindobona (modern Vienna)
fields: Government and Politics, Literature

Although renowned as the last of Rome's "good emperors," Marcus Aurelius is best remembered for the *Meditations*. These simply written private notes reflect the emperor's daily efforts to achieve the Platonic ideal of the philosopher-king and are the last great literary statement of Stoicism.

Marcuse, Herbert

b. July 19, 1898
Berlin, Germany
d. July 29, 1979
Starnberg, West Germany
fields: Philosophy

Herbert Marcuse had a political philosophy that was a synthesis of the ideas of Karl

Marx, Sigmund Freud, and G. W. F. Hegel. His books, such as *Eros and Civilization* (1955) and *One-Dimensional Man* (1964), attacked advanced industrial society as repressive. His *Soviet Marxism* (1958) was hostile to bureaucratic communism. After joining the faculty of the University of California at San Diego, he published a controversial essay, "Repressive Tolerance," which criticized the United States and for disrupting establishment persons. During the 1960's he came under attack for allegedly influencing campus rebellions, and an unsuccessful movement was begun to dislodge him from his teaching position.

Mares, Michael Allen

b. Mar. 11, 1945
Albuquerque, N.Mex
fields: Zoology

Latino Zoologist. Michael Allen Mares earned his Ph.D. in zoology from the University of Texas in 1973. In 1981, he began working as a professor of zoology and as director of the Stovall Museum at the University of Oklahoma at Norman. Mares has researched convergent evolution, adaptation and community organization of desert rodents, and the ecology, conservation, evolution, and systematics of South American mammals. Among his awards have been a Fulbright Residential Fellowship (1974) and a National Chicano Council Fellowship (1978).

Margaret of Denmark, Norway, and Sweden

b. 1353
Søborg, Denmark
d. October 28, 1412
Flensburg, Denmark
fields: Government and Politics, Monarchy

Scandinavian ruler, 1387-1412, named queen in 1389. Margaret was the first ruler to unite Scandinavia (under the Kalmar Union) and the first ruling queen of Denmark, Norway, and Sweden.

Marguerite of Navarre

né: Marguerite D'Angoulême
aka: Margaret of Navarre
b. April 11, 1492
Angoulême, France
d. December 1, 1549
Tarbes, France
fields: Philosophy, Monarchy, Church Reform

Both as a writer herself and as patroness of reformers and poets, Marguerite helped her brother, the king of France, introduce the new humanism into French culture. Her courts, first at Alençon and later in Navarre, were centers where educated women and men could discuss religion, literature, and politics. Marguerite single-handedly invented the *salon*, as it came to be known in the seventeenth century. She was the first society woman of learning—what the eighteenth century would call a "bluestocking."

Mari Brás, Juan

b. Dec. 2, 1927
Mayagüez, Puerto Rico
fields: Government and Politics

Puerto Rican political leader. Juan Mari Brás earned his law degree in 1954 and became a member of the Puerto Rican Bar Association and its Constitutional Law Commission. He also affiliated himself with the Ateneo Puertorriqueño, the oldest cultural institution in Puerto Rico. He later became a leader of the Puerto Rican Socialist Party.

Maria Agustina. *See* Saragossa, La

Maria Theresa

b. May 13, 1717
Vienna, Austria
d. November 29, 1780
Vienna, Austria
fields: Government and Politics, Monarchy

Queen of Hungary and Bohemia, 1740-1780. Beset by adversity, Maria Theresa proved herself to be the greatest ruler produced by the house of Habsburg. She initiated the reforms which transformed her vast holdings into a unified state and created modern Austria.

Marichal, Juan

full: Juan Antonio Marichal y Sanchez
b. October 20, 1937
Laguna Verde, Dominican Republic
fields: Sports (baseball)

Juan Marichal signed with the San Francisco Giants in 1958. He played two seasons in the minor leagues before he was called up to the Giants to throw a shutout in his first start. He led the National League in victories in 1963 and 1968, in winning percentage in 1966, in earned run average in 1969, and in shutouts in 1965 and 1969. He retired in 1975 with a career record of 243-142. He was inducted into the National Baseball Hall of Fame in 1983.

Marie-Antoinette

full: Marie-Antoinette-Josèphe-Jeanne D'Autriche-Lorraine
aka: Maria Antonia Josepha Joanna von Österreich-Lothringen
b. November 2, 1755
Vienna, Austria
d. October 16, 1793
Paris, France
fields: Government and Politics, Monarchy

Marie-Antoinette, through her exaggerated public image as a frivolous and extravagant woman, did much to undermine popular respect for the French monarchy. As queen of France (1774-1793), she opposed the revolutionary movement at every turn.

Marie de France

b. c. 1150
Île de France
d. c. 1215
probably England
fields: Literature

The earliest known French woman poet, Marie de France is still admired for her narrative and poetic skill and for her psychological insight.

Marín, Cheech

full: Richard Marín
b. July 13, 1946
Los Angeles, Calif.
fields: Theater and Entertainment (comedian and actor), Film, Television

Latino comedian and actor. Cheech Marín began his comedy work in partnership with Tommy Chong. As Cheech and Chong, the pair released several comedy albums and made such films as *Up in Smoke* (1978), *Cheech and Chong's Nice Dreams* (1981), and *Still Smokin'* (1983). Marín also acted in the films *It Came from Hollywood* (1982), *Yellowbeard* (1983), *Echo Park* (1986), *Ghostbusters II* (1989), *Rude Awakening* (1989), and *The Shrimp on the Barbie* (1990). He wrote, directed, and starred in the hit comedy *Born in East L.A.* (1987). In the 1990's he starred opposite Don Johnson in the television series *Nash Bridges*.

Marino, Eugene Antonio

b. May 29, 1934
Biloxi, Miss.
fields: Religion and Theology

African American religious leader; Eugene Antonio Marino was ordained priest of the Roman Catholic church in 1962; elected the vicar general of the Josephite Fathers in 1971; became one of three auxiliary bishops of the Catholic archdiocese of Washington, D.C., and the secretary of the National Council of Catholic Bishops in the United States; appointed to the seat of archbishop of Atlanta, Ga. (1988); the first African American to become a Roman Catholic archbishop in the United States; resigned from his position of archbishop of Atlanta in 1990.

Marion, Frances

full: Frances Marion Owens
b. November 18, 1887
San Francisco, California

d. May 12, 1973
Los Angeles, California
fields: Film

Described by *The New York Times* as "the dean of Hollywood screenwriters," Frances Marion helped forge the narrative conventions of the classic American cinema.

Mariotte, Edme

b. 1620
near Dijon, France
d. May 12, 1684
Paris, France
fields: Botany, Science, Physics, Physiology

Edme Mariotte determined the laws of impact of elastic collisions in 1673; connected barometric pressure to winds and the weather; proposed laws for the flow of fluids through pipes; examined human vision and the eye's blind spot; studied the color of rainbows and the movement of sap in plants.

Maris, Roger

full: Roger Eugene Maris
b. September 10, 1934
Hibbing, Minnesota
d. December 14, 1985
Houston, Texas
fields: Sports (baseball)

A baseball star best known for breaking Babe Ruth's single-season home run record, Roger Maris was voted American League Most Valuable Player in 1960 and 1961. Making his major league debut with the Cleveland Indians in 1957, he was traded to the Kansas City Athletics; two seasons later, the Athletics traded him to the New York Yankees. A slugging left-handed outfielder, Maris won the first of his consecutive Most Valuable Player awards in his first season with the Yankees, hitting thirty-nine home runs and driving in 112 runs for the league champions. In 1961, he entered the final day of the season tied with Babe Ruth for 60 season home runs. On October 1, 1961, Maris broke the record with a fourth-inning home run off Tracy Stallard of the Boston Red Sox. Maris played five more seasons with the Yankees and two with the St. Louis Cardinals before retiring from baseball following the 1969 season.

Maritain, Jacques

b. November 18, 1882
Paris, France
d. April 28, 1973
Toulouse, France
fields: Religion and Theology, Philosophy

Perhaps the most influential Catholic philosopher of the twentieth century, Maritain spearheaded a Catholic revival in France and, more broadly, the revival of philosophical Thomism in Europe and the United States. Although a traditionalist, philosophically speaking, he was one of the century's foremost proponents of Christian democracy, and his work helped pave the way for the reforms of Vatican II in the early 1960's.

Marius, Gaius

b. 157 B.C.E.
Cereatae
d. January 13, 86 B.C.E.
Rome
fields: Warfare and Conquest, Government and Politics

Marius was a successful Roman general whose military innovations created the professional army of the late Roman Republic and early empire. Representing the Popular Party, he was elected consul seven times.

Markham, Pigmeat

full: Dewey Markham
b. (April 18, 1904
Durham, N.C.
d. December 13, 1981
Bronx, N.Y.
fields: Theater and Entertainment (comedian)

African American comedian; Pigmeat Markham got his start in minstrel shows, carnivals, and medicine shows. Best known for the Broadway musical *Hot Rhythm* (1930), he was also the originator of the phrase, "Here come de judge," which was popularized in the 1970's on television's *Rowan and Martin's Laugh-In*, 1968-1973.

Marks, Phoebe Sarah. *See* Ayrton, Hertha Marks

Marlborough, first duke of

né: John Churchill
b. May 26, 1650
Devonshire, England
d. June 16, 1722
Windsor Lodge, Windsor, England
fields: Diplomacy, Military Affairs

Marlborough was a skillful diplomat and a brilliant general whose stunning victories over France in the War of the Spanish Succession established Great Britain as a major power and ended Louis XIV's dreams of French hegemony over Europe.

Marlowe, Christopher

b. February 6, 1564
Canterbury, England
d. May 30, 1593
Deptford, England
fields: Theater and Entertainment, Literature

An author concerned largely with the question of power and how it affects human beings, Marlowe was complex, lyrical, and frequently erotic in both his dramatic and his poetic writing.

Marqués, René

b. Oct. 4, 1919
Arecibo, Puerto Rico
d. Mar. 22, 1979
San Juan, Puerto Rico
fields: Literature

Playwright. René Marqués began writing in 1944 and won a Rockefeller Foundation Fellowship in 1948 to study playwriting in New York City. After returning to Puerto Rico, he started the Teatro Experimental de Ateneo. Among the plays he wrote were *La carreta* (1953; *The Oxcart*, 1969), *El hombre y sus sueños* (1948), *Palm Sunday* (1949), *Otro día nuestro* (1955), *Juan Boto y la dama del occidente* (1956), *Los soles truncos* (1959), *Un niño azul para esa sombra* (1959), and *La muerte no entrará en palacio* (1959).

Márquez, Gabriel García. *See* García Márquez, Gabriel

Marquis, Gail

b. November 18, 1956
New York, N.Y.
fields: Sports (basketball player)

African American basketball player; Gail Marquis was an outstanding collegiate player at Queens College of the City University of New York (CUNY) and a member of the U.S. women's basketball team that won a silver medal at the 1976 Olympic Games in Montreal.

Marr, Carmel Carrington

b. June 23, 1923?
Brooklyn, N.Y.
fields: Government and Politics, Law

African American lawyer, diplomat, and political appointee. During her term as legal adviser to the U.S. Mission to the United Nations in 1953, Carmel Carrington Marr served on a number of key committees in the General Assembly. She served as commissioner on the Human Rights Appeal Board of New York State from 1968 to 1971, Marr and on the New York State Public Service Commission from 1971 to 1986. Marr retired from legal practice in 1990 after working as an energy consultant for four years.

Marrow, Tracey. *See* Ice-T

Marsalis, Branford

b. August 26, 1960
Breaux Bridge, La.
fields: Music (soprano and tenor saxophonist)

African American soprano and tenor saxophonist; Branford Marsalis was part of the 1980's neotraditional jazz movement; influenced by Charlie Parker, Sonny Rollins, and John Coltrane; performed on *Wynton*

Marsalis (1981) and *Black Codes (from the Underground)* (1985); recorded *Decoy* (1983) with Miles Davis and *New Faces* (1984) with Dizzy Gillespie; recorded as leader *Scenes in the City* (1983), *Royal Garden Blues* (1986), and *Romances for Saxophone* (1986); performed with Sting on *Dream of the Blue Turtles* (1985); was chosen music director and arranger for *The Tonight Show with Jay Leno* (1992). He left the show in 1994 to pursue his own creative projects.

Marsalis, Wynton

b. October 18, 1961
New Orleans, La.
fields: Music (jazz trumpeter and composer)

African American jazz trumpeter and composer; Wynton Marsalis first gained national attention through performances with Art Blakey's Jazz Messengers in 1980; toured with musicians Herbie Hancock, Ron Carter, and Tony Williams, with whom he also made his first recordings in 1981; formed a quartet with his brother, saxophonist Branford Marsalis (1982); was the first musician to win Grammy Awards in both the classical and jazz categories; made a commitment to reinvigorate past styles and continue the modernist revolution. Some of the noteworthy albums he released include *Citi Movement* (1992) and *Joe Cool's Blues* (1994).

Marshall, George C.

full: George Catlett Marshall, Jr.
b. December 31, 1880
Uniontown, Pennsylvania
d. October 16, 1959
Washington, D.C.
fields: Government and Politics

General Marshall created the United States Army of World War II, picked the commanders who led it to victory, and exemplified the best in the American military tradition: civilian control, integrity, and competence.

Marshall, Jim

full: James Laurence Marshall
b. December 30, 1937
Danville, Ky.
fields: Sports (football player)

African American football player; Jim Marshall began his professional career with a year in the Canadian Football League in 1959. He then played two years with the Cleveland Browns of the National Football League (NFL), after which he was traded to the Minnesota Vikings. He set an NFL record for the most consecutive games played, 282, and was on the 1969 and 1970 Pro Bowl teams.

Marshall, John

b. September 24, 1755
Germantown (now Midland), Va.
d. July 6, 1835
Philadelphia, Pa.
fields: Law

Chief justice of the United States, 1801-1835. Widely regarded as the greatest chief justice the Supreme Court has ever known, John Marshall was responsible for consolidating the Court's power, making it into an instrument of American federalism. Significant decisions include *Marbury v. Madison* (1803), the Supreme Court's first clear expression of its power of judicial review, and *Dartmouth College v. Woodward* (1819).

Marshall, Paule

b. April 9, 1929
Brooklyn, N.Y.
fields: Literature

African American novelist and short-story writer; Much of Paule Marshall's writing deals with the West Indian African American community and draws on the culture of Barbados and the West Indies. Among her novels are *Brown Girl, Brownstones* (1959), *Praisesong for the Widow* (1983), and *Daughters* (1991).

Marshall, Penny

full: Carole Penny Marshall
b. October 15, 1942
Bronx, New York
fields: Film, Television

Achieving fame as a television actress, Penny Marshall made a successful transition to feature film direction with critically acclaimed hits such as *Big* (1988), *Awakenings* (1990), and *A League of Their Own* (1992).

Marshall, Thurgood

b. July 2, 1908
Baltimore, Maryland
d. January 24, 1993
Bethesda, Maryland
fields: Law

As an advocate and jurist, Marshall has had a sustained commitment to equal justice under the law. He was the lead lawyer of the NAACP and successfully argued *Brown v. Board of Education*, among others, before the Supreme Court; first African American Supreme Court justice, 1967-1991.

Marshall, William

b. August 19, 1924
Gary, Ind.
fields: Theater and Entertainment

African American actor; William Marshall's performance in the 1951 Broadway revival of *The Green Pastures* took him to Hollywood to perform in films such as *Lydia Bailey* (1952) and *Demetrius and the Gladiators* (1954), *The Boston Strangler* (1968), and *Blacula* (1972). His television credits include *Harlem Detectives* (1953-1954), *Othello, Bonanza, Star Trek, The Jeffersons, Frederick Douglass: Slave and Statesman*, and *Pee Wee's Playhouse*.

Martí, José Julián

b. January 28, 1853
Havana, Cuba
b. May 19, 1895
Dos Ríos, Cuba
fields: Government and Politics, Social Reform

By the age of seventeen José Martí was imprisoned for writing a treasonous letter to a friend. After being deported to Spain, he began a career of publicizing the call for Cuban liberty. He wrote and taught in Spain, Mexico, and Guatemala before returning to Cuba with his wife in 1878. Deported again (for conspiracy) in 1879, Martí settled in New York City in 1880, where he translated, taught, and wrote newspaper articles for both Spanish-language and English-language presses throughout the Americas. He retured to Cuba again to fight for Cuban independence in 1895 but died in battle. He was later generally hailed to be Cuba's most important national hero of the nineteenth century.

Martial

b. March 1, c. 40
Bilbilis, Spain
d. c. 104
Spain
fields: Literature

Martial perfected the epigram, the witty, sometimes salacious poem, typically of two to four lines, which points out the moral and social ills of the poet's day or lampoons prominent people.

Martin, Agnes

full: Agnes Bernice Martin
b. March 22, 1912
Maklin, Saskatchewan, Canada
fields: Art

A leading American artist of the style of minimalism in the 1960's and 1970's, Agnes Martin persevered in her commitment to art as a means of spiritual expression to become one of the few women artists of the twentieth century to achieve recognition and success.

Martin, Darnell

b. 1964?
New York, N.Y.
fields: Film

African American filmmaker; with her feature film, *I Like It Like That* (1994),

Darnell Martin became the first African American woman to direct a major studio film.

Martin, Louise

b. January 9, 1915
Brenham, Tex.
fields: Photography

African American photographer. After attending the Art Institute of Chicago, the American School of Photography, and Denver University, Louise Martin opened a portrait studio in Houston, Tex. (1946). She worked as a stringer for two black Houston newspapers, *Forward Times* and *The Informer* and founded the Louise Martin School of Photography (1973-1976).

Martin, Paul

full: Paul Edgar Philippe Martin, Jr.
b. August 28, 1938
Windsor, Ontario, Canada
fields: Government and Politics

Canadian political leader. Liberal Party member of Parliament Paul Martin was appointed minister of finance in 1993. Eliminated annual budget deficit by 1998. Coined the phrase "nationalism without walls."

Martin, Sallie

b. November 20, 1896
Pittfield, Ga.
d. June 18, 1988
Chicago, Ill.
fields: Music (gospel singer)

African American gospel singer; Sallie Martin joined Thomas A. Dorsey's choir at the Ebenezer Baptist Church in 1932 and began a professional relationship with Dorsey that would last more than thirty years. Martin toured singing gospel and organizing choruses. In 1940 she formed the Martin and Morris Publishing Company with Kenneth Morris. Two of their well-known songs are "Just for a Closer Walk with Thee" and "Dig a Little Deeper."

Martin, Tony

b. February 21, 1942
Port-of-Spain, Trinidad and Tobago
fields: Education

African American educator. In 1977 Tony Martin became a full professor at Wellesley College. Prior to that he had taught at St. Mary's College in Trinidad and at the University of Michigan at Flint. He is the author of several books about Marcus Garvey and Garveyism.

Martínez, Al

b. July 21, 1929
Oakland, Calif.
fields: Journalism

Journalist. Al Martínez worked at the *Oakland Tribune* from 1955 to 1971. In 1972, he moved to the *Los Angeles Times* as a feature writer-reporter for the Metro section. He has written several books—including *Rising Voices: Profiles of Hispano-American Lives* (1974), *Dancing Under the Moon* (1992), and *Rising Voices: A New Generation* (1994)—as well as scripts for television and film. Martínez has received numerous journalism awards, including the 1984 Pulitzer Prize Gold Medal for Meritorious Public Services as cowinner for the "Southern California Latino Community" series.

Martínez, Antonio. *See* Popovi Da

Martínez, Antonio José

b. Jan. 7, 1793
Abiquiu, N.Mex.
d. July 28, 1867
Taos, N.Mex.
fields: Religion and Theology

Latino religious figure. Antonio José Martínez, a Catholic priest, served in New Mexico's state legislature between 1830 and 1836. He fought against American influence in the region and may have instigated the Taos Rebellion of 1847. When the United States took over the area, Martínez worked to obtain political and educational benefits for native-born New Mexicans. His resistance to the new bishop's attempt to reintroduce tithing led to his excommunication, but he presided over his church until his death.

Martínez, Bob

full: Robert Martínez
b. Dec. 25, 1934
Tampa, Fla.
fields: Government and Politics

Cuban American educator and politician; Bob Martínez was Tampa's mayor from 1979 to 1986, and was governor of Florida from 1987 to 1991; as governor, led the National Governors Association in its efforts to stem drug trafficking and substance abuse; in 1991, was appointed to serve as director of Drug Control Policy under President Bush.

Martínez, César

b. 1944
Laredo, Tex.
fields: Art

Artist. César Martínez earned a B.A. in art education in 1968. He learned photography while serving in the U.S. Army, then returned to Texas and became involved with a Chicano activist organization called the Texas Institute for Educational Development and a Chicano visual arts group called Con Safos. He also helped found the periodical *Caracol*, serving as photographer, designer, and columnist. Martínez left Con Safos in the mid-1970's to concentrate on his art work and also shifted his concentration away from photography and back to painting.

Martínez, Crescencio

aka: Ta'e (Home of the Elk)
aka: Te E
b. c. 1890
San Ildefonso, N.Mex.
d. June 20, 1918
Santa Fe?, N.Mex.
fields: Art (painter)

A San Ildefonso Pueblo painter, Crescencio Martínez is considered by many to be the father of watercolor painting among Puebloan Indians, leading to the Southwestern school of Indian painting. Crescencio married Maximiliana (Anna) Martínez, sister of potter María Martínez and herself an accomplished potter. Crescencio painted Anna's pots, as well as those of his mother, sister, and sister-in-law. Other relatives were painters Alfonso Roybal, Romando Vigil, and Alfredo Montoya.

Martinez, Dennis

full: Jose Dennis Martinez y Emilia
b. May 14, 1955
Granada, Nicaragua
fields: Sports (baseball player)

Latino baseball player. Pitcher Dennis Martinez, the first Nicaraguan to play major league baseball, began playing with the Baltimore Orioles in 1977. In 1981, he led the American League with fourteen wins. A drinking problem led to his 1986 trade to the Montreal Expos, where he overcame his alcoholism and led the National League with a .733 winning percentage (11-4) in 1987. He was named to the All-Star Team in 1990, 1991, and 1992. On July 28, 1991, he became only the fifteenth pitcher in major league history to pitch a perfect game. At the end of 1993, he signed as a free agent with the Cleveland Indians. He played for the Seattle Mariners in 1997 and for the Atlanta Braves in 1998.

Martínez, Elizabeth

b. Apr. 14, 1943
Pomona, Calif.
fields: Scholarship (librarian)

Latina librarian. Elizabeth Martínez worked as a Los Angeles County Public librarian from 1966 to 1979, then taught at California State University, Fullerton. She helped the school obtain a federal grant for the Institute for Mexican American Librarians. From April, 1979, to June, 1990, Martínez was the county librarian for the Orange County public library system. During her tenure, eight new community libraries were built. In 1990, she became the city librarian for Los Angeles, supervising sixty-three branches in addition to the central library. In August, 1994, she became the executive director of the American Library Association.

Martínez, Julián

b. 1897
San Ildefonso, N.Mex.
d. c. 1943
San Ildefonso, N.Mex.
fields: Art (painter)

A San Ildefonso Pueblo (Tewa) painter, Julián Martínez collaborated with his wife, potter María Antonía Martínez, in making pottery prized by museums and collectors worldwide. After producing polychrome pottery for several years, María and Julián began to experiment with a firing technique which finally resulted in black-on-black ware (c. 1918-1920). Julián developed his two most innovative design elements, the *avanyu* (plumed serpent) and his own adaptation of the prehistoric Mimbres feather design, for use on the black pottery.

Martínez, María Antonía

aka: Poveka (Pond Lily)
b. Apr. 5, 1887
San Ildefonso, N.Mex.
d. July 20, 1980
San Ildefonso, N.Mex.
fields: Art (potter)

A San Ildefonso Pueblo potter, María Martínez revitalized the vanishing art of pottery among Pueblo peoples. Decorating her pots were Crescencio Martínez, her sister Maximiliana, husband Julián, daughter-in-law Santana, and son Popovi Da. In 1921, she and Julián revealed their technique for making black-on-black pottery. In 1923, she initiated the practice of signing her pottery.

Martínez, Vicente. *See* Tizol, Juan

Martínez, Vilma Socorro

b. Born Oct. 17, 1943
San Antonio, Tex.
fields: Civil Rights, Law

A Mexican American attorney, Vilma Socorro Martínez was on the staff of the National Association for the Advancement of Colored People Legal Defense and Educational Fund and worked for a Wall Street firm until she joined the legal staff of the Mexican American Legal Defense and Education Fund (MALDEF) after it formed in 1968. She was its leader from 1972 to 1981. In 1976 she was named to the University of California's Board of Regents.

Martínez-Cañas, María

b. May 19, 1960
Havana, Cuba
fields: Photography

Latino photographer. María Martínez-Cañas earned an undergraduate degree in photography from the Philadelphia College of Art (1982) and an M.F.A. from the School of Art Institute in Chicago, Illinois (1984). She has received several awards, including National Endowment for the Arts, Cintas Foundation, and Fulbright-Hays Fellowships. While Martínez-Cañas has experimented with photographic collages and various processes and materials, she has also taken more traditional photographs that reflect folktales, the culture of Cuba, and Spanish history.

Martínez Ybor, Vicente

b. Sept. 17, 1818
Valencia, Spain
d. Dec. 14, 1896
Tampa, Fla.
fields: Business and Industry

Latino businessman. Vicente Martínez Ybor contributed to the rise and modernization of the tobacco industry in Cuba. In the late 1860's, he supported Cuba's independence movement, then fled to Key West, Florida, in 1869 after Spanish authorities issued an order for his arrest. In 1885, Martínez Ybor moved east of Tampa and founded Ybor City, which, by 1890, had become a flourishing Latino colony and the center of cigar manufacturing in Florida.

Martini, Simone

b. c. 1284
Siena
d. 1344
Avignon, France
fields: Art

Through his innovative painting techniques and sophisticated use of color, Martini expanded on the French Gothic style.

Martorell, Antonio

b. 1939
Santurce, Puerto Rico
fields: Art

Latino artist. Antonio Martorell had several solo and group exhibitions in the early 1960's before founding the Taller Alacrán (scorpion workshop) in 1968. The workshop was established with the goal of training artists to create political graphic art at affordable prices. Martorell's satirical art—such as artworks based on playing cards that he created after the 1968 elections in Puerto Rico—has been acquired by several major museums in Puerto Rico and in the United States.

Martyn, Le Vardis Robert, Jr. *See* Burton, LeVar

Marutani, William

b. 1923
Kent, Wash.
fields: Law

William Marutani became the first Asian American to be named to the bench outside Hawaii or the western United States when he was appointed to the Court of Common Pleas in Philadelphia in 1975. He was interned at Tule Lake during World War II, then served in intelligence with the U.S. Army. He received a law degree from Chicago Law School in 1953.

Marx, Karl

b. May 5, 1818
Trier, Prussia
d. March 14, 1883
London, England
fields: Economics, Philosophy

Marx's ideas concerning modes of economic distribution, social class, and the developmental patterns of history have profoundly influenced theories in philosophical and economic thought and have helped shape the political structure of the modern world.

Mary I

aka: Mary Tudor
aka: Bloody Mary
b. February 18, 1516
Greenwich, England
d. November 17, 1558
London, England
fields: Government and Politics, Monarchy

Queen of England, 1553-1558. Mary was the first woman to rule England in her own right; she also restored Catholicism to her country.

Mary, Queen of Scots

aka: Mary Stuart
b. December 8, 1542
Linlithgow Palace, West Lothian, Scotland
d. February 8, 1587
Fotheringhay Castle, Northamptonshire, England
fields: Government and Politics, Monarchy

Queen of Scotland, 1542-1567. Through the misfortunes of her personal life, Mary precipitated a political and religious struggle in Scotland that ultimately led to her death in England as a Catholic martyr.

Mary Brant. *See* Brant, Molly

Mas Canosa, Jorge L.

b. Sept. 21, 1939
Santiago, Oriente, Cuba

d. Nov. 23, 1997
Miami, Fla.
fields: Social Reform

Latino community leader. Jorge L. Mas Canosa, who was born and educated in Cuba, was an advocate of democracy and the free market system. He was a successful businessman who became an unofficial spokesperson for the Cuban exile community in the United States. In 1993, Mas Canosa, who was an avowed enemy of Fidel Castro, helped Congressman Robert Torricelli of New Jersey pass the Cuban Democracy Act; critics complained that the legislation would cut off medical supplies and food for the impoverished people of Cuba.

Masaccio

né: Tommaso di Giovanni di Simone Guidi
b. December 21, 1401
Castel San Giovanni, Republic of Florence
d. 1428?
Rome
fields: Art

During a brief career, Masaccio became one of the major creators of the new Renaissance style of painting. His innovations utilizing perspective created a standard of realism admired and imitated by subsequent generations of artists.

Masaoka, Mike Masaru

b. Oct. 15, 1915
Fresno, Calif.
d. June 26, 1991
Washington, D.C.
fields: Social Reform, Civil Rights

Japanese American social activist, community leader; Mike Masaru Masaoka raised in Utah, where he became a Mormon; executive secretary of the Japanese American Citizens League, 1941; advised U.S. government on administration of World War II internment camps for Japanese Americans; fought for admission of Nisei (second-generation, U.S.-born Japanese Americans) into American armed forces; as a lobbyist, played a key role in Japanese American Evacuation Claims Act, 1948, and McCarran-Walter Immigration and Naturalization Act, 1952; wrote *They Call Me Moses Masaoka* (1987).

Masaryk, Tomáš

full: Tomáš Garrigue Masaryk
b. March 7, 1850
near Göding, Moravia, Austrian Empire (now Hodonín, Czech Republic)
d. September 14, 1937
Lány, Czechoslovakia
fields: Government and Politics, Philosophy

Masaryk was a professor of philosophy, an author, and a statesman who was the principal founder and first president of Czechoslovakia. He secured the support of the Western liberal powers during World War I for the Czechoslovakian cause and was awarded numerous honors including a D.C.L. from the University of Oxford in 1928.

Masinissa

b. c. 238 B.C.E.
Numidia, Northern Africa
d. 148 B.C.E.
Numidia, Northern Africa
fields: Government and Politics, Warfare and Conquest

Through his alliance with the Roman Republic, Masinissa helped to destroy the realm of Carthage, opening the way to Roman suzerainty over the Mediterranean.

Maslow, Abraham

full: Abraham Harold Maslow
b. April 1, 1908
Brooklyn, N.Y.
d. June 8, 1970
Menlo Park, Calif.
fields: Psychiatry and Psychology

Often called the father of modern humanism, Abraham Harold Maslow developed a theory of motivation and personality He developed a theory of motivation and personality based on his work with normal and creative people. His approach was novel, because it focused on healthy psychology. He also served as president of the American Psychological Association.

Mason, Biddy

full: Bridget Mason
b. August 15, 1818
Hancock County, Ga.?
d. January 15, 1891
Los Angeles, Calif.
fields: Business and Industry

African American community leader and entrepreneur; born a slave, Biddy Mason eventually became a wealthy woman through real-estate investments and an important leader in Los Angeles's African American community; in 1872, helped found the First African Methodist Episcopal (AME) Church in Los Angeles.

Mason, George

b. 1725
Dogue's Neck, Virginia
d. October 7, 1792
Gunston Hall, Virginia
fields: Government and Politics

Author of the Virginia Declaration of Rights, Mason also had a major role in shaping the Virginia constitution of 1776 and the United States Constitution.

Mass, Amy Iwasaki

b. July 5, 1935
fields: Social Reform

After receiving a master's degree in social work in 1958 from the University of Southern California, Amy Iwasaki Mass was a social worker for various agencies throughout Southern California and in San Francisco, then went into private practice as a clinical social worker in 1970. After receiving a Ph.D. in social work from the University of California, Los Angeles, in 1986, she became assistant professor in the Department of Sociology, Anthropology, and Social Work at Whittier College in Southern California. Mass specializes in the experiences of racially mixed individuals in the Asian American community in general and the Japanese American community in particular.

Massasoit

aka: Ousamequin (Yellow Feather)
b. c. 1580
near present-day Bristol, R.I.
d. 1661
near Bristol, R.I.
fields: Government and Politics, Diplomacy, Native American Affairs

Native American leader. A Wampanoag, Massasoit worked to preserve a peaceful relationship with the English colonists from the landing of the *Mayflower* in 1620 to his death in 1661. When the colonists held their first service of thanksgiving in November, 1621, they invited the Wampanoags. Massasoit and about ninety others went, taking with them five deer.

Massatamohtnock. *See* Opechancanough

Massé, Marcel

b. June 23, 1940
Montreal, Quebec, Canada
fields: Government and Politics

Canadian civil servant and Liberal Party politician. Marcel Massé was president of the Canadian International Development Agency; was undersecretary of state for external affairs (1982-1985); represented Canada on the Board of Directors of the International Monetary Fund (1985-1989); again president of Canadian International Development Agency until 1993. Elected to Parliament 1993; posts included presidency of the Treasury Board in late 1990's.

Massey, Vincent

b. February 20, 1887
Toronto, Canada
d. December 30, 1967
London, England
fields: Government and Politics

Massey's career, which culminated in his appointment as the first native-born governor-general in Canadian history, illustrates his constant striving to make Canadian nationalism compatible with continued Canadian ties to Great Britain and the Commonwealth.

Massey, Walter Eugene

b. April 5, 1938
Hattiesburg, Miss.
fields: Science, Physics

Walter Eugene Massey enjoyed a long association with the Argonne National Laboratory at the University of Chicago, serving as staff physicist (1966-1968), consultant (1968-1975), and director (1979-1984) before being named vice president for research in 1984. Massey's work contributed to the understanding of properties of materials at very low temperatures. He was also named president of Morehouse College in 1995.

Massey, William Ferguson

b. March 26, 1856
Limavady, County Londonderry, Ireland
d. May 10, 1925
Wellington, New Zealand
fields: Government and Politics

Massey's tenure as prime minister marked the coming-of-age and domination of the small farmer in New Zealand politics. Steadfastly steering his country through the trials of World War I, he combined conservative social values and fierce anti-Labour attitudes with a continuation of policies based on the intervention of the state to develop New Zealand as a prosperous outlying farm of the British Empire.

Massine, Léonide

né: Leonid Fyodorovich Miassin
b. August 8, 1895
Moscow, Russia
d. March 16, 1979
Cologne, West Germany
fields: Dance

Massine's career as a performer and creator of dance changed the nature of the art. His stage presence and dance style made a powerful impression in Europe and the United States and helped to establish the companies with which he worked as the leading forces in the renewal of ballet. His choreography was especially innovative in its collaboration with music and depth of characterization.

Mastai-Ferretti, Giovanni Maria. *See* Pius IX

Masters, William H.

b. December 27, 1915
Cleveland, Ohio
fields: Sociology

Using scientific equipment, William H. Masters and his wife, Virginia E. Johnson, recorded physiological responses to sexual stimulations in men and women engaging in sexual activity. In 1966 they published the results of a eleven-year research project in the best-selling *Human Sexual Response*. Their other books include *Homosexuality in Perspective* (1979), *Crisis: Heterosexual Behavior in the Age of AIDS* (1988), *The Pleasure Bond: A New Look at Sexuality and Commitment* (1975), and *Textbook of Sexual Medicine* (1979).

Masuda, Minoru

b. Apr. 10, 1915
Seattle, Wash.
fields: Psychiatry and Psychology

Minoru Masuda earned a Ph.D. in physiology from the University of Washington in 1956 and became a professor in the Department of Psychiatry there. He specialized in psychophysiology, a branch of psychology that attempts to explain the correlations between physiological processes and human behavior.

Masʿūdi, al-

full: Abū al-Ḥasan ʿAlī ibn Ḥusan al-Masʿūdi
b. c. 890
probably Baghdad, Iraq
d. 956
al-Fusṭaṭ (Old Cairo), Egypt
fields: Historiography, Geography, Exploration and Colonization

A pioneer Arab historian, geographer, and chronicler, al-Masʿūdi traveled extensively, gathering enormous quantities of information on poorly known lands. His work helped set the tone for future Arabic scholarship; he has been called the Herodotus of the Arabs.

Mata, Eduardo

b. Sept. 5, 1942
Mexico City, Mexico
fields: Music (orchestra conductor and composer)

Orchestra conductor and composer. Eduardo Mata has conducted for the Mexico Ballet Company (1963-1964), the Guadalajara Symphony Orchestra (1964-1966), the Philharmonic Orchestra of the National University of Mexico (1966-1976), the Phoenix Symphony Orchestra (1970), and the Dallas Symphony Orchestra (1977-1993). In 1990, he became principal guest conductor of the Pittsburgh Symphony Orchestra. Mata has also composed symphonies—including Symphony No. 1 "Classical" (1962), Symphony No. 2 "Romantic" (1963), Symphony No. 3 (1966/1967)—ballet music, and chamber works.

Mather, Cotton

b. February 12, 1663
Boston, Massachusetts
d. February 13, 1728
Boston, Massachusetts
fields: Religion and Theology, Scholarship

Devoted to God and to learning, Mather provided a distinctively American perspective to European thought and sought to reconcile New England Puritanism with the intellectual trends of his day.

Mather, Increase

b. June 21, 1639
Dorchester, Massachusetts
d. August 23, 1723
Boston, Massachusetts
fields: Religion and Theology, Education

Maintaining Puritan beliefs in seventeenth century Massachusetts, Mather led the Congregational churches of Boston to continue the status quo and sought to retain American independence from British political control. As president of Harvard College and a renowned writer, he aided in the development of higher education and culture in New England.

Mathis, Johnny

b. September 30, 1935
San Francisco, Calif.
fields: Music

African American singer; Johnny Mathis found success with his first album, *Wonderful, Wonderful* (1956), which sold in the millions, followed by *Chances Are* (1957), *The Twelfth of Never* (1957), and *Misty* (1959). His romantic ballads, rich tenor voice, and unconventional phrasing became very popular. Later in his career, he recorded several popular duet albums including *Too Much, Too Little, Too Late* (1978) with Deniece Williams and *Friends in Love* (1982) with Dionne Warwick.

Matihehlogego. *See* Hollow Horn Bear

Matisse, Henri

full: Henri-Émile-Benoî Matisse
b. December 31, 1869
Le Cateau-Cambrésis, France
d. November 3, 1954
Nice, France
fields: Art

Matisse became the leader of the French expressionists called Les Fauves, or wild beasts. When the artists of that unofficial movement dispersed, he steadfastly and daringly simplified painting to the point of abstract decoration.

Matney, William C., Jr.

b. September 2, 1924
Bluefield, W.Va.
fields: Journalism, Publishing

African American communications professional; William C. Matney, Jr., was managing editor with the *Michigan Chronicle* (1946-1961) and the first black network news correspondent for NBC Network Television (1966-1972). He worked for ABC Network News (1972-1978) and was a founding editor of *Who's Who Among Black Americans* (1974). Matney also worked as a public affairs coordinator for the U.S. Bureau of the Census (1979) and as deputy director of the Census Promotion Office (1989 and 1990).

Mato Tope

aka: Four Bears
b. c. 1795
d. July 30, 1837
fields: Government and Politics, Native American Affairs

There were two Mandan leaders known as Mato Tope, or Four Bears; they were father and son. Mato Tope the elder was born around 1795 and died in 1837; his son, who became chief after his father's death, died in 1861. Mato Tope the elder accused whites of genocide when an epidemic of smallpox decimated his tribe. Smallpox ultimately killed all but thirty-one of some sixteen hundred Mandan people. Mato Tope succumbed to the disease on July 30, 1837.

Mato Watakpe. *See* Grass, John

Matonabbee

b. c. 1736
near Fort Prince of Wales, Hudson Bay, Canada
d. 1782
Fort Prince of Wales, Hudson Bay, Canada
fields: Exploration and Colonization

A Chipewyan Indian, Matonabbee was a guide for the Hudson's Bay Company. He led the third Coppermine expedition in search of precious metals and the Northwest Passage in 1771-1772.

Matos Paoli, Francisco

b. Mar. 9, 1915
Lares, Puerto Rico
fields: Literature, Government and Politics

Poet and political activist. Although Francisco Matos Paoli taught at the University of Puerto Rico, he spent much of his time writing poetry and serving as secretary for the Puerto Rican Nationalist Party. He was imprisoned for five years for his political activism. He wrote several books of prize-winning poetry, including *Canto a Puerto Rico* (1952, canto to Puerto Rico), *Habitante del eco, 1937-41* (inhabitant of the echo), and *Canto a la locura* (1962; canto to madness).

Matsuda, Fujio

b. Oct. 18, 1924
Honolulu, Territory of Hawaii
fields: Engineering, Science, Education

Fuji Matsuda received a D.Sc. from the Massachusetts Institute of Technology (MIT) in 1952. He specialized in the response of structures to nuclear explosions and participated in tests conducted in Nevada and the Pacific Islands. He taught at the University of Illinois, Urbana, then the University of Hawaii, where he was department chair of the Civil Engineering Department. From 1963 to 1973, Matsuda headed the Hawaii State Department of Transportation. His administration's projects include the Interstate and Defense Highway system, the Honolulu Harbor acquisition and consolidation, and the Honolulu International Airport expansion. He became president of the University of Hawaii in 1974 and in 1984 became executive director of the Research Corporation of the University of Hawaii.

Matsuda, Mari

b. Apr. 8, 1956
Los Angeles, Calif.
fields: Law

A professor at Georgetown University School of Law, Mari Matsuda became known as an advocate of critical legal studied. She argued that the First Amendment right of free speech must be balanced with other constitutionally guaranteed rights, including the right of Asian Americans and other minorities to be protected from racist hate speech.

Matsudaira, Tadaatsu

b. 1855
d. 1888
fields: Engineering

Tadaatsu Matsudaira, who came the United States as a teenager, earned a degree in civil engineering from Rutgers University. He worked for the Union Pacific Railroad, then attended the Colorado School of Mines, eventually becoming the assistant inspector of mines for Colorado.

Matsudaira Takechiyo. *See* Tokugawa Ieyasu

Matsui, Robert Takeo

b. Sept. 17, 1941
Sacramento, Calif.
fields: Government and Politics

Robert Takeo Matsui received his J.D. from Hastings College of the Law in 1966, then practiced law in Sacramento. He became president of the Sacramento chapter of the Japanese American Citizens League (JACL) in 1969. He was elected to Sacramento's city council in 1971 and served as vice mayor from 1977 to 1978, when he won election to the U.S. House of Representatives from California's Third Congressional District. Matsui, reelected seven times, helped lead the fight for government reparations for Japanese Americans who had been interned in camps during World War II. Matsui declared his intention to run for a senate seat in 1992, but withdrew to spend time with his critically ill father.

Matsui, Teiko. *See* Tomita, Teiko

Matsumoto, Utaka. *See* Omura, James Matsumoto

Matsunaga, Masayuki

aka: Spark Matsunaga
b. Oct. 8, 1916
Kukuilula, Kauai, Hawaii
d. Apr. 15, 1990
Toronto, Ontario, Canada
fields: Government and Politics

Japanese American politician; Masayuki "Spark" Matsunaga was born in Hawaii; served in U.S. Army during World War II, earning bronze star and purple heart; earned law degree from Harvard University in 1952; representative to the Hawaiian territorial legislature, 1954-1959; U.S. representative (Democrat), 1963-1977; U.S. senator, 1977-1990; wrote *Rulemakers of the House* (1976).

Matsuo Bashō

né: Matsuo Kinsaku
b. 1644
Iga province, Ueno, Japan
d. October 12, 1694
Osaka, Japan
fields: Literature

Bashō is considered one of Japan's greatest poets, especially as master of the haiku. While the haiku was already established as a poetry form prior to the Tokugawa era, Basho is credited with reinvigorating the form at a time when it was in severe decline.

Matsura, Frank

b. 1874
d. June 16, 1913
Okanogan, Wash.
fields: Photography

After arriving in Washington State in 1903, Frank Matsura began photographing people and places he encountered in and around the old mining town of Conconully, in Okanogan County. He moved to Okanogan in 1907, opening his own photography studio. Many of his photographs have been archived at the Okanogan County Historical

Society and the Washington State University library.

Matsushita, Konosuke

b. November 27, 1894
Wasa, Wakayama Prefecture, Japan
d. April 27, 1989
Osaka, Japan
fields: Business and Industry

Matsushita was an energetic manufacturing and marketing genius who built the world's biggest multinational electric home appliance industry—Matsushita Electric Company. In the process, he developed a revolutionary management system that has influenced industry worldwide.

Matsuwaka-Maru. *See* Shinran

Matthews, Saul

b. ?
d. ?
fields: Warfare and Conquest

African American rifleman in the Continental Army and veteran of the American revolutionary war; Saul Matthews posed as a runaway slave in order to gather intelligence for the Continental Army. His abilities as a spy made him instrumental in sabotaging the campaign of British General Charles Cornwallis in Portsmouth. Matthews was freed because of his contribution to the Continental Army.

Matthews, Stanley Thomas

b. 1824
d. 1889
fields: Law

U.S. Supreme Court justice, 1881-1889 (died while in office); appointed by President Garfield. Closest Senate confirmation vote (24-23). Significant opinions: *Hurtado v. California*, 110 U.S. 516 (1884); *Yick Wo v. Hopkins*, 118 U.S. 356 (1886).

Matthews, Victoria

full: Ann Victoria Earle Matthews
b. May 27, 1861
Fort Valley, Ga.
d. March 10, 1907
Brooklyn Heights, N.Y.
fields: Journalism

African American journalist; Victoria Matthews contributed to many secular and religious papers, including short articles about dialect to the Associated Press, and was one of the most popular black female writers of her time. Founder of the White Rose Mission (1897), a training center and school for children from kindergarten age up, and the Home for Colored Women, a shelter and training facility, Mathews collected works of black literature, which she used to teach race history.

Matthias I Corvinus

né: Mátyás Hunyadi
b. February 24, 1443
Kolozsvár, Transylvania
d. April 6, 1490
Vienna, Austria
fields: Monarchy, Government and Politics, Military Affairs, Patronage of the Arts

King of Hungary, 1458-1490. Matthias I excelled as soldier, diplomat, and legal reformer. Most important, he moved Hungary from feudal particularism toward a more centralized state and through his lavish patronage promoted a remarkable Humanist literary and artistic achievement on the model of the Italian Renaissance.

Matzeliger, Jan Earnst

b. September 15, 1852
Paramaribo, Dutch Guiana
d. August 24, 1889
Lynn, Mass.
fields: Invention and Technology

African American inventor; Jan Earnst Matzeliger invented the lasting machine and a nailing machine. The original patent was granted in 1883. His machine formed the basis of the United Shoe Machinery Corporation. The mechanization of lasting, which involves adjusting the shoe, arranging leather over the sole, and driving in nails, cut shoe prices by about half.

Maugham, W. Somerset

full: William Somerset Maugham
b. January 25, 1874
Paris, France
d. December 16, 1965
Villa Mauresque, France
fields: Literature

Raised in France, W. Somerset Maugham, spent much of his life abroad and began writing during his twenties. After his first novel, *Liza of Lambeth* (1897), achieved some success, he opted to become a full-time writer. His next major success came with a series of plays, beginning with *Lady Frederick* (1911). During World War I, he served with British Intelligence in Switzerland and Russia. Afterward, he traveled to the South Seas, Southeast Asia, and America. In 1928 he settled on the French Riviera. His major fiction includes *Of Human Bondage* (1915), *The Moon and Sixpence* (1919), *Cakes and Ale* (1930), *The Razor's Edge* (1944), and *Catalina* (1948). Other significant works include *The Summing Up* (1938), *Great Novelists and Their Novels* (1948), and *A Writer's Notebook* (1949).

Maupassant, Guy de

full: Henri-René-Albert-Guy de Maupassant
b. August 5, 1850
Château de Miromesnil, near Dieppe, France
d. July 6, 1893
Passy, Paris, France
fields: Literature

Maupassant was one of the major literary figures at the end of the nineteenth century to help move short fiction away from the primitive folktale form to the short story of psychological realism. His most significant contributions to the form may be found in such affecting realistic stories as "Boule de Suif" and such powerful tales of psychological obsession as "The Horla."

Maupertuis, Pierre-Louis Moreau de

b. Sept. 28, 1698
Saint-Milo, France
d. July 27, 1759
Basel, Switzerland
fields: Mathematics (applied math)

Pierre-Louis Moreau de Maupertuis went to Lapland in 1736 to measure the terrestrial distance of one degree of arc of the meridian of longitude; worked in field of heredity.

Maurice, Frederick Denison

full: John Frederick Denison Maurice
b. April 29, 1805
Normanston, Suffolk, England
d. April 1, 1872
London, England
fields: Religion and Theology, Education

Maurice was the one of the most respected theologians in an age when religious crisis was a part of almost every person's life. His efforts to support educational and social reforms, specifically his involvement with the movement known as Christian Socialism, had significant beneficial impact on the working classes.

Maury, Antonia

full: Antonia Caetana De Paiva Pereira Maury
b. March 21, 1866
Cold Spring, New York
d. January 8, 1952
Dobbs Ferry, New York
fields: Astronomy

Maury's spectroscopic analysis of star systems contributed to the discovery and confirmation of a variety of astronomical phenomena.

Maury, Matthew Fontaine

b. January 14, 1806
Spotsylvania County, Virginia
d. February 1, 1873
Lexington, Virginia
fields: Oceanography, Meteorology, Geography (physical)

A universal scientist, Maury did not limit his endeavors to one area of science; instead, he researched the land, sea, and air and showed how they are inextricably linked to one another. Maury brought the study of physical geography and oceanography into the modern age.

Mauss, Marcel

b. May 10, 1872
Épinal, France
d. February 10, 1950
Paris, France
fields: Philosophy, Sociology

Combining strong philosophical training with sociological interests, Marcel Mauss was one of the key figures in twentieth century French sociology. Generally considered one of the pioneers of functionalist methodology, he made major contributions to sociological thought in the areas of the theory of religion, economic exchange, and primitive classification. His most important works are *Primitive Classification* (1963) and *The Gift: Forms and Functions of Exchange in Archaic Societies* (1923-1924).

Max, Peter

b. October 19, 1937
Berlin, Germany
fields: Art (graphic arts)

An artist whose works represented an unusual blending of cultural symbolism, Peter Max used an intense, vivid color palette to create bold, expressive, improvisational, cosmic landscapes in the 1960's. In 1967, he burst upon the art scene with his brilliantly colored cosmic imagery—stars, flowers, unusual lettering—that would become known as the "Max style" and spread across the United States and the world. His "psychedelic" images and graphics adorned mass-produced items such as posters, book jackets, and record covers, including the cover for the Beatles' *Yellow Submarine* album. In 1992, he created the official postage stamps commemorating the first Environmental Summit held in Rio de Janeiro, Brazil, and in 1995 he was named official artist for Earth Day. He has created numerous works celebrating freedom and democracy, including his famous Statue of Liberty paintings and series of U.S. flags.

Maximilian I

b. March 22, 1459
Wiener Neustadt, Austria
d. January 12, 1519
Wels, Austria
fields: Government and Politics, Monarchy

Holy Roman Emperor, 1493-1519. Maximilian I revived and strengthened both the concept and the actual position of Holy Roman Emperor by a great reform movement. These accomplishments were short-lived, however, and his enduring contribution lies in the development of German and Austrian nationalism.

Maxwell, Daphne. *See* Reid, Daphne Maxwell

Maxwell, James Clerk

b. June 13, 1831
Edinburgh, Scotland
d. November 5, 1879
Cambridge, England
fields: Physics

Both a theoretical and an experimental physicist as well as a notable mathematician, Maxwell founded modern field theory and statistical mechanics, mathematically describing interactions of electrical and magnetic fields that produce radiant energy, thus confirming the existence of electromagnetic waves that move at light speed. He also elaborated theories of the mechanics and kinetics of gases and a theory of Saturn's rings.

May, Scott Glenn

b. March 19, 1954
Sandusky, Ohio
fields: Sports (basketball player)

African American basketball player; Scott Glenn May was the star of the undefeated 1976 Indiana University team that won the National Collegiate Athletic Association (NCAA) title. He was a first-team All-American in 1975 and again in 1976, when he won the Naismith Award and earned a gold medal with the U.S. men's basketball team at the Montreal Olympics. May played with the Chicago Bulls, Milwaukee Bucks, and Detroit Pistons and averaged 10.4 points per game in his seven seasons in the National Basketball Association.

Mayakovsky, Vladimir

full: Vladimir Vladimirovich Mayakovsky
b. July 19, 1893
Bagdadi (now Mayakovsky), Georgia, Russian Empire
d. April 14, 1930
Moscow, U.S.S.R.
fields: Literature

Mayakovsky was the poet laureate of the Russian Revolution. Celebrating the modern technological age, he became the voice of the masses. Combining propaganda and innovative poetic techniques, he created sweeping epics, mass spectacles, and dramatic slogans that brought a vibrant literature to the people in the streets.

Mayer, Maria Goeppert

né: Maria Gertrude Goeppert
b. June 28, 1906
Kattowitz, Upper Silesia, Germany (now Katowice, Poland)
d. Feb. 20, 1972
San Diego, California
fields: Chemistry, Physics

Maria Goeppert Mayer, in 1947, proposed, with Edward Teller, a theory for the origin of the elements; in 1948, developed the nuclear shell model; work with molecular spectra provided a theoretical basis for important developments in laser physics and molecular orbital calculations; in 1963, won the Nobel Prize in Physics.

Mayfield, Curtis

b. June 3, 1942
Chicago, Ill.
fields: Music

African American singer, guitarist, songwriter, and record company executive; Curtis Mayfield came to prominance with the Impressions in 1964 with "I'm So Proud," "Keep on Pushing," and "Amen." Mayfield left the Impressions in 1970 to pursue a solo career and released *Curtis* and *Take It to the Streets* (1990). He wrote the sound track for *Super Fly* (1972), which contained two top-ten singles, "Freddie's Dead" and "Super Fly." An accident left Mayfield paralyzed from the neck down.

Mayfield, Julian

b. June 6, 1928
Greer, S.C.
d. October 20, 1984
Tacoma Park, Md.
fields: Literature

African American writer, editor, and educator; Julian Mayfield is known primarily for the novels he wrote during the 1950's and 1960's such as *The Hit* (1957), *The Long Night* (1958), and *The Grand Parade* (1961). Mayfield also wrote for the *Commentary, The Nation, Negro Digest,* and *Freedomways* and was editor of *Ten Times Black* (1972), a short story collection. He served as communications aide and speech writer for Ghanian president Kwame Nkrumah (1962-1966) and was senior political adviser to Prime Minister Forbes Burnham in Guyana (1971-1974).

Mayhew, Richard

b. April 3, 1934
Amityville, N.Y.
fields: Art

African American painter. Educated at the Brooklyn Museum Art School, Richard Mayhew won a National Institute of Arts and Letters Grant, a Tiffany Foundation Award, and a John Hay Whitney Fellowship. The Whitney Museum of American Art and the

Brooklyn Museum have exhibited his work in their permanent collections.

Maynard, Robert Clyve

b. June 17, 1937
Brooklyn, N.Y.
d. August 17, 1993
Oakland, Calif.
fields: Journalism, Publishing

African American journalist and newspaper publisher; in 1983, Robert Clyve Maynard became the first African American to own a major daily American newspaper, the *Oakland Tribune*, in general circulation; the paper was later sold in 1992.

Maynor, Dorothy

né: Dorothy Leigh Mainor
b. September 3, 1910
Norfolk, Va.
d. February 19, 1996
West Chester, Pa.
fields: Music (opera singer)

African American opera singer; Dorothy Maynor earned an international reputation with performances in Central and South America, Australia, and Europe. She retired after twenty-five years of performing and decided to devote her time to community outreach, especially to African American children. She founded the Harlem School for the Arts (1964) and was its director until 1979. In 1975 she was appointed to the Metropolitan Opera Board of Directors.

Mayo, Charles H.

full: Charles Horace Mayo
b. July 19, 1865
Rochester, Minnesota
d. May 26, 1939
Chicago, Illinois
fields: Medicine

In 1889, William W. Mayo and his two sons, William J. Mayo and Charles H. Mayo, with the Sisters of St. Francis founded St. Mary's Hospital in Rochester, Minnesota. From the "cooperative group clinic" which began at the hospital, the Mayo doctors founded the Mayo Clinic and, subsequently, the Mayo Foundation for Medical Education and Research (1915), a part of the University of Minnesota Graduate School in Rochester. The Mayo clinics and research facilities are considered among the best in the world.

Mayo, Whitman

b. November 15, 1930
New York, N.Y.
fields: Theater and Entertainment

African American actor. Best known for his role as Grady on the television series *Sanford and Son* (1973-1977) and the spin-off *Grady* (1975-1976), Whitman Mayo has also performed in numerous plays, including *The Amen Corner* (1964), *Goin' to Buffalo* (1969), and *What if It Had Turned Up Heads* (1972). In 1979 he appeared in the film *The Main Event*.

Mayo, William J.

full: William James Mayo
b. June 29, 1861
Le Sueur, Minnesota
d. July 28, 1939
Rochester, Minnesota
fields: Medicine

In 1889, William W. Mayo and his two sons, William J. Mayo and Charles H. Mayo, with the Sisters of St. Francis founded St. Mary's Hospital in Rochester, Minnesota. From the "cooperative group clinic" which began at the hospital, the Mayo doctors founded the Mayo Clinic and, subsequently, the Mayo Foundation for Medical Education and Research (1915), a part of the University of Minnesota Graduate School in Rochester. The Mayo clinics and research facilities are considered among the best in the world.

Mays, Benjamin Elijah

b. August 1, 1895
Epworth, S.C.
d. March 28, 1984
Atlanta, Ga.
fields: Education, Literature

African American educator and author. In 1940 Benjamin Elijah Mays was offered the presidency of Morehouse College which he directed until his retirement in 1967. Though Mays achieved some notoriety for his scholarly work, *The Negro's Church* (1933, in collaboration with Joseph Nicholson) and *The Negro's God as Reflected in His Literature* (1938), it is his invigoration of Morehouse College that is Mays's greatest legacy. Mays's autobiography, *Born to Rebel*, was published in 1971.

Mays, Willie

full: Willie Howard Mays, Jr.
b. May 6, 1931
Westfield, Alabama
fields: Sports (baseball)

Mays earned recognition as the classic "complete" baseball player, one who could do everything well. He hit for high averages with great home-run power, he was a fast and aggressive base runner, and he was perhaps the best defensive outfielder in the game's history. In the 1954 World Series, he made a spectacular running catch that is often cited as the best ever. In 1958, the Giants, for whom he played, moved from New York to San Francisco. In 1962, he led the Giants to another pennant, and in 1964 he was named the major leagues' first African American team captain. In 1965, he hit a career-high fifty-two home runs and won his second most valuable player award. In 1972, Mays returned to New York when the Giants traded him to the Mets in mid-season. He retired after the 1973 season and was inducted into the Baseball Hall of Fame in 1979.

Mazarin, Jules

b. July 14, 1602
Pescina, Papal States
d. March 9, 1661
Vincennes, France
fields: Government and Politics, Patronage of the Arts

Mazarin played a central role in stabilizing the French monarchy and laying the political foundations for French absolutism in the critical period between 1643 and 1661. Mazarin's patronage of the arts and letters was extravagant, and he exercised profound influence in shaping the foundations of modern French art, music, and drama.

Mazumdar, Sucheta

b. 1948
fields: Historiography

Sucheta Mazumdar earned undergraduate and advanced degrees at the University of California, Los Angeles, before becoming a professor in the Department of History at Duke University. She wrote numerous articles on Chinese history, comparative Asian history, and issues affecting both Asian Americans and women.

Mazzini, Giuseppe

b. June 22, 1805
Genoa, Ligurian Republic
d. March 10, 1872
Pisa, Italy
fields: Philosophy, Government and Politics

Mazzini was the most influential leader of the Risorgimento—the Italian national unification movement. His political activities and philosophy were carried beyond Italy and inspired fledgling nationalist and democratic reform movements throughout the world.

Mbiti, John S.

full: John Samuel Mbiti
b. November 30, 1931
Mulango (Kitui), Kenya
fields: Philosophy, Religion and Theology

Christian theologian and student of African culture John S. Mbiti collected and synthesized indigenous concepts of God, myths and stories, prayers, and proverbs into a religiously oriented "African worldview," exploring the complex relationship between African and Christian ontology, theology, and ethics. He holds that what remains of traditional Africa provides the fullest possible view of humans as spiritual beings. The tendency of Western critical philosophy has been to understand human beings politically, economically, scientifically, or historically, and each of these human types exists secularly, in the world and in time. Human beings existing in time are subject to ultimate dissolution and destruction; only if understood religiously and spiritually may human beings escape this temporal fate. His major works include novels, poems, stories, edited anthologies, and religious and philosophical studies such as *African Religions and Philosophy* (1969, rev. ed. 1990), *Love and Marriage in Africa* (1973), and *Bible and Theology in African Christianity* (1986).

Mead, George Herbert

b. February 27, 1863
South Hadley, Massachusetts
d. April 26, 1931
Chicago, Illinois
fields: Philosophy, Sociology, Psychiatry and Psychology

American pragmatist philosopher and psychologist George Herbert Mead earned wide acclaim as a social scientist, helping to establish sociology and social psychology as disciplines. Drawing on pragmatism and behaviorism, he formulated social behaviorism, a pragmatic philosophy that offered a radical view of mind and self as developing out of society, via the acquisition and the use of language, rather than the other way around. His major works include *The Philosophy of the Present* (1932), *Mind, Self, and Society* (1934), *Movements of Thought in the Nineteenth Century* (1936), and *The Philosophy of the Act* (1938).

Mead, Margaret

b. December 16, 1901
Philadelphia, Pennsylvania
d. November 15, 1978
New York, New York
fields: Anthropology

Through her best-selling books, her public lecturing, and her column in *Redbook* magazine, Mead popularized anthropology in the United States. She also provided American women with a role model, encouraging them to pursue professions while simultaneously championing their roles as mothers.

Means, Russell

b. Nov. 10, 1939
Pine Ridge Reservation, S.Dak.
fields: Native American Affairs, Civil Rights

Oglala Lakota (Sioux) activist; Russell Means served as director of the American Indian Center, 1969; met Dennis Banks in 1969, cofounder of the radical American Indian Movement (AIM), and established its second chapter in Cleveland, Ohio; a talented media strategist, Means engaged in confrontational tactics to attract attention to Native American concerns; by the time of the Trail of Broken Treaties occupation of the Bureau of Indian Affairs (BIA) headquarters building in Washington, D.C., in November, 1972, Means was one of AIM's primary leaders; widespread conflict over reservation abuses led to the armed occupation of the community of Wounded Knee from February to May, 1973; acquitted of murder charges in 1976; left AIM in 1988 to form the American Indian Anti-Defamation League; in 1995 Means published his autobiography, *Where White Men Fear to Tread.*

Medawar, Peter

full: Sir Peter Brian Medawar
b. Feb. 28, 1915
Rio de Janeiro, Brazil
d. Oct. 2, 1987
London, England
fields: Medicine, Science

Peter Medawar showed that rejection of transplants is under immunological control; in 1960, won the Nobel Prize in Physiology or Medicine.

Medici, Giovanni de'. *See* Leo X

Medici, Guilio de. *See* Clement VII

Medici, Lorenzo de'

b. January 1, 1449
Florence
d. April 8, 1492
Careggi, near Florence
fields: Banking and Finance, Government and Politics, Diplomacy, Literature

Florence's Lorenzo de' Medici was the most important statesman in Italy during the latter part of the fifteenth century. Lorenzo was also a noted banker, poet, and patron of the arts. He epitomized the concept of the Renaissance man.

Meek, Carrie Pittman

b. April 29, 1926
Tallahassee, Fla.
fields: Government and Politics, Education

African American educator and politician; in 1992, Carrie Pittman Meek became the first African American from Florida, and the first black female from that state, to be elected to Congress since Reconstruction.

Meese, Edwin, III

b. December 3, 1931
Oakland, California
fields: Government and Politics

Edwin Meese III began his career as a deputy district attorney in California's Alameda County, where he opposed antidraft and free speech protests in Oakland and Berkeley during the 1960's. He served as Ronald Reagan's executive assistant when Reagan was governor of California, then followed Reagan to Washington when the latter became president in 1981, and became Reagan's attorney general in 1985.

Mehmed II

b. March 30, 1432
Adrianople, Ottoman Empire
d. May 3, 1481
Hunkârçayırı, Ottoman Empire
fields: Government and Politics, Military Affairs

As Sultan of the Ottoman Empire (1451-1481), Mehmed II commanded armies that captured Constantinople, and under his rule control of the Balkans and Anatolia in substantial portions was extended as the Ottoman state became one of the most important powers of early modern times.

Mehta, Sonny

full: Ajay Singh Mehta
b. 1943
India
fields: Publishing

After graduating from Cambridge University, Sonny Mehta began working for paperback publishers such as Pan and Picador. In 1987, he joined New York publisher Alfred A. Knopf, a division of Random House. As editor in chief and president, Mehta maintained Knopf's reputation for literary excellence while producing best-sellers.

Mehta, Ved

full: Ved Parkash Mehta
b. Mar. 21, 1934
Lahore, Punjab, India, now Pakistan
fields: Literature

Ved Mehta, who joined *The New Yorker* as a staff writer in 1961, wrote autobiography, social commentary on India, articles and stories for magazines and newspapers, a documentary script, and a novel. His works provide Western audiences with an intimate and authentic portrait of the complexity of modern India. His major work was a multivolume autobiography, *Continents in Exile.*

Mehta, Zubin

b. Apr. 29, 1936
Bombay, India
fields: Music

Zubin Mehta studied at the State Academy of Music in Vienna from 1954 to 1960. He conducted student orchestras at the Vienna Academy, then won first prize in an international conductor's competition, a year as an assistant to the Liverpool Philharmonic Orchestra. Mehta was appointed director of the Montreal Symphony, a position he held from 1961 to 1967. He also was associate conductor for the Los Angeles Philharmonic Orchestra and became that orchestra's music director in 1962. In 1978, Mehta became director of the New York Philharmonic, a position he held until 1991. He became director of the Israel Philharmonic in 1969 and was appointed director for life in 1981.

Meighen, Arthur

b. June 16, 1874
near Anderson, Ontario, Canada
d. August 5, 1960
Toronto, Ontario, Canada
fields: Government and Politics

Arthur Meighen was elected Conservative member of Canadian Parliament in 1908. Two-time prime minister of Canada (1920-1921, 1926). Strong personal enmity between Meighen and Liberal leader William Lyon Mackenzie King, who replaced him as prime minister after both his defeats. Later served in Senate until 1941.

Meiklejohn, Alexander

b. February 3, 1872
Rochdale, England
d. September 16, 1964
Berkeley, California
fields: Education, Law

An educator and legal philosopher, Alexander Meiklejohn developed a two-level theory of free speech that would guarantee absolute protection to "public" speech but not to "private" speech, which he outlined in *Free Speech and Its Relationship to Self-Government* (1948). His has been credited with contributing to the U.S. Supreme Court's decision in *New York Times Co. v. Sullivan* (1964), but it was also criticized because of the difficulty in distinguishing between "public" and "private" speech.

Meir, Golda

né: Golda Mabovitch
aka: Golda Meyerson
b. May 3, 1898
Kiev, Ukraine, Russian Empire
d. December 8, 1978
Jerusalem, Israel
fields: Government and Politics

Meir was a leading Zionist and inspirational figure for world Jewry who rejected life in the United States to immigrate to Palestine in 1920. She became a major role player in Zionist organizations there, eventually rising to become Israel's first ambassador to the Soviet Union (1948), minister of labor (1949), foreign minister (1956), and prime minister (1969).

Meitner, Lise

b. November 7, 1878
Vienna, Austro-Hungarian Empire
d. October 27, 1968
Cambridge, England
fields: Physics

Working as a pioneer in a field to which few women were drawn—nuclear physics—Meitner's joint research with chemist Otto Hahn (and later Fritz Strassmann) yielded the discovery of new radioactive elements and their properties and paved the way for the discovery of uranium fission.

Melanchthon, Philipp

né: Philipp Schwartzerd
b. February 16, 1497
Bretten, Baden
d. April 19, 1560
Wittenberg
fields: Religion and Theology, Education

Melanchthon was a German Humanist scholar who became a close associate of Martin Luther in the Protestant Reformation. Known for his warm evangelical piety and his irenic, ecumenical spirit, he was the author of the Augsburg Confession of 1530, basically a summary of Luther's teachings, which remains as the fundamental confessional platform of worldwide Lutheranism. Melanchthon also is credited with having established the German school system.

Melbourne, Second Viscount

né: William Lamb
aka: William Lamb, Second Viscount Melbourne
b. March 15, 1779
Brocket Hall, Hertfordshire, England
d. November 24, 1848
Brocket Hall, Hertfordshire, England
fields: Government and Politics

A man of wit, urbanity, and cynicism, Melbourne was the stereotype of the aristocratic Whig politician. As prime minister in 1834 and from 1835 to 1841, he helped set the pattern for governmental reforms. He also was a crucial influence on the young Queen Victoria.

Meléndez, Edwin

b. Aug. 28, 1951
San Juan, Puerto Rico
fields: Scholarship

Latino scholar. Edwin Meléndez moved to the United States from Puerto Rico in 1978 and earned a Ph.D. from the University of Massachusetts at Amherst in economics. In 1984, he began teaching economics and Puerto Rican studies at Fordham University, taught in the department of urban studies and planning at the Massachusetts Institute of Technology from 1986 to 1992, and later directed the Mauricio Gaston Institute for Latino Community Development and Public Policy at the University of Massachusetts at Boston. He coedited *Hispanics in the Labor Force: Issues and Policies* (1993) and *Colonial Dilemma: Critical Perspectives on Contemporary Puerto Rico* (1993), among other books.

Meléndez, Rosalinda

b. ?
fields: Theater and Entertainment

Latina actor. In the 1940's, Rosalinda Meléndez starred with the Compañía de Revistas y Variedades el Niño Fidencio in the Los Angeles area. El Fidencio was a folk healer from Mexico who was later discredited. Meléndez's son was actor William Lanceford.

Mellon, Andrew

full: Andrew William Mellon
b. March 24, 1855
Pittsburgh, Pennsylvania
d. August 26, 1937
Southampton, New York
fields: Business and Industry

Through a combination of caution and shrewd investment, Mellon became one of the three richest men in the United States. He was called "the greatest Secretary of the Treasury since Alexander Hamilton."

Melville, Herman

b. August 1, 1819
New York, New York
d. September 28, 1891
New York, New York
fields: Literature

With great power and insight into man's ambiguous nature, Melville helped prove that American literature could equal that of England.

Melville, Margarita Bradford

né: Margarita Bradford
b. Aug. 19, 1929
Irapuato, Guanajuato, Mexico
fields: Scholarship, Social Reform

Latina scholar and activist. Margarita Bradford Melville taught in Guatemala until she was asked to leave in 1967 by the United States embassy and the Guatemalan government. She married Thomas Melville in the United States, then served nine months in federal prison for burning Selective Service records in Catonsville, Maryland, in an effort to increase American awareness of the presence of U.S. troops in Guatemala. She and her husband published *Whose Heaven,*

Whose Earth? in 1970 and *Guatemala: The Politics of Land Ownership* in 1971. Melville earned her doctorate in 1976 and became assistant professor of anthropology at the University of Houston. In 1986, she became an associate professor of the University of California, Berkeley, and in 1988 was named as associate dean in the graduate division.

Memphis Minnie

né: Minnie Douglas
aka: Lizzie Douglas
b. June 3, 1896
Algiers, La.
d. August 6, 1973
Memphis, Tenn.
fields: Music (blues musician)

African American blues musician. Though "Bumble Bee," Memphis Minnie's first major hit was released in 1939, she released the bulk of her work in Chicago, Ill., between 1934 and 1941. Among her most popular hits are "Bumble Bee," "Me and My Chauffeur Blues," and "Nothin' in Ramblin'." Noted for the individuality of her voice, expressed through the clarity of the details in her lyrics, Minnie's imagery and simple melodies allowed her voice to retain the flavor of her southern blues roots.

Memphis Slim

né: Peter Chatman
b. September 3, 1915
Memphis, Tenn.
d. February 24, 1988
Paris, France
fields: Music (blues singer and pianist)

African American blues singer and pianist; Memphis Slim was a well-known Chicago urban blues singer prominent in rhythm and blues in the 1940's and 1950's. In the 1960's he began recording honky-tonk and boogie woogie blues. He moved to the East Coast in 1959 and played Carnegie Hall and the Newport Jazz Festival. His most notable tunes include "Every Day I Have the Blues," "Beer Drinking Woman," and "Feel Like Screamin' and Cryin'." His lyrics are preoccupied with the meaning of the blues.

Menaechmus

b. c. 375 B.C.E.
on the island of Proconnesus (now Marmara, Turkey)
d. c. 325 B.C.E.
fields: Mathematics (geometry)

Menaechmus is responsible for the discovery of conic sections (the parabola, hyperbola, and ellipse); derived properties for them, geometrically; yielded their defining equations in analytic geometry.

Menander

b. c. 210 B.C.E.
probably Kalasi, Afghanistan
d. c. 135 B.C.E.
probably in northwest India
fields: Government and Politics, Religion and Theology

Menander extended the Greco-Bactrian domains in India more than any other ruler. He became a legendary figure as a great patron of Buddhism in the Pali book the *Milindapanha*.

Menander

b. c. 342 B.C.E.
Athens, Greece
d. c. 292 B.C.E.
Piraeus, Greece
fields: Theater and Entertainment

Noted for his careful plotting, his accurate depiction of middle-class society, and his sympathetic treatment of character, Menander is considered the finest writer of Greek New Comedy.

Mencius

aka: Meng-tzu
b. c. 372 B.C.E.
Tsou, China
d. c. 289 B.C.E.
China
fields: Philosophy

Through a lifetime of reflection, Mencius clarified and expanded the wisdom embodied in Confucius' *Analects*, rendering Confucian ideas more accessible. His *Meng-tzu* eclipsed other interpretations of Confucius and gained acceptance as the orthodox version of Confucian thought.

Mencken, H. L.

full: Henry Louis Mencken
b. September 12, 1880
Baltimore, Maryland
d. January 29, 1956
Baltimore, Maryland
fields: Journalism

Mencken, in his roles as editor, writer, and critic, kept an ever-watchful eye on American politics, letters, language, and ideas. He argued eloquently for an indigenous and independent American literature, and he encouraged and nurtured the authors who were striving to create it.

Mendel, Gregor Johann

b. July 22, 1822
Heinzendorf, Austria
d. January 6, 1884
Brno, Austria
fields: Genetics

Mendel demonstrated the rules governing genetic inheritance with his statistical approach to experiments in plant hybridization.

Mendeleyev, Dmitry Ivanovich

b. February 8, 1834
Tobolsk (now Tyumen Oblast), Siberia, Russia
d. February 2, 1907
St. Petersburg, Russia
fields: Chemistry

Although he did important theoretical work on the physical properties of fluids and practical work on the development of coal and oil resources, Mendeleyev is best known for his discovery of the periodic law, which states that the properties of the chemical elements vary with their atomic weights in a systematic way. His periodic table of the elements enabled him to predict accurately the properties of three unknown elements, whose later discovery confirmed the value of his system.

Mendelsohn, Erich

b. March 21, 1887
Allenstein, Germany
d. September 15, 1953
San Francisco, California
fields: Architecture

Mendelsohn did at least as much as such better-known contemporaries as Le Corbusier, Walter Gropius, and Ludwig Mies van der Rohe to develop and popularize modern architecture. Even more fully than the other founders of the so-called International Style, Mendelsohn was the representative architect of modern world industrialism—of machine, steel, concrete, and glass.

Mendelssohn, Felix

b. February 3, 1809
Hamburg
d. November 4, 1847
Leipzig, Saxony
fields: Music

Mendelssohn was one of the great composers of the Romantic period. His music is noted for its exceptionally melodic qualities and its ability to capture a mood. It has been continually performed and studied.

Mendenhall, Dorothy Reed

né: Dorothy Reed
b. September 22, 1874
Columbus, Ohio
d. July 31, 1964
Chester, Connecticut
fields: Medicine

Best known for her medical research identifying the cell responsible for Hodgkin's disease, Mendenhall spent most of her career as a physician interested in maternal and child health. As one of the first doctors employed by the U.S. Children's Bureau, she merged social welfare and preventive health strategies as the best approach for reducing maternal and infant mortality and morbidity.

Mendes, Sergio

b. Feb. 11, 1941
Niteroi, Brazil
fields: Music (jazz pianist and composer)

Jazz pianist and composer. As a teenager, Sergio Mendes joined the circle of musicians who created the bossa nova. In 1962, he appeared in Carnegie Hall with Antonio Carlos Jobim, João Gilberto, Charlie Byrd, Stan Getz, and Dizzy Gillespie. In 1968, he played with the National Symphony in Washington, D.C., and in 1970 he performed at the White House. In the mid-1960's, he toured and recorded with the group Brazil '66, which is known for the hit "Mas que Nada." Mendes's other hit songs include "So Many Stars" and "Song of No Regrets."

Mendès-France, Pierre

b. January 11, 1907
Paris, France
d. October 18, 1982
Paris, France
fields: Economics, Government and Politics

Mendès-France was a Left-leaning French politician of the Radical Party who is best remembered for negotiating an armistice with the Vietminh in 1954, which ended the French Indochina War, and for opening the negotiations which led to Tunisian independence. More generally, he acted as the conscience of the democratic non-Communist Left in France during the Fourth and early Fifth republics.

Mendez, José

b. Mar. 19, 1888
Cardena, Cuba
d. Oct. 31, 1928
Havana, Cuba
fields: Sports (baseball player and manager)

Latino baseball player and manager. Right-handed pitcher José Mendez played his first professional season in the Cuban winter league in 1908, compiling a 15-6 record. In 1909, he posted a 44-2 record with the U.S. Cuban Stars, then returned to Cuba for the 1910 and 1911 seasons. In 1912, Mendez returned to the United States, playing shortstop for the multiracial All-Nations of Kansas City and outfield for the Chicago American Giants and Detroit Stars. As a player-manager, Mendez led the Kansas City Monarchs to three straight Negro National League pennants from 1923 to 1925 and compiled a 20-4 pitching record. Although excluded from the major leagues by his color, Mendez outpitched such stars as Christy Mathewson and Eddie Plank in exhibition games.

Méndez, Miguel Morales

b. June 15, 1930
Bisbee, Ariz.
fields: Literature

Latino writer. Miguel Morales Méndez entered the United States as a migrant farmworker at the age of fifteen. In 1970, he began teaching at the Pima Community College in Tuscon and later taught at the University of Arizona. He published his first novel, *Peregrinos de Aztlán*, in 1974 and was awarded an honorary doctor of humanities degree by the University of Arizona in 1984.

Méndez, Rafael

b. Mar. 6, 1906
Jiquilpán, Michoacán, Mexico
d. Sept. 15, 1981
Encino, Calif.
fields: Music (composer and trumpeter)

Latino composer and trumpeter. At the age of ten, Rafael Méndez played the trumpet for Pancho Villa. After attending Mexico City Conservatory, he played in numerous bands in the United States. During the 1940's he was a studio musician in Hollywood and appeared in the films *Holiday in Mexico* (1946), *Fiesta* (1947), and *Luxury Liner* (1948). He recorded such classic songs as "Carnival in Venice," "The Flight of the Bumble Bee," and, with the Rafael Méndez Orchestra, "La Bamba" and "Tea for Two," among others. Méndez also composed many songs, including "The Elf Trumpeter" and "Valse Suriano." In 1964, he became the first trumpet player to perform solo at Carnegie Hall. F. E. Olds & Son named one of its trumpet models for him.

Mendieta, Ana

b. ?
d. 1985
fields: Art

Latina artist. Ana Mendieta immigrated to the United States in the early 1960's and attended the Center for the New Performing Arts at the University of Iowa. Mendieta's work centered on her own body; her early work, which dealt with blood, contained allusions to Santería rituals. She received numerous awards, including grants from the National Endowment for the Arts and a Guggenheim Fellowship. The New Museum of Contemporary Art in New York City held a posthumous exhibit of her work.

Mendoza, Hope

b. 1921
Miami, Ariz.
fields: Social Reform

Labor leader. Hope Mendoza dropped out of high school to work. After World War II, she became active in the International Ladies' Garment Workers' Union and the Central Labor Council. In 1948, she helped found the Community Service Organization and served on the executive board for seven years. Mendoza married in 1955, finished high school education, started her own deposition business, and worked with the Mexican American Youth Opportunities Foundation and the Council of Mexican American Affairs. President Lyndon Johnson appointed her to the National Advisory Council for the Peace Corps, after which she continued to work for the Los Angeles Mexican American community and the Democratic Party.

Mendoza, Lydia

b. May 13, 1916
Houston, Tex.
fields: Music (singer and composer)

Latina singer and composer. Lydia Mendoza, who first performed with her family group, El Cuarteto Carta Blanca, in 1920, released her first hit song, "Mal Hombre," in 1934. She recorded more than fifty albums during her sixty-year career, including the hit singles "Mal Hombre" and "Mujer Paseada." Mendoza performed for the president of Mexico in 1950 and for President Jimmy Carter's inauguration in 1977. She was inducted into the Texas Women Hall of Fame in 1984 and published *Lydia Mendoza: A Family Autobiography* in 1993.

Menelik II

né: Sahle Mariam
b. August 17, 1844
Ankober, Shoa
d. December 12, 1913
Addis Ababa, Ethiopia
fields: Monarchy, Government and Politics

Emperor of Ethiopia, 1887-1909. Menelik II unified Ethiopia after centuries of political fragmentation, consolidated the ancient Christian heritage against the growth of Muslim influence, and saved Ethiopia from European colonialism. He laid the foundations for Ethiopia's transformation from a medieval, feudal empire to a modern state.

Menem, Carlos Saúl

b. July 2, 1930
Anillaco, province of La Rioja, Argentina
fields: Government and Politics

A long-time opponent of Argentina's military governments, repeatedly harassed and arrested, Carlos Saúl Menem took office as president of Argentina in 1989; reelected 1995. Peronist. Stabilized economy; involved in forming Mercosur, a common market of

Argentina, Brazil, Uruguay, and Paraguay, in 1995.

Menéndez de Avilés, Pedro

b. February 15, 1519
Avilés, Spain
d. September 17, 1574
Santander, Spain
fields: Exploration and Colonization

Menéndez de Avilés developed the Florida peninsula as a colony of the Spanish crown.

Menes

b. c. 3100 B.C.E.
Thinis, Egypt
d. c. 3000 B.C.E.
Memphis, Egypt
fields: Government and Politics, Pharaohs

Menes is described in classical Greek and Roman sources and late-period Egyptian king lists as the ruler who was responsible for the unification of Egypt, the building of the capital city of Memphis, and the founding of the First Dynasty of Egypt.

Menewa

aka: Hothlepoya
aka: Crazy War Hunter
b. c. 1765
along the Tallopoosa River, present-day Ala.
d. 1865
Indian Territory, present-day Okla.
fields: Warfare and Conquest, Native American Affairs

Creek. As a leader of the Creek war faction (the Red Sticks), Menewa fought Andrew Jackson at the 1814 Battle of Horseshoe Bend during the Creek War. Joined the Red Sticks' principal leader, William Weatherford, aiding Tecumseh, leader of a pan-Indian rebellion. Executioner of William McIntosh.

Meng-tzu. *See* Mencius

Menno Simons

b. 1496
Witmarsum, Friesland
d. January 31, 1561
Wüstenfeld, Holstein
fields: Church Reform, Religion and Theology

Menno contributed a stabilizing influence to the Anabaptist movement of the sixteenth century and also to a defense of religious toleration. His most lasting contribution has been his emphasis on the Bible as the authority in religion and theology.

Menor, Benjamin

b. Sept. 27, 1922
San Nicolas, Philippines
fields: Law, Government and Politics

Benjamin Menor, who arrived in the United States in 1930, received an LL.B. degree in 1952 from Boston University and passed the bar examination in Hawaii in 1953. He became county attorney, then entered private practice in 1959. Menor's election to the Hawaii State Senate in 1962 marked the first time a Filipino American served in any U.S. legislature. In 1966, he returned to private practice and became as a judge on the Hawaii Circuit Court in 1969. In 1974, he was appointed to serve on the Hawaii State Supreme Court as an associate justice.

Menotti, Gian Carlo

b. July 7, 1911
Cadegliano, Italy
fields: Music

Gian Carlo Menotti is known primarily for his opera compositions, for which he composed the music and wrote the libretti. He is also a composer of ballets, concerti, and orchestral music. He founded the prestigious Spoleto Festival USA arts festival in 1976.

Menzies, Robert Gordon

b. December 20, 1894
Jeparit, Victoria, Australia
d. May 15, 1978
Melbourne, Victoria, Australia
fields: Government and Politics

As the leading conservative politician of Australia for more than a third of a century, and as prime minister from 1939 to 1941 and from 1949 to 1966, Menzies forged critical, lasting international commitments and national policies.

Mercator, Gerardus

né: Gerhard Kremer
b. March 5, 1512
Rupelmonde, Flanders
d. December 2, 1594
Duisburg, Duchy of Cleves
fields: Cartography, Geography

Mercator invented a map projection that is particularly useful for ocean navigation. He was the first person to use the name "atlas" for a volume of maps. His maps represented the best geographic knowledge available at his time.

Meredith, James

full: James Howard Meredith
b. June 25, 1933
Kosciusko, Miss.
fields: Civil Rights

African American civil rights activist; James Meredith became first African American to attend the University of Mississippi in 1962, generating riots and the stationing of federal troops on the campus; engaged in "march against fear" to encourage black voter registration in 1966 and was shot by a sniper, but recovered; others, including Martin Luther King, Jr., and Stokley Carmichael, continued Meredith's march; wrote *Three Years in Mississippi* (1966).

Mergenthaler, Ottmar

b. May 11, 1854
Hachtel, Germany
d. October 28, 1899
Baltimore, Maryland
fields: Invention and Technology (printing), Publishing

Mergenthaler invented Linotype, the most prominent typesetting device before the advent of computerized photocomposition, thus revolutionizing the production of printed matter.

Merian, Maria Sibylla

full: Anna Maria Sibylla Merian
b. Apr. 2, 1647
Frankfurt am Main, Hessen (now in Germany)
d. Jan. 13, 1717
Amsterdam, the Netherlands
fields: Zoology

Maria Sibylla Merian was the first scientist to record the metamorphosis of tropical insects: She raised their caterpillars and made drawings and engravings of them for book illustrations, showing both the insects and the plants on which they feed. In 1686, she was the first European scientist to describe the development of tadpoles into frogs.

Meriwether, Louise

b. May 8, 1923
Haverstraw, N.Y.
fields: Literature

African American novelist and biographer; Louise Meriwether is the author of novels, *Daddy Was a Number Runner* (1970), short stories, "A Happening in Barbados," and histories, *The Freedom Ship of Robert Smalls* (1971), *The Heart Man: Dr. Daniel Hale Williams* (1972), and *Don't Ride the Bus on Monday: The Rosa Parks Story* (1973).

Merkerson, S. Epatha

b. 1953?
fields: Theater and Entertainment, Television (actor)

African American actress; S. Epatha Merkerson's stage credits include *Lady Day at Emerson's Bar & Grill*, *The Piano Lesson*, and *I'm Not Stupid*; played Reba the mail lady on the television series *Pee-wee's Playhouse*; was cast as Lieutenant Anita Van Buren in the NBC drama series *Law & Order*

(1993). She appeared in such films as *Jacob's Ladder* (1990), *Terminator 2: Judgment Day* (1991), and *An Unexpected Life* (1997, a cable movie).

Merleau-Ponty, Maurice

b. March 14, 1908
Rochefort, France
d. May 4, 1961
Paris, France
fields: Philosophy

Merleau-Ponty, French philosopher and man of letters, was one of the most original and profound thinkers of the postwar French movement of existential phenomenology.

Merman, Ethel

né: Ethel Agnes Zimmerman
b. January 16, 1908
Astoria, New York
d. February 15, 1984
New York, New York
fields: Theatre and Entertainment (actor), Music

A leading actor of musical comedies on stage in the United States, Merman defined that theatrical form. She was known for her clarity of diction and strong vocal projection.

Merrell, Helen. *See* Lynd, Helen Merrell

Merriam, Eve

né: Eva Moskovitz
b. July 19, 1916
Philadelphia, Pennsylvania
d. April 11, 1992
New York, New York
fields: Literature

Poet, playwright, and prose writer Eve Merriam wrote many poems for children. Her public addresses and her essays about poetry made her an important influence on how children's literature was taught in the late twentieth century. Among her works are *The Double Bed from the Feminine Side* (1958), *Mommies at Work* (1961), *There Is No Rhyme for Silver* (1962), *It Doesn't Always Have to Rhyme* (1964), *Catch a Little Rhyme* (1966), *After Nora Slammed the Door* (1964), *Man and Woman* (1968), *Equality, Identity, and Complementarity* (1968), *The Inner City Mother Goose* (1969), *The Nixon Poems* (1970), *I Am a Man: Ode to Martin Luther King, Jr.* (1971), and *Boys and Girls, Girls and Boys* (1972). She wrote several plays, including the Obie Award-winning *The Club* (1976). In 1981, she was presented the National Council of Teachers of English Award for excellence in poetry for children.

Merritt, Emma Frances Grayson

b. January 11, 1860
Dumfries, Va.
d. June 8, 1933
Washington, D.C.
fields: Education

African American educator; Emma Frances Grayson Merritt, the principal of several elementary schools, introduced several innovations into her schools, including silent reading periods, field trips, and separation of classes within grades according to ability levels of students. She founded the Teacher's Benefit and Annuity Association and the Prudence Crandall Association, which provided for educational needs of poor children.

Mersenne, Marin

b. September 8, 1588
Soultière, France
d. September 1, 1648
Paris, France
fields: Physics, Mathematics, Music, Philosophy, Religion and Theology

Mersenne is best known as the priest-scientist who facilitated the cross-fertilization of the most eminent minds of his time. He is widely commemorated for helping to establish modern science by promoting the new ideas of Nicolaus Copernicus, Galileo, and René Descartes and by attacking the pseudosciences of alchemy, astrology, and natural magic.

Mesa-Bains, Amalia

b. 1943
fields: Art

Latina artist. Amalia Mesa-Bains earned an M.A. (1971) from San Francisco State University, then a second master's degree (1980) and a Ph.D. in psychology from the Wright Institute. Her art, which is filled with Mexican symbols and religious imagery, focuses on the way that gender roles and ethnic identity are created within the Latino community. Mesa-Bains has taught at various schools, worked with the United States Information Agency as a consultant and lecturer, served on the board of directors of the Galeria de la Raza in San Francisco, California, and was the commissioner of art for that city.

Messallina, Valeria

b. c. 20 C.E.
probably Rome
d. 48 C.E.
Rome
fields: Government and Politics

Empress of Rome for more than seven years, Valeria Messallina was intimately involved in the highest level of Roman politics.

Messiaen, Olivier

full: Olivier-Eugène-Prosper-Charles Messiaen
b. December 10, 1908
Avignon, France
d. April 28, 1992
Paris, France
fields: Music

Messiaen was the most important French composer of the twentieth century's second half. His catalog of compositions (which numbers more than seventy works) includes pieces for solo keyboard, chamber ensemble, electronic media, orchestra, oratorio, art song, and opera. He was the most significant composer for the organ since Johann Sebastian Bach.

Messner, Reinhold

b. September 17, 1944
Bressanone, Italy
fields: Exploration and Colonization, Sports (mountain climbing)

The first man to climb all fourteen mountains in the world over 8000 meters high, Messner revolutionized mountaineering through his advocacy of a climbing style that relied upon minimal equipment and his refusal to use bottled oxygen at high altitudes.

Mesta, Perle

né: Pearl Reid Skirvin
b. October 12, 1889
Sturgis, Michigan
d. March 16, 1975
Oklahoma City, Oklahoma
fields: Government and Politics

Perle Mesta, one of Washington's most celebrated hostesses, spent her life involved in politics. In 1949, Harry Truman appointed her to a diplomatic post in Luxembourg, where she served until 1953.

Mester, Jorge

b. Apr. 10, 1935
Mexico City, Mexico
fields: Music (orchestra conductor)

Orchestra conductor. Jorge Mester debuted as a conductor with the Orquesta Sinfónica Nacional de México in 1955 and went on to conduct numerous orchestras in the United States and Europe, including the British Broadcasting Corporation Symphony Orchestra and the Royal Philharmonic Orchestra in London. He won the Naumburg Award for conducting in 1968. Mester was associated with the Louisville Orchestra from 1967 to 1979, during which time they made approximately two hundred recordings of works by twentieth century composers.

Metacom. *See* Metacomet

Metacomet

aka: King Philip
aka: Metacom

aka: Philip of Pokanoket
b. c. 1639
Pokanoket, probably present-day Mass.
d. Aug. 12, 1676
near Bristol, R.I.
fields: Government and Politics, Warfare and Conquest, Native American Affairs

Native American leader, a son of Massasoit. Wampanoag leader Metacomet (also known as Metacom and as King Philip) is primarily known for waging King Philip's War against the English Puritan colonists in New England in 1675. More than six hundred colonists and hundreds more Indians are said to have died in the conflict.

Metcalf, Victor Howard

b. Oct. 10, 1853
Utica, N.Y.
d. Feb. 20, 1936
Oakland, Calif.
fields: Government and Politics

Victor Howard Metcalf, a graduate of Yale Law School, served as a California congressman from 1900 to 1904. Under President Theodore Roosevelt, he was secretary of commerce and labor, then secretary of the Navy. In 1906, Roosevelt sent Metcalf to investigate the conditions faced by Japanese under the policy of educational segregation developed by the San Francisco school board. Metcalf's report, *Japanese in the City of San Francisco* (1906), stated that California's Japanese community deserved full protection and urged that the segregation order be withdrawn.

Metcalfe, Ralph Horace

b. May 30, 1910
Atlanta, Ga.
d. October 10, 1978
Chicago, Ill.
fields: Sports, Government and Politics

African American track star and legislator; Ralph Horace Metcalfe broke or equaled every sprint record between 40 and 220 yards in the 1930's and was named Athletic Commissioner of Illinois in 1949. Afetr serving on the Chicago City Council from 1954 to 1970, Metcalfe was elected as representative of the Illinois First Democratic District; he was reelected in 1976.

Methodius, Saint

b. c. 825
Thessalonica, Greece
d. April 6, 884
probably near Velehrad in Great Moravia
fields: Religion and Theology, Language and Linguistics

Through their spiritual commitment, blood brothers Cyril and Methodius expanded Christianity in central and eastern Europe and established the foundations of Slavic culture and literature with the development of the Glagolitic alphabet.

Metternich

full: Clemens Wenzel Nepomuk Lothar von Metternich
b. May 15, 1773
Coblenz, Archbishopric of Trier
d. June 11, 1859
Vienna, Austro-Hungarian Empire
fields: Diplomacy, Government and Politics

As Europe's preeminent champion of post-French Revolution conservatism, Metternich was the chief architect in the reconstruction of the European map after the fall of Napoleon I. As minister of foreign affairs, and, later, as state chancellor to the Austrian emperor, Metternich presided for more than three decades over the political and diplomatic workings of the continent he had restored until the Revolutions of 1848 swept him from power and ushered in a new generation of leaders.

Metzger, Tom

b. 1938
fields: Television, Social Reform

The founder of the American white supremacist group White Aryan Resistance, Tom Metzger pioneered the use of cable-access television as a propaganda tool and recruiting tool. However, local communities have organized to oppose his broadcasts. In 1990 Metzger, his son John, and his organization were sued by the Southern Poverty Law Center and the Anti-Defamation League for inciting Oregon Skinheads who murdered an Ethiopian immigrant. In 1990 a jury ruled against Metzger and awarded the victim's family $12.5 million.

Mexican Spitfire. *See* Velez, Lupe

Meyer, Katharine. *See* Graham, Katharine

Meyer, Russ

full: Russell Albion Meyer
b. March 21, 1922
Oakland, California
fields: Film

Russ Meyer created sexually explicit films satirizing pornography. His first film, *The Immoral Mr. Teas* (1959), was the first soft-core pornographic film to make a lot of money. Its success launched Meyer's career and made him the target of censors. Later films included *Faster Pussycat, Kill, Kill* (1966), *The Vixen* (1969), *Supervixens* (1975), and *Beneath the Valley of the Ultravixens* (1979).

Meyerhold, Vsevolod Yemilyevich

né: Karl Theodor Kasimir Meyergold
b. February 9, 1874
Penza, Russia
d. February 2, 1940
Moscow, U.S.S.R.
fields: Theater and Entertainment (actor)

Meyerhold departed from the powerful naturalistic influences of Constantin Stanislavsky and the Moscow Art Theatre to experiment with more abstract forms of theater. Representing the other side of the universal duality in theater—expressionistic versus naturalistic—he dared to experiment with an ingenious stage language of his own invention and devised the constructivist principles of set design and the biomechanical approach to actor training.

Meyerson, Golda. *See* Meir, Golda

Mfume, Kweisi

né: Frizell Gray
b. October 24, 1948
Baltimore, Md.
fields: Civil Rights, Government and Politics

Kweisi Mfume served five terms as a U.S. congressman for Maryland's Seventh District, beginning in 1986. He served on the House Committee on Banking, Finance, and Urban Affairs; the House Committee on Small Business; and House select committees on hunger and narcotics abuse and control. He was also chair of the influential Congressional Black Caucus (CBC). He left Congress in 1996 to head the financially troubled and scandal-rocked National Association for the Advancement of Colored People (NAACP) in 1996. Mfume published his memoir, *No Free Ride: From the Mean Streets to the Mainstream* (1996).

Mi Fei

aka: Mi Fu
aka: Yuanzhang
aka: Yüan-chang
aka: Xiangyang
aka: Hsiang-yang
aka: Haiyue Waishi
aka: Hai-yüeh Wai-shih
b. 1052
Xiangyang, Hubei, China
d. 1107
Huaiyang, Jiangsu, China
fields: Art

An accomplished calligrapher and the paragon of Chinese artist-connoisseurs, Mi Fei played a pivotal role in the transmission of the classical tradition of Chinese calligraphy.

Miantonomo

b. c. 1600
d. 1643
fields: Government and Politics, Diplomacy, Native American Affairs

Narragansett leader Miantonomo attempted to build an anticolonial Indian alliance after he was briefly imprisoned by the Puritans in 1642. Mohegan leader Uncas turned Miantonomo over to the English, who sentenced him to die at the hands of Uncas' brother Wawequa in September, 1643.

Miassin, Leonid Fyodorovich. *See* Massine, Léonide

Miastashedekaroos. *See* White Man Runs Him

Micanopy

aka: Sint-Chakkee
b. c. 1780
St. Augustine region of Fla.
d. Jan. 2, 1849
Fort Gibson, Indian Territory
fields: Government and Politics, Native American Affairs

Native American leader. As principal chief of the Seminoles, Micanopy resisted removal during the Second Seminole War (1835-1842). Supported the resistance efforts of younger tribal leaders such as Osceola and Wildcat (Micanopy's nephew).

Micheaux, Oscar

b. January 2, 1884
d. 1951
fields: Film, Literature

African American novelist and film producer; Oscar Micheaux created and distributed some forty-eight features between 1918 and 1948, including *Birthright* (1918), considered to be the first full-length black film . Micheaux's films, *The Homesteader* (1919), *The Exile* (1932), and *The Betrayal* (1948), and novels, *The Wind from Nowhere* (1941) and *The Case of Mrs. Wingate* (1944), explore the theme of interracial love. Micheaux's other films, such as *Within Our Gates* (1920) and *Lem Hawkins' Confession* (1935), deal with the themes of wrongful accusation and racial prejudice.

Michelangelo

full: Michelangelo Buonarroti
b. March 6, 1475
Caprese, Tuscany
d. February 18, 1564
Rome
fields: Art, Architecture

Michelangelo was a true Renaissance man, excelling in sculpture, painting, architecture, and poetry. He was the supreme master of the human body, especially the male nude, and his idealized and expressive treatment of this theme was enormously influential, both in his own day and in subsequent centuries.

Michelena, Beatriz

b. ?
San Francisco, Calif.
d. ?
Spain
fields: Theater and Entertainmant, Music, Film

Latina actor and singer. By the early 1910's, Beatriz Michelena was performing on San Francisco's musical comedy stages. She made her screen debut in *Salomy Jane* (1914) and soon became the California Motion Picture Corporation's leading lady. Michelena appeared in eleven of the company's feature films before it went bankrupt in 1920. She then returned to the stage, touring widely with her own musical comedy group.

Michelet, Jules

b. August 21, 1789
Paris, France
d. February 9, 1874
Hyères, France
fields: Historiography, Philosophy

Michelet was France's greatest national historian and one of the guiding forces of modern historical writing.

Michelin, André

full: André Jules Michelin
b. January 16, 1853
Paris, France
d. April 4, 1931
Paris, France
fields: Business and Industry, Invention and Technology

The brothers André and Édouard Michelin pioneered the use of pneumatic tires on automobiles and were also leaders in the development of the radial-ply tire as well as steel-reinforced tire construction. They founded a motorist's travel guide company that produces handbooks for numerous tourist destinations throughout the world.

Michelin, Édouard

b. June 23, 1859
Clermont-Ferrand, France
d. August 25, 1940
Orcines, Puy-de-Dôme, France
fields: Business and Industry, Invention and Technology

The brothers Édouard and André Michelin pioneered the use of pneumatic tires on automobiles and were also leaders in the development of the radial-ply tire as well as steel-reinforced tire construction. They founded a motorist's travel guide company that produces handbooks for numerous tourist destinations throughout the world.

Michelson, Albert A.

full: Albert Abraham Michelson
b. December 19, 1852
Strelno, Prussia
d. May 9, 1931
Pasadena, California
fields: Physics

Michelson was the first American to win a Nobel Prize for Physics, which he received for determining the length of the standard meter in terms of wavelengths of light. His significant contributions to physics and optics include measurement of velocity of light, of the ether drift, of the rigidity of earth, and of the diameter of stars, as well as development of the interferometer.

Michener, James A.

full: James Albert Michener
b. February 3, 1907 (?)
New York, New York (?)
d. October 16, 1997
Austin, Texas
fields: Literature

Michener was a prolific writer who became known for his epic novels that explored the landscape, history, and culture of specific geographic regions in the United States and around the world.

Michikinikwa. *See* Little Turtle

Middleton, Herbert, Jr. *See* Blacque, Taurean

Midgley, Mary

né: Mary Scrutton
b. September 13, 1919
London, England
fields: Philosophy, Biology, Women's Rights

Mary Midgley combined critique and constructive commentary to bring philosophy to bear on contemporary issues. Her philosophy is marked by an emphasis on the importance of human nature and biology, the recognition and rejection of nonsense, and a resistance to smoothing out significant differences. Major works include *Beast and Man* (1978), *Animals and Why They Matter* (1983), *Women's Choices: Philosophical Problems Facing Feminism* (1983, with Judith Hughes), *Wickedness: A Philosophical Essay* (1984), *Evolution as a Religion* (1985), *Wisdom, Information, and Wonder* (1989), *Can't We Make Moral Judgements?* (1991), *Science as Salvation* (1992), *The Ethical Primate* (1994), *Utopias, Dolphins, and Computers* (1996).

Mies van der Rohe, Ludwig

né: Ludwig Mies
b. March 27, 1886
Aachen, Germany
d. August 7, 1969
Chicago, Illinois
fields: Architecture

One of the greatest architects and architectural educators of the twentieth century, Mies van der Rohe left a legacy of famous buildings and a legacy in furniture design unmatched by any other member of the Modern Movement.

Mijares, Jose Maria

b. 1921
Havana, Cuba
fields: Art

Latino artist. Jose Maria Mijares learned art at the Academia de Bellas Artes de San Alejandro in Cuba, which he attended in 1945 on a scholarship. He traveled to New York City in 1950 after winning the First National Prize in Painting and Sculpture, then returned to Cuba. In 1968, he fled the oppressive Cuban government and settled in Miami, Florida. Mijares won Cintas Foundation fellowships in 1970 and 1971.

Mikulski, Barbara

full: Barbara Ann Mikulski
b. July 20, 1936
Baltimore, Maryland
fields: Government and Politics

The first Democratic woman elected to the U.S. Senate on her own (in 1986), Mikulski is dedicated to the achievement of social and economic equity for working-class Americans.

Milburn, Amos

b. April 1, 1927
Houston, Tex.
d. January 3, 1980
Houston, Tex.
fields: Music (blues singer)

African American blues singer; Amos Milburn had his first hit with the single "Chicken Shack Boogie" (1947), which sold one million copies. Some of his other hits include "Rooming House Boogie" (1949), "Hold Me Baby" (1949), "Bad, Bad Whiskey" (1950), "Thinking and Drinking" (1952), "One Scotch, One Bourbon, One Beer" (1953), and "Let Me Go Home, Whiskey" (1953). Later songs, such as "Let's Rock Awhile" (1951) and "Rock, Rock, Rock" (1952), were precursors to the birth of rock and roll.

Milhaud, Darius

b. September 4, 1892
Aix-en-Provence, France
d. June 22, 1974
Geneva, Switzerland
fields: Music

Perhaps the most famous composer of the mythical "Les Six," Milhaud was undoubtedly the most prolific, his published works running to nearly 450. He did highly original work in such areas as polytonality and percussion music. His best work is characterized by a Gallic lyricism.

Milk, Harvey

b. May 22, 1930
New York, N.Y.
d. Nov. 27, 1978
San Francisco, Calif.
fields: Government and Politics, Civil Rights

An openly gay camera store owner who came to San Francisco in 1969, Harvey Milk got into city politics when Mayor George Moscone appointed him to an advisory group. In 1977 Milk was elected to the city/county board of supervisors and became the best-known openly gay public official in the United States. The following year he and Moscone were assassinated by Dan White, a mentally disturbed former supervisor.

Milken, Michael

b. 1946
Van Nuys, Calif.
fields: Banking and Finance

Securities broker. Michael Milken was a major figure in the controversial "junk" bond revolution of the 1980's. A broker with the firm of Drexel Burnham Lambert, he was implicated by fellow investor Ivan Boesky and charged with dozens of securities-law violations. In 1990, he pled guilty to six technical violations of securities laws, was ordered to pay more than a billion dollars in fines and restitution, and was sentenced him to ten years in prison. In 1993, he was released after having served twenty-two months.

Mill, James

b. April 6, 1773
Northwater Bridge, Logie Pert, Forfarshire, Scotland
d. June 23, 1836
Vicarage Place, Kensington, England
fields: Historiography, Philosophy, Economics

A utilitarian propagandist and theorist, Mill shattered neat boundaries of modern special scholarship with his intellectual and practical interests.

Mill, John Stuart

b. May 20, 1806
London, England
d. May 8, 1873
Avignon, France
fields: Philosophy, Economics

Desiring the greatest possible happiness for individual men and women and an England of the greatest possible justice and freedom, Mill questioned all assumptions about knowledge and truth and made what was observed the starting point of his discussions.

Millan, Felix

full: Felix Bernardo Millan y Martinez
aka: The Cat
b. Aug. 21, 1943
Yabucoa, Puerto Rico
fields: Sports (baseball player)

Latino Baseball player. Second baseman Felix Millan was nicknamed "The Cat" for his defensive reflexes. He made his major league debut in 1966 with the Atlanta Braves. He made three All-Star Teams and won Gold Glove Awards in 1969 and 1972. His career bating average was .279, his best year being 1970, when he hit .310 and scored 100 runs. He retired in 1977.

Millay, Edna St. Vincent

pseudo.: Nancy Boyd
b. February 22, 1892
Rockland, Maine
d. October 19, 1950
Austerlitz, New York
fields: Literature

Edna St. Vincent Millay was a symbol and spokeswoman for women's sexual liberation, particularly during the Roaring Twenties, and continues to be regarded as a pioneering American feminist.

Miller, Agatha Mary Clarissa. *See* Christie, Agatha

Miller, Arthur

b. October 17, 1915
New York, New York
fields: Theater and Entertainment

Considered one of the foremost dramatists in the United States, Miller has penetrated the American consciousness and gained worldwide recognition for his probing dramas of social awareness.

Miller, Bebe

né: Beryl Adele Miller
b. September 20, 1950
Brooklyn, N.Y.
fields: Dance (dancer and choreographer)

African American dancer and choreographer; in 1984, Bebe Miller established her own modern dance company in New York City; solo and group performances include *Spending Time Doing Things*, *Rain* (1989), *Trapped in Queens* (1984), *The Hendrix Project* (1991; performed to the music of Jimi

Hendrix), and *Hidden Boy: Incidents from a Stressed Memory* (1991).

Miller, Cheryl

full: Cheryl DeAnne Miller
b. January 3, 1964
Riverside, Calif.
fields: Sports (basketball player)

African American basketball player. At the University of Southern California (USC) Cheryl DeAnne Miller led her team to consecutive National Collegiate Athletic Association (NCAA) championships and was chosen as the NCAA tournament's outstanding player both years (1983, 1984). In 1984 Miller won a gold medal on the Olympic women's basketball team. Among her awards are the Broderick Award (1984, 1985), the Wade Trophy (1985), and the Naismith Trophy (1984, 1985, 1986). From 1993 to 1995, she was head coach of the women's basketball team at USC. During the 1990's, she also worked as a basketball analyst on television. In 1997, Miller was named head coach of the Women's National Basketball Association (WNBA) team the Phoenix Mercury.

Miller, Dorie

full: Doris Miller
b. October 12, 1919
Waco, Tex.
d. 1943
the Pacific
fields: Warfare and Conquest

African American military hero. During the attack on Pearl Harbor, December 7, 1941, Dorie Miller braved enemy fire to pull his wounded comrades to safety, then manned a machine gun, and shot down at least two Japanese planes. He received the Navy Cross for his heroism.

Miller, Earl B.

b. 1930
Seattle, Wash.
fields: Art (painter)

African American painter; Earl B. Miller received his training from many institutions, including the Illinois Institute of Technology, the Pratt Institute in Brooklyn, N.Y., the Brooklyn Museum School, the Art Students League, and the Akademie der Bildenden in Kunste, Germany. Several one-person shows of his abstract art followed his first exhibit in 1950.

Miller, Henry

b. December 26, 1891
New York, New York
d. June 7, 1980
Pacific Palisades, California
fields: Literature

Henry Miller wrote sexually explicit works that were long banned in English-speaking countries. His novel *Tropic of Cancer* (1934), established a distinction between Miller's often romantic yearnings and the mechanical lustful adventures of his male friends. It was followed by *Tropic of Capricorn* (1939). Both books drew critical praise, but were routinely seized by U.S. Customs agents because of their allegedly obscene content. Other books included *Sexus* (1949), *Plexus* (1953), and *Quiet Days in Clichy* (1956).

Miller, Kelly

b. July 18, 1863
Winnsboro, N.C.
d. December 29, 1939
Washington, D.C.
fields: Sociology, Education

African American sociologist and educator; Kelly Miller's well-known works include *Race Adjustment: Essays on the Negro in America* (1906), *Out of the House of Bondage* (1914), and *An Appeal to Conscience: America's Code of Caste a Disgrace to Democracy* (1918). He was a major contributor to the development of Howard University, as dean of the college of arts and sciences (1907-1918) among other positions. Miller was also one of the founders of the American Negro Academy (1897), a society of intellectuals.

Miller, Mary Boykin. *See* Chesnut, Mary Boykin

Miller, Reggie

full: Reginald Wayne Miller
b. August 24, 1965
Riverside, Calif.
fields: Sports (basketball player)

African American basketball player; Reggie Miller joined the the Indiana Pacers of the National Basketball Association (NBA) in 1987. His tremendous outside shooting ability helped Miller established himself as a powerful scorer; he played in his first NBA All-Star Game in the 1989-1990 season. During the 1990's, he was one of the most respected clutch shooting guards in the NBA.

Miller, Rice. *See* Williamson, Sonny Boy, II

Miller, Samuel F.

full: Samuel Freeman Miller
b. 1816
d. 1890
fields: Law

U.S. Supreme Court justice, 1862-1890 (died while in office); appointed by President Lincoln. Opposed using the Fourteenth Amendment to block state regulations of business activity and favored the use of individual rights to check the power of the federal government. Significant opinions: *Slaughterhouse Cases*, 83 U.S. 36 (1873); *Kilbourn v. Thompson*, 103 U.S. 168 (1881); *United States v. Lee*, 106 U.S. 196 (1882).

Miller, Thomas Ezekiel

b. June 17, 1849
Ferrebeeville, S.C.
d. April 8, 1938
Charleston, S.C.
fields: Government and Politics

African American U.S. representative;Thomas Ezekiel Miller was one of South Carolina's general assemblyman from 1874 until 1880, when he became a state senator. Though Miller ran for Congress in 1988, he did not take his seat untill September 24, 1890, because of election disputes. Miller was appointed to serve on the House Committee on the Library of Congress. In 1893, Miller returned to state politics, serving as a state representative from 1894 to 1896.

Millett, Kate

full: Katherine Murray Millett
b. September 14, 1934
St. Paul, Minnesota
fields: Women's Rights

Since the 1970 publication of her book *Sexual Politics*, a manifesto of the feminist movement, Millett has been an acknowledged leader of the modern women's movement.

Millikan, Robert Andrews

b. March 22, 1868
Morrison, Illinois
d. December 19, 1953
Pasadena, California
fields: Physics, Education

As a skilled and meticulous experimenter, Millikan made major contributions to twentieth century physics; as a textbook author, university teacher, and supervisor of research, he greatly influenced the way that physics was studied in the United States; as an administrator, he was responsible for the rise to prominence of the California Institute of Technology. He was awarded the 1923 Nobel Prize in Physics.

Millin, Henry Allan

b. May 17, 19??
St. Thomas, Virgin Islands
fields: Government and Politics

African American territorial official; Henry Allan Millin's first public posts were as chief clerk of the Police and Prison Department and as chief clerk of the tax assessor's office in the Virgin Islands. After serving as executive director of the Virgin Islands Housing Authority Millin became vice president of the First PA Bank of North America. In 1978 he was elected as lieutenant governor of the Virgin Islands.

Millinder, Lucky

full: Lucius Venable Millinder
b. August 8, 1900
Anniston, Ala.
d. September 28, 1966
New York, N.Y.
fields: Dance, Music

African American dancer, jazz composer, and bandleader; Lucky Millinder had a talent for remembering a musical arrangement and getting a band to perform it consistently. He was the leader of the Mills Blue Rhythm Band (1933-1938) and collaborated, as a composer, with Irving Mills on several of the the band's best-known pieces, including "Ride, Red, Ride" (1935). Millinder formed the Lucky Millinder Orchestra (1940), with vocalist Sister Rosetta Tharpe, which popularized the early rhythm-and-blues style in such hits as "When the Lights Go on Again" (1942) and "Apollo Jump" (1943).

Mills, Billy

full: William Mervin Mills
b. June 30, 1938
Pine Ridge, South Dakota
fields: Sports (track and field)

A Native American who stunned the world with a recordbreaking running performance, Billy Mills, with a tremendous burst of speed, sprinted to a ten-foot win, establishing an Olympic record for the 10,000-meter run in 1964. In 1972, he was named one of American's Ten Outstanding Young Men. In 1976, he was inducted into the National Track and Field Hall of Fame and in 1984 into the U.S. Olympic Hall of Fame.

Mills, Florence

b. January 25, 1895
Washington, D.C.
d. November 1, 1927
New York, N.Y.
fields: Theater and Entertainment

African American dancer, singer, and comedian; Florence Mills was a leading stage entertainer of the 1920's who starred in revues in New York City, London, and Paris. Her most popular song was "I'm a Little Blackbird Looking for a Bluebird," from the musical revue *Dixie to Broadway* (1924).

Mills, Stephanie

b. March 22, 1957
New York, N.Y.
fields: Theater and Entertainment, Music

African American actress and singer; Stephanie Mills had her first and greatest success on Broadway in the starring role in *The Wiz*. She is the recipient of seven Tony Awards for Broadway theater performance and has recorded two gold albums. She won a Grammy in 1980. During the 1990's, she continued to work in musical theater.

Milne, A. A.

full: Alan Alexander Milne
b. January 18, 1882
London, England
d. January 31, 1956
Hartfield, Sussex, England
fields: Literature

Milne wrote light comedy and drama but was most successful with his stories and poems for children, especially those featuring Winnie-the-Pooh.

Milner, Thirman L.

b. October 29, 1933
Hartford, Conn.
fields: Government and Politics

African American mayor of Hartford, Conn; Thirman L. Milner served as assistant majority leader in the Connecticut State House of Representatives during the 1981-1982 legislative session. He left his position as state representative to campaign for mayor of Hartford. Milner became the first African American to be popularly elected as a mayor in New England when he was elected on November 3, 1981. He served as first vice president of the National Conference of Black Mayors in 1985.

Milošević, Slobodan

b. August 29, 1941
Požarevac, Serbia, Yugoslavia
fields: Government and Politics

Slobodan Milošević became an ardent Serbian nationalist in 1980's. President of Serbia from 1989 to 1997 and of Yugoslavia beginning in 1997. Took charge of Serbian army to fight civil war in early 1990's when Bosnia, Macedonia, Slovenia, and Croatia all announced secession from Yugoslvian federation. In late 1990's, Milošević's ethinc cleansing policies against ethnic Albanians in Yugoslavian province of Kosovo provoked 1999 NATO air strikes and Yugoslavian troop withdrawal from the province.

Miltiades the Younger

b. c. 554 B.C.E.
probably Attica, Greece
d. 489 B.C.E.
probably Athens, Greece
fields: Government and Politics, Warfare and Conquest

Through innovative tactics and inspired battlefield leadership, Miltiades led Athens to victory over the Persians at the Battle of Marathon. He thus helped to secure Greek civilization from engulfment by Near Eastern influences and greatly enhanced Athenian prestige in the Greek world.

Milton, John

b. December 9, 1608
London, England
d. November 8, 1674
London, England
fields: Literature

An important writer of revolutionary prose during the English Commonwealth, Milton is also England's greatest heroic poet.

Milton, Little. *See* Little Milton

Mims, Madeline Manning

b. 1948
Cleveland, Ohio
fields: Sports (track and field)

African American runner. In 1968 Madeline Manning Mims won a gold medal in the 800-meter with an Olympic record time of 2:00.9 to become the first American woman to win that event in the Olympics. In the 1972 Olympics she won a silver medal for the 4 ⎱400-meter relay with a time of 3:25.2. Mims' American record for 800 meters (1:57.9) stood from 1976 to 1983. Named to the All-Time, All-Star Indoor Track and Field Team (1983), she is also a member of the U.S., National, and Olympics Track and Field Halls of Fame.

Min, Pyong Gap

b. 1942
fields: Sociology, Historiography

Pyong Gap Min received doctorates in education (1979) and sociology (1983), both from Georgia State. An associate professor of sociology at Queens College of the City University of New York, Min wrote *Ethnic Business Enterprise: Korean Small Business in Atlanta* (1988) and "Korean Immigrants in Los Angeles," in *Immigration and Entrepreneurship* (1993), edited by Ivan Light and Parminder Bhachu.

Min, Yong Soon

b. Apr. 29, 1953
Republic of Korea
fields: Art

Artist Yong Soon Min received a B.A., an M.A., and an M.F.A. from the University of California at Berkeley. She worked at the Asian American Arts Alliance in New York in the mid-1980's and received an artists fellowship grant from the National Endowment for the Arts in 1989-1990. She was named a National Printmaking Fellow at the Rutgers Center for Innovative Printmaking in 1990. Her installation pieces, including *Half Home*, *De-*

colonization, and *Ritual Labor of a Mechanical Bride*, look at gender stereotyping, the construction of Asian American identity, and Korean immigrant issues.

Minami, Dale

b. October 13, 1946
Los Angeles, Calif.
fields: Civil Rights, Law

Dale Minami, a third-generation Japanese American, cofounded the Asian Law Caucus in 1972. He was the lead attorney in the successful attempt to vacate, under a "writ of error coram nobis," the original conviction of Fred Korematsu, a Japanese American who resisted internment during World War II.

Mindszenty, József

b. March 29, 1892
Csehimindszenti, Austro-Hungarian Empire
d. May 6, 1975
Vienna, Austria
fields: Religion and Theology

József Mindszenty was a Hungarian Roman Catholic church leader who was harassed and imprisoned by both right-wing and communist regimes because of his political activism. Ordained a priest in 1915, he became a bishop in 1944. After World War II, he was appointed cardinal and prince primate of Hungary—titles he retained until 1973, when Pope Paul VI deprived him of both. Meanwhile, he helped lead the Christian-National movement that fought against the progressive Karolyi regime in late 1918 and the proletarian dictatorship of Béla Kun in 1919. During the 1930's and early 1940's he advocated of restoring Hungary's monarchy.

Miner, Myrtilla

b. Mar. 4, 1815
near Brookfield, N.Y.
d. Dec. 17, 1864
Washington, D.C.
fields: Education, Civil Rights, Social Reform

Myrtilla Miner was an educator and abolitionist; in 1851 opened the Colored Girls School in Washington, D.C. The school was closed in 1860 but reopened after Miner's death, a testament to the dire need for the abolition of slavery and the education of African Americans.

Mineta, Norman Yoshio

b. Nov. 12, 1931
San Jose, Calif.
fields: Government and Politics

Japanese American Norman Yoshio Mineta served as a U.S. Army intelligence officer from 1953 to 1956, when he returned to San Jose to join his father in the Mineta Insurance Agency. He became a member of the Human Relations Commission in 1962, then was appointed to the Housing Authority of San Jose and the City Council of San Jose in 1967. He became vice mayor in 1969 and served as mayor from 1971-1975. He was elected to the House of Representatives in 1974. A Democrat, he served on numerous committees and was one of the sponsors of the Civil Liberties Act of 1988, which provided reparations to Japanese Americans interned during World War II.

Mingus, Charlie

b. April 22, 1922
Nogales, Ariz.
d. January 5, 1979
Cuernavaca, Mexico
fields: Music (composer and bass violinist)

African American composer and bass violinist; Charlie Mingus, whose influences include musician Fats Waller, started playing with Louis Armstrong and later joined the Lionel Hampton band. Mingus became popular in the 1950's and 1960's.

Minh-ha, Trinh T.

b. 1950's
Vietnam
fields: Film, Music

Filmmaker, writer, and composer Trinh T. Minh-ha arrived in the United States in 1970. Her films include *Reassemblage* (1982), *Naked Spaces, Living Is Round* (1985), and *Surname Viet Given Name Nam* (1989). Her publications include *Un Art sans oeuvre* (1981), *African Spaces: Designs for Living in Upper Volta* (1985), *En Miniscules* (1987; poems), and *Woman, Native, Other: Writing, Postcoloniality and Feminism* (1989).

Minin, Nikita. *See* Nikon

Mink, Patsy

né: Patsy Takemoto
b. Dec. 6, 1927
Paia, Maui, Hawaii
fields: Government and Politics

Japanese American politician; Patsy Mink born Patsy Takemoto in Hawaii; earned law degree at the University of Chicago in 1951, returning to Hawaii to open private practice; territorial representative, 1956-1964; assistant secretary of state under President Jimmy Carter; U.S. representative, 1965-1977, since 1990 (Democrat); member of Honolulu city council, 1983-1987.

Minkowski, Hermann

b. June 22, 1864
Alexotas, Russian Empire (now Kaunas, Lithuania)
d. Jan. 12, 1909
Göttingen, Germany
fields: Mathematics (applied math, geometry, and number theory)

In 1909 Hermann Minkowski published *Raum und Zeit* (space and time), which demonstrated that relativity necessitates considering time as a fourth dimension; work was the foundation of modern functional analysis; worked with quadratic forms and developed the mathematical theory called the geometry of numbers; formed a mathematical description of Albert Einstein's special theory of relativity that helped Einstein to develop his general theory.

Minnick, Sylvia Sun

b. Apr. 26, 1941
Kuala Lumpur, Malaysia
fields: Publishing, Government and Politics

Sylvia Sun Minnick was the first Asian American to win a council seat in Stockton, California. Minnick founded the San Joaquin County Republican Asian Coalition and the consultant firm A Bridge to the Past. She is the publisher/owner of Heritage West Books in Stockton, California and the author of *Samfow: The San Joaquin Chinese Legacy* (1988).

Minoso, Minnie

b. November 29, 1922
Havana, Cuba
fields: Sports (baseball)

Minnie Minoso played professional baseball in Cuba and for the New York Cubans in the Negro Leagues in 1946 and 1947. He signed with the Cleveland Indians, making his major league debut with Cleveland in 1949. He was traded to the Chicago White Sox in 1951 but hit .326 and led the American League in triples and stolen bases. He also led the American League in steals in 1952 and 1953, in triples in 1954 and 1956, in doubles in 1957, and in hits in 1960. He was named to six All-Star teams, and won a Gold Glove Award (1957) for defensive excellence. He retired in 1964 after being traded between Chicago and Cleveland three times in the 1950's and playing briefly for the St. Louis Cardinals and Washington Senators. In 1976 and 1980, he was coaxed out of retirement for a small number of hitting appearances, making his career only the second in major league history to span five decades.

Minton, Sherman

b. 1890
d. 1965
fields: Law

U.S. Supreme Court justice, 1949-1956; appointed by President Truman. Consistently held for the government in criminal cases. Significant opinions: *United States v. Rabinowitz*, 339 U.S. 56 (1950); *United States ex rel. Knauff v. Shaughnessy*, 338 U.S. 537 (1950).

Mirabeau, comte de

né: Honoré-Gabriel Riqueti
b. March 9, 1749
the Estate of Mirabeau, Bignon, near Nemours, France
d. April 2, 1791
Paris, France
fields: Government and Politics

Mirabeau was a bridge between the aristocracy and the people, and between the variously named legislatures and the king. He led the fight to establish the National Assembly out of the Estates-General to bring order in the then-named National Constituent Assembly and to save the monarchy as one of the two agents of the people.

Miranda, Carmen

b. Feb. 9, 1909
Marco de Canaveses, Portugal
d. Aug. 5, 1955
Beverly Hills, Calif.
fields: Music, Theater and Entertainment

Latina singer and actor. Carmen Miranda's appearance in the Broadway musical *The Streets of Paris* (1939) singing "The South American Way" launched her Hollywood career. "The Brazilian Bombshell" made nineteen American films, appearing in secondary roles with such legends as Betty Grable, Groucho Marx, Don Ameche, and Alice Faye. Miranda made about 150 recordings, including the popular songs "I Yi Yi Yi Yi," "Chica Chica Boom Chic," "Boa Noite," and "Cuando Te Gusta." She also sang regularly with Xavier Cugat and Desi Arnaz.

Miranda, Rafael Cancel. *See* Cancel Miranda, Rafael

Miriam Simos. *See* Starhawk

Mirikitani, Janice

b. 1942
fields: Literature (poet)

Japanese American poet Janice Mirikitani was part of the Asian American ethnic pride movement in the late 1960's and early 1970's. Her socially conscious poetry is collected in *Awake in the River* (1978) and *Shedding Silence* (1987). Mirikitani edited the anthology *Making Waves: Writings by and About Asian American Women* (1989), which features short stories, essays, articles, and poems.

Miró, Joan

b. April 20, 1893
Barcelona, Spain
d. December 25, 1983
Palma, Majorca, Spain
fields: Art

The work of Miró, Spanish painter, sculptor, and ceramist, is acclaimed for its highly individualistic style, abstract as well as figurative, and is characterized by its vivacious fantasy. Many critics regard Miró as the greatest artist of the Surrealist movement.

Miruelo, Diego

b. ?
d. ?
fields: Exploration and Colonization

Spanish explorer. In 1516, three years after Juan Ponce de León made the first trip to the Florida coast, Diego Miruelo sailed a single vessel from Cuba to Florida and traded Spanish toys for the Native Americans' gold. His embellished accounts of the coast generating interest in the area in Cuba. A man named Diego Miruelo was a pilot in Pánfilo de Narváez's expedition to the Florida coast in 1528, during which all but four members of the party perished. Historians are uncertain whether this is the same Diego Miruelo.

Mises, Richard von

full: Richard Martin Edler von Mises
b. Apr. 19, 1883
Lemberg, Austro-Hungarian Empire (now Lvov, Ukraine)
d. July 14, 1953
Boston, Massachusetts
fields: Mathematics (applied math, probability, and statistics)

Richard von Mises generated ideas related to probability, such as sample space. In 1922, with Ludwig Prandtl, founded GAMM (Gesellschaft für Angewandte Mathematik und Mechanik), an organization for applied mathematicians; in 1939, formulated the birthday problem.

Mishima, Yukio

né: Kimitake Hiraoka
b. January 14, 1925
Tokyo, Japan
d. November 25, 1970
Tokyo, Japan
fields: Literature

Mishima was a writer of great power, whose life became a performance, ultimately a tragic performance. At the time of his suicide, he was widely regarded as a leading candidate for the Nobel Prize in Literature.

Mistahimaskwa. *See* Big Bear

Mistral, Gabriela

né: Lucila Godoy Alcayaga
b. Apr. 7, 1889
Vicuña, Chile
d. Jan. 10, 1957
Hempstead, N.Y.
fields: Literature

Poet. Gabriela Mistral wrote her first poems while attending the Escuela Superior de Niñas de Vicuña. In 1904, she began publishing her poems under various pseudonyms in *La voz de elqui*, a Vicuña periodical, and in *El Coquimbo*. In 1905, she moved to Campañía Baja to teach. She continued to publish in local papers, eventually collecting her poems in such books as *Desolación* (1922) and *Ternura* (1924). She also wrote the long narrative poem *Poema de Chile* (1967). She was awarded the Nobel Prize in Literature in 1945.

Mitchell, Abbie

b. September 25, 1884
Baltimore, Md.
d. March 16, 1960
New York, N.Y.
fields: Music (singer)

African American singer; Abbie Mitchell rose to prominence performing with vaudevillians Bert Williams and George Walker. Apart from her versatile performances in musical comedy, drama, and opera, Mitchell is remembered for nurturing many American talents when she taught and directed music at Tuskegee Institute.

Mitchell, Alice. *See* Rivlin, Alice

Mitchell, Arthur

b. March 27, 1934
New York, N.Y.
fields: Dance

African American dancer, choreographer, and dance company founder. In 1955 Arthur Mitchell, the first black principal dancer in a major company, made his debut with the New York City Ballet in George Balanchine's *Western Symphony*. He stayed with the company until 1969. He formed an interracial dance company and created the National Ballet Company of Brazil, acting as its artistic director and choreographer. He later formed his own dance school in Harlem, the Dance Theater of Harlem, which soon became one of the youngest companies to perform throughout the world.

Mitchell, Arthur Wergs

b. December 22, 1883
near Lafayette, Ala.
d. May 9, 1968
Petersburg, Va.
fields: Government and Politics

African American U.S. representative; Arthur Wergs Mitchell was the first black Democrat to be seated in Congress (January 3, 1935). He was chosen to serve on the House

Committee on Post Offices and Post Roads. Mitchell became the first African American to make an address at a Democratic National Convention when he was selected to give a seconding speech for Franklin D. Roosevelt's nomination in 1936. Mitchell also worked as western director of minority affairs in Roosevelt's reelection campaign.

Mitchell, Bobby

full: Robert Cornelius Mitchell
b. June 6, 1935
Hot Springs, Ark.
fields: Sports (football player)

African American football player. In 1958 Bobby Mitchell was drafted by the Cleveland Browns and played forty-eight consecutive games at halfback. He was traded to the Washington Redskins in 1961, becoming the team's first black player. He played wide receiver for the Redskins until 1968, when he joined their personnel staff. He made the All-Pro Team three consecutive years (1962-1964) and played in the Pro Bowl from 1961 through 1964. He was inducted into the Pro Football Hall of Fame in 1983.

Mitchell, Clarence M., Jr.

b. March 8, 1911
Baltimore, Md.
d. March 18, 1984
Baltimore, Md.
fields: Government and Politics

Clarence Mitchell was the director of the Washington, D.C., bureau of the National Association for the Advancement of Colored People (NAACP) from 1950 to 1978. He was director of the Fair Employment Practices Committee under President Franklin Roosevelt. In 1981 Governor Harry Hughes appointed Mitchell to the board of regents of the the University of Maryland.

Mitchell, Joni

né: Roberta Joan Anderson
b. November 7, 1943
Ft. Macleod, Alberta, Canada
fields: Music

Mitchell has been an influential figure in American folk and popular music since the release of her first album in 1968. She is an original and innovative songwriter who has enjoyed a distinguished recording career. Her songs have been widely recorded by other artists as well.

Mitchell, Leona Pearl

b. October 13, 1949
Enid, Okla.
fields: Music (opera singer)

African American opera singer; a noted soprano, Leona Pearl Mitchell's work includes performances in operas, with symphonies, and in films; sang for President Gerald Ford (1976) and President Jimmy Carter (1978 and 1979); named a member of the Oklahoma Hall of Fame in 1983.

Mitchell, Loften

b. April 15, 1919
Columbus, N.C.
fields: Literature

African American dramatist; Loften Mitchell's dramas concentrate on the struggles of African Americans and conflicts between violence and nonviolence. His first commercially successful play was *The Cellar* (pr. 1952). Others include *A Land Beyond the River* (pr. 1957), *Tell Pharaoh* (televised 1963, pr. 1967), *Star of the Morning* (pr. 1965), and *Bubbling Brown Sugar* (pr. 1976), which was nominated for a Tony Award as best musical. Mitchell's best-known work is an informal history, *Black Drama: The Story of the American Negro in the Theatre* (1967).

Mitchell, Maggie Lena. *See* Walker, Maggie Lena

Mitchell, Maria

b. August 1, 1818
Nantucket, Massachusetts
d. June 28, 1889
Lynn, Massachusetts
fields: Astronomy

A dedicated and meticulous observer of the sky, Mitchell discovered the comet that bears her name and trained future women astronomers in her position as professor of astronomy and director of the observatory at Vassar College.

Mitchell, Nellie E. Brown

b. 1845
Dover, N.H.
d. January, 1924
Boston, Mass.
fields: Music (concert soprano)

African American concert soprano; Nellie E. Brown Mitchell performed concerts in Baltimore, Md., Washington, D.C., Portland, Maine, and St. John, Neb., as well as in Canada. Brown was the leading soprano with James Bergen's Star Concert Company from the early to the mid-1880's. Mitchell established the Nellie Brown Mitchell Concert Company in Boston in 1886.

Mitchell, Parren James

b. April 29, 1922
Baltimore, Md.
fields: Government and Politics

African American U.S. representative; Parren James Mitchell, was the first African American representative from the state of Maryland (1971-1986). He served as a member of the House Committee on the Budget and the House Committee on Banking, Finance, and Urban Affairs. Mitchell pushed for legislation that would help minority-owned businesses in bidding for federal projects and called for strong sanctions to be imposed against new investments in South Africa by United States corporations. Mitchell became chairman of the House Committee on Small Business in 1981.

Mitchell, Peter D.

full: Peter Dennis Mitchell
b. Sept. 29, 1920
Mitcham, Surrey, England
d. Apr. 10, 1992
Glynn House, near Bodmin, Cornwall, England
fields: Medicine, Biology, Chemistry, Physiology

Peter D. Mitchell was a pioneer in understanding how living cells make and use energy; theories explained how electrical, chemical, and mechanical forms of biological energy are interconverted; won the Nobel Prize in Chemistry in 1978.

Mitchell, William

full: William Lendrum Mitchell
b. December 29, 1879
Nice, France
d. February 19, 1936
New York, New York
fields: Military Affairs

An advocate of air power in the armed forces, Mitchell worked to create a separate air force and to develop strategic doctrines that would utilize its potential in the conduct of modern war.

Mitford, Jessica

b. September 11, 1917
Batsford, Gloustershire, England
d. July 23, 1996
Oakland, California
fields: Social Reform

A civil rights activist, social critic, and muckraking journalist. Mitford's scathing attack on the mortuary business, *The American Way of Death* (1963), became a model of watchdog journalism and agitation on behalf of the consumer.

Mithradates the Great

né: Mithradates Dionysus Eupator
b. Probably 134 B.C.E.
probably Sinope, Kingdom of Pontus
d. 63 B.C.E.
Panticapaeum, Crimea
fields: Government and Politics

Mithradates fought three wars with Rome in the first half of the first century B.C.E., resulting in the destruction and transformation into a Roman province of his own Kingdom of Pontus.

Mitterrand, François

full: François Maurice Adrien Marie Mitterrand
b. October 26, 1916
Jarnac, France
d. January 8, 1996
Paris, France
fields: Government and Politics

Elected President of France in 1981 and again in 1988 with the backing of a coalition of the Left, which he had played a strong role in forging, Mitterrand was also a minister of several governments in the Fourth Republic and a Resistance leader in World War II.

Mittwer, Mary Oyama

b. 1907
Fairfield, Calif.
fields: Journalism

Mary Oyama Mittwer got her start in journalism with a string of jobs at well-known Japanese American newspapers as the *Kashu Mainichi*, *Rafu Shimpo*, and *Nichibei Shimbun*. From 1935 to 1941, she worked for the *New World-Sun*, a Japanese American newspaper in San Francisco. Her column, "I'm Telling You, Deirdre," guided Japanese Americans on topics such as marriage, dating, and careers as well as on the proper etiquette necessary for life in a society dominated and shaped by white Americans. She initiated public discussion on such topics as multiracial relations and gender roles for Japanese American women, and her works were also published in the mainstream American press.

Miyakawa, T. Scott

full: Tetsuo Scott Miyakawa
b. Nov. 23, 1906
Los Angeles, Calif.
d. August ?, 1981
Boston, Mass.
fields: Historiography, Sociology

T. Scott Miyakawa was one of the first scholars to study the history of Japanese Americans. In 1929, he worked as a manager for the New York office of the Southern Manchurian Railroad Company, a position that caused him to be blacklisted by the Federal Bureau of Investigation. After receiving a doctorate from Columbia University in 1951, he taught at Boston University and the University of Massachusetts in Boston. From 1962 to 1965, he directed the Japanese American Research Project. He wrote *Protestants and Pioneers: Individualism and Conformity on the American Frontier* (1964).

Miyama, Kanichi

b. 1847
Yamaguchi Prefecture, Japan
d. 1936
fields: Religion and Theology

Kanichi Miyama became a Christian while living in San Francisco. He pastored a church there, then moved to Hawaii in 1887 to spread Christianity among the Japanese laborers. He was the first Japanese-speaking Christian evangelist.

Miyamoto, Kazuo

b. 1897
Kauai, Hawaii
d. 1988
Honolulu, Hawaii
fields: Medicine, Literature

Kazuo Miyamoto received his medical degree from Washington University in St. Louis, Missouri. He conducted public health research in the Japanese American community in the 1930's. In 1941, after the Japanese attacked Pearl Harbor, Miyamoto was imprisoned for a year, then released to volunteer service as a physician at the Tule Lake relocation center. The journal he kept at the camp became the basis of his historical novel *Hawaii: End of the Rainbow* (1964). After the war, Miyamoto returned to Honolulu, where he resumed his medical practice and published various books, including *Vikings of the Far East* (1975).

Miyamoto, Shotaro Frank

b. 1912
fields: Sociology

Shotaro Frank Miyamoto received a master's degree in sociology rom the University of Washington. His thesis on the Japanese American community in Seattle, published as *Social Solidarity Among the Japanese in Seattle* (1939), was one of the first studies to examine the long-range impact of the restrictive Immigration Act of 1924 on Japanese Americans. He was working on his doctoral dissertation when the Japanese attacked Pearl Harbor in 1941. He was hired to work as a researcher on the Japanese Evacuation and Resettlement Study project in 1941 and conducted fieldwork at Tule Lake, where he was interned, and later in Chicago, a resettlement area. He was a member of the sociology department at the University of Washington from 1945 to 1980.

Miyamura, Hershey

né: Hiroshi Miyamura
b. 1926
fields: Warfare and Conquest

Japanese American Hershey Miyamura was a squadron leader attached to an infantry regiment in the Korean war. He displayed uncommon bravery in defending his men against advancing enemy troops. He spent more than two years as a war prisoner, and after his return to the United States, Miyamura was awarded the Congressional Medal of Honor.

Miyatake, Toyo

b. 1895
Takashinomura, Kagawa Prefecture, Japan
d. Feb., 1979
fields: Photography

Photographer Toyo Miyatake opened Toyo Miyatake Studio in Little Tokyo in Los Angeles in the 1930's. During World War II, he was removed to the Manzanar relocation center. Although cameras were forbidden, Miyatake had smuggled a lens into camp, and he used this to make a camera. When the camp director discovered the camera, he decided to make Miyatake the official Manzanar photographer for the U.S. War Relocation Authority. After the war, Miyatake reopened his studio in Little Tokyo, relinquishing control of the studio to his son in 1972. That year, he was honored as one of the Pioneers of the Year at the annual Nisei Week festival, and in 1976, he received a Distinguished Service Commendation from the Photographic Society of Japan. In 1978, he was Grand Marshal of the Nisei Week parade and was named the Japanese Artist of the Year.

Miyoshi, Masao

b. May 14, 1928
Tokyo, Japan
fields: Literature, Historiography

Masao Miyoshi, who received a Ph.D. from New York University in 1957, was a professor at the University of California, Berkeley, and the University of California, San Diego. He wrote extensively on literature, relations between Japan and the United States, and Asian Americans. His works include *Accomplices of Silence: The Modern Japanese Novel* (1974), *As We Saw Them: The First Japanese Embassy to the United States* (1979), and *Off Center: Power and Culture Relations Between Japan and the United States* (1991).

Möbius, August Ferdinand

b. Nov. 17, 1790
Schulpforta, Saxony (now Germany)
d. Sept. 26, 1868
Leipzig, Saxony
fields: Mathematics (geometry and topology)

August Ferdinand Möbius was a leader in the field of topology, a specialized branch of geometry. In 1858 he discovered the intriguing Möbius strip, which has a single surface without a reverse side.

Mobutu Sese Seko

aka: Joseph Désiré Mobutu
b. October 14, 1930
Lisala, Belgian Congo (now Zaire)
d. September 7, 1997
Rabat, Morocco
fields: Military Affairs, Government and Politics

Mobutu was one of the first major African leaders to come to power since the early 1960's. His Pan-Africanism gained for him much power in the Third World and his anticommunism pleased major Western powers. His long authoritarian presidency, however, ended in a coup.

Mochunozhin. *See* Standing Bear

Moctezuma II

b. c. 1480
Tenochtitlán, Mexico
d. 1520
Tenochtitlán, Mexico
fields: Monarchy

Aztec emperor. Moctezuma (also known as Montezuma) became emperor in 1503. When Hernán Cortés reached the Mexican coast in 1519, Moctezuma tried to convince the Spaniard to leave; failing that, Moctezuma decided to welcome Cortés in order to maintain peace. Moctezuma signed a vassalage treaty with Cortés, but some of his advisers rebelled and attacked the Spaniards. Moctezuma died in one of the following battles.

Moffitt, Billie Jean. *See* King, Billie Jean

Mohammad Reza Shah Pahlavi

né: Mohammad Reza
b. October 26, 1919
Tehran, Iran
d. July 27, 1980
Cairo, Egypt
fields: Government and Politics

Mohammad Reza ruled Iran from 1941 to 1979. His reign coincided with major changes in the social and economic life of Iran, although his despotic rule, sustained by brutal repression, and the corruption that accompanied his modernizing program contributed directly to the Islamic Revolution of 1979.

Mohammed I Askia

né: Mohammed Ture ibn Abi Bakr
b. c. 1442
probably near Gao, Songhai Empire
d. 1538
near Gao, Songhai Empire
fields: Monarchy, Government and Politics, Diplomacy

Askia of Songhai Empire, 1493-1528. Mohammed I Askia greatly expanded and consolidated the Songhai Empire, which dominated much of West Africa in the fifteenth and sixteenth centuries. His policies resulted in a rapid expansion of trade and the imposition of the stamp of Islamic civilization on Songhai.

Mohan, Anna Louisa. *See* Bryant, Louise

Mohanty, Chandra Talpade

b. Jan. 22, 1955
Bombay, Republic of India
fields: Women's Rights

Chandra Talpade Mohanty received a doctorate in education from the University of Illinois, Urbana-Champaign. A professor of feminist and international studies at Hamilton College, she coedited *Third World Women and the Politics of Feminism* (1991).

Mohorovicic, Andrija

b. Jan. 23, 1857
Volosko, Istria, Austrian Empire (now in Croatia)
d. Dec. 18, 1936
Zagreb, Yugoslavia (now in Croatia)
fields: Science

Andrija Mohorovicic, in 1909, discovered the Mohorovicic discontinuity as a result of an earthquake south of Zagreb, which led to the realization that the earth has a thin, brittle crust.

Mohr, Nicholasa

b. Nov. 1, 1935
New York, N.Y.
fields: Art, Literature

Latina artist and writer. Nicholasa Mohr studied at the Art Students League, the Brooklyn Museum of Art School, and the Pratt Center for Contemporary Printmaking between 1953 and 1969. During the 1970's, she taught art and writing at a variety of schools in New Jersey, New Hampshire, New York, Illinois, Wisconsin, and Connecticut. She also made videos about the cultural heritage of Caribbean Hispanic Americans. Mohr published several award-winning books about Puerto Ricans living in the United States, including *Nilda* (1973), *El Bronx Remembered* (1975), and *Going Home* (1986).

Moivre, Abraham de

b. May 26, 1667
Vitry, France
d. Nov. 27, 1754
London, England
fields: Mathematics (probability)

Abraham de Moivre was the first mathematician to examine the form and basic properties of the normal probability function; demonstrated that it could be used to approximate other types of probabilities.

Mojica, José

b. Sept. 14, 1895
Jalisco, Mexico
d. Sept. 20, 1974
Lima, Peru
fields: Music (singer)

Latino singer. In 1916, José Mojica made his opera debut as the tenor in *The Barber of Seville*. He recorded thousands of operatic and popular Mexican songs for the Edison recording company and appeared in several Hollywood films, including *El precio de un beso* (1928), *La cruz y la espada* (1937), and *El capitán aventurero* (1938). In 1940, Mojica retired to a Peruvian convent and was ordained as a priest in 1947. In 1949, he returned to singing to raise money for a convent in Arequipa, Peru. He also wrote *Yo pecador* (*I, a Sinner*, 1963), an autobiography that sold more than one million copies in Spanish.

Mo-jo, Kuo. *See* Guo Moruo

Moketavato. *See* Black Kettle

Molière

né: Jean-Baptiste Poquelin
b. January 15, 1622 (baptized)
Paris, France
d. February 17, 1673
Paris, France
fields: Theater and Entertainment

By grafting character study and social commentary upon traditional farce, Molière became the creator of modern French comedy and continues to be ranked as France's finest comic playwright.

Molina, Arturo, Jr. *See* Kid Frost

Molina, Gloria

b. May 31, 1948
Los Angeles, Calif.
fields: Government and Politics

Gloria Molina founded the Comision Femenil de Los Angeles in 1973. She was elected to the California State Assembly in 1984. In 1988 Molina was elected to the Los Angeles City Council.

Molina, Mario J.

full: Mario José Molina
b. Mar. 19, 1943
Mexico City, Mexico
fields: Chemistry

Mario Molina studied the effect of chlorofluorocarbons (CFCs) on the atmosphere; found that their decomposition destroys ozone; in 1995, shared the Nobel Prize in Chemistry with F. Sherwood Rowland and Paul Crutzen.

Molotov, Vyacheslav Mikhailovich

né: Vyacheslav Mikhailovich Skryabin
b. March 9, 1890
Kukarka, Vyatka Province, Russia
d. November 8, 1986
Moscow, U.S.S.R.
fields: Diplomacy, Government and Politics

As one of Joseph Stalin's most loyal subordinates, Molotov played a major role in the development of the Soviet Union's domestic and foreign policies, particularly the creation of the centralized command economy and the establishment of Soviet domination of Eastern Europe.

Molyneux, Tom

b. 1784
Washington, D.C.?
d. August 4, 1818
Dublin, Ireland
fields: Sports (boxer)

African American boxer. In 1810, in England, Tom Molyneux became the first African American to fight in a major championship bout. He fought for several years, and in 1958 he was inducted into the Boxing Hall of Fame.

Momaday, N. Scott

aka: Tsaoi-talee (Rock-Tree Boy)
b. Feb. 27, 1934
Lawton, Okla.
fields: Literature

Kiowa author; a professor of literature and Native American studies, N. Scott Momaday is best known for his innovative and extremely influential works of autobiography and fiction, including the novel *House Made of Dawn* (1968; winner of the 1969 Pulitzer Prize), *The Way to Rainy Mountain* (1969), *The Names: A Memoir* (1976; autobiography), *The Gourd Dancer* (1976; poetry, illustrated with Momaday's own sketches), and *Ancient Child* (1989); Momaday's disjointed narratives and his juxtaposition of prose, poetry, photographs, and sketches have exerted a powerful influence on many Indian authors.

Mommsen, Theodor

b. November 30, 1817
Garding, Schleswig
d. November 1, 1903
Charlottenburg, Germany
fields: Historiography

Mommsen transformed the study of Roman history by correcting and supplementing the literary tradition of the ancient historians with the evidence of Latin inscriptions. Going beyond the usual focus on the generals and emperors, Mommsen championed study in all aspects of ancient societies.

Moncado, Hilario Camino

aka: Hilarion Caminos Moncada
b. Nov. 3, 1895
Balamban, Philippines
d. Apr. 9, 1956
Aguascalientes, Mexico
fields: Government and Politics

Hilario Camino Moncado founded the Filipino Federation of America in Los Angeles in 1925 and served as its first president. The federation, which encouraged Filipino Americans to honor the U.S. constitution and flag and to adopt Christian practices, became a quasi-religious organization centered on faith in Moncado's divinity. Moncado, who earned a law degree from Southwestern University in 1928, failed to win election as the first president of the newly independent Republic of the Philippines in 1946. In 1948, Moncado moved back to Los Angeles, but left in 1954 rather than face threatened deportation.

Monck, George

b. December 6, 1608
Great Potheridge, Devonshire, England
d. January 3, 1670
London, England
fields: Government and Politics, Military Affairs

A consummate professional soldier, Monck served Parliament with distinction in Scotland and at sea against the Dutch after having begun the English Civil War as a Royalist. In the power struggles after Oliver Cromwell's death, he emerged as the central figure in the Restoration of Charles II. He was raised to the peerage as the Duke of Albemarle and served the king in a variety of roles until his death.

Moncrief, Sidney A.

b. September 21, 1957
Little Rock, Ark.
fields: Sports (basketball player)

African American basketball player. First-round draft pick of the Milwaukee Bucks of the National Basketball Association (NBA) in 1979, Sidney A. Moncrief established himself as one of the NBA's top guards in the 1980's. He excelled both as a scorer and as a defender and was named the NBA Defensive Player of the Year in 1983 and 1984. He played in NBA All-Star Games each year from 1982 through 1986.

Mondrian, Piet

né: Pieter Cornelis Mondriaan, Jr.
b. March 7, 1872
Amersfoort, The Netherlands
d. February 1, 1944
New York, New York
fields: Art

Mondrian was of paramount importance to the initiation of geometric abstraction for modern art during World War I. He was the principal voice and exemplar of neoplasticism in Dutch painting as well as one of the founders of the Dutch modern movement in architecture and design known as de Stijl, a movement that influenced the International style in building construction during the 1920's and 1930's.

Monet, Claude

full: Oscar-Claude Monet
b. November 14, 1840
Paris, France
d. December 5, 1926
Giverny, France
fields: Art

Monet is central to the development of Impressionist painting in the 1870's. In the 1890's, Monet developed the concept of multiple views of one subject, and in the 1940's and 1950's the abstract Impressionism of Monet's late water lily paintings provided a stimulus for the American abstract expressionists.

Monge, Gaspard

b. May 10, 1746
Beaune, France
d. July 28, 1818
Paris, France
fields: Mathematics, Chemistry, Physics, Engineering

Monge founded modern descriptive geometry (essential to mechanical and architectural drawing) and revitalized analytic geometry (essential to many fields of physics and mathematics). An enthusiastic supporter of the French Revolution, he helped establish the metric system and the École Polytechnique, an important engineering school.

Monk, Art

full: James Arthur Monk
b. December 5, 1957
White Plains, N.Y.
fields: Sports (football player)

African American football player; in 1980, Art Monk was drafted by the Washington Redskins; played in Super Bowl XVIII, XXII, and XXVI; played in the 1984, 1985, and 1986 Pro Bowls; played for the New York Jets in 1994 and the Philadelphia Eagles in 1995; relative of jazz musician Thelonious

Monk. He retired in 1997 after once again playing for the Washington Redskins.

Monk, Meredith

full: Meredith Jane Monk
b. November 20, 1942
Lima, Peru
fields: Dance, Music, Theater and Entertainment (drama)

A composer, choreographer, singer, and multimedia performance artist, Monk expands in her work the boundaries of dance performance by juxtaposing movement, sound, and theatrical images.

Monk, Thelonious

full: Thelonious Sphere Monk
b. October 10, 1917
Rocky Mount, N.C.
d. February 17, 1982
Englewood, N.J.
fields: Music (pianist and composer)

African American pianist and composer; Thelonious Monk creater of some of the most challenging and ultimately indispensable music of the twentieth century, was active during the formative stages of modern jazz, known as bebop. Monk was noted not for technique but for careful note selection and musical conception. Some Monk compositions that became jazz standards include "'Round Midnight," "Epistrophy," "Well, You Needn't," "Blue Monk," and "Rhythm-a-ning." The documentary film *Thelonious Monk: Straight No Chaser* was released to critical acclaim in 1988.

Monmouth, duke of

né: James Scott
b. April 9, 1649
Rotterdam, the Netherlands
d. July 15, 1685
London, England
fields: Government and Politics, Military Affairs, Monarchy

An illegitimate son of King Charles II, Monmouth became the hope of radical Protestants opposed to the succession of Charles's Catholic brother James II. The duke's ill-conceived invasion of England failed and led to his execution.

Monnet, Jean

b. November 9, 1888
Cognac, France
d. March 16, 1979
Montfort-l'Amaury, France
fields: Diplomacy, Economics, Government and Politics

Monnet has justly been called "the father of Europe," in recognition of the importance of his role in the foundation of the European Coal and Steel Community, Euratom, and the Common Market. He worked primarily as an adviser rather than as the holder of powerful political positions; his ideas and plans have been instrumental in shaping Europe's postwar moves toward economic and political integration.

Monod, Jacques Lucien

b. Feb. 9, 1910
Paris, France
d. May 31, 1976
Cannes, France
fields: Biology, Genetics, Medicine

Jacques Lucien Monod was an early biochemist and molecular biologistl explained how genes are expressed and how gene expression is controlled; in 1965, won the Nobel Prize in Physiology or Medicine jointly with André Lwoff and François Jacob.

Monroe, Earl

aka: Earl "the Pearl" Monroe
b. November 21, 1944
Philadelphia, Pa.
fields: Sports (basketball player)

African American basketball player; Earl Monroe played basketball at Winston-Salem State University in North Carolina before beginning his professional career with the Baltimore Bullets in 1967. He spent his thirteen seasons in the National Basketball Association playing with the Baltimore Bullets and the New York Knicks, retiring in 1980 with a career scoring average of 18.8 points per game.

Monroe, James

b. April 28, 1758
Westmoreland County, Virginia
d. July 4, 1831
New York, New York
fields: Government and Politics

As President of the United States (1817-1825) and author of the Monroe Doctrine, Monroe set forth one of the basic principles of American foreign policy

Monroe, Loren Eugene

b. ?
fields: Government and Politics

African American state official; Loren Eugene Monroe was the first African American to be elected treasurer for the state of Michigan.

Monroe, Marilyn

né: Norma Jeane Mortenson
b. June 1, 1926
Los Angeles, California
d. August 5, 1962
Los Angeles, California
fields: Film

Monroe rose from poverty to become one of the most famous film stars of the twentieth century. Despite the skepticism of studio executives, her Cinderella story touched filmgoers, and their reactions made her a cult figure rivaling Elvis Presley and the Beatles.

Montagu, Mary Wortley

né: Mary Pierrepont
b. Baptized May 26, 1689
London, England
d. August 21, 1762
London, England
fields: Literature, Medicine, Women's Rights

A writer, Montagu is best remembered for her epistolary literature—the letter as literature—and for her bold campaign to introduce the practice of smallpox inoculation into Europe.

Montaigne, Michel de

full: Michel Eyquem de Montaigne
b. February 28, 1533
Château de Montaigne, Périgord, near Bordeaux, France
d. September 13, 1592
Château de Montaigne, Périgord, near Bordeaux, France
fields: Philosophy, Government and Politics, Literature

In an age of violent religious and political struggles, Montaigne mediated for tolerance. His gift to literature was the invention of the essay.

Montalbán, Ricardo

b. November 25, 1920
Mexico City, Mexico
fields: Film, Television

Mexican American actor Ricardo Montalbán was a film actor in Mexico from 1942 to 1946. In the United States he appeared in more than twenty American films, including *Fiesta* (1947), *Sayonara* (1957), *Sweet Charity* (1969), *Star Trek II: The Wrath of Khan* (1982), and *The Naked Gun: From the Files of Police Squad!* (1988). He founded the Latino group Nosotros in 1969. He is best known for his role as the mysterious host Mr. Roarke on *Fantasy Island* (1978-1984), for which he won an Emmy Award in 1978, and as Chrysler's much-parodied pitchman for its Cordoba automobile.

Montale, Eugenio

b. October 12, 1896
Genoa, Italy
d. September 12, 1981
Milan, Italy
fields: Literature

Montale is the foremost Italian poet of the twentieth century and the recipient of the Nobel Prize in Literature in 1975. With his contemporaries Giuseppe Ungaretti and Salvatore Quasimodo, Montale created a modern Italian poetry of international significance: honest, poignant, serious, and wise.

Montano, Louis R.

b. Jan. 18, 1928
Roswell, N.Mex.
fields: Government and Politics

Latino public official. Louis R. Montano, a Mexican American, directed the Santa Fe Boys Club from 1957 to 1984. During that time, he was also elected to public office. In 1974, he was elected to the city council of Santa Fe. From 1978 to 1982, he served as mayor pro tem, and from 1982 to 1986, he was mayor. Montano then served as director of the Labor and Industrial Division of the New Mexico Department of Labor.

Montcorbier et des Loges, François de. *See* Villon, François

Montero, Frank

b. 1942
New York, N.Y.
fields: Government and Politics

African American political appointee; Frank Montero served as assistant executive director of the National Urban League for fifteen years before being appointed as adviser to the U.S. Mission to the United Nations in 1962. He was also the senior adviser on economic and social affairs for many United Nations committees.

Montesquieu

né: Charles-Louis de Secondat
full: Charles-Louis de Secondat, Baron de La Brède de Montesquieu
b. January 18, 1689
La Brède, near Bordeaux, France
d. February 10, 1755
Paris, France
fields: Philosophy, Political Science

Montesquieu's most lasting contribution was his defense and development of the theory behind separation of powers in government. His work in this area significantly influenced the framers of the United States Constitution. Philosophically, he is best known for positing history as the basis for normative judgment. Before Montesquieu, normative judgment had always been based on nature.

Montessori, Maria

b. August 31, 1870
Chiaravalle, Italy
d. May 6, 1952
Noordwijk aan Zee, The Netherlands
fields: Education, Science, Social Reform

The first woman to earn a medical degree and to practice medicine in Italy, Montessori became a spokesperson for human liberation and a pioneer in "scientific pedagogy." She developed an educational theory based upon children's spontaneous desire to learn in a prepared, free, child-centered environment that won international acclaim during her lifetime and enjoyed continued success after her death.

Monteverdi, Claudio

full: Claudio Giovanni Antonio Monteverdi
b. May 15, 1567
Cremona, Duchy of Milan
d. November 29, 1643
Venice
fields: Music

Monteverdi was the outstanding Italian composer of his age, which bridged the periods of the Renaissance and the Baroque. He made equally important contributions to the fields of sacred and secular music, especially in the genres of opera and the madrigal, and forged for himself and his successors an expressive musical style by combining the established techniques of his predecessors with the innovations of his contemporaries.

Montez, Lola

b. 1819
Limerick, Ireland
d. Jan. 17, 1861
New York, N.Y.
fields: Dance, Theater and Entertainment

Latina entertainer. Lola Montez gained fame in Spain as a dancer and for taking a series of lovers, including Ludwig I, King of Bavaria. She moved to the United States in 1851, eventually traveling to California, which offered tremendous opportunities to women with musical or theatrical abilities during the gold rush. In 1855, she traveled to Australia, only to return to California in July, 1856. In September of that year, Montez announced her retirement from the stage. In November, she moved to New York to become a lecturer.

Montez, María

né: María Africa Antonia Gracia Vidal de Santo Silas
b. June 6, 1920
Barahona, Dominican Republic
d. Sept. 7, 1951
Paris, France
fields: Theater and Entertainement (actor), Film

Latina actor. María Montez established herself as an exotic screen temptress in the film *The Invisible Woman* (1941). She starred in such Universal Technicolor "Easterns" as *Arabian Nights* (1942), *Ali Baba and the Forty Thieves* (1943), *Pirates of Monterey* (1947), and *Siren of Atlantis* (1948), in which she costarred with her husband, Jean-Pierre Aumont. Montez's most popular film was *Cobra Woman* (1944), in which she played the title role. Montez and Aumont later moved to Europe, where they acted in a number of French, Italian, and German films.

Montezuma II

b. 1467
Tenochtitlán, Aztec Empire
d. June 30, 1520
Tenochtitlán, Aztec Empire
fields: Monarchy

Emperor, 1503-1520. Montezuma II expanded the Aztec Empire to its greatest size and died as his empire crumbled under the pressures of Hernán Cortés.

Montezuma, Carlos

aka: Wassaja (Signaling or Beckoning)
b. c. 1867
Superstition Mountains of central Ariz.
d. Jan. 31, 1923
Fort McDowell Reservation, Ariz.
fields: Medicine, Civil Rights, Social Reform

Carlos Montezuma, a Yavapai, was one of the first American Indians to earn a physician's degree (in 1889) and practice European American medicine on reservations. Also an activist who attacked Bureau of Indian Affairs as a fraud and abomination; advocated citizenship rights and economic protection for Indians.

Montfort, Simon V de

aka: Simon de Montfort
b. c. 1208
Montfort, Île-de-France, France
d. August 4, 1265
Evesham, Worcestershire, England
fields: Government and Politics

A passionate, adventurous, and self-confident medieval nobleman who emerged as the leader of a group of English barons intent on curbing the abuses of power by the incompetent King Henry III, Simon de Montfort dramatically changed the relationship between king and Parliament in ways critical to the development of that institution as a force to limit and monitor the royal prerogative.

Montgolfier, Jacques-Étienne

b. January 6, 1745
Vidalon-les-Annonay, France
d. August 2, 1799
Serrières, France
fields: Aeronautics, Invention and Technology

Jacques-Étienne Montgolfier and his brother, Joseph-Michel, contributed to the invention, improvement, and flying of lighter-than-air craft. Their greatest achievement was their successful coordination in the invention and flying of the first balloon.

Montgolfier, Joseph-Michel

b. August 26, 1740
Vidalon-les-Annonay, Ardeche, France
d. June 26, 1810
Balaruc-les-Bains, France
fields: Aeronautics, Invention and Technology

Joseph-Michel Montgolfier and his brother, Jacques-Étienne, contributed to the invention, improvement, and flying of lighter-than-air craft. Their greatest achievement was their successful coordination in the invention and flying of the first balloon.

Montgomery, Bernard Law

b. November 17, 1887
London, England
d. March 24, 1976
near Alton, Hampshire, England
fields: Military Affairs

Montgomery will be remembered as Great Britain's best field general during World War II and one of the great military leaders of the twentieth century.

Montgomery, Thomasina. *See* Terrell, Tammi

Montgomery, Wes

full: John Leslie Montgomery
b. March 6, 1925
Indianapolis, Ind.
d. June 15, 1968
Indianapolis, Ind.
fields: Music (guitar player)

African American guitar player; Wes Montgomery was known for his unique style of plucking his guitar with his thumb, and many jazz greats were influenced by his personalized style of swing and improvisation.

Montini, Giovanni Battista. *See* Paul VI

Montoya, José

b. May 28, 1932
near Escoboza, N.Mex.
fields: Art

Latino artist. After serving in the U.S. Navy during the Korean War, José Montoya earned a bachelor of arts degree at the California College of Arts and Crafts in Oakland in 1962. He then worked on his master of fine arts degree and, in 1971, began teaching at Sacramento State University in California, where he helped develop a barrio art program. In addition to being an artist, Montoya also published poetry.

Montoya, Joseph

full: Joseph Manuel Montoya
b. Sept. 24, 1915
Pena Blanca, N.Mex
d. June 5, 1978
Washington, D.C.
fields: Government and Politics

Mexican American politician; Joseph Montoya was born in New Mexico; earned law degree from Georgetown University in 1938; New Mexico representative (Democrat), 1937-1941, senator, 1941-1947; lieutenant-governor, 1946-1950, 1954-1957; U.S. representative, 1957-1964; U.S. senator, 1962-1977; known for his work on the Senate Agricultural Committee and as a member of the Senate Watergate Committee.

Montoya, Juana Alicia. *See* Alicia, Juana

Montoya, Malaquías

b. June 21, 1938
Albuquerque, N.Mex.
fields: Art

Latino artist. While working toward his bachelor's degree in art at the University of California, Berkeley, in the 1960's, Malaquías Montoya became involved in the Chicano movement and other activist groups. He also designed the cover for *El Plan de Santa Bárbara: A Chicano Plan for Higher Education* (1969). During the 1970's, Montoya continued to work with various activist groups while making posters, silkscreens, murals, paintings, and drawings. He had numerous solo and group exhibitions in California and taught at the California College of Arts and Crafts in Oakland.

Montoya, María Teresa

b. ?
fields: Theater and Entertainment

Latina theater manager. María Teresa Montoya managed the Teatro Princesa in Los Angeles. Her own company, the Gran Compañía María Teresa Montoya, established in January of 1922, was poorly received and soon went bankrupt, a failure that she partially blamed on the Americanization of Mexicans in the United States. In 1956, she published her autobiography, *El teatro en mi vida* (the theater in my life).

Moody, Dwight L.

full: Dwight Lyman Moody
b. February 5, 1837
Northfield, Massachusetts
d. December 22, 1899
Northfield, Massachusetts
fields: Religion and Theology

In mass evangelistic campaigns, Moody preached a message of salvation and brought spiritual revival to the United States and England.

Moody, Helen Wills

né: Helen Newington Wills
b. October 6, 1905
Centerville, California
d. January 1, 1998
Carmel, California
fields: Sports (tennis)

Helen Wills Moody established a remarkable record in women's tennis in the Golden Age of Sports in the 1920's, one that might never be equaled in the sport. Her skills, determination, and record have remained as a model for women's tennis.

Moody, James

b. February 26, 1925
Savannah, Ga.
fields: Music (multi-instrumental jazz performer)

African American multi-instrumental jazz performer; James Moody, most famous for his recording of "I'm in the Mood for Love," (1949), sings and primarily plays alto and tenor saxophones and flute. He played sporadically with trumpeter Dizzy Gillespie beginning in the 1940's.

Moody, William Henry

b. 1853
d. 1917
fields: Law

U.S. Supreme Court justice, 1906-1910; appointed by President Theodore Roosevelt. Believed states were free to confer or withhold individual rights from criminal defendants. Significant opinion: *Twining v. New Jersey*, 211 U.S. 78 (1908); *Londoner v. Denver*, 210 U.S. 373 (1908).

Moon, Henry

b. Sept. 28, 1914
San Francisco, Calif.
d. Aug. 2, 1974
San Francisco, Calif.
fields: Medicine

Henry Moon graduated from the University of California School of Medicine in San Francisco in 1940 and later joined its faculty. He became chair of its Department of Pathology in 1956. Moon was a member of the scientific team that first isolated the adrenocorticotropic hormone (ACTH). He is known for his groundbreaking research on arteriosclerosis.

Moon, Sun Myung

né: Yong Myung Moon
b. January 6, 1920
Kwangju Sangsa Ri, Pyungan Bukedo Province, Korea
fields: Religion and Theology

Sun Myung Moon is the founder and spiritual leader of the Unification Church. His ideas were first published in 1952 in his *Divine Principle*. The church was established in Korea by 1954 but found a following in the United States by 1959. In the 1970's the church's membership expanded greatly but also drew the attention of government officials. Moon was convicted of tax evasion in 1982.

Moon, Warren

full: Harold Warren Moon, Jr.
b. November 18, 1956
Los Angeles, Calif.
fields: Sports, Journalism (professional football player)

African American professional football player; Warren Moon ranks as one of the most prolific passers in National Football League (NFL) history; in 1983, joined the Houston Oilers; traded to the Minnesota Vikings in the 1994-1995 season; launched a second career as a broadcaster with the Turner Network Television (TNT); cosponsored, with his wife, the Crescent Moon Foundation in Houston; traded to the Seattle Seahawks in 1998.

Moore, Alfred

b. 1755
d. 1810
fields: Law

U.S. Supreme Court justice, 1800-1804; appointed by President John Adams. Wrote only one opinion.

Moore, Archie

né: Archibald Lee Wright
b. December 13, 1913 or 1916
Benoit, Miss.
d. December 9, 1998
San Diego, Calif.
fields: Sports (boxer)

African American boxer; Archie Moore become champion in the light-heavyweight division in 1952 by defeating Joey Maxim. He was successful in defending his title eight times. He lost the title in 1961 because he failed to defend it. He was the oldest professional boxer to hold a world title at the time.

Moore, Bobby. *See* Rashad, Ahmad

Moore, Carry Amelia. *See* Nation, Carry

Moore, Emerson

b. May 16, 1938
New York, N.Y.
fields: Religion and Theology

African American religious figure. In addition to his degrees from Cathedral College and St. Joseph Seminary Emerson Moore earned a graduate degree in social work from Columbia University and was ordained as a Catholic priest in 1964. He was named auxiliary bishop of New York in 1982 and became vicar for the northwest Bronx, responsible for all Catholic church activities there.

Moore, G. E.

full: George Edward Moore
b. November 4, 1873
London, England
d. October 24, 1958
Cambridge, England
fields: Philosophy

With his meticulous and uncompromising analytic technique, Moore helped lead the movement away from the dominance of Idealism, establishing Analytic philosophy as a major methodology in modern philosophical thought.

Moore, George

b. February 24, 1852
County Mayo, Ireland
d. January 21, 1933
London, England
fields: Literature

Irish writer George Moore's first novel, *A Modern Lover* (1883), dealt with contemporary bohemian society, and made his work unpopular with circulating libraries. After publishing his next novel, *A Mummer's Wife* (1885), in an inexpensive edition, he won a reputation as an innovative, iconoclastic author. Nevertheless, libraries continued to shun his books, and his books also faced censorship in the United States.

Moore, Henry

b. July 30, 1898
Castleford, Yorkshire, England
d. August 31, 1986
Much Hadham, Hertfordshire, England
fields: Art

Through an elemental understanding of form and materials, Moore created sculpture of archetypal significance, universally recognized yet uniquely his.

Moore, James Isaac. *See* Harpo, Slim

Moore, Lenny

b. November 25, 1933
Reading, Pa.
fields: Sports (football player)

African American football player; Lenny Moore played football at Pennsylvania State University before joining the Baltimore Colts of the National Football League in 1956. He played twelve seasons with the Colts proving himself one of professional football's best runners and pass receivers. Moore caught 363 passes, rushed for 5,174 yards, and scored 63 touchdowns during his professional career. In 1975 he was inducted into the Pro Football Hall of Fame.

Moore, Marianne

full: Marianne Craig Moore
b. November 15, 1887
Kirkwood, Missouri
d. February 5, 1972
New York, New York
fields: Literature

An early leader in Modernist poetry, Moore eventually gained recognition as one of the half-dozen major poets in English of the middle twentieth century.

Moore, Melba

b. October 29, 1945
New York, N.Y.
fields: Theater and Entertainment, Music

African American actress and singer; Melba Moore, the first African American to give a solo concert at the Metropolitan Opera House in New York City (1972), acted in musicals on stage, *Hair* (1968) and *Purlie* (1970), for which she won a Tony Award, and on the screen, *Lost in the Stars* (1974) and the film version of *Hair* (1980). On television, Moore cohosted a variety series (1972), appeared in the television film *Ellis Island* (1984), and starred in *Melba* (1986), a situation comedy. In 1985 Moore was nominated twice for Grammy Awards for her albums *This Is It* and *Read My Lips*.

Moore, Sam

b. 1935
fields: Music (soul singer)

member of the African American vocal duo Sam and Dave, one of the most successful soul acts of the 1960's; Sam Moore had a gospel music background and his recordings with Dave Prater drew heavily on gospel singing techniques; the duo's hits included "You Don't Know Like I Know" (1966), "Hold On, I'm Comin'" (1966), "When Something Is Wrong With My Baby" (1967), and "Soul Man" (1967).

Moore, Sandra. *See* Faber, Sandra

Moore, Walter Louis

b. March 14, 1946
Pontiac, Mich.
fields: Government and Politics

Mayor of Pontiac, Mich. Moore attended Ferris State College from 1966 to 1968 and attended Oakland University. He worked as a fire fighter for the city of Pontiac, then, in 1978, became Oakland County commissioner from District Seven in Pontiac. He was the campaign manager for the Coalition for a Modern Charter for Pontiac. He was elected mayor of Pontiac in 1989 and took office in 1990. While in office, Moore helped found the I-75 Mayor's Conference. He was a member of the U.S. Conference of Mayors and the

National Conference of Black Mayors. Moore also served as director of Pontiac Youth Assistance and was a strong supporter of the Boys' and Girls' Clubs and other youth organizations.}}

Moore, William

b. Apr. 28, 1927
Binghampton, N.Y.
d. Apr. 23, 1963
Etowah County, Ala.
fields: Civil Rights

An African American civil rights activist, William Moore gained prominence when he staged a long pushcart march to the office of Mississippi governor Ross Barnett to deliver a letter complaining of government bigotry in 1963. He was fatally shot by an unknown sniper while passing through northeastern Alabama.

Moore, Winston E.

b. September 5, 1929
New Orleans, La.
fields: Social Reform

African American corrections official. From 1966 to 1968 Moore worked as a staff psychologist for the Youth Opportunity Center of the Illinois State Employment Service, after which he took over as superintendent of the Cook County Jail, where he remained into the 1990's. The Cook County Jail was known as one of the worst in the United States in terms of the violence, extortion, and drug dealing that occurred there. Moore began reforming the jail, and many of the problems were solved by the time he left.

Moorhead, Scipio

b. c. 1773
d.?
fields: Art (painter)

African American painter; Scipio Moorhead, probably the first African American artist in colonial America to receive formal training, studied with Mrs. Sarah Moorhead, an artist and art teacher. Phillis Wheatley dedicated a poem to Moorhead, and though no signed work by Moorhead has been found, it is possible that the engraved portrait used as a frontispiece in some of Wheatley's published poetry was done by him.

Mopope, Stephen

aka: Qued Koi (Painted Robe)
b. Aug. 27, 1898
near Red Stone Baptist Mission, Kiowa Reservation, Okla. Territory
d. Feb. 3, 1974
Fort Cobb, Okla.
fields: Art (painter)

Stephen Mopope was one of the Kiowa Five artists who helped to define and establish the Oklahoma style of Native American painting in the 1930's. Mopope drew from his background and his own performing abilities to paint portraits, traditional costumes, and dances. He frequently portrayed dancers doing the same steps that he himself danced. He painted or participated in the making of murals for a number of public buildings.

Mora, Pat

full: Patricia Mora
b. Jan. 19, 1942
El Paso, Tex.
fields: Literature, Education

Latina poet and educator. In 1967, Pat Mora earned a master's degree at the University of Texas at El Paso. After many years of teaching, she served as director of the El Paso Independent School District from 1988 to 1991, then became an English and communications instructor at El Paso Community College. She also served as judge for the Texas Institute of Letters and on the literary advisory council for the Texas Commission on the Arts. Mora has published several books, including *Chants* (1985), *Borders* (1986), and *Aunt Carmen's Book of Practical Saints* (1997).

Moraga, Cherríe

b. Sept. 25, 1952
Whittier, Calif.
fields: Publishing, Literature

Latina editor and writer. Cherríe Moraga earned her master's degree from San Francisco State University in 1981, then cofounded of the Kitchen Table/Women of Color Press. She served as playwright-in-residence at INTAR, a Hispanic American arts center in New York City, in 1984. In 1986, she became a writing instructor at the University of California at Berkeley. Moraga won the American Book Award from the Before Columbus Foundation for *This Bridge Called My Back: Writings by Radical Women of Color* (1981), which she coedited and to which she contributed.

Morales, Alejandro

b. Oct. 14, 1944
Montebello, Calif.
fields: Literature

Mexican American novelist. Alejandro Morales grew up in East Los Angeles and earned master's and doctoral degrees in Spanish from Rutgers University in New Jersey. he then become a professor in the department of Spanish and Portuguese at the University of California, Irvine. He has written several novels, including *Caras viejas y vino nuevo* (1975; *Old Faces and New Wine*, 1981) and *La verdad sin voz* (1979; *Death of an Anglo*, 1988), which were first published in Mexico, and *Reto en el paraíso* (1982; challenge in paradise), *The Brick People* (1988), and *The Rag Doll Plagues* (1992).

Morales, Esai

b. Oct. 1, 1962
Brooklyn, N.Y.
fields: Theater and Entertainement (actor), Film

Latino actor. After several stage appearances in New York City, Esai Morales made his film debut in *Bad Boys* (1983). He went on to play roles in *Rainy Day Friends* (1985), *La Bamba* (1987), *The Principal* (1987), *Bloodhounds of Broadway* (1989), *Naked Tango* (1990), and *Amazon* (1991), among others films. His television credits include the film *On Wings of Eagles* (1986) and the series *The Equalizer*, *Miami Vice*, and *Fame*. He won a Golden Eagle Award and a New York Image Award, and also established his own production company, Richport.

Morales, Noro

b. Jan. 4, 1911
San Juan, Puerto Rico
d. Jan. 4, 1964
San Juan, Puerto Rico
fields: Music (composer, conductor, and pianist)

Latino composer, conductor, and pianist. Noro Morales played piano in the Orquesta Hermanos Morales, a Puerto Rican band conducted by his father. After his father's death, Morales took over and led the band. Morales and several of his brothers moved to New York City in 1935. He formed his own band in 1939 and became one of the major names among Latin musicians. He recorded numerous songs for MGM, including "Bim Bam Bum," "Perfume de Amor," "If You Only Knew," "Walter Winchell Rumba," "Oye Negra," and "Rum and Soda."

Morales, Pablo

full: Pedro Pablo Morales, Jr.
b. Dec. 5, 1964
Chicago, Ill.
fields: Sports (swimmer)

Cuban American swimmer. Pablo Morales won the 50-yard butterfly national championship in the ten-and-under division at the age of ten. He repeated as national champion in the twelve-, fourteen-, and sixteen-year-old divisions. As a senior in high school, he broke Mark Spitz's record in the 100-yard butterfly. At Stanford University, he set the world record for the 100-meter butterfly. At the 1984 Los Angeles Olympics, Morales won a gold medal in the medley relay and silver medals in the 100-meter butterfly and 200-meter individual medley. He was named the U.S. team captain at the 1992 Barcelona Olympics, where he won his fourth Olympic medal, a gold in the 100-meter butterfly.

Morales, Sylvia

b. ?
fields: Film

Latino filmmaker. Sylvia Morales has made several films, both dramatic and documentary, that explore contemporary Latino and women's issues, including *Chicanas* (1979), *Los Lobos: And a Time to Dance* (1984), *Esperanza*, *SIDA Is AIDS*, *Values: Sexuality and the Family*, and *Faith Even to the Fire*.

Morawetz, Cathleen Synge

né: Cathleen Synge
b. May 5, 1923
Toronto, Ontario, Canada
fields: Mathematics (applied math)

Cathleen Synge Morawetz proved that it is impossible to design an airplane wing to avoid shock waves; first woman in the United States to head a mathematics institute; president of American Mathematical Society, 1995-1996.

Moré, Benny

full: Bartolomé Maximiliano Moré Gutierrez
b. Aug. 24, 1919
Cienfuegos, Cuba
d. Feb. 19, 1963
Havana, Cuba
fields: Music (singer and bandleader)

Cuban singer and bandleader. Benny Moré began his music career in Cuba, where he recorded with the group of Miguel Matamoros. In Mexico, he toured and recorded with Pérez Prado. Moré's big jazz band, Banda Gigante, which he formed in 1953 in Cuba, became popular in the Caribbean and in both South and North America. Among the collections of Moré's songs that have been released are *Magia Antillana*, *The Most from Benny Moré*, and the seven-volume collection *Benny Moré: Sonero Mayor*.

More, Thomas

aka: Sir Thomas More
b. February 7, 1478
London, England
d. July 6, 1535
London, England
fields: Literature, Government and Politics, Religion and Theology

Devoted to his faith and Renaissance learning, More served as the first lay Lord Chancellor of England, opposed Henry VIII's break with Rome, and forfeited his exalted position and his life rather than swear allegiance to the king as the supreme head of the Church of England.

Moreira Guimorva, Airto

b. Aug. 5, 1941
Itaiópolis, Brazil
fields: Music (jazz percussionist and singer)

Brazilian jazz percussionist and singer. Airto Moreira Guimorva began playing music and collecting instruments at a young age. In 1968, he helped form the unconventional jazz-rock group Weather Report. After moving to New York, he recorded with Miles Davis and played percussion for Chick Corea's group Return to Forever. During the 1970's, he became one of the best-known and influential jazz percussionists in the United States. Many consider the album *Identities* to be his best. He often sings and performs with his wife, Brazilian singer Flora Purim.

Moreno, Antonio

full: Antonio Garrido Monteagudo y Moreno
b. Sept. 26, 1887
Madrid, Spain
d. Feb. 15, 1967
Beverly Hills, Calif.
fields: Film (actor)

Actor. Antonio Moreno moved to the United States at the age of fourteen and made his motion-picture debut in 1912 in a D. W. Griffith film. He went on to become the prototype of the "Latin lover" and act in more than one hundred feature films, including *The House of Discord* (1913), *My American Wife* (1923, opposite Gloria Swanson), *The Exciters* (1923, opposite Bebe Daniels), and *Romance of the Rio Grande* (1929). The waning of Moreno's career paralleled the waning of silent film in the late 1920's and early 1930's. He continued to get smaller, stereotypically Latino character roles in such films as *Rose of the Rio Grande* (1938), *Captain from Castile* (1947), and *Creature from the Black Lagoon* (1954).

Moreno, Antonio Garrido Monteagudo y. *See* Moreno, Antonio

Moreno, Luisa

b. 1906
Guatemala
d. c. 1990
Mexico
fields: Labor Movement

Labor organizer; Luisa Moreno began organizing Hispanic garment workers in New York City in the 1930's; led a successful pecan sheller's strike of the United Cannery, Agricultural, Packing and Allied Workers of America, gaining favorable notice of the leadership and eventually rising to be international vice president; helped launch the National Congress of the Spanish Speaking People (also known as El Congresso) in 1938, the first Mexican American civil rights organization; suspected of being a communist and deported in the 1950's under terms of the McCarran-Walter Immigration Act; died in Mexico.

Moreno, Rita

né: Rosa Dolores Alverio
b. December 11, 1931
Humacao, Puerto Rico
fields: Film, Theater and Entertainment

Rita Moreno made her American film debut in 1950 in *So Young, So Bad*. Her other early films include *Singin' in the Rain* (1952), *The Fabulous Señorita* (1952), *The Ring* (1952), *Cattle Town* (1952), *Latin Lovers* (1953), and *Jivaro* (1953). Her Broadway credits include *The Sign in Sidney Brustein's Window* (1964), *Elmer Gantry* (1969), *The Ritz* (1975), and the female version of *The Odd Couple* (1985). Moreno awards include a 1962 Oscar as best supporting actress in *West Side Story*, a 1973 Grammy for best recording for an *Electric Company* sound track, a 1975 Tony for best supporting actress in *The Rink*, and 1977 and 1978 Emmys for appearances on *The Muppet Show* and *The Rockford Files*.

Morfi, Juan Agustín

b. c. 1710
Galicia, Spain
d. Oct. 20, 1783
Mexico
fields: Religion and Theology, Literature

Spanish priest and writer. In 1752, Juan Agustín Morfi traveled to the colony of New Spain and taught theology at Santiago de Tlatelolco. He is known for the extensive notes he took during his travels through the colonies of New Spain, New Galicia, and New Vizcaya and to territories north of the Rio Grande while trying to convert the natives to Christianity. His *History of Texas, 1673-1779* (English translation, 1935) is an important source of information about Texas during the colonial period.

Morgan, Garrett Augustus

b. March 4, 1875
Paris, Ky.
d. July 27, 1963
Cleveland, Ohio
fields: Invention and Technology

African American inventor. Famous for his contributions to public safety Garrett Augustus Morgan's inventions included a gas mask (patented in 1914) used by fire fighters, chemists, engineers, and World War I soldiers and the first automatic traffic-signal system (patented in 1923) used to regulate vehicular traffic at intersections.

Morgan, Sister Gertrude

b. 1900
Lafayette, Ala.
d. 1980
New Orleans, La.
fields: Art

African American self-taught artist; a painter in the "naive" style, Sister Gertrude Morgan's paintings reflect her commitment to the fundamentalist sect for which she was a street evangelist.

Morgan, J. P.

full: John Pierpont Morgan
b. April 17, 1837
Hartford, Connecticut
d. March 31, 1913
Rome, Italy
fields: Banking and Finance, Philanthropy

As an extraordinarily successful investment banker and a conspicuous philanthropist, and one of the most prominent art collectors of his day, Morgan symbolized an era of aggressive capitalism.

Morgan, Joe

b. September 19, 1943
Bonham, Tex.
fields: Sports (baseball player)

African American baseball player. Second baseman Joe Morgan played professional baseball for twenty-two years, primarily for the Houston Astros and Cincinnati Reds. He won Most Valuable Player awards with the Reds in 1975 and 1976. In 1976 Morgan had his best season when he batted .320 with 27 home runs, hit 111 runs batted in, and stole 60 bases. He was inducted into the baseball Hall of Fame in 1990 and held the record for most home runs by a second baseman (266).

Morgan, Joyce. *See* Morgan, Meli'sa

Morgan, Julia

b. January 26, 1872
San Francisco, California
d. February 2, 1957
San Francisco, California
fields: Architecture

One of the first female architects in the United States, Morgan designed nearly eight hundred buildings, including the magnificent Hearst Castle.

Morgan, Lee

b. July 10, 1938
Philadelphia, Pa.
d. February 19, 1972
New York, N.Y.
fields: Music (jazz trumpeter)

African American jazz trumpeter; Lee Morgan played with Dizzy Gillespie's orchestra and Art Blakey's Jazz Messengers. He recorded his own albums, *The Sidewinder* (1963), *Cornbread* (1965), and *The Rajah* (1966), and on other people's albums, John Coltrane's *Blue Train* (1957) and Hank Mobley's *Dippin'* (1965). In 1970 and 1971, Morgan was actively involved in the Jazz and People's Movement, an organization dedicated to promoting jazz music and African American performers on radio and television.

Morgan, Lewis Henry

b. November 21, 1818
Aurora, New York
d. December 17, 1881
Rochester, New York
fields: Anthropology, Natural History

Extending kinship studies, first among the Iroquois, then to cultures around the world, Morgan devised a theory of social and cultural evolution that provided both a theoretical paradigm for late nineteenth century anthropology and a theory of early family evolution that Karl Marx used in his interpretation of history.

Morgan, Meli'sa

né: Joyce Morgan
b. 1964
Queens, N.Y.
fields: Music (singer)

African American singer. After singing backup for such acts as Chaka Khan, Kashif, Whitney Houston, and Melba Moore Meli'sa Morgan decided to persue a solo career. Morgan wrote and produced a large portion of *Do Me Baby* (1985), her debut album. Her second album, *Good Love*, was released in 1987, her third, *The Lady in Me*, in 1990, and her fourth, *Still in Love with You*, in 1992.

Morgan, Michael

b. 1957
Washington, D.C.
fields: Music (music conductor)

African American music conductor; from 1980 to 1987, Michael Morgan served as assistant conductor for the Chicago Symphony; in 1987 accepted a new position as affiliate artist conductor.

Morgan, Norma Gloria

b. 1928
New Haven, Conn.
fields: Art (printmaker and painter)

African American printmaker and painter; Norma Gloria Morgan, who studied at the Hans Hofman School of Fine Art, the Art Students League in New York City, and the Whitney School of Art, is known for her intricate etchings and engravings. Her work reflects a fascination with Scottish moors, landscapes of northern England, or Biblical demons and prophets. Morgan has work in the permanent collections of museums in several major cities in the United States and in museums in Scotland.

Morgan, Robin

b. January 29, 1941
Lake Worth, Fla.
fields: Literature, Women's Rights

Robin Morgan is a pioneer writer on the subject of women's rights. A columnist and lecturer, Morgan received the prestigious Wonder Woman award for international peace and understanding. Her most important works include *Going Too Far: The Personal Chronicle of a Feminist* (1978) and *Sisterhood Is Global: The International Women's Movement Anthology* (1984).

Morgan, Thomas Hunt

b. September 25, 1866
Lexington, Kentucky
d. December 4, 1945
Pasadena, California
fields: Genetics

Through his ability to work closely with colleagues in unselfishly pursuing a scientific problem, Morgan's *Drosophila* research pioneered modern chromosome theory and genetic research. He was awarded the 1933 Nobel Prize in Physiology or Medicine.

Morgan, William

b. August 7, 1774?
probably Culpeper County, Virginia
d. September 12, 1826?
probably Fort Niagara, New York
fields: Literature

William Morgan wrote a book on Masonry but disappeared before it was published. In 1825 he joined the Royal Arch Mason lodge at Le Roy, New York. The next year he registered the title of a book, *Illustrations of Masonry, By One of the Fraternity Who Has Devoted Thirty Years to the Subject*, for copyright protection, and rumors spread through New York that his book would reveal the secret rituals of Masonry. Soon afterward, he was seized and spirited away, never to be seen again, and rumors spread that he had been murdered by Masons determined to prevent publication of his book. Accusations that members of Masonic lodges were shielding fellow members from prosecution for murder led to formation of the short-lived Anti-Masonic Party in New York.

Morganfield, McKinley. *See* Muddy Waters

Morgenthau, Henry, Jr.

b. May 11, 1891
New York, New York
d. February 6, 1967
Poughkeepsie, New York

fields: Government and Politics

Henry Morgenthau, Jr., was U.S. secretary of the treasury under President Franklin D. Roosevelt during New Deal era and World War II (1934-1945).

Mori, Toshio

b. Mar. 20, 1910
Oakland, Calif.
d. Apr. 12, 1980
San Leandro, Calif.
fields: Literature, Historiography

Writer and historian Toshio Mori's first book *Yokohama, California*, a collection of short stories, was published in 1949. Mori, interned at the Topaz relocation center in Utah, wrote about Japanese American life. His short stories appeared in anthologies such as *Best American Short Stories of 1943* (1944), *New Directions*, *Aiiieeeee! An Anthology of Asian-American Writers* (1974), and *The Big Aiiieeeee! An Anthology of Chinese American and Japanese American Literature* (1991). Mori also published a collection of short stories, *The Chauvinist and Other Stories* (1979) and a novel, *Woman from Hiroshima* (1979).

Morial, Dutch

full: Ernest Nathan Morial
b. October 9, 1929
New Orleans, La.
d. December 24, 1989
New Orleans, La.
fields: Government and Politics

African American mayor of New Orleans, Louisiana; Dutch Morial was elected president of the New Orleans chapter of the National Association for the Advancement of Colored People (1960); was appointed assistant U.S. attorney (1965), first black to hold this post in Louisiana; was elected to the Louisiana State House of Representatives (1968); served as a juvenile court judge (1970-1974); was elected judge on the Fourth Circuit Court of Appeals for Louisiana (1973-1977); was mayor of New Orleans (1977-1986).

Morial, Marc H.

b. January 3, 1958
New Orleans, La.
fields: Government and Politics

African American politician and mayor of New Orleans; in 1994, Marc H. Morial became mayor in the aftermath of a close and controversial election. He established the Mayor's Office of Tourism, Arts and Entertainment to help bring money into the economy.

Morimura, Toyo

b. 1854
Tokyo, Japan
d. 1899
fields: Business and Industry

Toyo Morimura, along with Momotaro Sato, founded the Hinode Company in New York in 1876. After Sato returned to Japan in 1879, Morimura reorganized the firm as Morimura Brothers and Company. After changing its focus to the importation of ceramics and porcelain, the company quickly expanded, achieving gross profits of $100,000 by 1880.

Morín, Raul R.

b. July 26, 1913
Lockhart, Tex.
d. 1967
fields: Literature, Social Reform

Mexican American author and civic leader. During his two-year recovery from a combat wound suffered during World War II, Raul R. Morín read extensively and took journalism classes. He wrote *Among the Valiant*, a book about Hispanic valor and service during the war. However, it remained unpublished for ten years. During the 1950's and 1960's, Morín became active in Mexican American Democratic politics, organizations, and veteran and civic groups. Among the commissions and boards to which he was appointed was the Mayor of Los Angeles' Advisory Committee. In 1968, the Raul R. Morín Memorial Square was dedicated in East Los Angeles.

Morison, Samuel Loring

b. October 30, 1944
London, England
fields: Historiography, Military Affairs

Samuel Loring Morison was the first American convicted of leaking classified information to the press. After serving in the U.S. Navy, he was employed by the Navy as a civilian Soviet ship analyst. He also worked part-time for *Jane's Fighting Ships*. In 1984 he sent the British *Jane's Defence Weekly* classified spy-satellite photographs of a Soviet nuclear-powered aircraft carrier under construction. After the pictures were picked up by a wire service, Federal Bureau of Investigation and naval intelligence officers arrested Morison. Charged with spying under the Espionage Act of 1917, he was tried in 1985 and sentenced to prison. Although many leading newspapers, broadcasting companies, and publishing groups urged that his conviction be reversed, it was upheld. The U.S. Supreme Court rejected his appeal without comment or dissent.

Morissette, Alanis

b. June 1, 1974
Ottawa, Ontario, Canada
fields: Music (pop)

In 1995 Alanis Morissette released her first American album, *Jagged Little Pill*, which won four Grammy Awards and went multiplatinum. Although some of Morissette's song lyrics have been considered too offensive to broadcast on radio stations or rock video television shows, she has enjoyed great commercial success. Her album *Supposedly Former Infatuation Junkie* was released in 1998.

Morita, Akio

b. January 26, 1921
Nagoya, Japan
fields: Business and Industry

Together with his mentor and business partner, Masaru Ibuka, Morita turned a tiny precision-instrument factory into the Sony Corporation, one of the largest industrial firms in the world and home of one of the best-known brand names in the world of business.

Morita, Pat

full: Noriyuki Morita
b. June 28, 1936
Berkeley, Calif.
fields: Film, Television

Pat Morita began work as a television and film actor in the mid-1960's, appearing in the films *Thoroughly Modern Millie* (1967), *The Shakiest Gun in the West* (1968), *Midway* (1976), and *Savannah Smiles* (1983), and *Captive Hearts* (1987). In 1984, Morita played the role of Miyagi in *The Karate Kid*, for which he was nominated for an Academy Award. On television, he appeared as a regular in a number of situation comedies, and in 1987 and 1988, he played the title character in the television crime drama *Ohara*.

Mornay, Philippe de

aka: Seigneur du Plessis-Marly
aka: Duplessis-Mornay
b. November 5, 1549
Buhy, Normandy, France
d. November 11, 1623
La Forêt-sur-Sèvre, France
fields: Diplomacy, Government and Politics, Military Affairs, Religion and Theology

Mornay was one of the formative influences within the early Huguenot movement in France. As the author of numerous religious and political tracts, he has had a lasting impact on liberal political theory; as a military leader and diplomat, he performed invaluable service toward securing the succession to the French throne for King Henry IV.

Morning Star. *See* Dull Knife

Moroles, Jesús Bautista

b. Sept. 22, 1950
Corpus Christi, Tex.
fields: Art (sculptor)

Latino sculptor. While enrolled at North Texas State University, Jesús Bautista Moroles strengthened his drafting, electronics, math, and woodworking skills, which would be useful in his later artistic work. After graduation, he studied stone sculptures in Italy, then returned to Texas and began working on his own sculptures. His work has been displayed at the Museum of Fine Arts in Santa Fe, New Mexico, and the University of Houston, among other locations.

Morris, Garrett

b. February 1, 1937
New Orleans, La.
fields: Theater and Entertainment

African American actor; Garrett Morris, best known for his membership in the original cast of the television comedy series *Saturday Night Live* (1975-1980), has appeared in numerous films and theater productions. His film credits include *Where's Poppa?* (1970), *Cooley High* (1975), and *Car Wash* (1976), and his plays include *Ain't Supposed to Die a Natural Death* (1971) and *What the Wine Sellers Buy* (1973).

Morris, Greg

b. September 27, 1934
Cleveland, Ohio
fields: Television

African American actor; Greg Morris, best known as Barney Collier, the technical wizard of television's *Mission: Impossible*, 1966 to 1973, was one of the few black actors to appear as a dramatic series regular in the 1960's. Other television credits include *Twilight Zone* (1963), *I Spy* (1966), *Sanford and Son* (1976), *Vega$* (1979-81), *The Jeffersons* (1983), and *The Jesse Owens Story* (1984). His film appearances include *The New Interns* (1964) and *Sword of Ali Baba* (1965).

Morris, Juanita. *See* Kreps, Juanita

Morris, Robert

b. January 31, 1734
Liverpool, England
d. May 8, 1806
Philadelphia, Pennsylvania
fields: Finance and Politics

Combining an intimate knowledge of the political workings of the early Revolutionary and Confederation periods with his experience as America's leading merchant, Morris saved the young United States from financial collapse and the consequent danger of losing its war for independence from Great Britain.

Morris, Steveland. *See* Wonder, Stevie

Morris, William

b. March 24, 1834
Walthamstow, near London, England
d. October 3, 1896
Hammersmith, near London, England
fields: Art, Architecture, Literature, Publishing, Government and Politics

Morris' influence on book design has been almost as profound as his impact on the decorative arts and the course of modern design; his key contribution to the growth of modern British socialism was practical, financial, and philosophical; he was also a powerful force in the revival of narrative poetry and the rediscovery of Norse literature, and an influential romantic and utopian writer.

Morrison, E. Frederick

aka: Sunshine Sammy
b. December 20, 1912
New Orleans, La.
fields: Theater and Entertainment, Film

First African American actor signed to a Hollywood studio (1919). Dubbed "Sunshine Sammy" by director Hal Roach, E. Frederick Morrison was known for his easy disposition and quick grasp of material. He was featured in silent movies but later made the transition to sound. A noted dancer, comedian, and singer, Morrison earned 146 film credits. In 1987 he was inducted into the Black Filmmakers Hall of Fame.

Morrison, Marion Michael. *See* Wayne, John

Morrison, Toni

né: Chloe Anthony Wofford
b. February 18, 1931
Lorain, Ohio
fields: Literature

Morrison was the first African American woman to win the Nobel Prize in Literature. Her work includes some of the most engaging contributions to American literature in the last hundred years.

Morrow, E. Frederic

full: Everett Frederic Morrow
b. April 20, 1909
Hackensack, N.J.
d. July 19, 1994
New York, N.Y.
fields: Government and Politics, Banking and Finance

African American political appointee and bank executive; E. Frederic Morrow was appointed business adviser to the Department of Commerce (1953-1955); was appointed as administrative officer for a White House special project group (1955); was the first African American to serve as a White House aide; left the White House to serve as vice president of the African American Institute in New York City (1961-1964); wrote *Black Man in the White House: A Diary of the Eisenhower Years by the Administrative Officer for Special Projects, the White House, 1955-1961* (1963).

Morrow, John Howard, Sr.

b. February 5, 1910
Hackensack, N.J.
fields: Education, Government and Politics

African American educator and political appointee; John Howard Morrow, Sr., joined the faculty of Talladega College in 1945; taught at Clark College in Atlanta (1954), Atlanta University (summers, 1950-1956), and North Carolina College (1956-1959); served as the first U.S. ambassador to the Republic of Guinea (1959-1961); was appointed alternate delegate to the United Nations (1961) and later U.S. permanent representative to the United Nations Educational, Scientific, and Cultural Organization (UNESCO) in Paris until 1963.

Morse, Samuel F. B.

full: Samuel Finley Breese Morse
b. April 27, 1791
Charlestown, Massachusetts
d. April 2, 1872
New York, New York
fields: Invention and Technology

Persevering through the trials of experimentation and the sluggishness of public approval, Morse developed and implemented a system of electric communication which revolutionized the availability of information and forever changed the sense of world distances.

Mortenson, Norma Jeane. *See* Monroe, Marilyn

Morton, Benny

full: Henry Sterling Morton
b. January 31, 1907
New York, N.Y.
d. December 28, 1985
New York, N.Y.
fields: Music (jazz trombonist)

African American jazz trombonist; Benny Morton played with Fletcher Henderson's Orchestra (1926-1928); performed in the bands of William "Chick" Webb (1930-1931), Don Redman (1932-1937), and Count Basie (1937-1940); played with pianist Teddy Wilson's sextet (1940-1943); formed own jazz group (1944-1946); worked in Broadway theater orchestras; worked as studio musician (late 1950's); toured Africa with Paul Taubman's concert orchestra (1964); performed with the Saints and Sinners (1967 and 1970), Wild Bill Davison (1968), Sy

Oliver (1970-1971), and the World's Greatest Jazz Band (1973-1974); resumed touring with the group in 1978.

Morton, Carlos

b. Oct. 15, 1947
Chicago, Ill.
fields: Literature

Latino playwright. Carlos Morton earned a master's degree in playwriting from the University of California, San Diego, in 1979 and a doctorate from the University of Texas at Austin in 1987. He then taught at the University of California, Riverside. Morton published a chapbook of poems called *White Heroin Winter* in 1971. His plays, which are written in urban dialects that combine English and Spanish, reflect the street life of Hispanic American communities. Among those that have been produced are *El Jardin* (1974) and *Pancho Diablo*. Other plays have been published in the collections *The Many Deaths of Danny Rosales and Other Plays* (1983) and *Johnny Tenorio and Other Plays* (1991).

Morton, Edna

b. ?
d. ?
fields: Film

African American silent-film actress; Edna Morton, "the black Mary Pickford," appeared in eight films from independent producers during the early 1920's, including *The Burden of Race* (1921), *The Call of His People* (1922), *Easy Money* (1922), and *Wildfire* (1925).

Morton, Jelly Roll

full: Ferdinand Joseph La Menthe Morton
b. October 20, 1890
Gulfport, La.
d. July 10, 1941
Los Angeles, Calif.
fields: Music (jazz pianist, composer, and arranger)

African American jazz pianist, composer, and arranger; Jelly Roll Morton first recorded in 1923, though his better-known recordings, with his band the Red Hot Peppers, began in 1926. Morton's reputation largely rests on this series of recordings. He was an innovator of the 1920's with songs such as "Grandpa's Spells" (1923), "Black Bottom Stomp" (1925), and "Cannonball Blues" (1926), and even earlier with "Jelly Roll Blues" (1905) and "King Porter Stomp" (1906). Remembered as a great piano player, composer, and arranger of his era, there have been many books written about him, including *Mister Jelly Roll* (1950), by Alan Lomax.

Morton, Joe

b. October 8, 1947
New York, N.Y.
fields: Film, Television (actor)

African American actor; Joe Morton, best known for his role in the cult film *The Brother from Another Planet* (1984), has appeared in a variety of film and television roles. His film credits include *Tap* (1989), *Between the Lines* (1977), *Crossroads* (1986), *Trouble in Mind* (1986), and *Stranded* (1987). On television, Morton portrayed an assistant district attorney on *Equal Justice* and Hal Marshall, one of the main characters, in the television sitcom *Grady* (1975-1976).

Morton, William Thomas Green

b. August 9, 1819
Charlton, Massachusetts
d. July 15, 1868
New York, New York
fields: Medicine (dentistry, anesthesiology)

Morton discovered anesthesia by ether inhalation. Rival claims to priority resulted in the most acrimonious debate in the history of medicine.

Mosca, Gaetano

b. April 1, 1858
Palermo, Sicily
d. November 8, 1941
Rome, Italy
fields: Political Science, Government and Politics

Mosca was one of the founders of modern political science. His writings on the concept of elite rule were crucial contributions to a modern theory of government. Mosca combined a university position with an active political life, serving in the Italian parliament for fifteen years and eventually opposing Benito Mussolini and Fascism.

Moses

b. c. 1300 B.C.E.
near Memphis, Egypt
d. c. 1200 B.C.E.
place unknown
fields: Religion and Theology

As the leader of tribal Israel who brought his people to the brink of nationhood in the thirteenth century B.C.E., Moses may be seen as the father of many governmental, social, and religious ideals that continue to influence the contemporary world. The codification of religious and ethical laws in the Pentateuch, the first five books of the Old Testament, is traditionally attributed to him.

Moses

aka: Quelatikan (The Blue Horn)
b. c. 1829
Wenatchee Flat, central Wash.
d. Mar. 25, 1899
near Wilbur, Wash.
fields: Government and Politics, Diplomacy, Native American Affairs

A Kowachinook tribal leader and diplomat, Moses was associated with a number of chiefs of the Northwest, including Chief Joseph (a lifelong friend) and Kamiakin, and he provided counsel during the wars of the 1850's.

Moses, Edwin

full: Edwin Corley Moses
b. August 31, 1955
Dayton, Ohio
fields: Sports (hurdler)

African American hurdler; Edwin Moses, considered to be the best 400-meter hurdler in history, won gold medals in the 1976 and 1984 Olympics and won the bronze medal in the 1988 Games. Moses was undefeated in seventy consecutive races from 1977 to 1981. He received the Sullivan Award as outstanding amateur athlete in the United States in 1983.

Moses, Grandma

né: Anna Mary Robertson
b. September 7, 1860
Washington County, near Greenwich, New York
d. December 13, 1961
Hoosick Falls, New York
fields: Art

A self-taught artist, Grandma Moses developed a distinctive style of painting, a form of Primitivism also referred to as naïve art or folk art.

Moses, Hilda Theresa. *See* Simms, Hilda

Moses, Phoebe Anne. *See* Oakley, Annie

Moses, Robert Parris

aka: Bob Parris
b. January 23, 1935
New York, N.Y.
fields: Civil Rights

A grassroots civil rights activist, Robert Moses began recruiting participants for the founding conference of SNCC in 1960. Moses then went to Mississippi where he directed the Council of Federated Organizations (COFO), a coalition of local civil rights organizations. Moses left SNCC in 1965 in opposition to the rise of militants in the organization. He was also active in the anti-Vietnam War effort, but by 1966 he had wearied of the movement's disunity. He moved to Canada to evade the draft, and there he joined various African freedom movements. In 1968 he moved to Tanzania until President Jimmy Carter pardoned draft resisters in 1977.

Moses de León

full: Rabbi Moses ben Shem Tov de León
b. 1250
probably León, Spain
d. 1305
Arévalo, Spain
fields: Religion and Theology, Philosophy

Through his lifework, the *Zohar*, Moses de León exercised the greatest influence on Judaic religious thought after the Talmud and the Bible.

Moskovitz, Eva. *See* Merriam, Eve

Moskowitz, Belle

né: Belle Lindner
aka: Belle Lindner Israels
b. October 5, 1877
New York, New York
d. January 2, 1933
New York, New York
fields: Social Reform, Government and Politics

A social reformer in the early 1900's, Moskowitz became the most politically influential woman in the United States when she served New York governor and 1928 presidential candidate Al Smith as a close adviser.

Mosley, Donna Lynn

b. 1964?
Willingboro, N.J.
fields: Sports (gymnast)

African American gymnast; Donna Lynn Mosley was the first African American to compete in the United States Gymnastics Federation Junior Olympic Nationals (1977). She was thirteen at the time.

Mosley, Roger E.

b. ?
Los Angeles, Calif.
fields: Television, Film (actor)

African American actor; from 1980 to 1988, Roger E. Mosley appeared as Theodore Calvin ("T.C."), one of Tom Selleck's sidekicks in the television series *Magnum, P.I.*; film credits include *Leadbelly* (1976), *Heart Condition* (1990), and *Unlawful Entry* (1992).

Mosley, Walter

b. January 12, 1952
Los Angeles, Calif.
fields: Literature (novelist)

African American novelist; Walter Mosley's protagonist, Ezekiel "Easy" Rawlins, is featured in a number of detective exploits set in and around South Central Los Angeles in the late 1940's, 1950's, and early 1960's, including *Devil in a Blue Dress* (1990; made into a film starring Denzel Washington in 1995), *A Red Death* (1991), *White Butterfly* (1992), *Black Betty* (1994), *A Little Yellow Dog* (1996), and *Blue Light* (1998).

Mossadegh, Mohammad

b. June 16, 1882
Tehran, Persia (now Iran)
d. March 5, 1967
Tehran, Iran
fields: Government and Politics

Mohammad Mossadegh became national Iranian hero when he led nationalization Iranian oil industry in 1951. Prime minister of Iran, 1951-1953. Attempted to define limits of shah's power. Driven from office by a CIA-assisted coup after U.S. came to view him as Marxist and dangerous to U.S. interests. Under house arrest until his death.

Mössbauer, Rudolf Ludwig

b. Jan. 31, 1929
Munich, Germany
fields: Chemistry, Physics

Rudolf Ludwig Mössbauer, at a quite young age, was awarded the Nobel Prize in Physics (1961) for developing the technique that allows resonance absorption of gamma rays to be studied—called Mössbauer spectroscopy.

Mossell, Gertrude Bustill

b. July 3, 1855
Philadelphia, Pa.
d. January 21, 1948
Philadelphia, Pa.
fields: Journalism

African American journalist. Gertrude Bustill Mossell initiated and edited the woman's department of *New York Age*, *Indianapolis World*, and edited *Woman's Era*, a national magazine for black women. Her first article, "Woman's Suffrage," was published in the *New York Freeman*. She continued to write about social and political matters and authored the biographical *The Work of the Afro-American Woman* (1894)

Mossell, Nathan Francis

b. July 27, 1856
Hamilton, Ontario, Canada
d. October 27, 1946
Philadelphia, Pa.
fields: Medicine

African American physician; Nathan Francis Mossell, the first African American to be graduated from the University of Pennsylvania Medical School, founded the Frederick Douglass Memorial Hospital in Philadelphia in 1895. He was president of the National Medical Association from 1907 to 1908.

Mota, Manny

full: Manuel Rafael Mota y Geronimo
b. Feb. 18, 1939
Santo Domingo, Dominican Republic
fields: Sports (baseball player)

Latino baseball player. Manny Mota's major league debut came with the San Francisco Giants in 1962, but he was traded to the Pittsburgh Pirates the following season. At different times, he played the outfield, second base, third base, and catcher. He also became known for the ability to deliver key pinch hits late in the game. Mota batted .332 in 1966 and better than .300 in six of the following seven seasons. He hit .600 as a pinch hitter for the Los Angeles Dodgers in three National League playoff series. He remained a remarkably effective pinch hitter past the age when most players have retired. After the 1980 season, he retired to become a full-time coach. His total of 150 career pinch hits is a major league record.

Moten, Bennie

full: Benjamin Moten
b. November 13, 1894
Kansas City, Mo.
d. April 2, 1935
Kansas City, Mo.
fields: Music (bandleader)

African American bandleader; Bennie Moten, instrumental in the development of big band jazz in the lower Midwest, spent most of his career in Kansas City. Part of Moten's style was the riff device, the repetition of a certain phrase. It added to the relaxed swing feeling of the Kansas City style. Moten's recording career blossomed in the 1920's with such releases as "Elephant's Wobble/Crawdad Blues" (1923), "The New Tulsa Blues" (1927), "Moten Stomp" (1927), and "Kansas City Breakdown" (1928). Recorded during the 1930's were "When I'm Alone" (1930), "Toby/Moten Swing" (1932), "Lafayette" (1932), and "Prince of Wales" (1932).

Motley, Archibald John, Jr.

b. October 7, 1891
New Orleans, La.
d. January 16, 1981
Chicago, Ill.
fields: Art

African American painter; Archibald John Motley, Jr., studied at the Art Institute of Chicago; there he was a Frank G. Logan Medalist and won the institute's J. N. Eisendrath Prize. Motley worked for the Illinois Federal Art Project, and his works were exhibited in many institutions and galleries in the United States. His ability to work in different styles influenced later generations of painters, who used his leadership to expand their own artistic horizons.

Motley, Constance Baker

b. September 14, 1921
New Haven, Conn.
fields: Law, Civil Rights

African American judge and civil rights activist; Constance Baker Motley won nine of her ten major civil rights cases before the U.S. Supreme Court as a lawyer with the National Association for the Advancement of Colored People Legal Defense and Educational Fund (1945-1965). She became the highest-ranking elected black woman in a major American city when she was elected Manhattan borough president in 1965. In 1966 she was named as the first black female district judge.

Motley, Willard Francis

b. July 14, 1912
Chicago, Ill.
d. March 5, 1965
Mexico City, Mexico
fields: Literature

African American writer; Willard Francis Motley wrote mostly about poor white people on the West Side of Chicago. *Knock on Any Door* (1947), his first novel, was made into a 1949 film starring Humphrey Bogart. Both *Knock on Any Door* and its sequel, *Let No Man Write My Epitaph* (1958), concerned juvenile delinquency. In 1960 *Let No Man Write My Epitaph* also was made into a film.

Moton, Robert

full: Robert Russa Moton
b. August 26, 1867
Amelia Co., Va.
d. May 31, 1940
Capahosic, Va.
fields: Education, Civil Rights

After his graduation Robert Russa Moton was asked to stay on as the highest ranking black administrator at Hampton Institute. In 1911 he became a founding sponsor of the National Urban League. In 1915 Moton was succeeded Booker T. Washington as president of Tuskegee Institute in Alabama. Moton acted as an African American representative to established white financial and political leadership circles, using his connections to oppose lynching and promote the appointment of public officials sypathetic to African Americans. He was a key figure in the construction of the Veterans Hospital at Tuskeegee and its staffing by African Americans.

Mott, John R.

full: John Raleigh Mott
né: John Mott
b. May 25, 1865
Livingston Manor, New York
d. January 31, 1955
Orlando, Florida
fields: Religion and Theology

The central figure in at least four worldwide Christian movements, Mott combined missionary zeal and personal piety with administrative efficiency. Cowinner of the Nobel Peace Prize in 1946, he is widely regarded as the father of the ecumenical movement, the most significant religious movement of the twentieth century.

Mott, Lucretia

né: Lucretia Coffin
b. January 3, 1793
Nantucket, Massachusetts
d. November 11, 1880
near Philadelphia, Pennsylvania
fields: Social Reform, Women's Rights

An eloquent advocate of the abolition of slavery and of equality for women, Mott devoted her life to working toward these goals.

Mott, Nevill

full: Sir Nevill Francis Mott
b. Sept. 30, 1905
Leeds, West Yorkshire, England
d. Aug. 8, 1996
Milton Keynes, Buckinghamshire, England
fields: Mathematics, Physics

Using the laws of quantum mechanics, Nevill Mott increased immeasurably the knowledge about solid-state physics; work on conduction in solids contributed to microelectronics; in 1977, was awarded the Nobel Prize in Physics.

Mountain Wolf Woman

aka: Xehaciwinga
aka: Haksigaxunuminka (Little Fifth Daughter)
b. April, 1884
East Fork River, Wis.
d. Nov. 9, 1960
Black River Falls, Wis.
fields: Literature, Anthropology

The autobiography of Mountain Wolf Woman, a Winnebago, is a unique account of the adaptation of traditional Winnebago lifeways to modern conditions. In 1958, Mountain Wolf Woman spoke into a tape recorder in the presence of her adopted kinswoman, Nancy Oestreich Lurie, who then edited a translation from Winnebago into English to produce the book *Mountain Wolf Woman, Sister of Crashing Thunder* (1961).

Mountbatten, Louis

né: Louis Francis Albert Victor Nicholas
aka: Prince Louis of Battenberg
aka: Louis, First Earl Mountbatten of Burma
b. June 25, 1900
Frogmore House, Windsor, England
d. August 27, 1979
off Mullaghmore, on Donegal Bay, Ireland
fields: Government and Politics, Military Affairs

A naval hero and military leader during World War II, the last viceroy of imperial India, and the first and only governor-general of an independent India, Mountbatten was a figure of great achievement, the most enduringly significant of which was perhaps the example of leadership he provided for his nephew and surrogate son Prince Philip, Duke of Edinburgh, and for his great-nephew and surrogate grandson Charles, Prince of Wales.

Mourning Dove

aka: Humishuma
aka: Christine Quintasket
aka: Cristal Quintasket
aka: Mrs. Fred Galler
b. c. 1885
near Bonner's Ferry, Idaho
d. Aug. 8, 1936
Medical Lake, Wash.
fields: Literature

Mourning Dove, an Okanagan, wrote *Cogewea, the Half-Blood: A Depiction of the Great Montana Cattle Range* (1927), one of the first novels by an American Indian to be published in the United States. (The novel was extensively edited by her mentor, friend, and agent, Lucullus Virgil McWhorter, who believed that the text provided a good platform to protest the mistreatment suffered by Indians.) Also wrote other works.

Mouskos, Mikhail Khristodolou. *See* Makarios III

Moutoussamy-Ashe, Jeanne

b. 1951
Chicago, Ill.
fields: Photography

African American photographer. After graduating from Cooper Union with a B.F.A. in photography, Jeanne Moutoussamy-Ashe-has went on to do free-lance work for *Ebony*, *World Tennis*, the Philip Morris company, International Business Machines, NBC television, and the Associated Press. Well known for her work documenting subjects living under apartheid in South Africa, her 1986 book, *Viewfinders: Black Women Photographers*, was well received.

Mowry, Jess

b. March 27, 1960
Mississippi

fields: Literature (young adult fiction writer)
African American young adult fiction writer; in 1990, Jess Mowry published a story collection, *Rats in the Trees*; novels include *Children of the Night* (1989), *Way Past Cool* (1992), and *Six Out Seven* (1993).

Moya del Pino, José

b. 1891
Cordova, Spain
d. 1969
Ross, Calif.
fields: Art
Latino artist. José Moya del Pino did much of his work under Works Progress Administration programs of the federal government during the 1930's. His murals were painted specifically for the locations at which they appeared and incorporated elements particular to the area. Moya del Pino painted murals at the Coit Tower in San Francisco and the Aztec Brewery in San Diego, and in Stockton, Redwood City, and Lancaster.

Mozart, Wolfgang Amadeus

full: Johan Crysostom Wolfgang Amadeus Mozart
b. January 27, 1756
Salzburg, Austria
d. December 5, 1791
Vienna, Austria
fields: Music
Along with Joseph Haydn and Ludwig van Beethoven, Mozart represents the fullest achievement of the Viennese classical style. Prolific and precocious, Mozart worked in a wide range of musical forms, from court dances and chamber music to symphonies and operas, producing some of the most enduring and masterful compositions in each.

Mozi

aka: Mo Di
aka: Mo Tzu
fl. fifth century B.C.E.
China
fields: Philosophy
Mozi's doctrines of universal love, the need to follow the will of Heaven, and the condemnation of offensive warfare, as passed on by his devoted followers, formed the foundations of the first and best organized alternative to the teachings of Confucius in China during the Warring States period (475-221 B.C.E.).

Mr. Excitement. *See* Wilson, Jackie

Mr. T

né: Lawrence Tureaud
or né: Lawrence Tero
b. May 21, 1952
Chicago, Ill.
fields: Theater and Entertainment
African American actor. In 1982 Mr. T starred in the Sylvester Stallone film *Rocky III* as boxer Clubber Lang. Previously Mr. T was a bodyguard for such celebrities as Muhammad Ali, Leon Spinks, and Donna Summer. He is best-known for his role as Sergeant Bosco "B.A." Baracus in the television series *The A-Team* (1983-1987).

Mubarak, Hosni

full: Mohammed Hosni Said Mubarak
b. May 4, 1928
Kafr el-Musaliha, Menufiyya Governorate, Egypt
fields: Government and Politics
Hosni Mubarak became vice president of Egypt in 1975; took office as president in 1981 after Anwar Sadat's assassination; reelected in 1987 and 1983. Generally maintained Sadat's policies; contended with unrest in army and among outlawed Muslim fundamentalists. Maintained good relations with U.S., for which criticized by other Arab countries and some Egyptians.

Muddy Waters

né: McKinley Morganfield
b. April 4, 1915
Rolling Fork, Miss.
d. April 30, 1983
Westmont, Ill.
fields: Music (blues singer)
African American Chicago blues singer; known for his deep and loudly resonant voice and for his electric slide technique of guitar playing, Muddy Waters helped create the rhythmically intense, highly amplified Chicago style blues; Waters's recordings include "I'm Your Hootchie Cootchie Man" (1954), "Mannish Boy" (1955), "Baby Please Don't Go," "Forty Days and Forty Nights," and "Got My Mojo Working."

Mugabe, Robert

full: Robert Gabriel Mugabe
b. February 21, 1924
Kutama, Southern Rhodesia (now Zimbabwe)
fields: Government and Politics
Mugabe rose rapidly in the struggle for independence in southern Africa during the 1960's to become a prominent nationalist leader and statesman during the later part of the 1970's and the 1980's. Mugabe participated actively in the Lancaster House negotiations that led Rhodesia (Zimbabwe) to majority rule in April, 1980, and became the first black prime minister of Zimbabwe and its first executive president.

Muḥammad

full: Muḥammad ibn ʿAbdallah
b. c. 570
Mecca, Arabia
d. June 8, 632
Medina, Arabia
fields: Religion and Theology, Government and Politics
Muḥammad received the revelation of the Qur'an and founded the religion of Islam, a monotheistic religion in which all facets of life, including communal life, are to be submitted to the will of God; the separation of church and state is alien to Islam. Muḥammad often retreated for contemplation to the cave at Hira, where, in 609, he began receiving the revelations that constitute the Qur'an. Muḥammad left Mecca in June, 622. This departure for Yathrib marks the beginning of the Islamic era, when Muḥammad's efforts turned away from worldly Mecca and toward building a new Muslim community. He devised a constitution for Yathrib, which later became known as Medina; it was often used as a model for proper Islamic political organization. Through his teachings and leadership, Islam was established as a religious system and a way of life which has possessed extraordinary influence and persuasive powers in many parts of the world.

Muhammad V

né: Sidi Muhammad Ben Yusuf
b. August 10, 1909
Fès, Morocco
d. February 26, 1961
Rabat, Morocco
fields: Government and Politics
Sultan (1927-1953) and king (1957-1961) of Morocco As sultan of Morocco (1927-1953), Muhammad V worked with French colonial authorities in 1930's and sided with Allies in World War II. In 1947 espoused nationalism and independence; deposed 1953. After unrest and threatened civil war, crowned king of Morocco in 1957 after end of French protectorate.

Muhammad, Elijah

né: Elijah Poole
b. Oct. 7, 1897
Sanderville, Ga.
d. Feb. 25, 1975
Chicago, Ill.
fields: Religion and Theology, Social Reform
African American religious leader and black nationalist; Elijah Muhammad was born Elijah Poole to a former slave; became chief assistant to W. D. Fard, founder of the Lost-Found Nation of Isalm, in 1930; upon Fard's disappearance in 1934, succeeded to leadership of the Nation of Islam; preached racial separatism, black integrity, and the need for economic independence from whites; support for Japan in World War II and

the conviction of three members of the Nation of Islam for the assassination of Malcolm X led to unfavorable press coverage, but the movement continued to grow, especially among the underemployed of the major cities; group splintered after his death with the best-known group being led by Louis Farrakhan.

Muhammad, Ozier

b. 1950
fields: Photography

African American photographer; the grandson of Elijah Muhammad, the founder of the Nation of Islam, Ozier Muhammad received the 1985 Pulitzer Prize for International Reporting for his photographic essay entitled "Africa: The Desperate Continent"; his internationally published photographs, many for *New York Newsday*, showcase his ability to capture emotions translated through gestures.

Muhammad, Wallace D.

aka: Imam Warith Deen Muhammad
b. October 30, 1933
Detroit, Mich.
fields: Religion and Theology

African American religious leader; succeeding his father, Muslim leader Elijah Muhammad, in 1975 as leader of the Nation of Islam, Wallace D. Muhammad brought about doctrinal and structural changes in the organization including preaching against separatism in religion, opening the American Muslim Mission, renamed in 1980, to white membership, and changing the name of the journal *Muhammad Speaks* to *Bilalian News*; his leadership, guiding the American Muslim Mission toward Orthodox Islam, led to full acceptance and recognition by international Islamic organizations and by the Islamic headquarters in Mecca, Saudi Arabia; in 1985 Muhammad decentralized the organization and removed himself as the national organization leader; he continued to be the imam (minister) of the Philadelphia Temple and maintained the Chicago headquarters.

Muhammad, Wallace Fard. *See* Fard, Wallace D.

Muhammad ʿAlī Pasha

b. 1769
Kavala, Macedonia
d. August 2, 1849
Alexandria, Egypt
fields: Military Affairs, Government and Politics

By applying strong-arm techniques so as to assure central-government control, Muhammad transformed Egypt from its eighteenth century status as an ungovernable and unproductive province of the Ottoman Empire into a largely autonomous state supported by an impressive military apparatus. That was done by combining Ottoman "new order" reform priorities with European technical contributions, especially in the areas of military and agricultural modernization.

Muir, John

b. April 21, 1838
Dunbar, Scotland
d. December 24, 1914
Los Angeles, California
fields: Exploration and Colonization, Conservation and Environmentalism

Combining his skills as a scientist, explorer, and writer, Muir played a significant role in the conservation movement and in the development of the United States National Park system.

Mukherjee, Bharati

b. July 27, 1940
Calcutta, West Bengal, India
fields: Literature

Writer; Bharati Mukherjee was born into the Brahman caste in India, settled first in Canada, then in the United States; most of her works deal with the location of identity when faced with a multiethnic experience; wrote novels: *The Tiger's Daughter* (1972), *Wife* (1975), *Jasmine* (1989), and *The Holder of the World* (1993); nonfiction: *Days and Nights in Calcutta* (1977) and *The Sorrow and the Terror* (1987), both cowritten with her husband, Clark Blaise; and short stories: *Darkness* (1985) and *The Middleman and Other Stories* (1988).

Muldoon, Robert

full: Robert David Muldoon
b. September 25, 1921
Auckland, New Zealand
d. August 5, 1992
Auckland, New Zealand
fields: Government and Politics

Robert Muldoon of the National Party was prime minister of New Zealand from 1975 to 1984. Charismatic and conservative. Created new government pension plan for people over sixty; internationally, staunch anticommunist.

Muldowney, Shirley

né: Shirley Roque
b. June 19, 1940
Schenectady, New York
fields: Sports (auto racing)

The first female driver in the male-dominated sport of drag-racing, Shirley "Cha Cha" Muldowney went on to win seventeen National Hot Rod Association titles. Her achievement of three Top Fuel world championships has not been matched by any other driver.

Muller, Hermann Joseph

b. December 21, 1890
New York, New York
d. April 5, 1967
Indianapolis, Indiana
fields: Genetics

The first scientist to induce mutations with X rays and the founder of the field of radiation genetics, Muller became a crusader for radiation protection. He was awarded the 1948 Nobel Prize in Physiology or Medicine.

Müller, Johann. *See* Regiomontanus

Müller, Lucas. *See* Cranach, Lucas, the Elder

Mulliken, Robert S.

full: Robert Sanderson Mulliken
b. June 7, 1896
Newburyport, Massachusetts
d. Oct. 31, 1986
Arlington, Virginia
fields: Chemistry, Physics

Robert S. Mulliken was one of the first scientists to apply quantum physics to the study of chemical bonds in molecules; developed the molecular orbital method; won the Nobel Prize in Chemistry in 1966.

Mulroney, Brian

full: Martin Brian Mulroney
b. March 20, 1939
Baie-Comeau, Quebec, Canada
fields: Government and Politics

Mulroney served as prime minister of Canada, won two general elections for the Progressive Conservative Party, and negotiated a significant free trade agreement with the United States.

Munch, Edvard

b. December 12, 1863
Løten, Norway
d. January 23, 1944
Ekely, Norway
fields: Art

The dramatic paintings and graphics of Munch not only reflected his inner torments and emotions but also proved highly influential on artistic developments in the late nineteenth and early twentieth centuries. In addition to becoming his native country's most famous artist, Munch served as one of the main progenitors of expressionism.

Munemori, Sadao

b. ?
Los Angeles, Calif.
d. Apr. 5, 1945
near Seravezza, Italy

fields: Warfare and Conquest

Sadao Munemori was awarded the Congressional Medal of Honor, the United States' highest military honor, for his bravery during World War II. He is the only second-generation Japanese American and one of only four Japanese Americans ever to receive the award. A member of the all-Japanese American 442nd Regimental Combat Team, Munemori threw himself atop a live German grenade, shielding two other U.S. servicemen but killing himself.

Mung, John. *See* Nakahama Manjiro

Muñoz, Anthony

full: Michael Anthony Muñoz
b. Aug. 19, 1958
Ontario, Calif.
fields: Sports (football player)

Mexican American football player. Anthony Muñoz, a 6-foot-6-inch, 285-pound offensive lineman, played at the University of Southern California (USC) before he was drafted by the Cincinnati Bengals in 1980. As a rookie, he won NFL Lineman of the Year and Cincinnati Bengal Man of the Year honors. Muñoz went on to earn ten Pro Bowl nominations in eleven seasons. He retired after thirteen seasons with the Bengals.

Muñoz, Carlos, Jr.

b. Aug. 25, 1939
El Paso, Tex.
fields: Education, Literature, Historiography

Latino educator, writer, and historian. Carlos Muñoz, Jr., earned a Ph.D. in government from Claremont Graduate School (1973), then worked as an instructor at California State University, Los Angeles, from 1968 to 1969, where he founded the first Mexican American Chicano Studies department in the United States (1968). In 1970, he became an assistant professor at the University of California, Irvine. In 1973, he cofounded of the National Association for Chicano Studies. In 1976, he became an associate professor at the University of California, Berkeley. He served as an adviser during Jesse Jackson's 1988 presidential campaign. In 1989, he wrote *Youth, Identity, Power: The Chicano Movement.*

Muñoz Marín, Luis

b. Feb. 18, 1898
San Juan, Puerto Rico
d. Apr. 30, 1980
San Juan, Puerto Rico
fields: Government and Politics, Journalism, Literature

Puerto Rican politician, journalist, and poet. Luis Muñoz Marín was educated in the United States and wrote for publications such as *The Nation* and *The American Mercury* during the 1920's. In Puerto Rico, he joined the Liberal Party in 1931 and was elected senator in 1932. He also took over *La Democracia*, which had been his father's newspaper. In 1938, he cofounded the Popular Democratic Party in an effort to strengthen the island's economy to prepare for independence. In 1940, he became president of the Puerto Rican Senate. In 1948, Muñoz Marín became governor of Puerto Rico. Under his leadership, in 1952 Puerto Rico became officially known as the Estado Libre Asociado or ELA (Free Associated State). In 1963, President John F. Kennedy awarded him the Presidential Medal of Freedom, the first Puerto Rican to receive it. Muñoz Marín served four consecutive terms before choosing not to run for re-election in 1964.

Muñoz Rivera, Luis

b. July 17, 1859
Barranquitas, Puerto Rico
d. Nov. 15, 1916
Santurce, Puerto Rico
fields: Government and Politics

Puerto Rican politician. While serving as resident commissioner (representative in Congress) in Washington, D.C., between 1910 and 1916, Luis Muñoz Rivera worked to obtain home rule for Puerto Rico from a reluctant U.S. Congress. Although he died in 1916, his efforts led to the passage of the 1917 Jones Act, which granted American citizenship to Puerto Ricans and instituted popularly elected houses of the legislature.

Munsch, Robert N.

b. June 11, 1945
Pittsburgh, Pennsylvania
fields: Literature

Canada's best-selling author of picture books for young children, Robert N. Munsch has seen many of his titles challenged and removed from schools. His books include *Love You Forever* (1986), *I Have to Go!* (1987) and *Pigs* (1989), *Thomas' Snowsuit* (1985), *The Paper Bag Princess* (1980), *Giant, or Waiting for the Thursday Boat* (1989), *A Promise Is a Promise* (1988), and *Good Families Don't* (1990).

Mura, David

full: David Alan Mura
b. June 17, 1952
Great Lakes, Ill.
fields: Literature

David Mura, a third-generation Japanese American, one of the emergent writers in Asian American literature. Mura's critically acclaimed collection of poems *After We Lost Our Way* (1989) won the National Poetry Series Contest. His *A Male Grief: Notes on Pornography and Addiction* was published in 1987, and his semiautobiographical travelogue *Turning Japanese* (1991) won the Oakland PEN Josephine Miles Book Award. That year he also cofounded Asian American Renaissance, a Minnesota-based Asian American arts group.

Murasaki Shikibu

b. c. 978
Kyoto, Japan
d. c. 1030
Kyoto, Japan
fields: Literature

The foremost writer of the Heian period, Murasaki authored *The Tale of Genji*, one of the greatest works in Japanese literature and the world's earliest novel, defining in it the aesthetic sensibility of the aristocratic courtier class whose lives and culture her writings reflected.

Murayama, Makio

b. Aug. 10, 1912
San Francisco, Calif.
fields: Medicine

Makio Murayama was a graduate student in biochemistry and nuclear physics at the University of California, Berkeley, when the Japanese bombed Pearl Harbor. Murayama's family was sent to a detention camp, but he was ordered to report to the Manhattan Project in Chicago as a physicist. He was rejected for being Japanese and was closely watched by the Federal Bureau of Investigation for the duration of the war. After receiving his doctorate in 1953, Murayama began postgraduate work at the California Institute of Technology, where, under Linus Pauling, he did research in sickle-cell disease.

Murayama, Milton

né: Atsushi Murayama
b. 1923
Lahaina, Territory of Hawaii
fields: Literature

Milton Murayama published his classic *All I Asking for Is My Body* in 1975. A second novel, *Five Years on a Rock*, about the mother of the family whose story is told in *All I Asking for Is My Body*, was published in 1994.

Murdoch, Iris

full: Jean Iris Murdoch
b. July 15, 1919
Dublin, Ireland
d. February 8, 1999
Oxford, England
fields: Philosophy, Literature

Schooled in philosophy, Iris Murdoch wrote more than twenty-five novels, many of them essentially philosophical, as well as several volumes that were overtly about philosophy. A prolific author, she wrote novels (including *Under the Net*, 1954; *The Unicorn*, 1963; *A Word Child*, 1975; *The Message to the Planet*, 1989), plays (*Art and Eros*, pr. 1980; *The One Alone*, pb. 1995), and philosophical works (*Metaphysics as a Guide to Morals*, 1992).

Murdoch, Rupert

full: Keith Rupert Murdoch
b. March 11, 1931
Melbourne, Australia
fields: Publishing, Business and Industry, Television

Media mogul. Rupert Murdoch created an Australian publishing empire in the 1960's before taking over several London papers, turning them into raucous tabloids. In the 1970's he extended the reach of his empire to the United States. His holdings include *The Times* of London, the *New York Post*, HarperCollins book publishers, the Fox television network, and the Los Angeles Dodgers baseball team.

Murdock, William

b. August 21, 1754
Bellow Mill, near Old Cumnock, Ayrshire, Scotland
d. November 15, 1839
Birmingham, England
fields: Engineering, Invention and Technology

Through his experimentation, Murdock helped to establish gas lighting in England and made improvements in the steam engine.

Murie, James

b. 1862
Grand Island, present-day Nebr.
d. 1921
fields: Anthropology (ethnographer)

A Skidi Pawnee, James Murie worked with anthropologists such as George A. Dorsey and later wrote his own anthropological works about the Pawnee.

Murieta, Joaquín

aka: Joaquín Murrieta
b. c. 1832
Sonora, Mexico
d. July, 1853
California
fields: Historical Figure (folk hero)

Folk hero. Joaquín Murieta was a legendary figure who is said to have migrated from Mexico to California during the gold rush. After enduring the insults of American miners for one year, he embarked on a series of robberies with a group of bandits in 1852. As vigilantes hunted him through the spring of 1853, the "Joaquín scare" spread across California. A special ranger company was created to capture him, and the governor offered a $1,000 reward. Just before the bounty expired, the ranger company produced a head pickled in a whiskey jar. Although it was never proved that the head belonged to Murieta, the legislature awarded $5,000 to the captain of the ranger company.

Muris, Johannes de

b. c. 1300
Lisieux diocese, Normandy
d. c. 1351
probably in or near Paris
fields: Music

De Muris was a leading proponent of the notational reform of music in the early fourteenth century.

Murphy, Calvin Jerome

b. May 9, 1948
Norwalk, Conn.
fields: Sports (basketball player)

African American basketball player; from 1970 to 1983, Calvin Jerome Murphy played guard for the San Diego/Houston Rockets in the National Basketball Association; in 1981 he set an NBA record for free throw percentage with a .958 success rate and, in 1983, he again led the NBA in free throw percentage.

Murphy, Carl

b. January 17, 1889
Baltimore, Md.
d. February 26, 1967
Baltimore, Md.
fields: Journalism

African American journalist; from 1918 to 1944, Carl Murphy worked for a Baltimore-based newspaper, the *Afro-American*, first as editor and then, beginning in 1922, as publisher and chairman of the board.

Murphy, Eddie

full: Edward Regan Murphy
b. April 3, 1961
Brooklyn, N.Y.
fields: Television, Film

African American actor and comedian; Eddie Murphy began his career as a stand-up comedian playing New York area comedy clubs; in January, 1981, Murphy became a permanent member of the television comedy series *Saturday Night Live* cast, earning $4,500 an episode; he made his film debut playing opposite Nick Nolte in the action comedy *48 Hrs.* (1982); Murphy's other film credits include *Trading Places* (1983), *Beverly Hills Cop* (1984; his first starring role and Paramount's highest-grossing winter release in history), *The Golden Child* (1986), *Beverly Hills Cop II* (1987), *Eddie Murphy Raw* (1987), *Coming to America* (1988), *Harlem Nights* (1989; which Murphy wrote, produced, and directed), *Another 48 Hrs.*(1990), *Boomerang* (1992), *The Nutty Professor* (1996), *Dr. Dolittle* (1998), *Life* (1999), and *Bowfinger* (1999); he has also produced two best-selling comedy albums and has recorded two music albums including *So Happy* (1989). In 1999, he helped to create the television claymation program *The PJs*.

Murphy, Frank

b. 1890
d. 1949
fields: Law

U.S. Supreme Court justice, 1940-1949 (died while in office); appointed by President Franklin D. Roosevelt. Argued vigorously for the availability of individual rights as checks on governmental power and opposed the expansion of the scope of warrantless searches and seizures. Significant opinions: *Thornhill v. Alabama*, 310 U.S. 88 (1940); *In re Yamashita*, 327 U.S. 1 (1946) (dissenting opinion); *Harris v. United States*, 331 U.S. 145 (1947) (dissenting opinion); *Wolf v. Colorado*, 338 U.S. 25 (1949) (dissenting opinion).

Murphy, Gardner

b. July 8, 1895
Chillicothe, Ohio
d. March 19, 1979
Washington, D.C.
fields: Psychiatry and Psychology

Gardner Murphy and his wife, Lois Murphy, together and separately wrote many books and articles topics relating to psychology, including world peace, parapsychology, and children's vulnerability and coping strategies. In 1947 Gardner Murphy published *Personality: A Behavioral Approach to Origins and Structure*, which was one of the first attempts to include the full range of issues necessary for a comprehensive theory of personality.

Murphy, Isaac

né: Isaac Burns
b. April 16, 1856
Frankfort, Ky.
d. February 12, 1896
Lexington, Ky.
fields: Sports (horse racing)

African American jockey; Isaac Murphy, a three-time winner of the Kentucky Derby (1884, 1890, and 1891), was victorious on 628 of 1,412 mounts; in 1956 he was inducted into the Jockey's Hall of Fame.

Murphy, John Henry, Sr.

b. December 25, 1840
Baltimore, Md.
d. April 5, 1922
Baltimore, Md.

fields: Publishing

African American publisher; John Henry Murphy, Sr., was born a slave; after being emancipated in 1863 and serving in the Union army during the Civil War, he worked at menial jobs until, at age fifty, he learned the printing trade; he then founded what would become one of the largest black newspapers in the United States, the Baltimore-based *Afro-American*.

Murphy, Lois

b. March 23, 1902
Lisbon, Iowa
fields: Psychiatry and Psychology, Education

Lois Murphy and her husband, Gardner Murphy, together and separately wrote many books and articles topics relating to psychology, including world peace, parapsychology, and children's vulnerability and coping strategies. Lois Murphy was one of the first to examine sympathy and coping strategies in children. As a child psychoanalyst, she treated, studied, and wrote about vulnerability and invulnerability in children and adolescents.

Murray, Albert

b. June 12, 1916
Nokomis, Ala.
fields: Scholarship, Literature

African American essayist and novelist; Albert Murray's publications include *The Omni-Americans: New Perspectives on Black Experience and American Culture* (1970), *South to a Very Old Place* (1971), *The Hero and the Blues* (1973), *Trainwhistle Guitar* (1974; a novel, part of a trilogy), and *Good Morning Blues: The Autobiography of Count Basie* (1985).

Murray, Charles

b. Jan. 8, 1943
Newton, Iowa
fields: Social Sciences

Social-science researcher and writer. Murray is a came to national attention in 1984 with his book *Losing Ground: American Social Policy, 1950-1980*, which argued that federal social-welfare programs had increased rather than alleviated poverty and should be eliminated. Another controversial explanation for social ills came in 1994's *The Bell Curve: Intelligence and Class Structure in American Life*, cowritten with Richard Herrnstein, which argued that intelligence is linked to achievement and that blacks as a group have lower intelligence test scores than whites.

Murray, Eddie

b. February 24, 1956
Los Angeles, Calif.
fields: Sports (baseball player)

African American baseball player; from 1977 to 1988, Eddie Murray played first base for the Baltimore Orioles, averaging close to 100 runs batted in and nearly 30 home runs per season; in 1982 he batted .316 (hitting 32 home runs and driving in 110 runs); he later played for the Los Angeles Dodgers, the New York Mets, the Cleveland Indians, the Baltimore Orioles again, and the Anaheim Angels. Retiring in 1997, Murray finished as one of only three players to collect at least 500 home runs and 3,000 hits in a career.

Murray, George Washington

b. September 22, 1853
near Rembert, S.C.
d. April 21, 1926
Chicago, Ill.
fields: Government and Politics

African American U.S. representative from South Carolina; George Washington Murray was voted the South Carolina Seventh District House representative (Republican) in 1892; after being defeated for reelection in 1894 and appealing the election results, the House Committee on Elections finally declared Murray the winner in the newly reapportioned First District, allowing him to commence his second term on June 4, 1896; Murray lost his 1896 bid for a third term.

Murray, Grace Brewster. *See* Hopper, Grace Murray

Murray, Madalyn. *See* O'Hair, Madalyn Murray

Murray, Pauli

b. November 20, 1910
Baltimore, Md.
d. July 1, 1985
Pittsburgh, Pa.
fields: Civil Rights, Women's Rights

African American civil rights activist; in 1946 Pauli Murray served as California's deputy attorney general; she taught law at Boston and Brandeis Universities and helped establish the National Organization for Women; she became the first African American woman to be ordained as an Episcopal priest in 1977; she also published fiction, poetry, and nonfiction works.

Murray, William. *See* Mansfield, first earl of

Murrow, Edward R.

né: Egbert Roscoe Murrow
b. April 25, 1908
Greensboro, North Carolina
d. April 27, 1965
Pawling, New York
fields: Journalism, Television

The pioneer of news broadcasting, Murrow set the standard for objective reporting while warning against the potential for manipulation by electronic journalism.

Mūsā, Mansa

aka: Kankan Musa
b. c. 1280
probably Niani, Mali
d. 1337
Niani, Mali
fields: Government and Politics

Ruler of Mali, 1307-1337. Mūsā was the ruler of the empire of Mali, the dominant political and cultural force in West Africa in the fourteenth century and a major influence in the development of an Islamic intellectual and religious environment in the region.

Musawi, Ruhollah. *See* Khomeini, Ayatollah

Muse, Clarence

b. October 7, 1889
Baltimore, Md.
d. October 13, 1979
Perris, Calif.
fields: Film

African American actor; in the 1930's, Clarence Muse played servant roles in films with great dignity; among his dozens of film roles, mostly during the 1930's and 1940's, were the role of Nappus in the all-black film *Hearts in Dixie* (1929), a dignified performance as Nigger Jim in *Huckleberry Finn* (1931; his first major film role), and a fiery performance in the role of Cato, the renegade slave, in the Civil War drama *So Red the Rose* (1935); Muse's last three film roles were in *Buck and the Preacher* (1972), *Car Wash* (1976), and *The Black Stallion* (1979); in 1973 Muse was inducted into the Black Filmmakers Hall of Fame.

Museveni, Yoweri Kaguta

b. 1944
Mbarara district, Uganda
fields: Government and Politics

Yoweri Kaguta Museveni of Uganda founded National Resistance Movement in 1981 and fought five-year guerrilla war against Milton Obote's government. Took office as president of Uganda in 1986. Privatized and stabilized economy and maintained peace among political factions. Led adoption of new Ugandan constitution in 1995. Held elections that same year and won nearly three-fourths of popular vote.

Musgrove, Mary

aka: Consaponaheeso
aka: Coosaponakeesa
aka: Creek Mary
aka: Mary Bosomworth

b. c. 1700
Coweta, Ala.
d. c. 1763
St. Catharine's Island, Ga.
fields: Diplomacy, Native American Affairs

A Creek Indian woman, Mary Musgrove was instrumental in the founding and development of the colony of Georgia. Married three times to Englishmen. It has been debated whether she helped or hurt the Creek people. At one point she and third husband jailed by Creeks for land schemes.

Muskie, Edmund

full: Edmund Sixtus Muskie
b. March 28, 1914
Rumford, Maine
d. March 26, 1996
Washington, D.C.
fields: Government and Politics

In 1958, Edmund Muskie became the first popularly elected Democratic senator from Maine. He supported bills providing for school aid, civil rights, antipoverty programs, Medicare, and establishment of the Department of Housing and Urban Development. He also introduced amendments to the Model Cities Act of 1966, part of President Lyndon B. Johnson's Great Society, and guided the legislation through the Senate. Muskie's greatest achievement, however, was in environmental regulation, on which he held hearings in major cities across the country in 1963, 1964, and 1965. He maneuvered through the Senate two important environmental laws: the Clean Air Act of 1963 and the Water Quality Act of 1965. Hubert Humphrey chose Muskie as his running mate in the 1968 presidential campaign; their campaign was unsuccessful. Muskie returned to the Senate, where he sponsored legislation that led to the establishment of the Environmental Protection Agency in 1970. His attempt to secure the Democratic presidential nomination in 1972 was unsuccessful. Between 1974 and 1980, Muskie was the first chairman of the Senate budget committee. As chairman, he developed a complex system to track federal spending. President Jimmy Carter appointed him secretary of state in 1980.

Mussolini, Benito

full: Benito Amilcare Andrea Mussolini
b. July 29, 1883
Predappio, Italy
d. April 28, 1945
Giulino di Mezzegra, near Dongo, Italy
fields: Government and Politics

Mussolini was the first Fascist dictator. He founded the Fascist Party in 1919 and led it to power in Italy in October, 1922.

Mussorgsky, Modest

full: Modest Petrovitch Mussorgsky
b. March 21, 1839
Karevo, Pskov, Russia
d. March 28, 1881
St. Petersburg, Russia
fields: Music

Mussorgsky, a major figure in the Russian national school, was the most original composer among the so-called Mighty Five. He excelled in creating dramatic works and songs in which natural speech inflections determined the vocal line, thus creating a striking realism, or naturalism.

Mustafa. *See* Atatürk, Kemal

Muzumdar, Haridas

full: Haridas Thakordas Muzumdar
b. Dec. 18, 1900
Gujarat, India
fields: Government and Politics

Haridas Muzumdar campaigned actively in the United States and India in the 1930's for India's independence from British colonial rule. In 1939, he went to India where he participated in discussions with Mahatma Gandhi, Jawaharlal Nehru, and other political leaders. He carried on his crusade in the United States from 1940 to 1947, when India was granted independence. Muzumdar, who became a U.S. citizen, wrote about the independence movement in *America's Contribution to India's Freedom* (1962). Other works include *India's Religious Heritage* (1986) and *Asian Indians' Contributions to America* (1986).

Myer, Dillon S.

b. Sept. 4, 1891
Hebron, Ohio
d. Oct. 21, 1982
Silver Spring, Md.
fields: Government and Politics

Dillon S. Myer became the director of the War Relocation Authority (WRA) in June, 1942. He was regarded as a benevolent father figure who was a friend to Japanese Americans by the Japanese American Citizens League (JACL), which had a policy of cooperation with the U.S. government. However, other internees resisted Myer's directives and were sent to Tule Lake or a prison camp in Moab, Utah. After the war, Myers became director of the Bureau of Indian Affairs, where he implemented the same policies toward American Indians as he had used with Japanese Americans.

Myers, Dwight. *See* Heavy D.

Myers, Walter Dean

b. August 12, 1937
Martinsburg, W.Va.
fields: Literature

African American writer; Walter Dean Myers authored more than twenty-five books for young adults and children; he also worked as an editor, publisher, and teacher.

Myrdal, Alva

né: Alva Reimer
b. January 31, 1902
Uppsala, Sweden
d. February 1, 1986
Stockholm, Sweden
fields: Diplomacy, Peace Advocacy

Swedish diplomat and nuclear-disarmament activist Alva Myrdal shared 1982 Nobel Peace Prize with a fellow disarmament advocate, Mexican diplomat Alfonso Garcia Robles. Worked with U.N. agencies, served as Sweden's ambassador to India (1955-1961).

Myrdal, Gunnar

b. December 6, 1898
Gustafs, Dalecarlia, Sweden
d. May 17, 1987
Stockholm, Sweden
fields: Economics, Sociology

Myrdal, who received the Nobel Prize in Economic Sciences, is among the most important intellectual figures of the twentieth century. He was one of the primary forces responsible for the development of the welfare state in his native Sweden, and his study of American racial relations contributed to the dismantling of legal segregation in the United States. His analyses of the Third World—its poverty and other problems—have been equally influential.

Nabokov, Vladimir

full: Vladimir Vladimirovich Nabokov
b. April 23, 1899
St. Petersburg, Russia
d. July 2, 1977
Montreux, Switzerland
fields: Literature

Nabokov established himself as one of the greatest novelists of the twentieth century. During the first half of his life, he wrote in Russian, while in his later years, he turned out a series of English-language masterpieces.

Nabrit, James

full: James Madison Nabrit, Jr.
b. September 4, 1900
Atlanta, Ga.
d. December 27, 1997
Washington, D.C.
fields: Civil Rights, Law, Education

James Nabrit was the director of public relations at Howard University, 1940-1950, 1955-1958, secretary of the university, 1939-1960, dean of the school of law, 1958-1960; and the university's president, 1960-1969. In 1954, he was legal adviser to the governor of the Virgin Islands. Nabrit's law career included a number of landmark civil rights cases, including *Nixon v. Herndon* (1927), *McLaurin v. Oklahoma State Regents* (1950), and *Bolling v. Sharpe* (1954), a companion case to *Brown v. Board of Education of Topeka*. Nabrit was appointed ambassador to the United Nations in 1965, and he served as a deputy representative on the United Nations Security Council.

Nabrit, Samuel

b. February 21, 1905
Macon, Ga.
fields: Education

African American educator; as the first African American to receive a Ph.D. from Brown University, Samuel Nabrit went on to serve as president of Texas Southern University (1955-1966), as executive director of the Southern Fellowships Fund of the Council of Southern Universities, and as chair of the Institute for Services to Education; he is also noted as the first African American appointed to the U.S. Atomic Energy Commission (1966).

Nabu-rimanni

b. early first century B.C.E.
probably Babylonia
d. late first century B.C.E.
probably Babylonia
fields: Astronomy

Nabu-rimanni was a Babylonian scribe who copied and preserved astronomical tables for the computation of lunar, solar, and planetary phenomena. By providing accurate numerical parameters for the prediction of astronomical phenomena, Babylonian astronomy furthered the development and success of Greek spherical astronomy, developed to its fullest in the Ptolemaic system.

Nader, Ralph

b. February 27, 1934
Winsted, Connecticut
fields: Government and Politics, Law, Social Reform

Using a variety of methods, including speech-making, writing, testifying before congressional committees, and establishing numerous public interest organizations, Nader has been the nation's leading advocate for the public interest in opposition to concentrations of unaccountable corporate and bureaucratic power.

Naess, Arne

b. January 27, 1912
Oslo, Norway
fields: Philosophy, Conservation and Environmentalism

Arne Naess, Norway's most prominent philosopher, achieved international recognition as the founder of a style of environmentalism known as deep ecology, which offers an alternative to Western civilization's traditional human-centered view of the world. Many of the ideas of the Green movement and of environmental counterculturalists have been drawn from Naess. He also pioneered an empirical approach to language with his 1938 work *"Truth" as Conceived by Those Who Are Not Professional Philosophers*. His most influential work is *Ecology, Community, and Lifestyle* (1974).

Nagae Lum, Peggy

b. 1951
Portland, Oreg.
fields: Law

Attorney Peggy Nagae Lum was lead counsel for the 1984 *coram nobis* case filed by Minoru Yasui against the U.S. government. She worked at the Seattle law firm of Betts, Patterson, and Mines from 1989 to 1991 and the University of Oregon School of Law. She was also adjunct professor at the University of Puget Sound School of Law in Tacoma, Washington, specializing in civil rights issues.

Nagano, Kent

b. 1948
Morro Bay, Calif.
fields: Music

Ken Nagano was musical director of L'Opera de Lyons, France, and of the Berkeley Symphony Orchestra in Berkeley, California. He won several recording awards, including the 1993 Gramophone Magazine Award for Best Opera Recording of the Year for his direction of L'Opera de Lyons performing Francis Poulenc's *Dialogues of the Carmelites*. He debuted at New York's Metropolitan Opera House in 1994. He received Grammy nominations for his recordings of John Adams' opera *The Death of Klinghoffer* and Sergei Prokofiev's *Love of Three Oranges*.

Nāgārjuna

b. c. 150
India
d. c. 250
India
fields: Religion and Theology, Philosophy

Nāgārjuna was an Indian Buddhist thinker who developed the Mādhyamaka school of Mahāyāna Buddhism and developed the concept *śūnyatā*, or "emptiness," which would influence Buddhism in Tibet, China, Korea, and Japan for the nearly two millennia since his death, particularly in the Zen tradition.

Nagasawa, Kanaye

né: Isonaga Hikosuke
b. 1852
Kagoshima, Japan,
d. 1934
Calif.
fields: Horticulture

In 1865, Kanaye Nagasawa arrived in the United States. He found work with a large New York vineyard owned by Thomas Lake Harris, leader of the Brotherhood of the New Life, a spiritualist sect. Harris taught Nagasawa the vintner's trade. Nagasawa became one of California's leading wine makers, producing wines under the Fountain Grove label near Santa Rosa.

Nagel, Thomas

b. July 4, 1937
Belgrade, Yugoslavia
fields: Philosophy

Thomas Nagel is one of the few twentieth century philosophers addressing nearly every area of philosophy, including ethics, political philosophy, the history of philosophy, the philosophy of mind, epistemology, and metaphysics. He tackles big and seemingly intractable issues, such as the nature of consciousness and the meaning of life. Holding a joint appointment in the Department of Philosophy and the School of Law at New York University, he founded the journal *Philosophy and Public Affairs* and with Robert Nozick began the Society for Ethical and Legal Philosophy (SELF). Best-known works include *The Possibility of Altruism* (1970), *Mortal Questions* (1979, including "What Is It Like to Be a Bat?"), *The View from Nowhere* (1986), *What Does It All Mean?* (1987), *Equality and Partiality* (1991), *Other Minds: Critical Essays, 1969-1994* (1995), and *The Last Word* (1997).

Nagumo, Shoji

b. 1890
Japan
d. 1976
fields: Horticulture

After arriving in the United States, Shoji Nagumo worked as a gardener's helper, then started his own business. He prospered by building and tending gardens for the new homes built in the Southern California construction boom in the 1920's. He cofounded the Japanese Gardeners' Association of Hollywood in 1933, which was absorbed four years later into the Southern California Gardeners Federation.

Nagy, Imre

b. June 7, 1896
Kaposvár, Hungary, Austro-Hungarian Empire
d. June 16, 1958
Budapest, Hungary
fields: Government and Politics

In the 1950;s, Imre Nagy was Hungary's minister of crop collection (1950-1952, deputy prime minister (1952-1953), then prime minister (1953-1955, 1956). Implemented liberal reforms, made concessions to Hungarian groups demanding change. Driven out of office by Soviet Union's invasion of Hungary in 1956 and executed two years later.

Nahm, Andrew C.

b. Mar. 3, 1919
Yonggang, Korea
fields: Historiography

Andrew C. Nahm received a doctoral degree from Stanford University in 1961. He was a research fellow with the Hoover Institution of Stanford in 1959-1960 and taught at the University of Nebraska (1961), Michigan State University (1964), and Western Michigan University (1960). His publications include *The United States and Korea: American-Korean Relations, 1866-1976* (1979), *Korea: Tradition and Transformation, a History of the Korean People* (1988), and *Historical Dictionary of the Republic of Korea* (1993).

Naiche

aka: Natchez
b. c. 1857
d. 1921
Mescalero, N.Mex.
fields: Government and Politics. Native American Affairs

Maiche, a Chiricahua Apache leader, was said to be Geronimo's closest associate in war and captivity. He led raiding parties in the 1880's, then was a leader of the Apache during their late nineteenth and early twentieth century interactions with the U.S. government.

Naidu, Sarojini

né: Sarojini Chattopadhyay
b. February 13, 1879
Hyderabad, India
d. March 2, 1949
Lucknow, India
fields: Government and Politics, Women's Rights, Education, Literature

Naidu demonstrated that strong-willed women can develop the statesmanship necessary to assume leadership of a nation. Her poetry, while overlooked in the West, is regarded as some of the most important in India.

Nakahama Manjiro

aka: John Mung
b. 1827
Nakanohama, Tosa Province, Japan
d. Nov. 12, 1898
Tokyo, Japan
fields: Diplomacy

In 1841, Nakahama Manjiro, a shipwrecked sailor, was rescued and brought to the United States, by William Whitfield, the captain of a whaling ship. Nakahama, whom Whitfield called John Mung, learned English before returning to Japan in 1851. He served as an interpreter between the Japanese feudal government and Commodore Matthew Perry, then in 1860 served as interpreter and navigational instructor on the *Kanrin Maru* goodwill mission to the United States. In 1869, Nakahama became a professor of English at Kaisei-jo Gakko (later Tokyo University). He visited the United States in 1870, visiting Whitfield, his rescuer and benefactor in the United States.

Nakahara, Ron

b. July 20, 1947
Honolulu, Territory of Hawaii
fields: Theater and Entertainment

As artistic associate for New York City's Pan Asian Repertory Theatre, Ron Nakahara directed works by Asian American dramatists Ed Sakamoto, Rosanna Alfaro Yamagiwa, Wakako Yamauchi, and Jon Shirota, as well as Asian playwrights Sha Yexin and Yukio Mishima. One of his more memorable performances as an actor was "The Child Who Becomes a Dictator" in the 1992 world premiere of Ernest Abuba's dance drama *Cambodia Agonistes*. Major theaters where Nakahara acted and directed include Hartford Stage, the Guthrie Theatre, and Actors Theatre of Louisville.

Nakaidoklini

b. c. mid-1800's
Ariz.
d. Aug. 30, 1881
Cibecue Creek, Ariz.
fields: Religion and Theology

Nakaidoklini was an Apache prophet whose murder by soldiers as Fort Apache in 1881 precipitated the final stage of the Apache Wars.

Nakamura, Gongoro

b. 1890
Hanechi, Okinawa, Japan
d. 1965
fields: Law, Social Reform

Gongoro Nakamura received a law degree from the University of Southern California, but because he was not a U.S. citizen, he could not become a lawyer. In the 1920's, he became active in community organizations and advised other Japanese Americans on legal matters. During World War II, he was interned at the Crystal City camp in southern Texas. After the war, Nakamura assisted Japanese Peruvians, Okinawans, and Japanese Americans displaced by the internment. In the early 1950's, he became a naturalized citizen.

Nakamura, Wakako. *See* Yamauchi, Wakako

Nakanishi, Don T.

b. Aug. 14, 1949
Los Angeles, Calif.
fields: Government and Politics

Don T. Nakanishi, who became director of the Asian American Studies Center of the University of California, Los Angeles (UCLA), in 1990, cofounded *Amerasia Journal*. UCLA denied him tenure in 1986, but with the support of students and others, he gained tenure at the Graduate School of Education three years later. He conducted research on a plethora of subjects including educational policy, electoral politics, international politics, and the impact of mass internment on Japanese Americans.

Nakano, Yosuke W.

b. 1887
Yamaguchi Prefecture, Japan

d. 1961
Kobe, Japan
fields: Architecture, Engineering

After studying at the University of Pennsylvania's architectural school, Yosuke W. Nakano was hired by Philadelphia architectural firm Wark and Company, where he rose to become chief engineer. He became an expert on the use of reinforced concrete in the building of large-scale structures. Nakano, who became a U.S. citizen in 1953, helped to construct more than two hundred buildings in the United States.

Nakaoka, Kiyoto Kenneth

b. Oct. 23, 1920
Los Angeles, Calif.
d. Aug. 12, 1980
Gardena, Calif.
fields: Government and Politics

Kiyoto Kenneth Nakaoka established a realty firm, the Ken Nakaoka Company, in Gardena, a Los Angeles suburb known for its large concentration of Japanese Americans. He was elected to the city council in 1966 and served three consecutive terms as mayor of Gardena, from 1968 to 1974, becoming the city's first Japanese American mayor. Nakaoka was active in numerous civic and community organizations and was named Rotarian of the Year in 1962 and 1968 by Rotary International.

Nakashima, George

b. 1905
Spokane, Wash.
d. 1990
New Hope, Pa.
fields: Business and Industry

Furniture maker George Nakashima received a master's degree in architecture in 1929 from the Massachusetts Institute of Technology. During World War II, he was interned in the Minidoka relocation center in southern Idaho. In 1943, Nakashima moved to Pennsylvania, where he opened his own furniture business in 1945. His handmade wooden furniture collected a number of prestigious honors and awards and was exhibited in the Museum of Modern Art in New York and the Renwick Gallery in Washington, D.C. In 1989, a retrospective of his work was staged by the American Craft Museum in Manhattan.

Nakayama, Joji

b. ?
fields: Business and Industry

Chief inspector Joji Nakayama was responsible for monitoring the health of the Japanese immigrant laborers on Hawaiian plantations and served as a liaison between the workers and plantation overseers. In 1886, Nakayama was appointed to serve as head of the Japanese section of the newly established Hawaiian Bureau of Immigration. Nakayama was supposed to represent the interests of the laborers, but his job was supported by the plantation owners, and he sided with them on all labor disputes.

Nakazawa, Ken

b. Dec. 18, 1883
Fukushima Prefecture, Japan
d. 1953
fields: Education

Ken Nakazawa, who arrived in the United States in 1908, became the first Japanese American to teach at a major American university when he was hired in 1926 by the University of Southern California to teach classes on Asian culture. He published a collection of short stories, *Weaver of the Frost*, in 1927. A post he had held with the Japanese consulate in Los Angeles resulted in his internment and eventual deportation to Japan in 1942. He was allowed back in the United States ten years later.

Namath, Joe

full: Joseph William Namath
b. May 31, 1943
Beaver Falls, Pennsylvania
fields: Sports (football)

Professional football quarterback Joe Namath was one of the first celebrity football stars, leading the New York Jets to a shocking upset victory in Super Bowl III on January 12, 1969. He was named Super Bowl Most Valuable Player and became a national celebrity. He retired from football in 1977 and was later inducted into the Pro Football Hall of Fame. He appeared in numerous commercials and several movies and television shows.

Nambu, Yoichiro

b. Jan. 18, 1921
Tokyo, Japan
fields: Physics

Yoichiro Nambu contributed to the Standard Model, which accounts for the fundamental interactions among elementary particles.

Nampeyo

b. c. 1860
Hano, First Mesa, Ariz. Territory
d. July 20, 1942
Hano, First Mesa, Ariz.
fields: Art (potter)

A Hano and Hopi potter, Nampeyo was inspired by prehistoric Sikyatki Polychrome pottery. She created her own style, known as Hano Polychrome, which revived the declining pottery tradition in the Hopi pueblos. She did not copy the Sikyatki patterns in her work but combined many of the elements and motifs, such as spiral bird beaks, wings, and feathers, with her own ideas to re-create the Sikyatki sense of form.

Namumpum. *See* Weetamoo

Nana

aka: Nané
aka: Nanay
b. c. 1810-1895?
Fort Sill, Okla.
fields: Warfare and Conquest, Native American Affairs

A Chiricahua Apache leader, Nana was said to have had the longest fighting career of any Apache warrior. Terrorized whites in New Mexico in 1881-1882 after surviving massacre by Mexican troops. In May, 1885, Nana and about 140 Chiricahuas broke away from the reservation on which they were living. Their flight into Mexico and subsequent raids ended March 25, 1886, when they negotiated a return to the reservation.

Nānak

aka: Gurū Nānak
né: Rā Bhoi dī Talvandī
b. April 15, 1469
Talwandi, Punjab
d. 1539
Kartārpur, Punjab, Mughal Empire
fields: Religion and Theology

Nānak was a religious reformer who synthesized the fundamental principles of Islam and the tradition of Hinduism into a new universal religion, Sikhism. His teaching emphasizes equality of all human beings and regards responsible social action as integral to true spiritual practice. Monism and the rejection of excessive ritual are the basic tenets of this religion.

Nansen, Fridtjof

b. October 10, 1861
Store-Frøen, Norway
d. May 13, 1930
Polhøgda, Norway
fields: Exploration and Colonization

Nansen was a major Arctic explorer, an accomplished scientist, an outstanding statesman, and world-renowned for his humanitarian services to advance the rights of the oppressed and war refugees.

Nantiotish. *See* Natiotish

Nanuntenoo. *See* Canonchet

Nanye-hi (One Who Goes About). *See* Ward, Nancy

Napier, John

aka: John Napier, eighth lord of Merchiston

b. 1550
Merchiston Castle (near Edinburgh), Scotland
d. April 4, 1617
Merchiston Castle, Scotland
fields: Mathematics, Religion and Theology

Working alone, without the benefit of earlier work and the encouragement of mentors, John Napier invented logarithms, the greatest boon to experimental science produced during the Renaissance.

Napoleon I

né: Napoleon Bonaparte
b. August 15, 1769
Ajaccio, Corsica
d. May 5, 1821
Saint Helena Island
fields: Government and Politics, Military Affairs

Emperor of France, 1804-1814. One of the greatest generals in history, Napoleon I also made lasting contributions to the laws and civil administration of France and other lands. His darker legacy is to have developed a dictatorial rule that is the precursor of modern Fascism.

Napoleon III

né: Louis Napoleon Bonaparte
b. April 20, 1808
Paris, France
d. January 9, 1873
Chislehurst, Kent, England
fields: Government and Politics

Napoleon III, nephew of Napoleon I, was president of the Second French Republic, 1848-1852, and emperor of the Second Empire, 1852-1870. He was one of the key figures, sometimes unwittingly, in the political unification of both Italy and Germany, and was also greatly responsible for the rebuilding of Paris.

Narendranath Datta. *See* Vivekananda

Narendranath Dutt. *See* Vivekananda

Narita, Jude

b. ?
fields: Theater and Entertainment

Actor Jude Narita is best known for *Coming into Passion: Song for a Sansei*, a solo show that explores issues of race and gender facing Asian American women of different ethnicities and generations. She has a loyal following among theater-goers of all ethnicities.

Narváez, Pánfilo de

b. c. 1470
Valladolid, Spain
d. 1528
Gulf of Mexico
fields: Exploration and Colonization

Spanish explorer and conquistador. Pánfilo de Narváez participated in the conquest and occupation of Jamaica and, in 1511, of Cuba. In 1520, Narváez was sent to Mexico to arrest Hernán Cortés, who, against orders, had claimed the land he conquered in his own name. However, Cortés captured and imprisoned Narváez until 1522. In 1528, Narváez set out to settle Florida. The expedition was attacked by Natives Americans, and Narváez and his party sailed west along the coast of the Gulf of Mexico in makeshift barges. Narváez's barge disappeared in a strong current, and he is believed to have died at sea.

Nascimento, Edson Arantes do. *See* Pelé

Nascimento, Milton

b. Oct. 26, 1942
Rio de Janeiro, Brazil
fields: Music (singer, songwriter, and bandleader)

Brazilian singer, songwriter, and bandleader. Milton Nascimento gained national attention in 1967, when he was the only artist allowed to perform three songs at the First International Pop Song Festival in Rio de Janeiro. Nascimento recorded several albums between 1970 and 1980, including *Travessia*, *Cravo E Canela*, *Native Dancer*, and *Geraes*. He recorded with the Chilean group Agua, singer Mercedes Sosa, Flora Purim, Airto Moreira, Paul Simon, and Herbie Hancock. He also wrote film scores and appeared in several films.

Nash, Charles Edmund

b. May 23, 1844
Opelousas, La.
d. June 21, 1913
New Orleans, La.
fields: Warfare and Conquest, Government and Politics

African American legislator and military hero; as an enlisted soldier in the Union army, Charles Edmund Nash lost the lower third of one leg during the battle of Fort Blakely, La.; beginning in 1874, he served one undistinguished term in the U.S. House of Representatives and lost his reelection bid.

Nash, John

b. 1752
London, England
d. May 13, 1835
East Cowes Castle, Isle of Wight, England
fields: Architecture

Nash designed Regent's Park and Regent Street in London, and he extensively redesigned and added to the Royal Pavilion at Brighton and to Buckingham Palace.

Nash, Johnny

b. August 19, 1940
Houston, Tex.
fields: Music (popular singer)

African American singer; Johnny Nash appeared as a regular on Arthur Godfrey's television and radio shows in the mid-1950's; he released *Johnny Nash* (1958), *Quiet Hour* (1959), *I Got Rhythm* (1959), *Let's Get Lost* (1960), *Studio Time* (1961), and *Composer's Choice* (1965), before his 1968 release *Hold Me Tight* reached the lower level of the charts; he received national acclaim with the release of the number-one hit "I Can See Clearly Now" (1972), followed by the hit "My Merry-Go-Round" (1973), and a second number-one hit "Tears on My Pillow."

Nash, Paul

b. May 11, 1889
London, England
d. July 11, 1946
Boscombe, England
fields: Art, Publishing

Nash's landscape paintings, aptly depicting the destruction of World Wars I and II, are among the best in the English tradition.

Nash, Philip

b. Dec. 3, 1956
New York, N.Y.
fields: Law

Attorney Philip Nash, born to a second-generation Japanese American mother and European American father, was executive director of the National Asian Pacific American Legal Consortium. He helped establish the National Asian Pacific American Law Student Association (NAPALSA), the first Asian Pacific American Heritage Week Festival in New York City (1979), and the AmerAsian League (1986). His poetry and articles were published in *The New York Nichibei*, *Bridge*, *Gidra*, and *The Asian Journal*.

Nashe, Thomas

b. November, 1567
Lowestoft, Suffolk, England
d. c. 1601
place unknown
fields: Literature, Theater and Entertainment

A versatile writer of satiric pamphlets, plays, lyric poetry, and a novel, Thomas Nashe had a marked influence on many of his contemporaries, including William Shakespeare and Ben Jonson, who admired his powers of wit and observation and his inventive use of language.

Nasmyth, James

full: James Hall Nasmyth
b. August 19, 1808
Edinburgh, Scotland
d. May 7, 1890
London, England
fields: Engineering (mechanical), Invention and Technology

Nasmyth developed and successfully marketed a pioneering class of industrial metal-working machines, principally the steam hammer, contributing to Great Britain's role as the fountainhead of the Industrial Revolution.

Nasrin, Taslima

b. August 25, 1962
Mymensingh, East Pakistan (later Bangladesh)
fields: Literature

Taslima Nasrin is a Bangladeshi author whose strong views on women's rights have provoked charges of blasphemy and calls for her death by Muslim fundamentalists. Her 1993 novel, *Lajja*, or *Shame*, sparked a campaign against her that led to rioting in Bangladesh and renewed calls for her murder. She sought refuge in Sweden and continued to attack Islamic fundamentalists and Bangladeshi reformers who she regarded as doing too little to oppose religious and political tyranny. An atheist, she argues for a modern, secular state to protect women's rights.

Nasser, Gamal Abdel

b. January 15, 1918
Alexandria, Egypt
d. September 28, 1970
Cairo, Egypt
fields: Government and Politics

A career army officer, Gamal Abdel Nasser served in Egypt's 1948 war against Israel, in which he saw the need for major reforms. Afterward he helped form the Free Officers Movement, which overthrew King Farouk in 1952. Two years later Nasser became president, remaining in office until he died in 1970. He outlined his political philosophy in *Egypt's Liberation: The Philosophy of the Revolution* (1955). While president, he worked to modernize Egypt's economy, nationalized the Suez Canal, and led Egypt into two more wars with Israel.

Nast, Thomas

b. September 27, 1840
Landau, Germany
d. December 7, 1902
Guayaquil, Ecuador
fields: Art, Government and Politics

As one of the greatest American cartoonists, Nast created lasting works of art that expressed his personal and political convictions while reflecting the hopes and dreams of a generation.

Natawista

aka: Natawista Iksana
aka: Madame Culbertson
b. c. 1825
Alberta, Canada
d. c. 1895
Alberta, Canada
fields: Diplomacy (interpreter, diplomat)

A Blood Indian. After marrying a white man, Major Alexander Culbertson (commander of Fort Union), Natawista became an interpreter, diplomat, and trading post hostess. They traveled and traded, amassing something of a fortune.

Natchez. *See* Naiche

Nation, Carry

né: Carry Amelia Moore
b. November 11, 1846
Garrard County, Kentucky
d. June 9, 1911
Leavenworth, Kansas
fields: Social Reform

An activist in the temperance and women's rights movements, Nation gained international notoriety by smashing saloons. She demonstrated the strength and place of women in temperance reform.

Natiotish

aka: Nantiotish
aka: Nantiatish
b. fl. mid-1800's
fields: Warfare and Conquest, Native American Affairs

White Mountain Apache leader. Bitter over the death of the Apache prophet Nakaidoklini, Natiotish led White Mountain Apache warriors in the Battle of Big Dry Wash, 1882.

Natividad, Irene

b. Sept. 14, 1948
Manila, Republic of the Philippines
fields: Government and Politics

Filipino American Irene Natividad became the first Asian American to head the bipartisan National Women's Political Caucus when she served as national chair from 1985 to 1988. Previous posts included chair of the New York State Asian Pacific Caucus (1982-1984), deputy vice chair of the Asian Pacific Caucus of the Democratic National Committee (1982-1984), representative to the Ferraro Campaign (1984), and Alternate Delegate of the Democratic Convention (1984). Natividad taught at Lehman College and City University, New York, and Columbia University. She was founding director of the National Network of Asian-Pacific American Women and the Child Care Action Campaign, founder and president of Asian-American Professional Women, executive director of The Philippine American Foundation, chair of the National Commission on Working Women, and director of Sallie Mae, the quasi-governmental corporation that administers student loans.

Natta, Giulio

b. February 26, 1903
Imperia, Italy
d. May 2, 1979
Bergamo, Italy
fields: Chemistry, Education, Invention and Technology

Natta was awarded the Nobel Prize in Chemistry in 1963 for his work on macromolecular synthesis with total control of the relative spatial orientation of groups of atoms that are bonded to the polymer chain. This important development revolutionized the plastics industry and made possible the use of polymers in widespread applications, such as plasticware, laundry detergents, and antiknock admixtures to high-octane fuels.

Nava-Villarreal, Hector Rolando

b. May 23, 1943
Nuevo Laredo, Tamaulipas, Mexico
fields: Medicine

Latino oncologist and medical researcher. Hector Rolando Nava-Villarreal earned his M.D. degree from the medical faculty of the Universidad de Nuevo León in 1967. He interned in Corpus Christi, Texas, and did his residency at the Roswell Park Cancer Institute in Buffalo, New York, where he also served as a fellow in surgical oncology from 1974 to 1976. Nava-Villarreal served in Vietnam in the U.S. Army as a battalion surgeon from 1968 to 1970, then began work as a cancer researcher at the Roswell Park Cancer Institute in 1976. He has helped pioneer the use of lasers to treat cancer.

Navarro, Fats

full: Theodore Navarro
b. September 24, 1923
Key West, Fla.
d. July 7, 1950
New York, N.Y.
fields: Music (jazz trumpeter)

African American jazz trumpeter; as a replacement for trumpeter Dizzy Gillespie in the band led by Billy Eckstine, Fats Navarro joined fellow instrumentalists in helping to create the modern jazz form known as bebop; his prolific recordings in the mid- and late 1940's included "Double Talk" (1948; with trumpeter Howard McGhee); other memorable performances by Navarro appear on Tadd

Dameron's recorded compositions "The Squirrel," "Our Delight," and "Good Bait"; Navarro died one week after performing at New York's Birdland with saxophonist Charlie Parker on June 30, 1950.

Navarro, Gabriel

b. ?
Guadalajara, Mexico
d. ?
fields: Literature, Journalism, Theater and Entertainment

Latino playwright, journalist, and actor. Gabriel Navarro started Compañía de Operetas, Dramas, Zarzuelas y Revistas Méxicanas after moving to Los Angeles in 1922. He then began writing more serious plays, including *Los emigrados* (1928), *El sacrificio* (1931), and *Alma yaqui* (1932). In 1923, Navarro started the magazine *La Revista de Los Angeles*. He wrote for *El Hispano Americano* in the late 1920's and was theater critic for *La Opinión* in the 1930's.

Navarro, José Antonio

b. Feb. 27, 1795
San Antonio, Tex.
d. Jan. 13, 1871
San Antonio, Tex.
fields: Government and Politics

Latino politician. José Antonio Navarro was elected to the Texas state legislature in 1821 and became one of three Tejanos who signed Texas' declaration of independence from Mexico in 1835. Navarro took part in Santa Fe Expedition of 1841, during which he was captured and condemned to death as a traitor. His sentence was commuted to life imprisonment, but he escaped and returned to Texas after Antonio López de Santa Anna's term as president of Mexico ended in 1845. Navarro retired from public life in 1849.

Navratilova, Martina

né: Martina Subertova
b. October 18, 1956
Prague, Czechoslovakia
fields: Sports (tennis)

As a leading figure in women's tennis since the mid-1970's, Martina Navratilova was one of the first women athletes to demonstrate that women's sports could be as exciting as men's and that professional women athletes deserved comparable financial rewards.

Nawat. *See* Left Hand the First; Left Hand the Second

Naylor, Gloria

b. January 25, 1950
New York, N.Y.
fields: Literature

African American novelist; Gloria Naylor's published works include *The Women of Brewster Place* (1982; winner of the American Book Award for best first novel), *Linden Hills* (1985), *Mama Day* (1988), and *Bailey's Café* (1992) ; these works are admired for their richness of characterization, although the symbolic settings reflect occasional straining for mythic dimensions.

Nazuha Hoksina. *See* Howe, Oscar

Neal, Larry

b. September 5, 1937
Atlanta, Ga.
d. January 6, 1981
Hamilton, N.Y.
fields: Literature, Education

African American writer and educator; Larry Neal wrote plays, screenplays, and television scripts; he coedited *Black Fire: An Anthology of Afro-American Writing* (1968; with LeRoi Jones); he also served as educational director of the Black Panther Party and acted as a spokesperson for the Black Arts movement.

Nebuchadnezzar II

b. c. 630 B.C.E.
place unknown
d. 562 B.C.E.
Babylon
fields: Warfare and Conquest, Government and Politics

One of the most ambitious and successful military leaders of ancient times, Nebuchadnezzar possessed excellent governing ability which made Chaldean Neo-Babylon the most powerful and feared nation in Western Asia.

Neckam, Alexander

b. 1157
St. Albans, Hertfordshire, England
d. Probably March 31, 1217
Kempsey, Worcestershire, England
fields: Science, Education, Religion and Theology

Neckam typifies the broadening humanistic interests of the twelfth century through his writing and teaching in many areas, including grammar, science, and theology.

Necker, Anne-Louise-Germaine. *See* Staël, Madame de

Necker, Jacques

b. September 30, 1732
Geneva
d. April 9, 1804
Coppet, Helvetia
fields: Business and Industry, Government and Politics

Necker was the best-known and perhaps most successful financier, financial writer, and reform minister during the reign of King Louis XVI—at a time when all three fields were in their pioneer stage. Controversies about his abilities and policies have not ceased, and he is a major figure in the continuing debates over mercantilism and Physiocracy.

Nee, Victor

b. 1945
fields: Historiography

Victor Nee coauthored *Longtime Californ': A Documentary Study of an American Chinatown* (1973), a collection of oral histories about San Francisco Chinatown residents. His other publications include *Remaking the Economic Institutions of Socialism: China and Eastern Europe* (1989) and *Social Exchange and Political Process in Maoist China* (1991).

Neel, Alice

full: Alice Hartley Neel
b. January 28, 1900
Merion Square, Pennsylvania
d. October 13, 1984
New York, New York
fields: Art

Described by some as a "collector of souls," Alice Neel spent six decades producing expressionistic, intense portraits, cityscapes, and still lifes that document the human condition. Often compared to works by Edvard Munch, Vincent van Gogh, Frida Kahlo, and other great artists, Neel's portraits reflect her belief in the importance of the human image to communicate values and beliefs.

Néel, Louis-Eugène-Félix

b. November 22, 1904
Lyons, France
fields: Physics

By applying revolutionary viewpoints to old ideas of physics, Néel discovered new forms of magnetism, including antiferromagnetic and ferrimagnetic materials. His work greatly strengthened modern magnetic theory and has added fundamentally to computer-memory techniques and to the use of high-frequency waves. For his scientific zeal, he was awarded the Nobel Prize in Physics in 1970. Additionally, he has had tremendous importance in the establishment of various research centers in Europe.

Nefertiti

b. c. 1366 B.C.E.
Thebes, Egypt
d. c. 1336 B.C.E.
probably Egypt

fields: Diplomacy, Government and Politics, Pharaohs, Religion and Theology

As queen of Egypt married to the iconoclastic Pharaoh Ikhnaton, Nefertiti helped in the temporary transformation of the culture's traditional religion into a monotheistic cult of sun worship. She also had an important role in ruling the empire and inspired standards of female beauty.

Negrete, Jorge

b. 1911
Guanajuato, Mexico
d. Dec. 5, 1953
Los Angeles, Calif.
fields: Theater and Entertainment, Music, Film

Singer and actor. Jorge Negrete's first film was *La madrina del diablo* (1938). He went on to appear in more than two dozen films, including *Juntos pero no revueltos* (1939), *¡Ay Jalisco no te rajes!* (1941), *Silk, Blood, and Sun* (1943), and *Tierra de pasiones* (1944).

Negrette, Lolita Dolores Martínez Asunsolo López. *See* Del Rio, Dolores

Nehru, Indira. *See* Gandhi, Indira

Nehru, Jawaharlal

b. November 14, 1889
Allahabad, India
d. May 27, 1964
New Delhi, India
fields: Government and Politics

Nehru led India through the difficult transition from colony to independence, providing the critical political skills for his close friend and mentor, Mahatma Gandhi. Upon India's being granted independence on August 15, 1947, Nehru became India's first prime minister. Following Gandhi's assassination in January, 1948, Nehru placed India firmly in a nonaligned, democratic path, ruling the country until his own death on May 27, 1964.

Nehru, Swarup Kumari. *See* Pandit, Vijaya Lakshmi

Neimark, Sof'ja Aleksandrovna. *See* Janovskaja, Sof'ja Aleksandrovna

Nell, William C.

b. 1816
Boston, Mass.
d. 1874
fields: Journalism, Historiography

African American historian, journalist, and abolitionist; William C. Nell assisted Frederick Douglass on his newspaper, the *North Star*; Nell led the Boston schools desegregation fight; after running unsuccessfully for the Massachusetts legislature, he compiled *Colored Patriots of the American Revolution* (1855; credited as the first serious history of African Americans); upon taking a position as a Boston postal clerk in 1861, Nell became the first African American to hold a federal position.

Nelson, Benjamin Earl. *See* King, Ben E.

Nelson, Jill

b. 1952
New York, N.Y.
fields: Journalism

African American journalist; Jill Nelson worked as a staff writer for *The Washington Post* in 1986 and later became a contributing editor with *Essence* magazine; in 1993, published a memoir entitled *Volunteer Slavery: My Authentic Negro Experience.*

Nelson, Lord

né: Horatio Nelson
aka: Viscount Nelson
b. September 29, 1758
Burnham Thorpe, Norfolk, England
d. October 21, 1805
off Cape Trafalgar, Spain
fields: Military Affairs

Nelson's innovative tactics in battle and his determination to achieve total victory over the enemy made him the most famous admiral in British history and helped to establish the tradition of British perseverance until final victory could be won.

Nelson, Prince Rogers. *See* Prince

Nelson, Samuel

b. 1792
d. 1873
fields: Law

U.S. Supreme Court justice, 1845-1872; appointed by President Tyler. Significant opinions: *Scott v. Sandford*, 60 U.S. 393 (1857) (concurring opinion); *Prize Cases*, 67 U.S. 635 (1863) (dissenting opinion); *Ex parte Milligan*, 71 U.S. 2 (1866) (dissenting opinion).

Nemerov, Diane. *See* Arbus, Diane

Nenekunat. *See* Ninigret

Neolin. *See* Delaware Prophet

Neri, Saint Philip

aka: Filippo Neri
b. July 21, 1515
Florence
d. May 26, 1595
Rome
fields: Religion and Theology

As a priest living in Rome during the Counter-Reformation, Saint Philip Neri stood apart from the religious politics of his time and influenced countless Catholics to reform their lives and return to traditional spirituality. Called the "Apostle of Rome," he founded the Congregation of the Oratory, which inspired both laymen and clergy to lead lives of holiness and charitable works. Canonized in 1622.

Nernst, Walther Hermann

b. June 25, 1864
Briesen, Prussia
d. November 18, 1941
near Bad Muskau, Germany
fields: Chemistry

Nernst won the Nobel Prize in Chemistry in 1920 for his statement of the third law of thermodynamics. Yet his equation for the electrode potential of a voltaic cell is his best-known contribution and appears in nearly all general chemistry texts.

Nero

né: Lucius Domitius Ahenobarbus
b. December 15, 37 C.E.
Antium (Anzio), Italy
d. June 9, 68 C.E.
Rome, Italy
fields: Government and Politics, Patronage of the Arts, Roman Emperors

As the fifth emperor of Rome, Nero continued the reign of terror of the Julio-Claudians while pursuing his own artistic career.

Neruda, Pablo

né: Neftalí Ricardo Reyes Basoalto
b. July 12, 1904
Parral, Chile
d. September 23, 1973
Santiago, Chile
fields: Literature

Neruda is the greatest modern poet to have combined a personal and lyrical mode with a political voice in a way that spoke to and for a popular mass readership. Rooted in Chile, his poetry has a universal human significance marked by the award of the Nobel Prize in Literature in 1971.

Nervi, Pier Luigi

b. June 21, 1891
Sondrio, Italy
d. January 9, 1979
Rome, Italy
fields: Architecture

Nervi was actually an engineer, but one whose goal was to create aesthetically pleasing structures. His importance lies in the fact that he was among the first in modern times to reunite architecture and engineering.

Neshapanasumin. *See* Journeycake, Charles

Netanyahu, Benjamin

aka: Bibi Netanyahu
b. October 21, 1949
Tel Aviv, Israel
fields: Government and Politics

Benjamin Netanyahu Prime minister of Israel from 1996 to 1999. As prime minister, Conservative Likud Party leader Benjamin Netanyahu moved slowly in peace agreemants with Palestinians but signed Wye River Agreement in 1998. Opposed Palestinian statehood; did not control increasing religious and social divisions within Israel. Had become widely unpopular by 1999 and was voted out of office by sizable margin.

Neumann, Hanna

né: Hanna von Caemmerer
b. Feb. 12, 1914
Berlin, Germany
d. Nov. 14, 1971
Ottawa, Canada
fields: Mathematics (algebra and mathematical logic)

Hanna Neumann is known for formulating theories in pure mathematics, especially concerning varieties of groups. She founded the Australian Association of Mathematics Teachers in 1966.

Neumann, John von. *See* von Neumann, John

Nevelson, Louise

né: Leah Berliawsky
b. Early Autumn of 1899 (possibly September 23 or October 16)
Kiev, Russia
d. April 17, 1988
New York, New York
fields: Art

Louise Nevelson's original and unusual view of sculpture as environmental and transforming, as well as her innovative use of materials, made her a leading sculptor of the twentieth century and a major role model for twentieth century women artists.

Neville, Aaron

b. 1941
New Orleans, La.
fields: Music (rhythm-and-blues singer)

African American rhythm-and-blues singer; winner of a 1990 Grammy Award for his duet with Linda Ronstadt, "Don't Know Much," Aaron Neville is recognized for his distinctive falsetto; "Tell It Like It Is" (1966) was his first major hit record; in 1977 he formed the Neville Brothers with his brothers Art, Cyril, and Charles. Some of the Neville Brothers' most acclaimed album releases include *Yellow Moon* (1989) and *Brother's Keeper* (1990). As a solo artist, Neville released such albums as *Warm Your Heart* (1991) and *The Tattooed Heart* (1995).

Neville, Richard. *See* Warwick, earl of

Newbery, John

b. July 19, 1713 (baptized)
Waltham St. Lawrence, Berkshire, England
d. December 22, 1767
London, England
fields: Publishing

Newbery was the first English publisher to profit from the publication and sale of books written especially for children.

Newcomb, Simon

b. March 12, 1835
Wallace, Canada
d. July 11, 1909
Washington, D.C.
fields: Science

Combining intellectual prowess and organizational ability, Newcomb, the best-known American scientist at the turn of the century, revolutionized dynamical astronomy.

Newcombe, Don

full: Donald Newcombe
b. June 14, 1926
Madison, N.J.
fields: Sports (baseball player)

African American baseball player; one of the first and most successful African American pitchers in the major leagues, Don Newcombe was the ace of the Brooklyn Dodgers pitching staff from 1949 to 1957; during his career he was named Rookie of the Year (1949), won twenty games in 1951 and 1955, and was named 1956 National League Most Valuable Player and received the 1956 Cy Young award for his record of 27-7.

Newcomen, Thomas

b. January or February, 1663
Dartmouth, Devonshire, England
d. August 5, 1729
London, England
fields: Invention and Technology, Engineering

Newcomen invented and developed the first commercially practical steam engine for pumping water out of British coal and tin mines. His work inaugurated the age of steam power, which made possible the rapid development of the Industrial Revolution.

Newhouse, Richard H.

b. January 24, 1924
Louisville, Ky.
fields: Government and Politics

African American state politician; in 1966 Richard H. Newhouse was elected to the Illinois State Senate as a representative from the Thirteenth Senate District; during his tenure there he founded and served as president of the Black Legislators Association, as director of Chicago's Black Legislative Clearing House, and, beginning in 1989, as chairman of the state senate Committee on Commerce and Economic Development.

Newman, Connie

full: Constance Berry Newman
b. July 8, 1935
Chicago, Ill.
fields: Government and Politics

African American political appointee; Connie Newman's political appointments included chief of the Midwest Section, Migrant Division, of the Office of Economic Opportunity (1967-1969), director of Volunteers in Service to America (VISTA; 1971-1973), commissioner and vice chair of the Consumer Products Safety Commission (1973-1976), assistant secretary for regulatory programs at the Department of Housing and Urban Development (appointed by President Gerald Ford, 1976); and director of the Office of Personnel Management (appointed by President George Bush, 1989).

Newman, John Henry

b. February 21, 1801
London, England
d. August 11, 1890
Edgbaston, England
fields: Religion and Theology

A leading figure in the Oxford Movement, which brought religious issues to the forefront of the Victorian consciousness, Newman, after his conversion to Catholicism, became the leading Catholic figure in Great Britain, writing eloquently about religion and education and influencing the course of theological and administrative practices within the Catholic church in Great Britain and throughout the world.

Newton, Huey P.

b. Feb. 17, 1942
Monroe, La.
d. Aug. 23, 1989
Oakland, Calif.
fields: Social Reform

African American activist; Huey P. Newton cofounded, with Bobby Seale, the Black Panther Party for Self-Defense in 1966, which became a major force in California politics; emphasized black nationalism and self-determination for the black community, campaigned against police brutality, and established an armed patrol to monitor police activities; later developed a class-based perspective turning to Marxist-Leninist political theory; convicted of manslaughter in the

1967 killing of an Oakland police officer, but the conviction was later overturned; helped elect Lionel Wilson as first black mayor of Oakland in 1977; frequently in legal trouble throughout the 1970's and 1980's; killed by a drug dealer.

Newton, Isaac

aka: Sir Isaac Newton
b. December 25, 1642
Woolsthorpe Manor, near Colsterworth, Lincolnshire, England
d. March 20, 1727
London, England
fields: Physics

With his three laws of mechanics and his theoretical basis for the concept of gravity, Newton pioneered the science of physics, establishing principles that remained current until the twentieth century.

Ney, Michel

b. January 10, 1769
Saarlouis, France
d. December 7, 1815
Paris, France
fields: Military Affairs

Ney was arguably the most celebrated of the twenty-six marshals who served Napoleon I and the French Empire throughout the 1804-1815 period. Ney is primarily remembered for his leadership during the retreat from Moscow and at Waterloo.

Nezahualcóyotl

b. 1402
probably Texcoco
d. 1472
Texcoco
fields: Government and Politics

Emperor, 1431-1472. Nezahualcóyotl, who was primarily responsible for the creation of the Aztec Empire, was a proponent of a religious vision which, if it had prevailed, might have made possible that empire's survival.

Ng, Fae Myenne

b. 1956
San Francisco, Calif.
fields: Literature

Chinese American Fae Myenne Ng, who received a master's degree in writing from Columbia University, published *Bone*, a novel about San Francisco's Chinatown in 1993. Critics praised the work, Ng's first.

Ng, Poon Chew

aka: Ng Poon Chew
b. March 14, 1866
Sun Ning, Guangdong Province, China
d. March 13, 1931
Oakland, Calif.
fields: Journalism, Civil Rights

In Los Angeles in 1899, Ng Poon Chew began editing and publishing *Hua Mei Sun Po* (*Chinese American Morning Paper*), the first daily Chinese newspaper in the United States. In 1900 he moved to San Francisco, where the paper was rechristened *Chung Sai Yat Po* (*Chinese American Daily Paper*) and became a leading forum for the Chinese American community. Ng was a popular speaker on the chautauqua and lyceum circuits and was one of the first Chinese Americans to achieve national recognition. In 1905 he spoke out against anti-Chinese discrimination.

Ng Sheung Chi

b. 1910
Taishan district, China
fields: Music

Folk singer Ng Sheung Chi sang as a child in rural China. He gradually collected folk songs, helping to preserve a rich local tradition that was threatened by modernity and the Cultural Revolution (1966-1976), when traditional arts came under attack. He moved to the United States in 1979 and continued to sing. The National Endowment for the Arts awarded Ng a National Heritage Fellowship in 1992, making him the first Chinese American recipient.

Ngengi, Kamau. *See* Kenyatta, Jomo

Ngo Dinh Nhu, Mme

né: Tran Le Xuan
b. 1924
fields: Diplomacy, Government and Politics

The wife of South Vietnam's chief of secret police, Ngo Dinh Nhu, Mme Ngo Dinh Nhu was effectively the country's "first lady" because her husband's brother, President Ngo Dinh Diem, never married. She saw herself as the reincarnation of legendary sisters who had led Vietnam's ancient independence struggle against China. She wielded power ruthlessly under Diem's regime and served as an international spokesperson for the South Vietnam government during the early 1960's. Abroad when her husband and brother-in-law were assassinated in late 1963, she settled in Italy.

Nguyen, Dustin

né: Nguyen Xuan Tri
b. Sept. 17, 1962
Saigon, South Vietnam
fields: Television, film

Actor Dustin Nguyen is known best for his role as Officer Harry Truman Ioki in the police drama *21 Jump Street* (1986-1990). Nguyen, a Vietnamese American who fled Saigon in 1975, was pursuing an engineering degree at Orange Coast College in California when he took an acting class and discovered his love for acting. His television debut was in 1984 in *Magnum, P. I.*, and he enjoyed a seven-month stint on *General Hospital*. In 1993, he was made a regular on the NBC television series *seaQuest DSV*. His film appearances include Oliver Stone's *Heaven and Earth* (1993) and *3 Ninjas Kick Back* (1994).

Nguyen That Thanh. *See* Ho Chi Minh

Nicandro, Glugio Gronk. *See* Gronk

Nichiren

né: Zennichi-maru
b. 1222
Kominato, Japan
d. 1282
Sochu-ji Temple, Ikegami, Japan
fields: Religion and Theology

Through extraordinary dedication, Nichiren founded the Lotus sect of Buddhism, which, in turn, gave rise to a fervent Japanese nationalism. He is the most famous of Japan's Buddhist leaders.

Nicholas I

né: Nikolay Pavlovich
b. July 6, 1796
Tsarskoye Selo, Russia
d. March 2, 1855
St. Petersburg, Russia
fields: Government and Politics, Monarchy

As Czar of the Russian Empire, 1825-1855, Nicholas I partially succeeded in restoring the historic power and position of the autocracy in Russian life and European affairs. His reign marks the high point of Russian conservative reaction to the French Revolution, Napoleonic Europe, and the Decembrist Revolt.

Nicholas II

né: Nicholai Aleksandrovich
b. May 18, 1868
Tsarskoye Selo (now Pushkin), near St. Petersburg, Russia
d. July 16 or 17, 1918
Yekaterinburg, Russia
fields: Government and Politics, Monarchy

Nicholas II, of the Romanov Dynasty, was the last czar of Russia. Ruled 1984-1917. Ill-prepared to govern; autocratic but largely ineffective. Widespread unrest in Russia, 1900-1917, exacerbated by defeat in Russo-Japanese War (1904-1905) and losses in World War I. Overthrown by 1917 Bolshevik revolution; he and family executed the following year.

Nicholas V

né: Tommaso Parentucelli

b. November 15, 1397
Sarzana, Republic of Genoa
d. March 24, 1455
Rome
fields: Diplomacy, Church Reform, Patronage of the Arts

Pope, 1447-1455. Nicholas V restored church unity by ending the schism between the Papacy and the conciliar party in Basel. He initiated serious efforts at church reform, helped bring peace to Italy, and sponsored architectural and literary projects in Rome.

Nicholas, Denise

b. July 12, 1944
Detroit, Mich.
fields: Television, Film

African American actress, producer, and writer; Denise Nicholas's television credits as a series regular include *Room 222* (1969-1974; for which she received three Emmy nominations), *Baby, I'm Back* (1978), and *In the Heat of the Night* (1989-1992); the public television programs in which Nicholas has appeared include *Voices of Our People: In Celebration of Black Poetry* (which she coproduced; received twelve Los Angeles Emmy Awards), *South by Northwest*, and *And the Children Shall Lead*; her film credits include *Blacula* (1972), *The Soul of Nigger Charley* (1973), *Let's Do It Again* (1975), *A Piece of the Action* (1977), *Capricorn One* (1978), *Marvin and Tige* (1983), and *Ghost Dad* (1990); Nicholas founded and was the co-owner of Masai Films, Inc., in Hollywood, through which she produced and directed short films.

Nicholas of Autrecourt

b. c. 1300
Autrecourt, near Verdun
d. After 1350
probably Metz, Lorraine
fields: Philosophy, Religion and Theology

A philosopher whose thinking reflected the intellectual themes of his time, Nicholas contributed to the end of High Scholastic thought by proposing a form of radical nominalism which was critical of the Aristotelian notions of substance and causation. Far ahead of its time, Nicholas' thought anticipated some of the discoveries of David Hume, later rationalists, and later empiricists.

Nicholas of Cusa

né: Nicholas Kryfts
aka: Nicholas Krebs
b. 1401
Kues, Upper Lorraine
d. August 11, 1464
Todi, Papal States
fields: Philosophy, Religion and Theology

Nicholas of Cusa contributed to preserving the hierarchical authority and unity of the Roman church while at the same time advocating Humanism and lay participation in both sacred and secular government during the early years of the Renaissance. His most lasting contribution has been to Western philosophy.

Nicholas the Great

aka: Saint Nicholas I
b. c. 819-822
Rome
d. November 13, 867
Rome
fields: Religion and Theology

Pope Nicholas I, 858-867. Nicholas strengthened the power of the Papacy by actively promoting the primacy of the Holy See in all Church matters and in secular cases of moral consequence.

Nichols, Barbara Lauraine

b. ?
Waterville, Maine
fields: Nursing, Government and Politics

African American nurse and political appointee; Barbara Lauraine Nichols is noted as the first African American president of the American Nursing Association (1978-1982); also noted as the first African American to hold a Wisconsin State cabinet-level post; received an Outstanding Woman of Color Award from the National Institute for Women of Color in 1984. In 1978, Nichols became the first African American to serve as president of the American Nursing Association (ANA);

Nichols, Nichelle

b. December 28, 1936
Robbins, Ill.
fields: Television, Film

African American actress; Nichelle Nichols is most well known for her role as Lieutenant Uhura in the *Star Trek* television series (1966-1969); although she played a glorified switchboard operator, she was the only African American and the only woman in a command position on the starship; between 1979 and 1991, Nichols appeared in six films based on the original television series; in 1978 the National Aeronautics and Space Administration (NASA) enlisted Nichols as a recruiter; she is on the National Space Society board of governors and was a founding member of the Kwanza Foundation.

Nichols, Terry

b. April 1, 1955
Lapeer County, Mich.
fields: Law (crime)

Suspect in the April 19, 1995, bombing of the Alfred P. Murrah Federal Building in Oklahoma City, Oklahoma. A Kansas farmer, Terry Nichols was charged with having abetted principal suspect Timothy McVeigh. Nichols denied knowledge of the bombing; his elder brother, James Nichols, was also held as a witness in the investigation. In December 1997, he was convicted of conspiracy to use a weapon of mass destruction and also convicted on eight counts of involuntary manslaughter.

Nicholson, Ben

b. April 10, 1894
Denham, Buckinghamshire, England
d. February 6, 1982
London, England
fields: Art

Influenced by such Continental innovators as Piet Mondrian, Joan Miró, and Pablo Picasso, Nicholson became the foremost exponent of abstract painting in twentieth century Great Britain.

Nicklaus, Jack

full: Jack William Nicklaus
b. January 21, 1940
Columbus, Ohio
fields: Sports (golf)

One of the greatest golfers of all time, nicknamed "the Golden Bear," Jack Nicklaus he won the U.S. Open in 1962, beginning a decade of friendly but intense rivalry between himself and the charismatic Arnold Palmer. Between 1959 and 1967, he won nine major championships and was in the top three in ten others while winning numerous lesser titles. Eventually he won each major at least three times. In 1968-1969, Nicklaus had a dry spell in the majors and was challenged by Gary Player and Lee Trevino for the number-one position, but his popularity grew as fans appreciated his sportsmanship and character. He regained his best form in the early 1970's and was again in great form in the 1980's. By 1986, he had won twenty major championships and many other victories worldwide. He always built his year around the majors, entering every professional major from 1962 to 1997. His moral legacy to golf includes a dignified demeanor and a well-lived, balanced life. In the 1990's, he became a leading golf-course architect, and his Golden Bear Corporation became a major producer of golf paraphernalia.

Nidetch, Jean

né: Jean Slutsky
b. October 12, 1923
Brooklyn, New York
fields: Business and Industry

As the founder of Weight Watchers International, the world's most successful diet plan corporation, Jean Nidetch has helped millions of people lose weight and keep it off.

Niebuhr, Barthold Georg

b. August 27, 1776
Copenhagen, Denmark
d. January 2, 1831
Bonn, Prussia
fields: Historiography, Philology

An extraordinarily able historian, Niebuhr, through meticulously researched as well as voluminous books and published lectures, founded the modern German school of critical historical scholarship, one objective of which was regeneration of the Prussian state.

Niebuhr, H. Richard

full: Helmut Richard Niebuhr
b. September 3, 1894
Wright City, Mo.
d. July 5, 1962
Greenfield, Mass.
fields: Religion and Theology

The author of important books such as *The Meaning of Revelation* (1941) and *Christ and Culture* (1951), Niebuhr became one of the leading Christian ethicists of the twentieth century, using insights from history, sociology, psychology, and philosophy to explore ways in which the Christian faith could help to transform and redeem the world. He believed that, to the degree that Christian communities made the "fitting response" to their world, they could spark a transformation that would bring the world closer to the kingdom of God.

Niebuhr, Reinhold

b. June 21, 1892
Wright City, Missouri
d. June 1, 1971
Stockbridge, Massachusetts
fields: Religion and Theology, Philosophy

The leading American formulator of Neoorthodox theology, Niebuhr used the political and social arenas to place the Christian faith in the center of the cultural and political world of his day.

Niemeyer, Oscar

full: Oscar Niemeyer Soares Filho
b. December 15, 1907
Rio de Janeiro, Brazil
fields: Architecture

Perhaps the most widely known of Brazilian architects, Niemeyer is one of a key group of architects who gave a distinctly Brazilian flavor to the modern international architectural style.

Niemöller, Martin

full: Friedrich Gustav Emil Martin Niemöller
b. January 14, 1892
Lippstadt, Germany
d. March 6, 1984
Wiesbaden, West Germany
fields: Church Reform, Social Reform

Niemöller, a leading religious opponent of the National Socialist regime, helped to organize the Confessing church in 1934, a body within the German Evangelical church that formed the center of Protestant resistance in the Third Reich. After his liberation from eight years in a concentration camp, he became a prominent figure in the restored German Evangelical church and the World Council of Churches, best known for his outspoken opposition to West German rearmament, nuclear armament, and his advocacy of pacifism.

Niépce, Nicéphore

b. March 7, 1765
Chalon-sur-Saône, France
d. July 5, 1833
Chalon-sur-Saône, France
fields: Invention and Technology

Niépce was a tenacious researcher who, despite rural isolation, succeeded in creating first a method of photomechanical reproduction and subsequently the earliest method of permanently recording the image of the camera obscura.

Nietzsche, Friedrich Wilhelm

b. October 15, 1844
Röcken, Saxony, Prussia (now in Germany)
d. August 25, 1900
Weimar, Germany
fields: Philosophy, Literature

Though mostly ignored during his lifetime, Nietzsche's writings became a bellwether in the twentieth century for radical philosophical, psychological, linguistic, and literary critiques of Western culture. Through a series of remarkable works of German prose, Nietzsche sought to smash the idol of Christian morality and liberate a few who might follow after him into a triumphant and tragic this-worldly life.

Niggli, Josephina

b. July 13, 1910
Monterrey, Nuevo León, Mexico
fields: Literature

Playwright and novelist. Josephina Niggli taught radio at the University of North Carolina, Chapel Hill, and drama at the University of North Carolina Women's College (1955-1956). She also worked as a writer at Metro-Goldwyn-Mayer Studios in 1951 and 1952. Niggli wrote one-act plays, two novels (*Mexican Village*, 1945; and *Step Down, Elder Brother*, 1947), and a children's book, *A Miracle for Mexico* (1964).

Nightingale, Florence

b. May 12, 1820
Florence, Italy
d. August 13, 1910
London, England
fields: Nursing, Social Reform

Following a deeply rooted passion to serve God and combining it with a strong will and intellect, Nightingale revolutionized the nursing profession and the design and conditions of medical care and hospital facilities.

Nijima Jo

b. 1843
Kanda, Edo, Japan
d. Jan., 1890
Oiso, Japan
fields: Historical Figure

Although Japanese laws prohibited citizens from leaving the country, in 1864 Nijima Jo secretly made his way out of the country and enrolled in school in the United States. He graduated from Amherst College in 1870. While studying at Andover Theological Seminary, from which he was graduated in 1874, he served as interpreter for the Japanese government's Iwakura Mission to Europe and the United States. He returned to Japan where he started a Christian college, Doshisha University in Kyoto.

Nijinsky, Vaslav

b. March 12, 1890
Kiev, Ukraine, Russian Empire
d. April 8, 1950
London, England
fields: Dance

With the impresario Sergei Diaghilev, who enlisted him as a premier dancer in the Ballet Russe company, Nijinsky established the popularity of Russian ballet throughout the Western world in the second decade of the twentieth century. As a choreographer, he was also very instrumental in adapting dance movements to the new music of the twentieth century, especially that of Russian composer Igor Stravinsky.

Nikon

né: Nikita Minin
b. 1605
Veldemanovo, Russia
d. August 27, 1681
en route to Moscow, Russia
fields: Religion and Theology, Government and Politics

Nikon contributed to the liturgical reforms in the Russian Orthodox church, the introduction of Western intellectualism in Russia, and the definition of the role of the church in the Russian state.

Nimitz, Chester W.

full: Chester William Nimitz
b. February 24, 1885
Fredericksburg, Texas
d. February 20, 1966
San Francisco, California
fields: Military Affairs

Nimitz commanded American forces in the Pacific during World War II and played a crucial role in winning the important and difficult Battle of Midway. After the war, he became Chief of Naval Operations.

Ninham, Daniel

b. c. 1710
d. Aug. 31, 1778
Kingsbridge, N.Y.
fields: Government and Politics, Native American Affairs

Mahican leader Daniel Ninham went to England, unsuccessfully seeking the return of Mahican lands. Returning to America, he fought on the colonial side in the American Revolution and died in battle in 1778.

Ninigret

aka: Ninicraft
aka: Nenekunat
b. c. 1600
d. c. 1678
Wequapaug, R.I.
fields: Government and Politics, Diplomacy, Native American Affairs

Ninigret was sachem (leader) of the eastern branch of the Niantic of southern Connecticut; he skillfully avoided being drawn into the seventeenth century wars between the Indians and the English settlers (such as King Philip's War of 1675-1676). Recognized the reality of British power and reluctantly accommodated himself to it.

Nirenberg, Marshall W.

full: Marshall Warren Nirenberg
b. Apr. 10, 1927
New York, New York
fields: Biology, Chemistry, Genetics

In 1964 Marshall W. Nirenberg announced a transfer RNA-binding technique for deciphering the genetic code; in 1968, won the Nobel Prize in Physiology or Medicine.

Nishida, Kitarō

b. June 17, 1870
Unoke, near Kanazawa, Japan
d. June 7, 1945
Kamakura, Japan
fields: Philosophy, Religion and Theology

Nishida is widely considered to be the foremost philosopher of modern Japan. He created his own highly original and distinctive philosophy, based upon his thorough assimilation of both Western philosophy and methodology and the Zen Buddhist tradition.

Nishikawa, Lane

b. Jan. 24, 1955
Honolulu, Territory of Hawaii
fields: Theater and Entertainment

As a solo performer, Lane Nishikawa won accolades for his pieces exposing and attacking Asian American stereotypes, *Life in the Fast Lane* (1981) and *I'm on a Mission from Buddha* (1989). A founding member of San Francisco's Asian American Theatre Company (AATC), he served as artistic director from 1986 to 1989 and also beginning in 1993. He directed world premieres of such major Asian American theater works as Milton Murayama's *All I Asking for Is My Body*, R. A. Shiomi's *Yellow Fever*, Philip Kan Gotanda's *A Song for a Nisei Fisherman*, and Laurence Yep's *Pay the Chinaman*.

Nishimoto, Richard Shigeaki

b. Aug. 23, 1904
Tokyo, Japan
d. 1956
fields: Sociology

Richard Shigeaki Nishimoto was the only foreign-born Japanese American on the Japanese American Evacuation and Resettlement Study, a special research commission that monitored and evaluated the incarceration of Japanese Americans during World War II. Although he was interned at the Poston relocation center in western Arizona, he conducted his fieldwork in secret, relaying reports to the commission. After the war ended, he coauthored *The Spoilage* (1946), which described the camp experiences of those prisoners labeled "disloyal." When the commission disbanded, Nishimoto was unable to find academic or research-oriented work; he was a night watchman for a San Francisco hotel when he died.

Nishitani, Keiji

b. February 27, 1900
Ishikawa Prefecture, Japan
d. November 24, 1990
Kyoto, Japan
fields: Philosophy, Religion and Theology

By synthesizing modern Western philosophy and Zen Buddhist thought, Keiji Nishitani sought to overcome the nihilism of the twentieth century and forge connections between Eastern and Western philosophy and religion. Taught ethics, German, Western philosophy, and Buddhist thought at universities in Japan, including Ōtani University, Kyoto Imperial College, and Kyoto University (1935). President, Eastern Buddhist Society; Conference on Religion in Modern Society; and International Institute for Japan Studies at the Christian Kansei Gakuin University. Major works include *The Self-Overcoming of Nihilism* (1949), and *Religion and Nothingness* (1961).

Nishiura, Michiko. *See* Weglyn, Michi

Nitobe, Inazo

b. Sept. 1, 1862
Morioka, Japan
d. Oct. 15, 1933
Victoria, British Columbia, Canada
fields: Literature

Inazo Nitobe, born in a samurai family, converted to Christianity and went to the United States in 1884 to study at Johns Hopkins University. He returned to Japan to teach in 1891 and published a number of books in English and Japanese intended to foster mutual understanding between Japan and the United States. The passage of the restrictive Immigration Act of 1924 angered Nitobe, and he refused to travel to the United States until the law was repealed, although he lectured in the United States in 1932.

Niwot. *See* Left Hand the First; Left Hand the Second

Nix, Robert Nelson Cornelius, Sr.

b. August 9, 1905
Orangeburg, S.C.
d. June 22, 1987
Philadelphia, Pa.
fields: Government and Politics

African American U.S. representative from Pennsylvania; on May 20, 1958, Robert Nelson Cornelius Nix, Sr., became the first black politician elected to the U.S. Congress from Pennsylvania; during his twenty year tenure, he served on the House Committee on Veterans' Affairs, the House Committee on Foreign Affairs, and the House Committee on Merchant Marine and Fisheries; he later served as chairman of the House Subcommittee on International Economic Policy (1975) and as chairman of the House Committee on the Post Office and Civil Service (1977).

Nix, Robert Nelson Cornelius, Jr.

b. July 13, 1928
Philadelphia, Pa.
fields: Law

African American judge; the son of Pennsylvania congressman Robert N. C. Nix, Sr., Robert Nelson Cornelius Nix, Jr., served as Pennsylvania deputy attorney general (1956-1958); served as an associate justice on the Pennsylvania Supreme Court (1972-1984); in

1984 appointed to serve as chief justice of the court.

Nixon, Norm

full: Norman Ellard Nixon
b. October 11, 1955
Macon, Ga.
fields: Sports (basketball player)

African American basketball player; Norm Nixon was chosen in the first round of the 1977 NBA draft by the Los Angeles Lakers; as a lightning-quick guard, Nixon played on the 1980 and 1982 NBA championship teams; from 1984 to 1989, Nixon played for the San Diego/Los Angeles Clippers; in 1982 and 1985, he played in NBA All-Star Games.

Nixon, Pat

né: Thelma Catherine Patricia Ryan
b. March 16, 1912
Ely, Nevada
d. June 22, 1993
Park Ridge, New Jersey
fields: Government and Politics

First Lady of the United States, 1969-1972, Pat Nixon supported her husband, Richard M. Nixon, throughout his political career, including during his resignation from the presidency in 1974. During her husband's first term as president, Nixon worked hard to make the White House more accessible. She suffered strokes in 1976 and 1983. In 1987, a malignant tumor was removed from her mouth. She died on June 22, 1993, of lung cancer at the age of eighty-one.

Nixon, Richard M.

full: Richard Milhous Nixon
b. January 9, 1913
Yorba Linda, California
d. April 22, 1994
New York, New York
fields: Government and Politics

Thirty-seventh president of the United States, 1969-1974. A realist in foreign policy, Nixon renewed American relations with the People's Republic of China, achieved détente with the Soviet Union, and ended the United States' involvement in Vietnam. Ironically, because of his "Watergate coverup," he aroused public and congressional opposition to the "imperial presidency."

Niza, Fray Marcos de

b. c. 1495
Nice, Savoy
d. Mar. 25, 1558
Mexico
fields: Religion and Theology

Priest. Fray Marcos de Niza went to the New World in 1531 and settled in New Galicia in 1538. In 1539, during an expedition north into unknown territories, Niza glimpsed an Indian pueblo that he believed to be Cíbola, a mythical complex of seven rich cities. His claim that he has seen a wealthy city filled with turquoise sparked the imagination of other explorers and conquistadores. In 1540, Niza was named provincial of his order and moved to Mexico City.

Niẓām al-Mulk

né: Abū ʿAli Ḥasan ibn ʿAlī
b. 1018 or 1019
Ṭūs, Iran
d. October 14, 1092
near Nahavand, Iran
fields: Government and Politics

The vizier, or principal minister, of the second and third Seljuk rulers of Iran, Niẓām was the virtual architect of the Seljuks' Middle Eastern empire, which he administered for thirty years between 1063 and 1092. His *Siyasat-nama* became a classic of medieval Muslim statecraft.

Nkrumah, Kwame

né: Francis Nwia Kofi
b. September 21, 1909
Nkroful, Gold Coast
d. April 27, 1972
Bucharest, Romania
fields: Government and Politics

Nkrumah was the first statesman to lead an African country to independence after World War II. As the first major proponent of Pan-Africanism, he gained both continental and international stature. He served as Prime Minister of the Gold Coast, Prime Minister of Ghana after its independence, and President of Ghana. After the coup that deposed him, he was named titular copresident of Guinea, a recognition of his status as an international leader and world statesman.

Nobel, Alfred

full: Alfred Bernhard Nobel
b. October 21, 1833
Stockholm, Sweden
d. December 10, 1896
San Remo, Italy
fields: Invention and Technology, Philanthropy

Although Nobel is remembered for inventing dynamite and the blasting cap that ignites it, and although he held 355 patents for his inventions, he will be most remembered for the provision he made in his last will for the distribution of the income from the bulk of his estate to provide annual prizes to those who confer upon humankind the greatest benefits in the fields of physics, chemistry, physiology or medicine, literature, and peace.

Noble, Gil

full: Gilbert E. Noble
b. February 22, 1932
New York, N.Y.
fields: Television, Journalism

African American television broadcaster and producer; after working as a part-time radio news announcer, Gil Noble became a correspondent for *Eyewitness News* on WABC-TV (1967); in April, 1968, he debuted his television show, *Like It Is*, which began as New York City local journalism, but expanded to profile black political figures, review historical accomplishments of black people, and feature interviews with black cultural and political leaders from around the world; in 1975, in addition to hosting the program, he began to produce it; by 1980 Noble had received six Emmy Awards; in 1981 he published *Black Is the Color of My TV Tube*.

Noble, Jeanne L.

b. July 18, 1926
Palm Beach, Fla.
fields: Education, Scholarship

African American educator; Jeanne L. Noble authored *The Negro Woman's College Education* (1956) and *Beautiful, Also, Are the Souls of My Black Sisters: A History of the Black Woman in America* (1978); in 1964 Noble served as head of a committee to develop the Girls' Job Corps; she also was involved with the Girl Scout organization.

Nock-ko-ist. *See* Bear's Heart, James

Noda, Steere Gikaku

b. 1892
d. 1986
fields: Law

Steere Gikaku Noda was a pitcher for the Asahis, the famous Japanese American baseball team that dominated Honolulu amateur leagues for many years. In 1917, he became the first second-generation Japanese American licensed to practice law in the state courts of Hawaii. He became a Hawaii state representative in 1948 and a state senator in 1959. Noda supported the sport of amateur wrestling and promoted various athletic events.

Noel-Baker, Philip John

né: Philip John Baker
b. November 1, 1889
London, England
d. October 8, 1982
London, England
fields: Government and Politics, Peace Advocacy

Philip John Noel-Baker was a British political leader and peace activist. A founder of League of Nations. Held many posts in British Labor government of 1945-1951. Wrote *The Private Manufacture of Armaments* (1936), warning of arms buildup in Europe, and *The Arms Race* (1958), urging nuclear weapons reduction. Awarded 1959 Nobel Peace Prize.

Noether, Emmy

full: Amalie Emmy Noether
b. Mar. 23, 1882
Erlangen, Germany
d. Apr. 14, 1935
Bryn Mawr, Pennsylvania
fields: Mathematics (algebra)

Emmy Noether worked for the development of abstract algebra.

Noguchi, Hideyo

b. Nov. 24, 1876
Inawashiro, Japan
d. May 21, 1928
Accra, Ghana
fields: Science

Bacteriologist, parasitologist, and immunologist Hideyo Noguchi advanced science through his research. He led the effort to stem the outbreak of bubonic plague in China as chief advisor to the International Sanitary Board. In the United States, he invented an innovative method for diagnosing syphilis, which led him to study Rocky Mountain spotted fever and yellow fever. He conducted a comparative study of the disease's effect on American Indians, Latin Americans, and Africans. In Africa, he contracted yellow fever and died.

Noguchi, Isamu

b. Nov. 17, 1904
Los Angeles, Calif.
d. Dec. 30, 1988
New York, N.Y.
fields: Art, Theater and Entertainment

Isamu Noguchi, son of Japanese poet Noguchi Yonejiro and Leonie Gilmour, an American teacher, combined the cultures of his parents in his work as an artist, stage designer, and builder of artificial landscapes. Between 1927 and 1929, Noguchi, trained as a sculptor, worked as a studio assistant to Constantin Brancusi in Paris. In the 1950's, Noguchi combined sculpture, architecture, and landscape in gardens he designed for the Beinecke Library at Yale University, the United Nations Educational, Scientific, and Cultural Organization (UNESCO) headquarters in Paris, and the Domon Ken Museum in Sakata, Japan. In 1982, he received the Edward MacDowell Medal for outstanding lifelong contribution to the arts. President Ronald Reagan presented Noguchi with the National Medal of Art in 1987, and the following year, the Japanese government gave him the Order of the Sacred Treasure.

Noguchi, Thomas

né: Tsunetomi Noguchi
b. Jan. 4, 1927
Fukuoka, Japan
fields: Medicine, Literature

Thomas Noguchi became deputy medical examiner of the Los Angeles County coroner's office in 1960 and chief medical examiner in 1967. Because he conducted the highly publicized investigations of actors Marilyn Monroe and Sharon Tate and Senator Robert F. Kennedy, the press dubbed him the "Coroner to the Stars." He was fired in 1969 amid accusations of unprofessional behavior but reinstated several months later. In 1982, Noguchi was demoted after a series critical articles appeared in the *Los Angeles Times*. He became deputy coroner at Los Angeles County-USC Medical Center and a professor of forensic pathology at the University of Southern California. He wrote *Coroner* (1983), *Coroner at Large* (1985), *Unnatural Causes* (1988), and *Physical Evidence* (1990).

Nolde, Emil

né Emil Hansen
b. August 7, 1867
Nolde, Germany
d. April 15, 1956
Seebüll, West Germany
fields: Art

Emil Nolde was a German expressionist painter who featured prominently in the Nazis' Degenerate Art Exhibition of 1937. He began painting during the first decade of the twentieth century, briefly joined the circle known as *Die Brücke* in 1906, and was a founding member of the New Berlin Secession in 1910. His ideas about art emphasized the spiritual and natural relation of race and landscape. His autobiography claims that he was persecuted by the Nazis for refusing to accept a position in the Ministry of Culture. In 1937 the government confiscated his work and displayed much of it in its Degenerate Art Exhibition. He continued to paint during and after the war.

Noloesca, La Chata. *See* Escalona, Beatriz

Nomkahpa. *See* Two Strike

Nomura, Gail

b. Apr. 5, 1948
Honolulu, Hawaii
fields: Sociology

Gail Nomura, who received a doctorate from the University of Hawaii in 1978, focused her research on Asian American women and communities in Hawaii and the Pacific Northwest. She taught at Washington State University and the University of Michigan.

Nonomura, Sōtatsu. *See* Sōtatsu

Noone, Jimmie

b. April 23, 1895
Cut-Off, La.
d. April 19, 1944
Los Angeles, Calif.
fields: Music (jazz clarinetist and bandleader)

African American clarinetist and bandleader; one of the most influential clarinetists in Chicago, Jimmie Noone played in various bands in the New Orleans area before moving to Chicago in 1917; from 1920 to 1926, he played clarinet and soprano sax with Doc Cooke's Dreamland Orchestra; Noone then formed his own small band, of which he was the star attraction with his smooth and agile style; their recordings for Vocalion included "Sweet Lorraine" and "Four or Five Times"; Noone continued to be musically active after moving to California in 1943.

Nordau, Max

né: Simon Maximilian Südfeld
aka: Max Simon Nordau
b. July 29, 1849
Pest (now Budapest), Hungary
d. January 22, 1923
Paris, France
fields: Art, Government and Politics, Literature

Nordau analyzed negative tendencies in late nineteenth century industrial society and its culture in terms understandable to the popular readers of his day. He also seconded Theodore Herzl in developing the World Zionist Organization, preparing international opinion for the rebirth of a Jewish state in Palestine.

Noriega, Manuel

full: Manuel Antonio Noriega Morena
b. February 11, 1938
Panama City, Panama
fields: Government and Politics

Manuel Noriega led Panama as commander of Panamanian Defense Forces between 1983 and 1989. In 1988 two indictments against Noriega for racketeering and drug trafficking were handed down by federal grand juries in Florida. The United States removed Noriega by force in December of 1989. He was sentenced to forty years in prison.

Norman, Jessye

b. September 15, 1945
Augusta, Georgia
fields: Music

Gifted with an extraordinary voice, Norman has established herself as one of the leading figures on the opera stage and as a recording artist with an unusually broad repertoire.

Norman, Marsha

né: Marsha Williams
b. September 21, 1947
Louisville, Kentucky
fields: Literature

The contention Marsha Norman's success has sparked among critics—either she is exploiting the status quo or candidly articulating the dilemma of women—suggests that expectations for female dramatists has remained a matter of debate well into the twentieth century's closing decades.

Normand, Mabel

full: Mabel Ethelreid Normand
b. November 9, 1892
Staten Island, New York
d. February 23, 1930
Monrovia, California
fields: Film

As a film actor and director during the heyday of the silent film era, Mabel Normand made lasting contributions to film comedy.

North, Frederick. *See* North, Lord

North, Lord

né: Frederick North
b. April 13, 1732
London, England
d. August 5, 1792
London, England
fields: Government and Politics

As Prime Minister of England from 1770 to 1782, North endeavored to keep the Crown and Parliament working together by adopting policies of moderation and consensus. The War of the American Revolution made it impossible for him to achieve this objective, and in 1782, when the House of Commons turned against the war, North resigned. In so doing, North helped establish the convention that the prime minister and cabinet can continue in office only with the support of a majority of the House of Commons.

North, Oliver

b. Oct. 7, 1943
San Antonio, Tex.
fields: Military Affairs, Government and Politics

Central figure in the Iran-Contra affair. Oliver North, a Marine officer working for the National Security Council, directed a secret U.S. operation to sell arms to Iran. He secretly diverted the profits to the Contras, a group trying to overthrow the government of Nicaragua. He was found guilty of crimes arising from the affair, but his conviction was overturned. In 1994, North ran for the U.S. Senate but was defeated.

Northcliffe, Viscount. *See* Harmsworth, Alfred

Northrop, John Howard

b. July 5, 1891
Yonkers, New York
d. May 27, 1987
Wickenberg, Arizona
fields: Biology, Chemistry, Invention and Technology, Medicine

John Howard Northrop studied enzymes; in 1929, crystallized pepsin; in 1930, proved that enzymatic action is a function of the crystallized protein; won the Nobel Prize in Chemistry in 1946, with Wendell Meredith Stanley and James Batcheller Sumner, for crystallizing pepsin and trypsin and for proving that enzymes are proteins.

Norton, Eleanor Holmes

b. April 8, 1938
Washington, D.C.
fields: Government and Politics

In 1970 Eleanor Holmes Norton became chairperson of the New York Commission on Civil Rights, a post she held while executive assistant to the mayor of New York City. President Jimmy Carter appointed her to head the Equal Employment Opportunity Commission (EEOC) in 1977. In 1990 Norton won a seat in Congress as the District of Columbia's nonvoting delegate to the House of Representatives.

Nostradamus

né: Michel Notredame
aka: Michel Nostredame
b. December 23 or 24, 1503
St. Rémy de Provence, France
d. July 1 or 2, 1566
Salon de Provence, France
fields: Astronomy, Government and Politics, Literature, Medicine

A prominent physician and political adviser, Nostradamus achieved widest fame with collections of veiled prophecies in poetical form.

Notredame, Michel. *See* Nostradamus

Novarro, Ramón

né: Ramón Samaniegos
b. Feb. 6, 1899
Durango, Mexico
d. Oct. 31, 1968
Hollywood, Calif.
fields: Theater and Entertainment (actor), Film

Latino actor. During the silent film era, Ramón Novarro played romantic leads in the "Latin lover" style in such films as *Ben Hur* (1926), *Mata Hari* (1931), and *The Cat and the Fiddle* (1934). His imperfect English limited his appeal in Hollywood "talkies." He appeared mostly in Spanish and French films in the 1930's and 1940's, then made two Westerns in 1950, *The Outriders* and *Crisis*. His last film was *Heller in Pink Tights* (1960). In 1968, he was murdered in his home in Hollywood.

Novello, Antonia Coello

b. August 23, 1944
Fajardo, Puerto Rico
fields: Education, Medicine

Latina physician and U.S. surgeon general; nominated by President George Bush, Antonia Coello Novello served as surgeon general of the United States (1989-1993), the first woman and the first Hispanic to hold that position; she concentrated on issues such as cigarette and alcohol advertisements that targeted children and pregnant women, teenage drinking, children infected with AIDS, and women's health issues.

Nozick, Robert

b. November 16, 1938
Brooklyn, New York
fields: Philosophy, Political Science

Robert Nozick is one of the foremost philosophers of the last quarter of the twentieth century, with few rivals in originality, diversity, and controversy. Best known for his *Anarchy, State, and Utopia* (1974), he writes on political theory, decision theory, rationality, and metaphysics, among other areas, attacking established doctrines and catalyzing dynamic philosophical debate. Taught at Princeton and Harvard Universities; at Harvard became legendary for refusing to teach the same course twice. Guggenheim Fellow (1996-1997); president-elect for the Eastern section of the American Philosophical Association. Other major works: *Philosophical Explanations* (1981), *The Examined Life* (1989), *The Nature of Rationality* (1993), *Socratic Puzzles* (1997).

Nubin, Rosetta. *See* Tharpe, Sister Rosetta

Nugent, Pete

b. 1910?
d. ?
fields: Dance

African American dancer; after dancing the Charleston in the male chorus of the all-black musical *Runnin' Wild* (1923) and appearing in the Broadway production of *Honeymoon Lane* (1926), Pete Nugent joined with Irving "Peaches" Beaman to form the tap dance duo called Pete and Peaches (1928); Duke Miller was added in 1931;

Pete, Peaches, and Duke performed in nightclubs until 1937, when Miller died of pneumonia; Nugent is credited as the choreographer who put together the group's remarkable teamwork and coordinated the continuity of the solos; in 1941 Nugent starred in the short-lived Duke Ellington musical *Jump for Joy*; in 1944 he danced with Billy Eckstine's bebop band.

Nunna Hidihi. *See* Ridge, John Rollin

Nussbaum, Martha Craven

né: Martha Craven
b. May 6, 1947
New York, New York
fields: Philosophy, Literature

Martha Craven Nussbaum taught philosophy and classics at Harvard (1980-1983), Wellesley College (1983-1984), and Brown University (1984-1995); law and ethics at the University of Chicago (1993); research adviser at the World Institute for Development Economics Research in Helsinki. Writings and projects examine works of philosophy and literature, inquiring into how to solve problems that require international cooperation and recognizing universal moral obligations. Major works include *The Fragility of Goodness* (1986), *Love's Knowledge* (1990), *The Therapy of Desire* (1994), *Poetic Justice* (1995), *For Love of Country* (1996), *Cultivating Humanity* (1997), and *The Feminist Critique of Liberalism* (1997).

Nutzhorn, Dorothea Margretta. *See* Lange, Dorothea

Nyerere, Julius

full: Julius Kambarage Nyerere
b. March, 1922
Butiama, Tanganyika (now Tanzania)
fields: Government and Politics

Nyerere peacefully brought an end to the British United Nations Trusteeship of Tanzania and became the founding father of independent Tanzania. Throughout the 1960's, 1970's, and 1980's, he opposed racial oppression and discrimination of all types.

Oakeshott, Michael

full: Michael Joseph Oakeshott
b. December 11, 1901
Chelsfield, Kent, England
d. December 19, 1990
Acton, near Langton Matravers, Dorset, England
fields: Philosophy, Education

Michael Oakeshott was a philosopher of skeptical and conservative disposition, a student of the history of political thought, especially known for his work on Thomas Hobbes and on the idea of history. He expounded a distinctive theory of the rule of law, of civil government, and of the concept of authority. Major works include *Experience and Its Modes* (1933), *The Social and Political Doctrines of Contemporary Europe* (1942), *Rationalism in Politics (and Other Essays* (1962, rev. ed. 1991), *Hobbes on Civil Association* (1975), *On Human Contact* (1975), *On History and Other Essays* (1983), *The Voice of Liberal Learning* (1989), *Morality and Politics in Modern Europe* (1993), *Religion, Politics, and the Moral Life* (1993), and *The Politics of Faith and the Politics of Scepticism* (1996).

Oakley, Annie

né: Phoebe Anne Moses
b. August 13, 1860
Darke County, Ohio
d. November 3, 1926
Greenville, Ohio
fields: Sports, Theater and Entertainment

An expert markswoman and consummate performer, Annie Oakley traveled throughout the United States and Europe demonstrating her expert shooting in an era when shooting was almost exclusively a man's sport.

Oates, Joyce Carol

b. June 16, 1938
Lockport, New York
fields: Literature

One of the United States' most distinguished authors, Joyce Carol Oates is critically acclaimed for both her fiction and her poetry. She is known for her prolific output. She is the recipient of numerous awards, including several O. Henry Awards, the Richard and Hinda Rosenthal Award of the National Institute of Arts and Letters (1968), the National Book Award for 1970 (for *them*), the Lotos Club Award of Merit (1975), the Alan Swallow Award for her 1988 short-story collection *The Assignation*, and the Rea Award for the short story (1990).

Oates, Titus

b. September 15, 1649
Oakham, Rutland, England
d. July 13, 1705
London, England
fields: Government and Politics

A miscreant throughout his life, Oates fabricated a conspiracy of Catholics, known as the Popish Plot, to murder King Charles II and replace him on the throne with his Catholic brother, James. This unleashed an anti-Catholic frenzy in England.

Obadele, Imari Abubakari

né: Richard B. Henry
pseudo.: Brother Imari
b. ?
fields: Civil Rights, Social Reform

One of the African American founders of the Republic of New Africa (RNA); Imari Abubakari Obadele advocated that African Americans should liberate through guerrilla warfare the geographical territories comprising the five states of the Deep South: Mississippi, Louisiana, Alabama, Georgia, and South Carolina as reparations for slavery; as president of the RNA, he published works including *War in America: The Malcolm X Doctrine* (1968) and *Revolution and Nation-Building* (1970; both written under the name Brother Imari), and *Free the Land!* (1984) and *America the Nation-State* (1988); as one of the RNA-11 tried for sedition and murder following a shoot-out between RNA members and the FBI and Mississippi state police, Obadele received a twelve-year sentence; in 1977 he filed a civil suit against the FBI alleging that he had been targeted by their COINTELPRO campaign.

O'Bail, John. *See* Cornplanter

Obata, Chiura

b. 1885
Sendai, Japan
d. 1975
fields: Art

Chiura Obata was already an artist when he arrived in San Francisco in 1903. He started teaching art at the University of California, Berkeley, in 1931. He was removed to the Tanforan assembly center in central California and the Topaz relocation center in central Utah during World War II. At the camps, he recorded his experiences in his paintings and taught art. After being released from the camp, he moved to St. Louis. In 1949, he returned to teaching art at Berkeley. Obata's art appears in *Beyond Words: Images from America's Concentration Camps* (1987), by Deborah Greensway and Mindy Roseman, and *Obata's Yosemite: The Art and Letters of Chiura Obata from His Trip to the High Sierra in 1927* (1993).

Oberth, Hermann

full: Hermann Julius Oberth
b. June 25, 1894
Hermannstadt, Siebenburgen, Transylvania
d. December 29, 1989
Nürnberg, West Germany
fields: Aviation and Space Exploration

Oberth is one of the three great pioneers of the sciences of astronautics and modern rocketry. Along with Konstantin Tsiolkovsky and Robert Goddard, he is credited with developing the principles behind rocket-powered flight beyond Earth's atmosphere, liquid-fueled rockets, a manned Earth orbital space station, and manned interplanetary flight.

Obledo, Mario Guerra

b. Apr. 9, 1932
San Antonio, Tex.
fields: Government and Politics

Public official. Mario Guerra Obledo was president of the League of United Latin American Citizens, served as an assistant attorney general in Texas beginning in 1965, and taught law at Harvard University. He also cofounded the Hispanic National Bar Association and the Mexican American Legal Defense and Education Fund, and he was a participant in the Southwest Voter Registration Education Project. Obledo worked as secretary of the California Department of Health and Welfare before becoming head of the agency in 1975.

Oboler, Eli M.

b. September 26, 1915
Chicago, Illinois
d. June 15, 1983
Pocatello, Idaho
fields: Education

Eli M. Oboler was a leading voice against censorship among academic librarians. He began a three-decade career as librarian at Idaho State College in Pocatello in 1949, served as president of the American Library Association, wrote hundreds of articles for journals and newspapers, conducted radio and television broadcasts about books and ideas, edited several library magazines, and published two books: *The Fear of the Word: Censorship and Sex* (1974) and *Defending Intellectual Freedom* (1980).

Obote, Milton

full: Apollo Milton Obote

b. December 28, 1928
Akoroko, Lango, Uganda
fields: Government and Politics

President of Uganda from 1966 to 1971 and 1980 to 1985. Uganda gained independence from Britain in 1962, and Milton Obote became Ugandan prime minister in 1963. Assumed presidency 1966, moved to consolidate power. Led Uganda through a period of relative stability and prosperity. Attempt in 1970 to create a one-party, socialistic state created unrest. Overthrown by Idi Amin in 1971. In 1979, Amin overthrown and Obote reelected president. Second term plagued by guerrilla attacks, his inability to control the army, tribal unrest, and economic instability. Forced from office again in 1985.

Obregón, Álvaro

b. February 17, 1880
Hacienda Siquisiva, Sonora, Mexico
d. July 17, 1928
Mexico City, Mexico
fields: Military Affairs, Government and Politics

Obregón emerged from humble beginnings to become the most successful and celebrated general of the Mexican Revolution. Elected President of Mexico after ten years of civil war, Obregón worked from 1920 to 1924 to pacify his country by a program of demilitarization, support for public education, and recognition by the U.S. government.

Ocampo, Silvina

b. 1906
Buenos Aires, Argentina
d. 1993
fields: Literature

Argentinean poet and short-story writer. Silvina Ocampo published several collections of short stories, including *Autobiografía de Irene* (1948), *Las invitadas* (1961), and *Leopoldina's Dream* (1988). With her husband, Adolfo Bioy Casares, she wrote the detective novel *Los que aman, odian* (1946). Ocampa, Bioy Casares, and Jorge Luis Borges co-edited the anthologies *Antología de la literatura fantástica* (1940; *The Book of Fantasy*, 1988) and *Antología poética argentina* (1941).

Occom, Samson

b. c. 1723
New London, Conn.
d. Aug. 2, 1792
New Stockbridge, N.Y.
fields: Religion and Theology (missionary)

A Mohegan Indian, Samson Occom was one of the first American Indians educated by whites who successfully bridged both cultures as a missionary and teacher. Taught by the Reverend Eleazor Wheelock, a prominent evangelical minister. Occom became a teacher and minister to the Montauk tribe on the eastern tip of Long Island from 1749 to 1764. Ordained a Presbyterian minister in 1759.

Ochoa, Ellen

b. May 10, 1958
Los Angeles, Calif.
fields: Aviation and Space Exploration

Mexican American astronaut. Ellen Ochoa obtained three patents in optical processing while working at the Imaging Technology Branch at Sandia National Laboratories in Livermore, California, from 1985 to 1988. In 1988, she began working as a researcher at NASA, then became head of the Intelligent Systems Technology Branch at the Ames Research Center. She received the 1989 Hispanic Engineer National Achievement Award. Ochoa earned her license to fly small-engine planes in 1988. In 1990, she completed the training necessary to become the first Latina astronaut.

Ochoa, Esteban

b. Mar. 17, 1831
Chihuahua, Mexico
d. Oct. 27, 1888
Tucson, Ariz.
fields: Business and Industry, Government and Politics

Businessman and politician. Esteban Ochoa was already a successful entrepreneur when he was elected chairman of a committee that sought to create an Arizona territory separate from New Mexico in 1859. After the Civil War, he organized the leading freight company in the Southwest and became a spokesman for the Spanish-speaking population of southern Arizona. He was elected to the Arizona territorial legislature and as mayor of Tucson, and he helped establish a public school system in the Arizona Territory.

Ochoa, Severo

b. Sept. 24, 1905
Luarca, Spain
d. Nov. 1, 1993
Madrid, Spain
fields: Medicine, Biology, Chemistry, Physiology

Spanish American biochemist; Severo Ochoa worked his way up the hierarchy at New York University Medical School, from research associate in 1942 to full professor and chair of the Department of Biochemistry in 1976; shared the 1959 Nobel Prize in Medicine and Physiology with Arthur Kornberg for their synthesis of RNA and DNA; received the National Medal of Science and Japan's Order of the Rising Sun.

Ochoa, Victor

b. 1948
Los Angeles, Calif.
fields: Art (muralist)

Muralist. Victor Ochoa was one of several Chicano artists who protested a highway project that displaced thousands of Chicano families in the Balboa Park area of San Diego during the mid-1960's. The San Diego Parks and Recreation department ceded a building to the artists, who, by 1969, had turned it into a cultural center and were painting murals. Ochoa also painted the mural Gerónimo in Balboa Park. Ochoa and others held an art exhibition in the cultural center in 1971. The artists later formed the Congreso de Arte Chicano en Aztlán in Logan Heights, California.

Ockham, William of

b. c. 1285
Surrey, England
d. 1347 or 1349
Munich, Bavaria (now in Germany)
fields: Philosophy, Religion and Theology

The most original and perhaps least understood of the late medieval philosophers, Ockham exercised a pervasive influence over his contemporaries and over thinkers for the next two centuries. He held that intuition was the only form of knowledge, and that God could only be approached through faith and revelation, not through the "proofs" of natural reason. Misconstrued, Ockham's nominalism—his rejection of the idea of abstract entities, or universals—had serious implications for the Church's teachings on the Eucharist.

O'Connell, Daniel

b. August 6, 1775
near Cahirciveen, County Kerry, Ireland
d. May 15, 1847
Genoa, Italy
fields: Law, Government and Politics, Social Reform

Once the leader of the struggle for Catholic emancipation in the British Empire, O'Connell is identified with the principles of religious freedom and separation of church and state, nonviolent reform movements, early democratic organizations, and the upholding of the rule of law.

O'Connor, Flannery

full: Mary Flannery O'Connor
b. March 25, 1925
Savannah, Georgia
d. August 3, 1964
Milledgeville, Georgia
fields: Literature

In her short lifetime, Flannery O'Connor created a small but significant body of fiction and nonfiction unique in American literature, Southern literature, Catholic literature, and feminist literature.

O'Connor, Sandra Day

né: Sandra Day
b. March 26, 1930
El Paso, Texas
fields: Law

U.S. Supreme Court justice, began tenure in 1981; appointed by President Reagan. First woman to serve on the Supreme Court. Significant opinions: *Strictland v. Washington*, 466 U.S. 668 (1984); *Oregon v. Elstad*, 470 U.S. 298 (1985); *Florida v. Bostick*, 501 U.S. 429 (1991).

O'Connor, Sinead

b. December 8, 1967
Dublin, Ireland
fields: Music

An Irish singer, Sinead O'Connor attracted strong public protests and was censored by a television network after shredding a picture of Pope John Paul II on *Saturday Night Live* in October, 1992, to express her opposition to the Roman Catholic Church's position on abortion.

O'Connor, Thomas Power

b. October 5, 1848
Athlone, Ireland
d. November 18, 1929
London, England
fields: Government and Politics, Journalism, Publishing

As a member of Parliament and as a journalist, O'Connor was able to advance the Irish cause and effect change without violence.

Oconostota

b. c. 1710
eastern Tenn.
d. 1783
Overhill Cherokee Territory
fields: Government and Politics, Diplomacy, Native American Affairs

Oconostota, a Cherokee leader, helped to shape early Cherokee policy toward British and French colonists in what became the southeastern United States. Until his death in 1783, Oconostota tried to protect the rights of the Cherokee while maintaining peaceful relations with the new nation that was emerging from the American Revolution.

Octavius, Gaius. *See* Augustus

Oda Nobunaga

b. June, 1534
Owari Province, Japan
d. June 21, 1582
Kyōto, Japan
fields: Military Affairs, Government and Politics

The greatest soldier of his time, Oda started a process through diplomacy and war that put an end to political fragmentation in Japan and paved the way for the unique feudal system that governed Japan during the Tokugawa period (1602-1867).

Odetta

né: Odetta Holmes Felious Gordon
b. December 31, 1930
Birmingham, Ala.
fields: Music (folk-blues singer)

African American folk-blues singer, actress, and self-taught guitarist; Odetta, who played an important role in the folk revival of the 1950's and 1960's, sang African American work songs, blues numbers, spirituals, and ballads; she was one of the few folk singers to find continued success after the folk music boom of the 1960's.

Odo, Franklin S.

b. 1940
Territory of Hawaii
fields: Sociology

Franklin S. Odo, former president of the Association for Asian American Studies, directed the ethnic studies program at the University of Hawaii, Manoa. He coauthored *A Pictorial History of the Japanese in Hawaii, 1885-1924* (1985) and coedited *Roots: An Asian American Reader* (1971).

Odoacer

aka: Odovacar
b. c. 435
Central Europe
d. About March 15, 493
Ravenna, Italy
fields: Government and Politics, Military Affairs

Although of uncertain ethnic background, Odoacer forged a powerful warband, deposed the last Western Roman emperor, and established the first German kingdom in an area that had been part of the Roman Empire.

O'Farrill, Alberto

b. 1899
Santa Clara, Cuba
fields: Literature, Theater and Entertainemt

Playwright and actor. Alberto O'Farrill began acting and writing in 1921 in Havana, where he also edited a literary journal called *Proteo*. He moved to New York City in the mid-1920's to continue his career. In 1927, he began edited the newspaper *El Gráfico*. During the 1930's, he worked with the companies of the Teatro Variedades and the Teatro Campoamor. Among the plays he wrote were *Un doctor accidental*, *Kid Chocolate*, *Un negro en Andalucía*, *Los misterios de Changó*, and *Una viuda como no hay dos*.

Offenbach, Jacques

né: Jacob Eberst
b. June 20, 1819
Cologne, Prussia
d. October 5, 1880
Paris, France
fields: Music

Over the course of one hundred operettas and a major opera, Offenbach virtually defined this form of musical theater through his characteristic mixture of gaiety, spontaneity, and infectious melody and thus became the first great influence in the process of internationalizing the operetta.

Officer, Carl E.

b. April 3, 1952
St. Louis, Mo.
fields: Government and Politics

African American mayor of East St. Louis, Illinois; in May of 1979, Carl E. Officer was elected the third African American mayor of East St. Louis with 95 percent of the vote; as mayor he created the Metro-East Conference of Black Mayors, Inc., to foster closer cooperation between himself and the mayors of four other predominantly black cities near East St. Louis; Officer was also a member of the U.S. Conference of Mayors, the National Conference of Black Mayors, and the National Urban League.

O'Flaherty, Katherine. *See* Chopin, Kate

Ogata Kōrin

b. 1658
Kyoto, Japan
d. 1716
Kyoto, Japan
fields: Art

Ogata Kōrin worked within traditional Japanese aesthetic forms to produce an art of originality and universality that for many epitomizes Japanese taste. His screen of irises is one of the most widely known of all Japanese paintings.

Ogawa, Dennis

b. Sept. 7, 1943
Los Angeles, Calif.
fields: Business and Industry

Dennis Ogawa, who has bachelor's, master's, and doctoral degrees from the University of California, Los Angeles, combines scholarship and business in his life. Part owner of the NGN cable television station in Hawaii, which features programs from Japan, he held a professorship in the American Studies department of the University of Hawaii. He also directed the Japanese American Research Center at the Honolulu Japanese Chamber of Commerce. His publications include *Jan Ken Po: The World of Hawaii's Japanese Americans* (1973) and *Kodomo No Tame Ni—For the Sake of the Children: The Japanese American Experience in Hawaii* (1978).

Ogawa, Hideki. *See* Yukawa, Hideki

Ogilvie, Ben

full: Benjamin Ambrosio Ogilvie
b. Feb. 11, 1949
Colon, Panama
fields: Sports (baseball player)

Latino baseball player. Outfielder Ben Ogilvie made his major league debut with the Boston Red Sox in 1971. He was traded to the Detroit Tigers and then, in 1978, to the Milwaukee Brewers. In his first season with the Brewers, he batted .303. In 1979, he hit 29 home runs. In 1980, he led the American League with 41 home runs. In 1982, he helped the Brewers become the American League champions by hitting 34 home runs and batting in 102 runs. Ogilvie made the All-Star Team three times before he retired after the 1986 season with a lifetime .273 batting average and 235 career home runs.

Oglethorpe, James Edward

b. December 22, 1696
London, England
d. June 30, 1785
Cranham Hall, Essex, England
fields: Exploration and Colonization

With his social vision, promotional genius, military ability, and personal guidance, Oglethorpe established the colony of Georgia and frustrated the Spanish effort to push the British out of southeastern North America.

Oh, Sadaharu

b. May 10, 1940
Tokyo, Japan
fields: Sports (baseball)

Oh hit more home runs, 868, than any other man in organized baseball while playing twenty-two years with the Yomiuri (Tokyo) Giants in the Central League in Japan. When he retired, he also held the Japanese career records in runs batted in, runs scored, and total bases as well as the second highest marks in doubles and games played.

O'Hair, Madalyn Murray

né: Madalyn Murray
b. April 13, 1919
Pittsburgh, Pennsylvania
1995?
fields: Social Reform

The self-proclaimed first lady of atheism, once known as the most hated woman in the United States. O'Hair was active in eliminating prayer and Bible studies from public schools. The case of *Murray v. Curlett* reached the United States Supreme Court, and on June 17, 1963, the Court held that by requiring students to recite a prayer and read aloud from the Bible, the school violated the ban on the establishment of religion created by the First and Fourteenth Amendments. She founded the American Atheist Center and the Society of Separationists. In September, 1995, O'Hair disappeared. It was reported that more than $627,000 had also disappeared from bank accounts belonging to two of the atheist societies O'Hair had founded. In 1999, investigators claimed that she and two relatives had been killed in a plot to steal the more than $627,000.

O'Hara, James Edward

b. February 26, 1844
New York, N.Y.
d. September 15, 1905
New Bern, N.C.
fields: Government and Politics

African American U.S. representative from North Carolina; James Edward O'Hara took his congressional seat as the North Carolina Republican representative from the Second Congressional District on March 4, 1883; he was reelected in 1884; during his tenure he served on the House Committee on Mines and Mining, the House Committee on Expenditures on Public Buildings, and the House Committee on Invalid Pensions; he lost his bid for reelection in 1886 and resumed his legal practice in North Carolina.

O'Hara, John

b. January 31, 1905
Pottsville, Pennsylvania
d. April 11, 1970
Princeton, New Jersey
fields: Literature

John O'Hara was a popular American novelist noted for frank treatments of contemporary sexual mores. His first novel, *Appointment in Samarra* (1934), was praised by many reviewers but castigated by others for its sexual outspokenness. His *Ten North Frederick* (1955) drew more censorship attempts than any of his other works.

O'Higgins, Bernardo

b. August 20?, 1778
Chillán, Chile
d. October, 1842
Peru
fields: Military Affairs, Social Reform

Widely regarded by Latin Americans as the George Washington of Chile, O'Higgins, inspired by both the American and the French revolutions, followed the lead of the great Argentine general José de San Martín and helped Martín liberate Chile from Spanish colonial rule. Although he was not a political administrator, O'Higgins was able to inspire both the troops under his command and the Chilean civilian population to overthrow a long-detested regime.

O'Higgins, Pablo

b. 1904
Salt Lake City, Utah
d. 1983
Mexico City, Mexico
fields: Art

Latino muralist and art historian. In 1924, Pablo O'Higgins was invited by Diego Rivera to visit Mexico, where he spent four years painting wall murals. In 1926, he began working for bilingual magazine *Mexico Folkways*. In 1927, he joined the Mexican Communist Party and later helped found the Liga de Escritores y Artistas Revolucionarios (LEAR). In 1931-1932, O'Higgins worked in Moscow on a grant. In 1937, he cofounded the anti-Fascist Taller de la Gráfica Popular (TGP).

Ohiyesa (The Winner). *See* Eastman, Charles Alexander

Ohkom Kakit. *See* Little Wolf

Ohnick, Hutchlon. *See* Onuki, Hachiro

Oiscoss. *See* Oshkosh

Okada, John

b. 1923
Seattle, Wash.
d. Feb., 1971
fields: Literature

John Okada, who received a master's in English from Columbia University in 1949, volunteered for military service during World War II and answered affirmatively to the loyalty and allegiance questions in the U.S. government's predraft questionnaire. His novel, *No-No Boy* (1957), addresses those who answered negatively to both questions and the deep and bitter divisions within members of the Japanese American communities. The book was not a success during Okada's lifetime, but five years after his death, it was reprinted and was widely read.

Okamura, Jonathan Y.

b. July 22, 1949
Wailuku, Hawaii
fields: Historiography

Jonathan Y. Okamura, who received a Ph.D. in anthropology from the University of London in 1983, researched and wrote extensively on Filipino immigration and the Filipino experience in Hawaii as well as the Philippines. In 1991, he published *The Filipino American Experience in Hawaii.*

Okazaki, Steven

b. Mar. 12, 1952
Los Angeles, Calif.
fields: Film

Japanese American filmmaker Steve Okazaki graduated from San Francisco State University in 1976. His *Days of Waiting* (1990), a documentary about a European American interned with Japanese Americans during World War II, won an Academy Award, and his documentary about Japanese American wartime internment resisters, *Unfinished Business* (1986), was nominated for an Oscar. Other films include *Living on Tokyo Time* (1987) and *Troubled Paradise* (1992).

O'Keeffe, Georgia

full: Georgia Totto O'Keeffe
b. November 15, 1887
Sun Prairie, Wisconsin
d. March 6, 1986
Santa Fe, New Mexico
fields: Art

Breaking with European traditionalism, Georgia O'Keeffe pointed to new ways to perceive the world about her, creating precise, sometimes stark depictions of nature and of urban scenes.

Okei

b. 1852
Japan
d. 1871
Gold Hill, Calif.
fields: Historical Figure

Okei was a teenage nursemaid who worked for John Henry Schnell's family in the Wakamatsu Tea and Silk Farm Colony in Gold Hill, California. Schnell brought a group of young immigrants from Kyushu to the United States with the intent of establishing an agricultural colony. Okei became a symbol of the colony's struggle and ultimate failure in 1871, the year of her death

O'Kelly, Seán T.

full: Seán Thomas O'Kelly
b. August 25, 1882
Dublin, Ireland
d. November 23, 1966
Dublin, Ireland
fields: Diplomacy, Government and Politics

O'Kelly was one of the pioneers of the Gaelic Revival and the Irish Independence movement. After independence had been secured for the southern twenty-six counties of Ireland, O'Kelly emerged as a mainstay of the Fianna Fail Party and a leading statesmen for the Irish Free State and the Republic of Ireland. He culminated his public career with two terms as president of Ireland.

Okihiro, Gary Y.

b. Oct. 14, 1945
Aiea, Hawaii
fields: Historiography

Historian Gary Y. Okihiro applied leftist theories of resistance to reexamine Japanese American history and World War II internment. His works include *Japanese Legacy: Farming and Community Life in California's Santa Clara Valley* (1985, with Timothy J. Lukes, *Cane Fires: The Anti-Japanese Movement in Hawaii, 1865-1945* (1991), and *Margins and Mainstreams: Asians in American History and Culture* (1994).

Okino, Betty

full: Elizabeth Okino
b. June 4, 1975
Entebbe, Uganda
fields: Sports (gymnast)

African American gymnast; Betty Okino won the vaulting, uneven bars, and all-around competitions at the 1991 McDonald's America Cup; she was a member of the 1991 silver medal-winning U.S. World Championship team and a member of the 1992 U.S. Olympic team which won a bronze medal; her original triple pirouette on the balance beam has been named the "Okino."

Okubo, Mine

b. 1912
Riverside, Calif.
fields: Art

In the 1930's, artist Mine Okubo was hired to produce murals for the U.S. Army through the federal Works Progress Administration, but after the bombing of Pearl Harbor, she was sent to the Tanforan assembly center and then to the Topaz relocation center in central Utah. While at the camp, she sketched her surroundings and taught art classes. She was released from the camp in 1944 to work at *Fortune* magazine. Okubo published a collection of ink on rice paper drawings of camp life as *Citizen 13660* in 1946.

Okumura, Takie

b. Apr. 18, 1864
Kochi, Japan
d. Feb. 10, 1951
Honolulu, Territory of Hawaii
fields: Religion and Theology

Christian minister Takie Okumura came to Hawaii in 1894 on a religious mission. He founded the Makiki Christian Church, formed a Japanese-language school, and ran a Christian dormitory for Japanese American high school and college students. Okumura, an outspoken accommodationist leader, assisted the Japanese immigrants in many ways, but he also worked with the plantation owners, encouraging the immigrants and their children to stay on the plantations and not seek work elsewhere.

Olaf I

né: Olaf Tryggvason
b. c. 968
in the area of the Oslo fjord, Norway
d. September 9, 1000
at Svold, probably near Rügen in the Baltic
fields: Military Affairs, Religion and Theology, Monarchy

King of Norway, 995-1000. His short reign as king brought about a temporary unification and Christianization of Norway, and his exploits later made him a national hero and legend for his people.

Olaf, Saint

né: Olaf Haraldsson
aka: Olaf II, King of Norway
b. c. 995
west of the Oslo fjord, Norway
d. July 29, 1030
Stiklestad, Norway
fields: Monarchy, Government and Politics, Law, Religion and Theology

King of Norway, 1015-1028. By consolidating and unifying Norway under a strong Christian monarchy, Olaf established his country's first national government and permanently influenced the political and religious development of his land. Declared a saint in 1041, the cult of Saint Olaf spread as miracles relating to Saint Olaf were reported throughout Western Europe.

Olah, George A.

full: George Andrew Olah
b. May 22, 1927
Budapest, Hungary
fields: Chemistry

George A. Olah developed synthetic methods; shaped the modern concept of carbocations; pioneered superacid chemistry; in 1994, won the Nobel Prize in Chemistry.

Olajuwon, Hakeem

b. January 21, 1963
Lagos, Nigeria
fields: Sports (basketball player)

African basketball player; recruited from Nigeria to play for the University of Houston,

Hakeem Olajuwon led that team into the National Collegiate Athletic Association tournament finals in his sophomore year, earning the tournament's Outstanding Player designation; in the 1984 NBA draft, he was the Houston Rockets first draft pick; as a center, he earned a reputation as one of the NBA's top scorers, shot blockers, and rebounders, becoming in 1990 the fourth player in NBA history to lead the league in rebounding in back-to-back seasons; he has been a regular All-Star selection. He led the Rockets to the NBA title in both 1994 and 1995. In 1994, he was named NBA Most Valuable Player for the season.

Oland, Warner

aka: Werner Ohlund
b. Oct. 3, 1880
Umea, Sweden
d. Aug. 5, 1938
Stockholm, Sweden
fields: Theater and Entertainment

Actor Warner Oland, a native of Sweden, portrayed detective Charlie Chan in the film series, beginning in 1931. He also worked as a set designer and Strindberg translator.

Olbers, Wilhelm

full: Heinrich Wilhelm Matthäus Olbers
b. Oct. 11, 1758
Arbergen, near Bremen, Germany
d. Mar. 2, 1840
Bremen, Germany
fields: Astronomy, Medicine

Wilhelm Olbers discovered numerous comets and asteroids; made a streamlined method for calculating cometary orbits; in 1802, confirmed the existence of Ceres, the first of several asteroids to be discovered between Mars and Jupiter; offered an explanation as to why the night sky is dark and not fully illuminated by the myriad stars in space.

Old Briton

b. ?
Wabash River area, northwestern Ind.
d. June 21, 1752
at Pickawillany, on the Miami River in Ohio
fields: Government and Politics, Business and Industry, Native American Affairs

Old Briton, a Miami Indian leader of the Piankashaw band, attempted to change Miami trading partners and allies from the French to the English in the mid-eighteenth century. Ultimately, after Old Briton's group started attacking French soldiers, the French attacked his town and trading center, Pickawillany, overwhelmed the Miami, and murdered Old Briton.

Oldenbarnevelt, Johan van

full: Johan Gerrit Reyerszoon van Oldenbarnevelt
b. September 14, 1547
Amersfoort, Bishopric of Utrecht
d. May 13, 1619
The Hague, United Provinces
fields: Government and Politics, Diplomacy

Oldenbarnevelt was the founder-lawgiver of the United Provinces of the Netherlands, whose statesmanship set the constitutional libertarian course that the modern Netherlands has followed. He was one of the greatest statesmen and diplomats in early modern Europe and in all Dutch history. Oldenbarnevelt served the United Provinces as Pensionary of Rotterdam and Advocate of Holland.

O'Leary, Hazel

né: Hazel Reid
full: Hazel Reid O'Leary
b. May 17, 1937
Newport News, Va.
fields: Government and Politics, Law

African American lawyer, administrator, and political appointee. Hazel O'Leary was secretary of energy in the cabinet of President Bill Clinton, 1993-1996. She was the first African American and the first woman to hold that post. She is president of the consulting firm O'Leary and Associates and serves on many boards of trustees, including Morehouse College (1998).

Oleinik, Olga

full: Olga Arsenievna Oleinik
b. July 2, 1925
the Soviet Union
fields: Mathematics (algebra, applied math, and geometry)

Olga Oleinik formulated complex mathematical theories about differential equations that had scientific applications.

Oliva, Tomas

b. 1930
Guanabacoa, Cuba
fields: Art

Tomas Oliva received his art education in Cuba, Spain, and France. He began showing his work in group exhibitions in the mid-1950's and had several one-man shows in Havana. By the 1960's, he was exhibiting around the world. In 1968, he left Cuba and settled in Miami, Florida.

Oliva, Tony

né: Pedro Oliva y Lopez
b. July 20, 1940
Pinar del Rio, Cuba
fields: Sports (baseball player)

Cuban baseball player; as perhaps the greatest baseball player to come from Cuba, Tony Oliva played for the Minnesota Twins from 1964 to 1976; during Oliva's playing career, he is noted as the first rookie to be American League batting champion (with a .323 batting average and 217 hits, including 32 home runs); in 1965 and 1971, he won two more batting titles; he became a Twins coach upon retiring in 1976.

Olivares, Julian

b. Dec. 6, 1940
San Antonio, Tex.
fields: Scholarship, Literature

Literary critic. Julian Olivares was an assistant professor of Spanish at Bridgewater State College in Bridgewater, Massachusetts, from 1978 to 1981, then an assistant professor at the University of Texas at Houston from 1981 to 1986, after which he was promoted to associate professor. In 1982, he began working as an associate editor of Arte Público Press, and he has edited *Chicano-Riquena*. Olivares has written many critical essays on the literature of Spain from the sixteenth and seventeenth centuries. His published works include *The Love Poetry of Francisco de Quevedo* (1983) and *The Sacred and Moral Verse of Francisco de Quevedo* (1988).

Olivares, Luis

b. 1934
San Antonio, Tex.
d. Mar. 18, 1993
fields: Religion and Theology

Roman Catholic priest. Luis Olivares served as pastor of La Placita, Los Angeles' oldest church, from 1981 to 1990. During that time, Olivares defended the rights of street vendors, proclaimed La Placita a sanctuary for the homeless and political refugees, and defied the 1986 Immigration Reform and Control Act by hiring undocumented workers. He also served as president of the United Neighborhoods Organization. Olivares died from complications of AIDS, contracted in El Salvador from a contaminated needle.

Olivárez, Graciela

b. May 9, 1928
near Phoenix, Ariz.
d. 1987
fields: Government and Politics

Mexican American public official. In 1970, Graciela Olivárez became the first woman to graduate from the University of Notre Dame's law school. In 1975, she became New Mexico's director of planning. In 1977, President Jimmy Carter appointed her director of the Community Services Administration. In 1980, she became a senior consultant with the United Way of America and continued to work with such nonprofit organizations as the American Cancer Society and the League of Women Voters. She also ran a television station.

Olivas, Michael

b. 1951
fields: Education, Law

Educator and attorney. Michael Olivas earned his law degree from Georgetown University in 1981. He served as the director of resources for the League of United Latin American Citizens (LULAC) Education Resource Center in Washington, D.C., from 1979 to 1982, then began teaching law at the University of Houston Law School. He later served as the director of the Institute for Higher Education, Law and Governance at that university and was named associate dean in 1990.

Olive, Milton L., III

b. November 7, 1946
Chicago, Ill.
d. October 22, 1965
near Phu Cuong, Vietnam
fields: Warfare and Conquest

African American Vietnam War hero; Milton L. Olive III became the first black soldier since the Korean War to receive the Congressional Medal of Honor when, on October 22, 1965, he fell on a grenade thrown into his group of five soldiers to absorb the blast, saving the lives of his four comrades.

Oliver, King

full: Joseph Oliver
b. May 11, 1885
Abend, La.
d. April 10, 1938
Savannah, Ga.
fields: Music (jazz cornetist)

African American cornetist and bandleader; remembered as one of the most influential and significant musicians of the classic jazz (New Orleans) style, King Oliver played in cabarets and bars around New Orleans before moving to Chicago; there he formed, led, recorded, and toured with several bands including the Creole Jazz Band and the Dixie Syncopators; his early recordings (1923) included "Canal Street Blues," "Weather Bird Rag," "Dippermouth Blues," "Snake Rag," "High Society Rag," "Zulu's Ball," and "Working Man Blues"; his recorded duets with pianist "Jelly Roll" Morton (1924) were "King Porter Stomp" and "Tom Cat Blues."

Oliver, Sy

full: Melvin James Oliver
b. December 17, 1910
Battle Creek, Mich.
d. May 27, 1988
New York, N.Y.
fields: Music (swing trumpeter, composer, and arranger)

African American trumpeter, composer, and arranger; Sy Oliver is best remembered for his brilliant arrangements, especially those he wrote during his years with Jimmie Lunceford's orchestra (1933-1939); classic recordings of this period include "For Dancers Only," "T'ain't Whatcha Do," "Margie," and "Stomp It Off"; during his time with Tommy Dorsey, Oliver penned the hit arrangements to "Well, Git It," "Swing High," and "On the Sunny Side of the Street"; Oliver moved on to musical direction and record production for several record companies, writing arrangements for such talents as Billie Holiday, Ella Fitzgerald, and Frank Sinatra.

Olivier, Laurence

full: Laurence Kerr Olivier
aka: Sir Laurence Olivier
aka: Baron Olivier of Brighton
b. May 22, 1907
Dorking, Surrey, England
d. June 11, 1989
near Ashurst, West Sussex, England
fields: Theater and Entertainment, Film

Widely considered the greatest twentieth century actor in the English-speaking world, Olivier has also been a distinguished theater manager and stage and film director and producer who has done more than anyone else to bring William Shakespeare's works to the screen.

Oller, Francisco

b. 1833
San Juan, Puerto Rico
d. 1917
San Juan, Puerto Rico
fields: Art (painter), Music

Puerto Rican painter and musician. Francisco Oller, considered to be the greatest Hispanic painter of the mid-nineteenth century, received his art training in Spain and France. In 1853, he exhibited and won local prizes in Puerto Rico. He submitted work to the Paris Salons of 1865, 1867, and 1875. In 1873, he received government funding to go to the Vienna Universal Exposition. Oller returned to France in 1874, where he became friends with Paul Cézanne, Camille Pissarro, Édouard Manet, Pierre-Auguste Renoir, and Claude Monet. He was inducted into the Order of King Charles III of Spain and served as court painter to King Amadeo.

Olmedo, Alex

full: Alejandro Olmedo
b. Mar. 24, 1936
Arequipa, Peru
fields: Sports (tennis player)

Peruvian tennis player. Alex Olmedo learned to play tennis as a child. He won National Collegiate Athletic Association (NCAA) singles titles in 1956 and 1958 while attending the University of Southern California (USC). He helped the United States team win the 1958 Davis Cup title. He won the singles and doubles titles at the 1959 U.S. Indoor Championship, the first by a South American. That same year, he won the Wimbledon and Australian Championship singles titles and reached the finals of the U.S. National Championship. In 1960, he began a successful professional career and became a national hero in Peru. He received his country's Order of Sports award and was indicted into the International Tennis Hall of Fame in 1987.

Olmos, Edward James

b. February 24, 1947
Los Angeles, Calif.
fields: Film, Theater and Entertainment

Mexican American actor, director, and producer Edward James Olmos had his first major Broadway role in Luis Valdez's *Zoot Suit*. He was nominated for a 1978 Tony Award for that role, a Los Angeles Drama Critics Circle Award, and a Theatre World Award. He starred in the film *Stand and Deliver* (1988) and was nominated for an Academy Award. He directed and coproduced *American Me* (1992). His other films include *Wolfen* (1981), *Blade Runner* (1982), *Saving Grace* (1986), *Triumph of the Spirit* (1989), *Maria's Story* (1990), and *A Talent for the Game* (1991). On television Olmos played *Miami Vice* (1984-1988), for which he won Golden Globe and Emmy Awards as best supporting actor.

Olmsted, Frederick Law

b. April 26, 1822
Hartford, Connecticut
d. August 28, 1903
Waverly, Massachusetts
fields: Social Reform, Landscape Architecture

Olmsted traveled extensively in the antebellum South and wrote some of America's best critical descriptions of slavery on the eve of the Civil War. He designed Central Park in New York City and other urban parks across the country. Olmsted is considered the father of the profession of landscape architecture in the United States.

Olson, Culbert L.

b. Nov. 7, 1876
Fillmore, Utah

d. April 13, 1962
Los Angeles, Calif.
fields: Government and Politics

Democrat Culbert L. Olson served as state senator before being elected governor of California in 1938. After the attack on Pearl Harbor, he devised a special internment plan that he proposed to the leaders of the Japanese American community on the West Coast. The plan was to incarcerate Japanese American men in concentration camps in the interior of the state, sending them to work in agriculture during the day. His plan was rejected, and he complied with the federal government's evacuation orders in 1942.

Omar Khayyám

b. 1048
probably Nishapur, Iran
d. 1131
Nishapur, Iran
fields: Mathematics, Literature (poetry)

Khayyám was a leading medieval mathematician and the author of Persian quatrains made world famous through Edward FitzGerald's *The Rubáiyát of Omar Khayyám.*

Omatsu, Glenn

b. ?
Cleveland, Ohio
fields: Journalism

Glenn Omatsu became a staff member of the Asian American Studies Center, University of California, Los Angeles (UCLA), in 1985. He served as associate editor of *Amerasia Journal* and as editor of *CrossCurrents*, the center's newsmagazine. Before working for UCLA, he was assistant editor of the English section of the *Hokubei Mainichi* from 1971 to 1976 and chief shop steward for Teamsters Local 986 at a small factor in Los Angeles from 1979 to 1985.

Omi, Michael Allen

b. Mar. 9, 1951
Berkeley, Calif.
fields: Sociology

Michael Allen Omi, who specializes in race relations and politics, coauthored *Racial Formation in the United States: From the 1960's to the 1980's* (1986). Omi, who taught ethnic studies at the University of California, Berkeley, received that institution's 1990 Distinguished Teaching Award.

Omura, James Matsumoto

né: Utaka Matsumoto
b. Nov. 17, 1912
Winslow, Bainbridge Island, Wash.
d. June 20, 1994
fields: Journalism

Japanese American journalist, activist; James Matsumoto Omura founded the magazine, *Current Life* (1940), which published poetry, fiction, and news articles by Japanese American writers; at the Tolan Committee hearings, spoke out against forcible removal of Japanese Americans from the West Coast.

Onassis, Jacqueline Kennedy

né: Jacqueline Lee Bouvier
aka: Jacqueline Kennedy
b. July 28, 1929
Southampton, New York
d. May 19, 1994
New York, New York
fields: Government and Politics

Jacqueline Kennedy was one of the most famous First Ladies of the twentieth century. The American people associate her with elegance, style, glamour and the excitement of her husband's brief presidency, his tragic death, and the troubled history of her celebrated family. She married multimillionaire Aristotle Onassis in 1968; after his death, she became an editor for Doubleday in 1975.

Oñate, Juan de

b. 1550
Guadalajara, Mexico
d. 1630
Spain
fields: Exploration and Colonization, Government and Politics

Explorer and administrator. Between 1595 and 1598, Juan de Oñate colonized the territory that became the modern state of New Mexico, then became its governor. During Oñate's rule, Franciscan priests converted many Pueblo Indians to Christianity and established missions in the pueblos. In 1607, Oñate resigned as governor after his enemies persuaded the king of Spain to recall him. He was tried and convicted of disobeying royal orders and of cruelty to the Pueblo Indians. Exiled from New Mexico, he settled in Spain.

O'Neal, Alexander

b. ?
fields: Music (popular vocalist)

African American pop vocalist; discovered by Prince, who helped promote his career, Alexander O'Neal performs in a cool yet steamy rhythm-and-blues style; his recordings include *Alexander O'Neal* (1985), *Hearsay* (1987; which included a number-one hit on the black contemporary singles chart, "Fake"), *My Gift to You* (1988), and *Lovers Again* (1997).

O'Neal, Frederick

b. August 27, 1905
Brooksville, Miss.
fields: Theater and Entertainment, Labor Movement

African American actor and labor leader; with playwright Abram Hill, Frederick O'Neal founded the American Negro Theatre (ANT; 1940-early 1950's) to train African Americans as actors, directors, playwrights, designers, and technicians; in 1948 O'Neal helped to organize the British Negro Theatre; he served as international president of the Associated Actors and Artists of America, president of Actors' Equity Association, and president of the American Federation of Labor-Congress of Industrial Organizations; for his performance in *Anna Lucasta* (1944-1945) he received the Clarence Derwent Award and the New York Drama Critics Circle Award; in 1975 he was inducted into the Black Filmmakers Hall of Fame.

O'Neal, Ron

b. September 1, 1937
Utica, N.Y.
fields: Film, Theater and Entertainment, Television

African American actor; best known for his leading role as a drug pusher in the film *SUPER Fly* (1972), Ron O'Neal has played smaller roles in the films *Brothers* (1977), *When a Stranger Calls* (1979), *The Final Countdown* (1980), *Red Dawn* (1984), *Mercenary Fighters* (1986), and *As Summers Die* (1987); his theater credits include the Negro Ensemble Company productions of *Ceremonies in Dark Old Men* (1969) and *Dream on Monkey Mountain* (1971), *Macbeth* (1974), and the New York Shakespeare Festival production of *Agamemnon* (1977); his television credits include recurring roles in *Bring 'Em Back Alive* (1982-1983; as the sultan of Johore) and in the action drama *The Equalizer* (1986; as Lieutenant Isadore Smalls).

O'Neal, Shaquille

full: Shaquille Rashaun O'Neal
b. March 6, 1972
Newark, N.J.
fields: Sports (basketball player)

African American professional basketball player; known for his "Shaq Attaq" shots and trademark slam dunks, Shaquille O'Neal became a dominant center in the National Basketball Association (NBA) when he entered the league in 1993; started playing for the Orlando Magic in 1989; became a marketing superstar and a multi-millionaire; starred in the film *Blue Chips* (1994) with Nick Nolte, released *Shaq Diesel*, a rap music album, selling more than a million copies; joined the Los Angeles Lakers in 1996.

O'Neil, Buck

full: John Jordan O'Neil
b. November 13, 1911
Carabelle, Fla.

fields: Sports (baseball player)

African American baseball player; from 1937 to 1950, Buck O'Neil played as a first baseman in the Negro Leagues, spending his entire career with the Kansas City Monarchs; managed the Monarchs from 1948 through 1955; hired by the Chicago Cubs in 1962, becoming the first African American to serve as a coach for a major league baseball team; scouted for the Kansas City Royals in the 1990's.

O'Neill, David. *See* Gallagher, Frank

O'Neill, Eugene

full: Eugene Gladstone O'Neill
b. October 16, 1888
New York, New York
d. November 27, 1953
Boston, Massachusetts
fields: Theater and Entertainment, Literature

O'Neill is commonly considered a great American playwright, honored as a writer who experimented ambitiously in a variety of dramatic modes. He won the 1936 Nobel Prize in Literature.

O'Neill, Gonzalo

b. 1867
d. 1942
fields: Literature

Puerto Rican poet and playwright. Gonzalo O'Neill worked with the magazine *El palenque de la juventud* (the young people's arena) before publishing his first book, *La indiana borinqueña* (1922; the Indians of Puerto Rico). In 1924, he published a book of nationalistic poetry titled *Sonoras bagatelas o sicilianas* (sonorous bagatelles or Sicilian verses). O'Neill also wrote several plays, including *Moncho Reyes* (1923), *Bajo una sola bandera* (1928; *Under Just One Flag*), and *Amoríos borincanos* (1938).

O'Neill, Tip

full: Thomas Philip O'Neill, Jr.
b. December 9, 1912
Cambridge, Massachusetts
d. January 5, 1994
Boston, Massachusetts
fields: Government and Politics

O'Neill was a lifelong defender of social legislation and an energetic leader of the House of Representatives whose ten years as Speaker saw a resurgence of congressional authority.

Onetti, Juan Carlos

b. July 1, 1909
Montevideo, Uruguay
d. May 30, 1994
Madrid, Spain
fields: Literature

Writer. Juan Carlos Onetti's first novel, *El Pozo* (1939; *The Pit*, 1991), prefigured the technical and narrative changes that would culminate in the "new novel" of the 1960's in Latin America. Subsequent novels include *Tierra de nadie* (1941), *Para esta noche* (1943; *Tonight*, 1991), *La vida breve* (1950; *A Brief Life*, 1976), *Los adioses* (1951; *Farewells*, 1992), *Una tumba sin nombre* (1959), *El astillero* (1961; *The Shipyard*, 1968), *Juntacadáveres* (1964; *Body Snatcher*, 1991), *La muerte y la niña* (1972), *Dejemos hablar al viento* (1979), and *Cuando entonces* (1987). His short stories are collected in *Un sueño realizado y otros cuentos* (1951) and *Tiempo de abrazar y los cuentos de 1933 a 1950* (1974).

Ong, Paul

b. Sept. 6, 1949
Sacramento, Calif.
fields: Architecture, Sociology

Paul Ong received his doctoral degree from the University of California in 1983. He taught in the Graduate School of Architecture and Urban Planning of the University of California, Los Angeles. His demographic analyses of Los Angeles played a significant role in that city's reapportionment, and he wrote many articles on issues affecting Asian Americans, including racism.

Ong, Wing Foon

b. Feb. 4, 1904
Wing On Li, Guangdong Province, China
d. Dec. 19, 1977
Phoenix, Ariz.
fields: Business and Industry

Wing Foon Ong was the first Chinese American to serve in a state legislature in the United States. He served two terms in the Arizona house of representatives (1946-1950) and one term in the state senate (1966-1968). His story appears as *Summer Wind: The Story of an Immigrant Chinese Politician* (1986), by Richard Nagasawa.

Ongwaterohiathe. *See* Shikellamy

Onizuka, Ellison

b. June 24, 1946
Kealakekua, Territory of Hawaii
d. January 28, 1986
Cape Canaveral, Fla.
fields: Science

Ellison Onizuka became an astronaut in 1978. He was the first Asian American astronaut, and he trained as a shuttle mission specialist. He was on the crew of the *Discovery* shuttle mission in January, 1985. Onizuka was killed in the explosion of the *Challenger*.

Ono, Yoko

b. February 18, 1933
Tokyo, Japan
fields: Art (multimedia), Music, Film

Avant-garde artist Yoko Ono's personal and professional partnership with Beatle John Lennon led to her widespread reputation as "the woman who broke up the Beatles." In the 1960's, she became a member of the conceptual art movement known as Fluxus; in 1968 she met Lennon, and their marriage a year later was soon followed by the breakup of the Beatles. Together, Lennon and Ono were influential in the counterculture of the 1970's, using their fame to stage events in the service of causes such as world peace. After a period of mourning following Lennon's murder in 1980, Yoko remained in New York, raising their son Sean and continuing to work on musical and artistic projects.

Onsager, Lars

b. Nov. 27, 1903
Kristiania (now Oslo), Norway
d. Oct. 5, 1976
Coral Gables, Florida
fields: Chemistry, Physics

Lars Onsager made important discoveries in statistical mechanics; was a pioneer in the field of nonequilibrium thermodynamics; in 1942, found an exact solution to the two-dimensional Ising model; won the Nobel Prize in Chemistry in 1968.

Onuki, Hachiro

né: Hutchlon Ohnick
b. 1849
Japan
d. 1921
fields: Business and Industry

Hachiro Onuki, who immigrated to the United States in 1876, moved to Phoenix where he was awarded a municipal contract to provide the city with light—gas, electric, or both. He became "Hutchlon Ohnick" and was named superintendent of the Phoenix Illuminating Gas and Electric Company. In 1901, Onuki moved to Phoenix, where he established the Oriental American Bank.

Oort, Jan Hendrik

b. April 28, 1900
Franeker, The Netherlands
d. November 5, 1992
Leiden, The Netherlands
fields: Astronomy

Oort was one of the most significant astronomers of the twentieth century. He was the first to postulate the vast swarm of comets known subsequently as the Oort cloud. He was one of the pioneers of radio astronomy, and he was one of the leaders in establishing the structure of the Milky Way Galaxy.

Oparin, Aleksandr Ivanovich

b. March 2, 1894
Uglich, Russia
d. April 21, 1980
U.S.S.R.
fields: Biochemistry, Botany, Biology

Oparin was the principal pioneer in theorizing on the origins of life on Earth from inorganic matter. Of major importance also were his works which dealt with the biochemistry of plant material, from which he successfully developed the principles of Soviet biochemistry based on biocatalysis.

Opechancanough

aka: Mangopeomen
aka: Massatamohtnock
b. c. 1544
Va.
d. 1644
Jamestown, Va.
fields: Native American Affairs, Warfare and Conquest

Powhatan Confederacy tribal chief; a brother of Powhatan, chief of a powerful Tidewater Virginia confederacy of tribes, Opechancanough confronted the English adventurer Captain John Smith on several occasions; it was Opechancanough who captured Smith and took the Englishman to his brother's village where Smith claimed that Powhatan's daughter, Pocahontas, saved his life; negotiated between English settlers and various Indian tribes, 1607-1618; shortly after Powhatan's death in 1618, Opechancanough became the chief of the Powhatan Confederacy; he led rebellions against English encroachment on native lands and culture in 1622 and 1644; was murdered while a prisoner.

Opeteca Hanawaywin. *See* Poundmaker

Opothleyaholo

aka: Apotheyahola
aka: Optothe Yoholo
aka: Good Shouting Child
b. c. 1798
Creek Nation, Ga.
d. 1862
near Leroy Creek, Kans.
fields: Government and Politics, Native American Affairs

Creek Indian leader. Opothleyaholo opposed an illegal treaty ceding twenty-five million acres of Creek land, signed by William McIntosh, leader of the Creek peace faction. In 1825-1826, Opothleyaholo led a Creek delegation to Washington, D.C., protesting removal. Signed the Treaty of Washington, ceding many, but not all, Creek lands. Signed a second treaty in Washington in 1832. He and his people were forcibly relocated to Indian Territory. There he became a head chief for temporarily reunited Creek factions, counseling peace with whites.

Oppenheimer, J. Robert

full: Julius Robert Oppenheimer
b. April 22, 1904
New York, New York
d. February 18, 1967
Princeton, New Jersey
fields: Physics

As director of the Los Alamos Laboratories, Oppenheimer was in charge of the team of scientists who developed the nation's first nuclear weapons.

Orcagna, Andrea

né: Andrea di Cione
b. c. 1308
Florence, Italy
d. c. 1368
Florence, Italy
fields: Art

In paintings and in sculptural and architectural projects combining religious intensity with naturalism, Orcagna extended the expressive range of Italian art in the mid-fourteenth century.

O'Ree, Willie

full: William Eldon O'Ree
b. October 5, 1935
Fredericton, New Brunswick, Canada
fields: Sports (hockey player)

African American hockey player; Willie O'Ree joined the Boston Bruins for a two-game trial in 1957, becoming the first black player in the National Hockey League; he played in forty-three games, making four goals and ten assists, in the 1960-1961 season; his subsequent nineteen years of play in the minor leagues included seven years with the Los Angeles Blades.

Orendaín, Antonio

b. May 28, 1930
Etzatlán, Jalisco, Mexico
fields: Social Reform

Labor leader. Antonio Orendaín helped establish and direct the National Farm Workers Association in 1962. In 1977, he founded and directed the Texas Farm Workers Union after he and hundreds of followers marched four hundred miles from the Rio Grande Valley to the state capital in Austin. Orendaín went on to organize packing house workers and electrical, radio, and machine workers. He also served as a consultant to a juvenile probation program and for a time hosted the television program *Contra Punto.*

Oresme, Nicole

b. c. 1325
possibly in Allemagne, France
d. July 11, 1382
Lisieux, France
fields: Mathematics (geometry)

Nicole Oresme created a two-dimensional graphing system. In 1377, he completed a translation from Latin to French of Aristotle's *De caelo et mundo* (the heavens and the world).

Origen

b. c. 185 C.E.
Alexandria, Egypt
d. c. 254 C.E.
probably Tyre (modern Sur, Lebanon)
fields: Religion and Theology

Origen is usually considered the greatest of the early Christian thinkers; he was the first not only to write extensive commentaries on most books of the Bible but also to study the main areas and problems within theology. He did so with such intelligence that often what he wrote determined the lines of all subsequent Christian thought.

Orlando, Tony

full: Michael Anthony Orlando Cassavitis
b. Apr. 3, 1944
New York, N.Y.
fields: Music (singer and composer)

Singer and composer. Tony Orlando recorded several hit songs in the early 1960's before he began working in promotions in the record industry. In 1970, Orlando formed a trio named Dawn and recorded "Knock Three Times," which became a number one hit in the United States and the United Kingdom. The group changed its name to Tony Orlando and Dawn and recorded more hits, including "Tie a Yellow Ribbon 'Round the Ole Oak Tree" (1973). From July, 1974, to December, 1976, the group starred in the prime time television series *Tony Orlando and Dawn.* Orlando retired from show business in 1977 but continued to give occasional solo performances.

Orléans, duc d'

né: Louis-Philippe-Joseph
aka: Philippe, duc d'Orléans
aka: Philippe Égalité
b. April 13, 1747
Saint-Cloud, France
d. November 6, 1793
Paris, France
fields: Government and Politics, Monarchy

Although a Bourbon prince, he encouraged opposition to royal absolutism and lent his support to the French Revolution of 1789.

Orozco, José Clemente

b. November 23, 1883
Ciudad Guzmán, Mexico
d. September 7, 1949
Mexico City, Mexico
fields: Art

Orozco was one of the greatest muralists of the twentieth century and was considered the foremost to work in fresco. He was among the earliest Mexican artists to break away from European conventionalism and treat purely Mexican themes: The silent, suffering masses became a recurring interest in his art, reflecting his deep humanitarian concern and empathy for his people.

Ørsted, Hans Christian

aka: Hans Christian Øersted
b. Aug. 14, 1777
Rudkøbing, Langeland, Denmark
d. Mar. 9, 1851
Copenhagen, Denmark
fields: Chemistry, Physics

Hans Christian Ørsted is sometimes called the founder of electromagnetism; in 1820, demonstrated that electric currents can produce magnetic effects; in 1825, prepared aluminum chloride and isolated metallic aluminum.

Ortega, Daniel

full: Daniel Ortega Saavedra
b. November 11, 1945
La Libertad, Chontales, Nicaragua
fields: Government and Politics

Sandinista revolutionary leader; president of Nicaragua from 1979 to 1990. Daniel Ortega joined the FSLN, a political group dedicated to overthrowing the Anastasio Somoza García dictatorship, in 1963. Imprisoned 1967-1974. In 1979 the Sandinistas (FSLN groups) and their allies overthrew Somoza, who went into exile. Ortega assumed leadership. Government aided by Cuba and Soviet Union, opposed by U.S., who put economic sanctions in place and funded "Contra" rebels. Ortega government failed to improve country's struggling economy and spent significant funds maintaining army. Defeated in 1990 election by Violeta Chamorro.

Ortega, José Benito

b. 1858
d. 1941
fields: Art

Artist. José Benito Ortega was an itinerant artist who traveled around New Mexico seeking Hispanic patrons for his simple and brightly painted santo figures.

Ortega, Katherine Davalos

b. July 16, 1934
Tularosa, New Mexico
fields: Government and Politics

As one of the first Latinas to hold a high government position, Ortega provided a role model and example for all women with political aspirations.

Ortega y Alberro, Malú

full: Maria Luisa Ortega y Alberro
b. ?
Chicago, Ill.
fields: Art

Mexican American muralist. Malú Ortega y Alberro is associated with the Chicano art/empowerment movement in Chicago, where she helped paint the monumental mural *To Hope* on Benito Juárez High School in the Pilsen neighborhood with Jaime Longoria, Marcos Raya, José Oscar Moya, and Salvador Vega.

Ortega y Gasset, José

b. May 9, 1883
Madrid, Spain
d. October 18, 1955
Madrid, Spain
fields: Philosophy, Journalism

Ortega's books, journalism, and lectures commanded attention throughout Europe. His renown helped to bring Spain out of a long period of cultural isolation, and his thought contributed greatly to his country's intellectual reawakening.

Ortego y Gasca, Philip D.

b. Aug. 23, 1926
Blue Island, Ill.
fields: Education, Literature, Publishing

Latino educator, poet, and publisher. Philip D. Ortego y Gasca taught at New Mexico State University (1964-1970) and the University of Texas at El Paso (1970-1972), where he founded the Chicano studies program. He then joined the faculty of the Mexican American graduate studies program at San Jose State University in California. Ortego was chair of the Hispanic Foundation from 1982 to 1986. He has written more than 150 poems, essays, short stories, and reviews. He has also written several books. He edited *We Are Chicanos: An Anthology of Mexican-American Literature* (1973) and wrote the play *Madre del Sol*. He has served as editor in chief of the *National Hispanic Reporter*, and in 1972 was named senior editor and literary director of the magazine *La Luz*.

Ortiz, Carlos

b. Sept. 9, 1936
Ponce, Puerto Rico
fields: Sports (boxer)

Carlos Ortiz began his professional boxing career by going undefeated in his first twenty-seven matches. He won the junior welterweight title and defended it twice before losing it to Duilio Loi in 1960. In April, 1962, he won the lightweight title, then defended it four times before losing it to Ismael Laguna in April, 1965. Ortiz won the rematch seven months later and held it until June, 1968. He retired in 1971 with a career record of 65-9-1, including thirty-seven knockouts. In 1991, he was inducted into the International Boxing Hall of Fame.

Ortiz, Francis V., Jr.

b. Mar. 14, 1926
Santa Fe, N.Mex.
fields: Diplomacy

Mexican American diplomat. Francis V. Ortiz, Jr., served in foreign service posts in Ethiopia, Mexico, Peru, Uruguay, Argentina, Barbados, and Grenada. He served as the U.S. ambassador to Guatemala in 1979, as ambassador to Peru from 1981 to 1983, and as ambassador to Argentina from 1983 to 1986.

Ortiz, Manuel

b. July 2, 1916
Corona, Calif.
d. May 31, 1970
San Diego, Calif.
fields: Sports (boxer)

Mexican American boxer. Manuel Ortiz turned professional in 1938 and won the bantamweight belt in his second title bout. After losing several matches, Ortiz regained his form and took the bantamweight title from Tony Olivera in 1943. He defended the title fifteen times over the next several years, then lost it in January, 1947, to underdog Harold Dade. Ortiz regained the title two months later and held it until 1950. He retired with a record of 97-28-3, including 49 knockouts.

Ortiz, Simon

b. May 27, 1941
Albuquerque, N.Mex.
fields: Literature (poet)

An Acoma Pueblo and member of the Eagle clan, Simon Ortiz became a respected and widely read American Indian poet in the 1970's and 1980's. Books of poems include *Going for the Rain* (1976), *A Good Journey* (1977), and *Fight Back: For the Sake of the People, for the Sake of the Land* (1980). Also writes fiction.

Ortiz, Vilma

b. Apr. 15, 1954
New York, N.Y.
fields: Scholarship

Latina scholar. Vilma Ortiz, whose research focuses on the social conditions of Latinos in the United States, joined the faculty of the University of California, Los Angeles

(UCLA), in 1988. She became involved in a thirty-year follow-up study of the landmark *The Mexican-American People: The Nation's Second Largest Minority* (1970), written by Leo Grebler, Joan W. Moore, and Ralph C. Guzmán. The purpose of the follow-up was to produce the first major intergenerational study of Mexican Americans.

Ortiz Cofer, Judith

b. Feb. 24, 1952
Hormigueros, Puerto Rico
fields: Literature

Puerto Rican poet and novelist. Judith Ortiz Cofer immigrated to the United States in 1956 and earned college degrees in English literature. She has published the poetry volumes *Latin Women Pray* (1980), *The Native Dancer* (1981), *Among the Ancestors* (1981), *Peregrina* (1986), and *Terms of Survival* (1987); a collection of personal essays titled *Silent Dancing* (1990); and a collection titled *The Latin Deli: Prose and Poetry* (1993). She received critical praise for her first novel, *The Line of the Sun* (1989).

Ortiz Montañez, Rafael

aka: Ralph Ortiz
b. Jan. 30, 1934
New York, N.Y.
fields: Art

Mexican American sculptor and video artist. Rafael Ortiz Montañez, known professionally as Ralph Ortiz, became the leading destructive artist in the United States. He performed "Piano Destruction Concert" for a British Broadcasting Corporation television broadcast in 1966 and later performed the same piece for national broadcast in the United States. He is known for sculpture, exhibitions, concerts, theater performances, and lectures at universities, on the radio, and on television. His best-known work is *Montezuma.*

Orwell, George

né: Eric Arthur Blair
b. June 25, 1903
Motihari, Bengal, India
d. January 21, 1950
London, England
fields: Literature

Orwell's uncompromising ideals, reflected consistently in the enormous and diverse body of his works, entitle him to be considered among the most personally courageous writers in the history of British letters, one whose social concern and distinctive style can be compared only to those of the eighteenth century political and social satirist Jonathan Swift.

Ory, Kid

full: Edward Ory
b. December 25, 1886
La Place, La.
d. January 23, 1973
Honolulu, Hawaii
fields: Music (jazz trombonist, composer, and singer)

Creole trombonist, composer, and singer; as the leading exponent of the New Orleans "tailgate" style of trombone playing, which involves the use of mutes to achieve various vocalizations, Kid Ory was a prominent musician in New Orleans (1912-1919; leading a band that at various times included Louis Armstrong, Mutt Carey, and King Oliver); the band he formed while living in California (1919-1925) became the first all-African American New Orleans-style jazz band to have recordings released; after moving to Chicago in 1925, Ory participated in recording sessions with Louis Armstrong's Hot Five and Jelly Roll Morton's Red Hot Peppers; in 1944, Ory performed weekly on a radio program hosted by Orson Welles and sponsored by Standard Oil; in 1954 Ory's jazz composition "Muskrat Ramble" (1926) became a hit when new lyrics were added; in 1966 Ory retired to Hawaii.

Osborne, Thomas. *See* Leeds, first duke of

Osborne, Thomas Mott

b. September 23, 1859
Auburn, New York
d. October 20, 1926
Auburn, New York
fields: Social Reform

Osborne's theories of limited self-government encouraged prisoners to be responsible for their own group discipline. His plan reduced problems within the American prisons where he worked and German prisons in the 1920's and 1930's.

Osceola

b. c. 1804
Tallassee on the Tallapoosa River near present-day Tuskegee, Alabama
d. Jan. 30, 1838
Fort Moultrie, Charleston, South Carolina
fields: Military Affairs, Native American Affairs

Allegedly a participant in the First Seminole War, Osceola (a Creek) became a leader of the Seminoles, who refused to be moved west of the Mississippi; he initiated the Second Seminole War.

Oshkosh

aka: Oshkusi
aka: Oiscoss (His Hoof, His Nail, or the Brave)
b. 1795
Old King's Village on the Fox River near present-day Green Bay, Wis.
d. Aug. 20, 1858
Keshena, Wis.
fields: Government and Politics, Native American Affairs

Menominee Indian leader Oshkosh was first appointed chief by federal agents during mediation of a land dispute; he helped to negotiate removal of the Menominee Indians. Urged Menominee compliance with white authority. Menominee land claims were continuously eroded, and removal was completed when Wisconsin became a state in 1848 and Oshkosh signed the Treaty of Lake Powahekone.

Osler, William

aka: Sir William Osler
b. July 12, 1849
Bond Head, Ontario, Canada
d. December 29, 1919
Oxford, England
fields: Medicine

Osler published the original *Principles and Practice of Medicine*, a classic text for many years, and he transformed medical education by extending it beyond the classroom to the patient's bedside.

Osman

b. c. 1258
Söğüt, Turkey
d. 1326
Söğüt, Turkey
fields: Government and Politics, Warfare and Conquest

Under Osman's patient and steady leadership, the influence and territorial extent of his principality were expanded until it arose as a regional power, which, as the Ottoman Empire, ultimately became one of the great powers of the early modern world.

Osorio, Carlos

b. 1927
Caguas, Puerto Rico
fields: Art

Puerto Rican cartoonist and illustrator. From 1956 to 1964, Carlos Osorio illustrated books and designed posters for the Division of community Education in San Juan, Puerto Rico, then moved the United States in 1964. In 1969, he joined the Taller Boricua in New York city and was a founding member of El Museo del Barrio in New York. He returned to Puerto Rico in 1980.

Ostwald, Wilhelm

full: Friedrich Wilhelm Ostwald
b. September 2, 1853
Riga, Latvia

d. April 4, 1932
Grossbothen, near Leipzig, Germany
fields: Chemistry, Physics, Philosophy

Ostwald's most notable work was in the field of chemistry, in which he is considered to be the "father" of physical chemistry and in which he was awarded the 1909 Nobel Prize. He was later nominated for a second Nobel Prize, this time in physics, for his work in the field of color science.

Oswald, Lee Harvey

b. October 18, 1939
New Orleans, Louisiana
d. November 24, 1963
Dallas, Texas
fields: Historical Figure

Lee Harvey Oswald was the alleged assassin of President John F. Kennedy and Texas governor John B. Connally, on November 22, 1963. When captured, Oswald denied everything; two days later, while being transferred to another holding facility, he was shot and killed by Dallas nightclub owner Jack Ruby. The Warren Commission, established by President Lyndon B. Johnson to investigate the events leading to Kennedy's death, reported in September, 1964, that Oswald had acted alone. However, a congressional committee that later reexamined the evidence concluded, in its 1979 report, that the assassination was probably a conspiracy. A multitude of books have been published on the topic, including *Oswald's Tale: An American Mystery* (1995), by Pulitzer Prize-winning author Norman Mailer.

Ota, Kamado

b. 1884
Yonagusuku, Okinawa, Japan
d. July 7, 1958
fields: Business and Industry

Kamado Ota worked in Mexico before moving to California in 1905 and becoming a farmer. Ten years later, he became a founding partner in the Star Produce Company of Los Angeles, which became one of the area's most prosperous produce businesses. Ota played important roles in associations serving the area's Okinawan community. During World War II, he was interned in a detention camp and the U.S. government closed his business.

Ota, Shelley Ayame Nishimura

b. 1911
fields: Literature

Shelley Ayame Nishimura Ota wrote *Upon Their Shoulders* (1951), the first English-language novel about the Japanese-American experience, in particular about the life of a Japanese immigrant in Hawaii.

Otherday, John

aka: Angpetu Tokecha
aka: Other Day
b. 1801
Swan Lake, Minn.
d. 1871
Sisseton Sioux Reservation, S.Dak.
fields: Warfare and Conquest

Wahpeton Sioux. As an army scout and protector of whites, Otherday was honored by the U.S. government. After the Spirit Lake Uprising of 1857, he rescued white female captives and assisted in the search for Sioux raiders. During Little Crow's uprising of 1862-1863, he led white settlers to safety. In retaliation, Little Crow burned Otherday's home.

Otis, Mercy. *See* Warren, Mercy Otis

Otóah-hastis. *See* Tall Bull

Otte, Eileen. *See* Ford, Eileen

Otto, Nikolaus August

b. June 10, 1832
Holzhausen, Nassau
d. January 26, 1891
Cologne, Germany
fields: Invention and Technology

Otto invented the first internal-combustion, four-stroke engine. His engine is the forerunner of modern gasoline automobile engines.

Otto the Great

aka: Otto I
b. November 23, 912
Saxony
d. May 7, 973
Memleben, Thuringia
fields: Government and Politics, Monarchy

King of Germany, 936-973; German emperor, 962-973. Otto's decisive victory over the Magyars shaped the fate of Europe; his coronation as emperor determined the course of German policy for centuries to come. Internally, he overcame tribalism by putting central administration in the unifying hands of the Church.

Oubre, Hayward Louis

b. ?
New Orleans, La.
fields: Art (painter and sculptor)

African American painter and sculptor; from 1950 to 1965, Hayward Louis Oubre chaired the art department at Alabama State College; from 1965 to 1981, he chaired the art department at Winston-Salem State College; in 1984 Oubre became curator of the Selma Burke Art Gallery.

Ouchi, William George

b. June 28, 1943
Honolulu, Territory of Hawaii
fields: Business and Industry

Japanese American William George Ouchi became a professor at the Graduate School of Management at the University of California, Los Angeles, in 1979. He received an M.B.A. from Stanford University in 1967 and a Ph.D. in business administration from the University of Chicago in 1972. He wrote about Japanese business practices and described their applications for American companies. His publications include *Theory Z* (1981), *The M-Form Society* (1984), and *Organizational Economics* (1986).

Oud, J. J. P.

full: Jacobus Johannes Pieter Oud
b. February 9, 1890
Purmerend, The Netherlands
d. April 5, 1963
Wassenaar, The Netherlands
fields: Architecture

Oud is one of the founders of functional modern architecture, which through subtle techniques he imbued with an elegance and style achieved by few other architects. With a pronounced social commitment, Oud specialized in handsome yet low-cost housing and public buildings.

Ouray

aka: Willie Ouray
aka: Ure
b. c. 1820
northern Mexico, in present-day southern Colo.
d. Aug. 24, 1880
Ignacio, Colo.
fields: Government and Politics, Diplomacy, Native American Affairs

Native American (Ute) leader. Ouray led central Colorado (Uncompaghre) Utes from the mid-1860's to 1880, convincing them to conciliate rather than fight with encroaching whites. In 1873 Ouray cooperated in obtaining the necessary signatures to ratify a new agreement ceding more Ute lands, for which he was given special concessions as well as a $1,000 annual salary, a home, and a 400-acre ranch at a new agency. Adopted white lifestyle.

Ousamequin. *See* Massasoit

Ousley, Curtis. *See* King Curtis

Outram, James

aka: Sir James Outram
b. January 29, 1803
Butterley Hall, Derbyshire, England

d. March 11, 1863
Pau, France
fields: Military Affairs, Colonial Administration

Using a mixture of military force and sound administrative techniques, Outram helped to complete the construction of the British imperial system in India.

Outterbridge, John Wilfred

b. March 12, 1933
Greenville, N.C.
fields: Art (assemblage artist)

African American assemblage artist; John Wilfred Outterbridge served as director of the Watts Towers Art Center until 1992; was an inaugural recipient of the Artist-Nominated Awards, voted on by artists throughout Los Angeles County, in 1995.

Ou-yang Hsiu

b. 1007
Mien-yang (modern Szechwan Province), China
d. 1072
Ying-chou (modern Anhwei Province), China
fields: Literature, Government and Politics

A political figure and innovative writer of prose and poetry, Ou-yang Hsiu substantially shaped the Confucian tradition which dominated China for almost a thousand years.

Overstreet, Joe

full: Joseph Overstreet
b. 1934
Conehatta, Miss.
fields: Art (painter)

African American painter; Joe Overstreet expressed ironic social protest in his early paintings; he presented his later work on shaped canvases; this work showed a concern with sculptural space and symbols derived from Native Americans and Africans.

Ovid

né: Publius Ovidius Naso
b. March 20, 43 B.C.E.
Sulmo, Italy
d. 17 C.E.
Tomis on the Black Sea
fields: Literature

While his contemporaries Vergil and Horace were glorifying the Roman Empire or harking back to sober republican virtues, Ovid wittily celebrated the senses. He also preserved for later generations many of the classical myths, although he treated the gods with the same irreverence as he did his fellow mortals.

Ow, George, Sr.

b. c. 1920
Canton, China
fields: Business and Industry

Entrepreneur George Ow, Sr., who arrived in the United States in 1937, helped establish the city of Capitola in California. He built a large supermarket called Ow's King's Market on what had formerly been a cow pasture in the 1960's. Ow developed Capitola and the surrounding Scots Valley, building several shopping centers.

Ow, George, Jr.

b. January 3, 1943
Santa Cruz, Calif.
fields: Film

Chinese American documentary filmmaker George Ow, Jr., has worked on films such as *A Dollar a Day, Ten Cents a Dance* (1984), *Mi vida: The Three Worlds of Maria Gutierrez* (1986), and *Chinese Gold: The Chinese of the Monterey Bay* (1987).

Owen, Robert

b. May 14, 1771
Newtown, Montgomeryshire, Wales
d. November 17, 1858
Newtown, Montgomeryshire, Wales
fields: Business and Industry, Social Reform

Best known for his Utopian community of New Harmony in Indiana, Owen was both one of the leaders of the early Industrial Revolution and one of its greatest critics. He developed the cotton-spinning factory while demonstrating the efficiency and productivity which resulted from the benevolent treatment of workers. He pioneered in educational reform and became the chief spokesman for the cooperative movement.

Owens, Dana. *See* Queen Latifah

Owens, Frances Marion. *See* Marion, Frances

Owens, Jesse

full: James Cleveland Owens
b. September 12, 1913
Oakville, Ala.
d. March 31, 1980
Tucson, Ariz.
fields: Sports (track and field athlete)

African American track and field athlete; Jesse Owens tied the world record in the 100-yard dash as a high school senior; while working his way through Ohio State University, Owens set three world records and tied a fourth at one track meet on May 25, 1935; he is best remembered for his performance at the 1936 Olympics held in Berlin, Germany, at which he earned gold medals in the 100-meter run (tying the Olympic record), the 200-meter run, the long jump, and the 400-meter relay, setting new Olympic records in the latter three events; as a result of racism, Owens was unable to find decent-paying work and thus was unable to finish his college education following his return from the Olympics; he was finally able to earn a living from his fame when, in 1955, the U.S. government sent him around the world as an "ambassador of sports"; Owens posthumously was awarded the Congressional Gold Medal in 1990.

Owens, Major Robert Odell

b. June 28, 1936
Memphis, Tenn.
fields: Government and Politics

African American U.S. representative from New York; from 1974 to 1982, Major Robert Odell Owens served as representative for the Brownsville and East New York sections of Brooklyn in the New York State Senate; in November, 1982, Owens was elected as U.S. representative from New York's Twelfth District and went on to serve four additional terms; during his tenure in Congress, Owens served as a senior member of the House Committee on Education and Labor, as a member of the House Committee on Government Operations, and as chairman of the House Subcommittee on Select Education (1987); from 1983 into the 1990's, Owens served as chairman of the Congressional Black Caucus Higher Education Brain Trust.

Oxenstierna, Axel

b. June 16, 1583
Fanö, near Uppsala, Sweden
d. August 28, 1654
Stockholm, Sweden
fields: Government and Politics

Combining intellect, courage, humor, and integrity, Oxenstierna mastered every aspect of state service and helped Gustavus II Adolphus to produce Sweden's age of greatness. As chancellor for Queen Christina, he was largely responsible for New Sweden on the Delaware.

Oyama, Joe

b. Sept. 8, 1912
Suisun, Calif.
fields: Journalism

Joe Oyama was a board member of the New York chapter of the Japanese American Citizens League (1944-1976) and the Japanese American Association of New York and president of the Japanese American News Corporation in New York City (1945). He moved to California in 1976, and his articles have appeared in numerous newspapers, including the *Pacific Citizen*, *Rafu Shimpo*, *Kashu Mainichi—California Daily News*,

San Francisco Nichibei, and *The New World Sun*.

Özal, Turgut

b. October 13, 1927
Malatya, Turkey
d. April 17, 1993
Ankara, Turkey
fields: Government and Politics

Turgut Özal was prime minister (1983-1989) and then president (1989-1993) of Turkey. A pro-Western conservative with a flamboyant personal style, he instituted economic reforms, lifting many economic controls and repealing import quotas. Gradually won government control away from Turkish military. In early 1990's began to lose popularity and faced a newly divided government. Died in office in 1993.

Ozawa, Seiji

b. September 1, 1935
Hoten, Manchuria
fields: Music (classical)

Seiji Ozawa began his conducting career in 1959 with the Japan Radio Orchestra and the Japan Philharmonic Orchestra. In 1960 he was made an assistant conductor for the New York Philharmonic Orchestra, making his debut with that orchestra on April 14, 1961. From 1966 until 1970 he was the Toronto Symphony Orchestra's permanent conductor, then moving to the San Francisco Orchestra as music director. In 1973 he took over the highly coveted musical directorship of the Boston Symphony Orchestra. In 1984, Ozawa formed the Saito Kinen Orchestra. In 1999 he announced that he would be leaving the Boston Symphony in 2002 to go to the Vienna State Opera.

P

Pace, Judy

b. 1946
Los Angeles, Calif.
fields: Television, Film

African American actress; Judy Pace's television credits include recurring roles in the series *Peyton Place* and *The Young Lawyers* (late 1960's and early 1970's), and guest appearances in *The Mod Squad* (1968) and *Sanford and Son* (1982); her film credits include *The Thomas Crown Affair* (1968), *Cotton Comes to Harlem* (1970), and *Frogs* (1972).

Pacelli, Eugenio Maria Giuseppe Giovanni.
See Pius XII

Pachacuti

aka: Cusi Inca Yupanqui
aka: Pachacutec Inca Yupanqui
b. c. 1391
probably Cuzco, Peru
d. 1471
near Cuzco, Peru
fields: Government and Politics, Warfare and Conquest

Inca emperor, 1438-1471. Pachacuti, through personal courage, brilliant political sense, and administrative genius, was primarily responsible for the creation of the Inca Empire in its final form.

Pacheco, Alex

b. ?
fields: Conservation and Environmentalism

Animal rights activist. Alex Pacheco cofounded People for the Ethical Treatment of Animals (PETA) in 1980 along with Ingrid Newkirk. The group has orchestrated laboratory break-ins and government office occupations in the name of animal rights..

Pacheco, Romualdo

b. Oct. 31, 1831
Santa Barbara, Calif.
d. Jan. 23, 1899
Oakland, Calif.
fields: Government and Politics

Latino politician. Romualdo Pacheco became a California senator as a Democrat in 1858. He served as brigadier general in a battalion of "Native Cavalry" formed by President Abraham Lincoln during the Civil War. In 1871, he was elected lieutenant governor as a Republican, then took the governorship in 1875 when the incumbent, Newton Booth, took an interim seat in the U.S. Senate. From 1879 to 1883, Pacheco served two terms as Santa Clara's congressman in Washington, D.C.

Packwood, Bob

full: Robert Packwood
b. Sept. 16, 1932
Portland, Oreg.
fields: Government and Politics

U.S. senator. Robert Packwood was first elected a U.S. senator from Oregon in 1968. He rose to the chairmanship of the Appropriations Committee and won a fifth term in 1992. Soon thereafter, evidence emerged that he had sexually harassed a number of women. In 1995, Senate Ethics Committee recommended his expulsion, and he resigned from the Senate.

Padilla, Amado Manuel

b. Oct. 18, 1942
Albuquerque, N.Mex.
fields: Education

Educator. Amado Manuel Padilla has taught at the State University of New York; the University of California, Santa Barbara; the University of California, Los Angeles; Stanford University; and Pontifica Universidad Catolica de Peru. He won the Distinguished Scholar Award by the American Educational Research Association in 1987 and the Distinguished Research Award by the same group in 1988. Padilla has written several books on bilingual education, Latino mental health and identity, and other topics. Among his publications are *Crossing Cultures in Therapy: Pluralistic Counseling for the Hispanic* (1980, coauthored with Elaine Levine) and *Chicano Ethnicity* (1987).

Padilla, Benjamín

aka: Kaskabel
b. ?
Guadalajara, Mexico
d. ?
fields: Literature

Writer. Benjamín Padilla, a Mexican who lived in the United States, wrote sketches of life in the Southwest between 1910 and 1929 and published them in newspapers under the name "Kaskabel" (rattlesnake).

Padilla, Heberto

b. Jan. 20, 1932
Pinar del Río, Cuba
fields: Literature

Cuban poet and novelist. Heberto Padilla left Cuba during the reign of Fulgencio Batista and returned when Fidel Castro took over in 1959. His second book of poetry, *Fuera de juego* (1968), won the first prize of the Cuban Union of Writers and Artists. On April 27, 1971, Padilla publicly denounced prominent writers, journalists, economists, friends, and even his wife as enemies of the Cuban Revolution. He was ostracized and moved to the United States in 1980. Among his books of poetry are *El justo tiempo humano* (1962), *Fuera del juego*, and *El hombre junto al mar* (1981; *Legacies*, 1982). He also published the novel *En mi jardin pastan los heroes* (1982; *Heroes Are Grazing in My Garden*, 1984).

Padilla, Juan de

b. c. 1500
Andalusia, Spain
d. 1542
Kansas
fields: Theology and Religion, Exploration and Colonization

Spanish priest and explorer. Juan de Padilla went on an expedition with Francisco Vázquez de Coronado to Cíbola. In 1539, he was sent on another expedition that occupied Hawikuh and Tiguex. Finding no gold or silver, another trip was organized, this time to Quivira, located in modern Kansas, where Padilla built a large cross. When the expedition returned to Mexico, Padilla stayed behind to convert the Indians to Catholicism. He then returned to Quivira and found his cross intact. He began missionary work but was killed by Indians in 1542.

Paganini, Niccolò

b. October 27, 1782
Genoa, Republic of Genoa (now Italy)
d. May 27, 1840
Nice, Kingdom of Sardinia (now France)
fields: Music

From his own time to the present, Niccolò Paganini has been considered one of the greatest violinists the world has ever known. He was the father of the freelance virtuosi—master musicians who made their living by giving public concerts. His astonishing feats of skill on the violin, his uncanny dramatic flair, and the compelling rumors and legends spawned by his colorful lifestyle all combined to captivate the imagination of audiences throughout early nineteenth century Europe and distinguish him as one of the most intriguing figures in music history.

Page, Alan

b. August 7, 1945
Canton, Ohio
fields: Sports (football player), Government and Politics

African American football player; Alan Page led the Minnesota Vikings to four Super Bowls and, in 1971, became the first defensive player ever to win the National Football League's Most Valuable Player Award; in 1987, he became Minnesota state assistant attorney general; in 1988 Page was inducted into the Pro Football Hall of Fame. In 1992, he became the first African American elected to the Minnesota Supreme Court.

Page, Clarence E.

b. June 2, 1947
Dayton, Ohio
fields: Journalism

African American journalist; Clarence E. Page, a nationally syndicated and award-winning columnist, also appeared as a regular panelist on *The McLaughlin Group* television news program; was a frequent guest on the PBS television program *The MacNeil/Lehrer News Hour* and the Black Entertainment Television (BET) program *Lead Story*; appeared on the National Public Radio program "Weekend Edition Sunday"; authored *Showing My Color: Impolite Essays on Race in America* (1996).

Page, Geraldine

b. November 22, 1924
Kirksville, Missouri
d. June 13, 1987
New York, New York
fields: Theater and Entertainment (actor), Film

A dedicated stage and screen actress of consummate skill, Geraldine Page first earned great critical acclaim for her interpretation of sensual, neurotic women in plays by Tennessee Williams. She was a brilliant method actress who, for thirty years, had few serious rivals in the mastery of that technique.

Page, Hot Lips

full: Oran Thaddeus Page
b. January 27, 1908
Dallas, Tex.
d. November 5, 1954
New York, N.Y.
fields: Music (blues trumpeter, singer, and bandleader)

African American trumpeter, singer, and bandleader; a talented blues instrumentalist and singer often compared to Louis Armstrong, Hot Lips Page worked the Theatre Owners Booking Association circuit before playing with other bands including Walter Page's Blue Devils (1928-1931), Bennie Moten's band (1931-1935), Count Basie's band (1936; billed as "the trumpet king of the West"), and Artie Shaw's band (1941-1942; releasing the hit recording "St. James Infirmary"); he also fronted a number of his own bands in New York, Boston, and Chicago and toured Europe; in 1949 he recorded with Pearl Bailey the single "Baby It's Cold Outside"/'The Hucklebuck' and attended the Paris Jazz Festival; Page worked as a featured soloist until suffering a heart attack in 1954.

Pagerie, Marie-Joséphe-Rose Tascher de la. *See* Joséphine

Paglia, Camille

b. April 2, 1947
Endicott, N.Y.
fields: Literature

Camille Paglia is known for her criticism of the feminist establishment. A controversial figure, she became popular with the publication of *Sexual Personae: Art and Decadence from Nefertiti to Emily Dickinson* (1990). Paglia believes feminists have presented a one-sided image of men and that there exist biological truths to sexual stereotypes.

Paiea. *See* Kamehameha I

Paige, Emmett, Jr.

b. February 20, 1931
Jacksonville, Fla.
fields: Military Affairs, Warfare and Conquest

African American military officer; during his thirty-year U.S. Army career, Emmett Paige, Jr., rose to the rank of Lieutenant General; his postings included combat duty in Vietnam (August, 1968-January, 1970), deputy chief of staff for the Army Communications Command and later commander of the Eleventh Signal Group, commanding general of the Army Communications Systems Agency in New Jersey and later commanding general of the Communications Research and Development Command there, and commanding general of the Information Systems Command at Fort Huachuca, Arizona; he retired on June 30, 1988.

Paige, Satchel

full: Leroy Robert Paige
b. July ?, 1906
Mobile, Ala.
d. June 8, 1982
Kansas City, Mo.
fields: Sports (baseball player)

African American baseball player; famous for a blistering fast ball and pinpoint control, Satchel Paige was one of baseball's greatest pitchers; Paige pitched on some of the best teams in Negro League history, including playing for the Pittsburgh Crawfords in the 1930's; in 1948 the major league ban on African American players was eased, and Paige helped the Cleveland Indians win the 1948 pennant (winning six games and losing one while posting a 2.48 earned run average) and the World Series (he retired the two batters that he faced as a relief pitcher in game five); from 1951 through 1953, he pitched with the St. Louis Browns and made the All-Star team in 1952; at almost sixty years old, Paige pitched three innings with the Kansas City Athletics in 1965 and allowed only one hit; in 1971 he was inducted into the Baseball Hall of Fame.

Paik, Hark-joon

b. 1935
Seoul, Korea
fields: Law

Hark-joon Paik received a B.A. degree from Stanford University in 1958 and a J.D. degree from Stanford Law School in 1961. His appointment as justice for the Superior Court of Monterey County in 1975 made him the first naturalized Korean American to become a California judge. He received the Freedom Foundation Award at Valley Forge. He is coauthor of the *California Complex Litigation Manual* (1991).

Paik, Naim June

b. July 20, 1932
Seoul, Korea
fields: Art, Theater and Entertainment

Naim June Paik was studying music in Germany in 1958 when he met experimental composer John Cage. Paik was impressed by the American's unpredictable public performances and began performing "action music"—collages of his own live piano playing, taped noises, and the sounds produced by such incongruous "instruments" as motorcycles and telephones, accompanied by outrageous onstage behavior. Paik worked with the Fluxus group, a loose confederation of avant-garde artists influenced by the principles of Dadaism. His later works, which use video technology as an art form, include *Global Groove* (1973) and *Guadalcanal Requiem* (1977).

Paine, Thomas

né: Thomas Pain
b. January 29, 1737
Thetford, England
d. June 8, 1809
New York, New York
fields: Government and Politics, Literature, Science

Paine was a participant in both the American and French revolutions, and, through his writings, he attempted to foment revolution in England as well. He was interested in the new scientific ideas of his age, spent considerable energy on the design of an iron-arch bridge, and tried to resolve the age-old conflicts between science and religion by espousing Deism.

Painter, Nell Irvin

b. August 2, 1942
Houston, Tex.
fields: Historiography

African American historian; Nell Irvin Painter's published works include *Exodus-*

ters: Black Migration to Kansas After Reconstruction (1977), *The Narrative of Hosea Hudson: His Life as a Negro Communist in the South* (1979), and *Sojourner Truth: A Life, a Symbol* (1996); her scholarship focuses on the Progressive and Reconstruction periods in the American South.

Paisley, Ian

full: Ian Richard Kyle Paisley
b. April 6, 1926
Armagh, Northern Ireland
fields: Government and Politics

Northern Ireland Protestant religious and political leader. Began rise to prominence in the late 1960's. Elected to the Northern Ireland parliament and then the United Kingdom parliament, both in 1970. Helped found the Democratic Unionist Party (DUP) in 1971; became its leader. By late 1970's, leading spokesman for radical Protestant unionism. Continued to be so in 1980's and 1990's.

Paiute Prophet. *See* Tavibo

Pak, Ty

b. 1938
Korea
fields: Journalism

Ty Pak had been a reporter in Korea for five years when he immigrated to the United States. He received a doctoral degree in English literature from Bowing Green State University, then taught in the English department at the University of Hawaii. In 1983, he published *Guilt Payment* (1983), a collection of short stories.

Pak Un-sik

b. 1861
d. 1926
fields: Historiography

Historian Pak Un-sik wrote two nationalist histories of Korea in the 1920's. Pak hoped to ignite a new sense of national pride and self-respect among the Korean people, who had been under Japanese occupation since before 1910.

Pak Yong-man. *See* Park Yong-man

Palacios, Monica

b. June 14, 1959
San Jose, Calif.
fields: Literature, Theater and Entertainment

Writer and performer. Monica Palacios began performing stand-up comedy at both mainstream and alternative clubs and events during the 1980's. In 1991, she developed a solo performance entitled *Latin Lezbo Comic*. In addition to writing short stories, Palacios has worked on a touring lecture/performance called *Greetings from a Queer Señorita*; one-act plays, including *La llorona loca* and *Seagullita*; a festival of Latina artists called *Fierce Tongues/Women of Fire*; and *Confessions*, a spoken-word and slide show. She has also worked as a producer, writer, and performer with VIVA, an association of lesbian and gay Latino artists.

Palés Matos, Luis

b. Mar. 20, 1898
Guayama, Puerto Rico
d. Feb. 23, 1959
Santurce, Puerto Rico
fields: Literature

Puerto Rican poet; Luis Palés Matos worked as a secretary, bookkeeper, and journalist as he developed his poetic craft; founded the short-lived San Juan avant-garde literary movement, Diepalismo in 1921; from the mid-1920's, developed (with Nicolas Guillen) the literary movement known as Negrismo, exalting black contributions to Latin American history and culture, which was controversial because he was white; abandoned Negrista poetry in the 1940's; wrote *Azaleas* (1915), *Sonetos del Campo* (1915), *Tuntún de pasa y grifería* (1937), *Drumbeats of Kink and Blackness* (1937), *Poesia 1915-1956* (1957).

Palladio, Andrea

né: Andrea di Pietro della Gondola
b. November 30, 1508
Padua, Republic of Venice
d. August, 1580
Vicenza, Republic of Venice
fields: Architecture

Palladio was the first great professional architect and one of the most influential the world has ever known. Possibly the most imitated architect in history, he was responsible for fusing classical proportions and harmony with Renaissance exuberance, thus creating an architectural manner that has endured into the twentieth century.

Palma, Tomás Estrada. *See* Estrada Palma, Tomás

Palmer, Alice Freeman

né: Alice Elvira Freeman
b. February 21, 1855
Colesville, New York
d. December 6, 1902
Paris, France
fields: Education

The second president of Wellesley College, Palmer championed the cause of educational reform for women, greatly influencing attitudes of educators and society at large concerning the need for quality education for women at every level.

Palmer, Arnold

full: Arnold Daniel Palmer
b. September 10, 1929
Youngstown, Pennsylvania
fields: Sports (golf)

By 1960, Arnold Palmer was the leading golf player on the professional tour, a role he shared with Jack Nicklaus after the mid-1960's. Their rivalry, as promoted by the media, initiated a golf boom. Palmer won sixty-one pro tournaments, not counting senior or non-U.S. wins. His dramatic victory in the 1960 U.S. Open and his Masters victories in 1958, 1960, 1962, and 1964 are among the leading events in the history of golf in the United States, and they helped to establish Palmer as a media celebrity and golf as a television attraction. In the 1980's however, he became one of the leading stars of the new PGA Senior Tour, which owed its success in large part to his continuing popularity.

Palmerston, Lord

né: Henry John Temple
aka: Henry John Temple, Third Viscount Palmerston
aka: Lord Pam
b. October 20, 1784
Westminster, London, England
d. October 18, 1865
Brocket Hall, Hertfordshire, England
fields: Government and Politics, Diplomacy

Lord Palmerston made aggressive use of military and naval power to ensure security for British commerce, while attempting to work closely with France to avoid any risk of war.

Palmieri, Charlie

full: Carlos Manuel Palmieri
b. Nov. 21, 1927
Manhattan, N.Y.
d. Sept. 12, 1988
Bronx, N.Y.
fields: Music (pianist, bandleader, and composer)

Latino pianist, bandleader, and composer. Charlie Palmieri attended the Juilliard School of Music in Manhattan and went on to play piano and record with Rafael Muñoz, Pupi Campo, Xavier Cugat, Tito Puente, and Vicentico Valdés, as well as with the Orquesta Ritmo Tropical, La Playa Sextet, and Conjunto Pin Pin between 1940 and the early 1950's. Palmieri, who contributed to the birth of salsa, recorded such singles as "Let's Dance La Charanga!," "Pachanga at the Caravana Club," "Viva Alegre," and "Salsa Na' Ma for Alegre," as well as the legendary Cuban Jam Session albums *El Gigante del Teclado*, *Vuelve el Gigante*, and *Adelante, Gigante*.

Palomino, Carlos

b. Aug. 10, 1949
San Luis, Mexico
fields: Sports (boxer)

Mexican boxer. Carlos Palomino won the World Boxing Council (WBC) welterweight title in 1976 and defended it seven times before losing to Wilfredo Benitez in 1979. He retired with a professional record of 27 wins, 3 losses, and 3 draws.

Palomino, Ernesto Ramírez

b. Dec. 21, 1933
Fresno, Calif.
fields: Art

Latino artist. Ernesto Ramírez Palomino has worked as a painter, sculptor, muralist, and filmmaker. His master's thesis project at San Francisco State University was a 450-minute film titled *My Trip in a '52 Ford* that used objects as characters. In the early 1960's, he concentrated on found-object art that had few references to the Chicano experience but subsequently began working with Luis Valdez of the Teatro Campesino in order to express his Chicano points of view. Palomino began teaching in the La Raza Studies department at Fresno State University in 1970. In 1978, he began directing summer programs in which young people painted murals.

Pan Ku

b. 32 C.E.
place unknown
d. 92 C.E.
Lo-yang, China
fields: Historiography

Through his compilation of the *Han shu*, Pan Ku preserved a full, well-documented record for this vital period of Chinese history and set the standard for all subsequent dynastic histories of China.

Pandit, Sakaram Ganesh

b. ?
Ahmadabad, Gujarat State, India
fields: Law

After the *United States v. Bhagat Singh Thind* (1923) decision declaring people of Asian Indian origin ineligible for citizenship, the U.S. Justice department brought denaturalization proceedings against attorney Sakaram Ganesh Pandit, naturalized in 1914. Pandit won a favorable legal opinion in 1924, but the opinion was challenged through appeals. In November, 1926, courts upheld the 1924 decision. In 1919, Pandit had successfully argued that Mohan Singh, an Asian Indian, was eligible for citizenship, but the Supreme Court's 1923 decision made Singh ineligible.

Pandit, Vijaya Lakshmi

né: Swarup Kumari Nehru
b. August 18, 1900
Allahabad, India
d. December 1, 1990
Dehra Dun, India
fields: Diplomacy, Government and Politics

Pandit served as post-independence India's foremost diplomatic representative, holding the highest positions in international councils and in many ways helping to reconcile the bitter and deep disputes between India, its neighbors, and its former rulers.

Pankhurst, Emmeline

né: Emmeline Goulden
b. July 14, 1858
Manchester, England
d. June 14, 1928
London, England
fields: Social Reform

Pankhurst fought to attain the vote for British women during the early years of the twentieth century, organizing the militant Women's Social and Political Union into an effective tool for obtaining women's rights.

Pantoja, Antonia

b. 1922
San Juan, Puerto Rico
fields: Education

Educator and administrator. Antonia Pantoja moved to the United States in 1943. In 1958, she cofounded the Puerto Rican Forum, which led to the 1961 founding of ASPIRA, which promotes higher education for Puerto Ricans. Between 1968 and 1970, she taught at the University of Puerto Rico and established ASPIRA clubs in that country. In 1970, Pantoja established the Universidad Boricua and Puerto Rican Research and Resource Center in Washington, D.C. She then cofounded the Graduate School for Community Development at San Diego State University. In the mid-1980's, Pantoja returned to Puerto Rico to develop Producir, a group that promotes self-sufficiency by creating jobs.

Paoli, Amalia

b. January 31, 1861
Ponce, Puerto Rico
fields: Music

Puerto Rican singer. Amalia Paoli, along with her brother, Antonio, moved to Spain in 1885 to pursue their studies. Amalia obtained a scholarship to study voice under baritone Napoleón Vergez, then made her operatic debut at the Teatro Real de Madrid in 1891, in the opera *Aida*. Two years later, she performed at the Teatro Manzoni in Milan, in Gaetano Donizetti's opera *La Favorita*. In 1895, she moved back to Spain to guide her younger brother's musical training. In 1897, they moved to Italy for further voice study.

Paoli, Antonio

b. April 14, 1871
Ponce, Puerto Rico
d. 1946
fields: Music

Puerto Rican singer. Antonio Paoli's early voice training was guided by his sister, Amalia Paoli. His operatic debut came at the Paris Opera in 1899, in the role of Arnold in Gioacchino Rossini's opera *Guillaume Tell.* He spent the 1900-1901 season at the Opera at Covent Garden in London. In 1901, he toured Puerto Rico, Cuba, and the United States. In 1907, he made the first complete recorded version of the leading role of Canio in the opera *I Pagliacci* by Ruggero Leoncavallo. His career peaked between 1908 and 1914, although he continued singing until 1928, when began teaching at the University of Puerto Rico.

Papandreou, Andreas

full: Andreas George Papandreou
b. February 5, 1919
Chios, Greece
d. June 23, 1996
Ekáli, near Athens, Greece
fields: Government and Politics

Prime minister of Greece from 1981 to 1989 and from 1993 to 1996. Andreas Papandreou was educated as an economist and spent many years living abroad; returned to Greece when military government fell in 1974. A leftist, he formed the Pasok Party in 1974. Criticized Greece's entrance into European Community (Common Market) in 1981. In 1981 became first socialist prime minister of Greece. Charged with financial wrongdoing; party lost the 1989 elections. Acquitted of the charges in 1992, and he again became prime minister in 1993. By 1995, his health had deteriorated so that he could no longer take an active role in governing. Resigned 1996.

Papen, Franz von

b. October 29, 1879
Werl, Westphalia, Germany
d. May 2, 1969
Obersasbach, Baden-Württemberg, West Germany
fields: Military Affairs, Government and Politics

After serving six months as German chancellor in 1932, Papen masterminded the backstairs appointment of Adolf Hitler to power on January 30, 1933. In the years that followed, he served the Third Reich as vice-chancellor (1933-1934) and ambassador to Austria (1934-1938) and Turkey (1939-1944).

Papin, Denis

b. August 22, 1647
near Blois, France
d. c. 1712
probably London, England
fields: Invention and Technology

Papin was one of the first to realize the potential of steam for the production of power in a piston engine.

Pappus

b. c. 300
Alexandria, Egypt
d. c. 350
place unknown
fields: Mathematics

Pappus provided a valuable compilation of the contributions of earlier mathematicians and inspired later work on algebraic solutions to geometric problems.

Paracelsus

né: Philippus Aureolus Theophrastus Bombast von Hohenheim
b. November 11 or December 17, 1493
Einsiedeln, Swiss Confederation
d. September 24, 1541
Salzburg, Austria
fields: Biochemistry, Chemistry, Medicine, Philosophy

Paracelsus has been hailed as the founder of biochemistry. He also made major contributions to the development of modern chemistry and made revolutionary changes in Renaissance medical theory and practice.

Pardo, Jorge

b. 1951
Havana, Cuba
fields: Art (sculptor)

Latino sculptor. Jorge Pardo moved to the United States with his parents when he was a child. His sculpture, which is influenced by French artist Marcel Duchamp, is characterized by the transformation of "found" objects into artworks. Among his sculptures are *A Skateboard Ramp* and *Six Bank of America Counters, Altadena Calif.*

Paredes, Américo

b. September 3, 1915
Brownsville, Tex.
fields: Scholarship

Folklorist, educator, and writer Américo Paredes served as editor of the *Journal of American Folklore* and the book *Folktales of Mexico* (1970). His best-known publication, *"With His Pistol in His Hand": A Border Ballad and Its Hero* (1958), concerns the ballad of Gregorio Cortez. His other publications include *George Washington Gómez: A Mexicotexan Novel* (1990) and *Between Two Worlds* (1991). His work drew scholarly attention to border culture and helped inspire the Chicano movement. With George I. Sánchez, he founded the University of Texas Mexican American studies program.

Parentucelli, Tommaso. *See* Nicholas V

Parish, Robert L., Jr.

b. August 30, 1953
Shreveport, La.
fields: Sports (basketball player)

African American basketball player; in the 1976 NBA draft, center Robert L. Parish, Jr., was the eighth draft pick of the Golden State Warriors; after four seasons, Parish was traded to the Boston Celtics; as a consistently effective scorer, rebounder, and defender, Parish joined Kevin McHale and Larry Bird to help the Celtics win NBA championships in 1981, 1984, and 1986. After playing for the Charlotte Hornets in 1994 and 1995, he finished his career in 1997 with another NBA championship playing for the Chicago Bulls.

Parizeau, Jacques

b. Aug. 9, 1930
Montreal, Québec, Canada
fields: Government and Politics, Economics

French-Canadian economist and politician. A longtime member of Québec's provincial legislature, Jacques Parizeau served as minister of finance and in 1994 was sworn in as premier of Québec. A member and onetime president of the Parti Québécois, Parizeau is dedicated to the separation of French-speaking Québec from Canada.

Park Chan Ho

b. June 30, 1973
Kong Ju City, South Korea
fields: Sports (baseball)

As an amateur pitcher playing college baseball in Korea, Park Chan Ho was scouted by U.S. major-league teams. The Los Angeles Dodgers of the National League signed him to a lucrative contract, and in April, 1994, Park became the first Korean to play in the major leagues.

Park Chung Hee

b. September 30 or November 14, 1917
near Taegu, Korea
d. October 26, 1979
Seoul, South Korea
fields: Government and Politics

Park Chung Hee staged a military coup on May 16, 1961, seizing power from Prime Minister Chang Myon. He made himself president of South Korea but was, in turn, assassinated in 1979 by Korean Central Intelligence Agency (KCIA) director Kim Jae Kyu.

Park, Joseph

b. Oct. 13, 1906
Honolulu, Territory of Hawaii
fields: Chemistry

Korean American Joseph Park, who received a doctorate from Ohio State University in 1937, was one of the leading American organic fluorine chemists. Park became a research supervisor for E. I. du Pont de Nemours and Company in 1944, and in 1947, joined the faculty of the University of Colorado, Boulder. He was made a professor of chemistry in 1953.

Park, Mungo

b. September 10, 1771
near Selkirk, Scotland
d. 1806
near Bussa on the Niger River
fields: Exploration and Colonization

Combining great ambition with tremendous courage and stamina, Park discovered and died in his efforts to traverse the Niger River in Western Africa.

Park, Robert E.

full: Robert Ezra Park
b. February 14, 1864
Harveyville, Pennsylvania
d. February 7, 1944
Nashville, Tennessee
fields: Sociology, Journalism

Robert Ezra Park was an early sociologist and journalist; reporter and editor in Minneapolis, Chicago, and Detroit, 1887-1898; on faculty at Harvard, 1904-1905, University of Chicago, 1914-1933, and Fisk University, 1936-1943; secretary to Booker T. Washington; became an expert in the study of African American sociology; wrote *The Immigrant Press and Its Control* (1922), *Race and Culture* (1950), *Human Communities* (1952).

Park Yong-man

né: Pak Yong-man
b. 1881
Kangwon Province, Korea
d. Oct. 17, 1928
Beijing, China
fields: Government and Politics

Korean nationalist Park Yong-man believed that independence from Japan required direct military confrontation, so in 1909, he established the Korean Youth Military Academy in Nebraska along with four other centers. The centers were consolidated in 1913 as the Korean National Brigade. Park went to Shanghai after the demonstrations that initiated the March First movement and briefly served as minister of foreign affairs in the Korean provisional government in exile. After clashing with Syngman Rhee, he trained a corps of Korean exiles in Manchuria. He was assassinated, probably by a rival faction in the independence movement, in 1928.

Parker, Barrington Daniels

b. November 17, 1915
Rosslyn, Va.
fields: Law

African American federal judge; in 1969 President Richard M. Nixon appointed Barrington Daniels Parker to the post of U.S. district judge for the District of Columbia; during his time on the federal bench, Parker also served as an adjunct professor at Washington College of Law at American University (1972-1977); he also served as a member of the District of Columbia Commission on Judicial Disabilities and Tenure.

Parker, Charlie

full: Charles Christopher Parker, Jr.
b. August 29, 1920
Kansas City, Kansas
d. March 12, 1955
New York, New York
fields: Music

Through mastery of the alto saxophone and broad knowledge of modern and contemporary music, Parker established himself as a virtuoso performer. He began as a bebop musician and soon earned, through his innovations in harmony and diverse improvisations, a lasting reputation as a key figure in the emergence of modern jazz.

Parker, Dave

full: David Gene Parker
b. June 9, 1951
Calhoun, Miss.
fields: Sports (baseball player)

African American baseball player; during his tenure with the Pittsburgh Pirates, Dave Parker won consecutive batting titles in 1977 and 1978; in 1978 he also received the National League's Most Valuable Player award; Parker has also played for the Cincinnati Reds and the Oakland Athletics, among other teams.

Parker, Dorothy

né: Dorothy Rothschild
b. August 22, 1893
West End, New Jersey
d. June 7, 1967
New York, New York
fields: Literature

Parker's ironic wit, astute observations, and acute verse, along with her place at the Algonquin Round Table, made her one of the twentieth century's most popular writers.

Parker, Ely Samuel

aka: Donehogawa
aka: Hasanoanda (the Reader, or Coming to the Front)
b. c. 1828
near Pembroke, N.Y.
d. Aug. 31, 1895
Fairfield, Conn.
fields: Native American Affairs, Government and Politics

Seneca tribal chief and government official; Ely Samuel Parker was chosen as a young man to assist Seneca delegations to the New York state and U.S. federal government; met and assisted Lewis Henry Morgan in the collection of data on the Seneca in 1844, leading to Morgan's anthropological study, *League of the Ho-de-no-sau-nee, or Iroquois* (1851); denied admittance to the New York bar because he was not a U.S. citizen; became an engineer, finally accepting a position in Galena, Illinois in 1857, where he met Ulysses S. Grant; commissioned a captain in the Union army in 1863, eventually becoming Grant's military secretary (1864-1866); transcribed the documents at Appomattox enumerating the surrender terms that ended the Civil War; first Indian appointed commissioner of Indian Affairs, 1869-1871.

Parker, Henry Ellsworth

b. February 14, 1928
Baltimore, Md.
fields: Government and Politics

African American state official; Henry Ellsworth Parker held the position of Connecticut state treasurer from 1976 to 1986 ; Parker was elected president of the National Association of State Treasurers in 1985.

Parker, James Thomas

b. April 2, 1934
Macon, Ga.
fields: Sports (football player)

African American football player; James Thomas Parker was the Baltimore Colts' first-round draft pick in 1957; in 1958, 1959, 1964, 1965, and 1967, Parker played central roles on the Colts' Western Conference championship teams; from 1959 through 1966, he participated in Pro Bowl games; in 1973 Parker was inducted into the Pro Football Hall of Fame.

Parker, Julius, Jr.

b. April 14, 1935
New Braunfels, Tex.
fields: Military Affairs

African American military officer; Julius Parker, Jr., retired from the U.S. Army on September 30, 1989, having achieved the rank of major general; he served in Vietnam as district senior adviser with the United States Military Assistance Command (1967-1968); other postings included commander of the 165th Military Intelligence Battalion with the U.S. Army Europe, deputy chief of staff for intelligence for the U.S. Army Europe and the Seventh Army, deputy director for management and operations in the Defense Intelligence Agency, and commanding general of the Army Intelligence Center and commandant of the Army Intelligence School at Fort Huachuca, Arizona.

Parker, Matthew

b. August 6, 1504
Norwich, Norfolk, England
d. May 17, 1575
London, England
fields: Religion and Theology

As the first Archbishop of Canterbury under Elizabeth I, Matthew Parker helped the queen achieve a truly national church, whose doctrine, ritual, and organization would be determined by Scripture, church tradition, and royal supremacy. Under Parker's archbishopric the Anglican church continued as a reformed branch of the Catholic Church rather than as a separate Protestant sect, maintaining religious peace in England.

Parker, Quanah

aka: Kwahnah (Sweet Odor)
b. c. 1845
near Cedar Lake, Tex.
d. Feb. 23, 1911
Fort Sill Reservation, near Lawton, Okla.
fields: Native American Affairs

Quohada Comanche tribal leader; after refusing to sign the Medicine Lodge Treaty of October, 1867, which required that the Plains Indians relocate their people to reservations in Oklahoma and Texas, Quanah Parker led raids on frontier settlements and against white buffalo hunters in the 1860's and 1870's; following a short war in 1874 targeting white settlers in Texas, Quanah surrendered to the U.S. government in 1875; although a fierce warrior and battle leader, became an outspoken advocate of Indian assimilation and aided his people in the transition from freedom to reservation life; in time, he became the principal chief of the Comanche nation and advocated Indian education in American-style schools and Indian technical education; recommended the leasing of reservation grazing lands to Texas cattlemen; shrewd businessman and negotiator.

Parker, Ray, Jr.

b. May 1, 1954
Detroit, Mich.
fields: Music (popular singer and songwriter)

African American singer and songwriter; during the early 1970's, Ray Parker, Jr., toured the world with Stevie Wonder and worked on Wonder's *Talking Book* (1972) and *Innervisions* (1973) albums; from 1977 to 1981, Parker worked with his own band, Raydio, and their gold debut album *Raydio* (1978) included the band's first top-ten single, "Jack and Jill"; as a solo artist Parker's biggest success was the title song to the film *Ghostbusters* (1984; reached number one on *Billboard*'s charts, went multiplatinum, and won a Grammy Award as best pop instrumental); later albums included *Sex and the Single Man* (1985) and the star-studded album, *After Dark* (1987).

Parker, Theodore

b. April 24, 1810
Lexington, Massachusetts
d. May 10, 1860
Florence, Italy
fields: Religion and Theology, Social Reform

A scholar with a strong social conscience, Parker was an influential Transcendentalist who helped shape American Unitarianism and was a leader in the abolitionist cause during the 1850's.

Parkes, Henry

aka: Sir Henry Parkes
b. May 27, 1815
Stoneleigh, Warwickshire, England
d. April 27, 1896
North Annandale, New South Wales, Australia
fields: Government and Politics

As Premier of New South Wales for five terms, Parkes successfully promoted immigration to Australia, established public education, and sponsored the movement for federation.

Parkman, Francis

b. September 16, 1823
Boston, Massachusetts
d. November 8, 1893
Jamaica Plain, Massachusetts
fields: Scholarship, Historiography

Parkman was the greatest of the nineteenth century American patrician historians. He combined extensive research with an unparalleled literary artistry that continues to excite the imagination of readers. For many years, Parkman's seven-part series *France and England in North America* (1865-1892) was regarded as the definitive history of the three-sided struggle among the Indians, French, and English for dominion over the continent.

Parks, Gordon, Sr.

b. November 30, 1912
Fort Scott, Kans.
fields: Photography, Literature, Film, Music

African American photographer, author, filmmaker, and composer; as a photographer, Gordon Parks, Sr., worked under the renowned Roy E. Stryker at the Farm Security Administration (1942; winning the first Julius Rosenwald Fellowship Award in photography), as a correspondent with the Office of War Information during World War II, and as a staff photographer/reporter for *Life* magazine; in 1963, Parks published the autobiographical novel *The Learning Tree*; in 1969 he became the first African American to produce a film for a major Hollywood studio when he turned his novel into a film released by Warner Bros./Seven Arts (Parks composed the musical score for the film as well); other feature films directed by Parks include the huge commercial hit *Shaft* (1971), *Shaft's Big Score* (1972), and *Leadbelly* (1976); other published works include *A Choice of Weapons* (1966), *To Smile in Autumn: A Memoir* (1979), the fictional *Shannon* (1981), and numerous books of photographs.

Parks, Henry Green, Jr.

b. September 29, 1916
Atlanta, Ga.
d. April 24, 1989
Towson, Md.
fields: Business and Industry

African American business executive; in 1951 Henry Green Parks, Jr., established his own company, H. G. Parks, Inc., which specialized in southern-style scrapple and sausage; in 1969 the company went public, and in 1977 Parks sold his interest for $1.58 million; at that time, the company's annual sales were about $10 million, and by 1989 they had reached $14 million; Parks remained with the company as a director and consultant until his death from Parkinson's disease.

Parks, Rosa

né: Rosa Lee McCauley
b. February 4, 1913
Tuskegee, Alabama
fields: Civil Rights

Rosa Parks, who is well known for her refusal to relinquish her bus seat to a white passenger in Montgomery, Alabama, on December 1, 1955, was a civil rights advocate before she committed her historic and heroic act.

Parmenides

b. c. 515 B.C.E.
Elea (also known as Velia)
d. Perhaps after 436 B.C.E.
possibly Elea
fields: Philosophy

By exploring the logical implications of statements which use apparently simple terms such as "one" or "is," Parmenides established metaphysics as an area of philosophy.

Parnell, Charles Stewart

b. June 27, 1846
Avondale, County Wicklow, Ireland
d. October 6, 1891
Brighton, Sussex, England
fields: Government and Politics

Parnell fused disparate peoples and organizations into a cohesive Irish Nationalist party for the purpose of achieving home rule for Ireland.

Parr, Catherine

aka: Catharine Parr
aka: Katherine Parr
aka: Katharine Parr
b. c. 1512
London, England
d. September 5, 1548
Sudeley Castle, Gloucestershire, England
fields: Monarchy

Catherine Parr was the sixth and last wife of King Henry VIII of Great Britain.

Parra, Catalina

b. ?
Chile
fields: Art (collage artist)

Chilean collage artist. Catalina Parra has created multimedia visual/word plays on advertising signs, such as *Plea-Sure* (1987), which examines the wording of cigarette ads. Some of her work, such as the collage *Who's Next*, addresses the emotional fallout of the AIDS epidemic and different kinds of victimization. She and her father made a video intended to shown on the Times Square light board in New York City. Her art often deals with the concepts of freedom and democracy.

Parra-Wa-Samen. *See* Ten Bears

Parrington, Vernon L.

full: Vernon Louis Parrington
b. August 3, 1871
Aurora, Illinois
d. June 16, 1929
Winchcombe, England
fields: Historiography, Literature

Parrington's three-volume *Main Currents in American Thought* (1927-1930) was a landmark work that not only helped shape how the generation coming to maturity in the 1930's viewed the United States' past but also did much to stimulate interest in American intellectual history as a field of study.

Parsons, Elsie Clews

né: Elsie Worthington Clews
b. November 27, 1875
New York, New York
d. December 19, 1941
New York, New York
fields: Anthropology

As a wealthy patron and an influential writer, Parsons contributed to feminism, sociology, and anthropology. In her own life and in her writings, she challenged traditional conventions of behavior for women.

Parsons, James Benton

b. August 13, 1913
Kansas City, Mo.
d. June 19, 1993
Chicago, Ill.
fields: Education, Law

African American educator, lawyer, and jurist; from 1934 to 1940, James Benton Parsons taught at Lincoln University and served as acting head of the music department; from 1940 to 1942, he served as a supervisor for the Greensboro, N.C. public schools; until 1951, Parsons served as assistant corporation counsel for Chicago; from 1960 to 1961, Parsons was assistant U.S. district attorney and a judge on the Cook County, Ill., Superior Court.

Partee, Cecil A.

b. April 10, 1921
Blytheville, Ark.
fields: Law, Government and Politics

African American attorney and state politician; Cecil A. Partee served as assistant state's attorney for Cook County, Illinois, from 1948 to 1956; from 1957 to 1966, he served in the Illinois State House of Representatives; from 1967 to 1977, Partee served on the state senate, winning awards as Most Outstanding Freshman Senator (1967) and as Most Effective Senator (1971).

Parton, Dolly

full: Dolly Rebecca Parton
b. January 19, 1946
rural Locust Ridge, Sevier County, Tennessee
fields: Music

A major force in bringing women to the forefront of country music, Parton also fashioned successful pop music as well as films and television.

Pascal, Blaise

b. June 19, 1623
Clermont-Ferrand, France
d. August 19, 1662
Paris, France
fields: Religion and Theology, Philosophy, Mathematics

Pascal was a man of genius in many areas, who made important contributions to mathematics and physics and invented an early form of the calculator. His major contribution, however, is the record of his religious and philosophical struggle to reconcile human experience, God, and the quest for happiness and meaning.

Pascual, Camilo Alberto

b. Jan. 20, 1934
Havana, Cuba
fields: Sports (baseball player)

Cuban Baseball player. Pitcher Camilo Alberto Pascual debuted with the Washington Senators in 1954 but did not gain attention until 1959, when he posted a 17-10 record and led the league in shutouts. In 1961, the season the Senators became the Minnesota Twins, Pascual led the American League in strikeouts, a feat he repeated the following two seasons. In 1961 and 1962, he led the league in shutouts, and, in 1962 and 1963, he had more than twenty wins. A five-time All-Star, Pascual retired in 1971 with a 174-170 record, a 3.63 earned run average, and 2,167 strikeouts

Pasha, İsmet. *See* Inönü, Ismet

Passaconaway

aka: Bear Cub
b. c. 1568
d. c. 1665
fields: Government and Politics, Native American Affairs

Native American leader. A Pennacook, Passaconaway was the principal Indian leader in southern New England during early English colonization.

Pasternak, Boris

full: Boris Leonidovich Pasternak
b. February 10, 1890
Moscow, Russia
d. May 30, 1960
Peredelkino, near Moscow, U.S.S.R.
fields: Literature

Pasternak was a leading Russian poet, a particularly gifted translator, and a writer of prose, most notably the novel *Doctor Zhivago*, for which he was offered the Nobel Prize in 1958. His highly cultured talent managed to find both expression and influence despite severe adversity in the Soviet literary climate.

Pasteur, Louis

b. December 27, 1822
Dôle, Jura, France
d. September 28, 1895
Villenueve-l'Étang, near Saint Cloud, France
fields: Chemistry, Biology

Pasteur, by his pioneering work in crystallography, established the discipline of stereochemistry (left-handedness and right-handedness in organic structures). He spent the bulk of his career founding modern microbiology and making exciting discoveries in immunology.

Pastorius, Jaco

né: John Francis Anthony III
b. Dec. 1, 1951
Norristown, Pa.
d. Sept. 21, 1987
Fort Lauderdale, Fla.
fields: Music (bass guitarist and bandleader)

Bass guitarist and bandleader. Jaco Pastorius first attracted attention in 1976 when he recorded with the band Weather Report on the album *Heavy Weather*. He went on to play in several bands and record with such artists as Herbie Hancock, Joni Mitchell, Pat Metheny, Albert Mangelsdorf, Ian Hunter, and Ira Sullivan. Pastorius's first two solo albums, *Jaco Pastorius* and *Word of Mouth*, established him as an international artist of note.

Patel, Marilyn

b. Sept. 2, 1938
Amsterdam, N.Y.
fields: Law

Federal judge Marilyn Patel wrote the opinion in the U.S. District Court *coram nobis* case *Korematsu v. United States* (1984). Through this case and two other *coram nobis* cases, the Japanese American community was attempting to vacate the criminal convictions of three Japanese American men who had violated the U.S. government's World War II exclusion and curfew orders. Patel vacated Korematsu's forty-year-old conviction in April, 1984.

Patel, Vallabhbhai Jhaverbhai

b. October 31, 1875
Nadiād, Gujerāt, India
d. December 15, 1950
Bombay, India
fields: Government and Politics

Patel's uncanny ability to inspire political cooperation among disparate personalities and groups served as the single most important element in the post-independence Indian government's successful integration of the various princely states into a single national unit.

Pater, Walter

full: Walter Horatio Pater
b. August 4, 1839
London, England
d. July 30, 1894
Oxford, England
fields: Literature, Art

His emphasis upon the importance of sensibility and feeling made Pater a central figure in the "art for art's sake" movement that marked the transition from Victorian realism to twentieth century modernism.

Paternosto, César Pedro

b. Nov. 29, 1931
La Plata, Buenos Aires, Argentina
fields: Art

Multimedia artist. In 1984, César Pedro Paternosto exhibited his art in the First Havana Biennial at the Museum of Modern Art in New York City. In 1996, he won first prize at the Third Biennial American Art (1966). His best-known work is *Recuay* (1983), a sixty-square-inch acrylic and sand painting on canvas. His work is in the Museum of Modern Art in New York and the National Fine Arts Museum in Argentina.

Paterson, Basil

b. April 27, 1926
New York, N.Y.
fields: Government and Politics

African American government official; from 1965 to 1970, Basil Paterson served as state senator for New York City's Twenty-sixth Senatorial District; in 1970 Patterson was the Democratic nominee for lieutenant governor; from 1979 to 1982, he was New York State's secretary of state.

Paterson, Katherine

b. October 31, 1932
Qing Jiang, China
fields: Literature

Katherine Paterson is a Chinese American author of popular children's books, many of which have been challenged or banned from classrooms and libraries. Her books include *Bridge to Terabithia* (1977) and *The Great Gilly Hopkins* (1978).

Paterson, William

b. April, 1658
Skipmyre, Dumfriesshire, Scotland
d. January, 1719
Queen Square, Westminster, England
fields: Business and Industry

Paterson was cofounder of the Bank of England, an active participant in the so-called Darien scheme—a project to establish a Scottish settlement in Panama—and an innovator in government finance.

Paterson, William

b. 1745
d. 1806
fields: Law

U.S. Supreme Court justice, 1793-1806 (died while in office); appointed by President Washington. Significant opinions: *Hylton v. United States*, 3 U.S. 171 (1796); *Stuart v. Laird*, 5 U.S. 299 (1803).

Patlán, Raymond M.

b. 1946
Chicago, Ill.
fields: Art (muralist)

Mexican American muralist. Raymond M. Patlán began to work at Casa Aztlán, a Pilsen community center, in 1965, and he started to paint and direct murals there on a volunteer basis in 1970. He was one of the founders of the Pilsen school of Chicano education/empowerment, a mural movement in the 1960's. Among the murals he painted were *Reform and Liberty*, *Culture in Our Community* (1971-1972), and *History of Mexican American Worker* (1975). Patlán codirected the Chicano Mural Workshop in Berkeley, California, in 1976. He also started the Chicago chapter of MARCH (the Chicano Artistic Movement) and spoke at the 1976 National Murals Conference in New York.

Paton, Alan

full: Alan Stewart Paton
b. January 11, 1903
Pietermaritzburg, Natal, South Africa
d. April 12, 1988
Botha's Hill, Natal, South Africa
fields: Literature, Social Reform

Alan Paton

Through his writings and political work, Paton both foresaw and helped to effect fundamental changes in the shape of South African society.

Paton, William

b. July 19, 1889
near Calumet, Mich.
d. April 26, 1991
Ann Arbor, Mich.
fields: Economics

Economist William Paton is best known for his 1952 volume *Shirtsleeve Economics*, in which he theorized that increased production results when people are encouraged to get out and hustle for self and family, with as little governmental interference as possible.

Patrick, Saint

b. Probably between 418 and 422
England
d. March 17, 493
Ireland or England
fields: Religion and Theology, Saints

Saint Patrick is a legendary figure who served as a missionary bishop to Ireland and converted large numbers of pagans to Christianity. He is the patron saint of Ireland.

Patterson, Floyd

b. January 4, 1935
Waco, North Carolina
fields: Sports (boxer)

African American Olympic middleweight and professional world heavyweight boxing champion. Floyd Patterson captured the 1952 Olympic middleweight gold medal, and in 1956 became the youngest world heavyweight champion ever. In a 1960 rematch, Patterson became the first man to regain the heavyweight championship. He twice defended his title before suffering first-round knockouts at the hands of Sonny Liston in 1962 and in a 1963. In 1965, he again attempted to recapture the title from new champion Muhammad Ali but was knocked out in the twelfth round. Patterson retired in 1972 with a professional record of 55-8-1.

Patterson, Frederick D.

full: Frederick Douglass Patterson
b. October 10, 1901
Washington, D.C.
d. April 26, 1988
New Rochelle, New York
fields: Education

Frederick D. Patterson was an educator; faculty member, and later president of, Tuskegee Institute from 1928; chair of the R. R. Moton Memorial Institute; organized United Negro College Fund in 1944 to aid historically black colleges and universities.

Patterson, Wayne

b. 1946
Philadelphia, Pa.
fields: Historiography

Wayne Patterson, professor of history at St. Norbert College and a Korea specialist, published works on Korea, the Korean diaspora, and U.S.-Korea relations. His publications include *The Koreans in America, 1882-1974: A Chronology and Fact Book* (1974, with Hyung-chan Kim), *The Koreans in America* (1977, with Hyung-chan Kim), *The Two Koreas in World Politics* (1983, with Tae-Hwan Kwak and Edward Olsen), *One Hundred Years of Korean-American Relations, 1882-1992* (1986, with Yur-Bok Lee), and *The Korean Frontier in America: Immigration to Hawaii, 1896-1910* (1988).

Patton, Charley

b. 1887
Edwards, Miss.
d. April 28, 1934
Indianola, Miss.
fields: Music (blues singer and guitarist)

African American blues singer and guitarist; regarded as one of the most influential of the early country blues singers and widely imitated, Charley Patton was not a professional musician in the contemporary sense—he played at local settings while working as a migrant plantation laborer; the first recordings of his vocal style, characteristic of the Mississippi Delta tradition (with vocal growls, a raspy voice, spoken beginnings and endings in the song, occasional falsetto, and other vocal effects), were made in 1929; his 1934 recordings for Vocalion included "Banty Rooster Blues," "Black Cow Blues," "High Sheriff Blues," "High Water Everywhere," "Magnolia Blues," "Pony Blues," "Snake Blues," "Screamin' and Hollerin' Blues," and "Shake It, Break It Blues"; Patton died of a heart attack.

Patton, George S.

full: George Smith Patton, Jr.
b. November 11, 1885
San Gabriel, California
d. December 21, 1945
Heidelberg, Germany
fields: Military Affairs

Though never a theoretician, Patton was a masterful tactician who demonstrated the advantages of mobility and aggressive offensive action as essential elements of modern warfare.

Paul III

né: Alessandro Farnese
b. February 29, 1468
Canino, Papal States
d. November 10, 1549
Rome
fields: Religion and Theology

Pope, 1534-1549. Pope Paul III was the last of the Renaissance popes, aristocratic, educated in the classics, with the concerns of his family often paramount. Yet he was also the first pope of the Catholic or Counter-Reformation, and it was he who summoned the Council of Trent, whose decisions governed the Church in subsequent centuries.

Paul IV

né Gian Pietro Carafa
b. June 28, 1476
Italy
d. August 18, 1559
Rome, Italy
fields: Religion and Theology

Paul IV was pontiff of the Roman Catholic church from 1555 to 1559. He was a member of the Church's original Inquisition and he intensified Roman Catholic censorship by creating the first *Index Librorum Prohibitorum* to ban books in 1559.

Paul VI

né: Giovanni Battista Montini
b. September 26, 1897
Concesio, near Brescia, Italy
d. August 6, 1978
Castel Gandolfo, Italy
fields: Religion and Theology, Church Reform

Pope Paul VI, 1962-1978. Paul VI convened the last three sessions of the historic Second Vatican Council (1962-1965), which brought the Roman Catholic church into constructive engagement with the modern world. His abiding concern for the poor and for human rights and social justice and his extensive travels reinforced the progressive influence of the Vatican Council.

Paul, Alice

b. January 11, 1885
Moorestown, New Jersey
d. July 9, 1977
Moorestown, New Jersey
fields: Women's Rights

The leader of the radical wing of the woman suffrage movement that helped pass the Nineteenth Amendment, Paul also introduced the Equal Rights Amendment.

Paul, Billy

né: Paul Williams
b. December 1, 1934
Philadelphia, Pa.
fields: Music (rhythm-and-blues singer)

African American rhythm-and-blues singer; before forming his own group, the Billy Paul Trio, Billy Paul sang with both the Flamingos and Harold Melvin and the Blue Notes in the early 1960's; Paul scored the multimillion-selling hit, "Me and Mrs. Jones" (1972) with the help of the songwriting and production team of Kenny Gamble and Leon Huff; later single recordings that made it onto the soul charts included "Am I Black Enough for You?" (1973), "Thanks for Saving My Life" (1974), and "Let's Make a Baby" (1976).

Paul, John. *See* Jones, John Paul

Paul, Saint

né: Saul
b. Date unknown
Tarsus, Cilicia (now Turkey)
d. c. 64 C.E.
Rome
fields: Religion and Theology

Through depth of conviction and force of personality, Paul spread the teachings of an obscure Jewish sect throughout the eastern Mediterranean and eventually to Rome. As the educated apostle, he gave Christianity a measure of intellectual credibility and formulated much of what would later become doctrine.

Paul, Thomas, Sr.

b. September 3, 1773
Exeter, N.H.
d. April 13, 1831
Boston, Mass.
fields: Religion and Theology

African American baptist clergyman; noted for his excellent preaching, Thomas Paul, Sr., organized and acted as founding pastor of two historic black churches: Boston's Joy Street Baptist Church (1805) and New York City's Abyssinian Baptist Church (1808); by the late 1830's, Abyssinian had grown to be the largest Baptist church in New York City.

Paul of Aegina

b. c. 607
Aegina, Greece
d. c. 690
place unknown
fields: Medicine

Paul of Aegina was a celebrated Byzantine physician, surgeon, and medical writer. His *Epitome* summarized nearly all medical knowledge of his time and had a profound influence on Western European, Arabic, and Persian medicine. His treatment of surgery is the best summary of ancient surgery that has survived.

Pauley, Jane

full: Margaret Jane Pauley
b. October 31, 1950
Indianapolis, Indiana
fields: Journalism, Television

Starting off as one of the youngest women to ever coanchor a major network morning show, Pauley parlayed her girl-next-door charm and solid journalistic skills into huge ratings at the *Today* show and left at the height of her popularity to launch her two successful prime-time newsmagazines: *Real Life with Jane Pauley* and *Dateline NBC.*

Pauli, Wolfgang

b. April 25, 1900
Vienna, Austria
d. December 14, 1958
Zurich, Switzerland
fields: Physics

Pauli's discovery of the exclusion principle, which asserts the individuality of electrons, revolutionized atomic physics. He is also responsible for the electron theory of metals, which led to the development of transistors, and for proposing the existence of neutrinos. He was awarded the 1945 Nobel Prize in Physics.

Pauling, Linus

full: Linus Carl Pauling
b. February 28, 1901
Portland, Oregon
d. August 19, 1994
Big Sur, California
fields: Chemistry, Biology, Medicine, Peace Advocacy

Pauling is the only person to have won two unshared Nobel Prizes, and these prizes, in chemistry (1954) and in peace, symbolize his contributions. In the 1930's and 1940's his scientific discoveries helped to make the United States an important center for structural chemistry and molecular biology. In the 1950's and 1960's his activities in the peace movement helped to mobilize the American public against the atmospheric testing of nuclear weapons.

Pavarotti, Luciano

b. October 12, 1935
Modena, Italy
fields: Music

Possessing a rigorously trained voice of exceptional beauty, Pavarotti became the leading lyric tenor of his time and a musical superstar who reached a larger audience than any classical artist who preceded him.

Pavlov, Ivan Petrovich

b. September 26, 1849
Ryazan, Russia
d. February 27, 1936
Leningrad, U.S.S.R.
fields: Physiology, Medicine

Pavlov is best known for developing the theory of conditioned reflexes, which he demonstrated by teaching a dog to salivate when it heard a bell. He also performed important experiments to determine the connection between human behavior and the nervous system; he won the Nobel Prize in Physiology or Medicine in 1904 for his work on the digestive tract.

Pavlova, Anna

full: Anna Pavlovna Pavlova
b. February 12, 1881
St. Petersburg, Russia
d. January 23, 1931
The Hague, The Netherlands
fields: Dance

Pavlova was widely regarded as the greatest embodiment of ballet in her lifetime, and she became a symbol of the best the ballet has known after her death. She spread knowledge of and interest in ballet through her worldwide tours.

Pavlovich, Nikolay. *See* Nicholas I

Pawhuska

b. c. 1760
Little Osage River in central Mo.
d. Aug. 25, 1825
present-day Vernon County, Mo.
fields: Government and Politics, Diplomacy, Native American Affairs

Native American leader. An Osage, Pawhuska was a tribal leader when Zebulon Pike established Camp Independence in Osage territory in 1806. Pawhuska also agreed to ceding all Osage lands in Missouri at the Treaty of Fort Clark in 1808. Later participated in 1818 and 1825 treaties ceding Osage land in Missouri and Arkansas.

Payne, Betty J.

b. 1950
Jackson, Miss.?
fields: Aviation and Space Exploration

African American pilot; after joining the United States Air Force in 1973, Betty J. Payne became the first African American woman to earn navigator wings; she was assigned to work on C-141 cargo aircraft.

Payne, Clarence H.

b. January 23, 1892
Hopkinsville, Ky.
d. July 7, 1965
fields: Medicine

African American physician; Clarence H. Payne is noted as one of a group of three physicians (with C. G. Roberts and Roscoe Giles) who successfully petitioned the American Medical Association to remove the entry "Col." following the names of black physicians in the *AMA directory*; for ten years Payne served as head of interns at Provident Hospital in Chicago, Ill.; during World War II, was called by President Franklin D. Roosevelt to participate in a conference on racial integration of the armed forces.

Payne, Daniel Alexander

b. 1811
Charleston, S.C.
d. Nov. 21, 1893
Wilberforce, Ohio
fields: Religion and Theology

African American educator, bishop; Daniel Alexander Payne was born to free parents; opened a school for blacks in Charleston, South Carolina, in 1829; after his school was closed by an act of the South Carolina legislature, traveled north to study, delivering powerful abolitionist speeches throughout the 1840's and 1850's; elected bishop of the African Methodist Episcopal Church in 1852; served as president of Wilberforce University into the 1870's and devoted the rest of his life to developing the university and overseeing missionary endeavors; wrote *Recollections of Seventy Years* (1888) and *History of the African Methodist Episcopal Church* (1891).

Payne, Dolley. *See* Madison, Dolley

Payne, Donald

b. July 16, 1934
Newark, N.J.
fields: Government and Politics

African American politician; first black president of the YMCA (1970-1973); served on the Newark city council (1982-1989); African American congressman from New Jersey. A strong leader on urban and minority issues and a chairman of the Congressional Black Caucus; Donald Payne served on the education and labor committee of the House of Representatives, on the Committee on Narcotics Abuse and Control, and, in 1991, he became a member of the foreign affairs committee. He was re-elected in 1998 for a sixth term.

Payne, Ethel

b. August 14, 1911
Chicago, Ill.
d. May 28, 1991
Washington, D.C.
fields: Journalism, Radio

African American journalist; known as "the first lady of the black press," Ethel Payne served as a White House correspondent from 1953 to 1973; in this capacity she earned a reputation for asking tough questions regarding civil rights; during her career she served as a regular columnist for newspapers including the *St. Louis Sentinel*, *Afro-American*, *Miami Herald*, and *Michigan Courier*; in 1967 she worked as the first African American female correspondent to cover the Vietnam War; in the late 1970's, Payne worked as the first black female commentator on the Columbia Broadcasting System radio network; she was also recognized as a broadcast journalist on television and radio stations throughout the Midwest and East; in 1988, elected to the Women's Hall of Fame in Washington, D.C.

Payne, Howard Marshall

b. August 18, 1907
Washington, D.C.
d. September 9, 1961
Boston, Mass.
fields: Medicine, Education

African American physician; after teaching on the the medical faculty at Howard University from 1937-1958, Howard Marshall Payne became superintendent and tuberculosis specialist at Middlesex County Sanitarium in Waltham, Mass.; from 1951 to 1952, he served as the first African American president of the National Tuberculosis Association.

Payne-Gaposchkin, Cecilia

né: Cecilia Helena Payne
b. May 10, 1900
Wendover, England
d. Dec. 6, 1979
Cambridge, Massachusetts
fields: Astronomy

Cecilia Payne-Gaposchkin studied stars and their structure; in 1925, was the first to propose that stars are composed mainly of hydrogen and helium; in 1956, became the first woman to be made a full professor at Harvard, was appointed head of the astronomy department.

Payton, Walter

b. July 25, 1954
Columbia, Miss.
fields: Sports (football player)

African American football player; a gifted runner, a punishing blocker, a talented pass receiver, and an accurate passer on halfback option plays, Walter Payton demonstrated his early talents at Jackson State University, where he set national collegiate athletic association football records by scoring sixty-six touchdowns and 464 points and earned his B.A. degree in only three and one-half years; a 1975 first-round draft pick of the Chicago Bears, Payton won the starting halfback job in his second season with the team; during his career with the Bears (1975-1987), Payton won five conference rushing titles, two NFL Player of the Year awards, a 1985 Super Bowl victory, and retired as the NFL's all-time career rushing leader with 16,726 yards; in 1978 he wrote *Sweetness*, his autobiography.

Paz, Octavio

b. March 31, 1914
Mexico City, Mexico
d. April 19, 1998
Mexico City, Mexico
fields: Literature

Writer. Octavio Paz published *Luna silvestre*, his first book of poems, in 1933. He worked as an editor for several literary magazines. In 1937, poet Pablo Neruda invited him to Spain for the Second Antifascist Writers Congress. During the trip, Paz met many famous writers who influenced his own work. Paz, who won the Nobel Prize in Literature in 1990, published many important books of poetry and essays in English, including *The Labyrinth of Solitude: Life and Thought in Mexico* (1961), *Collected Poems, 1957-1987* (1987), and *The Other Voice: Essays on Modern Poetry* (1991).

Peabody, Elizabeth Palmer

b. May 16, 1804
Billerica, Massachusetts
d. January 3, 1894
Jamaica Plains, Massachusetts
fields: Education

Elizabeth Palmer Peabody, who was independent, intellectual, and devoted to education, helped to introduce the kindergarten into the United States.

Peachey, Eleanor Margaret. *See* Burbidge, Margaret

Peale, Charles Willson

b. April 15, 1741
Queen Anne County, Maryland
d. February 22, 1827
Philadelphia, Pennsylvania
fields: Art (painting), Natural History

Peale combined a sense of patriotism in his portraits of revolutionary and early national leaders with a faith in democracy by establishing the first public museum of art and science in America.

Peano, Giuseppe

b. Aug. 27, 1858
Spinetta, Italy
d. Apr. 20, 1932
Turin, Italy
fields: Mathematics (calculus and mathematical logic)

In 1889 Giuseppe Peano developed a set of five axioms for the natural numbers, called the Peano postulates. He contributed to the development of the calculus with his discoveries of counterexamples to accepted theory, the most well known being a space-filling curve, which he discovered in 1890.

Pearson, Lester B.

full: Lester Bowles Pearson
b. April 23, 1897
Newtonbrook (now part of Toronto), Ontario, Canada
d. December 27, 1972
Ottawa, Ontario, Canada
fields: Diplomacy, Government and Politics

As Canada's secretary of state for foreign affairs, Lester B. Pearson helped lay groundwork for formation of United Nations and for 1948 establishment of state of Israel. A primary force in 1949 creation of NATO. Awarded 1957 Nobel Peace Prize for his role in defusing the 1956 Suez Crisis. Headed Liberal Party 1958-1963. As prime minister (1963-1968), helped create Canada's national health and pension plans.

Peary, Robert Edwin

b. May 6, 1856
Cresson, Pennsylvania
d. February 20, 1920
Washington, D.C.
fields: Exploration and Colonization

After several unsuccessful attempts, Peary became the first man to reach the geographic North Pole, on April 6, 1909.

Peay, Benjamin Franklin. *See* Benton, Brook

Pecci, Vincenzo Gioacchino. *See* Leo XIII

Pecham, John

aka: John Peckham
b. c. 1230
probably Patcham, Sussex, England
d. December 8, 1292
Mortlake, Canterbury, England
fields: Religion and Theology, Scholarship

Pecham was a scholar whose writings ranged from Augustinian theology to optics. As Archbishop of Canterbury between 1279 and 1292, he vigorously sought to remove abuses and to maintain the Church's independence from lay interference, resulting in confrontations with the king as well as with his own bishops and abbots.

Peck, Annie Smith

b. Oct. 19, 1850
Providence, R.I.
d. July 18, 1935
New York, N.Y.
fields: Sports (mountain climbing)

In 1885 Annie Smith Peck was the first woman to be admitted to the school of classics in Athens, Greece. In 1904 she climbed Huascaran, a peak in the Peruvian Andes, then the highest point climbed in the Western Hemisphere; in 1911, at sixty-one years old, she climbed Mount Coropun in Peru and planted a sign at the summit that read "Votes for Women." Peck wrote *A Search for the Apex of South America* (1911) and *Flying over South America* (1932).

Peckham, Rufus W.

full: Rufus Wheeler Peckham
b. 1838
d. 1909
fields: Law

U.S. Supreme Court justice, 1896-1909 (died while in office); appointed by President Cleveland. Author of best-known substantive due process case, *Lochner v. New York*, 198 U.S. 45 (1905). Believed states were not required to offer defendants all of the rights found in the Bill of Rights. Significant opinions: *Crain v. United States*, 162 U.S. 625 (1896); *White v. United States*, 164 U.S. 100 (1896); *Allegeyer v. Louisiana*, 165 U.S. 578 (1897); *Maxwell v. Dow*, 176 U.S. 581 (1900).

Peckinpah, Sam

b. February 21, 1925
Fresno, California
d. December 28, 1984
Inglewood, California
fields: Film, Television

Sam Peckinpah was an American filmmaker known for the graphic depiction of violence in his films. He began his career by writing episodes of television westerns, such as *The Rifleman*, *The Westerner*, *Zane Grey Theatre*, and *Tombstone Territory*. He later became a television director and then moved to film direction with *Major Dundee* in 1965. His films became known for their quirky style and odd slants on history, evidenced in such films as *Pat Garrett and Billy the Kid* (1973) and *Bring Me the Head of Alfredo Garcia* (1974). *The Wild Bunch* (1970) is considered his most poetical film.

Pedersen, Knut. *See* Hamsun, Knut

Pedreira, Antonio S.

b. June 13, 1898
San Juan, Puerto Rico
d. Oct. 23, 1939
San Juan, Puerto Rico
fields: Scholarship, Literature

Puerto Rican literary critic, biographer, and essayist. In 1927, Antonio S. Pedreira established the department of Hispanic studies at the University of Puerto Rico; he was chairman of the department until his death. He also headed the university's Social Research Center and cofounded the cultural journal *Indice*. Pedreira published biographies, including *Un hombre del pueblo: José Celso Barbosa* (1937) and *Hostos, cuidadano de América* (1932), and several volumes of essays, such as *Insularismo: Ensayo de interpretación puertorriqueña* (1934) and *La actualidad del jíbaro* (1935).

Peel, Robert

b. February 5, 1788
near Bury, Lancashire, England
d. July 2, 1850
London, England
fields: Government and Politics

Peel was a Tory who broke with party doctrine to reform the criminal code, create an effective police force, legalize labor unions, and repeal the Corn Laws, thereby ensuring the success of free trade.

Peery, Benjamin Franklin, Jr.

b. March 4, 1922
St. Joseph, Mo.
fields: Physics (astrophysics), Astronomy

African American astrophysicist and astronomist; as a graduate student and then as a professor on the astronomy faculty at Indiana University (1959-1976), Benjamin Franklin Peery, Jr., studied what happens in the interiors of stars that are close enough for changes in one star to affect the evolution of another star; in 1977 Peery chose to move to Howard University where he believed he could inspire young minority students to pursue career opportunities in scientific fields; he continued to teach at Howard into the 1990's.

Peete, Calvin

b. July 18, 1943
Detroit, Mich.
fields: Sports (golfer)

African American golfer; having taken up golf at the age of twenty-three, Calvin Peete turned pro in 1971 and, in 1975, qualified to join the Professional Golf Association Tour; he earned more than two million dollars on the links in less than fifteen years, becoming the first African American to earn more than one million dollars in golf; his prestigious victories included twice winning the Greater Milwaukee Open (1979, 1982) and winning the 1985 Twelfth Annual Tournament Players Championship by three strokes; consistently ranked among the top-ten golfers in driving accuracy, scoring, putting, and greens in regulation, Peete received the Ben Hogan Award (1983), and the Vardon Trophy for tournament low scoring (1984; he averaged 70.56 strokes per round). Injuries slowed his game in the late 1980's and early 1990's; he joined the senior tour in 1993.

Pei, I. M.

full: Ieoh Ming Pei
b. April 26, 1917
Canton (now Guangzhou), China
fields: Architecture

Through his designs for major public buildings, Pei helped shape architectural design in the second half of the twentieth century. Equally skilled in the conceptual process of design, urban development, and client and community politics, he succeeded in completing buildings under complicated and difficult urban situations.

Peirce, Charles Sanders

b. September 10, 1839
Cambridge, Massachusetts
d. April 19, 1914
Milford, Pennsylvania
fields: Philosophy

Largely unrecognized by contemporaries, except for his contribution to pragmatism, Peirce developed a system of philosophy that attempted to reconcile the nineteenth century's faith in empirical science with its love of the metaphysical absolute. His difficult and often confusing ideas anticipated problems central to twentieth century philosophy.

Peisistratus. *See* Pisistratus

Pelé

né: Edson Arantes do Nascimento
b. October 23, 1940
Três Corações, Minas Gerais, Brazil
fields: Sports (soccer)

Probably the greatest soccer player of all time, Pelé starred on the Brazilian national teams that won the World Cup in 1958, 1962, and 1970. Following his retirement, the New York Cosmos of the North American Soccer League lured him to the United States, where he did much to popularize soccer. After retiring from the field, Brazil's greatest goodwill ambassador also became his nation's Sports Minister.

Peletier, Jacques

aka: Jacques Peletier du Mans
b. 1517
Le Mans, France
d. 1582
fields: Literature

A member of la Pléiade (fl. 1549-1589), a group of loosely organized poets dedicated to raising the level of sophistication of the French language by adding words and genres derived from classical literature. Led by Pierre de Ronsard and Joachim du Bellay, they developed a new form of poetry based on forms such as the sonnet, the ode, epic, and elegy. They also worked to elevate the level of the poet to a position as an intermediary between humanity and the heavens.

Pelham, Henry

b. c. 1695-1696
place unknown
d. March 6, 1754
London, England
fields: Government and Politics

Pelham helped forge the British parliamentary system of government into one in which the cabinet is answerable to the House of Commons and not to the monarch.

Pell, Anna Johnson. *See* Wheeler, Anna Johnson Pell

Pelli, Cesar

b. Oct. 12, 1926
Tucuman, Argentina
fields: Architecture

Cesar Pelli, one of the first architects to use glass for nonstructural outer walls, created the innovative design for the Museum of Modern Art building (MOMA) in New York City. He served as dean of the School of Architecture at Yale University from 1977 to 1984.

Peltier, Leonard

b. September 12, 1944
Grand Forks, N. Dak.
fields: Historical Figure, Native American Affairs

Leonard Peltier, a member of the American Indian Movement (AIM), was convicted in the June 26, 1975, shooting deaths of two agents of the Federal Bureau of Investigation on the Lakota Indian Reservation in Pine

Ridge, South Dakota. During Peltier's appeals, the court found that the government had acted improperly in arresting and trying him. The case raised the question of whether it is right for a government to bend the law to convict someone believed to be guilty of a serious crime.

Peña, Amado Maurilio, Jr.

b. Oct. 1, 1943
Laredo, Tex.
fields: Art (painter)

Painter. During the 1960's, Amado Maurilio Peña, Jr., was involved in the Chicano movement and chose militant topics for his art. He also worked on naïve drawings and prints. He earned his M.A. from Texas Arts and Industries University in 1971. In 1973, he moved to Austin, Texas, to work as a high-school teacher and print instructor. His later began depicting Native American life in Santa Fe, New Mexico, where he spent his summers. One of his best-known works is *La Raza* (1974).

Peña, Elizabeth

b. Sept. 23, 1959
Elizabeth, N.J.
fields: Theater and Entertainment (actor), Film, Television

Latina actor. Elizabeth Peña appeared in stage performances in New York, Los Angeles, and San Francisco before making her film debut in *The Super* (1979). Her other films include *Down and Out in Beverly Hills* (1985), *La Bamba* (1987), *Batteries Not Included* (1987), *Vibes* (1988), *Blue Steel* (1989), *Jacob's Ladder* (1990), and *The Waterdance* (1992). Peña has appeared in such diverse television series as *One Life To Live*, *Tough Cookies*, *Shannon's Deal*, *Saturday Night Live*, *Hill Street Blues*, *Cagney and Lacey*, and *Crime and Punishment*. She also starred in the television film *Drug Wars: The Camarena Story*.

Peña, Federico

b. Mar. 15, 1947
Laredo, Tex.
fields: Government and Politics

Latino public official. Federico Peña was elected mayor of Denver, Colorado, at the age of thirty-six. In 1992, President Bill Clinton named Peña as the U.S. secretary of transportation. While serving in that office, Peña actively supported the president's economic package and the North American Free Trade Agreement. His efforts to redirect assets to improve the nation's transportation system were widely praised.

Peña, Tonita

aka: Quah Ah (Little Bead or Pink Shell)
b. June 10, 1893
San Ildefonso Pueblo, N.Mex.
d. Sept., 1949
Cochiti Pueblo?, N.Mex.
fields: Art (painter)

American Indian painter. A San Ildefonso and Cochiti, Tonita Peña was an influential artist who painted scenes of traditional dances and women's work. Archaeologist Edgar Hewett kept her supplied with good paper and watercolors and was her patron until his death. Also taught pottery at local Indian schools and collaborated on murals for the Works Progress Administration.

Peña, Tony

full: Antonio Francesco Peña y Padilla
b. June 4, 1957
Monte Cristi, Dominican Republic
fields: Sports (baseball player)

Baseball player. Catcher Tony Peña made his major league debut with the Pittsburgh Pirates in 1980. Over the next six seasons, he received four All-Star nominations and won three consecutive Gold Glove Awards. In 1987, he was traded to the St. Louis Cardinals and helped them win the National League pennant. In 1989, he made the National League All-Star team but was traded to the Boston Red Sox after the season. In 1991, he won another Gold Glove Award. In 1994, he signed as a free agent with the Cleveland Indians. He retired in 1997 while a member of the Houston Astros. The Astros named him to manage its minor league team in New Orleans in 1998.

Pendergrass, Teddy

full: Theodore D. Pendergrass
b. March 26, 1950
Philadelphia, Pa.
fields: Music (singer)

African American singer; in 1970 Teddy Pendergrass became a member of a Philadelphia rhythm-and-blues group, Harold Melvin and the Blue Notes, and participated in their major hit "If You Don't Know Me by Now" (1972); Pendergrass left the group to embark on a successful solo career in 1976; in 1982, he was rendered a quadriplegic as the result of an automobile accident.

Pendleton, Clarence

full: Clarence McLane Pendleton, Jr.
b. November 10, 1930
Louisville, Ky.
d. June 5, 1988
San Diego, Calif.
fields: Government and Politics

Clarence Pendleton served two years as director of the urban affairs department of the National Recreation and Parks Association before moving to San Diego, Calif., in 1972, to become the director of the Model Cities program there. On November 16, 1981, President Ronald Reagan appointed him chair of the U.S. Commission on Civil Rights. He was the first African American to serve in that position, but he drew controversy for his conservative opinions.

Peng Dehuai

aka: P'eng Te-huai
b. c. October 24, 1898
Xiangtan County, Hunan Province, China
d. November 29, 1974
Beijing, China
fields: Military Affairs, War and Conquest

Chinese revolutionary leader and politician; a leader of Communist Party beginning in 1930's. In October, 1934, Peng Dehuai was one of the leaders of the legendary Long March. Helped in communist takeover in 1949 and held many high government posts until 1959. Led Chinese forces in Korean War; they took at least 700,000 casualties, but Peng became a national hero. Criticism of Great Leap Forward in 1959 led to downfall; vilified during Cultural Revolution.

Penn, William

b. October 14, 1644
London, England
d. July 30, 1718
Ruscombe, England
fields: Government and Politics

A leading Quaker, Penn contributed to the early development of the sect through his traveling ministry, his numerous religious tracts, intervention with English authorities for toleration, and establishment of Pennsylvania as a refuge for dissenters.

Penniman, Richard. *See* Little Richard

Penpenhihi. *See* White Bird

Penrose, Roger

b. Aug. 8, 1931
Colchester, Essex, England
fields: Mathematics (applied math), Astronomy, Physics

Roger Penrose gave mathematical understandings for such astrophysical phenomena as black holes; found Penrose tiles, two geometric shapes that can cover a two-dimensional plane without any repeating pattern; shared Wolf Foundation Prize in Physics with Stephen Hawking in 1988.

Peopeo Kiskiok Hihih. *See* White Bird

Peoples, John Arthur, Jr.

b. August 26, 1926
Starkville, Miss.
fields: Education

African American educator and administrator; John Arthur Peoples, Jr., served as president of Jackson State University in Mississippi from 1967 to 1984; in 1977 he was also an education specialist with the State Department; served on the Advisory Committee on Accreditation and Institutional Eligibility for the Department of Health, Education, and Welfare.

Perales, Alonso S.

b. 1899
Alice, Tex.
d. May 9, 1960
fields: Civil Rights

Alonso S. Perales participated in the creation of the Order of Sons of America (1921) and the League of Latin American Citizens (1927), which eventually merged in 1929 as the League of United Latin American Citizens (LULAC). Perales served as a diplomat in the late 1920's and throughout the 1930's. As a result of his book *El Mexicano Americano y la politica del sur de Texas* (1931), Perales became an adviser on Mexican American concerns to President Franklin D. Roosevelt. He also published *En defensa de mi raza* (2 volumes, 1936 and 1937) and *Are We Good Neighbors?* (1948). He also published a newspaper column in a San Antonio, Texas, newspaper, *La Verdad*. In 1952, the Spanish government awarded Perales the rank of commander in the Spanish Order of Civil Merit in recognition of his unfailing quest for civil rights and social equality for all Spanish-speaking peoples.

Perales, César A.

b. Nov. 12, 1940
New York, N.Y.
fields: Government and Politics

Government official, lawyer; César A. Perales was director, Criminal Justice Coordinating Council, New York City Office of the Mayor, 1976-1977; regional director, Department of Health, Education and Welfare (HEW), 1977-1979; assistant secretary, HEW, 1979-1980; appointed assistant secretary for human development services by President Jimmy Carter in 1980; president, Puerto Rican Legal Defense and Education Fund, 1981-1983; New York City commissioner, 1983-1991; appointed deputy mayor for health and human services in New York, 1992.

Peregrinus de Maricourt, Petrus

aka: Pierre le Pèlerin de Maricourt
aka: Peter of Maricourt
b. Early thirteenth century
place unknown
d. Thirteenth century
place unknown
fields: Physics

Petrus was the author of the first Western scientific treatise on the principles of magnetism. His practical inventions included a floating compass and a pivoted compass, both of which were used for finding the meridian and the azimuths of heavenly bodies.

Perera Soto, Hilda

b. Nov. 11, 1926
Cuba
fields: Literature

Writer. Hilda Perera Soto was educated in both Cuba and the United States. She fled Fidel Castro's regime for good in 1964, smuggling out pages of what would become her most popular novel, *El sitio de nadie* (1972). She also wrote the novels *Mañana es 26* (1960), *Felices Pascuas* (1977), and *Plantado* (1981), as well as the short-story collection *Cuentos de Apolo* (1974). She has also written stories for children.

Peres, Shimon

né: Shimon Perski
b. August 21, 1923
Vishneva, Poland (now Belarus)
fields: Diplomacy, Government and Politics

Israeli statesman and two-time prime minister (1984-1986, 1995-1996). Shimon Peres held many government posts; as minister of defense, masterminded 1976 Entebbe rescue. Became prime minister in 1984; headed a national unity government, sharing power with Yitzhak Shamir, leader of Likud Party. Tried to resolve various problems resulting from Israel's incursion into Lebanon in 1982 and to rebuild Israel's struggling economy. Awarded 1994 Nobel Peace Prize, with Yitzhak Rabin and Palestine Liberation Organization (PLO) chairman Yasir Arafat, for role in Middle East peace accords. After Rabin's assassination in November, 1995, Peres was sworn in as prime minister and minister of defense. Held posts only until May, 1996, when he was defeated by Benjamin Netanyahu.

Perez, Anna

b. 1951
New York, N.Y.
fields: Government and Politics

African American press secretary to First Lady Barbara Bush; after working as congressional press aide for Washington State Senator Slade Gorton and as press secretary to Washington State Representative John Miller, Anna Perez was appointed in 1989 to serve as press secretary for Barbara Bush (the first African American to serve as a first lady's press secretary); Perez traveled extensively with President Bush and Mrs. Bush.

Pérez, Lisandro

b. c. 1949
Havana, Cuba
fields: Sociology

Sociologist. In 1960, at the age of eleven, Lisandro Pérez moved to the United States. He earned an M.A. and Ph.D. in sociology from the University of Florida, then worked at Louisiana State University for eleven years. In 1985, he moved to Florida International University and became director of the Cuban Research Institute. He has published essays on demographics and social change in Cuba and on the dynamics of the Cuban community in the United States. He has also served as contributing editor for *The Handbook of Latin American Studies*.

Perez, Pedro

b. 1951
Caibarien, Cuba
fields: Art

Artist. Pedro Perez's family moved to the United States in 1966. He received his M.F.A. in 1978 and began teaching at the Tyler School of Art in Philadelphia, Pennsylvania. Perez, who considers his work more American than Cuban, has produced paintings, sculptures, and drawings.

Pérez, Ruby Nelda

b. Feb. 17, 1954
Chicago, Ill.
fields: Theater and Entertainment (actor)

Latina actor. In 1977, Ruby Nelda Pérez cofounded the First Bilingual Theater of Houston. In 1979, she taught drama at the Plaza de la Raza in Los Angeles. In 1980, she joined Teatro de la Esperanza in Santa Barbara. In 1982, she became director of Houston's Bilingual Theater. In 1984, she and her husband moved to San Antonio to work at the Guadalupe Cultural Arts Center. In 1985, Pérez performed the one-woman show *A Woman's Work* at the Women's International Day Conference. In 1993, she premiered a second solo show, *Doña Rosita's Traveling Jalapeño Kitchen*, developed in collaboration with Teatro de la Ezperanza.

Perez, Selena Quintanilla. *See* Selena

Perez, Tony

full: Atanasio Perez y Rigal
b. May 14, 1942
Camagüey, Cuba
fields: Sports (baseball)

Tony Perez made his major league debut in 1964 with the Cincinnati Reds. From 1967 to 1975, Perez drove in more than 100 runs six times; he also hit as many as 40 home runs in a year and twice hit better than .300. In the 1975 World Series Perez hit three home runs. Perez was traded to the Montreal Expos after the 1976 season. A seven-time All-Star, Perez retired in 1986.

Pérez de Cuéllar, Javier

b. January 19, 1920
Lima, Peru
fields: Diplomacy, Government and Politics

Javier Pérez de Cuéllar served as Secretary-General of the United Nations from 1982 to 1992, focusing on the development of global social and economic policies and resolving a variety of international crises that emerged during his two terms in office.

Pérez-Méndez, Victor

b. Aug. 8, 1923
Guatemala City, Guatemala
fields: Physics

Physicist. Victor Pérez-Méndez earned a Ph.D. from Columbia University in 1951 and began work as a research scientist at the Lawrence Berkeley Laboratory. He became a professor of physics and radiology at the University of California, San Francisco, in 1969. He has researched nuclear and high-energy physics, radiation detectors, and medical imaging.

Pericles

b. c. 495 B.C.E.
Athens, Greece
d. 429 B.C.E.
Athens, Greece
fields: Government and Politics

The Age of Pericles was a crucial period in the history of Athens. Pericles' transformation of the Delian League into the Athenian empire provided the financial basis for the flowering of Athenian democracy.

Perkins, Charlotte Anna. *See* Gilman, Charlotte Perkins

Perkins, Edward Joseph

b. June 8, 1928
Sterlington, La.
fields: Diplomacy

African American diplomat; in 1967 Edward Joseph Perkins, a career diplomat, began his tenure with the U.S. Foreign Service working in the Agency for International Development; other diplomatic positions have included director of the Office of West African Affairs for the Bureau of African Affairs, ambassador to Liberia, the first African American ambassador to South Africa, director general and later director of personnel of the U.S. Foreign Service (1989-1992), United States ambassador to the United Nations (1992-1993), U.S. ambassador to Australia (1993-1996), when he retired.

Perkins, Frances

aka: Fannie Coralie Perkins
b. April 10, 1880
Boston, Massachusetts
d. May 14, 1965
New York, New York
fields: Government and Politics

Perkins, as secretary of labor for twelve years under President Franklin Delano Roosevelt, was the first woman to serve in a president's cabinet. As secretary of labor, she was instrumental in developing legislation to improve labor conditions for workers. Her most notable achievement was to chair the committee responsible for developing the social security system.

Perkins, Joseph

b. ?
fields: Journalism, Government and Politics

African American journalist and political appointee; Joseph Perkins worked as an editorial writer with a conservative point of view for *The Wall Street Journal* for four and one half years; appointed deputy assistant for domestic policy for the Office of the Vice President by President Ronald Reagan; in his article "Boom Time for Black America: The Middle Class Is Surging Under Reagan," published in *Policy Review* magazine, Perkins argued that the policies of the Reagan administration had fostered growth for members of the black middle class; editor of *A Conservative Agenda for Black Americans* (1987).

Perkins, M. Louise. *See* Grant, Micki

Perkins, Marion

b. 1908
Marche, Ark.
d. 1961
fields: Art (Sculptor)

African American sculptor; a student of Cy Gordon, Marion Perkins received a Purchase Award in 1951 from the Art Institute of Chicago, where her work resides in the permanent collection; her work was also exhibited at Howard University, Hull House in Chicago, and the American Negro Exposition in Chicago (1940).

Perkinson, Coleridge-Taylor

b. June 14, 1932
New York, N.Y.
fields: Music (composer and conductor)

African American composer and conductor; Coleridge-Taylor Perkinson was a guest conductor of the Albany, New York, and Dallas, Texas, symphony orchestras and served as conductor for the Brooklyn Community Orchestra (1959-1962); he was appointed the first composer-in-residence of the Negro Ensemble Company (1967); from 1966 to 1967, Perkinson worked for Jerome Robbins' American Theater Laboratory as music director; conductor of the Alvin Ailey American Dance Theater at the Brooklyn Academy of Music (beginning 1969); his works include *Sinfonietta for Strings* (1953), *Attitudes* (1964), *A Warm December* (1972), and *Freedom Road* (1979).

Perón, Eva

né: María Eva Duarte
full: Eva María Duarte de Perón
aka: Evita Perón
b. May 7, 1919
Los Toldos, Argentina
d. July 26, 1952
Buenos Aires, Argentina
fields: Government and Politics

Eva Perón's partnership with her husband, president Juan D. Perón, brought the laboring masses of Argentina into politics for the first time but also laid the foundation for a corrupt and brutal dictatorship.

Perón, Juan

full: Juan Domingo Perón
b. October 8, 1895
Lobos, Buenos Aires Province, Argentina
d. July 1, 1974
Buenos Aires, Argentina
fields: Government and Politics

More than any other figure, Perón dominated the history of twentieth century Argentina. He participated in coups that toppled the government in 1930 and 1943. With support from the armed forces and organized labor, he governed as president from 1943 to 1955 and 1973 to 1974. His legacy continued to divide Argentina long after his death in 1974.

Perot, H. Ross

full: Henry Ross Perot
b. June 27, 1930
Texarkana, Texas
fields: Business and Industry, Government and Politics

An immensely successful entrepreneur, Perot spent his first sixty years dedicated to improving American business. Thereafter he devoted his life to political reform and making government responsible to the people.

Pérotin

b. 1155-1160
possibly Paris, France
d. 1200-1205
probably Paris, France
fields: Music

Pérotin was a pioneer in the evolution of harmony as a principle of Western music. He transformed the nature of early music by first introducing three- and four-voice textures into church music, by developing polyphonic forms with semichordal sequences, and by adapting liturgical forms to secular purposes.

Perret, Auguste

b. February 12, 1874
near Brussels, Belgium
d. February 25, 1954
Paris, France
fields: Architecture

Perret's great contribution was the utilization, refinement, and promotion of reinforced concrete, or ferroconcrete, which he was convinced was the building material of the future.

Perrin, Jean-Baptiste

b. Sept. 30, 1870
Lille, France
d. Apr. 17, 1942
New York, New York
fields: Chemistry, Physics

Jean-Baptiste Perrin, in 1895, demonstrated that cathode rays are negatively charged; created an experimental proof for the existence of atoms, in 1908; in 1926, won the Nobel Prize in Physics.

Perry, Carrie Saxon

b. August 10, 1931
Hartford, Conn.
fields: Government and Politics

African American mayor of Hartford, Conn; an activist in matters of minority education and employment, Carrie Saxon Perry held office for eight years as state representative from Hartford to the Connecticut General Assembly; as state representative she sponsored the initiative that gave Connecticut's homeless citizens the right to vote; inaugurated mayor of Hartford on December 1, 1987.

Perry, Christopher James

b. September 15, 1859
Baltimore, Md.
d. 1921
fields: Publishing

African American publisher; Christopher James Perry published the Philadelphia *Tribune*, established in 1884, through which he campaigned for better working conditions and jobs for African Americans.

Perry, Fred

full: Frederick John Perry
b. May 18, 1909
Stockport, Cheshire, England
d. February 2, 1995
Melbourne, Australia
fields: Sports (tennis)

Between 1933 and 1936, Perry won all the world's major tennis championships and led the British team to victory in the Davis Cup, thereby restoring British tennis prestige.

Perry, Harold Robert

b. October 9, 1916
Lake Charles, La.
d. July 17, 1991
New Orleans, La.
fields: Religion and Theology

African American religious leader; Harold Robert Perry is noted as the first African American to head a Catholic religious order, to head a Catholic seminary, and to offer the opening prayer in the U.S. Congress; he served as an active pastor until his death.

Perry, Joe

full: Fletcher Joseph Perry
b. January 27, 1927
Stevens, Ark.
fields: Sports (football player)

African American football player; one of the first African Americans to play professional football, Joe Perry is known as one of the great running backs of professional football; he played for the San Francisco 49ers (1948-1960, 1963) and for the Baltimore Colts (1961-1962); he finished his fifteen-season career in 1963 as professional football's all-time rushing yardage leader; in 1969 elected to the Pro Football Hall of Fame.

Perry, Julia

b. March 25, 1924
Lexington, Ky.
d. April 24, 1979
Akron, Ohio
fields: Music (classical composer)

African American composer; after earning a master's degree from Westminster Choir College (1948), studying operatic conducting at Juilliard, and studying with Luigi Dallapiccola in Florence and Nadia Boulanger in Paris, Julia Perry produced such works as *Stabat Mater* (1951), *The Cask of Amontillado* (1954; an opera), *Homunculus, C. F.* (1969), and *Children's Symphony* (1978).

Perry, Lincoln Theodore Monroe Andrew Skeeter. *See* Fetchit, Stepin

Perry, Matthew C.

full: Matthew Calbraith Perry
b. April 10, 1794
Newport, Rhode Island
d. March 4, 1858
New York City
fields: Military Affairs, Diplomacy

In a naval career spanning almost half a century, Perry, besides commanding ships and fleets with distinction in peace and in war, proposed and accomplished reforms in naval architecture, ordnance, and organization, and through skillful negotiation introduced Japan into the modern community of nations.

Perry, Oliver Hazard

b. August 20, 1785
South Kingston, Rhode Island
d. August 23, 1819
near Port of Spain, Trinidad
fields: Military Affairs

Perry's skillful seamanship and tactical tenacity in the War of 1812 provided an example of leadership and courage to the officers and crews of the young republic's fledgling navy.

Perry, Shauneille

b. July 26, 1929
fields: Theater and Entertainment

African American theater director, actress, and playwright; Shauneille Perry was a foremost director for the Negro Ensemble Company; as coproducer for the National Black Touring Circuit she wrote the musical *Celebration*, which presented African American traditions; she has also penned several plays; recipient of an Audelco Award.

Pershing, John J.

full: John Joseph Pershing
b. January 13, 1860
Laclede, Missouri
d. July 15, 1948
Washington, D.C.
fields: Military Affairs

A career soldier, Pershing was ready when called upon to lead the American Expeditionary Force to Europe in World War I, helping to preserve democracy in the first global conflict.

Perske, Betty Joan. *See* Bacall, Lauren

Perski, Shimon. *See* Peres, Shimon

Persons, Truman Streckfus. *See* Capote, Truman

Perutz, Max

full: Max Ferdinand Perutz
b. May 19, 1914
Vienna, Austria
fields: Biology, Chemistry, Medicine

Max Ferdinand Perutz used X-ray crystallography to find the molecular structure of the protein hemoglobin. He won the 1962 Nobel Prize in Chemistry.

Peshkov, Aleksey Maksimovich. *See* Gorky, Maxim

Pestalozzi, Johann Heinrich

b. January 12, 1746
Zurich
d. February 17, 1827
Brugg, Switzerland
fields: Education

Pestalozzi spent his life seeking ways to help students improve their learning skills so that they could develop into effective adults. His method was based upon imparting an awareness of and encouraging direct interaction with objects, progressing from simple steps to more complex ones in an orderly pattern, thereby achieving harmonious organic development.

Pétain, Philippe

full: Henri-Philippe Pétain
b. April 24, 1856
Cauchy-à-la-Tour, France
d. July 23, 1951
Port-Joinville, Île d'Yeu, France
fields: Military Affairs, Government and Politics

During World War I, Pétain was one of the few prominent military commanders to discard the massive offensive as a desired operational method. His skill at defensive warfare contributed to the Allies' eventual defeat of Germany in 1918. Pétain later entered politics and served as the controversial Vichy chief of state during the entire German Occupation of France.

Petalésharo

b. c. 1797
d. c. 1833
fields: Government and Politics, Native American Affairs

"Petalésharo" seems to have functioned as a title, as well as a personal name, during the early eighteenth century among the Pawnee; several outstanding warriors used the name, and it is sometimes difficult to attribute biographical details to one individual. The best-known Petalésharo ended the use of human sacrifice in the Pawnee Morning Star Ceremony. Also toured the Northeast and spoke in Washington, D.C.

Peter III

né: Karl Peter Ulrich
aka: Grand Duke Peter Fedorovich
b. February 21, 1728
Kiel, Holstein
d. July 18, 1762
Ropsha, Russia
fields: Government and Politics, Monarchy

Czar of Russia for only 186 days in 1762, Peter III nevertheless influenced both Russia and the rest of Europe. He emancipated the Russian nobility from compulsory state service, secularized the property of the Russian Orthodox Church, and reversed Russia's traditional pro-Austrian foreign policy in favor of a Prussian orientation.

Peter, Saint

né: Simon
aka: Simeon
b. Early first century
Bethsaida of Galilee
d. 64 C.E.
Rome
fields: Religion and Theology

During Jesus' life, Peter was the most faithful and outspoken of the disciples; after Jesus' death he gave leadership to the early Church at Jerusalem and was active in missionary work. In Catholic tradition, he is the founder of the Christian Church and of the Papacy.

Peter the Great

b. June 9, 1672
Moscow, Russia
d. February 8, 1725
St. Petersburg, Russia
fields: Government and Politics, Social Reform, Monarchy

Czar of Russia, 1696-1725. Borrowing both ideas and technology from the West, Peter the Great modernized Russian society, introduced significant military reforms, and built a navy almost from scratch. He won important territories on the Baltic coast from Sweden and transformed Russia into a great European power.

Peters, Brock

né: Brock Fisher
b. July 2, 1927
New York, N.Y
fields: Theater and Entertainment, Film

African American actor; having debuted in the Broadway revival of *Porgy and Bess* (1943), Brock Peters went on to play in the touring productions of *Anna Lucasta* (1944-1945), *The Great White Hope* (1969), *Lost in the Stars* (1972), *Driving Miss Daisy* (1988), *The Importance of Being Earnest* (1992), and *Park Day* (1998); his film credits include the critically and popularly acclaimed role of a southern black man wrongly accused of raping a white woman in *To Kill a Mockingbird* (1962), *The Pawnbroker* (1965), *The Incident* (1967), the screen adaptation of the musical *Lost in the Stars* (1974), and *Star Trek IV: The Voyage Home* (1986); honors received include the L.A. Drama Critics Circle Award, lifetime achievement awards from the National Film Society and the Screen Actors Guild, and the NAACP Theater Award (1990).

Petersen, Frank E.

b. March 2, 1932
Topeka, Kans.
fields: Military Affairs, Warfare and Conquest

African American military officer; upon retiring as a lieutenant general from the U.S. Marine Corps in 1988, Frank E. Petersen's many firsts included being the first black aviator in the Marines, the first black officer to command a squadron in the U.S. Navy or Marine Corps, and the first black general in the Marine Corps (promoted February, 1979); his postings included flying sixty combat missions in Korea, commanding the Marine Fighter Attack Squadron 314 in Vietnam and flying three hundred missions, commanding general of the First Marine Aircraft Wing (1983), and commanding general of the Marine Corps Development and Education Command at Quantico, Va., (1986).

Peterson, Oscar

b. August 15, 1925
Montreal, Quebec, Canada
fields: Music (jazz pianist)

African American pianist; a classically trained pianist, Oscar Peterson found popular success with a trio which included Herb Ellis on guitar and Ray Brown on bass (1953-1958), later replacing Ellis with drummer Ed Thigpen (1958-1967); the trio's most well known recordings are probably those made while playing backup to Ella Fitzgerald and Louis Armstrong on an album of standards; Peterson established Toronto's Advanced School for Contemporary Music in 1960 and ran the school for a number of years; Peterson continued to perform with major symphony orchestras and as a soloist in the 1980's and 1990's.

Petrarch

né: Francesco Petrarca
b. July 20, 1304
Arezzo, Italy
d. July 18, 1374
Arquà, Italy
fields: Literature

Petrarch's scholarship stimulated a revival of interest in classical studies, and his vernacular poetry created a veritable Petrarchan school of sonneteers.

Petry, Ann

b. October 12, 1908
Old Saybrook, Conn.
d. April 28, 1997
Old Saybrook, Connecticut
fields: Literature

African American journalist and novelist; the work of Ann Petry, with its vivid depictions of ghetto life, is often compared to that of Richard Wright; her most well known work is *The Street* (1946), a portrayal of the life of a young woman struggling to raise her son.

Petty-Fitzmaurice, Henry Charles Keith. *See* Lansdowne, Lord

Pezi. *See* Grass, John

Pfeiffer, Jane Cahill

né: Jane Pennington Cahill
b. September 29, 1932
Washington, D.C.
fields: Business and Industry

Pfeiffer served as vice president of communications at International Business Machines in 1972 and chairman of the National Broadcasting Corporation in 1978, when she was the highest-paid female executive in the United States.

Phaedrus

b. c. 15 B.C.E.
Pieria, Thessaly, Macedonia
d. c. 55 C.E.
place unknown
fields: Literature

As a prolific writer of fables and reputed translator of Aesop, Phaedrus elevated the fable from a rhetorical device, used incidentally in writing and speaking, to a completely independent genre with a recognizable place in literature.

Pheidippides

b. probably c. 515 B.C.E.
Athens, Greece
d. perhaps 490 B.C.E.
perhaps Athens, Greece
fields: Warfare and Conquest

A courier commonly known as Pheidippides is famous for delivering a message, on foot and over a long distance, concerning the Battle of Marathon fought between Persia and Athens in 490 B.C.E.. Despite problems with the ancient tradition, Pheidippides' feat of running is still popularly associated with the announcement of the Athenian victory and also with the introduction of the "marathon" race in modern times.

Phelan, James D.

b. Apr. 20, 1861
San Francisco, Calif.
d. Aug. 7, 1930
Saratoga, Calif.
fields: Government and Politics

James D. Phelan was mayor of San Francisco (1897-1902), U.S. senator from California (1915-1921), and a regent of the University of California (1898-1899). He used the slogan Keep California White for his Senate reelection campaign and championed Chinese and Japanese exclusion, arguing that Chinese exclusion was the only way to preserve Western civilization. He supported California's Alien Land Law of 1913 and pushed for more stringent exclusionary legislation against the Japanese.

Phidias

b. c. 490 B.C.E.
Athens, Greece
d. c. 430 B.C.E.
Elis, Greece
fields: Art

Phidias' work embodied the high classical ideal in sculpture; his renditions of the gods became standards to which later artists aspired. Director of the sculpture program of the Parthenon in Athens, he was best known for his cult images of Athena in Athens and of Zeus in Olympia.

Philip II of Macedonia

b. 382 B.C.E.
Macedonia
d. 336 B.C.E.
Aegae, Macedonia
fields: Government and Politics, Warfare and Conquest

Philip inherited a backward kingdom on the verge of collapse and made it a powerful state. His military innovations revolutionized warfare and created the army that would conquer the Persian Empire.

Philip II

aka: Philip II Augustus
b. August 21, 1165
Paris
d. July 14, 1223
Mantes
fields: Government and Politics, Monarchy

King of France, 1180-1223. Philip II, the strongest of the Capetian kings of France, greatly expanded the royal domain and created an efficient system of political administration.

Philip II

b. May 21, 1527
Valladolid, Spain
d. September 13, 1598
El Escorial Palace, Spain
fields: Government and Politics, Religion and Theology, Monarchy

King of much of Europe and the New World, 1556-1598. Philip II was one of the most dominant monarchs in Europe during the late sixteenth century. Guided by his deep religious faith, Philip was involved in virtually every major event in the last half of the sixteenth century.

Philip IV the Fair

b. 1267 or 1268
Fontainebleau, France
d. November 29, 1314
Fontainebleau, France
fields: Government and Politics, Monarchy

King of France from 1285 to 1314, Philip steadfastly created a strong monarchy in France. He developed a bureaucracy that allowed for firmer central control of raising revenues in the kingdom. His efforts, by accelerating the departure from a feudal form of government, began to modernize the French state.

Philip, King. *See* Metacomet

Philip the Good

b. July 31, 1396
Dijon, Burgundy
d. June 15, 1467
Bruges, Flanders
fields: Government and Politics, Patronage of the Arts

Despite his failure to build a unified state between France and the German states, Philip created sound administrative policies throughout his territories and established one of the most brilliant and cultured courts in Europe.

Philip the Magnanimous

aka: Philipp der Grossmütige
b. November 13, 1504
Marburg, Hesse
d. March 31, 1567
Cassel, Hesse
fields: Monarchy, Church Reform

Ruler of Hesse, 1509-1567; proclaimed of age in 1518. Philip the Magnanimous was perhaps the most significant single political supporter of the Protestant Reformation during the critical early years of the movement in the sixteenth century.

Philippe, duc d'Orléans. *See* Orléans, duc d'

Phillip, Arthur

b. October 11, 1738
London, England
d. August 31, 1814
Bath, England
fields: Military Affairs, Government and Politics

An officer in the British Royal Navy, Phillip served as the first governor of Australia from 1788 to 1792. To this prudent and judicious head of the struggling convict colony, the modern nation owes its existence.

Phillips, Esther

né: Esther Mae Jones
b. December 23, 1935
Galveston, Tex.

d. August 7, 1984
Los Angeles, Calif.
fields: Music (Singer)

African American singer; a versatile performer who sang blues, pop, rhythm and blues, and skillfully merged soul music with jazz and country western, Esther Phillips recorded "Little Ester," her first number-one hit song, in 1950.

Phillips, Vel Rogers

b. February 18, 1924
Milwaukee, Wis.
fields: Government and Politics

African American city councilwoman and state politician; as the first African American and the first woman to serve on the Milwaukee, Wisconsin, city council (1956-1972), Vel Rogers Phillips was elected Wisconsin's secretary of state (1978-1982; the first African American elected to a statewide constitutional office in Wisconsin); served on the Democratic National Committee (1958-1964).

Phillips, Wendell

b. November 29, 1811
Boston, Massachusetts
d. February 2, 1884
Boston, Massachusetts
fields: Social Reform

Phillips was one of the foremost orators and writers in the American antislavery movement and other social movements from 1837 until 1884.

Philo of Alexandria

b. c. 20 B.C.E.
Alexandria, Egypt
d. c. 45 C.E.
possibly outside Alexandria
fields: Philosophy

Philo harmonized Old Testament theology with Greek philosophy, especially Platonism and Stoicism; his thought contributed much to that of Plotinus, originator of Neoplatonism, and to the ideas of the early church fathers.

Phung Thi Le Ly. *See* Hayslip, Le Ly

Piaget, Jean

b. August 9, 1896
Neuchâtel, Switzerland
d. September 16, 1980
Geneva, Switzerland
fields: Biology, Education, Philosophy

Piaget was awarded an honorary degree from Harvard University in 1936, the Sorbonne in 1946, and the University of Brussels in 1949 for his work on the evolution of intelligence in the human young. He found in developmental psychology a link between the biological adaptation of organisms to the environment and the philosophical quest for the source of knowledge.

Piankhi

b. c. 769 B.C.E.
place unknown
d. 716 B.C.E.
place unknown
fields: Warfare and Conquest, Government and Politics

Dynamic and forceful King of Kush, Piankhi invaded a divided Egypt, conquered it, and initiated an almost century-long Kushite rule over the entire Nile Valley.

Piazzola, Astor

b. March 11, 1921
Mar del Plata, Argentina
d. July 5, 1992
fields: Music

Musician and composer. Astor Piazzola, who grew up in New York City, performed and arranged music for tango bands and orchestras in Argentina before going to Paris to study music with Nadia Boulanger. He won prizes for his compositions and also gave the tango a new harmonic twist and rhythm character, sometimes referred to as the "new tango." In 1976, Piazzola formed El Quinteto Tango Nuevo, and they recorded the albums *Tango Zero Hour* and *The Rough Dancer and the Cyclical Night*. Piazzola's original works include more than 750 compositions and more than seventy recordings.

Picard, Émile

b. July 24, 1856
Paris, France
d. December 11, 1941
Paris, France
fields: Mathematics, Physics, Engineering

Picard's theories advanced research into analysis, algebraic geometry, and mechanics.

Picasso, Pablo

full: Pablo Ruiz Picasso
b. October 25, 1881
Málaga, Spain
d. April 8, 1973
Mougins, France
fields: Art

The most prolific and famous artist of his time, Picasso was crucial to the development of modern art. He was an inventor of cubism and one of the prime practitioners of academic realism, Postimpressionism, art nouveau, expressionism, Fauvism, abstract expressionism, Surrealism, and Futurism. A skilled craftsman, he was the master of many mediums.

Piccard, Auguste

b. January 28, 1884
Basel, Switzerland
d. March 24, 1962
Lausanne, Switzerland
fields: Aviation and Space Exploration, Oceanography, Physics

The twin brothers Auguste and Jean-Felix Piccard designed hot-air balloons and piloted them into the stratosphere to study cosmic rays and atmospheric electricity and to encourage high-altitude flight. Auguste also developed a bathyscaphe in which he reached unprecedented ocean depths.

Piccard, Jean-Felix

b. January 28, 1884
Basel, Switzerland
d. January 28, 1963
Minneapolis, Minnesota
fields: Aviation and Space Exploration, Physics

The twin brothers Auguste and Jean-Felix Piccard designed hot-air balloons and piloted them into the stratosphere to study cosmic rays and atmospheric electricity and to encourage high-altitude flight. Furthermore, Jean-Felix's discovery that certain types of molecules split apart in solution was named the Piccard Effect in his honor.

Piccolomini, Enea Silvio. *See* Pius II

Pickett, Bill

b. December 5, 1870
Williamson County, Texas
d. April 2, 1932
near Ponca City, Oklahoma
fields: Sports (cowboy and rodeo star)

African American cowboy and rodeo star; the first African American inducted into the National Cowboy Hall of Fame, Bill Pickett is noted for inventing the rodeo technique of "bulldogging" whereby the neck and horns of a steer are twisted downward while the range rider bites its upper lip, thus forcing the animal to the ground.

Pickett, Wilson

b. March 18, 1941
Prattville, Ala.
fields: Music (soul singer)

African American soul singer; known for such soul classics as "In the Midnight Hour" (1965) and "Funky Broadway" (1967), Wilson Pickett got his start in popular music as a member of the Falcons; he sang lead on that group's hit "I Found a Love" (1962).

Pickford, Mary

né: Gladys Louise Smith
b. April 8, 1892
Toronto, Ontario, Canada

d. May 29, 1979
Santa Monica, California
fields: Film (actor)

Early in the history of the film industry, Pickford established herself as the first name box-office draw, and hence the first star, of American cinema. While the attraction of her name and image shaped the economics of motion pictures for decades, Pickford also became an early role model for independent women who took charge of their own destinies.

Pico, Andrés

b. 1810
d. 1876
fields: Warfare and Conquest, Government and Politics

Andrés Pico, son of José María Pico, served as commander-in-chief of Mexican forces during the Mexican American War. He signed the Articles of Capitulation at Cahuenga on January 13, 1847, which served as Mexico's final surrender to the Americans. Pico remained in politics and was elected to the state assembly. In 1859, his plan to correct representation and taxation conflicts between Northern and Southern California was adopted. His offer to raise a regiment of native California cavalry to help the North in the U.S. Civil War was rejected.

Pico, José María

b. ?
d. ?
fields: Historical Figure

The Picos, who settled in Los Angeles in 1786, were a prominent family in early California history. Two of Santiago de la Cruz Pico's sons, José Dolores Pico and José María Pico, became important members in their communities. José María's sons included Pío de Jesús Pico and Andrés Pico. Several areas in Los Angeles still bear the Pico name, including Pico House, a hotel built by Pío Pico in 1870; Pico Rivera, a southeastern Los Angeles suburb; and Pico Boulevard, a major east-west Los Angeles artery.

Pico, Pío

full: Pío de Jesús Pico
b. 1801
d. 1894
fields: Government and Politics

Pío Pico, son of José María Pico, received a large land grant of property in Jamul, in what is now San Diego County. He was elected governor in 1832, but his term lasted only thirty-two days because of political strife. He served a second term from March of 1845 to July of 1846, during which he had no treasury. During this time, Pico ended the mission era by granting thousands of acres of mission land to friends and supporters.

Picotte, Susan La Flesche

né: Susan La Flesche
b. June 17, 1865
Omaha Indian Reservation, Nebraska
d. September 18, 1915
Walthill, Nebraska
fields: Medicine, Social Reform

As the first female Native American physician, Picotte served her tribe as medical missionary and community leader for twenty-five years.

Pierce, Elijah

b. 1892
near Baldwyn, Miss.
d. 1984
Columbus, Ohio
fields: Art (wood sculptor and painter)

African American wood sculptor and painter. Elijah Pierce was a self-taught artist who became best known for his boldly painted religious carvings. His singular, sometimes whimsical style is considered "naive."

Pierce, Franklin

b. November 23, 1804
Hillsborough, New Hampshire
d. October 8, 1869
Concord, New Hampshire
fields: Government and Politics

After service in his state's legislature and in both houses of Congress, Pierce became the nation's fourteenth president (1853-1857), serving during the turbulent years between 1853 and 1857.

Pierce, Lawrence Warren

b. December 31, 1924
Philadelphia, Pa.
fields: Law

African American federal judge; Lawrence Warren Pierce served as assistant district attorney for Kings County in Brooklyn, N.Y. (1954-1961), leaving this position to serve as deputy commissioner of the New York City police department; appointed U.S. district judge for the Southern District of New York by President Richard M. Nixon (1971); appointed U.S. circuit judge for the U.S. Court of Appeals in New York City by President Ronald Reagan.

Pierce, Ponchitta Anne

b. August 5, 1942
Chicago, Ill.
fields: Journalism

African American journalist; Ponchitta Anne Pierce has worked as a bureau chief of the New York office of *Ebony* (1967), as a television news special correspondent for the Columbia Broadcasting System (CBS), and as an editor for *McCall's* magazine and *Reader's Digest.*

Pierce, Richard. *See* Havens, Richie

Pierce, Samuel Riley, Jr.

b. September 8, 1922
Glen Cove, N.Y.
fields: Government and Politics, Law

African American attorney, judge, and government official; in 1980 President Ronald Reagan appointed Samuel Riley Pierce, Jr., to the position of secretary of the Department of Housing and Urban Development; under President Richard Nixon he served as general counsel to the U.S. Treasury; he has also held positions in New York State as a judge of the Court of General Sessions (New York City), as assistant U.S. attorney for the Southern District, and as assistant district attorney.

Pierce, Sarah

b. June 26, 1767
Litchfield, Conn.
d. Jan. 19, 1852
Litchfield, Conn.
fields: Education

Sarah Pierce started a school in Litchfield in her dining room, which became the Litchfield Female Academy in 1827; Harriet Beecher Stowe, Henry Ward, and Catherine Beecher attended.

Piercy, Marge

b. March 31, 1936
Detroit, Michigan
fields: Literature

A popular poet and novelist, Piercy writes about working- and middle-class men and women, chronicling their relationships to nature, to society, and with one another in the context of a radical historical and feminist critique of the political and economic system.

Piero della Francesca

b. c. 1420
Borgo San Sepulcro
d. October 12, 1492
Sansepulcro, Tuscany
fields: Art, Mathematics

Though admired selectively for centuries, Piero della Francesca's paintings were not placed among the world's masterpieces until the twentieth century. His *Baptism of Christ, Resurrection, Legend of the True Cross*, and *Nativity* are now seen as crucial to the development of the characteristic forms and methods of Italian Renaissance painting.

Pierrepont, Mary. *See* Montagu, Mary Wortley

Pietri, Pedro

full: Pedro Juan Pietri
b. Mar. 21, 1943
Ponce, Puerto Rico
fields: Literature

Puerto Rican poet. Pedro Pietri was raised in New York City. His published books includes the poetry collections *Puerto Rican Obituary* (1973) and *Traffic Violations* (1983), and the prose work *Lost in the Museum of Natural History* (1981).

Pietro, Guido di. *See* Angelico, Fra

Pike, Zebulon

full: Zebulon Montgomery Pike
b. January 5, 1779
Lamberton (Trenton), New Jersey
d. April 27, 1813
York (Toronto), Ontario, Canada
fields: Exploration and Colonization

Pike helped to open the American Southwest to U.S. interests, and he gave his name to the famous Pikes Peak in the state of Colorado.

Pilate, Pontius

b. Date and place of birth unknown
d. After 36 C.E.
place unknown
fields: Biblical Figures, Government and Politics, Religion and Theology

A provincial Roman official, Pontius Pilate became infamous as the magistrate who presided over the trial of Jesus Christ.

Pimentel, David

b. May 24, 1925
Fresno, Calif.
fields: Natural History

Ecologist and entomologist. David Pimentel served as chief of the Tropical Research Laboratory at the U.S. Public Health Service in San Juan, Puerto Rico, from 1951 to 1953. In 1955, he joined the staff of Cornell, where he became a professor in ecology. From 1964 to 1966 he served on the President's Science Advising Council. His areas of expertise include ecology, the genetics of insects and plants, environmental resource management and population, energy and land resources in the food system, ecosystems management, and pest control.

Pincay, Laffit, Jr.

b. Dec. 29, 1946
Panama City, Panama
fields: Sports (jockey)

Panamanian jockey. Pincay, Laffit, Jr., began racing in the United States in 1966. He broke numerous racing records, including highest single-season earnings ($13,353,299 in 1985) and highest career earnings (more than $116 million), and won the sport's richest one-race purse ($2 million, for winning the 1985 Jersey Derby). Pincay won more than 8,700 races, second only to Bill Shoemaker in career victories. Among his victories were three consecutive Belmont Stakes (1982-1984) and the 1984 Kentucky Derby. He was voted the sport's outstanding jockey five times (1971, 1973, 1974, 1979, and 1985) was elected to the National Museum of Racing Hall of Fame in 1975.

Pinchback, P. B. S.

full: Pinckney Benton Stewart Pinchback
b. May 10, 1837
Macon, Ga.
d. December 21, 1921
Washington, D.C.
fields: Government and Politics, Law

African American politician and lawyer; P. B. S. Pinchback's role in founding and organizing Louisiana's Republican Party led to his becoming a member of the state central committee and of the state's constitutional convention (1867); he went on to be elected president pro tempore of the state Senate, succeeded to the position of lieutenant governor when incumbent Oscar J. Dunn died, and, following the impeachment of the white carpetbag governor, Henry Clay Warmoth, he served as acting governor (December 9, 1872-January 13, 1873); while acting governor of Louisiana, Pinchback was elected congressman-at-large, and the members of the state legislature elected him to the U.S. Senate; although Democrats were successful in contesting the elections, the U.S. Senate voted to pay him three years senatorial salary that he would have earned while the election was contested.

Pinckney, Darryl

b. 1953
Indianapolis, Ind.
fields: Literature (novelist, literary critic, and essayist)

African American novelist, literary critic, and essayist; in 1992, Darryl Pinckney's novel, *High Cotton*, was published; received the Whiting Writers Award in 1986 and the Art Seidenbaum Award for first fiction from the *Los Angeles Times* for his novel *High Cotton*; published fiction and critical essays on African American literature in *The New York Review of Books*, *Granta*, *Vanity Fair*, *Vogue*, *The New Yorker*, and *The New York Times*.

Pindar

b. c. 518 B.C.E.
Cynoscephalae, near Thebes, Boeotia, Greece
d. c. 438 B.C.E.
Argos, Greece
fields: Literature, Music

Pindar proved through his poetry and music that creative aspirations raise humanity to near-perfection; as the greatest lyrical poet of classical times, he influenced literature and culture for centuries.

Piñero, Jesús T.

b. Apr. 16, 1897
Carolina, Puerto Rico
d. Nov. 9, 1952
San Juan, Puerto Rico
fields: Government and Politics

Puerto Rican public official. When Jesús T. Piñero was appointed to serve out the term of the last American governor of Puerto Rico, Rexford G. Tugwell, in 1946, he became the first Puerto Rican to occupy the position of governor. At the time of his appointment, Piñero, a member of the Popular Democratic Party (Partido Popular Democrático), was serving as resident commissioner. In January, 1949, Piñero was replaced by Luis Muñoz Marín, who took office as Puerto Rico's first elected governor.

Piñero, Miguel

b. Dec. 19, 1946
Gurabo, Puerto Rico
d. June 16, 1988
New York, N.Y.
fields: Literature, Theater and Entertainment

Playwright, actor, and poet. Miguel Piñero began writing in New York's Sing Sing Prison, where he served time for armed robbery. Among his plays were *Short Eyes* (1974), which won Obie and New York Drama Critics Circle Awards, *Eulogy for a Small-Time Thief* (1977), *Playland Blues* (1980), and *A Midnight Moon at the Greasy Spoon* (1981). He also published the poetry collection *La Bodega Sold Dreams* (1980) and coedited the anthology *NuYorican Poet* (1975). Piñero acted in the off-Broadway play *Steambath*; the films *Alambrista!* (1977) and *Fort Apache, the Bronx* (1981); and the television series *Baretta*, *Kojak*, and *Miami Vice*.

Pinkerton, Allan

b. August 25, 1819
Glasgow, Scotland
d. July 1, 1884
Chicago, Ill.
fields: Law

American private detective. Allan Pinkerton's detective agency was the first to collect and circulate photographs and detailed physical descriptions of criminals, anticipating the later work of the Federal Bureau of Investigation and Interpol. Formed the North-Western Police Agency, later the Pinkerton Agency, about 1850; its early motto, "The Eye That Never Sleeps," gave the term "private eye" to the language.

Pinkett, Jada

b. 1971
Baltimore, Maryland
fields: Film, Television (actor)

African American actress; in 1991, Jada Pinkett joined the cast of the NBC television series *A Different World* as the character Lena James; film credits include *Menace II Society* (1993), *The Inkwell* (1994), *A Low Down Dirty Shame*, *Jason's Lyric*, and *Scream 2* (1997).

Pinkham, Lucius Eugene

b. Sept. 19, 1850
Chicopee Falls, Mass.
d. Nov. 2, 1922
San Francisco, Calif.
fields: Business and Industry

Lucius Eugene Pinkham moved to Hawaii in 1898. As president of the Territorial Board of Health (1904-1908), he was praised for his effective handling of outbreaks of cholera and bubonic plague and was recognized for his efforts to improve living conditions at the leper colony on the island of Molokai. Pinkham and businessman Oswald A. Stevens began to recruit laborers from Hong Kong and the Philippines to work on Hawaii plantations in 1908. Pinkham was appointed governor of the Territory of Hawaii in 1913. As governor, he won praise for his administration's efforts to provide native Hawaiians with homesteads. He also worked to provide pensions to teachers and fund the reclamation of swampland in Waikiki through the construction of a canal that was completed between 1922 and 1924. Pinkham moved to San Francisco in 1918.

Pinkham, Lydia Estes

né: Lydia Estes
b. February 9, 1819
Lynn, Massachusetts
d. May 17, 1883
Lynn, Massachusetts
fields: Business and Industry

Lydia Estes Pinkham developed a thriving business based on her patent medicine, influencing advertising and women's struggle to gain economic power.

Pinkney, Jerry

b. December 22, 1939
Philadelphia, Pa.
fields: Art (designer and illustrator)

African American designer and illustrator; Jerry Pinkney, an award-winning illustrator of children books, designed commemorative stamps for the U.S. Postal Service "Black Heritage" series.

Pinochet Ugarte, Augusto

b. November 25, 1915
Valparaíso, Chile
fields: Government and Politics

Oppressive president of Chile from 1974 to 1990. A military commander, Augusto Pinochet Ugarte took control of the government of Chile in 1974, after a coup overthrew elected Marxist government of Salvador Allende. In 1977 the United Nations condemned Pinochet's regime for its human rights abuses, but the oppression continued unabated. The military and the police tortured and killed opponents. Many people were arrested and never seen again; they became know as *desaparecidos*—"disappeared" ones. Pinochet did bring higher level of economic prosperity, but the rich primarily benefited. Voted out of office in 1990. Remained head of army until 1998; appointed senator for life in 1998. That year, he was detained in England (he was there for medical treatment) as the Spanish government sought to have him extradited to Spain for trial on human rights abuses.

Piñon, Nélida

b. May 3, 1935
Rio de Janeiro, Brazil
fields: Literature

Brazilian writer. Nélida Piñon worked for the newspaper *O Globo*, then for the literary magazine *Cadernos Brasileiros*. She taught at Columbia University in New York City. In 1955, she began writing novels and short stories full time. Among her novels are *Guiamapa de Gabriel Arcanjo* (1961), *Madeira feita cruz* (1963), *Fundador* (1969), *A casa da paixao* (1972), *A república dos sonhos* (1984; *The Republic of Dreams*, 1989), and *A doce cancao de Caetana* (1987; *Caetana's Sweet Song*, 1992).

Pinquana. *See* Washakie

Pinzón, Martín

full: Martín Alonso Pinzón
b. c. 1440
probably near Palos, Spain
d. March, 20, 1493
Palos, Spain
fields: Exploration and Colonization

The brothers Martín Alonso and Vicente Yáñez Pinzón provided crucial assistance for Christopher Columbus' first voyage to the New World. The brothers helped Columbus obtain and outfit his three ships and served as captains of the *Pinta* (Martín) and the *Niña* (Vicente).

Pinzón, Vicente

full: Vicente Yáñez Pinzón
b. c. 1462
Palos, Spain
d. c. 1523
probably Spain
fields: Exploration and Colonization

The brothers Martín Alonso and Vicente Yáñez Pinzón provided crucial assistance for Christopher Columbus' first voyage to the New World. The brothers helped Columbus obtain and outfit his three ships and served as captains of the *Pinta* (Martín) and the *Niña* (Vicente).

Pippen, Scottie

b. September 25, 1965
Hamburg, Ark.
fields: Sports (basketball player)

African American professional basketball player; Scottie Pippen, one of the best players in the National Basketball League (NBA), was originally drafted by the Seattle Supersonics in 1987 and immediately traded to the Chicago Bulls; became a star in his fourth season; was named Most Valuable Player of the 1993-1994 All-Star game; played on the 1992 U.S. Olympic Dream Team alongside Michael Jordan, Magic Johnson, Charles Barkley to win a gold medal.

Pippin, Horace

b. February 22, 1888
West Chester, Pa.
d. July 6, 1946
fields: Art (Painter)

African American painter; as a self-taught artist, Horace Pippin often portrayed battle scenes as he recalled them from World War I; for his time, he was considered one of the leading African American artists.

Pirandello, Luigi

b. June 28, 1867
Girgenti (now Agrigento), Italy
d. December 10, 1936
Rome, Italy
fields: Literature

Pirandello revolutionized modern drama by creating innovative plays that explored the nature of drama itself. He created an intellectual drama that redefined the nature of the self and examined in detail the effects of relativity on the human psyche. He won the 1934 Nobel Prize in Literature.

Pire, Dominique

né: Georges Charles Clement Ghislain
Eugène François Pire

b. February 10, 1910
Dinant, Belgium
d. January 30, 1969
Louvain, Belgium
fields: Social Reform

Pire received the Nobel Peace Prize for his work among World War II refugees in Europe, particularly those who were aged, crippled, or without those skills that could assure them acceptance by a receiving country.

Pirelli, Alberto

b. April 28, 1882
Milan, Italy
d. October 19, 1971
Casciano, Italy
fields: Business and Industry, Government and Politics, Invention and Technology

The Pirelli family was a group of Italian industrialists who furthered the development, production, and trade of rubber goods, electric wire, and electric cables. The family also figured significantly in nineteenth and twentieth century Italian and international politics. Alberto Pirelli helped his brother, Piero, expand the business into international markets. He also served in several important appointed political positions; he was a trusted financial and economic adviser to Benito Mussolini.

Pirelli, Giovanni Battista

b. December 27, 1848
Varenna, Austrian Empire
d. October 20, 1932
Milan, Italy
fields: Business and Industry, Invention and Technology

Giovanni Battista Pirelli was the patriarch of the Pirelli family, which was a group of Italian industrialists who furthered the development, production, and trade of rubber goods, electric wire, and electric cables. The family also figured significantly in nineteenth and twentieth century Italian and international politics. Giovanni Battista established the first rubber factory in Italy, produced some of the earliest telegraph and telephone wires for Italy's army, and produced some of the first air-filled bicycle and automobile tires.

Pirelli, Piero

b. January 27, 1881
Milan, Italy
d. August 7, 1956
Milan, Italy
fields: Business and Industry, Invention and Technology

The Pirelli family was a group of Italian industrialists who furthered the development, production, and trade of rubber goods, electric wire, and electric cables. The family also figured significantly in nineteenth and twentieth century Italian and international politics. Piero Pirelli furthered the family business and followed his father in managing the now vast enterprise.

Pirenne, Henri

full: Jean Henri Otto Lucien Marie Pirenne
b. December 23, 1862
Verviers, Belgium
d. October 24, 1935
Ukkel, Belgium
fields: Historiography

Pirenne altered extant periodization of European history and altered the thinking of medievalists by reminders of the influences of Islam and Byzantium on Western history and of all historians by diverting them from undue emphasis on institutional (legal), political, and religious events. The "Pirenne Thesis" has been a major influence on professional historical thinking.

Pisano, Andrea

né: Andrea da Pontadera
b. c. 1270-1290
possibly Pisa, Italy
d. c. 1348
probably Orvieto, Italy
fields: Art

Bronze, unknown as a medium for sculpture in Florence prior to the 1330's, was brought to that city by Pisano, who made an important contribution to art with his baptistery door, which was to be the example to be matched and supremely surpassed during the Florentine Renaissance.

Pisano, Giovanni

b. c. 1250
Pisa, Italy
d. Between 1314 and 1318
probably Siena, Italy
fields: Art

By synthesizing Gothic and classical influences, Nicola and Giovanni Pisano created sculptural styles which are considered proto-Renaissance in their concern with expanded form and space and humanized narrative scenes.

Pisano, Nicola

b. c. 1220
Apulia, Italy
d. Between 1278 and 1284
Pisa, Italy
fields: Art

By synthesizing Gothic and classical influences, Nicola and Giovanni Pisano created sculptural styles which are considered proto-Renaissance in their concern with expanded form and space and humanized narrative scenes.

Pisistratus

aka: Peisistratus
b. c. 612 B.C.E.; near Athens, Greece
d. 527 B.C.E.
Athens, Greece
fields: Government and Politics, Patronage of the Arts

As benevolent tyrant of Athens, Pisistratus prepared the way for the birth of Athenian democracy by introducing social, religious, and political reforms that raised popular expectations and possibilities. He nurtured the nationalism and intellectual brilliance that became the hallmark of Athenian civilization.

Pissarro, Camille

full: Jacob Camille Pissarro
b. July 10, 1830
Charlotte Amalie, St. Thomas, Danish West Indies
d. November 12, 1903
Paris, France
fields: Art

Pissarro contributed to the formation of Impressionist techniques and thus to the Impressionist movement in France in the last half of the nineteenth century. In addition, he played an instrumental role in establishing a series of exhibitions to promote the work of the Impressionist artists.

Pistol Bullet. *See* Manuelito

Pitchlynn, Peter Perkins

aka: Hatchootucknee
b. Jan. 30, 1806
in present- day Miss.
d. 1881
in present-day Okla.
fields: Native American Affairs, Government and Politics

Choctaw tribal chief and statesman; Peter Perkins Pitchlynn helped create Choctaw constitution in 1826; moved to Oklahoma with Choctaws in 1831; established Choctaw national school system in 1840's; elected chief in 1864 and served in that capacity to 1866; Pitchlynn argued, unsuccessfully, for Choctaw neutrality during the Civil War, but as principal chief was able to sign an armistice ending Choctaw involvement in the war as a member of the Confederacy; the fact that the Choctaw had joined the Confederacy, against the counsel of Pitchlynn, lost them their claim to much of the U.S. government money paid to the Choctaw Nation from sales of ceded Choctaw land.

Pitney, Mahlon

b. 1858
d. 1924
fields: Law

U.S. Supreme Court justice, 1912-1922; appointed by President Taft. Rejected attempts to apply the Bill of Rights to state criminal justice systems and read the scope of those rights narrowly in federal criminal cases. Significant opinions: *Frank v. Mangum*, 237 U.S. 309 (1915); *Pierce v. United States*, 252 U.S. 239 (1920); *Berger v. United States*, 255 U.S. 22 (1921) (dissenting opinion).

Pitt the Elder, William

aka: first earl of Chatham
b. November 15, 1708
London, England
d. May 11, 1778
Hayes, Kent, England
fields: Government and Politics

With his brilliant administrative skill and his magnificent oratory, Pitt was the architect of Great Britain's success in the Seven Years' War against France, as a result of which she became the foremost maritime and commercial nation in the world.

Pitt the Younger, William

b. May 28, 1759
Hayes, Kent, England
d. January 23, 1806
Putney Heath, Surrey, England
fields: Government and Politics

One of the longest-serving prime ministers in British history, Pitt did much to restore stability to British politics in the aftermath of the American Revolution. He also strengthened the prime ministership, led the international opposition to Revolutionary and Napoleonic France, and changed the constitutional relationship between Great Britain and Ireland.

Pittacus of Mytilene

b. c. 645 B.C.E.
Mytilene, Lesbos, Greece
d. c. 570 B.C.E.
Mytilene, Lesbos, Greece
fields: Government and Politics

Elected tyrant by the people of Mytilene, Pittacus brought an end to his state's bitter aristocratic party struggles and established a government that remained stable for years after he had relinquished power. Though he was vilified by his political opponent Alcaeus, later Greeks considered Pittacus one of the "Seven Sages."

Pitts, Riley Leroy

b. October 15, 1937
Fallis, Okla.
d. October 31, 1967
near ApDong, Vietnam
fields: Warfare and Conquest

African American military hero; as a captain in the Twenty-seventh Infantry during the Vietnam War, Riley Leroy Pitts threw himself on a handgrenade to save his men but was spared when the grenade did not explode; several weeks later during a firefight with the enemy, Pitts was killed.

Pius II

né: Enea Silvio Piccolomini
aka: Aeneas Silvius Piccolomini
b. October 18, 1405
Corsignano, Republic of Siena
d. August 14/15, 1464
Ancona
fields: Religion and Theology, Government and Politics

Pope, 1458-1464. Through his elegant rhetoric and skilled diplomacy, Pius II reconciled differences among Christians to bring some peace to Western Christendom and tried vainly to mobilize a crusade to liberate Constantinople from the Turks.

Pius V

né: Antonio Ghislieri
b. January 17, 1504
Bosco, Duchy of Milan
d. May 1, 1572
Rome
fields: Religion and Theology, Church Reform

Cardinal Alessandrino, 1557-1566; Grand Inquisitor of the Roman Catholic Church, 1558-1566; Pope, 1566-1572. Pius V effected the reforms dictated by the Council of Trent, attempted to stem the spread of Protestantism, participated in the Inquisition, and was largely responsible for the naval defeat of the Ottoman Empire at Lepanto. His piety, religious zeal, and dedication to the Church eventually resulted in his canonization.

Pius IX

né: Giovanni Maria Mastai-Ferretti
b. May 13, 1792
Sinigaglia, Papal States
d. February 7, 1878
Rome
fields: Religion and Theology

Pius IX was elected pope in 1846, on the eve of the year of revolutions (1848). His was to be the longest papal reign in history. He led the Church through a difficult period into the era of Italian unity; in spite of the bitter conflict between church and state, he left the Church stronger at his death.

Pius XI

né: Ambrogio Damiano Achille Ratti
b. May 31, 1857
Desio, Italy
d. February 10, 1939
Vatican City, Italy
fields: Religion and Theology, Diplomacy

Pope Pius XI, 1922-1939. Pius XI was forced to deal with the problems emerging from World War I, especially the rise of communism and the various forms of right-wing totalitarianism (including Fascism and Nazism), along with the economic dislocation that affected Europe throughout the interwar period. His efforts not only allowed the Catholic church to regain respect but also restarted the Church's public involvement in social and political issues.

Pius XII

né: Eugenio Maria Giuseppe Giovanni Pacelli
b. March 2, 1876
Rome, Italy
d. October 9, 1958
Castle Gandolfo, near Rome, Italy
fields: Diplomacy, Religion and Theology

Pope Pius XII (1939-1958) preserved the Church as an institution during the crisis of World War II. He upheld traditional Catholic doctrine in an era of difficult economic, political, and social change.

Pizarro, Francisco

b. c. 1495
Trujillo, Spain
d. June 26, 1541
Lima, Peru
fields: Exploration and Colonization

Pizarro was a sixteenth century Spanish conquistador who experienced many frustrating years in the New World in search of fame and fortune before discovering and conquering the Incan Empire of Peru.

Pizi. *See* Gall

Place, Francis

b. November 3, 1771
London, England
d. January 1, 1854
London, England
fields: Government and Politics, Social Reform

Place worked for the advancement of organizations and legislation for the betterment of the workingman.

Planck, Max

full: Max Karl Ernst Ludwig Planck
b. April 23, 1858
Kiel, Schleswig
d. October 4, 1947
Göttingen, West Germany
fields: Physics, Philosophy, Religion and Theology

Planck's discovery in 1900 that light consists of infinitesimal "quanta" and his articulation of the quantum theory replaced classical physics with modern quantum physics. This work not only resulted in Planck's receiving the Nobel Prize in Physics for 1918 but also became a major enabling factor in the work of many other Nobel laureates.

Plantinga, Alvin

b. November 15, 1932
Ann Arbor, Michigan
fields: Philosophy, Religion and Theology

Best known for his philosophy of religion, Alvin Plantinga addresses the problem of how an omnipotent, omniscient God and evil can coexist. He uses the notion of possible worlds and possible persons as well as logical reasoning to argue for the existence of God. He published significant work on the philosophy of religion as well as metaphysics and knowledge theory (epistemology); he also offered theories in the philosophy of language and modal logic. One of his common themes, the nature of knowledge, was examined at length in his trilogy *Warrant: The Current Debate* (1993), *Warrant and Proper Function* (1993), and *Warranted Christian Belief* (1999). Plantinga's work in these areas influenced contemporary discussion on possible worlds, the problem of evil, the ontological argument, the notion of logical necessity, and the matter of when one is warranted in accepting something as true.

Plath, Sylvia

b. October 27, 1932
Boston, Massachusetts
d. February 11, 1963
London, England
fields: Literature

As both poet and novelist, Plath adopted a self-analytical style that helped to inspire the "confessional" school of literature in the decade following her death.

Platinum Prince. *See* Blow, Kurtis

Plato

né: Aristocles
b. c. 427 B.C.E.
Athens, Greece
d. 347 B.C.E.
Athens, Greece
fields: Philosophy

Plato used the dialogue structure in order to pose fundamental questions about knowledge, reality, society, and human nature—questions that are still alive today. He developed his own positive philosophy, Platonism, in answer to these questions, a philosophy which has been one of the most influential thought-systems in the Western tradition.

Plautus

né: Titus Maccius Plautus
b. c. 254 B.C.E.
Sarsina, Italy
d. 184 B.C.E.
Rome, Italy
fields: Theater and Entertainment

Plautus' action-packed, middle-class comedies, built from a dizzyingly contrived structure of disguises, mistaken identities, and the obligatory revelatory scene, were sensationally popular in his time; they have since influenced or been adapted by such comedic dramatists as William Shakespeare, Richard Brinsley Sheridan, Molière, and Jean Giraudoux.

Player, Gary

full: Gary Jim Player
b. November 1, 1935
Johannesburg, South Africa
fields: Sports (golf)

Player is one of only four men to achieve golf's Grand Slam, and at twenty-nine the youngest player to do so. He won numerous championships worldwide and helped to promote golf as an athletic sport.

Player, Willa Beatrice

b. August 9, 1909
Jackson, Miss.
fields: Education

African American educational administrator; as director of the division of institutional development in the office of education in the Department of Health, Education, and Welfare, Willa Beatrice Player used Title III of the Higher Education Act of 1965 to help secure funding for historically black and minority higher education institutions; was previously president of Bennett College, North Carolina.

Pleasant, Mary Ellen

b. August 19, 1814
Philadelphia, Pa.
d. January 11, 1904
San Francisco, Calif.
fields: Historical Figure, Business and Industry

African American entrepreneur and pioneer. Around 1850, Mary Ellen Pleasant opened a popular boardinghouse in San Francisco; may have helped finance John Brown's 1858 raid on Harpers Ferry; successfully sued two San Francisco railway companies for refusing passage to her and to other African Americans, in 1868.

Plekhanov, Georgi

b. November 29, 1856
Gudalovka, Russia
d. May 30, 1918
Terioki, Russia
fields: Government and Politics

Often dubbed the "Father of Russian Marxism," Georgi Plekhanov translated Karl Marx's and Friedrich Engels's *The Communist Manifesto* and embraced Marxism. In Russia he ranked second only to Karl Kautsky as a Marxist theorist until V. I. Lenin rose to power. Because of his hesitant support for Russia's 1905 Revolution and his support of Russian participation in World War I, Plekhanov's position as a leader weakened.

Plenty Coups

aka: Aleekchea'ahoosh (Many Achievements)
b. c. 1849
near Billings, Mont.
d. c. May 3, 1932
Pryor, Mont.
fields: Diplomacy, Government and Politics, Native American Affairs

Native American leader. Crow leader Plenty Coups allied the Crows with the U.S. Army against other Indian tribes. Crow warriors aided in the pursuit of Sitting Bull into Canada, the hounding of the Northern Cheyennes, and the surrender of Crazy Horse. Plenty Coups urged his people to become farmers and ranchers. Traveled to Washington, D.C., several times after 1880 to assure trade and aid for the Crows.

Plenty Kill. *See* Standing Bear, Luther

Plessis, Armand-Jean du. *See* Richelieu, Cardinal de

Plessis-Marly, Seigneur du. *See* Mornay, Philippe de

Pliny the Elder

né: Gaius Plinius Secundus
b. Probably 23 C.E.
probably Novum Comum, Italy
d. August 25, 79 C.E.
Stabiae, near Mount Vesuvius
fields: Science, Natural History

Pliny's *Natural History*, though not a work of original natural science, preserved for later times priceless information on the ancients' beliefs in countless areas. His work had great influence on later antiquity, the Middle Ages, and the early Renaissance, and he remains a major figure in the history of science.

Plotinus

b. 205
possibly Lycopolis, Upper Egypt
d. 270
Campania (now in Italy)
fields: Philosophy

As the founder of Neoplatonism, Plotinus has exerted a profound influence on Western philosophical and religious thought, from his own day to the present.

Plummer, Jewel. *See* Cobb, Jewel Plummer

Plunkett, Jim

full: James William Plunkett, Jr.
b. Dec. 5, 1947
Santa Clara, Calif.
fields: Sports (football player)

Football player. Jim Plunkett's college career at Stanford University included a Rose Bowl win and a Heisman Trophy. In 1971, he was drafted by the New England Patriots and earned the United Press International American Football Conference Rookie of the Year Award. Plagued by injuries, he did not live up to his promise until 1980, when he led the Oakland Raiders to a Super Bowl victory and was named both the Super Bowl Most Valuable Player and the Comeback Player of the Year. In the 1983, Plunkett led the Los Angeles Raiders to a Super Bowl win over the Washington Redskins. He retired after the 1986 season.

Plutarch

b. c. 46 C.E.
Chaeronea, Boeotia
d. After 120 C.E.
Chaeronea, Boeotia
fields: Literature

Plutarch was the greatest biographer of antiquity. He taught his successors how to combine depth of psychological and moral insight with a strong narrative that evokes the greatness and excitement of subjects' lives.

Poage, George Coleman

b. November 6, 1880
Hannibal, Mo.
d. 1962
Chicago, Ill.
fields: Sports (Hurdler)

African American hurdler; noted as the first black Olympian medalist, George Coleman Poage participated in the 1904 Olympics; he won one bronze medal in the 400-meter hurdles with a time of 54.8 seconds and a second bronze medal in the 200-meter hurdles with a time of 25.2 seconds; also set the collegiate record in the 220-yard high hurdles (25.0 seconds).

Pobedonostsev, Konstantin Petrovich

b. May 21, 1829
Moscow, Russia
d. March 23, 1907
St. Petersburg, Russia
fields: Government and Politics

As Director General of the Holy Synod and tutor to Czars Alexander III and Nicholas II, Pobedonostsev was a major contributor to the preservation of the autocratic governmental system in Russia against the forces of modernization.

Pocagin. *See* Pokagon, Leopold

Pocahontas

b. c. 1596
Virginia
d. March, 1617
Gravesend, Kent, England
fields: Diplomacy

One of the first women to influence the course of American history, Pocahontas was a critical figure in the survival of the first permanent English settlement.

Pochanaw-quoip. *See* Buffalo Hump

Podaladalte. *See* Zotom

Poe, Edgar Allan

b. January 19, 1809
Boston, Massachusetts
d. October 7, 1849
Baltimore, Maryland
fields: Literature

In addition to his achievements as one of the pioneering figures in American literature, Poe was influential in making magazine publishing an important force in the literary world of the nineteenth century.

Poggio

full: Giovanni Francesco Poggio Bracciolini
b. February 11, 1380
Terranuova, near Arezzo
d. October 30, 1459
Florence
fields: Literature

Through his tireless efforts, Poggio discovered and copied manuscripts of classical Latin authors that had been lost for centuries and which, if not for him, might have remained lost forever.

Poincaré, Henri

b. April 29, 1854
Nancy, France
d. July 17, 1912
Paris, France
fields: Mathematics, Physics

Poincaré was one of the most important mathematicians of the late nineteenth century. He developed the theory of automorphic functions (a method for expressing functions in terms of parameters), did extensive work in celestial mechanics and mathematical physics, was a codiscoverer of the special theory of relativity, and his writing style was so clear that he wrote books about the philosophy of science that were read widely by the general public and translated into many languages.

Poincaré, Raymond

b. August 20, 1860
Bar-le-Duc, France
d. October 15, 1934
Paris, France
fields: Government and Politics

Poincaré was perhaps the most important political figure of the French Third Republic (1871-1940). He had the distinction of moving from the premiership to the presidency before World War I and back to the premiership twice in the 1920's. He and Georges Clemenceau struggled to defend France against Germany during World War I and by the Treaty of Versailles, and Poincaré attempted to enforce or at least salvage part of the treaty during the postwar decade.

Poindexter, Joseph B.

b. Apr. 14, 1869
Canyon City, Oreg.
d. Dec. 3, 1951
Honolulu, Territory of Hawaii
fields: Government and Politics

Joseph B. Poindexter, a lawyer who had lived in Hawaii since 1917, was governor of the territory from 1934 until 1942, when martial law was imposed after the Japanese attacked Pearl Harbor on December 7, 1941. Major General Walter C. Short informed Poindexter that martial law was necessary to prevent a Japanese invasion of the islands, and following President Franklin D. Roosevelt's express approval, Short became military governor of Hawaii.

Poisson, Siméon-Denis

b. June 21, 1781
Pithiviers, France
d. Apr. 25, 1840
Sceaux, France
fields: Mathematics (applied math, calculus, and probability), Physics

Siméon-Denis Poisson described electrical phenomena—and other areas of physics, especially magnetism—mathematically.

Poitier, Sidney

b. February 20, 1924
Miami, Fla.
fields: Film, Theater and Entertainment

Sidney Poitier was the first African American male actor to be nominated for an Academy Award. His 1958 nomination for his role in *The Defiant Ones* was followed by an Academy Award for best actor for his 1963 role in *Lilies of the Field*. He became a top box office draw in the 1950's and 1960's with films such as *Blackboard Jungle* (1955), *Porgy and Bess* (1959), *In the Heat of the Night* (1967) and *To Sir with Love* (1967) and *Guess Who's Coming to Dinner* (1967). In the 1970's he teamed with Bill Cosby for a number of successful comedies, including *Uptown Saturday Night* (1974). He also directed a number of films, the most notable being *Stir Crazy* (1980), which starred Gene Wilder and Richard Pryor. In 1980 Poitier published his autobiography, *This Life*. In 1991 Poitier played Supreme Court Justice Thurgood Marshall in the made-for-television film *Separate but Equal*. He starred with Robert Redford in *Sneakers* in 1992. That year Poitier received a Life Achievement Award from the American Film Institute. His best-known theater role was as Walter Lee Younger in the first Broadway production of *A Raisin in the Sun* in 1959. In February of 1995, Poitier appeared in the CBS television miniseries *Children of the Dust*.

Pokagon, Leopold

aka: Pocagin
b. c. 1775
near Bertrand, Mich.
d. July 8, 1841
Cass County, Mich.
fields: Peace Advocacy, Diplomacy, Native American Affairs

Native American leader and powerful orator. A Potawatomi and Ojibwa (Chippewa), Leopold Pokagon was a forceful advocate of peace and a convert to Catholicism. Kept his people out of Tecumseh's uprising and the War of 1812. Sold the site of Chicago to whites in 1832

Pokagon, Simon

b. c. 1830
St. Joseph Valley, Mich.
d. Jan. 28, 1899
near Hartford, Mich.
fields: Government and Politics, Native American Affairs, Literature

Native American leader. A Potawatomi, Pokagon was widely regarded as one of the best-educated Indians of his generation; his writings on Indian culture were published in many magazines. Studied English at Notre Dame University, and Latin and Greek at Oberlin College. Mastered five languages and became an accomplished writer and organist.

Pol Pot

né: Saloth Sar
b. May 19, 1928
Kompong Thom Province, Cambodia
d. April 15, 1998
Dangrek Mountains, near Choam Ksant, Cambodia
fields: Government and Politics, Warfare and Conquest

In 1966, when the Cambodian communisty party, the Khmer Rouge, formed an army, Saloth Sar assumed the nom de guerre Pol Pot. After Prince Norodom Sihanouk was overthrown in 1970, Pol Pot's forces began a struggle against the new pro-American Khmer Republic, toppling it by 1975. Pol Pot's "reorganization" of Cambodian society resulted in the deaths of at least a million people. Vietnam sent troops in 1978 to drive Pol Pot's army out of Cambodia. Pol Pot remained the head of the Khmer Rouge from a base in Thailand, waging a guerrilla war against Vietnamese forces inside Cambodia. After a peace treaty was signed in Paris in 1991, political stability slowly returned to Cambodia, and Pol Pot was eventually placed under house arrest by his own Khmer Rouge. He died apparently of a heart attack in 1998.

Polite, Carlene Hatcher

b. August 28, 1932
Detroit, Mich.
fields: Literature, Social Reform, Education

African American novelist and educator; Carlene Hatcher, a political activist in the 1960's, organized the Northern Negro Leadership Conference; published *Les Flagellents* (1966) (*The Flagellants* 1967), and *Sister X and the Victims of Foul Play* (1975).

Polk, James K.

full: James Knox Polk
b. November 2, 1795
Mecklenburg County, North Carolina
d. June 15, 1849
Nashville, Tennessee
fields: Government and Politics

President of the United States, 1845-1849. A staunch nationalist, Polk used the authority of the presidency to bring about the expansion of the nation nearly to its continental limits. He added power as well as stature to the office.

Pollard, Fritz

full: Frederick Pollard, Sr.
b. January 27, 1894
Chicago, Ill.
d. May 11, 1986
Silver Spring, Md.
fields: Sports (football player and coach)

African American football player and coach; the first African American to play in a Rose Bowl game (1916, for Brown), Fritz Pollard left the collegiate scene to serve as player/coach for various professional football teams (again a first for an African American) including the Akron, Ohio, Indians (American Professional Football Association) and the Hammond, Ind., Pros (National Football League); after retiring from playing, Pollard founded (1935) and coached an African American football team called the Brown Bombers; in 1942 became vice president of the newly formed Negro Major Baseball League of America; in 1954 elected to the National Football Foundation College Football Hall of Fame.

Pollock, Jackson

full: Paul Jackson Pollock
b. January 28, 1912
Cody, Wyoming
d. August 11, 1956
East Hampton, Long Island, New York
fields: Art

A central figure in the New York School of Abstract Expressionists during the late 1940's and early 1950's, Pollock, through his "drip" painting, produced some of the most distinctive and unique work in the history of American art.

Polo, Marco

b. c. 1254
Venice?
d. January 8, 1324
Venice
fields: Exploration and Colonization

Through his Asian travels and his book recording them, Marco Polo encouraged a medieval period of intercultural communication, Western knowledge of other lands, and eventually the Western period of exploration and expansion.

Pólya, George

b. Dec. 13, 1887
Budapest, Austro-Hungarian Empire (now Hungary)
d. Sept. 7, 1985
Palo Alto, California
fields: Mathematics (applied math, calculus, geometry, number theory, and probability)

George Pólya is important for his work in mathematics education; his teaching style—sometimes called the "Pólya style"—is recorded on tape and presented as an example of masterful teaching to students at teachers' colleges; contributed to the language of mathematics; was the first to introduce the random walk and the central limit theorem; published *How to Solve It*, a popular book about mathematical problem solving, in 1945.

Polybius

b. c. 200 B.C.E.
Megalopolis, Arcadia, Greece
d. c. 118 B.C.E.
Greece
fields: Historiography

Through the advancement of sound historical methodology, Polybius contributed to the development of history as a significant area of inquiry having primarily a didactic rationale.

Polygnotus

b. c. 500 B.C.E.
Thasos, Greece
d. c. 440 B.C.E.?
Thasos, or Athens, Greece
fields: Art

Innovative, brash, confident in his skills, Polygnotus was the first great Greek painter. His murals at Delphi and in Athens established his reputation as the preeminent painter of the fifth century B.C.E. and probably the most famous in antiquity.

Pompa, Gilbert

b. Oct. 1, 1931
Devine, Tex.
d. April, 1990
Washington, D.C.
fields: Government and Politics

Mexican American government official. After earning his law degree, Gilbert Pompa worked as assistant city attorney in San Antonio (1960-1963) and assistant district attorney in Bexar County (1963-1967). In 1967, he began work as a field representative for the Community Relations Service of the U.S. Department of Justice. By 1978, he had worked his way up to director of the department. During his tenure, he was recognized for distinguished service during incidents at Wounded Knee, South Dakota, and Attica State Prison in New York.

Pompey the Great

aka: Gnaeus Pompeius
b. September 29, 106 B.C.E.
probably near Rome
d. September 28, 48 B.C.E.
Pelusium, Egypt
fields: Government and Politics, Warfare and Conquest

As a military leader and imperial proconsul, Pompey greatly extended the bounds of the Roman Empire during the late republic and, with Julius Caesar and Marcus Crassus, was one of the three leading figures whose careers and ambitions coincided with the final downfall of the Roman Republic.

Pompidou, Georges

b. July 5, 1911
Montboudif, France
d. April 2, 1974
Paris, France
fields: Government and Politics

Of the eighteen years during which Gaullism was in power in France, Pompidou was premier from 1962 to 1968 and president from 1969 to 1974. Gaullism stabilized France, renewed its pride, and restored its stature in the world.

Ponce, Mary Helen

b. Jan. 24, 1938
Southern California
fields: Literature

Latina writer. Mary Helen Ponce's published fiction, which explores such issues as bilingualism, biculturalism, and acculturation, includes the short-story collections *Recuerdo: Short Stories of the Barrio* (1983) and *Taking Control* (1987), and the novel *The Wedding* (1989).

Ponce de Léon, Juan

b. c. 1474
probably Santervás de Campos, Spain
d. July, 1521
Havana, Cuba
fields: Exploration and Colonization

Ponce de Léon discovered Florida and, more important, the Bahama Channel and the Gulf Stream, which proved invaluable to Spanish treasure ships making the passage from Mexico to Spain.

Ponce de León, Michael

b. July 4, 1922
Miami, Fla.
fields: Art (printmaker)

Printmaker. After serving in the U.S. Air Force during World War II, Michael Ponce de León began submitting drawings and cartoons to national magazines. His work appeared in *The Saturday Evening Post*, *The New Yorker*, and *American Legion*, among other publications. In 1978, he began teaching for the Art Students League, with whom he had studied previously. He also has taught at Pratt Graphic Center in New York City. His work is in the collections of the Museum of Modern Art, the Metropolitan Museum of Art, and the Smithsonian Institution.

Poncelet, Jean-Victor

b. July 1, 1788
Metz, France
d. Dec. 22, 1867
Paris, France
fields: Mathematics (geometry)

Jean-Victor Poncelet established projective geometry as a separate branch of mathematics.

Poniatowska, Elena

b. May 19, 1932
Paris, France
fields: Literature

Writer. Elena Poniatowska was educated in France, Mexico, and the United States. Her journalism career began in Mexico in 1955 with the newspaper *Excelsior*. In 1956, she began working for *Novedades*. Poniatowska is most well known for such journalistic books as *Hasta no verte, Jesús mío* (1969), *La noche de Tlatelolco* (1971; *Massacre in Mexico*, 1975), *Querido Diego, te abraza Quiela* (1978; *Dear Diego*, 1986), and *Gaby Brimmer* (1979, with Gabriela Brimmer). She also published the short-story collection *De noche nienes* (1979) and the novel *La "flor de Lis"* (1988).

Pontiac

b. c. 1720
on the Maumee River, Ohio
d. April 20, 1769
Cahokia, Illinois
fields: Native American Affairs, Diplomacy

Pontiac, of the Ottawa nation, was one of a series of great Indian leaders, including the Mohawk Joseph Brant, the Miami Little Turtle, the Shawnee Tecumseh, the Sac Black Hawk, and the Oglala Sioux Crazy Horse, who sought to maintain independence for the Indians in North America.

Pontiflet, Ted

b. June 19, 1932
Oakland, Calif.
fields: Photography, Literature, Education

African American photographer, writer, and teacher; after earning a B.F.A. at California College of Arts and Crafts and an M.F.A. at Yale University School of Art and Architecture, Ted Pontiflet began to write down and to photograph his experiences while living in Ghana during the 1960's; has taught courses on African American and African art at the college level; in 1978, published *Poochie*, a children's book.

Poole, Elijah. *See* Muhammad, Elijah

Poon, Wei Chi

b. ?
Canton, China
fields: Scholarship

Wei Chi Poon established the first Asian American library and Chinese American research collection at a U.S. university at the University of California, Berkeley. She wrote *The Directory of Asian American Collections in the United States* (1982) and *A Guide for Establishing Asian American Core Collections* (1989) and established Asian American subject headings that were recognized by the Library of Congress as national alternatives to standard subject headings.

Poor, Salem

b. 1758
Andover, Mass.

d. ?
fields: Warfare and Conquest

African American revolutionary War hero; born a free man, Salem Poor served in a primarily white Massachusetts militia company; several American officers petitioned the General Court of Massachusetts, asking that Poor be rewarded for his bravery during the Battle of Bunker Hill (June 17, 1775), but he received no commendation; on November 12, 1775, General George Washington issued instructions prohibiting African Americans from volunteering for military service or reenlisting; on December 30, 1775, Washington rescinded that order, and the Continental Congress approved reenlistment, thus enabling Poor to serve at both Valley Forge and White Plains.

Popé

b. 1630?
San Juan Pueblo
d. 1690
fields: Native American Affairs, Warfare and Conquest

San Juan Pueblo tribal leader and medicine man; Popé became an ardent opponent of the Spanish regime when Franciscan missionaries forced the Pueblos to abandon their own religion in favor of Christianity and *encomenderos* exploited Pueblo labor; in the 1670's, drought and famine brought Pueblo resentment and desperation to a peak; in 1675 Governor Juan Francisco Trevino arrested and flogged forty-seven Pueblo medicine men, including Popé; Popé inspired and led the Pueblo Revolt against Spanish colonists in New Mexico beginning on August 10, 1680; Franciscans living in the Pueblos were massacred, and Santa Fe was beseiged; by August 20, the surviving Spanish and a group of loyal Indians fled south to El Paso; the Spanish did not return to conquer the province until 1692.

Pope, Alexander

b. May 21, 1688
London, England
d. May 30, 1744
Twickenham, England
fields: Literature

The major English poet in the neoclassical tradition, Pope also wrote critical introductions to his edition of the works of William Shakespeare and his translation of Homer's *Iliad* and took up important critical concepts in *An Essay on Criticism* and certain others of his works in both verse and prose.

Popov, Aleksandr Stepanovich

b. March 16, 1859
Turinskiye Rudniki, Perm (now Krasnoturinsk), Russia
d. January 13, 1906
St. Petersburg, Russia
fields: Invention and Technology, Engineering

A Russian pioneer in the invention of radio and its application, Popov also contributed to the development of X-ray photography. Outside Russia, he contributed to the development of radio in France.

Popovi Da

aka: Antonio Martínez
b. April 10, 1923
San Ildefonso Pueblo, N.Mex.
d. Oct. 17, 1971
Santa Fe, N.Mex.
fields: Art (potter)

American Indian artist. A San Ildefonso Pueblo (Tewa), Popovi Da was the son of María and Julian Martínez. He continued the pottery renaissance that they had begun at San Ildefonso, adding many significant contributions of his own. From 1961 to 1964, he developed two new pottery types: sienna ware and black-and-sienna ware. Both types involved a complicated two-firing process. One of the most beautiful new finishes Popovi created was the gunmetal ware.

Popper, Karl Raimund

b. July 28, 1902
Vienna, Austria
d. September 17, 1994
Croydon, England
fields: Philosophy, Science

Karl Raimund Popper became well known in the 1930's for his rigorous analysis of the logic of scientific research, earning an international repubation with the publication of *The Logic of Scientific Discovery* (1935). Taught at Canterbury University College in New Zealand during World War II to escape Nazi persecution. *The Poverty of Historicism* (1944-1945) and *The Open Society and Its Enemies* (1945) established his reputation in history and politics, respectively. Joined the London School of Economics in 1946, where he continued there until 1969. Thereafter lectured widely, denouncing Marxism, and expanded and expounded his theories on the scientific method.

Poquelin, Jean-Baptiste. *See* Molière

Poquiam. *See* Uncas

Porphyry

né: Malchus
aka: Basileus
b. c. 234
Tyre, Phoenicia
d. c. 305
probably Rome
fields: Philosophy, Scholarship

As the loyal and devoted disciple of Plotinus, who is credited as the founder of Neoplatonic thought, Porphyry undertook to compile and edit his master's philosophical works, the *Enneads*, and to write a unique biography of his teacher. He also wrote extensive commentaries on Greek philosophers and on the allegorical interpretation, or exegesis, of the Homeric myths.

Porter, Cole

full: Cole Albert Porter
b. June 9, 1891
Peru, Indiana
d. October 15, 1964
Santa Monica, California
fields: Music

Porter was a composer and lyricist whose individuality and imagination brought a new facet to Broadway and Hollywood musicals.

Porter, Connie Rose

b. 1959
Buffalo, N.Y.
fields: Literature (novelist and children's book author)

African American novelist and children's book author; Connie Rose Porter's first novel was *All-Bright Court* (1991), followed by *Imani All Mine* (1999); in 1993, began publishing, for the Wisconsin-based Pleasant Company, an ongoing series of juvenile books featuring a nine-year-old black girl named Addy Walker living in the 1860's; titles include *Meet Addy: An American Girl* (1993), *Addy's Surprise: A Christmas Story* (1993), *Addy Learns a Lesson: A School Story* (1993), *Happy Birthday, Addy: A Springtime Story* (1993), *Addy Saves the Day: A Summer Story* (1994), and *Changes for Addy: A Winter Story* (1994).

Porter, James Amos

b. 1905
Baltimore, Md.
d. February, 1970
Washington, D.C.
fields: Art, Literature, Education

African American artist, author, and educator; James Amos Porter's artwork was exhibited at the American Negro Exposition in Chicago (1940) as well as in several other group exhibitions; his writings about black artists included *Modern Negro Art* (1943); for more than forty years, he taught at Howard University.

Porter, Katherine Anne

né: Callie Russell Porter
b. May 15, 1890
Indian Creek, Texas
d. September 18, 1980
Silver Spring, Maryland
fields: Literature

An important modernist writer, Porter was a fiercely independent and exacting artist whose life and work influenced many writers who followed her.

Porter, Liliana

b. Oct. 6, 1941
Buenos Aires, Argentina
fields: Art

Artist. Liliana Porter, who began studying art in Argentina, moved to New York City in 1964 to study printmaking at the Pratt Graphic Art Center. Her work has been shown at such major museums as the Museum of Modern Art in New York and the Museo de Bellas Artes in Caracas, Venezuela. She has won many awards, including first prize at the Latin American Graphic Arts Biennial in 1986 and a first prize at the VIII Latin American Print Biennial in San Juan, Puerto Rico, in 1986. Porter also cofounded the New York Graphic Workshop.

Porter, Pleasant

aka: Crazy Bear
aka: Talof Harjo
b. Sept. 26, 1840
Clarkesville, Ala.
d. Sept. 3, 1907
Okla.
fields: Native American Affairs, Education

Creek chief and educator; as a principal chief, Pleasant Porter sought acculturation and accommodation with whites; served in the Confederate army during the Civil War, rising from private to second lieutenant; appointed superintendent of schools in Creek nation in 1867 and, during the next twenty years, established an exemplary Creek educational system; defended Creek constitutionalism by commanding national militia in times of crisis, 1871, 1876, 1882-1883; Creek lobbyist in Washington, D.C., 1872-1890's; elected principal Creek chief, 1899, 1903; in 1889, Porter supported the Dawes Commission in ceding Creek lands to the United States for white settlers; in 1902, he ceded all Creek lands in support of the allotment policy by which individual tribal members would receive private allotments; president of constitutional convention that designed proposal for state of Sequoyah in 1905; died of a stroke.

Porter, Rodney Robert

b. Oct. 8, 1917
Newton-le-Willows, Lancashire, England
d. Sept. 7, 1985
Winchester, Hampshire, England
fields: Biology, Chemistry, Medicine

Rodney Robert Porter worked toward the determination of the chemical structure of antibodies; unraveled the way that the body's complement system destroys antigens; 1972, won the Nobel Prize in Physiology or Medicine jointly with Gerald M. Edelman.

Porter, William Sydney. *See* Henry, O.

Porter-Locklear, Freda

né: Freda Porter
b. Oct. 14, 1957
Lumberton, North Carolina
fields: Mathematics (applied math)

Freda Porter-Locklear is known for her research interests in environmental contamination and the predictive modeling of biodegradation rates of contaminants; is an advocate for American Indians and women in the scientific community; became Project Director of the AISES (American Indian Science and Engineering Society) Comprehensive Enrichment Program for the eastern portion of the United States in 1996.

Portes, Alejandro

b. Oct. 13, 1944
Havana, Cuba
fields: Education

Cuban educator. Alejandro Portes taught sociology at the University of Wisconsin-Madison in 1969 and 1970, then taught at the University of Illinois at Urbana for one year. In 1971, he became an associate professor of sociology at the University of Texas at Austin. In 1975, he became professor of sociology at Duke University. He has also worked at universities in Chile, Brazil, and Colombia. He has studied Spanish-language culture and urban culture in both the United States and developing countries.

Portillo Trambley, Estela

b. Jan. 16, 1936
El Paso, Tex.
fields: Literature

Writer. Estela Portillo Trambley began working for the Department of Special Services of the El Paso public schools in 1979. She has served as chairperson of the English department at the El Paso Technical Institute and as drama instructor, producer, and director at El Paso Community College. Portillo Trambley's published work, which focused on equality for women, includes the short-story collection *Rain of Scorpions and Other Writings* (1975), the drama *The Day of the Swallows* (1971), and the novels *Woman of the Earth* (1977) and *Trini* (1986). In 1972, she won the Quinto Sol Award.

Portolá, Gaspar de

b. c. 1723
Balageur, Spain
d. 1784
Mexico
fields: Warfare and Conquest, Exploration and Colonization

Spanish soldier and explorer. Gaspar de Portolá was a captain in the Spanish army when he was sent to California as its governor 1767. In 1769, he began a two-year expedition (which included Jesuit missionary Father Junípero Serra) that established a mission at San Diego and explored Monterey Bay. Portolá established the mission of Carmel and the city of Monterey in 1771. Portolá served governor of the Mexican city of Puebla from 1777 to 1784 before being ordered back to Spain.

Posener, Edith Claire. *See* Head, Edith

Posey, Alexander Lawrence

b. Aug. 3, 1873
near Eufaula, Creek Nation, present-day Okla.
d. May 27, 1908
Oktahutchee River
fields: Journalism

Native American journalist. A Creek (Tuskegee), Alexander Lawrence Posey wrote the Fus Fixico letters, which combined political satire, local color, and dialect humor in the tradition of Mark Twain. He was the first American Indian owner/editor of a daily newspaper; he published the weekly *Indian Journal* of Eufaula, Oklahoma.

Posidonius

b. c. 135 B.C.E.
Apamea of the Orontes, Syria
d. c. 51. B.C.E.
Rome
fields: Philosophy

Though virtually none of his writings survives, it is clear that Posidonius was one of the most influential thinkers of the ancient world. He made important contributions in the fields of philosophy, history, astronomy, mathematics, natural history, and geography.

Poston, Ersa Hines

b. May 3, 1921
Paducah, Ky.
fields: Government and Politics

African American government official; after working as a confidential assistant to Governor Nelson Rockefeller, Ersa Hines Poston became director of the New York State Office of Economic Opportunity (1964); from 1967 to 1975, she served as president of the New York Civil Service Commission; in 1977 she moved up to the position of commissioner of the U.S. Civil Service Commission; she became vice chairman of the U.S. Merit Systems Protection Board in 1979.

Potter, Beatrice. *See* Webb, Beatrice

Potter, Beatrix
full: Helen Beatrix Potter
b. July 28, 1866
South Kensington, Middlesex (now London), England
d. December 22, 1943
Near Sawrey, Lancashire, England
fields: Art, Literature, Social Reform

Potter, an English writer and illustrator of such children's books as *The Tale of Peter Rabbit*, was also an early member of England's National Trust for the preservation of properties of historic value or natural beauty. She donated four thousand acres of Lake District farmland to preserve the area's rural quality of life.

Poulenc, Francis
b. January 7, 1899
Paris, France
d. January 30, 1963
Paris, France
fields: Music

Poulenc gradually came to be recognized by many as perhaps the greatest twentieth century exponent of the art song and, toward the latter part of his career, as the composer of deeply felt religious music.

Pound, Ezra
b. October 30, 1885
Hailey, Idaho
d. October 30, 1972
Venice, Italy
fields: Literature

An American poet, Ezra Pound began writing after settling in England in 1908, and he later lived in France and Italy. During the 1930's Pound began preaching anti-Semitism in letters and in print. He opposed U.S. entry into World War II and offered his services to Benito Mussolini's Fascist government, which used him to write radio broadcasts. After the war, the U.S. government charged him with treason, but he was ruled insane and hospitalized, instead of being tried. In 1958 he was released, and he returned to Italy.

Pound, Roscoe
b. October 27, 1870
Lincoln, Nebr.
d. July 1, 1964
Cambridge, Mass.
fields: Law, Education

American jurist and educator; distinguished legal philosopher and prolific writer. Roscoe Pound's major contribution was his development and advocacy of "sociological jurisprudence," emphasizing that law should recognize the "social interests" of humanity and should attempt to deal with contemporary social issues.

Poundmaker
aka: Opeteca Hanawaywin
b. c.1842
near Battleford, Northwest Territory
d. July 4, 1886
near Gleichen, Alberta
fields: Native American Affairs, Government and Politics

Poundmaker was a Cree tribal leader in Canada; adopted by Blackfoot chief Crowfoot (c. 1873); named subchief of the Sipiwininiwug; signed Treaty Number 6 with the Canadian government, allocating land to the Indians and providing for education in farming; joined in the second Riel Rebellion in 1885; tried for treason and imprisoned for seven months in 1885.

Pous, Arquímides
b. ?
d. April, 1926
Mayagüez, Puerto Rico
fields: Theater and Entertainment, Literature

Cuban actor and playwright. Arquímides Pous, a popular Cuban blackface comedian of the 1920's organized the Compañía de Bufos Cubanos at New York's Leslie Theater in 1921. He wrote numerous *obras bufas cubanas*, social satires that criticized racism, explored Afro-Cuban culture, and incorporated Afro-Cuban music and religious belief. Pous also recorded music with Columbia Records. He was killed in a boating accident in Puerto Rico in 1926.

Poussaint, Alvin Francis
b. May 15, 1934
New York, N.Y
fields: Psychiatry and Psychology, Education

African American psychiatrist and educator; Alvin Francis Poussaint is noted for his analysis of mental and emotional health issues as they affect African Americans, and particularly for his "aggression-rage" theory of black behavior; his published works include *Why Blacks Kill Blacks* (1972) and *Black Child Care* (1975; with James P. Comer); he has served as associate professor of psychiatry and associate dean of students at Harvard Medical School.

Poussin, Nicolas
b. 1594
near Les Andelys, Normandy, France
d. November 19, 1665
Rome
fields: Art

Poussin was among the greatest French painters of the seventeenth century and one of the most influential artists of the Baroque era. His work reflects those qualities of rationality and high moral purpose which were so admired by the French classicists, and it profoundly influenced the subsequent development of painting, both in Rome, where he spent most of his life, and in France.

Poveka. *See* Martínez, María Antonía

Powderly, Terence V.
full: Terence Vincent Powderly
b. Jan. 22, 1849
Carbondale, Pa.
d. June 24, 1924
Washington, D.C.
fields: Labor Movement

Labor leader and immigration official Terence V. Powderly supported legislation barring immigrants from Europe and Asia, especially Chinese laborers. From 1874 to 1894, he was a member of the Order of Knights of Labor, and from 1897-1902, he served as head of the newly formed Bureau of Immigration. He vigorously supported the Chinese Exclusion Act of 1882 and feverishly sought out illegal Chinese immigrants already in the country. Dismissed by President Theodore Roosevelt in 1902, Powderly was reinstated and appointed chief of the Division of Information of the Bureau of Immigration from 1907 to 1921.

Powell, Adam Clayton, Sr.
b. May 5, 1865
Soak Creek, Va.
d. June 12, 1953
New York, N.Y.
fields: Religion and Theology

African American religious leader; from becoming a pastor in 1908 to his retirement in 1937, Adam Clayton Powell, Sr., helped build the Abyssinian Baptist Church membership from about sixteen hundred to about fourteen thousand; during the Depression, he directed the church in providing meals and social services.

Powell, Adam Clayton, Jr.
b. November 29, 1908
New Haven, Conn.
d. April 4, 1972
Miami, Fla.
fields: Government and Politics

African American congressman; Adam Clayton Powell, Jr., represented Harlem in the U.S. House of Representatives from 1944 to 1970; during the early 1960's, he served as chairman of the powerful House Committee on Education and Labor; Powell's inclination toward political radicalism as a solution to racism and his insistence on complete equality of the races garnered both admiration and hatred from whites and criticism from well known black leaders who had adopted a more gradual approach toward challenging racism; in 1967, expelled from Congress by a full House vote for allegations of misspending public funds and contempt of court; although reelected in a special election to fill the vacancy created by his expulsion, Powell did not take his seat and lived primarily on the Caribbean island of Bimini so as to avoid prosecution under U.S. laws; as a result he lost the 1970 primary election to Charles Rangel.

Powell, Art

full: Arthur L. Powell
b. February 25, 1937
Dallas, Tex.
fields: Sports (football player)

African American football player; Art Powell caught 469 passes during his career (1959-1968), making him one of professional football's all-time best receivers; he scored eighty-one touchdowns in eight seasons (1960-1967), establishing an American Football League record.

Powell, Bud

né: Earl Powell
b. September 27, 1924
New York, N.Y.
d. July 31, 1966
New York, N.Y.
fields: Music (jazz pianist)

African American jazz pianist; as an innovative and emotional bebop artist, Bud Powell played with saxophonist Charlie Parker, trumpeter Dizzy Gillespie, and drummer Max Roach; he pioneered transferring the sounds of various string instruments to the keyboard.

Powell, Colin

full: Colin Luther Powell
b. April 5, 1937
New York, New York
fields: Military Affairs

The first African American to become chairman of the Joint Chiefs of Staff, Colin Powell successfully organized and supervised American military operations in the Gulf War of 1991.

Powell, John Wesley

b. March 24, 1834
Mount Morris, New York
d. September 23, 1902
Haven, Maine
fields: Exploration and Colonization, Science

In 1869, Powell led the first party of exploration to descend the gorges of the Green and Colorado rivers by boat, stimulating interest in the geology and scenic wonders of the Grand Canyon. He also helped to establish the concepts of large-scale damming and irrigation projects as the keys to settlement and agricultural survival in the arid lands of the American West beyond the one hundredth meridian.

Powell, Lewis F., Jr.

full: Lewis Franklin Powell, Jr.
b. 1907
d. 1998
fields: Law

U.S. Supreme Court justice, 1972-1987; appointed by President Nixon. Author of modern "open fields" exception to the Fourth Amendment and of opinion cutting back access to federal *habeas corpus* for state prisoners. Significant opinions: *Barker v. Wingo*, 407 U.S. 514 (1972); *Doyle v. Ohio*, 426 U.S. 610 (1976); *Stone v. Powell*, 428 U.S. 465 (1976); *Solem v. Helm*, 463 U.S. 277 (1983); *Oliver v. United States*, 466 U.S. 170 (1984); *Batson v. Kentucky*, 476 U.S. 79 (1986).

Powell, Maud

b. August 22, 1867
Peru, Illinois
d. January 8, 1920
Uniontown, Pennsylvania
fields: Music

Widely acclaimed as a concert violinist, Powell advanced the cause of women on the concert stage and did much to introduce art music to audiences outside the major urban centers in the United States.

Powell, Mike

full: Michael Anthony Powell
b. November 10, 1963
Philadelphia, Pa.
fields: Sports (long jump competitor)

African American long jump competitor; in 1991, Michael Anthony Powell established one of the most remarkable records in the history of athletics by leaping 29 feet, 4 ½ inches in the long jump, besting teammate Carl Lewis and breaking the record set in the 1968 Summer Olympics by Bob Beamon; finished second to Carl Lewis in the 1992 Summer Olympics; dominated the long jump in international competition leading up to the 1996 Olympics, where an injury left in fifth place.

Powell, Renee

b. 1946
Canton, Ohio
fields: Sports (golfer)

African American golfer; Renee Powell was early on exposed to the game of golf because her father had built and maintained a golf course in Ohio; she joined the professional ranks in 1967 and played in the Ladies Professional Golf Association and at one time was the only African American on the Women's Professional Golf Association tour; she became a golf instructor in 1979 at an all-male club in England.

Powers, Georgia Montgomery Davis

b. October 29, 1923
Springfield, Ky.
fields: Government and Politics, Civil Rights

African American politician; in 1967, Georgia Montgomery Davis Powers became the first African American and the first woman to be elected to the upper house of Kentucky's legislature; worked closely with the Southern Christian Leadership Conference (SCLC) and participated in the 1965 Selma to Montgomery march; served as Kentucky state chair of Jesse Jackson's campaign for the Democratic presidential nomination in 1984 and 1988; published *I Shared the Dream* (1995).

Powers, Winston D.

b. December 19, 1930
Manhattan, N.Y
fields: Military Affairs, Warfare and Conquest

African American military officer; Winston D. Powers joined the U.S. Air Force in 1950 and had achieved the rank of lieutenant general by 1983; his postings included navigator instructor at Ellington Air Force Base, commander of the Space Communications Division for the North American Aerospace Defense Command, and director of the Defense Communications Agency in Washington, D.C.; his more than four thousand flying hours included flying seventy-five combat missions over Vietnam.

Powhatan

né: Wahunsenacawh
b. c. 1550
Powhata, near Richmond, Virginia
d. April, 1618
Powhata, Virginia
fields: Native American Affairs

Though better known in North American history as the father of the Indian princess Pocahontas, Powhatan made significant contributions to the English settlement in North America. Through his prudent leadership and goodwill, Powhatan provided the basis for a peaceful coexistence between the Indians and the English which ultimately enabled Jamestown, the first English colony in America, to thrive and expand.

Pozo y Gonzáles, Chano

full: Luciano Pozo y Gonzáles
b. Jan. 7, 1915
Havana, Cuba
d. Dec. 2, 1948
New York, N.Y.
fields: Music

Percussionist Chano Pozo y Gonzáles's collaboration with Dizzy Gillespie, which began during a concert at Carnegie Hall in 1947, helped change the direction of jazz music. Pozo and Gillespie were the first people to make a serious attempt to fuse elements of jazz and Latin music, a style that came to be referred to as "Cubop." They made several recordings together, including "Manteca," "Cubana Be, Cubana Bop," and "Afro-Cuban Suite."

Prado, Pedro

b. Oct. 8, 1886
Santiago, Chile
d. Jan. 31, 1952
Viña del Mar, Chile
fields: Literature

Writer. Although Pedro Prado experimented with free-verse poetry, his most well known verse is in sonnet form. Among his collections are *Camino de las horas* (1934), *No más que una rosa* (1946), and *Viejos poemas inéditos* (1949). He also published several novels, including *Alsino* (1920) and *Un juez rural* (1924).

Prado, Pérez

b. Nov. 13, 1922
Matanzas, Cuba
d. Dec. 4, 1983
Mexico City, Mexico
fields: Music (pianist, arranger, and bandleader)

Cuban pianist, arranger, and bandleader. During the 1940's, Pérez Prado played piano with the Orquesta Casino de la Playa and became a popular arranger for local mambo-style bands. He then recorded songs for RCA Mexico City Studios that were targeted to the Latin market in the United States, including "Mambo No. 5," "Caballo Negro," "Cherry Pink and Apple Blossom White," "Patricia," "Guaglione," and "Patricia Twist." His status as the best known mamba musician, largely because his music arrangements were accessible to large non-Latin American audiences, earned for him the title *el rey del mambo*, or "king of the mambo."

Pran, Dith

b. 1942
Cambodia
fields: Journalism

Dith Pran is a journalist; born in Cambodia; worked as an interpreter for U.S. military in 1960's; hired by *The New York Times* as photographer and assistant to Sydney Schanberg in covering the Vietnam War in the early 1970's; could not escape when United States evacuated Cambodia in 1975; miraculously survived during Pol Pot's regime, 1975-1979, emigrating to United States; actively involved in heightening awareness of Cambodian problems.

Prandtl, Ludwig

b. February 4, 1875
Freising, Germany
d. August 15, 1953
Göttingen, West Germany
fields: Physics, Aviation and Space Exploration

Prandtl was one of the fathers of theoretical aerodynamics and is credited with discovering many of the pivotal concepts upon which modern aviation is based. He was also the founder of the highly acclaimed school of aerodynamics and hydrodynamics at the University of Göttingen and the first director of what would become the Max Planck Institute for Fluid Mechanics.

Prasad, Rajendra

b. Dec. 3, 1884
Zeradei, Bihar, India
d. Feb. 28, 1963
Patna, Republic of India
fields: Government and Politics

Rajendra Prasad joined the noncooperation movement for independence against the British colonial rule, persuaded by nationalist leader Mahatma Gandhi. Prasad served as president of the Indian National Congress, then was elected national president, an office he held from 1950 until 1962.

Prater, Dave

b. 1937
d. 1988
fields: Music (soul singer)

member of the African American vocal duo Sam and Dave, one of the most successful soul acts of the 1960's; Dave Prater had a gospel music background, and his recordings with Sam Moore drew heavily on gospel singing techniques; the duo's hits included "You Don't Know Like I Know" (1966), "Hold On, I'm Comin'" (1966), "When Something Is Wrong With My Baby" (1967), and "Soul Man" (1967).

Prather, Ida. *See* Cox, Ida

Pratt, Awadagin

b. March 3, 1966
Pittsburgh, Pa.
fields: Music (classical pianist)

African American classical pianist; in 1992, Awadagin Pratt, known for his unconventional appearance (dreadlocks and jeans), was the first African American to win the Naumburg International Piano Competition; made his professional debut in 1995; released *A Long Way From Normal* (1994) and *Beethoven Piano Sonatas* (1996).

Pratt, Sharon. *See* Kelly, Sharon Pratt

Prawer, Ruth. *See* Jhabvala, Ruth Prawer

Praxiteles

b. c. 390 B.C.E.
Athens, Greece
d. c. 330 B.C.E.
place unknown
fields: Art

The subtle expression of personal emotions, such as tenderness and laziness, through marble statuary is the trademark of Praxiteles. His most famous work, the *Aphrodite of Knidos*, established Western civilization's standard of perfection in the female figure.

Prelog, Vladimir

b. July 23, 1906
Sarajevo, Bosnia
d. January 7, 1998
Zurich, Switzerland
fields: Chemistry

Vladimir Prelog worked on simple carbon rings and protein enzymes, among other topics; all of his studies emphasized the significance of molecular geometry; in 1975, won the Nobel Prize in Chemistry, jointly with John Warcup Cornforth.

Prescott, William Hickling

b. May 4, 1796
Salem, Massachusetts
d. January 28, 1859
Boston, Massachusetts
fields: Historiography

Prescott proved that historical writing could achieve the permanence of literature; he introduced into American historiography all the methods of modern scholarship, and he remains the most distinguished historian of sixteenth century Spain and Spanish America in the English language.

Presley, Elvis

full: Elvis Aron Presley
b. January 8, 1935
Tupelo, Mississippi

d. August 16, 1977
Memphis, Tennessee
fields: Music

Fusing the legacies of black and white American music, Presley helped create the cultural phenomenon of rock and roll and became its most famous and influential performer.

Preston, Ann

b. December 1, 1813
West Grove, Pennsylvania
d. April 18, 1872
Philadelphia, Pennsylvania
fields: Medicine, Women's Rights

Ann Preston, who became the first woman ever to be appointed dean of an American medical school, was instrumental in securing women's right to study and to practice medicine in the face of heated opposition from the male-dominated medical establishment.

Preston, Billy

b. September 9, 1946
Houston, Tex.
fields: Music (soul and gospel vocalist and organist)

African American soul and gospel vocalist and organist; Billy Preston developed a following touring with Sam Cooke, Little Richard, and Andrae Crouch; "Nothing from Nothing" (1974) was his best known pop hit; his work with the Rolling Stones and the Beatles garnered much public attention; he had a featured role in the 1978 film *Sergeant Pepper's Lonely Hearts Club Band.*

Price, H. H.

full: Henry Habberley Price
b. May 17, 1899
Neath, Glamorgan, Wales
d. November 26, 1984
place unknown
fields: Philosophy, Religion and Theology

H. H. Price expressed perhaps the most complex version of sense-data theory, articulated a sophisticated theory of concepts and a detailed account of belief, and discussed various key topics in the philosophy of religion, including the notion of an afterlife. Fellow at Magdalen College, Oxford (1922-1924), fellow and lecturer at Trinity College (1924-1935), professor of logic at New College (1935-1959); lecturer at Aberdeen University (1959-1960). Price was interested in psychical research, publishing articles in journals devoted to this topic and serving as president of the Society for Psychical Research, London, and a charter member of the Parapsychological Association as well as a member of the Aristotelian Society and the Mind Association. Major works: *Perception* (1932), *Hume's Theory of the External World* (1940), *Thinking and Experience* (1953), *Belief: The Gifford Lectures Delivered at the University of Aberdeen in 1960* (1969), *Essays in the Philosophy of Religion* (1972), *Philosophical Interaction with Parapsychology* (1995).

Price, Hugh

full: Hugh Bernard Price
b. November 22, 1941
Washington, D.C.
fields: Law, Social Reform

African American attorney and foundation executive; Hugh Bernard Price has worked for social reform through his positions as executive director of the Black Coalition of New Haven; consultant with Coger, Holt & Associates, where he focused on analyzing urban outreach programs; vice president of the Rockefeller Foundation in charge of the Special Initiative and Explorations grant fund, which dedicated its resources to serve minority groups and individuals; and chief executive officer and president of the National Urban League.

Price, Leontyne

né: Mary Violet Leontine Price
b. February 10, 1927
Laurel, Mississippi
fields: Music

Internationally acclaimed soprano of the operatic and concert stage, Leontyne Price paved the way for many subsequent black classical performers. The fifth black singer to appear at the Metropolitan Opera, she was the first to sustain a long career there. During her thirty-four-year history at the Met, she became the most sought after prima donna at the opera house.

Price, Lloyd

b. March 9, 1933?
New Orleans, La.
fields: Music (rhythm-and-blues singer and songwriter), Business and Industry

African American singer, songwriter, and businessman; Lloyd Price's hit recordings included "Lawdy Miss Clawdy" (1952; number one on the rhythm-and-blues charts, named record of the year, one of the first rhythm-and-blues songs to cross over onto the pop charts), "Oooh-Oooh-Oooh," "Restless Heart," "Ain't It a Shame," "Just Because" (1957; number four on rhythm and blues charts and number twenty on pop charts), and the traditional folksong "Stagger Lee" (1958; number one on the pop charts); formed recording labels Kent Record Company (KRC), Double L, and Turntable.

Prida, Dolores

b. Sept. 5, 1943
Caibarién, Cuba
fields: Literature

Latina writer. Dolores Prida moved from Cuba to New York City with her family in 1961. She worked in a variety of editorial positions in New York and London. Her poetry collections include *Treinta y un poemas* (1967) and *Women of the Hour* (1971). Her first play, *Beautiful Señoritas* (pb. 1991), was produced in New York in 1977. The play *La era latina* was produced in 1980. Prida's work deals with bilingualism and the problems of women in contemporary society.

Pride, Charley

b. March 18, 1938
Sledge, Miss.
fields: Music (country music singer)

African American country music singer; the first black country singer to perform at the Grand Ole Opry, Charley Pride has recorded more than fifty top-ten hits and received three Grammys.

Pride, Thomas

b. Date unknown, c. 1605
probably Ashcott near Glastonbury, England
d. October 23, 1658
Worcester House, Nonsuch, Surrey, England
fields: Military Affairs

A member of Parliament's New Model Army during the English Civil Wars (1642-1651), Pride saw action in significant battles but is best remembered for his excluding more than one hundred members of Parliament's House of Commons on December 6, 1648, in Pride's Purge and for serving as a member of the court that condemned Charles I to death.

Priestley, Joseph

b. March 13, 1733
Birstal Fieldhead, Yorkshire, England
d. February 6, 1804
Northumberland, Pennsylvania
fields: Religion and Theology, Science, Philosophy

One of the eighteenth century's important experimental scientists, Priestley was a supporter of civic and religious liberty who wrote extensively in a variety of scientific, educational, religious, and philosophical areas.

Prigogine, Ilya

b. Jan. 25, 1917
Moscow, Russia
fields: Chemistry, Physics

Ilya Prigogine contributed to the science of thermodynamics, which studies the interrelationships of heat, work, and energy; also worked in biological and social sciences; 1977, won the Nobel Prize in Chemistry.

Primas, Randy

full: Melvin Randolph Primas, Jr.
b. August 31, 1949
Camden, N.J.
fields: Government and Politics

African American mayor of Camden, N.J.; at age twenty-three, Randy Primas was elected to the Camden city council (1973), and in 1978 he became the city council president; in 1981, he took office as Camden's first African American mayor, serving until 1990; a job as commissioner of the New Jersey Department of Community Affairs followed.

Primus, Pearl

b. November 29, 1919
Trinidad, West Indies
d. October 29, 1994
New Rochelle, New York
fields: Dance, Anthropology

A pioneer in African American dance and an anthropologist specializing in the dances of western and central Africa and the Caribbean, Primus dedicated her life to demonstrating through dance the dignity, beauty, and strength in the heritage of peoples of African ancestry.

Prince

né: Prince Rogers Nelson
aka: Artist Formerly Known as Prince
b. June 7, 1958
Minneapolis, Minn.
fields: Music (Funk-rock musician, singer, and composer), Film

African American funk-rock musician, singer, and composer; Prince is noted for recordings that combine rock, funk, and pop music with erotic-themed lyrics that challenge mainstream norms and taboos and for his sexually ambiguous dress and hairstyles; his recordings, on which he played virtually all the instruments, include *Dirty Mind* (1980), *Controversy* (1981), the double album *1999* (1982; containing Prince's first significant popular hit, "Little Red Corvette"), and *Purple Rain* (1984; which accompanied the film *Purple Rain*, in which he starred); other film projects included *Under the Cherry Moon* (1986), *Graffiti Bridge* (1990), and *I'd Do Anything* (1993; for which he wrote the songs); in 1985, Prince founded Paisley Park Studios, a recording complex in Minneapolis; his 1992 album featured a glyph or figure representing a synthesis of the male and female gender symbols as its title; in 1993, Prince legally changed his name to this unpronounceable glyph symbol and began to be referred to as "the artist formerly known as Prince"; in 1994 Prince received a World Music Award for outstanding contributions to the pop music industry.

Prinze, Freddie

b. June 22, 1954
New York, N.Y.
d. Jan. 28, 1977
Los Angeles, Calif.
fields: Theater and Entertainment (actor), Television

Latino actor. Freddie Prinze began working on his provocative, ethnic-based comedy at New York's stand-up comedy clubs. He appeared on *The Jack Paar Show* and *The Tonight Show*, then landed the starring role in the television series *Chico and the Man* in 1974, which became an immediate success. In 1977, Prinze, who was twenty-two years old, died of a gunshot wound that may have been self-inflicted.

Priscian

b. Second half of the fifth century C.E.
Caesarea, Mauretania, Africa
d. First half of the sixth century C.E.
Constantinople
fields: Language and Linguistics

Priscian's *Institutiones grammaticae* preserved and abridged several earlier works of classical Latin grammar in a form so useful that it was copied and annotated and became the standard work in its genre until the end of the Middle Ages.

Priscillian

b. c. 340
Spain
d. 385
Trier
fields: Religion and Theology

Priscillian provides an example not only of the popularity of ascetic practices in the Christian church but also of what can happen when such activities are carried to extremes and challenge established Church beliefs and lines of authority.

Proclus

b. c. 410
Constantinople, Byzantine Empire
d. 485
Athens, Greece
fields: Philosophy

Proclus is known for his detailed systematization of the various theological and philosophical doctrines that he inherited from his predecessors and for his immense commentaries on the works of Plato, which consumed most of his activity.

Professor Longhair

né: Henry Roeland Byrd
b. December 19, 1918
Bogalusa, La.
d. January 30, 1980
New Orleans, La.
fields: Music (New Orleans blues piano player)

African American New Orleans blues piano player; Professor Longhair is remembered for his offbeat style which fused blues, jazz, and rock and roll, for his original piano playing, and for his often humorous lyrics; he loved Caribbean music and incorporated steel drums into some of his work; his recordings included "Mardi Gras in New Orleans," "Walk Your Blues Away," "Hadicol Bounce," and he performed on the live album of the New Orleans Jazz and Heritage Festival (1976).

Profet, Margie Jean

b. Aug. 7, 1958
Berkeley, California
fields: Biology, Medicine, Physiology

Margie Jean Profet worked in the developing field of evolutionary medicine; proposed theories about human adaptations to plant toxins and infectious organisms; delivered "pregnancy sickness" hypothesis in 1986.

Prokofiev, Sergei

full: Sergei Sergeyevich Prokofiev
b. April 23, 1891
Sontsovka, Ukraine, Russian Empire
d. March 5, 1953
Moscow, U.S.S.R.
fields: Music

Prokofiev is one of the two most successful Soviet composers of the twentieth century; he also ranks with the half dozen leading composers of the century. Although he first gained notice as an extraordinary pianist, he eventually created masterpieces in most major musical forms; in particular, in *Peter and the Wolf*, *Alexander Nevsky*, and *Romeo and Juliet*, he wrote three of the most celebrated works of his time.

Propertius, Sextus

b. c. 57-48 B.C.E.
Assisi?, Umbria
d. c. 16 B.C.E.-2 C.E.
place unknown
fields: Literature

Propertius expanded the scope and power of the Roman love poem in the passionate poems to and about Cynthia.

Prosser, Gabriel. *See* Gabriel

Protagoras

b. c. 485 B.C.E.
Abdera, Greece
d. c. 410 B.C.E.
place unknown
fields: Philosophy, Education

Protagoras was among the first and was possibly the greatest of the Greek Sophists, itinerant teachers who professed to be able to teach men virtue for a fee. His ideas on learning, morality, and the history of human society have influenced the system of education since the fifth century B.C.E.

Proudhon, Pierre-Joseph

b. January 15, 1809
Besançon, France
d. January 19, 1865
Paris, France
fields: Philosophy, Economics

Proudhon's greatest activity was as a journalist and pamphleteer. Hailed by his followers as the uncompromising champion of human liberty, Proudhon voiced the discontentment of the revolutionary period of nineteenth century France.

Proust, Marcel

b. July 10, 1871
Auteuil, France
d. November 18, 1922
Paris, France
fields: Literature

Proust is the most celebrated French writer of the twentieth century. His masterwork in seven volumes, the novel *À la recherche du temps perdu* (1913-1927; *Remembrance of Things Past*, 1922-1931, 1981) broke new ground in its explorations of the nature of individual identity, its psychology of space and time, and its stylistic and thematic expansiveness. Proust's fiction and his criticism have helped widen the traditional perspectives of literary criticism.

Prynne, William

b. 1600
Swainswick, Somerset, England
d. October 24, 1669
London, England
fields: Religion and Theology

An English Puritan pamphleteer, William Prynne opposed Roman Catholicism and a supposed decline in morals. His most famous work, *Histriomastix* (1632), attacked the theater and female actors, and he was tried in the Court of Star Chamber because it his play was thought critical of the queen. Heavily fined, he had his ears cropped and was imprisoned. After another trial in 1637, he was again fined, had the remainder of his ears cut off, and was exiled to the Channel Islands. He was released in 1640 and made a triumphal procession to London. His criticism of the Parliamentarian army opposing Charles I during the English civil war (1642-1648) got him ejected from Parliament. His protests against taxes earned him three years' imprisonment without trial.

Pryor, Rain

b. June, 1969
fields: Television, Film

African American actress; Rain Pryor, the daughter of comedian Richard Pryor, appeared as T. J. on the television sitcom *Head of the Class* (beginning 1989) and in *Rude Awadening* (1998); her film work includes the short film *Blackbird Fly* (1990).

Pryor, Richard

full: Richard Franklin Lennox Thomas Pryor
b. December 1, 1940
Peoria, Ill.
fields: Theater and Entertainment, Television, Film

African American comedian and actor; Richard Franklin Lennox Thomas Pryor first gained fame as a stand-up comic known for incorporating African American culture, particularly sex and racism, into his routines and for stretching the boundaries of acceptable entertainment; he struggled with cocaine addiction during the 1970's and was severely burned over 50 percent of his body in a fire at his residence in 1980; Pryor's work in recording, television, and film has garnered for him four Grammy Awards for comedy albums, four gold and one platinum record designations, two American Academy Humor awards, an American Writers Guild award, five Emmy Awards for screenplays, and an Academy Award nomination for his role in *Lady Sings the Blues* (1972); in 1984 he was elected to the Black Filmmakers Hall of Fame; Pryor was diagnosed with multiple sclerosis in August of 1986; on May 29, 1991, he suffered a heart attack resulting in quadruple by-pass surgery; Pryor published *Pryor Convictions: And Other Life Sentences*, his autobiography, in 1995.

Psamtik I

aka: Psammetichus I
b. c. 684 B.C.E.
place unknown
d. 610 B.C.E.
place unknown
fields: Government and Politics

Psamtik carved out political independence for Egypt after almost a century of foreign rule, inaugurating a renewal of its society and culture.

Psellus, Michael

né: Constantine Psellus
b. 1018
Nicomedia
d. c. 1078
Constantinople
fields: Government and Politics, Religion and Theology, Philosophy, Historiography

Psellus infused both Byzantine state theory and Orthodox theology with a revived classical tradition, while preserving a history of the personalities and events of his times.

Ptolemy

né: Claudius Ptolemaeus
b. c. 100
possibly Ptolemais Hermii, Egypt
d. c. 178
place unknown, possibly Egypt
fields: Astronomy, Mathematics, Geography

Ptolemy's scientific work in astronomy, mathematics, geography, and optics influenced other practitioners for almost fifteen hundred years.

Ptolemy Philadelphus

b. February, 308 B.C.E.
Cos, Greece
d. 246 B.C.E.
Alexandria, Egypt
fields: Government and Politics

Under Ptolemy, the domestic institutions and the foreign policy characteristic of Hellenistic Egypt matured. His patronage of the arts and sciences established Alexandria as the most important cultural center of the Greek world.

Ptolemy Soter

b. 367 or 366 B.C.E.
the canton of Eordaea, Macedonia
d. 283 or 282 B.C.E.
Alexandria, Egypt
fields: Government and Politics

A companion of Alexander the Great during the conquest of the Persian Empire, Ptolemy came to rule Egypt shortly after Alexander died—first as a satrap under Philip III and Alexander IV and after the extinction of the Argead royal family as a king in his own right. Ptolemy thereby founded the dynasty which ruled Egypt until the death of Cleopatra VII in 30 B.C.E.

Puccini, Giacomo

full: Giacomo Antonio Domenico Michele Secondo Maria Puccini
b. December 22, 1858
Lucca, Italy
d. November 29, 1924
Brussels, Belgium
fields: Music

Born into a Tuscan family with almost a dynastic tradition in musical composition and instruction, Puccini became a leading member of a talented group of Italian composers of opera in the generation succeeding Giuseppe Verdi. Many of Puccini's operatic works have proved to be among the most popular in the twentieth century operatic repertory.

Pucelle, Jean

b. c. 1290
Paris or northern France
d. 1334
Paris
fields: Art

Pucelle's manuscript illuminations, which depicted three-dimensional spatial settings and the emotional interaction of figures, influenced the direction of artistic developments in northern European painting in the late Middle Ages and the early Renaissance.

Puckett, Kirby

b. March 14, 1961
Chicago, Ill.
fields: Sports (baseball player)

African American baseball player; Kirby Puckett entered the American League in 1984 playing for the Minnesota Twins; in 1989 he batted an average of .339 and took the American League batting title; as a versatile player who could hit, run, and field well, Puckett became a regular on All-Star teams and frequently won the Gold Glove Award for defensive excellence; as a player on the Twins' 1987 and 1991 World Series championship teams, he was named 1991 American League playoffs Most Valuable Player. He lost the vision in his right eye and retired in July, 1996; became vice president for the Minnesota Twins.

Puente, Tito

full: Ernesto Antonio Puente
b. Apr. 20, 1923
New York, N.Y.
fields: Music (percussionist and bandleader)

Latino percussionist and bandleader. Tito Puente began his professional career by joining the Noro Morales orchestra around 1936. He then formed the Picadilly Boys, who toured and recorded for RCA in the 1940's. Puente went on to become an extremely popular arranger, composer, producer, and showman. He recorded more than one hundred albums, including *Dance Mania* (1958) and *The Mambo King: 100th LP* (1991). He has won numerous awards, including a Grammy.

Pufendorf, Samuel von

né: Samuel Pufendorf
b. January 8, 1632
Dorfchemnitz, Saxony
d. October 26, 1694
Berlin, Prussia
fields: Law, Philosophy

Pufendorf's teachings on jurisprudence, theology, and ethics made possible significant advances in the development of natural law theories in the Western world of the early modern age.

Pugin, Augustus Welby Northmore

b. March 1, 1812
London, England
d. September 14, 1852
London, England
fields: Architecture

Pugin wrote treatises promoting the Gothic revival in church architecture and built more than one hundred distinctive buildings during his short career.

Puig, Manuel

b. Dec. 28, 1932
General Villegas, Argentina
d. July 22, 1990
Cuernavaca, Mexico
fields: Literature

Argentinean writer. Manuel Puig was educated in Argentina and Italy, then lived in Paris and London, where he began writing film scripts. He was working as an assistant director in the Argentine movie industry when he completed *La traición de Rita Hayworth* (1968; *Betrayed by Rita Hayworth*, 1971), his first novel. His second novel, *Boquitas pintadas* (1969; *Heartbreak Tango: A Serial*, 1973), became an instant best-seller. His other novels include *El beso de la mujer araña* (1976; *Kiss of the Spider Woman*, 1984), *Pubis angelical* (1979; English translation, 1986), *Maldición eterna a quien lea estas páginas* (1980; *Eternal Curse on the Reader of These Pages*, 1982), and *Sangre de amor correspondido* (1982; *Blood of Requited Love*, 1984).

Pukui, Mary Abigail Kawena

b. 1895
Hawaii
d. May 21, 1986
Hawaii
fields: Linguistics, Music

Linguist, composer, and author Mary Abigail Kawena Pukui was the daughter of Henry Nathaniel Wiggin, a New Englander, and his wife Paahana, a Native Hawaiian. While working for Honolulu's Bishop Museum, she prepared several dictionaries, ethnographies, and lexicons of the Hawaiian language, many of which were published in collaboration with Samuel H. Elbert. Pukui also knew a great deal about native plants and traditional crafts and dances and was a talented composer of traditional Hawaiian songs. She received many honorary degrees and awards, was named Hawaiian of the Year, and was honored as a Living Treasure.

Pulitzer, Joseph

b. April 10, 1847
Mako, Hungary
d. October 29, 1911
Charleston, South Carolina
fields: Journalism

Combining a strong social conscience with a superb grasp of journalistic techniques, Pulitzer created with his *New York World* the prototype of the modern newspaper.

Punnett, Reginald Crundall

b. June 20, 1875
Tonbridge, Kent, England
d. Jan. 3, 1967
Bilbrook, Somerset, England
fields: Biology, Genetics, Zoology

Reginald Crundall Punnett performed breeding experiments, helping to establish Mendelian genetics as a new field in biology; in 1910, launched the *Journal of Genetics* with William Bateson.

Purcell, Henry

b. 1659
London, England
d. November 21, 1695
London, England
fields: Music

The greatest musical genius of the English Baroque period, Purcell composed a prodigious amount of music of high quality. Among his works are more than seventy anthems for the Anglican service, numerous odes for court and public ceremonies, more than two hundred vocal and instrumental pieces, incidental music for more than forty stage productions, five semioperas, and one opera.

Purim, Flora

b. Mar. 6, 1942
Rio de Janeiro, Brazil
fields: Music (singer, lyricist, and musician)

Brazilian singer, lyricist, and musician. Flora Purim performed in Brazil with the group Quarteto Novo, which included her husband, Airto Moreira. She moved to the United States in the 1960's and performed and recorded with Stan Getz's Latin jazz group (1968), Duke Pearson (1969-1970), Gil Evans (1971), and George Duke. Purim and Moreira both joined Chick Corea's quintet Return to Forever and performed on the albums *Light as a Feather* (1972) and *Return to Forever* (1973). In 1974, Purim recorded her first solo album, *Butterfly Dreams*, and won the *Down Beat* critics' poll. In 1976, she formed her own group.

Pusey, E. B.

full: Edward Bouverie Pusey
b. August 22, 1800
Pusey, Berkshire, England
d. September 16, 1882
Ascot Priory, Berkshire, England
fields: Religion and Theology

Pusey was a leader of the Oxford Movement to revive Anglo-Catholic doctrines and practices in the life of the Church of England, a defender of the Bible against attacks from higher criticism, and a distinguished scholar in Semitic languages.

Pushkin, Alexander

full: Alexander Sergeyevich Pushkin
b. June 6, 1799
Moscow, Russia
d. February 10, 1837
St. Petersburg, Russia
fields: Literature, Historiography

Revered by generations of Russian writers, Pushkin's largest legacy is in poetry, and his literary memory is compounded by the fact that his works inspired internationally celebrated operas, ballets, and films.

Pushmataha

aka: Apushamatahubib (Warrior's Seat Is Finished)
b. June, 1764
British Indian territory in present-day Noxubee County, Miss.
d. Dec. 24, 1824
Washington, D.C.
fields: Native American Affairs

Choctaw tribal chief; the most powerful Choctaw leader of the early nineteenth century, Pushmataha signed Treaty of Mount Dexter in 1805, ceding tribal lands in Alabama and Mississippi; opposed Tecumseh's confederation in 1811; allied with U.S. government during Creek War (1813-1814; he and his warriors later fought against the British at New Orleans and, as a reward, he was made a brigadier general in the United States Army) and the War of 1812; in 1820, at the Treaty of Doak's Stand, he agreed to the cession of a large portion of tribal lands in western and central Mississippi; in return the Choctaws received extensive lands west of the Mississippi River.

Putnam, Hilary

b. July 31, 1926
Chicago, Illinois
fields: Philosophy, Mathematics

Hilary Putnam is probably best known for his development and defense of Turing machine functionalism, for his concept of semantic externalism and the Twin Earth thought exercise, and for internal realism. Taught at Northwestern University (1952), Princeton (from 1953), the Massachusetts Institute of Technology (1961-1965), Harvard University (from 1965); vice president of the Eastern Division of the American Philosophical Association, 1975-1976; president, 1976-1977. Major works: *Philosophy of Logic* (1971), *Mathematics (Matter and Method* (1975), *Mind, Language, and Reality* (1975), *Meaning and the Moral Sciences* (1978), *Reason, Truth, and History* (1981), *Realism and Reason* (1983), *The Many Faces of Realism* (1987), *Representation and Reality* (1988), *Realism with a Human Face* (1990), *Renewing Philosophy* (1992), *Words and Life* (1994), *Pragmatism: An Open Question* (1995).

Pu-yi

aka: Xuanton
aka: Hsuan-tung
b. February 7, 1906
Beijing, China
d. October 17, 1967
Beijing, China
fields: Government and Politics

As small child, Pu-yi was the last emperor of China, from 1909-1911. In 1912, forced by government of Chinese Republic to vacate the imperial palace in Beijing; retained his title, received an annual allowance from the government, and retained the summer palace outside Beijing. Beginning in 1918, given modern education by an Englishman, Reginald Johnson. In 1934, installed by Japanese as figurehead emperor of Japan-occupied Chinese province of Manchuria, which they remaned Manchukuo. After World War II, imprisoned in Soviet Union, then China, until 1959.

Pym, John

b. May 20, 1584
Brymore, Somerset, England
d. December 8, 1643
London, England
fields: Government and Politics

Pym, a consummately skillful politician, was the leader of the majority in the Long Parliament, which in 1641 outlawed ship money and the other devices by which Charles I had maintained his government without calling a parliament. More than any other single individual, Pym preserved the institution of Parliament in England from destruction.

Pynchon, William

b. December, 1590
Springfield, London, England
d. October, 1662
Wraysbury, Buckinghamshire, England
fields: Literature

William Pynchon was an English philosopher who wrote against Puritan orthodoxy in the American colonies, where his writings became important expressions of enlightened inquiry. He helped found Massachusetts Bay Company, where he became a prominent farmer and trader. He also founded Springfield and served as treasurer and justice in the Connecticut and Bay colonies until 1651. Despite his position within the Puritan community, he diverged from the religious orthodoxy and commercial conservatism. Eventually, he and his works were formally denounced. In 1650 he published *The Meritorious Price of Our Redemption*, attacking central tenets of Puritan theology by suggesting that Jesus Christ did not pay for man's sins. His book was burned, and a day of fasting and humiliation was proclaimed to purge the colonies of his heresy.

Pyrrhon of Elis

b. c. 360 B.C.E.
Elis, Greece
d. c. 272 B.C.E.
buried in village of Petra, near Elis
fields: Philosophy

The founder of skepticism, Pyrrhon, a companion of Alexander the Great, taught that the nature of things is inapprehensible; his attitude greatly influenced science and philosophy throughout antiquity.

Pythagoras

b. c. 580 B.C.E.
Samos, Ionia, Greece
d. c. 500 B.C.E.
Metapontum, Lucania
fields: Philosophy, Mathematics, Astronomy, Music

Pythagoras set an inspiring example with his energetic search for knowledge of universal order. His specific discoveries and accomplishments in philosophy, mathematics, astronomy, and music theory make him an important figure in Western intellectual history.

Pytheas

aka: Pytheas of Massalia
b. c. 350-325 B.C.E.
Massalia, Gaul
d. After 300 B.C.E.
perhaps Massalia, Gaul
fields: Science, Exploration and Colonization

Pytheas undertook the first lengthy voyage to the North Atlantic and may have circumnavigated England. This knowledge of the West, together with his astronomical observations, provided the basis for centuries of study.

Q

Qaddafi, Muammar al-

b. 1942
near Surt, Libya
fields: Government and Politics

As the leader of the Free Unionist Officers, Qaddafi demolished the monarchical *ancien régime* of Libya, founded the Libyan Arab Republic, launched a relentless struggle against Western imperialism, and enunciated a sacred ideology by blending the precepts of Islam and Arab nationalism.

Qiu, Kong. *See* Confucius

Quah Ah. *See* Peña, Tonita

Quant, Mary

b. February 11, 1934
London, England
fields: Fashion

Creator of the miniskirt and recognized leader of the 1960's fashion world, British designer Mary Quant developed affordable, distinct styles defined the "mod" clothing of the decade. The British government recognized her achievements in fashion by making her an officer of the British Empire; she was the first female designer to be so honored. In 1990, she was named to the Hall of Fame of the British Fashion Council, and in 1994, at age sixty, she once again opened a London boutique, the Mary Quant Colour Shop.

Quarles, Benjamin

b. January 23, 1904
Boston, Mass.
d. November 16, 1996
Cheverly, Maryland
fields: Historiography, Education

African American historian and educator at historically black colleges and universities; Benjamin Quarles's studies of African American history include *Frederick Douglass* (1948), *The Negro in the Civil War* (1953), *The Negro in the American Revolution* (1961), *Lincoln and the Negro* (1962), *The Negro in the Making of America* (1969), *Black Abolitionists* (1969), and *Allies for Freedom: Blacks and John Brown* (1974); he taught at Shaw (1934-1939), served as professor of history and dean of instruction at Dillard University (1939-1953), and spent the next twenty-one years in the history department at Morgan State University, Baltimore; Quarles served on the Executive Council for the Association for the Study of Afro-American Life and History (1948-1984).

Quarles, Norma

b. November 11, 1936
New York, N.Y.
fields: Journalism, Television, Radio

African American broadcast journalist and disc jockey; after broadcasting as a Chicago radio newscaster and disc jockey (beginning 1965), Norma Quarles became an evening news coanchor for WNBC-TV in New York City; during her twenty-one years with the NBC network, Quarles won an Emmy for her reporting on WMAQ-TV's *Urban Journal* based in Chicago; in 1988 she became coanchor for the weekday news programs *Daybreak* and *Daywatch* on the Cable News Network.

Quayle, Dan

full: James Danforth Quayle
b. Feb. 4, 1947
Indianapolis, Ind.
fields: Government and Politics

U.S. legislator; vice president from 1989 to 1993. Indiana Republican Dan Quayle served in the U.S. House of Representatives from 1976 to 1980 and in the Senate from 1980 to 1988. In 1988, He was chosen by George Bush as his running mate in the 1988 presidential campaign. As vice president, Quayle became best known for clumsy public remarks, and he was regarded as a liability during Bush's unsuccessful 1992 reelection bid.

Qued Koi. *See* Mopope, Stephen

Queen Anne

b. c. 1650
junction of Pamunkey and Mattapony rivers, present-day Va.
d. c. 1725
fields: Government and Politics, Diplomacy, Native American Affairs

As leader of the Pamunkey tribe, which was part of the Powhatan Confederacy, Queen Anne aided white Virginia settlers against hostile tribes.

Queen Latifah

né: Dana Owens
b. March 18, 1970
Newark, New Jersey
fields: Music (Rap and hip-hop music artist)

African American rap and hip-hop music artist; Queen Latifah's music is a combination of hip-hop, house, jazz, and reggae styles of music; 1989 marked the beginning of her solo career; her albums include *All Hail the Queen* (1989), *Nature of a Sista'* (1991), *Juice* (1992), *Set It Off* (1996), *Living Out Loud* (1998), and *Sphere* (1998); she also appears as a regular on the television show *Living Single.*

Queiroz, Rachel de

b. Nov. 17, 1910
Fortaleza, Brazil
fields: Literature

Brazilian writer. Rachel de Queiroz's characters reflect her deep understanding of the situation of Brazilian women. She helped create the genre of the "novel of the northeast," whose stories are set in northeastern Brazil, in the 1930's. Queiroz's novels include *O Quinze* (1930), *O Caçador de Tatu* (1967), *João Miguel* (1932), *Caminho de Pedras* (1937), *As Três Marias* (1939; *The Three Marias*, 1963), and *Dôra, Doralina* (1975; English translation, 1984).

Quelatikan. *See* Moses

Quesada, Eugenio

b. 1927
Wickenburg, Ariz.
fields: Art

Latino artist. Educated in Arizona, California, and New York, Eugenio Quesada began teaching at Arizona State University in 1972. He has exhibited his work in Mexico and Arizona. Although he studied mural painting with Jean Charlot, a pioneer of Mexican muralism, much of his work takes the form of standard-size paintings. He mixes Hispanic and Native American elements in his art.

Quezon, Manuel

full: Manuel Luis Quezon y Molina
b. August 19, 1878
Baler, Philippines
d. August 1, 1944
Saranac Lake, N.Y.
fields: Government and Politics

Manuel Quezon was the first president of the Philippine Commonwealth and leader of the push for independence. Quezon moved to Washington, D.C., in 1909 to serve as resident commissioner for the Philippines, a post he left in 1916 following congressional passage of the Jones Act. Quezon won a seat in the Philippine senate, eventually becoming senate president. In 1934 Quezon again appealed to U.S. lawmakers to repeal the Hare-Hawes-Cutting Act of 1933. Quezon was elected commonwealth president in 1935. His autobiography, *The Good Fight*, was published posthumously, in 1946.

Quine, W. V. O.

full: Willard Van Orman Quine
b. June 25, 1908
Akron, Ohio
fields: Philosophy, Mathematics, Computer Science

Variously called the father of post-World War II American philosophy and the greatest philosopher of the second half of the twentieth century, W. V. O. Quine created a new framework of philosophy that describes the way knowledge is actually obtained. Teaching philosophy and mathematics at Harvard University (1938-1978), he lectured on six continents and visited approximately 113 countries. Through his articles, books, lectures, and textbooks on mathematical logic he taught several generations of philosophers and their students how to do logic and appreciate its power. Major works include "New Foundations for Mathematical Logic" (1937), *Methods of Logic* (1950), *Word and Object* (1960), *The Roots of Reference* (1974), *Quiddities* (1987), *Pursuit of Truth* (1992), and *From Stimulus to Science* (1995).

Quinequan. *See* Quinney, John W.

Quinlan, Karen Ann

b. March 29, 1954
Scranton, Pa.
d. June 11, 1985
Morris Plains, N.J.
fields: Historical Figure

On April 15, 1975, twenty-one-year-old Karen Ann Quinlan was taken to a hospital in a critical comatose state; in July, her parents asked that the respirator be removed and signed papers absolving the hospital from legal liability, but the doctors refused. In June, 1976, after she was weaned from the respirator, she was moved to a nursing home where lived for ten years in a persistent vegetative state. Her case is important in discussions of the right to die, the ordinary/extraordinary care distinction, the active/passive euthanasia distinction, and the need for a living will. The removal of her respirator helped the fight for the right to die, and her death is important in discussions regarding whether there is a difference between active and passive euthanasia.

Quinn, Anthony

full: Anthony Rudolph Oaxaca Quinn
b. April 21, 1915
Chihuahua, Mexico
fields: Film, Theater and Entertainment

Anthony Quinn began his acting career in 1936 in the play *Clean Beds*. Other stage performances include roles in a 1961 production of *A Streetcar Named Desire* and a 1983 production of *Zorba the Greek*. Quinn's film roles include *The Last Train from Madrid* (1937), *Blood and Sand* (1941), *Guadalcanal Diary* (1943), *Irish Eyes Are Smiling* (1944), *Back to Bataan* (1945), *Seven Cities of Gold* (1955), *The Man from Del Rio* (1956), *The Guns of Navarone* (1961), *Lawrence of Arabia* (1962), *Behold a Pale Horse* (1964), *The Secret of Santa Vittoria* (1969), *Mohammed: Messenger of God* (1976), *The Children of Sanchez* (1978), *The Greek Tycoon* (1978), and the 1985 television movie *Onassis: Richest Man in the World*. Quinn received Academy Awards for his supporting performances in *Viva Zapata!* (1952) and *Lust for Life* (1956).

Quinney, John W.

aka: Quinequan
b. 1797
New Stockbridge, N.Y.
d. July 21, 1855
Stockbridge, N.Y.
fields: Government and Politics, Native American Affairs

Native American leader. John W. Quinney was a Mahican (Stockbridge) leader at the time the tribe relocated from the East to the Great Lakes area in the early 1800's.

Quiñones, Wanda Maria

b. ?
New York, N.Y.
fields: Art

Latina artist. Wanda Maria Quiñones was educated at Adelphi University, the Fashion Institute of Technology, and Albany State University. She has taught craft classes for older people, art workshops for children for the Board of Education of New York City, and workshops at the Taller Boricua. Her batik costumes, banners, slide presentations, and demonstrations are inspired by Colombian and Caribbean designs. She created the logo for the television series *Visiones*. Quiñones has exhibited widely at venues specializing in Latin American art, including El Museo del Barrio in New York.

Quintasket, Christine. *See* Mourning Dove

Quirarte, Jacinto

b. Aug. 17, 1931
Jerome, Ariz.
fields: Art

Latino artist and art historian. Jacinto Quirarte was educated in the United States and Mexico. He directed cultural affairs for the Centro Venezolano Americano in Caracas, Venezuela, from 1964 to 1966. After one year of teaching at Yale, he began teaching art history at the University of Texas at Austin in 1967. In 1972, he moved to the University of Texas at San Antonio, where he served as dean of fine and applied arts until 1978 and developed a graduate art program. Quirarte has devoted his attention to Mexican American artists and has tried incorporate them into the art canon. He also wrote *Mexican American Artists* (1973).

R

Rabanus Maurus

b. c. 780
Mainz
d. February 4, 856
Winkel, Rhineland
fields: Religion and Theology, Monasticism, Government and Politics

As one of the leading scholars of the ninth century Carolingian revival of learning, Rabanus' voluminous writings interpreted and introduced generations of medieval students to the wisdom of the Bible and the church fathers and to the practical skills they would need as priests and monks. As abbot of Fulda and later as Archbishop of Mainz, he played a leading role in church governance at a time when the leaders of the Church helped to shape society.

Rabbit. *See* Rogers, Will

Rabelais, François

b. c. 1494
La Devinière, near Chinon, France
d. April, 1553
Paris, France
fields: Literature

Rabelais, although a physician by trade, is best known for his writings, which satirize the Church and its officials while capturing the spirit of the Renaissance through grandiose characters who have an insatiable thirst for knowledge. Rabelais' strong challenge to spiritual authority is representative of a new period in literary thought and action.

Rabi, Isidor Isaac

b. July 29, 1898
Rymanow, Austria-Hungary
d. January 11, 1988
New York, New York
fields: Physics, Government and Politics

Rabi developed the magnetic resonance method to measure with unprecedented accuracy the properties of atomic nuclei. After World War II, he used the international nature of science to bring peoples of the world together, himself becoming a world figure in the process. He was awarded the 1944 Nobel Prize in Physics.

Rābiʿah al-ʿAdawiyah

b. 712
Basra, Iraq
d. 801
Basra, Iraq
fields: Literature

Rābiʿah al-ʿAdawiyah composed numerous influential poems inspired by the absolute love of God and was one of the most important women in Islamic culture. She played an important part in transforming the severe asceticism of early Sufism into a mysticism focused on divine love. She inspired devotional poets such as al-Rūmī and was celebrated by ʿAṭṭār as "a second spotless Mary." She remains a popular ideal of devotion to God.

Rabin, Yitzhak

b. March 1, 1922
Jerusalem, Palestine (now Israel)
d. November 4, 1995
Tel Aviv
fields: Government and Politics, Diplomacy

Prime minister of Israel from 1974 to 1977, Yitzhak Rabin became famous for his efforts to make peace between Israel and the Palestinians and Arabs, for which he won the Nobel Peace Prize in 1994. He held a leadership position during Israel's 1948 war of independence, was an army chief of staff from 1964 to 1968, and was a key figure in Israel's victory in the 1967 Six-Day War. After serving as ambassador to the United States (1968-1973), he became head of Israel's Labor Party and the nation's first native-born prime minister (1974), Israeli defense minister (early 1980's), and then prime minister again (1992-1995). Assassinated by Yigal Amir, a right-wing Israeli opposed to the peace process, in 1995.

Raboteau, Albert Jordy

b. 1943
fields: Religion and Theology

African American professor of religion; Albert Jordy Raboteau authored *Slave Religion: The "Invisible Institution" in the Antebellum South* (1978); as a scholar of African American religious practices and beliefs, Raboteau has traced prejudice and discrimination in the Christian church; he maintains that church histories should include the development of black churches in the United States.

Rachmaninoff, Sergei

full: Sergei Vasilyevich Rachmaninoff
b. April 1, 1873
Semyonovo, Novgorod District, Russia
d. March 28, 1943
Beverly Hills, California
fields: Music

Rachmaninoff is best remembered as the composer who was the last great figure in the Romantic tradition and the leading pianist of his era. His music is noted for melancholy and long melodic line.

Racine, Jean

full: Jean Baptiste Racine
b. December, 1639
La Ferté-Milon, France
d. April 21, 1699
Paris, France
fields: Theater and Entertainment, Literature

Combining psychological insight, poetic power, and a profoundly pessimistic view of human life, Racine wrote the finest tragedies in French literature.

Radcliff, Callen, Jr. *See* Tjader, Cal

Radford, Rosemary. *See* Ruether, Rosemary Radford

Radhakrishnan, Sarvepalli

b. September 5, 1888
Tiruttani, India
d. April 17, 1975
Madras, India
fields: Government and Politics, Philosophy, Religion and Theology

Sarvepalli Radhakrishnan taught and wrote about Eastern religions and ethics at Oxford University (1936-1952) and Benares Hindu University (1939-1948); head of India's UNESCO delegation (1946-1952); India's ambassador to the Soviet Union (1949-1952); chancellor of the University of Delhi (1953-1962); president of India (1962-1967). Major works include *An Idealist View of Life* (1932), *Eastern Religions and Western Thought* (1939), *Is This Peace?* (1945), *Religion in a Changing World* (1967), *The Present Crisis of Faith* (1970), *Our Heritage* (1973).

Radishchev, Aleksandr

b. August 31, 1749
Moscow, Russia
d. September 24, 1802
St. Petersburg, Russia
fields: Literature, Social Reform

Aleksandr Radishchev achieved a posthumous reputation as the first radical Russian intellectual because of his published critique of serfdom. *A Journey from Saint Petersburg to Moscow* (1790), his critique of the Russian Empire, was banned by Empress Catherine II banned it and ordered Radischev's beheading—a sentence commuted to exile in Siberia. After Radishchev was fully pardoned in 1801, he was so demoralized that his later writings were deliberately noncontroversial. He eventually committed suicide.

Radnitz, Gerty Theresa. *See* Cori, Gerty T.

Raeburn, Henry

b. March 4, 1756
Stockbridge, Scotland

d. July 8, 1823
Edinburgh, Scotland
fields: Art

For nearly forty years, Raeburn reigned as the leading portrait painter in his native Scotland, leaving a valuable pictorial record of many prominent and affluent personages of late eighteenth and early nineteenth century Scottish society.

Rafsanjani, Hashemi

full: Ali Akbar Hashemi Rafsanjani
b. 1934
Rafsanjan, Iran
fields: Government and Politics

Hashemi Rafsanjani was president of Iran from 1989 to 1997. Student of Ayatollah Ruhollah Khomeini in 1950's. Pragmatic politician after 1979 Iranian revolution. As president, attempted economic reform, but with mixed results, including high inflation. Allowed suppressed Persian parts of Iran's culture to return discreetly. Elected to second term (the most allowable under Iranian constitution), which ended in 1997.

Ragle, Sarah. *See* Weddington, Sarah

Rai, Lala Lajpat

né: Sher-i-Punjab
b. 1865
Ludhiana, India
d. Nov. 17, 1928
Lahore, Pakistan
fields: Government and Politics

Lala Lajpat Rai, a prominent freedom fighter during India's independence movement, died from injuries received while participating in a freedom march in Lahore, becoming a martyr for the cause. He published *Young India*, a journal that presented an insider's view of the movement, from 1915 to 1919, when nationalist leader Mahatma Gandhi assumed the role of editor and publisher.

Rain in the Face

aka: Amarazhu
aka: Iromagaja
b. c. 1835
forks of the Cheyenne River, N.Dak.
d. Sept. 14, 1905
Standing Rock, N.Dak.
fields: Warfare and Conquest, Native American Affairs

Hunkpapa Sioux warrior. During the Sioux Wars of the 1860's and 1870's, Rain in the Face was a leading war chief. Participated in the war for the Bozeman Trail (1866-1868,), the war for the Black Hills (1876-1877), and in the last great Indian victory, the Battle of the Little Bighorn (1876)

Rainey, Joseph Hayne

b. June 21, 1832
Georgetown, S.C.
d. August 2, 1887
Georgetown, S.C.
fields: Government and Politics

African American U.S. representative from South Carolina during Reconstruction; Joseph Hayne Rainey served as a Republican delegate to the 1868 South Carolina constitutional convention; elected in an 1870 special election as the first black member of Congress, replacing Benjamin F. Whittemore who had resigned under scandalous circumstances; he was reelected in 1872, 1874, and 1876.

Rainey, Ma

né: Gertrude Rainey
aka: Madame Rainey
b. April 26, 1886
Columbus, Ga.
d. December 22, 1939
Columbus, Ga.
fields: Music (blues singer)

African American blues singer; generally recognized as the first professional blues singer, stylistically Ma Rainey employed many vocal effects (raspy voice, falsetto, and screams) that connected her to the male country blues tradition; she toured with Bessie Smith around 1915 in the Rabbit Foot Minstrels and recorded with many great blues and jazz musicians of the period, including Louis Armstrong; her ninety recordings (1923-1928) included "Bo Weevil Blues," "Brokenhearted Blues," "Gone Daddy Blues," "Louisiana Hoo Doo Blues," "Misery Blues," "Titanic Man Blues," and "Weepin' Woman Blues."

Raitt, Bonnie

full: Bonnie Lynn Raitt
b. November 8, 1949
Burbank, California
fields: Music

Raitt mingles the techniques of traditional, black country blues with lyrics that illuminate the spirit of her time, putting her gutsy voice and superb slide guitar to the service of issues that reflect her Quaker upbringing.

Ralegh, Walter

aka: Sir Walter Ralegh
aka: Sir Walter Raleigh
b. 1552 or 1554
Hayes Barton, Devon, England
d. October 29, 1618
London, England
fields: Exploration and Colonization, Government and Politics, Literature

Ralegh's vision and enterprise paved the way for English settlement in North America.

Ram, Kanshi

né: Pandit Kanshi Ram
b. ?
Maruli Kalan, Ambala district, Punjab Province, India
d. ?
Punjab Province
fields: Government and Politics

Kanshi Ram was one of the founding officers of the Ghadr Party. A successful labor contractor in Portland, Oregon, he supported Indian independence organizations such as the Indian Independence League, the Hindustani Association of the Pacific Coast, and the Ghadr Party, which he formed with fellow Asian Indians. In 1914, he returned to India, where he participated in the Ghadr-inspired uprising against the British. Arrested during the revolt, he was tried on sedition charges and sentenced to death by hanging.

Ramabai Sarasvati, Pandita

b. 1858
d. 1922
fields: Social Reform

Social worker Pandita Ramabai Sarasvati labored to improve conditions for women. In the early 1900's, she founded the Arya Mahila Samaj, an organization to assist young widows. She was a professor of Sanskrit and Marathi from 1884 to 1886 at Cheltenham College in England.

Ramakrishna

aka: Gadadhar Chatterji
aka: Gadadhar Chattopadhyaya
b. Feb. 18, 1836
Hooghly, Bengal, India
d. Aug. 16, 1886
Calcutta, India
fields: Religion and Theology

Ramakrishna was a Hindu ascetic and mystic. He devoted his life to the realization of God through a life of austerity and of service to humanity, particularly the poor and the suffering. He believed in the "oneness" of all world religions, and his ideas were embraced by thousands. Swami Vivekananda, his disciple and successor, disseminated Ramakrishna's work throughout the world.

Raman, Chandrasekhara Venkata

aka: Sir Chandrasekhara Venkata Raman
b. November 7, 1888
Trichinopoly (Tiruchirapalli), India
d. November 21, 1970
Bangalore, India
fields: Physics, Physiology, Education

Raman, the first internationally acclaimed Indian physicist to be entirely educated within India, was awarded the Nobel Prize in Physics in 1930 for his discovery of important characteristics of light scattering. Raman also made significant contributions to the education of Indian students, establishing the Raman Research Institute in Bangalore in 1948.

Rāmānuja

b. c. 1017
Śrīperumbūdūr, southern India, near Madras
d. 1137
Śrīraṇgam, southern India
fields: Religion and Theology

Rāmānuja expounded a theistic interpretation of Vedanta philosophy and led the Śrī Vaisnavas community in its formative period.

Ramanujan, Srinivasa Aiyangar

b. Dec. 22, 1887
Erode, Madras (now Tamil Nadu), India
d. Apr. 26, 1920
Chetput, Madras, India
fields: Mathematics (algebra and number theory)

Srinivasa Aiyangar Ramanujan contributed to elementary algebra, continued fractions, power series, number theory, hypergeometric series, and Bernoulli and Euler numbers.

Rameau, Jean-Philippe

b. 1683 (baptized September 25)
Dijon, France
d. September 12, 1764
Paris, France
fields: Music

Rameau was the outstanding French composer of his time. Particularly important as a composer of music for the stage, he was also an important theorist and can be said to have established the modern concept of harmonic practice.

Ramírez, Henry M.

b. May 29, 1929
Walnut, Calif.
fields: Government and Politics, Civil Rights, Social Reform

Mexican American politician and community activist appointed in 1968 director of the Mexican American Studies Division of the U.S. Commission on Civil Rights; in 1971, appointed chairman of President Richard M. Nixon's cabinet committee the Council on Opportunities for Spanish-Speaking People, where he worked for three years to secure the appointment of other qualified Mexican Americans to positions of power in the federal government. Ramírez then became a business consultant based in Washington, D.C.

Ramírez, Joel Tito

b. June 3, 1923
Albuquerque, N.Mex.
fields: Art

Although Joel Tito Ramírez attended the University of New Mexico in 1949 and 1960, he is largely self-taught as an artist. His paintings of the landscapes and history of New Mexico emphasize the light and the changing colors of the area. His works have been commissioned by such corporate clients as Ford Motor Company, Paramount Pictures, and Texas International Airlines.

Ramírez, Raul Carlos

b. June 20, 1953
Ensenada, Mexico
fields: Sports (tennis player)

Mexican tennis player. Raul Carlos Ramírez played tennis at the University of Southern California (USC) before turning professional and winning seventeen singles and sixty-two doubles titles. Ramírez reached the quarterfinals at Wimbledon and at the U.S. and French Opens, and he won the Italian Open in 1975. He played for the Mexican team in the Davis Cup from 1971 to 1983.

Ramírez, Ricardo

b. Sept. 12, 1936
Bay City, Tex.
fields: Religion and Theology, Scholarship, Education

Catholic bishop, scholar, and educator. Ricardo Ramírez was educated in the United States. He attended St. Basil's Seminary in Toronto, Canada, where he was ordained in 1966. He did missionary work in Mexico and the Philippines between 1968 and 1976, then taught at the Mexican American Cultural Center (MACC) in San Antonio, Texas. He was the executive director of MACC from 1976 to 1981, and he taught courses at Our Lady of the Lake University in San Antonio during the late 1970's. In 1981, he published *Fiesta, Worship, and Family*. In 1982, he was named auxiliary bishop of the new archdiocese of Las Cruces, New Mexico.

Ramirez, Sara Estela

b. 1881
Progreso, Coahuila, Mexico
d. Aug. 21, 1910
Tex.
fields: Literature, Government and Politics

Latino poet and political organizer. In 1898, Sara Estela Ramirez moved from Mexico to Laredo, Texas, to teach Spanish to Tejano children. She began publishing poems and poetic essays in the Laredo newspapers *El Demócrata Fronterizo* and *La Crónica*. In 1901, she founded the literary journal *La Corregidora*. Ramirez wrote romantic poetry as well as political essays in support of the Partido Liberal Mexicano. She demanded that feminist issues be part of the revolutionary agenda.

Ramón y Cajal, Santiago

b. May 1, 1852
Petilla de Aragón, Spain
d. Oct. 17, 1934
Madrid, Spain
fields: Biology, Physiology

Santiago Ramón y Cajal used Camillo Golgi's nerve tissue staining method to examine and illustrate the structure of animal nervous systems; in 1906, he and Golgi won the Nobel Prize in Physiology or Medicine.

Ramos, Fidel

full: Fidel Valdez Ramos
b. March 18, 1928
Lingayen, Philippines
fields: Government and Politics

President of the Philippines from 1992 to 1998. Fidel Ramos was head of national police under Ferdinand Marcos beginning in 1972. In unrest after 1986 elections, helped convince military to support Corazon Aquino's claim of victory over Marcos's. Marcos fled country, leaving Aquino as president. Ramos was military chief of staff from 1986 to 1988 and secretary of national defense from 1988 to 1991. Elected president 1992. Attempted to improve the Philippines' struggling economy and begin reforming the national police force. Reached a 1996 peace agreement with the rebel Moro Islamic Liberation Front.

Ramos Otero, Manuel

b. 1948
Manatí, Puerto Rico
fields: Literature

Puerto Rican writer. In 1968, Manuel Ramos Otero moved to New York City to study film and theater. The following year, he earned an M.A. in Spanish and Latin American literature from New York University and began working toward a doctorate at the same institution. In 1976, Ramos Otero founded the small press Editorial Libro Viaje, which published poetry books and Ramos Otero's experimental novel *La novelabingo* (1976).

Rampersad, Arnold

b. November 13, 1941
Port of Spain, Trinidad and Tobago
fields: Education, Scholarship

Educator, biographer, and literary historian; Arnold Rampersad authored *Melville's Israel Potter: A Pilgrimage and Progress* (1969); *The Art and Imagination of W. E. B. Du Bois* (1976); *The Life of Langston*

Hughes: Volume I: 1901-1941, I Too Sing America (1986) and *The Life of Langston Hughes: Volume II: 1941-1967, I Dream a World* (1988); compiled and edited *The Collected Poems of Langston Hughes* (1994); edited *Slavery and the Literary Imagination* (1989), *The Works of Richard Wright* (1991), and *Richard Wright: A Collection of Critical Essays* (1995); helped complete Arthur Ashe's 1993 autobiography *Days of Grace: A Memoir*.

Ramsay, James Andrew Broun. *See* Dalhousie, first marquess of

Ramses II

b. c. 1300 B.C.E.
probably the Eastern Delta of Egypt
d. 1213 B.C.E.
probably Pi-Ramesse (Qantir), Egypt
fields: Government and Politics

Renowned for his statesmanship, military leadership, administrative abilities, and building activity, Ramses set a standard by which subsequent rulers of Egypt measured themselves.

Rand, A. Barry

full: Addison Barry Rand
b. November 5, 1944
Washington, D.C.
fields: Business and Industry

African American corporate executive. In 1992, A. Barry Rand—who started out as the Xerox Corporation's first African American sales representative in the Washington D.C. area— was elected executive vice president of the company. He was inducted into the National Sales Hall of Fame in 1993. He resigned at the end of 1998; he serves on several boards.

Rand, Ayn

b. February 2, 1905
St. Petersburg, Russia
d. March 6, 1982
New York, N.Y.
fields: Literature, Philosophy

Novelist and philosopher; Ayn Rand pioneered a philosophy of self-interest called objectivism; graduated from the University of Leningrad in 1924; unable to adjust to Communism, emigrated to the United States in 1926, and became a naturalized citizen; an outspoken opponent of all forms of collectivism, she touted capitalism and believed in the victory of individualism over all forms of totalitarian government; Rand's philosophy is outlined in *The Virtue of Selfishness: A New Concept of Egoism* (1964) and *Capitalism: The Unknown Ideal* (1966); a screenwriter in Hollywood until 1949, Rand became a best-selling novelist with *The Fountainhead* (1943) and *Atlas Shrugged* (1957).

Randall, Dudley

b. January 14, 1914
Washington, D.C.
fields: Literature

African American poet; Dudley Randall, who has published several volumes of his own poetry, is the founder of the Detroit based independent publishing house Broadside Press; he edited *Black Poetry: A Supplement to Anthologies Which Exclude Black Poets* (1969).

Randolph, A. Philip

full: Asa Philip Randolph
b. April 15, 1889
Crescent City, Fla.
d. May 16, 1979
New York, N.Y.
fields: Labor Movement, Civil Rights

African American labor leader and civil rights activist; A. Philip Randolph is remembered as a key figure in the eventual integration of American labor who, beginning in 1925, led the successful fight to have the Brotherhood of Sleeping Car Porters recognized as an agent in negotiation with the Pullman Company; his actions led to the Pullman Company finally signing a contract with the porters in 1937; in 1941 Randolph was instrumental in convincing President Franklin D. Roosevelt to sign Executive Order 8802 which banned discrimination in employment by companies with defense contracts; in 1948 Randolph's threat to organize a black boycott of the military draft convinced President Harry S. Truman to sign Executive Order 9981 which ended segregation in the armed forces; Randolph was a symbolic and unifying force when he acted as chairman and provided opening remarks for the 1963 March on Washington; in 1968 Randolph retired as president of the Brotherhood of Sleeping Car Porters.

Randolph, Bernard P.

b. July 10, 1933
New Orleans, La.
fields: Military Affairs

African American military officer; from his beginnings as a flight crew instructor and evaluator with the Strategic Air Command at Lincoln Air Force Base, Nebraska (1956-1962), Bernard P. Randolph advanced to the rank of general in 1987; his postings included coordinator of airlift operations throughout the Republic of Vietnam (1969-1970), director of space systems and command, control, and communications, in the office of the deputy chief of staff for research, development, and acquisition in the headquarters of the U.S. Air Force in Washington, D.C. (1981-1983), and commander of Air Force Systems Command at Andrews Air Force Base, Md. (1987).

Rangel, Charles

b. June 11, 1930
New York, N.Y.
fields: Government and Politics

African American politician; it was during Charles Rangel's two terms as a New York state assemblyman (beginning 1966) that he first established his liberal voting record; during his first term as a Democratic representative from Harlem in the U.S. House (elected 1970), Rangel made destruction of the heroin trade his top priority; during the next thirty years as a House member, his main contribution would be continued work toward halting illegal drug shipments to the U.S.; in the U.S. House of Representatives Rangel became the first African American to be appointed to the powerful Ways and Means Committee, later becoming chairman of the health subcommittee of the Ways and Means Committee; in 1983 House Speaker Tip O'Neill appointed Rangel deputy whip and chairman of the Select Committee on Narcotics; top democrat on the Joint Committee on Taxation starting in 1995.

Ranger, Joseph

b. c. 1760
d. ?
fields: Warfare and Conquest

African American patriot; as a free black man, Joseph Ranger served in the American Navy during the Revolutionary War; as a member of the crew of the ship the *Patriot*, Ranger was taken prisoner by the British; when the British surrendered, Ranger was released; he continued to serve aboard Virginia ships until 1787.

Ranke, Leopold von

b. December 21, 1795
Wiehe, Thuringia
d. May 23, 1886
Berlin, Germany
fields: Historiography

Ranke is considered the father of modern historical scholarship and a founder of the German idea of history. His historical works rank as classics of modern historiography.

Rankin, Jeannette

b. June 11, 1880
near Missoula, Montana
d. May 18, 1973
Carmel, California
fields: Government and Politics, Social Reform

Rankin devoted her life to women's rights and peace. She was the first woman elected to Congress and the only member to vote against the entry of the United States into both world wars.

Ransier, Alonzo Jacob

b. 1834
Charleston, S.C.
d. August 17, 1882
Charleston, S.C.
fields: Government and Politics

African American politician; from 1868 until 1870, Alonzo Jacob Ransier served in the South Carolina state house of representatives; in 1870 he became lieutenant governor; from 1873 to 1875, Ransier was a member of the U.S. House of Representatives, serving during that time on the Committee on Manufactures; from 1875 to 1876, he worked as U.S. internal revenue collector for the Second District of South Carolina.

Raphael

né: Raffaello Sanzio
b. April 6, 1483
Urbino, Tuscany, Italy
d. April 6, 1520
Rome
fields: Art, Architecture, Archaeology

With Leonardo da Vinci and Michelangelo, Raphael was part of the great trio of High Renaissance masters. He became the most prolific and most widely celebrated painter of his time.

Rapier, James Thomas

b. November 13, 1837
Florence, Ala.
d. May 31, 1883
Montgomery, Ala.
fields: Government and Politics

African American U.S. representative from Alabama during Reconstruction; a wealthy cotton planter and founder of his own newspaper, James Thomas Rapier served as chairman of the Alabama Republican Party's first platform committee and was a delegate to the 1867 state constitutional convention; beginning in 1872 he served one term as an Alabama representative to the U.S. House, becoming a member of the House Committee on Education and Labor; he later used his income from cotton farming to support the Exoduster movement, sponsoring black migrants who were willing to settle lands in Kansas.

Rashad, Ahmad

né: Bobby Moore
b. November 19, 1949
Portland, Oreg.
fields: Sports (football player), Television

African American football player and sports announcer; during his eleven season career as a professional wide receiver (beginning 1972), Ahmad Rashad played for the St. Louis Cardinals, the Buffalo Bills, the Seattle Seahawks, and the Minnesota Vikings; as a Viking (traded just before the 1976 season), Rashad played in four Pro Bowls (1978-1981) and was named most valuable player in his first Pro Bowl appearance; during his career, Rashad scored forty-four touchdowns, averaged 13.8 yards per catch, and led the National Football League with 51 pass receptions in 1977 and 80 catches in 1979; in 1983 he began working as an announcer for NBC Sports; he married Phylicia Ayers-Allen in 1985.

Rashad, Phylicia

né: Phylicia Ayers-Allen
b. June 10, 1948
Houston, Tex.
fields: Television, Theater and Entertainment, Film

African American actress; after playing Courtney Wright on ABC's daytime series *One Life to Live*, Phylicia Rashad went on to play her best known role as Claire Huxtable on the television series *The Cosby Show* (1984-1992), for which she received two Emmy nominations; she would again team up with Bill Cosby on *Cosby* (1996-); her stage credits include on- and off-Broadway performances in *The Wiz*, *Into the Woods*, *Dreamgirls*, and *Ain't Supposed to Die a Natural Death*; her film credits include *Uncle Tom's Cabin* (1987), *False Witness* (1989), *Polly* (1989), *Polly Once Again* (1990), *Jailbirds* (1991), *Once upon a Time ... When We Were Colored* (1996), and the made-for-television *Free of Eden* (1999); recipient of two People's Choice awards, three Image Awards from the NAACP, and the Outstanding Achievement Award from Women in Film (1991); sister of Debbie Allen and wife of Ahmad Rashad.

Rasmussen, Knud Johan Victor

b. June 7, 1879
Jakobshavn, Greenland
d. December 21, 1933
Gentofte, Denmark
fields: Exploration and Colonization, Geography, Anthropology

A pioneer Arctic explorer, Rasmussen was best known for his seven Thule expeditions. In the fifth, the most famous of these, he crossed North America from Greenland to the Bering Strait. A celebrated ethnographer, Rasmussen studied the folkways of the Eskimos and published many works about the peoples and places of Arctic America.

Raspberry, William James

b. October 12, 1935
Okolona, Miss.
fields: Journalism

African American journalist and nationally syndicated columnist; William James Raspberry took over writing the column, "Potomac Watch," in 1966; was picked up for distribution by *The Washington Post* syndicate; was named Journalist of the Year in 1965 by the Capital Press Club for his coverage of the Watts riots in Los Angeles; published a collection of his columns in *Looking Backward at Us* (1991).

Rasputin, Grigori Yefimovich

b. c. 1870
Pokrovskoye, Siberia, Russian Empire
d. December 30, 1916
Petrograd (now St. Petersburg), Russia
fields: Government and Politics, Religion and Theology

Because of his mystic ability to improve the hemophilia of Alexei Nikolayevich, heir to the Russian throne, Rasputin ingratiated himself to Czar Nicholas II and Empress Alexandra. Rasputin's profligate ways and the refusal of the rulers to believe the scandal he consistently generated increased the estrangement between the rulers and their people, thus contributing to the Russian Revolution.

Rasulala, Thalmus

né: Jack Crowder
b. November 15, 1939
Miami, Fla.
fields: Theater and Entertainment, Film, Television

African American actor; Jack Crowder changed his name to Thalmus Rasulala in the early 1970's; his stage credits include *Fly Blackbird* (1962), *Hello, Dolly!* (1964-1969; for which he won a Theater World Award in 1968), and *One Is a Crowd* (1970); his film credits include *Cool Breeze* (1972), *The Last Hard Men* (1976), *Above the Law* (1988), and *Life on the Edge* (1992); he appeared on television as Lieutenant Jack Neal on ABC's daytime series *One Life to Live* (1969-1970) and on other programs including *T. J. Hooker*, *Cagney and Lacey*, *Simon and Simon*, *Duet*, and *Star Trek: The Next Generation*.

Ratramnus

b. Early ninth century
near Amiens, France
d. c. 868
Corbie, France
fields: Literature, Religion and Theology

Ratramnus was one of the leading theological writers of the first Eucharistic controversy, and his treatise on the subject has been cited in every subsequent occurrence of that debate.

Ratti, Ambrogio Damiano Achille. *See* Pius XI

Rattley, Jessie Meinfield

b. May 4, 1929
Birmingham, Ala.
fields: Business and Industry, Government and Politics

African American businesswoman and politician; beginning in 1952, Jessie Meinfield Rattley founded and directed Peninsula Business College in Newport News, Va.; she established a business department to train minority students while teaching at an all-black public high school in Newport News; she served as the first African American and the first woman on the Newport News city council (1970-1986) during which time she was also elected vice mayor (1976); she was elected mayor in 1986 and served until 1990.

Rauschenbusch, Walter

b. October 4, 1861
Rochester, New York
d. July 25, 1918
Rochester, New York
fields: Religion and Theology, Social Reform

Moving away from individualism, Rauschenbusch formulated a social gospel which influenced the Church and society to accept responsibility for social and economic injustice and to institute social reform.

Ravel, Maurice

full: Joseph Maurice Ravel
b. March 7, 1875
Ciboure, France
d. December 28, 1937
Paris, France
fields: Music

Ravel was one of the most important composers during the first third of the twentieth century, working in many styles and in many different forms.

Rawlings, Jerry John

b. June 22, 1947
Accra, Volta Region, Ghana
fields: Government and Politics

Jerry John Rawlings, a popular figure among the people of Ghana, seized power in 1982 coup. Elected president in a landslide in 1992 and reelected in 1996. Originally a Marxist, but soon aligned with the West.

Rawls, Betsy

né: Elizabeth Rawls
b. May 4, 1928
Spartanburg, South Carolina
fields: Sports (golf)

Over a professional golf career that spanned three decades, Betsy Rawls won fifty-five tournaments and more than $300,000. Her major victories included four U.S. Opens (1951, 1953, 1957, and 1960) and two Ladies' Professional Golf Association (LPGA) championships (1959 and 1969), these being the only women's majors at the time. In 1959, she won the Vare Trophy. She was LPGA Player of the Year in 1963, and she was twice LPGA president and was inducted into the LPGA Hall of Fame, confirming her status as a role model for two generations of women pro golfers. Her last victory was in 1972. In 1975, she left regular competition to become the LPGA's tournament director.

Rawls, John

full: John Bordley Rawls
b. February 21, 1921
Baltimore, Maryland
fields: Philosophy, Law, Political Science

John Rawls presented the basic political structure of democracy as a set of principles of justice obtained from a hypothetical social contract, a system of cooperation among equal citizens having a common allegiance. He caused a rethinking of the concept of justice as fairness and the protection of basic liberties. The philosophical liberal tradition shifted to considerations of communitarianism, emphasizing the group rather than the individual. His theories have been cited in dozens of state and federal court opinions. Taught at Princeton University (1950-1952), Fulbright fellow at Oxford University (1952-1953), assistant and associate professor at Cornell University (1953-1959), visiting professor at Harvard University (1959-1960), professor at the Massachusetts Institute of Technology (1960-1962) and Harvard University (1962-1993). Best known for *A Theory of Justice* (1971) and *Political Liberalism* (1993).

Rawls, Lou

b. December 1, 1935
Chicago, Ill.
fields: Music (popular singer)

African American pop singer; Lou Rawls started as a member of the Pilgrim Travelers gospel group (1950's), toured and recorded with Sam Cooke (late 1950's-early 1960's), and performed in Los Angeles nightclubs as a blues singer before scoring a hit record on both the pop and rhythm-and-blues charts with "Love Is a Hurtin' Thing" (1966); the album *Lou Rawls Live* garnered his first gold album and, in 1971, he received a Grammy Award for "A Natural Man"; in the mid-1970's he recorded "You'll Never Find Another Love Like Mine" and "Sit Down and Talk to Me," lushly orchestrated songs with a disco flavor; also became known as the television commercial voice of Budweiser beer.

Ray, Gene Anthony

b. May 24, 1962
New York, N.Y.
fields: Dance, Television, Film

African American dancer and actor; Gene Anthony Ray is best known for his role in the film *Fame* (1980) and reprised his role on the television series *Fame* (1982-1987); he then left Hollywood.

Ray, John

b. Nov. 29, 1627
Black Notley, Essex, England
d. Jan. 17, 1705
Black Notley, Essex, England
fields: Botany, Science, Zoology

John Ray composed comprehensive descriptions of plants and animals arranged according to their resemblances to one another, instead of alphabetically by name or according to their utility to humans—making him the first naturalist in England to do so.

Ray, Rammohan

b. May 22, 1772
Rādhānagar, Bengal
d. September 27, 1833
Bristol, England
fields: Religion and Theology, Social Reform

Ray's writings have become the putative source for almost all India's social and religious reformist ideals. Known as "the father of modern India," Ray saw the Hinduism of his day as a debased form of a purer monotheism practiced in India during a prehistoric Golden Age. He also found many social customs of his own day—the forced suicide of widows and child marriage, for example—as decadent, medieval accretions on the noble patterns of the Vedic age.

Ray, Satyajit

b. May 2, 1921
Calcutta, India
d. April 23, 1992
Calcutta, India
fields: Film

Ray was India's most distinguished film director, responsible for gaining Indian cinema international recognition and rescuing it from a reputation for indiscriminate productivity and vulgar escapism. For more than thirty years, his films not only established him as a moving force in world cinema but also provided Western audiences with profound insights into Indian life and inspired a generation of Indian filmmakers to follow his lead in producing films of serious social comment.

Raya, Marcos

b. 1948
Irapuato, Guanajuato, Mexico
fields: Art (muralist)

Muralist. Marcos Raya, a political muralist associated with the Pilsen neighborhood (Little Mexico) and the Casa Aztlán community center of Chicago, Illinois, helped paint Chicago's Benito Juárez High School mural and *Homage to Diego Rivera* (1972), a tribute to Rivera's *Man at the Crossroads*. He also changed some of Raymond Patlán's work at Casa Aztlán after a fire in the mid-1970's damaged the original.

Raymond of Peñafort

b. c. 1175
Peñafort, near Villafranca del Panadés, Catalonia
d. January 6, 1275
Barcelona, Catalonia
fields: Religion and Theology

Raymond of Peñafort compiled the decretals (the official code of church law) promulgated by Pope Gregory IX in 1234 and wrote a penitential handbook used throughout the Middle Ages.

Razi, al-

full: Abū Bakr Muḥammad ibn Zakariya al-Razi
b. c. 864
Rayy, Iran
d. c. 925
Rayy, Iran
fields: Medicine, Philosophy

The most original thinker and the keenest clinical observer of all the medieval Muslim physicians, al-Razi produced the first clinical account of smallpox and measles, a twenty-four-volume compendium of medical knowledge, and set new standards for medical ethics, the clinical observation of disease, and the testing of medical treatment.

Reagan, Ronald

full: Ronald Wilson Reagan
b. February 6, 1911
Tampico, Illinois
fields: Government and Politics

Fortieth president of the United States, 1981-1989. After a succession of failed presidencies over two decades, Reagan stemmed the general feeling of instability that had begun to surround the office. Almost by sheer personality and by effortlessly exuding an enormous self-confidence, Reagan reversed many of the negative images of the presidency.

Reagon, Bernice Johnson

b. October 2, 1942
Albany, Ga.
fields: Music, Historiography

African American singer, composer, museum curator, and historian; in 1973, Bernice Johnson Reagon founded the music group Sweet Honey in the Rock in Washington, D.C.; from 1976 to 1988 served as the program director and cultural historian of the program in Black American Culture at the Smithsonian Institution's Museum of American History;in 1988 became curator in the Division of Community Life at the museum.

Réaumur, René-Antoine Ferchault de

b. Feb. 28, 1683
La Rochelle, France
d. Oct. 17, 1757
Saint-Julien-du-Terroux, France
fields: Biology, Botany, Chemistry, Genetics, Invention and Technology, Mathematics, Physics, Physiology, Zoology

René-Antoine Ferchault de Réaumur applied science to technology; made precise, innovative studies of insects; in 1730, announced his invention of a new thermometer; in 1749, described his invention of an egg incubator.

Rebolledo, Tey Diana

b. Apr. 29, 1937
Las Vegas, N.Mex.
fields: Literature, Scholarship

Latina writer. Tey Diana Rebolledo, who has worked as editor of *Las mujeres hablan: An Anthology of Nuevo Mexicano Writers* (1988) and on the editorial board of Arte Público Press, has written numerous scholarly articles and has studied the bonds that Hispanic girls form with their grandmothers. She was named an eminent scholar by the New Mexico Commission on Higher Education in 1989.

Rechy, John Francisco

b. Mar. 10, 1934
El Paso, Tex.
fields: Literature

Novelist. John Francisco Rechy has taught creative writing at the University of California, Los Angeles; the University of Southern California; and Occidental College. In the early 1960's, he published several journalistic pieces in *Evergreen Review*, one of which formed the basis of *City of Night* (1963), his first novel. He subsequently published such books as *Numbers* (1967), *This Day's Death* (1969), *The Vampires* (1971), *The Fourth Angel* (1972), *The Sexual Outlaw: A Non-Fiction Account, with Commentaries, of Three Days and Nights in the Sexual Underworld* (1977), *Rushes* (1979), *Bodies and Souls* (1983), and *Marilyn's Daughter* (1988).

Rector, Eddie

b. late 1890's
Orange, N.J.
d. 1962
New York, N.Y.
fields: Dance

African American dancer; a forerunner of the sleek "class-act" style, Eddie Rector has been called the greatest soloist among soft shoe dancers; Rector is remembered for introducing full body motion and elegance to tap dancing; wearing gray top hat and tails, Rector combined expert footwork with graceful arm and hand movements to create a fluid style that would range across an entire stage; a soft shoe sand dance was his hallmark, but he also excelled in the waltz clog and is credited with inventing the traveling-time step known as the bambalina; his stage work included performing in *Dixie to Broadway* (1924), replacing Bill Robinson in an overseas tour of *Blackbirds of 1928*, working with bandleader Duke Ellington at the Cotton Club, playing the trumpet at the Sebastian Club in Los Angeles, and starring in such New York shows as *Hot Rhythm* (1930), *Rhapsody in Black* (1931), and *Yeah Man* (1932).

Red Bird

aka: Wanig Suchka
aka: Zitkaduta
b. c. 1788
near Prairie du Chien, Wis.
d. Feb. 16, 1828
Prairie du Chien, Wis.
fields: Warfare and Conquest, Native American Affairs

A Winnebago Indian and leader of the brief Winnebago Uprising of 1827, Red Bird was war chief of a small, militant group of Winnebagos.

Red Cloud

né: Makhpíya-Lúta
b. 1822
Blue Creek, near North Platte, Nebraska
d. December 10, 1909
Pine Ridge, South Dakota
fields: Military Affairs, Government and Politics

Red Cloud (born into the Oglala subtribe of the Teton branch of Dakota Sioux) led the Dakota Sioux Indians through a difficult period, effectively resisting the onrush of American westward advance and later helping the Sioux make the transition to reservation life under American rule.

Red Eagle. *See* Weatherford, William

Red Jacket

aka: Sagoyewátha (He Causes Them to Be Awake)
b. c. 1756
near Canoga, N.Y.
d. Jan. 20, 1830
Seneca Village, N.Y.
fields: Native American Affairs

Seneca tribal chief and orator; Red Jacket served as spokesperson for the British during the American Revolution; in 1780's assumed ceremonial title of council orator; after the revolution maintained a moderate stance, suggesting neutrality for the Iroquois in U.S.-Canadian disputes; an eloquent speaker known for his great wit and memory, Red Jacket participated in numerous treaty conferences, arguing against Seneca assimilation into white society (from 1790 to 1794, he was present at seven major negotiations between Iroquois and U.S. officials); at the same time, he signed treaties selling land and negotiated secretly with federal commissioners; this apparent hypocrisy earned him the enmity of the prophet Handsome Lake, who declared that Red Jacket would be undergoing eternal punishment for his role in the sale of Seneca land; in 1792, George Washington presented him with a silver medal.

Red Leaf. *See* Wapasha

Red Shoes

aka: Shulush Homa
b. c. 1700
New Stockbridge, N.Y.
d. June 22, 1748
fields: Peace Advocacy, Native American Affairs

Native American leader. A Choctaw, Red Shoes was an advocate of peace and trade with whites in the colonial era. Originally allied with French, but switched allegiance to English settlers. Received with ceremony by the English at Charleston in 1738. Attempted to sway other Choctaw towns away from their dependence on the French; killed by Choctaws at French urging.

Red Sleeves. *See* Mangas Coloradas

Red Walker. *See* Gall

Redding, Jay Saunders

b. October 13, 1906
Wilmington, Del.
d. March 2, 1988
Ithaca, N.Y.
fields: Literature

African American author and educator; Jay Saunders Redding's published works exploring the African American experience include *The Negro* (1967), *The Lonesome Road: The Story of the Negro's Part in America* (1958), *They Came in Chains: Americans from Africa* (1950), and *To Make a Poet Black* (1939).

Redding, Otis

b. September 9, 1941
Dawson, Ga.
d. December 10, 1967
Lake Monona, Wis.
fields: Music (soul singer)

African American soul singer; Otis Redding was at the height of his career when he was killed in a plane crash; prior to his death he had produced the hit recordings "Mr. Pitiful" (1965), "Respect" (1965), "I've Been Loving You Too Long" (1965), and "Tramp" (1967; a duet with Carla Thomas); released posthumously, "Dock of the Bay" topped the popular music charts.

Redman, Don

full: Donald Matthew Redman
b. July 29, 1900
Piedmont, W.Va.
d. November 30, 1964
New York, N.Y.
fields: Music (alto saxophonist, composer, arranger, and orchestra leader)

African American alto saxophonist, composer, arranger, and orchestra leader; noted for playing a major role in the development of big band orchestral jazz, Don Redman created such early musical arrangements for Fletcher Henderson's orchestra as "Shanghai Shuffle" (1924), "Go 'Long Mule" (1924), and "Copenhagen" (1924); as musical director of McKinney's Cotton Pickers, Redman created such arrangements as "Gee, Ain't I Good to You?" (1926), "Cherry" (1928), and "Rocky Road" (1930); from 1931 to 1940, Redman toured and recorded with his own orchestra; considered to be one of the premier orchestras of the day, it was one of the first black swing-era bands to be sponsored for a radio series; Redman's recordings as a leader included "Chant of the Weed/Shakin' the African" (1931), "Got the Jitters" (1934), and "Sweet Sue" (1937); Redman created arrangements for Fletcher Henderson, Count Basie, Paul Whiteman, and Jimmy Dorsey and, during the 1950's, served as musical director for vocalist Pearl Bailey.

Redmond, Eugene

b. December 1, 1937
East St. Louis, Ill.
fields: Literature

African American poet, critic, journalist, playwright, and educator who helped form the Black Arts movement of the 1960's; Eugene Redmond's poetry, which emphasizes his pride in his cultural heritage, includes *Songs from an Afro/Phone* (1972) and *In a Time of Rain and Desire* (1973); he has also published a critical survey, *Drumvoices: The Mission of African American Poetry* (1976), which looks at African American poetry from 1746 to 1976; Redmond edited the poetry of the late Henry Dumas.

Redon, Odilon

né: Bertrand-Jean Redon
b. April 22, 1840
Bordeaux, France
d. July 6, 1916
Paris, France
fields: Art

Through long years of artistic experimentation, Redon developed a mysterious, nostalgic, melancholy, and sometimes humorous fantasy world in his paintings, prints, and drawings. This world became his distinctive contribution to the allusive art movement of the end of the nineteenth century called Symbolism.

Reed, Dorothy. *See* Mendenhall, Dorothy Reed

Reed, Ishmael

b. February 22, 1938
Chattanooga, Tenn.
fields: Literature

African American author; a writer whose satiric novels, essays, and poems challenge accepted beliefs about politics, society, and the way literary works should be written, Ishmael Reed has published the novels *The Free-Lance Pallbearers* (1967), *Yellow Back Radio Broke-Down* (1969), *Mumbo Jumbo* (1972), *Flight to Canada* (1976), *Japanese by Spring* (1993), and *Airing Dirty Laundry* (1993); Reed began teaching at the University of California, Berkeley, in 1967 and finally received tenure in 1988; through the 1971 establishment of the Yardbird Publishing Company and the 1976 founding of the Before Columbus Foundation, Reed sought to widen the American literary canon to include a multiplicity of perspectives and ethnic groups; Reed's essays, which cover a variety of controversial social, literary, and political subjects, are collected in *Shrovetide in Old New Orleans* (1978), *God Made Alaska for the Indians* (1982), and *Writin' Is Fightin': Thirty-seven Years of Boxing on Paper* (1988).

Reed, Jimmy

full: James Mathis Reed
b. September 6, 1925
Dunleith, Miss.
d. August 29, 1976
Oakland, Calif.
fields: Music (blues musician)

African American blues musician; remembered as the teen idol who played guitar and harmonica at the same time and sang "Big Boss Man," Jimmy Reed was one of the few successful 1950's blues musicians; "You Don't Have to Go" (1955), his first hit, crossed over into popular music; between 1956 and 1961, Reed recorded eleven hits that reached the top twenty on the rhythm-and-blues charts; during the 1970's he performed at concerts and recorded in California.

Reed, John

b. October 22, 1887
Portland, Oregon
d. October 19, 1920
Moscow, U.S.S.R.
fields: Journalism

John Reed is best known for his reporting on the Mexican and Russian Revolutions. After traveling with Mexican rebel leader Pancho Villa in 1913 he published *Insurgent Mexico* (1914). On the outbreak of World War I, he went to Europe, reaching Saint Petersburg in time to witness Russia's October, 1917, Revolution. Afterward, he wrote a classic work on the revolution, *Ten Days That Shook the World* (1919). On his return to the United States, he joined the Socialist Labor Party but left it to help form the American Communist Labor Party. Indicted for sedition in 1919, he fled to the Soviet Union, where shortly thereafter he died.

Reed, Stanley

full: Stanley Forman Reed
b. 1884
d. 1980
fields: Law

U.S. Supreme Court justice, 1938-1957; appointed by President Franklin D. Roosevelt. Significant opinions: *McNabb v. United States*, 318 U.S. 347 (1943) (dissenting opinion); *Adamson v. California*, 332 U.S. 46 (1947); *Winters v. New York*, 333 U.S. 507 (1948); *Gallegos v. Nebraska*, 342 U.S. 55 (1951); *Carlson v. Landon*, 342 U.S. 524 (1952); *Brown v. Allen*, 344 U.S. 443 (1953).

Reed, Walter

b. September 13, 1851
Belroi, Virginia
d. November 22, 1902
Washington, D.C.
fields: Medicine

Reed served as the head of the commission that designed and conducted the experiments which revealed beyond a doubt that yellow fever was transmitted by the bite of an infected mosquito, thus making control of this terrible disease possible.

Reed, Willis, Jr.

b. June 25, 1942
Hico, La.
fields: Sports (basketball player and coach)

African American basketball player and coach; Willis Reed, Jr., was named Rookie of the Year for his 1964-1965 season with the New York Knickerbockers; for the 1969-1970 season, during which Reed played on the Knicks' NBA championship team, he was named Most Valuable Player for the All-Star game, the regular season, and the play-offs, the first player to receive all three honors in the same season; when he led the Knicks to the 1972-1973 championship, he was again named the play-offs' MVP; during his decade-long playing career, Reed averaged 18.7 points per game, scored 12,183 total points, and made 8,414 rebounds; he also appeared in seven All-Star games (1965-1971); he went on to coach college and professional teams; in 1981 he was inducted into the Basketball Hall of Fame.

Reese, Della

né: Dellareese Taliaferro
b. July 6, 1932
Detroit, Mich.
fields: Music (popular vocalist), Television

African American vocalist and actress; by age thirteen, Della Reese was touring with Mahalia Jackson; during the 1960's, 1970's, and 1980's, Reese achieved moderate success as a pop and cabaret singer; in the 1980's she moved into acting and, in 1991, was given her own television show, *The Royal Family*, costarring Redd Foxx. She also costarred in the popular television series *Touched by an Angel* (1994-). Her awards include Emmy, Golden Globe, and Screen Actors Guild nominations, and 1996 and 1998 NAACP Image Award for outstanding lead actress in a drama series.

Reeves, Dianne

b. 1956?
Detroit, Mich.
fields: Music (jazz vocalist)

African American jazz vocalist; Dianne Reeves gained early performing experience singing with a Latin jazz-rock group called Caldera, working as a principal vocalist with Sergio Mendes, and, beginning in 1983, performing for two and a half years with Harry Belafonte; her own work reflects the Brazilian, African, Caribbean, and Third World musical influences to which she was exposed while singing with Mendes and Belafonte; her album *Dianne Reeves* (1988), which includes material cowritten by Reeves with Herbie Hancock and Stevie Wonder and contains her hit single "Better Days," topped the jazz charts for eleven weeks. Other albums are *I Remember* (1991), *Quiet After the Storm* (1994), and *Grand Encounter* (1996).

Regiomontanus

né: Johann Müller
aka: Joannes de Regio monte
b. June 6, 1436
Königsberg, Archbishopric of Mainz (now Kaliningrad, Russia)
d. July 6, 1476
Rome, Papal States (now Italy)
fields: Mathematics (trigonometry)

Regiomontanus was the first European to systematize plane and spherical trigonometry as a discipline separate from astronomy; publishes *Ephemerides*, a navigational table, in 1474.

Regulus

né: Marcus Atilius Regulus
b. c. 300 B.C.E.
probably Rome
d. c. 249 B.C.E.
probably Carthage
fields: Warfare and Conquest

Through legendary embellishments on his actual exploits, Regulus has served as an example, variously, of moral courage and devotion to duty, of arrogance in the face of victory, and of the reversals of fortune that history records.

Rehnquist, William H.

full: William Hubbs Rehnquist
b. October 1, 1924
Milwaukee, Wisconsin
fields: Law

Rehnquist served as solicitor general, associate justice, and chief justice of the United States. He supported and presided over the Court's conservative shift during his tenure.

Reid, Daphne Maxwell

full: Daphne Maxwell
b. July 13, 1948
New York, N.Y.
fields: Television, Film

African American actress; Daphne Maxwell Reid's television credits include roles on the series *WKRP in Cincinnati*, *Simon and Simon*, *Frank's Place*, and *The Fresh Prince of Bel-Air* (1993-1996); her film credits include *The Long Journey Home* (1987). She is married to Tim Reid

Reid, George Houston

b. February 25, 1845
Johnstone, Renfrew, Scotland
d. September 12, 1918
London, England
fields: Government and Politics

George Houston Reid was prime minister of Australia from 1904 to 1905. In Australia's first federal Parliament (1901-1904), Reid led the Free Traders' opposition to the Liberal Party, led by Alfred Deakin. As prime minister, established an economic recovery program for Australia; strong advocate of free trade and opponent of protectionism. Helped establish the Commonwealth of Australia as an independent modern nation.

Reid, Hazel. *See* O'Leary, Hazel

Reid, Thomas

b. April 26, 1710
Strachan, Kincardineshire, Scotland
d. October 7, 1796
Glasgow, Scotland
fields: Philosophy

Famous for his criticism of "the way of ideas" and its attendant skepticism, Thomas Reid found the Scottis "common sense" school of philosophy. Pastor at New Machar (1737); taught at King's College, Aberdeen (1751-1764); helped organize the Aberdeen Philosophical Society (1758); succeeded Adam Smith as professor of moral philosophy at Glasgow (1764-1781). Major works are *An Inquiry into the Human Mind on the Principles of Common Sense* (1764), *Essays on the Intellectual Powers of Man* (1785), and *Essays on the Active Powers of Man* (1788; also known as *Essays on the Active Powers of the Human Mind*).

Reid, Tim

b. December 19, 1944
Norfolk, Va.
fields: Television (actor, producer), Film

African American actor; Tim Reid's television credits include his series roles as deejay Gordon "Venus Flytrap" Sims on *WKRP in Cincinnati* (1978-1982; for which he also wrote several episodes) and as detective Marcel "Downtown" Brown on the *Simon and Simon* (1983-1984); in addition to hosting CBS's *Summer Playhouse* (1987), Reid acted in and produced the series *Frank's Place* (1987-1988), created, produced, and acted in *Snoops* (1988-1989), stars in *Sister, Sister* (1996), and *Linc's* (1998); Reid's film credits include *Mother, Jugs, and Speed* (1976) and *Uptown Saturday Night* (1974).

Reifel, Ben

b. Sept. 19, 1906
Parmelee, S.Dak.
d. Jan. 2, 1990
Sioux Falls, S.Dak.
fields: Government and Politics, Native American Affairs

A Rosebud Sioux, Ben Reifel served five terms in the U.S. Congress (1961-1971 after several years in various capacities in the Bureau of Indian Affairs.

Reimer, Alva. *See* Myrdal, Alva

Reinecke, Aiko

né: Aiko Tokimasa
b. Jan. 9, 1907
Kahuku, Territory of Hawaii
fields: Education

Aiko Reinecke, along with her husband, John Reinecke, was charged on November 25, 1947, with violating the law that made it illegal for a public school teacher to be a member of the Communist Party. They were suspended without pay, and their hearing was held in August, 1948. They were found to be guilty and discharged without pay. In 1976, the State Board of Education expressed its regret at what happened and compensated them $250,000. Her husband was arrested in 1951 for allegedly advocating the overthrow of any government in the United States by force or violence. He was convicted but the guilty verdict was reversed in 1958 by the U.S. Ninth Circuit Court of Appeals.

Reinecke, John E.

b. July 2, 1904
near Devon, Kans.
d. June 11, 1982
Honolulu, Hawaii
fields: Education

John E. Reinecke, along with his wife, Aiko Reinecke, was charged on November 25, 1947, with violating the law that made it illegal for a public school teacher to be a member of the Communist Party. At their hearing, in August, 1948, the couple was found guilty and discharged without pay. Twenty-eight years later, the new board of education expressed regret its regret for what happened and awarded them compensation of $250,000. In August, 1951, John was among seven persons arrested in Honolulu on the charge of violating the Smith Act (1940), which makes it a criminal offense to advocate the overthrow of any government in the United States by force or violence. He and the others were found guilty. Their conviction was reversed in January, 1958.

Reischauer, Edwin O.

b. Oct. 15, 1910
Tokyo, Japan
d. Sept. 1, 1990
La Jolla, Calif.
fields: Diplomacy

Diplomat, scholar, and author Edwin O. Reischauer was the American ambassador to Japan (1961-1966) during the John F. Kennedy and Lyndon B. Johnson administrations. Reischauer served in various intelligence positions within the State Department, the War Department, and the U.S. Army during World War II. After the war, he became a professor in the Department of Far Eastern Languages and the Department of History at Harvard University, where he remained until he retired in 1982. His contributions to Japanese scholarship, Japan-America relations, and the establishment of Japanese studies programs in the United States are memorialized through the Reischauer Institute at Harvard University.

Reith of Stonehaven, First Baron

né: John Charles Walsham Reith
aka: John Charles Walsham, First Baron Reith of Stonehaven
b. July 20, 1889
Stonehaven, Kincardineshire, Scotland
d. June 16, 1971
Edinburgh, Scotland
fields: Radio, Theater and Entertainment

Reith created in the British Broadcasting Corporation the world's most famous radio broadcasting system, in which was combined high culture and moral uplift as well as entertainment.

Remarque, Erich Maria

né: Erich Paul Remark
b. June 22, 1898
Osnabrück, Germany
d. September 25, 1970
Locarno, Switzerland
fields: Literature

Remarque's novel *Im Westen nichts Neues* (1929; *All Quiet on the Western Front*, 1929), a realistic account of a soldier's life during World War I, is perhaps the most widely read and highly influential war novel of all time.

Rembrandt

né: Rembrandt van Rijn
b. July 15, 1606
Leiden, the Netherlands
d. October 4, 1669
Amsterdam, the Netherlands
fields: Art

Generally considered to be the greatest portrait painter of all time, Rembrandt is also renowned for his etchings and drawings. His works reflect his masterful ability to create realistic images which invite the viewer into his world, composed primarily of lower-class subjects living simple lives.

Remington, Frederic

full: Frederic Sackrider Remington
b. October 4, 1861
Canton, New York
d. December 26, 1909
Ridgefield, Connecticut
fields: Art, Literature

In his drawings and bronzes, Remington recorded the Old West before it vanished, thus preserving it for later generations.

Remond, Charles Lenox

b. February 1, 1810
Salem, Mass.
d. December 22, 1873
Boston, Mass.
fields: Civil Rights

African American abolitionist; as a free-born black, Charles Lenox Remond became the first black lecturer for the Massachusetts Anti-Slavery Society in 1838; in 1840 he traveled as one of four delegates to the World's Anti-Slavery Society meeting in London, England; after being warmly received by audiences throughout the British Isles, he returned to the United States carrying a petition signed by hundreds of Irish citizens demanding an end to slavery.

Renaldo, Duncan

full: Renault Renaldo Duncan
b. Apr. 23, 1904
Romania?
d. Sept. 3, 1980
Santa Barbara, Calif.
fields: Theater and Entertainment (actor), Film

Actor. Duncan Renaldo moved to the United States in the early 1920's and appeared in the films *Clothes Make the Woman* (1928) and *The Bridge of San Luis Rey* (1929). He had immigration problems during the 1930's until he was pardoned by President Franklin D. Roosevelt in 1936. During the 1930's and 1940's, Renaldo played in more than fifty Three Mesquiteers films. From 1945 to 1950, he played the Cisco Kid in twelve films and more than 150 television episodes. His other films include *Trapped in Tia Juana* (1932), *Down Mexico Way* (1941), *For Whom the Bell Tolls* (1943), *The Daring Caballero* (1949), and the serials *The Lone Ranger Rides Again* in the late 1930's and *Zorro Rides Again* in 1937 and 1959.

Renan, Ernest

full: Joseph-Ernest Renan
b. February 28, 1823
Tréguier, Côtes-du-Nord, France
d. October 2, 1892
Paris, France
fields: Religion and Theology, Historiography, Philosophy

Renan's writings encompass the areas of religion, history, science, and morality. His controversial biography of Jesus Christ illustrates Renan's ongoing theme of resolution of contradictions by emphasizing the problem of reconciling the historical and the spiritually divine Jesus.

Renault, Louis

fields: Diplomacy
b. May 21, 1843
Autun, France
d. February 8, 1918
Barbizon, France
fields: Law, Peace Advocacy, Diplomacy

French jurist and diplomat. Louis Renault was awarded the Nobel Peace Prize in 1907, along with Ernesto Teodoro Moneta, for his work at the Hague Conference of 1899; his contributions to the conference were extensive.

Reno, Janet

b. July 21, 1938
Miami, Florida
fields: Law, Government and Politics

As Florida's first female state attorney, Janet Reno focused on the root causes of criminal behavior, instituting programs to change the social and personal conditions that lead people to commit crimes. As the first woman attorney general of the United States, she declared her intention to reorient the national crime policy in the same way—toward prevention first, and then punishment.

Renoir, Jean

b. September 15, 1894
Paris, France
d. February 12, 1979
Los Angeles, California
fields: Film

Considered by many to be the world's greatest film director, Renoir explored his characters' relations to society and nature and their humanity during his forty-five-year career.

Renoir, Pierre-Auguste

b. February 25, 1841
Limoges, France
d. December 3, 1919
Cagnes, France
fields: Art

One of the major French Impressionists, Renoir painted in the open air, handling the paint loosely, dissolving masses, and abandoning local colors. He differed, however, from most of the other Impressionists in his concentration on the human figure and in his strong interest in portraiture.

Renville, Joseph

b. c. 1779
near present-day St. Paul, Minn.
d. c. 1846
Lac Qui Parle, Minn.
fields: Business and Industry, Diplomacy, Native American Affairs

A Sioux Indian, Joseph Renville was an influential white sympathizer among the Minnesota Sioux. Son of a French trader and a Sioux woman. Served as a captain for the British army during the War of 1812; interpreter for British in Canada.

Rescher, Nicholas

b. July 15, 1928
Hagen, Westphalia, Germany
fields: Philosophy

Nicholas Rescher contributed significantly to logic, philosophy of science, and the history of philosophy and developed a system of pragmatic idealism that placed him squarely in the mainstream of the history of American philosophy. Major works include *The Coherence Theory of Truth* (1973), *A System of Pragmatic Idealism* (1992-1994), *Objectivity: The Obligations of Impersonal Reason* (1997), and *Communicative Pragmatism and Other Philosophical Essays on Language* (1998).

Reuther, Walter P.

full: Walter Philip Reuther
b. September 1, 1907
Wheeling, West Virginia
d. May 9, 1970
Pellston, Michigan
fields: Labor Movement, Social Reform

Committed to politically active unionism, Reuther helped organize the automobile workers in the 1930's and led that union in the support of a broad range of social and economic reform in post-World War II United States.

Revels, Hiram Rhoades

b. September 27, 1822
Fayetteville, N.C.
d. January 16, 1901
Aberdeen, Miss.
fields: Government and Politics

African American politician; Hiram Rhoades Revels was elected to the Mississippi state senate in 1869; in 1870 Revels became the first African American to serve in Congress when the Mississippi legislature elected him to finish out Jefferson Davis's unexpired term of one year; following his Senate term, he became president of Alcorn College, near Lorman, Miss. (1871-1873 and 1876-1882); he served as Mississippi secretary of state for a brief period beginning in 1873.

Revere, Paul

b. January 1, 1735
Boston, Massachusetts
d. May 10, 1818
Boston, Massachusetts

fields: Business and Industry, Government and Politics, Military Affairs

American Revolutionary patriot and propagandist, Revere was a prominent silversmith, engraver, and industrialist.

Reverend Ike

né: Frederick Joseph Eikerenkoetter II
b. June 1, 1935
Ridgeland, S.C.
fields: Religion and Theology

African American clergyman; through the United Christian Evangelistic Association and the United Church and Science of Living Institute, of which Reverend Ike is founder and president, Reverend Ike espouses the philosophy that it is God's desire that humankind should prosper and that it is not money but the lack of it that underlies evil behavior and mischief among human beings; Reverend Ike encourages the positive use of mental power and urges his followers not to look only for an afterlife reward but to be productive and resourceful spiritually and materially.

Reyes, Alfonso

b. May 17, 1889
Monterrey, Mexico
d. Dec. 12, 1959
Mexico City, Mexico
fields: Literature, Education

Mexican poet, essayist, and educator. Alfonso Reyes moved to Mexico City in 1906 and became involved with a group of poets and scholars who initiated a cultural renewal and educational reform throughout the National Preparatory School and the National University. Reyes helped establish many cultural and educational institutions during his lifetime. Reyes wrote journalistic articles, poetry, essays, and short stories. His published books include *Visión de Anáhuac* (1917), *Ifigenia cruel* (1924), *Huellas, 1906-1919* (1922), *Romances del Río de Enero* (1933), and *El plano oblicuo* (1920).

Reyes Basoalto, Neftalí Ricardo. *See* Neruda, Pablo

Reyes, Mario Moreno. *See* Cantinflas

Reynolds, Barbara Ann

b. August 17, 1942
Columbus, Ohio
fields: Journalism, Literature

African American print and broadcast journalist; Barbara Ann Reynolds has worked as a reporter for the now-defunct *Cleveland Press* (1968), as assistant editor of *Ebony* magazine and, for a twelve-year period beginning in 1969, as a writer for the *Chicago Tribune*; she has also freelanced for such magazines as *Essence, Playboy, The New Republic*, and *Black Family*; cofounder of a magazine for black professionals called *Dollars and Sense*; her published books include the biography *Jesse Jackson: The Man, the Movement, the Myth* (1975), *And Still We Rise: Interviews with Fifty Black Role Models* (1988), *Dorothy L. Sayers: Her Life and Soul* (1993), and *No, I Won't Shut Up: Thirty Years of Telling It Like It Is* (1998); on the editorial board of the newspaper *USA Today* (beginning 1983).

Reynolds, Joshua

aka: Sir Joshua Reynolds
b. July 16, 1723
Plympton, Devonshire, England
d. February 23, 1792
London, England
fields: Art

Founder of the English School of painting, Reynolds served for more than two decades as the first president of the Royal Academy of Arts. His *Discourses* express the fundamental tenets of neoclassical art, while his paintings often anticipate the Romantic movement.

Reynolds, Mel

full: Melvin J. Reynolds
b. January 8, 1952
Mound Bayou, Miss.
fields: Government and Politics

African American politician; Mel Reynolds was first elected to the U.S. House of Representatives as a Democrat from the Second District in Illinois in 1992; was reelected in 1994; resigned October 1, 1995 after being sentenced to five years in prison for charges related to sexual misconduct involving a teenage campaign worker.

Reynoso, Cruz

b. May 2, 1931
Brea, Calif.
fields: Law, Government and Politics, Civil Rights, Social Reform

Mexican American government official. During the 1960's, assistant chief of the Division of Fair Employment Practices in California; deputy director, then director, of California Rural Legal Assistance; associate general counsel to the Equal Employment Opportunity Commission in 1967; taught at the University of New Mexico Law School, 1972-1974; appointed to the California Court of Appeals in Sacramento as an associate justice, 1976; appointed to the California Supreme Court in 1982, the first Latino to serve in that capacity; served on presidential commissions including the Select Commission on Immigration and Refugee Policy and the United Nations Commission on Human Rights.

Rhee, Syngman

b. March 26, 1875
P'yongsan, Korea
d. July 19, 1965
Honolulu, Hawaii
fields: Government and Politics

Rhee began his career as a student movement leader in the 1890's. In exile, he became the leader of an overseas movement to liberate Korea from Japanese rule between 1913 and 1945. He later became President of South Korea, holding that position throughout the Korean War.

Rhodes, Cecil

full: Cecil John Rhodes
b. July 5, 1853
Bishop Stortford, Hertfordshire, England
d. March 26, 1902
Muizenberg, Cape Colony, South Africa
fields: Business and Industry, Colonial Administration

Exponent of British colonization and domination in the world, Rhodes was a business tycoon who dominated the world's diamond supply and a benefactor who used wealth to establish the Rhodes scholarships.

Rhodes, J. B.

b. ?
d. ?
fields: Invention and Technology

African American inventor; J. B. Rhodes designed and patented a water closet for use in private homes.

Rhone, Sylvia M.

b. March 11, 1952
Philadelphia, Pa.
fields: Business and Industry

African American record company executive; from 1985 to 1988, Sylvia M. Rhone was the director of National Black Music Promotions for Atlantic Records, rising to the post of vice president and general manager of Black Music Operations in 1988; served as chairperson and chief executive officer of Atco-East West Records starting in 1991.

Ribbentrop, Joachim von

full: Ulrich Friedrich Willy Joachim Ribbentrop
b. April 30, 1893
Wesel, Germany
d. October 16, 1946
Nuremberg, Germany
fields: Diplomacy

A devoted follower of Hitler, Joachim von Ribbentrop was foreign minister of Nazi Germany from 1938 to 1945, helping bring Hitler's plans to fruition. The Nazi-Soviet Nonaggression Pact of August, 1939, is often said to be Ribbentrop's greatest foreign-policy success. Found guilty of war crimes at Nuremberg Trials and hanged.

Ribera Chevremont, Evaristo

b. 1896
San Juan, Puerto Rico
d. 1976
fields: Literature

Puerto Rican writer. In 1918, Evaristo Ribera Chevremont became a reporter for the newspaper *El Imparcial*. By 1927, he had created a new school of literature he called *Girandulismo*. In 1930, he went to Madrid, where he studied under Jose Ortega y Gasset. Back in Puerto Rico, he wrote a column titled "Paginas de vanguardia" for the newspaper *La Democracia* and wrote poems and essays for other periodicals. His poetry collections include *Color* (1938), *Antologia poetica, 1924-1950*, (1957) and *Nueva antologia* (1966).

Ricardo, David

b. April 18, 1772
London, England
d. September 11, 1823
Gatcombe Park, Gloucestershire, England
fields: Economics

Ricardo was the most influential of the early nineteenth century thinkers who formalized the growing science of economics. His impact on economics continues today, and Ricardo has been acknowledged as the father of political economy.

Rice, Condoleezza

b. November 14, 1954
Birmingham, Ala.
fields: Education, Diplomacy

African American educator and foreign policy expert; from 1989 to 1991, Condoleezza Rice served as a director of Soviet and East European Affairs with the National Security Council; also served as a strategic adviser to the Joint Chiefs of Staff; appointed by President George Bush as his assistant for national security affairs and, in 1990, sat at the bargaining table when he met Soviet premier Mikhail Gorbachev in Malta; named to the post of provost At Stanford University in 1993, becoming the first African American chief academic officer and budget officer at the university and one of the highest-ranking black college administrators in the entire nation; published *The Soviet Union and the Czechoslovakian Army, 1948-1983* in 1985.

Rice, James Edward

b. March 8, 1953
Anderson, S.C.
fields: Sports (baseball player)

African American baseball player; a right-handed power hitter playing for the Boston Red Sox, James Edward Rice hit the most home runs in the American League in 1977, 1978, and 1983; he retired in 1989 with 382 home runs, a career batting average of .298, 1,451 runs batted in, and 2,452 hits.

Rice, Jerry

full: Jerry Lee Rice
b. October 13, 1962
Starkville, Miss.
fields: Sports (football player)

African American football player; one of the most productive pass receivers in National Football League (NFL) history, Jerry Rice was drafted by the San Francisco 49ers (1985) and went on to become the National Football Conference rookie of the year; he was *Sports Illustrated's* NFL player of the year in 1986; he led the 49ers to Super Bowl victories in 1989 (winning the most valuable player award, 1990, and 1995; in 1993 was named Offensive Player of the Year, *Sports Illustrated* Player of the Year, and the NFL Players Association Most Valuable Player; Rice became the NFL's all-time leader in receiving yardage on October 29, 1995. He holds numerous NFL all-time records in receptions.

Rice, Norman Blann

b. May 4, 1943
Denver, Colo.
fields: Government and Politics

African American mayor of Seattle, Wash; beginning in 1978, Norman Blann Rice served for eleven years on Seattle's city council; in January, 1990, inaugurated as Seattle's first African American mayor (1990-1997); honored as Outstanding Public Citizen by the National Association of Social Workers in 1991. In 1997, he became executive vice president of Federal Home Loan Bak of Seattle.

Rich, Adrienne

b. May 16, 1929
Baltimore, Md.
fields: Literature, Women's Rights

Poet and essayist; Adrienne Rich explores women's lives and personal growth in feminist poetry and essays; her poetry and essays reflect her experiences as a fairly traditional 1950's wife and mother through her growing consciousness as a "woman-identified" feminist and lesbian; her poems voice conflicts, confusion, anger, and desire for wholeness; her published works include *A Change of World* (1951; her first books of poetry with a foreword by W. H. Auden), *Leaflets* (1969; including political poetry opposing the Vietnam War), *The Will to Change* (1971), and her books that center on women's issues such as *Diving into the Wreck* (1973; won the National Book Award), *Of Woman Born: Motherhood as Experience and Institution* (1976, essays), *On Lies, Secrets, and Silence: Selected Prose 1966-1978* (1979, essays), *The Dream of a Common Language* (1978), *A Wild Patience Has Taken Me This Far* (1981), *An Atlas of the Difficult World* (1991), and *Dark Fields of the Republic* (1995).

Rich, Matty

né: Matthew Satisfield Richardson
b. November 26, 1971
fields: Film

African American director, writer, producer, and actor; Matty Rich's first critically acclaimed film project, *Straight Out of Brooklyn* (1991), reflects the realities of life in a Brooklyn housing project; he funded the film with his and his sister's credit cards, funds from local black investors following a radio appeal, and veteran filmmaker Jonathan Demme helped secure additional money from the Public Broadcasting Service's American Playhouse Theatrical Films to finish all post-production work. His next project was *The Inkwell* (1994).

Richard I

aka: Richard the Lion-Hearted
b. September 8, 1157
Oxford, England
d. April 6, 1199
Chalus, the Limousin, France
fields: Government and Politics, Monarchy

King of England, 1189-1199. Although Richard I has not gone down in history as a particularly good king, he was the epitome of the literary medieval knight—brave, skilled, and chivalrous.

Richard II

né: Richard of Bordeaux
b. January 6, 1367
Abbey of St. André, Bordeaux, France
d. February, 1400
Pontefract Castle, Yorkshire, England
fields: Government and Politics, Monarchy

King of England, 1377-1399. Seeking to overcome his powerful uncles who dominated English government before he reached majority, Richard II harshly asserted his royal powers and became the second English monarch to be deposed by his subjects.

Richard III

aka: Richard Plantagenet
b. October 2, 1452
Fotheringay Castle, Northamptonshire, England
d. August 22, 1485
Bosworth Field, Leicestershire, England
fields: Government and Politics

King of England, 1483-1485. England's most maligned monarch, Richard III, in his attempt to restore order and dynastic stability to a nation torn by three decades of civil war by first serving his brother, Edward IV, loyally and then by accepting the throne himself, fell victim to the intrigues of those who were jealous of his loyalty and abilities and who coveted the Crown.

Richards, Ann

né: Dorothy Ann Willis
b. September 1, 1933
Lakeview, Texas
fields: Government and Politics

A longtime activist in Texas Democratic politics, Ann Richards became Texas' second woman governor in 1990 and was the first woman to be elected to that office based on her own merit.

Richards, Beah

b. July 1, c. 1928
Vicksburg, Miss.
fields: Theater and Entertainment, Film, Television

African American actress; Beah Richards's stage credits include the Broadway productions of *The Miracle Worker* (1959), Ossie Davis's *Purlie Victorious* (1961), and, as Sister Margaret—a black woman preacher, in James Baldwin's *The Amen Corner* (1965; for which she received the Theatre World Award for her performance); her film credits include *In the Heat of the Night* (1967), *Guess Who's Coming to Dinner?* (1967; for which she received an Oscar nomination as best supporting actress), *The Miracle Worker* (1962), *Gone Are the Days* (1963), *Mahogany* (1975), *Drugstore Cowboy* (1989), and *Beloved* (1998); her television credits include appearances on the series *The Bill Cosby Show* (1970-1971), *Sanford and Son* (1972), *Frank's Place* (1987; for which she received an Emmy Award in 1988), and *Murder, She Wrote* (1988), and in the miniseries *Roots: The Next Generations* (1979) and the made-for-television films *Palmerstown, U.S.A.* (1980) and *The Sophisticated Gents* (1981); Richards was inducted into the Black Filmmakers Hall of Fame in 1974.

Richards, Ellen Swallow

né: Ellen Henrietta Swallow
b. Dec. 3, 1842
Dunstable, Massachusetts
d. Mar. 30, 1911
Jamaica Plain, Boston, Massachusetts
fields: Chemistry

Ellen Swallow Richards began the fields of environmental, domestic, and sanitation chemistry; in 1900, published *Air, Water, and Food from a Sanitary Standpoint.*

Richards, Lloyd

b. 1922
Toronto, Ontario, Canada
fields: Theater and Entertainment

African American stage director; noted as the first African American Broadway director, Lloyd Richards directed Lorraine Hansberry's *A Raisin in the Sun* (1959); as artistic director of the National Playwrights Conference (1969-1999), he directed the work of more than two hundred dramatists; Richards directed the premiere productions of August Wilson's major works while he was artistic director of the Yale Repertory Theater (beginning in 1979).

Richardson, Barbara Rose. *See* Collins, Barbara-Rose

Richardson, Bill

full: William Richardson
b. Nov. 15, 1947
Pasadena, Calif.
fields: Government and Politics

Mexican American legislator. In 1978, Bill Richardson became executive director of the New Mexico State Democratic Committee. He later lost a congressional campaign against incumbent Manuel Luján, but redistricting created a majority Hispanic seat in 1982, allowing Richardson to emerge victorious. In the early 1990's, he was chief deputy whip for the House Democratic leadership and went on diplomatic missions abroad for Bill Clinton's administration.

Richardson, Henry Hobson

b. September 29, 1838
Priestley plantation, St. James Parish, Louisiana
d. April 27, 1886
Brookline, Massachusetts
fields: Architecture

By absorbing early medieval stylistic ideas, suffusing them with his own vision, and adapting them to the needs of his own time, Richardson earned his reputation as one of America's greatest architects.

Richardson, Matthew Satisfield. *See* Rich, Matty

Richardson, Scovel

b. February 4, 1912
Nashville, Tenn.
d. March 30, 1982
New Rochelle, New York
fields: Law

African American judge; Scovel Richardson worked as a lawyer and as a professor and dean at Lincoln University law school before becoming the chairman of the U.S. Board of Parole in 1954; he was appointed a judge on the U.S. Customs Court for New York State in 1957.

Richardson, W. H.

b. fl. 1800's
fields: Invention and Technology

African American inventor; W. H. Richardson is noted for inventing a device which kept baby carriages from tipping over; the "leveler" was patented in June, 1889.

Richardson, Willis

b. November 5, 1889
Wilmington, N.C.
d. November 8, 1977
Washington, D.C.
fields: Theater and Entertainment

African American dramatist; second only to Randolph Edmonds, Willis Richardson is recognized as the most produced and published African American dramatist before the 1960's; in 1923 Richardson became the first African American playwright to have a serious nonmusical play produced on Broadway with the premiere of his one-act play, *The Chip Woman's Fortune*.

Richelieu, Cardinal de

né: Armand-Jean du Plessis
b. September 9, 1585
Paris, France
d. December 4, 1642
Paris, France
fields: Government and Politics

As cardinal (1622-1642), prime minister, and head of the royal council of Louis XIII, Richelieu was the architect of centralized, absolutist government in France. In addition, his brilliant diplomacy in the Thirty Years' War helped to make France the foremost power in Europe.

Richet, Charles

b. Aug. 26, 1850
Paris, France
d. Dec. 4, 1935
Paris, France
fields: Medicine, Physiology

Charles Richet, in 1876, demonstrated that gastric acid is hydrochloric, not lactic; worked on anaphylaxis (1900), a manifestation of immunological hypersensitivity characterized by severe respiratory impairment and circulatory collapse; was awarded the Nobel Prize in Physiology or Medicine in 1913.

Richie, Lionel

b. June 20, 1949
Tuskegee, Ala.
fields: Music (popular singer and composer)

African American singer; a successful crossover artist into soul, country and western, and pop, Lionel Richie began his musical career singing and composing for the group the Commodores, with whom he stayed until 1982; some of his songs for the group included "Easy" (1977) and "Three Times a Lady" (1978; a number-one hit); as a solo artist and songwriter during the 1980's, he penned the number-one hits "Lady" (1980), for Kenny Rogers, and "Endless Love," which he recorded with Diana Ross; his 1984 album *Can't Slow Down* produced five hit singles including "All Night Long"; his song cowritten with Michael Jackson, "We Are the World," received a Grammy Award, and his song "Say You, Say Me" from the film *White Nights* received an Academy Award in 1985.

Richmond, June

b. July 9, 1915
Chicago, Ill.
d. August 14, 1962
Gothenburg, Sweden
fields: Music (big-band singer)

African American singer; June Richmond is remembered as one of the great swing era big-band singers; she toured the U.S. performing frequently with Kansas City-based Andy Kirk and Twelve Clouds of Joy; after moving to Paris in 1954, she continued to perform all over Europe.

Richter, Burton

b. Mar. 22, 1931
Brooklyn, New York
fields: Physics

In 1973 Burton Richter discovered a class of long-lived mesons by constructing a particle accelerator at Stanford; in 1976, won the Nobel Prize in Physics jointly with Samuel C. C. Ting.

Richter, Charles Francis

b. Apr. 26, 1900
near Hamilton, Ohio
d. Sept. 30, 1985
Pasadena, California
fields: Science, Physics

Working in seismology, Charles Francis Richter, in 1935 with Beno Gutenberg, created the Richter scale, for measuring the intensity of earthquakes; plotted earthquake-prone areas of the United States.

Rickover, Hyman G.

full: Hyman George Rickover
b. August 24, 1898, or January 27, 1900
Makow, Russian Empire (now Poland)
d. July 8, 1986
Arlington, Virginia
fields: Military Affairs

A specialist in electrical engineering, Rickover became a pioneer in nuclear propulsion after World War II. He headed the project that developed the *Nautilus*, the world's first nuclear-powered submarine, and remained a dominant personality in the navy and in public life for three decades.

Ricks, Willie

b. c. 1943
fields: Civil Rights

African American activist; while in high school in Chattanooga, Tennessee, Willie Ricks joined the Civil Rights movement; going against the wishes of Martin Luther King, Jr., Ricks tried to organize small-scale impromptu marches, as opposed to larger, more organized marches, during the March 7, 1965, demonstrations in Montgomery, Alabama; formerly affiliated with the student nonviolent coordinating committee, Ricks was the motivating force behind the Student Organization for Black Unity.

Riddle, Toby. *See* Winema

Ride, Sally

full: Sally Kristen Ride
b. May 26, 1951
Encino, California
fields: Aviation and Space Exploration, Physics (astrophysics)

An astronaut for the National Aeronautics and Space Administration (NASA) and the first American woman to fly in space.

Ridge, John Rollin

aka: Nunna Hidihi (Yellow Bird)
b. c. 1827
present-day Rome, Ga.
d. Oct. 5, 1867
Grass Valley, Calif.
fields: Journalism, Literature, Native American Affairs

A Cherokee, John Rollins Ridge became a leading journalist, a noted poet, and a spokesperson for the plight of Indians in the late nineteenth century. His pen name was Yellow Bird, a translation of his Indian name. Son of John Ridge, grandson of Major Ridge, both murdered in 1839.

Ridge, Major

aka: The Ridge
b. c. 1770
Hiwassee, present-day Tenn.
d. June 20, 1839
Indian Territory, present-day Ark.
fields: Government and Politics, Diplomacy, Native American Affairs

Native American leader. Major Ridge, an influential Cherokee orator, become a wealthy planter in Georgia. Led Cherokee forces against the Red Stick Creeks. At first resisted removal to Indian Territory but eventually concluded that moving was inevitable. In 1835, Major Ridge signed the treaty of New Echota. Doing so without the full consent of the Cherokee Nation made him liable to the Cherokee "blood law" decreeing death for anyone who sold Cherokee lands without full consent. Ridge and his family and followers moved west in 1836. Other Cherokees who still resisted removal, led by John Ross, were forced west on the Trail of Tears march. About one third of them died on the way. Blaming the Ridge party, militant followers of Ross condemned them to death and on June 22, 1839, murdered Major Ridge and his son (John Ridge) and nephew (Elias Boudinot).

Ridgway, Matthew B.

full: Matthew Bunker Ridgway
b. March 3, 1895
Fort Monroe, Virginia
d. July 26, 1993
Fox Chapel, near Pittsburgh, Pennsylvania
fields: Military Affairs, War and Conquest

U.S. military leader. During World War II Matthew B. Ridgway was commander of the Eighty-second Airborne Division and then deputy supreme commander of the Mediterranean theater of operations. Commanded Eighth Army in Korea; supreme NATO commander in early 1950's.

Ridley, Nicholas

b. c. 1500
probably at Willimotiswick Castle, South Tynedale, Northumberland, England
d. October 16, 1555
Oxford, England
fields: Church Reform, Religion and Theology

The English bishop and Protestant reformer Nicholas Ridley worked closely with Archbishop Thomas Cranmer to consolidate the reformation of the Church of England. Through his theological writings and by his martyrdom under Queen Mary Tudor, Ridley helped to further the development of the Anglican Church.

Riefenstahl, Leni

full: Helene Riefenstahl
b. August 22, 1902
Berlin, Germany
fields: Film

A controversial German film director, Leni Riefenstahl began her career as a dancer and switched to film acting after a knee injury. In 1932 she met Adolf Hitler, who asked her to film a Nazi Party rally. After she made *Sieg des Glaubens* (1933; Victory of Faith), she asked for fuller support to make another film. She then filmed the party's 1934 rally and made *Triumph des Willens* (1935; Triumph of the Will), which established her reputation. She also filmed the 1936 Olympic Games in Berlin. Her filmmaking career waned after the Nazi regime was destroyed in World War II.

Riel, Louis, Jr.

b. Oct. 23, 1844
Red River Colony, Northwest Territories, Canada
d. Nov. 16, 1885
Regina, Northwest Territories, Canada
fields: Native American Affairs

Metis revolutionary leader; Riel organized the Metis during two rebellions: fearing the destruction of Metis property rights following the sale of Hudson's Bay Company lands to the Canadian government, he led the Metis in a rebellion in 1869 which resulted in the Manitoba Act of 1870, which granted virtually everything that was petitioned and incorporated the eastern portion of Metis lands into the small new province of Manitoba; the Second Riel Rebellion in 1885, in which Riel insisted that the Northwest lands belonged to the half-breeds and the Metis and that the lands should be held in trust for future generations, ended with Riel's execution and transformed Riel into a heroic symbol of the oppressed.

Riemann, Bernhard

full: Georg Friedrich Bernhard Riemann
b. Sept. 17, 1826
Breselenz, Hanover (now Germany)
d. July 20, 1866
Selasca, Italy
fields: Mathematics (calculus, geometry, and number theory)

Bernhard Riemann was first to publish the concepts of geometric spaces with different curvatures and the properties needed to define the integral operator of integral calculus; contributed criteria for deciding when complex valued functions of a complex variable are differentiable; gave the Riemann hypothesis, which is used in the study of prime numbers.

Rienzo, Cola di

né: Nicola di Lorenzo
b. 1313
Rome
d. October 8, 1354
Rome
fields: Government and Politics

Though his reign as tribune of Rome was short-lived, Rienzo put in place genuine reforms that effectively broke the power of nobles and barons who had been plundering the city in the manner of warlords.

Riesz, Frigyes

b. Jan. 22, 1880
Györ, Austria-Hungary (now Hungary)
d. Feb. 28, 1956
Budapest, Hungary
fields: Mathematics (applied math, calculus, and topology)

Frigyes Riesz created an important new division of mathematics called functional analysis, with David Hilbert and Stefan Banach; published a fundamental theorem on the theory of real functions, called the Riesz-Fischer theorem, in 1907.

Riggs, Lynn

b. Aug. 31, 1899
near Claremore, Indian Territory
d. June 30, 1954
New York City
fields: Literature (dramatist, poet)

Cherokee writer Lynn Riggs is the best known of Native American playwrights. His work is deeply colored by Cherokee community observations. Among his plays are *Roadside* (later reworked as *Borned in Texas*) and *Green Grow the Lilacs*. He experienced his first commercial success with a 1933 production of *Green Grow the Lilacs*. Rodgers and Hammerstein later acquired rights to the play and transformed it into the Broadway musical *Oklahoma*!

Riggs, Marlon T.

b. 1957
Fort Worth, Tex.
d. April 5, 1994
Oakland, Calif.
fields: Film, Literature, Social Reform

African American filmmaker, poet, and gay activist; Marlon T. Riggs examined the relationships between race, sexuality, and political resistance in films such as *With Ethnic Notions* (1987), *Color Adjustment* (1991), and *Black Is . . . Black Ain't* (1995); pioneered black gay male expression in *Anthem* (1988), *Tongues Untied* (1989), *Affirmation* (1990), and *No Regrets* (1992).

Rijn, Rembrandt van. *See* Rembrandt

Riles, Wilson

full: Wilson Camanza Riles
b. June 27, 1917
Alexandria, Louisiana
d. April 1, 1999
Sacramento, California
fields: Education

African American educational administrator; from 1940 to 1954, Wilson Riles served as a teacher and administrator for the Arizona public school systems; during the presidency of Lyndon B. Johnson, Riles became chairman of the U.S. Commission on Urban Education; in 1970 Riles was elected California's superintendent of public instruction, the first African American to fill this position.

Riley, Pepsii

full: Cheryl Riley
b. 1962
New York, N.Y.
fields: Music (singer)

African American singer; Pepsii Riley is known for her message-filled lyrics and soulful voice; while attracting attention to the plight of single parents, Riley's first hit single, "Thanks for My Child," was at the same time criticized for supposedly advocating single parenthood; *Chapters* (1990), her second album, while also containing some funky dance tunes included a song dealing with child and wife abuse and another responding to her twenty-three-year-old brother's death from cancer; that album was followed by *All That!* (1993).

Rilke, Rainer Maria

b. December 4, 1875
Prague, Bohemia, Austro-Hungarian Empire
d. December 29, 1926
Valmont, Switzerland
fields: Literature

Rilke is generally considered the greatest German poet since Goethe, and his fame is by no means limited to his own country.

Rillieux, Norbert

b. March 17, 1806
New Orleans, La.
d. October 8, 1894
Paris, France
fields: Invention and Technology

African American inventor, instructor in applied mechanics at L'École Centrale in Paris; in 1846, patented a vacuum evaporating pan, widely used in the sugar-refining industry as it significantly reduced fuel and labor requirements and produced sugar of much higher quality than had been possible with traditional methods.

Rimbaud, Arthur

full: Jean-Nicholas-Arthur Rimbaud
b. October 20, 1854
Charleville, France
d. November 10, 1891
Marseilles, France
fields: Literature

Rimbaud became one of the most influential of the French Symbolist poets through his vigorous writings and his dramatic personal history.

Rimsky-Korsakov, Nikolay

b. March 18, 1844
Tikhvin, Russia
d. June 21, 1908
Lyubensk, St. Petersburg, Russia
fields: Music

One of the greatest and most prolific of Russian composers, Rimsky-Korsakov embodied in his music the nationalist spirit which was so important an element in late nineteenth century Russian culture. He composed fifteen operas, in addition to symphonies, concerti, chamber music, and solo pieces for piano and voice.

Ringgold, Faith

b. October 8, 1930
New York, N.Y.
fields: Art

African American artist, writer, and educator; Faith Ringgold's work, involving primarily nontraditional materials formed into soft sculpture and quilts, expresses her experiences as an African American woman; in 1991 the Museum of African American Art exhibited a twenty-five-year retrospective of her work; Ringgold helped found Women Students and Artists for Black Liberation.

Rios, Aurelio Alejandro Lopez y. *See* Lopez, Aurelio

Ríos, Hermínio

b. ?
fields: Publishing, Scolarship

Mexican American publisher and scholar. In the early 1970's, Hermínio Ríos worked to get microfilm copies of Spanish-language newspapers made at La Raza Library at the University of California, Berkeley. He has written on the history of the Spanish-language press, and he co-owned Quinto Sol Publications.

Riperton, Minnie

b. November 8, 1947
Chicago, Ill.
d. July 12, 1979
Los Angeles, Calif.
fields: Music (popular singer)

African American pop singer; remembered for her ability to sing in five different octaves, Minnie Riperton reached the height of her career with her album *Perfect Angel* (1974), which contained the number-one pop song "Lovin' You"; Stevie Wonder, with whose band Riperton had sung, produced two tracks on the album; Riperton died in her early 30's of breast cancer; the posthumously produced *Love Lives Forever* (1980) reached the Top Ten as an album.

Riqueti, Honoré-Gabriel. *See* Mirabeau, comte de

Ritschl, Albrecht

b. March 25, 1822
Berlin, Prussia
d. March 20, 1889
Göttingen, Germany
fields: Religion and Theology

Ritschl contributed to the liberalizing of nineteenth century Protestant theology by moving its concerns away from the speculative, neo-Scholastic abstractions that the faithful could not understand toward a renewal of a practical examination of the life of Jesus Christ as revealed in the New Testament. Since Christ was the perfect manifestation of the love of God, believers could have a model upon which to make proper value judgments.

Ritter, Mary. *See* Beard, Mary Ritter

Rivas, Marian Lucy

b. May 6, 1943
New York, N.Y.
fields: Genetics

Latina geneticist. From 1969 to 1971, Marian Lucy Rivas performed research at The Johns Hopkins University under a Johns Hopkins University Fellowship. From 1971 to 1975, she worked as an associate professor at Rutgers University and the Hemophilia Center of the Oregon Health Science University, then became a full professor at the Hemophilia Center in 1982. Rivas also worked at the Neurological Science Institute of Good Samaritan Hospital in Oregon, participated on genetics committees for the National Institutes of Health, and did genetics research in South America.

Rivas, Octavio Victor Rojas y. *See* Rojas, Cookie

Rivera, Chita

né: Dolores Conchita Figueroa del Rivero
b. Jan. 23, 1933
Washington, D.C.
fields: Theater and Entertaiment, Dance

Latina actor and dancer. In the 1950's, Chita Rivera appeared in such Broadway productions as *Seventh Heaven* (1955), *Mr. Wonderful* (1956), and *West Side Story* (1957). She was nominated for Tony Awards for *Bye Bye Birdie* (1961), *Chicago* (1976), and *Bring Back Birdie* (1981), finally winning for *The Rink* (1984) and *Kiss of the Spider Woman* (1993). She also appeared in *Zenda* (1963), *Threepenny Opera* (1966), *Kiss Me, Kate* (1974), and *Sing Happy!* (1978). Her film credits include *Sweet Charity* (1969) and *Sergeant Pepper's Lonely Hearts Club Band* (1978). She was also inducted into the Television Hall of Fame in 1985.

Rivera, Diego

b. December 8, 1886
Guanajuato, Mexico
d. November 25, 1957
Mexico City, Mexico
fields: Art

Rivera was a painter who at first transcended his native Mexico and its rich and diverse artistic heritage to embrace broader modern European movements. Eventually in his work, he fused the Mexican and European forms to become one of his country's greatest muralists and a giant in the world of art.

Rivera, Edward

b. 1944
Orocovis, Puerto Rico
fields: Literature

Autobiographer. Edward Rivera earned a master of fine arts degree from Columbia University has taught at the City College of New York. In 1982, he published *Family Installments*, an autobiography that traces the story of his coming of age in Spanish Harlem during the 1940's and 1950's.

Rivera, Geraldo

full: Geraldo Miguel Rivera
b. July 4, 1943
New York, N.Y.
fields: Journalism, Theater and Entertainment

Latino journalist and talk-show host; Geraldo Rivera earned a law degree at the University of Pennsylvania and a degree in journalism at Columbia University; began career as reporter for WABC-TV in New York City in 1970; wrote and produced award-winning documentaries including *Willowbrook: The Last Disgrace*; worked at *Eyewitness News* in New York City (1970-1974); contributor to *Good Morning America* (1974-1978); was senior correspondent with *20/20*; hosted the television talk show, *Geraldo*, (1987); hosted *Now It Can Be Told* (1991); wrote autobiography *Exposing Myself* (1991); has won a Peabody Award and ten Emmy Awards for broadcast journalism.

Rivera, Graciela

b. ?
Puerto Rico
fields: Music (opera singer)

Puerto Rican opera singer. In 1951, Graciela Rivera debuted with the New York City Opera. She went on to perform at the Metropolitan Opera House in *The Magic Flute* and the Puerto Rican opera *Nela* (1971). She was important to the development of opera in

Puerto Rico in the 1950's. Rivera taught music in New York City from 1970 to 1987.

Rivera, Henry Michael

b. Sept. 25, 1946
Albuquerque, N.Mex.
fields: Government and Politics

Mexican American government official. Henry Michael Rivera was appointed by President Ronald Reagan to serve on the Federal Communications Commission from 1981 to 1985. He was the first Latino commissioner. Rivera received a Public Service Award for Outstanding Leadership in Government, conferred by the National Association of Black-Owned Broadcasters.

Rivera, Tomás

b. Dec. 22, 1935
Crystal City, Tex.
d. May 16, 1984
Fontana, Calif.
fields: Literature

Latino short-story writer and poet. Tomás Rivera was appointed chancellor of the University of California at Riverside in 1979. His book . . . *y no se lo tragó la tierra* (1971; . . . *and the Earth Did Not Part*, 1971), which won the First Quinto Sol Literary Prize, is considered as a collection of fourteen short stories by some and as a novel by others. He has also published poetry in a number of literary journals.

Riverón, Enrique

b. Jan. 31, 1902
Cienfuegos, Las Villas, Cuba
fields: Art

Cuban caricaturist. Enrique Riverón began publishing his caricatures in newspapers and magazines in Havana. He organized a society of caricaturists in 1921 and had his first exhibition with them. He attended the San Fernando Academy in Madrid, Spain, on a scholarship, returned to Cuba in 1927, then settled in New York City in 1928. His work appeared in such magazines as *Life*, *The New Yorker*, *Modern Screen*, and *Cine Mundial*. Riverón gave up magazine illustration in 1950 when the latter magazine ceased publication. He moved to Kansas and taught cartooning at the Wichita Art Association from 1949 to 1953 and painting at Wichita University in 1958 and 1959.

Rivers, Conrad Kent

b. 1933
Atlantic City, N.J.
d. 1968
fields: Literature

African American poet; Conrad Kent Rivers's published works include the poetry collections *Perchance to Dream, Othello* (1959), *The Still Voice of Harlem* (1968), and a play *Dusk at Selma* (1965); his poetic themes focus on sadness, isolation, loneliness, and preoccupation with death.

Rivlin, Alice

né: Alice Mitchell
b. March 4, 1931
Philadelphia, Pennsylvania
fields: Economics, Government and Politics

A public affairs economist, Rivlin has found herself equally at home in government service, research institutions, and university teaching.

Rizal y Alonso, Jose Protasio. *See* Rizal y Mercado, Jose Protasio

Rizal y Mercado, Jose Protasio

aka: Jose Protasio Rizal y Alonso
b. June 19, 1861
Calamba, Philippines
d. Dec. 30, 1896
Manila, Philippines
fields: Government and Politics, Literature, Medicine

Writer, physician, and patriot, Jose Protasio Rizal y Mercado was a Philippine national hero whose life and writings helped inspire the country's nationalist reform movement against the Spanish occupation. Rizal began practicing medicine in the Philippines in 1887. He wrote *Noli me tangere* (1886; *The Social Cancer*, 1912) describing the Filipino people's suffering under the tyrannical rule of Spain and *El Filibusterismo* (1891; *The Reign of Greed*, 1912), which denounced Spanish rule in the Philippines. In July, 1892, Rizal was arrested, then exiled in Dapitan, where he conducted scientific investigations. In 1896, he was charged with and found guilty of sedition by the military court. On December 28, 1896, Rizal was shot to death.

Roa Bastos, Augusto

b. June 13, 1917
Asunción, Paraguay
fields: Literature

Writer. Augusto Roa Bastos began his career as a journalist in 1942, eventually becoming editor of the newspaper *El Pais*. He published the poetry collections *El ruiseñor de la aurora* (1942) and *El naranjal ardiente: Nocturno paraguayo, 1947-1949* (1960), the short-story collections *El trueno entre las hojas* (1953) and *Madera quemada* (1967), and the novels *Hijo de hombre* (1960; *Son of Man*, 1965) and *Yo, el Supremo* (1974; *I, the Supreme*, 1986).

Roach, Max

b. January 10, 1925
Elizabeth City, N.C.
fields: Music (bebop drummer)

One of the first outstanding African American bebop drummers; a pioneer in the use of modern choral backgrounds, Max Roach formed a famous quintet with saxophonists Sonny Rollins and Harold Land and trumpeter Clifford Brown; during his later career, Roach's work involved documentary films, plays, and videos and break dance and rap groups.

Roberts, Deborah A.

b. September 20, 1960
Perry, Ga.
fields: Journalism, Television

African American broadcast journalist; Deborah A. Roberts was hired by NBC News in 1990 and assigned to the network's Atlanta bureau as a general assignment correspondent; joined the staff of the network's popular newsmagazine, *Dateline NBC* in 1992 and later moved to ABC's *20/20*. She is married to the *NBC Today Show* weatherman Al Roker.

Roberts, Margaret Hilda. *See* Thatcher, Margaret

Roberts, Owen J.

full: Owen Josephus Roberts
b. 1875
d. 1955
fields: Law

U.S. Supreme Court justice, 1930-1945; appointed by President Hoover. Changed his vote and saved the Supreme Court from President Franklin D. Roosevelt's Court-packing plan, commonly known as a "switch in time that saved the nine." Consistent defender of individual rights in criminal cases. Significant opinions: *Grau v. United States*, 287 U.S. 124 (1932); *Herndon v. Lowry*, 301 U.S. 242 (1937); *Hague v. Committee for Industrial Organization*, 307 U.S. 496 (1939); *Cantwell v. Connecticut*, 310 U.S. 296 (1940); *Betts v. Brady*, 316 U.S. 455 (1942).

Roberts, Patricia

b. June 14, 1955
Monroe, Ga.
fields: Sports (basketball player)

African American basketball player; after being named a National Collegiate Athletic Association Division I women's first-team All-American (1977) while playing for the University of Tennessee, Patricia Roberts became a member of the 1976 silver medal-winning U.S. women's Olympic basketball team.

Roberts, Richard

b. December 7, 1910
Titusville, Pennsylvania

d. April 4, 1980
Washington, D.C.
fields: Chemistry, Biology, Invention and Technology, Physics

Richard Roberts discovered radioisotope beryllium 7 (1938) and delayed neutrons from fission (1939); helped design the proximity fuse (1940), an important weapon for the Allies in World War II; received the Presidential Medal of Merit (1947); determined the biosynthesis of *Escherichia coli* (culminating 1955); and studied the basis of long-term memory.

Roberts, Richard Samuel

b. 1881
d. 1936
fields: Photography

African American photographer Richard Samuel Roberts studied photography through reading and correspondence courses and, with his wife Wilhelmina, opened a studio in Columbia, South Carolina, where he developed his photographs of schools, churches, and other community organizations during the 1920's and 1930's.

Roberts, Wilhelmina Pearl Selena

b. 1887
d. 1976
fields: Art

African American artist; Wilhelmina Pearl Selena Roberts and her husband, photographer Richard Samuel Roberts, owned an art studio in Columbia, S.C.; in addition to tending the studio, working as her husband's assistant, and rearing their eight children, Roberts became known in her own right for her portraits of families and children.

Robertson, Anna Mary. *See* Moses, Grandma

Robertson, Benjamin. *See* Harney, Ben

Robertson, Oscar Palmer

b. November 24, 1938
Charlotte, Tenn.
fields: Sports (basketball player)

African American basketball player; co-captain of the 1960 gold medal-winning U.S. Olympic basketball team, Oscar Palmer Robertson was drafted that same year by the Cincinnati Royals as a guard; he took Rookie of the Year honors that same season and was the All-Star Game Most Valuable Player (MVP; the first of three times); in 1964 he was named the NBA's MVP; after he was traded to the Milwaukee Bucks, he and teammate Kareem Abdul-Jabbar led their team to the 1971 NBA championship; in 1979 Robertson was inducted into the NBA Hall of Fame.

Robertson, Pat

full: Marion Gordon Robertson
b. March 22, 1930
Lexington, Va.
fields: Government and Politics, Religion and Theology

Religious broadcaster and politician. Pat Robertson rose to prominence as the creator of *The 700 Club*, a Christian television show. Robertson was a pioneer of the "telechurch" phenomenon and formed the Christian Broadcasting Network (CBN). He campaigned unsuccessfully for the 1988 Republican presidential nomination.

Robertson, Stanley

b. ?
Los Angeles, Calif.
fields: Television, Film

African American television and film executive; from a position as a page at NBC Television in 1957, Stanley Robertson rose to the position of vice president for motion pictures for television by 1971; he moved up to director of programs by the late 1970's; Robertson became senior vice president of worldwide productions for Columbia Pictures by the mid-1980's.

Robeson, Eslanda Cardoza Goode

né: Eslanda Cardoza Goode
b. December 15, 1896
Washington, D.C.
d. December 13, 1965
New York, N.Y.
fields: Civil Rights, Government and Politics, Journalism, Photography

African American civil rights activist Eslanda Cardoza Goode Robeson was the first African American on the staff at Presbyterian Hospital of Columbia University as a histological chemist. She married actor Paul Robeson and managed his career; wrote his biography and books on colonialism (*Paul Robeson, Negro*, 1930; *African Journey*, 1945; *American Argument*, with Pearl S. Buck, 1949); studied photography; in 1945, attended the founding convention of the United Nations as a representative of the Council on African Affairs; in 1948, ran for secretary of state of Connecticut in 1948 as a Progressive; covered the U.N. as a journalist in the 1950's; drew attention for her criticism of U.S. foreign policy and her favorable view of the Soviet Union.

Robeson, Paul

full: Paul Bustill Robeson
b. April 9, 1898
Princeton, New Jersey
d. January 23, 1976
Philadelphia, Pennsylvania
fields: Music, Drama, Social Reform

A Renaissance man, Robeson made unprecedented contributions to American and world history as an athlete, intellectual, performer, and internationally renowned peace advocate. In politics, he championed the cause of human rights for black Americans and other oppressed people throughout the world.

Robespierre

full: Maximilien-François-Marié-Isidore de Robespierre
b. May 6, 1758
Arras, France
d. July 28, 1794
Paris, France
fields: Government and Politics

Alone among the leaders of the French Revolution, Robespierre was identified with every stage of the Revolution. In addition, he most clearly enunciated the ideals upon which the Revolution was to be based and fought most vigorously for its success.

Robinson, Aubrey E., Jr.

full: Aubrey Eugene Robinson, Jr.
b. March 30, 1922
Madison, N.J.
fields: Law, Civil Rights

African American civil rights attorney and judge Aubrey E. Robinson, Jr., practiced law in Washington, D.C. (1948-1965); was appointed to the bench on the juvenile court (1965); became a U.S. district court judge (1966), in which capacity he handed down rulings with important implications for civil rights; and assumed various positions in legal and social service agencies.

Robinson, Bill

né: Luther Robinson
aka: Bojangles Robinson
b. May 25, 1878
Richmond, Va.
d. November 25, 1949
New York, N.Y.
fields: Dance, Theater and Entertainment, Film

African American dancer and actor; creator of the famous stair dance, in which he produced a different sound with his feet on each step, Bill Robinson's stage credits include starring in the musical *Blackbirds of 1928*, on Broadway in *Brown Buddies* (1930), and in *The Hot Mikado* (1939); among the twenty-one films in which he was featured between 1930 and 1943 were the box office hits starring child actress Shirley Temple—*The Little Colonel* (1935), *The Littlest Rebel* (1935), and *Rebecca of Sunnybrook Farm* (1938)—and the lead role in *Stormy Weather* (1943).

Robinson, David

full: David Maurice Robinson
b. August 6, 1965
Key West, Fla.
fields: Sports (basketball player)

African American basketball player; as a college player for the U.S. Naval Academy, David Robinson was named college player of the year by United Press International, *The Sporting News*, and the U.S. Basketball Writers Association and received the Naismith, Wooden, and Rupp Awards; he played on three U.S. Olympic basketball teams in 1986 (gold medal), 1988 (bronze medal), and 1992 (gold medal with the "Dream Team"); he was the first pick of the San Antonio Spurs in the 1987 draft despite the fact that Robinson could not play for two years while completing his obligation to the Navy; in his 1989-1990 season as a center with the Spurs, he took NBA Rookie of the Year honors, leading the team to a Midwest Division title; 1991-1992 season, NBA Defensive Player of the Year; 1994-1995 season, NBA most valuable player; 1998-1999 season, Spurs are the NBA champions.

Robinson, Eddie

full: Edward Gay Robinson
b. February 12, 1919
Jackson, La.
fields: Sports (football)

African American college football player, athletic coach, and administrator; Eddie Robinson began coaching at Grambling State University, Louisiana, in 1941; on October 5, 1985, he became the coach with the most wins ever in college football history (324 wins).

Robinson, Elbert R.

b. ?
d. ?
fields: Invention and Technology

African American inventor; Elbert R. Robinson patented a railway trolley that used overhead electric wires to propel a passenger-carrying car; when two large corporations infringed on his patent, Robinson took his fight all the way to the Supreme Court but was unable to protect it; he was successful in a Supreme Court case involving his invention of the grooved railway wheel—he won a $31 million judgment.

Robinson, Frank, Jr.

b. August 31, 1935
Beaumont, Tex.
fields: Sports (baseball player and manager)

African American baseball player and manager; following a twenty-one year playing career (1956-1976), Frank Robinson, Jr., became the first African American to manage in the major leagues when he was named manager of the Cleveland Indians (1975-1977); he went on to manage the San Francisco Giants (named 1982 Manager of the Year) and the Baltimore Orioles; during his playing career as an outfielder who also played third base and first base, Robinson batted .294, hit 586 home runs, drove in 1,812 runs, and stole 204 bases; inducted into the Baseball Hall of Fame in 1982.

Robinson, Hilyard R.

b. 1899
Washington, D.C.
d. Summer, 1986
Washington, D.C.?
fields: Architecture

African American architect; in addition to working as a professor of architecture at Howard University, Hilyard R. Robinson took on many large projects including the Henry Hudson Hotel in Troy, N.Y., and the Langston Public Works Administration Housing Project.

Robinson, Hugh Granville

b. ?
Washington, D.C.
d. ?
fields: Military Affairs

African American military officer; Hugh Granville Robinson began service as a second lieutenant in 1954 and reached the rank of Army major general in 1981; his postings included Army assistant to the Armed Forces Aide to the President at the White House, executive officer of the Forty-fifth Engineer Group in Vietnam, and division engineer with the southwestern United States Army Engineer Division.

Robinson, Jackie

full: John Roosevelt Robinson
b. January 31, 1919
Cairo, Georgia
d. October 24, 1972
Stamford, Connecticut
fields: Sports, Civil Rights

Robinson was the first black to play in the major leagues and as such is known for breaking the "color line" in baseball. A hero for his brilliant career with the Brooklyn Dodgers, he was elected to the Baseball Hall of Fame.

Robinson, James

b. c. 1753
d. 1868
fields: Warfare and Conquest, Civil Rights

African American soldier; James Robinson won a gold medal for valor at Yorktown, but was forced to return to slavery even though he had been promised freedom; despite his ill-treatment, he again volunteered to fight, this time with Andrew Jackson's forces at the 1812 Battle of New Orleans; he returned to slavery after the battle and only received his freedom following the Emancipation Proclamation.

Robinson, Jo Ann Gibson

né: Jo Ann Gibson
b. April 17, 1912
near Culloden, Ga.
fields: Civil Rights

African American civil rights activist and educator Jo Ann Gibson Robinson was teaching in the English Department at Alabama State College in Montgomery when she became a key organizer of the Montgomery Bus Boycott (1955-1956), recording her experience in *The Montgomery Bus Boycott and the Women Who Started It* (1987).

Robinson, Julia Bowman

né: Julia Bowman
b. Dec. 8, 1919
St. Louis, Missouri
d. July 30, 1985
Oakland, California
fields: Mathematics (mathematical logic and number theory)

In 1970 Julia Bowman Robinson helped to solve Hilbert's tenth problem, which concerned finding a method to determine the solvability of Diophantine equations; was the first woman to be elected to the National Academy of Sciences, in 1976; served as president of the American Mathematical Society in 1983.

Robinson, Mary

né: Mary Teresa Winifred Bourke
b. May 21, 1944
Ballina, County Mayo, Ireland
fields: Government and Politics

Elected to the Irish Senate in 1969, Mary Robinson served for twenty years. Fought for rights for women and homosexuals and championed legalizing contraception. In 1990 became first woman to be elected president of Ireland, a largely ceremonial position. Visited Northern Ireland and shook hands with Sinn Féin leader Gerry Adams, an act that helped lead to Adams's acceptance by other leaders. Visited famine-stricken Somalia and publicized its predicament. Resigned in 1997 to become U.N. high commissioner for human rights.

Robinson, Max C.

b. May 1, 1939
Richmond, Va.
d. December 20, 1988
Washington, D.C.
fields: Television, Journalism

African American television newscaster; while working as a correspondent for WRC-TV (1965-1969), Max C. Robinson won a national Emmy Award (1967) and the Capital Press Club Journalist of the Year award; from 1978 to 1983, Robinson was one of three anchors on the American Broadcasting Company's (ABC) *World News Tonight*; for his election coverage during this time he won the Capital Press Club's national media award (1979) and a second Emmy Award (1981); assisted in the founding of the Association of Black Journalists; Robinson died of complications related to AIDS.

Robinson, Randall

b. July 6, 1941
Richmond, Va.
fields: Civil Rights

African American civil rights activist Randall Robinson became executive director of the human rights organization TransAfrica (Washington, D.C.), influential in Congress's eventual passage of the Comprehensive Anti-Apartheid Act of 1986, which implemented U.S. sanctions against South Africa until 1991, when South African leader Nelson Mandela was released from prison.

Robinson, Ray Charles. *See* Charles, Ray

Robinson, Robert

full: Sir Robert Robinson
b. Sept. 13, 1886
Rufford Farm, near Chesterfield, Derbyshire, England
d. Feb. 8, 1975
Grimm's Hill Lodge, Great Missenden, Buckinghamshire, England
fields: Chemistry

Robert Robinson added to the modern electronic theory of organic reactions; worked on the structure determination and chemical synthesis of natural products, especially alkaloids, plant pigments, and steroids; in 1947, won the Nobel Prize in Chemistry and the U.S. Medal of Freedom.

Robinson, Roscoe, Jr.

b. October 11, 1928
St. Louis, Mo.
d. July 22, 1993
Washington, D.C.
fields: Military Affairs

African American military officer; Roscoe Robinson, Jr., is remembered as the first African American to attain the rank of four-star general in the U.S. Army; he saw service in the Korean and Vietnam Wars and was a member of the NATO Military Committee.

Robinson, Rubye Doris Smith

né: Rubye Doris Smith
b. April 25, 1942
Atlanta, Ga.
d. October 7, 1967
Atlanta, Ga.
fields: Civil Rights

African American civil rights activist and a founder of the Student Nonviolent Coordinating Committee, Rubye Doris Smith Robinson played a key role in the student-led civil rights protests of the 1960's, becoming SNCC's executive secretary in 1966.

Robinson, Rudolph

b. ?
d. 1987
fields: Photography, Art

African American photographer, furniture designer, and graphic designer; a recipient of numerous awards for his photography, Rudolph Robinson was a faculty member at the Massachusetts College of Art, and served as artist-in-residence at Northwestern University.

Robinson, Smokey

full: William Robinson, Jr.
b. February 19, 1940
Detroit, Mich.
fields: Music (singer and songwriter)

African American singer and songwriter; as founder and lead singer of the Miracles, Smokey Robinson was signed by record producer Berry Gordy, Jr., before Gordy had established Motown Records; Robinson became a songwriter, producer, and, by 1962, a vice president for Motown, producing and writing songs such as "My Guy" (performed by Mary Wells), "My Girl," "Get Ready" (the Temptations), and "Ain't That Peculiar," "I'll Be Doggone" (Marvin Gaye); from 1960 to 1973, Smokey Robinson and the Miracles had more than forty songs on the rhythm-and-blues and national pop charts, with more than half of those reaching the top forty, including the songs "You've Really Got a Hold on Me" (1962), "Going to a Go-Go" (1965), "The Tracks of My Tears" (1965), "I Second That Emotion" (1967), and "The Tears of a Clown" (1970); Robinson left the Miracles in 1973 to devote his time to administrative duties at Motown; he was inducted into the Rock and Roll Hall of Fame (1986) and the Songwriter's Hall of Fame (1986); recipient of a Grammy Award (1987), as a soloist, for "Just to See Her."

Robinson, Spottswood W., III

b. July 26, 1916
Richmond, Virginia
d. October 11, 1994
Richmond, Virginia
fields: Law

African American judge and lawyer; Spottswood W. Robinson, III's diverse roles in the field of law included practicing attorney, dean of the Howard University Law School, district court judge, circuit court judge (appointed 1966), counsel for the Legal Defense and Educational Fund of the NAACP, and member of the U.S. Commission on Civil Rights.

Robinson, Sugar Ray

né: Walker Smith, Jr.
b. May 3, 1921
Detroit, Mich.
d. April 12, 1989
Culver City, Calif.
fields: Sports (boxer)

African American boxer; in a professional career that spanned the 1940's to 1965, Sugar Ray Robinson dominated the middleweight divisions, winning his first middleweight world championship in 1950; he defeated such opponents as Rocky Graziano and Jake Lamotta and, in 1990, was inducted into the International Boxing Hall of Fame.

Robusti, Jacopo. *See* Tintoretto

Rochambeau, comte de

né: Jean-Baptiste Donatien de Vimeur
b. July 1, 1725
Vendôme, France
d. May 10, 1807
Vendôme, France
fields: Military Affairs

Placed in command of French troops who came to assist the colonists in the American Revolutionary War, Rochambeau helped General George Washington plan the Battle of Yorktown and defeat the British under the command of Lord Charles Cornwallis in 1781.

Roche Rabell, Arnaldo

b. 1955
Santurce, Puerto Rico
fields: Art

Puerto Rican artist. Arnaldo Roche Rabell grew up in Puerto Rico but earned bachelor's and master's degrees in fine arts at the School of Art Institute of Chicago. While there, he experimented with "rubbings" of his models' bodies by placing them under the canvas and applying paint with his hands. In 1986, he began *Events, Miracles and Visions*, a series of self-portraits that address his Puerto Rican ethnicity. Roche Rabell continued exploring issues of ethnic identity with *You Have to Dream in Blue*.

Rock, Chris

b. 1968
Brooklyn, N.Y.

fields: Theater and Entertainment, Television, Film (actor and comedian)

African American actor and comedian; in 1990, Chris Rock joined the cast of *Saturday Night Live*, drawing national attention with his edgy, streetwise humor; appeared in films including *Beverly Hills Cop II* (1987), *I'm Gonna Git You Sucka* (1988), *New Jack City* (1991), *Boomerang* (1992), *CB4* (1993), and *Beverly Hills Ninja* (1997). In television, he earned two Emmy awards for his comedy special *Bring On the Pain!* (1996) and has been noted for his work as a television writer.

Rockefeller, Abby Aldrich

né: Abby Greene Aldrich
b. October 26, 1874
Providence, Rhode Island
d. April 5, 1948
New York, New York
fields: Patronage of the Arts

Abby Aldrich Rockefeller's most important contributions were the central role she played in the development of public interest in contemporary art, particularly American art, and the establishment of New York City's Museum of Modern Art. She also influenced family members, particularly her husband, John D. Rockefeller, Jr., and her son, Nelson Aldrich Rockefeller, to aid her in her endeavors.

Rockefeller, John D.

full: John Davison Rockefeller
b. July 8, 1839
Richford, New York
d. May 23, 1937
Ormond Beach, Florida
fields: Business and Industry, Philanthropy

One of the major industrialists and philanthropists in the history of the United States, Rockefeller pioneered in bringing a new scale to business organization through his phenomenally successful Standard Oil Company; he also brought a new scale to philanthropic giving.

Rockefeller, Nelson A.

full: Nelson Aldrich Rockefeller
b. July 8, 1908
Bar Harbor, Maine
d. January 26, 1979
New York, New York
fields: Government and Politics

After working in the administrations of Presidents Franklin D. Roosevelt Dwight Eisenower during the 1940's and 1950's, Nelson A. Rockefeller became governor of the state of New York throughout the 1960's, securing passage of much progressive social and welfare legislation for the state. He was frustrated in attempts to secure the Republican nomination for president; in 1964, he lost to Senator Barry Goldwater and in 1968 to Richard M. Nixon. He became more conservative in his last years as New York's governor, in 1971 presenting the legislature with an austerity budget that called for a tightening up of welfare payments and Medicaid allowances. Such actions and his tough suppression of the Attica prison riot in 1971 drew severe criticism from liberals. In 1973, he resigned as governor and in 1974, following the resignation of President Nixon, he became President Gerald Ford's vice president. After his term expired in January, 1977, his major activities included the heading of a White House Domestic Council and a special commission to investigate the Central Intelligence Agency. Turning from politics in 1977, he developed a lifelong interest in art: Shortly before his death, he was engaged in the creating and selling of reproductions from his collection of modern and primitive paintings, sculpture, and other art forms.

Rockwell

né: Kennedy W. Gordy
b. 1963?
fields: Music (popular vocalist)

African American pop vocalist; the son of Motown Records founder Berry Gordy, Jr., Rockwell submitted a demo tape anonymously to Motown Records and was signed to a recording contract; his top-ten hit single "Somebody's Watching Me," featuring guest vocals by Michael Jackson, caused his 1984 album to go platinum; his two subsequent albums did not equal the success of his first album, and he asked to be released from his Motown contract.

Rockwell, Norman

full: Norman Perceval Rockwell
b. February 3, 1894
New York, New York
d. November 8, 1978
Stockbridge, Massachusetts
fields: Art

Rockwell is one of America's most popular and best-known artists. His appeal lies in his ability to capture scenes of traditional American life in a way that needs no explanation.

Rocky Boy

aka: Stone Child
b. c. 1860
d. 1914
fields: Government and Politics, Native American Affairs

Rocky Boy became the leader of a group of nomad Chippewas (Ojibwas) who refused to live on a Wisconsin reservation, instead moving to Montana to hunt. As more land was fenced, the nomads' life became untenable and they were often reduced to begging. Rocky Boy lobbied Bureau of Indian Affairs, and eventually "Rocky Boy's Band" was granted a tract of land on the Fort Assiniboin military reserve in Montana. The land grant finally came in 1914, the year that Rocky Boy died.

Rodgers, Carolyn M.

full: Carolyn Marie Rodgers
b. December 14, 1945
Chicago, Ill.
fields: Literature

African American poet and short-fiction writer; Carolyn M. Rodgers's poetry explores love, religion, revolution, feminism, and African American male-female relationships; Rodgers received an award from the National Endowment for the Arts in 1970. Her books include *How I Got Ovah* (1975), *The Heart as Ever Green* (1978), *Morning Glory* (1989), *We're Only Human* (1994), *The Girl with Blue Hair* (1996), and *Salt* (1998).

Rodgers, Johnathan A.

b. January 18, 1946
San Antonio, Tex.
fields: Business and Industry

African American broadcast executive; Johnathan A. Rodgers, one of the highest ranking African Americans in broadcast management, became the president of the stations division of CBS Television in 1990; was named president of the Discovery Networks in 1996.

Rodgers, Johnny

full: John Rodgers
b. July 5, 1951
Omaha, Nebr.
fields: Sports (football player)

African American football player; Johnny Rodgers, considered to be one of the best punt returners in college football, won the 1972 Heisman Trophy playing for the University of Nebraska; he played for the Montreal Alouettes from 1973 to 1976 and received the Canadian Football League's Rookie of the Year Award; during his 1977 and 1978 seasons with the National Football League's San Diego Chargers, he was plagued by injuries. He retired in 1978 to persue business interests.

Rodgers, Richard

b. June 28, 1902
New York, New York
d. December 30, 1979
New York, New York
fields: Theater and Entertainment, Music

In the course of his sixty-year career as a Broadway composer, Richard Rodgers helped to establish the prototype of the American musical.

Rodham, Hillary Diane. *See* Clinton, Hillary Rodham

Rodin, Auguste

b. November 12, 1840
Paris, France
d. November 17, 1917
Paris, France
fields: Art

One of the greatest sculptors of all time, Rodin has been hailed for both the monumentality and the psychological penetration of his sculpture. Much of his work has a kinetic quality, a dynamism that takes over the solid material of his sculpture, transforming it into the expression of a towering personality.

Rodman, Dennis

aka: Worm
b. May 13, 1961
Dallas, Tex.
fields: Sports (basketball player)

African American basketball player; a defensive specialist with outstanding rebounding abilities, forward Dennis Rodman was a second-round draft pick for the Detroit Pistons in 1986; Rodman played on the 1989 and 1990 NBA championship teams, and in 1990 he was named NBA Defensive Player of the Year. Flamboyant, aggressive, explosive, attention-grabbing both on and off the court (hair-dying, body-piercing, cross-dressing), Rodman earned a reputation for being difficult. He moved from the San Antonio Spurs (1993-1995), to the Chicago Bulls (1995-1998), to a few months with the Los Angeles Lakers in 1999. He wrote two successful autobiographies, *Bad as I Wanna Be* (1996) and *Walk on the Wild Side* (1997).

Rodney, George

full: George Brydges Rodney
b. January, 1718
Middlesex, England
d. May 24, 1792
Hanover Square, London, England
fields: Military Affairs, Government and Politics

Utilizing both family connections and his own ability, Rodney advanced during this century of interest and place to the post of admiral, while leading England to naval victories during the Seven Years' War and the American Revolution.

Rodney, Walter

b. 1942
British Guiana
d. June 13, 1980
Georgetown, Guyana
fields: Scholarship

Guyanan scholar; Walter Rodney's published works include *The Groundings with My Brothers* (1969), *A History of the Upper Guinea Coast, 1545-1800* (1970), and *How Europe Underdeveloped Africa* (1972); he served as a leader in the Working Peoples Alliance; a car bomb explosion was responsible for his early death.

Rodriguez, Abraham, Jr.

b. 1961
New York, N.Y.
fields: Literature

Latino writer. Abraham Rodriguez, Jr., published his first book, a collection of short stories called *The Boy Without a Flag: Tales of the South Bronx*, in 1992. The story "Birthday Boy" was later expanded into *Spidertown: A Novel* (1993). Rodriguez's stories explore the experience of being a Puerto Rican in New York City.

Rodríguez, Armando M.

b. Sept. 30, 1921
Gómez Palacios, Durango, Mexico
fields: Education

Mexican American educator and administrator. Armando M. Rodríguez became a guidance consultant for the San Diego city schools in 1954 and vice principal of Gompers Junior High School in 1958. In 1965, he became principal of Wright Brothers High School and also became the first Chicano consultant to the California State Department of Education. In 1966, Rodríguez was named head of the department's Bureau of Intergroup Relations. He served as director of what became the Office for Spanish-Speaking American Affairs at the United States Office of Education in Washington, D.C. He became Regents' Lecturer at the University of California, Riverside, in 1970; president of East Los Angeles College in 1973; and a commissioner on the Equal Employment Opportunity Commission in 1978.

Rodríguez, Armando Osorio

b. 1929
fields: Law

Armando Osorio Rodríguez is a judge and social activist; directing attorney, California Rural Legal Assistance, 1965-1967; chairman and board member, California Rural Legal Assistance, 1969-1987; judge, Fresno Municipal Court, 1975-1978, since 1980; judge, Fresno Superior Court, 1978-1980; board chair and member, Migrant Legal Service Project since 1988.

Rodríguez, Arsenio

b. Aug. 30, 1911
Güira de Macurije, Cuba
d. Dec. 31, 1970
New York, N.Y.
fields: Music (percussionist and composer)

Arsenio Rodríguez, a blind Afro-Cuban percussionist and composer, moved to the United States around 1948 and made numerous recordings at Gabriel Oller's studio in midtown Manhattan, New York. He was instrumental in the development of Cuban *conjunto* music, the spread of salsa music, and the revival of the *banda típica* in New York in the 1960's. Rodríguez is also credited with popularizing the mambo in the United States and introducing conga drums as a major percussion instrument in the rhythm sections of salsa bands.

Rodríguez, Beatriz

b. Apr. 25, 1951
Ponce, Puerto Rico
fields: Dance

Latina ballet dancer. Beatriz Rodríguez began studying dance at the Newark Academy of Ballet at the age of nine. She danced with the company of the New Jersey School of Ballet and Richard England's Dance Repertory Company in New York City before joining the Joffrey Ballet in 1972. She became a principal dancer with the company, performing in such ballets as *Illuminations* (1980), *Le Sacré du Printemps* (1987), and *The Nutcracker* (1993). Rodríguez received the *Dance Magazine* Award for lifetime achievement in 1993.

Rodríguez, Chepita

b. ?
d. Nov. 13, 1863
San Patricio, Tex.
fields: Historical Figure

Rancher. In October, 1863, Chepita Rodríguez was found guilty of the murder of a man whose son she claimed she had borne years before. Despite the circumstantial evidence against her, the judge ordered her hanged. By the early 1990's, was one of the few women in Texas to be given the death penalty.

Rodriguez, Chi Chi

né: Juan Rodriguez
b. Oct. 23, 1935
Río Piedras, Puerto Rico
fields: Sports (golfer)

Puerto Rican golfer. Chi Chi Rodriguez joined the U.S. Professional Golfers' Association (PGA) Tour in 1960. Over the next twenty-five years, he won eight tournament titles and earned more than $1 million. In 1985, Rodriguez joined the PGA's Senior Tour and won more titles by 1987 than he had in twenty-five years on the PGA Tour. He continued to play into the 1990's.

Rodríguez, Clara Elsie

b. Mar. 29, 1944
New York, N.Y.
fields: Education

Educator. In 1973, Clara Elsie Rodríguez became an adjunct professor at Pace University, then served as assistant professor and chair of the Puerto Rican studies department from 1974 to 1976. She was dean of Fordham University from 1976 until 1981, when she became a professor at that university. Rodríguez was a visiting scholar at the Massachusetts Institute of Technology (1987-1988) and a visiting fellow at Yale University (1992). She wrote *Puerto Ricans: Born in the U.S.A.* (1989), and she coedited *The Puerto Rican Struggle: Essays on Survival in the U.S.* (1989) and *Hispanics in the Labor Force: Issues and Policies* (1991). Much of her work concerns immigration issues.

Rodriguez, Patricia

b. Nov. 8, 1944
Marfa, Tex.
fields: Art

Latina artist. When Patricia Rodriguez began attending school full-time at the age of thirteen, she could neither read nor write, so she encouraged to pursue art projects. She eventually earned a bachelor of fine arts degree (1972) from the San Francisco Art Institute and a master's degree in painting (1975) from Sacramento State University. She taught for five years at the University of California, Berkeley, where she developed the first course on Chicano art history. Her art is in the collections of the Mexican Museum in San Francisco, California, and the Museum of Modern Art in New York City.

Rodríguez, Paul

b. 1955
Mazatlán, Mexico
fields: Theater and Entertainment (comedian and actor), Television

Latino comedian and actor. After his early stand-up comedy success in Los Angeles, Paul Rodríguez appeared in the television series *AKA Pablo* (1984) and *Trial and Error* (1988). His other television credits include *The Newlywed Game with Paul Rodríguez, Paul Rodríguez Behind Bars, El Show de Paul Rodríguez,* and *I Need a Couch*. Rodríguez has also appeared in the films *Quicksilver* (1985) and *Born in East L.A.* (1987). In 1986, he produced the comedy album *You're in America Now, Speak Spanish.*

Rodríguez, Peter

b. June 25, 1926
Stockton, Calif.
fields: Art

Latino artist. Peter Rodríguez's art reflects his Northern California upbringing and the several years he spent in Mexico beginning in 1968. He is known for his altars and his abstract paintings. In 1972, Rodríguez founded the Mexican Museum in San Francisco, California.

Rodríguez, Richard

b. July 31, 1944
San Francisco, Calif.
fields: Journalism, Literature

Mexican American author and journalist; Richard Rodríguez reported for the *Los Angeles Times* and the Pacific News Service; his autobiographical *Hunger of Memory: The Education of Richard Rodríguez* earned the 1982 Anfield Wolf Award for Race Relations; in 1992, published *Days of Obligation: An Argument with My Mexican Father*; opposed to affirmative action and bilingual education.

Rodríguez de Tío, Lola

b. Sept. 14, 1843
San Germán, Puerto Rico
d. Nov. 10, 1924
Havana, Cuba
fields: Literature, Social Reform

Puerto Rican writer. Lola Rodríguez de Tío gained widespread acclaim in Puerto Rico when she published her first book of poems in 1876. In 1877, she was exiled and lived in Venezuela for one year. After returning to the island, she published more poems and became involved in trying to free people who had been imprisoned for supporting Puerto Rican autonomy from Spain. In 1889, Rodríguez de Tió was again banished from Puerto Rico. She spent three years in Cuba, then moved to New York City and helped José Martí create the Cuban Revolutionary Party. Rodríguez de Tió returned to Havana in 1924 and died shortly thereafter.

Roebling, John Augustus

b. June 12, 1806
Mühlhausen, Thüringen, Confederation of the Rhine
d. July 22, 1869
Brooklyn Heights, New York
fields: Engineering (civil)

An academically trained civil engineer who worked in the middle decades of the nineteenth century when such talents were rare in the United States, Roebling fully exploited the potentialities of the suspension bridge, placing the United States in the forefront in construction of long-span, stable, heavy-load-bearing bridges for generations.

Roebuck, John

b. 1718
Sheffield, England
d. July 17, 1794
Kenneil House, Scotland
fields: Invention and Technology

After learning chemistry as a medical student, Roebuck introduced a new method for manufacturing sulfuric acid on a large scale and a new method of smelting iron.

Rogers, Charles Calvin

b. September 6, 1929
Claremont, W. Va.
fields: Warfare and Conquest

African American military hero; Lieutenant Colonel Charles Calvin Rogers earned the Congressional Medal of Honor for bravely maintaining his fire support base during an attack by numerically superior forces during the Vietnam War; in 1975, he was promoted to major general.

Rogers, Ginger

né: Virginia Katherine McMath
b. July 16, 1911
Independence, Missouri
d. Paril 25, 1995
Rancho Mirage, California
fields: Film, Dance

A beloved film actress from Hollywood's classical studio era of the 1930's and 1940's, Rogers is most fondly remembered for her RKO musicals with Fred Astaire.

Rogers, Joel A.

b. September 6, 1883
Jamaica
d. March 26, 1965
New York, N.Y.
fields: Historiography, Journalism

African American historian and war correspondent; noted as the first African American war correspondent, in 1935 Joel A. Rogers reported on the invasion of Italy for the *Pittsburgh Courier*; his published works include *From Superman to Man* (1917), *As Nature Leads: An Informal Discussion of the Reason Why Negro and Caucasian Are Mixing in Spite of Opposition* (1919), *World's Greatest Men and Women of African Descent* (1935), and *Your History from the Beginning of Time to the Present* (1940).

Rogers, John W., Jr.

b. March 31, 1958
Chicago, Ill.
fields: Banking and Finance

African American investment broker and financier; John W. Rogers, Jr., founded the highly successful investment firm, Ariel Capital Management, Inc., in 1983; in 1988 was named Mutual Fund Manager of the Year by *Sylvia Porter's Personal Finance Magazine* and Entrepreneur of the Year by Arthur Young and *Venture Magazine*.

Rogers, Will

full: William Penn Adair Rogers
aka: Rabbit
b. November 4, 1879
near Oologah, Indian Territory (modern Oklahoma)
d. August 15, 1935
Walakpa Lagoon (near Point Barrow), Alaska
fields: Theater and entertainment, Journalism (humorist)

Cherokee humorist Will Rogers used homespun humor and satiric philosophy to point up the shortcomings of American society, government, and politics. His skill with a rope led him into work as a cowhand and then as a performer. Between rope tricks, he shared publicly the droll humor and philosophy for which he became famous.

Roh Tae Woo

b. Dec. 4, 1932
near Taegu, Korea
fields: Government and Politics

Roh Tae Woo became president of South Korea, 1988-1993. Roh, a four-star general, retired from the army in 1981 and became chairman of the ruling Democratic Justice Party in 1985. Outgoing South Korean president Doo Hwan Chun selected Roh as ruling party presidential candidate in 1987, and Roh won the direct presidential election that fall. He instituted democratic reforms and was considered a moderated and a balancing force. In 1996, he was convicted on charges of muting, sedition (from a 1979 coup he backed), and corruption (during his presidency); he was sentenced to 17 years in prison and severly fined. He was pardoned by his successor.

Rohmer, Sax

né: Arthur Sarsfield Wade
or as: Arthur Sarsfield Ward
b. February 15, 1883
Birmingham, England
d. June 1, 1959
London, England
fields: Literature

London reporter Sax Rohmer created the sinister Chinese criminal Fu Manchu, publishing *Dr. Fu Manchu*, the first in a series of popular books, in 1913. The character created by the adventure novelist was featured in films, television programs, and radio plays, which made Rohmer wealthy.

Rojas, Cookie

né: Octavio Victor Rojas y Rivas
b. Mar. 6, 1939
Havana, Cuba
fields: Sports (baseball player and manager)

Latino baseball player and manager. Second baseman Cookie Rojas played in the major leagues from 1962 to 1977 with the Cincinnati Reds, Philadelphia Phillies, St. Louis Cardinals, and Kansas City Royals. In 1968, he led National League second basemen with a .987 fielding percentage. He was named to five All-Star Teams and retired after the 1977 season with a .263 batting average. In 1981, he became a special assignment coach for the California Angels. In 1988, he became the team's manager but was fired after the team posted a 75-79 record.

Roland, Gilbert

né: Luis Antonio Dámaso de Alonso
b. Dec. 11, 1905
Juárez, Mexico
d. May 15, 1994
Beverly Hills, Calif.
fields: Film (actor)

Latino actor. Gilbert Roland's silent-era films include *The Plastic Age* (1925), *The Dove* (1927), *Man of the North* (1930), and *She Done Him Wrong* (1933, with Mae West). With the advent talkies, his accent forced him to take roles in Spanish-language films. Roland appeared in six episodes of the Cisco Kid film series in the 1940's. Other films include *Pirates of Monterey* (1947), *We Were Strangers* (1949), *The Bullfighter and the Lady* (1951), *The Treasure of Pancho Villa* (1955), *Cheyenne Autumn* (1964), *Islands in the Stream* (1977), and *Barbarosa* (1982). He appeared in many French and Italian films in the 1970's.

Rolle, Esther

b. November 8, 1922
Pompano Beach, Fla.
d. November 17, 1998
Los Angeles, Calif.
fields: Theater and Entertainment, Film, Television

African American actress; Esther Rolle's stage credits include *The Blacks* (1962; her debut), *Blues for Mister Charlie* (1964), *The Amen Corner* (1965), *MacBeth* (1977), *The River Niger* (1983), *A Raisin in the Sun* (1984), and the one-woman show *Ain't I a Woman* (1978); her film work includes *Cleopatra Jones* (1973), *How to Make an American Quilt* (1995), *Down in the Delta* (1998), and *Rosewood* (1997); her television credits include her role as Florida Evans on the CBS shows *Maude* (1972) and *Good Times* (1973-1979), and the NBC made-for-television movie, *Summer of My German Soldier*, for which she received an Emmy (best supporting actress in a limited series or special, 1978-1979); in 1991 Rolle was inducted into the Black Filmmakers Hall of Fame.

Rollins, Howard

full: Howard Ellsworth Rollins, Jr.
b. October 17, 1951
Baltimore, Md.
d. December 8, 1996
New York, N.Y.
fields: Television, Film

African American actor; although Howard Rollins has received rave reviews for his film performances, he has worked primarily on television, appearing in such programs as *King* (1978; in the role of Andrew Young), *Roots: The Next Generations* (1979), *A Member of the Wedding* (1982), the American Playhouse production *For Us, the Living* (1983; in the role of Medgar Evers), *The Wild Side* (1985), the NBC series *In the Heat of the Night* (1988-1993; in the role of Virgil Tibbs), and the made-for-television movie *With Murder in Mind* (1992); his film credits include *Ragtime* (1981; received an Oscar nomination as best supporting actor for his role as Coalhouse Walker, Jr.), *A Soldier's Story* (1984), and *Drunks* (1995).

Rollins, Sonny

full: Theodore Walter Rollins
b. September 7, 1930
New York, N.Y.
fields: Music (jazz saxophonist, recording artist, and producer)

African American free-style jazz saxophonist, recording artist, and producer; Sonny Rollins gained notice in the 1950's while playing with jazz greats Earl "Bud" Powell, Thelonious Monk, Max Roach, Charlie Parker, Clifford Brown, and Miles Davis; the film *Alfie* (1966) contained his musical work.

Rollo

aka: Hrolfr
b. c. 860
present-day Norway
d. c. 932
Normandy
fields: Government and Politics

Rollo established the Norman dynasty that ruled the lower Seine valley from 911 onward.

Rolls, Charles Stewart

b. August 28, 1877
London, England
d. July 12, 1910
Bournemouth, England
fields: Engineering (automotive), Business and Industry

Combining their talents, Sir Henry Royce produced and Charles Stewart Rolls marketed an automobile built to the highest standards of engineering excellence. Additionally, Royce designed a series of engines which powered many of the British aircraft of the two world wars.

Roman Nose

aka: Sauts (Bat)
aka: Wokini (Hook Nose)
aka: Woquini
b. c. 1830
d. Sept. 17, 1868
Beecher's Island, Colo.
fields: Native American Affairs, Warfare and Conquest

Southern Cheyenne warrior; Roman Nose was a fearless leader, though not a chief, during battles with white settlers and Union Pacific Railroad workers in the 1860's; it was generally believed that a protective war bonnet worn by Roman Nose could protect him against bullets and arrows in battle; legend recounts that the night before a battle at Beecher's Island on the Arickaree River against Major George A. Forsyth, Roman Nose was served food lifted with a metal fork, violating one of the laws that dictated the power of the war bonnet; Roman Nose announced his own death upon riding into the battle, and moments later he was struck down by gunfire.

Romano-V., Octavio

full: Octavio Ignacio Romano-Vizcarra
b. 1923
Mexico City, Mexico
fields: Literature, Publishing

Essayist and publisher. Octavio Romano-V. was born in Mexico and raised in the United States. In 1967, he cofounded *El Grito*, an influential journal that was founded to help overcome stereotypical representations of Chicanos. In the same year, Romano-V founded Quinto Sol Publications. He has worked as an assistant professor of behavioral sciences at the University of California, Berkeley, School of Public Health and has written numerous sociological and anthropological essays on the Chicano experience.

Romero, César

b. Feb. 15, 1907
New York, N.Y.
d. Jan. 1, 1994
Hollywood, Calif.
fields: Film, Television (actor)

Latino actor. Originally a dancer, César Romero's early film roles include *The Devil Is a Woman* (1935), *Wee Willie Winkie* (1937), and *Captain from Castile* (1947). During the 1940's, he appeared in six Cisco Kid adventure films, as well as a series of musicals with Carmen Miranda, including *Weekend in Havana* (1941), *Springtime in the Rockies* (1942), and *Carnival in Costa Rica* (1947). In the 1960's, Romero played Joker on the *Batman* series and appeared in such films as *Pepe* (1960), *Two on a Guillotine* (1964), *Sergeant Deadhead* (1965), and *A Talent for Living* (1969). In the 1980's, he appeared in the television series *Falcon Crest*.

Romero, Frank

b. 1941
East Los Angeles
fields: Art (painter)

Latino painter. Frank Romero met Carlos Almaraz at California State University, Los Angeles. In 1974, the two artists were joined by Roberto de la Rocha and Gilbert Luján in forming Los Four, a collective artist group that had major exhibitions in Los Angeles in the mid-1970's. Romero also worked on a large freeway mural for the 1984 Olympics in Los Angeles.

Romero, José Rubén

b. Sept. 25, 1890
Cotija de la Paz, Michoacán, Mexico
d. July 4, 1952
Mexico City, Mexico
fields: Literature

Mexican writer. José Rubén Romero worked for the newspaper *El Universal* in Mexico City. In 1930, he was appointed Mexican consul in Barcelona. He later became ambassador to Brazil (1937) and to Cuba (1939). Romero's early novels—*Apuntes de un lugareño* (1932; *Notes of a Villager*, 1988), *Desbandada* (1934), and *El pueblo inocente* (1934)—were regionalist in style. The novel *La vida inútil de Pito Pérez* (1938; *The Futile Life of Pito Pérez*, 1966), which used humor to examine and criticize Mexican culture, helped revive the picaresque form.

Rommel, Erwin

full: Erwin Johannes Eugen Rommel
b. November 15, 1891
Heidenheim an der Brentz, Württemberg, Germany
d. October 14, 1944
Herrlingen, near Ulm, Germany
fields: Military Affairs

A legendary commander of World War II, Rommel, known as "The Desert Fox" for his cunning, achieved distinction for his actions in France and North Africa. His successes on the battlefield resulted from his courage and determination, his aggressive leadership, and his mastery of military tactics.

Romney, George

b. December 26, 1734
Dalton-in-Furness, Lancashire, England
d. November 15, 1802
Kendal, Lancashire, England
fields: Art

Romney was one of the three leading portrait painters in eighteenth century England. At the height of his career his popularity was the equal of his great rival, Sir Joshua Reynolds.

Romo, Ricardo

b. June 23, 1943
San Antonio, Tex.
fields: Education

Educator. In 1970, Ricardo Romo earned his M.A. in history from Loyola University in Los Angeles and took a position as assistant professor at California State University, Northridge. In 1974, he began teaching at the University of California, San Diego. The following year, he earned his Ph.D. in history from the University of California, Los Angeles. In 1980, Romo began teaching history at the University of Texas at Austin. In 1988, he became director of the Tomás Rivera Center at that university. Romo wrote *East Los Angeles: History of a Barrio* (1983) and coedited *New Directions in Chicano Scholarship* (1978).

Romulo, Carlos Pena

b. Jan. 14, 1899
Manila, Luzon, Philippines
d. Dec. 15, 1985
Manila, Philippines
fields: Warfare and Conquest, Diplomacy, Journalism

General, diplomat, and journalist Carlos Pena Romulo, a newspaper publisher and editor when Japan invaded the Philippines in 1941, assisted the U.S. military effort by producing a series of anti-Japanese broadcasts. His prewar analyses of the Pacific region's political and military situation earned him the Pulitzer Prize in 1941. He became the first Asian to serve as president of the UN General Assembly in 1949 and became Philippine foreign affairs secretary in 1950. He was named ambassador to the United States in 1952. Romulo's autobiography, *I Walked with Heroes*, was released in 1961.

Roncalli, Angelo Giuseppe. *See* John XXIII

Rondon, Fernando E.

b. May 6, 1936
Los Angeles, Calif.
fields: Diplomacy

Mexican American diplomat. In 1976, Fernando E. Rondon served with the U.S. State Department as deputy director for the eastern coast of South America. In 1978, he became the deputy chief of mission in the U.S. embassy in Tegucigalpa, Honduras. He served as ambassador to Madagascar from 1980 to 1983, ambassador to Comoros in 1982 and 1983, and ambassador to Ecuador from 1983 to 1985. During the mid-1980's, a tumultuous period in the history of U.S.-Latin American relations, Rondon held several sensitive posts in South America.

Roney, Frank

b. Aug. 13, 1841
Belfast, Ireland
d. Jan. 24, 1925
Long Beach, Calif.
fields: Labor Movement

Irish immigrant Frank Roney moved to California in 1875, where he worked for San Francisco's Pacific Iron Works and joined Denis Kearney's Workingmen's Party of California and ardently supported its anti-Chinese politics. In 1882, Roney cofounded the League of Deliverance, which aimed to eventually exclude all Chinese immigration. It organized a boycott in San Francisco of all Chinese-made goods, printed and distributed handbills proclaiming the superior quality of American-made goods, and pressured employers to fire their Chinese workers. The Chinese Exclusion Act of 1882, passed shortly thereafter, halted all further immigration of Chinese laborers to the United States.

Ronsard, Pierre de

b. September 11, 1524
near Couture, Vendômois, France
d. December 27, 1585
Saint-Cosme, France
fields: Literature (poetry)

Ronsard enriched French poetry by adapting classical genres and styles to his native language. He wrote historically significant odes, hymns, and lyrics and one of the most important sonnet sequences in the history of literature. A member of la Pléiade (fl. 1549-1589), a group of loosely organized poets dedicated to raising the level of sophistication of the French language by adding words and genres derived from classical literature. Led by Ronsard and Joachim du Bellay, they developed a new form of poetry based on forms such as the sonnet, the ode, epic, and elegy. They also worked to elevate the level of the poet to a position as an intermediary between humanity and the heavens.

Ronstadt, Linda

full: Linda Marie Ronstadt
b. July 15, 1946
Tucson, Arizona
fields: Music

Linda Ronstadt became a pop-rock superstar in the 1970's, when the industry was primarily dominated by men. She continues to inspire vocalists with her increasingly controlled soprano voice and her commitment to diverse projects.

Röntgen, Wilhelm Conrad

b. Mar. 27, 1845
Lennep, Prussia (now Remscheid, Germany)
d. Feb. 10, 1923
Munich, Germany
fields: Chemistry, Physics

William Conrad Röntgen, in 1895, discovered X rays by a careful study of cathode emissions; studied the nature of gases, fluids, light, magnetism, and electricity; in 1901, won the first Nobel Prize in Physics.

Rooney, Andy

b. January 14, 1919
Albany, New York
fields: Television, Journalism

A long-time satirical commentator on its popular weekly news program, *60 Minutes*, Andy Rooney was suspended for three months in 1990 for having allegedly made racist statements in an interview. He was also accused of linking homosexual unions with the abuse of alcohol, drugs, overeating, and cigarettes as causes of premature death. Rooney was reinstated following strident protests from his loyal audience members.

Roosevelt, Alice Lee. *See* Longworth, Alice Roosevelt

Roosevelt, Eleanor

né: Anna Eleanor Roosevelt
b. October 11, 1884
New York, New York
d. November 7, 1962
New York, New York
fields: Social Reform

As First Lady and as a private citizen, Roosevelt worked for civil rights, women's rights, and domestic and international peace and justice.

Roosevelt, Franklin D.

full: Franklin Delano Roosevelt
b. January 30, 1882
Hyde Park, New York
d. April 12, 1945
Warm Springs, Georgia
fields: Government and Politics

Displaying extraordinary personal courage and perhaps the most astute political leadership America has ever witnessed, Roosevelt dominated American government for a longer period than has any other president of the United States. Thirty-second president of the United States, 1933-1945.

Roosevelt, Theodore

aka: Teddy Roosevelt
b. October 27, 1858
New York, New York
d. January 6, 1919
Oyster Bay, New York
fields: Government and Politics

As twenty-sixth president of the United States, 1901-1909, Roosevelt energetically led America into the twentieth century. Popular and effective, he promoted major domestic reforms and a larger role for the United States in world affairs. In so doing, he added power to the presidential office.

Root, Elihu

b. February 15, 1845
Clinton, New York
d. February 7, 1937
New York, New York
fields: Diplomacy, Government and Politics

As secretary of war under William McKinley and Theodore Roosevelt, Root administered territories gained at the end of the Spanish-American War and initiated reforms in army administration. He pursued a conservative line as secretary of state under Roosevelt and later as United States senator from New York, and argued for the value of international law as a political instrument.

Roque, Shirley. *See* Muldowney, Shirley

Rorschach, Hermann

b. November 8, 1884
Zurich, Switzerland
d. April 2, 1922
Herisau, Switzerland
fields: Psychiatry and Psychology

Rorschach is credited with only one major scientific achievement during his short career, but this achievement was important in the development of modern psychology and had far-reaching effects on other disciplines as well. In the early 1920's, Rorschach set forth a formal method of testing personality traits by recording, timing, and interpreting a subject's reactions to a series of inkblots. The test remains one of the most valuable testing tools of psychology.

Rorty, Richard

full: Richard McKay Rorty
b. October 4, 1931
New York, New York
fields: Philosophy

Richard Rorty revitalized the pragmatism and naturalism of William James and John Dewey by incorporating elements of linguistically oriented analytic philosophy, critiquing the quests for certainty and for the foundations of knowledge and championing creative individualism, political liberalism, and a consciousness of existential uncertainty. Major works: *Philosophy and the Mirror of Nature* (1979), *Consequences of Pragmatism* (1982),

Contingency, Irony, and Solidarity (1989), *Achieving Our Country*, (1998).

Ros-Lehtinen, Ileana

b. July 15, 1952
Havana, Cuba
fields: Government and Politics

Latina legislator. In 1982, Ileana Ros-Lehtinen became the first Latina elected to the Florida state legislature. In 1989, she became the first Cuban American elected to Congress. While serving in the U.S. House of Representative, Ros-Lehtinen focused on educational and environmental concerns, as well as U.S. policy toward Cuba. She has served on the House foreign affairs and government operations committees.

Rosario, Hector

b. ?
Puerto Rico
fields: Art (muralist)

Muralist. Hector Rosario, a member of the Puerto Rican Art Association in Chicago, Illinois, helped paint *La Crucifixion de don Pedro Albizu Campos* (1971), a mural measuring 28 feet by 50 feet that commemorates Albizu Campos and four others who attacked the U.S. House of Representatives in 1954 to bring attention to the Puerto Rican independence movement.

Rosca, Ninotchka

b. 1954
Manila, Philippines
fields: Journalism, Literature

Filipino American Ninotchka Rosca wrote two collections of stories, *Bitter Country and Other Stories* (1970) and *The Monsoon Collection* (1983), two novels, *State of War* (1988) and *Twice Blessed* (1992), and a nonfiction work, *Endgame: The Fall of Marcos* (1987). Rosca, a widely published journalist, had a regular column in *Filipinas* magazine.

Rose, Pete

full: Peter Edward Rose
b. April 14, 1941
Cincinnati, Ohio
fields: Sports (baseball)

Rose broke Ty Cobb's major league baseball record of 4,191 hits in 1985 and established a new record of 4,256 hits by the time he retired in 1986. He lost an assured place in baseball's Hall of Fame in 1989 when he was banned from the sport for allegedly betting on baseball games.

Rosenthal, Ida

né: Ida Kaganovich
aka: Ida Cohen
b. January 9, 1886
Rakov, Russia
d. March 28, 1973
New York, New York
fields: Business and Industry

Having created with her partner Enid Bissett in 1922 the first brassiere to give women a natural appearance, Rosenthal cofounded the Maiden Form Brassiere Company. Through sophisticated marketing and advertising, Rosenthal gave the Maidenform brand worldwide recognition and created what remains the largest privately held intimate apparel company in the United States.

Rosenzweig, Franz

b. December 25, 1886
Kassel, Germany
d. December 10, 1929
Frankfurt am Main, Germany
fields: Philosophy, Religion and Theology

German-Jewish philosopher and theologian Franz Rosenzweig, paralyzed with Lou Gehrig's disease (diagnosed in 1921), is best known for his work on Georg Wilhelm Friedrich Hegel's political philosophy and on his own existential philosophy of religion, which developed as he examined his identity as a Jew. His two major works, *Hegel und der Staat* and *The Star of Redemption*, deal with German Idealism and his coming to terms with the human immersion in and production of history.

Ross, Betsy

né: Elizabeth Griscom
aka: Betsy Ashburn
aka: Betsy Claypoole
b. January 1, 1752
Philadelphia, Pennsylvania
d. January 30, 1836
Philadelphia, Pennsylvania
fields: Art

Using an original idea presented to her by George Washington, Betsy Ross is reputed to have designed and sewn the first official American flag.

Ross, Diana

b. March 26, 1944
Detroit, Mich.
fields: Music, Film

African American popular singer; Diana Ross's work with the Supremes (1960-1969) produced such number-one hits as "Where Did Our Love Go" (1964); they were one of the top groups of the 1960's, breaking ground for both female and African American artists; the Supremes were inducted into the Rock and Roll Hall of Fame in 1988. Ross then launched an extremely successful solo career. Her film work included *Lady Sings the Blues* (1972; for which she earned an Academy Award nomination), the box-office success *Mahogany* (1975; the soundtrack of which contained the number-one hit "Do You Know Where You're Going To?"), and *The Wiz* (1978); her 1981 solo album *Diana: All the Great Hits* included the number-one pop single "Upside Down." She continued to perform and record through the end of the century; her autobiography is *Secrets of a Sparrow: Memoirs* (1993).

Ross, Edward Alsworth

b. Dec. 12, 1866
Virden, Ill.
d. July 22, 1951
Madison, Wis.
fields: Sociology

Edward Alsworth Ross, one of the founders of sociology as an academic discipline in the United States, advocated social engineering and scientific racism. He helped provide the rationale for the exclusion of Chinese and other Asian immigrants. He taught at Stanford University, the University of Nebraska, and the University of Wisconsin. His publications include *Social Control* (1901), *Foundations of Sociology* (1905), and *The Changing Chinese* (1911).

Ross, James Clark

b. April 15, 1800
London, England
d. April 3, 1862
Aylesbury, Buckinghamshire, England
fields: Exploration and Colonization

Through determined and efficient leadership, Ross discovered the North Magnetic Pole, mapped hundreds of miles of coastline, and discovered scores of geographical features.

Ross, John

né: Coowescoowe
b. October 3, 1790
Turkey Town, Alabama
d. August 1, 1866
Washington, D.C.
fields: Government and Politics, Diplomacy

As a leader of the Cherokee nation during its ordeal of forced removal and civil war, Ross is the supreme example of nineteenth century Native American statesmanship.

Ross, Nellie Tayloe

né: Nellie Davis Tayloe
b. November 29, 1876
St. Joseph, Missouri
d. December 19, 1977
Washington, D.C.
fields: Government and Politics

The first woman governor of a state (Wyoming) in the United States, Ross later served as an officer in the Democratic Party and as a director of the U.S. Mint, one of the first women to head a federal agency.

Ross, Ronald

b. May 13, 1857
Almora, India
d. September 16, 1932
Putney, London, England
fields: Medicine

Ross demonstrated the role of the mosquito in the transmission of malaria, proved the insect to be essential to the life cycle of the malarial parasite, and introduced the first effective preventive measures against malaria. He was awarded the 1902 Nobel Prize in Physiology or Medicine.

Rossby, Carl-Gustaf Arvid

b. Dec. 28, 1898
Stockholm, Sweden
d. Aug. 19, 1957
Stockholm, Sweden
fields: Science

Carl-Gustaf Arvid Rossby was a pioneer in the science of meteorology; studied atmospheric turbulence; discovered waves in the jet stream that influence weather on Earth.

Rossini, Gioacchino

b. February 29, 1792
Pesaro
d. November 13, 1868
Passy, France
fields: Music

Rossini was one of the greatest composers of Italian opera in the nineteenth century. In almost forty works for the operatic stage, Rossini composed some of the last and finest specimens of the *opera buffa* and also numerous serious operas which laid the foundation for the ensuing generation of Italian Romantic composers. His brilliant overtures have enjoyed a separate life as concert pieces.

Roth, Philip

b. March 19, 1933
Newark, New Jersey
fields: Literature

Writer; Philip Roth was the first major Jewish American writer to look frankly into middle-class Jewish life; won National Book Award (1963); most famous works include *Goodbye, Columbus and Five Short Stories* (1959), *Portnoy's Complaint* (1969), and *Operation Shylock* (1993); other comic novels are *Our Gang* (1971), *The Breast* (1972), and *The Great American Novel* (1973); novels involving Nathan Zuckerman, Roth's fictional projection of himself, include *My Life as a Man* (1974), *Zuckerman Bound* (1985), and *The Counterlife* (1986).

Roth, Samuel

b. November 17, 1894
Austria
d. July 3, 1974
New York, New York
fields: Publishing

An Austrian immigrant to the United States, Samuel Roth began publishing *Two Worlds Monthly*, a literary magazine, in 1925. In 1930 he was jailed for publishing uncensored portions of James Joyce's novel *Ulysses*. He also published the *Kama Sutra* and *The Perfumed Garden* and was again jailed for violating New York State's obscenity law. When he sold D. H. Lawrence's *Lady Chatterley's Lover* through the mail, he was jailed for three years. In 1957 Roth's name entered legal history in the U.S. Supreme Court's *Roth v. United States* decision, which established the Court's more liberal "Roth" standard for obscenity. However, Roth's five-year jail sentence and $5,000 fine were upheld.

Rothenberg, Susan

b. January 20, 1945
Buffalo, New York
fields: Art

As one of America's leading women artists, Rothenberg has pioneered new modes of imagination and vision in painting.

Rothermere, Viscount. *See* Harmsworth, Harold

Rothschild, Amschel Mayer

b. June 12, 1773
Frankfurt am Main
d. December 6, 1855
Frankfurt am Main
fields: Business and Industry

The Rothschild family developed one of the most successful banking and investment companies of all time. By locating branches in a number of major cities while keeping the business a family matter, they were able to coordinate international operations and provide services to clients and governments that were unavailable elsewhere. Amschel Mayer Rothschild, the oldest of Mayer Amschel's sons, followed his father in leading the business in Frankfurt, Germany.

Rothschild, Carl Mayer

aka: Karl Mayer Rothschild
b. April 24, 1788
Frankfurt am Main
d. March 10, 1855
Naples, Kingdom of the Two Sicilies
fields: Business and Industry

The Rothschild family developed one of the most successful banking and investment companies of all time. By locating branches in a number of major cities while keeping the business a family matter, they were able to coordinate international operations and provide services to clients and governments that were unavailable elsewhere. Carl Mayer Rothschild, the fourth son of Mayer Amschel, founded a branch of the family business in Naples.

Rothschild, Dorothy. *See* Parker, Dorothy

Rothschild, James Mayer

aka: Jacob Mayer Rothschild
b. May 15, 1792
Frankfurt am Main
d. November 15, 1868
Paris, France
fields: Business and Industry

The Rothschild family developed one of the most successful banking and investment companies of all time. By locating branches in a number of major cities while keeping the business a family matter, they were able to coordinate international operations and provide services to clients and governments that were unavailable elsewhere. James Mayer Rothschild, Mayer Amschel's youngest son and second only to Nathan in building the family's business, established the Rothschilds in Paris.

Rothschild, Lionel Nathan

b. 1808
d. 1879
fields: Business and Industry

The Rothschild family developed one of the most successful banking and investment companies of all time. Lionel Nathan Rothschild—son of Nathan Mayer Rothschild and part of the third generation of the Rothschild business—succeeded his father as a senior partner. He was elected to parliament seven times before the House of Lords allowed him to serve. He, thus, became the first practicing Jew ot be a Member of Parliament. He served two terms.

Rothschild, Mayer Amschel

b. February 23, 1744
Frankfurt am Main
d. September 19, 1812
Frankfurt am Main
fields: Business and Industry

The Rothschild family developed one of the most successful banking and investment companies of all time. By locating branches in a number of major cities while keeping the business a family matter, they were able to coordinate international operations and provide services to clients and governments that were unavailable elsewhere. Mayer Amschel Rothschild established the business in Germany by trading rare coins and dealing in luxury items. He had five sons and five daughters. His sons expanded the family business throughout Europe.

Rothschild, Nathan Mayer

b. September 16, 1777
Frankfurt am Main
d. July 28, 1836
Frankfurt am Main
fields: Business and Industry

The Rothschild family developed one of the most successful banking and investment companies of all time. By locating branches in a number of major cities while keeping the business a family matter, they were able to coordinate international operations and provide services to clients and governments that were unavailable elsewhere. Natha Mayer Rothschild, the third son of Mayer Amschel, is considered the most successful and dynamic of the second generation Rothschilds. Nathan expanded the family business into England.

Rothschild, Nathan Mayer

aka: Sir Nathan Mayer Rothschild
aka: Nathan Mayer, first baron Rothschild
aka: Natty Rothschild
b. 1840
d. 1915
fields: Business and Industry

The Rothschild family developed one of the most successful banking and investment companies of all time. Nathan Mayer Rothschild—son of Lionel Nathan Rothschild, grandson of his namesake, and part of the fourth generation of the Rothschild business—succeeded his father in running the London banking house. He served as a Member of Parliment, 1865-1885. He was the first Jew admitted to the House of Lords; he was made a peer in 1885.

Rothschild, Salomon Mayer

b. September 9, 1774
Frankfurt am Main
d. July 27, 1855
Paris, France
fields: Business and Industry

The Rothschild family developed one of the most successful banking and investment companies of all time. By locating branches in a number of major cities while keeping the business a family matter, they were able to coordinate international operations and provide services to clients and governments that were unavailable elsewhere. Salomon Mayer Rothschild, the second son of Mayer Amschel, founded a brank of the family business in Vienna.

Rotten Belly. *See* Arapoosh

Rouault, Georges

b. May 27, 1871
Paris, France
d. February 13, 1958
Paris, France
fields: Art

One of the greatest painters of the twentieth century, Rouault combined an existential philosophy and a strong Catholic faith with a prodigious artistic energy to amass a unique and distinctly identifiable body of work over fully seventy years of creativity.

Roundtree, Richard

b. July 9, 1942
New Rochelle, N.Y.
fields: Film, Television (actor)

African American actor; best known for his role as the assertive black detective John Shaft in the movie *Shaft* (1971), Richard Roundtree later appeared in the films *Shaft's Big Score* (1972), *Shaft in Africa* (1973), *Charley One-Eye* (1973), *Earthquake* (1974), *Diamonds* (1975), *Man Friday* (1976), and *City Heat* (1984); his television appearances included the short-lived series *Shaft* (1973-1974), the miniseries *Roots* (1977), the short-lived series *Outlaws* (1986-1987), and the NBC soap opera *Generations* (1988-1989).

Rous, Peyton

full: Francis Peyton Rous
b. Oct. 5, 1879
Baltimore, Maryland
d. Feb. 16, 1970
New York, New York
fields: Biology, Genetics, Medicine

Peyton Rous was the first to demonstrate that cancer in animals can be caused by viruses, in 1910, when he found that sarcomas in chickens are caused by a "filterable agent"; won the 1966 Nobel Prize in Physiology or Medicine.

Rousseau, Henri

full: Henri-Julien-Félix Rousseau
b. May 21, 1844
Laval, France
d. September 2, 1910
Paris, France
fields: Art

Rousseau was the best known of the "naïve" artists of the late nineteenth century. His deceptively primitive paintings possessed a mysterious poetry that transcended their often banal subject matter and childlike technique to inspire such later artistic movements as Surrealism.

Rousseau, Jean-Jacques

b. June 28, 1712
Geneva
d. July 2, 1778
Ermenonville, France
fields: Education, Literature, Political Science

Rousseau helped transform the Western world from a rigidly stratified, frequently despotic civilization into a predominantly democratic civilization dedicated to assuring the dignity and fulfillment of the individual.

Rowan, Carl Thomas

b. August 25, 1925
Ravenscroft, Tenn.
fields: Journalism, Literature

African American journalist and author; Carl Thomas Rowan advanced from copyreader to general reporter for the *Minneapolis Tribune* in 1950; his series written about the black experience in the South, *How Far from Slavery?*, elicited the largest volume of mail in the *Tribune*'s history; Rowan began his long-running Chicago Sun column in 1965; he produced *The Rowan Report*, a syndicated national affairs radio commentary, served as a commentator for the Post-Newsweek Broadcasting Corporation, and became a frequent panelist on *Meet the Press*; his published works included *The Pitiful and the Proud* (1956), *Go South to Sorrow* (1957), *Wait Till Next Year: The Life Story of Jackie Robinson* (1960), *Just Between Us Blacks* (1974), and *Breaking Barriers* (1991; memoirs). In 1952, *Look* magazine reprinted portions of *How Far from Slavery?*

Rowland, F. Sherwood

full: Frank Sherwood Rowland
b. June 28, 1927
Delaware, Ohio
fields: Chemistry

In 1974, F. Sherwood Rowland was first to realize that chlorine atoms released by the decomposition of chlorofluorocarbons in the stratosphere could damage the protective ozone layer of the earth; in 1986, published a paper explaining the formation of the ozone hole over Antarctica; in 1995, won the Nobel Prize in Chemistry jointly with Mario Molina and Paul Crutzen.

Roy, M. N.

full: Manabendra Nath Roy
né: Narendranath Bhattacharya
b. Mar. 21, 1887
Arbelia, West Bengal, India
d. Jan. 25, 1954
Dehra Dun, Uttar Pradesh, Republic of India
fields: Government and Politics

M. N. Roy was a Marxist revolutionary, writer, and founder of Radical Humanism. In 1905, he became involved with the underground nationalist movement in Bengal. Roy went to the United States, then Mexico, where he converted from a militant nationalist to a Marxist. Roy became involved with the Comintern and published *India in Transition* (1922), the first major Marxist analysis of conditions in India. He became unhappy with the Comintern and was expelled in 1929. He wrote *Revolution and Counter-Revolution in China* (1946) and returned to India. Disillusioned with political parties, in the 1940's Roy founded Radical Humanism, a movement that rejected all forms of dictatorship and authoritarianism. Its followers were to devote their energies toward the establishment of grassroots democracy and a philosophical revolution that was necessary to sustain and nurture a genuine democratic order.

Roy, Ram Mohun

b. May 22, 1772
Radhanagar, now in West Bengal, Republic of India
d. Sept. 27, 1833
Bristol, England
fields: Social Reform, Philanthropy

In 1815, Ram Mohun Roy began his crusade to reform Hindu society, concentrating his efforts of the practice of *sati*, the self-immolation by widows. The practice was made illegal in 1829 by the British government, probably as a result of Roy's crusade. Roy also attacked polygamy and the caste system. He strongly believed in the value of a Western education and freedom of the press. His reformist Hinduism brought criticism from orthodox Christians and Hindus. In 1828, he founded the Brahmo Samaj movement, which stood for a monotheistic Hinduism that believed in social justice and the ideals of reason.

Roybal, Alfonso. *See* Awa Tsireh

Roybal, Edward R.

b. Feb. 10, 1916
Albuquerque, N.Mex.
fields: Government and Politics

Latino politician; Edward R. Roybal was raised in Los Angeles, served in the Civilian Conservation Corps during the depression and in the army during World War II (1944-1945); cofounder, Community Service Organization, 1947; member, Los Angeles City Council, 1949-1962, the first Mexican American to serve there since 1881; opposed city development that adversely affected Mexican American families; U.S. representative (Democrat), 1963-1993; introduced legislation leading to the Bilingual Education Act of 1967; founding member of Congressional Hispanic Caucus, 1976, and the National Association of Latino Elected and Appointed Officials.

Roybal-Allard, Lucille

né: Lucille Roybal
b. June 12, 1941
Los Angeles, Calif.
fields: Government and Politics

Mexican American politician. Lucille Roybal-Allard, daughter of Edward Roybal, was elected to the California state assembly and served on the Rules Committee and the Ways and Means Committee. In 1992, as her father was retiring, Roybal-Allard was elected to Congress. With her election, she became the first Mexican American woman elected to Congress. She was reelected in 1994, 1996, and 1998.

Royce, Henry

full: Frederick Henry Royce
aka: Sir Henry Royce
b. March 27, 1863
Alwalton, England
d. April 22, 1933
West Wittering, England
fields: Engineering (automotive, aeronautical), Aviation and Space Exploration, Business and Industry

Combining their talents, Sir Frederick Henry Royce produced and Charles Steward Rolls marketed an automobile built to the highest standards of engineering excellence. Additionally, Royce designed a series of engines which powered many of the British aircraft of the two world wars.

Royce, Josiah

b. November 20, 1855
Grass Valley, California
d. September 14, 1916
Cambridge, Massachusetts
fields: Philosophy

Royce was the last major philosopher of the twentieth century to integrate theological or religious topics with idealistic philosophy and to present his system to the general reader in terms of community and loyalty. He advanced philosophic idealism and played a significant role in Harvard University's intellectual development.

Rozier, Jackson Evander, Jr.

b. March 21, 1936
Richmond, Va.
fields: Military Affairs

African American military officer; Jackson Evander Rozier, Jr., had achieved the rank of U.S. Army major general upon his retirement in 1990; his postings included executive officer in the division support command for the 801st Maintenance Battalion of the 101st Airborne Division and commanding general at the Army Ordnance Center and School at Aberdeen Proving Ground in Maryland.

Rubalcaba, Gonzalo

full: Gonzalo Julio Gonzales Fonseca Rubalcaba
b. 1963
Cuba
fields: Music (jazz pianist and composer)

Jazz pianist and composer. Gonzalo Rubalcaba made his triumphant American debut at Lincoln Center in New York City on May 14, 1993. By the late 1990's, Rubalcaba had recorded more than ten albums, including *Discovery*, *The Blessing*, and *Suite 4 y 20*. Rubalcaba has performed salsa music with his quartet but is also interested in Cuban music other than dance forms.

Rubbia, Carlo

b. Mar. 31, 1934
Gorizia, Italy
fields: Physics

Carlo Rubbia won the 1984 Nobel Prize in Physics, jointly with Simon van der Meer, for his proof of the existence of W^+, W^-, and Z^0 particles; in 1987-1996, led a team of a hundred scientists who designed, constructed, and used one of the world's largest superconducting supercolliders—a 2 million-electronvolt synchrotron, a large device for accelerating particles and directing them toward targets; in 1993, proposed the construction of an energy amplifier, a tool for producing neutrons and introducing them into atomic fuel.

Rubens, Peter Paul

b. June 28, 1577
Siegen, Westphalia
d. May 30, 1640
Antwerp, Brabant
fields: Art, Diplomacy

One of the most successful artists of his time, with a huge workshop of artists who completed many of his commissions, Rubens is regarded as the most important creator of Baroque art. As a distinguished diplomat, he used his cheerful personality and broad human interests to work for the cause of peace.

Rubenstein, Richard L.

full: Richard Lowell Rubenstein
b. January 8, 1924
New York, New York
fields: Philosophy, Religion and Theology

One of the first Jewish thinkers to explore deeply the ethical and religious implications of the Holocaust, Richard L. Rubenstein questioned the credibility of claims about God's presence in history and addressed overpopulation, modernization, bureaucracy, and the persistent threat of genocide in the modern world. Served as chaplain to Jewish students at Harvard (1956-1958), director of the B'nai B'rith Hillel Foundation and chaplain to Jewish students at the University of Pittsburgh and Carnegie Mellon University (1958-1970). In *After Auschwitz* (1966), Rubenstein contended that belief in a redeeming God is no longer credible, leading to the controversial death-of-God movement. Other major works include *The Cunning of History* (1975), the novel *Sophie's World* (1979), and *The Age of Triage* (1983).

Rubin, Vera C.

né: Vera Cooper
b. July 23, 1928
Philadelphia, Pennsylvania
fields: Astronomy, Physics

Vera C. Rubin studied the movement and rotation of galaxies; provided proof for the existence of the Local Supercluster, the Great Attractor, and dark matter.

Rubinstein, Arthur

b. January 28, 1887
Lodz, Poland
d. December 20, 1982
Geneva, Switzerland
fields: Music, Performance Art

Renowned concert pianist Arthur Rubinstein produced an enduring standard of virtuosity and a popular following worldwide. Early in his career, he toured throughout Europe, South America, and the United States, becoming a U.S. citizen in 1946. In the 1960's, in his seventies, he experienced one of his most active and productive periods of performances and recordings. Commanding a formidable repertoire of French, Spanish, German, Russian, and Brazilian composers, he enthralled audiences with his refined, assured technique and delicate yet vigorous interpretations, and he provided standard interpretations of Ludwig van Beethoven's, Johannes Brahms's, and especially Frédéric Chopin's compositions. Governments and organizations around the world bestowed awards, commendations, and honors upon him, and he performed well into his eighties. Becoming increasingly deaf and almost blind, he died of cancer in 1982. The Arthur Rubinstein International Music Society, in Tel Aviv, Israel, maintains a research center devoted to the pianist's life and work since 1980.

Rucker, Darius

b. 1966?
Charleston, S.C.
fields: Music (singer and songwriter)

African American singer and songwriter; Darius Rucker, lead singer and songwriter for the rock group Hootie and the Blowfish, is featured on albums including *Cracked Rear View* (1994), *Fairweather Johnson* (1996), and *Musical Chairs* (1998).

Rudkin, Margaret

né: Margaret Fogarty
b. September 14, 1897
New York, New York
d. June 1, 1967
New Haven, Connecticut
fields: Business and Industry

The founder of Pepperidge Farm, producer of high-quality bakery products, Margaret Rudkin achieved business success at a time when such accomplishments by women were rare. She wrote a best-selling autobiography/cookbook in 1963.

Rudolf I

b. May 1, 1218
Limburg-im-Breisgau
d. July 15, 1291
Speyer, Germany
fields: Government and Politics, Monarchy

King of Germany, 1272-1291. Rudolf, as the first of his family to achieve eminence, founded a dynasty that was to remain one of the most important royal families in Europe for more than six centuries.

Rudolph, Wilma

full: Wilma Glodean Rudolph
b. June 23, 1940
St. Bethlehem, Tennessee
d. November 12, 1994
Brentwood, near Nashville, Tennessee
fields: Sports (track and field)

Despite her early physical handicaps, Wilma Rudolph overcame much adversity to excel as one of the fastest runners the world of track has ever seen. She established many track records and garnered numerous medals and awards.

Ruef, Abraham

b. Sept. 2, 1864
San Francisco, Calif.
d. Feb. 29, 1936
San Francisco, Calif.
fields: Government and Politics

Abraham Ruef, a lawyer and leader of the Union Labor Party, became mayor of San Francisco in 1906 but shortly thereafter was brought down by a corruption scandal. The extremely anti-Japanese Ruef called for segregation of Japanese immigrant students in public schools and used anti-Asian sentiment to further his political career.

Ruether, Rosemary Radford

né: Rosemary Radford
b. November 2, 1936
St. Paul, Minnesota
fields: Religion and Theology, Social Reform

Positioning herself within the Roman Catholic church, Ruether has dedicated her life to fostering dialogue between opposites for the purpose of establishing "right relationships" in which all forms of oppression (racism, sexism, neocolonialism, anti-Semitism, classism, religious bias, and ecological destructiveness) are left behind.

Ruffin, David

b. January 18, 1941
Meridian, Miss.
d. June 1, 1991
Philadelphia, Pa.
fields: Music (soul singer)

African American singer; David Ruffin is remembered as one of the original members and the lead singer for the Temptations (beginning 1963); the group recorded scores of million-selling records; in 1989 Ruffin and four other members of the Temptations were inducted into the Rock and Roll Hall of Fame.

Ruggles, David

b. March 15, 1810
Norwich, Conn.
d. December 26, 1849
Northampton, Ma.
fields: Civil Rights, Journalism

African American abolitionist, journalist, and editor; through his work with the New York Vigilance Committee, David Ruggles helped hundreds of escaped slaves find shelter in the North; he edited *The Mirror of Liberty* (1838-1841) and *The Genius of Freedom* (1845) and also ran a bookshop.

Ruíz, Caribe

b. ?
d. 1988
fields: Art

Latino artist. Caribe Ruíz boosted the Puerto Rico mural movement in Chicago by serving as executive director of that city's Puerto Rican Congress. Beginning in 1972, he encouraged collaborative murals. He is associated with Mario Galán's mural *Símbolos* (1974), which features Taino (native Puerto Rican or Indian) designs.

Ruíz, Vicki L.

b. May 21, 1955
Atlanta, Ga.
fields: Education

Latina educator. From 1982 to 1985, Vicki L. Ruíz directed the Institute of Oral History at the University of Texas at El Paso. She began teaching at the University of California, Davis, in 1985. From 1988 to 1992, she was director of Mentorships for Undergraduate Researchers in Agriculture, Letters, and Science. She became the Andrew W. Mellon All-Claremont Professor in the Humanities at the Claremont Graduate School in 1992 and became chair of that school's history department in 1993. Ruíz's publications include *Cannery Women, Cannery Lives: Mexican Women, Unionization, and the California Food Processing Industry, 1930-1950* (1987). She coedited *Women on the U.S.-Mexico Border: Responses to Change* (1977) and *Unequal Sisters: A Multicultural Reader in U.S. Women's History* (1990).

Ruiz Belvis, Segundo

b. May 13, 1829
Hormigueros, Puerto Rico
d. Nov. 3, 1867
Valparaíso, Chile
fields: Government and Politics

Political reformer. In 1865, Segundo Ruiz Belvis was elected to travel to Spain to propose reforms dealing with the composition and extent of local administration in Puerto Rico. He helped draft the Bill for the Abolition of Slavery in Puerto Rico and contributed to a report advocating an autonomous form of government. However, political turmoil in Spain ended reform attempts. Ruiz Belvis publicly protested against this resolution. Forewarned of the decision by Spanish authorities to exile him, Ruiz Belvis went to New York City to promote Puerto Rican independence. He then went to Chile, where he died.

Ruiz-Conforto, Tracie

né: Tracie Lehuanani Ruiz
b. Feb. 4, 1963
Honolulu, Hawaii
fields: Sports (synchronized swimmer)

Synchronized swimmer. Duet team Tracie Ruiz-Conforto and Candace Costie swept the national championships as juniors. In 1981, they moved to the senior level and won the national title three straight years. At the 1982 World Championships, Ruiz and Costie finished second in the duet competition, while Ruiz won the solo competition with the highest score ever recorded in the sport. At the 1984 Los Angeles Olympics, Ruiz won the gold medal in the solo competition, and she and Costie won the gold medal in the duet competition. Ruiz won the silver medal in the solo event at the Seoul Olympics in 1988.

Ruiz de Burton, María Amparo

b. July 3, 1832
Loreto, Baja California
d. 1895
Chicago, Ill.
fields: Literature

Latina writer. María Amparo Ruiz de Burton and her mother moved from Baja to Moneterey in 1847. Ruiz de Burton wrote and produced a five-act comedy before publishing her first novel, *Who Would Have Thought It?* (1872). Her *The Squatter and the Don* (1885) was published under the ironic pseudonym C. Loyal, standing for *Ciudadano Leal*, or loyal citizen. The novel was critical of the American political structure. Ruiz de Burton later made an unsuccessful attempt to gain recognition of her claim to land in Ensenada, Baja California, that had been granted to her grandfather.

Rukeyser, Muriel

b. December 15, 1913
New York, New York
d. February 12, 1980
New York, New York
fields: Literature

Known as something of a veteran literary "freedom fighter," Rukeyser helped to promote social justice in many areas and showed women how they could improve their lives by improving the lives of others.

Rulfo, Juan

b. May 16, 1918
Apulco, Mexico
d. Jan. 7, 1986
Mexico City, Mexico
fields: Literature

Mexican writer. Juan Rulfo was raised in an orphanage run by the French Josephine nuns, went to high school and business school in Guadalajara, and began working in the migration archives in Mexico City in 1935. He published a collection of short stories called *El llano en llamas* (1953; *The Burning Plain and Other Stories*, 1967) and the novel *Pedro Páramo* (1955; English translation, 1959). Although he did not stop writing, he never published again, except for a few screenplays.

Rūmī, Jalāl al-Dīn

aka: Maulānā
b. c. Sept. 30, 1207
Balkh (now in Afghanistan)
d. Dec. 17, 1273
Konya, Asia Minor (now Turkey)
fields: Literature, Philosophy, Religion and Theology

Jalāl al-Dīn Rūmī was the eponymous founder of the Maulawiyah Sufi order and an extraordinarily prolific poet, best known for his *Mathnavî*, arguably the most important single work in Persian literature. Massive in scope (26,000 verses), it focuses on the longing of the soul for its beloved and the loss of self in a love for God so absolute that only God exists, emphasizing the cycle of the origination of all things from God and their return through extinguishing the self. Rūmī frequently reworked traditional stories or used metaphors of intoxication and/or human love. After his death, Sultan Walad organized the Mevlevî order of Sufis, in which dancing in circles is an important spiritual exercise. These "whirling dervishes" have been a significant popular, devotional alternative to more legalistic Islamic orthopraxy, and Rūmī's tomb remains a focus of popular religion and pilgrimage.

Rundstedt, Gerd von

full: Karl Rudolf Gerd von Rundstedt
b. December 12, 1875
Aschersleben, Germany
d. February 24, 1953
Hannover, West Germany
fields: Military Affairs

Rundstedt, though not an innovator, supported Manstein's revolutionary strategy, which led to victory over France in 1940. He did not participate in anti-Hitler conspiracies, though he disliked the Nazis and Hitler in particular. Prussian military honor and obedience guided his professional and personal life.

RuPaul

né: Rupaul Andre Charles
b. November 17, 1960
San Diego, Calif.
fields: Music, Theater and Entertainment, Film (singer and entertainer)

African American singer and entertainer. Drag persona RuPaul began appearing on stage in New York City in 1984; released debut album *Supermodel of the World* (1993), featuring the hit singles "Supermodel (You Better Work)" and "Back to My Roots"; in 1993, recorded "Don't Go Breaking My Heart" with Elton John for the British performer's *Duets* album and sang on the soundtrack for the film *Addams Family Values*; non-drag queen acting credits include *Crooklyn* (1995) and a made-for-television film *A Mother's Prayer* (1995); published *Lettin It All Hang Out: An Autobiography* (1995); became the first cross-dresser contracted to represent a major cosmetics company.

Ruppin, Arthur

b. 1876
Germany
d. 1943
Jerusalem, Palestine
fields: Scholarship

Arthur Ruppin was a scholar who helped establish the concept of Jewish studies in the United States; served as official in and adviser to many Zionist agencies; began teaching a course in sociology of the Jews in 1926 at Hebrew University; wrote *Die Juden der Gegenwart* (1904); *Die Soziologie der Juden* (1930-1931).

Rurik

b. Ninth century
Scandinavia

d. 879
probably in the vicinity of Novgorod, Russia
fields: Government and Politics, Military Affairs

According to tradition, Rurik established Kiev Rus, the first Russian state, and founded the ruling House of Rurik, which endured until 1598. He is still politically significant, both as the creator of an exemplary nondespotic government and as the inspiration for the controversial Norman Theory, which claims that Russia's very existence as a nation is the result of the political and military activities of Germanic peoples.

Rush, Benjamin

b. January 4, 1746
Byberry, Pennsylvania
d. April 19, 1813
Philadelphia, Pennsylvania
fields: Medicine, Psychiatry and Psychology, Chemistry

In his day, Rush was widely regarded as the most important American physician and professor of medicine; today he is more likely to be remembered as a signer of the Declaration of Independence and an enthusiastic supporter of the Constitution.

Rush, Bobby L.

b. November 23, 1946
Albany, Georgia
fields: Government and Politics; Social Reform

African American politician and radical activist; in 1969, Black Panther Party activist Bobby L. Rush surrendered to Jesse Jackson during an attempt by law enforcement officers to put him under arrest; became a successful businessman and served as associate dean of Daniel Hale Williams University; won a seat as an alderman on the Chicago city council in 1983; was elected as a Democratic house representative for Illinois' First Congressional District in 1992; reelected to Congress in 1998 to his fourth term.

Rush, Christopher

b. 1777
d. 1872
fields: Religion and Theology

African American successor to James Varick, the first bishop (1822) of the New York-based African Methodist Episcopal Zion church; Christopher Rush, who became bishop in 1828, published *A Short Account of the Rise and Progress of the African Episcopal Church in America* (1843); he lost his sight in 1852.

Rush, Otis

b. April 29, 1934
Philadelphia, Miss.
fields: Music (blues guitarist)

African American blues guitarist; Otis Rush, who was one of the first wave of Chicago musicians who rejected the Mississippi Delta tradition and played hard, tough ghetto blues, focused on electric guitar solos and on runs up and down the neck of the guitar; his recorded songs included "All Your Love," "Double Trouble," "Easy Go," "It Takes Time," "Right Place Wrong Time," "Take a Look Behind," and "Three Times a Fool."

Rushdie, Salman

full: Salman Ahmed Rushdie
b. June 19, 1947
Bombay, India
fields: Literature

Salman Rushdie's early novels, *Shame* and *Midnight's Children*, based on his experience as an Anglo-Indian, won him serious critical attention if not a wide readership. Publication of *The Satanic Verses* in 1988 won him generally positive reviews in the West, but the novel was condemned by Iranian Ayatollah Ruhollah Khomeini, who called on Muslims to execute him as a blasphemer. Rushdie lived in hiding under the protection of the British government until after the death of Khomeini and Iran lifted its sanctioning of the fatwa (1998). *The Moor's Last Sigh* (1995) was promptly banned by the government of India, allegedly for its insulting treatment of Hindu beliefs. In 1999, his novel *The Ground Beneath Her Feet* was published.

Rushen, Patrice

b. September 30, 1954
Los Angeles, Calif.
fields: Music (vocalist, film composer, and music director)

African American vocalist, film composer, and music director; Patrice Rushen, the first African American and the first woman to be the musical director of television's Emmy Awards (1991 and 1992), released several albums which produced the hit singles "Haven't You Heard," "Never Gonna Give You Up," "Don't Blame Me," "Remind Me," "Feels So Good," and "Forget Me Nots"; composed the score for the films *Without You I'm Nothing* (1990) and *HollyWOOD Shuffle* (1987).

Rushing, Jimmy

b. August 26, 1903
Oklahoma City, Okla.
d. June 8, 1972
New York, N.Y.
fields: Music (jazz/blues singer)

African American jazz/blues singer; an important member of the Walter Page (late 1920's), Bennie Moten (to 1935), and Count Basie (1935-1950) bands, Jimmy Rushing is remembered for his rough-textured voice, natural exuberance, and great rhythmic sense; "Harvard Blues" (1958) is one of his outstanding recordings; he also recorded with clarinetist Benny Goodman (1958), pianist Duke Ellington (1958 and 1959), and pianist Dave Brubeck (1960).

Rusk, Dean

full: David Dean Rusk
b. February 9, 1909
Cherokee County, Georgia
d. December 20, 1994
Athens, Georgia
fields: Government and Politics

Secretary of state from 1961 to 1969, under both John F. Kennedy and Lyndon B. Johnson. Rusk played an instrumental role in international relations, particularly U.S. involvement in the Vietnam War.

Ruskin, John

b. February 8, 1819
London, England
d. January 20, 1900
Coniston, Lancashire, England
fields: Art, Social Reform

Ruskin was the most influential critic of art and architecture in the nineteenth century, promoting the notion that art had a moral purpose; as a social critic, he worked to undercut notions of laissez-faire economics and utilitarianism, championing the dignity of individual workers and the need for national programs of education and welfare.

Russell, Bertrand

full: Bertrand Arthur William Russell
b. May 18, 1872
Trelleck, Monmouthshire, Wales
d. February 2, 1970
near Penrhyndeudraeth, Wales
fields: Philosophy, Mathematics, Government and Politics

Russell's original work in the areas of logic, mathematics, and the theory of knowledge was complemented by several important volumes of philosophical popularization, and in his later years Russell emerged as a major figure in the peace movement. He won the 1950 Nobel Prize in Literature.

Russell, Bill

full: William Felton Russell
b. February 12, 1934
Monroe, Louisiana
fields: Sports (basketball)

Revolutionizing the strategy of basketball, Russell introduced to the sport a style of play never before used or advocated.

Russell, Henry Norris

b. Oct. 25, 1877
Oyster Bay, New York
d. Feb. 18, 1957
Princeton, New Jersey
fields: Astronomy, Physics

Henry Norris Russell clarified the process of stellar evolution by studying the composition, structure, and dynamics of stars; discovered a fundamental relationship among their size, temperature, and intrinsic brightness.

Russell, Herman

b. December 23, 1930
Atlanta, Ga.
fields: Business and Industry

African American business proprietor and executive; the recipient of *Black Enterprise* magazine's annual achievement award (1978), Herman Russell ran businesses in land development, apartment management, mortgage brokerage, banking, and sports management.

Russell, John

b. August 18, 1792
London, England
d. May 28, 1878
Pembroke Lodge, Richmond Park, England
fields: Government and Politics

One of the leading Whig politicians of the nineteenth century, Russell held cabinet office for all but seven of the years between 1830 and 1866, and was twice prime minister.

Russell, Nipsey

b. October 13, 1923
Atlanta, Ga.
fields: Theater and Entertainment, Film

African American comedian and actor known for his humorous poetry; Nipsey Russell toured as a stand-up comic with Billy Eckstine, made many appearances in nightclubs and on television, and appeared in the 1978 film *The Wiz* as the Tin Man.

Russwurm, John Brown

b. October 1, 1799
Port Antonio, Jamaica
d. June 17, 1851
Liberia
fields: Journalism

African American journalist; John Brown Russwurm founded *Freedom's Journal* (1827-1829), the first black weekly newspaper in the United States; after traveling to the colony of Liberia, Africa, in 1829, he edited the *Liberia Herald* (1830-1835) and served as superintendent of schools, colonial secretary, and as the first black governor of a province in Liberia.

Rustin, Bayard

b. Mar. 17, 1910
West Chester, Pa.
d. Aug. 24, 1987
New York, N.Y.
fields: Civil Rights

Civil rights leader, war-resistance activist, pacifist; Bayard Rustin organized the Young Communist League, 1936-1941; imprisoned as a conscientious objector from 1943 to 1945; worked with James Farmer in the Chicago Committee of Racial Equality, which developed into the Congress of Racial Equality; was a founding member of the Southern Christian Leadership Conference, 1963; served as organizational coordinator of the 1963 March on Washington; was executive director of the A. Philip Randolph Institute, 1964-1979; founded Organization for Black Americans to Support Israel in 1975; consistent supporter of nonviolent change.

Ruth, Babe

né: George Herman Ruth
b. February 6, 1895
Baltimore, Maryland
d. August 16, 1948
New York, New York
fields: Sports (baseball)

A remarkably talented athlete with a great flair for showmanship, Babe Ruth has come to symbolize baseball, the American national pastime.

Rutherford, Ernest

b. August 30, 1871
Spring Grove (later known as Brightwater), near Nelson, New Zealand
d. October 19, 1937
Cambridge, England
fields: Physics

One of the pioneers of the atomic age, Rutherford investigated the nature of the atom and of radioactivity, laying the experimental basis of the new atomic physics. He won the 1908 Nobel Prize in Chemistry.

Rutherford, Joseph Franklin

b. November 8, 1869
near Boonville, Morgan County, Missouri
d. January 8, 1942
San Diego, California
fields: Religion and Theology

Joseph Franklin Rutherford became a both member of the Jehovah's Witness society and its legal counselor in 1906-1907. A decade later he became the organization's second president and began an extensive proselytizing campaign. In 1918 he and seven other Witnesses were arrested and charged with sedition. Found guilty on four counts of sedition, he six others were sentenced to twenty-year terms. After Supreme Court justice Louis Brandeis ordered their release on bail, all seven Witnesses were cleared of judgments on appeal. Rutherford's legal arguments based on the First and Fourteenth amendments were instrumental in strengthening civil liberties in the United States.

Rutledge, John

b. 1739
d. 1800
fields: Law

U.S. Supreme Court justice, 1790-1791; appointed by President Washington. Wrote no opinions and attended no sessions of the Supreme Court. Resigned to become chief justice of the South Carolina Court of Common Pleas. Took the oath to become chief justice in 1795 and presided over one session, where two cases were heard, before he was not confirmed by the Senate.

Rutledge, Wiley Blount, Jr.

b. 1894
d. 1949
fields: Law

U.S. Supreme Court justice, 1943-1949 (died while in office); appointed by President Franklin D. Roosevelt. Significant opinions: *Thomas v. Collins*, 323 U.S. 518 (1944); *In re Yamashita*, 327 U.S. 1 (1946) (dissenting opinion).

Ryan, Thelma Catherine Patricia. *See* Nixon, Pat

Rydberg, Johannes Robert

b. Nov. 8, 1854
Halmstad, Sweden
d. Dec. 28, 1919
Lund, Sweden
fields: Mathematics, Physics

Johannes Robert Rydberg found the fundamental pattern for spectral lines; in 1906, stated for the first time the rule that two, eight, and eighteen elements are found in the first three periods of the periodic table; in 1913, expanded his rule regarding the periodic table to include the rare earths.

Ryle, Gilbert

b. August 19, 1900
Brighton, Sussex, England
d. October 6, 1976
Whitby, North Yorkshire, England
fields: Philosophy, Language and Linguistics

Gilbert Ryle was a leader in the Oxford "ordinary language" movement. Taught at Oxford (1945-1968) and edited the journal

Mind (1948-1971), the premier philosophical journal of Great Britain. Major works: *Philosophical Arguments* (1945), *The Concept of Mind* (1949), *Dilemmas* (1954), *A Rational Animal* (1962), *Plato's Progress* (1966), *The Thinking of Thoughts* (1968).

Ryun, Jim

full: James Ronald Ryun

b. April 29, 1947
Wichita, Kansas

fields: Sports (track and field)

One of the world's greatest middle-distance runners, Jim Ryun in 1964 became the first high school student to break the four-minute mile, and he made the U.S. team for the 1964 Tokyo Olympics. Although outclassed at the Olympics, a year later Ryun beat gold medalist Peter Snell. In 1967, he broke the world record with a time of 3:51.1, a mark that would stand for eight years. He won the 1968 silver medal; in the 1972 Munich games, he was tripped 550 meters from the finish. In 1996, Ryun was elected to Congress as a Republican from the second district of Kansas.

Ryusai. *See* Hiroshige

S

Saavedra Lamas, Carlos

b. November 1, 1878
Buenos Aires, Argentina
d. May 5, 1959
Buenos Aires, Argentina
fields: Diplomacy, Law

Foreign minister of Argentina from 1932 to 1938 and winner of 1936 Nobel Peace Prize. Carlos Saavedra Lamas played instrumental role in the international Chaco Peace Conference, which ended the 1932-1935 Chaco War between Bolivia and Paraguay. Peace treaty was signed in 1938. Awarded Nobel Peace Prize in 1936 for the antiwar pact that he composed in his first year as foreign minister. Wrote several influential books, including books on international law.

Sábato, Ernesto

b. June 24, 1911
Rojas, Argentina
fields: Literature

Argentinean writer. Ernesto Sábato began writing while attending the School of Physical Sciences at the National University of La Plata. His first novel, *El túnel* (1948; *The Outsider*, 1950), became a best-seller and established his international reputation. His other novels include *Sobre héroes y tumbas* (1961; *On Heroes and Tombs*, 1981) and *Abaddón el exterminador* (1974). He has also written several collections of essays, including *Hombres y engranajes* (1951), *Heterodoxia* (1953), *El otro rostro del peronismo* (1956), *El escritor y sus fantasmas* (1963), *Tango: Discusión y clave* (1963), and *Tres aproximaciones a literatura de nuestro tiempo* (1968).

Sabin, Florence

b. November 9, 1871
Central City, Colorado
d. October 3, 1953
Denver, Colorado
fields: Medicine

A graduate of The Johns Hopkins University Medical School, Sabin actually had three careers: teacher of anatomy and histology at Johns Hopkins, researcher at the Rockefeller Institute for Medicine, and volunteer in public health in Colorado.

Sacagawea

aka: Sagagawea
aka: Sakakawea
b. c. 1788
central Idaho
d. December 20, 1812
Fort Manuel, Dakota Territory
fields: Exploration and Colonization

The only woman who accompanied the Lewis and Clark Expedition in exploring much of the territory acquired through the Louisiana Purchase, Sacagawea assisted as guide and interpreter. She was Northern Shoshone.

Sacco, Nicola

né: Ferdinando Sacco
b. April 22, 1891
Torremaggiore, Italy
d. August 23, 1927
Boston, Massachusetts
fields: Law

Along with Bartolomeo Vanzetti, Sacco was charged with a payroll robbery and murder in 1920. Their trial and execution, which led to worldwide protests, are considered examples of political and ethnic bias in the criminal justice system.

Sachs, Nelly

full: Nelly Leonie Sachs
b. December 10, 1891
Berlin, Germany
d. May 12, 1970
Stockholm, Sweden
fields: Literature

Sachs, primarily because of her focus upon the deaths of Europe's six million Jews in World War II and her anguished outcry against this ghastly event, has become known as the poet of the Holocaust. One who escaped Nazi horrors because of last-minute maneuvering on her behalf, Sachs was a witness who had to find a fitting way to commemorate the dead and engender hope despite the horror of the event; incredibly, given the difficulty of the task, Sachs succeeded brilliantly. She won the 1966 Nobel Prize in Literature.

Sadat, Anwar el-

b. December 25, 1918
Mit Abul-Kum, Egypt
d. October 6, 1981
Cairo, Egypt
fields: Government and Politics

Sadat was awarded the Nobel Peace Prize in 1978 for his role in preparing the first permanent peace between Israel and an Arab country (Egypt). Beyond this recognition for his efforts as a statesman, however, there is no doubt that Sadat was an excellent military strategist, a fact that was clearly illustrated in the first stage of the October, 1973, Arab-Israeli War.

Sade, Marquis de

b. June 2, 1740
Paris, France
d. December 2, 1814
Charenton, near Paris, France
fields: Literature, Philosophy

A Provençal aristocrat, Marquis de Sade began a career as an army but was repeatedly arrested for sexual assault, sodomy, and even murder. He was imprisoned in the Bastille from 1777 until the French Revolution. There he wrote his famous *Les 120 journées de Sodome* (published in the 1930's). After his release he wrote plays and novels, including *Justine* (1797), and *La Nouvelle Justine, suivie de l'historie de Juliette* (1797), then entered a second period of imprisonment, from 1801 to the end of his life. Sade's writings have always been controversial for extolling atheism and egoism and for extolling murder as a supreme act of virtue.

Saʿdī

probably né: Mosharrīf al-Dīn ibn Moṣliḥ al-Dīn
b. c. 1200
Shiraz, Iran
d. c. 1291
Shiraz, Iran
fields: Literature

Saʿdī's literary works, particularly his worldly-wise and entertaining classics, *The Orchard* and *The Rose Garden*, have made him one of the leading writers of Iran, where he is fondly known as "Shaykh Saʿdī" or simply "the Shaykh."

Safran, Roald. *See* Hoffmann, Roald

Sagan, Carl

full: Carl Edward Sagan
b. November 9, 1934
Brooklyn, New York
d. December 20, 1996
Seattle, Washington
fields: Astronomy, Education

One of the most well-known scientists in the twentieth century, Sagan had the unique ability to simultaneously conduct significant astronomical and planetary research and make science interesting and accessible to the general public.

Sagittinanda, Turiya. *See* Coltrane, Alice

Sagoyewátha (He Causes Them to Be Awake). *See* Red Jacket

Sahl, Mort

b. May 11, 1927
Montreal, Quebec, Canada
fields: Theater and Entertainment, Film

Comedian Mort Sahl introduced a hipster's view of Cold War politics to San Francisco audiences in 1953 and satirized the House Committee on Un-American Activities. Though never obscene and rarely even acerbic, Sahl was regarded as a dangerous comedian. From 1966 to 1970, he assisted New Orleans district attorney James Garrison's independent investigation of President John F. Kennedy's assassination and consequently lost television appearances and nightclub bookings. In 1994, he returned to the stage in a one-man show.

Sahle Mariam. *See* Menelik II

Saibara, Seito

b. 1861
Izuma, Shikoku, Japan
d. Apr., 1939
Tex.
fields: Government and Politics

Seito Saibara was a member of the Japanese parliament and university president when he left Japan to move to the United States at the beginning of the twentieth century. He went to Texas, where he established a rice-farm colony. The Saibara colony had grown to more than nine hundred acres by 1909. The colony prospered for a time, but Saibara was never able to acquire U.S. citizenship and the Immigration Act of 1924 prevented any more laborers from coming to the United States. In 1924, he and his wife moved to Brazil. In 1927, they returned to Texas.

Saigō Takamori

b. January 23, 1828
Kagoshima, Kyūshū, Japan
d. September 24, 1877
Kagoshima, Kyūshū, Japan
fields: Government and Politics

Saigō's military leadership and political support were instrumental in the events leading to the demise of Japan's last feudal government in 1868, while his championing of samurai ideals, culminating in the failed 1877 Satsuma Rebellion, during the early Meiji reform era earned for him the reputation as one of the last supporters of an honorable but outdated value system he helped destroy.

Saiki, Patricia Hatsue Fukuda

b. May 28, 1930
Hilo, Territory of Hawaii
fields: Government and Politics

U.S. representative and educator Patricia Hatsue Fukuda Saiki became secretary of the Hawaiian Republican Party in 1964 and served as the party's vice chair from 1966 to 1968. She was elected to a seat in the Hawaii state legislature in 1968. In 1974, Saiki won a seat in the state senate and was reelected four years later. She fought for the establishment of a teachers' union and for education and women's rights issues. In 1982, she became chair of the Hawaiian Republican Party. A year later, she was elected to the U.S. House of Representatives. President George Bush appointed her to head the Small Business Administration, a post she held until 1992. Ran, but lost, for governor of Hawaii in 1994.

St. Cyr, Johnny

full: John Alexander St. Cyr
b. April 17, 1890
New Orleans, La.
d. June 17, 1966
Los Angeles, Calif.
fields: Music (Dixieland jazz banjoist and guitarist)

African American early Dixieland jazz banjoist and guitarist; as an ensemble player, Johnny St. Cyr recorded and performed with such famous jazz artists as Joseph "King" Oliver, Louis Armstrong, Earl "Fatha" Hines, and Ferdinand "Jelly Roll" Morton.

St. Denis, Ruth

né: Ruth Emma Hull Dennis
aka: Ruth Dennis
b. January 20, 1879
Somerville, New Jersey
d. July 21, 1968
Hollywood, California
fields: Dance

One of the pioneers of American modern dance, St. Denis helped to popularize the art form in its infancy with exotic and lavish productions based on Asian and religious themes.

Saint-Gaudens, Augustus

b. March 1, 1848
Dublin, Ireland
d. August 3, 1907
Cornish, New Hampshire
fields: Art

Saint-Gaudens' memorial statues of America's greatest men and women are generally regarded as among the most beautiful and inspired examples of late nineteenth century artistic realism.

St. Hill, Shirley Anita. *See* Chisholm, Shirley

St. Jacques, Raymond

né: James Arthur Johnson
b. March 1, 1930
Hartford, Conn.
d. August 27, 1990
Los Angeles, Calif.
fields: Film

African American actor; Raymond St. Jacques's film credits include *The Comedians* (1967; in the role of Concasseur, the sadistic police captain) and *Cotton Comes to Harlem* (1970; as police detective Coffin Ed Johnson); he also appeared in guest roles on numerous television series (1960's and 1970's).

St. John, Henry. *See* Bolingbroke, First Viscount

Saint-Just, Louis de

full: Louis Antoine Léon de Saint-Just
b. August 25, 1767
Decize, France
d. July 28, 1794
Paris, France
fields: Government and Politics

An acute political theorist and insightful orator, Saint-Just dominated the executive councils of the National Convention at a time when internal anarchy and military invasions threatened social order in France.

St. Laurent, Louis

full: Louis Stephen St. Laurent
b. February 1, 1882
Compton, Quebec, Canada
d. July 25, 1973
Quebec City, Quebec, Canada
fields: Government and Politics

Prime minister of Canada from 1948 to 1957. Under prime ministership of Louis St. Laurent, the Trans-Canada Act authorized building of a trans-Canada highway; his government also signed agreement with U.S. for building the St. Lawrence Seaway. Instituted policy of equalization payments, under which financially well-off provinces contribute funds to be given to poorer provinces. Arguments over Trans-Canada Pipeline helped lead to Liberal Party's defeat in 1957.

Sakamoto, James Y.

b. 1903
Seattle, Wash.
d. 1955
Seattle, Wash.
fields: Publishing

James Y. Sakamoto became a boxer in the 1920's. He returned to Seattle where he became founder and publisher of the newspaper the *Japanese American Courier*. He used the paper to exhort Japanese readers to be loyal Americans. He was an influential member of the Japanese American Citizens League and served as the organization's president in 1938. His views reflected the organization's stance of cooperation with the U.S. government and acceptance of Japanese American internment.

Sakata, Harold T.

b. ?
Hawaii

d. July, 1982
Honolulu, Hawaii
fields: Theater and Entertainment, Sports

Harold T. Sakata became a champion weight lifter, capturing a silver medal in the 82.5-kilogram class at the London Olympics of 1948 and several U.S. championships. He also wrestled professionally as "Tosh Togo." In the early 1960's, Harry Saltzman, producer of the James Bond series, and British film director Guy Hamilton discovered Sakata, who cast him as the ruthless bodyguard Oddjob in the James Bond thriller *Goldfinger* (1964). He acted in commercials and television programs such as *Gilligan's Island* (1964-1967) and *Hawaii Five-O* (1968-1980).

Sakharov, Andrei

full: Andrei Dmitrievich Sakharov
b. May 21, 1921
Moscow, U.S.S.R.
d. December 14, 1989
Moscow, U.S.S.R.
fields: Physics, Civil Rights, Social Reform, Government and Politics

Sakharov's work as a scientist and human rights activist made him an important international figure. His scientific work played a key role in the production of the first hydrogen bomb and later in the study of the structure of the universe. His calls for civil rights in the Soviet Union commanded attention and respect throughout the world and earned for him the Nobel Peace Prize in 1975.

Śākyamuni. *See* Buddha

Saladin

full: al-Malik al-Nāṣir Ṣalāḥ al-Dīn aba ʿl-Mussafer Yūsuf ibn Ayyūb ibn Shadi
b. 1138
Tikrīt, Iraq
d. March 4, 1193
Damascus, Syria
fields: Government and Politics, Religion and Theology

Sultan of Egypt and Syria, 1174?-1193. In a period of disunity in the Muslim world, Saladin conquered and unified warring factions. Then, as Sultan of Syria, Saladin defeated King Richard I of England in the Third Crusade and drove the Christian rulers from Jerusalem.

Salas, Floyd

full: Floyd Francis Salas
b. Jan. 24, 1931
Walsenburg, Colo.
fields: Literature

Latino writer. Floyd Salas taught creative writing at several Bay Area colleges in the 1970's. In 1975, he was appointed assistant boxing coach at the University of California, Berkeley. He began teaching creative writing at that university in 1980. Salas's novels—including *Tattoo the Wicked Cross* (1967), *What Now My Love* (1970), *Lay My Body on the Line* (1978), and *State of Emergency* (1994)—view the ugly, marginal, criminal elements of society with a compassionate eye. Salas has also published *Buffalo Nickel: A Memoir* (1992) and *Color of My Living Heart* (1996).

Salazar, Alberto

b. Aug. 7, 1958
Havana, Cuba
fields: Sports (runner)

Latino runner. Alberto Salazar's family moved to the United States in 1960 after the Cuban Revolution. While at the University of Oregon, he won the 1978 National Collegiate Athletic Association and 1979 Amateur Athletic Union cross-country titles. In 1981, Salazar won his first marathon, the New York Marathon, in a record time. He defended the title in each of the next two years. In 1982, he also won the prestigious Boston Marathon.

Salazar, António de Oliveira

b. April 28, 1889
Vimiero, near Santa Comba Dão, Beira Alta province, Portugal
d. July 27, 1970
Lisbon, Portugal
fields: Government and Politics

António de Oliveira Salazar was authoritarian premier of Portugal from 1932 to 1968. His governing ideology was the "New State"-in Portuguese, *Estado Novo*. It strongly emphasized Portuguese nationalism. Widely popular until World War II; increasing dissatisfaction and high levels of emigration after World War II as regime failed to modernize Portuguese society. Education, in particular, remained backward.

Salazar, Rubén

b. Mar. 3, 1928
Ciudad Juárez, Chihuahua, Mexico
d. Aug. 29, 1970
Los Angeles, Calif.
fields: Journalism

Mexican American journalist. Rubén Salazar moved to the United States from Mexico with his family in 1929. He worked at the *El Paso Herald Post* from 1952 to 1954 and later worked at the *Santa Rosa Press Democrat* and the *San Francisco News*. From 1959 until his death in 1970, Salazar worked for the *Los Angeles Times*. He was a war correspondent in 1965 and 1966, then became bureau chief in Mexico City. In 1969, he became a columnist. He also served as news director of the Los Angeles television station KMEX until 1970, when he was hit in the head by a tear gas canister fired by a police officer during rioting surrounding the National Chicano Moratorium on Vietnam.

Salcedo, Manuel María de

b. Apr. 3, 1776
Malaga, Spain
d. Apr. 4, 1813
near San Antonio, Tex.
fields: Warfare and Conquest, Government and Politics

Spanish soldier and administrator. Manuel María de Salcedo was appointed governor of Texas in 1808. During the early years, he returned runaway black slaves to their owners and allowed many American army deserters to settle in Texas. In 1810, Miguel Hidalgo y Costilla began his Mexican revolution. He was defeated, but unrest continued. In early 1813, Salcedo surrendered Texas to rebel forces, which declared Texas to be an independent republic. Salcedo was then assassinated by the rebels.

Salem, Peter

b. 1750
Framingham, Mass.
d. Aug.16, 1816
Framingham, Mass.
fields: Warfare and Conquest

African American revolutionary war hero; because only freed blacks were allowed to serve, Peter Salem was freed so that he could join the Continental army; as a member of the First Massachusetts Regiment, he fought in battles at Lexington and Concord and is identified as the person who fired the shot that killed British General John Pitcairn at Bunker Hill (June 17, 1775); he served in the Continental army until 1783.

Salii, Lazarus Eitaro

b. Nov. 17, 1936
Anaguar, Palau, now the Republic of Belau
d. Aug. 20, 1988
Koror, Belau
fields: Government and Politics

Lazarus Eitaro Salii earned a degree in government from the University of Hawaii in 1961, then began a career in public service to his home country, a United Nations trust territory administered by the United States. Salii represented Palau in the newly formed Congress of Micronesia in 1964. He chaired the Future Political Status Commission in its negotiations with the United States from 1969 until 1979. He created a policy of "free association," which established Micronesian self-rule in domestic matters and continued U.S. control of military and foreign affairs. In 1981, Palau became the Republic of Belau, and Salii was elected president in 1985. In 1987, Salii admitted accepting a bribe, and in 1988, after the U.S. government announced plans to investigate allegations of corruption in Belau, Salii was found dead from a self-inflicted gunshot wound to the head.

Salimbene

né: Balian de Adam
b. October 9, 1221
Parma, Italy
d. c. 1290
Montefalcone, Italy
fields: Literature

A wandering Franciscan friar, priest, preacher, and writer, Salimbene met and wrote about the most important figures of his age—popes, emperors, kings, and prelates—as well as ordinary people and their daily lives.

Salinas, Baruj

b. July 6, 1935
Havana, Cuba
fields: Art

Latino artist. After moving to the United States, Baruj Salinas earned a bachelor's degree in architecture at Kent State University in Ohio in 1958. He became an American citizen in 1965. Salinas has had solo exhibits in various Latin American countries, across the United States, and in Canada, Spain, France, Switzerland, and, in 1976, Israel. In 1969, he won a Cintas Foundation Fellowship. Salinas, who is Jewish, was commissioned by the Sephardi School to paint a mural in Mexico's Federal District.

Salinas, Porfirio, Jr.

b. 1912
near Bastrop, Tex.
d. Apr. 18, 1973
fields: Art

Latino artist. Porfirio Salinas, Jr., who is known for painting Texas landscapes and bullfight scenes, was one of the first Mexican American artists to have work shown in the White House. At one time, five of his paintings were displayed there. He was President Lyndon Johnson's favorite painter.

Salinger, J. D.

full: Jerome David Salinger
b. January 1, 1919
New York, New York
fields: Literature

Although Salinger wrote only one novel and thirty-five stories, he attained a degree of international recognition and popularity that is unequaled by most twentieth century American authors.

Salisbury, first earl of

né: Robert Cecil
b. June 1, 1563
Westminster, England
d. May 24, 1612
Marlborough, Wiltshire, England
fields: Government and Politics, Diplomacy

As the principal secretary to both Queen Elizabeth and King James I, Cecil managed Parliament, supervised the peaceful transition from Tudor to Stuart rule, and negotiated a peace treaty with Spain.

Salisbury, third marquess of

né: Robert Cecil
full: Robert Arthur Talbot Gascoyne-Cecil
b. February 3, 1830
Hatfield, Hertfordshire, England
d. August 22, 1903
Hatfield, Hertfordshire, England
fields: Government and Politics

Serving as prime minister three times and foreign secretary four times, Salisbury guided Great Britain's domestic and foreign policies during the last quarter of the nineteenth century with a steady and firm hand.

Salk, Jonas

full: Jonas Edward Salk
b. October 28, 1914
New York, New York
d. June 23, 1995
La Jolla, California
fields: Medicine

Salk developed the first effective vaccine for polio, and he marshaled the nation's resources to help eradicate the disease.

Sallust

né: Gaius Sallustius Crispus
b. October 1, 86 B.C.E.
Amiternum (modern San Vittorino), Italy
d. 35 B.C.E.
probably Rome
fields: Historiography

Sallust's most important accomplishments were influential works of history composed after his retirement from a checkered political career. The tone, style, and subject matter of his writings reflect the perils and disenchantments of his earlier career.

Samaniegos, Ramón. *See* Novarro, Ramón

Samkara

aka: Shankara
aka: Śaṅkara
b. 788
Kaladi (now in Kerala, India)
d. 820
Himalayas
fields: Philosophy, Religion and Theology

Samkara was the greatest teacher and commentator of Advaita Vedanta Hinduism, a religious and philosophical tradition based on a nondualist, monistic reading of the Hindu sacred texts, the Upanishads. This perspective has been the dominant reading of these writings among Brahman teachers and a widely accepted perspective among Hindu philosophers. Founded monasteries at the four corners of India. Author of commentaries on the Bhaghavad Gita and the Upanishads; the *Vivekachudamani* (*The Crest Jewel of Wisdom*) is attributed to him.

Samora, Julian

b. Mar. 1, 1920
Pagosa Springs, Colo.
d. Feb. 2, 1996
Albuquerque, N. Mex.
fields: Sociology

Latino sociologist. Julian Samora taught at the University of Notre Dame from 1959 until 1985, when he was named professor emeritus. He wrote many important books, including *La Raza: Forgotten Americans* (1966), *Los Mojados: The Wetback Story* (1971), *A History of the Mexican-American People* (1977), and *Gunpowder Justice: A Reassessment of the Texas Rangers* (1979). He worked with the U.S. Commission on Civil Rights, the National Institute on Mental Health, and the President's Commission on Rural Poverty. He served as editor of the journals *Nuestro* and *International Migration Review*, directed the Mexican Border Studies Project at the University of Notre Dame, and won the 1979 La Raza Award from the National Council of La Raza.

Samoset

b. c. 1590
d. c. 1653
fields: Government and Politics, Native American Affairs

Native American leader. A Pemaquid (Abenaki), Samoset in 1621 was the first Indian to greet the Plymouth Pilgrims. He and the Wampanoag chief, Massasoit, had been clandestinely observing the Pilgrims since their arrival on Wampanoag land three months before. In 1625, Samoset and another Pemaquid Indian, Unongoit, signed the first deed between the British and the Indians for the sale of Pemaquid lands, thereby initiating the Plymouth practice of purchasing Indian lands.

Sampson, Edgar Melvin

aka: The Lamb
b. August 31, 1907
New York, N.Y.
d. January 16, 1973
Englewood, N.J.

fields: Music (saxophone and violin player, arranger, and composer)

African American saxophone and violin player, arranger, and composer; Edgar Melvin Sampson played in the bands of such notables as Duke Ellington, Arthur Gibbs, Charlie Johnson, Fletcher Henderson, and Chick Webb before leaving to work as a freelance arranger for such talent as Artie Shaw, Red Norvo, and Benny Goodman; from 1949 to 1951 Sampson led his own band in New York City; in the 1950's he arranged for several Latin bands, including that of Tito Puente.

Sampson, Edith

b. October 13, 1901
Pittsburgh, Pa.
d. 1979
fields: Law, Diplomacy

African American judge and diplomat; in 1947 Edith Sampson was appointed Illinois assistant state' attorney; she served as a Chicago municipal Court judge then went on to become the first African American woman to be elected as a judge (1964); she served as an associate judge of the Circuit Court of Cook County; in the field of diplomacy, Sampson was the first African American appointed a member of the U.S. delegation to the United Nations (1950).

Samuel

b. c. 1090 B.C.E.
Ramathaim-Zophim (or Ramah)
d. c. 1020 B.C.E.
Ramah
fields: Religion and Theology, Government and Politics

Though famed as a priest and prophet, Samuel is chiefly remembered as the instrument by which the monarchy was established in Israel.

Sánchez, George Isidore

b. Oct. 4, 1906
Barela, N.Mex.
d. Apr. 5, 1972
Austin, Tex.
fields: Education

Mexican American educator. After earning his doctorate in educational administration from the University of California, Berkeley, in 1934, George Isidore Sánchez worked for the New Mexico State Department of Education (1930-1935) and for Venezuela's Ministry of Education. He also served as president of the League of United Latin American Citizens (1941-1942). Sánchez began teaching in 1940 and spent most of his career at the University of Texas at Austin, where he taught Latin American education. He wrote many books on education and other topics, including *The Forgotten People: A Study of New Mexicans* (1940).

Sánchez, Luis Rafael

b. Nov. 17, 1936
Humacao, Puerto Rico
fields: Literature

Puerto Rican writer. Luis Rafael Sánchez began his writing career as a playwright. His plays include *La espera* (pr. 1959), *O casi el alma* (pr. 1964, pb. 1965), and *La pasión según Antígona Pérez* (pr., pb. 1968). He published *En cuerpo de camisa*, a collection of short stories, in 1966. Sánchez also wrote the novel *La guaracha del Macho Camacho* (1976; *Macho Camacho's Beat*, 1980).

Sánchez, Phillip Victor

b. July 29, 1929
Pinedale, Calif.
fields: Diplomacy, Publishing

Latino diplomat and publisher. Phillip Victor Sánchez worked in the U.S. Office of Economic Opportunity, first as assistant director (1971), then as director (1972). He served as ambassador to Honduras from 1973 to 1976, ambassador to Colombia until 1977, and vice president of the Pan American Bank from 1978 to 1982. Sanchez then became president of Woodside Industries. In 1987, he became publisher of *Noticias del Mundo* and the *New York City Tribune*. In 1990, he became vice president of New World Communications.

Sanchez, Poncho

full: Ildefonso Sanchez
b. Oct. 30, 1951
Laredo, Tex.
fields: Music (conga jazz drummer and bandleader)

Conga jazz drummer and bandleader. Poncho Sanchez started to play jazz with vibraphonist Cal Tjader in 1972. In 1980, he formed the Poncho Sanchez Latin Jazz Band, which mixed elements of Latin jazz, salsa, rhythm and blues, and pop music. He drew national and international attention after recording several albums for the Concord Jazz label. In 1980, he won his first Grammy, for the album *La Onda Va Bien*. Sanchez was honored with the Goodwill Ambassador Award in 1987 for his humanitarian efforts.

Sánchez, Ricardo

b. Mar. 29, 1941
El Paso, Tex.
fields: Literature

Latino poet. Ricardo Sánchez taught at the University of Massachusetts, Amherst, then directed the Itinerant Migrant Health Project in Denver, Colorado. He wrote while serving time in the U.S. Army and in prison, and, by 1971, he had published a volume of poetry, *Obras*, and founded a Chicano publishing house. He has written several volumes of poetry, including *Canto y grito mi liberación* (1971; expanded bilingual edition, 1973), *Hechizopspells* (1976), *Milhuas Blues and gritos norteños* (1978), *Brown Bear Honey Madness: Alaskan Cruising Poems* (1981), *Amsterdam Cantos y Poemas Pistos* (1983), and *Eagle-Visioned/ Feathered Adobes* (1990).

Sánchez, Robert Fortune

b. Mar. 20, 1934
Socorro, N.Mex.
fields: Religion and Theology, Education

Catholic archbishop and educator. Robert Fortune Sánchez was ordained to the priesthood in 1959. He taught high school in Albuquerque, New Mexico, and served as a pastor of two parishes. He was elected president of the archdiocesan Priests' Senate in 1973. In 1974, Sánchez became the first Mexican American archbishop and the highest-ranking American-born Latino to serve in the Catholic church when Pope Paul VI appointed him archbishop of the Santa Fe archdiocese. Sánchez later celebrated the first Mass to be delivered in three languages: English, Spanish, and Tewa.

Sánchez, Rosaura

b. Dec. 6, 1941
San Angelo, Tex.
fields: Education

Latina Educator. In 1972, Rosaura Sánchez became an assistant professor at the University of California, San Diego. In 1979, she became an associate professor. She served as chair of the National Council on Chicano Sociolinguistic Research. She has written on such topics as code switching and bilingualism in higher education. Among her publications is *Chicano Discourse: Socio-Historic Perspectives* (1983).

Sanchez, Sonia

né: Wilsonia Benita Driver
b. September 9, 1934
Birmingham, Alabama
fields: Literature

An African American poet of the 1960's Black Arts movement, Sonia Sanchez used black English, colloquial terminology, and dramatization of personal situations to capture her anger on behalf of the African American community. Her works include *Homecoming* (1969), *We a BaddDDD People* (1970), *It's a New Day: Poems for Young Brothas and Sistuhs* (1971). She also wrote children's books such as *The Adventures of Fathead, Smallhead, and Squarehead* (1973) and *A Sound Investment and Other Stories*

(1980). Her play Sister Son/ji was critical of treatment of women within the black revolutionary movement. Her *homegirls and homegrenades* (1984) received an American Book Award in 1985.

Sánchez Korrol, Virginia

b. ?
New York, N.Y.
fields: Historiography

Latina historian. Virginia Sánchez Korrol earned her Ph.D. from the State University of New York at Stony Brook in 1981. She has taught English in Chicago public high schools and Puerto Rican studies at Brooklyn College, where she chaired her department and helped direct the Center for Latino Studies. Sánchez Korrol also served as a consultant to the New York State Department of Education. She has published several books about Puerto Ricans living on the U.S. mainland, including *The Puerto Rican Struggle: Essays on Survival in the U.S.* (1980) and *From Colonia to Community: The History of Puerto Ricans in New York City, 1917-1948* (1983).

Sánchez Vilella, Roberto

b. Feb. 19, 1913
Mayagüez, Puerto Rico
d. Mar. 25, 1997
fields: Government and Politics

Puerto Rican government official. Roberto Sánchez Vilella helped to found the Popular Democratic Party (Partido Popular Democrático). In the 1940's, he served as administrator of the Transportation Authority, among other governmental administrative posts. In the 1950's, he was the executive secretary of Puerto Rico. In 1960, the Popular Democratic Party elected Sánchez Vilella to make recommendations to a board examining Puerto Rico's electoral structure. He also made recommendations to improve diplomatic relations with the United States. In 1964, he was elected governor. He served one term.

Sand, George

né: Amandine-Aurore-Lucile Dupin
aka: Baronne Dudevant
full: Amandine-Aurore-Lucile Dupin, Baronne Dudevant
b. July 1, 1804
Paris, France
d. June 8, 1876
Nohant, France
fields: Literature

Sand contributed to nineteenth century French literature a prodigious number of important romantic novels, travel writings, and political essays.

Sandage, Allan

full: Allan Rex Sandage
b. June 18, 1926
Iowa City, Iowa
fields: Astronomy

Allan Rex Sandage followed in Edwin Hubble's footsteps, using the 200-inch telescope on Mount Palomar to map the distances to galaxies in order to determine the rate of expansion of the universe and the decrease in that rate over time; in 1960, became the first person to identify a quasar; in 1961, published a paper suggesting that the universe began from a "big bang."

Sandburg, Carl

full: Carl August Sandburg
b. January 6, 1878
Galesburg, Illinois
d. July 22, 1967
Flat Rock, North Carolina
fields: Historiography, Literature

A prolific writer of verse and prose for adults and children, Sandburg extended the poetic techniques of free verse and glorified the American working person as its subject. He also sought to revitalize the biographical format by making it more human.

Sanders, Barry

b. July 16, 1968
Wichita, Kans.
fields: Sports (football player)

African American professional football player; Barry Sanders, one of the most gifted running backs in the history of the National Football League (NFL), won the Heisman Trophy in 1988 while at Oklahoma State University; drafted by the Detroit Lions and named NFL rookie of the year; awarded the Associated Press Offensive Player of the Year Award for 1994; he holds numerous all-time NFL rushing records.

Sanders, Deion

full: Deion Luwynn Sanders
b. August 9, 1967
Fort Myers, Fla.
fields: Sports (football and baseball athlete)

African American professional football and baseball athlete; Deion "Prime Time" Sanders excelled as a two-sport professional; won the Jim Thorpe Award as the nation's best defensive player in college football; drafted by the New York Yankees baseball team in 1988; picked in the 1989 National Football League (NFL) draft by the Atlanta Falcons; released from the Yankees (baseball) in 1990; signed with the Atlanta Braves baseball team in 1991; traded to the Cincinnati Reds (baseball) in 1994; traded to San Francisco Giants (baseball) in 1995, then back to Cincinnati in 1997; joined the NFL's San Francisco 49ers in 1994, helping to lead the team to a Super Bowl victory; signed with the NFL's Dallas Cowboys in 1995 as a star cornerback.

Sanders, Dori

full: Dorinda Sanders
b. c. 1935
near Filbert, S.C.
fields: Literature

African American novelist and farmer; Dori Sanders published her first novel, *Clover*, in 1990, receiving the Lillian Smith Award for Outstanding Writing About the South and the Best Book for Young Adults by the American Library Association; *Her Own Place* was published in 1993.

Sandino, Augusto César

b. May 18, 1895
Niquinohomo, Nicaragua
d. February 21, 1934
Managua, Nicaragua
fields: Government and Politics

Nicaraguan guerrilla leader. Beginning in 1926, Augusto César Sandino led a six-year guerrilla war against Conservative Party Nicaraguan leaders and American forces occupying the country to maintain the status quo. U.S. troops withdrew in 1932 and Sandino ended his campaign, pledging to work with new Nicaraguan government. In February, 1934, Sandino returned to the Nicaraguan capital to help finalize peace talks begun the previous year. Anastasio Somoza García, head of the country's new National Guard, had him shot.

Sandoz, Mari

full: Marie Susette Sandoz
b. May 11, 1896
Sheridan County, Nebraska
d. March 10, 1966
New York, New York
fields: Historiography, Literature

A western regional historian and novelist, Sandoz wrote extensively on frontier family life, white settlement, and American Indian resistance to white encroachment on the Central and Northern Great Plains.

Sands, Diana

b. August 22, 1934
New York, N.Y.
d. September 21, 1973
New York, N.Y.
fields: Theater and Entertainment, Film, Television

African American actress; Diana Sands's stage credits included the Off-Broadway productions of *Major Barbara* (1954), *A Land Beyond the River* (1957), and *The Egg and I* (1958; for which she received an Obie

Award) and the Broadway productions of *A Raisin in the Sun* (1959; her role as Beneatha Younger earned an Outer Circle Critics Award), *Tiger, Tiger, Burning Bright* (1962; received a Theatre World Award), *Blues for Mister Charlie* (1964), *The Owl and the Pussycat* (1964), *Gingham Dog* (1969), and Shakespeare's *Antony and Cleopatra* (1968; as Cleopatra); her film credits included *Ensign Pulver* (1964), *The Landlord* (1970), *Doctors' Wives* (1971), *Willie Dynamite* (1973), and *Honeybaby, Honeybaby* (1974); she made television guest appearances in *East Side/West Side* (1963), *The Nurses* (1964), *I Spy* (1966), *The Fugitive* (1967), and *Julia* (1970-1971); she died at the age of thirty-nine.

Sanford, Edward T.

full: Edward Terry Sanford
b. 1865
d. 1930
fields: Law

U.S. Supreme Court justice, 1923-1930 (died while in office); appointed by President Harding. Held that the First Amendment applied to the states through the due process clause of the Fourteenth Amendment. Significant opinions: *Gitlow v. New York*, 268 U.S. 652 (1925); *Fiske v. Kansas*, 274 U.S. 380 (1927).

Sanford, Isabel

b. August 29, 1917
New York, N.Y.
fields: Television, Film

African American actress; after developing her character of Louise Jefferson on the television sitcom *All in the Family* (1971-1975), Isabel Sanford earned an Emmy (1981) playing the same role on the black situation comedy *The Jeffersons* (1974-1985); her film credits include *Guess Who's Coming to Dinner?* (1967; in the role as the maid).

Sanford, John Elroy. *See* Foxx, Redd

Sanger, Frederick

b. Aug. 13, 1918
Rendcombe, Gloucestershire, England
fields: Chemistry, Genetics

Frederick Sanger determined the complete amino acid sequence of the protein insulin; was instrumental in the development and use of a novel method to sequence deoxyribonucleic acid (DNA); became the first person to receive two Nobel Prizes in Chemistry, in 1958 and 1980.

Sanger, Margaret

né: Margaret Higgins
b. September 14, 1879
Corning, New York
d. September 6, 1966
Tucson, Arizona
fields: Public Health, Social Reform

Through the establishment of low-cost birth control clinics, Sanger made birth control information and contraceptive devices available to American women of all social classes.

San Juan, E., Jr.

full: Epifanio San Juan, Jr.
b. Dec. 29, 1938
Manila, Philippines
fields: Literature

Scholar, critic, and writer E. San Juan, Jr., attracted worldwide renown for his work in comparative cultural studies. San Juan's *Racial Formations/Critical Transformations: Articulations of Power in Ethnic and Racial Studies in the U.S.* (1992) won the National Book Award of the Association for Asian American Studies in 1993. He received a Ph.D. from Harvard University in 1965 and began teaching at the University of Connecticut in 1967, eventually becoming professor of English and Comparative Literature. San Juan was awarded a Fulbright lectureship at the University of the Philippines in 1987-1988 and an honorary fellowship at the University of Edinburgh in 1993.

San Juan, Olga

b. Mar. 16, 1927
Brooklyn, N.Y.
fields: Theater and Entertainment (actor), Film

Latina actor. Olga San Juan established herself as a nightclub entertainer and radio personality in New York City, sometimes billed as "The Puerto Rican Pepper Pot." Her first film was *Rainbow Island* (1944), and she went on to act in such films as *Duffy's Tavern* (1945), *Out of This World* (1945), *Blue Skies* (1946), *Variety Girl* (1947), *One Touch of Venus* (1948), *Are You with It?* (1948), *The Countess of Monte Cristo* (1949), and *The Third Voice* (1960). She also appeared on Broadway in the stage musical *Paint Your Wagon*.

San Martín, José de

full: José Francisco de San Martín
b. February 25, 1778
Yapeyú, La Plata
d. August 17, 1850
Boulogne-sur-Mer, France
fields: Military Affairs

San Martín, against great odds, led the military forces that secured independence from Spain in Argentina, Chile, and Peru.

Sano, Roy

b. June 18, 1931
Brawley, Calif.
fields: Religion and Theology

Japanese American bishop Roy Sano received a M.Div. at Union Theological Seminary and taught at the Pacific School of Religion in Berkeley, California. From 1950 to 1969, he served in various pastoral roles in California and New York City, and from 1884 to 1992, he led the United Methodist Church in the Denver area. In 1992, he became affiliated with church in the Los Angeles area. He wrote the books *From Every Nation Without Number: Racial and Ethnic Diversity in United Methodism* (1982) and *Outside the Gate: A Study of the Epistle to the Hebrews* (1982).

Sanromá, Jesús María

b. Nov. 7, 1902
Carolina, Puerto Rico
d. Oct. 12, 1984
Guaynabo, Puerto Rico
fields: Music (classical pianist)

Puerto Rican classical pianist. From 1926 to 1944, Jesús María Sanromá served as the first official pianist of the Boston Symphony Orchestra. During that time, he established associations with such celebrated musicians as violinist Jascha Heifetz; conductors Serge Koussevitzky, Leonard Bernstein, and Arthur Fiedler; and composers Igor Stravinsky, Paul Hindemith, George Gershwin, and Heitor Villa-Lobos.

Sansovino, Jacopo

né: Jacopo Tatti
b. July 2, 1486
Florence
d. November 27, 1570
Venice
fields: Art, Architecture

Sansovino was the first architect to bring Renaissance classical ideas of architecture into a successful conjunction with the Venetian Byzantine-Gothic style, resulting in buildings in the Piazza San Marco which were to confirm its reputation as one of the greatest architectural developments in the world.

Santa Anna, Antonio López de

b. February 21, 1794
Jalapa, Veracruz, Mexico
d. June 21, 1876
Mexico City, Mexico
fields: Government and Politics, Military Affairs

Santa Anna dominated Mexican life during the first forty years of its independence. While his many presidencies and other power struggles were endemic to his time, he bears the greatest responsibility for the loss of territory to the United States and for retarding the development of political maturity in Mexico.

Santamaría, Mongo

full: Ramón Santamaría
b. Apr. 7, 1922
Havana, Cuba
fields: Music (percussionist, bandleader, and composer)

Cuban percussionist, bandleader, and composer. During the 1950's, Mongo Santamaría played with the *orquestas* of Gilberto Valdés, Pérez Prado, and Tito Puente in New York City. He quickly became a celebrity among Latinos and jazz musicians. In 1955, he recorded *Changó*, the album he considered his best. In California, Santamaría met Latin-jazz vibraphonist Cal Tjader, with whom he made such recordings as *Más Ritmo Caliente* (1957), *Yambú* (1958), *Mongo* (1959), and *Demasiado Caliente* (1960). He also recorded with such musicians as Joe Loco, La Lupe, Charlie Palmieri, Chick Corea, João Donato, and Dizzy Gillespie. By 1995 Santamaría had won two Grammy Awards.

Santana, Carlos

b. July 20, 1947
Autlan de Navarro, Jalisco, Mexico
fields: Music

Mexican American rock musician. Carlos Santana, who began his career by playing guitar in clubs in Tijuana, Mexico, moved to San Francisco in 1962 and four years later founded the band Santana. They played "Soul Sacrifice" at the Woodstock Festival (1969), and the group's first album, *Santana* (1969), immediately followed. Santana's more than thirty albums including *Abraxas* (1970), *Caravanserai* (1972), *Amigos* (1976), and *Viva Santana!*(1988). He is credited with being instrumental in the creation of Latin rock.

Santayana, George

b. Dec. 16, 1863
Madrid, Spain
d. Sept. 26, 1952
Rome, Italy
fields: Philosophy, Literature

George Santayana wrote *The Life of Reason: Or, The Phases of Human Progress* (1905-1906), *Scepticism and Animal Faith* (1923), and *The Realms of Being* (1927-1940). Perhaps best remembered for his aphorism "Those who cannot remember the past are condemned to repeat it."

Santiago, Benito

full: Benito Santiago y Rivera
b. Mar. 9, 1965
Ponce, Puerto Rico
fields: Sports (baseball player)

Puerto Rican baseball player. Catcher Benito Santiago made his major league debut with the San Diego Padres in 1986. He won the 1987 National League Rookie of the Year Award and also set a major league rookie record with a 34-game hitting streak. He won three consecutive Gold Glove Awards beginning in 1988 and was selected to the National League All-Star Team for four consecutive seasons beginning in 1989. He signed as a free agent with the Florida Marlins for the 1993 season. After playing for Florida through the 1994 season, Santiago played for various teams including the Toronto Blue Jays and the Chicago Cubs.

Santiago, Isaura

b. Jan. 19, 1946
Brooklyn, N.Y.
fields: Education

Educator and administrator. In 1969, Isaura Santiago earned her master's degree in education from Brooklyn College. In 1972, she began teaching elementary education at the City University of New York, eventually developing a graduate bilingual education program. While working on her doctorate, she became involved in *Aspira of New York v. Board of Education of the City of New York*, a legal case that concerned rights of non-English-speaking children within the city's school system. Her dissertation, which documented the case, was published in 1977 as *Aspira Versus Board of Education of the City of New York: A History*. In 1979, Santiago began teaching at Columbia University, where she served until she became president of Hostos Community College.

Santiesteban, Tati

full: Humberto Santiesteban
b. Nov. 3, 1943
El Paso, Tex.
fields: Government and Politics

Latino public official. In 1962, Tati Santiesteban earned his LL.B. from the University of Texas Law School. He was elected to serve in the Texas House of Representatives from 1967 to 1972 and then went on to serve in the Texas State Senate.

Santorio, Santorio

aka: Sanctorius Sanctorius
b. March 29, 1561
Capodistria, Venice
d. February 22 or March 6, 1636
Venice
fields: Medicine

Santorio was in the vanguard of innovators in the late sixteenth and early seventeenth centuries in physiology, applied medicine, and medical instruments. By quantitative experimentation, he encouraged the use of mathematics and experimentation as analytical tools in the study of physiology and pathology. He also worked against the strong cult of astrology in Italy, which had blocked progress in the advancement of medicine for centuries.

Santos, Beinvenido N.

b. Mar. 22, 1911
Manila, Philippines
fields: Literature

Filipino American writer; Beinvenido N. Santos' books, short stories, and novels deal with the cultural difficulties of Filipinos who are unable to fully recover their culture because of contact with the United States; novels include *Villa Magdalena* (1965), *The Praying Man* (1982), *What the Hell for You Left Your Heart in San Francisco* (1987); short-story collections include *You Lovely People* (1955), *Brother My Brother* (1960), *Scent of Apples: A Collection of Stories* (1979), and *Dwell in the Wilderness* (1985); poetry volumes include *The Wounded Stag* (1956) and *Distance in Time* (1983).

Santos-Dumont, Alberto

b. July 20, 1873
Palmira, Brazil
d. July 24, 1932
Guarujá, Brazil
fields: Aviation and Space Exploration, Invention and Technology

Santos-Dumont, a leading European aviator during the period of early development of manned flight, is recognized as an inventor and innovative designer in both major categories of flight: lighter than air (airships) and heavier than air (airplanes). Working with semirigid airships, he adapted the internal-combustion engine as a source of power for lighter-than-air vehicles, and he was the first to design, build, and fly a heavier-than-air machine in Europe. Two of the airplanes he designed and built played a major role in the development of European aviation.

Sanzio, Raffaello. *See* Raphael

Sappho

b. c. 612 B.C.E.
Mytilene or Eresus, Lesbos, Asia Minor
d. c. 580 B.C.E.
probably Mytilene, Lesbos, Asia Minor
fields: Literature

Regarded by ancient commentators as the equal of Homer, Sappho has poetically expressed the human emotions with honesty, courage, and skill.

Sar, Saloth. *See* Pol Pot

Saragossa, La

né: Maria Agustina Saragossa y Domenech
aka: Maria Agustina
b. 1786
Tortosa, Catalonia, Spain
d. 1857
Saragossa, Spain
fields: Military Affairs

By her legendary act of courage during the French siege of Saragossa, Maria Agustina (La Saragossa) symbolized Spanish resistance to Napoleon's forces during a crucial period of invasion in the Peninsular War.

Sardiñas, Eligio

aka: Kid Chocolate
b. Oct. 28, 1910
Havana, Cuba
d. Aug. 8, 1988
Miami, Fla.
fields: Sports (boxer)

Latino boxer. Eligio Sardiñas, known as "Kid Chocolate," won his first junior lightweight title in July of 1931. In October of 1932, he also won the featherweight title. Sardiñas lost the junior lightweight title in December, 1933, and lost the featherweight title in February, 1934. He retired in 1938 with a 132-10-6 record and 50 knockouts. In 1959, he was inducted into the Boxing Hall of Fame.

Sarduy, Severo

b. Feb. 25, 1937
Camagüey, Cuba
d. August, 1993
France
fields: Literature

Latino novelist. Severo Sarduy began publishing poetry, short stories, and art criticism while working in an advertising agency in Havana. In 1959, he moved to Paris with a scholarship from the Cuban government to study art history and eventually became a citizen of France. Among the novels he wrote were *Gestos* (1963), *De donde son los cantantes* (1967; "From Cuba with a Song," in *Triple Cross*, 1972), *Cobra* (1972; English translation, 1975), *Maitreya* (1978; English translation, 1987), and *Colibrí* (1984). He also wrote several books of essays and poetry.

Sargent, Frank Pearce

b. Nov. 18, 1854
East Orange, Vt.
d. Sept. 4, 1908
Washington, D.C.
fields: Government and Politics

Frank Pearce Sargent, commissioner-general of the U.S. Bureau of Immigration from 1902 to 1908, campaigned vehemently for restrictions and controls curtailing immigration from Southern Europe and Asia. In 1881, he was initiated into the Brotherhood of Locomotive Firemen, thus beginning his long career in the American labor movement. As commissioner-general, Sargent strongly enforced the Chinese exclusion laws, prevented the illegal migration of Chinese from Mexico and Canada, and encouraged immigration officials to harass and abuse the Chinese in the United States, wrongly arresting or deporting many Chinese.

Sargent, John Singer

b. January 12, 1856
Florence, Italy
d. April 15, 1925
London, England
fields: Art

Sargent was renowned for his magnificent portraiture, which earned for him a reputation as a modern Van Dyck.

Sargon II

b. Second half of eighth century B.C.E.
Assyria
d. 705 B.C.E.
north of Assyrian empire
fields: Warfare and Conquest, Government and Politics

Through incessant, successful warfare and widespread resettlement of conquered populations, Sargon II brought an embattled Assyria to a late zenith of power and reshaped the structure of its empire; the dynasty he founded would last until the fall of Assyria.

Sarkisian, Cherilyn. *See* Cher

Saro-Wiwa, Ken

b. October 10, 1941
Bori, Rivers State, Nigeria
d. November 10, 1995
Port Harcourt, Nigeria
fields: Literature, Conservation and Environmentalism

Ken Saro-Wiwa was a Nigerian author and environmentalist who was executed for his outspoken opposition to oil extraction in eastern Nigeria. His writings include children's books, poetry and short story collections, and his last book, *A Month and a Day: A Detention Diary*. In 1990 he helped found the Movement for the Survival of the Ogoni People (MOSOP), claiming that oil revenue from eastern Nigeria's Ogoniland was enriching the Nigerian elite, while Ogoniland was being ruined by pollution. He was later arrested for allegedly obstructing electoral politics and was hanged.

Sarraute, Nathalie

né: Nathalie Tcherniak
b. July 18, 1900
Ivanovo-Voznessensk, Russia
fields: Literature

Sarraute is often called the mother of the French New Novel. The New Novel rejected nineteenth century novelistic concerns of character and plot and changed the face of French literature. After a thirty-year career of novel writing, Sarraute began playwriting and found new success on the Parisian stage.

Sartre, Jean-Paul

b. June 21, 1905
Paris, France
d. April 15, 1980
Paris, France
fields: Philosophy, Literature, Social Reform

A powerhouse of intellectual energy, French existentialist Sartre poured out novels, plays, screenplays, biographies, criticism, political essays, and philosophy. Journalist, teacher, and perennial activist, he served in the first rank of worldwide liberal causes. He won the 1964 Nobel Prize in Literature.

Sassacus

b. c. 1560
near Groton, Conn.
d. c. July, 1637
N.Y.
fields: Warfare and Conquest, Government and Politics, Native American Affairs

Native American leader. Sassacus was the principal Pequot sachem when the tribe was virtually destroyed in war with the English during 1636-1637. His short period as sachem was marked by continuing conflict with the Narragansetts to the east, a war with the English, and the secession of many dissatisfied Pequots, including Uncas. His forces devastated in 1937, Sassacus journeyed west to the Mohawk country in a desperate attempt to win military support from the Mohawks, the Pequots' traditional enemies. Instead, the Mohawks killed Sassacus and his men and sent Sassacus's scalp to the English.

Sassen, Saskia

b. Jan. 5, 1945
The Hague, The Netherlands
fields: Education

Saskia Sassen taught at the City University of New York and Queens College and Graduate School before becoming a professor at the Columbia University Graduate School of Architecture in 1985. She served as the school's director of urban planning (1987-1990), chair of the division of urban planning (1988-1990), and director of Ph.D. program beginning in 1989. She served as a member of the Ford Foundation Hispanic Research

Task Force (1983-1985) and was part of the Stanford University Project on U.S.-Mexico Relations (1984-1986). her books include *Exporting Capital and Importing Labor: The Role of Caribbean Immigration to New York City* (1981), *The Mobility of Labor and Capital: A Study in International Investment and Labor Flow* (1988), and *The Global City* (1991).

Sastaretsi. *See* Adario

Satanta
aka: Guaton-bain (Big Ribs)
b. c. 1830
d. Oct. 11, 1878
Huntsville, Tex.
fields: Government and Politics, Native American Affairs

Kiowa. Satanta was one of the major Kiowa leaders to sign the Medicine Lodge Treaty of 1867; later, he led raids against whites. In 1874, the Kiowa, joined by the Comanche, Cheyenne, and Arapaho, went to war against the whites to protect the remaining buffalo herds from slaughter.

Satcher, David
b. March 2, 1941
Anniston, Ala.
fields: Medicine (physician)

African American physician; a highly respected medical professional, David Satcher came to national attention in 1994, when he became the first African American director of the Centers for Disease Control and Prevention (CDC), an Atlanta-based federal agency; also served as an adviser to Hillary Rodham Clinton's task force on health care reform.

Satie, Erik
b. May 17, 1866
Honfleur, France
d. July 1, 1925
Paris, France
fields: Music

Satie was a unique figure in French music at the beginning of the twentieth century. In the 1890's he played an important role in turning French music away from the influence of nineteenth century German Romanticism. During and after World War I, he was the major composer of the French avant-garde; he turned away from Impressionism, in which he never really took part, and prefigured the neoclassicism of the 1940's and 1950's.

Sato, Eisaku
b. March 27, 1901
Tabuse, Japan
d. June 2, 1975
Tokyo, Japan
fields: Government and Politics

Satō served consecutively as Prime Minister of Japan longer than any other individual. He is the only modern Japanese politician to expand the country permanently. One of the founders of the Liberal-Democratic Party, he not only followed its traditional probusiness policy but also tripled the per capita income of the Japanese. In 1974, he became the first Asian to receive the Nobel Peace Prize.

Sato, Eunice N.
b. June 8, 1921
Livingston, Calif.
fields: Government and Politics, Education

Eunice N. Sato earned an M.A. from Columbia University in 1958 before becoming an educational missionary in Japan from 1948 to 1951. She was a member of the Long Beach, California, city council (1975-1986) and then served as mayor (1980-1982). Sato was president of the American Red Cross and the National Conference of Christians and Jews.

Satow, Masao
b. February 14, 1908
San Mateo, Calif.
d. March 3, 1977
fields: Government and Politics

National director of the Japanese American Citizens League (JACL). A Nisei, Massa Satow, became active in the JACL in the 1930's. Following his release from the Japanese American internment camp Granada in 1942, he gained a national position with the Young Men's Christian Association and in 1946 became national secretary—and subsequently director—of the JACL until 1973.

Saud, Sulaimon. *See* Tyner, McCoy

Saund, Dalip Singh
b. Sept. 20, 1899
Chhajalwadi, near Amritsar, India
d. Apr. 23, 1973
Hollywood, Calif.
fields: Government and Politics

Politician; Dalip Singh Saund came to the United States in 1920; after earning a Ph.D. in mathematics, raised produce in California; wrote memoir, *My Mother India* (1930); organized the Indian Association of America (1942); went to Washington, D.C., to fight laws denying citizenship to Indian immigrants; naturalized in 1946; first mainland Asian immigrant to win a seat in the U.S. House of Representatives (Democrat, California), 1957-1963; appointed to the House Committee on Foreign Relations.

Saunders, Raymond
b. October 28, 1934
Pittsburgh, Pa.
fields: Art (painter)

African American painter; Raymond Saunders's work can be found in the collections of many museums in the United States, Mexico, and Europe including the Whitney Museum of American Art and the Pennsylvania Academy of Fine Arts; among the awards received by Saunders are the Prix de Rome, a Guggenheim award, and a National Endowment for the Arts award.

Saunders, Richard
b. 1922
Bermuda
d. 1987
fields: Photography

African American photographer; with a background working as a portrait and wedding photographer in Bermuda, Richard Saunders moved to the U.S. in 1947 and obtained work as a photographer for such magazines as *Life, Look, Ebony*, and *Fortune*; he went on to become international editor for *Topic*, a magazine published by the U.S. Information Service for distribution in Africa.

Saussure, Ferdinand de
b. November 26, 1857
Geneva, Switzerland
d. February 22, 1913
Vufflens, near Geneva, Switzerland
fields: Language and Linguistics

Primarily through a book written by colleagues after his death, Saussure established the foundations of twentieth century linguistics. His focus on the systematic structure of language is the fundamental principle of structuralism in linguistics, anthropology, and literary criticism, and he provided the theoretical basis of semiology—the study of signs.

Saussure, Horace Bénédict de
b. Feb. 17, 1740
Conches, near Geneva, Switzerland
d. Jan. 22, 1799
Geneva, Switzerland
fields: Botany, Science

Horace Bénédict de Saussure was a leading researcher of the structure and physical environment of mountains; in 1771-1773, toured Mount Vesuvius and climbed Mount Etna; in 1787, climbed to the summit of Mont Blanc and carried out scientific measurements there.

Sauts (Bat). *See* Roman Nose

Sauvé, Jeanne
né: Jeanne Mathilde Benoît

b. April 26, 1922
Prud'Homme, Saskatchewan, Canada
d. January 26, 1993
Montreal, Quebec, Canada
fields: Government and Politics

As Canada's first female governor-general, Sauvé was a pioneer for women and for French-Canadians.

Savage, Augusta

né: Augusta Christine Fells
b. February 29, 1892
Green Cove Springs, Florida
d. March 26, 1962
New York, New York
fields: Art

A black sculptor, Augusta Savage earned a reputation as an inspiring and devoted teacher. A central figure in the Harlem Renaissance, especially in the 1930's, Savage became nationally known when she courageously exposed racial discrimination.

Savage, Gus

full: Augustus F. Savage
b. October 30, 1925
Detroit, Mich.
fields: Government and Politics

African American U.S. representative from Illinois; as Illinois' Second Congressional District representative (1981-1992), Gus Savage served on and then chaired the House Committee on Public Works and Transportation; he also served on the House Subcommittee on Economic Development and the House Committee on Small Business.

Savigny, Friedrich Karl von

b. February 21, 1779
Frankfurt am Main
d. October 25, 1861
Berlin, Prussia
fields: Law

Savigny was a leading historian of Roman law. In the field of legal philosophy, he is considered generally to be either the founder or the leading exponent of the so-called historical or Romantic school of jurisprudence, which means that the content of a given body of law can only be understood through a process of historical research.

Savitzky, Bella. *See* Abzug, Bella

Savonarola, Girolamo

b. September 21, 1452
Ferrara
d. May 23, 1498
Florence
fields: Religion and Theology, Government and Politics

Savonarola set in motion the greatest religious revival of his day, turning a materialistic and worldly city into a democratic theocracy. He inspired many Florentines with a new, simple faith. He began the tide of Reformation soon to sweep over Europe.

Sawyer, Eugene

b. September 4, 1934
Greensboro, Ala.
fields: Government and Politics

African American mayor of Chicago, Ill; Eugene Sawyer served as the second African American mayor of Chicago from late 1987 through April of 1991.

Saxo Grammaticus

b. c. 1150
probably Zealand, Denmark
d. c. 1220
place unknown
fields: Historiography, Literature

Saxo Grammaticus, who wrote one of the earliest chronicles of Danish legend and history, was Denmark's most prominent medieval scholar. The only great writer of Latin prose in Denmark before the Reformation, and acclaimed as that country's first national historian, Saxo is the most important source of information about early Danish literature and history.

Saxton, Alexander P.

full: Alexander Plaisted Saxton
b. July 16, 1919
Great Barrington, Mass.
fields: Historiography

Alexander P. Saxton, who received a Ph.D. degree from the University of California, Berkeley in 1967, was professor of history at the University of California, Los Angeles, until he retired in 1991. He was awarded a National Endowment for the Humanities Fellowship and wrote *The Indispensable Enemy: Labor and the Anti-Chinese Movement in California* (1971).

Say, Allen

b. August 28, 1937
Yokohama, Japan
fields: Literature

Allen Say is a prizewinning writer and illustrator of books for children and young adults who received the Caldecott Award for his book *Grandfather's Journey* (1993). Say spent his childhood in Japan and is the son of a Korean father and a Japanese American mother. He first came to the United States in the early 1950's and spent most of his life since then in that country. His other works include *The Ink-Keeper's Apprentice* (1979), *El Chino* (1990), and *Tree of Cranes* (1991).

Sayers, Gale Eugene

b. May 30, 1943
Wichita, Kans.
fields: Sports (football player)

African American football player; twice voted All-American as a halfback for the University of Kansas, Gale Eugene Sayers played for the Chicago Bears as a running back from 1965 to 1971; during his seven-year professional career Sayers carried 991 times for 4,956 yards and scored fifty-six touchdowns, was named Rookie of the Year, was voted the greatest halfback in the first fifty years of professional football (1969) by the Professional Football Writers of America, and held nine National Football League records; in 1977 Sayers was inducted into the Pro Football Hall of Fame.

Sayre, Zelda. *See* Fitzgerald, Zelda

Scales, Jeffrey Charles

b. 1954
fields: Photography

African American photographer; Jeffrey Charles Scales's photography focuses on documenting U.S. black communities; he has also worked as a freelance photojournalist for magazines such as *Time*, *Paris Photo*, and *New York Magazine*.

Scalia, Antonin

b. March 11, 1936
Trenton, N.J.
fields: Law

U.S. Supreme Court justice. A 1960 graduate of the Harvard University Law School, Scalia served in private practice and in public-service positions during the Richard Nixon and Gerald Ford administrations; he also taught at the University of Chicago and the University of Virginia. In 1986, he was nominated to the Supreme Court by President Ronald Reagan and was subsequently confirmed by the Senate.

Scaliger, Joseph Justus

b. August 5, 1540
Agen, France
d. January 21, 1609
Leiden, United Provinces
fields: Literature, Historiography

Educated by a learned father and through study with leading scholars, Scaliger became the foremost scholar of Greek and Latin in his time. His editions of Latin authors set high critical standards; his research on ancient chronology established the study of ancient history on a firm foundation and introduced to Europe the literature and history of Byzantium.

Scarborough, William Sanders

b. February 16, 1852
Macon, Ga.
d. September 9, 1926
Wilberforce, Ga.
fields: Education

African American educator; known as a scholar of languages (including Latin, Greek, Hebrew, and Sanskrit), William Sanders Scarborough served as president of a small South Carolina denominational college before joining the faculty at Wilberforce University; he was president of Wilberforce from 1908 to 1920.

Scarface Charlie

aka: Chichikam Lupalkuelatko (Wagon Scarface)
b. c. 1837
near the Rogue River, Calif.
d. Dec. 3, 1896
Seneca Station, Indian Territory
fields: Warfare and Conquest, Native American Affairs

A Modoc warrior, Scarface Charlie was the chief adviser, interpreter, and battlefield tactician to Modoc chief Captain Jack; he performed honorably and brilliantly during the Modoc War of 1872-1873. Under his command, the Modocs never lost a battle. The only battle the Modocs lost, which caused their defeat and surrender, occurred when Captain Jack displaced Scarface Charlie as commander. Several Modocs, including Captain Jack, were executed for their role in the war, but Scarface Charlie was spared

Scarlatti, Alessandro

full: Pietro Alessandro Gaspare Scarlatti
b. May 2, 1660
Palermo, Sicily
d. October 22, 1725
Naples
fields: Music

Scarlatti was the outstanding Italian composer of operas and cantatas active at the end of the seventeenth and beginning of the eighteenth centuries. His work brought fame to Naples as a center for operatic composition and performance, and provided the foundation for the so-called Neapolitan school of composers, though he and his musical style had little direct influence on them.

Scharnhorst, Gerhard Johann David von

b. November 12, 1755
Bordenau, Lippe
d. June 28, 1813
Prague, Bohemia, Austrian Empire
fields: Military Affairs

Scharnhorst's modernization of the Prussian army made it the model for the armies of the nineteenth century. Among the reforms which he either initiated or helped to push through were the development of the general staff, the abolition of army corporal punishment, a scheme for training large numbers of recruits, and the overhaul of Prussian tactical training.

Schawlow, Arthur L.

full: Arthur Leonard Schawlow
b. May 5, 1921
Mount Vernon, New York
d. April 28, 1999
Stanford, California
fields: Physics, Invention and Technology

Arthur L. Schawlow was a pioneer in the field of spectroscopy; in 1958 with his colleague Charles H. Townes, first proposed a theory of operation and a structure for the laser; in 1981, won the Nobel Prize in Physics.

Schechter, Soloman

b. December 7, 1847
Focsani, Romania
d. November 19, 1915
New York, New York
fields: Religion and Theology

Soloman Schechter was a leader of Conservative Judaism; born in Romania and educated in Vienna, Berlin, and London; appointed lecturer in Talmudics at Cambridge University in 1890; moved to the United States to become president of the Jewish Theological Seminary of America in Philadelphia in 1902; supported the Zionist movement as a check on assimilation; founded the United Synagogue of America in 1913; wrote *The Wisdom of Ben Sira* (1899).

Scheler, Max

b. August 22, 1874
Munich, Germany
d. May 19, 1928
Frankfurt, Germany
fields: Philosophy, Sociology, Religion and Theology

Scheler was one of the most brilliant and creative moral philosophers of the twentieth century. His system of ethics, in sharp disagreement with Kantian ethics as well as with positivism, attempts to give the emotional life its due as an epistemologically reliable response to objective values.

Schelling, Friedrich Wilhelm Joseph

b. January 27, 1775
Leonberg in Württemberg
d. August 20, 1854
Bad Ragaz, Switzerland
fields: Philosophy

Schelling contributed to the development of German Idealism and to the rise of German Romanticism. His later ontological and mythological speculations, though unpopular among his contemporaries such as G. W. F. Hegel, have influenced modern existentialism and philosophical anthropology.

Schildkret, Lucy. *See* Dawidowicz, Lucy S.

Schiller, Friedrich

b. November 10, 1759
Marbach, Württemberg
d. May 9, 1805
Weimar, Saxe-Weimar
fields: Theater and Entertainment, Literature, Historiography, Philosophy

Schiller's main contribution to German literature was in the field of drama, especially historical drama. In philosophy, his contributions were mainly in the areas of ethics and aesthetics. Belonging to the school of German classicism, he was one of the leading contributors to German Idealism in literature and philosophy.

Schlafly, Phyllis

b. August 15, 1924
St. Louis, Mo.
fields: Government and Politics, Literature

Profamily, antifeminist activist; the mother of six children, Phyllis Schlafly organized an influential antifeminist movement and has been an effective proponent of ultraconservative political causes; an articulate, persuasive voice against liberal politics and the National Organization for Women (NOW), she was instrumental in the 1982 defeat of the Equal Rights Amendment (ERA); Schlafly ran unsuccessfully for Congress in 1952, 1960, and 1970; her published works include *A Choice Not an Echo* (1964; in support of Barry Goldwater's presidential bid), *The Phyllis Schlafly Report* (1967; a newsletter), *Kissinger on the Couch* (1975), and *The Power of the Positive Woman* (1977); Schlafly has founded organizations to promote the ultraconservative agenda, including the Eagle Trust Fund, Stop ERA, and the highly influential Eagle Forum and has hosted a nationally syndicated radio show.

Schleiden, Matthias Jakob

b. Apr. 5, 1804
Hamburg, Germany
d. June 23, 1881
Frankfurt am Main, Germany
fields: Biology, Botany

Matthias Jakob Schleiden was a pioneering microscopist, theorist, and popularizer; helped to unify the biological sciences, focusing them on cellular processes.

Schleiermacher, Friedrich

full: Friedrich Daniel Ernst Schleiermacher

b. November 21, 1768
Breslau, Silesia
d. February 12, 1834
Berlin, Prussia
fields: Religion and Theology, Philosophy

Schleiermacher helped Christian theology address the challenges and opportunities that were offered theological thought by modern historical consciousness. His most lasting contribution has been his theological system.

Schliemann, Heinrich

né: Julius Schliemann
b. January 6, 1822
Neu Bockow, Mecklenburg-Schwerin
d. December 26, 1890
Naples, Italy
fields: Archaeology

A stunningly successful merchant in his early years, Heinrich Schliemann began a new career in his middle age as an archaeologist. Relying on an unwavering faith in Homer, he found and excavated Troy and unearthed the riches of Mycenae, and thus singlehandedly brought the splendors of the Greek Bronze Age to the the attention of both amateurs and professionals.

Schlumberger, Dominique. *See* de Menil, Dominique

Schmidt, Bernhard Voldemar

b. March 30, 1879
Island of Naissaar, Estonia
d. December 1, 1935
Hamburg, Germany
fields: Astronomy, Invention and Technology, Physics

In 1930, Schmidt invented an optical system that revolutionized astronomy by significantly widening the field of vision of the largest telescopes then in use. The Schmidt photographic telescope used a spherical mirror in combination with a glass plate to capture celestial images on photographic plates. For the first time, wide areas of the sky could be photographed with sharp definition across the entire field, edge to edge.

Schmidt, Käthe. *See* Kollwitz, Käthe

Schmidt, Maarten

b. Dec. 28, 1929
Groningen, the Netherlands
fields: Astronomy

In 1963 Maarten Schmidt noticed a shift toward the red end of the spectrum for two stellar objects, thereby discovering quasars, highly energetic quasi-stellar objects at great distances from the Milky Way.

Schmidt-Rottluff, Karl

né: Karl Schmidt
b. December 1, 1884
Rottluff, Germany
d. August 10, 1976
West Berlin, West Germany
fields: Art

The period 1905-1915 marked the beginning of twentieth century artistic principles. This was the decade of *Die Brücke*, an organized group of European artists and art lovers whose common interest was to encourage revolutionary methods of artistic expression. Schmidt-Rottluff, as a founding member of this influential group, maintained a lifelong dedication to its purposes.

Schmoke, Kurt Liddell

b. December 1, 1949
Baltimore, Md.
fields: Government and Politics

African American mayor of Baltimore, Md. (1987-1999); Kurt Liddell Schmoke was selected to serve on President Jimmy Carter's White House Domestic Policy Staff (1977) and later was appointed as assistant director of the Department of Transportation; holding a J.D. degree from Harvard Law School, Schmoke returned to his hometown and was elected to the office of Baltimore state's attorney (1982) and served for four years; in 1987 he was elected mayor of Baltimore.

Schoenberg, Arnold

né: Arnold Franz Walter Schönberg
b. September 13, 1874
Vienna, Austro-Hungarian Empire
d. July 13, 1951
Los Angeles, California
fields: Music

Schoenberg was the leading composer of the second Viennese school, a manifestation of the expressionist movement in music. By breaking from the tradition of tonality, a process he later codified in his twelve-tone method, Schoenberg introduced compositional techniques and aesthetic principles that became pervasive throughout the first half of the twentieth century.

Scholder, Fritz

b. Oct. 6, 1937
Brekenridge, Minn.
fields: Art (painter, sculptor)

Native American artist. A Luiseño, Fritz Scholder broke the bounds of traditionalist Indian painting with his brightly colored portraits of contemporary Indians. In 1967, he launched his famous "Indian series," which eventually included groups of pictures of monster Indians, Indians and horses, Dartmouth portraits, American portraits, contemporary Indians in Gallup, and Indian postcards. With these paintings, he began what one critic called the postmodern interrogation of the historically circumscribed image of the Indian, using Postimpressionist, expressionist, and pop art styles. The series was concluded in 1980, whereupon he vowed never to paint another Indian.

Schomburg, Arthur

full: Arthur Alfonso Schomburg
b. January 24, 1874
San Juan, Puerto Rico
d. June 10, 1938
New York, N.Y.
fields: Historiography, Scholarship

Bibliophile and curator. Arthur Schomburg's collection of Africana formed the core of what is now known as the Schomburg Center for Research in Black Culture at the New York Public Library. He began collecting Africana while a college student, believing that preserving tradition was an antidote for the persecution experienced by black Americans. He was the curator at Fisk University (1930-1932) and then at the New York Public Library (1932-1938). Satow Memorial Building.

Schopenhauer, Arthur

b. February 22, 1788
Danzig (now Gdań), Poland
d. September 21, 1860
Frankfurt am Main (now in Germany)
fields: Philosophy

In the tradition of Immanuel Kant, Schopenhauer developed a pessimistic system of philosophy based upon the primacy of will.

Schröder, Gerhard

full: Gerhard Fritz Kurt Schröder
b. April 7, 1944
Mossenberg, Germany
fields: Government and Politics

Social Democrat Gerhard Schröder was elected chancellor of Germany in 1998, defeating long-time prime minister Helmut Kohl. (Kohl had faced high unemployment, a faltering economy, and gridlock in the legislature in his last term.) The major problem facing Schröder's government—a coalition government with the much smaller Green Party—was high employment—about 12 percent nationally in 1998.

Schrödinger, Erwin

b. August 12, 1887
Vienna, Austro-Hungarian Empire
d. January 4, 1961
Alpbach, Austria
fields: Physics, Philosophy

Schrödinger invented wave mechanics in 1926, for which he received the Nobel Prize in Physics (along with Paul Adrien Maurice Dirac) in 1933, and he helped to develop the formal equations that are central to quantum mechanics. His pioneering work on the relationship between physics and living systems influenced the growth of molecular biology.

Schroeder, Pat

né: Patricia Nell Scott
aka: Patricia S. Schroeder
b. July 30, 1940
Portland, Oregon
fields: Government and Politics

As a leader of the liberal wing of the Democratic Party, Schroeder has given direction to the important issues of foreign and military policy, women's rights, and the American family.

Schubert, Franz

b. January 31, 1797
Himmelpfortgrund, near Vienna, Austria
d. November 19, 1828
Vienna, Austro-Hungarian Empire
fields: Music

Schubert created the *Lied* (art song) and set models for subsequent ones in his more than six hundred *Lieder*. His larger instrumental works, in their freedom of form and enhanced key relationships, became models for the lyrical Romantic sonatas and symphonies of the later nineteenth century. The expressively songful character of his shorter piano pieces was equally influential.

Schultz, Michael A.

b. November 10, 1938
Milwaukee, Wisc.
fields: Film, Theater and Entertainment, Television

African American film, television, and theater director; Michael A. Schultz, a theater director with New York City's Negro Ensemble Company since 1964, received a 1967-1968 Obie Award, and a Tony nomination for his efforts as the first African American to stage a Broadway play, *Does a Tiger Wear a Necktie*, in 1969; directed *Cooley High* (1974), *Car Wash* (1975), *Greased Lightning* (1977), *Which Way Is Up?* (1977), *Krush Groove* (1985), and *Livin' Large* (1991); inducted into the Black Filmmakers Hall of Fame in 1991; television credits include episodes of the crime series *The Rockford Files*, *Baretta*, *Starsky and Hutch*, *For Us, the Living* (1983), a made-for-television film about Medgar Evers, and *Picket Fences*.

Schumann, Robert

full: Robert Alexander Schumann
b. June 8, 1810
Zwickau, Saxony
d. July 29, 1856
Endenich, near Bonn, Prussia
fields: Music

Schumann was important not only as a composer of music during the Romantic period but also as an editor of *Neue Zeitschrift für Musik*, which did much to establish standards of musical criticism.

Schurz, Carl

b. March 2, 1829
Liblar, Prussia (now Germany)
d. May 14, 1906
New York, New York
fields: Government and Politics

Recognized as a leader of the German-American community in the United States, this partisan of liberty fled Germany after the revolutions of 1848 and made a career as a journalist and politician, serving as a Union general in the Civil War, a senator from Missouri, and a secretary of the interior.

Schutz, Alfred

b. April 13, 1899
Vienna, Austro-Hungarian Empire
d. May 20, 1959
New York, New York
fields: Philosophy, Sociology

Drawing on Edmund Husserl's phenomenology and Max Weber's sociology, Alfred Schutz developed an account of meaning and action that addressed the actor's knowledge, intersubjectivity, and the nature of sociological analysis. In 1939, emigrated from Nazi Germany to the United States; taught at the New School for Social Research. Main ideas expressed in "Concept and Theory Formation in the Social Sciences" (1954); author of *The Phenomenology of the Social World* (1932).

Schütz, Heinrich

b. October, 1585
Köstritz, Reuss
d. November 6, 1672
Dresden, Saxony
fields: Music

Heinrich Schütz was the most important German composer of his era, and his works and pupils had an immense influence on the subsequent development of music in Germany. He is especially noted for his combining of the German church music traditions with the newer Italian styles developing in the early seventeenth century.

Schuyler, George Samuel

b. February 25, 1895
Providence, R.I.
d. August 31, 1977
New York, N.Y.
fields: Literature

African American novelist and journalist; the writing of George Samuel Schuyler satirized white's prejudices and the political and social problems present in African American communities; his novels include *Black No More: Being an Account of the Strange and Wonderful Workings of Science in the Land of the Free* (1931) and *Slaves Today: A Story of Liberia* (1931); in his later life he became known for his assimilationist politics.

Schuyler, Philippa Duke

b. 1931
Harlem, N.Y.
d. May 9, 1967
Vietnam
fields: Music (pianist, composer), Journalism

African American pianist, composer, and journalist; Philippa Duke Schuyler, the daughter of black journalist George Schuyler and white artist and writer Jody Cogdell, was a musical child prodigy; she spent most of her life traveling and performed for dignitaries around the world, but was not invited to perform in the U.S.; she worked as a journalist and wrote four books of nonfiction; while on assignment for the *Manchester Union Leader*, she died in a helicopter crash in Vietnam.

Schwartzerd, Philipp. *See* Melanchthon, Philipp

Schwarzkopf, H. Norman

b. Aug. 22, 1934
Trenton, N.J.
fields: Military Affairs, Warfare and Conquest

U.S. Army general. The son of a brigadier general, A 1956 graduate of the U.S. Military Academy at West Point, Schwarzkopf served two tours of duty in Vietnam in the 1960's. In 1983, he was promoted to general; that year, he oversaw the U.S. invasion of Grenada. In 1988, Schwarzkopf was made commander in chief of the U.S. Central Command. He rose to fame in January and February of 1991, when he directed U.S. forces during the Persian Gulf War. He retired from the Army in August, 1991.

Schwarzschild, Karl

b. October 9, 1873
Frankfurt am Main, Germany
d. May 11, 1916
Potsdam, Germany
fields: Astronomy

Schwarzschild developed a new use for photography, as a tool for measuring the brightness of stars, particularly variable objects. He was the first scientist to develop a solution for Albert Einstein's general relativity field equations, dealing with gravity around a star of such intensity that it becomes a black hole, surrounded by a boundary known as the Schwarzschild radius.

Schweitzer, Albert

b. January 14, 1875
Kaysersberg, Germany
d. September 4, 1965
Lambaréné, Gabon
fields: Religion and Theology, Peace Advocacy, Philosophy, Music, Medicine

Schweitzer, a renowned organist, student of the music of Bach, and an unorthodox biblical scholar, dedicated himself as a medical missionary to the natives of Africa, a decision that led to a fifty-year career that captured the admiration of many people and led to his receiving the Nobel Peace Prize. He also actively urged the public, politicians, and statesmen to come to grips with the threat of nuclear war and work for peace.

Schwerner, Michael

b. ?
d. June 21, 1964
Neshoba County, Miss.
fields: Civil Rights

Michael Schwerner was one of three civil rights workers murdered by members of the Ku Klux Klan in Mississippi in June, 1964. The outrage over their murders brought unprecedented publicity and pressure for the federal government to enforce civil rights of African Americans in the southern states. On October 20, 1967, an all-white Mississippi jury found seven men guilty of the murder, marking the first time a Mississippi jury ever found a white person guilty of crimes perpetrated on a black person or civil rights worker. After exhausting their appeals, the guilty men all served lengthy prison sentences at various federal penitentiaries.

Schwinger, Julian Seymour

b. Feb. 12, 1918
New York, New York
d. July 16, 1994
Los Angeles, California
fields: Physics

Julian Seymour Schwinger, in 1948, presented a relativistic quantum field theory; in 1951, developed a quantum action principle for quantum field theory; in 1965, won the Nobel Prize in Physics.

Scipio Aemilianus

né: Publius Cornelius Scipio Aemilianus Africanus Numantinus
aka: Scipio the Younger
b. 185 B.C.E.
probably Rome
d. 129 B.C.E.
Rome
fields: Warfare and Conquest, Government and Politics, Patronage of the Arts

Combining a genius for military conquest with an appreciation for literature and the arts, Scipio Aemilianus embodies—perhaps better than any other figure of his day—the paradoxical forces which swept through Rome during the central years of the Republic.

Scipio Africanus

né: Publius Cornelius Scipio
aka: Scipio the Elder
b. 236 B.C.E.
Rome
d. 184 or 183 B.C.E.
Liternum, Campania
fields: Warfare and Conquest, Government and Politics

Scipio's military victory over Carthaginian forces in Spain and North Africa, brought about by his genius as strategist and innovator of tactics, ended the Second Punic War and established Roman hegemony in the Western Mediterranean.

Scopas

aka: Scopas of Paros
b. Possibly as early as 420 B.C.E.
Paros, Greece
d. c. late fourth century B.C.E.
place unknown
fields: Art

A leader of the evolution in late classical sculpture away from the powerful but emotionally detached balance of fifth century art, Scopas created works of relaxed gracefulness on the one hand and strong emotion, stress, and turbulence on the other. With Praxiteles of Athens and Lysippus of Sicyon, his work dominated the art of the fourth century B.C.E.

Scott, Bobby

full: Robert Cortez Scott
b. April 30, 1947
Washington, D.C.
fields: Government and Politics

African American politician; Bobby Scott served in the Virginia State Senate from 1983 to 1993; elected to the U.S. House of Representatives in 1992, and served in Congress as one of the group of fifteen African Americans newly elected in 1993.

Scott, Byron

b. March 28, 1961
Odgen, Utah
fields: Sports (basketball player)

African American basketball player; Byron Scott began playing as a shooting guard for the Los Angeles Lakers in 1983; he was the starting shooting guard for the Lakers during the "Showtime" era in the second half of the 1980's; he led the Lakers in scoring during the 1987-1988 season and was known for his three-point shooting ability. He was with the Lakers from 1983-1993 and 1996-1997, winning three world championships with them (1985, 1987, 1988); with the Indiana Pacers, 1993-1995; with the Vancouver Grizzliers, 1995-1996; and joined the coaching staff of the Sacramento Kings for the 1998-1999 season.

Scott, Charlie

full: Charles Thomas Scott
b. December 15, 1948
New York, N.Y.
fields: Sports (basketball player)

African American basketball player; a member of the 1968 U.S. gold-medal winning Olympic basketball team, Charlie Scott joined the Virginia Squires and was named the 1971 American Basketball Association (ABA) Rookie of the Year; he led the ABA in scoring the following season with a 34.6-points-per-game average; at the end of the 1971-1972 season, Scott moved to the National Basketball Association (NBA) and played through the 1979-1980 season with the Phoenix Suns, Boston Celtics, Los Angeles Lakers, and Denver Nuggets.

Scott, Charlotte Angas

b. June 8, 1858
Lincoln, England
d. Nov. 10, 1931
Cambridge, England
fields: Mathematics (algebra and geometry)

Charlotte Angas Scott studied the relationship between geometry and algebra; introduced many, especially women, to the careful study of mathematics; became the only woman elected to the Council of the American Mathematical Society, in 1891; was the only female mathematician noted as outstanding in *American Men of Science*, 1906.

Scott, Dred

b. c. 1795
Virginia
d. September 17, 1858
St. Louis, Missouri
fields: Civil Rights

Born a slave, Dred Scott instigated a legal challenge to the definition of "citizenship" for black people in the United States. His challenge led to the Supreme Court's 1857 *Dred Scott v. Sandford* decision, which became a step toward Civil War and the end of slavery.

Scott, George Gilbert

aka: Sir George Gilbert Scott
b. July 13, 1811
Gawcott, Buckinghamshire, England
d. March 27, 1878
London, England
fields: Architecture

Because of his designs for the Foreign Office, St. Pancras Hotel, and the Albert Memorial, as well as his restoration of many important medieval buildings throughout Great Britain, Scott became one of the most highly regarded architects in nineteenth century England.

Scott, Hazel

b. June 11, 1920
Port of Spain, Trinidad
d. October 2, 1981
New York, N.Y.
fields: Music (blues and jazz singer)

African American singer; identified as a prodigy, Hazel Scott studied at Juilliard and later appeared in Broadway musicals; Scott recorded many of her own jazz and blues compositions and accompanied small jazz groups on the piano; during the 1940's she had her own radio show and appeared in several films; she was married to Adam Clayton Powell, Jr., from 1945 to 1960, when they divorced.

Scott, James. *See* Monmouth, duke of

Scott, Nathan Alexander, Jr.

b. April 24, 1925
Cleveland, Ohio
fields: Scholarship

African American author; Nathan Alexander Scott, Jr., a priest in the Episcopal Church, served at the University of Virginia as the William R. Kenan, Jr., professor of religious studies and professor of English; his scholarly publications include *Samuel Beckett* (1965), *The Broken Center: Studies in the Theological Horizon of Modern Literature* (1966), *Ernest Hemingway* (1966), *Negative Capability: Studies in the New Literature and the Religious Situation* (1969), *The Poetry of Civic Virtue: Eliot, Malraux, and Auden* (1976), *Mirrors of Man in Existentialism* (1978), and *Visions of Presence in Modern American Poetry* (1993).

Scott, Patricia Nell. *See* Schroeder, Pat

Scott, Rodney Cline Carew y. *See* Carew, Rod

Scott, Walter

aka: Sir Walter Scott
b. August 15, 1771
Edinburgh, Scotland
d. September 21, 1832
Abbotsford, Scotland
fields: Literature

Scott's narrative poems about the stirring events in Scottish and medieval history were immensely popular in the nineteenth century, and in fiction he created the genre of the historical novel.

Scott, Wendell

b. 1921?
d. December 22, 1990
Detroit, Mich.
fields: Sports (stock car racer)

African American stock car racer; as the first important black driver in stock car racing, Wendell Scott played an integral part in Winston Cup Grand National racing from 1961 to 1973; although he was regularly harassed by spectators and promoters, Scott raced in 495 Winston Cup races, winning one (1963; the promoter did not want to give a black man the $1,000 purse so Scott filed a protest and received his winnings, but he never got his trophy), finishing in the top five 20 times, and finishing in the top ten 147 times; in 1966 Scott finished sixth in National Association for Stock Car Auto Racing (NASCAR) points, in 1967 he finished tenth, and in 1968 he finished ninth; in 1973 he retired from racing after he broke his pelvis in a crash during the Winston 500.

Scott, William Edouard

b. 1884
Indianapolis, Ind.
d. 1964
fields: Art (painter, illustrator, and muralist)

African American painter, illustrator, and muralist; known as the dean of African American artists, William Edouard Scott spent a year portraying the people in Haiti—his trip was funded by a 1931 Rosenwald Foundation grant; upon his return to the U.S., Scott painted murals on the walls of public buildings and hospitals in New York, Indiana, Illinois, and West Virginia.

Scott, Winfield

full: Winfield Mason Scott
b. June 13, 1786
Petersburg, Virginia
d. May 29, 1866
West Point, New York
fields: Military Affairs

Scott, whose military career spanned more than fifty years, left his mark by showing the power of volunteer troops fighting in a republican army.

Scott-Heron, Gil

b. April 1, 1949
Chicago, Ill.
fields: Music

African American novelist, poet, and musician; many consider popular performer Gil Scott-Heron's compositions, fusing jazz stylings with a running dialogue depicting racial and social issues, to be the precursors of the rap and hip-hop styles of the 1990's; he is also a published author.

Scripps, Edward Wyllis

b. June 18, 1854
near Rushville, Illinois
d. March 12, 1926
at sea, off the coast of Monrovia, Liberia
fields: Journalism, Publishing

Through delegating responsibility but maintaining control of his holdings, Scripps established a publishing empire that eventually included newspapers, the United Press Association, Acme Newsphotos, and the United Feature Syndicate. Late in life he founded, with his half-sister Ellen, the Scripps Institute of Oceanography, the Scripps Foundation for Research in Population Problems, and the Science News Service.

Scruggs, Faye. *See* Adams, Faye

Scrutton, Mary. *See* Midgley, Mary

Scullin, James Henry

b. September 18, 1876
Trawalla, Victoria, Australia
d. January 28, 1953
Melbourne, Victoria, Australia
fields: Government and Politics

James Henry Scullin was Labor Party prime minister of Australia from 1929 to 1931, during the onset of the Depression. Ultimately his economic policies split the party, leading to his defeat in 1931.

Seaborg, Glenn Theodore

b. April 19, 1912
Ishpeming, Michigan
d. February 25, 1999
Lafayette, California
fields: Science (nuclear), Education

Codiscoverer of ten transuranium elements and numerous radioisotopes with wide applications in research, medicine, and industry, Seaborg served under five United States presidents in establishing policy regarding the role of science and uses of atomic energy. He won the 1951 Nobel Prize in Chemistry.

Seale, Bobby

b. Oct. 22, 1936
Dallas, Tex.
fields: Social Reform

African American activist; Bobby Seale cofounded, with Huey P. Newton, the Black Panther Party for Self-Defense in 1966; helped implement Panther programs such as the breakfast program for schoolchildren and free clinics for people unable to pay for medical assistance; mistrial declared in his 1971 trial for the kidnapping and killing of a suspected police informant; disenchanted with revolutionary politics, left the Panthers in 1974 to form the Advocates Scene; wrote *Seize the Time: The Story of the Black Pan-*

ther Party (1970) and *A Lonely Rage: The Autobiography of Bobby Seale* (1978).

Seals, Son

né: Frank Seals
b. August 11, 1942
Osceola, Ark.
fields: Music (blues musician)

African American blues musician; initially a drummer, Son Seals moved to Chicago in 1966 and performed in the modern Chicago electric style as a guitarist and vocalist; Seals formed his own group after a short stint as a drummer for guitarist Albert King's band.

Sealth, Noah. *See* Seattle

Seaman, Elizabeth Cochrane. *See* Bly, Nellie

Searle, John R.

full: John Rogers Searle
b. July 31, 1932
Denver, Colorado
fields: Philosophy, Language and Linguistics

John R. Searle elaborated on speech act theory and developed theories of intentionality and consciousness. His famous "Chinese room" thought experiment is the most influential argument against artificial intelligence. Major works include *Speech Acts* (1969), *Expression and Meaning* (1979), *Intentionality* (1983), *Minds, Brains, and Science* (1984), *The Rediscovery of the Mind* (1992), *The Construction of Social Reality* (1995), *The Mystery of Consciousness* (1997).

Sears-Collins, Leah Jeanette

b. June 13, 1955
Heidelberg, West Germany
fields: Law (judge)

African American judge; Leah Jeanette Sears-Collins completed her law degree at Emory University in Atlanta, Ga., and passed the bar exam in 1980. She served as a judge in the City Court of Atlanta from 1985 to 1988. She was elected to a judgeship on the Superior Court of Fulton County (serving Atlanta) in 1989 and received an appointment to the Georgia Supreme Court in 1992.

Seathl. *See* Seattle

Seattle

aka: Noah Sealth
aka: Seathl
b. c. 1788
near Seattle, Wash.
d. June 7, 1866
Port Madison Reservation, Wash.
fields: Native American Affairs

Suquamish, Duwamish tribal chief; as chief of the Suquamish, Duwamish, and other allied Puget Sound tribes, Seattle urged peaceful coexistence with U.S. settlers; resisted encroachment by the Hudson's Bay Company; converted to Catholicism in 1838; appointed by U.S. leaders as head chief of the region following settlement of U.S.-Canadian land dispute; Seattle won the support of the tribes for the Point Elliott Treaty (January 22, 1855) which provided for the creation of a reservation, submission to agency authorities, and land cessions; at his death Chief Seattle, much beloved and admired by white settlers, was mourned by all; the city of Seattle, which bears his name, erected a monument over his gravesite in 1890.

Sebree, Charles

b. 1914
Madisonville, Ky.
d. 1985
fields: Art

African American painter, illustrator, set designer, and playwright; from 1936 to 1938, Charles Sebree worked for the Illinois Federal Art Project in the easel division; he was a product of the little-known but significant art scene of the 1930's in Chicago.

Secada, Jon

né: Juan Secada
b. 1964
Cuba
fields: Music (singer and composer)

Cuban singer and composer. Jon Secada moved from Cuba to Miami, Florida, at the age of eight. He graduated from the University of Miami and worked as a music teacher, then joined the chorus of Gloria Estefan's group Miami Sound Machine. With Estefan, he recorded "Coming Out of the Dark" and "Can't Forget You." He gained attention with is version of "Siempre hay algo." Secada's debut album *Jon Secada*, which included the song "Otro Día Mas Sin Verte" (also recorded in English as "Another Day Without You"), won the Grammy Award for best Latin pop album in 1993. He also released the albums *Amor* (1995) and *Secada* (1997).

Secondat, Charles-Louis de. *See* Montesquieu

Seddon, Richard John

b. June 22, 1845
Eccleston, St. Helens, Lancashire, England
d. June 10, 1906
on board SS *Oswestry Grange*, off Sydney, Australia
fields: Government and Politics

The first New Zealand prime minister who was not a "gentleman," Seddon completely dominated politics between 1893 and 1906. Astute, domineering, and incredibly popular, Seddon laid the foundation of the first social democratic, egalitarian welfare state in the world.

Seeckt, Hans von

full: Johannes Friedrich Leopold von Seeckt
b. April 22, 1866
Schleswig, Prussia
d. December 27, 1936
Berlin, Germany
fields: Military Affairs

Seeckt reshaped Germany's small post-1918 *Reichswehr* on modern lines, emphasizing the principles of mobility and combined attack later employed in the Blitzkrieg victories of 1940.

Seeger, Pete

b. May 3, 1919
New York, New York
fields: Music (folk)

In 1940 Pete Seeger formed the Almanac Singers with Woody Guthrie, Lee Hays, and Millard Lampell, and began performing songs such as "Which Side Are You On?" before occasionally violent audiences at labor rallies. During World War II he performed his overtly procommunist shows. Afterward, along with Guthrie, he created the immensely popular "hootenanny" sing-alongs. In 1948 Seeger formed the Weavers, the most important and influential of the American folk revivalists. Seeger was blacklisted in 1955 after refusing to testify before the House Committee on Un-American Activities. Although he later dropped his membership in the Communist Party and was acquitted of all charges in 1962, Seeger was banned from network television, including the American Broadcasting Company's *Hootenanny*. During the 1960's Seeger wrote or popularized such anthems as "We Shall Overcome," "If I Had a Hammer," "Where Have All the Flowers Gone?" and "Little Boxes."

Segovia, Andrés

b. Probably February 17, 1893
Linares, Spain
d. June 2, 1987
Madrid, Spain
fields: Music

Renowned as one of the foremost concert performers of the twentieth century, Segovia is responsible for establishing the guitar as a serious musical instrument. In addition to adapting works of Mozart, Haydn, Bach, and others for the classical guitar, Segovia stimulated modern composers to write new works for his instrument.

Segovia, Josefa

b. ?
d. July 5, 1851
Downieville, Calif.
fields: Historical Figure

Josefa Segovia was brought to trial in 1851 after she stabbed a miner named Fred Cannon to death for calling her a whore. Cannon had broken the door of her cabin on the night of July 4, 1851, and had refused to pay for its repair. Segovia was condemned to death by hanging.

Segrè, Emilio Gino

b. Feb. 1, 1905
Tivoli, Italy
d. Apr. 22, 1989
Lafayette, California
fields: Chemistry, Physics

Emilio Gino Segrè, in 1937, used a cyclotron to discover the new element technetium; in 1938, discovered element astatine; in 1941 with Glenn Seaborg, discovered plutonium; in 1955 discovered the antiproton, the subnuclear antiparticle of the proton; in 1959 won the Nobel Prize in Physics, with colleague Owen Chamberlain.

Segura, Pancho

full: Francisco Segura
b. June 20, 1921
Gua-yaquil, Ecuador
fields: Sports (tennis player)

Latino tennis player. Pancho Segura attended the University of Miami on a scholarship and won three consecutive National Collegiate Athletic Association singles titles from 1943 to 1945. He turned professional in 1946 and won national professional singles titles in 1950, 1951, and 1952 and doubles titles in 1948, 1954, 1955, and 1958. Segura was inducted into the International Tennis Hall of Fame in 1984.

Seidelman, Susan

b. December 11, 1952
Abington, Pennsylvania
fields: Film

A leading director of offbeat comedies, Seidelman broke through the ranks of independent filmmakers to work successfully in commercial cinema.

Seingalt, Jean-Jacques, chevalier de. *See* Casanova, Giovanni Giacomo

Seldes, George

b. November 16, 1890
Alliance, New Jersey
d. July 2, 1995
Windsor, Vermont
fields: Journalism

George Seldes began a long journalism career as a cub reporter for the *Pittsburgh Leader* in 1909. After the *Chicago Tribune* paper failed to publish articles he wrote on Mexico in 1927, he quit in disgust and became a freelancer, launching his career with the first of twenty-one books, *You Can't Print That* (1929). In 1937 he covered the Spanish Civil War for the *New York Post*. After the *Post* dropped his reports, Seldes quit newspaper reporting completely and launched *In Fact*, a weekly newsletter that castigated the mainstream media for not covering important issues. Ironically, Seldes' greatest popular acclaim came from his brief appearance in Warren Beatty's film, *Reds* (1981) and his best-known book, *The Great Quotations* (1961).

Selena

né: Selena Quintanilla Perez
b. Apr. 16, 1971
Lake Jackson, Tex.
d. Mar. 31, 1995
Corpus Christi, Tex.
fields: Music

Latina singer. Selena, known as "the Mexican Madonna" because of her suggestive clothing and stage presence, won the 1994 Grammy for best Mexican American album for *Selena Live*. At the 1994 Tejano Music Awards, she won for female entertainer of the year, female vocalist of the year, best record of the year, and best album. She was about to release her first English-language album when she was murdered by Yolanda Saldivar, a former president of Selena's fan club, on March 31, 1995.

Seleucus I Nicator

b. 358 or 354 B.C.E.
Europus or Pella, Macedonia
d. Summer, 281 B.C.E.
near Lysimachia, Thrace
fields: Government and Politics, Warfare and Conquest

By his courage and practical common sense, Seleucus created the Seleucid Empire, maintaining the loyalty of a heterogeneous population by fair government.

Selika, Marie

né: Marie Smith
b. c. 1849
Natchez, Miss.
d. May 19, 1937
New York, N.Y.
fields: Music (concert singer)

African American concert singer; promoted as the "Queen of Staccato" because of the precision of her coloratura, Marie Selika was one of several renowned nineteenth century African American concert singers; in 1878 she became the first African American to sing at the White House; she toured Europe several times, her performances including one for Queen Victoria in 1883; in 1916 Selika retired to teach at the Martin-Smith School of Music.

Sellars, Wilfrid S.

full: Wilfrid Stalker Sellars
b. May 20, 1912
Ann Arbor, Michigan
d. July 2, 1989
Pittsburgh, Pennsylvania
fields: Philosophy

Wilfrid S. Sellars is best known for his attack on the "myth of the given," his attempt to synthesize the "manifest" and the "scientific images," and his philosophy of mind. Taught at the University of Minnesota (1946) and at Yale University in (beginning 1959). Founded *Philosophical Studies* (1950), which he edited until 1975. President of the Eastern Division of the American Philosophical Association 1970-1971. Major works: *Science, Perception, and Reality* (1963), *Philosophical Perspectives* (1967), *Science and Metaphysics* (1968), *Essays in Philosophy and Its History* (1974), *Naturalism and Ontology* (1979), *Pure Pragmatics and Possible Worlds* (1980), *The Metaphysics of Epistemology* (1989), *Empiricism and the Philosophy of Mind* (1997).

Sellers, Cleveland, Jr.

b. November 8, 1944
Denmark, S.C.
fields: Civil Rights

African American political activist; from November, 1965, to May, 1967, Cleveland Sellers, Jr., served as the Student Nonviolent Coordinating Committee (SNCC) program secretary; he was SNCC's state coordinator for South Carolina during the Orangeburg massacre in February, 1968. on September 28, 1970, he was convicted of participating in the riot and sentenced to a year in prison; in 1973 Sellers published his autobiography, *The River of No Return*.

Semenov, Nikolai

full: Nikolai Nikolayevich Semenov
b. Apr. 15, 1896
Saratov, Russia
d. Sept. 25, 1986
Moscow, Soviet Union
fields: Chemistry, Physics

Nikolai Semenov worked on branched chain chemical reactions in combustion processes, which are important in the development of internal combustion engines and plastic polymerization processes; won the 1956 Nobel Prize in Chemistry.

Semmelweis, Ignaz Philipp

b. July 1, 1818
Buda, Hungary, Austrian Empire
d. August 13, 1865
Vienna, Austrian Empire
fields: Medicine

Semmelweis, a Hungarian physician, was the first to recognize the infectious nature of puerperal fever (childbed fever). His use of antiseptic techniques in obstetric practice greatly reduced deaths from the fever and paved the way for the development of modern surgery.

Senanayake, D. S.

full: Don Stephen Senanayake
b. Oct. 20, 1884
Colombo, Ceylon, now Sri Lanka
d. Mar. 22, 1952
Colombo, Ceylon
fields: Government and Politics

D. S. Senanayake was the first prime minister of Ceylon after it gained independence in 1948. As prime minister, Senanayake initiated efforts toward the development of hydroelectric power. Before becoming prime minister, he was a Ceylonese legislator for thirty years and held government ministerial posts for more than twenty. Appointed minister for agriculture and lands in 1931, he instituted land development measures, attempted agricultural modernization, and urged the development of cooperatives.

Sendak, Maurice

full: Maurice Bernard Sendak
b. June 10, 1928
Brooklyn, New York
fields: Art

Sendak was one of the twentieth century's best-known illustrators of children's books. He received the international Hans Christian Andersen Award in 1970 in recognition of his major contribution to children's literature.

Seneca the Younger

b. c. 4 B.C.E.
Córdoba
d. April, 65 C.E.
Rome
fields: Government and Politics, Philosophy, Literature

An influential intellectual, Seneca also showed great abilities as coadministrator of the Roman Empire during the first years of Nero. In literature, Seneca's essays and tragedies were influential from the Middle Ages to the Renaissance, when English playwrights took his dramas as models.

Senghor, Léopold

full: Léopold Sédar Senghor
b. October 9, 1906
Joal, Senegal
fields: Literature, Government and Politics

Senghor, one of Africa's leading poets and intellectuals, is best known for having helped create and having greatly contributed to the *négritude* movement begun in the 1930's. A writer of rich, complex poems illuminating his love for his native Senegal as well as that for his beloved France, Senghor was also both a diplomat representing colonial Senegal in the French National Assembly and the President of Senegal after its independence in 1960. He has been a forceful, intelligent, influential pro-African leader respected throughout the world.

Sengstacke, John

b. November 25, 1912
Savannah, Georgia
d. May 28, 1997
Chicago, Illinois
fields: Publishing

African American publisher; John Sengstacke acquired the *Courier* newspapers of Pittsburgh and Miami and the *Chronicle* in Detroit after having inherited a publishing company from his uncle, Robert Sengstacke Abbott; he founded the Negro Newspaper Publishers Association and directed the National Newspaper Publishers Association.

Sequoyah

aka: Sikwaji
aka: Siwayi
aka: Sogwili
b. c.1770
Taskigi, near Fort Loudon, Tennessee
d. August, 1843
near San Fernando, Tamaulipas, Mexico
fields: Language and Linguistics, Native American Affairs

Sequoyah single-handedly devised a Cherokee syllabary that allowed his tribal nation to become literate in their own indigenous language—a first for American Indian cultures located north of the advanced pre-Columbian civilizations of Mexico and Central America.

Serequeberhan, Tsenay

b. May 18, 1952
Teheran, Iran
fields: Philosophy, Political Science

Employing intellectual tools fashioned by phenomenology, existentialism, and hermeneutics, Tsenay Serequeberhan sought to articulate a postcolonial African philosophy rooted in the "lived experience" of African political liberation. He wrote about African politics, particularly issues concerning Eritrea. Following Eritrean independence in 1993, Serequeberhan in 1999 began an association with the Research and Documentation Center of the People's Front for Democracy and Justice, Asmara, Eritrea. Major works include "The Idea of Colonialism in Hegel's Philosophy of Right" (1989), *The Eritrean People's Liberation Front* (1989), *The Hermeneutics of African Philosophy* (1994), "Reflections on *In My Father's House*" (1996), and "Africanity at the End of the Twentieth Century" (1998).

Sergius I

aka: Patriarch Sergius of Constantinople
b. Date unknown
place unknown
d. Early December, 638
Constantinople
fields: Religion and Theology

Patriarch of Constantinople, 610-638. As head of the Orthodox Christian Church, Patriarch Sergius of Constantinople made a major if unsuccessful effort to resolve the vexing Monophysite controversy by advancing the Monothelete doctrine. At the same time, he became the loyal and invaluable partner of the Emperor Heraclius, helping him save the Late Roman (or Byzantine) state in a time of dire crisis.

Sergius I, Saint

b. 635
Palermo, Sicily
d. September 8, 701
Rome, Italy
fields: Religion and Theology

Pope Sergius I, 687-701. During his reign as pope, Sergius greatly strengthened relations between Rome and the churches in the Anglo-Saxon west and maintained the Western church's independence from the emperors of Constantinople. He introduced the Agnus Dei into the Mass and was responsible for the restoration and embellishment of churches throughout Rome.

Serra, Junípero

né: Miguel José Serra
b. November 24, 1713
Petra, Majorca, Spain
d. August 28, 1784
Carmel, Calif.
fields: Religion and Theology, Exploration and Colonization

Franciscan monk who oversaw the founding of California's Spanish missions. Born Miguel José Serra, Serra entered the Roman Catholic Church's Franciscan order in 1731, taking the name Junípero from a companion of Saint Francis. During the late eighteenth century he worked in California, where he personally founded missions at San Diego, Carmel, San Antonio de Padua, San Gabriel, San Luis Obispo, San Francisco, San Juan

Capistrano, Santa Clara, and San Buenaventura (now Ventura). Some critics have denounced him as a representative of Spanish imperialism who helped to enslave and mistreat American Indians. Others have praised him as a man who made great personal sacrifices to bring Christianity to an unenlightened land. In 1988, Serra was beatified for his work.

Serra, Richard

b. Nov. 2, 1939
San Francisco, Calif.
fields: Art (sculptor)

Sculptor. Richard Serra, who earned an M.F.A. at Yale University, works with such "unorthodox" materials as vulcanized rubber, heavy steel and lead sheets, and molten lead. Objects are often stacked, leaned, or propped against walls or on top of one another. He has constructed landscape-scale works such as steel sheets set in earth. He has also made film that investigate processes and perceptions in art. His work has been displayed in many cities around the world, including Los Angeles; New York City; Bern, Switzerland; Amsterdam, The Netherlands; Rome, Italy; and Cologne, Germany.

Serrano, Andres

b. August 15, 1950
New York, New York
fields: Art

Andres Serrano strives to present repulsive images, such as body fluids and corpses, and portray them in a way that transcends superficial revulsion. In 1989 Serrano's photograph *Piss Christ*, depicting a crucifix submerged in an effervescent veil of urine, became a catalyst of politically motivated actions intended to suppress public funding for projects deemed immoral.

Sert, José Luis

b. July 1, 1902
Barcelona, Spain
d. Mar. 15, 1983
Barcelona, Spain
fields: Architecture, Art

Spanish American architect and urban designer; José Luis Sert worked with the Swiss architect Le Corbusier; came to the United States in 1939 and cofounded Town Planning Associates, which designed plans for established cities and new towns in Cuba, Colombia, Peru, Venezuela, and Brazil; opened his own firm in 1955; designed the U.S. Embassy in Baghdad, Iraq, Harvard's Holyoke Center, and the Foundation Maeght in St. Paul de Vence, France; authored *Can Our Cities Survive?* (1942) and *Antoní Gaudí* (1960).

Servetus, Michael

b. 1511?
Villanueva de Sixena, Spain
d. October 27, 1553
Geneva
fields: Religion and Theology, Medicine

Servetus was the first to provide a systematic account of Unitarian ideas. As a doctor, Servetus' greatest achievement was the discovery of the pulmonary circulation of the blood.

Sesostris III

b. Date unknown
place unknown
d. 1843 B.C.E.
place unknown
fields: Government and Politics

Sesostris' egocentric nature inspired him to be the first king of ancient Egypt to pursue a truly imperialistic policy, conducting war in the Levant and extending Egypt's southern border. His lasting impact was on Egypt's social structure, where he eliminated the vestiges of the indigenous nobility.

Sesshū

b. 1420
Akahama, Bitchu Province, Japan
d. 1506
Yamaguchi, Suho Province, Japan
fields: Art

Sesshū is considered the greatest of Japanese landscape painters and a major ink painter whose genius pushed Japanese art toward its apex at the beginning of the sixteenth century.

Seth, Vikram

b. June 20, 1952
Calcutta, West Bengal, India
fields: Literature

Poet, novelist, and travel writer Vikram Seth published his first work, *Mappings: A Chapbook of Poems*, in 1981. His *From Heaven Lake: Travels Through Sinkiang and Tibet* (1983) won the Thomas Cook Travel Award for 1983. Other works include a collection of poems, *The Humble Administrator's Garden* (1985); two novels, *The Golden Gate* (1986) and *A Suitable Boy* (1993); a volume of translations, *Three Chinese Poets* (1993); and fables in verse, *Beastly Tales from Here and There* (1993). Seth, who received a master's degree in philosophy, politics, and economics from the University of Oxford in 1978, received the Commonwealth Poetry Prize and a Guggenheim Fellowship (1986).

Setimkia. *See* Stumbling Bear

Seton, Saint Elizabeth

né: Elizabeth Ann Bayley Seton
b. August 28, 1774
New York, New York
d. January 4, 1821
Emmitsburg, Maryland
fields: Religion and Theology, Education

Through her resourceful, independent, and pioneering spirit, Elizabeth Seton had a profound influence on nineteenth century American education, laying the foundations of the Catholic parochial school system. Proclaimed a saint in 1975, the first American-born saint of the Catholic Church.

Seurat, Georges

b. December 2, 1859
Paris, France
d. March 29, 1891
Paris, France
fields: Art

Seurat became one of the most perceptive imagists of the modern city and its inhabitants in the late nineteenth century. His great curiosity about new developments in technology and the sciences transformed his art into one based increasingly upon scientific and pseudoscientific theories, something valued highly by twentieth century modern movements. His work may be seen also as a prophecy of surface abstraction and grand decoration.

Seuss, Dr.

né: Theodor Seuss Geisel
b. March 2, 1904
Springfield, Massachusetts
d. September 24, 1991
La Jolla, California
fields: Art, Literature

Through his unusual drawings and unique use of language, Geisel introduced generations of children to the joys of reading and the wonders of the imagination.

Sewall, Samuel

b. March 28, 1652
Bishopstoke, Hampshire, England
d. January 1, 1730
Boston, Massachusetts
fields: Law, Religion and Theology, Social Reform

Author of one of the first antislavery tracts in America, and the only judge at the infamous Salem witchcraft trials to speak out against the proceedings, Samuel Sewall became a voice of social conscience in Puritan New England.

Seward, William H.

full: William Henry Seward
b. May 16, 1801
Florida, New York

d. October 10, 1872
Auburn, New York
fields: Diplomacy, Government and Politics

As an antislavery leader who helped to found the Republican Party during the 1850's, Seward, who contested Lincoln for the presidential nomination in 1860, went on to become one of the United States' greatest secretaries of state.

Sexton, Anne

né: Anne Gray Harvey
b. November 9, 1928
Newton, Massachusetts
d. October 4, 1974
Weston, Massachusetts
fields: Literature

Despite a modest education and her lifelong struggle with mental illness, Anne Sexton became a poet who was celebrated by critics, academics, and the public as a new voice in literature and the cause of feminism.

Sextus Empiricus

b. c. 140-160 C.E.
Greece
d. c. 220-230 C.E.
Greece or Alexandria, Egypt
fields: Philosophy

Promoting Pyrrhonian radical Skepticism, Sextus compiled arguments against dogmatic philosophers of Stoicism, Epicureanism, and Academic Skepticism, and in doing so he laid the foundation for modern philosophy. Author of *Pyrrōneiōn Hypotypōseōn*, *Pros Mathēmatikous.*

Sforza, Ludovico

b. July 27, 1452
Vigevano, Republic of Milan
d. May 27, 1508
Loches, Toubrenne, France
fields: Government and Politics, Patronage of the Arts

One of the most spectacular and significant statesmen and political manipulators of the High Renaissance in Italy, Sforza directed the Duchy of Milan during a crucial period of European history. His political maneuvers determined the following century of Italian affairs.

Shabazz, Qubilah Bahiyah

b. December 25, 1960
New York, N.Y.
fields: Law (accused conspirator)

African American accused conspirator; on January 12, 1995, Shabazz Qubilah Bahiyah Shabazz, daughter of Malcolm X and Betty Shabazz, was arrested for hiring Michael Fitzpatrick to assassinate Louis Farrakhan, the spiritual leader of the Nation of Islam. The alleged assassination plot was in revenge for Farrakhan's purported involvement in the 1965 assassination of Malcolm X. Plea bargaining arrangements resulted from the revelation of Fitzgerald's criminal record and countercharges of entrapment

Shábona

aka: Chambly
b. c. 1775
Ohio or Ill.
d. c. July 17, 1859
Morris, Ill.
fields: Government and Politics, Native American Affairs

Native American leader. Initially a loyal follower of Tecumseh, Potawatomi leader Shábona advocated peace and accommodation with whites following the War of 1812.

Shackelford, Lottie Holt

b. April 30, 1941
Little Rock, Ark.
fields: Government and Politics

African American mayor of Little Rock, Ark.; following Lottie Holt Shackelford's tenure on the Little Rock city council (1978-1986) and her tenure as mayor (1987-1989), Shackelford gained membership on the city board of directors; her activities in state politics have included serving on the Arkansas State Democratic Committee (1976-1982; rising to vice chair in 1982), as board member of the National League of Cities (1984-1986), and as vice chair of the Democratic National Committee; appointed by President Bill Clinton to the board of directors of the Overseas Private Investment Corp in 1994.

Shadd, Mary Ann

b. October 9, 1823
Wilmington, Del.
d. June 5, 1893
Washington, D.C.
fields: Education, Journalism, Civil Rights, Law

African American teacher, journalist, abolitionist, and lawyer; in 1839 Mary Ann Shadd organized and taught at a private school for blacks in Delaware; from 1854 to 1858, she served as *The Provincial Freeman*'s chief editor and published essays and news articles of interest to the Canadian provinces' black communities; she later became a regular contributor to several leading black newspapers, including Frederick Douglass' *New National Era* and John Wesley Cromwell's *The Advocate*; during 1855, Shadd lectured to U.S. audiences on the benefits of black emigration to Canada; Shadd became the first woman to enroll in the Howard University law department, and she was the third woman to graduate from the school (1883); she ran a successful private law practice well into her sixties.

Shaftesbury, first earl of

né: Anthony Ashley Cooper
b. July 22, 1621
Wimborne St. Giles, Dorset, England
d. January 21, 1683
Amsterdam, the Netherlands
fields: Government and Politics

After serving several Interregnum regimes, Shaftesbury played an important role in the restoration of Charles II and then served in several administrative capacities. In the 1670's, he broke with Charles II over foreign and religious policies and became the leading opposition figure. In this capacity he organized an effective political organization, the Whigs, that provided the foundation for party politics in England.

Shaftesbury, third earl of

aka: Anthony Ashley Cooper
b. February 26, 1671
Dorset, England
d. February 15, 1713
Naples, Italy
fields: Philosophy

During the Interregnum period, Shaftesbury served in several regimes; he played an important role in the restoration of Charles II to the English throne; and in the 1670's he became the leading opposition figure, organizing the Whigs, which provided the foundation for party politics in England; at the end of the century, he served in both the House of Commons and House of Lords. As a philosopher, he emphasized common sense as opposed to logical systems and introduced the theory of the moral sense as an influential element of ethical theory. Among his most important works are *An Inquiry Concerning Virtue* (1699), *A Letter Concerning Enthusiasm* (1708), *Sensus Communis* (1709), *The Moralists* (1709), *Characteristics of Men, Manners, Opinions, Times* (1711).

Shagal, Moishe. *See* Chagall, Marc

Shah Jahan

né: Khurram
b. January 5, 1592
Lahore, India (now Pakistan)
d. January 22, 1666
Agra, India
fields: Government and Politics, Patronage of the Arts

Shah Jahan ruled the Mughal Empire (1628-1658) at the culminating phase of its wealth and power, enabling him to act as an unequaled patron of Muslim art and architecture in the Indian subcontinent.

Shaka

b. c. 1787
Mtetwa Empire
d. September 22, 1828
Zulu Empire
fields: Monarchy, Military Affairs

Shaka revolutionized the military and political organization of the Zulus and their neighboring peoples, transforming the systems from the traditional to what might have developed into a modern nation-state, had not colonialism intervened. His achievements enabled the Zulus to resist European conquest until the late nineteenth century and preserved Zulu national identity.

Shakespeare, William

b. April 23, 1564
Stratford-upon-Avon, Warwickshire, England
d. April 23, 1616
Stratford-upon-Avon, Warwickshire, England
fields: Literature

The leading playwright in the great flowering of Renaissance English drama, Shakespeare created some of the world's most enduring literary and dramatic masterpieces.

Shakur, Assata Olugbala

né: JoAnne Deborah Byron
later: JoAnne Deborah Chesimard
b. July 16, 1947?
New York, N.Y.
fields: Civil Rights

African American political activist; after Assata Olugbala Shakur joined the Black Liberation Army, she was involved in a shoot-out that occurred on the New Jersey Turnpike on May 2, 1973; at the time of her arraignment, Shakur was on the FBI's Most Wanted List in connection with a bank robbery and also stood accused of other crimes including kidnapping and attempted murder; on March 25, 1977, she was convicted as an accomplice in the murder of New Jersey state trooper Werner Foerster and of atrocious assault with intent to kill state trooper James Harper; Shakur escaped from prison in 1979 and was granted political asylum in Cuba.

Shakur, Tupac

full: Tupac Amaru Shakur
b. June 16, 1971
New York, New York
b. September 13, 1996
Las Vegas, Nevada
fields: Music (rap)

Tupac Shakur's solo debut album *2Pacalypse Now* (1991) went gold. He was sued, however, by the wife of a slain Texas state trooper who claimed that the lyrics on the album inspired her husband's killer. In March, 1993, Shakur was convicted of assaulting a film director who had fired him from a film. In February, 1995, he was convicted of assaulting a woman in a New York hotel room. His third album, *Me Against the World*, became a number-one seller while he was serving time in prison on his 1995 assault conviction. His fourth and last album *All Eyez on Me*, recorded after his release from prison, sold more than five million copies. Shakur also acted in several films, including *Juice* (1992), *Poetic Justice* (1993), and *Above the Rim* (1994). In September, 1996, he died from gunshot wounds inflicted by an unknown assailant.

Shalala, Donna

full: Donna Edna Shalala
b. February 14, 1941
Cleveland, Ohio
fields: Education, Government and Politics

Shalala served as head of two educational institutions, Hunter College in New York City, and the University of Wisconsin, where she was the first woman to lead a Big Ten University and one of the first to head a major research university before being named secretary of Health and Human Services by President Bill Clinton.

Shange, Ntozake

né: Paulette Williams
b. October 18, 1948
Trenton, N.J.
fields: Literature, Theater and Entertainment

African American playwright and feminist Ntozake Shange gained attention for her play *for colored girls who have considered suicide/ when the rainbow is enuf* (1976), a "choreopoem" that celebrated the strengths and struggles of black women. Other published works include *Sassafrass* (novella, 1976); *Nappy Edges* (poetry, 1978); *Three Pieces* (plays, 1981); *See No Evil: Prefaces, Essays, and Accounts, 1976-1983* (1984); *I Live in Music* (poetry, 1994); and *Liliane* (novel, 1994).

Shankar, Ravi

b. Apr 7, 1920
Varanasi, Uttar Pradesh, India
fields: Music

Ravi Shankar, perhaps the most internationally well-known of twentieth century Indian classical musicians, was not only a virtuoso soloist and a versatile composer but also a cultural ambassador. He interpreted classical *ragas* and explored new forms, fusing Indian melodic styles with European orchestrational concepts to produce film scores, symphonic works, and chamber music. As a sitarist, he is featured on many recordings, collaborating with European musicians such as violinist Yehudi Menuhin and conductor Andre Previn. Shankar wrote *My Music, My Life* (1969).

Shankara. *See* Samkara

Shannon, Claude Elwood

b. Apr. 30, 1916
Gaylord, Michigan
fields: Mathematics (algebra, applied math, and probability)

Claude Elwood Shannon added to information theory; applied Boolean algebra to the theory of switching circuits.

Shao-hyowa. *See* General, Alexander

Shapley, Harlow

b. Nov. 2, 1885
Nashville, Missouri
d. Oct. 20, 1972
Boulder, Colorado
fields: Astronomy

Harlow Shapley measured the Milky Way's dimensions and located its center and the earth's position in it, in 1918, by developing a means of determining distances within the solar system.

Shapur II

b. c. 309
Iran
d. 379
Iran
fields: Government and Politics, Warfare and Conquest

Shapur was one of the greatest rulers of the Sassanid Dynasty in pre-Islamic Iran. Succeeding to the throne after a period of internal confusion, he restored the fortunes of the Sassanid Empire and extended its frontiers in all directions.

Sharp, Granville

b. November 19, 1735
Durham, England
d. July 6, 1813
Fulham, England
fields: Social Reform

A Radical pamphleteer who championed several humanitarian causes, Sharp had his greatest success in securing the abolition of the slave trade.

Sharpton, Al

full: Alfred Sharpton, Jr.
b. Oct. 3, 1954
Brooklyn, N.Y.
fields: Civil Rights

Pentecostal minister, social activist; after gaining prominence for his preaching in Brooklyn, Al Sharpton became active in the Civil Rights movement; appointed youth director of Jesse Jackson's Operation Breadbasket; briefly served as a bodyguard for singer James Brown and became involved with fight promoter Don King; founded the National Youth Movement (later the United African Movement) in 1971; involved with many high-profile racial incidents in New York City, including the Bernhard Goetz murder trial in 1984, the Howard Beach killing in 1986, the Tawana Brawley affair in 1987, and the Bensonhurst killing in 1989; cowrote *Independent Black Leadership in America* (1990) with Lenora Fulani and Louis Farrakhan; controversial figure whose motives have been questioned.

Shaw, Anna Howard

b. February 14, 1847
Newcastle upon Tyne, Northumberland, England
d. July 2, 1919
Moylan, Pennsylvania
fields: Women's Rights

The first American woman to hold divinity and medical degrees simultaneously, the Reverend Shaw was a central figure in the crusades for political equality and women's rights.

Shaw, Bernard

b. May 22, 1940
Chicago, Ill.
fields: Journalism

African American television journalist; in 1964 Bernard Shaw began his journalism career as an anchor for Chicago's WNUS; his subsequent assignments included correspondent in the Washington Bureau of CBS News, senior Capitol Hill correspondent for ABC News, and chief Washington anchor for the Cable News Network.

Shaw, George Bernard

aka: G. B. Shaw
b. July 26, 1856
Dublin, Ireland
d. November 2, 1950
Ayot St. Lawrence, Hertfordshire, England
fields: Literature, Theater and Entertainment, Philosophy (social)

Shaw was not only England's greatest modern playwright but also a dazzlingly versatile and witty showman of ideas.

Shaw, Herbert Bell

b. 1908
Wilmington, N.C.
d. ?
fields: Religion and Theology

African American clergyman; ordained as an elder in the African Methodist Episcopal Zion Church (1928), Herbert Bell Shaw served as presiding bishop of the Third Episcopal District from 1943 to 1952.

Shaw, Marlena

b. ?
New Rochelle, N.Y.
fields: Music (rhythm-and-blues and jazz singer)

African American singer; Marlena Shaw's recordings include the albums *Out of Different Bags, Spice of Life* (1967; containing the rhythm-and-blues hit "Mercy, Mercy, Mercy"), *Sweet Beginnings* (containing the hit song "Go Away Little Boy"), and *Take a Bite*; as the first female artist to be signed to Blue Note Records (1972), where she cut an album per year for five years, she released a rhythm-and-blues hit single, "It's Better than Walking Out" (1976); in addition to recording for various labels, Shaw has performed jazz vocals with the Count Basie Orchestra; she performed with Joe Williams at Carnegie Hall in 1989.

Shawnee Prophet. *See* Tenskwatawa

Shays, Daniel

b. c. 1747
probably in Hopkinton, Massachusetts
d. September 29, 1825
Sparta, New York
fields: Government and Politics, Military Affairs

In 1787, Shays led farmers in a rebellion against the state government of Massachusetts, protesting unfair debtor laws and inequitable taxation. The rebellion raised fears of anarchy among political leaders throughout the United States, motivating them to meet in Philadelphia, where they would draft the Constitution.

Sheehy, Gail

b. November 27, 1937
Mamaroneck, N.Y.
fields: Journalism, Sociology

A journalist and editor, Gail Sheehy, extended developmental psychology to adulthood, discerning and later exploring predictable stages of adult growth. She is best known for her best-selling book, *Passages: Predictable Crises of Adult Life* (1976). Her other books include *Pathfinders* (1981), *The Silent Passage: Menopause* (1992), and *New Passages: Mapping Your Life Across Time* (1995). Her biography *Gorbachev: The Man Who Changed the World* (1990), won the Washington Journalism Review Award.

Sheen, Charlie

né: Carlos Estevez
b. September 3, 1965
New York, N.Y.
fields: Film (actor)

Charlie Sheen, born Carlos Estevez, is the youngest son of Martin and Janet Sheen. He made his film debut in *Grizzly II* (1984) and went on to appear in such films as *Red Dawn* (1984), *Ferris Bueller's Day Off* (1986), *Lucas* (1986), and *Platoon* (1986), *Wall Street* (1987), *Eight Men Out* (1988), *Major League* (1989), *Hot Shots!* (1991), and *Money Talks* (1997). He won the Hollywood Women's Press Club Discovery of the Year Award in 1987. He also wrote a poetry collection called *A Peace of My Mind* (1988).

Sheen, Martin

né: Ramón Estevez
b. August 3, 1940
Dayton, Ohio
fields: Theater and Entertainment (actor), Film, Television

Martin Sheen, born Ramón Estevez, appeared in numerous major stage roles before his film debut in *The Incident* (1967). His other films include *Catch-22* (1970), *Badlands* (1973), *Apocalypse Now* (1979), *Gandhi* (1982), and *Firestarter* (1984). On television, he appeared on the soap opera *As the World Turns* (1967-1968) and the miniseries *Blind Ambition* (1979) and *Kennedy* (1983). He is also a director, producer, and playwright. He won an Emmy for *Babies Having Babies* (1986) and was nominated for Emmy Awards for *The Execution of Private Slovak* (1974) and *The Atlanta Child Murders* (1985). Sheen and his wife, Janet, have had three sons: Emilio, Ramón, and Carlos.

Sheffey, Fred Clifton, Jr.

b. August 27, 1928
McKeesport, Pa.
fields: Military Affairs

African American military officer; during his U.S. Army career (1950-1980), Fred Clifton Sheffey, Jr., rose from second lieutenant to the rank of major general (1976); his postings included director of materiel management at the U.S. Army Materiel Development and Readiness Command in Alexandria, Va. (1975) and commanding general of the U.S. Army Quartermaster Center and commandant of the U.S. Army Quartermaster School in Fort Lee, Va. (1977).

Shell, Art

full: Arthur Shell
b. November 26, 1946
Charleston, S.C.
fields: Sports (football player and coach)

African American football player and coach; Art Shell was an offensive lineman for the Oakland Raiders from 1968 to 1982; he played on numerous Pro Bowl teams (1973-1979, 1981) and played in Superbowl XI (the

Raiders beating the Minnesota Vikings) and in Superbowl XV; in 1983 Shell was named offensive line coach for the Raiders and, in 1989, was named head coach—the first African American to be designated a head coach in National Football League history; that same year, Shell was inducted into the Pro Football Hall of Fame.

Shelley, Mary Wollstonecraft

né: Mary Godwin
b. August 30, 1797
London, England
d. February 1, 1851
London, England
fields: Literature

As an innovative and politically subversive writer of novels, tales, and stories, Shelley was a significant contributor to the history of women's writing and the development of prose fiction.

Shelley, Percy Bysshe

b. August 4, 1792
Field Place, near Horsham, Sussex, England
d. July 8, 1822
At sea off Leghorn, Italy
fields: Literature

In his zeal to renew the human spirit and to reform society, Shelley produced an impassioned, philosophically complex poetry suffused with prophetic vision.

Shelton, Christopher

b. 1933
New Orleans, La.
fields: Art (sculptor)

African American sculptor; Christopher Shelton experimented with multidimensional sculpture, combining painting with the manipulation of space. To realize his concept of a new vision for African American artists, Shelton drew on his rich cultural heritage and his own creative energy to express himself through various media. He constructed his work where it would be displayed which conveyed a sense that environment and sculptural form are inextricably wedded. His works compose the artistic sequence entitled *Air Afrique*.

Shen, Catherine

b. Oct. 31, 1947
Boston, Mass.
fields: Publishing

Catherine Shen became the first Asian American publisher of a mainstream daily when she assumed the post of publisher of *Star Bulletin*, a major daily afternoon newspaper in Honolulu, Hawaii. Other posts include assistant managing editor of the "Life" section of *USA Today* and associate publisher of *Marin Independent Journal* in California. She received a master's degree from Claremont Graduate School in California.

Sheng, Yuan. *See* Assing, Norman

Shepard, Alan

full: Alan Bartlett Shepard, Jr.
b. November 18, 1923
East Derry, New Hampshire
d. July 21, 1998
Monterey, California
fields: Aviation and Space Exploration

Shepard flew the first U.S. manned space flight in 1961 and became the only Mercury astronaut to walk on the Moon.

Shepherd, Harry

b. ?
d. ?
fields: Photography

African American photographer; Harry Shepherd's principal photographic subjects were portraits taken at and scenes of Tuskegee Institute; he showed some of these photographs at the Paris Exposition in 1900; in 1887 he opened his first gallery; in 1891 he won first prize at the Minnesota State Fair.

Shepp, Archie

b. May 21, 1934
Ft. Lauderdale, Fla.
fields: Music (jazz tenor saxophonist)

African American jazz tenor saxophonist and playwright; with a musical sound strongly influenced by the styles of Sonny Rollins and John Coltrane, Archie Shepp is noted for incorporating social themes into his music; as one of the first jazz musicians to do this, Rollins included songs containing poetry about Malcolm X.

Sheppard, Sam

b. Nov. 5, 1923
Fort Sheridan, Ill.
d. April 6, 1970
Columbus, Ohio
fields: Historical Figure

On July 4, 1954, Marilyn Reese Sheppard, four months pregnant, was found stabbed to death in her bed. Although her husband, Sam Sheppard, insisted that an intruder had murdered his wife and then attacked him when he came to his wife's aid, he was convicted of the murder and sentenced to life in prison in one of the longest-running criminal trials of that era. Almost ten years after his conviction, Sheppard retained attorney F. Lee Bailey, who succeeded in having the decision reversed by the U.S. Supreme Court. After a retrial, the jury returned a not-guilty verdict on November 16, 1966. The case inspired a television series, *The Fugitive*, and a feature film of the same name. Sheppard resumed his medical practice but resigned after malpractice suits were filed against him and became a professional wrestler. He died in 1970.

Sher-i-Punjab. *See* Rai, Lala Lajpat

Sherman, Edward Forrester

b. January 17, 1945
New York, N.Y.
fields: Photography

African American photographer; during the 1960's, Edward Forrester Sherman worked as a freelance photographer, contributing work to *Freelance Photographer* from 1969 on; in 1971 Sherman served as cochair of Collective Black Photographers; in 1973 he became associate editor of the *NCA New Journal*.

Sherman, Roger

b. April 19, 1721
Newton, Massachusetts
d. July 23, 1793
New Haven, Connecticut
fields: Government and Politics

Sherman's political wisdom and facility for compromise helped create the United States Constitution. He also served ably as a Colonial leader in Connecticut during the American Revolution.

Sherman, William Tecumseh

né: Tecumseh Sherman
b. February 8, 1820
Lancaster, Ohio
d. February 14, 1891
New York, New York
fields: Military Affairs

One of the architects of the Union victory in the Civil War and a father of modern warfare, Sherman was also a leader in the nation's late nineteenth century Indian wars in the West.

Sherrington, Charles Scott

full: Sir Charles Scott Sherrington
b. Nov. 27, 1857
London, England
d. Mar. 4, 1952
Eastbourne, Sussex, England
fields: Medicine, Physiology

Charles Scott Sherrington worked to understand reflexes and the nervous system; in 1932, won the Nobel Prize in Physiology or Medicine.

Sherwood, Kenneth N.

b. August 10, 1930
New York, N.Y.
d. July 28, 1989
Kingston, Jamaica
fields: Business and Industry

African American business executive; in 1965 when Kenneth N. Sherwood bought Reter's Furniture Store from a white owner, he became the first African American to own a business in Harlem's economic hub; his Kenwood Company soon branched out into areas, including supermarkets and liquor stores; among the government and public service positions Sherwood held were commissioner and treasurer of the New York State Parks Commission (1968-1973), commissioner of the New York State Athletic Commission (1972-1975; taking the place of Jackie Robinson), and member of the Business Council for Urban Development; he moved his family to Jamaica in 1976 and held the Burger King franchise for Jamaica.

Shevardnadze, Eduard

full: Eduard Amvrosiyevich Shevardnadze
fields: Government and Politics
b. January 25, 1928
Mamati, Georgia, U.S.S.R.
fields: Diplomacy, Government and Politics

When Mikhail Gorbachev came to power in the Soviet Union in 1985, he named reform-minded Eduard Shevardnadze as Soviet foreign minister, replacing long-time minister Andrei Gromyko. The second most important figure in the Soviet Union, Shevardnadze served 1985-1990, then briefly in 1991. After breakup of Soviet Union, he became chairman of parliament of the Republic of Georgia in 1992 and was elected Georgia's president in 1995. Faced numerous problems and crises. Rebels launched guerrilla attacks on the Shevardnadze government, and he reluctantly sought assistance from the Russian army. Struggled with Georgian nationalists angered at continuing Russian influence and with ethnic separatist movements that threatened to become violent.

Shigeta, James

b. 1933
Territory of Hawaii
fields: Theater and Entertainment, Music, Film

Actor and singer James Shigeta starred or had a major role in films such as *The Crimson Kimono* (1959), *Walk Like a Dragon* (1960), *Cry for Happy* (1961), *Bridge to the Sun* (1961), and *Flower Drum Song* (1961). Later film credits include *The Yakuza* (1975) and *Die Hard* (1988). Shigeta served in the U.S. Marine Corps in the Korean War then became a singer, entertainer, and actor in Japan before starting his film career in the United States.

Shi Huangdi

aka: Ch'in Shih Huang-ti
aka: Shih huang-ti
b. c. 259 B.C.E.
Qin, China
d. 210 or 209 B.C.E.
China
fields: Government and Politics

The first emperor to rule a unified China, Shih Huangdi came to power in 246 B.C.E. as ruler of Qin feudal state that unified China in 221 B.C.E. Both the Qin state and its royal dynasty were governed by Legalism, a totalitarian philosophy emphasizing discipline and complete obedience to the ruler.

Shikellamy

aka: Ongwaterohiathe
aka: Takashwangarous
b. ?
d. Dec. 6, 1748
Shamokin, present-day Sunbury, Pa.
fields: Government and Politics, Diplomacy, Native American Affairs

Shikellamy was born either French or Cayuga, or possibly a mixture of the two. He was kidnapped by the Oneidas when he was two years old and later adopted by them. As representative for the Pennsylvania Iroquois, Shikellamy helped negotiate their admittance into the Iroquois Confederacy in 1763. James Logan, a leader of the Ohio Oneidas who became known as Mingos, was Shikellamy's son.

Shima, George

né: Kinji Ushimura
b. 1864
Fukuoka Prefecture, Japan
d. March 27, 1926
Hollywood, Calif.
fields: Business and Industry

Japanese American agriculturist and businessman. George Shima arrived in California in 1887 and began picking potatoes near Stockton. In time he acquired acreage of his own and became the "Potato King" of that state. By 1920, he owned an estimated 85 percent of California's potato crop and was worth $16 million. He was the first president of the Japanese American Association.

Shimoda, Yuki

b. early 1920's
Sacramento, Calif.
d. May 21, 1981
Los Angeles, Calif.
fields: Theater and Entertainment, Film, Television

Yuki Shimoda, interned in the Tule Lake relocation center during World War II, appeared in numerous Broadway plays and more than two dozen feature films. He appeared in long-running Broadway productions such as *South Pacific* (1949), *The King and I* (1951), *Teahouse of the August Moon* (1953), and *Auntie Mame* (1956). His film credits include *Auntie Mame* (1958), *A Majority of One* (1961), *Midway* (1976), *MacArthur* (1977), and *Hito-Hata: Raise the Banner* (1980). Shimoda had roles on the television shows *Ironside* (1967-1975), *Hawaii Five-O* (1968-1980), and *Kung Fu* (1972-1975) and on the television movie *Farewell to Manzanar* (1976).

Shines, Johnny

aka: Shoe Shine Johnny
b. April 26, 1915
Frayser, Tenn.
d. April 20, 1992
Tuscaloosa, Ala.
fields: Music (blues musician)

African American blues musician; known as a highly skilled bottleneck guitarist, Johnny Shines had difficulty obtaining recording contracts because he resisted changing his style to suit popular fashion, preferring instead to play primitive country blues in the Delta blues tradition; his lyrics conjured up striking images reflecting a Mississippi theme, and his music was emotionally intense and rhythmic; "Blues to Texas" and "Moon Is Rising" are two of his more well known songs.

Shinran

né: Matsuwaka-Maru
b. 1173
near Kyōto, Japan
d. November 28, 1262
Kyōto
fields: Religion and Theology

Shinran founded the Japanese Mahāyānist Buddhist sect Jōdo Shinshū, or the True Pure Land Sect. Taught that real truth (faith) refers to the gift of salvation in the next world, while common truth (morality) refers to one's duty to society in this world.

Shiomi, Rick A.

b. May 25, 1947
Toronto, Ontario, Canada
fields: Theater and Entertainment, Literature

Japanese Canadian Rick A. Shiomi wrote for Canadian television and created works that became Asian American theater standards, *Yellow Fever* (1982) and *Rosie's Cafe* (1987). Other works include *Play Ball* (1989) and *Uncle Tadao* (1992). Shiomi became artistic director of Theatre Mu in Minneapolis in 1993. He was instrumental in nurturing young Asian American playwrights, actors, and designers.

Shiras, George

b. 1832
d. 1924
fields: Law

U.S. Supreme Court justice, 1892-1903; appointed by President Harrison. Dissenting opinions offered modern view of the protections offered by the Fifth Amendment. Significant opinions: *Mattox v. United States*, 156 U.S. 237 (1895) (dissenting opinion); *Wong Wing v. United States*, 163 U.S. 228 (1896); *Brown v. Walker*, 161 U.S. 591 (1896) (dissenting opinion).

Shirley, George

b. April 18, 1934
Indianapolis, Ind.
fields: Music (opera)

African American opera lead tenor; the initiator of a radio program on African Americans in classical music, George Shirley is noted as the New York Metropolitan Opera Company's first African American male lead; his performances in *Die Fledermaus, The Magic Flute, La Boheme*, and *Madame Butterfly* gained international recognition.

Shirota, Jon

b. 1928
Peahi, Maui, Territory of Hawaii
fields: Literature

Japanese American Jon Shirota moved to Los Angeles after graduating from Brigham Young University in 1952. A former treasury agent for the Internal Revenue Service, he finished his first novel at the Louwney Handy Colony, a writing-school retreat in Marshall, Illinois. His works include the novels *Lucky Come Hawaii* (1965) and *Pineapple White* (1972).

Shivers, Robert L.

b. 1894?
Ashland City, Tenn.
d. June 28, 1950
Honolulu, Territory of Hawaii
fields: Government and Politics

Robert L. Shivers was agent-in-charge of the Honolulu office of the Federal Bureau of Investigation (FBI) from 1939 to 1943. His job was to determine how to handle Hawaii's large Japanese population if hostilities occurred. Shivers's approval was required for any person to be interned or released from internment. He developed a deep faith in the loyalty and patriotism of Hawaii's Japanese, with the result that only 980 of the 160,000 Japanese Americans in Hawaii were detained. Because of a heart ailment, Shivers returned to the mainland in 1943.

Shocklee, Hank

né: Hank Boxley
b. 1960?
fields: Music (rap music producer)

Early African American rap music producer; Hank Shocklee helped develop the rap acts Public Enemy (produced their debut album, 1987), Ice Cube, and many other artists on the Def Jam Records label; founded S.O.U.L. (Sound of Urban Listeners), his own record label distributed through MCA Records, in 1990; scored, assembled, and produced the sound track to the film *Juice* (1992).

Shoong, Joe

b. 1879
Longtouhuan Village, Zhongshan, Guangdong Province, China
d. Apr. 13, 1961
San Francisco, Calif.
fields: Business and Industry, Philanthropy

Joe Shoong cofounded a dry goods store in 1901 and built it into a corporation, National Dollar Stores, in 1920. By 1961, the corporation had fifty-four outlets. Shoong was also successful in real estate and the stock market., acquiring a majority interest in national Shoe Company. He built and supported a primary school in his native village, helped support a middle school near his village, and established a scholarship fund for Chinese students at the University of California. In 1946, he created the Joe Shoong Foundation, which increased the University of California scholarship fund and dropped racial restrictions.

Short, Alonzo Earl, Jr.

b. ?
Greenville, North Carolina
fields: Military Affairs

African American military officer; Alonzo Earl Short, Jr.'s Army service has included appointments at the Armed Forces Staff College and the Defense Communications Agency; served as commanding general of the Army Information Systems Engineering Command, Fort Huachuca, Arizona. He retired with the rank of Army general; he serves on the board of directors of Promise Keepers, a national organization dedicated to overcoming racial barriers.

Short, Bobby

b. September 15, 1926
Danville, Ill.
fields: Music (singer and pianist)

African American singer and pianist; most often associated with New York's sophisticated Cafe Society, Bobby Short spent more than two decades singing and playing piano at the Carlyle Hotel in New York City; noted as an important interpreter of Cole Porter and of the more obscure works of Lorenz Hart and Richard Rodgers.

Short Bull

b. c. 1845
Niobrara River, northern Nebr.
d. c. 1915
Pine Ridge Reservation, S.Dak.
fields: Religion and Theology, Government and Politics, Native American Affairs

Brule Sioux leader Short Bull introduced the Ghost Dance religion, begun by Paiute prophet Wovoka, to the Sioux in 1889 and preached a holy war against whites. The new religion found many converts, especially on the Rosebud and Pine Ridge reservations. Oglala and Brule Sioux leaders spoke a fiery rhetoric and danced themselves into a trancelike condition. White settlers and the Pine Ridge agent began to panic and called for troops to restore order. Three thousand troops arrived. Short Bull was arrested and imprisoned, and Hump was pacified. Sitting Bull was ordered arrested but was killed in the attempt.

Shorter, Wayne

b. August 25, 1933
Newark, N.J.
fields: Music (jazz saxophonist, composer, and bandleader)

African American jazz saxophonist, composer, and bandleader; with a preference for including a multiplicity of styles from various traditions in his music, Wayne Shorter has been influenced by soul, rock, bebop, blues, and Latin American forms; he played with Art Blakey's Jazz Messengers (1959-1963) and Miles Davis's quintet (1964-1970; taking up the soprano saxophone in 1968) and, along with pianist Joe Zawinul, founded the jazz-rock fusion group Weather Report (1970-1985); after leaving Weather Report he formed a new band and toured Japan, Europe, and the United States; he plays in an understated style, preferring a short song or short improvisation with simple, clear phrases rather than a lengthy and complicated piece.

Shostakovich, Dmitri

full: Dmitri Dmitrievich Shostakovich
b. September 25, 1906
St. Petersburg, Russia
d. August 9, 1975
Moscow, U.S.S.R.
fields: Music

Shostakovich was a first-rank composer in the Soviet Union for a full five decades. He adroitly balanced the insistent requirements of totalitarian political dictatorship over artistic culture with his own irrepressible inspiration for superb creativity to win worldwide acclaim.

Shōtoku Taishi

b. 573
Honshu, Japan
d. 621
Kauga, Honshu, Japan
fields: Government and Politics, Religion and Theology

As regent for his aunt, Empress Suiko, Shōtoku is credited with strengthening the central government, solidifying the rule of the imperial family, and transforming Japan's civilization through adoption of Confucian and Buddhist institutions and values.

Shouren. *See* Wang Yangming

Showa. *See* Hirohito

Shridharani, Krishnalal

b. Sept. 16, 1911
Umrala, Bhavnagar, Republic of India
d. July 23, 1960
New Delhi, India
fields: Journalism

Krishnalal Shridharani was arrested and imprisoned for participating in Mahatma Gandhi's March to the Sea in 1930 to protest the British government's salt monopoly. Arriving in the United States in 1934, he earned an M.A. degree in sociology from New York University and, from Columbia University, an M.S. degree in journalism and a Ph.D. degree in sociology and political theory. He traveled throughout the United States speaking about India's independence movement and in 1946 returned to India. His works include *The Banyan Tree* (1930), *I Shall Kill the Human in You* (1932), *Spring Flowers* (1933), *These Earthen Lamps* (1934), *War Without Violence* (1939), *My India, My America* (1941), and *The Mahatma and the World* (1946).

Shtern, Sholem

b. 1906
d. ?
fields: Literature

Sholem Shtern is a writer who developed a distinctively Jewish Canadian literature, with heavy Marxist overtones; wrote *In Kanade* (1960, 1963), detailing the Jewish immigrant experience.

Shufeldt, Robert W.

b. Feb. 21, 1822
Red Hook, N.Y.
d. Nov. 7, 1895
Washington, D.C.
fields: Diplomacy

Commodore Robert W. Shufeldt, in 1882, as U.S. special representative, along with China's foreign-relations representative Li Hongzhang, initiated and directed Korea's first treaty with the West, the Treaty of Chemulpo.

Shulush Homa. *See* Red Shoes

Shunrō. *See* Hokusai

Shuttlesworth, Fred L.

b. March 18, 1922
Mt. Meigs, Ala.
fields: Civil Rights

African American baptist minister and civil rights leader. Fred Shuttlesworth, a close friend of Martin Luther King, Jr., was a key participant in the efforts to abolish segregation in the South during the 1950's and 1960's. He helped organize and was named president of the Alabama Christian Movement for Human Rights; he also helped organize the Southern Christian Leadership Conference (SCLC). During the 1960's he moved to Cincinnati, Ohio, to serve as pastor of a Baptist church there. By the mid-1990's he was pastor of the Greater New Light Baptist Church and director of the Shuttlesworth Housing Foundation, an organization that assisted low-income families to purchase homes.

Si Tanka. *See* Big Foot

Siad Barre, Muhammad

b. c. 1910
Shiilaabo, Ogaden, Abyssinian Somaliland (now Ethiopia)
d. January 2, 1995
Lagos, Nigeria
fields: Government and Politics

Muhammad Siad Barre was dictatorial ruler of Somalia, 1969-1991. Started and lost war with Ethiopia in 1977-1978. Open rebellion began in 1988; regime collapsed in 1991, and Siad Barre fled. Country fell into anarchy and clan warfare; a severe famine caused death of at least 300,000 people.

Sib. *See* Williamson, Sonny Boy, II

Sibelius, Jean

full: Johan Julius Christian Sibelius
b. December 8, 1865
Tavastehus, Finland
d. September 20, 1957
Järvenpää, Finland
fields: Music

Closely identified with Finnish nationalism, Sibelius not only is a national hero in his own country but also is considered by many to have been the greatest symphonic composer of the twentieth century.

Sibley, Charles

full: Charles Gald Sibley
b. Aug. 7, 1917
Fresno, California
fields: Biology, Zoology

Charles G. Sibley was an ornithologist and educator who championed the use of biochemical methods to determine the phylogenetic relationships among groups of organisms, primarily birds.

Siddhārtha. *See* Buddha

Sidgwick, Henry

b. May 31, 1838
Skipton, Yorkshire, England
d. August 28, 1900
Cambridge, Cambridgeshire, England
fields: Philosophy, Education

A proponent of higher education for women and an advocate of research into paranormal phenomena, Sidgwick attempted in philosophy to reconcile an intuitive approach to morality with that of utilitarianism. His reasoned defense of the resulting ethical method produced one of the most significant works on ethics in English, the capstone of nineteenth century British moral philosophy.

Sidney, Philip

aka: Sir Philip Sidney
b. November 30, 1554
Penshurst, England
d. October 17, 1586
Arnhem, the Netherlands
fields: Literature, Government and Politics, Military Affairs

Known during his lifetime as the perfect example of a Renaissance courtier because of his learning, nobility, and chivalry, Sidney was also a poet of the first rank whose sonnet sequence *Astrophel and Stella* is a classic of English literature.

Siemens, Friedrich

b. December 8, 1826
Lübeck, Prussia
d. May 24, 1904
Berlin, Germany
fields: Invention and Technology

The four Siemens brothers—Werner, William, Friedrich, and Karl—were notable for their many contributions to applied technology in nineteenth century electrical and steel industries, including telegraphy, the electric dynamo, and the open-hearth steel furnace. Friedrich pioneered the work on the application of the regenerative furnace into the smelting of steel, thus creating the famous

Siemens-Martin open-hearth furnace (with French engineer Pierre-Émile Martin).

Siemens, Karl
b. March 3, 1829
Lübeck, Prussia
d. March 21, 1906
St. Petersburg, Russia
fields: Invention and Technology

The four Siemens brothers—Werner, William, Friedrich, and Karl—were notable for their many contributions to applied technology in nineteenth century electrical and steel industries, including telegraphy, the electric dynamo, and the open-hearth steel furnace. Karl Siemens' contribution was in keeping a rapport between all the brothers. He helped to extended the technology developed by the firm of Siemens and Halske into telegraph and electric systems sold, installed, and maintained by the company across the Western world.

Siemens, Werner
full: Ernst Werner von Siemens
b. December 13, 1816
Lenthe, Prussia
d. December 6, 1892
Berlin, Germany
fields: Invention and Technology

The four Siemens brothers—Werner, William, Friedrich, and Karl—were notable for their many contributions to applied technology in nineteenth century electrical and steel industries, including telegraphy, the electric dynamo, and the open-hearth steel furnace. Werner Siemens invented an electroplating process in 1842; formed the firm of Siemens and Halske, with the physical mechanic Johann Georg Halske; invented the dial telegraph in 1847; manufactured and laid telegraph cable.

Siemens, William
né: Karl Wilhelm Siemens
aka: Sir Charles William Siemens
b. April 4, 1823
Lenthe, Prussia
d. November 19, 1883
London, England
fields: Invention and Technology

The four Siemens brothers—Werner, William, Friedrich, and Karl—were notable for their many contributions to applied technology in nineteenth century electrical and steel industries, including telegraphy, the electric dynamo, and the open-hearth steel furnace. William Siemens' career was mostly devoted to invention and advancing the realm of the electric telegraph. William emigrated to England and became a naturalized citizen in 1859. He holds 113 English patents. Among other accomplishments, he invented the regenerative steam engine, opened a cable factory in England, improved the steel making process, and laid cable across the Atlantic Ocean.

Sierra, Paul Alberto
b. July 30, 1944
Havana, Cuba
fields: Art

Cuban American artist. Paul Alberto Sierra began as a minimalist. In the 1970's, he moved into a more expressionist style that explored images and subjects from Cuba and Africa. His work is hung in major collections including the Museum of Contemporary Art in Chicago and the Anheuser-Busch Corporate Collection. Sierra was included in *Cuba-U.S.A.: The First Generation*, the first traveling group exhibition of Cuban and American artists.

Sierra, Rubén
b. Dec. 6, 1946
San Antonio, Tex.
fields: Literature, Theater and Entertainment

Latino director, playwright, and actor. Rubén Sierra's first play, *La Raza Pura: Or, Racial, Racial* (1968), was later produced for public television. Sierra worked with the political Teatro de Piojo (Theater of the Louse) from 1972 to 1977, during which time he wrote *Manolo* (1976), one of the first full-length Chicano dramas. He was artistic director of the Seattle Group Theater from 1978 to 1992. In 1989, he moved to Los Angeles and taught at the California Institute for the Arts and the University of Southern California before becoming full professor at California State University in 1993. That year, he helped to found the East L.A. Classical Theater Company.

Sierra, Ruben Angel
b. Oct. 6, 1965
Rio Piedras, Puerto Rico
fields: Sports (baseball player)

Puerto Rican baseball player. Outfielder Ruben Angel Sierra made his major league debut with the Texas Rangers in 1986. The following year, at the age of twenty-one, he became the youngest player since 1965 to hit thirty home runs in a season. In 1989, Sierra led the American League with 119 runs batted in and 14 triples; he finished second in the voting for the American League Most Valuable Player Award. He was named to the All-Star Team three times with the Rangers before being traded to the Oakland Athletics in 1992. He won All-Star honors again in 1994.

Sifford, Charlie
b. June 2, 1922
fields: Sports (golfer)

African American golfer; six-time winner of the Negro National Open, Charlie Sifford was not allowed to become a PGA member until 1961; Sifford became the first African American to win a regular PGA tour event when he won the 1967 Hartford Open; in the period from 1960 to 1969, he was among the top sixty money winners on the PGA tour.

Siger of Brabant
b. c. 1235
probably Brabant
d. c. 1282
Orvieto
fields: Philosophy

By combining his mastery of Latin Averroistic philosophy with his intention to remain loyal to the institution and doctrines of the Roman Catholic church, Siger was able to help clarify the enduring questions concerning the relationship of philosophy to theology and of reason to revelation.

Sihanouk, Norodom
full: Norodom Sambeth Preah Sihanouk
b. October 31, 1922
Phnom Penh, Cambodia
fields: Government and Politics

King of Cambodia from 1941 to 1955, then alternately prime minister, head of state, and leader of various opposition movements, Sihanouk could for many years be found at the center of Cambodia's fractious and highly controversial politics.

Silas, María Africa Antonia Gracia Vidal de Santo. *See* Montez, María

Silex, Humberto
b. ?
fields: Social Reform

Mexican American labor leader. Humberto Silex moved from Mexico to the United States in 1921 and served in the United States Army. He organized the workers at the American Smelting and Refining Company in El Paso, Texas, into Local 509 and became president of that union. Silex successfully fought the efforts of angry industrial and government leaders to have him deported. He remained in the United States and continued to work for the rights of workers.

Silko, Leslie Marmon
b. March 5, 1948
Albuquerque, New Mexico
fields: Literature

A Laguna pueblo writer who gained prominence for her poetry, fiction, and essays. Her works include *Laguna Woman*

(1974), a book of poetry, *The Man to Send Rain Clouds* (1974) and *Storyteller* (1981), short story collections, and *Ceremony* (1977) and *Almanac of the Dead* (1991), novels.

Sills, Beverly

né: Belle Miriam Silverman
b. May 25, 1929
Brooklyn, New York
fields: Music

Beverly Sills ranks among the most successful opera stars of the twentieth century. She also served as a director of the New York City Opera Company.

Siloé, Diego de

b. c. 1495
near Burgos, Spain
d. October 22, 1563
Granada, Spain
fields: Architecture, Art

Siloé ranks as one of Spain's greatest architects for his exquisite translations and combinations of Roman, Moorish, and High Renaissance Italian style into a Spanish idiom, most evident, despite his many other works, in the great Cathedral of Granada.

Silver, Horace

b. September 2, 1928
Norwalk, Conn.
fields: Music (jazz pianist and composer)

African American jazz pianist and composer; Horace Silver plays a funk style of jazz based on emotion-filled melodies and gospel-inspired harmonies which would influence such later musicians as Chick Corea and Herbie Hancock; in the early 1950's, Silver performed in the Stan Getz quintet and in drummer Art Blakey's Jazz Messengers; in 1956 he formed his own quintet.

Silverman, Belle Miriam. *See* Sills, Beverly

Silverstein, Shel

full: Shelby Silverstein
b. 1932
Chicago, Illinois
May 10, 1999
Key West, Florida
fields: Art, Literature

Well known as a cartoonist for *Playboy* and other magazines, Shel Silverstein became a popular American children's book author. His most successful books have been eccentric collections of light verse, such as *Where the Sidewalk Ends: The Poems and Drawings of Shel Silverstein* (1974), *A Light in the Attic: Poems and Drawings* (1981), and *The Giving Tree* (1964). His children's books were widely criticized and even banned on charges of sexism, sexual suggestiveness, and bad taste. He also wrote a number of songs including "A Boy Named Sue."

Simeon Stylites, Saint

b. c. 390
Sis, near Nicopolis, Syria
d. 459
Telneshae (Telanissos), Syria
fields: Religion and Theology

An ascetic who spent the greater part of his career perched in prayer atop a sixty-foot pillar, Simeon was one of the most controversial figures of the fifth century. Although he left behind no works of enduring value, he was the conscience and spiritual example for Syrian Christians in the patristic period.

Simmons, Paul A.

b. August 31, 1921
Monangahela, Pa.
fields: Law

African American federal judge; after teaching law at law schools in North and South Carolina (1949-1956), practicing private law (1956-1970), and becoming a law firm partner (1970-1973), Paul A. Simmons was appointed judge of the Court of Common Pleas of Washington County, Pa., in 1973; President Jimmy Carter appointed him to serve as U.S. district judge for the Western District of Pennsylvania in 1978; Simmons retired from the federal bench in 1981.

Simmons, Russell

b. October 4, 1957
Hollis, Queens, N.Y.
fields: Music (rap music manager, producer, and record executive)

African American rap music manager, producer, and record executive; cofounder with Rick Rubin of Def Jam Records (1985), Russell Simmons has maintained creative control of the majority of artists signed to Def Jam Records and has served as associate producer of the rap films *Krush Groove* (1985) and *Tougher than Leather* (1988); Simmons's multimillion-dollar entertainment company, which encompasses music, film, and television, grew to become the largest black-owned music business in the United States. He was executive producer for *The Nutty Professor* (1996; starring Eddie Murphy), and *Def Jam's How to be a Player* (1997).

Simms, Hilda

né: Hilda Theresa Moses
b. April 15, 1920
Minneapolis, Minnesota
d. February 6, 1994
Buffalo, New York
fields: Theater and Entertainment, Television

African American stage and television actress; Hilda Simms is most remembered for her more than two thousand performances (in New York, Chicago, and London) of the title role in the American Negro Theatre production of *Anna Lucasta* (1944); from 1962 to 1965 Simms appeared as Miss Ayres in the prime-time dramatic series *The Nurses*.

Simon. *See* Peter, Saint

Simon, Neil

full: Marvin Neil Simon
b. July 4, 1927
Bronx, New York
fields: Theater and Entertainment, Film, Literature

One of the most popular American playwrights of the 1960's, Neil Simon wrote comedies that captured and at times even created the archetypal images of modern life in the United States. After writing comedy for radio and then television (receiving Emmy Awards for *Your Show of Shows* in 1957 and for the *Sergeant Bilko* show in 1959), he wrote his first full-length play, *Come Blow Your Horn*, produced in 1960, followed by a string of successful comedies including *Barefoot in the Park* (1963), *The Odd Couple* (1965), *Sweet Charity* (1966), *Promises, Promises* (1968), *Plaza Suite* (1968), and *The Last of the Red-Hot Lovers* (1969). Through the 1970's, he averaged nearly two plays per year, eight stage comedies and eleven screenplays. The 1980's saw his plays become increasingly serious, particularly the autobiographical trilogy *Brighton Beach Memoirs* (1982), *Biloxi Blues* (1984), and *Broadway Bound* (1986). Critical acceptance came at last with these plays, as well as *Lost in Yonkers,* which won the 1991 Pulitzer Prize for Drama. Late twentieth century American comedy was largely shaped by Simon.

Simone, Nina

né: Eunice Waymon
b. February 21, 1933
Tryon, N.C.
fields: Music (singer and pianist/organist)

African American singer and pianist/organist; with a style that mixes blues, pop, jazz, rock, classical, and African music, Nina Simone incorporated black pride and other social themes into her music; in the 1960's she was involved in the Civil Rights movement.

Simonides

b. c. 556 B.C.E.
Iulis, Greece
d. c. 467 B.C.E.
Syracuse, Sicily

fields: Literature

Having advanced the quality of Greek lyric poetry through his elegies and epigrams, Simonides brought the dithyramb and Epinician ode to a level of perfection comparable only to that of Pindar.

Simpson, Carole

b. December 7, 1940
Chicago, Ill.
fields: Journalism

African American broadcast journalist; from 1971 to 1974, Carole Simpson taught journalism at Northwestern University's Medill School of Journalism; she is noted as Chicago's first black female television reporter; she started news reporting with ABC in 1982; beginning in 1988, Simpson served as an anchor on ABC's *World News Saturday*; she earned an Emmy nomination for her 1988 ABC News *American Agenda* report on children with acquired immunodeficiency syndrome; she won an Emmy for her coverage of Nelson Mandela's release from prison in 1990.

Simpson, Coreen

b. 1942
New York, N.Y.
fields: Photography

African American photographer; Coreen Simpson has had several one-person exhibitions of her photography, which focuses on journalistic subjects and photographs of people; for a time she served as associate curator of photography at the Studio Museum of Harlem.

Simpson, Lorna

b. 1960
fields: Photography

African American photographer; Lorna Simpson is known for her large photographs, usually forty by sixty inches, which often include short captions printed on the photographs.

Simpson, O. J.

full: Orenthal James Simpson
aka: The Juice
b. July 9, 1947
San Francisco, Calif.
fields: Sports (football player)

African American football player; in 1967 O. J. Simpson won the job as the University of Southern California (USC) Trojans' starting tailback; in 1968 Simpson was awarded the Heisman Trophy; he was drafted by the Buffalo Bills of the American Football League in 1969 and, during his nine seasons with the Bills, Simpson won four league rushing titles and three AFL Player of the Year awards; he was inducted into the Pro Football Hall of Fame in 1985; Simpson went on to act in films and television and he also worked as a television sportscaster for ABC and NBC. Beginning in October, 1994, Simpson was tried for the June, 1994, murders of his former wife, Nicole Brown Simpson, and her friend, Ronald Goldman; on October 3, 1995, Simpson was acquitted on both murder charges; in February, 1997, he was found guilty in the civil trial that followed and was ordered to pay $33.5 million to the Brown and Goldman families.

Simpson, Richard. *See* Chubb Rock

Simpson, William

b. 1830
Buffalo, N.Y.
d. 1872
Boston, Mass.
fields: Art (painter)

African American portrait artist; trained by local artist Matthew Wilson, William Simpson became a famous portrait painter of children and family groups; he is particularly noted for his paintings of Charles Sumner and John L. Hilton.

Sims, Naomi

b. March 30, 1949
Oxford, Miss.
fields: Fashion

African American fashion model; from 1967 until her retirement in 1973, Naomi Sims was the most prominent African American model; in 1969 Sims became the first African American to reach the top rung of fashion modeling when she was named Model of the Year; she has authored several books on beauty and success and has developed her own line of beauty products.

Sims, Sandman

full: Howard Sims
b. 1918
fields: Dance

African American tap dancer; after dancing on L.A. street corners in the 1940's, Sandman Sims moved to New York and, through the 1950's and 1960's, became a regular at the Apollo Theater dancing as a headliner, working Amateur Night from the box (he would signal for untalented performers to be removed), and mentoring backstage; Sims's television and film credits include guest appearances on *The Cosby Show*,and appearances in the video documentaries *No Maps on My Taps* (1979) and *Tappin': The Making of Tap* (1989), and in the feature film *Tap* (1989).

Sinatra, Frank

full: Francis Albert Sinatra
b. December 12, 1915
Hoboken, New Jersey
d. May 14, 1998
Los Angeles, California
fields: Music

Perhaps the most popular singer of his generation, Sinatra recorded definitive renditions of many popular American songs. His personal sense of style extended to performances on stage and screen, making him an icon of American culture.

Sinbad

né: David Atkins
b. 1957
Benton Harbor, Mich.
fields: Theater and Entertainment (comedian and actor), Television

African American comedian and actor; Sinbad started as a stand-up comedian, worked as an opening act for musicians, and did a stint as a warm-up comedian for studio audiences watching the taping of *The Cosby Show*. This led to his television debut as a member of the ensemble cast of the show's spinoff series *A Different World* in 1986. Sinbad hosted the syndicated variety show *It's Showtime at the Apollo* beginning in 1989. He became known for his outrageous yet family-oriented comedy. Sinbad starred in *The Sinbad Show*, his own situation comedy, in the 1994-1995 television season; he continued to do stand-up comedy and cut comedy albums.

Sinclair, Madge

né: Madge Walters
b. April 28, 1940
Kingston, Jamaica
d. December 20, 1995
Los Angeles, California
fields: Film, Television

African American actress; Madge Sinclair's film credits include *Conrack* (1974; for which she won an NAACP Image Award), *Star Trek IV: The Voyage Home* (1986), *Coming to America* (1988), and a lead voice in Disney's *The Lion King* (1994); her television credits include *Gabriel's Fire* (for which she won an Emmy Award as best supporting actress in 1991), and *Trapper John, M.D.* (1980-1986; for which she received three Emmy nominations and two additional Image Awards, 1981 and 1983).

Sinclair, Upton

full: Upton Beall Sinclair, Jr.
b. September 20, 1878
Baltimore, Maryland
d. November 25, 1968
Bound Brook, New Jersey
fields: Government and Politics, Literature, Social Reform

Sinclair was a prolific writer, a champion of social justice, a socialist reformer, and a 1934 Democratic candidate for governor of California. His greatest impact came from his muckraking novel *The Jungle* (1906), which stirred America's conscience, strengthened the Progressive reform movement, and brought about national consumer legislation.

Sing, Lillian K.

b. Nov. 13, 1942
Shanghai, China
fields: Law

Lillian K. Sing became a San Francisco municipal court judge in 1981, the first Asian American woman judge in Northern California. She served as board member of the Chinese Newcomers Service Center and the Chinese Cultural Foundation, and as president of the Chinese American Democratic Club; cochaired the Asian American Task Force on University Admissions; and cofounded Chinese for Affirmative Action, Wah Mei Bilingual Pre-School, and the Chinese Elected Officers Association.

Singer, Isaac Bashevis

b. July 14, 1904
Leoncin, Poland
d. July 24 1991
Surfside, Florida
fields: Literature

Isaac Bashevis Singer was an American Jewish journalist, writer; born in Poland, withdrew from rabbinical seminary to work as a translator and proofreader for a Warsaw newspaper; moved to United States in 1935 and began working for the *Jewish Daily Forward*, a Yiddish-language newspaper; naturalized as a U.S. citizen in 1943 but continued to write in Yiddish; attempted to blend his old-world Jewish heritage with modern sensibilities; earned Nobel Prize in Literature in 1978; wrote many books, including *Satan in Goray* (1935), *The Family Moskat* (1950), *The Slave* (1962), and *Enemies, a Love Story* (1972).

Singer, Peter

full: Peter Albert David Singer
b. July 6, 1946
Melbourne, Australia
fields: Philosophy, Social Reform

Blending classical and preference utilitarianism, Peter Singer has applied his theory to animal welfare, environmental ethics, famine relief, euthanasia, abortion, civil disobedience, and aid to refugees. He helped introduce the concept of speciesism—discrimination grounded on the morally irrelevant characteristic of membership in a particular species—that characterizes scientific experimentation, the wearing furs and leather goods, and the commercail production of meats. Among his best-known works are *Animal Liberation* (1975, 1990), *Practical Ethics* (1979, 1993), *Should the Baby Live? The Problem of Handicapped Infants* (1985, with Helga Kuhse), *How Are We to Live? Ethics in an Age of Self-Interest* (1993), and and *Rethinking Life and Death* (1994).

Singh, Jag Jeet

b. May 20, 1926
Rohtak, India
fields: Physics

Asian Indian American physicist; Jag Jeet Singh worked for the National Aeronautical and Space Administration (NASA) from 1964 to 1980; won its 1990 Medal for Exceptional Scientific Achievement; established radiation damage thresholds for semiconductor devices; developed techniques for safety monitoring in aerosols, polymeric materials, and aviation fuels.

Singh, Jane

b. ?
fields: Historiography

Jane Singh, who is descended from one of the original Sikh families that immigrated to California in the early 1900's and settled in the Sacramento Valley, was a specialist in Asian Indian American history at the University of California, Berkeley. She served as coordinating editor of *South Asians in North America: An Annotated and Selected Bibliography* (1988), on the editorial board of *Making Waves: Writings By and About Asian American Women* (1989), and as curator of "People of South Asia in America," a national pictorial exhibit.

Singh, Jawala

b. 1859?
Thatian, Amritsar District of Punjab State, India
d. 1938?
fields: Business and Industry

Jawala Singh, born to a poor peasant family in Indian, eventually became one of the wealthiest farmers in the United States. Singh's success earned him the nickname "the potato king." Singh and other Stockton area Sikh settlers organized and built the first *gurdwara*, or Sikh temple, in the United States in 1912. The temple, a community center, later became a center of revolutionary activities aimed at the expulsion of British imperialism from India. Singh, a founder of the Ghadr Party, a group working toward armed revolution against the British in India, went to India in 1914 in order to set off a revolt. Arrested and sentenced to life in prison, Singh was released in 1933. Shortly thereafter, Singh served a year in jail because of his activities on behalf of peasant farmers.

Singletary, Mike

full: Michael Singletary
b. October 9, 1958
Houston, Tex.
fields: Sports (football player)

African American football player; drafted by the Chicago Bears of the National Football League (NFL) in 1981, Mike Singletary, at only six feet tall, was considered too small to play successfully at the linebacker position. Singletary worked to hone his skills as a middle linebacker year round and proved his detractors wrong. Singletary served as the Bears' field coach: he was the team's defensive captain and signal caller. He helped lead the Bears to a 46-10 victory over the New England Patriots in Super Bowl XX, in 1986.

Singleton, John

b. January 6, 1968
Los Angeles, Calif.
fields: Film

African American film director; immediately after being graduated from the University of Southern California's School of Cinema/Television (1990; where he received the Jack Nicholson Award for writing and was signed by the Creative Arts Agency based on his student screenplays), John Singleton signed a three-year film deal with Columbia Pictures; his first film, *Boyz 'N the Hood*, debuted at the 1991 Cannes Film Festival to rave reviews; Singleton received Academy Award nominations for best screenplay and best director (at age 24, the youngest person ever to receive an Oscar nomination for best director) and the New York Film Critics voted him Best New Director; his second film entitled *Poetic Justice* (1993), for which he also wrote the screenplay, was a box office and critical disappointment; other film credits include *Higher Learning* (1995) and *Rosewood* (1997).

Sint-Chakkee. *See* Micanopy

Siqueiros, David Alfaro

b. Dec. 29, 1896
Santa Rosalía de Camargo, Chihuahua, Mexico
d. Jan. 6, 1974
Cuernavaca, Mexico
fields: Art (muralist)

Mexican muralist. David Alfaro Siqueiros began painting murals in Mexico in the 1920's. From 1930 to 1934, he painted several murals in the United States. His first exhibition was in Mexico City in 1932, and he later had others in New York City; Venice, Italy; and Mexico. He founded the Siqueiros

Experimental Workshop in New York in 1935, the Centro Realista de Arte Moderno in Mexico in 1944, and the Mexican Art Academy in 1968. Siqueiros was involved with Mexican Communist Party and was jailed and exiled several times for his political activity. He was awarded the Mexican national art prize in 1966 and the Lenin Peace Prize by the Soviet Union in 1968.

Siricius, Saint

b. c. 335 or 340
probably in or near Rome
d. November 26, 399
Rome
fields: Religion and Theology

Siricius was the first pope to exercise his authority throughout the Roman Empire. In the process, he set precedents which were to be used to great effect by his successors.

Sissle, Noble

b. July 10, 1889
Indianapolis, Ind.
d. December 17, 1975
Tampa, Fla.
fields: Music (jazz composer and bandleader)

African American composer and bandleader; Noble Sissle, in collaboration with composer Eubie Blake, wrote and directed the all-African American musicals *Shuffle Along* (1921) and *Chocolate Dandies* (1924); for nearly half a century, Sissle toured widely with his own jazz bands.

Sisson, Tack

b. c. 1743
d. 1821
fields: Warfare and Conquest

African American soldier; during the Revolutionary War, Tack Sisson served as a commando; on July 9, 1777, Sisson and two other soldiers captured British general Richard Prescott in his own headquarters; Prescott was later exchanged for Major General Charles Lee, an American prisoner.

Sitting Bull

né: Tatanka Iyotake
b. March, 1831
near the banks of the Grand River, Dakota Territory
d. December 15, 1890
Standing Rock Agency, South Dakota
fields: Native American Affairs

Sitting Bull led his people (part of the Sioux Confederation) from their zenith in the middle of the nineteenth century to the decline of their culture in the face of superior technology and numbers of the whites.

Śivajī

né: Śivajī Bhonsle
b. April 6, 1627
Poona, India
d. April 3, 1680
Rajgarh, India
fields: Government and Politics

The founder of an independent Maratha kingdom, Śivajī was a pioneer of guerrilla warfare, a great general, and a fiery Hindu nationalist. He became a symbol of Hindu statesmanship for twentieth century Indians.

Skinner, B. F.

full: Burrhus Frederic Skinner
aka: Fred Skinner
b. March 20, 1904
Susquehanna, Pennsylvania
d. August 18, 1990
Cambridge, Massachusetts
fields: Psychiatry and Psychology, Literature

By developing a variety of effective techniques for behavioral modification, Skinner radically transformed the science of psychology and thereby exerted a profound influence in the fields of psychiatry and pedagogy. His ideas, moreover, have been popularized through nontechnical writings of his own, including a utopian novel entitled *Walden Two*.

Skinner, Elliott Percival

b. June 20, 1924
Port of Spain, Trinidad
fields: Anthropology

African American anthropologist; Elliott Percival Skinner has spent most of his teaching career, beginning in 1957, at Columbia University; from 1966 to 1969 he served as ambassador to the West African country of Upper Volta (now Burkina Faso); the appointment, made by President Lyndon B. Johnson, was considered appropriate because Skinner's scholarly research had focused on the Mossi people of that region; upon return to his position as Franz Boas Professor of Anthropology at Columbia University, he not only chaired the department but also served as an outstanding mentor and teacher specializing in ethnological and cultural history, cultural change and political anthropology in Africa, and urbanization in Africa; he has authored, coauthored, or edited numerous books including *Beyond Constructive Engagement: U.S. Foreign Policy Toward Africa* (1986).

Skirvin, Pearl Reid. *See* Mesta, Perle

Sklarek, Norma Merrick

b. April 15, 1928
New York, N.Y.
fields: Architecture

African American architect; in 1954 Norma Merrick Sklarek became the first African American woman to be licensed as an architect in New York and in California in 1962. She has served on the faculties of the City College of New York and the University of California, Los Angeles. The American Embassy in Tokyo and Terminal One of the International Airport in Los Angeles are among Sklarek's principal works.

Skłodowska, Marya. *See* Curie, Marie

Skolem, Thoralf Albert

b. May 23, 1887
Sandsvaer, Norway
d. Mar. 23, 1963
Oslo, Norway
fields: Mathematics (mathematical logic and number theory)

Thoraf Albert Skolem stated that certain concepts in mathematics cannot have absolute meaning—they must be interpreted relative to the underlying structure; introduced the *p*-adic method in Diophantine analysis in 1935.

Skryabin, Vyacheslav Mikhailovich. *See* Molotov, Vyacheslav Mikhailovich

Slater, Samuel

b. June 9, 1768
near Belper, England
d. April 21, 1835
Webster, Massachusetts
fields: Business and Industry

In the early years of America's modern economic history, Slater almost single-handedly established the basis upon which the country's industrial development would be built by effectively founding textile manufacturing in New England.

Slaughter, John Brooks

b. March 16, 1934
Topeka, Kans.
fields: Physics, Engineering

African American physicist and electrical engineer; named scientist of the year in 1965, John Brooks Slaughter has served as an administrator with the U.S. government naval electronics laboratory center (1960-1975), as director of the applied physics laboratory at the University of Washington (1957-1977), and as assistant director (1977-1980) and then director (1980-1982; the first African American to hold this position) of the National Science Foundation; he later served as chancellor of the University of Maryland at College Park.

Sledge, Percy

b. 1941
Leighton, Ala.
fields: Music (soul singer)

African American soul singer; Percy Sledge's debut single, "When a Man Loves a Woman" (1966), was the first soul recording to reach number-one on the popular music charts; as a singer of soul ballads, Sledge released subsequent lesser hits including "Warm and Tender Love," "Any Day Now," and "Take Time to Know Her."

Sleet, Moneta, Jr.

b. February 14, 1926
Owensboro, Ky.
fields: Photography

African American photographer; in 1969 Moneta Sleet, Jr., became the first black male to earn a Pulitzer Prize; his photos of Coretta Scott King and her daughter, taken at the funeral of Martin Luther King, Jr., won the Pulitzer for feature photography.

Slim, First Viscount

né: William Joseph Slim
aka: William Joseph, First Viscount Slim
b. August 6, 1891
Bishopston, near Bristol, England
d. December 14, 1970
London, England
fields: Military Affairs

After conducting a fighting retreat from Burma in early 1942, Slim was chosen to command the British Fourteenth Army, which in the succeeding years defeated the Japanese invasion of India, destroyed the main Japanese army of Southeast Asia, and reconquered Burma.

Slipher, Vesto Melvin

b. Nov. 11, 1875
Mulberry, Indiana
d. Nov. 8, 1969
Flagstaff, Arizona
fields: Astronomy

Vesto Melvin Slipher, in 1908, found calcium gas in space; in 1912, identified the Pleiades nebula as dust reflecting local starlight; in 1912-1913, discovered that the Andromeda nebula is rapidly moving toward the sun, leading him to state that spiral nebulas are receding into space at extremely high speeds and that, therefore, nebulas are independent galaxies and the universe is expanding.

Slocum, John

b. 1830's
d. c. 1896
fields: Religion and Theology, Native American Affairs

Native American leader. A Northwest Salish, John Slocum founded the Indian Shaker Church in the early 1880's.

Sluter, Claus

b. c. 1340-1350
probably Haarlem, Netherlands
d. c. 1405-1406
Dijon, France
fields: Art

Sluter's innovations in creating individually distinct and expressively sculptured figures brought to Western art a new realism. Credited with bridging the late Gothic and the early Renaissance in northern Europe, Sluter and his name are synonymous with the Burgundian school of sculpture.

Slutsky, Jean. *See* Nidetch, Jean

Slyde, Jimmy

né: James Godbolt
b. 1927
Atlanta, Georgia
fields: Dance

African American tap dancer; Jimmy Slyde, with his trademark sliding, joined with Jimmy "Sir Slide" Mitchell to form the Slyde Brothers; they performed throughout the United States in burlesque houses, nightclubs, and theaters; Slyde was most active from the 1940's through the 1950's.

Smalley, Richard E.

full: Richard Errett Smalley
b. June 6, 1943
Akron, Ohio
fields: Chemistry

Richard E. Smalley discovered fullerenes, a family of highly symmetrical carbon cage molecules; won the 1996 Nobel Prize in Chemistry with Robert F. Curl, Jr., and Sir Harold W. Kroto.

Smalls, Robert

b. April 5, 1839
Beaufort, S.C.
d. February 23, 1915
Beaufort, S.C.
fields: Warfare and Conquest, Government and Politics

African American sailor; Robert Smalls, although impressed into the Confederate navy during the Civil War, became a naval hero for the Union; he and a small group of other African Americans took over the *Planter*, the Confederate ship on which they were serving, and turned it over to the Union; in 1863, Smalls became the *Planter*'s captain; Smalls went on to serve in the U.S. House of Representatives.

Smallwood, Joseph Roberts

b. December 24, 1900
Gambo, Bonavista Bay, Newfoundland (now part of Canada)
d. December 17, 1991
St. John's, Newfoundland, Canada
fields: Government and Politics

Joseph Roberts Smallwood led the island of Newfoundland into confederation with Canada; it became a province in 1949, and Smallwood was its premier from 1949 to 1971.

Smedley, Agnes

b. February 23, 1892
Campground, Missouri
d. May 6, 1950
Oxford, England
fields: Journalism, Social Reform, Women's Rights

As a newspaper correspondent and writer, Smedley reported on the Chinese Communist revolutionary movement and the Sino-Japanese War during the 1930's and 1940's.

Smith, Abigail. *See* Adams, Abigail

Smith, Adam

b. June 5, 1723 (baptized)
Kirkcaldy, Fifeshire, Scotland
d. July 17, 1790
Edinburgh, Scotland
fields: Philosophy, Economics

Smith was one of the major luminaries of the eighteenth century Scottish Enlightenment. His *The Wealth of Nations* became the bible of nineteenth century liberals, and twentieth century conservatives are similarly animated by his vision of the beneficent results of the free marketplace. Economists, whatever their personal ideologies, continue to pay homage to Smith for his contribution to the study of economic development.

Smith, Alfred E.

full: Alfred Emanuel Smith
b. December 30, 1873
New York, New York
d. October 4, 1944
New York, New York
fields: Government and Politics

Smith was a leading figure in the Democratic Party during the Progressive Era and the 1920's. He represented the urban, immigrant Roman Catholic, and relatively liberal interests of the party at a time when it was deeply divided along regional, cultural, and ideological lines.

Smith, Anna Deavere

b. September 18, 1950
Baltimore, Md.
fields: Theater and Entertainment

African American actor, director, and writer; from 1974 to 1976, Anna Deavere Smith worked with the American Conservatory Theatre in San Francisco, California, debuting in *Horatio* (1974); among the plays she has authored are *On the Road* (1983) and *Aye, Aye, Aye, I'm Integrated* (1984); she has written and appeared in one-woman shows including *A Birthday Card and Aunt Julia's Shoes*, the Obie Award-winning *Fires in the Mirror: Crown Heights, Brooklyn, and Other Identities*, the highly acclaimed *Twilight: Los Angeles, 1992* (1992; written in response the to Rodney King beatings and subsequent riots), and *House Arrest: An Intorgression* (1999). She wrote the libretto for and performed in *A Hymn for Alvin Ailey* (1995; choreographed by Judith Jamison).

Smith, Arthur Lee, Jr. *See* Asante, Molefi Kete

Smith, Barbara

b. November 16, 1946
Cleveland, Ohio
fields: Social Reform, Women's Rights, Scholarship

African American feminist editor and essayist; a founding member of a black feminist group in Boston, the Combahee River Collective, and a cofounder of the publishing company Kitchen Table: Women of Color Press, Barbara Smith advocates for the inclusion of black women writers and black lesbian writers in feminist and black literary studies; Smith co-edited *Conditions V: The Black Women's Issue* (with Lorraine Bethel, 1979) and *All the Women Are White, All the Blacks Are Men, but Some of Us Are Brave: Black Women's Studies* (with Gloria T. Hull and Patricia Bell Scott, 1982); edited *Home Girls: A Black Feminist Anthology* (1983); and coauthored of *Yours in Struggle: Three Feminist Perspectives on Anti-Semitism and Racism* (with Elly Bulkin and Minnie Brue Patt, 1984); since 1973, she has been an active organizer of black feminist causes.

Smith, Bessie

b. April 15, 1894
Chattanooga, Tennessee
d. September 26, 1937
Clarksdale, Mississippi
fields: Music

The first internationally popular female blues singer, Bessie Smith paved the way for later female blues and gospel singers such as Billie Holiday, Ella Fitzgerald, and Mahalia Jackson.

Smith, Beuford

b. 1939
Cincinnati, Ohio
fields: Photography

African American photographer; in 1966 Beuford Smith began freelance photography; in 1968 he began working as a cinematographer; he has held many exhibitions of his work.

Smith, Cecil Lewis Troughton. *See* Forester, C. S.

Smith, Emmitt

full: Emmitt J. Smith III
b. May 15, 1969
Pensacola, Fla.
fields: Sports (football player)

African American football player; a talented running back, Emmitt Smith was selected by the Dallas Cowboys in the first round of the 1990 NFL draft; for three consecutive years he captured the NFL rushing title; he was named the NFL's 1993 Most Valuable Player; he was instrumental in bringing the Cowboys to Super Bowl championships in 1993, 1994, and 1996 and was voted most valuable player for his performance in Super Bowl XXVIII; he has established the "I Have a Dream" Foundation, a charitable organization dedicated to assisting African American youngsters; he holds several NFL rushing records.

Smith, Gerald L. K.

full: Gerald Lymann Kenneth Smith
b. February 27, 1898
Pardeeville, Wisconsin
d. April 15, 1976
Los Angeles, California
fields: Religion and Theology

An American fascist spokesperson, Gerald Smith was ordained a Disciples of Christ minister while young but left the ministry to work for Louisiana governor Huey Long's "Share Our Wealth" movement. After Long was assassinated in 1935, Smith allied himself with Francis E. Townsend, the director of the Old Age Pension Movement, and later with Father Charles E. Coughlin and William Lemke to campaign against Franklin D. Roosevelt. While traveling through the country, he made religio-political harangues and threatened to seize control of the government. He wrote hundreds of books and pamphlets and founded the periodical *Cross and the Flag* in 1942 and contributed most of its contents.

Smith, Gladys Louise. *See* Pickford, Mary

Smith, Hale

b. June 29, 1925
Cleveland, Ohio
fields: Music (jazz composer)

African American composer; Hale Smith's compositions include *Epicedial Variations* (1956), *By Yearnings and by Beautiful* (1961), and *Contours for Orchestra* (1962); Smith also has written and arranged works for jazz artists Quincy Jones, Eric Dolphy, and Ahmad Jamal; Smith has served on the faculties of C. W. Post College (1968-1970) and the University of Connecticut at Storrs (beginning 1970).

Smith, Ian

full: Ian Douglas Smith
b. April 8, 1919
Selukwe, Rhodesia (now Shurugwi, Zimbabwe)
fields: Government and Politics

Prime minister of Southern Rhodesia from 1964 to 1979. Ian Smith headed the white minority government of Southern Rhodesia for fifteen years. England refused to grant independence to Rhodesia as long as a white government ruled and gave the majority black population no voice. All attempts at negotiation and compromise eventually failed, and Smith was forced out of office in 1979. Southern Rhodesia became Zimbabwe in 1980.

Smith, Isaac Dixon

b. May 2, 1932
Wakefield, La.
fields: Military Affairs

African American military officer; during Isaac Dixon Smith's thirty years of military service with the U.S. Army, he achieved the rank of major general; his postings have included primarily artillery division command with some reserve officer training; in 1974 Smith was deputy director of the Army's equal opportunity program.

Smith, James McCune

b. April 18, 1813
New York, N.Y.
d. November 17, 1865
Williamsburg, N.Y.
fields: Medicine

African American medical doctor; after being refused admission to an American medical college, James McCune Smith became the first African American to receive a medical degree when he subsequently obtained a medical degree from the University of Glasgow in Scotland (1837); he later worked as a practitioner in New York City and operated two drugstores; he also edited *The Colored American*, in which he supported the abolitionist movement and voiced his antislavery views.

Smith, James Todd. *See* L.L. Cool J.

Smith, Jedediah

full: Jedediah Strong Smith
b. January 6, 1799
Jericho (Bainbridge), New York

d. May 27, 1831
near Cimmaron River en route to Santa Fe, New Mexico
fields: Exploration and Colonization

The most adventurous of the nineteenth century mountain men, Smith charted trails through the Rockies that opened the American West to settlement by the pioneers who followed the fur traders.

Smith, Jimmy

full: James Oscar Smith
b. December 8, 1925
Norristown, Pa.
fields: Music (jazz organist)

African American jazz organist; Jimmy Smith, one of the most popular and acclaimed jazz organists since the mid-1950's, has influenced many organists such as Jimmy McGriff and Joey DeFrancesco; Smith has made frequent recordings.

Smith, John

b. January 9, 1580 (baptized)
Willoughby, England
d. June 21, 1631
London, England
fields: Exploration and Colonization

Smith's strong leadership in early Virginia and his promotional literature on North America helped ensure the success of England's efforts at colonization.

Smith, Joseph

b. December 23, 1805
Sharon, Vermont
d. June 27, 1844
Carthage, Illinois
fields: Religion and Theology

Smith founded the first indigenous American religion, the Church of Jesus Christ of Latter-day Saints. He developed a novel exegesis of the traditional Protestant Bible and provided new scriptures, including the Book of Mormon.

Smith, Linda Jane. *See* Ellerbee, Linda

Smith, Lula Carson. *See* McCullers, Carson

Smith, Mamie

b. 1883
d. 1946
fields: Music (blues singer)

African American singer; Mamie Smith's "Crazy Blues" (1920) is considered to be the first blues ever recorded; she sang with many legendary artists and, from the late 1930's through the early 1940's, appeared in a number of films.

Smith, Margaret Chase

né: Margaret Madeline Chase
b. December 14, 1897
Skowhegan, Maine
d. May 29, 1995
Skowhegan, Maine
fields: Government and Politics

As the first leading American stateswoman to be elected in her own right to both houses of the United States Congress, Margaret Chase Smith focused her attention on improving the status of women, military preparedness, and defense of free speech and democratic values.

Smith, Marie. *See* Selika, Marie

Smith, Mary Alice. *See* Alice, Mary

Smith, Ozzie

full: Osborne Earl Smith
b. December 26, 1954
Mobile, Ala.
fields: Sports (baseball player)

African American baseball player; the winner of many Gold Glove awards while playing for the San Diego Padres (1978-1981) and the St. Louis Cardinals (1980-1992). Ozzie Smith is known for his acrobatic plays at shortstop. He retired from baseball in 1996.

Smith, Patricia. *See* Churchland, Patricia Smith

Smith, Reggie

full: Carl Reginald Smith
b. April 2, 1945
Shreveport, La.
fields: Sports (baseball player)

African American baseball player; Reggie Smith is noted as the only switch-hitter to hit more than one hundred home runs in both the National and the American Leagues; during his playing career (1966-1982), Smith played for four teams and became one of only five players to hit World Series home runs in both leagues (in 1967 for the Boston Red Sox and in 1977 and 1978 for the Los Angeles Dodgers).

Smith, Robert Weston. *See* Wolfman Jack

Smith, Rubye Doris. *See* Robinson, Rubye Doris Smith

Smith, Susan Maria. *See* Steward, Susan Maria Smith McKinney

Smith, Theobald

b. July 31, 1859
Albany, New York
d. December 10, 1934
New York, New York
fields: Biology (microbiology), Medicine

Considered to be the most distinguished American microbiologist and probably the leading comparative pathologist in the world, Smith made discoveries fundamental to theoretical biology, public health, and veterinary medicine, and opened new vistas in disease control.

Smith, Tommie

b. June 5, 1944
Clarksville, Tex.
fields: Sports (sprinter)

African American sprinter. During a 1968 Olympics award ceremony, 200-meter gold medalist Tommie Smith, along with bronze medalist John Carlos refused to acknowledge the American flag and raised their fists in a black power salute. They were protesting the treatment of African American athletes but were expelled from the Olympic village. Smith held eleven world records. One of the best sprinters of all time, Smith gained world rankings in the 100-, 200-, and 400-meter races, as well as in the long jump. His best time in the 100-yard dash was 9.35 seconds; it was 10.1 seconds in the 100 meters.

Smith, Vincent DaCosta

b. December 12, 1929
Brooklyn, N.Y.
fields: Art (painter and printmaker)

African American painter and printmaker; award-winning artist Vincent DaCosta Smith has exhibited his work, which explores the aspirations of black youth and the rise of black militancy, in numerous one-man shows; he has taught painting at various museums including the Whitney Museum of Art in New York City and the Brooklyn Museum.

Smith, Walker, Jr. *See* Robinson, Sugar Ray

Smith, Will

aka: Fresh Prince
full: William Smith III
b. September 25, 1968
Wynnefield, Pa.
fields: Television, Film, Music (rap vocalist)

African American actor and vocalist; Will Smith's success as a rap artist (teaming with Jeffrey Townes as Jazzy Jeff and Fresh Prince and winning the first-ever rap music Grammy Award, 1989, for the single "Parents Just Don't Understand") led to a starring role in his own television series *The Fresh Prince of Bel-Air* (1990-1996); his film credits include dramatic roles in *Where the Day Takes You* (1992) and *Six Degrees of Separation* (as a gay con man; 1993), the comedy *Made in America* (1993), the action film *Bad Boys* (1995), the science fiction films *Independence Day* (1996) and *Men in Black* (1997), and *Wild, Wild West* (1999); Smith has also continued his rap career, he and Townes receiving the 1991 Grammy for "Summer Time."

Smith, Willi

b. February 29, 1948
Philadelphia, Pa.
d. April 17, 1987
New York, N.Y.
fields: Fashion

African American fashion designer; known for his fun, comfortable, and free-flowing Willi Wear fashions, made with natural fibers, Willi Smith came into prominence in the late 1960's; his full-cut pants and big and boxy jackets were designed and priced for everyday people; Smith designed Caroline Kennedy's wedding dress and, as a result, Willi Wear gained renewed popularity; Smith died at age thirty-nine of AIDS-related complications.

Smith, William

b. Mar. 23, 1769
Churchill, Oxfordshire, England
d. Aug. 28, 1839
Northampton, Northamptonshire, England
fields: Science

William Smith discovered that beds of the same rock type can be distinguished by the types of fossils found in them, in 1796; in 1802-1812, prepared a series of geological maps of England and Wales, the first geologic maps of an entire country; was the first to recognize that fossils occur in a definite, consistent, vertical order, referred to as the principle of fossil succession.

Smith, Willie

né: William Henry Joseph Bonaparte Bertholoff
aka: The Lion
b. November 25, 1897
Goshen, N.Y.
d. April 18, 1973
New York, N.Y.
fields: Music (jazz pianist)

African American jazz pianist; with his signature bowler hat and cigar, Willie Smith had legendary New York stride piano performance skills; Smith participated in the recording of "Crazy Blues" (1920) with blues artist Mamie Smith, with whom he also toured; his solo recordings included "Concentrating/ Sneak Away" (1939), "Echoes of Spring/ Fading Star" (1939), "Rippling Waters/ Finger Buster" (1939), and "Morning Air/Passionatte" (1939); he also released the album *The Lion Roars* (1957; containing a tribute to Duke Ellington) and a book *Music on My Mind: The Memoirs of an American Pianist* (1964; with a foreword by Duke Ellington); Smith toured Europe in the late 1940's and mid-1960's and appeared in the film *Jazz Dance* (1954).

Smith, Willie Mae Ford

b. 1906
Rolling Fork, Mississippi
d. February 2, 1994
St. Louis, Missouri
fields: Music (gospel singer), Religion and Theology

African American gospel singer and evangelist; Willie Mae Ford Smith became a serious gospel singer in 1926; in 1936 Thomas Dorsey appointed Smith as the director of the Soloists Bureau of the National Convention of Gospel Choirs and Choruses, in which capacity she demonstrated the proper gospel song style and delivery to younger singers; Smith left the Baptist Church in 1939 to become ordained as an evangelist with the Holiness Church of God Apostolic; instead of pursuing a professional gospel singing career, Smith devoted herself to evangelizing and limited her singing to religious revivals and similar appearances; she was the subject of the gospel documentary, *Say Amen, Somebody* (1982).

Smits, Jimmy

b. July 9, 1955
Brooklyn, N.Y.
fields: Film, Television

Latino actor. Jimmy Smits made his film debut in *Running Scared* (1986) and went on to appear in *Old Gringo* (1989), *Switch* (1991), and *The Tommyknockers* (1993). From 1986 to 1991, Smits played on the television series *L.A. Law*, a role for which he won the Emmy as best supporting actor in a dramatic series in 1990. In 1994, he was cast to appear in the television series *NYPD Blue.* He left *NYPD Blue* in 1998.

Smohalla

aka: Smóqula (the Preacher)
aka: Smokeller
aka: Waipshwa (Rock Carrier)
b. c. 1815
Wallula, Wash.
d. c. 1907
fields: Religion and Theology, Native American Affairs

Smohalla was a Wanapam relilgious leader. His teachings formed the basis of the Dreamer religion, which flourished among the tribes of the Pacific Northwest well into the twentieth century. He preached that all native peoples should reject the whites' beliefs and artifices. He counseled native peoples to stay away from reservations and to restore traditional ways of life. The Dreamer religion included dances done in hypnotic rhythm to bells, drums, and other musical instruments.

Smokeller. *See* Smohalla

Smóqula. *See* Smohalla

Smuts, Jan Christian

b. May 24, 1870
Bovenplaats, near Riebeeck West, Cape Colony (now part of South Africa)
d. September 11, 1950
Doornkloof, Irene, near Pretoria, South Africa
fields: Government and Politics

Jan Christian Smuts was twice prime minister of South Africa: from 1919 to 1924 and from 1939 to 1948. Helped write South African constitution in 1910; a founder of League of Nations following World War I. Became prime minister again after outbreak of World War II; collaborated with Winston Churchill and other leaders; played a major role in drafting the charter of the United Nations.

Smythe, Hugh H.

b. August 19, 1913
Pittsburgh, Pa.
d. 1977
fields: Government and Politics, Education

African American government official and educator; as an anthropologist, Hugh H. Smythe taught at New York's Brooklyn College and at the State Department's Foreign Service Institute; he also trained Peace Corps volunteers; from 1965 to 1967, he served as ambassador to Syria (appointed by President Lyndon B. Johnson); Smythe also served as special counsel to the Senate Foreign Relations Committee, as a member of the U.S. delegation to the United Nations General Assembly, and as a research consultant to the State Department.

Snell, George D.

full: George Davis Snell
b. Dec. 19, 1903
Bradford, Massachusetts
d. June 6, 1996
Bar Harbor, Maine
fields: Biology, Genetics, Medicine

George D. Snell was a pioneer in immunogenetic research; discovered the major histocompatibility complex, a genetic group that controls tissue graft rejection in mice; in 1980, won the Nobel Prize in Physiology or Medicine.

Snipes, Wesley

b. July 31, 1962
Orlando, Florida
fields: Film

African American actor; Wesley Snipes studied drama, dance, and singing at the High School for the Performing Arts in New York; Snipes's film credits include his debut role in

Wildcats (1986), *Major League* (1989), *Mo' Better Blues* (1989; as jazz saxophonist Shadow Henderson), *New Jack City* (1991), *Jungle Fever* (1991; Snipes's role as architect Flipper Purify brought him national exposure), *White Men Can't Jump* (1992), *Passenger 57* (1992; his debut as an action-adventure hero), *Mondy Train* (1995), *The Fan* (1996; with Robert De Niro), *One Night Stand* (1997; winning the Venice Film Festival's best actor award), and *Blade* (1998); Snipes was also featured in Michael Jackson's video *Bad* (1987).

Snoop Doggy Dogg

né: Calvin Broadus
aka: Snoop
b. October 20, 1971
Long Beach, Calif.
fields: Music (rap vocalist and lyricist)

African American rap vocalist and lyricist; known for his relaxed, low-pitched delivery of hard-edged, explicit lyrics expressing casual attitudes toward violence and sex, West Coast rapper Snoop Doggy Dogg wrote the number one single "Nuthin' but a 'G' Thang" on Dr. Dre's solo album *The Chronic*; he released a solo debut album, *Doggystyle* (1993), that entered *Billboard* magazine's pop album chart at number one; in 1993 Snoop Doggy Dogg was charged as an accomplice in a murder allegedly committed by his bodyguard; in February of 1996 he was found not guilty of murder and conspiracy and was acquitted on charges of being an accessory after the fact to the 1993 shooting death of Philip Woldemariam. His next album, *Doggfather* (1996) did half as well as his first, which caused Snoop to change his image, as reflected in *Da Game Is to Be Sold Not to be Told* (1998).

Snorri Sturluson

b. 1178 or 1179
Hvamm, Iceland
d. September 23, 1241
Reykjaholt, Iceland
fields: Historiography, Literature

Snorri preserved the myths, poetry, history, and culture of the early Germanic people; in doing so, he created an original literature of permanent significance and renown for himself as one of the foremost authors of the Middle Ages.

Snow, Phoebe

b. July 17, 1952
New York, N.Y.
fields: Music (singer, guitarist, and composer)

African American singer, guitarist, and composer; Phoebe Snow was known in the 1970's for songs such as "I Don't Want the Night to End," "No Show Tonight," "Poetry Man," "Shine, Shine, Shine," and "Harpo's Blues"; she filed lawsuits against Shelter Records on the grounds that they allegedly tried to restrict her advancement. She returned to charts in 1998 with *I Can't Complain*.

So Jae-pil. *See* Jaisohn, Philip

Socrates

b. c. 470 B.C.E.
Athens, Greece
d. 399 B.C.E.
Athens, Greece
fields: Philosophy

Socrates combined his professional philosophical life with his private life in an exemplary fashion. He was a leader in the intellectual advancement that drew attention to human and social questions (in addition to physical questions) and bequeathed to posterity the Socratic method of learning by question and answers.

Soddy, Frederick

b. Sept. 2, 1877
Eastbourne, Sussex, England
d. Sept. 22, 1956
Brighton, Sussex, England
fields: Chemistry

Working with Ernest Rutherford, Frederick Soddy developed the disintegration theory of radioactive transformation; in 1903, showed that helium is produced in the disintegration of radium; explored other concepts crucial to the subsequent understanding of radioactivity; in 1913, proposed the term "isotope"; in 1921, won the Nobel Prize in Chemistry.

Söderblom, Nathan

full: Lars Olaf Jonathan Söderblom
b. January 15, 1866
Trönö, Sweden
d. July 12, 1931
Uppsala, Sweden
fields: Religion and Theology, Peace Advocacy

Söderblom, as Archbishop of Uppsala, was a principal promoter of the Universal Christian Conference on Life and Work. He was awarded the Nobel Peace Prize for his work in promoting international understanding through the ecumenical movement. He is also noted for his work on behalf of war prisoners and displaced persons following World War I. A prolific writer, he emphasized the need to reunite Christianity and make it a practical, humanitarian movement.

Soeharto. *See* Suharto

Soga, Yasutaro

b. 1873
d. 1957
fields: Publishing

Yasutaro Soga published the *Nippu Jiji*, a Japanese-language daily newspaper in Hawaii, to which he added an English section in 1919. In the late 1890's, Soga got a job with the *Hawaii Shimpo*, then in 1905, he took control of the *Yamato Shimbun* and used the publication to advance support of the pro-labor movement in Hawaii. In 1906, the publication changed its name to *Nippu Jiji* and became an influential paper.

Soiga, Gaspar. *See* Adario

Sokabe, Shiro

b. June 26, 1865
Fukuoka Prefecture, Japan
d. July 3, 1949
fields: Religion and Theology

Shiro Sokabe arrived in Hawaii in 1894 to pastor the Honomu Church, where he stayed for almost fifty years. One of his first activities was to build a Christian school for the children of the plantation workers. The Honomu Gijuku, a Japanese-language boarding school, opened after 1897. Sokabe was favorably disposed toward the plantation owners, which angered some of the laborers.

Solís, Gloria

b. ?
fields: Art (muralist)

Latina muralist. Gloria Solís worked with José G. González, José Maldonado, Nancy Marrero, Sergio Zambrano, and seven assistants on the first eight panels of the thirty-two-panel, one-mile-long *La Raza de Oro* mural on West Hubbard Street in Chicago, Illinois. The mural honors pre-Columbian cultures.

Solis, Hilda L.

b. ?
fields: Government and Politics

Public official. Hilda L. Solis worked in Washington, D.C., as a management analyst in the federal government's Office of Management and Budget, then served as director of the California Student Opportunity and Access Program in a California high school district. She also served as vice president and president of the Rio Hondo Community College Board. In 1992, she was elected to the state assembly from the Fifty-seventh Assembly District of California. She was elected to the California State Senate in 1994.

Solomon

b. c. 991 B.C.E.
Jerusalem, Israel

d. 930 B.C.E.
Jerusalem, Israel
fields: Government and Politics, Religion and Theology

Through the application of his famous wisdom and the construction of the Temple, Solomon not only made a major contribution to the Judeo-Christian tradition but also forged the twelve tribes of Israel into a true nation, giving them an identity that would survive succeeding dispersions and persecutions.

Solomon, Aubrey. *See* Eban, Abba

Solon

b. c. 630 B.C.E.
probably Athens, Greece
d. c. 560 B.C.E.
probably Athens, Greece
fields: Government and Politics, Law, Literature

Through his law code, Solon averted a civil war at Athens and established the political and social foundations for the development of classical Athenian democracy.

Solzhenitsyn, Aleksandr

full: Aleksandr Isayevich Solzhenitsyn
b. December 11, 1918
Kislovodsk, U.S.S.R.
fields: Literature, Government and Politics, Social Reform

One of three persons to hold honorary U.S. citizenship, Solzhenitsyn has produced a striking body of literature and has led a long, heroic life, working for freedom in the Soviet Union. His nomination for the Lenin Prize affected de-Stalinization, and his Nobel Prize in Literature (1970) has positively influenced East-West relations.

Sommerfeld, Arnold

full: Arnold Johannes Wilhelm Sommerfeld
b. Dec. 5, 1868
Königsberg, Prussia (now Kaliningrad, Russia)
d. Apr. 26, 1951
Munich, Germany
fields: Physics

Arnold Sommerfeld proposed elliptical orbits for particular electrons by modifying the circular electron orbits in Niels Bohr's model of the atom; used Albert Einstein's relativity theory to account for the fine structure of lines observed in atomic spectra.

Sommerville, Duncan McLaren Young

b. Nov. 24, 1879
Beawar, Rajasthan, India
d. Jan. 31, 1934
Wellington, New Zealand
fields: Mathematics (geometry)

Duncan McLaren Young Sommerville worked in Euclidean and non-Euclidean geometry; researched tessellations, the study of how geometric shapes fit together to fill a plane; found applications of tessellations in crystallography.

Somoza García, Anastasio

aka: Tacho Somoza García
b. February 1, 1896
San Marcos, Nicaragua
d. September 29, 1956
Ancón, Panama Canal Zone (now Panama)
fields: Government and Politics

Dictatorial leader of Nicaragua from 1937 to 1956. Named head of paramilitary National Guard in 1932; used position to eliminate opponents and consolidate power; eventually forced President Sacasa to resign in June, 1936. Assumed presidency in 1937. Amassed a fortune; suppressed dissent. Assassinated in 1956. His sons then ruled the country until 1979.

Son Pyong-hui

b. 1861
d. 1922
fields: Religion and Theology, Government and Politics

Son Pyong-hui served as the third leader of the Tonghak (Eastern learning) religious movement, as a Korean independence movement activist, and as chairman of the thirty-three signatories to the Korean Declaration of Independence (1919). Son also was elected chief executive of the Korean left-wing Manchuria group, one of several provisional governments that arose after the 1919 March First uprising.

Sone, Monica

b. 1919
Seattle, Wash.
fields: Literature

Monica Sone's *Nisei Daughter* (1953) was the first published account of the Japanese American search for identity and the World War II internment experience as seen through a second-generation Japanese American woman's eyes. Sone grew up in a cultured and intellectual environment and had more contact with whites than with other Japanese Americans. Her book does not dwell on the hardships Japanese Americans suffered in the detention camps and ends with Sone's happy assimilation into the mainstream Anglo culture. Sone received a master's degree in clinical psychology from Western Reserve University in Cleveland, Ohio, in 1949.

Song, Cathy

b. Aug. 20, 1955
Honolulu, Territory of Hawaii
fields: Literature (poet)

Poet Cathy Song, who is of Korean and Chinese ancestry, grew up in Hawaii, and this upbringing is evident in her poetry. Her first book of poetry, *Picture Bride* (1983), won the prestigious Yale Series of Younger Poets Award in 1982. Her second collection, *Frameless Windows, Squares of Light*, was published in 1988, followed by *School Figures* in 1994. Her poems are anthologized in *Breaking Silence: An Anthology of Contemporary Asian American Poets* (1983), *Poetry Hawaii: A Contemporary Anthology* (1979), and *Talk Story: An Anthology of Hawaii's Local Writers* (1978).

Song Qingling. *See* Sun Yat-sen, Madame

Song Ziwen. *See* Soong, T. V.

Sontag, Susan

b. January 16, 1933
New York, New York
fields: Literature

One of the first American women to achieve eminence as a critical essayist, Sontag became a spokesperson for 1960's radical intellectuals and a leader in the antiwar movement that forced the United States to withdraw from Vietnam.

Soo, Jack

né: Goro Suzuki
b. b. 1915
Oakland, Calif.
d. Jan. 11, 1979
Los Angeles, Calif.
fields: Theater and Entertainment

Japanese American Goro Suzuki, a successful performer interned for two years at the Topaz relocation center, adopted a Chinese stage name, Jack Soo, to gain employment as an actor in the anti-Japanese climate that prevailed after the war. He appeared in the original 1958 production of Rodgers and Hammerstein's Broadway musical *Flower Drum Song* and in films such as *Thoroughly Modern Millie* (1967), *Flower Drum Song* (1961), *Who's Been Sleeping in My Bed?* (1963), *The Oscar* (1966), *The Green Berets* (1968), and *Return from Witch Mountain* (1978). He also played Sergeant Yemana on the popular television series *Barney Miller*, which premiered in 1975.

Soong Mei-ling. *See* Chiang Soong Mei-ling

Soong, T. V.

né: Song Ziwen

b. Dec. 4, 1894
Shanghai, China
d. Apr. 25, 1971
San Francisco, Calif.
fields: Banking and Finance, Government and Politics

T. V. Soong was from a prominent Chinese family with family connections to three of the most powerful men in Republican China: Sun Yat-sen, H. H. Kung, and Chiang Kai-shek. He studied in the United States then returned to Shanghai where he became a wealthy banker and entrepreneur. In 1923, he first assumed an official position in the Chinese Nationalist regime. He served as minister of finance (1928-1933), minister of foreign affairs, and president of the Soong became president of the Executive Yuan (or cabinet). After the 1949 Communist victory, Soong went to the United States.

Sophocles

b. c. 496 B.C.E.
Colonus, near Athens, Greece
d. 406 B.C.E.
Athens, Greece
fields: Literature

One of the most important ancient Greek tragedians, Sophocles was an innovative and skilled master of character development and dramatic irony.

Sorel, Georges

full: Georges-Eugène Sorel
b. November 2, 1847
Cherbourg, France
d. August 30, 1922
Boulogne-sur-Seine, France
fields: Social Reform, Philosophy

Sorel was the leading spokesman for revolutionary syndicalism in the first two decades of the twentieth century.

Sori, Susana

b. 1949
Camagüey, Cuba
fields: Art

Latina artist. In 1961, Susana Sori moved from Cuba to Chicago, Illinois, with her family. She attended the Art Institute of Chicago in 1977 and was awarded a Cintas Foundation Fellowship in 1981. In 1987, her work appeared in the group exhibition "Latin American Drawing at the Art Institute of Chicago" and at the First Biennial at the Museum of Contemporary Hispanic Art in New York City. Her work is held in the collections of such major museums as the Art Institute of Chicago, the Brooklyn Museum, and the Cuban Museum of Art and Culture in Miami, Florida.

Sosa, Dan, Jr.

b. Nov. 12, 1923
Las Cruces, N.Mex.
fields: Law

Latino judge. Dan Sosa, Jr., earned his law degree at the University of New Mexico in 1951 and became an assistant district attorney for New Mexico. In 1952, he became a city judge in Las Cruces. From 1956 to 1964, Sosa was district attorney for the Third Judicial District in New Mexico. In 1973, he became chief justice of the New Mexico Supreme Court. Sosa founded the Mexican American Legal Defense and Education Fund, joined the Hispanic Bar Association, and chaired the Freedom Foundation National Jury Awards Committee.

Sosa-Riddell, Adaljiza

b. Dec. 12, 1937
Colton, Calif.
fields: Education

Latina educator. Adaljiza Sosa-Riddell earned her Ph.D. in political science from the University of California, Riverside, in 1974. In 1971, she began teaching in the department of political science at the University of California, Davis, and later became director of the Chicano studies program. She also helped found the National Association for Chicano Studies in 1971. Sosa-Riddell served as chair of the Committee on Status of Chicanos of the Western Political Science Association from 1972 to 1974. In 1981, she cofounded Mujeres Activas en Letras y Cambio Social with the goal of fostering the development of Latina scholarship.

Sosigenes

b. c. 90 B.C.E.
place unknown
d. First century B.C.E.
place unknown
fields: Astronomy, Mathematics

Sosigenes advised Julius Caesar on the development of the Julian calendar, which, with only slight modification, is still in use today.

Sōtatsu

aka: Tawaraya Sōtatsu
aka: Sōtatsu Kitagawa
aka: Sōtatsu Nonomura
b. Date unknown
Noto Province, Japan
d. c. 1643
Kanagawa, Kaga Province, Japan
fields: Art

In collaboration with the artist and calligrapher Honami Kōetsu, Sōtatsu founded the Rimpa school of painting. This style, characterized by the use of traditional Japanese themes, bold colors, and innovative paint and ink techniques, would influence Japanese art for nearly two hundred years.

Soto, Gary

b. Apr. 12, 1952
Fresno, Calif.
fields: Literature

Latino poet. In 1976, Gary Soto earned a master of fine arts degree in creative writing from the University of California at Irvine. In 1977, he became a lecturer in the Chicano studies department at the University of California at Berkeley. Soto has written several volumes of poetry, including *The Elements of San Joaquin* (1977), *The Tale of Sunlight* (1978), *Father Is a Pillow Tied to a Broom* (1980), *Where Sparrows Work Hard* (1981), and *Neighborhood Odes* (1992). In 1978, he was nominated for the National Book Award and became one of the first Chicanos to be nominated for the Pulitzer Prize.

Soto, Hernando de

b. c. 1496
Jérez de los Caballeros?, Spain
d. May 21, 1542
near modern Ferriday, Louisiana
fields: Exploration and Colonization, Warfare and Conquest

After playing a prominent role in the conquest of Nicaragua and Peru, de Soto led the 1539-1542 expedition which explored what became the southeastern United States and discovered the Mississippi River.

Soto, Jorge

b. 1947
New York, N.Y.
fields: Art

Latino artist. Jorge Soto, a self-taught artist, was involved in the formation of the Taller Boricua (Puerto Rican Workshop) in New York City in the early 1970's. Other artists associated with the Taller Boricua are Carlos Osorio, Ralph Ortiz Montañez (Ralph Ortiz), Rafael Colón Morales, Marcos Dimas, and Nitza Tufiño.

Soto, Pedro Juan

b. July 11, 1928
Cataño, Puerto Rico
fields: Literature

Puerto Rican writer. Pedro Juan Soto moved to New York City when he was eighteen years old. After serving in the U.S. Army, he earned a master's degree in education at Columbia University and a doctorate in Latin American studies from the University of Toulouse in France. He then began teaching at the University of Puerto Rico. Soto published several novels about the experience of rootlessness and alienation in a foreign culture, including *Usmaíl* (1959), *Ardiente suelo, fría estación* (1961; *Hot Land, Cold Season*, 1973), *El francotirador* (1969), *Temporada de duendes* (1970), and *Un oscuro pueblo sonriente* (1982).

Soto Vélez, Clemente

b. 1905
Lares, Puerto Rico
d. April 15, 1993
fields: Literature, Social Reform

Puerto Rican writer and political activist. Clemente Soto Vélez worked as a journalist and editor at the newspaper *El Tiempo*. He cofounded a literary group, El Hospital de los Sensitivos, in 1928, then formed another group in 1929. In 1936, he was sentenced to seven years in federal prison for conspiring to overthrow the United States government. Soto Vélez was not allowed to return to Puerto Rico, so he moved to New York City and helped unite the political, creative, and economic resources of the Puerto Rican community. He published several poetry collections, including *Abrazo interno* (1954), *Arboles* (1955), *Caballo de Palo* (1959), and *La tierra prometida* (1979).

Souljah, Sister

né: Lisa Williamson
b. 1964
Bronx, N.Y.
fields: Music (rap singer), Social Reform

African American rap singer and social activist; through her guest vocals with the group Public Enemy and her cameo appearances on their videos, Sister Souljah became active on the rap music scene; in 1992 she released her debut rap album *360 Degrees of Power*; during the early 1990's, she frequently spoke at U.S. college campuses and has also lectured in the former Soviet Union and Western Europe; in 1994 she published the book *No Disrespect*.

Sour Belly. *See* Arapoosh

Sousa, John Philip

b. November 6, 1854
Washington, D.C.
d. March 6, 1932
Reading, Pennsylvania
fields: Music, Literature

Sousa profoundly affected the development of American musical taste. One of his era's finest bandmasters, he was renowned as a composer of infectious marches and other musical pieces and was, at one time, the most popular musician in the world.

Souter, David

full: David Hackett Souter
b. September 17, 1939
Melrose, Mass.
fields: Law

U.S. Supreme Court justice. A Rhodes Scholar and 1966 graduate of Harvard Law School, David Souter served as New Hampshire deputy attorney general and as a justice on the New Hampshire Supreme Court. In 1990, he was made a justice on the U.S. Court of Appeals for the First Circuit. In July, 1990, President George Bush nominated Souter to the Supreme Court, and he was subsequently confirmed by the Senate.

Southern, Terry

b. May 1, 1926
Alvaredo, Texas
d. October 29, 1995
New York, New York
fields: Literature, Film

Terry Southern was a novelist and screenwriter whose satirical writings mocked pornography, attacked religious complacency, and explored fascist tendencies in the United States. His books included *Candy* (1959), a parody of Voltaire's *Candide*; *The Magic Christian* (1960), and *Blue Movie* (1970). His film writing credits include *The Loved One* (1965), *Easy Rider* (1969), and *Dr. Strangelove, or, How I Learned to Stop Worrying and Love the Bomb* (1964).

Sowell, Thomas

b. June 30, 1930
Gastonia, N.C.
fields: Economics, Education, Scholarship

African American economist, author, and educator; Thomas Sowell served as an economist for the U.S. Department of Labor; he has taught at various institutions including Rutgers, Howard, Cornell, Brandeis, and UCLA; his published works, many of which focus on the economics of discrimination, include *Civil Rights: Rhetoric or Reality?* (1984), *Education: Assumptions Versus History, Collected Papers* (1986), and *Compassion Versus Guilt, and Other Essays* (1987).

Soyinka, Wole

full: Akinwande Oluwole Soyinka
b. July 13, 1934
Abeokuta, Nigeria
fields: Literature

The first African ever to win the Nobel Prize in Literature (1986), Soyinka is generally held to be Nigeria's foremost contemporary dramatist and possibly the most influential of all black African playwrights. Although he has earned high praise equally for his poetry, fiction, and literary criticism, it is as a playwright that Soyinka has distinguished himself.

Spaak, Paul-Henri

full: Paul-Henri Charles Spaak
b. January 25, 1899
Schaerbeek, Belgium
d. July 31, 1972
Brussels, Belgium
fields: Government and Politics

A Socialist member of the Belgian Chamber of Deputies, Spaak was prime minister on three occasions and foreign minister in many cabinets. He successfully opposed the return of King Leopold III to the Belgian throne following World War II. The implementor of Belgium's policy of voluntary neutrality before the war, Spaak subsequently advocated European integration and international cooperation. He shaped treaties and served in multiple international posts in service to this goal.

Spahecha. *See* Isparhecher

Spallanzani, Lazzaro

b. January 12, 1729
Scandiano, Duchy of Modena
d. February 11, 1799
Pavia, Cisalpine Republic
fields: Biology, Physiology, Chemistry, Geology, Natural History

Spallanzani is famous for his acute scientific observation and experimentation. Although he tackled problems in geology, volcanology, meteorology, chemistry, and physics, Spallanzani's studies of infusoria, circulation of the blood, as well as biological reproduction, digestion, and respiration are of great scientific significance.

Spand, Charlie

b. ?
d. ?
fields: Music (barrelhouse pianist)

African American pianist in the barrelhouse tradition in the 1920's and 1930's; as a fluent, technically sound, but not overly flashy pianist, Charlie Spand was in great demand as a session musician; for most of his career he lived in Detroit, Michigan, although many of his lyrics referred to his southern upbringing; his twenty-four sides recorded in 1929 and 1930 included the moderately successful "Soon This Morning".

Spartacus

b. c. 100 B.C.E.
Thrace (modern Bulgaria)
d. 71 B.C.E.
Lucania Province, southern Italy
fields: Warfare and Conquest

A gladiator of great courage and capacity for leadership, Spartacus was the main leader of the largest and most violent slave insurrection in the history of Roman civilization.

Spaulding, Asa T.

b. July 22, 1902
Columbus County, N.C.
d. 1990
fields: Business and Industry

African American business executive Asa Spaulding was president of North Carolina Mutual Life Insurance, the largest insurance company in the world owned by African Americans; in addition he ran a chain of advisory and consulting services for U.S. corporations.

Spaulding, Charles C.

b. August 1, 1874
Clarkton, N.C.
d. August 1, 1952
Durham, N.C.
fields: Business and Industry

African American business leader; one of the founders of the Mutual, a company founded in 1898 by ex-slaves, asked Charles C. Spaulding to become manager of the company in 1900; Spaulding was elevated to vice president in 1908; in 1923, the board of the Mutual asked Spaulding to lead the North Carolina Mutual Life Insurance Company, and he developed it from a tiny operation to a firm with millions of dollars in policies; it became one of the most successful black-owned businesses in American history.

Spearman, Leonard Hall O'Connell

b. July 8, 1929
Tallahassee, Fla.
fields: Education, Government and Politics

African American political appointee and educator; beginning in 1970, he was appointed to serve as director of the division of student special services at the U.S. Office of Education; after being promoted several times, Spearman received the Superior Service Award (1975) for his work in the U.S. Office of Education; in 1978 he became associate deputy commissioner for higher and continuing education and, in 1980, was promoted to associate deputy secretary for higher and continuing education; Spearman received the Distinguished Service Award for his work from the Department of Health, Education, and Welfare but left public service in 1980 to serve as president of Texas Southern University.

Spears, Charlotta. *See* Bass, Charlotta Spears

Speer, William

b. Apr. 24, 1822
New Alexandria, Pa.
d. 1904
fields: Religion and Theology

William Speer became a pastor in 1846 and served as a Presbyterian missionary in Canton, China, from 1846 to 1850, returning to the United States because of poor health. In 1852, Speer, who spoke Chinese and was sensitive to Chinese culture, opened a mission in San Francisco. In 1853, the first Chinese church was created with four charter members. Speer helped obtain the repeal of California laws of 1854-1855 that excluded Chinese workers from the mines and spoke out against the anti-Chinese racist assaults. Ill health forced him to retire in 1856. In 1879, he wrote *China and the United States.*

Speke, John Hanning

b. May 4, 1827
Orleigh Court, Devon, England
d. September 15, 1864
Neston Park, near Bath, England
fields: Exploration and Colonization

Speke traveled extensively in East and Central Africa and during the course of his explorations discovered Lake Victoria, the source of the Nile River.

Spellman, Francis Joseph

aka: Cardinal Spellman
b. May 4, 1889
Whitman, Massachusetts
d. December 2, 1967
New York, New York
fields: Religion and Theology

Francis Joseph Spellman was the Roman Catholic archbishop of the New York diocese from 1939 until his death in 1967, and was made a cardinal in 1946. In the early 1940's he began condemning the American film industry. He used his political influence to restrict film and play showings in his diocese. However, after the U.S. Supreme Court affirmed the appeal of the producers of *The Miracle* (1953)—which he had tried to ban—U.S. filmmakers ceased to be troubled by condemnations of the Roman Catholic church.

Spencer, Diana Frances. *See* Diana, Princess of Wales

Spencer, Herbert

b. April 27, 1820
Derby, England
d. December 8, 1903
Brighton, England
fields: Philosophy

Best known as the leading Social Darwinist of the nineteenth century, Spencer was a broad-ranging thinker who epitomized the scientific mentality of his age. He coined the phrase "survival of the fittest" and attempted to build a comprehensive philosophical synthesis based on evolution.

Spencer, James Wilson

b. ?
fields: Government and Politics

African American politician; from 1967 to 1968, James Wilson Spencer served in the Missouri House of Representatives from the state's Thirteenth District; after his tenure there he practiced law as an assistant prosecuting attorney for Jackson County, Missouri, and then as a law firm partner.

Spenser, Edmund

b. c. 1552
London, England
d. January 13, 1599
London, England
fields: Literature

Reflecting both Renaissance and Reformation ideals in his Christian humanism, Spenser incorporated classical, Continental, and native English poetic traditions to create in his epic *The Faerie Queene*, the quintessential statement of Elizabethan national and moral consciousness.

Speransky, Mikhail Mikhaylovich

b. January 12, 1772
Cherkutino, Russia
d. February 23, 1839
St. Petersburg, Russia
fields: Government and Politics, Law

A career bureaucrat, Speransky sought to liberalize and modernize the Russian government by limiting the power of the autocracy, reforming local government, and codifying Russian law.

Spielberg, Steven

b. Dec. 18, 1947
Cincinnati, Ohio
fields: Film

Film director and producer. Steven Spielberg has directed many of the highest-grossing motion pictures in history, including *Jaws* (1975), *Close Encounters of the Third Kind* (1977), *E.T.* (1982), *The Color Purple* (1985), the Indiana Jones adventure trilogy, *Schindler's List* (1993), for which he received an Academy Award as best director, and *Saving Private Ryan* (1998).

Spikes, Richard B.

b. 18??
d. 1962
fields: Invention and Technology

African American inventor; Richard B. Spikes is noted for inventing directional signals for automobiles (first used on the 1913 Pierce Arrow) and for obtaining patents on the automatic gear shift and its transmission (early 1930's) and on a combined hydraulic and electric brake system.

Spinks, Leon

b. July 11, 1953
St. Louis, Mo.
fields: Sports (boxer)

African American boxer; Leon Spinks defeated Muhammad Ali in 1978 to win the title of World Heavyweight Boxing Champion; in a rematch later that year, Ali won; prior to his professional boxing career, Spinks was three-time All-Marine light heavyweight champion; he was also a gold medal winner at the 1976 Olympics in Montreal in the heavyweight division.

Spinks, Michael

b. July 29, 1956
St. Louis, Mo.
fields: Sports (boxer)

African American boxer; after earning a gold medal in boxing at the 1976 Montreal Olympics (middleweight division), Michael Spinks went on to win three professional boxing titles: the World Boxing Association's Light Heavyweight Championship (1981), the World Boxing Council's Light-Heavyweight Championship (held from 1983 to 1985), and the International Boxing Federation's Heavyweight Championship (1985; defeating Larry Holmes).

Spinoza, Baruch

b. November 24, 1632
Amsterdam, United Provinces
d. February 21, 1677
The Hague, United Provinces
fields: Philosophy

Spinoza was a major figure among seventeenth century philosophers. Though he inspired few open disciples, Spinoza helped to lay the groundwork for future developments in philosophy and letters. He also contributed much to the emergence of political and religious tolerance. He is one of a handful of philosophers who can be said to have lived an exemplary life.

Spivak, Gayatri Chakravorty

né: Gayatri Chakravorty
b. Feb. 24, 1942
Calcutta, West Bengal, India
fields: Literature

Scholar, writer, and translator Gayatri Chakravorty Spivak received her M.A. (1962) and Ph.D. (1967) degrees in English and comparative literature from Cornell University. She taught at the University of Iowa, the University of Texas, Austin, and the University of Pittsburgh. Spivak's translation of the French philosopher Jacques Derrida's *De la Grammatology* (1967; *Of Grammatology*, 1976) played a pivotal role in disseminating Derrida's ideas. Her other works include *Myself Must I Remake: The Life and Poetry of W. B. Yeats* (1974) and *In Other Worlds: Essays in Cultural Politics* (1987). Twelve interviews with Spivak, collected and edited by Sarah Harasym, were published in 1990 as *The Post-Colonial Critic: Interviews, Strategies, Dialogues*.

Spock, Benjamin

full: Benjamin McLane Spock
b. May 2, 1903
New Haven, Connecticut
d. March 15, 1998
San Diego, California
fields: Education, Medicine, Social Reform; Psychiatry and Psychology

Through his advocacy, publications, and activities related to child care and developmental psychology, Spock sought to advise parents on matters and issues previously ignored by mainstream pediatric medicine. As a social activist, he called for socialized medicine, an end to U.S. military police action abroad, and nuclear disarmament.

Spotted Elk. *See* Big Foot

Spotted Tail

aka: Sinte Gleska
b. c. 1823 or 1824
near present-day Pine Ridge, S.Dak.
d. Aug. 5, 1881
Rosebud, S.Dak.
fields: Native American Affairs

Brule Sioux tribal chief; After a youth spent fighting whites, Spotted Tail came to realize the number and power of whites and advocated peace; in 1870, at a conference in Washington with President Ulysses S. Grant, Spotted Tail complained about the Sioux territory lost despite the Laramie Treaty (1868); throughout the plains war of 1876-1877, Spotted Tail remained the most popular spokesman of the Sioux people; in 1877, he negotiated the final surrender of hostile Sioux bands at Fort Robinson, Nebraska, and Spotted Tail and the Brule Sioux moved to the Rosebud Reservation in South Dakota; Spotted Tail's last years were spent in advocating Brule social and economic needs; on August 5, 1881, Spotted Tail was shot and killed by Crow Dog, a political opponent; the Dakota court sentenced Crow Dog to hang; the case was appealed to the Supreme Court (*Ex parte Crow Dog*, 1883), and the Court concluded that state courts have no jurisdiction on Indian reservations; Crow Dog was released.

Spottswood, Stephen Gil

b. July 18, 1897
Boston, Mass.
d. December 1, 1974
Washington, D.C.
fields: Religion and Theology

African American bishop of the African Methodist Episcopal Zion church; Stephen Gil Spottswood was chairman of the board of the NAACP (1961-1974).

Spybuck, Ernest

aka: Mahthela
b. 1883
on the Potawatomi and Shawnee Reservation, Oklahoma Territory
d. 1949
near Shawnee, Okla.
fields: Art (painter)

Native American painter. Ernest Spybuck, a Shawnee, was one of the first Native American artists of the twentieth century to create a narrative style of painting depicting tribal culture. Spybuck is known for genre painting that is illustrative of cultural life in the early twentieth century. He depicted clothing, housing, and activities in detail, portraying the acculturation between the Native American and white worlds.

Squanto

aka: Tisquantum
b. c. 1580
d. 1622
fields: Diplomacy, Native American Affairs

Native American leader. Squanto, a Patuxet and Wampanoag, helped the first English settlers survive in America. He was taken to Spain as a slave, but traveled to England and then back to New England in 1619. In March, 1621, instrumental in helping the Pokanoket and Plymouth English set up a treaty. Squanto then lived among the Pilgrims and acted as a diplomat and interpreter. He also helped in obtaining seed corn and teaching planting techniques. Behind the scenes he also tried to put the epidemic-ravaged remnants of his Patuxet tribe back together, incurring some English wrath.

Ssu-ma Ch'ien

b. c. 145 B.C.E.
Lung-men, Han-ch'eng hsien, China
d. c. 86 B.C.E.
China
fields: Historiography

As principal author of the *Shih chi*, a monumental historical work of 130 chapters which covers the history of the Chinese people from earliest times to the late first century B.C.E., Ch'ien is the chief source of nearly all subsequent historical knowledge of the dynasties of ancient China. For helping to fill this gap in scholarship, Ch'ien ranks with Thucydides and Herodotus as an important ancient historian.

Ssu-ma Kuang

b. 1019
Hsia, Hunan, China
d. 1086
Pien Lian, Hunan, China
fields: Literature, Historiography, Government and Politics

Ssu-ma Kuang was a scholar, statesman, and poet who compiled the *Tzu-chih t'ung-chien*, one of the outstanding works in Chinese historiography. He was also a significant political figure in the Northern Sung Dynasty.

Stadler, Joseph F.

b. ?
d. ?
fields: Sports (track and field athlete)

African American track and field athlete; Joseph F. Stadler was one of two black athletes to participate in the 1904 Olympics; won a bronze medal for standing triple jump.

Staël, Madame de

né: Anne-Louise-Germaine Necker
b. April 22, 1766
Paris, France
d. July 14, 1817
Paris, France
fields: Literature, Philosophy, Government and Politics

Madame de Staël publicly articulated the liberal, rational opposition to the injustices and corruption of the French government during the Revolution and under Napoleon I. Her social and literary criticism, as well as her colorful personal life, placed her in the vanguard of the Romantic movement, and her two major novels constitute early treatments of the concerns of women.

Stahl, Georg Ernst

b. October 21, 1660
Ansbach, Franconia
d. May 14, 1734
Berlin, Prussia
fields: Chemistry, Medicine

Stahl was a physician who developed the phlogiston theory, modern chemistry's first great explanatory system. It provided chemists with a deeper understanding of such reactions as combustion and the smelting of metal ores, and it guided research into such productive discoveries as new gases and the composition of the chemical molecule.

Stalin, Joseph

né: Joseph Vissarionovich Dzhugashvili
b. December 21, 1879
Gori, Georgia, Russian Empire
d. March 5, 1953
Kuntsevo, U.S.S.R.
fields: Government and Politics

Stalin succeeded Lenin as leader of the Soviet Union. During Stalin's twenty-five years in power, the Soviet Union was transformed from a backward agricultural society into one of the world's superpowers. This was achieved through a combination of Marxist-Leninist ideology, police terror, and sheer political will.

Stallings, George Augustus, Jr.

b. March 17, 1948
New Bern, N.C.
fields: Religion and Theology

African American religious leader; George Augustus Stallings, Jr. founded the Imani Temple African American Catholic Congregation (1989).

Stand Watie

aka: Uwatie
b. Dec. 12, 1806
near Rome, Ga.
d. Sept. 9, 1871
Honey Creek Indian Territory (later Delaware County, Okla.)
fields: Native American Affairs

Cherokee leader who counseled acquiescence in removal of the Cherokee tribe to Indian Territory (Oklahoma); Stand Watie signed the Treaty of New Echota (1835), which ceded all Cherokee lands to the United States for $5,600,000 and was to provide for free transportation to Indian Territory; instead led to forced removal in 1838 along the Trail of Tears; in 1861 raised a regiment of Cherokee mounted riflemen for Confederate service; was made a brigadier general in 1864.

Standing Bear

aka: Mochunozhin
b. c. 1829
d. Sept., 1908
fields: Law, Government and Politics, Native American Affairs

The Poncas, with Standing Bear as their leader, were treated abysmally by the U.S. government in the 1870's, and out of this mistreatment came the 1879 civil rights case *Standing Bear v. Crook*. In this case Judge E. S. Dundy rendered the decision that an Indian was a person "within the meaning of U.S. law." To prevent other tribal peoples from using the decision as precedent to leave other reservations, the commissioner of Indian affairs ruled that the decision applied only to Standing Bear and his people. In the winter of 1879-1880, Standing Bear toured the East with correspondent Thomas H. Tibbles and interpreters Francis and Susette La Flesche.

Standing Bear, Luther

aka: Plenty Kill
b. c. 1868
Pine Ridge, S.Dak.
d. Feb. 20, 1939
Huntington Park, Calif.
fields: Literature, Anthropology

An Oglala Sioux author, Luther Standing Bear was one of the few early twentieth century Indians to provide accounts of the transition from the old ways to reservation life and to offer a first-hand account of Sioux history and traditions. *My People, the Sioux* (1928) is an autobiography highlighting his youth, Carlisle Indian School years, the Ghost Dance, and his Wild West Show experiences. *Land of the Spotted Eagle* (1933) is an ethnographic description of traditional Sioux life and customs, criticizing whites' efforts to "make over" the Indian into the likeness of the white race.

Standish, Miles

b. c. 1584
Ellenbane, Isle of Man, England
d. October 3, 1656; Duxbury, Massachusetts
fields: Exploration and Colonization, Government and Politics, Military Affairs

Standish made his greatest contribution by providing the Pilgrims of Plymouth Colony with basic military training, by making their settlement defensible, and by helping to organize a practical system of militia and government for the colony.

Stanford, John Henry

b. September 14, 1938
Darby, Pa.
fields: Military Affairs

African American military officer; John Henry Stanford achieved the rank of major general in the U.S. Army.

Stanford, Leland

full: Amasa Leland Stanford
b. March 9, 1824
Watervliet, New York
d. June 20, 1893
Palo Alto, California
fields: Business and Industry, Government and Politics, Education

As president of the Central Pacific Railroad, Stanford guided the project which produced the nation's first transcontinental railroad; he also founded Stanford University, in Palo Alto, California.

Stanhope, First Earl

né: James Stanhope
b. 1673
Paris, France
d. February 5, 1721
London, England

fields: Government and Politics, Diplomacy

The leading minister in the government of King George I, Stanhope was responsible for a series of measures that solidified support for the new Hanoverian dynasty, and his successful diplomacy enabled England to launch an extended period of peace, so necessary to the political and economic reforms of his successor, Sir Robert Walpole.

Stanislavsky, Konstantin

né: Konstantin Sergeyevich Alekseyev
b. January 17, 1863
Moscow, Russia
d. August 7, 1938
Moscow, U.S.S.R.
fields: Theater and Entertainment (acting)

The founder (with Vladimir Nemirovich-Danchenko) of the Moscow Art Theater, director of the plays of Anton Chekhov, and writer of the most influential acting lessons in modern times, Stanlislavsky is the father of modern acting techniques; all modern actors, directors, and acting schools owe a great debt to Stanislavsky's methods, which revolutionized the theater in the early twentieth century.

Stanley, Edward George Geoffrey Smith. *See* Derby, fourteenth earl of

Stanley, Henry Morton

b. January 28, 1841
Denbigh, Denbighshire, Wales
d. May 10, 1904
London, England
fields: Exploration and Colonization

Best known for finding and resupplying Dr. David Livingstone in 1871, Stanley was the first white man to chart a number of the great lakes in central Africa and follow the Congo River to its mouth. His exploration opened much of Africa to European commerce and colonization.

Stanley, Wendell Meredith

b. Aug. 16, 1904
Ridgeville, Indiana
d. June 15, 1971
Salamanca, Spain
fields: Biology, Chemistry

Wendell Meredith Stanley was the first person to isolate and characterize a virus, in 1935, with the isolation of tobacco mosaic virus (TMV), proving that it was a macromolecule; in 1943, developed the first effective influenza vaccine; in 1946, won the Nobel Prize in Chemistry.

Stanton, Edwin M.

full: Edwin McMasters Stanton
b. December 19, 1814
Steubenville, Ohio
d. December 24, 1869
Washington, D.C.
fields: Government and Politics, Law, Military Affairs

Stanton as secretary of war made a major contribution to Union victory during the Civil War. In 1869, he was appointed a U.S. Supreme Court justice by President Ulysses S. Grant. He died four days after confirmation by the Senate.

Stanton, Elizabeth Cady

né: Elizabeth Cady
b. November 12, 1815
Johnstown, New York
d. October 26, 1902
New York, New York
fields: Women's Rights, Government and Politics

Stanton was one of the founders of the organized women's rights movement in the United States, and she served as one of its chief leaders during the second half of the nineteenth century.

Stanton, Gertrude. *See* Käsebier, Gertrude

Staples, Brent A.

b. September 13, 1951
Chester, Pa.
fields: Journalism, Literature

African American journalist and author; an editorial writer at *The New York Times*, Brent A. Staples recounted his escape from a poverty-ridden youth and adolescence into success in college and graduate school in a memoir entitled *Parallel Time: Growing Up in Black and White* (1994).

Stargell, Willie

full: Wilver Dornel Stargell
b. March 6, 1941
Earlsboro, Okla.
fields: Sports (baseball player)

African American baseball player; Willie Stargell played for the Pittsburgh Pirates; member of the Baseball Hall of Fame.

Starhawk

né: Miriam Simos
b. June 17, 1951
St. Paul, Minn.
fields: Religion and Theology

Starhawk (Miriam Simos) is known for practicing witchcraft, a pre-Christian, Goddess-centered religion that is similar in practice and spirit to American Indian and African religions. She is codirector of Reclaiming, a center offering classes in the tradition of Goddess religion. She published *The Spiral Dance: A Rebirth of the Ancient Religion of the Great Goddess* (1979) and *Dreaming in the Dark: Magic, Sex, and Politics* (1982), which explore the influence of witchcraft on the feminist and ecology movements.

Stark, Johannes

b. April 15, 1874
Schickenhof, Germany
d. June 21, 1957
Traunstein, West Germany
fields: Physics

Stark's detection of the Doppler effect in a terrestrially generated light source led to his discovery that a strong electric field will split the spectral lines of chemical elements. Stark's experiments provided confirmation of Albert Einstein's special theory of relativity and evidence for the controversial quantum theories of Max Planck. He was awarded the 1919 Nobel Prize in Physics.

Starkey, Richard. *See* Starr, Ringo

Starling, Ernest Henry

b. April 17, 1866
London, England
d. May 2, 1927
near Kingston, Jamaica
fields: Medicine

Starling discovered the mechanisms that regulate the output of the heart and the flow of lymphatic fluid and discovered the role of hormones in the control of organ function.

Starr, Edwin

né: Charles Hatcher
b. January 21, 1942
Nashville, Tenn.
fields: Music (singer)

African American singer; Edwin Starr made a number of moderately successful recordings for Motown in the 1960's and 1970's, including "Twenty-five Miles" (1969); also had some success in disco.

Starr, Ringo

né: Richard Starkey
b. July 7, 1940
Liverpool, England
fields: Music (popular)

Ringo Starr was best known as the drummer for the Beatles. More than any other English band before it, the Beatles popularized American rock-and-roll and became not only the major exponent of British rock-and-roll to the world but also one of the greatest popular bands ever.

Starved Bear. *See* Lean Bear

Staudinger, Hermann

b. March 23, 1881
Worms, Germany
d. September 8, 1965
Freiburg im Breisgau, West Germany

fields: Chemistry

Staudinger became the father of a novel branch of chemistry when he conceived of and proved the existence of macromolecules. This work laid the foundation for the technological achievements in the plastics and high polymer synthetics industries. In addition, Staudinger contributed to the fields of organic chemistry and molecular biology. He won the 1953 Nobel Prize in Chemistry.

Steele, Shelby

b. January 1, 1946
Chicago, Ill.
fields: Literature, Education

African American writer and educator; Shelby Steele, a professor of English at San Jose State University, received the 1990 National Book Critics Circle Award for his collection of essays focusing on his personal journey toward understanding the issue of race, *The Content of Our Character: A New Vision of Race in America* (1990); he has stirred controversy with his arguments that African Americans sometimes use racism as an excuse for not taking the initiative to succeed, continued with his next book, *A Dream Deferred: The Second Betrayal of Black Freedom in America* (1998); Steele and Thomas Lennon collaborated on the 1990 documentary *Seven Days in Bensonhurst.*

Stefan Dušan

aka: Stefan Uroš IV Dušan
aka: Stephen Dusan
b. 1308
central Serbia
d. December 20, 1355
near Prizren, Serbia
fields: Government and Politics, Monarchy

King of Serbia, 1331-1355. The greatest ruler of medieval Serbia, Stefan Dušan extended his kingdom's borders at the expense of the Byzantine Empire. He successfully defended Serbia against its enemies, promulgated an important law code, and was crowned Czar of the Serbs and the Greeks in 1346.

Steffens, Lincoln

b. April 6, 1866
San Francisco, California
b. August 9, 1936
Carmel, California
fields: Journalism

Considered one of the most talented journalists to emerge from the muckraking era of the early 1900's, Lincoln Steffens found it difficult to publish in the United States because of his identification with leftist causes. In 1901 he became managing editor of *McClure's Magazine*, writing and publishing his famous series detailing municipal corruption, "The Shame of the Cities." After he visited the Soviet Union in 1919, he wrote "I have seen the future and it works." This statement led to a blacklisting of his writings in the United States. *The Autobiography of Lincoln Steffens*, published in 1931, was widely read for many years but fell out of favor during the Red Scare of the 1950's.

Steichen, Edward

né: Éduard Jean Steichen
b. March 27, 1879
Luxembourg
d. March 25, 1973
West Redding, Connecticut
fields: Photography

Steichen was a gifted and remarkably versatile photographer and a visionary editor, who did more than any single individual in developing the range of photography's possibilities as an expressive medium.

Stein, Edith

b. October 12, 1891
Breslau, Germany (now Wrocław, Poland)
d. August 9, 1942
Auschwitz, Poland
fields: Philosophy, Religion and Theology, Women's Rights

Stein, a disciple of the phenomenologist Edmund Husserl, became herself a leading proponent of his method of philosophy. Alongside her spiritual evolution from Judaism to atheism to Catholicism, she tried, in her writings, to relate phenomenology to personalism, Thomism, the Catholic tradition on women, and the mystical theology of Saint John of the Cross.

Stein, Freiherr vom

full: Heinrich Friedrich Karl, Freiherr vom und zum Stein
b. October 26, 1757
Nassau, Holy Roman Empire
d. June 29, 1831
Cappenberg, Prussia
fields: Government and Politics, Social Reform

Stein was the architect of the reform movement in Prussia, during the period from 1806 to 1808, that altered the authoritarian nature of the Prussian state in the direction of modern liberalism and resulted in fundamental changes in Prussian institutions.

Stein, Gertrude

b. February 3, 1874
Allegheny, Pennsylvania
d. July 27, 1946
Neuilly-sur-Seine, France
fields: Literature

A literary innovator, Gertrude Stein captured the dialogue of common people and significantly influenced the writing of post-World War I authors.

Steinbeck, John

full: John Ernst Steinbeck
b. February 27, 1902
Salinas, California
d. December 20, 1968
New York, New York
fields: Literature

Steinbeck has given to the American consciousness a permanent portrait of America's rural and immigrant underclasses, especially during the years of the Great Depression. He won the 1962 Nobel Prize in Literature.

Steinberger, Jack

b. May 25, 1921
Bad Kissingen, Germany
fields: Physics

Jack Steinberger made the first laboratory-made beam of neutrinos; discovered a new type of neutrino, contributing to the development of the "Standard Model" classification of matter; in 1988, won the Nobel Prize in Physics jointly with Leon Max Lederman and Melvin Schwartz.

Steinem, Gloria

b. March 25, 1934
Toledo, Ohio
fields: Women's Rights, Journalism

A leading proponent of the twentieth century feminist movement, Steinem was also a founder of *Ms.* magazine. Her outspoken advocacy for women has made her a nationally known figure.

Steiner, Jakob

b. March 18, 1796
near Utzendorf, Canton of Bern, Switzerland
d. April 1, 1863
Bern, Switzerland
fields: Mathematics

Steiner was one of the greatest geometers of the first half of the nineteenth century. His major geometrical books and dozens of articles established him as a chief authority on isoperimetric geometry and as the founder of modern synthetic geometry in Germany.

Steinmetz, Charles Proteus

né: Carl August Steinmetz
b. April 9, 1865
Breslau, Germany
d. October 16, 1923
Schenectady, New York
fields: Engineering, Education

Steinmetz helped lay the engineering foundations for the large-scale use of electric power through his technical achievements, his role as an educator and inspirer of other engineers, and his creation of research and engineering institutions. In the process, he came to personify electrical engineering to a public that understood little of its technical details.

Stendhal

né: Marie-Henri Beyle
b. January 23, 1783
Grenoble, France
d. March 23, 1842
Paris, France
fields: Literature

Stendhal combined the themes of Romanticism with the style of realism. His insistence on telling the truth about emotions in simple, stark terms resulted in novels that, although not very popular during his lifetime, have become classics.

Stephen I

aka: Saint Stephen
aka: Stephen the Apostle of Hungary
b. 975
Esztergom, Hungary
d. August 15, 1038
Royal Alba, Hungary
fields: Religion and Theology, Government and Politics, Monarchy

King of Hungary, 997-1038. Stephen I zealously spread the Christian faith to his largely pagan people, taking a great interest in the welfare of the poorest of his subjects and establishing numerous churches and monasteries both at home and abroad to place Christianity at the center of Hungarian life.

Stephen, Adeline Virginia. *See* Woolf, Virginia

Stephen, King

né: Stephen of Blois
b. c. 1097
place unknown
d. October 25, 1154
Dover, Kent, England
fields: Government and Politics, Monarchy

Stephen was king of England (1135-1154) and duke of Normandy during a period of civil war and anarchy. He proved to be a weak king, unable to sustain the peace created by Henry I. On his death, the throne passed to his cousin, Henry Plantagenet.

Stephen, Saint

b. c. 5 C.E.
Samaria
d. c. 36 C.E.
Jerusalem
fields: Religion and Theology

By means of his innovative theology, his personal courage, and his martyrdom, Stephen helped to universalize the early Christian Church by encouraging its expansion beyond the doctrinal confines of Judaism and the political confines of Jerusalem.

Stephens, Alexander H.

full: Alexander Hamilton Stephens
b. February 11, 1812
Wilkes County, Georgia
d. March 4, 1883
Atlanta, Georgia
fields: Government and Politics

Stephens, called "Little Aleck" by his colleagues because he only weighed one hundred pounds, was a member of the United States Congress from 1843 to 1859 and vice president of the Confederate States of America during the Civil War. Following the war, he again served in Congress and as governor of Georgia.

Stephenson, George

b. June 9, 1781
Wylam, Northumberland, England
d. August 12, 1848
Chesterfield, Derbyshire, England
fields: Engineering (civil)

By constructing and equipping the Stockton and Darlington and the Liverpool and Manchester railways, Stephenson demonstrated the economic viability of the steam railway, guaranteeing its rapid development as Great Britain's basic transportation system.

Stern, Howard

b. January 12, 1954
Roosevelt, Long Island, New York
fields: Radio

A pioneer in "shock jock" or "topless" radio, Howard Stern has been the target of numerous listener complaints and has been investigated by the Federal Communications Commission. His initially conventional radio program, which began broadcasting in New York in 1976, evolved as Stern mixed music with more and more candid telephone conversations with guests and listeners. In the fall of 1986 he began syndicating his weekday morning show. Charges of racism, misogyny, homophobia, and unmitigated vulgarity only made his show more popular. By the mid-1990's the show reached more than thirty stations across the United States. He also wrote the bestsellers *Private Parts* (1993) and *Miss America* (1995).

Stern, Otto

b. Feb. 17, 1888
Sohrau, Upper Silesia, Germany (now Zory, Poland)
d. Aug. 17, 1969
Berkeley, California
fields: Physics

Otto Stern developed molecular beam methods to verify the wave nature of particles, to show that the orbital angular momentum of atomic electrons is quantized, and to measure the magnetic moments of the proton and the deuteron; in 1943, awarded the Nobel Prize in Physics.

Sterne, Laurence

b. November 24, 1713
Clonmel, Ireland
d. March 18, 1768
London, England
fields: Literature

A free-thinking, iconoclastic novelist and Anglican cleric, Laurence Sterne was a critic of the Roman Catholic Church. His novel *A Sentimental Journey Through France and Italy by Mr. Yorick* (1768), published shortly before his death, received the church's censure in 1819. Ironically, *Sentimental Journey* expresses significantly more tolerance for Catholicism than much of Sterne's earlier work, including his collection of sermons, published as *Sermons of Mr. Yorick* (1760), and his first novel, *The Life and Opinions of Tristram Shandy, Gentleman* (1759-1767).

Stevens, Durham White

b. Feb. 1, 1852
Washington, D.C.
d. Mar. 25, 1908
San Francisco, Calif.
fields: Government and Politics

Durham White Stevens became foreign affairs adviser in Korea after Japan forced the Korean government to sign an agreement giving Japan almost complete control over all domestic and foreign matters. Korea had to accept Japanese advisers in key ministries and foreign affairs advisers who handled all diplomatic affairs in consultation with Japanese officials. When Stevens returned to San Francisco in 1908, he was confronted by an angry Korean expatriate, Chang In-hwan. Chang shot Stevens, who died of his wounds two days later.

Stevens, John Paul

b. April 20, 1920
Chicago, Ill.
fields: Law

U.S. Supreme Court justice, began tenure in 1975; appointed by President Ford. Significant opinions: *Payton v. New York*, 445 U.S. 573 (1980); *United States v. Jacobsen*, 466 U.S. 109 (1984); *Maryland v. Garrison*, 480 U.S. 79 (1987).

Stevens, Nettie Maria

b. July 7, 1861
Cavendish, Vermont
d. May 4, 1912
Baltimore, Maryland
fields: Biology, Genetics

Nettie Maria Stevens demonstrated that sex is determined by a particular chromosome, when she published a monograph in 1905 identifying the X and Y chromosomes; was the first to establish that chromosomes exist as paired structures in body cells; was the first to realize that certain insects have supernumerary chromosomes.

Stevens, Thaddeus

b. April 4, 1792
Danville, Vermont
d. August 11, 1868
Washington, D.C.
fields: Civil Rights, Government and Politics

Although greatly disliked during his lifetime and by some later historians, Stevens was the leading advocate of a just policy for former slaves; his program was only a part of his larger commitment to equality for all people.

Stevens, Williamina Paton. *See* Fleming, Williamina Paton Stevens

Stevens, Yvette Marie. *See* Khan, Chaka

Stevenson, Adlai E.

full: Adlai Ewing Stevenson II
b. February 5, 1900
Los Angeles, California
d. July 14, 1965
London, England
fields: Government and Politics

Although unsuccessful in his repeated bids for the presidency, Stevenson inspired a new generation of liberals who would write the agenda for the New Frontier and Great Society during the 1960's; he brought to the American political scene an all too uncommon blend of integrity, high intelligence, and humane values.

Stevenson, Robert Louis

full: Robert Louis Balfour Stevenson
b. November 13, 1850
Edinburgh, Scotland
d. December 3, 1894
Vailima, near Apia, Samoa
fields: Literature

The author of thirty-two books during his brief lifetime, Stevenson created various classics in the field of children's literature as well as several popular adult works, including *The Strange Case of Dr. Jekyll and Mr. Hyde*, which has exerted a powerful influence on Western cultural imagination.

Steward, Susan Maria Smith McKinney

né: Susan Maria Smith
b. 1847
Brooklyn, N.Y.
d. March 7, 1918
Wilberforce, Ohio
fields: Medicine, Social Reform

African American physician and activist; Susan Maria Smith McKinney Steward was the first African American woman in New York State and the third in the United States to graduate from a medical school; she maintained a private medical practice in Brooklyn and, in 1881, cofounded the Brooklyn Woman's Homeopathic Hospital and Dispensary; from 1898 to 1918, she taught at Wilberforce University, Ohio; as an advocate of women's rights and civil liberties, she addressed local, national, and international audiences on social and medical issues.

Stewart, Bennett McVey

b. August 6, 1914
Huntsville, Ala.
d. April 26, 1988
Chicago, Ill.
fields: Government and Politics

African American U.S. representative from Illinois; Bennett McVey Stewart became a member of Congress in 1979, having been selected to serve out the remainder of the deceased Ralph Metcalf's term; was not reelected in 1980.

Stewart, Chuck

b. 1927
fields: Photography

African American photographer; Chuck Stewart photographed most major jazz musicians active between 1950 and 1980.

Stewart, David Keith

b. February 19, 1957
Oakland, Calif.
fields: Sports (baseball player)

African American baseball player; David Keith Stewart pitched for the Oakland Athletics.

Stewart, Frank

b. 1949
Nashville, Tenn.
fields: Photography

African American photographer; Frank Stewart was one of the ten photographers commissioned by the Los Angeles Olympic Committee.

Stewart, Isabella. *See* Gardner, Isabella Stewart

Stewart, James

full: James Maitland Stewart
b. May 20, 1908
Indiana, Pennsylvania
d. July 2, 1997
Beverly Hills, California
fields: Film, Military Affairs, Theater and Entertainment

Stewart was one of the most successful and enduring actors in the history of American motion pictures.

Stewart, Maria Miller

b. 1803
Hartford, Conn.
d. December 17, 1879
Washington, D.C.
fields: Civil Rights, Social Reform

African American abolitionist; Maria Miller Stewart was a proponent of abolitionist William Lloyd Garrison; publicly challenged the role of women; matron of the Freedman's Hospital.

Stewart, Martha

né: Martha Kostyra
b. 1941 or 1942
Jersey City, New Jersey
fields: Business and Industry

Known as the "guru" of home entertainment, Stewart has written books on entertaining, gardening, and cooking in addition to books on weddings and home remodeling.

Stewart, Potter

b. 1915
d. 1985
fields: Law

U.S. Supreme Court justice, 1958-1981; appointed by President Eisenhower. Leader in development of Supreme Court's approach to interpreting the scope of the Fourth Amendment in modern times. Famous for his quip concerning attempts to define obscenity: "[P]erhaps I could never succeed in intelligibly [defining obscenity]. But I know it when I see it; and the motion picture involved in this case is not that." *Jacobellis v. Ohio*, 378 U.S. 184, 197 (1964) (concurring opinion). Significant opinions: *Massiah v. United States*, 377 U.S. 201 (1964); *Stoner v. California*, 376 U.S. 483 (1964); *Katz v. United States*, 389 U.S. 347 (1967); *Chimel v. California*, 395 U.S. 752 (1969); *Gregg v. Georgia*, 428 U.S. 153 (1976) (plurality opinion); *Brewer v. Williams*, 430 U.S. 387 (1977); *Rhode Island v. Innis*, 446 U.S. 291 (1980).

Stewart, Robert. *See* Castlereagh, Viscount

Stieglitz, Alfred

b. January 1, 1864
Hoboken, New Jersey
d. July 13, 1946
New York, New York
fields: Photography

Stieglitz was a central figure in the development of early twentieth century photography, in the introduction of modern art to the

American people, and, most important, in the discovering and fostering of an indigenous American culture.

Stieltjes, Thomas Jan

b. Dec. 29, 1856
Zwolle, the Netherlands
d. Dec. 31, 1894
Toulouse, France
fields: Mathematics (calculus and number theory)

Thomas Jan Stieltjes published "Recherches sur les fractions continues," in 1894, in which he introduced the Stieltjes integral, a generalization of definite integrals that led to many advances in mathematics and statistics.

Stilicho, Flavius

b. c. 360
Eastern Roman Empire, perhaps near Constantinople
d. August 22, 408
Ravenna, Italy
fields: Warfare and Conquest

For a period of some fifteen years, Stilicho acted as the generalissimo of the Western Roman Empire (and as much of the Eastern as he was allowed), repeatedly staving off barbarian assaults on Rome and on Constantinople.

Still, William

b. 1821
Shainong, N.J.
d. 1902
fields: Civil Rights, Social Reform

African American abolitionist; William Still, the son of slaves, became chairman of Pennsylvania Society for the Abolition of Slavery; active in the Underground Railroad.

Still, William Grant

b. May 11, 1895
Woodville, Miss.
d. December 3, 1978
Los Angeles, Calif.
fields: Music (composer)

African American composer; William Grant Still was the most famous African American composer; conducted the New Orleans Philharmonic Symphony; first African American to conduct a major U.S. orchestra, the Los Angeles Philharmonic, in 1936; wrote the *Afro-American Symphony* (1931).

Stimson, Henry L.

full: Henry Lewis Stimson
b. September 21, 1867
New York, New York
d. October 20, 1950
Huntington, New York
fields: Diplomacy, Government and Politics

Serving as secretary of war during the years 1909 to 1913 and again during World War II, and serving as secretary of state from 1929 to 1933, Stimson helped to define the United States' transition from isolationism to world responsibility.

Stirling, James

b. 1692
Garden, Stirling, Scotland
d. Dec. 5, 1770
Edinburgh, Scotland
fields: Mathematics (applied math, calculus, and geometry)

James Stirling found a formula that approximates $n!$, the product of the first n positive integers; invented the Stirling engine in 1745.

Stitt, Sonny

full: Edward Stitt
b. February 2, 1924
Boston, Mass.
d. July 22, 1982
Washington, D.C.
fields: Music (saxophonist)

African American saxophonist; Sonny Stitt was a major figure in bebop; played with Dizzy Gillespie and Norman Granz; was frequently compared with Charlie Parker.

Stoakes, Louise

b. ?
Malden, Mass.
d. ?
fields: Sports (track sprinter)

African American track sprinter; Louise Stoakes was known as "The Malden Meteor"; replaced with a white runner on both the 1932 and 1936 Olympic teams; the first African American woman to make an Olympic team, though not allowed to compete.

Stockhausen, Karlheinz

b. August 22, 1928
Mödrath, near Cologne, Germany
fields: Music

Stockhausen is one of the most innovative and influential composers of his time, successfully bridging the gap between technology and creative endeavor and integrating a wide spectrum of musical and nonmusical concepts into his work.

Stokes, Carl Burton

b. June 21, 1927
Cleveland, Ohio
d. April 2, 1996
Cleveland, Ohio
fields: Government and Politics

African American politician; Carl Burton Stokes served two terms in the Ohio state legislature, beginning in 1962; was the first African American elected mayor of a major American city (Cleveland) in 1967; won reelection in 1969; became a newscaster in 1972; became a Cleveland municipal court judge in 1980; U.S. Ambassador to the Republic of Seychelles, 1994-1996.

Stokes, Louis

b. February 23, 1925
Cleveland, Ohio
fields: Government and Politics

African American politician; Louis Stokes, brother of Carl Stokes, represented Charles P. Lucas, a black Republican, in a suit against the Ohio legislature that charged gerrymandering to dilute black voting strength; first African American to be elected to Congress from Ohio; chairman of the Congressional Black Caucus; served on a number of important committees; embroiled in House check-bouncing scandal; retired in 1998.

Stone, Harlan Fiske

b. October 11, 1872
Chesterfield, New Hampshire
d. April 22, 1946
Washington, D.C.
fields: Education, Law

As Associate and then Chief Justice of the United States Supreme Court, Stone advocated a philosophy of moderation that combined judicial restraint and liberal nationalism with a concern for civil and political liberties. His integrity and persistence contributed significantly to the Court's dramatic shift in 1937 from hostility to sympathy for the liberal nationalism of New Deal legislation, thereby avoiding a major constitutional crisis over the Court's powers.

Stone, I. F.

full: Isidor Feinstein Stone
b. December 24, 1907
Philadelphia, Pennsylvania
d. June 18, 1989
Boston, Massachusetts
fields: Journalism

A journalist from his teens, I. F. Stone published his independent newsletter, *I. F. Stone's Weekly*, in which he spoke his mind on virtually any subject from 1953 until 1972. Stone curtailed operations somewhat in 1969, when the *Weekly* became *I. F. Stone's Bi-Weekly*. At its peak, the newsletter had more than seventy thousand subscribers by the end of 1971.

Stone, Lucy

b. August 13, 1818
Coy's Hill, near West Brookfield, Massachusetts
d. October 18, 1893
Dorchester, near Boston, Massachusetts

fields: Social Reform, Women's Rights

Stone committed her life to the struggle for woman suffrage and equal rights.

Stone, Oliver

b. September 15, 1946
New York, New York
fields: Film

A Yale University dropout, Oliver Stone traveled in Vietnam and Mexico and joined the Army to fight in Vietnam, where he received a Bronze Star for Valor. After returning home, he studied film at New York University. His first big success was the screenplay for *Midnight Express* (1978), for which he won an Academy Award. His own films all carried strong and emotionally charged political messages. This include *Salvador* (1986); *Platoon* (1986), about the Vietnam War; *Born on the Fourth of July* (1988), also about the war; *The Doors* (1990); and *JFK* (1991), about the assassination of President John F. Kennedy; and *Nixon* (1995).

Stone, Toni

né: Marcenia Lyle
b. 1921
St. Paul, Minnesota
d. November 10, 1996
Alameda, California
fields: Sports (female baseball player)

African American female baseball player; Toni Stone played second base for the Indianapolis Clowns of the Negro Leagues.

Stone Child. *See* Rocky Boy

Stopes, Marie

full: Marie Charlotte Carmichael Stopes
b. October 15, 1880
Edinburgh, Scotland
d. October 2, 1958
Norbury Park, near Dorking, Surrey, England
fields: Social Reform, Psychiatry and Psychology

A pioneer in sex education and birth control, Stopes emphasized the importance of happiness in human relationships.

Storni, Alfonsina

b. May 29, 1892
Sala Capriasca, Switzerland
d. Oct. 25, 1938
Mar del Plata, Argentina
fields: Literature (poet)

Poet Alfonsina Storni, an independent single mother, lived in Argentina and wrote most of her work there. She committed suicide at the age of forty-six after being stricken with cancer. Two periods of work; first includes *La inquietude del rosal* (1916), *El dulce daño* (1918), *Irremediablemente* (1919), and *Languidez* (1920). Second includes *Mundo de siete pozos* (1934) and *Mascarilla y trébol* (1938). Called Argentina's first feminist poet.

Story, Joseph

b. September 18, 1779
Marblehead, Massachusetts
d. September 10, 1845
Cambridge, Massachusetts
fields: Law

U.S. Supreme Court justice, 1812-1845 (died while in office); appointed by President Madison. Intellectual leader of the Supreme Court who also wrote many of the most significant early commentaries on American law. Significant opinions: *Martin v. Hunter's Lessee*, 14 U.S. 304 (1816); *Charles River Bridge v. Warren Bridge Co.*, 36 U.S. 420 (1837) (dissenting opinion); *United States v. Schooner Amistad*, 40 U.S. 518 (1841); *Swift v. Tyson*, 41 U.S. 1 (1842). Other writings: *Commentaries on the Constitution of the United States* (1833) (3 volumes); *Commentaries on Equity Jurisprudence* (1834); and numerous other books and articles.

Stott, Alicia Boole

né: Alicia Boole
aka: Alice Stott
b. June 8, 1860
Cork, Ireland
d. Dec. 17, 1940
London, England
fields: Mathematics (geometry)

Alicia Boole Stott aided the understanding and visualization of certain four-dimensional geometric figures that she named polytopes.

Stowe, Harriet Beecher

né: Harriet Beecher
b. June 14, 1811
Litchfield, Connecticut
d. July 1, 1896
Hartford, Connecticut
fields: Social Reform, Women's Rights

Stowe's popular novel *Uncle Tom's Cabin* attacked slavery as a threat to the Christian family and helped to end this institution in the United States. In this and later novels, Stowe wrote as an early advocate for women—one who wished to help them by creating a "women's sphere" in the home.

Strabo

b. 64 or 63 B.C.E.
Amasia, Pontus, Asia Minor
d. After 23 C.E.
probably Amasia or Rome
fields: Geography, Historiography

Building on the work of his predecessors, Strabo wrote a description of the known inhabited world, valuable for its philosophy of geography, its historical digressions, and the current scientific notions it contains. Although not always accurate in details, the seventeen books of the *Geography* stand out for their diverse subjects, encyclopedic scope, and contemporary view of the ancient world at the dawn of the Christian era.

Stradivari, Antonio

b. 1644?
Cremona?, Duchy of Milan
d. December 18, 1737
Duchy of Milan
fields: Music

Stradivari, the most famous violin maker in history, modified the traditional design of the violin as it had developed for one hundred years in Cremona. He created instruments during his lifetime that are renowned for their superb tonal quality and have been the models for violin making ever since.

Strafford, first earl of

né: Thomas Wentworth
b. April 13, 1593
London, England
d. May 12, 1641
London, England
fields: Government and Politics

Strafford was one of the principal advisers of Charles I during the era of personal rule, from 1629 to 1640. As such, he became the focus for the dissatisfaction and resentments of nearly all segments of society against arbitrary royal rule. To an unusual degree, his role in and contribution to seventeenth century history have remained controversial.

Straus, Murray

b. June 18, 1926
New York, N.Y.
fields: Sociology

Am authority on family violence, Murray Straus began teaching in the sociology and anthropology department at the University of New Hampshire in the 1960's. His research provided evidence of links between family violence and male dominance of the family. Around 1989-1990, he began some of his most controversial work, studying corporal punishment in families. By the late 1990's he had become a leading critic of corporal punishment.

Strauss, Johann

b. October 25, 1825
Vienna, Austria
d. June 3, 1899
Vienna, Austria
fields: Music

Strauss built upon the musical achievements of his father and Austrian dance composer Joseph Lanner to raise the waltz to its highest level of development, a point at which it passed from dance music to symphonic music. His achievements in the operetta were less dramatic, for only two of his operettas have received lasting acclaim.

Strauss, Leo

b. September 20, 1899
Kirchhain, Hessen, Germany
d. October 18, 1973
Annapolis, Maryland
fields: Philosophy, Political Science

Fleeing Nazi Germany in 1937, Leo Strauss settled in the United States, teaching at Columbia University, at the New School for Social Research, and (beginning in 1949) at the University of Chicago. A political philosopher, he searched the texts of both the ancients and the moderns to construct his vision of a viable politics that included the rule of the wise. He decried sociologists and political scientists who tried to describe society and politics in value-neutral terms, seeing their moral relativism as a dereliction of the thinker's responsibility. He believed that social scientists should draw on the wisdom of past philosophers to assess the contemporary world and, as the titles of some of his works suggest, was acutely conscious of writing in a world full of danger for philosophers. Among his major works are *On Tyranny* (1948, rev. 1963), *Persecution and the Art of Writing* (1952), *Natural Right and History* (1953), *What Is Political Philosophy?* (1959), and *The City and Man* (1964).

Strauss, Richard

b. June 11, 1864
Munich, Bavaria, Germany
d. September 8, 1949
Garmisch-Partenkirchen, West Germany
fields: Music

The symphonic poems composed by Strauss in the last years of the nineteenth century won for him early fame and fortune. He was widely regarded by the music community as one of the brilliant young men destined to lead music into the twentieth century.

Stravinsky, Igor

full: Igor Fyodorovich Stravinsky
b. June 17, 1882
Oranienbaum, Russia
d. April 6, 1971
New York, New York
fields: Music

Summarizing and consummating the history of Western music, Stravinsky, reacting against the growing chaos of late nineteenth century Romanticism, reintroduced principles of order and expanded the horizons of music.

Strawberry, Darryl

full: Darryl Eugene Strawberry
b. Mar 12, 1962
Los Angeles, California
fields: Sports (baseball player)

African American baseball player; Darryl Strawberry started his major league career with the New York Mets, setting a home run record in 1983; joined the Los Angeles Dodgers as free agent, earning an annual salary in excess of $4 million (1991-1994); 1994-1995 season with the San Francisco Giants; 1995-1998 with the New York Yankees. In 1998 he had a successful operation for colon cancer. His career has been tarnished by drug and financial problems.

Strawson, Peter

full: Peter Frederick Strawson
b. November 23, 1919
London, England
fields: Philosophy

Peter Strawson developed a relatively informal logic in comparison to W. V. O. Quine' s unrelentingly formal approach, offered a chastened and influential account of Immanuel Kant's metaphysics and epistemology, and presented an account of the general conceptual scheme as an exercise in descriptive metaphysics. Strawson's best-known works are *Introduction to Logical Theory* (1952), *Individuals* (1959), and *The Bounds of Sense* (1966).

Strayhorn, Billy

b. November 29, 1915
Dayton, Ohio
d. May 31, 1967
New York, N.Y.
fields: Music (pianist, arranger, and composer)

African American pianist, arranger, and composer; Billy Strayhorn was a seminal jazz figure, linked closely to Duke Ellington, with whom he worked between 1939 and 1965; his best known composition is "Take the A Train" (1941), Ellington's signature piece.

Streep, Meryl

né: Mary Louise Streep
b. June 22, 1949
Summit, New Jersey
fields: Film (actor)

Streep is a highly acclaimed actress who, in order to break stereotypes of women as weak, will only appear in films that depict women characters of many dimensions.

Street, George Edmund

b. June 20, 1824
Woodford, England
d. December 18, 1881
London, England
fields: Architecture

Street designed and built the Law Courts in London, and he was a leading builder of churches in England and Europe during the Gothic Revival.

Streicher, Julius

b. February 12, 1885
Fleinhausen, Germany
d. October 16, 1946
Nuremberg, Germany
fields: Journalism, Government and Politics

A journalist, Julius Streicher was a leading anti-Semitic propagandist for Germany's Nazi Party. After helping to form the German Socialist (Nazi) Party in the early 1920's, he published the virulently anti-Jewish *Der Stürmer.* When Adolf Hitler came to power in 1933, he appointed Streicher chairman of an anti-Jewish boycott. Streicher also played a leading role in the November 9, 1938, pogrom known as *Kristallnacht* (Crystal Night). In 1940 he was dismissed as *Gauleiter*, but he continued to publish articles advocating the extermination of Jews. In 1946 the Nuremberg Tribunal found him guilty of crimes against humanity, and he was hanged.

Streisand, Barbra

full: Barbara Joan Streisand
b. April 24, 1942
Brooklyn, New York
fields: Music, Film, Theater and Entertainment

As a critically acclaimed and commercially successful actress, singer, director, and producer, Streisand has paved the way for women in industries traditionally controlled by men.

Stresemann, Gustav

b. May 10, 1878
Berlin, Germany
d. October 3, 1929
Berlin, Germany
fields: Government and Politics

Although unenthusiastic in his support for a German republic, Stresemann nevertheless served the Weimar Republican government as chancellor and foreign minister during the 1920's. As foreign minister, he was able to revise portions of the Treaty of Versailles and help to bring Germany into the mainstream of European diplomacy.

Strindberg, August

full: Johan August Strindberg

b. January 22, 1849
Stockholm, Sweden
d. May 14, 1912
Stockholm, Sweden
fields: Literature

Sweden's Strindberg stands, with the Norwegian Henrik Ibsen, as Scandinavia's greatest dramatist. He introduced both naturalism and expressionism to the modern European stage; considered to be the father of Swedish literature, with dozens of novels, essays, and scientific treatises as well as more than fifty plays to his credit, he never received that country's Nobel Prize but permanently influenced the shape of twentieth century world theater.

Stroessner, Alfredo

b. November 3, 1912
Encarnación, Paraguay
fields: Government and Politics

Alfredo Stroessner was dictatorial president of Paraguay from 1954 to 1989. Maintained control through military and powerful Colorado Party. Regime's anticommunism gained support of U.S.; Stroessner tolerated considerable illegal activities by military and political leaders and opposed land reform. In 1982 inaugurated the Itaipú Dam, built in conjunction with Brazil. Ousted by commander of army in 1989.

Strong, William

b. 1808
d. 1895
fields: Law

U.S. Supreme Court justice, 1870-1880; appointed by President Grant. Author of opinions opening jury service to African Americans. Significant opinions: *Strauder v. West Virginia*, 100 U.S. 303 (1880); *Ex parte Virginia*, 100 U.S. 339 (1880); *Virginia v. Rives*, 100 U.S. 313 (1880).

Stuart, Gilbert

full: Gilbert Charles Stuart
b. December 3, 1755
North Kingstown, Rhode Island
d. July 9, 1828
Boston, Massachusetts
fields: Art

More than any other person, Stuart has shaped the American image of George Washington. He also acquainted Americans with many others, both men and women, of the generation which founded the United States. His great artistic achievements were important in launching the cultural life of the new nation.

Stubbs, John

b. 1541?
Norfolk, England
d. 1591
Havre, France
fields: Religion and Theology

John Stubbs was an English Puritan pamphleteer who lost a hand in 1579 for criticizing Queen Elizabeth I's proposed marriage to the Duke of Alencon—the brother of France's king. The Crown's brutal response to his criticism clearly exposed the limits on free speech in Elizabethan England.

Stumbling Bear

aka: Setimkia (Charging Bear)
b. c. 1832
d. 1903
Fort Sill, Indian Territory, present-day Okla.
fields: Diplomacy, Government and Politics, Peace Advocacy, Native American Affairs

Initially a fierce warrior, Kiowa leader Stumbling Bear was principal war chief against Colonel Christopher "Kit" Carson at the first Battle of Adobe Walls in 1864. Stumbling Bear subsequently embraced peace after signing the Treaty of Medicine Lodge in 1867, which established reservations in Kansas.

Sturtevant, Alfred H.

full: Alfred Henry Sturtevant
b. Nov. 21, 1891
Jacksonville, Illinois
d. Apr. 5, 1970
Pasadena, California
fields: Biology, Genetics, Zoology

Alfred H. Sturtevant, in 1920, discovered the first reparable gene defect, the vermillion eye color mutation in fruit flies; in 1925, presented the concepts of position effect and of unequal crossing-over at meiosis; discovered the principles of gene mapping.

Stuyvesant, Peter

né: Petrus Stuyvesant
b. c. 1610
Scherpenzeel, Friesland, the Netherlands
d. February, 1672
Manhattan Island, New York
fields: Government and Politics

As the last Dutch governor of New Netherland, Stuyvesant brought order and prosperity to the fledgling colony and facilitated the rapprochement between Dutch and English settlers.

Su Dongpo

aka: Su Tung-p'o
né: Su Shi
b. December 19, 1036
Meishan, Sichuan, China
d. July 28, 1101
Zhangzhou, China
fields: Government and Politics, Literature, Art

One of China's most famous poets and scholars, Su Dongpo was also an important government official during the Song Dynasty (960-1279). He figured prominently in the political controversies surrounding the attempted imposition of state capitalist programs.

Suárez, Mario

b. Jan. 12, 1925
Tucson, Ariz.
d. Feb. 27, 1998
San Dimas, Calif.
fields: Literature (short-story writer)

Mario Suárez was a Latino writer of short fiction. First published stories appeared in the *Arizona Quarterly* in 1947; centered on Chicanos living in barrios of the 1940's. Suárez was an early writer to offer an accurate and detailed view of Chicano life.

Suárez, Virgil

b. 1962
Havana, Cuba
fields: Literature (fiction writer)

Latino writer Virgil Suárez emigrated from Cuba to U.S. at age of eight with his family. *Latin Jazz* (1989), his first novel, depicts a family that leaves Cuba and settles in Los Angeles. Other works include the novel *The Cutter* (1991); a collection of short stories, *Welcome to the Oasis and Other Stories* (1992); and en edited anthology, *Iguana Dreams: New Latino Fiction* (1992).

Suarez, Xavier

b. May 21, 1949
Las Villas, Cuba
fields: Government and Politics

Cuban American politician. Xavier Suarez, a 1975 Harvard graduate, practiced law and served on Miami's Affirmative Action Commission and Downtown Development Authority during the early 1980's. In 1985, he became Miami's first Cuban American mayor. He was reelected to second and third terms in 1987 and 1989, and was later appointed by President George Bush to the board of directors of the Legal Services Corporation.

Suárez y Romero, Anselmo

b. Apr. 21, 1818
Havana, Cuba
d. Jan. 7, 1878
Havana, Cuba
fields: Literature (writer and critic)

Cuban writer Anselmo Suárez y Romero held a law degree from the University of Havana and taught at a number of Cuban universities. Wrote the novel *Francisco* in 1839, but it was not published until 1880; it presents a grim picture of slavery in Cuba and is one of the earliest works of fiction written in the Americas. Also published critical essays.

Subba Row, Yellapragada

b. July, 1896
Madras State, India
d. Aug. 9, 1948
Pearl River, N.Y.
fields: Medicine

Physician and researcher Yellapragada Subba Row was inspired by his brother's death of sprue to conquer tropical diseases. With Harvard biochemistry professor Cyrus Fiske, Subba Row developed the Fiske-Subba Row method of detecting small amounts of phosphorus in muscle tissue. After receiving a doctorate in biochemistry in 1930, Subba Row conducted research in pellagra and pernicious anemia at Harvard and at Lederle Laboratories. His experiments with liver extract led to the isolation of critical substances in animal and bacterial nutrition, leading to the synthesis of folic acid. At Lederle, he developed several drugs, teropterin (cancer), aminopterin (leukemia), and hetrazan (filariasis).

Subertova, Martina. *See* Navratilova, Martina

Sublett, John William. *See* Bubbles, John

Sucre, Antonio José de

b. February 3, 1795
Cumaná, New Granada (now Venezuela)
d. June 4, 1830
in the Berruecos Mountains, near Venta Quemada, Ecuador
fields: Military Affairs

Sucre was a leading military and political leader in the struggle of South American patriots to achieve independence from Spain. The republics of Venezuela, Colombia, Ecuador, Peru, and Bolivia were created as a result of this conflict.

Sudarkasa, Niara

né: Gloria Marshall Clark
b. August 14, 1938
Fort Lauderdale, Fla.
fields: Education

African American university professor and administrator; Niara Sudarkasa was the first woman to be president of Lincoln University, the oldest historically black college in the United States.

Südfeld, Simon Maximilian. *See* Nordau, Max

Sue, Stanley

b. Feb. 13, 1944
Portland, Oreg.
fields: Psychology

Stanley Sue received a doctoral degree from the University of California, Los Angeles (1971), where he later became professor of psychology and director of the National Research Center on Asian American Mental Health. One of the United States' foremost experts on Asian American mental health issues, Sue consulted with and advised many agencies and institutions across the nation .

Sugahara, Kay

full: Keiichi Sugahara
b. 1909
Seattle, Wash.
d. 1988
fields: Business and Industry

Kay Sugahara founded the Universal Exchange Customs Brokerage House in 1932, becoming the first Japanese American customs broker in the continental United States. He amassed a fortune by age twenty-nine but lost most of it when he was forcibly evacuated to the Granada relocation center in southeastern Colorado during World War II. After serving with the Office of Strategic Services, Sugahara became board chair of the Fairfield Maxwell shipping and oil empire and chaired the nonprofit United States-Asia Institute.

Suger

b. 1081
Saint-Denis, near Paris
d. January 13, 1151
Saint-Denis
fields: Government and Politics, Architecture

A lover of peace, order, and political harmony, Suger defined and popularized the centralizing and peacekeeping mission of the Capetian monarchy, increasing its prestige and assisting its rise to dominance in medieval France. As abbot of Saint-Denis he rebuilt the abbey church according to principles which make him the founder of the Gothic style.

Sugimoto, Etsu

b. 1874
Echigo, Japan
d. June 20, 1950
Tokyo, Japan
fields: Literature

Japanese immigrant Etsu Sugimoto wrote of life during the early Meiji era in Japan and of the early immigrant experience in the United States. Her works include *A Daughter of the Narakin* (1932) and a memoir, *Daughter of the Samurai* (1934).

Sugimoto, Henry

b. 1901
Wakayama, Japan
fields: Art

Henry Sugimoto traveled to Paris to study art in 1929, after receiving a B.F.A. from the California College of Arts and Crafts the previous year. He returned to the United States and continued to paint, exhibiting his artwork in numerous galleries and museums. During World War II, Sugimoto was sent to the Jerome and Rohwer relocation centers in Arkansas where he produced paintings and drawings of camp conditions on bedsheets, pillow cases, and mattress covers. He illustrated children's books and designed fabrics before becoming a full-time artist in 1962. In 1984, internment camp artwork donated by Sugimoto became part of the Smithsonian National Museum of American History.

Suharto

aka: Soeharto
b. June 8, 1921
Kemusu, Argamulja, Java, Dutch East Indies (now Indonesia)
fields: Government and Politics

President of Indonesia from 1968 to 1998. As army general, Suharto wrested power from Sukarno after a year of chaos in 1966; elected president in 1968; reelected in 1973, 1978, 1983, 1988, 1992, and 1997. Achieved great success in improving food production, expanding economy, and reducing poverty and illiteracy. Suharto and his family also accrued tremendous wealth. Indonesian economy crashed in 1997 and his support disappeared; resigned the next year.

Sui, Anna

b. 1955?
Dearborn Heights, Mich.
fields: Fashion

Chinese American fashion designer Anna Sui displayed an interest in fashion at an early age. She attended the Parsons School of Design in New York, where she formed a creative collaboration with Steven Meisel, who would later achieve fame as a fashion photographer. In 1980, after selling six original pieces to a Macy's department store, she launched her own business, which developed into a million-dollar company. Her first runway showing was in 1991, and in 1992, she opened her own boutique in the SoHo district of Manhattan.

Sui Sin Far

né: Edith Maud Eaton
b. 1865
England

d. Apr. 7, 1914
Montreal, Quebec, Canada
fields: Literature

Sui Sin Far, born Edith Maud Eaton of a British father and Chinese mother, was one of the first Chinese American fiction writers. Far (as she referred to herself) struggled with her Eurasian identity and was never fully accepted by either the whites or Chinese. Far earned a living as a stenographer and journalist, and wrote fiction on the side. Many of her stories appeared in such periodicals as *Good Housekeeping*, *The New York Evening Post*, and *Sunset* from 1900 to 1908. Thirty-seven of her stories was published as *Mrs. Spring Fragrance* in 1912.

Sukarno

b. June 6, 1901
Surabaya, Dutch East Indies (now Indonesia)
d. June 21, 1970
Jakarta, Indonesia
fields: Government and Politics

A superb orator and a charismatic leader, Sukarno raised Indonesian national consciousness while providing a rudimentary administrative infrastructure under Dutch colonial and Japanese occupational forces. After the Japanese defeat in 1945, he declared his nation's independence and served as president and strongman until 1965, when involvement in a Communist-inspired coup undermined his authority.

Süleyman the Magnificent

aka: Süleyman I
aka: Süleyman Kanuni
b. 1494 or 1495
probably in Istanbul, Ottoman Empire
d. September 5 or 6, 1566
near Sziget, Hungary
fields: Government and Politics, Law

Sultan of the Ottoman Empire, 1520-1566. Süleyman I was undoubtedly the best-known Ottoman Turkish sultan: He extended the domains of the Ottoman Empire eastward, establishing a long-lasting border between the Sunni Turks and the Shiʿite realm under the Safavid shahs. His reign marked a period of internal stability, primarily through an ordered system of laws.

Sulla, Lucius Cornelius

b. 138 B.C.E.
Rome
d. 78 B.C.E.
Puteoli
fields: Government and Politics, Warfare and Conquest

Sulla played an extremely important historical role in the transformation of the Roman Republic into the Roman Empire. While attempting to prevent others from using force to influence Roman politics, Sulla became the first Roman to use the military to gain a political end.

Sullivan, Anne Mansfield. *See* Macy, Anne Sullivan

Sullivan, Arthur

full: Arthur Seymour Sullivan
aka: Sir Arthur Sullivan
b. May 13, 1842
London, England
d. November 22, 1900
London, England
fields: Music, Theater and Entertainment

One of the foremost British composers of the nineteenth century, Arthur Sullivan displayed an amazing range, from overtures and oratorios to operettas and hymns; he is primarily remembered for his collaborations with W. S. Gilbert in light opera.

Sullivan, Harry Stack

b. February 21, 1892
Norwich, New York
d. January 14, 1949
Paris, France
fields: Psychiatry and Psychology

The life of Sullivan, the formulator of the interpersonal theory of psychiatry, marks an outsider's triumph over personal adversity. A former schizophrenic, Sullivan broke through his loneliness to deliver rich insights into the human psyche and schizophrenia.

Sullivan, Leon Howard

b. October 16, 1922
Charleston, W.Va.
fields: Religion and Theology, Civil Rights

African American religious leader and community organizer; Leon Howard Sullivan was pastor of Zion Baptist Church in Philadelphia, Pa. (1950-1988); organized the Opportunities Industrialization Centers of America as a means of providing African Americans with skills and training; member of the board of directors of General Motors (1971); chair named for him at the University of Wisconsin.

Sullivan, Louis

full: Louis Henry Sullivan
b. September 3, 1856
Boston, Massachusetts
d. April 14, 1924
Chicago, Illinois
fields: Architecture

Known as the father of the skyscraper, Sullivan was a pioneer in the artful design of the tall building and in the development of distinctly American architecture.

Sullivan, Louis Wade

b. November 3, 1933
Atlanta, Ga.
fields: Education, Government and Politics

African American educator and government official; as Morehouse College dean, Louis Wade Sullivan was cofounder of Morehouse School of Medicine; secretary of health and human services under George Bush.

Sullivan, Maxine

né: Marietta Williams
b. May 13, 1911
Homestead, Pa.
d. April 7, 1987
New York, N.Y.
fields: Music (singer)

African American singer; Maxine Sullivan was a popular singer, appearing in film and on Broadway; introduced the song "Jeepers Creepers" in the film musical *Going Places* (1938).

Sumida, Stephen H.

b.?
fields: Literature

Stephen H. Sumida, an associate professor in the department of English at the University of Michigan, Ann Arbor, did pioneering work on the literature of Hawaii. He coauthored *Asian American Literature in Hawaii: An Annotated Bibliography* (1979) and coedited *Talk Story: Big Island Anthology* (1979). He wrote the widely acclaimed *And the View from the Shore: Literary Traditions of Hawaii* (1991).

Summer, Cree

b. July 7, 1970
Saskatchewan, Canada
fields: Television, Music (singer, songwriter)

African American actress; Canadian-born Cree Summer acted in films, on stage, and on television in Canada (she started at the age of thirteen doing cartoon voices) before joining the cast of the television series *A Different World* (began 1989; in the role of Freddie Brooks); from 1994 to 1995 she joined the cast of *Sweet Justice*; she released her first solo album, *Street Faerie*, in 1999. She continued to do commercial voice over and cartoon voices, notably Susie Charmichael on *Rugrats*, Penny on *Inspector Gadget*.

Summer, Donna

né: LaDonna Gaines
b. December 31, 1948
Boston, Mass.
fields: Music (singer and composer)

African American singer and composer; Donna Summer was a disco star in the 1970's; among her big hits are "Love to Love

You Baby," "I Feel Love" (1977), "MacArthur Park" (1978), "Bad Girls" (1979), and "Hot Stuff" (1979).

Summers, Edna White

b. September 4, 1919
Evanston, Ill.
fields: Government and Politics

African American supervisor of Evanston, Ill; Edna White Summers became supervisor (similar to a mayor) for Evanston Township, 1985-1992, the first African American woman to attain this post in Illinois.

Sumner, Charles

b. January 6, 1811
Boston, Massachusetts
d. March 11, 1874
Washington, D.C.
fields: Civil Rights, Government and Politics

For a quarter of a century, Sumner was the most significant proponent in high public office of equal rights and equal opportunities for black Americans.

Sumner, John

b. September 22, 1876
Washington, D.C.
d. June 20, 1971
Floral Park, New York
fields: Social Reform

John Sumner succeeded Anthony Comstock as the last head of the New York Society for the Suppression of Vice in 1915, holding the post until he retired in 1950. During his first year in his new office he forced Theodore Dreiser's novel *The Genius* to be withdrawn from sale. Later he directed SSV efforts to initiate obscenity charges against such works as James Branch Cabell's *Jurgen* (1919), James Joyce's *Ulysses* (1922), D. H. Lawrence's *Lady Chatterley's Lover* (1928), and Edmund Wilson's *Memoirs of Hecate County* (1946). In 1927 Sumner helped get Mae West jailed for directing and acting in the play *Sex*.

Sun Fo

aka: Sun K'o
b. Oct. 20, 1891
Xiangshan, Guangdong Province, China
d. Sept. 13, 1973
Taipei, Republic of China
fields: Government and Politics

Sun Fo, the only son of Sun Yat-sen, leader of Nationalist China, moved to Honolulu in 1896. He received an M.A. degree in economics from Columbia University in 1917 before returning to China. Sun served in various positions in the Guomindang (Nationalist Party of China), including posts as minister of railways, vice president of the Examination Yuan, president of the China National Aviation Corporation, and president of the Legislative Yuan between 1932 and 1948. When the Nationalists were defeated by the Communists in 1949, Sun went to France, then the United States, returning to Taiwan in 1965.

Sun Yat-sen

aka: Sun Yixian
aka: Sun Wen
b. November 12, 1866
Cuiheng, Xiangshan county, Guangdong Province, China
d. March 12, 1925
Beijing, China
fields: Government and Politics

Sun founded the Kuomintang (Chinese Nationalist Party) and led the Republican Revolution of 1911. He is honored by both the Communists and the Nationalists as the founding father of the Chinese republic.

Sun Yat-sen, Madame

né: Song Qingling
b. Jan. 27, 1893
Shanghai, China
d. May 29, 1981
Beijing, People's Republic of China
fields: Government and Politics

In 1914, Song Qingling married Sun Yat-sen, father of the Chinese republican revolution of 1911 and leader of the Nationalist Party. Madame Sun Yat-sen was her husband's secretary and chief confidant until his death in 1925. She later opposed Chiang Kai-shek, her sister's husband and the eventual successor to her husband. When the Communists took over in 1949 and Chiang's forces fled to Taiwan, Madame Sun remained in China. She later assumed several positions in the Chinese government.

Sunday, Billy

full: William Ashley Sunday
b. November 19, 1862
Ames, Iowa
d. November 6, 1935
Chicago, Illinois
fields: Religion and Theology

Sunday was the most flamboyant and colorful of the many Christian revivalists of early twentieth century America. Born in poverty in a log cabin, he was a successful major league baseball player before becoming an evangelist. Sunday preached to more than a million persons in the days before radios and speaker systems; approximately one million of these persons came "down the sawdust trail" and were "saved" as a result of his efforts.

Sunday, Elisabeth

b. ?
fields: Photography

African American photographer; Elisabeth Sunday was an active Oakland, California, photographer in the 1980's; produced a number of limited edition portfolios of her work.

Sundjata

b. c. 1215
near the confluence of the Niger and Sankarani rivers in Guinea, West Africa
d. c. 1255
near Niani, Guinea, West Africa
fields: Government and Politics

Founder of the thirteenth century empire of Mali in the western Sudan, Sundjata has become the unifying cultural figure for the Mandingo peoples of West Africa.

Sung, Betty Lee

b. Oct. 3, 1924
Baltimore, Md.
fields: Sociology

Betty Lee Sung, who earned a Ph.D. degree in sociology from the Graduate Center of the City University of New York in 1983, became a full professor of Asian American studies at the City College of New York, retiring in 1992. She wrote the prize-winning books *Mountain of Gold* (1967) and *Survey of Chinese American Manpower and Employment* (1976); *The Chinese in America* (1973), a children's book; and *Chinese American Intermarriage* (1990).

Sunoo, Brenda Paik

b. Feb. 13, 1948
Los Angeles, Calif.
fields: Journalism

Brenda Paik Sunoo, the former news editor of the *Korea Times* English edition in Los Angeles, frequently spoke on the role of the ethnic press and race relations. Sunoo also worked as a reporter for the *Modesto Bee* and the *Orange County Register*, both in California, and a features editor at *Rice* magazine, an Asian American monthly. A member of the Community Media Advisory Board for *Amerasia Journal*, she received a John Swett Award for excellent news coverage of education.

Sunshine Sammy. *See* Morrison, E. Frederick

Susann, Jacqueline

b. August 20, 1918
Philadelphia, Pennsylvania
d. September 21, 1974
New York, New York
fields: Literature

A best-selling author of the 1960's, Jacqueline Susann wrote popular novels about sex and drug use among the rich and famous and garnered an unprecedented three number-one spots on *The New York Times* best-seller list for *Valley of the Dolls* (1966), *The Love Machine* (1969), and *Once Is Not Enough* (1973). Two more novels—*Dolores* (1976), loosely based on the life of Jacqueline Kennedy Onassis, and the science-fiction fantasy *Yargo* (1979)—appeared after Susann's death from cancer. Although her work was disdained by critics, her success was undisputed; *Valley of the Dolls* was credited by the *Guinness Book of World Records* as the best-selling novel of all time, a record that held for almost three decades.

Sussman, Rosalyn. *See* Yalow, Rosalyn

Sutherland, George

b. 1862
d. 1942
fields: Law

U.S. Supreme Court justice, 1922-1938; appointed by President Harding. Intellectual leader of the Supreme Court's opposition to New Deal regulatory measures; supported selective application of the Bill of Rights to state criminal justice systems. Significant opinions: *Powell v. Alabama*, 287 U.S. 45 (1932); *Berger v. United States*, 295 U.S. 78 (1935); *Carter v. Carter Coal Co.*, 298 U.S. 238 (1936).

Sutherland, Graham Vivian

b. August 24, 1903
London, England
d. February 17, 1980
London, England
fields: Art

Creatively fusing the English tradition of painting by the light of nature with the European practice of art, Sutherland earned his place as the most distinguished and original English artist of the mid-twentieth century.

Sutter, John Augustus

né: Johann August Suter
b. Feb. 15, 1803
Kandern, Germany
d. June 18, 1880
Washington, D.C.
fields: Historical Figure

John Augustus Sutter established the colony of Nueva Helvetia (New Switzerland), which would later become Sacramento, in California in 1839. In 1841, he built "Sutter's Fort," founded frontier industries, and brought Hawaiians over to cultivate farms on his estate. During the construction of a sawmill on his land in 1848, gold was discovered, and the California gold rush of 1849 began. The gold drew thousands of Chinese immigrants seeking their fortune in California.

Suttner, Bertha von

né: Bertha Félice Sophie, Countess Kinsky of Wchinitz and Wettau
aka: Bertha Félice Sophie, Countess Kinsky von Chinic und Tettau
aka: Countess Kinsky
full: Bertha Félice Sophie, baroness von Suttner
aka: Baroness von Suttner
b. June 9, 1843
Prague, Austro-Hungarian Empire
d. June 21, 1914
Vienna, Austro-Hungarian Empire
fields: Literature, Social Reform

Suttner inspired and organized peace movements and was instrumental in persuading Alfred Nobel to establish the Peace Prize named for him. Her novel *Die Waffen nieder!* (1889; *Lay Down Your Arms*, 1892) was a clarion call for disarmament.

Sutton, PePe

full: Pierre Montea Sutton
b. February 1, 1947
New York, N.Y.
fields: Business and Industry

African American broadcasting company executive; PePe Sutton was chairman of the Inner City Broadcasting Corporation, taking over in 1990 from his father, Percy Sutton, who founded the company.

Sutton, Percy Ellis

b. November 24, 1920
San Antonio, Texas
fields: Government and Politics

African American politician; Percy Ellis Sutton was a New York state assemblyman (1964-1966); president of the borough of Manhattan (1966-1977); owner and chairman of the board of the Inner City Broadcasting Corporation (1977-1990).

Suvorov, Aleksandr Vasilyevich

b. November 24, 1729
near Moscow, Russia
d. May 18, 1800
his estate, Kobrin, near St. Petersburg, Russia
fields: Military Affairs

By abandoning the defensive tactics of the period, Suvorov created a new type of army in which speed, mobility, and independence of judgment by junior officers were valued more than drills and sieges.

Suzuki, Bob H.

b. January 2, 1936
Portland, Oreg.
fields: Education

Bob H. Suzuki was the first U.S.-born Japanese American to be made president of a major university—California State Polytechnic University, Pomona—in the continental United States after being an administrator with the California State University system for ten years. He earned a doctoral degree in aeronautics from the California Institute of Technology. He also did work in Asian American studies at the University of Massachusetts, Amherst. He published a paper criticizing the application of the Model Minority label to Asian Americans in 1977.

Suzuki, D. T.

full: Daisetz Teitaro Suzuki
b. October 18, 1870
Kanazawa, Japan
d. July 12, 1966
Kamakura, Japan
fields: Philosophy, Religion and Theology

Through his teaching, lectures, and many writings and translations, D. T. Suzuki is credited with bringing Buddhism to the Western world. Emphasizing the unity of spiritual thought and synthesizing Eastern and Western religions, he defined the nature of Buddhism in Western philosophy and widened the influence of Zen Buddhism internationally. His doctrine of unifying the separate schools of Buddhism redefined the importance of Zen in Japan and created the climate for unity later favored by Tibet's spiritual leader, the Dalai Lama. Before Suzuki, Zen was a narrowly structured school of thought; after him, it became synonymous with enlightenment, awareness, and spiritual awakening. Among his many works are *Outlines of Mahayana Budddhism* (1907), *Mysticism: Christian and Buddhist Essays in Zen Buddhism* (1927) *Zen Buddhism and Psychoanalysis* (1960, with Erich Fromm), and the posthumous *Sengai, the Zen Master* (1971).

Suzuki, Goro. *See* Soo, Jack

Suzuki, Pat

full: Chiyoko Suzuki
b. 1931
Cressy, Calif.
fields: Theater and Entertainment

Actor and singer Pat Suzuki, who was interned in a detention camp in Granada, Colorado, during World War II, began to sing in nightclubs while still in college. She appeared in the Rodgers and Hammerstein musical *Flower Drum Song* in 1958. Suzuki and fellow *Flower Drum Song* performer Miyoshi Umeki were featured on the cover of *Time* magazine in December, 1958. Suzuki also appeared in the 1969 Burt Reynolds movie *Skullduggery* and in the television series *Mr. T and Tina*.

Suzuki, Peter T.

b. Nov. 22, 1928
Seattle, Wash.
fields: Anthropology

Peter T. Suzuki, incarcerated at the Puyallup assembly center and in Minidoka detention camp during World War II, later attended Columbia, Yale, and Leiden (Holland) universities. An anthropologist, Suzuki joined the faculty at the University of Nebraska, Omaha, in 1973, and published numerous articles in anthropological journals.

Swados, Elizabeth

b. February 5, 1951
Buffalo, New York
fields: Music, Theater and Entertainment

An innovative composer, Swados has combined world music with modern European compositional techniques to create important works at the famed La Mama Experimental Theatre in New York and other venues. She has adapted works as varied as classical Greek theater and *Alice in Wonderland* to create productions, and she has based works on current social themes.

Swallow, Ellen Henrietta. *See* Richards, Ellen Swallow

Swan, Joseph Wilson

b. October 31, 1828
Sunderland, Durham, England
d. May 27, 1914
Warlingham, Surrey, England
fields: Invention and Technology

Swan's invention and business leadership helped launch the electric lighting industry. He pioneered in artificial fibers. His technical contributions enriched a wide range of other fields, from photography to batteries to tanning.

Swanson, Howard

b. August 18, 1907
Atlanta, Ga.
d. November 12, 1978
New York, N.Y.
fields: Music (composer)

African American composer; Howard Swanson was a nationally recognized composer whose works include "The Negro Speaks of Rivers" (1949) and *Short Symphony* (1950), which was performed by the New York Philharmonic Orchestra.

Swayne, Noah Haynes

b. 1804
d. 1884
fields: Law

U.S. Supreme Court justice, 1862-1881; appointed by President Lincoln. Most consistent supporter of President Lincoln's orders concerning prosecution of the Civil War. Significant opinion: *Slaughterhouse Cases*, 83 U.S. 36 (1873) (dissenting opinion).

Swedenborg, Emanuel

b. January 29, 1688
Stockholm, Sweden
d. March 29, 1772
London, England
fields: Invention and Technology, Physiology, Religion and Theology

Swedenborg was first a mechanical prodigy, then a scientist and philosopher, then an anatomist, and finally a theologian. Recognition of his achievements has followed a similar time line. His peers saw him as a genius in science and invention, but it was much later before his anatomical studies were appreciated. His many contributions to Christian religious thought are still not widely known.

Sweezy, Carl

aka: Wattan (Black)
b. c. 1879
near Darlington, Okla. Territory
d. May 28, 1953
Lawton, Okla.
fields: Art, Anthropology (painter)

Native American painter. Carl Sweezy, an Arapaho, was one of the earliest to use the Native American narrative genre style of painting, and he developed it beyond ledger-book-style drawings. Sweezy's paintings are important ethnographically and represent important values. He portrayed such events as hunting buffalo, riding horseback, the defeat of Custer, ceremonies, and portraits, including details of costumes. His paintings of the Sun Dance are some of the best early visual documentation of that ceremony.

Swift, Jonathan

b. November 30, 1667
Dublin, Ireland
d. October 19, 1745
Dublin, Ireland
fields: Literature

Perhaps the greatest prose satirist in the history of English literature, Swift was also a champion of Irish and Anglo-Irish rights against the colonial impositions of Great Britain.

Swinburne, Algernon Charles

b. April 5, 1837
London, England
d. April 10, 1909
Putney, England
fields: Literature

English poet Algernon Charles Swinburne wrote sadomasochistic and homoerotic poetry that shocked Victorian society. His first collection of poetry, *Poems and Ballads* (1866) scandalized Victorian England. the controversy surrounding his collection made Swinburne a household name. In pushing the limits of public tolerance, he became known as the English Charles Baudelaire.

Sydenham, Thomas

b. September 10, 1624 (baptized)
Wynford Eagle, Dorset, England
d. December 29, 1689
London, England
fields: Medicine

Hailed as the "English Hippocrates," Sydenham was indeed the father of modern medicine: His practice and writings laid the foundations for modern clinical, scientific, and public-health medicine, and he has been credited with the invention of the modern conception of disease as a morbid entity in nature with its own natural history, instead of the archaic notion of disease as peculiar events in people's lives with only particular case histories.

Sydenstricker, Pearl. *See* Buck, Pearl S.

Sykes, Brenda

b. June 25, 1949
Shreveport, La.
fields: Film, Television (actor)

African American actress; Brenda Sykes appeared in a number of television programs, including *Ozzie's Girls* (1973) and *Executive Suite* (1976-1977); also starred in the film *Mandingo* (1975).

Sylvester

né: Sylvester James
b. c. 1946
Los Angeles, Calif.
d. December, 1988
Oakland, Calif.
fields: Music (singer)

African American singer; Sylvester was a high-camp gay disco star whose flambouyant style allowed him to cross over to the mainstream at the high point of the disco craze.

Sylvester II

né: Gerbert of Aurillac
b. c. 945
Aurillac, Aquitaine
d. May 12, 1003
Rome
fields: Education, Government and Politics

Gerbert was the most outstanding teacher of the tenth century; his brilliant pedagogy contrasted sharply with the cultural darkness of his age. After he became pope under the name Sylvester II (999-1003), he furthered papal-imperial cooperation during his short pontificate.

Sylvester, James Joseph

b. Sept. 3, 1814
London, England
d. Mar. 15, 1897
London, England
fields: Mathematics (algebra and number theory)

James Joseph Sylvester, with Arthur Cayley, developed the theory of invariants; discovered and coined the term "discriminant" for quadratic and higher-order equations; was the first to use the term "matrix"; founded the *American Journal of Mathematics* in 1878.

Synge, Cathleen. *See* Morawetz, Cathleen Synge

Syreeta

né: Syreeta Wright
b. 1946
Pittsburgh, Pa.
fields: Music (singer)

African American singer; Syreeta recorded a number of albums for Motown; briefly married to Stevie Wonder and collaborated with him on writing songs; duet album with Billy Preston produced her biggest hit, "With You I'm Born Again."

Szent-Györgyi, Albert

full: Albert Imre Szent-Györgyi von Nagyrapolt
b. Sept. 16, 1893
Budapest, Austro-Hungarian Empire (now Hungary)
d. Oct. 22, 1986
Woods Hole, Massachusetts
fields: Chemistry, Physiology

Albert Szent-Györgyi isolated vitamin C; discovered vitamin P; studied the molecular structure of muscles and the physiology of muscle contraction; in 1937, won the Nobel Prize in Physiology or Medicine.

Szold, Henrietta

b. December 21, 1860
Baltimore, Maryland
d. February 13, 1945
Jerusalem, Israel
fields: Social Reform, Education

An author, teacher, Zionist, and health activist, Szold was the first president of Hadassah (the American women Zionists' organization), a founder of Hadassah Hospital in Jerusalem, and the director of Youth Aliyah, an agency devoted to saving Jewish children from Nazi Germany.

T

Taaffe, Ellen. *See* Zwilich, Ellen Taaffe

Ṭabarī, al-

full: Abū Jaʿfar Muḥammad ibn Jarīr al-Ṭabarī
b. c. 839
Āmol, Tabaristan (modern Iran)
d. 923
Baghdad, Iraq
fields: Historiography, Religion and Theology

The premier historian on the first century of the Islamic empire and a renowned commentator on Koranic tradition, al-Ṭabarī established a model of universal history and a corpus of religious tradition crucial to the development of later Islamic theology and scholarship.

Tacitus, Cornelius

b. c. 56 C.E.
place unknown
d. c. 120 C.E.
probably Rome
fields: Government and Politics, Historiography

Combining a successful career in the Roman civil service with a lifelong interest in his nation's past, Tacitus devoted his mature years to exploring the many facets of history. His portraits of the famous and the infamous, especially during the early years of the Roman Empire, are among the most vivid and influential descriptions in all Roman literature.

Tacla, Jorge

b. ?
Santiago, Chile
fields: Art (painter)

Painter Jorge Tacla moved to New York City from Chile in 1981 and held a number of solo shows in the following decade. Painted figurative images until 1991, when he began to do more abstract work. Also paints large, somewhat Chinese-influenced landscapes. Known for the lines of dots and dashes that cross many of his paintings.

Tadlock, Robert

b. ?
fields: Theater and Entertainment

African American costume designer; Robert Tadlock worked Off-Broadway designing costumes beginning in the 1950's.

Tadodaho. *See* Atotarho

Ta'e. *See* Martínez, Crescencio

Taewon-gun

né: Yi Ha-ung
b. 1821
d. 1898
fields: Government and Politics

The father of King Kojong, regent Taewon-gun ruled Choson Korea from 1864 to 1873. Yi Ha-ung's son was selected as successor to King Cholchong Chuljong, who died in 1863, and Yi became regent. He rejected modernization in favor of traditional Confucianism and refused to establish diplomatic relations with the West. This destructive anti-Western stance hastened the demise of the regime. He was removed from power by his enemies, including his daughter-in-law, Queen Min, when the king reached adulthood in 1873.

Taft, Robert A.

full: Robert Alphonso Taft
b. September 8, 1889
Cincinnati, Ohio
d. July 31, 1953
New York, New York
fields: Government and Politics

A third-generation member of one of America's most enduring political dynasties, Taft entered the United States Senate from Ohio in 1939 and there achieved a position of leadership as a spokesman for conservative Republicanism.

Taft, William Howard

b. September 15, 1857
Cincinnati, Ohio
d. March 8, 1930
Washington, D.C.
fields: Law, Government and Politics

After serving as the twenty-seventh president of the United States, 1909-1903, Taft finally achieved his personal goal and found both his greatest happiness and his greatest success as chief justice of the United States.

Tagaskouita, Catherine. *See* Tekakwitha, Kateri

Tagore, Rabindranath

b. May 7, 1861
Calcutta, India
d. August 7, 1941
Calcutta, India
fields: Literature

The prolific author of more than one hundred books of verse, fifty dramas, forty works of fiction, and fifteen books of essays, Nobel laureate (1913) Tagore is recognized as a pioneer in Bengali literature, particularly the short story, and is internationally acclaimed as one of the world's finest lyric poets. The foundation for Tagore's literary achievements is his vision of the universal man, based on his unique integration of Eastern and Western thought.

Tahatan Wakan Mini. *See* Little Crow

Tahca Ushte. *See* Lame Deer

Tahgahjute. *See* Logan, James

Taine, Hippolyte

full: Hippolyte-Adolphe Taine
b. April 21, 1828
Vouziers, France
d. March 5, 1893
Paris, France
fields: Art, Literature, Historiography, Philosophy

As a critic and historian of the arts and society, Taine dominated much of the intellectual life in France in the last half of the nineteenth century. Influential in England and the United States, much of his history and literary theory has fallen into disrepute in this century. Yet his method and his appreciation of literary works continue to engage critics and historians.

Taira Kiyomori

b. 1118
Japan
d. March 21, 1181
Heian-kyo, Japan
fields: Government and Politics

A warrior who rose to power in the last years of aristocratic government in Japan, Kioyomori used political connections and the marriages of his daughters to control the imperial court. Shortly after his death, his family was destroyed, marking the most dramatic rise and fall in Japanese history.

Taira, Linda

b. ?
Tokyo, Japan
fields: Journalism

Broadcast journalist Linda Taira became the Cable News Network's congressional correspondent in 1985. She won the National Headliner Award for her coverage of the U.S. Senate's Iran-Contra hearings in 1987. The Japanese American grew up in Kaneohe, Hawaii, and received her bachelor's degree from the University of Hawaii.

Taizong

né: Li Shimin
aka: T'ai Tsung
aka: Tang Tai Zong
b. January 23, 599
Wohong County, Shaanxi Province, China

d. May, 649
Changun, Shaanxi Province, China
fields: Government and Politics

The second rule of the Tang Dynasty (627-649), Taizong brilliantly consolidated his regime through administrative reorganization and centralization, codification of laws, extension of hegemony over domestic enemies and menacing foreign powers, stabilization of commerce, and cultivation of the arts. Throughout East Asia, his regime continues to be regarded as the exemplar of civic order and military might.

Tajima, Renee

b. Sept. 11, 1958
New York, N.Y.
fields: Film

Documentary filmmaker Renee Tajima is best known for *Who Killed Vincent Chin?* (1989), which she made with Christine Choy. The film, which was nominated for an Academy Award, was originally intended to be a five-minute video supporting the mother of Vincent Chin, who was beaten to death by two men who were merely placed on probation and fined for their actions. Tajima paired with Choy to make *Fortune Cookie: The Myth of the Model Minority*, which examines the idea of Asian Americans as a "model minority."

Tajiri, Larry

b. 1914
Los Angeles, Calif.
d. 1961
fields: Journalism

Journalist Larry Tajiri got his start on his high school newspaper. After a year of college, Tajiri became editor of the *Kashu Mainichi*'s English-language section and, in 1934, joined the staff of the *Nichibei Shimbun*. In 1940, he became a staff writer for the Tokyo and Osaka *Asahi*. When war was declared against Japan in 1941, Tajiri lost his job and became editor of the *Pacific Citizen*, the official paper of the Japanese American Citizens League, which they continued to edit from Salt Lake City beginning in 1942. In 1952, Tajiri became art and literary critic for the *Denver Post*.

Tajtelbaum, Alfred. *See* Tarski, Alfred

Takaezu, Toshiko

b. June 17, 1922
Pepeeko, Territory of Hawaii
fields: Art

Ceramist, sculptor, and weaver Toshiko Takaezu learned sculpture and ceramics at the Honolulu School of Art, beginning in 1948. She studied art in Michigan, taught at the University of Wisconsin, then studied pottery and Zen philosophy in Japan. She began teaching at Princeton in 1967. Takaezu has staged solo exhibitions at galleries across the country and her works can be found in museums in Boston, New York, and Baltimore. She won the Dickson College Award in 1982..

Takagi, Paul

b. May 3, 1923
Auburn, Calif.
fields: Education, Sociology

Paul Takagi, who received a Ph.D. degree from Stanford University in 1967, was professor of education and criminology at the University of California, Berkeley, until his retirement in 1989. He was the first Asian American to receive a doctoral degree in sociology from Stanford and the first Asian American tenured professor in the social sciences at Berkeley. Takagi was also the first in criminology to advance the theory that racism played an important role in police brutality.

Takahashi, Sakae

b. Dec. 8, 1919
Makaweli, Kauai, Territory of Hawaii
fields: Government and Politics

Sakae Takahashi served as a first lieutenant, then a captain, in World War II. He earned a degree from Rutgers University Law School and entered the field of politics, joining the emergent Democrats in Hawaii. In 1950, Takahashi won a seat on the Board of Supervisors of Hawaii, was appointed treasurer of the Territory in 1951, and a won a Senate seat in 1954. He was the first Japanese American in a cabinet positoin in the territorial government. In 1969, Takahashi fought development of Magic Island. Although Takahashi lost to the developers, the next year legislation prevented the lands from being developed.

Takaki, Ronald

b. Apr. 12, 1939
Honolulu, Hawaii
fields: Historiography, Education

Japanese American historian; Ronald Takaki was born in Honolulu, Hawaii; involved in the Free Speech movement in 1964; joined faculty of University of California, Los Angeles (UCLA), 1967; helped establish a multicultural atmosphere at UCLA, developing a course on the history of racial inequality and establishing centers for Chicano, Asian American, Native American, and African American studies; joined faculty at University of California, Berkeley, in 1972; an award-winning author, he has produced many works on ethnic studies, including *A Pro-Slavery Crusade* (1970); *Iron Cages: Race and Culture in Nineteenth Century America* (1979), *Strangers from a Different Shore: A History of Asian Americans* (1989), and *A Different Mirror: The Making of a Multicultural America* (1993); received a Distinguished Teaching Award as a professor of ethnic studies at Berkeley.

Takamine, Jokichi

b. November 3, 1854
Takaoka, Japan
d. July 22, 1922
New York, N.Y.
fields: Science, Invention and Technology

Japanese American chemist Jokichi Takamine settled in the United States in 1890, about the time he developed the amylase enzyme Taka-diastase, which changes starch to sugar. In 1901 he isolated adrenaline from the adrenal gland. He cofounded the Japanese Association of New York and operated the Takamine Laboratories and the International Takamine Ferment Company.

Takashwangarous. *See* Shikellamy

Takei, George

b. April 20, 1939
Los Angeles, Calif.
fields: Television, Film

George Takei was the first Japanese American actor to receive a star on the Hollywood Walk of Fame. He is best known for his role as Lieutenant Sulu on the television series *Star Trek* (1966-1969), a role he reprised in a string of films that were released beginning in 1979.

Talbot, Marion

b. July 31, 1858
Thun, Switzerland
d. October 20, 1948
Chicago, Illinois
fields: Education, Sociology, Women's Rights

A leading authority on women's higher education, an author, the first dean of women in a coeducational institution, a cofounder of the American Association of University Women, and a charter faculty member at the University of Chicago, Talbot was also a significant leader of women in sociology and home economics.

Taliaferro, Dellareese. *See* Reese, Della

Tall Bull

aka: Hotóakhihoois
aka: Hotúaeka'ash Tait
aka: Otóah-hastis
b. c. 1830
d. July 11, 1869
fields: Warfare and Conquest, Native American Affairs

Central Cheyenne. Tall Bull, the most noted Dog Soldier chief and leader, featured prominently in the Plains Wars of the late 1860's. Tall Bull led 165 lodges of Dog Soldiers and their families to establish a village on the Republican River. The village was attacked in the spring of 1869 by Major Eugene Carr, in which twenty-five of Tall Bull's five hundred warriors were killed. During the retaliation that ensued, Tall Bull was killed.

Tallchief, Maria

né: Elizabeth Marie Tall Chief
aka: Betty Marie Tall Chief
b. January 24, 1925
Fairfax, Oklahoma
fields: Dance

Prima ballerina of the New York City Ballet for fifteen years, Tallchief symbolized American ballet for an entire generation of theater and television audiences.

Talleyrand

full: Charles-Maurice de Talleyrand-Périgord
b. February 2, 1754
Paris, France
d. May 17, 1838
Paris, France
fields: Government and Politics

Talleyrand directed the foreign relations of his country in a time of changing principles and changing regimes—the Directory, the Consulate, the Empire, and the Restoration Monarchy—trying to adjust his French patriotism with the establishment of a viable balance of power that formed the basis of European relations for a century.

Talmadge, Eugene

b. September 23, 1884
Forsyth, Georgia
d. December 21, 1946
Atlanta, Georgia
fields: Government and Politics

Eugene Talmadge was governor of Georgia from 1933 to 1937 and 1941 to 1943. He advocated removing advocating racial equality from public schools and universities. However, controversy over his interference in state schools led to his defeat in the 1942 gubernatorial primary. After he lost the election, the pressures for censorship of books in Georgia's schools and universities diminished considerably.

Tamamoto, T.

full: Tsunetaro Tamamoto
b. ?
Japan?
d. ?
fields: Theater and Entertainment

Actor T. Tamamoto was touted as the first English-speaking Japanese actor in the United States. A well-known veteran of theater and film, he planned to pursue directing and theater management. However, he was relegated to playing "stage Orientals" in Broadway comedies and melodramatic potboilers between 1909 and 1923. Silent films in which he appeared include *Paid in Full* (1914) and *The Innocence of Ruth* (1916).

Tamanend. *See* Tammany

Tamayo, Rufino

b. 1899
Oaxaca, Mexico
d. June 24, 1991
Mexico City, Mexico
fields: Art (painter, muralist)

A Mexican painter and muralist, Rufino Tamayo held his first solo exhibition in 1926. From 1936 to 1956, Tamayo spent some of his time living in New York; taught at the Dalton School in 1936 and at the Brooklyn Museum in 1946. Executed murals at Smith College (1943), on the UNESCO building in Paris (1958), on walls in Israel (1963), and for the Mexican Pavilion at Expo 67 in Montreal, Canada (1967). Won numerous international prizes and awards.

Tamayo, William R.

b. Sept. 4, 1953
San Francisco, Calif.
fields: Law

As managing attorney of the Asian Law Caucus, a San Francisco-based public interest law office, William R. Tamayo wrote extensively on the practice of immigration and nationality law, fought against housing discrimination, and proposed redistricting efforts aimed at giving Asian Americans a greater voice in government. He served as a member of the board of directors of the American Civil Liberties Union of California and chair of the National Network for Immigrant and Refugee Rights.

Tambiah, S. J.

full: Stanley Jeyaraja Tambiah
b. Jan. 16, 1929
Ceylon, now Sri Lanka
fields: Religion and Theology

S. J. Tambiah, a professor at Harvard University, was best known for his volumes on Thai Buddhism: *Buddhism and the Spirit Cults in Northeast Thailand* (1970), *World Conqueror and World Renouncer: A Study of Buddhism and Polity in Thailand Against a Historical Background* (1976), and *The Buddhist Saints of the Forest and the Cult of Amulets: A Study in Charisma, Hagiography, Sectarianism, and Millennial Buddhism* (1984). Tambiah, who earned hi doctoral degree from Cornell University in 1954, was an expert on the political and social economy of Sri Lanka.

Tamela Pashme. *See* Dull Knife

Tamerlane

b. 1336
Kesh (modern Shahr-i Sabz), Transoxiana, Central Asia
d. 1405
Otrar, Turkistan, Central Asia
fields: Government and Politics, Patronage of the Arts

Tamerlane combined extraordinary military talent with strong administrative leadership to create the first large independent Central Asian state to throw off the domination of the Mongols. In the process, he altered the regional balance of power and revived Central Asia's main cities as international trading and cultural centers.

Tamm, Igor Yevgenyevich

b. July 8, 1895
Vladivostok, Siberia
d. Apr. 12, 1971
Moscow, Soviet Union
fields: Physics

Igor Yevgenyevich Tamm, in 1934, predicted that the neutron, although uncharged, would have a magnetic moment; in 1937-1939 with Ilya Frank, explained Cherenkov radiation, the light emitted by a particle moving through a medium faster than the local speed of light; in 1958, won the Nobel Prize in Physics with Frank and Pavel Cherenkov.

Tammany

aka: Tamanend (the Affable)
b. c. 1625
d. c. 1701
fields: Government and Politics, Native American Affairs

Native American leader. A Lenni Lenape (Unami Delaware), Tammany sold the Delawares' homeland to William Penn, who dubbed the land "Pennsylvania". Tammany's name appears on two 1683 treaties (one of which sold to William Penn the land between Neshaminy and Pennypack creeks) and on another signed in 1697.

Tampa Red

né: Hudson Woodbridge
b. December 25, 1900
Smithville, Ga.
d. March 19, 1981
Chicago, Ill.
fields: Music (blues guitarist)

African American blues guitarist; Tampa Red began his career in the 1920's, playing slide guitar in Florida's gulf coast; in the mid-1920's, moved to Chicago; teamed with Georgia Tom Dorsey as the Hokum Boys; played with a number of established blues artists, including Ma Rainey and Victoria Spivey; formed his own group, the Chicago Five, in the 1930's; career declined with popularity of electric guitar music; played sporadically during 1960's blues revival.

Tan, Amy

b. February 19, 1952
Oakland, California
fields: Literature

A superb storyteller, Amy Tan provides her readers with a portrait of the Chinese American experience, especially that of emigrant Chinese women and their American daughters.

Tanacharison. *See* Half-King

Tanaka, Seiichi

b. June 18, 1943
Tokyo, Japan
fields: Music

Musician Seiichi Tanaka introduced taiko (a kind of drum) as an art form into the United States and was the first taiko grand master in the United States. He moved to the United States in 1968. He performed more than one thousand times throughout the United States, Europe, Japan, Canada, and Mexico and appeared or was featured in films such as *The Right Stuff* (1983), *Apocalypse Now* (1979), and *Rising Sun* (1993).

Tanaka, Togo William

b. Jan. 7, 1916
Portland, Oreg.
fields: Banking and Finance

Financial executive Togo William Tanaka was the English-language editor of the *Kashu Mainichi* newspaper from 1936 to 1941, when he was hired as the historian at the Manzanar relocation center in California by the War Relocation Authority. After the war, he was successful in the finance industry, serving on many boards, most notably those of the Los Angeles Wholesale Produce Market Development Corporation and the Federal Reserve Bank in San Francisco, both from 1979 to 1989.

Tancred

b. c. 1078
place unknown
d. December 12, 1112
Antioch
fields: Military Affairs

Through his leadership and political sense, Tancred contributed greatly to the success of the First Crusade, spreading Christian influence and establishing a firm Christian presence in the Near East that lasted for decades.

Tandy, Jessica

b. June 7, 1909
London, England
d. September 11, 1994
Easton, Connecticut
fields: Theater and Entertainment (actor), Film

An extremely versatile actress, Jessica Tandy has repeatedly shown that a superb talent, compelling stage presence, and dedication to craft can more than compensate for a lack of superficial glamour.

Taney, Roger Brooke

b. March 17, 1777
Calvert County, Maryland
d. October 12, 1864
Washington, D.C.
fields: Law

During his tenure as Chief Justice of the United States for twenty-eight years, Taney successfully used his considerable talents to adjust the law to the new egalitarian political and economic currents and states' rights concerns of Jacksonian democracy, while preserving the essentials of both property rights and the authority of the federal government. In dealing with the volatile issue of the expansion of slavery in the territories, Taney also sought moderation until the *Dred Scott* case, when he unsuccessfully attempted to resolve judicially what Congress and the president were unable to decide legislatively.

Tang, Julie M.

b. Oct. 22, 1949
Hong Kong
fields: Law

Julie M. Tang was elected in 1990 as a San Francisco municipal court judge. In 1980, 1984, and 1988, she served three terms as the president of the San Francisco Community College Board. In 1973, she cofounded the Wah Mei Bilingual Pre-School in San Francisco.

Tang Qinghua. *See* Tongg, Ruddy F.

Tang, Thomas

b. Jan. 11, 1922
Phoenix, Ariz.
fields: Law

Thomas Tang received his LL.B. from the University of Arizona in 1950. He became a member of the Arizona state bar in 1950, then began a career in public service. He was appointed to the Arizona Superior Court in 1963, then returned to private practice in 1971. In 1977, he was named a judge of the U.S. Ninth Circuit Court of Appeals—the first Asian American ever appointed to a federal appellate court

Tang Tingzhi. *See* Tong K. Achik

Tanguma, Leo

b. c. 1945
fields: Art (muralist)

Chicano muralist Leo Tanguma, inspired by David Alfaro Siqueiros's work, began painting his monumental murals in the 1970's. His work is highly controversial, containing radical political content, and some of his murals have been destroyed because of this. Works include *The People's Judgement Against Institutionalized Brutality and Racism: Rebirth of Our Nationality* (1973); *Towards a Humanitarian Technology for la Raza* (1972, destroyed); *Americanization of a Chicano* (1974, destroyed); and *Humanity in Harmony with Nature* (1981).

Tanizaki, Jun'ichiro

b. July 24, 1886
Tokyo, Japan
d. July 30, 1965
Yugawara, Japan
fields: Literature

Tanizaki admired Western literature early in his career but was drawn increasingly to traditional values and forms with the passage of time. His work is characterized by both intricate narratives and stylistic elegance.

Tanner, Henry Ossawa

b. June 21, 1859
Pittsburgh, Pa.
d. May 25, 1937
Etaples, France
fields: Art (painter)

African American painter; Henry Ossawa Tanner was an important late nineteenth century painter; studied under Thomas Eakins and later in France, where he took up residence; works include sensitive portrayals of African Americans such as *The Banjo Lesson* and biblical subjects such as *Christ and Nicodemus on a Rooftop*.

Tanner, Jack Edward

b. November, 1919
fields: Law (federal judge)

African American federal judge; Jack Edward Tanner was appointed by Jimmy Carter to the Western District of Washington State.

Tao Qian

aka: T'ao Ch'ien
b. 365 C.E.
Xinyang, China
d. 427 C.E.
Xinyang, China

fields: Literature

Tao Qian's insistence upon directness and simplicity in both form and content, although largely unappreciated during his lifetime, was in subsequent generations recognized as a major contribution to the development of Chinese poetry.

Taoyateduta. *See* Little Crow

Tapia, Luis

b. 1950
Santa Fe, N.Mex.
fields: Art

Latino artist Luis Tapia began making santos (traditionally, carved and painted representations of holy persons) around 1970 after becoming aware of Latino civil rights issues. Used bright colors, shocking some traditionalists. Also involved in restoration projects, including the church at Ranchos de Taos.

Tarango, Yolanda

b. Sept. 26, 1948
El Paso, Tex.
fields: Government and Politics, Church Government, Religion and Theology

Civic and church leader and administrator in the Hispanic community. Among her positions in the 1980's, Yolanda Tarango was director of pastoral education of the Mexican American Cultural Center, founder and director of the Visitation House Homeless Shelter, and director of volunteers for the Sisters of Charity of the Incarnate Word. Author of *Hispanic Women: Prophetic Voice in the Church* (1988).

Tarbell, Ida

full: Ida Minerva Tarbell
b. November 5, 1857
Erie County, Pennsylvania
d. January 6, 1944
Bridgeport, Connecticut
fields: Journalism

Ida Tarbell became a prominent leader in American magazine journalism in a period when women were almost entirely absent from the field.

Tarhe

aka: Crane
aka: Le Chef Grue
aka: Monsieur Grue
b. 1742
near Detroit, Mich.
d. Nov., 1818
Crane Town, near Upper Sandusky, Ohio
fields: Warfare and Conquest, Native American Affairs

Tarhe was a Wyandot (Huron) leader. Although initially resisting westward white settlement, Tarhe became an ally of the Americans. Fought beside Shawnee leader Cornstalk against the whites during Lord Dunmore's War in 1744 and fought in Battle of Fallen Timbers, during Little Turtle's War (1790-1794). Refused to join Tecumseh in his attempts to organize a pan-Indian resistance to whites. During the war of 1812, led his warriors in several battles against the British.

Tarrant, Caesar

b. 1755?
d. 1796?
fields: Warfare and Conquest

African American sailor; Caesar Tarrant was a Chesapeake Bay pilot who served in the American Navy during the Revolutionary War; is believed to have been at the wheel of the *Patriot* when it was captured by the British; freed by the Virginia legislature in 1789 in recognition of his service.

Tarry, Ellen

b. September 26, 1906
Birmington, Ala.
fields: Literature

African American author; Ellen Tarry was a journalist who published a number of books, including *The Runaway Elephant* (1950), *The Third Door: The Autobiography of an American Negro* (1955), *Martin de Porres: Saint of the New World* (1963), and *Pierre Toussaint: Apostle of Old New York* (1998).

Tarski, Alfred

né: Alfred Tajtelbaum
b. Jan. 14, 1902
Warsaw, Poland, Russian Empire (now Poland)
d. Oct. 26, 1983
Berkeley, California
fields: Mathematics (algebra and mathematical logic)

Alfred Tarski worked on establishing the equivalence between certain problems in logic and related problems in algebra; used mathematical rules to establish if the mathematical problem, and by implication the equivalent logical problem, was solvable or not.

Tartaglia, Niccolò Fontana

b. 1500
Brescia, Republic of Venice (now Italy)
d. Dec. 13, 1557
Venice, Republic of Venice
fields: Mathematics (algebra)

Niccolò Fontana Tartaglia found a formula to solve cubic equations and published it in 1545 in Girolamo Cardano's *Ars Magna.*

Tashunca-uitko. *See* Crazy Horse

Tasman, Abel Janszoon

b. c. 1603; Lutjegast, The Netherlands
d. 1659
place unknown
fields: Exploration and Colonization, Geography

Tasman was a Dutch navigator who discovered New Zealand, Australia, Tonga, the Fiji Islands, and Tasmania, which bears his name.

Tasso, Torquato

b. March 11, 1544
Sorrento, Kingdom of Naples
d. April 25, 1595
Rome
fields: Literature

Tasso—considered to be one of the greatest Italian poets—reflects the crisis of his age, and his writings seek to reconcile classical ideals with the renewed religious fervor arising from the Counter-Reformation. In this attempt to synthesize the vision of perfection and human dignity of the classics with Christian spiritual values lies the significance of his major works.

Tasunka Kokipapi. *See* Young Man Afraid of His Horses

Tatanka Cante Sica. *See* Bad Heart Bull, Amos

Tatanka Iyotake. *See* Sitting Bull

Tatapanum. *See* Weetamoo

Tatti, Jacopo. *See* Sansovino, Jacopo

Tatum, Art, Jr.

b. October 13, 1909
Toledo, Ohio
d. November 5, 1956
Los Angeles, Calif.
fields: Music (jazz pianist)

African American jazz pianist; Art Tatum, Jr., was a seminal jazz pianist by the 1940's who was critically acclaimed and respected by his fellow musicians; nevertheless, popular success eluded him; remains one of the most influential figures in early jazz.

Tatum, Edward Lawrie

b. Dec. 14, 1909
Boulder, Colorado
d. Nov. 5, 1975
New York, New York
fields: Chemistry, Biology

With George Wells Beadle, Edward Lawrie Tatum led the study of gene function through the use of biochemical mutations; in

1958, won the Nobel Prize in Physiology or Medicine.

Tatum, Goose

full: Reese Tatum
b. May 3, 1921
Calion, Ark.
d. January 18, 1967
El Paso, Tex
fields: Sports (basketball player)

African American basketball player; Goose Tatum played for the Harlem Globetrotters until 1955, when he formed the Harlem Magicians.

Taub, Edward Arnold

b. Oct. 22, 1931
Brooklyn, N.Y.
fields: Medicine, Physiology, Psychiatry and Psychology

Specialist in functional relations between mind and body. Edward Taub's experiments with monkeys have shown that animals with nerve damage can regain some control over affected limbs. He has applied his techniques to human victims of stroke and other traumatic brain injuries with some success, but his experimental methods have been decried by animal rights activists.

Taube, Henry

b. Nov. 30, 1915
Neudorf, Saskatchewan, Canada
fields: Chemistry

Henry Taube is universally recognized as the founder of the modern study of inorganic mechanisms; worked on electron transfer reactions; won the 1983 Nobel Prize in Chemistry.

Taubman, George Dashwood Goldie. *See* Goldie, George

Taussig, Helen Brooke

b. May 24, 1898
Cambridge, Massachusetts
d. May 20, 1986
Kennett Square, Pennsylvania
fields: Medicine, Physiology

Helen Brooke Taussig created a surgical procedure to treat blue baby syndrome; worked to prevent thalidomide, a drug that causes severe birth defects, from being used in the United States.

Taussky-Todd, Olga

né: Olga Taussky
b. Aug. 30, 1906
Olmütz, Austro-Hungarian Empire (now Olomouc, Czech Republic)
d. Oct. 7, 1995
Pasadena, California
fields: Mathematics (algebra and number theory)

Olga Taussky-Todd modernized and made popular matrix theory, used for the resolution of mathematical problems involved in technological development.

Tavibo

aka: the Paiute Prophet
b. c. 1810
Mason Valley, Nev.
d. c. 1870
fields: Religion and Theology, Native American Affairs

Tavibo, a Paiute, delivered prophecies about the destruction of whites. His prophecies formed the basis for the Ghost Dance religion of the 1890's, created by Tavibo's son, Wovoka.

Tawaquaptewa

b. c. 1882
Oraibi, Third Mesa, Ariz.
d. April 30, 1960
Oraibi, Third Mesa, Ariz.
fields: Government and Politics, Native American Affairs

A Hopi (Bear Clan) leader, Tawaquaptewa tried to lead his clan and the Hopi Progressive faction through major civil strife in the Hopi Nation; he is blamed for the degradation of the ancient pueblo of Oraibi. After rival Yukioma was jailed in 1912, Tawaquaptewa was the undisputed leader of the Hopi, a role for which he was unqualified and unprepared. Having received a routine American education from 1906 to 1910 in California, he could not reconcile his newfound knowledge with Hopi spiritual traditions. Oraibians began to abandon traditional ceremonies and, by 1933, the pueblo numbered only 112 people. At his death in 1960 the Bear Clan disintegrated, and Oraibi was in ruins.

Tawaraya Sōtatsu. *See* Sōtatsu

Tayloe, Nellie Davis. *See* Ross, Nellie Tayloe

Taylor, Billy

full: William Taylor
b. July 24, 1921
Greenville, N.C.
fields: Music (jazz pianist)

African American jazz pianist; Billy Taylor studied classical piano but became the longest-running house pianist at Birland; working with the likes of Ben Webster, Dizzy Gillespie, and Charlie Parker, Taylor received critical praise; led the orchestra for the *David Frost Show* (1969-1972); served as general manager for black-owned radio station WLIB; hosted *Jazz Alive* for National Public Radio in the 1980's.

Taylor, Brook

b. Aug. 18, 1685
Edmonton, Middlesex, England
d. Dec. 29, 1731
London, England
fields: Mathematics (calculus and geometry), Physics

Brook Taylor established a famous formula for expanding functions; created a mathematical theory of perspective.

Taylor, Charley

full: Charles Robert Taylor
b. September 28, 1942
Grand Prairie, Tex.
fields: Sports (football player)

African American football player; Charley Taylor played running back for the Washington Redskins in 1964; switched to wide receiver the next year and retired in 1977; inducted into the Pro Football Hall of Fame in 1984.

Taylor, Elizabeth

full: Elizabeth Rosemond Taylor
b. February 27, 1932
London, England
fields: Film (actor)

An international film star from childhood, Elizabeth Taylor dominated headlines in the early 1960's with her film successes and the scandals of her private life. She appeared in *National Velvet* (1944), won an Academy Award for her performance in *Butterfield Eight* (1960), and received an unprecedented payment of $1 million for starring in *Cleopatra* (1963). Perhaps her most notable film, *Who's Afraid of Virginia Woolf?* (1966), based on the play by Edward Albee, garnered her second Academy Award. During the 1980's and 1990's, she continued to appeared in television and feature films, also developing her own successful line of perfumes. Her courage and compassion remained in the public eye as she did extensive charitable work, especially on behalf of AIDS, and overcame challenges to her health (including brain surgery), remaining admired and respected into her later years.

Taylor, Frederick Winslow

b. March 20, 1856
Germantown, Pennsylvania
d. March 21, 1915
Philadelphia, Pennsylvania
fields: Business and Industry

Taylor studied the functions and practices of men and machinery in minute detail and drew up detailed plans for saving time and increasing productivity. Many of the principles upon which he worked have formed the basis of modern managerial practice.

Taylor, Gardner Calvin
b. June 18, 1918
Baton Rouge, La.
fields: Religion and Theology
African American baptist clergyman; Gardner Calvin Taylor was pastor of the Concord Baptist Church in Brooklyn for forty-two years (retiring in 1990); the first Baptist and the first African American to serve as head of the Protestant Council.

Taylor, Hobart, Jr.
b. December 17, 1920
Texarkana, Texas
d. April 2, 1981
the Bahamas
fields: Business and Industry, Government and Politics
African American businessman and governmental appointee; Hobart Taylor, Jr., was executive vice chairman of Lyndon Johnson's Committee on Equal Employment Opportunity; served on numerous boards of directors of major U.S. firms.

Taylor, John Baxter, Jr.
b. November 3, 1882
Washington, D.C.
d. December 2, 1908
fields: Sports (runner)
African American runner; John Baxter Taylor, Jr., won a 1908 Olympic gold medal for the 400-meter relay, but died five months later of typhoid pneumonia.

Taylor, Johnnie
b. May 5, 1938
Crawfordsville, Ark.
fields: Music (singer)
African American singer; Johnnie Taylor took Sam Cooke's place with the Soul Stirrers in 1957 and later recorded for Cooke's label, achieving minor success; after another artist attempted to capitalize on Taylor's name by recording a modestly successful single, "Part Time Love," under the name Little Johnny Taylor, Taylor assumed the imposter's moniker and rerecorded "Part Time Love," making it a big rythm-and-blues hit; recorded number one single "Who's Making Love" in 1968; recorded one of the first certified platinum singles, "Disco Lady," in 1976.

Taylor, Koko
né: Cora Walton
b. September 28, 1935
Memphis, Tenn.
fields: Music (blues singer)
African American blues singer; Koko Taylor began her career in 1953, garnering nearly every honor awarded to blues singers; hits include "Wang Dang Doodle" (1965).

Taylor, Kristin Clark
b. March 26, 1959
Detroit, Michigan
fields: Government and Politics
African American political appointee; Kristen Clark Taylor was assistant press secretary (1987-1988) and director of media relations (1989-1990) under George Bush; served on the start-up staff of *USA Today*; vice president of external affairs for the Student Loan Marketing Association (Sallie Mae), starting in 1994.

Taylor, Lawrence
aka: L. T.
b. February 4, 1959
Williamsburg, Va.
fields: Sports (football player)
African American football player; Lawrence Taylor played linebacker for the New York Giants from 1981 to 1994; won numerous awards, including Player of the Year in 1986; tested positive for illegal drug use in 1985 and 1988; embarked on a post-footfall career in professional wrestling, with his first match in 1995; inducted into the Professional Football Hall of Fame, 1999.

Taylor, Major
full: Marshall W. Taylor
b. November 26, 1878
Indianapolis, Ind.
d. June 21, 1932
Chicago, Ill.
fields: Sports (bicycle racer)
African American bicycle racer; Major Taylor was the first well-known black athlete from the United States; considered the best sprinter in the U.S. in 1900; retired from cycling in 1910 and wrote his autobiography, *The Fastest Bicycle Rider in the World* (1928).

Taylor, Meshach
b. April 11, 1947
Boston, Mass.
fields: Television, Film
African American actor; Meshach Taylor's television credits include made-for-television films and the comedy series *Designing Women* (as Anthony Bouvier, a role for which he received a 1989 Emmy Award nomination) and *Dave's World*; his film credits include *Damien—Omen II* (1978), *The Howling* (1981), *House of Games* (1987), *Mannequin* (1987), *Mannequin II* (1991), *Class Act* (1992), and *The Secret of NIMH II* (1998).

Taylor, Mildred D.
b. 1943
Jackson, Miss.
fields: Literature (author of children's novels)
African American author of children's novels; Mildred D. Taylor wrote a number of popular books for young people, including Newbery Medal winner *Roll of Thunder, Hear My Cry* (1976), and *Let the Circle Be Unbroken*.

Taylor, Moddie Daniel
b. Mar. 3, 1912
Nymph, Alabama
d. Sept. 15, 1976
Washington, D.C.
fields: Chemistry
Moddie Daniel Taylor worked on the Manhattan Project during World War II, the U.S. program to build an atomic bomb.

Taylor, Noel C.
b. July 15, 1924
Bedford City, Va.
fields: Government and Politics
African American mayor of Roanoke, Va; Noel C. Taylor was a pastor of High Street Baptist Church in Roanoke when he was elected to the city council in 1970; elected mayor in 1975.

Taylor, Susan L.
b. January 23, 1946
New York, N.Y.
fields: Journalism
African American journalist; Susan L. Taylor became beauty editor of *Essence* magazine in 1971; became editor in chief of *Essence* in 1981 and vice president of Essence Communications in 1986.

Taylor, Theodore
b. June 23, 1921
Statesville, N.C.
fields: Literature
African American author; Theodore Taylor's best known work is the children's novel *The Cay* (1969).

Taylor, Valerie E.
full: Valerie Elaine Taylor
b. May 24, 1963
Chicago, Illinois
fields: Mathematics (applied math)
Valerie E. Taylor was leading computer architect who applied mathematics to design high-speed computers.

Taylor, Victoria. *See* Draves, Vickie

Taylor, Zachary
b. November 24, 1784
Orange County, Virginia
d. July 9, 1850
Washington, D.C.
fields: Government and Politics, Military Affairs

Climaxing a military career of nearly forty years with major victories in the Mexican War, Taylor used his popularity as a war hero to win office as twelfth president of the United States (1849-1850).

Tchaikovsky, Peter

full: Peter Ilich Tchaikovsky
b. May 7, 1840
Votkinsk (Vyatka district), Russia
d. November 6, 1893
St. Petersburg, Russia
fields: Music

Tchaikovsky is one of the most popular Western composers. His soaring melodies, expressive supporting harmonies, and lush orchestration have made his concertos and later symphonies the epitome of late Romantic musical opulence.

Tchekhov, Anton. *See* Chekhov, Anton

Tchen, John Kuo Wei

b. 1951
Madison, Wis.
fields: Sociology

John Kuo Wei Tchen, professor of the Department of Urban Studies at Queens College, City University of New York, served as director of the Asian/American Center. He wrote many studies of Asian American communities, including the text for *Genthe's Photographs of San Francisco's Old Chinatown* (1984). Tchen cofonded the New York Chinatown History Project, later renamed the Chinatown History Museum.

Tcherniak, Nathalie. *See* Sarraute, Nathalie

Te E. *See* Martínez, Crescencio

Teague, Bob

full: Robert Teague
b. January 2, 1929
Milwaukee, Wisc.
fields: Journalism, Television

African American newscaster; Bob Teague began work with NBC in 1963, appearing on a number of late-night news programs.

Teasdale, Sara

full: Sara Trevor Teasdale
b. August 8, 1884
St. Louis, Missouri
d. January 29, 1933
New York, New York
fields: Literature

One of the best-selling poets of the early twentieth century, Teasdale used traditional verse forms to express her own attitudes toward love, beauty, and solitude.

Tecumseh

b. c. 1768
Old Piqua, western Ohio
d. October 5, 1813
Thames River, southeastern Canada
fields: Native American Affairs

A popular Shawnee war chief who led Indians of the Old Northwest in a united defense against the intrusion of white settlers, Tecumseh contributed significantly to the development of pan-Indianism in American history.

Teedyuscung

b. c. 1705
near present-day Trenton, N.J.
d. 1763
Wajomick, Pa.
fields: Diplomacy, Warfare and Conquest, Native American Affairs

Lenni Lenape (Delaware). Teedyuscung was an eloquent defender of Indian land rights. In 1754 the Lenni Lenape were expelled, with Iroquois cooperation, to Wajomick, near Wilkes-Barre, Pennsylvania. During the Seven Years' War (1755-1763), Teedyuscung was a leader of a group of warriors from several tribes living in Wajomick. Teedyuscung appeared at a number of important meetings, including the Albany Conference of 1754. He became a symbol of the unfairness of proprietary policy toward Indian land rights, and his speeches were published by Benjamin Franklin.

Tegakwith. *See* Tekakwitha, Kateri

Teilhard de Chardin, Pierre

full: Marie-Joseph-Pierre Teilhard de Chardin
b. May 1, 1881
Sarcenat, France
d. April 10, 1955
New York, New York
fields: Religion and Theology, Philosophy, Geology, Anthropology

Through his work as a geologist on the evolution of the earth and as a paleontologist on the evolution of life, Teilhard, a devout Jesuit priest, came to see human beings progressing toward a new consciousness and spiritual unity called the "Omega Point," which he identified with Jesus Christ.

Tei-Shin. *See* Fenollosa, Ernest Francisco

Tejada, Raquel. *See* Welch, Raquel

Tekahionwake. *See* Johnson, Emily Pauline

Tekakwitha, Kateri

né: Tekakwitha
aka: Tegakwith (She Pushes with Her Hands)
aka: Catherine Tagaskouita
b. 1656
Ossernenon, Mohawk Valley (near present-day Auriesville, New York)
d. April 17, 1680
Sault St. Louis, Canada (near present-day Montreal)
fields: Native American Affairs, Religion and Theology

Because of her heroic practice of prayer, chastity, mortification, and Christian virtue, this Iroquois virgin became the first Native American woman to be beatified by the Roman Catholic Church. Devotion to Kateri Tekakwitha is responsible for establishing Native American Ministries in Catholic churches throughout the United States and Canada.

Telemann, Georg Philipp

b. March 14, 1681
Magdeburg, Brandenburg
d. June 25, 1767
Hamburg
fields: Music

In addition to creating a vast quantity of beautiful music, Telemann championed the development of simpler, more readily accessible forms of composition, expanded the control of the composer over his works, and paved the way for the transition from the Baroque to the classical style.

Telford, Thomas

b. August 9, 1757
Glendinning, Scotland
d. September 2, 1834
London, England
fields: Engineering (civil)

By building an extraordinary number of bridges, canals, harbors, roads, and waterways, Telford became one of the great engineers of his day and helped to establish the profession of civil engineering in Great Britain.

Teller, Edward

b. January 15, 1908
Budapest, Hungary
fields: Physics (nuclear), Government and Politics

Teller helped to establish the theoretical groundwork for the production of the first atom bomb; he was also instrumental in the development of the hydrogen bomb in the United States. In the public policy arena, Teller promoted the peaceful uses of nuclear energy and urged the United States to develop new technologies to assure a strong defense.

Telles, Raymond L., Jr.

b. Sept. 15, 1915
El Paso, Tex.

fields: Government and Politics

A Mexican American, Raymond L. Telles, Jr., served two terms as mayor of El Paso, beginning in 1957. At the federal level, served as ambassador to Costa Rica (beginning 1961), chaired the U.S. Section of the Joint U.S.-Mexico Commission for Border Development and Friendship (beginning 1967), and was on the Equal Employment Opportunity Commission (1971-1976).

Temple, Henry John. *See* Palmerston, Lord

Temple, Lewis

b. 1800
Richmond, Va.
d. 1854
New Bedford, Mass.
fields: Invention and Technology

African American inventor; Lewis Temple invented the toggle whaling harpoon in 1848.

Temple, Shirley

aka: Shirley Temple Black
b. April 23, 1928
Santa Monica, Calif.
fields: Film, Government and Politics

Actor and politician. Shirley Temple was making films by age four; appeared in *The Red-haired Alibi* (1932), *Little Miss Marker* (1934), *Heidi* (1937), and *Rebecca of Sunnybrook Farm* (1938); film career ended abruptly when she became a teenager; retired from films in 1950; married businessman Charles A. Black in December of that year, thereafter using the name Shirley Temple Black. She became a representative to the United Nations in 1969; served as American ambassador to Ghana from 1974 to 1976; in 1973 served on the U.S. Commission for the United Nations Educational, Scientific, and Cultural Organization (UNESCO); in 1989 was ambassador to Czechoslovakia.

Ten Bears

aka: Parra-Wa-Samen
b. 1792
southern Great Plains
d. Nov. 23, 1872
near Fort Sill, Okla.
fields: Diplomacy, Government and Politics, Native American Affairs

A Comanche leader, Ten Bears led efforts to preserve peace between the Comanche and white settlers moving into Comanche territory. His peacemaking twice took him to Washington, D.C. Ten Bears's most famous speech, a masterpiece of oratory, was delivered in 1867 at the Council of Medicine Lodge Creek in Barber County, Kansas. He forcefully defended the Comanche, declaring that most conflicts were initiated by U.S. soldiers. The most emotional part of the address was Ten Bears' appeal that the Comanche be allowed to live as their ancestors had lived—on the open plains, unrestricted by walls or fences. The treaty signed at the conclusion of the council, however, the last treaty ever made with the Comanche, restricted them to a reservation.

Tenayuca, Emma

aka: Emma Tenayuca Brooks
b. 1916
San Antonio, Tex.
fields: Labor Movement

Latino labor organizer Emma Tenayuca was a leader of the Pecan Shellers' Strike (1938) in Texas before being replaced by Luisa Moreno. Well educated, charismatic, and a devoted Communist. Founded militant Workers Alliance and led demonstrations in Texas. Moved to California and had faded from public eye by 1940's.

Tendoy

b. c. 1834
Boise River area in Idaho
d. 1907
Fort Hall, Idaho
fields: Diplomacy, Government and Politics, Native American Affairs

Native American leader. A Bannock, Tendoy influenced his people to work peaceably with the white settlers of Wyoming. Unlike many Bannocks, who became destitute with the demise of their hunting economy, Tendoy and his band prospered by maintaining a trading relationship with white settlers, miners, and others.

Tene-angop'te. *See* Kicking Bird

Tennyson, Alfred, Lord

b. August 6, 1809
Somersby, Lincolnshire, England
d. October 6, 1892
Alderworth, near Haslemere, Sussex, England
fields: Literature

Generally considered to be the quintessential Victorian poet, Tennyson grappled with grief in the midst of the most profound theological crisis in the history of the modern world, caused by the emergent theory of evolution. Tennyson's poetry of spiritual struggle and affirmation captured the soul of his generation.

Tenskwatawa

aka: Lalawethika (the Rattle)
aka: the Shawnee Prophet
b. Mar. 1768
Piqua, Ohio
d. Nov., 1837
Argentine, Kans.
fields: Religion and Theology, Native American Affairs

Tenskwatawa, the Shawnee Prophet, led a spiritual and cultural revival among the tribes of the Old Northwest during the first decade of the nineteenth century. From 1804 until 1811, agents of the U.S. government negotiated numerous treaties with various tribes of the Old Northwest, under which the government purchased millions of acres of Indian land. Tenskwatawa and his brother Tecumseh challenged the validity of many treaties signed between 1804 and 1811. Tenskwatawa attracted followers from many Indian nations to his village, Prophetstown. Convinced that Tenskwatawa and Tecumseh posed a serious threat, Indiana Governor William Henry Harrison raised an army and marched to Prophetstown. Harrison arrived near the Indian village while Tecumseh was on a southern journey. Tenskwatawa encouraged his multitribal army to strike first. He promised them that the power of his magic would lead to victory. They were defeated in what came to be known as the Battle of Tippecanoe. Following the battle, Prophetstown was burned, and Tenskwatawa was discredited as a religious leader.

Teraoka, Masami

b. Jan. 13, 1936
Onomichi, Japan
fields: Art

Painter and sculptor Masami Teraoka is best known for rendering contemporary subjects in the style of classical Japanese paintings and prints, particularly ukiyo-e. Many of these paintings combine the comic and the erotic. Teraoka received an M.F.A. from the Otis Art Institute in 1968.

Terence

né: Publius Terentius Afer
b. c. 190 B.C.E.
Carthage
d. 159 B.C.E.
en route to Greece
fields: Literature

As a Roman comic playwright whose innovative adaptations of Greek dramas depicted in graceful Latin the social realities operating in his ancient world, Terence strongly influenced the development of sophisticated theater in the West. His psychologically accurate portraits brought integrity to his craft.

Teresa, Mother

né: Agnes Gonxha Bojaxhiu

b. August 26, 1910
Shkup, Albania, Ottoman Empire (now Skopje, Macedonia)
d. September 5, 1997
Calcutta, India
fields: Religion and Theology, Social Reform

Mother Teresa spent most of her life caring for the "poorest of the poor." Her Missionaries of Charity have expanded their scope from the humblest beginnings on the streets of Calcutta to locations on every continent, including, in the United States, New York's South Bronx. By 1987, the International Association of Co-Workers of Mother Teresa, formally established eighteen years before, numbered more than three million people. Mother Teresa was awarded the Nobel Prize in 1979.

Teresa of Ávila, Saint

b. March 28, 1515
Ávila, Spain
d. October 4, 1582
Alba, Spain
fields: Church Reform, Religion and Theology

This patron saint of Spain and doctor of the Church was active in reforming monasticism in Spain. She is also known for her mystic writings, which describe how mental prayer can bring the soul through successive stages to union with God. Named patroness of Spain in 1617; canonized in 1622.

Tereshkova, Valentina

full: Valentina Vladimirovna Nikolayeva Tereshkova
b. March 6, 1937
Maslennikovo, Yaroslavl region, Russia, U.S.S.R.
fields: Aviation and Space Exploration, Government and Politics

On June 16, 1963, Tereshkova became the first woman in space. During her 71-hour flight, she achieved an altitude of over 143.2 miles and traveled a distance of 1,222,020 miles. Upon her return to the Soviet Union, she became a national heroine who traveled the world extolling the virtues of the communist system.

Tero, Lawrence. *See* Mr. T

Terrell, Mary Church

b. September 23, 1863
Memphis, Tenn.
d. July 24, 1954
Annapolis, Md.
fields: Civil Rights, Women's Rights

Mary Church Terrell was a prominent African American born to wealthy parents and highly educated. She gained appointment as one of the first black women on the District of Columbia school board (1895-1901 and 1906-1911), headed the prestigious Bethel Literary and Historical Society, and co-founded the Washington Colored Women's League. She was the first president of the National Association of Colored Women (1896-1901). She was also active in the women's suffrage movement and Republican Party politics. Terrell's autobiography, *A Colored Woman in a White World*, was published in 1940.

Terrell, Tammi

né: Thomasina Montgomery
b. 1946
Philadelphia, Pa.
d. March 16, 1970
Philadelphia, Pa.
fields: Music (singer)

African American singer; Tammi Terrell had a moderately successful solo career during the 1960's; paired by Motown with Marvin Gaye, resulting in a number of hits, including "Ain't No Mountain High Enough" and (1967) and "Ain't Nothing Like the Real Thing" (1968).

Terry, Ellen

full: Alice Ellen Terry
b. February 27, 1847
Coventry, Warwickshire, England
d. July 21, 1928
Smallhythe, Kent, England
fields: Theater and Entertainment

As the leading Shakespearean actress and one of the most liberated women of her time, Terry left an indelible impression on the artistic and social worlds of Victorian England.

Terry, Lucy

b. 1730
West Africa
d. 1821
Sunderland, Vt.
fields: Literature

African American poet; Lucy Terry is considered to be the first African American poet; authored only one known poem, "Bars Flight" (published in 1893), which she narrated to a second party in 1746.

Terry, Megan

né: Marguerite Josephine Duffy
b. July 22, 1932
Seattle, Washington
fields: Theater and Entertainment, Literature

A founding member of the Open Theatre in the 1960's and playwright-in-residence at the Omaha Magic Theatre since 1974, Megan Terry is one of the most prolific American dramatists, having written more than sixty successful plays. She is one of the major pioneers in the development of transformational drama and is also considered one of America's first feminist dramatists.

Terry, Randall

b. April 25, 1959
Rochester, N.Y.
fields: Social Reform

Antiabortion activist. In 1988, Randall Terry founded Operation Rescue, which blockades abortion clinics to prevent access. The organization grew out of Project Life, created by Terry and his wife in Binghamton, N.Y.

Tertullian

né: Quintus Septimius Florens Terullianus
b. c. 155-160 C.E.
at or near Carthage, North Africa
d. After 217 C.E.
probably near Carthage, North Africa
fields: Religion and Theology, Literature

Eloquent and aggressive, Tertullian was the most outstanding spokesman for Christianity in the Latin West before Saint Augustine; his polemical treatises set the direction for much of Western theology.

Teruya, Albert

b. 1913
Hakalau, Territory of Hawaii
fields: Business and Industry

Albert Teruya, along with his brother Wallace Teruya, was an entrepreneur who owned the Times Super Market Chain, which, with fourteen locations on Oahu, is one of the largest supermarket chains in Hawaii. The Teruyas worked in restaurants before opening a small lunchroom in downtown Honolulu. Their first supermarket opened in 1949.

Teruya, Wallace

b. 1915
Hakalau, Territory of Hawaii
fields: Business and Industry

Wallace Teruya, in partnership with his brother Albert Teruya, founded the Times Super Market Chain. The chain, which started with a single supermarket in 1949, grew to fourteen locations on Oahu, making it one of the largest supermarket chains in Hawaii. The brothers left the family plantation to work in restaurants. After a number of years, they opened a small lunchroom in downtown Honolulu before going into the supermarket business.

Tesla, Nikola

b. July 9, 1856
Smiljan, Croatia
d. January 7, 1943
New York, New York
fields: Engineering (electrical)

With his brilliant, intuitive insight and endless creative imagination, Telsa laid the foundations for many of the technological developments of the twentieth century.

Thales of Miletus

b. c. 624 B.C.E.
Miletus, Ionia, Asia Minor
d. c. 548 B.C.E.
Miletus, Ionia, Asia Minor
fields: Philosophy, Science

Through his various theories, Thales countered supernatural and mythical explanations of nature, attempting to replace them with empirically derived answers. He became a transitional figure between the worlds of philosophy and science.

Thant, U

né: Thant
b. January 22, 1909
Pantanaw, Burma
d. November 25, 1974
New York, New York
fields: Diplomacy

U (an honorific) Thant took over as acting secretary-general of the United Nations when Dag Hammarskjöld was killed in an airplane crash in 1961 and served until 1971. Thant therefore was the speaker for the United Nations during the many crises of the 1960's and early 1970's, including the Cuban Missile Crisis, the Arab-Israeli conflict, the crisis in the Congo and other parts of Africa, and the U.S. involvement in Vietnam, providing the U.N. with a strong neutral voice.

Thaonawyuthe. *See* Blacksnake

Tharp, Twyla

b. July 1, 1941
Portland, Indiana
fields: Dance

An important choreographer in the field of modern dance, Tharp established an individualistic style that was unique in its combination of various dance and musical genres. Her commercial work included film and Broadway performances as well as the work of her company.

Tharpe, Sister Rosetta

né: Rosetta Nubin
b. March 20, 1915
Cotton Plant, Ark.
d. October 9, 1973
Philadelphia, Pa.
fields: Music (vocalist, guitarist, and pianist)

African American vocalist, guitarist, and pianist; Sister Rosetta Tharpe began her career as a gospel singer; her rough voice and spirited guitar playing contrasted with the sophisticated stage presence of her partner Madam Marie Knight; played in a number of jazz venues but was shunned by gospel audiences after dabbling with the blues.

Thatcher, Margaret

né: Margaret Hilda Roberts
b. October 13, 1925
Grantham, Lincolnshire, England
fields: Government and Politics

Through fiscally conservative economic policies, Thatcher, the first woman prime minister in British history, has lessened public dependence on government and moved the nation in the direction of more competition and self-reliance.

Thaxton, Hubert Mach

b. Dec. 28, 1912
Lynchburg, Virginia
d. Jan. 3, 1974
New York, New York
fields: Mathematics, Physics, Invention and Technology

Hubert Mach Thaxton was a leader in the theoretical analysis of proton-proton scattering.

Thayendanegea. *See* Brant, Joseph

Thayer, Sylvanus

b. June 9, 1785
Braintree, Massachusetts
d. September 7, 1872
South Braintree, Massachusetts
fields: Education, Engineering, Military Affairs

Thayer, known as the "Father of West Point," is remembered for reorganizing the administration and curriculum of the U.S. Military Academy at West Point and for firmly establishing a scientific and theory-based system of engineering education in the United States.

Themistocles

b. c. 524 B.C.E.
Athens, Greece
d. c. 460 B.C.E.
Magnesia, Asia Minor
fields: Government and Politics, Military Affairs

Themistocles engineered the naval defeat of the Persians at Salamis and thus made possible the subsequent Age of Pericles in ancient Athens.

Theodora

b. c. 497
Constantinople
d. June 28, 548
Constantinople
fields: Government and Politics, Women's Rights, Monarchy

Empress of Byzantium (Augusta), 527-548. Theodora used her privileged position as consort of the great Byzantine emperor Justinian to demonstrate the ability of a woman to administer the complex political machinery of an empire. Although a formidable political opponent, she was sympathetic to the needs of women in an age when this was unheard of, and she succeeded in defending the religious rights of the persecuted Monophysite religious sect against the Orthodox majority in the early Christian era. An empress in more than title, she took an active part in political decision making and social reform.

Theodore of Mopsuestia

b. c. 350 C.E.
Antioch (modern Turkey)
d. 428
Mopsuestia, Cilicia
fields: Religion and Theology

The most important representative of the Antiochene school of biblical exegesis and theology, Theodore served as Bishop of Mopsuestia from 392 until his death in 428. Primarily because of alleged similarities with Pelagianism and Nestorianism, Theodore's theological views were condemned by the Emperor Justinian and by the Fifth Council of Constantinople in 553.

Theodoret of Cyrrhus

b. c. 393 C.E.
Antioch, Roman Syria
d. c. 458 C.E.
Cyrrhus, Roman Syria
fields: Religion and Theology

Theodoret served as the Bishop of Cyrrhus for forty-one years. Aside from carrying out an effective and sensitive bishopric, he authored works on practically every aspect of Christian thought and practice. He is perhaps best remembered for his contribution to the Christological debates that led to the Council of Chalcedon.

Theodoric the Great

b. c. 454
probably Hungary
d. August 30, 526
Ravenna, Italy
fields: Government and Politics, Monarchy

King of the Ostrogoths, 471-526. For a third of a century, Theodoric gave Italy strong, stable governance and its longest period of peace and prosperity in more than a century. His promotion of Roman ideals of justice and civic virtue led to the preservation of Roman law, administration, learning, and urban life. These formed the groundwork for the structure of medieval Italian society.

Theodosius the Great
né: Flavius Theodosius
b. January 11, 346 or 347 C.E.
Cauca, Gallaecia
d. January 17, 395 C.E.
Milan
fields: Government and Politics

Theodosius restored peace to the Eastern Roman Empire after the Roman defeat at Adrianople and established a dynasty that held the throne for more than seventy years. His settlement of Visigoths as *federati* inside the Empire may have contributed to the fall of the western part of the Empire, and his religious policies were a major step in the development of a theocratic state in the East.

Theoleptus of Philadelphia
b. c. 1250
Nicaea (modern İznik, Turkey)
d. c. 1326
Philadelphia (modern Alasehir, Turkey)
fields: Religion and Theology

As a spiritual writer, dynamic speaker, and respected teacher among medieval Greeks, Theoleptus played a major role in preventing the reunion of the Roman Catholic and Greek Orthodox churches. He also was influential in promoting Hesychasm, a mystical form of prayer and meditation.

Theophanes the Confessor
b. c. 752
Constantinople
d. c. 818
Samothrace
fields: Historiography

Theophanes the Confessor was a monk and author whose chronicle, *Chronographia*, is for modern scholars the main source for the history of the Eastern Roman (or Byzantine) Empire from about 600 to 813.

Theophrastus
né: Tyrtamus
b. c. 372 B.C.E.
Eresus, Lesbos, Greece
d. c. 287 B.C.E.
Athens?, Greece
fields: Science, Philosophy, Literature

Successor of Aristotle as head of his school, the Lyceum, Theophrastus became father of the sciences of botany, ecology, and mineralogy. He also wrote *Characters*, literary sketches of human psychological types.

Theorell, Hugo
full: Axel Hugo Teodor Theorell
b. July 6, 1903
Linköping, Sweden
d. August 15, 1982
Stockholm, Sweden
fields: Biochemistry

Theorell received the 1955 Nobel Prize in Physiology or Medicine for his work on the nature and action of oxidation enzymes. He was the first to produce a pure enzyme in the laboratory and the first to produce myoglobin in a pure form.

Theotokópoulos, Doménikos. *See* Greco, El

Thespis
b. Before 535 B.C.E.
probably Icarios (Icaria) or Athens, Greece
d. After 501 B.C.E.
probably Athens, Greece
fields: Theater and Entertainment

Though perhaps more legendary than historical, since none of his plays have survived, Thespis is credited with introducing the first actor into the Dionysian festival of song and dance. Thus, he is the traditional originator of Greek drama.

Theus, Lucius
b. October 11, 1922
near Bells, Tenn.
fields: Military Affairs

African American Air Force officer; Lucius Theus was commissioned as a second lieutenant in 1946; achieved the rank of major general in 1975; retired in 1979.

Thibault, Anatole François. *See* France, Anatole

Thiers, Adolphe
full: Marie-Joseph-Louis-Adolphe Thiers
b. April 15, 1797
Marseilles, France
d. September 3, 1877
Saint-Germaine-en-Laye, near Paris, France
fields: Government and Politics, Historiography

Thiers was a central figure among the moderate politicians who in the early nineteenth century created the July Monarchy and, forty years later, the Third Republic. He also wrote important multivolume histories of the revolutionary and Napoleonic eras.

Thigpen, Lynne
b. December 22, c. 1948
Joliet, Illinois
fields: Film, Theater and Entertainment

African American actress; Lynne Thigpen appeared in the stage and film versions of *Godspell*; also had roles in *Lean on Me* (1989) and *Tootsie* (1982); in television she played a district attorney on *L.A. Law* and The Chief on *Where in the World is Carmen Sandiego?*, which she also directed.

Thoc-me-tony. *See* Winnemucca, Sarah

Thomas, Bettye Collier
b. 1943
Macon, Ga.
fields: Historiography

African American historian, museum director, and educator; Bettye Collier Thomas is best known for her scholarly endeavors in African American women's history; administered the Bethune Museum and archives in Washington, D.C.; became the first director of Temple University's Center for African American History and Culture in 1989.

Thomas, Carla
b. 1942
Memphis, Tenn.
fields: Music (soul singer)

African American soul singer; Carla Thomas dominated female soul music until being eclipsed by Aretha Franklin; "Cause I Love You," her first record, was also the first Memphis soul hit, and it helped establish Memphis' Stax Records as the dominant soul music label.

Thomas, Clarence
b. June 23, 1948
Pin Point, Georgia
fields: Government and Politics, Law

Confirmed by a narrow 52-48 Senate vote, Thomas became the second African American to serve as an associate justice of the United States. After his controversial nomination by President Bush and a brutal 1991 confirmation battle marked by accusations of sexual harassment against him in Anita F. Hill's testimony before the Senate Judiciary Committee, Thomas remained a controversial justice because of his refusal to support positions many believed were essential to African American well-being.

Thomas, Debi
b. March 25, 1967
Poughkeepsie, N.Y.
fields: Sports (figure skater)

African American figure skater; Debi Thomas was the first African American figure skater to win an Olympic medal, the bronze in 1988.

Thomas, E. Donnall
full: Edward Donnall Thomas
b. Mar. 15, 1920
Mart, Texas
fields: Biology, Medicine

E. Donnall Thomas developed the techniques that made the transplantation of bone marrow possible, which resulted in a means to treat blood diseases; in 1990, won the Nobel Prize in Physiology or Medicine.

Thomas, Frank Edward

b. May 27, 1968
Columbus, Ga.
fields: Sports (baseball player)

African American baseball player; selected by the Chicago White Sox in the first round of the 1989 free-agent draft, Frank Edward Thomas led the Sox with thirty-two home runs in 1991 and, in 1993, achieved a career high of forty-one home runs; became a full-time designated hitter for the Sox in the 1998 season.

Thomas, Franklin A.

b. May 27, 1934
Brooklyn, N.Y.
fields: Law, Business and Industry

African American corporate executive and attorney; Franklin A. Thomas served as assistant U.S. attorney for the Southern District of New York (1964-1965); served as New York City deputy police commissioner in charge of legal matters (1965-1967); was appointed by Senator Robert F. Kennedy to serve as president and chief executive officer of the Bedford-Stuyvesant Restoration Corporation (1967-1977); beginning in 1979, served as president of the Ford Foundation, reducing the foundation's staff so as to free up resources to be used to support charitable causes; served as a member of the Secretary of State's Advisory Commission on South Africa (1985-1987).

Thomas, Gerald Eustis

b. June 23, 1929
Natick, Mass.
fields: Military Affairs

African American U.S. Navy officer. Gerald Eustis Thomas achieved the rank of rear admiral of the U.S. Navy; highly decorated, he retired in 1981.

Thomas, Isiah

full: Isiah Lord Thomas III
b. April 30, 1961
Chicago, Ill.
fields: Sports (basketball player)

African American basketball player; Isiah Thomas was the first round draft pick of the Detroit Pistons in 1981; leading the Pistons to a succession of successful seasons, including NBA championships in 1989 and 1990; he retired in 1994 to become the executive vice president of the Toronto Raptors.

Thomas, Martha Carey

b. January 2, 1857
Baltimore, Maryland
d. December 2, 1935
Philadelphia, Pennsylvania
fields: Education, Women's Rights

As dean and president of Bryn Mawr College, Thomas helped to build an institution dedicated to providing nineteenth century women with an education equal to that available in the best men's colleges.

Thomas, Norman

full: Norman Mattoon Thomas
b. November 20, 1884
Marion, Ohio
d. December 19, 1968
Huntington, New York
fields: Social Reform, Government and Politics

Often called "the conscience of America," Thomas ran six times for president on the Socialist Party ticket and became one of the country's greatest critic-reformers.

Thomas, Philip Michael

b. May 26, 1949
Los Angeles, Calif.
fields: Television

African American actor; Philip Michael Thomas's television credits include the series *Miami Vice* (1984-1989; in the role of Detective Ricardo "Rico" Tubbs), several made-for-television films, and infomercials; he has also worked as a television director.

Thomas, Piri

b. Sept. 30, 1928
New York, N.Y.
fields: Literature

Piri Thomas, born in New York, was the first Puerto Rican writer to break into mainstream publishing, and he became a spokesman for Puerto Ricans. Served seven years in prison, where he earned high school equivalency diploma and began writing. Autobiography, *Down These Mean Streets*, published in 1967. Also wrote *Saviour, Saviour Hold My Hand* (1972) and *Seven Long Times* (1974), both autobiographical, as well as plays, poetry, and short stories.

Thomas, Rufus

b. March 26, 1917
Casey, Miss.
fields: Music (soul singer)

African American soul singer; Rufus Thomas is best known for his hits "Walking the Dog" (1963), and "Do the Funky Chicken" (1970); also recorded duets with his daughter Carla Thomas.

Thomas, Saint

aka: Didymus
b. c. early first century C.E.
Galilee, Palestine
d. Second half of the first century
possibly Mylapore, India
fields: Religion and Theology

As one of the handpicked followers of Jesus, Thomas played a role in the epoch-making spread of the Christian message in the first century. He continues to be venerated in Christendom, especially among Christians of India, who plausibly claim that Thomas first brought the word of Jesus Christ to their ancestors and others in the Orient.

Thomas, Theodore

full: Theodore Christian Friedrich Thomas
b. October 11, 1835
Esens, East Friesland, Germany
d. January 4, 1905
Chicago, Illinois
fields: Music

A professional musician from childhood, Thomas pioneered the then new role of virtuoso conductor, markedly raising standards of orchestral performance both in light and in serious works. With the Chicago Orchestra, he also perfected the means of supporting and maintaining ensembles of the highest quality. He was virtually the father of the modern American symphony orchestra.

Thomas, Thurman

b. May 16, 1966
Houston, Tex.
fields: Sports (football player)

African American football player; as a member of the Buffalo Bills since 1988, Thurman Thomas, a top NFL all-purpose running back, led the Bills to four straight Super Bowl appearances (1991-1994); he gained more than one thousand yards in six consecutive seasons (1989-1994) and was selected as the NFL's Most Valuable Player in 1992. By the end of the 1997 season, he was among the NFL's all-time top rushers and receivers.

Thomas à Kempis

né: Thomas Hemerken
b. 1379
Kempen, The Rhineland (now in Germany)
d. August 8, 1471
monastery of St. Agnietenberg, near Zwolle, Bishopric of Utrecht (now in The Netherlands)
fields: Religion and Theology

Thomas is credited by most historians with writing *The Imitation of Christ*, the most important piece of devotional literature produced by the late medieval pietistic movement called the *devotio moderna* and one of the most influential religious works in history. Some scholars claim that this work has been more widely read than any Christian work other than the Bible.

Thomas Aquinas, Saint

aka: Tommaso d'Aquino

b. 1224 or 1225
Roccasecca, north of Naples, Italy
d. March 7, 1274
Fossanova, Italy
fields: Religion and Theology, Philosophy

By adapting pagan philosophy as a handmaiden to Christian doctrine, Thomas created both a magisterial systematization of medieval Catholic faith and a philosophical system with implications for ethics, law, psychology, semantics, and the nature of reason itself. Canonized in 1323.

Thompson, Bob

full: Robert Thompson
b. June 26, 1937
Louisville, Ky.
d. 1966
Rome, Italy
fields: Art (painter)

African American painter; Bob Thompson's works are characterized by areas of brilliant color, depicting inner feeling rather than objective form.

Thompson, David

b. July 13, 1954
Shelby, N.C.
fields: Sports (basketball player)

African American basketball player; David Thompson was drafted by the Denver Nuggets and was that team's Rookie of the Year (1975-1976); traded to the Seattle Supersonics in 1982; retired because of a knee injury during the 1983-1984 season.

Thompson, Dorothy

b. July 9, 1893
Lancaster, New York
d. January 30, 1961
Lisbon, Portugal
fields: Journalism

Thompson was one of the first female political columnists. Her fiery interpretations of world events kept the masses informed.

Thompson, Era Bell

b. August 10, 1906
Des Moines, Iowa
d. December 30, 1986
Chicago, Ill.
fields: Journalism

African American journalist; Era Bell Thompson is best known as editor of both *Negro Digest* and *Ebony* magazines.

Thompson, Hunter S.

full: Hunter Stockton Thompson
b. July 18, 1937
Louisville, Kentucky
fields: Journalism

One of the first practitioners of "gonzo journalism," Hunter S. Thompson pioneered a style of reporting in which political and social occurrences are presented in the format of realistic fiction. Between 1959 and 1965, he served as a correspondent for *Time* magazine, the *New York Herald Tribune*, and the *National Observer*. In a 1964 article for *The Nation*, "Motorcycle Gangs: Losers and Outsiders," he challenged the media's representation of the Hell's Angels; after riding with and living with the motorcycle gang until 1966, he completed *Hell's Angels: A Strange and Terrible Saga*, one of the best examples of the New Journalism participant-observer reporting for which he became famous. His best-known work, *Fear and Loathing in Las Vegas* (1972), was widely read by 1970's remnants of the counterculture.

Thompson, John Robert, Jr.

b. September 2, 1941
Washington, D.C.
fields: Sports (basketball coach)

African American basketball coach; John Robert Thompson, Jr., played for the Boston Celtics from 1964 to 1966; head coach of the 1988 U.S. Olympic basketball team.

Thompson, Smith

b. 1768
d. 1843
fields: Law

U.S. Supreme Court justice, 1824-1843 (died while in office); appointed by President Monroe. Significant opinion: *Cherokee Nation v. Georgia*, 30 U.S. 1 (1831) (dissenting opinion).

Thompson, William H.

b. ?
Brooklyn, N.Y.
d. August 6, 1950
Korea
fields: Warfare and Conquest

William H. Thompson was one of two African American infantry soldiers to receive the Congressional Medal of Honor for service in the Korean War, for keeping his machine-gun post even as his fellow soldiers retreated.

Thomson, Joseph John

full: Sir Joseph John Thomson
aka: J. J. Thomson
b. Dec. 18, 1856
Cheetham Hill, near Manchester, England
d. Aug. 30, 1940
Cambridge, England
fields: Physics

Joseph John Thomson, in 1987, discovered that cathode rays consist of a stream of negatively charged particles now called electrons; in 1906, won the Nobel Prize in Physics.

Thomson, Tom

full: Thomas John Thomson
b. August 4, 1877
Claremont, Ontario, Canada
d. c. July 8, 1917
Canoe Lake, Ontario, Canada
fields: Art

In landscape paintings of vibrant color and energetic brushwork, Thomson helped steer a course toward an indigenous Canadian artistic expression.

Thomson, Virgil

full: Virgil Garnett Thomson
b. November 25, 1896
Kansas City, Missouri
d. September 30, 1989
New York, New York
fields: Music

American composer Virgil Thomson wrote serious music that was simple in structure, harmonically diatonic, and melodically traditional in its evocation of American life. He collaborated with Gertrude Stein to write the opera *Four Saints in Three Acts* (1927); composed the music for two documentaries, *The Plow That Broke the Plains* and *The River* (1936-1937); won a Pulitzer Prize for the score to *Louisiana Story* (1948); was music critic for the *New York Herald Tribune* (1940-1954); was appointed to the French Legion of Honor; published *Music Reviewed* (1967); composed the opera *Lord Byron* (1961-1968); scored John Houseman's film *Journey to America* (1964); wrote for solo voice (*The Feast of Love*, 1964) and chorus (*The Nativity*, 1966-1967); published *American Music Since 1910* (1971) and continued composing and writing music criticism until his death in 1989.

Thomson, William. *See* Kelvin, Lord

Thoreau, Henry David

b. July 12, 1817
Concord, Massachusetts
d. May 6, 1862
Concord, Massachusetts
fields: Literature

As essayist, naturalist, social critic, and editor, Thoreau has come to be recognized as a major figure in the Transcendentalist movement.

Thorndike, Edward L.

full: Edward Lee Thorndike
b. August 31, 1874
Williamsburg, Massachusetts
d. August 9, 1949
Montrose, New York

fields: Psychiatry and Psychology, Education

Often referred to as the "Father of Modern Educational Psychology," Thorndike incorporated measurement into education and psychology, as well as developing testing of animals and studies of learning in humans.

Thornton, Big Mama

full: Willie Mae Thornton
b. December 11, 1926
Montgomery, Ala.
d. July 25, 1984
Los Angeles, Calif.
fields: Music (singer)

African American singer; Big Mama Thornton was a seminal blues figure connected for much of her career with Johnny Otis; recorded the hit "Hound Dog" in 1953.

Thorpe, Jim

full: James Francis Thorpe
aka: Wa-tho-huck (Bright Path)
b. May 22, 1888
near Prague, Okla.
d. Mar. 28, 1953
Lomita, Calif.
fields: Sports (football, track and field, baseball)

Jim Thorpe, a Sauk and Fox, was one of the greatest and most versatile athletes in American history. Thorpe's versatility was revealed at the 1912 Summer Olympics in Stockholm, Sweden, where he won both the pentathlon and the decathlon. Although his gold medals were taken away because of his earlier professional baseball career, they were eventually returned to his family in 1982. After many years of professional baseball and football, Thorpe retired from athletics in 1929.

Thrash, Dox

b. March 22, 1893
Griffin, Georgia
d. 1965
fields: Art (painter, printmaker)

African American painter, printmaker, and coinventor of the carborundum print process; Dox Thrash worked for the Pennsylvania Federal Art Project.

Thucydides

b. c. 459 B.C.E.
probably Athens, Greece
d. c. 402 B.C.E.
place unknown
fields: Historiography

For the methods he employed in his account of the Peloponnesian War, Thucydides is considered one of the founders of the discipline of history.

Thurber, James

full: James Grover Thurber
b. December 8, 1894
Columbus, Ohio
d. November 2, 1961
New York, New York
fields: Art, Literature, Theater and Entertainment

Thurber pioneered an urbane and sophisticated style of humor that was markedly different from the bucolic, provincial, and often self-conscious American humor of the nineteenth century and that was far more appropriate to the complex, anxiety-ridden America being thrust into world leadership in the twentieth century.

Thurman, Howard

b. November 18, 1900
Daytona Beach, Fla.
d. April 10, 1981
San Francisco, Calif.
fields: Religion and Theology

African American theologian and educator; Howard Thurman cofounded the Church for the Fellowship of All Peoples in San Francisco in 1944 and served as pastor until 1953; taught theology in a number of universities, including Howard, Morehouse, and Spelman; dean of Marsh Chapel at Boston University (1953-1964).

Thurman, Wallace Henry

b. August 16, 1902
Salt Lake City, Utah
d. December 22, 1934
New York City
fields: Literature

African American novelist and editor; Wallace Henry Thurman satirized a number of Harlem Renaissance figures in his controversial book *Infants of the Spring* (1932); best known for his novel; *The Blacker the Berry* (1929).

Thurmond, Nate

full: Nathaniel Thurmond
b. July 25, 1941
Akron, Ohio
fields: Sports (basketball player)

African American basketball player; Nate Thurmond was drafted by the San Francisco Warriors in 1963; began playing center in 1967 and established his rank as one of the best players of his era; traded to the Chicago Bulls in 1974 and to the Cleveland Cavaliers in 1975; retired, with his number, in 1977.

Thurmond, Strom

b. December 5, 1902
Edgefield, South Carolina
fields: Government and Politics

An archetypal prosegregation, anti-civil rights Southern politician, Strom Thurmond was elected governor of South Carolina in 1946. Thurmond opposed the efforts of President Harry S Truman to end segregation, and in 1948 Thurmond became the Dixiecrats' presidential candidate. After becoming the only U.S. senator elected by a write-in vote in 1954, Thurmond, in 1957, made a record filibuster of twenty-four hours and eighteen minutes to defeat a civil rights bill. In keeping with his conservative, states' rights principles, he switched from the Democratic to the Republican Party in 1964. He tempered his segregationist positions in the 1970's and continued to serve in Congress through the 1980's and 1990's. He was reelected to the Senate in 1996 at the age of ninety-three.

Thutmose III

b. Late sixteenth century B.C.E.
near Thebes, Egypt?
d. 1450 B.C.E.
near Thebes, Egypt?
fields: Government and Politics

During a reign of nearly fifty-four years, Thutmose III consolidated Egypt's position as primary power in the ancient Near East and North Africa. He laid the groundwork for some two hundred years of relative peace and prosperity in the region.

Tiant, Luis

full: Luis Clemente Tiant y Vega
b. November 23, 1940
Marianao, Cuba
fields: Sports (baseball)

Pitcher Luis Tiant was the son of one of Cuban baseball's great pitchers. In nineteen seasons (1964-1982), Tiant won 229 games. He had four twenty-win seasons (1968, 1973, 1974, 1976) and twice led the American League in earned run average (1968, 1972). Tiant's best years were with the Boston Red Sox, whom he helped win the 1975 World Series.

Tiberius

né: Tiberius Claudius Nero
b. November 16, 42 B.C.E.
Rome, Italy
d. March 16, 37 C.E.
Misenum, Italy
fields: Government and Politics

As the second emperor of Rome, Tiberius solidified and firmly established the new system of power—but not without devastating impact on his personal life and the Roman upper classes.

Tien, Chang-lin

b. July 24, 1935
Wuhan, Hubei Province, China

fields: Science, Education

After serving as the chair of the Department of Mechanical Engineering from 1974 to 1981, Chang-lin Tien became vice chancellor in charge of research (1983-1985) at the University of California, Berkeley. In 1990 Tien assumed the office of Berkeley's seventh chancellor, becoming the first Asian American to head a major research university in the United States. He is also an internationally respected scientist working in the field of heat-transfer technology.

Tienda, Marta

b. Aug. 10, 1950
Donna, Tex.
fields: Education, Sociology

Hispanic educator and sociologist Marta Tienda wrote widely on immigrant workers. Edited *Hispanics in the U.S. Economy* (1985), coedited *The Hispanic Population of the United States* (1987, with Frank Bean). Served as editor of the *American Journal of Sociology*. Joined the faculty of the University of Wisconsin at Madison in 1976; served as a visiting professor at Stanford University in 1987; became a professor at the University of Chicago in 1989.

Tiepolo, Giovanni Battista

b. March 5, 1696
Venice
d. March 27, 1770
Madrid, Spain
fields: Art

The last important painter of the Venetian school, Tiepolo was the most versatile of the Italian ceiling painters. Although he worked primarily in the Baroque tradition, his work shares some qualities of the rococo.

Tiger, Jerome R.

aka: Kacha (Tiger)
b. July 8, 1941
Tahlequah, Okla.
d. Aug. 13, 1967
Eufaula, Okla.
fields: Art (painter)

Native American painter. A Creek and Seminole, Jerome R. Tiger added emotion, subtle colors, and delicate strokes to traditional Indian painting. From 1962 until 1967, produced hundreds of paintings and sketches of the Creek stomp dance, of Seminole individuals, of windswept Indians on the Trail of Tears, and of contemporary Indians. By 1966, his distinctive style—a delicate line on blue or brown posterboard using one or two tempera colors—was established.

Tigranes the Great

b. c. 140 B.C.E.
Armenia
d. c. 55 B.C.E.
Armenia
fields: Government and Politics

As King of Armenia between 95 and 55 B.C.E., Tigranes the Great defied the growing power of Rome and carved out a vast but short-lived empire which stretched from upper Mesopotamia to the Mediterranean.

Tijerina, Reies López

b. September 21, 1926
near Falls City, Tex.
fields: Civil Rights

In the early 1950's Reies López spent time in Mexico researching Spanish and Mexican land grants of the American Southwest. On February 2, 1962, he organized the Alianza Federal de Mercedes (Federal Alliance of Land Grants) and the land-grant movement. By 1965 the Alianza claimed twenty thousand members, many of which favored militant confrontation. On June 5, 1967, the Tierra Amarilla courthouse was raided by Alianza members. Tijerina was charged with kidnapping and assault to commit murder, destruction of federal property, and assault on two officials.

Tilak, Bal Gangadhar

b. July 23, 1856
Ratnāgiri, India
d. August 1, 1920
Bombay, India
fields: Government and Politics

Through his oratorical skill, political savvy, and editorship of several newspapers, Tilak showed the Hindu masses a connection between ancient tradition and twentieth century nationalism. His politics also were considerably more radical than those of other contemporary Indian leaders, giving the *swaraj* (self-government) movement a strong push forward.

Tillich, Paul

full: Paul Johannes Tillich
b. August 20, 1886
Starzeddel, Germany
d. October 22, 1965
Chicago, Illinois
fields: Philosophy, Religion and Theology

Tillich introduced a unique and challenging approach to the area of theology.

Timerman, Jacobo

b. January 6, 1923
Bar, Ukraine, U.S.S.R.
fields: Journalism

Jacobo Timerman came to Argentina from the Ukraine when he was five years old. In 1947 he became a newspaper reporter and later became a prominent radio and television news commentator, as well as publisher of two weekly news magazines. After selling his magazines in 1971, he cofounded the daily newspaper *La Opinión*. Through a violent era in Argentinean history, his paper was a voice for moderation. In 1977 agents of a new military junta arrested him, later charging him with supporting an antigovernment conspiracy. He was cleared of all charges later that year but was not released until the following year. He later described his experiences in *Prisoner Without a Name, Cell Without a Number* (1981).

Tindley, Charles Albert

b. July 7, 1856
Berlin, Md.
d. July 26, 1933
Philadelphia, Pa.
fields: Music, Religion and Theology

African American minister and gospel composer; Charles Albert Tindley was longtime pastor to the Bainbridge Street Church in Philadelphia, beginning in 1902; composed many well-known gospel songs and hymns.

Ting, Samuel

full: Samuel Chao Chung Ting
b. January 27, 1936
Ann Arbor, Mich.
fields: Science

In 1969 Samuel Ting was made full professor in physics at the Massachusetts Institute of Technology and became program consultant of the Division of Particles and Fields of the American Physics Society in 1970. He discovered a long-lived product particle, the J/psi particle and in 1976 received the Nobel Prize in Physics.

Tintoretto

né: Jacopo Robusti
b. c. 1518-1519
Venice
d. May 31, 1594
Venice
fields: Art

Tintoretto was a leading exponent of the mannerist movement in painting, a style which parted with the rational symmetry of the Renaissance and moved toward dramatic imbalance and tension and the creation of mysterious moods by means of chiaroscuro, radical foreshortening, and unorthodox brushwork.

Tiny Tim

né: Herbert Khaury
b. April 12, 1922?
New York, New York
d. November 30, 1996
Minneapolis, Minnesota
fields: Theater and Entertainment

A performer famous for his novelty act singing "Tiptoe Through the Tulips" in a falsetto voice while playing the ukulele, Tiny Tim provided moments of comic relief during the turbulent 1960's. His record *God Bless Tiny Tim* (1968) sold more than two hundred thousand copies, and he became a regular act on American television. Some thirty-five million viewers saw his wedding to his first wife, Miss Vicky (Victoria May Budinger), on Johnny Carson's *The Tonight Show*. By mid-1970, his career was in decline; he made a few recordings and took whatever gigs he were offered, from circuses to benefits. In the 1990's, he released a few compact discs and again appeared on television.

Tirado, Romualdo

b. ?
Spain
d. ?
fields: Theater and Entertainment (actor, producer, and writer)

Born in Spain, Romualdo Tirado spent fifteen years acting in Mexico, then moved to Los Angeles shortly before 1920. He generally played a stock *peladito* (a sympathetic underdog) comic persona. A well-known figure in early theater in Los Angeles, he sought to present work of Hispanic dramatists. Adapted Mariano Azuela's epic 1916 novel of the Mexican Revolution, *Los de abajo*, for the stage in 1938.

Tirpitz, Alfred von

né: Alfred Peter Friedrich Tirpitz
b. March 19, 1849
Küstrin, Brandenburg, Prussia
d. March 6, 1930
Ebenhausen, Germany
fields: Military Affairs

Tirpitz, one of the ablest naval administrators in modern history, was the architect of the German High Seas Fleet that fought in World War I.

Tisquantum. *See* Squanto

Titian

né: Tiziano Vecellio
b. c. 1490
Pieve di Cadore, Venetian Republic
d. August 27, 1576
Venice
fields: Art

Titian is considered one of the greatest artists of the Italian High Renaissance. During his long and prolific career, he developed an oil-painting technique of successive glazes and broad paint application which influenced generations of future artists.

Tito

né: Josip Broz
b. May 7, 1892
Kumroveć, Croatia, Austro-Hungarian Empire
d. May 4, 1980
Ljubljana, Yugoslavia
fields: Military Affairs, Government and Politics

Tito built and led the Yugoslav Communist Partisan army, which was the most successful guerrilla resistance force against the Nazis and Fascists in World War II. After the war, he broke away from Joseph Stalin and until his death led the country on an independent Communist path.

Tizol, Juan

né: Vicente Martínez
b. Jan. 22, 1900
San Juan, Puerto Rico
d. Apr. 23, 1984
Inglewood, Calif.
fields: Music (jazz trombonist and composer)

Puerto Rican musician Juan Tizol moved to the U.S. in 1920, having already played the valve trombone extensively in Puerto Rico. Played with Duke Ellington beginning in late 1929. He and Ellington collaborated on writing pieces such as "Caravan," "Pyramid," "Conga Brava," and "Perdido." Also played with the Harry James band and recorded with others.

Tjader, Cal

né: Callen Radcliff, Jr.
b. July 16, 1925
St. Louis, Mo.
d. May 5, 1982
Manila, Philippines
fields: Music (Latin jazz vibrophonist)

Vibrophonist Cal Tjader, a Swedish American, was a leading player and bandleader in the Latin jazz scene from the 1950's to the 1970's. Also played piano and percussion and composed. Played with such influential musicians as Willie Bobo, Mongo Santamaría, Eddie Palmieri, Tito Puente, Scott Hamilton, and Ray Barretto. Albums include *Mambo with Tjader*, *Ritmo Caliente*, *Mas Ritmo Caliente*, *Cal Tjader Plays Mucho*, *The Cal Tjader Sextet*, *La Onda Va Bien* (a 1980 Grammy winner), and *Good Vibes* (1982), his final album.

Tocqueville, Alexis de

full: Alexis-Henri-Charles-Maurice Clérel, comte de Tocqueville
b. July 29, 1805
Paris, France
d. April 16, 1859
Cannes, France
fields: Political Science, Sociology

A political and social analyst, Alexis de Tocqueville was the earliest, the greatest, and surely the most percipient observer of the initial growth and increasing persuasiveness of democracy in all areas of American culture.

Todd, Thomas

b. 1765
d. 1826
fields: Law

U.S. Supreme Court justice, 1807-1826 (died while in office); appointed by President Jefferson. Never disagreed with Chief Justice Marshall on any constitutional issue.

Todorov, Tzvetan

b. Sofia, Bulgaria
March 1, 1939
fields: Philosophy, Literature

Tzvetan Todorov's greatest influence was in structuralism; a synthesizer and organizer, he helped to define the program of structuralist poetics by providing it with its most coherent and comprehensive manifesto in his *An Introduction to Poetics* (1973), and he helped to give structuralist poetics its most important forum as a cofounder and coeditor of the journal *Poétique*. In the 1980's and 1990's, Todorov turned his attention increasingly to questions of ethics and morality in such works as *On Human Diversity* (1989), *The Morals of History* (1991), *Les Abus de la mémoire* (1995), and *La Vie commune* (1995). One of his most influential of these later works is *Facing the Extreme: Moral Life in the Concentration Camps* (1996), in which he examined the heroic virtues that maintain humanity during the toughest times.

Togasaki, George Kiyoshi

b. 1895
San Francisco, Calif.
d. ?
fields: Business and Industry

After serving in the U.S. Army during World War I, George Kiyoshi Togasaki and a group of Japanese Americans founded the American Loyalty League, a precursor of the Japanese American Citizens League. He moved to Tokyo to serve as president of the English-language newspaper *Japan Times* and as the first board chair of International Christian University. He also was president of the 600,000-member Rotary International.

Tohauson. *See* Dohasan

Tojo, Hideki

b. December 30, 1884
Tokyo, Japan
d. December 23, 1948
Tokyo, Japan
fields: Government and Politics

Hideki Tojo was war minister (1940-1941), then prime minister of Japan during World War II (1941-1944). Approved 1941 surprise attack on Pearl Harbor. Personally assumed control of important government ministries. Allowed military commanders to formulate policies in occupied territories. Therefore, although not directly responsible for various atrocities, he never made any attempt to curtail such behavior. After Japan's defeat, hanged for war crimes in 1948.

Tokimasa, Aiko. *See* Reinecke, Aiko

Tokioka, Masayuki

b. May 22, 1897
Okayama, Japan
fields: Business and Industry

Hawaii-based investor Masayuki Tokioka helped finance half of the Japan Center complex in San Francisco but later sold his interest in the center. He served as president of National Braemer and owned the National Mortgage and Finance Company.

Tokuda, Kip

b. October 8, 1946
Seattle, Wash.
fields: Social Reform

Social worker Kip Tokuda was appointed executive director of the Washington Council on Child Abuse Prevention in 1986 by Washington governor Booth Gardner. Tokuda, who received a master's degree in social work in 1973 from the University of Washington, served on the boards of several community-based agencies.

Tokuda, Wendy

b. 1950
Seattle, Wash.
fields: Journalism

Third-generation Japanese American Wendy Tokuda is an Emmy Award-winning news anchor. Tokuda first worked in broadcast journalism in Seattle, moving to San Francisco's KPIX in 1978. She became KPIX's lead anchor for the 6 o'clock and 11 o'clock news in 1980. In December, 1991, Tokuda moved to Los Angeles, where she became a coanchor at KNBC. With her husband, Richard Hall, Tokuda wrote two children's books, *Humphrey the Humpback Whale* (1987) and *Shiro in Love* (1989).

Tokugawa Ieyasu

né: Matsudaira Takechiyo
b. January 31, 1543
Okazaki, Mikawa Province, Japan
d. April 17, 1616
Sumpu, Suruga Province, Japan
fields: Government and Politics, Military Affairs

Ieyasu united Japan under a feudal administration and brought it to the height of its cultural tradition in a closed society which lasted for more than two centuries.

Tokyo Rose

né: Iva Toguri
aka: Iva Toguri d'Aquino
b. July 4, 1916
Los Angeles, Calif.
fields: Historical Figure

Iva Toguri (later d'Aquino), a Californian, was in Japan when war broke out and was unable to return. She was recruited as a broadcaster for a Japan Broadcasting Corporation program called "Zero Hour" organized by three Allied prisoners of war. She and other Japanese American women played popular music interspersed with light banter that frequently addressed the fears and loneliness of American armed forces members. The propaganda was subtle rather than overt. U.S. military personnel referred to Toguri and the other women as Tokyo Rose. After the war, two reporters seeking Tokyo Rose offered d'Aquino two thousand dollars for her story. Arrested in October, 1945, on suspicion of treason, she was released in 1946. In 1948, she was prosecuted for treason and convicted. President Gerald R. Ford formally pardoned her in 1977.

Tolan, John H.

b. Jan. 15, 1877
St. Peter, Minn.
d. June 30, 1947
Oakland, Calif.
fields: Government and Politics

Democrat John H. Tolan was elected to the House of Representatives in 1935. During World War II, he headed a committee that attempted to solicit public opinion concerning Japanese Americans on the West Coast. The Tolan Committee concluded that it was advisable to remove all persons of Japanese ancestry from the coast.

Toler, Sidney

b. Apr. 28, 1874
Warrensburg, Mo.
d. February 12, 1947
Beverly Hills, Calif.
fields: Film (actor)

In 1938, actor Sidney Toler replaced the late Warner Oland as Chinese sleuth Charlie Chan in the popular series of detective films. Toler's films were less successful than Oland's. They included *Charlie Chan in Honolulu* (1938), *Charlie Chan in Reno* (1939), *Murder over New York* (1940), *Charlie Chan in Panama* (1940), and *The Scarlet Clue* (1945). After Toler died, he was replaced by Roland Winters.

Tolkien , J. R. R.

full: John Ronld Reuel Tolkien
b. January 3, 1892
Bloemfontein, South Africa
d. September 2, 1973
Bournemouth, England
fields: Literature

Tolkien communicated the sensibility of medieval epic and romance in his widely read mythopoetic fiction. With influential articles on the Anglo-Saxon epic *Beowulf* and the standard edition of the fourteenth century English Arthurian fantasy romance *Sir Gawain and the Green Knight*, he was an important medievalist long before he became much more famous and beloved for his widely read fantasy novels *The Hobbit*, *The Lord of the Rings*, and *The Silmarillion*.

Tolliver, Melba

b. 1939
Rome, Ga.
fields: Television

African American television broadcaster; Melba Tolliver worked in television journalism for a number of years before hosting her own show *Melba Tolliver's New York*.

Tolson, M. B.

full: Melvin Beaunorus Tolson
b. February 6, 1898
Moberly, Mo.
d. August 29, 1966
Guthrie, Okla.
fields: Literature

African American poet; M. B. Tolson was poet laureate of Liberia in 1947; a modernist, Tolson explored the relationship of the artist and community.

Tolstoy, Leo

full: Count Lev Nikolayevich Tolstoy
b. September 9, 1828
Yasnaya Polyana, Russia
d. November 20, 1910
Astapovo, Russia
fields: Literature, Social Reform

During the first half of his long and active life, Leo Tolstoy brought universal fame to Russian literature through his fiction. In later years, he achieved worldwide renown as a pacifist, social activist, and moralist. He is equally significant as a novelist and moral philosopher.

Tom, Maeley L.

b. Dec. 10, 1941
San Francisco, Calif.
fields: Government and Politics

Maeley L. Tom became the first Asian American woman to serve as both chief administrative officer in the California Assembly and chief of staff to the California Senate president pro tempore. She organized the first national Conference of Asian Pacific Democrats and helped form the first Asian Pacific Affairs Office in the California Legislature.

Tomah

aka: Thomas Carron
b. c. 1752
near present-day Green Bay, Wis.
d. c. 1817
Mackinaw, Wis.
fields: Government and Politics, Warfare and Conquest, Native American Affairs

Native American leader. A Menominee, Tomah resisted Tecumseh's call for armed resistance. Tomah also feared white encroachment, however, and when it appeared that the Americans might be defeated in the War of 1812, he aided the British. Along with his protégé, Oshkosh, Tomah and approximately one hundred braves helped defeat the Americans at Fort Mackinaw, Michigan, and Fort Stephenson, Ohio.

Tombaugh, Clyde William

b. February 4, 1906
Streator, Illinois
d. January 17, 1997
Las Cruces, New Mexico
fields: Astronomy

After a systematic search based on the predictions of earlier astronomers, Tombaugh discovered the planet Pluto in 1930. He also discovered several star clusters and galaxies, studied the distribution of extragalactic nebulas, searched for small natural earth satellites, and made observations of the surfaces of several planets and of the Moon.

Tomita, Teiko

né: Teiko Matsui
aka: Yukari
b. Dec. 1, 1896
Osaka Prefecture, Japan
d. 1990
fields: Literature (poet)

Teiko Tomita, an immigrant from Japan, wrote *tanka* describing her experiences in the United States and providing a glimpse of life in the rugged Pacific Northwest of the 1920's. When Japan attacked Pearl Harbor in 1941, Tomita, who wrote under the pen name of Yukari, destroyed most of her work, fearing that Japanese poems might cause authorities to suspect disloyalty. During internment at the Tule Lake relocation center, she began writing again, re-creating some of her old work. Some of Tomita's poems appear in *Renia no yuki* (snow of Rainier), a poetry anthology published in 1956.

Tomlin, Lily

né: Mary Jean Tomlin
b. September 1, 1939
Detroit, Michigan
fields: Theater and Entertainment (actor), Film

An award-winning actress who has had success on television, in films, and in the theater, Tomlin is especially known for her portraits of eccentric but sympathetic characters.

Tomochichi

b. c. 1650
Apalachukla, Ala.
d. Oct. 15, 1739
Yamacraw, Ga.
fields: Diplomacy, Government and Politics, Native American Affairs

Native American (Creek) leader. So great was Tomochichi's importance in the eyes of colonial English and Creek leaders that he was chosen, with both English and Indian approval, to head a diplomatic party of Creeks to England. The visit lasted from June 19 to October 31, 1734. He inspired much public sympathy for Indian issues.

Tomonaga, Shin'ichiro

b. Mar. 31, 1906
Tokyo, Japan
d. July 8, 1979
Tokyo, Japan
fields: Physics

Shin'ichiro Tomonaga aided the development of quantum electrodynamics, simultaneously and concurrently with Julian Schwinger and Richard P. Feynman; shared the 1965 Nobel Prize in Physics with his American colleagues.

Tong K. Achik

aka: Tong A-chick
aka: Tang Tingzhi
aka: Tong Mow-chee
b. 1827
Tangjia village, Xiangshan, Guangdong Province, China
d. 1897
Shanghai, China
fields: Business and Industry

Tong K. Achik was an interpreter, community leader, and comprador. He attended English-language schools as a child and worked as an interpreter before going to California in 1852. A Christian, Tong became involved with local churches. He acted as interpreter and translator for the Chinese community, representing the Chinese position. He returned to China around 1857 to work with the Chinese customs service, becoming a comprador for Jardine, Matheson and Company in Tianjin in 1871.

Tongg, Ruddy F.

né: Tang Qinghua
b. 1905
Territory of Hawaii
d. Aug., 1988
fields: Business and Industry

Chinese American Ruddy F. Tongg got his start in business in 1926, when he founded the bilingual weekly *Hawaii Chinese News* and a small printing firm. After the bombing of Pearl Harbor in 1941, some fearful islanders fled to the mainland, and Tongg bought their properties, which included a glass bottle factory, a small travel business in a tourist area, an insurance company, and a ranch, becoming wealthy in the process. Tongg and several other investors established Trans-Pacific Airlines in 1946, but this venture faltered because of delays. The airline was reorganized as Aloha Airlines and survived. Tongg, a land developer, served as board chairman of Honolulu Trust, American Finance, Tongg Publishing, and an officer or director of numerous other local firms.

Tönnies, Ferdinand Julius

b. July 26, 1855
Oldenswort, Schleswig, Denmark
d. April 9, 1936
Kiel, Germany
fields: Sociology

Tönnies was one of the founders of sociology as a field of scientific study. His major contribution lay in the distinction that he drew between two fundamentally different types of social orders—the realm of *Gemeinschaft* contrasted with that of *Gesellschaft*, or, in what has become the standard English translation, "community" versus "society." The continuing influence of this dichotomy upon sociological thought is shown in contemporary development theory with its distinction between traditional and modern societies.

Toomer, Jean

full: Nathan Eugene Toomer
b. December 26, 1894
Washington, D.C.
d. March 30, 1967
Doylestown, Pa.
fields: Literature

African American writer; Jean Toomer was a major figure of the Harlem Renaissance; best known works are the novel *Cane* (1923) and the poem "Blue Meridian" (1936).

Toote, Gloria E. A.

b. November 8, 1931
New York, N.Y.
fields: Business and Industry, Government and Politics

African American businesswoman and political appointee; Gloria E. A. Toote was president of Toote Town Publications, Inc.; member of the editorial staff of the national affairs section for *Time* magazine; appointed assistant secretary of the Department of Housing and Urban Development (HUD) (1973-1975).

Torquemada, Tomás de

b. 1420
Torquemada, near Valladolid, Spain
d. September 16, 1498
Avila, Spain
fields: Church Reform, Government and Politics, Religion and Theology

A Dominican prior in Segovia, Tomás de Torquemada shaped the Spanish Inquisition, which led ultimately to the expulsion of the Jews from Spain in 1492. Between 1484 and 1498 he issued the orders that became the foundation for future inquisitors to investigate and punish Jews. During the eighteen years he controlled the Inquisition, more than two thousand people were burned, and thirty-seven thousand were tortured into accepting conversion.

Torrence, Gwen

full: Gwendolyn L. Torrence
b. June 12, 1965
Atlanta, Ga.
fields: Sports (track and field athlete)

African American track and field athlete; Gwendolyn L. Torrence won sixteen straight races in 1987 and thirty-eight victories in indoor races in 1988. Her determination to succeed helped her regain her world-class status after a complicated pregnancy in 1989, and she finished second in both the 100- and 200-meter races at the 1991 World Championships. Torrence won three medals at the 1992 Summer Olympic Games in Barcelona, Spain: an individual gold medal in the 200-meter dash (21.81 seconds)and as a member of the women's 400-meter and 1600-meter relay teams, a gold medal and a silver medal, respectively. She achieved her goal of making the 1996 Summer Olympic Games, held in her hometown of Atlanta; she won a bronze medal in the 100-meter dash and gold in the 400-meter relay.

Torres, Art

b. Sept. 24, 1946
Los Angeles, Calif.
fields: Government and Politics

Mexican American California state legislator born and raised in East Los Angeles. Art Torres was elected to the California State Assembly in 1974; served until his election to the state senate in 1982. Advocated the improvement of education and proposed legislation to address the problem of high dropout rates in state schools. In 1994, he decided to leave the state senate and run for California Insurance Commissioner. Although he was not elected Insurance Commissioner, Torres became chair of the California Democratic Party in 1997.

Torres, Esteban Edward

b. Jan. 27, 1930
Miami, Ariz.
fields: Government and Politics

Esteban Edward Torres founded antipoverty organization The East Los Angeles Community Union (TELACU). Named U.S. ambassador to the United Nations Educational, Scientific, and Cultural Organization (UNESCO) by President Jimmy Carter. Served in the U.S. Congress from 1983 to 1999; named to California Transportation Commission in 1999.

Torres, José Luis

b. May 3, 1936
Playa de Ponce, Puerto Rico
fields: Sports (boxer)

Puerto Rican boxer José Luis Torres knocked out Willie Pastrono to win 1965 light-heavyweight title. Successfully defended his title four times and became a hero in Puerto Rico. Career ended in 1966 with loss to Dick Tiger.

Torres-Gil, Fernando

b. June 24, 1948
Salinas, Calif.
fields: Government and Politics

Fernando Torres-Gil became a nationally known expert on health-care policy issues, including long-term care, rehabilitation, disabilities, and the effects of ethcnicity on care and policy. Served Clinton administration as member of White House Working Group on Welfare Reform and as assistant secretary for aging in Department of Health and Human Services.

Torricelli, Evangelista

b. October 15, 1608
Modigliano
d. October 25, 1647
Florence
fields: Physics, Mathematics, Invention and Technology

Torricelli extended Galileo's system of mechanics to fluids, developed Torricelli's theorem, which mathematically calculates the velocity of liquid emerging from an opening in a vessel, and invented the barometer. He also stands among the founders of modern integral and differential calculus.

Torstenson, Lennart

b. August 17, 1603
Torstena, Vastergotland, Sweden
d. April 7, 1651, Stockholm, Sweden
fields: Military Affairs

Torstenson has been called the "father of field artillery." He ably advanced the reforms in artillery introduced by King Gustavus II Adolphus of Sweden and made standardized, mobile, rapid-firing field artillery the decisive factor in several Swedish victories of the Thirty Years' War, thereby introducing these reforms to the rest of Europe.

Toscanini, Arturo

b. March 25, 1867
Parma, Italy
d. January 16, 1957
New York, New York
fields: Music

A genius among classical orchestral conductors, Toscanini is considered by many to be the most influential conductor of the twentieth century. His interpretive insights into the classical orchestral repertory and his development of the conductor's art made him a pivotal figure in the history of musical performance.

Tótsohnii Hastiin. *See* Ganado Mucho

Toulmin, Stephen

full: Stephen Edelston Toulmin
b. March 25, 1922
London, England
fields: Philosophy

Beginning as a physicist, Stephen Toulmin became a philosopher of remarkable breadth and interests, Stephen Toulmin believed that the idea of rationality has been too closely tied to issues of formal logic and therefore analyzed rationality afresh in numerous fields of theory and practice. A student at Oxford whose mentor was Ludwig Wittgenstein, Toulmin taught at Oxford, then Brandeis University, and finally the University of Southern California. His major works include *An Examination of the Place of Reason in Ethics* (1950), *Philosophy of Science* (1953), *The Uses of Argument* (1958), *Human Understanding* (1972), and *Cosmopolis: The Hidden Agenda of Modernity* (1990).

Toulouse-Lautrec, Henri de

full: Henri Marie Raymond de Toulouse-Lautrec Monfa
b. November 24, 1864
Albi, France
d. September 9, 1901
Château de Malromé, France
fields: Art

By means of more than seven hundred paintings, sketches, lithographs, and posters,

Toulouse-Lautrec recorded vividly the people and activities of Paris in the last decades of the nineteenth century. He elevated color lithography and the poster to major art forms.

Touré, Ahmed Sékou

b. January 9, 1922
Faranah, Guinea
d. March 26, 1984
Cleveland, Ohio
fields: Government and Politics

A lifelong revolutionary nationalist, Touré led Guinea in 1958 to independence from French colonial rule by securing, in all of Francophone Africa, the only no vote against affiliation with the French Community. Guinea's president from independence in 1958 until his death twenty-six years later, he implemented radical sociopolitical transformations. A leading revolutionary African ideologue, Touré left the imprint of his socialist vision on all aspects of Guinean life.

Toure, Kwame. *See* Brown, H. Rap

Toussaint, Allen

b. January 14, 1938
New Orleans, La.
fields: Music (songwriter, producer, and arranger)

African American songwriter, producer, and arranger; Allen Toussaint wrote and produced songs for many artists, including Joe Cocker, Dr. John, and the Pointer Sisters.

Toussaint-Louverture

né: François Dominique Toussaint Bréda
b. May 20, 1743
near Cap Français, Saint-Domingue
d. April 7, 1803; Fort-de-Joux, France
fields: Government and Politics, Military Affairs

Born in slavery to African parents, Toussaint-Louverture seized leadership of a chaotic revolution and transformed it into a successful struggle that ended slavery in Saint-Domingue. He politically united the island of Hispaniola (modern Haiti and the Dominican Republic) and brought France's richest colony one step away from independence.

Towns, Ed

full: Edolphus Towns
b. July 21, 1934
Chadbourn, N.C.
fields: Government and Politics

African American politician; Ed Towns was elected to Congress representing New York's eleventh district in 1982; chairman of the Congressional Black Caucus (1991).

Townsend, Robert

b. February 6, 1957
Chicago, Ill.
fields: Film

African American actor, comedian, director, producer, and writer; Robert Townsend directed comedian Eddie Murphy's concert film, *Raw* (1987); cowrote, directed, and starred in *Hollywood Shuffle* (1987); also wrote, directed, and produced *The Five Heartbeats* (1990). Other credits include *The Meteor Man* (1993) and the television series *Townsend Television* (1993).

Townsend, Willard Saxby

b. December 4, 1895
Cincinnati, Ohio
d. February 3, 1957
Chicago, Ill.
fields: Labor Movement

African American labor union official; Willard Saxby Townsend was president of the United Transport Service Employees of America (UTSEA) (1940-1957); vice president of the American Federation of Labor-Congress of Industrial Organizations (AFL-CIO) (beginning in 1955).

Toyama Kyuzo

b. 1868
Okinawa
d. 1910
fields: Business and Industry

Toyama Kyuzo helped organize emigration from Okinawa to Hawaii. The governor of Okinawa, who was not an Okinawan, initially opposed this emigration because he felt the distinctive linguistic and cultural patterns of the Okinawans made them poor representatives of Japan. He relented, and on January 8, 1900, the first group of Okinawan immigrants reached Hawaii. Toyama continued to promote emigration until 1907, when the Gentleman's Agreement restricted immigration into the United States.

Toyama, Tetsuo

b. 1883
Okinawa, Japan
d. May, 1971
Honolulu, Hawaii
fields: Journalism

Japanese American journalist Tetsuo Toyama was the founder and editor of the *Jitsugyono Hawaii Journal*. During World War II, was evacuated to a mainland U.S. internment camp. After passage of the 1952 McCarran-Walter Act allowing naturalization of Japanese Americans, Toyama was, on February 26, 1953, among the first small group of Issei to become American citizens; in 1954, founded *The Citizen*, a bilingual newspaper that provided information and encouragement for potential citizens.

Toynbee, Arnold

full: Arnold Joseph Toynbee
b. April 14, 1889
London, England
d. October 22, 1975
York, North Yorkshire, England
fields: Historiography

His challenge and response theory of history, set forth in his twelve-volume *A Study of History*, made Toynbee an important twentieth century philosopher of history.

Toyoda, Eiji

b. September 12, 1913
Nagoya, Japan
fields: Business and Industry

For more than a half century, Toyoda has been a central management figure and a driving force in the development of a small family enterprise into one of the world's most successful corporate empires.

Toyota, Tritia

b. ?
Oregon
fields: Journalism

Through the 1980's and 1990's, broadcast journalist Tritia Toyota was a high-profile news anchor in Los Angeles. She received a master's degree in journalism from the University of California, Los Angeles, in 1970. She began as copyperson at KNX 1070 Newsradio and became on-air reporter before becoming a weekend anchor at KNBC-TV Channel 4 in 1972. She moved to KCBS-TV Channel 2 in 1985, where she coanchored one of the station's weekday newscasts. She was one of the founders of the Asian American Journalists Association.

Toyotomi Hideyoshi

né: Toyotomi Hideyoshimaru
b. February 6, 1537
Nakamura, Owari Province, Japan
d. August 18, 1598
Fushimi, Yamashiro Prefecture, Japan
fields: Government and Politics, Military Affairs

Hideyoshi was one of the pivotal figures in the unification of Japan out of a welter of competing feudal domains at the end of the sixteenth century. As an astute general and canny power broker and lawgiver, Hideyoshi was to go a long way toward establishing the political foundations that brought Japan from the middle ages into its early modern period.

Trajan

né: Marcus Ulpius Traianus

b. c. 53 C.E.
Italica, Baetica
d. c. August 8, 117 C.E.
Selinus, Cilicia
fields: Government and Politics, Warfare and Conquest

The first of the adoptive emperors of Rome, Trajan became one of the most successful, in both war and politics. During his reign, the Roman Empire reached its maximum territorial extent.

Trask, Haunani-Kay

b. ?
fields: Government and Politics

Haunani-Kay Trask, who received a Ph.D. degree in political science from the University of Wisconsin, Madison, was an active member of Ka Lahui Hawaii, one of several groups seeking self-government for native Hawaiians. She was also director of the Center for Hawaiian Studies at the University of Hawaii. She wrote *Eros and Power: The Promise of Feminist Theory* (1986), *From a Native Daughter: Colonialism and Sovereignty in Hawaii* (1993), and a collection of poems, *Light in the Crevice Never Seen* (1994).

Travis, Dempsey Jerome

b. February 25, 1920
Chicago, Ill.
fields: Business and Industry

African American business executive; Dempsey Jerome Travis owned numerous companies involved in the real estate, securities, and mortgage industries.

Tresvant, Ralph

b. 1967 or 1968
Boston, Mass.
fields: Music (soul vocalist)

African American soul vocalist; Ralph Tresvant began his career as a junior high school student, singing in the group New Edition; went solo in 1990.

Treviño, Jesús Salvador

b. Mar. 26, 1946
El Paso, Tex.
fields: Film (filmmaker)

Latino documentary filmmaker Jesús Salvador Treviño made *Yo Soy Chicano* (1985), the first nationally televised Hispanic documentary; examined Chicano social and political progress during the 1970's and 1980's. Also directed *La Raza Unida* (1972), *Have Another Drink, Ese* (1977), *Raíces de Sangre* (1977), *One Out of Ten* (1979), and *Seguín* (1982), which gives a Hispanic perspective on the Alamo's history.

Trevino, Lee

full: Lee Buck Trevino
b. December 1, 1939
Dallas, Tex.
fields: Sports (golf)

Lee Trevino emerged as a golf star when he won the 1968 U.S. Open, becoming the first golfer to shoot four subpar rounds in the tournament's history. In 1971, he captured won the U.S., British, and Canadian Opens. His other wins include the 1972 British Open, 1977 and 1979 Canadian Open, and 1974 and 1984 PGA Championship titles. In 1970, 1971, 1972, 1974, and 1980, Trevino won the Vardon Trophy as the PGA player with the lowest yearly scoring average. Trevino was struck by lightning at the 1975 Western Open and was left with severe back problems. Once on the PGA Senior Tour he came to dominate it. In 1981, he was inducted into the PGA/World Golf Hall of Fame.

Trevithick, Richard

b. April 13, 1771
Illogan, Cornwall, England
d. April 22, 1833
Dartford, Kent, England
fields: Engineering (civil)

Trevithick developed the high-pressure steam engine. The importance of his invention was not merely its efficiency—it made steam engines applicable for many uses. Trevithick is known as "the father of the locomotive engine," as his engines were used for road and rail locomotives, for powering dredgers and steam ships, and in agricultural threshing machines.

Trillo, Manny

full: Jesus Manuel Marcano y Trillo
b. Dec. 25, 1950
Caridito, Venezuela
fields: Sports (baseball player)

Venezuela-born baseball player Manny Trillo was a respectable right-handed hitter and an extremely effective defensive player at second base. Won three Gold Glove Awards in four seasons with Philadelphia Phillies; named the Most Valuable Player of the National League playoffs in 1980. A three-time All-Star while with the Phillies. Major-league debut in 1973; retired in 1987.

Trimble, Robert

b. 1777
d. 1828
fields: Law

U.S. Supreme Court justice, 1826-1828 (died while in office); appointed by President John Q. Adams. Significant opinions: *The Antelope Case*, 25 U.S. 546 (1827); *Ogden v. Saunders*, 25 U.S. 213 (1827).

Trimiar, Tyger

full: Marian Trimiar
b. 1953
fields: Sports (boxer)

Tyger Trimiar was an African American woman boxer who began competing in the 1970's.

Trist, Nicholas

b. June 2, 1800
Charlottesville, Va.
d. Feb. 11, 1874
Alexandria, Va.
fields: Diplomacy

Nicholas Trist was chosen by President James K. Polk as peace commissioner to Mexico in 1847 to conclude a treaty that would end Mexican-American War. Polk ordered him home after U.S. troops captured Mexico City, but Trist (fearing renewed hostilities) instead stayed and negotiated the Treaty of Guadalupe Hidalgo, which was signed in February, 1848.

Troeltsch, Ernst

full: Ernst Peter Wilhelm Troeltsch
b. February 17, 1865
Haunstetten, near Augsburg, Bavaria
d. February 1, 1923
Berlin, Germany
fields: Religion and Theology, Philosophy, Historiography, Sociology

Troeltsch pioneered in making the study of religion a phenomenon amenable to social and scientific analysis in contrast to the standard theological approach. His sociological method stimulated in turn the comparative study of religions and helped gain acceptance for sociology as an academic discipline. His reflections on the philosophy of religion also helped establish the credibility of that field of inquiry.

Trogdon, William. *See* Heat-Moon, William Least

Tromp, Cornelis

b. September 9, 1629
Rotterdam, Holland
d. May 29, 1691
Amsterdam, Holland
fields: Military Affairs

While Cornelis Tromp, his father Maarten, and other Dutch heroes, such as Michiel Adriaanszoon de Ruyter, were in command, the Netherlands came close to being the chief naval power in Europe. The competition between the elder Tromp and the English commanders resulted in a revolution in naval tactics.

Tromp, Maarten

b. April 23, 1598
Brielle, South Holland
d. August 10, 1653
at sea, near Scheveningen, Holland
fields: Military Affairs

While Maarten and his son Cornelis Tromp, and other Dutch heroes such as Michiel Adriaanszoon de Ruyter, were in command, the Netherlands came close to being the chief naval power in Europe. The competition between Maarten Tromp and the English commanders resulted in a revolution in naval tactics.

Trotsky, Leon

né: Lev Davidovich Bronstein
b. November 7, 1879
Yanovka, Ukraine, Russian Empire
d. August 20, 1940
Coyoacán, Mexico City, Mexico
fields: Military Affairs, Journalism, Government and Politics

Trotsky was a preeminent leader of the 1917 Russian Revolution. Along with Vladimir Ilich Lenin, he directed and guided the revolution and became one of its leading political, military, and intellectual figures. Ousted from political power by Joseph Stalin in 1927 and exiled from the Soviet Union two years later, Trotsky continued to publish on a wide variety of political issues until his murder by a Soviet secret police agent in 1940.

Trotter, William Monroe

b. April 7, 1872
Chillicothe, Ohio
d. April 7, 1934
Boston, Mass.
fields: Civil Rights

William Monroe Trotter founded the militant newspaper the *Boston Guardian* in 1901 to promote socioeconomic and political rights for African Americans. Trotter helped organize the Niagara Movement (1905), the predecessor of the National Association for the Advancement of Colored People—an organization he did not join because he found it too accommodationist. He pushed for civil rights on every front and pressed President Woodrow Wilson to eliminate discrimination in the federal government and the military. Denied a passport, he arranged passage to Paris for the 1919 Peace Conference by posing as a ship's cook; there, he lobbied for legislation outlawing racial discrimination.

Trudeau, Pierre

full: Pierre Elliott Trudeau
b. October 18, 1919
Montreal, Canada
fields: Government and Politics

Through force of will and through his energetic efforts, Trudeau preserved the Canadian Confederation against the threat of Quebecois separatism.

Truffaut, François

b. February 6, 1932
Paris, France
d. October 21, 1984
Neuilly-sur-Seine, France
fields: Film

A film critic whose auteur theory helped revolutionize film analysis, Truffaut was a leader of the New Wave directors who changed filmmaking itself.

Trujillo, Rafael

full: Rafael Leónidas Trujillo Molina
b. October 24, 1891
San Cristóbal, Dominican Republic
d. May 30, 1961
Ciudad Trujillo (now Santo Domingo), Dominican Republic
fields: Government and Politics

Dictatorial head of the Dominican Republic from 1930 to 1961. After coming to power, secure recognition of his administration by the United States. Ruthlessly eliminated any Dominican whom he saw as an enemy. Maintained absolute control in a manner similar to Adolf Hitler and Joseph Stalin. Dominated the country's economy and enriched himself, his family, and his supporters. In 1937, unleashed a massacre along the Haitian border that resulted in the deaths of an estimated fifteen thousand to twenty thousand Haitians. Ruled more than thirty-one years; assassinated in 1961.

Trujillo Herrera, Rafael

b. 1897
Durango, Mexico
fields: Theater and Entertainment, Literature

Mexican-born playwright Rafael Trujillo Herrera immigrated to Los Angeles in 1926. He wrote nearly a hundred plays, including full-length, one-act, and radio plays. Among his full-length plays are *Revolución*, *Estos son mis hijos*, *La hermana de su mujer*, *A la moda vieja*, *Juan Tenorio*. *Una luz en las tinieblas*, and *Cuando la vida florece*. Founded Teatro Intimo in 1974.

Truman, Harry S

b. May 8, 1884
Lamar, Missouri
d. December 26, 1972
Kansas City, Missouri
fields: Government and Politics

As the thirty-third president of the United States, 1945-1953, Truman defended and institutionalized the New Deal reform program of Franklin D. Roosevelt and established the doctrine of containment that guided American policymakers in the Cold War era.

Trumbo, Dalton

pseud., Robert Rich
b. December 9, 1905
Montrose, Colorado
d. September 10, 1976
Los Angeles, California
fields: Literature, Film

A screenwriter and novelist, Dalton Trumbo ranked as Hollywood's highest paid screenwriter in 1943. The following year he joined the Communist Party and participated in film industry labor disputes. In 1947 the House Committee on Un-American Activities (HUAC) summoned him and nine others to testify in Washington, D.C. When Trumbo refused to answer questions, HUAC cited him for contempt. Afterward, the film industry blacklisted him, forcing him to write under assumed names. His script for *The Brave One* (1956), written under the pseudonym Robert Rich, won an Academy Award; Trumbo's authorship was not publicly known for years. After blacklist ended in 1960, Trumbo again wrote under his own name, for such films as *Exodus* and *Spartacus* (1960), *Lonely Are the Brave* (1962), *Hawaii* (1966), and *Papillon* (1973).

Trump, Donald

b. June 14, 1946
New York, N.Y.
fields: Business and Industry

Entrepreneur and real-estate tycoon. Donald Trump became famous for his business deals and his flamboyant lifestyle in the 1980's, as he amassed an empire that included the opulent Trump Tower in New York City and several casinos and hotels in Atlantic City, New Jersey. In 1989, he took over Eastern Airlines' bankrupt shuttle business. In the 1990's, his empire verged on collapse. His relationships with his first wife, Ivana, and his second wife, Marla Maples, have been frequent tabloid fodder.

Truth, Sojourner

né: Isabella Baumfree
b. c. 1797
Hurley, Ulster County, New York
d. November 26, 1883, Battle Creek, Michigan
fields: Social Reform

Born into slavery, Sojourner Truth was a featured speaker at abolitionist meetings before the Civil War. Truth worked initially to expose the immorality of the practice of slavery and later to ensure to welfare of emancipated African Americans.

Tsai, Gerald, Jr.

b. Mar. 10, 1929
Shanghai, China
fields: Banking and Finance

Gerald Tsai, Jr., earned an M.A. degree in economics from Boston University in 1949, then became a securities analyst with Bache Securities in New York. An employee of Fidelity Management and Research Company of Boston from 1952 until 1965, he was one of the firm's star stock analysts in the mutual funds department. Tsai created his own mutual fund, which he later sold at a profit of millions of dollars. He founded G. Tsai & Company in 1965, enlarging his portfolio by buying other businesses. In 1982, he was appointed a director of American Can Company and helped build the company into a prosperous financial investment house, Primerica. He served as chairman and chief executive officer from 1987 until 1988.

Tsai, Shih-shan Henry

b. February 1, 1940
Chia-yi, Taiwan
fields: Historiography

Shih-shan Henry Tsai was a professor of history and chair of the Asian Studies program at the University of Arkansas. His specialty is the study of the Chinese diaspora. His works include *China and the Overseas Chinese in the United States, 1868-1911* (1983) and *The Chinese Experience in America* (1986).

Tsang King-man. *See* Kingman, Dong Moy Shu

Tsaoi-talee (Rock-Tree Boy). *See* Momaday, N. Scott

Tsatoke, Monroe

b. Sept. 29, 1904
near Saddle Mountain, Okla.
d. Feb. 3, 1937
fields: Art (painter)

Native American painter. Tsatoke, a Kiowa, was a member of the Kiowa Five group of painters who contributed to the formation of the twentieth century Oklahoma styles of Native American painting. Although he painted standard images, such as warriors, he was best known for paintings of dance scenes, drummers, and peyote cult subjects.

Tse-min, Chiang. *See* Jiang Zemin

Tseng Kuo-fan. *See* Zeng Guofan

Tshombe, Moïse

full: Moïse Kapenda Tshombe
b. November 10, 1919
Musamba, Katanga, Belgian Congo
d. June 29, 1969
under house arrest in a secret location near Algiers, Algeria
fields: Government and Politics

Tshombe believed that a confederation of provinces held together by a weak central government comprised the key to national unity in the postcolonial Congo. In spite of formidable opposition, Tshombe tried to carry out his unification program by emphasizing ethnicity over pan-Africanism and by using European money, men, and material.

Tsiolkovsky, Konstantin

full: Konstantin Eduardovich Tsiolkovsky
b. September 17, 1857
Izhevskoye, Russia
d. September 19, 1935
Kaluga, U.S.S.R.
fields: Aviation and Space Exploration

Tsiolkovsky was the first scientist to discover the mathematical theories of rocketry and astronautics on which modern space travel is based. Along with contemporary scientists Hermann Oberth of Germany and Robert Goddard of the United States, he pioneered the concepts of reaction propulsion as a means to lift a rocket into space, liquid-fueled rocket engines, and manned space travel.

Tsuji, Kenryu Takashi

b. Mar. 14, 1919
Mission City, British Columbia, Canada
fields: Religion and Theology

Buddhist clergyman Kenryu Takashi Tsuji arrived in the United States in 1959 and became a citizen in 1964. He was ordained as a minister in the Buddhist church in 1941 and subsequently served in temples in the United States and Canada. From 1968 until 1981, he was bishop of the Buddhist Church of America.

Tsukiyama, Wilfred Chomatsu

b. 1897
d. Jan., 1965
Honolulu, Hawaii
fields: Law

Wilfred Chomatsu Tsukiyama was one of the earliest Japanese American lawyers in Hawaii and the first chief justice of the Hawaii Supreme Court. After graduating from the University of Chicago Law School, he won appointment in 1929 as deputy attorney for the City and County of Honolulu and in 1933 was made chief attorney. He went into private practice during World War II. Tsukiyama was elected to a Hawaii state legislative seat in 1946, leaving in 1959 to become chief justice.

Tsungunsini. *See* Dragging Canoe

Tsutakawa, George

b. Feb. 22, 1910
Seattle, Wash.
d. December 18, 1997
Seattle, Wash.
fields: Art, Education

A long-time resident of Seattle, George Tsutakawa enjoyed a lengthy career as a painter, sculptor, and art professor at the University of Washington. Shortly after World War II broke out, Tsutakawa was inducted into the U.S. Army. After the war, he taught at the University of Washington, becoming a full professor in 1955 and achieving emeritus status in 1976. Tsutakawa's 1956 visit to Japan became the inspiration behind his specialty, water fountains. He created more than sixty public fountains in the United States. A sixty-year retrospective exhibition of his work staged at the Bellevue Art Museum in 1990 displayed his paintings, prints, sculptures, and furniture.

Tsvetayeva, Marina

full: Marina Ivanovna Tsvetayeva
b. October 9, 1892
Moscow, Russia
d. August 31, 1941
Yelabuga, U.S.S.R.
fields: Literature

Tsvetayeva, whose life and work bridged the Bolshevik Revolution, was one of the greatest Russian poets of the twentieth century. Her poetry and her correspondence illuminate the time in which she lived, and her mastery of the technique of writing poetry led to innovative poetic forms and rhythms.

Tu Fu. *See* Du Fu

Tuan, Yi-Fu

b. December 5, 1930
Tianjin, China
fields: Sociology

Yi-Fu Tuan, a professor of geography at the University of Wisconsin, Madison, conducted a number of innovative interdisciplinary studies. Tuan, who came to the United States in 1951, received an M.A. from Oxford in 1955 and a Ph.D. from the University of California, Berkeley, in 1957. His publications include *Space and Place: The Perspective of Experience* (1977), *Landscapes of Fear* (1980), *Dominance and Affection: The Making of Pets* (1984), *The Good Life* (1986), and *Morality and Imagination: Paradoxes of Progress* (1989).

Tubman, Harriet

né: Araminta
b. c. 1820
Bucktown, Dorchester County, Maryland

d. March 10, 1913
Auburn, New York
fields: Civil Rights, Nursing

A fugitive slave herself, Tubman was called the "Moses" of her people for rescuing numerous slaves from bondage and leading them to freedom.

Tubman, William V. S.

full: William Vacanarat Shadrach Tubman
b. November 29, 1895
Harper, Liberia
d. July 23, 1971
London, England
fields: Government and Politics

Tubman, who was President of Liberia for twenty-seven years, held that office longer than anyone else in the history of Africa's first republic. During his tenure, he instituted several political, economic, and social reforms, which had important consequences for Liberian society.

Tuchman, Barbara

né: Barbara Wertheim
b. January 30, 1912
New York, New York
d. February 6, 1989
Greenwich, Connecticut
fields: Historiography

Recipient of two Pulitzer Prizes in history and one of the most widely read American historians, Tuchman helped reintroduce history as an art to the reading public.

Tucker, Cynthia Delores Nottage

b. October 4, 1927
Philadelphia, Pa.
fields: Government and Politics

African American politician; Cynthia Delores Nottage Tucker served in a variety of Democratic Party posts, including vice chair of the Pennsylvania State Democratic Party; president of the Federation of Democratic Women; first African American woman secretary of state for Pennsylvania (1971-1977); chair of the National Political Congress of Black Women; collaborated with conservative Republican William Bennett to pressure music labels to reevaluate marketing of gangsta rap.

Tucker, Lem

full: Lemuel Tucker
b. May 26, 1938
Saginaw, Mich.
d. March 2, 1991
Washington, D.C.
fields: Television, Science

African American broadcaster; Lem Tucker was medical and science correspondent for *CBS Evening News with Dan Rather* from 1984 until his retirement in 1988.

Tucker, Sophie

né: Sophie Kalish
b. January 13, 1884
Russia
d. February 9, 1966
New York, New York
fields: Music, Theater and Entertainment

Tucker's six-decade career as a comedian and singer centered on bawdy songs, live audiences, and ethnic humor.

Tucker, Walter, III

b. May 28, 1957
Los Angeles, Calif.
fields: Government and Politics

African American politician; Walter Tucker III succeeded his father, who had died, as mayor of Compton, Calif., in a special election in 1991.

Tu-hsiu, Ch'en. *See* Chen Duxiu

Tull, Jethro

b. March 30, 1674 (baptized)
Basildon, Berkshire, England
d. February 21, 1740 or 1741
Prosperous Farm, near Hungerford, Berkshire, England
fields: Invention and Technology

Tull's publications describing his farming experiments and inventions spread knowledge of new agricultural techniques, thereby contributing to the network of changes which constituted the Agricultural Revolution.

Tunnell, Em

full: Emlen Tunnell
b. March 29, 1925
Bryn Mawr, Pa.
d. July 23, 1975
Pleasantville, N.Y.
fields: Sports (football player)

African American football player; Em Tunnell played eleven seasons for the New York Giants, beginning in 1948, and three seasons for the Green Bay Packers.

Tupolev, Andrei Nikolayevich

b. November 10, 1888
Pustomazovo, Russia
d. December 23, 1972
Moscow, U.S.S.R.
fields: Aviation and Space Exploration

Tupolev was among the world's leading designers of military and civilian aircraft. He worked in the Soviet aircraft industry for half a century and designed more than 120 planes, many of which have held world records for being the heaviest, fastest, or largest built. He was first in the U.S.S.R. to build all-metal aircraft, was a member of the Academy of Sciences of the U.S.S.R., and was a recipient of many state prizes.

Tureaud, Lawrence. *See* Mr. T

Turgenev, Ivan

full: Ivan Sergeyevich Turgenev
b. November 9, 1818
Orel, Russia
d. September 3, 1883
Bougival, France
fields: Literature

Turgenev combined the lyrical with the realistic in fiction that had a powerful influence on social conditions in his own time and on later writers such as Anton Chekhov and Henry James, who truly ushered in the modern period in literature.

Turgot, Anne-Robert-Jacques

aka: Baron de l'Aulne
b. May 10, 1727
Paris, France
d. March 18, 1781
Paris, France
fields: Government and Politics, Economics

Turgot was perhaps the most important reform-minded minister to serve the French monarchy in the last generation before the Revolution of 1789. He is best known as an economic theorist. He championed the laissez-faire precepts of the "classical" economic school and strove to remove obsolete or artificial barriers to the free flow of trade in prerevolutionary France.

Turing, Alan Mathison

b. June 23, 1912
London, England
d. June 7, 1954
Wilmslow, Cheshire, England
fields: Mathematics, Computer Science

Through his research on computable functions and artificial intelligence, Turing prepared the foundation for modern computer science. His work during World War II breaking German codes for the British government was of major value to the Allied effort in Europe.

Turman, Glynn

full: Glynn Russell Turman
b. January 31, 1947
New York, N.Y.
fields: Theater and Entertainment (actor), Film, Television

African American actor; Glynn Russell Turman appeared in the 1959 production of *A Raisin in the Sun* starring Sidney Poitier; appeared on the television series *Peyton Place* (1968-1969); appeared in films such as *The River Niger* (1975), *Cooley High* (1975), *A Hero Ain't Nothin' but a Sandwich* (1977), and the made-for-television film *Buffalo Soldiers* (1997); received an NAACP Image Award for his achievements as an actor

(1978); was cast in reoccurring role on television series *A Different World* (1988); was married to and later divorced from Aretha Franklin.

Turner, Benjamin S.

b. March 17, 1825
near Weldon, N.C.
d. March 21, 1894
Selma, Ala.
fields: Government and Politics

African American politician; Benjamin S. Turner served in Congress as a representative from Alabama (1871-1873).

Turner, Darwin Theodore Troy

b. May 7, 1931
Cincinnati, Ohio
d. 1991
Iowa City, Iowa
fields: Education

African American educator; Darwin Theodore Troy Turner was a university teacher, literary critic, anthologist, and pioneer of the study of african american history and culture within higher education.

Turner, Debbye

b. 1965
Ark.
fields: Theater and Entertainment

Miss America 1990; Debbye Turner was the second African American woman to win the Miss America title.

Turner, Frederick Jackson

b. November 14, 1861
Portage, Wisconsin
d. March 14, 1932
Pasadena, California
fields: Historiography

Developing a unique thesis based on the influence of the frontier in American history, Turner became the most dominant figure among professional historians in the United States for the first three decades of the twentieth century.

Turner, Henry McNeal

b. Feb. 1, 1834
Abbeville, S.C.
d. May 8, 1915
Windsor, Ontario, Canada
fields: Religion and Theology, Civil Rights

African American religious leader and activist; Henry McNeal Turner was born to free parents; tutored by lawyers for whom he worked as a janitor; served as Georgia state representative, 1868-1869, 1870; elected AME bishop (1880- 1892); served twelve years as president of Morris Brown University; supported voting rights for blacks and advocated a return to Africa when the Civil Rights Act was overturned by the Supreme Court in 1883; founder and editor of publications such as *The Southern Recorder* (1886-1888), *The Voice of Missions* (1893-1900), and *The Voice of the People* (1901-1907); wrote *The Negro in All Ages* (1873), *The Genius and Theory of Methodist Polity: Or, the Machinery of Methodism* (1885), and *Turner's Catechism* (c. 1917); proclaimed that "God is a Negro"; forerunner of modern black theology.

Turner, Ike

b. November 5, 1931
Clarksdale, Miss.
fields: Music (rhythm-and-blues pianist)

African American rhythm-and-blues pianist; Ike Turner began his career in the 1950's with his band, the Kings of Rhythm; worked as a talent scout for Sun and Modern Records and the Memphis Recording Studio; best known for his work with his wife, Tina Turner.

Turner, J. M. W.

full: Joseph Mallord William Turner
b. April 23, 1775
London, England
d. December 19, 1851
London, England
fields: Art

Turner, the outstanding revolutionary painter of landscapes, was a Romantic. With the vast complexity of his work, he has been called the Shakespeare of English art. An artist far ahead of his time, he is without equal in depicting the sea in all of its moods.

Turner, James Milton

b. May 16, 1840
St. Louis County, Mo.
d. November 1, 1915
Ardmore, Okla.
fields: Education, Government and Politics

African American educator and government official; James Milton Turner helped develop Missouri's Lincoln Institute, which later became Lincoln University; as assistant state superintendent of schools, was responsible for establishing free public education for African Americans in Missouri; appointed minister resident and consul-general for Liberia by Ulysses Grant, though he came to oppose colonization of Africa by African Americans; acted as attorney for black members of American Indian tribes that were denied compensation by the U.S. government.

Turner, John Napier

b. June 7, 1929
Richmond, Surrey, England
fields: Government and Politics

Prime minister of Canada briefly in 1984. Minister of justice, then minister of finance, in Pierre Trudeau's government. John Napier Turner became Liberal leader and prime minister upon Trudeau's 1984 retirement. Prime minister only eighty days; in elections, he and the Liberals soundly defeated by Brian Mulroney and the Progressive Conservative Party. Liberal Party leader until 1990.

Turner, Nat

b. October 2, 1800
Southampton County, Virginia
d. November 11, 1831
Jerusalem, Virginia
fields: Civil Rights, Religion and Theology

Nat Turner led the largest slave revolt in the history of the United States. As a slave preacher, he linked religion, liberation, and black militancy, thus providing a model for many future black liberation movements.

Turner, Ted

full: Robert Edward Turner III
b. Nov. 19, 1938
Cincinnati, Ohio
fields: Business and Industry, Television

Media tycoon. In 1976, Ted Turner became one of the first broadcasters to use a communications satellite to relay programs to local cable companies. His Turner Broadcasting System (TBS) owns the Cable News Network (CNN), Turner Network Television (TNT), and the Atlanta Braves baseball and Atlanta Hawks basketball teams. Both Turner and his wife, actress Jane Fonda, have been active in support of peace movements and environmental causes.

Turner, Thomas Wyatt

b. April 16, 1877
Hughesville, Md.
d. April 21, 1978
Washington, D.C.
fields: Religion and Theology

African American scientist and religious activist; Thomas Wyatt Turner founded the Federation of Colored Catholics (1924), which opposed racism in the Roman Catholic Church.

Turner, Tina

né: Anna Mae Bullock
b. November 26, 1939
Brownsville, Tennessee
fields: Music

One of the most exciting and durable female rock singers, Turner first came to prominence during the 1960's and continued to have songs on the Top-10 charts in the 1970's, 1980's and 1990's. She had a major role in the 1985 film *Mad Max: Beyond Thunderdome*, and the popular 1993 film *What's*

Love Got to Do with It was based on her bestselling autobiography, *I, Tina* (1986).

Tustennugee Hutkee. *See* McIntosh, William

Tustennugee Thlucco. *See* Big Warrior

Tutankhamen

b. c. 1370 B.C.E.
probably Tell el-Amarna, Egypt
d. c. 1352 B.C.E.
place unknown
fields: Government and Politics, Pharaohs

Tutankhamen is one of the best-known and most studied of the Egyptian pharaohs because his tomb lay undisturbed and intact until its discovery in the early twentieth century. Although he was a relatively minor figure in the course of Egyptian history, the gold-laden contents of his tomb have captured the imagination of the world and contributed much to the knowledge of ancient Egyptian life, culture, and religion.

Tutu, Desmond

full: Desmond Mpilo Tutu
b. October 7, 1931
Klerksdorp, South Africa
fields: Religion and Theology, Civil Rights, Social Reform

Tutu became the first black Anglican Bishop of Johannesburg and head of the South African Anglican church. He is a leader of the antiapartheid movement, and his 1984 Nobel Peace Prize was a recognition of his contributions to nonviolent resistance to apartheid.

Twain, Mark

né: Samuel Langhorne Clemens
b. November 30, 1835
Florida, Missouri
d. April 21, 1910
Redding, Connecticut
fields: Literature

In the *Adventures of Huckleberry Finn* (1884), Twain gave America the prototypical initiation novel, but his humor and nostalgia for the past increasingly gave way to his pessimism about man's technological "progress."

Tweed, William Marcy

aka: Boss Tweed
b. April 3, 1823
New York City
d. April 12, 1878
New York City
fields: Government and Politics

William Marcy "Boss" Tweed's name is synonymous with corruption and dishonesty in urban government. Through the power waged by Tweed's Tammany Hall political machine, New York City and its citizens were systematically bilked of millions of dollars in taxes meant for civic projects. Tweed was eventually brought down by his own greed and the combined efforts of a reform coalition of prominent citizens, ordinary people, The New York Times, and political cartoonist Thomas Nast.

Tweedsmuir, Lord. *See* Buchan, John

Twiggy

né: Leslie Hornby
b. September 19, 1949
London, England
fields: Fashion

Twiggy, a Cockney teenager who became the world's top model during the 1960's, had a waiflike appearance that popularized the Mod look in fashion. Photographed by Richard Avedon and profiled by several magazines, she brought out a line of clothing bearing her name and endorsed a wide range of products. By the close of the decade, she had given up modeling to pursue a career as an actor, singer, and dancer; she appeared in Ken Russell's film *The Boyfriend* in 1971 and on Broadway in 1983 in *My One and Only*. She achieved her greatest impact in fashion, however, having ushered in a new level of desirable thinness for models and the women who emulated them.

Two Leggings

aka: Big Crane
aka: His Eyes Are Dreamy
b. c. 1844
along the Bighorn River, Mont.
d. April 23, 1923
Hardin, Mont.
fields: Anthropology

Two Leggings, a Crow, provided invaluable insights regarding his life as a Crow warrior to anthropologist William Wildschut. Wildschut recorded Two Leggings' detailed observations regarding everyday Crow life and the life cycles of a Crow warrior. Wildschut's manuscript, entitled *Two Leggings: The Making of a Crow Warrior*, was edited by anthropologist Peter Nabokov and published in 1967.

Two Moon

aka: Ishi'eyo
aka: Ishaynishus
b. c. 1847
d. c. 1917
fields: Warfare and Conquest, Government and Politics, Native American Affairs

A Cheyenne and an ally of Sitting Bull and Crazy Horse in the Sioux Wars of the 1870's; a leader in the war for the Black Hills of 1876-1877. Two Moon also distinguished himself as an informant to the writer Hamlin Garland.

Two Strike

aka: Two Strikes
aka: Nomkahpa (Knocks Two Off)
b. 1832
southern Nebr.
d. c. 1915
Pine Ridge Reservation, S.Dak.
fields: Warfare and Conquest, Native American Affairs

A Brule Sioux, Two Strike was a prominent leader of the Sioux during the time before the closing of the frontier at Wounded Knee in 1890. During the 1870's, Two Strike allied with Spotted Tail and tried to insulate his people from the European American invasion. In the 1880's, Two Strike became an advocate of the Ghost Dance. A month before the massacre at Wounded Knee, however, Two Strike heeded whites' advice to give up the dance and its promised delivery from white domination.

Two Strikes. *See* Two Strike

Two Tails. *See* Little Wolf

Ty-Casper, Linda

b. Sept. 17, 1931
Manila, Philippines
fields: Literature

Award-winning novelist and short-story writer Linda Ty-Casper earned a law degree from Harvard 1957. The Filipino American writer's books include *The Peninsulars* (1964), *The Secret Runner and Other Stories* (1974), *The Three-Cornered Sun* (1979), *Wings of Stone* (1986), *Ten Thousand Seeds* (1987), *A Small Party in a Garden* (1988), and *Common Continent: Selected Stories* (1991).

Tyard, Pontus de

aka: Pontus de Thyard
b. c. 1522
d. 1605
fields: Literature

A member of la Pléiade (fl. 1549-1589), a group of loosely organized poets dedicated to raising the level of sophistication of the French language by adding words and genres derived from classical literature. Led by Pierre de Ronsard and Joachim du Bellay, they developed a new form of poetry based on forms such as the sonnet, the ode, epic, and elegy. They also worked to elevate the level of the poet to a position as an intermediary between humanity and the heavens.

Tyler, Anne

b. October 25, 1941
Minneapolis, Minnesota
fields: Literature

Known for her gentle humor and eccentric characters, Anne Tyler writes fiction that depicts confining family situations, characters desiring their separate identities yet needing to be connected, and the circling journey narrative she continued to use in her later works. Calling herself a "southern writer," Tyler skillfully selects details and conveys small-town speech to evoke setting and character. Major themes include movement without change or change without movement and the sense of remoteness from present life. In 1977, she received the American Academy and Institute of Arts and Letters Award for Literature. Her 1980 novel, *Morgan's Passing*, brought wide recognition and the Janet Heidinger Kafka Prize. For *Dinner at the Homesick Restaurant* (1982), she won the PEN/Faulkner Award for Fiction. *The Accidental Tourist* (1985) received the National Book Critics Circle Award and *Breathing Lessons* (1988) the Pulitzer Prize. Her novels of the 1990's, including the best-selling *Ladder of Years* (1996), feature familiar themes.

Tyler, John

b. March 29, 1790
Greenway, Charles City County, Virginia
d. January 18, 1862
Richmond, Virginia
fields: Government and Politics

Upon the death of President William Henry Harrison, Tyler became the first vice president to succeed to the presidency following the death of a chief executive. Tyler established the precedent that in such circumstances the new president holds the office in both fact and name. President of the United States, 1841-1845.

Tyler, Wat

b. Fourteenth century
England
d. June 15, 1381
Smithfield, near London, England
fields: Civil Rights, Social Reform

Wat Tyler led a popular uprising, which, though suppressed, speeded the end of serfdom and focused the attention of the English people on the importance of personal freedom.

Tyndale, William

b. c. 1494
probably Gloucestershire, England
d. October 6, 1536
Vilvorde, Belgium
fields: Religion and Theology, Literature

During the Reformation, Tyndale translated the New Testament and the first five books of the Old Testament into English.

Tyner, McCoy

full: Alfred McCoy Tyner
aka: Sulaimon Saud
b. December 11, 1938
Philadelphia, Pa.
fields: Music (pianist)

African American pianist; McCoy Tyner played with the Benny Golson-Art Farmer Jazztet (1959) and with John Coltrane's quartet (1960-1965); released a number of solo recordings, including *The Real McCoy* (1967) and *Sahara* (1972).

Tyson, Cicely

b. December 19, 1939(?)
East Harlem, New York, New York
fields: Theater and Entertainment (actor), Film

An actress of remarkable talent and conviction, Tyson brought perfection and idealism to the theater, by showing great sensibility to her characters, and by refusing to accept roles that are stereotypical and degrading to women and to African Americans.

Tyson, Mike

full: Michael Gerard Tyson
b. June 30, 1966
Brooklyn, N.Y.
fields: Sports (boxer)

In 1984 Mike Tyson won the National Golden Gloves heavyweight championship, but he lost a spot on the 1984 U.S. Olympic Team when he was defeated by Henry Tillman at the Olympic trials. Tyson turned professional the following year. He won twenty-three of his first twenty-five professional fights by knockout. In 1986, he won the World Boxing Council (WBC) heavyweight title, becoming the youngest heavyweight champion in history. He was indicted in 1991 for rape. He and was paroled in 1995. He returned to the ring and won several bouts before losing to Evander Holyfield in 1996. In a highly touted rematch against Holyfield in 1997, Tyson bit off pieces of both his opponent's ears before the fight was stopped. He was fined by the Nevada state boxing commission and his boxing license was revoked. Tyson got his license reinstated and began fighting again in 1999.

Tyus, Wyomia

b. August 29, 1945
Griffin, Ga.
fields: Sports (sprinter)

African American sprinter; Wyomia Tyus was the first athlete to win an Olympic sprint title (the 100 meters, in 1964 and 1968) twice; won a number of other Olympic medals and set 2 world records; undefeated in professional track events between 1974 and 1976.

Tz'u-hsi. *See* Cixi

Tzu-yang, Chao. *See* Zhao Ziyang

U Thant. *See* Thant, U

Uchida, Yoshiko

b. November 24, 1921
Alameda, California
d. June 21, 1992
Berkeley, California
fields: Literature

An acclaimed writer, particularly of fiction, for both adults and young readers, Uchida is best known for her representations of the experiences of Japanese Americans in internment camps during World War II.

Ugarte y Loyola, Jacobo

b. c. 1721
the Basque Provinces, Spain
d. Aug. 20, 1798
Guadalajara, Mexico
fields: Warfare and Conquest, Military Affairs

Jacobo Ugarte y Loyola was a Spanish military officer who had a thirty-one year career serving in Spanish America in the eighteenth century. Governor of various provinces, including Coahuila, Sonora, and Pueblo; commandant general of Nueva Galica from 1791 to 1798.

Uggams, Leslie

b. May 25, 1943
New York, N.Y.
fields: Television, Theater and Entertainment

African American actor; Leslie Uggams was a regular performer on the 1960's television show *Sing Along with Mitch*; won a Tony in 1968 for her performance in *Hallelujah, Baby!*; won an Emmy in 1977 for playing Kizzy in the miniseries *Roots* (1977).

Ugolino of Segni. *See* Gregory IX

Ulam, Stanislaw

b. April 3, 1909
Lwów, Poland, Austrian Empire (now Lvov, Ukraine)
d. May 13, 1984
Santa Fe, New Mexico
fields: Mathematics, Science

Stanislaw Ulam helped develop the Monte Carlo method of data analysis, which he used to simulate the fission process in the hydrogen bomb. He also helped to establish new branches of graph theory, biomathematics, and probability theory.

Ulbricht, Walter

b. June 30, 1893
Leipzig, Germany
d. August 1, 1973
East Berlin, East Germany
fields: Government and Politics

As Moscow's loyal ally, Ulbricht helped to found East Germany and make it into the most stable and prosperous socialist state in Eastern Europe during his lifetime. His oppressive rule in the 1950's and 1960's, including the building of the Berlin Wall in 1961, prolonged the Cold War and cemented the political division of Germany.

Ulfilas

b. 311
the region of modern Rumania
d. 383
Constantinople
fields: Religion and Theology

An apostle to the Goths, Ulfilas developed an alphabet for the Gothic language and made the first Gothic translation of the Bible. He was also instrumental in converting the Goths to Arianism, leading to conflicts once these peoples settled inside the predominately Nicene Roman Empire.

Ulibarrí, Sabine

b. Sept. 21, 1919
Tierra Amarilla, N.Mex.
fields: Literature

Sabine Ulibarrí, a Chicano writer and scholar, earned a doctorate in Spanish from UCLA, where he also taught for a time. Books include poetry (such as *Al cielo se sube a pie* and *Amor y Ecuador*, both 1966) and collections of short stories (including *Tierra Amarilla*, 1964, English translation, 1971, and *Mi Abuela Fumaba Puros: My Grandmother Smoked Cigars*, bilingual edition, 1977).

Ulica, Jorge. *See* Arce, Julio

Ulrich, Karl Peter. *See* Peter III

Ulrich, Master. *See* Zwingli, Huldrych

Ulyanov, Vladimir Ilich. *See* Lenin, Vladimir Ilich

Umeki, Miyoshi

b. 1929
Otaru, Hokkaido, Japan
fields: Theater and Entertainment, Film

After World War II, Miyoshi Umeki began to sing at clubs established for American servicemen and on Japanese radio and television. She went to the United States in the 1950's to work as a nightclub singer and was discovered after an appearance on the Arthur Godfrey television show. She won an Academy Award as best supporting actress for her role in *Sayonara* (1957) in 1958. Umeki appeared on Broadway in the *Flower Drum Song* (1958) and reprised her role as Mei Li in the film adaptation in 1961. Other films in which she appeared include *Cry for Happy* (1961), *The Horizontal Lieutenant* (1961), and *A Girl Named Tamiko* (1963). Umeki also played the housekeeper on the television series *The Courtship of Eddie's Father* from 1969 to 1972.

Unáduti. *See* Bushyhead, Dennis Wolf

Unamuno y Jugo, Miguel de

b. September 29, 1864
Bilbao, Spain
d. December 31, 1936
Salamanca, Spain
fields: Literature

One of the outstanding Spanish men of letters of the twentieth century, Unamuno wrote everything from poetry and novels to philosophy, drama, and cultural criticism; he served the cause of Spanish republicanism, was a key figure in the expression of the existentialist tension between reason and faith, and influenced two generations of Spanish students at the University of Salamanca.

Uncas

aka: Wonkas (the Fox)
aka: Poquiam
b. c. 1606
d. c. 1682
fields: Government and Politics, Warfare and Conquest, Diplomacy, Native American Affairs

Seventeenth century Mohegan leader Uncas protected his people's interests in a period of conflict and change in seventeenth century New England by skillfully allying himself with the English. Assisted English during the Pequot War of 1636-1637. In a battle in 1643 near Norwich, Connecticut, Uncas and four hundred Mohegans defeated a thousand Narragansetts and took prisoner their principal sachem, Miantonomo, executing him at English urging. During King Philip's War (1675-1676), Uncas again assisted the English.

Underwood, Blair

b. 1964
Tacoma, Wash.
fields: Television

African American actor; Blair Underwood starred in the NBC television show *L.A. Law* as the fictional law-firm's first African American associate.

Unkei

b. c. 1150
probably Nara, Japan
d. 1223
probably Nara, Japan

fields: Art

Unkei established a new style of Buddhist sculpture during the Kamakura period in Japan. He is the best-known sculptor in Japanese history.

Uno, Edison

b. Oct. 19, 1929
Los Angeles, Calif.
d. Dec. 24, 1976
fields: Civil Rights

Japanese American educator, social activist; interned in Colorado and Texas during World War II; at age eighteen became president of the East Los Angeles chapter of the Japanese American Citizens League (JACL); taught in the ethnic studies department of San Francisco State College; worked to repeal Title II of the Internal Security Act of 1950 which had authorized retention camps; played a major role in the redress movement; received the Hearst Award as outstanding civil libertarian.

Uno, Roberta

b. May 12, 1956
Honolulu, Hawaii
fields: Theater and Entertainment

Roberta Uno, a director and theatrical producer, directed plays by African American, Asian American, and Hispanic American playwrights. In 1979, she established the New World Theatre in Amherst, Massachusetts. Drawing on her knowledge of the theater, Uno edited an anthology devoted to Asian American playwrights, *Unbroken Thread: An Anthology of Plays by Asian American Women* (1993).

Unseld, Wes

full: Westley Sissel Unseld
b. March 14, 1946
Louisville, Ky.
fields: Sports (basketball player and coach)

African American basketball player and coach; Wes Unseld set scoring and rebounding records for the St. Louis Cardinals between 1962 and 1964; 1968 first draft choice for the Baltimore Bullets; five-time All-Star; retired in 1981 and became vice president of the Washington Bullets; head coach of the Bullets beginning in 1988.

Updike, John

b. March 18, 1932
Shillington, Pennsylvania
fields: Literature

An author who captured the American middle class in its private moments, John Updike is known for his tales of the changing sexual mores of suburbia and the emptiness of American society. His most noted work began with his 1960 novel *Rabbit, Run*, the first of a four-volume series (followed by *Rabbit Redux*, 1971; *Rabbit Is Rich*, 1981; and *Rabbit at Rest*, 1990) that would span some forty years of Updike's career and become a landmark of contemporary American fiction. Updike's 1963 novel *The Centaur* earned the National Book Award and the writer's election to the National Institute of Arts and Letters.

Urban II

né: Odo of Lagery
aka: Otto of Lagery
aka: Otho of Lagery
aka: Eudes of Lagery
b. c. 1042, Châtillon-sur-Marne, France
d. July 29, 1099
Rome
fields: Government and Politics, Religion and Theology

Pope Urban II, 1088-1099. Through the practice of a quiet, astute diplomacy, Urban II laid the foundation for papal supremacy within the medieval church and lifted the papacy to the leadership of Western Christendom during the High Middle Ages.

Ure. *See* Ouray

Urey, Harold C.

full: Harold Clayton Urey
b. April 29, 1893
Walkerton, Indiana
d. January 5, 1981
La Jolla, California
fields: Science, Chemistry, Astronomy

Urey discovered deuterium, the heavy isotope of hydrogen, as well as methods of isotope separation. He founded the modern science of cosmochemistry, devoted to understanding the origin and development of the solar system. He won the 1934 Nobel Prize in Chemistry.

Urista-Heredia, Alberto Baltazar. *See* Alurista

Urrea, Teresa

b. Oct. 15, 1873
Rancho Santana, Sinaloa, Mexico
d. Jan. 11, 1906
Clifton, Ariz.
fields: Government and Politics, Medicine

Teresa Urrea was a Mexican curandera (healer) who gathered a local following in village of Tomochic, Chihuahua. Exiled to U.S. in 1892 after villagers revolted against Mexican government of Porfirio Díaz in 1891 and said that her teachings had inspired them. Later rebels against the Díaz regime invoked her name, even after her death, so she may be considered an inspiration for the beginning of the Mexican Revolution in 1910.

Urueta, Cordelia

b. Sept. 16, 1908
Coyoacán, Mexico
fields: Art (painter), Diplomacy

Cordelia Urueta's paintings are largely portraits and landscapes, done in oils on canvas. First exhibition was in New York in 1929. Taught painting and drawing in 1930's and 1940's. Appointed art producer at Mexican National Institute of Fine Arts in 1955. Her work gained international attention in the 1960's. Exhibited at the Museum of Modern Art in Mexico City (1964), Biennale of São Paulo, Brazil (1969), at the museums of modern art in Kyoto, Japan, and Mexico City (1975), and at the Petit Palais in Paris. Also served Mexico as a diplomat in Paris in 1938 and in New York in 1939.

Ushimura, Kinji. *See* Shima, George

Usry, James L.

full: James Le Roy Usry
b. February 2, 1922
Macon, Georgia
fields: Government and Politics

African American politician; James L. Usry was mayor of Atlantic City (1984-1990).

Uwatie. *See* Stand Watie

Uyeda, Clifford

b. Jan. 14, 1917
Olympia, Wash.
fields: Medicine, Civil Rights

A second generation Japanese American, Clifford Uyeda served in the U.S. Air Force during the Korean War as a medical officer between 1951 and 1953. After returning from war, he established a private practice and settled in the San Francisco area. In the 1970's, Uyeda assisted in forming a chapter of the Japanese American Citizens League and served as the organization's president from 1977 to 1980. He strongly lobbied for a presidential pardon to be granted to accused collaborator Iva Toguri d'Aquino ("Tokyo Rose") and strove to assuage tensions between Japanese Americans who had opposed the draft during World War II and JACL supporters. Uyeda also served as president of the National Japanese American Historical Society from 1988 to 1992.

Uyemoto, Holly

b. c. 1976
fields: Literature

Japanese American Holly Uyemoto was a teenager when her first novel, *Rebel Without a Clue*, was published in 1989. A resident of Northern California, Uyemoto was only fifteen when she decided to become a writer. She explores concerns facing Asian American youths, as well as youths of all races. Her themes include family relations, friendship, love, and pop culture.

Valadez, John

b. 1951
Los Angeles, Calif.
fields: Art (painter, muralist)

John Valadez is a Mexican American painter and muralist who came to prominence in the 1970's and 1980's. Most of his work has been done in and around Los Angeles and reflects the culture around him rather than imitating the Mexican muralists. Most of his work is figurative and deals with Chicano self-identity. His *Broadway Mural* (1982) appears beside a busy Los Angeles street. In the 1980's Valadez also began to paint smaller studio works, including narrative paintings and portraits in pastel and oil.

Valcárcel, Emilio Díaz. *See* Díaz Valcárcel, Emilio

Valdemar II

aka: Waldemar II
b. May 9, 1170; Denmark
d. March 28, 1241
Vordingborg, Denmark
fields: Government and Politics, Warfare and Conquest, Monarchy

King of Denmark, 1202-1241. Valdemar II was a warrior, lawgiver, builder, and Crusader. He extended Danish control over North Germany, Scandia, and Estonia, leaving to his successors the dream of an empire extending over the Baltic Sea.

Valdés, Jorge E.

b. Apr. 18, 1940
Matanzas, Cuba
fields: Government and Politics

Cuban-born Jorge E. Valdés was elected mayor of Sweetwater, Florida, in 1978, the first Cuban American mayor in the state. In 1981, he was elected a county commissioner for Metro-Dade County, the first Cuban American to hold the position of county commissioner in Florida.

Valdez, Luis Miguel

b. June 26, 1940
Delano, Calif.
fields: Theater and Entertainment, Film, Television

Playwright and director; Luis Miguel Valdez founded El Teatro Campesino in 1965, the political plays of which were intended to drum up support for the United Farm Workers Union; his plays include *Zoot Suit* (1978) and *I Don't Have to Show You No Stinking Badges* (1986); they explore such issues as stereotypes, prejudice, and Chicano gangs; his film directing credits include *I Am Joaquín* (1969), *Zoot Suit* (1982, for which he also wrote the screenplay adaptation), and *La Bamba* (1987, in which he also performed); Valdez wrote a dramatization of traditional Mexican narrative ballads, *Corridos!* (1987), for public television; among awards received are an Obie and an Emmy; Valdez has edited several anthologies of Chicano writing.

Valens, Ritchie

né: Richard Valenzuela
b. May 13, 1941
Pacoima, Calif.
d. February 3, 1959
near Mason City, Iowa
fields: Music (rock and roll singer)

Latino singer; the first major Hispanic American rock and roll star, Ritchie Valens produced hits such as "Come On, Let's Go" (1958; his debut), "Donna," "That's My Little Susie," "La Bamba," and "Little Girl"; Valens was killed in a plane crash along with singer Buddy Holly and disc jockey J. P. "Big Bopper" Richardson.

Valentinus

b. Probably early second century
Lower Egypt
d. c. 165
Cyprus or Rome
fields: Religion and Theology, Philosophy

A second century religious genius, Valentinus synthesized concepts drawn from such disparate sources as Christian theology, rabbinic mysticism, Neopythagoreanism, Neoplatonism, Hellenistic mystery religions, and theosophy into an elaborate system of Gnostic thought that attracted large numbers of converts in the patristic period. His influence was so great that the patristic heresiologists singled him out as one of the most formidable enemies of orthodox Christianity.

Valenzuela, Fernando

full: Fernando Valenzuela y Anguamea
b. November 1, 1960
Etchohuaquila, Mexico
fields: Sports (baseball player)

After receiving the Mexican League Rookie of the Year Award (1979), Fernando Valenzuela entered the Los Angeles Dodgers' farm system (1979-1980); he moved up to the big-league team at the end of the 1980 season and debuted with eighteen scoreless innings of relief pitching; drawing capacity crowds as a particularly popular player with Los Angeles' Mexican American community, Valenzuela helped the Dodgers to win the 1981 World Series and, in the same year, won the Rookie of the Year and Cy Young awards; played on National League All-Star Teams (1981-1986); earned 1986 Gold Glove Award; shoulder injuries diminishing his effectiveness, Valenzuela was released by the Dodgers in 1991, and he went on to play with a series of clubs through the 1990's.

Valenzuela, Luisa

b. Nov. 26, 1938
Buenos Aires, Argentina
fields: Literature, Journalism

An Argentinean journalist and novelist, Luisa Valenzuela worked for Argentina's foremost newspaper, *La Nación*, in the 1960's; studied writing in the U.S. in early 1970's. Considered a Magical Realist novelist; works include *El gato eficaz* (1972), *Como en la guerra* (1977; *He Who Searches*, 1979), *El señor de Tacuru* (1983; *The Lizard's Tail*, 1983), and *Novela negra con argentinos* (1990; *Black Novel with Argentines*, 1992).

Valenzuela, Richard. *See* Valens, Ritchie

Valéry, Paul

b. October 30, 1871
Sète, France
d. July 20, 1945
Paris, France
fields: Literature

Valéry was one of the most important French poets of the early twentieth century; he also made significant contributions to literary criticism.

Valla, Lorenzo

b. 1407
Rome
d. August 1, 1457
Rome
fields: Religion and Theology, Philosophy

By means of his careful scholarship, Valla helped to legitimize Renaissance Humanism, reorganize philosophical methodology, and expose certain prevalent Roman Catholic beliefs and practices to critical scrutiny, thus helping to prepare the way for the rise of Protestantism.

Vallejo, César

b. Mar. 16, 1892
Santiago de Chuco, Peru
d. Apr. 15, 1938
Paris, France
fields: Literature (poet)

César Vallejo was Peru's leading poet of the early twentieth century. Published his first book of poetry, *Los heraldos negros*, in 1918 (translated as *The Black Heralds*, 1990). Major collections include *Poemas en prosa* (1930) and *Poemas humanos* (1939; *Human Poems*, 1968). Also wrote plays, essays, and a novel, *El tungesteno* (1931; *Tungsten*, 1988).

Vallejo, Ignacio Vicente

b. 1748
Mexico
d. 1832
fields: Exploration and Colonization

Ignacio Vicente Vallejo of Jalisco, Mexico, was given a large land grant near modern Watsonville, California, for his services in the Rivera y Moncada California expedition in 1774. The grant established the Vallejo lands in the region. Father of Mariano Guadalupe Vallejo. The Vallejos became extremely influential in nineteenth century California.

Vallejo, José de Jesus

b. January 20, 1798
San Jose, Calif.
d. 1882
San Jose, Calif.
fields: Colonial Administration, Military Affairs

José de Jesus Vallejo was granted California land known as the Arroyo de la Alameda. Military commander of San Jose and of an artillery battery at Monterey. Served as government administrator and postmaster of San Jose. Brother of Mariano Guadalupe Vallejo.

Vallejo, Mariano Guadalupe

b. July 7, 1808
Monterey, Calif.
d. January 18, 1890
Sonoma, Calif.
fields: Government and Politics, Colonial Administration, Military Affairs

Mariano Guadalupe Vallejo supported the Californios in opposition to the Mexican governor in 1830. In 1830's he was made a general in command of northern California to guard against Russian encroachment. Administrator of Solano mission during secularization. Created a fiefdom within the new pueblo of Sonoma; established vineyards and made the first wine in the region. In 1849, Mariano Vallejo was one of eight Californios elected to the state's constitutional convention and was elected to the new state's first senate. Brother of Rosalia Vallejo, José de Jesus Vallejo, and Salvador Vallejo.

Vallejo, Rosalia

full: Maria Paula Rosalia Vallejo
b. January 25, 1811
Monterey, Calif.
d. July 30, 1889
Monterey, Calif.
fields: Historical Figure

Rosalia Vallejo (sister of Mariano Guadalupe Vallejo, José de Jesus Vallejo, and Salvador Vallejo) married Jacob Primer Leese, an early California trader and shipowner. Disliked American nationalism, particularly after her brothers were involved in the Bear Flag incident in Sonoma.

Vallejo, Salvador

b. January 1, 1813
Monterey, Calif.
d. 1876
Sonoma, Calif.
fields: Colonial Administration, Warfare and Conquest

Salvador Vallejo (brother of Mariano Guadalupe Vallejo, José de Jesus Vallejo, and Rosalia Vallejo) was appointed a California militia captain in the 1830's. Commanded a post in Sonoma; served as colonial administrator of the Solano mission. Successful rancher. Led California volunteers against Indians in Arizona in 1836; known as a hard-drinking and reckless soldier.

Van Allen, James

full: James Alfred Van Allen
b. Sept. 7, 1914
Mount Pleasant, Iowa
fields: Physics

James Van Allen developed the proximity fuse in 1942-1946; experimented with captured German V-2 rockets during World War II. In 1958 he analyzed information from early satellites to discover a region around the earth possessing a high density of fast-moving charged particles, now called the Van Allen belts.

Vanbrugh, John

aka: Sir John Vanbrugh
b. January 24, 1664 (baptized)
London, England
d. March 26, 1726
London, England
fields: Theater and Entertainment, Literature, Architecture

The most versatile of the English gentlemen-amateurs, Vanbrugh has an equally distinguished reputation as a playwright and an architect, having produced two of the finest Restoration comedies and at least three of the finest English Baroque buildings.

Van Buren, Martin

b. December 5, 1782
Kinderhook, New York
d. July 24, 1862
Kinderhook, New York
fields: Government and Politics, Law

Van Buren played a central role in the development of the modern party system. As president from 1837 to 1841, he kept the peace, eased sectional tensions over slavery, and formally separated the Treasury from private banks.

Vancouver, George

b. June 22, 1757
King's Lynn, Norfolk, England
d. May 10, 1798
Petersham, England
fields: Exploration and Colonization

This British navigator surveyed and mapped the west coast of North America; studied and charted the Hawaiian Islands, befriending the natives; established Great Britain's claim to western Canada; and determined that the long-sought Northwest Passage through North America did not exist.

Vanderbilt, Cornelius

b. May 27, 1794
Port Richmond, Staten Island, New York
d. January 4, 1877
New York, New York
fields: Business and Industry, Philanthropy

Vanderbilt created a worldwide shipping and railroad business that was both efficient and profitable. Vanderbilt endowed Central University (later renamed Vanderbilt University) with one million dollars.

Vanderbilt, Gertrude. *See* Whitney, Gertrude Vanderbilt

Vanderbilt, Gloria

full: Gloria Laura Vanderbilt
b. February 20, 1924
New York, New York
fields: Fashion, Art

Gloria Vanderbilt, an innovative designer and brilliant entrepreneur, used her artistic abilities to create apparel and many other products and her business acumen to market her name and trademarks, thus gaining great wealth and worldwide name recognition.

Van Der Zee, James Augustus Joseph

b. June 29, 1886
Lenox, Mass.
d. May 15, 1983
Washington, D.C.
fields: Photography

African American photographer; James Augustus Joseph Van Der Zee is best known for his portraits of celebrities and common people during the Harlem Renaissance of the 1920's.

Van Devanter, Willis

b. April 17, 1859
Marion, Indiana
d. February 8, 1941
Washington, D.C.
fields: Law

U.S. Supreme Court justice, 1911-1937; appointed by President Taft. Significant opinion: *McGrain v. Daugherty*, 273 U.S. 135 (1927).

Vando, Gloria

b. ?
New York, N.Y.
fields: Literature (poet)

Nuyorican poet. One of the few woman Nuyorican (New York Puerto Rican) poets, Gloria Vando moved to Missouri after marrying writer Bill Hickok. First book, *Promesas: Geography of the Impossible*, published in 1993. Vando's poetry explores the disparity between American promises and the reality lived by Puerto Ricans.

Vando Rodriguez, Erasmo

b. June 2, 1896
Ponce, Puerto Rico
d. ?
fields: Government and Politics, Journalism, Theater and Entertainment

Puerto Rican-born Erasmo Vando Rodriguez moved to New York in 1919. Helped found the Puerto Rican Association of Writers and Reporters in 1939; founding member of many organizations, including the Pro Puerto Rican Independence Association, Spanish Workers' Center, and Club Pomarrosas, which distributed toys to children at Christmas. Served a number of times as president of Puerto Rican Nationalist Party. Theatrical director, producer, actor, and playwright. Presented Hispanic-themed musicals and plays in New York and elsewhere. Returned to Puerto Rico in 1945, where he continued working in journalism and theater.

Vandross, Luther

b. April 20, 1951
New York, N.Y.
fields: Music (singer)

African American singer; Luther Vandross, known widely simply as "Luther," gained recognition for his smooth balladeering; works include *Never Too Much*, *Forever, for Always, for Love*, *Busy Body*, and *The Night I Fell in Love*.

Vang Pao

b. 1932?
Laos
fields: Military Affairs, Government and Politics

A military leader in his native Laos, in 1975, after the collapse of the government, Vang Pao fled to Thailand and then to the United States. He founded Lao Family Community, a social service agency which played a vital part in the resettlement of Hmong refugees during the 1980's. He served as president of the agency until 1988, when he resigned because of divisions among the Hmong people. During this period, Vang also founded the United Lao National Liberation Front (Neo Hom), which advocated the overthrow of the Communist government in Laos.

Vanier, Georges

full: Georges Philias Vanier
b. April 23, 1888
Montreal, Quebec, Canada
d. March 3, 1967
Ottawa, Ontario, Canada
fields: Diplomacy, Government and Politics

Canadian statesman; represented Canada internationally from 1920's to 1950's in a number of posts. Georges Vanier was later the first French Canadian governor-general, serving from 1959 to 1967.

Vanier, Jean

b. Sept. 10, 1928
Geneva, Switzerland
fields: Religion and Theology

French-Canadian spiritual writer and founder of l'Arche (The Ark), a community for the handicapped. Vanier, a Roman Catholic layman, began the first l'Arche community in Trosly-Breuil, France, in 1964. L'Arche communities can be found throughout the world; they are communal attempts to live out the simplicity of love and hope witnessed in the Bible.

Van Peebles, Mario

b. January 15, 1957
Mexico City, Mexico
fields: Film

African American actor and director; Mario Van Peebles followed his well-known filmmaker father, Melvin Van Peebles, into the film industry; had supporting roles in a number of films and television shows; directed hit film *New Jack City* (1991).

Van Peebles, Melvin

b. August 21, 1932
Chicago, Ill.
fields: Film

African American director, producer, writer, actor, and composer; Melvin Van Peebles's films alerted the film industry to the substantial earnings potential from black filmgoers; directed *Watermelon Man* (1970) and *Sweet Sweetback's Baadasssss Song* (1971); also worked on Broadway and in television.

Van Reed, Eugene Miller

b. ?
d. 1873
Pacific Ocean
fields: Business and Industry, Government and Politics

An American businessman who resided in Japan, Eugene Miller Van Reed recruited the initial group of Japanese laborers to Hawaii. In 1865, he was named Hawaii's consul general to Japan. Van Reed resigned his post as consul general in 1871, but was requested to remain as acting consul general. He died at sea returning to the United States in 1873.

van't Hoff, Jacobus Henricus

b. Aug. 30, 1852
Rotterdam, the Netherlands
d. Mar. 1, 1911
Steglitz (now Berlin), Germany
fields: Chemistry, Physics

Jacobus Henricus van't Hoff researched chemical dynamics and osmotic pressure in solutions; won the first Nobel Prize in Chemistry in 1901.

Van Vleck, John H.

full: John Hasbrouck Van Vleck
b. Mar. 13, 1899
Middletown, Connecticut
d. Oct. 27, 1980
Cambridge, Massachusetts
fields: Physics

A theoretical physicist, John H. Van Vleck worked in both the old quantum theory and the subsequent quantum mechanics—in the latter, he studied its application to magnetism, the theory of solids, and chemical physics; in 1977, shared the Nobel Prize in Physics with Philip W. Anderson and Sir Nevill Mott.

Vardhamāna

b. c. 599 B.C.E.
Kundagrama, Bihar, India
d. 527 B.C.E.
Papa, Bihar, India
fields: Religion and Theology, Monasticism

By the example of his ascetic life and his charismatic leadership, Vardhamāna revived and systematized the religious tradition of Jainism.

Varèse, Edgard

né: Edgar Victor Achille Charles Varèse
b. December 22, 1883
Paris, France
d. November 6, 1965
New York, New York
fields: Music

Varèse was one of the first composers to appreciate the opportunities presented by electronic music and advanced recording techniques. His influence has been felt by many modern composers and has percolated into the rock music field.

Vargas, Diego de

né: Diego de Vargas Zapata Luján y Ponce de Leon
b. Nov. 8, 1643
Madrid, Spain
d. Apr. 4, 1704
Bernalillo, N.Mex.
fields: Government and Politics, Warfare and Conquest

Diego de Vargas was a Spanish soldier and adventurer of noble birth. Immigrated to New Spain and served two terms as governor of New Mexico (1692-1696; 1703-1704). Vargas regained Spanish control of New Mexico, which had been lost after Indian revolts in the early 1680's. Spent much of his time conquering and "pacifying" the Indians of the region. A 1696 Indian revolt was blamed on Vargas, and he was imprisoned; freed and exonerated by 1701, he spent a short second term as governor, dying in office.

Vargas, Getúlio

full: Getúlio Dorneles Vargas
b. April 19, 1883
São Borja, Brazil
d. August 24, 1954
Rio de Janeiro, Brazil
fields: Government and Politics

Dominant figure of modern Brazilian political history. Getúlio Vargas was dictatorial president of Brazil from 1930 to 1945 and again from 1950 to 1954. Seized power in 1930. Closed congress and abolished political parties; governed by decree. In 1937, following the development of fascist regimes in Europe, Vargas abrogated his own constitution of 1934. Established himself as the head of an authoritarian regime known as the "New State." Government censored newspapers, films, and radio. Political critics were jailed and persecuted. Espousing Brazilian nationalism was a primary tool of the regime. Ousted by military coup in 1945. Returned to presidency in 1950; committed suicide to avoid being ousted a second time.

Vargas Llosa, Mario

b. Mar. 28, 1936
Arequipa, Peru
fields: Literature (novelist)

Peruvian novelist. To a large extent, Mario Vargas Llosa's work represents a passionate rebellion against the problems of Peruvian society. Novels include *La cuidad y los perros* (1963; *The Time of the Hero*, 1966), *La casa verde* (1966; *The Green House*, 1968), *Conversación en la catedral* (1969; *Conversation in the Cathedral*, 1975), *La tía Julia y el escribidor* (1977; *Aunt Julia and the Scriptwriter*, 1982), *La guerra del fin del mundo* (1981; *The War at the End of the World*, 1984), and *¿Quien mato a Palomino Molero?* (1986; *Who Killed Palomino Molero?* 1987).

Varmus, Harold E.

full: Harold Eliot Varmus
b. Dec. 18, 1939
Oceanside, Long Island, New York
fields: Biology, Medicine

Harold E. Varmus found the genes that cause cancer; won the Nobel Prize in Physiology or Medicine in 1989, with J. Michael Bishop.

Varo, Remedios

b. 1913
Spain
d. 1963
fields: Art (painter)

Painter Remedios Varo left Spain during the Spanish Civil War. She worked as a commercial artist, interior decorator, costume designer, and nature illustrator in France and Venezuela in 1930's and 1940's. Began to paint her serious work—oils on masonite and canvas—in 1953. Combined feminism, nature imagery, and surrealism.

Varona, Francisco

b.?
fields: Government and Politics, Labor Movement

In 1920, labor mediator Francisco Varona investigated labor conditions suffered by Filipino laborers on Hawaiian sugar plantations. He negotiated the "Honolulu Contract," which stated plantation owners must provide ways for workers without guaranteed return passage to secure means to return to the Philippines. In a report to the governor-general of the Philippines, Varona blamed labor discord on racial tensions between white owners, Filipino, and Japanese laborers. After being appointed to the Philippine Resident Commissioner's Office, Varona served as the mediator of disputes between Filipino laborers and employers.

Varro, Marcus Terentius

aka: Marcus Terentius Varro Reatinus
b. 116 B.C.E.
Reate
d. 27 B.C.E.
Rome
fields: Scholarship

Varro contributed to every field of abstract and practical knowledge extant in his day, established the worthiness of intellectual pursuits such as linguistic study and encyclopedism, and left a body of knowledge that, directly or indirectly, has informed and influenced writers and scholars ever since.

Vasari, Giorgio

b. July 30, 1511
Arezzo, Republic of Florence
d. June 27, 1574
Florence
fields: Literature, Art, Architecture

Modern knowledge of the lives and works of the principal, as well as a number of lesser, artists of the Renaissance derives almost exclusively from Vasari's *Lives of the Most Eminent Painters, Sculptors, and Architects*. Vasari was also a minor painter and architect.

Vasconcelos, José

b. Feb. 28, 1882
Oaxaca, Mexico
d. June 30, 1959
Mexico City, Mexico
fields: Philosophy, Literature

Mexican philosopher and writer José Vasconcelos wrote autobiography, history, biography, sociology, and fiction. He was involved in the Mexican Revolution, at different times an ally of Francisco Madero and Venustiano Carranza. Exiled from Mexico for a time, he traveled in Central America and lived in the U.S. In 1938 Mexico allowed him to return. He directed the National Library and the Library of Mexico. Vasconcelos was a founding member of El Colegio de México, wrote regularly for various periodicals, and lectured in Latin America and the United States. Wrote a five-volume autobiography that stands as an excellent study of Mexico in the first half of the twentieth century.

Vasquez, Luis

b. Oct. 3, 1795
St. Louis, Mo.
d. 1868
Westport, Mo.
fields: Business and Industry

Luis Vasquez was a frontier trader and businessman in the West in the first half of the nineteenth century. With his partner, Jim Bridger, he established Fort Bridger in Wyoming in 1842. It was an active trading center and was later a strategic stop for the Pony Express.

Vásquez, Richard

b. June 11, 1928
Southgate, Calif.
fields: Literature, Journalism

Richard Vásquez wrote the epic novel *Chicano* (1970), one of the best-selling Chicano novels ever written. It is frequently taught in high schools and universities in literature, Chicano literature, and sociology classes. Other novels include *The Giant Killer* (1978) and *Another Land* (1982). Vasquez also wrote hundreds of articles on Chicano folklore and history and worked as a journalist.

Vásquez, Tiburcio

b. Aug. 11, 1835
Monterey, Calif.
d. Mar. 19, 1875
San Jose, Calif.
fields: Historical Figure

Bandit; Tiburcio Vásquez was allegedly driven to crime by white injustice, became a Mexican American folk hero as he stole cattle and robbed California Anglos; many Californios feared Vásquez' crimes would cause racial violence against them; betrayed and captured near La Brea in 1874 and executed the following year.

Vásquez de Coronado, Francisco. *See* Coronado, Francisco Vásquez de

Vassa, Gustavas. *See* Equiano, Olaudah

Vauban, Sébastien Le Prestre de

b. May 15, 1633
Saint-Léger de Foucherest, France
d. March 30, 1707
Paris, France
fields: Military Affairs, Engineering

Vauban is chiefly remembered as Europe's best and most prolific military engineer at a time when siege works and fortifications were crucial to the art of military affairs.

Vaughan, Sarah

full: Sarah Lois Vaughan
b. March 27, 1924
Newark, New Jersey
d. April 3, 1990
Hidden Hills, California
fields: Music

With her rich voice, Vaughan incorporated bebop into jazz singing.

Vaughan Williams, Ralph

b. October 12, 1872
Down Ampney, Gloucestershire, England
d. August 26, 1958
London, England
fields: Music

Through the use of folk songs and native idioms, Vaughan Williams helped bring about the twentieth century revival of English music and established himself as its foremost composer.

Vavilov, Nikolai Ivanovich

b. November 26, 1887
Moscow, Russia
d. January 26, 1943
Saratov, U.S.S.R.
fields: Genetics, Botany

Vavilov is noted for his pioneering work on the origins, distribution, and genetics of crop plants. He postulated a law of homologous series in variation whereby variation (and thus characteristics of possible cultivars) of a plant could be predicted from variation in related species. He also mapped centers of origin and genetic diversity of cultivated plants on a worldwide scale as well as personally organizing and leading numerous botanical expeditions and establishing a network of agricultural experiment stations in the Soviet Union.

Vázquez de Ayllón, Lucas

b. c. 1475
Toledo, Spain
d. Oct. 18, 1526
Winyah Bay, S.C.
fields: Exploration and Colonization

Spanish explorer and colonist Lucas Vázquez de Ayllón became a wealthy judge in the colonial administration of Santo Domingo. He led an expedition from there northward in 1526, landing on the coast of what is now South Carolina. Founded the settlement of San Miguel de Guadalupe, but conditions were so bad that Ayllón himself died there in October of 1526 and the survivors abandoned the settlement.

Veblen, Thorstein

full: Thorstein Bunde Veblen
b. July 30, 1857
Cato Township, Manitowoc County, Wisconsin
d. August 3, 1929
Palo Alto, California
fields: Economics, Social Science

Rejecting the classical view of economics as governed by "laws" of supply and demand, Veblen conceived a system in which production and distribution of goods would be controlled by engineers, foreshadowing a "technocracy."

Vecellio, Tiziano. *See* Titian

Vega, Ana Lydia

b. Dec. 6, 1946
Santurce, Puerto Rico
fields: Literature (short-story writer)

Ana Lydia Vega, a Puerto Rican writer of short stories, earned her master's and doctoral degrees in comparative literature in France at the University of Provence. Books include *Virgenes y mártires* (1981, with Carmen Lugo Filippi), *Encancaranu-blado y otros cuentos de naufragio* (1981), and *Pasión de historia y otras historias de pasión* (1987). Her irreverent and sometimes humorous stories, centering on Puerto Rico, often blend history and fiction.

Vega, Bernardo

b. 1885
Puerto Rico
d. 1965
fields: Literature

In 1940, Puerto Rican-born writer and cigar maker Bernardo Vega wrote his picaresque *Memorias de Bernardo Vega*, which was not published until 1977. It tells of his emigration from Puerto Rico to the United States, of life in New York, particularly in the cigar factories, and of liberation movements. Vega also wrote for New York's Spanish-language newspapers; active in Puerto Rican Socialist Party.

Vega, Ed

full: Edgardo Vega Yunqué
b. May 20, 1936
Ponce, Puerto Rico
fields: Literature (fiction writer)

Puerto Rican-born fiction writer Ed Vega moved to New York with his family at age thirteen. Books include *Mendoza's Dreams* (1987, short stories), *The Comeback* (1985, novel), and *Casualty Report* (1991, short stories). Draws on English- and Spanish-language traditions and depicts everyday events in the lives of Puerto Ricans in the barrios.

Vega, Lope de

full: Lope de Vega Carpio
b. November 25, 1562
Madrid, Spain
d. August 27, 1635
Madrid, Spain
fields: Theater and Entertainment, Literature

Lope de Vega was the creator of the Spanish national theater of the Golden Age. He established the norms that would characterize Spanish theater until the late seventeenth century.

Vega, Salvador

b. ?
fields: Art (painter)

Chicano painter Salvador Vega broke stylistically with the Chicano mural tradition and executed abstract works such as *Man Enjoying the Sun*. In 1981 his show "Birth of the Earth" was featured at Chicago's Museum of Contemporary Art.

Velasco Ibarra, José María

b. March 19, 1893
Quito, Ecuador
d. March 30, 1979
Quito, Ecuador
fields: Government and Politics

Five-time president of Ecuador between 1934 and 1972. José María Velasco Ibarra's populist rhetoric attracted and maintained his following. A conservative, he presented himself as a supporter of the poor and downtrodden. Once in office, Velasco Ibarra tended to become autocratic and dictatorial, alienated the people. Forcibly removed from office four times; served a full term only 1952-1956.

Velasquez, Baldemar

b. Feb. 15, 1947
Pharr, Tex.
fields: Labor Movement

Labor activist Baldemar Velasquez worked with migrant laborers throughout the U.S. Founded (1967) and led the Farm Labor Organizing Committee (FLOC); negotiated with large food companies to obtain better conditions for migrant workers they employed. Led 1980's boycott of Campbell's products. Granted a John D. and Catherine T. MacArthur Foundation Fellowship in 1990.

Velasquez, Jorge Luis, Jr.

b. Dec. 28, 1946
Panama City, Panama
fields: Sports (jockey)

Panamanian-born Jorge Luis Velasquez, Jr., was a leading jockey in the 1970's and 1980's. Began racing in the United States in 1965. Leading money-winner in 1969. In 1981, won the Kentucky Derby and the Preakness riding Pleasant Colony.

Velásquez, William

b. May 8, 1944
Orlando, Fla.
d. June 15, 1988
San Antonio, Tex.
fields: Civil Rights

Mexican American civil rights activist; William Velásquez worked as field director of the Southwest Council of La Raza, Phoenix (1970); in 1971 became assistant director for the National Council of La Raza in charge of fund-raising and organizing; founded the nonprofit Southwest Voter Registration Education Project (1972) and for fourteen years served as its executive director; this organization increased Latino voter registration nationwide and is credited with increasing the number of Latino elected officials.

Velázquez, Diego

b. June, 1599
Seville, Spain
d. August 6, 1660
Madrid, Spain
fields: Art

In his role as court painter to King Philip IV, Velázquez produced a series of masterly works that made him the preeminent artist in his native Spain and one of the greatest painters of the entire Baroque era in Europe.

Velázquez, Juan Ramon

b. 1865
d. 1899
fields: Art (santero artisan and painter)

Santero artisan and painter Juan Ramon Velázquez was one of the few nineteenth century creators of santos (carved and painted representations of holy persons) known by name. Lived in the southwestern United States.

Velázquez, Loreta Janeta

b. June 26, 1842
Havana, Cuba
d. ?
fields: Warfare and Conquest, Military Affairs

Cuban-born Loreta Janeta Velázquez passed herself off as a man in order to fight in the Confederate army. Her American husband, an army officer, was stationed in Kansas at outbreak of Civil War, and he joined Confederate forces. Calling herself Lieutenant Harry T. Buford, she formed and temporarily commanded a volunteer unit under General Barnard Bee. Fought in a number of battles before her secret was discovered in 1863.

Velázquez de Cuéllar, Diego

b. c. 1465
Cuéllar, Spain
d. June 11, 1524
Santiago de Cuba, Cuba
fields: Exploration and Colonization

Diego Velázquez de Cuéllar sailed to Hispaniola with Christopher Columbus in 1493 and became a wealthy colonist there. Appointed to found Cuban colony in 1511; his soldiers (including Pánfilo de Narváez) used brutal tactics to subdue natives. Sent Hernán Cortés to explore Mexico and search for rumored rich civilization. Colonial governor of Cuba from 1511 until his death in 1524.

Velez, Eddie

b. June 4, 1958
New York, N.Y.
fields: Film, Theater and Entertainment (actor)

Actor Eddie Velez made his major film debut in *Repo Man* (1984); other films include *Doin' Time* (1985), *Extremities* (1986), *The Women's Club* (1987), *Rooftops* (1989), and *Romero* (1989). Worked extensively in Los Angeles and San Francisco theaters. Also wrote works for theater and performed standup comedy.

Velez, Lupe

full: María Guadalupe Velez de Villalobos
aka: Mexican Spitfire
b. July 18, 1908
San Luis Potosí, Mexico
d. Dec. 14, 1944
Beverly Hills, Calif.
fields: Film (actor)

Mexican-born actress Lupe Velez's career spanned silent and sound motion pictures. Possessing an unusual deep voice, she played a variety of ethnicities and screen sirens. Became known as the "Mexican Spitfire," a strong, comic persona, in a series of films that included *The Girl from Mexico* (1939), *The Mexican Spitfire's Party* (1941), *The Mexican Spitfire's Elephant* (1942), and *The Mexican Spitfire's Blessed Event* (1943). Married to actor Johnny Weissmuller.

Velez, Ramón S.

b. 1933
Mayagüez, Puerto Rico
fields: Government and Politics

Born a farmer's son in Puerto Rico, Ramón S. Velez became a political power broker in New York's South Bronx. Administrator of a range of antipoverty programs and nonprofit organizations, he began building a network of business allies and interests, politicians, and family members in the 1960's. Velez underwent numerous investigations into his various dealings with government agencies.

Vélez-Ibañez, Carlos G.

b. Oct. 27, 1936
Nogales, Ariz.
fields: Anthropology

The books of anthropologist Carlos G. Vélez-Ibañez include *Rituals of Marginality: Politics, Process, and Culture Change in Urban Central Mexico* (1983) and *Bonds of Mutual Trust: The Cultural Systems of Rotating Credit Associations Among Urban Mexicans and Chicanos* (1983). He served on the faculty of University of California, Los Angeles (UCLA), in the 1970's, then taught at the University of Arizona beginning in 1982.

Venegas, Daniel

b. c. 1900
Mexico
fields: Journalism, Theater and Entertainment, Literature

Spanish-language journalist and playwright Daniel Venegas emigrated from Mexico as a laborer and made his way to Los Angeles. He remained proud of his origins even as he became a member of Los Angeles's Latino cultural elite. Journalist for the newspaper *El Pueblo* in Los Angeles; founded the weekly newspaper *El Malcriado* in 1924 and edited it for a number of years. Founded a theatrical company and wrote plays, all of which have been lost. Also wrote a novel, *Las aventuras de Don Chipote; O,*

Cuando los pericos mamen (1928), about Mexican immigrant workers.

Venette, Jean de

b. 1307 or 1308
probably the village of Venette, near Compiègne
d. 1368 or 1369
probably Paris
fields: Literature, Religion and Theology

A friar who wrote a chronicle recording the political and social events of northern France between 1340 and 1368, Jean captured the sense of urgency and distress of the times in which he lived, while criticizing those whom he thought to be partially responsible for the troubles.

Venizélos, Eleuthérios

b. August 23, 1864
Mournies, Crete, Ottoman Empire
d. March 18, 1936
Paris, France
fields: Government and Politics

Venizélos is the outstanding national figure of modern Greece. In and out of power he was the country's leading statesman in the first part of the twentieth century.

Venn, John

b. Aug. 4, 1834
Hull, Humberside, England
d. Apr. 4, 1923
Cambridge, England
fields: Mathematics (mathematical logic and probability)

John Venn is responsible for Venn diagrams, visual representations of geometrical figures used to interpret propositions of logic; wrote *Symbolic Logic* in 1881.

Vera Cruz, Philip Villamin

b. December 25, 1904
Saoang, Philippines
d. June 11, 1994
Bakersfield, Calif.
fields: Labor Movement

Filipino American labor union official; Philip Villamin Vera Cruz became active in efforts to organize farm labor while working in the vineyards of California's San Joaquin Valley; during the 1950's, he became a leader in the National Farm Labor Union; during the 1960's, he served as a leader in the Filipino-dominated Agricultural Workers Organizing Committee (AWOC); in 1965 the AWOC led strikes against the grape growers of Coachella and Delano; after the National Farm Workers Association, led by César Chávez, joined the effort, the strikes gained national media attention; the two groups merged in 1971 to become the United Farm Workers (UFW) Organizing Committee, with Vera Cruz as second vice president; he resigned from the UFW in 1977 because of interethnic and ideological conflicts.

Vercingetorix

b. Probably c. 75 B.C.E.
central Gaul (modern France)
d. Possibly c. 46 B.C.E.
Rome
fields: Diplomacy, Government and Politics, Warfare and Conquest

As leader of the Arverni, a Celtic tribe in Gaul, Vercingetorix fashioned a coalition of Gallic tribes to expel their Roman conquerors. Although he was captured at his capital of Alesia by Julius Caesar and more than likely executed in Rome, Vercingetorix has long been identified as an early French national hero.

Verdi, Giuseppe

b. October 10, 1813
Le Roncole, Duchy of Parma
d. January 27, 1901
Milan, Italy
fields: Music

Verdi, one of the giants of nineteenth century opera, was an innovator who during a long career evolved his own form of music drama and contributed at least half a dozen of the most enduringly popular operas in the international repertory.

Verdon, Gwen

full: Gwyenth Evelyn Verdon
b. January 13, 1925
Culver City, California
fields: Dance

As a Broadway dancer and actress, Gwen Verdon refined musical theater dance to an art. She spent five years training film performers at Twentieth Century-Fox before rising to Broadway stardom in 1953. A versatile performer, Verdon has had a career encompassing television, theater, and film.

Verdugo, Elena

b. Apr. 20, 1926
Hollywood, Calif.
fields: Film, Television (actor)

Mexican American actress Elena Verdugo acted in numerous films from 1940 to the 1960's; she also performed television roles throughout the 1950's and 1960's. Verdugo perhaps became best known in the 1970's, playing Nurse Consuelo in the television series *Marcus Welby, M.D.*

Vereen, Ben

b. October 10, 1946
Miami, Fla.
fields: Theater and Entertainment, Television

African American singer, dancer, and actor; Ben Vereen came to national attention with his portayal of Chicken George on the television miniseries *Roots* (1977), though his career was already well established on Broadway for his roles in such productions as *Hair* (1968-1969), *Jesus Christ Superstar* (1971), *Pippin* (1972), and *Cabaret* (1975); appeared in a number of short-lived television programs; critically acclaimed for his role in *Jelly's Last Jam* (1993).

Vergil

né: Publius Vergilius Maro
b. October 15, 70 B.C.E.
Andes, Cisalpine Gaul
d. September 21, 19 B.C.E.
Brundisium
fields: Literature

Author of an epic poem celebrating the beginnings of the Roman race (the *Aeneid*), pastoral poems (the *Eclogues*), and a poem about the farmer's life (the *Georgics*), Vergil is among the greatest poets of all time.

Vermeer, Jan

b. October 31, 1632
Delft, United Provinces
d. December, 1675
Delft, United Provinces
fields: Art

Although most scholars firmly attribute fewer than thirty-five paintings to the hand of Vermeer, he is considered a master of seventeenth century Dutch painting and a major artist of the Western world.

Verne, Jules

b. February 8, 1828
Nantes, France
d. March 24, 1905
Amiens, France
fields: Literature

Verne was a popular and prolific French novelist whose works were immediately translated into other major languages. He is credited with being the father of the literary genre now known as science fiction.

Veronese, Paolo

né: Paolo Caliari
b. 1528
Verona, Republic of Venice
d. 1588
Venice
fields: Art

Veronese was one of the greatest painters in sixteenth century Venice and, along with Titian and Tintoretto, was responsible for the countermannerism which characterized the style of that school of art. His luminous colors and dynamic, decorative compositions foreshadow the artistic concerns of the next century's painters.

Verrett, Shirley

b. May 31, 1933
New Orleans, La.
fields: Music

African American opera singer; Shirley Verrett made her debut at the Metropolitan Opera House in 1968 in the role of Carmen; one of the best known African Americans in opera.

Verrius Flaccus, Marcus

b. c. 60 B.C.E.
place unknown
d. c. 22 C.E.
place unknown
fields: Education

Emerging from a slave background, Verrius established at Rome an innovative method for the teaching of Latin language and literature and, through his studies of Roman antiquities, contributed to modern understanding of Latin literature and Roman history.

Verrocchio, Andrea del

né: Andrea di Michele di Francesco Cione
b. 1435
Florence
d. October 7, 1488
Venice
fields: Art

Verrocchio was one of the best sculptors of the later part of the fifteenth century and a great favorite of the Medici family. He was able to work in silver, bronze, and terracotta as well as marble and was also active as a painter. It was in Verrocchio's workshop that Leonardo da Vinci received his first training.

Versalles, Zoilo

full: Zoilo Casanova Versalles y Rodriguez
b. Dec. 18, 1939
Havana, Cuba
d. June 9, 1995
Bloomington, Minn.
fields: Sports (baseball player)

Shortstop Zoilo Versalles began his major-league career in 1959 with the Washington Senators (who became the Minnesota Twins in 1961). His best season was in 1965: He led the American League in doubles, triples, and runs scored and helped the Minnesota Twins to the pennant. Won the league's Most Valuable Player Award, the first Latino to do so. Versalles won Gold Glove Awards in 1963 and 1965. Retired in 1971.

Vesalius, Andreas

b. December 31, 1514
Brussels
d. October 15, 1564
Zacynthus (modern Zante), Greece
fields: Medicine, Physiology

Vesalius, a physician and anatomist of the Renaissance, was one of the most important figures in the history of medicine. He published the first modern comprehensive text of human anatomy. His accurate description of the structure of the human body, the result of firsthand dissection, is the basis of the modern scientific study of human anatomy.

Vesey, Denmark

b. 1767
d. July 2, 1822
Charleston, S.C.
fields: Historical Figure

African American slave insurrectionist; in 1800 Denmark Vesey purchased his own freedom after years of serving as a slave at sea; he then opened a successful carpenter's shop in Charleston, S.C.; wishing to liberate blacks who were still enslaved, he began to plan an uprising in 1818; his plan to attack city infrastructure and arsenals during the summer of 1822 was revealed by several black informants; Vesey and thirty-four others were hanged; as a result of the plot, black gatherings were subject to new restrictions.

Vespasian

né: Titus Flavius Vespanianus
b. 9 C.E.
Reate (modern Rieti, Italy)
d. June 23, 79 C.E.
Aquae Cutilae (modern Bagni di Paterno, Italy)
fields: Government and Politics

After the chaos and civil war which followed the downfall of Nero, Vespasian restored peace and order to the Roman Empire and secured its survival as an enduring political and cultural institution.

Vespucci, Amerigo

b. March 14, 1454
Florence
d. February 22, 1512
Seville, Spain
fields: Exploration and Colonization, Cartography

The first European credited with persuading his contemporaries that what Christopher Columbus had discovered was a "New World," Vespucci revolutionized geographic thinking when he argued that this region, now bearing his name, was a continent distinct from Asia.

Vial, Pedro

b. 1746
Lyons, France
d. 1814
Santa Fe, N.Mex.
fields: Exploration and Colonization

Pedro Vial, a Spanish explorer, cleric, and adventurer, was born in France. The first record of Vial in the New World appears in the Spanish Southwest about 1780. In 1792-1793, for the Spanish governor of Texas, he found the route between St. Louis and Santa Fe that became known as the Santa Fe Trail. Liked Indian life and lived with the Comanches for periods of time. Also lived and traded in Santa Fe and, for Spain, explored Missouri River.

Vico, Giambattista

b. June 23, 1668
Naples
d. January 23, 1744
Naples
fields: Philosophy, Historiography

Vico founded the philosophical study of history and elaborated the theoretical basis for sociological study.

Victoria, Queen

né: Alexandrina Victoria
b. May 24, 1819
Kensington Palace, London, England
d. January 22, 1901
Osborne House, Osborne, England
fields: Government and Politics, Monarchy

While striving to assert a greater role for the sovereign in British constitutional government, Queen Victoria accepted a gradually diminishing role. Her personal moral force lent such prestige to the Crown, however, that she made it possible for her successors to play a creative part in the continuity of government.

Victorio

aka: Bidu-ya
aka: Beduiat
aka: Lucero
b. c. 1825
present-day southwestern N.Mex.
d. Oct. 16, 1880
Tres Castillos, Mexico
fields: Warfare and Conquest, Native American Affairs

Mimbreño Apache leader. Victorio led his band in raids against U.S. and Mexican forces; his death and the destruction of his band marked the midpoint of the Apache Wars.

Viereck, George Sylvester

b. December 31, 1884
Munich, Germany
d. March 18, 1962
Holyoke, Massachusetts
fields: Journalism

A German immigrant to the United States, George Sylvester Viereck became a respected journalist. During World War I the German embassy employed him to organize anti-British and pro-German propaganda. During the 1920's Viereck wrote for the Hearst newspapers. During the following decade he enthusiastically supported Adolf Hitler; however, he refused to write anti-Semitic or anti-American propaganda. In 1943 he was convicted for violating the Foreign Agents Registration Act and served four years in prison. His writings include several books: *Confessions of a Barbarian* (1910), *My First Two Thousand Years: The Autobiography of the Wandering Jew* (1928), and *Men into Beasts* (1952).

Viète, François

aka: Franciscus Vieta
b. 1540
Fontenay-le-Comte, Poitou (now Vendée), France
d. Feb. 23, 1603
Paris, France
fields: Mathematics (algebra and trigonometry)

François Viète carried on the development of algebra begun by Italian mathematicians; added new techniques of solution of equations using trigonometry and a significant improvement in notation; attacked the Copernican theory in 1600; attacked the Gregorian calendar reforms in 1602.

Vigée-Lebrun, Élisabeth

né: Élisabeth Vigée
b. April 16, 1755
Paris, France
d. March 30, 1842
Paris, France
fields: Art

Vigée-Lebrun was one of the most celebrated artists of her time and is ranked with the best portraitists of the late eighteenth and early nineteenth centuries. By concentrating on the personalities of her sitters, she broke with the tradition of the empty ceremonial portrait.

Villa, José García

b. Aug. 5, 1914
Manila, Philippines
fields: Literature

José García Villa, a self-exile from the Philippines, was a renowned writer of short stories and poetry. In 1973, he was proclaimed National Artist, the first Filipino writer in English to receive the honor. He published the literary magazine *Clay* while a student at the University of New Mexico, from which he graduated in 1932. Villa's third volume of verse, *Have Come, Am Here* (1942), was praised as worthy of the Pulitzer Prize. He became associate editor of the avant-garde New Directions Publishing Corporation of New York and led numerous poetry workshops.

Villa, Pancho

aka: Francisco Villa
né: Doroteo Arango
b. June 5, 1878
Hacienda de Río Grande, San Juan del Río, Mexico
d. July 20, 1923
near Parral, Mexico
fields: Military Affairs

Villa played a central role in the Mexican Revolution as a rough, crude, and sometimes brilliant general from 1910 to 1920. Villa's exploits on and off the battlefield have broadened into legends that remain an integral part of Mexican history and folklore.

Villa-Lobos, Heitor

b. March 5, 1887
Rio de Janeiro, Brazil
d. November 17, 1959
Rio de Janeiro, Brazil
fields: Music

Villa-Lobos' compositions number more than two thousand in authentic Brazilian style, which he cultivated and popularized throughout the world. He has also been a champion of Brazilian folk melodies, traveling through all areas of Brazil in search of melodies and rhythms that he has published and used as bases for compositions.

Villagrá, Gaspar Pérez de

b. 1555
Puebla de Los Angeles, New Spain
d. 1620
fields: Historiography, Literature (poet)

Gaspar Pérez de Villagrá, the son of Spanish immigrants to New Spain, was part of Juan de Oñate's 1596 expedition to the northern region of New Spain (present-day New Mexico). Became a captain and the expedition's legal officer. Later, probably in Spain, Villagrá wrote the epic poem *Historia de la Nueva Mexico* (1610), telling of the experiences of the Oñate expedition. The poem was the first history of New Mexico to be published.

Villalongín, Carlos

b. ?
d. ?
fields: Theater and Entertainment (actor and director)

Carlos Villalongín, with his Mexican theatrical troop, fled the Mexican Revolution in 1910, moving north to San Antonio, Texas. The troop was called the Gran Compañía Lirico Dramatica de Carlos Villalongín and emphasized serious dramatic performances. To make ends meet during the Depression, the group toured other cites in Texas and the Southwest. Villalongín remained a presence in San Antonio theater into the 1950's.

Villalpando, Catalina Vasquez

b. Apr. 1, 1940
San Marcos, Tex.
fields: Government and Politics

Catalina Vasquez Villalpando became a senior vice president with Communications International, in charge of marketing and public relations in the Northeast. Entered government service in Reagan administration as an assistant liaison. Served in the Bush administration as U.S. treasurer from 1989 to 1993. (The treasurer oversees U.S. Mint operations, the Bureau of Engraving and Printing, and the U.S. Savings Bond Division.) In 1994, she was found guilty of evading more than $47,000 in federal taxes.

Villani, Giovanni

b. c. 1275
Florence, Italy
d. 1348
Florence, Italy
fields: Historiography

In his *Chronicle*, Villani conveys an empirical account of the Italian communes and lays the foundation for a historiography based on human will and action.

Villanueva, Danny

full: Daniel Villanueva
b. 1937
Tucumcari, N.Mex.
fields: Sports (football player), Television

Danny Villanueva, a punter and kicker, played in the National Football League from 1960 to 1967 for the Los Angeles Rams and the Dallas Cowboys. Became station manager (1969), eventually president of Spanish-language station KMEX-TV in Los Angeles. Organized the Spanish International Network-West (SIN-West).

Villanueva, Tino

b. Dec. 11, 1941
San Marcos, Tex.
fields: Literature (poet)

Poet Tino Villanueva earned his Ph.D. in Spanish from Boston University in 1981, and he went on to teach at Wellesley College for a number of years. Much of his poetry is concerned with Chicano cultural identity. Major collections include *Hay otra voz: Poems, 1968-1971* (1972), *Shaking Off the Dark* (1984), *Scene from the Movie Giant* (1993), and *Crónica de mis años peores* (1987; *Chronicle of My Worst Years*, 1994). Also edited the Chicano anthology *Chicanos: Antología histórica y literaria* (1980).

Villarreal, Andrea

b. ?
d. ?
fields: War and Conquest, Government and Politics

A figure in the 1910 Mexican Revolution. In the years immediately preceding the revolution, the Villarreal sisters, Andrea and Teresa, along with their father Próspero, led a campaign that attempted to secure release of Mexican revolutionaries imprisoned in the United States. In 1910 they published *La Mujer Moderna*, a militant newspaper, in San Antonio, Texas.

Villarreal, Antonio

b. 1875
Monterrey, Nuevo Leon, Mexico
fields: War and Conquest, Government and Politics

A leader in the 1910 Mexican Revolution. Antonio Villarreal joined Francisco Madero in his 1910 attempt to overthrow the Díaz government. An associate of Ricardo Flores Magón, an architect of the revolution. The Villarreals became advisers to revolutionary leaders such as Francisco Madero and Venustiano Carranza. Respected for his ability to plan and execute complicated military operations. Worked to end civil war; served as president pro tem of the 1914 constitutional convention.

Villarreal, Felicitás

b. 1875
Monterrey, Neuvo Leon, Mexico
d. 1917
Mexico City, Mexico
fields: War and Conquest, Government and Politics

A leader in the 1910 Mexican Revolution. Felicitás Villarreal was a financial expert in prerevolutionary Mexico. After 1910, the Villarreals became advisers to revolutionary leaders such as Francisco Madero and Venustiano Carranza. Felicitás was later a cabinet member and finance minister of the Military Convention of Aguascalientes.

Villarreal, José Antonio

b. July 30, 1924
Los Angeles, Calif.
fields: Literature (novelist)

Mexican American novelist José Antonio Villarreal moved to Mexico in the early 1970's and became a Mexican citizen; he later returned to U.S. to teach. Novels include *Pocho* (1959) and *The Fifth Horseman* (1974). *Pocho* depicts the dilemmas of a Mexican family living in the United States, highlighting questions of identity.

Villarreal, Leonardo

b. ?
d. ?
fields: War and Conquest, Government and Politics

A leader in the Mexican Revolution. Leonardo and his brother Marcelimo Villarreal led prorevolutionary groups in Arizona and Texas, as well as in Sonora, Mexico, between 1910 and 1920.

Villarreal, Marcelimo

b. ?
d. ?
fields: War and Conquest, Government and Politics

Marcelimo Villarreal was a leader in the Mexican Revolution. Marcelimo and his brother Leonardo Villarreal led prorevolutionary groups in Arizona and Texas, as well as in Sonora, Mexico, between 1910 and 1920.

Villarreal, Teresa

b. ?
d. ?
fields: War and Conquest, Government and Politics

A figure in the 1910 Mexican Revolution. In the years immediately preceding the revolution, the Villarreal sisters, Andrea and Teresa, along with their father Próspero, led a campaign that attempted to secure release of Mexican revolutionaries imprisoned in the United States. In 1910 they published *La Mujer Moderna*, a militant newspaper, in San Antonio, Texas. Teresa also founded *El Obrero*, a socialist publication that was widely read in the Latino community.

Villaseñor, Victor Edmundo

b. May 11, 1940
Carlsbad, Calif.
fields: Literature

Victor Edmundo Villaseñor's first novel was *Macho!* (1973), about conflict between two generations of Mexicans; it had the Mexican Revolution as a cultural backdrop. *Macho!* was one of the first Chicano novels to be published by a mainstream publisher. Other books include *Jury: The People versus Juan Corona* (1977, nonfiction) and *Rain of Gold* (1991). Villaseñor was raised near Riverside, California, in a Spanish-speaking home.

Villehardouin, Geoffroi de

b. c. 1150
near Bar-sur-Aube, France
d. c. 1213
possibly Greece
fields: Warfare and Conquest, Literature

After playing a significant role in the organization and conduct of the Fourth Crusade, Villehardouin wrote an original and valuable history of it.

Villiers, George. *See* Buckingham, First Duke of

Villon, François

né: François de Montcorbier et des Loges
b. 1431
Paris, France
d. 1463?
place unknown
fields: Literature

In his intensely personal, forthright verse, sordidly realistic yet devout, Villon was the greatest poet of medieval France.

Vimeur, Jean-Baptiste Donatien de. *See* Rochambeau, comte de

Vincent, Edward

b. June 23, 1934
Stubenville, Ohio
fields: Government and Politics

African American politician; Edward Vincent was elected mayor of Inglewood, California, in 1986.

Vincent, Marjorie

b. November 21, 1964
Chicago, Ill.
fields: Theater and Entertainment

Marjorie Vincent, an African American, was crowned Miss America in 1991.

Vincent de Paul, Saint

b. April 24, 1581
Pouy, France
d. September 27, 1660
Paris, France
fields: Education, Religion and Theology, Social Reform

Most renowned for his charitable and educational work, Saint Vincent de Paul founded the Congregation of the Mission, the Confraternities of Charity, and, with Saint Louise de Marillac, the Daughters of Charity. He also helped in the revival of French Catholicism, and the Roman Catholic church has named him the universal patron of its charitable institutions. Canonized in 1737.

Vincent of Beauvais

b. c. 1190
Beauvais, Oise, France
d. 1264
Beauvais, Oise, France
fields: Literature, Historiography

Vincent compiled the most comprehensive encyclopedia of the Middle Ages, encompassing natural science, history, theology, philosophy, and the liberal and mechanical arts.

Vincent of Lérins, Saint

b. Late fourth century
probably in or near Toul
d. c. 450
Lérins, Marseilles, or Troyes
fields: Religion and Theology

In his own time, Vincent was one of the leaders in the Gallic opposition to the concept of Augustinian predestination. After his death, Vincent came to be known primarily for his formula for distinguishing orthodoxy from heresy.

Vinson, Fred M.

b. January 22, 1890
Louisa, Ky.
d. September 8, 1953
Washington, D.C.
fields: Law

Chief justice of the United States, 1946-1953. Fred M. Vinson was appointed by President Harry S Truman to heal deep divisions within the Supreme Court. He has been criticized as being one of the weakest leaders in the Court's history. Believed that overwork had contributed to some justices' early deaths and succeeded in reducing the Court's increasingly heavy workload.

Viramontes, Helena María

b. Feb. 26, 1954
East Los Angeles, Calif.
fields: Literature (short-story writer)

Chicana writer Helena María Viramontes grew up in East Lost Angeles. The stories in her 1985 collection *The Moths and Other Stories* show her political and sociological awareness as well as her flair for experimentation in narrative. Coedited *Chicana Creativity and Criticism: Charting New Frontiers in American Literature* (1988).

Virchow, Rudolf

full: Rudolf Ludwig karl Virchow
b. October 13, 1821
Schivelbein, Pomerania
d. September 5, 1902
Berlin, Germany
fields: Medicine, Government and Politics, Anthropology

Virchow received worldwide recognition for his contribution to medical science, anthropology, archaeology, and public health. His greatest contribution to medical science was in establishing the principles of cellular pathology.

Virgin Mary

b. 22 B.C.E.
unknown
d. unknown
probably Israel, perhaps Ephesus
fields: Biblical Figures, Religion and Theology

Though little is known about the historical Mary, the virgin mother of Jesus Christ has been revered throughout the ages.

Visconti, Luchino

aka: Don Luchino Visconti, count of Modrone
b. November 2, 1906
Milan, Italy
d. March 17, 1976
Rome, Italy
fields: Film, Theater and Entertainment

Visconti helped create the neorealist movement in Italian cinema, by which Italians came to grips with the post-World War II world.

Vitoria, Francisco de

b. c. 1483
Vitoria, Álava, Spain
d. August 12, 1546
Salamanca, Spain
fields: Philosophy, Religion and Theology, Law

Vitoria was a Spanish theologian and pioneer in the field of international law. He is principally associated with his idea that the nations of the world constitute a community based on natural law.

Vitry, Philippe de

b. October 31, 1291
Vitry, Champagne, France
d. June 9, 1361
Meaux, France
fields: Music, Literature

De Vitry, whose reputation as a musician and poet was well known among his contemporaries, is remembered as the author of the treatise *Ars nova*. De Vitry proposed a solution to notational problems that was ultimately adopted in France and Italy in the fourteenth century.

Vivaldi, Antonio

full: Antonio Lucio Vivaldi
b. March 4, 1678
Venice
d. July 28, 1741
Vienna, Austria
fields: Music

As the most influential and original Italian composer of the early eighteenth century, Vivaldi developed the basic form of the Baroque concerto and made it the standard for instrumental music throughout much of Europe. He was a pioneer of program music, and his techniques of orchestration and lyrical violin style anticipated the Romanticism of the nineteenth century.

Vivekananda

né: Narendranath Datta
aka: Narendranath Dutt
aka: Swami Vivekananda
b. Jan. 12, 1863
Calcutta, West Bengal, India
d. July 4, 1902
Calcutta, West Bengal, India
fields: Religion and Theology, Philosophy

Vivekananda, Ramakrishna's disciple and successor, spent his life spreading the teachings of his former master. He dedicated his life to social reform and urged the modernization of Indian tradition. He introduced Vedanta tenets to Americans and the British and started several Vedanta societies in the United States. The Vedanta Society of the City of New York, incorporated in 1898, is the oldest American branch of the Ramakrishna Mission, established a year earlier near Calcutta, India.

Vivó, Paquita

b. ?
San Juan, Puerto Rico
fields: Government and Politics

Paquita Vivó held a number of positions with government agencies and private organizations in Puerto Rico. A public affairs officer for the Organization of American States (1962-1980), member and officer of National Conference of Puerto Rican Women (1972-1989), president of ISLA (1980-1990), president of the Institute for Puerto Rican Affairs (beginning in 1988). Also served on the boards of directors of National Urban Coalition (1986-1991) and National Puerto Rican Coalition (1976-1979). Compiled *The Puerto Ricans: An Annotated Bibliography* (1973).

Vizenor, Gerald R.

full: Gerald Robert Vizenor
b. Oct. 22, 1934
Minneapolis, Minn.
fields: Literature, Education

A White Earth Chippewa (Ojibwa) writer and professor, Gerald Vizenor is known for his provocative and theoretically sophisticated works of fiction, nonfiction, and poetry. Vizenor has published numerous volumes of poetry; his novels include the autobiographical *Darkness in Saint Louis Bearheart* (1978, revised as *Bearheart: The Heirship Chronicles*, 1990) and *Griever: An American Monkey King in China* (1987). The novel *Dead Voices: Natural Agonies in the New World* (1992) draws on traditions of oral narrative to look at the trickster figure of Native American myth in the context of contemporary society. Works of nonfiction include an edited volume of literary criticism, *Narrative Chance: Postmodern Discourse on American Indian Literatures* (1989).

Vladimir I

full: Saint Vladimir I, Grand Prince of Kiev
b. 955?
Kiev (in modern Ukraine)
d. July 15, 1015
Berestova, near Kiev
fields: Government and Politics, Warfare and Conquest, Religion and Theology

Vladimir expanded the territorial base of Kiev, the first Russian state, to unite the East Slavs and Finno-Baltic peoples into a large nation. He linked the cultural fortunes of the Rus with the Byzantine world by his conversion of the East Slavs to Orthodox Christianity in 988.

Vo Nguyen Giap

b. 1911 or 1912
An Xa, Vietnam, French Indochina
fields: Military Affairs, Government and Politics

As chief Vietnamese Communist military strategist and expert guerrilla warfare tactician, Giap was architect of the Viet Minh victory over the French in 1954 (which ended French colonialism in Southeast Asia). Afterward he officially served as North Vietnam's defense minister and directed the military campaigns of the 1960's and 1970's that led to final victory over U.S. and South Vietnamese forces in 1975.

Voit, Carl von

b. Oct. 31, 1831
Amberg, Bavaria (now Germany)
d. Jan. 31, 1908
Munich, Germany
fields: Biology, Physiology

Carl von Voit used experimental methodology and equipment to study the metabolism of different types of food; explained how the body derives energy from proteins, carbohydrates, and fats.

Volta, Alessandro

full: Alessandro Giuseppe Antonio Anastasio Volta
b. February 18, 1745
Como, Duchy of Milan
d. March 5, 1827
Como, Duchy of Milan
fields: Physics, Chemistry

Volta contributed to the development of concepts and techniques in electrostatics, including the inventions of the electrophorus and the condensing electrometer. His most important contributions were the discovery of contact electricity and the invention of the electric battery.

Voltaire

né: François-Marie Arouet
aka: François-Marie Arouet de Voltaire
b. November 21, 1694
Paris, France
d. May 30, 1778
Paris, France
fields: Literature, Philosophy

Voltaire encompasses in his work the extremes of rationalism during the Enlightenment. Until he was middle-aged, he was an optimist, but in his sixties, he rejected this philosophy in disgust and brilliantly argued the limitations of reason. He wrote prolifically in all literary forms during his lifetime, making critical commentary on prevailing social conditions and conventions.

Volterra, Vito

b. May 3, 1860
Ancona, Papal States (now Italy)
d. Oct. 11, 1940
Rome, Italy
fields: Mathematics (applied math and calculus)

Vito Volterra formulated the idea of functionals in differential calculus; made important contributions to integral calculus; applied his integro-differential equations to the study of elastics.

von Braun, Wernher. *See* Braun, Wernher von

von Neumann, John

aka: Johnny von Newmann
b. December 28, 1903
Budapest, Hungary
d. February 8, 1957
Washington, D.C.
fields: Mathematics, Physics (mathematical), Computer Science

A brilliant mathematician who laid the mathematical foundations of modern physics and computer science, von Neumann affirmed the importance of autonomous scientific research during the anti-Communist McCarthy era.

Vonnegut, Kurt

né Kurt Vonnegut, Jr.
b. November 11, 1922
Indianapolis, Indiana
fields: Literature

Kurt Vonnegut grew up in the Midwest, where his family suffered severe emotional and financial setbacks during the Depression years. He began college in 1940, ordered by his father to study science, for career job security. In 1943 Vonnegut joined the army. Less a year later he was captured by the Germans and was being held in Dresden at the moment the Allies firebombed the city in 1945. After the war, Vonnegut became a publicist with General Electric. Meanwhile, he began writing what would told more than a dozen novels, numerous essays, a Broadway play, and a musical work. His novels include *Player Piano* (1952), *The Sirens of Titan* (1959), *Mother Night* (1961), *Cat's Cradle* (1963), *God Bless You, Mr. Rosewater* (1965), *Slaughterhouse-Five* (1969), *Breakfast of Champions* (1973), *Slapstick* (1976), *Jailbird* (1979), *Deadeye Dick* (1982), *Galapagos* (1985), *Bluebeard* (1987), *Hocus Pocus* (1990), and *Timequake* (1997).

Voorhees, Donald

b. July 30, 1916
Leavenworth, Kans.
d. July 7, 1989
Seattle, Wash.
fields: Law

Federal judge Donald Voorhees, a graduate of Harvard Law School, was appointed by President Richard M. Nixon. He presided in the 1988 *coram nobis* rehearing of the Gordon Hirabayashi wartime internment and curfew case of 1943, ruling in favor of Hirabayashi. In another case, Voorhees ordered a forced busing plan to achieve racial balance in the Seattle school system.

Voznesensky, Andrey Andreyevich

b. May 12, 1933
Moscow, Soviet Union
fields: Literature

Poet Andrey Andreyevich Voznesensky first appeared on the Soviet literary scene in 1958 and quickly became known as one of the "angry young men" of Russian letters. He excited listeners with poems of rebellion and hope for renewal. Meanwhile, he was kept under police surveillance and was officially reprimanded for his politics. However, he couched his poems in such obscure metaphors and allusions that authorities found it difficult to charge him with treason. Voznesensky was instrumental in the struggle for democracy in the late 1980's and early 1990's.

Vreeland, Diana

né: Diana Dalziel
b. c. 1903
Paris, France
d. August 22, 1989
New York, New York
fields: Fashion

As fashion editor at *Harper's Bazaar* and editor-in-chief at *Vogue*, Vreeland directed America's fashion sensibility; as special consultant to the Metropolitan Museum's Costume Institute, she arranged enormously popular exhibits.

Vries, Hugo de

full: Hugo Marie de Vries
b. Feb. 16, 1848
Haarlem, the Netherlands
d. May 21, 1935
Lunteren, the Netherlands
fields: Botany, Genetics

Hugo de Vries was responsible for rediscovering Gregor Johann Mendel's laws of heredity and advancing the idea that mutations are the chief source of genetic variation and the major method by which new species formed.

Vuillard, Édouard

full: Jean-Édouard Vuillard
b. November 11, 1868
Cuiseaux, France
d. June 21, 1940
La Baule, France
fields: Art

Vuillard's wide experience in graphic art for the theater taught him to paint large-scale decorations, and, through his experiments with the formal elements of painting, he helped the Nabis school of painting to fulfill its primary ambition: to gain acceptance for decorative paintings.

Waals, Johannes Diderik van der

b. Nov. 23, 1837
Leiden, the Netherlands
d. Mar. 8, 1923
Amsterdam, the Netherlands
fields: Physics

Johannes Diderik van der Waals studied the states of matter and the intermolecular forces affecting their behavior; received the Nobel Prize in Physics in 1910.

Waban

b. c. 1604
present-day Concord, Mass.
d. c. 1677
present-day Newton, Mass.
fields: Government and Politics

Waban, a Nipmuck Indian, adapted his tribal leadership capabilities to serve as town clerk and justice of the peace in the earliest of the Massachusetts missionary John Eliot's "praying towns," Natick. The town prospered from circa 1650 until difficulties caused by the outbreak of King Philip's War in 1675.

Wabanaquot. *See* White Cloud

Wach, Joachim

b. January 25, 1898
Chemnitz, Germany
d. August 27, 1955
Orselina, Switzerland
fields: Religion and Theology

Wach distilled the descriptive requirements for a scientific definition of religious experience from his general theory of knowledge and understanding. He created the modern academic field of the history of religions out of and in contrast to preceding notions of comparative religion.

Waddles, Mother

né: Charleszetta Lina
full: Mrs. Payton Waddles
b. October 7, 1913
St. Louis, Mo.
fields: Social Reform

African American mission director and charity leader; Mother Waddles, called "Detroit's Black Angel" in recognition of her charity work in that city, served as mission director and founder of the nonprofit, nondenominational, charitable organization "Waddles' Perpetual Mission for Saving Souls of All Nations, Inc.," which began operation in 1956.

Waddy, Joseph C.

b. 1911
Louisa, Va.
fields: Law

African American judge; Joseph C. Waddy became a judge on the U.S. District Court for the District of Columbia (1967).

Wade, Arthur Sarsfield. *See* Rohmer, Sax

Wagner, Mary Kathlyn. *See* Ash, Mary Kay

Wagner, Richard

b. May 22, 1813
Leipzig, Saxony
d. February 13, 1883
Venice, Italy
fields: Music, Theater and Entertainment

Wagner wrote the librettos and scores of some of the world's greatest operas, most notably *Tristan und Isolde* (1859) and the tetralogy *Der Ring des Nibelungen* (1874; the ring of the Nibelungs). A conductor, musical director, and writer as well as a composer, he raised standards for musical performances and developed the aesthetic of the *Gesamtkunstwerk* (total work of art), using compositional techniques based on chromaticism, variable meter, the leitmotif (a musical phrase with dramatic import), and an "infinite melody" of continuous expressiveness and significance.

Wahiev. *See* Dull Knife

Wahunsenacawh. *See* Powhatan

Waihee, John David, III

b. May 19, 1946
Honokaa, Hawaii
fields: Government and Politics

Native Hawaiian John David Waihee III worked with school districts in Michigan from 1968 to 1971, then returned to Hawaii to work with the planners and directors of the Honolulu Model Cities Program. He became senior planner for the city and county of Honolulu, then program manager for the city's Office of Human Resources. He received a law degree in 1976 from the University of Hawaii and became a partner in his own firm in 1979. The next year, Democrat Waihee was elected to the Hawaiian House of Representatives, and in 1982, he was elected as the state's lieutenant governor. He was elected governor in 1986, the first governor of native Hawaiian descent., and reelected in 1992. After his term ended in 1994, he went on to head a law firm in Hawaii.

Waipshwa. *See* Smohalla

Wairasuap. *See* Bear Hunter

Waite, Morrison Remick

b. November 29, 1816
Lyme, Conn.
d. March 23, 1888
Washington, D.C.
fields: Law

Chief justice of the United States, 1874-1888. Assuming leadership of the Supreme Court in the wake of the *Scott v. Sandford* debacle of 1857 (the Dred Scott decision) and the political maneuverings of his predecessor, Salmon P. Chase, Waite restored a measure of authority to the judicial branch of government.

Wakabayashi, Ron

b. Nov. 13, 1944
Reno, Nev.
fields: Government and Politics

Administrator and activist Ron Wakabayashi served as executive director of the Los Angeles City Human Relations Commission. Earlier posts include a stint as the national director of the Japanese American Citizens League and a key position with the United Way.

Wakatsuki, Jeanne Toyo. *See* Houston, Jeanne Wakatsuki

Wake, Lloyd

b. Jan. 12, 1922
Reedley, Calif.
fields: Religion and Theology

Lloyd Wake, who was interned at Poston, Arizona, during World War II, became the first Asian American pastor (1967-1989) to serve at Glide Memorial United Methodist Church in San Francisco, California. He was a board member of the Bay Area Asian American Service Committee (1976-1978), the Asian Law Caucus (beginning in 1976), and the Ohana Cultural Center of Oakland, California (1985-1987). Wake was a member of the Asian American United Methodist goodwill team to South Korea (1974) and Taiwan (1980).

Wakefield, Edward Gibbon

b. March 20, 1796
London, England
d. May 16, 1862
Wellington, New Zealand
fields: Government and Politics, Social Reform

An enthusiastic champion of the British Empire and colonization during the early Victorian decades, when such enthusiasm was out of general favor in many circles in and out of Parliament, Wakefield promoted emigration and anticipated notions of self-government that had significance for the development of the later British Commonwealth.

Waksman, Selman Abraham

b. July 22, 1888
Priluka, Russia
d. August 16, 1973
Hyannis, Massachusetts
fields: Medicine, Biology (microbiology)

Waksman's painstaking research into the nature of soil microorganisms, culminating in the discovery of streptomycin, helped to bring about the antibiotic age. He was awarded the 1952 Nobel Prize in Physiology or Medicine.

Wakukawa, Seiei

b. Aug. 18, 1947
Okinawa, Japan
fields: Journalism

Seiei Wakukawa, former editor of the *Hawaii Times*, was executive director of the Okinawa Relief and Rehabilitation Foundation. He wrote a book about Toyama Kyuzo, a pioneer Okinawan who emigrated to Hawaii, and taught the Japanese language at the University of Chicago.

Walcott, Jersey Joe

né: Arnold Raymond Cream
b. January 31, 1914
Merchantville, New Jersey
d. February 25, 1994
Camden, New Jersey
fields: Sports (boxer)

African American boxer; Jersey Joe Walcott won the heavyweight championship in 1951, defeating Ezzard Charles.

Walcott, Louis Eugene. *See* Farrakhan, Louis

Wald, Lillian D.

b. March 10, 1867
Cincinnati, Ohio
d. September 1, 1940
Westport, Connecticut
fields: Nursing, Social Reform

Founder of the Henry Street Settlement and organizer of the first public health nursing system, Wald was a major social reformer during the Progressive Era.

Waldemar II. *See* Valdemar II

Waldheim, Kurt

full: Kurt Josef Waldheim
b. December 21, 1918
Sankt Andrä-Wördern, Austria
fields: Diplomacy

Austrian diplomat Kurt Waldheim was secretary-general of the United Nations from 1972 to 1982. He had previously served the United Nations in various capacities. Elected to the Austrian presidency in 1986. Campaign and succeeding governance were seriously marred, however, by an international examination into his military past. Allegations and some documentation surfaced that Waldheim had facilitated criminal warfare for the Nazi regime. There were public calls for his prosecution; Waldheim repeatedly stated his innocence throughout. He lost his bid for reelection in 1992.

Waldon, Alton Ronald, Jr.

b. December 31, 1936
Lakeland, Fla.
fields: Government and Politics

African American U.S. representative from New York. Alton Ronald Waldon served in the New York state assemly between 1982 and 1986; elected to fill Congressional seat of Joseph Addabbo, who died in 1986; elected to state Senate in 1991.

Wałęsa, Lech

full: Lech Michal Wałęsa
b. September 29, 1943
Popowo, Poland
fields: Labor Movement, Government and Politics

Lech Wałęsa's receipt of the Nobel Peace Prize in 1983 underlined his contributions to peaceful political evolution in the Eastern Bloc. Wałęsa's role since 1980 as leader of Solidarnost (Solidarity) in pressuring the Polish leadership for recognition of proletariat demands that were not addressed by the country's government-controlled trade unions was capped by the Polish authorities in 1989 with the holding of free elections and the subsequent victory of the Solidarity-led ticket.

Walker, Alice

b. February 9, 1944
Eatonton, Georgia
fields: Literature

Walker, winner of the Pulitzer Prize and the American Book Award, has dedicated her life to establishing a literary canon of African American women writers and to encouraging the "survival whole" of all women. She has actively sought to win recognition for literary "foremothers" such as Zora Neale Hurston and to place their contributions within the fabric of her own artistry.

Walker, Chet

full: Chester Walker
b. February 22, 1940
Benton Harbor, Mich.
fields: Sports (basketball player)

African American basketball player; Chet Walker was known as a well-rounded player who reached the play-offs in each of his thirteen seasons as a professional; part of the Philadelphia 76ers front court trio that included Luke Jackson and Wilt Chamberlain and won the 1966-1967 championship.

Walker, David

b. September 28, 1785
Wilmington, North Carolina
b. June 28, 1830
Boston, Massachusetts
fields: Civil Rights, Social Reform

Walker wrote one of the most powerful condemnations of slavery ever published in U.S. history; it was violently opposed by Southern slave states, and Walker himself died mysteriously. *Appeal to the Colored People of the World* (1829) urged slaves to armed revolt. It was widely distributed and had great influence on African American social and political thought in the North and the South.

Walker, George

b. 1873
Lawrence, Kans.
d. 1911
Lawrence, Kans.
fields: Theater and Entertainment (singer and comedian)

African American singer and comedian; George Walker teamed with Bert Williams to form a popular act in the late 1890's; brought into vogue the cakewalk; coproduced musical plays *In Dahomey* (1903), the first African American production ever to open on Broadway, *Abyssinia* (1906), and *Bandanna Land* (1908).

Walker, Herschel

b. March 3, 1962
Wrightsville, Ga.
fields: Sports (football player)

African American football player; Herschel Walker won the 1982 Heisman Trophy and set ten NCAA records before joining the United States Football League's New Jersey Generals; played with the National Football League's Dallas Cowboys and Minnesota Vikings, leading the league in rushing in 1988.

Walker, Jimmie

full: James Carter Walker
b. June 25, 1948
New York, N.Y.
fields: Television

African American comedian and actor; Jimmie Walker was cast in the role of J. J. Evans on the CBS television series *Good Times*; also well known as a stand-up comedian.

Walker, Kurt. *See* Blow, Kurtis

Walker, Madam C. J.

né: Sarah Breedlove

full: Sarah Breedlove McWilliams Walker
b. December 23, 1867
Delta, Louisiana
d. May 25, 1919
Irvington-on-Hudson, New York
fields: Business and Industry

Vastly successful as a self-made entrepreneur, Walker provided African American women with effective hair-care techniques and products as well as less arduous, higher paying employment as Walker Agents. She also made sizeable contributions to African American charities and educational institutions, supported African American architects, artists, and literary figures, and spoke out against injustices suffered by her people.

Walker, Maggie Lena Draper

b. July 15, 1867
Richmond, Va.
d. December 15, 1934
Richmond, Va.
fields: Business and Industry

African American banker and organizer; the first woman bank president, Maggie Lena Draper Walker founded the Saint Luke Penny Savings Bank in 1903 and reorganized it in 1934 as the Consolidated Bank and Trust Company.

Walker, Margaret Abigail

b. July 7, 1915
Birmingham, Alabama
d. November 30, 1998
Chicago, Illinois
fields: Literature

African American author and educator; Margaret Abigail Walker etablished a reputation as a poet in 1942 with *For My People*; published the novel *Jubilee* (1966).

Walker, Moses Fleetwood

b. October 7, 1857
Mt. Pleasant, Ohio
d. May 11, 1924
Cleveland, Ohio
fields: Sports (baseball)

First African American to play major league baseball, Moses Fleetwood Walker played with the Toledo Blue Stockings of the American Association in 1884.

Walker, T-Bone

full: Aaron Thibeaux Walker
b. May 28, 1910
Linden, Tex.
d. March 16, 1975
Los Angeles, Calif.
fields: Music (blues singer and guitarist)

African American blues singer and guitarist; T-Bone Walker is credited with being the first blues guitarist to use electric amplification; a powerful influence on later blues and rock and roll artists, toured widely and recorded between the 1930's and 1970's.

Wallace, C. Everett

b. August 16, 1951
Chicago, Ill.
fields: Government and Politics

African American attorney and political appointee; C. Everett Wallace became cofounder and vice chairman of the Black Republican Congressional Staffers Association and served as counsel secretary of the 1980 Republican National Convention; appointed by Ronald Reagan as deputy assistant secretary of Fair Housing for the Department of Housing and Urban Development.

Wallace, George

b. ?
Atlanta, Georgia
fields: Theater and Entertainment

African American comedian; George Wallace was a popular comic on late night television talk shows and on the nightclub circuit during the 1980's.

Wallace, George C.

full: George Corley Wallace
b. August 25, 1919
Clio, Alabama
d. September 13, 1998
Montgomery, Alabama
fields: Government and Politics

A four-time governor of Alabama and twice a candidate for the presidency, Wallace during the 1960's became a leading spokesman for continued segregation and southern conservativism.

Wallace, Henry A.

full: Henry Agard Wallace
b. October 7, 1888
Adair County, Iowa
d. November 18, 1965
Danbury, Connecticut
fields: Government and Politics, Journalism

Wallace was an outspoken critic of post-World War II American foreign policy. He was also one of the principal architects of American farm policy and an eloquent spokesman for some of the most important ideas of twentieth century American liberalism.

Wallace, Michele

b. January 4, 1952
New York, N.Y.
fields: Journalism

African American journalist, cultural critic, and feminist; Michele Wallace's most influential work, *Black Macho and the Myth of the Superwoman* (1979), explored the double injustice of racism and sexism faced by black women.

Wallace, Ruby Ann. *See* Dee, Ruby

Wallace, Sippie

full: Beulah Wallace
b. November 11, 1898
Houston, Tex.
d. November 1, 1986
Detroit, Mich.
fields: Music (blues singer and musician)

African American blues singer and musician; Sippie Wallace is most remembered as a blues singer with strong ties to gospel music, having served as director of the National Convention of Gospel Choirs and Choruses for most of the 1930's.

Wallace, William

aka: Sir William Wallace
b. c. 1272/1273, Ellerslie (now Elderslie), Ayrshire, Scotland
d. August 23, 1305
London, England
fields: Military Affairs

With a combination of valor, ferocity, and tenacity, Sir William Wallace galvanized the Scottish will to rise against English invaders and thus sparked the Scots' determination to be an independent nation once again.

Wallach, Meier Moiseevich. *See* Litvinov, Maksim Maksimovich

Wallenstein, Albrecht Wenzel von

b. September 24, 1583
Heřmanice, Bohemia
d. February 25, 1634
Eger, Bohemia
fields: Military Affairs, Government and Politics

A master of recruiting and logistics, Wallenstein raised and commanded the armies that saved the Catholic Habsburgs from losing the Thirty Years' War to their Protestant opponents. He was able to amass great wealth and power and may even have aspired to an independent crown of his own.

Waller, Calvin Augustine Hoffman

b. December 17, 1937
Baton Rouge, La.
fields: Military Affairs

African American military officer; Calvin Augustine Hoffman Waller retired from the United States Army on November 30, 1991, with the rank of lieutenant general.

Waller, Fats

full: Thomas Wright Waller
b. May 21, 1904
Waverley, N.Y.

d. December 15, 1937
Kansas City, Mo.
fields: Music (stride composer and pianist)

African American composer and pianist; Fats Waller was a legendary performer of New York stride piano; known for such solo recordings of his own works as "Handful of Keys" (1929), Waller recorded for Okeh during the 1920's; coauthored, with Andy Razaf, the music for *Keep Shufflin'* (1928) and *Hot Chocolates* (1929), both of which were Broadway productions; in the 1930's, recorded with Les Hite's band and his own Fats Waller and His Rhythm; appeared in a number of Hollywood films, including *Stormy Weather* (1943) with Lena Horne.

Wallis, John

b. Nov. 23, 1616
Ashford at Kent, England
d. Nov. 8, 1703
Oxford, England
fields: Mathematics (algebra, calculus, and geometry)

John Wallis expressed the principal geometric results of the ancient Greeks as algebraic results; made significant contributions to finding areas bounded by plane curves; became a founding member of the Royal Society of London in 1662.

Walls, Josiah Thomas

b. December 30, 1842
Winchester, Virginai
d. May 15, 1905
Tallahassee, Flordia
fields: Government and Politics

African American politician; Josiah Thomas Walls was the first African American U.S. representative from Florida; he served in the Forty-second through Forty-fourth Congresses (1871-1875); served in the Florida assembly (1868) and state senate (1868, 1876).

Walpole, Robert

aka: Sir Robert Walpole
b. August 26, 1676
Houghton Hall, Norfolk, England
d. March 18, 1745
London, England
fields: Government and Politics

As chief minister of England from 1722 to 1742, Walpole gave his country the longest period of peace and political stability in the eighteenth century. He also raised the status of the House of Commons to that of principal partner in government.

Walras, Léon

full: Marie-Esprit-Léon Walras
b. December 16, 1834
Évreux, France
d. January 5, 1910
Clarens, near Montreux, Switzerland
fields: Economics

Walras, along with Herman Heinrich Gossen, William Stanley Jevons, and Carl von Menger, discovered the concept of marginal utility. His long-term influence rests on his system of general equilibrium; which was a far more comprehensive analysis of value and price, demand and supply than any postulated up to his time. Many economists, however, believe that his pioneering use of mathematics in economic theory is his most lasting contribution to the science.

Walrond, Eric

b. 1898
Georgetown, British Guiana
d. 1966
London, England
fields: Literature

African American author; Eric Walrond was one of the most important figures associated with the Harlem Renaissance; wrote as a journalist for the National Urban League's publication, *Opportunity*; published his collection of ten stories, *Tropic Death*, in 1926.

Walsh, Richard J.

b. Nov. 20, 1886
Lyons, Kans.
d. May 28, 1960
near Doylestown, Pa.
fields: Publishing, Social Reform

Richard J. Walsh, a Harvard graduate, served consecutively as editor for *Collier's Weekly, Judge, Asia Magazine*, and *United Nations World* from 1917 to 1949. In 1930, Walsh's publishing firm, John Day, printed Pearl S. Buck's first book, *East Wind: West Wind*. Walsh and Buck married and spent much time promoting understanding of Asian and advocating racial equality. They fought to repeal the Chinese Exclusion Act of 1882. In 1949, Buck and Walsh founded Welcome House in Bucks County, Pennsylvania, to care for and find foster homes for children of mixed blood who has been abandoned by their parents. The institution placed many unwanted children fathered by U.S. servicemen in countries such as Japan and Korea.

Walter, John, II

b. February 23, 1776
London, England
d. July 28, 1847
London, England
fields: Publishing, Journalism

The son of John Walter I, founder of *The Times* of London, John Walter II fought to establish some of the principles and practices that are fundamental to modern journalism, above all the freedom to report and interpret the news independent of financial sponsorship or government pressure. Under his leadership, *The Times* became the leading newspaper of Europe and created a body of informed public opinion that had the power to move government.

Walters, Alexander

b. August 1, 1858
Bardstown, Ky.
d. February 2, 1917
New York, N.Y.
fields: Civil Rights

Alexander Walters was appointed pastor of a newly organized African Methodist Episcopal Zion church in Indianapolis after his ordination in 1877. He eventually became pastor at the historic Mother Zion Church in New York, N.Y., and in 1892 he was elected bishop of the Seventh District by the General Conference of the AMEZ church. Walters asked African American publisher Thomas T. Fortune to call a meeting of black leaders, which resulted in the formation of the National Afro-American Council was formed in Rochester, N.Y., with Walters as president. He was elected president seven times. He also was elected president of the Pan-African Association at the 1990 Pan-African Congress. His autobiography, *My Life and Work*, was published in 1917.

Walters, Barbara

full: Barbara Jill Walters
b. September 25, 1931
Boston; Massachusetts
fields: Journalism

As the first female cohost of the *Today Show* and the first female network news anchor, Walters broke ground for women in the top echelons of network news.

Walters, Madge. *See* Sinclair, Madge

Walters, Ricky

aka: Slick Rick Walters
b. January 14, 1965
London, England
fields: Music (rap vocalist)

African American rap vocalist; Ricky Walters an early rap act to be managed by Russell Simmons, who signed him as Slick Rick to his Def Jam rap label; appeared on Doug E. Fresh's hit "The Show"; released a compilation of singles as *The Great Adventures of Slick Rick* (1988); convicted of attempted murder in the early 1990's.

Walters, Ronald

b. July 20, 1938
Wichita, Kans.
fields: Education

African American educator, writer, and activist; Ronald Walters taught at Syracuse and Brandeis universities prior to joining the political science department at Howard University; served as senior foreign affairs consultant for Congressman Charles Diggs (1976) and for Congressman William Gray (1977-1979); was deputy campaign manager for issues for Jesse Jackson's 1984 presidential campaign and consultant for platform and convention operations for the 1988 campaign; authored four research monographs on the subjects of African affairs and American black politics and several books, including *South Africa and the Bomb: Responsibility and Deterrence* (1987), *Black Presidential Politics in America* (1988), and *Jesse Jackson's 1984 Presidential Campaign: Challenge and Change in American Politics* (1989, with Lucius Barker).

Walther von der Vogelweide

b. c. 1170
probably lower Austria
d. c. 1230
near Würzburg, Bavaria
fields: Literature

Walther von der Vogelweide was the greatest lyric poet of the German High Middle Ages; his writings set high standards of artistic quality in the genre of the courtly love lyric as well as that of political poetry.

Walton, Cora. *See* Taylor, Koko

Walton, William

full: William Turner Walton
aka: Sir William Walton
b. March 29, 1902
Oldham, Lancashire, England
d. March 8, 1983
Ischia, Italy
fields: Music

In the field of concert music, Walton created a small but remarkably effective group of masterpieces, heard throughout the world in public performances and by means of recordings. A wider public has heard his church music, his stirring ceremonial music, and his scores for radio and film—the latter including Sir Laurence Olivier's *Hamlet*, *Henry V*, and *Richard III*.

Wang, An

b. February 7, 1920
Shanghai, China
d. March 24, 1990
Boston, Mass.
fields: Business and Industry, Invention and Technology

In 1945 An Wang came to the United States as one of hundreds of Chinese engineers selected to study American technology. In 1948 Wang helped develop magnetic core memory. He sold patent for his magnetic memory core device to International Business machines in 1956. In 1951 he founded Wang Laboratories. Wang pioneered the development of calculators in the 1960's, word processors in the 1970's, and minicomputers. Wang Industries became one of the largest computer companies in the world, and Wang was believed to be the fifth wealthiest man in the United States.

Wang Anshi

aka: Wang An-shih
b. 1021
Lin-chuan, China
d. 1086
Nanking, China
fields: Government and Politics

A writer and statesman during the Northern Song Dynasty, Wang Anshi introduced sweeping reforms in government, affecting particularly the state financial system and the bureaucracy.

Wang, Art

b. Feb. 4, 1949
Boston, Mass.
fields: Government and Politics

Art Wang, who received a J.D. degree from the University of Puget Sound's law school in Washington, was elected in 1981 to the Washington State House of Representatives. He served on a number of committees, including Revenue, Capital Facilities and Financing, and House Appropriations. Wang taught courses on legislation and state and local taxation at the University of Puget Sound.

Wang Bi

aka: Wang Pi
b. 226
possibly in modern Shandong Province, China
d. 249
China
fields: Philosophy

Wang was a major creative force behind the most important philosophical school of his day, and his commentaries on some of the most revered Chinese classics still help shape their interpretation.

Wang Ching-wei. *See* Wang Jingwei

Wang Chong

aka: Wang Ch'ung
b. 27
Shangyu, Kuaiji, China
d. c. 100
Shangyu, Kuaiji, China
fields: Philosophy

During the later Han Dynasty, apocryphal literature became popular, supplementing humanistic and rationalistic Confucianism and supporting the belief in portents and prophecies. Amid this change, Wang Chong became a rationalistic, naturalistic, and materialistic thinker; his philosophy subsequently contributed to clearing the atmosphere of superstition and occultism and to enhancing the spirit of skepticism, rationalism, and naturalism, which later bloomed in the form of Neo-Taoism during the Wei-Chin period.

Wang Hsi-chih. *See* Wang Xizhi

Wang Jingwei

aka: Wang Ching-wei
b. May 4, 1883
Canton, China
d. November 10, 1944
Nagoya, Japan
fields: Government and Politics

Wang, an early disciple of Sun Yat-sen and a founding member of the Tongmeng hui, was contender for leadership of the Kuomintang after Sun's death in 1925. He was initially identified with the left wing of the party, then became an anticommunist and favored appeasement of Japan as leader of the government between 1932 and 1936; in 1937, he defected to form a puppet government in Japanese-occupied China in 1940.

Wang, L. Ling-chi

b. 1938
Xiamen, Fujian, China
fields: Sociology, Historiography

L. Ling-chi Wang chaired the Department of Ethnic Studies and served as coordinator of Asian American Studies at the University of California, Berkeley. Wang's received two bachelor's degrees, one in music from Hope College and the other in Old Testament studies from Princeton Seminary, as well as a master's degree in Semitic studies from the University of California. He cofounded Chinese for Affirmative Action, a civil-rights group based in San Francisco. He wrote and spoke on Asian American history, civil rights, and educational issues affecting Asian Americans.

Wang Pi. *See* Wang Bi

Wang, Taylor Gunjin

b. June 16, 1940
Shanghai, China
fields: Science (physics)

Physicist Taylor Gunjin Wang invented the acoustic levitation and manipulation chamber and holds twenty other patents in his field. From 1972 to 1988, he served as a manager of the microgravity science and applications program at the Jet Propulsion Lab in Pasadena, California, and afterward served as director of the Center for Microgravity Research and Applications at Vanderbilt University in Nashville, Tennessee. Wang was a Space Shuttle astronaut-scientist for the National Aeronautics and Space Administration (NASA) from 1983 to 1985.

Wang, Wayne

b. January 12, 1949
Hong Kong
fields: Film

In 1993, Wayne Wang directed the critically and commercially successful film, *The Joy Luck Club*, based on the 1989 best-seller of the same title by Chinese American novelist Amy Tan. His first work on an American film was directin the Chinese sequences of *Golden Needles* (1974). In 1982 he shot *Chan Is Missing*—the first American feature film with a completely Asian American cast. His films, including *Dim Sum: A Little Bit of Heart* (1984) and *Eat a Bowl of Tea* (1989) generally depict Chinese Americans caught between competing cultures. The offbeat *Life Is Cheap . . . but Toilet Paper Is Expensive*, made in Hong Kong, appeared in 1990.

Wang Wei

b. 701
district of Qi, prefecture of Taiyuan, China
d. 761
Changan, prefecture of Jingzhao, China
fields: Literature, Art, Music, Government and Politics

A major Tang poet, Wang Wei left a body of some 370 poems that can be considered authentic; his nature poetry has been particularly admired, and it accounts for his preeminence in Chinese literature. He was credited with founding the Southern school of landscape painting. Wang Wei was also a highly skilled musician and an unusually competent government official.

Wang Xizhi

aka: Wang Hsi-chih
aka: Yi-shao
b. c. 307 C.E.
Langye, Linxi, Shandong Province, China
d. c. 379 C.E.
near Shanyin, Zhejiang Province, China
fields: Art

By refining the styles of earlier calligraphers and developing new ones, Wang Xizhi, through his innovative brushwork, set the aesthetic standards for all subsequent calligraphers in China, Korea, and Japan.

Wang Yangming

né: Shouren
aka: Boan
b. November 30, 1472
Youyao, Zhejiang, China
d. January 9, 1529
Nanen, Jiangxi, China
fields: Philosophy, Government and Politics

As a high official, holding many governmental offices from magistrate to governor, Wang suppressed rebellions and created a reign of peace in China that lasted a century. As a Neo-Confucian philosopher, he exercised tremendous influence in both China and Japan for 150 years.

Wanig Suchka. *See* Red Bird

Wankel, Felix

b. August 13, 1902
Lahr, Germany
d. October 9, 1988
Lindau, West Germany
fields: Invention and Technology

As early as 1924, Wankel began to sketch models for rotary piston engines; in 1929, he obtained his first patent for an engine that has a reciprocating piston housed in a horizontal cylinder, the earliest Wankel engine, that has since been perfected to the point that it can power automobiles and other motorized vehicles.

Wapasha

b. c. 1718
present-day Minnesota
d. ?
fields: Government and Politics, Native American Affairs

Several prominent Mdewakanton (Eastern Dakota or Santee) Sioux chiefs in the eighteenth and nineteenth centuries (between roughly 1750 and 1870) were named Wapasha; they were members of the same family. The eldest known to the historical record was born in about 1718 in present-day Minnesota. Made contact with the English when they withdrew trading relations following the murder of a merchant. He had a strong reputation and his band roamed from the upper Iowa River to the Root River in southeastern Minnesota.

Wapasha II

aka: Red Leaf
b. 17??
Wapasha's Prairie (now Winona, Minnesota)
d. 18??
fields: Government and Politics, Native American Affairs

Several prominent Mdewakanton (Eastern Dakota or Santee) Sioux chiefs in the eighteenth and nineteenth centuries (between roughly 1750 and 1870) were named Wapasha; they were members of the same family. Wapasha II ("Red Leaf"), son of the elder Wapasha, was born on the site of present-day Winona, Minnesota. He met Zebulon Pike's 1805 expedition. Though he was generally an ally of immigrating Americans, the British claimed his loyalty in the War of 1812. He Lost Wapasha's Prairie to the white settlers in the Mendota Treaty of 1851.

Wapasha, Joseph

b. ?
d. 1876
Santee Agency, Nebraska
fields: Government and Politics, Native American Affairs

Several prominent Mdewakanton (Eastern Dakota or Santee) Sioux chiefs in the eighteenth and nineteenth centuries (between roughly 1750 and 1870) were named Wapasha; they were members of the same family. In 1862, a third Wapasha, Joseph Wapasha, became the Mdewakanton Sioux's principal chief. Reluctantly, he joined the Great Sioux Uprising that began in 1862 under Little Crow. Wapasha and his people did their best to stay out of the actual hostilities, but after the war vigilantes drove Wapasha and his people to a reservation on the upper Missouri. They later moved to the Santee Agency in Nebraska, where Joseph Wapasha died in 1876.

Warbourg, Eugene

b. c. 1825
New Orleans, La.
d. 1867
fields: Art (sculptor)

African American sculptor; Eugene Warbourg is most famous for his portrait bust of John Young Mason, a United States minister to France.

Warburg, Otto Heinrich

b. Oct. 8, 1883
Freiburg, Germany
d. Aug. 1, 1970
West Berlin, West Germany
fields: Biology, Chemistry, Physiology

Otto Heinrich Warburg was a pioneer in biochemistry; identified the enzymes that enable living cells to obtain energy from food; in 1920-1924, discovered the quantum requirements of photosynthesis; in 1931, was awarded the Nobel Prize in Physiology or Medicine, but not allowed to accept it; in 1954-1968, found enzymes for fermentation and photosynthesis; studied the causes of cancer.

Ward, Arthur Sarsfield. *See* Rohmer, Sax

Ward, Clara
b. April 21, 1924
Philadelphia, Pa.
d. January 16, 1973
Los Angeles, Calif.
fields: Music (gospel singer and composer)

African American gospel singer and composer; Clara Ward was one of the best known gospel singers of her era; began her career as a gospel singer and pianist for the Ward Trio, a family group that included her mother, Gertrude, and her sister, Willa; her move to secular music in the 1960's cost her much of her gospel following, but in 1963 she performed in the first gospel musical written by Langston Hughes, *Tambourines to Glory*.

Ward, Douglas Turner
b. May 5, 1930
Burnside, La.
fields: Theater and Entertainment

African American actor, director, and playwright; Douglas Turner Ward cofounded the Negro Ensemble Company (1967) and was its artistic director; authored the one-act plays *Happy Ending* (1965) and *Day of Absence* (1965).

Ward, Julia. *See* Howe, Julia Ward

Ward, Lester Frank
b. June 18, 1841
Joliet, Illinois
d. April 18, 1913
Washington, D.C.
fields: Sociology

Ward's concern for the enduring features of social life caused him to become one of the founders of the discipline of sociology. As a result of his contributions, the first systematic examinations of the complexities of the market economy, the social role of women, social and intrapersonal conflict, and social planning became core parts of social explanation.

Ward, Montgomery
full: Aaron Montgomery Ward
b. February 17, 1844
Chatham, New Jersey
d. December 7, 1913
Highland Park, Illinois
fields: Business and Industry, Conservation and Environmentalism

Combining extraordinary business foresight with innovative technical methods and a genuine concern for his fellow citizens, Ward revolutionized the history of trade by founding the first mail-order business and introduced the concept of environmental protection by beautifying the Chicago lakefront.

Ward, Nancy
aka: Nanye-hi (One Who Goes About)
b. c. 1738
Chota, Tenn.
d. c. 1824
Polk County, Tenn.
fields: Native American Affairs

Cherokee tribal chief; as a young woman, Nancy Ward led Cherokees in battle against the Creeks in 1755; she was accorded the title Ghigau (Beloved or Most Honored Woman); shortly after being widowed in 1755, married Bryant Ward, an Irish trader; negotiator of the Treaty of Hopewell in 1785, first Cherokee treaty with the newly formed country; urged Cherokee to sell no more land to U.S. government in 1808; she was a staunch advocate of peace between the Cherokees and the white settlers.

Ward, Samuel Ringgold
b. October 17, 1817
eastern shore of Maryland
d. 1866
St. George Parish, Jamaica
fields: Civil Rights, Social Reform

African American congregational minister, orator, and abolitionist; Samuel Ringgold Ward was cofounder of the Liberty Party and helped to organize the Free Soil Party in New York State.

Ward, Theodore
b. September 15, 1902
Thibodaux, La.
d. May 8, 1983
Chicago, Ill.
fields: Theater and Entertainment

African American dramatist; Theodore Ward was among the first African Americans to have a play produced on Broadway, *Our Lan'* (1947); his play *Big White Fog* (pr. 1938), was produced by the Chicago unit of the Federal Theatre Project.

Warfield, Marsha
b. March 5, 1955
Chicago, Ill.
fields: Theater and Entertainment, Television

African American comedian and actress; Marsha Warfield began her comedy career doing stand-up, which eventually led to her roles on such television comedy series as *The Richard Pryor Show* (1977-1978), *Night Court* (1986-1991), and *Empty Nest* (1993-1995). She also appeared as a semi-regular on the television drama *Riptide* (1983) and in 1990, she hosted *Marsha*, her own celebrity morning talk series. Her stand-up act has been televised on such specials as *Comic Relief* (1987), *Just for Laughs* (1987) and *On Location* (1987), and her film credits include *The Marva Collins Story* (1981), *Mask* (1985), *D.C. Cab* (1985), *Caddyshack II* (1988), and the made-for-television film *Doomsday Rock* (1997).

Warfield, Paul D.
b. November 28, 1942
Warren, Ohio
fields: Sports (football player)

African American football player; Paul D. Warfield was a premier wide receiver of the National Football League (NFL); was a (1964) first-round draft choice for the Cleveland Browns; traded to the Miami Dolphins in 1969; signed with the Memphis Southmen of the World Football League in 1974; retired in 1977.

Warfield, William
b. January 22, 1920
West Helena, Ark.
fields: Music (singer)

African American singer; William Warfield made his recital debut in New York City in 1950, thereafter making recordings and international tours; highly regarded for his interpretations of spirituals and for his performances of Porgy in George Gershwin's *Porgy and Bess*.

Warhol, Andy
né: Andrew Warhola
b. August 6, 1928
Pittsburgh, Pennsylvania
d. February 22, 1987
New York, New York
fields: Art

More than any other artist of his time, Warhol created the world of American Pop Art. His many paintings and sculptures reflect the commercialism, affluence, and materialism of postwar American society, serving both as legitimate works of art and as artifacts of an era in America's development as a consumerist nation.

Waring, Laura Wheeler
b. 1887
Hartford, Conn.
d. February 3, 1948
Philadelphia, Pa.
fields: Art (painter)

African American artist; Laura Wheeler Waring was known for her portraits of wealthy Americans and also several famous African Americans, including W. E. B. Du Bois and James Weldon Johnson.

Warren, Earl
b. March 19, 1891
Los Angeles, California
d. July 9, 1974
Washington, D.C.
fields: Law

Warren was Chief Justice of the United States between 1953 and 1969; under his leadership, landmark decisions were reached striking down existing practices in the areas of racial segregation, limitations on political association, voting apportionment, the investigation of criminal suspects, and other controversial issues.

Warren, Mercy Otis

né: Mercy Otis
b. September 25, 1728
Barnstable, Massachusetts
d. October 19, 1814
Plymouth, Massachusetts
fields: Literature

Warren was a leading figure during the American Revolution. As a pamphleteer and propagandist for the patriot cause, she wrote satirical plays attacking the corruption of the British government. She also wrote *A History of the Rise, Progress, and Termination of the American Revolution.*

Warren, Michael

b. March 5, 1946
South Bend, Ind.
fields: Television

African American actor; Michael Warren is best known for his role on the television series *Hill Street Blues* (1981-1987).

Warren, Robert Penn

b. April 24, 1905
Guthrie, Kentucky
d. September 15, 1989
West Wardsboro, near Stratton, Vermont
fields: Literature

Warren, one of the foremost figures in twentieth century American literature, was widely admired for his novels, poetry, literary criticism, and writings on history and current events.

Warren, William W.

b. May 27, 1825
LaPointe, Mich.
d. June 1, 1853
St. Paul, Minn.
fields: Historiography

William W. Warren, an Ojibwa (Chippewa) educated in both the English and Chippewa languages, wrote a detailed history of the Ojibwa. He was employed as a U.S. government interpreter and was elected to the Minnesota State Legislature in 1850. Interviewed many tribal elders. His *History of the Ojibways, Based upon Traditions and Oral Statements* was published posthumously in 1885.

Warrick, Meta Vaux. *See* Fuller, Meta Vaux Warrick

Warwick, Dionne

b. December 12, 1941
East Orange, N.J.
fields: Music (pop singer)

African American singer; Dionne Warwick is best known for her work in collaboration with songwriter Burt Bacharach, including "Then Came You" (1974).

Warwick, earl of

né: Richard Neville
b. November 22, 1428
probably Wessex, England
d. April 14, 1471
Barnet, Hertfordshire, England
fields: Military Affairs

Warwick's activities during the Wars of the Roses proved that the accumulation of wealth and power in the hands of the nobles led only to chaos and destruction. New techniques of government—nationalism and diplomacy—were needed in a more modern world.

Wasechun-tashunka. *See* American Horse

Washakie

aka: Pinquana
b. c. 1804
Bitterroot Valley, Mont.
d. Feb. 10, 1900
Bitterroot Valley, Mont.
fields: Diplomacy, Warfare and Conquest, Government and Politics, Native American Affairs

Washakie, a Shoshone leader, led the Eastern Shoshone in numerous battles against tribal enemies but remained friendly to whites, offering assistance to settlers and allying with the U.S. Army against other tribes. Washakie's band dominated the Upper Green and Sweetwater rivers in southwestern Wyoming and later laid claim to the Wind River country. Tribal disputes soon arose over this game-rich area. In 1866, the Crow fought against Washakie's band in a bloody five-day battle; Chief Washakie emerged from the fight with the Crow chief's heart on the end of his lance. In 1874, joined with the U.S. Cavalry against the Arapaho; in 1876, fought with the cavalry against the Sioux.

Washington, Booker T.

full: Booker Taliaferro Washington
b. April 5, 1856
near Hale's Ford, Virginia
d. November 14, 1915
Tuskegee, Alabama
fields: Social Reform

The son of a slave and an unknown white man, Booker T. Washington provided leadership and a program to American blacks during an era of segregation by combining an optimistic outlook with a spirit of accommodation in race relations.

Washington, Bushrod

b. 1762
d. 1829
fields: Law

U.S. Supreme Court justice, 1789-1829 (died while in office); appointed by President John Adams. Almost always agreed with Chief Justice Marshall's views. Significant opinion: *Ogden v. Saunders*, 25 U.S. 213 (1827).

Washington, Craig Anthony

b. October 12, 1941
Longview, Tex.
fields: Government and Politics

African American U.S. representative from Texas. Craig Anthony Washington was elected to the Texas state house of representatives in 1973; elected to the state senate in 1983; succeeded his friend and former colleague Mickey Leland to the U.S. Congress after Leland's death.

Washington, Denzel

full: Denzel Washington, Jr.
b. December 28, 1954
Mt. Vernon, N.Y.
fields: Film

African American actor; Denzel Washington's first major role was as Private Melvin Peterson in Charles Fuller's *A Soldier's Play*; played Dr. Phillip Chandler in the television show *St. Elsewhere* for five years, until 1987, the same year in which he appeared in the film *Cry Freedom*; won an Academy Award for his role in the film *Glory* (1989); starred in Spike Lee's *Mo' Better Blues* (1990); played the title role in *Malcom X* (1992); continued his career as one of Hollywood's top male actors in such films as *Philadelphia* (1993), *Crimson Tide* (1995), *The Preacher's Wife* (1996), *Courage Under Fire* (1996), and *He Got Game* (1998).

Washington, Dinah

né: Ruth Lee Jones
b. August 29, 1924
Tuscaloosa, Ala.
d. December 14, 1963
Detroit, Mich.
fields: Music (jazz, blues, and soul singer)

African American jazz, blues, and soul singer; Dinah Washington was known as "The Mother of Soul"; became lead singer for the Lionel Hampton band in 1943.

Washington, Fredi

full: Fredricka Carolyn Washington
b. December 23, 1903
Savannah, Georgia

d. June 28, 1994
fields: Theater and Entertainment, Film

African American actress; Fredi Washington appeared opposite Paul Robeson in the play *Black Boy* (1926); played Peola in the film *Imitation of Life* (1934); cofounded in 1937 the Negro Actors Guild and served as its executive secretary.

Washington, George

b. February 11, 1732
Westmoreland County, Virginia
d. December 14, 1799
Mount Vernon, Virginia
fields: Government and Politics, Military Affairs

As commander in chief of the Continental army during the American Revolution, as president of the Constitutional Convention of 1787, and as first president of the United States (1789-1797), Washington was the principal architect of the nation's independence and its federal political system.

Washington, George

b. 1817
Frederick County, Va.
d. 1905
fields: Historical Figure

African American pioneer. George Washington moved to what is now Washington State, bought land, and established the town now known as Centralia.

Washington, Grover, Jr.

b. December 12, 1943
Buffalo, N.Y.
fields: Music (jazz saxophonist)

African American jazz saxophonist; Grover Washington, Jr., recorded his debut album, *Inner City Blues*, in 1971; known as one of the best reed players in the world, Washington was awarded a Grammy for best jazz fusion performance in 1981.

Washington, Harold

b. April 15, 1922
Chicago, Ill.
d. November 25, 1987
Chicago, Ill.
fields: Government and Politics

African American politician; Harold Washington was elected to the Illinois house of representatives in 1964; elected to the U.S. Congress in 1980; was mayor of Chicago from 1982-1987.

Washington, Kenny

full: Kenneth S. Washington
b. August 31, 1918
Los Angeles, Calif.
d. June 24, 1971
Los Angeles, Calif.
fields: Sports (football player)

African American football player; Kenny Washington starred at halfback for the UCLA Bruins (1937-1939); with UCLA teammate Woody Strode became the first post-World War II black players in the National Football League; played for the Los Angeles Rams (1946-1948).

Washington, Lula

b. c. 1951
fields: Dance

African American dancer and choreographer; Lula Washington was artistic director of the Los Angeles Contemporary Dance Theater; choreographed the 1989 film *The Little Mermaid*; her own works include "Urban Man," "Reggae Suite," and "Lift Every Voice."

Washington, MaliVai

b. June 20, 1969
Glen Cove, N.Y.
fields: Sports (tennis player)

African American professional tennis player; when MaliVai Washington turned professional in 1989, he was named Rookie of the Year. He reached Wimbledon in 1991 and was ranked eleventh on the international men's circuit in 1992. In 1993 he was named to the United States Davis Cup team. At the 1994 Australian Open, Washington played in his first Grand Slam quarterfinal; made the Wimbeldon finals in 1996 and achieved his career best ranking of number 11 that same year.

Washington, Martha

né: Martha Dandridge Custis
b. June 2, 1731
Chestnut Grove plantation, Va.
d. May 22, 1802
Mount Vernon, Va.
fields: Government and Politics

First American First Lady; Martha Washington married George Washington in 1759, lived at Mt. Vernon, Virginia, until George was inaugurated as first president of the United States in 1789; accused of having an excessively opulent lifestyle in New York and, later, Philadelphia, when the capital was moved there (Martha Washington chose to ignore the comments); wished to have no part in politics, but her graciousness and warmth defined the role of the American First Lady for generations to come.

Washington, Mary Helen

b. January 21, 1941
Cleveland, Ohio
fields: Education

African American educator; Mary Helen Washington was director of the University of Detroit's Center for Black Studies, beginning in 1975.

Washington, Ora

b. 1898
Philadelphia, Pennsylvania
d. May 28, 1971
Philadelphia, Pennsylvania
fields: Sports (tennis and basketball player)

African American tennis and basketball player; Ora Washington was undefeated in tennis from 1924 until 1936; starred for eighteen years as the center on the *Philadelphia Tribune* women's basketball team and later played for the Germantown Hornets.

Washington, Walter E.

b. April 15, 1915
Dawson, Georgia
fields: Government and Politics

First mayor of Washington, D.C. Walter E. Washington was appointed by Lyndon Johnson to the post of commissioner of the District of Columbia; served in that post until 1975, when the post became the elected office of mayor; elected mayor in 1975, serving until 1979.

Wassaja. *See* Montezuma, Carlos

Watanabe, Gedde

né: Gary Watanabe
b. June 26, 1955
Ogden, Utah
fields: Film, Theater and Entertainment

Actor Gedde Watanabe appeared in several major films in the 1980's, including *Sixteen Candles* (1984) and *Gung Ho* (1986). The roles played by Watanabe, particularly in *Sixteen Candles*, were criticized for perpetuating stereotypical roles depicting Asian Americans as nerds and foreigners.

Waters, Ethel

b. October 31, 1900
Chester, Pa.
d. September 1, 1977
Chatsworth, Calif.
fields: Music, Film, Theater and Entertainment

African American singer and actress; Ethel Waters began her career in vaudeville, then at nightclubs; debuted on Broadway in *Africana*, a revue she put together with Donald Hayward and Earl Dancer; other Broadway roles include *Blackbirds*, *Rhapsody in Blue*, *As Thousands Cheer*, and *At Home Abroad*; for the Federal Theatre Project, performed in George Bernard Shaw's *Androcles and the Lion* and in DuBose and Dorothy Heyward's *Mamba's Daughters*, and Carson McCullers's *The Member of the Wedding*; appeared in films such as *Pinky* (1949), *Tales of*

Manhattan (1942), and *Cabin in the Sky* (1943) and in the television show *Beulah*.

Waters, Maxine

b. 1938
St. Louis, Mo.
fields: Government and Politics

African American politician; the fifth of thirteen children reared by a single mother, Maxine Waters was a member of the California State Assembly (1976-1990) before her election to the U.S. House of Representatives in 1990; became the first nonlawyer to serve on the House Judiciary Committee; 1997-1998, Chair of the Congressional Black Caucus. Elected in 1998 to her fifth term, she is an outspoken advocate for women, children, the poor, and peole of color.

Wa-tho-huck. *See* Thorpe, Jim

Watie, Stand

aka: Dagataga
aka: Degadoga (He Stands on Two Feet)
b. Dec. 12, 1806
near Rome, Ga.
d. Sept. 9, 1871
Indian Territory, present-day Okla.
fields: Diplomacy, Journalism, Warfare and Conquest, Native American Affairs

Stand Watie, a Cherokee, helped establish the *Cherokee Phoenix*, was a signer of the treaty accepting removal to Indian Territory, and was a Confederate brigadier general in the Civil War. In 1835, he joined his brother Elias Boudinot, their cousin John Ridge, and their uncle Major Ridge in signing the Treaty of New Echota, which required the Cherokees to give up their lands in Georgia and "remove" to what is now Oklahoma. The signers were liable to the "blood law," which decreed death for anyone selling Cherokee land without the full consent of the nation. Militant followers of Cherokee leader Ross murdered the Ridges and Watie's brother Boudinot. Watie himself was marked for death but escaped, offered $10,000 for the murderers of his brother, and became leader of the anti-Ross party. When the Cherokees joined the Confederacy at the beginning of the Civil War, Watie raised the first regiment of Cherokee volunteers, the "Cherokee Mounted Rifles."

Watkins, Bruce R., Sr.

b. March 20, 1924
Parkville, Mo.
d. Sept.13, 1980
Kansas City, Mo.
fields: Civil Rights, Government and Politics

Bruce Watkins cofounded a civil rights group in Kansas City called Freedom, Inc., in 1962. He was elected to the Kansas City city council in 1963 and served as clerk for Jackson county from 1969 to 1974. He was later reelected to the city council. He ran for mayor in 1979 and won the primary, but he lost in the general election. Watkins served as an executive assistant to the regional director for the Department of Housing and Urban Development (HUD).

Watkins, Gloria. *See* Hooks, Bell

Watkins, Joseph Philip

b. August 24, 1953
New York, N.Y.
fields: Government and Politics

African American minister, journalist, and political appointee; Joseph Philip Watkins first worked in Washington, D.C., as an aide to Senator Dan Quayle of Indiana (1981-1984); appointed by George Bush to serve as associate director of the White House Office of Public Liaison.

Watkins, Perry

b. 1907
d. 1974
Newburgh, N.Y.
fields: Theater and Entertainment

African American theater scenic designer, costume designer, producer, and film director; Perry Watkins became famous for his production designs for the Harlem Unit of the Federal Theatre Project.

Watley, Jody

b. January 30, 1961
Chicago, Ill.
fields: Dance, Music

African American singer and dancer; Jody Watley was a Soul Train dancer before cofounding the groug Shalamar; solo career included *Larger than Life*, which produced six top-ten singles and a 1988 Grammy as best new artist, and *Affairs of the Heart* (1991); released an exercise video, *Dance to Fitness*, in 1991.

Watohkonk. *See* Kicking Bird

Watson, Barbara M.

b. November 5, 1918
New York, New York
d. February 17, 1983
Washington, D.C.
fields: Government and Politics

African American political appointee; Barbara M. Watson served in a number of minor government posts before becoming the first woman to attain the rank of assistant secretary of state at the State Department (1977-1980); appointed ambassador to Malaysia (1980).

Watson, James D.

full: James Dewey Watson
b. Apr. 6, 1928
Chicago, Illinois
fields: Biology, Genetics

James D. Watson, with Francis Crick, discovered the structure of deoxyribonucleic acid (DNA), the genetic material; won the Nobel Prize in Physiology or Medicine in 1962.

Watson, James L.

b. May 21, 1922
New York, N.Y.
fields: Law

African American federal judge; James L. Watson was elected to the New York state senate as a representative from the Twenty-first Senatorial District (1954-1963); elected to the post of judge of the Civil Court of New York City (1963), becoming the first African American judge to be elected in the history of New York State; President Lyndon B. Johnson appointed Watson to serve as judge on the U.S. Customs Court (1966), which later was renamed the U.S. Court of International Trade.

Watson, John B.

b. January 9, 1878
near Greenville, S.C.
d. September 25, 1958
New York, N.Y.
fields: Psychiatry and Psychology

Considered the father of behaviorist psychology, John B. Watson defined psychology as the science of behavior in 1913, arguing for an objective science based on observable events and behaviors and emphasizing environment in shaping behavior. His academic career ended 1920 because of a divorce scandal. Afterward became a successful executive in an advertising agency and continued *Psychological Care of the Infant and Child* (1928).

Watt, James

b. January 19, 1736
Greenock, Renfrewshire, Scotland
d. August 25, 1819
Heathfield, near Birmingham, England
fields: Engineering (mechanical), Invention and Technology

Recognized as a great inventor in his own day, Watt developed a practical steam engine that virtually powered the early Industrial Revolution.

Watteau, Antoine

b. October 10, 1684
Valenciennes, France
d. July 18, 1721
Nogent-sur-Marne, France

fields: Art

Watteau was one of the finest French painters of the early eighteenth century and was the originator and perhaps the most successful practitioner of the *fête galante*, the idealized, romantic representation of love and sexual liaison.

Wattleton, Faye

full: Alyce Faye Wattleton
b. July 8, 1943
St. Louis, Mo.
fields: Medicine

As president of Planned Parenthood from 1978 until 1992, Wattleton not only changed the organization's image but also made it better known to the American public.

Watts, Andre

b. June 20, 1946
Nuremberg, Germany
fields: Music (concert pianist)

African American concert pianist; internationally respected, Andre Watts came to national prominence at age sixteen, when he played with the New York Philharmonic.

Watts, J. C., Jr.

b. November 18, 1957
Eufaula, Okla.
fields: Government and Politics, Sports (football player)

African American politician and former professional football player; J. C. Watts, Jr., played as a quarterback for the Ottawa Roughriders (1981-1985) before playing for the Toronto Argonauts (1986). After retiring from professional football, Watts served as president and owner of Watts Energy Corporation in Oklahoma (1981-1989). He served on the Environmental Protection Agency Board on National Drinking Water, as commissioner on the Oklahoma State Corporation Commission, and as honorary chairman of the March of Dimes in 1991. In 1994, Watts campaigned for Congress as a Republican candidate and took office in 1995; he was re-elected in 1998. He headed a task force encouraging more African Americans to register to vote as Republicans.

Watts, Rolanda

b. b. July 12, 1959
Winston-Salem, N.C.
fields: Television, Journalism

African American broadcast journalist and talk show host. Before becoming a nationally syndicated talk show host, Rolanda Watts worked as a reporter and news anchor at the television station WNBC in New York City. In 1992 Watts was hired to host *Rolanda*, and a new talk show was launched into the highly competitive syndicated television talk show market. In February of 1995, the show's producers altered the format, switching the focus from news-oriented topics to issues with a more youthful, commercial appeal. With this change the low-rated show became one of the most widely distributed programs in syndication.

Watumull, G. J.

full: Gobindram Jhamandas Watumull
b. June 26, 1891
Hyderabad, Sind, now Pakistan, India
d. Aug., 1959
Honolulu, Hawaii
fields: Business and Industry, Philanthropy

In 1917 G. J. Watumull's brother Jhamandas asked him to come to Honolulu to help manage the East India Store. Under G. J.'s management, the East India Store in downtown Honolulu grew from a small bazaar to a major department store chain that sold the first raw silk and Hawaiian aloha shirts offered in the islands. By 1957 the Watumull brothers' properties included ten stores, a Waikiki apartment house, and assorted commercial developments. Watumull used his wealth to support Indian independence and the work of Syed Hussain, Krishnalal Shridharani, and Anup Singh who publicized India's cause. In 1942 Gobindram established the Watumull Foundation.

Watumull, Jhamandas

b. February 14, 1885
Hyderabad, Sind, now Pakistan, India
d. 198?
Honolulu, Hawaii
fields: Business and Industry

Jhamandas Watumull started a retail business in Manila that specialized in imports from the Orient. He moved to Hawaii in 1913 and, with a partner, opened the East India Store. In 1917 his partner returned to India and his brother Gobindram (or G. J.) took over management of the store. Jhamandas traveled in Asia in search of imports. In 1937 the Watumull Building was erected in Honolulu to house the headquarters of the growing Watumull Brothers business enterprise. Jhamandas returned to Honolulu in 1956, and after Gobindram's death in 1959, Jhamandas continued to expand operations. By 1973 there were twenty-nine Watumull stores. Jhamandas established a hospital in Bombay named for his wife, who had died in 1955. Jhamandas also established two family foundations, the Rama Watumull Fund (named for his late son) and the J. Watumull Estate, to benefit local charitable and educational institutions.

Wauneka, Annie Dodge

né: Annie Dodge
b. April 10, 1910
Navajo Nation, near Sawmill, Arizona
d. November 10, 1997
Flagstaff, Arizona
fields: Social Reform, Public Health

A Navajo health educator and leader in the implementation of Navajo health programs, Annie Dodge Wauneka helped to educate her people about how to eradicate tuberculosis, which was rampant on her reservation. Her advocacy of health reforms led to an expanded crusade to help improve the Navajo way of life.

Wayans, Damon

b. 1960
New York, N.Y.
fields: Television, Film

African American comedian; Damon Wayans, the brother of Keenen Ivory Wayans, was part of the original cast of television's *In Living Color* from 1990-1992; appeared in a number of films, including *Beverly Hills Cop* (1984), *The Last Boy Scout* (1991), and *Mo' Money* (1992), for which he wrote the screenplay.

Wayans, Keenen Ivory

b. June 8, 1958
New York, N.Y.
fields: Film

African American writer, director, producer, and actor; Keenen Ivory Wayans cowrote and starred in several Robert Townsend productions, including *Hollywood Shuffle* (1982) and *Robert Townsend's Partners in Crime*, produced for Home Box Office; also worked with Townsend as coproducer and cowriter on *Eddie Murphy Raw* (1987); was executive producer, writer, director, and star of *I'm Gonna Git You Sucka* (1989); created Fox Network's comedy series *In Living Color*.

Waymon, Eunice. *See* Simone, Nina

Wayne, James Moore

b. 1790
d. 1867
fields: Law

U.S. Supreme Court justice, 1835-1867 (died while in office); appointed by President Jackson. Significant opinion: *Louisville, Cincinnati and Charleston Railroad Co. v. Letson*, 43 U.S. 497 (1844).

Wayne, John

né: Marion Michael Morrison
aka: the Duke
b. May 26, 1907
Winterset, Iowa
d. June 11, 1979
Los Angeles, California

fields: Film

Wayne, one of the most popular film actors of all time, achieved his greatest work in Westerns, many of which are among the finest Western films ever made. He also came to embody what many people saw as basic American values, such as strength, courage, patriotism, and willingness to accept personal responsibility.

Weatherford, William

aka: Lamochattee
aka: Lumhe Chate
aka: Red Eagle
b. c. 1780
near Montgomery, Ala.
d. Mar. 9, 1822
Polk County, Tenn.
fields: Warfare and Conquest, Native American Affairs

Native American leader. As principal leader of the Creek war faction, the Red Sticks, William Weatherford fought the Americans during the Creek War, 1813-1814. Approximately one thousand warriors under Weatherford's command successfully assaulted Americans at Fort Mims on August 13, 1813, killing five hundred settlers and releasing their black slaves. Subsequently, federal and state troops were mobilized under the command of General Andrew Jackson. At the Battle of Horseshoe Bend, March 27, 1814, Weatherford's forces suffered their final defeat.

Weathers, Carl

b. January 14, 1948
New Orleans, La.
fields: Film, Television

African American film and television actor; Carl Weathers is best known as the boxer Apollo Creed in the first four *Rocky* films; starred the television series *Fortune Dane* (1986).

Weaver, George Leon-Paul

b. June 18, 1912
Pittsburgh, Pa.
fields: Government and Politics

African American political appointee and business consultant; George Leon-Paul Weaver was appointed by John F. Kennedy to serve as special assistant to the secretary of labor; served as assistant secretary of labor international affairs and special assistant to the director general of the International Labor Organization in Geneva from 1969 until his retirement; became a consultant to the World ORT Union in 1975.

Weaver, Michael S.

b. November 26, 1951
Baltimore, Md.
fields: Literature (poet, playwright), Education

African American poet, playwright, and educator; Michael S. Weavern began teaching and later received tenure as an associate professor of English at the Camden campus of Rutgers University. He authored several poetry collections, including *Water Song* (1985), *My Father's Geography* (1992), *Stations in a Dream* (1993), and *Timber and Prayer: The Indian Road Poems* (1995). Several of his poems and short stories have been anthologized; his feature articles, reviews, and editorials have appeared in several Baltimore and Philadelphia newspapers. Among the numerous awards and fellowships Weaver has received are a Pennsylvania Arts Council Fellowship in 1994 and a National Endowment for the Arts fellowship in 1985. His plays *Rosa* and *Elvira and the Lost Prince* were produced professionally.

Weaver, Robert Clipton

b. December 29, 1907
Washington, D.C.
d. July 17, 1997
New York, N.Y.
fields: Government and Politics

African American government official; Robert Clipton Weaver was the first African American to be a cabinet member when Lyndon Johnson appointed him secretary of housing and urban development (1966); was a member of Franklin D. Roosevelt's "black cabinet."

Webb, Beatrice

né: Beatrice Potter
b. January 22, 1858
Gloucester, Gloucestershire, England
d. April 30, 1943
Liphook, Hampshire, England
fields: Economics, Sociology, Social Reform, Historiography

Beatrice and Sidney Webb were leading figures in the Fabian Society and in the development of Labour Party policies. Founders of the London School of Economics and *New Statesman*, they also authored several important texts on trade unions, local government, and the Poor Laws.

Webb, Chick

full: William Henry Webb
b. February 10, 1909
Baltimore, Md.
d. June 16, 1939
Baltimore, Md.
fields: Music (drummer, bandleader, and composer)

African American drummer, bandleader, and composer; Chick Webb was resident bandleader, with his Harlem Stompers, at the Savoy Ballroom in Harlem for ten years, beginning in the 1920's; in 1935 he recruited Ella Fitzgerald into his band; wrote a number of hit songs, including "Stompin' at the Savoy," "Lonesome Moments," "Holiday in Harlem," and "Heart of Mine."

Webb, Clifton

b. August 7, 1950
New Orleans, La.
fields: Art (painter and sculptor)

African American painter and sculptor; Clifton Webb is known for his work synthesizing African and Central American approaches to the senses and conveying a sense of musical order.

Webb, Loretta. *See* Lynn, Loretta

Webb, Sidney

b. July 13, 1859
London, England
d. October 13, 1947
Liphook, Hampshire, England
fields: Economics, Sociology, Social Reform, Historiography

Beatrice and Sidney Webb were leading figures in the Fabian Society and in the development of Labour Party policies. Founders of the London School of Economics and *New Statesman*, they also authored several important texts on trade unions, local government, and the Poor Laws.

Webb, Spud

né: Anthony Jerome Webb
b. July 13, 1963
Dallas, Texas
fields: Sports (basketball player)

African American basketball player; Spud Webb played basketball for North Carolina State University until 1985; only 5′7″ tall he signed by the Atlanta Hawks in 1985 and played with them until 1991; 1991-1995 with the Sacramento Kings and led the NBA in free-throw shooting (93.4%) in the 1994-1995 season; 1995-1996 with the Atlanto Hawks then Minnesota Timerwolves; joined the Orlando Magic in 1997.

Webb, Wellington Edward

b. February 17, 1941
Chicago, Ill.
fields: Government and Politics

African American mayor and city official; Wellington Edward Webb who is best known as the mayor of Denver, Colorado, also served as the city auditor until he was elected mayor in 1991. He was a representative in the Colorado state legislature (1973-1977) and also served as the principal regulation official of the U.S. Department of Health and Human Services (1977). Webb was the director of the Colorado State University Manpower Laboratory (1969-1974) and served as the chairman of the United Negro College Fund (UNCF) (1973-1975). In 1976 he was awarded the Barney Ford Award for Political Action.

Webber, Chris

b. March 1, 1973
Detroit, Mich.
fields: Sports (basketball player)

African American professional basketball player; Chris Webber, National Basketball Association (NBA) Rookie of the Year (1993-1994), was the number one pick in the National Basketball Association draft in 1993. Webber played with the Golden State Warriors (1993-1994 season), before being traded to the Washington Bullets. He led the Bullets in scoring, rebounding, steals, and minutes played in the 1994-1995 season. As a member of the University of Michigan "Fab Five" basketball team, Webber gained national attention and led the Michigan Wolverines to two straight National Collegiate Athletic Association finals (1992 and 1993).

Weber, Carl Maria von

b. November 18, 1786
Eutin, Oldenburg
d. June 5, 1826
London, England
fields: Music

Weber was the principal founder of German Romantic music. Best known as an opera composer, he made many significant contributions to piano music and wrote some of the staples of the wind instrument player's repertoire.

Weber, Lois

full: Florence Lois Weber
b. June 13, 1881
Allegheny, Pennsylvania (later incorporated into Pittsburgh)
d. November 13, 1939
Hollywood, California
fields: Film

As an actor, writer, and director, Lois Weber was the first American woman "auteur," the author of her own melodramatic films.

Weber, Max

b. April 21, 1864
Erfurt, Prussia
d. June 14, 1920
Munich, Germany
fields: Sociology

A German social scientist and theorist widely acclaimed as the "father of sociology," Weber is best known for his thesis of the Protestant ethic, which links the psychological effects of Calvinism with the development of modern capitalism.

Webern, Anton von

full: Anton Friedrich Wilhelm von Webern
b. December 3, 1883
Vienna, Austro-Hungarian Empire
d. September 15, 1945
Mittersill, Austria
fields: Music

Webern brought to the second Viennese school a unique and highly individual compositional approach. Like his mentor Arnold Schoenberg, Webern broke with existing musical traditions and developed a new compositional language and perspective. His adaptation of Schoenberg's twelve-tone method, based upon his own contrapuntal proclivity and concise musical rhetoric, proved to be the major influence on the subsequent generation of composers.

Webster, Ben

b. March 27, 1909
Kansas City, Mo.
d. September 20, 1973
Amsterdam, The Netherlands
fields: Music (jazz tenor saxophonist)

African American jazz tenor saxophonist; Ben Webster was already an established musician when he joined Duke Ellinton's band in 1939; enjoyed a successful recording career in the 1950's, releasing *Soulville* (1957) and playing on singer Jimmy Witherspoon's *At the Renaissance* (1959); moved to Europe in the 1960's but continued to play until the end of his life.

Webster, Daniel

b. January 18, 1782
Salisbury, New Hampshire
d. October 24, 1852
Marshfield, Massachusetts
fields: Law, Oratory, Government and Politics, Diplomacy

The greatest orator of his time, Webster, more than any other individual, articulated a near-mystical devotion to the Union which would define Northern patriotism during the Civil War.

Webster, Noah

b. October 16, 1758
West Hartford, Connecticut
d. May 28, 1843
New Haven, Connecticut
fields: Language and Linguistics (lexicography), Law, Education

Webster helped to turn English into a universal language by compiling the first major dictionary of American English. He was a leader in bringing about the passage of copyright laws, and he was one of the founders of Amherst College.

Weddington, Sarah

né: Sarah Ragle
b. February 5, 1945
Abilene, Texas
fields: Law, Government and Politics, Women's Rights

As a twenty-six-year-old attorney, Weddington argued *Roe v. Wade* before the Supreme Court and has continued to work diligently as an advocate for women's rights.

Wedgwood, Josiah

b. July 12, 1730 (baptized)
Burslem, Staffordshire, England
d. January 3, 1795
Etruria, England
fields: Business and Industry, Invention and Technology, Art

Wedgwood's genius and innovations helped not only to convert pottery making from a peasant's craft to a major industry but also to bring about the Industrial Revolution in England.

Weems, Carrie Mae

b. 1953
Portland, Oregon
fields: Photography

African American photographer; Carrie Mae Weems's work concentrates on showing African American culture from an insider's perspective.

Weetamoo

aka: Namumpum
aka: Tatapanum
b. c. 1650
southwestern Mass.
d. Aug. 6, 1676
near Taunton, Mass.
fields: Government and Politics, Native American Affairs

Native American leader. Weetamoo was a "squaw sachem," or female chief, of the Pocasset (a branch of the Wampanoag). When King Philip's War broke out in June, 1675, she joined Metacomet (King Philip), sachem of the Wampanoag, with whom the Pocasset were affiliated, in the war. In August, 1676, her band was taken by surprise on the bank of the Taunton River, near Taunton, Massachusetts, and Weetamoo drowned while trying to escape across the river on a raft. Her head was cut off and set on a pole in Taunton.

Wegener, Alfred

full: Alfred Lothar Wegener
b. November 1, 1880
Berlin, Germany

d. Winter of 1930
Greenland
fields: Geology, Physics

Wegener was a German meteorologist and Arctic explorer who received credit for the first clear statement of the hypothesis of continental drift. Although his ideas were scornfully dismissed by most geologists in his own time, they were enthusiastically revived by oceanographers in the mid-1960's as the precursor to the well-known plate tectonics theory.

Weglyn, Michi

né: Michiko Nishiura
b. Nov. 29, 1926
Stockton, Calif.
fields: Historiography

Japanese American Michi Weglyn, a theatrical costume designer by profession, wrote *Years of Infamy: The Untold Story of America's Concentration Camps* (1976), after extensive research. Weglyn's book documented the process by which the U.S. government decided to intern Japanese Americans during World War II.

Wei, William

b. c. 1948
New York, New York
fields: Sociology, Historiography

William Wei, a professor at the University of Colorado, Boulder, wrote *The Asian American Movement* (1993). Wei, who taught Asian American studies, produced the first full-scale history of the Asian American movement.

Weierstrass, Karl

full: Karl Theodor Wilhelm Weierstrass
b. Oct. 31, 1815
Ostenfelde, Bavaria (now Germany)
d. Feb. 19, 1897
Berlin, Germany
fields: Mathematics (calculus)

Karl Weierstrass established a firm theoretic foundation for the calculus; constructed a continuous function having no tangents in 1861.

Weil, Simone

b. February 3, 1909
Paris, France
d. August 24, 1943
Ashford, Kent, England
fields: Philosophy, Religion and Theology

Perhaps even more than her writing, the life of Weil, twentieth century French mystic and philosophical thinker, has for several generations both fascinated and perplexed many. Weil's passion and originality, her intense sense of commitment toward eternity and her fellowman, and her willingness to sacrifice her life for her truths remain her principal legacy.

Weill, Kurt

full: Kurt Julian Weill
b. March 2, 1900
Dessau, Germany
d. April 3, 1950
New York, New York
fields: Music

Weill was one of the outstanding composers of the generation that came to maturity after World War I. He broke away from the Romantic, emotional style of Wagnerian opera to create a revolutionary new form: the opera of sharp social satire. After his emigration to the United States, Weill turned away from his earlier "serious" works to become one of the top composers of Broadway musicals in the 1940's.

Weinberg, Steven

b. May 3, 1933
New York, New York
fields: Astronomy, Mathematics, Physics

With Sheldon Glashow and Abdus Salam, Steven Weinberg tried to construct a mathematical model that would unify all the known forces and particles of matter; in 1979, received the Nobel Prize in Physics, with Salam and Glashow.

Weismann, August

full: August Friedrich Leopold Weismann
b. January 17, 1834
Frankfurt am Main
d. November 5, 1914
Freiburg im Breisgau, Germany
fields: Biology, Natural History, Zoology, Genetics

Weismann is most noted for his development and refinement of the theory of the continuity of the germ plasm, for his devout support of Darwinism and the principle of natural selection, and for his discrediting the idea of the inheritance of acquired characteristics.

Weizmann, Chaim

full: Chaim Azriel Weizmann
b. November 27, 1874
Motol, Poland, Russian Empire
d. November 9, 1952
Rehovot, Israel
fields: Government and Politics, Chemistry

Although a world-class chemist and scientific researcher, Weizmann's greatest contributions and achievements must be regarded as his leadership of the World Zionist Organization for twelve years and his central role in helping to forge the new State of Israel. He was the first president of that new nation from 1949 through 1952.

Welch, James

b. Nov. 18, 1940
Browning, Mont.
fields: Literature (novelist, poet)

Native American writer. A Blackfoot and Gros Ventre (Atsina), James Welch grew up in an Indian environment, and the traditions and religion especially of the Blackfoot inform his writing. He attended the University of Montana. Much of Welch's fiction pivots on the interaction between the American Indian and white America. Novels include *Winter in the Blood* (1974), *The Death of Jim Loney* (1979), *Fools Crow* (1986), and *The Indian Lawyer* (1990). The early poetry collection *Riding the Earthboy 40* (1971) includes protest poetry and deals with reservation life in Montana.

Welch, Raquel

né: Raquel Tejada
b. Sept. 5, 1940
Chicago, Ill.
fields: Film (actor)

Raquel Welch was born to a Bolivian American father and an English mother. She became a celebrity before appearing in any major film roles. Subsequently, roles in *A Swingin' Summer* (1965), *Fantastic Voyage* (1966), and *One Million Years B.C.* (1966) established her as a film sex symbol. Other films include *Bandolero!* (1968), *One Hundred Rifles* (1969), *Myra Breckenridge* (1970), *Bluebeard* (1972), *Kansas City Bomber* (1972), *The Three Musketeers* (1974), *Mother, Jugs, and Speed* (1977), and *The Prince and the Pauper* (1977).

Welles, Orson

full: George Orson Welles
b. May 6, 1915
Kenosha, Wisconsin
d. October 10, 1985
Hollywood, California
fields: Film, Theater and Entertainment

As an actor, director, and writer, Welles breathed fresh life into all the media he explored: stage, radio, and film. Most important, his innovative cinematic techniques in such areas as lighting, camera angles and focus, and sound continue to influence film directors.

Wellesley, Arthur. *See* Wellington, duke of

Wellington, duke of

né: Arthur Wesley
later: Arthur Wellesley
aka: Viscount Wellington of Talavera
aka: Iron Duke
b. May 1, 1769
Dublin, Ireland

d. September 14, 1852
Walmer Castle, near Dover, Kent, England
fields: Military Affairs, Government and Politics

One of Great Britain's finest military leaders, Wellington, through victories in the Peninsular War and at Waterloo, hastened the downfall of Napoleon and the end of the Napoleonic Wars.

Wells, H. G.

full: Herbert George Wells
b. September 21, 1866
Bromley, Kent, England
d. August 13, 1946
London, England
fields: Literature

Through his writings—both fiction and nonfiction—Wells became a significant shaper of liberal social thought in the first half of the twentieth century.

Wells, Junior

né: Amos Blackmore
b. December 9, 1934
Memphis, Tenn.
d. January 15, 1998
Chicago, Ill.
fields: Music (blues harmonica player and singer)

African American blues harmonica player and singer; Junior Wells began his professional career as a teenager, joining Muddy Waters band in the early 1950's; made a number of recordings while serving in the military, including "Eagle Rock" (1953), "Hoodoo Man" (1953), "Lawdy, Lawdy" (1954), and "So All Alone" (1954); played the college circuit during the 1960's blues revival; departed from the Chicago blues in the 1970's toward a soul/funk style influenced by James Brown.

Wells, Mary

b. May 13, 1943
Detroit, Mich.
d. July 26, 1991
Los Angeles, Calif.
fields: Music (pop and soul singer)

African American pop and soul singer; Mary Wells was one of Motown's first stars; recorded a number of hits between 1961 and 1964, including "You Beat Me to the Punch" (1962), "Two Lovers" (1962), and "My Guy" (1964); recorded popular duets with Martin Gaye in 1964.

Wells-Barnett, Ida B.

né: Ida Bell Wells
b. July 16, 1862
Holly Springs, Mississippi
d. March 25, 1931
Chicago, Illinois
fields: Civil Rights, Women's Rights, Journalism

An organizer of the antilynching movement, Ida B. Wells was an indefatigable crusader for equal rights for African Americans in the violent decades around the turn of the century, working on issues of education, social services, woman suffrage, and racial violence.

Welsing, Frances Cress

b. March 18, 1935
Chicago, Ill.
fields: Psychiatry and Psychology

African American psychiatrist; Frances Cress Welsing wrote *The Cress Theory of Color-Confrontation and Racism* (1970) and *The Isis Papers* (1991).

Wenceslaus

aka: Wenceslaus IV, King of Bohemia
b. February 26, 1361
Nuremberg
d. August 16, 1419
Prague
fields: Government and Politics, Monarchy

King of Bohemia, 1363-1419; German king, 1378-1400; Through his incompetence and hesitation, Wenceslaus contributed to the weakening of central authority in Germany and Bohemia, but he also encouraged the development of a Czech national consciousness.

Wentworth, Thomas. *See* Strafford, first earl of

Wentworth, W. C.

full: William Charles Wentworth
b. Probably August 7, 1790
probably at sea, between Sydney and Norfolk Island, Australia
d. March 20, 1872
Wimborne, Dorset, England
fields: Government and Politics

Wentworth contributed both to egalitarian and conservative forces in Australian life.

Wertheim, Barbara. *See* Tuchman, Barbara

Wertheimer, Max

b. April 16, 1880
Prague, Austro-Hungarian Empire
d. October 12, 1943
New York, New York
fields: Psychiatry and Psychology

Wertheimer pioneered the development of Gestalt psychology, which he and his coworkers Kurt Koffka and Wolfgang Köhler introduced to the European and American psychological communities.

Wesley, Arthur. *See* Wellington, Duke of

Wesley, Charles Harris

b. December 2, 1895
Louisville, Ky.
d. August 16, 1987
Washington, D.C.
fields: Education

African American historian; Charles Harris Wesley was president of Central State University in Arkansas (1942 until mid-1960's); professor and dean at Howard University; director for the Association for the Study of Afro-American Life and History.

Wesley, John

b. June 17, 1703
Epworth, Lincolnshire, England
d. March 2, 1791
London, England
fields: Religion and Theology

Wesley founded the Methodist church and presaged the entire Evangelical movement which followed in England and America.

West, Cornel

b. June 2, 1953
Tulsa, Okla.
fields: Education, Philosophy, Social Reform

Cornel West taught at Yale, but moved to Princeton in 1986 to become director of its African American studies department. His commentaries on race relations include the best-selling, controversial *Race Matters* (1993). His other books include *Prophesy Deliverance!: An Afro-American Revolutionary Christianity* (1982) and *The Ethical Dimensions of Marxist Thought* (1991).

West, Dorothy

b. June 2, 1907
Boston, Massachusetts
d. August 16, 1998
Boston, Massachusetts
fields: Literature (novelist, editor, and short-story writer)

African American novelist, editor, and short-story writer. A member of the literary elite of the Harlem Renaissance, Dorothy West was founder and editor of the literary magazines *Challenge* and *New Challenge* during the 1930's. West wrote about the obsessive color consciousness within the black middle class and their loss of moral and spiritual values while emulating white ideals. The novels *The Living Is Easy* (1948) and *The Wedding* (1995) satirize the pretensions of the black bourgeoisie of Boston and the resort community of Oak Bluffs on Martha's Vineyard. Many of West's short stories were first published in *Opportunity*, the *Messenger*, the *Saturday Evening Quill*, and *The*

New York Daily News. The Richer, the Poorer (1995) is a collection of these stories.

West, Lightfoot Allen

b. ?
d. 1942
fields: Medicine

African American physician; Lightfoot Allen West was president of the National Medical Association (1929-1930); founded the National Hospital Association; founded Mercy Hospital in Memphis, Tenn., in 1917.

West, Mae

b. August 17, 1893
Brooklyn, New York
d. November 22, 1980
Los Angeles, California
fields: Film, Theater and Entertainment (actor)

A memorable screen presence and wit, Mae West was also a breakthrough playwright in the handling of taboo subjects and a role model as a woman in control of her own sexuality.

West, Roy A.

b. ?
fields: Government and Politics

African American mayor of Richmond, Va.; Roy A. West was elected to serve on the city council from Richmond's Third District; was elected by his fellow council members as the city's mayor (1985-1986).

Westerfield, Samuel Z.

b. 1919
Chicago, Ill.
fields: Government and Politics

African American political appointee and economist; Samuel Z. Westerfield was made senior adviser to the Treasury Department's Office of International Affairs; appointed by Lyndon Johnson to serve on the staff of the Bureau of African Affairs of the U.S. Department of State (1964); U.S. ambassador to Liberia (1969).

Westinghouse, George

b. October 6, 1846
Central Bridge, New York
d. March 12, 1914
New York, New York
fields: Invention and Technology

Both an ingenious inventor and a shrewd entrepreneur, Westinghouse developed both mechanical and electrical inventions that permitted America to emerge as a major industrial nation in the late nineteenth century. As an inventor, he designed the air brake, signaling systems, and other key inventions for railroads, and as an entrepreneur he supported the creation of electric light and power systems, using alternating current.

Weyden, Rogier van der

b. 1399 or 1400
Tournai, the Netherlands
d. c. June 18, 1464
Brussels
fields: Art

One of the greatest of the fifteenth century Netherlandish painters, Rogier influenced other painters of the Christian altarpiece, stylistically and tonally, and dominated northern European painting throughout the period.

Weyl, Hermann

b. Nov. 9, 1885
Elmshorn, near Hamburg, Germany
d. Dec. 8, 1955
Zurich, Switzerland
fields: Mathematics (algebra, applied math, calculus, geometry, mathematical logic, number theory, set theory, and topology)

Hermann Weyl contributed to the development of point set topology and differential geometry.

Wharton, Clifton Reginald, Sr.

b. May 11, 1899
Baltimore, Md.
d. April 23, 1990
Phoenix, Ariz.
fields: Diplomacy

Clifton Reginald Wharton, Sr. entered the foreign service of the U.S. government in 1925 and was the first black diplomat to head a U.S. delegation to a European country (Romania), in 1958. He was also ambassador to Norway (1961-1964).

Wharton, Clifton Reginald, Jr.

b. September 13, 1926
Boston, Mass.
fields: Education

Clifton Wharton, Jr., was elected as the president of Michigan State University in 1969, the first African American to lead a major, predominantly white university. He was chancellor of the State University of New York in Albany and was appointed to the President's Commission on World Hunger by Jimmy Carter in 1975. In 1992 Bill Clinton chose Wharton to serve as deputy secretary of state.

Wharton, Edith

né: Edith Newbold Jones
b. January 24, 1862
New York, New York
d. August 11, 1937
St.-Brice-sous-Forêt, France
fields: Literature

Edith Wharton was a novelist who was noted for her portrayal of the decline of New York aristocracy and for her characters' trapped sensibilities.

Wheat, Alan Dupree

b. October 16, 1951
San Antonio, Tex
fields: Government and Politics

U.S. representative from Missouri. Alan Dupree Wheat, an African American, served in the Missouri general assembly (1977-1982) before being elected to the U.S. Congress in 1982, leaving in 1994; became vice president of public policy and governmental relations for the CARE Foundation in 1995; continued to persue business interests.

Wheatley, Phillis

b. 1753?
Gambia, Africa
d. December 5, 1784
Boston, Mass.
fields: Literature

Phillis Wheatley was the first African American to publish a volume of poetry. *Poems on Various Subjects, Regious and Moral* was published in 1773 and made her a celebrity in the American colonies and in England, where she was sent to meet Benjamin Franklin and other dignitaries. On the early deaths of her owners, Wheatley was freed, though she fell into poverty and obscurity. She died in childbirth and was buried in an unmarked grave.

Wheatstone, Charles

b. February, 1802
Gloucester, England
d. October 19, 1875
Paris, France
fields: Invention and Technology (telegraphy), Engineering (electrical), Physics

From the joining of William Fothergill Cooke's entrepreneurial skills and Charles Wheatstone's scientific knowledge came the world's first commercial telegraph network. Wheatstone also made valuable contributions to later developments in telegraph as well as dynamo technology, electrical engineering, and the physics of sound, light, and electricity.

Wheeler, Anna Johnson Pell

né: Anna Johnson
later: Anna Johnson Pell
b. May 5, 1883
Calliope (now Hawarden), Iowa
d. Mar. 26, 1966
Bryn Mawr, Pennsylvania
fields: Mathematics (algebra, calculus, and set theory)

Anna Johnson Pell Wheeler worked on the theory of integral equations and functional analysis.

Wheeler, John Archibald

b. July 9, 1911
Jacksonville, Florida
fields: Astronomy, Physics

John Archibald Wheeler, in 1942, joined the Manhattan Project; in 1944, diagnosed the first case of reactor "poisoning" by the by-products of fission; in 1950, began working to develop a hydrogen bomb; in 1957, used the MANIAC computer to determine the result of the collapse of a star; in 1967, coined the term "black hole."

Whipple, George Hoyt

b. August 28, 1878
Ashland, New Hampshire
d. February 1, 1976
Rochester, New York
fields: Medicine, Physiology

Using anemic dogs, Whipple studied the effects of many foods on the regeneration of hemoglobin. Along with two others, he won the Nobel Prize in Physiology or Medicine in 1934 for the discovery that liver was valuable in the treatment of pernicious anemia.

Whipple, Henry B.

full: Henry Benjamin Whipple
b. February 15, 1822
Adams, New York
d. September 16, 1901
Faribault, Minnesota
fields: Religion and Theology

Henry B. Whipple was a Christian bishop; Episcopal bishop of Minnesota, 1859; convinced of government cruelty and corruption in dealing with Indians, appealed to Presidents James Buchanan, Abraham Lincoln, and Ulysses S. Grant, leading eventually to Indian Appropriations Act of 1869 and an ostensible peace policy.

Whirling Bear. *See* Conquering Bear

Whistler, James McNeill

full: James Abbott McNeill Whistler
b. July 10, 1834
Lowell, Massachusetts
d. July 17, 1903
London, England
fields: Arts, Literature

Aside from producing one of the most popular and best-known paintings in the world, Whistler developed an artistic style and ideas about the role of the artist which were to influence art and art criticism throughout the world.

Whitaker, Forest

b. July 15, 1961
Longview, Tex.
fields: Film

African American actor; Forest Whitaker has appeared in a number of popular films, including *Fast Times at Ridgemont High* (1982), *The Color of Money* (1986), *Platoon* (1986), *Good Morning, Vietnam* (1987), and *Bird* (1988), for which he won the Best Actor Award at the Cannes Film Festival; also appeared in *A Rage in Harlem* (1991), *The Crying Game* (1992), *Jason's Lyric* (1994), and *Phenomenon* (1996); he has directed such films as *Waiting to Exhale* (1995) and *Hope Floats* (1998).

Whitaker, Louis Rodman

b. May 12, 1957
Brooklyn, N.Y.
fields: Sports (baseball player)

African American baseball player; Louis Rodman Whitaker played for the Detroit Tigers, beginning in 1977.

White, Barry

b. September 12, 1944
Galveston, Tex.
fields: Music (singer, songwriter, and record producer)

African American singer, songwriter, and record producer; Barry White wrote "The Harlem Shuffle," a rhythm-and-blues hit recorded by Bob and Earl; known for his deep, husky voice and lush orchestral arrangements, pioneered disco; big hit was "Love's Theme" (1973), written for the Love Unlimited Orchestra.

White, Bill

full: William DeKova White
b. January 28, 1934
Lakewood, Fla.
fields: Sports (baseball player)

African American baseball player and president of the National League; Bill White played for the New York Giants in the late 1950's until being traded to the St. Louis Cardinals in 1959, with whom he played until 1965.

White, Byron R.

full: Byron Raymond White
b. June 8, 1917
Fort Collins, Colo.
fields: Law

U.S. Supreme Court justice, 1962-1993; appointed by President Kennedy. Critical of the exclusionary rule and expansive view of the scope of protection offered by the Fourth Amendment. Significant opinions: *Miranda v. Arizona*, 384 U.S. 436 (1966) (dissenting opinion); *Camara v. Municipal Court of the City and County of San Francisco*, 387 U.S. 523 (1967); *Duncan v. Louisiana*, 391 U.S. 145 (1968); *Chambers v. Maroney*, 399 U.S. 42 (1970); *United States v. Matlock*, 415 U.S. 164 (1974); *Stone v. Powell*, 428 U.S. 465 (1976) (dissenting opinion); *United States v. Leon*, 468 U.S. 897 (1984); *New Jersey v. T.L.O.*, 469 U.S. 325 (1985); *California v. Greenwood*, 486 U.S. 35 (1988).

White, Charles

b. April 2, 1918
Chicago, Illinois
d. October 3, 1979
Los Angeles, California
fields: Art (painter)

African American painter; Charles White is considered an eminent leader in social art; best known work is his mural *The Contribution of the Negro to American Democracy.*

White, Cheryl

b. 1954
Rome, Ohio
fields: Sports (jockey)

African American jockey; Cheryl White became the first recognized female jockey in 1971.

White, Edward Douglass

b. November 3, 1845
near Thibodaux, La.
d. May 19, 1921
Washington, D.C.
fields: Law

U.S. Supreme Court justice, 1894-1910; ninth chief justice of the United States, 1910-1921. Appointed by President Cleveland. Significant opinion: *Rasmussen v. United States*, 197 U.S. 506 (1905). White provided moderately conservative leadership to the Supreme Court during the Progressive era.

White, Ellen G.

né: Ellen Gould Harmon
b. November 26, 1827
Gorham, Maine
d. July 16, 1915
St. Helena, California
fields: Religion and Theology

Cofounder of the Seventh-day Adventist church, Ellen G. White was a charismatic religious leader, a health reformer, and an educator.

White, George Henry

b. December 18, 1852
Rosindale, N.C.
d. December 28, 1918
Philadelphia, Pa.
fields: Government and Politics

U.S. representative from North Carolina. White was born into slavery but was elected to the North Carolina state senate in 1884; was elected to the U.S. Congress in 1896 and was the only African American to serve in the fifty-fifth Congress; founded Whitesboro, a black township in New Jersey; founded the People's Savings Bank, which served African American homeowners and entrepreneurs.

White, Maurice

b. December 19, 1941
Memphis, Tenn.
fields: Music (singer, percussionist, songwriter)

African American singer, percussionist, songwriter, and leader of Earth, Wind, and Fire; Maurice White worked successfully as a session musician before forming the popular rock/soul band.

White, Michael Reed

b. August 13, 1951
Cleveland, Ohio
fields: Government and Politics

African American mayor and politician; Michael Reed White served on the Cleveland city council (1977-1984) and was a member of the Ohio state senate (1984-1989). He received an Outstanding Young Leader Award from the Cleveland Jaycees in 1979 and also a Service Award from the East Side Jaycees. White was presented with an Outstanding Service Award by the Cleveland Chapter of the National Association of Black Veterans in 1985. He took office as the mayor of Cleveland, Ohio, in 1990.

White, Reggie

full: Reginald Howard White
b. December 19, 1961
Chattanooga, Tenn.
fields: Sports (football player), Religion and Theology

African American professional football player and ordained minister. In 1984 Reggie White was signed by the Memphis Showboats of the United States Football League (USFL). In 1985 he was released by the Showboats and began playing as a defensive end for the Philadelphia Eagles of the National Football League (NFL) that year. With Philadelphia White played in the Pro Bowl in seven consecutive seasons and established a record in the NFL for all-time sacks. White signed to the Green Bay Packers for the 1993-1994 season and continued with them through the end of the decade as a premier defensive end. White, an ordained minister, organized a program—through local churches—that provides inner-city residents with low-interest loans.

White, Ruth

b. 1951 or 1952
fields: Sports (fencer)

African American fencer; Ruth White was the youngest national fencing champion and the first African American to win a major American fencing title (1969); competed in the 1972 Olympics.

White, Slappy

full: Melvin White
b. 1921
Baltimore, Maryland
d. November 7, 1995
Brigantine, New Jersey
fields: Theater and Entertainment

African American comedian; Slappy White was the comedy partner of Redd Foxx in the 1950's; remained a popular live performer and appeared in a number of television programs in the 1970's, including *Sanford and Son* (1972-1977); he also appeared in the Billy Crystal film *Mr. Saturday Night* (1992).

White, Walter

b. July 1, 1893
Atlanta, Georgia
d. March 21, 1955
New York, New York
fields: Civil Rights

As the chief administrator of the NAACP during many of its formative years, White helped pave the way for the monumental changes that advanced U.S. civil rights and race relations in the second half of the twentieth century.

White, Willye B.

b. January 1, 1939
Money, Mich.
fields: Sports (long jumper and runner)

African American long jumper and runner; Willye B. White won a silver medal in the 1956 Olympics in the long jump; became the first female track and field athlete to represent the United States in five Olympics (1956-1972); was the first individual to be awarded the Pierre de Coubertin International Fair Play Trophy (1965).

White Bird

aka: Penpenhihi
aka: Peopeo Kiskiok Hihih (White Goose)
b. c. 1807
Idaho
d. c. 1882
Canada
fields: Warfare and Conquest, Religion and Theology, Native American Affairs

Native American leader. A skilled Nez Perce negotiator and marksman, White Bird was a leader in the Nez Perce War of 1877. Along with Chief Joseph (Joseph the Elder), White Bird refused to sign the Treaty of 1863, by which the Nez Perce would move to the Lapwai Reservation in Idaho. In the Nez Perce War, the retreating Nez Perce were overtaken in the Bear Paw Mountains (Montana), only 30 miles from Canada, and defeated. After a six-day siege at the Battle of Bear Paw, beginning September 30, White Bird, with approximately twenty other Nez Perce leaders and two hundred followers, managed to retreat to Canada.

White Cloud

aka: Wabanaquot
b. c. 1830
Gull Lake, Minn.
d. 1898
White Earth Reservation, Minn.
fields: Diplomacy, Government and Politics, Native American Affairs

Native American leader. An Ojibwa (Chippewa), White Cloud was a renowned peace chief, diplomat, and orator. He led his people to the White Earth Reservation in 1868, where they adopted sedentary agriculture and settled into a life of peace. White Cloud became dependent on alcohol and earned a reputation as a chief who accepted bribes and acted against the best interests of his tribe in favor of feeding his own addiction.

White Eyes

aka: Koquethagechton
b. c. 1730
western Pa.
d. Nov., 1778
Pa.
fields: Government and Politics, Warfare and Conquest, Diplomacy, Native American Affairs

White Eyes, a Delaware (Lenni Lenape), became principal chief of the Ohio Delawares in 1776. At the beginning of the American Revolution he counselled neutrality, but he took up the Patriot cause after the Delaware leader Hopocan sided with the British.

White Man Runs Him

aka: Batsida Karoosh
aka: Beshayeschayecoosis
aka: Miastashedekaroos (White Man Runs Him)
b. c. 1855
d. c. 1925
fields: Warfare and Conquest, Native American Affairs

Crow warrior White Man Runs Him, in his youth, participated in numerous horse-stealing raids against the Sioux. In the 1870's, he was chief Indian scout in Custer's Seventh Cavalry. While on a scouting foray,

White Man Runs Him and four other scouts, in search of Sioux who had left the reservation, spotted them encamped on the banks of the Little Bighorn River. The sighting was reported to Custer, and the stage was set for the Battle of the Little Bighorn (1876).

Whitehead, Alfred North

b. February 15, 1861
Ramsgate, Isle of Thanet, Kent, England
d. December 30, 1947
Cambridge, Massachusetts
fields: Philosophy, Mathematics

Striving for a more comprehensive and unified system of human knowledge, Whitehead made major contributions to mathematical logic and produced a wholly original and modern metaphysics.

Whitfield, Lynn

b. May 6, 1953
Baton Rouge, Louisiana
fields: Film, Television

African American film and television actress; Lynn Whitfield won an Emmy Award for her title role in the film *The Josephine Baker Story* (1991); was featured in such television films as *Johnnie Mae Gibson: FBI* (1986) and *The Women of Brewster Place* (1989), and in the series *Heartbeat* (1989) and *The Wedding* (1998); her film roles include *Jaws: The Revenge* (1987), *Dead Aim* (1988), *Eve's Bayou* (1997), and *The Color of Courage* (1998).

Whitfield, Norman

b. 1943
New York, N.Y.
fields: Music (songwriter and producer)

African American songwriter and producer; Norman Whitfield cowrote, with Barrett Strong, the Marvin Gaye hit "I Heard it Through the Grapevine" (1968); helped Motown transition to the "psychedelic soul" sound.

Whitlam, Gough

full: Edward Gough Whitlam
b. July 11, 1916
Kew, Victoria, Australia
fields: Government and Politics

Prime minister of Australia from 1972 to 1975. Gough Whitlam became Labor Party leader in 1967; reformed party. As prime minister, instituted social reforms: made college education free for those who were academically qualified, introduced welfare payments for single-parent families and homeless people, and abolished the death penalty for federal crimes. Also led movement to acknowledge cultural contributions of Australian Aborigines. Liberal Party in Senate opposed his policies. Because of increases in inflation and unemployment, Labor Party fell out of favor and was voted out in 1975.

Whitman, Walt

full: Walter Whitman, Jr.
b. May 31, 1819
West Hills, New York
d. March 26, 1892
Camden, New Jersey
fields: Literature

The first real poet of American English, Whitman created a language to express the spirit of American democracy and used that language to shape a vision of a new continent that still fires the American imagination.

Whitney, Eli

b. December 8, 1765
Westborough, Massachusetts
d. January 8, 1825
New Haven, Connecticut
fields: Invention and Technology

Whitney, the inventor of the cotton gin, which revolutionized agriculture in the South, also contributed to the nation's industrial development by founding one of its first manufacturing establishments.

Whitney, Gertrude Vanderbilt

né: Gertrude Vanderbilt
b. January 9, 1875
New York, New York
d. April 18, 1942
New York, New York
fields: Art, Patronage of the Arts

Whitney was a distinguished American sculptor of figures, monuments, and reliefs for the public domain and an art patron and founder of the Whitney Museum of American Art in New York.

Whittaker, Charles Evans

b. 1901
d. 1973
fields: Law

U.S. Supreme Court justice, 1957-1962; appointed by President Eisenhower. Supplied the critical vote in a series of 5-4 decisions in which the Supreme Court rejected individual rights claims in state criminal cases. Significant opinions: *Draper v. United States*, 358 U.S. 307 (1959).

Whitten, Jack

b. 1939
Bessemer, Ala.
fields: Art (painter)

African American painter; Jack Whitten's works were featured in a one-man show at the Allan Stone Gallery in 1970; has taught at the Pratt Institute.

Whittier, John Greenleaf

b. December 17, 1807
Haverhill, Massachusetts
d. September 7, 1892
Hampton Falls, New Hampshire
fields: Literature

Over a career spanning more than sixty years, Whittier produced a large body of poetry that was not only extremely popular in its own day but also reflected with remarkable clarity and consistency some of the cultural and social attitudes of nineteenth century America.

Whittle, Frank

aka: Sir Frank Whittle
b. June 1, 1907
Coventry, Warwickshire, England
d. August 8, 1996
Columbia, Maryland
fields: Engineering (aeronautical)

With a background that included flight experience, training in power-plant design, and metalworking skills, Whittle designed and built the first jet engine in Great Britain.

Wide Mouth. *See* Flat Mouth

Wideman, John Edgar

b. June 14, 1941
Washington, D.C.
fields: Literature (novelist, short-story writer, and scholar)

African American novelist, short-story writer, and scholar; John Edgar Wideman's best known work is his Homewood trilogy, comprising *Hiding Place* (1981), *Damballah* (1981), and *Sent for You Yesterday* (1983).

Widukind

b. Eighth century
probably Saxony (modern Germany)
d. c. 807
place unknown
fields: Government and Politics, Military Affairs, Religion and Theology

As a pivotal military and spiritual leader of the Saxons in their numerous struggles against the expanding Frankish empire, Widukind organized several pagan rebellions that repeatedly forced Charlemagne to re-establish his supremacy within the region of Saxony.

Wiebe, Rudy

b. October 4, 1934
Fairholme, Saskatchewan, Canada
fields: Literature

Rudy Wiebe is a writer; born in Saskatchewan to Russian immigrants; briefly edited the *Mennonite Brethren Herald* in the early 1960's; wrote widely on encounters between Anglo-Canadians and Mennonites, the Metis, and native Canadians; began teaching at the University of Alberta in 1967; wrote *Peace Shall Destroy Many* (1962), *The Blue Mountains of China* (1970), *The Temptations of Big Bear* (1973), *My Lovely Enemy* (1983), and *A Discovery of Strangers* (1994).

Wien, Wilhelm

b. Jan. 13, 1864
Gaffken, near Fischhausen, East Prussia (now Primorsk, Russia)
d. Aug. 30, 1928
Munich, Germany
fields: Physics

Wilhelm Wien researched the laws of heat radiation, making possible the development of quantum theory; won the Nobel Prize in Physics in 1911.

Wiener, Norbert

b. November 26, 1894
Columbus, Missouri
d. March 18, 1964
Stockholm, Sweden
fields: Mathematics, Computer Science

Wiener was a distinguished American mathematician credited with a founding of cybernetics, a science which facilitates comparison of biological and electronic systems by focusing on communication, feedback, and control.

Wiesel, Elie

b. September 30, 1928
Sighet, Romania
fields: Literature, Philosophy, Religion and Theology, Civil Rights

Wiesel is not only a prizewinning novelist, dramatist, and religious philosopher, but by writing and speaking out on behalf of the world's victims, he has become the conscience of modern times. For his work in this area he was awarded the Nobel Peace Prize.

Wiesengrund, Theodor. *See* Adorno, Theodor

Wiesenthal, Simon

b. December 31, 1908
Buczacz, Galicia, Austro-Hungarian Empire (now Buchach, Ukraine)
fields: Law

Wiesenthal, a survivor of a dozen Nazi concentration and death camps, became the world's leading independent Nazi hunter. Between 1945 and 1989, Wiesenthal investigated and brought charges against eleven hundred Nazi war criminals. Through his highly publicized cases and publications, he added significantly to the documentary record of the Holocaust—the Nazi destruction of the European Jews—and contributed more than any other individual to bringing the Nazi perpetrators to justice and keeping the historical memory of the Holocaust alive.

Wightman, Hazel

né: Hazel Virginia Hotchkiss
aka: Hazel Hotchkiss Wightman
b. December 20, 1886
Healdsburg, California
d. December 5, 1974
Chestnut Hill, Massachusetts
fields: Sports (tennis)

Labeled the "Queen Mother" of American tennis, Hazel Hotchkiss Wightman was a four-time national singles champion of the United States Lawn Tennis Association who paved the way for the acceptance of women's tennis as a reputable sport in the United States.

Wigner, Eugene P.

full: Eugene Paul Wigner
b. Nov. 17, 1902
Budapest, Hungary
d. Jan. 1, 1995
Princeton, New Jersey
fields: Physics, Mathematics, Invention and Technology

Eugene P. Wigner studied atomic, nuclear, and particle physics using symmetry principles and group theory; described neutron absorption; designed the first large nuclear reactors; in 1963, won the Nobel Prize in Physics.

Wilberforce, William

b. August 24, 1759
Hull, Yorkshire, England
d. July 29, 1833
London, England
fields: Social Reform

Guided by his Evangelical views, Wilberforce led the fight to end the slave trade and later slavery in the British Empire. He also sought to reform the morals of his country. As a result of his struggles throughout a long parliamentary career, he and his supporters developed a number of techniques designed to mobilize public opinion which have become a standard part of modern British political life.

Wildcat

aka: Coacoochee
b. c. 1810
Yulaka, Fla.
d. 1857
Coahuila, Mexico
fields: Warfare and Conquest, Native American Affairs

Seminole leader Wildcat, beginning with the Second Seminole War in 1835, was known as the most aggressive of the Seminole chieftains during their crusade against the U.S. Army; he was known for carrying a rifle and a scalping knife. In 1841 he urged his followers, including escaped slaves, or Black Seminoles, to give up the fight, and the war ended.

Wilde, Oscar

full: Oscar Fingal O'Flahertie Wills Wilde
b. October 16, 1854
Dublin, Ireland
d. November 30, 1900
Paris, France
fields: Literature, Theater and Entertainment

Wilde's comedies, including such masterpieces as *The Importance of Being Earnest*, were the finest seen on the English stage for many years and have endured as witty testaments to his artistic credo that art is superior to life.

Wilder, L. Douglas

full: Lawrence Douglas Wilder
b. January 17, 1931
Richmond, Va.
fields: Government and Politics

L. Douglas Wilder received a bronze star for extraordinary bravery during the Korean War and became a highly successful Virginia trial lawyer. In the 1950's and 1960's, Wilder was active in the Civil Rights movement, eventually becoming a director of the board of the Richmond National Urban League. In 1969 Wilder ran for the state senate and became the first African American elected to the Virginia senate since Reconstruction. In 1985 he became Virginia's lieutenent governor, and four years later became governor—the first African American to be elected governor of an American state. In 1991 he launched an unsuccessful presidential campaign as a conservative Democrat.

Wilder, Laura Ingalls

né: Laura Ingalls
b. February 7, 1867
Pepin, Wisconsin
d. February 10, 1957
Mansfield, Missouri
fields: Literature

As a newspaper columnist in the 1910's and 1920's, Wilder espoused traditional values. Through the widely acclaimed fictionalized account of her youth in the "Little House" novels, she presented a picture of pioneer and homesteading life from the 1860's to the 1880's.

Wiley, George

b. February 26, 1931
Bayonne, N.J.
d. August 8, 1973
Chesapeake Beach, Md.
fields: Civil Rights

George Wiley left his post as a chemistry professor at Syracuse University to serve as associate director of the Congress of Racial Equality (CORE) from 1964 to 1966. In 1966 he established the National Welfare Rights Organization (NWRO) to lobby on behalf of welfare recipients. He died in 1973, shortly after founding the Movement for Economic Justice.

Wilkens, Lenny

full: Leonard Randolph Wilkens
b. October 28, 1937
Brooklyn, N.Y.
fields: Sports (basketball player and coach)

African American basketball player and coach; Lenny Wilkens was the 1960 first-round draft choice of the St. Louis Hawks; traded to the Seattle Supersonics, then to the Cleveland Cavaliers; became player-coach for the Portland Trail Blazers, retiring as a player in 1975; continued to coach for all three teams.

Wilkes, Charles

b. April 3, 1798
New York, New York
d. February 8, 1877
Washington, D.C.
fields: Exploration and Colonization

Wilkes's determination and leadership as commander of the United States Exploring Expedition of 1838-1842 ensured the success of this major step in the emergence of the United States as a naval and scientific power.

Wilkes, John

b. October 17, 1725
London, England
d. December 26, 1797
London, England
fields: Government and Politics, Journalism

The most famous British radical of the second half of the eighteenth century, Wilkes became the era's preeminent symbol of liberty. His influence was felt in struggles to extend the freedom of the press, in the Wilkite movement that agitated for parliamentary reform, and in the strengthening of American opposition to British policy in the decade preceding the Revolutionary War.

Wilkins, Dominique

full: Jacques Dominique Wilkins
b. January 12, 1960
Paris, France
fields: Sports (basketball player)

African American basketball player; Dominique Wilkins signed with the Atlanta Hawks; was on the NBA All-Star team every season from 1983 to 1991, except for 1984-1985.

Wilkins, George Hubert

aka: Sir George Hubert Wilkins
b. October 31, 1888
East Mount Bryan, South Australia, Australia
d. December 1, 1958
Framingham, Massachusetts
fields: Natural Science, Film, Exploration and Colonization

Wilkins was able to utilize new technological developments and to apply aviation, cinematography, and meteorology in order to understand the diverse conditions of the polar regions during his explorations.

Wilkins, Maurice H. F.

full: Maurice Hugh Frederick Wilkins
b. December 15, 1916
Pongaroa, New Zealand
fields: Physics (biophysics)

Wilkins' X-ray diffraction studies were instrumental in the structure determination of DNA. He was awarded the 1962 Nobel Prize in Physiology or Medicine.

Wilkins, Roger Wood

b. March 25, 1932
Kansas City, Mo.
fields: Journalism, Government and Politics, Education

African American journalist, government official, and educator; President Lyndon B. Johnson named Roger Wood Wilkins director of the Community Relations Service (CRS) in 1966, thus Wilkins became the first black to served as assistant attorney general of the United States. Wilkins joined the Ford Foundation in 1969. He directed funding of programs for job training, education, and drug rehabilitation within poor communities. Wilkins worked for *The Washington Post*, *The New York Times*, and *The Washington Star*. He became a senior fellow at the Institute for Policy Studies in 1982; joined the faculty of George Mason University; named Clarence J. Robinson Professor of History and American Culture in 1987. Wilkins' publications include *A Man's Life: An Autobiography* (1982) and *Quiet Riots: Race and Poverty in the United States* with Fred Harris (1988). He wrote scripts for two documentaries that aired on PBS television: *Keeping the Faith* (1987) and *Throwaway People* (1990).

Wilkins, Roy

b. Aug. 30, 1901
St. Louis, Mo.
d. Sept. 8, 1981
New York, N.Y.
fields: Journalism, Civil Rights

African American journalist, civil rights leader; Roy Wilkins was on the staff of the *Kansas City Call*, 1923-1931; served as assistant executive secretary of the National Association for the Advancement of Colored People (NAACP), 1931-1955; succeeded W. E. B. Du Bois as editor of *The Crisis*, 1934-1949; was executive secretary of the NAACP, 1955-1964; served as executive director of the NAACP, 1964-1977; chairman of the Leadership Conference on Civil Rights; helped organize the March on Washington (1963), at which he was a featured speaker; served on 1967 Presidential Commission on Civil Disorders; fought for political equality and equal economic opportunity within the American democratic tradition.

Wilkinson, Frederick D., Jr.

b. January 25, 1921
Washington, D.C.
d. November 15, 1998
Mount Vernon, New York
fields: Business and Industry

African American business executive; Frederick D. Wilkinson, Jr., served as executive officer for the New York City Transit Authority until he was made vice president for travel by the American Express Company in 1977, where he was made senior vice president in 1985.

Wilkinson, Geoffrey

full: Sir Geoffrey Wilkinson
b. July 14, 1921
Springside, near Todmorden, Yorkshire, England
d. Sept. 26, 1996
London, England
fields: Chemistry

Geoffrey Wilkinson led the field in analyzing the chemistry of organometallic "sandwich" compounds; in 1973, won the Nobel Prize in Chemistry.

Wilkinson, John

b. 1728
Clifton, Cumberland, England
d. July 14, 1808
Bradley, Staffordshire, England
fields: Business and Industry, Invention and Technology

Wilkinson was a pioneer of the Staffordshire iron trade, and he contributed to the perfection of the first steam engine with his inventions for boring cylinders. He aided Abraham Darby III in building the first cast-iron bridge, and he also built the first iron barge and the Paris waterworks.

Wilks, Samuel Stanley

b. June 17, 1906
Little Elm, Texas
d. Mar. 7, 1964
Princeton, New Jersey

fields: Mathematics (probability and statistics)

Samuel Stanley Wilks established improved statistical methods to understand relationships among several variables and how these variables influence one another; president of the Institute of Mathematical Statistics in 1940; president of the American Statistical Association in 1950.

Will, George

b. May 4, 1941
Champaign, Ill.
fields: Journalism, Government and Politics

Conservative columnist and political commentator. A former Michigan University and University of Toronto political science professor with a 1964 doctorate from Princeton University, George Will left academia in 1970. From 1973 to 1975, he served as the Washington editor of the conservative journal *National Review* and earned a national reputation as a syndicated columnist. In 1977, he won a Pulitzer Prize; his many books include *Statecraft as Soulcraft: What Government Does* (1983).

Willard, Emma

né: Emma Hart
b. February 23, 1787
Berlin, Connecticut
d. April 15, 1870
Troy, New York
fields: Education

A strong belief in the need for women to be properly educated influenced Willard to develop new methods of training teachers and to work for the professionalization of teaching.

Willard, Frances

full: Frances Elizabeth Caroline Willard
b. September 28, 1839
Churchville, New York
d. February 18, 1898
New York, New York
fields: Education, Social Reform (temperance), Women's Rights

Advocating a "do everything" policy for reformers in the late nineteenth century, Willard helped advance the causes of temperance and women's rights as president and the most famous and symbolic leader of the Woman's Christian Temperance Union.

William II

né: Prince Friedrich Wilhelm Viktor Albert
b. January 27, 1859
Berlin, Prussia
d. June 4, 1941
Doorn, The Netherlands
fields: Government and Politics, Monarchy

Emperor of Germany and king of Prussia, 1888-1918. After a quarter of a century of straining the patience and tolerance of his fellow rulers with his ill-advised antics, it was William II's misfortune to lead the German Empire during World War I. Although certainly not solely responsible for that conflict, it is hard to deny that his inability to cope with the demands of the modern state helped to create the climate of instability that eventually led to the rise of Adolf Hitler.

William III

né: William of Orange
b. November 14, 1650
the Hague, the Netherlands
d. March 19, 1702
Kensington Palace, London, England
fields: Government and Politics, Diplomacy

As chief executive officer (*stadholder*, 1672-1702) of the United Provinces of the Netherlands and as joint sovereign (1689-1702), with his wife, Mary II, of England, Scotland, and Ireland, William III organized the Grand Alliance of European powers, which eventually defeated Louis XIV and prevented the establishment of French domination over Europe.

William IV

né: William Henry
b. August 21, 1765
Buckingham House, London, England
d. June 20, 1837
Windsor Castle, near London, England
fields: Government and Politics

The Reform Bill of 1832, which may well have averted a revolution, could not have been passed without King William IV's support. His reign also witnessed the continued increase of the House of Commons' power and the continued erosion of the power of the Crown.

William of Auvergne

b. c. 1190
Aurillac, Auvergne, France
d. March 30, 1249
Paris, France
fields: Philosophy

As the first European medieval scholar to attempt to integrate Aristotelian philosophy and Christian theology, William encouraged the growth of philosophy as a discipline distinct from theology and paved the way for the great synthesis of faith and reason of the later Middle Ages.

William of Auxerre

b. c. 1150
Auxerre, France
d. November 3, 1231
Rome
fields: Religion and Theology, Philosophy

As one of the first European medieval scholars to use the methods of philosophy to answer theological questions, William ranks as a pioneer in the growth of Scholasticism and the centuries-long attempt to harmonize Aristotelian philosophy with the theology of Saint Augustine.

William of Moerbeke

b. c. 1215
Moerbeke, near Gent, Flanders
d. c. 1286
Corinth, Greece
fields: Scholarship

Along with many translations of classical works by other authors, William provided Europe with its first Latin translations from the Greek of Aristotle's major works.

William of Rubrouck

aka: Willem van Ruysbroeck
b. c. 1215
Rubrouck, French Flanders
d. c. 1295
place unknown
fields: Exploration

William provided the first accurate account of the geography of Central Asia and of its people, the Mongols. He thus helped to fill in a blank space on the map and opened up a new era of exploration.

William of Saint-Amour

b. c. 1200
Saint-Amour, Jura, France
d. September 13, 1272
Saint-Amour, Jura, France
fields: Religion and Theology

By opposing the papal and royal support of the newly created Franciscan and Dominican orders, William laid the foundations of later Gallican—and even Protestant—opposition to the Papacy.

William of Saint-Thierry

b. Probably between 1075 and 1080
Liège
d. September 8, 1147 or 1148
Signy Abbey, Diocese of Reims, France
fields: Religion and Theology

William of Saint-Thierry, whose name is forever linked with that of Saint Bernard of Clairvaux, was one of the greatest of twelfth century monks, mystics, and theologians of the spiritual life. His writings on love, monastic friendship, and the Trinity were particularly influential.

William the Conqueror

b. Probably c. 1028
Falaise, Normandy, France

d. September 9, 1087
Rouen, France
fields: Government and Politics, Military Affairs

Through his conquest of the English at Hastings in 1066, William made it possible for his Anglo-Norman successors to develop a strong feudal monarchy which flourished for several centuries.

William the Silent

aka: William I
b. April 24, 1533
Dillenburg Castle, Nassau
d. July 10, 1584
Delft, Holland
fields: Government and Politics

Stadholder of the Netherlands, 1579-1584. William, Prince of Orange and Count of Nassau, led the revolt of the Netherlands against Spain despite overwhelming difficulties. His leadership proved decisive to the Dutch independence movement at its crucial beginnings in the late sixteenth century.

Williams, Albert P.

b. ?
Savannah, Georgia
fields: Law

African American judge; Albert P. Williams began to serve as an associate justice on the New York State Supreme Court in 1978.

Williams, Ann Claire

b. August 16, 1949
Detroit, Mich.
fields: Law

African American federal judge; Ann Claire Williams was appointed by Ronald Reagan to the post of U.S. district judge for the Northern District of Illinois in 1985.

Williams, Bert

full: Egbert Austin Williams
b. November 12, 1874
Antigua, West Indies
d. March 4, 1922
New York, N.Y.
fields: Theater and Entertainment

African American vaudeville star; Bert Williams is widely considered among the finest comedians in the history of American show business; appeared in two films, *Darktown Jubliee* (1914) and *A Natural Born Gambler* (1916); recorded such hit songs as "It's Nobody's Business but My Own," "Oh Death Where Is Thy Sting," and "It's Getting So You Can't Trust Nobody"; best known for his work with the Ziegfeld Follies and for his partnership with song-and-dance man George Walker; Walker and Williams created and starred in *In Dahomey*, a Broadway hit in 1903 that also had a successful run in London; the team was responsible for the cakewalk craze that swept England, France, and the United States.

Williams, Billy Dee

b. April 6, 1937
New York, N.Y.
fields: Film

African American actor; Billy Dee Williams played on stage and television before landing the role of Gayle Sayers in the television film *Brian's Song*; starred in a number of films, including two with Diana Ross—*Lady Sings the Blues* (1972) and *Mahogany* (1975)—before playing Lando Calrissian in *The Empire Strikes Back* (1980) and *Return of the Jedi* (1983).

Williams, Billy Leo

b. June 15, 1938
Whistler, Ala.
fields: Sports (baseball player and coach)

African American professional baseball player and coach. A star outfielder for the Chicago Cubs (1961-1974) and the Oakland Athletics (1974-1976) Billy Leo Williams was selected as the National League Rookie of the Year in 1961 and National League and Major League Player of the Year in 1972. Williams played in six All-Star games and holds the National League record for most consecutive games played (1,117). He was elected as a member of the Baseball Hall of Fame in 1987. After he retired as a player Williams served as a coach and hitting instructor for the Chicago Cubs, the Oakland Athletics, and the Cleveland Indians.

Williams, Chancellor

b. December 22, 1905
Bennettsville, S.C.
fields: Historiography

African American historian; Chancellor Williams attempted to determine the independent achievements of African people and the nature of civilization in Africa before Asian and European influence; *The Destruction of Black Civilization: Great Issues of a Race from 4500 b.c. to 2000 a.d.* (1971) won the 1971 Book Award from the Black Academy of Arts and Letters.

Williams, Charles Edward

b. August 8, 1938
Wedgeworth, Ala.
fields: Military Affairs

African American military officer; Charles Edward Williams retired from the United States Army in 1989 with the rank of major general.

Williams, Clarence, III

b. August 21, 1939
New York, N.Y.
fields: Television, Film

African American actor; Clarence Williams III is best known for his role as Linc Hayes on the television series *The Mod Squad* (1968-1973); also appeared on a number of other television shows, including *Daktari* (1967) and *Miami Vice* (1985); film credits include *Purple Rain* (1984), *I'm Gonna Git You Sucka* (1988), *Deep Cover* (1992), and *Sugar Hill* (1994).

Williams, Daniel Hale

b. January 18, 1856
Hollidaysburg, Pa.
d. August 4, 1931
Idlewild, Mich.
fields: Medicine

African American doctor Daniel Hale Williams was one of the best-known physicians in the United States at the end of the nineteenth century. In 1889 he was appointed to the Illinois State Board of Health. Two years later he founded Provident Hospital for African Americans in Chicago. He performed the first successful heart surgery in 1893.

Williams, David Welford

b. March 20, 1910
Atlanta, Ga.
fields: Law

African American attorney and jurist; David Welford Williams became a judge on the Los Angeles Municipal Court in 1956; joined the Superior Court in 1962; was elevated to the federal bench in 1969.

Williams, Deniece

b. June 3, 1951
Gary, Ind.
fields: Music (pop and gospel singer)

African American singer; Deniece Williams was recruited in 1969 by Stevie Wonder as a backup singer for his group Wonderlove; sang backup on albums by Wonder, Roberta Flack, Minnie Ripperton, and others; wrote a number of hit songs performed by other artists; first solo album, *This Is Niecey*, was released in 1977, with a worldwide hit single, "Free"; released a number-one hit with Johnny Mathis, "Too Much, Too Little, Too Late," in 1978; released a number of pop and gospel albums in the 1980's and 1990's.

Williams, Douglas Lee

b. August 9, 1955
Zachary, La.
fields: Sports (football player)

African American football player; Douglas Lee Williams was drafted by the struggling Tampa Bay Buccanneers expansion team, which he led to its first three play offs; signed as a backup quarterback with the Washington Redskins in 1986 after several seasons in the short-lived United States Football League; was essentially sidelined until an injury to the Redskins' quarterback allowed Williams to lead the team to a come-from-behind victory; was the second African American quarterback to be a first round draft choice and the first to start as quarterback in a Super Bowl; retired in 1989.

Williams, Eddie Nathan

b. August 18, 1932
Memphis, Tenn.
fields: Government and Politics, Journalism

African American political scientist; Eddie Nathan Williams became president of the Joint Center for Political Studies (1972), which assists minority elected officials associated with the National Black Caucus with information on voting patterns and on proposed legislation, among other data; served on the U.S. Senate Committee on Foreign Relations staff and as a foreign service officer in the state department (1961-1968); became vice president for public service at the University of Chicago (1968-1972); was also an editorial columnist for the *Chicago Sun-Times* (1970-1972); served on a number of boards, including for the National Children's Television Workshop and the National Coalition on Black Voter Participation.

Williams, Eleazar

b. May, 1788
St. Regis, N.Y.
d. Aug. 28, 1858
near Hogansburg, N.Y.
fields: Diplomacy, Religion and Theology

Mohawk missionary Eleazar Williams was an influential missionary who tried to use his position to persuade the Iroquois to establish a new empire west of Lake Michigan in the 1820's.

Williams, Fess

full: Stanley R. Williams
b. April 10, 1894
Danville, Ky.
d. December 17, 1975
New York, N.Y.
fields: Music (jazz clarinetist and bandleader)

African American jazz clarinetist and bandleader; Fess Williams was a dance band leader between 1919 and the mid-1940's; his Royal Flush Orchestra played in Harlem and attracted a national following through recordings, tours, and radio broadcasts.

Williams, Franklin H.

b. October 22, 1917
Flushing, N.Y.
fields: Government and Politics, Diplomacy

Franklin H. Williams was appointed to serve as assistant attorney general for the state of California in 1959. He left that post in 1960 to become African regional director for the United States Peace Corps. In 1963 Williams was appointed to serve as U.S. representative to the United Nations Economic and Social Council. From 1965 to 1968 Williams was U.S. ambassador to Ghana.

Williams, George Washington

b. October 16, 1849
Bedford Springs, Pennsylvania
d. August 2, 1891
Blackpool, England
fields: Historiography, Government and Politics

As the author of the first reliable history of black Americans and a prominent political spokesman and observer, Williams contributed to the development of African American identity and racial pride.

Williams, Harvey Dean

b. ?
Whiteville, N.C.
fields: Military Affairs

African American military officer; Harvey Dean Williams retired from the United States Army in 1982 with the rank of major general.

Williams, Hosea

b. January 5, 1926
Attapulgus, Ga.
fields: Civil rights

Hosea Williams was a key figure in the Civil Rights movement, participating in boycotts, sit-ins, and marches. He began publishing the *Crusader* newspaper in 1961 and served as organizer and president of the Atlanta chapter of the Southern Christian Leadership Conference (1967-1969), as SCLC national executive director (1969-1971), and as regional vice president (1970-1971). He was elected to the Georgia state legislature in 1974. He also served on the Atlanta City Council and the De Kaib County Commission. In 1980, he served as an adviser to President Ronald Reagan.

Williams, Joe

b. December 12, 1918
Cordele, Ga.
d. March 29, 1999
Las Vegas, Nev.
fields: Music (jazz singer)

African American singer; Joe Williams was best known for his work with the Count Basie band (1954-1961), including the hit, "All Right, Okay, You Win" (1955); his album *Nothin' but the Blues* won a Grammy Award in 1984.

Williams, John Alfred

b. December 5, 1925
Jackson, Miss.
fields: Literature

African American novelist, journalist, social critic, and educator; John Alfred Williams worked as a correspondent in Africa for Newsweek (1964-1965), after having written for *Ebony* and *Jet* as a correspondent based in Spain (1958-1959); best known for his work as a novelist, including *The Angry Ones* (1961), *Night Song* (1961), *Sissie* (1963), *The Man Who Cried I Am* (1967), *Sons of Darkness, Sons of Light* (1969), *Captain Blackman* (1972), *Mothersill and the Foxes* (1975), *The Junior Bachelor Society* (1976), *!Click Song* (1982), and *Jacob's Ladder* (1987).

Williams, Maggie

full: Margaret Ann Williams
b. December 25, 1954
Kansas City, Mo.
fields: Government and Politics

African American political appointee; Maggie Williams was appointed to serve as chief of staff to First Lady Hillary Rodham Clinton in 1993. Williams was in charge of scheduling, matters of protocol, and press contacts for the First Lady. As a member of the inner circle at the White House, Williams became one of the top-ranking African American officials in the Clinton Administration. In 1994, Williams and other high-level administrators were questioned at a congressional hearing concerning the involvement of the Clintons in the Whitewater investment partnership. Williams was questioned again in 1995.

Williams, Marietta. *See* Sullivan, Maxine

Williams, Marsha. *See* Norman, Marsha

Williams, Mary Lou

né: Mary Elfrieda Scruggs
b. May 8, 1910
Atlanta, Georgia
d. May 28, 1981
Durham, North Carolina
fields: Music

One of the great pianists in the history of jazz, Mary Lou Williams was one of the few jazz musicians to master all the major styles of music that developed during the fifty-year period in which she was an active player. Equally at home playing ragtime, boogie-woogie, swing, and bebop, she was also a gifted composer and arranger. In her later years, she created the Bel Canto Foundation, which was dedicated to caring for jazz musicians who had fallen victim to alcohol and drug addiction.

Williams, Montel B.

b. July 3, 1956
Baltimore, Md.
fields: Television

African American television talk show host. In the summer of 1991 Montel B. Williams began his talk show, *The Montel Williams Show*; it was in its seventh year of national syndication by 1999. Some of Williams' shows dealt with controversial topics such as racism and the growth of hate crimes. He developed a new television series called *Matt Waters* in 1995. In the show, Williams played a former naval officer.

Williams, Ozzie

né: O. S. Williams
b. 1921
fields: Aviation and Space Exploration, Engineering (aeronautical engineer)

African American aeronautical engineer. At Greer Hydraulics, Inc., Ozzie Williams served as a group project engineer and helped to develop the first airborne radar beacon for locating crashed aircraft. Being a specialist in small rocket engine design, Williams was also associated with the Reaction Motors Division of Thiokol Chemical Corporation. He joined Grumman International in 1961 to develop and produce the control rocket systems for the National Aeronautics and Space Administration (NASA) that guided lunar modules during moon landings. He also was the engineer manager responsible for developing the lunar module's reaction control rocket system during the Apollo space program. These maneuvering engines on the lunar landing module helped to save the crew of the Apollo 13 mission. In the 1990's, Williams served as vice president of Grumman International.

Williams, Patricia J.

b. 1951
fields: Law, Literature, Education

African American attorney, educator, and author; Patricia J. Williams is best known for her autobiographical work, *The Alchemy of Race and Rights: Diary of a Law Professor* (1991). It portrays varied instances of racial, gender, and class injustices. With powerful allegories and personal experiences, Williams critically documents conflicting legal theories and practices. Williams taught as an associate professor of law at the University of Wisconsin. Later she became a law professor at Columbia University. Williams' other essays include "Hate Radio" and "Inside the Black Middle Class."

Williams, Paul. *See* Paul, Billy

Williams, Paul Revere

b. February 1894
Los Angeles, Calif.
d. January 23, 1980
Los Angeles, Calif.
fields: Architecture

African American architect; Paul Revere Williams was a popular and respected architect who contributed many landmark buildings in Los Angeles; won a Spingarn Medal in 1953 for his contributions as an architect and designer; designed homes for many of Los Angeles' rich and famous, including Frank Sinatra, Lon Chaney, and Julie London; also designed many buildings for organizations in Los Angeles such as the Young Men's Christian Association and several fraternity and sorority houses at UCLA.

Williams, Paulette. *See* Shange, Ntozake

Williams, Robert Franklin

b. 1925
fields: Civil Rights

In the late 1950's Robert Franklin Williams was president of the National Association for the Advancement of Colored People (NAACP) chapter in Monroe, N.C. Williams organized a rifle corps of fifty African Americans, who responded to a Ku Klux Klan attack on an SCLC officer's home. Williams's militant approach to self-defense and protest resulted in his expulsion from the SCLC in 1959. In 1962, he published *Negroes with Guns.*

Williams, Roger

b. c. 1603
London, England
d. between January 16 and March 15, 1683
Providence, Rhode Island
fields: Religion and Theology

Williams argued for separation of Church and State, freedom of conscience in religious matters, and the possibility of social order in the absence of state regulation of religion.

Williams, Tennessee

né: Thomas Lanier Williams
b. March 26, 1911
Columbus, Mississippi
d. February 24, 1983
New York, New York
fields: Literature

Williams' plays, to a large extent drawn from his own experiences, brought new realism and compelling originality to the American theater.

Williams, Vanessa

b. March 18, 1963
Millwood, N.Y.
fields: Theater and Entertainment, Music

Former Miss America and pop singer; Vanessa Williams was the first African American to win the title of Miss America (in 1983), though she relinquished the title in 1984 after *Penthouse* magazine announced it would print nude photos of her in an upcoming issue; went on to release a number of highly successful albums, including *The Right Stuff* (1989), *The Comfort Zone* (1991) and *The Sweetest Days* (1994); recorded "Colors of the Wind," for the soundtrack of the Walt Disney animated film, *Pocahontas* (1995); Williams also appeared as a host on the VH-1 cable music program *The Soul of VH-1*, among other television, stage, and film appearances.

Williams, Venus

b. June 17, 1980
Lynwood, Calif.
fields: Sports (tennis athlete)

African American tennis athlete. In 1990 Venus Williams began her formal tennis training with Rick Macci in Florida. She entered the ranks of women's professional tennis at fourteen. Williams' professional career is managed by her father, who places emphasis on her formal education and has encouraged her to make public service appearances at schools. In 1997-1998 her world ranking rocketed from number 211 to number 12; in 1998-1999, she made at least the quarterfinals in six of eight Grand Slam tournaments; she is also a top-ranked doubles player with her sister, Serena.

Williams, Vesta

b. 1963
Coshocton, Ohio
fields: Music (pop vocalist)

African American pop vocalist; Vesta Williams's work includes her 1986 album *Vesta*, which contained the hit single "Once Bitten Twice Shy," and her follow-up album, *Special* (1991), which was also a best-seller.

Williams, Walter Edward

b. March 31, 1936
Philadelphia, Pa.
fields: Education, Economics

African American educator and conservative economist; Walter Edward Williams taught at Temple University and later joined the faculty at George Mason University; there he became the John M. Olin Distinguished Professor of Economics. In articles and books such as *America: A Minority Viewpoint* (1982) and *The State Against Blacks* (1982), Williams argues that government social programs hamper a free market society and do not encourage self-reliance, but rather perpetuate poverty, dependency, and immorality.

Williams, Wayne Bertram

b. May 27, 1958
fields: Law (crime)

African American accused serial killer; Wayne Bertram Williams was convicted of killing two young men in 1981 and was strongly suspected of murdering twenty-eight African American children in a series of killings known as the Atlanta Child Murders; the killings stopped after Williams's arrest.

Williams, William Thomas

b. July 17, 1942
Cross Creek, N.C.
fields: Art (painter)

African American painter. Considered a member of the lyrical Expressionist school from the early 1970's, William Thomas Williams acknowledges a debt to jazz improvisation; color and brushwork is interwoven in his painting in a way that allows countless variations on a theme. Williams' concern is primarily with the surface and materials of his painting. Though landscapes are suggested by his work, the emphasis remains the artist's memory and experience, rather than an accurate depiction of nature.

Williams, Willie

full: Willie Lawrence Williams
b. October 1, 1943
Philadelphia, Pa.
fields: Law (law enforcement)

African American law enforcement executive; Willie Williams became Philadelphia's city police commissioner in 1988. He established police mini-stations in strategic locations throughout the city to respond more effectively in crime-ridden areas and encouraged the concept of community policing. Based on his success in Philadelphia, Williams filled the post of Los Angeles police chief. As police chief, Williams had to contend with incidents such as negative publicity in the wake of the Rodney King beating, the 1992 Los Angeles riots, and the highly publicized trial of O. J. Simpson. Williams published a book entitled *Taking Back Our Streets: Fighting Crime in America* in 1996. He left the LAPD in 1997.

Williams, Willie. *See* Williamson, Sonny Boy, II

Williamson, Fred

b. March 5, 1938
Gary, Ind.
fields: Film

African American actor, director, and producer; Fred Williamson is best known for his starring roles as the hero of action movies during the Blaxploitation era of the 1970's.

Williamson, Lisa. *See* Souljah, Sister

Williamson, Sonny Boy

né: John Lee Williamson
b. March 30, 1914
Jackson, Tenn.
d. June 1, 1948
Chicago, Ill.
fields: Music (blues)

Sonny Boy Williamson was a blues harmonica player. In the 1930's he relocated to Chicago, Ill., where he recorded a number of songs on the Bluebird label, including the classics "Good Morning, Little Schoolgirl" and "Stop Breakin' Down." In 1946, Williamson formed a new band that recorded for the Victor label.

Williamson, Sonny Boy, II

né: Aleck Ford
aka: Rice Miller
aka: Willie Miller
aka: Willie Williams
aka: Little Boy Blue
aka: Sib
b. December 5, 1899
Glendora, Miss.
d. May 25, 1965
Helena, Ark.
fields: Music (blues)

Sonny Boy Williamson II was an itinerant blues musician throughout the 1930's. In 1941 he and Robert Lockwood, Jr., began appearing on "King Biscuit Time," an afternoon radio show broadcast daily on KFFA in Helena, Ark. It was probably for this show that Miller adopted the name "Sonny Boy Williamson," though John Lee Williamson, a Chicago-based blues harmonica player, was already using that name. In 1951 he recorded for the Trumpet label such classics as "Eyesight to the Blind," "Mighty Long Time," "Pontiac Blues," and "Nine Below Zero." In 1955 Williamson to Milwaukee, Wis., and began recording for the Checker-Chess label. He was a popular figure in the 1960's blues revival.

Willie, Charles Vert

b. October 8, 1927
Dallas, Tex.
fields: Sociology

African American researcher, writer, and social scientist; Charles Vert Willie has authored or edited more than a dozen books, including *The Family Life of Black People* (1970); *Black Students at White Colleges* (1972); *A New Look at Black Families* (1976); *Five Black Scholars: An Analysis of Family Life, Education, and Career* (1986); *African Americans and the Doctoral Experience: Implications for Policy* (1991 with Michael Grady and Richard Hope), and *The Education of African Americans* (1990 with Antoine Garibaldi and Wornie Reed).

Willis, Dorothy Ann. *See* Richards, Ann

Willis, Thomas

b. Jan. 27, 1621
Great Bedwyn, Wiltshire, England
d. Nov. 11, 1675
London, England
fields: Medicine

Thomas Willis was an anatomist; clarified the circulation in the brain; region of the brain now called the circle of Willis in his honor.

Willke, Jack

full: John Charles Willke
b. April 5, 1925
Maria Stein, Ohio
fields: Social Reform

Pro-life author and leader. Jack Willke is the coauthor (along with his wife Barbara) of pro-life materials including *Handbook on Abortion* (1971) and *Abortion: Questions and Answers* (1985). He served as president of the National Right to Life Committee (NRLC) from 1980 to 1983 and again from 1984 to 1991 and became president of the International Right to Life Federation in 1985. He founded the Life Issues Institute in 1991.

Willoughby, Charles A.

b. Mar. 8, 1892
Heidelberg, Germany
d. Oct. 25, 1972
Naples, Fla.
fields: Warfare and Conquest

Charles A. Willoughby was chief of intelligence on General Douglas MacArthur's staff in the Philippine campaign in 1941. He served in the southwest Pacific from 1941 to 1946 and was a veteran of Bataan and Corregidor. Willoughby was MacArthur's representative in negotiations to receive the surrender of the Imperial Japanese delegation in August, 1945. His published works include *The Economic and Military Participation of the United States in the World War* (1931) and *Maneuver in War* (1939).

Wills, Frank

b. ?
fields: Historical Figure

African American security guard; Frank Wills detained the Watergate burglars when he discovered them installing surveillance equipment in the offices occupied by the Democratic Party National Headquarters.

Wills, Harry

b. May 15, 1892
New Orleans, La.
d. December 21, 1958
New York, N.Y.
fields: Sports (boxer)

African American boxer; Harry Wills, nicknamed "The Brown Panther," Wills was one of the top heavyweight contenders through much of the 1920's; was not allowed to fight white champion Jack Dempsey, but retired in 1932 after losing only 8 of 102 official fights.

Wills, Maury

full: Maurice Morning Wills
b. October 2, 1932
Washington, D.C.
fields: Sports (baseball player)

African American baseball player; Maury Wills was an All-Star shortstop for the Los Angeles Dodgers for five years in the 1960's, reviving the stolen base as an offensive weapon.

Wilson, August

b. April 27, 1945
Pittsburgh, Pa.
fields: Literature

African American playwright; August Wilson wrote a number of critically acclaimed plays, including *Ma Rainey's Black Bottom* (pr. 1984), *Fences* (1985), *Joe Turner's Come and Gone* (pr. 1986), and *The Piano Lesson* (pr. 1988).

Wilson, Demond

b. October 13, 1946
Valdosta, Ga.
fields: Television

African American actor and evangelist; Demond Wilson is best known as Lamont Sanford on the television series *Sanford and Son*, costarring Redd Foxx (1972-1977); also starred in *The New Odd Couple* (1982-1983); retired from acting to become an evangelist in Southern California.

Wilson, Edmund

b. May 8, 1895
Red Bank, New Jersey
d. June 12, 1972
Talcottville, New York
fields: Literature

Combining an acute literary sensibility with both a social and a historical point of view, Wilson became an influential force in twentieth century literature and literary criticism.

Wilson, Edward O.

full: Edward Osborne Wilson
b. June 10, 1929
Birmingham, Alabama
fields: Biology, Zoology

Edward O. Wilson worked on ants; produced important sociobiology theories about many species, including humans; in 1979, won the Pulitzer Prize for his 1978 book *On Human Nature*.

Wilson, Ellis

b. April 30, 1899
Mayfield, Kentucky
d. January 1, 1977
New York, New York
fields: Art

African American painter; Ellis Wilson's work is represented in many museums and private collections, including the Schomburg Collection of the New York Public Library.

Wilson, Flip

full: Clerow Wilson
b. December 8, 1933
Jersey City, New Jersey
d. November 25, 1998
Malibu, California
fields: Theater and Entertainment

African American comedian; Flip Wilson was one of the most popular comedians of the 1970's; was a regular at the Apollo Theater and, in 1965, began appearing on *The Tonight Show*; hosted the NBC television variety program *The Flip Wilson Show* from 1970-1974.

Wilson, Harold

full: James Harold Wilson
aka: Sir Harold Wilson
b. March 11, 1916
Huddersfield, Yorkshire, England
d. May 24, 1995
London, England
fields: Government and Politics

As prime minister for eight years, from 1964 to 1976, Wilson became the most successful politician of the postwar era, winning four general elections of the five he contested as leader of the Labour Party.

Wilson, Jack. *See* Wovoka

Wilson, Jackie

full: Jack Wilson
b. January 17, 1918
Spencer, N.C.
d. March 10, 1956
fields: Sports (boxer)

African American boxer; Jackie Wilson was defeated only once as an amateur, in the finals of the 1936 Olympics; boxed professionally for thirteen years without competing for a championship, though he fought a number of the great boxers of his era; retired in 1949 with a professional record of 69 wins, 19 losses, and 5 draws.

Wilson, Jackie

aka: Mr. Excitement
b. June 9, 1934
Detroit, Mich.
d. January 21, 1984
Mount Holly, N.J.
fields: Music (singer)

African American singer; Jackie Wilson was an influential figure in the development of rhythm and blues and pop music in the 1950's and 1960's; replaced Clyde McPhatter in the Dominoes until going solo with a string of top-forty hits; in 1960, released two number one hits: "Doggin' Around" and "A Woman, A Lover, A Friend"; after recovering from wounds accidentally inflicted by a suicidal fan in 1961, continued to record pop and rhythm and blues hits throughout the 1960's.

Wilson, James

b. September 14, 1742
Carskerdo, Scotland
d. August 21, 1798
Edenton, North Carolina
fields: Law

Wilson was a leader in the movement for American independence, one of the most important members of the Philadelphia Convention, which created the United States Constitution, and a powerful advocate in Pennsylvania for its ratification. He was renowned for his learning in law and political theory, and George Washington appointed him to the first United States Supreme Court.

Wilson, John

b. April 14, 1922
Boston, Mass.
fields: Art

African American painter, printmaker, illustrator, and educator; John Wilson's work is in many collections in the United States and abroad, including those held by the Bezalel Museum in Jerusalem and by the French government.

Wilson, Lance Henry

b. July 5, 1948
New York, N.Y.
fields: Government and Politics

African American political appointee and attorney; Lance Henry Wilson was appointed by Ronald Reagan to serve as executive assistant to Secretary Samuel R. Pierce, Jr., of the Department of Housing and Urban Development (1981-1984); served as president of the New York City Housing Development Corporation (1984).

Wilson, Lionel J.

b. March 14, 1915
New Orleans, La.
d. January 23, 1998
Oakland, Calif.
fields: Government and Politics

African American mayor of Oakland, Calif; Lionel J. Wilson was appointed by California governor Edmund "Pat" Brown appointed Wilson to the Oakland Piedmont Municipal Court in 1960 and then to the Superior Court in 1964; became presiding judge of the Alameda County Superior Court in 1973; was elected mayor of Oakland in 1977, becoming the first African American mayor of Oakland; reelected mayor in 1981, serving until 1990.

Wilson, Margaret Bush

b. January 30, 1919
St. Louis, Mo.
fields: Civil Rights

Margaret Bush Wilson was the first African American woman to be named as national chair of the National Association for the Advancement of Colored People (NAACP), beginning in 1975. She served with numerous community organizations, including the St. Louis Model City Agency, the Missouri Council on Criminal Justice, and St. Louis Lawyers for Housing.

Wilson, Mary

b. March 6, 1944
Greenville, Miss.
fields: Music (singer)

African American singer; Mary Wilson, with Florence Ballard and Diana Ross, formed the Supremes; took a back up role in the group under the direction of Barry Gordy, who chose to enhance Ross's role; objected to light pop lyrics of the Supreme's material, but stayed with the group even after the departure of Ballard; released *Supreme Faith: Someday We'll Be Together* (1990), a critical remembrance of the group and her relationship with Motown.

Wilson, Nancy

b. February 20, 1937
Chillicothe, Ohio
fields: Music (jazz singer)

African American jazz singer; Nancy Wilson had a hit with "Guess Who I Saw Yesterday" in the 1950's and continued recording and performing; coheads Wil-Den Enterprises, an organization that manages and publishes the works of other entertainers, with her husband Kenny Dennis.

Wilson, Olly

b. September 7, 1937
St. Louis, Mo.
fields: Music (composer)

African American composer; Olly Wilson's works include *Structure for Orchestra* (1960), *Sextet* (1963), *Cetus* (1967), *In Memoriam—Martin Luther King, Jr.* (1969), *Voices* (1970), and *Akwan* (1974).

Wilson, Pete

b. Aug. 23, 1933
Lake Forest, Ill.
fields: Government and Politics

U.S. politician. Pete Wilson served in the California Assembly, as the mayor of San Diego, and as a U.S. senator before becoming governor of California in 1991. In 1994, he won a second term as governor. He opposed affirmative action programs and called for cuts in government spending. He sought the 1996 Republican presidential nomination but withdrew from the race in September, 1995.

Wilson, Shanice

b. 1973
fields: Music (pop vocalist)

African American pop vocalist; Shanice Wilson's first album, *Discovery*, was critically acclaimed but failed to achieve commercial success; her second album, *Inner Child*, was released in 1991.

Wilson, Teddy

full: Theodore Shaw Wilson
b. November 24, 1912
Austin, Tex.
d. July 31, 1986
New Britain, Conn.
fields: Music (jazz pianist)

African American pianist; Teddy Wilson was a important swing-era pianist, playing with many of the greatest figures of his era; joined the Benny Carter band in 1933; played in the Benny Goodman trio, one of the first integrated groups, from 1935 to 1939; was closely associated with the careers of Billie Holiday and Lester Young; his recordings include *Blue Interlude* (1933), *Body and Soul* (1935), *Between the Devil and the Deep Blue Sea* (1937), *Jim* (1941), *Pres and Teddy* (1956 with Lester Young), *Three Little Words* (1976), *With Billie in Mind* (1972), *Striding After Fats* (1974), and *Cole Porter Classics* (1977).

Wilson, William G.

full: William Griffith Wilson
aka: Bill Wilson
b. November 26, 1895
East Dorset, Vt.
d. January 24, 1971
Miami Beach, Fla.
fields: Medicine

William G. Wilson played a major role in developing the twelve-step recovery program used by Alcoholics Anonymous (AA), and other recovery organizations. He began his career as a successful stockbroker but had a drinking problem that worsened when the 1929 stockmarket crash left him in debt. In 1935, after undergoing a spiritual conversion, he and a fellow alcoholic founded AA as forum for people with dependencies to talk about their experiences. Wilson's publications include *Alcoholics Anonymous* (1939), a compendium of individual alcoholics' experiences in recovery, and *Twelve Steps and Twelve Traditions* (1953), which outlined the organization's philosophy and procedure.

Wilson, William Julius

b. December 20, 1935
Derry Township, Pa.
fields: Sociology

African American professor of sociology and public policy. William Julius Wilson taught at the University of Chicago from 1971 to 1975, becoming a full professor in 1975. While at Chicago Wilson held several distinguished professorships. He also held a post at the University of Massachusetts, Amherst, from 1965 to 1971. Wilson served on the board of directors for the Center for National Policy and the Center for Advanced Study of Behavioral Sciences. Wilson's published works include *Power, Racism, and Privilege* (1973), *The Declining Significance of Race: Blacks and Changing American Institutions* (1979), and *The Truly Disadvantaged* (1987). Wilson's key theory was that neither the vestiges of institutionalized racism nor the existence of a persistent culture of poverty had as great an effect on the socioeconomic status of African Americans as America's changing economic structure in the late twentieth century.

Wilson, Woodrow

full: Thomas Woodrow Wilson
b. December 28, 1856
Staunton, Virginia
d. February 3, 1924
Washington, D.C.
fields: Government and Politics

As twenty-eighth president of the United States (1913-1921), Wilson was responsible for American entry into World War I, was one of the formulators of the Paris peace settlement, and was the principal architect of the League of Nations.

Wiltshire, George

b. ?
d. ?
fields: Theater and Entertainment

African American comedian; George Wiltshire is known for his work as a straight man for other comedians from the 1920's through the 1950's; performed in Noble Sissle and Eubie Blake's musical *Shuffle Along*; was teamed with comedian Dewey "Pigmeat" Markham, with whom he played the Alhambra Theater in the late 1920's and the Apollo Theater beginning in the 1930's; Wiltshire and Markham were featured with singer Edith Wilson in the Broadway cast of *Hot Rhythm* (1930).

Winans, BeBe

full: Benjamin Winans
b. ?
Detroit, Michigan
fields: Music (gospel singer)

African American gospel singer; BeBe Winans is part of the gospel-singing Winans clan, though frequently partnered with CeCe Winans.

Winans, CeCe

full: Priscilla Winans Love
b. ?
Detroit, Michigan
fields: Music (gospel)

African American gospel singer; CeCe Winans is part of the gospel-singing Winans clan, though frequently partnered with BeBe Winans; her voice is regarded as one of the best in the music business, both gospel and secular.

Winbush, Angela

b. 195?
St. Louis, Missouri
fields: Music (pop vocalist, songwriter, and producer)

African American pop vocalist, songwriter, and producer; Angela Winbush first received recognition for her performance on Stevie Wonder's album *Songs in the Key of Life* (1976); has written, arranged, and produced songs for other artists, including the Isley Brothers, Stephanie Mills, and Janet Jackson; solo albums include *Sharp* and *The Real Thing*; cofounded Angela Winbush Productions in order to promote her performing and producing talents and to assist other young African Americans interested in album production.

Winckelmann, Johann Joachim

b. December 9, 1717
Stendal, Prussia
d. June 8, 1768
Trieste
fields: Art, Archaeology, Historiography

Winckelmann's studies of ancient Greek art profoundly influenced the development of the European neoclassical period in the late eighteenth century. His work helped to shape the areas of literature, the fine arts, art history, and classical archaeology.

Windsor, duke of

né: Prince Edward Albert Christian George Andrew Patrick David
aka: Edward VIII
b. June 23, 1894
Richmond, Surrey, England
d. May 28, 1972
Paris, France
fields: Monarchy, Government and Politics

King Edward VIII of Great Britain and Ireland was crowned in 1936 but abdicated the throne later that same year. He had fallen love with a divorced American woman named Wallis Simpson, and in December he declared his intention to marry her. Facing public disapproval and, worse, a constitutional crisis, he formally abdicated the throne. The duke of Windsor seriously tested the resilience of the British monarchy and created a modern romantic myth known the world over as "the love story of the century."

Winema

aka: Toby Riddle
b. c. 1836
Link River, Calif.
d. May 10, 1932
Klamath Reservation, Oreg.
fields: Diplomacy, Native American Affairs

A Modoc fluent in English, Winema became an interpreter and mediator during the Modoc War of 1873. She was shunned by her cousin, Captain Jack, leader of the Modoc rebellion, after trying to convince him to return to Oregon. In February of 1873, Winema warned a white peace commission of a murder plot by Captain Jack. Ignoring her warning, two members of the commission were killed; Winema rescued a third, Alfred Meacham. Following the war that ensued, Winema became a celebrity, touring cities in a theatrical production about her life.

Winfield, Dave

full: David Mark Winfield
b. October 3, 1951
St. Paul, Minn.
fields: Sports (baseball player)

African American baseball player; Dave Winfield was drafted by four professional teams in three different sports; signed with the San Diego Padres of the National League in 1973; was chosen to NL All-Star teams in 1977, 1978, 1979, and 1980 and earned NL Gold Glove awards in 1979 and 1980; signed a ten-year contract with the New York Yankees of the American League (AL) (1980) and was chosen to AL All-Star teams every year from 1981 to 1988 and won AL Gold Gloves in 1982, 1983, 1984, 1985, and 1987; moved to the California Angels in 1990 and to the Toronto Blue Jays in 1991; in 1992, helped lead the Blue Jays to the World Series title; with the Minnesota Twins, 1993-1994; with the Cleveland Indians, 1994-1996; became an analyst for *Baseball on Fox* in 1996.

Winfield, Hemsley

b. 1907
Yonkers, N.Y.
d. 1934
fields: Dance

African American dancer and choreographer; Hemsley Winfield founded the New Negro Art Theater Dance Group; began as an actor in the 1920's but switched to dance after filling in for an actress in the role of Salome; formed the Negro Art Theater in Harlem to expand black dance beyond vaudeville and musical comedy, incorporating tribal African dance forms and African American themes into a formal concert form.

Winfield, Paul

full: Paul Edward Winfield
b. May 22, 1940
Los Angeles, California
fields: Film, Television

African American actor; Paul Winfield's film career includes roles in *Sounder* (1972), *The Greatest* (1977), *A Hero Ain't Nothin' But a Sandwich* (1977), *Star Trek II: The Wrath of Khan* (1982), *The Serpent and the Rainbow* (1988), *Presumed Innocent* (1990), and *Relax ... It's Just Sex* (1998); also appeared in a number of television programs, including *Backstairs at the Whitehouse*, *Roots: The Next Generations* and *Roots: The Gift*, and *The Women of Brewster Place*; won a 1995 Emmy for a guest appearance on dramatic series *Picket Fences*.

Winfrey, Oprah

full: Oprah Gail Winfrey
b. January 29, 1954
Kosciusko, Mississippi
fields: Film, Television

A talk-show host, actor, producer, and one of the richest women in the entertainment business, Winfrey is the first African American to own a television and film studio.

Wingate, Henry T.

b. ?
fields: Law

African American federal judge; Henry T. Wingate was appointed to serve as a judge on the U.S. District Court in Mississippi in 1985 by President Ronald Reagan.

Winkfield, Jimmy

b. ?
d. ?
fields: Sports (jockey)

African American jockey; Jimmy Winkfield rode winning horses in the 1901 (on His

Eminence) and 1902 (on Alan-a-Dale) Kentucky Derbys.

Winnemucca, Sarah

né: Thoc-me-tony
b. c. 1844
Humboldt Sink, Nevada Territory
d. October 17, 1891
Henry's Lake, Idaho
fields: Civil Rights, Social Reform

A Paiute Indian, Sarah challenged American officials and their policies as she sought to maintain peace and ensure human rights for her people.

Winthrop, John

b. January 12, 1588
Edwardstone, Suffolk, England
d. March 26, 1649
Boston, Massachusetts
fields: Government and Politics

Winthrop was committed to the ideal of creating a Christian commonwealth, and his determined leadership was crucial to the establishment of the Massachusetts Bay Colony.

Wirth, Louis

b. Aug. 28, 1897
Gemunden, Germany
d. May, 1952
Chicago, Ill.
fields: Sociology

Sociologist and social activist; Louis Wirth was the first Jewish president of the American Sociological Association; first president of the International Sociological Association; his first major work, *The Ghetto* (1928), viewed the Jewish community as retrograde and urged assimilation of Jews; founder and director of the American Council on Race Relations; member of the National Resources Planning Board (1935-1944).

Wisdom, John

full: Arthur John Terence Dibben Wisdom
b. September 12, 1904
London, England
d. December 9, 1993
Cambridge, England
fields: Philosophy

John Wisdom was a British analytic philosopher who originally came to prominence as a presenter of Ludwig Wittgenstein's ideas to the public. His writings, in vivid conversational style, deal especially with the nature of philosophy and with the philosophy of mind. Taught at Cambridge University from the 1950's to the 1960's. His best-known works are *Other Minds* (1952, 1965) and *Philosophy and Psycho-Analysis* (1953).

Wise, Isaac Mayer

b. March 29, 1819
Steingrub, Bohemia
d. March 26, 1900
Cincinnati, Ohio
fields: Religion and Theology, Education

As a pioneering Reform rabbi with the avowed goal of uniting American Jewry, Wise became the greatest organizer of Reform Jewish institutions. He was the architect of and prime mover in the establishment of the Union of American Hebrew Congregations (1873), Hebrew Union College (1875), and the Central Conference of American Rabbis (1889), and he served as the first president of each of those three organizations.

Wise, Stephen Samuel

b. March 17, 1874
Budapest, Austro-Hungarian Empire (now Hungary)
d. April 19, 1949
New York, New York
fields: Religion and Theology, Social Reform

One of the most influential rabbis in U.S. history, Wise was a social and moral reformer, a Zionist, a leader in Jewish-Christian relations, and the founder of the Free Synagogue.

Witherspoon, John

b. February 15, 1723
Gifford, Scotland
d. November 15, 1794
at his home, Tusculum, near Princeton, New Jersey
fields: Education, Government and Politics, Religion and Theology

A leading pastor in the Church of Scotland, Witherspoon, as president of the College of New Jersey (later Princeton University), led its development into a major center of education for the arts and sciences and for the preparation of Presbyterian ministers. As a delegate from New Jersey to the Second Continental Congress, he championed American independence and signed the Declaration of Independence.

Wittgenstein, Ludwig

full: Ludwig Josef Johann Wittgenstein
b. April 26, 1889
Vienna, Austro-Hungarian Empire
d. April 29, 1951
Cambridge, England
fields: Philosophy

Wittgenstein is one of the most important and influential philosophers of the twentieth century and perhaps of all time. In his later, mature period, he did not produce a systematic philosophy or even claim to teach new doctrines. Instead, he professed to offer new methods and techniques for work in philosophy.

Wittig, Georg

b. June 16, 1897
Berlin, Germany
d. Aug. 26, 1987
Heidelberg, West Germany
fields: Chemistry

George Wittig was an organic chemist; developed a versatile method for joining carbon units—the Wittig reaction, which has provided a means of introducing double bonds in specific locations and is extensively used in the synthesis of pharmaceuticals and other complex molecules; in 1979, won the Nobel Prize in Chemistry jointly with Herbert C. Brown.

Władysław II Jagiełło

né: Jagiełło
b. c. 1351
place unknown
d. June 1, 1434
Gródek, near Lvov, Lithuania
fields: Government and Politics, Religion and Theology, Monarchy

King of Poland, 1386-1434. Jagiełło's marriage to the crown princess of Poland, Jadwiga, brought about the unification of Lithuania and Poland and the conversion of the Lithuanian people from paganism to the Roman Catholic faith.

Wodehouse, P. G.

full: Pelham Grenville Wodehouse
b. October 15, 1881
Guildford, Surrey, England
b. February 14, 1975
Southampton, Long Island, New York
fields: Literature

P. G. Wodehouse was the most popular English humorist of the early twentieth century. He wrote genial stories about English upper-class dimwits. The popularity of his *Jeeves* and *Blandings* stories declined because of his apparent collaboration after he was interned by the Nazis during World War II. Wodehouse made several humorous radio broadcasts for the Nazis that led to attacks on him and his writings in Great Britain. After his release from the German prison he moved to the United States. He took U.S. citizenship and continued to write until his death in 1975.

Wofford, Chloe Anthony. *See* Morrison, Toni

Wöhler, Friedrich

b. July 31, 1800
Eschersheim, near Frankfurt am Main
d. September 23, 1882
Göttingen, Germany
fields: Chemistry

Wöhler synthesized urea in 1828 and thus first demonstrated that organic materials, heretofore believed to possess a vital force, need not be made exclusively within living organisms. He also isolated aluminum metal in 1827 and discovered the elements beryllium and yttrium.

Wojtyła, Karol Jozef. *See* John Paul II

Wokini (Hook Nose). *See* Roman Nose

Wolf, Blanche. *See* Knopf, Blanche Wolf

Wolf, Max

b. June 21, 1863
Heidelberg, Baden
d. October 3, 1932
Heidelberg, Germany
fields: Astronomy

Wolf was the first astronomer to use an astronomical camera to discover asteroids by combining the camera with a mechanical telescope. During his very full career, Wolf discovered 582 asteroids with 228 of these receiving general recognition. This figure is a personal record of discoveries in astronomy which has been difficult to surpass.

Wolfe, George C.

b. September 23, 1954
Frankfort, Ky.
fields: Theater and Entertainment

African American playwright, director, and theater manager; George C. Wolfe became known with his satirical comedy *The Colored Museum* (1986). He won acclaim for his musical *Jelly's Last Jam* (1991) and as the director of *Angels in America: A Gay Fantasia on National Themes*, *Angels in America: Millenium Approaches* (for which he won a 1993 Tony Award as best director). Wolfe's many awards and honors include an Obie Award in 1990, the Dorothy Chandler Award in 1992, and a Drama Desk Award in 1992. In 1986 he received the Hull-Warriner Award, and his production of *Jelly's Last Jam* garnered three Tony Awards in 1992 (lighting design, best featured actress, and best actor). He also conceived and produced the highly acclaimed *Bring in 'da Noise, Bring in 'da Funk* (1995), which ran for nearly three years on Broadway before going on national tour.

Wolfe, James

b. January 2, 1727
Westerham, Kent, England
d. September 13, 1759
Quebec City, Canada
fields: Military Affairs

Using a daring maneuver, Wolfe was largely responsible for the defeat of the French at Quebec in 1759, preparing the way for the subsequent French loss of Canada to the British in the French and Indian War.

Wolfe, Thomas

full: Thomas Clayton Wolfe
b. October 3, 1900
Asheville, North Carolina
d. September 15, 1938
Baltimore, Maryland
fields: Literature

Wolfe was a master of characterization who, particularly in his first two novels, created memorable characters drawn directly from his family. He was an effusive, gargantuan writer, often uncontrolled, often poetic, but always imbued with the sense of what it meant to be American; he sought to achieve in prose what Walt Whitman had achieved in poetry.

Wolfman Jack

né: Robert Weston Smith
b. January 21, 1938
Brooklyn, New York
d. July 1, 1995
Belvidere, North Carolina
fields: Theater and Entertainment

Wolfman Jack was one of the most famous disc jockeys in the history of broadcasting. Through his trademark wolf howls, raspy voice, and unconventional style, he became a spokesperson for rock and roll in the 1960's. By 1972, he had produced the first syndicated rock-and-roll program on the air, eventually broadcasting on twenty-two hundred stations in forty-three countries. In 1973, he played himself in the award-winning film *American Graffiti*, finally revealing the face that matched the voice and catapulting him from cult figure to mainstream celebrity. From 1973 to 1981, the Wolfman hosted *Midnight Special*, a National Broadcasting Company (NBC) television program that featured live rock-and-roll performances. By 1995, he had amassed countless television and personal appearances, including a live show from Planet Hollywood in Washington, D.C.

Wolfram von Eschenbach

b. c. 1170
probably Eschenbach bei Ansbach, Franconia
d. c. 1217
probably Eschenbach bei Ansbach, Franconia
fields: Literature

In the era of the High Middle Ages, Wolfram was a master in the tradition of the courtly epic; his works constitute one of the high points of the narrative writing produced during this first golden age of German literature.

Wollstonecraft, Mary

b. April 27, 1759
London, England
d. September 10, 1797
London, England
fields: Literature, Social Reform

In challenging British institutions to extend the political liberties of the American and French Revolutions to women, Wollstonecraft developed a comprehensive feminist program.

Wolsey, Thomas

aka: Cardinal Thomas Wolsey
b. 1471 or 1472
Ipswich, Suffolk, England
d. November 29, 1530
Leicester Abbey, Leicester, England
fields: Government and Politics

By combining in himself the highest lay administrative post of chancellor and the religious position of papal legate *a latere* (1515-1529), Wolsey paved the way for the combining of church and state under Henry VIII.

Womack, Bobby

b. March 4, 1944
Cleveland, Ohio
fields: Music (singer, guitarist, and songwriter)

African American singer, guitarist, and one of the most prolific songwriters in rock-and-roll history; Bobby Womack was recruited by Sam Cooke to join the Soul Stirrers; moved to Memphis in 1964 and became a prolific songwriter and session musician; popular success for his own solo recordings eluded him, though he attracted a strong following in Europe during the 1970's; performed on the 1986 release "The Harlem Shuffle," by the Rolling Stones, whose second U.S. hit, "It's All Over Now," was written by Womack.

Wonah'ilayhunka. *See* Cloud, Henry Roe

Wonder, Stevie

né: Steveland Judkins
or né: Steveland Morris
b. May 13, 1950
Saginaw, Mich.
fields: Music

African American entertainer and songwriter. Though Stevie Wonder lost his eye sight shortly after birth, he went on to become a singer, pianist, and composer. Wonder started his career with Motown Records in Detroit. By the mid-1970's Wonder had twelve gold records to his credit and had received more awards than any other American pop singer—including fourteen Grammys (1973-1976) and the American Music Award

(1978). His hits include "Superstition," "You Are the Sunshine of My Life," and "Living for the City." In 1984 he received the Academy Award for the best original song, "I Just Called to Say I Love You." During the 1980's Wonder was influential in the movement to make the birthday of Dr. Martin Luther King, Jr., a national holiday.

Wong, Anna May

né: Wong Liu Tson
b. January 3, 1905
Los Angeles, California
d. February 3, 1961
Santa Monica, California
fields: Film

As one of the first Asian Americans to break through the film industry's general policy of racial exclusion Anna May Wong enjoyed a film career that spanned more than forty years. Especially for Chinese Americans, Wong came to represent opportunity and tangible success.

Wong, B. D.

b. Oct. 24, 1962
San Francisco, Calif.
fields: Film, Theater and Entertainment

For his performance as Song Liling in David Henry Hwang's *M. Butterfly*, in 1988, B. D. Wong became the first Asian American actor to receive a Tony Award. Also in recognition for that performance, Wong received the Drama Desk, Theatre World, Outer Critics' Circle, and Clarence Derwent awards. In 1992, he became the first man and first minority member to star in the musical *Peter Pan*, at Kansas City's Starlight Theatre. Wong led the 1990 protest against casting policies for the Broadway production of *Miss Saigon* and cofounded the Asian Pacific Alliance for Creative Equality. He has appeared in films such as *Family Business* (1989), *The Freshman* (1990), *Father of the Bride* (1991), *Jurassic Park* (1993), *And the Band Played On* (1993), and his voice was used in *Mulan* (1998).

Wong, Bernard P.

b. Feb. 12, 1941
Guangdong Province, China
fields: Historiography, Sociology

Bernard P. Wong, faculty member at San Francisco State University, became the first Chinese American to chair its Department of Anthropology in 1991. He wrote *A Chinese American Community: Ethnicity and Survival Strategies* (1979), *Chinatown* (1982), and *Patronage, Brokerage, Entrepreneurship, and the Chinese Community of New York* (1988). He studied the Chinese in the Philippines, China, Peru, Singapore, and the United States.

Wong, Diane Yen-Mei

b. Feb. 12, 1950
Seattle, Wash.
fields: Journalism, Publishing

Diane Yen-Mei Wong wrote on Asian American issues in her column for the *Hawaii Herald* newspaper and as a contributor to *USA Weekend Magazine*. She wrote two question-and-answer books, *Dear Diane: Questions and Answers for Asian American Women* (1983) and *Dear Diane: Letters from Our Daughters* (1983), and coedited *Making Waves: An Anthology of Writings By and About Asian American Women* (1989). She was executive director of the Asian American Journalists Association (1987-1992) and edited *East/West*, a San Francisco-based Asian American newspaper.

Wong, Dickie

full: Richard S. H. Wong
b. June 10, 1933
Honolulu, Territory of Hawaii
fields: Government and Politics

Dickie Wong, part Hawaiian and part Chinese, was a Hawaii state senator for twenty-six years, retiring in 1992. His first job with the state was as a detention home counselor for the juvenile court in 1962. He was elected to the state house in 1966 and to the senate in 1974. From 1979 to 1992, Wong served as Hawaii senate president.

Wong, Elizabeth

b. June 6, 1958
South Gate, Calif.
fields: Theater and Entertainment

Elizabeth Wong became a playwright after a successful journalism career. She wrote the first American script to consider the 1989 Tiananmen Square incident, *Letters to a Student Revolutionary* (pr. 1991), which won the 1990 Playwrights' Forum Award and a 1992 Margo Jones New Play Citation. Wong has written other plays, including *Bu and Bun* (pr. 1991), *Reveries of an Amorous Woman* (pr. 1991), and *Kimchee and Chitlins* (pr. 1992), about conflicts between African Americans and Korean Americans.

Wong, H. K.

full: Henry Kwock Wong
b. Apr., 1907
San Francisco, Calif.
d. Jan. 13, 1985
fields: Social Reform

Community advocate H. K. Wong created the Miss Chinatown USA pageant in 1958 and served as executive secretary of the Chinese Consolidated Benevolent Association. He established the Chinese Historical Society of America in 1963 and was technical director for the film *Flower Drum Song* (1961). Wong edited the book *San Francisco Chinatown on Parade in Picture and Story* (1961).

Wong, Jade Snow

b. January 21, 1922
San Francisco, Calif.
fields: Literature

Chinese American writer. Jade Snow Wong graduated from Mills College in 1942. After owning a ceramics gallery—winning several pottery awards and having her worked displayed at several museums—she turned to writing. Wong's autobiographical work, *Fifth Chinese Daughter* (1950), about assimilation into American culture, was well received and subsequently translated into several languages. *The Immigrant Experience* (1971) and *No Chinese Stranger* (1975) followed. In 1976 Wong received a Silver Medal for nonfiction from the Commonwealth Club of San Francisco. She was a member of the California Council for the Humanities (1978-1981) and director of the San Francisco Chinese Cultural Center (1978-1981). Wong was also a columnist for the *San Francisco Examiner* and a regular contributor to several periodicals.

Wong, Nellie

b. 1934
Oakland, Calif.
fields: Literature (poet)

The poems of Chinese America Nellie Wong were collected in *Dreams in Harrison Railroad Park* (1977) and *The Death of Long Steam Lady* (1986) and in such anthologies as *This Bridge Called My Back: Writings by Radical Women of Color* (1981) and *Breaking Silence: An Anthology of Contemporary Asian American Poets* (1983). She and Japanese American poet Mitsuye Yamada were featured in the 1981 documentary film *Mitsuye and Nellie, Asian-American Poets*.

Wong, Sau-ling Cynthia

b. ?
fields: Sociology, Literature

Chinese American Sau-ling Cynthia Wong, an associate member of the Department of Ethnic Studies at the University of California, Berkeley, was director of the Asian American Studies program. She wrote *Reading Asian American Literature: From Necessity to Extravagance* (1993).

Wong, Shawn

b. 1949
Oakland, Calif.
fields: Literature

Shawn Wong's first novel, *Homebase* (1979) received critical acclaim. The director of the Asian American Studies program at the University of Washington, he coedited *Aii-*

ieeeee! An Anthology of Asian-American Writers (1974), *The Big Aiiieeeee! An Anthology of Chinese American and Japanese American Literature* (1991), *The Before Columbus Foundation Fiction Anthology: Selections from the American Book Awards, 1980-1990* (1992), and *The Before Columbus Foundation Poetry Anthology: Selections from the American Book Awards, 1980-1990* (1992).

Wong, Stella

b. Mar. 30, 1914
Oakland, Calif.
fields: Art

Painter Stella Wong studied at the California College of Arts and Crafts, at the University of California, Berkeley, in Mexico City, and in Dublin, Ireland. Before returning to the San Francisco Bay Area in 1940, she designed jewelry for Helena Rubinstein in New York City. As part of the Chinese Art Association, she exhibited at the M. H. de Young Memorial Museum in 1935.

Wong Tung Jim. *See* Howe, James Wong

Wonkas. *See* Uncas

Woo, Gilbert Gang Nam

né: Hu Jingnan
b. Dec. 25, 1911
Taishan, China
d. Nov. 17, 1979
San Francisco, Calif.
fields: Journalism

Gilbert Gang Nam Woo wrote columns in the Chinese American press for forty years. He wrote propaganda during the war between China and Japan in the 1930's, then became an editor for the *Chinese Times* under Walter U. Lum. A column condemning the internment of Japanese Americans created controversy, and Woo quit after arguing with Lum. After World War II, Woo addressed racial discrimination in the United States, founding the *Chinese Pacific Weekly*, which was neither Nationalistic or Communistic. Because of his paper's objective stance, Woo was accused of being procommunist. The paper was granted membership in the San Francisco Press Club in 1960. After Woo's death, the *Chinese Pacific Weekly* suffered and was gradually subsumed into *East-West*, a bilingual weekly.

Woo, John

b. 1946
Canton, China
fields: Film, Theater and Entertainment

Hong Kong director John Woo creates stylishly violent, artistic, and often comic action-adventure films. His martial-arts films and slapstick comedies of the 1970's matured into bloodier, darker works, as evidenced by the gangster epic *A Better Tomorrow* (1986) and *Bullet in the Head* (1989), a Vietnam War film that carried an antiviolence message. Other films include *The Killer* (1989) and *Hard-Boiled* (1991). After Woo moved to Los Angeles in 1992, he directed a film featuring Jean-Claude Van Damme, *Hard Target* (1993), which was criticized for its violent scenes. Some of his other films include *Broken Arrow* (1996) and *Face/Off* (1997).

Woo, Michael

b. Oct. 8, 1951
Los Angeles, Calif.
fields: Government and Politics

Michael Woo became the first Asian American on the Los Angeles City Council in 1981. Woo, who received an M.A. degree in urban planning at the University of California, Berkeley, was hired by state senate majority leader David Roberti as a key speechwriter and policy adviser. In 1993, he lost the Los Angeles mayoral election to Richard Riordan. A Democrat, as city councilman for Hollywood Wood led the fight to strengthen tenants' rights and pushed for a new law extending sick-leave benefits to city employees who are members of nontraditional families. He helped limit development on Ventura Boulevard and helped preserve Fryman Canyon.

Woo, S. B.

b. Aug. 13, 1937
Shanghai, China
fields: Government and Politics

S. B. Woo was the highest-ranking Asian American state official in the continental United States as lieutenant governor of Delaware (1985-1989). He served as national board member (1977-1979) and later national president (1990-1991) of the Organization of Chinese Americans. Other positions include principal of the Chinese School of Delaware (1973) and board chair and chief executive officer of the Chinese American Community Center (1982-1983). Woo, who received a doctoral degree from Washington University in St. Louis, Missouri, taught physics at the University of Delaware.

Woo Yee-bew

b. 1864
Fat San, near Canton, China
d. 1930
fields: Religion and Theology

Woo Yee-bew enrolled at a Lutheran school in Canton after becoming a Christian. After attending St. Stephen's College in Hong Kong in the 1880's, he went to San Francisco and then Hawaii. He established a camp for Chinese plantation workers and began to evangelize the Chinese community at Kohala, Hawaii, in 1887. He helped found the St. Paul Chinese Mission. After moving to Honolulu in 1915, Wood continued mission work.

Wood, Annie. *See* Besant, Annie

Wood, Grant

full: Grant Devolson Wood
b. February 13, 1891
near Anamosa, Iowa
d. February 12, 1942
Iowa City, Iowa
fields: Art

Wood was one of the central figures of Midwestern regionalism, a visual and literary arts movement in the United States during the 1920's and 1930's that emphasized the history, lifestyles, and folkways of specific geographic areas.

Wood, Thomas Alexander

b. January 26, 1926
New York, N.Y.
fields: Business and Industry

African American business executive; Thomas Alexander Wood founded TAW Development Corporation in 1966 and TAW International Leasing Corporation in 1968; the leasing company was owned principally by African Americans, leasing capital equipment in Africa, and was the first leasing company to get a guarantee from the Agency for International Development; Wood was elected to the board of directors of Chase Manhattan Bank and Chase Manhattan Corporation in 1970, making him the first African American director of a major U.S. bank not owned by African Americans.

Woodard, Alfre

b. November 8, 1953
Tulsa, Okla.
fields: Theater and Entertainment (actor)

African American actress; Alfre Woodard made her film debut in Alan Rudolph's *Remember My Name* (1978). She next appeared in Robert Altman's *H.E.A.L.T.H.* (1979) and in Marjorie Kinnan Rawlings critically acclaimed *Cross Creek* (1983), for which she received an Oscar nomination for best supporting actress. Her television appearances include *Tucker's Witch* (1982-1983), *Hill Street Blues* (for which she earned her first Emmy Award in 1984), *Sara* (1985), and *St. Elsewhere* (1985-1987). Woodard won her second Emmy for her performance in the 1987 pilot episode *L.A. Law*. Woodard's television film credits include *Go Tell It on the Mountain* (1984) and *Mandela* (1987). She has appeared in feature films such as *Miss Firecracker* (1989), *Grand Canyon* (1991),

Passion Fish (1992), *Bopha!* (1993), *Crooklyn* (1994), *Miss Evers' Boys* (1997), and *Funny Valentines* (1999).

Woodard, Lynette

b. August 12, 1959
Wichita, Kans.
fields: Sports (basketball player)

African American basketball player; Lynette Woodard became the NCAA's all-time women's scoring leader and won the Wade Trophy as the outstanding female college player in the nation in 1981; in 1979 she was a member of the U.S. team that won the gold medal at the World University Games, and she was selected for the 1980 U.S. Olympic team, though she did not play because of the U.S.-led boycott of the Moscow Olympics; played for a year professionally in an Italian women's league; in 1983 she played for U.S. teams that won the gold medal in the Pan-American Games and the silver medal in the World University Games; in 1984 was captain of the gold-medal winning U.S. Olympic team; was the first woman to play for the Harlem Globetrotters; retired to concentrate on a teaching and coaching career.

Woodbridge, Hudson. *See* Tampa Red

Woodbury, Levi

b. 1789
d. 1851
fields: Law

U.S. Supreme Court justice, 1845-1851 (died while in office); appointed by President Polk. Rejected abolitionists' arguments for limiting the impact of the fugitive slave clause of the Constitution. Significant opinion: *Jones v. Van Zandt*, 46 U.S. 215 (1847).

Wooden Leg

aka: Kummok'quifiokta
b. 1858
Cheyenne River, Black Hills of Dakota
d. 1940
Mont.
fields: Historiography

The autobiography of Wooden Leg, a Northern Cheyenne, documents some of the most important events in Cheyenne history, including the Battle of the Little Bighorn, the Fort Robinson breakout, the Ghost Dance movement, and the difficult transition to reservation life.

Woodhull, Victoria

b. September 23, 1838
Homer, Ohio
d. June 10, 1927
Norton Park, Bremons, Worcestershire, England
fields: Journalism, Women's Rights

From 1870 through 1872 Victoria Woodhull and her sister, Tennessee Claflin (1845-1923), published *Woodhull and Claflin's Weekly*, a newspaper supporting sexual equality, woman suffrage, and other reforms. Woodhull's outspoken advocacy of sexual liberation made her a frequent target of critics. In 1872, after she published an article accusing Protestant clergyman Henry Ward Beecher of having committed adultery, Anthony Comstock appealed to federal authorities in New York to arrest her for violating U.S. postal regulations banning obscene materials from the mail. Woodhull and Claflin were tried on federal obscenity charges but acquitted. In 1877 Woodhull moved to England.

Woodruff, Hale

b. August 26, 1900
Cairo, Ill.
d. September 15, 1980
New York, N.Y.
fields: Art (painter)

African American painter; Hale Woodruff's works include *Ancestral Remedies*, *The Amistad Mutiny*, *The Art of the Negro*, *Founding of Talladega*, and *Summer Landscape*. His *Shantytown* and *Mudhill Row*, done in connection with the Depression-era Work Projects Administration.

Woods, Granville T.

b. April 23, 1856
Columbus, Ohio
d. January 30, 1910
New York, N.Y.
fields: Invention and Technology

Granville T. Woods moved to Cincinnati and opened Woods Electric Company, which manufactured telephones, telegraphs, and other electrical equipments. Woods was the inventor of more than fifty patented devices. In 1884, his first patent was granted for a steam boiler system. His other inventions include a telephone transmitter, a system for pulling electricity from overhead power lines into the motor of a train or trolley, a dimmer switch for theater lights (1896) that used 40 percent less electricity than its forerunners, an egg incubating system, an automatic air brake for trains, a regulation device for electric motors that conserved electricity because it used smaller resistances, and a third-rail system for trains which is still in use today in New York City's subway system. One of his most important inventions was the synchronous multiplex railway telegraph (patented 1887), which permitted members of train crews to send messages to each other and to railroad stations, decreasing the chance of collisions.

Woods, Howard B.

b. 1917
Perry, Okla.
fields: Journalism

African American journalist, public official, and publisher; Howard B. Woods founded, edited, and published the *St. Louis Sentinel*; was St. Louis bureau chief for the *Chicago Defender* (1942-1949) and executive editor of the *St. Louis Argus* (1954); was appointed by Lyndon B. Johnson to the Community Relations Service established under the 1964 Civil Rights Act and was appointed associate of the United States Information Agency in 1965.

Woods, Tiger

né: Eldrick Woods
b. December 30, 1975
Cypress, California
fields: Sports (golf)

Woods has laid the foundation for the sport of golf to open its doors to minorities and has a chance to become the best golfer and ambassador of the game in its history.

Woods, William Burnham

b. 1824
d. 1887
fields: Law

U.S. Supreme Court justice, 1881-1887 (died while in office); appointed by President Hayes. Significant opinions: *United States v. Lee*, 106 U.S. 196 (1882) (dissenting opinion); *United States v. Harris*, 106 U.S. 629 (1883); *Presser v. Illinois*, 116 U.S. 252 (1886).

Woodson, Carter G.

full: Carter Godwin Woodson
b. December 19, 1875
New Canton, Va.
d. April 3, 1950
Washington, D.C.
fields: Historiography

African American historian; Carter G. Woodson published *The Education of the Negro Prior to 1861: A History of the Education of the Colored People of the United States from the Beginning of Slavery to the Civil War* (1915), the first of nineteen works; established the Association for the Study of Negro Life and History (ASNLH) in 1915; was editor of the ASNLH's *Journal of Negro History* and the *Negro History Bulletin*; organized Associated Publishers in 1921, which enabled him to publish full-length manuscripts and studies; inaugurated the first Negro History Week in 1926.

Woodson, Lewis

b. c. 1805
Virginia

d. 1878
fields: Social Reform
African American reformer; Lewis Woodson was supporter of William Lloyd Garrison in the 1830's, but argued that the oppressive conditions under which African Americans had rendered them a distinct class; in letters published under the pseudonym "Augustine" in the *Colored American* in the late 1830's, Woodson advocated separate black moral reform societies and black communities in the West; sometimes called "the father of black nationalism," though he believed that whites and blacks shared an interest in advancing American economic prosperity and political ideals.

Woodson, Robert L.

b. April 8, 1937
Philadelphia, Pa.
fields: Government and Politics
African American public servant; Robert L. Woodson was director of the National Urban League, director of the American Enterprise Institute Neighborhood Revitalization Project, a fellow at the American Enterprise Institute for Public Policy Research, chair of the Council for a Black Economic Agenda, and president of the National Center for Neighborhood Enterprise, an organization he founded in 1981.

Woodward, Joanne

full: Joanne Gignilliat Woodward
b. February 27, 1930
Thomasville, Georgia
fields: Film, Theater and Entertainment (actor)
A talented, award-winning character actress, Woodward has achieved critical and commercial success in films, on television, and on the stage. She is also an outspoken advocate for various social causes and is an important patron of regional theater and the ballet.

Woodward, Robert Burns

b. April 10, 1917
Boston, Massachusetts
d. July 8, 1979
Cambridge, Massachusetts
fields: Chemistry
Woodward was the preeminent organic chemist in the postwar United States. Renowned for the total synthesis of complex natural products, for more than thirty years he achieved syntheses of unparalleled creativeness and elegance. He won the 1965 Nobel Prize in Chemistry.

Woolf, Virginia

né: Adeline Virginia Stephen
b. January 25, 1882
London, England
d. March 28, 1941
near Rodmell, Sussex, England
fields: Literature
Woolf contributed significantly to prose fiction through her experiments with stream of consciousness and characterization; she also influenced critical thought through her analytical essays and reviews.

Woquini. *See* Roman Nose

Wordsworth, William

b. April 7, 1770
Cockermouth, Cumberland, England
d. April 23, 1850
Grasmere, Westmoreland, England
fields: Literature
As one of the first and probably the greatest of the English Romantic poets, Wordsworth redirected the literary trends of the time. His most important poems present a vision of the expanded human mind in creative interplay with the external world.

Workman, Fanny Bullock

né: Fanny Bullock
b. January 8, 1859
Worcester, Massachusetts
d. January 22, 1925
Cannes, France
fields: Exploration and Colonization, Geography, Women's Rights
A tireless explorer and geographer, writer, accomplished linguist, feminist, and suffragist, Fanny Bullock Workman set international mountain-climbing records for women. Her enormous contribution to the body of geographical knowledge was acknowledged by numerous geographical societies around the world.

Worm. *See* Rodman, Dennis

Wormley, James

b. January 16, 1819
Washington, D.C.
d. October 18, 1884
Boston, Mass.
fields: Business and Industry
African American hotel proprietor; James Wormley operated a notable Washington, D.C., hotel known for hosting the capital's elite, beginning in the 1870's until his death (his son continued to operate the Wormley Hotel until 1893).

Worthy, James

full: James Ager Worthy
b. February 27, 1961
Gastonia, N.C.
fields: Sports (basketball player)
African American basketball player; James Worthy, with Michael Jordan, led the Tar Heels to a regular-season number-one ranking and their first National Collegiate Athletic Association (NCAA) championship in twenty-five years; signed with the Los Angeles Lakers as their first overall pick and played with them through the "Showtime" era of the 1980's; won three world championships with the Lakers (1985, 1987, 1988); was named Most Valuable Player Award for the 1988 NBA play-offs; retired from the Lakers and professional basketball in 1994.

Wovoka

aka: Jack Wilson
b. c. 1858
Mason Valley, Nev.
d. Sept. 20, 1932
Schurz, Nev.
fields: Native American Affairs, Religion and Theology
Northern Paiute religious leader; Wovoka originated the messianic Ghost Dance religion, which was embraced by nearly sixty thousand Indians from 1889 to 1890; he prophesied that as a result of performing the sacred Ghost Dance and practicing pacifism, within two years the earth would be regenerated and returned to the Indians, that the whites would disappear, that buffalo herds would reappear, and that all Indians—including their dead ancestors—would live forever in paradise; the phenomenal expansion of the Ghost Dance among the Plains Indians alarmed the white authorities, who began to round up many of its promoters; the Ghost Dance movement faded following the massacre at Wounded Knee, during which an estimated three hundred Sioux were killed by federal government troops; the discredited prophet lived out his remaining forty-two years in Mason Valley as "Jack Wilson."

Wren, Christopher

aka: Sir Christopher Wren
b. October 20, 1632
East Knoyle, Wiltshire, England
d. February 25, 1723
London, England
fields: Architecture
Combining his skill as an engineer with a thorough knowledge of the classical principles of art, Wren became one of the greatest architects of all time, influencing not only the designers and builders of his own era but also those of successive generations.

Wright, Allen

aka: Kiliahote (Let's Kindle a Fire)
b. Nov. 28, 1825
Attala County, Miss.

d. Dec. 2, 1885
Boggy Depot, Okla.
fields: Scholarship

A highly regarded Choctaw scholar, Allen Wright earned a B.A. at Union College, Schenectady, New York, in 1853 and an M.A. at Union Theological Seminary, New York, in 1855. He became a noted scholar in Latin, Greek, Hebrew, and English. Ordained by the Presbyterian Church in 1865, Wright returned to Indian Territory to work among his people. Wright served in several elected tribal offices; he gave Oklahoma its name.

Wright, Archibald Lee. *See* Moore, Archie

Wright, Betty

b. December 21, 1953
Miami, Fla.
fields: Music (rhythm-and-blues singer)

African American rhythm-and-blues singer; Betty Wright released her first album, *My First Time Around*, which reached number fifteen on the rhythm-and-blues chart and number thirty-three on the pop chart; her single "Clean Up Woman" (1971), from Wright's album *I Love the Way You Love Me*, went gold and reached number two on the rhythm-and-blues chart and number six on the pop chart; won Grammy for "Where Is the Love" (1975); *Betty Wright* (1981) contained a single "What Are You Going to Do with It," which she recorded with Stevie Wonder.

Wright, Bruce McMarion

b. December 19, 1918
Princeton, N.J.
fields: Law, Literature

African American judge, attorney, educator, and author; Bruce McMarion Wright was general counsel for the Human Resources Administration (HRA) in New York City before being appointed to the bench. Wright served as a judge on New York's criminal court bench and was known for his practice of setting low bail for indigent minority defendants. Because of his criticism of the criminal court system Wright was transferred from criminal court to the civil court bench. These criticism were recorded in his 1987 book *Black Robes, White Justice*. Wright was appointed as a justice on the New York State Supreme Court in 1983; he retired in January of 1995.

Wright, Eric. *See* Eazy-E

Wright, Frank Lloyd

b. June 8, 1867
Richland Center, Wisconsin
d. April 9, 1959
Phoenix, Arizona
fields: Architecture

Strongly individualistic, flamboyant, and arrogant, Wright designed and built more than four hundred structures which reflect his architectural genius. Wright, directly and indirectly, heavily influenced twentieth century architecture with his diverse use of geometry in his designs.

Wright, Isaac. *See* Coker, Daniel

Wright, Jay

b. May 25, 1934 or 1935
Albuquerque, N.Mex.
fields: Literature

African American poet; Jay Wright's poetry is informed by his studies in history, anthropology, and primitive religions and is also infused with allusions to early Christian and Renaissance writers; publications include *The Homecoming Singer* (1971), *Dimensions of History* (1976), and *The Double Invention of Komo* (1980).

Wright, Louis Tompkins

b. July 23, 1891
La Grange, Ga.
d. October 8, 1952
New York, N.Y.
fields: Medicine

African American medical researcher; Louis Tompkins Wright is known for his studies of the intradermal method of smallpox vaccination and for being the first to use chlortetracycline, an antibiotic, on humans.

Wright, Marian. *See* Edelman, Marian Wright

Wright, Mickey

full: Mary Kathryn Wright
b. February 14, 1935
San Diego, California
fields: Sports (golf)

The biggest women's professional golf star of the early 1960's, Mickey Wright by 1960 was the top player on the Ladies' Professional Golf Association (LPGA) tour. In 1965, she reduced her schedule and returned to college at Southern Methodist University, but she remained competitive as a part-time player. Although Wright's full-time professional career was brief, no other player, with the short-term exception of Nancy Lopez in the late 1970's, has rivaled her level of dominance on the LPGA tour. She won more than eighty tournaments and set a number of scoring and money-winning records. Her major victories included four U.S. Opens (1958, 1959, 1961, 1964) and four LPGA Championships (1958, 1960, 1961, 1963), the only women's majors of the time. She led the money winners four times (1961-1964).

Wright, Nathan, Jr.

b. August 5, 1923
Shreveport, La.
fields: Education

African American educator; Nathan, Jr. Wright taught urban affairs at the State University of New York, beginning in 1969, and was chair of the department of Afro-American studies; chaired the 1967 and 1968 National Conferences on Black Power.

Wright, Orville

b. August 19, 1871
Dayton, Ohio
d. January 30, 1948
Dayton, Ohio
fields: Invention and Technology, Aviation and Space Exploration

The brothers Wilbur and Orville Wright invented the first practical manned powered aircraft, thereby initiating the Air Age. Their first successful attempt at motor-powered flight occurred on December 17, 1903, near Kitty Hawk, North Carolina.

Wright, Richard

b. Sept. 4, 1908
Natchez, Miss.
d. Nov. 28, 1960
Paris, France
fields: Literature

African American novelist; Richard Wright became a member of the Communist Party, 1933-1944; used personal experience from his Mississippi youth to dramatize the brutal effects of racism in books such as *Uncle Tom's Children* (Best Work of Fiction by a Works Progress Administration writer, 1938), *Native Son* (1940), and the largely autobiographical *Black Boy* (1945); moved to Paris in 1946; there continued writing, including *The Outsider* (1953), *Black Power* (1954), *White Man Listen* (1957), *Eight Men* (1961); *American Hunger* (1977) was a continuation of his autobiography.

Wright, Robert Courtlant

b. November 5, 1944
Chester, Pa.
fields: Government and Politics

African American state politician and attorney; Robert Courtlant Wright served as president of the Republican Council of Delaware County (1977); elected to the Pennsylvania state legislature as a representative from District 159 for Chester County (1981); treasurer of the Pennsylvania Legislative Black Caucus; served on the executive boards of the National Black Caucus of State Legislators and the Pennsylvania Minority Business Development Authority.

Wright, Sarah E.

full: Sarah Elizabeth Wright
b. December 9, 1928
Wetipquin, Md.
fields: Literature (writer, poet), Civil Rights

African American writer, poet, educator, and activist; Sarah Elizabeth Wright, a dedicated activist within the black community, became involved in the Harlem Writers' Guild in the late 1950's and helped organize the Cultural Association for Women of African Heritage in the mid-1960's. In 1955, Wright published *Give Me a Child* (with Lucy Smith), a collection of poetry focused on the theme of African American survival in the face of racism and prejudice. Her best-known novel, *This Child's Gonna Live* (1969), was hailed for its stream-of-consciousness narrative and its handling of folk dialect and speech rhythms.

Wright, Syreeta. *See* Syreeta

Wright, Wilbur

b. April 16, 1867
near Millville, Indiana
d. May 30, 1912
Dayton, Ohio
fields: Invention and Technology, Aviation and Space Exploration

The brothers Wilbur and Orville Wright invented the first practical manned powered aircraft, thereby initiating the Air Age. Their first successful attempt at motor-powered flight occurred on December 17, 1903, near Kitty Hawk, North Carolina.

Wright-Jones, Jane Cooke

b. November 30, 1919
New York, N.Y.
fields: Medicine, Education

African American surgeon and educator; Jane Cooke Wright-Jones was associate dean and professor of surgery at New York Medical College; member of the board of trustees at Smith College; member of the President's Commission on Heart Disease; director of the Harlem Hospital Cancer Research Foundation.

Wu, Chien-Shiung

b. May 31, 1912
Liuho, China
d. February 16, 1997
New York, New York
fields: Physics

Wu made significant contributions in the research of nuclear forces and structure, including experiments that overthrew the principle of parity, a basic principle of physics. She was one of the world's leading experimental physicists.

Wu Dingfang

b. July 9, 1842
Singapore
d. 1922
fields: Diplomacy

Wu Dingfang's first job in the service of the Chinese government was a post at Tianjin in 1882. He helped negotiate a treaty between China and France in 1885, and at the conclusion of the Sino-Japanese War (1894-1895), he assisted in the drafting of the treaty with Japan. Wu served as Chinese minister to the United States from 1897 to 1902 and 1907 to 1909. He traveled to various cities trying to persuade the American public to end all discriminatory practices against the Chinese.

Wu, Harry

né: Wu Hongda
b. February 8, 1937
Shanghai, China
fields: Government and Politics

Chinese American activist. An outspoken critic of human rights abuses by the government of the People's Republic of China, Harry Wu was imprisoned and spent nineteen years in labor camps after he criticized the Soviet Union in 1960. After his release he emigrated to the United States. He became a U.S. citizen and began a campaign to publicize human rights abuses in China. He made secret trips to China on several occasions to document abuses. In June, 1995, on one such trip, he was arrested at a remote border crossing. Wu was held for more than two months, before being tried on espionage charges, convicted, and sentenced to fifteen years imprisonment. U.S. officials strongly protested Wu's detention and trial, and he was expelled from China shortly after his conviction.

Wu, Robin

b. June 3, 1956
New York, N.Y.
fields: Art

Robin Wu promoted Asian American performing arts to mainstream American and numerous overseas Chinese communities. She prepared an exhibition called "The Chinese of America, 1785-1980" and cochaired a national symposium on Chinese American performance arts held in San Francisco in 1984. Wu also promoted cultural exchanges of artists between China and the United States.

Wundt, Wilhelm

b. August 16, 1832
Neckerau, Baden
d. August 31, 1920
Grossbothen, Germany
fields: Psychiatry and Psychology, Physiology

Wundt did much to develop psychology as an independent discipline. Beginning in 1879, Wundt established a psychological institute at the University of Leipzig, where he directed many experiments in which subjects studied their sensations and feelings.

Wyatt, Hattie Ophelia. *See* Caraway, Hattie

Wyclif, John

b. c. 1328
Wiclif-on-Tees, Yorkshire, England
d. December 31, 1384
Lutterworth, Leicestershire, England
fields: Religion and Theology

Wyclif's ideas became the rallying point for demands for religious reform in England and influenced the Hussite movement in Bohemia, preparing the way for the Reformation. Wyclif's emphasis on the authority of Scripture and the priesthood of the believer inspired the first translation of the entire Bible into English.

Wyeth, Andrew

full: Andrew Newell Wyeth
b. July 12, 1917
Chadds Ford, Pennsylvania
fields: Art

Wyeth, one of the most famous and best-loved American painters throughout the world, created a body of work that many consider to embody the essence of American representational art.

Wyeth, Henriette

full: Ann Henriette Wyeth
b. October 22, 1907
Wilmington, Delaware
d. April 3, 1997
Roswell, New Mexico
fields: Art

As a member of the first rank of contemporary American artists, Henriette Wyeth is noted for her murals, her landscape and still life paintings, and her portraits.

Wynepuechsika. *See* Cornstalk

Wynfrith. *See* Boniface, Saint

Wynn, Albert R.

b. September 10, 1951
Philadelphia, Pa.
fields: Government and Politics, Law

African American politician and attorney; Albert R. Wynn was elected to serve as a member of the Maryland State Senate in 1987, and after the state of Maryland redrew its congressional districts in the wake of 1990 census figures he declared his candidacy for Maryland's newly created Fourth Congressional District. In 1992 Wynn won election as a Democrat; he was re-elected in 1994 and in 1998.

Xanthippe

b. c. 445 B.C.E.
Athens, Greece
d. Early to middle fourth century B.C.E.
probably Athens, Greece
fields: Women's Rights

Through her aggressive behavior, Xanthippe forced men to reflect upon and reconsider conventional assumptions about women's nature and social roles. She was married to Socrates.

Xavier, Saint Francis

b. April 7, 1506
the Castle of Xavier, Navarre
d. December 3, 1552
Island of Sancian, China
fields: Religion and Theology

Francis, who suffered many physical and mental hardships in order to bring the Christian message to countries of the Far East, was one of the first seven members of the Roman Catholic Church's Jesuit Order as well as its most successful missionary. Canonized in 1622.

Xehaciwinga. *See* Mountain Wolf Woman

Xenakis, Iannis

b. May 29, 1922
Braila, Romania
fields: Music, Architecture, Engineering, Mathematics

Xenakis is one of Europe's most prestigious avant-garde composers. His works exhibit a new and individual kind of musical thinking based on physics, mathematics, and architecture. Especially important for Xenakis has been the mathematics of probability. He introduced the term "stochastic music" for music utilizing probabilistic processes, and he has sometimes used computers to aid in the elaborate calculations demanded.

Xenophanes

b. c. 570 B.C.E.
Colophon, near the coast of Asia Minor
d. c. 478 B.C.E.
western Greece
fields: Philosophy, Literature, Religion and Theology

Xenophanes' critique of the Homeric gods marks the beginning of both systematic theology and the rational interpretation of myth in ancient Greek society.

Xenophon

b. c. 431 B.C.E.
near Athens
d. c. 354 B.C.E.
probably Corinth or Athens
fields: Literature, Philosophy

Through his writings on subjects ranging from the practical to the philosophical, Xenophon, a pupil of Socrates, sought in the fourth century B.C.E. to instruct and improve Greek society. His works provide the modern reader with a clearer picture of the ancient world.

Xerxes I

b. c. 519 B.C.E.
place unknown
d. 465 B.C.E.
Persepolis
fields: Warfare and Conquest, Architecture

Xerxes mobilized the largest army ever assembled in ancient times and marched against Greece; he crossed Thessaly and annexed Attica to the Persian Empire. Posterity remembers him for capturing Athens and burning the Acropolis and for building the magnificent Palace of Xerxes at Persepolis.

Ximenes, Vicente Treviño

b. Dec. 5, 1919
Floresville, Tex.
fields: Government and Politics

Vicente Treviño Ximenes worked for the United States Agency for International Development in Ecuador (1961-1964) and Panama (1965-1967); led Latino segment of President Lyndon Johnson's 1964 reelection campaign. Johnson named him cabinet committee chairman for Mexican American affairs (1967-1968). Also a member of the Equal Employment Opportunity Commission (1967-1977), the first Mexican American on the commission.

Xuan, Tran Le. *See* Ngo Dinh Nhu, Mme

Xunzi

aka: Hsün-tzu
b. c. 313 B.C.E.
Zhao, China
d. After 238 B.C.E.
Lanling, China
fields: Philosophy

Considered the third of the great Chinese philosophers (after Confucius and Mencius), Xunzi built a synthesized and realistic foundation for Confucian ideology that was influential throughout China during the Han Dynasty (207 B.C.E.-220 C.E.). His chief work, *Xunzi*, consists of essays on Confucian ethics, music, and philosophy. Xunzi is important not only because of his startling proposition that humanity is naturally evil but also because his views influenced a disciple, Han Feizi, whose work became a masterpiece of Chinese philosophy.

Yalow, Rosalyn

né: Rosalyn Sussman
full: Rosalyn Sussman Yalow
b. July 19, 1921
New York, New York
fields: Biochemistry, Medicine

Yalow was instrumental in the development of the radioimmunoassay technique for the measurement of minute quantities of biological materials. For her work, Yalow was awarded a 1977 Nobel Prize in Physiology or Medicine.

Yamada, Mitsuye Yasutake

b. July 5, 1923
Kyushu, Japan
fields: Education, Literature (poet)

Mitsuye Yasutake Yamada, along with her family, was interned at the Minidoka relocation center in Idaho. She studied at the University of Cincinnati and then New York University before completing a master's degree at the University of Chicago. Yamada, a professor at Cypress College in Southern California, taught courses in literature and creative writing. She published *Camp Notes and Other Poems*, a book of poetry based on her wartime experiences, in 1976. She and poet Nellie Wong were featured in the 1981 film *Mitsuye and Nellie: Asian American Poets*. Yamada's publications include *The Webs We Weave* (1986) and *Desert Run: Poems and Stories* (1988).

Yamada, Waka

né: Asaba Waka
b. Dec. 1, 1879
Kanagawa Prefecture, Japan
d. Sept. 6, 1956
Japan
fields: Social Reform

After arriving in the United States in the late 1890's, Waka Yamada was forced into prostitution in a Seattle brothel. She escaped to San Francisco and soon entered the Presbyterian Mission House for Chinese Girls, where she converted to Christianity. Yamada married and returned to Tokyo with her Japanese American husband, Yamada Kakichi. Yamada joined a feminist organization, the Seitosha, and wrote for its journal form 1914 to 1916. She later formed her own magazine, *Women and the New Society*, and in 1931, became an advice columnist for the *Tokyo Asahi Shimbun*. She championed the cause of maternalism, working for special laws favorable to mothers.

Yamaguchi, Kristi

full: Kristi Tsyua Yamaguchi
b. June 12, 1971
Hayward, California
fields: Sports (figure skating)

Yamaguchi's athleticism and artistry earned for her the gold medal in woman's figure skating at the 1990 Olympics in Albertville, France, making her the fifth American woman to win this honor. In 1992, she became the first American woman since Peggy Fleming in 1968 to defend her World Championship title.

Yamamoto, Hisaye

b. 1921
Redondo Beach, Calif.
fields: Journalism, Literature

Japanese American Hisaye Yamamoto was interned with her parents and siblings during World War II at the Poston relocation center. After World War II, she worked as a journalist for several years. She received a John Hay Whitney Foundation Opportunity Fellowship in 1950, and her short story, "Yoneko's Earthquake" was included in *Best American Short Stories, 1952*. This story was later adapted for a 1991 American Playhouse production (PBS), *Hot Summer Winds*. Yamamoto's stories were collected and published in 1988 as *Seventeen Syllables and Other Stories*. Her 1952 story was adapted

Yamamoto, Isoroku

b. April 4, 1884
Nagaoka, Niigata Prefecture, Japan
d. April 18, 1943
Solomon Islands
fields: Military Affairs, War and Conquest

Japanese admiral. Isoroku Yamamoto was commander of the Japanese fleet in the early years of World War II. Warned Japanese leaders against going to war with the United States. Prepared fleet for war after being named chief of combined fleet in 1939. Planned 1941 surprise attack on Pearl Harbor. Killed on inspection tour of South Pacific when his plane was shot down.

Yamani, Ahmad Zaki

b. June 30, 1930
Mecca, Saudi Arabia
fields: Diplomacy, Government and Politics

Between 1962 and 1986, Yamani was the best-known spokesman for Middle Eastern oil producing countries' interests in the Organization of Petroleum Exporting Countries (OPEC). He built a considerable reputation as a moderate interested in reconciling strong nationalist demands among producers and the expectations of Western industrialist consuming countries.

Yamasaki, Minoru

b. Dec. 1, 1912
Seattle, Wash.
d. Feb. 6, 1986
Detroit, Mich.
fields: Architecture

Japanese American architect. Chief designer of the World Trade Center's twin towers in New York, the world's two tallest buildings at the time of their construction, Minoru Yamasaki gained fame as head of his own firm. During his career, Yamasaki produced well in excess of 250 residential, commercial, and industrial buildings. Some notable examples of Yamasaki's structures include the St. Louis Airport Terminal (completed in 1956), the Federal Science Pavilion at the World's Fair in Seattle (1962), the Woodrow Wilson School of Public and International Affairs at Princeton University (1965), and the Century Plaza Hotel (1966) and the Century Plaza Towers (1975), both in Los Angeles. The Japanese American Citizens League (JACL) honored him as its Nisei of the Biennium (1962) for "artfully blending" Japanese art and culture with the architecture of the West.

Yamashita, Karen Tei

b. 1951
fields: Literature

The writings of Karen Tei Yamashita explore environmental, cultural, and political issues from a Japanese Brazilian perspective. *Through the Arc of the Rainforest* (1990), her first published book, earned for her widespread recognition. Yamashita's novel *Brazil-Maru* (1992) portrays the experience of the Japanese in Brazil.

Yamashita, Soen

b. 1898
Yasuura, Hiroshima Prefecture, Japan
fields: Journalism

Soen Yamashita, who arrived in the United States in 1914, became a reporter for the *Nippu Jiji*, a Hawaii Japanese newspaper, becoming its Japan correspondent in 1933. While in Japan, he worked on behalf of Japanese Americans who were living in the country. His 1942 book supported Japan's claim to the Hawaiian Islands and advocated colonization of the islands as part of the formation of a new order uniting the nations of East Asia.

Yamauchi, Wakako

né: Wakako Nakamura
b. Oct. 25, 1924
Westmoreland, Calif.
fields: Theater and Entertainment, Literature

Playwright and writer Wakako Yamauchi was interned at the Poston relocation center in Arizona during World War II. She worked as a staff artist on the camp newspaper. Yamauchi turned her short story, "And the Soul Shall Dance," depicting the struggles of Japanese immigrant farmers, into a full-length drama, which premiered in 1977 at East West Players. It was named best new play of the year by the Los Angeles Critics Circle and developed for public television. Recipient of three Rockefeller Foundation grants and an American Theatre Critics Award for Outstanding Playwriting, Yamauchi's other works include *The Music Lessons* (1980), *12-1-A* (1982), *The Memento* (1984), *The Chairman's Wife* (1990), and *Not a Through Street* (1991).

Yampoochee. *See* Antonio, Juan

Yan Liben

aka: Yen Li-pen
b. c. 600
Wannian, Shaanxi, China
d. 673
Siking, China
fields: Art

Yan Liben introduced a new sense of realism to portrait painting, a genre which he did much to develop during the period of the Tang Dynasty.

Yan, Martin

b. 1949
Guangzhou, China
fields: Theater and Entertainment, Television

Chinese American Martin Yan is a chef, television personality, and writer. He is best known as the host of the syndicated television program *Yan Can Cook*. Yan's books include *The Yan Can Cook Book* (1981), *The Joy of Wokking: A Chinese Cookbook* (1983), *Martin Yan: The Chinese Chef* (1985), *A Wok for All Seasons* (1988), *Everybody's Wokking* (1991), and *The Well-Seasoned Wok* (1993).

Yanagisako, Sylvia

b. July 11, 1945
Honolulu, Territory of Hawaii
fields: Anthropology

Sylvia Yanagisako obtained her Ph.D. degree in anthropology from the University of Washington and began teaching in 1975. The director of Feminist Studies Program at Stanford University from 1988 to 1991, she is best known for her study of kinship among Japanese Americans. Her publications include *Transforming the Past: Kinship and Tradition Among Japanese Americans* (1985) and *Towards a Unified Analysis of Gender and Kinship* (1987, coedited with Jane F. Collier).

Yancey, Jimmy

full: James Edward Yancey
b. February 20, 1889
Chicago, Ill.
d. September 17, 1951
Chicago, Ill.
fields: Music (piano player)

African American piano player; Jimmy Yancey is widely considered the father of the boogie-woogie piano style; began his career as a vaudeville performer; enjoyed a revival of his career in the 1930's after Lux Lewis released "The Yancey Special" (1936); made a number of recordings in the 1940's until illness ended his career.

Yanehiro, Jan

b. Jan. 4, 1948
Honolulu, Territory of Hawaii
fields: Journalism

Jan Yanehiro became the first Asian American to host a magazine-style entertainment television show at KPIX, the Columbia Broadcasting System affiliate in San Francisco, California as cohost of *Evening Magazine* (1976-1990). The winner of numerous Emmy awards for on-air talent and entertainment programming, Yanehiro was a member of the Asian American Journalists Association and the San Francisco chapter of the Japanese American Citizens League.

Yañez, Agustín

b. May 4, 1904
Guadalajara, Mexico
d. Jan. 17, 1980
Mexico City, Mexico
fields: Literature, Government and Politics

Agustín Yañez was a Mexican writer, editor, publisher, and government official. Served for a time as Mexico's secretary of public education; governor of Jalisco from 1953 to 1959. Books include *Genio y figuras de Guadalajara* (1941) and *Flor de juegos antiguos* (1941), two short narratives about Guadalajara; *Archipiélago de mujeres* (short stories, 1943); and *Al filo del agua* (novel, 1947; translated as *The Edge of the Storm*, 1963). Yañez also edited a variety of literature, philosophy, and history journals.

Yang, Chen Ning

aka: Franklin Yang
b. Sept. 22, 1922
Hefei, Anhui Province, China
fields: Physics

Physicist Chen Ning Yang studied under Enrico Fermi at the University of Chicago, earning a doctoral degree in 1948. In 1955, he became a professor at the Institute of Advanced Study in Princeton. In 1957, Yang and Tsung-Dao Lee shared the Novel Prize in Physics for their penetrating investigations of the parity laws, which disproved a principle that had been accepted for three decades and which led to revolutionary discoveries regarding subatomic particles. Other awards include the Albert Einstein Commemorative Award (1957), Rumford Prize (1980), National Medal of Science (1986), and Liberty Award (1986). Yang became Albert Einstein Professor of Physics and director of the Institute of Theoretical Physics at the State University of New York at Stony Brook in 1966.

Yang, Linda Tsao

b. Sept. 5, 1926
Shanghai, China
fields: Economics

Economist Linda Tsao Yang was the first Asian American to serve on the Board of Administration of the California Public Employees Retirement System (1977-1980). She was also the first minority and woman to serve as California Savings and Loan commissioner (1980-1982). Yang was a board member of California Blue Cross and a three-time delegate to the Democratic National Convention (1984, 1988, and 1992). She regularly contributed to the *Hong Kong Economic Journal*.

Yano, Rodney J. T.

b. 1943
Kona, Territory of Hawaii
d. 1969
Vietnam
fields: Warfare and Conquest

Vietnam War hero Rodney J. T. Yano was one of only four Japanese Americans ever awarded the Congressional Medal of Honor. He was a sergeant attached to the Air Cavalry Troop when a grenade detonated aboard the helicopter in which he was flying. He bravely attempted to jettison the rest of the explosives before they could explode, despite suffering severe wounds, which later caused his death.

Yaqut

full: Yaqut ibn 'Abdallah
b. 1179
probably Syria
d. 1229
Aleppo, Syria
fields: Historiography

A major compiler of geographical, historical, and ethnographic information, Yaqut was the first Muslim scholar to use an encyclopedic organization for his material. His work gives modern scholars the most comprehensive insight on the state of knowledge in the thirteenth century Islamic world.

Yaratev. *See* Irateba

Yarbrough, Camille

b. 1938
Chicago, Ill.
fields: Literature (children's book writer, educator)

African American children's book writer, educator; Camille Yarbrough received a Coretta Scott King Award in 1980 for her first children's book, *Cornrow* (1979). She is also the author of two juvenile novels: *The Shimmershine Queens*,1989, about young fifth-grade girls who convince their classmates to take pride in their urban neighborhood, and *Tamika and the Wisdom Rings*, 1994, about a young girl learning to cope with her father's death at the hand of drug dealers. Yarbrough also served on the faculty of the Black Studies department at the City College of New York (CCNY).

Yashima, Taro

né: Iwamatsu Jun Atsushi
b. Sept. 21, 1908
Kagoshima, Japan
d. June 30, 1994
Glendale, Calif.
fields: Literature, Art

Taro Yashima is an internationally acclaimed author and illustrator of children's books. His children's publications include *Crow Boy* (1955), *Umbrella* (1958), *The Golden Footprints* (1960), *Youngest One* (1962), and *Seashore Story* (1967). He also wrote powerful autobiographical books *The New Sun* (1943) and *Horizon Is Calling* (1947), using a comic book format.

Yasui, Minoru

b. Oct. 19, 1916
Hood River, Oreg.
d. Nov. 14, 1986
Denver, Colo.
fields: Historical Figure, Law

Minoru Yasui, who was trained as a lawyer, challenged the curfew order placed on Japanese Americans in 1942. In November, 1942, a judge found the curfew order to be unconstitutional for American citizens, but he argued that Yasui had forfeited his U.S. citizenship by working at the Japanese consulate, and therefore, Yasui was guilty of violating the curfew order. Yasui was sentenced to one year in prison and a fine of $5,000. In 1943, the cases of Yasui and fellow resisters Fred T. Korematsu and Gordon K. Hirabayashi came before the court of appeals. The appeals court asked the U.S. Supreme Court to rule. In 1943, the Court reversed the lower court ruling that the curfew order was unconstitutional in its application to American citizens. It also found that the trial judge had wrongly decided that Yasui forfeited his citizenship by working at the Japanese consulate. In 1984, Yasui's conviction was vacated by the U.S. district court upon a motion by the government.

Yatabe, Thomas T.

b. 1897
San Francisco, Calif.
d. ?
fields: Social Reform

Japanese American community leader and administrator; Thomas T. Yatabe was one of the first Japanese Americans born on the mainland; ordered to attend racially segregated schools in San Francisco in 1906; cofounder of the American Loyalty League in 1918, forerunner of the Japanese American Citizens League (JACL); first president of the JACL, 1934; interned during World War II but continued to preach loyalty to the U.S. government; founded Chicago chapter of JACL following resettlement there, 1943.

Yau, John

b. 1950
Lynn, Mass.
fields: Art, Literature (poet)

Poet and art critic John Yau published his first collection of poetry, *Crossing Canal Street*, in 1976. Some of Yau's later poetry collections are *Corpse and Mirror* (1983), *Radiant Silhouette: New and Selected Work 1974-1988* (1989), and *Edificio Sayonara* (1993). His works in art criticism include *In the Realm of Appearances: The Art of Andy Warhol* (1993) and *A. R. Penck* (1993). He received the Academy of American Poets' Lavan Award for Younger Poets (1988) and the General Electric Foundation Award for Younger Writers (1988).

Yeats, William Butler

b. June 13, 1865
Sandymount, near Dublin, Ireland
d. January 28, 1939
Cap Martin, France
fields: Literature

Yeats transformed himself from a minor late Romantic poet into the complex artist who became the greatest poet of the twentieth century. He won the 1923 Nobel Prize in Literature.

Yeh Wei-lien. *See* Yip, Wai-lim

Yellow Wolf

aka: Hermene Moxmox (Yellow Wolf)
aka: Heinmot Hikkih (White Thunder or White Lightning)
b. 1856
Wallowa Valley, Oreg.
d. Aug. 21, 1935
Colville Indian Reservation, Wash.
fields: Warfare and Conquest, Native American Affairs

Yellow Wolf was an important Nez Perce warrior, exhibiting loyalty, courage, and skill during the Nez Perce War of 1877. In September, 1877, Yellow Wolf was moved from a rear guard position to advance guard in order to deal with straggling soldiers before them. This change was recognition from his fellow warriors of their confidence in Yellow Wolf's ability to take care of the enemy singlehandedly.

Yeltsin, Boris N.

full: Boris Nikolayevich Yeltsin
b. February 1, 1931
Butka, Sverdlovsk region, U.S.S.R.
fields: Government and Politics

From within the Soviet establishment, Yeltsin led the increasingly radical forces that first sought to reform the Soviet Union then engineered its demise. Yeltsin became the first president of the post-Soviet Russian Federation.

Yen Li-pen. *See* Yan Liben

Yep, Laurence Michael

b. June 14, 1948
San Francisco, Calif.
fields: Literature

Chinese American writer. Laurence Michael Yep was a graduate student and teaching fellow at the State University of New York at Buffalo when he received a Book-of-the-Month Club writing fellowship in 1970. He began writing science fiction stories aimed primarily at children. Yep won the International Reading Association Children's Book Award in 1976 for *Dragonwings* (1975). Some of his other titles include *Sweetwater* (1973), *Seademons* (1977), *Child of the Owl* (1977), *Sea Glass* (1979), and *Dragon of the Lost Sea* (1982). Aside from his science fiction novels, Yep has retold traditional Chinese folktales in two collections, *Rainbow People* (1989) and *Tongues of Jade* (1991), and edited the anthology *American Dragons: Twenty-Five Asian American Voices* (1993). Yep has taught in the University of California system beginning in 1987 and was a National Endowment for the Arts Literature Fellow in 1990. He published his autobiography, *The Lost Garden*, in 1991.

Yepes y Álvarez, Juan de. *See* John of the Cross, Saint

Yerby, Frank

né: Frank Garvin
b. September 5, 1916
Augusta, Georgia

d. November 29, 1991
Madrid, Spain
fields: Literature
African American author; Frank Yerby wrote short stories and novels with racial themes; best known for a series of plantation romances that began with *The Foxes of Harrow* in 1946.

Yevtushenko, Yevgeny

full: Yevgeny Alexandrovich Yevtushenko
b. July 18, 1933
Zima, Soviet Union
fields: Literature
Poet Yevgeny Alexandrovich Yevtushenko gained national stature in the Soviet Union in the early 1960's through poetry readings to large audiences. Wile many of his poems praised Soviet economic achievements, criticized United States involvement in the Vietnam War, and portrayed the Soviet Union as a peaceful nation, his poetry also criticized Russian anti-Semitism and warned of the dangers of latent Stalinism. After unauthorized Western publication of Yevtushenko's autobiography in 1963, Soviet authorities temporarily forbade him to leave the country. The Mikhail Gorbachev years raised Yevtushenko's hopes for genuine reform. Following the Soviet Union's dissolution in 1991, Yevtushenko he urged Russians to break with the old servile obedience to those in power.

Yew, Virginia. *See* Lee, Virginia

Yi Ha-ung. *See* Taewon-gun

Yi Myong-bok. *See* Kojong

Yi Tae-wi. *See* Lee, David

Yi Wan-yong

b. 1858
d. 1926
fields: Government and Politics
Yi Wan-yong, born to a family of *yangban*, the scholar-official ruling class of traditional Korea, served the Korean government in a variety of posts during the later years of the Yi Dynasty (1392-1910). He became ambassador to the United States in 1888 and foreign minister in 1896. Yi, who was strongly pro-Japanese, signed the Protectorate Treaty of 1905. He became prime minister in 1907 and helped negotiate the Treaty of Annexation of 1910.

Yip, Wai-lim

né: Yeh Wei-lien
b. June 20, 1937
Guangdong Province, China
fields: Literature (poet)
Wai-lim Yip, one of the leading contemporary Chinese poets of Taiwan, was a translator and literary scholars. He became a professor of Chinese and comparative literature at the University of California, San Diego, in 1967. He wrote more than thirty books in Chinese and English, including *Ezra Pound's "Cathay"* (1969), *Chinese Poetry: Major Modes and Genres* (1976), and *Diffusion of Distances: Dialogues Between Chinese and Western Poetics* (1993).

Yi-shao. *See* Wang Hsi-chih

Yo Fei

aka: Yüeh Fei
b. 1103
China
d. 1141
Hangzhou, China
fields: Warfare and Conquest
The Chinese general Yo Fei was killed in prison by members of his own government during a war against an external army. Since that time he has been hailed as a symbol of patriotic resistance to foreign invaders.

Yoholo, Optothe. *See* Opothleyaholo

Yonaguska

b. c. 1760
near the Tuckaseigee River, N.C.
d. c. 1839
Quallatown, N.C.
fields: Government and Politics, Diplomacy, Native American Affairs
Native American leader. Under Yonaguska's leadership, a small band of Cherokees successfully resisted removal to Indian Territory and eventually became known as the Eastern Band of the Cherokee. In 1829, Yonaguska led fifty-one men and their families to a new home at the juncture of the Soco Creek and the Oconaluftee River in western North Carolina. They had separated from the Cherokee Nation through a provision in a treaty that allowed them to settle on an independent reservation. There they made a claim for United States citizenship. Through the aid of William Holland Thomas, a white lawyer and adopted son of Yonaguska, their small tribe successfully fought removal.

Yoneda, Karl Goso

b. July 15, 1906
Glendale, Calif.
d. May 9, 1999
Fort Bragg, Calif.
fields: Journalism
Karl Goso Yoneda, born in the United States and educated in Japan, joined the Communist Party and became active in the California labor movement in the 1920's. After the Japanese bombed Pearl Harbor in 1941, Yoneda was interned at the relocation center in Manzanar, California. At the camp, he took a cooperative stance, which resulted in threats against his life. Removed from the camp, he served as volunteer intelligence officer and translator with the U.S. Army. He rejoined the Communist Party after the war, working with the International Longshoreman's and Warehouseman's Union. Yoneda was an active participant in the redress movement during the 1970's and 1980's. His autobiography, *Ganbatte: Sixty-Year Struggle of a Kibei Worker*, was published in 1983.

Yonglo

né: Chu Ti
aka: Yung-lo
b. 1363
Nanking, China
d. 1424
Beijing, China
fields: Government and Politics, Monarchy
Ming emperor, 1402-1424. Combining traditional Chinese and Mongol ideas of imperial rule, Yonglo brought the Ming Dynasty to its height, making it notable for the caliber of its ministers, internal improvements, support of the arts, and domestic stability.

York

b. c. 1770
d. c. 1806
fields: Exploration and Colonization
African American explorer; York was a slave held by William Clark, who accompanied the 1804-1806 Lewis and Clark expedition; freed by Clark and set up in the freight business on his return from the expedition.

Yoshida, Jim

b. July 28, 1921
Seattle, Wash.
fields: Historical Figure
In April, 1941, second-generation Japanese American Jim Yoshida and his family went to Japan to return his father's ashes and for a short visit. After the Japanese attacked Pearl Harbor on December 7, 1941, his family was unable to return to the United States. Conscripted into the Japanese Imperial Army, Yoshida served in central China. In the postwar years, he found work as a translator for the U.S. Army in Korea. In April, 1954, he succeeded in regaining U.S. citizenship. Yoshida, with the help of Bill Hosokawa, wrote his autobiography, *The Two Worlds of Jim Yoshida* (1972).

Yoshimura, Wendy

b. Jan., 1943
Manzanar, Calif.

fields: Art, Government and Politics

Wendy Yoshimura, born in the detention camp at Manzanar, became involved in anti-Vietnam War activities while studying art in Oakland. She was arrested along with Patty Hearst, daughter of the head of the Hearst Corporation, in San Francisco in 1975. Hearst, who went from kidnap victim to member of the Symbionese Liberation Army, claimed that Yoshimura was a member of the group, but Yoshimura was not charged with anything related to Hearst. However, Yoshimura was arrested and charged with felony possession of explosives and a machine gun, charges stemming from a March, 1972, raid on a garage in Berkeley. After Yoshimura's arrest, the Japanese American community supported her, providing funds to secure a fair trial. Yoshimura was convicted and served six months in state prison and eight months in a work-release program.

Young, Al

b. May 31, 1939
Ocean Springs, Miss.
fields: Literature

African American short-story writer, poet, novelist, and editor; Al Young published four volumes of poetry, the most successful being *The Blues Don't Change: New and Selected Poems* (1982).

Young, Andre. *See* Dr. Dre

Young, Andrew

full: Andrew Jackson Young, Jr.
b. 1932
fields: Civil Rights

African American civil rights activist, politician, diplomat; Andrew Young was an aide and confidant of Martin Luther King, Jr., in the early 1960's; was executive vice president of the Southern Christian Leadership Conference, 1967; instrumental in organizing the Birmingham Children's Crusade and the first march on Selma; helped draft the Civil Rights Act of 1964 and the Voting Rights Act of 1965; served as Georgia state representative, 1973-1977; was U.S. ambassador to the United Nations, 1977-1979; served as mayor of Atlanta, 1982-1989; chair of the Atlanta Committee for the Olympic Games.

Young, Brigham

b. June 1, 1801
Whitingham, Vermont
d. August 29, 1877
Salt Lake City, Utah
fields: Religion and Theology

Young's leadership of the Church of Jesus Christ of Latter-day Saints (the Mormons) in the Utah territory influenced both the religious and the secular development of the American West.

Young, Buddy

full: Claude Henry Young
b. January 5, 1926
Chicago, Ill.
d. September 4, 1983
Terrell, Tex.
fields: Sports (football player)

African American football player; Buddy Young played with the New York Yankees (1947-1949), then with the New York Yanks (1950-1951) and the Dallas Texans (1952); joined the Baltimore Colts (1953-1955); compiled 9,601 total yards and scored 44 touchdowns in nine seasons, retiring with a record 27.7-yard average on kickoff returns.

Young, Charles

b. Mar. 12, 1864
Mayslick, Ky.
d. Jan. 18, 1922
Lagos, Nigeria
fields: Military Affairs

African American army officer. Charles Young was the third black graduate of the U.S. Military Academy at West Point in 1889. He had a career with black units in Haiti, the Philippines, Mexico, Liberia, and Nigeria. Young was a skilled mapmaker and served in the Spanish American War. For his work in Liberia Young received the NAACP's SPINGARN MEDAL (1916). His forced retirement during World War I—purportedly because of high blood pressure—was controversial. Following the Armistice, Young was returned to active duty. After his death in 1922, Young was buried with full honors in Arlington National Cemetery near Washington, D.C.

Young, Coleman Alexander

b. May 24, 1918
Tuscaloosa, Ala.
d. November 29, 1997
Detroit, Mich.
fields: Government and Politics

African American mayor of Detroit, Mich; Coleman Alexander Young was one of the Tuskeegee Airmen during World War II; in the 1950's founded the National Negro Labor Council, which drew the attention of HUAC, before whom he refused to testify; elected as a delegate to the Michigan Constitutional Convention in 1960; elected to the Michigan state senate in 1964; ran for the office of mayor in 1973 and served five consecutive terms in office.

Young, Grace Chisholm

né: Grace Chisholm
b. Mar. 15, 1868
Haslemere, England
d. Mar. 29, 1944
Croydon, England
fields: Mathematics (calculus, geometry, and set theory)

Grace Chisholm Young earned a Ph.D. magna cum laude from the University of Göttingen, the first woman to do so in Germany, in 1895; worked independently, but most important work was with her husband, William Henry Young; in 1906, they published *The Theory of Sets of Points*, the first book on set theory.

Young, Lester

aka: Pres or Prez Young
b. August 27, 1909
Woodville, Miss.
d. March 15, 1959
New York, N.Y.
fields: Music (jazz tenor saxophonist)

African American tenor saxophonist; Lester Young was nicknamed "Prez" (short for "president") by Billie Holiday, with whom he was closely associated; played with many greats of his era, including Count Basie, and was influential on the styles of saxaphonists Charlie Parker and Dexter Gordon.

Young, Mavis de Trafford. *See* Gallant, Mavis

Young, Nathan Benjamin

b. September 15, 1862
Newbern, Ala.
d. 1933
fields: Education

African American educator; Nathan Benjamin Young was the first president (1921-1927, 1929-1931) of Lincoln University after its conversion to a university from Lincoln Institute.

Young, Thomas

b. June 13, 1773
Milverton, Somerset, England
d. May 10, 1829
London, England
fields: Invention and Technology, Physics

Thomas Young gave the first experimental support for the wave theory of light. Because of his principle of interference, many phenomena associated with light from multiple sources could be understood.

Young, Victor Sen

b. 1915
San Francisco, Calif.
d. Nov. 9, 1980
North Hollywood, Calif.
fields: Film, Television

Victor Sen Young became an actor after working on *The Good Earth* (1937). He landed the role of Charlie Chan's number-two son in *Charlie Chan in Honolulu* (1938) and spent the next forty years as a Hollywood actor. Young appeared in many Chan movies and in films such as *The Letter* (1940), *Across the Pacific* (1942), and *Flower Drum Song* (1961). He played the part of Hop Sing, the Chinese cook at the Cartwright ranch, in *Bonanza* (1959-1973) and had a recurring role (1961-1962) on *Bachelor Father* (1957-1962). He also appeared in *Hawaii Five-O* (1968-1980) and *Kung Fu* (1972-1975).

Young, Whitney

full: Whitney Moore Young, Jr.
b. July 31, 1921
Lincoln Ridge, Ky.
d. March 11, 1971
Lagos, Nigeria
fields: Civil Rights, Education

African American educator, civil rights leader; Whitney Young was executive director of the Omaha Urban league, 1950-1954; was dean of Atlanta University School of Social Work, 1954-1961; served as executive director of National Urban League, 1961-1971; called for a "domestic Marshall Plan" to end black poverty, and helped President Lyndon B. Johnson craft his war on poverty; received Medal of Freedom in 1969; wrote *To Be Equal* (1964) and *Beyond Racism: Building an Open Society* (1969).

Young Bear

aka: Maqui-banasha
b. c. 1868
Iowa
d. 1933
Tama County, Iowa
fields: Government and Politics, Social Reform, Native American Affairs

Native American (Fox) leader. During the late nineteenth and early twentieth centuries, when official government policy called for Indian assimilation, Young Bear advocated revitalization of Indian traditions. Recorded tribal legends and sponsored a revival of traditional arts and crafts.

Young M. C.

né: Marvin Young
b. 1968
London, England
fields: Music (rap music artist)

African American rap music artist; Young M.C. had a million-selling single with "Bust a Move"; a recipient of an American Music Award and a Grammy Award (both in 1990), his albums include *Stone Cold Rhymin'* (1989) and *Brainstorm* (1991).

Young Man Afraid of His Horses

aka: Tasunka Kokipapi (Young Man of Whose Horses They Are Afraid)
b. c. 1830
d. 1900
Pine Ridge Reservation, S.Dak.
fields: Warfare and Conquest, Government and Politics, Diplomacy, Native American Affairs

Oglala Sioux warrior and leader. Young Man Afraid of His Horses was instrumental in helping to delay white expansion during the 1860's. Various tribes respected his leadership abilities; in 1865, the Cheyenne inducted him into their Crooked Lances clan. A realist, Young Man Afraid of His Horses tried unsuccessfully to warn his people of the falseness of the Ghost Dance prophesies. Seeing the futility of further resistance to white expansionism, he worked for improved conditions on the Pine Ridge Reservation. The English rendition of his name is an inaccurate translation; his Sioux name is intended to convey the idea that, in war, he is so powerful that even the sight of his horses inspires fear in others.

Youngblood, Johnny Ray

b. June 23, 1948
New Orleans, La.
fields: Religion and Theology

African American baptist minister; Johnny Ray Youngblood, the senior pastor of Saint Paul Community Baptist Church in Brooklyn, N.Y., used his dynamic leadership skills as a pastor and community organizer to transform a depressed neighborhood in Brooklyn. Part of this transformation included the construction of 2,200 single-family homes as part of the Nehemiah Housing Project. The church has grown from 84 members in 1974 to a congregation of more than 7,000. Youngblood's church operates 13 stores, a reading center, and an elementary and junior high school; it has a staff of 57 employees and an operating budget of more than $3 million. Youngblood was the subject of 1993 biography, *Upon This Rock: The Miracles of a Black Church* (Samuel G. Freedman).

Younger, Tank

full: Paul Younger
b. June 25, 1928
Grambling, Louisiana
fields: Sports (football player)

African American football player; Tank Younger was considered one of the best players in the black college system, scoring sixty touchdowns; joined the Los Angeles Rams in 1949 as the first player from a black college to be signed by a National Football League team; he played with the Rams until 1957.

Ypsilanti, Alexander

full: Alexander Ypsilanti
b. 1792
d. January 31, 1828
Vienna, Austria
fields: Government and Politics

In their individual ways, the Ypsilanti brothers (Alexander and Demetrios), idealistic aristocratic Greek revolutionaries of the Byzantine Phanariote class, demonstrated the problems as well as the possibilities of the Greek movement toward national autonomy and independence.

Ypsilanti, Demetrios

b. December 25, 1793
d. 1832
fields: Government and Politics

In their individual ways, the Ypsilanti brothers (Alexander and Demetrios), idealistic aristocratic Greek revolutionaries of the Byzantine Phanariote class, demonstrated the problems as well as the possibilities of the Greek movement toward national autonomy and independence.

Yu, Connie Young

b. June 19, 1941
Los Angeles, Calif.
fields: Historiography

Connie Young Yu, who earned an English degree from Mills College in 1963, published numerous materials on Chinese American history in various books and journals and lectured widely. Yu's publications include *Chinatown, San Jose, USA* (1991) and *Profiles in Excellence: Chinese Americans on the Peninsula* (1986). In 1987, 1990, and 1993, she was honored for her service to the Asian American community.

Yuan Shikai

aka: Yüan Shih-kai
b. September 16, 1859
Xiangcheng, Henan Province, China
d. June 6, 1916
Beijing, China
fields: Government and Politics, War and Conquest

Chinese military leader and head of Chinese government from 1912 to 1916. Yuan Shikai was a military leader for Chinese monarchy (the Qing or Manchu Dynasty). In 1911, asked by monarchy to subdue rebellion, but he ultimately sought rebels' support. Monarchy forced to abdicate 1912. Yuan named provisional president in 1912 and refused to relinquish power after losing election; outlawed opposition party, the Kuomintang (KMT), and had some party leaders killed. As leader of so-called Chinese Republic, had no interest in democracy or other Western reforms. Sought unsuccessfully to have himself named emperor; died while in office.

Yüan-chang. *See* Mi Fei

Yuey, Joe

b. 1906
Hoiping, China
fields: Business and Industry

Entrepreneur Joe Yuey was detained at the Angel Island immigration station in San Francisco Bay for almost a month after immigrating to the United States in July, 1923. For more than twenty terms, he chaired the Suey Sing Tong. In 1963, Yuey founded the Chinese Culture Foundation of San Francisco. He became owner of the Imperial Palace Restaurant, one of the first elegant dining establishments in San Francisco's Chinatown.

Yukari. *See* Tomita, Teiko

Yukawa, Hideki

né: Hideki Ogawa
b. Jan. 23, 1907
Tokyo, Japan
d. Sept. 8, 1981
Kyoto, Japan
fields: Physics

Hideki Yukawa first predicted a fundamental particle (the meson) with a mass about two hundred times that of the electron, in 1935, twelve years before its discovery; in 1949, won the Nobel Prize in Physics.

Yun Chi-ho

b. 1865
d. 1945
fields: Social Reform

Korean nobleman Yun Chi-ho studied in Japan, returning in 1883 to serve as interpreter for the first American minister to Korea. He converted to Christianity in 1887. He served in a succession of key posts at the Korean royal court, using his impressive skill with languages. He founded the Tongnip Hyophoe, an independence club, in 1896, and the government reassigned him. He served as general secretary of the Young Men's Christian Association from 1915 to 1920.

Yune, Johnny

b. ?
Choongbook Province, Korea
fields: Theater and Entertainment, Film

Korean American comedian Johnny Yune enjoyed popularity after an appearance on *The Tonight Show Starring Johnny Carson*. Yune, who became a U.S. citizen in 1968, also played roles in feature films.

Yung, Judy

b. ?
San Francisco, Calif.
fields: Historiography

Judy Yung was a faculty member of the American Studies department at the University of California, Santa Cruz, and the coordinator of the Asian American Studies program. She wrote *Chinese Women of America: A Pictorial History* (1986) and coedited *Island: Poetry and History of Chinese Immigrants on Angel Island, 1910-1940* (1980), with Him Mark Lai and Genny Lim. Yung also was the project director for *Making Waves: An Anthology of Writings By and About Asian American Women* (1989).

Yung Wing

b. Nov. 17, 1828
Nam Ping, Pedro Island, China
d. Apr. 21, 1912
Hartford, Conn.
fields: Government and Politics, Education

In 1847 Yung Wing became one of the first three Chinese to come to study in the United States. He also converted to Christianity and became a naturalized U.S. citizen (1852). Yung earned his degree at Yale University in 1854 becoming the first Chinese to graduate from an American university. Eventually, Yung returned to China and went into government service; he was the first Chinese to conduct a cultural exchange between the two nations. The first commissioner of the Chinese Educational Mission (1872-1881), Yung brought 120 Chinese to study in the United States. Yung and his colleague Chen Lanbin also engaged in diplomatic negotiations for China with Spain and Peru. Their efforts eventually resulted in the abolishment of the infamous "coolie trade" to Cuba and Peru, and they were later appointed the first Chinese foreign ministers to the United States, Spain, and Peru. Yung's autobiography, *My Life in China and America*, was published in 1909.

Yung-lo. *See* Yonglo

Yuriko

né: Yuriko Kikuchi
b. Feb. 2, 1920
San Jose, Calif.
fields: Dance

After internment at Gila River relocation center, Japanese American dancer Yuriko became a major soloist in Martha Graham's Dance Company. She originated significant roles in the Graham repertory, including *Appalachian Spring* (pr. 1944) and *Cave of the Heart* (pr. 1946). Another role she created was that of Eliza in the original Broadway production of *The King and I* (pr. 1951), and in numerous revivals of that play, she restaged Jerome Robbins's original choreography. Yuriko served as director to The Martha Graham Ensemble and gave classes at the Martha Graham School of Contemporary Dance. She also choreographed more than forty original modern dance works.

Yusuf, Sidi Muhammad Ben. *See* Muhammad V

Z

Zaghlūl, Saʿd

full: Saʿd Zaghlūl Pasha ibn Ibrāhīm
b. July, 1857
Ibyānah, Egypt
d. August 23, 1927
Cairo, Egypt
fields: Government and Politics

Egyptian nationalist leader, prime minister of Egypt in 1924. Saʿd Zaghlūl formed activist groups during World War I with goal of Egyptian independence from Great Britain. Founded Waft Party in 1918. Imprisoned 1921-1923; during this period, the British granted partial independence to Egypt. Became the first prime minister of Egypt in January of 1924. Violent conflicts continued between the British and the Egyptians; Zaghlūl unable to restore order. When the British commander in chief of the Egyptian army was assassinated in November of 1924, Zaghlūl was forced to resign under British pressure.

Zaharias, Babe Didrikson

né: Mildred Ella Didriksen
aka: Babe Didrikson
b. June 26, 1914
Port Arthur, Texas
d. September 27, 1956
Galveston, Texas
fields: Sports (track and field, basketball, track and field, golf, softball)

Participating in numerous sports in which she excelled and set several records, Zaharias is recognized as the greatest woman athlete of the first half of the twentieth century. She is still considered by many to be the greatest woman athlete of all time.

Zambrano, Sergio

b. ?
fields: Art (muralist)

Chicago-based Mexican American muralist Sergio Zambrano participated in the mile-long mural story on the walls on Chicago's West Hubbard Street. Also collaborated on eight panels of *La Raza de Oro* that pay homage to pre-Columbian cultures.

Zamyatin, Yevgeny Ivanovich

b. February 1, 1884
Lebedyan, Russia
d. March 10, 1937
Paris, France
fields: Literature

A Russian writer and romantic visionary, Yevgeny Ivanovich Zamyatin is best known for his anti-utopian novel *We*, which was never published in the Soviet Union. From 1917 to 1921 he was a leading figure in Leningrad intellectual circles, respected as a creative artist and critic. After the introduction of the New Economic Policy in 1921, however, communists denounced him as an apolitical individualist hostile to the Revolution. With the purge of the All-Russian Union of Writers consequent to the adoption of the First Five Year Plan in 1929, Zamyatin was heavily criticized for the romantic individualism of his major work, the anti-utopian novel *My*, completed in 1921 and first published as a whole, in English translation, as *We* (1924). His books were removed from many libraries. In 1931 went to France and never returned to Russia.

Zanuck, Darryl F.

full: Darryl Francis Zanuck
b. September 5, 1902
Wahoo, Nebraska
d. December 22, 1979
Palm Springs, California
fields: Film

As the head of production at two major Hollywood studios, Zanuck was the youngest, fiercest, and most flamboyant of the tycoons who controlled the American film industry.

Zapata, Carmen

b. July 15, 1927
New York, N.Y.
fields: Film, Television (actor and director)

Actress, director, and acting coach Carmen Zapata helped found the Bilingual Foundation for the Arts in 1973 to give experience to Latino actors and help introduce them to the film industry. Won Emmy Award in 1973; in 1983 received the Ruben Salazar Award of the National Council of La Raza and the Women in Film Humanitarian Award. In 1985, she was chosen Woman of the Year by the Hispanic Women's Council in 1985; received a Dramalogue Award for Best Actress in 1986.

Zapata, Emiliano

b. August 8, 1879
Anenecuilco, Morelos, Mexico
d. April 10, 1919
Hacienda Chinameca, Morelos, Mexico
fields: Social Reform, Military Affairs

Zapata was a notable rebel leader of peasant guerrillas in the Mexican Revolution who became a legendary folk hero among the poor Mexican farmers of Morelos because of his idealistic devotion to land reform and his brilliant guerrilla tactics during the Revolution.

Zappa, Frank

full: Frank Vincent Zappa
b. December 21, 1940
Baltimore, Maryland
d. December 4, 1993
Los Angeles, California
fields: Music

An acclaimed and unique composer of rock music, Frank Zappa provided scathing commentary on both the establishment and the counterculture during the 1960's. Founder in 1964 of the group that eventually became the Mothers of Invention, he and that band produced such albums as *Freak Out!* (1966), *Absolutely Free* (1967), *We're Only in It for the Money* (1967), *Lumpy Gravy* (1967), *Cruisin' with Ruben and the Jets* (1968), *Mothermania* (1969), and *Uncle Meat* (1969). Zappa continued to produce distinctive music until his death from prostate cancer in 1993, with more than fifty albums, a feature film (*200 Motels*, 1971), and countless live performances. His serious compositions were recorded by world-renowned orchestras, his live guitar solos were anthologized, and he won a 1988 Grammy Award. He not only expanded the technical and intellectual limits of rock music, crossing barriers between musical forms, but also remained a proponent of free expression, opposing censorship in testimony before the U.S. Congress.

Zavala, Lorenzo de

b. Oct. 3, 1788
Mérida, Yucatán, Mexico
d. Nov. 16, 1836
Texas Point, Tex.
fields: Government and Politics

Lorenzo de Zavala was one of Mexico's most distinguished liberal and republican statesmen in the early nineteenth century. He helped draft the 1824 federal constitution, and he served as governor of the state of Mexico and as minister to France. Advocated such radical policies as the redistribution of wealth. In 1835, he helped Texas colonists achieve independence, and in 1836 he was briefly interim vice president of the new Lone Star Republic.

Zavella, Patricia

b. Nov. 28, 1949
near Tampa, Fla.
fields: Anthropology

Anthropologist and Chicana activist Patricia Zavella received her Ph.D. from the University of California, Berkeley, in 1982, with her dissertation research focusing on a discrimination suit filed by California cannery workers. In 1983 she began teaching at the University of California, Santa Cruz; became associate professor in 1989. Books include

Women's Work and Chicano Families: Cannery Workers of the Santa Clara Valley (1987) and *Sunbelt Working Mothers: Reconciling Family and Factory* (1993).

Zeami Motokiyo

b. 1363
Nagaoka, Yamishiro Province, Japan
d. 1443
Kyoto, Honshu Province, Japan
fields: Theater and Entertainment

A great actor and a great dramatist, Zeami was also an outstanding teacher of acting and a theoretician of theatrical aesthetics. He established the No (*sarugaku*) form of drama, which has survived to modern times.

Zedillo, Ernesto

full: Ernesto Zedillo Ponce de León
b. December 27, 1951
Mexico City, Mexico
fields: Government and Politics

Took office as president of Mexico in 1994. Ernesto Zedillo was educated as an economist. In 1993 the choice of the PRI (Mexico's dominant party) for presidential candidate was Luis Donaldo Colosio Murrieta. Colosio named Zedillo as his campaign manager. When Colosio was assassinated, Zedillo became his replacement, even though few Mexicans were familiar with him and he was not a charismatic figure. Zedillo won the 1994 election. Faced pressures to reform the PRI and Mexico's electoral system in general as well as an insurrection in the state of Chiapas in 1994. Devalued the peso December, 1994, pushing country into recession in 1995. With international aid, implemented economic reforms in 1995.

Zeeman, Pieter

b. May 25, 1865
Zonnemaire, Isle of Schouwen, Zeeland, the Netherlands
d. Oct. 9, 1943
Amsterdam, the Netherlands
fields: Physics

Pieter Zeeman proved that the spectral lines of an atom broaden when it is placed in a magnetic field; won the 1902 Nobel Prize in Physics with Hendrik Antoon Lorentz.

Zeiger, Larry. *See* King, Larry

Zeng Guofan

aka: Tseng Kuo-fan
b. November 26, 1811
Xiang-xiang, Hunan, China
d. March 12, 1872
Nanking, China
fields: Government and Politics, Military Affairs

Zeng Guofan directed the Ch'ing Dynasty's extraordinary suppression of the Taiping Rebellion. His strategy used locally recruited but professional armies and required twelve years to succeed. He continued to serve in high office and is recognized as a key figure in the Ch'ing restoration that began in the 1860's. Renowned for his probity, Zeng recruited men who became the dynasty's chief ministers after his death, but few approached his talents or his upright character.

Zenger, John Peter

b. 1697
The Palatinate, Germany
d. July 28, 1746
New York, New York
fields: Journalism

Zenger printed attacks on Governor William Cosby of the colony of New York in the *New York Weekly Journal*, for which he was indicted for libel. His celebrated trial became a landmark in establishing a free press in America.

Zeno Gandía, Manuel

b. Jan. 10, 1855
Arecibo, Puerto Rico
d. Jan. 30, 1930
San Juan, Puerto Rico
fields: Literature

Puerto Rican fiction writer Manuel Zeno Gandía studied medicine in Spain, then practiced in Paris, where he explored the works of contemporary French novelists. Returned to Puerto Rico in 1876; active in medicine, journalism, literature, and politics. The tetralogy *Crónicas de un mundo enfermo* (1894-1925) is his major achievement in fiction. The first part, *La charca* (1894; English translation, 1982), is considered his finest work.

Zeno of Citium

b. c. 335 B.C.E.
Citium (modern Larnaca), Cyprus
d. Probably fall, 261 B.C.E.
Athens
fields: Philosophy

Zeno founded Stoicism, the leading Hellenistic school of philosophy. Though not the school's greatest thinker, he created its unified, systematic teaching and guided it to prominence.

Zeno of Elea

b. c. 490 B.C.E.
Elea
d. c. 440 B.C.E.
Elea
fields: Philosophy

Although Zeno cannot be said to have succeeded in defending Paramenides' doctrine of the one, his paradoxes are still remembered, and his method of argument influenced all later philosophy.

Zeppelin, Ferdinand von

b. July 8, 1838
Konstanz, Baden
d. March 8, 1917
Charlottenburg, Germany
fields: Aviation and Space Exploration

Zeppelin developed the concepts and designs for the construction of the first practical airships capable of navigating over long distances. The success of Zeppelin's rigid dirigibles served to stimulate experimentation in all areas of aeronautics and paved the way for military and commercial applications of airships.

Zermelo, Ernst

full: Ernst Friedrich Ferdinand Zermelo
b. July 27, 1871
Berlin, Germany
d. May 21, 1953
Freiburg im Breisgau, Germany
fields: Mathematics (applied math, calculus, mathematical logic, and set theory)

Ernst Zermelo proved the well-ordering theorem and published "Beweis, dass jede Menge wohlgeordnet werden kann" ("Proof That Every Set Can Be Well-Ordered," 1967) in 1904, introducing the first collection of axioms for set theory.

Zetkin, Clara

né: Clara Eissner
b. July 5, 1857
Wiederau, Saxony
d. June 20, 1933
Arkhangelskoye, near Moscow, U.S.S.R.
fields: Women's Rights, Government and Politics, Social Reform, Labor Movement

With Friedrich Engels and August Bebel, Zetkin pioneered a Marxist analysis of women's status in a capitalist society. Her objective was to create a new social order free of political and economic oppression.

Zhao Ziyang

aka: Chao Tzu-yang
b. October 17, 1919
Hua County, Henan Province, China
fields: Government and Politics

Premier of China from 1980 to 1987 and secretary-general of Chinese Communist Party from 1987 to 1989. Zhao Ziyang attempted to revitalize Chinese industry and, with approval of Deng Xiaoping, to streamline vast governmental bureaucracy. Faced considerable resistance from conservatives and hard-liners. Fell from power in 1989 after failing to take strong position against student demonstrators—he refused to crack down or to impose martial law in Beijing. Placed under house arrest and stripped of chairmanships.

Zhdanov, Andrei

b. February 26, 1896
Mariupol, Ukraine, Russian Empire
d. August 31, 1948
Moscow, Soviet Union
fields: Government and Politics

As commissar of Soviet arts, Andrei Zhdanov presided over the purging of the arts in the last years of Joseph Stalin's rule. At Stalin's bidding, he was the driving force behind four ideological resolutions imposed by the Central Committee of the Communist Party. Zhdanov intimidated the artistic communities until his sudden death in 1948. He issued three resolutions in 1946 dealing with literature, theater, and film, warning artists not to challenge the ideology of the Communist Party.

Zhogaxe. *See* La Flesche, Francis

Zhou Enlai. *See* Chou En-Lai

Zhu De

aka: Chu Teh
b. December 12 or 18, 1886
Yilong County, Sichuan Province, China
d. July 6, 1976
Beijing, China
fields: Military Affairs, Government and Politics

Zhu De is one of the great military figures of the Communist Revolution in modern China. He is acclaimed as the "Father of the Red Army." His service as commander of the Communist Army in the 1930's and 1940's attests that he was respected for his military ability as well as for his unflagging commitment to the Communist movement. In addition to his military contributions, Zhu helped establish the Chinese soviets, and he served in the Politburo and was Chairman of the Standing Committee of the National People's Congress.

Zhuangzi

aka: Chuang Tzu
b. c. 365 B.C.E.
Meng, Kingdom of Song, China
d. c. 290 B.C.E.
Nanhua Hill, Caozhou, Kingdom of Chi, China
fields: Philosophy

Zhuangzi was the greatest interpreter of the Chinese Daoist school of philosophy. He went much beyond its founder, Laozi, in constructing an apolitical, transcendental philosophy designed to promote an individual's spiritual freedom, as expounded in his major work, *Zhuangzi*.

Zhukov, Georgy Konstantinovich

b. December 2, 1896
Strelkovka, Russia
d. June 18, 1974
Moscow, U.S.S.R.
fields: Military Affairs, Government and Politics

Zhukov was the most important Soviet staff and field commander throughout World War II and was involved in the planning and/or execution of all the primary battles and campaigns against the Germans. Zhukov was the first career military man to be selected as a member of the Presidium (Politburo) of the Communist Party, came to be feared as a rival by both Joseph Stalin and Nikita S. Khrushchev, and was decisive in preventing Khrushchev's ouster in 1957.

Zia-ul-Haq, Mohammad

b. August 12, 1924
Jullundur, Punjab (now India)
d. August 17, 1988
near Bahāwalpur, Pakistan
fields: Government and Politics

President of Pakistan from 1978 to 1998. Mohammad Zia-ul-Haq took over government of Pakistan in 1977 bloodless coup and declared martial law. Assumed presidency in 1978. Promoted nationalism and strict adherence to Islam; banned union activities; forbade banks to charge or pay interest. Banned political activity in 1978, political parties in 1979. Cultivated U.S. support. High rate of economic growth under his leadership. Allowed elections in 1985 and was officially elected to presidency. Killed in 1988, along with thirty other passengers, when the military plane they were aboard exploded and crashed in an apparent act of sabotage.

Zilliacus, Konni

b. September 13, 1894
Kobe, Japan
d. July 6, 1967
London, England
fields: Journalism, Government and Politics

Konni Zilliacus was a leading peace propagandist at the League of Nations in the 1920's and 1930's. During World War I he supported creation of the League of Nations. Using pseudonyms, he wrote hundreds of letters to newspaper editors and articles in support of the league. In 1945 he was elected to Britain's Parliament, where he became the Labour government's most vocal foreign policy critic and opposed his own government's pro-American Cold War policy. Writing in journals, he campaigned for peaceful coexistence with communism. Eventually, the Labour Party expelled him for holding communist sympathies, but he returned to Parliament in 1955. Until his death he continued to lobby and write about the dangers of the Cold war. His books included *The League of Nations Today* (1923) and *Inquest on Peace* (1935).

Zimmerman, Ethel Agnes. *See* Merman, Ethel

Zimmerman, Robert Allen. *See* Dylan, Bob

Zinzendorf, Graf von

né: Nikolaus Ludwig
full: Nikolaus Ludwig, Graf of Zinzendorf and Pottendorf
b. May 26, 1700
Dresden, Saxony
d. May 9, 1760
Herrnhut, Saxony
fields: Religion and Theology, Church Reform

Zinzendorf revived and transformed the nearly extinct Moravian Church by infusing it with an evangelical Pietistic theology. In so doing he also became a pioneer of ecumenism among Christians and gave birth to the modern Protestant missionary movement.

Zipkoheta. *See* Big Bow

Zitkaduta. *See* Red Bird

Zitkala Sa (Red Bird). *See* Bonnin, Gertrude Simmons

Žižka, Jan

aka: Count Jan Žižka
b. c. 1360
Trocnov, Bohemia
d. October 11, 1424; Přibyslav, Bohemia
fields: Warfare and Conquest

Žižka's innovations in military organization and weapons were directly responsible for the success of the Hussite revolution; they spelled the end of the medieval system of mounted knights.

Zola, Émile

b. April 2, 1840
Paris, France
d. September 28, 1902
Paris, France
fields: Literature

Zola's major contributions were in three areas: literature, as a writer of poetry, drama, novels, and essays; literary theory, as one of the major forces in defining naturalism as a literary school; and human rights, as a defender of Alfred Dreyfus, who was falsely accused of treason and sentenced to Devil's Island.

Zoroaster

b. c. 628 B.C.E.
probably Rhages, northeastern Iran
d. c. 551 B.C.E.
probably northern Iran
fields: Religion and Theology

The founder of one of the great ethical religions of the ancient world, Zoroaster exerted direct and indirect influence on the development of three other great religions: Judaism, Christianity, and Islam.

Zoser

b. c. 2700 B.C.E.
probably Memphis, Egypt
d. c. 2650 B.C.E.
Memphis, Egypt
fields: Government and Politics, Architecture

Zoser was the first great king of the epoch known as the Old Kingdom, Third through Sixth dynasties. His outstanding achievement was the construction of the Step Pyramid at Saqqara near Memphis, the earliest of the great pyramids.

Zotom

aka: Podaladalte (Snake Head)
aka: the Biter
b. 1853
southern Plains
d. Apr. 27, 1913
Okla.
fields: Art, Warfare and Conquest

Zotom was a Kiowa warrior and artist. His pictographs on ladies' fans, his model tipis, and his shield covers provide valuable ethnographic and artistic data. Zotom was a graceful dancer, a gifted painter, and an accomplished orator. His drawing books chronicle Indian activities on the Plains and at Fort Marion, Florida, where he was held for three years in the 1870's.

Zwicky, Fritz

b. Feb. 14, 1898
Varna, Bulgaria
d. Feb. 8, 1974
Pasadena, California
fields: Astronomy, Physics

Fritz Zwicky helped discover neutron stars; found the first proof of dark matter in the universe, in the mid-1930's; led indirectly to the theory of black holes, extremely dense material from which no light or gravitation escapes.

Zwilich, Ellen Taaffe

né: Ellen Taaffe
b. April 30, 1939
Miami, Florida
fields: Music

One of America's foremost composers of art music, Zwilich became the first woman to win the Pulitzer Prize in music.

Zwingli, Huldrych

aka: Ulrich Zwingli
aka: Master Ulrich
b. January 1, 1484
Wildhaus, Swiss Confederation
d. October 11, 1531
near Kappel, Swiss Confederation
fields: Church Reform, Religion and Theology

Zwingli led the Swiss Reformation against Roman Catholic ecclesiastical abuses, sharing both the rhetoric and the theology of Germany's own reformer, Martin Luther, until the two disagreed over the nature of the Eucharist. Overshadowed in church history by both Luther and John Calvin, Zwingli's most lasting contribution to Church history is his incipient Reformed theology and his recognition of the role that secular government might play in ecclesiastical matters.

Zworykin, Vladimir

full: Vladimir Kosma Zworykin
b. July 30, 1889
Mourom, Russia
d. July 29, 1982
Princeton, New Jersey
fields: Invention and Technology, Television

Frequently called the "father of television," Zworykin invented both the iconoscope camera tube and the kinescope picture tube, which together form the electronic television system.